THE ALL ENGLAND LAW REPORTS 1983

Volume 2

Editor
PETER HUTCHESSON LL M
Barrister, New Zealand

Assistant Editor
BROOK WATSON
of Lincoln's Inn, Barrister
and of the New South Wales Bar

Consulting Editor
WENDY SHOCKETT
of Gray's Inn, Barrister

London
BUTTERWORTHS

ENGLAND	Butterworth & Co (Publishers) Ltd 88 Kingsway, **London** WC2B 6AB
AUSTRALIA	Butterworths Pty Ltd, **Sydney, Melbourne, Brisbane, Adelaide** and **Perth**
CANADA	Butterworth & Co (Canada) Ltd, **Toronto** Butterworth & Co (Western Canada) Ltd, **Vancouver**
NEW ZEALAND	Butterworths of New Zealand Ltd, **Wellington**
SINGAPORE	Butterworth & Co (Asia) Pte Ltd, **Singapore**
SOUTH AFRICA	Butterworth Publishers (Pty) Ltd, **Durban**
USA	Mason Publishing Co, **St Paul**, Minnesota Butterworth Legal Publishers, **Seattle**, Washington, **Boston**, Massachusetts and **Austin**, Texas D & S Publishers, **Clearwater**, Florida

ISBN 0 406 85148 4

Typeset by CCC, printed and bound in Great Britain by William Clowes Limited, Beccles and London

REPORTERS

House of Lords

Mary Rose Plummer Barrister

Privy Council

Mary Rose Plummer Barrister

Court of Appeal, Civil Division

Mary Rose Plummer Barrister
Frances Rustin Barrister
Diana Procter Barrister
Henrietta Steinberg Barrister
Diana Brahams Barrister
Patricia Hargrove Barrister
Sophie Craven Barrister

Court of Appeal, Criminal Division

N P Metcalfe Esq Barrister
Sepala Munasinghe Esq Barrister
Dilys Tausz Barrister
Jacqueline Charles Barrister
April Weiss Barrister
Raina Levy Barrister
Martine Kushner Barrister

Chancery Division

Jacqueline Metcalfe Barrister
Evelyn M C Budd Barrister
Hazel Hartman Barrister
Vivian Horvath Barrister

Queen's Bench Division

David Bartlett Esq Barrister
M Denise Chorlton Barrister
J M Collins Esq Barrister
K Mydeen Esq Barrister

Family Division

Bebe Chua Barrister

Admiralty

N P Metcalfe Esq Barrister

Revenue Cases

Rengan Krishnan Esq Barrister
Edwina Epstein Barrister

Courts-Martial Appeals

N P Metcalfe Esq Barrister

SUB-EDITORS

Radhika Edwards Barrister
Robert Brennan Esq Barrister, New Zealand

MANAGER

John W Wilkes Esq

House of Lords

The Lord High Chancellor: Lord Hailsham of St Marylebone

Lords of Appeal in Ordinary

Lord Diplock
Lord Fraser of Tullybelton
Lord Keith of Kinkel
Lord Scarman
Lord Roskill
Lord Bridge of Harwich
Lord Brandon of Oakbrook
Lord Brightman
Lord Templeman

Court of Appeal

The Lord High Chancellor

The Lord Chief Justice of England: Lord Lane
(President of the Criminal Division)

The Master of the Rolls: Sir John Francis Donaldson
(President of the Civil Division)

The President of the Family Division: Sir John Lewis Arnold

The Vice-Chancellor: Sir Robert Edgar Megarry

Lords Justices of Appeal

Sir John Frederick Eustace Stephenson
Sir Frederick Horace Lawton
Sir George Stanley Waller
Sir James Roualeyn Hovell-Thurlow-Cumming-Bruce
Sir Edward Walter Eveleigh
Sir Desmond James Conrad Ackner
Sir Robin Horace Walford Dunn
Sir Peter Raymond Oliver
Sir Tasker Watkins VC
Sir Patrick McCarthy O'Connor
Sir William Hugh Griffiths
Sir Michael John Fox
Sir Michael Robert Emanuel Kerr
Sir John Douglas May
Sir Christopher John Slade
Sir Francis Brooks Purchas
Sir Robert Lionel Archibald Goff
Sir George Brian Hugh Dillon

Chancery Division

The Lord High Chancellor

The Vice-Chancellor

Sir Peter Harry Batson Woodroffe Foster
Sir John Norman Keates Whitford
Sir Ernest Irvine Goulding
Sir Raymond Henry Walton
Sir Nicolas Christopher Henry Browne-Wilkinson
Sir John Evelyn Vinelott
Sir Martin Charles Nourse
Sir Douglas William Falconer
Sir Jean-Pierre Frank Eugene Warner
Sir Peter Leslie Gibson
Sir David Herbert Mervyn Davies
Sir Jeremiah LeRoy Harman

Queen's Bench Division

The Lord Chief Justice of England

Sir Joseph Donaldson Cantley
Sir Hugh Eames Park
Sir Bernard Caulfield
Sir Hilary Gwynne Talbot
Sir William Lloyd Mars-Jones
Sir Ralph Kilner Brown
Sir Peter Henry Rowley Bristow
Sir Hugh Harry Valentine Forbes
Sir David Powell Croom-Johnson
Sir Leslie Kenneth Edward Boreham
Sir Alfred William Michael Davies
Sir John Dexter Stocker
Sir Kenneth George Illtyd Jones
Sir Haydn Tudor Evans
Sir Peter Richard Pain
Sir Kenneth Graham Jupp
Sir Stephen Brown
Sir Roger Jocelyn Parker
Sir Ralph Brian Gibson
Sir Walter Derek Thornley Hodgson
Sir James Peter Comyn
Sir Anthony John Leslie Lloyd
Sir Frederick Maurice Drake
Sir Brian Thomas Neill
Sir Michael John Mustill
Sir Barry Cross Sheen
Sir David Bruce McNeill
Sir Harry Kenneth Woolf
Sir Christopher James Saunders French
Sir Thomas Patrick Russell
Sir Peter Edlin Webster
Sir Thomas Henry Bingham
Sir Iain Derek Laing Glidewell
Sir Henry Albert Skinner
Sir Peter Murray Taylor
Sir Murray Stuart-Smith
Sir Christopher Stephen Thomas Jonathan Thayer Staughton
Sir Donald Henry Farquharson
Sir Anthony James Denys McCowan
Sir Iain Charles Robert McCullough
Sir Hamilton John Leonard
Sir Alexander Roy Asplan Beldam
Sir David Cozens-Hardy Hirst
Sir John Stewart Hobhouse
Sir Michael Mann
Sir Andrew Peter Leggatt
Sir Michael Patrick Nolan
Sir Oliver Bury Popplewell
Sir William Alan Macpherson

Family Division

The President of the Family Division

Sir John Brinsmead Latey
Sir Alfred Kenneth Hollings
Sir Charles Trevor Reeve
Dame Rose Heilbron
Sir Brian Drex Bush
Sir Alfred John Balcombe
Sir John Kember Wood
Sir Ronald Gough Waterhouse
Sir John Gervase Kensington Sheldon
Sir Thomas Michael Eastham
Dame Margaret Myfanwy Wood Booth
Sir Anthony Leslie Julian Lincoln
Dame Ann Elizabeth Oldfield Butler-Sloss
Sir Anthony Bruce Ewbank
Sir John Douglas Waite
Sir Anthony Barnard Hollis

CITATION

These reports are cited thus:

[1983] 2 All ER

REFERENCES

These reports contain references to the following major works of legal reference described in the manner indicated below.

Halsbury's Laws of England

The reference 39 Halsbury's Laws (3rd edn) 860, para 1303 refers to paragraph 1303 on page 860 of volume 39 of the third edition, and the reference 26 Halsbury's Laws (4th edn) para 577 refers to paragraph 577 on page 296 of volume 26 of the fourth edition of Halsbury's Laws of England.

Halsbury's Statutes of England

The reference 5 Halsbury's Statutes (3rd edn) 302 refers to page 302 of volume 5 of the third edition of Halsbury's Statutes of England.

The Digest

References are to the blue band replacement volumes and the green band reissue volumes of The Digest (formerly the English and Empire Digest), and to the continuation volumes.

The reference 47 Digest (Repl) 781, *25* refers to case number 25 on page 781 of Digest Blue Band Replacement Volume 47.

The reference 36(2) Digest (Reissue) 764, *1398* refers to case number 1398 on page 764 of Digest Green Band Reissue Volume 36(2).

The reference Digest (Cont Vol E) 640, *2392a* refers to case number 2392a on page 640 of Digest Continuation Volume E.

Halsbury's Statutory Instruments

The reference 20 Halsbury's Statutory Instruments (4th reissue) 302 refers to page 302 of the fourth reissue of volume 20 of Halsbury's Statutory Instruments; references to subsequent reissues are similar.

Cases reported in volume 2

Digest of cases reported in volume 2

CORRIGENDA

228

[1983] 1 All ER

229 p 754. **Ford v Warwickshire CC.** Line *j*3 should read '. . . an interval that could *not* be characterised as
230 short . . .'

231

[1983] 2 All ER

232 p 245. **Ashcroft v Mersey Regional Health Authority.** Counsel for the plaintiff: read '*John Rowe*
233 *QC* and *Norman A Wright*'.

234 p 735. **Astro Exito Navegacion SA v Southland Enterprise Co Ltd**. Line *h*6 should read '. . . But I
234 do *not* intend by my use of that phrase . . .'

236 p 762. **Kuwait Minister of Public Works v Sir Frederick Snow & Partners (a firm).** Line *h*5
237 should read 's 1(2)(*c*) of the Foreign Judgments (Reciprocal Enforcement) Act 1933.'

240

Resolute Maritime Inc and another v Nippon
b Kaiji Kyokai and others
The Skopas

QUEEN'S BENCH DIVISION (COMMERCIAL COURT)
MUSTILL J
c 3, 6 DECEMBER 1982

Misrepresentation – Agent – Liability – Agent's liability for misrepresentation inducing another to enter into contract – Whether liability for agent's misrepresentation attaching to principal only – Whether agent personally liable to innocent party for misrepresentation – Misrepresentation Act 1967, s 2(1).

d
Where a person has entered into a contract after a misrepresentation has been made to him by 'another party thereto' and has suffered loss as a result, the liability imposed by s 2(1)[a] of the Misrepresentation Act 1967 on that other party attaches only to a principal who is a party to the contract, since the 1967 Act is concerned with the parties to a contract and with representations made in the particular context of the contract.
e Accordingly, where the misrepresentation is made by an agent of the principal acting under his express or ostensible authority, or by a person on behalf of the agent, neither the agent nor any person acting on his behalf is personally liable under s 2(1) of the 1967 Act to the person who has entered into the contract with the principal on the strength of the misrepresentation (see p 3 *g* to *j* and p 4 *a b*, post).

f
Notes

For the liability of the principal for misrepresentation of his agent, see 1 Halsbury's Laws (4th edn) paras 848–849 and 31 ibid para 1029, and for cases on the subject, see 1(2) Digest (Reissue) 801–807, *5208–5238*.

For damages under the Misrepresentation Act 1967, see 31 Halsbury's Laws (4th edn) para 1103.

g For the Misrepresentation Act 1967, s 2, see 22 Halsbury's Statutes (3rd edn) 676.

Case referred to in judgment

Hedley Byrne & Co Ltd v Heller & Partners Ltd [1963] 2 All ER 575, [1964] AC 465, [1963] 3 WLR 101, HL, 36(1) Digest (Reissue) 24, *84*.

h

Preliminary issue

The first plaintiff, Resolute Maritime Inc, and the second plaintiff, Dashwood Co Ltd, issued a writ against Nippon Kaiji Kyokai and twelve other defendants, including the thirteenth defendants, J C O'Keefe Ltd, claiming damages for misrepresentation. On 16
j July 1982 Staughton J granted the plaintiffs leave to join the fourteenth defendant, John C O'Keefe, as a party to the action and also ordered, inter alia, that a preliminary issue be tried, namely whether the thirteenth and fourteenth defendants could in law be liable to

---

a Section 2(1) is set out at p 2 *j*, post

the plaintiffs under s 2(1) of the Misrepresentation Act 1967. The facts are set out in the judgment. a

Gordon Pollock QC for the plaintiffs.
Roger Buckley QC and *Bruce Reynolds* for the thirteenth defendants.
Peter Gross for the fourteenth defendant.
The other defendants did not appear.

Cur adv vult b

6 December. The following judgment was delivered.

MUSTILL J. Pursuant to an order made on 16 July 1982 this matter comes before the court as a preliminary issue of law stated in an action brought by Resolute Maritime Inc and Dashwood Co Ltd against a total of 14 defendants, of whom the thirteenth and c fourteenth are parties to the issues stated.

The dispute arises from a transaction whereby the plaintiffs purchased from the third defendants their vessel Skopas. The plaintiffs claim that they were misled into making the purchase by incorrect representations about the passing of a special survey in the comparatively recent past, and about maintenance and repair said to have been performed d on behalf of the sellers. The plaintiffs have sued the sellers, their managers and their respective employees, and the Classification Society and its local surveyor. In addition, they have joined as thirteenth defendants, J C O'Keefe Ltd, who acted as brokers in respect of the transaction, and as fourteenth defendant, Mr John C O'Keefe, who controls the thirteenth defendants and was the person individually concerned in broking the contract.

e By their reamended point of claim, the plaintiffs seek damages on the basis that representations were made (a) fraudulently or (b) negligently. In addition, the plaintiffs rely on s 2(1) of the Misrepresentation Act 1967. It is this latter claim which raises the issue now for consideration, it being common ground that the kindred claims in fraud and negligence turn on matters of fact which will have to be tried. It has, however, been though appropriate to decide in advance of the trial a question of law under the 1967 f Act. It is this: if an agent, acting in his express or ostensible authority, makes a statement which is untrue in circumstances where he did not have reasonable ground to believe that it was true, can he be held liable under the 1967 Act? There is a subsidiary question which affects the fourteenth defendant alone and will arise if the answer to the question is affirmative, namely whether the person who actually makes the statement on behalf of the agent incurs a similar liability.

In order to make the questions intelligible it is necessary to set out the first three g sections of the 1967 Act:

> '**1.** Where a person has entered into a contract after a misrepresentation has been made to him, and—(*a*) the misrepresentation has become a term of the contract; or (*b*) the contract has been performed; or both, then, if otherwise he would be entitled to rescind the contract without alleging fraud, he shall be so entitled, subject to the h provisions of this Act, notwithstanding the matters mentioned in paragraphs (*a*) and (*b*) of this section.
>
> **2.**—(1) Where a person has entered into a contract after a misrepresentation has been made to him by another party thereto and as a result thereof has suffered loss, then, if the person making the representation would be liable to damages in respect thereof had the misrepresentation been made fraudulently, that person shall be so j liable notwithstanding that the misrepresentation was not made fraudulently, unless he proves that he had reasonable ground to believe and did believe up to the time the contract was made that the facts represented were true.
>
> (2) Where a person has entered into a contract after a misrepresentation has been made to him otherwise than fraudulently, and he would be entitled, by reason of the misrepresentation, to rescind the contract, then, if it is claimed, in any

> proceedings arising out of the contract, that the contract ought to be or has been
> a rescinded, the court or arbitrator may declare the contract subsisting and award damages in lieu of rescission, if of opinion that it would be equitable to do so, having regard to the nature of the misrepresentation and the loss that would be caused by it if the contract were upheld, as well as to the loss that rescission would cause to the other party.
>
> (3) Damages may be awarded against a person under subsection (2) of this section
> b whether or not he is liable to damages under subsection (1) thereof, but where he is so liable any award under the said subsection (2) shall be taken into account in assessing his liability under the said subsection (1).
>
> **3.** If any agreement . . . contains a provision which would exclude or restrict—(*a*) any liability to which a party to a contract may be subject by reason of any misrepresentation made by him before the contract was made; or (*b*) any remedy
> c available to another party to the contract by reason of such a misrepresentation; that provision shall be of no effect except to the extent (if any) that . . . the court or arbitrator may allow reliance on it as being fair and reasonable . . .'

(Section 3 has since been substituted by s 8(1) of the Unfair Contract Terms Act 1977.)

It is sensible to approach the problem by looking at the words of s 2(1) in isolation to
d see whether they point so clearly towards one conclusion that there is no need for consideration of the Act as a whole or of the purpose which it was intended to achieve. Counsel for the plaintiffs says that they do. The draftsman has, he points out, chosen the word 'party' to describe the representee in the opening words of the subsection, and has then chosen 'person' to describe the representor in the remainder of the subsection. This shift in language demonstrates, so it is contended, that the person intended to be liable is
e not the obligor under the contract, but the individual who actually makes the representation. To this, counsel for the thirteenth defendant replies that the alteration in language was for the purpose of euphony. One could not speak of 'another person thereto'. This argument itself prompts the response that, if the intention had been to make the obligor liable to the exclusion of the agent, the draftsman would have continued to use 'party' throughout the remainder of the subsection, instead of reverting to the
f word 'person'. Finally, the defendants can reply by pointing out that, since an agent who incurs no personal liability under a contract is not 'a party thereto', the agent can only be brought within the description of the representor if the words 'by another party thereto' are read as meaning 'by or on behalf of another party thereto', which is not what they say.

In my judgment, none of these arguments is sufficiently clinching to provide an
g immediate answer to the problem, and one must look elsewhere for a solution. The key is, in my view, to be found by looking at the position of the principal, in a case where he has authorised his agent to make the representation, and had no reasonable grounds to believe that the representation was true. Common sense suggests that if anyone is liable under a statute concerned with representations inducing a contract it ought to be a principal as party to the contract. That this is, indeed, the case is shown by s 2(3), which
h contemplates that credit will be given as between the recoveries under sub-ss (1) and (2); and these relate to liabilities of the same person, as witness the words 'he' and 'his'. The liabilities under s 2(2) must attach to the principal, for they are conferred as an alternative to rescission, a remedy which is available only against a party to the contract. It follows, therefore, that the word 'person' in s 2(1) must be read as including the principal.

It may, however, be objected that even if this is so there is still room to read s 2(1) as
j creating an additional liability in the agent. I do not agree. The 1967 Act is concerned with representations made in the particular context of a contract, and it seems to me that it was aimed at the position of the parties to the contract. It was therefore natural that there should be created under sub-ss (1) and (2) rights which are prima facie absolute, and independent of any general duty of care, a concept which plays no part in the law of contract. The purpose of the 1967 Act was to fill a gap which existed, or was believed to exist, in the remedies of one contracting party for an innocent representation by the

other. But there was no such gap in the case of the agent; he was already subject to the ordinary liabilities in fraud and negligence, the doctrine of *Hedley Byrne & Co Ltd v Heller* a *& Partners Ltd* [1963] 2 All ER 575, [1964] AC 465 having been recognised before the 1967 Act was passed. What purpose would there be in creating an entirely new absolute liability, independent of proof that the representee fell within the scope of a duty of care, simply because the representor happened to be an agent, concerned in the making of a contract, but not himself a party to it? I can see none; and, since, as I have suggested, the words of s 2(1) must be read as extending to the principal, I consider that their operation b should be confined to him alone.

In arriving at this conclusion, I recognise that the opposite view has been expressed in *Chitty on Contracts* (24th edn, 1976) para 379 and *Spencer Bower and Turner on Actionable Misrepresentations* (3rd edn, 1974). I can only say that this is the kind of short point on which opinions may very well differ, and having reached my own I must put it into effect by answering the issue No, the thirteenth and fourteenth defendants cannot in law c be liable to the first or second plaintiffs, by reason of s 2(1) of the Misrepresentation Act 1967.

An interesting argument was addressed by counsel for the fourteenth defendant to the effect that his client as sub-sub-agent could not be liable under the 1967 Act, even if the thirteenth defendants did incur liability, but in the circumstances it is unnecessary to express an opinion on it. d

Order accordingly.

Solicitors: *Holman Fenwick & Willan* (for the plaintiffs); *Sinclair Roche & Temperley* (for the thirteenth defendants); *McHale & Co* (for the fourteenth defendant).

e

K Mydeen Esq Barrister.

Burgess and another v Purchase & Sons (Farms) Ltd and others f

CHANCERY DIVISION
NOURSE J
6, 7, 26 OCTOBER 1982

g

Valuer – Valuation – Mistake – Speaking valuation – Shares – Private company – Valuation for purposes of sale – Price to be fixed by valuer – Valuer's decision to be final, binding and conclusive – Basis of valuation stated on face of valuation – Transfer of shares effected on basis of valuation – Transferor seeking declaration that valuation fundamentally erroneous – Whether statement of claim disclosing reasonable cause of action – Whether party to a contract can impugn contract if speaking valuation shows valuation to be erroneous – Whether completion of transaction before h *proceedings are commenced a bar to declaratory relief.*

The articles of association of a private company gave members of the company a right of pre-emption, at a fair value, over the issued shares in the capital of the company, the fair value of shares to be fixed by the company's auditors, whose decision was to be final, binding and conclusive. On the death of a shareholder his executors, the plaintiffs, gave j the company notice of sale as required by the company's articles of association in respect of the deceased's shareholding. Thereupon, under the articles, the company became the plaintiffs' agents for the sale of the deceased's shares to a member of the company. The company's auditors, by a letter to the directors of the company, purported to fix the fair value of the deceased's shares for the purposes of the sale and explained in the letter how they had arrived at their valuation. Because the auditors gave reasons for their valuation

it was therefore a 'speaking' valuation. The plaintiffs informed the company that they
a did not accept the auditors' valuation because it was excessively low and was computed on wrong principles. Nevertheless the company notified the plaintiffs that pursuant to the articles of association it had declared a contract between the plaintiffs and a member of the company for the sale of the deceased's shares to that member at the valuation fixed by the auditors. The plaintiffs maintained their objection to the auditors' valuation but the company, pursuant to the articles, effected a compulsory transfer of the shares to the
b member and registered him as the holder of the shares. A cheque for the price of the shares valued in accordance with the auditors' valuation was deposited in an account in the company's name on behalf of the plaintiffs. The plaintiffs, though conceding that a sale and purchase of the shares to the member had been duly completed in accordance with the articles, refused to accept payment for the shares and issued a writ against the company, the member and the auditors alleging that on several grounds the auditors'
c valuation was fundamentally erroneous, contrary to the articles and was negligently prepared. The plaintiffs sought declarations as against the company and the member that the valuation was not binding on the plaintiffs, that they were entitled to a new valuation of the shares and that the member was bound to purchase the shares at the price fixed by the new valuation, and in the alternative claimed damages for negligence against the auditors. The company and the member applied to strike out the plaintiffs' action under
d RSC Ord 18, r 19 or under the court's inherent jurisdiction on the ground that the statement of claim did not disclose any cause of action against them, contending that, just as a non-speaking valuation could not be impugned by a party to the contract pursuant to which it was made, so a speaking valuation could not be impugned, even if the valuation was fundamentally erroneous.

e **Held** – A speaking valuation which was made by an expert pursuant to a contract to have a valuation made and which demonstrated on its face that it had been made on a fundamentally erroneous basis could be impugned by a party to the contract. Moreover, the fact that the transaction dependent on the valuation had been completed before the plaintiff commenced proceedings to impugn the valuation did not automatically constitute a bar to his obtaining declaratory relief in the proceedings to declare the
f valuation invalid, the question whether such relief should be granted being a matter for the court's discretion at the trial. Accordingly, on the assumption that the auditors' valuation could be impugned on the grounds put forward in the statement of claim, it followed that the statement of claim could not be struck out as failing to disclose a reasonable cause of action against the company and the member who had purchased the shares (see p 10 *c g h*, p 11 *b c j* and p 12 *b c e*, post).

g *Johnston v Chestergate Hat Manufacturing Co Ltd* [1915] 2 Ch 338 and *Frank H Wright (Constructions) Ltd v Frodoor Ltd* [1967] 1 All ER 433 applied.

Campbell v Edwards [1976] 1 All ER 785 distinguished.

Dean v Prince [1954] 1 All ER 749, *Arenson v Arenson* [1975] 3 All ER 901, *Sutcliffe v Thackrah* [1974] 1 All ER 859 and *Baber v Kenwood Manufacturing Co* [1978] 1 Lloyd's Rep 175 considered.

h Per curiam. The fact that a plaintiff may have a remedy against the valuer is irrelevant to the question of his remedy against the other party to the valuation contract (see p 11 *g*, post).

Notes

j For the valuation of shares by auditors on a compulsory transfer, see 7 Halsbury's Laws (4th edn) para 399.

Cases referred to in judgment

Arenson v Arenson [1973] 2 All ER 235, [1973] Ch 346, [1973] 2 WLR 553, CA; *rvsd* [1975] 3 All ER 901, [1977] AC 405, [1975] 3 WLR 815, HL, Digest (Cont Vol D) 1016, *26a*.

Baber v Kenwood Manufacturing Co [1978] 1 Lloyd's Rep 175, CA.
Campbell v Edwards [1976] 1 All ER 785, [1976] 1 WLR 403, CA, Digest (Cont Vol E) **a** 643, *5a*.
Dean v Prince [1954] 1 All ER 749, [1954] Ch 409, [1954] 2 WLR 538, CA; *rvsg* [1953] 2 All ER 636, [1953] Ch 590, [1953] 3 WLR 271, 9 Digest (Reissue) 605, *3609*.
Gouriet v Union of Post Office Workers [1977] 3 All ER 70, [1978] AC 435, 3 WLR 300, HL, 16 Digest (Reissue) 265, *2528*.
Johnston v Chestergate Hat Manufacturing Co Ltd [1915] 2 Ch 338, 9 Digest (Reissue) 592, **b** *3540*.
Jones v Jones [1971] 2 All ER 676, [1971] 1 WLR 840, Digest (Cont Vol D) 1016, *12b*.
Sutcliffe v Thackrah [1974] 1 All ER 859, [1974] AC 727, [1974] 2 WLR 295, HL, 7 Digest (Reissue) 455, *2626*.
Wright (Frank H) (Constructions) Ltd v Frodoor Ltd [1967] 1 All ER 433, [1967] 1 WLR 506, Digest (Cont Vol C) 1051, *12a*. **c**

Motion

By a writ and statement of claim dated 22 December 1981 the plaintiffs, Sylvia Burgess and William James Milligan Richards, as executors of the will of William Purchase deceased, who died on 18 July 1978, claimed against the defendants, Purchase & Sons (Farms) Ltd, Angus Henry Lewis Purchase (Mr Purchase) and Edwards & Keeping, a firm **d** of chartered accountants, (1) a declaration that the valuation prepared by Edwards & Keeping of the ordinary £1 shares and the 3% non-cumulative preference £1 shares in the company registered in the name of William Purchase at the date of his death was not binding on the plaintiffs for the purposes of art 7 of the company's articles of association; (2) a declaration that the plaintiffs were entitled to a new valuation of the shares in accordance with art 7(h) of the articles of association; (3) a declaration that Mr Purchase **e** was bound to purchase the shares at a price per share determined in accordance with such new valuation; (4) an order that Mr Purchase should pay to the plaintiffs such sum as equalled the aggregate price of the shares purchased by him from the plaintiffs determined according to the new valuation; and (5) alternatively, against the accountants, damages for negligence. By a notice of motion dated 31 March 1982 the company and Mr Purchase sought an order, under RSC Ord 18, r 19 or the court's inherent jurisdiction, **f** striking out those parts of the statement of claim whereby the plaintiffs claimed against them, on the ground that the statement of claim disclosed no reasonable cause of action against them. The facts are set out in the judgment.

Lionel Levine for the company and Mr Purchase.
David A S Richards for the plaintiffs. **g**

Cur adv vult

26 October. The following judgment was delivered.

NOURSE J. The question in this case is whether it is still the law that a valuation made **h** by an expert and not an arbitrator and so expressed as to demonstrate that it has been made on a fundamentally erroneous basis can be impugned by a party to the contract pursuant to which it was made. The question arises on an application by two of three defendants to strike out an action relating to the shares in a family farming company called Purchase & Sons (Farms) Ltd. It is said that the statement of claim discloses no reasonable cause of action against those two defendants and that the action is otherwise **j** an abuse of the process of the court.

The company was incorporated in 1954 for the purpose of acquiring a business which had been carried on for many years previously near Wimborne in Dorset, originally by two brothers, Mr W J Purchase and Mr Henry Purchase. Mr W J Purchase died some years ago. In due course the 6,000 ordinary shares in the company came to be held as to

2,750 by his son, Mr William Purchase, as to 284 by Mr Henry Purchase and as to the remaining 2,966 by the latter's son Mr Angus Purchase who is the second defendant in these proceedings. The 8,334 issued preference shares were held by Mr William Purchase and Mr Henry Purchase in equal shares. Mr William Purchase died on 18 July 1978. It is following his death that the dispute in this action has arisen. The executors of his will are the plaintiffs, Mrs Sylvia Burgess and Mr W J M Richards. On 25 September 1978, within three months of Mr William Purchase's death, the plaintiffs, pursuant to art 7(b) and (g) of the company's articles of association, gave the company notice that they desired to sell Mr William Purchase's shares in the company. The effect of that was to constitute the company the agent of the plaintiffs for the sale of those shares to any member of the company 'at the fair value'. Article 7(h) is in these terms:

> 'The fair value of the shares of the company shall be fixed by the auditor of the company whose decision shall be final, binding and conclusive.'

In a letter to the directors of the company dated 29 December 1978 the company's auditors fixed the values of each of the plaintiffs' ordinary and preference shares at £10·50 and 10p respectively. That letter explained how the valuation of the ordinary shares had been arrived at. It is therefore agreed that it was in the modern parlance a 'speaking' as opposed to a 'non-speaking' valuation.

In a letter dated 7 February 1979 the plaintiffs' solicitors informed the company's solicitors that the plaintiffs did not accept the value put on the shares by the auditors. They said that the value appeared to them to be inordinately low and computed on wrong principles. They added that they would be taking steps for a declaration that the plaintiffs were not bound by the value determined by the auditors, and in the alternative, if such value was binding on them, for damages against the auditors in negligence.

By a letter dated 19 February 1979 the company gave notice to the plaintiffs that pursuant to art 7(c) it had declared a contract between the plaintiffs and Mr Angus Purchase for the sale of Mr William Purchase's shares to him at a price of £10·50 per ordinary share and 10p per preference share. The plaintiffs maintained their objection and thereafter steps were taken, pursuant to other provisions of art 7, to effect a compulsory transfer of the shares to Mr Angus Purchase and to register him as the holder of them. A cheque for £29,291·70, being the correct amount of the purchase price of the shares as valued by the auditors, was deposited in an account in the name of the company on behalf of the plaintiffs. It remains there to this day, the plaintiffs having refused to accept payment. However, they accept for the purposes of this application that the sale and purchase were duly completed in accordance with the provisions of art 7 before the commencement of these proceedings.

This action was commenced by a writ endorsed with a statement of claim issued on 22 December 1981. The defendants are the company, Mr Angus Purchase and the auditors. Paragraph 17 of the statement of claim alleges that the auditors prepared the valuation of the shares on a fundamentally erroneous basis and contrary to art 7(h) in four respects, which are then particularised. Paragraph 18 alleges that in the premises the auditors failed to fix the fair value of the shares in accordance with art 7(h) and that the valuation is not binding on the plaintiffs. Paragraph 19 alleges that the auditors owed a duty (amongst others) to the plaintiffs to exercise due skill and care in the preparation of the valuation, and para 20 that they acted in breach of that duty in the four respects particularised in para 17 and also in five additional respects which are then themselves particularised. Paragraph 21 alleges that if, contrary to their primary contention, the valuation is binding on the plaintiffs, then they have suffered loss and damage by reason of the auditors' breaches of duty. Particulars of damage are given which proceed on the basis that the fair value of each ordinary share at the material date was £65 and not £10·50. The prayer for relief claims declarations that the valuation is not binding on the plaintiffs, that they are entitled to a new valuation, and that Mr Angus Purchase is bound to purchase the shares at a price per share determined in accordance with such new valuation; and also an order that he pay the plaintiffs (in effect) the difference between what he has already paid and the amount which the new valuation discloses that he ought to pay. There is then an alternative prayer against the auditors for damages for *a* negligence.

The plaintiffs' case can therefore be summarised as follows. They say that the valuation was prepared both on a fundamentally erroneous basis and negligently, but they recognise that if they can get a new valuation their cause of action against the auditors in negligence will not be perfected because they will not have suffered any damage. The company is evidently a necessary party to the proceedings, because if the plaintiffs are *b* entitled to have the art 7 procedures reopened it is important that it should be bound by any order which is made. However, it is clear that the effective defendants are Mr Angus Purchase and the auditors.

In support of their claim that the statement of claim discloses no reasonable cause of action as against them, the company and Mr Angus Purchase contend that as a result of certain recent cases in the Court of Appeal it is no longer the law, if indeed it was before, *c* that a speaking valuation made by an expert on a fundamentally erroneous basis can be impugned by a party to the contract pursuant to which it was made. They say that there is now no difference in this respect between a speaking and a non-speaking valuation.

I was referred to a number of authorities on this point. The cases in the present century are *Johnston v Chestergate Hat Manufacturing Co Ltd* [1915] 2 Ch 338; *Dean v Prince* [1953] 2 All ER 636, [1953] Ch 590; [1954] 1 All ER 749, [1954] Ch 409, CA; *Frank H Wright* *d* *(Constructions) Ltd v Frodoor Ltd* [1967] 1 All ER 433, [1967] 1 WLR 506; *Jones v Jones* [1971] 2 All ER 676, [1971] 1 WLR 840; *Arenson v Arenson* [1973] 2 All ER 235, [1973] Ch 346, CA; [1975] 3 All ER 901, [1977] AC 405, HL; *Campbell v Edwards* [1976] 1 All ER 785, [1976] 1 WLR 403, CA; and *Baber v Kenwood Manufacturing Co* [1978] 1 Lloyd's Rep 175, CA.

The judgment of Sir David Cairns in the last case contains a most helpful review of all *e* but one of these authorities and also four others decided in the old Court of Chancery between 1753 and 1869. The exception is *Johnston v Chestergate Hat Manufacturing Co Ltd* on which Harman J based his decision in *Dean v Prince* [1953] 2 All ER 636, [1953] Ch 590 that a speaking valuation made on a fundamentally erroneous basis can be impugned. It is a case which may have been overlooked in recent times. It had to be considered in the present case because counsel who appears for the defendants was disposed to suggest *f* that Harman J's view of a speaking valuation depended on a false analogy with trustees and directors, who, having a fiduciary duty to consider whether they should or should not do a particular act, give reasons for their decision. However in *Johnston v Chestergate Hat Manufacturing Co Ltd* Sargant J held that on the face both of an auditor's certificate and of a balance sheet which had to be read with it the certificate had obviously been based on a wrong principle and was therefore not binding. That case was therefore a *g* sound basis for Harman J's decision, whether his analogy was a good one or not. The decision of Roskill J in *Frank H Wright (Constructions) Ltd v Frodoor Ltd* is a third decision at first instance to the same effect.

Counsel for the defendants relied strongly on judgments of Lord Denning in three of the cases to which I have referred. In *Dean v Prince* [1954] 1 All ER 749 at 758–759, [1954] Ch 426–427, as Denning LJ, he thought that a valuation made by an expert and *h* not an arbitrator could be impeached not only for fraud but also for mistake or miscarriage. He made no distinction between a speaking and a non-speaking valuation. He said that in considering the matter the cases about the personal liability of a valuer ought to be put on one side. They showed that he was not liable to an action unless he was dishonest. In 1954 it was certainly understood to be the law that the valuer could not be liable in negligence. That, however, was shown to have been a misunderstanding by *j* the decision of the House of Lords in *Arenson v Arenson*, a case of a non-speaking valuation of shares in a private company. The disappointed shareholder sued the other shareholder and the valuers in proceedings in which the relief claimed was substantially the same as that claimed in the present action. On the basis of the law as then understood the valuers applied to have the action struck out as against them. In that, they were successful up to the Court of Appeal, where Lord Denning MR dissented, holding that the auditors should be kept in the action because there was a doubt whether the valuation could be a impeached for mistake. Lord Denning MR referred to the decision of Harman J in *Dean v Prince* in relation to a speaking valuation and said ([1973] 2 All ER 235 at 242, [1973] Ch 346 at 363): 'This may be right, though I am not quite sure about it.' Neither Buckley LJ nor Sir Seymour Karminski considered the point at all, since they did not think that the question what remedy, if any, the purchaser might have against the vendor had any relevance to the question whether the valuers were liable in negligence or not. It would b seem that the same view was taken by the House of Lords, since none of their Lordships made any reference to it. *Campbell v Edwards*, the third of Lord Denning's cases, was another case of a non-speaking valuation, in which the plaintiff and the defendant had been the landlord and tenant respectively of a flat in Mayfair. The lease required the tenant not to assign without first offering a surrender to the landlord at a price fixed by a chartered surveyor to be agreed between them. A surveyor was agreed and the price c fixed at £10,000. The tenant then went out of possession and the landlord went into possession in circumstances where there was clearly a surrender by operation of law. The landlord afterwards obtained two much lower valuations, £3,500 and £1,250, and claimed that he was not bound by the £10,000 valuation. On those facts it is hardly surprising that the tenant's application to strike out the landlord's statement of claim was successful at all stages of the litigation. I would think that the modern law of promissory d estoppel would have been well up to the task of defeating the landlord, although presumably not before trial. In any event the Court of Appeal proceeded primarily on the ground of contract. Lord Denning MR said that the law on the subject had been transformed by *Arenson v Arenson* and *Sutcliffe v Thackrah* [1974] 1 All ER 859, [1974] AC 747, which dealt with architects. A valuer could now be sued in negligence. He said that in former times (when it was thought that the valuer was not liable for negligence) the e courts used to look for some way of upsetting a valuation which was shown to be wholly erroneous. He then referred to his own judgment in *Dean v Prince*. He said that the earlier cases had now to be reconsidered and that he had reconsidered them in *Arenson v Arenson*. Lord Denning MR said ([1976] 1 All ER 785 at 788, [1976] 1 WLR 403 at 407):

> 'I stand by what I there said. It is simply the law of contract. If two persons agree f that the price of property should be fixed by a valuer on whom they agree, and he gives that valuation honestly and in good faith, they are bound by it. Even if he has made a mistake they are still bound by it. The reason is because they have agreed to be bound by it. It there were fraud or collusion, of course, it would be very different. Fraud or collusion unravels everything. It may be that if a valuer gives a speaking valuation—if he gives his reasons or his calculations—and you can show on the face g of them that they are wrong, it might be upset. But this is not such a case. Messrs Chesterton simply gave the figure. Having given it honestly, it is binding on the parties. It is no good for either party to say that it is incorrect.'

That was not a concluded view, far less a decision in relation to a speaking valuation. Geoffrey Lane LJ agreed in terms which also left the point open.

h *Campbell v Edwards* was followed in *Baber v Kenwood Manufacturing Co* by another Court of Appeal consisting of Megaw, Lawton LJJ and Sir David Cairns. That was another case of a non-speaking valuation in which the status of a speaking valuation was again left open. It is nevertheless an authoritative decision which requires careful consideration in this court. All three members of the court emphasised that the question depended on the terms of the contract between the parties. Sir David Cairns considered implied as j well as express terms. There are some differences of emphasis, but no disagreements, to be found in the three judgments. At this stage I need only refer to two passages in the judgment of Megaw LJ. He said ([1978] 1 Lloyd's Rep 175 at 179) that if the valuers had in error valued the shares of some different company or had given their valuation by reference to the wrong number of shares, the plaintiffs would not have been bound by the valuation because it would then be shown to have been a valuation which was not in accordance with the express terms of the contract. I think it clear that the position would be exactly the same if the valuation were to be made by someone other than him on whom the parties had agreed: cf *Jones v Jones*. Then Megaw LJ (at 180) said that he would have regarded it as a question for careful consideration whether, if there had been any earlier authority to the contrary, it would continue to be properly regarded as binding, because of the possible effect on the whole basis of such earlier authority of the decisions of the House of Lords in *Sutcliffe v Thackrah* and *Arenson v Arenson*.

Counsel for the defendants accepted that neither *Campbell v Edwards* nor *Baber v Kenwood* was a decision in regard to a speaking valuation. The general effect of his argument was that those cases demonstrate that the Court of Appeal would now make no distinction between a speaking and a non-speaking valuation and that I should act on that demonstration. It seems to me that I could not tread that path without trespassing on the rarest ethers of speculation. The function of a judge of first instance is to apply the law as it stands. He is not to speculate on what some higher court may one day declare it to be. If the law is declared by earlier decisions at first instance he ought to follow them unless he is satisfied that they are wrong. In this case the law is declared by three earlier decisions at first instance. I am certainly not satisfied that they are wrong. I must therefore follow and apply them.

Counsel also relied strongly on the fact that the transaction in the present case had been completed before the proceedings were commenced. That was a point which was expressly considered by the Court of Appeal in *Campbell v Edwards* [1976] 1 All ER 785 at 788, [1976] 1 WLR 403 at 407, where Lord Denning MR said:

> 'But even if the valuation could be upset for mistake, there is no room for it in this case. The premises have been surrendered to the landlord. He has entered into occupation of them. Months have passed. There cannot be restitutio in integrum.'

Geoffrey Lane LJ said ([1976] 1 All ER 785 at 789, [1976] 1 WLR 403 at 408):

> 'The parties here had agreed on a valuer. They had agreed as to the terms on which the valuer was to value the property and on which he was to be instructed. The valuation took place, it was acted on, and the tenant surrendered the lease. It is a common law situation in which there is no room for an equitable remedy.'

I agree with Sir David Cairns in *Baber v Kenwood Manufacturing Co* [1978] 1 Lloyd's Rep 175 at 183 in thinking that these passages show that it was an alternative ground of the decision in *Campbell v Edwards* that the valuation had been acted on and the transaction completed. It is, however, very important to note that not merely had the transaction been completed but the valuation acted on and acted on by both parties. I have already expressed the tentative view that the landlord might well have been defeated by the doctrine of promissory estoppel at trial, but whether that be right or wrong the facts of that case are a long way removed from those of the present. It is no doubt true that the transaction here was technically completed, but the valuation has not been acted on by the plaintiffs who have consistently maintained their objection and refused to accept the purchase moneys. In my view it is impossible to say now that the completion of the transaction before the proceedings were commenced will be an automatic bar to the plaintiffs' obtaining declaratory relief at trial. It is true that such relief, although not equitable, is to an extent discretionary. Nevertheless the question whether it should be granted or not is essentially one for the trial when all material considerations, and not just one, can be taken into account. I should add that this question was not one which had to be considered in any of the three earlier decisions on speaking valuations.

There is a further point in regard to uncompleted transactions which I have found very difficult. Since it relates to non-speaking valuations and does not arise in this case, I will deal with it as briefly as I can. In *Baber v Kenwood Manufacturing Co* one of the grounds on which counsel for the plaintiff sought to distinguish *Campbell v Edwards* was that in the latter case the shares had not been transferred and the transaction remained uncompleted. All three members of the court clearly thought that that was not a valid distinction on the facts of that case. However, it does seem to me to be possible to read the judgments, and in particular that of Sir David Cairns, as not having wholly excluded

the power of equity to refuse specific performance (or an injunction) in the case of an
a uncompleted transaction relating to a non-speaking valuation. That would mean that the party who wished to sustain the valuation would be left to his remedy in damages. I have been unable to decide with confidence whether that is a correct reading of *Baber v Kenwood* or not. On balance I think it is. But even supposing that that is so it is still very uncertain in what circumstances the valuation would nowadays be sustained but the equitable relief refused.

b In my judgment the present state of the law can be summarised as follows. The question whether a valuation made by an expert on a fundamentally erroneous basis can be impugned or not depends on the terms expressed or to be implied in the contract pursuant to which it is made. A non-speaking valuation made of the right property by the right man and in good faith cannot be impugned, although it may still be possible, in the case of an uncompleted transaction, for equitable relief (as opposed to damages) to
c be refused to the party who wishes to sustain the valuation. On the other hand, there are at least three decisions at first instance to the effect that a speaking valuation which demonstrates that it has been made on a fundamentally erroneous basis can be impugned. In such a case the completion of the transaction does not necessarily defeat the party who wishes to impugn the valuation.

Whether this will hereafter be found to be the law to be applied to speaking valuations
d by some higher court is not for me to say. I merely proffer the following observations. It may be that the rule can be justified on the footing that a valuation made on a fundamentally erroneous basis is no more that for which the parties have contracted than one made of the wrong property or by the wrong man or in bad faith. The possibility of there being an implied term to that effect was discussed by Sir David Cairns in *Baber v Kenwood Manufacturing Co* [1978] 1 Lloyd's Rep 175 at 181. Where the contract provides
e for the valuation to be fair it might often be said that there was a breach of an express term. In either event there must remain something of an anomaly in that the right to impugn a valuation for fundamental error, as opposed to bad faith for example, depends solely on whether the evidence which makes the attack possible is or is not voiced by the valuation itself. The reconciliation may be that the law ought not to shrink from an anomaly where the court can see for itself a fundamental error on the face of the very
f exercise for which the parties have contracted. It may be that Harman J's analogy with trustees and directors is after all a sound basis for the rule.

As for the suggestion that the rule, if otherwise soundly based, ought now to be reconsidered in the light of *Arenson v Arenson* and *Sutcliffe v Thackrah* I must, with the greatest respect to the views of Lord Denning MR and Megaw LJ, if indeed they went that far, express my own view that that cannot be correct. Like Buckley LJ and Sir
g Seymour Karminski in *Arenson v Arenson* when dealing with the converse, I do not think that the question of what remedy, if any, the plaintiff may have against the valuers has any relevance to the question of what is his remedy against the other party to the contract. That course is charted between the Scylla of leaving the plaintiff with no remedy at all and the Charybdis of assuming that every valuation made on a fundamentally erroneous basis involves negligence on the part of the valuer, an assumption which no court of
h justice could make. Take for example the valuer who proceeds on a fundamentally erroneous construction of the agreement which it is not within his professional competence to detect. In such case there could be no invariable rule that the valuer was liable in negligence. Of greater practical significance, take the valuer who only agrees to act on terms that he is not to be liable in negligence, a protection which the law does not deny him. That example seems to me to be the clearest exposure of the plaintiff's plight
j and the surest ground for saying that the suggestion cannot be correct.

I have already said that para 17 of the statement of claim alleges that there were four respects in which the valuation of the shares was prepared on a fundamentally erroneous basis and contrary to art 7(h). It is neither necessary nor desirable that I should go into those matters in detail. It is enough for me to say that if made out, as I must assume that they will be, they would be capable of making good the plaintiffs' claim. Without prejudice to any other arguments which may be available to him, counsel who appears

for the plaintiffs and to whose argument I am much indebted submits that in the first and second respects and possibly the fourth there were breaches of express provisions of a
art 7. In the third respect he was disposed to rely solely on fundamental error, but it appears that if that point were to be made good it would necessarily follow that the valuation was unfair, since, without going into detail, it would have resulted in Mr Angus Purchase's acquiring the ordinary shares at a price roughly equivalent to half their resultant value to him.

The test to be applied in determining whether a statement of claim discloses a b
reasonable cause of action has been expressed by different judges in differing terms. I respectfully adopt the formulation of Lord Wilberforce in *Gouriet v Union of Post Office Workers* [1977] 3 All ER 70 at 76, [1978] AC 435 at 472 and ask myself whether, as the law stands, the plaintiffs' claim against the company and Mr Angus Purchase is manifestly ill founded in law. I answer that question in the negative.

The alternative claim is that the action is otherwise an abuse of the process of the court. c
As I understood his argument, counsel for the defendants relied first on the plaintiffs' delay in commencing their action and allowing the transfer and registration of the shares to proceed in the meantime. There is nothing in that point. Assuming, without deciding, that delay falling short of a relevant period under the Limitation Act 1980 could in extreme circumstances make the commencement of proceedings an abuse of process, I cannot see anything special, far less extreme, in the circumstances of the present case. d
Secondly, counsel submitted that the commencement of an action to which the auditors were joined as defendants as well as the company and Mr Angus Purchase was an abuse of process vis-à-vis Mr Angus Purchase because the attack on the auditors would prejudice the chances of their producing a second valuation of an acceptable nature. I am far from certain that I have recognised the true worth of that point, but if I have I am certain that there is no more in it than the first. All other considerations aside, I could not possibly e
assume that professional men would not in those circumstances be able and willing to make a fresh valuation on a correct basis.

The application is dismissed.

Application dismissed.

f

Solicitors: *Maxwell Batley & Co* (for the company and Mr Purchase); *Sharpe Pritchard & Co* (for the plaintiffs).

Hazel Hartman Barrister.

g

R v Tan and others

COURT OF APPEAL, CRIMINAL DIVISION
MAY LJ, PARKER AND STAUGHTON JJ
7, 8 DECEMBER 1982, 10 FEBRUARY 1983

h

Criminal law – Disorderly house – House used by one prostitute for provision of sexual services – Prostitute advertising that such services available there – Prostitute seeing only one client at a time – No one else present when prostitute providing services for client – Whether prostitute keeping a 'disorderly house'.

Criminal law – Prostitution – Living on earnings of prostitution – Man living on earnings of j
prostitution – Offence for a 'man' to live on earnings of prostitution – Accused a male at birth but subsequently undergoing sex change operation – Accused living on earnings of prostitution – Whether accused a 'man' living on earnings of prostitution – Sexual Offences Act 1956, s 30.

Criminal law – Prostitution – Living on earnings of prostitution – Male prostitution – Prostitute a male at birth but subsequently undergoing sex change operation and working as female prostitute – Accused living on prostitute's earnings – Whether accused living on earnings of prostitution of 'another man' – Sexual Offences Act 1967, s 5(1).

A single prostitute who provides services in private premises to one client at a time
a without spectators is guilty of the common law offence of keeping a disorderly house if it is proved that the services provided are open to the public and are of such a character and are conducted in such a manner (whether by advertisement or otherwise) that their provision amounts to an outrage of public decency or is otherwise calculated to injure the public interest to such an extent as to call for condemnation and punishment (see p 18 *g h*, post).

b *R v Higginson* (1762) 2 Burr 1232, *R v Rogier* (1823) 2 Dow & Ry KB 431, *R v Berg, Britt, Carré and Lummies* (1927) 20 Cr App R 38, *Shaw v DPP* [1961] 2 All ER 446, *R v Quinn* [1961] 3 All ER 88 and *R v Brady* [1964] 3 All ER 616 considered.

A person who was born a male and remains biologically a male but who has undergone a sex change operation is neverthelesss capable of being convicted under s 30[a] of the Sexual Offences Act 1956 of being 'a man' who lives on the earnings of prostitution.
c Similarly, if such a person engages in prostitution, a man or woman who lives on that person's earnings as a prostitute is guilty of the offence of living on the earnings of the prostitution 'of another man' contrary to s 5(1)[b] of the Sexual Offences Act 1967 (see p 19 *f* to *j*, post).

Corbett v Corbett (orse Ashley) [1970] 2 All ER 33 applied.

d **Notes**

For the common law offence of keeping a disorderly house, see 11 Halsbury's Laws (4th edn) para 1057, and for cases on the subject, see 15 Digest (Reissue) 1054–1055, 9076–9078.

For living on the earnings of prostitution, see 11 Halsbury's Laws (4th edn) paras 1068, 1070.

e For the Sexual Offences Act 1956, s 30, see 8 Halsbury's Statutes (3rd edn) 433.

For the Sexual Offences Act 1967, s 5, see ibid 580.

Cases referred to in judgment

Corbett v Corbett (orse Ashley) [1970] 2 All ER 33, [1971] P 83, [1970] 2 WLR 1306, 27(1) Digest (Reissue) 29, *137*.

f *Jenks v Turpin* (1884) 13 QBD 505, DC, 8(2) Digest (Reissue) 644, *176*.

R v Berg, Britt, Carré and Lummies (1927) 20 Cr App R 38, CCA, 14(2) Digest (Reissue) 507, *4150*.

R v Brady, R v Ram [1964] 3 All ER 616, CCA, 15 Digest (Reissue) 1055, *9078*.

R v Higginson (1762) 2 Burr 1232, 97 ER 806, 15 Digest (Reissue) 1055, *9080*.

R v Quinn, R v Bloom [1961] 3 All ER 88, [1962] 2 QB 245, [1961] 3 WLR 611, CCA, 15
g Digest (Reissue) 1055, *9077*.

R v Rogier (1823) 2 Dow & Ry KB 431.

Shaw v DPP [1961] 2 All ER 446, [1962] AC 220, [1961] 2 WLR 897, HL, 14(1) Digest (Reissue) 139, *965*.

Appeals and applications for leave to appeal

h On 28 September 1982 in the Crown Court at Inner London Sessions, before Mr R U Thomas sitting as an assistant recorder and a jury (1) the appellant Moira Tan was convicted of keeping a disorderly house at 89b Warwick Way, London SW1 (count 1), was sentenced to six months' imprisonment and was deprived of property rights in

---

j *a* Section 30 provides:

'(1) It is an offence for a man knowingly to live wholly or in part on the earnings of prostitution.

(2) For the purposes of this section a man lives who lives with or is habitually in the company of a prostitute, or who exercises control, direction or influence over a prostitute's movements in a way which shows he is aiding, abetting or compelling her prostitution with others, shall be presumed to be knowingly living on the earnings of prostitution, unless he proves the contrary.'

b Section 5(1), so far as material, provides: 'A man or woman who knowingly lives wholly or in part on the earnings of prostitution of another man shall be liable . . . (*b*) on conviction on indictment to imprisonment for a term not exceeding seven years.'

apparatus found on the premises, (2) the appellant Gloria Gina Greaves was convicted (i) of keeping a disorderly house at 89b Warwick Way, London SW1 (count 1), (ii) of a keeping a disorderly house at 15 Clarendon Street, London SW1 (count 2) and (iii) of living on the earnings of prostitution (of the applicant Tan) contrary to s 30 of the Sexual Offences Act 1956 (count 3), was sentenced to six months' imprisonment, concurrent, on counts 1 and 2, and to twelve months' imprisonment, consecutive, on count 3, and was also fined £10,000 on count 3 (or six months' consecutive imprisonment in default of payment) and deprived of property rights in apparatus found at 89b Warwick Way and b 15 Clarendon Street, (3) the appellant Brian Greaves was convicted of living on the earnings of prostitution (through his association with Gloria Greaves) contrary to s 30 of the 1956 Act (count 4), and of living on the earnings of male prostitution (of the appellant Gloria Greaves), contrary to s 5 of the Sexual Offence Act 1967 (count 5). Each of the appellants appealed against conviction on points of law. The appellant Tan appealed against sentence by leave of Bush J. The appellants Gloria Greaves and Brian Greaves c applied for leave to appeal against sentence. Their applications were referred by Bush J to the full court. The facts are set out in the judgment of the court.

Nicholas Freeman for the appellant Tan.
Andrew Patience for the appellants Gloria Greaves and Brian Greaves.
John P V Bevan for the Crown. d

At the conclusion of the hearing of the appeals May LJ announced that for reasons to be given later the court (1) would allow the appeal of Brian Greaves against his conviction on count 4 and would quash that conviction, but that all the other appeals against conviction would be dismissed, (2) would grant the applications for leave to appeal against sentence, treating the hearing as the hearing of the appeals against sentence, and e (3) would allow all the appeals against sentence inasmuch as all sentences would be suspended for two years.

10 February. The following judgment of the court was delivered.

PARKER J. On 28 September 1982 the appellants were convicted in the Crown Court f at Inner London Sessions on an indictment containing five counts. On count 1, Tan and Gloria Greaves were convicted of keeping a disorderly house at 89b Warwick Way, London SW1, and were each sentenced to six months' imprisonment. Both were, in addition, deprived of property rights in apparatus found at such premises. On count 2, Gloria Greaves was convicted of keeping a disorderly house at 15 Clarendon Street, London SW1, and was sentenced to six months' imprisonment, concurrent with the g sentence on count 1, and was also deprived of property rights in apparatus found there. On count 3, Gloria Greaves was convicted of living on the earnings of prostitution contrary to s 30 of the Sexual Offences Act 1956, and was sentenced to twelve months' imprisonment, consecutive to the sentences imposed on counts 1 and 2, was fined £10,000 or six months' consecutive in default of payment and was ordered to pay the prosecution's costs. The total custodial sentence imposed on her thus amounted to h eighteen months' imprisonment. On count 4, Brian Greaves was convicted of living on the earnings of prostitution contrary to s 30 of the 1956 Act, and was sentenced to twelve months' imprisonment. On count 5, Brian Greaves was also convicted of living on the earnings of male prostitution contrary to s 5 of the Sexual Offences Act 1967, and was sentenced to twelve months' imprisonment, concurrent with the sentence on count 4.

All the appellants appealed on points of law. Tan appealed against sentence by leave of j the single judge. Applications by Gloria Greaves and Brian Greaves for leave to appeal against sentence were referred by the single judge to the full court. The single judge also granted all three defendants bail, pending the hearing of their appeals and applications.

The appeals against conviction, the appeal against sentence and the applications for leave to appeal against sentence were heard on 7 and 8 December 1982. On the conclusion of the hearing, the appeal of Brian Greaves against his conviction on count 4 was allowed and that conviction was quashed, but all other appeals against conviction were dismissed.

The applications for leave to appeal against sentence were granted and the hearing treated as the hearing of the appeals against sentence. All the appeals against sentence were allowed, to the extent only that all sentences of imprisonment were suspended for two years. We then said that we would give our reasons later. This we do now. We deal first with counts 1 and 2.

At 89b Warwick Way, Tan, and at 15 Clarendon Street, Gloria Greaves, provided sexual services for reward to those wishing to receive them. Tan rented 89b Warwick Way from Greaves. The services provided were of a like nature in each case. They involved the use of much equipment of a similar kind and were provided in the case of Warwick Way by Tan alone and in the case of Clarendon Street by Gloria Greaves alone. They were provided in private, in that there were no other participants than the client or customer and, in the one case, Tan, and, in the other, Greaves. In no case were there any observers. There might, however, from time to time, be a customer waiting in a neighbouring room whilst a previous customer was in receipt of the services for which he had come to the premises.

The services provided at both premises were of a particularly revolting and perverted kind. Straightforward sexual intercourse was not provided at all. With the aid of a mass of equipment, some manual (such as whips and chains), some mechanical and some electrical, clients were subjected, at their own wish and with their full consent, to a variety of forms of humiliation, flagellation, bondage and torture, accompanied often by masturbation.

The availability of the services provided at both premises was advertised extensively, including by insertion in what are known as 'contact magazines', which are published and available to the public. An example of such an advertisement, in relation to each of the premises, is as follows. 89b Warwick Way:

> 'Humiliation enthusiast, my favourite pastime is humiliating and disciplining mature male submissives, in strict bondage, lovely tan coloured mistress invites humble applicants, T.V., C.B., B., D. and rubber wear, 12 p.m. to 7 p.m. Mon. to Fri. 89 Basement Flat, Warwick Way, Victoria, SW1.'

15 Clarendon Street:

> 'The most equipped mistress in Town, report now for C.P., W.S., D.H.N. Racks, stocks, pillory, dungeon, T.V.'s wardrobe, stiletto heels, boots, rubber, leather, E-shocks, Maid training etc. etc. You name it? Madam has it, also madam does nursing treatments, intimate examinations, Victorian and modern enemas. Bottle and breast feeding. Nappy changing by Nanny. Report to Madam Stern, 15 Clarendon Street, Basement Flat, Victoria, London, SW1.'

It will be noted that in these two cases, addresses but not telephone numbers are given. In other cases, there were telephone numbers provided and appointments could be made either by telephone or by going to the premises. The advertisements constitute a clear invitation to any member of the public so inclined to resort to the premises and there submit himself to perverted practices.

At the close of the prosecution case at the trial, it was submitted that there was no case to answer, on the ground that, where a single prostitute provided sexual services to a single client at a time in private in certain premises, such premises were incapable in law of being a disorderly house. That submission was rejected. The case was left to the jury, who duly convicted on both counts. No complaint is made of the summing up and it was indeed accepted that if premises are, despite the fact that the sexual services are always provided to a single client in private, capable of being a disorderly house, then both the premises here in question were virtually certain to be found by a jury to be within that description. The submission made at the trial was repeated before us as the only ground of appeal on counts 1 and 2.

Keeping a disorderly house is a common law offence, albeit that it received limited statutory attention in the Disorderly Houses Act 1751 in two respects, namely, first, that by s 2 places kept for public dancing, music or other public entertainment within or within 20 miles of the cities of London and Westminster were, unless licensed, deemed to be disorderly houses and, second, that by s 5 prosecutions were encouraged against those keeping bawdy-houses, gaming houses or other disorderly houses. We can find *a* little assistance in this Act on the question whether, as was submitted on behalf of the appellants, an essential ingredient of a disorderly house is a plurality of either participants or spectators. Such indication as there is suggests, however, that such plurality is not required. A bawdy-house would clearly cover a house in which two prostitutes operated entirely in separate rooms, never saw more than one client at a time and were never observed by anyone else, and the wording accepts or recognises that a bawdy-house is or *b* may be a disorderly house.

Two early cases were cited in argument, namely *R v Higginson* (1762) 2 Burr 1232, 97 ER 806 and *R v Rogier* (1823) 2 Dow & Ry KB 431. In the first of such cases, a motion in restraint of judgment on the ground that the indictment on which the defendant had been convicted was too general failed, but the court held the indictment good without giving reasons and without hearing argument. The particulars in the indictment certainly *c* alleged that 'certain evil and ill-disposed persons . . . come together . . . fighting of cocks, boxing, playing at cudgels and misbehaving themselves', but there is nothing to indicate that, had the indictment alleged that a succession of 'evil and ill-disposed persons' had resorted to the premises and there separately and successively indulged with the proprietor in 'cock-fighting, boxing, playing at cudgels and misbehaving', the indictment would have been bad. *d*

R v Rogier (1823) 2 Dow & Ry KB 431 is more helpful. The defendants were convicted of keeping a common gaming house and permitting an unlawful game called 'Rouge et Noir'. As in *R v Higginson*, there was a motion in restraint of judgment. In his judgment Abbott CJ said (at 433):

> 'If a common gaming house be so conducted that it becomes a receptacle for idle *e* and disorderly persons, who are permitted to assemble there and enter into play for sums of an illegal amount, it becomes a public nuisance, and the maintaining it is an offence indictable at common law; and if the game of "Rouge et Noir," or any other game, however innocent in itself, is played at by such persons, and to an excessive amount, it becomes an illegal game, and those who hold out to others the means of so playing at it are guilty of a common law offence.'

f

This case is of importance for two reasons. First, it shows that a game innocent in itself may become unlawful if it is played for stakes which a jury consider to be excessive. Second, it contains the plain statement that those who hold out to others the means of playing such a game are guilty of a common law offence. The reference to people being permitted to assemble was said to indicate that a plurality of persons was necessary. In its context, however, we have no doubt that it contains no such indication. It is no more *g* than a reference to the facts of the particular case. We should also mention that, if and in so far as this case appears to indicate that there can be no conviction for keeping a gaming house or indeed other disorderly houses unless there is a public nuisance, it has since been decided that this is unnecessary (see *R v Quinn, R v Bloom* [1961] 3 All ER 88, [1962] 2 QB 245, to which we revert hereafter).

h

The first case in which the definition of what constitutes a disorderly house was expressly considered was *R v Berg, Britt, Carré and Lummies* (1927) 20 Cr App R 38. The appellants in that case were convicted of a 'conspiracy to corrupt the morals of and to debauch persons resorting to a certain disorderly house', and two of them were convicted of keeping a disorderly house. The recorder, in directing the jury, had used the definition of 'disorderly' in *Webster's Dictionary*, namely 'Not regulated by the restraints of morality; unchaste; of bad repute, as a *disorderly* house'. In his judgment Avory J said (at 41–42): *j*

> 'The Recorder's definition, from Webster is somewhat vague, but would be correct if the element of keeping open house is present and there is added "being so conducted as to violate law and good order." . . . The argument that unless the house is open to the public at large its disorderliness is not indictable is refuted by *Rogier* ((1823) 2 Dow & Ry KB 431) cited by Hawkins J. in *Jenks* v. *Turpin* ((1884) 13 QBD

505): those cases referred to gaming houses, but the decisions equally apply to the practices here in question . . . The gist of the indictment was that the accused were lewd and immoral persons assembled for the purpose of unnatural practices.'

The facts of the case are not set out in the report, but it may be inferred that the accused and others took part in exhibitions of a perverted nature for the edification of those resorting to the premises. The case provides clear authority that (a) there must be some element of keeping open house, albeit the premises need not be open to the public at large, (b) the house must not be regulated by the restraints of morality, or must be unchaste or of bad repute, and (c) it must be so conducted as to violate law and good order.

The definition of disorderly house was further considered in *R v Quinn, R v Bloom* [1961] 3 All ER 88, [1962] 2 QB 245. The premises there in question were used for the performance of acts of strip-tease, some of which acts were, on the evidence, seriously indecent and, in some respects, revolting. The appellants were convicted of keeping a disorderly house and the convictions were upheld. The court, subject to two comments, accepted a definition which was advanced by the prosecution and derived, at least in part, from observations of the House of Lords in *Shaw v DPP* [1961] 2 All ER 446, [1962] AC 220. That definition was in the following terms ([1961] 3 All ER 88 at 91, [1962] 2 QB 245 at 255):

> 'A disorderly house is a house conducted contrary to law and good order in that matters are performed or exhibited of such a character that their performance or exhibition in a place of common resort (a) amounts to an outrage of public decency or (b) tends to corrupt or deprave or (c) is otherwise calculated to injure the public interest so as to call for condemnation and punishment.'

The two comments made by the court were, first, that the essence of the charge in that case was that indecent performances had taken place, and that the charge might be based on some other ground. The definition must therefore be taken as limited to cases in which indecent exhibitions are alleged. Second, although the elements specified in (a), (b) and (c) of the definition were expressed as alternatives, they should not be regarded as mutually exclusive.

In addition to accepting, subject to the two comments, the definition advanced by the prosecution, the court also rejected in short shrift both the argument that a public nuisance was a necessary ingredient of the offence and the argument that, since those resorting to the premises did not themselves take part in any indecent behaviour, the premises could not be a disorderly house.

The last case to which it is necessary to refer is *R v Brady, R v Ram* [1964] 3 All ER 616, where the court accepted without deciding that, in order to constitute the common law offence of keeping a disorderly house, some element of persistent use was required.

If the definition in *R v Berg, Britt, Carré and Lummies* is taken, there can be no doubt that there was evidence in the present case on which the jury could find that the premises were in each case not regulated by the restraints of morality. It is said, however, that it was not so conducted as to violate law and good order, since what took place between the defendants and each client was not itself a criminal offence and that there was not the necessary element of open house.

Both contentions we reject. A strip-tease performance is not itself a criminal offence, but *R v Quinn, R v Bloom* shows that it may so overpass what is acceptable, that it may become unlawful just as gaming may be excessive and thus unlawful. It is for the jury to set the standard. As to the element of open house, there was clearly a public invitation to resort to the premises for the purpose of indulging in perverted and revolting practices. This invitation by advertisement was equally clearly part of the conduct of the premises, and we have no doubt that it was open to the jury to find both that this constituted a sufficient element of open house and that, as a result, the premises were conducted in violation of law and good order.

In *Shaw v DPP* [1961] 2 All ER 446 at 460, [1962] AC 220 at 281 Lord Reid, in his minority opinion, said:

> 'The evidence shows that the invitations were to resort to certain of the prostitutes for the purpose of certain forms of perversion. That I would think to be an offence a for a different reason . . . the authorities . . . establish that it is an indictable offence to say or do or exhibit anything in public which outrages public decency . . . In my view, it is open to a jury to hold that a public invitation to indulge in sexual perversion does so outrage public decency as to be a punishable offence.'

Lord Reid was not prepared to go as far as other members of the House of Lords but, even on the basis of his minority opinion, it would have been open to the jury to hold b that the advertisements in the present case alone constituted an offence and thus that the premises were conducted contrary to law and good order.

Turning to the definition in *R v Quinn, R v Bloom*, it clearly cannot be applied in terms to the present case, for here there were no performances or exhibitions as such. If, however, *R v Berg, Britt, Carré and Lummies* and *R v Quinn, R v Bloom* are taken together, in the light of what was said in *Shaw v DPP*, we have no hesitation in rejecting the c submission made. Were it correct, it would mean that it would be open to anyone (so long as perverted practices were conducted with one client at a time) to advertise such services without restriction, no matter how revolting they might be, thereby encouraging the public to indulge in them and to allow others (so long as they did not observe or take part) to await their turn to partake of such practices.

No doubt a prosecution in circumstances like the present is novel. It was submitted d that the trend is for the criminal law to withdraw from concern with what takes place between consenting adults in private (with the single exception of buggery between a man and a woman) and that the courts should not create a new offence. We accept that the prosecution is novel, that the courts should not or should at least be slow to create new offences and that the tendency alleged exists. Novelty is, however, no valid objection (see *Berg* and *Shaw*) and to reject the submission is not to create a new offence but to hold e that a certain set of circumstances, not hitherto made the subject of the charge, fall squarely within the scope of an existing offence.

In *Quinn* the court did not seek to lay down an exhaustive definition. Nor do we. Many forms of conduct may fall within the scope of the offence, and to attempt to establish a universal definition with precision is both undesirable and impossible. It is, however, both desirable and possible to indicate how a jury should be directed, where the ground f on which the charge is based is that the premises are being used for the provision of sexual services. In such cases, the direction, adapting the definition in *R v Quinn, R v Bloom* [1961] 3 All ER 88 at 91, [1962] 2 QB 245 at 255, would in our judgment be that, in order to convict, the jury must be satisfied that the services provided are open to those members of the public who wish to partake of them and are of such a character and are conducted in such a manner (whether by advertisement or otherwise) that their provision g amounts to an outrage of public decency or is otherwise calculated to injure the public interest to such an extent as to call for condemnation and punishment. They should further be directed that the fact, if it be a fact, that the services are provided by a single prostitute to one client at a time and without spectators does not prevent the house being a disorderly house.

Finally, with regard to the appeal on counts 1 and 2, we observe that acceptance of the h submission would involve results that fly in the face of common sense. Premises would, for example, be incapable of being a disorderly house if there was a large notice in neon lights over the door containing an open invitation to be whipped or subjected to any form of perversion, with the tariff set out. Yet the law would be powerless to intervene, save, perhaps, under the Indecent Displays (Control) Act 1981, so long as the service itself was provided successively to those resorting to the premises and this would be so, j notwithstanding that the adjoining premises had similar notices and provided similar services. To hold that the law was powerless in such a case, but could act in the case of a much more discreet invitation so long as there was in addition to the prostitute and her client a watcher or watchers, offends against common sense.

In *Shaw v DPP* [1961] 2 All ER 446 at 453, [1962] AC 220 at 268 Viscount Simonds said:

> 'Let it be supposed that at some future, perhaps, early, date homosexual practices

> between adult consenting males are no longer a crime. Would it not be an offence
> a if, even without obscenity, such practices were publicly advocated and encouraged by pamphlet and advertisement? Or must we wait until Parliament finds time to deal with such conduct? I say, my Lords, that if the common law is powerless in such an event, then we should no longer do her reverence.'

It may well be that in the circumstances supposed by Viscount Simonds a jury would not now convict, but it is for the jury and not the judges to decide whether conduct exceeds
b the limits of what, at any period of time, is acceptable. For the judges to adopt the stance that no matter how it may be advertised or provided anything, except heterosexual buggery, is permissible between consenting adults in private would be for the judges partially to usurp the functions of juries. The judges' task is to determine whether conduct is capable of being a crime. It is for the jury to decide in an individual case whether it is.

c In the case of the two counts presently under consideration, the recorder rightly decided that it was open to the jury to convict. On the evidence, the jury did convict and it could not be and was not suggested that, if the legal submission failed, there was otherwise than ample evidence to justify the convictions in both cases.

For the above reasons, the appeals on counts 1 and 2 were dismissed.

An essential ingredient of the offences charged in counts 3 and 5 was that Gloria
d Greaves was a man. It was accepted that Gloria Greaves was born a man and remained biologically a man, albeit he had undergone both hormone and surgical treatment, consisting in what are called 'sex change operations', consisting essentially in the removal of the external male organs and the creation of an artificial vaginal pocket.

In *Corbett v Corbett (orse Ashley)* [1970] 2 All ER 33, [1971] P 83 it was held that a person who was born a man and remained biologically a man was a man for the purposes of
e marriage, and thus that a form of marriage between a man and another person born a man was a nullity, no matter that such last-mentioned person had undergone operative and other sex change treatment.

It was, however, contended that for the purposes of s 30 of the Sexual Offences Act 1956 and s 5 of the Sexual Offences Act 1967 another test should be applied; that, if the person had become philosophically or psychologically or socially female, that person
f should be held not to be a man for the purposes of the sections and that, on this basis, the evidence was inconclusive and the counts ought to have been withdrawn from the jury.

We reject this submission without hesitation. In our judgment, both common sense and the desirability of certainty and consistency demand that the decision in *Corbett v Corbett* should apply for the purpose, not only of marriage, but also for a charge under s 30 of the Sexual Offences Act 1956 or s 5 of the Sexual Offences Act 1967. The same
g test would apply also if a man had indulged in buggery with another biological man. That the *Corbett v Corbett* decision would apply in such a case was accepted on behalf of the appellant. It would, in our view, create an unacceptable situation if the law were such that a marriage between Gloria Greaves and another man was a nullity, on the ground that Gloria Greaves was a man; that buggery to which she consented with such other person was not an offence for the same reason; but that Gloria Greaves could live on the
h earnings of a female prostitute without offending against s 30 of the 1956 Act because for that purpose he/she was not a man and that the like position would arise in the case of someone charged with living on his earnings as a male prostitute.

A further ground of appeal was raised in relation to count 3, namely that the jury were incorrectly, or insufficiently, directed as to the ingredients of the offence. As to this we need say no more than that having carefully considered the summing up we can discern
j no insufficiency of directions or any misdirection. The appeals on counts 3 and 5 were accordingly dismissed.

There remained, so far as the convictions were concerned, only the appeal of Brian Greaves against his conviction on count 4, which was allowed. We can deal with this very shortly.

When directing the jury on this count, the recorder stated initially that the prosecution relied on the presumption in s 30(2) of the Sexual Offences Act 1956. This was not in fact the case. The recorder mistakenly thought that count 4 charged Greaves with living on the earnings of Gloria Greaves and thus that the presumption would arise if he was living with Gloria Greaves or was habitually in the latter's company. He carefully and properly directed the jury as to the effect of the section and the burden of proof, but it was then pointed out to him by the prosecution that count 4 did not relate to Brian Greaves living on the earnings of Gloria Greaves, but of Tan and another prostitute, with neither of whom was he living, and thus that no question of a presumption under s 30(2) arose. The recorder then withdrew his direction to the jury with regard to that subsection, but gave no further direction, other than to say that the prosecution had to prove everything.

We are satisfied that, on withdrawal of his earlier direction, the recorder should, however shortly, have reminded the jury of the precise matters of which they had to be satisfied before they could convict Greaves of living on the earnings of either Tan or the other prostitute. In the absence of such a direction, the jury may well have been left in a state of some confusion and uncertainty. This being so, the verdict on this count could only be regarded as unsafe and unsatisfactory. It follows, therefore, that the conviction had to be quashed.

We turn now to the sentences. Apart from the custodial sentences, no point was pressed before us and we do not, therefore, find it necessary to deal with the orders for deprivation of property rights against Tan and Gloria Greaves, or the £10,000 fine and costs awarded against Gloria Greaves. We need only say that they were fully justified. As to the custodial sentences, we have no doubt that custodial sentences of the lengths imposed were also fully justified. Indeed, they exhibit a degree of leniency, no doubt flowing from the fact that in the case of Tan and Gloria Greaves they genuinely believed that they were not offending against the law. We considered, however, that the uncertainties in the law justified the exercise of further leniency and that it would be appropriate to suspend the sentences. It should, however, be known that in the case of others offending in like manner immediate custodial sentences of greater length can be expected.

In the case of Brian Greaves the position is different. He was undoubtedly living on the earnings of Gloria Greaves, whether a man or a woman, and can have been in no doubt on the subject. On the other hand, on count 5, which is the only conviction against him which survives and the only charge of living on the earnings of Gloria Greaves, it is said and we accept, first, that he had gone through a ceremony of marriage with and regarded Gloria Greaves as a female and, second, that there was no element of coercion involved. This being so, we considered it right in this case also to suspend the sentence.

This judgment and the sentences likely to be imposed in the future will, we hope, serve as a warning to others that to invite the public to resort to premises and there indulge in conduct going beyond the limits which a jury regard as tolerable is criminal conduct, even if those responding are attended to in succession and in private, and that such criminal conduct may well result in immediate custodial sentences.

All appeals against conviction dismissed with the exception of Brian Greaves's appeal against his conviction on count 4, which was allowed. All appeals against sentence allowed to the extent that all the sentences of imprisonment were suspended for two years.

The court refused leave to appeal to the House of Lords but extended, under s 34 of the Criminal Appeal Act 1968, the time in which application for leave to appeal might be made to the House by 14 days and certified, under s 33(2) of that Act, that the following point of law of general public importance was involved in the decision: whether premises could be a disorderly house, notwithstanding that every sexual act that took place therein was between a single prostitute and a single customer unobserved by any other person.

14 April. The Appeal Committee of the House of Lords (Lord Diplock, Lord Bridge of Harwich and Lord Brandon of Oakbrook) dismissed petitions by the appellants Tan, Gloria Greaves and Brian Greaves for leave to appeal.

Solicitors: *Coles & Stevenson* (for the appellant Tan); *Knapp-Fishers* (for the appellants Gloria Greaves and Brian Greaves); *D M O'Shea* (for the Crown).

April Weiss Barrister.

a

Hill and others v Rochard and another

COURT OF APPEAL, CIVIL DIVISION
EVELEIGH AND DUNN LJJ
24, 25 JANUARY 1983

b *Rent restriction – Alternative accommodation – Suitable to needs of tenant as regards extent and character – Character – Tenant's life-style in old accommodation – Amenities incidental to accommodation – Tenant occupying large period country house in isolated position with outbuildings, stable and adjoining field – Tenants able to keep open house for family and friends – Tenants keeping pony and numerous house pets – New accommodation consisting of detached modern house on estate near country village – New accommodation not having stable or field – Whether 'needs' of tenant restricted to housing needs – Whether tenant's personal life-style in old* c *accommodation and enjoyment of incidental amenities relevant considerations – Rent Act 1977, s 98(1)(a), Sch 15, para 5(1)(b).*

The tenants, a husband and wife, held a lease of a large period country house in an isolated position and which had a staff flat, outbuildings, stable, large garden and an d adjoining field on which they kept a pony. The tenants paid a rent of £2,100 per annum. The staff flat enabled them to have live-in help, and the size of the house enabled them to keep numerous pets and open house for their family and friends. They enjoyed the isolated position of the house, the life-style which its size enabled them to have, and the use of the amenities ancillary to the house, i e the stable and the field etc. When the lease expired they held over as statutory tenants. The landlords wished to sell the house, which e was worth nearly £100,000, and invest the proceeds in order to get a better return on its capital value. They purchased for the sum of £52,500 a modern detached house with four bedrooms, two living rooms, a double garage and garden, situated on a pleasant estate on the outskirts of a country village, and offered it to the tenants as suitable alternative accommodation. The tenants considered that they would not be able to enjoy in the alternative accommodation either their existing life-style or the amenities that f went with their existing accommodation and refused to give up possession of the house. The landlords brought an action against the tenants, contending that they had offered the tenants alternative accommodation which was reasonably suitable 'to the needs of the [tenants] as regards extent and character', for the purposes of para 5(1)(*b*)[a] of Sch 15 to the Rent Act 1977, and were therefore entitled to a possession order under s 98(1)(*a*)[b] of that Act on the ground that the tenants had been offered 'suitable alternative accommodation'. g The judge held that the test of suitable alternative accommodation was whether it met the needs of an ordinary reasonable tenant as regards extent and character, and found that the offered accommodation, both in regard to its extent and character, met that standard. The judge accordingly made an order for possession against the tenants. The tenants appealed, contending that the proper test of suitable alternative accommodation was whether it met the needs of the particular tenant in question, having regard, inter h alia, to its 'character', which meant taking into account whether the tenants would be able to continue the life-style and enjoy the same amenities which they had in the existing accommodation.

Held – In determining for the purposes of para 5(1)(*b*) of Sch 15 to the 1977 Act whether j alternative accommodation offered to a tenant was suitable to his 'needs' as regards 'character' the court could only have regard to the housing needs of the particular tenant in question, i e his needs for accommodation for habitation, which did not include his ability to enjoy the life-style and incidental amenities (such as a stable) which he enjoyed

a Paragraph 5(1), so far as material, is set out at p 26 *h*, post
b Section 98(1), so far as material, is set out at p 26 *a*, post

in his existing accommodation. The environment and the standard of living to which the tenant was accustomed in his existing accommodation were, however, relevant *a* factors, but since the alternative accommodation offered to the tenants was in a country environment which would enable them to enjoy the amenities of country life and since it was of a sufficiently high standard to provide for their particular housing needs it was 'suitable alternative accommodation' for the purposes of s 98(1)(*a*) of the 1977 Act. The landlords were accordingly entitled to possession. The tenants' appeal would therefore be dismissed (see p 26 *j*, p 27 *b* to *j* and p 28 *c* to *f*, post). *b*

Dicta of Edmund Davies LJ in *MacDonnell v Daly* [1969] 3 All ER at 854 and of Buckley LJ in *Redspring Ltd v Francis* [1973] 1 All ER at 643 considered.

Notes

For suitable alternative accommodation, see 27 Halsbury's Laws (4th edn) para 664, and for cases on the subject, see 31(2) Digest (Reissue) 1106–1112, *8581–8628*. *c*

For the Rent Act 1977, s 98, Sch 15, para 5, see 47 Halsbury's Statutes (3rd edn) 504, 614.

Cases referred to in judgments

Briddon v George [1946] 1 All ER 609, CA, 31(2) Digest (Reissue) 1110, *8616*.
Christie v Macfarlane 1930 SLT (Sh Ct) 5. *d*
Clark v Smith (16 July 1920, unreported).
MacDonnell v Daly [1969] 3 All ER 851, [1969] 1 WLR 1482, CA, 31(2) Digest (Reissue) 1109, *8611*.
Middlesex CC v Hall [1929] 2 KB 110, [1929] All ER Rep 398, DC, 31(2) Digest (Reissue) 1108, *8598*.
Redspring Ltd v Francis [1973] 1 All ER 640, [1973] 1 WLR 134, CA, 31(2) Digest (Reissue) *e* 1111, *8264*.

Appeal

John Vivian Rochard and his wife, Peggie Rochard, the statutory tenants of a house called The Grange, The Street, Alveston, Avon, appealed against the judgment of her Honour Judge Counsell given on 30 July 1982 in the Bristol County Court in an action for *f* possession brought against them by John Charles Cathorne Hill and Peter Kirwan-Taylor (the landlords), the freeholders of the house, whereby the judge ordered the tenants to give up possession of the house on or before 30 October 1982 on the ground that it was reasonable to make a possession order within s 98(1) of the Rent Act 1977 and suitable alternative accommodation was available for the tenants, within s 98(1)(*a*). The ground of the appeal was that the judge misdirected herself in regard to the test to be applied in *g* determining whether the accommodation offered by landlords was suitable alternative accommodation within the 1977 Act. The facts are set out in the judgment of Dunn LJ.

Richard Gordon for the tenants.
Paul Morgan for the landlords.

h

DUNN LJ (delivering the first judgment at the invitation of Eveleigh LJ). This is an appeal from an order of her Honour Judge Counsell sitting in the Bristol County Court when, on 30 July 1982, she made an order for possession of premises known as The Grange, The Street, Alveston, Avon, such possession to be given on 30 October 1982. This court granted a stay pending this appeal.

The judge held that a house at 2 Chestermaster Close, Almondsbury, about three and *j* a half miles from The Grange, constituted suitable alternative accommodation and that it was reasonable to make an order. She made the order under s 98(1) of and Part IV of Sch 15 to the Rent Act 1977.

The tenants now appeal to this court. Section 108 of the County Courts Act 1959, as amended by the Supreme Court Act 1981, provides, in effect, that where an order is

made under the provisions to which I have referred, which include the question of
a reasonableness, no appeal lies on any question of fact. So the only effective ground of appeal is that the judge misdirected herself in respect of the test to be applied in determining whether or not the accommodation offered by the landlords constituted suitable alternative accommodation.

The tenants are husband and wife. They are now aged 63 and 64 respectively. On 20 February 1967 they took an assignment of the residue of a lease of The Grange for 14
b years from 4 April 1962. The rent was originally £400 a year, but as a result of various increases it is now some £2,100 a year. The lease expired on 28 September 1975, and the tenants then held over as statutory tenants.

The Grange was described by the judge as a handsome period country house with a large number of rooms, a staff flat, outbuildings, stable and a large garden. On the assignment the lease was varied to include a field across the road, and the total amount of
c land is some one and a half acres. The house is centrally heated by solid fuel, but the heating is not used by the tenants as they prefer to use the numerous open fires. The tenants have become very attached to the house and do not wish to move. The judge described it as not being in superb condition. It costs up to £1,000 a year to maintain.

In 1976 the original landlord, Mr Charles Hill, died, and The Grange vested in his executors and the trustees of his estate, who are the plaintiffs in the action. The property
d has been valued at between £90,000 and £100,000 and the trustees formed the view that the rent of £2,100 a year constituted an unreasonably low return on that asset. They wish to sell the house and invest the proceeds so as to obtain a greater return on the capital for the benefit of the beneficiaries under the will. They offered the tenants, as alternative accommodation, a cottage nearby. The tenants refused the offer, so the landlords started the present proceedings.

e In November 1980 Judge Counsell saw The Grange and also the cottage, and after the viewing indicated, before even hearing the evidence of the tenants, that she did not regard the cottage as suitable alternative accommodation, and she adjourned the case. Thereafter the landlords offered the tenants some six other premises as alternative accommodation. They were all refused.

In October 1981 the landlords bought the house, 2 Chestermaster Close, for £52,500
f specifically for the purpose of rehousing the tenants. Again the tenants refused the offer. 2 Chestermaster Close is a modern detached house with four bedrooms, a bathroom, a downstairs shower room, a modern kitchen, a utility room, a communicating living and dining room, and an integral double garage. The judge described it as a convenient to run house set in a pleasant estate in a cul-de-sac on the outskirts of the village of Almondsbury. It has oil-fired central heating, no open fires, and one-eighth of an acre of
g garden, including a lawn, flower beds and vegetable garden.

The judge visited 2 Chestermaster Close, and she also visited The Grange again, before she reached her decision that Chestermaster Close constituted suitable alternative accommodation.

Numerous reasons were advanced by the tenants why 2 Chestermaster Close did not constitute suitable alternative accommodation. Although the tenants live alone they very
h much enjoy their life-style at The Grange. They like living in a large country house with no houses, apart from cottages, anywhere near. They do not want to live on an estate with other houses on either side. They particularly like a bit of land, which they have been accustomed to for some time, not only for the unimpeded view it affords them but also because they keep an old pony and want room for another to keep it company. They have two dogs and ten cats. They say that they could keep none of these animals, or at
j any rate not nearly so many of them, in Almondsbury because of possible annoyance to the neighbours. They like the spacious rooms of The Grange and say that the rooms at Chestermaster Close would not accommodate their furniture. They like living-in help and want the necessary accommodation. They like to keep open house for their friends and relatives. Their daughter lives nearby. Her marriage is difficult and they want enough room to accommodate her and her two children if necessary. Mrs Rochard is a

follower of the Krishnamurti Foundation and she wants room to hold meetings at her home. Finally, Mr Rochard was said to be claustrophobic and did not want to live in suburbia, as he described Chestermaster Close.

The judge, in a careful judgment, dealt at length with these various points and made findings of fact on them. She concluded that the tenants did not wish to move from The Grange and would use any permissible reason to prevent this coming about. These findings of fact cannot be disturbed; but complaint is made of her direction as to the law. In her judgment she said:

> 'The standard I have to adopt is that of an ordinary tenant and not one which will gratify to the full "all the fads and fancies and preferences of the tenant". The Rochards are not ordinary tenants and for the past 15 years they have not been ordinarily housed. They are both now in their sixties and resist a change. The accommodation offered is modern, easy to run, and by ordinary standards generous accommodation. The accommodation at Chestermaster Close does not compare exactly with that at The Grange but it does not have to. The test is: does it meet the standards of the needs of an ordinary and reasonable tenant? I am satisfied that it does, both as to extent and as to character.'

It is said by counsel for the tenants that that passage constituted a misdirection. The test, he said, is not whether the alternative accommodation offered meets the standard of needs of an ordinary and reasonable tenant: the test is whether the accommodation meets the standard of needs of these particular tenants. In considering that question regard may be had to the life-style of the tenants in their present accommodation, and if that life-style cannot be continued in the alternative accommodation offered, then that alternative accommodation is not suitable to the needs of the tenant.

In support of that submission counsel relied on two decisions of this court, the first of which is *MacDonnell v Daly* [1969] 3 All ER 851, [1969] 1 WLR 1482. That was a case in which the alternative accommodation offered was two of three rooms which had previously been occupied by the tenant. The judge dismissed the landlord's claim, holding that the two rooms were not suitable alternative accommodation. This court upheld the judge's finding, but counsel for the tenants relies, in particular, on certain obiter dicta of Edmund Davies LJ in relation to *Briddon v George* [1946] 1 All ER 609, which was a case where the landlord was offering the tenant alternative accommodation which did not include a garage, whereas the premises occupied by the tenant did include a garage. Edmund Davies LJ said ([1969] 3 All ER 851 at 854, [1969] 1 WLR 1482 at 1487):

> 'This court there held that the dwelling-house itself was the unit which fell to be considered throughout the Rent Restriction Acts, that these Acts were concerned with the provision only of a suitable habitation, and that the absence of a garage could not, therefore, be taken into consideration in deciding the suitability of the alternative accommodation offered. I venture respectfully to doubt whether the same decision would be arrived at by this court under the circumstances prevailing, not in 1946, but in 1969. One thinks of the common case of the man who went into the premises originally because they had a garage, without which they would be wholly unsuitable to him. Is it to be said in these days that to offer him premises which lack that which was an essential requirement for him when he initially went into possession and so remains, constitutes the provision of suitable alternative accommodation? Circumstances have changed so much that considerable doubts arise in my mind whether such question would be answered today as it was 23 years ago.'

Counsel for the tenants submits that that case indicates that, in considering the suitability of needs, the court is not simply confined to the provision of suitable habitation but can also have regard to other amenities enjoyed by the tenant in his present accommodation.

He also referred us to *Redspring Ltd v Francis* [1973] 1 All ER 640, [1973] 1 WLR 134, which he said established the same point. In that case the tenant, who occupied a flat in a quiet residential road, was offered alternative accommodation in a flat which, unlike the first flat, had no garden and was in a busy traffic thoroughfare with a fried fish shop next door. The county court judge made the order for possession and this court allowed the appeal, holding that what a tenant needed was somewhere he could live in reasonably comfortable conditions suitable to the style of life which he led. Counsel relied particularly on a passage in the judgment of Buckley LJ where, after referring to a concession which had been made by counsel for the landlord, he said ([1973] 1 All ER 640 at 643, [1973] 1 WLR 134 at 138):

> 'That concession was, in my judgment, properly made. For if a tenant who occupies accommodation in a residential area is offered other accommodation which may be physically as good as or better than the accommodation which he is required to vacate but is situated in an area which is offensive as the result of some industrial activity in the neighbourhood, which perhaps creates offensive smells or noises, or which is extremely noisy as a result of a great deal of traffic passing by, or in some other respect is clearly much less well endowed with amenities than the accommodation which the tenant is required to vacate, then it seems to me that it would be most unreal to say that the alternative accommodation is such as to satisfy the needs of the tenant with regard to its character. What he needs is somewhere where he can live in reasonably comfortable conditions suitable to the style of life which he leads, and environmental matters must inevitably affect the suitability of offered accommodation to provide him with the sort of conditions in which it is reasonable that he should live.'

Sachs LJ said ([1973] 1 All ER 640 at 645, [1973] 1 WLR 134 at 140):

> 'In each case it is a question of fact having regard to the needs of the tenant in the circumstances as a whole. The view which I have just expressed coincides with the tenor of those sparsely reported decisions of the court (eg in the Estates Gazette) to which reference has already been made. Any other view of the meaning of the relevant words would, indeed, produce astonishing results, some of which were canvassed in the course of argument. It would result in accommodation on the third floor of premises facing on to Edgware Road being necessarily held to be equivalent in character to a quiet third floor flat in nearby Montagu Square. Another example was put of a cottage in a quiet country lane which has one character and that of a cottage of identical construction which finds itself implanted in or entangled with a new M-road.'

Counsel for the tenants submitted that those two cases supported his proposition, to which I have referred, and he also drew attention to the fact that *Christie v Macfarlane* 1930 SLT (Sh Ct) 5 had been cited in argument in *Redspring Ltd v Francis*. He pointed out that *Christie v Macfarlane* had been cited to the judge in this case and that it contains a reference to the ordinary tenant, and includes the phrase used by the judge taken from *Clark v Smith* (16 July 1920, unreported):

> 'The alternative accommodation need not be a dwelling-house in which all the fads and fancies and preferences of the tenant shall be gratified to the full.'

(See 1930 SLT (Sh Ct) 5 at 10.)

This citation, he said, misled the judge.

He submitted that the two cases of *MacDonnell v Daly* and *Redspring Ltd v Francis* show that the court is not concerned, as might appear from *Christie v Macfarlane*, with the needs of the ordinary tenant, but is concerned with the needs of the tenant in question, and those needs include the ability of the particular tenant, in his new accommodation, to follow the life-style which he had enjoyed in the old accommodation.

For myself I prefer to go first to the relevant statutory provisions before considering how they have been construed. Section 98(1) of the Rent Act 1977 provides as follows:

> 'Subject to this Part of this Act, a court shall not make an order for possession of a dwelling-house which is for the time being let on a protected tenancy or subject to a a statutory tenancy unless the court considers it reasonable to make such an order and either—(*a*) [and this is the material provision] the court is satisfied that suitable alternative accommodation is available for the tenant or will be available for him when the order in question takes effect . . .'

Then sub-s (4):

> b 'Part IV of Schedule 15 shall have effect for determining whether, for the purposes of subsection (1)(*a*) above, suitable alternative accommodation is or will be available for a tenant.'

So we turn to Part IV of Sch 15. Paragraph 3 provides:

> 'For the purposes of section 98(1)(*a*) of this Act, a certificate of the housing c authority for the district in which the dwelling-house in question is situated, certifying that the authority will provide suitable alternative accommodation for the tenant by a date specified in the certificate, shall be conclusive evidence that suitable alternative accommodation will be available for him by that date.'

No certificate has been issued in this case, but that paragraph may have some relevance when one comes to construe para 5 which is the material paragraph in this case. d Paragraph 4 provides:

> 'Where no such certificate as is mentioned in paragraph 3 above is produced to the court, accommodation shall be deemed to be suitable for the purposes of section 98(1)(*a*) of this Act if it consists of either—(*a*) premises which are to be let as a separate dwelling such that they will then be let on a protected tenancy [and that is e the situation in this case. But the paragraph goes on:] . . . and, in the opinion of the court, the accommodation fulfils the relevant conditions as defined in paragraph 5 below.'

Then para 5(1):

> 'For the purposes of paragraph 4 above, the relevant conditions are that the f accommodation is reasonably suitable to the needs of the tenant and his family as regards proximity to place of work, and either—(*a*) similar as regards rental and extent to the accommodation afforded by dwelling-houses provided in the neighbourhood by any housing authority for persons whose needs as regards extent are, in the opinion of the court, similar to those of the tenant and of his family . . .'

There was, in fact, a certificate from the local housing authority. It was a certificate g certifying that 'the needs of a family of two comprising a husband and wife would be a one- or two-bedroom flat or house including one or at the most two living rooms'. The certificate had been issued some years before in, we were told, 1979. The judge did not purport to rely on sub-para (1)(*a*) of para 5, but in a rider to her judgment she said that she thought that the fairest way of dealing with it was to use the certificate as a guide.

Then para 5(1)(*b*) provides— h

> '. . . or (*b*) reasonably suitable to the means of the tenant and to the needs of the tenant and his family as regards extent and character . . .'

It was para 5(1)(*b*) which was the material provision in this case.

In my judgment the word 'needs' means 'needs for housing', and the question is whether the accommodation offered is reasonably suitable for the tenant's housing needs j as regards extent and character. Paragraph 3, to my mind, with its reference to the local housing authority, reinforces the construction that I have put on sub-para (1)(*b*) of para 5.

It has not been seriously suggested, in this appeal, that 2 Chestermaster Close is not suitable as regards extent. A four-bedroomed house with two living rooms is perfectly extensive enough for an elderly couple living alone, as these tenants are.

The argument in this court has revolved around the word 'character'. The sub-paragraph does not provide, and it is not necessary, that the character of the alternative accommodation should be similar to that of the existing premises. Indeed, there are, in this case, certain obvious differences between the character of The Grange and the character of 2 Chestermaster Close. 2 Chestermaster Close is a modern house and not a period house. It stands in a housing estate and does not stand alone. But the question is whether 2 Chestermaster Close is reasonably suitable to the tenants' housing needs as regards its character. In considering those needs the cases to which I have referred show that it is permissible for the court to look at the environment to which the tenants have become accustomed in their present accommodation, and to see how far the new environment differs from that. The new house is on the outskirts of a village, and the tenants will, in ordinary parlance, still be living in the country. It is not as if they have been offered accommodation on a housing estate in a town. In so far as their style of life is relevant they will still be able to enjoy the amenities of country life. Indeed, looked at from the point of view of reasonable suitability, as this court is required to do by the paragraph, many people would say that a modern house in a country village is more suitable to the needs of people of the ages of these tenants than a large isolated country house such as The Grange.

In my view the judge was right to say that these tenants were not ordinary tenants. By that I take her to mean that, accommodation aside, the present tenancy enabled them to enjoy the use of certain amenities, including the paddock and outbuildings, so that they could keep their animals. Even on a liberal construction of the statutory provisions I do not think that the Rent Acts were intended to protect incidental advantages of that kind. The Rent Acts are concerned with the provision of housing and accommodation. In her judgment the judge said:

> 'I accept Lower Almondsbury is not precisely similar to The Street, but it is a country village, many would say a pleasant country area which in my judgment will permit the Rochards to live reasonably comfortably in the life-style they like to lead. Not precisely in the way they can at The Grange but in a reasonably similar way. Accordingly I find the plaintiffs have satisfied me that suitable alternative accommodation is available to the Rochards.'

That crucial finding followed immediately after a citation by the judge from *Redspring Ltd v Francis*, when she cited Buckley LJ's observations about the tenant needing somewhere where he can live in conditions suitable to the style of life which he leads. The judge must have had those observations of Buckley LJ in mind when she made her finding, which is directed not to the ordinary tenant but to these particular tenants. I find no fault in that finding. Nor can this court interfere with the judge's finding that it was reasonable to make an order. That was essentially a matter for the judge. She balanced the detriments, if I may so describe them, to the landlords on the one side if no order was made, against the position of the tenants if an order was made, and she came down plainly in favour of the landlords.

This court cannot interfere with a determination of that kind. I would accordingly dismiss this appeal.

EVELEIGH LJ. I agree. Paragraph 5(1)(*b*) of Part IV of Sch 15 to the Rent Act 1977 requires the court to consider whether the accommodation is reasonably suitable to the means of the tenant and to the needs of the tenant and his family as regards extent and character. Like Dunn LJ I would not seek to introduce words which would reformulate that test but to work from the words of the statute itself.

However, those words have to be considered in the context of housing accommodation. The protection of the Acts relates to a dwelling house. In *Briddon v George* [1946] 1 All ER 609 at 613 Scott LJ referred to *Middlesex CC v Hall* [1929] 2 KB 110, [1929] All ER Rep 398 and said:

> 'The headnote says that the court consisting of TALBOT, J., and HUMPHREYS, J.,

came to the conclusion that: "The alternative accommodation which must be offered to the tenant by an applicant for possession under the Rent Restriction Acts of a premises used as a dwelling-house and also as business premises, need only be as regards their user as a dwelling-house, and not as regards their user as business premises." In the judgment of the court delivered by TALBOT, J., there is this sentence ([1929] 2 KB 110 at 114, [1929] All ER Rep 398 at 400): "But the court, having regard to the scope and object of the Act, which protected dwelling-houses only, considered that the words 'alternative accommodation available for the tenant' b must be confined to accommodation for the purposes of habitation." That case was decided under sect. 5(1)(*d*) of the Act of 1920, but that principle, I have no doubt, was in the mind of the Legislature in determining the details of subsect. (3) of sect. 3 of the Act of 1933.'

I myself have no doubt that that consideration was in the minds of the legislature in relation to the Rent Act 1977. Therefore you consider the needs of the tenant for the c purposes of habitation. Proximity to place of work is specifically made an independent consideration by Sch 15 itself and the inductory words to para 5. Proximity to entertainment, recreation or sport is not relevant to the test of suitability, and proximity to a paddock or stable is, in my view, also not relevant.

The court must apply, as Dunn LJ has said, para 5(1)(*b*), and the word is 'needs', that is to say the needs of the tenant for accommodation for the purpose of habitation. Of course d you consider the actual tenant and his standard of living, but from the point of view of accommodation needs. We are asked to consider, among other factors, the peculiarly personal desires and interests of these tenants, which go far beyond anything covered by the word 'needs'. It seems to me that in the argument which has been addressed to us in relation to the character of the house, at the end of the day, we are also being asked to say that the character is unsuitable, not from the point of view of these tenants' needs but in e relation to their peculiar wishes and desires, their own particular taste for amenities, which go again beyond their needs even for persons who are entitled to sustain a high standard of living.

I agree with the judgment which Dunn LJ has just delivered.

I would just add one point. In the course of argument, in response probably to a question put by the court (I have forgotten what), the court was told that the rent of these f premises was higher than that which had been thought to be the case in the court below, and counsel has asked this court to have regard to that fact also. No formal application had been made, no notice had been given of any application to adduce further evidence, and there is nothing on the facts of this case to indicate that the rent, whatever it is, is unsuitable to the means of this particular tenant. So that all we have been told in effect is that the rent is higher than it was thought to be, and is higher than the rent that was g being paid for The Grange. That is not enough to make it a relevant consideration in a decision whether or not the possession order was right in this case.

So, for myself, I do not regard that additional information as affecting this appeal in any way at all.

Appeal dismissed. Order for possession within 28 days. Leave to appeal to the House of Lords refused. h

Solicitors: *Lyons Davidson & Co*, Bristol (for the tenants); *Burges Salmon*, Bristol (for the landlords).

Henrietta Steinberg Barrister.

Lister v Quaife

a

QUEEN'S BENCH DIVISION
MAY LJ AND STEPHEN BROWN J
30 APRIL 1982

Criminal evidence – Written statement – Evidential value – Prosecution serving on defendant
b *copy of statement to be used at trial – Defendant not serving any notice requiring maker of*
statement to attend trial – Statement of prosecution witness read to court – Evidence given by
defendant contradicting evidence in prosecution witness's statement – Whether prosecution
witness's statement conclusive evidence of matters stated in it – Whether defendant entitled to
contradict statement – Criminal Justice Act 1967, s 9.

c On 24 July 1981 the defendant was stopped just after leaving a branch of a chain store
carrying a dress bearing one of the chain store's reduced price labels. She was unable to
produce any evidence that she had bought it and was taken to a police station where she
made a voluntary statement saying that she had bought it on 2 July at another branch of
the chain store and intended changing it. An information was preferred against her
charging her with theft of the dress. Before she appeared before the magistrates, the
d prosecutor notified her that he would be tendering in evidence under s 9[a] of the Criminal
Justice Act 1967 two written statements to the effect that it was not until 22 July, when
there had been a direction from the chain store's head office, that any such dress would
have been on sale at any of the store's branches at a reduced price, and that, in any event,
the branch where she claimed to have bought the dress had never stocked that particular
type of dress and even if it had accepted one returned by a customer of another branch
e the dress would have been marked with a different kind of label. The defendant's legal
advisers did not serve any notice under s 9(2)(*d*) requiring the makers of the statements
to attend and give evidence in person at the trial. At the defendant's trial the statements
were read out by the prosecutor. The defendant gave evidence to the effect that she had
bought the dress on 2 July and that a mistake must have been made by the chain store.
The prosecutor submitted to the magistrates that once they accepted the statements
f which had been tendered under s 9, it was not open to the defendant to give evidence
contradicting those statements. The magistrates held that the defendant's explanation of
what had happened was reasonable and that they were entitled to accept her evidence
despite the statements adduced by the prosecutor under s 9. They dismissed the
information on the ground that there was a reasonable doubt about the alleged theft.
The prosecutor appealed, contending that the magistrates' opinion was inconsistent and
g that their decision was perverse.

Held – On the true construction of the 1967 Act, a statement tendered under s 9 was not
deemed to be conclusive evidence of the matters stated in it but was to be treated in the
same way as if the maker of the statement had been called as a witness and given the
evidence contained in it. Although at the hearing of the charge against the defendant the
h proper procedure of putting the defence case to prosecution witnesses had not been
followed, the burden of proof nevertheless remained throughout on the prosecution, and
therefore even if the makers of the statements had been called as witnesses the magistrates
were still entitled to conclude that the prosecution had not established beyond reasonable
doubt that the defendant had stolen the dress. Accordingly the appeal would be dismissed
(see p 31 *d*, p 32 *h* to p 33 *c g h* and p 34 *a*, post).

j Per curiam. If the prosecution is confronted by a defendant who gives evidence
inconsistent with evidence set out in s 9 statements which have not been the subject of a
notice under s 9(2)(*d*) of the 1967 Act, they always have the right, under s 9(4)(*a*), to apply

a Section 9, so far as material, is set out at p 30 *h j* and p 31 *b*, post for an adjournment in order that the maker of the statement may attend to give evidence (see p 33 *c d* and *h*, post).

Per Stephen Brown J. Section 9 of the 1967 Act is a provision designed to save expense and trouble in many instances but, where evidence central to the issues in the case is in written statements served under s 9, the prosecution should give very careful consideration to calling the actual witness so that the proper impact of that evidence can be made on the court (see p 33 *h j*, post).

Notes

For proof by written statement, see 11 Halsbury's Laws (4th edn) para 433.

For the Criminal Justice Act 1967, s 9, see 8 Halsbury's Statutes (3rd edn) 585.

Case stated

Barry Spencer Lister appealed, by way of case stated by the justices for the county of Norfolk, acting in and for the petty sessional division of King's Lynn, against a decision of the justices whereby they dismissed an information preferred by him against the respondent, Elaine Margaret Quaife, alleging that on 24 July 1981 in the parish of King's Lynn in the county of Norfolk she stole one brassière valued at £3·50 and a dress valued at £11·99, the property of Marks & Spencer Ltd, contrary to ss 1 and 7 of the Theft Act 1968. The questions for the opinion of the High Court were (i) whether, when the respondent had accepted evidence adduced on behalf of the appellant under s 9(1) of the Criminal Justice Act 1967, it was open to the court to consider evidence from the respondent on the same point which contradicted that evidence already read out to the court under s 9(6) of the Act without first exercising the power under s 9(4)(*b*) to require the witnesses whose evidence had been read to attend and give evidence, (ii) if it was not open to the court to receive evidence as above, whether the justices should have invited the appellant to ask for an adjournment so that the witnesses whose evidence was being contradicted by the respondent could appear before them. The facts are set out in the judgment of May LJ.

Michael Lewer for the appellant.
Anthony Brigden for the respondent.

MAY LJ. This is a prosecutor's appeal by way of case stated from a decision of the Norfolk justices sitting at King's Lynn on 12 November 1981. By that decision the justices acquitted the respondent of a charge of theft, the goods allegedly stolen being a brassière and a dress from Marks & Spencer on 24 July 1981. The justices expressed the view that the evidence in relation to the alleged theft of the brassière was equivocal. This view the appellant realistically appreciates cannot be and is not challenged in this court and, accordingly, that article of clothing plays no further part in this appeal.

The appeal is concerned with the provisions and effect of s 9 of the Criminal Justice Act 1967. That is an extremely useful and very well-known section. So familiar have practitioners become with it and with its operation that its precise effect may not on occasions have been fully appreciated. By sub-s (1) it is provided:

> 'In any criminal proceedings, other than committal proceedings, a written statement by any person shall, if such of the conditions mentioned in the next following subsection as are applicable are satisfied, be admissible as evidence to the like extent as oral evidence to the like effect by that person.'

Subsection (2) sets out the various conditions, which need not be repeated here, except for para (*d*) which is to this effect:

> 'none of the other parties or their solicitors, within seven days from the service of the copy of the statement, serves a notice on the party so proposing objecting to the statement being tendered in evidence under this section.'

Thus if a party to criminal proceedings, other than committal proceedings, is served with a a statement which it is proposed to read in evidence in the proceedings, that party so served has the power under that provision in para (*d*) of sub-s (2) to object to the statement being tendered in evidence. The consequence will, of course, be that the maker of the statement will be called in person to give the evidence which would otherwise have been contained in the statement.

I ought also to refer to s 9(4) which provides:

b 'Notwithstanding that a written statement made by any person may be admissible as evidence by virtue of this section—(*a*) the party by whom or on whose behalf a copy of the statement was served may call that person to give evidence; and (*b*) the court may, of its own motion or on the application of any party to the proceedings, require that person to attend before the court and give evidence.'

c The provisions of s 9 of the 1967 Act may be contrasted with those in s 10, which is the other familiar section permitting proof of facts by formal admission. It provides that where there has been a formal admission that shall be conclusive evidence of the fact admitted. There is no such equivalent provision in s 9 of the Act. That merely provides that a written statement shall be admissible in evidence as if the person who had made the statement had gone into the witness box and given that evidence. There is no d statutory provision that any such statement is to be deemed to be conclusive evidence of the matters stated in it.

In this particular case the facts are, as I have said, that it was alleged that the respondent had stolen a dress from the King's Lynn store of Marks & Spencer Ltd on 24 July 1981. This was a grey dress found in her possession when she was stopped after leaving the store, and was marked with a reduced price label stating a price of £11·99. When she e was asked about it, she said, and case before the justices was, that she had bought it at the Marks & Spencer's store in Portsmouth when she, with her husband, had been on holiday in Hayling Island during a period from the end of June to 4 July 1981. In an earlier statement, after she had been arrested, she had said that she had got it from the Bournemouth store of Marks & Spencer Ltd, but the error is understandable and, at any rate, no point was taken on it in the court below.

f That being the respondent's case, at any rate prior to trial, in those voluntary statements which she had made to the police, before the hearing before the justices the prosecution gave notice to the respondent or her legal advisers of two statements under s 9 of the Criminal Justice Act 1967, which, taken briefly, had the combined effect of evidence that until after 22 July 1981, when there had been a head office direction from Marks & Spencer, no such grey dress as the subject matter of the charge would have been on sale g anywhere in this country at the reduced price of £11·99. The original price of such a dress was £19·99. There was then a national direction from head office on 22 July that its price should be reduced to £11·99, and that a special reduced price label should be attached to such a dress. Further, the statements contained evidence to the effect that although the Bournemouth store of Marks & Spencer had had one such dress at a reduced price, this was not until after the head office direction of 22 July. In so far as Portsmouth h was concerned, that branch had had no stocks at all of this particular dress, although following the known practice of this particular organisation, if anyone had sought to return to the Portsmouth store a dress of this nature which they had bought elsewhere, it would have accepted it and refunded the price. Any such dress, however, returned to the Portsmouth store before 22 July would have been priced with a large white swing label and marked as an oddment. The dress which was recovered from the respondent in this case was not so marked.

j The appellant no doubt took the view that by adducing that evidence by those statements, unless and until they were objected to and the makers required to attend to give evidence, the material in those statements would be sufficient to satisfy the justices that the respondent's voluntary statement to the police that she had bought the dress, be it at Portsmouth or in Bournemouth on 2 July at the price of £11·99, could not be true.

If it could not be true then the case against her would, the prosecution might have thought, have been strong.

No notice was given requiring the attendance of the makers of those statements prior to the hearing before the King's Lynn justices. They were read. They thus constituted evidence to the effect of their contents. When the prosecution's case was closed the respondent gave evidence. Her evidence was entirely in accordance with the voluntary statements that she had given to the police, namely that she had bought this dress on 2 July at £11·99 at Portsmouth.

In those circumstances it is perhaps not surprising that the contentions of the respective parties, as set out in the case stated, were to this effect. In so far as the appellant prosecutor was concerned, the submission was that if the court accepted the s 9 statements which had been tendered, it was not open to the respondent to give evidence to the effect that she had bought the dress on an occasion before 22 July. Further that it was not open to her to allege that a mistake may have been made in the arrangements at Marks & Spencer Ltd so that, notwithstanding what was said in the statements, there was a possibility that she had in fact bought the dress at Portsmouth well before the head office direction reducing the price.

In answer to those contentions, the respondent by her representative contended that even if the justices accepted the evidence comprised in the s 9 statements it did not preclude her from giving evidence that she had bought it in Portsmouth on 2 July and that a mistake had been made, that notwithstanding that the court had received and had read to it the s 9 statements, there was a reasonable doubt about the alleged appropriation of the dress on 24 July and that, accordingly, the respondent should be acquitted, her evidence disclosing, it was submitted, a reasonable explanation of her actions when she was stopped.

The justices, by reason of the procedure which was followed in this case must have found themselves in a difficulty. Here they had s 9 statements which, on their face, made it quite clear that the respondent could not have bought the dress on 2 July. No notice had been given requiring the makers of the statements to attend at the trial. Yet here was the respondent giving evidence that she had bought the dress on 2 July. In the end, despite the difficulty which they were in, and with which we fully sympathise, the justices expressed their view in this way:

> 'We were of the opinion that . . . The Respondent's explanations that the items had been purchased on an earlier occasion at another branch of the store and had been brought to King's Lynn on the 24th July, 1981 were reasonable and we could accept that evidence despite that adduced by the Appellant under Section 9 of the Criminal Justice Act, 1967 to the effect that the dress could not have been on sale at that reduced price until after the 22nd July, 1981 . . .'

In his submission to us on this appeal, counsel for the appellant contends that the two halves of that finding by the justices are inconsistent, that this is a perverse decision and that the matter should go back to the justices for rehearing.

We have not found this at all an easy case but in the end we have come to the clear conclusion that the answer really lies in a proper appreciation of what s 9 in fact achieves. As I have already said, this is that the contents of the statements read are evidence in the case just as if, and only to to the extent as if, the makers of those statements had been called as witnesses in the trial and given the evidence contained in the statements. If that had happened at the hearing before the King's Lynn justices in this case, and there had been no cross-examination about the possibility of mistake, or their evidence had not been challenged in any way, then when the respondent went into the witness box no doubt strong comment could have been made that nothing had been put to the witnesses about the possibility that the respondent might indeed have been able to and did buy the dress somewhere else, in Portsmouth in particular, on 2 July 1981.

Although any such comment by those representing the Crown would have had substantial force and might well have led the justices to view the respondent's evidence with a degree of scepticism, the position remains that the burden throughout was on the prosecution and although the proper procedure of putting a defence case to prosecution witnesses had not been followed, it would have been open to the justices, having heard all three witnesses, to have said: 'Well, it may be that that procedure laid down by Marks & Spencer was what should have happened, and it may have happened in at least the majority, if not every other case concerning a dress of this nature, but we have also seen the respondent. She has given evidence. We cannot say that her evidence cannot be true, and in those circumstances there must be a doubt in our minds and accordingly we must acquit.'

If one realises that that is all that is achieved by a s 9 statement, then notwithstanding that criticism may be made of the fact that the respondent's legal advisers did not give any appropriate notice requiring the makers of the statements to attend at the trial, we do not think that in the end it is right to say that the two halves of that opinion of the justices are necessarily inconsistent and their decision perverse.

It will be readily appreciated that under sub-s (4) of s 9 of the 1967 Act, which I read at the start of this judgment, if the Crown in the circumstances of or in similar circumstances to those which obtain in the present case finds a defendant giving evidence which is inconsistent with evidence set out in the s 9 statements which have not been the subject of a notice under para (*d*) of sub-s (2), they always have the right, as does the court of its own motion, to apply for, or to order, an adjournment in order that the maker of the statement shall attend to give evidence. It is unnecessary for us to give any examples either way, but in certain circumstances it may very well be that a court would take the view that if such an application was made by the prosecution, not only would justice require that such an adjournment should be granted but that justice would also require that the costs thrown away by any such adjournment should be paid by the defendant or perhaps by the defendant's legal advisers, it having been their failure to take appropriate steps to ensure that the proper procedure, namely that a defendant's case is put to prosecution witnesses, was followed in the circumstances of that case.

We take the view that legal representatives of defendants in criminal cases, whether before the justices or indeed in the Crown Court, should observe the well-known practice that you do put your case to witnesses for the prosecution, and the failure to give a notice under s 9(2)(*d*) is not to be used as any sort of device whereby you can have the defendant present, giving evidence in person, and avoid the presence of the witnesses whose statements under s 9 have been served and merely hear those statements read out in court. Everyone knows that there is a natural tendency for evidence given in person by a witness to have more impact than statements read out by counsel or solicitors under s 9 of the 1967 Act. We would deprecate any deliberate reluctance to give a notice under s 9(2)(*d*) of the 1967 Act in order to achieve such an advantage.

Nevertheless, for the reasons which I have given in the circumstances of the present case, I do not think that it can be said that the justices came to a perverse conclusion. They were entitled to say that the respondent's evidence had raised a doubt in their minds and if there was such a doubt then she has to be acquitted. Accordingly, in my judgment, this appeal must be dismissed.

STEPHEN BROWN J. I agree, and would only add that this case illustrates the desirability of calling oral evidence on issues which are central to a contested case. Section 9 of the Criminal Justice Act 1967 is a very valuable provision designed to save expense and trouble in very many instances, but where the evidence, which is in written statements, served under the provisions of the notice, is central to the issues in the case, prosecutors should give very careful consideration whether or not they should call the actual witness so that the proper impact of that evidence can be made on the court.

This case has very many unsatisfactory features, but I have great sympathy with the justices in the position into which they were put, not through their own fault. In the end, however, it is they who had the duty of weighing the evidence which had been properly admitted before them and the decision of fact was entirely for them. Whilst it may be that this court might itself have come to a different conclusion, none the less it seems to me to be impossible to interfere with the decision of the justices, which was fully within their competence. Therefore, I agree with May LJ that this appeal must be dismissed.

Appeal dismissed.

Solicitors: *Sharpe Pritchard & Co*, agents for *D I Tomlinson*, Norwich (for the appellant); *Metson Bradford & Clements*, Cambridge (for the respondent).

Sepala Munasinghe Esq Barrister.

Practice Note

COURT OF APPEAL, CIVIL DIVISION
SIR JOHN DONALDSON MR, DUNN AND PURCHAS LJJ
12 APRIL 1983

Court of Appeal – Practice – Civil Division – Presentation of appeals – Skeleton arguments – Notes for hearings.

SIR JOHN DONALDSON MR made the following statement at the sitting of the court. As is well known, the judges of the Court of Appeal have been seeking new ways in which appeals can be presented and decided more quickly and at less expense to the parties. One innovation which has proved very successful in more complex appeals is the submission by counsel of what have been called 'skeleton arguments'.

It would be quite inappropriate to issue a practice direction in this context since whether skeleton arguments should be submitted, what form they should take and how they should be used will depend on the peculiarities of the appeal concerned. However, it may assist both branches of the profession if I mention the result of such experience as we have had of their use.

Skeleton arguments are, as their name implies, a very abbreviated note of the argument and in no way usurp any part of the function of oral argument in court. They are an aide-mémoire for convenience of reference before and during the hearing and no one is inhibited from departing from their terms. Nevertheless experience shows that they serve a very real purpose.

Before the appeal is called on, the judges will normally have read the notice of appeal, any respondent's notice and the judgment appealed from. The purpose of this prereading is not to form any view of the merits of the appeal, but to familiarise themselves with the issues and scope of the dispute and thereby avoid the necessity for a lengthy, or often any, opening of the appeal. This process is assisted by the provision of skeleton arguments, which are much more informative than a notice of appeal or a respondent's notice, being fuller and more recently prepared.

During the hearing of the appeal itself, skeleton arguments enable much time to be saved because they reduce or obviate the need for the judges to take a longhand note, sometimes at dictation speed, of the submissions and authorities and other documents referred to. Furthermore in some circumstances a skeleton argument can do double duty not only as a note for the judges but also as a note from which counsel can argue the appeal.

The usual procedure is for the skeleton argument to be prepared shortly before the hearing of the appeal at the same time as counsel is getting it up. It should contain a numbered list of the points which counsel proposes to argue, stated in no more than one or two sentences, the object being to *identify* each point, not to argue it or to elaborate on it. Each listed point should be followed by full references to the material to which counsel will refer in support of it, ie the relevant pages or passages in authorities, bundles of documents, affidavits, transcripts and the judgment under appeal. It should also contain anything which counsel would expect to be taken down by the court during the hearing, such as propositions of law, chronologies of events, lists of dramatis personae and, where necessary, glossaries of terms. If more convenient, these can of course be annexed to the skeleton argument rather than being included in it. Both the court and opposing counsel can then work on the material without writing it down, thus saving considerable time and labour.

The document should be sent to the court as soon as convenient before the hearing or, if for some reason this is not possible, handed in when counsel rises to address the court. It is however more valuable if provided to the court in advance. A copy should of course at the same time be sent or handed to counsel on the other side.

It cannot be over-emphasised that skeleton arguments are not formal documents to the terms of which anyone will be held. They are simply a tool to be used in the interests of greater efficiency. Experience shows that they can be a valuable tool. The judges of the court all hope that it will be possible to refine and extend their use.

Finally, even in simple appeals where skeleton arguments may be unnecessary, counsel should provide notes (preferably typed) of any material such as I have mentioned which would otherwise have to be taken down by the court more or less at dictation speed, thereby saving considerable time and labour.

Frances Rustin Barrister.

Practice Direction

QUEEN'S BENCH DIVISION

Practice – Funds in court – Transfer to short-term investment account – Revocation of earlier direction – Supreme Court Funds (Amendment) Rules 1983.

Attention is drawn to the Supreme Court Funds (Amendment) Rules 1983, SI 1983/290.

As from 1 April 1983, Masters' Practice Direction 15A made on 23 March 1973 ([1973] 2 All ER 64, [1973] 1 WLR 500; see also *The Supreme Court Practice* 1982 vol 2, p 216, para 916A) is revoked.

JOHN ELTON

30 March 1983 Senior Master, Queen's Bench Division.

Re a company

CHANCERY DIVISION
LORD GRANTCHESTER QC SITTING AS A DEPUTY JUDGE OF THE HIGH COURT
10, 11, 12 NOVEMBER 1982

Company – Member – Unfair prejudice to member's interests – Conduct of company 'unfairly prejudicial' to interests of member – Minority shareholder in private family company – Minority shareholder wishing to sell shareholding within family rather than to outsider because better price obtainable – Company members not wishing to purchase shareholding – Company refusing to propound scheme for reconstructing company to facilitate realisation of shares – Company refusing to purchase shares itself – Company proposing to embark on new business unrelated to existing business – Minority shareholder alleging company's conduct unfairly prejudicing his interests – Whether company's refusal to propound reconstruction scheme or to purchase shares amounting to conduct unfairly prejudicial to shareholder's interests – Whether proposal to apply assets in new business unfairly prejudicial to shareholder – Companies Act 1948, s 287 – Companies Act 1980, s 75(1) – Companies Act 1981, ss 46(1), 47.

A deceased testator's minority shareholding in a private family company was held by his executors for the benefit of the testator's two young children. The shareholding was the only asset from which the executors could obtain money to maintain and educate the children. The company had substantial assets and proposed but had not finally decided to apply part of its liquid assets in financing a wine bar and restaurant business, which was a type of business wholly unrelated to the company's existing business interests. The executors wished, in the interests of the children, to realise their shareholding and considered that a better price for the shares would be realised by selling them within the family rather than to an outsider. However, none of the members of the company wished to increase their shareholdings, nor were they willing to propound a scheme of reconstruction of the company to facilitate the realisation of the executors' shares. Furthermore, the company was unwilling to purchase the shares pursuant to ss 46[a] and 47[b] of the Companies Act 1981, although it was willing to assist the executors to effect a sale of the shares to an outsider and to lend the executors money to pay any capital transfer tax consequent on a sale. The executors presented a petition under s 75[c] of the Companies Act 1980 alleging that the company's affairs were 'being . . . conducted in a manner which [was] unfairly prejudicial to the interests' of the executors, because the company's failure either to formulate a scheme of reconstruction under s 287[d] of the

---

a Section 46(1), so far as material, provides: 'Subject to the following provisions of this Part of this Act, a company limited by shares or limited by guarantee and having a share capital may, if authorised to do so by its articles, purchase its own shares (including any redeemable shares).'

b Section 47, so far as material, provides:

'(1) This section applies to an off-market purchase by a company of any of its own shares.

(2) A purchase by a company of any of its own shares is an off-market purchase for the purposes of this section if . . . (*a*) the shares are purchased otherwise than on a recognised stock exchange . . .

(4) A company may only make an off-market purchase of its own shares in pursuance of a contract approved in advance in accordance with the following provisions of this section or under section 48 of this Act.

(5) The terms of the proposed contract of purchase must be authorised by a special resolution of the company before the company enters into the contract . . .'

c Section 75, so far as material, is set out at p 42 *j* to p 43 *b*, post

d Section 287, so far as material provides:

'(1) Where a company is proposed to be, or is in course of being, wound up altogether voluntarily, and the whole or part of its business or property is proposed to be transferred or sold to another company . . . (in this section called "the transferee company"), the liquidator of the first-mentioned company (in this section called "the transferor company") may, with the sanction of a special resolution of that company, conferring either a general authority on the liquidator or an

(*Continued on p 37*)

Companies Act 1948 or to purchase the shares under ss 46 and 47 of the 1981 Act prevented the executors from realising the true value of the shares and was thereby unfairly prejudicial to the executors' interests. The executors also alleged that the proposed use of the company's assets to finance the wine bar business was unfairly prejudicial to the executors' interests because if the proposal succeeded the company's liquid resources might be insufficient to buy out the executors' shareholding. Accordingly, the petition sought orders, pursuant to s 75 of the 1980 Act, requiring the directors of the company either to formulate a reconstruction scheme under s 287 of the 1948 Act or to purchase the executors' shareholding pursuant to ss 46 and 47 of the 1981 Act at a price to be determined as directed by the court. The company applied to strike out the petition on the ground that it disclosed no reasonable cause of action or was frivolous or vexatious or an abuse of the court's process.

Held — The petition would be struck out for the following reasons—

(1) A company's conduct was 'unfairly prejudicial' to the interests of a member of the company, so as to make the company's conduct actionable under s 75 of the 1980 Act, only where the company's conduct resulted in the member being unfairly prejudiced in his capacity as a member of the company. Section 75 was not intended to enable a minority shareholder in a company to require the company to buy him out at a price which he considered adequately reflected the value of his shareholding (see p 44 *e f* and p 45 *h j*, post); *Ebrahimi v Westbourne Galleries Ltd* [1972] 2 All ER 492 considered.

(2) Applying that principle, (a) the mere failure, omission or refusal of the company to propound a reconstruction scheme under s 287 of the 1948 Act could not amount to unfair prejudice to the executors' interests within s 75 of the 1980 Act, since a member of a company had no rights, as a member, in a reconstruction scheme until the scheme was proposed, (b) the company's refusal, failure or omission to proceed to purchase the shares under ss 46 and 47 of the 1981 Act did not amount to conduct which unfairly prejudiced the executors' interests, since a member of a company had no rights in regard to a purchase of his shares under ss 46 and 47 until an agreement by the company to purchase the shares had been made, and even then the member's rights were rights arising out of the contract and not from the fact that he was a member of the company, and (c) although a member of a company could be unfairly prejudiced within s 75 by the directors of the company making, or omitting to make, a decision relating to the conduct of the company's business, the mere proposal of the company regarding the wine bar business could not amount to unfair prejudice to the interests of the executors since it was the directors' duty in managing the company to consider all proposals for using the company's assets which were put forward (see p 44 *j* to p 45 *h*, post).

(3) Alternatively, if the basis of 'unfair prejudice' to a member's interests within s 75 of the 1980 Act was that the value or quality of his shares was adversely affected by the company's conduct of its business, the refusal or failure of the company to proceed with a reconstruction scheme or with the purchase of the executors' shareholding under ss 46 and 47 of the 1981 Act had not unfairly prejudiced the executors' interests, because the value of their shares had not been adversely affected (see p 45 *d e h*, post).

Notes

For the power of the court to grant relief where members are unfairly prejudiced, see 7 Halsbury's Laws (4th edn) paras 1010–1012, and for cases on the subject, see 10 Digest (Reissue) 943–945, 5526–5530.

(Continued from p 36)

authority in respect of any particular arrangement, receive, in compensation or part compensation for the transfer or sale, shares, policies or other like interests in the transferee company for distribution among the members of the transferor company, or may enter into any other arrangement whereby the members of the transferor company may, in lieu of receiving cash, shares, policies or other like interests, or in addition thereto, participate in the profits of or receive any other benefit from the transferee company.

(2) Any sale or arrangement in pursuance of this section shall be binding on the members of the transferor company . . .'

For the Companies Act 1948, s 287, see 5 Halsbury's Statutes (3rd edn) 329.
For the Companies Act 1980, s 75, see 50(1) ibid 167.
For the Companies Act 1981, ss 46, 47, see 51 ibid 296, 297.

Cases referred to in judgment

Drummond-Jackson v British Medical Association [1970] 1 All ER 1094, [1970] 1 WLR 688, CA, 32 Digest (Reissue) 139, 969.
Ebrahimi v Westbourne Galleries Ltd [1972] 2 All ER 492, [1973] AC 360, [1972] 2 WLR 1289, HL, 10 Digest (Reissue) 916, 5354.
Hubbuck & Sons Ltd v Wilkinson, Heywood & Clark Ltd [1899] 1 QB 86, [1895–9] All ER Rep 244, CA, 50 Digest (Repl) 49, 381.
Scottish Co-op Wholesale Society Ltd v Meyer [1958] 3 All ER 66, [1959] AC 324, [1958] 3 WLR 404, HL, 10 Digest (Reissue) 943, 5526.

Cases also cited

Forte (Charles) Investments Ltd v Amanda [1963] 2 All ER 940, [1964] Ch 240, CA.
Loch v John Blackwood Ltd [1924] AC 783, [1924] All ER Rep 200, PC.

Motion

By a petition presented on 20 September 1982 under s 75 of the Companies Act 1980 by the executors of a deceased minority shareholder in a private company (the company), who held the deceased's shareholding, the petitioning executors prayed for orders pursuant to s 75 of the 1980 Act, (1) requiring the directors of the company forthwith to formulate either (a) a scheme for the reconstruction of the company pursuant to s 287 of the Companies Act 1948 or (b) proposals for the purchase by the company of the shareholding pursuant to ss 46 and 47 of the Companies Act 1981, (2) requiring the directors as soon as practicable to convene an extraordinary general meeting of the company and to submit to it resolutions requisite to carry into effect either a reconstruction of the company or proposals to purchase the petitioners' shareholding and (3) requiring the members of the company other than the petitioners to vote in favour of the said resolutions. By an application dated 27 October 1982 the company applied for an order under RSC Order 18, r 19, or under the court's inherent jurisdiction, that the petition should be removed from the file of proceedings, i e be struck out, on the ground that it disclosed no reasonable cause of action and/or was frivolous or vexatious and/or was otherwise an abuse of the court's process. The facts are set out in the judgment.

Eben Hamilton QC and *Martin Mann* for the company.
Ralph Instone for the petitioning executors.

LORD GRANTCHESTER QC. This is an application by the company, supported by two of its members (to whom I shall refer as Miss Audrey and Mr Stephen) for an order that a petition presented to this court by the executors of their late brother (to whom I shall refer as the testator) be removed from the file and struck out. The petition seeks relief under s 75 of the Companies Act 1980. The grounds of this application to strike out the petition are that it discloses no reasonable cause of action or is otherwise an abuse of the process of the court, thereby relying on the provisions of RSC Ord 18, r 19.

The company was formed in 1932 as a company limited by shares to carry on the business of advertising agents and commercial artists and other objects in its memorandum. It is a family company. The share capital is £13,700 divided into 13,700 shares of £1 each, all issued and fully paid. Of these shares 6,324 (approximately 46%) are held by and registered in the name of Miss Audrey. Her surviving brother, Mr Stephen, and her two sisters, each held a further 1,844 shares (approximately 13·5%). The remaining 1,844 shares were held by, and are still registered in the name of, the testator, who was another brother of Miss Audrey. The testator died on 28 July 1980 and the petitioners are his executors. The 1,844 shares passed under the will of the testator to his former wife, but she died intestate on 7 July 1981. As a result the shares are now held for the two children of the testator, who are aged 15 and 11 years old.

The directors of the company are Miss Audrey and two other individuals who are not members of the family. One was appointed in 1979, the other in 1981. The testator was also a director until his death. Miss Audrey is the chairman of meetings of the directors and of the company in general meeting, and its managing director, for which responsibilities in the year ending 31 December 1981 she received a salary of £14,000. She received £25,000 in the previous year.

The shares in the company are not quoted or dealt in on any stock exchange. The articles of the company adopt, in the main, Table A in Sch 1 to the Companies Act 1929. Thereunder the directors may refuse to register the transfer of any share, but no shareholder is subject to any pre-emption provisions requiring him, if he desires to sell or transfer a share, to offer it to the other members or any of them for purchase by them.

On the death of the testator his 1,844 shares were included in the Inland Revenue affidavit at £20 each, so as to total £36,880. The total value of his net estate, according to such affidavit, was £38,102. However, the value of the testator's shares at his death was subsequently agreed with the Inland Revenue at £29 per share, or £53,476. The widow left no other substantial asset. The shares are now the only asset from which the executors can obtain moneys for the maintenance, education and general upbringing of the testator's two children, and for the payment of any capital transfer tax for which they or the administrator of the estate of the former wife of the testator are liable.

The company has substantial assets. In June 1981 the company sold two of its subsidiaries for £381,000 plus a dividend reserved to itself of £30,000 and payment of an amount equal to certain book debts then outstanding. As a result, on 31 December 1981, the date to which its latest accounts have been made up, the company had short term deposits of £611,441 included in its current assets of £926,289, and current liabilities of £339,161. The shareholders' funds are therein stated to be £722,552. One asset of the company consists of the freehold of its main premises in the West End of London which appears in such accounts at £45,659 but which have been professionally revalued as at that date at £625,000. A calculation of the net value of the assets of the company as at 31 December 1981, taking account of such revaluation of the freehold premises, has been made by its auditors, and their figure came out at £1,284,513, or £93·76 per share. On that basis, the 1,844 shares held by the executors come out at £172,893.

Both in 1980 and 1981 the company paid dividends totalling £40,000. If such sum had been divided amongst the members in proportion to the number of shares held by them respectively, Miss Audrey would have received £18,464 and the executors £5,384. But Miss Audrey waived £15,464 of the dividend otherwise payable to her, and the amount so waived was distributed amongst the other members in proportion to their shares. As a result the executors received a further £3,866 so as to make their total dividend for that year up to the sum of £9,250.

Following the sale of such subsidiaries, it has been proposed that the company should devote part of its liquid resources to the establishment of a wine bar and restaurant at its premises in the West End of London. It has been proposed that a new company should be formed to set up and carry on such business, and that new company should be partly-owned subsidiary. The proposals further envisage that the remaining shares of such new company would be taken by the individual to whom the day-to-day management of the wine bar and restaurant would be entrusted. It appears that no formal decision thereon has yet been taken.

In the circumstances it was in the interests of the two children of the testator that his shares should be sold, and it was the duty of the executors to realise the best price possible for such a sale. From October 1981 down to the date of the presentation of this petition correspondence passed between the advisers of the company and the executors relating to the way in which the executors might realise cash for their shares. No member of the company wished to increase his or her holding, and the executors took the view that they would obtain a better price for the shares from a realisation within the family than to an outsider. In October 1981 the auditors of the company wrote to the executors suggesting that a realisation might be possible as part of a scheme of reconstruction under s 287 of the Companies Act 1948. However, by January 1982 they intimated that this suggestion was not acceptable to the other members. In response the executors suggested a purchase of the shares by the company itself under ss 46 and 47 of the Companies Act 1981. In February 1982 the executors threatened proceedings against the company, which in March 1982 was repeated as a threat of proceedings under s 75 of the Companies Act 1980. This threat was thereafter repeated from time to time until the petition herein was actually presented.

On 1 June 1982 the auditors advanced a valuation of the 1,844 shares of the executors at £95,091 (being a computation of net asset value discounted at 45%). On 10 June the auditors rejected that valuation as a basis of a sale, and put forward a figure of £175,000 (or £95 per share, being slightly more than such earlier computation of net asset value). In July 1982 the auditors increased their valuation and offered £112,000 (or £60·94 per share) to the executors, but this offer was not accepted. The petition was then presented on 20 September 1982. Whilst I have picked out the salient features of the correspondence, it can be noted that the auditors acting for the company indicated that they would assist the executors in any negotiations for a sale of their shares to an outsider, other than a business competitor, and that the company would lend moneys to the executors to pay any capital transfer tax.

In the petition there are two allegations of the executors being unfairly prejudiced. After referring to the suggested scheme of reconstruction under s 287 of the 1948 Act and the suggestion of share purchases under ss 46 and 47 of the 1981 Act, the petition proceeds:

> '17. The interests of your Petitioners as the persons to whom the said shares of the Testator have been transmitted are being unfairly prejudiced because they are unable to realise the value of the said shares or a substantial proportion thereof and to account for the proceeds of realisation to the administrator of the estate of ... deceased in order that he may provide for her children by her marriage to the Testator. The continuing failure of the Directors of the Company to formulate and recommend proposals for that purpose constitutes conduct of the affairs of the Company (by virtue of such failure or omission) which is unfairly prejudicial as aforesaid.
>
> 18. Since the Company now has liquid resources which are substantially in excess of the requirements of its remaining business, such failure cannot be justified as being necessary in the interests of the Company or of any of its members.'

There follows a paragraph which was intended to be included in the petition originally, but inadvertently was omitted on filing and has subsequently been added:

> '19. The Directors of the Company are proposing without any consent or sanction from its members to devote a substantial part of its liquid resources in financing the business of a wine bar and restaurant to be conducted by a partly-owned subsidiary formed or to be formed for that purpose on the ground floor and basement of the Company's premises ... The said Directors are further considering the purchase of another property at Harrow Middlesex for the conduct of a similar business at a cost of upwards of £200,000. Such a business is wholly unrelated to the existing businesses of the Company and the Directors have no experience as managers or owners of such a business. The foregoing proposals are unfairly prejudicial to the interest of your Petitioners as the persons to whom the said shares of the Testator have been transmitted.'

On that basis the relief sought is as follows:

> '... an Order or Orders pursuant to Section 75 of the Companies Act 1980:—(1) Requiring the Directors of the Company forthwith to formulate either: (a) A scheme for the reconstruction of the Company pursuant to Section 287 of the Companies Act 1948 whereunder all its undertakings and assets (other than the cash required to purchase the shares of your Petitioners pursuant to Sub-Section (3) of the

> said Section) shall be transferred to a successor Company... (b) Proposals for the
> a purchase by the Company of all the said shares of your Petitioners pursuant to Sections 46 and 47 of the Companies Act 1981 at a price to be determined in such manner as the Court may direct.'

There follows certain other ancillary relief designed to put those provisions into effect.

It is to be noted that the petition does not allege any act of impropriety on the part of the directors or shareholders, but that what has not been done in relation to any scheme
b under s 287 the 1948 Act or purchase under ss 46 and 47 of the 1981 Act, and the actual making of the proposals relating to the wine bar and restaurant, has resulted in unfair prejudice to the executors.

I must refer to two passages in the affidavits in support of the petition. The first was sworn on 20 September 1982. I read para 11:

> c 'The failure of the Directors to propound and circulate a scheme to enable my co-petitioner and myself to realise our holding in order to provide for the Testator's children is a serious injustice, and in our submission constitutes unfair prejudice to our interests as members justifying the intervention of the Court under Section 75 of the Companies Act 1980. It may be preferable from the point of view of the Company and the other members, and their respective tax situations, for our
> d interests to be purchased by the Company pursuant to Sections 46(1) and 47(5) of the Companies Act 1981, instead of under a scheme of reconstruction, or by means of a purchase by one or more of the other shareholders. Accordingly the relief sought in our Petition provides for either of these remedies in the alternative.'

In the second affidavit sworn on 6 October 1982, para 4:

> e '... The proper course is for the Company to be reconstructed in the manner indicated in paragraph 1(a) of the prayer to our Petition, so as to enable my co-petitioner and I (and any other non-assenting shareholder) to exercise our statutory rights of dissent and be bought out in cash, leaving those who favour the new venture to embark their own money in it, or else for us to be bought out on the same basis under the provisions of sections 46 and 47 of the Companies Act 1981.'

f The summons herein is dated 27 October 1982. It is supported by an affidavit of Miss Audrey. I read a short passage from that affidavit, para 13(c):

> 'The Petitioners appear to pin their hopes for the success of the Petition on the amendment at paragraph 19. The position remains however as recorded in the letter dated 13th August 1982... which is to say that the board of directors is considering
> g certain options for the advancement of the Company's members' and employees' interests, but has yet to decide which option it wishes to put to the members in general meeting. The board of directors considered that it would be imprudent and wrong in principle to regard the present cash surplus as other than a capital fund with which to underwrite the Company's future prospects. Be that as it may, no steps will be taken to implement any major policy decision, whether or not
> h involving a requirement to alter the Memorandum of Association of the Company, without first fully informing the members and submitting to their judgment in general meeting. Therefore it is right to observe that even if the proposals currently under consideration are capable of being unfairly prejudicial (which is not conceded) there is in reality as yet no such actual or proposed act capable of implementation.'

j The petitioning executors accept the statement made in that paragraph that it is intended that no step will be taken to implement any of the proposals without first fully informing the members and submitting to their judgment in general meeting.

In addition to the foregoing, in order to complete the picture, I will mention that counsel for the company has informed me that the proposal mentioned in para 19 of the petition for the purchase of another property outside of London at which the company would carry on a similar business to the business proposed for the company's premises in the West End of London, has been dropped. a

Counsel for the applicant company referred me to s 75 of the Companies Act 1980 under which the petition has been brought, and to RSC Ord 18, r 19. Order 18, r 19 provides:

> '(1) The Court may at any stage of the proceedings order to be struck out or amended any pleading or the indorsement of any writ in the action, or anything in any pleading or in the indorsement, on the ground that—(*a*) it discloses no b
> reasonable cause of action or defence, as the case may be; or (*b*) it is scandalous, frivolous or vexatious; or (*c*) it may prejudice, embarrass or delay the fair trial of the action; or (*d*) it is otherwise an abuse of the process of the court; and may order the action to be stayed or dismissed or judgment to be entered accordingly, as the case may be . . . c
> (3) This rule shall, so far as applicable, apply to an originating summons and a petition as if the summons or petition, as the case may be, were a pleading.'

And in the notes to that rule in *The Supreme Court Practice* 1982, vol 1, it is stated as follows. Paragraph 18/19/3 reads:

> 'It is only in plain and obvious cases that recourse should be had to the summary process under this Rule, *per* Lindley, M.R. in *Hubbuck* v. *Wilkinson* ([1899] 1 QB 86 d
> at 91, [1895–9] All ER Rep 244 at 247) . . . The summary procedure under this Rule can only be adopted when it is clearly seen that the claim or answer is, on the face of it "obviously unsustainable"... The summary remedy under this Rule is only to be applied in plain and obvious cases when the action is one which cannot succeed or is in some way an abuse of the process or the case unarguable. . . It cannot be exercised by a minute and protracted examination of the documents and the facts of the case, e
> in order to see whether the plaintiff really has a cause of action.'

In para 18/19/5, under 'No Reasonable Cause of Action or Defence', the note reads:

> '"There is some difficulty in affixing a precise meaning to" this term. "In point of law . . . every cause of action is a reasonable one"... A reasonable cause of action means a cause of action with some chance of success when only the allegations in f
> the pleadings are considered (*per* Lord Pearson in *Drummond-Jackson* v. *British Medical Association* ([1970] 1 All ER 1094 at 1101, [1970] 1 WLR 688 at 696)).'

Paragraph 18/19/10A says:

> 'The Court has inherent jurisdiction to stay an action which must fail; as, for instance, an action brought in respect of an act of State . . . or an action brought by g
> an infant suing by a next friend which clearly is brought in the interests of the next friend and not of the infant . . . It is not limited to cases in which the facts are not in dispute . . . A judicial discretion must be used as to what proceedings are vexatious; for the Court must not prevent a suitor from exercising his undoubted rights on any vague or indefinite principle . . . The jurisdiction will not be exercised except with great circumspection and unless it is perfectly clear that the plea cannot succeed h
> . . .'

So I apply those principles to the petition in this case which is based on s 75 of the 1980 Act. This section provides:

> '(1) Any member of a company may apply to the court by petition for an order j
> under this section on the ground that the affairs of the company are being or have been conducted in a manner which is unfairly prejudicial to the interests of some part of the members (including at least himself) or that any actual or proposed act or omission of the company (including an act or omission on its behalf) is or would be so prejudicial . . .

> (3) If the court is satisfied that a petition under this section is well founded, it
> a may make such order as it thinks fit for giving relief in respect of the matters complained of.
>
> (4) Without prejudice to the generality of subsection (3) above an order under this section may . . . (*d*) provide for the purchase of the shares of any members of the company by other members or by the company itself and, in the case of a purchase by the company itself, the reduction of the company's capital
> b accordingly . . .'

This section replaces s 210 of the 1948 Act, which entitled a shareholder to bring proceedings where he could establish, inter alia, that the affairs of the company were being conducted 'in a manner oppressive to some part of the members (including himself)', and that the facts would justify the making of a winding-up petition on just
c and equitable grounds, and that to wind up the company would unfairly prejudice that part of the members. Clearly, therefore, the new s 75 is intended to have a wider ambit and applicability than the old s 210. This case involves the question as to the extension thereby effected.

Counsel for the company advanced four submissions as follows. (1) Under s 75, the petitioning executors must show that the value of their shareholding has been impaired
d by the conduct of the others, which conduct is 'unfair'. (2) There is no duty or obligation on the company or the other shareholders to buy out the petitioning executors, or to assist them to realise their shares in any way. (3) The object of s 75 is not to assist a shareholder who wished to sell his shares to do so at a better price than is obtainable in the open market, and so give such a shareholder preferential treatment. (4) The petitioning executors have failed to put forward any tangible evidence to show that the
e value of their shareholding has been impaired by the conduct of the company and other shareholders. There is therefore, so he submits, in this case no question of exploitation or unfair prejudice so as to come within the section at all. It is, he argues, an abuse of the process of the court to call in aid s 75 in order to obtain a price for a shareholding in excess of that which otherwise could be obtained in the open market. Having regard to the refusal of the other shareholders to buy, the executors must find an outside purchaser,
f but such a purchaser would only buy a minority holding at a discount. Notwithstanding such position, the petitioners are using these proceedings in order to obtain payment from the company for their shares at their asset value.

Counsel for the petitioning executors argues that it is not necessary for an applicant under s 75 to show that the value of his shareholding has been impaired. He submits that, by enacting s 75 in place of s 210 of the 1948 Act, Parliament was intending to
g extend assistance to personal representatives, whose usual complaint was either that they were refused registration or found it difficult to realise their holding at an appropriate price. He submitted that under s 75 there was no need to establish any wrongdoing, but only to show that by reason of some difference between the interests of the petitioners on the one hand and the interests of those determining managerial policy on the other hand, some act or omission on the part of the latter, whether actual or proposed, operated or
h will operate unfairly and to the prejudice of the interests of the petitioners. Thus if a failure or refusal to recommend and pay proper dividends is actionable under s 75, so, on the same basis, is a failure or refusal to procure a capital payment, where such failure or refusal was unfairly prejudicial. If a company or shareholders omit to do what it is within their power to do, then such failure may unfairly prejudice another so as to give a right to proceed under s 75.

j Turning back to s 75 of the 1980 Act, the section operates where 'the affairs of the company are being or have been conducted in a manner which is unfairly prejudicial to the interests of some part of the members'. In relation thereto, *Gore-Brown on Companies* (43rd edn, 1977) contains two passages in para 28–13. First:

> 'Clearly, a "dictionary definition" of "unfairly prejudicial" conduct of the affairs

of the company (to adapt Lord Simonds' approach [in *Scottish Co-op Wholesale Society Ltd v Meyer* [1958] 3 All ER 66 at 71, [1959] AC 324 at 342] to the definition of a
"oppressive" as "burdensome, harsh and wrongful") will require a more liberal approach to the problems of minority shareholders in small companies. If "prejudicial" may be defined, in dictionary terms, as "causing prejudice, detrimental to rights, interests etc.", and "unfair" as that which is *not* "just, unbiased, equitable, legitimate", then clearly the new standard (as the Jenkins Report (Cmnd 1749 (1962), para 204) intended) will be less demanding of the petitioning shareholder in b
respect of the burden of proof and of the kind of conduct of which he is entitled to complain. Seemingly, what he must show is that the value of his shareholding in the company has been seriously impaired as a consequence of the conduct of those who control the company in a way that is "unfair".'

The second passage is as follows: c

'However, the language of section 75(1) still seems to require the interpretation that he must be so prejudiced in his capacity as "member *qua* member". This, of course, was how the courts interpreted section 210. In a small private company it is legalistic to segregate the separate capacities of the same individual as shareholder, director or employee. His dismissal from the board or from employment by the company will inevitably affect the real value of his interest in the company expressed d
by his shareholding. It is precisely this recognition which makes the House of Lords decision in *Re Westbourne Galleries* ([1972] 2 All ER 492, [1973] AC 360) so notable.'

In my view, these two passages are most germane to the problem which arises at this hearing. To my mind, in passing s 75 of the 1980 Act, Parliament did not intend to give a right of action to every shareholder who considered that some act or omission by his e
company resulted in unfair prejudice to himself. In argument, an example was advanced of a shareholder who objected to his company carrying out some operation on land adjoining his dwelling house, which resulted in that house falling in value. It is not difficult to envisage an act or omission on the part of a company rendering an asset of a shareholder, other than his shares, of lesser value. In my judgment s 75 is to be construed as confined to 'unfair prejudice' of a petitioner 'qua member'; or, put in another way, the f
word 'interests' in s 75 is confined to 'interests of the petitioner as a member'. I do not consider that *Ebrahimi v Westbourne Galleries Ltd* [1972] 2 All ER 492, [1973] AC 360, which was a decision involving s 210 in very different circumstances, requires a wider scope to be given to s 75. The decision in that case was primarily concerned with the rights of a member to obtain a winding-up order on just and equitable grounds, and not on what constituted 'oppression' for s 210 purposes. g

If the foregoing be correct, then what I have now to consider is whether or not the matters of which the petitioning executors complain in the petition and the evidence in support can amount to conduct of the affairs of the company 'in a manner which is unfairly prejudicial to' them as shareholders. The matters of which complaint is made are: (1) the failure by the company and its management to propound a s 287 scheme of reconstruction; (2) the failure by the company and its management to propound a h
purchase scheme under ss 46 and 47 of the 1981 Act; and (3) the making of the proposal for the establishment of a wine bar and restaurant through the medium of a partly-owned subsidiary.

Let me take the first two together. The argument proceeds on this basis. The petitioning executors require cash for the benefit of the two infant children. They can obtain cash under a suitable scheme in respect of their shares. Therefore the failure to j
propound such a scheme is 'unfairly prejudicial' to them as members. I do not accept that line of reasoning because I do not consider that a refusal to propound a scheme does affect or prejudice a member as a member. I take the view that under s 287 of the 1948 Act and, to take a similar type of provision, s 206 of the same Act, a member of a company has certain statutory rights if and when a scheme is proposed. In relation to an

article empowering a reconstruction in terms similar to s 287 aforesaid, a member has
a certain contractual rights as and when a scheme is proposed by analogy with s 287. But to my mind, these rights and any concomitant interests only arise on and by virtue or by reason of the scheme. I do not accept that a member of a company has an interest 'as a member' in a non-existent hypothetical scheme which could be proposed or in having such a scheme proposed for his benefit. It follows that I do not consider that a member can be affected or prejudiced, unfairly or otherwise, by a failure or omission or refusal to
b propose or propound such a scheme.

I take the view that similar reasoning applies to the complaint of the failure to propose a scheme of purchase under ss 46 and 47 of the 1981 Act. To my mind, on an agreement being made for the purchase of shares by a company, contractual rights arise, subject to and with the benefit of the provisions of the two sections. In such a case, however, such rights, and any interests of the vendor shareholder, arise ex contractu and not qua
c member. Accordingly I have come to the conclusion that the sections do not create interests for members qua members, and that a refusal, failure, or omission to proceed under the section before any agreement on price has been reached cannot be conduct 'unfairly prejudicial' of the prospective vendors as members.

The first extract which I read from *Gore-Browne* seems to arrive at a similar solution, but by another route. It suggests that to constitute 'unfair prejudice', the value or the
d quality of the shareholder's interest, i e his shares in a company limited by shares, must be adversely affected. Certainly the refusals or failure by the company to proceed in this case with a s 287 scheme or a purchase under ss 46 and 47, do not adversely affect the value of the shares of the petitioning executors; instead, the propounding of such a scheme or purchase would or might have brought about a benefit to them.

I am therefore left with the third complaint, the fact that a proposal has been advanced
e for the establishment of a wine bar and restaurant in the company's premises through the medium of a subsidiary. The reasoning behind this complaint is that if the proposal proceeds, the liquid resources may then be insufficient to buy out the 1,844 shares of the petitioning executors. In my judgment, a decision of the directors, or even the omission of the directors to come to a decision relating to the conduct of its business, may amount to conduct which comes within s 75 of the 1980 Act, so as to be actionable by a member
f who is thereby unfairly prejudiced as a member. But I cannot accept that the foregoing extends to a consideration by directors of a company of proposals or suggestions similar to the one with which I am now concerned and at the stage at which the proposal or suggestion now stands. It is the duty of the directors to manage the business of the company, and to put its assets to the best use, or realise them to the best advantage for the benefit of the company as a whole. For such purposes they must duly consider all
g proposals and suggestions put forward. In my view, in relation to this aspect of the proceedings, I agree with counsel for the company that the petition now presented is premature. The wine bar proposal or suggestion may, or may not, be adopted but, if it is adopted, the petitioning executors accept that the correct procedures will then be followed.

In the outcome I have accepted the submission that the petition cannot succeed. I do
h not consider that s 75 was enacted so as to enable a 'locked-in' minority shareholder to require the company to buy him out at a price which he considered adequately to reflect the value of the underlying assets referable to his shareholding, providing the company held sufficient resources so to do. I will order the petition to be removed from the file and struck out accordingly.

j *Order accordingly.*

Solicitors: *Taylor Tyrrell Lewis & Craig* (for the company); *T J James & Sarch* (for the petitioning executors).

Hazel Hartman Barrister.

R v Jenner

COURT OF APPEAL, CRIMINAL DIVISION
WATKINS LJ, CANTLEY AND HIRST JJ
27 JANUARY 1983

Town and country planning – Stop notice – Using land in contravention of stop notice – Criminal prosecution – Defence that notice invalid – Whether validity of stop notice can be challenged in criminal proceedings – Town and Country Planning Act 1971, s 90(1)(2)(7).

The local planning authority served on the appellant a 'stop notice' under s 90(1)[a] of the Town and Country Planning Act 1971 requiring him to discontinue certain activities on his land within three days. When he failed to comply with the notice he was committed for trial in the Crown Court on an information alleging that he was using his land in contravention of the stop notice, contrary to s 90(7) of the 1971 Act. At his trial he wished to put forward the defence that the stop notice was invalid because the activities complained of had been commenced more than 12 months earlier and consequently were exempted by s 90(2) from the prohibition contained in the stop notice. The trial judge ruled that it was not open to the appellant to challenge the validity of the stop notice in the Crown Court and that the validity of such a notice could only be challenged on an application to the Divisional Court for judicial review. The appellant was convicted and fined. He appealed against his conviction.

Held – A person who appeared before a court to answer a charge of using his land in contravention of a stop notice, contrary to s 90(7) of the 1971 Act, was not prevented by the provisions of s 90 or the other associated provisions of that Act from attempting to establish in criminal proceedings that he was not in fact subject to the prohibition contained in the notice. It followed that the trial judge had erred in denying the appellant the right to put forward the defence that the stop notice was invalid. The appeal would accordingly be allowed and the conviction quashed (see p 50 *e* to *g*, post).

Notes

For stop notices, see Supplement to 37 Halsbury's Laws (3rd edn) para 448A.

For the Town and Country Planning Act 1971, s 90 (as substituted by the Town and Country Planning (Amendment) Act 1977, s 1), see 47 Halsbury's Statutes (3rd edn) 1357.

Case referred to in judgment

Smith v East Elloe RDC [1956] 1 All ER 855, [1956] AC 736, [1956] 2 WLR 888, HL, 26 Digest (Reissue) 793, *5320*.

Cases also cited

London & Clydeside Estates Ltd v Aberdeen DC [1979] 3 All ER 876, [1980] 1 WLR 182, HL.

Miller-Mead v Minister of Housing and Local Government [1963] 1 All ER 459, [1963] 2 QB 196, CA.

O'Reilly v Mackman [1982] 3 All ER 1124, [1982] 3 WLR 1096, HL.

Scott Markets Ltd v Waltham Forest London Borough Council (1979) 77 LGR 565, CA.

---

a Section 90, so far as material, is set out at p 49 *d* to *f* and *h*, post

Appeal

a On 18 May 1982 in the Crown Court at Southend, before Mr Recorder G V Owen QC and a jury, the appellant, Walter Rupert Jenner, was convicted of using land in contravention of a stop notice, contrary to s 90(7) of the Town and Country Planning Act 1971, fined £500 and in default sentenced to three months' imprisonment and ordered to pay the costs of the prosecution in a sum not exceeding £350. He appealed with leave against conviction. The facts are set out in the judgment of the court.

b

Raymond Sears QC (who did not appear in the court below) and *Tobias Davey* for the appellant.
Stephen Aitchison for the local planning authority.

c

WATKINS LJ delivered the following judgment of the court. On 18 May 1982 in the Crown Court at Southend before Mr Recorder G V Owen QC and a jury, the appellant, Walter Rupert Jenner, was convicted of using land in contravention of a stop notice, contrary to s 90(7) of the Town and Country Planning Act 1971. He was thereupon fined £500 with an alternative in default of three months' imprisonment and ordered to pay
d the costs of the prosecution in a sum not exceeding £350. He appeals against that conviction on a point of law to this court.

What in fact brings him here is this. He lived at 23 Wickford Road, Westcliff-on-Sea. He carried on at his premises, it is said, activities for which he had neither sought nor obtained planning permission. Accordingly, the local planning authority served on him an enforcement notice, the effect of which was to order him to cease his activities at those
e premises within the time limit contained in the enforcement notice, which was 28 days. The appellant appealed against the enforcement notice to the Secretary of State for the Environment.

The planning authority, having regard to the objections of the appellant's neighbours to the use he was making of his land, was determined to try and bring those activities to an end before the appeal was heard and decided. So it resorted to the use of the provisions
f of s 90 of the Town and Country Planning Act 1971 and served on the appellant a stop notice. This was dated 11 December 1981 and was served on that day. It was specified to take effect three days later, namely on 15 December, and was thus expressed at the most material part:

> '... the Council do hereby prohibit each and every person on whom this Stop
> g Notice is served from carrying out or continuing on the said land the following activity namely the parking of lorries, the storage and hire of skips, the use of the caravan sited on the said land as an office and the tipping of rubbish.'

The stop notice when served on him was accompanied, as is usual, with a copy of ss 90
h and 177 of the Act. The appellant was thereby informed of the powers of the local planning authority contained in s 90 and the provisions for the payment of compensation in certain circumstances contained in s 177. He was apparently unimpressed by the prohibition contained in the stop notice. He did not obey it. He carried on two of the activities referred to in the stop notice, namely the parking of lorries and the storage and hire of skips. So on 16 December 1981 the local planning authority took out an
j information before the justices at Southend, in which it was alleged that the appellant had on 11 December 1981, having received a stop notice, contravened that notice contrary to s 90(7) of the Act. The appellant applied to the Divisional Court for leave to challenge the stop notice. He was given leave by Glidewell J. There is a time limit for the entry of an application for a judicial review of four weeks. The appellant did not apply within the required time, or at all, consequent on the leave given therefor by Glidewell J.

Meanwhile his appeal against the enforcement notice was extant and due to be heard some time in the future, either by an inspector appointed by the Secretary of State to report to him, so that the Secretary of State could make his own decision on the challenge to the enforcement notice, or by the delegation of power by the Secretary of State to the inspector so that he (the inspector) could make that decision. Those procedures were not undergone, for the reason that the appellant was committed for trial at the Crown Court at Southend from the magistrates' court on an indictment which contained two counts, the first of which was not proceeded with, the jury being directed by the recorder that they were not required to return a verdict on it. It was, however, otherwise, as has been said, with the second count in the indictment.

The trial did not take an ordinary course. What happened was that the recorder at the outset of the proceedings was invited to and did listen to submissions from counsel for the local planning authority and counsel for the appellant. The burden of the submission on behalf of the local planning authority was that the appellant had no defence because it was not open in that court for him to challenge the validity of the stop notice. The stop notice must be presumed by the court to be valid unless proven otherwise. The only court in which an argument could be raised in order to establish the invalidity of a stop notice was, so it was contended, the Divisional Court on a judicial review. The appellant's counsel endeavoured strongly to resist that argument and sought to prove by evidence that the appellant was not in contravention of the stop notice. We do not feel it necessary to rehearse, even in the most summary form, the rival submissions then made to any greater extent than that. Suffice it to say that the arguments on behalf of the local planning authority prevailed, the recorder ruling as follows:

> 'I have come to the conclusion that the defendant is not allowed in these proceedings to challenge the validity of the stop notice. As I say, it is a difficult decision to come to, but I must give great weight to what Lord Radcliffe said in similar proceedings, albeit in civil proceedings (see *Smith v East Elloe RDC* [1956] 1 All ER 855 at 871, [1956] AC 736 at 769–770). But, it is said, in itself the notice bears no brand of invalidity on its forehead, on the face of it. Therefore since no proceedings have been taken at law, although there are no extant proceedings at the moment to establish the cause of invalidity and to get it quashed or otherwise upset, it will remain effective until, as a preliminary ruling of law, I rule it is not open for the defendant in these proceedings, although it might sound illogical or unfair; but that is my reading of the statute and my reading of the indictment: it deals with, "served with a stop notice"; it does not say, "with a legal stop notice or a valid stop notice". So there has been no challenge at the moment to any civil court to challenge that validity, and without going into any Latin tags or legal niceties, my judgment is that that stop notice is effective today in these proceedings and cannot be challenged in these courts.'

The recorder thereupon commenced the trial, put the defendant (as he then was) in the charge of the jury, allowed the stop notice to go before them, told them that the defendant had no defence and bade the jury to convict him of count 2 of the indictment.

The appellant, following on that conviction, seems to have thought that it would be imprudent, for reasons which do not concern us, to carry on the activities complained of any longer, so he withdrew his appeal against the enforcement notice, ceased these activities and sold his premises.

Counsel for the appellant, who did not appear in the court below, has represented him here. He argues that the recorder was wrongly persuaded by counsel for the local planning authority into reaching a wholly erroneous decision in denying the defendant the right to defend himself at the Crown Court. It is, he argues, a misconception of the provisions of s 90 of the Act to contend that by those provisions, and other associated parts of the Act, a person on whom a stop notice is served is disabled at all times and in all circumstances from endeavouring to establish, either in a magistrates' court or in a Crown Court, that a stop notice has no application to him. It would, he says, be unfair and nonsensical to hold that a defendant, faced with a criminal information, is disallowed from raising a defence, so that for example magistrates could find on the facts that he had not at any relevant time carried on activities in contravention of the penal provisions of s 90. He referred to the code which exists for the service of enforcement notices, and for enabling a person on whom such a notice is served, to appeal against that notice to the Secretary of State and thereafter to the Divisional Court and upwards. He compares that comprehensive code with all the provisions which relate to stop notices in the 1971 Act, as amended. I have referred to all the provisions. They are contained in ss 90 and 177. Nowhere in s 90 is there to be found a right of appeal against a stop notice. Likewise in s 177, which deals exclusively with the right, in certain circumstances, of a person who has been the recipient of a stop notice to claim compensation for the effects of it upon him. If, so counsel for the appellant submits, it was intended that an appellate procedure of the kind which is provided for in relation to enforcement notices was contemplated by Parliament as applying to stop notices, then suitable and like provisions would have been included in the Act as amended. But, as has been said, nothing of the sort appears there.

How then is a person who receives a stop notice to defend himself against the effects of it? Is he to be utterly powerless in this respect, or is he entitled to go to the magistrates' court, or a Crown Court (if the complaint has become an indictment) to raise the defence of not in fact being in contravention of the prohibition set out in the stop notice?

Section 90(1) and (2) (as amended), so far as material, provides:

> '(1) Where in respect of any land the local planning authority—(*a*) have served a copy of an enforcement notice requiring a breach of planning control to be remedied; but (*b*) consider it expedient to prevent, before the expiry of the period allowed for compliance with the notice, the carrying out of any activity which is, or is included in, a matter alleged by the notice to constitute the breach, then, subject to the following provisions of this section, they may at any time before the notice takes effect serve a further notice (in this Act referred to as a "stop notice") referring to, and having annexed to it a copy of, the enforcement notice and prohibiting the carrying out of that activity on the land, or any part of it specified in the stop notice.
> (2) . . . and where the period during which an activity has been carried out on land (whether continuously or otherwise) began more than twelve months earlier, a stop notice shall not prohibit the carrying out of that activity on that land unless it is, or is incidental to, building, engineering, mining or other operations or the deposit of refuse or waste materials.'

It is not disputed that if the appellant had been permitted to he could have given evidence to the Crown Court which, if accepted, would have brought him within the exempting provisions of the tailpiece of s 90(2) and outside the prohibitions contained elsewhere in s 90 and in the stop order, in which event he could not have been convicted, as he was, of such a contravention.

By s 90(7) (as amended), it is provided:

> 'If any person contravenes, or causes or permits the contravention of, a stop notice . . . then, subject to subsection (8) of this section, he shall be guilty of an offence and liable on summary conviction to a fine not exceeding [£1,000], or on conviction on indictment to a fine; and if the offence is continued after conviction he shall be guilty of a further offence and liable on summary conviction to a fine not exceeding £100 for each day on which the offence is continued, or conviction on indictment to a fine.'

This being a penal provision, it follows that the court in fining a person found guilty of a contravention of s 90(7) would, as was the case here, have ordered him, on a failure to pay the fine within a given time, to serve a term of imprisonment.

Counsel for the local planning authority nevertheless submitted that we have to apply, in examining the right of this appellant to defend himself, the principles pertaining to challenges to orders (such as stop notices, enforcement orders and the like) in civil proceedings. We should therefore take cognisance of various pronouncements which have been made in the Court of Appeal and the House of Lords in a number of cases on the permissible manner in which challenges may be made to the validity of notices and orders of that kind. We feel it unnecessary in this judgment to refer either to the cases in which those pronouncements appear or to the circumstances which gave rise to them. Needless to say, they are wholly different from those which confront this court. So far as we know, this is the first time that a point of this kind has been the subject of an appeal. It matters not, so counsel for the local planning authority says, that the proceedings taken against the appellant were of a criminal nature, the notice is sacrosanct. It is unchallengeable, except in a conventional way. The only conventional way available to the appellant here was to challenge the validity of the notice by judicial review in the Divisional Court, pursuant to the leave given. We do not agree. The process of judicial review, which rarely allows of the reception of oral evidence, is not suited to resolving the issues of fact involved in deciding whether activity said to be prohibited by it is caught by s 90. These issues could not possibly be decided on the contents of affidavits, which is the form of evidence usually received by the Divisional Court.

With those few observations on it, we leave the question of the propriety of seeking, and likely effectiveness of, in such a matter as this, a judicial review and return to examine the precise nature of the proceedings in hand. They were criminal proceedings, as is self-evident from the penal provisions of s 90. The tailpiece to s 90(2) makes it abundantly plain that a stop order does not inevitably prohibit the activities complained of from being carried on. Is a person, against whom is laid an information of the kind already referred to, not permitted to say: 'I am not prohibited by the stop notice from carrying on the activities you object to'? In fact the defence relied on here was that what the appellant was doing when the stop order was served on him, he had been doing for well over 12 months.

In the view of this court, when a person appears to answer an information or an indictment on a charge of this nature, he is entitled to attempt to establish that he is not in fact prohibited from carrying on his activities by the terms of the prohibition contained on the face of the stop order. To find otherwise in criminal proceedings would be to create a unique situation for a defendant, who is, if convicted, liable to be fined or imprisoned in default of payment of it. We cannot think that Parliament can have contemplated that it was, by ss 90 and 177 or otherwise, denying the usual right of a defendant in a criminal case to defend himself other than by seeking to quash a stop notice. We do not think it is either appropriate or relevant to import into criminal proceedings the ways in which notices or orders, of the kind previously mentioned, can be challenged in civil procedures. What happens to a stop notice once magistrates or a jury have found that a defendant is not subject to its prohibitions is no concern of a criminal court. Its concern is the guilt or otherwise of an accused person and not with whether a notice should be declared valid, or invalid or be quashed. This appeal is allowed and the conviction quashed.

Appeal allowed. Conviction quashed.

Solicitors: *Gregson Owles & Roach*, Southend-on-Sea (for the appellant); *David G Preddy*, Southend-on-Sea (for the local planning authority).

Raina Levy Barrister.

White v White

COURT OF APPEAL, CIVIL DIVISION
CUMMING-BRUCE LJ AND REEVE J
7, 8 FEBRUARY 1983

Injunction – Domestic violence – Attachment of power of arrest to injunction – Jurisdiction – Application to be made by party to marriage – Former wife applying for power of arrest to be attached to injunction excluding former husband from former matrimonial home – Whether 'party to a marriage' including party to a former marriage – Domestic Violence and Matrimonial Proceedings Act 1976, s 2(1)(2).

In April 1981 the applicant was granted a decree absolute dissolving her marriage to the respondent. In May the respondent moved out of the former matrimonial home which was then put into the applicant's name. In October the applicant obtained an injunction from the county court excluding the respondent from the former matrimonial home. When the respondent persisted in visiting the former matrimonial home and started striking the applicant she applied to the court under s 2(1)[a] of the Domestic Violence and Matrimonial Proceedings Act 1976 for a power of arrest to be attached to the injunction. The court refused the application on the ground that the applicant was not 'a party to a marriage' since she was no longer married to the respondent nor was she cohabiting with him as man and wife, and therefore there was no jurisdiction under s 2 to entertain her application. The applicant appealed.

Held – On the true construction of s 2 of the 1976 Act 'a party to a marriage' included only a party to a subsisting marriage or a man and a woman who were living with each other in the same household as husband and wife at the time of the incidents giving rise to the application under s 2. The applicant came within neither category and therefore the county court had no jurisdiction under s 2(1) to attach a power of arrest to the injunction excluding the respondent from the former matrimonial home. The applicant's appeal would therefore be dismissed (see p 56 *h j*, p 57 *b c* and *g* to *j* and p 58 *a* to *d e f h*, post).

Per curiam. If after a decree absolute the former husband and the former wife are living together in the same household as husband and wife, the county court does have jurisdiction under s 2(2) of the 1976 Act to attach a power of an arrest to an injunction excluding the other party from the home (see p 57 *h j* and p 58 *f*, post).

Notes

For the jurisdiction of the county court to grant matrimonial injunctions, see Supplement to 13 Halsbury's Laws (4th edn) para 1228.

For the Domestic Violence and Matrimonial Proceedings Act 1976, s 2, see 46 Halsbury's Statutes (3rd edn) 714.

Cases referred to in judgments

B v B [1978] 1 All ER 821, [1978] Fam 26, [1978] 2 WLR 160, CA, Digest (Cont Vol E) 279, *7683c*.

Davis v Johnson [1978] 1 All ER 1132, [1979] AC 264, [1978] 2 WLR 553, HL; *affg* [1978] 1 All ER 841, [1979] AC 264, [1978] 2 WLR 182, CA, Digest (Cont Vol E) 279, *7683Ce*.

McLean v Nugent (1979) 1 FLR 26, CA.

Cases also cited

G (a minor), Re (1982) Times, 6 November, CA.

Lewis (A H) v Lewis (R W F) [1978] 1 All ER 729, [1978] Fam 60, CA.

O'Malley v O'Malley [1982] 2 All ER 112, [1982] 1 WLR 244, CA.

---

a Section 2, so far as material, is set out at p 52 *d* to *f*, post

Quinn v Quinn (1982) Times, 24 June, CA.
Spencer v Camacho (1983) Times, 26 January, CA. a

Interlocutory appeal

Jean White appealed against that part of an order made by his Honour Judge Clapham in the Bromley County Court on 17 November 1982 whereby he refused her application for a power of arrest to be attached to an earlier order of the court restraining the respondent, David Henry White, from assaulting, molesting or otherwise interfering b with her or the children of the family and from entering the former matrimonial home or approaching within 50 yards thereof. The facts are set out in the judgment of Cumming-Bruce LJ.

Franklin Evans for the petitioner.
Gayle Hallon for the respondent. c

CUMMING-BRUCE LJ. This appeal raises a short point of construction of s 2 of the Domestic Violence and Matrimonial Proceedings Act 1976. Subsections (1), (2) and (3) read as follows:

> '(1) Where, on an application by a party to a marriage, a judge grants an d injunction containing a provision (in whatever terms)—(*a*) restraining the other party to the marriage from using violence against the applicant, or (*b*) restraining the other party from using violence against a child living with the applicant, or (*c*) excluding the other party from the matrimonial home or from a specified area in which the matrimonial home is included, the judge may, if he is satisfied that the other party has caused actual bodily harm to the applicant or, as the case may be, to e the child concerned and considers that he is likely to do so again, attach a power of arrest to the injunction.
>
> (2) References in subsection (1) above to the parties to a marriage include references to a man and a woman who are living with each other in the same household as husband and wife and any reference in that subsection to the matrimonial home shall be construed accordingly. f
>
> (3) If, by virtue of subsection (1) above, a power of arrest is attached to an injunction, a constable may arrest without warrant a person who he has reasonable cause for suspecting of being in breach of such a provision of that injunction as falls within paragraphs (*a*) to (*c*) of subsection (1) above by reason of that person's use of violence or, as the case may be, of his entry into any premises or area.'

The phrase in s 2(1), 'on an application by a party to a marriage', also appears in s 1 of g the same Act, which again I set out in this judgment in extenso:

> '(1) Without prejudice to the jurisdiction of the High Court, on an application by a party to a marriage a county court shall have jurisdiction to grant an injunction containing one or more of the following provisions, namely—(*a*) a provision restraining the other party to the marriage from molesting the applicant; (*b*) a h provision restraining the other party from molesting a child living with the applicant; (*c*) a provision excluding the other party from the matrimonial home or a part of the matrimonial home or from a specified area in which the matrimonial home is included; (*d*) a provision requiring the other party to permit the applicant to enter and remain in the matrimonial home or a part of the matrimonial home; whether or not any other relief is sought in the proceedings.' j

The question for decision is a short one. Does the phrase 'a party to a marriage' have the meaning 'a party to a subsisting marriage' or, alternatively, does it extend to 'a party to a former marriage'?

I set out the facts. The parties were married in 1968. There were four children of the family, two of them being children who were born to the husband and wife; the other two being children of whom the wife had custody. The wife, the petitioner, brought proceedings for dissolution, seeking custody of all the children, with reasonable access to the respondent husband after the divorce. Both parties at that time were still living in the matrimonial home.

On 11 March 1981 a decree nisi was granted, together with an order confiding the custody of the two youngest children of the family to the petitioner, with reasonable access to their father. A decree absolute was made on 24 April 1981 at a time when the parties were still living under the same roof.

On 18 May 1981 the husband left the former matrimonial home and went to live in a council flat. The former matrimonial home was transferred to the wife as the tenant. From that date the former wife, as tenant, had the exclusive right of possession of the hereditament which had been the former matrimonial home and her former husband was living elsewhere in his own premises.

On 11 November 1981 the court made an order for financial provision.

For some 18 months after the parting the former husband habitually returned to the former matrimonial home. He used to come nearly every day and his visits and attentions were annoying and embarrassing, but there was no violence. For some reason, perhaps out of politeness on the part of the mother, there had been no definition of the father's rights of access.

For eight weeks ending 14 October 1982, the former husband's behaviour became worse. It was described in the former wife's affidavit dated 14 October 1982:

> '... unfortunately, this behaviour has increased in intensity in the course of the last eight weeks or so during which the respondent has refused his usual medication.'

I interpolate that the trouble in this case is that the former husband has for long been afflicted with mental disease which is apparently totally controlled, provided he takes his prescribed injection. But, during the period with which the former wife was dealing, he had stopped taking his injections and therefore had become exceedingly erratic and eccentric. The affidavit continues:

> 'As some illustration of his present behaviour, on 30 September, 1982 (on his own account) he was intending to kill himself by jumping from a balcony when he heard a message from God telling him not to kill himself but to kill his wife instead. On Monday, 4 October 1982 he came to the house and told me that he would obtain a shotgun (giving details of how he intended to do this) and would blow my head off and play football with it thereafter. I have tried to be sympathetic or to dissuade the respondent from his actions but he takes no notice whatsoever. I have also tried to interest his own general practitioner on his behalf but with minimal success. The respondent's conduct causes me extreme anxiety and distress. The constant and persistent visits, letters, etc, have been so wearing on my nervous system that they have had a physical effect only equal to an outright assault. Moreover, I greatly fear that if the respondent's condition continues to deteriorate he may actually become physically violent towards me and that if such violence arises it will be of a serious nature.'

On 14 October 1982 the former wife sought an injunction prohibiting the former husband from assaulting, molesting or otherwise interfering with her or with the family, and for an order restricting him from entering or even approaching the house where she was living in Muirkirk Road, London SE6. That application was made ex parte to his Honour Ian Fife, sitting as a deputy circuit judge, who made the order sought by injunctions as requested, and gave liberty to the former husband to apply to vary or discharge the order. He attached to the order a penal notice that 'unless you obey the directions contained in this order you will be guilty of contempt of court and will be liable to be committed to prison'.

The former wife applied again to the court on 10 November, accompanied by an affidavit dated the same date. By the notice of her application she sought a power of arrest to attach to the order of 19 October 1982 in these terms;

> 'Take notice that the petitioner hereby applies to this Honourable Court for an order that a power of arrest attach to the Order made by His Honour Judge Fife on *a* 19th October 1982. The grounds upon which the petitioner claims to be entitled to this order are set out in her accompanying affidavit.'

I observe that that notice, like the other applications made by her, was made in the number described as the plaint number on the matrimonial proceedings.

One turns to the affidavit of the petitioner dated 9 November 1982 in support of her *b* application for a power of arrest to be attached to the injunction. She described a distressing history in which, in spite of the injunction, the respondent in a quite irrational way was still coming into the house, persuading the children in the absence of the mother to let him in and, when he got in, making a formidable nuisance of himself by abuse and eccentric behaviour. On one occasion he became very excitable. He actually hit his former wife and had to be restrained from hitting her again. Later the same day he turned up at midnight, shouted through the letter box making an awful noise, and a *c* day or two later there was a repetition of the same kind of behaviour: getting into the house, threatening his former wife, and on that occasion had to be carried off by the police, struggling so violently that the police had to call reinforcements. After that incident he came up before the justices and was bound over in the sum of £50 for a period of one year.

d That history was what prompted her application for the urgent remedy of a power of arrest to be attached to the order of 19 October. On 10 November she appeared before his Honour Judge Clapham, again ex parte. There were obvious reasons: the urgency of the situation, the anxiety that unless she obtained the power of arrest there might be difficulties as soon as he received notice of the application, and so on.

In those ex parte proceedings the judge made an order that the order of Judge Fife would have attached to it a power of arrest, effective to 17 November, provided that such *e* power of arrest would not become operative until after the order had been served on the respondent. He continued the injunctions and prohibited the respondent from entering the former matrimonial home or approaching within 50 yards thereof without further order of the court, with liberty to the respondent to apply. Again that order had indorsed on it a penal notice for committal in the event of contempt of the order. The power of arrest was indorsed in the appropriate words on that ex parte order. The return day was *f* 17 November, when the parties appeared before the same judge. The respondent was represented by a solicitor who called no evidence and filed no evidence. Counsel appeared for the applicant. The order made by the judge enjoined and restrained the respondent by injunctions from assaulting, molesting or otherwise interfering with the petitioner or the children of the family and from entering the house in Muirkirk Road or approaching within 50 yards thereof, which order superseded the order the judge made on 19 October. *g* The order continued:

> 'The power of arrest attached to the order herein of the 10th November 1982 do now cease to be effective and that the police be notified accordingly.'

On that order was indorsed a penal notice giving him notice that he was liable to be committed to prison in the event of a contempt by breach of the order. The judge gave *h* leave to appeal in respect of his refusal to continue the power of arrest and in a careful judgment the judge has explained the reason why he took that course. He said:

> 'It is in my view most important that the power of arrest should not be attached to an injunction unless the court is certain that it has power to do so, as the consequences may be serious. I am not satisfied on the evidence before me that I *j* have jurisdiction to order a power of arrest and therefore the power attached on 10 November 1982 will no longer apply. I think it would be helpful to have a ruling from the Court of Appeal on the question and I therefore give leave to the petitioner, if so advised, to pursue the matter further. Having said that, the power of arrest is only to be attached in exceptional circumstances and . . . I do not think that this is a case where I would have attached a power of arrest even if I had jurisdiction.'

In this court counsel for the petitioner has submitted that, if this court takes the view that it should not uphold the judge's view on jurisdiction, in spite of what the judge said it would be appropriate to send the case back to him because counsel, in the light of the observations of the judge at the hearing on jurisdiction, forbore from calling evidence which he would have called in order to substantiate his submission that, there being jurisdiction, it was an appropriate case to exercise it. On the view that I have formed of the point of law on the question of jurisdiction, it becomes unnecessary to consider the question whether to send the case back.

I come to the point which arises for decision. Counsel for the petitioner, in a very helpful argument, has submitted that once a party to a marriage, always a party to a marriage, for the purposes of ss 1 and 2 of the Domestic Violence and Matrimonial Proceedings Act 1976. He submits that jurisdiction in relation to the sections, and in particularly s 2, with which we are concerned, should not and does not depend on status, namely the status of the applicant as husband or wife under the matrimonial law, because the matter is to be approached by reference to the relationship of the parties and, if the relationship of the parties has been that of husband and wife, the fact of that relationship should be that they are in this statute regarded as parties to the marriage, namely parties to a marriage which once subsisted but which no longer continues, having been determined by a decree absolute of dissolution. Counsel derives support for his submission from consideration of judgments and observations made in cases which have been primarily concerned with the construction of s 1(2) of the 1976 Act. Subsection (2) reads:

> 'Subsection (1) above shall apply to a man and a woman who are living with each other in the same household as husband and wife as it applies to the parties to a marriage and any reference to the matrimonial home shall be construed accordingly.'

According to the literal construction of the language of that subsection, it applies only to a man and woman who are at the moment of the application which invokes the jurisdiction of the court, or even at the moment when the court is called on to exercise its power, actually living with each other in the same household. Having regard to the mischief to which that subsection was directed, the court has had little difficulty in deciding that a literal construction does not give effect to the intention of Parliament, for such a construction would have the effect that the very persons whom the Act was designed to provide with an urgent and practical remedy would, in the nature of things, usually be unable to invoke the jurisdiction. For example (and it is a common situation) the situation of the girl living with a cohabitee and with a child being the child of the young man and young lady, the young man returns to the house, knocks her about and thrusts her from the matrimonial home in the sense in which the term is used in the statute; from that moment she has ceased to live with the other party. She invokes the protection of the 1976 Act and the court, as a matter of construction, has decided that in spite of the literal words of the subsection, it applies to parties who are not living with each other at the time when the matter came to court and who were not living with each other at the time of the application to the court, but who had been living together and were living together at the time of the incidents which give rise to the claim for relief.

Fortified by that construction of s 1(2) of the 1976 Act, counsel for the petitioner submits that likewise a liberal construction should be given to the phrase 'a party to a marriage' in ss 1 and 2 in order to afford to parties who have been married but whose marriage has been dissolved the protection of the urgent and almost instant remedy afforded by the power of arrest which is derived from s 2 of the statute. He submits that there is a common sense about that. For example, on the facts of the present case, at the date of the decree absolute the parties were still living together in the matrimonial home and, if the respondent had failed to take his injections at that time and had become subject to the dangerous eccentricities to which he later became subjected, surely the statute would have afforded to her the remedy of obtaining a power of arrest attached to an injunction which she could, on any view, have obtained a week before when the parties were living together after decree nisi but before the marriage had been dissolved by decree absolute. So, counsel submits, as the court has done in relation to s 1(2), do not look at status, look at the relationship of the parties, the reality of their situation and the *a* mischief to which this statute was aimed, and give that phrase 'a party to a marriage' a liberal construction so that it comprehends not only parties to a subsisting marriage but also parties of a former marriage.

Counsel for the petitioner derives support from the judgments in *McLean v Nugent* (1979) 1 FLR 26. That was a case which came before the court on an application under s 1(2) of the 1976 Act and counsel derived assistance from the judgment of Ormrod LJ, *b* in particular where, in relation to that subsection, he said (at 31):

> 'In my judgment the test, as it emerges from the passages I have cited [which were passages from *Davis v Johnson* [1978] 1 All ER 841 at 850, 859, 874, [1979] AC 264 at 275, 285, 303–304 per Lord Dening MR, Baker P and Goff LJ, [1978] 1 All ER 1132 at 1145, [1979] AC 264 at 334 per Viscount Dilhorne, and which included a reference to *B v B* [1978] 1 All ER 821, [1978] Fam 26], depends essentially on the *c* existence at some time of a relationship which is that of "a man and a woman living together as man and wife". In other words, if the evidence shows that they have been living together as man and wife, they are, within limits which are not easy to define, to be treated as though they were married at that time. The question of fact which arises, of course, in such a situation will be: when has that relationship come to an end? How long after it comes to an end is a party entitled to take advantage of *d* [s 1(2) of the 1976 Act]?'

Having stated the advantages in that way Ormrod LJ proceeded to examine this application to the facts of the appeal before him. Eveleigh LJ said (at 32):

> 'Section 1(1) [of the 1976 Act] gives jurisdiction to the court to provide four different kinds of relief to people who complain of harmful conduct during a *e* relationship. That relationship under subs. (1) is marriage. When subs. (2) says that: "Subsection (1) above shall apply to a man and a woman who are living with each other in the same household as husband and wife . . ." it is saying that the court's jurisdiction shall extend to govern such a case . . . In the present case there was conduct at the time when the relationship between the parties could perfectly properly be described as that of a man and a woman who were living with each *f* other.'

If that is the correct approach to the construction of sub-s (2) (as undoubtedly it is, and I would respectfully affirm all that Ormrod LJ said in his judgment) is not that a reason for taking the same approach to the phrase 'a party to a marriage' in ss 1 and 2, to discard the submission that that sets up a test of status, namely the subsistence of the status of husband and wife, and to substitute the test 'are these two parties parties who had a *g* relationship of husband and wife, though that relationship may have ended'? If that approach is right it would, of course, become a matter for consideration of the facts on each case whether the time and circumstances which have elapsed since the date of decree absolute are such as to make the court conclude that the relief afforded by the 1976 Act was intended by Parliament still to be available to the aggrieved party.

Attractive though the submission of counsel for the petitioner was, I do not accept it. *h* It appears to me that this Act, in ss 1 and 2, provides relief for two quite different classes of person. The first class of person which Parliament was contemplating were persons who were parties to a subsisting marriage, either of whom could claim relief provided by s 1 or s 2 during the continuance of the marriage. One of the factors which, in my view, point to that conclusion is that the Act was clearly contemplating throughout a situation where a man and a woman were cohabiting, or at any rate sharing *j* accommodation, in an actual or quasi matrimonial home. In the case of married persons being parties to a subsisting marriage each, subject to the provisions of the 1976 Act, have a right to enter the matrimonial home by reason of their status as husband or wife, and while they continue to enjoy those rights which flow from that status the 1976 Act affords urgent and instant remedy for parties (usually the wives) to acquire protection. But when their marriage is dissolved by a decree absolute, their rights in relation to the matrimonial home and in relation to consortium and access to each other and to the children of the family are thereafter entirely dependent on the orders made by the court in the jurisdiction under the Matrimonial Causes Acts and Matrimonial Proceedings and Property Act 1970. In those statutes there is to be found a code by which either former spouse can regulate all matters relating to access to children and access to property or rights to occupy property. In that code it is to be expected, and there is nothing in my experience to doubt it, that former spouses have at their disposal machinery which enables them to obtain relief with the requisite celerity because, in virtually every case, the parties have ceased to live in the same matrimonial home and if they do, as the parties did in this case for a short time continue so to live, it is usually by agreement and not from any compulsion of circumstances. Looking at the need for the remedies provided by the Domestic Violence and Matrimonial Proceedings Act 1976, I see no reason, having regard to the mischief, to give an extended meaning to the phrase 'a party to a marriage' which is wider, in my view, than a literal construction would require or point to. There is a significant and important distinction between the class of husbands and wives, which is the first class with whom the section deals, and the second class being a man and a woman who are living together in the same household as husband and wife. In their case, as was explained in the speeches and judgments in *Davis v Johnson* [1978] 1 All ER 1132, [1979] AC 264, HL; [1978] 1 All ER 841, [1979] AC 264, CA, their cohabitation, their rights, their needs and their obligations, are not controlled by any matrimonial or quasi matrimonial legislation, but are dependent entirely on the common law or such equities as may arise from contractual arrangements between them. So there was every reason, in order to find a construction that afforded a remedy, for the courts to have taken the course that they did in giving a liberal construction to the present tense in the phrase 'who are living together' so as to extend it in the way that has been done.

In the case of husband and wife, while they are married and have mutual rights and obligations, there is every reason for providing the remedy which the 1976 Act affords, but when the relationship of husband and wife has ended, they no longer share rights of occupation in the matrimonial home. Access to children and access to property may all be regulated by proceedings taken after the filing of the petition up to decree nisi, after decree nisi and after decree absolute, and I would expect it unlikely that after decree absolute a situation of such urgency should arise between the parties (the former husband and former wife) which made it necessary to contemplate the use of a power of arrest annexed to an injunction, pursuant to the 1976 Act. Indeed the only occasion that I can see, would arise on an occasion in which the former wife had been belated, by herself or her solicitors, in obtaining protection by injunction accompanied by a penal notice afforded to her under the existing law, other than the 1976 Act. I would go further and say that I would regard such an extension of the jurisdiction of the 1976 Act as carrying with it positive disadvantages. I therefore find no reason, looking at the mischief to which the Act is aimed, and the circumstances of the first class of person which the Act is designed to protect, to extend that class beyond parties to a subsisting marriage to the class of former husbands and former wives being parties to a marriage which once subsisted but which has ceased to exist.

For those reasons I would move that the doubts expressed by Judge Clapham were well founded and the order that he made, excluding the power of arrest from the injunction of Judge Fife, was right. I would dismiss this appeal.

I would only add this. If after decree absolute the former husband and former wife are living together in the same household as husband and wife, there is jurisdiction to attach a power of arrest under s 2(2) of the 1976 Act. That is not the instant case.

REEVE J. I agree and would only add very few words of my own.

It is not disputed that the court has power to attach a power of arrest under s 2 of the Domestic Violence and Matrimonial Proceedings Act 1976 to an injunction which has been granted under some section other than s 1 of that Act. That power, of course, is in any event subject to the conditions contained in s 2(2) of the 1976 Act. In effect what the court can do is to graft a power of arrest on to an injunction which itself has been granted under whatever jurisdiction, and thereby produce what I ventured to call during argument a 'hybrid order'. But the court has no jurisdiction to graft a power of arrest on to an injunction, except where there is an application by a 'party to a marriage'. I take those words from s 2(1). To my mind the plain and ordinary meaning of that phrase is a person who is still married; but in view of the arguments which have been addressed to us, it is necessary to ask whether there is anything to indicate that the words should be construed more liberally so as to include 'a party to a former marriage'. To my mind the Act was intended to give protection to one of a couple against the other when they are either married to each other, or are or have been living with each other in the same household. So far as unmarried couples are concerned, the words 'are living with each other in the same household' cannot be construed literally or the purpose of the Act would be largely thwarted.

For the reasons given by Ormrod LJ in *McLean v Nugent* (1979) 1 FLR 26 at 31 by reference to a number of reported cases which have been decided under this Act, it is plain that much of the usefulness of the 1976 Act would be destroyed by a literal construction of s 2(2). If unmarried couples not actually cohabiting were unable to avail themselves of the relief afforded by the Act, they would have the greatest difficulty in obtaining any legal relief whatever. But in the case of married couples, there is relief potentially available under the legislation dealing with matrimonial causes. It is unnecessary in their case to depart from a strict construction of the Act; but of course they may wish to avail themselves of the provisions of the 1976 Act by way of immediate first aid in certain instances, particularly when they are cohabiting or where matrimonial proceedings have not been instituted between them. Where there have been divorce proceedings, as ex hypothesi there must have been if a decree absolute has been pronounced, the court has power in those proceedings to grant injunctions for the protection of children and, in exceptional cases, may have power in ancillary proceedings to grant injunctions regulating the occupation of the former matrimonial home. But where the parties are not actually cohabiting, there is little or no necessity for a power of arrest to be added to the injunction. References in ss 1(1)(*c*) and (*d*) and 2(1)(*c*) to a matrimonial home reinforce my view that the Act contemplates some degree of cohabitation between the parties before this part of the Act can be invoked. If, after the marriage has been dissolved by decree absolute, the parties continue to cohabit or resume cohabitation, recourse can be had to the Act under the provisions of s 2(2). In those circumstances I do not find it necessary to depart from a strict construction of the plain and ordinary use of the words.

Counsel for the respondent, in a most helpful argument, took us through a number of previous statutes where the same phrase 'party to a marriage' was used. I do not derive any real assistance from that review which was undertaken by counsel. Alternative words are used in certain Acts, such as 'husband and wife', 'petitioner and respondent' and sometimes even 'spouses', but it seems to me that the use of those various expressions in their different and varying contexts does not throw any real light on the proper construction of the phrase 'party to a marriage' in the 1976 Act.

I can conceive that there might be exceptional circumstances in which it would be desirable for the court to have jurisdiction to add a power of arrest to an injunction granted after a decree absolute when the parties were not cohabiting, but I cannot find on a true construction of this Act that such jurisdiction has been conferred.

Appeal dismissed. Leave to appeal to the House of Lords refused.

Solicitors: *William J Stoffel & Co*, Beckenham (for the petitioner); *Bryan Lewis & Co*, Sydenham (for the respondent).

Bebe Chua Barrister.

a Epsom and Ewell Borough Council v C Bell (Tadworth) Ltd

CHANCERY DIVISION
HIS HONOUR JUDGE RUBIN SITTING AS A JUDGE OF THE HIGH COURT
20, 21 OCTOBER 1982

b

Agricultural holding – Tenancy – Agreement whereby land let for interest less than tenancy from year to year – Agreement to take effect as agreement for tenancy from year to year – Exception where minister approving the letting before agreement was made – Minister approving letting of land for 364 days – No tenancy agreement executed – 364-day tenancy arising by implication – Whether minister's approval could cover such a tenancy – Whether tenancy taking effect as
c *tenancy from year to year – Agricultural Holdings Act 1948, s 2(1).*

By s 2(1)[a] of the Agricultural Holdings Act 1948, where any land was let under an agreement to a person for use as agricultural land for any interest less than a tenancy from year to year in circumstances such that the person would be a tenant of an agricultural holding if his interest were a tenancy from year to year, then, 'unless the
d letting . . . was approved by the Minister before the agreement was entered into', the agreement was to take effect as if it were an agreement for the letting of the land for a tenancy from year to year, thereby giving the tenant security of tenure under the 1948 Act. On 1 February 1977 the plaintiff, with the minister's prior approval given under s 2(1) of the 1948 Act, granted the defendant a tenancy of certain land for agricultural purposes for a period of 364 days expiring on 30 January 1978. The plaintiff anticipated
e that when that period expired the defendant would want a further term of 364 days. Accordingly, on 3 October 1977, the plaintiff obtained the minister's approval to 'the letting [of the land] by an agreement to be entered into after the date hereof . . . for the period of 364 days commencing on 31 January 1978'. Negotiations between the parties as to the further term broke down and no new tenancy agreement was executed. The defendant held over after the existing term expired and at the end of each quarter during
f the ensuing year tendered to the plaintiff the rent payable for a quarter under the terms of the previous agreement. The plaintiff accepted the rent for the first two quarters, so that by implication a tenancy was created for a term of 364 days expiring on 30 January 1979. When that tenancy expired and the defendant refused to deliver up possession the plaintiff brought an action against the defendant claiming an order for possession. The defendant contended that, by virtue of s 2(1), the tenancy created by the holding over
g and payment of rent took effect as a tenancy from year to year, giving it security of tenure, because (i) the minister had no power under s 2(1) to approve the grant of a tenancy by implication and (ii) even if he had such power, the approval which he had given on 3 October 1977 did not cover such a tenancy.

Held – The defendant did not have security of tenure and the plaintiff was entitled to an
h order for possession, because on the true construction of s 2(1) of the 1948 Act the minister merely had, before any agreement was made, to approve the letting of the particular piece of land which was ultimately the subject of the agreement, and not the terms of the particular agreement as to rent and other conditions, since ex hypothesi the agreement had not then been entered into and the terms and conditions might not by then have been finally settled. Furthermore, on the facts, the minister's approval did in
j fact cover the particular 364-day tenancy which arose by implication from the defendant holding over and paying rent (see p 63 *d* to *h* and p 64 *c d*, post).

Reid v Dawson [1954] 3 All ER 498 and *Finbow v Air Ministry* [1963] 2 All 647 considered.

---

a Section 2(1), so far as material, is set out at p 62 *a* to *c*, post

Notes

For tenancies from year to year and for security of tenure, see 27 Halsbury's Laws (4th edn) paras 177, 875.

For the Agricultural Holdings Act 1948, s 2, see 1 Halsbury's Statutes (3rd edn) 689.

Cases referred to in judgment

Finbow v Air Ministry [1963] 2 All ER 647, [1963] 1 WLR 697, 2 Digest (Reissue) 7, *14*.

Reid v Dawson [1954] 3 All ER 498, [1955] 1 QB 214, [1954] 3 WLR 810, CA, 2 Digest (Reissue) 9, *19*.

Action

The plaintiff, Epsom and Ewell Borough Council, brought an action against the defendant, C Bell (Tadworth) Ltd (the company), claiming (i) an order for the delivery up of possession of the property known as Long Grove Farm, which formed part of Horton Country Park and Buffer land in the borough of Epsom and Ewell, (ii) arrears of rent down to 29 January 1979, amounting to £1,506·45, (iii) mesne profits in respect of Long Grove Farm at the rate of £8·15 per day from 30 January 1979 down to the date of the hearing, (iv) mesne profits at the rate of £8·15 per day from the date of the hearing until the delivery up of possession, and (v) such further or other relief as the court considered the council was entitled to have. The facts are set out in the judgment.

Ernest Scamell for the council.
Anthony Dinkin for the company.

HIS HONOUR JUDGE RUBIN. The plaintiff, the Epsom and Ewell Borough Council, is the owner of certain land in the borough described as the Horton Country Park and Buffer land which it acquired for amenity purposes. It has for some time past allowed the defendant company to use a substantial part of that land for carrying on various agricultural activities.

I can start the story for the purposes of these proceedings with a tenancy agreement which was dated 9 January 1976. It was an agreement under which the council let the relevant land to the company for a term of more than 12 months and less than two years, a term which did not then create a secure tenancy for the purposes of the Agricultural Holdings Acts. I need say no more about that tenancy agreement. It expired by effluxion of time on 31 January 1977, and on the next day a new tenancy agreement was granted to the company for a period of 364 days. Prior to the grant of that tenancy agreement, the approval of the minister had been obtained under s 2 of the Agricultural Holdings Act 1948. Again I need say no more about that term because nothing turns on it, other than it expired in due course by effluxion of time on the expiration of the 364 days created by that term.

In the mean time certain events had occurred. It is clear that the appropriate officers of the council contemplated that at the end of that term a further like term of 364 days would be granted to the company, because the officers of the council applied to the minister for a further consent and that was granted on 3 October 1977, well before the original term of 364 days had expired. As so much turns on that permission perhaps I should read it in full:

'THE AGRICULTURAL HOLDINGS ACT 1948.

Approval by the Minister of a short-term letting of land.

In exercise of the powers conferred upon him by section 2 of the Agricultural Holdings Act 1948, the Minister of Agriculture, Fisheries and Food hereby approves (but only for the purposes of the said Section) the letting by an agreement to be entered into after the date hereof of the land, the particulars of which are as follows [it then sets out the particulars:] 259 acres (approximately) forming part of the Horton Country Park and Buffer land and shown edged red on the plan annexed

> hereto signed by the undersigned for use as agricultural land for the period of 364
> a days commencing on 31 January 1978.'

It is signed on behalf of the minister. There is no issue in this case about the identity of the land. Nobody suggests that the 259 acres referred to in that permission are not the land with which I am concerned in this case.

After the grant of that approval by the minister, negotiations took place between the council and the company's advisers in contemplation of the grant of a further term of
b 364 days at the expiration of the then existing term. Certainly the council had that in mind. What was in the mind of the company and its advisers is not so clear from the correspondence. The council went to the extent of even preparing a lease, or a draft of a lease, in which they included the date of execution, which is somewhat unusual in a draft, being of course the very day after the expiration of the existing 364-day term.

Be that as it may, those negotiations were fruitless and no new tenancy agreement was
c executed at all. However, on the expiration of the existing term of 364 days the company remained in possession of the land, and indeed remain in possession, as far as I am aware, to this day. At the end of what would be a quarter of either a new year or a new term of 364 days, the company tendered a quarter of what would have been the full rent payable under a 364-day lease on the terms of the previous 364 days' term, and that rent was accepted by the council. At the end of the second quarter a like sum was tendered and
d again accepted by the council. For the remaining two quarters like sums were tendered, but by now somebody in the council no doubt realised the dangers involved and rejected those two tenders of rent. So, out of the 364 days which came into being on the expiration of the original 364 days, one-half of the rent has been paid.

Now, it is common ground between the parties that the effect of the company holding over, and the acceptance of rent by the council was by implication to create a new term
e of 364 days. Now, perhaps it is convenient at this stage that I refer shortly to one case which was cited during the course of argument, that being the decision of the Court of Appeal in *Reid v Dawson* [1954] 3 All ER 498, [1955] 1 QB 214. That was a case under the proviso to s 2(1) of the 1948 Act which deals with short tenancies let in contemplation of grazing of land. It is not directly a point in the present case but I think it is interesting to look at part of the judgment of Morris LJ where he dealt with the decision of the
f county court judge on the facts of that case that the holding over had in fact created a tenancy of one further period of 364 days. At the end of his judgment he said ([1954] 3 All ER 498 at 501, [1955] 1 QB 214 at 220–221):

> 'In regard to that part of the case, however, an additional argument has been addressed to us, that inasmuch as this further period was a period that arose by
> g implication, then it was not for some specified period of the year; for it is said that if the period arises by implication it cannot be "specified". In my judgment, that reasoning is not sound. For the later period there was a necessity to resort to some extent to implication, but that merely means that, in the absence of a new agreement in writing, or in the absence of terms wholly and completely orally expressed, the judge found that there was material from which he could infer or imply what the
> h new contract was. It is quite clear what the new contract was and what were the terms that the parties agreed. They were terms similar to those that they had previously agreed. Therefore, in the new contract they agreed to terms one of which was that the period was to be 364 days, which in my judgment is a specified period within the meaning of the words of [the proviso].'

j Now, of course, I am not troubled with that sort of problem in this case because the parties agree that the term to be implied was indeed one further term of 364 days. It is said, of course, on behalf of the company that the effect of this grant of a term by implication was to create an agricultural holding and, accordingly, that the company has security of tenure. Let me go straight to the section concerned, since at the end of the day the problems which I have to solve to a very large extent depend on the true construction of it, namely s 2 of the Agricultural Holdings Act 1948. I shall read the relevant part of it:

> '(1) Subject to the provisions of this section, where under an agreement made on or after the first day of March, nineteen hundred and forty-eight [and of course the agreement which arose by implication is quite clearly one made after that date], any land [and I emphasise those words and will come back to them later in this judgment] is let to a person for use as agricultural land for an interest less than a tenancy from year to year [and that quite clearly is this case], or a person is granted a licence to occupy land for use as agricultural land, and the circumstances are such that if his interest were a tenancy from year to year he would in respect of that land be the tenant of an agricultural holding [and that is clearly so in this case, and then one comes to the vital part of the section], then, unless the letting or grant was approved by the Minister before the agreement was entered into, the agreement shall take effect, with the necessary modifications, as if it were an agreement for the letting of the land for a tenancy from year to year [with the inevitable consequence, of course, that it would be a protected tenancy under the Act] . . .'

The section then goes on in the proviso to deal with short tenancies of land let in contemplation of the use of the land only for grazing or mowing during some specified period of the year. There, one clearly has to look at the contemplation of the parties at the time of the letting to see whether it was for the use for that particular purpose in the sense that one is there looking at a possible future event.

Now, it is argued by counsel for the company, first of all that as a matter of law the minister had no power under that section to authorise or to approve the grant of a tenancy by implication of this land which arose in the events which occurred. It is secondly argued on behalf of the company that, if that is wrong, the particular approval granted by the minister did not approve that particular type of tenancy. Now, the first point, of course, is essentially a question of construction of the section. I was referred to one case, *Finbow v Air Ministry* [1963] 2 All ER 647, [1963] 1 WLR 697; as far as I am aware it is the only case which deals with the construction of this part of the section. Counsel for the company argues that that case was wrongly decided, and that as it is a case of the first instance, the decision is not binding on me. I need not go into the rather complicated facts of that case, other than to note that the permission granted by the minister in that case was an approval stating that he approved of the grant to any of the government departments or the persons specified in the schedule (so, in a sense, it was a block approval granted to a large number of people) 'of every licence to occupy and use as agricultural land any land which belongs to any of the scheduled authorities [those are the persons I have mentioned] for any estate or interest [therein] whatever'. Now, the relevant part of the judgment of McNair J is as follows ([1963] 2 All ER 647 at 656–657, [1963] 1 WLR 697 at 710):

> 'It is next submitted on behalf of the plaintiff that s. 2 does not contemplate a blanket approval but requires an approval given ad hoc after consideration of the terms of the proposed agreement or at least the circumstances relating to the particular letting or grant. It was argued that, if a blanket approval to letting or grants by the named service authorities were held to be valid, the minister would equally have power in advance to approve all lettings or grants by whomsoever made and that this, in effect, would enable the minister to deprive s. 2 of any effect at all. This argument seems to me to be fallacious, since, if a blanket approval of all lettings and grants were attempted, it would be clear that the minister had not applied his mind to any relevant circumstances. In the present case by confining his approval to lettings or grants by specific named authorities it is clear that he had applied his mind to the general circumstances relating to such grants.'

Then he dealt with two authorities which I need not mention. McNair J then went on to say:

> 'I can find nothing in the language used in s 2(1) or in the policy of the Act of 1948 to be deduced from its provisions which requires or supports the submission that the approval must be given ad hoc. If anything, the use of the words requiring the approval of "the letting or grant" rather than "of the terms of the proposed agreement" seems to point the other way and suggests that the minister may approve lettings or grants of particular types without considering the particular proposed letting or grant. The form of words used follows a very familiar statutory form . . .'

and then he went on to deal with some other matters with which I am not concerned in this case. Now, counsel for the company criticises that judgment, primarily by looking at the section itself, saying and submitting that the judgment is inconsistent with the language used by the draftsman of the section. Now, with all respect to McNair J, I can see considerable force in that argument, but I think there is a danger of carrying that argument too far. What the words of the section are, are these:

> '. . . then, unless the letting [and counsel for the company emphasises these words] or grant was approved by the Minister before the agreement was entered into . . .'

Now, it seems to me that one cannot have a letting or grant in the abstract. It has got to be a letting or grant of something, and, in my judgment, one has got to look back to the earlier part of the section to see what letting or grant was in the contemplation of the draftsman when he used those words. The only reference, of course, could be to the 'any land' at the beginning of the section. Therefore, it seems to me that on its true construction one here has to read this section as if it read, 'unless the letting or grant of the land which was ultimately let was approved by the Minister before the agreement was entered into . . .'

I find myself driven to a conclusion that what the minister has to apply his mind to is the letting or grant of a particular piece of land. However, I agree with McNair J when he decided that the minister was not concerned with the particular terms of the agreement to be entered into. Again, as a matter of construction of the section, what is required is that, 'unless the letting or grant should be approved by the Minister'. There is nothing there which requires the minister to approve of the terms of the agreement which, ex hypothesi, have not then been entered into and, indeed, may not by then have been finally settled. That seems to me, again, to be consistent with the general policy of the Act, and in particular this section which is dealing with security of tenure in respect of particular land, and the minister is concerned with that aspect of the matter only. He is not concerned with other aspects of the agreement of letting, the rent, or anything else of that nature and, therefore, in my judgment, on the true construction of this section the minister has to apply his mind to the circumstances of the particular land, and to the letting or the grant in respect thereof. He is not concerned with the terms of the particular agreement.

It seems to me, therefore, that applying that to the present case, when the application ultimately came before the minister on the 3 October 1977 what he had to apply his mind to was the letting of a particular piece of land; that he duly applied his mind to that subject one can see from the very nature of the approval itself. I have, therefore, come to the conclusion that the minister had power under the section to grant the approval which he did grant.

The next question, of course, is: did that approval in fact apply to the particular tenancy which in fact came into being by the implication arising from the holding over, and of the payment of rent? Now, again, it seems to me that when one looks at the section, as the minister is not concerned with any particular agreement, one has got to look from the section to his approval, see what it means, and see whether it can fairly be said to apply to the events which, in fact, occurred. What the minister, in fact, approved was this: 'the letting by an agreement to be entered into after the date hereof . . .' Now, of course, when one sees those words, an immediate reaction to them may be that the agreement was to be an agreement in writing.

It is accepted that one can create a tenancy of agricultural land for 364 days or, indeed, for any other period, by an agreement in writing, by an agreement under seal, orally or, *a* indeed, by implication arising from a holding over and a payment of rent, and that the agreement which comes into being, whatever way it comes into being, is none the less an agreement, and what is more it is none the less an agreement which is entered into after the date of the approval, so I can see, at the end of the day, no difficulty over that. There is certainly no difficulty over the land, because it is common ground that the 259 acres, referred to in the minister's approval, is indeed the land occupied by the company. *b* 'For use as agricultural land': again, there is no dispute over that; that that amply fits the land which was indeed let. Then the minister in his approval has limited his approval to a particular type of tenancy: 'for the period of 364 days commencing on 31 January 1978.' Again, the tenancy which in fact came into effect by implication was, it is agreed between the parties, a tenancy for 364 days. Moreover such tenancy must have commenced on 31 January, because the previous tenancy expired by effluxion of time *c* on the day before. For these reasons, in my judgment, without looking at the correspondence or the intention of the parties or what was in their contemplation, what in fact happened was the creation of the precise tenancy which is indicated by the minister's approval, and is, indeed, a letting approved by the minister, and accordingly, as a result of s 2 of the Agricultural Holdings Act 1948, it is exempt from taking effect as a tenancy from year to year, and accordingly is not an agricultural holding and there is *d* no security of tenure. It follows from this (we will have to look at the precise terms of relief in a moment) that the council is entitled to its order for possession.

Order for delivery up of possession on date to be agreed by parties, for payment of arrears of rent and for payment of mesne profits at agreed rate from 30 January 1979 to date of delivery up of possession.

Solicitors: *Sharpe Pritchard & Co* (for the council); *Downs,* Dorking (for the company).

Hazel Hartman Barrister.

Oceanica Castelana Armadora SA v Mineralimportexport (Barclays Bank International Ltd intervening) The Theotokos and related applications

QUEEN'S BENCH DIVISION (COMMERCIAL COURT)
LLOYD J
21, 27 JANUARY 1983

Injunction – Interlocutory – Danger that defendant may transfer assets out of jurisdiction – Protection of interests of innocent third parties – Banks – Assets covered by injunction held by bank – Variation of injunction to protect bank – Protection of bank's usual rights of set-off against a customer's funds – Bank making loans to defendant prior to injunction – Whether bank entitled to variation of injunction to enable it to exercise usual rights of set-off in respect of loans – Whether bank required to make disclosures regarding state of defendant's accounts with it and existence of other assets of defendant available to meet repayment of principal and interest under loans.

A foreign defendant had funds (amounting to less than $US2m) deposited with a bank in England. The bank had made substantial loans to the defendant which were still outstanding. Interest on the loans was payable monthly. Subsequent to the loans the plaintiff, who had a claim against the defendant under a contract, obtained a Mareva injunction against the defendant restraining it from removing out of the jurisdiction assets within the jurisdiction in the sum of $US2m. The bank applied to the court to have the injunction varied to enable it to exercise in respect of the funds held by it its ordinary rights of set-off in respect of the principal and the interest under the loans. The bank made no disclosure to the court regarding the state of the defendant's accounts with it or regarding the existence of any other assets of the defendant within the jurisdiction which might be available to meet the defendant's obligations under the loans.

Held – Although a bank which held funds which were subject to a Mareva injunction could not, having regard to the current wording of Mareva injunctions, exercise a banker's usual rights of set-off against the funds without first applying to the court to vary the injunction, once the bank had so applied it was entitled to a variation of the injunction to enable it to exercise over the funds subject to the injunction its usual rights of set-off in connection with any facilities it had granted to the defendant before it received notification of the injunction, since a Mareva injunction was not intended to interfere with contractual rights between a third party and the defendant, and a bank which held funds which were subject to such an injunction ought not, merely because it held the funds, to be in a worse position than the defendant's other creditors (in respect of whom the defendant could apply for a variation of the injunction to enable him to draw on his bank account to pay them). Moreover, the bank was entitled to a variation of the injunction without having to disclose information about the state of the defendant's accounts with the bank or the existence within the jurisdiction of other free assets of the defendant, because to require such disclosures would be to interfere with contractual rights between the bank and the defendant. Accordingly, a bank holding funds which were subject to a Mareva injunction was not required to accept, in lieu of the bank's usual rights of set-off, an indemnity from the plaintiff in respect of the sums owing or likely to be owed in the future to the bank from the defendant. It followed that the bank was entitled to a variation of the Mareva injunction issued against the defendant to enable the bank to exercise a right of set-off in connection with the loans made to the defendant, the right of set-off being exercisable in respect of both the interest on the loans already accrued due at the date of notification of the injunction and interest accruing due in the future (see p 70 *a b c* to *e* and *g* to p 71 *a* and *e*, post).

Galaxia Maritime SA v Mineralimportexport, The Eleftherios [1982] 1 All ER 796 applied. *a*

Dictum of Kerr LJ in *Galaxia Maritime SA v Mineralimportexport, The Eleftherios* [1982] 1 All ER at 799–800 and *Project Development Co Ltd SA v KMK Securities Ltd (Syndicate Bank intervening)* [1983] 1 All ER 465 considered.

A v C (No 2) [1981] 2 All ER 126 distinguished.

Per curiam. (1) Where a defendant has assets in a bank within the jurisdiction which *b* exceed the amount of his assets which are covered by a Mareva injunction issued against him, he is entitled to payment from the bank of the balance of the assets after deduction of the amount covered by the injunction, since the balance constitutes free assets and, accordingly, the bank is only entitled to retain the amount of the assets covered by the injunction. It follows that any right of set-off the bank may have against the defendant will be exercisable only over the assets covered by the injunction retained by the bank *c* and that those assets are therefore liable to be reduced if the bank exercises its right of set-off (see p 71 *d e*, post).

(2) As the greatest burden of policing Mareva injunctions falls on banks, and because the necessity of banks having to apply to the court for variation of Mareva injunctions (to enable them to exercise their usual rights of set-off) should be avoided if possible, it is desirable that in future all Mareva injunctions intended to be served on banks should *d* contain a proviso to the effect that nothing in the injunction shall prevent the bank from exercising any rights of set-off it may have in respect of facilities it has afforded to the defendant prior to the date of the injunction (see p 71 *g h*, post).

Notes

For an injunction restraining the disposition of property, see 24 Halsbury's Laws (4th *e* edn) para 1018, and for cases on the subject, see 28(2) Digest (Reissue) 1091–1094, *918–960*.

Cases referred to in judgment

A v C (No 2) [1981] 2 All ER 126, [1981] QB 961, [1981] 2 WLR 634.

Galaxia Maritime SA v Mineralimportexport, The Eleftherios [1982] 1 All ER 796, [1982] 1 *f* WLR 539, CA.

Project Development Co Ltd SA v KMK Securities Ltd (Syndicate Bank intervening) [1983] 1 All ER 465, [1982] 1 WLR 1470.

Z Ltd v A [1982] 1 All ER 556, [1982] QB 558, [1982] 2 WLR 288, CA.

Summonses

g

In November and December 1981 a number of shipowners, including Ataka Navigation Inc Panama (Ataka) and Oceanica Castelana Armadora SA (Oceanica), obtained ex parte Mareva injunctions against the defendants, Mineralimportexport, a Romanian state trading organisation, in respect of various claims against the defendants as charterers of the shipowners' vessels, restraining the defendants from removing from the jurisdiction their assets, up to a stated maximum amount, within the jurisdiction. Barclays Bank *h* International Ltd (Barclays Bank) held money within the jurisdiction which had been deposited with it by the Romanian Bank for Foreign Trade (the Romanian bank) as security for guarantees which Barclays Bank were intending to issue on behalf of the defendants but which, in the event, it became unnecessary to issue. Barclays Bank contended that that money belonged to the Romanian bank and not to the defendants and was not therefore subject to the Mareva injunctions against the defendants. On 28 *j* September 1982 another shipowner, Seawind Maritime Inc (Seawind), who had a claim against the Romanian bank under a shipbuilding contract, obtained a Mareva injunction against the Romanian bank restraining it from removing from the jurisdiction its assets, up to a stated maximum amount, within the jurisdiction. Prior to that injunction Barclays Bank had made loans in favour of the Romanian bank on which interest was payable monthly by the Romanian bank. Barclays Bank wished to be entitled to exercise against the money deposited by the Romanian bank a right of set-off in respect of the principal and interest payable under the loans. By two summonses dated 18 November 1982 Barclays Bank, as interveners, sought directions from the court in respect of the Mareva injunctions against the defendants, and the Mareva injunction against the Romanian bank. The summonses were heard in chambers but judgment was given by Lloyd J in open court. The facts are set out in the judgment.

Peter Cresswell for Barclays Bank.
Giles Caldin for Ataka and Oceanica.
Alan Pollock QC and *Roderick Cordara* for Seawind.

Cur adv vult

27 January. The following judgment was delivered.

LLOYD J. In these two summonses, Barclays Bank International Ltd, as interveners, seek directions from the court in relation to Mareva injunctions obtained by Holman Fenwick & Willan on behalf of various clients. Both applications illustrate the difficulties in which banks, and other third parties, may find themselves unless there is great care in formulating the original ex parte order, and unless there is subsequent co-operation between the parties in working out the order once it has been granted.

On the second application the bank seeks general guidance from the court as to the exercise of a bank's right of set-off when a customer's account has become subject to a Mareva injunction. But, before coming to that, I must first give a short account of the background which is common to both applications.

Mineralimportexport is a Romanian state trading organisation. Towards the end of November 1981 a number of shipowners had claims against Mineralimportexport as charterers. Oceanica Castelana Armadora SA (Oceanica) of Panama had a claim for demurrage in respect of their vessel Theotokos. Ataka Navigation Inc (Ataka) of Panama had a claim for hire in respect of their vessel Minoan Bull. In each case the owners wished to pursue their claims in arbitration. Mineralimportexport, who I shall refer to as the defendants, have few, if any, assets outside Romania. But it was known that they had an agreement with the National Coal Board under which they bought regular cargo loads of coke for shipment from South Wales to Romania. On 27 November 1981, Ataka obtained a Mareva injunction over the defendants' assets within the jurisdiction, including in particular a cargo of coke loaded on board a vessel called Tirgu Frumos. The Tirgu Frumos had just completed loading her cargo at the port of Barry. Oceanica obtained a similar injunction; and other owners obtained injunctions in relation to cargo on board other vessels.

Negotiations then took place between the defendants, represented by Thomas Cooper & Stibbard, and various plaintiffs represented by Holman Fenwick & Willan. The defendants were anxious to obtain the release of their cargo. They put forward a form of guarantee to be furnished by Anglo-Romanian Bank. Eventually it was agreed that the guarantees (there were five in all) would be provided by Barclays Bank International, against a cash deposit furnished by the Romanian Bank for Foreign Trade. The guarantees were duly prepared. But they were never issued; for at the last moment the defendants got what they wanted by a side wind.

On 17 December 1981 there was an application to discharge one of the other injunctions obtained against the defendants in respect of their cargo on board another vessel called the Eleftherios. The effect of this injunction had been, of course, to prevent the vessel from sailing. The application to discharge that injunction was made, not by the defendants themselves, but by the owners of the vessel.

The matter went to the Court of Appeal: see *Galaxia Maritime SA v Mineralimportexport, The Eleftherios* [1982] 1 All ER 796, [1982] 1 WLR 539. Eveleigh LJ said that it was absolutely intolerable that the vessel should be prevented from sailing because of a claim with which the owners of the vessel were in no way concerned. Kerr LJ described it as a clear abuse of the Mareva jurisdiction. Accordingly, on 18 December 1981 the Court of Appeal discharged the injunction against the defendants so far as it related to the cargo on board the Eleftherios.

Four days later, on 22 December, the owner of the Tirgu Frumos followed suit. The injunctions were discharged so far as they related to the cargo on board that vessel as well. Thereafter the need for the guarantees was gone.

However, the plaintiffs were not to be so easily deterred. Although the cargoes had been released, there was still the injunction over the remaining assets, if any, of the defendants within the jurisdiction; and there was still the cash deposit held by Barclays Bank International as cover for the abortive guarantees. The plaintiffs were evidently advised that the cash deposit was caught by the existing Mareva injunction. On Christmas Eve they telexed the bank as follows:

> 'We have reason to believe that sums of money have been deposited with Barclays Bank International as security for a number of bank guarantees which were to be issued by the bank on behalf of Mineralimportexport to our clients. The Mareva injunctions apply to all assets of Mineralimportexport which will therefore include the above-mentioned deposited sums and we have therefore served copies of the injunctions upon Barclays Bank International at 168 Fenchurch Street.'

The bank made inquiries. On 30 December 1981 they were given clear and specific instructions by Thomas Cooper & Stibbard that the funds which had been deposited with the bank belonged to the Romanian Bank for Foreign Trade, and *not* to the defendants. If that was so, then obviously the injunction would not bite. But the plaintiffs were unwilling to accept that position. The matter dragged on.

On 11 March 1982 the bank's solicitors wrote as follows:

> 'As you are aware, a sum of money was deposited with our clients to serve as security for guarantees which in fact never became effective. That money, however, was not deposited by Mineralimportexport, and our clients have been informed by the depositor that it is not an asset of Mineralimportexport. We have advised our clients that in our opinion the deposit is not subject to your injunctions. However, as you have made the allegation that the injunctions do cover this money, we would ask you to confirm, having heard our explanation, that you now accept that they do not.'

On 18 March the plaintiffs replied:

> 'You say that the funds deposited at Barclays Bank International were not remitted by Mineralimportexport. This does not, of course, exclude the probability that the funds were deposited by way of security for the guarantees issued in favour of our various clients [and then it gives their names] in respect of claims against Mineralimportexport. In our view, they are thereby covered by the Mareva injunctions obtained on behalf of our clients. The depositor has no doubt taken adequate counter security from Mineralimportexport and we are of the view that the funds deposited with your clients by way of security for the guarantees fall within the definition of an asset belonging to Mineralimportexport.'

Thereafter the correspondence continued all summer. On 12 August the bank asked the plaintiffs for copies of the injunctions which were said to affect the bank. There was no reply. The bank sent a chaser on 1 September, but still there was no reply.

Then on 28 September came a fresh development. Holman Fenwick & Willan obtained yet another Mareva injunction, this time acting on behalf of Seawind Maritime Inc. This time the claim was not against Mineralimportexport, but against the Romanian Bank for Foreign Trade. By their writ, issued in the Queen's Bench Division, the plaintiffs in the new action claimed against the Romanian Bank for Foreign Trade as guarantors of a shipbuilding contract entered into with a firm of Romanian shipbuilders. The bank was notified of the new injunction. On 1 October 1982 the bank applied ex parte for directions. They were particularly concerned as to their right of set-off. It seemed to me that that was a matter on which I ought to hear both sides. So the application was adjourned. It is the second of the two applications before me today. I will return to it when I have completed dealing with the Mineralimportexport matter.

Counsel for Oceanica and Ataka invited me to infer that the money deposited with Barclays Bank International belonged to Mineralimportexport. He submits that since the guarantees were going to be put up to secure the release of the defendants' cargo, the natural inference is that it was the defendants' funds which were being used as cover for the guarantees. I cannot accept counsel's argument. If the request had come direct from the defendants to Barclays Bank International, then that might have provided some basis for the inference which I am asked to draw. But here the request came via the Romanian Bank for Foreign Trade. In those circumstances it seems to me just as likely, if not more likely, that the money belonged to the Romanian bank. The fact that the Romanian bank may have taken counter-security from its customers, as envisaged in the plaintiffs' letter of 18 March 1982, does not make the funds actually deposited the assets of the defendants.

But even if I were otherwise minded to draw the suggested inference, I could not do so in the light of the clear statement contained in Thomas Cooper & Stibbard's letter of 30 December 1981 that the funds in question do not belong to the defendants. This was confirmed by what Mr Bateson of Thomas Cooper & Stibbard repeated in court. Mr Bateson found himself in an unusual position, since the defendants have never been served with the originating summons in the proceedings, and therefore Thomas Cooper & Stibbard are not on the record. The originating summons has now lapsed. Nevertheless, I took the view that I was entitled to hear Mr Bateson. In the light of what he told me on instructions, it would be quite wrong for me to draw the inference that the money still belongs, or ever did belong, to the defendants.

Accordingly, my directions are that the funds deposited with Barclays Bank International as cover for the guarantees are not subject to the Mareva injunctions obtained by the plaintiffs in December 1981.

I would only add my concern that it has taken so long to reach this obvious result. When the bank wrote to the plaintiffs as long ago as March 1982 asking for their confirmation that the funds might be released, the answer should have come back promptly, 'Yes.' There could be no other answer in the light of Thomas Cooper & Stibbard's letter to which I have already referred. But the plaintiffs did not give that answer. As a result it has been left to the bank to make this application. Banks and other third parties are sufficiently harassed by applications for Mareva injunctions as it is. It is important that they should be able to look to plaintiffs for greater co-operation than they have received in this case.

I now turn to the second application, arising out of the injunction obtained by Seawind Maritime Inc (Seawind) in September 1982. The effect of the injunction is to restrain the Romanian Bank for Foreign Trade from removing or disposing of its assets within the jurisdiction save in so far as they exceed $US2,190,060. Since I have already held that the funds deposited with Barclays Bank International do not belong to Mineralimportexport, it follows (and I would if necessary infer) that they must belong to the Romanian Bank for Foreign Trade. Prima facie, therefore, the injunction attaches to the funds so deposited. I assume that they amount to a good deal less than the sum for which Seawind have now obtained their injunction. The question is what, if any, rights of set-off the bank can exercise against the deposit, now that the injunction has been obtained.

It appears from the evidence that Barclays Bank International has well over fifty substantial term loans outstanding in favour of the Romanian Bank for Foreign Trade. I was not given the total amount of these loans, and I do not need to know. Interest becomes due on the loans from month to month, and in due course they will presumably fall to be repaid. Barclays Bank International wish to know whether they are entitled to exercise their right of set-off in respect of interest falling due under the loans from time to time, as well as interest which had already fallen due before notification of the injunction.

By a telex of 1 October 1982 Barclays Bank asked for confirmation that they were entitled to exercise their normal rights of set-off in respect of all interest, whether accrued or accruing due, on what I will call the pre-Mareva facilities afforded by Barclays Bank to the Romanian Bank for Foreign Trade. The plaintiffs gave a somewhat guarded reply.

Now that the matter has been argued out, I see no possible answer to the bank's submission. It is now firmly established that a defendant who is subject to a Mareva injunction can apply to the court to vary the injunction, so as to enable him to pay his ordinary debts as they fall due. If the defendant can thus, in a suitable case, draw on his bank account to pay his ordinary creditors, notwithstanding a Mareva injunction, why should he not be free to pay his bank? Why should the bank be in a worse position than other ordinary creditors, just because it is the bank which holds the funds in question?

Counsel for Seawind argues that if it were the defendants who were making the application to vary the injunction they would have to satisfy the court that they had no other free assets, i e assets *not* caught by the Mareva injunction, out of which to pay the debt in question: see *A v C (No 2)* [1981] 2 All ER 126, [1981] QB 961. By the same token, he submits, Barclays Bank International should give full disclosure of the number of term loans advanced by the bank, how they have been repaid in the past, whether the Romanian Bank for Foreign Trade has any other assets within the jurisdiction out of which to meet interest as it falls due, and so on; instead of which Barclays Bank has, as counsel submits, disclosed nothing. It has played its cards very close to its chest.

I cannot accept this criticism of the bank. There is a world of difference between a defendant who is seeking to vary a Mareva injunction and a third party, such as a bank, which is exercising its ordinary rights and remedies in the ordinary course of its business. A Mareva injunction was never intended to interfere with the rights of third parties in this way. In a passage I have already referred to from *Galaxia Maritime SA v Mineralimportexport* [1982] 1 All ER 796 at 799, [1982] 1 WLR 539 at 542, Eveleigh LJ said that he regarded it as intolerable that the freedom of shipowners to trade their ships should be restricted, or that 'third parties should be inconvenienced in this way'. It seems to me that in exercising a right of set-off against their customers, banks are in the same position as any other third party.

It is true that in the *Galaxia Maritime* case [1982] 1 All ER 796 at 799–800, [1982] 1 WLR 539 at 542 Kerr LJ said:

> 'In this connection, it is crucial to bear in mind not only the balance of convenience and justice as between plaintiffs and defendants, but above all also as between plaintiffs and third parties. Where assets of a defendant are held by a third party incidentally to the general business of the third party (such as the accounts of the defendant held by a bank, or goods held by a bailee as custodian, for example in a warehouse) an effective indemnity in favour of the third party will adequately hold this balance, because service of the injunction will not lead to any major interference with the third party's business.'

I do not read that passage as affecting the bankers' right of set-off, or as requiring the bank to accept an indemnity from the plaintiffs in lieu of its right of set-off against its customer. Kerr LJ continued:

> 'But where the effect of service must lead to interference with the performance of a contract between the third party and the defendant which relates specifically to the assets in question, the right of the third party in relation to his contract must clearly prevail over the plantiff's desire to secure the defendant's assets for himself against the day of judgment.'

It seems to me that to require a bank to disclose the state of its customer's accounts, or provide other information about its customer, as a condition of being able to exercise its ordinary right of set-off, would indeed be 'to interfere with the performance of a contract between the third party and the defendant which relates specifically to the assets in question'.

On the second application, therefore, I hold that Barclays Bank International is entitled to a variation of the Mareva injunction granted in September 1982 so as to enable it to exercise any right of set-off it may have in connection with facilities granted to the Romanian Bank for Foreign Trade before they received notification of the injunction.

Any such right of set-off may be exercised in respect of interest accruing due in the future as well as interest which had already accrued due at the date of the notification. Parker J reached the same conclusion in *Project Development Co Ltd SA v KMK Securities Ltd (Syndicate Bank intervening)* [1983] 1 All ER 465, [1982] 1 WLR 1470, although his reasoning is not reported. For completeness I should add that the bank will also be allowed to meet any liabilities which it may incur on confirmed letters of credit opened at the request of the defendants before notification of the injunction, and to debit the defendants accordingly: see *Z Ltd v A* [1982] 1 All ER 556 at 563, 576, [1982] QB 558 at 574, 591 per Lord Denning MR and Kerr LJ.

Next, counsel for Seawind argued that in calculating the amount which is *not* caught by the Mareva injunction, the bank should make provision for all future instalments of interest and, presumably, repayment of the principal. The point can be illustrated by an example. Suppose the defendants' assets held by the bank amounted to $10m. Suppose future instalments of interest and repayment of principal amount to $3m. The injunction is, as I have already mentioned, for just over $2m. Counsel argued that the bank should, as it were, set $3m on one side as well as $2m, leaving only $5m as free assets available for immediate repayment to the customer. If the bank were to repay $8m instead of $5m, then any subsequent set-off of interest and principal would reduce and eventually extinguish the $2m altogether. This would be, according to counsel for Seawind, contrary to the policy underlying the operation of Mareva injunctions.

I do not agree. I can see no ground on which the bank could, in the example given, refuse to repay $8m to its customer, in respect of which, ex hypothesi, it would have no existing right of set-off. It is true that the $2m subject to the Mareva injunction would then gradually be reduced as the bank exercised its right of set-off in the future. But this is an inevitable consequence of a defendant who is subject to a 'maximum sum' Mareva injunction (to use the language of Kerr LJ), and who has no other free assets, being allowed to pay his debts as they fall due.

Finally, I come to what, from the bank's point of view, is perhaps the most important question of all. Can banks exercise their right of set-off without coming back to the court for a variation? On the current form of wording, I think the answer must be No. At the very least, there is a doubt. I agree with counsel for the bank that this is unsatisfactory. Counsel for Seawind argued that it is no great hardship for banks to have to apply for variations of Mareva injunctions; but, against that, they may have to move in a hurry. In any case, as was pointed out by Kerr LJ in *Z Ltd v A*, it is unsatisfactory that courts should be 'cluttered up' with Mareva applications more than is strictly necessary.

The solution lies in finding a form of wording which can be incorporated in the original ex parte order, which would enable banks to exercise their ordinary rights of set-off notwithstanding the injunction. Counsel for Seawind objected that if a special provision were made in favour of banks, then why not in the case of other third parties? I am not much impressed by that objection. There is no doubt that by far the greatest burden of policing Mareva injunctions falls on banks. In order to avoid the necessity of their coming back for variations, and in order to save court time, it is desirable that in future all Mareva injunctions which are intended to be served on banks should contain a suitable proviso. The language suggested by counsel for Barclays Bank International is as follows: 'Provided that nothing in this injunction shall prevent [the bank] from exercising any rights of set-off it may have in respect of facilities afforded by [the bank] to the defendants prior to the date of this injunction.' It seems to me that that wording is satisfactory and produces the desired result.

Directions accordingly.

Solicitors: *Durrant Piesse* (for Barclays Bank); *Holman Fenwick & Willan* (for Ataka, Oceanica and Seawind).

K Mydeen Esq Barrister.

Smith Kline & French Laboratories Ltd and others v Bloch

COURT OF APPEAL, CIVIL DIVISION
LORD DENNING MR, ACKNER AND O'CONNOR LJJ
15, 16, 17, 18 MARCH, 13 MAY 1982

Conflict of laws – Foreign proceedings – Restraint of foreign proceedings – Circumstances in which court will restrain foreign proceedings – Defendant resident in Britain making licensing agreement with English subsidiary of American company based in Pennsylvania – Agreement made and performed in England – Defendant bringing action in Pennsylvania for breach of contract and damages against English subsidiary and American company – Defendant seeking in Pennsylvanian proceedings advantages of costs based on contingency fee, higher damages, jury trial and more extensive discovery – English subsidiary seeking injunction to restrain defendant from continuing proceedings in Pennsylvania – Whether court should grant injunction – Whether advantages of Pennsylvanian forum relied on by defendant amounting to legitimate juridical advantages.

The first plaintiffs (the English company) were a pharmaceutical company in England and were a wholly-owned subsidiary of the second plaintiffs (the US company), a multinational corporation based in Pennsylvania. The defendant was a research worker resident in England. In 1974, by a written agreement made in England, the defendant granted the English company the sole licence to develop and market a drug which he had invented. Under the terms of the agreement the English company had exclusive responsibility for registration and marketing of the drug and also the right to terminate the agreement if they decided not to proceed with the drug's further development. In 1975 the defendant was appointed a consultant to the English company. Clinical trials of the drug were subsequently carried out in hospitals throughout the United Kingdom under the defendant's supervision. In 1976 it was decided that the drug should not be developed any further and as a result the defendant left the English company's employment. In 1980 the English company terminated the licensing agreement with the defendant. The defendant brought an action for damages in Pennsylvania against both the English company and the US company contending, inter alia, (i) that the English company were in breach of contract for which the US company, as the principal in his contract with the English subsidiary, were liable, (ii) that the US company and the English company had been guilty of false representation in saying that they intended to market the defendant's drug whereas they intended to keep it out of the market so that it would not compete with their own products, (iii) alternatively that the US company had improperly interfered with the contract between the English subsidiary and the defendant, and (iv) that the US company and the English company had intentionally inflicted emotional distress on the defendant. The English company sought an injunction in the English court to restrain the defendant from further proceeding with his claim in Pennsylvania or from making any further claims outside the jurisdiction of the English court and further sought declarations that the proper law of the agreement was that of England and that the English company were not liable for the breaches complained of. In the course of the hearing in England, the US company were joined as plaintiffs to the action. The defendant contended that Pennsylvania was the natural forum for the action because of the overriding involvment of the US company and that if the injunction was granted he would be deprived of legitimate juridical advantages, namely (a) the contingency fee basis of remuneration in the United States, under which payment of legal fees was contingent on his action being successful, (b) the practice in the United States of awarding higher damages and also damages for mental distress, (c) the availability of trial by jury and (d) the fuller discovery procedures in Pennsylvania. He further contended that the English court should not restrain a litigant in foreign proceedings unless it could be shown that those proceedings themselves were in breach of contract or

against equity and good conscience, nor should it restrain him if the foreign proceedings
a had been started first. The judge granted the injunction sought. The defendant appealed.

Held – The appeal would be dismissed for the following reasons—

(1) The court had jurisdiction to grant an injunction restraining a litigant from continuing proceedings in a foreign court where the parties were amenable to the English jurisdiction and where it was satisfied (a) that justice could be done between the parties
b in the English forum at substantially less inconvenience and expense, and (b) that the stay of proceedings did not deprive the litigant in the foreign proceedings of any legitimate personal or juridical advantage which would otherwise have been available to him. The jurisdiction was nevertheless to be exercised with great caution, but (per O'Connor LJ), subject to the overriding requirement of caution, the court's jurisdiction to restrain a litigant from continuing proceedings in a foreign court was not confined to
c instances where those proceedings were themselves in breach of contract or against equity and good conscience, nor should the court refrain from granting such relief merely because the foreign proceedings had been started first (see p 78 *b c j*, p 79 *f*, p 82 *h*, p 84 *d e* and p 85 *a b* and *j* to p 86 *b* and *h j*, post); *MacShannon v Rockware Glass Ltd* [1978] 1 All ER 625 and dictum of Lord Scarman in *Castanho v Brown & Root (UK) Ltd* [1981] 1 All ER at 149 followed; *Piper Aircraft Co v Reyno* (1981) 454 US 235 considered.

d (2) England was the natural forum for litigating the dispute because the defendant and the English company were both amenable to the English jurisdiction and the US company had made themselves amenable, the licence agreement had been entered into and performed in England and a large number of witnesses were in England where the clinical trials were carried out. Furthermore, there were no decisive or legitimate juridical advantages to the defendant in pursuing the foreign proceedings because (a) the fact that
e in the United State the case could be prosecuted with minimal risk of costs because of the contingency fee system was not a juridical advantage and in any event the defendant was at no disadvantage in England because he had legal aid, (b) there was evidence that the Pennsylvanian court would apply English law to the issue of damages and the possible advantage that it would apply Pennsylvanian law was highly speculative and therefore not a real advantage, (c) there was no real advantage for the case to be tried by jury since
f jury trial was inappropriate for such a claim, and (d) although English discovery procedures were different from those in Pennsylvania they were wholly adequate to ensure that the defendant suffered no injustice. Accordingly, the injunction had been properly granted (see p 77 *d* to *h*, p 78 *g* to p 79 *a* and *e f*, p 80 *g* to *j*, p 81 *f*, p 82 *j* to p 83 *f* and *j* to p 84 *a d e h j* and p 86 *b* to *j*, post).

g **Notes**

For the general principles governing the stay of foreign proceedings, see 8 Halsbury's Laws (4th edn) para 787–788, and for cases on the subject, see 11 Digest (Reissue) 637–641, 1720–1746.

Cases referred to in judgments

h *Atlantic Star, The, Atlantic Star (owners) v Bona Spes (owners)* [1973] 2 All ER 175, [1974] AC 436, [1973] 2 WLR 795, HL.
Bushby v Munday (1821) 5 Madd 297, [1814–23] All ER Rep 304, 56 ER 908.
Castanho v Brown & Root (UK) Ltd [1981] 1 All ER 143, [1981] AC 557, [1980] 3 WLR 991, HL; *varying* [1980] 3 All ER 72, [1980] 1 WLR 833, CA.
Ellerman Lines Ltd v Read [1928] 2 KB 144, [1928] All ER Rep 415, CA.
j *Guaranty Trust Co of New York v Hannay & Co* [1915] 2 KB 536, [1914–15] All ER Rep 24, CA.
James v Grand Trunk Western Railroad Co (1958) 152 NE 2d 858.
MacShannon v Rockware Glass Ltd [1978] 1 All ER 625, [1978] AC 795, [1978] 2 WLR 362, HL; *rvsg* [1977] 2 All ER 449, [1977] 1 WLR 376.
Piper Aircraft Co v Reyno (1981) 454 US 235.
Portarlington (Lord) v Soulby (1834) 3 My & K 104, [1824–34] All ER Rep 610, 40 ER 40.

St Pierre v South American Stores (Gath & Chaves) Ltd [1936] 1 KB 382, [1935] All ER Rep 408, CA. a
Teheran-Europe Co Ltd v S T Belton (Tractors) Ltd [1968] 2 All ER 886, [1968] 2 QB 545, [1968] 3 WLR 205, CA.
Trendtex Trading Corp v Crédit Suisse [1980] 3 All ER 721; *affd* [1980] 3 All ER 721, [1980] QB 629, [1980] 3 WLR 367, CA; *affd* [1981] 3 All ER 520, [1982] AC 679, [1981] 3 WLR 766, HL. b

Cases also cited

Camilla Cotton Oil Co v Granadex SA [1976] 2 Lloyd's Rep 10, HL.
Cohen v Rothfield [1919] 1 KB 410, [1918–19] All ER Rep 260, CA.
Connolly Bros Ltd, Re, Wood v Connolly Bros Ltd [1911] 1 Ch 731, CA.
Diamond v Bank of London and Montreal Ltd [1979] 1 All ER 561, [1979] 1 QB 333, CA.
Settlement Corp v Hochschild [1965] 3 All ER 486, [1966] Ch 10. c

Appeal

The defendant, Maurice Bloch, appealed against the order of Sir Douglas Frank QC, sitting as a deputy judge of the High Court, made on 30 November 1981 whereby he ordered, inter alia, that the defendant be restrained until judgment of the action or until further order whether acting by himself, his servants or agents from further prosecuting d in respect of the first plaintiffs, Smith Kline & French Laboratories Ltd (the English subsidiary), and the second plaintiffs, Smith Kline Corp (the American parent company), or either of them the claim which had been filed against them and which was pending in the Court of Common Pleas of Philadelphia County, Pennsylvania in the United States of America and from making any claim whatsoever outside the jurisdiction of the court in respect of the licensing agreement entered into between the English subsidiary and e the defendant on 10 April 1974. The facts are set out in the judgment of Lord Denning MR.

Colin Ross-Munro QC and *Robert Englehart* for Mr Bloch.
Anthony Walton QC and *David Eady* for the English subsidiary and the American parent company. f

Cur adv vult

13 May. The following judgments were delivered.

LORD DENNING MR. As a moth is drawn to the light, so is a litigant drawn to the g United States. If he can only get his case into their courts, he stands to win a fortune. At no cost to himself, and at no risk of having to pay anything to the other side. The lawyers there will conduct the case 'on spec' as we say, or on a 'contingency fee' as they say. The lawyers will charge the litigant nothing for their services but instead they will take 40% of the damages, if they win the case in court, or out of court on a settlement. If they lose, the litigant will have nothing to pay to the other side. The courts in the United States h have no such costs deterrent as we have. There is also in the United States a right to trial by jury. These are prone to award fabulous damages. They are notoriously sympathetic and know that the lawyers will take their 40% before the plaintiff gets anything. All this means that the defendant can be readily forced into a settlement. The plaintiff holds all the cards. If you wish to know how it is all done, you should read *Castanho v Brown & Root (UK) Ltd* [1981] 1 All ER 143, [1981] AC 557. There a Portuguese sailor was badly j injured at Great Yarmouth in England. It was an American ship. He started an action in England but was persuaded by American lawyers to take proceedings in the United States. I was against it (see [1980] 3 All ER 72 at 76–83, [1980] 1 WLR 833 at 849–858). But when it got to the House of Lords they allowed the litigant to go ahead in the United States (see [1981] 1 All ER 143, [1981] AC 557). His American lawyers won a huge settlement to the profit of the litigant and of course for themselves as well. You should also read *Piper Aircraft Co v Reyno* (1981) 454 US 235 decided on 8 December 1981 by the Supreme Court of the United States. A small commercial aircraft crashed in Scotland, killing all six Scottish people on it. The propellers had been manufactured in the United States. The widows and children were persuaded by lawyers in the United States to bring proceedings there against the manufacturers of the propellers, alleging that they were faulty. No doubt the lawyers had their eyes on the heavy damages and their contingency fees. The Supreme Court of the United States refused to allow the proceedings to continue in the United States. They should have been brought in Scotland, which was the only appropriate forum.

Now we have another case of that ilk. Dr Maurice Bloch lives in England. He has a complaint against an English company. He says that they broke their contract with him. It was an English contract governed by English law. The obvious place where it should be tried is in England. Yet he has gone to American lawyers and they have found an excuse for bringing it in the United States. It is because the English company was a wholly-owned subsidiary of an American corporation. So the American lawyers for Dr Bloch have brought an action in the United States courts against the English subsidiary and its American parent, hoping, no doubt, to get a good settlement out of it, both for themselves and Dr Bloch, at no cost to him.

Now here is the twist in the story. The English company and its American parent wish to stop the proceedings in the United States courts. They want to nip them in the bud. They have applied to the United States courts to stop them. But with no success so far there. An American judge has made an order allowing Dr Bloch to go ahead with the proceedings in the United States court.

Having been thus rebuffed in America, the English subsidiary (and now its American parent) have applied to the English court. They ask us to issue an injunction against Dr Bloch to restrain him from proceeding in the United States. They say that he is quite at liberty to sue them in England if he is so advised, in which case they will defend themselves. But he should not be allowed to go on in the United States. I may say that, even in England, Dr Bloch is 'sitting pretty' anyway. He has got legal aid with the result that all his costs here will be paid by the legal aid fund.

At the moment the English High Court has acceded to the request of the English subsidiary and its American parent. It has issued an injunction against Dr Bloch stopping him from going on with his proceedings in the United States court; he now appeals to this court.

Now there is yet a further twist. Dr Bloch has asked the United States court to issue a counter-injunction against the American parent to stop it from coming to the English court; and an American judge has made the order.

It is apparent from this account of proceedings that there is a conflict of jurisdiction between our courts here in England and the courts in the United States. This is much to be regretted. In the interests of comity, one or other must give way. I wish that we could sit together to discuss it. But, as that is not possible, I propose to put the case forward, as we see it here, in the hope that we may come to an agreed solution.

Let me first give the background. It arises out of the use of drugs in medicine. Doctors prescribe drugs for diseases of all kinds. These drugs are made by pharmaceutical multinational companies. One of them is the Smith Kline group. The parent company is incorporated in Pennsylvania with its head office in Philadelphia. It has wholly-owned subsidiaries all over the world. One of them is the English subsidiary, Smith Kline & French Laboratories Ltd.

In order to keep ahead, the Smith Kline group are much concerned to promote research and development into new drugs. One of the drugs they developed was called 'Dyazide' in America. Another drug they developed was called 'Tagamet' in England. They have proved very successful in treating stomach ulcers.

Now in England there is a research worker called Dr Maurice Bloch. He has worked in hospitals and for drug companies. From 1971 to 1973 he was employed by the well-known firm of May & Baker on clinical research. After leaving them, he approached the English subsidiary of Smith Kline. He told them that he had a good idea. It was to use magnesium compounds for treating stomach complaints. The English subsidiary thought he was worth a trial. So they engaged him as a medical adviser. They agreed to treat all his ideas and information as confidential. He showed such promise that he ceased to be their employee and became a consultant. By a written agreement of 10 April 1974 he gave them a licence to use his information worldwide. They agreed to pay him a royalty of 2% on worldwide net sales for 15 years from the date of first marketing of any drugs. They paid him £10,000 cash down as an advance against future royalties. The agreement contained this important provision:

> '*Registration and Marketing* All decisions on registration and marketing of products will be the exclusive responsibility of SK&F [the English subsidiary]. (a) If SK&F make a decision not to proceed with further development in the U.K. or not to apply for a product licence under the Medicines Act, they will hand over to M.B. [Dr Bloch] the development work to date, and give up their exclusive rights under this agreement . . .'

From 1973 to July 1976 Dr Bloch did research work for the English subsidiary. He developed many drugs made of magnesium compounds and arranged for them to be tried out in leading hospitals in London, Bristol, Southampton, Manchester, Salisbury, Glasgow and Dundee. Dr Bloch was himself in control.

In July 1976 there was an important meeting in Philadelphia of a committee which advised the group on the development of various products. They decided that Dr Bloch's products were not likely to be a success. The managing director of the English subsidiary told Dr Bloch that, as he stated—

> 'the committee had decided that the development of the products should not be supported financially and that the products were not a commercial proposition. After this . . . I ceased to work for the English subsidiary . . .'

The English subsidiary did, however, continue the trials in hospitals.

After leaving the English subsidiary, Dr Bloch went back to May & Baker. He worked for them as a senior clinician from October 1976 to November 1979. He was then dismissed by May & Baker because he did not apply himself to the tasks allotted to him. He spent too much time in lengthy argument. He complained to an industrial tribunal that he had been unfairly dismissed by May & Baker. The hearing took nine days. The tribunal rejected his complaint. They held unanimously that 'having given him very great latitude over a long period, his conduct was sufficient to justify his dismissal'.

Meanwhile the English subsidiary had been receiving reports of the trials. They proved disappointing. So on 5 February 1980 the English subsidiary wrote to Dr Bloch:

> 'I write with reference to the Magnesium containing compounds, the subject of our Agreement dated the 10th April 1974. We have now received a report that the last ongoing trial has been finished, which proved disappointing. In view of the fact that it was not possible for clinical trialists to find enough patients with Magnesium deficiency and the data is not sufficient to justify a further application for a product licence, we have decided not to continue further development work. Accordingly, we are giving up our exclusive rights under the Agreement. This will allow you to enter into other arrangements.'

So here was Dr Bloch dismissed by May & Baker and his products discarded by Smith Kline. What was he to do? He had been in touch with English solicitors as far back as 1976, but they foresaw difficulties in litigation in England. So he turned to American lawyers. They advised him to bring an action in the United States, both against the English subsidiary and the American parent. He instituted it on 16 May 1980. He is quite frank about his reasons:

> '. . . there were financial considerations in that litigation in this Country would undoubtedly involve me in substantial expense; on the other hand, if American lawyers agreed to take on my case, they would be prepared to do so in accordance with American legal practice for a contingency fee so that they would be remunerated out of any damages which I might recover.'

If Dr Bloch had attempted to sue the English subsidiary alone in America, the United States courts would not have entertained it for one moment. So he had to bring in the American parent as a defendant to the American proceedings. He alleged that:

(1) The American parent was the principal in his contract with the English subsidiary and liable for a breach of contract by the English subsidiary. For this he claimed damages of $US40,000,000.

(2) The American parent and English subsidiary had been guilty of false representation in saying that they intended to market the plaintiff's product whereas they never intended to do so. They intended to keep it out of the market so that it should not be in competition with their own existing product, 'Dyazide'. For this he claimed another $US40,000,000 damages.

(3) The American parent had improperly interfered with the contract by the English subsidiary with Dr Bloch. More damages of $US40,000,000.

(4) The American parent and the English subsidiary had intentionally inflicted emotional distress on Dr Bloch for which he was entitled to punitive damages of another $US40,000,000.

If you consider each of those four claims, you will see at once that if Dr Bloch had any cause of action at all he could perfectly well have started it in England against the English subsidiary alone and got all the damages to which he was justly entitled. If he had sought to sue the American parent in England, he would not have got leave to serve it out of the jurisdiction, because he had no semblance of a cause of action against them. At any rate he would not have a good arguable case for these reasons:

(1) The contract was made by Dr Bloch with the English subsidiary in its own name. That is a factor showing that it was intended that the English subsidiary should be the party to the contract. When that is coupled with the additional factor that 'all decisions on registration and marketing of products will be the exclusive responsibility of SK&F' (that is of the English subsidiary), it is plain that only the English subsidiary is liable for the breach, if any, of the contract. The American parent is not liable. The latest case on this subject here is *Teheran-Europe Co Ltd v S T Belton (Tractors) Ltd* [1968] 2 All ER 886, [1968] 2 QB 545.

(2) There is nothing to warrant the suggestion that the English subsidiary and the American parent were from 1974 guilty of conspiracy and fraud, or that they intentionally duped Dr Bloch with the belief that they would develop his project, when they intended never to do so. That is a suggestion made without any evidence to support it. It is decisively refuted by the fact that from 1974 onwards Dr Bloch was himself in control of the research and development of his product at the many hospitals and so forth. No doubt he developed it to the best of his ability.

(3) and (4) The claims for inducing breach of contract and emotional distress have no substance whatever.

To my mind this claim of Dr Bloch against the American parent is a device, adopted by American lawyers, so as to get the case into the United States courts, where they will get contingency fees and force a settlement. Such a device ought not to be allowed to succeed. I trust that our courts on both sides of the Atlantic will not allow it.

The law

It often happens that a plaintiff is entitled to bring proceedings in two or more jurisdictions. Sometimes it is said that the choice is his. He can choose whichever of them suits him best. If he can get more damages in one than he can in the other, then good luck to him. Let him go there. If he will be met by a time bar in one and not in the other, let him go to the one where he is not barred. If it is more convenient for the plaintiff in one than it is for the defendant, then the plaintiff can choose. You need not spin a coin between the two contestants. It always comes down in favour of the plaintiff, so it is said, unless the defendant can prove that it would work an injustice to him. That was the way the English Court of Appeal approached the problem in *St Pierre v South American Stores (Gath & Chaves) Ltd* [1936] 1 KB 382, [1935] All ER Rep 408 and the Supreme Court of Illinois approached it in *James v Grand Trunk Western Railroad Co* (1958) 152 NE 2d 858. Once a plaintiff institutes an action in accordance with this prior claim of his, then no court in a rival jurisdiction should grant an injunction to prevent the plaintiff from exercising and pursuing his action to its determination. This is the *a* only way, it is said, to avoid unseemly conflict and to ensure comity.

The basis of all this reasoning has now been removed. In England by the House of Lords in *MacShannon v Rockware Glass Ltd* [1978] 1 All ER 625, [1978] AC 795. In the United States by the Supreme Court in *Piper Aircraft Co v Reyno* (1981) 454 US 235. The plaintiff has no longer an inborn right to choose his own forum. He no longer wins the toss on every throw. The decision rests with the courts. No matter which jurisdiction is *b* invoked, the court must hold the balance between the plaintiff and the defendant. It must take into account the relative advantages and disadvantages to each of them: not only the juridical advantages and disadvantages, but also the personal conveniences and inconveniences: not only the private interests of the parties but also the public interests involved. The court decides according to which way the balance comes down. This was the approach of the House of Lords in *MacShannon v Rockware Glass Ltd*, where it was *c* much to the juridical advantage of the plaintiff to bring his action in England, where he would get higher damages, but the natural forum was Scotland. It was in the public interest that a Scottish case should be tried in Scotland. So he was bound to go to Scotland. His action in England was stayed. It was also the approach of the Supreme Court of the United States in *Piper Aircraft Co v Reyno*, where it was much to the juridical advantage of the plaintiffs that they should sue in Pennsylvania, where they would get higher *d* damages and the lawyers would get contingency fees. But the public interest was against trial in the United States. If claims such as these aircraft claims were all to be brought in the United States, it would involve far too great a commitment of judicial time and resources. Scotland was the natural forum. The public interest favoured Scotland. So the trial should take place there.

By contrast, in *Castanho v Brown & Root (UK) Ltd* [1981] 1 All ER 143, [1981] AC 557 *e* the plaintiff had an undisputed claim for damages against a Texan-based group of companies. The only question at issue was quantum. The plaintiff had a legitimate advantage in suing in Texas where he could get such damages as a Texan court thought appropriate. Although I took the other view, the House of Lords held that the balance came down clearly in the plaintiff's favour (see [1981] 1 All ER 143 at 152, [1981] AC 557 at 577). *f*

Holding the balance

In our present case Dr Bloch is resident in England. He works in England. He sues on a contract with an English company which was made in England and is governed by English law. The witnesses are mostly in England. The natural forum is England beyond any doubt. The public interest requires that so English a dispute should be tried in *g* England, to which it belongs rather than in the United States.

It would, no doubt, be an advantage to Dr Bloch to sue in the United States, because he would there get higher damages, trial by jury and lawyers on contingency fees. But that is not a legitimate advantage. It is an illegitimate advantage. Even putting it into the scale, the balance comes down clearly in favour of England.

h

Injunction

Once the English court decides that the dispute should be tried in England and not in the United States, then it is open to the court to issue an injunction against Dr Bloch restraining him from continuing his proceedings in the courts of the United States. No doubt this jurisdiction should be exercised with caution, but that it can be done there is no doubt. It was affirmed by the House of Lords in the *Castanho* case [1981] 1 All ER 143 *j* at 149, [1981] AC 557 at 572–573.

I have no doubt that this is a case where the court should grant an injunction against Dr Bloch so as to restrain him from continuing with the proceedings in the United States courts. He will, of course, be able to make his claim in the English courts, either by a fresh action, or by a counterclaim in the present action. He has the benefit of legal aid; so he can get justice in this country beyond all doubt. That is the right way of it.

Further twist

a It now appears that as long ago as 21 July 1975 Dr Bloch assigned his rights under the agreement of 10 April 1974 to a trust of which the trustees were domiciled in England and resident in England. This assignment was made in England and was governed by English law. Due notice of it was given to the English subsidiary. As a result of this twist, it is quite clear that Dr Maurice Bloch had no right himself whatever to sue for breach of the agreement.

b On this assignment being discovered, the American lawyers sought to rectify the error. They started a second action in the United States courts, but this time in the name of the trustees, making the same claims that Dr Maurice Bloch had done against the American parent and the English subsidiary.

The American lawyers also started in the United States courts an anti-trust suit in the names of the trustees and Dr Bloch against the American parent, the English subsidiary
c and an American subsidiary.

In answer, the American parent, the English subsidiary and an American subsidiary started in the English courts a second English action. This time it was aginst the trustees, claiming an injunction to stop them going on with the second American action.

All these writs and proceedings disclose a very regrettable state of affairs, financed on the Bloch side in the United States by contingency fees and in England by legal aid. In
d one country or another it is an abuse of the process of the courts. To my mind it is high time that all this litigation should be brought to an end, save that Dr Bloch and his trustees should be permitted to make a claim in England against the English subsidiary if so advised. Everything else should be stopped.

Conclusion

e Seeing that England is the natural and proper forum for any proceedings that Dr Maurice Bloch is advised to bring, I would grant an injunction against him personally to stop him from going on with any proceedings in the United States. I would grant it at the instance not only of the English subsidiary but also of the American parent. Seeing that both are being harassed in the United States courts, both should be able to come to these courts to stop it. The like is the position with regard to the trustees.

f I would thus uphold the decision of Sir Douglas Frank and dismiss the appeal.

ACKNER LJ. The foundation of this litigation is an agreement made in England on 10 April 1974 between an English company, the first respondents to this appeal, referred to hereafter as 'the English subsidiary', and Dr Maurice Bloch, the appellant, who is a British subject resident in this country and employed at the time by the English
g subsidiary. Dr Bloch is a doctor of medicine and a research clinician, having worked for many years in the pharmaceutical industry for different drug companies. Before Dr Bloch became employed by the English subsidiary, he had done work on the pharmaceutical uses of magnesium-containing compounds, referred to as the 'products' in the agreement. In August 1973 he entered into a confidential agreement to enable the English subsidiary to investigate his work, with a view to entering into a licensing
h agreement and this is referred to in the recitals to that agreement. Under the agreement Dr Bloch licensed the English subsidiary to produce and market the products worldwide in consideration of the payment of a royalty on sales. The agreement also provided for the termination of his employment with the English subsidiary and his appointment as a consultant. There is only one clause in the agreement to which I need make specific reference, and that is cl 8:

j

> '*Registration and Marketing* All decisions on registration and marketing of products will be the exclusive responsibility of SK&F [the English subsidiary]. (a) If SK&F make a decision not to proceed with further development in the U.K. or not to apply for a product licence under the Medicines Act, they will hand over to M.B. [Dr Bloch] the development work to date, and give up their exclusive rights under this agreement. (b) If SK&F obtain a product licence but do not market a product

> in the U.K. covered by this agreement within twelve months of the grant of such a licence, they will hand the technical data to M.B. on which the application was based and give up their exclusive rights under this agreement. (c) If within three years from the date of marketing in the U.K. a company in the SK&F group has not marketed or applied for registration of a product covered by this agreement in any overseas country, nor sub-licensed such a product resulting in its marketing in the country, SK&F will give up their exclusive rights to such country under this agreement.'

In September 1975, pursuant to the terms of the agreement, Dr Bloch's employment was terminated and he was appointed a consultant to the English subsidiary. In 1976 his consultancy was terminated. Thereafter he became employed by May & Baker Ltd, in whose employment he remained for the next three years. On 5 February 1980 the English subsidiary wrote to Dr Bloch as follows:

> 'I write with reference to the Magnesium containing compounds, the subject of our Agreement dated the 10th April 1974. We have now received a report that the last ongoing trial has been finished, which proved disappointing. In view of the fact that it was not possible for clinical trialists to find enough patients with Magnesium deficiency and the data is not sufficient to justify a further application for a product licence, we have decided not to continue further development work. Accordingly, we are giving up our exclusive rights under the Agreement. This will allow you to enter into other arrangements.'

Dr Bloch alleges that the English subsidiary broke the terms of the agreement. He maintains that there was an implied obligation on them to develop and market the products within a reasonable time and that this obligation remained in force until the exclusive rights were returned under cl 8(a) of the agreement. He further maintains that there was an implied obligation that the English subsidiary would act in good faith and would not carry out 'merely token development in order to preserve its exclusive rights for a collateral purpose, such as protecting other Group products from competition'. He asserts that in breach of the implied obligations the English subsidiary did not develop the products, nor did it ever intend so to do, but at the most carried out merely token developments in order to retain its exclusive rights and to preserve the market for a highly profitable drug, marketed by the group, called Dyazide. The English subsidiary deny that they have committed any breaches of the agreement, either as alleged or at all.

England is undoubtedly the natural forum for litigating this dispute. To adopt and slightly to adapt the observation made by Stephenson LJ in *MacShannon v Rockware Glass Ltd* [1977] 2 All ER 449 at 453, [1977] 1 WLR 376 at 382 (when that case was heard in the Court of Appeal) and repeated in the House of Lords by Lord Salmon ([1978] 1 All ER 625 at 634 [1978] AC 795 at 817): 'Anyone with nothing but common sense to guide him would say the action ought to be tried in England.' In addition to the points already made, it is common ground that the proper law of the contract is English law and the deputy judge was satisfied that a large number of doctors at various hospitals in England and Scotland engaged in clinical trials and a number of officials of the Department of Health and Social Security would be required to be called. How then does the problem arise?

On 16 May 1980 Dr Bloch caused a complaint to be filed in the Court of Common Pleas of Philadelphia County, Pennsylvania, USA, not only against the English subsidiary but against the parent company, a Philadelphian company, the second respondents to this appeal. The basis of the claim against the parent company is that the English subsidiary in entering into the licensing agreement was acting solely as agent for the American parent which controlled the Smith Kline group of companies; alternatively, if the contract was with the English subsidiary, the American parent produced and/or induced the breach. As counsel for the appellant succinctly put it, the English subsidiary were merely puppets who were operated by the American parent company, with whom the contract was in fact and in law made and who dictated the decisions which caused the breaches of contract relied on.

Dr Bloch, in his affidavit, has given a number of reasons for commencing the proceedings in America, some of which are more convincing than others. The first reason he puts forward is that it was the American parent which was effectively controlling the development of the products and which had taken the major decisions. This cannot in itself be a reason on its own, but must be connected with his second reason, which was that his former English solicitors advised him that litigation would and should involve the American parent, but that there might be difficulties of jurisdiction over the American parent in this country. Such difficulties are, and always have been, more imaginary than real, since the American parent is entirely content to accept the jurisdiction of the English courts.

His third reason sounds a more acceptable note. He says:

> '... there were financial considerations in that litigation in this Country would undoubtedly involve me in substantial expense; on the other hand, if American lawyers agreed to take on my case, they would be prepared to do so in accordance with the American legal practice for a contingency fee so that they would be remunerated out of any damages which I might recover.'

He might well have added, since this is well known, that in America the costs which an unsuccessful party has to pay his successful opponent are limited virtually to court fees. He does, however, under the heading of 'Substantial Juridical Advantages' refer to the exemplary damages and the damages for mental distress which he claims are recoverable in the American courts and which, in the American proceedings, are set as \$US160,000,000 (that is \$40,000,000 in respect of each of four separate causes of action).

He also points out that in Philadelphia the action would be tried before a judge and jury, which he considers to be more appropriate as his case, he claims, essentially depends on an assessment of the good faith of the conduct of the various persons involved. However, in the next but one paragraph in the same affidavit, while accepting that English law may well be the proper law of the contract, he states that his case does not raise any difficult questions of English law, but 'rather depends on detailed factual analysis'. This, I would have thought, is a clear contra-indication of its suitability for jury trial.

I can thus well understand and sympathise with the view expressed by Sir Douglas Frank, who said:

> 'I suspect that the parent company has been joined solely for the purpose of providing a pretext for instituting proceedings in the United States.'

He concluded that the alleged juridical advantages to Dr Bloch of a trial in Pennsylvania, to which I will refer later in greater detail, were, at the best, speculative and that the true advantage to him was extra-juridical, namely that the prospect of having to meet a very heavy bill of costs might coerce the companies into negotiating the payment of a large sum in settlement.

The English subsidiary issued a writ on 7 November 1980 claiming:

> '1. An injunction to restrain the Defendant [Dr Bloch] whether acting by himself, his servants or agents or otherwise howsoever from further prosecuting in respect of the Plaintiff companies or either of them the claim which has been filed against them and which is currently pending in the Court of Common Pleas of Philadelphia County, Pennsylvania, United States of America and from making any claim whatsoever outside the jurisdiction of this Court in respect of the licensing agreement ...
>
> 2. Declarations to the following effect:—that the proper law of the said agreement is that of England; and that the First Plaintiffs [the English subsidiary], having acted in good faith and having taken all proper steps in accordance with the said agreement

> towards the development of the Defendant's product but without success, were entitled to determine the said agreement and that they have validly and lawfully determined the same in accordance with their letter dated 5th February 1980.'

Counsel for Dr Bloch accepts that the court has power to grant the two declarations sought, but he claims that they are artificial declarations which are unlikely to be granted. They provide only, he claims, a procedural hook on which to hang the claim for the injunction. I cannot accept this submission. Dr Bloch having commenced his proceedings in Philadelphia, the only declaration which the English subsidiary can then properly seek must be in the nature of a declaration of non-liability. That such a declaration is permissible is clearly established in *Guaranty Trust Co of New York v Hannay & Co* [1915] 2 KB 536, [1914–15] All ER Rep 24.

It is common ground that the court has power to make the order sought. In *Castanho v Brown & Root (UK) Ltd* [1981] 1 All ER 143 at 149, [1981] AC 557 at 572–573 Lord Scarman, with whose speech Lord Wilberforce, Lord Diplock, Lord Keith and Lord Bridge agreed, dealt with the question of jurisdiction in these terms:

> 'Injunction, being an equitable remedy, operates in personam. It has been used to order parties amenable to the court's jurisdiction "to take, or to omit to take, any steps and proceedings in any other court of justice whether in this country or in a foreign country": Leach V-C in *Bushby v Munday* (1821) 5 Madd 297 at 307, [1814–23] All ER Rep 304 at 306. The English court, as Leach V-C went on to say, "does not pretend to any interference with the other court; it acts upon the defendant by punishment for his contempt in his disobedience to the order of the court". The jurisdiction, which has been frequently exercised since 1821, was reviewed by the Court of Appeal in *Ellerman Lines Ltd v Read* [1928] 2 KB 144, [1928] All ER Rep 415. Scrutton LJ in that case quoted with approval a passage from the judgment of Lord Brougham LC in *Lord Portarlington v Soulby* (1834) 3 Myl & K 104 at 107, [1824–34] All ER Rep 610 at 611, where Lord Brougham LC affirmed that "the injunction was not directed to the foreign Court, but to the party within the jurisdiction here". I would not, however, leave *Ellerman*'s case without a reference to the warning of Eve J ([1928] 2 KB 144 at 158, [1928] All ER Rep 415 at 422): "No doubt, the jurisdiction is to be exercised with caution . . ."'

Counsel for Dr Bloch very properly does not suggest that to grant an injunction in the circumstances of this case against Dr Bloch would be useless, a mere brutum fulmen. We are clearly entitled to proceed on the basis that Dr Bloch will obey the order of the court.

It is further common ground that the principles governing the exercise of the court's discretion are the same whether the remedy sought is a stay of English proceedings or a restraint on foreign proceedings: see again per Lord Scarman in the *Castanho* case [1981] 1 All ER 143 at 150, [1981] AC 557 at 575. In my judgment, Sir Douglas Frank has rightly transposed into the context of this case Lord Diplock's formulation of the principle to be found in the *MacShannon* case [1978] 1 All ER 625 at 630, [1978] AC 795 at 812. To justify the grant of the injunction it has to be established (a) that the English court is the forum to whose jurisdiction Dr Bloch is amenable and in which justice can be done at substantially less inconvenience and expense, and (b) that the injunction must not deprive Dr Bloch of a legitimate personal or juridical advantage which would be available to him in the American proceedings.

I have avoided any reference to the question of onus, which is discussed in some little detail by Robert Goff J in *Trendtex Trading Corp v Crédit Suisse* [1980] 3 All ER 721 at 734, since the answers to questions raised by this formulation are quite clear.

I have already pointed out that England has an overwhelming connection with the dispute. It is the natural forum, to whose jurisdiction not only the English subsidiary and Dr Bloch are amenable, but whose jurisdiction, as stated above, has been accepted by the American parent. I entirely accept the judge's view that justice can be done here at substantially less inconvenience and expense.

I have already referred to some of the alleged juridical advantages to Dr Bloch of proceeding in Philadelphia. I need make no further reference to jury trial. As regards his claim to punitive damages and damages for mental distress, Professor Gorman, a professor of law and associate dean at the University of Pennsylvania Law School, rejects the proposition that the amount of damages recoverable in England is likely to be considerably less than in Philadelphia. For the reasons he gives in his impressive affidavit, he concludes that the Pennsylvanian courts would apply English law to the measure of damages, including the availability of exemplary damages and damages for emotional distress, both in the contract claim and in the tort claims asserted by Dr Bloch. Like the judge, I do not consider that the professor's evidence is diminished by the suggestion made by Mr O'Neill, an experienced lawyer practising in Philadelphia, that there could be additional evidence, of an unspecified kind, which could give rise to the possibility of applying Pennsylvanian law of damages.

As to the conduct of the proceedings in this country, Dr Bloch's concern that he would be in the position of a counterclaiming defendant and could be prejudiced by a plea of the Limitation Acts is no longer a practical problem in view of the undertaking not to invoke those Acts. Dr Bloch can, if he desires, start separate proceedings, seek consolidation and claim the conduct of those proceedings. The only other juridical advantage claimed is the pre-trial procedure, which he maintains will be a great assistance in the prosecution of his claims. If there is validity in the claims made by Dr Bloch, the provisions for discovery and interrogatories in the English procedure should be wholly adequate for his purposes. Maybe the American provisions for pre-trial depositions, enabling what these courts might characterise as a 'fishing operation', will establish somewhat earlier, if this were to be the case, that the claims have little or no validity, but I cannot attribute to this juridical advantage a decisive weight in this 'critical equation', as so described by Lord Wilberforce in *The Atlantic Star, Atlantic Star (owners) v Bona Spes (owners)* [1973] 2 All ER 175 at 194, [1974] AC 436 at 468. If they are to be resorted to merely to enable Dr Bloch to 'try his luck', I cannot accept such an advantage is a legitimate one.

I therefore wholly agree with the judge that, if the American parent company were not a party to the English proceedings for the injunction and declaration, there would be no need for hesitation before granting the injunction.

It is important to have regard to what happened shortly before the conclusion of the proceedings in the court below. Counsel for Dr Bloch drew attention to the fact that, although the claim was only made by the English subsidiary, the injunction sought was to restrain not only the prosecution of the American proceedings, but also 'making any claim whatsoever outside the jurisdiction in respect of the licensing agreement'. Counsel for Dr Bloch submitted to Sir Douglas Frank that this part of the injunction was aimed at preventing Dr Bloch from proceeding not only against the English subsidiary in America, but also against the parent company. He accordingly submitted that the parent company ought to be added as a plaintiff in the English proceedings and this suggestion was then adopted by the English subsidiary. Hence the very late amendment to the writ, which took place shortly before the judge reserved his judgment.

In my judgment, it was unnecessary to add the American parent as an additional plaintiff to the English proceedings. It has provided Dr Bloch with the cri de coeur: how can it be right for an English court to seek to prevent the continuance of proceedings in Philadelphia against a Philadelphian company, when it is accepted that the Philadelphian court has jurisdiction to entertain the suit? The answer to that question is that what Dr Bloch, a British subject resident in this country, is seeking to do in relation to a contract which he made in England with an English company, to be performed in England and allegedly broken in England, is to enforce that contract in proceedings in Philadelphia, where on the available material it appears that the American parent company had been joined solely for the purpose of providing a pretext for instituting proceedings in that jurisdiction. The judge was thus wholly entitled to grant an injunction in favour of the English subsidiary in the terms sought, restraining Dr Bloch from further prosecuting the claim currently pending in Philadelphia against the English subsidiary and from making any claim whatsoever outside the jurisdiction in respect of the licensing agreement. Thus Dr Bloch, who is amenable to the English courts, is obliged to confine

his litigation in respect of the licensing agreement to the English courts. The American
parent having accepted the jurisdiction of the English courts and Dr Bloch having been a
granted legal aid, he has no legitimate complaint in being obliged to resort to the natural
forum for this litigation.

I should just say a word or two about one of the other actions pending in the
Philadelphian courts. It became apparent in the course of the English proceedings that,
on 21 July 1975, Dr Bloch had assigned the benefit of his interest under the licensing
agreement to trustees, namely Sidney Bloch and Simon Myers Olswang. We were told b
that Mr Olswang has been replaced by Mr Anthony John Epstein as a trustee and that the
beneficiaries under the trust are Dr Bloch and Draydown Finance Ltd, from which
company Dr Bloch had obtained a loan. From the above facts it would appear that such
rights of action as Dr Bloch may have under the licence agreement have passed to his
trustees. This point does not seem to have been appreciated until very recently by the
American lawyers. They have not sought to substitute the trustees for Dr Bloch in the c
action which he commenced in May 1980, but they have taken what counsel for Dr
Bloch describes as 'protective proceedings' by the issue, last month in the Philadelphian
Court of Common Pleas, of a complaint on behalf of the trustees. This, to my mind,
substantially reduces the force of Dr Bloch's contention that the Philadelphian court was
thus the court of prior jurisdiction. However, the existence of these proceedings has of
course this particular relevance, that, if the trustees are to be the plaintiffs, then a similar d
order to that originally claimed in the English proceedings, mutatis mutandis, should be
made against them. I understand that there are pending proceedings before Sir Douglas
Frank to achieve this end.

I would accordingly dismiss this appeal. Dr Bloch should have no difficulty in
discharging the injunction which *he* has obtained in Philadelphia against the American
parent. He will thus be able, if he so desires, to claim or counterclaim against the English e
subsidiary *and* the American company in the same proceedings in this country.

O'CONNOR LJ. This is an appeal by the defendant, Dr Bloch, against an order of Sir
Douglas Frank QC, sitting as a deputy judge of the High Court, restraining him from
prosecuting any proceedings arising out of an agreement in writing dated 10 April 1974 f
made between Dr Bloch and Smith, Kline & French Laboratories Ltd outside England.

Dr Bloch is a doctor of medicine and an inventor. Smith, Kline & French Laboratories
Ltd is the English subsidiary of an American multinational pharmaceutical corporation
Smith Kline Inc based in Philadelphia, Pennsylvania. The 1974 agreement between Dr
Bloch and the English subsidiary was made in England; Dr Bloch had invented a drug,
but it needed a great deal of development and clinical testing. The agreement gave the g
English subsidiary a sole licence to do this work and to market any resulting product,
paying royalties to Dr Bloch. In February 1980 the English subsidiary terminated the
agreement, as they were entitled to do. Dr Bloch alleges that the English subsidiary put
his invention into cold storage in order to protect the sale of another drug marketed by
its American parent and was thus in breach of the agreement. He further alleges that the
breach was induced by the American parent; alternatively that the American parent was h
party to the contract as undisclosed principal of the English subsidiary.

I do not think that there can be any doubt that England is the natural forum for any
litigation arising out of this contract. Dr Bloch thought otherwise. He persuaded
American lawyers to accept his instructions to pursue a claim against the English
subsidiary and the parent company on a contingency fee basis, and on his behalf they
commenced proceedings in the Court of Common Pleas for Philadelphia County, j
Pennsylvania. He claimed $US160,000,000. This was in May 1980. The English
subsidiary moved to have the proceedings against them struck out on the ground that
the court had no jurisdiction to entertain them, and both the English subsidiary and the
parent company asked for a stay on the ground that the forum conveniens for the
litigation was England.

In November 1980 the English subsidiary issued a writ asking for a declaration that the agreement with Dr Bloch had been properly determined and an injunction to restrain a him from proceeding further with his action in Pennsylvania.

It is not disputed that the court has power to make such an order. The authorities show that it is a jurisdiction which should be exercised with very great caution because, although the injunction operates in personam against someone over whom the English court has jurisdiction, the effect inevitably is to hamstring the proceedings in the foreign jurisdiction: see *Castanho v Brown & Root (UK) Ltd* [1981] 1 All ER 143 at 149, [1981] AC b 557 at 572–573.

Counsel for Dr Bloch submitted that, if an English plaintiff brought an action in a foreign court of competent jurisdiction against a foreign resident therein, the English court should not force him to stay those proceedings and proceed in England unless either the foreign proceedings were brought in breach of contract or the institution of those proceedings is a breach of equity or good conscience. In support of this submission c we were referred to *Ellerman Lines Ltd v Read* [1928] 2 KB 144 at 151–152, [1928] All ER Rep 415 at 417. In that case the court was asked to enjoin the defendant from enforcing a judgment obtained in a foreign court in breach of contract and by fraud. Not suprisingly, in granting the injunction, Scrutton LJ said:

> 'In such a case, as I understand the decisions, the English Courts have always d professed, and asserted, their power to act. They do not, of course, grant an injunction restraining the foreign Court from acting; they have no power to do that; but they can grant an injunction restraining a British subject who is fraudulently breaking his contract, and who is a party to proceedings before them, from making an application to a foreign Court for the purpose of reaping the fruits of his fraudulent breach of contract . . . The English Courts have therefore clearly jurisdiction to restrain a person who is subject to the English jurisdiction from e taking proceedings in a foreign Court in breach of contract and in fraud.'

I can find nothing in that case limiting the jurisdiction to breach of contract and/or fraud; the court was simply dealing with the facts of the case.

Counsel for the Dr Bloch submitted further that, if the foreign proceedings had been started first, the English court ought not to grant the injunction, relying on dicta in f *Castanho*'s case. Brandon LJ in the Court of Appeal said ([1980] 3 All ER 72 at 92, [1980] 1 WLR 833 at 870):

> 'It would always have been open to the plaintiff, if he had been so advised early enough to sue the JMC group [the defendants] in Texas first, and never to have brought any action against them in England at all. If he had done so, the JMC group could not, so far as I can see, have compelled him to sue in England, and would have g had to incur the inconvenience and expense of contesting the claim in Texas in any event.'

Lord Scarman in the House of Lords said ([1981] 1 All ER 143 at 152, [1981] AC 557 at 576):

> 'My Lords, on this aspect of the case I find the judgment of Brandon LJ convincing. h He found that to restrain the plaintiff from proceeding in Texas would deprive him of a legitimate personal or juridical advantage. I agree. If he had been advised early enough to sue the JMC group in Texas first, they could not have compelled him to sue in England.'

These passages were appropriate to the facts of *Castanho*'s case, but cannot be taken as j laying down a rule that the injunction can never be granted against a plaintiff who starts first in the foreign jurisdiction.

I do not think that there are any good grounds for not adhering to what I believe to be the true principle found in the cases. The jurisdiction is to be exercised with caution: see per Eve J in *Ellerman Lines Ltd v Read* [1928] 2 KB 144 at 158, [1982] All ER Rep 415 at 422, approved by Lord Scarman in *Castanho*'s case [1981] 1 All ER 143 at 149, [1981] AC 557 at 573. The court should look to see in which jurisdiction the cause can be more conveniently tried, that is having regard to expense of time and money; that includes the distribution of necessary witnesses and having regard to the proper law of the contract. The court must not deprive the plaintiff by injunction of any legitimate personal or juridical advantage which he would enjoy in the foreign jurisdiction: see per Lord Diplock in *MacShannon v Rockware Glass Ltd* [1978] 1 All ER 625 at 630, [1978] AC 795 at 812.

In the present case the first criterion must be decided in favour of England as the forum. English law applies, the parties are English (save for the American parent) and there are a large number of witnesses, many of them doctors, engaged in research who are all in England where the clinical trials were carried out.

I do not regard the fact that in the United States the case can be prosecuted with minimal risk of costs because of the contingency fee as a juridical advantage. Even if I am wrong about this, Dr Bloch is at no disadvantage in this country because he has legal aid.

It is said that in Pennsylvania exemplary damages could be awarded, which would certainly not be so in England. The affidavits of the American lawyers show that one is reasonably sure that the Pennsylvanian court would apply the English law to the issue of damages and the other only suggests that it is arguable that the court would apply the American rule. I think that the plaintiff must show a real and not a highly speculative possible advantage. Next it is said that discovery, certainly against the American parent, is more thorough and extensive in Pennsylvania than it would be in England (remember that the American parent has undertaken to submit to the jurisdiction in England and not to rely on any time bar); the rules as to discovery are different, but in a case such as this I cannot think that the English rules could or would work any injustice to Dr Bloch.

I thought at one time during the argument that it would not be right to prevent Dr Bloch from prosecuting his suit against the American parent in Pennsylvania. On further consideration I do not think that in so far as that suit arises out of the contract with the English subsidiary it would be right to permit him to do so. I think that Sir Douglas Frank may well be right in thinking that the only reason the American parent is sued is to try and give the Pennsylvanian court jurisdiction in a suit which really has nothing to do with Pennsylvania.

Finally, it is said that it would be an advantage to Dr Bloch to have the case tried by a jury, as it would be in Pennsylvania, and that the damages, if recovered, would be much higher than in England. I do not accept that it is an advantage to have a case like this tried by a jury, and I am not persuaded that the damages that an English court might award would be in any way unfair to Dr Bloch, relieved as he would be of having to pay perhaps 40% of what he recovered to his lawyers.

Lastly, I have considered whether it would be of any help to relieve any dispute between the American court and ourselves if the American parent were removed as a plaintiff in the English suit.

As I have come to the conclusion that the order made by Sir Douglas Frank was right, I do not think it is of any use to remove the American parent. The result of the injunction is that Dr Bloch cannot proceed in Pennsylvania. He is entirely free to proceed in England: he can either proceed by counterclaim in the present action or bring fresh proceedings and consolidate. He is free to ask the court in Pennsylvania to discharge the injunction against the American parent and if he thinks he has any worthwhile claim against it to pursue it in this country.

I would dismiss this appeal.

Appeal dismissed with costs. Leave to appeal to the House of Lords refused. Order for costs not to be enforced except on application to the court. Liberty to apply.

Solicitors: *Manches & Co* (for Dr Bloch); *Woodham Smith* (for the English subsidiary and the American parent company).

Diana Procter Barrister.

R v Braithwaite
R v Girdham

COURT OF APPEAL, CRIMINAL DIVISION
LORD LANE CJ, MICHAEL DAVIES AND FRENCH JJ
10 FEBRUARY 1983

Criminal law – Corruption – Presumption of corruption – Gift or consideration received by employee of public body – Consideration – Employee receiving goods or services from company holding contract with public body – Whether receipt of goods or services constituting 'consideration' – Whether Crown required to prove whether value given for goods or services – Whether receipt of goods or services raising presumption that they were received corruptly – Prevention of Corruption Act 1906, s 1 – Prevention of Corruption Act 1916, s 2.

The defendants, two employees of a public body, were each charged with corruption, contrary to s 1[a] of the Prevention of Corruption Act 1906, by having corruptly received, from a company which held a contract with the public body, a gift or consideration as an inducement or reward for showing favour to the company in relation to the public body's affairs or business. At their respective trials each defendant admitted to having received goods or services from the company but alleged that he had paid for or intended to pay for them. In each case the trial judge directed the jury that the receipt of goods or services from the company (which was admitted) amounted to the receipt of 'consideration' within s 2[b] of the Prevention of Corruption Act 1916 and therefore, under s 2, the burden of proof lay on the defendant to prove on the balance of probabilities that the consideration had not been paid and received corruptly. The defendants were convicted. Each appealed against conviction on the ground that since s 2 was directed towards the receipt of 'any money, gift, or other consideration', the term 'consideration' referred to a gratification similar to, but other than, a gift, or alternatively a benefit not including money or a gift which was capable of being an inducement or reward. The defendants further submitted that the burden lay on the Crown to prove that the defendants had not given value for the goods or services received and only then did the burden arise under s 2 for the defendant to prove that he had not acted corruptly.

Held – Since the word 'consideration' was defined in both the 1906 and the 1916 Acts as including valuable consideration it was used in those Acts in its legal sense as connoting the existence of some kind of contract or bargain between the parties, in contrast to the situation envisaged by the word 'gift', namely where there was no such contract or bargain between the parties and therefore no consideration. It followed that, once it was proved or admitted that the defendants had received the goods or services from the companies under a bargain or contract, the goods or services were presumed under s 2 of the 1916 Act to have been received corruptly and the burden of proof then lay on the defendants to explain the receipt of the goods or services. Accordingly, in each case the judge had directed the jury correctly. The appeals would therefore be dismissed (see p 92 *a c* to *e* and *g* to *j*, post).

Dictum of Lush J in *Currie v Misa* (1875) LR 10 Exch at 162 applied.

Public Prosecutor v Yuvaraj [1970] AC 913 considered.

Notes

For corruption relating to official contracts, see 11 Halsbury's Laws (4th edn) para 924, and for cases on the subject, see 15 Digest (Reissue) 937–940, *8071–8086*.

---

a Section 1, so far as material, is set out at p 90 *b* to *d*, post

b Section 2 is set out at p 90 *e f*, post.

For the Prevention of Corruption Act 1906, s 1, see 8 Halsbury's Statutes (3rd edn) 236.
For the Prevention of Corruption Act 1916, s 2, see ibid 291. a

Cases referred to in judgment

Currie v Misa (1875) LR 10 Exch 153, Ex Ch; *affd Misa v Currie* (1876) 1 App Cas 554, [1874–80] All ER Rep 686, HL.
Public Prosecutor v Yuvaraj [1970] AC 913, [1970] 2 WLR 226, PC. b

Cases also cited

Carlill v Carbolic Smoke Ball Co [1893] 1 QB 256, [1891–4] All ER Rep 127, CA.
R v Carr [1956] 3 All ER 979, [1957] 1 WLR 165, C-MAC.
R v Mills (Leslie) (1978) 68 Cr App R 154, CA.
R v Smith [1960] 1 All ER 256, [1960] 2 QB 423, CCA. c
R v Wellburn, Nurdin and Randel (1979) 69 Cr App R 254, CA.

Appeals

R v Braithwaite

On 26 May 1982 in the Crown Court at Lincoln before his Honour Judge Hutchinson d and a jury Frank Wilson Braithwaite was convicted on a majority verdict of 10 to 2 of four counts of corruption contrary to s 1 of the Prevention of Corruption Act 1906 in that whilst he was an agent of the British Steel Corp (BSC), a public body, he corruptly accepted from Doughty Webb & Co Ltd for himself a gift or consideration, namely motor car tyres supplied and fitted by F J Wilson (Tyre Specialists) Ltd, as an inducement or reward for showing favour or forbearing to show disfavour to Doughty Webb & Co e Ltd in relation to the affairs or business of the BSC. He was fined £250 on each count to be paid within six months, with two months' imprisonment in default of payment on any count, and was ordered to pay £1,000 towards his legal aid he having already paid £500 in legal aid contribution. He appealed against the convictions on the ground, inter alia, that the trial judge had erred in directing the jury that the transfer of the tyres to him notwithstanding his payment for them amounted to acceptance of a consideration f contrary to s 1 of the 1906 Act. The facts are set out in the judgment of the court.

R v Girdham

On 27 October 1981 in the Crown Court at Lincoln before Forbes J and a jury Ralph Girdham was convicted on a majority verdict of 11 to 1 of four counts of corruption contrary to s 1 of the Prevention of Corruption Act 1906 in that whilst he was an agent of the British Steel Corp (BSC) he corruptly accepted from Leyden (Scunthorpe) Ltd, a g company which provided labour for construction works for the BSC, for himself and his wife work done on cars owned by him and his wife, as an inducement or reward for showing favour or forbearing to show disfavour to Leyden (Scunthorpe) Ltd in relation to the affairs or business of the BSC. He was acquitted on two similar counts. Girdham was fined £75 on each of the four counts with three months' imprisonment in default of h payment on any count. He appealed against the convictions on the ground, inter alia, that the trial judge had erred in directing the jury that he had received a consideration within s 1 of the 1906 Act and that, therefore, the presumption of corruption under s 2 of the Prevention of Corruption Act 1916 operated and the burden of proof passed thereunder to the defendant, because as he paid or always intended to pay for the services which were rendered to him and his wife, no consideration, for the purposes of the 1906 j and 1916 Act, was received by him. The facts are set out in the judgment of the court.

The two appeals were called on and heard together by consent.

B A Farrer QC (assigned by the Registrar of Criminal Appeals) for the first appellant.
Timothy Barnes for the second appellant.
Peter Baker QC and *Roy Ashton* for the Crown.

LORD LANE CJ delivered the following judgment of the court. These are two appeals which, as a matter of convenience, we have heard together with the consent of the parties, because they raise what is essentially the same point. The names of the appellants are Frank Wilson Braithwaite and Ralph Girdham.

The appellant Braithwaite appeared in the Crown Court at Lincoln before his Honour Judge Hutchinson and a jury and after a trial, on 26 May 1982, was convicted of four counts of having corruptly received from a company called Doughty Webb & Co Ltd, a gift or consideration, namely motor car tyres, as an inducement or reward for showing or forbearing to show favour or disfavour, contrary to s 1 of the Prevention of Corruption Act 1906. There were in fact some nine motor car tyres in all of a value of something over £100: the precise amount does not matter. The allegation was that those offences had been committed between August 1973 and October 1975.

The facts which lay behind those allegations, in so far as they are material, were these. The appellant was employed by the British Steel Corp (BSC). There was no dispute that that is a public body within the meaning of s 2 of the Prevention of Corruption Act 1916. There is equally no doubt but that Doughty Webb was a person holding a contract from the BSC within the meaning of that same subsection. It was admitted that the appellant had taken delivery of the tyres which I have mentioned from a firm of wholesalers and it was also admitted that Doughty Webb paid for those tyres through their own account with these motor accessory wholesalers. The appellant's contention was that he had paid one of the company directors, a man called Webb, for the tyres. The Crown conceded that if the appellant had paid for those tyres that would be evidence, and indeed clear evidence, that they had not been received corruptly as an inducement or reward. On the other hand it is right to say that the Crown expressly abandoned as any basis for their allegations that the admitted discounts on the tyres of between 5% and 10% adversely affected the appellant in any way.

The only live issue in the case consequently was whether payment had or had not been made. If it was, he was not guilty; if not, he was guilty.

So far as the other appellant Girdham is concerned, he was convicted on 27 October 1981 in the Crown Court at Lincoln before Forbes J and a jury by a majority of 11 to 1 on four counts of corruption. Counts 1, 3, and 5 related to work alleged to have been done on his own motor car, and count 9 related to work which, it was alleged, had been done on the motor car of his wife. He was acquitted of two other counts. He was jointly tried with a number of other people, both human and companies.

He appeals, as does the first appellant, on a point of law which is of the same nature.

The facts which gave rise to these allegations were these. Between April 1975 and August 1976 this appellant was an engineer at one of the steel works belonging to the BSC. It was a senior post with a good deal of responsibility. There was a company called Leyden (Scunthorpe) Ltd, which was employed extensively on BSC sites providing labour for construction work. The work done on the motor vehicles owned by the appellant and his wife was authorised and paid for by Leydens at a total cost of some £443. Here again the appellant's defence was that he had made arrangements for the work to be done by Leydens purely as a matter of convenience, and that he had intended wholly to repay them. In the upshot he did produce an invoice, which contained no items on it, for £890 and some pence from Leydens, which he claimed included the amount of £443 in respect of the repairs. He said that he paid that invoice in full. He denied that he was in a position to influence the allocation of contracts or providing any benefits for Leydens, but the Crown disputed these contentions.

There is no need to go into the details of the defence, save to say that there were certain features about it which were extremely suspicious. The cheque by which he said he had paid this amount was dated 27 September 1977, which was just before a press release about police investigations into widespread alleged corruption at the BSC at Scunthorpe. The bank receipt stamp was dated 17 November 1977, and the evidence of the gentleman who received the cheque was that it had been received on 10 November, after the press release about the police activity. It is perhaps unnecessary to go into any great detail.

In each of these cases, Judge Hutchinson in the first and Forbes J in the second, the judge directed the jury that the burden of proof under s 2 of the 1916 Act moved to the defendant, and in each case the appellant submits that that direction was wrong. It is necessary therefore first of all to go to the Acts to see their wording.

Section 1 of the Prevention of Corruption Act 1906 reads as follows:

> '(1) If any agent corruptly accepts or obtains, or agrees to accept or attempts to obtain, from any person, for himself or for any other person, any gift or consideration as an inducement or reward for doing or forbearing to do, or for having after the passing of this Act done or forborne to do, any act in relation to his principal's affairs or business, or for showing or forbearing to show favour or disfavour to any person in relation to his principal's affairs or business; or If any person corruptly gives or agrees to give or offers any gift or consideration to any agent as an inducement or reward for doing or forbearing to do, or for having after the passing of this Act done or forborne to do, any act in relation to his principal's affairs or business, or for showing or forbearing to show favour or disfavour to any person in relation to his principal's affairs or business; or If any person knowingly gives to any agent, or if any agent knowingly uses with intent to deceive his principal, any receipt, account, or other document in respect of which the principal is interested, and which contains any statement which is false or erroneous or defective in any material particular . . . he shall be guilty of [an offence], and shall be liable on conviction . . .
>
> (2) For the purposes of this Act the expression "consideration" includes valuable consideration of any kind . . .'

I then turn to s 2 of the 1916 Act, which deals with the presumption of corruption in certain cases. It reads as follows:

> 'Where in any proceedings against a person for an offence under the Prevention of Corruption Act, 1906 [which is this case], or the Public Bodies Corrupt Practices Act, 1889, it is proved that any money, gift, or other consideration has been paid or given to or received by a person in the employment of Her Majesty or any Government Department or a public body by or from a person, or agent of a person, holding or seeking to obtain a contract from His Majesty or any Government Department or public body, the money, gift, or consideration shall be deemed to have been paid or given and received corruptly as such inducement or reward as is mentioned in such Act unless the contrary is proved.'

The effect of that is that when the matters in that section have been fulfilled, the burden of proof is lifted from the shoulders of the prosecution and descends on the shoulders of the defence. It then becomes necessary for the defendant to show, on a balance of probabilities, that what was going on was not reception corruptly as inducement or reward. In an appropriate case it is the judge's duty to direct the jury first of all that they must decide whether they are satisfied so as to feel sure that the defendant received money or gift or consideration, and then to go on to direct them that if they are so satisfied, then under s 2 of the 1916 Act the burden of proof shifts.

In the present case each judge, to put the matter shortly, on the view that he took of the law, directed the jury that since in each case there had admittedly been a receipt of goods or service, that amounted in law to consideration, and therefore, on the very concessions made by the defence, without further ado the burden of proof shifted. It is quite unnecessary in those circumstances for us to read the passages in the directions to the jury, in which each judge set out that matter and directed the jury. The sole question in the appeal is whether that interpretation of the word 'consideration' in s 2 of the 1916 Act is correct. The appellants submit it is not.

We were referred to the wording of the earlier Act, the Public Bodies Corrupt Practices Act 1889. Section 1(1) of that Act, which counsel for the second appellant in particular prays in aid in order to test the interpretation of the word 'consideration', runs as follows:

> 'Every person who shall by himself or by or in conjunction with any other person,

> corruptly solicit or receive, or agree to receive, for himself, or for any other person,
> a any gift, loan, fee, reward, or advantage whatever as an inducement to, or reward for, or otherwise on account . . .'

Those words, counsel points out, are a great deal fuller than the words which appear in the 1906 Act, and he seeks by that means to elicit the meaning of the word 'consideration' in the 1906 Act.

b This line of argument he advances further by drawing our attention to a Privy Council case, *Public Prosecutor v Yuvaraj* [1970] AC 913. The passage to which he draws our attention is in the speech of Lord Diplock. Their Lordships were considering the Prevention of Corruption Act 1961 which was in force in Malaysia, which corresponds with s 2 of the 1916 Act which we are considering here today. The headnote reads (at 915):

> c '. . . the burden of rebutting such presumption is discharged if the court considers that on the balance of probabilities the gratification was not paid or given and received corruptly as an inducement or reward as mentioned in sections 3 or 4 of the Prevention of Corruption Act, 1961 . . .'

Drawing on that particular wording, counsel for the second appellant suggests,
d plausibly, that the word 'consideration' should be read in the light of the word 'gratification', and should be construed as if it were gratification. He refers to the passage in the speech of Lord Diplock (at 922):

> 'The policy which underlies section 14 of the Prevention of Corruption Act, 1961, is, in their Lordships' view, clear. The section is limited to persons "in the employment of any public body". No similar presumption applies to agents of
> e private principals. Corruption in the public service is a grave social evil which is difficult to detect, for those who take part in it will be at pains to cover their tracks. The section is designed to compel every public servant so to order his affairs that he does not accept a gift in cash or in kind from a member of the public except in circumstances in which he will be able to show clearly that he had legitimate reasons for doing so.'

f It seems to us that that is precisely the reason likewise for the existence of s 2 in the 1916 Act. It is, one scarcely needs emphasise, extremely difficult, if not impossible, for the Crown to prove that any person did not give value for a favour which he received, and that must, in our judgment, have been the reason for the 1916 Act which supplemented the 1906 Act. It does not need very much imagination to see that between
g the two Acts it must have become apparent that the difficulties of bringing home these allegations were insurmountable in the absence of such a provision as s 2 of the 1916 Act.

It is submitted by the appellants that the word 'consideration' therefore means a gratification which does not include money or a gift, or alternatively, as counsel for the first appellant put it after prompting by French J in argument, any benefit not including money or a gift which is capable of being an inducement or reward. Secondly it is
h submitted on behalf of the appellants that the word 'gift' in s 2 of the 1916 Act is pointless if the argument of the Crown is correct. Thirdly it is submitted that where there is an ambiguity it must be resolved in favour of the defendant. We have been referred to *Maxwell on the Interpretation of Statutes* (12th edn, 1969). It is perhaps unnecessary for us to refer to the specific passage which counsel for the second appellant drew to our attention. Finally it is submitted on behalf of both appellants that the onus of proof in
j cases such as this should only shift where there is something which emerges from the prosecution case which calls for or demands an explanation from the defendant.

First of all what is the meaning of the word 'consideration', particularly in the light of the definition contained in the 1906 Act, namely '"consideration" includes valuable consideration of any kind'? That is picked up in s 4(3) of the 1916 Act as follows: '. . . "consideration" in this Act [has] the same meaning as in the Prevention of Corruption

Act, 1906 . . .' In our view the meaning of the word 'consideration' must be the legal meaning of it and not any common or garden meaning; that really goes without saying. On that basis one turns to the classic definition which is to be found in *Currie v Misa* (1875) LR 10 Exch 153 at 162 per Lush J delivering the judgment of the Court of Exchequer Chamber:

> 'A valuable consideration, in the sense of the law, may consist either in some right, interest, profit, or benefit accruing to the one party, or some forbearance, detriment, loss, or responsibility, given, suffered, or undertaken by the other . . .'

If one turns, as we think we are entitled, to see what the *Shorter Oxford English Dictionary* has to say about consideration, the only meaning of it which is relevant to the present circumstances is meaning no 6:

> '*Law.* Anything regarded as recompense or equivalent for what one does or undertakes for another's benefit; *esp.*, in the law of contracts, "the thing given or done by the promisee in exchange for the promise".'

In our judgment the word 'consideration' connotes the existence of something in the shape of a contract or a bargain between the parties. In the context of the present case, take E as the employee of the public body and A as the agent of the contractor. E the employee, promises to pay A, the agent of the contractor, £x. The consideration for that promise is that the contractor will supply tyres for E's car, or will do work on E's car, as the case may be. That is the consideration, namely the work done on the car or the supplying of the tyres for the car. If that is correct, then on proof of the receipt of the tyres or the doing of the work, the defendant is called on for an explanation. In our view the word 'gift', according to the Crown's argument, is not otiose. The word 'gift' is the other side of the coin, that is to say it comes into play where there is no consideration and no bargain. Consideration deals with the situation where there is a contract or a bargain and something moving the other way. Indeed if one looks at the word 'money' in the 1916 Act, although it does not appear in the 1906 Act, it would be a very strange thing if the receipt of money was to bring s 2 into play even though value is given for it, whereas the receipt of goods did not bring s 2 into play where there was value given for the receipt of goods. Consequently the first submission on behalf of the appellants, in our opinion, fails.

Likewise it seems to us that there is no ambiguity which would bring into operation the principles set out in *Maxwell on the Interpretation of Statutes.* As suggested earlier in this judgment, it seems to us that this case demonstrates the very reason for the passing of the 1916 Act. Given that the advantage of the tyres or the repairs work is proved, it is almost impossible for the Crown to prove that no payment was ever made in return. Indeed in answer to the appellants' final point, in our view there was indeed something which called for an explanation in these circumstances, and that is the reason for s 2 of the 1916 Act.

For these reasons we have come to the conclusion that on this main point the judge in each case was correct.

Counsel for the second appellant, in his attractive, terse and concise argument raised two subsidiary points. We are sure he will acquit us of any discourtesy if we say we have considered them carefully and do not think there is anything in either of them and those grounds of appeal also fail.

Consequently both appeals must be dismissed.

Appeals dismissed.

24 March. The court refused leave to appeal to the House of Lords but certified, under s 33(2) of the Criminal Appeal Act 1968, that the following point of law of general public importance was involved in the decision: whether the word 'consideration' in s 1 of the Prevention of Corruption

Act 1906 and s 2 of the Prevention of Corruption Act 1916 included a benefit received by the defendant for which the Crown did not prove that he did not give full value.

Solicitors: H M *Winocour*, Scunthorpe (for the second appellant); *Director of Public Prosecutions.*

N P Metcalfe Esq Barrister.

Attorney General of New Zealand v Ortiz and others

HOUSE OF LORDS

LORD FRASER OF TULLYBELTON, LORD SCARMAN, LORD ROSKILL, LORD BRANDON OF OAKBROOK AND LORD BRIGHTMAN

7, 8, 9 MARCH, 21 APRIL 1983

Conflict of laws – Foreign law – New Zealand statute providing that historic articles unlawfully removed 'shall be forfeited' to Her Majesty – Whether goods so removed automatically forfeited on removal from New Zealand – Whether forfeiture dependent on seizure of goods – Whether Crown's title accruing only on seizure – Historic Articles Act 1962 (NZ), s 12(2).

New Zealand – Statute – Interpretation – Statute providing that historic articles unlawfully removed 'shall be forfeited' to Her Majesty – Whether goods so removed automatically forfeited on removal from New Zealand – Whether forfeiture dependent on seizure of goods – Whether Crown's title accruing only on seizure – Historic Articles Act 1962 (NZ), s 12(2).

In 1973 the third defendant, an art dealer, purchased a valuable Maori carving in New Zealand, which was a historic article within the meaning of the New Zealand Historic Articles Act 1962. By s 5(1)[a] of that Act, it was unlawful to remove such an article, knowing it to be a historic article, from New Zealand without a certificate of permission from the Minister of Internal Affairs. Section 12(2)[b] of that Act further provided that 'An historic article knowingly exported . . . shall be forfeited to Her Majesty' and that the provisions of the New Zealand Customs Act 1913 relating to forfeited goods were to apply 'subject to the provisions' of the 1962 Act. Section 251[c] of the 1913 Act provided that 'forfeiture [was to] take effect' on seizure and was then 'for all purposes [to] relate back to the date' when the cause of forfeiture arose. Section 251 of the 1913 Act was replaced by s 274[d] of the Customs Act 1966, which provided that when any goods were forfeited and the goods were seized 'the forfeiture [was] for all purposes [to] relate back to the date of the act or event from which the forfeiture accrued'. The third defendant exported the carving from New Zealand without obtaining a certificate of permission and sold it to the first defendant, a collector of Polynesian art. In 1978 the first defendant placed the carving for sale by auction in England with the second defendant. The plaintiff, the Attorney General of New Zealand suing on behalf of Her Majesty in right of the government of New Zealand, applied in the Queen's Bench Division for an injunction restraining the sale of the carving and for an order for its delivery up on the ground that it had been forfeited automatically to Her Majesty by its removal from New Zealand in breach of s 5(1) of the 1962 Act. By an order of a master a preliminary issue was ordered to be determined, namely, inter alia, whether Her Majesty had become the

a Section 5(1) is set out at p 96 *b c*, post
b Section 12(2) is set out at p 96 *e f*, post
c Section 251 is set out at p 97 *j* to p 98 *a*, post
d Section 274 is set out at p 97 *e*, post

owner and was entitled to possession of the carving pursuant to the 1962 Act and the 1913 and 1966 Acts. The judge found for the plaintiff. The defendants successfully *a* appealed to the Court of Appeal. On appeal to the House of Lords the plaintiff accepted that under the 1966 Act forfeiture did not normally occur until seizure but contended that, since the 1966 Act was subject to the provisions of the 1962 Act, s 12(2) of the 1962 Act had modified the forfeiture provisions in the 1966 Act so as to make forfeiture automatic at the point when a historic article was exported with knowledge that it was a historic article. *b*

Held – Although the forfeiture provisions contained in the 1966 Act took effect subject to the 1962 Act, on its true construction there was nothing in the 1962 Act when taken as a whole to alter those provisions so as to render a historic article automatically forfeited at the moment it was exported with knowledge that it was a historic article. Instead the act of knowingly exporting a historic article merely made it liable to be forfeited on *c* seizure and, since the carving had not been seized by the New Zealand customs or police, forfeiture had not occurred. Accordingly the Crown did not have title to the carving and the appeal would be therefore dismissed (see p 94 *j* to p 95 *b*, p 100 *g* to *j* and p 101 *a*, post).

Decision of the Court of Appeal [1982] 3 All ER 432 affirmed.

Notes *d*

For the general rights of the Crown in relation to property, see 8 Halsbury's Laws (4th edn) paras 1076–1082, and for cases on the subject, see 11 Digest (Reissue) 776–777, *891–900*.

Appeal *e*

The plaintiff, the Attorney General of New Zealand suing on behalf of Her Majesty the Queen in right of the government of New Zealand, appealed with leave of the Court of Appeal against the decision of the Court of Appeal (Lord Denning MR, Ackner and O'Connor LJJ) ([1982] 3 All ER 432, [1982] 3 WLR 570) on 21 May 1982 allowing the appeal by the first defendant, George Ortiz, and the third defendant, Lance Entwistle, from the decision of Staughton J ([1982] 3 All ER 432, [1982] QB 349) given on 1 July *f* 1981 holding, on the trial of two preliminary issues, that on the assumed facts (1) Her Majesty the Queen had become the owner and was entitled to possession of a Maori artifact pursuant to the provisions of the New Zealand Historic Articles Act 1962 and the Customs Acts 1913 and 1966 and (2) that the provisions of those Acts, although enactments of the New Zealand Parliament, were none the less enforceable in England. Pursuant to a consent order the second defendants, Sotheby Parke Bernet & Co, retained *g* possession of the artifact pending the outcome of the action and proceedings against them were stayed. The facts are set out in the opinion of Lord Brightman.

Andrew Morritt QC and *Charles Gray* for the New Zealand government.
Paul V Baker QC and *Nicholas Patten* for Mr Ortiz.
Colin Ross-Munro QC and *Gerald Levy* for Mr Entwistle. *h*

Their Lordships took time for consideration.

21 April. The following opinions were delivered.

LORD FRASER OF TULLYBELTON. My Lords, I have had the advantage of *j* reading in draft the speech prepared by my noble and learned friend Lord Brightman and I agree with it. For the reasons there stated I would dismiss this appeal.

LORD SCARMAN. My Lords, I have had the advantage of reading in draft the speech to be delivered by my noble and learned friend Lord Brightman. I agree with it. For the reasons he gives I would dismiss the appeal.

LORD ROSKILL. My Lords, I have had the advantage of reading in draft the speech
a prepared by my noble and learned friend Lord Brightman. For the reasons he gives I too
would dismiss the appeal.

LORD BRANDON OF OAKBROOK. My Lords, I have had the advantage of
reading in draft the speech prepared by my noble and learned friend Lord Brightman. I
agree with it, and for the reasons which he gives would dismiss the appeal.

b

LORD BRIGHTMAN. My Lords, this appeal arises out of the trial of a preliminary
issue in a suit brought by the New Zealand government against the exporter and
purchaser of a tribal antiquity. The facts as pleaded in the amended statement of claim,
on the basis of which the issue fell to be tried, are as follows. In or about 1972 one
c Manukonga found in a swamp in the province of Taranaki a valuable Maori relic,
described as a series of five carved wood panels that formed the front of a food store. In
1973 Manukonga sold the carving to the third defendant, Mr Entwistle, who was a dealer
in primitive works of art. The carving was to the knowledge of Mr Entwistle a historic
article within the meaning of the Historic Articles Act 1962 of New Zealand. Later in
the same year the carving was exported from New Zealand by or on behalf of Mr
d Entwistle. No permission under the Historic Articles Act 1962 authorising the removal
of the carving from New Zealand had been obtained by him. In the same year Mr
Entwistle sold the carving to the first defendant, Mr Ortiz, for $65,000. In 1978 Mr Ortiz
consigned the carving to Messrs Sotheby Parke Bernet & Co (Sothebys) in England for
sale by auction.

In June 1978 the Attorney General of New Zealand (suing on behalf of Her Majesty
e the Queen in right of the government of New Zealand) issued proceedings against Mr
Ortiz and Sothebys and (by amendment) Mr Entwistle. The New Zealand government
claims a declaration that the carving is the property of Her Majesty the Queen, as against
Mr Ortiz and Sothebys an order for delivery up of the carving, and as against Mr
Entwistle damages for conversion.

Under a consent order Sothebys retain possession of the carving pending the outcome
f of the action, and proceedings against them have been stayed.

In 1980 the Queen's Bench master, whose decision was upheld on appeal, ordered the
trial of two preliminary issues, first, whether on the facts pleaded—

> 'Her Majesty the Queen has become the owner and is entitled to possession of the
> carving . . . pursuant to the provisions of the Historic Articles Act 1962 and the
> Customs Acts 1913 and 1966.'

g

And, second—

> 'whether in any event the provisions of the said Acts are unenforceable in England
> as being foreign penal, revenue and/or public laws.'

It is not in dispute for the purposes of the preliminary issues that the carving was
h exported in breach of the 1962 Act. The resolution of the first issue depends on whether,
on the true construction of s 12 of the 1962 Act, incorporating certain provisions of the
Customs Act, the carving was forfeited immediately it was unlawfully exported, so that
it thereupon became vested in the Crown, or whether the unlawful export of the carving
merely rendered it liable to forfeiture in the future, the forfeiture taking effect only on
the seizure by the New Zealand customs or police, which has not taken place. There is an
j express provision in the Customs Act 1913, and it is a necessary implication from a
provision in the Customs Act 1966, that forfeiture under those Acts is not complete until
seizure.

I turn in more detail to the statutory provisions. The Historic Articles Act 1962
repealed the Maori Antiquities Act 1908, which itself consolidated earlier enactments.
The 1962 Act is described in the long title as 'An Act to provide for the protection of
historic articles and to control their removal from New Zealand'. Section 2 contains a

definition of 'historic article'. It is not in dispute that the carving falls within this definition. The definition is a wide one, and includes not only artifacts but also *a* documentary matter and certain specimens of animals, plants and minerals. Section 4 enables the Minister of Internal Affairs to acquire a historic article by purchase or gift. Section 5 describes what acts are unlawful in particular relation to a historic article, and it is the only section to do so. Unless a person transgresses s 5, he is at liberty to dispose of or deal with a historic article in the same manner as he may dispose of or deal with any other article. This section, which is crucial to the construction of s 12, reads as follows, so *b* far as relevant:

> '(1) It shall not be lawful after the commencement of this Act for any person to remove or attempt to remove any historic article from New Zealand, knowing it to be an historic article, otherwise than pursuant to the authority and in conformity with the terms and conditions of a written certificate of permission given by the Minister under this Act. *c*
>
> (2) Every person who contrary to the provisions of this section removes or attempts to remove any article from New Zealand, knowing it to be an historic article, commits an offence, and shall be liable on summary conviction to a fine not exceeding two hundred pounds . . .'

Sections 6 to 11 deal with applications for permission to remove a historic article from *d* New Zealand and incidental matters. Section 12, which is the section that falls to be construed, reads as follows:

> '(1) Subject to the provisions of this Act, the provisions of the Customs Act 1913 shall apply to any historic article the removal from New Zealand of which is prohibited by this Act in all respects as if the article were an article the export of which had been prohibited pursuant to an Order in Council under section 47 of the *e* Customs Act 1913.
>
> (2) An historic article knowingly exported or attempted to be exported in breach of this Act shall be forfeited to Her Majesty and, subject to the provisions of this Act, the provisions of the Customs Act 1913 relating to forfeited goods shall apply to any such article in the same manner as they apply to goods forfeited under the Customs Act 1913. *f*
>
> (3) Where any historic article is forfeited to Her Majesty pursuant to this section, it shall be delivered to the Minister and retained in safe custody in accordance with his directions: Provided that the Minister may, in his discretion, direct that the article be returned to the person who was the owner thereof immediately before forfeiture subject to such conditions (if any) as the Minister may think fit to impose.'

g Section 16 empowered the Governor General by Order in Council to make regulations for certain purposes, including regulations providing for such matters as are contemplated by or necessary for giving full effect to the provisions of the Act. Your Lordships have not been made aware of any relevant regulations.

The 1962 Act is no longer in force. It was repealed by the Antiquities Act 1975 as from 1 April 1976. However, the New Zealand government do not claim that they are able to *h* base the Crown's claim to ownership on any provision of the 1975 Act, which therefore can be disregarded.

Section 12 of the 1962 Act was expressed to operate by reference to the Customs Act 1913. The provisions of that Act are to apply to a historic article the removal from New Zealand of which is prohibited by the 1962 Act as if the article were an article the export of which had been prohibited pursuant to an Order in Council under s 47 of the 1913 *j* Act. The 1913 Act was repealed by the Customs Act 1966, which came into operation for all relevant purposes on 1 January 1967. Section 70 of the 1966 Act is the section which corresponds to s 47 of the 1913 Act. It is common ground (although at one time disputed) that, in consequence of s 21 of the Acts Interpretation Act 1924, s 12 of the 1962 Act must for present purposes be read as referring to the Customs Act 1966, and in particular to s 70 thereof.

The immediate effect of notionally including, without qualification, a historic article as a prohibited export under s 70 of the 1966 Act is that a contravention of the prohibition would render the exporter liable to a fine and would render the article subject to forfeiture, in the terms of sub-ss (6) and (7), which read as follows:

> '(6) If any person exports, or ships with intent to export, or conspires with any other person (whether within New Zealand or not) to export any goods contrary to the terms of any such prohibition in force with respect thereto he commits an offence and shall be liable to a fine not exceeding five hundred pounds or three times the value of the goods, whichever sum is the greater.
>
> (7) All goods shipped on board any ship or aircraft for the purpose of being exported contrary to the terms of any such prohibition in force with respect thereto, and all goods waterborne for the purpose of being so shipped and exported, shall be forfeited.'

A further effect of notionally including without qualification a historic article in s 70 would be to bring into operation in relation thereto all the other provisions of the Customs Act 1966 which are incidental to sub-ss (1), (6) and (7). For instance, s 69 defines the time at which goods on board a ship or aircraft are deemed to be exported. Section 212 confers on a person in the employment of the customs the right to question a person who is on board a ship or aircraft whether he has in his possession restricted or forfeited goods; 'restricted goods' includes prohibited exports. Sections 213 to 218 confer rights of search and discovery of documents. Section 225 regulates the sale of forfeited goods. Section 254 prescribes a penalty for concealing restricted goods on a ship or aircraft. Of particular significance are ss 274 and 275, which read as follows, so far as material:

> '274. When it is provided by this Act or any other of the Customs Acts that any goods are forfeited, and the goods are seized in accordance with this Act or with the Act under which the forfeiture has accrued, the forfeiture shall for all purposes relate back to the date of the act or event from which the forfeiture accrued.
>
> 275. (1) Any officer of Customs or member of the Police may seize any forfeited goods or any goods which he has reasonable and probable cause for suspecting to be forfeited . . .
>
> (4) No goods shall be so seized at any time except within two years after the cause of forfeiture has arisen.'

Section 278 requires immediate notice of seizure to be given to a person known or believed to have an interest in the goods. Section 279 provides that goods seized as forfeited shall be deemed to be condemned unless forfeiture is disputed in the prescribed manner. Section 280 deals with proceedings instituted in the Supreme Court for the condemnation of goods seized as forfeited. Section 282 is to the like effect in relation to a magistrate's court. Section 283 provides that conviction of an offence which gives rise to forfeiture shall have effect as condemnation, without suit or judgment, of any goods that have been seized and in respect of which the offence was committed. Section 286 provides that 'all forfeited goods shall, on forfeiture, become the property of the Crown . . .' Section 287 empowers the Governor General to waive a forfeiture.

It follows from the wording of s 274 of the 1966 Act, and from the definition of 'forfeited goods' in s 2 as goods 'in respect of which a cause of forfeiture has arisen', that goods which are declared by the Act to be forfeited are in most instances more accurately described as 'liable to forfeiture', and that no actual forfeiture takes place and there is accordingly no transfer of ownership until the goods have been seized. This was, perhaps, more clearly expressed in the corresponding section of the 1913 Act, which reads as follows:

> '251. When it is provided by this Act or any other Customs Act that any goods are forfeited, the forfeiture shall take effect without suit or judgment of condemnation so soon as the goods have been seized in accordance with this Act or with the Act under which the forfeiture has accrued, and any such forfeiture so

> completed by seizure shall for all purposes relate back to the date of the act or event from which the forfeiture accrued.' a

Counsel for the New Zealand government conceded before your Lordships (although it was at one time disputed) that there is no relevant distinction between these two sections.

The two preliminary issues were tried by Staughton J ([1982] 3 All ER 432, [1982] QB 349). The first issue raised a question of foreign law. A question of foreign law is a question of fact on which the trial judge requires the assistance of evidence from foreign b lawyers. The judge had the advantage of expert evidence from Dr Inglis QC on behalf of the New Zealand government and Mr Thomas QC on behalf of Mr Ortiz. The witnesses were divided whether the Customs Act 1966 provided for automatic forfeiture or whether seizure was a necessary preliminary. On this issue the judge accepted the evidence of Mr Thomas that the Act did not provide for automatic forfeiture. That view of the effect of the Act is no longer challenged. There was a similar divergence of view c between the experts whether or not there was automatic forfeiture under s 12(2) of the 1962 Act. On that aspect, the judge expressed himself as follows ([1982] 3 All ER 432 at 443, [1982] QB 349 at 362):

> 'My conclusions on this issue are therefore as follows: (1) the words "shall be forfeited" are equally capable of meaning shall be forfeited automatically or shall be d liable to forfeiture; (2) the reference to the Customs Act 1913 and now to the Customs Act 1966 where the same words mean "shall be liable to be forfeited", points to the words having that meaning in the 1962 Act; (3) that is not conclusive because s 12 of the Historic Articles Act 1962, when it refers to the Customs Act, does so "subject to the provisions of this Act"; (4) the purpose of the 1962 Act may properly be taken into account by a New Zealand court and points firmly in favour e of automatic forfeiture. On these grounds I accept the evidence of Dr Inglis that it does so provide.'

The judge then turned to the second issue, which he decided in favour of the New Zealand government for reasons which need not be recounted.

Mr Ortiz and Mr Entwistle appealed. In reserved judgments the Court of Appeal f unanimously decided that there was no ambiguity in s 12(2) of the 1962 Act, that forfeiture under that section took effect only on seizure, and that, since the carving had not been forfeited, the Crown was neither the owner nor entitled to possession of the carving (see [1982] 3 All ER 432, [1982] 3 WLR 570).

That decision was sufficient to dispose of the preliminary issues. If the first issue were decided against the New Zealand government, there was no need to discuss and decide g the second issue, as O'Connor LJ pointed out. The court did, however, deal with the second issue, and expressed opinions thereon. I imagine that this course was taken for the assistance of your Lordships' House, in case your Lordships should form a contrary view on the first issue, in which event it would have been helpful to have had the opinions of the Court of Appeal. It was perhaps with this sort of consideration in mind that the order made by the master directed a trial of the second issue 'in any event'. My h Lords, I take the view that the opinions expressed by the Lords Justices on the second issue were, in truth, obiter. Indeed, that would also seem to have been the view of the Lords Justices themselves, because in the report of the case in the Weekly Law Reports, which, as your Lordships know, will have been seen in proof by the Lords Justices, the appeal is treated in the headnote as disposed of on the first issue alone. Your Lordships have heard no argument on the second issue, and I venture to think that, in any event, j your Lordships would not wish to be taken as expressing any conclusion on the correctness or otherwise of the opinions so expressed.

My Lords, I am in respectful agreement with the decision on the first issue reached by the Court of Appeal, although I express my reasons differently.

Section 12(1)of the 1962 Act says: 'Subject to the provisions of this Act, the provisions

of the Customs Act 1913 shall apply to any historic article the removal from New Zealand
a of which is prohibited by this Act . . .' That raises the question: what articles are forbidden to be removed from New Zealand by the Act? In my opinion, the answer is those articles defined by s 2 the removal of which is not authorised by a certificate of permission given by the Minister of Internal Affairs, although there is no offence unless the removal is done knowingly. I shall refer to a historic article the removal of which is forbidden by s 5(1) as a 'protected chattel'.

b Continuing with my analysis of s 12(1), I find that the provisions of the Customs Act 1913 are to apply to a protected chattel 'in all respects as if the article were an article the export of which had been prohibited pursuant to an Order in Council under section 47 of the Customs Act 1913'. This formula, if unqualified, would have the effect of applying to a protected chattel all the provisions of the 1966 Act which are appropriate. I have already suggested a number of provisions of the 1966 Act which are thus introduced,
c notably s 69 (time of exportation), sub-ss (4) and (5) of s 70 (fine and forfeiture for contravention) and s 274 (relation back of forfeiture and necessity for seizure). The interpretation section is also introduced, the most important definition being that of 'forfeited goods—goods in respect of which a cause of forfeiture has arisen under the Customs Acts'. The definition of 'restricted goods', as inclusive of goods the exportation of which is prohibited by the Customs Acts, is also important as it provides the lead-in to
d a number of sections of the 1966 Act.

However, this application of the 1966 Act takes effect 'Subject to the provisions of this Act'. The provisions of the 1962 Act are, therefore, paramount, and in consequence the incorporated provisions of the 1966 Act are subject to the provisions of ss 5 and 12(2) and (3) of the 1962 Act.

Section 5(1) of the 1962 Act creates the one and only offence which is peculiar to a
e historic article, namely the removal of it or an attempt to remove it from New Zealand, with knowledge that it is a historic article, otherwise than pursuant to a written certificate of permission. For that offence s 5(2) imposes a liability on summary conviction to a fine not exceeding £200. It is at that point that we find the first qualification on the general application of the provisions of the 1966 Act to a protected chattel. Under s 70(6) of the 1966 Act, the pecuniary penalty for exporting, or shipping with intent to export, any
f goods contrary to the prohibition in s 70(1) is a fine not exceeding £500 or three times the value of the goods if greater. Only the lesser penalty prescribed by the 1962 Act can be imposed for the unlawful removal or attempted removal from New Zealand of a protected chattel.

The application of the 1966 Act is also subject to s 12(2) of the 1962 Act. There are two limbs to this subsection. The first limb provides that a historic article 'knowingly'
g exported or attempted to be exported in breach of the 1962 Act shall be forfeited to the Crown. It is clear from s 5 that the adverb 'knowingly' applies not to knowledge of the fact of export or attempt thereat, but to knowledge that the article is a historic article as defined. What the first limb of sub-s (2) does is to introduce the penalty of forfeiture for committing an offence under s 5(1), as a penalty which is additional to the fine that can be imposed under s 5(2). But, as in the case of the fine, there is no penalty of forfeiture
h unless it can be said of the exporter (remover) that he knew at the time the offence was committed that the article was a historic article.

The second limb of s 12(2) provides, again subject to the provisions of the 1962 Act, that 'the provisions of the Customs Act 1966 relating to forfeited goods shall apply to any such article in the same manner as they apply to goods forfeited under the Customs Act 1966'. The effect is to apply to a historic article, known to be such, which is exported or
j attempted to be exported in breach of s 5(1), the whole range of provisions of the Customs Act 1966 relating to 'forfeited goods', but subject again to the paramountcy of the 1962 Act. These provisions include, most importantly, s 274, which implies that forfeiture takes effect only on seizure and provides that the forfeiture then relates back to the date when the cause of forfeiture arose.

Since the application of such forfeiture provisions is expressed to be 'Subject to the provisions of this Act', and since s 12(2) of the 1962 Act is the enactment which imposes forfeiture for an offence under s 5(1) of the 1962 Act, it seems to me that sub-s (7) of s 70 of the 1966 Act is overridden by s 12(2) of the 1962 Act. A further minor result of the paramountcy of the 1962 Act is that the power conferred on the Governor General by s 287 of the Customs Act 1966 to waive a forfeiture will not apply in the case of the forfeiture of a historic article; such power is vested by s 12(3) of the 1962 Act in the Minister of Internal Affairs.

So, as it seems to me, the position of the Crown and the wrongdoer under the 1962 Act is clear. The offence is created by s 5(1). The pecuniary penalty is defined by s 5(2). The penalty 'in rem' is created by s 12(2). The process of forfeiture is regulated in accordance with the provisions of the 1966 Act, in particular, the necessity of seizure (to be followed by actual or deemed condemnation) before the forfeiture is completed, at which stage it relates back to the accrual of the right to forfeit. There being no seizure in the instant case, the conclusion is inescapable that the ownership of the carving and the right to possession thereof have not become vested in the Crown.

Counsel for the New Zealand government sought to argue that sub-s (2) of s 12 imposed automatic forfeiture for a 'knowing' export of a historic article, as a remedy additional to conditional forfeiture for an 'unknowing' but illegal export under the Customs Act 1966 as applied by sub-s (1). He accepted that there could be no forfeiture without seizure in the case of an 'unknowing' export or attempted export, but he argued that there was no reason in the case of a 'knowing' export or attempted export to introduce into a sub-s (2) forfeiture the requirement of seizure before the forfeiture takes effect. He sought to bolster the argument by reference to the supposed effect of the earlier Maori Antiquities Act 1908, which was said by both expert witnesses to have had the result of imposing immediate forfeiture without seizure if a Maori antiquity were 'entered for export' contrary to the Act. It was said that it would be unlikely that the repealing Act, with its stated object of protecting historic articles and controlling their removal from New Zealand, would have deliberately reduced that protection, and lessened the chances of reversing an unlawful removal by requiring seizure before forfeiture. I am, however, by no means convinced that the 1908 Act on its true construction did provide for forfeiture without seizure, which would be quite contrary to the general pattern of a Customs Act. Reference to the 1908 Act is of limited value in this case, and I express no opinion on the point. Counsel also referred to s 5(*j*) of the Acts Interpretation Act 1924, which bids the court to give to a statute 'such fair, large and liberal construction and interpretation as will best ensure the attainment of the object of the Act . . . according to its true intent, meaning and spirit'. Counsel submitted, and I am disposed to agree, that the recovery of unlawfully exported historic articles would be best ensured if title thereto were to vest in the Crown independently of seizure.

In my opinion there is a fatal flaw in the argument of counsel. There is no offence committed under the 1962 Act by the export of a historic article unless it is done 'knowingly'. No cause of forfeiture is capable of arising by reason of an 'unknowing' export of a historic article, apart from a forfeiture for an offence under the Customs Act which has nothing to do with the fact that the subject matter of the export is a historic article. There are not two possible causes of forfeiture of a historic article, one cause arising under the Customs Act 1966 based on an 'unknowing' export or attempt thereat and the other arising under s 12(2) of the 1962 Act based on a 'knowing' export or attempt thereat. It is only to s 12(2) of the 1962 Act that one can look in order to find a cause of forfeiture of a historic article as such. Then, to ascertain the process of forfeiture, one turns to the 1966 Act. There one finds that s 274 requires seizure as a preliminary to forfeiture. The contingent nature of the forfeiture is underlined by the reference in s 12(2) to 'the provisions of the Customs Act 1913 relating to forfeited goods', which must inevitably be read as 'the provisions of the Customs Act 1966 relating to goods in respect of which a cause of forfeiture has arisen under the Customs Act'. It is not in my opinion possible to reach any conclusion save that (a) the penalty of forfeiture of a historic article as such is imposed only for an offence under s 5(1) of the 1962 Act and (b) such forfeiture is not complete until seizure.

I have every sympathy with the New Zealand government's claim. If the statement of a claim is correct, New Zealand has been deprived of an article of value to its artistic heritage in consequence of an unlawful act committed by the second respondent. I do not, however, see any way in which, on a proper construction of the 1962 Act and in the events which here happened, the Crown is able to claim ownership thereof.

I would dismiss the appeal.

b *Appeal dismissed.*

Solicitors: *Allen & Overy* (for the New Zealand government); *Joelson Wilson & Co* (for Mr Ortiz); *Samuels & Green* (for Mr Entwistle).

Mary Rose Plummer Barrister.

c

Fraser and others v Thames Television Ltd and others

d QUEEN'S BENCH DIVISION
HIRST J
14–17, 21–25, 28–30 JUNE, 1, 2, 5–9, 12–16, 19–23, 26–29 JULY, 4–8, 11, 12, 20, 21 OCTOBER 1982

Equity – Breach of confidence – Damages – Use of information obtained in confidence – Actresses e developing idea for television series in which they proposed to appear – Actresses disclosing idea orally and in confidence to defendants – Defendants using idea to create television series with other actresses – Test to be applied to determine whether a breach of confidence – Whether law relating to protection of confidential information extending to protection of an idea communicated orally.

f *Contract – Implied term – First refusal – Agreement giving defendants option to use plaintiffs' idea for television series in which plaintiffs wished to appear – Agreement providing that if plaintiffs unable to appear in series defendants entitled to produce series with other actresses – Defendants using other actresses to produce series without first offering parts to plaintiffs – Whether negative covenant to be implied into agreement that if plaintiffs willing to appear defendants would not use plaintiffs' idea for series without using plaintiffs as actresses – Whether g defendants' failure to offer parts to plaintiffs a breach of contract.*

In 1973 the second plaintiffs, three female actresses, formed a rock group with the assistance of the first plaintiff, who was their manager and also their composer. The actresses and the manager developed an idea for a television series which was to portray the formation of a three-girl rock group and the members' subsequent experiences. The h series was to be part fact and part fiction, the factual part being based on the actresses' own experiences, and was to focus on both the group and the individual members' lives to contrast their collective character with their individual characters. The three actresses intended that they would appear in the series as the three singers and that their manager would compose music for the series. Oral discussions took place between the actresses, the manager, a representative of the first defendant, a television company (Thames), the j second defendant, the scriptwriter, and the third defendant, the producer, in which the idea for the series was disclosed to the defendants in confidence with a view to its realisation. As a result of those discussions and in consideration of a payment by Thames of £500 the actresses and the manager granted Thames an oral option which was later confirmed in writing. The confirming letter stated that Thames was to 'acquire an option on your services in connection with a possible new series', that the actresses were to have first refusal should the series be proceeded with, and that if they declined the offer

Thames was to have the right to make the series with three other actresses. In January
1975 one of the actresses, A, was engaged to play in a musical which was to begin in *a*
April. In February Thames renewed the option and commissioned the scriptwriter to
write scripts for the series after deciding to make the series in September 1975.
Unsuccessful efforts were made by A's agent to obtain her release from the musical. The
actresses and the manager by letter agreed to participate in the series in accordance with
the terms of the option. A stormy meeting between Thames, the producer and the
manager followed and soon after that Thames informed the manager by letter that unless *b*
A was free of all other work commitments by the next morning the parts in the series
would be recast. The release from the musical was not obtained in time and the series
was subsequently made with three other actresses in the leading roles. The actresses and
the manager sued Thames, the scriptwriter and the producer claiming damages (i) for
breach of contract, contending that there was an implied negative covenant in the option
agreement that if the three actresses were willing to perform in the series Thames would *c*
not go ahead with the series using their idea without also using their services as actresses,
and (ii) for breach of confidence. The defendants contended (i) that the manager had
acted merely as agent for the three actresses and not as a principal party to the agreement
and was therefore not entitled to sue in his own right, (ii) that the contract related only
to the services of the actresses and did not embrace rights in the idea for the series, (iii)
that the actresses' and the manager's conduct amounted to a constructive refusal of an *d*
offer of parts, and (iv) that the law of confidence did not extend to an idea which had
been expressed orally.

Held – (1) On the facts, the manager was a joint owner of the idea and a member of the
group so that in addition to being agent for the three actresses he was himself a principal
party to the agreement. He was therefore entitled to sue in his own right (see p 112 *h j* *e*
and p 113 *h j*, post).

(2) It was an express term of the contract between the group and Thames created by
the granting of the option that Thames was to acquire the right to the idea which
belonged to the group and furthermore there was implied into the agreement a negative
covenant that if the three actresses were willing to appear in the series Thames would not
make use of the idea without also employing them as the actresses in the series on terms *f*
to be negotiated later. Accordingly, Thames's failure to offer the three actresses the parts
was a breach of that implied negative covenant, and its use of the idea with three other
actresses in the absence of a refusal by the plaintiff actresses was a wrongful repudiation
of the contract (see p 114 *a* to *g* and *j* to p 115 *b g* and *j* to p 116 *b*, post).

(3) The court would prevent a person who had received an idea expressed in oral or
written form from disclosing it for an unlimited period or until that idea became general *g*
public knowledge provided (*a*) that the circumstances in which it was communicated
imported an obligation of confidence and (*b*) that the content of the idea was clearly
identifiable, original, of potential commercial attractiveness and capable of reaching
fruition. Applying that test to the facts, the communication of the idea for the series had
been made in confidence and the idea was a distinct concept having sufficient originality,
commercial attractiveness and likelihood of realisation so as to fix Thames, the scriptwriter *h*
and the producer with an obligation of confidence which they had breached when they
used the idea as the basis for their own television series. Accordingly the actresses and the
manager were entitled to damages (see p 117 *g*, p 121 *d* to *j* and p 122 *a* to p 123 *c*, post);
dictum of Lord Upjohn in *Boardman v Phipps* [1966] 2 All ER at 759, *Seager v Copydex
Ltd* [1967] 2 All ER 415, *Ansell Rubber Co Pty Ltd v Allied Rubber Industries Pty Ltd* [1967]
VR 37, *Coco v A N Clark (Engineers) Ltd* [1969] RPC 41, *Carl-Zeiss-Stiftung v Herbert Smith* *j*
& Co (a firm) (No 2) [1969] 2 All ER 367, *Mense and Ampere Electrical Manufacturing Co
Pty Ltd v Milenkovic* [1973] VR 784, *Thomas Marshall (Exports) Ltd v Guinle* [1978] 3 All
ER 193 and *Talbot v General Television Corp Pty Ltd* [1981] RPC 1 applied; *Kelly v Cinema
Houses Ltd* (1932) MacG Cop Cas (1928–35) 362, *Donoghue v Allied Newspapers Ltd* [1937]
3 All ER 503 and dictum of Latham CJ in *Federal Comr of Taxation v United Aircraft Corp*
(1943) 68 CLR at 534 distinguished; *Gilbert v Star Newspapers Co Ltd* (1894) 11 TLR 4
explained.

Notes

a For the right of an agent to enforce a contract, see 1 Halsbury's Laws (4th edn) para 864, and for cases on the subject, see 1(2) Digest (Reissue) 839–845, *5429–5468*.

For terms implied by the courts, see 9 Halsbury's Laws (4th edn) para 355, and for cases on the subject, see 12 Digest (Reissue) 751–753, *5395–5402*.

For equitable relief for breach of confidence, see 16 Halsbury's Laws (4th edn) para 1455.

b

Cases referred to in judgment

Albert (Prince) v Strange (1849) 1 Mac & G 25, 41 ER 1171, LC.
Ansell Rubber Co Pty Ltd v Allied Rubber Industries Pty Ltd [1967] VR 37.
Bagge v Millar (1920) MacG Cop Cas (1917–23) 179.
Bickerton v Burrell (1816) 5 M & S 383, 105 ER 1091.
c *Boardman v Phipps* [1966] 3 All ER 721, [1967] 2 AC 46, [1966] 3 WLR 1009, HL.
Carl-Zeiss-Stiftung v Herbert Smith & Co (a firm) (No 2) [1969] 2 All ER 367, [1969] 2 Ch 276, [1969] 2 WLR 427, CA.
Coco v A N Clark (Engineers) Ltd [1969] RPC 41.
Deta Nominees Pty Ltd v Viscount Plastic Products Pty Ltd [1979] VR 167.
Donoghue v Allied Newspapers Ltd [1937] 3 All ER 503, [1938] Ch 106.
d *Federal Comr of Taxation v United Aircraft Corp* (1943) 68 CLR 525.
Fisher v Marsh (1865) 6 B & S 411, 122 ER 1247.
Franchi v Franchi [1967] RPC 149.
Fraser v Edwards (1905) MacG Cop Cas (1905–10) 10.
Gilbert v Star Newspapers Co Ltd (1894) 11 TLR 4.
Kelly v Cinema Houses Ltd (1932) MacG Cop Cas (1928–35) 362.
e *Marshall (Thomas) (Exports) Ltd v Guinle* [1978] 3 All ER 193, [1979] Ch 227, [1978] 3 WLR 116.
Mense and Ampere Electrical Manufacturing Co Pty Ltd v Milenkovic [1973] VR 784.
Moore v Edwards (1903) MacG Cop Cas (1901–04) 44.
Nichrotherm Electrical Co Ltd v Percy [1957] RPC 207.
Rayner v Grote (1846) 15 M & W 359, 153 ER 888.
f *Rees v Melville* (1914) MacG Cop Cas (1911–16) 168, CA.
Saltman Engineering Co Ltd v Campbell Engineering Co Ltd (1948) 65 RPC 20.
Schmaltz v Avery (1851) 16 QB 655, 117 ER 1031.
Seager v Copydex Ltd [1967] 2 All ER 415, [1967] 1 WLR 923, CA.
Seager v Copydex Ltd (No 2) [1969] 2 All ER 718, [1969] 1 WLR 809, CA.
Smith v Morgan [1971] 2 All ER 1500, [1971] 1 WLR 803.
g *Sutton Vane v Famous Players Film Co Ltd* (1928) MacG Cop Cas (1928–35) 6, CA.
Talbot v General Television Corp Pty Ltd [1981] RPC 1.
Tudor Marine Ltd v Tradax Export SA, The Virgo [1976] 2 Lloyd's Rep 135, CA.

Action

h By a writ issued on 8 August 1975 and an amended statement of claim the first plaintiff, Donald Alexander Fraser, and the second plaintiffs, Gabrielle Elizabeth Brown, Diane Shirley Maria Langton, and Judith Annabel Leventon claimed, inter alia, damages against the first defendant, Thames Television Ltd, for breach of contract and breach of confidence, and damages against the second defendant, Howard Schuman, and the third defendant, Andrew Brown, for breach of confidence consequent on the first, second and j third defendants' use of the first and second plaintiffs' idea for a television series about the experiences of a rock group composed of three female artistes. A summary of the findings of fact is set out in the judgment.

John Wilmers QC and *Nicholas Strauss* for the plaintiffs.
Jeremiah Harman QC and *Graeme Williams* for the defendants.

Cur adv vult

20 October. The following judgment was delivered.

HIRST J. In this action the plaintiffs claim damages and other relief against the first *a* defendants for breach of contract and against all three defendants for breach of confidence. The present trial is limited to issues of liability.

The case concerns the origination and development of, and the rights in relation to, a television programme entitled 'Rock Follies', which was transmitted in two series with considerable success in 1976 and 1977 by the first defendants, Thames Television Ltd.

The four plaintiffs were together concerned in a rock group called 'Rock Bottom'. *b*

The first plaintiff, Mr Donald Fraser, who is now aged 35, was a successful student at the Royal College of Music. He has since divided his musical activity between classical and popular music. In the former field he is the composer of a number of works and has also conducted well-known orchestras; in the latter field, with which this case is concerned, he has composed a number of works, produced records, and also acted as musical director and accompanist. *c*

Miss Annabel Leventon comes from a middle-class professional background. She is an exhibitioner and graduate of St Anne's College, Oxford, where she read English. While at Oxford she performed in a number of plays with the Oxford University Dramatic Society and also sang in university pop groups and in cabarets. After leaving Oxford she studied acting at London Academy of Music and Dramatic Art. Thereafter in her career as an actress she performed in repertory, in serious drama and in musicals, including the *d* musical 'Hair' in 1968. She also undertook a number of television roles.

From about 1971 until 1977 (which covers the whole period relevant in this case) Miss Leventon and Mr Fraser lived together. In April 1973 she became pregnant and underwent an abortion, which caused considerable emotional distress.

Miss Gaye Brown was privately educated and after leaving school did a London season as a debutante. Thereafter she went to the Guildhall School of Music and Drama, but at *e* first found difficulty in obtaining parts as she is very tall. In 1963 she joined Miss Joan Littlewood's Company at Stratford East and thereafter for the next ten years performed in a number of plays in that theatre, including 'Oh What A Lovely War'. She also appeared on television and in small film parts.

Miss Diana Langton comes from a working-class family and has been on the stage since the age of twelve. She was trained at the Corona Academy Stage School in drama *f* and classical ballet. Her main career has been in musicals (including 'Hair') where she first met Miss Leventon. She also worked under Miss Joan Littlewood at Stratford East, where she first met Miss Brown.

The first defendants, Thames Television Ltd (Thames), are and were at all material times programme contractors for midweek in the London area. From July 1974 onwards the Head of Drama has been Miss Verite Lambert, who was an important witness in the *g* case. Their casting director is Miss Elizabeth Sadler, who was also an important witness.

The second defendant, Mr Howard Schuman, was born in New York City and graduated with honours in political science from Brandeis University in 1961. From 1962 onwards he wrote a number of plays and also a number of comedy monologues and song-scripts for cabaret. He settled in England in 1968. From 1973 onwards he wrote a number of successful television plays, including 'Verite' and 'Captain Video's *h* Story'. He also wrote a television play called 'Censored Scenes from King Kong' ('King Kong') for the BBC, which was made but never screened, though later shown at the Edinburgh Festival. This last-named television play, and to a lesser extent 'Verite', has considerable importance in the case, and the scripts of all of them were produced in evidence. In 1973 Mr Schuman worked with Franco Zefferelli on the adaptation of 'Much Ado About Nothing' as a film. *j*

The third defendant, Mr Andrew Brown, is a New Zealander by birth. He first came to England in 1966, where he worked first on television commercials and then as a script editor. He worked with Miss Lambert at the BBC in the late 1960s, and thereafter they became very close friends. By the early 1970s he was established as a successful producer of television plays. Mr Brown was the producer of 'Verite' in 1973. Thereafter he and Mr Schuman became friends.

The hearing lasted a total of eight working weeks, of which the bulk was taken up by extensive evidence from both sides. This demonstrated very numerous, deep, contentious and sometimes bitter conflicts of fact which it is my function to resolve. There are also several important differences to be resolved as to the applicable principles of law. Before proceeding to these matters, I shall first set the scene by summarising the framework of relevant facts and outlining the main issues at stake.

In order to alleviate Miss Leventon's distress following her abortion, she and Mr Fraser sought a new focus for her professional career. Mr Fraser suggested that they should form an all-girl rock group with Mr Fraser as the composer and Miss Leventon as one of the singers. They regarded three as the right number of singers harmonically as a result of a previous experience of making a record produced by Mr Fraser with Miss Leventon as one of the singers.

At the end of July 1973 Miss Leventon met Miss Brown at an audition. They discussed the rock group project, and Miss Brown agreed to participate and suggested Miss Langton as the third member of the group. Miss Langton was approached and agreed to join. The group was thus formed by the late summer of 1973 and shortly afterwards was entitled Rock Bottom.

At the time of the formation of the Rock Bottom group, Mr Fraser discussed first with Miss Leventon, and later with the other two girls, its potential aims and objectives. Mr Fraser put forward a plan which envisaged: (1) giving live concerts in London, avoiding the provincial tours conventionally undertaken when a rock group is launched; (2) seeking a record contract which would hopefully lead to the issue of records by the group; (3) seeking the production of a television series which would portray the backgrounds of the three Rock Bottom girls, the formation of the group and their subsequent activities, the stories to be part fact and part fiction.

The extent to which this idea was formulated, its degree of novelty and the nature and format of the projected television series are disputed. It is the plaintiffs' case that the Rock Bottom group was novel in concept, since it comprised three experienced actresses of different character and background with well established individual careers coming together to form a rock group, and that the idea of portraying this, together with both their individual lives and their group activities (part fact, part fiction) in a television series, was novel. The defendants contend that the idea lacked both form and novelty.

Meanwhile Miss Leventon had been cast to play the leading part of 'Shirley' in Mr Schuman's television play 'Verite'.

By chance in August 1973 Mr Fraser and Miss Leventon met Mr Schuman, accompanied by Mr Tim Curry (who was also cast in 'Verite'), at the Casserole Restaurant in the Kings Road. Miss Leventon suggested Mr Fraser as composer for the songs in 'Verite'. As a result she, Mr Fraser and Mr Schuman met for lunch the following day to discuss the project further. Afterwards Mr Fraser and Mr Schuman together went on to the offices of Messrs Breitkopf and Hartel Ltd, a firm of music publishers whose managing director, Mr Larry Fenton, is a close friend and supporter of Mr Fraser, who Mr Fraser described as his 'mentor'.

The upshot was that Mr Fraser was selected as composer for the 'Verite' songs, and thereafter Mr Schuman and Mr Fraser collaborated on this and other work, including a song called 'Memory Lane', which was later performed by the Rock Bottom group. Mr Schuman, Mr Fraser and Miss Leventon also became friends and met on a number of occasions throughout 1973 and early 1974, though the closeness of the friendship and the frequency of the meetings are in issue.

'Verite' was rehearsed and taped in August/September 1973. 'King Kong' was accepted by the BBC in October 1973 and rehearsed and taped in December 1973. It is Mr Schuman's case (which the plaintiffs contest) that during this period, quite independently, he conceived the idea of a television series which was to be developed from a sub-plot in 'King Kong'. The germ of the idea as he described it was the experiences of an all-female rock group being subjected to exploitation by male managers and eventually ending in failure. The idea, according to both Mr Schuman and Mr Brown, was further developed in early January 1974 by suggestions from Mr Brown derived from a number of 1930's American film musicals which were revived in a London season in January 1974 and seen by Mr Brown.

In December 1973 Mr Fraser and Miss Leventon approached Mr Jack Rosenthal, a well-known television writer, with a view to his writing their proposed television series. They explained their idea to Mr Rosenthal and to his wife, who is a well-known actress, known professionally as Maureen Lipman. However, on 20 January 1974 Mr Rosenthal turned down this suggestion, mainly because he was unfamiliar with the rock music scene.

On 22 January 1974 Miss Leventon and Mr Schuman met for lunch at an Italian restaurant and a lengthy discussion took place as to a prospective television series. The course of the discussion, and in particular the nature and origination of the ideas discussed, is in fundamental dispute. Mr Schuman contends that his ideas were discussed with only a passing reference to the plaintiffs' idea. Miss Leventon contends that the plaintiffs' idea for a Rock Bottom television series was discussed with a view to Mr Schuman being the writer, Mr Rosenthal having declined, and that there was no mention of any ideas of Mr Schuman's.

During late 1973 and early 1974 the Rock Bottom group made a number of demonstration tapes and entered into negotiations with Polydor Ltd for a recording agreement, which by February 1974 had reached the stage of draft agreements, though the negotiations subsequently fell through. Thereafter negotiations took place with RCA, which led to the signing of a record agreement in August 1974.

During the summer of 1974 the Rock Bottom group received some press and radio publicity, including an extensive article by Miss Molly Parkin in the Evening Standard in June 1974.

By April 1974 Miss Lambert had accepted the appointment of Head of Drama at Thames, though this was not announced until subsequently, and she did not take up her post until July. Mr Brown meantime had accepted a post as consultant with Stella Richman Productions Ltd, a television production company formed mainly to collect ideas and take them to television companies. Following a meeting between Mr Brown and Miss Lambert in April 1974, Mr Brown introduced Mr Schuman to Miss Lambert on 14 May 1974, where a preliminary discussion took place concerning a possible television series. Both Mr Schuman and Mr Brown firmly maintain that the projected idea discussed was Mr Schuman's as developed in collaboration with Mr Brown and had nothing whatever to do with any idea of the plaintiffs.

On 14 July 1974 the Rock Bottom group performed at a concert in the Kings Road Theatre. This is a crucial event in the story and is the first occasion on which all the main protagonists (Mr Fraser, the three Rock Bottom girls, Mr Schuman, Mr Brown and Miss Lambert) were all present together. The circumstances in which Mr Brown and Miss Lambert attended and the course of events immediately after the concert are in dispute and are of considerable importance. In essence the defendant's case is that Miss Lambert and Mr Brown attended, to the knowledge of the plaintiffs, simply and solely for audition purposes to evaluate the Rock Bottom girls as potential actresses in Mr Schuman's television series. The plaintiffs contend that they had no idea that Miss Lambert was present, and that Mr Brown attended at Mr Schuman's invitation as a potential producer of their series, and was introduced by Mr Schuman to Mr Fraser after the concert with this role in mind.

On 5 August Miss Lambert, Mr Brown and Mr Schuman met again, and the projected television series was discussed in more detail, still, according to Mr Schuman and Mr Brown, simply and solely based on Mr Schuman's idea. The defendants' case is that the Rock Bottom girls only came into the discussion as potential actresses, Miss Lambert having liked their Kings Road performance, with Miss Lambert also favouring Rock Bottom as the title for the series. It is also the defendants' case that Mr Schuman was provisionally offered a commission to write a pilot script for the series.

Meantime in May 1974 Mr Fraser and Miss Leventon had approached another television producer, Mr Brian Degas, with a view to his producing a Rock Bottom television series. This was subsequently discussed with Mr Schuman in circumstances which are in issue.

On 12 August 1974 Mr Schuman, Miss Leventon, Miss Brown and Miss Langton met for lunch at La Tavernetta restaurant in Soho and were joined towards the end by Mr

Fraser. This was an important meeting. There was extensive conversation as to a projected
a television series, though the purpose and the course of the discussion is strongly in dispute. In essence it is Mr Schuman's case that he explained his own idea to the three girls, told them that he had been provisionally commissioned by Miss Lambert to write a pilot script and inquired whether the three girls would be interested in taking part in his series as actresses. The plaintiffs' case on the other hand is that the purpose of the meeting was for Mr Schuman to seek their authority to take their idea to Miss Lambert
b with a view to its production as a television series, that they agreed and that Mr Schuman told them nothing concerning his provisional commission to write a pilot script.

On 4 October 1974 there was a meeting at Thames attended by Miss Lambert and Miss Sadler for Thames and by the three Rock Bottom girls and, towards the end, by Mr Fraser. At the conclusion an oral contract relating to a projected television series was entered into. The terms of the contract were supposedly confirmed by letter dated 16
c October 1974. I say 'supposedly' because both sides from their respective viewpoints contend that the letter did not fully or accurately reflect the oral terms. It is common ground that Thames agreed to pay £500 for, and obtained, an option for a possible television series in 1975 to be exercised by 31 December 1974 and that the three girls were given a right of first refusal for the parts if Thames decided to proceed, but the nature of the option, the rights, if any, ceded by the plaintiffs and purchased by Thames
d and the restrictions on activities accepted by the three Rock Bottom girls are in fundamental conflict. Whether Mr Fraser was a party to the contract is also in question.

The plaintiffs' case is that they were all parties to the agreement, that the whole meeting proceeded on the underlying assumption that the idea for the television series was theirs, and that the option related both to the use of their idea and to the services of the three girls as actresses, with the qualification that if Thames decided to go ahead but
e the plaintiffs decided not to participate, Thames should still be free to use the idea. The plaintiffs contend that there was no restriction on their other activities, apart from the fact that they agreed not to perform as a group in a television series during the option period.

Thames's case on the other hand is that the option simply and solely related to the services of the three girls as actresses and had nothing to do with the idea; that Mr Fraser
f was not a party to the agreement at all, save as agent for the three girls; and that in addition to the restriction on any group television series during the option period, it was expressly made clear to the girls that once rehearsals and taping of the projected series started, they would have to make themselves exclusively available for that purpose.

Meantime in August 1974 Miss Lambert had entered into negotiations with Stella Richman Productions, on the footing that they had an interest in the idea having regard
g to Mr Brown's consultancy. These eventually resulted in a contract under which Thames agreed to pay royalties on the series to Stella Richman.

A formal agreement was entered into between Thames and Mr Schuman on 28 October 1974 commissioning the pilot script and giving Thames an option to commission Mr Schuman to write further episodes.

In late October 1974 Mr Schuman, who was also busy on other projects, started writing
h the pilot script of episode one of the series and submitted it via Mr Brown to Miss Lambert in December 1974. It was rejected at a meeting in the first week of December on artistic grounds, and Mr Schuman agreed to rewrite it. Shortly afterwards Mr Brown went abroad and did not return until mid-March 1975.

During the autumn of 1974 Rock Bottom appeared in approximately six to seven live concert performances in London and were also interviewed on the BBC television
j programme 'Nationwide'. They were also written up in a number of press articles.

Shortly before the end of December, when the option was about to expire, it was orally agreed between Miss Sadler on behalf of Thames and Mr Fraser that it should be extended for a further month until 31 January 1974 on payment of a further £250.

In January 1975 Mr Schuman and Mr Fraser met by chance in the Kings Road, and an important discussion took place at Habitat as to the characterisation in the series, the terms of which are in issue between them.

On 7 February Miss Sadler telephoned Mr Fraser and said that the decision by Thames concerning the series was imminent. It is the plaintiffs' case that during the conversation, as confirmed by subsequent conduct, the option was in effect reinstated, though without further payment from Thames. This is disputed by Thames.

At about the same time the second version of the script of episode one was submitted by Mr Schuman, and in mid-February Thames exercised their option for a further five episodes.

Meantime in January 1975 an intended London production of the musical 'A Little Night Music', which had been abandoned in the previous year, was revived. Miss Langton, who had been retained to play a leading part the previous year, was approached again in early 1975 and accepted the part. 'A Little Night Music' was due to start its run at the Adelphi Theatre with previews in April 1975. The producers were Forum Ventures, a company of which Mr Richard Pilbrow was a director.

On 3 March 1975 Mr Schuman dined with Mr Fraser and Miss Leventon at the latter's flat. A very important conversation took place concerning which there is serious conflict. All agree that 'A Little Night Music' was discussed, but Mr Schuman's version (which the plaintiffs deny) is that this became a major issue, Mr Fraser reiterating time and again that he was entitled to and would get Miss Langton out of the show.

It is the plaintiffs' case that throughout February and March they made a number of efforts, without avail, to get a copy of the pilot script from Thames.

In March Mr Brown and Miss Leventon had a chance meeting in West Kensington at which 'A Little Night Music' was discussed, but they disagree about what was said.

Towards the end of March 1975 Thames finally decided to go ahead with the series in September 1975. Miss Sadler therefore notified the three girls' respective agents, offering them parts in the series. During her conversation with Miss Langton's agent, Miss Hilda Physick, Miss Sadler was informed of Miss Langton's retainer to play in 'A Little Night Music'. At Miss Sadler's request, Miss Physick approached the theatre management seeking Miss Langton's release, but the request was refused.

Thereafter the Little Night Music problem developed into a major issue between the two sides. The defendants maintained that Miss Langton's appearance in the show precluded her also participating in the series. The plaintiffs maintained that the defendants could and should work round her, or themselves seek suitable arrangements with the Little Night Music management.

On about 4 April there was a conversation on the telephone between Miss Sadler and Mr Fraser at which 'A Little Night Music' was discussed, but there is disagreement as to what was said.

On 8 April 1975 Miss Lambert telephoned Mr Fraser and raised the problem of 'A Little Night Music' direct with him. Mr Fraser for his part asked for sight of the pilot script. On the following day Miss Lambert despatched a copy of the pilot script to Mr Fraser under cover of a letter which also expanded on the Little Night Music difficulties. Miss Lambert then left for a two weeks holiday.

Meantime in March Mr Fraser had attended a merchandising meeting with representatives of Thames, and this was followed by another meeting in April.

By letter dated 29 April 1975 Mr Fraser notified to Thames the three girls' agreement to participate in the series.

On 5 May Mr Fraser attended a meeting at Thames with Miss Lambert, Miss Sadler and Mr Brown. The topic was 'A Little Night Music'. There is considerable dispute between the plaintiffs on the one hand and Mr Fraser on the other as to the terms of the conversation; in particular whether Mr Fraser gave firm assurances as to his ability to get Miss Langton out of the show. A further meeting was arranged for a week later.

During the ensuing week there were a number of conversations or alleged conversations between parties on both sides which are seriously in dispute.

Finally, on 12 May there was another meeting at Thames with the same persons present. It is not in dispute that this was a very unpleasant and contentious meeting. Miss Lambert became very angry, lost her temper and subjected Mr Fraser to severe and abusive censure. Matters were made worse after an attempted telephone call to Miss

Langton herself and a conversation on the telephone with Miss Physick. By the end Miss
a Lambert said Mr Fraser was a liar and made it clear that she could not work any longer
with him. The meeting broke up in total disharmony.

The same day Miss Lambert addressed a letter to Mr Fraser giving him an ultimatum
to get an agreement for Miss Langton's release from the show by the following morning.
This requirement was not met (as indeed it never could have been), and the final
breakdown between the two sides ensued.

b By this stage Mr Schuman had completed the drafts of the first two episodes of the
series, the second being delivered at the end of the first week of May.

During the next few days there were some acrimonious conversations that got
nowhere, and the letter before action, addressed to Thames only, was sent on 19 May
1975.

Auditions for the three girls to replace the three Rock Bottom girls took place later in
c May, and three actresses were chosen: Miss Charlotte Cornwell, Miss Julie Covington and
Miss Rula Lenska (the three new actresses). They were subsequently approached under
remarkable circumstances on behalf of Mr Schuman and Mr Brown with a view to the
latter forming a company to undertake their management in relation to their group
activities.

The first series of Rock Follies, comprising six parts, was made in the autumn of 1975
d and transmitted in 1976. A second series, also comprising six parts, was made in late
1976, and five parts were transmitted in 1977, the sixth being lost due to industrial
action. Both series were extremely successful.

The plaintiffs contend that both series used their original idea and that the characters
of the three girls (called respectively 'Anna Wynd' played by Miss Cornwell, 'Q' played
by Miss Lenska and 'Dee' played by Miss Covington) are in several key respects similar to
e the real life Annabel Leventon, Gaye Brown and Diane Langton respectively; and
furthermore that a number of actual incidents in which one or more of them were
involved are portrayed, particularly in the first two episodes. The plaintiffs also contend
that the manager of the three girls in the series, called Derek Hyper Huggins, is similarly
based on the real life Donald Fraser. This is firmly denied by the defendants and by Mr
Schuman, the author, in particular. The defendants' case is that this was a most original
f series which broke new ground on television in its subject matter (particularly the
contemporary topical setting of the 1970's rock music scene), in its style (particularly Mr
Schuman's unique blend of surrealism and uninhibited writing) and in its techniques of
presentation (particularly the use of new video techniques). They contend that the idea
is entirely Mr Schuman's own and in no way derived from the plaintiffs and that the
characters of the three girls and Huggins are entirely original creations of Mr Schuman's,
g quite unlike the plaintiffs, apart from certain immaterial trace elements. The defendants
also deny that any of the incidents are derived from the plaintiffs' actual experiences,
apart again from a few incidental trace elements.

The plaintiffs' case in contract is in essence that the defendants were in breach of
contract by using the plaintiffs' idea without also using their services as actresses; and
that they were also in breach of contract by failing to make a contractual offer of the parts
h in the series to the three girls, and by going ahead with the series with the three new
actresses, notwithstanding the plaintiffs' exercise of their right of first refusal after
Thames had exercised their option under the agreement. The defendants' case in essence
is that they were fully entitled to use the idea since it formed no part of the contract; that
they did in fact make a contractual offer of the parts; and that in any event the plaintiffs'
conduct in relation to the Little Night Music episode constituted a constructive refusal of
j the parts.

The plaintiffs' case in confidence is in essence that all three defendants were subject to,
but broke, an obligation of confidence by using the plaintiffs' idea in relation to the Rock
Follies series. The defendants deny that the plaintiffs' idea had the necessary quality to
attract a right of confidence, and they further deny that the Rock Follies series was in any
way based on the plaintiffs' idea.

The writ was issued on 8 August 1975, joining Thames only as defendants. Mr Schuman and Mr Brown were added as defendants by amendment on 5 June 1980.

It will be seen that, running through the many detailed conflicts of evidence I have already foreshadowed, there are the following main issues of fact, or at least part fact, to be decided. (1) Whose was the original idea at the outset? (2) What knowledge did Miss Lambert and Mr Brown have of the authorship of the idea? (3) What were the terms of and who were the parties to the contract of October 1974? (4) Was the option reinstated in February 1975? (5) What are the rights and wrongs of the controversy about 'A Little Night Music', which was certainly the occasion (whether or not it was the root cause) of the breakdown? (6) If the original idea was the plaintiffs', was that idea in fact embodied in the Rock Follies series? (7) Were the characters of the three girls and Huggins in Rock Follies derived at least in part from the real life characters of the plaintiffs?

[His Lordship then considered the evidence in detail relating to each of the issues set out above and in the course of his judgment made the following findings of fact where appropriate:

1. *Whose was the original idea at the outset?*

His Lordship found that from the formation of the Rock Bottom group in the summer of 1973 Mr Fraser, with the assistance of Miss Leventon, was developing his own idea for a television series and that by December 1973, the date of the first meeting with Mr Rosenthal, they had developed a well-formed idea for a television series, based on the Rock Bottom group, whose essentials were: (1) that the series should be part fact and part fiction, the fact part being based on the actual experiences of the plaintiffs; the balance between the two would depend on the approach of the chosen writer; (2) it would highlight the unusual feature of a three girl rock group, where each of the three girls was an established actress of wit and intelligence with a life of her own; (3) it would portray the formation of the group and their subsequent experiences, trials and tribulations, focusing both on the group as such and on the girls' separate lives, and bringing out the contrast between their collective characters as members of the group and their separate characters outside it.

2. *What knowledge did Miss Lambert and Mr Brown have of the authorship of the idea?*

His Lordship found that Mr Schuman knew that the idea originated from the plaintiffs from his meeting with Miss Leventon on 22 January 1974; that Mr Brown learnt of that from Mr Schuman shortly afterwards; and that Miss Lambert learnt of that either from Mr Schuman or from Mr Brown or from both at the latest by the date of a Kings Road concert on 14 July and possibly as early as 14 May.

3. *What were the terms of and who were the parties to the contract of October 1974?*

His Lordship set out the letter of 16 October to the plaintiffs from Thames:

Thames Television
Teddington Studios
Teddington Lock
Teddington
Middlesex

16th October 1974.

The Rock Bottom Group
c/o Fenette Music
8 Horse and Dolphin Yard, W1V 7LG

ATT: DON FRASER ESQ.

Dear Mesdames,

Re: UNTITLED SERIES *By Howard Schuman*

We write to confirm the understanding between us whereby in consideration of the payment by us to you of the agreed sum of FIVE HUNDRED POUNDS (£500) we shall acquire an option on your services in connection with a possible new series of

programmes to be undertaken in 1975 during the period commencing from the
a date hereof until 31st December 1974. *It is understood and agreed that*: 1. During the aforestated period you (i.e. THE ROCK BOTTOM GROUP consisting of the three artistes GAYE BROWN, DIANE LANGTON and ANNABEL LEVENTON) will not appear on television in any drama production(s) or in any situation comedy series. 2. Should THAMES decide to proceed with the new series project you will have first refusal in connection therewith but in the event of your deciding against such a project your decision
b shall in no way jeopardize THAMES' right to undertake the series with three other artistes. 3. In the event of your participation in the said series such participation shall be on terms to be negotiated on the further understanding that such terms shall not be in excess of what would be deemed to be a fair fee for the services of the said artistes in a television drama production at the time of negotiation. We shall be obliged if you will please confirm your agreement with the foregoing by signing
c and returning to us the enclosed copy hereof.

Yours faithfully
for and on behalf of
THAMES TELEVISION LIMITED
N. T. MUSTOE
Copyright/Contracts Manager

d

WE AGREE TO THE ABOVE
SIGNED D. FRASER (MANAGER) DATE 25/10/74
for and on behalf of THE ROCK BOTTOM GROUP.'

His Lordship held that that letter did not fully or accurately set out the terms of the contract, which was essentially oral.

e His Lordship found that at the meeting of 4 October which preceded the sending of the letter of 16 October Miss Lambert expressly sought, and was expressly granted, as a contractual term, permission to go ahead with the series if the girls decided not to take part. Such a request presupposed that the idea was the plaintiffs' and could not be used by Thames with other actresses without the plaintiffs' consent. His Lordship referred to the last three and a half lines of para 2 of the letter of 16 October: 'in the event of your
f *deciding against* such a project'. His Lordship stated that had the contract been limited to the girls' services as actresses, he would have expected the next stage of any discussion to be handled not by Mr Fraser, but by the girls' agents. On the other hand the arrangement that Mr Fraser should act was fully appropriate to an agreement of the wider scope for which the plaintiffs contended. His Lordship further found that Miss Lambert did not say, let alone insist, that during the making of the series the three girls must keep
g themselves free of other engagements.

4. *Was the option reinstated in February 1975?*

His Lordship found that various telephone conversations between Mr Fraser and Miss Sadler of Thames, acting on Miss Lambert's instructions, and all the subsequent conduct of the parties on both sides up to the breakdown between the two sides was consistent
h with the option having been reinstated on 7 February.

5. *What are the rights and wrongs about the controversy about 'A Little Night Music'?*

His Lordship stated that the factual issue was whether Miss Langton's appearance in 'A Little Night Music' effectively precluded her taking a part in the series, as the defendants contended or whether, as the plaintiffs contended, Thames could or should have worked
j round Miss Langton's commitment to 'A Little Night Music', or at least made an effort themselves to secure some other workable arrangement, such as her temporary release from the show during the making of the series. His Lordship found that Thames never made any attempt themselves to negotiate direct with the management of 'A Little Night Music' for either a 'working-round' arrangement or an arrangement for Miss Langton's release. His Lordship referred to evidence by Miss Lambert that she did not go to the management of 'A Little Night Music' because her patience was exhausted, and found

that by May 1975 Miss Lambert was not averse to a breakdown with the plaintiffs and was not prepared to do anything herself to avert it. His Lordship found that Thames *a* could and should have taken a hand themselves by a direct approach to the management of 'A Little Night Music' to seek Miss Langton's release and should have explored the alternative of a satisfactory 'working-round' arrangement, difficult though that would have been.

6 and 7. *Was the plaintiffs' idea used in Rock Follies and were characters in Rock Follies derived from the real life characters of the plaintiffs?* *b*

His Lordship held that there were very substantial similarities between the plaintiffs and characters portrayed in Rock Follies, that the similarities were far more extensive and significant than mere trace elements and that the similarities could not have occurred otherwise than through Mr Schuman seeking to portray the actual characters of the three Rock Bottom girls and Mr Fraser on the basis of his knowledge and observation of them. *c*

His Lordship continued:]

All these considerations drive me to the conclusion that the Rock Follies series as a whole, and especially the first two episodes, were substantially based on the characters and actual experiences of the Rock Bottom girls and Mr Fraser. This was part of the plaintiffs' own idea. Furthermore, all the other aspects of the plaintiffs' idea feature in the series, namely an all-girl rock group made up of girls of very different character and *d* social background with well-established careers in the theatre (or at least in show business), the formation of the group and their experiences as a group, interwoven with their contrasting private lives.

Consequently, I hold that Rock Follies did use the plaintiffs' idea.

I now proceed to consider the plaintiffs' two causes of action in the light of my findings of fact. *e*

The claim in contract

1 *The parties*

The plaintiffs contend that all four of them were parties to the contract of 4 October. The defendants say that only the three girls were parties and not Mr Fraser. *f*

Counsel for the defendants' first contention was based on the proposition that Mr Fraser was not in truth a member of Rock Bottom at all, but merely their manager and composer. He relied on a number of documents, especially (i) two very early home-made agreements which certainly support his contention, (ii) an agreement with one of Mr Fenton's companies in which the three girls signed as Rock Bottom, and (iii) a minute of a Rock Bottom meeting which is, I think, more ambiguous about membership. He also *g* relied on documents which suggest that outsiders perceived the group as consisting of only the three girls.

All four plaintiffs testified that so far as they were concerned Mr Fraser was a full member of the group. Counsel for the plaintiffs relied on a number of documents supporting this view, especially the form proposing registration of Rock Bottom as a business name, including Mr Fraser as a proprietor, Rock Bottom bank statements, *h* including Mr Fraser as an account holder, and a proposed agency agreement showing Mr Fraser as a member of the group. He also relied on the undoubted fact that the Rock Bottom income was divided equally between the four of them.

Taking the matter as a whole, I find that, so far as the four plaintiffs' own internal arrangements within the group were concerned, Mr Fraser was a member of the group, at all events by 4 October 1974. But I accept that in the eyes of outsiders, especially the *j* press, the three girls (who were always in the forefront of the group's public performances) might well be seen as constituting the group.

Without question Mr Fraser was in fact a joint owner of the plaintiffs' idea.

In my judgment the question whether Mr Fraser was a party to the agreement of 4 October turns mainly on the course of conversations, the understanding of the parties and the terms of the letter from Thames dated 16 October 1974, all viewed in the light of the applicable principles of law.

Counsel for the defendants' argument rests on two main contentions: first that nothing *a* was said at the meeting to suggest that Mr Fraser was a party; second that the terms of the letter, and particularly the description of Rock Bottom as consisting of the three girls and the form of signature by Mr Fraser as agent for Rock Bottom, rule out any possibility of Mr Fraser being a principal party.

Counsel for the plaintiffs places considerable reliance on passages in Miss Lambert's evidence as showing that she regarded Mr Fraser as having a commercial interest in the *b* series. She said that she saw Mr Fraser as occupying a managerial role, but was happy that he should write the music for the series, provided details could be sorted out. In cross-examination she stated that one purpose of the series was to advance Mr Fraser's commercial interests. Counsel for the plaintiffs submitted that the description of Mr Fraser's position in the letter had only limited potency, since all sides agreed that the letter was defective.

c Counsel for the plaintiffs also relied on a number of authorities in support of his argument.

In *Tudor Marine Ltd v Tradax Export SA, The Virgo* [1976] 2 Lloyd's Rep 135 it was held that a description in one part of a charterparty of the defendants as agents was not conclusive as to their status and that the court must have regard to all relevant contractual provisions wherever they might appear in the contractual documents. The broad *d* principle is that 'you must look at the contract as a whole in relation to the particular provisions of the particular contract that may be relevant; contracts are infinitely various in subject-matter, content, word and form—and, indeed, in surrounding circumstances': per Megaw LJ (at 145). In the result the defendants were held to have contracted as principals.

In *Bickerton v Burrell* (1816) 5 M & S 383, 105 ER 1091 it was held that the plaintiff, *e* having signed a contract unequivocally as agent, could not sue as principal, at all events unless he had given notice to the defendant of such status in advance.

In *Rayner v Grote* (1846) 15 M & W 359, 153 ER 888 the plaintiff had signed a contract for the sale of goods as agent for a named principal. Subsequently he gave notice to the defendant that he was in truth the principal and was paid part of the purchase price. It was held he was entitled to sue. The court contrasted a case where the skill or solvency of *f* the person named as principal was a material ingredient of the contract. Some doubt was cast on the authority of *Bickerton*'s case.

In *Fisher v Marsh* (1865) 6 B & S 411 at 416, 122 ER 1247 at 1249 Blackburn J stated that 'the general rule is that when an agent makes a contract, naming his principal, the contract is made with the principal and not with the agent'. But the court nonetheless held that on the facts of the particular case the plaintiff auctioneer was entitled to sue as *g* there were reasons in the facts of the case why he should have entered into the contract as a principal.

In *Schmaltz v Avery* (1851) 16 QB 655, 117 ER 1031 it was held that the plaintiff who had signed a charterparty as agent for an unnamed principal was entitled to sue as principal, there being no prejudice to the defendant in respect of any supposed reliance on the solvency of the principal.

h In all these cases the question was whether the agent signatory was entitled to substitute himself as principal. They do not deal directly with the instant problem, where the agent signatory seeks to add himself to the three named principals as a party to the contract.

I have not found this an easy point to decide. However, taking all the circumstances into account, in the light of the applicable principles of law, I hold that Mr Fraser was a party to the contract and is entitled to sue. The form of signature on the letter dated 16 *j* October is clearly not conclusive; it must be viewed in the light of the surrounding circumstances of the contract as a whole, which was essentially an oral contract. Miss Lambert regarded Mr Fraser as having some commercial interest in the agreement, which cannot, in my judgment, be interpreted as merely his interest qua agent, especially as she saw him as a potential composer for the series. Mr Fraser was in fact one of the joint owners of the idea, so that there are reasons in fact why he should have been a party. The question of reliance on the skill of solvency of the three girls cannot arise, since Mr Fraser is not seeking to be substituted for them.

2 *The disputed terms*

The first issue between the parties is whether, and if so to what extent, the contract embraced rights in the idea in addition to services. In my judgment the plaintiffs' evidence (which I have accepted) clearly demonstrates that the whole underlying basis on which the conversation took place was that the idea belonged to Rock Bottom. This evidence also demonstrates that the series under discussion was to be based on them and their experiences. For the series to go ahead it was necessary for Thames to acquire the right to the idea, which, as I have already held, Miss Lambert knew belonged to Rock Bottom. Indeed, in her evidence Miss Lambert never sought to contest the necessity of acquiring the right to the idea, if, contrary to her firm contention, it was not Mr Schuman's.

It is for this reason that Miss Lambert sought, and was granted, the right to use the idea if the plaintiffs decided not to take part in the series. This stipulation only makes sense if the option related to the combined use of the idea and of the three girls' services as actresses. In this connection I think it is also significant that Miss Sadler testified that it is very unusual for a television company to pay any money for a mere option on actresses' services.

In my judgment the option did embrace the idea as well as the services of Rock Bottom. Even though not precisely spelt out, I am prepared to hold that it was sufficiently clearly imported by reference to constitute an express term. In any event, such a term was clearly implied, since, for the reasons I have given, it was necessary to give the agreement business efficacy and went without saying: see *Chitty on Contracts* (24th edn, 1977) paras 784–786.

The plaintiffs next contend that there is to be implied in the agreement a negative covenant that if the three girls were willing to perform in the series, Thames would not go ahead with the series using their idea without also using their services as actresses. This, say the plaintiffs, is a necessary corollary to the stipulation as to Thames's right to use the idea if the three girls decided not to perform. Counsel for the plaintiffs cited in this connection *Nichrotherm Electrical Co Ltd v Percy* [1957] RPC 207 at 213, 215 per Lord Evershed MR and per Romer LJ, where an implied term was upheld in not dissimilar circumstances, albeit as a result of a concession by counsel.

Counsel for the defendants contended that if, contrary to his main submission, the option agreement did embrace the idea as well as the girls' services it was in the nature of a licence to use the idea, which, he argued, did not import a negative covenant. However, in this case the licence was of a peculiar double-edged character, namely a licence to use the idea in combination with the girls' services if they agreed to perform, or to use the idea alone if the girls decided not to perform. To give the latter business efficacy, it seems to me necessary to imply the negative covenant. I therefore hold that the negative covenant also forms part of the agreement.

I have already held that there was no stipulation that the three girls would have to agree to keep themselves free from other engagements during the making of the series. It is, as already noted, common ground that the agreement did contain a term that the three girls should not appear as a group on television in any drama production or situation comedy during the option period. Counsel for the plaintiffs contended that the effect of this term was that there was no other restriction whatsoever on the girls' freedom to work. I do not accept this contention. The agreed restriction related solely to the option period and had no bearing on any later relevant period.

Counsel for the plaintiffs further submitted that, Thames having exercised the option and the girls having exercised their right of first refusal, Thames were not entitled to impose any additional terms in relation to other work by the girls during the making of the series. In my judgment this is putting the case too high. At the appropriate stage the detailed working arrangements during the making of the series had to be negotiated, and this might well involve stipulations as to other work. These detailed matters had, quite reasonably, not been worked out at the time of the agreement.

However, I do accept counsel for the plaintiffs' alternative argument that Thames were at this stage obliged to make to the girls a contractual offer of parts, in terms not inconsistent with what had been agreed on 4 October and not less favourable than they were in fact prepared to accept: see *Smith v Morgan* [1971] 2 All ER 1500, [1971] 1 WLR 803. I think that counsel for the plaintiffs is also right in submitting that they would have been obliged to keep such offer open for as long as was reasonable in the circumstances prevailing at the time. Inevitably time would be needed to try to agree the detailed terms of the engagement (involving no doubt some give and take on both sides if any agreement was to be reached). It was at this juncture, after the making of the contractual offer, that I think it was appropriate to endeavour to settle these details, including any arrangements as to other work.

3 *Other terms*

There is no dispute as to the other terms, namely the payment of £500, the duration of the option until 1 January 1976, the first refusal granted to the three girls, the date for the projected series being 1975, and the limitation of the scale of fees to be paid to the three girls to an appropriate level for a television drama production.

4 *Reinstatement of option*

I have already held that in the conversation of 7 February Miss Sadler asked, and Mr Fraser agreed, that the option should be kept open without further payment until there was further news from Thames, the plaintiffs agreeing to keep Thames informed if they were offered a drama or light entertainment series in the mean time. In my judgment this had the effect of reinstating the option and also the three girls' right of first refusal, the only variation being that the previous obligation not to take part in a competing series was replaced by the obligation to keep Thames informed. This is in all respects consistent with the subsequent conduct of the parties. I should add that counsel for the defendants does not dispute there was consideration moving from Thames to support a contractual reinstatement of the option even though no further payment was stipulated.

5 *Breaches of contract*

Counsel for the defendants contended that Thames did in fact make a contractual offer of parts to the three girls by Miss Sadler's approach to the agents in March and by letters dated 9 April and 2 May. He argued that a contractual offer did not require any detailed spelling out of the terms. I do not accept these contentions. In my judgment a contractual offer must contain at least the salient terms proposed, including most importantly terms as to remuneration. On none of the occasions relied on by counsel were any terms whatsoever spelt out. Furthermore, in my judgment, the first two occasions relied on were premature, since they preceded the exercise of the right of first refusal.

Consequently I hold that no contractual offer was made prior to Thames's precipitation of the breakdown on 12 May.

Counsel for the defendants further contended that in any event, irrespective of whether or not a contractual offer was made, the plaintiffs' conduct in relation to 'A Little Night Music', and in particular Mr Fraser's conduct, constituted a constructive refusal of the parts, thus justifying Thames's precipitation of the breakdown. I reject this contention. I hold that Mr Fraser, far from giving any indications of refusal, was to the knowledge of Thames doing his utmost to solve the problem, and that his efforts were summarily cut off by Thames just at the moment they were likely to succeed. The reason that he did not start earlier was no fault of his, but stemmed from Thames's delay in furnishing the script, compounded by the confusion engendered by Miss Sadler about the dates. Thames were also at fault in failing to take any steps themselves to solve the matter by an approach to Mr Pilbrow. If, as I think, the test of constructive refusal is whether a reasonable man acquainted with the facts would so regard the conduct relied on, then, in my judgment, no reasonable man would regard the conduct of Mr Fraser, or of any of the other plaintiffs, as constituting a constructive refusal.

I hold that the following breaches of contract were committed by Thames: (1) the use of the plaintiffs' idea with the three new actresses in the two Rock Follies series constituted a breach of the implied negative covenant; (2) under the reinstated option agreement, the plaintiffs, having exercised their right of first refusal in response to Thames's exercising their option, were entitled to a contractual offer of the parts. This they never received. There was no constructive refusal by the plaintiffs. By Miss Lambert's conduct on 12 May and the letter of the same date, Thames intimated that they intended to recast all three parts. This constituted a wrongful repudiation by Thames. Thames then proceeded to recast and to make and screen the two series with the new actresses, all of which constituted breaches of contract.

The claim in confidence

The basic principles of the law of confidence are conveniently set out in *Copinger and Skone-Jones on Copyright* (12th edn, 1980) para 711 as follows:

> 'There is a broad and developing equitable doctrine that he who has received information in confidence shall not take unfair advantage of it or profit from the wrongful use or publication of it. He must not make any use of it to the prejudice of him who gave it, without obtaining his consent or, at any rate, without paying him for it . . . If, therefore, a defendant is proved to have used confidential information, directly or indirectly obtained from a plaintiff, without his consent, express or implied, he will be guilty of an infringement of the plaintiff's rights.'

It is well settled that the obligation of confidence rests not only on the original recipient, but also on any person who received the information with knowledge acquired at the time or subsequently that it was originally given in confidence: see *Copinger and Skone-James on Copyright*, para 731.

Counsel for the defendants accepted that as a matter of principle the law of confidence is capable of protecting the confidential communication of an idea. But he argued that a literary or dramatic idea cannot be protected unless it is fully developed in the form of a synopsis or treatment and embodied in permanent form (ie in writing or on film or tape). His argument relied substantially on analogies with the law of copyright.

He further submitted that considerations of legal policy require that anything so ephemeral and so subject to contradictory recollection as an oral idea should not be protected; that such protection would unduly stultify an author's freedom to develop ideas; and that such protection would be unfair to third parties confronted with rival claims to the origination of an idea, since he says it would be impossible for them to decide which claimant was right in the absence of any written formulation of the idea in question.

Counsel for the defendants further argued that where an idea is capable of development in more than one format (eg situation comedy or drama) it is not entitled to protection.

I consider first the argument by analogy with the law of copyright, which may be summarised as follows. (1) It is trite law that there is no copyright in an idea as such. How anomalous would it be, argued counsel for the defendants, if the originator of an idea was in a better position under the law of confidence than under the law of copyright with its strict time limits and carefully defined limitations. (2) The authorities on the law of copyright clearly establish that a plaintiff can only succeed if his work is in a developed written form. The same, argued counsel for the defendants, should apply in confidence. (3) Decided copyright cases in relation to dramatic works, with particular reference to s 1(2) of the Copyright Act 1911 (now incorporated in s 2 of the Copyright Act 1956) establish that mere reproduction of a plot (i e an idea) is not an infringement. Infringement only arises if there is substantial reproduction of actual dramatic incidents or situations (*Copinger and Skone-James on Copyright*, paras 539–540).

In support of his arguments counsel for the defendants relied on a number of copyright cases.

In *Donoghue v Allied Newspapers Ltd* [1937] 3 All ER 503, [1938] Ch 106 the plaintiff, a well-known jockey, who had furnished the defendants' reporter with material for a number of published articles, failed in a claim for infringement of copyright by republication of similar articles in another newspaper, because he was held not to be a joint owner of the copyright in the original article. Farwell J stated ([1937] 3 All ER 503 at 507, [1938] Ch 106 at 109):

> 'It is necessary in considering whether Mr. Donoghue is the owner or part owner of the copyright in this book, to see what it is in which copyright exists under the Copyright Act, 1911. This, at any rate, is clear, and one can start with this beyond all question, that there is no copyright in an idea or in ideas. A person may have a brilliant idea for a story, or for a picture, or for a play, and one which so far as he is concerned, appears to be original, but, if he communicates that idea to an author or a playright or an artist, the production which is the result of the communication of the idea to the author or the artist or the playwright is the copyright of the person who has clothed the idea in a form, whether by means of a picture, a play, or a book, and the owner of the idea has no rights in that product.'

Counsel for the defendants relied on this passage and also commented that it was extraordinary that no claim of breach of confidence was raised if such a right existed. In my judgment, however, this comment is ill-founded, since confidentiality had already been lost by the publication in the first series of articles.

Moore v Edwards (1903) MacG Cop Cas (1901–04) 44, *Bagge v Millar* (1920) MacG Cop Cas (1917–23) 179, *Rees v Melville* (1914) MacG Cop Cas (1911–16) 168 and *Sutton Vane v Famous Players Film Co Ltd* (1928) MacG Cop Cas (1928–35) 6 were all cited in support of the proposition that in relation to dramatic works there must be substantial reproduction of incidents or scenes from an earlier written work to support a claim for infringement.

Finally under this head, counsel for the defendants cited *Kelly v Cinema Houses Ltd* (1932) MacG Cop Cas (1928–35) 362 where the court rejected a claim for infringement by alleged reproduction in a film of part of a plaintiff's novel which had been based, with permission, on a play by another author. It was held that there could be no infringement as there was no novelty in the characters, scenes or situations in the relevant part of the novel, nor was there any substantial reproduction in the film of that part of the novel.

With all respect to counsel for the defendants, I do not find the argument by analogy with copyright cases helpful. The law of copyright is about copying. It is of the very essence of copyright that it protects material in permanent form. The very first sentence of *Copinger and Skone-James on Copyright*, para 1 states: 'Copyright law is, in essence, concerned with the negative right of preventing the copying of physical material existing in the field of literature or the arts.'

It is therefore an essential ingredient of every copyright action that the plaintiff should start with a work in permanent form.

On the other hand, under the general law of confidence the confidential communication relied on may be either written or oral (see eg *Seager v Copydex Ltd* [1967] 2 All ER 415, [1967] 1 WLR 923).

Copyright is good against the world generally, whereas confidence only protects against those who receive information or ideas in confidence. Although copyright has a fixed (albeit extensive) statutory time limit, and confidence, at all events in theory, no time limit, in practice the obligation in confidence ceases the moment information or idea becomes public knowledge.

Furthermore, although the law of copyright protects unpublished as well as published works, it is no part of its purpose to protect confidentiality as such. Indeed s 46(4) of the 1956 Act expressly provides that 'nothing in this Act shall affect the operation of any rule of equity relating to breaches of . . . confidence'.

Of much more assistance are the cases cited by counsel for the defendants which deal directly with breaches of confidence in the field under consideration. In *Gilbert v Star Newspapers Co Ltd* (1894) 11 TLR 4 Chitty J granted an ex parte injunction restraining the defendants from publishing the plot of Mr W S Gilbert's comic opera 'His Excellency', which was due to open a few days later. It was argued that an actor or employee at the theatre must have communicated the information to the newspaper contrary to an established custom in the theatrical profession that such information was confidential. Chitty J based his decision on the principles of the law of confidence as enunciated in *Prince Albert v Strange* (1849) 1 Mac & G 25, 41 ER 1171. Counsel for the defendants submitted that this case supported his argument that there must be a written libretto in existence before the law of confidence can apply to such a situation; but there is no indication in the report that the libretto as such was ever passed to the newspaper, and Chitty J did not base his decision on any such consideration. It is, however, noteworthy that the confidential information in *Gilbert's* case related to the plot of the opera, which (as the copyright authorities cited above show) would not be protected as such under the law of copyright. This case therefore seems to establish a wider protection under the law of confidence than under the law of copyright.

In *Fraser v Edwards* (1905) MacG Cop Cas (1905–10) 10 the defendant was held liable for breach of confidence by appropriation of the character, plot and idea from a scenario which had earlier been submitted by the plaintiff to the defendant's theatre manager. Counsel for the defendants pointed out that this case concerned a fully developed written scenario.

Finally in this group of cases, counsel for the defendants cited the very recent Australian decision of *Talbot v General Television Corp Pty Ltd* [1981] RPC 1, a case which on the facts has some remarkable similarities with the present case. The judgment reported is that of Harris J at first instance in the Supreme Court of Victoria. The decision was affirmed by the Full Court, but the appellate decision is not reported, so I am informed, either here or in Australia. In this case the plaintiff, a film producer, developed an idea for a television series, which he submitted in the form of a written submission to the defendants. He heard no more about his proposal. The defendants subsequently broadcast the first segment of a series of programmes which they claimed were their own idea, but which the plaintiff claimed were derived from his. The plaintiff sought an injunction on the ground of breach of confidence, and the hearing of the application was treated as the trial of the action. The learned judge found in favour of the plaintiff. He said (at 8–9):

> 'It is clear that an obligation of confidence may exist where there is no contractual relationship between the parties. Where a plaintiff sues, relying upon breach of confidence, he must establish three elements. These are: (1) that the information was of a confidential nature; (2) that the information was communicated in circumstances importing an obligation of confidence; and (3) that there has been an unauthorised use of the information to the detriment of the person communicating it (i.e. the plaintiff). Those statements of law are taken from the judgment of Megarry J. in *Coco* v. *A. N. Clark (Engineers) Ltd.* ([1969] RPC 41 at 47–48): see also *Ansell Rubber Co. Pty. Ltd.* v. *Allied Rubber Industries Pty. Ltd.* ([1967] VR 37); *Mense and Ampere Electrical Manufacturing Co. Pty. Ltd. v Milenkovic* ([1973] VR 784 at 800–801); and *Deta Nominees Pty. Ltd.* v. *Viscount Plastic Products Pty. Ltd.* ([1979] VR 167). Both counsel agreed that the three elements that I have referred to were the relevant principles to be applied in this case. Mr. Gillard [counsel for the defendant] submitted that none of those elements had been established by the plaintiff, and further submitted that, even if they were, there were two other reasons why the plaintiff's claim should be dismissed. Mr. Archibald [counsel for the plaintiff] submitted that the plaintiff had made out his case for relief and that none of the matters raised by Mr. Gillard afforded any reason why relief should be denied to the plaintiff. Mr. Gillard began by submitting that the information which the plaintiff alleged had been misused by the defendant did not have the necessary quality of confidence. He put it that the plaintiff was seeking to protect an idea for a programme about millionaires, how they succeeded and what viewers could learn from them, and that this was not original. He pointed to evidence that there had been programmes before on the careers of successful men and that it was a usual practice for interviewers to ask such people the secret of their success. He also put it that there was authority for the proposition that there is "no property in an idea" (or in knowledge) and that as all the plaintiff had conveyed to the network was an idea, it was not susceptible of protection. The authorities he referred to were *F.C. of T.* v. *United Aircraft Corp.* ((1943) 68 CLR 525 at 534 per Latham CJ) and *Halsbury*, 4th ed., vol. 9, para. 829. But the passages referred to deal with the point in different contexts (those of the construction of the word "idea" in a statute and in copyright law) and do not support Mr. Gillard's submission in this case. What Mr. Archibald

said was that this abstract proposition could only divert one from the real problem, and he referred to what Lord Upjohn said in *Boardman* v. *Phipps* ([1966] 3 All ER 721 at 759, [1967] 2 AC 46 at 127) where his Lordship pointed out that "the real truth is that it [i.e. information] is not property in any normal sense but equity will restrain its transmission to another if in breach of some confidential relationship". The real problem, Mr. Archibald said, was to decide whether the idea, or concept, had been sufficiently developed. Where it had been developed to the point of setting out a format in which it could be presented, so that it was apparent that the concept could be carried into effect, then, said Mr. Archibald, it was something that was capable of being the subject of a confidence. Without deciding that it is always necessary for a plaintiff to go that far, I am satisfied that where a concept or idea has been developed to the stage where the plaintiff had developed his concept, it is capable of being the subject of a confidential communication. The plaintiff had developed his concept so that it would be seen to be a concept which had at least some attractiveness as a television programme and to be something which was capable of being realised as an actuality.'

Counsel for the defendants accepted, indeed contended, that this case was rightly decided, and, though not binding on me, I find it of great assistance. He submitted that the decision rested essentially on the fact that the material submitted by the plaintiff included a substantial written submission (see [1981] RPC 1 at 5). However, it is clear that the judge expressly refrained from deciding that any less elaborately worked idea would not qualify for protection.

Counsel for the plaintiffs also accepted the correctness of *Talbot's* case. He drew attention to the twist or slant which was held to be original (at 9); and he submitted that this twist or slant was the kernel of the idea to which, he submitted, the written submission added nothing of substance. He also drew attention to the fact that this kernel may have been communicated orally (at 10).

Counsel for the plaintiffs submitted that, as a matter of general principle, an obligation of confidence is implied in law if the communication is made in circumstances where the parties understand the recipient will treat it as confidential. He argued that this arises either (1) where the information or idea is given in a situation where both parties recognise an ethical obligation of confidence or (2) where information or an idea is communicated by one party to another with a view to a possible joint commercial venture or contractual relationship.

So far as ideas specifically are concerned, counsel for the plaintiffs submitted that there is no requirement that the idea must be developed to any particular degree, still less that it must be embodied in writing. He accepted that it must be specific in the sense that it must be clear and identifiable and that it must be original, at least to the extent that it is distinguishable from the ordinary run of ideas in common use. While he accepted it must have potential commercial merit, he argued that there is no requirement that it should have been developed to a state where it was ready for commercial exploitation.

On the general principles of the law of confidence, counsel for the plaintiffs relied on *Saltman Engineering Co Ltd v Campbell Engineering Co Ltd* (1948) 65 RPC 203, and in particular on the statements of principle in the judgment of Lord Greene MR (at 213):

> 'If a defendant is proved to have used confidential information, directly or indirectly obtained from a plaintiff, without the consent, express or implied, of the plaintiff, he will be guilty of an infringement of the plaintiff's rights.'

And (at 215):

> 'The information, to be confidential, must, I apprehend, apart from contract, have the necessary quality of confidence about it, namely, it must not be something which is public property and public knowledge. On the other hand, it is perfectly possible to have a confidential document, be it a formula, a plan, a sketch, or something of that kind, which is the result of work done by the maker upon materials which may be available for the use of anybody; but what makes it

> confidential is the fact that the maker of the document has used his brain and thus produced a result which can only be produced by somebody who goes through the same process.'

Counsel for the plaintiffs also relied on a passage in the judgment of Somervell LJ (at 218), recognising the importance of the defendants' own perception that it would have been wrong to use the information for their own purposes.

With regard to the requirements of form and degree of development of information or ideas, counsel for the plaintiffs placed strong reliance on *Seager v Copydex Ltd* [1967] 2 All ER 415, [1967] 1 WLR 923. In this case the plaintiff, in the course of discussion with the defendants of a carpet grip which he had invented, orally volunteered to the defendants what Salmon LJ described as 'the germ of the idea' for a different form of carpet grip which the plaintiff had devised. Later the defendants developed and marketed a carpet grip which was unwittingly based on the plaintiff's alternative type of grip. The Court of Appeal concluded that the plaintiff's idea was the 'springboard' which enabled the defendants to devise their own grip and held that the defendants were liable for breach of confidence. Counsel for the plaintiffs submitted that this case is a strong authority (albeit in a different field) that confidence can attach to an oral idea and that even comparatively undeveloped ideas are capable of protection. I find this case of great assistance.

This same case returned to the Court of Appeal two years later on the issue of damages: *Seager v Copydex Ltd (No 2)* [1969] 2 All ER 718, [1969] 1 WLR 809. Counsel for the plaintiffs submitted that the judgments of Lord Denning MR and Salmon LJ show that the degree of originality need not be high (see [1969] 2 All ER 718 at 719–720, 721, [1969] 1 WLR 809 at 813, 814).

Counsel for the plaintiffs also relied on two decisions of Sir Robert Megarry V-C: *Coco v A N Clark (Engineers) Ltd* [1969] RPC 41 and *Thomas Marshall (Exports) Ltd v Guinle* [1978] 3 All ER 193, [1979] Ch 227. These are both industrial cases.

In the former case he stated (at 47):

> 'Something that has been constructed solely from materials in the public domain may possess the necessary quality of confidentiality: for something new and confidential may have been brought into being by the application of the skill and ingenuity of the human brain. Novelty depends on the thing itself, and not upon the quality of its constituent parts. Indeed, often the more striking the novelty, the more commonplace its components.'

And (at 48):

> 'From the authorities cited to me, I have not been able to derive any precise idea of what test is to be applied in determining whether the circumstances import an obligation of confidence . . . It may be that that hard-worked creature, the reasonable man, may be pressed into service once more; for I do not see why he should not labour in equity as well as at law. It seems to me that if the circumstances are such that any reasonable man standing in the shoes of the recipient of the information would have realised that upon reasonable grounds the information was being given to him in confidence, then this should suffice to impose upon him the equitable obligation of confidence. In particular, where information of commercial or industrial value is given on a business-like basis and with some avowed common object in mind, such as a joint venture or the manufacture of articles by one party for the other, I would regard the recipient as carrying a heavy burden if he seeks to repel a contention that he was bound by an obligation of confidence.'

In the latter case the Vice-Chancellor stated obiter ([1978] 3 All ER 193 at 209–210, [1979] Ch 227 at 248):

> 'If one turns from the authorities and looks at the matter as a question of principle, I think (and I say this very tentatively, because the principle has not been argued out) that four elements may be discerned which may be of some assistance in

identifying confidential information or trade secrets which the court will protect. I speak of such information or secrets only in an industrial or trade setting. First, I think that the information must be information the release of which the owner believes would be injurious to him or of advantage to his rivals or others. Second, I think the owner must believe that the information is confidential or secret, ie that it is not already in the public domain. It may be that some or all of his rivals already have the information: but as long as the owner believes it to be confidential I think he is entitled to try and protect it. Third, I think that the owner's belief under the two previous heads must be reasonable. Fourth, I think that the information must be judged in the light of the usage and practices of the particular industry or trade concerned.'

Counsel for the plaintiffs recognised, of course, that both these cases related to industrial information. Nevertheless, he submitted, and I accept, that by analogy they support his submissions.

Counsel for the defendants sought to invoke *Seager v Copydex Ltd* on the ground that at least some written material was in existence embodying Mr Seager's idea (see [1967] 1 WLR 923 at 937; cf [1967] 2 All ER 415 at 418–419 per Winn LJ). But I consider the written material was so vestigial as to be of no significance.

In my judgment there is no reason in principle why an oral idea should not qualify for protection under the law of confidence, provided it meets the other criteria I discuss below. Neither the originality nor the quality of an idea is in any way affected by the form in which it is expressed. No doubt both the communication and the content of an oral idea may be more difficult to prove than in the case of a written idea, but difficulties of proof should not affect the principle any more than in any other branches of the law where similar problems arise (eg contract and defamation).

I do not accept counsel for the defendants' argument that this will cause unfairness to third parties, since it is clear that, in order to be fixed with an obligation of confidence, a third party must know that the information was confidential; knowledge of a mere assertion that a breach of confidence has been committed is not sufficient: see *Carl-Zeiss-Stiftung v Herbert Smith & Co (a firm) (No 2)* [1969] 2 All ER 367, [1969] 2 Ch 276.

Nor do I accept counsel for the defendants' argument that an idea which is capable of development in more than one format is not entitled to protection. In my judgment the precise format is a matter for the writer to decide, and the fact that it is developable in more than one format in no way diminishes its intrinsic value.

I accept that to be capable of protection the idea must be sufficiently developed, so that it would be seen to be a concept which has at least some attractiveness for a television programme and which is capable of being realised as an actuality (see per Harris J in *Talbot*'s case [1981] RPC 1 at 9). But I do not think this requirement necessitates in every case a full synopsis. In some cases the nature of the idea may require extensive development of this kind in order to meet the criteria. But in others the criteria may be met by a short unelaborated statement of an idea. In *Talbot*'s case itself I do not think the detailed submission (at 5) added very much of substance to the idea which is set out in one sentence (also at 5).

Unquestionably, of course, the idea must have some significant element of originality not already in the realm of public knowledge. The originality may consist in a significant twist or slant to a well-known concept (see *Talbot*'s case). This is, I think, by analogy, consistent with the statements in *Saltman*'s case and *Coco*'s case that novelty in the industrial field can be derived from the application of human ingenuity to well-known concepts.

To the best of my recollection, every witness in the theatre or television business on both sides agreed that if he or she received an idea from another it would be wrong to make use of it without the consent of the communicator. They of course were expressing their views in the context of a moral usage in their profession rather than of a strict legal obligation. However, the authorities, and in particular *Saltman*'s case per Somervell LJ and *Marshall*'s case, strongly support counsel for the plaintiffs' argument that the existence of such a usage is a factor of considerable force in deciding whether a legal obligation exists. I think the law as laid down in the authorities I have cited clearly establishes that the obligation which the witnesses saw as moral is in fact also legal in character.

This of course does not mean that every stray mention of an idea by one person to another is protected. To succeed in his claim the plaintiff must establish not only that the occasion of communication was confidential, but also that the content of the idea was clearly identifiable, original, of potential commercial attractiveness and capable of being realised in actuality. With these limitations, I consider there is no basis for the fears of counsel for the defendants that authors' freedom to develop ideas will be unduly stultified.

Applying these principles to the facts of the present case, Miss Leventon's communication of the idea to Mr Schuman, in particular at the meeting on 22 January 1974, was clearly in confidence; indeed it was in the nature of a professional occasion, since she was sounding out Mr Schuman's willingness to write a series based on the idea, Mr Rosenthal having declined (cf *Coco*'s case). I reject counsel for the defendants' attempt to distinguish *Coco*'s case on the grounds that there was no joint enterprise between Miss Leventon and Mr Schuman, because each had their separate role as actress and author respectively. I think that on 22 January 1974 they were jointly concerned commercially in the possible use of the idea.

That the idea could be seen as a concept which had commercial attractiveness for a television programme and was something which was capable of being realised as an actuality is clearly proved by Mr Rosenthal's evidence. Its originality is also clearly proved by Mr Rosenthal, supported by the evidence of Mrs Rosenthal, Mr Sizer and Mr Edwards. This originality, as Mr Rosenthal indicated, lies in the slant or twist the plaintiffs' idea gave to well-known concepts. It is difficult to think of anybody in a better position to prove this aspect than a television writer of Mr Rosenthal's stature. Quite apart from all this evidence, Mr Schuman's own success in turning the idea into a much-acclaimed television series is eloquent testimony of its commercial attractiveness, its ability to be realised in actuality and its originality.

Consequently, I hold that Mr Schuman owed an obligation of confidence in relation to the plaintiffs' idea.

Mr Brown knew from Mr Schuman that the idea was the plaintiffs' and had been imparted to Mr Schuman in confidence. He is therefore fixed with an obligation of confidence.

Thames, through Miss Lambert, knew, either from Mr Schuman or Mr Brown or both, that the idea was the plaintiffs' and had been imparted to Mr Schuman in confidence, and so Thames also are fixed with an obligation of confidence. I reject counsel for the defendants' argument that any obligation of confidence resting on Thames was 'washed out' once the contract of 4 October 1974 was entered into. I see no reason in principle why this result should ensue; nor was there any such provision in the contract. Furthermore, in this particular case, if Thames had declined to exercise their option, as they were perfectly free to do, they would then (on counsel for the defendants' argument) have been free of any obligation of confidence in relation to the idea. Such a result would be absurd.

I also reject counsel for the defendants' argument that, whatever its original status, the plaintiffs' idea lost its confidentiality once they disclosed it to others (eg Mr Degas). Since such disclosure to others was plainly also in confidence, confidentiality remained intact (see *Franchi v Franchi* [1967] RPC 149).

Counsel for the defendants accepts that, in relation to the claim in confidence, all four plaintiffs stand or fall together, so that there is no distinction to be drawn between Mr Fraser and the other three plaintiffs.

Counsel for the plaintiffs accepts that, on the plaintiffs' own case, the communication of the idea by Mr Schuman and Mr Brown to Thames in the spring or summer of 1974 was legitimate, since it was done with the plaintiffs' consent. His claim for breach of confidence is therefore confined to the user of the idea after the breakdown.

I hold that Mr Schuman was in breach of confidence in using the idea in his writing of the two Rock Follies series after May 1975.

I hold that Mr Brown was in breach of confidence in using the plaintiffs' idea in his production of the two Rock Follies series after May 1975. I reject counsel for the defendants' argument that Mr Brown can escape liability, because his activity as producer was under Thames's aegis, and added nothing to the harm caused to the plaintiffs by Thames's breach of confidence. In my judgment Mr Brown's liability falls to be judged by reference to his conduct on its own separate merits, irrespective of Thames's position.

I hold that Thames were in breach of confidence in using the idea in the making and screening of the two Rock Follies series, all of which took place after May 1975.

There will therefore be judgment for all four plaintiffs against Thames on their claim in contract.

On the claim in confidence there will be judgment for all four plaintiffs against all three defendants.

Judgment for the plaintiffs on issue of liability. Damages ordered to be assessed by a judge.

Solicitors: *Wright & Webb Syrett & Sons* (for the plaintiffs); *David I P Kent* (for the defendants).

K Mydeen Esq Barrister.

Dowse v Government of Sweden

HOUSE OF LORDS

LORD DIPLOCK, LORD WILBERFORCE, LORD KEITH OF KINKEL AND LORD BRIGHTMAN

2 MARCH, 21 APRIL 1983

Extradition – Committal – Evidence – Evidence sufficient to justify committal – Evidence relied on given in requesting state not under oath – Affirmation – Statement made before judge not under oath – Witness not liable to penal sanction for giving false statement – Whether witness's statement amounting to affirmation – Whether statement admissible in extradition proceedings – Extradition Act 1870, s 14 – Extradition Act 1873, s 4.

The appellant was accused of committing certain drug offences within the jurisdiction of Sweden. The Swedish government sought his extradition under the Extradition Acts 1870 and 1873 and the relevant extradition treaty between Sweden and the United Kingdom. In the course of the extradition proceedings before the magistrate the Swedish government produced in evidence a statement made by an accomplice in the alleged crime in evidence before a Swedish court. In the statement the accomplice confirmed previous statements made to the Swedish police implicating the appellant and identified the appellant. In accordance with Swedish law the accomplice's evidence was not given on oath and he was not liable to be punished for perjury if he gave false evidence. However, he was liable to imprisonment if the statements made to the police were false and he was reminded of that fact when giving evidence before the Swedish court. The magistrate found that there was a case to answer and committed the appellant to await extradition to Sweden. The appellant applied for a writ of habeas corpus on the ground that the accomplice's evidence was inadmissible in the extradition proceedings since it was not given on oath or by 'affirmation' as required by s 14[a] of the 1870 Act and s 4[b] of the 1873 Act. The application was refused by the Divisional Court. The appellant appealed to the House of Lords, contending that a statement made before a judicial

a Section 14 is set out at p 126 *b c*, post

b Section 4, so far as material, is set out at p 126 *d*, post authority in the extraditing state, not under oath, was not admissible in extradition proceedings as an affirmation unless the maker of the statement was liable to incur penal *a* sanctions from the judicial authority if the statement was untrue.

Held – Where the affirmation of a statement was made and recorded in legal proceedings before a foreign judge or magistrate who certified the correctness of the record, that was itself sufficient to make the certified statement admissible as evidence of the facts contained in the statement in extradition proceeding brought under the 1870 and 1873 *b* Acts since all that was required by way of affirmation was a confirmation or declaration that the statement was true. The absence of penal sanctions for making a false affirmation before the foreign judge or magistrate merely affected the weight to be given to the statement and not its admissibility as an affirmation. The accomplice's statement was therefore admissible in the extradition proceedings against the appellant. The appeal would accordingly be dismissed (see p 127 *d* to *j* and p 128 *b* to *g*, post). *c*

Dictum of Ackner LJ in *R v Governor of Pentonville Prison, ex p Singh* [1981] 3 All ER at 27 distinguished.

Decision of the Divisional Court of the Queen's Bench Division sub nom *R v Governor of Pentonville Prison, ex p Passingham* [1982] 3 All ER 1012 affirmed.

Notes *d*

For evidence required for extradition, see 18 Halsbury's Laws (4th edn) para 225 and for cases on the subject, see 24 Digest (Reissue) 1137–1138, *12,055–12,074*.

For the Extradition Act 1870, s 14, see 13 Halsbury's Statutes (3rd edn) 259.

For the Extradition Act 1873, s 4, see ibid 270.

Case referred to in opinions *e*

R v Governor of Pentonville Prison, ex p Singh [1981] 3 All ER 23, [1981] 1 WLR 1031, CA.

Appeal

The appellant, Neil Bernard Dowse, appealed with leave of the House of Lords granted on 28 July 1982 against the decision of the Divisional Court of the Queen's Bench Division (Griffiths LJ and Forbes J) (sub nom *R v Governor of Pentonville Prison, ex p* *f* *Passingham* [1982] 3 All ER 1012, [1982] 3 WLR 981) on 22 June 1982 dismissing the application by the appellant for a writ of habeas corpus directed to the Governor of Pentonville Prison where the appellant was detained under a warrant of committal issued by the Metropolitan Stipendiary Magistrate (L Robbins Esq) at Bow Street on 17 February 1982. The respondents to the appeal were the prison governor and the government of Sweden, which had sought the applicant's extradition under the Extradition Acts 1870 *g* and 1873 in respect of drug offences committed within the jurisdiction of the government of Sweden. The facts are set out in the opinion of Lord Diplock.

Clive Stanbrook for the appellant.

Ann Goddard QC and *David Paget* for the respondents.

Their Lordships took time for consideration. *h*

21 April. The following opinions were delivered.

LORD DIPLOCK. My Lords, the appellant, Dowse, was committed to prison by a metropolitan stipendiary magistrate to await extradition to Sweden for various offences *j* in connection with the possession and smuggling into Sweden of heroin. These are extraditable offences under art 3 of the extradition treaty with that country which is scheduled to the Sweden (Extradition) Order 1966, SI 1966/226.

Dowse applied to the Divisional Court under s 11 of the Extradition Act 1870 for a writ of habeas corpus, on the ground that the magistrate had wrongly admitted in evidence against him statements made by an accomplice in Sweden which were not taken on oath nor by way of affirmation, and that without those statements there was *a* insufficient evidence to justify his committal under s 10 of the Act.

The statements that were objected to were made by one Michalski in the course of his interrogation by the police in a pre-trial investigation of drug offences which he was charged with having committed in concert with Dowse and others. In these statements Michalski confessed to having been engaged in Sweden as a dealer in heroin and stated that on two occasions in February 1981 he had employed Dowse as a courier to smuggle *b* parcels of heroin from Holland to Sweden, and had paid him for doing this at the rate of £1,000 a trip. Under Swedish law it is an offence punishable by a maximum of two years imprisonment to make in the course of interrogation by the police in a pre-trial investigation into a suspected crime a false accusation that another person has committed a criminal offence.

On 2 November 1981, while the interrogation of Michalski was still proceeding, the *c* public prosecutor applied to the District Court at Huddinge in Sweden for evidence to be taken from Michalski (who was then in custody) for the purpose of obtaining from the court an order for the arrest of Dowse as one of those suspected of having acted in concert with Michalski in some of the drug offences to which the latter had confessed. On 9 November Michalski appeared before the Huddinge District Court to confirm the statements which inculpated Dowse. An English translation of the relevant part of the *d* record of those proceedings is as follows:

> 'RICHARD Florian Michalski, born 11 February, 1959, came before the court. He was informed by the Judge that if the statement he had made about the involvement of other persons in narcotic drugs trafficking were untrue, he could be sentenced under Swedish law for false incrimination to imprisonment for a maximum of two years. He was also reminded that it was not an offence under Swedish law to make *e* false statements before a court concerning a crime committed by another person if the statements were not made on oath. Finally, he was told that notwithstanding he should keep to the truth in his statements before the court. The interpreter read out the translation into the English language of the following police interrogations of Michalski at Visby. Interrogations took place: (1) 28 October 1981 commencing 10.40 hrs; (2) 2 November 1981 commencing 17.00 hrs; (3) 3 November 1981 *f* commencing 15.55 hrs... When asked, Michalski confirmed that the particulars he had given at the police interrogation were correct and that one of the signatures on each page of the interrogation record was his. Wallberg [the public prosecutor] asked Michalski: "Have you during these proceedings understood that if you have lied at the police interrogations about Passingham's and Dowse's complicity in crime, that you are guilty of an offence under Swedish law? Have you been aware *g* of this?" Michalski answered: "Yes". Michalski was shown one copy of each of the enclosed photographs ... and stated that one was a photograph of Dowse ... and the other a photograph of Passingham ..., and wrote on the back of both photographs the place, date and his signature.'

At the conclusion of the proceedings, the court ruled that there were probable grounds *h* for suspecting Dowse of the drug offences alleged against him, and made an order for his detention.

The requisition by the Swedish government for the extradition of Dowse was accompanied by a certificate of the Swedish Ministry of Foreign Affairs that the decision of the Huddinge District Court constituted in Swedish law a warrant of arrest for the purposes of art 10(3) of the Swedish extradition treaty. The requisition was also *j* accompanied by certified copies and translations into English of the record of the Huddinge District Court proceedings signed by the presiding judge, which included as annexes the statements made by Michalski which he had confirmed at the hearing and also a statement by a Swedish lawyer as to the relevant Swedish law, including the law as to the offence of 'false incrimination' and as to an accused person not being permitted to give evidence on oath in proceedings brought to add another party as co-defendant with him in a prosecution that has already been commenced against him. It would seem that

in Sweden, as in a number of civil law countries, a defendant in a criminal trial when he gives evidence is not allowed to do so on oath, and he incurs no penal sanction if he does a
not tell the truth. The rule about not giving evidence on oath inculpating a proposed co-defendant as a participant with the accused in the offence, would appear to be a corollary of this rule.

My Lords, to justify an order for committal under s 10 of the Extradition Act 1870, such evidence must be produced before the committing magistrate as would be sufficient to justify the committal for trial of the prisoner if the crime of which he is accused had b
been committed in England; but this is subject to the provisions of ss 14 and 15. Section 14 provides as follows:

> 'Depositions or statements on oath, taken in a foreign state, and copies of such original depositions or statements, and foreign certificates of or judicial documents stating the fact of conviction, may, if duly authenticated, be received in evidence in proceedings under this Act.' c

Section 15 deals with the authentication, inter alia, of 'depositions or statements on oath, and copies thereof'. It provides that these documents are to be received in evidence without further proof if they 'purport to be certified under the hand of a judge, magistrate or officer of the foreign state where the same were taken'.

The provisions of ss 14 and 15 relating to depositions and statements on oath have d
been extended by s 4 of the Extradition Act 1873 to 'affirmations taken in a foreign state, and copies of such affirmations'. (I shall refer to the 1870 Act as so extended by the 1873 Act as 'the Extradition Act'.)

The Extradition Act is made applicable to a particular state by an Order in Council made under s 2. Section 5 provides that by such Order in Council 'limitations, restrictions, conditions, exceptions and qualifications' of the provisions of the Act may be imposed in e
the application of the Act to extradition to and from the particular state. This does not permit of any extension of the powers conferred on magistrates to make committal orders under s 10. So what it falls to your Lordships to construe as respect the admissibility of the documentary evidence challenged by Dowse in this appeal is s 14 of the Extradition Act, subject to any restrictions that may be imposed by any provision of the Swedish extradition treaty dealing with the admissibility of evidence. The relevant provision is to f
be found in art 13 and reads as follows:

> 'The authorities of the requested High Contracting party shall admit as evidence, in any proceedings for extradition, a sworn deposition or affirmation taken in the territory of the requesting Party, any certificate of, or judicial document stating the fact of, a conviction, any warrant, and any copy of any of the foregoing documents, if it is authenticated—(*a*) in the case of a warrant by being signed, or in the case of g
> any other original document by being certified, by a judge, magistrate or officer of the requesting Party or, in the case of a copy, by being so certified to be a true copy of the original, and (*b*) either by the oath of some witness or by being sealed with the official seal of the appropriate Minister of the requesting Party; or in such other manner as may be permitted by the law of the requested Party.'

h

This is a reciprocal provision. It applies in Sweden when extradition is requested by the United Kingdom and in the United Kingdom when extradition is requested by Sweden. It differs from s 14 of the Extradition Act only by omitting any separate reference to 'statements on oath', other than 'sworn depositions'.

My Lords, s 14 of the Extradition Act where it speaks of 'affirmations' and 'depositions' and 'statements on oath' is dealing with documentary evidence. It makes admissible in j
evidence in extradition proceedings written statements of fact which fall within any of those descriptions and are duly authenticated in manner provided for by s 15, notwithstanding that under English laws of evidence what appears in the statement would only be admissible in the form of oral testimony given on oath by the maker of the statement. The manifest purpose of the section, as has frequently been stated, is to

obviate the necessity of bringing witnesses from one country that is a party to an extradition treaty to give oral evidence in the other.

The only question in this appeal is whether the confirmation that was given by Michalski before the District Court at Huddinge of statements inculpating Dowse that he had previously made at the police interrogation, constitutes an 'affirmation' within the meaning of s 14 of the Act and art 13 of the treaty so as to render admissible as evidence of the facts contained in the statements the duly authenticated record of the proceedings of the court which incorporated copies of the statements and recorded Michalski's confirmation of them before the judge.

It is rightly conceded that the expression 'affirmation' appearing in an Act of Parliament which provides for the entry by the United Kingdom into extradition treaties which make reciprocal arrangements for the surrender of fugitive criminals to and by foreign countries whose legal procedures in criminal cases may differ widely from one another and in particular from those of England cannot be confined to the narrow technical meaning of a statement made after reciting the form of words that was permitted as a substitute for an oath in 1873 and is now set out in s 6 of the Oaths Act 1978. Since it is to be applied to procedures which take place in a country other than England, in casu Sweden, where certain categories of witnesses of fact are not permitted to give evidence before a court on oath, it must be understood in some wider sense. The primary and natural meaning of an 'affirmation' in ordinary speech is a confirmation or declaration that something is true; and I see no reason for not giving to the word, where it appears in s 14 of the Act and art 13 of the treaty, its primary and natural meaning.

The reference in ss 14 and 15 of the Act and art 13 of the treaty to affirmations and statements 'taken' in the state that is requesting extradition and the requirement in s 15(2) that they should be authenticated by being 'certified under the hand of a judge, magistrate or officer of the foreign state where the same were taken' indicate that an affirmation, to be admissible in evidence, must be one the making of which involved some formality of an official character; and, in my view, make it clear that where the formality consists of the affirmation being made in proceedings before a judge or magistrate who gives a certificate to that effect that is sufficient to make the statement certified by the judge or magistrate as having been made in those proceedings admissible in evidence in extradition proceedings brought under the Extradition Act.

It was contended on behalf of Dowse that on the true construction of s 14 no statement that had not been made on oath in the country by which extradition was requested was admissible in evidence as an affirmation unless not only was it declared to be true by the maker on an appearance before a judicial authority, but also the maker of the statement would incur penal sanctions if the statement were not true. For my part I can see no grounds on which, as a matter of construction, the absence of a penal sanction for making an affirmation before a judicial authority that is false prevents it from being an affirmation within the meaning of s 14. Absence of penal sanctions may go to weight; it cannot go to admissibility where the affirmation is made before a judge or magistrate—and I would remind your Lordships that this appeal is not concerned with affirmations taken by a non-judicial officer of the foreign state, to which different considerations might apply.

So, in the instant case the fact that under Swedish law Michalski could not give evidence on oath incriminating Dowse but could make an unsworn statement because the purpose of the proceedings in which he was brought before the Huddinge District Court was to initiate criminal proceedings against Dowse as a co-defendant with Michalski in the same proceedings as had already been commenced against the latter cannot make inadmissible the duly authenticated record of the proceedings of the Huddinge District Court incorporating Michalski's statements to the police and recording his confirmation of their accuracy before the judge.

In the instant case, while it is the fact, as was pointed out to him by the judge at the hearing, that Michalski, since he would not be on oath, would commit no additional offence in Swedish law if he confirmed false statements incriminating Dowse that he had previously made to the police in the course of the pre-trial investigation, the making of false statements of this nature to the police was itself a criminal offence the gravity of *a* which, if Michalski had indeed committed it, would obviously be enhanced if he were to affirm the false statements in proceedings before the district judge himself brought for the purpose of obtaining the arrest of those whom he had implicated as participants with him in drug offences with which he was charged. So there must have been present to Michalski's mind the risk of incurring an increased penalty if he now confirmed as being true previous statements to the police that had been to his knowledge false; so *b* apart from the solemnity of the occasion there was this additional inducement to Michalski not to repeat a lie.

In their judgment in the instant case the Divisional Court treated as the criterion of the admissibility of an affirmation that it was made in circumstances of solemnity and gravity, a requirement that they held to have been fulfilled (see [1982] 3 All ER 1012, [1982] 3 WLR 981). In adopting this criterion they were following what had been said *c* by Ackner LJ in *R v Governor of Pentonville Prison, ex p Singh* [1981] 3 All ER 23 at 27, [1981] 1 WLR 1031 at 1036:

> 'What is required, where the statement has been made, is its adoption in circumstances which recognise the gravity and importance of the truth being told on the particular occasion.' *d*

I would agree, my Lords, that this may be the appropriate criterion to apply to an affirmation taken otherwise than on oath by a non-judicial officer of a foreign state; but for the reasons given earlier, based on the language of ss 14 and 15 of the Extradition Act, I am of opinion that where the affirmation of a statement is made and recorded in legal proceedings before a foreign judge or magistrate who certifies the correctness of the record, duly certified copies and translations of the record are admissible as evidence of *e* the facts contained in the statement so affirmed.

For these reasons I would dismiss this appeal.

LORD WILBERFORCE. My Lords, I have had the advantage of reading in draft the speech by my noble and learned friend Lord Diplock. I agree with it and for the reasons he gives I would dismiss the appeal. *f*

LORD KEITH OF KINKEL. My Lords, for the reasons given in the speech of my noble and learned friend Lord Diplock, which I have had the benefit of reading in draft and with which I agree, I too would dismiss the appeal.

LORD BRIGHTMAN. My Lords, I would dismiss this appeal for the reasons given by *g* my noble and learned friend Lord Diplock.

Appeal dismissed.

Solicitors: *Simons Muirhead Allan & Burton* (for the appellant); *Director of Public Prosecutions.*

Mary Rose Plummer Barrister.

Tracomin SA v Sudan Oil Seeds Co Ltd and another (No 2)

QUEEN'S BENCH DIVISION (COMMERCIAL COURT)
LEGGATT J
1, 2, 3, 17 FEBRUARY 1983

Conflict of laws – Foreign proceedings – Restraint of foreign proceedings – Circumstances in which court will restrain foreign proceedings – Contract providing for arbitration in London – Contract between Swiss buyers and Sudanese sellers – Buyers commencing proceedings in Swiss court for breach of contract – Sellers asking Swiss court to stay proceedings in view of arbitration agreement – Swiss court giving judgment for buyers on basis of Swiss law in absence of evidence of English law – Sellers seeking injunction from English court to restrain buyers from proceeding further with Swiss proceedings – Whether court having jurisdiction to restrain buyers from instituting or maintaining foreign proceedings in breach of arbitration agreement – Whether sellers' failure to inform Swiss court of relevant English law a reason for English court to refuse injunction – Whether duplicity of proceedings sufficient reason to restrain buyers from proceeding in Swiss court.

A dispute arose between the Swiss buyers and the Sudanese sellers of a consignment of peanuts. The contract of sale was evidenced by a sold note which stated that the conditions of the contract were to be 'as per' a standard form. The standard form stated that disputes were to be referred to arbitration in London. The buyers, however, brought an action in the Swiss court claiming damages for breach of contract. The sellers entered what was in effect a plea in bar in the Swiss court, asking for a stay of proceedings on the ground that the dispute should be settled under the arbitration clause incorporated into the contract. The Swiss court dismissed the sellers' application because, in the absence of the citation of English law by either party, it assumed English law to be the same as Swiss law and held that the arbitration clause was not to be regarded as having been incorporated into the contract. The sellers then sought to have arbitrators proceed with arbitration in London. The buyers brought an action seeking an order to restrain the sellers from proceeding with the arbitration, and the sellers counterclaimed for an order to restrain the buyers from proceeding further with the Swiss action. On the counterclaim,

Held – (1) Where a contract contained an agreement to submit disputes to arbitration in London, and especially where that agreement provided that the making of an award was to be considered a condition precedent to any right of action in respect of any of the matters agreed to be referred, the parties to the contract had sufficient connection with England to give the English courts jurisdiction to grant an injunction restraining either party, even though resident abroad, from instituting or maintaining proceedings abroad in breach of the arbitration agreement. The jurisdiction was, however, discretionary and was to be exercised with great caution; and the more remote the connection with England and the more that the foreign court had become involved in the matter, the greater was the caution called for (see p 136 *d* to *f*, post); *Pena Copper Mines Ltd v Rio Tinto Co Ltd* [1911–13] All ER Rep 209, *Ellerman Lines Ltd v Read* [1928] All ER Rep 415, *Royal Exchange Assurance Co Ltd v Compania Naviera Santi SA, The Tropaioforos (No 2)* [1962] 1 Lloyd's Rep 410 and dictum of Dunn LJ in *Mike Trading and Transport Ltd v R Pagnan & Flli, The Lisboa* [1980] 2 Lloyd's Rep at 551 applied.

(2) The Swiss courts, like the English courts, could only be informed of foreign law by appropriate evidence, and a party who failed to produce it could not afterwards impeach a judgment obtained against him in a Swiss court on account of an error into which that court had fallen in consequence of the admitted default of that party. Since it had been the duty of the sellers to bring to the knowledge of the Swiss courts the provision of the English law on which for the first time they relied in the English court, since they had failed in that duty and since the Swiss court had behaved with perfect

propriety and had only reached what to an English lawyer was the wrong conclusion on account of the negligence of the sellers, the sellers did not merit the assistance of the a
English court but had to submit to the consequences of their own negligence. The fact that that might result in duplicity of proceedings was not a sufficient reason for the English court to attempt to restrain the buyers from proceeding in the Swiss court even if the sellers continued to pursue the contractual remedy of arbitration. It followed that the counterclaim would be dismissed (see p 137 *e* to *j* and p 138 *f*, post); dictum of Hannen J in *Godard v Gray* (1870) LR 6 QB at 154 followed. b

Notes

For injunctions to restrain foreign proceedings, see 8 Halsbury's Laws (4th edn) paras 730, 787, and for cases on the subject, see 11 Digest (Reissue) 637–642, *1713–1753*.

Cases referred to in judgment c

Castanho v Brown & Root (UK) Ltd [1980] 3 All ER 72, [1980] 1 WLR 833, CA; *varied* [1981] 1 All ER 143, [1981] AC 557, [1980] 3 WLR 991, HL.

Cohen v Rothfield [1919] 1 KB 410, [1918–19] All ER Rep 260, CA.

Ellerman Lines Ltd v Read [1928] 2 KB 144, [1928] All ER Rep 415, CA.

Godard v Gray (1870) LR 6 QB 139.

Marazura Navegacion SA v Oceanus Mutual Underwriting Association (Bermuda) Ltd [1977] 1 d
Lloyd's Rep 283.

Mike Trading and Transport Ltd v R Pagnan & Flli, The Lisboa [1980] 2 Lloyd's Rep 546, CA.

Pena Copper Mines Ltd v Rio Tinto Co Ltd (1911) 105 LT 846, [1911–13] All ER Rep 209, CA.

Royal Exchange Assurance Co Ltd v Compania Naviera Santi SA, The Tropaioforos (No 2) e
[1962] 1 Lloyd's Rep 410.

Settlement Corp v Hochschild [1965] 3 All ER 486, [1966] Ch 10, [1965] 3 WLR 1150.

Tracomin SA v Sudan Oil Seeds Co Ltd [1983] 1 All ER 404.

Counterclaim

By an order dated 9 December 1982 Bingham J, sitting as the Commercial judge in f
chambers, ordered to stand as the counterclaim of the first defendants, Sudan Oil Seeds Co Ltd (the sellers), the claim set out in an affidavit of Charles Howard Deans, a solicitor having the conduct of the sellers' case. By that claim the sellers sought an order that, inter alia, the plaintiffs, Tracomin SA (the buyers), their directors, officers, solicitors, advocates, servants or agents be restrained from continuing or prosecuting proceedings commenced by the buyers against the sellers in the canton of Vaud, Switzerland, or from commencing g
any further or other proceedings there or elsewhere, directed to obtaining any order for the payment of moneys alleged to be due or damages or compensation for breach of contract or otherwise concerning or arising from or in relation to a contract no 4–80/81 dated 30 November 1980 by which the sellers agreed to sell to the buyers 2,000 tonnes, 5% more or less, Sudanese HPS groundnut kernels (Spanish type) 70/80 count per ounce 1980–81 crop pure basis. The second defendant, George J Bridge, one of two arbitrators h
in references to arbitration pursuant to arbitration agreements contained in the contract, took no part in the counterclaim. The counterclaim was heard in chambers but judgment was given by Leggatt J in open court. The facts are set out in the judgment.

Nicholas Merriman for the sellers.
David Grace for the buyers. j

Cur adv vult

17 February. The following judgment was delivered.

LEGGATT J. I wish I could say that this is a case about peanuts. Unhappily, however,

the basic dispute between the parties has become overlaid through the ingenuity of
a lawyers in this country and in Switzerland by a series of procedural wrangles, of which this is one.

The basic dispute is between Swiss buyers, who are the plaintiffs in these proceedings, and Sudanese sellers, who are the defendants in these proceedings, of consignments of peanuts. The contracts of sale, of which there were two, were made towards the end of 1981. Each was evidenced by a 'sold note'. The sold note referred to conditions of
b contract, which were to be 'as per' a standard form. The standard form stated that disputes were to be referred to arbitration in London. The buyers, however, brought an action in the Swiss court claiming damages for breach of contract. The sellers entered what is variously translated as a plea in bar or an application for a stay in the Swiss court, asking for a stay of proceedings on the ground that the dispute should be settled under the arbitration clause incorporated into the contract. The Swiss court dismissed the
c application. It did so because, assuming English law to be the same as Swiss law, the arbitration clause was not to be regarded as having been incorporated into the contract. The sellers are seeking to have the arbitrators proceed with the arbitration in London.

In an associated action the buyers claimed before Staughton J that the sellers were estopped by the Swiss judgment from asserting that the arbitration clause was incorporated into the contract. Staughton J concluded that, had the common law applied,
d that claim that the sellers were estopped would have been successful. But before he gave judgment the Civil Jurisdiction and Judgments Act 1982 had come into force. Applying the provisions of s 33 of that Act, the judge held that the sellers were to be deemed not to have submitted to the jurisdiction of the Swiss court merely because they had entered a plea requesting a stay of proceedings on the ground that the dispute should be decided under the arbitration agreement. The judge further held, applying the provisions of s 32
e of the same Act, that the court could not recognise or enforce the judgment of the Swiss court because under English law there was a valid arbitration agreement, and the bringing of proceedings in the Swiss court by the buyers was contrary to that agreement.

Staughton J has succinctly summarised the majority of the facts which are relevant for present purposes. I gratefully adopt the first part of his judgment (see *Tracomin SA v Sudan Oil Seeds Co Ltd* [1983] 1 All ER 404 at 406–409). All I need do by way of
f supplement is to bring the matter up to date.

Shortly before judgment was given by Staughton J on 6 October 1982 there had been an application made to the Swiss court by the sellers for a stay under art 120 of the Swiss Code of Civil Procedure on the ground of lis alibi pendens. The issue was whether there was a pending arbitration in London. The judge held that he was not satisfied that there was a pending arbitration in London and he refused a stay.

g On 15 November the originating summons, one part of which is now before me, was issued. It was issued by the buyers and by its terms they sought to revoke the authority of the arbitrators in the reference to arbitration in England.

On 9 December the matter came before Bingham J. In consequence of what then ensued the sellers' arbitrator has been replaced, but the arbitration to which the proceedings related is still in being. For purposes of the hearing before Bingham J there
h was sworn on behalf of the sellers an affidavit of Mr Deans (the sellers' solicitor). By the terms of Bingham J's order that affidavit was ordered to stand as a counterclaim, and the issues raised by it were ordered to be tried on a date to be fixed as expeditiously as possible. The particular relief sought was an order that—

> 'the Plaintiffs [that is to say the buyers], their directors, officers, solicitors, advocates, servants or agents be restrained from continuing or prosecuting
> j proceedings commenced by the Plaintiffs against the First Defendants in the Canton of Vaud, Switzerland or from commencing any further or other proceedings there or elsewhere, directed to obtaining any order for the payment of moneys alleged to be due or damages or compensation for breach of contract or otherwise concerning or arising from or in relation to a contract No. 4–80/81 dated 30th November 1980 by which the First Defendants agreed to sell to the Plaintiffs 2,000 metric tonnes,

5% more or less, Sudanese H.P.S. Groundnut Kernels (Spanish Type) 70/80 Count per ounce 1980/1981 Crop pure basis.'

The contract referred to was the first of two between the sellers and buyers, the second having been made on 6 December 1981 for another 2,000 tonnes of peanuts.

For purposes of the hearing before Bingham J there was a continuing cross-fire of affidavits between the solicitors. There was also sworn, on behalf of the buyers, an affidavit of their Swiss lawyer, Maître Rusconi, dealing with the proceedings current in Switzerland. In his affidavit he explained that if an injunction is granted in England, restraining the buyers from prosecuting their action against the sellers in Switzerland, and if that injunction were respected by the buyers, the consequence would be that when nothing had happened for one year the action in Switzerland would automatically expire, and with it there would expire also the sequestration order which has been obtained there by the buyers against the sellers in relation to their shipping documents. Once the sequestration order was lifted, the buyers would lose such security as is afforded them by that order, whatever tribunal might eventually deal with the basic dispute between the parties. Maître Rusconi indicates that in the normal way the security effected by the sequestration order would have been available to meet a London arbitration award, but, now that the Swiss courts have decided that the arbitration clause is not incorporated, that cannot occur. He uses the phrase 'the Swiss courts' because, not content with the judgment at first instance, the sellers appealed to the Cantonal Court of Appeal and confronted once more with an adverse finding they have pursued their remedy to the ultimate court of appeal in Switzerland, namely the Federal Supreme Court. Maître Rusconi deposes that in resisting the various applications of the sellers in Switzerland the buyers had incurred legal costs exclusive of court fees of about 100,000 Swiss francs. Two matters he mentions particularly in relation to what the sellers have done or sought to do in Switzerland, apart from their application for a stay. The first is that through their Swiss lawyer, Maître Vanner, the sellers elected domicile at his law office for the purposes of the action, without in so doing including any protest or reservation in relation to the jurisdiction of the court. It is Maître Rusconi's opinion that by electing domicile without any reservation the sellers chose to put themselves in the position that they would be in if they were resident in Lausanne at Maître Vanner's office. Maître Rusconi secondly refers to the fact that, having failed in their appeal to the Cantonal Court of Appeal, the sellers issued an application for a temporary stay or suspension of the action. That is the application to which I have already referred under art 120 of the Code of Civil Procedure. According to Maître Rusconi, such an application acknowledges that the action pending is validly brought, in the sense that the court has and should exercise jurisdiction to determine it, but also asks that it should suspend judgment until the result of the first action elsewhere is known. If the application is granted, says Maître Rusconi, the court does not decline jurisdiction, it temporarily suspends the exercise of it.

He concludes his affidavit by expressing surprise that the sellers saw fit before Staughton J to offer to make the security in Switzerland available to meet a London arbitration award in circumstances where, according to Maître Rusconi, the sellers have formally admitted in the Swiss proceedings that the banks through whom the documents were or were to be processed and not the sellers themselves are entitled to the security.

That affidavit was sworn and served only a few days before the present proceedings began, and that put the sellers at some disadvantage in seeking to answer it. Accordingly, I ought not to be too much affected by the paucity of the response. It was made by Maître Vanner apparently by telex in the form of a comment only on the question of electing domicile at his offices. He says that the sellers, having raised a plea of incompetence, as he describes it, cannot be taken to have submitted to the jurisdiction of the Swiss court, and he makes the point that the election of domicile at his office does not indicate that the sellers accept the Swiss jurisdiction for the reason in particular that domicile and submission to the jurisdiction are fundamentally different concepts in Swiss law.

The dismissal by the Federal Supreme Court of the sellers' final appeal occurred on 22 December. The sellers are accordingly able to declare that they have exhausted all the steps open to them in Switzerland to restrain the buyers' proceedings in Switzerland, in a circumstances where the effect of Staughton J's decision is that the judgment of the Swiss court is not enforceable here. The sellers now seek an injunction in this court to restrain the prosecution of the Swiss action, and the matter may be summarised in this way.

The buyers started proceedings in Switzerland to validate the sequestration. The sellers appeared there in order to contest the jurisdiction on the ground that the arbitration clause in the contracts applies. Neither side cited English law. If English law had been b cited, the Swiss courts would have applied it. If it had been applied, the courts would have held that the arbitration clause applies and would have stayed the Swiss proceedings. Because English law was not cited, the Swiss courts applied the same principle as an English court would apply. They assumed English law to be the same as Swiss law. According to Swiss law, the arbitration clause was not incorporated into the contracts. They therefore held that the jurisdiction of the Swiss court was not ousted.

c Staughton J has held that this decision is not binding on the English court, so far as concerns the recognition and enforcement of the Swiss judgment.

Counsel for the buyers has not advanced any convincing reason why Staughton J's judgment is wrong. But the buyers have appealed against it. The sellers took proceedings in Switzerland, partly to prevent the buyers from seizing their assets. An English court might well have not interfered to stop the seizure of assets in aid of the arbitration d proceedings. But the effect of what the sellers have done in the Swiss proceedings is that assets seized there cannot be held in aid of arbitration proceedings but only in aid of proceedings in Switzerland. The sellers now seek to restrain the buyers from proceeding with the Swiss proceedings in Switzerland (that is from enforcing the Swiss judgment in Switzerland). The position has therefore now been reached that the buyers are intending to proceed in Switzerland on an entirely false basis, namely that the arbitration clause e does not apply, despite the fact that both contracting parties agree that it does or should.

Meanwhile, because the Swiss judgment is not recognised here, arbitration proceedings will proceed in England unless the Court of Appeal reverses Staughton J. That may result in conflicting decisions in different jurisdictions.

The sellers argue that the buyers should be restrained now by injunction here from proceeding with the Swiss action in breach of the arbitration clause. The difficulty is that f the Swiss court is only seised of the action because of the sellers' failure to take the point in the Swiss proceedings that English law is the proper law of the contract and to prove what it is. It is right to record that counsel for the buyers did not argue whether there was power or jurisdiction in this court to prevent a foreigner resident abroad from proceeding in the court of his own residence by an injunction issued here. That is a point which he expressly reserves should this matter go further.

g A convenient preface to the law which I have to apply is provided by Mustill and Boyd *The Law of Commercial Arbitrations in England* (1982) p 410, which both counsel read to me with no variations except of emphasis, a fact which may indicate that there is no real dispute between them as to the law applicable but rather as to the manner in which I should exercise the relevant discretion. The passage reads as follows:

> h 'The textbooks state that an injunction will not be granted to restrain a party from bringing proceedings in the English courts in breach of an agreement to submit disputes to arbitration. Different principles apply where the action is brought abroad. In such a case, the English Court can provide no alternative remedy in the shape of a stay, nor does any principle of English public policy arise, as regards ousting the jurisdiction of the foreign court. Accordingly, there seems no reason in principle why the Court should not grant an injunction restraining the parties from j proceeding in breach of their agreement to arbitrate. The Court will, no doubt, be cautious in granting the remedy, given that it might be regarded as an unacceptable infringement of the prerogatives of the foreign court; and it is in any event unlikely to be granted unless the claimant is or has assets within the jurisdiction, and hence [is] amenable to coercion if he acts in defiance of the order, or has at least submitted to the jurisdiction. Where the case falls within the New York Convention, and

possibly in other cases as well, we suggest that the right course is for the aggrieved party to exhaust his local remedies by seeking a stay or kindred relief from the local courts, before asking the English Court to intervene. It is only in cases where something has plainly gone badly wrong in the local courts that the English Court should grant the extreme remedy of an injunction.'

Counsel for the sellers contends that something 'has plainly gone badly wrong' in the Swiss courts with the result that, since the sellers have exhausted their remedies there, they should now be entitled to an injunction in this court.

To that counsel for the buyers responds that, if it be right to say that something has plainly gone badly wrong in the Swiss courts, it only has so on account of the acts or omissions of sellers.

The cases relevant to this matter are summarised in the judgment of Dunn LJ in *Mike Trading and Transport Ltd v R Pagnan & Flli, The Lisboa* [1980] 2 Lloyd's Rep 546 at 551:

> 'Although the English Court has jurisdiction to restrain a party to English proceedings from proceeding in a foreign Court, the jurisdiction will be exercised with great caution especially when the defendant to the English proceedings is plaintiff in the foreign proceedings, and the injunction should not normally be granted unless the foreign proceedings are vexatious or oppressive (see *Cohen v. Rothfield* ([1919] 1 KB 410, [1918–19] All ER Rep 260), per Lord Justice Scrutton, and *Castanho v. Brown & Root (U.K.) Ltd.* ([1980] 3 All ER 72, [1980] 1 WLR 833)). [I should interpolate there that the majority judgment of the Court of Appeal in that case has since been upheld in the House of Lords.] This is so even if the parties have agreed not to proceed in a foreign Court (*Settlement Corporation v. Hochschild* ([1965] 3 All ER 486 at 490–491, [1966] Ch 10 at 17–18), per Mr. Justice Ungoed-Thomas) or if they have agreed that all disputes shall be submitted to arbitration in England (*Marazura v. Oceanus* ([1977] 1 Lloyd's Rep 283)). There may however be cases in which the court will exercise the jurisdiction, but as a matter of discretion and not of right (see *Pena Copper Mines Ltd. v. Rio Tinto Co. Ltd.* ((1911) 105 LT 846, [1911–13] All ER Rep 209); *Ellerman v. Read* ([1928] 2 KB 144, [1928] All ER Rep 415); and *The Tropaioforos (No. 2)* ([1962] 1 Lloyd's Rep 410)). It is always a relevant consideration whether or not the party seeking the injunction will be adequately protected by an award of damages.'

For present purposes it suffices to look a little more closely at the last three cases cited by Dunn LJ. The first is *Pena Copper Mines Ltd v Rio Tinto Co Ltd.* That was a case in which the contract contained (as does the present contract) an arbitration clause fortified by a Scott v Avery clause. It was held that the court had discretionary jurisdiction to restrain the prosecution of proceedings in a foreign court by an English person if the bringing of those proceedings is in breach of a contract made in this country. The injunction granted was held by the Court of Appeal to have been rightly granted. It was granted in a form which counsel for the sellers has adapted or sought to adapt for present purposes. In the judgment of Cozens-Hardy MR, he said (105 LT 846 at 850–851, [1911–13] All ER Rep 209 at 212), referring to the argument of counsel for the appellants:

> '[Counsel], with some courage, asserted boldly that there was no jurisdiction and that the Spanish action ought to be allowed to go on until the defendants to that action—that is to say, the Pena Company—had put in a plea which he says would be admitted according to Spanish law and which might then have the effect—I rather gather from his view—of rendering further proceedings in Spain nugatory and void. I can see no foundation at all for that. The jurisdiction of the Court of Chancery acting *in personam* is too well known and too plain to admit of any contest. It is beyond all doubt that this court has jurisdiction to restrain the Rio Tinto Company from commencing or continuing proceedings in a foreign court if those proceedings are in breach of contract . . . But to contend that as regards any breach of a clear contract made between the plaintiffs and the defendants the court cannot

> restrain the defendants—who have contracted that they will not sue in a foreign court—from so suing is a proposition to which I think no sanction ought to be given by this court and which is certainly quite unwarranted by any authority that I am aware of.'

The second of this group of cases (and the case on which counsel for the sellers most strongly relies) is *Ellerman Lines Ltd v Read* [1928] 2 KB 144, [1928] All ER Rep 415. That was a case in which a steamship had gone aground in Romania. A salvage vessel belonging to the defendants and commanded by one of them, named Landi, who was a naturalised British subject, entered into an agreement with the master of the vessel for its salvage. The agreement was in standard Lloyd's form and provided in the event of dispute as to salvage for arbitration in London. It also provided that the vessel was not to be arrested if satisfactory security were given in London. After salvaging the vessel Mr Landi sought to arrest it against payment of the sum demanded by way of salvage. The vessel was by then in Turkey, and in proceedings in the Turkish court Mr Landi swore, contrary to the truth, that solicitors had not been authorised by him to accept the guarantee that had been proffered in respect of the sums due by way of salvage. The owners of the vessel in these circumstances sought an injunction to restrain the defendants, including Mr Landi, from enforcing their judgment in the Turkish court. MacKinnon J found at first instance that Mr Landi committed a deliberate and shameless breach of contract when he caused the vessel to be arrested, and that when he swore that he had not authorised his London solicitors to take a guarantee he told a lie. On appeal the judgment of Scrutton LJ, so far as is directly material, read as follows ([1928] 2 KB 144 at 151; cf [1928] All ER Rep 415 at 416-417):

> 'Here we have an English contract, considerable portions of which were to be performed in England, entered into by a naturalized British subject; that naturalized British subject is proved to have broken that contract and by fraud obtained a foreign judgment which he proposes to enforce against the property of the other contracting party. He has been properly served with the writ in this action and is a party to the proceedings. In such a case, as I understand the decisions, the English Courts have always professed, and asserted, their power to act. They do not, of course, grant an injunction restraining the foreign Court from acting; they have no power to do that; but they can grant an injunction restraining a British subject who is fraudulently breaking his contract, and who is a party to proceedings before them, from making an application to a foreign Court for the purpose of reaping the fruits of his fraudulent breach of contract.'

It is to observed that as in the previous case, the *Pena Copper Mines* case, the party sought to be restrained was a British subject. It is also to be observed that Scrutton LJ uses in the passage which I have read from his judgment references to breach of contract and fraud, but although he specifies them separately it is not necessarily to be supposed that the same result would have ensued in that case had there been mere breach of contract without fraud.

Counsel for the sellers also refers to a passage from the judgment of Atkin LJ, where he says ([1928] 2 KB 144 at 155; cf [1928] All ER Rep 415 at 420):

> 'The principle upon which an English Court acts in granting injunctions is not that it seeks to assume jurisdiction over the foreign Court, or that it arrogates to itself some superiority which entitles it to dictate to the foreign Court, or that it seeks to criticize the foreign Court or its procedure; the English Court has regard to the personal attitude of the person who has obtained the foreign judgment. If the English Court finds that a person subject to its jurisdiction has committed a breach of covenant, or has acted in breach of some fiduciary duty or has in any way violated the principles of equity and conscience, and that it would be inequitable on his part to seek to enforce a judgment obtained in breach of such obligations, it will restrain

> him, not by issuing an edict to the foreign Court, but by saying that he is in
> conscience bound not to enforce that judgment.' a

I read that passage in particular for the light that it sheds on the submission of counsel
for the buyers that to suggest that the Swiss court is not being baulked in its ability to
proceed on its own judgment by any injunction issued in this court is mere hypocrisy, or
worse.

The third of the cases referred to by Dunn LJ was *Royal Exchange Assurance Co Ltd v
Compania Naviera Santi SA, The Tropaioforos (No 2)* [1962] 1 Lloyd's Rep 410. In that case b
the assured, under a contract of insurance relating to a ship which was a total loss, made
an agreement with one of his insurers that he would be bound, not only in relation to
that insurer but in relation to all the others, by the result of an action brought in this
country in respect of the loss of the vessel. In the action it was held that the claim must
fail for the reason that the ship was scuttled. None the less, in breach of the bargain that
he had made with the first insurer, the assured sought to bring fresh proceedings in c
Greece. It was held by Megaw J that, having regard to the agreement to be bound, the
assured's proceedings in Greece were vexatious and oppressive and that the facts warranted
a conclusion that the assured had sufficient connection with this country to give the
English courts jurisdiction to grant an injunction restraining the assured, albeit resident
elsewhere, from instituting proceedings whether in England or elsewhere in relation to
the same subject matter. It is to be noted that for reasons which no doubt seemed good d
to him the assured, in the action before Megaw J, had refrained from entering an
appearance.

From those cases I conclude that, where a contract contains an agreement, especially
where it is supported by a Scott v Avery clause, to submit disputes to arbitration in
London, the parties to the contract have sufficient connection with this country to give
the English courts jurisdiction to grant an injunction restraining either party, even e
though resident abroad, from instituting or maintaining proceedings abroad in breach
of the arbitration clause. This is, however, a discretionary jurisdiction to be exercised
with great caution. The more remote the connection with this country, and the more
that foreign courts have become involved in the matter, the greater is the caution called
for.

Counsel for the sellers argues that there was clear breach here by the buyers in starting f
proceedings in Switzerland. The sellers had to challenge the proceedings to validate the
sequestration or alternatively do nothing and allow the buyers to obtain judgment by
default. He contends that the sellers have not waived their right to enforce the arbitration
clause. He remarks that the Swiss proceedings have not as yet been concerned with the
merits of the claims for damages, for those claims depend in particular on certificates of
quality which the Federation of Oils, Seeds and Fats Associations Ltd (FOSFA) arbitrators g
are peculiarly fitted to assess. In the result, says counsel, I should exercise my discretion
to grant an injunction for the reason in particular that the security would remain in
Switzerland for one year. The security is in any event of doubtful value, and in so far as
the buyers have incurred costs in Switzerland, they took their chance by electing to
proceed there in breach of the arbitration agreement.

Against this, counsel for the buyers argues that there has at all times been available in h
Switzerland what he calls a 'swift, effective remedy' for the sellers. That which they
applied for, known as a 'requête de déclinatoire', is the exact equivalent of a stay in the
English courts. It is available in aid of a Swiss or foreign action or arbitration. Switzerland,
he reminds the court, is a party to the New York Convention (Convention of the
Recognition and Enforcement of Foreign Arbitral Awards (New York, 31 December
1958, TS 20 (1976); Cmnd 6419)). The remedy afforded by the Swiss courts was swift j
and also convenient. Moreover, counsel asserts, the Swiss court, if it had been told what
the English law is, would have applied it. The factors which he urges on me in exercising
my discretion are these. First, he says that the security is not to be treated as being of
little worth. If it had been, those proceedings which are known to be on foot, involving

not only these parties but also the banks in Switzerland in respect of the security, would hardly have been warranted. Second, he says that the obedience of the buyers to any injunction issued in this court is not to be assumed,. because even though they may continue in the peanut trade it is not to be supposed that they would be successfully ostracised altogether in the event that they sought to disregard the order of the court. Third, counsel urges that the buyers have real merit in relation to what I have called the basic dispute, however little those merits have been allowed to emerge on either side in the present proceedings. Finally, he reminds me of what the attitude of the Swiss court might be expected to be to any injunction issued in this court.

The question therefore is whether in the exercise of my discretion I should hold that the buyers are entitled to pursue what they acknowledge is the wrong procedure because the sellers failed to take the point in Switzerland which would have demonstrated that the arbitration clause was incorporated into the contract. On the one hand, it is said that the sellers, having unsuccessfully sought a stay in Switzerland, ought still to be able to obtain an injunction in the English court to stop Swiss proceedings which would otherwise run parallel with the English arbitration and in which no judgment would be recognised by the English court. On the other hand, the remedy which the sellers elected to pursue in Switzerland only failed there because of the sellers' own error, and so the buyers argue that the sellers should not be entitled to prevent the Swiss action from proceeding.

Over a hundred years ago, in *Godard v Gray* (1870) LR 6 QB 139 at 154, one member of the court, Hannen J, gave reasons for his decision which appear to me to be apposite in the present case. It is not necessary for present purposes to refer to the facts of that case but only to cite the passage which is applicable here, if for 'French' where it is there used one substitutes 'Swiss':

> 'It does not appear upon the face of the proceedings, nor at all, that the French Court was informed of what the English law was. It was the duty of the defendants to bring to the knowledge of the French Court the provision of the English law on which they now for the first time rely, and having failed to do so, they must submit to the consequences of their own negligence. The French Courts, like our own, can only be informed of foreign law by appropriate evidence, and the party who fails to produce it cannot afterwards impeach the judgment obtained against him on account of an error into which the foreign Court has fallen presumably in consequence of his own default.'

For that passage to be applicable here, one must also substitute for the word 'presumably' in the last sentence the word 'admittedly'. In my judgment the sellers have forfeited their right to expect that the English court would intervene to protect their interests. At the outset they would have had the opportunity of applying for an injunction if they had had any reason to doubt the availability of the remedy they sought in Switzerland, or if they had been able to point to any prospective deficiency in the administration of justice in the foreign court. Their alternative was to apply for a stay in the foreign court. They chose that alternative course. If the foreign court had, without fault on the sellers' part, reached a palpably wrong conclusion then this court might have been justified in intervening. But, where, as here, the foreign court has behaved with perfect propriety and has only reached what to an English lawyer was the wrong conclusion on account of the negligence of the sellers, it seems to me that they no longer merit the assistance of the English court. True it is that this may result in duplicity of proceedings, but that is not a sufficient reason in my judgment for the court to attempt to restrain the plaintiffs from proceeding in their own court, even if the defendants continue to pursue the contractual remedy of arbitration.

In case I was not in his favour on that point counsel for the buyers relied on two subsidiary arguments with which in the circumstances I need not fully deal. The first such argument was to this effect, that the consequence of the Civil Jurisdiction and

Judgments Act 1982 is that the court is prevented from recognising or enforcing a foreign judgment notwithstanding that a party has entered a plea requesting a stay of proceedings on the ground that the dispute should be decided under an arbitration agreement. But although that is the effect of the statute counsel contends that the position at common law remains the same. The result is that if there is left untouched by the 1982 Act a voluntary submission to the jurisdiction, albeit in the form of the entry of a plea requesting a stay of proceedings on the ground that the dispute should be decided under an arbitration agreement, that still precludes the court from making such an injunction as is here sought. About that argument I need only say that it would indeed be an unfortunate result if, where a person appears in the foreign court for a purpose which would not relieve the court from its duty not to recognise or enforce a foreign judgment, the court could not in the same circumstances issue an injunction to prevent the prosecution of proceedings abroad which could only result in a judgment of that character.

Counsel's second subsidiary argument for the buyers was simply that the sellers were guilty of delay, not having pursued their remedy diligently. For present purposes I would regard delay as the avoidable time during which proceedings last longer than they should last. An action having been initiated by the buyers in Switzerland, it seems to me that the sellers were entitled to object to the jurisdiction there in the manner that they have and that they have not made those proceedings or any proceedings more protracted than they should have been.

Before parting with this case let me add one comment. As I said at the beginning, the dispute between the parties is or ought to be about peanuts. It reflects little credit on the lawyers in this country or in Switzerland on either side that the matter has so far been before the courts of this country on about ten different days, before three different Commercial judges, and has engaged the courts of Switzerland probably for a similar number of days up to and including their ultimate court of appeal. What the parties ought now to do, as it appears to the detached observer, with or without the assistance of their lawyers, is to decide on a forum for the trial of their dispute. On the face of it that should be by arbitration in London but with suitable safeguards no doubt as to the sequestrated assets. The parties would of course be entitled to make any other arrangement they chose, but they should bear in mind that if they make no arrangement at all it is only the lawyers who will continue to benefit, or perhaps I should say 'profit'. Meanwhile in these proceedings the counterclaim is dismissed.

Counterclaim dismissed.

Solicitors: *William A Crump & Son* (for the sellers); *Richards Butler & Co* (for the buyers).

K Mydeen Esq Barrister.

a

Note
Unilever Computer Services Ltd v Tiger Leasing SA

COURT OF APPEAL, CIVIL DIVISION
b SIR JOHN DONALDSON MR, DILLON LJ AND SIR GEORGE BAKER
9 MARCH 1983

Practice – Hearing – Date – Fixed date – Vacation of date fixed for hearing – Matters on which court must be satisfied before it will allow date to be vacated.

c **Summons**

By a summons dated 8 March 1983 the plaintiffs, Unilever Computer Services Ltd, applied to vacate the date fixed for the hearing on an appeal by the plaintiffs against the decision of Staughton J on 13 July 1981 whereby he ordered judgment for £190,787·80 to be entered for the defendants, Tiger Leasing SA (formerly National Equipment Rental SA), on the plaintiffs' claim and on the defendants' counterclaim.

d

Michael Turner QC for the plaintiffs.
Christopher Moger for the defendants.

SIR JOHN DONALDSON MR. This is an application on behalf of the appellant plaintiffs to vacate the date for the hearing of the appeal, which has been fixed for e Monday, 14 March 1983. That date was fixed last autumn. The basis of the application is that counsel for the plaintiffs has been overcome by the misfortunes of litigation in that he undertook a brief which could not reasonably have been anticipated to conflict with this appeal; but Parkinson's law, or some other law, has operated, and the case is going on for a very long time.

The application is opposed on good commercial grounds because this is a very stale f appeal and the respondent defendants wish to enter into various transactions, for the purpose of which it is necessary for them to know what their position is in relation to the plaintiffs' claim. In those circumstances, this application cannot be granted.

I would like to make it clear that, where this court has fixed dates, it will require cogent reasons why a date shall be vacated. This is not a matter of the judges being tiresome or standing on their dignity or anything of that sort. It is that we have a very g large backlog of appeals, and it is quite impossible to get through them if fixed dates are to be vacated and we are to be permanently juggling with lists. I understand that it is generally believed amongst barristers' clerks that there is no problem at all about vacating a date if both parties are agreed. I should like to make it clear that that is not the case. There will still be problems. Certainly in such a case the court will normally require to be satisfied that the lay clients on both sides fully understand the consequences of the h date being vacated, and both agree. In that situation it may very well be that the court will be prepared to vacate the date, although it by no means follows that an early substitute date will be able to be provided.

So far as this application is concerned, it must be refused.

Application refused.

Solicitors: *Stanleys & Simpson North* (for the plaintiffs); *Cameron Markby* (for the defendants).

Frances Rustin Barrister.

Prasad and another v Wolverhampton Borough Council

COURT OF APPEAL, CIVIL DIVISION
STEPHENSON, FOX AND KERR LJJ
20, 21 DECEMBER 1982, 21 FEBRUARY 1983

Housing – Compulsory purchase – Compensation – Compensation for disturbance – Displacement from land 'in consequence of' compulsory acquisition – In consequence of – Claimants' house subject to compulsory purchase order – Claimants vacating house shortly before notice to treat served by local authority – Whether claimants displaced 'in consequence of' compulsory acquisition – Whether claimants entitled to compensation for disturbance – Land Compensation Act 1973, s 37(1)(a).

In December 1977 the appellants purchased a house which was in an area declared by the local council to be a clearance area under s 42 of the Housing Act 1957 and which was subject to a compulsory purchase order made under s 43 of that Act. The appellants lived in the house until October 1979 when they vacated it. On 2 November the council served a notice to treat on the appellants, who then lodged a claim against the council for, inter alia, compensation for disturbance under s 37(1)(*a*)[a] of the Land Compensation Act 1973. The question arose whether, for the purposes of s 37(1)(*a*), the appellants had been 'displaced from . . . land in consequence of . . . the acquisition of the land' by the council. The council took the view that because the appellants had vacated the land before the notice to treat was served they had not been displaced 'in consequence of' the compulsory acquisition of the land and were therefore not entitled to compensation under s 37(1) for disturbance. The appellants appealed to the Lands Tribunal, which held that the appellants were not entitled to compensation for disturbance. The appellants appealed to the Court of Appeal. At the hearing of the appeal the council contended that there could be no acquisition unless and until a notice to treat was served and therefore there could be no displacement 'in consequence of' the acquisition until after the notice to treat was served.

Held – On the true construction of s 37 of the 1973 Act the requirement that a claimant must be displaced from land 'in consequence of' the compulsory acquisition of that land before he was entitled to compensation for disturbance was a causal, and not necessarily a temporal, requirement. Accordingly, a person was displaced 'in consequence of' the compulsory acquisition if he was displaced by reason of the acquisition, and he was therefore entitled to compensation for disturbance for all losses naturally and reasonably incurred by reason of the acquisition, including losses incurred in anticipation of, and prior to, the land actually being acquired. In any event, the disturbance had to be related to the 'acquisition' of the land rather than to the notice to treat, which was but one step in the prolonged process of 'acquisition'. The appellants were therefore entitled to compensation for loss reasonably incurred by reason of the council's acquisition of their house and the case would be remitted to the Lands Tribunal for assessment of such compensation (see p 146 *b c*, p 150 *c* to *e*, p 151 *h j*, p 152 *a*, p 153 *a* to *g*, p 155 *d f*, p 156 *b* to *j* and p 157 *c* to *g*, post).

Smith v Strathclyde Regional Council (1980) 42 P & CR 397 and *Sim v Aberdeen City DC* (1982) 264 EG 621 followed.

Per curiam. Loss of trade or business which results not from quitting a particular property but because, for example, the threat of impending compulsory purchase and demolition in the area has caused trade to fall away is not compensatable under s 37 of the 1973 Act (see p 155 *e* to *g*, post).

---

a Section 37(1) is set out at p 142 *j* to p 143 *b*, post

Notes

a For the right to compensation for disturbance, see 8 Halsbury's Laws (4th edn) paras 341–342.

For the Housing Act 1957, ss 42, 43, see 16 Halsbury's Statutes (3rd edn) 150, 151.

For the Land Compensation Act 1973, s 37, see 43 ibid 203.

Cases referred to in judgments

b *Adams v London and Blackwall Rly Co* (1850) 2 Mac & G 118, 42 ER 46, LC.
Bailey v Derby Corp [1965] 1 All ER 443, [1965] 1 WLR 213, CA.
Birmingham City Corp v West Midland Baptist (Trust) Association (Inc) [1969] 3 All ER 172, [1970] AC 874, [1969] 3 WLR 389, HL.
Bloom (Kosher) & Sons Ltd v Tower Hamlets London Borough (1977) 35 P & CR 423, Lands Tribunal.
c *Bostock Chater & Sons Ltd v Chelmsford Corp* (1973) 26 P & CR 321, Lands Tribunal.
Capital Investments Ltd v Wednesfield UDC [1964] 1 All ER 655, [1965] Ch 774, [1964] 2 WLR 932.
Harding v Metropolitan Rly Co (1872) 7 Ch App 154, LC.
Harvey v Crawley Development Corp [1957] 1 All ER 504, [1957] 1 QB 485, [1957] 2 WLR 332, CA.
d *Haynes v Haynes* (1861) 1 Drew & Sm 426, 62 ER 442.
Horn v Sunderland Corp [1941] 1 All ER 480, [1941] 2 KB 26, CA.
Lanarkshire and Dumbartonshire Rly Co v Main (1895) 22 R (Ct of Sess) 912.
Newham London Borough Council v Benjamin [1968] 1 All ER 1195, [1968] 1 WLR 694, CA.
R v Stone (1866) LR 1 QB 529.
Rugby Joint Water Board v Shaw-Fox [1972] 1 All ER 1057, [1973] AC 202, [1972] 2 WLR
e 757, HL.
Sim v Aberdeen City DC (1982) 264 EG 621, CS; *affg* (1981) 258 EG 451, Lands Tribunal for Scotland.
Smith v Strathclyde Regional Council (1980) 42 P & CR 397, Lands Tribunal for Scotland.
Tiverton and North Devon Rly Co v Loosemore (1884) 9 App Cas 480, HL.
Venables v Dept of Agriculture for Scotland 1932 SC 573.
f *Walters Brett and Park v South Glamorgan CC* (1976) 32 P & CR 111, Lands Tribunal.
Webb v Stockport Corp (1962) 13 P & CR 339.
Widden (G E) & Co Ltd v Kensington and Chelsea London Borough Council (1970) 10 RVR 160, Lands Tribunal.

Case stated

g Sachindra Prasad (Dr Prasad) and his wife, Bindu Prasad, appealed by way of case stated from a decision of the Lands Tribunal (W H Rees Esq) given on 31 March 1981 awarding the appellants £150 compensation, being the site value of the freehold property at 38 Salisbury Street, Wolverhampton acquired from the appellants by the Wolverhampton Borough Council (the acquiring authority) under a compulsory purchase order. On 10 November 1982 the Court of Appeal (Stephenson, Fox and Kerr LJJ) dismissed all but
h one of the appellants' grounds of appeal and adjourned the appeal for further hearing of that ground, namely whether the appellants were entitled to compensation for disturbance under s 37 of the Land Compensation Act 1973. In the course of giving judgment in the Court of Appeal on 10 November Stephenson LJ found the following facts. What the Lands Tribunal had to decide was the disputed question of compensation, referred to it under s 6 of the Compulsory Purchase Act 1965, and to decide how much
j compensation was payable by the acquiring authority for its compulsory acquisition of the Prasads' property, 38 Salisbury Street, Wolverhampton, under ss 42 and 43 of the Housing Act 1957. On 16 March 1977 the acquiring authority had passed a resolution declaring the area in which the subject property of the appellants was to be a clearance area under s 42 of the 1957 Act. On 11 November 1977 the acquiring authority included no 38 in a compulsory purchase order, the Wolverhampton Borough Council (Salisbury

Street) Compulsory Purchase Order 1977, an order made under s 43 of the 1957 Act. Both in declaring it a clearance area and in making the compulsory purchase order, the appellants' property was declared to be unfit for human habitation. On 6 December 1977 the appellants bought the property, the previous owner having died not long before, and they bought the freehold from an intermediate owner. They lived there from 5 December 1977 until a date which was not precisely ascertained but which appeared to have been October 1979, although it was contended by Dr Prasad that it was the end of 1979. From October 1978 until about that time, Dr Prasad used part of the premises as his surgery, he being a general practitioner. On 21 August 1979 the Secretary of State confirmed the compulsory purchase order. On 2 November 1979 the acquiring authority served a notice to treat and a notice of entry on Dr Prasad only, and not on his wife, and on 16 November entry was made. On 19 November the acquiring authority ordered a building company to demolish the property. On 1 January 1980, as found by the tribunal, the acquiring authority changed its mind and decided to include no 38 in an industrial improvement area, not in a slum clearance area; and on 12 June 1980 the acquiring authority reallocated the subject property from residential to industrial use. In those circumstances the appellants claimed a sum of compensation in excess of £90,000 (including £39,000 for loss of business), while the acquiring authority maintained that they were only entitled to £150, the site value, plus a sum of £28·75 surveyor's fee. The bulk of the appellants' claim related to the value of the site as industrial land, the cost of modernising the house, the loss of business suffered by Dr Prasad through losing patients when demolition was in the air, and compensation for the failure of the acquiring authority to provide him and his wife with any alternative accommodation. The Lands Tribunal rejected all the appellants' claims and held that they were only entitled to the site value, which was given in evidence by a Mr Powis, an associate of the Royal Institute of Chartered Surveyors and a member of the valuation department of the Inland Revenue. His evidence was that the site value was £150; that was accepted by the tribunal and, in so far as other evidence was directed by two surveyors called by Dr Prasad to that issue, the tribunal preferred the evidence of Mr Powis to the evidence of those surveyors.

Dr Prasad appeared in person representing both appellants.
Alan Fletcher for the acquiring authority.
Simon D Brown as amicus curiae.

Cur adv vult

21 February. The following judgments were delivered.

STEPHENSON LJ. I have stated the nature of this appeal and the facts of the case in the judgment which I gave, with the agreement of Fox and Kerr LJJ, on 10 November 1982 ([1982] CA Bound Transcript 443). I incorporate what I then said without repeating it in the judgment which I now give.

We then rejected all the appellants' grounds of appeal save one, and we adjourned the hearing of the appeal on the one ground only, as Dr Prasad was appearing in person for his wife and himself without legal assistance or qualifications and it appeared to us and to counsel on behalf of the respondent council (the acquiring authority) to raise a point of law which had been the subject of conflicting decisions in England and Scotland and which called for the help of an amicus curiae.

This remaining head of claim is made under s 63 of the Housing Act 1957, now replaced by ss 37 and 38 of the Land Compensation Act 1973, the statute which now deals with what it calls 'disturbance payments' as follows:

> '**37.**—(1) Where a person is displaced from any land in consequence of—(*a*) the acquisition of the land by an authority possessing compulsory purchase powers; (*b*) the making, passing or acceptance of a housing order, resolution or undertaking in respect of a house or building on the land; (*c*) where the land has been previously

acquired by an authority possessing compulsory purchase powers or appropriated
a by a local authority and is for the time being held by the authority for the purposes for which it was acquired or appropriated, the carrying out of redevelopment on the land, he shall, subject to the provisions of this section, be entitled to receive a payment (hereafter referred to as a "disturbance payment") from the acquiring authority, the authority who made the order, passed the resolution or accepted the undertaking or the authority carrying out the redevelopment, as the case may be.

b (2) A person shall not be entitled to a disturbance payment—(*a*) in any case, unless he is in lawful possession of the land from which he is displaced; (*b*) in a case within subsection (1)(*a*) above, unless either—(i) he has no interest in the land for the acquisition or extinguishment of which he is (or if the acquisition or extinguishment were compulsory would be) entitled to compensation under any other enactment; or (ii) he has such an interest as aforesaid but the compensation is
c subject to a site value provision and he is not (or if the acquisition were compulsory would not be) entitled in respect of that acquisition to an owner-occupier's supplement; (*c*) in a case within subsection (1)(*b*) above, if he is entitled to an owner-occupier's supplement by reference to the order, resolution or undertaking. In this subsection "site value provision" means section 29(2) or 59(2) of the Housing Act 1957, section 20 of the Housing (Scotland) Act 1966 or section 10 of the Housing
d (Scotland) Act 1969 and "owner-occupier's supplement" means a payment under Part II of Schedule 2 to the said Act of 1957, Schedule 5 to the Housing Act 1969 or sections 18 to 20 of the Housing (Scotland) Act 1969.

(3) For the purposes of subsection (1) above a person shall not be treated as displaced in consequence of any such acquisition or redevelopment as is mentioned in paragraph (*a*) or (*c*) of that subsection unless he was in lawful possession of the
e land—(*a*) in the case of land acquired under a compulsory purchase order, at the time when notice was first published of the making of the compulsory purchase order prior to its submission for confirmation or, where the order did not require confirmation, of the preparation of the order in draft; (*b*) in the case of land acquired under an Act specifying the land as subject to compulsory acquisition, at the time when the provisions of the Bill for that Act specifying the land were first published;
f (*c*) in the case of land acquired by agreement, at the time when the agreement was made; and a person shall not be treated as displaced in consequence of any such order, resolution or undertaking as is mentioned in paragraph (*b*) of that subsection unless he was in lawful possession as aforesaid at the time when the order was made, the resolution was passed or the undertaking was accepted . . .

(6) A disturbance payment shall carry interest, at the rate for the time being
g prescribed under section 32 of the Land Compensation Act 1961 or, in Scotland, section 40 of the Land Compensation (Scotland) Act 1963, from the date of displacement until payment . . .

(10) This section applies if the date of displacement is on or after 17th October 1972.

38.—(1) The amount of a disturbance payment shall be equal to—(*a*) the
h reasonable expenses of the person entitled to the payment in removing from the land from which he is displaced; and (*b*) if he was carrying on a trade or business on that land, the loss he will sustain by reason of the disturbance of that trade or business consequent upon his having to quit the land.

(2) In estimating the loss of any person for the purposes of subsection (1)(*b*) above, regard shall be had to the period for which the land occupied by him may reasonably
j have been expected to be available for the purposes of his trade or business and to the availability of other land suitable for that purpose. This subsection has effect subject to section 46(7) below . . .

(4) Any dispute as to the amount of a disturbance payment shall be referred to and determined by the Lands Tribunal or, in Scotland, the Lands Tribunal for Scotland.'

The items of this claim are not precisely defined either in Dr Prasad's notice of appeal or in his so-called pleadings. But it is the sort of loss specified in s 38(1), expenses of moving and loss of patients and consequent financial loss, for which Dr Prasad seeks compensation. In his claim to the Lands Tribunal he put the amount of that loss at no less than £39,000. That was item 5 of his claim; the Lands Tribunal dealt with that in this way:

> 'With regard to item 5, Mr Powis' evidence that Dr Prasad vacated the subject premises at the end of 1979 [and it looks as if that means October 1979] before he had received notice to treat, was not contested. Having regard to that, the acquiring authority's solicitor [Mr Webb] submitted that the claimant was not entitled to compensation for disturbance and in that connection he referred me to *Walters Brett and Park v South Glamorgan CC* (1976) 32 P & CR 111 and *Bloom (Kosher) & Sons Ltd v Tower Hamlets London Borough* (1977) 35 P & CR 423. The claimant said that he had had to move because large numbers of houses close to his surgery had been demolished and he lost his patients in consequence. I accept the submission made by the acquiring authority's solicitor and determine that no compensation is payable in respect of item 5 of the claim; in any event the figure of £39,000 is quite unsupported.'

Counsel for the acquiring authority I think ultimately conceded that that was simply a conclusion by the member that the claim was bad in law, not that it was unsupported by any facts. He was following the authorities cited to him and indicating that if he had felt able to depart from them he could not think that the appellants' loss and expenses before the notice to treat could come to anything like £39,000.

The acquiring authority acted under Part III of the Housing Act 1957. The relevant provisions of that part are ss 42, 43, 47 and 59, as follows:

> '**42.**—(1) Where a local authority ... are satisfied as respects any area in their district—(*a*) that the houses in that area are unfit for human habitation ... the authority shall cause that area to be defined on a map ... and shall pass a resolution declaring the area so defined to be a clearance area, that is to say, an area to be cleared of all buildings in accordance with the subsequent provisions of this Part of this Act ...
>
> **43.**—(1) So soon as may be after a local authority have declared any area to be a clearance area, they shall, subject to and in accordance with the provisions of this Part of this Act, proceed to secure the clearance of the area in one or other of the following ways, or partly in one of those ways and partly in the other of them, that is to say—(*a*) by making one or more orders (in this Act referred to as "clearance orders") for the demolition of the buildings in the area; or (*b*) by purchasing the land comprised in the area and themselves undertaking, or otherwise securing, the demolition of the buildings on that land ...
>
> **47.**—(1) Subject to the provisions of the next following section, a local authority who have under this Part of this Act purchased any land comprised in, or surrounded by, or adjoining, a clearance area shall, so soon as may be, cause every building thereon to be vacated and shall deal with that land in one or other of the following ways, or partly in one of these ways and partly in the other of them, that is to say—(*a*) they shall demolish every building thereon before the expiration of six weeks from the date on which it is vacated, or before the expiration of such longer period as in the circumstances they deem reasonable ...
>
> **59.**—(1) Where land is purchased compulsorily by a local authority under this Part of this Act, the compensation payable in respect thereof shall be assessed in accordance with the Acquisition of Land (Assessment of Compensation) Act, 1919, subject to the following provisions of this section.
>
> (2) The compensation to be paid for the land, including any buildings thereon, purchased as being land comprised in a clearance area shall be the value at the time

the valuation is made of the land as a site cleared of buildings and available for development in accordance with the requirements of the building byelaws for the time being in force in the district . . .'

The right to compensation seems limited until inspection of the 1919 Act reveals that it preserves what has been called the common law right to compensation for disturbance. Section 2 of that Act provides rules for compensation, including rr (2) and (6):

> '(2) The value of land shall, subject as hereinafter provided, be taken to be the amount which the land if sold in the open market by a willing seller might be expected to realise: Provided always that the arbitrator shall be entitled to consider all returns and assessments of capital value for taxation made or aquiesced in by the claimant . . .
>
> (6) The provisions of Rule (2) shall not affect the assessment of compensation for disturbance or any other matter not directly based on the value of land.'

The effect of that last provision was stated by Greene MR in *Horn v Sunderland Corp* [1941] 1 All ER 480 at 485, [1941] 2 KB 26 at 34, as follows:

> 'Rule (6) does not confer a right to claim compensation for disturbance. It merely leaves unaffected the right which, before the Act of 1919, the owner would have had in a proper case to claim that the compensation to be paid for the land should be increased on the ground that he had been disturbed.'

That section is now re-enacted in s 5 of the Land Compensation Act 1961 with the same numbered rules.

The appellants were displaced, apparently in October 1979, from their house, 38 Salisbury Street, Wolverhampton, which was acquired by an authority possessing compulsory purchase powers. But were they displaced 'in consequence of its acquisition'? The answer depends on the true construction of those words in their context. For unless they were displaced in consequence of the council's acquisition of their land they were not entitled to disturbance payments under s 37 as defined in s 38. Counsel for the acquiring authority contended, and contends, that they were not so displaced because they left house and land before the notice to treat on 2 November 1979: no acquisition till notice to treat; no displacement in consequence of acquisition till after notice to treat, because 'in consequence of' means 'following in point of time', 'after as well as because of'. So they have no right to a disturbance payment and the member was right to confine their compensation to the site value of the land under s 59(2) of the Housing Act 1957.

That is the normal rule of the Lands Tribunal in England laid down in 1962 and followed in other cases decided before and after the Land Compensation Act 1973, including this case: see *Webb v Stockport Corp* (1962) 13 P & CR 339; *G E Widden & Co Ltd v Kensington and Chelsea London Borough Council* (1970) 10 RVR 160; *Bostock Chater & Sons Ltd v Chelmsford Corp* (1973) 26 P & CR 321; *Walters Brett and Park v South Glamorgan CC* (1976) 32 P & CR 111; *Bloom (Kosher) & Sons Ltd v Tower Hamlets London Borough* (1977) 35 P & CR 423. In the last of these cases Mr V G Wellings QC put the matter clearly and succinctly in different ways (at 430, 434):

> 'I cannot accept that a loss is consequent upon an acquisition if it is incurred before there *is* an acquisition . . . loss which precedes an acquisition cannot, in my view, be regarded as a consequence of it.'

If loss precedes acquisition, a fortiori displacement which causes loss precedes acquisition and cannot be consequent on it or a consequence of it.

But counsel for the acquiring authority drew our attention, in discharge of his duty as counsel, to two decisions of the Lands Tribunal for Scotland, one of which had been affirmed by the Court of Session, which allowed losses or expenses incurred before a notice to treat; and it was to resolve the apparent conflict between the two countries that we invited the assistance of an amicus curiae. The basis for allowing such losses was that they are caused by the dispossession caused by the compulsory acquisition and in that sense, though not in time, both dispossession and the losses caused by it are consequences of the acquisition.

Counsel for the acquiring authority submits that the Scottish decisions are wrong and have no application to the construction of s 37 of the English statute, and that the appellants are not entitled to any disturbance payment by reason of the fact that before service of the notice to treat they have removed themselves from the premises compulsorily acquired by the council.

Counsel as amicus curiae, in discharge of his duty to help the court, has felt bound to resist counsel for the acquiring authority's support of the English decisions, including that under appeal, and to argue for a generous construction of ss 37 and 38 in support of the appellants' case on this point. He submits that the requirement that a claimant must be displaced from land in consequence of the compulsory acquisition is to be treated as a causal but not necessarily a temporal qualification; the requirement is satisfied if the displacement is caused by, occurs by reason of, a compulsory acquisition; it does not have to follow the acquisition temporarily, in temporal sequence, in point of time.

If the argument of counsel as amicus curiae on the meaning of 'consequent on' be right, there is no need to consider the meaning of 'the acquisition' and whether it means, as counsel for the acquiring authority argues, the completion of the acquisition by notice to treat. It is admittedly not till notice to treat is given that a relationship analogous to that of vendor and purchaser is established: see *Tiverton and North Devon Rly Co v Loosemore* (1884) 9 App Cas 480. Admittedly also, many years may elapse between an authority's resolution to acquire, or the threat of it, and confirmation of a compulsory purchase order, and subsequent notice to treat. And it cannot be disputed that it is often wise, and not always risky, for a person threatened with the compulsory acquisition of his property to find alternative accommodation which may put him to expense and which may cause disturbance and loss of trade or business. Such prudent anticipation may mitigate the loss resulting from losing the property, whereas waiting to move till the last moment may increase the dispossessed person's loss.

At the time when the Land Compensation Act 1973 was passed, compensation for disturbance was payable to landowners dispossessed by compulsory acquisition of their land. Such landowners had to find other property on which to live or to carry on their business, and that might be expensive and cause them compensatable loss. Lord Reid said in *Birmingham City Corp v West Midland Baptist (Trust) Association (Inc)* [1969] 3 All ER 172 at 175, 178, [1970] AC 874 at 893, 896–897 of the compensation payable under the Lands Clauses Consolidation Act 1845 to such a landowner with a business or trade:

> 'If he wishes to continue his activities he will not only have to obtain other premises but he will have to pay costs of removal and if he is carrying on business the move may cause loss of profits and other loss. He will not be fully compensated unless all this is taken into account.'

And again that an owner's claim—

> 'might include costs of removal, loss of profits or other consequential loss and there appears to be no suggestion in the authorities that these elements in the value of land to the owner must be valued as at the date of the notice to treat. The actual costs or losses following an actual dispossession have been taken, and that appears to be the accepted practice today with regard to claims under r. (6) [of the 1919 Act].'

That decision removed the date for assessing compensation from the date of the service of the notice to treat to the date on which the work of equivalent reinstatement pursuant to s 2, r (5) of the 1919 Act might normally have been commenced. In deciding that case the House of Lords was not concerned with loss incurred *in anticipation of* compulsory acquisition, but Lord Reid refers to full compensation for costs and losses 'following an actual dispossession' and leaves open the question we have to consider and indeed the question when that dispossession 'actually' takes place. The same is true of the Court of

Appeal in decisions including *Harvey v Crawley Development Corp* [1957] 1 All ER 504, [1957] 1 QB 485 and *Bailey v Derby Corp* [1965] 1 All ER 443, [1965] 1 WLR 213.

In the former case Mrs Harvey received compensation from the Lands Tribunal and this court for removal expenses, solicitors' and surveyors' costs and travelling expenses all incurred after notice to treat. Denning LJ said ([1957] 1 All ER 504 at 506, [1957] 1 QB 485 at 492):

> 'It seems to me that, as these costs of £241 10s. 1d. were reasonably incurred by the freeholder [Mrs Harvey] in getting another house, they can fairly be regarded as a direct consequence of the compulsory acquisition. Prima facie, therefore, they fall within the heading of compensation for disturbance.'

Romer LJ said ([1957] 1 All ER 504 at 507–508, [1957] 1 QB 485 at 494–495):

> 'The authorities to which our attention was drawn establish that any loss sustained by a dispossessed owner (at all events one who occupies his house) which flows from a compulsory acquisition may properly be regarded as the subject of compensation for disturbance, provided, first, that it is not too remote and, secondly, that it is the natural and reasonable consequence of the dispossession of the owner . . . The natural thing for a dispossessed owner-occupier to do is to buy another home of a comparable kind, and that in fact is what the freeholder [Mrs Harvey] did . . . I would only add that the tribunal's decision in this case seems to me not only to be right in law but to accord with common sense. I cannot help feeling that the contrary view would lead to a great deal of discontentment on compulsory acquisitions. It is bad enough in itself for a person to be compulsorily dispossessed of his home, but it is worse if he has himself to bear expenses of the kind which are in issue in the present case in finding another house in which to live.'

Sellers LJ said ([1957] 1 All ER 504 at 508, [1957] 1 QB 485 at 496):

> 'The evidence in this case would seem to show that the tribunal were entirely justified in saying that this particular expenditure in relation to the acquirement of new premises—it may be that the abortive expenditure was a misfortune, but no distinction is made between the two—is expenditure which was directly arising from the circumstance that this lady had to find another house in which to live by reason of being compulsorily dispossessed of her home.'

In *Bailey*'s case [1965] 1 All ER 443 at 445, [1965] 1 WLR 213 at 219 Lord Denning MR said:

> 'You must first ascertain the value of the land. That must be taken as at the date of the notice to treat. Next, you must ascertain the compensation for disturbance, as it is called. That must be ascertained by looking at what has in fact happened since the notice to treat. He can get compensation for his loss due to the acquisition; provided, in the words of ROMER, L.J., in *Harvey* v. *Crawley Development Corpn.*: ". . . first, that it is not too remote, and, secondly, that it is the natural and reasonable consequence of the dispossession of the owner." '

And he spoke of the compensation to which Mr Bailey was entitled as 'compensation for his loss by reason of the acquisition of the land'. In *Bailey*'s case Lord Denning MR's statement was made before the *West Midland Baptist (Trust) Association* case [1969] 3 All ER 172, [1970] AC 874 had shifted the date for valuation (although not the date for ascertaining the nature of the owner's interest: see *Rugby Joint Water Board v Shaw-Fox* [1972] 1 All ER 1057, [1973] AC 202) from the date of the notice to treat. In *Harvey*'s case the language of Romer and Sellers LJJ is general enough not to exclude costs and loss reasonably incurred in anticipation of a notice to treat leading to final or legal dispossession. So also is the judgment of the Lord Justice Clerk (Alness) in the Court of Session in *Venables v Dept of Agriculture for Scotland* 1932 SC 573 at 581 (a decision approved in *Harvey*'s case [1957] 1 All ER 804, [1957] 1 QB 485) where Lord Alness

quoted with approval the dictum of Lord Kinnear (cited later) in *Lanarkshire and
Dumbartonshire Rly Co v Main* (1895) 22 R (Ct of Sess) 912 at 919 and went on to say: a

> 'The sound principle would seem to be that the person dispossessed should get
> compensation for *all* loss occasioned to him by reason of his dispossession. The Act
> of 1845 recognises that; the text-books recognise it; judicial authority recognises it;
> and the Act of 1919 continues to the evicted owner all claims formerly open to him
> ...' (My emphasis.) b

The principle stated by Romer LJ in *Harvey*'s case and by Lord Alness in *Venables*'s case
was applied by the Lands Tribunal for Scotland (Lord Elliott and William Hall Esq
FRICS) to fees of a quantity surveyor, an architect, a valuer and a solicitor amounting to
£3,663·78 reasonably incurred, some of them before the date of the deemed notice to
treat, in *Smith v Strathclyde Regional Council* (1980) 42 P & CR 397. In *Sim v Aberdeen City
DC* (1981) 258 EG 451 on 18 February 1981 the Lands Tribunal for Scotland (Mr Hall c
sitting alone) followed that decision in allowing as compensation for disturbance
solicitors' fees incurred in the owners' purchase of an alternative house when it was
indicated that the compulsory purchase of their own house was likely in the near future,
though in fact they had been incurred nearly five years before the deemed notice to treat,
and even before any resolution of the acquiring authority; and that decision was upheld
by the Court of Session (the Lord Justice Clerk (Lord Wheatley), Lord Robertson and d
Lord Dunpark) on 9 July 1982 (see 264 EG 621). It was there conceded that the appellants'
expenses, if incurred after notice to treat, would have been reasonable and that if it was
legitimate to look at the period before notice to treat it was natural and reasonable to buy
the other house and the expenses of buying it were not too remote.

In these cases no mention is made of the Land Compensation (Scotland) Act 1973, in
which ss 35 and 36 were enacted in terms identical with ss 37 and 38 of the English Act, e
probably because the houses acquired were not unfit. But there the Lands Tribunal, and
now the Court of Session, have refused to follow *Bloom (Kosher) & Sons Ltd v Tower Hamlets
London Borough* (1977) 35 P & CR 423, the last of the line of decisions of the Lands
Tribunal in England to which I have already referred. The Court of Session in *Sim v
Aberdeen City DC* 264 EG 621 at 623–624 said: f

> 'When the issue was debated in this court the argument advanced by counsel,
> although presented from different angles, came to this. The legal position between
> the parties did not come into existence until the notice to treat—or the deemed
> notice to treat—was served. Accordingly the date of the notice to treat was the
> earliest date from which expenses incurred in consequence of the disturbance
> occasioned by the acquisition of the property could legally be claimed, as was g
> decided in *Bloom* ... In the instant case, the expenses claimed were incurred some
> five years prior to the notice to treat, and years prior to the compulsory purchase
> order itself and even prior to the resolution of the appellants' predecessors to
> promote a compulsory purchase order. It was only on the promulgation of the
> compulsory purchase order that the act of acquisition had begun. That submission
> having been advanced and stoutly supported, counsel for the appellants conceded h
> that if the tests adumbrated in *Harvey* ... were applied, and it was legitimate to look
> at the period before the notice to treat was served, the circumstances here were
> sufficient to warrant the decision at which the tribunal arrived ... We could have
> contented ourselves with a simple approval of the decision of the tribunal in *Smith*'s
> case and the reasons given therefor, and holding that this was sufficient to warrant
> the tribunal's decision. However, in recognition of the careful argument put j
> forward by counsel for the appellants we shall express our own reasons, albeit
> somewhat briefly. There appears to be no provision for disturbance in the Land
> Compensation (Scotland) Act 1963 apart from what appears in section 12(6) thereof,
> namely: "The provisions of rule (2) shall not affect the assessment of compensation
> for disturbance or any other matter not directly based on the value of land". Nor is

there any definition of "disturbance" in that Act. In *Venables* . . . Lord Justice Clerk
a Alness quoted with approval the dictum of Lord Kinnear in *Lanarkshire and Dumbartonshire Railway Co v Main* ((1895) 22 R (Ct of Sess) 912 at 919): "It is a well-settled rule in the construction of the Lands Clauses Act (1845) that when lands have been taken in the exercise of [powers of] compulsory purchase, the owner or occupier, as the case may be, is entitled not only to the market value of his interest but to full compensation for *all* the loss which he may sustain by being deprived of
b his land". The italics are ours. Lord Alness went on to say: "If that be sound—and the language is quite general, and the authority of its author unimpeachable—*cadit quaestio*". He summed up the position thus: "The sound principle would seem to be that the person dispossessed should get compensation for *all* loss occasioned to him by reason for his dispossession". Again the italics are ours, and it is to be observed that the words used are "occasioned to him by reason of his dispossession" and not
c "in consequence of his dispossession". He went on to indicate that in these circumstances the onus would be on the person maintaining a restriction to that unqualified statement to establish it. *Venables* is a decision which is binding on this court, and with respect we agree with it. It is a decision which has been accepted, cited with approval and followed in England, as in *Harvey* . . . We accordingly turn to consider whether the appellants have successfully circumvented the generality of
d *Venables.* We start by recalling the concession that if the *tempus inspiciendi* in relation to the expense incurred extends prior to the date of the notice to treat, the circumstances here present satisfy the two tests laid down by Romer LJ in *Harvey* as a matter of fact. The argument for the defenders was based on the use of the word "consequence" by Romer LJ and Denning LJ (as he was then) in *Harvey.* In laying down the second of his conditions, Romer LJ said that the loss had to be the natural
e and reasonable consequence of the dispossession of the owner. Denning LJ said: "Legal costs reasonably incurred in acquiring another house can fairly be regarded as a direct consequence of the compulsory acquisition". It was accordingly argued that "consequence" could only mean "following" in the temporal sense, and that placed the *terminus a quo* of the qualification for compensation as the date of the notice to treat at the earliest. It was only then that dispossession became a reality and
f not just possibly a threat. We have several observations to make on this. The word "consequence" was used in *Harvey* in the circumstances of that case. It would appear that the expenditure in connection with the acquisition of alternative accommodation had been incurred after the development corporation had decided to acquire the plaintiff's house compulsorily and the plaintiff was faced with the request for acquisition. In that situation the word "consequence" could be used both in the
g temporal and in the causal sense. It does not follow that the judges were confining its use to the temporal sense. Such a restriction does not seem to us to march with the broader concept stated by Lord Kinnear and Lord Justice Clerk Alness. The phrase used by the latter was "all loss occasioned by reason of his dispossession". Circumstances might prevail when the threat of dispossession was such that prudence would demand that steps be taken to obtain alternative accommodation
h before the notice to treat was served, since the time available between the service of that notice and the physical dispossession was so short that reasonable alternative accommodation could not be acquired in that period of time. In fact it was said that the period could be restricted to 28 days. The Lord Justice Clerk in *Venables* regarded the claim for disturbance as one of equity. In the absence of any statutory definition or restriction, we regard that as a proper test. It seems to us to be inequitable if a
j claim which satisfies the tests of Romer LJ should be denied the right to compensation because the expenditure was incurred prior to the service of the notice to treat, when similar expenditure incurred subsequent to the service of the notice would be admitted. Provided the tests are satisfied the former situation seems to us to be "a loss *occasioned by reason of his dispossession*". We accordingly take the view that the decision in *Smith* was right and that the tribunal took the right course in following

it in the circumstances of the case. Consequently we do not consider that *Bloom* should be followed. That being so, we reject the submission of the appellants that *a* the date of the notice to treat or indeed any of their alternatives is the necessary *datum* line. As Sellers LJ said, it is a question of fact in each case. Any suggestion that such an extension of the time-limit would expose the appellants to extensive and unjustified liability is countered by the restriction imposed by the tests adumbrated by Romer LJ.'

b The Scottish cases appear to be cases of compensation for disturbance under the law as it existed in England and Scotland from 1845 until 1973, the Land Compensation (Scotland) Act 1963 having the same rules for assessing compensation, including r (6) which preserves the existing right to compensation for disturbance, as the 1919 Act, which applied to both countries, and the English Land Compensation Act 1961. These cases are not therefore authorities on the interpretation of the provisions for statutory *c* disturbance payments in the 1973 Acts. But they do interpret differently, and purport to follow with differing results, from the Lands Tribunal in England the language of judges in both countries, which is sometimes close to the language of those provisions, and I find their reasoning as to the compensation payable for disturbance apart from those statutes compelling. I make no apology for citing also at some length from the earlier decision of the Lands Tribunal for Scotland in *Smith v Strathclyde Regional Council* (1980) *d* 42 P & CR 397, because it exactly expresses better than I can my opinion of the authorities and the principle to be drawn from them and applied to costs and loss incurred in obtaining alternative accommodation to that which is threatened with compulsory acquisition. The tribunal said of the date of the deemed notice of treat (at 405–406):

'The question now arises whether this date [ie the date of the deemed notice to treat] constitutes a dividing line on one side of which "disturbance or other matters" *e* mentioned in rule 6 may be claimed; and on the other side of which they may not even if the items of expenditure were "naturally and reasonably incurred" or "the natural thing for a dispossessed owner-occupier to do"—to quote other passages from the same page of Lord Romer's judgment in *Harvey* v. *Crawley* ([1957] 1 All ER 504, [1957] 1 QB 485). Both Romer L.J. and Denning L.J. in *Harvey* relied on the Scottish case of *Venables* (1932 SC 573) which was one of the first cases in which *f* the nature of a disturbance claim was reconsidered following the passing of the Acquisition of Land (Assessment of Compensation) Act 1919 and in which the so-called rule 6 first appears. In *Venables* the Court of Session emphasised that claims for disturbance do not arise *totidem verbis* from section 2(6) itself but are really based on the original provisions of the Lands Clauses Acts. Lord Justice Clerk Alness referred in particular to sections 17, 19, 71 and 114 of the Lands Clauses *g* Consolidation (Scotland) Act 1845. These sections, which have their English counterparts, will be seen to refer variously to compensation for damage or for any loss or injury that may be sustained. Hence rule 6 gives no new right but merely preserves the existing right to be compensated not only for the taking of the land but also for consequential loss caused by the compulsory acquisition. Lord Justice Clerk Alness said: "The sound principle would seem to be that a person dispossessed *h* should get compensation for all loss occasioned to him by reason of his dispossession." He also quoted with approval a dictum of Lord Kinnear in *Lanarkshire and Dumbartonshire Railway Company* ((1895) 22 R (Ct of Sess) 912 at 919): "It is a well-settled rule in the construction of the Lands Clauses Act that when lands have been taken in the exercise of powers of compulsory purchase, the owner or occupier, as the case may be, is entitled not only to the market value of his interest but to full *j* compensation for all the loss which he may sustain by being deprived of his land." The Tribunal do not consider that the reference to "full compensation" can be read as supporting the view that loss, injury or expense reasonably incurred prior to the date of a notice or deemed notice to treat is not to be compensated. On the contrary it is couched in language apt to embrace prior loss provided always that it is naturally

> and reasonably incurred and can truly be described as loss or expenditure incurred through the claimant being deprived of his land as opposed to something extraneous or due to some independent business decision of his own. *Harvey* followed *Venables* without criticism and we can find no contrary statement of principle therein. Romer L.J. plainly regarded the main test to be that of remoteness saying ([1957] 1 All ER 504 at 507–508, [1957] 1 QB 485 at 494–495): "[objection] might have been raised with regard to the expenditure which was incurred by Mrs. Harvey in connection with the abortive purchase of a house which she was advised by her surveyor was not a reasonable residence for her." But he concluded by saying: "It is bad enough in itself for a person to be compulsorily dispossessed of his house, but it is worse still if he has himself to bear expenses of the kind which are in issue in the present case in finding another house in which to live." In the light of that dictum, we cannot think that his Lordship, by using the words "in consequence of" rather than by "by reason of" in a case in which all the expenditure incurred was after the notice to treat can have intended that expenditure by a displaced householder should be disallowed if it preceded that date; nor can we see any reason why there should be such disallowance if the dispossessed claimant is to receive full compensation for all loss and injury sustained by reason of the compulsory acquisition. [Then after a sentence which I do not follow, and counsel were unable to explain, the tribunal proceeded:] The principle in assessing compensation is that of equivalence described by Scott L.J. in *Horn* v. *Sunderland Corporation* ([1941] 1 All ER 480 at 491, [1957] 2 KB 26 at 42) as: "The right to receive a money payment not less than the loss imposed on him in the public interest, but on the other hand, no greater." Why then, more particularly since the decision of the House of Lords in *Birmingham Corporation* v. *West Midland Baptist Church Ltd* ([1969] 3 All ER 172, [1970] AC 874) should the service of a notice to treat operate so as to prevent full compensation for loss or expenditure reasonably incurred? As appears from the modern textbooks dealing with the subject, the point is still in law an open one.'

The tribunal stated its conclusion thus (at 408):

> 'The main question, however, recurs namely whether expenditure in furtherance of mitigation is only compensatable if incurred after the date of service of the notice to treat or whether the claimant is entitled to have prior expenditure incurred in endeavours to mitigate his loss also taken into consideration. We consider that he can. In our opinion, following *Venables, Harvey* and the *Birmingham Corporation* case we therefore reject the legal submissions based upon the alleged significance of the deemed notice to treat. In our judgment it is simply a question of circumstances in each case whether particular losses or expenditure claimed as items of compensation under rule 6 were naturally and reasonably incurred by reason of the compulsory acquisition; or, in contrast, were too remote as being independently incurred. And, where questions of anticipatory mitigation of damage arise, whether the steps taken to avoid what would otherwise be greater loss were reasonable steps to take in all the circumstances.'

Like the Court of Session in *Sim v Aberdeen City DC* (1982) 264 EG 621, I could have contented myself with a simple approval of that decision and the reasons given therefor, but like them have not done so. I regard both the Scottish decisions as of high persuasive authority on a point of law which affects many inhabitants on each side of the border and ought to be decided in the same way in all the courts of this island. These decisions have the support of counsel acting as amicus curiae, who submits that they apply to this case, and I would apply them in favour of the appellants unless satisfied that the 1973 Act has altered the law.

If the Scottish decisions are wrong, then the decision under appeal on the construction of the 1973 English Act is right and this appeal fails. For nobody contended, or could contend, that a displaced person who can avail himself of this statute can be better off in his compensation for disturbance than he would have been if he had not come within those classes whom the statute is intended to benefit. But if the Scottish decisions are right, as I think they are, the remaining question is whether the language of ss 37 and 38 of the English Act (and ss 35 and 36 of the Scottish Act, for we have to decide whether Parliament has altered the law of Scotland as well as of England) gives those entitled to the compensation it provides for the same or a more restricted right. If those who do not need the Act to obtain compensation for disturbance are entitled to be compensated for such costs and loss as may have been incurred by the appellants on moving house before notice to treat, are those who do need it entitled to the same compensation or does the Act on its true construction exclude such costs and loss from a right to disturbance payments? Does this 'new provision for the benefit of persons displaced from land by public authorities', as the preamble to the Act describes it, apply to such costs and loss?

Counsel as amicus curiae accepts, as does counsel for the acquiring authority, that the object of the new section (s 37) we have to understand and apply is correctly stated in the general note to this part of the Act which is to be found in 43 Halsbury's Statutes (3rd edn) 205 and reads:

> 'This section institutes a new right to a payment known as a disturbance payment in favour of persons displaced from land other than agricultural land. The claimant must have been in lawful possession of the land, but need not have had any further interest in it. The payment is, in fact, intended primarily to benefit those who do not otherwise qualify for compensation because they have no interest requiring to be purchased. It is also available to those whose compensation under existing legislation is limited to the value of the land as a cleared site.'

The appellants are admittedly members of the second of those two classes, being under s 59(2) of the Housing Act 1957 entitled to compensation limited to the site value of their land, as the member of the Lands Tribunal has held on their application. They are accordingly capable of benefiting from this new provision, as are those in the first class with minor interests, such as monthly tenants, statutory tenants and licensees.

Part III of the 1973 Act makes 'Provisions for Benefit of Persons Displaced from Land' under the heads of home loss payments (ss 29–33), farm loss payments (ss 34–36) and rehousing (ss 39–43).

I have already read the relevant provisions of ss 37 and 38. The language of these provisions is, to my mind, like enough to the language in which judges have stated the principle of fully compensating owners dispossessed by compulsory acquisition of their property to indicate the intention of Parliament to give to those classes of persons not previously entitled to compensation for disturbance the same right as those previously entitled to it enjoyed, not a reduced or lesser right. As those previously entitled had a right to be paid as compensation for disturbance their expenses or loss reasonably incurred before given notice to treat, actual or deemed, so the newly favoured are now to obtain disturbance payments which include those expenses and loss.

Section 37(1) provides that the displacement of the person from the land must be in consequence of the acquisition by the authority (or of the housing order, resolution or undertaking or the redevelopment). Section 38(1) equates the amount of the payment with (a) the reasonable expenses of the person in removing from the land from which he is displaced, (b) the loss he will sustain by reason of the disturbance of his trade or business consequent on his having to quit the land.

I note first the use of the word 'displaced', a word which I think came into familiar use at the end of the last war when what had been loosely called 'refugees' were more accurately included in a large, new category of 'displaced persons'. 'Displaced' is used once in *Smith v Strathclyde Regional Council* (1980) 42 P & CR 397 in the first passage which I have quoted, instead of the more usual 'dispossessed', but as far as I know it makes its first appearance in a statute in Part III of this Act. If its use instead of 'dispossessed' has any significance, it is to get rid of the notion which 'dispossessed' might convey, that what is being considered is the termination of legal possession as opposed to actual possession, the ending of rights and interests in the land as opposed to occupation of it. A man may be dispossessed when he gives up his right to possession; the date of dispossession may readily be considered the date when he receives notice to treat. A man is displaced when he gives up actual possession; the date of displacement may more easily be said to be the date when he leaves the place, removes from the land, quits the land. And that is what counsel as amicus curiae submits that displacement and the date of displacement are. If the person threatened with inevitable dispossession, displacement, removal, having to quit the land, call it what you will, because of compulsory acquisition acts reasonably in moving to other accommodation before he is given notice to treat, or before his land is actually acquired by compulsory purchase, he is then displaced in consequence of the acquisition; he then has to quit his land and quits it; his reasonable expenses are expenses in moving from land from which he is already displaced and the loss he will sustain thereafter by reason of the disturbance then of his trade or business is consequent on his having to quit the land.

Another way of reaching the same result is to regard acquisition as a process, often prolonged, which begins with a resolution by an authority (or perhaps even before, if *Sim v Aberdeen City DC* (1981) 258 EG 451; *affd* (1982) 264 EG 621 was rightly decided and applies to s 37, for there the fees were incurred in the purchase of alternative accommodation before the authority had ever passed a resolution) and is completed by the authority's entry under a confirmed compulsory purchase order. That is not the ratio of the Scottish decisions, but, if it be right, then the temporal as well as the causal connection between the loss and expense and the acquisition is established. When the completion has to be, as here under Part III of the Housing Act 1957, 'so soon as may be', this wide interpretation of the words 'the acquisition of land' is less strained. By whichever route the construction of the sections leads to the inclusion of expenses and loss reasonably incurred before acquisition is completed, it does not contradict any provision that acquisition means acquisition by notice to treat, or that the date of displacement means the date of the notice to treat, because there is no reference to the notice to treat or its date in the sections. It is hardly ever conclusive against the implication of clarifying words in an Act of Parliament that they could have been expressed, and the draftsman might not have had an altogether easy task in incorporating references to the notice to treat in these provisions. But he has not done so and I am not persuaded after the full and helpful arguments we have heard that the Lands Tribunal in England has been right to imply them, more especially as there may be more than one notice to treat and more than one date for the notices to treat in respect of the same land or landowner.

In support of the Lands Tribunal's decision in this and earlier cases, counsel for the acquiring authority points first to the anomaly created by overturning those decisions: s 37(2) then gives mere licensees a more generous compensation than is available to holders of short tenancies under s 121 of the Land Clauses Consolidation Act 1845 and, since 1965, s 20 of the Compulsory Purchase Act 1965 which replaced it. Those sections give those entitled to compensation under them a right to compensation, not after notice to treat, because they are not entitled to a notice to treat, but after being required to give up possession by notice to quit: *R v Stone* (1866) LR 1 QB 529; *Newham London Borough Council v Benjamin* [1968] 1 All ER 1195, [1968] 1 WLR 694. There is, counsel for the acquiring authority submits, no reason why Parliament should have created this anomaly, and he also submits that the language of the sections reads more naturally to exclude compensation for any loss or expense incurred before the date of the notice to treat.

What he says about some of the tenses, eg 'is displaced', 'will sustain', is, I think, met by the interpretation counsel as amicus curiae advises us to put on 'displaced' and 'displacement'. So also the references to 'in lawful possession' do not tell against the construction of counsel as amicus curiae because the displaced person entitled to compensation is of necessity always in lawful possession actually and legally at the time he quits or removes and is in legal possession thereafter.

Section 37(6) and its provision for interest have caused me more difficulty, but Parliament may have considered that most persons disturbed in their residence or business by compulsory acquisition would wait to move until given notice to treat or later, and that those prudent few who moved in anticipation of acquisition should be *a* rewarded by interest over a longer period on unpaid compensation. And, as counsel as amicus curiae reminded us, the payment of compensation for loss and expenses incurred in anticipation of acquisition would only be required where they were reasonable and reasonably incurred, and persons who claimed them might often have difficulty in proving that they were reasonably incurred and compensatable accordingly.

I have also considered and reconsidered other provisions of the 1973 Act, such as *b* s 29(2) and (3), to which counsel for the acquiring authority referred us, and s 46(7), to which, as Kerr LJ pointed out, s 38(2) is made subject. Section 29(2) and (3) tell, if they tell any way, against counsel for the acquiring authority, as I think he appreciated before he felt it his duty as counsel to call our attention to it after counsel as amicus curiae had finished his reply. Section 29(2) and (3) provides:

> '(2) A person shall not be entitled to a home loss payment unless throughout a *c* period of not less than five years ending with the date of displacement—(*a*) he has been in occupation of the dwelling, or a substantial part of it, as his only or main residence; and (*b*) he has been in occupation as aforesaid by virtue of an interest or right to which this section applies.
>
> (3) For the purposes of this section a person shall not be treated as displaced from *d* a dwelling in consequence of the compulsory acquisition of an interest therein if he gives up his occupation thereof before the date on which the acquiring authority were authorised to acquire that interest, but, subject to that, it shall not be necessary for the acquiring authority to have required him to give up his occupation of the dwelling.'

Subsection (3) seems to cut out of displacement from a dwelling, for the purposes of *e* dating it, any giving up of occupation of it before acquisition or authorisation. If the date of such prior abandonment of occupation could not be the date of displacement, why was it necessary to provide that it should not be so treated, and for the purposes of this section? Why not for the purposes of s 37 as well as for s 29? Section 46 provides:

> '(1) Where a person is carrying on a trade or business on any land and, in *f* consequence of the compulsory acquisition of the whole of that land, is required to give up possession thereof to the acquiring authority, then if—(*a*) on the date on which he gives up possession as aforesaid he has attained the age of sixty; and (*b*) on that date the land is or forms part of a hereditament the annual value of which does not exceed the prescribed amount; and (*c*) that person has not disposed of the goodwill of the whole of the trade or business and gives to the acquiring authority the undertakings mentioned in subsection (3) below, the compensation payable to *g* that person in respect of the compulsory acquisition of his interest in the land or, as the case may be, under section 121 of the Lands Clauses Consolidation Act 1845 or section 20 of the Compulsory Purchase Act 1965 (tenants from year to year etc.) shall, so far as attributable to disturbance, be assessed on the assumption that it is not reasonably practicable for that person to carry on the trade or business or, as the *h* case may be, the part thereof the goodwill of which he has retained, elsewhere than on that land...
>
> (7) This section shall apply in relation to any disturbance payment assessed in accordance with section 38(1)(*b*) above as it applies in relation to the compensation mentioned in subsection (1) above, and shall so apply subject to the necessary modifications and as if references to the giving up of possession of land to the acquiring authority in consequence of its compulsory acquisition were references to *j* displacement as mentioned in section 37 above...'

If requiring sexagenarians to give up possession of land on which they carry on a trade or business be treated as the equivalent of giving notice to treat, then there is in sub-s (7) an indication that the date of assessment of compensation for disturbance under s 38 is assumed to be the date of the notice to treat. But I see no compelling need to take the intermediate step of treating the one as equivalent to the other, and the same reasoning might more naturally lead to the conclusion that the date of displacement and assessment of disturbance payments is the date when possession is required by notice of entry.

Counsel as amicus curiae accepts that his construction of s 37 involves the anomaly relied on by counsel for the acquiring authority, but submits that it accords better with the language used by Parliament and its likely intention. Being unable to attribute a priori to the legislature an intention to give new qualifiers for disturbance payments or compensation less than those who qualified for full compensation for all that they spent and lost as the natural and reasonable result of compulsory acquisition, I interpret the sections as entitling those new qualifiers to be compensated under those heads. After all, the local authority is acquiring the house of such persons as the appellants as unfit for human habitation; and, as Kerr LJ suggested, that makes it unreasonable that they should go on occupying it any longer than it takes them to find alternative accommodation, and reasonable that the authority should compensate them for leaving as soon as they can. Parliament may well have recognised their situation and intended to promote their leaving unfit premises of their own accord by requiring the authority to compensate them for so doing.

I would therefore allow the appeal and remit the application to the Lands Tribunal to decide whether either appellant has reasonably incurred any reasonable expenses, or loss of business, in and in consequence of moving to other premises. This will involve a more explicit finding as to the exact date when the appellants acquired other premises and vacated the compulsorily purchased premises and Dr Prasad ceased to carry on his medical practice there.

Loss of practice due not to his quitting no 38 but to the threat of impending compulsory purchase and demolition of no 38 will not be compensatable. It will be for the member to decide, on the evidence which he has heard and will hear, whether there is any disturbance payment to be made to the appellants in respect of expenses and loss incurred by reason of the compulsory purchase.

I should like to hear what Fox and Kerr LJJ and counsel have to say about the precise form of the order.

FOX LJ. I agree. The issue is whether the appellants were 'displaced from . . . land in consequence of . . . the acquisition of the land by an authority possessing compulsory purchase powers'.

It is said that because they withdrew from the land before the service of a notice to treat (although after the compulsory purchase order) the displacement was not 'in consequence of' the compulsory acquisition. It is agreed that, had they remained until after the service of the notice to treat, they would have come within the wording which I have quoted.

That seems to me to give undue weight to the mere service of a notice to treat in the process of compulsory acquisition. It is, of course, quite true that, in the authorities, the service of a notice to treat has long been described as producing a situation analogous to that of vendor and purchaser. But in relation to the present question it is, I think, of some value to analyse the position further. It is clear that until the parties have agreed the price there is no contract giving rise to a true vendor and purchaser relationship (see *Adams v London and Blackwall Rly Co* (1850) 2 Mac & G 118, 42 ER 46 and *Harding v Metropolitan Rly Co* (1872) 7 Ch App 154). The position, as I understand it, is as stated by Wilberforce J in *Capital Investments Ltd v Wednesfield UDC* [1964] 1 All ER 655 at 667, [1965] Ch 774 at 794 as follows:

> 'There is, by the mere service of a notice to treat, no consensus between the parties because at this point the price has not been fixed. A notice to treat does nothing more than establish conditions in which a contract might come into existence, either a voluntary contract or a statutory contract. As a matter of authority, it seems

> to me that the position is clearly established in *Haynes* v. *Haynes* ((1861) 1 Drew & Sm 426, 62 ER 442) ... It has been said that for certain purposes and to a certain extent the notice to treat constitutes the relation of vendor and purchaser but in the same passages in which this statement has been made it has also been made clear that the notice does not constitute a contract ...'

It was, therefore, held in the *Capital Investments* case that, until ascertainment of the price, there was no estate contract capable of registration under the Land Charges Act 1925, even though notice to treat had been given.

The result, it seems to me, is that where there is merely a service of a notice to treat (the purchase price not yet having been determined) there is no 'acquisition' of the land by the acquiring authority. Once the purchase price has been determined and in consequence a specifically enforceable contract has come into existence, the position is otherwise. The acquiring authority becomes the owner of the land in equity and the vendor's interest is transferred to the purchase money. That was the point in *Haynes v Haynes*. The testator on whom a notice to treat had been served died before the price was ascertained. By his will he gave the land in one way and his personalty in another. It was held that, there being no contract, the land devolved as land and was not converted into personalty.

The service of a notice to treat is not, therefore, an 'acquisition' of the land any more than is the compulsory purchase order. It certainly has important consequences (the landowner, for example, can insist on the purchase price being determined) but it is simply a step in the process of acquisition just as the order is.

It was stated in this court in *Harvey v Crawley Development Corp* [1957] 1 All ER 504 at 506, 507, [1957] 1 QB 485 at 492, 494 that compensation for disturbance under r (6) of s 2 of the 1919 Act includes all damages directly consequent on the taking of the land under statutory powers (per Denning LJ) and that any loss sustained by a dispossessed owner which flows from a compulsory acquisition 'may properly be regarded as the subject of compensation for disturbance, provided, first, that it is not too remote and, secondly, that it is the natural and reasonable consequence of the dispossession of the owner (per Romer LJ).'

It is difficult to see why, in giving effect to those principles of compensation, loss should be disallowed by reason of the fact that the loss was suffered before rather than after the mere notice to treat. In neither case can one say, in temporal terms, that it was 'in consequence of the acquisition' because in neither case, at the date of the loss, had any acquisition occurred. The property interests remain unaltered. What has happened is that the process of compulsory acquisition has caused the displacement. In practical terms it could not be a sensible rule that only loss arising after the completion of the acquisition could be recoverable, because in most cases a landowner would have to make necessary arrangements, which would involve him in monetary loss, before the completion. Some earlier date must therefore be chosen. As between the date of the publication of the compulsory purchase order, or an earlier date such as the date of the authority's resolution which initiates the process of acquisition, and the date of the notice to treat I see no decisive consideration, in law or in convenience, in favour of the last. That is not to say that the date when the alleged loss is suffered is wholly irrelevant for all purposes. It may have some evidential significance in that the earlier the date of the loss the more difficult it might be to establish that the damage does in fact come within the principle of *Harvey*'s case.

I would allow the appeal and make the appropriate order.

KERR LJ. I have found this a difficult case in a field with which I have little familiarity. In the upshot, however, I am left in no doubt that this appeal should be allowed for the reasons indicated in both the foregoing judgments, and I will only add a short summary of my own conclusions.

In the ultimate analysis the issue turns on the question whether the wording of s 37(1) of the Land Compensation Act 1973 compels the conclusion that Parliament intended, in making 'new provision for the benefit of persons displaced from land by public authorities' in this Act, that the qualification for disturbance payments should be narrower than the basis for analogous rights to compensation under legislation which has been in force since 1845 and which has been interpreted by the courts in a wider sense both in England and Scotland. It is said, however, that this is the effect of the words 'displaced . . . in consequence of . . . the acquisition . . .' in s 37(1)(*a*). It is said that there can be no 'acquisition' before a notice to treat has been served, and that the words 'in consequence of' must therefore, or perhaps in any event, be construed restrictively in a purely temporal sense: unless the (subsequently) displaced person has remained in occupation until the service of the notice to treat, he has not been 'displaced' and is therefore disqualified from any entitlement to any disturbance payment.

In the same way as Stephenson and Fox LJJ, there are a number of reasons why I cannot accept this construction. As shown by the authorities reviewed in the judgment of Stephenson LJ, it is in itself highly improbable that Parliament intended in 1973 that the words 'in consequence of' should, in this context, have a purely temporal, as opposed to a causative, meaning. Moreover, as pointed out in the judgment of Fox LJ, the service of the notice to treat is no more than one, albeit essential, step in the total process of 'acquisition of the land by an authority possessing compulsory purchase powers'. Unlike, for instance, s 53 of this Act in relation to agricultural land, ss 37 and 38 contain no reference to notices to treat but refer merely to 'acquisition' in the present context. However, 'acquisition' is a process which in itself is not completed by the service of a notice to treat. So why should the service of this notice be the crucial moment by reference to which only a subsequent displacement would qualify for compensation under these provisions? I think that this construction gives an unduly narrow meaning both to 'acquisition' and 'in consequence of', and that the correct interpretation of s 37 is in line with the Scottish case to which Stephenson LJ has referred.

In rejecting the acquiring authority's narrow construction I am also influenced by the consideration that its implications appear to fly in the face of common sense when one has regard to the practicalities. Long before October 1979, when Dr Prasad removed himself, his wife and his practice from this house, its occupation by anyone was doomed: see in particular ss 43 and 47 of the Housing Act 1957. Counsel for the acquiring authority expressly conceded, as I took down his words, that 'under Part III of this Act [ie the 1957 Act] it was inevitable that the authority had to proceed to notice to treat, entry and demolition'. Why, then, should the owners' entitlement to a disturbance payment depend on their remaining in occupation of an unfit house right up to the moment of an inevitable notice to treat, to be followed inevitably thereafter by a compulsory displacement? I can see no sense, let alone merit, in a construction of s 37 which leads to this result, and I do not think its wording compels this conclusion.

I therefore agree that this appeal should be remitted to the Lands Tribunal to assess any disturbance payment to which the appellants may be entitled.

Appeal allowed. Case remitted to the Lands Tribunal to assess any disturbance payment to which the appellants might be entitled.

Solicitors: *Sharpe Pritchard & Co* (for the acquiring authority); *Treasury Solicitor.*

Diana Brahams Barrister.

PCW (Underwriting Agencies) Ltd v Dixon and another a

QUEEN'S BENCH DIVISION (COMMERCIAL COURT)
LLOYD J
17, 20 JANUARY 1983 b

Injunction – Interlocutory – Danger that defendant may transfer assets out of jurisdiction – Injunction restraining removal of assets out of the jurisdiction – Variation of injunction – Variation to increase defendant's allowance for living expenses, to meet outstanding debts and to pay defendant's legal costs – Whether injunction should be varied.

Injunction – Interlocutory – Preservation of subject matter of cause – Injunction restraining c
removal of assets out of jurisdiction – Application to vary injunction to enable defendant to pay debts and legal expenses and meet reasonable living expenses – Whether injunction should be maintained to preserve trust fund and plaintiff's tracing rights if successful in action.

The plaintiffs were a company which acted as the managing agent for numerous insurance underwriting syndicates. The defendant was a director and major shareholder d
of the plaintiffs. The plaintiffs brought an action against him claiming that reinsurances effected on behalf of the syndicates had been arranged with reinsurers in which the defendant had beneficial interests and on terms which were bound to result in substantial profits to the reinsurers so that the defendant had made secret profits from the plaintiffs' affairs. The plaintiffs obtained, inter alia, a Mareva injunction over the whole of the defendant's assets within the jurisdiction save that he was permitted to draw reasonable e
living expenses not exceeding £100 per week. The defendant maintained that he needed £1,000 per week for reasonable living expenses and that he also needed to have access to £77,500 to meet outstanding debts and pay legal expenses incurred in defending the action. He applied for a variation of the injunction on those terms. The plaintiffs contended that the existing injunction could be justified on the established principles applicable to Mareva injunctions or, alternatively, on the wider ground that the plaintiffs f
were laying claim to a trust fund which should be preserved so that if the plaintiffs were successful in the action they could have recourse to that fund by tracing in equity.

Held – (1) The sole purpose of a Mareva injunction was to prevent a plaintiff being cheated out of the proceeds of an action, should it be successful, by a defendant transferring his assets abroad or dissipating his assets within the jurisdiction. The remedy g
was not intended to give a plaintiff priority over those assets, or to prevent a defendant from paying his debts as they fell due, or to punish him for his alleged misdeeds, or to enable a plaintiff to exert pressure on him to settle an action. Applying those principles to the facts, the injunction would be varied to allow the defendant sufficient funds to meet his reasonable living expenses, pay his outstanding debts and defend himself in the proceedings brought by the plaintiffs (see p 162 *d* to p 163 *d*, p 164 *e f* and p 165 *b c*, h
post); *Iraqi Ministry of Defence v Arcepey Shipping Co SA, The Angel Bell* [1980] 1 All ER 480 and dicta of Lord Denning MR and Kerr LJ in *Z Ltd v A* [1982] 1 All ER at 561, 571 applied; *A v C (No 2)* [1981] 2 All ER 126 distinguished.

(2) Moreover, the injunction could not be maintained in its original form on the wider ground that the plaintiffs were laying claim to a trust fund, since it was unlikely that the whole of the defendant's assets could be a trust fund. Even if all his assets could j
be subject to a trust, injunctions were a discretionary remedy and in the exercise of its discretion the court would not continue the injunction in its original form because to do so would cause injustice to the defendant by (a) compelling him to reduce his living standards, (b) preventing him from paying his bills and (c) denying him the means to defend himself properly (see p 164 *g* to *j* and p 165 *b c e*, post); *A v C* [1980] 2 All ER 347 and *Chief Constable of Kent v V* [1982] 3 All ER 36 distinguished.

Notes

For injunctions restraining the disposition of property, see 24 Halsbury's Laws (4th edn) para 1018.

Cases referred to in judgment

A v C [1980] 2 All ER 347, [1981] QB 596, [1981] 2 WLR 629.
A v C (No 2) [1981] 2 All ER 126, [1981] QB 961, [1981] 2 WLR 634, CA.
Bankers Trust Co v Shapira [1980] 3 All ER 353, [1980] 1 WLR 1273, CA.
Bekhor (A J) & Co Ltd v Bilton [1981] 2 All ER 565, [1981] QB 923, [1981] 2 WLR 601, CA.
Carl-Zeiss-Stiftung v Herbert Smith & Co (a firm) (No 2) [1969] 2 All ER 367, [1969] 2 Ch 276, [1969] 2 WLR 427, CA.
Chief Constable of Kent v V [1982] 3 All ER 36, [1983] QB 34, [1982] 3 WLR 462, CA.
Iraqi Ministry of Defence v Arcepey Shipping Co SA (Gillespie Bros & Co Ltd intervening), The Angel Bell [1980] 1 All ER 480, [1981] QB 65, [1981] 2 WLR 488.
MBPXL Corp v Intercontinental Banking Corp Ltd [1975] CA Transcript 411.
Third Chandris Shipping Corp v Unimarine SA, The Pythia, The Angelic Wings, The Genie [1979] 2 All ER 972, [1979] QB 645, [1979] 3 WLR 122, QBD and CA.
Z Ltd v A [1982] 1 All ER 556, [1982] QB 558, [1982] 2 WLR 288, CA.

Application and cross-application

The plaintiffs, PCW (Underwriting Agencies) Ltd, issued a writ dated 3 December 1982 against the first defendant, P S Dixon, and the second defendant, P E J Cameron-Webb, and by an ex parte application made on 3 December 1982 obtained a Mareva injunction granted by Mustill J against the first defendant over the whole of the first defendant's assets within the jurisdiction, save that he was entitled to draw reasonable living expenses not exceeding £100 per week. The judge further ordered the first defendant to disclose the whereabouts of his bank accounts, whether within the jurisdiction or abroad, and to disclose within 14 days the precise identity and whereabouts of all assets, wherever located, representing or derived from premiums paid under any reinsurance effected on behalf of underwriting syndicates managed by the plaintiffs. By a summons issued on 7 January 1983 the first defendant applied to vary the order to enable him (a) to draw reasonable living expenses not exceeding such sum as was as just but not less than £1,000 per week, (b) to pay certain liabilities not exceeding £27,404, and (c) to pay his solicitors on account of the costs of the action a sum or sums not exceeding £50,000. The first defendant further sought to have the order varied to enlarge the time for compliance with the order that he supply information as to his assets. By a cross-summons issued on 12 January 1983, the plaintiffs applied, inter alia, for the time for compliance with the order to supply information not to be extended beyond 4 pm on 21 January 1983 and also applied to restrain the first defendant from in any way tampering with the documentation in relation to the reinsurances in question. The applications were heard in chambers and the judgment was given by Lloyd J in open court with the consent of the parties. The facts are set out in the judgment.

Nicholas Chambers and *Stephen Ruttle* for the plaintiffs.
Charles Gibson for the first defendant.
The second defendant did not appear.

Cur adv vult

20 January. The following judgment was delivered.

LLOYD J. This is an application by the first defendant to vary an order for a Mareva injunction granted ex parte by Mustill J on 3 December 1982. The summons was issued on 7 January 1983. There is a cross-application by summons dated 12 January 1983 in which the plaintiffs seek additional relief. Since some of the points involved are of general importance I am giving my judgment in open court with the consent of the parties. a

Before coming to the substance of the matter I may perhaps refer to the recent decision of the Court of Appeal in *Z Ltd v A* [1982] 1 All ER 556, [1982] QB 558. In that case Kerr LJ drew attention to the importance of plaintiffs in Mareva applications ensuring so far as possible that the order made on the original ex parte application is in appropriate terms. Otherwise the courts will, as he put it, become cluttered up with hearings on Mareva injunctions even more than they already are (see [1982] 1 All ER 556 at 573– b 574, [1982] QB 558 at 587–588).

The history and the practice in relation to the granting of Mareva injunctions was described by Mustill J in *Third Chandris Shipping Corp v Unimarine SA, The Pythia* [1979] 2 All ER 972, [1979] QB 645 and by Ackner LJ in *A J Bekhor & Co Ltd v Bilton* [1981] 2 All ER 565, [1981] QB 923. From having been regarded at first as an exceptional remedy (see *MBPXL Corp v Intercontinental Banking Corp Ltd* [1975] CA Transcript 411 per c Stephenson LJ) they had by 1979 become commonplace. Mustill J estimated that in 1979 applications were being made at the rate of 20 per month. Since 1979 that number has doubled. In the Commercial Court alone applications for Mareva injunctions are now running at the rate of 40 a month; in the Queen's Bench list the number of ex parte applications has increased from 785 in 1979 to double that figure in 1983. No doubt a large part of this increase is due to applications for Mareva relief. There is no division of d the High Court in which Mareva injunctions are not now regularly granted. The statutory basis for the jurisdiction is contained in s 37(3) of the Supreme Court Act 1981. As Lord Denning MR observed in *Z Ltd v A* Mareva injunctions have become an established feature of the English law.

Only a very small proportion of Mareva injunctions granted ex parte ever come back for hearing before the court. In many cases that will be because the terms of the original e order have proved appropriate. Where the terms of the original order have proved inappropriate they are usually varied or discharged by consent. Consent orders are placed before the judge for initialling; no court appearance is necessary; little time is taken up. But there are exceptional cases where a further hearing is necessary, either because the jurisdiction has been abused, or for some other reason.

In the present case it must have been obvious to the plaintiffs from the start, for reasons f which I will explain later, that the terms proposed for the ex parte order were inappropriate. It would have been obvious to the court as well, if the application had been on summons, even at short notice, instead of ex parte. There does not appear to be any reason why the application in this case should not have been made on summons. The plaintiffs had no ground for thinking that the defendant would be likely to remove his assets from the jurisdiction. Be that as it may, one would have thought that, at any g rate once the plaintiffs had obtained their ex parte relief, they would have been able to agree sensible and appropriate terms by way of variation of the original order. Unfortunately that has not proved to be the case.

Turning to the facts of the present case, the plaintiffs carry on business as managing agents at Lloyd's. As such they manage the underwriting business of numerous Lloyd's syndicates. The first defendant was one of two controlling shareholders and directors of h the plaintiff company from its incorporation in 1966. He subsequently became chairman. He is a member of Lloyd's and a wealthy man. The second defendant is or was the other controlling shareholder and director of the plaintiff company. He also acted as underwriter on behalf of the syndicates until his retirement in 1981. He has taken no part in the hearing before me. It is said that he is now living abroad.

In the mid-1970s a number of Lloyd's syndicates, owing perhaps to the explosion of j business, found themselves near the top of or over their premium income limits. In such cases it was the normal practice to reduce the syndicate's net retention by effecting re-insurance. Reinsurances were effected in this way on behalf of the syndicates managed by the plaintiffs. From 1975 onwards these reinsurances were broked by Alexander Howden (Insurance Brokers) Ltd.

The plaintiffs' case is that these reinsurances were placed on terms which were bound to result in substantial profits to the reinsurers, or were otherwise unduly favourable to them. Thus, for the period 1975 to 1980 they say that total reinsurance premiums amounted to \$53m, whereas total claims paid amounted only to \$17m, thus resulting in a profit ratio of about 75%. These profits ultimately accrued, so the plaintiffs say, to six companies carrying on reinsurance business in Gibraltar. The first defendant is alleged to have, or to have had, a beneficial interest in those companies. In this way he is said to have made secret profits out of the conduct of the plaintiffs' affairs. I will read the last three paragraphs of the affidavit which was filed in support of the ex parte application:

> '(11) I now seek to justify the relief sought. I submit that the facts set out above clearly indicate that the defendants have been party in some degree to a scheme designed to channel reinsurance premiums emanating from syndicates managed by the plaintiffs to a number of off-shore companies created or adapted specifically for this purpose and without significant assets other than those derived from the reinsurance business.
>
> (12) Further the defendants have concealed from the plaintiffs' syndicates their interest in the reinsurance business. In the result large sums of money originating from the syndicates have been channelled abroad. Some has been returned to meet claims. The balance is said to be available to meet claims in so far as it has not been distributed as profits.
>
> (13) Even if the terms on which the various reinsurance contracts have been concluded can be justified as fair and reasonable I submit that the defendants have acted improperly and in breach of duty in seeking to channel our clients' business into companies in which they are interested. There are, however, grounds for suspicion that at least some of the reinsurance business was effected on terms that were unduly favourable to the reinsurers. Should this prove to be the case the conduct of the defendants would be more serious.'

On the strength of that affidavit and various unsworn statements which are exhibited Mustill J made an order which contains three paragraphs. By para 1 he granted a Mareva injunction over the whole of the first defendant's assets which were within the jurisdiction, save that he was to be entitled to draw reasonable living expenses not to exceed £100 per week. By para 2 the first defendant was ordered to disclose the whereabouts of his bank accounts, whether at home or abroad. By para 3 he was ordered to disclose within 14 days the precise identity and whereabouts of all his assets, wherever located, representing or derived from the premiums paid under any reinsurances effected on behalf of the syndicates managed by the plaintiffs.

The first defendant complied fully with the order under para 2 within a day or so of being served with the order. By his summons he seeks a variation of the order made under para 1 and para 3. I will take para 1 first.

At a meeting on 15 December 1982 the first defendant's solicitors gave the plaintiffs' solicitors an outline of the first defendant's financial requirements. Instead of £100 per week which had been allowed by the ex parte order they said he needed £750 a week for himself and family, and £250 a week for nursing his old mother, making £1000 in all. In addition there were substantial sums due to the Inland Revenue and others. The first defendant's solicitors also asked to be allowed to be paid £50,000 on account of their own costs, in addition to the £20,000 which they had already received. These requests were confirmed in a letter of the same date, in which they asked for the plaintiffs' consent.

In their reply of 21 December 1982 the plaintiffs either did not deal with these questions at all or, if they did, said they did not anticipate receiving instructions to agree any variation. The first defendant was thus to be left with £100 a week.

On 6 January there was a telephone conversation between the two firms of solicitors. This would have afforded the plaintiffs' solicitors a further opportunity to agree a variation of the order as requested by the first defendant, but no such agreement was reached and as a result a summons was issued the next day.

In his affidavit in support of the summons the first defendant sets out his financial obligations in considerable detail. The affidavit shows first that the first defendant had a pressing need to pay, either at once or in the immediate future, bills amounting to £27,404. Second, it showed how the figure of £1,000 a week had been arrived at. The first defendant has a flat in Grosvenor House Hotel. In addition he has five children to educate and other general expenses. I need not go into the details; they are all contained in the affidavit and the supporting vouchers. The affidavit appears on its face to be candid and truthful. There was no application to cross-examine the first defendant on his affidavit, although he was known by the plaintiffs to have been sitting in court throughout the hearing.

The affidavit in reply consists of 11 paragraphs. The first 10 deal with the application to vary para 3 of Mustill J's order, to which I will come later. The last paragraph deals with the living expenses. The figures are not challenged. What is said is that the first defendant may have some other source of income or capital assets at home or abroad which could be used to meet his liabilities within the jurisdiction. But so far as assets within the jurisdiction are concerned they are all, of course, caught by the existing Mareva injunction. So far as other sources of income are concerned the first defendant has always accepted, whether necessarily or not does not matter, that his income as an underwriting member of Lloyd's will be caught by the Mareva injunction when it is received. So far as assets outside the jurisdiction are concerned the first defendant says in a further affidavit that his only moneys are £50 in the Bank of Bermuda, an account which he had already disclosed.

What should be the correct approach for the court to take in these circumstances? The first reported case in which a similar question was considered is *Iraqi Ministry of Defence v Arcepey Shipping Co SA, The Angel Bell* [1980] 1 All ER 480, [1981] QB 65. In that case Robert Goff J held that it was consistent with the policy underlying the Mareva jurisdiction that the defendant should be allowed to pay his debts as they fall due. The purpose of the jurisdiction is not to secure priority for the plaintiff; still less, I would add, to punish the defendant for his alleged misdeeds. The sole purpose or justification for the Mareva order is to prevent the plaintiffs being cheated out of the proceeds of their action, should it be successful, by the defendant either transferring his assets abroad or dissipating his assets within the jurisdiction: see *Z Ltd v A* [1982] 1 All ER 556 at 561, 571, [1982] QB 558 at 571, 584 per Lord Denning MR and Kerr LJ.

I am not going to attempt to define in this case what is meant by dissipating assets within the jurisdiction or where the line is to be drawn; but wherever the line is to be drawn this defendant is well within it. It could not possibly be said that he is dissipating his assets by living as he has always lived and paying bills such as he has always incurred. I say nothing about the cost of defending himself in these proceedings. The Mareva jurisdiction was never intended to prevent expenditure such as this or to produce consequences such as would inevitably follow if this ex parte order is upheld.

Counsel for the plaintiffs relied on *A v C (No 2)* [1981] 2 All ER 126, [1981] QB 961. But in that case there was no evidence whether the defendant had other assets freely available, that is to say not caught by the Mareva injunction, to meet the relevant debt. Here all the assets within the jurisdiction are caught by the Mareva, and according to the first defendant no more than £50 in moneys is available elsewhere.

Applying what I believe to be the correct approach in Mareva cases it is clear that the first defendant's application to vary para 1 of the ex parte order must succeed. At first I was concerned by the sum of £50,000 for the first defendant's solicitors costs in addition to the £20,000 they had already received; that might seem excessive at this stage; but the figures as such, as I have said, have not been challenged by the plaintiffs and the figure has been put forward by the first defendant's solicitors themselves. So I say no more about it.

What concerns me more in this case is why the figure of £100 was ever put forward by the plaintiffs in the first place. Here was a man who was known to be wealthy. He had been a founder member and chairman of the plaintiff company. The plaintiffs must have known his salary. No doubt it was considerable. They must therefore have known that the figure of £100 a week put forward was wholly unrealistic if he was to maintain his standard of living. Inevitably I have been led to wonder whether the real purpose in putting forward so low a figure and in failing or refusing to agree any increase was to exert pressure on the first defendant to settle the action. If so then this case would fall within one of the two abuses mentioned by Kerr LJ in *Z Ltd v A*.

In their affidavit in reply the plaintiffs complain that unlike others (who, incidentally, they have also sued) the first defendant has not offered to return any money to which he may not be entitled. I cannot understand the relevance of that assertion unless it be in relation to a possible settlement. In any event it does not seem to be true, for in para 16 of his affidavit the first defendant says:

> 'If, in the course of an exercise designed to avoid the incidence of tax, I have become liable to the plaintiffs, and through them to the syndicates which they represent, I am anxious that the true extent of my liability should be determined and that I should discharge it, and I shall make every endeavour to discharge it.'

The plaintiffs may well feel strongly in the justice of their case and they may in the end prove right. But until the matter is tried they are not entitled to exercise undue pressure on the first defendant. In my view that is what they have been doing. They are entitled to a Mareva injunction. There is no dispute about that. But they were not entitled to put forward a figure, and still less to continue to insist on a figure, as low as £100. They must have known that if the figure £100 a week was maintained it could only result in the first defendant's capitulation.

But counsel for the plaintiffs seeks to support the ex parte injunction on another ground. He submits that this is a case in which there is a fund which in equity belongs to the members of the syndicates. The plaintiffs are, he says, entitled to restrain the first defendant from using other people's money to meet his bills or pay for his defence. The fact that some of his own money may be mixed with the money which belongs to the 'names' is, it is said, no answer to the plaintiffs' claim for an injunction. Counsel for the plaintiffs conceded that if this way of putting the plaintiffs' case is correct the first defendant would not even be entitled to £100 a week.

I may say in passing that there is nothing in the original affidavit to support counsel's submission along these lines. The original affidavit looks like an ordinary application for a Mareva injunction, together with ancillary relief which I will come to later. The new way of putting the case only emerges in the affidavit filed in reply, where it is said that though the injunction may be characterised as a Mareva injunction it is justifiable on wider grounds.

In support of his argument on this wider ground counsel relied on *A v C* [1980] 2 All ER 347, [1981] QB 596, *Bankers Trust Co v Shapira* [1980] 3 All ER 353, [1980] 1 WLR 1273 and *Chief Constable of Kent v V* [1982] 3 All ER 36, [1983] QB 34. *A v C* was, so far as I know, the first case to highlight the distinction between the ordinary Mareva jurisdiction and the right to trace in equity in pursuance of a proprietary claim. In that case there was a fund amounting to £383,871 which had been paid into an account at a bank. The plaintiffs said that the fund was the proceeds of fraud committed on the plaintiffs by the first five defendants, and that the fund belonged in equity to them. The bank was named as the sixth defendant. Robert Goff J held that the plaintiffs were entitled to an injunction to restrain the defendants from disposing of the trust fund, or what remained of it, quite apart from the Mareva jurisdiction. Otherwise the trust fund might have disappeared before the action came on for trial and equity would have been invoked in vain. As Templeman LJ said in an earlier case, it is the concern of any court of equity to see that the stable door is locked before the horse has gone. See also the same distinction drawn by Ackner LJ in *A J Bekhor & Co Ltd v Bilton* [1981] 2 All ER 565 at 573, [1981] QB 923 at 936.

In *Chief Constable of Kent v V* the defendant was charged in effect with stealing the proceeds of 21 cheques which he had paid into his own account. The total amount of the cheques was £16,001. The Chief Constable of Kent applied for an injunction to restrain the defendant from drawing on the account. The main question in the case (on which

Slade LJ dissented) was whether the chief constable had any standing to maintain the claim, since he was not asserting that the money belonged to him. A similar question might have arisen in the present case, since the plaintiffs are not asserting that the trust fund belongs to them; if it exists at all it belongs to 'the names', not to the plaintiffs, although it is said that the plaintiffs may have an interest in the trust fund as managers. But that question was not pursued at the present hearing, so I need not mention it further.

The relevance of *Chief Constable of Kent v V* to the present application is that the Court of Appeal held that the chief constable was entitled to an injunction, even though the bank account contained money which admittedly belonged to the defendant. Lord Denning MR said ([1982] 3 All ER 36 at 42, [1983] QB 34 at 44):

> 'There remains the final question: suppose the bank account contains moneys which the thief has come by honestly, so that they are really his own moneys, and are then mixed with moneys which he has come by dishonestly, by theft or fraudulent obtaining. At the time of his arrest, the police discover that to be the state of his bank account. It is quite plain that he paid the stolen money into his own bank account so as to avoid detection. It follows that under s 43 of the Theft Act 1968 the court of trial, on his conviction, can make an order depriving him of his rights in the stolen money. He cannot avoid such an order by mixing it with his own moneys. In order to make the power under s 43 effective, it is essential that the court should have power to grant an injunction meanwhile to stop him disposing of any moneys in his account; because, until trial, it cannot be known how much of it belongs to him personally and how much was stolen.'

Donaldson LJ did not go so far as Lord Denning MR. He held that the injunction which had been granted was much too wide; it should be confined to moneys in the account which were traceable as having come from the account of the true owner.

The distinction between the ordinary Mareva plaintiff (to use Ackner LJ's phrase) and the case where the plaintiff is laying claim to a trust fund on the so-called wider ground, is thus clear. In the latter case the whole object is to secure the trust fund itself so that it should be available if the plaintiff should prove his claim. In the former case by contrast the plaintiff is not entitled to any security. The purpose of the jurisdiction, as is now clearly established, is not to provide the plaintiffs with any form of pre-trial attachment. It is simply to prevent the injustice of a defendant removing or dissipating his assets so as to cheat the plaintiff of the fruits of his claim.

Can the plaintiffs then bring the present case within the wider jurisdiction? I have grave doubts. Both in *A v C* and *Chief Constable of Kent v V* the claim related to specific identifiable bank accounts. It is difficult to regard the whole of a man's assets as a fund in that sense, even though his assets may in part contain or be derived from money improperly come by. But even if I could regard the whole of the defendant's assets as a trust fund, I would be quite unwilling to uphold the ex parte order in the present case on that basis. All injunctions are, or course, in the end discretionary. I would regard it as unjust in the present case if the defendant were compelled to reduce his standard of living, to give up his flat or to take his children away from school, in order to secure what is as yet only a claim by the plaintiffs. I would regard it as even more unjust that he should be prevented from defending himself properly (for that is what it would amount to), merely because the plaintiffs say that in doing so he is using somebody else's money.

A not dissimilar point arose in *Carl-Zeiss-Stiftung v Herbert Smith & Co (a firm) (No 2)* [1968] 2 All ER 367, [1969] 2 Ch 276. In that case the East German foundation asserted that the West German foundation were using moneys which belonged in equity to the East German foundation for the purpose of defending themselves in the main action. They brought a subsidiary action against the defendants' solicitors. The Court of Appeal ordered a preliminary issue whether the statement of claim against the defendants' solicitors disclosed a cause of action. Pennycuick J held that the subsidiary action was contrary to public policy, on the ground that it obstructed the course of justice. The Court of Appeal decided the case in favour of the defendants' solicitors on different

grounds. But Danckwerts LJ said obiter that there was a good deal to be said for the
a contention that had found favour with Pennycuick J (see [1969] 2 All ER 367 at 375, [1969] 2 Ch 276 at 293).

I further note that at the end of his judgment in *Chief Constable of Kent v V* [1982] 3 All ER 36 at 42, [1983] QB 34 at 44–45 (the case which can be regarded as the strongest authority in favour of the plaintiffs' submission) Lord Denning MR specifically reserved the right of the defendant to apply to the court for release of such sum as he might need
b for his defence or otherwise.

In my view justice and convenience require in the present case that the first defendant should be allowed the means of defending himself, even if it could be said that the plaintiffs had laid claim to the whole of his assets as a trust fund. Similarly justice and convenience require that he should be able to pay his ordinary bills and continue to live as he has been accustomed to live heretofore. So whether the case is put on the basis of
c the Mareva jurisdiction or the so-called wider jurisdiction to trace in equity I reach the same conclusion.

Counsel for the plaintiffs also submitted that the ex parte injunction should be maintained at least until the first defendant has disclosed what part of his assets can be traced to the original reinsurance premiums so that the trust fund can then be limited and identified. I can see no merit at all in that submission. The tracing of assets back to
d the reinsurance premiums will be one of the main issues to be investigated at the trial. It will obviously be a task of great complexity, including much work to be done by accountants and others. I can see no good reason why the first defendant should be required to do that work on the plaintiffs' behalf at this stage. As will appear later the first defendant has agreed to co-operate in carrying out the necessary work once the plaintiffs have, so to speak, started the ball rolling. There would be no justice in requiring
e him to carry out all the work on his own without the ability to pay his lawyers or his accountants as a condition of being able to pay his ordinary bills and maintain his ordinary standard of living.

Finally it is said that the first defendant is already in breach of the order in certain respects to which I shall now be coming. I attach little weight to that consideration. The order was made ex parte; the first defendant is entitled to apply to have it set aside or
f varied. The fact that the first defendant has found it difficult or impossible to comply with para 3 of the order, even though his solicitors thought at one stage that he could, is no ground for resisting a sensible variation of para 1. It is said that, unlike others, this defendant is making no effort to assist the plaintiff in the preparation of their case. My impression from reading the affidavits is to the contrary. The first defendant is not being difficult or evasive. He is prepared to co-operate so far as he can while preserving his
g right to defend himself. For the reasons which I have mentioned I would hold that the first defendant is entitled to the variation which he seeks in para 1 of his summons.

I now turn to para 3 of Mustill J's order under which it will be remembered the first defendant was ordered to disclose within 14 days the identity and whereabouts of all his assets, wherever located representing or derived from the reinsurance premiums. The first defendant has admittedly failed to comply with this order. Fortunately I can deal
h with the matter briefly, since agreement between the parties has now been reached.

On the face of it para 3 of the order goes beyond anything which any court has ever ordered before at so early a stage of the proceedings. Counsel for the plaintiffs rightly did not seek to justify the order under para 3 as discovery in aid of Mareva. Rather it was justified, as I understood the argument, on the ground that the first defendant had been chairman of the plaintiff company and that he ought therefore to be in a good position
j to help the plaintiffs prepare their claim or discover what their claim truly is.

The answer to that argument, if I have correctly understood it, is contained in the first defendant's affidavit. The first step of the tracing process is to identify the reinsurance premiums in question. This depends on the documents, all of which are in the plaintiffs' possession or within their access. The relevant documents are no longer in the first defendant's possession, if they ever were, since they were the subject of an Anton Piller order in other proceedings. It seems to me obvious in those circumstances that it is and

always was for the plaintiffs to start the tracing process by identifying the relevant reinsurance premiums which they say have been misappropriated. This is what has now *a*
been agreed. Thereafter the first defendant will take the tracing process through the next stage in accordance with the ex parte order, but with an extended time limit.

Whether the plaintiffs were ever strictly entitled to an order in the form of para 3 does not therefore now matter. By para 2 of his summons the first defendant asks for para 3 of the order to be varied in accordance with what I have just outlined. The extended time limit will be three months from the date when the plaintiffs serve a schedule *b*
identifying the relevant reinsurance premiums. I will vary para 3 of the order accordingly.

Counsel for the plaintiffs wished to protect the plaintiffs in the event of the schedule subsequently turning out to be incomplete. I can see no difficulty on that score. There will be liberty to apply.

Finally I turn to the plaintiffs' cross-summons for additional relief. Paragraph 1 is now no longer relevant. Paragraphs 2, 3 and 4 are all conceded in principle, and are the sort of *c*
orders which might have been applied for in the first place. By para 5 the plaintiffs ask for an affidavit of all the first defendant's assets within the jurisdiction or outside. This again is an ordinary application for discovery in aid of Mareva which could have been asked for on the original application and is in marked contrast with para 3 of the order actually made. Again it is conceded in principle. If necessary I will hear further argument on the additional para 3(a), if the plaintiffs wish to pursue it. *d*

Application allowed. Order varied accordingly.

Solicitors: *Clifford-Turner* (for the plaintiffs); *Kingsley Napley & Co* (for the first defendant).

K Mydeen Esq Barrister. *e*

Power Packing Casemakers Ltd v Faust and others *f*

COURT OF APPEAL, CIVIL DIVISION
STEPHENSON, PURCHAS LJJ AND SIR GEORGE BAKER
17, 18 JANUARY 1983

Unfair dismissal – Dismissal in connection with strike or other industrial action – Other industrial *g*
action – Refusal to work overtime because of dispute over wage increase – Refusal to work overtime not constituting breach of contract – Whether refusal to work overtime amounting to taking part in 'other industrial action' – Whether industrial tribunal having jurisdiction to hear complaint of unfair dismissal – Employment Protection (Consolidation) Act 1978, s 62(1)(b).

The employers' workforce at their factory banned overtime working because they were *h*
in dispute with the employers over a wage increase. The employers received an export order which required overtime work if the order was to be completed in time. The employers therefore threatened the workforce with dismissal if they refused to work overtime. All but three employees complied with the request to work overtime. The three employees were dismissed. On a complaint to an industrial tribunal of unfair dismissal, the tribunal held that the employees had not been in breach of their contracts *j*
of employment or guilty of misconduct in refusing the employers' request to work overtime and that they had therefore been unfairly dismissed. The employers appealed to the Employment Appeal Tribunal, contending that under s 62[a] of the Employment Protection (Consolidation) Act 1978 the industrial tribunal had no jurisdiction to

a Section 62, so far as material, is set out at p 168 *j* to p 169 *a*, post

entertain the employees' complaint. The employers conceded that the employees were
a not in breach of their contracts of employment in refusing the request to work overtime. The appeal tribunal held that in refusing the request to work overtime the employees were taking part in 'other industrial action' (apart from a strike) for the purposes of s 62(1)(*b*) of the 1978 Act, and that since there were no other 'relevant employees' who had not been dismissed or who had been re-engaged after dismissal there had been no victimisation of the dismissed employees and therefore, by virtue of s 62(2), the industrial
b tribunal had no jurisdiction to entertain the complaint. The employees appealed to the Court of Appeal, contending that an employee's action had to involve a breach of his contract of employment for it to constitute 'other industrial action' within s 62(1)(*b*).

Held – On the ordinary and natural meaning of the phrase 'strike or other industrial action' in s 62(1)(*b*) of the 1978 Act 'other industrial action' meant industrial action of the same kind as a strike. Once it was established that at the date of his dismissal an employee
c was taking part in industrial action with the object of applying pressure on his employer or of disrupting the employer's business, then, irrespective of whether his action was in breach of his contract of employment, he was at the date of his dismissal taking part in 'other industrial action' within s 62(1)(*b*). It followed that, unless the employee could show that he had been victimised within s 62(2)(*a*) or (*b*), an industrial tribunal had no
d jurisdiction to entertain his complaint of unfair dismissal. The industrial tribunal had therefore not had jurisdiction to determine the employees' complaint, and their appeal would accordingly be dismissed (see p 168 *g h*, p 169 *b*, p 170 *e f*, p 173 *h j*, p 174 *d e* and *j* to p 175 *a f* and p 176 *f g*, post).

Secretary of State for Employment v Associated Society of Locomotive Engineers and Firemen (No 2) [1972] 2 All ER 949 considered.

e **Notes**

For dismissal for taking part in a strike or other industrial action, see 16 Halsbury's Laws (4th edn) para 633.

For the Employment Protection (Consolidation) Act 1978, s 62, see 48 Halsbury's Statutes (3rd edn) 514.

f **Cases cited in judgments**

NWL Ltd v Woods, NWL Ltd v Nelson [1979] 3 All ER 614, [1979] 1 WLR 1294, HL.
Rasool v Hepworth Pipe Co Ltd [1980] ICR 494, EAT.
Secretary of State for Employment v Associated Society of Locomotive Engineers and Firemen (No 2) [1972] 2 All ER 949, [1972] 2 QB 455, [1972] 2 WLR 1370, NIRC and CA.

g **Appeal**

The employees, Philip G Faust, James Cullinan and Robert G MacQuillan, appealed from a decision of the Employment Appeal Tribunal dated 17 December 1980 (May J, Mr A J Ramsden and Mr R Thomas) ([1981] ICR 484) whereby the appeal tribunal allowed the appeal of the employers, Power Packing Casemakers Ltd, from a decision of an industrial tribunal sitting at Bury St Edmunds, published on 21 April 1980, deciding that the
h employees had been unfairly dismissed. The appeal tribunal held that by virtue of s 62(2) of the Employment Protection (Consolidation) Act 1978, the industrial tribunal did not have jurisdiction to hear the employees' complaint of unfair dismissal because at the date of their dismissal they were taking part in 'other industrial action' within s 62(1)(*b*) of the 1978 Act. The grounds of the employees' appeal were that the appeal tribunal erred in law in its construction of s 62 because 'other industrial action' within s 62(1)(*b*) was
j limited to conduct of an employee which amounted to a breach of his contract of employment. The employers had conceded before the appeal tribunal that the industrial action taken by the employees did not amount to a breach of their contracts of employment. The facts are set out in the judgment of Stephenson LJ.

Geraint Jones for the employees.
Christopher Carr for the employers.

STEPHENSON LJ. This appeal raises a new point of law on the construction of a statute, the Employment Protection (Consolidation) Act 1978, the point being taken for the first time before the Employment Appeal Tribunal on appeal from an industrial tribunal.

On 17 December 1980 the appeal tribunal decided that the three appellant employees had been dismissed by the respondent employers for taking part in 'other industrial action' than a strike within s 62(1)(*b*) of the Employment Protection (Consolidation) Act 1978; and as no other relevant employees had not been dismissed or offered re-engagement, the industrial tribunal had no jurisdiction to determine whether their dismissal was fair or unfair by virtue of s 62(2). The appeal tribunal therefore allowed an appeal from the industrial tribunal, who had heard the employees' claims for compensation for unfair dismissal and had determined on 2 April 1980 by a majority that their dismissal was unfair, and on 5 March 1981 the appeal tribunal gave the employees leave to appeal.

The employees were dismissed without notice on 26 November 1979 for refusing to work overtime at the employers' request. The employers are a small company employing a staff of only 15, nine of them on the shop floor. They make packing cases for goods for despatch and they got a rush order for an export job, which they claimed, and the employees denied, required their workmen to work overtime to get the goods packed and on board ship before a deadline. All the workmen, when threatened with dismissal, complied with the request to work overtime, except the three appellants. They refused and were dismissed.

The only point taken before the industrial tribunal was whether it was a term of their contracts of employment that they should work overtime when requested. That depended on whether an appendix to a recognition and procedure agreement between the employers and the Transport and General Workers' Union incorporated such a term into their contracts. The majority of the tribunal decided that it did not. The dissenting member thought that it did, and further that an employer may have a right to dismiss a workman who will not co-operate by working overtime to help the employer out of a temporary difficulty. The decision of the majority was that, as the employees were not in breach of contract or guilty of misconduct in refusing to work overtime, they were unfairly dismissed.

The employers' challenge to this decision on the ground that there was a term of the employees' contracts obliging them to work overtime if reasonably requested was abandoned at the start of the employers' appeal to the appeal tribunal. The only point taken before the appeal tribunal was a point on s 62 of the 1978 Act not taken below. The appeal tribunal allowed it to be taken because it went to jurisdiction, then decided it in the employers' favour, and decided that it was unnecessary to remit the case to the industrial tribunal, and allowed the appeal. Counsel for the employees, to whom the court is indebted for the manner in which he has argued the appeal before us, concedes that the appeal tribunal were right to hear and decide the point and not to remit the case if it was correct to decide it as the appeal tribunal did. The sole question for us, therefore, is whether the appeal tribunal did decide the point rightly.

In my opinion they did. I agree with the reasons given by May J in giving the judgment of the appeal tribunal with one exception, but in view of the importance of the case and of the arguments addressed to us, I shall state my opinion in my own way, though using many of the words of May J.

Section 62 provides as follows:

> '(1) The provisions of this section shall have effect in relation to an employee who claims that he has been unfairly dismissed by his employer where at the date of dismissal—(*a*) the employer was conducting or instituting a lock-out, or (*b*) the employee was taking part in a strike or other industrial action.
>
> (2) In such a case an industrial tribunal shall not determine whether the dismissal was fair or unfair unless it is shown—(*a*) that one or more relevant employees of the

> same employer have not been dismissed, or (*b*) that one or more such employees have been offered re-engagement, and that the employee concerned has not been offered re-engagement . . .'

Subsection (4) defines 'date of dismissal' and 'relevant employees'.

All the relevant employees were dismissed because only the appellant employees refused to work overtime. So the question is: in refusing to work overtime, were the appellants taking part in 'other industrial action' than a strike within s 62(1)(*b*)?

It has not been suggested, except from the Bench, that they were taking part in a strike. But were they taking part in the same kind of industrial action as a strike? For that is the question prompted by what I regard as the natural and ordinary meaning of the words in their context. There was, according to the findings of the industrial tribunal, a history of a dispute about wages after an increase in November 1978. The employers half promised a further increase, but refused to implement the increase. I quote from the industrial tribunal's decision: 'The men through Mr Cullinan [the second appellant] stated that they would take industrial action.' According to the industrial tribunal, they did. In passages from paras 6 and 9 of the industrial tribunal's decision, which the appeal tribunal quoted, the industrial tribunal found, first—

> 'that the ban on overtime which was indulged in by the workforce was in connection with wage negotiations. Undoubtedly the workforce used it as a weapon. It was industrial action but it was industrial action which did not amount to a breach of contract and was not therefore misconduct. That is the firm view of the majority of this tribunal.'

Second, they found that—

> 'the fact remains that these three [employees] were dismissed for taking industrial action by refusing to work overtime.'

The written grounds of each employee's complaint were these:

> 'For some time before my dismissal, I and the other men employed at the factory had been asking our employers for an increase in wages. We approached them both directly through our shop steward and through the local officer of our union. The management avoided meaningful negotiations and the workforce decided on limited industrial action. For taking part in this I was dismissed without any warning or operation of the ACAS code of conduct or the discplinary procedure set out in the terms and conditions of our contract of employment. The circumstances leading to the dismissal were artificially created by the management and were not bona fide.'

The opinion which each appellant gave as to the reason for his dismissal was:

> 'The company wished to get rid of us because we had several times asked for increased wages or at least to intimidate us so that we would drop our claim for increased wages.'

The appeal tribunal stated their view in this way ([1981] ICR 484 at 489–490):

> '. . . first, it is clear from the evidence and from the reasons the industrial tribunal gave for their decision that the material refusals to work overtime occurred at a time when the employees generally were in dispute with their employers about wages. We refer back to the sentence which we have already quoted from paragraph 6 of the reasons for the decision of the industrial tribunal. It is also clear, we think, that this was the situation from the evidence of the three employees themselves, and the chairman's notes of evidence. One of the witnesses said: "No rise came . . ." that is no rise in pay came ". . . in spite of redundancies. We had no alternative but to ban overtime." Later: "I made clear that over refusal to do overtime we were taking industrial action." Later still: "All refused to work overtime. A ban because of the

> pay rise dispute." Then another witness: "We were told that in no way could they afford to give us a rise so we said we would take industrial action." Then the last quotation which I need incorporate in this judgment; "We all agreed to ban overtime until we heard about our pay rise."'

To that I would add two answers by the third appellant:

> 'I think management created a confrontation over overtime because a dispute over wages had been going on for some time . . . [and in cross-examination:] It seemed to me that management brought about the confrontation. We were wanting to negotiate a wage rise but management produced the deadlock.'

The industrial tribunal were not addressing their minds to s 62 of the 1978 Act and the meaning of the words 'industrial action' there. But I find that that makes the material provided by the evidence quoted, and the findings based on it, all the more impressive. An industrial tribunal and the lay members of the appeal tribunal may be trusted to recognise industrial action when they see it, and that was how both tribunals, as well as one appellant and one other witness, described the employees' refusal to work overtime.

Now counsel submits on the employees' behalf that they ought not to have described it so, because it was not a breach of contract. His point on construction is this: to constitute 'industrial action' in the natural meaning of those words on the part of an employee there must be action in breach of his contract of employment. If he merely refuses to do something which he is not contractually bound to do, he cannot be taking part in industrial action. I would agree that if he refuses because he has a private commitment to visit a sick friend, or a personal preference for a football match, he is not taking industrial action. But that is not this case. If he refuses because he and others who refuse with him hope to extract an increase of wages out of his employers because their business will be disrupted if they do not grant it, that continued application of pressure is industrial action in the common sense of the words. I do not feel able to say any more about that argument of counsel for the employees that that is *not* the natural meaning of 'industrial action'. And when the words come at the end of the phrase 'taking part in a strike or other industrial action', they seem to me to cover even more clearly a refusal used as a bargaining weapon, whether it is a breach of contract or not.

As the appeal tribunal said, this may be thought at first sight a somewhat startling result, a gift to employers which requires careful examination. Counsel agree that there is no authority on the question whether industrial action must involve a breach of contract, but that in all reported cases the industrial action considered has in fact involved a breach of contract. As I read *Secretary of State for Employment v Associated Society of Locomotive Engineers and Firemen (No 2)* [1972] 2 All ER 949, [1972] 2 QB 455 that case is no exception, though the judgments of this court there suggest that what the employees did in the instant case may have constituted a breach of an implied contractual obligation such as the dissenting member of the industrial tribunal adumbrated. We were asked by counsel for the employers to support the judgment of the appeal tribunal on that additional and alternative ground without a respondents' notice, and to hold, if necessary, as a point going to jurisdiction, that the employees' industrial action was a breach of contract. I express no opinion on that point, because I think the appeal can and should be decided on the grounds on which it was argued below by other counsel for the employees and by counsel for the employees in this court.

Both counsel rely for the interpretation of the words in s 62 of the 1978 Act on a certain amount of statutory history. In 1971 began a series of statutes following the immunity from liability for unlawful actions conferred since 1906 on certain types of industrial action. I begin with s 26 of the Industrial Regulations Act 1971, which provided as follows:

> '(1) The provisions of this section shall have effect in relation to an employee who claims that he has been unfairly dismissed by his employer, where on the date of

dismissal he was taking part in a strike or in any irregular industrial action short of a strike.

(2) If the reason or principal reason for the dismissal was that the claimant took part in the strike or other industrial action, the dismissal shall not be regarded as unfair unless it is shown—(*a*) that one or more employees of the same employer (in this section referred to as "the original employer"), who also took part in that action, were not dismissed for taking part in it, or (*b*) that one or more such employees, who were dismissed for taking part in it, were offered re-engagement on the termination of the industrial action and that the claimant was not offered such re-engagement, and that the reason (or, if more than one, the principal reason) for which the claimant was selected for dismissal, or not offered re-engagement, was his having taken action to which the next following subsection applies.'

In s 33(4) there was contained a definition of 'irregular industrial action short of a strike'. It provided:

'In this Act "irregular industrial action short of a strike" means any concerted course of conduct (other than a strike) which, in contemplation or furtherance of an industrial dispute,—(*a*) is carried on by a group of workers with the intention of preventing, reducing or otherwise interfering with the production of goods or the provision of services, and (*b*) in the case of some or all of them is carried on in breach of their contracts of employment or (where they are not employees) in breach of their terms and conditions of service.'

It is to be noted that in sub-s (2), as in the sidenote to the section, a 'strike or other industrial action' were referred to, and the full words of sub-s (1), 'irregular industrial action short of a strike' were not repeated. But the first phrase must be shorthand for the second, because it is sub-s (1) which governs the whole of the rest of the section.

The second thing to be noted is that by s 33(4)(*b*) industrial action short of a strike must be action carried on in breach of a contract of employment, and that presumably, at any rate in part, was an elucidation of the word 'irregular' in s 26(1).

Next comes the Trade Union and Labour Relations Act 1974, which by s 1(1) repealed the whole of the Industrial Relations Act 1971. Section 1(2) went on to provide:

'Nevertheless, Schedule 1 to this Act shall have effect for re-enacting, with amendments consequential on the following sections of this Act and other amendments, the under-mentioned provisions of that Act, that is to say . . . (*b*) Part II of that Schedule so re-enacts sections 22 to 33 (unfair dismissal) . . .'

That schedule, and that part of it, Part II, 'so re-enacts' s 26 in para 8, and s 33 in para 15. Paragraph 8, headed 'Dismissal in connection with a strike or other industrial action [Section 26]', provided:

'(1) The provisions of this paragraph shall have effect in relation to an employee who claims that he has been unfairly dismissed by his employer, where on the date of dismissal he was taking part in a strike or other industrial action.

(2) If the reason or principal reason for the dismissal was that the employee took part in the strike or other industrial action, the dismissal shall not be regarded as unfair unless it is shown . . .'

And then there were the same two provisions against discrimination or victimisation, paras (*a*) and (*b*). Paragraph 15, headed 'Pressure on employer to dismiss unfairly [Section 33],' provided:

'In determining, for the purposes of this Part of this Schedule any question as to the reason, or principal reason, for which an employee was dismissed or any question whether the reason or principal reason for which an employee was dismissed was a reason fulfilling the requirements of paragraph 6(1)(*b*) above or whether the employer acted reasonably in treating it as a sufficient reason for dismissing him,—

(*a*) no account shall be taken of any pressure which, by calling, organising, procuring or financing a strike or other industrial action, or threatening to do so, was exercised on the employer to dismiss the employee, and (*b*) any such question shall be determined as if no such pressure had been exercised.'

The interesting feature of that limited re-enactment of sections of an Act which had been totally repealed is that it contained no repetition of the requirement of the industrial action being a breach of contract, and no repetition of the qualification of the other industrial action being irregular and short of a strike.

Next comes the Employment Protection Act 1975, an Act which amended the law relating to workers' rights. Section 125(1) provided that the provisions of, inter alia, the Trade Union and Labour Relations Act 1974 specified in Part III of Sch 16, should 'have effect subject to the amendments so specified ... being minor amendments and amendments consequential on any provisions of this Act'. These amendments included that made by para 13 of Part III of Sch 16. That paragraph provided:

'For paragraphs 7 and 8 of Schedule 1 (dismissal in connection with industrial action) substitute the following paragraph:—

"7.—(1) The provisions of this paragraph shall have effect in relation to an employee who claims that he has been unfairly dismissed by his employer where at the date of dismissal—(*a*) the employer was conducting or instituting a lock-out; or (*b*) the employee was taking part in a strike or other industrial action.

(2) In such a case an industrial tribunal shall not determine whether the dismissal was fair or unfair unless it is shown—(*a*) that one or more relevant employees of the same employer have not been dismissed, or (*b*) that one or more such employees have been offered re-engagement, and that the employee concerned has not been offered re-engagement."'

The paragraph went on to provide, with one additional paragraph, exactly the same things as s 62 of the 1978 Act.

So, by this so-called minor consequential amendment, Parliament introduced a bar to an industrial tribunal's deciding whether a dismissal was fair or unfair when it took place at a time when the employee was on strike or engaged in other industrial action, unless there is victimisation as in the previous statutes. So the bar, now re-enacted in s 62 of the 1978 Act, is new; the no-victimisation provisions remain.

Paragraph 13 was repealed by s 159(3) of the 1978 Act, to the extent specified in Sch 17 to that Act but, as is plain from what I have read from the two Acts, para 13 was reproduced in s 62 of the 1978 Act, with the omission of one paragraph.

So, industrial tribunals presented with a complaint of unfair dismissal by an employee alleged to have taken part in industrial action had, from 1971 to 1974, to consider that action and the provisions against victimisation, in the course of determining whether he had proved his complaint, but had, from 1975 to 1978 and since, to consider them in order to determine whether he could even try to prove it.

Since the repeal in 1974 of the 1971 Act there are no references in these statutory provisions to the requirement that the 'other industrial action' should be 'irregular' or in breach of contract, or, for that matter, 'short of a strike'; and I respectfully agree with the view of Waterhouse J in giving the judgment of the appeal tribunal in *Rasool v Hepworth Pipe Co Ltd* [1980] ICR 494 at 509 that it is impermissible to import the earlier definition into the later provisions.

Why were those words left out? Why should they be put back? When they were put in, I agree with counsel for the employers that Parliament was thereby indicating that without them 'other industrial action' extended to action involving no breach of contract or irregularity. I would assume that the qualifying words and the definition of them were not accidentally omitted, that there was some reason for deliberately omitting them. I cannot take the words now used as shorthand for the words no longer used or for the now absent definition, and I can find no compelling reason for putting those in after

their four years' absence. Subsequent statutes of 1980 and 1982 have not reinserted them.
a I can infer that the words 'short of a strike' were left out as unnecessary or otiose, but why leave out 'irregular' or the restriction to breaches of contract? Why, furthermore, should the industrial tribunal have to embark on an inquiry into the terms of a claimant's contract of employment, express and implied, in order to decide whether he was taking part in industrial action when he was dismissed?

Counsel for the employees submits that to give these words the extended (and what,
b contrary to his first submission, I have held to be the natural) meaning which they bear if not confined to breaches of contract, would do injustice and defeat the purpose and object of s 62 and its predecessor in the 1975 Act, namely to deprive an employee of his right to complain to an industrial tribunal of unfair dismissal if, and only if, he has been guilty of misconduct or has broken the terms of his contract. If counsel's gloss (for such, contrary to his submission, it clearly is) on the language of the section is rejected,
c unscrupulous employers will be allowed, so he submits, to dismiss unfairly and unjustly those who take legitimate industrial action, without any fear of the circumstances being investigated by the statutory tribunals, or of having to pay compensation or reinstate those unfairly dismissed employees. He calls attention to an obvious misunderstanding by the appeal tribunal of the effect of their interpretation of s 62. In his judgment May J said ([1981] ICR 484 at 489):

d
> 'In our view, the phrase "other industrial action" in section 62 of the Act of 1978 does not necessarily have to be conduct in breach of contract on the part of the employee and we are, for present purposes, only concerned with the employee. We do not propose to define the phrase "other industrial action" in section 62. As we have already said there is no definition in the relevant section of the Act nor in the definition section, and we think that the decision whether or not something was
e "other industrial action" within section 62 can and should be left to the good sense of industrial tribunals. They are locally situated. They know the local employment position. They know, for instance, the area's industries. They know what conditions are in the area. They no doubt know, in some cases at any rate, the parties involved. They will be able to ascertain all the relevant facts. They will be able to make findings about what perhaps may be one of the most important aspects of such a
f case, namely, the motives actuating both sides, that is to say, both employer and employee in the dispute concerned. Having considered these and all other matters which they think pertinent and relevant they will be able to decide whether or not the employees were taking "other industrial action" within section 62 and were dismissed in consequence. When one stresses, as we do, that industrial tribunals should, in considering this part of the relevant legislation, look at not merely the
g actions but also the motives of both sides of the dispute, employer and employee, we feel quite happy that this judgment will not provide the licence for many uncompensated dismissals, which [counsel for the employees] suggested would follow our decision.'

Now with all that I respectfully agree, except with the statement that tribunals will be
h able to ascertain all the relevant facts, including the motives actuating *the employer* and the question whether or not the employees were dismissed in consequence of their industrial action. For once an industrial tribunal, in the exercise of its good sense, decides that an employee was, at the date of his dismissal, taking part in industrial action, whether in breach of his contract or not, with the object of applying pressure on his employer or of disrupting his business, the tribunal must refuse to entertain the
j complaint or to go into the questions of the employer's motive or reasons for dismissing. And this is a result which requires plain language. If there was any ambiguity in the words of the section, I would reject the appeal tribunal's construction of the phrase, their refusal to define it and their leaving its application to the good sense of industrial tribunals.

Counsel for the employers concedes that the criticisms of this part of May J's judgment are well founded, but counters the potential injustice relied on by counsel for the employees by submitting that the purpose and object of the section is to avoid courts of law and tribunals being required to investigate the rights and wrongs, or to adjudicate on the merits, of trade disputes in the context of unfair dismissal applications. He referred us to what Lord Scarman said in *NWL Ltd v Woods* [1979] 3 All ER 614 at 630, [1979] 1 WLR 1294 at 1312 about the policy of the 1974 Act to exclude trade disputes from judicial review by the courts and to substitute an advisory, conciliation and arbitration process; and he pointed out that such disputes are often complex and to give the determination of them to industrial tribunals would defeat the legislative aim of providing cheap and speedy hearings of unfair dismissal complaints by such tribunals. These considerations must, he submitted, have outweighed with the legislature the potential injustice created by the statutory ban imposed not only on determining complaints by strikers or those engaged in industrial action by s 62(1)(*b*), but imposed by s 62(1)(*a*) on determining complaints by employees locked out by employers at the date of dismissal.

I feel the force of these submissions, but no certainty as to the intention of the legislature in enacting this provision.

In threading my way from section and subsections to schedule and paragraphs, and from schedule back to section, I may have lost the way, or the thread, or sight of Parliament's aim and object, even if Parliament itself did not. But of this I have no doubt, that as there is no compelling reason why the words of the provision should not be given their natural and ordinary meaning, and good reason why they should not now be defined as once they were, we ought to give them that meaning and apply them, as the appeal tribunal did, to the undisputed facts of the case in favour of the respondent employers.

I would accordingly affirm their decision and dismiss this appeal.

PURCHAS LJ. I agree with all that has fallen from Stephenson LJ. I only add a few words of my own out of respect for the forceful argument proposed by counsel for the employees and because we are told that the point central to this appeal has not specifically been considered in this court.

I hope that I do justice to the main submission of counsel for the employees if I summarise it in this way: in order to mitigate the effect of the words 'strike or other industrial action' in s 62(1)(*b*) of the Employment Protection (Consolidation) Act 1978, it is necessary to add by way of definition or implication the words 'in breach of contract of employment or service'; otherwise, industrial action could, and in this case did, extend to an employee declining to do something which he was not in any event obliged to do under his contract of employment or service. In such a context an unscrupulous employer could dismiss an employee for his own purposes, and the industrial tribunal would be prevented from inquiring into the matter.

In this context I respectfully agree with what Stephenson LJ has said about the one part of the finding of the Employment Appeal Tribunal which counsel for the employers found himself unable to support. This, submitted counsel for the employees, would open the floodgates of abuse and strike at the whole object of the legislation providing employment protection. Counsel for the employees submitted that, however the statute might be worded, this could not have been the intention of Parliament.

Counsel for the employers contended that the submissions of counsel for the employees were based on a fallacy and that the true intention of the legislation was to keep the industrial tribunals and the courts away from the complicated, and sometimes extensive, areas of dispute involved in cases of strikes or other industrial action. Counsel for the employers submitted that once this intention was appreciated, then the question whether or not the industrial action involved also amounted to a breach of contract was irrelevant, and that therefore the words of s 62 of the 1978 Act could be given their plain and ordinary meaning, namely once it was established that the employee was, at the date of his dismissal, engaged in a strike or other industrial action, the industrial tribunal could only enter on a consideration of the merits of the case if it could be shown that the *a* employee had been subjected to discriminatory treatment in the matter of dismissal or re-engagement.

I agree with this submission. In order to find a reference to breach of contract, it is necessary to go back to the Industrial Relations Act 1971. Section 26 of that Act referred to 'irregular industrial action short of a strike'. Subsection (1) depended on the necessity of the employee being shown at the date of his dismissal to be taking part in a strike or *b* any irregular industrial action short of a strike. Although s 26(2) did not specifically repeat the word 'irregular', I accept the submission of counsel for the employers that, taking the section as a whole, the omission of the word 'irregular' from sub-s (2) was of no import; the whole of the provisions of s 26 were geared to sub-s (1) where the word 'irregular' was included.

In s 33(4) of the 1971 Act there was a definition of 'irregular industrial action short of *c* a strike'; it was defined as—

> 'any concerted course of conduct other than a strike which, in contemplation or furtherance of an industrial dispute, is carried on by a group of workers with the intention of preventing, reducing or otherwise interfering with the production of goods or the provision of services . . .'

d I pause at this point before continuing to note that there was no mention of breach of contract in s 33(4)(*a*). Section 33(4)(*b*) added a further qualification to the definition of 'irregular industrial action short of a strike' and referred, for the first and only time in this legislation so far as this particular aspect is concerned, to breach of contract.

It may well be that, as has been mentioned by Stephenson LJ, some guidance can be obtained, if it is necessary to define 'industrial action', from s 33(4)(*a*), where it was *e* dealing with concerted actions by groups of workers, with a certain intention defined.

It was in the context of the provisions of s 6 and s 33 of the Industrial Relations Act 1971 that in *Secretary of State for Employment v Associated Society of Locomotive Engineers and Firemen (No 2)* [1972] 2 All ER 949, [1972] 2 QB 455 this court was specifically concerned with the question of whether or not a breach of contract was established. But as I have indicated in this judgment already, once one departs from the provisions of the *f* 1971 Act, in my judgment the question of breach of contract is no longer relevant to the definition of 'other industrial action'.

The Trade Union and Labour Relations Act 1974, by s 1(1), repealed the whole of the 1971 Act. By sub-s (2)(*b*) of s 1 of the 1974 Act, certain parts of the 1971 Act were re-enacted with amendments. The relevant re-enactment is to be found in para 8 of Sch 1, where reference is made to the phrase 'strike or other industrial action'. It is to be noted *g* that the word 'irregular' has gone, but the words 'other industrial action' have remained.

Paragraph 15 of Sch 1, which re-enacted certain parts of s 33 of the 1971 Act, did not re-enact the definition of 'irregular industrial action'; nor did it make any reference to breach of contract. As Stephenson LJ has already indicated, it is not, certainly in my judgment, open to this court to assume that the alterations and amendments in the re-enactments involved in Sch 1 to the 1974 Act were not deliberate in their particular *h* omissions, to which I have made reference.

So far as the duties and powers of an industrial tribunal are concerned, until the enactment of the Employment Protection Act 1975, the respective sections merely provided the circumstances in which the tribunal should, or should not, find a dismissal to be unfair. In the Employment Protection Act 1975 there was, in my judgment, an important change of attitude. That Act, in Part I, which is headed 'Machinery for *j* Promoting the Improvement of Industrial Relations', provided for the Advisory, Conciliation and Arbitration Service (in the Act referred to as 'the Service') in s 1.

I only mention the provisions of Part I of the 1975 Act as part of the background to the effect of s 125, which is the specific section introducing what are described in the margin as 'minor and consequential amendments', etc, and which in the body of the section, dealing with Part III of the schedule, which relates to the provisions of the 1974

Act specifically, provides for enactments, minor amendments and amendments consequential on any provisions of the Act; and of course one of the provisions of the Act a is the establishment of what is now known as ACAS in Part I of the Act.

Paragraph 13 of Sch 16 to the 1975 Act replaces what had previously been paras 7 and 8 of Sch 1 to the 1974 Act. In effect it provides for the continuation of the provisions excluding the consideration of matters by the industrial tribunal where it is established that at the date of dismissal the employee was taking part (I quote now from para 13 and s 7(*b*)) in 'a strike or other industrial action'. b

Again there is the proviso that the industrial tribunal shall not consider the merits of the case once it is established or shown that the employee was, at the date of his dismissal, engaged or taking part in a strike or other industrial action. The significant difference is to be found in the words 'In such a case an industrial tribunal shall not determine whether the dismissal was fair or unfair unless' (see para 13 and s 7(2) of Sch 16 to the 1975 Act) and then the previous provisions relating to discriminatory treatment are c repeated.

There is by the words of this schedule, for the first time in this legislation so far as I can see, a total withdrawal of jurisdiction from the industrial tribunal, as opposed to a direction as to the nature of their finding in certain circumstances. It was on that basis that the Employment Appeal Tribunal were, in my judgment rightly, prepared to deal with the matter on a ground that had not been deployed before the industrial tribunal; d but there is nothing that I wish to add on this aspect of the case to that which has already fallen from Stephenson LJ.

It is clear that the intention of Parliament was to remove, as counsel for the employers has submitted, from the areas of consideration of the industrial tribunal, saving only the special aspects of discriminatory treatment, any question which arose out of a strike or industrial action. e

I refer to the speech of Lord Scarman in *NWL Ltd v Woods* [1979] 3 All ER 614 at 630, [1979] 1 WLR 1294 at 1312 where Lord Scarman referred to the court of inquiry into the Grunwick affair, where reference was made to the intentions of Parliament in this legislation.

In the light of the history of the Acts, to which I have made reference, which led to the passing of the 1978 Act, I have no doubt that there is no justification, let alone a mandate, f to import, by interpretation or implication, the words 'breach of contract' to qualify the meaning of 'other industrial action', and that the words must be given their plain and ordinary meaning, namely where it is shown that an employee was taking part in a strike or other industrial action, the industrial tribunal can only deal with individual discriminatory action within the provisions of s 62(2) of the 1978 Act.

Accordingly, I agree that this appeal must fail. g

SIR GEORGE BAKER. I agree with both judgments, and have nothing further to add.

Appeal dismissed. Leave to appeal to the House of Lords refused.

Solicitors: *Burnett Barker*, Bury St Edmunds (for the employees); *Peter Blackmore*, Sutton (for the employers).

Diana Brahams Barrister.

National Westminster Bank Ltd v Hart

COURT OF APPEAL, CIVIL DIVISION
WALLER LJ AND SIR DAVID CAIRNS
13, 14, 27 JANUARY 1983

Landlord and tenant – Title – Right of tenant to question landlord's title – Estoppel – Tenant paying rent to landlord in ignorance of fact that landlord's title previously determined – Tenant refusing to pay rent on discovering true facts about landlord's title – Tenant unable to show that there was a third party who had a better title than landlord – Whether tenant estopped from denying landlord's title.

The freeholders granted the tenant's predecessor in title a lease of a house for 99 years from March 1868. The tenant acquired the residue of the lease in 1921 and subsequently sublet the house to subtenants. The headlease expired in March 1967 but the subtenants were not informed of that and continued to pay rent to the tenant until he died in August 1978. Thereafter they paid the rent to a bank which was appointed as the tenant's executor, until they discovered later in 1978 that the headlease had long since expired. The subtenants then refused to pay any further rent to the bank until it satisfied them that it had good title to the house and was accordingly entitled to receive the rent. No heirs or assignees of the original freeholders could be traced. The bank informed the subtenants that they were not in a position to deny the bank's title and brought an action against them to recover the arrears of rent. The judge gave judgment for the bank on the grounds (i) that by continuing to pay rent after the headlease had expired the subtenants had acknowledged the tenant's title and (ii) that they were estopped from challenging that title because they could not show that there was anyone who had a better title than the bank as the tenant's executor. On appeal by the subtenants,

Held – A lessee who paid rent to a lessor after the lessor's title had been determined was subsequently estopped from disputing the lessor's title only if it was shown that at the time at which the rent was paid the lessee knew, or had notice of, the true facts about the lessor's title. Accordingly, the subtenants were not estopped from denying the bank's title merely because they could not show that there was a third party who had a better title than the bank. Since there was no evidence that they knew that the headlease had expired when they paid the rent, it followed that they were entitled to resist the bank's claim for the arrears of rent. The appeal would therefore be allowed (see p 180 *e f*, p 181 *b* to *f* and *h* and p 183 *g* to p 184 *b*, post).

Fenner v Duplock (1884) 2 Bing 10 and *Serjeant v Nash Field & Co* [1900–3] All ER Rep 525 followed.

Carlton v Bowcock (1884) 51 LT 659 and *Hindle v Hick Bros Manufacturing Co Ltd* [1947] 2 All ER 825 considered.

Notes

For estoppel by the payment of rent, see 16 Halsbury's Laws (4th edn) para 1629.

For cases on what amounts to admission of lessee's title, see 31(1) Digest (Reissue) 44–45, 269–280.

Cases referred to in judgments

Carlton v Bowcock (1884) 51 LT 659.
Doe d Higginbotham v Barton (1840) 11 Ad & El 307, 113 ER 432.
England d Syburn v Slade (1792) 4 Term Rep 682, 100 ER 1243.
Fenner v Duplock (1824) 2 Bing 10, 130 ER 207.
Hindle v Hick Bros Manufacturing Co Ltd [1947] 2 All ER 825, CA.

Rogers v Pitcher (1815) 6 Taunt 202, 128 ER 1012.
Serjeant v Nash Field & Co [1903] 2 KB 304, [1900–3] All ER Rep 525, CA. a
Walton v Waterhouse (1671) 2 Wm Saund 420, 85 ER 1233.

Cases also cited
Industrial Properties (Barton Hill) Ltd v Associated Electrical Industries Ltd [1977] 2 All ER 293, [1977] QB 580, CA.
Mountnoy v Collier (1853) 1 E & B 630, 118 ER 573. b
Robertson's Application, Re [1969] 1 All ER 257, [1969] 1 WLR 109.

Appeal
The defendants, Alfred Ernest Hart and Dulcie Marjorie Hart, appealed against a judgment of his Honour Judge Barr, given on 11 January 1982 at Brentford County Court, whereby he held that the plaintiffs, National Westminster Bank Ltd, were entitled c
to arrears of rent, totalling £1,347, from the defendants who were occupying the property known as 42 Haggard Road, Twickenham. The facts are set out in the judgment of Waller LJ.

Jonathan Parker QC and *Nicholas Asprey* for the defendants. d
J Anthony Moncaster for the plaintiffs.

Cur adv vult

27 January. The following judgments were delivered. e

WALLER LJ. This is an appeal from the decision of his Honour Judge Barr sitting at Brentford County Court and given on 11 January 1982. The actual decision was that the respondent bank, executors of C W Cowles (the plaintiffs), were entitled to arrears of rent from the defendants, who live at 42 Haggard Road, Twickenham. On the decision not only does payment of rent depend, but in all probability the ownership of the freehold f
of that house.

C P and C W Cowles were long leaseholders of that house, and Mr and Mrs Hart, the defendants, had been in possession of the house as protected tenants paying rent to the Cowles for a number of years. Unknown to the defendants, the long lease under which C P and C W Cowles held the house expired on 25 March 1967. Thereafter they had no legal title to the premises or to rent. When C W Cowles died on 4 August 1978, the g
defendants discovered that the lease had determined in 1967 and wrote to the plaintiffs asking for confirmation that the plaintiffs were entitled to receive rent. The plaintiffs replied saying that the defendants were not in a position to deny their present landlord and therefore were not entitled to withhold rent. Nevertheless, the defendants withheld the rent, putting it aside so that the money would be available if the plaintiffs were h
entitled to receive it.

The history, so far as is relevant, was that the house was built in 1867 and was let on a 99-year lease expiring 25 March 1967. The residue of the lease was acquired by C P and C W Cowles in 1921, and in 1947 Mrs Hart moved in as a tenant of a sublease of C P and C W Cowles, but that sublease expired in March 1965. Thereafter the defendants were requested to pay rent to Messrs Cowles, but C P Cowles died on 4 March 1967, leaving C W Cowles as the sole survivor. In January 1973, the agents for C P and C W Cowles j
(who were a partnership) asked the defendants to agree a new rent, and a new rent was fixed in March. In the particulars of agreement, C P and C W Cowles described themselves as the landlord. The judge held that this was an adjustment of rent and was not a new tenancy, and no appeal is made against that part of his decision.

In March 1978 the defendants wrote asking for some work to be done, and said: 'It is

within your power as holders of the lease to have a grant from the local council.' So at
a that date, the defendants had no doubts about the tenancy, and the Cowles made no denial of this.

On 4 August 1978 C W Cowles died, leaving the plaintiffs as executors, and there then followed correspondence from the defendants saying that they were not going to pay the rent until they were satisfied that the plaintiffs had good title, but that they would put the money aside to be paid as soon as they were so satisfied. The plaintiffs did not provide
b any further information, and in due course these proceedings were started.

There can be no question but that the Cowleses' title as lessees expired on 25 March 1967. Furthermore, no heir or assignee of Mr James Haggard, the original freeholder, has been discovered. The judge held that the defendants were estopped from denying the title of the plaintiffs as executors of C W Cowles to recover the rent, and gave judgment for the rent outstanding.

c The defendants submit that they became tenants of this house before 1965, at which time they became the tenants of the Cowleses, and that the Cowleses made no communication to them in 1967 when the headlease expired. The defendants cannot be estopped by the fact that they paid rent from March 1967 until August 1978, because they did not know the facts, and the plaintiffs did not tell them. They submit that neither the Cowleses nor their personal representatives have title to 42 Haggard Road.
d They rely on *Fenner v Duplock* (1824) 2 Bing 10, 130 ER 207 and *Serjeant v Nash Field & Co* [1903] 2 KB 304, [1900–3] All ER Rep 525, and submit that the judge was in error in his conclusions.

The plaintiffs submit that the defendants are not entitled to succeed because the defendants are unable to prove an adverse claim by a third party. They rely on *Carlton v Bowcock* (1884) 51 LT 659 and *Hindle v Hick Bros Manufacturing Co Ltd* [1947] 2 All ER
e 825.

The judge, being of opinion that the reasoning in *Carlton* and *Hindle* was inconsistent with *Fenner* and *Serjeant*, preferred *Carlton* and *Hindle*, and since there was no adverse claim by a third party on the facts of this case, gave judgment for the plaintiffs.

Estoppel between landlord and tenant is estoppel by convention and arises when two parties agree to become landlord and tenant, and do so become. The landlord cannot
f derogate from his grant and the tenant cannot dispute the landlord's title:

> 'When the parties have acted in their transaction upon the agreed assumption that a given state of facts is to be accepted between them as true, then as regards that transaction each will be estopped against the other from questioning the truth of the statement of facts so assumed.'

g (See *Spencer Bower and Turner on Estoppel by Representation* (3rd edn, 1977) p 157.)

In *Fenner v Duplock* Duplock having bought premises from Collins, who had taken them under Brooks' will, let them to Fenner. When Brooks died, his heir at law claimed the rent. The question was whether Fenner, who had been paying rent to Duplock for such premises, was estopped from denying Duplock's title when a third party claimed that Duplock's title was based on a life interest which had determined, and where Fenner
h had made a number of payments of rent after he should have known about the defective title.

Best CJ said (2 Bing 10 at 11–12, 130 ER 207 at 208):

> 'According to the case of *England d. Syburn* v. *Slade* ((1792) 4 Term Rep 682, 100 ER 1243), a tenant, though he cannot dispute the right of his landlord to demise, may shew that his title has expired, and the rule is founded on good sense and
> j justice; because if it were otherwise, the tenant might be called on to pay his rent twice over. Although, however, a tenant may shew that his landlord's title has expired, yet if he enters on a new tenancy, he shall be bound; but before he can be so bound, it must appear that he was acquainted with all the circumstances of the landlord's title: the landlord, before he enters into any new contract, must say openly, "My former title is at an end; will you, notwithstanding, go on?" The

> Defendant in the present case knew that his title was at an end; was it honest in him to persist in his claim, and to call for rent under such circumstances?' a

In *Serjeant v Nash Field & Co* [1903] 2 KB 304 at 312, [1900–3] All ER Rep 525 at 529 Collins MR said:

> 'It is clear law that though a tenant cannot deny the title of his landlord to deal with the premises, he may prove that the title has determined. The fact was abundantly proved, and there was certainly no estoppel arising from any act of the b tenant which could induce the mortgagees to suppose that they were acting on an admission that the relation of landlord and tenant existed when the distress was put in.'

Stirling LJ said ([1903] 2 KB 304 at 314, [1900–3] All ER Rep 525 at 530):

> 'Though a tenant is precluded from denying his landlord's title at the time of the c demise, yet it is open to him to show that his landlord's interest had determined. The cases on this point are collected in the notes to *Walton* v. *Waterhouse* ((1671) 2 Wm Saund 420, 85 ER 1233). In *Doe* v. *Barton* ((1840) 11 Ad & El 307, 113 ER 432), which was a case of a tenant holding under a mortgagor, the law is thus stated by Lord Denman C.J.: "That rule is fully established: viz., that a tenant cannot deny that the person by whom he is let into possession had title at that time; but he may d show that such title is determined".'

Mathew LJ said ([1903] 2 KB 304 at 315–316, [1900–3] All ER Rep 525 at 532):

> 'It is further said that there is an estoppel between the parties to this action, based on a supposed representation made by the plaintiff to the mortgagees that he was still their tenant. Upon the facts of the case that is not so.' e

It is to be observed that, although there was in each of these cases a third party claimant, in none of the judgments is it suggested that a third party claimant is necessary before the tenant can deny his landlord's title. Indeed, it is clear from the judgments of Collins MR and Stirling LJ, and from the passage quoted from Lord Denman CJ that it was not so regarded.

f

Carlton v Bowcock (1884) 51 LT 659 was not a case of the landlord's title determining. It was a case where the landlord, one Watson, died, and the agent gave to the defendant tenants a receipt for the payment of rent, at first stated to be on behalf of Watson's executors, then on behalf of his representatives, and finally on behalf of his trustees. When there appeared doubts about the title, the tenants stopped paying. The judge was satisfied that, if asked, the agents would have said they were claiming on behalf of the plaintiff. Cave J said (at 660–661): g

> 'Receipt of the rent is *prima facie* evidence of the title as assignee of the reversion of the person to whom it is paid; but the tenant may show, if he can, that there is a third person who is in fact the assignee of the reversion, and that he paid rent by mistake or in ignorance of the facts relating to the title. Thus, in *Rogers* v. *Pitcher* ((1815) 6 Taunt 202, 128 ER 1012), which was an action of replevin, the plaintiff, h notwithstanding that he had paid rent to the defendant as assignee of the reversion, was allowed to prove that in fact one Mrs. Baker was the assignee of the reversion, and that he had paid rent to the defendant in ignorance of the true state of the title . . . I think the conclusions to be drawn from these cases are: (1) That where a person claiming to be assignee of the reversion obtains payment of rent from the tenant by fraud or misrepresentation, such payment is no evidence of title, but that j receipt of the rent is *prima facie* evidence of title where there is no such fraud or misrepresentation; (2) that where rent is paid by the tenant under such circumstances as to amount to *prima facie* evidence of title, the person receiving the rent is in as good a position as if he were actually in possession; and that, although it is open to the tenant to prove, if he can, that he paid the rent in ignorance of the true state of

the title, and that some third person is the real assignee of the reservation, yet he must show such a title in that third person as would entitle him to a verdict in ejectment, and that it is not enough to show that the person to whom the rent was paid has no title, his receipt of the rent being sufficient until a better title is shown.'

This case was followed in *Hindle v Hick Bros Manufacturing Co Ltd* [1947] 2 All ER 825, another case of an assignment of the reversion where the Court of Appeal followed and approved the decision in *Carlton v Bowcock*.

Can the reasoning of these two lines of cases be reconciled? The plaintiffs submit that they are not inconsistent because in *Fenner v Duplock* and in *Serjeant v Nash Field & Co*, although in neither case did the judges mention it, there was in each case a third party claimant. There was in each case a possible third party claimant, but in my judgment the existence of such a person was not regarded by the judge as important. In *Fenner*'s case, Best CJ, having said that a tenant may show that his title has expired, said that the rule was founded on good sense, 'because if it were otherwise the tenant might be called on to pay his rent twice over'. And in *Serjeant v Nash Field & Co* the observations of each member of the court were quite specific, and I cannot believe that the necessity would have gone unmentioned by each member of the court if it was regarded as a requirement.

Counsel for the defendants submits that the decisions are quite consistent because when considering estoppel there is a great difference between the case of the landlord's title determining without informing a tenant so that the tenant in ignorance continues to pay rent, and the case of the landlord assigning his interest and the tenant, aware that there has been an assignment, paying rent to the assignee. In the latter case he is on notice that there has been a change of landlord and it is for him to decide whether to pay his rent to the assignee or not. If he does, he cannot be heard to complain about the assignee's title unless there is somebody else claiming title. It is clear from the care with which Cave J set out the receipts in his judgment that he regarded them as important because they gave notice of the change. In the former case of the landlord's title determining, the tenant does not know because nothing has happened to give him notice of the change. There can be no estoppel unless the tenant knows the facts or he has had notice which should have warned him.

As counsel for the defendants pointed out, there is a logical difference between the assignee and the landlord whose title has determined. When the tenant has freely entered into a tenancy agreement with the landlord and has as a consequence entered into possession, so long as he is in possession he is estopped from denying his landlord's title. However, the tenant whose landlord has assigned the tenancy and he, with notice, has accepted the assignee, he cannot challenge the assignee's title unless there is a third party claiming to be the landlord.

Finally, in the case of the landlord whose title has determined and who has not informed the tenant, 'it is clear law that though a tenant cannot deny the title of his landlord to deal with the premises, he may prove that the title has determined' (see per Collins MR in *Serjeant*'s case [1903] 2 KB 304 at 312, [1900–3] All ER Rep 525 at 529).

In the present case in my opinion if the plaintiffs had told the defendants in 1967 that their title had determined, the defendants would have been under no obligation to pay rent to them. The plaintiffs not having disclosed the fact that their title had determined, the defendants cannot now be estopped from relying on that determination. I have come to the conclusion that the defendants are not liable to pay rent to the plaintiffs, and I would allow this appeal.

SIR DAVID CAIRNS. There are two lines of authority on the question of the effect of the payment of rent by 'A' to 'B' when it may be that 'B' has no estate in the land. The question that has arisen in each set of cases is whether 'B' can claim later rent because of the payment of the earlier rent. The two lines seem to have developed independently without any cross-reference between one and the other. Cases in one line are more favourable to the tenant, and in the other more favourable to the landlord. (I use these terms without prejudice to the issue of whether there is a tenancy or not.) a

A pair of cases from each set were cited to the judge below, and to us. The judge held that the two lines were inconsistent with each other and, considering that the cases more favourable to the landlord laid down the correct rule of law, he gave judgment for the plaintiffs. The defendants appeal, contending that the cases which favour the tenant are the cases that govern the present case. The plaintiffs resist the appeal, making the converse contention. b

Counsel on both sides before us submitted that all the cases were consistent with each other, but each submitted that the facts brought the matter within the cases favouring his clients.

The cases favouring the tenant are *Fenner v Duplock* (1824) 2 Bing 10, 130 ER 207 and *Serjeant v Nash Field & Co* [1903] 2 KB 304, [1900–3] All ER Rep 525. They are both cases where there was a letting by a lessee to a tenant who occupied the premises and paid rent c after the lessee's title had expired.

In *Fenner* the head lessor, Collins, had only an estate for life, but after he died the tenant, Fenner, continued to pay rent to the lessee, Duplock. When rent had twice been demanded of him by Judge, the heir to the lead lessor, Fenner refused to pay any more to Duplock, who then distrained on him. Fenner brought a replevin and it was found by a jury that Duplock knew that he held only for the life of Collins; that Fenner knew of d Judge's claim but had paid in ignorance of its nature and in ignorance that Collins had only an estate for life. On those findings he was held by the court sitting in banc to be entitled to succeed because, as it was put by Best CJ, payment of rent was evidence of attornment only if the tenant knew all the circumstances.

In *Serjeant* the original landlord's title was ended by the forfeiture of his lease, after he had been made bankrupt and a receiver had been appointed by mortgagees of his lease. e The tenant made a payment of rent to the receiver after he knew of the forfeiture, but did not know the ground of it. He refused the next quarter's rent, the receiver distrained, and the tenant sued him for wrongful distress. The tenant succeeded in the action, tried with a jury, and the receiver appealed, contending that the tenant was estopped from denying the title of the receiver because of his last payment of rent. The appeal was dismissed. f

It was held by Collins MR that the estoppel broke down because (1) it was doubtful whether payment of rent was ever enough to raise an estoppel, and (2) if it was, there was no estoppel at the time of the distress because a tenant was entitled to prove that his landlord's title had come to an end. There was no act of his which could have induced the mortgagees to believe that they were acting on an admission of his that the relation of landlord and tenant still existed (see [1903] 2 KB 304 at 312, [1900–3] All ER Rep 525 g at 529).

Stirling LJ said that, though a tenant is precluded from denying the landlord's title at the time of the demise, he is not precluded from denying that the title has expired (*Doe d Higginbotham v Barton* (1840) 11 Ad & El 307, 113 ER 432). He held further that the payment did not estop because the tenant did not know the ground of the forfeiture, and he cited *Fenner v Duplock* (see [1903] 2 KB 304 at 314, [1900–3] All ER Rep 525 at 530). h Mathew LJ agreed, saying that there was no representation by the tenant to raise an estoppel (see [1903] 2 KB 304 at 316, [1900–3] All ER Rep 525 at 532).

The cases favouring the landlord are not cases where a lessee landlord's lease had been determined by effluxion of time or forfeiture or otherwise, but where a person claiming as assignee of a lease did not establish that he had any estate in the land but relied on the payment of rent. The first is *Carlton v Bowcock* (1884) 51 LT 659 and the second is *Hindle* j *v Hick Bros Manufacturing Co Ltd* [1947] 2 All ER 825.

In *Carlton* one Watson had let premises to the defendants for five years. During the currency of that lease he died, having left the reversion to the plaintiff, his executor. Agents for the plaintiff collected rents from the defendants giving receipts on behalf of 'Watson's executors', 'Watson's representatives' and 'Watson's trustees'. The defendants

made no inquiry, and Cave J found that if they had done so they would have been told
a that the rents were being collected for the plaintiff. The agents then discovered that there was a doubt whether Watson's will, made in Scotland, was validly witnessed so as to pass the property in England to the plaintiff. For the purposes of the case the judge was asked to assume that it was not. It was argued for the defendants that there was no attornment, or if there was, it was by mistake and in ignorance of the facts. Cave J held that it was unnecessary to decide whether there was an attornment, that payment of rent to one
b claiming as assignee was not an estoppel, but was prima facie evidence that the landlord was entitled to the rent unless the payments were made by mistake or in ignorance of facts relating to the title. He went on to say that in the absence of fraud or misrepresentation, the tenant could only defeat the landlord's claim by showing that when he paid the rent he was ignorant of the true state of the title, and that some third person was the real assignee.

c In *Hindle* there was a claim for possession and rent by assignees from persons purporting to convey as trustees for sale. Prior to the alleged assignment, the defendants had been paying rent to agents for the landlords 'whoever they might be'. After the alleged assignment, the defendants paid rent to the plaintiffs. Then they stopped. It was uncertain how the tenancy had been created. The defence was that the plaintiffs had no title. The plaintiffs relied on the payments of rent to them. The county court judge held that there
d was 'a good deal of knowledge by the defendants'. He decided in favour of the plaintiffs, and his decision was upheld by the Court of Appeal. Tucker and Bucknill LJJ both held expressly that the rules laid down by Cave J in *Carlton* were correct. Tucker LJ based his decision on the finding that the defendants had not paid in ignorance but he went on to say that if the defendants had established a prima facie case that the estate was in A or B, neither of whom had made any claim, it was doubtful if that was sufficient; that part of
e his judgment shows that he was upholding Cave J's view that, to succeed, the defendants had to prove both ignorance and that there was some person who was the true assignee.

Roxburgh J's short judgment indicates by implication that he was taking the same view (see [1947] 2 All ER 825 at 828). Bucknill LJ simply said that for the defendants to succeed would be unjust.

The contention of counsel for the defendants before us was that the critical question in
f both types of case was whether the tenant, when paying rent, was making a deliberate choice between two possible claimants. On that basis the present defendants would succeed because so long as they were paying rent, they had nothing to put them on notice that the lease had expired. But it does not appear to me that there was any less a deliberate choice in *Fenner* and *Serjeant* than in *Carlton* and *Hindle*. Fenner chose to pay Duplock rather than Judge after he knew of Judge's claim, and Serjeant chose to pay the receiver
g after he knew of the action for forfeiture.

Counsel for the plaintiffs submitted that the tenant could only succeed if he could show that there was some existing person who was really entitled to the estate, like Judge in *Fenner*'s case, and the head lessor in *Serjeant*'s. On that basis the defendants would fail here because they could not point to anybody who had a better title to the land than the plaintiffs. But there is no suggestion in the judgment in either of the cases in which
h tenants were successful that this was a factor which turned the scales in their favour.

I cannot understand why *Fenner* and *Serjeant* were treated by the courts as cases where, if the landlords were to succeed, it would be on the ground of estoppel, whereas in *Carlton* and *Hindle* the basis on which the landlords did succeed was that the payment of rent was prima facie evidence of title which could only be rebutted in a particular way.

For my part I agree with the trial judge that the two lines of authority are in conflict
j with each other in the sense that there is no apparent doctrine to justify the different judgments in the different cases. But I do not feel able to go on, as the judge did, to prefer the reasoning in one line to the other. I have to fall back on the fact that the two cases of *Fenner* and *Serjeant* are directly relevant to the instant case in that they are cases of the landlord's lease having come to an end, whereas the other two cases are not directly relevant in that they are concerned with assignments. For that reason I consider that this

court should apply the principles established in the first two cases, and decide in favour of the tenants.

I would add that it seems to me that the plaintiffs in this case might have contended that they and their predecessors had been in possession of the rents and profits for more than 12 years, paying no rent and in no way recognising the rights of whoever may have been the freeholder, and that in that way they might have acquired a possessory title. But no such case was open to them on the pleadings, nor discussed in the court below.

For the reasons I have given, I agree that the appeal should be allowed.

Appeal allowed. Declaration made as claimed.

Solicitors: *David Baker & Co*, Isleworth (for the defendants); *Routh Stacey* (for the plaintiffs).

Sophie Craven Barrister.

Hillesden Securities Ltd v Ryjak Ltd and another

QUEEN'S BENCH DIVISION
PARKER J
3 DECEMBER 1982, 19 JANUARY 1983

Conversion – Damages – Measure of damages – Profit-earning chattel – Sale of profit-earning chattel by lessee without title – Defendant purchaser admitting liability – Plaintiffs claiming hire charge from date of conversion until return of chattel as damages – Defendant contending damages should be value of chattel at date of conversion plus interest – Whether assessment of damages for interference with goods the same under statute as damages at common law for conversion – Torts (Interference with Goods) Act 1977, s 3.

In 1979 the owner of a motor vehicle leased it for three years as part of his business activities. While the agreement was still in force the lessee purported to sell the vehicle to the second defendant, who was a director of and shareholder in the first defendant, a company. The owner, on learning of the sale, made formal written demand of both defendants for delivery up of the vehicle, but after that failed he assigned all his rights and title in the vehicle to the plaintiffs, a finance company. The finance company commenced proceedings against the defendants in August 1981 for conversion. In March 1982 the first defendant sold his shares in the company and resigned as a director. The vehicle was retained by the company. At the trial of the action it was agreed that the value of the vehicle at the date of its sale was £7,500 and that the value of its use and enjoyment thereafter was £115 per week. The first defendant admitted liability for damages and the vehicle was thereafter returned to the finance company. On the issue of quantum of damages, the finance company contended that s 3[a] of the Torts (Interference with Goods) Act 1977 and the common law relief preserved by s 3 entitled them to damages at the agreed weekly rate from the date of the sale until the date of the return of the vehicle. The first defendant contended (i) that his liability commenced to run only from the date when formal demand was made for the vehicle's return, (ii) that s 3 only applied when a defendant retained possession of goods up to the date of judgment and, since he had already relinquished control over the vehicle, s 3 did not apply, and (iii) that

a Section 3, so far as material, is set out at p 187 *d* to *f*, post

instead the damages should be no more than the value of the vehicle at the date of
a conversion plus interest up to the date either when he ceased to be a director or when the company returned the vehicle.

Held – The finance company was entitled to judgment against both defendants, who were jointly liable, for the agreed hire value of the vehicle from the time the lessee purported to sell it until it was returned to the finance company, since (a) on its true
b construction s 3 of the 1977 Act applied when a defendant was in possession of goods at the time proceedings were commenced, (b) the courts' discretion to grant relief pursuant to s 3 and at common law included a power to award a plaintiff commercial hire charges for the period that a profit-earning chattel was wrongfully in a defendant's possession, and (c) the return of the vehicle to the finance company made the alternative method of calculating damages based on the value of the vehicle at the date of conversion plus
c interest untenable (see p 186 *h* and p 187 *f* to p 188 *h*, post).

Dictum of Denning LJ in *Strand Electric and Engineering Co Ltd v Brisford Entertainments Ltd* [1952] 1 All ER at 801 applied.

Notes

For measure of damages in detinue and conversion for wrongful detention of chattels,
d see 2 Halsbury's Laws (4th edn) para 1583 and 12 ibid paras 1160–1161, and for cases on the subject, see 3 Digest (Reissue) 491, *3234–3235*, and 46 Digest (Repl) 514–515, *595–606*.

For the Torts (Interference with Goods) Act 1977, s 3, see 47 Halsbury's Statutes (3rd edn) 1343.

e **Case referred to in judgment**

Strand Electric and Engineering Co Ltd v Brisford Entertainments Ltd [1952] 1 All ER 796, [1952] 2 QB 246.

Action

By a writ issued on 7 August 1981 the plaintiffs, Hillesden Securities Ltd, sought as
f against the first defendant, Ryjak Ltd, and the second defendant, William James Edwards, (1) the delivery to the plaintiffs of a Rolls-Royce motor car, registration LCS 514F, (2) alternatively, a declaration that the plaintiffs were entitled to possession of the motor car, (3) damages for wrongful interference with and detention of the motor car and (4) interest pursuant to statute or to the leasing agreement. The facts are set out in the judgment.

g

Richard Hone for the plaintiffs.
Charles Flint for the second defendant.
The first defendant was not represented.

Cur adv vult

h

19 January. The following judgment was delivered.

PARKER J. In June 1979 one Mr H J Rayment was the owner of a Rolls-Royce motor car, registration LCS 514F, which he had purchased in that month for £10,250. On 11 June he leased the car to a Mr Vigus for a term of 36 months. On 13 September 1980,
j during the currency of the leasing agreement, Mr Vigus purported to sell the car to the second defendant, Mr Edwards, or the first defendants, Ryjak Ltd, of which company Mr Edwards was both a director and shareholder. The price paid was £5,750, and was paid, as to £1,000, in cash on 13 September 1980 and, as to the balance of £4,750, also in cash, on 15 September 1980.

At that time Mr Vigus was in financial difficulties and Mr Rayment had been having

trouble obtaining payment of the hire under the leasing agreement at the time when it fell due. It appears from the documents that, despite the purported sale, Mr Vigus did a
pay the instalment of hire due in October 1980 and was then up to date with payments under the leasing agreement, but he paid no further amounts and Mr Rayment therefore took steps to ascertain the whereabouts of the car with a view to recovering possession. Early in 1981 it was found to be in the possession of Mr Edwards or Ryjak Ltd, and, after verbal demands for delivery up, Mr Rayment's solicitors, by letter dated 23 February 1981 to Mr Edwards, made written demand for such delivery. On 16 July 1981 Mr b
Rayment, having failed in his efforts to obtain the return of the vehicle, assigned to the plaintiffs the legal title therein, the benefit of the leasing agreement and all rights of action against the defendants. Notice was given by the plaintiffs' solicitors to the defendants' solicitors on the same day and the letter giving such notice demanded delivery up of the vehicle. This achieved no result and as a result this action was launched on 7 August 1981. The statement of claim was delivered on the following day and the c
defendants delivered their defence on 6 November 1981. A third party notice was issued by the defendants against Mr Vigus on 10 December 1981 and the third party proceedings have already been disposed of by order dated 30 June 1982. Directions in the action were given on 21 December 1981 and the action came on for trial on 30 November 1982. In the mean time Mr Edwards, on 11 March 1982, had entered into an agreement for the sale of his shares in Ryjak Ltd and resigned, or purported to resign, as a director of that d
company.

At the trial Mr Edwards was represented but Ryjak Ltd was not. Mr Edwards originally contended that he was not a party to the sale by Mr Vigus, that this was a sale to Ryjak Ltd only and that Ryjak Ltd and not he had throughout been in possession of the car. He admitted, however, that the sale by Mr Vigus was wholly ineffective and that Mr Vigus had no title to sell. Subject to liability it was also agreed between both the defendants and e
the plaintiffs that the value of the car at the date of sale was £7,500 and that a proper figure for its use and enjoyment thereafter was £115 per week.

Despite his initial stand, Mr Edwards finally admitted liability for damages but raised a number of contentions with regard to the amount of such damages. It is with these contentions only that the court is therefore now concerned.

It is necessary to say, however, that I am satisfied on the evidence that the sale was f
made to Mr Edwards albeit that he may have been acting as agent for Ryjak Ltd and that the car was subsequently detained and used jointly by Mr Edwards and the company for profit.

The first contention as to damages, which was advanced on what may be described as a somewhat tentative or unenthusiastic basis, was that Mr Edwards's liability stems from a failure to respond to the first written demand of 23 February 1981 and not from the g
earlier purported sale by Mr Vigus. This contention was based on the fact that the statement of claim alleged no earlier wrongful act by the defendants. The lack of enthusiasm with which this point was taken is not surprising. Although, when dealing with the sale the plaintiffs do not, in the statement of claim, expressly say that the defendants converted the vehicle or acted wrongfully in the matter of the sale, the facts alleged clearly constitute a conversion of the car, and that is all that is required. Mr h
Edwards plainly converted it on 13 September 1980 and is liable for that conversion.

The second contention advanced by Mr Edwards is that his liability is at maximum the value of the car at the date of conversion, namely £7,500, plus interest thereafter pursuant to statute, either up to 11 March 1982, when he ceased to be a director or have any connection with Ryjak Ltd, or until the date of judgment or return of the vehicle. Before dealing with this contention as such, it is necessary to deal with the factual matters j
which it raises. First, despite the fact that Mr Edwards was a most unsatisfactory witness, much of whose evidence I reject without hesitation, I accept that from 11 March 1982 he ceased to have any connection with Ryjak Ltd and that he could not thereafter have returned the car, which remained in their possession, even if he had wished to do so. Second, the car was in fact returned to the plaintiffs by Ryjak Ltd on Friday 3 December

1982, pursuant to order of the court made on 30 November. Third, the car was an income- or profit-earning asset which was hired out by Mr Rayment as part of his business and was from 13 September 1980 used by Mr Edwards and the defendant company in the course of their business for reward.

In *Strand Electric and Engineering Co Ltd v Brisford Entertainments Ltd* [1952] 1 All ER 796, [1952] 2 QB 246 the plaintiffs were held to be entitled, in an action in detinue, to recover as damages the full market hire of such a profit-earning chattel of which the defendants had made use during the whole period of detention.

The plaintiffs contend that this is what they are entitled, in the present case, to recover against the defendants. Damages at the agreed rate of £115 per week would result in a total of £8,970 up to 11 March 1982 and £13,282 up to 3 December 1982 when the car was returned. Although the tort of detinue was abolished by the Torts (Interference with Goods) Act 1977, s 3 of that Act, in effect, preserves the remedies for what previously would have constituted detinue and their claim is, they say, within such remedies. It is, however, submitted on behalf of Mr Edwards that s 3 has no application in the present case since Mr Edwards has not been in possession or control of the car since 11 March 1982.

Section 3 provides:

> '(1) In proceedings for wrongful interference against a person who is in possession or in control of the goods relief may be given in accordance with this section, so far as appropriate.
>
> (2) The relief is—(*a*) an order for delivery of the goods, and for payment of any consequential damages, or (*b*) an order for delivery of the goods, but giving the defendant the alternative of paying damages by reference to the value of the goods, together in either alternative with payment of any consequential damages, or (*c*) damages.
>
> (3) Subject to rules of court—(*a*) relief shall be given under only one of paragraphs (*a*), (*b*) and (*c*) of subsection (2), (*b*) relief under paragraph (*a*) of subsection (2) is at the discretion of the court, and the claimant may choose between the others.
>
> (4) If it is shown to the satisfaction of the court that an order under subsection (2)(*a*) has not been complied with, the court may—(*a*) revoke the order, or the relevant part of it, and (*b*) make an order for payment of damages by reference to the value of the goods . . .'

It is submitted for Mr Edwards that this section only applies where a defendant is in possession or control of the chattel at the time of judgment, and that, since he has not been in possession or control of the chattel since 11 March 1982, the damages recoverable against him are limited to common law damages in conversion which are not more than the value of the car at the date of conversion plus interest thereafter.

If this is correct it would lead to strange results. For example, the hire charge recoverable in this case, on the basis of the *Strand Electric* case, is £115 per week or £5,980 per annum. If the defendants retained the car until judgment the plaintiffs would therefore be entitled, if judgment were given two years after the original wrong, to the return of the car plus £11,960 or to that sum plus the value of the car at the date of judgment. Suppose, however, that he returned the car the day before judgment. Could it be said that the whole basis of the plaintiffs' entitlement changed and that instead of £11,960 and the value of the car at that time he was entitled instead to some wholly different damages for the two-year detention? Or suppose that, instead of returning the car the day before judgment he disposed of it. Is the plaintiff then to be relegated to recovering the value at the date of the original sale plus two years' interest, which, in the present case, would be a much lesser sum? In common sense it should make no difference and, in my judgment, it makes no difference in law either.

In the first place, s 3 of the 1977 Act refers to the relief which may be given 'in proceedings . . . against a person who is in possession or in control of goods'. Such words are apt to describe proceedings such as the present where the defendants were in possession or control of the goods when such proceedings were launched. It is true that if, before judgment, the goods have been returned or disposed of, an order for delivery *a* up, with or without the alternative of damages, would not be possible, but s 3 covers such a situation for it provides that the relief specified may be given 'so far as appropriate'.

Secondly, in the case of a profit-earning chattel, Denning LJ said in the *Strand Electric* case [1952] 1 All ER 796 at 801, [1952] 2 QB 246 at 255:

> 'If the goods are retained by the wrongdoer up till judgment, the hiring charge *b* runs up to that time, and in addition the owner will get the return of the goods or their value at the time of judgment . . . If the goods have been disposed of by the wrongdoer, the hiring charge will cease at the time of such disposal, but the owner will get in addition damages for the loss he has sustained by the conversion, which is usually the value at the time of conversion.'

The action in that case was in detinue and not conversion, but there will in almost all *c* cases of detinue have been an original act of conversion also, and what was in effect held in that case was that, in the case of conversion of a profit-earning chattel which a defendant has used for his own benefit, the owner can recover by way of damages a hire charge plus either the return of the chattel or, if there has been a subsequent conversion by disposal, the value of the chattel at the date of such conversion.

Thirdly, although damages for conversion normally consist of the value of the goods *d* at the date of conversion, consequential damages are always recoverable if not too remote.

Finally, there is clearly no basis on which damages could be assessed as being the value at the date of the original conversion plus interest, for the car has in the end been returned.

What the plaintiffs have lost is the use of the car over the whole period from the original conversion until the ultimate return. Until 11 March 1982 both the defendants *e* are without doubt liable for the hire charge. On that date Mr Edwards may have put it out of his power to return the car, but he cannot by so doing have terminated his liability. He must either be liable for the hire charge to the date of return or he must be liable, in addition to the hire charge up to 11 March, for the value of the car at that date on the basis that he then disposed of it. He cannot be heard to say that by putting it out of his power to return the car he terminated his liability. It was not submitted, as it would have *f* been open to Mr Edwards to do, that the value of the car at 11 March was less than the agreed hire charge between that date and the date of return, nor was it submitted by the plaintiffs that they were entitled to recover more than the hire charge. Accordingly, there will be judgment against Mr Edwards for the hire charge over the whole period, ie for $115\frac{1}{2}$ weeks at £115 per week. This, as I have already said, amounts to £13,282·50. The question of interest was not argued at the trial and I will hear submissions on that *g* matter at the conclusion of this judgment if the plaintiffs seek any interest in addition.

As to the defendants Ryjak Ltd, there must also be judgment against them on a like basis for they plainly were jointly liable with Mr Edwards up to 11 March 1982 and continued thereafter to use the car for their own purposes until they returned it on 3 December 1982.

h

Judgment against both defendants for £13,282·50 with interest from 23 February 1981 on half that amount at the short-term investment account rate from time to time in force.

Solicitors: *W T Jones* (for the plaintiffs); *H Davis & Co* (for the second defendant).

K Mydeen Esq Barrister.

Merkur Island Shipping Corp v Laughton and others

HOUSE OF LORDS

LORD DIPLOCK, LORD EDMUND-DAVIES, LORD KEITH OF KINKEL, LORD BRANDON OF OAKBROOK AND LORD BRIGHTMAN

14, 15, 16 MARCH, 21 APRIL 1983

Tort – Inducement to commit breach of contract – Indirect inducement – Interference with performance of contract – Whether interference with performance of contract giving rise to cause of action at common law – Preconditions for cause of action.

Trade dispute – Acts done in contemplation or furtherance of trade dispute – In contemplation or furtherance of – Secondary action in furtherance of dispute – Immunity of secondary action from suit in tort – Contract for supply of services between employer who is party to dispute and employer to whom secondary action relates – Vessel let on time charter by owners to charterers and sub-let to sub-charterers – Sub-charterers contracting with tug company for towage services to enable vessel to leave port – Vessel blacked while in port – Employees of tug company persuaded by seamen's union to take secondary action to prevent vessel leaving port – Whether contract for supply of services between shipowners and tug company – Whether secondary action directly preventing supply of services by shipowner under time charter – Whether secondary action by seamen's union actionable in tort – Trade Union and Labour Relations Act 1974, s 13(1) – Employment Act 1980, s 17(3)(6).

The shipowners were the registered owners of a cargo vessel sailing under a Liberian flag of convenience and manned by an Asian crew who were paid below the rates approved by the International Transport Workers Federation (the ITF). The ship was time chartered to charterers who had in turn sub-chartered it to sub-charterers. Both the charter and the sub-charter required the captain, acting on behalf of the owners, to 'prosecute his voyages with the utmost despatch' and required the charterers or sub-charterers to provide and pay for towage into and out of berths when the ship docked. Under the terms of the time charter hire was not payable to the shipowners in the event of time being lost because of a labour dispute. The ship docked at Liverpool to load and when it was ready to sail the sub-charterers arranged with a tug company, with which they had a running contract, for the tug company to move the ship out of dock. In the mean time the ITF decided to black the ship because of the low wages paid by the shipowners to the crew and persuaded the tugmen employed by the tug company to refuse to operate tugs assigned to move the ship, with the result that it was unable to leave port. The tugmen's refusal to take the vessel out was a breach of their contracts of employment with the tug company. Three days later the shipowners served a copy of the time charter on the ITF and then applied for, and were granted, an interlocutory injunction requiring the ITF to lift the blacking. The shipowners also issued a writ against the defendants, three officials of the ITF, seeking damages in tort for, inter alia, unlawful interference with their charter contract with the charterers. The defendants appealed against the injuction, contending that the part of the shipowners' writ relating to unlawful interference with the charter disclosed no cause of action at common law and that even if it did they were protected from an action in tort by the immunity provided by s 13(1)[a] of the Trade Union and Labour Relations Act 1974 since their action had been in furtherance of a trade dispute with the shipowners and therefore was not actionable 'on the ground . . . that it induces another person to break a contract or interferes or induces any other person to interfere with its performance'. The shipowners conceded that the defendants' actions came within s 13(1) and would be protected if s 13(1) applied, but they contended that the immunity from

a Section 13(1) is set out at p 193 *h*, post

action provided by s 13(1) had been removed by s 17[b] of the Employment Act 1980
because the defendants' action did not fall within the category of secondary action a
exempted from liability in tort by s 17(3) since there was no 'supply of . . . services . . . in
pursuance of a contract', within s 17(6), between 'an employer who is a party to the
dispute [ie the shipowners] and the employer under the contract of employment to
which the secondary action relates [ie the tug company]', because the shipowners were
not a party to the contract by which the tug company were to supply towage services.
The Court of Appeal dismissed the appeal and the defendants appealed to the House of b
Lords.

Held – (1) The question whether blacking or other disruptive action in connection with
a trade dispute was lawful in any particular case involved a three-stage approach: stage 1
was whether the plaintiffs had a cause of action at common law; if they did, stage 2 was
whether that cause of action had been removed by s 13 of the 1974 Act; if it had not been c
so removed, the plaintiffs were entitled to sue, but if it had been so removed, stage 3 was
whether that cause of action had been restored by s 17 of the 1980 Act; if it had been so
restored, the plaintiffs were entitled to sue (see p 193 *a b* and p 199 *a* to *d*, post); dictum
of Brightman LJ in *Marina Shipping Ltd v Laughton* [1982] 1 All ER at 489 approved.

(2) On the stage 1 issue of whether the shipowners had a cause of action at common
law, the tort of actionable interference with contractual rights was not restricted to d
procuring a breach of contract between the plaintiff and a third party but extended to
actions which interfered with the performance of the contract by the third party. On the
facts, the four essential preconditions for a cause of action based on interference with the
performance of a contract were present, since (a) the defendants knew of the existence of
the time charter or were sufficiently familiar with the shipping industry to know that
such a contract would almost certainly have existed, and they intended to prevent the e
shipowners from carrying out their contractual obligation under the charter to prosecute
voyages with the utmost dispatch, (b) the defendants procured the tugmen to break their
contracts of employment with the intention of preventing the shipowners from
performing their obligation under the charter contract, (c) the tugmen did in fact break
their contracts of employment, and (d) the fact that the shipowners were prevented from
performing their obligation under the charter contract was a necessary consequence of f
the tugmen breaching their contracts of employment. The shipowners had therefore
made out a strong prima facie case that they had a cause of action at common law.
However, on the stage 2 issue, that cause of action based on interference with the charter
had been removed by s 13(1)(*a*) of the 1974 Act and therefore the shipowners had to
show that it had been restored by s 17 of the 1980 Act (see p 195 *e* to *g*, p 196 *a* to *c* and *e*
to *j*, p 197 *b* and p 199 *a* to *d*, post); dicta of Jenkins LJ in *D C Thomson & Co Ltd v Deakin* g
[1952] 2 All ER at 379–380 and of Lord Denning MR in *Torquay Hotel Co Ltd v Cousins*
[1969] 1 All ER at 530 applied.

(3) On the stage 3 issue of whether the shipowners' cause of action had been restored
by s 17 of the 1980 Act, the effect of s 17(3), read with s 17(6), was that secondary action
in relation to a trade dispute was not immune from action in tort if the contract for the
supply of goods and services which the secondary action was aimed at preventing or h
disrupting was not made between the employer who was a party to the trade dispute and
the employer affected by the secondary action. Since the tug company (the employer
affected by the secondary action) was not a party to the contract for the supply of services
under the time charter and since the shipowners (the employer who was a party to the
trade dispute with the ITF) were not party to any contract with the tugowners, the
defendants' secondary action was not immune from action in tort under s 17(3). j
Accordingly, the shipowners' cause of action at common law in respect of the interference
with their contractual rights by the defendants' unlawful secondary action had been
restored by s 17 of the 1980 Act. The defendants' appeal would therefore be dismissed
(see p 197 *d* and *j* to p 198 *b e* and p 199 *a* to *d*, post).

Per curiam. Section 17 of the 1980 Act, by which s 17(1)(*a*) brings in s 17(2) which in

---

b Section 17, so far as material, is set out at p 194 *b* to *f*, post turn brings in s 17(3) which in turn brings in s 17(6), is most regrettably lacking in clarity in an area of law, namely the field of industrial relations, where the law ought to be plain and where the absence of clarity is destructive of the rule of law (see p 197 *d* and p 198 *j* to p 199 *d*, post).

Decision of the Court of Appeal [1983] 1 All ER 334 affirmed.

Notes

For the legal liability of trade unions, see Supplement to 38 Halsbury's Laws (3rd edn) para 677B.3.

For the Trade Union and Labour Relations Act 1974, s 13, see 44 Halsbury's Statutes (3rd edn) 1769, and for s 13(1) of that Act (as substituted by the Trade Union and Labour Relations (Amendment) Act 1976, s 3(2)), see 46 ibid 1941.

For the Employment Act 1980, s 17, see 50(2) ibid 2635.

Cases referred to in opinions

Marina Shipping Ltd v Laughton [1982] 1 All ER 481, [1982] QB 1127, [1982] 2 WLR 569, CA.

NWL Ltd v Woods, NWL Ltd v Nelson [1979] 3 All ER 614, [1979] 1 WLR 1294, HL.

Thomson (D C) & Co Ltd v Deakin [1952] 2 All ER 361, [1952] Ch 646, CA.

Torquay Hotel Co Ltd v Cousins [1969] 1 All ER 522, [1969] 2 Ch 106, [1969] 2 WLR 289, CA.

Interlocutory appeal

The defendants, Brian Laughton, Harry Shaw and Harold Lewis (officials of the International Transport Workers' Federation (the ITF)), appealed with leave of the Appeal Committee of the House of Lords granted on 21 December 1982 against the decision of the Court of Appeal (Sir John Donaldson MR, O'Connor and Dillon LJJ) ([1983] 1 All ER 334, [1983] 2 WLR 45) on 4 November 1982 dismissing an appeal by the defendants from an order of Parker J dated 23 July 1982 whereby he granted the plaintiffs, Merkur Island Shipping Corp, interlocutory injunctions, in effect requiring the defendants to lift the blacking of the plaintiffs' vessel Hoegh Apapa at Liverpool which was chartered to Leif Hoegh & Co A/S and sub-chartered to Ned Lloyd which had arisen in the course of a trade dispute between the plaintiffs and the ITF. The facts are set out in the opinion of Lord Diplock.

Cyril Newman QC and *Nicholas Merriman* for the appellants.
Roger Buckley QC and *T R Charlton* for the respondents.

Their Lordships took time for consideration.

21 April. The following opinions were delivered.

LORD DIPLOCK. My Lords, this appeal (in which I shall refer to the individual appellants collectively as 'the ITF') is concerned with yet another skirmish in the war that has for some years past been waged by the International Transport Workers' Federation against the use of vessels under flags of convenience in maritime trade to and from ports in Western Europe. The objects of this campaign, its consequences on the employment of Asian seamen and the way in which it has hitherto been conducted are explained in *NWL Ltd v Woods* [1979] 3 All ER 614 at 617, [1979] 1 WLR 1294 at 1297. The present appeal, however, differs from the previous ITF cases because it is the first to have come before this House, and only the second to have come before the Court of Appeal, in which the 'blacking' of a flag-of-convenience vessel by preventing it from leaving a port in the United Kingdom took place after the coming into force of s 17 of the Employment Act 1980, which withdraws from certain kinds of secondary action taken in furtherance of a trade dispute the wide immunity from liability in tort conferred by s 13 of the Trade Union and Labour Relations Act 1974 as amended in 1975 and 1976.

Such facts as it is necessary to recount in order to dispose of this appeal can be stated briefly. The respondents (the shipowners) own the Hoegh Apapa, a Liberian registered ship, of which the majority of the crew were Filipinos. On 15 July 1982 she arrived at a dock in Liverpool for loading. The ITF (of which the individual appellants are officials), having previously learnt that the shipowners were paying less than the rate of wages approved by the ITF, persuaded the tugmen employed by a company known as Rea Towing (the tugowners) to refuse, in breach of their contracts of employment with the tugowners, to move the ship out of the dock so as to enable her to sail.

The ship was let by the shipowners to Leif Hoeg & Co A/S (the charterers) under a time charter (the charter) in the New York Produce Exchange form with certain additional clauses, to two of which it will be necessary to refer. The charterers in turn had sub-chartered the ship to Ned Lloyd under a six months' time charter (the sub-charter) containing similar clauses. Both the charter and sub-charter provided that the charterers thereunder should—

> 'provide and pay for all . . . Port Charges, normal Pilotages, Agencies, Commissions, Consular Charges . . . and all other usual expenses . . . but when the vessel puts into a port for causes for which the vessel is responsible, then all such charges incurred shall be paid by the owners.'

Pursuant to this clause in the sub-charter, the sub-charterers, who have a running contract with the tugowners for the provision of tugs to all their vessels using the port of Liverpool, made through their agent a specific contract with the tugowners for the provision of tugs to take the ship into and out of the dock at which the ship was to be loaded. As a result of the blacking of the vessel, however, on completion of the loading on 16 July the tugmen employed by the tugowners, in breach of their contracts of employment, refused to move the ship except to a lay berth.

While the ship was thus immobilised, on 21 July the shipowners applied ex parte to Parker J, sitting in the Commercial Court, for an order requiring the ITF to lift the blacking of the ship. The hearing, at which the ITF were represented and adduced affidavit evidence, took place on 23 July when Parker J granted the injunction.

On the very same day as the injunction was granted an extraordinarily high tide in the Mersey made it necessary for the lock keepers to leave the dock gates open and the ship, dispensing with the use of tugs, seized the opportunity to escape from the dock under her own power and to proceed to sea. The result was that the injunction came too late to have practical consequences unless the ship should return to Liverpool on another voyage under the sub-charter, an event which did not in fact occur. But the question whether Parker J misdirected himself in law in holding that the shipowners had a cause of action against the ITF has not been thereby rendered wholly academic. The shipowners' writ includes claims in tort for damages under two alternative heads:

> '(1) damages for deliberate interference with and/or threat to the performance of a time charter dated 12th February 1982 between the Plaintiffs and Leif Hoegh and Co. Aktieselskab, such interference and/or threat being brought about by unlawful means, namely wrongfully procuring and/or inducing and/or threatening to procure or induce lock keepers and/or tugmen and/or pilots and/or boatmen and/or linesmen and/or others concerned with the free passage and operation of vessels at Liverpool to refuse to assist the free passage or working of the "HOEGH APAPA" at Liverpool.
>
> (2) Damages for deliberate interference with and/or threat to the trade and business of the Plaintiffs, such interference and/or threat being brought about by unlawful means namely wrongfully procuring and/or inducing and/or threatening to procure or induce lock keepers and/or tugmen and/or pilots and/or boatmen and/or linesmen and/or others concerned with the free passage and operation of vessels at Liverpool to refuse to assist the free passage or working of the "HOEGH APAPA" at Liverpool.'

It was under the first head that Parker J held that on the evidence before him the shipowners had shown a cause of action at common law in respect of which it was unlikely that the ITF would succeed in establishing an immunity from liability under the 1974 Act as modified by the 1980 Act.

Before the 1980 Act came into force the question whether blacking was lawful in any particular case involved a two-stage approach. Stage 1 was to determine whether the plaintiff had established that what was done in the course of the blacking would, if the 1974 Act had not been passed, have given him a cause of action in tort. If so, stage 2 was to determine whether that cause of action was removed as against individual defendants by s 13 of the 1974 Act. To that two-stage process the 1980 Act added one further stage, stage 3. This was to determine whether that cause of action which had been removed by the 1974 Act was restored by s 17 of the 1980 Act. In adopting this three-stage approach I gratefully follow the lead of Brightman LJ in *Marina Shipping Ltd v Laughton* [1982] 1 All ER 481 at 489, [1982] QB 1127 at 1143.

In the instant case there were two separate questions of law on which it was contended by the ITF that Parker J had erred. The first, which I shall call the stage 1 point, was that Parker J was wrong in holding that there was any such tort at common law as was alleged in head (1) of the writ. The second, which I shall call the stage 3 point, was that the judge had misconstrued s 17 of the 1980 Act, a question of construction on which he had regarded himself as bound by the judgments in the *Marina Shipping* case.

Desirous of clarifying the law about blacking as affected by s 17 of the 1980 Act, the ITF appealed to the Court of Appeal from Parker J's order. In their notice of appeal in addition to the stage 1 point and the stage 3 point they raised several other points with which your Lordships need not be concerned. The Court of Appeal (Sir John Donaldson MR, O'Connor and Dillon LJJ) acceded to the ITF's request for clarification of the law; since, as Sir John Donaldson MR put it, 'lack of clarity posed problems for a judge who is asked, at short notice and as a matter of urgency, to grant an injunction' (see [1983] 1 All ER 334 at 347, [1983] 2 WLR 45 at 61). The Court of Appeal were unanimous in upholding the judgment appealed from on the stage 1 point. On the stage 3 point, the Court of Appeal too regarded themselves as bound by the decision in the *Marina Shipping* case, although both Sir John Donaldson MR and O'Connor LJ did state briefly in their own words reasons for agreeing with the interpretation of s 17 of the 1980 Act that had commended itself to the Court of Appeal in that case.

My Lords, although the stage 1 point is one of common law, the importance of the shipowners' being able to establish a cause of action at common law under head (1) of the writ rather than, or as well as, a cause of action at common law under head (2), is a consequence of the language used in s 13 of the 1974 Act and s 17 of the 1980 Act, since it is rightly not contested by the shipowners that if their only cause of action at common law lay under head (2) of the writ, it would be removed at stage 2 by s 13(2) of the 1974 Act and would not be restored at stage 3 by s 17 of the 1980 Act. It is therefore convenient to start by setting out these sections in extenso omitting only, as irrelevant, sub-ss (4) and (5) and part of sub-s (7) of s 17 of the 1980 Act:

1974 Act

'**13.** *Acts in contemplation or furtherance of trade disputes.*—(1) An act done by a person in contemplation or furtherance of a trade dispute shall not be actionable in tort on the ground only—(*a*) that it induces another person to break a contract or interferes or induces any other person to interfere with its performance; or (*b*) that it consists in his threatening that a contract (whether one to which he is a party or not) will be broken or its performance interfered with, or that he will induce another person to break a contract or to interfere with its performance.

(2) For the avoidance of doubt it is hereby declared that an act done by a person in contemplation or furtherance of a trade dispute is not actionable in tort on the ground only that it is an interference with the trade, business or employment of another person, or with the right of another person to dispose of his capital or his labour as he wills.

(3) For the avoidance of doubt it is hereby declared that—(*a*) an act which by reason of subsection (1) or (2) above is itself not actionable; (*b*) a breach of contract in contemplation or furtherance of a trade dispute; shall not be regarded as the

doing of an unlawful act or as the use of unlawful means for the purposes of establishing liability in tort. a

(4) An agreement or combination by two or more persons to do or procure the doing of any act in contemplation or furtherance of a trade dispute shall not be actionable in tort if the act is one which, if done without any such agreement or combination, would not be actionable in tort.'

1980 Act b

'**17.** *Secondary action.*—(1) Nothing in section 13 of the 1974 Act shall prevent an act from being actionable in tort on a ground specified in subsection (1)(*a*) or (*b*) of that section in any case where—(*a*) the contract concerned is not a contract of employment, and (*b*) one of the facts relied upon for the purpose of establishing liability is that there has been secondary action which is not action satisfying the requirements of subsection (3), (4) or (5) below. c

(2) For the purposes of this section there is secondary action in relation to a trade dispute when, and only when, a person—(*a*) induces another to break a contract of employment or interferes or induces another to interfere with its performance, or (*b*) threatens that a contract of employment under which he or another is employed will be broken or its performance interfered with, or that he will induce another to break a contract of employment or to interfere with its performance, if the employer d under the contract of employment is not a party to the trade dispute.

(3) Secondary action satisfies the requirements of this subsection if—(*a*) the purpose or principal purpose of the secondary action was directly to prevent or disrupt the supply during the dispute of goods or services between an employer who is a party to the dispute and the employer under the contract of employment to which the secondary action relates; and (*b*) the secondary action (together with e any corresponding action relating to other contracts of employment with the same employer) was likely to achieve that purpose . . .

(6) In subsections (3)(*a*) and (4)(*a*) above—(*a*) references to the supply of goods or services between two persons are references to the supply of goods or services by one to the other in pursuance of a contract between them subsisting at the time of the secondary action, and (*b*) references to directly preventing or disrupting the supply f are references to preventing or disrupting it otherwise than by means of preventing or disrupting the supply of goods or services by or to any other person.

(7) Expressions used in this section and in the 1974 Act have the same meanings in this section as in that Act . . .

(8) Subsection (3) of section 13 of the 1974 Act shall cease to have effect.'

The stage 1 point g

The common law tort relied on by the shipowners under head (1) of the writ is the tort of interfering by unlawful means with the performance of a contract. The contract of which the performance was interfered with was the charter; the form the interference took was by immobilising the ship in Liverpool to prevent the captain from performing the contractual obligation of the shipowners under cl 8 of the charter to 'prosecute his voyages with the utmost despatch'. The unlawful means by which the interference was h effected was by procuring the tugmen and the lockmen to break their contracts of employment by refusing to carry out the operations on the part of the tugowners and the port authorities that were necessary to enable the ship to leave the dock.

The reason why the shipowners relied on interference with the performance of the charter rather than procuring a breach of it was the presence in the charter of cll 51 and 60 which were in the following terms: j

'Clause 51. Blockade/Boycott. In the event of loss of time due to boycott of the vessel in any port or place by shore labour or others, or arising from Government restrictions by reason of the vessel's flag, or arising from the terms and conditions on which the members of the crew are employed, or by reason of the trading of this vessel, payment of hire shall cease for time thereby lost.

> Clause 60. Cancellation. Should the vessel be prevented from work for the reasons as outlined in Clauses 49/50/51 and 52 for more than ten days, Charterers shall have the option of cancelling this contract.'

My Lords, your Lordships have had the dubious benefit during the course of the argument in this appeal of having been referred once more to many of those cases, spanning more than a century, that were the subject of analysis in the judgment of Jenkins LJ in *D C Thomson & Co Ltd v Deakin* [1952] 2 All ER 361, [1952] Ch 646 and led to his statement of the law as to what are the essential elements in the tort of actionable interference with contractual rights by blacking that is cited by Sir John Donaldson MR and, at rather greater length, by O'Connor LJ in their judgments in the instant case. That statement has, for 30 years now, been regarded as authoritative, and for my part, I do not think that any benefit is gained by raking over once again the previous decisions. The elements of the tort as stated by Jenkins LJ were ([1952] 2 All ER 361 at 379–380, [1952] Ch 646 at 697):

> '... first, that the person charged with actionable interference knew of the existence of the contract and intended to procure its breach; secondly, that the person so charged did definitely and unequivocally persuade, induce or procure the employees concerned to break their contracts of employment with the intent I have mentioned; thirdly, that the employees so persuaded, induced or procured did in fact break their contracts of employment; and, fourthly, that breach of the contract forming the alleged subject of interference ensued as a necessary consequence of the breaches by the employees concerned of their contracts of employment.'

D C Thomson & Co Ltd v Deakin was a case in which the only interference with contractual rights relied on was procuring a *breach* by a third party of a contract between that third party and the plaintiff. That is why in the passage that I have picked out for citation Jenkins LJ restricts himself to that form of actionable interference with contractual rights which consists of procuring an actual breach of the contract that formed the subject matter of interference; but it is evident from the passages in his judgment which precede the passage I have cited and are themselves set out in the judgment of O'Connor LJ that Jenkins LJ, though using the expression 'breach', was not intending to confine the tort of actionable interference with contractual rights to the procuring of such non-performance of primary obligations under a contract as would necessarily give rise to secondary obligations to make monetary compensation by way of damages. All prevention of due performance of a primary obligation under a contract was intended to be included even though no secondary obligation to make monetary compensation thereupon came into existence, because the secondary obligation was excluded by some force majeure clause.

If there were any doubt about this matter, it was resolved in 1969 by the judgments of the Court of Appeal in *Torquay Hotel Co Ltd v Cousins* [1969] 1 All ER 522, [1969] 2 Ch 106. That was a case in which the contract the performance of which was interfered with was one for the delivery of fuel. It contained a force majeure clause excusing the seller from liability for non-delivery if delayed, hindered or prevented by, inter alia, labour disputes. Lord Denning MR stated the principle thus ([1969] 1 All ER 522 at 530, [1969] 2 Ch 106 at 138):

> '... there must be *interference* in the execution of a contract. The interference is not confined to the procurement of a *breach* of contract. It extends to a case where a third person *prevents* or *hinders* one party from performing his contract, even though it be not a breach.' (Lord Denning's emphasis.)

Parliamentary recognition that the tort of actionable interference with contractual rights is as broad as Lord Denning MR stated in the passage I have just quoted is, in my view, to be found in s 13(1) of the 1974 Act itself, which refers to inducement not only 'to break a contract', but also 'to interfere with its performance', and treats them as being pari materia.

So I turn to the four elements of the tort of actionable interference with contractual rights as Jenkins LJ stated them, but substituting 'interference with performance' for 'breach', except in relation to the breaking by employees of their own contracts of employment where such breach has as its necessary consequence the interference with the performance of the contract concerned.

The first requirement is actually twofold: (1) knowledge of the existence of the contract concerned and (2) intention to interfere with its performance.

As respect knowledge, the ITF had been given an actual copy of the charter on 19 July 1980, three days after the blacking started but two days before the application to Parker J was made. Quite apart from this, however, there can hardly be anyone better informed than the ITF as to the terms of the sort of contracts under which ships are employed, particularly those flying flags of convenience. I agree with what was said by Sir John Donaldson MR on the question of the ITF's knowledge ([1983] 1 All ER 334 at 349, [1983] 2 WLR 45 at 63):

> 'Whatever the precise degree of knowledge of the defendants at any particular time, faced with a laden ship which, as they well knew, was about to leave port, the defendants must in my judgment be deemed to have known of the almost certain existence of contracts of carriage to which the shipowners were parties. The wholly exceptional case would be that of a ship carrying the owner's own goods. Whether that contract or those contracts consisted of a time charter, a voyage charter or one or more bill of lading contracts or some or all of such contracts would have been immaterial to the defendants. Prima facie their intention was to immobilise the ship and in so doing to interfere with the performance by the owners of their contract or contracts of carriage; immobilising a laden ship which had no contractual obligation to move would have been a pointless exercise, since it would have brought no pressure to bear on the owners.'

The last sentence of this citation deals also with intention. It was the shipowners on whom the ITF wanted to bring pressure to bear, because it was they who were employing seamen at rates of pay lower than those it was the policy of the ITF to enforce. The only way in which income could be derived by the shipowners from the ownership of their ship was by entering into contracts with third parties for the carriage of goods under which a primary obligation of the shipowners would be to prosecute the contract voyages with the utmost dispatch, and their earnings from their ship would be diminished by its immobilisation in port. Diminishing their earnings under the contract of carriage was the only way in which pressure could be brought to bear on the shipowners.

The fulfilment of the second and third requirements, that the ITF successfully procured the tugmen and lock keepers to break their contracts of employment and that the ITF's intention in doing so was to interfere with the performance by the shipowners of their primary obligations to the charterers under the charter, is beyond dispute. So is the fulfilment of the fourth requirement, that the prevention of the performance by the shipowners of their primary obligation under the charter to secure through the captain that the ship, as soon as she had completed loading should proceed from the port of Liverpool on her voyage with the utmost dispatch, was a necessary consequence of the breaches by the tugmen and the lock keepers of their contracts of employment.

On the stage 1 point I accordingly agree with the Court of Appeal that the shipowners, on the evidence that was before Parker J, have made out a strong prima facie case that the ITF committed the common law tort of actionable interference with contractual rights.

Clauses 51 and 60 of the charterparty do not assist the ITF any more than did the force majeure clause in the *Torquay Hotels* case; but cl 51 does show that the ITF's action did in fact succeed in causing damage to the shipowners.

In anticipation of an argument that was addressed to your Lordships on the stage 3 point, I should mention that the evidence also establishes a prima facie case of the common law tort, referred to in s 13(2) and (3) of the 1974 Act, of interfering with the trade or business of another person by doing unlawful acts. To fall within this genus of torts the unlawful act need not involve procuring another person to break a subsisting contract or to interfere with the performance of a subsisting contract. The immunity granted by s 13(2) and (3) I will call the 'genus immunity'. Where, however, the procuring of another person to break a subsisting contract *is* the unlawful act involved, as it is in s 13(1), this is but one species of the wider genus of tort. This I will call the 'species immunity'.

The stage 3 point

My Lords, the acts done by the ITF in the instant case, like those in *NWL Ltd v Woods*, clearly fell within the immunity conferred by s 13 of the 1974 Act on persons acting in furtherance of a trade dispute before that immunity was cut down by the provisions of s 17 of the 1980 Act. To that section I now turn.

The first thing to note is the opening words: 'Nothing in section 13 of the 1974 Act shall prevent . . .' Not only the species immunity under sub-s (1) of s 13, but also the genus immunity under sub-ss (2) and (3), form the subject matter with which s 17 of the 1980 Act is dealing, although it is only from a sub-species of the species of tort dealt within s 13(1) that immunity is removed by the subsequent provisions of the section.

Section 17(1) lays down two conditions which must be satisfied in order to bring an act within the sub-species from which immunity is withdrawn. The first, in para (*a*), is simple. The subsisting contract of which the non-performance of a primary obligation is procured must not be a contract of employment. A charterparty, whether a time charter or a voyage or consecutive voyage charter, is not a contract of employment. The second condition, in para (*b*), is highly complex since it brings in also sub-s (2) which in turn, for the purposes of the instant case, brings in sub-s (3), which in its turn brings in sub-s (6).

To start with there must be 'secondary action' as defined in sub-s (2). That subsection, in effect, defines secondary action in such a way as to single out from the species of torts referred to in s 13(1) of the 1974 Act a sub-species in which the means of interference with the performance of a contract is to procure employees of an employer who is not a party to a trade dispute to break their contracts of employment with that employer. Withdrawal of immunity is confined to this sub-species. Subsection (3), however, then goes on to limit the withdrawal of immunity to a sub-species of secondary action that is defined by reference to its purpose and the likelihood of achieving that purpose; but the description of the purpose incorporates two phrases, 'supply of goods or services' between two persons and 'directly to prevent or disrupt' such supply. The meaning of these phrases is to be found in sub-s (6).

Reading into sub-s (3)(*a*) the definitions of those phrases from sub-s (6) the paragraph would run (inelegantly) as follows:

> 'Secondary action satisfies the requirements of this subsection if the purpose or principal purpose of the secondary action was to prevent or disrupt, during the trade dispute, the supply of goods or services between parties to a contract where (i) the contract pursuant to which such services are agreed to be supplied is a contract then subsisting between the employer who is a party to the trade dispute and the employer under the contract of employment to which the secondary action relates and (ii) the prevention or disruption of the supply of goods or services between those parties is brought about by some means other than by preventing or disrupting the supply of goods or services by or to any other person than a party to such contract.'

My Lords, in the instant case the contract concerned was the charter. The employers who were parties to the trade dispute were the shipowners. The charter was a contract for the supply of services, to which the shipowners and the charterers alone were parties. The shipowners were not parties to any subsisting contract with the tugowners. The tugowners were the employers under the contract of employment to which the secondary action related. So the requirements of sub-s (3)(*a*) were not satisfied; nor would those requirements have been satisfied if the contract with the tugowners had been made directly between the tugowners and the charterers pursuant to cl 8 of the charter instead of being made between the tugowners and the sub-charterers. Neither the charterers nor the sub-charterers were parties to the trade dispute, of which the subject matter was the terms and conditions on which the shipowners employed the ship's crew and, in *a* particular, the wages paid by the shipowners to them.

So, I agree with the Court of Appeal that in the instant case there was secondary action within the meaning of s 17(2) which did not satisfy the requirements of sub-s (3) (the only relevant subsection), with the result that the immunity from liability in tort granted by s 13 of the 1974 Act was withdrawn by s 17(1) of the 1980 Act. It is a very winding path that leads to this conclusion but the maze through which it winds has only one *b* centre, which, when one reaches it, is unmistakable.

It was submitted on behalf of the ITF, although counsel was at a loss to find any justification for this submission in the language of s 17 itself, that Parliament cannot have intended that the employer who was an actual party to the trade dispute should be included in the beneficiaries of the withdrawal of immunity from liability in tort from those who procured the interference with the performance of a contract to which he was *c* himself a party. For my part, in the absence of any words expressing such a limitation on the withdrawal of immunity for liability, I can see no reason for supposing that Parliament nevertheless sub silentio intended such a limitation to be understood. On the contrary, as a matter of legislative history, the employer who was the party to the trade dispute was the obvious plaintiff whose right of action in tort for procuring a breach of a contract of employment by his own employees was taken away by s 3 of the Trade *d* Disputes Act 1906. There is no compelling reason for supposing that if a contract into which he himself had entered satisfied the criteria laid down in s 17(1) for withdrawal of immunity from liability in tort on the part of anyone who procured an interference with its performance, Parliament intended to deprive the employer who was party to the dispute of the benefit of the withdrawal of that immunity.

So, on the true construction of s 17 of the 1980 Act, I would decide the stage 3 point in *e* favour of the shipowners, for what are substantially the same reasons as were given in the *Marina Shipping* case and in the judgments of Sir John Donaldson MR and O'Connor LJ in the instant appeal. I would therefore dismiss this appeal.

I appreciate that this will have the consequence of making it more difficult for the ITF to continue to apply its policy of blacking vessels sailing under flags of convenience without a blue certificate from the ITF. It may also make blacking more difficult in other *f* industries where contracts and sub-contracts are common, but your Lordships have not needed to go into that in the instant appeal. One thing is plain as to the intention of Parliament in enacting s 17 of the 1980 Act; it was to impose restrictions on the circumstances in which blacking could be procured without incurring liability in tort. The only function of this House in its judicial capacity is to ascertain from the language that the draftsman used the extent of those restrictions. *g*

My Lords, the 1974 Act and the 1980 Act, to which must now be added the Employment Act 1982, deal with industrial relations. They lay down what can and what cannot lawfully be done in connection with industrial disputes, not only as a result of decisions that are taken by the controlling body or the top officials of large trade unions or federations of trade unions like the ITF with ready and immediate access to expert legal advice, but also as a result of decisions taken by the steward on the shop floor in *h* circumstances of urgency and under pressure from his fellow workers. I see no reason for doubting that those on whom the responsibility for deciding whether and if so what industrial action shall be taken in any given circumstances wish to obey the law, even though it be a law which they themselves dislike and hope will be changed through the operation of this country's constitutional system of parliamentary democracy. But what the law is, particularly in the field of industrial relations, ought to be plain. It should be *j* expressed in terms that can be easily understood by those who have to apply it even at shop floor level. I echo everything that Sir John Donaldson MR has said in the last three paragraphs of his judgment in this case. Absence of clarity is destructive of the rule of law; it is unfair to those who wish to preserve the rule of law; it encourages those who wish to undermine it. The statutory provisions which it became necessary to piece together into a coherent whole in order to decide the stage 3 point are drafted in a manner which, having regard to their subject matter and the persons who will be called on to apply them, can in my view, only be characterised as most regrettably lacking in the requisite degree of clarity.

LORD EDMUND-DAVIES. My Lords, I have had the advantage of reading in draft form the speech prepared by my noble and learned friend Lord Diplock, and for the reasons he gives I also would dismiss this appeal.

LORD KEITH OF KINKEL. My Lords, for the reasons given in the speech of my noble and learned friend Lord Diplock, which I have had the benefit of reading in draft and with which I agree, I too would dismiss the appeal.

LORD BRANDON OF OAKBROOK. My Lords, I have had the advantage of reading in draft the speech prepared by my noble and learned friend Lord Diplock. I agree with it, and for the reasons which he gives I would dismiss the appeal.

LORD BRIGHTMAN. My Lords, I also would dismiss this appeal for the reasons given by my noble and learned friend Lord Diplock.

Appeal dismissed.

Solicitors: *Clifford-Turner* (for the appellants); *Holman Fenwick & Willan* (for the respondents).

Mary Rose Plummer Barrister.

Practice Note

COURT OF APPEAL, CIVIL DIVISION
SIR JOHN DONALDSON MR, DUNN AND PURCHAS LJJ
5 MAY 1983

Court of Appeal – Practice – Applications for leave to appeal – Applications to single judge – Applications to be heard in open court.

SIR JOHN DONALDSON MR made the following statement at the sitting of the court. In October 1982 I made a statement concerning changes being made in the procedure of the court (see *Practice Note* [1982] 3 All ER 376, [1982] 1 WLR 1312). In the course of the 'informal commentary' which I issued at the same time, I drew attention to the fact that a single judge of the Court of Appeal would in future be able to consider incidental applications, such as those for leave to appeal, thus saving the time of the full court. I added that he would sit in chambers.

It has recently been suggested to us that, on the true construction of the Supreme Court Act 1981 and RSC Ord 59, the sole exception to the general rule that the single judge will normally sit in chambers is the case where he is considering an application for leave to appeal and that he should then sit in open court. The practice has been altered accordingly and applications for leave to appeal are now being heard in open court.

Although it is now considered that the previous practice of hearing such applications otherwise than in open court was a procedural irregularity, the only result of such irregularity is that orders previously made in chambers could, in theory, be set aside if application were made for that purpose. As the merits will have been fully considered before the order was made, the applicant, on any such application, would be unlikely to succeed unless he satisfied the court that he had been prejudiced by the hearing having taken place in chambers rather than in open court.

Frances Rustin Barrister.

Moran v Lloyd's a

COURT OF APPEAL, CIVIL DIVISION

SIR JOHN DONALDSON MR, DILLON LJ AND SIR GEORGE BAKER

1, 2 MARCH 1983

Court of Appeal – Leave to appeal – Necessity – Appeal against order refusing to set aside arbitration award or to remit it to umpire – Whether order refusing to set aside or remit award b *an interlocutory or a final order.*

Arbitration – Award – Leave to appeal against award – Setting aside or remitting award – Allegation of misconduct of umpire by reason of inconsistency in findings – Whether inconsistency amounting to misconduct by umpire – Whether leave to appeal ought to be granted – Arbitration Act 1950, ss 22, 23 – Arbitration Act 1979, s 1. c

Arbitration – Award – Leave to appeal against award – Setting aside or remitting award – Allegation of misconduct of umpire – Whether 'misconduct' applying to procedural errors by umpire – Arbitration Act 1950, s 23.

The applicant, an underwriting member of Lloyd's, was the respondent in an arbitration d between himself and the Committee of Lloyd's. The arbitration was constituted under the Lloyd's Act 1871, but was subject to the provisions of the Arbitration Act 1950 and the Arbitration Act 1979. By s 20 of the 1871 Act a member of Lloyd's could be excluded from membership if he had been guilty, inter alia, of 'any act or default discreditable to him as an underwriter or otherwise in connection with the business of insurance', provided that such guilt had first been determined by arbitration proceedings. The e Committee of Lloyd's made ten allegations of discreditable conduct against the applicant and at the ensuing arbitration the umpire found him guilty of five of the complaints. The applicant applied for leave to appeal against the award pursuant to s 1 of the 1979 Act, and for an order under ss 22(1)[a] or 23(2)[b] of the 1950 Act remitting the award to the umpire or setting it aside on the ground that the umpire had misconducted himself in the proceedings. The judge dismissed the applications and also refused leave to appeal f from his refusal to make an order under s 22 or s 23 of the 1950 Act. The applicant appealed to the Court of Appeal, contending (i) that leave to appeal to the Court of Appeal was not required because the judge's refusal was not an interlocutory but a final order since it finally determined the rights of the parties in relation to the award, and (ii) that alternatively, if the judge's order was interlocutory, leave to appeal ought to be granted because the applicant could show an arguable case of misconduct on the part of the g umpire, namely that the umpire had made a finding of guilt in relation to one complaint which was inconsistent with his failure to find guilt in relation to other complaints, and had found against the applicant on a basis which had not been put forward by Lloyd's, thereby depriving him of an opportunity of properly defending himself.

Held – (1) The question whether an order was interlocutory or final was to be determined h by the nature of the application and not by the nature of the order which the court eventually made. Since an order made on an application to set aside an award was interlocutory it followed that an order made on an application to remit an award was also interlocutory. Accordingly, since the applications under s 22 and s 23 of the 1950 Act were both interlocutory, leave to appeal was required (see p 203 *c* to *f*, post); *Re Croasdell* j

a Section 22(1), so far as material, provides: 'In all cases of reference to arbitration the High Court or a judge thereof may from time to time remit the matter referred . . . to the reconsideration of the arbitrator or umpire.'

b Section 23(2), so far as material, provides: '(2) Where an arbitrator or umpire has misconducted himself or the proceedings . . . the High Court may set the award aside.'

and Cammell Laird & Co Ltd [1906] 2 KB 569 followed; *Salter Rex & Co v Ghosh* [1971] 2 All ER 865 considered.

(2) Leave to appeal would not be granted, however, for the following reasons—

(a) the applicant had failed to make out an arguable case of misconduct under s 23 of the 1950 Act. It was doubtful whether inconsistency between one part of an award and another could ever constitute or evidence misconduct by an arbitrator or umpire and the overwhelming likelihood was that it would merely show error of law or of fact, or both, which in themselves did not amount to misconduct (see p 204 *f g* and p 205 *c*, post);

(b) when considering a claim for remitting an award under s 22 of the 1950 Act on the ground of inconsistency, a distinction was to be drawn between the operative parts of the award and the reasoning for it. While inconsistency of reasoning would at most give rise to a right of appeal if it showed an error of law, inconsistency or ambiguity in the operative parts of an award might require remission to the arbitrator or umpire to enable him to resolve such inconsistency, since it would not be right to enforce an award in an ambiguous or inconsistent form. However, the applicant had shown no arguable ground for remission either on the basis of any internal inconsistency or for inconsistency in the reasoning (see p 204 *h* to p 205 *c*, post); *Oleificio Zucchi SpA v Northern Sales Ltd* [1965] 2 Lloyd's Rep 496 considered;

(c) failure by an arbitrator or umpire to allow a party a reasonable or proper opportunity to put forward his case could constitute misconduct for the purposes of setting aside an award or for exercising discretion to remit it, but on the facts there were no arguable grounds for alleging that there had been such misconduct (see p 205 *b c*, post).

Per curiam. (1) Since the 1979 Act has created restrictions on the powers of the court to intervene in arbitration proceedings, ss 22 and 23 of the 1950 Act are not to be used as a means of circumventing those restrictions (see p 204 *e f*, post).

(2) The terminology of s 23 of the 1950 Act, which provides remedies where an arbitrator or umpire has 'misconducted himself or the proceedings', can give rise to a wholly misleading impression of the complaint made against the arbitrator or umpire since s 23 is not confined to dishonesty or breach of business morality, which the terminology more usually implies, but can also apply to procedural errors (see p 203 *f* to *j*, post).

Notes

For what constitutes misconduct, see 2 Halsbury's Laws (4th edn) para 622, and for cases on the subject, see 3 Digest (Reissue) 279–285, *1853–1880*.

For the Arbitration Act 1950, ss 22, 23, see 2 Halsbury's Statutes (3rd edn) 451, 452.

For the Arbitration Act 1979, s 1, see 49 ibid 59.

Cases referred to in judgment

Ames v Milward (1818) 8 Taunt 637, 129 ER 532.
Bozson v Altrincham UDC [1903] 1 KB 547, CA.
Croasdell and Cammell Laird & Co Ltd, Re [1906] 2 KB 569, CA.
Oleificio Zucchi SpA v Northern Sales Ltd [1965] 2 Lloyd's Rep 496.
Salaman v Warner [1891] 1 QB 734, CA.
Salter Rex & Co v Ghosh [1971] 2 All ER 865, [1971] 2 QB 597, [1971] 3 WLR 31, CA.

Cases also cited

Becker v Marion City Corp [1977] AC 271, [1976] 2 WLR 728, PC.
Steinway & Sons v Broadhurst-Clegg (1983) Times, 25 February, CA.

Application for leave to appeal

The applicant, Christopher John Moran applied for leave to appeal against the order of Lloyd J dated 16 October 1982 dismissing his application for an order that the award dated 24 September 1982 made by Andrew Leggatt QC, the umpire in proceedings brought against the applicant pursuant to s 20 of the Lloyd's Act 1871, be set aside or remitted. The facts are set out in the judgment of the court. a

Mark Littman QC, *John Finnis* and *Julian Burling* for the applicant.
Peter Scott QC and *Anthony Boswood* for Lloyd's.

Cur adv vult b

2 March. The following judgment of the court was delivered.

SIR JOHN DONALDSON MR. The applicant, Christopher John Moran, an underwriting member of Lloyd's, was the respondent in an arbitration between him and the Committee of Lloyd's. The umpire was Mr Andrew Leggatt QC. The arbitration was c constituted under the Lloyd's Act 1871 (34 & 35 Vict c xxi), but the Arbitration Act 1950 and the Arbitration Act 1979 applied to it.

Section 20 of the 1871 Act, as amended, renders a member of Lloyd's liable to exclusion from membership by the votes of four-fifths of such members of the society as are present at a meeting specially convened for the purpose, if the member has violated any of the fundamental rules of the society or been guilty of an act or default discreditable to d him as an underwriter or otherwise in connection with the business of insurance. However, this power of exclusion can only be exercised if the fact that the member has violated such a rule or has been guilty of such an act has first been determined by arbitral award and, in making such an award, the arbitrators and umpire are bidden to take into account all the circumstances of the case, moral as well as legal.

The Committee of Lloyd's alleged ten specific counts of discreditable conduct and by e his award dated 24 September 1982 the umpire found the applicant guilty under nos 3, 4, 7, 8 and 9.

The applicant then moved the Commercial Court for (a) leave to appeal against the award pursuant to s 1 of the Arbitration Act 1979, and (b) an order setting aside the award or remitting it to the umpire on the grounds that the umpire had misconducted himself or the proceedings. The latter order was sought under ss 22 and 23 of the f Arbitration Act 1950.

On 18 October 1982 Lloyd J dismissed both applications. His decision to refuse leave to appeal to the High Court cannot be questioned in this court, since such an appeal does not lie without the leave of Lloyd J and he refused it. Lloyd J also refused leave to appeal against his refusal to set the award aside or to remit it. Section 1(6)(*a*) of the 1979 Act does not apply to such an application and we now have to consider (a) whether leave to g appeal is required, (b) if so, whether it should be granted, and (c) if leave to appeal is not required or we grant it, whether the appeal should be allowed.

Is leave to appeal required?

One might well have thought that this was no longer an open question, but it is a fact that I personally can never remember an occasion when I have appeared before or sat in h the Commercial Court where it has been explored in the context of a motion to set aside or remit an award. Invariably when such a motion was considered, counsel said something along the lines of, 'No one seems to know whether leave to appeal is required and whether my client has 14 days or six weeks in which to appeal. Would you therefore give leave to appeal and extend my time to six weeks de bene esse?', and the judge agreed. A series of judgments by McNair J, to which we were referred by counsel for Lloyd's, j bears out this recollection. The time for appealing is no longer in doubt following the amendment of RSC Ord 59, r 4. It is four weeks from the date on which the judgment or order of the court below was signed, entered or otherwise perfected. However the question of whether leave to appeal is needed remains and has now to be determined.

In the absence of an order under s 18(1)(*h*)(vi) of the Supreme Court Act 1981 the question depends on whether the order sought to be appealed was or was not an interlocutory order. This also determines whether the Court of Appeal is properly constituted for the hearing of the appeal if it consists only of two judges (see s 54(4)). One might, therefore, have expected there to be clear rules for the determination of what is and what is not an interlocutory order, but that is not yet the case, although there is power to make rules to this effect under s 60(1) of the 1981 Act.

In *Salter Rex & Co v Ghosh* [1971] 2 All ER 865, [1971] 2 QB 597 Lord Denning MR, with the agreement of Edmund Davies and Stamp LJJ, drew attention to the two different tests which have from time to time been applied in deciding whether a judgment or order is final or interlocutory. In one (that adopted by Lord Alverstone CJ in *Bozson v Altrincham UDC* [1903] 1 KB 547 at 548) the yardstick was whether the judgment or order *as made* finally disposed of the rights of the parties. In the other (that adopted by Lord Esher MR in *Salaman v Warner* [1891] 1 QB 734) the yardstick was the nature of the *application* to the court, from which it follows that the order had always to be interlocutory or final whether or not the application was successful. Lord Denning MR adopted Lord Esher MR's test, adding that in case of difficulty it was important to look to previous decisions of the court.

An order made on an application to set an award aside for misconduct has in fact been the subject of a previous decision of this court. In *Re Croasdell and Cammell Laird & Co Ltd* [1906] 2 KB 569, a court consisting of Collins MR and Vaughan Williams, Romer, Cozens-Hardy, Fletcher Moulton and Farwell LJJ held that an order setting an award aside was interlocutory. While it is true that a court of six has no greater jurisdiction, and its decision no greater force as a precedent, than a court consisting of a lesser number of judges, this was, without doubt, a very strong court. Counsel for the applicant seeks to distinguish this decision on various grounds, the principal ground being that there had been important changes in the law of arbitration since 1906. However, in our judgment the decision is quite indistinguishable. An order made on an application to remit an award is at least as interlocutory as one made on an application to set the award aside and the decision in *Croasdell* would therefore apply equally to such an order. Accordingly we ruled during the course of the argument that the applicant must seek leave to appeal before the merits of his complaints against the judge's order could be considered in depth.

Should leave to appeal be granted?

Counsel for the applicant wishes to argue, as he did before Lloyd J, that the umpire misconducted himself or the proceedings and that, on that account, the award should be set aside or remitted to the umpire for further consideration.

In para 67 of its 1978 Report on Arbitration (Cmnd 7284) the Commercial Court Committee drew attention to the fact that the term 'misconduct' can give a wholly misleading impression of the complaint being made against an arbitrator or umpire. It said:

> '"*Misconduct*"
>
> 67. Section 23 of the 1950 Act provides certain remedies if the arbitrator or umpire has "misconducted himself or the proceedings". Few would object to this terminology if what was referred to was dishonesty or a breach of business morality upon the part of the arbitrator or umpire. But the section has been held to apply to procedural errors or omissions by arbitrators who are doing their best to uphold the highest standards of their profession. In this context the terminology causes considerable offence, even in a permissive society. The Committee would like to see some other term substituted for "misconducted" which reflects the idea of irregularity rather than misconduct. It may be said that this point is merely cosmetic, but arbitrators are not to be criticised for their sensitivity and the Courts should not be required to use opprobrious terminology about arbitrators and be obliged to take time explaining that when they have found that the arbitrator has misconducted himself, they were not using the words in any ordinary sense.'

Unfortunately no effect was given to this recommendation in the 1979 Act.

This is just such a case as the committee had in mind. Counsel for the applicant expressly disavows any intention of impugning the honour, integrity or professional competence of the umpire, but is forced to use the term 'misconduct' because the only relevant power to set the award aside is contained in s 23 of the 1950 Act which uses this term. In fact what he wishes to argue in this court is that the umpire erred in two respects, namely that his finding of guilt in relation to complaint no 3 is inconsistent with his failure to find the applicant guilty in relation to complaints nos 1 and 2 and that, in relation to complaints nos 4 and 9, the umpire found against the applicant on a basis which had not been put forward by Lloyd's, thereby inadvertently depriving the applicant of an opportunity of adequately defending himself.

Section 22 of the 1950 Act differs from s 23 in that it gives a power of remission, as contrasted with a power to set aside, and in that its exercise does not depend on a finding of misconduct on the part of the arbitrator or umpire. It is in terms wholly discretionary, but that discretion has to be exercised in accordance with established principles.

For present purposes it is only necessary to say, as counsel for the applicant fully accepted, that the authorities established that an arbitrator or umpire does not misconduct himself or the proceedings merely because he makes an error of fact or of law. Similarly the power of remission under s 22 has never been exercisable merely on the basis that the arbitrator or umpire has made such an error. Prior to the passing of the 1979 Act, the only occasion on which an error of fact could be used to justify the intervention of the court was when it appeared on the face of the award. This power of intervention has been abrogated by s 1(1) of the 1979 Act. Similarly the only occasion on which an error of law could be used to justify the intervention of the court was where it appeared on the face of the award or where the question of law was raised by a special case stated for the opinion of the court. Again this power of intervention has been abrogated by s 1(1) of the 1979 Act, although a new right of appeal on questions of law has been created. This was the right which the applicant sought to exercise, but for which he failed to obtain leave from Lloyd J, a decision from which he is unable to appeal.

We stress this aspect in order to make it clear to all who are concerned in and with arbitration that neither s 22 nor s 23 of the 1950 Act is available as a back-door method of circumventing the restrictions on the court's power to intervene in arbitral proceedings which have been created by the 1979 Act.

Returning to the complaint of inconsistency, we doubt whether, as such, inconsistency between one part of an award and another could ever constitute or evidence misconduct on the part of an arbitrator. The overwhelming likelihood is that it would merely constitute or evidence error of law or of fact or both and these do not amount to misconduct. Halsbury's Laws of England suggests the contrary and cites *Ames v Milward* (1818) 8 Taunt 637, 129 ER 532 as authority (see 2 Halsbury's Laws (4th edn) para 622). But that was a case not of misconduct, but of error of law on the face of the award at a time when this was a ground for setting aside.

If the applicant's notice of motion is to be strictly construed, we need not go beyond a consideration of whether an arguable case of 'misconduct' has been made out. So far as that is concerned, we are quite clear that it has not. However, in view of the seriousness of the matter from the point of view of the applicant, we do not think that it would be right to take so narrow a view of the proceedings. We have therefore considered the possibility of a claim for remission under s 22 in the absence of any misconduct. In this context we think that a distinction has to be drawn between the award itself (the operative or decisive part of the award) and the reasons for that award. Inconsistency of *reasoning* may betray an error of fact, but it is in the nature of arbitral proceedings that this must be accepted by the parties. Alternatively it may betray an error of law. That may give rise to a right of appeal, but it has no other effect. Inconsistency or ambiguity in the operative parts of the award, the parts which would 'be enforced in the same manner as a judgment or order to the same effect' if application were made under s 26 of the 1950 Act, may be another matter. The executive power of the state to enforce an award is not to be invoked in an inconsistent or ambiguous form and in such an event it

might well be right to remit the award to the arbitrator or umpire under s 22 to enable
a him to resolve the ambiguity or inconsistency.

This was the view of the law expressed by McNair J in *Oleificio Zucchi SpA v Northern Sales Ltd* [1965] 2 Lloyd's Rep 496. There have been few judges more experienced in the law of arbitration and we respectfully agree with his view. Applying this to the award under consideration we can detect no arguable grounds for remitting the award on the basis of any internal inconsistency. Indeed we can detect no arguable grounds for alleging
b inconsistency even in the reasoning.

This brings us to the submission in relation to complaints nos 4 and 9. Any failure to give a party a reasonable and proper opportunity to put forward his own case and to rebut that of the opposite party is undoubtedly capable of constituting 'misconduct' of the proceedings justifying the court in setting the award aside pursuant to s 23 of the 1950 Act or, alternatively, of constituting a circumstance which would justify the court
c in remitting the award to the arbitrator or umpire for further consideration pursuant to s 22. But in the present case we can again detect no arguable grounds for submitting that this occurred.

For these reasons the application for leave to appeal will be dismissed.

Application dismissed.

d

Solicitors: *Goodman Derrick & Co* (for the applicant); *Freshfields* (for Lloyd's).

Diana Procter Barrister.

e

Export Credits Guarantee Department v Universal Oil Products Co and others

QUEEN'S BENCH DIVISION
f STAUGHTON J
7 SEPTEMBER 1982

COURT OF APPEAL, CIVIL DIVISION
WALLER, SLADE LJJ AND SIR SEBAG SHAW
25, 26, 27 OCTOBER, 23 NOVEMBER 1982

g

HOUSE OF LORDS
LORD DIPLOCK, LORD ELWYN-JONES, LORD KEITH OF KINKEL, LORD ROSKILL AND LORD BRIGHTMAN
23 FEBRUARY, 24 MARCH 1983

Contract – Penalty – Indemnity clause – Enforceability – Defendants agreeing to construct oil
h *refinery for oil companies – Bankers agreeing to provide finance for project – Oil companies issuing promissory notes – Plaintiffs guaranteeing notes to bankers – Contract made between plaintiffs and defendants providing for defendants to indemnify plaintiffs if defendants in breach of contractual obligations to other parties – Whether indemnity provision a penalty clause.*

In 1970 a number of interlocking multilateral contracts were concluded between three
j Newfoundland companies, the three defendant companies and a consortium of bankers for the design, construction and installation of an oil refinery in Newfoundland and the financing of those operations. One of the contracts was a construction contract for the refinery made between one of the Newfoundland companies (the building company) and the third defendant by which the third defendant agreed to construct the refinery. The third defendant was a subsidiary of the second defendant which in turn was a

subsidiary of the first defendant which, by separate agreement, gave a number of undertakings as to the performance of the refinery when completed. The financing of *a* the project was partly effected by an arrangement whereby the Newfoundland companies issued promissory notes maturing on different dates in return for the banking consortium providing the requisite funds to the building company to enable it to pay the third defendant for the building work as it proceeded. Payment of the promissory notes issued by the Newfoundland companies to the banking consortium was guaranteed by the plaintiffs in consideration of a premium of over £1m paid by the defendants to the *b* plaintiffs under a premium agreement which further provided, by cl 7(1), that the defendants would reimburse the plaintiffs in respect of any sums paid by the plaintiffs to the banking consortium under the guarantee in the event of the Newfoundland companies dishonouring the promissory notes at a time when the defendants were in breach of the agreements, including the construction contract. Many of the promissory notes were subsequently dishonoured by the Newfoundland companies on presentation *c* and the plaintiffs were required to pay the banking consortium some £39m under the guarantee. The plaintiffs then brought an action against the defendants alleging that at the time the plaintiffs made payment under the guarantee the third defendant was in default under the construction contract and claiming reimbursement of the £39m by the defendants under cl 7(1) of the premium agreement. The defendants pleaded by way of defence, inter alia, that cl 7(1) was a penalty clause and unenforceable, since it imposed *d* on the defendants an obligation to make repayment to the plaintiffs no matter how trivial the third defendant's breach of the construction contract might be and therefore the sums payable by the defendants might be out of all proportion to any damage which the plaintiffs suffered as a result of a trivial breach of the construction contract. On the trial of a preliminary issue whether cl 7(1) was a penalty clause, both the judge and the Court of Appeal held that it was not and was therefore enforceable. The defendants *e* appealed.

Held – A provision in a contract providing for the payment of money by one party on the occurrence of a specified event, rather than on breach of a contractual duty owed by that party, could not be a penalty because the doctrine relating to the unenforceability of penalties was confined to payments which were agreed in advance to be made in respect *f* of, but which were not a genuine pre-estimate of the damage arising from, a breach of obligation by one party. Since the third defendants owed no contractual duty to the plaintiffs under the construction agreement any breach of that agreement by the third defendants was, vis-à-vis cl 7(1) of the premium agreement, merely the occurrence of a specified event and not a breach of duty by them. The amount claimed by the plaintiffs was therefore not damages for breach of contract but a debt due under an indemnity which was made operative by the occurrence of an event provided for; but in any event *g* the plaintiffs were only seeking to recover their actual loss, namely the amount they had been obliged to pay under the guarantee, and not a sum which bore no relation to the damage suffered by them. Clause 7(1) was therefore not a penalty clause and the defendants' appeal would accordingly be dismissed (see p 222 *d* to *f*, p 223 *f* and p 224 *a* to *h*, post). *h*

Notes

For the rules for distinguishing between damages and penalties, see 12 Halsbury's Laws (4th edn) para 1117, and for cases on the subject, see 17 Digest (Reissue) 176–186, *547–598*.

j

Cases referred to in judgments and opinions

Alder v Moore [1961] 1 All ER 1, [1961] 2 QB 57, [1961] 2 WLR 426, CA.

Apex Supply Co Ltd, Re [1941] 3 All ER 473, [1942] Ch 108.

Bernstein (Philip) (Successors) Ltd v Lydiate Textiles Ltd [1962] CA Transcript 238, sub nom *Sterling Industrial Facilities Ltd v Lydiate Textiles Ltd* 106 SJ 669.

Bridge v Campbell Discount Co Ltd [1962] 1 All ER 385, [1962] AC 600, [1962] 2 WLR 439, HL.

Clydebank Engineering and Shipbuilding Co Ltd v Don Jose Ramos Yzquierdo y Castaneda [1905] AC 6, [1904–7] All ER Rep 251, HL.
Dunlop Pneumatic Tyre Co Ltd v New Garage and Motor Co Ltd [1915] AC 79, [1914–15] All ER Rep 739, HL.
Gilbert-Ash (Northern) Ltd v Modern Engineering (Bristol) Ltd [1973] 3 All ER 195, [1974] AC 689, [1973] 3 WLR 421, HL.
Schuler (L) AG v Wickman Machine Tool Sales Ltd [1973] 2 All ER 39, [1974] AC 235, [1973] 2 WLR 683, HL.

Preliminary issue

By writs issued on 30 July 1980 and 20 March 1981 and subsequently consolidated the plaintiffs, the Export Credits Guarantee Department (the ECGD), brought an action against the defendants, Universal Oil Products Co, Procon Inc and Procon (Great Britain) Ltd, claiming the sum of £39,571,001·54 and interest due to the ECGD by the defendants and each of them under the terms of an agreement in writing dated 16 October 1970 (the premium agreement). On 6 April 1982 Robert Goff J ordered to be tried as a preliminary issue before all other questions in the action the question raised in the defence and counterclaim and the reply and defence to counterclaim, ie whether cl 7 of the premium agreement, which imposed on the defendants an obligation to pay the ECGD, in certain circumstances, a sum equal to that paid by the ECGD to Kleinwort Benson Ltd under two contracts of guarantee both dated 14 October 1970, operated as a penalty and was accordingly null, void and of no effect and gave rise to no liability in the defendants thereunder. The facts are set out in the judgment.

Nicholas Phillips QC and *Ian Glick* for the ECGD.
James Fox-Andrews QC, *Richard Yorke QC* and *Stuart Isaacs* for the defendants.

STAUGHTON J. The preliminary point which has been argued in this case is in my view difficult. But it is also short, and there is little authority which bears directly on it. The skilled argument on both sides has taken less than a day. In those circumstances it seems to me, as a judge of first instance, that I must decide it now, leaving the parties, if they wish, to embark on a more leisurely course to the Court of Appeal.

There were three Newfoundland companies, called Provincial Holding Co Ltd, Provincial Building Co Ltd and Provincial Refining Co Ltd. They are all now in liquidation. In 1970 they wanted a refinery built at Come-by-Chance, in Newfoundland; so one of them, Provincial Building Co Ltd, entered into a construction contract with the third defendant in the present action, Procon (Great Britain) Ltd. It is a subsidiary of the second defendant, Procon Inc, which in turn is a subsidiary of the first defendant, Universal Oil Products Co. I shall call the three defendants the 'Procon companies'. Under that construction contract Procon (Great Britain) Ltd was to build a refinery. By separate agreement Universal Oil Products Co gave a number of undertakings as to the performance of the refinery when completed.

There was a problem about finance, or rather two problems. First, the Newfoundland companies either did not have or did not wish to part with the money to pay for the building work as it proceeded, but only over an extended period. That was solved by an arrangement whereby a consortium of banks led by Kleinwort Benson Ltd (Kleinworts) would lend the money. I am told that the details were immensely complicated; but in essence, with sufficient accuracy for present purposes, it amounted to this. The Newfoundland companies made and issued promissory notes for various sums that were part of the price, maturing on different dates. Kleinworts in return for the promissory notes provided money to Provincial Building Co Ltd, in order that it in turn should pay Procon (Great Britain) Ltd. Kleinworts would claim payment on them from the makers. The second problem was that Kleinworts wanted an assurance that the notes would be paid on maturity; so it was arranged that the present plaintiffs, the Export Credits Guarantee Department (the ECGD), should issue guarantees for the notes to Kleinworts.

That required an agreement between the ECGD and the Procon companies, which was called the 'premium agreement', and is the agreement sued on in this action. It provided a
that the Procon companies should pay to the ECGD sums totalling £1,008,826 17s 10d being the premiums for the guarantees that the ECGD had issued or were to issue to Kleinworts. It also contained the following clause, cl 7(1):

> 'The premiums hereby payable are not intended to and do not cover payments made by the Guarantors under the Sterling Guarantee Agreement nor the Eurodollar Guarantee Agreement by reason of any default by Building Company and Operating b
> Company at any time when UOP shall be or is in default in the performance of its obligations under any or all of the UOP Guarantees or Procon is in default under the terms of the Contract. Upon payment by the Guarantors to Kleinworts of any sum under the Sterling Guarantee Agreement and/or the Eurodollar Guarantee Agreement in the above circumstances the Companies will on demand pay to the Guarantors a sum equal to that paid by the Guarantors to Kleinworts as aforesaid.' c

The 'Contract' in that clause means the construction contract.

I have been told that the refinery was built and that the Procon companies left the site in November 1974 with the job completed. A large number of the promissory notes maturing on various dates between 30 September 1973 and 30 September 1981 have been dishonoured. In value they total £39,571,000·54. The equivalent amounts have d
been paid by the ECGD to Kleinworts. The ECGD now claim in these consolidated actions to be reimbursed by the Procon companies under cl 7(1) of the premium agreement. They say that at the time when payments were made by them to Kleinworts under their guarantees Procon (Great Britain) Ltd were in default in many respects under the construction contract, so as to bring cl 7(1) into operation.

The Procon companies have pleaded a large number of defences to that claim, or at e
any rate a number of defences at very great length. By order of Robert Goff J made on 6 April 1982 one only has been tried before me as a preliminary issue. It is as follows:

> 'IT IS HEREBY ORDERED that questions or issues raised in paragraphs 24 and 131 of the Defence and Counterclaim and paragraph 86 of the Reply and Defence to Counterclaim, namely, that the clause 7 of the Premium Agreement operates as a penalty and is accordingly null, void and of no effect and gives rise to no liability in f
> the Defendants thereunder, be tried as preliminary questions or issues before all other question or issues in this action.'

The issue is thus whether cl 7(1) of the premium agreement is unenforceable on the ground that it provides for a penalty.

Meanwhile, another action of considerable dimensions is wending its way to trial in g
this court. In that action Procon (Great Britain) Ltd are plaintiffs and the defendants are Provincial Building Co Ltd, Provincial Refining Co Ltd, the Newfoundland Refining Co Ltd, the Clarkson Co Ltd and Kleinworts. I have not been referred to the pleadings in detail; but it seems that the claim is for a balance of the contract price under the construction agreement together with some items of extras and certain other remedies. What matters is the counterclaim by which two of these Newfoundland companies, that h
is the first and second defendants in that action, allege that Procon (Great Britain) Ltd defaulted under the construction contract. If the counterclaim succeeds because there was default, part at least of the proceeds will ultimately reach the ECGD by means of the liquidation of the Newfoundland companies and the security which the ECGD and Kleinworts hold on their property. Thus Mr Yorke QC for the defendants submits that, if I hold cl 7(1) of the premium agreement to be unenforceable as providing for a penalty, j
the ECGD will not be left altogether without remedy. If it can be established that there was default by Procon (Great Britain) Ltd under the construction contract, damages appropriate to the extent of that default will reach the ECGD. They may well not amount to £39m; indeed it is the underlying premise of Mr Yorke's case that they will not come to anything like that sum, so that an order for payment of £39m in this action would be totally disproportionate to any default of the Procon companies.

Attention was drawn to two other clauses in the premium agreement which were said
a to be relevant. They are as follows:

> '6. Provided that none of the Companies is in breach of any of its obligations to the Guarantors under this Premium Agreement and Procon is not in breach of any of its obligations to Building Company under the Contract and circumstances have arisen in which, in accordance with the provisions of paragraph 13 of the Sterling
> b Financial Agreement or of paragraph 12 of the First Eurodollar Agreement, Kleinworts cease to be under any obligation to make further sums available or to buy Notes as defined therein the Guarantors hereby undertake that they will procure Kleinworts to exercise their option to continue to buy such Notes . . .
>
> 8. In the event of any breach of this Agreement by the Companies (meaning in relation to paragraph 2 the Companies as defined in that paragraph) or any of them
> c at a time when the Guarantors are obliged to pay any sum to Kleinworts under the Sterling Guarantee Agreement and/or the Eurodollar Guarantee Agreement the Companies shall on demand pay to the Guarantors a sum equal to that sum paid to Kleinworts by the Guarantors provided that the amount so paid shall be taken into account when the extent and amount of the damages suffered by the Guarantors and which flow from the said breach of this Agreement by the Companies as so
> d defined or any of them has been assessed by agreement judgment or otherwise. If the amount paid by the Companies under this paragraph shall exceed the amount of damages suffered by the Guarantors and assessed as aforesaid the amount of such excess shall be repaid by the Guarantors to the Companies.'

Clause 6 was relied on by counsel for the ECGD as illustrating the point that the law as to penalties depends on form rather than substance. The obligation of the ECGD under that
e clause is conditional on Procon (Great Britain) Ltd not being in breach of the construction contract. The valuable rights which it confers melt away if Procon (Great Britain) Ltd are in breach, no matter how trivial their misdemeanour. Nobody suggests that the court can reform that clause. I accept the illustration, which was not contradicted by Mr Yorke, for what it is worth.

Clause 8 was relied on by Mr Yorke as showing that the draftsman of the premium
f agreement knew how to provide for a punishment to fit the crime, in other words, for damages commensurate with the breach from which they flow, when he wanted to do so. It does indeed show that, but I do not see how it helps me to resolve the present dispute.

Then I turn to cl 7(1), on which the preliminary issue must be decided. Mr Yorke invited me to decide the issue on the basis that the default to which it refers may be any
g breach of the relevant contracts however trivial and whether or not causally connected with the failure of the Newfoundland companies to honour their promissory notes. Counsel for the ECGD did not dissent from that suggestion, since it is his clients' case that a breach of contract is a default within the clause, however trivial it may be and whether or not it may have cause the dishonour of the notes. So I decide that issue on that basis. I do not know whether Mr Yorke, if he fails on this preliminary issue, will
h later seek to contend that default in cl 7(1) has some other and narrower meaning, and I certainly do not intend to indicate one way or the other whether I would be inclined to accept a narrower construction of the clause if one were put forward. No argument whatsoever has been put before me on that point. However, I must go so far as to say this. If the contractual provision leads to an apparently absurd and unjust result, one's first inclination is to consider whether any other possible construction is available: see
j the speech of Lord Reid in *L Schuler AG v Wickman Machine Tool Sales Ltd* [1973] 2 All ER 39 at 45, [1974] AC 235 at 251:

> 'The fact that a particular construction leads to a very unreasonable result must be a relevant consideration. The more unreasonable the result the more unlikely it is that the parties can have intended it, and if they do intend it the more necessary it is that they shall make that intention abundantly clear.'

Only second, and in my view a long way second, does one consider whether equity will rewrite the contract so as to relieve one of the parties from an improvident bargain. *a*
In the present case the first stage has never arisen. I have not been invited to consider whether 'default' has any narrow meaning. I am asked to decide the issue and do decide it on the hypothesis that 'default' means any breach of contract, however trivial and whether or not it caused the Newfoundland companies to dishonour the promissory notes.

On that assumption it is as plain as can be, to my mind at any rate, that cl 7(1) was a *b*
foolish and improvident term for the Procon companies to agree to. It also produces an adventitious benefit for the ECGD, in the sense that they recover what they have lost, being what they have paid to Kleinworts, but the reason why they were required to pay may well be wholly unconnected with breaches of contract by the Procon companies. Of course breaches of a building contract may be trivial, just as they may be serious. Mr Yorke spent some time giving examples, but he was pushing at an open door. A claim *c*
must be tested by its weakest link, as Lord Dunedin observed in *Dunlop Pneumatic Tyre Co Ltd v New Garage and Motor Co Ltd* [1915] AC 79 at 89, [1914–15] All ER Rep 739 at 743. Mr Yorke also submitted that in practice it is inevitable that a building contractor will break some term or terms of his contract, and I suspect that in practice he is right. So the upshot is that, under cl 7(1), the ECGD will be entitled, if they think fit, to claim reimbursement of sums that they have paid to Kleinworts under circumstances which *d*
are almost certain to occur. Their premium of £1m is taken for loss that they may suffer if not one but two conditions are fulfilled: first, the Newfoundland companies dishonour their promissory notes and become insolvent; second, the Procon companies prove unable to meet the inevitable claim under cl 7(1). Mr Yorke submits that the second condition was most unlikely, since the Procon companies had an immensely wealthy oil company as their ultimate parents. That is not disputed; but so at one time had the *e*
subsidiaries of Dome Petroleum.

Clause 7(1) is not only capricious because it may inflict a loss on the Procon companies which is altogether disproportionate to the gravity of the default of which they are guilty. In passing I would mention that the Harter Act 1893 of the United States may produce a similar result: see *Carver's Carriage by Sea* (12th edn, 1971) vol 1, paras 240 to 243. Counsel for the ECGD also mentioned that some insurance contracts contain warranties *f*
which, if they are broken, will defeat a claim, even though the breach is wholly unconnected with the circumstances which gave rise to the claim.

The clause also contains the possibility of some strange accidents in its temporal provisions. It was, I think, the common submission of both parties that the words 'at any time when' referred to the time when payment is made by the ECGD. In other words, three conditions have to be fulfilled before the clause operates: (1) the ECGD makes *g*
payment to Kleinworts; (2) they do so by reason of a dishonour by the Newfoundland companies of a promissory note; (3) they do so at a time when either United Oil Products Co is in default under its undertaking or Procon (Great Britain) Ltd is in default under the construction contract. The promissory notes may have been made and issued at a time when there was no default whatever by the Procon companies. They may even have been dishonoured at a time when there was no such default. But, if there was any *h*
default at the time when the ECGD paid Kleinworts, then the ECGD are entitled to be reimbursed by the Procon companies.

Counsel for the ECGD submits that, if there is default on the part of the Procon companies, that may well encourage the Newfoundland companies to dishonour promissory notes, and that this was a risk which the ECGD did not wish to assume. Equally, Kleinworts would not wish to bear it. He may well be right. But the *j*
sledgehammer which the ECGD took to crack this nut has, if I may say so, thrown out the baby with the bath water.

All these considerations lead me without hesitation to conclude that, if cl 7(1) has to be justified as a genuine pre-estimate of damages for breach of contract, it fails at the first and all subsequent fences. But the whole issue here is whether it does have to be so justified. Counsel for the ECGD starts from the proposition that Chancery mends no a man's bargain, apart from certain well-defined exceptions. Once it is established what a contract means (and I proceed on the hypothesis as already explained, that there is only one possible interpretation of cl 7(1)) and that the parties are of full age and discretion then the courts will not rewrite it for them, however improvident it may seem. There are exceptions in the case of penalty and forfeiture clauses as well as fraud and duress. There may be others, but none was mentioned in argument. To succeed here, counsel b for the ECGD submits that the Procon companies must show cl 7(1) to be a penalty clause. He referred me to the speech of Lord Radcliffe in *Bridge v Campbell Discount Co Ltd* [1962] 1 All ER 385 at 397, [1962] AC 600 at 626:

> '"Unconscionable" must not be taken to be a panacea for adjusting any contract between competent persons when it shows a rough edge to one side or the other . . .'

c Mr Yorke did not dissent from that analysis of the problem. Indeed, his whole argument was directed to the point that it was a penalty clause. The real question here is well described in Meagher, Gummow and Lehane *Equity: Doctrines and Remedies* (1975) para 1820.

> d '. . . it remains of crucial importance to isolate the criteria for a penalty because without these there can be no equitable relief on a general basis. In other words, granted Equity's reason for its relief against penalties is bottomed in considerations of policy and improper use of legal power, that does not mean there is any general dispensation in that behalf. It is always a question of bringing a case within an established head of relief: *Campbell Discount Co Ltd* v *Bridge* ([1962] 1 All ER 385 at 388, [1962] AC 600 at 614 per Viscount Simonds) . . .'

e The general test for determining whether a clause provided a penalty or not is set out in the speech of Lord Dunedin in the *Dunlop* case [1915] AC 79 at 86–88, [1914–15] All ER Rep 739 at 741–742. It is well known and was not in controversy between the parties to this case. I need not set it out again. Counsel for the ECGD submits that one does not reach that test in the present case for three reasons. First, the claim here does not arise by f reason of breach of contract sued on, but by reason of a breach or breaches of other and different contracts. Second, the contractual duty alleged to be broken here was not owed to the plaintiffs, the ECGD, but to other and different parties. Third, the remedy sought here is not compensation for breach of contract but a sum which the contract makes payable on the occurrence of a specified event, or rather three specified events as set out above. Adopting the metaphor used by Diplock LJ in *Philip Bernstein (Successors) Ltd v* g *Lydiate Textiles Ltd* [1962] CA Transcript 238 (sub nom *Sterling Industrial Facilities Ltd v Lydiate Textiles Ltd* 106 SJ 669), counsel for the ECGD submits that the penalty area is a narrow field.

In my judgment the first two points of counsel for the ECGD, while relevant to the determination of the issue, are not, either individually or taken together, conclusive of it. Thus the first point as to separate contracts cannot in itself by sufficient to avoid the h doctrine of penalty clauses. Suppose that by one contract A agrees to build a refinery for B and by another contract he agrees to pay B $1m if he shall commit any breach of the first contract. Nobody would suppose that this was not a penalty. Mr Yorke had another answer to the point, which was that all the contracts here were part of one comprehensive arrangement. That argument will be open to him if the issue goes further. So, although perhaps less clearly, with the second point. Suppose that A Ltd agrees to build a refinery j for B Ltd, and also agree with X, the sole shareholder of B Ltd, to pay him £1m if they should commit any breach of that obligation. Counsel for the ECGD demurred, but I would not myself doubt that this was a penalty.

Although I reject both those points as insufficient in themselves to avoid the application of the doctrine of penalty clauses, I still consider that they are relevant when one comes to the third point, that this contract merely provides for payment of a sum of money on

a specified event. There is authority which I consider binding on me, that a clause
providing for payment of money on a specified event which is not a breach of contract is *a*
not a penalty clause: see *Alder v Moore* [1961] 1 All ER 1, [1961] 2 QB 57, the *Philip
Bernstein* case and see also *Re Apex Supply Co Ltd* [1941] 3 All ER 473, [1942] Ch 108 and
the cases there cited. Some difference of view on the point can be detected obiter in the
Campbell Discount case, but for the present I must follow the Court of Appeal.

The nearest of those cases to the present is the *Philip Bernstein* case. There a finance
company extracted from dealers a recourse agreement, which provided that if customers *b*
introduced by the dealers should fail to pay the whole of the instalments contemplated
by their agreements the dealers would do so. This was greater than any amount which
the customers themselves could lawfully have been compelled to pay. Diplock LJ said:

> 'In the ordinary way a penalty is a sum which, by the terms of a contract, a
> promisor agrees to pay to the promisee in the event of non-performance by the *c*
> promisor of one or more of the obligations and which is in excess of the damage
> caused by such non-performance. When there is such a stipulation in a contract,
> then the question arises whether that provision is a genuine pre-estimate of the
> damages which will be sustained on a breach, in which case it is enforceable, or
> whether it is a penalty, in which case the court will grant relief against it and refuse
> to allow the promisee to recover more than the actual damage which he has *d*
> sustained. It is apparent from what I have read of the clause that no case here arises
> of any breach by the defendants, the parties to the contract, of an obligation under
> their contract. They are being sued in respect of sums payable on an event defined
> in the contract, namely the default by the hirers in the payment of instalments
> under the quite separate contracts of hire purchase which those hirers entered into
> with the plaintiffs. Gorman J in a careful and considered judgment referred to the *e*
> cases, starting with *Re Apex Supply Co Ltd* [1941] 3 All ER 473, [1942] Ch 108, in
> which a distinction has been drawn by the courts between payment which by the
> terms of the contract a party undertakes to make in a specified event and payments
> which he undertakes to make on breach of a contract. Those cases, which I need not
> repeat, for they are set out in the judgment, in the view of Gorman J, and in my
> view rightly, draw a distinction between those two types of payment, and, to use *f*
> the words I think [counsel for the second defendant] adopted from Hodson LJ in an
> earlier case, hold that the former type of payment does not fall within the penalty
> area. [Counsel for the second defendant] concedes that there is no case in which it
> has been held that a payment to be made on a specified event not being a breach by
> the promisor of his own contract is a penalty or can be treated by the courts in the
> same way as a penalty. The ordinary rule which the courts apply is that contracts *g*
> should be enforced, pacta sunt servanda, unless they can be brought within that
> limited category of cases in which, for reasons of public policy, the court refused to
> give effect to the agreement of the parties. One limited class and well-known class is
> the class of penalty, but up till now it has been restricted to cases where there is a
> prior agreement by the parties to the contract as to an amount to be paid by a party
> in breach to the other party in respect of that breach. Since the judgment of Gorman *h*
> J there has been some discussion of the nature of penalties in the recent case in the
> House of Lords of *Bridge v Campbell Discount Co Ltd* [1962] 1 All ER 385, [1962] AC
> 600, but speaking for myself I can find nothing in the decision in that case and
> nothing in the speeches of any of their Lordships, with the possible exception of
> Lord Denning, which throws any doubt on the rule accepted by Gorman J that the
> penalty area is limited to the narrow field which I have described. There are, it is *j*
> true, in the speech of Lord Denning certain observations which suggest that that
> field should be extended (see [1962] 1 All ER 385 at 399–400, [1962] AC 600 at
> 628–629). But those observations find, so far as I can see, no support in any other of
> the speeches of their Lordships, and, for my part, I think the law is well settled as to
> what the penalty area is. What, in effect, the parties agreed here, and this was a

dealer bargaining with a hire-purchase company, was that in certain events, namely a failure by a hirer to pay an instalment, the dealer should pay a sum specified in the contract and the finance company should assign its rights to the dealer. It may be that that was an improvident bargain. Whether it was depends on all the terms and not on an isolated clause. But one does not relieve against bargains merely because they are improvident when they are entered into between parties at arm's length, as these two were. In my view, the judgment of Gorman J was right. This was not a penalty and clearly, I think, did not fall within the penalty area. I, for my part, am not prepared to extend the law by relieving against an obligation in a contract entered into between two parties which does not fall within the well-defined limits in which the court has in the past shown itself willing to interfere.'

The crucial question here is whether it makes any difference that the specified event or events are to include a breach of some contract made with some other party. In the *Philip Bernstein* case the dealers were not in breach of any contract with anybody, and it may be that even the customers would not necessarily have been in breach. Here, however, the Procon companies are assumed to be in breach of their contracts with the Newfoundland company. In my judgment that distinction does not make any difference. Clause 7(1) here is not and does not purport to be a genuine pre-estimate of damage suffered by reason of the breach of contract, but equally it is not a threat imposed in terrorem to discourage non-performance of a contract. I appreciate that Lord Radcliffe in the *Campbell Discount* case [1962] 1 All ER 385 at 395, [1962] AC 600 at 622 disliked the phrase 'in terrorem'; and it does not occur in the summary of the *Dunlop* case set out in 12 Halsbury's Laws (4th edn) para 1117. But it still seems to me, with great respect, to serve some useful function in pointing the contrast between what is a genuine pre-estimate of damages and what is not, even though, as Lord Radcliffe said, it adds nothing of substance to the test. The clause here is neither of those things, because it is not in any way concerned either with a remedy or compensation for breach of a contractual duty owed by the Procon companies to the ECGD or with punishment for breach of such contract (see *Clydebank Engineering and Shipbuilding Co Ltd v Don Jose Ramos Yzquierdo y Castaneda* [1905] AC 6 at 15, [1904–7] All ER Rep 251 at 254 per Lord Davey). It is concerned to define three specified events which will together entitle the ECGD to recover moneys from the Procon companies. Only one of those events happens to be the breach of a contractual duty owed by the Procon companies to others.

I therefore conclude that the clause does not provide for a penalty and is not on that ground unenforceable. That conclusion is rendered somewhat less unpalatable by the fact that the ECGD might otherwise have considerable difficulty in finding any alternative remedy, even in the case of catastrophic default by the Procon companies. In other penalty cases (except *The Merchant of Venice*) the plaintiff has been able to recover his actual loss, even if he could not recover his penalty. Here it is open to question whether the ECGD can even do that. Mr Yorke's answers to this point, although not in the order he gave them, were as follows. (1) Too bad. The ECGD, like Shylock, have lost all by seeking too much. (2) The ECGD can recover their actual loss indirectly by the round-the-house route mentioned earlier in this judgment. (3) If Lord Denning was right in the *Campbell Discount* case [1962] 1 All ER 385 at 401, [1962] AC 600 at 632, the Procon companies may be required in this action, as a condition of relief against the penalty, to pay the ECGD the damages actually sustained by reason of the Procon companies' breach of contract. If the non-payment of the notes were clearly and beyond question shown to be caused by breaches of contract on the part of the Procon companies, none of these answers would provide as copper-bottomed a remedy to the ECGD as that contained in cl 7(1) of the premium agreement.

There will be judgment for the ECGD on the preliminary issue.

Judgment for the ECGD. Leave to appeal.

Appeal
The defendants appealed.

James Fox-Andrews QC, *Richard Yorke QC* and *Stuart Isaacs* for the defendants.
Nicholas Phillips QC and *Ian Glick* for the ECGD.

Cur adv vult

23 November. The following judgments were delivered.

WALLER LJ. This is an appeal against a decision of Staughton J on a preliminary point in an action between the Export Credits Guarantee Department (the ECGD) and the Universal Oil Product companies (the UOP). The action arises out of a large scale building operation of an oil refinery in Newfoundland at Come-by-Chance. There were three Newfoundland companies concerned with the purchase and operation of the refinery and the three defendant companies who were concerned with the design and erection of the refinery and its installation. Part of the financing was an arrangement whereby the Newfoundland companies issued promissory notes maturing on different dates. Kleinwort Benson Ltd (Kleinworts), acting for themselves and a number of other banks, in return for the promissory notes provided money which was paid to the third defendants, Procon (Great Britain) Ltd. These promissory notes were guaranteed by the ECGD, the plaintiffs. In turn there was a premium agreement between the three defendant companies and the ECGD. This provided that the Procon company should pay sums totalling over £1m as premiums for the guarantees. Paragraph 2 of the statement of claim sets out briefly the financial arrangements.

In due course the refinery was built and put into operation, but because of a variety of circumstances which in the middle 1970s completely altered the oil market the Newfoundland companies went into liquidation leaving 17 batches of promissory notes each totalling over £3m dishonoured on presentation. The banks had to be reimbursed by the guarantees and the ECGD had to pay to the banks a total of £39,100,000.

This case is concerned with cl 7(1) of the premium agreement. The plaintiffs claim that they are entitled to be reimbursed by the defendants because the defendants were in default in the performance of their obligations. The defendants have pleaded that this clause was a penalty clause and on 6 April 1972 Robert Goff J ordered that this question be determined as a preliminary issue. On 7 September 1982 Staughton J held that it was not a penalty clause and the defendants now appeal.

Before this court Mr Yorke QC's case was that this clause was a penalty clause because it could operate against Procon in circumstances where Procon's liability was out of all proportion to the default of which they were guilty. He instanced defaults of minor character, eg faulty lighting, causing a liability for millions of pounds. He submitted that the fact that the breach of duty of Procon was not a direct breach of duty to the ECGD did not prevent this being a penalty clause because when all the contracts are considered together the duties are owed directly to the Newfoundland companies who in turn owe a duty to the ECGD and therefore the duty is owed via the Newfoundland companies to the ECGD. Although it could not be said that the relationship of Procon to the ECGD was sufficiently close for the sum payable to be 'in terrorem' nevertheless recent authorities did not rely on this principle but relied largely on disparity and therefore the court should be ready to extend the doctrine of penalty to a case such as this. He submitted that the observations of Lord Denning in *Bridge v Campbell Discount Co Ltd* [1962] 1 All ER 385, [1962] AC 600 and the decision in *Gilbert-Ash (Northern) Ltd v Modern Engineering (Bristol) Ltd* [1973] 3 All ER 195, [1974] AC 689 where the temporary withholding of money due was held to be a penalty indicate that there is a tendency to widen the area where the courts will interfere.

The ECGD accept that the various contracts covering the relationship of the parties should be considered together in this case. The plan was to build a refinery. The

Newfoundland companies were going to operate it and wished to have it built for them but finance was required. A consortium of banks were prepared to provide the finance provided they had security. Since Procon (Great Britain) Ltd was an English company the ECGD were prepared to provide security and so they had to consider the risks and then state the appropriate terms. Those terms were that for roughly 2½% of the total liability and with the security of a mortgage on the refinery they would accept the risk provided that Procon were not in default. If however Procon were in default then they would not accept the risk and Procon would have to accept it. The ECGD submit that in those circumstances no question of penalty arises.

The premium agreement was the contract by which the ECGD agreed with Procon to enter into guarantee agreements guaranteeing payments on promissory notes issued by the Newfoundland companies. It is unnecessary to set out the earlier parts of the premium agreement save to mention that those clauses provide for payment of the premium. Clause 7(1) however is the clause with which this case is concerned. It reads:

> 'The premiums hereby payable are not intended to and do not cover payments made by the Guarantors under the Sterling Guarantee Agreement nor the Eurodollar Guarantee Agreement by reason of any default by Building Company and Operating Company at any time when UOP shall be or is in default in the performance of its obligations under any or all of the UOP Guarantees or Procon is in default under the terms of the Contract. Upon payment by the Guarantors to Kleinworts of any sum under the Sterling Guarantee Agreement and/or the Eurodollar Guarantee Agreement in the above circumstances the Companies will on demand pay to the Guarantors a sum equal to that paid by the Guarantors to Kleinworts as aforesaid.'

The principles governing the decision whether or not a clause is a penalty clause are set out in the well-known passage in the speech of Lord Dunedin in *Dunlop Pneumatic Tyre Co Ltd v New Garage and Motor Co Ltd* [1915] AC 79 at 86–89, [1914–15] All ER Rep 739 at 741–742. Diplock LJ in *Philip Bernstein (Successors) Ltd v Lydiate Textiles Ltd* [1962] CA Transcript 238 (sub nom *Sterling Industrial Facilities Ltd v Lydiate Textiles Ltd* 106 SJ 669) in the Court of Appeal summarised the law in this way:

> 'In the ordinary way a penalty is a sum which, by the terms of a contract, a promisor agrees to pay to the promisee in the event of non-performance by the promisor of one or more of the obligations and which is excess of the damage caused by such non-performance. When there is such a stipulation in a contract, then the question arises as to whether provision is a genuine pre-estimate of the damages which will be sustained on a breach, in which case it is enforceable, or whether it is a penalty, in which case the court will grant relief against it and refuse to allow the promisee to recover more than the actual damage which he has sustained.'

No case has been cited to us in which these principles have been departed from.

A distinction is drawn in the cases, however, where the sum of money is payable on the happening of an event: see for example *Re Apex Supply Co Ltd* [1941] 3 All ER 473, [1942] Ch 108, *Alder v Moore* [1961] 1 All ER 1, [1961] 2 QB 57 and the *Philip Bernstein* case. Where the contract provides for a sum of money payable on the happening of an event no question of a penalty arises and the court will not grant any relief. See also *Bridge v Campbell Discount Co Ltd* [1962] 1 All ER 385, [1962] AC 600, where the distinction was drawn between the exercise of an option and a genuine pre-estimate of damage for breach of contract. If the sums payable are by reason of the exercise of an option the penalty clause provisions would not apply.

The facts of the present case show that Procon owed no contractual duty to the ECGD to perform the construction contract properly. That duty was contained in a contract between Procon and the Newfoundland companies. Second, the breach of contract by Procon was only one of three events giving right of recourse. First of all there had to be dishonour by the Newfoundland companies, second, there had to be payment by the ECGD to Kleinworts to compensate for such dishonour and, third, Procon had to be in default at the time of payment. Procon's breach of contract alone did not give rise to any claim. Lastly, the claim under cl 7 was not a claim for damages suffered by reason of Procon's breach of contract; it was a claim for recourse by the ECGD under their guarantee to recover payments which had been made by the ECGD.

The situation in this case is entirely different from any of the cases dealing with penalty clauses which are clauses put into a contract to cover breach of that contract. This was quite different, this was a clause in a contract by which the ECGD had undertaken to guarantee against certain risks but they had specifically excluded from the guarantee liability for those risks when there was the additional risk created by the fact that Procon were in default. It was a clause providing for the payment (in fact the repayment) of certain sums of money on the happening of an event, namely default of the Newfoundland companies causing payment by the ECGD to the banks at the time when Procon were in default. Procon entered into this contract in 1970 with their eyes open and they were prepared to divide the risk in that way. I see no reason whatever for saying that, because in the events that have followed the risk has turned out to be a very expensive one, they were entitled to any relief. I would dismiss this appeal.

SLADE LJ. I agree. It is common ground that it is necessary to look at the other interrelated transactions, of which the premium agreement of 16 October 1970 formed one part, for the purpose of determining the construction and effect of cl 7(1). My understanding of the substance of these somewhat complicated transactions is as follows.

On 30 August 1970 a contract (the contract) was concluded between Provincial Building Co Ltd (the building company) and Procon (Great Britain) Ltd (Procon), whereby Procon agreed to construct an oil refinery. It was contemplated that the refinery when built would be operated by Provincial Refining Co Ltd (the operating company), which was associated with the building company. By separate contracts (the UOP guarantees) Universal Oil Products Co (UOP) (the parent company of Procon Inc, which was itself the parent company of Procon), entered into guarantees with the operating company in relation to the provision of services to be provided by UOP to the operating company. However, the effective operation of the contract and the UOP guarantees was made conditional on the building company and the operating company raising the necessary finance. In due course the building company and the operating company made appropriate arrangements for this purpose with Kleinwort Benson Ltd (Kleinworts), which agreed to enter into three agreements (the sterling financial agreement, the first Eurodollar agreement and the second Eurodollar agreement) with the building company acting jointly with the operating company. These agreements provided, inter alia, for the making and issue of promissory notes in favour of Kleinworts, maturing on different dates, and intended to provide for repayment of the contemplated loans. Kleinworts, however, required further security to be given to it for the performance of the obligations of the building company and the operating company under their contractual arrangements with Kleinworts, since it would be likely to find itself in difficulty if any of the contemplated promissory notes were not met on maturity. Kleinworts therefore requested that additional security should be procured for it in the form of two further agreements which were to be executed in its favour by the plaintiffs (the ECGD) and were to be known as 'the sterling guarantee agreement' and 'the Eurodollar guarantee agreement'. In these circumstances Procon, UOP and Procon Inc (the Procon companies) requested the ECGD to enter into these two agreements, so as to enable the package deal to go through.

As must have been obvious to all parties, the ECGD, in entering into them, would be undertaking substantial contingent risks, in particular the risk that the building company or the operating company might default in the performance of its obligations to Kleinworts and that in consequence the ECGD might be called on to pay very large sums to Kleinworts under its guarantees. In these circumstances, as one might have expected, the ECGD demanded payment from the Procon companies of substantial premiums to cover the sums which it might be called on to pay to Kleinworts, by reason of any default

of the building company or the operating company. Payment of such premiums was
a provided for by cl 1 of the premium agreement. Equally not surprisingly, the ECGD, by way of limiting the risk which it was undertaking, required that in certain contingencies the Procon companies should indemnify it against moneys which it might find itself obliged to pay to Kleinworts. Clauses 7(2) and 8 of the premium agreement contained provisions to this effect. So did cl 7(1), which began by expressly stating that the premiums payable under the premium agreement were not intended to and did not
b cover payments made by the ECGD under the sterling guarantee agreement, or the Eurodollar guarantee agreement, by reason of any default by the building company and the operating company at any time when either (i) UOP was in default in the performance of its obligations under any of the UOP guarantees or (ii) Procon was 'in default under the terms of the Contract'. It then continued with the sentence with which this appeal is principally concerned:

c

> 'Upon payment by the Guarantors to Kleinworts of any sum under the Sterling Guarantee Agreement and/or the Eurodollar Guarantee Agreement in the above circumstances the Companies will on demand pay to the Guarantors a sum equal to that paid by the Guarantors to Kleinworts as aforesaid.'

In the event both the building company and the operating company defaulted under
d the terms of their financial agreements with Kleinworts. As a result the ECGD became liable to pay and did pay to Kleinworts sums totalling £39·1m under the sterling guarantee agreement and the Eurodollar guarantee agreement. ECGD claims that Procon was at all material times 'in default under the terms of the Contract', within the meaning of cl 7(1) of the premium agreement, though this is strongly denied by the Procon companies.

e In these circumstances the ECGD has demanded that the Procon companies should repay it the sum of £39·1m (and interest) by virtue of the indemnity provisions contained in cl 7(1) of the premium agreement. This the Procon companies have declined to do on the ground (among other grounds) that cl 7(1) is void and of no effect, as being a penalty clause. The present question for decision is whether that contention is correct.

There is no dispute that the wording of cl 7(1), if it is a valid provision, imposed on the
f Procon companies the obligation to make repayment to the ECGD, in the contingencies there stated, however trivial might be the relevant default of UOP under the terms of the UOP guarantees or of Procon under the terms of the contract. Accordingly, it is common ground that the very nature of cl 7(1) was such that the sums which the Procon companies might find themselves bound thereunder to repay to the ECGD might be largely out of all proportion to any damage which the ECGD would have actually suffered as a result of
g the relevant breach of contract by UOP or Procon. This is a point which has naturally featured in the forefront of Mr Yorke's argument on their behalf.

Nevertheless, the mere fact that a person contracts to pay another person, on a specified contingency, a sum of money which far exceeds the damage likely to be suffered by the recipient as a result of that contingency does not by itself render the provision void as a penalty. This is shown quite clearly for example by the decisions of Simonds J in *Re Apex*
h *Supply Co Ltd* [1941] 3 All ER 473, [1942] Ch 108 and of this court in *Alder v Moore* [1961] 1 All ER 1, [1961] 2 QB 57.

The type of provision for payment in a contingency which the court will or may regard as a penalty is to be found conveniently summarised in the passage from the judgment of Diplock LJ in *Philip Bernstein (Successors) Ltd v Lydiate Textiles Ltd* [1962] CA Transcript 238 (sub nom *Sterling Industrial Facilities Ltd v Lydiate Textiles Ltd* 106 SJ 669)
j in the Court of Appeal, which Waller LJ has already quoted. It is implicit in this statement of principle that, in the ordinary way, a penalty is a sum which, by the terms of a contract made between A and B, A agrees to pay to B in the event of non-performance by A of one or more of A's obligations under that contract with B, and which is not a genuine pre-estimate of the damage which is likely to be suffered by B in the event of such breach.

If, however, the doctrine of penalties is limited in this way, it cannot avail the Procon companies on the facts of the present case. For the relevant contingencies which give rise *a* to their obligation to make payments to the ECGD under cl 7(1) of the premium agreement do not include any breach of contractual obligations owed by them to the ECGD. It is common ground that none of the Procon companies have contracted with the ECGD itself to observe the provisions of the contract of 30 August 1970, entered into by Procon with the building company.

Put shortly, therefore, a question of principle raised by this appeal is whether the *b* doctrine of penalties is capable of applying in a case where the terms of a contract between A and B provide that A is to pay to B a stated sum in the event of non-performance by A of one or more of the contractual obligations owed by A not to B himself but to a third party, C.

Unless more recent authorities point in a different direction, in my opinion a conclusive negative answer to this question is to be found in the *Bernstein* case itself. The facts of that *c* case, as appearing from the judgment of Diplock LJ, were these. The plaintiffs were a finance company financing hire-purchase agreements. The agreement under which the action was brought was a 'recourse' agreement, under which the defendant dealers had undertaken to procure offers from hirers to enter into hire-purchase agreements with the plaintiffs, on a commission basis. Clause 6 contained a provision to the effect that, if the hirer was in default in respect of instalments payable under a hire-purchase agreement, *d* the dealers would pay to the plaintiffs an amount equal to the total balance of the instalments which the hirer would have had to pay if the hire-purchase agreement had continued throughout the term, and which had not been received by the plaintiffs. The amount payable under cl 6 by the dealers in the event of default by a hirer was greater than any amount which would have been payable by the hirer on such default. In these circumstances the defendants submitted that the court should treat cl 6 as a penalty *e* clause and accordingly relieve them against it, by not allowing the plaintiffs to recover from them any greater sum than the actual loss sustained as a result of the default by the hirer.

The Court of Appeal unanimously rejected this argument. Diplock LJ, with whose judgment Ormerod LJ agreed without adding any observations of his own, said this in the course of his judgment: *f*

> 'The ordinary rule which the courts apply is that contracts should be enforced, pacta sunt servanda, unless they can be brought within the limited category of cases in which, for reasons of public policy, the court refuses to give effect to the agreement of the parties. One limited class and well-known class is the class of penalty, but up till now it has been restricted to cases where there is a prior *g* agreement by the parties to the contract as to an amount to be paid by a party in breach to the other party in respect of that breach. Since the judgment of Gorman J there has been some discussion of the nature of penalties in the recent case in the House of Lords of *Bridge v Campbell Discount Co Ltd* [1961] 1 All ER 385, [1962] AC 600, but speaking for myself I can find nothing in the decision in that case and nothing in the speeches of any of their Lordships, with the possible exception of *h* Lord Denning, which throws any doubt on the rule accepted by Gorman J that the penalty area is limited to the narrow field which I have described. There are, it is true, in the speech of Lord Denning certain observations which suggest that that field should be extended (see [1962] 1 All ER 385 at 399–400, [1962] AC 600 at 628–629). But those observations find, so far as I can see, no support in any other of the speeches of their Lordships, and, for my part, I think the law is well settled as to *j* what the penalty area is. What, in effect, the parties agreed here, and this was a dealer bargaining with a hire-purchase company, was that in certain events, namely a failure by a hirer to pay an instalment, the dealer should pay a sum specified in the contract and the finance company should assign its rights to the dealer. It may be that was an improvident bargain. Whether it was depends on all the terms and not

> on an isolated clause. But one does not relieve against bargains merely because they
> a are improvident when they are entered into between parties at arm's length, as these two were.'

I think that, mutatis mutandis, almost every word of this passage from Diplock LJ's judgment is applicable in the present instance.

Mr Yorke, as I understand him, submitted that the *Bernstein* case is distinguishable
b from the present case on the grounds that the relevant contingency envisaged by cl 7(1) of the premium agreement is a breach of a contractual duty owed by the Procon companies themselves, albeit a duty owed to persons other than the ECGD. In the *Berstein* case, as he pointed out, it was the breach of contract by persons other than the dealers that gave rise to the obligation on the dealers to pay. With due respect to the argument, this is in my opinion a distinction without any difference. The passage from Diplock LJ's judgment which I have read makes it plain that the court regarded the 'penalty area' as
c restricted to the 'narrow field' where there has been *'a prior agreement by the parties to the contract as to an amount to be paid by a party in breach to the other party in respect of that breach'*, in substitution for the amount of damages which would otherwise have been payable in respect of it. It is, I think, necessarily implicit in the decision that the court would *not* have regarded the 'penalty area' as extending to a case where there is no
d question of the agreed stipulated sum taking the place of an award of damages, and that it would not have been prepared to extend the law to cover such a case.

Accordingly, subject to the effect of any subsequent cases, I regard the decision of this court in the *Berstein* case as by itself affording conclusive authority which compels the rejection of the company's submissions.

The subsequent case on which Mr Yorke principally, and strongly, relied was *Gilbert-Ash (Northern) Ltd v Modern Engineering (Bristol) Ltd* [1973] 3 All ER 195, [1974] AC 689.
e In that case the House of Lords had to consider a provision which, according to its natural meaning, would have enabled the contractors concerned to have—

> '[suspended or withheld] payment of very large sums of money due by them to the sub-contractors in the event of the sub-contractors committing some minor breach of contract causing only trivial damage in no way comparable to the amount
> f owed to the sub-contractors.'

(See [1973] 3 All ER 195 at 220, [1974] AC 689 at 723 per Lord Salmon.)

The House of Lords held that this provision was unenforceable on the grounds that it provided for the exaction of a penalty.

Mr Yorke submitted in effect that this decision represented a significant extension of
g the doctrine of penalties, inasmuch as the relevant clause provided for the withholding, rather than the payment, of money, and indeed of a sum which was not specifically quantified. Thus, he suggested, the decision shows that, notwithstanding what was said in the *Bernstein* case, the boundaries of the penalty area are by no means closed. In the present case, as he put it, any breach of contract occurring within the transaction as a whole should suffice to attract equitable relief, if the sum consequentially claimed is not
h a genuine pre-estimate of the damage suffered, and a fortiori where there is no demonstrable causal link between the breach and the damage. Common law and equity, he submitted, are constantly evolving to meet modern conditions. So far as necessary, in his submission, the penalty area should be extended to cover cl 7(1), just as it was extended to cover the relevant clause in the *Gilbert-Ash* case.

I do not regard that decision as embodying any significant extension of the penalty
j area. For many years now, the courts, in considering whether contractual provisions fall within it, have had regard to substance rather than to form. If the effect of a provision in a contract between A and B is to entitle B *to receive* sums at the expense of A in the event of non-performance by A of one or more of his obligations under that contract and those sums are not a genuine pre-estimate of the damage which is likely to be suffered by B in the event of such breach, then the provision must, I think, prima facie fall within the

penalty area; it cannot make any difference whether B is to receive such sums by way of direct payment by A or by way of retention at A's expense.

In my judgment, however, neither the *Gilbert-Ash* decision nor any other decision subsequent to the *Bernstein* case which has been cited to this court lends any support whatever to the proposition that it should or can extend the penalty area so as to cover cases where the breach of contract which is expressed to give rise to the obligation to pay the alleged penalty is the breach of a contractual duty owed to a third party other than the person who is to receive it. Mr Yorke submitted that the building company and the operating company are not properly to be regarded as 'third parties' for any such purpose, bearing in mind the close, interlocking nature of the relevant contracts, and regarding them all as part of one composite transaction. Even so regarding them, I cannot accept this submission. The contracts could no doubt have been drafted so as to impose on the Procon companies a specific contractual obligation, *owed to the ECGD*, to observe the provisions of the contract and the UOP guarantee. But they did not do so and cannot now be read as if they did.

Staughton J, as I read his judgment, rejected the Procon companies' submission essentially on the grounds that a provision cannot amount to a penalty if it provides for the payment of money on a specified event other than a breach of a contractual duty owed by the contemplated payer to the contemplated payee. For the reasons which I have given, I agree with this conclusion.

Therefore it is not necessary to consider two other points which might otherwise have been particularly significant on this appeal. First, the relevant breaches of contract by the Procon companies are on any footing only one of three contingencies which *all* have to occur before their obligations to pay sums to the ECGD under cl 7(1) can arise. They may commit regular and gross breaches of their obligations to the building company and the operating company, but this will expose them to no liability to the ECGD until the building company and the operating company themselves are in breach of their obligations to Kleinworts, and in consequence Kleinworts call on the ECGD to pay up. If, therefore, the true commercial purpose of cl 7(1) were to be regarded as that of deterring the Procon companies from breaking their contractural obligations to the building company and the operating company, or of punishing them for so doing, its deterrent or punitive effect would have been somewhat limited, to say the least. Second, as I understand the position, Procon Inc, though one of the indemnifying parties under cl 7(1), was not itself a party to the relevant contracts with the building company and the operating company; cl 7(1) itself seems to be drafted on this assumption. At present therefore I find it rather difficult to see how Procon Inc could properly invoke the penalty doctrine on any possible footing.

Mr Yorke eloquently elaborated on the hardship which he said his clients might suffer, if the clause were to be held valid, and on the alleged unconscionable attitude of the ECGD in seeking to enforce it. However, in the absence of any claim for rectification or rescission of the premium agreement, I do not think that general considerations such as this are relevant. The question in issue is simply a question of construction of cl 7(1), falling to be decided in the light of the authorities, on the terms and surrounding circumstances of that agreement, judged as at the time of its execution (see *Snell's Principles of Equity* (28th edn, 1982) p 528). I would merely record that it has not been suggested that there is anything in the least obscure in the language of the indemnity provisions of cl 7(1) or that the Procon companies were misled in any way when they agreed to enter into the premium agreement, or indeed that they did not have the benefit of the full legal advice which one would expect them to have received before entering into an agreement of this magnitude. It is understandable that in the events which have happened they may regret having entered into a transaction which has proved such an unfortunate one. But there is no general principle of equity which entitles the court to relieve a party to a bargain merely because in the event it operates hardly against him. In my view the relevant question is simply whether cl 7(1) does or does not fall within the well-established boundaries of the 'penalty area'. As I have indicated, no authority has

been cited which in my opinion would compel or even permit this court to hold that it
a does.

In all the circumstances, I think that the principle pacta sunt servanda applies to cl 7(1). I would dismiss this appeal.

SIR SEBAG SHAW. I agree with the judgments and with the reasons stated by Waller and Slade LJJ.

b The structure of the contractual situation out of which this appeal arises is extremely complicated, as Slade LJ has demonstrated; but Mr Yorke's argument is of limited scope and is of necessity confined to the doctrine of penalty. He acknowledges that as the law stands he cannot contend in this court for a wider principle of amelioration by way of equitable relief on the ground that the strict enforcement of a contractual provision results in oppression or undue hardship or the imposition of unforeseen and intolerable
c burdens in regard to a contracting party.

The first difficulty that confronts Mr Yorke arises from the nature of the connection between the parties concerned. There are contracts and collateral contracts and cross-contracts relative to the construction of the Come-by-Chance oil refinery, to the financing of the project and to securing payment in the course of the development. Mr Yorke put before the court a diagrammatic representation as to how the different contractors were
d linked in contracts, which was between different combinations of the various parties involved, in different capacities, in the overall project. The diagram was designed to demonstrate that the various parties, though not all contractually related, were intimately bound together in a common project. Hence, submitted Mr Yorke, when their contractual obligations came to be defined, they must be considered having regard to the involvement of all those represented in his diagram. There is, in appropriate
e circumstances, support for this proposition; but the intricate interconnection of the different and distinct contracts which are involved in the overall transaction make such unification in the present case incongrous, impracticable and illogical.

However, Mr Yorke goes on to contend that, looking at the outcome of the strict enforcement of cl 7(1) of the premium agreement, it is manifest that Procon has been penalised. What may have been an insignificant or readily remedied breach of the
f building contract (with which, of course, the ECGD had no direct connection) has brought on Procon an enormous and immediate liability. The conjunction of the contracting parties involved in the whole complicated scheme was never designed or intended to expose Procon to such a peril. So the argument ran. Unfortunately, however, that is just what cl 7(1) did. In such case, Mr Yorke contended, the clause provided for what was in truth a penalty notwithstanding that the indemnity it made operative arose
g from no breach of contract as between Procon and the ECGD. The outcome was harsh and unconscionable. The fact that such a result was possible demonstrated that cl 7(1) was a penalty clause. The argument demonstrates no more than that it was from Procon's standpoint an improvident clause, but it does not begin to show that it comes within what has been described as 'the penalty area'. In general, parties to a contract must perform their respective obligations according to their tenor. If a party defaults he must
h pay compensation for the damages suffered by the other party; but he cannot be made to pay more than proper compensation; not even if he has in the contract itself undertaken to do so. Where a contract fixes the amount to be paid in damages in the event of breach, the court will consider whether at the time it was so fixed it represented a genuine pre-estimate of the damage which would result from a breach. If it did, it will be upheld although in the outcome the actual damage may be less. If it appeared unrelated to the
j probable damage, the court would relieve against it and the true damage would have to be ascertained.

These considerations have never been applied save between parties to a contract which one of them has broken. Relief against enforcement of the provisions of a contract is by way of exception to the principle pacta sunt servanda. In general, contracts are enforceable without gloss or modification even if they are onerous to a party and show him to have been rash in his undertakings. Mr Yorke seeks to graft a new exception on that principle.

His attractive and interesting argument really involved a facile legalistic sidestep from a well-established and defined penalty area into an artificial extension of it which the law does not recognise.

The sum claimed by the ECGD from Procon is not damages for breach of contract. It is a debt due under an indemnity which was made operative by an event provided for and which occurred.

I would dismiss the appeal.

Appeal dismissed. Leave to appeal to the House of Lords refused.

Appeal

The defendants appealed to the House of Lords with leave of the Appeal Committee of the House of Lords granted on 20 January 1983.

James Fox-Andrews QC, *Richard Yorke QC* and *Stuart Isaacs* for the defendants.
Nicholas Phillips QC and *Ian Glick* for the ECGD.

Their Lordships took time for consideration.

24 March. The following opinions were delivered.

LORD DIPLOCK. My Lords, I have had the advantage of reading in draft the speech of my noble and learned friend Lord Roskill. I agree with it, and for the reasons he gives I would dismiss the appeal.

LORD ELWYN-JONES. My Lords, I have had the benefit of reading in draft the speech to be delivered by my noble and learned friend Lord Roskill. I agree with it, and for the reasons he gives I too would dismiss the appeal.

LORD KEITH OF KINKEL. My Lords, I have had the benefit of reading in draft the speech to be delivered by my noble and learned friend Lord Roskill. I agree with it, and for the reasons he gives I too would dismiss the appeal.

LORD ROSKILL. My Lords, this appeal involves a very large sum of money but a very short, and I venture to think, simple question of construction of cl 7(1) of an agreement dated 16 October 1970 and concluded between the defendants and the ECGD. This agreement, known as the 'premium agreement', was one of a number of interlocking agreements concluded between, inter alios, a group of Newfoundland companies, the defendants, and a group of bankers headed by Kleinwort Benson Ltd (Kleinworts), and the ECGD, regarding the design, construction and installation of a refinery in Newfoundland, and the financing of those operations. It is unnecessary to relate the details of those highly complex agreements in order to determine the present issue, which is whether the obligation seemingly clearly imposed on the defendants by the ECGD by cl 7(1) is a penalty, so that the sum of £39,571,001·54 which the ECGD seek to recover from the defendants in the events which occurred is for that reason irrecoverable in law. It is sufficient to say that the Newfoundland companies made and issued a series of promissory notes for different sums maturing on different dates, and Kleinworts, in return for the promissory notes, provided the requisite funds to one of the Newfoundland companies. The ECGD guaranteed those promissory notes but as part of the interlocking transactions required the premium agreement to be entered into by the defendants. The defendants paid a premium of over £1m sterling in consideration of the guarantee given by the ECGD to Kleinworts. A large number of those promissory notes which matured between 30 September 1973 and 30 September 1981 were dishonoured. Kleinworts claimed the sum due on the dishonoured notes from the ECGD who duly discharged their obligations and now seek to have recourse against the defendants under the premium agreement by reason of cl 7(1).

My Lords, the question whether the obligation imposed by cl 7(1) is a penalty is not the only issue raised in the present action. The dimensions of the action can perhaps best be gauged by the fact that the present issue was raised in paras 24 and 131 of the defence and counterclaim and in para 86 of the reply and defence to counterclaim. There is another action of equally large dimensions proceeding between various of the parties to these interlocking agreements with which happily your Lordships are not concerned.

Robert Goff J ordered the question whether cl 7(1) operated as a penalty to be tried as a preliminary issue. Both Staughton J and the Court of Appeal (Waller, Slade LJJ and Sir Sebag Shaw) had no difficulty in concluding that it was not, and for substantially the same reasons. The Court of Appeal refused leave to appeal but your Lordships' House subsequently gave leave on being told that this challenge to the efficacy of cl 7(1) as an effective recourse provision was of great general importance since the ECGD had issued guarantees involving many thousands of millions of pounds sterling on the basis of recourse provisions either the same as, or very similar to, cl 7(1). Your Lordships therefore thought it right that the issue which thus assumed an importance beyond that directly involved in this appeal should be finally and authoritatively determined by this House.

For ease of reference I set out the whole of cl 7(1):

> 'The premiums hereby payable are not intended to and do not cover payments made by the Guarantors under the Sterling Gaurantee Agreement nor the Eurodollar Guarantee Agreement by reason of any default by Building Company and Operating Company at any time when UOP shall be or is in default in the performance of its obligations under any or all of the UOP Guarantees or Procon is in default under the terms of the Contract. Upon payment by the Guarantors to Kleinworts of any sum under the Sterling Guarantee Agreement and/or the Eurodollar Guarantee Agreement in the above circumstances the Companies will on demand pay to the Guarantors a sum equal to that paid by the Guarantors to Kleinworts as aforesaid.'

My Lords, the reason why the defendants' submissions failed in the courts below can be simply stated. The clause was not a penalty clause because it provided for payment of money on the happening of a specified event other than a breach of a contractual duty owed by the contemplated payer to the contemplated payee: see, in particular, the judgment of Slade LJ (see pp 216ff, ante).

Mr Yorke QC, for the defendants, conceded that he could not point to an authority whereby the law regarding penalty clauses in contracts as enunciated by this House in *Dunlop Pneumatic Tyre Co Ltd v New Garage and Motor Co Ltd* [1915] AC 79, [1914–15] All ER Rep 739 had been extended as far as he invited your Lordships now to extend it. But he explained this absence of authority by contending that the law evolved at a time when contractual situations were simple, and few contracts were other than bilateral. Today, he urged, complex interlocking, multilateral contracts of the kind presently involved were commonplace in this field of international financing of contracts of many kinds, especially construction contracts, and that the premium agreement and cl 7(1) in particular could not be interpreted simply as a single contract between the defendants and the ECGD, but was an essential part of the multilateral contracts, so that, in determining whether or not the obligations arising under cl 7(1) were penal in character, it was necessary to have regard to the totality of the contractual provisions involved, not just to a single provision in a single bilateral contract. He urged that, if his submission were wrong, the slightest breach of contract by Procon (Great Britain) Ltd in the performance of its obligations under the construction contract, could bring cl 7(1) into play irrespective of the actual loss which the ECGD had suffered.

Mr Yorke invited your Lordships to look at the number of authorities in support of his proposition that the relevant law should now be extended, and contended that those authorities showed that the way remained open for such extension. Those cases are referred to in the judgments of the courts below and I shall not refer to them again for, with respect, I am unable to find the slightest support in any of them for Mr Yorke's submissions. a

My Lords, one purpose, perhaps the main purpose, of the law relating to penalty clauses is to prevent a plaintiff recovering a sum of money in respect of a breach of contract committed by a defendant which bears little or no relationship to the loss actually suffered by the plaintiff as a result of the breach by the defendant. But it is not and never has been for the courts to relieve a party from the consequences of what may in the event prove to be an onerous or possibly even a commercially imprudent bargain. b The defendants could only secure the finance from Kleinworts if the ECGD were prepared to give Kleinworts the guarantee which Kleinworts required. The ECGD were only prepared to give their guarantee to Kleinworts on the terms of the premium agreement which included the stringent right of recourse provided for in cl 7(1). The defendants accepted those terms which provided for the right of recourse to arise on the happening of a specified event, and that specified event has now happened. But, as my c noble and learned friend Lord Keith observed during the argument, this is not a case where the ECGD are seeking to recover more than their actual loss as compensation by way of damages for breach of a contract to which they were a party. They are seeking, and only seeking, to recover their actual loss, namely the sums which they became legally obliged to pay and have paid to Kleinworts. I am afraid I find it impossible to see how on these facts there can be any room for the invocation of the law relating to penalty clauses. d

My Lords, I have arrived at this conclusion in complete agreement with the courts below and for the same reasons, simply as a matter of the construction of the premium agreement, and that is sufficient to dispose of this appeal. But both courts below relied on a virtually unreported decision of the Court of Appeal in *Philip Bernstein (Successors) Ltd v Lydiate Textiles Ltd* [1962] CA Transcript 238 (sub nom *Sterling Industrial Facilities Ltd v Lydiate Textiles Ltd* 106 SJ 669). The court consisted of Ormerod, Danckwerts and e Diplock LJJ. Your Lordships' House has recently, and since the judgments given in the courts below, strongly deprecated the citation of unreported decisions of the Court of Appeal, and *Bernstein*'s case is such a decision. I therefore only refer to it because the judgments below contain substantial extracts from the judgment of Diplock LJ, who spoke for all the members of the court. Those extracts show that the view then taken by the Court of Appeal is in entire conformity with the view of the law which I understand f all your Lordships to take and which I have endeavoured to express without reference to that unreported decision. I would only add that I entirely agree with the concluding observation of Diplock LJ in that case.

> 'I, for my part, am not prepared to extend the law by relieving against an obligation in a contract entered into between two parties which does not fall within the well-defined limits in which the court has in the past shown itself willing to g interfere.'

I would respectfully and gratefully adopt that statement as my own.

I would dismiss this appeal with costs.

LORD BRIGHTMAN. My Lords, I would dismiss this appeal for the reasons given by h my noble and learned friend Lord Roskill.

Appeal dismissed.

Solicitors: *Davies Arnold & Cooper* (for the defendants); *Treasury Solicitor*.

Mary Rose Plummer Barrister.

a
Marshall v Osmond and another

COURT OF APPEAL, CIVIL DIVISION
SIR JOHN DONALDSON MR, DILLON LJ AND SIR DENYS BUCKLEY
16 MARCH 1983

Negligence – Duty to take care – Driver of motor vehicle – Police officer – Police officer pursuing b *person attempting to avoid arrest for arrestable offence – Extent of policeman's duty of care to that person.*

The plaintiff was travelling as a passenger in a car which he knew to be stolen and which was being pursued by a police vehicle driven by a police officer. The car stopped and the plaintiff tried to escape in order to avoid arrest. As he attempted to do so, he was struck c and injured either by the police vehicle itself or by some part of the stolen car after it had been hit by the police vehicle. He brought an action for damages against the police officer, claiming that his injuries had been caused by the officer's negligent driving. The judge dismissed the claim, holding that a police officer driving a motor vehicle in hot pursuit of a person whom he rightly suspected of having committed an arrestable offence did not owe the same duty of care which he owed to innocent and law-abiding users of d the highway and that, although a police officer was not entitled deliberately to injure such a person unless it was reasonably necessary to do so in order to arrest him, the officer's actions were not to be judged on the same standards as those which would apply if he had time to consider all possible alternative courses of action which he could take to enable him to discharge his duty successfully. The plaintiff appealed.

e
Held – Although a police officer was entitled to use such force in effecting a suspected criminal's arrest as was reasonable in all the circumstances, the duty owed by the police officer to the suspect was in all other respects the standard duty of care owed to anyone else, namely to exercise such care and skill as was reasonable in all the circumstances. On the facts, the police officer had made an error of judgment, but the evidence did not f show that he had been negligent. The appeal would accordingly be dismissed (see p 227 *b* to *g*, post).

Per curiam. Since the duty owed by a police driver to a suspect is the same duty as that owed by anyone else, a defence of volenti non fit injuria is not applicable in the case of the police pursuing a suspected criminal (see p 227 *b* and *g*, post).

Decision of Milmo J [1982] 2 All ER 610 affirmed.

g
Notes

For the duty to take care and the standard of care, see 34 Halsbury's Laws (4th edn) paras 5–11, and for cases on the subject, see 36(1) Digest (Reissue) 17–46, *34–148*.

For negligence in relation to the performance of statutory functions, see 34 Halsbury's Laws (4th edn) para 4.

h
Cases cited

Gaynor v Allen [1959] 2 All ER 644, [1959] 2 QB 403.
Woods v Richards (1977) 65 Cr App R 300, DC.

j **Appeal**

The plaintiff, Victor Marshall, appealed against the decision of Milmo J ([1982] 2 All ER 610, [1982] QB 857) given on 1 February 1982 whereby he dismissed the plaintiff's claim against the first defendant, Sir Douglas Osmond, the Chief Constable of Hampshire, and the second defendant, Maximilian Anthony Needham, a police constable of the Hampshire Police Force, for damages for personal injuries arising out of the negligent driving of the second defendant on the C11 road in the vicinity of Wilverley Plain on 2 May 1976. The facts are set out in the judgment of Sir John Donaldson MR.

John Spokes QC and *C H E Gabb* for the plaintiff.
Ian Kennedy QC and *Richard Dening* for the first and second defendants.

SIR JOHN DONALDSON MR. This is an appeal from a judgment of Milmo J given in London on 1 February 1982 following a hearing which took place in Winchester in the autumn of the previous year. By that judgment the judge dismissed the plaintiff's claim for damages for personal injuries which he sustained in what can loosely be described as a motor accident. It was, however, an unusual motor accident arising out of unusual facts.

The first defendant is Sir Douglas Osmond, the Chief Constable of Hampshire, and he features by virtue of his vicarious liability for the second defendant, Pc Needham.

The second defendant was the driver of an unmarked red Mini in the early hours of the morning of 2 May 1976. He had been dispatched to the Brockenhurst area together with a Pc Ford to keep special observation because there had been a spate of stealing and taking and driving away motor cars without the consent of the owner.

Whilst on duty, at 1.10 am, he saw a Mk II Cortina being driven past with a number of youths inside. Bearing in mind the time of night and the previous history of the area, this aroused his suspicions and he started to pursue the Cortina. His plan was not to stop the Cortina at that stage, but to find out which road it was going to take and then radio ahead for assistance from uniformed officers in marked cars to stop it.

However, the Cortina pulled into a lay-by, possibly to ascertain the nature of the car which was following it, and the second defendant pulled his car up slightly in front of the Cortina. Pc Ford got out. At that stage the Cortina reversed at considerable speed. It then drove forward, passing the Mini, and continued down the road Pc Ford got back into the Mini, and the second defendant set off in pursuit of the Cortina.

After the Cortina had travelled about four hundred yards, it crossed to the offside of the road and stopped in a lay-by. The youths then got out with a view to making themselves scarce. I should say that the whole incident took place on one of the open New Forest roads where there were no houses, and the youths were intending to make their escape across open country.

The second defendant's intention was to draw up alongside the Cortina. He braked, and as he braked he skidded slightly sideways, and his car came into contact with the Cortina, causing damage to his car and no doubt to the Cortina. When he got out he found the plaintiff lying on the lay-by between the two cars. He had a seriously injured leg.

That is a bare outline of the background facts. Against that background, the judge made certain specific findings. He found ([1982] 2 All ER 610 at 614, [1982] QB 857 at 862):

> '(1) at all material times the plaintiff was willingly being carried in the Cortina motor car knowing that it had been taken and driven away without the consent of the owner; (2) at the time when he sustained his injury the plaintiff was fully aware of the fact that the police were in hot pursuit of the Cortina and were seeking to stop, question and [the word is 'inevitably' but perhaps 'hopefully' is what he meant] arrest its occupants; (3) the other occupants of the Cortina had already made their getaway into the bushes and it was the plaintiff's intention to do so himself as quickly as possible; (4) the whole incident between the high-speed chase from the first lay-by until the Cortina stopped by the second lay-by took a very short time and the events thereafter occurred in a matter of seconds; (5) when he was endeavouring to make his escape and avoid arrest, the plaintiff sustained the injuries in respect of which he how claims damages by reason of being struck by some part of the police vehicle or by some part of the Cortina after it had been struck by the police vehicle;

(6) the defendant did not intend to injure the plaintiff or any of the occupants of the car . . .'

Those are findings of fact. He then reached his conclusion, which was that the defendant was not guilty of any want of reasonable care in all the circumstances of the case.

In the course of his judgment the judge adverted to the line of cases which is concerned with spectators attending sporting events. This suggests that the spectator voluntarily takes the risk of injury where a competitor is competing carefully in accordance with the rules but nevertheless causes him injury. There was a plea in this case of volenti non fit injuria. For my part I am bound to say that I do not believe that the defence of volenti non fit injuria is really applicable in the case of the police pursuing a suspected criminal. I think that the duty owed by a police driver to the suspect is, as counsel on behalf of the plaintiff, has contended, the same duty as that owed to anyone else, namely to exercise such care and skill as is reasonable in all the circumstances. The vital words in that proposition of law are 'in all the circumstances', and of course one of the circumstances was that the plaintiff bore all the appearance of having been somebody engaged in a criminal activity for which there was a power of arrest.

Counsel for the plantiff put forward four propositions, the first of which I have just mentioned. The second was that the police driver might use such force as was reasonable in the circumstances to effect the plaintiff's arrest. Third, the police driver was in breach of his duty as set out in the first proposition, and, on the facts, there was a foreseeability of injury which in fact occurred. Fourth, there should be no finding of volenti non fit injuria.

From what I have said it will be apparent that I accept propositions 1, 2 and 4. As I see it, the sole issue in this appeal is whether there was a breach of the duty of care in all the circumstances.

The judge, who heard and saw the witnesses, held that there was not. We have been taken through the evidence. As I see it, what happened was that this police officer pursued a line in steering his car which would, in the ordinary course of events, have led to his ending up sufficiently far away from the Cortina to clear its open door. He was driving on a gravelly surface, at night, in what were no doubt stressful circumstances. There is no doubt that he made an error of judgment because, in the absence of an error of judgment, there would have been no contact between the cars. But I am far from satisfied on the evidence that the police officer was negligent.

It follows that I would dismiss the appeal.

DILLON LJ. I agree.

SIR DENYS BUCKLEY. I also agree.

Appeal dismissed with costs not to be enforced without the leave of the court. Legal aid fund to pay costs on usual order.

Solicitors: *Blatch & Co*, Southampton (for the plaintiff); *Theodore Goddard & Co*, agents for *R A Leyland*, Winchester (for first and second defendants).

Diana Procter Barrister.

Gordon v Douce

COURT OF APPEAL, CIVIL DIVISION
FOX LJ AND BUSH J
13, 14, 17 JANUARY 1983

Trust and trustee – Constructive trust – Unmarried couple – House acquired by joint efforts for joint benefit – Date of valuation of shares – House purchased by man for purpose of family home for mistress and children – House conveyed into sole name of man – Couple separating – Mistress and children remaining in occupation – Intention that no order for sale while children living in house – Mistress claiming share in property – Whether mistress's share to be valued at date of separation or date of sale.

The parties met in 1962 and the plaintiff became the defendant's mistress. From 1964 they started to live together as man and wife, and from 1968 did so on a permanent basis. As a result of their association two children were born. In 1977 the defendant bought a house for £4,500 which was conveyed into his sole name, the purchase price being paid partly by joint savings of £1,000 and the balance by loans from a bank and the defendant's relatives. The property was intended to be a family home for the couple and the children. Both parties worked, the defendant discharging the various loans by weekly instalments and the plaintiff contributing towards the housekeeping expenses and paying for certain repairs, improvements and outgoings. In September 1980 the relationship broke down and the defendant left the house. The plaintiff remained in occupation with the children and she sought a declaration that she was entitled to a half share of the property. At the hearing, the defendant indicated that he would not seek an order for sale while the children were still living in the house. The judge found that the plaintiff's earnings had enabled the defendant to save and discharge the various loans on the property and declared that the plaintiff was entitled to a 25% share of the property. He further ordered that the value of the shares be calculated as at 30 September 1980, being the date of the separation of the parties. The plaintiff appealed against that part of the order which directed that her share should be valued at the date of the termination of the relationship, contending, inter alia, that the judge had failed to take into account the terms of the trust under which the property was held, that the plaintiff and the children were continuing to live in the property and that it was the intention of the parties that the house should provide a home for the plaintiff and the children.

Held – The appeal would be allowed for the following reasons—

(1) Whether a party was entitled to a share in property vested in the other party by reason of an implied or resulting trust was dependant on whether the parties had so conducted themselves that it would be inequitable to permit the party in whom the property was vested in law to deny that the other party had a beneficial interest in it. In deciding that question, the same principles applied whatever the relationship between the parties, although the court could, in drawing inferences as to the intention of the parties, take into account the nature of the relationship (see p 230 *e* to *h* and p 232 *f*, post); dicta of Lord Dilhorne in *Gissing v Gissing* [1970] 2 All ER at 785 and of Lord Denning MR in *Bernard v Josephs* [1982] 3 All ER at 167 applied.

(2) Prima facie, if persons were entitled to property in aliquot shares as tenants in common under a trust for sale, the value of their respective shares was to be determined at the date when the property was sold, but that might be subject to the circumstances of the case, as for example where one of the parties wished to buy out the other, in which case the value of that party's share might have to be determined at a different date. There was no rigid rule that in a mistress case the valuation was to be at the date of the termination of the relationship, since the date of valuation was a matter of discretion for the court. Since the relationship between the parties had been of long duration, since there were children who were living in the house with the plaintiff and since there was

no intention to seek an order for sale while the children were still living in the house, the purpose of the trust had not come to an end. Furthermore, the plaintiff might have to incur expenditure on the property to enable the children and herself to live there and that would have to be taken into account as between the plaintiff and the defendant at a later date. In the circumstances there was no reason to determine the plaintiff's share at the date of separation (see p 230 *h j* and p 231 *a e f* and *j* to p 232 *f*, post); *Cooke v Head* [1972] 2 All ER 38 followed; *Hall v Hall* (1982) 3 FLR 379 distinguished.

Notes

For resulting trusts arising out of joint transactions, see 38 Halsbury's Laws (3rd edn) 868, para 1462, and for cases on the subject, see 47 Digest (Repl) 127, *925–927*.

For a trustee's powers of sale generally, see 38 Halsbury's Laws (3rd edn) 1016–1019, paras 1750–1754, and for cases on the subject, see 47 Digest (Repl) 398–400, *3586–3596*.

For the determination of property rights between husband and wife, see 22 Halsbury's Laws (4th edn) para 1030, and for cases on the subject, see 27(1) Digest (Reissue) 305–315, *2267–2330*.

Cases referred to in judgments

Bernard v Josephs [1982] 3 All ER 162, [1982] Ch 391, [1982] 2 WLR 1052, CA.
Cooke v Head [1972] 2 All ER 38, [1972] 1 WLR 518, CA.
Gissing v Gissing [1970] 2 All ER 780, [1971] AC 886, [1970] 3 WLR 255, HL.
Hall v Hall (1982) 3 FLR 379, CA.

Appeal

By an order dated 8 December 1981 his Honour Judge Paul Hughes directed that the property known as 121 St Giles Road, Derby be transferred into the joint names of the plaintiff, Alice Gordon, and the defendant, Vincent Lloyd Douce, on trust for sale to be held for the benefit of the plaintiff and the defendant in the ratio of 25% to the plaintiff and the balance of the equity to the defendant and that the value of the shares was to be calculated as at the date of the separation of the parties, ie 30 September 1980. The plaintiff appealed, contending that the value of the plaintiff's share should be valued at the date of the sale of the property and not at the date of separation. The facts are set out in the judgment of Fox LJ.

Stephen Hockman for the plaintiff.
Giles Harrison-Hall for the defendant.

Cur adv vult

17 January. The following judgments were delivered.

FOX LJ. This is an appeal from a decision of his Honour Judge Paul Hughes at Derby County Court.

The parties met in 1962. They have two children, born in 1963 and 1966, but they never married. They lived together from 1964 from time to time and from 1968 to 1980 on a permanent basis, though they parted now and again resulting in a temporary separation. For a time they lived at a property called 94 Stanhope Street, Derby where the plaintiff had a tenancy of some rooms.

In 1977 the defendant bought the property with which this case is concerned, 121 St Giles Road, Derby (I will call it 'St Giles Road'). It was conveyed into his name alone. The plaintiff gave up her tenancy at Stanhope Street at the same time. She has lived at St Giles Road ever since with the two children. The defendant lived there with them until the relationship broke up in September 1980. The house cost £4,500. The defendant borrowed £2,000 from a bank and probably about £1,500 or so from relatives, an uncle and a brother, and £1,000 was provided from savings, which were described by the judge as a pool. Over a substantial period the plaintiff was in employment. She paid for certain repairs and improvements to St Giles Road, and various outgoings. In the present proceedings she claimed a declaration that she was entitled to a half share in the property which, at the time of the hearing before the judge, was of the value of about £9,250. The value is increasing.

The mortgage has been paid off, as has the defendant's debt to his brother. At the time of the trial a comparatively small sum of £500 was still due to the uncle but is being paid off at £15 a week.

After a full review of the evidence the judge held that the plaintiff was entitled to a 25% share in St Giles Road. He ordered that the property be transferred into joint names on trust for sale 'in the ratio of 25% of the value of the equity of the property on 30th September 1980 to the Plaintiff and the balance of the equity to the Defendant'.

The plaintiff appeals from that part of the order which provides that her share of the equity be valued as at 30 September 1980, which was the date of the termination of the relationship between her and the defendant. There is no appeal by the defendant as to the finding of the plaintiff's entitlement to a 25% share.

The judge does not deal with the matter concerning the date of valuation in the notes of judgment, which are with the court papers, but it is common ground that he made a statement in the following terms or to the following effect:

> 'I declare the plaintiff to be beneficially entitled to a 25% share. I declare that that share is to be valued on 30th September 1980. That is the date when they separated. That is an area where, on authority, it is quite clear this point is different between a husband and wife case and a mistress case.'

The judge evidently thought he was bound to make the order which he did because this is a case between a man and his mistress. I think in considering the matter it is necessary to distinguish between the questions, first in what shares is the property held in equity, and second is there a need for any special direction as to the date of valuation about the shares?

As to the first question, what the court is concerned with in such a case as this is whether, by reason of an implied or resulting trust the applicant is entitled to a share in property vested in the other party. That is dependant on whether the parties have so conducted themselves that it would be inequitable to permit the party in whom the property is vested in law to deny that the other party has a beneficial interest. In deciding that matter, it seems to me that exactly the same principles would apply, whatever the relationship between the parties. As Lord Dilhorne observed in *Gissing v Gissing* [1970] 2 All ER 780 at 785, [1971] AC 886 at 899, there is not one law of property applicable where a dispute as to property is between spouses or former spouses and another law of property where the dispute is between others.

I refer also to the observations of Lord Denning MR in *Bernard v Josephs* [1982] 3 All ER 162 at 167, [1982] Ch 391 at 399, where he said:

> 'In my opinion in ascertaining respective shares, the court should normally apply the same consideration to couples living together (as if married) as they do to couples who are truly married.'

The court may, in drawing inferences as to the intentions of the parties, be influenced by the relationship. What might be sensible between husband and wife might not be so between two brothers, but in general the principles applicable must be the same, whatever the relationship.

I now come to the second question, the date at which the shares are to be valued. Prima facie, if persons are entitled to property in aliquot shares as tenants in common under a trust for sale, the value of their respective shares must be determined at the date when the property is sold, but that may have to give way to circumstances. For example, one of the parties may buy out the other, in which case the value of that party's share may have to be determined at a different date. Thus, in *Bernard v Josephs* [1982] 3 All ER 162 at 168, [1982] Ch 391 at 400 Lord Denning MR said:

> 'After ascertaining the shares, the next problem arises when it is to be turned into a money. Usually one of the parties stays in the house, paying the mortgage instalments and the rates and other outgoings. The house also increases in value greatly owing to inflation. None of that alters the shares of the parties in the house itself. But it does mean that when the house is sold, or the one buys the other out, there have to be many adjustments made.'

b *Bernard v Josephs* was a mistress case in which the judge held that the parties were entitled in equal shares. The relationship broke up in 1976 and the woman left the house. The man stayed in the house and subsequently in 1978 he married. He was still living in the house with his wife at the hearing of the appeal in March 1982. The judge made an order for sale. The Court of Appeal upheld the judge's decision as to the shares of the parties. The court decided that it would be a hardship on Mr Josephs and his new wife if they were compelled to leave the house to enable it to be sold, without an opportunity to c buy the plaintiff out. Accordingly the court ordered that the property be sold but the order was not to be enforced if Mr Joseph paid £6,000 to Miss Bernard, the plaintiff, within four months, in return for which she should transfer all her share in the property to him. It is clear that the £6,000 was calculated as being the value of Miss Bernard's share at the date of the hearing of the appeal: see the judgment of Griffiths LJ ([1982] 3 All ER 162 at 171–172, [1982] Ch 391 at 405–406).

d *Hall v Hall* (1982) 3 FLR 379 is another example of a case where the valuation of a share may be at a date other than sale. We understand that the short report in that case was read to the judge and I think it must have led him to his conclusion that in a mistress case the valuation should be at the date of the termination of the relationship. I do not think that *Hall v Hall* laid down such a principle. The parties lived together for about seven years. They had both previously been married. There were no children of the e relationship. They did not marry and never intended to. The woman (the plaintiff) left in 1978, a year after the house was bought, and the man lived with another woman, and another after that. After the plaintiff left she lived with another man and when that relationship ended she lived with yet another. The defendant continued to live in the house after the relationship ended. The judge held that the plaintiff was entitled to one-f fifth of the equity valued at the date when the relationship ended, to carry 10% interest until realisation.

This court upheld that decision. Lord Denning MR plainly did not proceed on the basis that there was a hard and fast rule that in a mistress case the valuation must be at the date of the determination of the relationship. He stated (at 382) that he regarded the matter as one for the discretion of the judge. Dunn LJ said (at 385):

> g 'So far as the date for the assessment or valuation of the share is concerned, as Lord Denning MR said in *Cooke v Head*, in the case of a mistress that fell to be assessed at the date of separation. I respectfully agree that, although there may be different considerations when dealing with a resulting trust as between husband and wife, in the case of a mistress the trust comes to an end at the termination of the relationship which gave rise to the trust in the first place.'

h Lord Denning MR in *Cooke v Head* [1972] 2 All ER 38 at 42, [1972] 1 WLR 518 at 521 said:

> 'In the light of recent developments, I do not think it is right to approach this case by looking at the money contributions of each and dividing up the beneficial interest according to those contributions. The matter should be looked at more j broadly, just as we do in husband and wife cases. We look to see what the equity is worth at the time when the parties separate. We assess the shares as at that time. If the property has been sold, we look at the amount which it has realised and say how it is to be divided between them. Lord Diplock in *Gissing v Gissing* [1970] 2 All ER 780 at 793 [1971] AC 886 at 909 intimated that it is quite legitimate to infer that, "the wife should be entitled to a share which was not to be quantified immediately

on the acquisition of the home but should be left to be determined when the mortgage was repaid or the property disposed of". Likewise with a mistress.' *a*

That passage suggests to me a flexible rather than a rigid approach to the matter. In my opinion *Hall v Hall* cannot, as a matter of authority, be regarded as establishing a rigid rule that the date of valuation of the shares in cases concerned with mistresses must be the date of separation. Lord Denning MR thought it was a matter of discretion and there is nothing to suggest that O'Connor LJ, who agreed with the reasons of both the other *b* members of the court, disagreed with it.

I agree, however, that in *Hall v Hall* the court took the view that the trust came to an end at the time of the separation and regarded that as a matter of importance: see per Lord Denning MR and Dunn LJ (3 FLR 379 at 382, 385). It was I think primarily on that basis that the court reached a decision as to the date of valuation.

This case, however, in my opinion is far removed from *Hall v Hall* on its facts. In this *c* case the relationship between the parties was of much longer duration. There were children and the woman (the plaintiff) is still living in the house with the children. Further, in his evidence the defendant stated that he expected the house 'to be a home for her and the children'. It is not his intention, so I understand, to seek an order for sale while the children are still living in the house. In my opinion, therefore, the purposes of the trust have not come to an end. They are still very much in existence. *d*

The expenditure of money by the plaintiff, which was the basis of her entitlement to a share in the property, was therefore for a purpose which has not yet come to an end. I see no reason, in the circumstances, why the valuation of the plaintiff's share should be at the date of separation. The plaintiff may make expenditure on the property to enable the children and herself to live there, which will have to be taken into account as between the plaintiff and the defendant at a later date. *e*

As a matter of law it seems to me that there is no rule which would have compelled the judge to decide that the valuation must be at the date of separation. If he regarded himself as exercising a discretion (and I doubt if he did), I see no reason to suppose that he took into account the very important circumstances that the purpose of the trust had not been determined. In my opinion there was no good reason in the present case for directing the valuation to be at the date of separation. *f*

Accordingly I would allow the appeal and vary the order of the judge by deleting the references to valuation on 30 September 1980 contained in the order. The precise form of the order we can discuss with counsel.

BUSH J. I agree with everything Fox LJ has said and have nothing to add.

Appeal allowed. Costs in the Court of Appeal and below, payment of such costs suspended until sale of property or further order of the county court.

Solicitors: *Barrs,* Derby (for the plaintiff); *Partridge Haldenby & Cawdron,* Derby (for the defendant).

Bebe Chua Barrister.

a

R v Secretary of State for Trade and others, ex parte Anderson Strathclyde plc

QUEEN'S BENCH DIVISION
DUNN LJ AND McCULLOUGH J
1, 2, 3 FEBRUARY 1983

b

Monopolies and mergers – Report of Monopolies and Mergers Commission – Order of Secretary of State on merger reference – Discretion of Secretary of State – Reference of takeover bid to Monopolies and Mergers Commission – Majority report by commission that takeover against public interest – Commission's recommendation overruled by Secretary of State – Whether Secretary of State entitled to permit takover – Fair Trading Act 1973, s 73(2)(3).

c

Judicial review – Evidence in support of claim for relief – Record of proceedings in Parliament – Admissibility – Applicant claiming relief in respect of something done outside Parliament – Applicant relying on statements made in Parliament and recorded in Hansard to support his claim – Whether Hansard can be used to support claim for judicial review.

d The Secretary of State for Trade, acting under Part V of the Fair Trading Act 1973, referred a takeover bid for the applicant company to the Monopolies and Mergers Commission. The commission investigated the takeover and recommended, by a majority of four to two, that the takeover would not be in the public interest and should not be permitted to proceed. The Secretary of State had a small shareholding in the bidding company and accordingly considered that the actual decision on the commission's
e report and the takover should be made by his deputy, the Minister of State. Both ministers made statements in Parliament regarding the matter. The Minister of State later announced that he had decided that the takeover should be allowed to proceed. The applicant company sought (i) an order of certiorari to quash the Minister of State's decision, on the grounds that, since under s 73(2)[a] of the 1973 Act the minister 'may by order' exercise certain powers 'for the purpose of remedying or preventing the adverse
f effects specified in the report' of the commission and that since under s 73(3) the minister was required to 'take into account any recommendations' included in the commission's report, the minister was bound to accept and give effect to the majority view expressed in the report, and in any event even if the minister had a discretion to overrule the majority conclusion he had taken into account irrelevant considerations in exercising that discretion, and (ii) an order of mandamus requiring the Secretary of State to consider
g the commission's report in accordance with his statutory obligation to give effect to it. At the hearing of the application the question arose whether the applicant company could rely on the ministers' statements in Parliament and reported in Hansard to support its claim that the Secretary of State had wrongly divested himself of his decision-making powers under the 1973 Act by delegating them to the Minister of State.

h **Held** – On the true construction of s 73 of the 1973 Act the minister had an unfettered discretion in deciding whether to approve a takeover bid. In particular, the minister was not bound by the majority view of the Monopolies and Mergers Commission and was entitled to evaluate the majority's view for himself and to take into account the minority's view and also advice and representations from others before reaching his decision. Furthermore, applying accepted principles, it had not been established that the minister
j had taken into account irrelevant considerations in reaching his decision. The application for certiorari and mandamus would therefore be refused (see p 241 *h* to p 242 *b*, p 243 *f* to *j* and p 244 *c* to *e*, post).

Associated Provincial Picture Houses Ltd v Wednesbury Corp [1947] 2 All ER 680 applied.

---

a Section 73 is set out at p 240 *f* to *j*, post

Per curiam. A report in Hansard of what has been said and done in Parliament cannot be used to support a ground for relief in proceedings for judicial review in respect of a
something which occurred outside Parliament (see p 239 *b* to *d* and p 243 *h j*, post); *Church of Scientology of California v Johnson-Smith* [1972] 1 All ER 378 applied.

Notes

For merger references, see Supplement to 38 Halsbury's Laws (3rd edn) para 102D(2).

For privilege in respect of proceedings in Parliament and of reports thereof, see 28 b
Halsbury's Laws (4th edn) para 119, and for cases on the subject, see 32 Digest (Reissue) 275–276, *2252–2259*.

For the Fair Trading Act 1973, s 73, see 43 Halsbury's Statutes (3rd edn) 1683.

Cases referred to in judgments

Associated Provincial Picture Houses Ltd v Wednesbury Corp [1947] 2 All ER 680, [1948] 1 c
KB 223, CA.

Carltona Ltd v Comrs of Works [1943] 2 All ER 560, CA.

Church of Scientology of California v Johnson-Smith [1972] 1 All ER 378, [1972] 1 QB 522, [1971] 3 WLR 434.

Farrell v Alexander [1976] 2 All ER 721, [1977] AC 59, [1976] 3 WLR 145, HL.

IRC v Joiner [1975] 3 All ER 1050, [1975] 1 WLR 1701, HL. d

Maunsell v Olins [1975] 1 All ER 16, [1975] AC 373, [1974] 3 WLR 835, HL.

Wason, Ex p (1869) LR 4 QB 573.

Application for judicial review

Anderson Strathclyde plc (Anderson) applied, with the leave of Glidewell J granted on 12 January 1983, for (i) an order of certiorari to bring up and quash the decision of the e
second respondent, the Minister of State for Trade, made on 21 December 1982, not to prohibit the acquisition by the third respondents, Charter Consolidated plc (Charter), of the whole of the undertakings or assets of Anderson, (ii) an order of mandamus requiring the first respondent, the Secretary of State for Trade, to consider according to law the report of the Monopolies and Mergers Commission (Cmnd 8771) laid before Parliament on 21 December 1982 and to exercise his discretion under s 73(3) of the Fair Trading Act f
1972 according to law, (iii) a declaration that the discretion conferred on the Secretary of State under s 73(3) of the Act had been exercised by the Minister of State in a manner which was not in accord with the intention of the Act, (iv) a declaration that in exercising his discretion under s 73 the Minister of State was not entitled (a) to disregard the conclusions of two-thirds of the members of the Monopolies and Mergers Commission as to the effects adverse to the public interest that a merger situation might be expected g
to have and/or (b) to have regard to any conclusions as to such effects of fewer than two-thirds of the members of the Commission and/or (c) to substitute for the conclusions of two-thirds of the members of the Commission as to such effects conclusions of the minister, (v) a declaration that, on the basis of the conclusions of the Monopolies and Mergers Commission as to its particular effects adverse to the public interest which the creation of the merger situation might be expected to have the discretion of the minister h
was to be exercised for the purpose of remedying or preventing such adverse effects, (vi) a declaration that for the purpose of remedying or preventing the adverse effects specified in the commission's report the Minister of State erred in law in seeking only an assurance from Charter that Anderson would remain a Scottish company with its registered office in Scotland, (vii) a declaration that the exercise of the minister's discretion according to law required the exercise of such one or more powers under Sch 8 to the Act as would j
prohibit the acquisition by Charter of Anderson, (viii) such further or other relief as the court might consider appropriate. The facts are set out in the judgment of Dunn LJ.

J A Swift QC, *Raymond Jack QC* and *Richard Fowler* for Anderson.

Simon D Brown for the Secretary of State and the Minister of State.

Richard Southwell QC and *Peter Roth* for Charter.

DUNN LJ. This is an application by leave on behalf Anderson Strathclyde plc
a (Anderson) for judicial review of the decision of the Minister of State for Trade made on 21 December 1982 not to exercise one or more of the powers specified in Parts I and II of Sch 8 to the Fair Trading Act 1973 so as to prohibit the acquisition by Charter Consolidated plc (Charter) of the whole of the undertaking or assets of Anderson the Monopolies and Mergers Commission having concluded, pursuant to s 72 of the Fair Trading Act 1973 that such an acquisition may be expected to operate against the public
b interest.

The relief sought is first an order for certiorari to bring up and quash the decision of the Minister of State for Trade made on 21 December 1982, second an order of mandamus to require the Secretary of State for Trade to consider, according to law, the report of the commission, and five declarations.

Although the notice before the court contains numerous grounds for the relief, only
c two grounds were persisted in in this court: (1) that the minister misdirected himself in law as to the proper separation of functions as between the commission and the Secretary of State, in that he failed to appreciate that he was bound to accept the conclusion of the majority of the commission that the proposed merger may be expected to operate against the public interest; (2) in the alternative if, contrary to (1), the minister had a discretion to consider the majority conclusion of the commission and to overrule it, he took into
d account irrelevant considerations, namely that it was common ground that the proposed merger would not prejudice competition, and that it was no more than speculative to conclude that the merger might harm the public interest.

Before considering the two grounds on which relief is sought, I must deal with the background. In February and May 1980, by two separate purchases, Charter brought a total of 10,775,000 shares in Anderson, giving Charter a total holding of 28·4% of the
e equity.

On 30 April 1982 Charter informed Anderson of its intention to make a bid for Anderson's remaining shares in the afternoon of that day. On 4 May 1982 Anderson informed Charter that its board had unanimously decided to reject Charter's proposal that discussions should take place leading to an agreed bid. Charter's Stock Exchange announcements were made immediately after and the offer documents were posted on
f 13 May 1982. On 2 June 1982 the Secretary of State for Trade, in exercise of his powers under s 75 of the Fair Trading Act 1973, referred the matter to the commission for investigation and report within six months. Thereupon the offer lapsed, though Charter are still interested in acquiring Anderson.

After the reference the commission took evidence from numerous witnesses and reported on 22 November 1982. The commission sat in a group of six. A majority of
g four was against the merger. At para 9.20 of the report (Cmnd 8771) they set out a summary of the adverse effects:

> 'We conclude that the proposed merger may be expected to have an adverse effect upon the management, effectiveness and labour relations of Anderson Strathclyde, and that this would tend to diminish effective competition in the supply of goods,
> h would be contrary to the interests of purchasers of goods in the United Kingdom and would not promote competitive activity by Anderson Strathclyde in markets outside the United Kingdom. We also conclude that both because it would affect employment within Anderson Strathclyde and because it would detract from the dynamism of business in the region, it may be expected to have an adverse effect upon employment in a relatively depressed part of the United Kingdom. These
> j effects may be expected to operate against the public interest unless offset by some advantages.'

Their recommendation appears at para 9.24:

> 'The adverse effects which we set out in paragraph 9.20 are not offset by any advantages which the proposed merger would confer. Therefore, on balance we consider that the merger may be expected to operate against the public interest. The

adverse effects arise directly from the proposed merger, and we cannot devise any action which could be taken for the purpose of remedying or preventing them if the merger took place. We therefore recommend that the merger should not be permitted.'

A minority of two, including the chairman, on the same day signed a statement of dissent. They found no reason why the merger should not go forward. The statement of dissent forms part of the report. In para 9.42 the minority said:

'In our judgment, the evidence does not justify such a conclusion [that is to say the conclusion of the majority] on any point in this inquiry. The Fair Trading Act confers upon the Secretary of State far-reaching powers exercisable in case of a report of the Commission that a proposed merger may be expected to operate against the public interest. The Commission is required to base such a report on "particular effects, adverse to the public interest, which in the opinion of the Commission [the proposed merger] may be expected to have": s 73(1)(*b*). If the intention of Parliament is judged, as it must be, from the language of the Fair Trading Act, we do not consider that the general possibilities and risks upon which the recommendation in this case is based amount to such material as Parliament intended should lead to ministerial intervention.'

On 21 December 1982 a letter was sent from the Scottish Economic Planning Department, Industrial Development Division, which is part of the Scottish Office, to the chief executive and deputy chairman of Anderson. The letter reads:

'You will wish to know what decision the Government has come to on the recommendation of the Monopolies and Mergers Commission. The following is the relevant extract from the public announcement made at 10.30 a.m. today: "Ministers have considered this Report with great care. The decision has been taken that, in all the circumstances of this case, it would not be right to stop the merger. But in leaving Charter to renew their bid, an assurance is being sought from them that Anderson Strathclyde will remain a Scottish Company with its registered office in Scotland." A full copy of the Press notice will be available later today and we shall forward a copy to you as soon as possible thereafter.'

The press notice, which was dated the same day, is in the following terms:

'*The proposed merger between Charter Consolidated plc and Anderson Strathclyde plc. Monopolies and Mergers Commission report published.*

The proposed merger between Charter Consolidated plc and Anderson Strathclyde plc should be allowed to go ahead. Mr Peter Rees, Minister for Trade, announced this today on the publication of the Monopolies and Mergers Commission report on the proposed merger. An assurance is however to be sought that Anderson Strathclyde will remain a Scottish company, with its registered office in Scotland. Mr Rees said: "The Monopolies and Mergers Commission concluded by a majority of four to two that the proposed merger might be expected to operate against the public interest and recommended that it should not be allowed. Careful consideration has been given to the majority report, together with the powerful dissenting report of the minority, which included the Chairman of the MMC. The Director General has also given advice, which the Fair Trading Act requires to be taken into account: he has strongly recommended against preventing the merger. It is common ground that the merger would not prejudice competition. The sole question is whether the merger would harm other aspects of the public interest. In this connection the arguments based on possible industrial implications in Scotland require a particularly sensitive approach. But, taking all these matters into account, it is no more than speculative to conclude that the merger might harm the public interest. It is for these reasons that the decision has been reached that, in all the circumstances of this case, it would not be right to stop the merger. But in case Charter renew their bid an assurance is being sought from them that Anderson Strathclyde will remain a Scottish company with its registered office in Scotland."'

On 12 January Anderson made an ex parte application for leave to apply for judicial review, which was granted by Glidewell J.

A fundamental point was taken in the course of the proceedings in this court by Mr Jack QC, one of the counsel for Anderson. He submitted that the Secretary of State had wrongly divested himself of his function under s 73 of the Fair Trading Act 1973 and had purported to transfer that function to the Minister of State for the Department of Trade. It was said that in those circumstances the case could be distinguished from the line of authority starting with *Carltona Ltd v Comrs of Works* [1943] 2 All ER 560, in that in this case the Minister of Trade was not purporting to stand in the shoes of the Secretary of State, who would retain responsibility for the decision, but was purporting himself to exercise powers that could only be exercised by the Secretary of State and to take full responsibility for the decision. Mr Jack said that consequently the decision was not the decision of the Secretary of State and was null and void and of no effect.

Mr Jack said that if he was wrong and the Secretary of State had retained responsibility for the decision, at the time that it was made he himself possessed a shareholding in Charter and it might be possible to submit that this was enough to vitiate the decision, although Mr Jack did not in fact make any such submission. If it had been made it would have been unsound. Before the decision could be vitiated it would be necessary to show that the Secretary of State had allowed his shareholding to influence his decision. Every action which the Secretary of State took in this case demonstrates to the contrary.

Mr Jack conceded that the evidence in support of the necessary factual basis of his fundamental submission, namely that the Secretary of State had divested himself of his decision-making function and referred it to the minister, was contained in the true meaning of certain statements made and answers given by ministers in both Houses of Parliament and reported in Hansard.

Neither the Secretary of State nor the minister filed an affidavit in this court, but counsel for both of them made an admission of the following facts for the purpose of these proceedings. Counsel admitted that because of the Secretary of State's small shareholding in Charter, which, together with other share certificates, he had deposited with his bank with instructions not to deal in any of them so long as he holds ministerial office, the Secretary of State felt that he had disqualified himself from personally taking the decision in this case, concluding that it was more appropriate and in accordance with the recognised proprieties for the decision to be taken by the minister. In making that admission counsel made it plain that he did not accept either that the Secretary of State had divested himself of his statutory function by transference to the minister or otherwise, or that the Secretary of State had declined Parliamentary responsibility for the decision.

The question then arose whether this court could refer to Hansard so that Mr Jack could make good the factual basis of his submission. Counsel for the Secretary of State and the minister left that decision to the court, while pointing out the difficulty caused by the decision in *Church of Scientology of California v Johnson-Smith* [1972] 1 All ER 378, [1972] 1 QB 522. Counsel said that he was quite prepared to take the court through the relevant entries in Hansard which, he said, on a fair reading of all of them demonstrated that, taken as a whole, they formed no factual basis for Mr Jack's submission.

The *Church of Scientology* case was a libel action. The defendant was a member of Parliament. The libel was alleged to have been published in the course of a television broadcast. The defendant pleaded fair comment on a matter of public interest and privilege. The plaintiffs, in reply, sought to rely on certain statements by the defendant in Parliament as showing malice. In order to prove those statements the plaintiffs applied to the judge to introduce the relevant extracts from Hansard as evidence at the trial.

Browne J excluded the evidence. In his judgment he reviewed the authorities and said that in his view the two relevant sub-paragraphs of the reply—

> 'must involve a suggestion that the defendant was, in one way or another, acting improperly or with an improper motive when he did and said in Parliament the things referred to in those sub-paragraphs. I accept the Attorney-General's argument that the scope of Parliamentary privilege extends beyond excluding any cause of action in respect of what is said or done in the House itself. And I accept his proposition which I have already tried to quote, that is, that what is said or done in the House in the course of proceedings there cannot be examined outside Parliament for the purpose of supporting a cause of action even though the cause of action itself arises out of something done outside the House. In my view, this conclusion is supported by both principle and authority.'

(See [1972] 1 All ER 378 at 381, [1972] 1 QB 522 at 529–530.)

The judge then went on to cite *Ex p Wason* (1869) LR 4 QB 573, which shows that the same principle applies to criminal proceedings as to civil proceedings. The judge added ([1972] 1 All ER 378 at 382, [1972] 1 QB 522 at 531):

> 'But the Attorney-General limited what he said about the probable attitude of Parliament to the use of Hansard by agreement by saying that Hansard could be used only for a limited purpose. He said it could be read simply as evidence of fact, what was in fact said in the House, on a particular day by a particular person. But, he said, the use of Hansard must stop there and that counsel was not entitled to comment on what had been said in Hansard or to ask the jury to draw any inferences from it.'

Citations from Hansard in the courts have always been a delicate area, because of the constitutional importance of Parliament retaining control over its own proceedings and because of the extent of Parliamentary privilege. It was formerly necessary for a petition to be presented to the House for reference to be made to reports of proceedings of the House of Commons in Hansard. No such petition was necessary before reports of proceedings in the House of Lords were referred to in court. But on 31 October 1980 the House of Commons passed the following resolution:

> 'That this House while reaffirming the status of proceedings in Parliament, confirmed by Article 9 of the Bill of Rights, gives leave for reference to be made in future Court proceedings to the Official Report of Debates and to the published Reports and evidence of Committees in any case in which, under the practice of the House, it is required that a petition for leave should be presented and that the practice of presenting petitions for leave to refer to Parliamentary papers be discontinued.'

So it is not now necessary for a petition for leave to be presented before extracts from Hansard are referred to in court. But the question remains: for what purpose may Hansard be used in court?

Article 9 of the Bill of Rights (1688) provides:

> 'That the freedome of speech and debates or proceedings in Parlyament ought not to be impeached or questioned in any court or place out of Parlyament.'

That article has been widely construed, as Browne J showed in *Church of Scientology of California v Johnson-Smith* [1972] 1 All ER 378 at 381, [1972] 1 QB 522 at 530. He said:

> 'It will be observed, and, indeed, the Attorney-General said, that the basis on which Blackstone puts it is that anything arising concerning the House ought to be examined, discussed, and adjudged in that House and not elsewhere (1 Bl Com (17th edn, 1830) 163). The House must have complete control over its own proceedings and its own members. I also accept the other basis for this privilege which the Attorney-General suggested, which is, that a member must have a complete right of free speech in the House without any fear that his motives or intentions or reasoning will be questioned or held against him thereafter. So far as the authorities are

concerned it will be seen that the words used are very wide. In the Bill of Rights a (1688) itself the word is "questioned": "freedome of speech and debates or proceedings in Parlyament ought not to be impeached or questioned in any court or place out of Parlyament." Blackstone uses the words "examined discussed or adjudged": they ought not to be examined discussed or adjudged elsewhere than in the House.'

b In my judgment there is no distinction between using a report in Hansard for the purpose of supporting a cause of action arising out of something which occurred outside the House, and using a report for the purpose of supporting a ground for relief in proceedings for judicial review in respect of something which occurred outside the House. In both cases the court would have to do more than take note of the fact that a certain statement was made in the House on a certain date. It would have to consider the c statement or statements with a view to determining what was the true meaning of them, and what were the proper inferences to be drawn from them. This, in my judgment, would be contrary to art 9 of the Bill of Rights. It would be doing what Blackstone said was not to be done, namely to examine, discuss and adjudge on a matter which was being considered in Parliament. Moreover, it would be an invasion by the court of the right of every member of Parliament to free speech in the House with the possible adverse effects d referred to by Browne J.

On those grounds we refused Mr Jack's application to refer to the extracts from Hansard, although we had already read them de bene esse since they were exhibited to an affidavit and proved themselves.

Mr Jack then applied for an adjournment to enable him to adduce further evidence, and to consider an application under RSC Ord 73, r 8 for leave to administer interrogatories e to the Secretary of State. We also refused this application. It was made at an extremely late stage, at the close of the applicants' case, and the applicants must or should have known, from the very outset, the difficulties of proof with which they were faced, having regard to the decision in the *Church of Scientology* case.

The Fair Trading Act 1973 contains provisions which emphasise the importance of expedition on a reference by the Secretary of State to the commission in respect of a f merger. The reason is almost too obvious to mention. Take this case. It is in the interests of the shareholders of both Anderson and Charter that a decision should be made, one way or the other, in the shortest possible time. The Take-Over Panel of the City of London are concerned that the legal position should be defined without delay. Proceedings for judicial review are not designed for detailed inquiry into contested facts. It is for the applicants to take all proper steps to put the facts on which they rely in g support of the relief claimed before the court at the first opportunity. There is no reason to suppose that in view of their failure, after nearly six weeks from the announcement of the decision, to adduce further evidence on this issue they should be able to do so after a further adjournment, which would inevitably have to be a short one, and there is no reason to suppose that there is any ground for allowing an application to interrogate the Secretary of State.

h After we announced our decision refusing the adjournment, Mr Jack conceded that he could not support his submissions as there was no factual basis on which he could do so.

I now turn to consider the submissions of leading counsel for Anderson. This involves a consideration of the detailed provisions of the Fair Trading Act 1973. Part V of the Act deals with mergers. The Secretary of State may refer a merger to the commission where it appears to him that it is or may be the fact that arrangements are in contemplation j which, if carried into effect, will result in a merger situation qualifying for investigation: see s 75. A merger situation qualifying for investigation is defined in s 64(1) as being either (and I use a shorthand expression) a 'monopoly situation', or when the value of the assets taken over exceeds £15m, which has been increased by statutory instrument from the £5m mentioned in the Act. There is no monopoly situation here. The only ground for the reference is that the assets of Anderson to be taken over exceed £15m.

On a merger reference the commission is required to investigate and report on two questions: (a) whether a merger situation qualifying for investigation has been created, *a* and (b) if so, whether the creation of that situation may be expected to operate against the public interest: see s 69.

The reference is required to specify a date, not exceeding six months, within which the report is to be made. No action is to be taken in relation to the report unless it is made before the end of the specified period or as extended by the Secretary of State up to a further three months: see s 70. Section 72 of the Act, so far as is material, is in the *b* following terms:

> '(1) In making their report on a merger reference, the Commission shall include in it definite conclusions on the questions comprised in the reference, together with—(*a*) such an account of their reasons for those conclusions, and (*b*) such a survey of the general position with respect to the subject-matter of the reference, and of the developments which have led to that position, as in their opinion are *c* expedient for facilitating a proper understanding of those questions and of their conclusions.
>
> (2) Where on a merger reference the Commission finds that a merger situation qualifying for investigation has been created and that the creation of that situation operates or may be expected to operate against the public interest . . . the Commission shall specify in their report the particular effect, adverse to the public interest, which *d* in their opinion the creation of that situation . . . have or may be expected to have; and the Commission—(*a*) shall, as part of their investigations, consider what action (if any) should be taken for the purpose of remedying or preventing those adverse effects, and (*b*) may, if they think fit, include in their report recommendations as to such action.'

e

I need not read sub-s (3).

Section 73 is in the following terms:

> '(1) The provisions of this section shall have effect where a report of the Commission on a merger reference has been laid before Parliament in accordance with the provisions of Part VII of this Act, and the conclusions of the Commission set out in the report, as so laid,—(*a*) include conclusions to the effect that a merger *f* situation qualifying for investigation has been created and that its creation, or particular elements in or consequences of it specified in the report, operate or may be expected to operate against the public interest, and (*b*) specify particular effects, adverse to the public interest, which in the opinion of the Commission the creation of that situation, or (as the case may be) those elements in or consequences of it, have or may be expected to have. *g*
>
> (2) In the circumstances mentioned in the preceding subsection the Secretary of State may by order made by statutory instrument exercise such one or more of the powers specified in Parts I and II of Schedule 8 to this Act as he may consider it requisite to exercise for the purpose of remedying or preventing the adverse effects specified in the report as mentioned in the preceding subsection; and those powers may be so exercised to such extent and in such manner as the Secretary of State *h* considers requisite for that purpose.
>
> (3) In determining whether, or to what extent or in what manner, to exercise any of those powers, the Secretary of State shall take into account any recommendations included in the report of the Commission in pursuance of section 72(2)(*b*) of this Act and any advice given by the Director under section 88 of this Act.' *j*

Section 82(3) provides:

> ' . . . if . . . (*b*) on a reference to the Commission . . . a member of the . . . Commission . . . dissents from any conclusions contained in the report on the reference as being conclusions of the . . . Commission, the report shall, if that member so desires, include a statement of his dissent and his reasons for dissenting.'

Section 84 provides:

> a '(1) In determining for any purposes to which this section applies whether any particular matter operates, or may be expected to operate, against the public interest, the Commission shall take into account all matters which appear to them in the particular circumstances to be relevant and, among other things, shall have regard to [and there are then set out five matters].
>
> b (2) This section applies to the purposes of any functions of the Commission under this Act . . .'

So that relates back to the previous sections to which I have referred which set out the functions of the commission, in particular s 72. Section 86(1) provides:

> '. . . a copy of every report of the Commission . . . on a merger reference . . . shall c be transmitted by the Commission to the Director [ie the Director General of Fair Trading]; and the Minister or Ministers to whom any such report is made shall take account of any advice given to him or them by the Director with respect to a report of which a copy is transmitted to the Director under this section.'

Section 88 deals with action by the Director General in consequence of a report of the d commission on a merger reference. I need do no more than refer to it. Section 91(2) provides:

> 'Before making any order under . . . section 73 of this Act . . . the Minister proposing to make the order shall publish, in such manner as appears to him to be appropriate, a notice [It then sets out what the notice has to contain, which includes e a statement:] that any person whose interests are likely to be affected by the order, and who is desirous of making representations in respect of it, should do so in writing . . . before a date specified in the notice . . . and the Minister shall not make the order before the date specified in the notice . . . and shall consider any representations duly made to him in accordance with the notice before that date.'

f Schedule 8 lists the powers exercisable by orders under s 73. Part 1 of the schedule contains the relevant powers. Those are orders which the Secretary of State is empowered to make.

The submission of leading counsel for Anderson was that on the true construction of the Act, if the commission or the majority of the commission conclude, as they did in this case, that a merger situation may be expected to operate against the public interest, g and if they specify in their report, as they did, the particular effects adverse to the public interest which in their opinion the creation of the merger situation may be expected to have, then the Secretary of State is bound by that conclusion and his discretion is limited to a choice of which order may be made under Sch 8.

I cannot accept that submission. The words 'the Secretary of State may by order' in s 73(2), and the words 'in determining whether, or to what extent or in what manner' in h s 73(3) indicate that the Secretary of State has a complete discretion whether to make any order or whether to make no order at all. Counsel's construction would have required quite different words in sub-ss (2) and (3) to the words that we find.

His construction would also give power to the majority of the commission to decide whether a merger situation was adverse to the public interest, and is inconsistent with the provision in s 82(3) that a statement of dissent should be included in the report, j indicating that the Secretary of State is entitled to take into account the whole report including the statement of dissent. It is also inconsistent with the duty placed on the Secretary of State, under s 86(1), to take account of the advice of the Director General and with his duty, under s 91(2), to consider representations made after notice and before making his order. As counsel for the Secretary of State and the minister said, if leading counsel for Anderson is right the Secretary of State would be unable to take action if there were a change of circumstances after publication of the report.

In my judgment, the Act read as a whole shows that the Secretary of State is not bound by the conclusions of the majority of the commission, that he has a wide discretion in *a* deciding whether to make any order at all, and in exercising that discretion he is entitled to take into account all the relevant circumstances, and to consider the opinion of the minority of the commission, and also representations and advice from persons other than members of the commission.

There is another point. Leading counsel for Anderson urged on us a purposive construction of this statute. The Act itself places a limitation on freedom of contract. On *b* counsel's construction the right to limit freedom of contract would be vested in a majority of the commission, who are not directly responsible to Parliament, rather than in the Secretary of State who is directly responsible to Parliament. I cannot believe that that was the intention of Parliament.

Counsel sought to support his construction by reference to the Monopolies and Mergers Act 1965, which was the forerunner of the 1973 Act. He drew attention to the *c* differences in wording of certain of the sections of that Act as compared with the provisions of the 1973 Act. He submitted that the 1973 Act showed a development in competition law so as to give more power to the commission. I do not find any assistance to be derived from looking at a different Act in order to construe the Act with which we are concerned. Indeed, I am doubtful if we should do so.

In *Farrell v Alexander* [1976] 2 All ER 721 at 725–726, [1977] AC 59 at 72 Lord *d* Wilberforce said:

> 'Lord Diplock and Lord Simon of Glaisdale [in *Maunsell v Olins* [1975] 1 All ER 16, [1975] AC 373] thought the word was clear and for that reason considered that it was not legitimate to go back into the legislative history. If I may say so, on that hypothesis I would agree with them. I would agree and endorse the principle that it *e* is quite wrong that, in every case where a consolidation Act is under consideration, one should automatically look back through the history of its various provisions, and the cases decided on them, and minutely trace the language from Act to Act—a process, which, incidentally, has led to an argument of four days' length in this House. In recent times, because modern statutes have become so complicated, the courts, myself included, (cf *Inland Revenue Comrs v Joiner* [1975] 3 All ER 1050, *f* [1975] 1 WLR 1701) rather too easily accept this process, whether under persuasion of counsel or from their own scholarly inclinations. But, unless the process of consolidation, which involves much labour and careful work, is to become nothing but a work of mechanical convenience, I think that this tendency should be firmly resisted; that self-contained statutes, whether consolidating previous law, or so doing with amendments, should be interpreted, if reasonably possible, without recourse *g* to antecedents, and that the recourse should only be had when there is a real and substantial difficulty or ambiguity which classical methods of construction cannot resolve.'

I find no difficulty, using what I believe to be 'classical methods of construction', in resolving the question which arises in this case from the words of the statute itself. *h*

Assuming, however, that he was wrong on his first point of construction, leading counsel for Anderson nevertheless sought to challenge the exercise of the minister's discretion on *Wednesbury* principles, by saying that the minister had taken into account two matters which he should not have taken into account: see *Associated Provincial Picture Houses Ltd v Wednesbury Corp* [1947] 2 All ER 680 at 682–683, [1948] 1 KB 223 at 228–229. *j*

The first was the sentence in the press notice where it is stated: 'It is common ground that the merger would not prejudice competition.' What the majority in their report said was that there would be no direct prejudice to competition, but because of the adverse effects which the merger might be expected to have, both on the management and labour of Anderson, there was likely to be an indirect effect on competition.

Counsel submitted that the press notice showed that the minister had misunderstood *a* that and had proceeded on a wrong basis, namely that the merger would not prejudice competition. In fact, on the second page of the press notice the minister summarised the conclusions of the majority. He referred to certain paragraphs of the report by number, and he said:

> 'The majority concluded that the proposed merger might be expected to be against the public interest, to the extent that the management of the two companies *b* might not mix well, which might lead to a loss of management effectiveness in Anderson, with an accompanying loss of morale. Labour relations could also be affected to the extent that conditions were created in which the present degree of co-operation of the labour force was not forthcoming. From that the majority also took the view that if the proposed merger had these effects, there might be consequential effects on employment in Scotland, both in Anderson's own works *c* and possibly among suppliers. Even if these effects were not to materialise, there remains the possibility of adverse effects on the region.'

He was, it seems to me, saying that the business of Anderson would be adversely affected by the merger which would inevitably make it less competitive.

In my view there is no ground for saying that the minister did not understand the *d* basis on which the majority reported.

The second ground on which it is said that he took into account a matter which he should not have taken into account was to be inferred from the statement, 'it is no more than speculative to conclude that the merger might harm the public interest'.

Leading counsel for Anderson referred us to passages in their report in which the majority specifically refer to the evidence in support of their conclusions, and he said in *e* those circumstances the minister was wrong to say that their conclusion was 'no more than speculative'. But on the basis which I have held to be the true basis, that the Secretary of State was entitled to have regard to the note of dissent, it is necessary to look at that. The two dissenting members of the commission said, in effect, that the evidence was insufficient to support the conclusion to which the majority had come.

In my view, it was a matter for the minister, in his unfettered discretion, to choose *f* between those two views, taking into account any other relevant matters including the advice which he received from the Director General. He preferred the view of the minority. Whether he was right or wrong about that is a matter of political judgment, and not a matter of law.

No reason has been shown which would entitle this court, on well-established principles, to interfere with his decision on a matter of that kind. We have not gone into, *g* and it is no part of the function of this court to go into, the merits of whether or not this proposed merger should be allowed. Our sole function is to consider whether the minister, in refusing to stop the merger, acted lawfully. That involves answering two questions and two questions only. (1) Did the minister have the power under the Fair Trading Act 1973 to take the course he did? He did have that power. (2) In exercising the power, did he take into consideration any matter which he should not have taken *h* into consideration? He did not. Accordingly, this application, in my view, must fail and be dismissed.

McCULLOUGH J. I agree with each of Dunn LJ's conclusions and with his reasoning. I shall, however, put into a few words of my own the view which I have formed about the construction of s 73 of the Fair Trading Act 1973, which is the one point on which *j* my mind hesitated during the course of the argument.

Section 72(1) requires the Monopolies and Mergers Commission to reach 'definite conclusions'. Although the word 'opinion' is to be found in s 72(2) in relation to particular effects perceived to be adverse to the public interest, the same subsection contemplates that the commission will 'find' that a merger situation may be expected to operate against the public interest.

Further, s 84(1) treats the function of the commission in this respect as one of 'determining' whether a particular matter may be expected to operate against the public interest. 'Definite conclusions', 'find', 'determining', these are all strong words.

I have in addition been exercised by the fact that s 73(3) provides that the advice given by the Director General, to which the Secretary of State has to have regard, is not the general advice which he may give in the circumstances contemplated by s 86 after a copy of the commission's report has been transmitted to him, but the more limited advice which he must give under s 88, which deals primarily with the question of whether the adverse effects contemplated by the commission may satisfactorily be overcome by the obtaining of undertakings.

These features lend, I think, a measure of support to the argument of leading counsel for Anderson.

Be that as it may, the options given to the Secretary of State by s 73(2), and recognised by s 73(3), are expressed in the most unfettered terms. He may exercise one or more of his powers under Sch 8. He may obtain a suitable undertaking or undertakings. Or he may do nothing, that is nothing to prevent the adverse effects foreseen by the commission. This in turn implies that he may evaluate for himself the conclusions and opinions reached by the commission. Indeed, not only may he do so, he must.

I am fortified in this view by s 82(3), which contemplates that the Secretary of State shall be provided with a statement of dissent from any member of the commission who dissents from any 'conclusion' contained in the report, the word is not 'recommendation' but 'conclusion', and he may be provided with a statement of the reasons for his dissent. What purpose can lie behind this other than that the Secretary of State should evaluate both the conclusions and the reasoning of the minority? This must imply that the conclusions and reasoning of the majority must, likewise, be evaluated.

Had the intention of Parliament been as leading counsel for Anderson contends, I cannot accept that s 73(2) and (3) would have been worded as they have been. I would have expected to see a provision along the following lines (and I am not drafting): 'In the circumstances mentioned the Secretary of State shall exercise such one or more of his powers under Sch 8 as he may consider it requisite to exercise for the purpose of remedying or preventing the adverse effects specified in the report, unless he is of the opinion that the said purpose will be achieved by such one or more undertakings as he has obtained.'

Despite the other provisions to which I have referred, I regard s 73(2) as unambiguous. If, contrary to my opinion, there is an ambiguity, in my judgment, it should be resolved in the way least calculated to lead to ministerial interference with the rights of private citizens, individual or corporate, to contract as they please.

If it were permissible to draw any conclusion from a comparison of the wording of s 73 of the 1973 Act with that of s 3 of the Monopolies and Mergers Act 1965, the conclusion which I would draw would be that whereas by the earlier Act the Board of Trade was permitted to interfere to remedy or prevent mischiefs which it itself foresaw, the later Act cut down that power to interfere, confining it to the remedying and prevention of adverse effects which had been foreseen by the commission after investigation.

Finally, I would underline, as has Dunn LJ, the importance of remembering that this court has not been called on to decide whether or not the proposed merger would have adverse effects on the public interest. That evaluation was not for us. Our function was to see whether it has been demonstrated that the Secretary of State, if I may put it colloquially, broke the law in deciding as he did. In my judgment, he did not.

Application dismissed.

Solicitors: *Clifford-Turner* (for Anderson); *Treasury Solicitor*; *Linklaters & Paines* (for Charter).

April Weiss Barrister.

a Ashcroft v Mersey Regional Health Authority

QUEEN'S BENCH DIVISION AT LIVERPOOL
KILNER BROWN J
17, 18, 21, 29 MARCH 1983

b *Negligence – Professional person – Duty to exercise reasonable skill and care – Proof of negligence – Question for consideration by court – Failure on balance of probabilities to exercise care required of professional person – Whether additional burden of proof on person alleging negligence.*

In an action for negligence against a professional person in connection with his calling, the question for consideration by the court is whether on a balance of probabilities it has been established that the defendant failed to exercise the care required of a man possessing c and professing special skill in circumstances which require the exercise of that special skill. If there is an added burden of proof, that burden does not rest on the person alleging negligence; on the contrary, the more skilled a person is the more the care which is expected of him. The test should however be applied without gloss either way (see p 247 *d* to *f*, post).

Whitehouse v Jordan [1981] 1 All ER 267 considered.

d

Notes

For the duty to exercise the special skill required in the practice of a profession, see 34 Halsbury's Laws (4th edn) para 12, and for cases on the subject, see 36(1) Digest (Reissue) 49–50, *149–158*.

e **Case referred to in judgment**

Whitehouse v Jordan [1981] 1 All ER 267, [1981] 1 WLR 246, HL; *affg* [1980] 1 All ER 650, CA.

Action

The plaintiff, Mary Joyce Ashcroft, brought an action against the defendants, Mersey f Regional Health Authority, claiming damages for personal injury caused to her by the negligent carrying out of an operation performed on her in one of the defendants' hospitals. The facts are set out in the judgment.

John Rowe QC and *Norman A Wright* for the plaintiff.
Michael Kershaw QC and *David Clarke* for the defendants.

g

Cur adv vult

29 March. The following judgment was delivered.

h **KILNER BROWN J.** On 20 January 1978 the plaintiff submitted herself to an operation on her left ear. It was performed by Mr Joseph Siegler, a surgeon of long experience, great skill and the highest reputation. The operation proved to be disastrous, for the plaintiff was left with a partial paralysis of the left side of the face, an injury for which she claims damages alleging that the operation was carried out negligently. The paralysis was caused by damage to the facial nerve. Now, the operation in question was j for the removal of granulated tissue adhering to part of the ear drum and is regarded as routine and perfectly safe. Mr Siegler himself has performed this operation hundreds of times and in his experience and in his study of the relevant literature it has never before resulted in damage to the facial nerve. Mr Smith, the eminent surgeon called as a witness for the defence, has come across only two cases where damage has been caused to the facial nerve and agreed that this operation must have been performed many hundred thousand times. Plainly, therefore, something must have gone badly wrong. But was Mr

Siegler negligent? As I observed during the course of the evidence, this claim reveals a
disgraceful state of affairs. Where an injury is caused which never should have been a
caused, common sense and natural justice indicate that some degree of compensation
ought to be paid by someone. As the law stands, in order to obtain compensation an
injured person is compelled to allege negligence against a surgeon who may, as in this
case, be a careful, dedicated person of the highest skill and reputation. If ever there was a
case in which some reasonable compromise was called for, which would provide some
amount of solace for the injured person and avoid the pillorying of a distinguished b
surgeon, this was such a case. I make these observations without knowing whether or
not efforts were made and rejected by the plaintiff. If so, the moral obloquy would rest
with her. As it is, my findings, even if short of proof of negligence, will do no good to
Mr Siegler or his reputation and may result in failure to obtain compensation on the
plaintiff's side. There are no winners in such circumstances. The only persons who
emerge with credit, and also, no doubt, with profit, are leading counsel on either side, c
who have conducted their respective cases with skill, moderation and courtesy.

The plaintiff had a long history of trouble with both ears and had been under the care
of the Liverpool Ear, Nose and Throat Infirmary since 1957. From the preserved records
relating to this patient, it is plain even to me, as it would be much more so to any
qualified ear surgeon, that the left ear in particular was by the year 1975 in urgent need
of treatment. An operation was performed in January 1976 which revealed not only that d
there was persistent discharge through what is described as an attic perforation, but that
granular tissue had formed to such an extent that the ear drum was adherent to the inner
wall of the middle ear. It is unnecessary for the purpose of this judgment to describe all
that makes up the remarkable structure of the human ear. It is, however, necessary to
bear in mind that the facial nerve, which is a motor nerve controlling movements of lips,
cheeks, eyelids and skin, descends from the brain through the middle ear and is, or e
should be, covered by a fibrous sheath and enclosed by a bone covering which should
exist as protection throughout its passage through the middle ear. The nerve complete
lies in and continues along a canal, so that part of it is exposed and even the exposed part
lies behind the little bones, the malleus (hammer), the incus (anvil) and stapes (stirrup).
The cavity of the middle ear is about 8 mm in width and 6 mm in depth, which registers
with an instructed layman as a cavity one-third of an inch by one-sixth of an inch, which, f
in other words, is even smaller in size than the inside of a lady's wrist watch. Granular
tissue found in the ear is formed as a result of chronic infection and consists of small
masses of cells, blood vessels and other tissue. Granulation is much the same as a soft scab
which forms on a healing abrasion and those granulations which form in the ear vary in
consistency and may be removed by gentle scraping or by picking off with a forceps. The
forceps are extremely fine and delicate, as they have to be in order to pass through a g
perforation in the drum into the middle ear and then to operate in this very small
confined area. It is regarded as important to keep the middle ear free from granulation
as far as possible because it may, as in this lady's case, build up and act as a bonding tissue
causing adherence of one part of the middle ear to another.

So it was that an operation was performed in January 1976. On examination, extensive
attic granulations were seen to be present and the ear drum was found to be adherent to h
the inner wall of the middle ear. The drum was mobilised and granulations were safely
removed. There is no suggestion in the written notes or the diagrammatic sketch that
the facial nerve was affected by erosion or necrosis or was in any way displaced or
anatomically abnormal. Throughout the year 1976 and the first half of 1977 both the
right ear and the left ear gave rise to complaint of infection, discharge and discomfort.
Constant and regular visits to the ENT hospital are noted and recorded. Remedial j
treatment was applied. The notes and the diagrammatic sketches show persistent and
increasing granulation, but no anatomic abnormality of the facial nerve.

As there had been little improvement, it was decided on 19 January 1978 that
examination of the ear and appropriate treatment should be carried out under general
anaesthesia. This was done the next day and it is common ground that whilst removing

granulations with the use of forceps Mr Siegler damaged the facial nerve. Mr Siegler himself, whilst deeply regretting the accident, is satisfied that he did nothing which could be categorised as negligent. Mr Smith, an eminent ear surgeon who was called on behalf of the defendants, was also of the opinion that Mr Siegler had not been negligent. He was not, however, as confident in his opinion as was Mr Peter Taylor, another eminent ear surgeon, who gave evidence to the effect that the accident could only have happened because of negligence on the part of Mr Siegler. Faced with such an acute division of opinion amongst experts, it becomes necessary to analyse their opinions and to assess the strength of the reasons given in support. My findings and conclusions must have regard to the state of the law. From time to time judges at first instance receive helpful guidance from the superior courts. At other times, guidelines in the Court of Appeal need clarification in the House of Lords. In *Whitehouse v Jordan* [1981] 1 All ER 267, [1981] 1 WLR 246 their Lordships were constrained to differ from certain observations in the Court of Appeal made by Lord Denning MR and Lawton LJ ([1980] 1 All ER 650). Thus, the medical and social consequences of medical men being found guilty of negligence on insufficient evidence may be appropriate as a statement of probable consequences, but beg the question which has to be decided. And the proposition that an error of judgment by a medical man is not negligence is an inaccurate statement of the law. It may be; it may not. Furthermore, the suggestion that a greater burden rests on a plaintiff alleging negligence against a doctor is plainly open to question. The fallacies inherent in this mode of approach were analysed and exposed in the dissenting judgment of Donaldson LJ in the Court of Appeal. The question for consideration is whether on a balance of probabilities it has been established that a professional man has failed to exercise the care required of a man possessing and professing special skill in circumstances which require the exercise of that special skill. If there is an added burden, such burden does not rest on the person alleging negligence; on the contrary, it could be said that the more skilled a person is the more the care that is expected of him. It is preferable in my judgment to concentrate on and to apply the test which has long been established in the law and to avoid all commentary or gloss. I propose therefore to examine the evidence and the expert opinions in the limited context which the law requires.

Mr Siegler based his denial of negligence partly on his recollection of the manner in which he carried out the actual operation of removing granular tissue and partly on his findings in a second operation the same day to try and repair the damaged nerve. In a letter to the plaintiff's solicitors dated 23 February 1979 Mr Siegler wrote as follows:

> 'The findings were that during its course within the middle ear there was no boney covering of the facial nerve normally. The facial nerve itself was found to be adherent to the under surface of the ear drum by granulations.'

Then, after referring to the damage to the nerve and the treatment to the nerve, he went on to add the following observations which are supported and illustrated by diagrammatic sketches:

> 'Diagram number 1 shows the profile view of the middle ear and the relationship of the facial nerve to the ear drum. Note that the recognised distance between the facial nerve and the ear drum in a normal ear should be about 5mm. The nerve should be surrounded by a boney covering . . . Diagram number 3 is an endeavour to show what had happened in this particular case as the facial nerve was adherent to the under surface of the ear drum exposing it to the risk of being damaged even by the simple process of removal of granulation. There was no warning that such an eventuality might take place because she had had a previous removal of granulations without any untoward effect and at the time of operation just by looking at the ear through a microscope and at the marginal perforation filled with granulations there was no way of knowing the position and state of the underlying facial nerve.'

Thus Mr Siegler was emphasising two points: one, that the ear drum had become joined to the nerve by granular tissue and, two, that the boney covering of the nerve was missing. In the witness box he added a third point, namely that the nerve was displaced and was for that reason in an abnormal position closer to the ear drum. I regret to say that I cannot accept this third matter. If the nerve had become displaced, a very unusual thing, I should have expected some reference to this fact in his post-operation notes and in his letter of February 1979. I do, however, accept that there was no boney covering to the nerve, that the ear drum was close to the nerve and that the granulations extended to the nerve. It is clear to me that he got the forceps to bite on the nerve because he was searching for granulations which extended that far. I cannot accept the proposition that he removed the boney covering during the operation, There was necrosis and disappearance of other boney structure, particularly the long process of the incus due to long-standing infection. And by the same token the boney covering of the nerve may have disappeared.

Mr Taylor was able to deliver a formidable argument in support of the allegation of negligence and his evidence was impressive. His criticism began with the fact that there was clear evidence in the recorded hospital notes that the ear was in a bad condition, was much affected by granulation and that, the drum having moved, there was much less space than normal in which to manipulate the forceps. Thus the situation called for especial care and gentleness. Then he maintained, and was supported by documentary evidence, that even if the boney covering was absent, the nerve sheath and the nerve itself is tough in construction. He maintained therefore that the damage to the nerve was done by excessive force in the use of the forceps. It requires much more force to damage the nerve than to remove granulation and in his opinion Mr Siegler, no doubt thinking he was removing granular tissue and finding that the tissue was not coming away easily, went on with the forceps too long and too strongly because in fact he was attacking the nerve. At the end of Mr Taylor's evidence I would have said that the case against Mr Siegler was established. However, Mr Siegler was, as one would expect from a man of his calibre, careful, moderate and convincing. He was quite satisfied that he was using the forceps as he always did and certainly did not use excessive force. The injury was an unforeseeable accident.

In consequence, albeit on a balance of probabilities, I am faced with the agonising question of deciding whether the probabilities are such that I am driven to say of Mr Siegler that he has convinced himself that he did not use too much force when in fact he must have done so. It is not an easy problem and is a question of whether the proper inferences to be drawn from the primary facts are such that on this occasion Mr Siegler's belief in his carefulness is misplaced and that he did fall below the standard of care expected of him. In the end I have come to the conclusion that I cannot go so far. I fully recognise that other judges might take a different view.

If I had found in favour of the plaintiff I would have held that the cosmetic blemish of an apparent sunken and half closed left eye was much worse than the medical reports indicate. In other respects the medical reports accurately describe the disability from which this lady suffers. In consequence, I would have assessed the damages at £15,000 for pain and suffering and loss of amenities, to which of course would have to be added the agreed figure for special damage. However, for the reasons I have given, there must be judgment for the defendants.

Judgment for the defendants.

Solicitors: *Benjamin Kay & Co*, Liverpool (for the plaintiff); *A Gibbons*, Liverpool (for the defendants).

Mark Eldridge Esq Barrister.

Stanfield Properties Ltd v National Westminster Bank plc (London and County Securities Ltd, third party)

CHANCERY DIVISION
SIR ROBERT MEGARRY V-C
27, 28 JANUARY 1983

Discovery – Interrogatories – Interrogatories to company – Duty of company in answering interrogatories – Whether duty to make inquiries of former officers, servants and agents of company.

A director, liquidator or other officer of a limited company who answers interrogatories administered to the company in the course of proceedings is under a duty to make all reasonable inquiries which are likely to, or may, reveal what is known to the company relevant to the interrogatories; for the question is not what is known to the individual but what is known to the company. In order to show that that duty has been complied with, the person answering the interrogatories should include in the answers a statement in general terms that he has attempted to discharge the duty by making diligent inquiries of all officers, servants and agents of the company who might reasonably be expected to have some knowledge relevant to the interrogatories (though he need not set out details of the inquiries made), and if such a statement is not included in the answers the party administering the interrogatories may justifiably question whether the company has complied with the duty and require that reasons be given on affidavit why relevant inquiries have not been made. Moreover, since inquiries should be made of a person by the company whenever it is reasonable to do so, inquiries should be made of former (as well as present) officers, servants or agents of the company even though the company may no longer have control over them. It is not a sufficient answer to say that the officer, servant or agent is no longer employed by the company, although it may well be unreasonable to expect inquiries to be made of former officers and others where they have left the company a long time ago, especially if their whereabouts are unknown (see p 250 *h* to p 251 *f* and p 253 *a* to *c*, post).

Dictum of Brett LJ in *Bolckow Vaughan & Co v Fisher* (1882) 10 QBD at 169 not followed.

Notes

For interrogatories to a company, see 13 Halsbury's Laws (4th edn) paras 129–130.

For the extent of the duty to answer interrogatories, see ibid paras 132, 137, and for cases on the subject, see 18 Digest (Reissue) 231–233, *1837–1860*.

Cases referred to in judgment

Alliott v Smith [1895] 2 Ch 111.
Bolckow Vaughan & Co v Fisher (1882) 10 QBD 161, CA.
Southwark and Vauxhall Water Co v Quick (1878) 3 QBD 315, CA.

Interlocutory appeal

In an action by the plaintiffs, Stanfield Properties Ltd, against the defendants, National Westminster Bank plc, claiming £900,000 as damages for conversion of a cheque or as money had and received by the defendants to the plaintiffs' use, in which London and County Securities Ltd were joined as third party, interrogatories were served by the defendants on the plaintiffs and the third party, pursuant to an order made on 13 November 1981. The plaintiffs were in compulsory liquidation and the third party was in a creditors' voluntary winding up. The answers to the interrogatories were made by the respective liquidators of the plaintiffs and the third party. By summonses dated 19 October 1982 the defendants sought an order under RSC Ord 26, r 5 requiring the plaintiffs and the third party to make further answer to the interrogatories, on the ground that the respective liquidators had failed to make any or all proper inquiries of servants and agents or former servants or agents of the plaintiffs and the third party respectively in answering the interrogatories. On 7 December 1982 Master Gowers refused to make the order sought. The defendants appealed. The appeal was heard in chambers but judgment was given by Sir Robert Megarry V-C in open court. The facts are set out in the judgment.

Anthony Mann for the defendants.
David Oliver for the plaintiffs and the third party.

SIR ROBERT MEGARRY V-C. This is an appeal from a decision by Master Gowers. On 7 December 1982 he refused to make an order under RSC Ord 26, r 5 requiring the plaintiffs and the third party to make further answers to interrogatories. All three parties are limited companies. The plaintiffs are in compulsory liquidation, and the third party is in a creditors' voluntary winding up. In each case the answers to the interrogatories were made by the liquidator of the respective companies. What is in issue is a cheque for £900,000 drawn on the third party, who are bankers, under an alleged conspiracy to get money out of the third party for a Mr Pepperell. In the action, the plaintiffs are claiming that the defendants, who are well-known bankers, are liable to the plaintiffs for £900,000 either for conversion of the cheque or as money had and received to the use of the plaintiffs. There has plainly been much dishonesty and, in January 1974, inspectors were appointed under the Companies Act 1948, s 165, in respect of both the plaintiffs and the third party. In March 1975, the inspectors duly reported with findings, I was told, of serious dishonesty.

The interrogatories and the answers to them are substantial documents, 16 pages long in the case of the plaintiffs and 25 pages long in the case of the third party. The essence of the complaint of the defendants is that the liquidators, in giving their answers, appear to have failed to make inquiries of existing and past officers and servants of the companies, and in the main have confined their answers to what they have discovered in the company documents, and what appears in the inspectors' report and in the evidence given to them. Within those limits, the answers appear to be quite full, and they have not been stigmatised as being perfunctory. In particular, counsel on behalf of the defendants complains that the answers to the interrogatories ought to reveal what inquiries have been made of past and present officers and directors of the companies, and that if inquiries have not been made of any of them, the reasons ought to be stated. Although it was for the companies and not the defendants to state these matters, he pointed to certain men who appear to be possible sources of knowledge, yet who appear to have been asked nothing by the plaintiffs and the third party. These men were a Mr Wade and a Mr Pepperell, who were directors of the plaintiffs and might still be, and a Mr Perry, a Mr McMenemy, and a Mr Caplan, who had been directors of the third party but who had resigned, I was told, on 5 December 1973. All of them, it was said, had given evidence to the inspectors.

From the authorities put before me, I think it is clear that a limited company in answering interrogatories must procure the making of proper inquiries from the company's officers, servants and agents: see, for example, *Southwark and Vauxhall Water Co v Quick* (1878) 3 QBD 315 at 321. The position about inquiries to be made from former officers, servants or agents is less clear. In *Bolckow Vaughan & Co v Fisher* (1882) 10 QBD 161 at 169 Brett LJ suggested that such inquiries need not be made; but this was plainly obiter, and with all due respect I cannot agree with it. I do not think that any categorical answer can be given, simply turning on whether the employment has ended. I do not see why inquiries should not be made of a servant who left or retired a few days or a few weeks before the interrogatories are being answered, even though the company no longer has any control over him; the lack of any power to compel an answer is no reason why the question should not be asked. But if the departure or retirement was a long while ago, it might well be unreasonable to expect inquiries to be made, especially if the company does not know where the officer or servant is. The making of reasonable inquiries is one thing, pursuit of ancient history may be another: consider *Alliott v Smith* [1895] 2 Ch 111. In the end, I think it came to be accepted on all hands that the test was one of reasonableness, and not whether or not the employment had been terminated; and this plainly seems to be right.

Interrogatories administered to a company have, of course, the special feature that as the company is an artificial person they must be answered not by the litigant but by some human being who holds a position in relation to the company which enables him to give the answers, such as a director, or, here, a liquidator. Yet throughout, the question is not what is known to the individual but what is known to the company. A director or liquidator who answers that he does not know is not answering the question; for the question is what the company knows, not merely what the director or liquidator knows. The person answering the interrogatories is accordingly bound to make all reasonable inquiries which are likely to reveal, or may reveal, what is known to the company. In order to show that this has been done, it is obviously desirable that the answers should include some statement which shows that the person swearing the answers has applied his mind to this duty and has attempted to discharge it. This, however, is all that I think is required. I do not think that there is any duty to set out the details of the inquiries made, giving the names and addresses of all persons questioned, and specifying what questions were asked, and so on. If the answers do not at least state in general terms that the person swearing to them has made diligent inquiries of all officers, servants and agents of the company who might reasonably be expected to have some knowledge relevant to the questions, the party administering the interrogatories may justifiably question whether the company has discharged its obligations in answering the questions. In particular, if any person is an obvious source of knowledge, he must be questioned. If he is not, the company should say why. As Lindley LJ said in the *Bolckow* case 10 QBD 161 at 171:

> 'Of course, the servant or agent may die, or may be at some place or other where he cannot be got at; but if that be the case let the defendants say so.'

Viewed in this light, I do not think that the answers given in this case are satisfactory. Many of the answers are to the effect that the liquidator has no personal knowledge of the matters in question, and they then go on to refer to evidence given to the inspectors and what appears from that evidence. Some answers also refer to various documents, and there are references to information given by a Mr Gillett, who was an assistant branch manager employed by the third party. But there is no general assertion to the effect that diligent inquiries have been made of all persons likely to have information, or, indeed, that inquiries had been made of anyone except Mr Gillett. In particular, there is nothing to reveal that any inquiries have been made of Messrs Wade, Pepperell, Perry, McMenemy and Caplan, whom I have already mentioned, and nothing to explain why no such inquiries have been made.

It will be seen that I do not regard the answers given to the interrogatories as being satisfactory. That, however, is not the real question that I have to decide. Under RSC Ord 26, r 5, if the court considers that any interrogatories have been answered insufficiently the court 'may' order the person answering them to make a further answer. The jurisdiction is thus plainly discretionary. Even if the answers are insufficient, the court may decide that no answers need be given.

The question is thus whether I ought to exercise this discretionary power to order further answers to be given. On behalf of the plaintiffs and the third party, counsel said that the answer was No. He said that of the five persons named, Mr McMenemy died in August 1982, after the interrogatories had been served in May but before the hearing before the master. Even if counsel for the defendants is right in saying that inquiries should have been made of Mr McMenemy while he was still alive, it would obviously now be futile to require inquiries to be made of him. I was also told Mr Caplan was last known to be in California, having successfully resisted extradition, that Mr Perry, after acquittal at the Old Bailey, was last known of practising as a chiropodist in North London, and that Mr Pepperell was in prison. As I have said, I was told that all these, as well as Mr Wade, gave evidence before the inspectors. I was also told that some inquiries had been made of Mr Wade, though this was not until December 1982, after the interrogatories had been answered and just before the hearing before the master, and that these inquiries had yielded no information. In those circumstances, counsel for the plaintiffs and the third party said, the liquidators had taken all reasonable steps to answer the interrogatories properly. They should not be required to take expensive steps, at the cost of the creditors, to trace and interrogate Mr Caplan and Mr Perry when they had been fully questioned before the inspectors, whose report had at least some evidential value (see the Companies Act 1948, s 171). Nor, for similar reasons, would it be worth while to seek to interrogate Mr Pepperell again; and Mr Wade had in fact been questioned, though belatedly and fruitlessly.

It will be observed that all this material has been put before me by counsel, speaking on instructions. Most of it is factual, yet it is wholly unsupported by any affidavit, as counsel for the defendants forcefully pointed out. I have heard no reason why it should not have been put before the court on affidavit, nor why it should not have been revealed to the defendants in correspondence. The solicitors for the defendants expressed their dissatisfaction with the answers to interrogatories in a letter dated 30 July 1982, and in subsequent letters, but they got no answer from the solicitors for the plaintiffs and the third party until 25 November 1982. All that a letter of this date said was that the solicitors were satisfied that all avenues of inquiry had been pursued, that proper answers to the interrogatories had been given, and that if the defendants' solicitors indicated the basis of their allegations, they would consider the position further and pursue any unexplored avenues of inquiry which were indicated, though they could not conceive of any. It was shortly after that that they wrote their fruitless letter of inquiry to Mr Wade.

It is in those circumstances that I have to consider what course to take. On the whole, on the facts stated on instructions by counsel for the plaintiffs and the third party, I do not consider that there is any point in requiring the plaintiffs and the third party to make any further inquiries. As counsel pointed out, the liquidators are in a position of conflict with those formerly in control of the companies, and they are most unlikely to elicit any more from them than has already been elicited before the inspectors. At the same time, counsel for the defendants is fully entitled to say, as he has said, that this appeal ought not to be decided on the basis of facts which have never been proved but have merely been stated by counsel on instructions. I wish, too, to avoid any unnecessary costs being incurred on this point. Accordingly, what I propose to do is to dismiss this appeal on certain terms. Those terms are, first, that within a limited time the plaintiffs and the third party are to file an affidavit for each company, verifying (with any necessary corrections and amplifications) the facts that counsel for the plaintiffs and the third party has put before me which explain why no further inquiries were made before answering the interrogatories. That affidavit should state in general terms (if it be the fact) that the liquidators have made diligent inquiries from all sources likely to provide any information that is required to answer the interrogatories, and state what exceptions there are to this and the reasons for the exceptions. Second, my order dismissing the appeal is not to take effect until a stated period after the affidavits have been filed and counsel for the defendants has been able to consider them, with liberty to all parties to apply to me, when I shall make such order as may be appropriate. If on the expiration of the stated period no such application has been made, then my order will take effect. Third, subject to anything counsel for the plaintiffs and the third party has to say, I think there must be consequences in costs for the plaintiffs and the third party. Their solicitors have been far from forthcoming in the matter, and it is at least possible that some timely explanation would have made these proceedings unnecessary.

I would add this. I am not laying down that answers to interrogatories by a company
a must always include information and explanations as to the inquiries made, though in many cases it will be convenient to include them, at least in outline. What I am saying is that a company which is interrogated and gives answers which give no indication whether there has been any attempt to tap obvious sources of information must be prepared, on inquiry made, to give explanations of reasonable amplitude and, if required, verify them by affidavit. What it should not do is to withhold this information until the
b matter is brought before the court and then supply the information in unverified form in the course of counsel's submissions. A company which does this has only itself to blame if the court takes an unfavourable view of this mode of proceeding, both generally and in relation to costs. All concerned must seek to avoid the evils of unnecessary litigation and unnecessary costs; and those advising a company should never forget that the answers to interrogatories administered to the company are the answers of that
c company itself, using all the internal sources of the company to discover what the company collectively knows, and not merely the answers of the person, whether officer, liquidator or anyone else, who swears to the answers.

Appeal dismissed on terms.

d Solicitors: *Wilde Sapte* (for the defendants); *Herbert Smith & Co* (for the plaintiffs and the third party).

Vivian Horvath Barrister.

e

f

Practice Direction

FAMILY DIVISION

g

Child – Removal from jurisdiction – Injunction – Notification of Passport Office.

In matrimonial, wardship and guardianship cases the court may grant an injunction restraining the removal of a child from the court's jurisdiction. In cases in which the apparent threat comes from the holder of a foreign passport this may be the only safe
h course. In cases in which the child holds, or the threat comes from the holder of, a British passport the court sometimes orders the surrender of any passport issued to, or which contains particulars of, that child.

Unless the Passport Office is aware that the court has ordered a British passport to be surrendered, there may be nothing to prevent a replacement passport from being issued. Accordingly in such cases the court will in future notify the Passport Office in every case
j in which the surrender of a passport has been ordered.

Issued with the concurrence of the Lord Chancellor.

J L ARNOLD
President.

29 April 1983

Land Securities plc v Receiver for the Metropolitan Police District a

CHANCERY DIVISION
SIR ROBERT MEGARRY V-C
31 JANUARY, 1, 4 FEBRUARY 1983 b

Landlord and tenant – Breach of covenant to repair – Leave to institute proceedings – Discretion of court – Standard of proof required – Prima facie case sufficient – Court having discretion to refuse leave even though prima facie case made out – Circumstances in which discretion will be exercised – Leasehold Property (Repairs) Act 1938, s 1(5).

By a lease dated 5 November 1965 the landlord's predecessor in title granted a tenancy of c
a building to the tenant for a term of 99 years. The lease contained a full repairing
covenant on the part of the tenant. A dispute arose between the parties concerning the
cladding on the building, which consisted of polished granite panels measuring about
2 ft by 4 ft. Cracks had appeared in many of the panels and it appeared that some were
not satisfactorily fixed to the frame of the building. The tenant wished to replace all the
granite panels with stainless steel, at a cost of some £5m. The landlord wanted only those d
granite panels that were defective to be replaced by new granite panels, at a cost of some
£½m. In November 1979 the tenant brought an action against, inter alios, the architect
and consulting engineer employed in the construction of the building and also against
the landlords, alleging negligence in the construction of the building. In July 1982, while
that action was still pending, the tenant issued an originating summons under the
Landlord and Tenant Act 1927 against the landlord, seeking, inter alia, declarations that e
the removal of the granite cladding and its replacement by stainless steel would amount
to an improvement under that Act, that the landlord had unreasonably withheld its
consent to the improvement, and that the tenant was entitled to carry out the work
without the landlord's consent. In October 1982 the landlord issued an originating
summons under s 1[a] of the Leasehold Property (Repairs) Act 1938, applying for leave to
bring an action for forfeiture of the lease and for damages in respect of the tenant's breach f
of the repairing covenant. The landlord's reason for applying for leave was his desire to
ensure that all the various points in dispute were resolved in binding form by the court,
even though, as was conceded, most of the matters in dispute arose under the originating
summons issued in July 1982 under the 1927 Act. The landlord further contended that
an action for forfeiture and damages was the normal way to resolve disputes over a
repairing covenant, since the ensuing tenant's application for relief from forfeiture would g
bring all the matters into issue. On the hearing of the summons issued under the 1938
Act the master granted the landlord leave to proceed up to the close of pleadings. The
tenant appealed against that grant of leave.

Held – On an application for leave under s 1 of the 1938 Act to bring an action for
forfeiture the requirement imposed on the landlord to prove that one of the matters h
stated in s 1(5) was satisfied was merely to make out a prima facie case to that effect, in
the sense that the court was not required to evaluate any rebutting evidence put forward
by the tenant. On the facts, the landlord had made out a prima facie case for the purposes
of s 1(5)(*a*) and (*d*) that immediate remedying of the breach was required to prevent the
value of the landlord's reversion being diminished and could be achieved at much less
expense than if the repairs were postponed. However, in order to obtain leave the j
landlord also had to show that the court ought to exercise its discretion by granting leave.
Since all the matters which the landlord wanted resolved could be resolved more
conveniently and in less time at less cost in the proceedings under the 1927 Act it was
unnecessary for the landlord to sue for forfeiture and damages under the 1938 Act and

a Section 1, so far as material, is set out at p 256 *j* to 257 *a*, post

therefore leave to bring the forfeiture proceedings would be refused. The appeal would
a accordingly be allowed (see p 257 *j*, p 258 *f h*, p 259 *b f g* and p 260 *a b* and *f g*, post).

Sidnell v Wilson [1966] 1 All ER 681 applied.

Re Metropolitan Film Studios Ltd v Twickenham Film Studios Ltd (Intended Action), [1962] 3 All ER 508 considered.

b **Notes**

For leave to institute forfeiture proceedings, see 27 Halsbury's Laws (4th edn) para 302, and for cases on the subject, see 31(2) Digest (Reissue) 832, *6888–6889*.

For the Landlord and Tenant Act 1927, see 18 Halsbury's Statutes (3rd edn) 451.

For the Leasehold Property (Repairs) Act 1938, s 1, see ibid.

c **Cases referred to in judgment**

Metropolitan Film Studios Ltd v Twickenham Film Studios Ltd (Intended Action), Re [1962] 3 All ER 508, [1962] 1 WLR 1315.

Sidnell v Wilson [1966] 1 All ER 681, [1966] 2 QB 67, [1966] 2 WLR 560, CA.

Cases also cited

d *Yat Tung Investment Co Ltd v Dao Heng Bank Ltd* [1975] AC 581, PC.

Interlocutory appeal

By an originating summons dated 22 October 1982 and subsequently amended, the plaintiff, Land Securities plc (the landlord), applied for leave under s 1 of the Leasehold Property (Repairs) Act 1938 to issue proceedings against the defendant, the Receiver for
e Metropolitan Police District (the tenant), to enforce the right of re-entry or forfeiture in respect of breach of a repairing convenant contained in a lease dated 5 November 1965 made between the parties, and damages. The grounds of the application were (1) that immediate remedying of the breaches of covenant was requisite for preventing substantial diminution in value of the landlord's reversion, (2) that the breaches could be immediately remedied at a lesser expense, and (3) that there were special circumstances which rendered
f it just and equitable that leave be given. On 21 December 1982 Master Chamberlain granted the landlord leave to proceed up to the close of pleadings and until other pending proceedings had been set down and a date fixed for hearing. The tenant appealed against the grant of leave. The appeal was heard in chambers but judgment was given by Sir Robert Megarry V-C in open court at the parties' request. The facts are set out in the judgment.

g

Derek Wood QC and *Kim Lewison* for the tenant.

Ronald Bernstein QC and *Benjamin Levy* for the landlord.

Cur adv vult

h 4 February. The following judgment was delivered.

SIR ROBERT MEGARRY V-C. In this case there has been an application by originating summons under the Leasehold Property (Repairs) Act 1938, as amended, for leave to bring an action for forfeiture of a lease and for damages in respect of breaches of a repairing covenant. The application is made by Land Securities plc (which I shall call
j 'the landlord') against the Receiver for the Metropolitan Police District (whom I shall call 'the tenant'). The property in question is New Scotland Yard, and the tenant holds it under a lease dated 5 November 1965 made between a predecessor in title of the landlord and the tenant. The lease is for a term of 99 years from 5 November 1965, so that it has some 82 years to run. The building was originally intended to be erected to a different design, but this design was varied during the course of construction by agreement between the landlord's predecessor in title and the tenant. The lease was granted at a

premium of £6m, in return for which the tenant was to pay a rent of £570,000 a year but from 4 November 1986 a rent which, as revised from time to time, would be some *a*
37·6% less than the rack rent as computed under the terms of the lease. The lease contains a full repairing covenant. The originating summons initially came before Master Chamberlain, who gave the landlord leave to proceed up to the close of pleadings, and until other proceedings between the parties under the Landlord and Tenant Act 1927 had been set down and a date fixed for the hearing. From this decision the tenant has appealed, and as requested by the parties I am delivering judgment in open court. *b*

The dispute centres on the cladding on the building. This consists of polished granite panels measuring about 2 ft by 4 ft, and weighing about 165 lb each. Some six years ago it was found that this cladding was in an unsatisfactory condition. There were reports that cracks were appearing in many of the panels, and there were questions whether they were satisfactorily fixed to the concrete of the building. It is common ground that the building is out of repair as regards the cladding, but it is in dispute how extensive that *c*
want of repair is, and in particular there is a sharp divergence on what is the proper action to take in order to make good the lack of repair. Put broadly, the tenant wishes to replace all the granite panels with stainless steel, as a cost of some £5m, whereas the landlord wishes only those granite panels which are defective to be replaced by new granite panels, at a cost of some £½m. It is not the least curious feature of the case that the landlord is objecting to the tenant spending ten times as much on repairing the *d*
premises as the landlord wishes to have spent, and that the tenant is objecting to the modesty of the figure which the landlord says is all that the tenant need spend on repairs. Of course, that way of putting it must not be allowed to conceal the underlying grounds of dispute, which are as to the unsuitability of the material and the methods proposed by the tenant.

Now as I have indicated, the proposed action here in question is not the only litigation *e*
which affects the parties. On 30 November 1979, I was told, the tenant issued a writ in the Queen's Bench against the architect, the consulting engineer, the developers (the landlord now being included under this head) and the GLC. The general basis of this action is a claim for damages for negligence in the erection of the building and for breach of the provisions of the development agreement. Pleadings in this action have not yet closed, and at this stage not much more can be said than that the action is expected to be *f*
ripe for hearing in 1985, and will be heard by a judge exercising the functions of an Official Referee. The estimated duration is some four months.

Second, there are the Chancery proceedings under the Landlord and Tenant Act 1927 which I have already mentioned. They were commenced by originating summons on 2 July 1982. In these, the tenant claims various declarations as against the landlord. One is that the removal of the granite cladding and its replacement by stainless steel cladding *g*
according to certain plans in the specification would amount to an improvement within the Landlord and Tenant Act 1927; and the tenant asks for a certificate that the work would be a proper improvement within s 3 of the Act. Then declarations are sought that the landlord has unreasonably withheld its consent to carrying out this work and is unreasonably withholding it. Last, there is a declaration that, despite cl 3(17) of the lease, the plaintiff is entitled to carry out the work without the landlord's consent. *h*

On 22 October 1982, a little less than four months after the tenant issued his originating summons, the landlord issued the originating summons which is now before me. In this, counsel for the landlord claims that the case falls within three of the five heads in s 1(5) of the Leasehold Property (Repairs) Act 1938, namely paras (*a*), (*d*) and (*e*); and to these I must turn in a moment. The mechanics of operating the Act are not in dispute. The landlord wishes to sue for forfeiture of the lease and damages; a notice *j*
under s 146 of the Law of Property Act 1925 has been duly served; the tenant has duly served a counter-notice; more than three years of the lease remains unexpired; the landlord cannot therefore commence its action without the leave of the court; and 'Leave for the purposes of this section shall not be given unless the lessor proves' that one of the paragraphs in s 1(5) is satisfied. The heads on which counsel relies are:

'(*a*) that the immediate remedying of the breach in question is requisite for preventing substantial diminution in the value of his reversion, or that the value thereof has been substantially diminished by the breach . . . (*d*) that the breach can be immediately remedied at an expenses that is relatively small in comparison with the much greater expense that would probably be occasioned by postponement of the necessary work . . . (*e*) special circumstances which in the opinion of the court, render it just and equitable that leave should be given.'

During the argument it was accepted by counsel for the landlord and by counsel for the tenant that on an application under the 1938 Act the landlord had to leap three hurdles. The first was that there was a breach of a repairing covenant; and it was not disputed that there was. The second was that s 1(5) of the Act was satisfied; and that was in issue. The third was that as all that resulted from satisfying s 1(5) was merely that a prohibition against the granting of leave by the court was removed, there still remained the question whether the court ought to exercise its discretion in favour of granting leave to the landlord to bring the action. I must therefore consider the second and third heads.

On the second head, there was considerable argument about what was decided in *Sidnell v Wilson* [1966] 1 All ER 681, [1966] 2 QB 67. Counsel for the tenant adopted the approach appearing in the headnote ([1966] 2 QB 67). On an application for leave under the 1938 Act, a landlord did not have to 'satisfy' the court that there had been a breach of the repairing covenant which invoked s 1(5); for the application was merely of an interlocutory nature, and as the question whether or not there had been such a breach would have to be determined at the trial, it would be wrong to determine it on the interlocutory application, and so try it twice over. Instead, the landlord merely had to establish that there was a 'prima facie case' that there had been such a breach. That was the view of Lord Denning MR and Harman LJ. Diplock LJ, on the other hand, held that the landlord merely had to establish an 'arguable case' that one or more of the conditions in s 1(5) had been satisfied.

Counsel for the tenant's contention was that the difference in these two views was not merely whatever difference there might be between a 'prima facie' case and an 'arguable' case, but that there was in some way a difference between the process of establishing a breach of covenant and the process of establishing that one of the paragraphs of s 1(5) had been satisfied. On the first process, the requirement was only that there should be a prima facie case. But this did not apply to the second, since the question whether one of the heads of s 1(5) was satisfied would have to be determined once and for all on the application for leave to bring the proceedings, and so, unlike the question whether there was any breach of covenant, would not arise for a second time at the trial. I pressed counsel for the tenant to discover what had to be shown in establishing that one of the paragraphs of s 1(5) had been satisfied, but although he readily proffered a collection of the matters that had to be taken into consideration, he put forward no clear standard in place of the 'prima facie' or 'arguable' case that had to be shown on establishing a breach of covenant. The standard was different, he said, but the difference was not explained, beyond being one that was more exacting than was indicated by the words 'prima facie' and 'arguable'.

I do not think that this contention is right. One must begin with the words of s 1(5). There is no separate requirement of establishing a breach of covenant; instead, the existence of a breach is clearly assumed under each head in s 1(5) except the last. Thus under para (*a*), what the lessor must prove is that 'the immediate remedying of the breach in question is requisite for preventing substantial diminution in the value of his reversion', and so on. The word 'proves' governs a compound requirement which includes the immediate remedying of the breach, and this being requisite to prevent substantial diminution in the value of the reversion. I do not see how the existence of the breach can be segregated out of this compound requirement and given a different standard of proof from the rest of it. Instead, all that I think that Lord Denning MR and Harman LJ were doing was to say that as the existence of the breach would have to be determined at the trial, at this interlocutory stage only a prima facie case for the existence of such a breach need be shown, with the result that this must be the standard required for the whole of each paragraph of s 1(5) in which a breach of covenant lay embedded. It is plain from *Sidnell v Wilson* [1966] 1 All ER 681 at 684, [1966] 2 QB 67 at 77 that Lord Denning MR was considering not merely whether there was a breach of covenant but whether the landlord had brought himself within s 1(5)(*a*), which must mean the whole of s 1(5)(*a*); and on the facts of that case Lord Denning MR was holding that the landlord had done this, provided he had sufficiently established a breach. Accordingly the thrust of the judgment was on this latter point rather than on the whole of para (*a*); but that does not mean that the rest of para (*a*) was being ignored.

Counsel for the tenant contended that this view was wrong. He said that s 1 of the 1938 Act nowhere in terms refers to proving that a breach of a repairing covenant has been committed; and that indeed is the case. Section 1(1) refers to the service under the Law of Property Act 1925 of 'a notice that relates' to a breach of a repairing covenant; s 1(2) refers to a 'right to damages for a breach of such a covenant' and a notice served under the Law of Property Act 1925, s 146(1), and a counter-notice; s 1(3) refers to proceedings for forfeiture or damages 'for breach of the covenant or agreement in question'; s 1(4) refers back to notices served under sub-ss (1) and (2). Thus when s 1(5)(*a*) refers to the immediate remedying of 'the breach in question', it appears to be assuming that there is a breach. Yet obviously the court should give no leave to bring proceedings within the section if there has in fact been no breach of covenant, even though not until s 1(5) is reached does there seem to be anything to raise the question whether a breach has in fact been committed. Counsel for the defendant, however, contended that this issue arose under s 1(3), and that in deciding in *Sidnell v Wilson* what standard of proof should be applied in determining whether or not there had been a breach of covenant, the Court of Appeal was really construing s 1(3) and not s 1(5). He had to accept, however, that there was not a word in any of the judgments about s 1(3), although all the members of the court considered s 1(5)(*a*); and I do not see how the decision could possibly be treated as a decision on the meaning and effect of a subsection that the judgments do not even mention. If any emphasis is needed, it is supplied by the terms of s 1(3); for as I have indicated, this is expressed in terms of imposing a prohibition on taking proceedings for forfeiture under a proviso or stipulation in the lease, or for damages, for breach of the covenant or agreement, and not in terms of whether or not there has in fact been such a breach.

In the end, I think that all that a landlord has to do on an application for leave is to make out a prima facie case (or perhaps a bona fide arguable case) that at least one of the paragraphs of s 1(5) is satisfied; and this includes making out such a case for there being a breach of the repairing covenant. I think that this includes para (*e*), even though it does not mention any breach of covenant; for I do not see how a landlord could establish that there are special circumstances making it just and equitable for leave to be given unless he has established a prima facie, or arguable, case that there has been a breach of covenant. *Sidnell v Wilson* is a decision on the word 'proves' in s 1(5), and the standard of proof that it lays down applies to the whole of the contents of paras (*a*) to (*e*). If the term 'prima facie case' is used, I think that this is to be understood in the sense of a case made out by the landlord, without the need to go into any rebutting evidence put forward by the tenant. That is why Diplock LJ used the term 'bona fide arguable case' (see [1966] 1 All ER 681 at 686, [1966] 2 QB 67 at 80); and the unanimous view of the court that the point ought not to be tried twice over seems to point strongly to the phrase 'prima facie case' bearing the meaning that I have indicated.

In the case before me, in contrast with *Sidnell v Wilson*, there is no difficulty about the lack of repair, for that is clear, and it has not been disputed. On the other hand, counsel for the tenant has contended that the evidence put forward to support the other elements of paras (*a*), (*d*) and (*e*) does not amount to even a prima facie case, or an arguable case. The evidence is not impressive. Expressions of opinion by a chartered surveyor employed by the landlord which do little more than apply to the building something of the

language of paras (*a*) and (*d*), and wind up with a watered-down version of para (*e*),
a obviously leave a good deal to be desired. On the other hand, the primary facts of the
case by themselves go far towards satisfying paras (*a*) and (*d*). Given the nature and
position of the building, and the state of at least some of the granite slabs, it is difficult
not to infer that the case falls within these paragraphs. Looking at the evidence as a
whole, and allowing for the fact that much is in dispute, I nevertheless reach the
conclusion that, on the lowly standards of proof that apply, paras (*a*) and (*d*) are
b sufficiently satisfied, and s 1(5) imposes no prohibition on the granting of leave to the
landlord.

That brings me to the third hurdle, that of the discretion of the court. For some while
during the argument I remained completely in the dark why it was that the landlord
wished to sue for forfeiture and damages for breach of the repairing covenant when a
tenant of unquestionable responsibility was seeking to spend far more on repairs than
c the landlord claimed. Counsel for the tenant could not enlighten me, but ultimately
counsel for the landlord intervened to give an explanation which he amplified later.
None of this explanation appears to have been put before the master or, indeed, told to
the tenant until counsel for the landlord made his intervention. The reason, counsel said,
was to ensure that various points in dispute between the parties were resolved in binding
form by the court. Most of these points, he agreed, arose in the originating summons
d issued in July 1982 under the Landlord and Tenant Act 1927; but the judge who tried
that case might not find it necessary to decide all of the points, and the landlord wished
to ensure that they were all resolved. For this reason the landlord had launched the
present application for leave to sue for forfeiture and damages, with the intention of
having the action (if leave was given) brought on at the same time as the proceedings
under the 1982 originating summons. An action for forfeiture and damages was, counsel
e for the landlord said, the normal way in which to get disputes over a repairing covenant
resolved, since the tenant's application for relief from forfeiture would bring all the
matters into issue. Counsel put in a list of the points that he wished to have resolved, and
later added to the list.

I can well see that it is desirable to have resolved at one and the same time all the
matters in dispute between the parties. What I found it hard to follow was why this had
f to be done by a separate action for a forfeiture of the lease that the landlord is most
unlikely to want. Counsel never in terms accepted that the landlord had no desire for
forfeiture, though he accepted that this was not the landlord's primary object. From start
to finish, I may say, nobody has suggested that there has been any impropriety or lack of
good faith on either side. I do not intend to disturb this happy abstinence, and I make no
imputations; but I must say that I cannot see in the proposed new proceedings anything
g but a somewhat inappropriate and expensive means of obtaining decisions on the
meaning and effect of the repairing covenant which may more suitably and more cheaply
be obtained by other means. I cannot see why the whole apparatus of a new set of
proceedings, claiming an unwanted forfeiture, with the attendant costs in time and
money, should have to be launched instead of having the points in issue resolved in the
existing proceedings. True, the existing proceedings are brought by originating summons
h and not by writ; but even if the landlord, in putting in evidence under the originating
summons (which has yet to be done), cannot procure that the points are raised for
decision, and the originating summons cannot be amended to raise the points, I do not
see why the landlord should not raise the points by counterclaim. True, the landlord
ought to have done this promptly (see RSC Ord 28, r 7(2)); but I think the court has
ample powers under Ord 2, r 1 and Ord 3, r 5 to cure any defect of this kind; and counsel
j for the tenant made it plain, as soon as this point arose, that he would welcome rather
than oppose such a course of action. In short, of the course of taking new proceedings for
forfeiture and damages instead of using the existing proceedings, I would simply say,
'Cui bono?'

As for the nature of any counterclaim, I see no reason why it should be for forfeiture
and damages. There appears to be no real difficulty in the points raised by counsel for the

landlord (which I forbear from setting out) being cast into the form of declarations. Counsel at one stage argued that to do this would in some way circumvent the 1938 Act; but he failed to sustain this contention, and I reject it. If the matter is dealt with by a claim for declarations, then if the grossly improbable later occurs, and the tenant refuses to act on the declarations, it would still be open to the landlord to seek leave to sue for forfeiture and damages, and at that stage the 1938 Act would apply. But the remote possibility of that being necessary at some time in the future is no reason for granting leave to bring such proceedings today.

It is not for me to determine exactly how the questions should be raised and decided. It suffices for me to say that I am satisfied that it is unnecessary and undesirable for the landlord to sue for forfeiture and damages at this stage, since all that the landlord wants can be resolved more conveniently and with greater economy of time and money in the proceedings under the 1982 originating summons. Accordingly, I feel no hesitation in saying that in my judgment my discretion ought to be exercised by refusing leave under the 1938 Act.

In reaching this conclusion, I do not overlook *Re Metropolitan Film Studios Ltd v Twickenham Film Studios Ltd (Intended Action)* [1962] 3 All ER 508 at 517, [1962] 1 WLR 1315 at 1324, where Ungoed-Thomas J said that the discretion under the 1938 Act is—

> 'of an interlocutory nature, not to be exercised to exclude the lessor from his rights subject to the wide discretion given to the court under s. 146 [that is, of the Law of Property Act 1925], unless the court is clearly convinced that, despite compliance with the requirements specified in the paragraphs of sub-s. (5), the application should be refused.'

In so far as this suggests that, once sub-s (5) is satisfied and the discretion of the court is opened, leave should always be given unless the court is 'clearly convinced' that it should not, I would have some difficulty in agreeing with it. Proceedings for forfeiture and damages are burdensome on tenants, even though relief from forfeiture may be granted, and the 1938 Act was plainly passed so as to prevent oppression from the threat of such proceedings. With all respect, I would have thought that the discretion of the court was much less fettered than is suggested by subjecting it to the words 'clearly convinced'. The fact that one of the paragraphs of sub-s (5) must have been satisfied before the discretion is opened does of course of itself point towards the landlord being given leave to bring the proceedings; but there may be many other factors present which ought to be considered in deciding whether or not to grant leave, including the fact that only prima facie evidence is required under sub-s (5), and I do not see why in balancing all the relevant matters nothing save a clear conviction that leave should be refused should suffice for refusing leave. However, even if I accept the *Metropolitan Film Studios* case to the full, I would still refuse leave because I am in fact 'clearly convinced' that it ought to be refused. I therefore allow the appeal; and that is all that I have to decide.

At the same time I should say that I will readily accede to any application for directions or orders which will make it possible to have all matters in dispute between the parties under the repairing covenant resolved in the most convenient way, either now, or after counsel have had an opportunity of discussing matters between themselves. For this purpose I will, of course, be willing to treat the 1982 originating summons as being before me.

Appeal allowed.

Solicitors: *Winckworth & Pemberton* (for the tenant); *Nabarro Nathanson* (for the landlord).

Vivian Horvath Barrister.

Practice Direction

LORD CHANCELLOR'S DEPARTMENT

Crown Court – Bail – Applications – Bail in course of proceedings in magistrates' court – Procedure – Certificate to accompany application – Venue for application – Legal aid – Bail Act 1976, s 5(6A) – Crown Court Rules 1982, rr 19, 20.

The Lord Chancellor's Department has issued the following notice.

1. From 24 May 1983, when s 60 of the Criminal Justice Act 1982 comes into force, it will for the first time be possible to apply to the Crown Court for bail before committal. So that these applications may be dealt with as expeditiously as possible, practitioners are asked to note the following points.

Procedure

2. Rules 19 and 20 of the Crown Court Rules 1982, SI 1982/1109, apply to these applications. The application form for bail has been amended to cover the new procedure.

3. Before the Crown Court can deal with an application it must be satisfied that the magistrates' court has issued a certificate under s 5(6A) of the Bail Act 1976 (as added by s 60(3) of the Criminal Justice Act 1982) that they heard full argument on the application for bail before they refused the application. A copy of the certificate will be issued to the applicant and not sent directly to the Crown Court. It will therefore be necessary for applicants' solicitors to attach a copy of the certificate to the bail application form. If the certificate is not enclosed with the application form it will be difficult to avoid some delay in listing.

Venue

4. Applications should be made to the court to which the case will be or would have been committed for trial. In the event of an application in a purely summary case it should be made to the Crown Court centre which normally receives class 4 work. The hearing will be listed as a chambers matter unless a judge has directed otherwise.

Legal aid

5. If the applicant is legally aided in the magistrates' court (either under an ordinary order or under an order limited to a bail application) the legal aid order covers applications under this new procedure. If he is not legally aided neither the Crown Court nor the magistrates' court has power to grant a legal aid order for the purpose of applications for bail to the Crown Court alone.

6. Legal aid for this purpose is limited to representation by a solicitor only unless the legal aid order granted by the magistrates' court specifically includes representation by counsel. This does not preclude a solicitor from instructing counsel to act on his behalf if he wishes, though any costs determined cannot exceed those which would be allowed had the solicitor undertaken the case without counsel. The legal aid costs will be determined by the Law Society as part of the magistrates' court costs under the legal aid order.

26 April 1983

R v London Transport Executive, ex parte Greater London Council a

QUEEN'S BENCH DIVISION
KERR LJ, GLIDEWELL AND NOLAN JJ
18, 19, 20, 21, 24, 27 JANUARY 1983

b

Public authority – Statutory powers – Excessive exercise of statutory powers – Greater London Council – Reduction of fares on London Transport – GLC requiring London Transport to reduce fares – London Transport required 'so far as practicable' to make up operating deficits in subsequent years – Whether GLC entitled to make grant to London Transport to reduce or eliminate deficit – Whether fact that London Transport only required to make up deficit 'so far as practicable' enabling GLC to make grant to London Transport – Whether GLC acting within legal c *powers in directing London Transport to reduce fares – Transport (London) Act 1969, ss 1, 5(1), 7(3)(b)(6).*

London Transport Executive – Fares – Reduction – Greater London Council requiring LTE to reduce fares – Whether GLC acting in excess of statutory power – Transport (London) Act 1969, ss 1, 5(1), 7(3)(b)(6). d

By s 1[a] of the Transport (London) Act 1969 the Greater London Council (the GLC) was under a general duty to develop policies and encourage measures which promoted 'the provision of integrated, efficient and economic transport facilities and services for Greater London'. The responsibility for implementing those policies was, by s 4, conferred on the London Transport Executive (the LTE). By s 5(1)[b] the LTE was under a general duty e to provide public passenger transport services which best met the needs of Greater London and to exercise and perform its functions in accordance with principles laid down by the GLC and with due regard to 'efficiency, economy and safety of operation'. By s 7(3)(*b*)[c] if at the end of an accounting period there was a deficit in the LTE's revenue account the LTE was required, 'so far as practicable', to make up that deficit in the next accounting period. Under s 7(6) the GLC was entitled to 'take such action', after having f regard to the LTE's duty under s 7(3)(*b*) to balance its accounts, as was necessary and appropriate to enable the LTE to comply with that duty. The GLC was further empowered by s 3(1)[d] to make grants to the LTE 'for any purpose'. The GLC gave a direction to the LTE under s 11[e] to implement a restructuring of its fares which, it was anticipated, would lead to a decrease in revenue and a consequent increase in the GLC grant to cover operating costs. The LTE considered the direction was unlawful and g declined to comply with it. The GLC applied to the court for declarations that it was within its powers in giving the direction and that the LTE would be within its powers in implementing it. The LTE contended (i) that the requirement in s 7(3) that the LTE balance its accounts was a paramount duty for the LTE, and a primary consideration for the GLC, which required the LTE to impose the highest practicable level of fares while discharging its duties under s 5(1), (ii) that grant support could only arise after, and as an h unavoidable consequence of, compliance with the LTE's duties under s 5(1), and (iii) that the direction would impose fares which were not set at the highest practicable level with the result that avoidable losses would be incurred.

Held – Although the LTE's duties under s 5(1) of the 1969 Act and the GLC's duties under s 7(6) of that Act were subject to the requirement in s 7(3) that any deficit incurred j

a Section 1, so far as material, is set out at p 264 *j*, post
b Section 5(1) is set out at p 265 *f*, post
c Section 7, so far as material, is set out at p 265 *j* to p 266 *d*, post
d Section 3(1) is set out at p 265 *d*, post
e Section 11, so far as material, is set out at p 266 *e* to *g*, post

by the LTE in an accounting period was, so far as practicable, to be made up in a
a subsequent accounting period, the GLC could nevertheless make a grant to the LTE, pursuant to the GLC's wider duties under s 1, in order to reduce or eliminate an existing or expected deficit, since (a) on its true construction s 7(3) permitted such grants to be included in the LTE's revenue account and thereby to reduce or eliminate a deficit incurred in an accounting period and (b) the fact that under s 7(3) the LTE was only required to make up a deficit 'so far as practicable' meant that the GLC had a discretion
b to make such grants in furtherance of the duties imposed on it by s 1 whenever it was not practicable to require the LTE to eliminate a deficit by self-generated income alone while still maintaining transport services to the requisite standard, provided that the GLC acted in accordance with the well-established principles applicable to the exercise of such a discretion and, in particular, after balancing the interests of the general body of ratepayers against the competing interests of the travelling public. Accordingly, the court
c would grant a declaration that on the true construction of the 1969 Act it was within the legal powers of the GLC to give the LTE a direction to implement the restructuring of fares and it was within the legal power of the LTE to comply with that direction; but, in the absence of any argument on behalf of the general body of ratepayers, it was not for the court to say whether in exercising those powers the GLC had considered all relevant factors and no irrelevant factors or had in all the circumstances acted reasonably (see
d p 267 *e* to *g*, p 271 *d* to *j*, p 273 *c* to p 274 *c*, p 275 *b* and *d* to *g*, p 277 *d e*, p 280 *f*, p 281 *d* to *j*, p 28 *a b* and *g* to *j*, p 283 *c* to *g* and *j* to p 284 *b* and *f g*, p 285 *d* to *j* and p 288 *e* and *g*, post).

Associated Provincial Picture Houses Ltd v Wednesbury Corp [1947] 2 All ER 680, *Prescott v Birmingham Corp* [1954] 3 All ER 698, *Dedman v British Building and Engineering Appliances Ltd* [1974] 1 All ER 520 and *Bromley London Borough Council v Greater London Council*
e [1982] 1 All ER 129 applied.

Notes

For the general duty and powers of the Greater London Council, see 29 Halsbury's Laws (4th Edn) paras 100–101.

For the Transport (London) Act 1969, ss 1, 3, 4, 5, 7, 11, see 20 Halsbury's Statutes (3rd
f Edn) 822, 824, 825, 829, 833.

Cases referred to in judgments

Associated Provincial Picture Houses Ltd v Wednesbury Corp [1947] 2 All ER 680, [1948] 1 KB 223, CA.

Bromley London Borough Council v Greater London Council [1982] 1 All ER 129, [1982] 2
g WLR 62, CA and HL.

Dedman v British Building and Engineering Appliances Ltd [1974] 1 All ER 520, [1974] 1 WLR 171, CA.

Prescott v Birmingham Corp [1954] 3 All ER 698, [1955] Ch 210, [1954] 3 WLR 990, CA.

University College, Oxford v Durdy [1982] 1 All ER 1108, [1982] Ch 413, [1982] 3 WLR 94, CA.

h

Application for judicial review

The Greater London Council (the GLC) applied, with the leave of Leonard J granted on 23 December 1982, for declarations (i) that the proposal described as 'option II' for the simplification and reduction of fares for London Transport submitted by the London Transport Executive (the LTE) to the GLC on 11 November 1982 was within the legal
j powers of the LTE to implement, and that the GLC was within its legal powers in giving approval to option II on 14 December 1982, (ii) that a direction under s 11 of the Transport (London) Act 1969 to the LTE by the GLC pursuant to a resolution made on 14 December 1982 that the LTE implement option II was a lawful direction, (iii) that it would be within the GLC's and the LTE's legal powers for the direction to be implemented on or after 3 April 1983, and (iv) that in so far as the LTE had decided that to implement the direction on 3 April 1983 would be unlawful it had misdirected itself

in law. The respondent to the application was the LTE. The facts are set out in the judgment of Kerr LJ. a

Roger Henderson QC and *Charles George* for the GLC.
John Drinkwater QC and *Christopher Lockhart-Mummery* for the LTE.

Cur adv vult

27 January. The following judgments were delivered. b

KERR LJ.

Introduction

This is an application for judicial review, for which the necessary leave has been given, c whereby the Greater London Council (the GLC) seeks various declarations from the court to the effect that its most recent proposals under the heading of 'option II' or the 'balanced plan' for the restructuring of fares, services and expenditure in relation to public passenger transport in Greater London constitute a lawful exercise of the GLC's powers under the Transport (London) Act 1969, and that the GLC is accordingly entitled to maintain a direction which it has given to the London Transport Executive (the LTE) to d put these proposals into operation. The LTE welcomes the proposals in principle, as I explain later. However, on the advice which it has received, it considers that the proposals are unlawful under the 1969 Act in the light of the decision of the House of Lords in *Bromley London Borough Council v Greater London Council* [1982] 1 All ER 129, [1982] 2 WLR 62, which unanimously affirmed a unanimous decision of the Court of Appeal ([1982] 1 All ER 129, [1982] 2 WLR 62) that earlier proposals under the heading of Fares e Fair were clearly unlawful. This difference of view, to put it broadly for the moment, turns on the question to what extent it is lawful for the GLC to subsidise the operations of the LTE, by a grant which must ultimately come out of the pockets of the ratepayers of Greater London, in order to enable the LTE to provide passenger services of a standard, and at a cost to the users in terms of fares, which the GLC considers to be appropriate in discharging the overall functions which are laid on it by the 1969 Act. In the view of the f LTE, the 'balanced plan' proposals, which have now been evolved after much thought and consultation, still involve a breach of the LTE's financial duties under the 1969 Act, because they still strike an impermissible balance between, again to put it broadly, the levels of fares on the one hand and of grant support out of rates on the other. This is the issue which falls to be decided on this application and the answer depends on the true construction of the 1969 Act, in particular of s 7, and on an analysis of the grounds of the g decision in the *Bromley* case in so far as these affect this issue.

The Transport (London) Act 1969

It is convenient at this point to set out or refer to those provisions of the 1969 Act (as amended from time to time) which are most important for present purposes, and then to bear them in mind later in conjunction with their analysis in the *Bromley* case. h

Following the establishment of the GLC, the purpose of the 1969 Act, as shown by its long title, was to lay on the GLC the overall responsibility for transport in and around Greater London, whereas this responsibility had not previously been integrated under the authority of a single body. Thus Part I of the Act deals with the general powers of the GLC in that regard, Part II established the LTE to exercise functions with respect to passenger transport services in Greater London, Part IV deals with public service vehicles j and railway closures and Part V deals with highways and road traffic, including car parks, parking meters, pedestrian crossings etc. Section 1 of the Act, after a reference to the GLC's duties under the Road Traffic Regulation Act 1967, provides that:

> '... it shall be the general duty of the Greater London Council ... to develop policies, and to encourage, organise and, where appropriate, carry out measures,

which will promote the provision of integrated, efficient and economic transport facilities and services for Greater London.'

Section 2(1) provides:

'... the Council shall from time to time prepare, and cause to be published in such manner as seems to the Council appropriate for informing persons appearing to the Council to be concerned, plans relating to transport in Greater London with due regard to the relationship and interaction between transport facilities and services within, and such facilities and services outside, Greater London ...'

and requires the GLC to send to the Minister of Transport a copy of any such plan.

Section 2(2) requires the GLC, in preparing any such plan, to consult with the minister, the railways board, the LTE and any local authority which may be particularly concerned, and also to have regard, inter alia, to the Greater London development plan, to which statutory effect was subsequently given. Section 5 of that plan provides for a 'unified strategy' concerning every aspect of transportation (including pedestrians, or, to give them their statutory name, foot passengers), which has regard not only to the nature, quality and frequency of public transport services, but also to all the manifold environmental factors and amenities, including traffic congestion, of which account is to be taken in planning the various public transport services and the integration between them.

Section 3(1) of the Act requires to be set out in full in its amended form as follows:

'Without prejudice to any other power of the Council to make grants for transport purposes, the Council shall have power to make grants—(*a*) to the Executive for any purpose; or (*b*) to the Railways Board in respect of passenger transport services or other passenger transport amenities or facilities provided or to be provided by them which appear to the Council to be required to meet the needs of Greater London.'

Part I of the Act having dealt with the functions of the GLC, which can properly be described as an overall strategy, one then comes to Part II, which deals with the establishment of the LTE 'For the purpose of implementing the policies which it is the duty of the Council under section 1 of this Act to develop' (see s 4(1)), and with its functions under the direction of the GLC. In this connection s 5(1) must also be set out in full:

'Subject always to the requirements of section 7(3) of this Act, it shall be the general duty of the Executive to exercise and perform their functions, in accordance with principles from time to time laid down or approved by the Council, in such manner as, in conjunction with the Railways Board and the Bus Company, and with due regard to efficiency, economy and safety of operation, to provide or secure the provision of such public passenger transport services as best meet the needs for the time being of Greater London.'

Section 6 lists the numerous powers of the LTE, including certain purely commercial activities which are to be carried on as if the LTE was 'a company engaged in a commercial enterprise'. However, it is unnecessary to elaborate on this phrase for present purposes, since it is clear from the decision in *Bromley*, again to put it broadly for the moment, that the LTE must act generally in accordance with ordinary business principles, though obviously bearing in mind that, in the nature of things, and having regard to the interests of the community as a whole, it cannot on any view wind up its operations and disappear from the scene. I will have to return to this aspect later in this judgment.

Section 7, dealing with the financial duty of the LTE, requires to be set out largely in full since it is crucial for present purposes:

'*Financial duty of Executive.*—(1) In respect of each accounting period of the Executive, the Executive shall charge to revenue account, and secure that any subsidiary of theirs so charges, all charges which are proper to be made to revenue account, including, in particular, proper provision for the depreciation or renewal of assets. a

(2) Without prejudice to the power of the Executive to establish specific reserves, they shall establish and maintain a general reserve, and the Council may give to the Executive directions as to any matter relating to the establishment or management of that general reserve, or the carrying of sums to the credit thereof, or the application thereof; but no part of the moneys comprised in that general reserve shall be applied otherwise than for purposes of the Executive or a subsidiary of b
theirs.

(3) The Executive shall so perform their functions as to ensure so far as practicable—(*a*) that at the end of each such period as may from time to time be agreed for the purpose of this paragraph between the Executive and the Council the aggregate of the net balance of the consolidated revenue account of the Executive and any subsidiaries of theirs and the net balance of the general reserve of the c
Executive is such (not being a deficit) as may be approved by the Council with respect to that period, and (*b*) that, if at the end of any accounting period of the Executive the said aggregate shows a deficit, the amount properly available to meet charges to revenue account of the Executive and their subsidiaries in the next following accounting period of the Executive exceeds those charges by at least the amount of that deficit . . . d

(6) The Council, in exercising or performing their functions under this Act, shall have regard—(*a*) to the duty imposed on the Executive by subsection (3) of this section; and where the requirements of paragraph (*b*) of the said subsection (3) fall to be complied with by the Executive, the Council shall take such action in the exercise and performance of their functions under this Act as appears to the Council to be necessary and appropriate in order to enable the Executive to comply with e
those requirements . . .'

Finally, it is necessary to set out a good deal of s 11:

'(1) In addition to any power of the Council under any other provision of this Act to give directions to the Executive as respects any matter, the Council may give to the Executive general directions as to the exercise and performance by the Executive f
of their functions . . . in relation to matters appearing to the Council to affect the policies and measures which it is the duty of the Council under section 1 of this Act to develop, organise or carry out . . .

(2) Without prejudice to any requirement as to the approval or consent of the Council in any other provision contained in or applied by this Act, the Executive shall submit to the Council and obtain the Council's approval of . . . (*d*) the general g
level and structure of the fares to be charged for the time being for the carriage of passengers by the Executive or any subsidiary of theirs on railway services [ie including the Underground] or London bus services . . .

(3) . . . the Council may direct the Executive to submit proposals for an alteration in the Executive's fare arrangements to achieve any object of general policy specified by the Council in the direction . . .' h

These are the main provisions of the 1969 Act which fall to be considered on this application in the light of the decision in *Bromley*.

The duty of local and other authorities in exercising discretionary powers and the role of the courts

It is necessary to refer to this aspect at the outset, since it was crucial to the decision in j
the *Bromley* case concerning the Fares Fair proposals. It is also necessary to do so because the basis of that decision was widely misunderstood and indeed misrepresented. Briefly, the position is as follows. Authorities invested with discretionary powers by an Act of Parliament can only exercise such powers within the limits of the particular statute. So long as they do not transgress their statutory powers, their decisions are entirely a matter for them, and, in the case of local authorities, for the majority of the elected representatives; subject however, to one important proviso. This is, again to put it

broadly, that they must not exercise their powers arbitrarily or so unreasonably that the exercise of the discretion is clearly unjustifiable. This is an imperfect and generalised paraphrase of the well-known statement of Lord Greene MR in *Associated Picture Houses Ltd v Wednesbury Corp* [1947] 2 All ER 680 at 682, [1948] 1 KB 223 at 229, which has come to be known as the *Wednesbury* principle and applied in countless cases.

If an authority misdirects itself in law, or acts arbitrarily on the basis of considerations which lie outside its statutory powers, or so unreasonably that its decisions cannot be justified by any objective standard of reasonableness, then it is the duty and function of the courts to pronounce that such decisions are invalid when these are challenged by anyone aggrieved by them and who has the necessary locus standi to do so. This was the position of the London borough of Bromley against the background of the 1969 Act in relation to the proposals labelled Fares Fair.

The interpretation of the intention of Parliament as expressed in our statutes is a matter for the courts. Once the meaning of an Act of Parliament has been authoritatively interpreted, at any rate by the House of Lords at a judicial sitting as our highest tribunal, that interpretation is the law, unless and until it is thereafter changed by Parliament. Thus, in the present case the basic law is the 1969 Act, but, to the extent that it has been interpreted by the House of Lords in the *Bromley* case in a manner which governs the present issue, that interpretation is the law of the land for present purposes. This does not involve any substitution of the views of the judges on questions of policy or discretion for those of the authority concerned, but merely the interpretation of the will of Parliament as expressed in its enactments. Thereafter any change in the law from its definition by the courts again devolves to Parliament alone. Thus, we were informed in the present case that a Transport Bill is presently under consideration by Parliament which may fundamentally affect the issues raised by s 7 of the 1969 Act and the decision in *Bromley*. But on the present application we are in no way concerned with any change in the law which may be enacted hereafter.

In relation to the present issue there is also another important aspect which must be borne in mind. When it comes to the proper exercise of powers concerning services such as public transport, which fall to be financed partly out of self-generated revenue (ie fares and other ancillary income such as advertising) and usually as to the balance by funds provided by the local ratepayers, the foregoing principles have a further particular application. This is that the local authority may not strike an unfair balance between passengers and ratepayers. Subject to the true construction of the 1969 Act, as interpreted in the *Bromley* case and discussed hereafter, the place where this balance is to be struck is a matter for the discretion of the GLC as the authority charged with the implementation of the Act. But, if the balance is arbitrary or clearly unfair, then it will be invalid under the *Wednesbury* principle, and indeed ultra vires, and it will then be the duty of the courts so to hold. An important illustration of this principle was the decision of the Court of Appeal in *Prescott v Birmingham Corp* [1954] 3 All ER 698, [1955] Ch 210, which was unanimously affirmed by the House of Lords in *Bromley*. In times before the introduction by Parliament of cheap or free travel for old people, the corporation introduced a scheme of free travel for them. This was held to be invalid because it favoured one section of the community at the expense of the rest. Having rejected an argument to the effect that the corporation could have financed its transport undertaking entirely out of the rates Jenkins LJ, giving the judgment of the court, said in a crucial passage ([1954] 3 All ER 698 at 706–707, [1955] Ch 210 at 236):

> 'We think it is clearly implicit in the legislation, that while it was left to the defendants to decide what fares should be charged within any prescribed statutory maxima for the time being in force the undertaking was to be run as a business venture, or, in other words, that fares fixed by the defendants at their discretion, in accordance with ordinary business principles, were to be charged. That is not to say that in operating their transport undertaking the defendants should be guided by considerations of profit to the exclusion of all other considerations. They should, no doubt, aim at providing an efficient service of omnibuses at reasonable cost, and it may be that this objective is impossible of attainment without some degree of loss.

But it by no means follows that they should go out of their way to make losses by giving away rights of free travel.' a

In the *Bromley* case both the Court of Appeal and the House of Lords clearly decided that the same principles apply to the true construction of the 1969 Act, and I will have to refer hereafter to what was held in this context.

The main issue for present purposes, however, is to what extent the discretionary powers of the GLC and of the LTE may be fettered, more specifically having regard to the correct interpretation of the 1969 Act in the light of that decision. b

The history of events and the factual background

In 1980 the LTE was running at a deficit of about £136m. In November 1980 it submitted to the GLC a budget designed to achieve a break-even by a possible increase in fare revenue, increased productivity, and an assumed GLC grant of £80m. I take the latter facts from the speech of Lord Wilberforce in *Bromley* [1982] 1 All ER 129 at 158, c
[1982] 2 WLR 62 at 98 where he went on to say:

'Its budget contains a careful review of the measures taken, by way of economy and better fare collection, to keep the deficit down as far as practicable. Obviously this was not the only possible budget at the time, but in its preparation and structure it represents a serious attempt to comply with the Act.' d

However, this budget never came into force. The local elections in 1981 resulted in a narrow Labour majority on the GLC and, almost within a matter of days, without consultation and apparently without legal advice, a decision was made that the whole level of fares was to be radically changed as a matter of political policy.

In October 1981 fares were cut by 25% on average and the burden on the ratepayers was doubled. This was done on the basis of one of the statements in the election manifesto e
and, as was unanimously held by the Court of Appeal and the House of Lords in the *Bromley* case, without any regard to the powers of the GLC under the 1969 Act and arbitrarily, without any regard to the interests of ratepayers but solely in the interests of passengers. (Of course these overlap in many cases, as they do for two of the three members of this court.) Watkins LJ described Fares Fair in his judgment as a 'hasty, ill-considered, unlawful and arbitrary use of power' (see [1982] 1 All ER 129 at 149, [1982] f
2 WLR 62 at 87).

This exercise of the GLC's discretionary powers was accordingly set aside as clearly unlawful. There is no need to discuss it further other than to mention that the basis of the unanimous decision of the three members of the Court of Appeal and of the five members of the Appellate Committee of the House of Lords was widely misunderstood, and, in many cases, obviously misrepresented. Some of the public comments gave the g
misleading impression that Lord Denning MR was sitting alone in the Court of Appeal (where each member of the court gave a full judgment), and that the judgments at both levels were designed to thwart the wishes of the majority on the GLC for political motives. Such reactions, whether based on ignorance or whatever, can only be described as total rubbish. If the GLC succeeds in the present application it would be equally ignorant, or deliberately misleading, if the cry were to be, 'Judges slash fares,' or, h
unfortunately more likely, 'Judges increase rates.' It is to be hoped that nothing like that will happen again.

However, it took about six months from the implementation of Fares Fair before the *Bromley* case was decided in the House of Lords and the implications of the decision could be fully assessed and dealt with on the basis of a new policy. Meanwhile the resulting deficit was increasing hugely. Accordingly, following the decision which declared Fares j
Fair to be invalid, and on the basis of legal advice as to its implications, the GLC decided in March 1982 to increase fares by just under 100% across the board. The legality of that decision was subsequently challenged in a letter from the London borough of Camden, but there have been no proceedings. This remains the position today, when fares have reached record levels.

The issue is now where the balance between fare levels and rate support should be
a struck in the medium-term future. The so-called 'balanced plan' put forward by the GLC strikes this balance at one point, whereas a draft budget presented by the LTE, as mentioned below, although welcoming the 'balanced plan' in principle strikes the balance at another point. The reason is that the LTE has been advised that the 'balanced plan' is ultra vires the 1969 Act as interpreted by the House of Lords in *Bromley*.

It is necessary to explain briefly the descriptions 'balanced plan' or 'option II' which
b have been given to the GLC's present proposals. During 1982, after the average level of fares was virtually doubled in March, a number of proposals were considered by the GLC under different labels, as mentioned later and embodied in a 'draft medium-term plan'. This was designed to arrive at a conclusion how the GLC should properly discharge its functions under the 1969 Act in the foreseeable future, having regard to the decision in *Bromley* and the possible different interpretations of it.

c After full consultation, two options were presented by the GLC to the LTE. 'Option I' would have involved a reduction in fare revenue of £95m below present levels, whereas 'option II' involves a reduction of £100m. As between the two, the LTE preferred 'option II' and submitted a proposal to this effect on 11 November 1982. The GLC agreed to this choice, but on condition that the LTE would find means of cutting expenditure by the difference of £5m, and the LTE has evidently agreed to endeavour to do so. Accordingly,
d the 'balanced plan' now incorporates 'option II'. On 15 December 1982 the GLC thereupon gave a direction to the LTE under s 11 of the 1969 Act to implement the 'balanced plan' on this basis, having adopted a resolution to this effect on 14 December 1982. However, the LTE felt obliged to decline to comply with this direction because, on the basis of the legal advice which it had received as to the effect of the decision in *Bromley*, it considered that the direction was unlawful. Instead, it has presented its own
e draft budget for 1983, with a different 'policy mix' which involves higher fare levels and lower grant support than the 'balanced plan'. The budget envisages keeping fares at their present levels, without increasing them with inflation, and the cost figures allow for lower bus services, marginally lower Underground services and higher unit costs. In the view of the GLC, however, the draft budget is unduly restrictive on the basis of the legal advice which the GLC has now received and the GLC is accordingly maintaining its
f direction to the LTE. The issue on this application is, therefore, whether or not the GLC is entitled to a declaration against the LTE to the effect that its direction to the LTE to implement the 'balanced plan' and 'option II' is lawful.

The first point to be mentioned in this connection is that it is quite clear, and in no way disputed, that the 'balanced plan' is a totally different exercise from the arbitrary decision in 1981 to introduce Fares Fair. It derives from a 'draft medium-term plan'
g which was carefully researched and subjected to full consultation, as required by s 2(2) of the 1969 Act. The decision in favour of the 'balanced plan' was made in October 1982 and the plan was then circulated to, inter alia, all other local authorities in Greater London. We understand that some comments on it have been received, and in principle it remains open to challenge as mentioned hereafter. To the extent to which the GLC has been advised that the law so permits, its proposals are claimed to represent an appropriate
h strategic policy for transport within and around Greater London which takes account of the Greater London development plan and traffic congestion and amenities generally. However, for the reasons mentioned hereafter, whether this is so or not, whether the balance has been struck at the best point, or even at a permissible point, is not a matter which this court can evaluate or which it is any part of our function to assess in any way. But, subject to the question of its legality under the 1969 Act, which is the issue in
j dispute, its evaluation by the LTE has been expressed as follows:

> 'The Executive believes that this is a unique opportunity to introduce a radical restructuring of the fare structure as a major plank in a programme to generate extra use of the system and to retain existing markets. This approach would offer major advantages in transport terms and constitute a significant step towards the development of a more integrated and efficient public transport system for London.'

The second matter is that the 'balanced plan' has been evolved as one of a range of possible options under different labels following the *Bromley* decision. It is far from being the option which is preferred by the majority of the members of the GLC, but has been evolved as a matter of reluctant compromise in the light of the legal advice received by the GLC. The 'balanced plan' was adopted by resolution of the GLC on the basis of full and detailed legal advice. All of this material has been exhibited by the GLC in the evidence before us, covering many hundreds of pages.

I must briefly refer to the range of options which were considered in the 'draft medium-term plan' and which have now led to the adoption of the compromise of the 'balanced plan'. Taking Fares Fair at one extreme, the options considered by the GLC fall under the headings of 'minimum needs', 'restrained needs', then the 'balanced plan', the 'cash limits' (which is evidently the preferred option of the Secretary of State for Transport), and finally 'break even' which would lead to the highest level of fares with no revenue support at all. However, no one now contends that the 'break even' option, which would make London Transport entirely self-supporting, is either practicable or the correct answer in law. This could only be achieved by cutting down the present services to an 'inner core' and would effectively destroy the transport system for Greater London as we know it, which everyone agrees would be clearly unacceptable from the point of view of the community as a whole and in no way required under the 1969 Act or the decision in *Bromley*.

I will give a few comparative figures with which we were supplied on which both parties were agreed. However, it is also agreed that these cannot be taken at face value, because they clearly cannot in themselves reflect the 'policy mix' for the overall strategic structure of transport in and around Greater London, and the capital investment and operational details, which are involved in the different alternatives. Accordingly, the figures merely serve as a broad indication in terms of money.

First, looking at the position historically and then in terms of the LTE's draft budget and the 'balanced plan', there emerges the following picture on the basis of the price levels ruling in October 1981 (thus in cash terms ignoring inflation), before Fares Fair was introduced and taking fare levels at the figure of 100 for October 1981:

Full year effect at various times	Fare levels (October 1981 = 100)	Fares and other income	Grant support
(1) Immediately before Fares Fair	100	465	136
(2) Fares Fair, October 1981	68	350	259
(3) Fares doubled (March 1981 following the decision in *Bromley*)	133	545	57
(4) The LTE's draft 1983 budget	133	540	111
(5) Immediately before 'balanced plan' (April 1983)	133	540	100
(6) The GLC's 'balanced plan' (April 1983)	100	440	210

I also set out, for the purpose of broad comparison, an agreed projection to 1987, again using October 1981 prices, of the middle of the range of options mentioned above, ie ignoring Fares Fair 'minimum needs' and 'restrained needs' at one end of the spectrum, and 'break even' at the other. In this connection I must briefly refer to the 'cash limits' option which is evidently favoured by the government. On the basis of the summary of it in the evidence before us, it differs from the LTE's draft budget by increasing fares in line with inflation. Bus and train mileage would be cut in comparison with the other proposals and there would be about ten station closures. It would also involve a lower level of grant support than the LTE's 1981 budget, which Lord Wilberforce had regarded as 'a serious attempt to comply with the Act' in the passage which I have already quoted.

Turning then to the 1987 figures, the same index figure for fare levels as at October 1981 has been taken. All the figures relate to 1987 (though the LTE's draft budget has necessarily been included on an estimated basis, since it does extend to 1987) and have been multiplied by a factor of 0·94 to bring them back to 1981 prices:

	Fare levels (October 1981 = 100)	Fares and other income (ignoring OAP subsidy) £m	Costs £m	Grant support £m
'Cash limits' option	128	466	554	32
The LTE's draft budget	120	442	572	76
The GLC's 'balanced plan'	90	370	573	158

What emerges from these figures at a glance is that both parties before us have been advised (and are acting on advice which we have seen, since its consideration by them is highly relevant under the *Wednesbury* principle and the decision in *Prescott v Birmingham Corp*, to which I have already referred) that their discretionary powers under the 1969 Act do not require them to strike the balance between passengers and ratepayers at the point of the 'cash limits' option, although the LTE's proposals lie much closer to this than to the GLC's 'balanced plan'. The difference between these three options is therefore one of degree, but nevertheless a very considerable difference. In view of the respective contentions of the GLC and the LTE, the argument before us has therefore not involved any consideration of the 'cash limits' option as being one which is mandatory under the 1969 Act and the decision in the *Bromley* case, although, on the basis of the conclusion which we have reached, this would in no way be mandatory. We have only had occasion to consider the differences of view on the legal position as between the GLC and the LTE. These ultimately turn on the true construction and effect of s 7(3) and (6) of the 1969 Act in the context of that Act as a whole and in the light of the decision of the House of Lords in *Bromley*. If one were to refine the difference even further, one might say that in the final analysis it turns on the words 'so far as practicable' in s 7(3).

Before attempting to set out the parties' respective contentions in this regard, it is necessary to emphasise two points.

First, unlike the *Bromley* case, the interests of the ratepayers have not, as such, been represented before the court. We have only heard the arguments as between the GLC and the LTE, which both claim to have given due regard to the ratepayers, though they are widely apart in terms of money. It is therefore common ground that the order which we will ultimately make in the form of a declaration has only been reached on this basis and we have heard no argument, nor have we considered, to what extent it may bind anyone other than the parties before us.

Second, it has been expressly conceded before us that both the view of the GLC and that of the LTE as to the point at which the balance should be struck remains open to challenge, at any rate in theory, by reference to the broad *Wednesbury* principle. All that we can say on this aspect is that both parties before us are in agreement, that the proposals of neither of them infringe that principle, and that nothing has emerged in the evidence and argument presented to us which has led us to think the contrary. Both the GLC's 'balanced plan' and the LTE's draft budget clearly appear to have been carefully considered by reference to the relevant factors and, needless to say, neither is in the least arbitrary, nor obviously unfair or unreasonable, in the way in which Fares Fair was unanimously held to be in the *Bromley* case. However, all that we can do on this application is to decide between the respective contentions of the parties on the limited basis of the 1969 Act and its interpretation in *Bromley*. This is the reason why the wording of the declarations, which I set out at the end of this judgment, has been framed by reference to the true construction of the Act and not on any wider basis.

The contentions of the parties

On behalf of the GLC the submission made by counsel can broadly be summarised as follows.

(i) The references in *Prescott* and *Bromley* to the requirement that a transport system must be conducted on business principles were primarily intended to exclude philanthropic considerations and to emphasise the need for the proper and cost-effective use of resources. This does not mean, in the context of a public transport system, that fare revenue requires to be maximised on ordinary business principles of profit and loss. There is also no overriding obligation to avoid losses if such avoidance would have the effect, in the context of s 1 of the 1969 Act, that the system will, in the reasonable view of the GLC, cease to be 'integrated, efficient and economic', the latter word meaning 'cost-effective'. The interpretation of the Act and of *Bromley* are consistent with the making of continuous losses when such losses are the minimum losses necessary to maintain an integrated, efficient and economic (cost-effective) system. However, within these parameters, due regard must equally be had by the GLC to the obligation of the LTE under s 7(3) to break even in successive accounting periods 'so far as practicable'. To that extent the GLC is restricted by s 7(6), and also in securing the achievement by the LTE of the objectives in s 5(1) 'to provide or secure the provision of such public passenger transport services as best meet the needs for the time being of Greater London'.

(ii) However, while due regard must be had to all the foregoing matters, there is also an overall strategic function which is imposed on the GLC by s 1 of the Act, to which equal regard must be given, 'to develop policies, and to encourage, organise and, where appropriate, carry out measures, which will promote the provision of integrated, efficient and economic transport facilities and services for Greater London'. These cover a considerably wider range of responsibilities (as I have already indicated earlier in this judgment) than those of the LTE under the direction of the GLC pursuant to Part II of the Act, since the LTE is only concerned with public passenger transport services. Although the LTE's duties under s 5(1) are clearly and expressly subject to s 7(3), as are the GLC's duties and powers under ss 7(6) and 11, s 1 in Part I of the Act is not subject to these restrictions in Part II. What the GLC must do is to strike a strategic balance which takes proper account of all these factors.

(iii) There is nothing in the Act, nor in its interpretation in the *Bromley* case, which leads to any different conclusion. The ratio of the decision of the House of Lords in *Bromley* can be summarised as follows. Although the GLC has power under the Act to make grants in aid of past and prospective revenue deficits in order to permit the LTE to discharge its duty to break even so far as practicable in consecutive accounting periods, it is beyond the powers of the GLC to do so in aid of a policy of generalised low fares which was not intended to further any statutory purpose, and which ignored the LTE's duty to operate on business lines and the GLC's own fiduciary duty to the general body of ratepayers. In this connection it was also clearly impermissible simply to follow the election manifesto. On the other hand, the case did not decide whether or not a statutory policy under s 1 of the Act, and the promulgation of a plan for such policy under s 2, could justify the acceptance of losses or increased losses; nor did the case decide what is meant by 'so far as practicable' in s 7(3). Finally, although this was not decided expressly, there are strong indications in the speeches in the House of Lords that, if the promotion of an 'integrated, efficient and economic' (cost-effective) transport system under s 1 inevitably involves increased losses, then such promotion would nevertheless be a lawful exercise of the GLC's powers, provided that this is not done without proper regard to the fact that ss 5(1) and 7(6) are subordinated to s 7(3).

On behalf of the LTE the submissions of counsel can be summarised as follows (indeed I am stating them almost verbatim).

(i) The duty in s 7(3) to 'break even' so far as practicable is a paramount duty for the LTE and is also 'a primary consideration' for the GLC. The policies of the GLC, in their formulation and implementation, must be consistent with such duty.

(ii) Such duty requires the LTE to assess the highest practicable level of fares, while discharging its duties to meet transport needs under s 5(1). However, the former duty need not 'expunge' the latter duties; thus, there is no requirement to go so far as to reduce the level of the present transport services substantially in quality or frequency, let alone to reduce them to a mere 'inner core', as I have already mentioned.

(iii) Accordingly, the question of grant support out of rates can only arise after, and as an unavoidable result of, compliance with (ii) above; it may not be planned for as part of a transport policy.

(iv) The ratio of the decision in *Bromley* can be summarised as follows. (a) Both the LTE and the GLC are under a duty to conduct London Transport on business principles. (b) Grants may be made by the GLC to the LTE in aid of present and prospective deficits which are unavoidable. (c) However, such grants cannot be made unless and until the fares have been, or are to be, set at the maximum practicable level. (d) The powers of the GLC, including the powers of direction under s 11, cannot be used inconsistently with such duties. (e) It is the function of the LTE, as the operator of the transport system, to decide at what point fares are at the 'maximum practicable level'. This has been done in the LTE's draft budget, but not in the GLC's 'balanced plan'. Accordingly the 'balanced plan' is ultra vires the 1969 Act.

My conclusions

I am in broad agreement with all of counsel for the GLC's submissions, but on examining those of counsel for the LTE, which appear to me to have been framed with great care and very succinctly, it seems to me that they do not present any tenable analysis of the 1969 Act or of the ratio of the decision in *Bromley* which can be set against those of counsel for the GLC. I have also had the advantage of reading in advance the judgments about to be delivered by Glidewell and Nolan JJ and broadly also agree with their reasons for reaching the same conclusion, although there may well be nuances of difference between us in approach and as to the best way of analysing some of the passages in the speeches of the House of Lords in *Bromley*. I will therefore only make further observations on points which appear to me of particular importance.

(1) The general and primary duty of the GLC is clearly that stated in s 1 of the Act. In my view this section, and Part I of the Act as a whole, apply to 'transport' in and around Greater London in the wide sense of all aspects of transport comprised within the Act, ie in particular not only Part II but also Parts IV and V. Although Lord Diplock was clearly of the contrary view (see [1982] 1 All ER 129 at 159, [1982] 2 WLR 62 at 100), I do not think that this was the view of the majority. On the contrary, I think that this is in line with the views of Oliver LJ in the Court of Appeal (see [1982] 1 All ER 129 at 141, [1982] 2 WLR 62 at 77) and that none of the speeches in the House of Lords expressly or impliedly dissented from this passage. Accordingly, the GLC's power under s 3(1)(*a*) to make grants to the LTE 'for any purpose', includes power to make grants designed to further the GLC's overall strategy pursuant to s 1.

The words 'for any purpose' are of course confined to purposes which are consistent with the GLC's functions under the Act as a whole and must not be abused so as to infringe the principles of *Wednesbury* and *Prescott*. That was the case in relation to the GLC's Fares Fair policy, but neither party before us had suggested (in my view prima facie clearly rightly) that any similar criticism can be made of any of the proposals which arise for consideration in the context of the present proceedings.

(2) Sections 5(1) and 7(6) are expressly subject to s 7(3). The achievement by the LTE, under the direction or guidance of the GLC, of the objectives in s 5(1), and the GLC's duties and powers under s 7(6), are therefore clearly constrained to this extent. But in this connection it must be borne in mind that s 7(3) is itself qualified by the words 'so far as practicable'.

(3) It is clear that the majority of the House of Lords in *Bromley* (with only Lord Brandon dissenting) have held that the LTE's budgeting duties under s 7(3) may properly take into account any grants which the GLC may be willing to make and that such grants may cover prospective deficits as well as past deficits. This, as it seems to me, is the giant step inherent in *Bromley* which goes a long way towards compelling a conclusion in favour of the GLC's contentions. Once this step has been taken, and having regard to my conclusion in (1) above, one is really only left with the words 'so far as practicable'. The flexibility inherent in these words does not appear to me to exclude consideration of the GLC's overall strategic functions under Part I of the Act, with the result that grants made

in part for Part I purposes are not necessarily to be excluded. An example of this, which
was repeatedly given by counsel for the GLC, would be the determination of the proper *a*
level of fares not only in the context of s 7(3) and its restriction on the LTE's functions
under s 5(1), but also bearing in mind the desirability of getting people to use public
transport so as to relieve congestion on the roads, which falls within the ambit of s 1
rather than of s 5(1).

(4) Once one has reached this point, the whole matter comes down to a proper
balancing exercise as indicated in submissions (i) and (ii) of counsel for the GLC. On this *b*
basis, while the powers of the LTE, viewed in isolation, are undoubtedly more limited,
the powers of the GLC under the 1969 Act are not effectively, or at any rate substantially,
narrower than is inherent in the obligation to comply with the principles laid down in
Wednesbury and, in particular, *Prescott* in the present context. These, however, admit of
the possibility of continuing losses: see in particular per Lord Keith ([1982] 1 All ER 129
at 168, [1982] 2 WLR 62 at 111). *c*

(5) I think that all analysis of any of the judgments and speeches in *Bromley* for the
purposes of the present case must proceed with the greatest caution. One must always
bear in mind that every word and phrase was formulated against a wholly different
background, ie the policy inherent in Fares Fair, the manner in which this was
introduced, and all the derogatory adjectives in the sense of *Wednesbury* and *Prescott*
which were applicable to it. I feel the greatest reluctance in having to extract an *d*
authoritative interpretation of a statute from judgments dealing with the statute in
another context: see eg *University College, Oxford v Durdy* [1982] 1 All ER 1108, [1982]
Ch 413, although on that aspect I was in a minority in that case. Thus, in the instant case
I have had great difficulty in making up my mind what the effect of Lord Scarman's
speech should be taken to be for the purposes of the present proceedings. I feel reasonably
confident that he took what I have described as the giant step in (3) above, but he was *e*
nevertheless explicitly strict in his analysis of s 7(3) (see [1982] 1 All ER 129 at 173, 176–
177, [1982] 2 WLR 62 at 118, 122–123). However, all the references to 'transport need'
in the latter passages appear to derive from his introduction, where 'transport need' is
clearly adopted as a phrase designed to indicate the performance of duties in favour of
passengers to the exclusion of those concerning ratepayers (see [1982] 1 All ER 129 at
170, [1982] 2 WLR 62 at 114). For this reason, and because none of the other speeches *f*
(apart from Lord Brandon's) compel the contrary conclusion, and indeed Oliver LJ
supports this view (see [1982] 1 All ER 129 at 141, [1982] 2 WLR 62 at 77), I reach the
conclusion which is summed up in (4) above, subject only to considering whether the
submissions of counsel for the LTE compel the contrary.

(6) As already indicated in (1) above, I feel considerable difficulty about the submissions
of counsel for the LTE and I will mention some of the main points in this connection. *g*

(a) His formulation in (i) of his submissions appears to shrink, in my view rightly,
from treating the duty in s 7(3) to 'break even' as equally 'paramount' for the GLC as it is
for the LTE; as regards the GLC he only submits that it is 'a primary consideration',
which approaches a balancing exercise such as I have indicated.

(b) What standard determines 'the highest practicable level of fares' in (ii) and 'the
maximum practicable level of fares' in (iv)(d) and (e) of his submissions? Thus, it appears *h*
from para 47 of the affidavit of Mr Stonefrost, the Comptroller of Finance to the GLC,
that both the GLC and the LTE are in agreement that the level of fares proposed by the
GLC is 'the highest practicable if the policies in the medium term plan, and in particular
its provisions in relation to integration of services, were to be achieved'. Why is the LTE's
highest or maximum practicable level determinative?

(c) Counsel for the LTE also shrank from submitting, in my view again rightly, that *j*
whatever may at any particular time be the level of fares or the level of deficit is in any
way sacrosanct in the sense that fares may not be reduced or the deficit increased. Thus, I
put to him in particular the question whether he submitted that the test was that, once
the LTE was 'in the red' at the end of an accounting period under s 7(3)(*a*), so that sub-s
(3)(*b*) and the latter part of sub-s (6) come into operation, the budget for the following

accounting period could never go 'into the red' to a greater extent. However, he was
a evidently not prepared to go as far as this. In this connection it should be mentioned for the record, although it does not affect the true construction of the 1969 Act, that at the end of the present accounting period there is in fact no deficit, although a small one had been anticipated. At the present moment, accordingly, sub-s (3)(*b*) and the latter part of sub-s (6) do not appear to be applicable.

(d) On the other hand, the submissions of counsel for the LTE appeared to imply that,
b if at any time there is a deficit, then the quality and frequency of public transport services *must* remain static, or *must* be reduced below the then existing level, until the deficit has been eliminated or at any rate reduced. In my view this would go too far as a mandatory part of any balancing exercise.

(e) Finally, counsel for the LTE appeared to regard *any* budget for the future which is bound to result in a deficit, let alone an increased deficit, as something analogous to what
c Lord Scarman described as a 'policy . . . to accept loss-making as an object of transport policy' or so as to 'erect grant financing of deficit into an object of policy' (see [1982] 1 All ER 129 at 176, 177, [1982] 2 WLR 62 at 121, 123). This was held to be so in *Bromley* in relation to Fares Fair, and Lord Scarman was of course speaking in that context. But in my view this is clearly not so in the case of the 'balanced plan'.

d *The order*

I have already explained that the declarations which we can properly make on this application must in my view be limited by reference to the construction of the 1969 Act and not on any wider basis, and this was accepted by both parties. An agreed formulation was placed before us for this purpose, but the latter part of this should in my view be slightly modified for the same reason. On this basis I consider that the GLC is entitled to
e the following declarations: on the true construction of the Transport (London) Act 1969, and without otherwise making any declaration as to the lawfulness of the matters hereinafter referred to, (i) the proposal described as option II in the LTE's submission to the GLC of 11 November 1982 and the decision of the GLC on 14 December 1982 in relation thereto were within the legal powers of the LTE and the GLC respectively; (ii) it would be within the powers of the LTE under the 1969 Act to implement the direction
f given to the LTE on 15 December 1982 following and in accordance with the resolution so to direct of the GLC of 14 December 1982.

GLIDEWELL J. I agree with Kerr LJ's reasoning and that we should grant declarations in the form he proposes. I shall, however, set out my own approach to the issues before
g us, both because of the importance which the parties attach to the matter and out of deference to the clear and careful arguments which have been addressed to us.

By a letter dated 7 October 1982 the Greater London Council (the GLC) requested the London Transport Executive (the LTE) to 'submit to the Council and obtain the Council's approval of . . . (d) the general level and structure of the fares to be charged for the time being for the carriage of passengers by the Executive . . .' under s 11(2) of the Transport
h (London) Act 1969. By its submissions of 11 November 1982 the LTE complied with that request.

If it had declined to do so, the GLC would no doubt have issued a direction under s 11(3), but this was not necessary. The direction issued by the GLC on 15 December 1982, which is the subject of these proceedings, was therefore a direction under s 11(1), under which—

j 'the Council may give to the Executive general directions as to the exercise and performance by the Executive of their functions . . . in relation to matters appearing to the Council to affect the policies and measures which it is the duty of the Council under section 1 of this Act to develop, organise or carry out.'

By s 45(1) of the Act 'functions' includes powers, duties and obligations. It follows that, in exercising the power under s 11(1) to give a direction, the GLC was obliged by s 7(6) to have regard to the duty imposed on the LTE by s 7(3). The LTE's general duties are to be found set out in s 5 of the Act, which starts, '(1) Subject always to the requirements of section 7(3) of this Act . . .'

It follows, therefore, from the wording of the statute that consideration of the question whether the direction given by the GLC was within the powers of the Act requires attention to be given to ss 1, 5(1), 7(3) and 7(6) of the Act. It also follows that, in exercising their power under s 3 to make to the LTE any grant which may be necessitated by the direction, the GLC is again subject to the requirement of s 7(6). Our decision obliges us to consider the meaning to be given to, and the interaction of, the sections of the Act to which I have referred and which Kerr LJ has set out in his judgment.

We must, of course, interpret the relevant provisions of the 1969 Act in the light of the speeches in the House of Lords in *Bromley London Borough Council v Greater London Council* [1982] 1 All ER 129, [1982] 2 WLR 62. However, although their Lordships were all agreed that the resolution of the GLC which was then in issue was outside the powers of the 1969 Act, they did not all reach that conclusion by the same route or, if they did, they described it in different words.

In order to ascertain what I conceive to be the ratio decidendi of the *Bromley* case I have sought to analyse shortly the reasoning in each of the speeches (despite Kerr LJ's cautionary words about such an analysis). Lord Wilberforce said ([1982] 1 All ER 129 at 154–155, [1982] 2 WLR 62 at 94):

> 'Section 3 gives the GLC power to make grants to the LTE "for any purpose" and no doubt these words are wide enough to cover grants to revenue as well as for capital purposes. The section cannot, however, be read in isolation, and it is necessary to examine the rest of the Act in order to ascertain the framework in which this power is exercisable. Its extent and the manner in which it is to be exercised must be controlled by the fact that the GLC owes a duty to two different classes. First, under its responsibility for meeting the needs of Greater London, it must provide for transport users: these include not only the residents of London, but persons travelling to and in London from outside (eg commuters) and tourists. Most of these will not pay rates to the GLC. Second, it owes a duty of a fiduciary character to its ratepayers who have to provide the money. These, it is said, represent 40% only of the electorate and probably a smaller proportion of the travelling public; they would themselves, most likely, also be travellers. Most of the rates (62%) have to be found from commercial ratepayers. For the extent of this fiduciary duty see *Prescott v Birmingham Corp* [1954] 3 All ER 698, [1955] Ch 210, a decision which remains valid in principle although free travel for selected categories has since been authorised by statute. These duties must be fairly balanced one against the other . . .'

His opinion of the relevant powers of the GLC and the LTE under the Act is contained in the following passage ([1982] 1 All ER 129 at 157–158, [1982] 2 WLR 62 at 97–98):

> 'In my opinion there are two clear provisions in the Act. The first is in s 7(3)(*b*). This states the obligation of the LTE to make good a deficit in the year following a deficit year. This is an obligation the meeting of which the LTE is to ensure as far as practicable. In my opinion this points to the taking of action which it is in the power of the LTE to take. On the other hand, though I feel less confident about this, particularly since it was not an argument accepted by Oliver LJ, I am willing to accept that, subject to the LTE discharging the responsibilities cast on it, it may make provision in its revenue account for grants in aid of revenue, actual or assumed. The corresponding provision as regards the GLC is s 7(6) which dovetails with s 7(3). This recognises that the duty stated in s 7(3)(*b*) (to make up a deficit in year two) is one which "falls to be complied with by the Executive", and then obliges the GLC in performing its functions to have regard to that duty and take action which will enable the LTE to comply with those requirements. Such actions might

take several forms: the GLC might direct fares to be raised or services to be adjusted. Or the GLC could decide to make a grant. But it can only to that after it has "had regard" to the LTE's duty under s 7(3). The respective statutory obligations of the GLC and the LTE fit in with one another: the LTE must carry out its duty as defined in s 7(3): the GLC cannot exercise its powers unless and until the LTE carries out that duty and must then do so with proper regard to its fiduciary duty to its ratepayers. If these constraints were not to exist, there would be no limit on the power of the GLC to make grants in aid of revenue, since the Act provides for no governmental control. I find it impossible, in the light of the previous history and of the far from definite language used, to accept that Parliament could have intended that this should be so. To say this is not to impose on the LTE a rigid obligation to balance its accounts every year, or, as it was at one time put in argument, to maximise fares. There is flexibility in the words "so far as practicable", and the obligatory establishment of a reserve gives room for manoeuvre (as indeed the LTE accounts from 1970 onwards show). But given this, it appears to me clear that neither the LTE in making its proposals, nor the GLC in accepting them, could have power totally to disregard any responsibility for ensuring, so far as practicable, that outgoings are met by revenue, and that the LTE runs its business on economic lines.'

Thus his opinion was that, if the LTE anticipates a deficit on its revenue account and seeks to avoid it 'so far as practicable', it may make provision in the accounts to remove the deficit by the receipt of a grant from the GLC to add to its income from fares (by the phrase 'income from fares' I mean to include income from all aspects of the LTE's operations). The phrase 'so far as practicable' introduces flexibility. The GLC owes duties to two classes of persons, to transport users and to ratepayers, which must be balanced.

Lord Diplock agreed that 'receipts to be credited to LTE's revenue account may be derived from such grants [ie by the GLC] as well as from income earned by the LTE from the operation of its undertaking . . .' (see [1982] 1 All ER 129 at 163, [1982] 2 WLR 62 at 105). It is clear that the purpose and effect, in his view, of s 7(3) and (6) is to hold the balance equitably between present and future ratepayers, by preventing the LTE from accumulating deficits over the years. Section 7(6) is not a restraint in Lord Diplock's opinion on the power of the GLC to make such a grant. On this point s 7(6) is neutral (see [1982] 1 All ER 129 at 164, [1982] 2 WLR 62 at 106). However, there is a limitation on the exercise of that power in the GLC's fiduciary duty to its ratepayers.

He said ([1982] 1 All ER 129 at 165, [1982] 2 WLR 62 at 108):

'My Lords, the conflicting interests which the GLC had to balance in deciding whether or not to go ahead with the 25% reduction in fares, notwithstanding the loss of grant from central government funds that this would entail, were those of passengers and the ratepayers. It is well established by the authorities to which my noble and learned friend Lord Wilberforce has already referred that a local authority owes a fiduciary duty to the ratepayers from whom it obtains moneys needed to carry out its statutory functions, and that this includes a duty not to expend those moneys thriftlessly but to deploy the full financial resources available to it to the best advantage, the financial resources of the GLC that are relevant to the present appeals being the rate fund obtained by issuing precepts and the grants from central government respectively.'

Lord Keith also agreed that the LTE's revenue account may include a grant from the GLC as a receipt. He said ([1982] 1 All ER 129 at 169, [1982] 2 WLR 62 at 112):

'I would accept that the GLC has power to make grants to the LTE, for revenue purposes, and that these may be made to meet either actual or prospective deficits, and also that such grants may be taken into account in the balancing exercise required by s 7(3)(*b*). But this does not, in my opinion, properly lead to the conclusion that the LTE is empowered, either on its own initiative or as a result of a

suggestion or directive from the GLC, to carry on its undertaking, so far as the fixing of fares is concerned, without due regard to ordinary business principles. In a
the first place, if that were the intention of Parliament, I would have expected, in view of the radical departure from previous principle which would have been involved, a clear indication of such intention, but I can find none. In the second place, acceptance of the argument would reduce the LTE's obligation under s 7(3)(*b*) to a mere bookkeeping exercise. I do not think that can be right, because the subsection is one of the key provisions of the Act, which takes its place in s 5(1) as b
the overriding consideration of the LTE and to which, by virtue of s 7(6), the exercise of the GLC's functions under the Act, and that must mean the whole of such functions, is in a sense subordinated. So far as the concluding words of s 7(6) are concerned, it is to be kept in view that a variety of courses of action in addition to the making of revenue grants (which is not specifically mentioned) appear to be in contemplation as available to the GLC to enable the LTE to comply with s 7(3)(*b*), c
for example directions to raise fares or trim services. Section 11 of the Act contains additional provisions as to control of the LTE by the GLC. There is nothing in these provisions, in my opinion, which is inconsistent with the LTE being required to operate its transport undertaking in accordance with ordinary business principles, or which empowers the GLC to direct the LTE to depart therefrom, whether for the purposes of achieving some object of social policy, or for other reasons.' d

The expression that the exercise of the GLC's functions under the Act is in a sense subordinate to s 7(3) is a reference, in my view, to the requirement in s 7(6) that, in exercising or performing its functions under the Act, the GLC shall have regard to the duty imposed on the LTE by s 7(3).

Lord Keith's reference to 'ordinary business principles' was derived from the judgment e
of Jenkins LJ in *Prescott v Birmingham Corp* [1954] 3 All ER 698, [1955] Ch 210, in a passage which is set out in Lord Keith's speech (see [1982] 1 All ER 129 at 167, [1982] 2 WLR 62 at 109). Kerr LJ has already read it so I will not repeat it. Lord Keith said of that decision (ie *Prescott*) ([1982] 1 All ER 129 at 168, [1982] 2 WLR 61 at 111):

'As was made clear in the passage quoted above from the judgment in *Prescott*'s f
case, a public transport undertaking may be carried on in accordance with ordinary business principles even though it does not and cannot make a profit and some degree of loss may be inevitable, so that if it were a company engaged in a commercial enterprise it would be obliged to close down.'

In his conclusion, Lord Keith said ([1982] 1 All ER 129 at 169, [1982] 2 WLR 62 at 113): g

'I am of opinion, for the reasons I have endeavoured to express, that it was contrary to the LTE's duties under the Act to submit proposals which involved an arbitrary reduction of this nature in the existing general level of fares, which it is not suggested had been fixed otherwise than in accordance with ordinary business principles.' h

I note that the 'existing general level of fares' there referred to, ie those in force before the introduction of Fares Fair, resulted in a disparity on the LTE's revenue account between fare income and expenditure of some £136m per annum, which was made up by a grant from the GLC. It is apparent, therefore, both from the quotation from *Prescott* and from the passages I have quoted, that it was Lord Keith's view that the LTE may j
operate on ordinary business principles while still incurring a substantial loss on fare income alone.

Lord Scarman was also of the opinion that s 7(3) permits a grant from the GLC to be included in the LTE's revenue account. He said ([1982] 1 All ER 129 at 176–177, [1982] 2 WLR 62 at 122–123):

'My Lords, when first I studied the judgment of Oliver LJ, I was persuaded by him that sub-s (3) must be construed as excluding grant from revenue account. I still believe that the construction has great force. But I have been driven to the conclusion that it must be rejected. Nevertheless, that construction, though it must, for the reasons which I shall give, be rejected, captures the spirit of the section. And the spirit is that the LTE must, under the direction of the GLC, conduct its operations so as, so far as practicable, to avoid loss, a spirit which accords well with the fiduciary duty owed by the GLC to the ratepayers. I reject Oliver LJ's construction because, as counsel for the GLC urged and the learned Lord Justice (as I think) recognised, it is inconsistent with "advance budgeting": counsel's phrase to emphasise that s 7(3) imposes a duty of financial planning which may well envisage the possibility, or probability, of loss, on a balance of fares income and expenditure, having to be made good by grant. Subsection (3) does, in my view, envisage financial planning, ie budgeting. Paragraph (*a*) requires the LTE to ensure, so far as practicable, that, at the end of such period as it and the GLC agree (it could be a quinquennium), the aggregate of the balance on revenue account and the balance of the general reserve will be such as to avoid a deficit. There is nothing to suggest that in such planning the LTE should not bring into account any grants which the GLC plans to make during the period under review: and there is nothing in s 3 of the Act (which confers on the GLC its power to make grants) to suggest that grants in support of revenue may be made only to make good deficits which have already arisen. Indeed, it is sensible that in planning ahead the LTE should take account not only of the prospective earnings from its services but also of prospective grant income. I conclude, therefore, that the GLC may make grants to provide not only for past, but for anticipated losses. It follows that the GLC and the LTE are entitled to anticipate a trading loss and to bring into their accounts a grant to offset the resulting deficit.'

In the following passage from his speech Lord Scarman said ([1982] 1 All ER 129 at 177, [1982] 2 WLR 62 at 123):

'The subsection [ie s 7(3)] is, however, capable of another interpretation which is consistent with that duty. This interpretation, which I accept, is that, while permitting advance budgeting, it nevertheless requires the LTE so to provide its services as to ensure, so far as practicable, that deficit is avoided. Though the LTE may be compelled by circumstances to budget for a loss which will have to be made good by grant, the subsection requires it to avoid it, if it can. Its principal weapon is fares income. The subsection, though it envisages budgeting for a deficit, permits it not as an object of social or transport policy, but as a course of action which it may not be practicable or possible to avoid. Loss may be unavoidable: but it does not thereby become an acceptable object of policy . . . To conclude, s 7(3), in my judgment, requires the LTE to follow, so far as practicable, a financial policy of "break-even". Grants in support of revenue from fares are envisaged: but as a necessity, and not as an object of social or transport policy.'

These passages, and thus his speech generally, are capable of two interpretations. A possible interpretation is that s 7(3) and (6) requires the LTE to break even on fare income alone and the GLC not to make any grant, if it is possible so to operate, whatever the consequences for public transport in London. The GLC and the LTE both accept that, if the bus and Underground train services were vastly reduced, in number and frequency, to what is called a 'core system', London Transport could be run at a small profit. But such a reduction would clearly be in direct conflict with the LTE's duty under s 5 'to provide or secure the provision of such public passenger transport services as best meet the needs for the time being of Greater London'.

An alternative interpretation of Lord Scarman's speech is, however, urged on us by counsel for the GLC and is, I believe, accepted by counsel for the LTE. Counsel for the

GLC points out that earlier in his speech Lord Scarman defined the term 'transport need' when he said ([1982] 1 All ER 129 at 170–171, [1982] 2 WLR 62 at 114):

> 'The Act recognises, it is said, not merely a duty owed to the travelling public (transport need) but also a duty owed to the ratepayers (business principles)'.

Lord Scarman then went on to consider the decision in *Prescott*, concluding that it was correctly decided and the decision remains in law. In the course of reaching that conclusion he said ([1982] 1 All ER 129 at 172, [1982] 2 WLR 62 at 116): '... if an efficient operation is impossible of attainment without some degree of loss, it does not follow that the transport authority may "go out of their way" to make losses.'

In a later passage Lord Scarman said ([1982] 1 All ER 129 at 174, [1982] 2 WLR 62 at 119):

> 'The GLC owes not only a duty to the travelling public of Greater London but also a duty to the ratepayers from whose resources any deficit must largely be met. Understandably, the appellants have emphasised the first, and Bromley the second. But they co-exist. Where, therefore, the general duty of the GLC is spelt out in s 1, it is necessary to bear in mind that it breaks down into two duties owed to two different, though overlapping, classes. "Economic" in s 1 must, therefore, be construed widely enough to embrace both duties. Accordingly, I conclude that in s 1(1) of the Act "economic" covers not only the requirement that transport services be "cost-effective" but also the requirement that they be provided so as to avoid or diminish the burden on the ratepayers so far as it is practicable to do so. Section 1(1), therefore, requires the GLC to strike a balance between the interest of the travelling public and the interest of the ratepayers. But, apart from affirming by the use of the word "economic" the existence of the two obligations which I have described, the section gives no further guidance. The section, however, in no way excludes the *Prescott* principle. Indeed, it is drafted in terms which are wholly consistent with its continuance in full force and effect, and I so construe it.'

Counsel for the GLC therefore submits, and I agree, that Lord Scarman was saying that so far as practicable the LTE is required by s 7(3) to break even. If however the proper carrying out of the respective duties of the LTE and the GLC under ss 1 and 5 necessarily results in the LTE incurring a level of overall costs which cannot wholly be met out of fares income, it is then not practicable to break even. Thus, if that situation arises, the GLC may lawfully make a grant to the LTE to cover the potential deficit.

So understood, Lord Scarman's speech is in agreement, save perhaps in emphasis, with those of Lord Wilberforce and Lord Keith.

I would add that both Lord Wilberforce and Lord Scarman expressed general approval of the approach adopted and the views expressed by Oliver LJ in the Court of Appeal (see [1982] 1 All ER 129 at 154, 173, [1982] 2 WLR 62 at 93, 117–118). They differed from the Lord Justice only in not accepting his view that the grant from the GLC cannot be treated as income in the LTE's revenue account for the purposes of s 7(3). This approval, therefore, extends to the following passage from Oliver LJ's judgment ([1982] 1 All ER 129 at 141, [1982] 2 WLR 62 at 77):

> 'Granted that the power in s 11(3) can embrace *some* increase in the subsidy provided from the rates (and the provisions of sub-s (5) seem to indicate that this was within the legislature's contemplation), how can it be said to permit a total departure from any ordinary business principle by an arbitrary and deliberate increase in the operating deficit, having particular regard, as I say, to the provisions of s 7(6)? If the word "economic" in s 1 has the meaning ascribed to it by counsel for Bromley, which I rather think in the circumstances it has having regard to the general framework of the Act, counsel for the GLC has to concede that his difficulty is insuperable. But even on his own construction of s 1, he cannot bring that which he relies on, or would have to rely on, as a direction within his client's powers. It is

a step which involves compelling the LTE to exercise its power to charge and collect fares in a way which conflicts with its statutory duty under s 7(3), and I can see the argument in favour of such a course if it is a course adopted on a direction for achieving one or other of the overriding policy considerations referred to in s 1. But, whatever else may be said about the general object of reducing fares by 25%, the one thing that is perfectly clear is that at the time when the proposals with which this application is concerned were first formulated they had nothing whatever to do with integration, efficiency or cost-effectiveness.'

Lord Brandon was with Oliver LJ in concluding that 'the LTE are only entitled to include on the credit side of the consolidated revenue account self-generated income, in particular fares charged for passenger services' (see [1982] 1 All ER 129 at 180, [1982] 2 WLR 62 at 126). With respect, I therefore do not find it necessary to consider his speech further.

While Lord Diplock differed from Lord Wilberforce, Lord Keith and Lord Scarman in considering that s 7 did not govern the GLC's power to make grants to the LTE it seems nevertheless that the majority regarded the duty of the GLC under s 7(6) as being a statutory example of its general fiduciary duty to its ratepayers. Thus in the event I discern little difference, save perhaps in emphasis, between Lord Diplock's conclusion and that of the majority.

Whether that is correct or not, in my judgment the ratio decidendi derived from the speeches of Lord Wilberforce, Lord Keith and Lord Scarman can be expressed as follows.

(1) The LTE is obliged by s 7(3) to ensure so far as practicable that it breaks even on fare income alone.

(2) If it is not practicable for the LTE so to break even, giving proper weight to s 7(3), the resultant deficit in the LTE's revenue account may be made good by a grant from the GLC under s 3, and the LTE may budget for such a grant so that it forms a part of its income in its revenue account in any relevant period.

(3) In deciding whether or not it is practicable to break even, and if not how large a departure is justifiable, the GLC and the LTE must balance (a) the LTE's duty under s 7(3) to break even, as above, and the GLC's duties under s 7(6) to have regard to that duty imposed on the LTE and its fiduciary duty to its ratepayers against (b) the respective duties of the GLC and the LTE under ss 1 and 5(1) of the Act 'to develop policies, and to encourage, organise and ... carry out measures, which will promote the provision of integrated, efficient and economic transport facilities and services for Greater London' and 'with due regard to efficiency, economy and safety of operation, to provide or secure the provision of such public passenger transport services as best meet the needs for the time being of Greater London'.

(4) Fares Fair was outside the powers of the 1969 Act because in introducing it the GLC acted arbitrarily, without regard to its duty under s 7(6) or to its fiduciary duty to its ratepayers or to the LTE's duty under s 7(3). Thus it was not in any sense a proper striking of a balance. Moreover, the gain to passengers on London Transport in total was, because of the resultant loss of block grant, appreciably less than the total burden cast on the rates, which illustrated the lack of any proper regard to the interests of ratepayers.

I should perhaps add that that last point, which was relevant when considered in relation to Fares Fair, may not now, we are told, be relevant because, as a result of other steps taken, it is likely that no further loss of block grant will arise.

It is perhaps not surprising, but it is regrettable, that the reasons for the decision in *Bromley London Borough Council v Greater London Council* have been, as I believe, widely misunderstood. As I hope I have shown, it is not an authority for the proposition that the GLC may never make a grant to the LTE out of the rates which will have the effect of enabling the bus or Underground train fares to be reduced. What it does establish is that the GLC's power to make such grants may only be exercised within strict limits, and the method by which and the purposes for which the Fares Fair scheme was introduced fell outside these limits.

It follows, in my judgment, that a proposal by the LTE to introduce a new structure and scale of fares for its services which results in a larger difference between overall costs *a* and fare income than does the current fare scale and the GLC's approval and subsequent direction to adopt that proposal are within the powers of the 1969 Act provided that (a) having regard to the LTE's duty under s 5(1), which imports as a prime consideration s 7(3), it is not practicable for the LTE to charge higher fares than those to which the proposal and direction refer and (b) the purpose of the GLC's approval and direction is to secure the implementation of policies developed and to carry out measures in accordance *b* with s 1 of the Act.

In reaching their decision that the introduction of the Fares Fair scheme was outside the powers of the Act, it was not necessary for their Lordships in the *Bromley* case to decide the proper meaning of the phrase 'as far as practicable' in s 7(3). In the different circumstances of the present case, I apprehend that it is necessary for our decision to embark on this exercise. *c*

On this point we were referred to the decision of the Court of Appeal in *Dedman v British Building and Engineering Appliances Ltd* [1974] 1 All ER 520, [1974] 1 WLR 171. That case concerned a claim for wrongful dismissal. The issue was whether it was 'not practicable' for the employee's complaint to be presented within the time limit of four weeks laid down by the relevant statutory regulation. In his judgment Lord Denning MR said ([1974] 1 All ER 520 at 525, [1974] 1 WLR 171 at 176): 'In my opinion the *d* words "not practicable" should be given a liberal interpretation in favour of the man [ie the employee].' Scarman LJ, agreeing, said ([1974] 1 All ER 520 at 528, [1974] 1 WLR 171 at 179):

> 'On the point of construction of "the escape clause" I agree with Lord Denning MR. The word "practicable" is an ordinary English word of great flexibility: it takes *e* its meaning from its context. But, whenever used, it is a call for the exercise of common sense, a warning that sound judgment will be impossible without compromise. Sometimes the context contemplates a situation rarely to be achieved, though much to be desired: the words then indicate one must be satisfied with less than perfection: see, for example, its use in s 5 of the Matrimonial Proceedings and Property Act 1970. Sometimes, as is submitted in the present case, what the context *f* requires may have been possible, but may not for some reason have been "practicable". Whatever its context, the quality of the word is that there are circumstances in which we must be content with less than 100 per cent: and it calls for judgment to determine how much less.'

The phrase is not 'so far as possible' or 'unless it be impossible'. There must, therefore, *g* be some difference in meaning between 'practicable' and 'possible', reflecting Lord Wilberforce's words, 'There is flexibility in the words "so far as practicable" ...' (see [1982] 1 All ER 129 at 157, [1982] 2 WLR 62 at 98). Thus 'practicable' does not in my view mean 'capable of attainment come what may'.

In my judgment, in the context in which it is used in s 7(3), the phrase requires the LTE to adopt the highest structure and level of fares which still enable the LTE to fulfil, *h* or to come reasonably close to fulfilling, its duties (a) to accord with principles laid down or approved by the GLC (by which I understand policies under s 1), (b) to have 'due regard to efficiency, economy and safety of operation and (c) 'to provide ... such public passenger transport services as best meet the needs for the time being of Greater London'.

In this formulation, it matters not in my view whether the words 'efficiency' and 'economy' relate to 'of operation' or are of general application, since the obligation *j* imposed on the LTE will be much the same on either interpretation. In so interpreting the phrase, I am adopting, though considerably expanding, the formulation advanced by counsel for the LTE at an early stage.

Counsel for the LTE makes the following submissions as to the application in this case of the phrase 'so far as practicable'. (i) The existing levels of service have been and still are regarded by the LTE as fulfilling its duty under s 5(1). Thus the obligation under s 7(3) a is to maximise fares while broadly maintaining that level of service. (ii) It follows that, save in exceptional circumstances, total fare revenue may never be reduced below the existing level when there is already a deficit which will necessarily be increased by the reduction in fares. (iii) The decision as to what is practicable is a matter primarily for the LTE.

As to the third point, while I agree that in the first place one would expect a possible b alteration in the structure or scale of fares to be the subject of consideration and report by the LTE, as was the case here, I do not accept that the final decision on the subject will necessarily rest with the LTE. Indeed, the power of the GLC to give to the LTE a direction requiring the LTE to submit proposals for an alteration of fares, which (as I have already said) necessarily requires the GLC to have regard to the LTE's duty under s 7(3), suggests to my mind that, in the event of disagreement, the eventual decision as to what is or is c not practicable is vested in the GLC.

The first and second of the points raised by counsel for the LTE stand or fall together. The issues they raise are, it seems to me, essentially questions of fact. If I am right in my view that both the GLC and the LTE may decide what is or is not 'practicable', with the GLC if necessary having the last word, that decision involves an exercise of discretion, which can only be challenged in this court on the well-known principles enunciated in d *Associated Provincial Picture Houses Ltd v Wednesbury Corp* [1947] 2 All ER 680, [1948] 1 KB 223.

However, counsel for the GLC has made it clear that he is not inviting us to rule whether what the GLC has done offends against the *Wednesbury* principles, but to leave that matter open. All he asks us to do is to decide whether the GLC has acted within its statutory powers. The reason is that, though the LTE disagreed with the GLC on the e proper construction of the statute, and has through its counsel tenaciously and clearly advanced its argument in this court, the LTE will be well satisfied if we tell it that it was wrong in law. It, like the GLC, regards the adoption of the 'balanced plan' as highly desirable. Though all relevant local authorities have been informed of this hearing, we have not had opposition from any who wish to take a *Wednesbury* point, e g that the GLC, even though acting within the statute, has failed to take some relevant consideration into f account. Thus, if there is such a point which could be made, our decision must not prevent it being made in future.

For these reasons it is unnecessary to decide whether, in considering what in the circumstances *was* practicable, the GLC has taken into account relevant considerations or has in other words complied with the *Wednesbury* tests. I do, however, think it right to comment that I can see no particular sanctity in the present structure and level of fares. g As Kerr LJ has made clear, after the decision of the House of Lords in the *Bromley* case was announced, the rapid reaction of the GLC was to double the fares current under Fares Fair. It took this step (a) because the finding that Fares Fair was unlawful inevitably meant that, since it was introduced, the LTE had been accumulating a deficit, which had to be made good as soon as possible, and (b) as a result of the legal advice it received initially as to the effect of their Lordships' decision.

h Since the effect of Fares Fair on average was to reduce fares in money terms to 68% of the levels current before October 1981, an approximate doubling in March 1982 resulted in fares (again in money terms) being 33% on average above those obtaining before October 1981. The effect, we are told, of the present 'balanced plan' proposals is to return fares, in money terms, to the same average level as pre-October 1981, or some 10% less when inflation is taken into account. Without in any way deciding the matter, I can see j that there may well be an argument that a return to an overall level of fares similar to that obtaining before October 1981 is as likely to satisfy the test of practicability as does the present level.

In general, therefore, I would answer the question, 'Is the proposal for alteration of the structure and level of fares approved by the GLC in December 1982 within the powers of the 1969 Act?' in favour of the GLC.

Conclusion

Kerr LJ has already explained the reasons for granting the second declaration sought
by the GLC in a form slightly different from that proposed by it. In agreement with a
him, I too would grant to the GLC declarations in the form he proposes.

NOLAN J. I agree that the Greater London Council (the GLC) is entitled to declarations
in the form proposed by Kerr LJ. I will state my reasons as shortly as possible in my own
words, although my reasons do not differ in substance from those already given. b

The issue raised by these proceedings arises out of the direction which the GLC
resolved on 14 December 1982 to give to the London Transport Executive (the LTE),
under s 11(1) of the Transport (London) Act 1969. The effect of the direction, so far as
material, if implemented by the LTE, will be to produce an overall reduction in the fares
charged to passengers of some 25% and a reduction of some 17% in the LTE's fares
revenue. The deficit on the LTE's revenue account will be correspondingly increased. c
The deficit, it is anticipated, will be made good by means of a grant from the GLC under
s 3 of the Act. The burden of the grant will, of course, fall on the ratepayers.

The LTE has objected to the direction on the ground that it fails to have regard to the
LTE's duty to break even so far as practicable. This duty, it is said, requires the LTE to
assess the highest practicable level of fares, (which I assume to be at or near the level in
fact charged at present). To this, the GLC replies that the level of fares proposed in the d
direction is, in its opinion, the highest practicable if the policies in the medium-term
plan, and in particular its provisions in relation to integration of services, are to be
achieved: see para 47 of the affidavit of Mr Stonefrost, the Comptroller of Finance to the
GLC.

It is not in dispute, in these proceedings, that those policies fall within the scope of the
general duty laid on the GLC by s 1 of the Act. So the critical question is whether the e
powers conferred on the GLC by the Act are wide enough to enable it, for the purpose of
carrying out its duty under s 1, to impose on the LTE a reduced fare structure and to
make a grant to the LTE in compensation for the loss of revenue to which the reduction
in fares will give rise.

As has been made clear, we are not concerned with the question whether those powers,
assuming them for the moment to exist, have been exercised in the right manner: the f
sole question for us is whether they exist at all. I would say at the outset that, unless I am
constrained by what was said in *Bromley London Borough Council v Greater London Council*
[1982] 1 All ER 129, [1982] 2 WLR 62 to take a different view, I would regard the
argument for the GLC as finding ample support in the language of the Act. I have already
referred to s 1, which provides for the GLC, not as a matter of choice but as a matter of
duty, 'to develop policies, and to encourage, organise and, where appropriate, carry out g
measures, which will promote the provision of integrated, efficient and economic
transport facilities and services for Greater London'. Section 3 authorises the GLC to
make grants to the LTE 'for any purpose', a phrase which plainly embraces the purposes
specified in s 1. Section 4, to my mind a most important section, provides that 'For the
purpose of implementing the policies which it is the duty of the Council under section 1
of this Act to develop, there shall be constituted a public authority to be called the h
London Transport Executive . . .'

I pause there to add that the exercise by the GLC of the powers conferred on it by s 3
is controlled as a matter of general law and, irrespective of the precise meaning of the
word 'economic' in s 1, by the fact that the GLC owes a fiduciary duty to ratepayers as
well as a duty to transport users. As Lord Wilberforce observed in *Bromley London Borough
Council v Greater London Council* [1982] 1 All ER 129 at 155, [1982] 2 WLR 62 at 94: j
'These duties must be fairly balanced one against the other.'

Section 5(1) carries the matter a stage further. It describes the general duty of the LTE
as being subject always to the (financial) requirements of s 7(3) of the Act. I would regard
the effect of this overriding requirement as twofold. In the first place, it emphasises the
duty of the LTE to practise economy in its operations, and thus to avoid imposing

unnecessary burdens on the ratepayers. Secondly, it incorporates into that duty of the LTE the precise requirements of s 7(3). It is to be observed, however, that subject to the overriding requirement, the general duty of the LTE is stated in s 5(1) as being '. . . to exercise and perform their functions, in accordance with principles from time to time laid down or approved by the Council . . .' I find it difficult to see how these principles could be formulated by the GLC otherwise than in accordance with the provisions of s 1.

Section 7(3) reads as follows:

> 'The Executive shall so perform their functions as to ensure so far as practicable—(*a*) that at the end of each such period as may from time to time be agreed for the purpose of this paragraph between the Executive and the Council the aggregate of the net balance of the consolidated revenue account of the Executive and any subsidiaries of theirs and the net balance of the general reserve of the Executive is such (not being a deficit) as may be approved by the Council with respect to that period, and (*b*) that, if at the end of any accounting period of the Executive the said aggregate shows a deficit, the amount properly available to meet charges to revenue account of the Executive and their subsidiaries in the next following accounting period of the Executive exceeds those charges by at least the amount of that deficit.'

In construing the word 'practicable' I find welcome assistance in the judgment of Scarman LJ in *Dedman v British Building and Engineering Appliances Ltd* [1974] 1 All ER 520 at 528, [1974] 1 WLR 171 at 179, where he said:

> 'Whatever its context, the quality of the word is that there are circumstances in which we must be content with less than 100 per cent: and it calls for judgment to determine how much less.'

Section 11(1) of the Act authorises the GLC to give to the LTE directions in relation to matters appearing to the GLC to effect the policies and measures which it is the duty of the GLC under s 1 of the Act to develop, organise or carry out; and it is clear by inference from s 11(2)(*d*) that these matters may include 'the general level and structure of the fares to be charged for the time being for the carriage of passengers by the Executive'.

These provisions, read together, seem to me to bear a reasonably clear and consistent meaning. By s 1, the GLC is obliged to develop policies and carry out measures which will promote the wide objects of providing integrated, efficient and economic transport facilities and services for Greater London. The LTE has been brought into existence for the purpose of implementing those policies.

The functions and responsibilities of the LTE are, of course, narrower than those of the GLC. In particular, the provision of integrated transport facilities and services is plainly a matter for the GLC, and not for the LTE. But, as is repeatedly emphasised, the functions of the LTE must be carried out in conformity with the duty laid on the GLC by s 1, and with the directions lawfully given by the GLC to the LTE in furtherance of its duty. The LTE, for its part, is under a strict obligation to conduct its operations in such a manner that, so far as practicable, it pays its own way. If it is not practicable for the LTE to do so, because of the effects of a direction given to it by the GLC in pursuance of the GLC's wider responsibilities under s 1, then the LTE will lawfully operate at a deficit, and the GLC can lawfully make good the deficit by means of a grant under s 3. Granted that the direction given in the present case was truly made in pursuance of the GLC's general duty under s 1, then it was within the powers conferred on the GLC by the Act.

Is there anything in the *Bromley* case which invalidates this conclusion? Before coming to the judgments and speeches, I would refer to the obvious but important fact, already stressed by Kerr LJ and Glidewell J, that the reduced fares policy effectively imposed on the LTE by the GLC in May 1981, which was the subject of the complaint by Bromley, was a very different creature from the policy enjoined by the direction in the present case.

By way of example, the GLC had not on that occasion, though it has on this, obtained the advice of leading counsel a number of times, including advice specifically addressed to the legality of the proposed direction before giving it. I am far from suggesting that *a* consultation with leading counsel is a statutory requirement for the GLC or any other local authority, but it is noteworthy that in the *Bromley* case the evidence did not disclose any consideration by the GLC of the legality of the policy which it imposed. More generally, the Court of Appeal and the House of Lords were not concerned with a direction such as that in the present case, which the LTE accepts, and which we are invited to assume, is designed to serve the purposes of s 1. These considerations do not, *b* of course, in any way detract from the binding force of what was said in the *Bromley* case about the construction of the Act. They do, however, explain some of the phrases used by their Lordships to illustrate what is, and what is not, within the powers conferred by the Act. They also show why it was not necessary for their Lordships in the *Bromley* case, though it is necessary for us, to reach a concluded view on the effect of the words 'so far as practicable' in s 7(3).

c I turn again to the speech of Lord Wilberforce. I note, in particular, his rejection of the argument that the LTE is under a rigid obligation to maximise fares and his reference to the flexibility in the words 'so far as practicable'. He concludes this part of his speech by saying ([1982] 1 All ER 129 at 158, [1982] 2 WLR 62 at 98):

> 'But given this, it appears to me clear that neither the LTE in making its proposals, nor the GLC in accepting them, could have power totally to disregard any *d* responsibility for ensuring, so far as practicable, that outgoings are met by revenue, and that the LTE runs its business on economic lines.'

On the basis of the assumptions which we are invited to make, there could be no suggestion of any such total disregard of its responsibilities by the GLC in the present case.

e I also note Lord Wilberforce's adoption of the views expressed by Oliver LJ, save that in one respect (namely the propriety of the LTE in taking prospective GLC grants into account when framing its budget) Lord Wilberforce took a view more favourable to the GLC than that of Oliver LJ. Thus Lord Wilberforce may be taken to have approved the observation of Oliver LJ where he said (commenting on the argument of the GLC in that case) that it—

f

> 'involves compelling the LTE to exercise its power to charge and collect fares in a way which conflicts with its statutory duty under s 7(3), and I can see the argument in favour of such a course if it is a course adopted on a direction for achieving one or other of the overriding policy considerations referred to in s 1.'

(See [1982] 1 All ER 129 at 141, [1982] 2 WLR 62 at 77.)

g This observation was made on the hypothesis that the word 'economic' in s 1 meant 'cost-effective', a hypothesis which Oliver LJ was inclined to doubt. But Lord Wilberforce said that he was prepared to take 'economic' as meaning 'cost-effective' (see [1982] 1 All ER 129 at 154, [1982] 2 WLR 62 at 94). Thus Oliver LJ's observation, read in the light of the speech of Lord Wilberforce, provides some support for the submissions of the GLC in the present case. Additional and direct support for those submissions is to be found in *h* the observations of Watkins LJ (see [1982] 1 All ER 129 at 153, [1982] 2 WLR 62 at 92). These observations were not cited by Lord Wilberforce or by the other members of their Lordships' House, but there is nothing to suggest that they were regarded with disapproval.

Lord Keith made plain his view that the LTE is not empowered, either on its own initiative or as a result of a suggestion or directive from the GLC, to carry on its *j* undertaking, so far as the fixing of fares is concerned, without due regard to ordinary business principles. He expressed this view in the context of s 7(3)(*b*), with which we are not directly concerned, but I would respectfully accept his Lordship's general proposition as applying to the whole of the subsection. His Lordship went on to say that the subsection—

> 'is one of the key provisions of the Act, which takes its place in s 5(1) as the overriding consideration of the LTE and to which, by virtue of s 7(6), the exercise of the GLC's functions under the Act, and that must mean the whole of such functions, is in a sense subordinated.'

(See [1982] 1 All ER 129 at 169, [1982] 2 WLR 62 at 112.)

By this I take his Lordship to mean that the primary duty of the LTE is to pay its own way, so far as practicable, in carrying out its duties under s 5(1). The GLC has no power to relieve the LTE of that primary duty. But did his Lordship intend to convey, by his reference to the whole of the GLC's function under the Act, that the GLC was prohibited from subsidising the LTE in pursuit of its own wider policies and responsibilities under s 1 of the Act? I think not.

Lord Keith went on to say, after referring to s 11 of the Act ([1982] 1 All ER 129 at 169, [1982] 2 WLR 62 at 112–113):

> 'There is nothing in these provisions, in my opinion, which is inconsistent with the LTE being required to operate its transport undertaking in accordance with ordinary business principles, or which empowers the GLC to direct the LTE to depart therefrom, whether for the purpose of achieving some object of social policy, or for other reasons. The concluding words of s 11(3) provide that the GLC "may direct the Executive to submit proposals for an alteration in the Executive's fare arrangements to achieve any object of general policy specified by the Council in the direction". "Any object of general policy" is a very wide expression, but clearly it is confined to the field of transport policy, and within that field it cannot, having regard to s 7(6), be invoked to justify a direction to the LTE to ignore its financial obligation under s 7(3).'

He went on to express disapproval of the reduction of fares imposed in May 1981 as involving 'an arbitrary reduction . . . in the existing general level of fares, which it is not suggested had been fixed otherwise than in accordance with ordinary business principles'. So he made it clear, to my mind, that the Act conferred no power on the GLC to direct reductions of fares for purposes falling outside the field of transport policy (which I take as a reference to s 1), and that, even within that field, the GLC could not justify a direction to the LTE to ignore its financial obligation under s 7(3).

Does the direction given in the present case call on the LTE to ignore its financial obligations under s 7(3)? These words would seem to me to be inappropriate to the declared object of the GLC in the present case which is, as I have said, to prescribe a level of fares which is the highest practicable if the policies in the medium-term plan and its provisions in relation to integration of services are to be achieved.

Lord Scarman's speech appears to me to come closest to providing support for the LTE's objection to the GLC direction. He says ([1982] 1 All ER 129 at 173, [1982] 2 WLR 62 at 118):

> 'Part II of the Act spells out the duties and powers of the LTE, in aid of which the grant-making power is given to the GLC. The words in s 3, "for any purpose", fall to be construed in the light not only of s 1 which declares the general duty of the GLC but of Part II of the Act which declares the duties and powers of the LTE.'

He continues to say of s 7(3) ([1982] 1 All ER 129 at 175, [1982] 2 WLR 62 at 120):

> 'It is a paramount obligation not only for the LTE but for the GLC. For s 5(1) does not make sense save on the basis that the principles which the GLC may lay down are themselves to be consistent with the financial duty imposed by s 7(3).'

I pause there to note that Lord Scarman uses the phrase that the principles laid down by the GLC must be 'consistent with' the financial duty imposed by s 7(3); he does not say that they must be subordinate to it. But, if s 7(3) is indeed paramount, there seems to me to be little to choose between these expressions. Is his Lordship therefore saying that the LTE's duty to break even as far as practicable must take precedence over the GLC's duty to perform its s 1 obligations? I repeat that this is not a question which, on the facts before them, their Lordships had to consider, but is that the fair inference to be drawn from his Lordship's speech? At the end of the day, I reach the conclusion that the answer to these questions is No.

Lord Scarman summarises his views on s 7(3) by saying ([1982] 1 All ER 129 at 177, [1982] 2 WLR 62 at 123):

> 'Though the LTE may be compelled by circumstances to budget for a loss which will have to be made good by grant, the subsection requires it to avoid it, if it can. Its principal weapon is fares income. The subsection, though it envisages budgeting for a deficit, permits it not as an object of social or transport policy, but as a course of action which it may not be practicable or possible to avoid. Loss may be unavoidable: but it does not thereby become an acceptable object of policy.'

The words 'transport policy' in this context must, I think, refer back to the phrase 'transport need' which Lord Scarman had earlier adopted and explained (see [1982] 1 All ER 129 at 170, [1982] 2 WLR 62 at 114). It refers to a policy of satisfying the need of the fare-paying passengers considered in isolation. As such, like 'social policy', it does not fall within the ambit of s 1. In other words, Lord Scarman too was construing the relevant provisions of the Act in the light of the facts before him and was concerned to make it plain that the May 1981 proposals for fare reductions had no statutory basis. He does not rule out the expenditure by the GLC of ratepayers' money to make good deficits which are the unavoidable result of policies properly formulated under s 1.

To put it another way, his Lordship's use of the word 'unavoidable' appears to me to reflect his use of the statutory word 'practicable'. What is practicable and what is avoidable cannot be decided in the abstract: the decision must depend on the circumstances of the particular case which include, of course, the statutory duties laid on the GLC and the LTE. In absolute terms, any loss made by the LTE is avoidable, since it could operate profitably by confining its passenger services to the rush hours, but no one contends for that. The GLC's declared object of aiming at the highest practicable level of fares (and thus minimising the unavoidable loss) which is consistent with its duty under s 1 appears to me to fall within the permissible limits laid down by Lord Scarman.

I have not referred to the speech of Lord Diplock because his approach to the statute, though generally favourable to the GLC argument in the present case, was, as he acknowledged, different from that of the other members of their Lordships' House. Nor have I referred to Lord Brandon's speech because he, like Oliver LJ, but unlike the other members of their Lordships' House, took the view that grants under s 3 must be left out of account in the performance of the budgeting exercise under s 7(3).

I conclude, in short, that the applicants are entitled to the declarations proposed.

Declarations granted accordingly.

Solicitors: *J R Fitzpatrick* (for the GLC); *I E King* (for the LTE).

N P Metcalfe Esq Barrister.

R v Immigration Appeal Tribunal, ex parte Kotecha

COURT OF APPEAL, CIVIL DIVISION
LORD LANE CJ, WATKINS LJ AND SIR ROGER ORMROD
23 NOVEMBER 1982

Immigration – Appeal – Evidence of facts coming into existence after entry clearance officer's decision – Whether adjudicator or appeal tribunal can admit evidence of facts occurring after entry officer's decision – Immigration Act 1971, s 19(2) – Immigration Appeals (Procedure) Rules 1972, rr 18(1), 29(1).

Where an immigrant appeals under the Immigration Act 1971 to an adjudicator or the Immigration Appeal Tribunal against an entry clearance officer's refusal to grant him an entry certificate into the United Kingdom, neither s 19(2)[a] of the 1971 Act nor rr 18(1)[b] and 29(1)[c] of the Immigration Appeals (Procedure) Rules 1972 permit him to adduce to the adjudicator or to the tribunal evidence of events which have taken place since the hearing before the entry clearance officer, because the appeal system under the 1971 Act is not an extension of the entry officer's administrative function but is simply a process which enables the entry officer's decision to be reviewed in the light of events as they stood at the time of his decision (see p 293 *d* to *j*, post).

R v Immigration Appeal Tribunal, ex p Weerasuriya [1983] 1 All ER 195 applied.

Notes

For the procedure in immigration appeals, see 4 Halsbury Laws (4th edn) paras 1024–1026.

For the Immigration Act 1971, s 19, see 41 Halsbury's Statutes (3rd edn) 40.

For the Immigration Appeals (Procedure) Rules 1972, rr 18, 29, see 2 Halsbury's Statutory Instruments (4th reissue) 33, 36.

Cases referred to in judgments

Chattopadhyay v Headmaster of Holloway School [1982] ICR 132, EAT.
R v Immigration Appeal Tribunal, ex p Amirbeaggi (1982) Times, 25 May.
R v Immigration Appeal Tribunal, ex p Rashid [1978] Imm AR 71.
R v Immigration Appeal Tribunal, ex p Tong (1981) Times, 8 December.
R v Immigration Appeal Tribunal, ex p Weerasuriya [1983] 1 All ER 195.
Secretary of State for the Home Dept v Thaker [1976] Imm AR 114.

Appeal

The appellant, Deepak Valji Khetsi Kotecha, appealed against the judgment of Glidewell J given on 4 February 1982 in the Divisional Court (1) refusing the appellant's application for an order of certiorari to quash a decision of the Immigration Appeal Tribunal dismissing his appeal from an adjudicator's decision, which had dismissed his appeal from the refusal of an entry clearance officer to grant him an entry certificate into the United Kingdom, and (2) refusing the appellant's application for an order of mandamus ordering the appeal tribunal to determine the appeal according to law. The facts are set out in the judgment of Lord Lane CJ.

K S Nathan for the appellant.
Alan Moses for the appeal tribunal.

---

a Section 19(2) is set out at p 291 *c*, post
b Rule 18(1) is set out at p 291 *d*, post
c Rule 29(1) is set out at p 291 *f*, post

LORD LANE CJ. This is an appeal from a refusal by Glidewell J on 4 February 1982 of an application for an order of certiorari to quash a decision of the Immigration Appeal *a* Tribunal given on 21 October 1981, and also for an order of mandamus, ordering the tribunal to determine the appeal according to law.

Only one point arises on the appeal in the upshot, and that is whether an adjudicator or an Immigration Appeal Tribunal should admit evidence relating to events which have occurred since the date of the decision by the entry clearance officer or the immigration officer, as the case may be. *b*

The facts of the case may be stated comparatively briefly. The proposed immigrant and the appellant is a youth called Deepak, who was born on 3 December 1965 in India, of which country he is a citizen. He is now 16 years of age, rising 17. He is an orphan. His mother died in 1968, when he was two, and his father died in 1969, the year following.

His father had been a merchant in Tanzania. But in 1964 or 1965, it matters not *c* which, the whole family took themselves off to India, where Deepak himself was born shortly afterwards. He has two brothers. One of the brothers is named (although it is not his full name) Kishor. He is the sponsor of this young man and he lives in the United Kingdom. The other brother is now in Tanzania. There are five sisters: three in the United Kingdom, one in Tanzania and one in India. The grandmother, we are told, who was alive when the matter was before the entry clearance officer, has died. His uncle and *d* aunt are still alive. For a number of years Kishor and the two sisters supported Deepak and they continued to do so after the parents had died.

In August 1978 the appellant came to the United Kingdom with Kishor. He was in the United Kingdom for 42 days, while representations that he should be allowed to stay longer were being considered by the relevant government department. On 6 September 1978 the sponsor was told that Deepak would have to go back to India because he had no *e* entry certificate, and it was only fair to other applicants in the queue for such certificates that he should go back to India. There is no appeal against that. He went back to India and there he applied for an entry certificate.

On 17 January 1979 the matter came before the entry clearance officer and on 7 February 1979 he refused to grant a certificate. There is no question, as counsel for the appellant has pointed out, of any deception on the part of Deepak. The applicant told the *f* entry clearance officer that the grandmother was still alive, that the uncle and aunt were living not very far away from him in India and the three sisters and the remaining brother were there in India. That was the basis of fact on which the entry clearance officer came to his conclusion.

On 24 March 1981 there was an appeal to the adjudicator. That appeal was dismissed. But by this time the years had rolled by and there had been changes in the material facts. *g* The grandmother had died of advanced age. The sponsor, Kishor, had been appointed in India as the legal guardian of this young man, and had become therefore responsible for the boy's welfare.

Then on 21 October 1981 there was a further appeal to the Immigration Appeal Tribunal. By this time there had been further changes in the circumstances surrounding this young man. As has already been pointed out, there had been two sisters in India. *h* The elder one was by this time said to have gone to Tanzania, although there was no concrete evidence that that was the fact. One sister had come to the United Kingdom and the other brother had also gone to Tanzania, but the uncle and aunt had remained in India, still living close at hand. The Immigration Appeal Tribunal in its turn refused the appeal.

Now we are asked by counsel on behalf of the appellant to say that the adjudicator and *j* the Immigration Appeal Tribunal were both wrong in declining, as they no doubt did, to pay attention to the evidence of facts which had taken place since the determination by the entry clearance officer. It is necessary to go through the relevant provisions, both of the statute and the rules, to see what assistance can be given in this matter.

One starts off with s 13 of the Immigration Act 1971, sub-s (2) of which reads:

> 'Subject to the provisions of this Part of this Act, a person who, on an application duly made, is refused a certificate of patriality or an entry clearance may appeal to an adjudicator against the refusal.'

There is only one limitation to that, s 13(4), which has no application to the present case.

Then one turns to s 19 of the 1971 Act, which reads:

> '(1) Subject to sections 13(4) and 16(4) above, and to any restriction on the grounds of appeal, an adjudicator on an appeal to him under this Part of this Act—(*a*) shall allow the appeal if he considers—(i) that the decision or action against which the appeal is brought was not in accordance with the law or with any immigration rules applicable to the case; or (ii) where the decision or action involves the exercise of a discretion by the Secretary of State or an officer, that the discretion should have been exercised differently; and (*b*) in any other case, shall dismiss the appeal.
>
> (2) For the purposes of subsection (1)(*a*) above the adjudicator may review any determination of a question of fact on which the decision or action was based . . .'

The relevant rule is r 18 of the Immigration Appeals (Procedure) Rules 1972, SI 1972/1684. It is headed 'Evidence', and reads:

> '(1) In any proceedings on an appeal the Tribunal shall receive as evidence the summary or record taken or kept in accordance with Rule 40 of any evidence received—(*a*) by the adjudicator in the course of the proceedings to which the appeal relates, or (*b*) by an adjudicator to whom the appeal has been remitted in pursuance of paragraph (3)(*c*)(i) below.
>
> (2) If any party to the appeal wishes to adduce evidence before the Tribunal further to that to be received in accordance with paragraph (1) above, he shall give notice in writing to that effect to the Tribunal indicating the nature of the evidence; any such notice shall—(*a*) in the case of the appellant, be given with the notice of appeal or as soon as practicable after notice of appeal is given or is deemed to have been given . . .
>
> (3) In any proceedings on an appeal—(*a*) the Tribunal may, in its discretion, receive or decline to receive further evidence of which notice has been given in accordance with paragraph (2) above . . .'

Rule 29(1) of the 1972 rules, again under the heading 'Evidence', reads:

> 'An appellate authority may receive oral, documentary or other evidence of any fact which appears to the authority to be relevant to the appeal, notwithstanding that such evidence would be inadmissible in a court of law.'

It is on that basis that counsel for the appellant invites us to say that those provisions permit the appellant to adduce evidence of events which have taken place since the hearing before the entry clearance officer, and he has referred us to a number of cases. Some of them, we are bound to say, with respect to counsel, do not seem to advance the argument or to be relevant to the question at all; some are certainly relevant.

The first to which our attention was drawn, which was so relevant, was *Secretary of State for the Home Dept v Thaker* [1976] Imm AR 114. It seems to us, having looked at this decision, that it is a decision the effect of which is contrary to the arguments of counsel for the appellant. It enables us to turn on to *R v Immigration Appeal Tribunal, ex p Rashid* [1978] Imm AR 71. That was a decision of Lord Widgery CJ in the Divisional Court, and the headnote reads:

> 'Where an application for entry as a returning resident . . . was refused by an immigration officer, because the applicant had not substantiated his contention that he was a "returning resident", additional evidence tendered to support the applicant's claimed status would be relevant and admissible on an appeal against the refusal; the adjudicator's power on such an appeal would not be restricted to a consideration of the facts which had been established before the immigration officer.'

What is made clear by the judgment in that case is that Lord Widgery CJ is confining himself to evidence of events which had happened before the original hearing, evidence a
which had not been adduced at the original hearing. This case is no support for the proposition which counsel for the appellant has advanced.

One then turns to a decision by Glidewell J on 1 December 1981 in *R v Immigration Appeal Tribunal, ex p Tong* (1981) Times, 8 December. That was a case which involved a tribunal of fact endeavouring to determine what the expectation of success or failure of a particular business might be. It will be clear from that short synopsis that it is very far b
removed from the circumstances of the present case. Let me read part of the judgment of Glidewell J (of which we have seen the full transcript), which reads:

> 'I should say that one of [counsel for the appeal tribunal's] subsidiary points was that the adjudicator was obliged to look at the position as it was in May 1978, at the time of the notice of refusal, and in so far as he was entitled to look at anything that c
> had happened since he was only entitled to do so as a guide to what could have been expected to happen viewed from the standpoint of May 1978. In other words, what has actually happened is to be taken into account in deciding what, had one been looking forward from two years back, would have been likely to happen. That, I think, is right. I think that if, for instance, as I suggested in argument, this young man had won a large sum on the football pools some time between 1978 and 1980 d
> and had then invested that in the business, that is not a matter that could reasonably have been expected and so ought not to have entered into the adjudicator's conclusion because he was not deciding the matter on the facts in 1980, he was deciding whether the immigration officer had reasonable grounds for his decision.'

Another case with a similar sort of situation was a decision of Woolf J in *R v Immigration* e
Appeal Tribunal, ex p Amirbeaggi (1982) Times, 25 May. There, in the course of the judgment (and we have again seen a full transcript) Woolf J said:

> 'The primary submission that [counsel for the applicant] made on this application, and the matter with which I am mainly concerned, is that the tribunal went wrong because they failed to have regard to the events which took place subsequent to the f
> Secretary of State's decision on 21 August 1979. This is a matter on which there is now developing a number of decisions of the courts. At first sight, [counsel for the applicant's] submission appears to be inconsistent with the approach laid down by Glidewell J in the recent case of *R v Immigration Appeal Tribunal, ex p Kotecha* [the case with which we are concerned today] which was given on 4 February 1982, but which has not yet been reported except in The Times newspaper for 9 February. It g
> also, on first sight appears to be inconsistent with the case very recently decided by Webster J, *R v Immigration Appeal Tribunal, ex p Weerasuriya* [1983] 1 All ER 195. Those cases lay down that whereas a tribunal, be it an adjudicator or an Immigration Tribunal, which is hearing oral evidence, is entitled to hear fresh evidence which was not before the Secretary of State at the time he gave his decision, it is not concerned with the subsequent events, at least in so far as those subsequent events h
> refer to new factual matters.'

Then he cited a passage from Glidewell J's judgment in the present case where, dealing with the final point, the judge said:

> 'What in my view s 19(2) does not entitle the adjudicator to do is to say: "I am not concerned with the facts at the date of the entry clearance officer's decision. I will j
> consider the facts as they exist before me today." Or, perhaps not quite so strongly: "I will consider not only the facts as they were, but the facts as they are today." In my judgment, he is not entitled to do that. He must deal with the appeal on the basis of the factual situation that existed when the original decision against which the appeal lies was made. That is true both of the adjudicator and of the appeal tribunal.'

What that case and the earlier case of *R v Immigration Appeal Tribunal, ex p Tong* (1981)
a Times, 8 December seem to decide is this, that the situation may be different where the original decision involves making an inspired guess as to the future prospects of, for example, a business. It may be that within a very limited sphere it is proper in these limited circumstances to have regard to what happened subsequent to the original hearing. That is, as I say, very far from the present case.

We have also been referred to a decision of the Employment Appeal Tribunal,
b *Chattopadhyay v Headmaster of Holloway School* [1982] ICR 132, a decision of Browne-Wilkinson J. There the facts were so far away from the present case that I feel it is not helpful to refer to them, save to mention the name of the case out of courtesy to counsel for the appellant who cited it to us.

Finally, to bring this up to date, is the decision already mentioned, by Webster J in *R v Immigration Appeal Tribunal, ex p Weerasuriya* [1983] 1 All ER 195. There the issues are
c conveniently encapsulated in the judgment (at 201), where Webster J sets out the contentions of the Secretary of State. It reads (at 201–202):

> 'The submission of counsel for the Secretary of State is to the contrary effect and it is that although, as I have already said, it is common ground that an appellate tribunal may take into account evidence which was not available at an earlier stage
> d of the proceedings in question, it may not take into account evidence of any fact which was not in existence at the date when the Secretary of State made his decision. He relies, primarily as matters of construction, on the use of the past tense in s 19(1)(*a*)(i) and (ii), and on the words, in (ii), "should have been exercised differently". If it were to be purely a question of construction I would be persuaded, I think, by that argument, namely that those words which I have just quoted would, if there were no other assistance to be gained as to the answers to this question, be
> e determinant of it in favour of counsel for the Secretary of State. But it seems to me that there are other considerations which reinforce that conclusion. The decision which is effectively under appeal is the decision of the Secretary of State, that is to say an administrative decision. In judgments on applications for judicial review of administrative decisions it has often been stated that the function of the court is not to substitute its own decision for the decision of the department or tribunal under
> f review. Of course it is not possible to apply that principle directly to the appellate structure which is attached to the Secretary of State's decision in this case and in similar cases; but it is, as it seems to me, necessary to look at that appellate structure in order to ask oneself the question whether that appellate structure has to be regarded as an extension of the original administrative decision-making function or whether it is to be regarded as simply a process for enabling that decision to be
> g reviewed. As it seems to me it falls into the latter category rather than into the former category.'

With that conclusion I would respectfully agree. It puts the matter succinctly and in my judgment puts it accurately. Indeed were the situation to be otherwise, and were the submissions of counsel for the appellant to be accepted as correct, it would mean a never-
h ending system of appeal, each court up the line being obliged to review the facts in the light of events as they stood, not at the time of the original decision but as they stood at each stage of the appellate system, and the system would become even more unmanageable than some people believe it to be at present.

For my part I would dismiss this appeal.

j **WATKINS LJ.** I agree.

SIR ROGER ORMROD. I agree.

Appeal dismissed.

Solicitors: *Nazerali & Co* (for the appellant); *Treasury Solicitor.*

Sophie Craven Barrister.

Chubb Cash Ltd v John Crilley & Son (a firm)

COURT OF APPEAL, CIVIL DIVISION
FOX LJ AND BUSH J
20 JANUARY 1983

Hire purchase – Damages – Disposal of goods by hirer – Sale of goods by convertor – Measure of damages in conversion – Amount outstanding on hire-purchase agreement exceeding value of goods – Whether amount outstanding on agreement or value of goods recoverable.

By a hire-purchase agreement made in October 1977, the plaintiffs, who were manufacturers of cash registers, sold a cash register to the purchaser. The hire-purchase price was £1,755 plus VAT, which was to be paid by monthly instalments of £27·39 over a period of 60 months. Under the terms of the agreement the property in the register would not pass to the purchaser until the final instalment was paid. In November 1977 the plaintiffs entered into an agreement with a credit company whereby the hire-purchase instalments were assigned to the credit company in consideration of payment of a cash sum by them to the plaintiffs. The agreement provided that, if the purchaser defaulted on payment of an instalment, the plaintiffs were to repay to the credit company the amount of the cash sum paid by the credit company less any sum paid to them by the purchaser. The plaintiffs were to retain the property in the goods. The defendants, who were bailiffs acting on behalf of the Commissioners of Customs and Excise, were instructed to execute a judgment obtained by the commissioners against the purchaser. They accordingly executed a distraint warrant against the purchaser's goods and on 30 July 1979, on the purchaser's assurance that the cash register was his, the defendants took possession of it and on 11 September sold it at a public auction for the sum of £178·25. As agreed under the assignment, the plaintiffs paid the credit company £951·55 by reason of the default of the purchaser to pay the instalments. The plaintiffs then brought an action for damages for conversion against the defendants. At the trial of the action the defendants submitted to judgment for damages for conversion of the cash register and the only issue to be determined was the amount of damages. The judge assessed damages at £951·55 being the amount the plaintiffs had to pay to the credit company under the assignment by reason of the purchaser's default in paying the instalments. The defendants appealed, contending that the proper measure of damages was £178·25 being the value of the goods at the time of the conversion. The plaintiffs contended that they were entitled to recover the amount which they had failed to recover from the purchaser, being some £1,200, or alternatively the £951·55 which they had had to pay the credit company under the assignment in consequence of the default.

Held – The appeal would be allowed for the following reasons—

(1) Prima facie the measure of damages for conversion was the market value of the goods at the date of conversion. Where goods were subject to a hire-purchase agreement the measure of damages for conversion was therefore the market value of the goods or the amount still owing under the agreement at the date of the conversion, whichever was the lesser amount (see p 296 *d*, p 297 *c*, p 298 *c* and *j* and p 299 *f*, post); *Wickham Holdings Ltd v Brooke House Motors Ltd* [1967] 1 All ER 117 and *Belvoir Finance Co Ltd v Stapleton* [1970] 3 All ER 664 distinguished.

(2) On the facts, the best evidence of the market value of the cash register on the date of the conversion, namely 30 July 1979 when the cash register was distrained, was the price it fetched at auction on 11 September, there being no evidence of any change in the market or in the condition of the cash register between those dates, and no evidence that the price was artificially low by reason of the forced sale. The sum claimed by the plaintiffs corresponding to the balance of the hire-purchase price outstanding was not consequential damage flowing from the conversion, since it was caused by the failure of

the purchaser to perform his obligations under the hire-purchase agreement with the a plaintiffs, and an award to the plaintiffs of that sum would therefore lead to the recovery by them of a sum far in excess of the value of the goods and would have the unacceptable effect of making the innocent convertors guarantors of the debt for the benefit of the plaintiffs. The proper measure of damages for the plaintiffs was therefore the price realised at the auction, ie £178·25, which represented the market value of the cash register at the date of the conversion (see p 297 *e* to p 298 *d f g* and p 299 *c* to *f*, post).

b

Notes

For the measure of damages for conversion, see 38 Halsbury's Laws (3rd edn) 792–795, paras 1318–1320, and for cases on the subject, see 46 Digest (Repl) 512–515, *583–606*.

Cases referred to in judgments

c *Acatos v Burns* (1878) 3 Ex D 282, CA.

Belvoir Finance Co Ltd v Stapleton [1970] 3 All ER 664, [1971] 1 QB 210, [1970] 3 WLR 530, CA.

Ewbank v Nutting (1849) 7 CB 797, 137 ER 316.

Hall (J & E) Ltd v Barclay [1937] 3 All ER 620, CA.

Wickham Holdings Ltd v Brooke House Motors Ltd [1967] 1 All ER 117, [1967] 1 WLR 295, d CA.

Cases also cited

Arpad, The [1934] P 189, [1934] All ER Rep 326, CA.

Clarke v Nicholson (1835) 1 Cr M & R 724, 149 ER 1272.

e

Appeal

The defendants, John Crilley & Son (a firm), appealed against the judgment of his Honour Judge Wilson at the Birmingham County Court given on 19 November 1981 whereby it was adjudged that the plaintiffs, Chubb Cash Ltd, should recover from the defendants the sum of £951·55 in damages. The facts are set out in the judgment of Fox LJ.

f

John Wait for the defendants.

Jeremy Cousins for the plaintiffs.

FOX LJ. This is a claim for damages for conversion. A hire-purchase agreement was made on 21 October 1977. The plaintiffs let to the purchaser (I will call him the 'debtor' g for convenience) a cash register. The period of payment was 60 months. The hire-purchase price was £1,755 plus VAT; the monthly instalments were £27·39. The property in the cash register did not pass to the debtor under the agreement until the final instalment was paid.

In November 1977 the plaintiffs entered into an agreement (which I will call 'the assignment') with Barclay Masterloan Ltd, whereby the hire-purchase instalments were h assigned to Masterloan in consideration of payments by them to the plaintiffs of a cash sum. It was provided by the assignment that, if the debtor defaulted on payment of an instalment, the plaintiffs would repay Masterloan the amount of the cash sum paid by Masterloan less any payments made by the debtor to Masterloan. The plaintiffs retained the property in the goods under the assignment.

The plaintiffs manufacture cash registers and they have no difficulty in meeting the j demand for them. There is a large profit element in the sale price, though we have not been told precisely what it is, nor is there any evidence of the cost of manufacture.

The defendants are bailiffs. On 30 July 1979, they acted on behalf of the Commissioners of Customs and Excise to execute a judgment obtained by the commissioners against the debtor, and for that purpose they executed a distraint warrant against the debtor's goods. The debtor assured the defendants that the cash register was his and they distrained on it.

They removed it to their own premises where they stored it until it was auctioned in September, as I will mention in a moment. a

The defendants put the cash register into a public auction sale on 11 September 1979 at Clare's Auction Rooms in Birmingham. Cash registers were regularly sold there. On 11 September 1979 other cash registers were being offered. Clare's, it seems, had a weekly auction of up to 500 lots. The attendance was about 50 to 100 dealers and members of the public. The cash register was sold at the auction for £155 plus VAT. The defendants received net £126·50 which they duly paid over to the Customs and Excise. b

Under the terms of the assignment, the plaintiffs paid Masterloan £951·55 by reason of the default of the debtor to pay instalments.

This action was commenced by the plaintiffs in the Birmingham County Court where they sought damages for the conversion. At the trial the defendants submitted to judgment for damages for conversion of the cash register, so the only question was and is the amount of damages. c

The judge assessed the damages at £951·55, which was the amount the plaintiffs had to pay Masterloan under the assignment by reason of the debtor's default in paying the instalments.

The defendants appeal. They say that the proper measure of damages is £178·25 being, it is said, the value of the goods at the time of the conversion.

Prima facie, the measure of damages for conversion is the value of the goods at the d date of the conversion. I refer, for example, to the observations of Lord Denning MR in *Wickham Holdings Ltd v Brook House Motors Ltd* [1967] 1 All ER 117 at 120, [1967] 1 WLR 295 at 299. The judge, however, was influenced by two decisions of this court, namely the *Wickham Holding* case, to which I have just referred, and the later decision in *Belvoir Finance Co Ltd v Stapleton* [1970] 3 All ER 664, [1971] 1 QB 210. In both of those cases the measure of damages permitted was held to be the actual loss to the plaintiffs which, on e the facts, was the amount still owing under the hire-purchase agreement at the date of conversion.

I do not think those cases are of assistance here. The object of the court in those decisions was not to give the plaintiff more than the value of the chattel at the date of the conversion, but less. The court regarded it as unjust that, if the hire-purchase owner had only a limited interest in the goods (ie the outstanding instalments), he should recover f their full value. The damage, therefore, was limited to the actual amount of the loss, that is to say the amount still outstanding under the hire-purchase agreement.

The plaintiffs assert in the present case, on evidence that I will mention in a moment, that the value of this property to them was £875. That, however, is less than the amount which they are claiming as damages.

At this point I should mention the evidence that was relied on by the plaintiffs as to g the value of the chattel. First of all, in the agreed statement of facts, it is stated that, on 30 July 1979—

> 'the Plaintiffs had the right to re-possess the register, if they had done so they would have put a new case on it at a cost of £25 and would have offered it for sale at a price of approximately £900.'

h

It appears from the judge's notes of evidence that the credit controller of the plaintiffs, gave evidence to this effect:

> 'On repossession, either sell as it stood or put new case on and re-sell. We do sell second-hand. £900 with new case costing £25—nett £875.'

j

He then produced an agreement in relation to a transaction in December 1979. The judge's note continued: '£950 discount £50—nett £900. Identical machine.'

In those circumstances the contention of the plaintiffs is that, on the basis of the decisions in *Wickham Holdings* and *Belvoir Finance*, and the principles there annunciated in relation to the right of the plaintiffs to recover what they had in fact lost, the amount which they had lost is the amount which they had failed to recover from the debtor which is about £1,200 or alternatively it must be the £951·55 which they had to pay to Masterloan under the assignment in consequence of the default by the debtor (which was the sum actually awarded by the judge). I do not think that that can be correct. The *Wickham Holdings* and the *Belvoir Finance* cases are quite different as they are concerned solely with the problem which arises where the hire-purchase company seeks to recover in respect of the conversion an amount which is more than the amount still outstanding under the hire-purchase agreement, which the court in those cases thought to be unfair. The cases are not authorities for the proposition that the hire-purchase company can recover the value of the chattel at the date of conversion or the outstanding instalments, whichever is the greater. Their purpose was to limit the damages.

In my opinion, in the present case, the ordinary rule applies and the measure of damages is the value of the cash register at the date of conversion which, it is common ground, was 30 July 1979. I see no reason for displacing that rule here.

I therefore approach the matter to consider what, on the evidence before the court, was the value of this chattel at the date of conversion (30 July 1979). In approaching that, I observe that the chattel was sold at a public auction in rooms which hold auctions weekly, where cash registers are regularly sold, where cash registers were in fact sold on the same day as this was sold (11 September 1979) and which are well attended by dealers and by the public and where there seem regularly to be substantial lots of varying sorts, not all necessarily cash registers, available for sale. It may be that there are cases where the amount obtainable at a forced sale is not to be regarded as reliable, and we were referred by counsel for the plaintiffs in his helpful argument to two cases, *Acatos v Burns* (1878) 3 Ex D 282 and *Ewbank v Nutting* (1849) 7 CB 797, 137 ER 316.

I need not examine that problem further, in the circumstances of this case, because I think we have sufficient evidence before us to determine the value of this chattel. There is no specific evidence that the sale was at an undervalue.

The position can be summarised in relation to the question of determining the value as follows. First, there is no question here of consequential damage, or of damage in relation to some special use to which the chattel could be put. Second, the plaintiffs say that, if they had recovered possession, they would have expended £25 on it and then offered it for sale at £900. As to that, I observe that this was not a new article. It was a year and a half old. There is no independent valuation of any kind, by reference to comparables, of its value as at 30 July 1979. There is indeed no evidence as to the state of the market at that date. Further, there is no evidence as to the condition of the cash register on 30 July 1979.

Third, what we do know is that at the public auction on 11 September it fetched £155.

Fourth, that sale, I think, is prima facie good evidence of the value of the chattel on 11 September 1979, and there is nothing to indicate that its condition on 11 September 1979 was any different from its condition on 30 July.

In those circumstances, it seems to me that the market having been tested at such an auction as I have mentioned, on 11 September, the proper inference is that the value on 30 July was the same as that fetched at the auction because we have no evidence of any change in the market between the two dates, and we have no evidence of any change in the condition of the article between the two dates. It is perfectly true, as I have indicated by references to the judge's notes of evidence, that evidence was given on behalf of the plaintiffs at the trial of the sale of what was described as an identical machine, in December 1979, for £900 but that evidence by itself, in my view, cannot take us very far, because we do not know, and it is manifestly of importance, what was the condition of the machine on 30 July 1979. It may or may not have borne any real resemblance to the condition of the machine which the plaintiffs sold in December 1979. Nor, indeed, does it show whether there had been much movement in the market between July and December.

It comes to this, that it seems to me that the best evidence that we have on the facts before us, of the value of this chattel on 30 July 1979 is the auction price of £178·25 and, in my opinion, it is that amount which the plaintiffs are entitled to recover.

I only add, that in relation to the contention in support of a larger sum, which was put forward by counsel on behalf of the plaintiffs, that seems to me to be unsatisfactory in two respects. First, it would enable the plaintiffs in such a case to recover an amount in respect of the value of a chattel which is, in fact, far in excess of the value of the chattel. Second, it would in effect make persons in the position of the present defendants, who have inadvertently converted, guarantors of the debt for the benefit of the plaintiffs. I do not think in practical terms that result would be acceptable.

Looking at the whole matter and assessing the value as best we can on the evidence before us, I conclude that the proper answer is that the value at the date of conversion was the amount realised at the auction sale.

I would award damages accordingly and vary the judge's order.

BUSH J. I agree. As we are differing from the decision of the circuit judge, I would add a few observations of my own.

The plaintiffs contended that the measure of damages for the admitted conversion of the defendants was the value of the goods as at the date of the conversion, or the amount outstanding on a hire-purchase agreement, whichever was the greater. Put another way, they said that the value of the goods to the plaintiffs at the time of the conversion was the amount outstanding on the hire-purchase agreement.

The defendants, on the other hand, contended that the damages were the market price of the goods, as evidenced by the auction sale price.

The judge found that the sale by auction was not a proper market place for those goods and went on to say:

> 'The question is what damage has resulted to the plaintiff by the conversion that is admitted. The answer is, because of the conversion the plaintiff had to pay out £951·55.'

(That is, the amount that had to be paid to Barclay Masterloan Ltd.) The judge went on: 'I shall take that figure, it is smaller than the sum claimed, that is the measure of loss and damage.'

The £951·55, as I have said, was in fact the amount the plaintiffs had to pay Barclay Masterloan Ltd. They did not have to pay it because of the defendants' conversion; they had to pay it under the agreement because of the debtor's default on the payments under his hire-purchase agreement with the plaintiffs. As Fox LJ has said, the judge was purporting to make a converting tortfeasor a guarantor for the debtor's contract with the plaintiffs. However, the plaintiffs contend that the decisions of this court in *Wickham Holdings Ltd v Brooke House Motors Ltd* [1967] 1 All ER 117, [1967] 1 WLR 295 and *Belvoir Finance Co Ltd v Stapleton* [1970] 3 All ER 664, [1971] 1 QB 210 meant that the plaintiffs were entitled to either the market value, or the amount due under the hire-purchase agreement.

In fact, these cases decided that the measure of damages was the market value of the goods, or the amount still owing under the hire-purchase agreement, whichever was the lower as at the date of the conversion. It was a limited decision, not a decision which entitled the plaintiffs, if the amount outstanding on the hire-purchase agreement was greater than the value of the goods, to claim that.

The Torts (Interference with Goods) Act 1977 abolished the tort of detinue, but it did not interfere with the common law rules relating to damages for conversion, with which we are at present concerned. The normal measure of damages for conversion is the market value of the goods converted. This, as is pointed out in *McGregor on Damages* (13th edn, 1972) at p 987 is because, as Greer LJ in *J & E Hall Ltd v Barclay* [1937] 3 All ER 620 at 623 said:

> 'Where you are dealing with goods which can be readily bought in the market, a
> a man whose rights have been interfered with is never entitled to more than what he would have to pay to buy a similar article in the market.'

If there is no market for the goods, as in *Hall v Barclay*, then the cost of a replacement may be obtained.

The matter does not rest there because in all actions in conversion the plaintiff may
b recover any additional damage he may suffer which is not too remote.

The plaintiffs' argument is that they have suffered further damage because the amount outstanding on the hire-purchase agreement, or alternatively the amount due on a similar basis to Barclay Masterloan Ltd, is greater than the value of the goods and remains unpaid.

This damage does not in this case flow from the conversion, but flows from the failure
c of the debtor to perform his obligations under the agreement. In this case, though there may be other cases on different facts where different considerations might apply, the defendants' tortious act did not affect the hire-purchase agreement itself and the relationship between the debtor (the hirer) and the plaintiffs. The plaintiffs, however, go on to say, 'On 30th July 1979, the date of the conversion, we had the right to repossess this cash register and if we had done so we would have put a new case on it for £25 and
d sold it for approximately £900.' However, at that time the plaintiffs were manufacturing cash registers, but they could have mitigated their damage by purchasing a secondhand cash register and done the same with that, purchasing it, that is to say, in the market.

Having regard to the agreed facts, to which Fox LJ has already referred, it is plain that there was a market in cash registers, though the judge was not satisfied that the auction itself produced the fair market price.

e I find it difficult to accept that finding because the only independent evidence of the value of the cash register that the judge had before him was the evidence of the sum recovered on the sale of it at the auction. In my view the judge misdirected himself by treating the amount outstanding to Barclay Masterloan Ltd as being damage which flowed from the conversion.

So far as the quantum of damage is concerned, I do not need to repeat the matters to
f which Fox LJ has already referred under that head and with which I agree.

I, too, agree that this appeal should be allowed.

Appeal allowed.

Solicitors: *Sharpe Pritchard & Co*, agents for *Bosworth Bailey Cox & Co*, Birmingham (for the defendants); *Kent Jones & Done*, Stoke-on-Trent (for the plaintiffs).

Patricia Hargrove Barrister.

R v Inland Revenue Commissioners, ex parte Preston a

QUEEN'S BENCH DIVISION (CROWN OFFICE LIST)
WOOLF J
23, 24 FEBRUARY 1983

b

Judicial review – Availability of remedy – Exercise of discretion on behalf of Crown – Inland Revenue Commissioners – Powers to initiate machinery for cancellation of tax advantage – Assurance given to taxpayer by Revenue in 1978 that no further investigation would be made into sale of certain shares – Taxpayer forgoing claims for tax relief in reliance on assurance – Revenue deciding in 1982 to reopen investigation into sale of shares – Whether Revenue bound to investigate alleged tax advantage – Whether court may review decision to reopen investigation – Whether c *decision to reopen investigation an unreasonable exercise of discretion – Income and Corporation Taxes Act 1970, ss 460, 465.*

In January 1977 the taxpayer sold certain shares for £24,375 to a company controlled by a group of companies by which he had been employed since 1974. He left that employment in March 1977. In May 1978 the taxpayer received a letter from the Special d Investigation Section of the Inland Revenue requesting a meeting to discuss his tax returns for the years 1975–76 to 1977–78. After an exchange of correspondence, however, an agreement was reached whereby the taxpayer, after furnishing certain information relating to the sale of the shares, agreed to withdraw claims for relief which he had made in respect of certain capital losses and interest payments if all his tax affairs relating to the years in question were agreed by the Revenue and no further inquiries e were made. In reliance on that agreement the taxpayer withdrew his claims for relief and discharged a liability to capital gains tax in respect of the shares. Four years later the Revenue sought to carry out further investigations into the sale of the shares. In July 1982 the taxpayer received a notice issued by a different inspector of the Special Investigation Section under s 465 of the Income and Corporation Taxes Act 1970 requiring him to furnish information relating to the sale of the shares. He supplied the f information required by the notice but pointed out that he considered that the Revenue were bound by the 1978 arrangement. In September the Revenue issued a notice under s 460 of the 1970 Act putting into operation the machinery for the cancellation of a tax advantage. The taxpayer applied for judicial review seeking, inter alia, a declaration that the Revenue were not entitled further to assess or attempt to assess him in respect of the sale of the shares. The taxpayer contended that it would be unfair for the Revenue to g seek to exercise their powers in the circumstances, that the Revenue had a discretion whether to exercise those powers and that the discretion was to be exercised reasonably and fairly taking into account all relevant considerations. The Crown contended that the 1978 arrangement did not include possible proceedings under s 460, which were not contemplated at that time, and that in any event s 460 did not create a discretion but imposed a duty on the Revenue to put the anti-avoidance machinery into operation as h long as, in their judgment, the facts were such that it would lead to the recovery of tax.

Held – (1) Since the Crown could not put itself in a position where it was prevented from performing its public duty, it could not, by entering into an arrangement or agreement, estop itself from exercising in the future a discretion which it was its duty to exercise, and, if the Crown sought to make an agreement which had that consequence, j that agreement was of no effect (see p 306 g, post).

(2) However, where a statutory body or officers of the Crown had a statutory discretion, they were to exercise that discretion reasonably, and in deciding whether a course of conduct was reasonable it was incumbent on the individual or individuals exercising the discretion to have regard to the fairness or otherwise of what they were

doing. Whereas it was not open to an officer of the Revenue to make it impossible at a
a later date for a statutory discretion to be exercised, it was possible for the Revenue to behave in such a manner that the results of their conduct at one stage had to be taken into account at a later stage when it became necessary to assess whether to take or not to take a particular course of conduct. It followed that the court could intervene if it found that there was a statutory discretion which was to be exercised by the Revenue and that that discretion had been exercised unreasonably. In all the circumstances, what occurred
b in 1978 was that the taxpayer had indicated to the Revenue that in order to have his affairs dealt with simply and straightforwardly he was prepared to co-operate with the Revenue by assisting them with providing information which they required and forgoing two claims which he then had, and he had surrendered those two claims only after he had been told by the tax inspector that the inspector did not intend to raise any further inquiries in the form of special investigations of the taxpayer's tax affairs. Accordingly,
c before the Revenue exercised their discretion to reopen their investigation in connection with the shares sold by the taxpayer, they were required to have regard to what had happened previously. On the facts it was clear, when the Revenue decided to reopen their investigation, either that they did not consider that what had happened in 1978 was relevant to their decision whether to take action in 1982 or that they exercised their discretion unreasonably, since on the evidence of what had happened in 1978 there was
d nothing which would justify a decision to initiate further inquiries in 1982. The court would accordingly grant the taxpayer the declaration sought (see p 306 *j* to p 307 *b*, p 308 *b c f g*, p 309 *h j* and p 310 *a b* and *d h*, post); dictum of Lord Scarman in *IRC v National Federation of Self-Employed and Small Businesses Ltd* [1981] 2 All ER at 111–112 applied.

Notes

e For the abuse of the exercise of a discretion or power, see 1 Halsbury's Laws (4th edn) paras 60–62.

For the power of the Inland Revenue Commissioners to counteract tax advantages, see 23 ibid paras 1462–1464, and for cases on the subject, see 28(1) Digest (Reissue) 489–494, *1753–1762*.

For the Income and Corporation Taxes Act 1970, ss 460, 465, see 33 Halsbury's Statutes
f (3rd edn) 591, 599.

Cases referred to in judgment

IRC v National Federation of Self-Employed and Small Businesses Ltd [1981] 2 All ER 93, [1982] AC 617, [1981] 2 WLR 722, HL.

R v Treasury Lords Comrs (1872) LR 7 QB 387, DC.

g *Williams (Inspector of Taxes) v Grundy's Trustees* [1934] 1 KB 524, [1933] All ER Rep 875.

Cases also cited

A-G of Hong Kong v Ng Yuen Shiu [1983] 2 All ER 346, [1983] 2 WLR 735, PC.

HTV Ltd v Price Commission [1976] ICR 170, CA.

IRC v Garvin [1981] 1 WLR 793, HL.

h *Olin Energy Systems Ltd v Scorer (Inspector of Taxes)* [1982] STC 800.

Application for judicial review

Michael David Preston (the taxpayer), applied, with the leave of Woolf J granted on 25 November 1982, for (i) an order of prohibition prohibiting the Commissioners of Inland
j Revenue from taking any further steps under Part XVII of the Income and Corporation Taxes Act 1970 for the purpose of investigating or assessing him to further tax in connection with the affairs of Gymboon Ltd and/or (ii) an order of prohibition prohibiting a tribunal constituted under s 463 of the 1970 Act from considering and making any determination on a notice dated 14 September 1982 to the taxpayer pursuant to s 460(6) of the 1970 Act and (iii) a declaration that the commissioners were not entitled further

to assess or attempt to assess the taxpayer in respect of the affairs of Gymboon Ltd. The facts are set out in the judgment. a

Stanley Brodie QC and *Stephen Nathan* for the taxpayer.
Robert Carnwath for the Crown.

WOOLF J. This is an application for judicial review against the Commissioners of b Inland Revenue in respect of action which has been taken by the Revenue under the provisions of Part XVII of the Income and Corporation Taxes Act 1970, which are the provisions of the Act which deal with tax avoidance.

It is contended by the taxpayer, who is Michael David Preston, that because of an arrangement which was reached between himself and the Revenue it would be unfair and arbitrary and unreasonable for the Revenue to take advantage of those provisions. It c is also contended by the taxpayer that, in fact, a contract or agreement was reached between himself and the Revenue which prevents the Revenue from taking that action. However, it is conceded by counsel for the taxpayer that before this court he cannot argue the latter point, although he reserves the right to do so in a higher court if that should prove necessary.

The facts of the matter are as follows. The taxpayer is a chartered accountant. However, d he is not a chartered accountant who has specialised in tax affairs. In April 1974 he acquired 50% of the share capital of a company called Gymboon Ltd. Having disposed of part of his share capital to a third party, in January 1977 he sold the remainder of the shares in the company to another company, Broadforth Ltd, and in respect of that sale he received £24,375.

In November 1974, that is after he had acquired his shareholding in Gymboon Ltd, he e became employed by what I will call the Rossminster group of companies. As has become very much public knowledge as a result of proceedings in which the Revenue has been engaged, Rossminster did carry on certain activities which were aimed at saving tax for their clients by schemes of tax avoidance. In March 1977 the taxpayer left the employment of the Rossminster group, having received what is sometimes described as 'a golden handshake'. f

While he was employed by the Rossminster group it is his contention that he was solely engaged in the corporate finance activities of the group and that he was not engaged in their activities in the revenue field.

In May 1978 he made his returns to the Revenue for the years ending 1975, 1976 and 1977, those being years during which he had been working for the Rossminster group. On 4 May 1978 he received a letter from a Mr Thomas of the Special Investigations Section of the Revenue, Mr Thomas being one of Her Majesty's Inspectors of Taxes. The g letter said:

> 'I have seen your recent tax returns and correspondence addressed to [another inspector] and I note in particular that you are claiming relief for interest paid to Rossminster Acceptances Limited during the 2 years ended 5 April 1976. I should welcome the opportunity of discussing with you your [and then he sets out the tax h years] tax returns and I should therefore be grateful if you would suggest 2 alternative dates and times when it would be convenient for you to call at my office.'

The taxpayer, on 15 May, replied to that letter saying, among other things, that he would be happy to attend at the inspector's office but that he would be grateful if he could be told in advance what matters in particular the inspector wished to discuss and j what information, if any, the inspector would like him to provide.

On 18 May Mr Thomas replied to that letter. He pointed out that he had reserved a time for a meeting and then went on:

> 'The particular matters that I should like to discuss with you are: a. your claims to relief for interest paid to Rossminster Acceptances Ltd, b. the loss which you have

claimed in respect of the purchase and sale of shares in Jurby Raven Ltd and allied operations, c. your transactions in the shares of Gymboon Ltd, Jacksons Bourne End Ltd, The Telbex Group Ltd, Powerstem Ltd, Alanvale Securities Ltd, and First London Securities Ltd, d. the leaving payment which you received from Rossminster Management Services Ltd. It would be very helpful if you would bring to the meeting the documents, correspondence and other papers in your possession which are relevant to these matters.'

That letter was replied to in the following terms (and I read out those passages in the letter of 24 May which are relevant):

'Upon receipt of your first letter in which you referred to my claims for relief in respect of interest paid to Rossminster Acceptances Limited . . . I inferred that the proposed discussion would surround such claims and their circumstances. On that basis, and in a spirit of co-operation which I still preserve, I felt able to attend. It is clear, however, from your second letter, and particularly from your request for detailed documentation, that you wish the discussions to be of a more detailed and technical nature. In such circumstances, I must point out that although a Chartered Accountant, I am by no means well-versed in highly-complex taxation matters, and feel that I am not competent to converse with you on equal terms. Subject to my comments below, therefore, if the interview is still considered necessary I feel that I must now seek professional advice. In the meantime, however, in order to facilitate the finalisation of my affairs I set out below certain information and observations on the matters specified in your letter of 18 May. In this regard it seems to me that your questions fall into two main categories. Dealing first with the claims for relief for interest paid to Rossminster Acceptances Limited (in connection solely with which the holding of shares in First London Securities Limited arose) and for loss on disposal of shares in Jurby Raven Limited, the following background information may be relevant. In November 1974, I was invited to join The Rossminster Group Limited . . . which was then a small company engaged in taxation advice and financial services, with a view to developing a commercial and corporate financial activity for the group, and with the ultimate aim of making such activity the principal, if not sole, activity of the group.'

Then he goes on to deal with his role in the company and he concludes that part of his letter by saying:

'As measured however, against the financial success of Rossminster's other activities, my department's relative importance within Rossminster was not increasing in the way which its own success seemed to justify. Two consequences flowed from this development and began to manifest themselves towards the latter part of 1976. On the one hand the substance of Rossminster's current financial well-being clearly now depended very little on my department and in commercial terms we were no longer an essential ingredient of the group's future well-being. At the same time, from a personal viewpoint, I had become progressively less sympathetic towards the nature and aims of Rossminster's main field of activity. Accordingly, I left Rossminster at the end of March 1977 since which time I have developed my own business interests. The ex-gratia payment from Rossminster may be seen in the light of the brief history set out above. As you will appreciate, as the head of the corporate financial and commercial activity at Rossminster I would have displayed a considerable lack of confidence in my employers if I had failed to enter into the transactions in question and into which all other senior employees of Rossminster had evidenced their intention to enter. The foregoing deals adequately, I hope, with the first category. Turning to the second category of matter raised by your enquiries, these involve commercial investments of business substance, and need not, in my view, be considered other than as capital transactions. As things stand today it is not a matter of great concern to me whether or not I proceed with my claims for relief for interest or capital loss. What is most certainly of greater importance is that my taxation affairs are maintained on a current basis. Accordingly, without prejudice to any claim which may have to be made for interest relief or capital loss, I am prepared to forgo such claims for the years in question on the basis that by so doing I shall facilitate the agreement of my tax affairs.'

I emphasise the sentence I have just read. The letter concludes by saying:

'In the light of the above you may feel that a discussion is no longer necessary. However, if you still wish to proceed with such a meeting, perhaps you will provide me with a list of specific questions on which I can obtain professional advice. I look forward to hearing from you.'

Having received that letter, on 25 May (the following day) Mr Thomas telephoned the taxpayer, and there is a note made by Mr Thomas of that telephone conversation. It is necessary for me to read the relevant parts of that note.

'Thomas asked Preston to confirm that he wished to withdraw his claims to relief for interest paid to Rossminster Acceptances Ltd and for the loss of the disposal of shares in Jurby Raven Ltd. Preston said that this was indeed his wish—he had incorporated in his letter the phrase "without prejudice to any claim which may have to be made for interest relief or capital loss" solely to protect his position should the Revenue not be prepared to accept his proposal. [I emphasise the word 'proposal'.] Regarding the agreement of Preston's tax affairs generally, Thomas told Preston that he could not speak for the local District to whom Preston made his Returns—the Inspector might wish to raise points with Preston in the normal course of dealing with his returns. However, so far as the Special Investigations Section was concerned there seemed just one point on which further information was now required, namely the purchase and sale of shares in Gymboon Ltd. Would Preston clarify the details regarding the acquisition and subsequent disposal of these shares by providing the names and addresses of the persons from whom they were acquired and to whom they were sold, the relevant dates and numbers of shares involved. Preston replied that whilst he could not supply this information over the telephone, he would certainly provide it if Thomas cared to send him a letter setting out precisely what was required. Thomas then asked Preston to indicate why the value of the shares rose so quickly between September 1976 and the date of sale in January 1977. Preston replied that the rise in value reflected the success of Gymboon Ltd's trading activities. Thomas then enquired precisely what was Gymboon Ltd's trade and Preston replied that the company had traded in commodities. Thomas told Preston that he would write a letter asking him to confirm the position with regard to the claim for relief on the Rossminster Acceptances Ltd interest and the Jurby Raven Ltd's shares, and setting out the factual information required with regard to Gymboon Ltd. Thomas added that he thought it should be possible to dispense altogether with the proposed interview.'

In accordance with that telephone conversation, a letter was written by Mr Thomas on 26 May to Mr Preston. I am afraid it is necessary for me to read that letter as well.

'If I understand the penultimate paragraph of your letter correctly, you are withdrawing your claims to relief for interest paid to Rossminster Acceptances Ltd during the two years ended 5 April 1976, and you are not pursuing the inclusion in the computation of your gains chargeable to Capital Gains Tax a loss on the disposal of shares in Jurby Raven Ltd. For the avoidance of doubt would you please let me have a note confirming these amendments to your Income Tax Returns. I have considered your comments regarding the subjects mentioned in subparagraphs c. and d. of my letter of 18 May 1978. [I interpose to say that those are the matters dealing with the transactions, among others, in respect of the shares of Gymboon Ltd.] As stated on the telephone I should like the following factual information regarding the shares in Gymboon Ltd: a. full details of the acquisition and disposal of these shares, including the names and addresses of the person from whom they were acquired and to whom they were sold, the relevant dates and numbers of shares involved b. a note of the circumstances in which the value of the shares increased so quickly between September 1976 and the date of disposal. What was the precise nature of Gymboon Ltd's business activities? I look forward to hearing from you on these points. I confirm that I should not wish to trouble you with an interview if you withdraw your claim to relief for interest paid to Rossminster Acceptances Ltd and for the loss on the disposal of the shares in Jurby Raven Ltd.'

There was then a request for a reply to that letter, and on 23 June 1978 the taxpayer wrote to Mr Thomas setting out details with regard to the shares in Gymboon Ltd. He finished up by saying:

'I trust that the above is sufficient for your requirements, and upon hearing from you that you have no further questions on my tax affairs, I shall be happy to write formally to you withdrawing my claims to relief for interest paid to Rossminster Acceptances Limited and for loss on the disposal of shares in Jurby Raven Limited. I look forward to hearing from you.'

The reply came on 21 July 1978:

'Thank you for your letter of 23 June 1978 and I have noted the information supplied regarding the shares in Gymboon Ltd. On receipt of your note formally withdrawing your claims to relief for interest paid to Rossminster Acceptances Ltd during the two years ended 5 April 1976 and confirming that you are not pursuing the inclusion in the computation of your gains chargeable to Capital Gains Tax a loss on the disposal of shares in Jurby Raven Ltd, I propose to return your tax papers to HM Inspector of Taxes North East 5 (London) [that is the local inspector] as I do not intend to raise any further enquiries on your tax affairs.'

Thereafter, the taxpayer gave the formal notice that was requested, and in due course he paid the capital gains tax on the disposal of his shares in Gymboon Ltd, having forgone any right to set off his alleged losses on the disposal of the shares in the other company.

Thereafter, so far as the taxpayer was concerned, everything proceeded as he no doubt envisaged it would, until four years later. In July 1982 he received a notice from another inspector of taxes, also of the Special Investigations Section of the Inland Revenue, that notice being dated 26 July 1982. It referred to the powers conferred on the Commissioners of Inland Revenue by s 465 of the Income and Corporation Taxes Act 1970 and required him, on or before 27 August 1982, to furnish certain information. The body of the document made it clear that the information which was required was in relation to his dealings in the shares in Gymboon Ltd and, in particular, in respect of the sale by him to Broadforth Ltd of his shares. He was asked, among other things, for copies of all correspondence relating to the disposal of the shares in Gymboon Ltd between himself and Broadforth Ltd.

Having received that document, the taxpayer wrote to the named inspector in these terms:

'In your letter dated 21st July, 1978 and sent to me by Special Investigations Section you stated [and I interpose to say it was not of course this particular inspector but a different one] "I do not intend to raise any further enquiries on your tax affairs". If you refer to this letter and to the correspondence which led up to it, you will see that this latter statement was a consequence of and in consideration for the withdrawal by me of certain claims for tax relief. I would contend accordingly that this correspondence constituted a binding legal agreement which estops you from now raising enquiries on Gymboon Limited or any other matters covered by the correspondence.'

Thereafter, further correspondence took place between the Revenue and the taxpayer. For the purposes of this judgment it is not necessary to refer to that correspondence. a

The machinery provided in Part XVII of the 1970 Act was put into operation by the taxpayer, while making it clear that he was doing so without prejudice to his contentions. He did so, in particular, because he did not want to fall foul of the time limits provided in those provisions.

He first of all provided the information which was requested from him pursuant to s 465 and, when, having received that information, the Revenue then purported to bring b
into force the provisions contained in that Part of the Act with a view to cancelling an alleged tax advantage from a transaction in securities, he, as he was entitled to, took the matter to a tribunal specially set up to protect the taxpayer with regard to those provisions.

I should, perhaps, interpose here to say that that protection clearly emphasises the fact that the provisions, which are contained in this Part of the 1970 Act, give the Revenue very extensive and wide powers to deal with tax avoidance. They are clearly a very c
important part of the Revenue's machinery for dealing with schemes and arrangements which are designed to avoid the normal implications of the tax legislation. They are clearly ones which can have a very serious impact on the taxpayer, and it is because of that that the tribunal is there to protect the individual from the misuse of those provisions.

Before the tribunal, the taxpayer did raise certain of the matters which I have to d
consider, but it is not suggested before me that that in any way debars him from seeking judicial review in the present circumstances.

In his submissions on behalf of the taxpayer, counsel has put his case in a number of different ways, but he accepts that his submissions to a substantial extent overlap. However, his primary submission, which is that, having regard to the arrangement which was made, the Revenue are not entitled to issue the notices which they have, he e
accepts amounts to no more than seeking by the back door to achieve what he accepts he cannot achieve by the front door. He accepts that before this court, as I have already indicated, he cannot set up the contract or an arrangement which estops the Crown from seeking to take the action that they have.

However, by his principal submission, he contends that in any event the identical result is achieved because what the Crown is seeking to do is to exercise a discretion, and f
as a matter of public as opposed to private law it cannot be entitled to exercise that discretion in a manner which would be inconsistent with the arrangement or agreement which had been made.

Put in the primary way which counsel for the taxpayer advances his submission, I would not be prepared to accede to it. The reason underlying the rule that the Crown cannot be estopped in matters of this nature has, as its justification, the fact that the g
Crown cannot put itself in a position where it is prevented from performing its public duty and here the Crown has a duty to exercise its discretion. If it seeks to make an agreement which has that consequence, that agreement is of no effect.

However, there is a secondary manner in which counsel for the taxpayer puts his submission, of which I form a much more favourable view. He submits in effect that, because of the arrangement which was made between the taxpayer and the Revenue, it h
would be unfair for the Revenue to seek to exercise the powers which they have, that the Revenue have a discretion whether or not to exercise those powers and that that discretion must be exercised in accordance with the well-known principles.

Conventionally, it is accepted that in the administrative field, where a statutory body or officers of the Crown have a statutory discretion, they must exercise that discretion reasonably, and in doing so must not misdirect themselves as to the law, take into account j
irrelevant considerations or fail to take into account relevant considerations.

It seems to me that, in deciding whether or not a course of conduct is reasonable, it is incumbent on the individual or individuals exercising the discretion to have regard to the fairness or otherwise of what they are doing. Whereas it is not open to an officer of the Revenue to make it impossible at a later date for a statutory discretion to be exercised, what it is possible for the Revenue to do is to behave in such a manner that the results of

their conduct at one stage have to be taken into account at a later stage when it becomes
a necessary to assess whether or not to take a particular course of conduct. I will turn in a moment to the effect, as I find it from the papers that are put before me, of the arrangement which was made between the taxpayer and Mr Thomas. However, even without considering in detail the effect of that arrangement, it seems to me clear that, before the Revenue exercised a discretion to reopen the affairs of Gymboon Ltd, they were required to have regard to what had happened previously.

b It must be remembered, in considering an attack of the sort which is advanced by the taxpayer on the Revenue in this application, that the Revenue have very much to bear in mind the public duty which they owe to the public in respect of the collection of revenue. If they unreasonably grant an indulgence to one taxpayer, that can have the consequence of placing a greater burden on other taxpayers. It is because of this that it is inappropriate to look at their activities as though they were to be governed by the considerations which
c normally apply in the private law sphere. Their conduct has to be judged by the approach, which I would respectfully adopt, indicated by Lord Scarman in *IRC v National Federation of Self-Employed and Small Businesses Ltd* [1981] 2 All ER 93 at 111–112, [1982] AC 617 at 650–651:

> 'The Taxes Management Act 1970 places income tax under their care and
> d management and for that purpose confers on them and inspectors of tax very considerable discretion in the exercise of their powers. It also imposes on them the very significant duty of confidence in investigating, and dealing with, the affairs of the individual taxpayers. Indeed, the Lord Advocate relied on the existence of this duty as an indication that the statute imposed no duty owed to a taxpayer (or the general body of taxpayers) in respect of the collection of taxes due from another taxpayer, and he made particular reference to ss 1 and 6 of and Sch 1 to the Act. He
> e rightly observed that in the daily discharge of their duties inspectors are constantly required to balance the duty to collect "every part" of due tax against the duty of good management. This conflict of duties can be resolved only by good managerial decisions, some of which will inevitably mean that not all the tax known to be due will be collected. On this analysis of the statutes the Lord Advocate submitted that the law neither imposes nor recognises a duty owed to an individual taxpayer or a
> f group of taxpayers to collect from other taxpayers all the tax due from them. He supported his submission by a reference to *R v Lords Comrs of the Treasury* (1872) LR 7 QB 387; and he emphasised that Parliament and, since 1967, the Parliamentary Commissioner exist to redress the sort of grievance asserted by the federation in this case. His ultimate characterisation of the Revenue's failure in this case, if it was a failure, was "maladministration", not breach of any public duty owed at law to the
> g general body of taxpayers. While I reject his conclusion, I accept much, but not all, of his submission. The analysis of the statutory provisions is clearly correct. They establish a complex of duties and discretionary powers imposed and conferred in the interest of good management on those whose duty it is to collect the income tax. But I do not accept that the principle of fairness in dealing with the affairs of taxpayers is a mere matter of desirable policy or moral obligation. Nor do I accept
> h that the duty to collect "every part of inland revenue" is a duty owed exclusively to the Crown. Notwithstanding the *Treasury* case in 1872, I am persuaded that the modern case law recognises a legal duty owed by the Revenue to the general body of the taxpayers to treat taxpayers fairly, to use their discretionary powers so that, subject to the requirements of good management, discrimination between one group of taxpayers and another does not arise, to ensure that there are no favourites
> j and no sacrificial victims. The duty has to be considered as one of several arising within the complex comprised in the care and management of a tax, every part of which it is their duty, if they can, to collect.'

That, of course, was a case which raised very different issues from the present application. However I attach particular importance to the reference made by Lord Scarman to the principle of fairness in dealing with the affairs of taxpayers. He returned to that subject later in his speech but I do not propose to lengthen this judgment by referring to that passage. a

The approach which I have sought to indicate is very different from the considerations which were before the court in *Williams (Inspector of Taxes) v Grundy's Trustees* [1934] 1 KB 524, [1933] All ER Rep 875. That case was dealing with a situation where, under the taxing statutes, the judge had to consider the right of the Revenue to raise additional assessments. Whereas I do not dissent from anything said by the judge in that case, in my view what was said becomes relevant only if and when an argument is advanced to b the effect that the Crown can be estopped by the activities of an inspector.

The consequence of my view of the obligations of the Revenue with regard to statutory discretions means that this court can intervene if it finds, first, that there is a statutory discretion and, second, that that discretion has been exercised in a manner which contravenes the conventional principles to which I have already made reference. Approaching this case in this way, before it could be shown that there was a right to c intervene, it is necessary to decide whether or not the Revenue had any discretion.

Counsel for the Crown submits that s 460 creates not a discretion but a duty, and that where the circumstances for the application of that section arise then the Revenue are under a duty to put the machinery into operation as long as, in their judgment, the facts are such that it will lead to a recovery of tax and it is not bad management to make use of those provisions. He would submit that, in so far as the Revenue have any discretion d under s 460, it is much more limited than the sort of discretion which is necessary to bring into play the principles to which I have made reference.

With regard to that, I would draw attention to the fact that in this particular case the machinery contained in that part of the 1970 Act was initiated by making use of the powers contained in s 465 to obtain information. That section, at any rate, quite clearly gives the Revenue a discretion whether or not to seek to obtain information, a discretion e which clearly falls within the type of discretion which brings into operation the principles to which I have made reference.

I have the gravest reservations as to the submission that there is not, under s 460, a like discretion. I would be surprised indeed if the provisions of s 460 have to be construed in such a manner that the Revenue have to avail themselves of those draconian powers even if they come to the conclusion that it would be unreasonable, arbitrary and unfair to do f so. However, as I hope to make clear hereafter, it is not necessary for me to express any concluded view on that subject. Since in any event s 465 contains a clear discretion and the procedure was initiated in this case in consequence of the use of that section, it seems to me that, if an unlawful use was made of s 465 in this case, it would be appropriate and proper to use the powers of this court in a way which, in the circumstances which exist here, prevents the Revenue taking advantage of that misuse of their powers. g

Returning to the facts of the matter, the evidence initially filed on behalf of the Revenue consisted of an affidavit by Mr Owston, who explained that it was when he was considering, in October 1979, a tax avoidance scheme known as the Rossminster company purchase scheme that there were referred to him the accounts of Gymboon Ltd for the year ended 13 September 1977, those having been submitted by a party independent from the taxpayer. He says that it was apparent to him from those accounts h that the provisions of s 460 could be invoked to counteract tax advantages.

He concludes his affidavit by saying:

> '... [the taxpayer] sold his shares in Gymboon Ltd on 11 January 1977 and that action under Section 460 has been commenced with a view to the necessary preliminaries being completed ... in time for an assessment to be made by 5 April 1983 to counteract the tax advantage which it is contended [the taxpayer] obtained j in the year 1976/77.'

There is also an affidavit by Mr Thomas, the inspector to whom I have made reference. In that affidavit the only comment which he makes with regard to the taxpayer's conduct to which I draw attention is that 'the [taxpayer] did not tell me that the sale price of the shares was based on an asset value which excluded a provision for Corporation Tax on those profits'. He says: 'At no time did I say or imply that the Board of Inland Revenue would not contemplate proceedings under these provisions', 'these provisions' being the anti-avoidance provisions contained in the 1970 Act. He says that he only told Mr Preston 'that so far as the Special Investigations Section was concerned, the only point on which further information was at that time required related to the purchase and sale of shares in Gymboon Ltd.'

Counsel for the taxpayer criticised the contents of that affidavit in so far as they contained matters of information and belief. Counsel for the Crown justified the form of the affidavit by indicating that it set out material which indicated the manner in which the Revenue had come to the conclusion to invoke the s 460 provisions in this case.

It is pertinent to say that there is no reference in either of the affidavits which were filed indicating that specific consideration had been given to the question whether or not it was unfair to the taxpayer, having regard to what had happened in and prior to 1978, to initiate the procedure which commenced with the application under s 465 of the 1970 Act.

As a result of my questioning of counsel for the Crown during the course of his helpful submissions, it became apparent that the evidence filed on behalf of the Revenue had been filed without regard to the possibility of there being in issue a question whether or not the Revenue had taken into account all relevant considerations before making use of the statutory provisions. In consequence of that, I agreed to an application by counsel for the Crown to allow the Revenue to put further material before the court as to what matters were taken into account by the Revenue before the machinery contained in the 1970 Act was initiated by the notice under s 465.

That evidence is contained in an informal statement by Mr Hobson, who is the inspector of principal grade who was responsible for supervising the activities of the Revenue which are now called into question. He says in that statement that he issued the s 465 notice to the taxpayer. He says:

> 'At that time I was aware of the correspondence [exhibited before me]. I think I saw this correspondence in [the taxpayer's] District File, but in any event copies of it were in a Section File. I did not consider that this correspondence inhibited me in any way from initiating action under section 460. That matter was not under consideration in 1978 and all the facts were not then known.'

On the material which has been placed before me by the Crown, it seems that the Revenue's approach to this matter was not that indicated by Lord Scarman in the speech to which I have referred. Mr Hobson's statement approaches the matter on the basis of what was under consideration in 1978 and the facts which were then known. That is an approach which is understandable when considering whether or not there are circumstances which, in the ordinary way, would justify a further assessment or a fresh approach to the liability of a taxpayer. It is not an approach which I would regard as being appropriate when you have the sort of special circumstances which are disclosed by the facts of this case.

It seems to me that the only proper interpretation of what occurred in 1978 was that the taxpayer was indicating to the Revenue that, in order to have his affairs dealt with simply and straightforwardly and on a current basis, he was prepared to co-operate with the Revenue by assisting them with providing information which they required and forgoing two claims which he then had. He surrendered those two claims after he had been told by the tax inspector that he did not intend to raise any further inquiries on his, the taxpayer's, tax affairs. The assurance which he received was obviously a limited one. It may not create a contract. It did not apply to the sort of conventional inquiries that the taxpayer's local inspector might make, but it was clearly intended to apply with regard to the type of special investigations which the Special Investigations Section of the Revenue would be engaged on which includes investigations into tax avoidance schemes.

Those inquiries clearly included the sale of the shares by the taxpayer in Gymboon
Ltd, and, whereas I of course accept that the Revenue at that time were not contemplating *a*
the operation of s 460, this would not be known to the taxpayer and they were making
it clear that they were not going to raise further inquiries into the Gymboon transaction.
The taxpayer was entitled to assume, as he said he did, that that was going to be a matter
which was going to be treated as one where he would have a liability for capital gains tax,
a liability which he was prepared to meet and which he did in fact meet in 1978, but was
a matter in respect of which no further inquiries were going to be made by the Special *b*
Investigations Section. What happened four years later was clearly quite contrary to what
the taxpayer had been led to believe was going to happen. It could have the consequence
of making him liable for a very substantial amount of additional tax.

Counsel for the Crown conceded that he would have to be given credit for the tax that
he had already paid. It was contended by counsel for the Crown that what had been
given up by the taxpayer was probably not of much substance and that may well be *c*
right. It did however, I was told, amount in total to something in the order of a claim for
relief of £40,000, and there would be no way in which the taxpayer could now raise
those matters except with the assistance and co-operation of the Revenue as a matter of
concession.

Certainly, it seems to me that those were matters which required very careful
consideration by the Revenue before they launched their application under s 465. I do *d*
not say that there would not be some circumstances which would justify the Revenue
saying that in performance of their public office they were entitled to initiate the
procedure under s 465. What I do say is that there is nothing in the papers before me
which indicates that that matter received the sort of consideration which it should have
received before the machinery in s 465 was initiated. Indeed the clear implication from
the evidence is that the Revenue did not consider what happened in 1978 was relevant to *e*
their decision whether to take action in 1982.

If, however, I am wrong in expressing that view and, although the material does not
indicate this clearly, in fact the matter was given proper consideration, then I am bound
to say I would be forced to the conclusion that the discretion was exercised unreasonably.
Having regard to my interpretation of what happened in 1978, in the circumstances of
this case I can find nothing which would justify deciding to initiate further inquiries in *f*
1982. On my reading of the material, the taxpayer was led to believe that the 1978
Gymboon share transaction was closed when he paid the capital gains tax on those shares.
For him to now be faced with a new claim in respect of that transaction would be wrong
and improper unless there were circumstances, of which I have no evidence and of which
I know not, which would alter the normal implication to be drawn from such a situation.
It is because of that that I come to the conclusion that in this case the Revenue were *g*
acting in a manner not permitted by the statutory provisions contained in Part XVII of
the 1970 Act when they made an application to the taxpayer for the information which
was set out in the notice of 26 July 1982.

It seems to me that everything that thereafter happened was linked and connected to
the initiation of the procedure by the service of that notice and that being the case it
would be proper for the court to come to the conclusion that the whole machinery is *h*
affected by what happened when it was put into motion.

Judgment for the taxpayer. Declaration granted.

Solicitors: *Landau & Scanlan* (for the taxpayer); *Solicitor of Inland Revenue.*

Edwina Epstein Barrister.

a
Blackshaw v Lord and another

COURT OF APPEAL, CIVIL DIVISION
STEPHENSON, DUNN AND FOX LJJ
13, 14, 15, 16, 17 DECEMBER 1982, 17 FEBRUARY 1983

Libel and slander – Qualified privilege – Report of notice issued by public authority for information
b *of public – Notice or other matter issued by government department – Fair and accurate report of notice or other matter issued by government department – Report in newspaper – What constitutes matter issued by government department – Whether statement given by government official to journalist over telephone can constitute 'matter issued' by government department – Whether statement made without authority by government official in answer to journalist's questions can constitute 'matter issued' by government department – Defamation Act 1952, s 7(1),*
c *Sch, para 12.*

Libel and slander – Qualified privilege – Protection at common law – Report in newspaper – When newspaper report entitled to protection at common law – Journalist inferring from statement made to him by government official that plaintiff dismissed from Civil Service for incompetence – Allegations against plaintiff not substantiated at time of publication – Whether
d *public at large having legitimate interest in publication of inference – Whether newspaper having duty to publish inference – Whether fair information on matter of public interest a defence open to newspaper at common law.*

Libel and slander – Damages – Appeal – Power of Court of Appeal – New trial or substitution of award – Test – No reasonable jury properly directed and properly considering evidence could
e *have made award – No power to order new trial or substitute different award merely because Court of Appeal considering award to be excessive – £45,000 damages awarded to former civil servant for libel that he was dismissed from Civil Service for incompetence – Whether award so high that no reasonable jury properly directed and properly considering evidence could have made award.*

f
A government department operated through one of its divisions in Scotland a scheme to provide finance, within stated guidelines, for companies developing oil and gas resources in the North Sea. A House of Commons committee investigated payments which had been made under the scheme. On 23 July 1979 the head of the government department gave evidence before the committee that there had been irregularities in operating the scheme and that several people, including an under-secretary responsible for operating
g the scheme, had been reprimanded, but he did not give their names. The press were not present at the committee's proceedings but on 12 September 1979 the chairman of the committee held a press conference in the House of Commons which was attended by the first defendant, a journalist on a national newspaper. At the press conference it was stated on behalf of the committee that subsequently to the evidence given on 23 July a senior official in the government department had been dismissed. However the chairman of
h the committee stated that fraud was not involved although there had been inefficiency, incompetence, inadequate staff and inadequate supervision in operating the scheme, and substantial sums had been disbursed outside the guidelines. The first defendant wished to know the name of the official who had been dismissed and the amount of the over-payments, and on the same day he telephoned a press officer in the government department to make inquiries. The press officer told the first defendant that £52m had
j been overpaid under the scheme and read out the evidence given to the committee by the head of the government department, but he denied that anyone in the department had been dismissed or reprimanded and refused to give the first defendant any names on the ground that he was not authorised to do so. The first defendant pressed the officer to name the person who had been dismissed or reprimanded and eventually the officer

informed the first defendant over the telephone that the plaintiff had held the post of
under-secretary in the department and had been head of the division operating the a
scheme, but he also stated that the plaintiff had left that division in July 1978 to go to a
position of equal rank as head of another division of the department and that in July
1979 he had resigned from the Civil Service for personal reasons, namely to pursue a
writing career. Although two under-secretaries had been involved in the scheme the first
defendant inferred that it was the plaintiff who had been dismissed and that evening
filed an article with his newspaper which appeared in the first edition of the paper the b
next morning, 13 September. The article was headed '"Incompetence" at Ministry' and
stated that the government department had paid £52m to North Sea oil companies
which they should not have received, that the investigations of the House of Commons'
committee had led to a number of civil servants being reprimanded, that the plaintiff
was the official in charge of the department's scheme when the overpayments were
made, that the plaintiff had resigned from the Civil Service the previous month and that c
the chairman of the House of Commons committee had described the events as 'a story
of inefficiency, incompetence, inadequate staff and inadequate supervision'. The article
did not state that the plaintiff had left the Civil Service for personal reasons, and, although
in later editions of the newspaper on 13 September the defendants published the
plaintiff's own explanation of his resignation from the Civil Service, the defendants
refused to publish an apology to the plaintiff and did not publish vindications of the d
plaintiff issued by the government department, by the minister in the House of
Commons and by the House of Commons committee. The plaintiff brought an action
for libel against the first defendant and the publishers of the newspaper. The defendants
denied that the article was defamatory of the plaintiff and in the alternative alleged that
the article was the subject of qualified privilege as being, inter alia, a fair and accurate
report of a matter issued on behalf of a government department (ie the information e
given by the press officer to the first defendant) and therefore privileged by virtue of
s 7(1)[a] of, and para 12[b] of the schedule to, the Defamation Act 1952, and/or at common
law. The trial judge ruled that, if the article was a fair and accurate report such as was
alleged, it would be the subject of qualified privilege under the 1952 Act and at common
law, but he left to the jury the question whether in fact the article was a fair and accurate
report of the information given by the press officer to the first defendant. At the trial, f
counsel for the defendants, on instructions, sought to besmirch the plaintiff's credit and
reputation. The jury found that the article was defamatory of the plaintiff and that it was
not a fair and accurate report of the information given to the first defendant by the press
officer, and awarded the plaintiff damages of £45,000 for the libel. The defendants
appealed, contending (i) that the question whether the article was a fair and accurate
report of the information given to the first defendant ought not to have been left to the
jury once the judge had ruled as he did on qualified privilege because, in the absence of a g
plea of malice, there was then no issue left to go to the jury, (ii) that the jury's verdict
that the article was not a fair and accurate report should be reversed, and (iii) that the
award of damages was excessive and the Court of Appeal should substitute its own award.
By a respondent's notice the plaintiff sought to affirm the jury's verdict on the additional
grounds that, even if the article was a fair and accurate report of the information given h
to the first defendant, it was not the subject of qualified privilege under s 7(1) of and para
12 of the schedule to the 1952 Act because the information obtained from the press
officer was not a 'notice or other matter issued . . . by or on behalf of a government
department' within para 12, and neither was the article the subject of qualified privilege
at common law.

Held – The appeal would be dismissed for the following reasons— j

(1) There was material on which the trial judge had been entitled to leave to the jury
the issue whether the article was a fair and accurate report of the information given to

a Section 7, so far as material is set out at p 325 *a b*, post

b Paragraph 12 is set out at p 325 *c*, post

the first defendant notwithstanding his ruling on qualified privilege, and furthermore
a there was material on which the jury had been entitled to find that the article was not a
fair and accurate report of the information given by the press officer (see p 322 *h*, p 323 *g*
to *j*, p 332 *a b*, p 338 *d e* and p 341 *a b*, post).

(2) In any event, even if (contrary to the jury's verdict) the article was to be regarded
as a fair and accurate report of what the press officer had said to the first defendant, the
article was not protected by qualified privilege under s 7(1) of and para 12 to the schedule
b to the 1952 Act because, for information given to the press by an official of a government
department to constitute a 'notice or other matter issued ... by or on behalf of [the]
government department', within para 12, so as to entitle a fair and accurate report of the
information to the protection of qualified privilege afforded by s 7(1), the information
had to be of a formal nature issued on the initiative of the government department and
with its authority. It followed that, even though para 12 was not confined to written
c 'hand-outs' or pictorial representations, not every statement of fact made to a journalist
by a government official in the course of his employment was entitled, by virtue of para
12, to the privilege afforded by s 7(1). In particular, a government official's ex parte
statement made without authority in reply to a journalist's questioning was outside the
statutory privilege, since it could not be said to be a formal statement released to the press
on the initiative of the government department concerned. Likewise, any assumption,
d inference or speculation made on the part of a journalist from a statement made to him
by a government official was outside the statutory privilege. Accordingly, even if the
article had been a fair and accurate report of what the press officer had said to the first
defendant, then regardless of whether the press officer himself had said that it was the
plaintiff who had been dismissed, or whether that was merely the first defendant's
inference from what the press officer had said, the article would not have been protected
e by qualified privilege as a fair and accurate report of 'matter issued ... by ... [a]
government department', within para 12, since if the press officer had stated that the
plaintiff had been dismissed he had made that statement without authority, and if he
had not it was merely the first defendant's inference (see p 324 *f*, p 325 *d* to p 326 *a*,
p 332 *a b*, p 336 *d e*, p 337 *a b*, p 338 *e* to *g* and p 341 *a b*, post); dictum of Jordan CJ in
Campbell v Associated Newspapers Ltd (1948) 48 SR (NSW) at 303 and *Boston v W S Bagshaw*
f *& Sons* [1966] 2 All ER 906 applied.

(3) Furthermore, for a newspaper report to be protected by qualified privilege at
common law (as preserved by s 7(4) of the 1952 Act), it was not enough that the report
was of general interest to the public. The public at large had to have a legitimate interest
in receiving the information contained in the report and the publisher had to have a
corresponding duty to publish the report to the public at large. Accordingly, a plea of
g fair information on a matter of public interest did not constitute a defence at common
law. Whether the public had a legitimate interest in receiving a report in a newspaper
and the publisher had a corresponding duty to publish it depended on the particular
circumstances. It followed that, since at the time the first defendant wrote his article any
allegation of incompetence against the plaintiff had not been made good, the public at
large could not be said to have had a legitimate interest in receiving either the press
h officer's statement or the first defendant's inference or speculation that it was the plaintiff
who had been dismissed for incompetence and at that stage the defendants had no duty
to publish what was then mere rumour about the plaintiff. Therefore, even if (contrary
to the jury's verdict) the article was to be regarded as a fair and accurate report of what
the press officer had said, it would not be protected at common law by qualified privilege
(see p 324 *f*, p 327 *a* to *h*, p 328 *a b*, p 332 *a b h*, p 334 *b c e f*, p 336 *e f*, p 338 *g*, p 339 *h j*
j and p 341 *a b*, post); *Purcell v Sowler* (1877) 2 CPD 215, dicta of Buckley LJ in *Adam v
Ward* (1915) 31 TLR at 304 and of Cantley J in *London Artists Ltd v Littler* [1968] 1 All ER
at 1085 applied; *Perera v Peiris* [1949] AC 1 and *Webb v Times Publishing Co Ltd* [1960] 2
All ER 789 considered.

(4) On the issue of damages, the Court of Appeal, when considering whether to allow
an appeal against a jury's award of damages for defamation, had to apply a stricter test
than it applied to an appeal against a judge's award of damages and could only reduce a

jury's award if the sum they had awarded was one which no reasonable jury, properly
directed by the judge and properly considering the evidence, could have awarded. a
Moreover, there was little value in comparing an award for defamation with awards for
personal injuries since the difference between the two kinds of award was too great to be
of real value. It followed that the Court of Appeal could not substitute its own award for
a libel merely because it considered that the jury's award was excessive. In all the
circumstances, in particular having regard to the defendants' conduct before and during
the trial which had aggravated the injury to the plaintiff's feelings caused by the b
publication of the libel, the court could not say that £45,000 was a sum that no reasonable
jury properly directed and properly considering the evidence before it could have
awarded, even though in the court's view the award was far too high (see p 328 *b* to *e*,
p 331 *c d* and *j* to p 332 *b*, p 337 *b c g* to *j*, p 339 *j* to p 340 *c* and *e* to p 341 *b*, post); dictum
of Lord Esher MR in *Praed v Graham* (1889) 24 QBD at 55 and *Cassell & Co Ltd v Broome*
[1972] 1 All ER 801 applied; dictum of Holroyd Pearce LJ in *Lewis v Daily Telegraph Ltd* c
[1962] 2 All ER at 717 followed; dictum of Diplock LJ in *McCarey v Associated Newspapers
Ltd* [1964] 3 All ER at 960 not followed.

Notes

For privileged publications and the defence of qualified privilege generally, see 28
Halsbury's Laws (4th edn) paras 108–111, 115, and for cases on the subject, see 32 Digest
(Reissue) 228–232, *1934–1958*. d

For the statutory privilege accorded to reports in a newspaper of matter issued by or on behalf of a government department, see 28 Halsbury's Laws (4th edn) paras 128, 130.

For the Defamation Act 1952, s 7, Sch, para 12, see 19 Halsbury's Statutes (3rd edn) 38, 45.

Cases referred to in judgments e

Adam v Ward (1915) 31 TLR 299, CA; *affd* [1917] AC 309, [1916–17] All ER Rep 157, HL.
Boston v W S Bagshaw & Sons [1966] 2 All ER 906, [1966] 1 WLR 1126, CA.
Campbell v Associated Newspapers Ltd (1948) 48 SR (NSW) 301.
Cassell & Co Ltd v Broome [1972] 1 All ER 801, [1972] AC 1027, [1972] 2 WLR 645, HL.
Chapman v Lord Ellesmere [1932] 2 KB 431, [1932] All ER Rep 221, CA. f
Cox v Feeney (1863) 4 F & F 13, 176 ER 445, NP.
Croke v Wiseman [1981] 3 All ER 852, [1982] 1 WLR 71, CA.
Dunford Publicity Studios Ltd v News Media Ownership Ltd [1971] NZLR 961.
Gillard v Goldsmith [1981] CA Bound Transcript 102.
Gilpin v Fowler (1854) 9 Exch 615, 156 ER 263, Ex Ch.
Hayward v Thompson [1981] 3 All ER 450, [1982] QB 47, [1981] 3 WLR 470, CA. g
Jones v Brough [1981] CLY 600.
Lewis v Daily Telegraph Ltd [1962] 2 All ER 698, [1963] 1 QB 340, [1962] 3 WLR 50, CA; *affd* [1963] 2 All ER 151, [1964] AC 234, [1963] 2 WLR 1063, HL.
London Artists Ltd v Littler [1968] 1 All ER 1075, [1968] 1 WLR 607; *on appeal* [1969] 2 All ER 193, [1969] 2 QB 375, [1969] 2 WLR 409, CA.
McCarey v Associated Newspapers Ltd [1964] 3 All ER 947, [1965] 2 QB 86, [1965] 2 WLR 45, CA. h
Mangena v Wright [1909] 2 KB 958.
Perera v Peiris [1949] AC 1, PC.
Praed v Graham (1889) 24 QBD 53, CA.
Purcell v Sowler (1877) 2 CPD 215, CA.
Stuart v Bell [1891] 2 QB 341, CA. j
Webb v Times Publishing Co Ltd [1960] 2 All ER 789, [1960] 2 QB 535, [1960] 3 WLR 352.
Youssoupoff v Metro-Goldwyn Mayer Pictures Ltd (1934) 50 TLR 581, CA.

Appeal

By a writ dated 26 October 1979 the plaintiff, Alan Blackshaw, claimed against the defendants, Rodney Lord, the economics correspondent of the Daily Telegraph newspaper, and the Daily Telegraph Ltd, the publishers of the newspaper, damages for a libel on the plaintiff contained in an article published in the Daily Telegraph on 13 September 1979. By their defence the defendants denied that the words complained of bore a meaning defamatory of the plaintiff and in the alternative alleged that the words complained of were privileged as an accurate report of Parliamentary proceedings or as a fair and accurate report of matter issued on behalf of a government department under para 12 of the schedule to the Defamation Act 1952 and/or at common law. At the trial of the action, before Caulfield J and a jury, the judge ruled, inter alia, that if the article was a fair and accurate report of what was said to the first defendant by an officer in a government department it was subject to qualified privilege by virtue of para 12 of the schedule to the 1952 Act and at common law. The jury found that the words complained were defamatory of the plaintiff and were not a fair and accurate report of what was said to the first defendant by the officer in the government department, and awarded the plaintiff damages of £45,000 for libel. On 26 February 1981 Caulfield J on the jury's verdict entered judgment for the plaintiff. The defendants appealed against the verdict and judgment, asking that they be set aside, alternatively that a new trial be ordered or, in the further alternative, that the award of damages be set aside and a new trial be ordered as to the quantum of damages. By a respondent's notice the plaintiff contended that the verdict and judgment should be affirmed on the grounds, additional to those relied on in the court below, that if the words complained of were a fair and accurate report of what was said to the first defendant (1) they were not subject to qualified privilege under the 1952 Act because they did not constitute a fair and accurate report or summary of any 'notice or other matter issued for the information of the public by or on behalf of any government department' within para 12 of the schedule to the 1952 Act and (2) nor were the words complained of subject to qualified privilege at common law. The facts are set out in the judgment of Stephenson LJ.

Peter Bowsher QC and *James Price* for the defendants.
David Eady for the plaintiff.

Cur adv vult

17 February. The following judgments were delivered.

STEPHENSON LJ. This is an appeal by the defendants, the Daily Telegraph Ltd and their economics correspondent, Mr Lord, against a verdict of a jury and judgment entered thereon by Caulfield J on 26 February 1981 for £45,000 damages for a libel on the plaintiff, Mr Blackshaw.

The libel complained of is contained in the heading and the first four paragraphs of an article written by Mr Lord, the first defendant, and published by the second defendant in the first edition of the Daily Telegraph for 13 September 1979. The whole article reads thus:

'"Incompetence" at Ministry cost £52m

By *RODNEY LORD, Economics Correspondent*

A GOVERNMENT Department has paid North Sea oil companies £52 million in grants which they should not have received. The money is unlikely to be repaid.

Investigations by the Exchequer and Audit Department and the Public Accounts Committee of the House of Commons have led to a number of senior civil servants being reprimanded.

Mr Alan Blackshaw, the official in charge of Offshore Supplies Office when the payments were being made, resigned from the civil service last month.

Mr Joel Barnett, Labour MP for Heywood and Royston and chairman of the Public Accounts Committee yesterday described the events as "a story of inefficiency, incompetence, inadequate staff and inadequate supervision."

But he emphasised that there had been no fraud.

> In so far unpublished evidence to the committee Sir Jack Rampton, Permanent Secretary of the Energy Department, admitted that there had been "a number of irregularities. a
>
> He added: "By that I mean on the one hand mistakes and, on the other, decisions to depart from the guidelines which were agreed with the Treasury and published for the benefit of industry without the necessary consultation" within the Department or with the Treasury as was necessary in certain cases.
>
> "That is a fact and I'm not attempting to argue with that at all." b
>
> Late applications
>
> The money paid consisted of grants, under a scheme to provide interest relief on goods and services supplied for North Sea operations by British companies. Under the scheme introduced in 1973, companies are entitled to grants of 3 per cent. a year on 80 per cent. of the value of qualifying contracts.
>
> Until last November there was a time limit of three months to apply for interest c
> rate relief. But relief was paid on applications which fell outside the about a third of the total relief period.
>
> The £52 million constitutes of £150–160 million.
>
> The scheme is to be terminated at the end of this present financial year.
>
> Sir Jack in his evidence said that an under secretary and a number of assistant secretaries had been reprimanded. Their promotion prospects are understood to d
> have been affected.'

The plaintiff does not complain of the last paragraph or of anything but the first four paragraphs. They are alleged to mean—

> 'that by reason of the Plaintiff's incompetence and inefficiency as the official in charge of the Offshore Supplies Office £52 million of public money had been lost e
> or improperly paid and in consequence the Plaintiff had been reprimanded and compelled to resign from the civil service.'

The defendants denied that those paragraphs were defamatory, and alternatively alleged that they were privileged in as many as three different ways. The jury found in answer to the first question put to them by the judge that the words complained of were f
defamatory of the plaintiff and from that finding there is no appeal. The second question they were asked was, 'Are the words complained of in the context of the Daily Telegraph article as a whole a fair and accurate report or summary of what was said by Mr Martyn Smith, the Department of Energy press officer, to Mr Rodney Lord, the Daily Telegraph journalist?' They answered that 'No', and in answer to the third question, 'What sum do you all propose as damages?' they gave the answer, '£45,000.' g

The second question follows a ruling of the judge which is the subject of criticism by the plaintiff in a respondent's notice contending that the verdict and judgment should be affirmed on additional grounds. The defendants contend that the judge should not have left the question to the jury and the jury should not have answered it as they did. The judge should have entered judgment for the defendants because after his ruling on qualified privilege there was, in the absence of any plea of malice, no issue to go to the h
jury. To explain the rulings and the contentions of the parties on the issues of privilege to which the unusual facts of the case gave rise, it is necessary to state those facts in some detail.

The plaintiff had a distinguished scholastic career and distinguished service in the Royal Marines before he entered the Home Civil Service in 1956, in which he served until 10 August 1979. During those years he wrote and published a standard handbook j
on mountaineering and worked at another on skiing, two activities in which he is a recognised expert. In 1974 he was promoted at the early age of 41 to the rank of under-secretary in the newly created Department of Energy and was posted to Glasgow as deputy director general of the Offshore Supplies Office set up there when that office was moved from London. In 1977 he succeeded another under-secretary as director general and occupied that responsible position until November 1978, when he was transferred

to London to be head of the coal division in the Department of Energy. But he found
a living in Scotland and working in London expensive and tiring; he wanted to devote more time to complete his book on skiing and other works. So he resigned, as has been said, in August 1979 for a career as business consultant and author, and was presented with a silver tankard on behalf of the department by the Permanent Under-Secretary of State for the department, Sir Jack Rampton, to whom he had given notice of his resignation a month earlier.

b The Offshore Supplies Office had the task of assisting British industry in developing oil and gas resources in the North Sea. To that end the Department of Energy arranged a scheme for granting interest relief. I take this account of it from the opening paragraphs of the Third Report from the Committee of Public Accounts (HC Paper (1979–80) no 286), ordered by the House of Commons to be printed 26 November 1979:

> '1. In 1973 the Treasury approved arrangements made by the Department of
> c Energy for giving financial assistance under section 8 of the Industry Act 1972 in the form of interest relief grants to reduce the cost to companies developing oil and gas resources on the UK continental shelf of credit obtained to finance the supply of United Kingdom goods and services. These supplies do not qualify for Export Credits Guarantee Department assistance and the interest relief grant scheme was intended to compensate in some measure for the preferential export credit rates
> d available to overseas suppliers. Under the arrangements the Department pay grants at three per cent per annum on not more than 80 per cent of the value of qualifying contracts for fixed offshore installations, equipment, goods or services of not less than £100,000. Applicants must have obtained credit to finance their contracts through specified banks and the Department issue the grants as periodic payments for up to eight years, allowing three years for drawing loans and five years for their
> e repayment. Applicants are subject to corporation tax on the grants they receive.
>
> 2. In 1974 the Department issued a Guide for Industry setting out the detailed rules and procedures approved by the Treasury for submission of claims and calculation of grants. The Guide formed the written operating instructions which staff in the Department's Offshore Supplies Office were required to follow when considering applications for grants under the interest relief grants scheme. It
> f provided for the initial application to cover a period not exceeding 12 months, and subsequent applications periods of 6 or 12 months, and allowed three months from the end of each period for the submission of claims.'

The committee, under the chairmanship of Mr Joel Barnett MP, heard evidence in public on 23 July 1979 and again on 31 October 1979. Paragraph 3 of the report shows that the committee was investigating after a report by the Comptroller and Auditor
g General. That paragraph reads:

> 'A test examination by the C & AG's staff of claims and supporting documents relating to grants paid up to June 1978 showed that a number of payments had been approved which differed from those allowable on a strict interpretation of the Guide. The Department accepted that there had been six cases involving the rules for
> h reckoning the amount of borrowing qualifying for grant and resulting in overpayments totalling £1,912,000, a further six cases where grants totalling £640,000 had been paid in respect of claims rendered after expiry of the three months period allowed for submission, and other cases of failure to convert foreign currency borrowing to sterling in the manner specified in the Guide. In some cases excessive grant payments had been caused by clerical error in calculations but in
> j other cases there had been conscious departures from the terms of the Guide.'

On 23 July 1979 the chairman asked Sir Jack Rampton this question:

> '118. There seems to have been a rather disturbing failure of public expenditure control as far as one can see, which no doubt you will have been looking into very carefully. What weaknesses have you identified, and who were responsible for those weaknesses?'

In a long answer Sir Jack explained that there had been irregularities including 'decisions to depart from the guide lines which were agreed with the Treasury . . . without the necessary consultation within the Department or with the Treasury . . .' He gave as reasons the unforeseen complexity of the scheme, the lack of continuity when the Department of Energy was split off from the Department of Trade and Industry, the move of the Offshore Supplies Office from London to Glasgow with consequent taking of decisions by the operating staff without reference to senior officers and without sufficient supervision of the operating staff, an unlucky failure of internal audits to reveal the irregularities. He concluded his answer by saying:

> 'The decisions—and they will be detailed here—which were taken by those running the scheme, and which resulted in decisions which were not in line with the guide lines, were not, in my view, stupid decisions. They were sensible decisions, apart from a limited number of mistakes. They were sensible decisions which might, in my view, have led to adjustments and changes in the scheme at an earlier stage had they been pursued in the proper way. After all, in a scheme of this kind, one has reason to expect that there would be modifications of guide lines in the light of experience which, because of the events that I have just been talking about, did not, of course, happen.'

In the examination of Sir Jack Rampton the following question and answer is to be found in the report:

> '172. Has there been any talk of disciplinary action against the people responsible?—All the people involved have been reprimanded. Of course, it will stand to their account for the future. A number of the people concerned were immediately transferred elsewhere and clearly this will be a serious disadvantage for them in future years.'

The following questions addressed to Sir Jack Rampton and his answers to them are printed in the report:

> '225. What is the most senior level of civil servant who has been reprimanded?—It goes to under-secretary.*
>
> 226. That would be the under-secretary based in Glasgow?—Yes.*
>
> 227. So that in the opinion of the Department there is no blame to be attached to anyone based in London?—No, I did not say that. Within that, yes, assistant secretaries as well.
>
> 228. But not enough blame to justify a reprimand? It is the people in Glasgow who have been held responsible?—No, I was talking about all the people involved, whether they were in London or not, or in Glasgow. That concerns people in London, too.
>
> 229. But the most senior level would be somebody at Glasgow who has been reprimanded?—That is right.'

The asterisks call attention to a footnote in these terms:

> '*Note*: The witness subsequently submitted the following note to the Chairman of the Committee: On checking the proof of the evidence given on 23 July, I am afraid I find with the greatest regret that I misinformed the Public Accounts Committee in my reference to the reprimand of an Under-Secretary of the Offshore Supplies Office in Glasgow (paras. 225–226 of the draft evidence). In fact no Under-Secretary has been reprimanded and I ask the Committee to accept my most sincere apologies for this mistake.'

The date of the note submitted to the chairman was 17 September 1979, four days after the publication of Mr Lord's article in the Daily Telegraph.

When the committee reported in November, they referred to the Treasury's agreement in 1978 to extend the period for making claims to interest relief grants from three months to six months and added:

> '8. Nevertheless the Department accepted that there had been poor administration and lack of judgment by various officers but gave us assurances, which we accept, that no question of dishonesty or collusion on the part of the Department's staff had been involved. We appreciate that where conscious decisions to depart from the time-limits or other aspects of the Guide were involved, the staff who took them thought that they were acting in accordance with the intentions and policy objectives of the scheme. This is borne out by the subsequent Treasury decision to extend the time-limit. But the fact remains that clear guidelines governing the disbursement of substantial sums of public money, which had been carefully worked out by the Department and approved in detail by the Treasury, were not followed. We agree with the Accounting Officer that there has been poor administration and lack of judgement by those responsible for the execution and supervision of this scheme.'

In para 15 the committee made these comments:

> '15. We wish to emphasise our great concern and amazement that during our investigations grossly inaccurate and misleading evidence was given by those who must be presumed to be fully and accurately briefed beforehand. For example, in July the Department's initial answers implied that about a dozen persons involved in operating the scheme had been reprimanded, including an Under Secretary. We were told by letter in September that an Under Secretary had not been reprimanded and later that two officers only had been reprimanded. Again in July, after examination of less than half of the paid claims, the Department had estimated that the value of payments and commitments outside the Guide totalled £52 million. In October we were told that this figure had been overstated through an arithmetical error of no less than £11 million. We were also told in July that none of the eight sample cases examined by internal audit in 1976–77 had included irregularities, but in October the Department admitted that special re-examination had identified underlying irregularities in three of the eight cases.'

Now the proceedings of the committee on 23 July 1979 had not been attended by the press; but at noon on 12 September Mr Barnett held a press conference in the House of Commons, which was attended by Mr Lord and nine other journalists, and at that conference among other less newsworthy matters emerged, as a result of an intervention by a member of the committee, some of the recorded evidence which had been given to the committee by Sir Jack Rampton in July about interest relief grants, and a statement from the chairman that after that evidence had been given a senior official of the Department of Energy in Scotland had been dismissed.

Mr Lord gave unchallenged evidence, refreshing his memory from notes which he made at the time, of what Mr Barnett told the press at that interview. Referring to those notes his evidence was this:

> 'It was said that the grants were being paid for interest relief when the grants should not have been being paid if the rules had been properly followed. "Test check showed tens of millions of pounds"—that was a check by the Comptroller and Auditor General which showed that tens of millions of pounds had been paid outside the proper rules. Joel Barnett then emphasised that there was no fraud involved, that it was a matter of inefficiency, incompetence, inadequate staff and inadequate supervision of those paying out the money. I think the "£9 million" figure is a reference—I am not totally sure, but it may be a reference to the amount that had actually been paid out at that stage. "More written evidence has been requested", that is, more written evidence had been requested by the Public Accounts Committee from the Department of Energy and was in process of being supplied by the Department. And tens of millions of pounds had been committed

> but had not yet been actually paid over. The Public Accounts Committee believed that it was in their power to request the repayment of the money. And the final sentence is a reference, I suppose, to Sir Jack Rampton's evidence when, at any rate, the members of the PAC suggested that one reason given for these irregular payments was that one part of the Offshore Supplies Office was in Glasgow—or one part of the Department was in Glasgow and one was in London. So there was not perhaps proper co-ordination between the two.'

Mr Lord had been given the name of the secretary of the Public Accounts Committee, Mrs Helen Irwin, as a source of additional information about the interest relief grants. He wrote down a number of questions for her including 'How much money paid or to be paid?' and 'Who was the official?' 'Was he dismissed?' 'Any others?' and the names of press officers and an assistant secretary at the Department of Energy, headed by Mr Martyn Smith. Having failed to get in touch with Mrs Irwin by telephone, he got a telephone call through to Mr Martyn Smith in the press office of the department that afternoon. It is what Mr Smith told him in that conversation which he claims to have reported or summarised fairly and accurately in the article of which the plaintiff complains and for which the defendants claim privilege. Mr Lord gave the jury his version of this all-important conversation and so did Mr Smith. There was no material difference in their two accounts except on one small, but, in the opinion of the judge crucial, point. Mr Lord again had his contemporary notes to rely on; Mr Smith had only his recollection, which he said was not detailed. Both accounts were concisely and correctly summed up by the judge to the jury.

Mr Lord asked Mr Smith questions including those he had written down. To 'How much money paid or to be paid?' Mr Smith answered that '£52 million out of £150–160 million' was overpaid because of the unauthorised practices. Asked about his evidence given to the committee, Mr Smith read out from the print which he had of the evidence taken by the committee, question 118 and Sir Jack Rampton's long answer which I have quoted in part from the committee's report. He read out other passages from the evidence including questions and answers 225, 226 and 227, which I have read. When he heard those answers, Mr Lord asked who was the official who had been reprimanded. His evidence of what followed was this:

> '*Q.* So you are saying that at this point you said, "Who was the official?" *A.* And I think that then it transpired that Mr Blackshaw was the official in charge of the OSO for most of the relevant period, but that he had actually left the OSO and gone to the coal division about a year before the evidence was taken.
>
> *Q.* That is what Mr Smith told you? *A.* That is right.
>
> *Q.* Then there is a reference in your note to *Who's Who*. How did that come up? *A.* Mr Smith told me that he had an entry in *Who's Who*.
>
> *Q.* Would you turn over to p 21 of the bundle. You see the reference to mountaineering. What was that? *A.* Mr Smith told me that Mr Blackshaw had written a Penguin book on mountaineering.
>
> *Q.* And how did the conversation go on? *A.* I asked "Was he dismissed?" which is the next question on my list of questions at p 18, and Martyn Smith said, as I have written down, "No one was dismissed as a result of this business" and that Mr Blackshaw left the Civil Service for personal reasons. But he said words to the effect that the person who was reprimanded must have been Mr Blackshaw.
>
> *Caulfield J.* That is an important point on which to finish today.'

The conversation ended with a few more questions, in answer to one of which Mr Smith told Mr Lord that the plaintiff lived in Linlithgow, Scotland. Then Mr Lord telephoned Mrs Irwin again and asked her to confirm that Sir Jack Rampton had given evidence to the Public Accounts Committee. And she said (I quote from his evidence)—

> 'that he had and I think she said that written evidence had been given to the committee on various occasions and on 23 July Sir Jack had appeared to give oral evidence before the committee. I asked her whether it was true that someone had

> been dismissed from the Civil Service, as Mr Joel Barnett, the chairman of the committee, had said, and she said that she couldn't confirm that and that she couldn't say anything that was on the record. But she did say that someone had left the Civil Service since, and that that person was the head of the Offshore Supplies Office.
>
> Q. Do those square brackets round that sentence have any significance? *A.* They indicate that she had said that she couldn't be quoted on that matter, that it was off the record.
>
> Q. Yes, I see. Then how did the conversation continue? *A.* Well, I asked her who the person was who had left the Civil Service. I think I said, "Was it Alan Blackshaw, the under-secretary in Glasgow?" and she confirmed that it was. I then asked her one or two details about the scheme and she elaborated slightly, saying that the interest relief grants were only payable to British companies, to UK companies.'

The sentence in square brackets was as follows in Mr Lord's note: 'One bloke has left Civil Service since—boss of Offshore Supplies Office.'

He then, at about 5.30 pm, telephoned the plaintiff's Linlithgow number, which he got from *Who's Who*, was told by the plaintiff's wife that he was flying home, typed out some details about him from *Who's Who*, then went home himself and wrote and filed the story which appeared in the article of 13 September. After another telephone call to the plaintiff before he had reached home, Mr Lord at last on a final call spoke at 11 pm to the plaintiff and asked him whether he had been reprimanded. The plaintiff said, 'No'. I quote again from Mr Lord's evidence:

> 'Mr Blackshaw told me that he had left the Offshore Supplies Office in the normal way last summer. He said that the audit report prepared by the Comptroller and Auditor General on which the Public Accounts Committee's investigations were based had been during the autumn. He said that he had not been consulted about the report but that he had spoken, I think, about it, I think primarily to give details of the lines of communication in the department. I wanted to be absolutely certain that he had not been reprimanded and that I had got that right and that there was no connection between his departure from the Civil Service and the payments outside the rules. And he said that there was absolutely no connection whatsoever. He said, "I came up to Scotland in 1974 with my family and I like it up here." He explained that, in dealing with the North Sea, he had been away an average of 110 nights a year and he said, "I decided it was a rational decision to concentrate on my mountaineering writing in these circumstances."'

Mr Lord then telephoned the gist of this conversation to the Daily Telegraph newsroom and it was incorporated in all later editions of his article.

Now the only question which the judge could and did leave to the jury on the defendants' liability to pay the plaintiff something, apart from the question whether the article was defamatory, was whether it was a fair and accurate report or summary of what Mr Smith had told Mr Lord on the telephone, not of what Mrs Irwin, or the plaintiff, had told him. The only challenge was to what Mr Smith had said and whether Mr Lord had fairly and accurately reported or summarised his conversation with Mr Smith. The jury's attention was accordingly directed to Mr Smith's version of that conversation and the respects in which it differed from Mr Lord's.

Mr Smith had a busy day on 12 September 1979. From the forenoon till 6 pm he had a great many telephone calls from journalists, all wanting to know who was the under-secretary of the department who had, according to Sir Jack Rampton's evidence, been reprimanded. Mr Smith naturally could not remember which journalist had asked him which question or had been given which answer, but of one thing he was certain: he stuck rigidly to standard practice in all government departments at the time 'that you do not name specific civil servants unless there are names given in evidence', and as none was given in evidence here he could not have named the plaintiff as the reprimanded under-secretary. He admitted that he had named the plaintiff to Mr Lord as one of those

who had held the post of under-secretary, but there were according to his evidence four
such, and always two in Glasgow. Indeed, he does not seem to have disputed Mr Lord's a
evidence that he had mentioned the plaintiff's name three times, telling Mr Lord that he
had left the Offshore Supplies Division a year before 23 July 1979 to go to a position of
equal rank as head of the coal division, and that he had left the Civil Service altogether a
month before 12 September for personal reasons, namely to write about mountaineering.
But he could not accept that he said to Mr Lord that the reprimanded under-secretary
must be Blackshaw. He frankly admitted that it would be 'an inevitable conclusion' by a b
process of elimination on the part of a reporter who consulted *Who's Who* or *Whitaker's
Almanack* or the *Civil Service Year Book*, because he was under the mistaken impression
that *Whitaker's Almanack* gave the plaintiff that rank and that he was the only man with
the specific title of under-secretary. But he had referred Mr Lord and others to such
works of reference in the course of performing his duty not to name any civil servant not
named in the evidence about which they were inquiring. The 'Must be Blackshaw' which c
Mr Lord had put in his notes was therefore a record of what Mr Lord inferred or
concluded, not of what Mr Smith had said. And that was perhaps confirmed by the
absence of quotation marks round those three words, though in the immediately
preceding notes Mr Lord had put quotation marks round such words as 'No-one was
dismissed as result of this business' and 'for personal reasons'. It was this difference about
'Must be Blackshaw' which the judge told the jury was the main issue raised by the d
second question they had to answer, namely whether Mr Lord's article was a fair and
accurate report or summary of what Mr Smith had told him.

There is no appeal from the jury's answer to the first question, whether the words
complained of were defamatory of the plaintiff. The defendants do not now maintain
that they were not defamatory. That was not always their attitude. At the trial Mr Lord
maintained that they were not defamatory. He told the jury that he had simply reported e
neutral facts, including the plaintiff's resignation, and had nothing to apologise for.
Hence the defendants had never apologised to the plaintiff and had been less than
enthusiastic, as I shall point out later, in reporting the efforts of others to vindicate the
plaintiff's reputation before trial. But the defendants still contend that the paragraphs
complained of in the context of the whole article are a fair and accurate report or
summary of what Mr Smith said to Mr Lord and they appeal against the jury's verdict on f
the second question. I have already stated that they have a prior contention, namely that
the judge should not have left that question to the jury. But, if the jury's answer to it
stands, it does not matter to the parties, or at least to the plaintiff, whether the jury should
or should not have had to consider it, because the plaintiff is entitled to damages and the
only remaining question is the third question, 'How much?' It is of interest to the
defendants, and it may be to the press generally, that the judge's rulings should be g
reversed or disapproved; but, if the defendants cannot succeed in upsetting the jury's
verdict against the fairness and accuracy of Mr Lord's report of his conversation with Mr
Smith, the plaintiff succeeds in getting judgment against them for the libel complained
of.

In my judgment, there was material on the issue whether the report was fair and
accurate which entitled the judge to leave the question to the jury and entitled the jury h
to find that it was not.

It is not altogether easy to keep the question whether the report was defamatory
separate from the question whether it was fair and accurate, for Mr Lord's denials that it
was defamatory imply that it was fair because it was not defamatory and that if it was
defamatory it was not fair. But there was more than that in favour of the jury's view.
Counsel for the plaintiff relied at the trial, as he did in this court, on what the judge called j
'gaps and silences' in the report, which were not fair and accurate. Mr Lord referred to
the plaintiff's resignation but left out that it was 'for personal reasons', though he
admitted that Mr Smith had made that plain and that he himself had written those words
down in his notes in quotation marks. Mr Lord quoted part of Sir Jack Rampton's
evidence, but he left out his evidence that 'sensible decisions' were made by the civil

servants who departed from the guidelines, although that part of his evidence was fully quoted in Mr Lord's notes. He left out all reference to the plaintiff's transfer to head of the coal division, though there was a reference in his notes to the plaintiff's going to the coal division. Finally, there was the contradictory evidence of Mr Lord and Mr Smith on 'Must be Blackshaw' with its bearing on the introduction into the article of the plaintiff's name, an introduction made only in the Daily Telegraph and the Daily Mail in reporting the matter. On this question the judge told the jury:

> 'Now that article, in substance, apart from the quotation from Mr Joel Barnett, is, according to Lord, a fair and accurate report of the information obtained from Smith. You will see that the main issue between Smith and Lord is on the words, "Must be Blackshaw." Was that a conclusion reached without authority and without foundation by Lord, or was it a conclusion conveyed to him by Mr Smith? You might think, although that is a brief way of putting the issue, that that is really the issue between Smith and Rodney Lord.'

Of the article he said:

> 'He [Mr Lord] would not accept from [counsel for the plaintiff] the interpretation put on his article by [counsel for the plaintiff]. He did have to accept, and you must consider it, that he did not include in his article that Mr Blackshaw had resigned for personal reasons. Mind you, Mr Blackshaw in his own evidence said even if that had been included it would not have cleared the article from his point of view. He did not include in this article, though it is included in his notes, that sensible decisions were made by the civil servants involved who had departed from the guidelines. That does not appear from the article.'

Counsel for the defendants made much of Mr Smith's 'inevitable conclusion' that the plaintiff was the reprimanded under-secretary and the failure of counsel for the plaintiff to get Mr Smith to recede in re-examination from what he had said in cross-examination. Counsel for the plaintiff conceded that there might be cases in which what a press officer said without naming a culprit might be tantamount to identifying the culprit, and when there is only one holder of an office at all material times its holder would be identified without naming him and the press officer, not the reporter, would be responsible for whatever the reporter attributed to the holder. But that is not this case, though it may come near it. Here there was always one other under-secretary than the plaintiff who might have been named as the culprit, and, however probable the inference that the plaintiff was the man, it was not in fact a necessary inference. He only became more likely to be the man if his position was coupled with his resignation from it, and the jury were entitled to accept Mr Smith's evidence that that coupling was something he resolutely refused to make.

The jury were, in my opinion, entitled to conclude, as their answer to the second question shows they did, that in the telephone conversation Mr Smith had not blamed the plaintiff and had indeed been studiously careful to avoid implicating him in the maladministration or in connecting his resignation with it, but that Mr Lord in his article reporting the conversation was blaming the plaintiff and inserted his name and the reference to his resignation, and left out what was favourable to him, so as to give his readers the impression that the plaintiff, in the judge's words in directing the jury on the first question, 'was got rid of because of incompetence arising out of the Offshore Supplies Office interest grant maladministration'. We have not heard Mr Smith and Mr Lord in the witness box; but on reading the transcript of their evidence I see no reason to suppose that the jury, who did see and hear them examined and cross-examined, came to a wrong conclusion about either of them, let alone an impossible conclusion. I would dismiss the defendants' appeal on liability on that ground.

Counsel for the defendants complained of certain misdirections and non-directions in the judge's summing up, in particular (1) that he twice told the jury that Mr Lord's notes did not constitute evidence, (2) that he omitted to refer to the standard of proof and (3) that he failed to correct certain misleading suggestions in the closing speech of counsel for the plaintiff. As to (1), the judge was admittedly wrong, as counsel for the defendants had made the notes an exhibit after Mr Lord had been cross-examined and re-examined on them. But the judge in his summing up invited the jury to regard the notes as 'rather good' and referred to them more than once. As to (2), counsel for the plaintiff referred to the correct standard of proof in addressing the jury, and I cannot agree with counsel for the defendants that the jury may have decided the case on the higher standard made familiar to them in broadcasts on radio and television. As to (3), we have examined the forensic eloquence which led counsel for the plaintiff at one point to confuse fair reporting with fair play generally, before he directed the minds of the jury correctly, for the second time, to answering the second question by comparing the article with the evidence of what Mr Smith said.

We have to remember that RSC Ord 59, r 11(2) provides:

> 'The Court of Appeal shall not be bound to order a new trial on the ground of misdirection, or of the improper admission or rejection of evidence . . . unless in the opinion of the Court of Appeal some substantial wrong or miscarriage has been thereby occasioned.'

I shall consider another part of this rule in connection with the defendants' appeal on damages, but I hold that these alleged misdirections in the summing up have not occasioned any wrong or miscarriage and the verdicts of the jury in favour of the plaintiff on the first two questions cannot be impugned on the ground of misdirection. Indeed, the misdirections come within those which Lord Denning MR dismissed in *Gillard v Goldsmith* [1981] CA Bound Transcript 102 at p 14, decided on 19 January 1981, and in *Hayward v Thompson* [1981] 3 All ER 450 at 459, [1982] QB 47 at 63 as niceties of analysis not plainly leading to a substantial miscarriage or invalidating a jury's verdict.

That is the end of the defence on liability and it might be thought enough to leave it there and undesirable to say more before going on to consider the appeal against the quantum of damages. But counsel for the plaintiff has mounted a strong challenge to the judge's rulings in the defendants' favour and counsel for the defendants agrees that these are important rulings on a subject on which there is a dearth of authority. He has submitted that it is important for the freedom of the press to uphold them. We have therefore heard interesting arguments on them. I am of opinion that both rulings were wrong and, as I understand Dunn and Fox LJJ are of the same opinion, we should say so.

The judge gave three rulings on qualified privilege. First, he rejected a plea in para 5 of the defence that—

> 'the article . . . was a fair and accurate report of proceedings in Parliament, namely the examination of witnesses by the Committee of Public Accounts on 23rd July 1979, and accordingly the said article is privileged.'

He held that the defendants' article was not a report of Parliamentary proceedings. The defendants' challenge to that ruling in their notice of appeal has not been pursued by counsel for the defendants in this court.

Next he upheld a plea, or rather two pleas, in para 6 of the defence that—

> 'the . . . article . . . was a fair and accurate report of matter issued on behalf of a government department and/or on behalf of the members of a Parliamentary Committee and accordingly the . . . article is privileged by virtue of paragraph 12 of Part II of the Schedule of the Defamation Act, 1952 and/or at common law.'

The second plea of common law privilege was added to the first plea of statutory privilege by reamendment of the amended defence on the first morning of the trial. It ran:

> 'In the premises [which included particulars added at the same time] the Defendants had a legitimate duty or interest to publish the words complained of and the readers of The Daily Telegraph had a corresponding or common interest therein.'

Section 7 of the Defamation Act 1952 provides:

a '(1) Subject to the provisions of this section, the publication in a newspaper of any such report or other matter as is mentioned in the Schedule to this Act shall be privileged unless the publication is proved to be made with malice . . .

(3) Nothing in this section shall be construed as protecting the publication of any matter the publication of which is prohibited by law, or of any matter which is not of public concern and the publication of which is not for the public benefit.

b (4) Nothing in this section shall be construed as limiting or abridging any privilege subsisting (otherwise than by virtue of section four of the Law of Libel Amendment Act, 1888) immediately before the commencement of this Act . . .'

Part II of the schedule to the 1952 Act lists a number of 'Statements Privileged Subject to Explanation or Contradiction' under five heads, ending with para 12, which provides:

c 'A copy or fair and accurate report or summary of any notice or other matter issued for the information of the public by or on behalf of any government department, officer of state, local authority or chief officer of police.'

To come therefore within the statutory protection of the privilege provided by para 12, the defendants had to prove first that what Mr Smith said to Mr Lord was matter, other d than a notice, issued for the information of the public by or on behalf of the Department of Energy. The judge ruled that it was. I am of the opinion that it was not.

The judge approached the words of the paragraph 'in not a strictly literal sense but in a fairly liberal way', to include information painfully extracted by journalists, like a tooth, from an official of a government department acting in the course of his employment, as well as formal statements released to the press by the government e department. That seems to me to pay too little attention to the word 'issued' and to the language's indication that the matter issued must be of the same kind as a notice. It would unduly restrict the words to confine them to written 'hand-outs', including photographs, sketches or other pictorial representations, which are given as examples in the revised version of para 12 suggested in the Report of the Committee on Defamation of 1975, presided over by Faulks J (still unimplemented) ((Cmnd 5909) App XI, p 273, f para 17); but it is right to confine them to official notices and the like, such as, for example, the police message broadcast on television in *Boston v W S Bagshaw & Sons* [1966] 2 All ER 906, [1966] 1 WLR 1126, the only reported case on the paragraph, statements 'of a genuinely official nature' formally 'issued for the information of the public', in the words accepted by Jordan CJ considering a statutory provision in similar terms in *Campbell v Associated Newspapers Ltd* (1948) 48 SR (NSW) 301 at 303. It may be g right to include in the paragraph's ambit the kind of answers to telephoned interrogatories which Mr Lord, quite properly in the discharge of his duty to his newspaper, administered to Mr Smith. To exclude them in every case might unduly restrict the freedom of the press and I did not understand counsel for the plaintiff to submit the contrary. But information which is put out on the initiative of a government department falls more easily within the paragraph than information pulled out of the mouth of an unwilling h officer of the department, and I accept the argument of counsel for the plaintiff that not every statement of fact made to a journalist by a press officer of a government department is privileged, and what is certainly outside the privilege is assumption, inference, speculation on the part of the journalist. That is not authorised; that is not official. If the assumption, inference, speculation were the press officer's, it would not be within the paragraph; Mr Smith was not speaking on behalf of his department if he told Mr Lord j the reprimanded official was or must have been the plaintiff. And the defendants' case both as pleaded and as put in evidence alleged no more than that Mr Smith stated assumptions and/or it was inevitably to be inferred from what he said that the plaintiff was the man. A fortiori the reporter's own assumption, inference, speculation could not be attributed to the press officer's department. That would be to accord to investigative journalism the protection provided for reporting of official information. The question

whether what Mr Smith said was matter within the paragraph is closely connected with the question whether Mr Lord's article was a report of it or a fair and accurate report of a
it. But in my judgment Mr Lord's version of what Mr Smith told him, put at its highest, did not bring it or his report of it in his article within the paragraph.

Was the judge also wrong in ruling that the article might be a privileged publication at common law? This point the judge found more difficult, and I have not found it easy. He derived the principles to be applied from the judgment of Buckley LJ in *Adam v Ward* (1915) 31 TLR 299 at 304 as summarised by Cantley J in *London Artists Ltd v Littler* b
[1968] 1 All ER 1075 at 1085, [1968] 1 WLR 607 at 619. He then stated his conclusion in these words:

> '... if the facts be these, and I stress, if the facts be these because they are not yet found by the jury, that Mr Lord on his interrogation of Mr White, who was an official at the [Department] of Energy, concluded that there had been maladministration in the Civil Service in the administration of the grants and that a substantial c
> sum of money was involved and, further, that the person who was responsible, I do not mean directly but right at the top of the whole administration, for administering the scheme was the plaintiff and it had been conveyed to Mr Lord that it must be Alan Blackshaw who would be the person who was referred to in the Public Accounts Committee, that is a matter which, I think, it is beyond argument would be for the ordinary English person who would be interested in the workings of d
> government, a matter which is so important, in my judgment, that it would be the duty of the press to bring it to the attention of the public, and any right-thinking person who wanted good administration in this country, and who was interested in the running of the country, would want to know those facts, not only want to know them, but he would be keen to know them, and, furthermore, a newspaper proprietor, in my judgment, of any proper standing, I mean of integrity and of e
> independence, would have a strict duty to bring those matters to the attention of the public. In those circumstances, though this ruling, I am told, is novel in the sense that there has not been any similar ruling, I would conclude, and do conclude, that the common law privilege would attach to this particular article.'

There is no doubt that 'the general law of qualified privilege is available to newspapers f
... as much as to any other person' (see the Report of the Faulks Committee on Defamation, p 55, para 215(*f*); cf Duncan and Neill *Defamation* (1978) p 109, para 14.29; *Gatley on Libel and Slander* (8th edn, 1981) pp 251, 277, paras 591, 649). The common law privilege subsists and is not limited or abridged by the statute: see s 7(4) of the 1952 Act, which I have read. But I approach with caution the application of common law privilege to an occasion, or more correctly a publication, which tries and fails to come within g
statutory privilege, and find no very clear guidance in such authorities as there are on the circumstances in which a newspaper report has the necessary qualifications for the protection of the common law. I make that approach bearing in mind Lord Denning MR's observation in *Boston v W S Bagshaw & Sons* [1966] 2 All ER 906 at 910, [1966] 1 WLR 1126 at 1132 that 'The case of *Chapman* v. *Lord Ellesmere* ([1932] 2 KB 431, [1932] All ER Rep 221) made it very difficult for a newspaper to claim privilege' and that the h
Defamation Act 1952, ss 7 and 9(2) gave a privilege to newspapers for many matters of public concern.

The principal authorities are: *Cox v Feeney* (1863) 4 F & F 13, 176 ER 445; *Purcell v Sowler* (1877) 2 CPD 215; *Adam v Ward* (1915) 31 TLR 299, [1917] AC 309, [1916–17] All ER Rep 157, both in the Court of Appeal and in the House of Lords; *Chapman v Lord Ellesmere* [1932] 2 KB 431, [1932] All ER Rep 221; *Perera v Peiris* [1949] AC 1; *Webb v* j
Times Publishing Co Ltd [1960] 2 All ER 789, [1960] 2 QB 535; *Dunford Publicity Studios Ltd v News Media Ownership Ltd* [1971] NZLR 961; and the judgment of Cantley J in *London Artists Ltd v Littler* [1968] 1 All ER 1075, [1968] 1 WLR 607 (appealed on another point [1969] 2 All ER 193, [1969] 2 QB 375).

The question here is, assuming Mr Lord recorded Mr Smith's conversation with him fairly and accurately, did Mr Lord (and his newspaper) publish his report of that conversation in pursuance of a duty, legal, social or moral, to persons who had a corresponding duty or interest to receive it? That, in my respectful opinion, correct summary of the relevant authorities is taken from the Report of the Faulks Committee, p 47, para 184(*a*), repeated in *Duncan and Neill* p 98, para 14.01. I cannot extract from any of those authorities any relaxation of the requirements incorporated in that question. No privilege attaches yet to a statement on a matter of public interest believed by the publisher to be true in relation to which he has exercised reasonable care. That needed statutory enactment which the Faulks Committee refused to recommend (See pp 53–55 paras 211–215). 'Fair information on a matter of public interest' is not enough without a duty to publish it and I do not understand Pearson J's ruling in *Webb v Times Publishing Co Ltd* [1960] 2 All ER 789, [1960] 2 QB 535, that a plea of a fair and accurate report of foreign judicial proceedings was not demurrable, was intended to convey that it was enough. Public interest and public benefit are necessary (cf s 7(3) of the 1952 Act), but not enough without more. There must be a duty to publish to the public at large and an interest in the public at large to receive the publication; and a section of the public is not enough.

The subject matter must be of public interest; its publication must be in the public interest. That nature of the matter published and its source and the position or status of the publisher distributing the information must be such as to create the duty to publish the information to the intended recipients, in this case the readers of the Daily Telegraph. Where damaging facts have been ascertained to be true, or been made the subject of a report, there may be a duty to report them (see eg *Cox v Feeney* (1863) 4 F & F 13, 176 ER 445, *Perera v Peiris* [1949] AC 1 and *Dunford Publicity Studios Ltd v News Media Ownership Ltd* [1971] NZLR 961), provided the public interest is wide enough (*Chapman v Lord Ellesmere* [1932] 2 KB 431, [1932] All ER Rep 221). But where damaging allegations or charges have been made and are still under investigation (*Purcell v Solwer* (1877) 2 CPD 215), or have been authoritatively refuted (*Adam v Ward* (1915) 31 TLR 299; *affd* [1917] AC 308, [1916–17] All ER Rep 157), there can be no duty to report them to the public.

In this case, as counsel for the plaintiff points out, there is, when Mr Lord types his article, no allegation against the plaintiff which had been made good. He may have been reprimanded, he may have been dismissed, he may have been compelled to resign. Mr Lord is in effect still investigating the nature and the truth of the allegations and is in no position to reach or state any conclusion when he thinks it his duty not, as he says, to state neutral facts but, as the jury has found, to dot the i's and cross the t's and give his defamatory conclusions to the public. He may have been under a duty to inform the public of the £52m loss, but not to attribute blame to the plaintiff or to communicate information about his resignation, even if it was of public interest. The general topic of the waste of taxpayers' money was, counsel for the plaintiff concedes, a matter in which the public, including the readers of the Daily Telegraph's first edition, had a legitimate interest and which the press were under a duty to publish; but they had no legitimate interest in Mr Lord's particular inferences and guesses, or even in Mr Smith's, and the defendants had certainly no duty to publish what counsel for the plaintiff unkindly called 'half-baked' rumours about the plaintiff at that stage of Mr Lord's investigations.

There may be extreme cases where the urgency of communicating a warning is so great, or the source of the information so reliable, that publication of suspicion or speculation is justified; for example, where there is danger to the public from a suspected terrorist or the distribution of contaminated food or drugs; but there is nothing of that sort here. So Mr Lord took the risk of the defamatory matter, which he derived from what he said were Mr Smith's statements and assumptions, turning out untrue.

Again, the question whether Mr Lord's article was a fair and accurate report of the information he got from Mr Smith is not always easy to separate from the question whether if it were fair and accurate it was the subject of qualified privilege at common law. But only one other newspaper appears to have thought it its duty to publish the plaintiff's name in a defamatory connection with the loss of millions of pounds sterling in unauthorised interest relief grants, and I have come to the conclusion that, even on Mr Lord's version of what Mr Smith had told him, its publication was not privileged at common law.

What of the £45,000 damages to compensate the plaintiff for the hurt to his feelings and the injury to his reputation from being falsely accused of being reprimanded and having to resign for being in charge of an office which was so incompetently administered that millions of pounds sterling in public money were wrongly granted to those who were not entitled to them?

I confess that I regard the sum as very high and if it was an award of a judge I should be disposed to reduce it substantially. But it is an award of a jury, and in spite of the recommendations of the Faulks Committee and the considerations which led them to make those recommendations (ch 17 and in particular p 143, para 516), juries still have the function of assessing damages for defamation and this court has no power, simply because it thinks their assessment wrong, to substitute such sum as in its view should have been awarded, except with the consent of all parties concerned (which has in this case been given): RSC Ord 59, r 11(4). We cannot reduce (or increase) the sum awarded by this jury unless it was one which no twelve reasonable jurors could have awarded if they had properly directed their minds to the evidence and been properly directed as to the relevant considerations and principles by the judge. In considering whether to allow an appeal against a jury's award of damages, this court applies an even stricter principle than to an appeal against a judge's award; the note to RSC Ord 59, r 10, in *The Supreme Court Practice 1982* vol 1, p 945, para 59/10/11 is misleading in so far as it suggests the contrary, and ought to be corrected. As Lord Hailsham LC said in *Cassell & Co Ltd v Broome* [1972] 1 All ER 801 at 825–826, [1972] AC 1027 at 1073:

> 'In awarding "aggravated" damages the natural indignation of the court at the injury inflicted on the plaintiff is a perfectly legitimate motive in making a generous rather than a more moderate award to provide an adequate solatium.'

Though a defendant's conduct does not entitle a jury to punish him in addition to compensating the plaintiff, it does increase the injury and widen the brackets which Lord Reid in the same case was able to assume must exist—

> 'between the sum which on an objective view could be regarded as the least and the sum which could be regarded as the most to which the plaintiff is entitled as compensation.'

(See [1972] 1 All ER 801 at 836, [1972] AC 1027 at 1085.)

The extent of the subjective element in such injury as a libelled plaintiff may suffer, where, as here, the defendants' conduct does not mitigate but aggravates the damage, and the impossibility of ascertaining how wide and deep and long-lasting will be the damage to the libelled plaintiff's reputation, and the impossibility of converting either into money, have been so stressed by judges in that and other cases that counsel were unable to point to any case in the last 18 years since *McCarey v Associated Newspapers Ltd* [1964] 3 All ER 947, [1965] 2 QB 86 where this court had interfered with a jury's award of damages for defamation. We still have the power to reduce an excessive award, but can we ever exercise it, at any rate in the absence of any plain misdirection by the trial judge? Are there any circumstances in which the size of the sum awarded is by itself so clearly and ridiculously disproportionate to the injury, even when aggravated, that this court can exercise its apparently obsolescent power and order a new trial, as it did in *Lewis v Daily Telegraph Ltd* [1962] 2 All ER 698, [1963] 1 QB 340, with the approval of the House of Lords ([1963] 2 All ER 151, [1964] AC 234), in the hope that another jury may not award the same sum, as well they may, an objection pointed out, for example, by

Scrutton LJ in *Youssoupoff v Metro-Goldwyn Mayer Pictures Ltd* (1934) 50 TLR 581 at 585? Is this a case in which this court ought to take that risk?

Any defendant challenging a jury's award of damages for defamation has an uphill task, as counsel for the defendants recognised, and there is not much in the judge's summing up of this case to help him up the hill to a reduction of these damages. The judge referred to the plaintiff's own evidence about his consternation and distress when he read the article, and to the vindications of his reputation that he had had from others but never from the defendants. He then gave the jury this direction:

> 'Your damages, you may think, will not be small. Newspapers cannot expect a small award if they defame a man who has an important position in the country and who has a high reputation. These matters you will take into account if you come to consider the question of damages. I hope that I have given you some guidance on damages. I do not have to, I am not permitted, indeed, to mention any figures to you. Juries are independent to reach their own conclusions as to what is proper compensation in a case such as this. But what you will consider when you come, if you come, to the question of damages is the injured and hurt feelings of the plaintiff, the damage to his reputation as measured by you. Your sum will probably reflect this principle: he has been libelled and our award will show that he was libelled, and that he should be vindicated. So there is an element of vindication in any award which you reach. But in assessing damages, you might like to say to yourselves, "What is the wrong complained of? How serious is the wrong done?" You might ask yourselves what other degrees of defamation could there be which would demand very high damages. Dishonesty has not been alleged by the plaintiff. Indeed, in the article published by the Daily Telegraph, quoting from Mr Smith's telephone call, Mr Lord has included in his article that there was no question of any irregularity; nothing dishonest. So this man, Mr Blackshaw, is not seeking to have himself vindicated because of any charge of dishonesty. If that had been the case, would it have brought a higher award than what you will bring in, assuming you award damages? The charge here, you may think, is a false charge of incompetence, that is if the plaintiff succeeds. All defamations are hurtful but you might consider in what league or division, using football terms, you would put this false charge of incompetence. You will know that the plaintiff does not have to prove that he has suffered any actual loss and he has not sought to prove, in this action, that he has suffered any specific loss, in other words, proving specific amounts. But remember that, if you do award damages for a libel which you say has been published, actual financial loss need not be proved by the plaintiff, because certainly some damage is presumed. You will also consider the degree of dissemination of the alleged libel. You will consider the parts of the kingdom which certainly received the first edition of the Daily Telegraph. You will consider what has happened since publication. There have been the press notice of the ministry and the mention in Parliament. You will also consider the £4,000 ex gratia payment. But do not think of a figure and then say to yourselves, "We will deduct £4,000." But if there is some element of loss suffered only once by the plaintiff, which he has already recovered, you would not think it right to include that again in any award you make. You will also consider that he is claiming damages for a similar libel against the Daily Mail. You do not need any words from me to enable you to assess the Daily Mail, but he is seeking damages from the Daily Mail in respect of a similar article. So I have to tell you, and I do tell you, that in considering that evidence, namely that there has been and will be a claim against the Daily Mail, you should consider how far the damage suffered by the plaintiff can reasonably be attributed solely to the libel which you are concerned with, namely the Daily Telegraph, and how much has been suffered by the plaintiff as regards the joint result of the two libels. If you think that some part of the damage is the joint result of the two libels, you should bear in mind that the plaintiff ought not to be compensated twice for the same loss. You can deal with

> this of course only, as a jury, on very broad lines. You can take it that if another judge is trying the action between the plaintiff and the Daily Mail he will probably a
> say to the jury what I am saying to you. You must do your best to ensure, on the question of damages, that the sum that you will award the plaintiff, assuming he succeeds, will fully compensate for the damage that has been caused to him by the particular libel in the particular edition of the Daily Telegraph. You will not take into account that part of the total damage suffered by him which ought to enter into an assessment of damages in his action against the Daily Mail. So my final b
> request to you is to use your common sense and, pooling your wisdom and your dispassionate views, come to a conclusion on the three questions which are going to be left for you.'

I cannot find anything wrong with that clear and careful direction. The judge did not tell the jury that the damages must be moderate and fair to the defendants as well as to the plaintiff; but was he bound to do that or do more than he did in favour of defendants c
who had aggravated the injury to the plaintiff and consequently the compensation the jury were entitled to award him by their conduct in a number of ways, forcefully put before us as before the jury by counsel for the plaintiff as the four 'smears' with which counsel for the defendants, on their instructions, had sought to besmirch the plaintiff's credit and reputation?

They were (1) that the plaintiff was responsible for the office which had lost £3m in a d
£40m oil scandal and might properly be compensated by the smallest coin of the realm, (2) that he had not been frank in his evidence that the article complained of came as a bolt from the blue in spite of some earlier criticism of the Offshore Supplies Office, (3) that the plaintiff had concocted with Lord Taylor of Gryfe a false version of a letter Lord Taylor had written to him on 26 October 1979, revised to eliminate any suggestion that the damage done to his reputation came from an article in the Scotsman and not from e
the articles in the Daily Mail and the Daily Telegraph, (4) that his object in bringing the action was simply to make money. The plaintiff, his counsel submitted, told the jury of the shattering effect on him, when just starting a new career and hoping to become a director of Morgan Grenfell (Scotland) Ltd with Lord Taylor's help, of Mr Lord's article in its first form. From September 1979 to February 1981 he suffered the strain of litigation, while the defendants, after publishing in later editions his own explanation of f
his resignation, rejected his solicitors' efforts to obtain any apology or vindication from them. On the contrary, the second defendant published only a brief summary of a press notice of 18 September 1979 vindicating the plaintiff by correcting the inference and the evidence which defamed him, and followed a further vindication by the Secretary of State for Energy in answers given in the House of Commons on 26 November 1979 and 3 June 1980 with a report more likely to revive than destroy the implications of its first g
article in these terms:

> 'MAN IN £44M OIL SCANDAL GIVEN £4,000
>
> A senior civil servant who left after a scandal in which £44 million was overpaid to North Sea oil firms is to receive a £4,000 ex-gratia payment from the Department of Energy, Mr Howell, Energy Secretary, disclosed yesterday. In a Commons written h
> reply Mr Howell told Mr Jeff Rooker (Lab., Perry Barr) that the resignation last August of Mr Alan Blackshaw, a former director-general of Offshore supplies, was for domestic reasons. The overpayment was disclosed in evidence in the Public Accounts Committee in July of that year. Then, the Energy Department's Permanent Under-Secretary, Sir Jack Rampton, said that a dozen officials had been reprimanded over the situation.' j

All the correspondence between the plaintiff's solicitors and the two defendants (which I need not read) revealing their intransigence, the jury was entitled to take into account as requiring a resounding vindication in damages by their verdict. It was not until the plaintiff got that verdict in the teeth of the defendants' persistent opposition that they vindicated him by publishing the fair and accurate report by a High Court reporter of the trial and verdict on 27 February 1981. That kind of 'neglect born of indifference', as Sir George Baker described the defendants' conduct in *Hayward v Thompson* [1981] 3 All ER 450 at 465, [1982] QB 47 at 70, justified (said counsel for the plaintiff) the jury's large award, which was by no means too high.

Counsel for the defendants tried to demonstrate that it was ludicrously and inordinately high by comparison with awards in personal injury cases for pain and suffering and loss of amenities: in *Jones v Brough* [1981] CLY 600 Glidewell J on 10 July 1981 awarded a badly brain-damaged man of 48 at the time of his accident £45,300, of which no more than £22,000 was for pain and suffering and loss of amenities; in *Croke v Wiseman* [1981] 3 All ER 852, [1982] 1 WLR 71 a majority of this court upheld a judge's award of £35,000 to a totally disabled child under the same head, though Lord Denning MR would have reduced it by £10,000. For my part I find little assistance in comparing awards for defamation with awards for personal injuries, in this respect following Holroyd Pearce LJ in *Lewis v Daily Telegraph Ltd* [1962] 2 All ER 698 at 717, [1963] 1 QB 340 at 381, though not quite for the same reason, and not following Diplock LJ in *McCarey v Associated Newspapers Ltd* [1964] 3 All ER 947 at 960, [1965] 2 QB 86 at 109. The differences are too great for a comparison of any real value. We were also pressed with other awards in defamation cases, both reported, like *Cassell & Co Ltd v Broome* [1972] 1 All ER 801, [1972] AC 1027 and *Hayward v Thompson* [1981] 3 All ER 450, [1982] QB 47, and unreported but recollected, no doubt accurately, by counsel from the experience of themselves and their instructing solicitors. We were also asked to consider what house or motor car or annuity £45,000 would buy, and we were told that it would purchase an annuity of £5,000 gross, £1,675 of it tax free. Counsel for the defendants also called our attention to the injury and damage caused by the Daily Mail article, which was the subject of another action not concluded at the date of trial, by articles in other newspapers which did not name the plaintiff, and by the last paragraph of Mr Lord's article, of which the plaintiff made no complaint; and he submitted that the jury's award showed that they must have taken into account more than the injury and damage specifically referable to the words complained of in Mr Lord's article. It is, of course, easier for a jury to give a reasonable award if they try two actions like this and the plaintiff's action in respect of the Daily Mail article together, as was done with consolidated actions in the *Lewis* and *McCarey* cases.

These considerations, many of them complicated by inflation, have left me uncertain what, if there are brackets for aggravated damages, is the top bracket; but I am bound to say that they have reinforced the doubts I felt before hearing any argument whether this £45,000 has not gone over the top. I may have been influenced in my reaction to the figure by asking the irrelevant questions: 'Why, if the maladministration of the Offshore Supplies Office was so serious, no senior civil servant there was reprimanded or dismissed or compelled to resign?' 'If, on the other hand, most of the maladministration consisted in sensible decisions being taken locally by junior civil servants to benefit British industry without reference to higher authority and in disregard of guidelines which were later relaxed to permit such decisions to be taken without such reference, why should those responsible for those decisions be criticised in the strong terms used by Sir Jack Rampton, or why should that criticism have been accepted by the Public Accounts Committee at its face value?' But those are not questions the jury had to consider. They saw and heard the plaintiff, as well as Mr Smith and Mr Lord, and they obviously felt that the defendants' conduct was, as counsel for the plaintiff suggested to them, disgraceful and the plaintiff required to be vindicated by a really substantial sum of money.

I have come to the conclusion that the defendants have brought this large award of damages on themselves by the course of action which they have chosen to take, in the perhaps understandable belief that they were exposing a 'cover-up' in and by a department of the Civil Service. The jury have shown their disapproval of that course, as they were entitled to do, and have assessed the damages at a figure which will adequately console the plaintiff and restore his reputation beyond doubt.

Though my own opinion is that that could have been achieved by a considerably lower award, I am not able to regard this as one of those rare and exceptional cases in which this *a* court can and should order a new trial on the issue of damages or substitute a lower sum of its own.

I would accordingly dismiss the appeal.

DUNN LJ (read by Stephenson LJ). I agree that the appeal should be dismissed for the reasons given by Stephenson LJ. Although not necessary for our decision, I would add *b* some words of my own in relation to the respondent's notice, since the matters raised by it have been fully argued. The judge ruled that the article in question was subject to qualified privilege under para 12 of the schedule to the Defamation Act 1952 and also at common law if, so far as material, it was a fair and accurate report of information conveyed on 12 September 1979 by Mr Smith to Mr Lord on the telephone. The respondent by notice in this court seeks to uphold the verdict and judgment on the *c* additional grounds that no qualified privilege attached to the article either by statute or at common law.

It is convenient to deal first with the plea of qualified privilege at common law. The basis of his ruling was that the judge held that any matters discussed between Mr Smith and Mr Lord which involved maladministration in the civil service were so important that any right-thinking person would have an interest in knowing them, and that it was *d* the duty of a newspaper proprietor of integrity to publish them. The judge equated the duty to publish with the degree of public interest and held that the public interest was so great that the duty arose. He based himself on the following statement of Buckley LJ in *Adam v Ward* (1915) 31 TLR 299 at 304:

> 'But the following proposition, I think, is true—that if the matter is a matter of public interest and the party who publishes it owes a duty to communicate it to the *e* public, the publication is privileged, and in this sense duty means not a duty as matter of law, but, to quote Lord Justice Lindley's words in Stuart v. Bell ([1891] 2 QB 341 at 350), "a duty recognised by English people of ordinary intelligence and moral principle, but at the same time not a duty enforceable by legal proceedings, whether civil or criminal".'

f

The judge also founded himself on a statement by Cantley J in *London Artists Ltd v Littler* [1968] 1 All ER 1075 at 1085, [1968] 1 WLR 607 at 619 that a publication was privileged at common law 'where the defendant has a legal, social or moral duty to communicate it to the general public'.

It is true that in some cases of high authority (eg *Adam v Ward* [1917] AC 309, [1916–17] All ER Rep 157 in the House of Lords and *Perera v Peiris* [1949] AC 1 in the Privy *g* Council) the duty has been expressed in very wide terms. In *Webb v Times Publishing Co Ltd* [1960] 2 All ER 789 at 801–802, [1960] 2 QB 535 at 565 Pearson J held that qualified privilege attached to reports of foreign judicial proceedings when such reports were of public interest in England, and suggested that a plea of 'fair information on a matter of public interest' could constitute a defence even if the information was defamatory. For reasons I shall give later in this judgment, although wholly unexceptionable in relation *h* to their particular facts, these wide statements of principle taken out of context are misleading, and I do not think there is any defence of 'fair information on a matter of public interest' in defamation proceedings. In *London Artists Ltd v Littler* [1968] 1 All ER 1075 at 1085, [1968] 1 WLR 607 at 619 Cantley J, rightly in my view, declined to follow the wide principle stated by Pearson J in *Webb v Times Publishing Co Ltd* and founded himself on Buckley LJ in *Adam v Ward.* The interesting argument of Sir Valentine *j* Holmes KC in *Perera v Peiris* [1949] AC 1 at 9 shows that in the eighteenth century privilege afforded no defence to a defamatory publication. During the nineteenth century the judges were using the word 'privilege' as meaning the existence of a set of circumstances in which the presumption of malice was negatived. It was said in *Gilpin v Fowler* (1854) 9 Exch 615 at 623–624, 156 ER 263 at 266 that 'instead of the expression

"privileged communication" it would be more correct to say that the communication
a was made on an occasion which rebutted the presumption of malice'. The judges, having to face the problem of what would be the circumstances in which the presumption of malice would be negatived, went on two lines, duty and interest, and the public good and for the public interest.

By the end of the ensuing 100 years it had been established that certain categories of documents by their very nature rebutted the presumption of malice, and publication of
b them was accordingly privileged. These included fair and accurate reports of judicial proceedings and of proceedings in Parliament. But the courts stressed that the categories were not closed, and in each case it was necessary to determine whether the occasion was privileged not only by reference to the subject matter of the information published but also to its status, and whether that gave rise to the duty to publish. In *Perera v Peiris* the Privy Council, in considering whether the duty arose, drew attention to the circumstances
c in which the report in question was produced, stressing that it was a public document which came into existence after a full investigation of the facts.

In *Purcell v Sowler* (1877) 2 CPD 215 the Court of Appeal held that the publication by a newspaper of a report of proceedings at a meeting of poor law guardians was not privileged by the occasion, notwithstanding that the administration of the Poor Laws, including the conduct of medical officers mentioned in the report, was a matter of public
d interest. In that case Mellish LJ said (at 221–222):

> 'The law on the subject of privilege is clearly defined by the authorities. Such a communication as the present ought to be confined in the first instance to those whose duty it is to investigate the charges. If one of the guardians had met a person not a ratepayer or parishioner, and had told him the charge against the plaintiff,
> e surely he would have been liable to an action of slander. I do not mean to say that the matter was not of such public interest as that comments would not be privileged if the facts had been ascertained. If the neglect charged against the plaintiff had been proved, then fair comments on his conduct might have been justified. But this is a very different thing from publishing ex parte statements, which not only are not proved but turn out to be unfounded in fact. I am, therefore, clearly of opinion that
> f the occasion of the publication was not privileged, and that the judgment for the plaintiff ought to be affirmed.'

And Bramwell JA said (at 222–223):

> 'This is a case in which the defendants have published a true and bona fide report of a statement of facts charged against the plaintiff, but a statement which shews
> g that the person making it was making it in the absence of the plaintiff and without any knowledge on the part of the person making it. There was no duty to report such ex parte proceedings; if the guardians did not exclude strangers, as they might well have done, the reporter ought to have taken care what he was about, and not to have reported libellous matter; and the defendants, having published it, must take the consequences.'

h

Purcell v Sowler was referred to by Buckley LJ in *Adam v Ward* (1915) 31 TLR 299 at 304 in the following passage:

> 'In Cox v. Feeney ((1863) 4 F & F 13 at 18, 176 ER 445 at 447) a dictum of Chief Justice Tenterden is quoted in the following terms:—"A man has a right to publish, for the purpose of giving the public information, that which it is proper for the
> j public to know." With great respect, I doubt whether there is contained in those words an accurate statement of the circumstances in which a privileged occasion arises for the publication of matter interesting to the public. I am not prepared to hold that the publication even by a public body of its proceedings or conclusions in a matter of public interest is on that account and without more privileged. Purcell v. Sowler is, I think, an authority to the contrary. I doubt whether in Mangena v.

> Wright ([1909] 2 KB 958 at 978) Mr. Justice Phillimore was right in saying . . . that "where the communication is made by a public servant as to a matter within his a province, it may be the subject of privilege in him" if those words are intended to convey that those facts without more will create a privileged occasion. More, I think, is wanted.'

As I read him, Buckley LJ was saying that the mere fact that the communication was made by a public servant in respect of a matter of public interest does not mean that the communication is made on a privileged occasion. There must be more, and *Purcell v* b *Sowler* shows that the court must look at the circumstances of the particular communciation to the newspaper in deciding whether or not the occasion is privileged.

Purcell v Sowler was cited in the House of Lords in *Adam v Ward* [1917] AC 309, [1916–17] All ER Rep 157 but not referred to in the speeches. In *Perera v Peiris* [1949] AC 1 counsel suggested that *Purcell v Sowler* should be overruled, but no reference was made to the case in the judgment. So *Purcell v Sowler*, which has stood for over 100 years, c remains good law.

In *Webb v Times Publishing Co Ltd* [1960] 2 All ER 789 at 804, [1960] 2 QB 535 at 568 Pearson J accepted that there must be an appropriate status for the report as well as the need for appropriate subject matter, which must be of interest to the public concerned. He held in that case that there was the ready-made status of a fair and accurate report of foreign judicial proceedings, and I think that his judgment can be supported on the d narrower ground that the privilege was analogous to the well-established privilege attaching to reports of English judicial proceedings, once he had found (as he did) that the report in the newspaper was a matter of legitimate and proper interest to English readers. As in so many of the cases there was no question as to the status of the report, and the only question was whether there was sufficient public interest.

This review of the authorities shows that, save where the publication is of a report e which falls into one of the recognised privileged categories, the court must look at the circumstances of the case before it in order to ascertain whether the occasion of the publication was privileged. It is not enough that the publication should be of general interest to the public. The public must have a legitimate interest in receiving the information contained in it, and there must be a correlative duty in the publisher to publish, which depends also on the status of the information which he receives, at any f rate where the information is being made public for the first time. Different considerations may arise in cases such as *Adam v Ward* (1915) 31 TLR 299; *affd* [1917] AC 309, [1916–17] All ER Rep 157 and *Dunford Publicity Studios Ltd v News Media Ownership Ltd* [1971] NZLR 961, where the matter has already been made public, and the publication in question is by way of defence to a public charge, or correction of a mistake made in a previous publication. g

As Cantley J pointed out in *London Artists Ltd v Littler* [1968] 1 All ER 1075 at 1081, [1968] 1 WLR 607 at 615, if the law were otherwise, and if the wider principle on which Pearson J decided *Webb*'s case were applicable, then there would be no need for a plea of fair comment, and anyone could publish any untrue defamatory information provided only that he honestly believed it, and honestly believed that the public had an interest in receiving it. h

Apart from *Adam v Ward*, no case before 1952 was cited to us in which a statement issued by or on behalf of a government department was held to be privileged. It may be that in the circumstances of a particular case privilege might have been held to cover such a statement, but it is significant that in that year the position was apparently sufficiently unclear to require legislation. It is true that the Defamation Act 1952 preserved the common law, and included within its provisions some categories of j documents which were already privileged at common law. But the absence of authority before 1952 indicates that the inclusion of such statements would have involved the extension of the doctrine of qualified privilege as it was understood at that date.

I turn to consider statutory privilege. Section 7(1) of the Defamation Act 1952
a provides:

> 'Subject to the provisions of this section, the publication in a newspaper of any such report or other matter as is mentioned in the Schedule to this Act shall be privileged unless the publication is proved to be made with malice.'

Paragraph 12 of Part II of the schedule, headed 'Statements Privileged Subject to
b Explanation or Contradiction', is in these terms:

> 'A copy or fair and accurate report or summary of any notice or other matter issued for the information of the public by or on behalf of any government department, officer of state, local authority or chief officer of police.'

The plea of privilege in this case, on which the judge ruled, was until an amendment on
c the first day of the trial confined to a plea in reliance on para 12, and was based on an assumption by Mr Smith that the reprimand must have been delivered to the plaintiff since there was no one else to whom it could refer. However by an amendment made at the conclusion of the evidence it was averred that—

> 'Smith ... stated ... that the official in charge of the Offshore Supplies Office during most of the relevant period was the Plaintiff and that the person who was
> d reprimanded must have been the Plaintiff and that the Plaintiff had since left the Civil Service for personal reasons and/or it was inevitably to be inferred from what Smith said that the Plaintiff was the Under-Secretary in question and the person who was reprimanded.'

In ruling on the plea of privilege, the judge said:

e

> 'I have no doubt at all that, if a journalist seeks information openly as a journalist from a government department and an official in a government department, that is somebody who is acting in the course of his employment, discloses information to the press which the press then utilise, that information, provided it becomes the subject of a fair and accurate report or summary, deserves the cloak of privilege
> f conferred by para 12.'

The question, it seems to me is: was what was said by Mr Smith to Mr Lord a notice or other matter issued for the information of the public? The context of the telephone conversation is important. It arose out of the evidence of Sir Jack Rampton before the Public Accounts Committee on 23 July 1979, in particular paragraphs of the report which have been read by Stephenson LJ. No journalists were present at the time. No
g name was given in the evidence. On 12 September 1979 a press conference was held by the Public Accounts Committee. A number of journalists including Mr Lord were present. It was stated on behalf of the Public Accounts Committee that a senior official had been dismissed after the evidence of 23 July 1979, and Mr Joel Barnett, the chairman of the committee, stated, 'No fraud was involved but inefficiency, incompetence, inadequate staff, and inadequate supervision of those paying out the money.' This was
h the first Mr Lord knew of the matter; at that stage he did not know of the evidence which had been given on 23 July, but obviously there were the makings of a newsworthy story. I suspect he had two priorities: (1) to find out exactly what was said on 23 July, and (2) to find out the name of the official who had been dismissed. As a result he naturally rang Mr Smith, a public relations officer at the Department of Energy. Mr Smith read out the material parts of the evidence from a transcript, including para 225,
j and told Mr Lord that no one had been dismissed. So Mr Lord pressed him for the name of the under-secretary who had been reprimanded. Mr Smith made it perfectly plain that he could not name names; public relations officers and ministry spokesmen are not allowed to name civil servants without express authority, and Mr Lord must have known

this. All the same he continued to press Mr Smith and eventually the name of Blackshaw was mentioned. Mr Smith said that Blackshaw had left Glasgow to go to the coal division *a*
a year before the evidence, ie in 1978, and had subsequently resigned for personal reasons. A great deal of the evidence at the trial was directed to the phrase 'Must be Blackshaw' recorded in Mr Lord's notes. The jury by their verdict must have held that those words were not said by Mr Smith, but for the purpose of considering the judge's ruling I am content to assume that they were.

Mr Lord's efforts to obtain the name were described by the judge as akin to the *b*
extraction of a tooth. The fact of the matter was that Mr Lord had got two-thirds of a story; he had the material parts of Sir Jack Rampton's evidence; he had the comments by Mr Joel Barnett at the press conference; and he wanted the remaining one-third, namely the name of the civil servant who had been said to have been reprimanded, in order to complete his story. This is a situation which must be frequently experienced by journalists. They have a hard fact here, and a hard fact there, and in order to produce a *c*
complete and newsworthy story they have to fill out the remaining facts by using intelligent deduction, drawing inferences, or just speculating. Whether the phrase 'Must be Blackshaw' resulted from the mental process of Mr Lord (as the jury must have found) or that of Mr Smith (as Mr Lord alleged) or was a joint effort between them, it would, it seems to me, be a misuse of words to describe the result as 'matter issued for the information of the public'. One thing is clear, namely that Mr Smith was not prepared *d*
to take responsibility on behalf of the ministry for giving the name; he was not giving it or purporting to give it on behalf of his department. Not every piece of information given by a spokesman acting in the course of his employment is necessarily information given on behalf of his department. What Mr Smith did was to give a series of facts, including the fact that Mr Blackshaw had resigned of his own accord, from which more than one inference could be drawn. Mr Lord chose not to mention that fact in the article, *e*
and drew an inference defamatory of Mr Blackshaw which turned out to be wrong.

If that analysis of the facts be correct, in my view the Daily Telegraph was under no duty at common law to publish the article in the form in which it did. The status of the conversation between Mr Smith and Mr Lord was not such as to give rise to the duty and so attract the common law privilege. Taken at its most favourable to Mr Lord, what Mr Smith said about Mr Blackshaw was no more than an ex parte statement based on *f*
inference, into the truth of which Mr Smith had made no investigation, and on which Mr Blackshaw had had no opportunity to comment.

Nor do I think that what was said by Mr Smith to Mr Lord could be described as 'matter issued for the information of the public by or on behalf of [a] government department' so as to attract the statutory privilege. I adopt the statement of Jordan CJ when considering a similar Australian provision in *Campbell v Associated Newspapers Ltd* *g*
(1948) 48 SR (NSW) 301 at 303:

> 'The notice or report must be of a genuinely official nature, and must be issued in such circumstances that it may fairly be regarded as issued for the information of the public. It is not, of course, for this Court to assume to lay down rules for what is, and what is not, proper to be made the subject of a governmental or police notice *h*
> or report. I see no reason for doubting that an authoritative announcement of an official character made or handed to members of the press for publication in their respective newspapers would, or at least could, constitute a notice or report issued for the information of the public, and if published in the form in which it was supplied would be published with the consent of the department, etc., supplying it. On the other hand, if the matter so supplied was such as to admit of a reasonable *j*
> inference that it was mere gossip and not an official notice or report, or that an official report so supplied was not published in substantially the form in which it was issued, it would be competent to the tribunal of fact to find that the defence had not been made out. And, if the trial judge was satisfied that the matter was incapable of constituting a notice or report within the meaning of s. 29 (1) (g) [of the Defamation Act 1912 (NSW)], or that, if it was, it was incapable of being regarded

as published substantially in the form in which it was issued, it would be his duty
a to direct a verdict for the plaintiff on the plea.'

What Mr Smith said to Mr Lord was not a notice or other matter of a genuinely official nature. Put at its highest it was an inference which Mr Smith had drawn from facts known to him, made in reply to a series of questions which Mr Smith had no authority to answer, and which Mr Lord must have known he had no authority to answer. I
b accordingly hold that the judge was in error in holding that the publication was made on a privileged occasion.

I now turn to damages. Speaking for myself I think that the award of £45,000 was much too high even for this serious libel, especially if one compares it with awards for pain and suffering and loss of amenity which are currently awarded for personal injuries. But that is not the test. A series of decisions which are binding on us show that this court
c must not interfere with such an award unless the damages are so large that no reasonable jury could have given them, or unless the jury were misled, or took into account matters which they ought not to have considered. Counsel for the defendants submitted that the judge should have warned the jury in his summing up to be moderate in their award of damages, in order to correct some suggestions made in his final speech by counsel for the plaintiff as to the conduct of Mr Lord and the Daily Telegraph, which counsel for the
d defendants said were irrelevant to any issue in the case, there being no plea of malice. These comments related to the conduct of Mr Lord in omitting in his article some parts of what Mr Smith had said to him which were favouable to the plaintiff, and also to the conduct of the Daily Telegraph in not publishing any of the vindications of the plaintiff which had been issued not only by the Department of Energy but also by the Public Accounts Committee and the minister in the House of Commons, and on the contrary
e in publishing a further article on 4 June 1980 referring to an 'oil scandal', in terms which could be linked to the article of 13 September 1979. Counsel for the plaintiff also criticised the Daily Telegraph's conduct of the trial, including certain aspects of the cross-examination of the plaintiff and the defendants' counsel's final speech when he suggested that the jury should, if they found for the plaintiff, award him the smallest coin of the realm by way of damages.

f In my judgment in our adversary system it is a matter for the trial judge how he deals with allegations and cross-allegations of that kind. He is in a better position than anyone to get the atmosphere of the case. He will know better than anyone whether the jury have been unreasonably inflamed by anything said or done by either side during the trial. This very experienced judge gave no special warning to the jury, although at the beginning and end of the summing up he told them to act dispassionately. He summed
g up quite neutrally, summarising the evidence and the material facts on both sides. In no way could the jury have been misled. They were specifically warned only to give damages for the Daily Telegraph article, and that the plaintiff was not entitled to be compensated for injury to his reputation caused by similar articles in other newspapers. Nothing was left to the jury which it was wrong for them to take into account and in my view no criticism can properly be made of the judge's clear and succinct summing up.

h The speeches of Lord Hailsham LC and Lord Reid in *Cassell & Co Ltd v Broome* [1972] 1 All ER 801, [1972] AC 1027 show that in defamation proceedings compensatory damages include damages for injury to the plaintiff's feelings, aggravating factors as they are called, and that these may be increased by any high-handed, malicious, insulting or oppressive conduct of the defendant at any time including during the trial down to the date of the award. There were certainly aggravating factors in this case, and I cannot for
j my part say that no twelve men with knowledge of the world and of the value of money today could reasonably have come to the figure of £45,000, high though I think it is.

Before leaving the case I would add that I think that it is the greatest pity that none of the recommendations in the Report of the Committee on Defamation (the Faulks Committee) (Cmnd 5909) which was presented to Parliament in March 1975 have been implemented by legislation. In particular the amendments to the schedule to the Defamation Act 1952 prepared in a revised schedule appended to the report as App XI

would, as this case has demonstrated, serve to clarify an obscure and technical branch of the law. Further, although in this case both parties agreed that if this court allowed the *a*
appeal against damages the court should itself assess the figure, implementation of the recommendation of the report at pp 143–144, para 516(*e*) would save the costs of a retrial if the parties did not consent.

FOX LJ. At the trial the defendants asserted that if, contrary to their contention, the article published by the Daily Telegraph on 13 September 1979 was defamatory of the *b*
plaintiff, it was published on a privileged occasion. The privilege claimed was that conferred by para 12 of the schedule to the Defamation Act 1952 or, in the alternative, common law privilege. There was also a plea of parliamentary privilege. The latter was rejected by the judge as a matter of law, and is not pursued.

The privilege conferred by para 12 of the schedule to the 1952 Act is confined to—

> 'A copy or fair and accurate report or summary of any notice or other matter *c*
> issued for the information of the public by or on behalf of any government department . . .'

The question whether the material part of the article was a fair and accurate report of what was said by Mr Smith to Mr Lord was put to the jury. They answered it in the negative. Since, as it seems to me, there was no material misdirection by the judge on *d*
any aspect of the case and there was material which entitled the judge to leave the matter to the jury, and evidence on which they could find as they did (on all of which matters I agree with the judgment of Stephenson LJ), that verdict of the jury concludes the question for the purpose of this case. But, as we have heard argument as to the ambit of para 12, I add this (though it is not necessary for our decision). The paragraph is, I think, only concerned with information issued with the authority of the government *e*
department or other body; in other words it must be information for which the department or body accepts responsibility. As I read Mr Smith's evidence (which in substance must, I think, have been accepted by the jury) he was not prepared, in his capacity as an official of the department, to name Mr Blackshaw or anybody else as the official who had been reprimanded. 'My entire line that afternoon,' he said, 'was not to name people specifically.' But, even if it were the case that Mr Lord succeeded in the end *f*
in extracting from Mr Smith some such words as 'It must have been Blackshaw', it still does not follow that that was anything more than the personal inference of Mr Smith; and if that is all it was I do not think it could properly be regarded as a 'notice or other matter issued . . . by or on behalf of any government department'.

As regards common law privilege, that is specifically preserved by s 7 of the 1952 Act. I agree with Stephenson and Dunn LJJ that, for the purposes of the present case, the *g*
matter is concluded against the defendants by the jury's finding on the second question. Here again, however, we have heard argument and I will express my view though it is not necessary for the determination of the appeal.

I take the correct principle of common law privilege to be that stated by Buckley LJ in the Court of Appeal in *Adam v Ward* (1915) 31 TLR 299 at 304:

> '. . . if the matter is of public interest and the party who publishes it owes a duty *h*
> to communicate it to the public, the publication is privileged, and in this sense duty means not a duty as matter of law, but, to quote Lord Justice Lindley's words in Stuart v. Bell ([1891] 2 QB 341 at 350), "a duty recognised by English people of ordinary intelligence and moral principle, but at the same time not a duty enforceable by legal proceedings . . ."'

j
There is not, I think, anything in the speeches in the House of Lords in *Adam v Ward* [1917] AC 309 at 318, 321, 324, 334, [1916–17] All ER Rep 157 at 160, 164, 165–166, 170 per Lord Finlay LC, Earl Loreburn, Lord Dunedin and Lord Atkinson which is inconsistent with the formulation of Buckley LJ, and it was accepted and applied by Cantley J in *London Artists Ltd v Littler* [1968] 1 All ER 1075 at 1085, [1968] 1 WLR 607 at 619 after a review of the authorities.

No doubt the privilege may also attach if the statement is made for the protection of some lawful interest of the person who makes it, for example for the protection of his own property; but that is not this case. Again, an allegation of improper or negligent conduct against a public servant may be privileged if made to persons having a proper interest to receive it, such as the police or senior officials. That is not this case either.

There are, however, statements in the books which put the principle differently. In *Perera v Peiris* [1949] AC 1 at 21 Lord Uthwatt, giving the advice of the Privy Council, said: 'If it appears that it is to the public interest that the particular report be published, privilege will attach.' The case was primarily concerned with the Roman-Dutch law rather than English law, though I think the Board was stating principles which it considered applicable to both systems (see [1949] AC 1 at 20). I do not think that the case really advances the matter for present purposes. It was concerned with a newspaper report of extracts from the Official Report of the Bribery Commission set up by the Governor of Ceylon under statutory powers to inquire into allegations that bribes had been paid to members of the then State Council to influence their decisions. I should have thought that in those circumstances there was a public duty on the newspaper to publish the material. Indeed, although the Board put the matter in terms of public interest, they state (at 21): '... the public interest of Ceylon demanded that the contents of the Report be widely communciated to the public.' That, I think, is the recognition of a duty. They added (though they say it is 'perhaps' irrelevant in law) that the ordinary member of the community of Ceylon would conceive it to be part of the duty of a public newspaper in the circumstances to furnish at least a proper account of the substance of the report. The case is, on its facts, far removed for the present.

A wider principle is stated by Pearson J in *Webb v Times Publishing Co Ltd* [1960] 2 All ER 789 at 805, [1960] 2 QB 535 at 570:

> 'As the administration of justice in England is a matter of legitimate and proper interest to English newspaper readers, so also is this report [of foreign proceedings], which has so much connection with the administration of justice in England. In general, therefore, this report is privileged.'

I think that states the principle rather too widely. It is necessary to a satisfactory law of defamation that there should be privileged occasions. But the existence of privilege involves a balance of conflicting pressures. On the one hand there is the need that the press should be able to publish fearlessly what is necessary for the protection of the public. On the other hand there is the need to protect the individual from falsehoods. I think there are cases where the test of 'legitimate and proper interest to English newspaper readers' would tilt the balance to an unacceptable degree against the individual. It would, it seems to me, protect persons who disseminate—

> '[any] untrue defamatory information of apparently legitimate public interest, provided only that they honestly believed it and honestly thought it was information that the public ought to have.'

(See *London Artists Ltd v Littler* [1968] 1 All ER 1075 at 1081, [1968] 1 WLR 607 at 615.)

If, as in my opinion the law requires, it is necessary for the defendants to establish that they had a duty to publish the article if they are to be entitled to common law privilege in respect of it, I do not think that the defendants have done so. Mr Smith was not prepared to give the authority of the Department of Energy to the naming of Mr Blackshaw. In so far as the article implied that Mr Blackshaw had been reprimanded or forced to resign from the Civil Service it was based on inference or conjecture derived from insufficient knowledge of the facts. In my opinion the defendants were under no duty to the public to publish the article in the form in which it appeared, having regard to the actual degree of knowledge available to them. Accordingly, in my view the defence of common law privilege fails.

There remains the question of damages. It is said that they were excessive. Certainly I would not myself have awarded so much. But the assessment of the damages was committed by our law to the jury and not to judges. This court is not entitled to seize the matter from the jury and set aside the award merely because our opinion as to the a proper amount of damages differs from that of the jury. If we are to interfere it can only be on the basis that no reasonable jury, properly directed, could have reached the conclusion which this jury did; or, as the same principle is sometimes put, that the damages are so high 'that twelve sensible men could not reasonably have given them' (see per Lord Esher MR in *Praed v Graham* (1889) 24 QBD 53 at 55).

The test thus propounded is a severe one. It is the more so because the assessment of b damages for defamation involves a large subjective element in consequence of the subject matter with which the inquiry is concerned, namely the injury to a man's reputation. We were pressed by counsel for the defendants, in his helpful argument, with comparisons with the damages awarded in personal injury cases for the loss of a limb or a sense. The comparison is not satisfactory because of the subjective element to which I have referred and which, in a financial sense, may leave a plaintiff better off than he was before the c libel. Thus in *Cassell & Co Ltd v Broome* [1972] 1 All ER 801 at 824, [1972] AC 1027 at 1071 Lord Hailsham LC said:

> 'Not merely can he recover the estimated sum of his past and future losses, but, in case the libel, driven underground, emerges from its lurking place at some future date, he must be able to point to a sum awarded by a jury sufficient to convince a bystander of the baselessness of the charge ... Quite obviously, the award must d include factors for injury to the feelings, the anxiety and uncertainty undergone in the litigation, the absence of apology, or the reaffirmation of the truth of the matters complained of, or the malice of the defendant ... What is awarded is thus a figure which cannot be arrived at by any purely objective computation.'

Against that background, I think that, in considering whether the award was one e which no reasonable jury could have decided on, the following considerations are material. (1) It was a serious libel. The plaintiff was a distinguished public servant. The implication of the libel was, in effect, that by reason of his incompetence as the civil servant in charge of the Offshore Supplies Office some £50m of public money had been paid away improperly and that as a consequence the plaintiff had been reprimanded and compelled to resign from the public service. (2) The reporting by the Daily Telegraph of f the £4,000 ex gratia payment to the plaintiff by the Department of Energy did not ameliorate the position. It was headed, 'Man in £44m Oil Scandal given £4,000.' (3) The newspaper gave no publicity to the fact that in November 1979 the Secretary of State for Energy confirmed in the House of Commons that the plaintiff had left the department with an unblemished reputation and a record of excellent service and that there was no question of any blame attaching to him. (4) No apology was ever offered. Mr Lord in g cross-examination at the trial confirmed that he still said he had done nothing which called for any apology to the plaintiff. And counsel for the defendants, in his address to the jury, told them that if they felt compelled to award some sort of damages it should be 'the smallest coin in the realm'. (5) Not merely was the plaintiff subjected to the anxiety of litigation but allegations were made against him in that litigation. Firstly, it was suggested that his evidence that he knew little about the investigation by the h Comptroller and Auditor General until he read of it in the papers was 'pretty curious and a bit difficult to swallow'. Secondly, the second letter from Lord Taylor was described as 'the false version' which the plaintiff used to support a claim against the Department of Energy. Thirdly, it was suggested that the action was little more than a money-seeking expedition by the plaintiff. The jury were entitled, if they thought fit, to reject those complaints.

At the time of the trial the plaintiff had left the government service and was seeking j work in new fields. His reputation was of considerable practical importance to him. The perpetuation of a belief that he had, by his incompetence, lost huge sums of public money could do him very great harm. If the jury felt that a strong vindication of his reputation was necessary they would, I think, be entitled to that view. As regards quantum, the case was not one for small damages, as the very experienced trial judge

told the jury. That being so, and having regard to the circumstances which I have
a mentioned, I do not feel able to say that no reasonable jury could have awarded £45,000. My own opinion is that it was too much, but I do not think it is beyond the bounds of reason.

I would dismiss the appeal.

Appeal dismissed. Leave to appeal to House of Lords refused.

b

Solicitors: *Simmons & Simmons* (for the defendants); *Trower Still & Keeling* (for the plaintiff).

Diana Brahams Barrister.

c

Austin and others v Hart

PRIVY COUNCIL

LORD FRASER OF TULLYBELTON, LORD SIMON OF GLAISDALE, LORD KEITH OF KINKEL, LORD BRIDGE OF HARWICH AND LORD TEMPLEMAN

d 11, 12 JANUARY, 21 FEBRUARY 1983

Time – Persons entitled to bring action – Fatal accident – Action – Dependant of deceased entitled to sue if no action commenced by executor within six months of death – Executors appointed by will – Action commenced by dependants three months after death – No action commenced by executors – Whether claim commenced prematurely – Whether action a nullity – Compensation
e *for Injuries Ordinance (Trinidad and Tobago), s 8.*

The deceased was involved in a motor accident while he was a passenger in a car driven by the defendant, and as a result of injuries received in the accident he died the following day, 4 May 1974. Under the Trinidad and Tobago Compensation for Injuries Ordinance a plaintiff had the right to maintain an action for damages against any tortfeasor who
f caused death by his wrongful act, neglect or default provided that such an action was commenced within twelve months of the date of death. Section 8(1)[a] of the ordinance provided that where the injuries received resulted in death such an action was to be for the benefit of specified relatives of the deceased, including the parents and children of the deceased, and was to be brought in the name of the executor or administrator of the deceased. Section 8(2) further provided that in the absence of an executor or administrator,
g or where there was an executor or administrator but no action had been brought within six months after the death of the deceased, the action could be brought by all or any of the specified relatives. The deceased had appointed two executors, one of whom subsequently renounced probate, but by 2 August 1974 there had been no grant of probate or letters of administration. On that date the plaintiffs, who were the mother and children of the deceased, issued a writ against the defendant claiming damages for
h negligence in causing the death of the deceased. The defendant served a defence denying liability without questioning the right of the plaintiffs to commence the action. No action was brought by the remaining executor within the six-month period after the death. In July 1975, over a year after the death, the defendant amended his defence with the leave of the court pleading that the court had no jurisdiction to entertain the plaintiffs' claim on the ground that, since the right to sue under s 8 was vested in the executor, the
j plaintiffs were not competent parties to commence the action until after the expiration of the six-month period following the death. On appeal by the plaintiffs, the Trinidad and Tobago Court of Appeal held that the plaintiffs had not been entitled to issue the writ when they did and that accordingly the action was and remained a nullity. The plaintiffs appealed to the Privy Council.

---

a Section 8 is set out at p 343 *c d*, post

Held – Assuming that by the law of Trinidad and Tobago an executor who had not proved the will was nevertheless an executor within the meaning of s 8 of the ordinance, a
the issue of the writ was premature. However, further assuming that a premature writ was irregular, where the irregularity was of a kind which could be cured without amendment by the mere lapse of time and which caused no prejudice to the defendant, there was no reason for the court to insist that the irregularity nullified and invalidated the whole proceedings unless it caused substantial injustice. Furthermore, s 8(2) of the ordinance did not expressly invalidate any action brought within the six-month period b
if at the date of the writ there was in fact an executor, and accordingly the plaintiffs were entitled to sue in the capacity in which they brought their claim provided that no action was brought within that period by an executor. It followed that since the premature issue of the writ did not cause any injustice and since no action had been commenced by the executor within the six-month period the plaintiffs were entitled to sue. The appeal would accordingly be allowed (see p 344 *h* to p 345 *b* and *g* to *j*, post). c

Marsh v Marsh [1945] AC 271 followed.

Ingall v Moran [1944] 1 All ER 97, *Hilton v Sutton Steam Laundry* [1945] 2 All ER 425 and *Finnegan v Cementation Co Ltd* [1953] 1 All ER 1130 considered.

Notes

For actions under the Fatal Accidents Act 1976 by an executor or administrator, see 34 d
Halsbury's Laws (4th edn) paras 14–15, and for cases on the subject, see 36(1) Digest (Reissue) 342–343, *1366–1376*.

For actions begun before the grant of probate, see 17 Halsbury's Laws (4th edn) para 737.

Section 8 of the Trinidad and Tobago Compensation for Injuries Ordinance corresponds to ss 1 and 2 of the Fatal Accidents Act 1976. For ss 1 and 2 of the 1976 Act, see 46 e
Halsbury's Statutes (3rd edn) 1115, 1118.

Cases referred to in judgment

Finnegan v Cementation Co Ltd [1953] 1 All ER 1130, [1953] 1 QB 688, [1953] 2 WLR 1015, CA.

Hilton v Sutton Steam Laundry [1945] 2 All ER 425, [1946] KB 65, CA. f

Ingall v Moran [1944] 1 All ER 97, [1944] 1 KB 160, CA.

Marsh v Marsh [1945] AC 271, PC.

Seward v The Vera Cruz, The Vera Cruz (1884) 10 App Cas 59, [1881–5] All ER Rep 216, HL.

g

Appeal

Alexandrine Austin and Deborah Austin, Sharlene Austin and Richard Austin (infants suing by their mother and next friend, Maria Lezama) appealed with leave of the Court of Appeal of Trinidad and Tobago granted on 2 December 1980 from the judgment of that court (Corbin and Hassanali JJA, Kelsick JA dissenting) dated 22 July 1980 dismissing the appeal of the appellants against the order of Warner J dated 25 July 1977 whereby, h
on the hearing of a preliminary point, he dismissed the appellants' action against the respondent, Gene Hart, for damages under the Trinidad and Tobago Compensation for Injuries Ordinance. The facts are set out in the judgment of the Board.

George Newman QC and *James Guthrie* for the appellants.
Stuart McKinnon QC and *Mark Strachan* for the respondent.

j

21 February. The following judgment of the Board was delivered.

LORD TEMPLEMAN. In these proceedings the respondent has so far successfully argued that the appellants were too hasty by three months and too tardy by six months in the issue of proceedings.

By his last will dated 12 September 1970 Simon Austin appointed his brother William Austin and one Ramesh L Maharaj to be his executors. The dispositions of the estate of Simon Austin contained in his will are not material to this appeal.

On 3 May 1974 Simon Austin was a passenger in a motor car driven by the respondent Gene Hart. The car ran off the road and collided with a bridge. Simon Austin received injuries from which he died the following day, 4 May 1974.

Section 3 of the Compensation for Injuries Ordinance of Trinidad and Tobago creates the right to maintain an action against and to recover damages from any tortfeasor who causes death by his wrongful act, neglect or default. By s 6 of the ordinance such an action can only be commenced within 12 months from the time of death.

Section 8 of the ordinance is in these terms:

> '(1) Every action in respect of injury resulting in death shall be for the benefit of the wife, husband, parent, and child, as the case may be, of the person whose death shall have been so caused, and shall be brought by and in the name of the executor or administrator of the person deceased.
>
> (2) If there be no executor or administrator of the person deceased, or if although there be such executor or administrator no such action shall, within six months after the death of such deceased person, have been brought by and in the name of his executor or administrator, then and in every such case such action may be brought by and in the name or names of all or any of the persons (if more than one) for whose benefit such action would have been if it had been brought by and in the name of such executor or administrator.'

The benefit of a right of action for injuries resulting in death thus belongs to the specified dependants who are relatives of the deceased. The benefit of the right of action does not form part of the estate of the deceased or devolve under the provisions of his will. The ordinance provides machinery for the action to be brought by personal representatives of the deceased as trustees for the dependants or, in certain circumstances, for one or more of the dependants themselves to bring the action as trustee or trustees for all the dependants.

Simon Austin was survived by four dependants entitled to the benefit of any action maintainable against the respondent for causing the death of Simon Austin by negligent driving. Those dependants were the first appellant, who was the mother of Simon Austin, and the remaining appellants who were the children of Simon Austin.

On 8 May 1974 Ramesh L Maharaj renounced probate of the will of Simon Austin.

By writ dated 2 August 1974 issued in the Trinidad and Tobago High Court and accompanied by a statement of claim, the appellants asserted their rights as dependants of Simon Austin under the ordinance and claimed damages from the respondent for negligently causing the death of Simon Austin. At the date of that writ no one had proved the will or taken out letters of administration to the estate of Simon Austin.

By a defence dated 28 October 1974 the respondent denied negligence. He did not question the right of the appellants to bring the proceedings.

During the six months after the death of Simon Austin, ending on 3 November 1974, no executor or administrator of Simon Austin brought proceedings against the respondent. On and from 4 May 1975, the first anniversary of the death of Simon Austin, s 6 of the ordinance barred the right of any executor or administrator or dependant to commence proceedings against the respondent in respect of the death of Simon Austin.

The respondent applied for and was granted leave to amend his defence which was amended on 9 July 1975. By the amendment the respondent contended that—

> 'the Court has no jurisdiction in terms of Section 8 of the ... Ordinance ... to entertain the claim herein or to enter any judgment thereon for the reason that by his Will dated 12th September, 1970, the deceased Simon Austin appointed two executors in one of whom namely, William Austin, the right to bring an action under the said Ordinance was vested at all material times'.

Unless the only material time was the date of the issue of the writ that amendment was plainly inaccurate or at any rate incomplete because on any footing a right to bring an *a* action under the ordinance was vested in the appellants from 4 November 1974 to 4 May 1975. Probate of the will of Simon Austin was eventually granted to William Austin on 28 May 1976 but any right vested in him to bring an action against the respondent in respect of the death of Simon Austin had ceased on 4 May 1975.

If there was any substance in the amendment to the defence made by leave on 9 July 1975 and if such an amendment was necessary to defeat the claims put forward by the *b* appellants then it is surprising that the amendment was only put forward after the limitation period had expired and even more surprising that leave to amend was granted. The respondent by his initial defence served on 28 October 1974 had led the appellants to assume that the respondent only intended to defend the proceedings on their merits. Accidentally or by design the respondent delayed putting forward any claim that the proceedings were invalid until, by the expiration of the limitation period, the appellants *c* were no longer able to institute fresh proceedings.

In the High Court of Trinidad and Tobago Warner J dismissed the appellants' action against the respondent, holding on a preliminary point that the court had no jurisdiction to entertain the appellants' claim. At the date of the writ on 2 August 1974 there was an executor of Simon Austin, namely William Austin, and six months had not elapsed since the death of the deceased. The judge, supported by a majority of the Court of Appeal of *d* Trinidad and Tobago (Corbin and Hassanali JJA, Kelsick JA dissenting), concluded that the action was and remained a nullity because the appellants were not entitled to issue a writ when they did so on 2 August 1974.

For the purposes of this appeal their Lordships are content to assume, without deciding, that by the law of Trinidad and Tobago an executor who has not proved the will is nevertheless an executor within the meaning of s 8 of the ordinance. The issue of the *e* writ by the appellants was therefore premature. If before 4 November 1974 William Austin had brought valid proceedings against the respondent, the appellants would have been unable to maintain their action. But William Austin did not issue a writ and by 4 November 1974 the appellants were persons who were entitled to bring and had brought proceedings against the respondent under the ordinance. In *Seward v The Vera Cruz* (1884) 10 App Cas 59 at 67, [1881–5] All ER Rep 216 at 219 the Earl of Selborne LC *f* pointed out that s 1 of Lord Campbell's Act (the Fatal Accidents Act 1846), which corresponded to s 3 of the ordinance, created a new cause of action—

> 'given in substance not to the person representing in point of estate the deceased man, who would naturally represent him as to all his own rights of action which could survive, but to his wife and children, no doubt suing in point of form in the name of his executor.' *g*

It would be unfortunate if the existence of an executor, known or unknown to the dependants, invalidated an action which at all times belonged in equity to the dependants merely because the dependants did not sue in point of form in the name of the executor but sued in their own names. Of course if the dependants were supplanted by the executor, if, for example, William Austin had himself brought proceedings within six *h* months of the death of Simon Austin, then the action by the dependants could have been stayed or dismissed. That possibility is no reason for the court to refuse to entertain an action which the dependants in fact became entitled to initiate and pursue before their right to do so was challenged.

Section 8(2) of the ordinance does not expressly invalidate any action by a dependant within six months of the death if at the date of the writ there exists an executor or *j* administrator. By 4 November 1974 it was certain that the dependants were entitled to bring proceedings, because it was certain that no executor or administrator had brought an action within that period of six months. Their Lordships are not convinced that a premature action is irregular although it may be stayed or dismissed if within six months of the death another action is brought by the executor or administrator. Their Lordships are satisfied that, if a premature action is irregular and the irregularity is of a kind, which, as in the instant case, was cured without amendment by the mere lapse of time and which causes no prejudice to the defendant, there is no reason for the court to insist that the irregularity nullifies and invalidates the whole proceedings. The modern approach is to treat an irregularity as a nullifying factor only if it causes substantial injustice: see *Marsh v Marsh* [1945] AC 271 at 284. The premature issue of the writ in the present case did not cause any injustice at all. A bizarre and unjust result would follow if a writ issued on 2 November 1974 and served on 4 November 1974 were held to be a nullity whereas a writ issued and served on 4 November 1974 would plainly have been effective.

On behalf of the respondent reliance was placed on authority for the proposition that proceedings are a nullity unless the plaintiff is entitled to sue at the date of the writ. In *Ingall v Moran* [1944] 1 All ER 97, [1944] 1 KB 160 the plaintiff sued as administrator and claimed damages under the Law Reform (Miscellaneous Provisions) Act 1934. The plaintiff was not an administrator at the date of the writ and did not obtain letters of administration until the limitation period had expired. It was held that the proceedings were a nullity. But in that case the plaintiff did not become entitled to sue until it was too late.

In *Hilton v Sutton Steam Laundry* [1945] 2 All ER 425, [1946] KB 65 the plaintiff claimed as administratrix under the provisions of the Fatal Accidents Act 1846 which correspond to s 8 of the ordinance. The plaintiff was not an administratrix at the date of the writ and sought to amend so as to sue as a dependant widow. The Court of Appeal refused to allow the amendment and, following *Ingall v Moran*, held that the plaintiff was not entitled to continue her action as administratrix. In *Finnegan v Cementation Co Ltd* [1953] 1 All ER 1130, [1953] 1 QB 688 the plaintiff claimed in the writ as administratrix, though in the statement of claim she pleaded that she was both the widow and the administratrix. The Court of Appeal, following their earlier decisions, held that the plaintiff was not entitled to continue the action or to amend. The plaintiff was not the administratrix and never became entitled to sue in that capacity. None of the other authorities cited by counsel for the respondent carries the matter any further.

In the cited cases the plaintiff did not have any right to sue in the capacity claimed. In the present case the appellants were entitled to sue in the capacities in which they claimed provided, as happened, no executor or administrator intervened to bring an action within six months of the death of the deceased. In *Ingall v Moran* [1944] 1 All ER 97 at 102, [1944] 1 KB 160 at 169 Luxmoore LJ could not help 'feeling some regret'. In *Hilton v Sutton Steam Laundry* [1945] 2 All ER 425 at 429, [1946] KB 65 at 73 Lord Greene MR was not 'averse to discovering any proper distinction which would enable this unfortunate slip to be corrected'. In *Finnegan v Cementation Co Ltd* [1953] 1 All ER 1130 at 1136, [1953] 1 QB 688 at 699 Singleton LJ lamented 'that these technicalities are a blot on the administration of the law, and everyone except the successful party dislikes them'. Accepting, without approving, the decisions of the Court of Appeal which have been cited, their Lordships see no reason to encourage any extension of their ambit. In the present case the appellants were entitled to sue in the capacities named in the writ, they were entitled at the date of the writ to sue unless the executor or administrator intervened within six months of the death, no such intervention took place and the appellants without needing or seeking any amendment are entitled to proceed with the action which they have launched.

Their Lordships allow the appeal and direct that the order of Warner J should be set aside and that the action should proceed to trial on its merits. The respondent must pay the costs of the appellants relating to the preliminary point in the courts below and before the Board.

Appeal allowed. Order of Warner J set aside. Action to proceed to trial on its merits.

Solicitors: *Philip Conway Thomas & Co* (for the appellants); *Ingledew Brown Bennison & Garrett* (for the respondent).

Diana Procter Barrister.

Attorney General of Hong Kong v Ng Yuen Shiu

PRIVY COUNCIL

LORD FRASER OF TULLYBELTON, LORD SCARMAN, LORD BRIDGE OF HARWICH, LORD BRANDON OF OAKBROOK AND SIR JOHN MEGAW

15, 16 DECEMBER 1982, 21 FEBRUARY 1983

Hong Kong – Natural justice – Hearing – Duty to hear parties – Illegal immigrant – Government announcement that each illegal immigrant's case would be dealt with on its own merits – Order made for removal of applicant as an illegal immigrant without giving him a hearing – Whether announcement creating legitimate or reasonable expectation of a hearing – Whether applicant entitled to hearing before removal.

Natural justice – Hearing – Duty to hear parties – Hong Kong immigration authority – Illegal immigrant – Government announcement that each illegal immigrant's case would be dealt with on its own merits – Order made for removal of applicant as an illegal immigrant without giving him a hearing – Whether announcement creating legitimate or reasonable expectation of a hearing – Whether applicant entitled to hearing before removal.

In 1976 the respondent entered Hong Kong illegally. He remained there without being detected and became part owner of a factory which employed several workers. On 28 October 1980 a change in immigration policy was announced by the Hong Kong government to the effect that illegal immigrants would be interviewed in due course and that, although no guarantees could be given that they would not subsequently be removed, each case would be treated on its merits. The following day the respondent reported to an immigration officer and after being interviewed he was detained until a removal order was made against him by the Director of Immigration. He appealed to the immigration tribunal, which dismissed his appeal without a hearing, as it was entitled to do. The respondent then applied for judicial review. The Court of Appeal of Hong Kong granted him an order of prohibition against the director, prohibiting the execution of the removal order until an opportunity had been given to the respondent to put the circumstances of his case before the director. The Attorney General of Hong Kong appealed to the Privy Council.

Held – Assuming that there was no general right in an alien to have a hearing in accordance with the rules of natural justice before the making of a removal order against him, a person was nevertheless entitled to a fair hearing before a decision adversely affecting his interests was made by a public official or body if he had a legitimate or reasonable expectation of being accorded such a hearing. Such an expectation might be based on some statement or undertaking by, or on behalf of, the public authority which had the duty of making the decision if the authority had, through its officers, acted in a way which would make it unfair or inconsistent with good administration to deny the person affected an inquiry into his case. That principle was as much applicable where the person affected was an alien as where he was a British subject, because a public authority was bound by its undertakings as to the procedure it would follow, provided those undertakings did not conflict with its statutory duty. It followed that the government undertaking that each case would be treated on its merits had not been implemented, since the respondent had been given no opportunity to explain the humanitarian grounds on which he might have been allowed to remain in Hong Kong, in particular that he was a partner in a business which employed several workers. Accordingly the Attorney General's appeal would be dismissed, although an order of certiorari to quash the removal order made against the respondent would be substituted for the order of prohibition (see p 350 *c d h j* and p 351 *g* to p 352 *b* and *d* to *g*, post).

R v Criminal Injuries Compensation Board, ex p Lain [1967] 2 All ER 770, dictum of Lord Denning MR in *Schmidt v Secretary of State for Home Affairs* [1969] 1 All ER at 909, *Re Liverpool Taxi Owners' Association* [1972] 2 All ER 589, *R v Hull Prison Board of Visitors, ex p St Germain (No 2)* [1979] 3 All ER 545 and dictum of Lord Diplock in *O'Reilly v Mackman* [1982] 3 All ER at 1126–1127 applied.

Dictum of Barwick CJ in *Salemi v Minister for Immigration and Ethnic Affairs (No 2)* (1977) 14 ALR at 7 not followed.

Notes

For the right to a hearing, see 1 Halsbury's Laws (4th edn) para 76, and for cases on the subject, see 1(1) Digest (Reissue) 200–201, *1172–1176*.

Cases referred to in judgment

Birkdale District Electric Supply Co Ltd v Southport Corp [1926] AC 355, HL.
Liverpool Taxi Owners' Association, Re [1972] 2 All ER 589, [1972] 2 QB 299, [1972] 2 WLR 1262, CA.
O'Reilly v Mackman [1982] 3 All ER 1124, [1982] 3 WLR 1096, HL.
R v Criminal Injuries Compensation Board, ex p Lain [1967] 2 All ER 770, [1967] 2 QB 864, [1967] 3 WLR 348, DC.
R v Hull Prison Board of Visitors, ex p St Germain (No 2) [1979] 3 All ER 545, [1979] 1 WLR 1401, DC.
Salemi v Minister for Immigration and Ethnic Affairs (No 2) (1977) 14 ALR 1, Aust HC.
Schmidt v Secretary of State for Home Affairs [1969] 1 All ER 904, [1969] 2 Ch 149, [1969] 2 WLR 337, CA.

Appeal and cross-appeal

The Attorney General of Hong Kong appealed by leave of the Court of Appeal of Hong Kong given on 2 December 1981 from an order of the Court of Appeal (McMullin VP, Li JA and Baber J) dated 13 May 1981 which allowed in part the appeal by the respondent, Ng Yuen Shiu (also known as Ng Kam Shing), from an order of the Full Bench of the High Court of Justice of Hong Kong (Roberts CJ and Rhind J) dated 4 December 1980 quashing a writ of habeas corpus issued by Rhind J on 6 November 1980 and dismissing applications for orders of certiorari and prohibition. The Court of Appeal allowed the appeal to the extent of setting aside the order of the Full Bench and ordering that an order of prohibition issue prohibiting the Director of Immigration of Hong Kong from executing a removal order made against the respondent on 31 October 1980 until the respondent had been given the opportunity of making further representations to the Director of Immigration on his case. The respondent cross-appealed from that part of the judgment of the Court of Appeal which rejected his claim to be a Chinese resident with seven years' residence, or otherwise immune from removal under the provisions of s 19(1)(*b*) of the Immigration Ordinance, and also from the refusal to issue a writ of habeas corpus or order of certiorari. The facts are set out in the judgment of the Board.

Neil Kaplan QC and *Barrie Barlow* (both of the Hong Kong Bar) for the Attorney General.
Louis Blom-Cooper QC and *Richard Drabble* for the respondent.

21 February. The following judgment of the Board was delivered.

LORD FRASER OF TULLYBELTON. The question in this appeal is whether an alien, who has entered Hong Kong without permission and contrary to the laws of the colony, has a right to a hearing by the Hong Kong authorities, conducted in accordance with the rules of natural justice, either in every case or in the particular circumstances of this case.

The appeal arises out of the serious immigration problem which faced the government of Hong Kong in 1980. Immigrants from mainland China were pouring into the colony in increasing numbers. Some of the immigrants had permission to enter, but the majority did not. For some years up until 23 October 1980 the government of Hong Kong followed the 'reached base' policy, under which illegal immigrants from China were not repatriated if they managed to reach the urban areas without being arrested. Counsel for the Attorney General informed their Lordships that the number of illegal immigrants from China who reached base was in 1978 about 9,000 and in 1979 over 88,000. In 1980 up until 23 October, 58,400 illegal immigrants from China reached base, a further 80,700 failed to reach base and were repatriated to China, and in addition 58,000 immigrants entered from China legally. That makes a total for the ten months of over 197,000, which was not far short of the population of the city of Aberdeen. The total population of Hong Kong rose from 4·4 million in 1976 to 5·5 million in 1982, and the government had to take urgent measures to stem the flood of immigrants. On 23 October 1980 it announced that the 'reached base' policy would be discontinued forthwith, and on the same day it issued the Immigration (Amendment) (No 2) Ordinance 1980 which amended the Immigration Ordinance 1971 (the principal ordinance) so that it (i) required all residents of Hong Kong to carry proof of identity, (ii) prohibited the employment of illegal immigrants and (iii) conferred on the Director of Immigration a power to make removal orders under s 19.

There is no doubt that the Director of Immigration had power under s 19 (in the substituted form provided for in the 1980 ordinance) to order removal of illegal immigrants. There is also no doubt that neither that section, nor any other statutory provision, expressly requires an inquiry to be held before such an order is made. The only question raised in the appeal is whether, at common law, the respondent was entitled to have a fair inquiry held before a removal order was made against him. It is therefore unnecessary to do more than refer briefly to the substituted s 19, which provides, inter alia, as follows:

> '(1) A removal order may be made against a person requiring him to leave Hong Kong—(*a*) subject to subsection (3), by the Governor if it appears to him that person is an undesirable immigrant who has been ordinarily resident in Hong Kong for less than three years; or (*b*) subject to subsection (2), by the Director if it appears to him that that person . . . (ii) has committed or is committing an offence under section 38(1) or section 41, whether or not that person has been convicted of such offence and whether or not the time within which any prosecution may be brought has expired . . .'

Under s 38(1) of the principal ordinance a person commits an offence if, having landed in Hong Kong unlawfully, he remains in Hong Kong without the authority of the Director of Immigration.

The respondent was born in China on 16 May 1951. He was taken to Macau by his parents at the age of three. He entered Hong Kong from Macau illegally in 1967. He came to the notice of the authorities in Hong Kong only in 1976, when he applied for an identity card, and he was removed to Macau under a removal order in March 1976. In April 1976 he re-entered Hong Kong illegally and he has remained there until the present time. He was apparently an industrious worker and by 1980 he had become part owner of a small garment factory along with the registered proprietor.

The change of policy announced on 23 October 1980 was followed by a series of television announcements explaining that all illegal immigrants from China would be liable to be repatriated. Although the announcement only applied to illegal immigrants from China, it naturally caused anxiety to illegal immigrants of Chinese origin who had entered Hong Kong from Macau, including the respondent. On 28 October 1980 a group of illegal immigrants who had entered from Macau submitted a petition to the Governor of Hong Kong outside Government House, where a senior immigration official read out to them a series of questions and answers which had been prepared in the office of the Secretary for Security, dealing with the position of such persons and the actions which they should take. One of the questions, with its answer, was:

> 'Q. Will we be given identity cards? *A.* Those illegal immigrants from Macau will be treated in accordance with procedures for illegal immigrants from anywhere other than China. They will be interviewed in due course. No guarantee can be given that you may not subsequently be removed. Each case will be treated on its merits.'

The promise that each case would be treated on its merits is at the root of the respondent's argument before the Board.

The respondent was not present outside Government House and did not hear the announcement and the questions and answers, but he did see a television programme about the subject on the evening of 28 October. Earlier that day he had gone to an office of the Immigration Department to register with the department and had been told to report to the immigration clearance office on 29 October. He did so and, after being interviewed by an immigration officer there, he was detained under powers contained in s 26(*a*) of the principal ordinance, pending inquiry for the purpose of the ordinance. He was detained until 31 October. On 31 October the Director of Immigration made a removal order against the respondent. The respondent appealed to the immigration tribunal under s 53A of the principal ordinance, but the tribunal dismissed his appeal without hearing him, as it was entitled to do. He was notified of the tribunal's decision on 3 November. The respondent applied for a writ of habeas corpus, and he was released on bail on 6 November. At the hearing of his application for the writ, he was allowed to apply for judicial review, including orders of certiorari to quash the removal order dated 31 October and also the removal order of 1976, to quash the decision of the appeal tribunal, and an order of prohibition to restrain the director from executing the removal order of 31 October.

His application was heard by the Full Bench of the High Court (Roberts CJ and Rhind J), which quashed the writ of habeas corpus and refused the application for certiorari and prohibition. But the court ordered that the removal order be stayed on condition that the respondent's appeal from its decision was entered within seven days. The respondent appealed to the Court of Appeal. On 13 May 1981 the Court of Appeal (McMullin VP, Li JA, and Baber J) allowed the appeal in part. It allowed it to the extent of granting an order of prohibition against the Director of Immigration prohibiting him from executing the removal order of 31 October 1980 before an opportunity had been given to the respondent of putting all the circumstances of his case before the director. All the other orders made by the High Court were affirmed.

Against that very limited order of prohibition, the Attorney General of Hong Kong has appealed to this Board. The respondent cross-appealed on the issue of whether he was an illegal immigrant. He contended that he was a 'Chinese resident' as defined in the principal ordinance and that he was entitled to live in Hong Kong. The contention was stated on behalf of the respondent in his printed case and was not formally abandoned by his counsel, who submitted no oral argument in support of it. Their Lordships, not having heard argument on the question, express no opinion on it, and the decision of the Court of Appeal to the effect that the respondent was an illegal immigrant therefore stands.

The argument for the Attorney General raised two questions, one of wide general importance, the other of more limited scope. The general question, which both the High Court and the Court of Appeal decided in favour of the Attorney General, is whether an alien who enters Hong Kong illegally has, as a general rule, a right to a hearing, conducted fairly and in accordance with the rules of natural justice, before a removal order is made against him. The narrower question is whether, assuming that the answer to the general question is in the negative, nevertheless the respondent has a right to such a hearing in the particular circumstances of this case. The Court of Appeal answered the latter question in favour of the respondent and therefore made the limited order of prohibition now under appeal. Having regard to the view which their Lordships have formed on the narrower question, it is unnecessary for them to decide the general question. They will therefore assume, without deciding, that the Court of Appeal rightly decided that there was no general right in an alien to have a hearing in accordance with the rules of natural justice before a removal order is made against him.

The narrower proposition for which the respondent contended was that a person is entitled to a fair hearing before a decision adversely affecting his interests is made by a public official or body, if he has 'a legitimate expectation' of being accorded such a hearing. The phrase 'legitimate expectation' in this context originated in the judgment of Lord Denning MR in *Schmidt v Secretary of State for Home Affairs* [1969] 1 All ER 904 at 909, [1969] 2 Ch 149 at 170. It is in many ways an apt one to express the underlying principle, though it is somewhat lacking in precision. In *Salemi v Minister for Immigration and Ethnic Affairs (No 2)* (1977) 14 ALR 1 at 7 Barwick CJ construed the word 'legitimate' in that phrase as expressing the concept of 'entitlement or recognition by law'. So understood, the expression (as the learned Chief Justice rightly observed) 'adds little, if anything, to the concept of a right'. With great respect to the learned Chief Justice, their Lordships consider that the word 'legitimate' in that expression falls to be read as meaning 'reasonable'. Accordingly 'legitimate expectations' in this context are capable of including expectations which go beyond enforceable legal rights, provided they have some reasonable basis: see *R v Criminal Injuries Compensation Board, ex p Lain* [1967] 2 All ER 770, [1967] 2 QB 864. So it was held in *R v Hull Prison Board of Visitors, ex p St Germain (No 2)* [1979] 3 All ER 545, [1979] 1 WLR 1401 that a prisoner is entitled to challenge, by judicial review, a decision by a prison board of visitors, awarding him loss of remission of sentence, although he has no legal right to remission, but only a reasonable expectation of receiving it.

The decision of the Court of Appeal in *St Germain* was approved by the House of Lords recently in *O'Reilly v Mackman* [1982] 3 All ER 1124 at 1126–1127, [1982] 3 WLR 1096 at 1100–1101, where Lord Diplock, with whose speech the other Law Lords present agreed, said this:

> 'It is not, and it could not be, contended that the decision of the board awarding him forfeiture of remission had infringed or threatened to infringe any right of the appellant derived from private law, whether a common law right or one created by a statute. Under the Prison Rules remission of sentence is not a matter of right but of indulgence. So far as private law is concerned all that each appellant had was a legitimate expectation, based on his knowledge of what is the general practice, that he would be granted the maximum remission, permitted by r 5(2) of the Prison Rules, of one-third of his sentence if by that time no disciplinary award of forfeiture of remission had been made against him. So the second thing to be noted is that none of the appellants had any remedy in private law. In public law, as distinguished from private law, however, such legitimate expectation gave to each appellant a sufficient interest to challenge the legality of the adverse disciplinary award made against him by the board on the ground that in one way or another the board in reaching its decision had acted outwith the powers conferred on it by the legislation under which it was acting; and such grounds would include the board's failure to observe the rules of natural justice: which means no more than to act fairly towards him in carrying out their decision-making process, and I prefer so to put it.'

The expectations may be based on some statement or undertaking by, or on behalf of, the public authority which has the duty of making the decision, if the authority has, through its officers, acted in a way that would make it unfair or inconsistent with good administration for him to be denied such an inquiry.

One such case was *Re Liverpool Taxi Owners' Association* [1972] 2 All ER 589, [1972] 2 QB 299. Liverpool Corporation had the duty of licensing the number of taxis which they thought fit, and for some years the number had been fixed at 300. In 1971 a sub-committee of the council recommended increases in the number of licensed taxis for 1972 and again in 1973, and no limitation on numbers thereafter. The chairman of the relevant committee gave a public undertaking on 4 August 1971 that the number would not be increased beyond 300 until a private Bill had been passed by Parliament and had

come into effect, and his undertaking was confirmed by him orally and by the town
a clerk in a letter to two associations representing the holders of existing taxi licences. In November 1971 the sub-committee resolved that the number of licences should be increased in 1972, before the private Bill had been passed, and the resolution was approved by the full committee and by the council in December. The association of licence holders applied to the court for an order of prohibition and certiorari. The Divisional Court refused the application, but the Court of Appeal granted an order of
b prohibition against the corporation from granting any increased number of licences without first hearing any representations which might be made by or on behalf of persons interested therein, including the appellant association. It is important to notice that the court order was limited to ensuring that the corporation followed a fair procedure by holding an inquiry before reaching a decision: provided such procedure was followed the decision was left with the corporation to whom it had been entrusted by Parliament.
c Lord Denning MR said ([1972] 2 All ER 589 at 594, [1972] 2 QB 299 at 308):

> '... the corporation were not at liberty to disregard their undertaking [not to increase the number without holding an inquiry]. They were bound by it so long as it was not in conflict with their statutory duty. It is said that a corporation cannot contract itself out of its statutory duties. In *Birkdale District Electric Supply Co Ltd v Southport Corpn* [1926] AC 355 at 364 the Earl of Birkenhead said that it was—"a
> d well established principle of law, that if a person or public body is entrusted by the Legislature with certain powers and duties expressly or impliedly for public purposes, those persons or bodies cannot divest themselves of these powers and duties. They cannot enter into any contract or take any action incompatible with the due exercise of their powers or the discharge of their duties." But that principle does not mean that a corporation can give an undertaking and break it as they please.
> e So long as the performance of the undertaking is compatible with their public duty, they must honour it.'

Roskill LJ said ([1972] 2 All ER 589 at 596, [1972] 2 QB 299 at 310):

> 'It is for the council and not for this court to determine what the future policy should be in relation to the number of taxi licences which are to be issued in the city
> f of Liverpool. It is not for this court to consider population growths or falls or the extent of the demand for taxis within or without the city ... All those are matters for the council. This court is concerned to see that whatever policy the corporation adopts is adopted after due and fair regard to all the conflicting interests. The power of the court to intervene is not limited, as once was thought, to those cases where the function in question is judicial or quasi-judicial. The modern cases show that
> g this court will intervene more widely than in the past.'

Their Lordships see no reason why the principle should not be applicable when the person who will be affected by the decision is an alien, just as much as when he is a British subject. The justification for it is primarily that, when a public authority has promised to follow a certain procedure, it is in the interest of good administration that it
h should act fairly and should implement its promise, so long as implementation does not interfere with its statutory duty. The principle is also justified by the further consideration that, when the promise was made, the authority must have considered that it would be assisted in discharging its duty fairly by any representations from interested parties and as a general rule that is correct.

In the opinion of their Lordships the principle that a public authority is bound by its
j undertakings as to the procedure it will follow, provided they do not conflict with its duty, is applicable to the undertaking given by the government of Hong Kong to the respondent, along with other illegal immigrants from Macau, in the announcement outside Government House on 28 October 1980, that each case would be considered on its merits. The only ground on which it was argued before the Board that the undertaking had not been implemented was that the respondent had not been given an opportunity to put his case for an exercise of discretion, which the director undoubtedly possesses, in

his favour before a decision was reached. The basis of the respondent's complaint is that, when he was interviewed by an official of the Immigration Department who a
recommended to the director that a removal order against him should be made, he was not able to explain the humanitarian grounds for the discretion to be exercised in his favour. In particular he had no opportunity of explaining that he was not an employee but a partner in a business which employed several workers. The evidence of the respondent, contained in an affidavit to the High Court, was that at the interview he was not allowed to say anything except to answer the questions put to him by the official b
who was interviewing him. Roberts CJ, giving the judgment of the Full Bench, concluded that the respondent—

> 'should have been asked whether there were any humanitarian reasons or other special factors which he would like to be taken into account before a decision was reached. If this had been done, he would not have been able to claim that he had no opportunity of making it clear that he was a proprietor of a business and not just a c
> technician.'

When the appeal was before the Court of Appeal McMullin VP pointed out that 'this is the narrow factual basis on which the appeal stands'. It was emphasised by Baber J in two striking sentences as follows:

> 'It is a pity that he was not expressly asked at his interview on 29 October 1980 d
> "have you anything to say as to why you should be allowed to remain in Hong Kong?" and his answer recorded. This would have been an adequate opportunity to state his case and had this been done these proceedings would have been unnecessary.'

Their Lordships consider that this is a very narrow case on its facts, but they are not disposed to differ from the view expressed by both the courts below, to the effect that the e
government's promise to the respondent has not been implemented. Accordingly the appeal ought to be dismissed. But in the circumstances their Lordships are of opinion that the order made by the Court of Appeal should be varied. The appropriate remedy is not the conditional order of prohibition made by the Court of Appeal, but an order of certiorari to quash the removal order made by the director on 31 October against the respondent. That order of certiorari is of course entirely without prejudice to the making f
of a fresh removal order by the Director of Immigration after a fair inquiry has been held at which the respondent has been given an opportunity to make such representations as he may see fit as to why he should not be removed.

Their Lordships will humbly advise Her Majesty that the appeal ought to be dismissed and that, in substitution for the order of prohibition made by the Court of Appeal, an order of certiorari should be made quashing the removal order dated 31 October 1980 g
by the Director of Immigration. There will be an order for costs to the respondent. There will be no order on the cross-appeal.

Appeal dismissed. Order of certiorari substituted for order of prohibition. No order on cross-appeal.

Solicitors: *Macfarlanes* (for the Attorney General); *Hewitt Woollacott & Chown* (for the respondent).

Diana Procter Barrister.

R v Police Complaints Board, ex parte Madden
R v Police Complaints Board, ex parte Rhone

QUEEN'S BENCH DIVISION (CROWN OFFICE LIST)
McNEILL J
29, 30 NOVEMBER, 1, 2, 21 DECEMBER 1982

Police – Complaint against police – Police Complaints Board – Discharge of board's function – Board required to 'have regard' to guidance given by Secretary of State – Secretary of State's guidance stating that disciplinary proceedings should not be taken if Director of Public Prosecutions deciding that evidence against police officer insufficient for criminal prosecution – Whether board bound to comply with Secretary of State's guidance – Whether board abdicating statutory function by not considering complaint if Director deciding not to prosecute – Whether board unlawfully fettering its discretion – Police Act 1976, s 3(2).

When a member of the public made a complaint regarding a police officer the police were required to investigate the complaint and, by virtue of s 2(1) of the Police Act 1976, were required to send a copy of the report of the investigation to the Police Complaints Board. If the police decided not to prefer disciplinary charges against the officer concerned following their investigation and the board disagreed with that decision, the board was entitled, under s 3(2)[a] of the 1976 Act, to recommend and if necessary direct the chief officer of police to bring such charges as the board considered appropriate. In discharging that function, the board was required by s 3(8)[b] of the 1976 Act to 'have regard' to guidance given to it by the Secretary of State in regard to preferring disciplinary charges. The Secretary of State had indicated to both the police and the board, by way of guidance, that where the Director of Public Prosecutions had decided on evidential grounds not to institute criminal proceedings against a police officer then the police should normally not take disciplinary proceedings against the officer if the evidence required to substantiate the disciplinary charge was the same as that required to substantiate a corresponding criminal charge. The board adopted a policy that it was precluded by the guidance from recommending disciplinary proceedings if the Director of Public Prosecutions had decided that there was insufficient evidence to bring criminal charges, because fairness required that a police officer should not be put in double jeopardy by having to face disciplinary proceedings founded on evidence which the Director of Public Prosecutions thought insufficient to secure a conviction on a corresponding criminal charge. The applicants each made a complaint to the police about the conduct of certain police officers. The complaints were treated as alleging criminal offences against the officers and were referred to the Director of Public Prosecutions, who decided that the evidence was insufficient to justify criminal proceedings. The police then decided not to prefer disciplinary charges because the evidence to substantiate them was the same as the evidence considered by the Director of Public Prosecutions and submitted reports of the investigations into the complaints to the board for its consideration. The board decided that it was not open to it, because of the guidance, to question the police decision not to prefer disciplinary charges, and therefore declined to consider the complaints further. The applicants applied for judicial review of the board's decisions, seeking certiorari to quash the decisions, on the grounds (i) that the board, in considering itself bound by s 3(8) to comply with the Secretary of State's guidance and therefore precluded from further considering the complaints, had abdicated its statutory function under s 3(2) to

a Section 3(2) is set out at p 357 *j*, post
b Section 3(8) is set out at p 358 *d*, post

consider the complaints, and (ii) that alternatively the board had thereby unlawfully fettered the discretion which it had under s 3(2). *a*

Held – The applicants were entitled to certiorari to quash the board's decisions, for the following reasons—

(1) The board had erred in law in declining jurisdiction to consider the complaints further and had thereby unlawfully abdicated its statutory function under s 3(2) of the 1976 Act, because on the true construction of s 3(8) the requirement that the board 'shall *b* have regard' to the guidance given by the Secretary of State meant no more than that the board was required to take the guidance into account when exercising its functions under s 3(2) and did not mean that it was obliged to comply with the guidance. Furthermore, although the 1976 Act and the Secretary of State's guidance were to be considered against the background of the rule against double jeopardy, that rule, properly understood, meant that a person was not to be tried twice for the same offence. Accordingly, the rule *c* against double jeopardy did not apply where an officer had not been tried but evidence which the Director of Public Prosecutions considered to be insufficient to convict on a criminal charge was sought to be used in disciplinary proceedings against him. Thus, although the board was required to be 'fair' to an officer when considering a complaint made against him, the rule against double jeopardy was not to be equated with the concept of 'fairness'. In any event a policy of fairness did not entitle the board to limit its *d* statutory obligation to consider complaints and did not of itself justify the board declining to consider a complaint because the Director of Public Prosecutions had advised against criminal proceedings (see p 367 *c* to *e*, p 371 *d* to *f*, p 373 *c* to *f* and p 374 *f g*, post); *Connelly v DDP* [1964] 2 All ER 401, *Lewis Shops Group v Wiggins* [1973] ICR 335, *Laker Airways Ltd v Dept of Trade* [1977] 2 All ER 182 and *De Falco v Crawley BC* [1980] 1 All ER 913 applied. *e*

(2) The board had unlawfully fettered the discretion which it had under s 3(2) of the 1976 Act by regarding itself as bound to comply with the Secretary of State's guidance and thereby to accept the police decision not to institute disciplinary proceedings, since the object for which the board was created was the consideration of complaints against police officers and natural justice required the board itself to consider such complaints rather than to accept as binding the decision of another person, namely the Director of *f* Public Prosecutions, not to prosecute an officer (see p 374 *d* to *g*, post).

Notes

For investigation of complaints against a police officer, see 36 Halsbury's Laws (4th edn) para 275.

For the Police Act 1976, s 3, see 46 Halsbury's Statutes (3rd edn) 1182. *g*

Cases referred to in judgment

Alexander v Immigration Appeal Tribunal [1982] 2 All ER 766, [1982] 1 WLR 1076, HL.
Associated Provincial Picture Houses Ltd v Wednesbury Corp [1947] 2 All ER 680, [1948] 1 KB 223, CA.
Bates Farms and Dairy Ltd v Scott [1976] IRLR 214, EAT.
Bhandari v Advocates Committee [1956] 3 All ER 742, [1965] 1 WLR 1442, PC. *h*
British Oxygen Co Ltd v Minister of Technology [1970] 3 All ER 165, [1971] AC 610, [1970] 3 WLR 488, HL.
Connelly v DPP [1964] 2 All ER 401, [1964] AC 1254, [1964] 2 WLR 1145, HL.
Cumings v Birkenhead Corp [1971] 2 All ER 881, [1972] Ch 12, [1971] 2 WLR 1458, CA.
De Falco v Crawley BC [1980] 1 All ER 913, [1980] QB 460, [1980] 2 WLR 664, CA.
DPP v Nasralla [1967] 2 All ER 161, [1967] 2 AC 238, [1967] 3 WLR 13, PC. *j*
Edwards (Inspector of Taxes) v Bairstow [1955] 3 All ER 48, [1956] AC 14, [1955] 3 WLR 410, HL.
IRC v National Federation of Self-Employed and Small Businesses Ltd [1981] 2 All ER 93, [1982] AC 617, [1981] 2 WLR 722, HL.
Laker Airways Ltd v Dept of Trade [1977] 2 All ER 182, [1977] QB 643, [1977] 2 WLR 234, CA.
Lewis Shops Group v Wiggins [1973] ICR 335, NIRC.

Maynard v Osmond [1977] 1 All ER 64, [1977] QB 240, [1976] 3 WLR 711, CA.
Padfield v Minister of Agriculture, Fisheries and Food [1968] 1 All ER 694, [1968] AC 997, [1968] 2 WLR 924, HL.
Perry v Wright [1908] 1 KB 441, CA.
R v Disciplinary Board of the Metropolitan Police, ex p Borland (20 July 1982, unreported), DC.
R v London County Council, ex p Corrie [1918] 1 KB 68, DC.
R v Port of London Authority, ex p Kynoch Ltd [1919] 1 KB 176, CA.
R v Rochdale Metropolitan BC, ex p Cromer Ring Mill Ltd [1982] 3 All ER 761.
R v Secretary of State for the Environment, ex p Brent London Borough Council [1982] QB 593, [1982] 2 WLR 693, DC.
Sagnata Investments Ltd v Norwich Corp [1971] 2 All ER 1441, [1971] 2 QB 614, [1971] 3 WLR 133, CA.
Weddel (W) & Co Ltd v Tepper [1980] ICR 286, CA.
Zamir v Secretary of State for the Home Dept [1980] 2 All ER 768, [1980] AC 930, [1980] 3 WLR 249, HL.

Cases also cited

Currie v Chief Constable of Surrey (1981) Times, 10 June.
Hotel and Catering Industry Training Board v Automobile Pty Ltd [1969] 2 All ER 582, [1969] 1 WLR 697, HL.

Applications for judicial review

R v Police Complaints Board, ex p Madden

Errol Patrick Madden applied, with the leave of Webster J granted on 29 April 1982, for: (1) a declaration that the Police Complaints Board misdirected themselves (a) in considering themselves bound in law by the guidance by the Secretary of State on the Preferring and Withdrawing of Disciplinary Charges, (b) in misinterpreting the guidance as precluding the institution of disciplinary proceedings where the Director of Public Prosecutions (the director) had determined not to bring criminal proceedings on the same or similar evidence required to substantiate a corresponding disciplinary charge and (c) in concluding that the Police Act 1974 precluded the institution of disciplinary proceedings where the director had determined not to bring criminal proceedings on the same or similar evidence required to substantiate a corresponding disciplinary charge, (2) further or in the alternative a declaration that if the guidance in fact precluded the institution of disciplinary proceedings in the above circumstances, that the guidance was in breach of the 1976 Act, (3) an order of certiorari to quash the decision of the board given in letters dated 18 and 19 November 1981 not to recommend or direct the institution of disciplinary charges in respect of complaints made by the applicant against Pc Stephen Hollowell and Pc David Charles Wildbore of the Metropolitan Police. The facts are set out in the judgment.

R v Police Complaints Board, ex p Rhone

Trevor Clive Rhone applied, with the leave of Webster J granted on 29 April 1982, for similar relief to that claimed by the applicant Madden in respect of a decision of the board given in a letter dated 31 March 1982 not to recommend or direct the institution of disciplinary charges in respect of complaints made by the applicant against Police Sgt Brian Cheeseman and Police Sgt Norman McGowan of the Metropolitan Police. The facts are set out in the judgment.

Michael Beloff QC and *Edward Fitzgerald* for the applicant Madden.
Michael Beloff QC for the applicant Rhone.
John Laws for the board.
John Ungley for Pc Hollowell, Pc Wildbore, Police Sgt Cheeseman and Police Sgt McGowan.

Cur adv vult

21 December. The following judgment was delivered.

McNEILL J. These are two applications for judicial review of decisions of the Police Complaints Board which have been heard together by consent. Each raises the same point of law. Each applicant claims relief in the following terms:

> '(1) A Declaration that the Police Complaints Board misdirected themselves in that they (a) considered themselves bound in law by the Guidance by the Secretary of State on the Preferring and Withdrawing of Disciplinary Charges, hereinafter referred to as the "Guidance"; (b) misinterpreted the "Guidance" as precluding the institution of disciplinary proceedings where the Director of Public Prosecutions has determined not to bring criminal proceedings on the same or similar evidence; (c) concluded that the Police Act 1976 precludes the institution of disciplinary proceedings where the Director of Public Prosecutions has determined not to bring criminal proceedings on the same or similar evidence. (2) Further or in the alternative A Declaration that if the "Guidance" in fact precludes the institution of disciplinary proceedings in the circumstances outlined above then the "Guidance" does so in breach of the said Act. (3) Certiorari of the said decision of the Police Complaints Board. (4) Costs and that all necessary and consequential directions be given.'

Each applicant had made a complaint about the conduct of police officers. The relevant decision of the board in each case is as follows. In the case of Madden, in a letter from the chairman of the board to the applicant's solicitor, dated 19 November 1981, the relevant passage reads:

> 'The available evidence was first referred to the Director of Public Prosecutions who informed you on 23rd June of his decision that the evidence then available was insufficient to justify the institution of criminal proceedings against any police officer. As you know the Secretary of State's guidance means that it is not open to the Deputy Commissioner or to the Board to question this decision or to bring about disciplinary charges on the same evidence.'

In the case of Rhone, in a letter from the secretary of the board to the applicant, care of his solicitors, dated 31 March 1982, the relevant passage reads:

> 'The Director concluded that the evidence of the further investigation was insufficient to justify the institution of criminal proceedings against the officers for any offence and the report of the investigation has now been submitted to the Police Complaints Board. The Board have considered the report of this further investigation very carefully. You will know from the Board's earlier letter that they may not use the same facts and evidence to recommend a disciplinary charge which is in substance the same as the offence considered by the Director and they are satisfied that the investigation has not revealed other matters which would merit disciplinary proceedings against any officer.'

The statutory framework within which the board operates is to be found, firstly, in s 49 of the Police Act 1964. It reads:

> '(1) Where the chief officer of police for any police area receives a complaint from a member of the public against a member of the police force for that area he shall (unless the complaint alleges an offence with which the member of the police force has then been charged) forthwith record the complaint and cause it to be investigated and for that purpose may, and shall if directed by the Secretary of State, request the chief officer of police for any other police area to provide an officer of the police force for that area to carry out the investigation.
>
> (2) A chief officer of police shall comply with any request made to him under subsection (1) of this section.

(3) On receiving the report of an investigation under this section the chief officer
a of police, unless satisfied from the report that no criminal offence has been committed, shall send the report to the Director of Public Prosecutions.'

Section 50 of the 1964 Act states the position prior to the Police Act 1976. It deals with information as to the manner of dealing with complaints. It states:

'Every police authority in carrying out their duty with respect to the maintenance
b of an adequate and efficient police force, and inspectors of constabulary in carrying out their duties with respect to the efficiency of any police force, shall keep themselves informed as to the manner in which complaints from members of the public against members of the force are dealt with by the chief officer of police.'

The Police Complaints Board was set up by the Police Act 1976. Section 1 reads:

c '(1) For the purposes of this Part of this Act there shall be a board known as the Police Complaints Board consisting of not less than nine members appointed by the Prime Minister . . .'

It then goes into more detail, saying that members of the board shall not include any person who is or has been a constable in any part of the United Kingdom. It also states that the Prime Minister shall appoint one of the members of the board to be chairman
d and either one or two members of the board to be deputy chairman or deputy chairmen.

The scheme of the Act can be seen from the next following sections. Section 2(1) provides:

'Where a chief officer of police receives the report of an investigation into a complaint under section 49 of the Police Act 1964 . . . he shall, subject to subsection
e (2) and section 5 below, send to the Police Complaints Board a copy of the report together with—(*a*) a copy of the complaint; and (*b*) a memorandum signed by him stating—(i) his opinion on the merits of the complaint; (ii) whether he has preferred disciplinary charges in respect of the matter or matters complained of and, if not, his reasons for not doing so; and (iii) if he has preferred such disciplinary charges, particulars of the charges and of any exceptional circumstances affecting the case by
f reason of which he considers that section 4 below should apply to the hearing of them.'

Section 2(2) provides that sub-s (1) shall not apply where disciplinary charges have been preferred and where the accused has admitted the charges and not withdrawn his admission; or where the complaint has been withdrawn or the complainant has indicated that he does not wish any further steps to be taken; or where the officer holds a rank
g above superintendant and the regulations do not apply. Subsection (3) is procedural and I do not need to read the remainder of that section.

Section 3(1) and (2) reads:

'(1) Where the report of an investigation into a complaint is sent to the Police Complaints Board under section 2(1) above the following provisions shall have effect
h in relation to disciplinary charges in respect of the matter or matters complained of; and for the purpose of discharging their functions under those provisions the Board may request the chief officer of police to furnish them with such additional information as they may reasonably require.

(2) Where the chief officer of police has not preferred disciplinary charges the Board may, if they disagree with his decision, make recommendations to him as to
j the charges which they consider should be preferred; and if, after the Board have made such recommendations and consulted the chief officer, he is still unwilling to prefer such charges as the Board consider appropriate they may direct him to prefer such charges as they may specify.'

Subsection (3) provides that where the board have given a chief officer a direction under sub-s (2) they shall furnish him with a written statement of their reasons for doing so. Subsection (4) provides that where disciplinary charges have been or are preferred, they shall not be withdrawn except with the leave of the board. Subsection (5) provides:

> 'Where disciplinary charges have been or are preferred (otherwise than in pursuance of a direction under subsection (2) above) the Board may direct that section 4 below shall apply to the hearing of the charges if they consider that to be desirable by reason of any exceptional circumstances affecting the case; and that section shall also apply to the hearing of any charges preferred in pursuance of a direction under that subsection.'

Subsection (6) provides that notwithstanding sub-s (5), s 4 shall not apply in any case where the accused admits the charges and does not withdraw his admission before the beginning of the hearing. Subsection (7) provides that a chief officer of police shall comply with any direction given to him under sub-s (2) and, subject to any regulations made by the Secretary of State under s 6, with any request under sub-s (1). Section 3(8) provides:

> 'In discharging their functions under subsections (2) and (4) above the Board shall have regard to any guidance given to them by the Secretary of State with respect to such matters affecting the preferring and withdrawing of disciplinary charges as are for the time being the subject of guidance by him to chief officers of police, including in particular the principles to be applied in cases that involve any question of criminal proceedings and are not governed by section 11 below.'

I need not read s 4, which applies to the hearing of a disciplinary charge. I pass to s 5(1) and (2) which provides:

> '(1) Where the report of an investigation into a complaint is sent to the Director of Public Prosecutions in pursuance of section 49(3) of the Police Act 1964 (cases where criminal offences may have been committed) section 2(1) above shall not apply to the complaint until the question of criminal proceedings has been dealt with by the Director.
>
> (2) Where it appears to the Police Complaints Board that any information furnished to them under section 2 or 3 above—(*a*) may be relevant to the question of criminal proceedings against the member of a police force against whom the complaint in question is made; but (*b*) has not been furnished to the Director of Public Prosecutions, the Board may request the chief officer of that force to transmit that information to the Director; and the chief officer shall transmit that information accordingly unless it has already been furnished to the Director or the chief officer is satisfied that it cannot be relevant as aforesaid.'

Subsection (3) is not relevant. Section 6 deals with the procedure to be followed by chief officers of police and the Police Complaints Board in relation to complaints.

I can now pass to s 11 which deals with disciplinary charges in criminal cases. It provides:

> '(1) Where a member of a police force has been acquitted or convicted of a criminal offence he shall not be liable to be charged with any offence against discipline which is in substance the same as the offence of which he has been acquitted or convicted.
>
> (2) Subsection (1) above shall not be construed as applying to a charge in respect of an offence against discipline which consists of having been found guilty of a criminal offence.'

The crucial words for the purposes of these applications are found in s 3(8). They are: 'In discharging their functions . . . the Board *shall have regard* to any guidance etc' (my emphasis). The subsection contemplates two types of guidance: (1) that given by the Secretary of State to them, and (2) that given by the Secretary of State to chief officers of police. It was common ground at the Bar that in May 1977 the then Secretary of State wrote to the board (no copy of the letter has been exhibited and I did not see one) indicating his wishes that the board should have regard to the guidance he had given to the chief officers and to avoid 'double jeopardy'. It appears that he drew particular attention to what in the current Guidance to Chief Officers on Police Complaints and Discipline Procedures (Home Office circular 32/1980, as amended by Home Office circular 15/1982) would be certain parts of ss 5 and 9 of the guidance.

As will appear, it may be that the board treated the Secretary of State's expression of wishes as a direction to *follow* the guidance. The Secretary of State is not a party to this application and I should not be prepared, in his absence, to determine whether or not he gave a direction and if so whether or not it was within his powers. The issue here is that of the powers of the board and the way in which it exercised them or declined to exercise them. All this must be seen in the statutory context of an obligation on the board 'to have regard' to the guidance. I accept, for the purposes of this judgment, that the Secretary of State did no more than indicate his wishes, as I have set out above.

It is also fair to observe that the board appears to have regarded para 6.13 of the guidance as obliging it to 'follow' the guidance. That paragraph reads:

> 'The Complaints Board are required under section 3(8) of the 1976 Act to have regard to any guidance given to them by the Secretary of State with respect to such matters affecting the preferring and withdrawing of disciplinary charges as are the subject of current guidance by him to the police. The Secretary of State has issued guidance to the Board to follow the criteria set out in paragraphs 5.4, 5.9–5.14, 9.2–9.4, 9.6 and 9.9–9.11.'

This passage appears in s 6 of the guidance, which is a section advising chief officers of the functions of the board. Section 5, for completeness, is headed 'Consideration of and action on investigation report' and s 9 is headed 'Disciplinary arrangements for officers up to and including chief superintendent'. I note that in the last sentence of para 6.13, the Secretary of State does not suggest that he has included s 6 (or, in particular, para 6.13) in his guidance to the board. In any event, and even if he had done, the last sentence of para 6.13 is erroneous in that whatever guidance he did issue to the board, it did not include guidance 'to follow the criteria'. The statutory obligation on the board is solely 'to have regard' to the guidance. It is unnecessary to read out paras 9.2 to 9.4 and 9.9 to 9.11 as they are part of the discipline code. I need not read para 5.4 as it has no bearing on the relevant events. Paragraphs 5.9 to 5.14 are in a subsection headed 'The relationship between criminal and disciplinary proceedings' and I read them in full:

> '5.9 Section 11 of the 1976 Act states the principle that no officer who has been charged with and either acquitted or convicted of a criminal offence should be charged with a disciplinary offence which is in substance the same as that criminal offence. Apart from this it is not practicable to lay down absolute rules but there are a number of other considerations which may be relevant to the avoidance of double jeopardy in a case which has both criminal and disciplinary aspects.
>
> 5.10 Where it seems that a police officer has committed a criminal offence, the fact that he is a police officer subject to a discipline code is no sufficient reason to refrain from prosecuting him, particularly if the case is one in which proceedings would be taken against a member of the public. It therefore follows that misconduct which amounts to a criminal offence should not be dealt with under the discipline code as an alternative to criminal proceedings when the latter are clearly justified. Nor would it be proper to appear to have recourse to disciplinary proceedings simply because it was thought impossible to establish a criminal charge to the satisfaction of a court of law.
>
> 5.11 In some cases the alleged criminal offence is in itself unimportant and not serious enough to justify prosecution, but it would be entirely proper in the public interest that the misconduct should be dealt with as a matter of internal discipline.

An instance of such misconduct might be a technical assault upon another member of the force (which is particularly specified as an offence against discipline in the discipline code).

5.12 There are cases in which, in addition to the circumstances pointing to a criminal offence, there are other elements which involve a breach or breaches of discipline. For example, a constable may have left his beat or other place of duty without authority or good cause, in circumstances which suggest that he was responsible for breaking into adjoining property. The evidence may be insufficient to justify prosecution for the criminal offence of, say, burglary, but there is no reason why the officer should not be dealt with for disobedience to orders, or neglect of duty in respect of his action in leaving his beat. Again, a man may be suspected of having misappropriated money or property entrusted to him, but evidence which is essential to support a criminal charge may be lacking. There may, however, be evidence that he has failed to account properly for the money or property, and in such circumstances it would be right to deal with the matter as a disciplinary charge. It is important in such cases that the charge is not framed in such a way as to suggest that the disciplinary authority is purporting to decide whether or not a criminal offence has been committed.

5.13 In some cases, the decision (of the Director or of the deputy chief constable) whether to bring proceedings may turn on the willingness of a complainant to give evidence in a criminal court. Generally speaking, disciplinary proceedings should not be brought in cases where a finding of guilt would depend upon the evidence of a complainant who was unwilling to give it in criminal proceedings; but where other evidence to prove a disciplinary offence is available proceedings should not be ruled out solely because the complainant's attitude prevents the possibility of criminal prosecution.

5.14 Where an allegation against a police officer has first been the subject of criminal investigation and it has been decided after reference to the Director (or otherwise), that criminal proceedings should *not* be taken, there should normally be no disciplinary proceedings if the evidence required to substantiate a disciplinary charge is the same as that required to substantiate the criminal charge. There will be cases, however, in which disciplinary proceedings would be appropriate as in the circumstances described in paragraphs 5.11 and 5.12. It must not be assumed that when the Director has decided not to institute criminal proceedings this must automatically mean that there should be no disciplinary proceedings. It is important that, notwithstanding a decision taken by the Director on evidential grounds not to prosecute, the possible grounds for action under the discipline code are fully examined.'

The approach of the board to its responsibilities, summarised in the two decision letters to which I have already referred, is set out in detail in the affidavits of Sir George Ogden, the deputy chairman of the board, in each of these applications, his affidavit in the Rhone application being adopted by his affidavit in the Madden application, save in so far as the particular facts of the latter application required. I need only refer to one paragraph in his affidavit in the Madden application which referred to a letter written by the chairman to Madden's member of Parliament, dated 18 November 1981, the day before the decision letter. The relevant passage in the letter reads:

'... the available evidence was not sufficient to permit the Director of Public Prosecutions to conclude that criminal proceedings would be justified against the officers concerned and because of the Secretary of State's guidance within which this Board is required to work, we are precluded from recommending disciplinary charges on the same evidence.'

It is the use of the word 'precluded' on which counsel for the applicants relies, which is dealt with in the affidavit at para 7. That reads as follows:

'I am aware that Sir Cyril's letter . . . asserts that the Board is "precluded" from
a recommending disciplinary charges in the circumstances to which he had adverted; and his letter . . . to Miss Harman asserts that the "Guidance means that it is not open to the Deputy Commissioner or to the board to question this decision or to bring about disciplinary charges on the same evidence". The position is that I have dealt with this matter in the manner which I have described in this Affidavit. As I have said in the Affidavit sworn by me in Mr. Rhone's case, the Board has adopted,
b in the interests of fairness and the proper administration of its statutory functions, a policy that, after making its own full appraisal of the evidence in every case, it will not recommend a disciplinary charge in any case where the *only* basis for doing so is the existence of factual allegations as regards which the Director of Public Prosecutions has decided that there is insufficient evidence properly to mount a prosecution if the disciplinary charge is substantially the same as the criminal
c charge. It was only with this approach, and this policy, in mind that the letter in question was written; I respectfully say that the policy is one which the Board rightly adopts and in no sense has it fettered its own powers and duties in relation to its functions under the Police Act. Nor is there any misunderstanding as to the proper meaning of the Guidance; and I refer to the letter exhibited by me from Sir Cyril Philips of 27th October, 1981 to Miss Harman.'

d I now read the relevant passages from Sir George Ogden's affidavit in the Rhone case. They state:

'7. I desire now to deal with the substantive approach of the Board to problems of this kind, so that the particular matters of which complaint is made in these proceedings may be viewed against this background. It is necessary to explain how
e the Board regards its duty especially in circumstances which potentially give rise to the risk that a police officer might be put upon double jeopardy, in relation to any given allegations. (a) Section 11(1) of the Police Act 1976 provides that where a police officer has been acquitted or convicted of a criminal offence he shall not be liable to be charged with a disciplinary offence which is in substance the same as the offence of which he has been acquitted or convicted—although this is subject to a
f necessary exception in section 11(2) which allows a convicted offender to be charged with the disciplinary offence of being found guilty of a criminal offence. (b) Section 3(8) of the 1976 Act requires the Board in discharging their functions to have regard to any guidance given to them by the Secretary of State with respect to such matters affecting the preferring and withdrawing of disciplinary charges as are for the time being the subject of guidance by him to chief officers of police, including in
g particular the principles to be applied in cases that involve any question of criminal proceedings and are not governed by section 11. (c) The current guidance to chief officers on police complaints and disciplinary procedures is contained in a lengthy memorandum which was circulated to chief officers of police and clerks to police authorities under cover of Home Office Circular No. 32/1980 on 15th May 1980 a true copy of which is now produced and shown to me . . . This is a consolidated
h version, incorporating subsequent amendments, of a similar memorandum circulated in 1977, though the principles were to be found in guidance issued by the Home Office to police forces long before that. The relevant paragraphs of the guidance dealing with the relationship between criminal and civil disciplinary proceedings are paragraphs 5.9–5.14, and a later paragraph in the memorandum—paragraph 6.13—makes it clear that the Secretary of State has issued guidance to the
j Board to follow the criteria set out in, inter alia, paragraph 5.9–5.14. The important paragraph in the guidance is paragraph 5.14 in which a principle analogous to that in section 11 is stated namely, that where an allegation against a police officer has been the subject of a criminal investigation and it has been decided after reference to the Director (or otherwise) that criminal proceedings should not be taken, there should normally be no disciplinary proceedings if the evidence required to

substantiate a disciplinary charge is the same as that required to substantiate the criminal charge. The paragraph goes on to state that there will be cases, however, in which disciplinary proceedings would be appropriate as in the circumstances described in paragraphs 5.11 and 5.12, and that it must not be assumed that where the Director has decided not to institute criminal proceedings this must automatically mean that there will be no disciplinary proceedings. (d) The general principle underlying paragraph 5.14 is dictated by fairness. The punishments available when a police officer is found guilty of a disciplinary offence can be severe since they include dismissal from the force, a requirement to resign with possible loss of valuable pension rights or reduction in rank. By long-standing practice, therefore, the standard of proof required in police disciplinary cases, is the same as that required in criminal cases, ie. proof beyond reasonable doubt; and the Home Secretary has stated in successive Home Office Circulars that cases on appeal to him are decided on this basis. That being so, it would be unfair, in a case in which the Director has decided that the evidence is insufficient to justify criminal proceedings, if a disciplinary charge which is in substance the same as a possible criminal charge considered by the Director could be preferred where the evidence required to substantiate it is the same as that required to substantiate the criminal charge and was before the Director at the time he made his decision. (e) In interpreting the Secretary of State's guidance in paragraph 5.14, the Board have always had regard to the injunction in the last sentence of the paragraph and have never taken the view that where the Director has decided not to institute criminal proceedings, this must automatically mean that there should be no disciplinary proceedings. It has been the consistent practice of the Board in every case to examine carefully the evidence assembled in the investigating officer's report so that they can consider all possible grounds for action under the discipline code arising from the complaint. In some cases, for example, the evidence discloses that disciplinary offences quite unconnected with the criminal matters considered by the Director may have been committed, and it goes without saying that the Board has an entirely free hand in relation to charges of this kind. But, even where the possible disciplinary offences are closely connected with the criminal matters considered by the Director, that, as the Board are aware, is far from being the end of the matter. (f) There are cases, for example, in which the Director's decision is taken on other than evidential grounds. Where this is so, it is the Director's practice to indicate in his decision letter to the police that in his view a prosecution would not be justified on public interest or merit grounds. In such cases, which are exemplified in paragraph 5.11 of the guidance, the Board regard themselves as free to recommend that disciplinary charges should be preferred, if they consider that course appropriate, notwithstanding that the evidence required to prove the disciplinary charge is the same as that required to prove the criminal charge. (g) The position is that the Board do not regard the guidance in paragraph 5.14 as applying unless the Director's decision is made on evidential grounds and he has stated in terms that in his view there is insufficient evidence to justify the institution of criminal proceedings. Even then the guidance is subject to the important qualification described in paragraph 5.12. Accordingly in cases which the Director has ruled out prosecution on the grounds that the evidence is insufficient to justify criminal proceedings for any offence, the Board scrutinise the Investigating Officer's report to see if there is evidence which would justify the preferment of a disciplinary charge which would not correspond to a criminal charge considered by the Director and would not require to be proved by evidence which is in substance the same. Instances of such cases in which disciplinary charges would be appropriate are given in paragraph 5.12, and the Board have from time to time recommended such disciplinary charges notwithstanding that the Director has taken a decision on evidential grounds not to prosecute. (h) It will be noted, therefore, that paragraph 5.14 of the guidance, while stating the general principle designed to protect against double jeopardy, identifies only two types of

case in which it is not to be regarded as applying. First, as pointed out in paragraph
a (f) above, there are the cases in which, although the Director has decided not to prosecute, his decision is made on public interest or merit grounds. Secondly, as pointed out in paragraph (g) above, paragraph 5.14 of the guidance covers cases in which, although the decision not to prosecute is made on evidential grounds, there are elements in the evidence which show that in the course of the activities complained of the officer has committed a disciplinary offence (eg. disobedience to
b orders or neglect of duty which though closely connected with the alleged criminal matters, is different in substance from any criminal offence to which the Director's decision is related.) As the guidance makes clear in paragraphs 5.11 and 5.12 in neither of these two classes of cases is there any reason why the officer should not be proceeded against for the appropriate disciplinary offence. In the Board's view, the word "normally" in the first sentence of paragraph 5.14 of the guidance and the
c injunction in the last sentence are directed at cases of this type and do not justify a construction of paragraph 5.14 which would leave the Board free, in a case in which the Director has taken the view that there is insufficient evidence to justify the institution of criminal proceedings, to recommend the preferment of a charge for a corresponding disciplinary offence if the Board take a different view from the Director on the sufficiency of the evidence and consider that there is a reasonable
d prospect that a disciplinary hearing, involving the same evidence and the same standard of proof, will result in a finding of guilt. Such a construction would appear to undermine the basis of the principle which paragraph 5.14 of the guidance, and the statutory obligation on the Board to have regard to it, are designed to give effect, ie. that the officer should not be at risk of being tried and punished in disciplinary proceedings on evidence which the Director does not consider sufficient to give a
e reasonable prospect of securing a conviction on substantially the same charge before a criminal court. (i) Police disciplinary authorities stand in a different position from the Board in relation to the guidance since in their case, unlike that of the Board, there is no statutory provision which requires them to have regard to advice of this kind given by the Secretary of State. If, by inadvertence or design therefore, they prefer a disciplinary charge in disregard of the guidance in paragraph 5.14, the
f officer would seem to have no remedy other than his ordinary appeal on the merits if he is found guilty of the charge. (The Board have no jurisdiction in relation to a disciplinary charge preferred by the police disciplinary authority except that of deciding under section 3(4) of the 1976 Act, whether there are exceptional circumstances which make it desirable that the charge should be heard by a tribunal.) While there have been, to the knowledge of the Board, one or two instances in
g which charges have been preferred by police disciplinary authorities in disregard of the Secretary of State's guidance in paragraph 5.14, the general experience of the Board is that the police do scrupulously have regard to the guidance in deciding whether or not to prefer a disciplinary charge. In practice, therefore, the question of compliance with the guidance will usually arise for the Board only in cases in which the police are seeking to justify their decision not to prefer a disciplinary charge by
h reference to the Secretary of State's guidance. In such a case it has been the Board's consistent view over the years that provided they are satisfied that the police decision not to prefer a disciplinary charge accords with the Secretary of State's guidance in paragraph 5.14 as read with paragraphs 5.11 and 5.12, the Board's obligation under section 3(8) of the 1976 Act to have regard to that guidance leaves them with no alternative but to accept the police decision. As indicated in paragraph (h) above, in
j the Board's view the context and underlying purpose of the guidance and of the statutory obligation to have regard to it exclude a construction which would allow the Board, in effect, to disregard the guidance in any case in which they disagreed with the Director's view as to the sufficiency of the evidence. (j) The view the Board have consistently taken since they were first set up about the restrictive effect on the Board's powers of the guidance and of the statutory obligation to have regard to it

has been clearly set out in successive reports which the Board are required to make to the Secretary of State under sections 8(3) and 8(6) of the 1976 Act and which are presented to Parliament and published; see, eg. paragraphs 49 to 55 of the 1978 report set out in Annex 4. While critics of the present complaints system have cited this restriction on the Board's powers as one among a number of reasons they put forward for calling for reform of the present system, no one has hitherto challenged in the courts the way in which the Board apply the guidance to which they are required by section 3(8) of the 1976 Act to have regard. (k) Some of the critics of the present system appear to take the view that there is something wrong in principle about a restriction of this kind on disciplinary proceedings which stems from a decision on the part of the Director that there is insufficient evidence to justify prosecution (as distinct from a verdict in a criminal court as in section 11 of the 1976 Act) and that the police are being afforded a special and unusual degree of protection in this respect. While there may be no corresponding formal restriction in relation to other occupations, it is perhaps doubtful whether in practice other employees would be treated all that differently. (1) On 4th May 1982, the Home Office issued a circular (No. 15/1982) making a slight amendment to paragraph 5.14 of the guidance by adding at the end a further sentence:—"It is important that notwithstanding a decision taken by the Director on evidential grounds not to prosecute, the possible grounds of action under the discipline code are fully examined". While this amendment is in any event inapplicable to this case, its effect is merely to confirm the existing practice of the Board as set out in paragraphs (e) to (g) above and it would seem to be in no way inconsistent with the construction of paragraph 5.14 which the Board have consistently adopted and which is explained in paragraph (h) above.

8. It was my duty to consider this Applicant's case upon its second referral to the Board in 1982. In considering whether there was now further evidence which would justify the Board in recommending the preferment of a disciplinary charge, I took note of the Director's decision that the evidence was insufficient to justify the institution of criminal proceedings; in view of all the circumstances of the case, as disclosed both in 1978 and in 1982, and including the course of the civil trial, the finding of the jury and the comments of the Judge, it was plain to me that the Director must have given consideration to the possibility of bringing charges of perjury, assault and false imprisonment, and that he concluded that in view of the conflict of evidence upon the facts of the case as to what happened when the Applicant was arrested, and his then conduct and condition, that there was not in truth a sufficient or reasonable prospect of securing a conviction for any of these offences in a criminal Court. Thus, having regard to the Guidance, and in the light of the approach which I have hereinbefore sought to describe, I took the decision that the Board should not recommend disciplinary charges. It was very clear to me that the case was basically one in which, as paragraph 5.14 of the Guidance has it, "The evidence required to substantiate a disciplinary charge is the same as that required to substantiate the criminal charge" (as contemplated by the DPP). Nor did the investigation reveal evidence of other matters, which would justify disciplinary proceedings. Consonant with the policy set out in the Guidance, I made the decision to which I have referred.

9. Following that decision, the letters of 31st March 1982 and 15th April 1982, exhibited . . . to Mr. Grosz' affidavit, were written.

10. In relation to these letters which as I apprehend lie at the heart of this application, and in relation to this challenge itself, I desire to emphasise that the Board has adopted, purely in the interests of fairness and the proper administration of its statutory functions, a policy to the effect that once it has made its own full appraisal of the evidence in every case, it will not recommend a disciplinary charge in any case where the *only* basis for doing so is the existence of factual allegations as regards which the Director of Public Prosecutions has decided that there is

insufficient evidence properly to mount a prosecution, if the disciplinary charge is substantially the same as the criminal charge. That leaves open other circumstances in which disciplinary process may readily be appropriate; but this policy is one which, I respectfully say, fairness requires; its implementation in every case to which as a matter of fact it applies, does not diminish or stultify, but rather fulfils, the proper use of its powers by the Board. It was only with this approach, and this policy, in mind that the particular letters in March and April 1982 . . . were written.'

Next, I propose to summarise the material facts of the two cases. Errol Madden was, on 9 October 1980, an 18-year old art student, born in the United Kingdom of Caribbean parentage. There is a suggestion that he was suffering from some mental handicap. At 3 am on that day he was stopped in St John's Road, London SW11 by two constables of the Metropolitan Police, named Stephen Hollowell and David Charles Wildbore. For no reason other, so far as I can see from their statements, than that when they drove along in a Panda car he, to use their words, 'appeared to speed up and walk away' or 'quickened his pace and walked', they stopped him and inquired his business. He was found to have in a holdall two Dinky toy cars. The holdall contained various other toys, including old Dinky toys. According to the police, after some conversation, Madden was told that if he refused to answer the constables' questions he would be arrested on suspicion of theft. He told them that it was nothing to do with them.

It is common ground that he was thereupon arrested and taken to Battersea police station. Madden's version differed. He alleged that the two constables were hostile and menacing, abused him, calling him a 'fucking black cunt' and maligning his mother. They used some force on him and they wanted him to confess to stealing the two toy cars.

At the police station, Madden complained that he was interrogated under pressure, that other officers were involved and that he was forced to make a statement. He did make a statement: a confession to stealing the two toy cars. The constables say that this was made between 4.55 am and 5.15 am under caution, and after proper questioning, in the course of which Madden admitted theft.

It is now common ground, and was so recognised by the police when Madden appeared before the magistrates on 25 February 1981, that not merely had Madden not stolen the two toy cars, but they had not been stolen at all. He had consulted solicitors shortly after his release on bail on 9 October. He had a receipt for the purchase of one of the cars but later that month, his solicitors had a statement from a witness who was present when Madden bought the other one. The solicitor also obtained a statement from the proprietor of the shop confirming that no theft had occurred.

It is hardly surprising that when Madden appeared before the magistrates, no evidence was offered against him. He was acquitted and his complaint was formally made on 13 March 1981.

I hope that it is not inappropriate to observe that this is precisely the sort of situation which has given rise, over recent years, to a great deal of public anxiety.

So far as Rhone is concerned, the facts were very different. Trevor Clive Rhone was, on 6 November 1977, a Jamaican-born self-employed fruit broker, aged about 40, residing in Inglewood Road, London NW6. At about 2.30 am on that day, he was in Belsize Lane, London NW3, having been to a party. He was stopped by two sergeants of the Metropolitan Police, Brian Cheeseman and Norman McGowan. They arrested him and took him to Hampstead police station, where he was charged with being disorderly whilst drunk. He was detained until about 5.20 am. He alleges, and the sergeants deny, that he was assaulted and humiliated by them.

Within an hour of his release, namely at 6.05 am, he wrote out a statement of the events in question. On 12 November 1977, having pleaded not guilty on his first appearance before the magistrates, he was tried by a magistrates' court sitting at Hampstead. Having heard the evidence of the two sergeants and the applicant, the magistrates dismissed the charge and awarded the applicant £15 costs against the police.

On 17 February 1978 the applicant, who is a man of good character, made a formal complaint through his solicitors about the conduct of the two sergeants.

By a letter dated 20 October 1978 the secretary of the board wrote to the solicitors, as far as is material, as follows:

> 'As you know the Deputy Commissioner arranged for your client's complaints to be investigated by a senior officer under Section 49 of the Police Act 1964. Since your client's complaint of assault might have constituted a criminal offence, the report of the investigation was sent to the Director of Public Prosecutions. The Director, who is an independent authority, has decided that the evidence is not such as to justify criminal proceedings. The papers have now been sent to the Police Complaints Board. The Board provide an independent element in the disciplinary, as opposed to the criminal, aspects of a complaint. In the case of your client's complaints the Deputy Commissioner has decided not to take disciplinary action against the officers concerned and the Board have to decide whether or not to accept this view. The Board have no other function in the matter. The Board have studied the papers. In the matter considered by the Director, the facts and evidence required to prove a disciplinary offence are the same as those which the Director has decided do not justify criminal proceedings and there are no separate matters arising from this complaint calling for disciplinary action. So far as your client's other complaints are concerned the Board have accepted the Deputy Commissioner's decision not to prefer disciplinary charges against the officer concerned. You will appreciate that the Board's decision related solely to the question of whether disciplinary charges should be preferred; they have no other function in relation to your client's complaints.'

Nothing daunted, this applicant then launched proceedings in the county court and after a contested hearing was, on 27 January 1981, awarded by a jury a total sum of £673·56 with costs, in respect of the false imprisonment and malicious prosecution of him by the two sergeants on 6 November 1977. The complaint was referred back to the board but was effectively concluded by the letter of 31 March 1982, to which I have already referred. His solicitors did request yet further reconsideration and received a letter dated 15 April 1982. I read the material passages. They are:

> 'I can understand your concern that the Board appeared to have reached a decision which seems incompatible with the decision of the jury but there are a number of reasons why this is so. The first of these is that the decision of the Board on whether disciplinary charges should be preferred does not depend on the Board being satisfied that, on the balance of probabilities, a disciplinary offence has been committed. The Board has to be satisfied that there is sufficient evidence to secure a finding of guilt at a disciplinary hearing. The standard of evidence required at a disciplinary hearing is the same as that required in a criminal court, that is to say proof beyond reasonable doubt. It follows that evidence which is sufficient to secure success in a civil action may still be insufficient to satisfy a disciplinary hearing that an officer has been guilty of a disciplinary offence. The second point is that the Board is required under section 3(8) of the Police Act 1976 to have regard to any guidance given to them by the Secretary of State with respect to such matters affecting the preferring and withdrawing of disciplinary charges as are for the time being the subject of guidance by him to chief officers of police. The relevant part of the current guidance (contained in paragraph 5.14 of the Annex to Home Office Circular No 32/1980 to chief officers of police) is that where an allegation against a police officer has first been the subject of criminal investigation and it has been decided after reference to the Director of Public Prosecutions (or otherwise), that criminal proceedings should not be taken, there should normally be no disciplinary proceedings if the evidence required to substantiate disciplinary charges is the same as that required to substantiate the criminal charge. In effect, the Secretary of State's guidance prevents the Board recommending disciplinary charges for offences which are in substance

> the same as offences considered by the Director in a criminal context. In this case
> a the Director has informed the Deputy Commissioner that the evidence of the second investigation is insufficient to justify proceedings against any officer for any offence. In the circumstances it is not open to the Board to recommend charges of abuse of authority (for assault or for making an arrest without good and sufficient cause) under the Police Discipline Code. The remaining matters of the original complaint were that Mr Rhone was subjected to verbal abuse both at the time of his arrest and
> b at the police station and that he was refused telephone facilities at the police station. The Board are satisfied that subsequent developments and the further investigation have provided no further information about these matters.'

The use of the words 'The Secretary of State's guidance *prevents* the Board recommending' confirms beyond question the attitude of the board towards its jurisdiction and authority. There is, in my view, no question that the background to this legislation and guidance is
c that a police officer should not be put in double jeopardy in the sense in which those words are properly understood. It is also clear from the opening and introductory words of para 7 of Sir George Ogden's affidavit that the board puts a different and an erroneous interpretation on the words 'double jeopardy'. I read Sir George's words again:

> 'It is necessary to explain how the Board regards its duty especially in circumstances
> d which potentially give rise to the risk that a police officer might be put upon double jeopardy in relation to any given allegations.'

Double jeopardy, properly understood, is best described in the phrase 'No man should be tried twice for the same offence.' I emphasise the word 'tried'. The point was made plain by Lord Morris in *Connelly v DPP* [1964] 2 All ER 401 at 412, [1964] AC 1254 at 1305, in the following words:

> e 'In my view, both principle and authority establish:—(i) that a man cannot be tried for a crime in respect of which he has previously been acquitted or convicted; (ii) that a man cannot be tried for a crime in respect of which he could on some previous indictment have been convicted; (iii) that the same rule applies if the crime in respect of which he is being charged is in effect the same or is substantially the
> f same as either the principal or a different crime in respect of which he has been acquitted or could have been convicted or has been convicted; (iv) that one test whether the rule applies is whether the evidence which is necessary to support the second indictment, or whether the facts which constitute the second offence, would have been sufficient to procure a legal conviction on the first indictment either as to the offence charged or as to an offence of which, on the indictment, the accused
> g could have been found guilty.'

This passage was followed in *DPP v Nasralla* [1967] 2 All ER 161 at 166, [1967] 2 AC 238 at 249 per Lord Devlin.

This is precisely translated into the terms of police discipline by s 11(1) of the 1976 Act, subject to the saving in s 11(2) of the principle that a conviction of a criminal offence may itself be a disciplinary offence. Further, the machinery laid down in s 5 is, to my
h mind, designed precisely to prevent any risk of double jeopardy.

It is convenient now to look at the whole process of investigating complaints against members of police forces. The complaint itself may be made originally either to the board itself or to the police (either the authority or a senior officer). Whichever it is, the first investigation is that directed by the chief officer of police under s 49(1) of the 1964 Act. When he receives the report of that investigation he shall, unless satisfied that no
j criminal offence has been committed, send the report to the Director of Public Prosecutions under s 49(3). He shall also send a copy of the report to the board with the other material referred to in s 2(1) of the 1976 Act unless disciplinary charges have been preferred and have been admitted, or the complaint has been withdrawn, or the officer is over the rank of superintendant.

Further, by s 5(1), if the matter has been referred to the Director of Public Prosecutions, the report and material shall not be sent to the board until the question of criminal proceedings has been dealt with by the Director.

Section 3 then sets out the powers of the board on receipt of the report. For present purposes, it is sufficient to record that if the chief officer has not preferred disciplinary charges, the board may 'recommend' that he do so and, if he is still unwilling to do so, 'direct' him to do so: s 3(2). By s 3(4): 'Where disciplinary charges have been or are preferred, they shall not be withdrawn except with the leave of the Board.' This leads to the problem presently for my consideration, arising from s 3(8), the 'shall have regard' subsection. It is right, first, to exclude from the general rule expressed in the two decision letters, cases where the criminal offence is, in itself, unimportant and not serious enough to justify prosecution and cases where, in addition to the circumstances pointing to a criminal offence, there are other elements pointing to a breach of discipline not being a criminal offence. In these cases, the board does consider disciplinary charges and follows the guidance in paras 5.11 and 5.12. These cases are specifically dealt with in the concluding sentence of para 7(c) and in para 7(e), (f) and (g) and the first full sentences of para 7(h) of Sir George Ogden's affidavit.

It is also clear, by definition, that the board does not regard its powers as in any way limited where the papers have not been referred to the Director at all.

Apart from those matters, the board does regard its powers as limited: quite apart from the two decision letters themselves, this is made plain in para 7(c), (d), the latter part of para 7(h), passages in para 7(i) and (j), and in paras 8 and 10 of Sir George's affidavit. I extract only a few words from some of these. In para 7(h) he says:

> 'It will be noted, therefore, that paragraph 5.14 of the guidance, while stating the general principle designed to protect against double jeopardy, identifies only two types of case in which it is not to be regarded as applying' (indicating paras 5.11 and 5.12).

In sub-para (i) it says:

> '... in the Board's view the context and underlying purpose of the guidance and of the statutory obligation to have regard to it exclude a construction which would allow the Board, in effect, to disregard the guidance in any case in which they disagreed with the Director's view as to the sufficiency of the evidence.'

In sub-para (j) reference is made to 'the restrictive effect on the Board's powers of the guidance and of the statutory obligation to have regard to it.' Paragraph 10 states:

> 'I desire to emphasise that the Board has adopted, purely in the interests of fairness and the proper administration of its statutory functions, a policy to the effect that once it has made its own full appraisal of the evidence in every case, it will not recommend a disciplinary charge in any case where the *only* basis for doing so is the existence of factual allegations as regards which the Director of Public Prosecutions has decided that there is insufficient evidence properly to mount a prosecution, if the disciplinary charge is substantially the same as the criminal charge. That leaves open other circumstances in which disciplinary process may readily be appropriate; but this policy is one which, I respectfully say, fairness requires; its implementation in every case to which as a matter of fact it applies, does not diminish or stultify, but rather fulfils, the proper use of its powers by the Board. It was only with this approach, and this policy, in mind that the particular letters in March and April 1982 ... were written.'

It is thus clear that the board regards itself as bound in the terms of the two decision letters and, in particular, by para 5.14 of the guidance. I refer once more to the last sentence of para 5.9, a reference to the avoidance of double jeopardy, and to para 5.14, only to stress the use of the words 'normally' and 'automatically'. I have already read Sir George's understanding of the thrust of the word 'normally'.

Each of the applicants made a complaint which was treated as if alleging criminal offences and each was referred to the director. In Madden's case, he declined, on counsel's a advice, to be interviewed by the investigating officer. He then contemplated taking civil proceedings and these were commenced on 26 October 1981 but they have not yet been heard. His statement of complaint was, however, sent to the commissioner on 15 April 1981.

Rhone was at first unwilling to be interviewed. He, too, was taking civil proceedings. However, after the conclusion of those proceedings in his favour, he was interviewed by b a chief inspector, as were, I understand, three witnesses, two of whom had given evidence for Rhone at the county court (the third not being available at the time of the hearing).

In each case, the Director concluded, as I have already said, that there was insufficient evidence to justify the institution of criminal proceedings against any one of the officers, Sgt Cheeseman, Sgt McGowan, Pc Wildbore and Pc Hollowell.

On this material, counsel for the two applicants put his submissions, I trust I c sufficiently summarise them, in what are essentially two ways: (1) that on his construction of s 3(8) and the guidance, the board has refused and declined jurisdiction to consider any complaint where criminal offences may have been committed and where the Director of Public Prosecutions has concluded that the evidence is insufficient to justify the institution of criminal proceedings against the police officer or officers concerned and, accordingly, has made an error of law as to its statutory powers, duties and d responsibilities; (2) that, alternatively, the board has, for the same reason, fettered the discretion vested in it to consider complaints against police officers. It is to be noted that the applicants do not wish any particular conclusion of the investigation of the complaints. They only ask that the complaints be investigated. If the board, said counsel for the applicants, directed themselves correctly in law, they could and should exercise their statutory authority, having regard to but not being bound by the guidance.

e The first consideration is the force to be conveyed by the words 'shall have regard'. Counsel for the applicants submitted that this could properly be paraphrased as 'take account of' but not, as the board's construction of its powers implied, 'comply with'. He drew attention to the use of the latter phrase in s 3(7): 'A chief officer of police shall comply . . .' and submitted that the use in the same section of the two different phrases indicated that Parliament intended them to have different meanings.

f Further, he submitted that his construction of the words fitted in with the construction by the court of similar words in similar statutes. In *Perry v Wright* [1908] 1 QB 441 where the material provision of the Workmen's Compensation Act 1906 said that in computing a workman's wages, where there had been only a short period of employment, 'regard may be had to the average weekly amount' which had been earned by a workman in the same trade over the previous 12 months, Fletcher Moulton LJ approved a description of g the phrase as 'a guide, and not a fetter' (at 458). I note, however, that this was a 'may' and not a 'shall' provision.

However, the phrase 'shall have regard to' has been used in a number of modern statutes. For example, in s 12 of the Housing (Homeless Persons) Act 1977 wording very like that in the instant case is to be found. It says:

> h 'In relation to homeless persons . . . a relevant authority shall have regard in the exercise of their functions to such guidance as may from time to time be given by the Secretary of State.'

In *De Falco v Crawley BC* [1980] 1 All ER 913 at 921, [1980] QB 460 at 478 Lord Denning MR, dealing with a submission that the authority did not observe the code of guidance, said:

> j 'But I am quite clear that the code should not be regarded as a binding statute. The council, of course, had to have regard to the code (see s 12 of the 1977 Act) but, having done so, they could depart from it if they thought fit. This is a case in which they were perfectly entitled to depart from it.'

Bridge LJ put it in this way ([1980] 1 All ER 913 at 925, [1980] QB 460 at 482):

> '... although the authority must "have regard" to the guidance given under s 12, that guidance is of no direct statutory force or effect and the local authority are not a
> bound to follow it in any particular case.'

Notes for or a code of guidance can be distinguished from such statements or rules as are laid before Parliament under s 3(2) of the Immigration Act 1971 as to the practice to be followed in the administration of that Act for regulating entry into the United Kingdom, which are subject to disapproval by Parliament. Although without statutory force, and amounting to guidance (see Lord Wilberforce in *Zamir v Secretary of State for* b
the Home Dept [1980] 2 All ER 768 at 771, [1980] AC 930 at 947) they seem to be accepted as having greater force than that (see eg *Alexander v Immigration Appeal Tribunal* [1982] 2 All ER 766, [1982] 1 WLR 1076).

In the Employment Protection Act 1975, s 6 provides for 'Codes of Practice'. In *Lewis Shops Group v Wiggins* [1973] ICR 335 at 338, in a decision under the Industrial Relations Act 1971, Sir Hugh Griffiths, giving the judgment of the National Industrial Relations c
Court, said:

> 'But even in a case in which the code of practice is directly in point, it does not follow that a dismissal must as a matter of law be deemed unfair because an employer does not follow the procedures recommended in the code ... The code is, of course, always one important factor to be taken into account in the case, but its d
> significance will vary according to the particular circumstances of each individual case.'

In the Civil Aviation Act 1971, s 3(2) empowers the Secretary of State to 'give guidance to the Authority' and continues:

> 'and it shall be the duty of the Authority to perform [its] functions in such a manner as it considers is in accordance with the guidance for the time being given e
> to it ...'

Here, the draft guidance had to be approved by a resolution of Parliament.

In *Laker Airways Ltd v Dept of Trade* [1977] 2 All ER 182 at 188, [1977] QB 643 at 699 Lord Denning MR distinguished such 'guidance' from 'direction', saying that the former did not whereas the latter did denote 'an order or command'. He said that guidance 'can f
only be used so as to explain, amplify or supplement' the provisions of the statute (see also [1977] 2 All ER 182 at 199, 208, [1977] QB 643 at 714, 724–725 per Roskill and Lawton LJJ). At a later stage, I shall return to a recent decision of this court relied on by counsel for the applicants. It is *R v Disciplinary Board of the Metropolitan Police, ex p Borland* (20 July 1982, unreported).

Counsel for the board contended that if and in so far as it was alleged that the board g
had, as a matter of policy, unlawfully decided to 'comply' with the guidance, it would be equally unlawful and in plain breach of the statutory obligation for the board, as a matter of policy and of practice, to 'disregard' the guidance. This, I accept. It does not, however, go to the fundamental question of whether or not the board abdicated its statutory function.

On the point of the use of comparable terms in other statutes, counsel for the board h
drew attention to s 25 of the Matrimonial Causes Act 1973 and s 33 of the Limitation Act 1980 both of which, for the purposes of the determinations to be made thereunder, direct the court to have regard to certain listed matters. Here, of course, the 'code' is in the statute but again there is no suggestion that having had regard to the listed matters, the court may not look at other factors, if relevant in the individual case.

Counsel for the board submitted that as the guidance was neither statutory nor j
contractual, it was for the board to decide how to approach and follow it. The court's power, therefore, would be limited to its normal reviewing jurisdiction under the principles in *Associated Provincial Picture Houses Ltd v Wednesbury Corp* [1947] 2 All ER 680, [1948] 1 KB 223 and *Edwards (Inspector of Taxes) v Bairstow* [1955] 3 All ER 48, [1956] AC 14.

I do not think that this can be right. Here, the court has to consider first whether the
a board's view of its own jurisdiction is correct or not and this, as a point of construction, is a matter of law and not of review; so, too, would be the conclusion whether or not the board had fettered the discretion reposed in it, if that be the real question.

In dealing with the argument of counsel for the applicants on double jeopardy, counsel for the board contended that this principle, or a necessary extension of or gloss on it, rendered unfair a second attempt, on the same evidence and in the same circumstances,
b to put a police officer at risk of sanctions even if under the disciplinary and not under the criminal code. Indeed, he said, repeated investigation of the same facts could be oppressive and could bring the scheme into disrepute. One should remember that the standard of proof of police disciplinary charges is the same as that of criminal offences. He said the board ought not to be able to say on a point of sufficiency or reliability of evidence that the Director of Public Prosecutions may have got it wrong. I accept that the criminal
c standard of proof does apply to disciplinary charges. This seems to follow from cases such as *Bhandari v Advocates Committee* [1956] 3 All ER 742, [1956] 1 WLR 1442 and *Maynard v Osmond* [1977] 1 All ER 64, [1977] QB 240 and from the wording of the Police (Discipline) Regulations 1977, SI 1977/580, which reflects a 'criminal style' approach to disciplinary charges.

I do not think that such charges can properly be established on a 'reasonable belief in
d guilt' basis such as may be acceptable in the 'unfair dismissal' aspect of employment law: see eg *W Weddel & Co Ltd v Tepper* [1980] ICR 286 and *Bates Farms and Dairy Ltd v Scott* [1976] IRLR 214.

Counsel for the applicants has not contended that the board had acted capriciously, still less in bad faith but, to my mind, the concept of 'fairness', even a policy of 'fairness' (and it is quite plain from Sir George Ogden's affidavit that the board regarded itself as
e motivated by 'fairness', although confusing that with the double jeopardy principle), cannot limit the board's statutory obligation to consider complaints. It goes without saying that the board should and would be 'fair' in considering complaints but, in my view, it could not treat fairness as a justification for declining to consider complaints further when the Director of Public Prosecutions has advised against criminal proceedings, save in the exceptional paras 5.11 and 5.12 situations.

f That is nearly sufficient to conclude this case but the first and second propositions are so closely linked that I must go on to consider the second, lest it be said that if the board has not abdicated its function, it has fettered its discretion in the stated circumstances.

This submission by counsel for the applicants begins with the proposition illustrated, for example, by *Laker Airways Ltd v Dept of Trade* [1977] 2 All ER 182 at 187, [1977] QB 643 at 699 per Lord Denning MR. Guidelines cannot, by an administrative device,
g reverse or contradict statutory powers. Guidelines must be applied to further the purposes of the statute and not to frustrate them. Accordingly, counsel for the applicants submitted, where, as here, a statute reposes in a body a responsibility to 'recommend' or 'direct' a chief officer of police to bring disciplinary charges, that body may not fetter its discretion by accepting that the decision of another body or authority is conclusive in its own determinations: see, for an analogous proposition, Lord Reid in *British Oxygen Co
h Ltd v Minister of Technology* [1970] 3 All ER 165 at 170–171, [1971] AC 610 at 625. The board, counsel for the applicants said, is an independent body set up to exercise its own independent judgment. It would, I agree, be surprising if this were not so, bearing in mind that in 1976 Parliament determined to replace the existing procedure for dealing with complaints against the police by machinery in which the board, a new jurisdiction, is endowed with important functions. Further, the importance which Parliament
j attached to the board is signified by the fact that the Prime Minister has the power of appointment.

Counsel for the board invited me to say that the principle of natural justice that an administrative body should not fetter a discretion vested in it was derived from two lines of authority. The first was what is conveniently called the audi alterem partem principle: the principle being that such a body must not shut the door on or shut its ears to representations made to it by those concerned with the consequences of its decisions. This, he said, was illustrated by the *British Oxygen* case, citing, and also relied on by counsel for the applicants, the judgment of Bankes LJ in *R v Port of London Authority, ex p Kynoch Ltd* [1919] 1 KB 176 (also cited by Lord Denning MR in *Sagnata Investments Ltd v Norwich Corp* [1971] 2 All ER 1441 at 1447, [1971] 2 QB 614 at 626), an older authority by Sankey J in *R v London County Council, ex p Corrie* [1918] 1 KB 68 at 75 and a recent authority by Forbes J in *R v Rochdale Metropolitan BC, ex p Cromer Ring Mill Ltd* [1982] 3 All ER 761. These cases show that, although an authority may have a fixed policy, it can do so only 'so long as it allows people to come forward and to say that the policy does not apply to them for various reasons: per Forbes J (at 766), following the *Sagnata* case; see also the recent observations of Ackner LJ in the judgment of the Divisional Court in *R v Secretary of State for the Environment, ex p Brent London Borough Council* [1982] QB 593 at 641.

The second line of authority is that an authority must act so as 'to promote the policy and objects of the Act': per Lord Reid in *Padfield v Ministry of Agriculture* [1968] 1 All ER 694 at 699, [1968] AC 997 at 1030; see also Lord Upjohn ([1968] 1 All ER 694 at 718–719, [1968] AC 997 at 1060). This, too, is the principle followed in *Cumings v Birkenhead Corp* [1971] 2 All ER 881 at 884–885, [1972] 1 Ch 12 at 36–38 per Lord Denning MR.

Accordingly, counsel for the board submitted that the discretion of the board, if such it be, is already limited by the statute by its remit to promote the policy and objects of the statute. To that extent, it is a 'fettered' discretion. Further, in so far as carrying out that exercise, it is required by the Act to have regard to the guidance, the board cannot systematically disregard the guidance. Thus, even if not impelled by the Act to 'comply' with the guidance, what the board does must be consistent with the objects of the Act. This, he said, entitled the board to 'follow' the guidance, save in those instances (paras 5.11 and 5.12) where the guidance itself provided exceptions; those exceptions should be regarded as exhaustive. The board should not substitute its own view of the sufficiency and reliability of the evidence for that of the Director of Public Prosecutions and the board is right, he contended, in declining to do so.

This is particularly the case, counsel for the board went on to submit, when a complainant has no right, under the Act, to make representations to the board, other than making the complaint itself. A complainant has no right to be heard and the board has no function to hear him. All investigation is carried out by the police on the instructions of the chief officer. The only question which the board has to answer is whether or not it agrees with the decision of the chief officer not to prefer disciplinary charges in cases in which no question of criminal proceedings arises. A complainant has, of course, a right to be present at disciplinary proceedings under reg 20 of the 1977 disciplinary regulations but he is given no such right before the board. Although he made no concession, counsel for the board did not argue that the applicants had no locus standi to take the present proceedings. For my part, I think they had, as persons aggrieved by the failure to consider their complaints. However, counsel for the board pointed out that just as complainants have no right to be heard, even a finding of guilt against the police officer concerned confers no right on a complainant, no damages, no award, nothing of that sort. Counsel for the board drew attention to what is now apparently known generally as the 'Fleet Street casuals case', *IRC v National Federation of Self-Employed and Small Businesses Ltd* [1981] 2 All ER 93, [1982] AC 617, pointing out that decisions based on 'good management' would be in order whereas decisions made for extraneous or ultra vires reasons would amount to a breach of duty and would be ultra vires: see Lord Diplock ([1981] 2 All ER 93 at 101, [1982] AC 617 at 637). However, counsel for the board was not, as I have said, contending that neither applicant had locus standi and, in my view, they clearly came within the ambit of the statutory duty here in point: see Lord Wilberforce ([1981] 2 All ER 93 at 96–98, [1982] AC 617 at 630–632). It would follow, according to the argument of counsel for the board, that if in a particular case it cannot be shown that a party has been deprived of a right to be heard and if in the same case the tribunal has fairly administered the statute according to its purpose in law, there is no room for the application of the rule, if such it be, that in the particular circumstances, *a* the tribunal has 'fettered its discretion'. Those considerations, he said, apply here.

Counsel for the board further submitted that, in the Madden complaint, the chief officer gave the two constables 'advice' as to their duties and directed disciplinary charges on collateral matters against the station sergeant and others. Instances of these are in paras 5.11 and 5.12. This indicates, he said, that the whole matter was not concluded on and in compliance with the director's views.

b For my part, subtle and attractive though the argument of counsel for the board was, I am not persuaded that the great web of natural justice (or that aspect of it making unlawful the fettering of discretion) can be canalised and systematised in the way he suggests. Although there are attractions jurisprudentially and pragmatically in isolating and identifying from decided cases different strands which make up the web, it is the web of natural justice itself which is infinite in its capacity to cater for infinitely varying *c* factual situations and decision-making procedures. Reduced to its crudest elements in the instant case, the board has a duty to receive a complaint. Since the object for which it was created was the consideration of complaints and the receipt of reports of investigation into those complaints I cannot see that that object is pursued if, in relation to certain complaints, it accepts as binding on it the decision of another body, even so distinguished a person as the Director of Public Prosecutions. As I see it, far more public concern would *d* be likely if it were known that the board regarded itself as so bound than if, as counsel for the board suggested, it were known that the board, on occasions, disagreed with the director. I do not accept that the 'fettered discretion' rule should be as narrowly applied as counsel for the board suggests. The rule itself is strictly only a label for one aspect of natural justice, as the law stands.

In the end, it may be that the fettering of discretion adds nothing to the first point, *e* namely that the board was in error in law in declining jurisdiction further to consider a complaint which might give rise to criminal proceedings if the director advised against such proceedings. The board, as an independent body, ought to be asserting its independence. I am reinforced in the conclusions to which I have come by observations made recently in the Divisional Court in *R v Disciplinary Board of the Metropolitan Police, ex p Borland* (20 July 1982, unreported).

f In that case, the applicant, a sergeant in the Metropolitan Police force, sought judicial review of a decision of a disciplinary board finding him guilty of two disciplinary offences. It was a case in which the director had decided not to institute criminal proceedings. Ormrod LJ, giving the first judgment, with which McCullough J agreed, observed that it was therefore not a 'double jeopardy' case and that s 11 of the 1976 Act did not apply. He continued:

g

> '[Counsel for the applicant] put considerable reliance on what he called the "non-statutory double jeopardy rule". That may be a convenient phrase; it may be a misleading one. The basis of it is that a Home Office circular to chief officers of police has been in circulation in one form or another for a long time. The relevant one in this case is Home Office circular 63/1977, and para 56 is the paragraph in *h* question. That reads: "Where an allegation against a police officer has first been the subject of criminal investigation and it has been decided after reference to the director (or otherwise), that criminal proceedings should not be taken, there should normally be no disciplinary proceedings if the evidence required to substantiate a disciplinary charge is the same as that required to substantiate the criminal charge. There will be cases, however, in which disciplinary proceedings would be appropriate *j* as in the circumstances described in paragraphs 53 and 54 above. It must not be assumed that when the director has decided not to institute criminal proceedings this must automatically mean there should be no disciplinary proceedings." Assuming, which I think is a doubtful assumption, that it is open to this court in these sort of proceedings to construe that Home Office circular, which is intended to be no more than a guidance to the chief officer of police, one could say, that it is

> somewhat misleading; it is misleading in the sense that it is a little ambiguous. It was not at all easy to see what effect is to be given to the word "normally", or to the concluding sentence of the paragraph. It might be regarded by the chief officers of police as not very helpful guidance, but the one thing that is absolutely clear is that it is no more than a guidance to the chief officer of police, or in this case, the commissioner, in the exercise of his discretion whether or not to institute disciplinary proceedings. To my mind it is a matter for him to decide how to deal with the situation which arises when the director has decided not to institute criminal proceedings because the evidence is insufficient. I leave the matter there because I do not think that it helps the applicant in any way in the present case. Suffice it to say that the commissioner exercised his discretion to proceed with disciplinary charges notwithstanding the decision of the director not to prosecute, and that until the exercise of that discretion is attacked in appropriate proceedings (and it would have to be attacked on the *Wednesbury* principles [see *Associated Provincial Picture Houses Ltd v Wednesbury Corp* [1947] 2 All ER 680, [1948] 1 KB 223]) the matter does not seem to me to have any further relevance to this particular case.'

This is clearly of persuasive authority, for Ormrod LJ is there saying not that the guidance is binding on the complaints board, or indeed on the chief officer of police, but that, on the contrary, it leaves it to the chief officer's discretion whether or not to institute disciplinary proceedings of this kind; a fortiori the board. Just as Ormrod LJ recognised that the exercise of that discretion could be reviewed, so too could the discretion of the board. However, more importantly, the decision reinforces my view that the board was in error in regarding the guidance as something with which it was obliged to comply.

In the end, I accept that the board's statutory obligation to have regard to the criteria means precisely that, no more and no less. If, having had regard to the guidance, the board is persuaded that it should accept the director's view and determines accordingly, so be it. If, on the other hand, the board determines that despite the director's view, and bearing in mind the standard of proof required, disciplinary proceedings should be recommended or directed, it would, it seems to me, be doing precisely the task which Parliament created it to do. It is not in itself a disciplinary body. It is not concerned with the result of disciplinary proceedings. It is concerned with the investigation of complaints and the recommendation or direction of disciplinary proceedings when it, and it alone, in the last resort, thinks that only in this way is the purpose ultimately spelt out in s 3 of the Act effected.

In those circumstances, the applicants are entitled to relief. The proper relief was canvassed in argument and counsel for the board indicated that if I reached such a finding as I have done, it is unnecessary to grant mandamus and, subject to argument, it seems to me that the appropriate relief is certiorari to quash the two decisions. There will be leave to apply if necessary.

Applications granted. Orders of certiorari.

Solicitors: *Harriet Harman* (for the applicant Madden); *Bindman & Partners* (for the applicant Rhone); *Gregory Rowcliffe & Co* (for the board); *Russell Jones & Walker* (for Pc Hollowell, Pc Wildbore, Police Sgt Cheeseman and Police Sgt McGowan).

Sepala Munasinghe Esq Barrister.

Skips A/S Nordheim and others v Syrian Petroleum Co Ltd and another
The Varenna

QUEEN'S BENCH DIVISION (COMMERCIAL COURT)
HOBHOUSE J
12, 26 NOVEMBER 1982

Shipping – Bill of lading – Incorporation of terms of charterparty – Arbitration clause – Bill of lading providing that 'all conditions and exceptions of [the] charterparty' deemed to be incorporated in bill of lading – Charterparty providing for bill of lading to incorporate 'all terms and conditions of [the] charter including . . . the arbitration clause' – Whether arbitration clause a 'condition' incorporated in bill of lading – Whether arbitration clause incorporated in bill of lading by charterparty or bill of lading.

The shipowners chartered their vessel to the charterers for the shipment of a cargo of crude oil on behalf of the shippers for delivery to the consignees under a bill of lading which stated that 'all conditions and exceptions of [the] Charter party' were deemed to be incorporated in the bill of lading. The charterparty provided, inter alia, that disputes under the charter were to be settled by arbitration in London and that all bills of lading issued pursuant to the charter were to 'incorporate by reference all terms and conditions of [the] charter including the terms of the Arbitration clause, and shall contain [a stated] Paramount clause'. The bill of lading did not contain the stated paramount clause and did not specifically provide for the arbitration of disputes. When the charterers defaulted in payment of demurrage the shipowners brought an action against the shippers and the consignees claiming the amount of the demurrage. The consignees applied, under s 1 of the Arbitration Act 1975, for the shipowners' action to be stayed, contending that the arbitration clause in the charterparty had been incorporated into the bill of lading and that therefore any dispute between the shipowners and the consignees arising out of the bill of lading was to be settled by arbitration.

Held – The consignee's application for a stay of the shipowner's action would be refused, for the following reasons—

(1) The arbitration clause in the charterparty was not incorporated into the bill of lading by the incorporation clause in the bill of lading, because on the true construction of the bill of lading the 'conditions' of the charterparty deemed to be incorporated in the bill of lading were only conditions properly so called, namely conditions to be performed by the consignee on the arrival of the vessel, and did not include a 'clause' or 'term' such as the arbitration clause (see p 380 *f* to *j*, p 381 *e f* and p 383 *f g*, post); dicta of Cave J in *Allen v Coltart* (1883) 11 QBD at 785, of Lord Esher MR in *Serraino & Sons v Campbell* [1891] 1 QB at 290 and of Bailhache J in *Fort Shipping Co Ltd v Pederson & Co* (1924) 19 Ll L Rep at 27 applied; *Astro Valiente Compania Naviera SA v Pakistan Ministry of Food and Agriculture (No 2)* [1982] 1 All ER 823 not followed.

(2) Furthermore, the arbitration clause was not incorporated into the bill of lading by the terms of the charterparty itself, because it was to be inferred from the antithesis between the two documents arising out of the different wording used in each that the parties intended to incorporate less into the bill of lading than was provided for in the charterparty (see p 377 *h j*, p 382 *f g* and p 383 *d* to *g*, post).

Notes

For the incorporation of an arbitration clause from a charterparty in a bill of lading, see 2 Halsbury's Laws (4th edn) para 522, and for cases on the subject, see 3 Digest (Reissue) 31–34, *160–172*.

For the Arbitration Act 1975, s 1, see 45 Halsbury's Statutes (3rd edn) 33.

Cases referred to in judgment

Allen v Coltart (1883) 11 QBD 782.
Annefield, The, Annefield (owners) v Annefield (cargo owners) [1971] 1 All ER 394, [1971] P 168, [1971] 2 WLR 329, CA.
Astro Valiente Compania Naviera SA v Pakistan Ministry of Food and Agriculture (No 2), The Emmanuel Colocotronis (No 2) [1982] 1 All ER 823, [1982] 1 WLR 1096.
Crossfield & Co v Kyle Shipping Co Ltd [1916] 2 KB 885, [1916–17] All ER Rep 906.
Diederichsen v Farquharson Bros [1898] 1 QB 150, CA.
Fort Shipping Co Ltd v Pederson & Co (1924) 19 Ll L Rep 26.
Gray v Carr (1871) LR 6 QB 522.
Heyman v Darwins Ltd [1942] 1 All ER 337, [1942] AC 356, HL.
Hogarth Shipping Co Ltd v Blyth Greene Jourdain & Co Ltd [1917] 2 KB 534, CA.
Manchester Trust v Furness [1895] 2 QB 539, CA.
Merak, The, T B & S Batchelor & Co Ltd (cargo owners) v SS Merak (owners) [1965] 1 All ER 230, [1965] P 223, [1965] 2 WLR 250, CA.
Northumbria, The [1906] P 292, DC.
Rena K, The [1979] 1 All ER 397, [1979] QB 377, [1978] 2 WLR 431.
Russell v Niemann (1864) 17 CBNS 163, 144 ER 66.
Schuler (L) AG v Wickman Tool Sales Ltd [1973] 2 All ER 39, [1974] AC 235, [1973] 2 WLR 683.
Serraino & Sons v Campbell [1891] 1 QB 283, CA.
Thomas (T W) & Co Ltd v Portsea Steamship Co Ltd [1912] AC 1, HL.

Summons

By a writ issued on 1 March 1982 pursuant to an order of Parker J, the plaintiffs, Skips A/S Nordheim, A/S Vestheim, Skips A/S Vaarheim, and Marit Ditlev Simonsen, Halfdan Ditlev-Simonsen and Guttorm Fossen (all trading as Sameiet Varenna), claimed against the defendants, Syrian Petroleum Co Ltd and Petrofina SA, demurrage amounting to $US104,527·04 and/or damages and interest. The second defendants applied by summons for a stay of the action under s 1 of the Arbitration Act 1975 claiming that a bill of lading dated 17 March 1976 issued and signed by the master of the vessel 'Varenna' owned by the plaintiffs contained a contract between the parties for the arbitration of disputes between them. The application was heard in chambers but judgment was given by Hobhouse J in open court. The facts are set out in the judgment.

Timothy Young for the plaintiffs.
Jeffrey Gruder for the second defendants.
The first defendants were not represented.

Cur adv vult

26 November. The following judgment was delivered.

HOBHOUSE J. This is a summons for a stay under s 1 of the Arbitration Act 1975. The contract relied on in support of the application is contained in a bill of lading dated 17 March 1976 at Tartou, issued and signed by the master of the Varenna. It names the Syrian Petroleum Co as the shippers of a cargo of crude oil. It was for the carriage of that cargo to Wilhelmshaven and delivery there to the order of Petrofina SA. The parties to the present application are Petrofina SA (the named consignees) and the owners of the Varenna (on whose behalf the bill of lading was issued and signed by the master). For present purposes there is no dispute that this bill of lading contains a contract between these two parties. What is in dispute is whether the contract includes an agreement to refer disputes arising under it to arbitration. If it does this application must succeed; if it does not it must fail.

The action has been brought by the shipowners as plaintiffs against two defendants, the Syrian Petroleum Co and Petrofina. So far as I am aware, the first defendants have to date taken no part in the action. They do not appear before me. The stay is concerned only with the proceedings against the second defendants. The claim in the action is for demurrage. The second defendants will, if the action against them proceeds, contend that there is no such liability under the bill of lading contract or that, if there is, it has been discharged by either the lapse of time or by payments made by them to Colocotronis Greece SA. Colocotronis Greece SA were, on the relevant voyage, the charterers of the vessel from the shipowners and have defaulted on their demurrage liability under that charterparty. Hence the present action against the shippers and the consignees.

The charterparty was dated London 16 February 1976 and was on the Finavoy form. It contained an arbitration clause:

> 'This charter shall be construed and the relations between the parties determined in accordance with the Laws of England and any dispute arising under this charter shall be settled in London by arbitration in accordance with the provisions of the Arbitration Act 1950 or any statutory modifications or re-enactment thereof for the time being in force. Owners and Charterers shall each appoint an arbitrator and the two so chosen shall immediately appoint an umpire whose sole decision shall be final if the two arbitrators cannot agree on the dispute.'

This clause only refers to 'disputes under this charter'. However, there was also a clause (cl 44) which provided:

> 'All Bills of Lading issued pursuant to this charter shall incorporate by reference all terms and conditions of this charter including the terms of the Arbitration clause, and shall contain the following Paramount clause.'

If the bill of lading had been issued in accordance with the provisions of this clause, matters would have been easy. But, as we will see, it was not.

There is another clause of the charterparty which should be referred to as well. It is cl 33, which provides (in part):

> 'Bills of Lading are to be signed as Charterers direct, without prejudice to this charter. Charterers hereby indemnify Owners: (*a*) against all liabilities that may arise from the signing of Bills of Lading in accordance with the directions of Charterers to the extent that the terms of such Bills of Lading impose more onerous liabilities than those assumed by Owners under the terms of this charter . . .'

This clause expressly contemplates that the bills of lading which the charterers, through the shippers, present to the master for signature may not conform in all respects to the charterparty.

The bill of lading, which is before me, was on the form used by the Syrian Petroleum Co. It provides that the cargo is—

> 'to be delivered (subject to the undermentioned conditions and exceptions) . . . unto ORDER Petrofina SA or to their assigns upon payment of freight as per Charterparty, all conditions and exceptions of which Charter party including the negligence clause, are deemed to be incorporated in Bill of Lading.'

It is agreed between the present parties that the charterparty referred to must be that dated 16 February 1976 at London. The wording 'all conditions and exceptions including the negligence clause' must be contrasted with the wording of cl 44 of the charterparty, 'all terms and conditions including the terms of the arbitration clause'. Also, the bill of lading did not set out the paramount clause called for by cl 44. Accordingly, on the face of the two documents there is already an antithesis which suggests an intention of the parties to the bill of lading not to follow the provisions of the charterparty.

The argument of the second defendants is that the words of incorporation in the bill of lading incorporate the charterparty arbitration clause into the bill of lading so as to make it an agreement between the shipowners and the second defendants to arbitrate disputes between them arising under the bill of lading. The second defendants contend that the inclusion of the word 'conditions' is enough to incorporate an arbitration clause and that cl 44 of the charterparty removes any difficulty which might arise from the restrictive wording of the actual arbitration clause itself. In developing the argument the second defendants' counsel in his careful and full submissions did not feel that he could support the actual ratio decidendi of the recent case *Astro Valiente Compania Naviera SA v Pakistan Ministry of Food and Agriculture (No 2), The Emmanuel Colocotronis (No 2)* [1982] 1 All ER 823 at 831, [1982] 1 WLR 1096 at 1106, that 'specific words in the charterparty will suffice, provided that the bill of lading has once directed the reader to look at the charterparty'. (See also [1982] 1 All ER 823 at 831, 832, [1982] 1 WLR 1096 at 1105, 1107.)

Counsel accepted that a necessary first step is to construe the actual words used in the bill of lading. He has advanced and developed an argument, advanced but not accepted in that case, that the word 'condition' must, in the context, be read as 'term' (see [1982] 1 All ER 823 at 828, 833, [1982] 1 WLR 1096 at 1101, 1107).

The plaintiffs submitted that the word 'condition' has, in the context of an incorporation clause in a bill of lading, a well-recognised limited meaning and does not suffice to incorporate an arbitration clause and, secondly, that in any event the provisions of this charterparty are not clear enough. Counsel for the plaintiffs submitted that the *Astro Valiente* decision was wrong and should not be followed.

The question of the incorporation of charterparty provisions, and specifically arbitration clauses, into bills of lading has been the subject of many cases. The problems discussed in these cases arise primarily for the simple fact that charterparties by their nature normally contain many more provisions and stipulations than are relevant to the simple contract of bailment between a bill of lading holder and a shipowner. The courts have therefore recognised that prima facie only provisions directly germane to the subject matter of the bill of lading, that is the shipment, carriage and delivery of goods, should be incorporated (see *The Annefield* [1971] 1 All ER 394, [1971] P 168). A charterparty arbitration clause is not normally germane to the bill of lading contract and therefore a clear intention to incorporate it has to be found. Although earlier cases may have disclosed an element of judicial prejudice against arbitration clauses (see *T W Thomas & Co Ltd v Portsea Steamship Co Ltd* [1912] AC 1) that element is wholly absent from the more recent authorities and is not the basis on which they have proceeded. Some decisions have also reflected the principle that exclusions of liability, if they are to be relied on by the carrier, must be clearly expressed.

Another point which is apparent from the authorities, and indeed from any consideration of principle, is that the primary task of the court is to construe the bill of lading. The bill of lading contract is the contract between the parties before the court and it is in that document that their intention must be found (see *The Rena K* [1979] 1 All ER 397, [1979] QB 377; *Gray v Carr* (1871) LR 6 QB 522 at 537 per Brett J). The breadth of the intention disclosed by the bill of lading is critical. There are many gradations of such intention. These are fully documented in the well-known textbooks *Scrutton on Charterparties* (18th edn, 1974) and *Carver on Carriage by Sea* (13th edn, 1982), and were illustrated in the cases cited to me by counsel for the second defendants. The oldest and narrowest form of wording was 'he or they paying freight as per charterparty' (see *Abbott on Merchant Ships and Seamen* (5th edn, 1827) p 286). Then there was a wider form, 'paying freight and all other conditions as per charterparty' (see, for example, *Russell v Niemann* (1864) 17 CBNS 163, 144 ER 66). Express reference to 'exceptions' or to 'negligence clause' were introduced (see, for example, *The Northumbria* [1906] P 292). Also in this century much wider expressions came into use, such as, 'The terms, conditions and exceptions contained in the charterparty' (see, for example, *Crossfield & Co v Kyle Shipping Co Ltd* [1916] 2 KB 885, [1916–17] All ER Rep 906) or 'all the terms, conditions, clauses and exceptions contained in the said charterparty' (see, for example, *The Merak, T B & S Batchelor & Co Ltd (cargo owners) v SS Merak (owners)* [1965] 1 All ER 230, [1965]

P 223). For many years it has been commonplace to find bills of lading using any of these various alternatives. Sometimes wider forms are used, sometimes narrower ones. It certainly cannot be said that anyone who takes even cursory steps to inform himself about the interrelation of charterparty and bills of lading contracts need remain in ignorance of the choices open to him. The documents in the present case illustrate this. Both cl 44 of the charterparty and the bill of lading have been drafted using wording which reflects a consciousness of decisions of the English courts.

In this type of situation there are well-established principles of English law to be applied. They arise from the respect which English law has for the commercial bargain which the parties have made rather than that which the court thinks they might more reasonably have made.

As Scrutton LJ said in *Hogarth Shipping Co Ltd v Blythe Greene Jourdain & Co Ltd* [1917] 2 KB 534 at 552:

> '... I have come to the conclusion that the Court is not justified in straining the terms of a well-known clause to get a meaning, however reasonable, which the parties might quite well have expressed in plain language but have not.'

Accordingly, where a particular type of clause has received a certain judicial interpretation and become established as such in commercial law, a later tribunal will not substitute its own view of that clause's meaning for that previously stated.

This proposition is essential to the proper recognition of contractual intention in commercial transations. In the present context of bill of lading clauses this principle has been expressly stated and acted on in more than one case: see, for example, *Diederichsen v Farquharharson Bros* [1898] 1 QB 150 and per Lord Denning MR in *The Annefield* [1971] 1 All ER 394 at 405, [1971] P 168 at 183:

> 'Once a court has put a construction on commercial documents in standard form, commercial men act on it. It should be followed in all subsequent cases.'

It is also a well-recognised principle that courts do not distinguish between similar forms of wording unless there are significant differences between them. Mere verbal changes in the way a well-known clause is expressed do not form the basis for attributing a different meaning to the clause. Thus in the *Diederichsen* case a shortened version of the incorporation clause was held to have the same meaning as the fuller version which had been the subject of the decision in *Serraino & Sons v Campbell* [1891] 1 QB 283.

The use of the word 'conditions' in bill of lading charterparty incorporation clauses has a long history, going back to at least the middle of the last century. It has throughout been consistently interpreted as meaning the conditions which have to be performed on the arrival of the ship by the consignee who is asserting his right to take delivery of the goods. Typically such a condition is the discharge of any lien on the goods or the performance of any unloading obligations.

The commercial situation which this reflects is well stated by Cave J in *Allen v Coltart* (1883) 11 QBD 782 at 785:

> '... where goods are deliverable to the holder of a bill of lading on certain conditions being complied with, the act of demanding delivery is evidence of an offer on his part to comply with those conditions, and the delivery accordingly by the master is evidence of his acceptance of that offer.'

Where the Bills of Lading Act 1855 applies there is no need to infer such an offer and acceptance, but the relevance and nature of the conditions incorporated into the bill of lading remain the same.

The nineteenth century decisions on the words 'deliver unto order or assigns they paying freight for the goods and all other conditions as per charterparty' were undoubtedly based on an ejusdem generis construction derived from the reference to freight (see *Serraino & Sons v Campbell* and the cases cited therein). In the present century the emphasis has simply been on the use of the word 'conditions' as opposed to the wider words 'terms' or 'clauses'. In *Diederichsen v Farquharson Bros* the difference between the majority and minority judgments clearly points the contrast between construing a 'conditions' as 'conditions' (the majority view) or as 'terms' (the minority view). Collins LJ ([1898] 1 QB 150 at 162) quotes and adopts Lord Esher MR's observations in *Serraino & Sons v Campbell* [1891] 1 QB 283 at 290 that exceptions 'are not conditions which are to be performed by the consignee—indeed they are not conditions which have to be performed by any one'. In *Hogarth Shipping Co Ltd v Blyth Greene Jourdain & Co Ltd* [1917] 2 KB 534 at 548, 551–552, 556 the emphasis is clearly on the word 'condition'. Bray J b said of the charterparty clause there in question (a conclusive evidence clause): 'It is not really a condition to be performed by any one. It is a term of the contract—a stipulation' (see [1917] 2 KB 534 at 556).

The same view is reflected in a judgment of Bailhache J in *Fort Shipping Co Ltd v Pederson & Co* (1924) 19 Ll L Rep 26. The case was like *Hogarth Shipping Co Ltd v Blyth Greene Jourdain & Co Ltd* in that it concerned a charterparty conclusive evidence clause c but unlike it in that instead of the incorporating words in the bill of lading being 'freight and all other conditions and exceptions as per charterparty', they were 'all terms and exceptions contained in this charterparty are herewith incorporated'. Bailhache J was also faced with the fact that in *Hogarth v Blyth* the Court of Appeal had held that the clause was not incorporated whereas a short while before in *Crossfield & Co v Kyle Shipping Co Ltd* [1916] 2 KB 885, [1916–17] All ER Rep 906, the Court of Appeal had assumed that d the clause was incorporated by the phrase 'terms conditions and exceptions'. Bailhache J, having referred to these matters continued (19 Ll L Rep 26 at 27–28):

> 'My judgment proceeds on the use of the words "terms". If the words here had been "conditions and exceptions", and those alone, I should obviously have been bound by the decision in the Hogarth case: but it seems to me that the word "terms" e is a very much wider word than the word "conditions" . . . Inasmuch as I cannot help thinking that the earlier cases all turned on the strict interpretation and construction of the words of incorporation used, for instance, interpreting "conditions" strictly to mean conditions and "exceptions" strictly to mean exceptions, it seems to me that I am entitled and ought to give the word "term" its ordinary and usual signification. Giving it that signification, it does include the conclusive f evidence clause.'

The position is that over some 150 years the question whether the word 'condition' should be construed as a synonym for 'term' or 'clause' has been before the courts on many occasions and on every occasion the wider construction has been rejected. There can be no doubt that the narrower construction represents the established meaning in g the present context of bills of lading and charterparties.

It is in recognition of this meaning of the word 'conditions' that the alternative wider words 'terms' and 'clauses' have been and are used by parties when they wish to effect a wider incorporation.

However, the second defendants argued against this conclusion by saying that the court should distinguish between wording such as 'deliver to order or assigns upon their h paying freight and all other conditions as per charterparty', and wording such as 'all conditions of the charterparty are to be incorporated in this bill of lading'. It is argued that the second shows an intention to use the word 'conditions' in a more general sense. I cannot accept such an argument. It might have been worthy of consideration in the formative stage of this branch of the commercial law in the nineteenth century (see *Gray v Carr* (1871) LR 6 QB 522). I suspect that even then the better view would have been j that it should be rejected. But in the present century it clearly would be contrary to the authorities I have referred to. Bailhache J did not consider it material. The argument is an example of the error of seeking to derive a different contractual intention from insignificant changes in wording. Staughton J in the *Astro Valiente* case [1982] 1 All ER 823 at 833, [1982] 1 WLR 1096 at 1107 appears to have been of the same opinion:

> 'Counsel for the shipowners had an alternative argument which was said to lead to the same result. This was that, in the authorities where a limited meaning had been given to the word 'conditions', that word had always occurred in the same sentence as and directly connected with the payment of freight, whereas here the two topics are in separate sentences. I perhaps did not hear counsel for the shipowners on this point as fully as he would have wished. So I say nothing more about it, except that such a distinction seems to me implausible and undesirable.'

In any event the wording of the present bill of lading is at best a hybrid between the two extremes and does not provide a basis for finding an intention to depart from the established meaning of 'conditions'.

Another argument was that the phrase 'all conditions including negligence clause', which is sometimes found, shows that 'conditions' can have a wider connotation: see, for example, per Scrutton LJ in *Hogarth v Blyth* [1917] 2 KB 534 at 552, commenting on *The Northumbria* [1906] P 292. However, this again in my judgment is an over-subtle argument. The verbal differences are not, in reality, significant nor does the present bill of lading provide a basis for its acceptance; here the phrase 'including the negligence clause' is coupled with 'conditions and *exceptions*'.

It was also argued that *L Schuler AG v Wickman Tool Sales Ltd* [1973] 2 All ER 39, [1974] AC 235 provided a basis for departing from the established meaning of 'conditions'. But at best that case is authority for the proposition that the word 'condition' can be ambiguous or 'equivocal', and that where the usual meaning is manifestly unreasonable the court is at liberty to adopt another meaning. In the present context there is an established meaning. There is nothing unreasonable in the result it produces. Further, as clearly laid down in *The Annefield* [1971] 1 All ER 394, [1971] P 163, ambiguity is no basis for the incorporation of an arbitration clause into a bill of lading.

The correct construction of the present bill of lading therefore is that when it refers to conditions it refers only to conditions properly so called to be performed by the consignee on the arrival of the vessel. On no view is an arbitration clause such a condition. An arbitration clause is a collateral provision (see *Heyman v Darwins Ltd* [1942] 1 All ER 337, [1942] AC 356). It is a clause or a term. It is not a condition.

If, as I hold, this was the meaning of the word 'conditions' in this bill of lading, counsel for the second defendants did not feel able to support the reasoning of Staughton J in the *Astro Valiente* case. I consider counsel was right. The contractual intention must be found in the first instance in the bill of lading. The charterparty does not as such have a contractual force except as between the parties to it (see *Manchester Trust v Furness* [1895] 2 QB 539). Staughton J accepted that an intention to incorporate 'exceptions' cannot incorporate an arbitration clause (see [1982] 1 All ER 823 at 825, [1982] 1 WLR 1096 at 1101). Nor can a simple reference to freight; no more can a reference to 'conditions'. Staughton J derived a contrary conclusion from four cases. But in each of the cases he cites the words of incorporation were wider than simply a reference to 'conditions'. In *The Northumbria* [1906] P 292 the words were 'all other conditions as per charterparty including negligence clause'. The question in that case was whether the words 'negligence clause' referred to the whole of the charterparty exceptions clause or only part of that clause. In *The Merak* [1965] 1 All ER 230, [1965] P 223 and *The Annefield* [1971] 1 All ER 394, [1971] P 168 the bills of lading expressly incorporated not only 'all conditions' but also 'all the terms' or 'all the terms and clauses'. In each case it was this wide wording which formed the basis of the decision. In the former case Sellers LJ referred to 'the all-embracing words of the incorporation clause' (see [1965] 1 All ER 230 at 235, [1965] 223 at 253); in the latter Brandon J (whose judgment was affirmed on appeal) said ([1971] 1 All ER 394 at 399, [1971] 1 P 168 at 173):

> 'First, in order to decide whether a clause under a bill of lading incorporates an arbitration clause in a charterparty it is necessary to look at both the precise words in the bill of lading alleged to do the incorporating, and also the precise terms of the arbitration clause in the charterparty alleged to be incorporated.'

In *The Rena K* [1979] 1 All ER 397, [1979] QB 377 the words of incorporation were wider again: 'All terms, clauses conditions and exceptions including the arbitration clause, the negligence clause and the cesser clause.' It was this express wording which formed the basis of the decision (see [1979] 1 All ER 397 at 404–405, [1979] QB 377 at 389–391).

None of these decisions or the judgments in them is authority for disregarding the contractual intention expressed in the bill of lading. On the contrary, they are authority for the proposition that the contractual intention as expressed in the bill of lading must be given effect to. Furthermore I do not agree that when Brandon J in *The Rena K* [1979] 1 All ER 397 at 404, [1979] QB 377 at 389 refers to 'general words' of incorporation he is referring to the narrow incorporation of 'conditions'. Brandon J refers to cases each of which contained the wider formulae that included at least 'terms' and he gives examples of such wider formulae. He again says ([1979] 1 All ER 397 at 405, [1979] QB 377 at 390):

> 'It was an essential element in the facts of the *cases referred to* that the words of incorporation in the bill of lading were general words without specific reference to the arbitration clause in the charterparty . . .' (My emphasis.)

It is clear that Brandon J was in no way seeking to upset or qualify the authorities on the meaning of 'conditions', none of which he referred to or were cited to him. He was dealing with the contrast between words such as 'all terms, conditions and clauses' and words such as 'all terms including the arbitration clause'. It was the former he was indicating when he referred to 'general words'.

There is a hybrid argument which also might have influenced the conclusion of Staughton J in the *Astro Valiente* case [1982] 1 All ER 823 at 832, [1982] 1 WLR 1096 at 1107. It might be argued that when one reads the bill of lading and the charterparty together one may find that the word 'conditions' has been given some special meaning. Thus the bill of lading might say 'conditions as per charterparty'; and the charterparty might say 'the conditions to be included in the bill of lading are the following', and then set out various clauses including an arbitration clause. However, that was not in truth the case even in the *Astro Valiente* case where the bill of lading referred to 'the conditions and exceptions' and the charterparty to the wider word 'clauses'. In the present case there is an even stronger antithesis between the wider words of cl 44 of the charterparty, 'all terms and conditions of this charter including the terms of the arbitration clause', and the narrower words of the bill of lading, 'all conditions and exceptions including the negligence clause'. The present case is not a case in which such an argument could be advanced. I will therefore not comment further on it.

What I have said is enough to dispose of the application, but counsel for the plaintiffs also argued that in any event the charterparty was not clear enough to satisfy the requirement of clarity stated by the Court of Appeal in *The Annefield* [1971] 1 All ER 394 at 405–406, [1971] P 168 at 184:

> '. . . it should not be incorporated into the bill of lading contract unless it is done explicitly in clear words either in the bill of lading or in the charterparty.'

It was submitted that this meant that there must be an arbitration clause like that in *The Merak* [1965] 1 All ER 230, [1965] P 233, which said expressly 'any dispute arising out of this charter or any bill of lading issued hereunder shall be referred to arbitration'. Clause 44 of the present charterparty, it was said, was not enough to remedy this omission. I was referred to what Russell LJ said ([1965] 1 All ER 230 at 239, [1956] P 223 at 259):

> 'The agreement between charterer and shipowner that bills issued under the charter ought to take a particular form cannot be regarded as incorporated in the bill; as a contractual term it is irrelevant to the contract constituted by the bill itself.'

This dictum is directly contrary to the reasoning of Gorell Barnes P in *The Northumbria*

[1906] P 292 at 300. In that case as well the charterparty contained a provision (cl 25) as
a to what should be included in the bill of lading. Gorell Barnes P said:

> 'Clause 25 of the charterparty required that the exceptions in clause 11, which is the one I have just referred to, should be incorporated in the bill of lading, and I think that there is not the smallest doubt that Mr Weiler, when he put the bill of lading forward in the printed form, containing reference to this negligence clause, intended to comply with the terms of the charterparty. I am afraid I cannot
> b appreciate the argument of counsel for the plaintiffs on this part of the case. It seems to me that any reasonable person, reading this bill of lading and having notice of the charterparty, because it is expressly referred to, would undoubtedly infer, and would be right in inferring, that the whole of clause 11 was included, and that, that being so, unseaworthiness is a matter for which the shipowner is not responsible, unless it results from want of due diligence by the owners of the steamer or the ship's
> c husband or manager.'

With respect, although I appreciate the logic of what Russell LJ said, I find the reasoning of Gorell Barnes P, which represented the ratio decidendi of a Divisional Court decision by which I am bound, more persuasive.

However, this difference of approach will rarely be critical with regard to the
d incorporation of arbitration clauses because one still has to look for a clear, explicit intention to incorporate the charterparty arbitration clause into the bill of lading. If, as in the present case, the bill of lading wording specifically creates an antithesis with the charterparty wording so that one must infer, reading the two documents together, an intention of the parties to the bill of lading to incorporate less into the bill of lading than the charterparty had provided, then the charterparty clause cannot (as I have held) effect
e the incorporation proprio motu. On the other hand, if the bill of lading wording does follow that of the relevant provision in the charterparty, they must both, ex hypothesi, disclose a clear, explicit intention to make the bill of lading subject to an arbitration clause and no problem arises. If the bill of lading wording in the present case had followed the wording of cl 44 of the charterparty the arbitration clause would clearly have been incorporated.

f I consider that the present case is essentially a very simple one. The bill of lading uses a well-established form of wording of well-known and limited effect. It demonstrates that the bill of lading parties did not intend the wide incorporation provided for by cl 44 of the charterparty. Reading the two documents together reinforces this clear conclusion. I have only felt it necessary to give a lengthy judgment discussing the authorities because I am declining to follow the decision in *Astro Valiente* and am, at the invitation of the
g parties, giving my decision in open court.

The second defendants' application accordingly is dismissed.

Application dismissed. Leave to appeal.

Solicitors: *Sinclair Roche & Temperley* (for the plaintiffs); *Ince & Co* (for the second defendants).

K Mydeen Esq Barrister.

Sheffield Area Health Authority v Sheffield City Council

QUEEN'S BENCH DIVISION (COMMERCIAL COURT)

LLOYD J

23, 24, 25, 26 NOVEMBER, 2 DECEMBER 1982

National health service – Reorganisation – Transfer to Secretary of State of property held by local authorities for their former health functions – Determination of question whether property was held for health functions of a local authority – Whether determination can be made by local authority which only came into existence on reorganisation of local government – National Health Service Reorganisation Act 1973, s 16 – National Health Service (Transferred Local Authority Property) Order 1974, art 3(1).

On the true construction of art 3(1)[a] of the National Health Service (Transferred Local Authority Property) Order 1974, the question whether property was held or used by a local authority for one of its health functions immediately before 1 April 1974 (ie immediately before the appointed day for the transfer of such property to the Secretary of State pursuant to s 16[b] of the National Health Service Reorganisation Act 1973) may be determined under art 3(1) on or after 1 April 1974 and therefore may be determined by a 'local authority' which only came into existence on 1 April 1974 on the reorganisation of local government effected by the Local Government Act 1972 (see p 388 *j* to p 389 *j*, post).

Notes

For the transfer to the Secretary of State from a local authority of property held by it for the purposes of its health functions, see 33 Halsbury's Laws (4th edn) para 10.

For the Local Government Act 1972, see 42 Halsbury's Statutes (3rd edn) 841.

For the National Health Service Reorganisation Act 1973, s 16, see 43 ibid 786.

Cases referred to in judgment

Jungheim Hopkins & Co v Foukelmann [1909] 2 KB 948.

Rahcassi Shipping Co SA v Blue Star Line Ltd [1967] 3 All ER 301, [1969] 1 QB 173, [1967] 3 WLR 1382.

Preliminary issue

By a writ issued on 4 July 1980 the plaintiffs, Sheffield Area Health Authority, as the area health authority on behalf of the Secretary of State for Social Services, claimed against the defendants, Sheffield City Council, damages for trespass on premises known as 8 Orchard Place, Sheffield, alleging that prior to 1 April 1974 the premises were occupied by Sheffield County Borough Council (the old local authority) as the lessees of the premises for the purpose of carrying out their statutory functions as a health authority, that by reason of the National Health Service Reorganisation Act 1973 the premises were transferred to and vested in the Secretary of State for Social Services as from 1 April 1974, that at all material times after 31 March 1974 the defendants (the new local authority

a Article 3(1) is set out at p 386 *g h*, post

b Section 16, so far as material, provides:

'(1) ... on the appointed day [ie 1 April 1974] there shall by virtue of this subsection be transferred to and vest in the Secretary of State—(*a*) all property which immediately before that day—(i) was held by a local authority solely for the purposes of one or more of its health functions, or (ii) was held by a local authority otherwise than as mentioned in the preceding sub-paragraph and was used by the authority wholly or mainly for the purposes there mentioned ...

(2) The Secretary of State may by order ... (*b*) make provision as to the manner of determining ... whether immediately before the appointed day any property was held or held and used as mentioned in the preceding subsection ...'

under the Local Government Act 1972) wrongly maintained that the premises had not vested in the Secretary of State and denied the plaintiffs, as the area health authority, use of them and instead used the premises for the defendants' own purposes, and that by a decision of a duly appointed arbitrator dated 8 December 1979 it was declared that the defendants' contention that the premises had not vested in the Secretary of State on 1 April 1974 was wrong and that as from that date the premises were the plaintiffs' premises. By their defence the defendants denied that the premises had vested in the Secretary of State on 1 April 1974 pursuant to the 1973 Act, alleging, inter alia, that on 14 August 1973 the health committee of the old local authority had determined that on and after 1 April 1974 the premises would vest in the defendants and not in the plaintiffs, that that determination was confirmed by the old local authority on 5 September 1973, further that that determination of the old local authority was a 'determination' by the appropriate 'local authority' within art 3(1) of the National Health Service (Transferred Local Authority Property) Order 1974, SI 1974/330, and was the only effective determination made under art 3(1) in regard to the premises and that, as the Secretary of State had not given notice of dissatisfaction of that determination under art 3(2) of the order, the arbitrator's determination of 8 December 1979 was not a valid determination for the purpose of art 3(2) and was on no effect. By an order dated 18 February 1982 Mustill J ordered that the question whether the parties were bound by the arbitrator's award dated 8 December 1979 be tried as a preliminary issue and by a further order dated 25 June 1982 Parker J ordered that the preliminary issue be tried in the Commercial Court. The facts are set out in the judgment.

Conrad Dehn QC and *Ian A B McLaren* for the plaintiffs.
Anthony Cripps QC and *Robert Denman* for the defendants.

Cur adv vult

2 December. The following judgment was delivered.

LLOYD J. This dispute concerns premises at 8 Orchard Place, Sheffield, formerly used as a maternity clinic. By the National Health Service Reorganisation Act 1973, the duty to provide services which had formerly been provided by local health authorities under Part III of the National Health Service Act 1946 was transferred to the Secretary of State for Social Services. Section 16 of the 1973 Act makes provision for the transfer by local authorities to the Secretary of State of property held or used by local authorities for one or more of its health functions. The detailed provisions are set out in the National Health Service (Transferred Local Authority Property) Order 1974, SI 1974/330. Article 3 contains machinery for the settlement of disputes. A question arose between the Secretary of State and the defendants, Sheffield City Council, whether the premises at Orchard Place were being held or used as a maternity clinic immediately before 1 April 1974, the date appointed for transfer of property to the Secretary of State. The Secretary of State said the premises were being so held or used. The local authority said they were not.

On 27 February 1979 the Lord Chancellor appointed Mr David Savill QC to resolve the dispute. By his award, dated 8 December 1979, Mr Savill answered all questions in favour of the Secretary of State. The local authority accepted his decision. At least they did not dispute it. On 22 February 1980 the building was duly handed over. Then, on 4 July 1980, the plaintiffs, Sheffield Area Health Authority, exercising functions on behalf of the Secretary of State, issued a writ claiming damages for trespass by reason of the local authority's wrongful occupation of the building from 1 April 1974 onwards. The total claim amounts to £203,960. They claim compound interest on top, with quarterly rests, from the date of the issue of the writ. Not surprisingly, the defendants have sought to defend themselves against a claim which, I was told, they regard as unmeritorious. As part of their defence, they allege that Mr Savill's award is not binding on them and has no legal effect. The grounds for that assertion are technical in the extreme. On 18

February 1982 Mustill J ordered that the question whether the award is binding on the parties should be dealt with as a preliminary issue. On 25 June 1982 Parker J ordered that the preliminary issue be tried in the Commercial Court.

On the trial of the issue I am not, of course, concerned with the underlying merits. But the prospect of two public authorities fighting it out in the courts at public expense is never gratifying, especially where, as here, what is said to be a wholly unmeritorious claim is met by a highly technical defence. I would hope that, once the preliminary issue is decided, the parties will succeed in reaching agreement, so as to avoid any further litigation.

I must now relate the history of the matter in somewhat greater detail. For many years the local authority has had plans to redevelop the area surrounding the maternity clinic. These plans began to crystalise in the early 1970s. On 12 June 1973 the health committee of Sheffield County Borough Council (the old authority) resolved that, in the light of the proposals for the development of the Orchard Place area, 'approval in principle be given to a proposal to transfer the facilities at present provided at the Orchard Place Maternity and Child Welfare Clinic to alternative accommodation in Wilks Building, Norfolk Street . . .' Planning permission for the use of Wilks Building as a maternity clinic had been given on 25 April 1973. On 14 August 1973, the health committee recommended that Orchard Place should be excluded from the list of premises to be transferred to the Secretary of State under the 1973 Act. On 5 September 1973 the old local authority resolved that the recommendation of its health committee be approved and confirmed.

When 1 April 1974 came, a number of properties were transferred to the Secretary of State without any problem arising. But there were some properties which were still in dispute, including Orchard Place. On 5 April 1975 the plaintiffs wrote to the defendants (the new local authority) asking for Orchard Place to be transferred. On 1 October 1975 the defendants declined. On 14 October the Department of Health and Social Security wrote that they did not wish to stand in the way of the redevelopment of the Orchard Place area, but nevertheless insisted on transfer of 8 Orchard Place. On 18 November 1975 the defendants again declined, setting out their reasons at some length. They maintained that the premises had ceased to be held or used as a clinic prior to 1 April 1974, and, as proof, that the staff had moved into Wilks Building during the weekend of 29–31 March 1974. The move into Wilks Building had, they said, been carried out in the ordinary course of business.

Matters came to a head at the beginning of 1976. On 25 February the defendants suggested that the only course now open was to resort to the disputes procedure under art 3 of the 1974 order. Article 3 provides:

> '(1) Any question—(*a*) whether any property was held or held and used as mentioned in section 16(1) of the Act; or (*b*) whether any property is or is not transferable by virtue of the provisions of section 16(2)(*a*) of the Act; or (*c*) whether any local authority was entitled to rights, or subject to liabilities, as mentioned in section 16(1) of the Act, shall, subject to the next following paragraphs, be determined by the local authority in which that property was vested immediately before 1st April 1974, or which, as the case may be, was entitled to those rights or subject to those liabilities immediately before that date.
>
> (2) If the Secretary of State gives notice before 1st April 1975 that he is dissatisfied with any such determination, the question shall be determined by agreement between the Secretary of State and the local authority, or failing such agreement shall be determined by a person to be appointed by agreement between the Secretary of State and the local authority or in default of such agreement by a single person appointed by the Lord Chancellor.
>
> (3) If a local authority fails to make a determination under paragraph (1) of this article, the Secretary of State may before 1st April 1975 give notice to the appropriate local authority that a question exists and the question shall be determined as if it were a question to which paragraph (2) of this article applied and the provisions of that paragraph shall apply accordingly . . .'

In their reply dated March 1976, the department said that they assumed that the *a* defendants had never made any determination as envisaged by art 3(1). The department, therefore, invited the defendants to make such a determination so that the Secretary of State could give notice of dissatisfaction under art 3(2). The defendants answered that a determination had already been made on 5 September 1973 when, it will be remembered, the old local authority approved the recommendation of its health committee that Orchard Place be excluded from the list of properties to be transferred. The department *b* would not accept that as being a 'determination' within the meaning of art 3, since it was made before the date when the 1974 order came into operation, namely 11 March 1974. Accordingly, the department asked the defendants to make another determination, which it did, on 7 July 1976. The resolution reads:

> 'NATIONAL HEALTH SERVICE REORGANISATION—TRANSFER OF PROPERTY
>
> *c* The Chief Executive reported further concerning the disputes between the City Council and the Sheffield Area Health Authority on the question of the vesting of the ownership of the Firth Park and Manor Welfare Centres and Orchard Place Clinic and he submitted a letter from the Department of Health and Social Security stating that the confirmation by the former Sheffield City Council of a resolution passed by its Health Committee concerning the three properties could not be *d* accepted as a determination under Article 3(1) of the National Health Service (Transferred Local Authority Property) Order 1974 and accordingly requesting that the council should now make its formal determinations regarding the three properties. RESOLVED: That it be hereby determined that . . . (b) the Orchard Place Clinic although held for health purposes on 16th November, 1972, ceased to be so held prior to 1st April 1974, consequent upon events taking place in the ordinary *e* course of business.'

The defendants asked the department to confirm that the resolution was satisfactory for the purpose of art 3(1). Nothing more happened until 17 March 1977, when the Secretary of State gave notice of dissatisfaction as follows:

> 'NOTICE BY THE SECRETARY OF STATE FOR SOCIAL SERVICES UNDER ARTICLE 3(2).
>
> *f* To the Sheffield Metropolitan District Council.
>
> The Secretary of State for Social Services in pursuance of article 3(2) of the above-mentioned order hereby gives notice that he is dissatisfied with the determination dated 7th July 1976, of the Sheffield District Council that the property described below was not held or held and used as mentioned in section 16(1) of the National Health Service Reorganisation Act 1973.'

g And the property described below is clearly Orchard Place Clinic, Sheffield.

There was then protracted correspondence between the parties in the course of which they tried to agree on the name of an arbitrator. Numerous names were suggested, including the names of distinguished Queen's Counsel. But each side rejected names suggested by the other, either because they were said to have a 'local authority background', whatever that may mean, or because they were said to have 'connections *h* with health authorities'. Eventually, on 27 February 1979, the Lord Chancellor appointed Mr David Savill. He invited the parties to state their cases in writing. There was a hearing on 26 and 27 November 1979. It was never suggested at any stage by the defendants that Mr Savill had not been validly appointed.

Mr Savill found that the maternity clinic was being *held* by the local authority for the purpose of its health functions immediately before 1 April 1974. That was sufficient for *j* a decision in favour of the Secretary of State. He also found that it was being *used* for health purposes, despite the rapid evacuation of staff during the weekend of 29–31 March 1974 to the new, and as yet unfinished, premises at Wilks Building. Finally, he found that, if, contrary to his view, the premises had ceased to be used for health purposes before 1 April 1974, then the change had not taken place in the ordinary course of business. The only explanation for the rapid evacuation of the staff during the weekend

29–31 March 1974 was to prevent transfer of the premises to the Secretary of State under the 1973 Act.

Those being the facts, I now turn to the argument of counsel for the defendants. It involves three steps. First, it was common ground that Mr Savill was appointed as arbitrator to resolve a dispute arising out of the 'determination' made by the defendants on 7 July 1976. That was the determination in respect of which the Secretary of State had given notice of dissatisfaction on 17 March 1977. The Secretary of State never gave notice that he was dissatisfied with the earlier 'determination', in September 1973, because he believed (wrongly, in counsel's submission) that no determination was possible prior to the 1974 order coming into operation.

Second, the 1976 determination was itself a nullity, because it was a determination made by the *new* local authority (the defendants), which only came into existence on 1 April 1974 under the Local Government Act 1972. The 1974 order draws a distinction between the old local authority and the new local authority, and provides, on its true construction, for all determinations to be made by the *old* local authority. Since the old local authority had ceased to exist on 31 March 1974, that was the last day on which a valid determination could be made. The purported determination by the new local authority (the defendants) in July 1976 was therefore far too late and was not a 'determination' within the meaning of art 3(1) of the 1974 order at all. Accordingly, there was nothing in respect of which the Secretary of State could express his dissatisfaction under art 3(2).

Third, since the Secretary of State has never given valid notice of dissatisfaction in respect of the 1976 'determination', there was never a question to be determined under art 3(2) of the 1974 order, and Mr Savill was never therefore effectively appointed as arbitrator to determine such question. His award is, therefore, a nullity or, at any rate, is not binding on the parties under the 1974 order. In support of this third step counsel for the defendants relies on *Jungheim Hopkins & Co v Foukelmann* [1909] 2 KB 948 and *Rahcassi Shipping Co SA v Blue Star Line Ltd* [1967] 3 All ER 301, [1969] 1 QB 173.

Counsel for the defendants readily accepted that his argument had no merit. But he justified it on the ground that it was no more unmeritorious than the claim it was designed to meet.

Counsel for the plaintiffs had several answers to the argument of counsel for the defendants. I shall mention only two. First, he submitted that, having taken part in the arbitration without any question having been raised as to the validity of Mr Savill's appointment, it was not now open to the defendants to challenge the award. Second, he contended, contrary to the second step of counsel for the defendants' argument, that there was nothing in the 1974 order which required a determination to be made before 1 April 1974. He submitted that the 1976 determination was a valid and effective determination within the meaning of the order.

Logically, it seems to me that counsel for the plaintiffs' second submission comes first. If he is right on that, then the rest of counsel for the defendants' argument falls to the ground. It would then be unnecessary to consider any question of waiver or estoppel, questions which can always give rise to difficulty, even when the answer seems obvious at first sight.

The strength of the argument of counsel for the defendants is that 'local authority' and 'new local authority' are separately defined in art 1(1) of the order. Prima facie, therefore, 'local authority' in art 3(1) means the old local authority. Where the draftsman means 'new local authority' he says so: see, for example, arts 5 and 9.

I cannot accept the argument of counsel for the defendants. When one looks at the order as a whole, I am convinced that Parliament must have intended that determinations should still be capable of being made after 31 March 1974. Thus, art 3(1), which follows the language of s 16(2)(*b*) of the 1973 Act, requires the local authority to determine whether any property was held or used for one of the local authority's health functions 'immediately before the appointed day', ie 1 April 1974. Furthermore, the regulations contemplate that changes in the ordinary course of business might take place at any time up to and including 31 March 1974, or at any rate up to and including the last working day prior to 31 March 1974. If that be so, then it follows that Parliament must have contemplated that a determination might be made by a local authority which only came into existence after 31 March 1974. As counsel for the plaintiffs submitted, it is little short of ludicrous to imagine the old local authority, in its dying moments, engaged in determining what, if any, changes were taking place in the ordinary course of business around its deathbed.

The matter becomes even clearer when one looks at art 3(2), which provides that the Secretary of State may give notice of dissatisfaction at any time before 1 April 1975, subsequently extended to 1 April 1976, and thereafter without limit of time. Article 3(2) goes on to provide that any question between the Secretary of State and the local authority should be determined by agreement between the parties, and in default of agreement by a person to be appointed by agreement between the parties. 'The parties' means the Secretary of State and the local authority. 'Local authority' in art 3(2) must mean, therefore, or at any rate include the new local authority. For there would be no other local authority after 31 March 1974 with whom the Secretary of State could attempt to reach agreement. If local authority can mean or include the new local authority in art 3(2) despite the separate definition of new local authority in art 1(1), then there is no reason why it should not bear or include the same meaning in art 3(1).

Similarly, in art 3(3) there is a reference to 'appropriate local authority' which must, for the same reason, be capable of including the appropriate *new* local authority. Finally, there is art 4, which sets out the factors to be taken into account or disregarded by local authorities in making their determinations under art 3. There is reference in art 4(2)(*c*)(iii) to the period of three months ending on 31 March 1974, and in art 4(2)(*e*)(i) to the accounts of the local authority for the year ending on 31 March 1974. These references to a period of time ending on 31 March all indicate that Parliament must have contemplated determinations being made after 31 March 1974.

I would only add, as further small pointers in the same direction, that if Parliament had intended all determinations to be made before 1 April 1974 it would surely have said so, particularly in art 3(3), which deals with the case where the authority fails to make any determination at all. Moreover, if the Secretary of State was right that a local authority could not make a valid determination before the coming into operation of the 1974 order on 11 March 1974 or perhaps before the making of the order (because until then the local authority would not know what factors to take into account or disregard), it seems unlikely that Parliament intended *all* determinations to be made in the short period of a month or less leading up to 31 March 1974.

For the above reasons, I conclude that Parliament intended that determinations should still be capable of being made after 31 March 1974, and therefore should be capable of being made by the new local authorities. I accept that the separate definition of 'new local authority' in art 1(2) creates a difficulty. I accept also that, if one carries counsel for the plaintiffs' argument to its logical conclusion, it would mean that no determination could be made before 1 April 1974. These difficulties would be serious if the regulations as a whole gave the impression of having been drafted with meticulous care. But that is not my impression. In art 3(1) there would, in any event, have been a drafting problem, for it would not have been possible simply to insert 'new' before 'local authority', because of the words which follow, viz 'in which that property was vested immediately before 1st April 1974'. It would have been necessary to add some such words as 'or by the appropriate new local authority, as the case may be'. Be that as it may, I am satisfied that 'local authority' must be given a meaning wide enough to include the new local authority where, as in art 3(1), the sense demands it.

If I am right on that point, then the foundation of counsel for the defendants' argument goes, and I need not consider the alternative argument of counsel for the plaintiffs that it is not now open to the defendants to challenge the award. All I would say is that, as a matter of common sense, the argument has much to commend it.

I will, therefore, answer the preliminary issue in favour of the plaintiffs. Mr Savill's award is valid and binding on the parties. In the course of the argument I indicated that, should I reach that result, the case should be brought back before me at the earliest opportunity for further directions. If, as I earnestly hope, the case now settles, that will not be necessary.

Determination accordingly.

Solicitors: *John D Evans*, Sheffield (for the plaintiffs); *Roger Pensam*, Sheffield (for the defendants).

K Mydeen Esq Barrister.

Paula Lee Ltd v Robert Zehil & Ltd

QUEEN'S BENCH DIVISION
MUSTILL J
21 APRIL, 27 MAY 1982

Contract – Damages for breach – Alternative obligations – Defendant free to choose method of fulfilling contractual obligation – Basis for assessment of damages – Damages to be assessed according to method of performance least unfavourable to defendant – Defendant's freedom of choice limited to reasonable methods of performance.

The plaintiffs, who were dress manufacturers, appointed the defendants to act as their sole distributors for the sale of their range of garments in a territory consisting of certain Middle Eastern countries. Under the terms of the agreement the defendants undertook to purchase not less than 16,000 garments each season and by cl 7 of the agreement it was agreed that the defendants were to have complete discretion on the marketing and selling policy to be adopted in the territory. Thus, provided the defendants ordered not less that 16,000 garments per season, they were entitled to sell or market the plaintiffs' products to whoever and on such terms as they wished within the territory. The agreement did not make any stipulation as to the sizes or styles of the garments comprising the minimum obligation under the agreement. The defendants prematurely terminated the agreement while it still had two seasons to run, and in an action brought by the plaintiffs for breach of contract the defendants were held to have wrongfully repudiated the contract. On the issue of the quantum of damages there arose the question of how the plaintiffs' loss attributable to the premature termination of the agreement was to be computed. The defendants contended that since cl 7 of the agreement gave them complete freedom of marketing in the territory they were entitled under the agreement to fulfil the whole order by choosing 32,000 of the plaintiffs' cheapest garments and therefore the damages should be the plaintiffs' loss of profits on 32,000 of their cheapest garments. The plaintiffs contended that the appropriate yardstick by which the damages were to be measured was the average price of all garments in the plaintiffs' range which were suitable for sale in the territory since the defendants would have chosen 32,000 garments of varying styles, prices and quality from throughout the range.

Held – (1) Where damages were required to be calculated for breach of contract in a situation where the defendant could fulfill his part of the contract by performing his obligation by alternative methods and had a freedom of choice which method to use, damages were to be assessed by reference to that method of performance which was least unfavourable to the defendant. However, in making that assessment the contract was to be read subject to an implied term in the contract that the defendant's freedom of choice

was limited to those methods of performance which could be regarded as reasonable in
a all the circumstances (see p 394 *c d* and p 396 *d*, post); *Abrahams v Herbert Reiach Ltd* [1922] 1 KB 477 applied; *Thomas v Clarke and Todd* (1818) 2 Stark 450, *Capper v Forster* (1837) 3 Bing NC 938 and *Cockburn v Alexander* (1848) 6 CB 791 considered.

(2) Although the agreement gave the defendants a wide discretion as to the sale of the garments in regard to volume, price and outlets, it could not have been in the contemplation of the parties when they made the agreement that the defendants would
b order 32,000 garments of the same size, style and colour, since a one-garment range would have been unsaleable and would have alienated the defendants' wholesalers, deprived the plaintiffs of a realistic presence in the territory and killed the market. Accordingly, the purchase of 32,000 of the plaintiffs' cheapest garments was not, in the circumstances, a reasonable method by which the defendants could fulfill their obligation under the contract. Instead, the agreement was to be construed as being subject to an
c implied term that the 32,000 garments would be selected in a reasonable manner, and the damages were to be assessed in terms of that reasonable selection which yielded the lowest and therefore least unfavourable price to the defendants (see p 396 *g* to p 397 *c*, post).

Notes

d For the measure of damages in contract where the defendant has contracted to do one of a number of things and does neither, see 12 Halsbury's Law (4th edn) para 1177, and for cases on the subject, see 17 Digest (Reissue) 105, *127–129*.

Cases referred to in judgment

Abrahams v Herbert Reiach Ltd [1922] 1 KB 477, CA.
e *Bold v Brough Nicholson & Hall Ltd* [1963] 3 All ER 849, [1964] 1 WLR 201.
British Westinghouse Electric and Manufacturing Co Ltd v Underground Electric Rlys Co of London Ltd [1912] AC 673, [1911–13] All ER Rep 63, HL.
Capper v Forster (1837) 3 Bing NC 938, 132 ER 672.
Cockburn v Alexander (1848) 6 CB 791, 136 ER 1459.
Lavarack v Woods of Colchester Ltd [1966] 3 All ER 683, [1967] 1 QB 278, [1966] 3 WLR
f 706, CA.
Maredelanto Compania Naviera SA v Bergbau-Handel GmbH, The Mihalis Angelos [1970] 3 All ER 125, [1971] 1 QB 164, [1970] 3 WLR 601, CA.
Thomas v Clarke and Todd (1818) 2 Stark 450, 171 ER 702.

Action

g By a writ issued on 26 October 1979 the plaintiffs, Paula Lee Ltd, claimed against the defendants, Robert Zehil & Co Ltd, damages for wrongful repudiation of a contract made between the parties on 21 August 1978 and amended by a supplemental agreement dated 26 June 1979 whereby the defendants agreed to act as the sole distributors of the plaintiffs' garments in Kuwait and Saudi Arbia. The action was first tried on the issue of liability of the parties and on 21 December 1981 Mustill J held that the defendants were
h liable for anticipatory breach of contract for having wrongfully repudiated the contract with the plaintiffs. The matter was adjourned on the issue of quantum of damages. The case is reported only on the question of damages. The facts are set out in the judgment.

Peter Millett QC and *David di Mambro* for the plaintiffs.
Leslie Joseph QC and *Victor Levene* for the defendants.

j

Cur adv vult

27 May. The following judgment was delivered.

MUSTILL J. This is the second stage of an action brought by Paula Lee Ltd against Robert Zehil & Co Ltd. The dispute raises issues of principle on both liability and quantum. It was therefore arranged that the first part of the trial should deal with the question of liability, and with two issues relating to the quantum of damage, leaving the remainder of the dispute for decision at a second hearing if the plaintiff succeeded in establishing liability. In the event, shortage of time made it impossible to give adequate consideration to the second issue on quantum, and I therefore confined my judgment to the question of liability and to one of the points raised on quantum. At a second hearing full argument was addressed on this outstanding question and I now state my decision on it, by way of guidance to those who will conduct the matter when the facts relating to the issues of damages are explored.

The history of the dispute is set out fully in my previous judgment, and it is sufficient for present purposes to recall that the matter arose under a contract whereby the plaintiffs appointed the defendants to act as their sole distributors for the sale of their dresses in certain Middle Eastern countries, that the agreement was prematurely terminated in the manner which I have held to be a wrongful repudiation by the defendants, and that there remained, according to the interpretation which I have placed on the contract, two seasons of the arrangement left to run, at the time when it was repudiated.

It is convenient to set out again certain clauses material to the present stage of the argument. The agreement, as subsequently amended, provided:

> '1. The Company hereby appoints the Distributor to be its sole and exclusive Distributor for the sale of its merchandise (hereinafter called "the merchandise") in the Countries Kuwait and Saudi Arabia (hereinafter called "the territory") subject to the terms and conditions hereinafter set out . . .
>
> 3. The Company hereby undertakes that all its exports to other Middle Eastern Countries including North Africa (excluding the territory) will be made directly by the Company and not through any agent and the Company shall refuse to supply any agent if it knows or ought to know that that agent is supplying customers in other Middle Eastern Countries including North Africa
>
> 4. (a) The Company will prepare two ranges per year of Girls dresses of a type traditionally made by it—the first range available in March/April and the second available, in September/October of each year (b) The Distributor undertakes to purchase or procure the purchase of not less than Sixteen thousand (16,000) garments each Season from the Company for the Territory by the end of the sixth week of the date that the Distributor is informed by the Company in writing or by Telex that the Company's complete range of garments is available for showing . . .
>
> 7. The Distributor shall have the sole discretion on marketing and selling policy in the territory so that provided the Distributor is ordering not less than the said Sixteen thousand (16,000) garments per season the Distributor shall be able to sell or market the Company's products to whom they shall desire within the territory and upon such terms and conditions as the Distributor shall solely determine . . .'

The question now for consideration is this. Given that the contract provides only for the purchase by the defendants of at least 16,000 dresses, without saying anything about the sizes and styles of the dresses composing the minimum obligation, what assumption should be made as to the nature of the hypothetical purchase when computing the plaintiffs' loss attributable to the premature termination of the agreement? For example, should it be assumed that the whole quantity would have been composed of the cheapest dresses? If this is so, the plaintiffs will recover no damages for they sold sufficient of the more expensive models by way of mitigation to overtop the loss of profit on the larger quantity of the cheaper kind. Or should the putative sales be related to an average, and, if so, what kind of average, price for the range as a whole? Or should a forecast be made of the dresses which would have been sold if the contract had gone ahead?

There are two reasons why this is a difficult question to answer. First, the scheme of the contract is not fully worked out in the document, and it is not easy to complete the scheme by implication. Second, the principles on which damages are to be calculated in situations where the defendant has some freedom of choice as to the manner of performance are not so clearly established that they can easily be applied to the novel situation now arising.

At first sight, it must seem a surprising assertion that the theory of damages in relation to alternative obligations is still open to doubt. In commercial disputes, damages are so often calculated in terms of the minimum quantity of goods to be delivered or cargo to be shipped that this mode of assessment has become a matter of routine, and the principles rarely have to be considered. The principles are, however, less clear cut than might be thought. For example, a dictum of Maule J which is very often cited from *Cockburn v Alexander* (1848) 6 CB 791 at 814, 136 ER 1459 at 1468–1469 to the effect that when assessing damages the presumed mode of performance is that which is least profitable to the plaintiff and the least burdensome to the defendant is a possible source of difficulty. Unless this is only an elaborate way of saying that the performance is assumed to be that which will yield the least award, the two halves of the rule are capable of leading to different answers, for the position of the defendant might be better overall if he chose a mode of performance which involved a greater than minimum liability in damages but avoided losses in other directions. Again, the foundation of the doctrine is very often sought in the statement of Scrutton LJ in *Abrahams v Herbert Reiach Ltd* [1922] 1 KB 477 at 482 that a defendant is not liable in damages for not doing that which he is not obliged to do. This dictum looks to minimum performance, not to minimum recovery (although the two will often be the same), nor to minimum detriment for the defendant. Furthermore, the principle is expressed solely in terms of the defendant's obligations, considered in the abstract. Yet there are circumstances where the court has paid regard to evidence of what the defendant would actually have done if the contract had gone ahead: see, for example, *Bold v Brough Nicholson & Hall Ltd* [1963] 3 All ER 849, [1964] 1 WLR 201, *Maredelanto Compania Naviera SA v Bergbau-Handel GmbH, The Mihalis Angelos* [1970] 3 All ER 125, [1971] 1 QB 164 and perhaps also *Abrahams v Herbert Reiach Ltd* itself.

I believe that some at least of the difficulties which arise in this branch of the law can be minimised if it is kept in mind that inquiry always involves a comparison between the plaintiff's actual position in face of the breach, and the position which he would have occupied if the contract had been performed. This must involve an identification of the promise, followed by a valuation of its promised worth to the promisee. Each part of the inquiry may involve considering a choice which would have been open to the promisor. Thus:

1. The promisor may have a right of election which fixes the content of his obligation. This can take more than one form. It may, for example, give the vendor the option to deliver 1,500 to 2,000 tons of goods. Here, in accordance with the dictum of Scrutton LJ, the damages are assessed on the basis that the quantity delivered would have been 1,500 tons, for the seller could not have been compelled to deliver more than this amount. Where the obligation is to deliver at A or B, the dictum does not always work so well, for it cannot necessarily be said that A represents more of an obligation than B. So here the presumption is explained in different terms, by looking for the obligation which would have been least detrimental to perform.

2. Even where the obligation has been fixed in advance, or determined by election, the value of it to the promisee, and hence the amount which he has lost through non-performance, may be determined by contingencies. Sometimes, it is possible to be sure what would have happened if the contract had been performed, and (if so) this finding is used to estimate the worth of the promise. More often, the fact that the repudiation has prevented the time for performance from arising means that the best that can be done is to make an estimate of the likelihood that the contingent event would occur, and adjust the damages accordingly. For this purpose it makes no difference that the contingency is one which is under the control of the defendant. Although it is not legitimate to look at what the promisor would have done, but only what he could have done, when identifying the promise, the position is different when, as in *The Mihalis Angelos* and *Bold v Brough Nicholson & Hall Ltd* the inquiry concerns the valuation of the promise itself: see especially

per Diplock LJ in *Lavarack v Woods of Colchester Ltd* [1966] 3 All ER 683 at 691, [1967] 1 QB 278 at 295–296.

There is one further distinction which must be mentioned, namely that which exists between (a) an obligation expressed in terms of a range of alternatives from which the promisor may choose and (b) a single obligation expressed in an indefinite way. A duty of the latter kind may often be construed as an obligation to act reasonably, and the damages will be assessed on the basis of what would have been reasonable. That this distinction does exist cannot, I think, be disputed, and it presents no serious theoretical difficulty when it is possible to say that there is one reasonable mode of performance, and one alone. But what of the case where there is more than one reasonable method, or a whole range of reasonable methods, shading into one another? One possible view is that the court should try to forecast how the defendant would have performed but for the repudiation. In my opinion this approach is inconsistent with principle, since the defendant may in the event have done no more than was necessary to qualify as reasonable, and to assess damages on any other basis would be to penalise him for failing to do something which he was not obliged to do. The answer must, in my judgment, be that the court is to look at the range of reasonable methods, and select the one which is least unfavourable to the defendant, bearing in mind, of course, that in deciding what methods qualify as reasonable the question must be approached with the interests of both parties in mind. This is, I believe, the way to account not only for the decision in *Abrahams v Herbert Reiach Ltd*, but also for the divergencies of approach which might seem to exist between the various judgments, and within the individual judgments, delivered in that case.

I now turn to the present contract. One thing at least is clear, that so far as quantity is concerned this is not a case of optional obligations. There was a single obligation, to purchase 16,000 dresses, coupled with a liberty to purchase more if the defendants so wished. The problem is to determine the content of the obligation in the absence of any provision as to the ratios in which the dresses were to be ordered.

Before discussing this question it is convenient to deal with an argument addressed by the plaintiffs to the effect that the damages should be computed by applying to the shortfall the average price of all of those dresses which were of a style and size suitable for sale in the territory. There are, I believe, two ways in which this argument could be advanced.

The first is by the orthodox route of construing the contract first, and then measuring the damages in terms of the obligation thus arrived at. If the argument proceeds in this way, it is in my judgment bound to fail. Assuming for the moment that the plaintiffs are contending for a simple arithmetical average, the only obligation which would produce the desired award of damages would be one to order the minimum 16,000 dresses with every size and style in exactly the same quantities across the entire range. This would be commercial nonsense, and could not be a tenable interpretation of the contract. The proposition is not made more attractive by adopting some kind of weighted average, because there is nothing in the contract to fix the method of weighting. It was suggested that a weighting might be arrived at by looking at past experience; but this would not be practicable for the first season, and in any event to suggest that in each season the defendants were obliged to buy the minimum quantity of dresses in the same proportions as in the previous season, no matter how different the conditions (or for that matter the dresses) might be, is not a commercially feasible solution. One further proposition, namely that the damages should be assessed by reference to the plaintiffs' own experience when selling in mitigation, plainly cannot be justified by means of any argument which takes the identification of the obligation as its starting point.

The plaintiffs do, however, have another basis for their argument in support of an average price. This is founded on a small group of nineteenth century decisions relating to the computation of damages for breach with an obligation to load under a charterparty. When approaching these rather difficult cases it is necessary to bear in mind that there are three questions which are distinct, although they appear to have become intertwined:

(a) what goods and in what proportions is the charterer obliged to ship; (b) how is the freight to be calculated; (c) how are the damages to be calculated?

The first case was *Thomas v Clarke and Todd* (1818) 2 Stark 450, 171 ER 702, a decision at nisi prius. The charterer had the option to ship various types of merchandise, for each of which a separate rate of freight was fixed. In answer to a claim for a complete failure to ship, the charterer argued that the damages should be assessed on the basis of the cargo which yielded the least amount of freight. Lord Abbott CJ did not accept this, and directed the jury that 'the proper course would be to estimate the freight by means of an average, so as to take neither the greatest possible freight nor the least'.

The second case is *Capper v Forster* (1837) 3 Bing NC 938, 132 ER 672. The charter here was different from the one considered in *Thomas v Clarke and Todd* since it stipulated for the loading of 'a full and complete cargo of lawful merchandise', and then went on to enumerate freights for various types of goods. The ship brought home a part cargo of goods which were not of the type described. Holding that the damages should be assessed on the basis of an average of the stipulated rates, Tindal CJ cited *Thomas v Clarke and Todd*, and said (3 Bing NC 938 at 949–950, 132 ER 672 at 677):

> '... the original intention and expectation of the parties at the time the charter was entered into as to the amount of freight which would become payable for the voyage, must have been founded upon the assumption, that the ship would bring home a cargo consisting of all or some of the enumerated articles; in both cases, therefore, there exists the same necessity of applying the rule above laid down, which necessity is grounded on the consideration, that unless you adopt this rule, you have no other guide whatever; the liberty, "to fill up with other lawful merchandises," being understood by us to mean other lawful merchandises, ejusdem generis, at least so far as the calculation of the freight is involved in that construction.'

Finally, there was *Cockburn v Alexander* (1848) 6 CB 791, 136 ER 1459, where the charter stipulated for a full and complete cargo of wool, tallow, bark or other lawful merchandise 'with separate rates of freight for wool, pressed and unpressed, tallow, bark and hides with stated maximum quantities of bark, tallow and hides'. The ship in fact loaded cargo which included quantities of tallow and bark greater than the stipulated maximum, and also certain other goods for which no rate of trade was fixed. The question was whether, as the defendants asserted, freight should be paid in an amount which would have resulted from applying the market rate to all the unenumerated articles, whereas the plaintiffs said that the assumption should be made that the ship had carried the maximum of bark, tallow and hides, and had filled up the remainder with wool. The Court of Common Pleas upheld the plaintiffs' argument.

The first two cases are not easy to explain, but I believe the reasoning to be as follows. The courts concerned themselves not with the charterer's obligation to ship, but with his obligation to pay freight. They held that whatever the charterer might choose to ship, and in whatever proportions, he was obliged, on the true construction of the charterparty, to pay freight calculated on the basis of an average of the enumerated articles. *Cockburn v Alexander* was, however, to a different effect. Here, the court did not assume any kind of average. Instead the reasoning proceeded by two stages. First, the freight clause was understood as requiring the calculation to assume that the unenumerated articles were ejusdem generis to those for which freight was fixed, and that the whole scheme for the calculation of freight must be found in the contract itself, without recourse to rates derived from the market. Second, it was held that the freight for the notional full cargo composed of enumerated goods and nothing else should, for the purpose of assessing damages, be computed on the basis of a cargo distribution which would yield the lowest recovery to the plaintiff. It was in relation to the first stage of the reasoning that recourse was had to *Capper v Forster*, as pointing out a solution to the problem of 'lawful merchandise' not expressly catered for in the freight clause. The second stage of the argument was quite different, and indeed it seems to have been uncontroversial. At this stage, the court departed from the precedent of the two earlier cases. The question of striking an average does not appear even to have been considered. Instead an approach was adopted which was entirely in line with modern doctrines. *a*

In these circumstances, it seems to me plain that *Cockburn v Alexander* provides no authority for the plaintiffs' argument in the present case. There remain the two earlier decisions. I find it hard to be sure how these are to be understood. Perhaps they are cases on the computation of freight. If so, the subject matter of the contract was far too distant from the present to allow any reliable analogy to be drawn. Perhaps again they were decisions which show that in that particular context the ordinary process of proceeding *b* to construe the obligation before assessing the damages could be short-circuited by the application of a conventional measure of damage. If so, I venture to doubt, notwithstanding the high authority of the judges concerned, whether even in its own limited sphere the convention can now be regarded as good law. Even if it could, I see no reason to transfer it afresh into the present very different context.

It appears to me, therefore, that the choice must be made between two alternatives. *c* Either the contract is read precisely as written, requiring the defendants to buy at least 16,000 dresses each season, with the whole range of dresses to choose from without restriction, in which case the application of the ordinary rules demands that the cheapest dresses must form the yardstick for the entire computation. Or it must be subject to an implied term that the choice must be made in a manner which is reasonable in all the circumstances. If so, *Abrahams v Herbert Reiach Ltd* [1922] 1 KB 477 shows that a selection *d* must be made from those methods of performance which can be regarded as reasonable, on whatever basis yields the result least unfavourable to the defendants.

Although the choice between these alternatives lies at the heart of the present dispute, it is not one which admits of lengthy discussion. The plaintiffs say that, whatever its formal structure, the contract set up an arrangement in the nature of a joint venture, requiring the parties to co-operate in the effective exploitation of the plaintiffs' garments *e* within the territory, an exploitation which would involve the protection of the plaintiffs' goodwill. This objective would not be promoted by the sale of any random collection of dresses, far less a collection which by no stretch of the imagination could possibly have been sold, and which (it might well be) could not even have been manufactured in time. On the defendants' side, cl 7 is relied on to show that they were given such a freedom of action that the plaintiffs must be taken to have ceded the control and protection of their *f* goodwill, for so long as the contract was in force. Again, the defendants say that the minimum obligation would, ex hypothesi, come into play at a time when the defendants would be unable to sell the purchased goods and could therefore not be expected to buy at any but the lowest possible prices.

I do not think that either of these arguments is an answer to the plaintiffs' claim. Certainly, cl 7 did give a wide discretion as to volume, outlets and retail price, and the *g* taking of a wrong view on these matters could cost both parties dear, and damage the goodwill for the future. Nevertheless, I find it hard to accept as being in the contemplation of the parties, when the agreement was made, that the defendants could permissibly order 16,000 garments of the same size, style and colour, and no others at all, a configuration which would alienate their wholesalers, deprive the plaintiffs of anything but a ludicrous presence in the territory, and kill the market not only for the current *h* seasons but for those which were to follow. Even taking into account the very stringent tests imposed under English law for the implication of a term, some constraint on the defendants' freedom of choice must be assumed, in order to make sense of the agreement.

Nor in my judgment is it correct to answer that an implication cannot be made in face of the fact that the defendants would only be in breach of the minimum obligation clause if sales within the territory could not be made in the quantities which the clause *j* required. In my judgment, this approaches the problem from the wrong end. The implication of terms must be assessed on the assumption of performance, not breach. Performance consists of the purchase of 16,000 dresses, or more, if the defendants wanted them. It was explicitly provided that the purchases were to be 'for the territory', not that the dresses were to be left in a warehouse, or put on a bonfire. A purchase of 16,000 garments, and no more, would not be a measure of distress, but would be a full

performance of the contract, and there is in my view no justification for distorting what
a would otherwise be a businesslike interpretation of the agreement, by assuming that the defendants would want, and should be allowed, to carry out that performance in a way which would do nothing but harm to the joint interests of the parties, and which would serve only the self-contradictory purpose of minimising damages which in a case of full performance would never fall due.

Accordingly I consider that the agreement must be construed as subject to an implied
b term that the garments would be selected in a reasonable manner. Since selection would be a matter of judgment, this leaves open the very strong possibility that there would not be a unique reasonable selection, but a range of such selections, some yielding a greater total price than others for the 16,000 chosen garments. On this basis, the damages should, as I have already suggested, be assessed in terms of that reasonable selection which would yield the lowest price. I am very conscious of the problem which will face the court in
c establishing the boundaries of the range, since the sales in mitigation go some way towards showing what a reasonable selection would have been, but they do not show what other selections might also have been made which would qualify as reasonable. I can only say that a similar, although less complex, task is one which the Court of Appeal found itself able to perform in *Abraham v Herbert Reiach Ltd*, on the basis of evidence much less comprehensive that is likely to be available at the hearing of the references to
d damages.

I now turn to a separate issue which relates to the manner in which the sales in mitigation should be brought into account. I can deal with this quite briefly.

It was argued that the sales made by the plaintiffs directly should be treated as performance, pro tanto, by the defendants, and that only the balance of the 16,000 dresses should be the subject of a notional distribution and calculation of damages. I do not
e accept this. Sales by the plaintiffs were not in the nature of a substituted performance, for there was nothing left to perform. There was a completed anticipatory breach of the whole obligation, followed by partial mitigation. As in every case of damages, the correct approach is to compare the position which the plaintiff would have occupied if the contract had been fully performed, and the position which he actually occupied in face of the breach. For the first half of the computation it is necessary to look at the whole of
f the 16,000 garments to see how the sizes, and so on, would have been distributed, and to work out the total price which would have been payable. The second half of the computation must be made of those garments which were sold, or (if failure properly to mitigate is in issue) could have been sold in the territories reopened to the plaintiffs by the termination of the contract.

It seems to me that the two seasons for this purpose should be treated as a whole. True,
g the court may have to look separately at the seasons when deciding what would have been a reasonable choice, but there was a single anticipatory breach in relation to the entire quantity of 32,000 dresses. Both the breach and the subsequent mitigation must be looked at as a whole. I can see nothing inconsistent here with the decision or the reasoning of *British Westinghouse Electric and Manufacturing Co Ltd v Underground Electric Rlys Co of London Ltd* [1912] AC 673, [1911–13] All ER Rep 63.

h I hope in the judgment just delivered that I have given sufficient guidance to enable the parties now to proceed to the concluding stage of the dispute. I cannot part with the matter without expressing the earnest wish that these respectable parties should now, having got so far, find it possible in the light of the guidance provided by the court to compromise their dispute rather than fight it to a conclusion.

Judgment for the plaintiffs for assessment of damages by a master.

Solicitors: *Martin Clore & Co* (for the plaintiffs); *Michael Goldstone & Co*, Woodford (for the defendants).

K Mydeen Esq Barrister.

Garner v Cleggs (a firm)

COURT OF APPEAL, CIVIL DIVISION
LAWTON, OLIVER AND ROBERT GOFF LJJ
3, 4 MARCH 1983

Practice – Payment into court – Withdrawal of payment in – Defendant withdrawing payment in on ground of change of circumstances – Plaintiff succeeding in action but recovering less than sum previously in court – Defendant seeking costs incurred after date of payment in – Whether fact of payment in should be taken into account in awarding costs of action.

In 1978 the plaintiff, who had fairly extensive experience of running proprietary clubs, received particulars of the sale of a club from which he inferred that what was being offered for sale was a licensed proprietary club. Having agreed a price with the vendor he instructed the defendant firm of solicitors to do the conveyancing for him. The contract sent by the vendor's solicitors to the defendant firm showed that what was being offered was not a proprietary club but a members' club, which would have precluded the plaintiff from making any profit on the sale of alcoholic drinks and was therefore not a good business proposition for him. However, the solicitor in the defendant firm who dealt with the matter failed to appreciate the difference between a members' club and a proprietary club, and the conveyance was completed. On discovering the mistake the plaintiff brought an action against the defendants claiming damages for negligence. In August 1981 the defendants paid into court the sum of £25,655 in satisfaction of the claim. The plaintiff did not take the money out of court within the 21-day period laid down by RSC Ord 22, r 3(1)[a] within which he was entitled as of right to take the money out of court. On 13 October 1981 the defendants received information that the vendor was claiming that the plaintiff had known all along that what he was buying was a members' club. On 22 January 1982, before the date of the trial, the defendants applied to withdraw their payment in on the ground of a change of circumstances and on 26 February the court made the order sought. At the trial the defendants admitted their mistake but contended that the mistake had not caused damage to the plaintiff. The judge found that the evidence of the vendor was untrue and he gave judgment for the plaintiff for £23,224·70, which was less than the amount which had previously been in court. The defendants submitted that in the circumstances they should be given their costs incurred after the date of the payment in, having regard to the failure of the plaintiff to take out the sum previously in court. The judge rejected that submission, holding that by taking out the money they had paid into court the defendants had nullified the payment in and that accordingly costs should follow the event. The defendants appealed against the order for costs.

Held – (1) Where, more than 21 days after paying money into court but before the commencement of the trial of the action, the defendant withdrew the money with the leave of the court, it was wrong in principle to order the plaintiff to bear all the costs of the action from the date of payment in if, in the outcome, the plaintiff succeeded in the action but recovered less than the sum previously paid in, since, althought the plaintiff had at one time had the opportunity of taking the money out of court so that no further costs would have been incurred by either party, the result of the defendant's taking the money out of court was that the plaintiff then had no option but either to abandon his claim or to take the risks of litigation at a trial (see p 405 *c d* and *g* to p 406 *d* and p 407 *e* to *h*, post).

(2) Since the plaintiff would not, after 13 October 1981, have been able to take the money out of court had it been left in court, because the defendants could then have

a Rule 3(1), so far as material, is set out at p 403 *g h*, post

objected that there had been a change of circumstances when they learned of the likely
a evidence of the vendor, it followed that the plaintiff had been at risk as to costs only in respect of the period from the expiration of 21 days after the payment in August 1981 until 13 October when he could no longer have taken the money out of court. However, although the costs for that period ought ordinarily to be borne by the plaintiff, the judge had not, in the circumstances, erred in the exercise of his discretion. The appeal would accordingly be dismissed (see p 405 *e* to *j*, p 406 *c d*, p 407 *h j* and p 408 *a*, post).

b

Notes

For payment into and out of court, see 37 Halsbury's Laws (4th edn) paras 285–297, for court's discretion to award costs, see ibid para 714, and for cases on the subject, see 51 Digest (Repl) 576–599, *2091–2255*.

c **Cases referred to in judgments**

Findlay v Rly Executive [1950] 2 All ER 969, CA.

Gaskins v British Aluminium Co Ltd [1976] 1 All ER 208, [1976] QB 524, [1976] 2 WLR 6, CA.

Cases also cited

d *Barker v Barker* [1950] 1 All ER 812, CA.

Gooday v Gooday [1968] 3 All ER 611, [1969] P 1, CA.

Ward v James [1965] 1 All ER 563, [1966] 1 QB 273, CA.

Appeal

The defendants, Cleggs, a firm of solicitors, appealed against an order for costs made by
e his Honour Judge Roy Ward QC sitting as a judge of the High Court at Nottingham on 25 March 1982 at the trial of an action in which the plaintiff, Graham Edward Garner, claimed damages against the defendants arising out of a breach of contract and/or negligence on the part of the defendants, their servants or agents between May and September 1978 whilst acting as solicitors for the plaintiff in connection with his purchase of the New Office Club at Brighton, Sussex. The judge found that the only
f damage the plaintiff had suffered was under three heads of para 14 of his statement of claim, viz that the defendants failed to make any or any adequate inquiry as to the nature of the licence in force at the said premises (sub-para (i)), that they failed to advise the plaintiff as to the fundamental difference between a proprietary club and a registered members club (sub-para (iii)), and that they exchanged contracts without having any answer to their inquiries before contract (sub-para (iv)). The judge directed that judgment
g should be entered for the plaintiff for the sum of £23,224·70, being £15,000 for special damages and £8,224·70 agreed interest thereon and costs. The judge granted the defendants leave to appeal. The facts are set out in the judgment of Lawton LJ.

E Anthony Machin QC and *Hedley Marten* for the defendants.

Ian A B McLaren for the plaintiff.

h

LAWTON LJ. This is an appeal by the defendants, a firm of solicitors practising under the name of Cleggs, against an order for costs made by his Honour Judge Roy Ward QC, sitting as a judge of the High Court at Nottingham in March 1982.

The appeal is brought by the leave of the judge. It raises a point about payment into court which, as far as the thorough researches of counsel have revealed, is a novel one.

j The order for costs, which was an order against the defendant firm, was made in the trial of an action brought against them by the plaintiff, Mr Graham Edward Garner, for damages for professional negligence in the handling of a property transaction for him in the year 1978.

The background of the case can be stated shortly, because it is of only marginal relevance to the facts of this appeal.

The plaintiff was a businessman who had had fairly extensive experience of running proprietary clubs. Some time in 1978 he received particulars of a club known as the Office Club at 2 St George's Place, Brighton. He inferred from the particulars that what was being offered for sale was a proprietary club. The subject matter of the sale was to be the assignment of a lease together with the furnishing of the premises. He then consulted the defendant firm, with a view to their doing the conveyancing for him. He himself was willing to negotiate the business side of the sale with the vendor, a Mr Talty. He did so, and agreed with Mr Talty a price of £8,000, made up as to £5,000 premium on the assignment of the lease and £3,000 for the furnishings on the premises. He gave those figures to the defendant firm.

When the plaintiff had approached the defendant firm, he had given instructions to one of the partners. Understandably, as the proposed conveyancing seemed to be of a comparatively minor and simple kind, the defendant firm asked one of their assistant solicitors to do the necessary work. That assistant solicitor was a young man, recently qualified. Most unfortunately he seems not to have had much knowledge of the law relating to clubs. It is understandable that he should not have had much knowledge because, in the ordinary way of professional training and examinations for solicitors, clubs and all the complications relating to them do not figure very prominently.

The vendor's solicitors sent the defendant firm a contract. If the assistant solicitor had appreciated what was meant by the contract he would also have appreciated that what was being offered was not a proprietary club at all but a members' club, that is to say the client was being offered a lease of the premises, together with fixtures and fittings, on which a members' club was being conducted.

Members' clubs are not attractive as business propositions to men like the plaintiff, because the law provides that those who own the premises cannot take any profits from the sale of alcoholic liquor by a members' club carried on there. It is the profit from the sale of alcoholic liquors which is the main attraction for men like the plaintiff in running clubs.

The failure to appreciate the difference between a members' club and a proprietary club was fatal to the plaintiff's business objectives.

The conveyance was completed. The plaintiff parted with £8,000. Inevitably there were costs involved in the conveyancing, and there were other costs involved as an almost inevitable part of the taking over of the club. So, at the end, the judge at the trial came to the conclusion that, as a result of the mistake made by the assistant solicitor, the plaintiff had lost the sum, by way of capital investment, of £15,000.

When the plaintiff did take possession of the premises he seems to have appreciated fairly quickly that he had taken over a members' club. That did not discourage him from continuing to run it, but it did arouse the interest of the Brighton police. By October 1978 the police had made it clear to him that he would have to stop managing the club. By this time he had come to the conclusion that he had suffered a grievous loss at the hands of his solicitors. He claimed that he had suffered a breakdown in mental health, due to the worry. He also claimed that as a result of their negligence he had been prevented from earning profits as a club owner, either on the premises at Brighton or alternatively in other premises which he would have taken over had he not acquired those in Brighton.

He considered that he had a very substantial claim against the defendants. As a result, he instructed his solicitors to issue a writ in September 1979. A statement of claim was delivered, which was amended from time to time. That statement of claim sets out lengthy particulars of damage. I will enumerate them shortly. There was an allegation of capital loss; an allegation of loss of profit; an allegation of non-recurring expenses; there was an allegation of expenses incurred in attempting to mitigate part of the loss; and an allegation that he had suffered interest charges. The whole claim, according to what counsel for the defendants has told us in this court, if one put a money tag on it, came to about £80,000.

The defendants delivered a defence. They, of course, had the sense to consult another

firm of solicitors, experienced in this class of litigation. By their defence, the defendants
a denied any liability. But they must have appreciated from early on that they were at considerable risk of being found liable on the plaintiff's claim, because there clearly had been a mistake by the young assistant solicitor which ought not to have been made. Indeed, it looks to me as if for a long time during the early part of this litigation the only issue which was likely to be fought out in the contest was causation in relation to some of the damage claimed and the quantum of what was likely to be proved.

b As a result, no doubt, of advice, the defendant firm decided to pay into court the sum of £25,655. They did so by notice to the plaintiff, which was in the appropriate form, and it reads as follows:

> 'The Defendants Cleggs have paid £25,655·00 into Court. The said £25,655·00 is in satisfaction of all the causes of action in respect of which the Plaintiff claims including any claim for interest pursuant to Order 22 Rule 1 (8).'

c
The notice was dated 5 August 1981, but we have been told by counsel that it was not in fact served on the plaintiff's solicitors until 11 August. (When I say 'served on 11 August', it was sent off to the plaintiff's solicitors by letter dated 10 August, and I assume that in the ordinary course of post it is likely to have arrived on 11 August.)

The plaintiff, as I shall point out later, had 21 days in which to make up his mind
d whether to take that money out of court. He did not take it out. He went on with preparations for trial, as did the defendants.

In October the defendants' solicitors got to know that the Mr Talty, who had been the plaintiff's vendor, claimed to be in a position to give them information about the transaction into which the plaintiff had entered. The solicitor who got the information was a Mr Maybury. He later swore an affidavit, on 27 January 1982, in which he dealt
e with what he had learnt from Mr Talty. The substance of his affidavit was that he had met Mr Talty on 13 October 1981, and Mr Talty had then told him (untruthfully, as it turned out at the trial) that the plaintiff had known all along that he (Mr Talty) was proposing to sell a members' club; that Mr Talty had alleged that the plaintiff had visited the premises, had looked round them, and had seen the books of the club from which it was obvious that what was being offered was not a proprietary club but a members' club.

f Mr Maybury, as one would expect from a responsible solicitor, was keen to get a written statement from Mr Talty. Mr Talty, for reasons which became only too obvious at the trial, was not anxious to give a written statement. He was pressed by the solicitor to do so, and in the end he sent a letter to the solicitor setting out the substance of what he had said in the interview with the solicitor on 13 October 1981.

Leading counsel (it was not Mr Machin), who had been taken in to advise, took the
g view that it would be prudent to get Mr Talty to swear an affidavit setting out what he had told the solicitor, and that Mr Talty did. That affidavit was sworn on 15 January 1982.

Once that affidavit had been obtained, there seems to have been a consultation between the solicitor representing the defendant firm and leading counsel, as a result of which certain advice was given. Following that advice, on 22 January 1982 the defendants
h arranged to take the money which they had paid into court in August 1981 out of court, on the ground that there had been a change of circumstance in that their case had been considerably strengthened by what Mr Talty had told them. The way the case had been strengthened was this: the defendant firm were willing to accept that there had been a mistake by the assistant solicitor, but that mistake had not caused any damage to the plaintiff because, so they then believed, the plaintiff knew perfectly well that he was
j buying a members' club.

The summons was heard by the district registrar at Nottingham on 26 February 1982. Both sides were represented, and he ruled that the defendants should be allowed to take the money out of court; this they did.

At the time when the application to take the money out of court was heard by the registrar the parties were under notice from the court administrator that the trial was likely to begin within a comparatively short time; in fact it began on 16 March 1982 and lasted eight days.

A number of issues were canvassed. On the sixth day of the trial Mr Machin (who by this time had been taken in to represent the defendant firm in court) made a formal admission that the defendants accepted that they had been in breach of duty to the plaintiff, but went on to say that they were continuing to contest the case on the ground that the damage which the plaintiff sustained had not been caused by that breach of duty. The plaintiff's claims in various respects were challenged. The plaintiff had the advantage of being represented by Mr McLaren, who has had extensive experience of common law litigation. He sensibly did not pursue some of the more exaggerated aspects of the plaintiff's claim. But he did canvass the proposition that the illness which the plaintiff had had, following his failure to be allowed to carry on this club as a result of police intervention, had been caused by the defendants' negligence. The judge was not impressed by that argument. In the end the judge found that the only damage which the plaintiff had suffered was under three heads, namely para 14(i), (iii) and (iv), and he assessed the damages, as I have already said, at £15,000.

The plaintiff was clearly entitled to interest on that sum. There was some discussion about the amount of the interest. Counsel between them agreed the rate at which it should be calculated and, although they did not in court do the arithmetic, they were both agreed that the amount of the interest would leave the plaintiff with a total sum by way of damages which would not be more than £24,000. That was at least £1,655 less than the amount which had been paid into court on 11 August 1981.

This situation presented the judge with an unusual problem. Counsel for the plaintiff asked for his costs; he put the matter very succinctly (as is his wont) in this way. After having called the judge's attention to the history of the payment in, he said:

> 'But my position is clear in my submission. There was no money in court at the date of the trial. There was no money which the plaintiff could take to avoid the trial and he is entitled to his costs.'

Counsel for the defendants was then asked to make his comments, and he did so with his usual succinctness and clarity. He said, after having set out the history:

> 'So, in my submission, there is no reason why the usual consequences should not follow from a failure to take out of court moneys in excess of the sum recovered.'

We have been told by counsel that these submissions with regard to costs took place just before the midday adjournment and, through no fault of the trial judge, it was clear to everybody that he would have to give a ruling quickly, and he did so in these terms:

> 'Well I take the view that if the defendant pays a sum of money into court and then takes it out, he nullifies the payment into court and it is then as if it never happened and accordingly it seems to me the normal order must follow that costs follow the event and there will be costs in favour of the plaintiff.'

That was an order which would inevitably lead to the defendants having to pay a very substantial sum by way of costs, by reason of the fact that the trial had lasted eight days. Counsel for the defendants at once asked for leave to appeal on the question of costs and, as I have said, the judge granted it.

The defendants then gave notice of appeal, and it is relevant to call attention to the way in which they put their case in their notice of appeal. They asked:

> 'FOR AN ORDER that the said Order for costs may be varied and that the Respondent may be ordered to pay the costs of the said action from the 5th day of August 1981 and that the Appellant may be ordered to pay the costs of the said action up to the 5th day of August 1981 and for an order that the Respondent pay to the Appellant the costs of this Appeal to be taxed.'

What they were asking for was that the successful plaintiff should pay the costs on the

normal basis on which orders for costs are made when money is paid into court, is not
a taken out, and the plaintiff, at the trial, obtains less than what has been paid into court. That form of order received approval in this court in *Findlay v Rly Executive* [1950] 2 All ER 969 at 972. In the course of his judgment in that case, Denning LJ said:

> 'The public good is better secured by allowing plaintiffs to go on to trial at their own risk generally as to costs. That is the basis of the rules as to payment into court, and I think we should implement them here, even though it means that the plaintiff
> b has to pay out much of her damages in costs to the defendants. The only issue in the case was the amount of the damages. The defendants paid a reasonable sum into court. The plaintiff took her chance of getting more, and, having failed, she must pay the costs.'

The argument of counsel for the defendants in this court when he opened this case
c was as follows: that the plaintiff, for 21 days after the money had been paid into court, had his chance of settling the case for a reasonable sum. He decided not to. He took the chance of getting more, and he must take the consequences of getting less.

It is now necessary for me to look in some detail at the rules of court relating to money paid into court. Those rules are set out in RSC Ord 22, and it seems to me that the draftsman of the rules did not contemplate the particular problem which has arisen in
d this case. There appears to be a gap in the rules to which the Rule Committee might perhaps pay some attention at the next revision of the rules. Order 22, r 1(1) reads as follows:

> 'In any action for a debt or damages any defendant may at any time pay into Court a sum of money in satisfaction of the cause of action in respect of which the plaintiff claims or, where two or more causes of action are joined in the action, a
> e sum or sums of money in satisfaction of any or all of those causes of action.'

Paragraph (3) is as follows:

> 'A defendant may, without leave, give notice of an increase in a payment made under this Rule, but, subject to that and without prejudice to paragraph (5), a notice of payment may not be withdrawn or amended without the leave of the Court
> f which may be granted on such terms as may be just.'

It is pertinent to point out that what that paragraph refers to is the withdrawal of a notice of payment. It does not specifically deal with what happens to the money which has been paid in; and, as far as I can see, there is no specific provision in the rule to deal with the payment out of moneys in court to defendants. Indeed, as I shall show in a moment,
g there is another rule under Ord 22 which provides that money can only be paid out in satisfaction of claims. Order 22, r 3(1) is as follows:

> 'Where money is paid into Court under Rule 1, then subject to paragraph (2), within 21 days after receipt of the notice of payment or, where more than one payment has been made or the notice has been amended, within 21 days after receipt of the notice of the last payment or the amendment notice but, in any case,
> h before the trial or hearing of the action begins, the plaintiff may . . .'

and then there are set out details as to what he may do, and the substance of it comes to this: he can take the money out of court.

The difficulty, however, which the rules create arises under r 5, which has the heading 'Money remaining in court', and it is in these terms:

j

> 'If any money paid into court in an action is not accepted in accordance with Rule 3, the money remaining in court shall not be paid out except in pursuance of an order of the Court which may be made at any time before, at or after the trial or hearing of the action; and where such an order is made before the trial or hearing the money shall not be paid out except in satisfaction of the cause or causes of action in respect of which it was paid in.

That seems to me to be mandatory in its terms, and to be in conflict with r 1(3) unless there is read into para (3), by implication, a provision that, if the notice of payment is withdrawn, the money in court may also be withdrawn. We understand from counsel that the practice has been that defendants are allowed, on application to the court, to withdraw money in court. But *Gaskins v British Aluminium Co Ltd* [1976] 1 All ER 208, [1976] QB 524 seems to indicate that the money can only be paid out to the defendants if they show a change of circumstance. In *Gaskin*'s case the application for the money to be paid out was made by the plaintiff during the course of the trial, so that case is not directly in point to the instant case. But the court did consider the general application of the rules relating to payments into court, and Lord Denning MR said ([1976] 1 All ER 208 at 211, [1976] QB 524 at 530):

> 'I think a distinction must be drawn between an application made *before* the trial, and one made at or after it. When the application is made *before* the trial, it will usually be made to the master. He *can* make an order allowing it. If the chances of success or failure—or of greater or less damages—are substantially the same as they were at the time of the payment into court, the master may allow the payment out to the plaintiff, but he will usually allow it only on the terms that the plaintiff pays all the costs from the date of the payment into court. If the chances have substantially altered, then the master should not allow the plaintiff to take the payment out: for the same reason that it would be unfair to hold the defendant to a sum which he offered in different circumstances. He can say: "Non haec in foedera veni." I think the defendant should indicate to the master the circumstances which have altered the position, such as a decision of the courts which has changed the way in which damages are to be assessed, or the discovery of further evidence or information affecting the chances . . .'

He then referred to a series of cases. He went on:

> 'But I do not think the defendant should be required to state circumstances which, if disclosed to the plaintiff at this stage, would affect the conduct of the case at the trial, as, for instance, by making the plaintiff aware of the questions which he might be asked in cross-examination.'

There is one other rule which is relevant to this appeal; it is RSC Ord 62, r 5. This is the order which deals with costs. Rule 5 is as follows:

> 'The Court in exercising its discretion as to costs shall, to such extent, if any, as may be appropriate in the circumstances, take into account . . . (*b*) any payment of money into court and the amount of such payment.'

In the ordinary course of litigation, where money is paid into court and is not taken out there is no difficulty about applying Ord 62, r 5(*b*). But the complication arises in this case where the money was in court, was not taken out by the plaintiff but after some time was taken out by the defendant. To what extent, if any, should the court take into account the fact that money had been paid into court and the plaintiff had had an opportunity of taking the money out but had lost it before the trial began?

It is important, in my judgment, that we should bear in mind that these rules are rules of practice. They have got to be complied with, but the court should apply them in the light of what tends to happen. We have had the benefit in this case of admirable arguments both by counsel for the defendants and by counsel for the plaintiff about the practice with regard to payments into court. It is impossible, in my judgment, to lay down any general propositions as to what happens in practice, because circumstances differ. But by and large, in the majority of cases where money is paid into court by a defendant in settlement of a case and it is not taken out fairly soon after it is paid in, it remains in court. Counsel for the plaintiff told us that this is the first case he has ever come across in which money has been taken out by the defendants; and I, personally, have never myself come across a similar case. But those of us who have had experience of a payments into court know that fairly frequently plaintiffs reject the offer when the money is first paid into court and then, at a later stage of the litigation, they may get advice, usually from counsel, about the adequacy of the payment and their prospects of getting any more; and when that advice is given and is accepted by the plaintiff it is common for the plaintiff to apply to the court for leave to take the money out. In such circumstances, the usual order which is made (as is reflected in what Lord Denning MR b said in *Gaskin*'s case) is that they are allowed to do so on condition that they pay all the costs after the payment in which the defendants have incurred.

It is against that background that I look at the facts of this case.

The first problem is to try to interpret, as best one can, the very short statement which the judge made when giving his ruling. I am alive to the fact that he had to give a short ruling because of circumstances which were beyond his control, and I would not like to c construe it as if it were a deed or a statute. But I am driven to the conclusion that what he was saying was that, in the circumstances of this case, he felt impelled to disregard altogether the fact that at any time there had been a payment into court. In my judgment, he was not justified in doing that. On the other hand, what he was justified in doing was to bear in mind these facts: once that money had been taken out of court, the plaintiff had no option but either to abandon his claim or to take the risks of litigation at a trial. d He had been put into that position by the defendants. Without criticising the defendants in any way, and with hindsight, one can see that they would have been better advised, in the circumstances of this case, having regard to the evidence which they thought they had got from Mr Talty, to leave the money in court. Then if, at the court door, the plaintiff had decided that perhaps he would be wise to take the money out, they could have objected on the ground that since they had knowledge of Mr Talty's likely evidence e there had been a change of circumstance. If they had taken that attitude, they would not have found themselves in the difficulty in which they did find themselves at the trial.

What is the reality of the situation? The reality, as I see it, is this: that, after the money had been paid into court, the plaintiff had to make up his mind whether he was going to go on with his claim. For some time he deliberately decided to go on with it and to take the risk of being awarded less than he thought he was likely to get. But there did come a f time when he would not have been able to take the money out of court; that time came when Mr Maybury, the solicitor who was representing the defendant firm, heard about Mr Talty. That was on 13 October 1981. If, after 13 October 1981, the plaintiff had tried to take the money out of court, the defendant firm would have been entitled to say, on the authority of *Gaskin*'s case: 'You can't have the money now, because our case has changed. Before we heard of Mr Talty we were in considerable difficulties on liability, g but now, although we will probably have to accept at the trial that we were in breach of duty, we can show that the damage which the plaintiff has suffered was not caused by that breach of duty.' In other words, from 13 October 1981 onwards the plaintiff probably would not have been able to take the money out of court. By their summons, which they issued on 22 January, and the district registrar's ruling on 26 February, the defendants put it completely beyond the power of the plaintiff to do anything about the h money in court, and, as I have said, he had to fight the action or abandon it.

So I have come to this conclusion: that if the judge meant, as I think he must be taken as meaning, that he had to disregard altogether the fact that the payment into court had been made, he was wrong. What he should have done was to have paid regard to the fact that from the beginning of September until 13 October the plaintiff was taking a gamble, and during that period there may have been some costs incurred which he might have j been ordered by the judge to pay, but only for that period, because after that period the plaintiff was not in a position to take a gamble at all, for the reasons I have stated.

What, then, is to be done on this appeal?

There are two or three factors which I feel we must bear in mind. The first is that, again understandably, counsel for the defendants never asked the judge to approach the matter in the way that I think was the right way of approaching the position which had arisen in this case. Had the matter rested there, that would have been an omission which a was not even venial, merely a slip of a very minor character. But the defendant firm have not approached this appeal in that way at all. As I have already pointed out, they have asked this court, on the hearing of the appeal, to make the same kind of order as is usually made when money is paid into court and remains in court. For the reasons which I have already stated, they were not entitled to that form of order at all. Counsel for the defendants did not, even in argument in opening, submit that there was an alternative b way of looking at this matter. It was not until the point was canvassed from the Bench that he accepted that what I have said was a possible way of approaching this case. Had the matter been brought to the attention of the trial judge, he might very well have come to the conclusion which I have come to.

In those circumstances, I find difficulty in seeing why this court should interfere with his discretion. It is some consolation to me to think that the quantum of costs which was c involved between the beginning of September and 13 October must be very small indeed. I would not like to approach the matter, as counsel for the plaintiff suggested, on a de minimis basis, because we have no information what costs were incurred during that period, but the likelihood is that they were comparatively small.

In all the circumstances of this case, I would dismiss the appeal.

d

OLIVER LJ. I agree.

ROBERT GOFF LJ. The question in this case can be simply stated. A sum is paid into court by a defendant, notice being duly given to the plaintiff. Subsequently, after the expiry of the 21-day period during which the plaintiff is entitled as of right to take the e money out of court in satisfaction of his claim but some time before the beginning of the trial of the action, the defendant is given leave to withdraw his notice of payment in, and indeed the payment in itself, on the ground of a material change of circumstances. The action is then fought. The plaintiff succeeds but is given judgment in a sum smaller than the amount previously in court. What weight, if any, is in such circumstances to be given by the judge, when making his award of costs, to the fact that there had at one f time been a payment into court?

Counsel for the defendants submitted to the judge that the fact that there had been a payment into court should not merely be taken into account but should persuade the court to award to the defendants the costs of the action. Counsel for the plaintiff submitted to the judge that the payment in, having been withdrawn before the trial began, was irrelevant. It was the latter view which the judge accepted. He said: g

> '... I take the view that if the defendant pays a sum of money into court and then takes it out, he nullifies the payment into court and it is then as if it never happened and accordingly it seems to me the normal order must follow that costs follow the event and there will be costs in favour of the plaintiff.'

In my judgment, the language used by the judge was too sweeping, although he was h certainly right to reject the argument advanced on behalf of the defendants.

The position is this. A payment into court has some of the characteristics of an offer, but it is not identical with an offer because, once the payment is made into court, it is subject to all the relevant provisions of the Rules of the Supreme Court, and in particular, for present purposes, the provisions of rr 1, 3 and 5 of Ord 22 to which Lawton LJ has already referred. The effect of the relevant parts of these provisions is, in summary, as j follows. First, once money has been paid in, the plaintiff has the right to take the money out of court in satisfaction of his claim, without leave, at any time within 21 days after receipt of the notice of the payment in and before the trial or hearing of the action begins (see r 3). Second, after the expiry of the 21-day period the money in court may only be paid out to the plaintiff in pursuance of an order of the court (see r 5). Third, notice of payment in (and, by implication, a payment in itself) may only be withdrawn by the defendant by leave of the court (see r 1(3)). In practice such leave will only be given where the defendant has shown good reason, and that ordinarily means a material change of circumstances.

It follows from these rules that a payment into court lacks one of the most important characteristics of a simple offer, viz that it can be withdrawn at any time at the will of the offeror. Still less is it like an offer which is expressed to be open for acceptance within a specified period so that it lapses at the end of that period. On the contrary, a plaintiff, faced with a payment into court, has time to consider his position. Obviously the 21-day period is important to him, because he should know that if he does not take the money out in satisfaction of his claim within that period he will thereafter be on risk as to costs. But, subject to his taking that risk, and subject to his also taking the risk that there may thereafter be some good reason, in particular a material change of circumstances, to prompt an application by the defendant for leave to withdraw his notice of payment in and to justify the granting of such leave, the plaintiff knows that the money will remain in court. Until the tempo of preparation for trial increases as the time for trial approaches, the amount expended in costs may not be extravagant. The plaintiff may wish for further time of consideration. He may wish to study the defendant's discovery of documents; he may wish to search for further evidence; he may anticipate an increased payment into court by the defendant; and he has the right to change his mind. Subject to the two risks I have mentioned, he can delay his decision whether or not to take the money out of court, in the knowledge that the money will still be available to him for that purpose until the time of the commencement of the trial.

That being so, if, before the commencement of the trial, the defendant does in fact withdraw (with leave) his notice of payment into court, it appears to me that it would be wrong in principle to order that the plaintiff should bear all the costs of the action from the date of payment in if the plaintiff, in the outcome, wins but recovers less than the sum previously paid in. True, the plaintiff had at one time the opportunity of taking the money out of court and, if he had done so, no further costs would have been incurred by either party. But he was entitled to wait and consider his position after the expiry of the 21-day period, though on risk as to costs incurred meanwhile. After all, it is open to the defendant to leave the money in court. If the defendant does so, and the plaintiff does not take it out, then the usual consequences will ordinarily follow if the plaintiff recovers no more than the sum paid in. But that was a course which, in the present case, the defendants decided not to take.

However, the payment into court will, in such circumstances, ordinarily be relevant in respect of costs incurred during the period between the date of payment in and the date when the defendant's notice of payment in is withdrawn by leave of the court, or more accurately, in the circumstances of the present case, the date after which the defendant would have been likely to oppose, and to oppose successfully, an application by the plaintiff to take the money out of court. Of course, if the money had been left in court and available to the plaintiff, and had been taken out by him with leave, in satisfaction of his claim, the plaintiff would ordinarily have had to bear the costs incurred by the defendant after the date of payment in.

It is only right, therefore, that even where notice of the payment into court is withdrawn by the defendant with leave after the expiry of the 21-day period, the costs previously incurred by the defendant during the period which has elapsed since the payment in, during which the money was in reality available to the plaintiff to be taken out, should ordinarily be borne by the plaintiff. It was during that period, and that period alone, that the plaintiff was, by reason of the payment in, truly at risk as to costs. That point was not, however, taken before the judge. He was simply faced with two stark alternatives: whether the plaintiff should pay the defendants' costs, or the defendants should pay the plaintiff's costs. He chose the latter alternative. In these circumstances, in agreement with Lawton and Oliver LJJ, I do not consider that it would be right for this court to hold that the judge erred in the exercise of his discretion.

I would, therefore, also dismiss the appeal.

Appeal dismissed with costs.

Solicitors: *Pinsent & Co*, Birmingham (for the defendants); *R A Young & Pearce*, Nottingham (for the plaintiff).

Mary Rose Plummer Barrister.

Bradburn v Lindsay
Bradburn and another v Lindsay

CHANCERY DIVISION AT MANCHESTER
HIS HONOUR JUDGE BLACKETT-ORD V-C SITTING AS A JUDGE OF THE HIGH COURT
25, 26, 27 MAY, 16, 17, 24 SEPTEMBER 1982

Easement – Support – Interference – Demolition of adjoining house – Demolition pursuant to demolition order – Owner of house neglecting to keep it in repair – Local authority ordering demolition of house – Local authority demolishing house after owner failing to comply with order – Demolition resulting in loss of support for neighbour's house – Whether owner owing duty to neighbour to prevent damage occurring – Whether owner liable to neighbour for loss of support occasioned by demolition – Whether fact that demolition carried out by local authority freeing owner from liability to neighbour.

Nuisance – Neglect – Neglect of house – Neglect interfering with easement of support – Neglect resulting in loss of support for neighbouring house – Owner of neighbouring house having right to enter neglected house and abate nuisance – Whether owner of neglected house owing duty to neighbour to prevent damage occurring to neighbour's house – Whether right to enter and abate nuisance freeing owner of neglected house from liability to neighbour for nuisance.

Two semi-detached properties, no 53 and no 55, were built as a unit, with a dividing wall between them. The properties were in common ownership until 1919, when one was sold off, the conveyance containing a declaration that the dividing wall was a party wall belonging to and repairable by the respective owners in equal shares. By virtue of the Law of Property Act 1925, Sch 1, Pt V, para 1[a] the party wall was divided medially between the two owners with cross-rights of support. The plaintiffs bought no 55 in 1970, at a time when no 53 appeared to be in a somewhat derelict condition. By 1972 no 53, which was owned by the defendant, was being vandalised. The plaintiffs complained to the defendant about the general dereliction of no 53 and also about the fact that no 53 was suffering from dry rot which might come through the party wall. The defendant did nothing. In early 1977 the local authority made a demolition order and in November, the defendant having taken no action, it demolished no 53, with the defendant's consent, leaving the party wall standing but largely unsupported. The plaintiffs brought an action against the defendant based on negligence and nuisance and claiming damages, contending that the defendant was in breach of her duty to take reasonable care of no 53

a Paragraph 1 provides: 'Where, immediately before the commencement of this Act, a party wall or other party structure is held in undivided shares, the ownership thereof shall be deemed to be severed vertically as between the respective owners, and the owner of each part shall have such rights to support and of user over the rest of the structure as may be requisite for conferring rights corresponding to those subsisting at the commencement of this Act.'

and that her failure to repair it had led to its demolition and caused loss to the plaintiffs
a by way of loss of support and exposure of the side of no 55 to dry rot and decay. The
defendant denied liability, contending that, although she could not herself have pulled
down no 53, she had not been liable to repair it, and the fact that her neglect of it had led
to its demolition by the local authority did not give the plaintiffs any cause of action. The
defendant further contended that the plaintiffs should themselves have entered no 53
and taken appropriate steps to prevent damage occurring to no 55.

b

Held – Since the defendant should reasonably have appreciated the danger to no 55 from
the dry rot and from the lack of repair of no 53 and since there were steps which she
could reasonably have taken to prevent the damage occurring, she owed a duty to the
plaintiffs to take those steps, and because she had failed to do so she was liable for the
damage caused. Neither the possibility that the plaintiffs might have a right to enter on
c no 53 and abate the nuisance nor the fact that the actual demolition had been carried out
with the defendant's consent by the local authority when she had herself neglected to
comply with the demolition order freed the defendant from her liability to the plaintiffs.
In the circumstances the plaintiffs were entitled to support for the party wall in the form
of buttresses and to have the wall treated to prevent the spread of dry rot, and to have
that work done to a reasonable specification so as to make good, within reason, the
d damage caused by the defendant's neglect (see p 413 *e f* and *j* to p 414 *e* and *j* and p 415 *b*
c, post).

Leakey v National Trust for Places of Historic Interest or Natural Beauty [1980] 1 All ER 17
applied.

Dicta of Parker J in *Jones v Pritchard* [1908–10] All ER Rep at 83–84 and of Greene MR
in *Bond v Norman* [1940] 2 All ER at 18 considered.

e

Notes

For the easement of support and for interference therewith and repair thereof, see 14
Halsbury's Laws (4th edn) paras 174–182, and for cases on the subject, see 19 Digest
(Reissue) 170–174, *1242–1276*.

For abatement of and actions for nuisance, see 34 Halsbury's Laws (4th edn) paras 349–
f 365, and for cases on the subject, see 36(1) Digest (Reissue) 471–479, *499–579*.

For the Law of Property Act 1925, Sch 1, Pt V, para 1, see 27 Halsbury's Statutes (3rd
edn) 657.

Cases referred to in judgment

Batty v Metropolitan Property Realizations Ltd [1978] 2 All ER 445, [1978] QB 554, [1978]
2 WLR 500, CA.
g
Bond v Norman, Bond v Nottingham Corp [1940] 2 All ER 12, [1940] Ch 429, CA.
Jones v Pritchard [1908] 1 Ch 630, [1908–10] All ER Rep 80.
Leakey v National Trust for Places of Historic Interest or Natural Beauty [1980] 1 All ER 17,
[1980] QB 485, [1980] 2 WLR 65, CA.
Phipps v Pears [1964] 2 All ER 35, [1965] 1 QB 76, [1964] 2 WLR 996, CA.
h *Wheeldon v Burrows* (1879) 12 Ch D 31, [1874–80] All ER 669, CA.

Actions

By a summons issued on 22 November 1977 out of the Stockport County Court the
plaintiff, James Bradburn, claimed damages of £2,000 against the defendant, Mary
Lindsay, for negligence and/or nuisance. By an order made on 4 February 1981 by his
j Honour Philip Curtis, sitting as a deputy circuit judge, in the Stockport County Court
the proceedings were transferred to the Manchester District Registry of the Chancery
Division of the High Court. By a writ issued from the Manchester District Registry of
the High Court on 27 March 1981 the plaintiffs, James Bradburn and Eileen Bradburn
(his wife), claimed damages, costs and further or other relief arising out of breaches by
the defendant, Mary Lindsay, of the obligations incumbent on her by virtue of an
agreement and declaration as to a party wall contained in a conveyance of 53 Kennerley

Road, Stockport, Cheshire dated 19 February 1919 and made between Lucy Mary Good and Charles William Kenyon. The facts are set out in the judgment. a

M S Johnson and *Andrew Gilbart* for the plaintiffs.
P W Watkins for the defendant.

HIS HONOUR JUDGE BLACKETT-ORD V-C. The plaintiffs in these proceedings (there are two actions), Mr and Mrs Bradburn, own a semi-detached property, 55 b Kennerley Road, Stockport, which was built towards the end of the last century. The defendant, Mrs Lindsay, owned no 53 and, it having been pulled down, still owns the site.

The two properties were built as a unit. The dividing wall between them was not carried up into the roof space. The two front doors were in the middle, side by side facing the road, and when you went through either front door you saw in front of you the stair c well with an arch at the foot of the stairs. The wall above the arch in each property was carried by a single bressumer passing through the dividing wall. The properties were in common ownership until 1919, and when one of them was sold off the conveyance contained a declaration that the dividing wall should be a party wall belonging to and repairable by the respective owners in equal shares. By the operation of para 1 of Pt V of Sch 1 to the Law of Property Act 1925 the result was that the party wall was divided d medially between the two owners with cross-rights of support.

The story can be taken up in August 1970 when the plaintiffs bought no 55. At that time the adjoining property, no 53, appeared to be in a somewhat derelict condition, and I think it was Mr Bradburn who said he was told it belonged to an eccentric lady and that her relatives were going 'to do it up'. When he had completed his purchase, Mr Bradburn set to work to install central heating. He got into his roof space to put in a header tank e and was surprised to find firstly that there was no physical division between the roof space of no 55 and the roof space of no 53 and secondly that this roof space had been clearly used as a roosting place for pigeons for very many years, they gaining access on no 53's side. It showed all the obvious signs.

He again investigated no 53 in about 1972. Number 53 was being vandalised. Mr Bradburn said that he could hear 'drop outs' going up the stairs in the middle of the f night. He got the police to investigate. He saw the defendant (which he did not very often do because she seems only to have showed herself perhaps annually) and complained to her about the pigeons and the general dereliction of the property and also complained of the fact that no 53 was suffering from dry rot which might come through the party wall. He was told by the defendant on one occasion that 'it would be all right' and on another occasion, after he had had the police round, to 'mind his own business and not to do it again'. The important point is that I find, as a fact, that in the early 1970s Mr g Bradburn complained to the defendant about the risk of dry rot infestation.

He pressed the local council to take some action to get the defendant to put her property in order, but initially without very much success. In 1975 he called in a surveyor who confirmed an outbreak of dry rot on the ground floor of no 55 along the party wall, and he was advised that it must have come through from no 53. He had it dealt with by h Rentokil Ltd. At about the same time the council was considering making a compulsory purchase of no 53, and the machinery for a compulsory purchase order was set in motion. The defendant objected and a public inquiry was ordered. The council, it seems, then had second thoughts because the property at no 53 was in such a bad state that repairs would cost more than the property was worth. But it seems that the machinery once set in motion cannot be stopped and there was a public inquiry in April 1976 which resulted j in an inspector's report in August 1976. This is not strictly evidence in the case but some of what the inspector says summarises conveniently the evidence of Mr Bradburn and his surveyor. The inspector said:

> 'The house is in a ruinous condition, open to wind and rain. The brick shell looks sound but dry rot is widespread. There is extensive dilapidation to internal wall

> plaster and ceilings . . . The dry rot infestation is extensive, it has penetrated the main walls. All woodwork will have to be removed and burnt. The walls will have to be irrigated.'

I find that that was the position in the middle of 1976. In the next year, in the spring, the council made a demolition order under the Housing Act 1957. Predictably the defendant took no action, but in September she telephoned the council and agreed to the council carrying out demolition and this the council did in November 1977. The front and rear walls of no 55 were left with a jagged edge of largely unsupported brickwork. The whole of the party wall between the two houses, consisting of two leaves of brick, one belonging to no 53 and the other to no 55, was left standing in its entirety except for a little damage. At the rear a chimney breast of no 53 was left sticking out, largely unsupported, into space.

Although the main part of the two properties front on to the public road, there was in the original design a projection at the rear with a hipped roof which looks as though it contained the kitchens with perhaps a room above each and with a chimney stack. The whole of this chimney stack was left. Number 55's half of the projection and the roof of that half was left, but no 53's half was removed so that the ridge-tiles on no 53's side were sticking out into space. At the rear as well as in the main part of the house, the party wall did not go fully up to the apex of the roof and the gaps were apparently filled by the local authority with some temporary material such as canvas or felt. The bressumer, which I have mentioned, was simply broken off where it came through the wall. Other joists which had also come through the wall were broken off and the ends were left exposed.

The next year, in 1978, some work was carried out apparently on behalf of the defendant in that the roof voids were bricked up. The canvas or felt was replaced by brickwork, a hole in the party wall made by the demolition contractors was also bricked up and some sort of waterproof covering was put over the ends of the joists, but no attempt was made to support the front or rear corners of no 55 adjoining the party wall or to point up or support the party wall itself. There are two photographs in the bundle. They were taken in 1979 and indicate the high-water mark of the defendant's work on the party wall. It appears that a lot of old plaster was left adhering to it.

Mr Bradburn, in September 1978, began proceedings in the Stockport County Court based on negligence and nuisance claiming damages for dry rot. I should say that the defendant put in a defence to that. I only mention it because it is in manuscript and perhaps reflects her own views. The particulars of claim had said in para 3 that Mr Bradburn had spoken to her and informed her of the rot and that it would spread if the defendant did nothing about it. The defence states:

> 'Paragraph 3 is untrue dry rot was never mentioned the subject under discussion was entirely different. I do not consider myself under any liability for damages to his property.'

I do not know whose writing that really is. It is in a somewhat uneducated hand, and I only mention that point because the defendant has not appeared in court or given evidence.

The county court action was transferred to the High Court in 1981. I think Mrs Bradburn, who is a joint tenant with Mr Bradburn, must also have been made a plaintiff. I am not sure about that because the papers before me seem to have differing views on the subject, but it does not I think matter. The second action was taken in the High Court by writ of 27 March 1981 and the amended statement of claim of 4 April 1982 alleges a breach of duty by the defendant to take reasonable care of her property by failing to repair it. The statement of claim says that this led to the demolition of the property and has caused loss to the plaintiffs by way of loss of support and exposure of the side of the property to rot and decay.

The pleadings are based on the assumption that the party wall, or no 53's half of the party wall, had been demolished, which appeared from the evidence not to have been the case, but the burden of the claim is, I think clear: that a breach of duty by the

defendant had occurred, a duty owed by her to the plaintiffs to keep her property in
repair. The case was put on the footing that she should have taken steps to prevent the a
dry rot spreading through to no 55, and also should have maintained it so as to provide
support and protection for no 55.

The party wall declaration which I mentioned to begin with has not really featured in
the case because the case has proceeded on the footing that it is not applicable if one party
in breach of duty makes the repairs necessary. The joint obligation to repair is only
imposed where neither side is to blame. Counsel for the defendant conceded that in the b
present case no 55 enjoys a right of support from no 53 on the principle in *Wheeldon v
Burrows* (1879) 12 Ch D 31, [1874–80] All ER Rep 669. The question therefore is the
extent of the right of support, or conversely of the duty of the defendant to provide
support. Counsel for the defendant relies on *Jones v Pritchard* [1908] 1 Ch 630, [1908–10]
All ER Rep 80. That was a case where Mr Jones's predecessor had built a house and,
contemplating there would be a house built next door on vacant land, he provided c
chimney openings and flues which such a house could use. Later Mr Pritchard bought
the land next door, built a house, and bought half the existing wall with the right to use
the flues. The case concerned the smoke from Mr Pritchard's house which found its way
into Mr Jones's rooms through cracks in Mr Jones's half of the flues. Mr Pritchard was
held not to be liable. But Parker J made some general observations first dealing with the
rights of the parties in respect of their flues ([1908] 1 Ch 630 at 637, [1908–10] All ER d
Rep 80 at 83–84):

> 'Apart from negligence or want of reasonable care and precaution, neither party
> is, in my judgment, subject to any liability to the other in respect of nuisance or
> inconvenience caused by an exercise of the rights or easements so impliedly granted
> or reserved.' e

Then, a little lower down:

> '... the general principles of the common law relating to easements are, I think,
> sufficiently defined to afford assistance in dealing with the question now at issue. In
> the first place, it appears to me that on principle the owner of a servient tenement
> cannot so deal with it as to render the easement over it incapable of being enjoyed
> or more difficult of enjoyment by the owner of the dominant tenement. On this f
> principle neither party can in the present case pull down his half of the wall or stop
> up his half of any flue used for the purpose of his neighbour's house ... neither
> party is in the present case subject to any liability if, by reason of natural decay or
> other circumstances beyond his control, his half of the wall falls down or otherwise
> passes into such a condition that the easement thereover becomes impossible or
> difficult of exercise.' g

Counsel concedes that the defendant could not pull down the property, but he says she
is not liable to repair it and, therefore, the fact that her neglect of the property led to the
demolition of the property by the local authority (which was in my view the position)
does not give the plaintiffs any cause of action. The damage was, as Parker J said, beyond
her control, that is unless she carried out repairs which counsel says she was not bound to h
do. He also referred to *Bond v Norman, Bond v Nottingham Corp* [1940] 2 All ER 12 at 18,
[1940] Ch 429 at 438–439, where Greene MR said:

> 'The nature of the right of support is not open to dispute. The owner of the
> servient tenement is under no obligation to repair that part of his building which
> provides support for his neighbour. He can let it fall into decay. If it does so, and
> support is removed, the owner of the dominant tenement has no cause for complaint. j
> On the other hand, the owner of the dominant tenement is not bound to sit by and
> watch the gradual deterioration of the support constituted by his neighbour's
> building. He is entitled to enter and take the necessary steps to ensure that the
> support continues by effecting repairs and so forth to the part of the building which

gives the support. What the owner of the servient tenement is not entitled to do, however, is by an act of his own to remove the support without providing an equivalent. There is the qualification upon his ownership of his own building that he is bound to deal with it subject to the rights in it which are vested in his neighbour, and can deal with it subject only to those rights.'

In the present case I have already said that I find the defendant knew of the dry rot at an early stage. In the *Bond* case Greene MR was dealing with the nature of the right of support, but the plaintiffs put their case on the wider ground of negligence or nuisance, and rely on the case of *Leakey v National Trust for Places of Historic Interest or Natural Beauty* [1980] 1 All ER 17, [1980] QB 485. Reading the headnote ([1980] QB 485 at 485–486):

'The plaintiff's two houses had been built to the west and at the foot of a large mound on the defendants' land. Over a period of many years, soil and rubble had fallen from the bank of the mound on to the plaintiff's lands. Falls were due to natural weathering and the nature of the soil. From 1968 at the latest, the defendants knew that the instability of their land was a threat to the plaintiff's properties because of the real possibility of falls from it of soil and other material. After a very dry summer followed by wet autumn in 1976, a large crack opened in the mound above the house of the first two plaintiffs. They drew the defendants' attention to the danger to their house from a major fall of soil, but the defendants replied that, as it was a natural movement of land, they had no responsibility for any damage caused. A few weeks later, a large quantity of earth and some tree stumps fell from the bank on to the plaintiff's land. The plaintiffs brought an action in nuisance claiming orders for abatement of the nuisance and damages.'

To put is shortly, they succeeded. I find that the defendant should reasonably have appreciated the danger to no 55 from the dry rot and from the lack of repair of no 53, and that there were steps which she could reasonably have taken to prevent the damage occurring. In my judgment she owed a duty to the plaintiffs to take reasonable steps. She failed to do so and, therefore, she is liable for the damage caused.

Counsel for the defendant urged, relying on *Bond v Norman*, that the plaintiffs should have entered on no 53 and themselves taken appropriate steps to prevent any damage occurring to no 55. This argument, I think, is effectively dealt with by Megaw LJ in *Leakey*'s case [1980] 1 All ER 17 at 34, [1980] QB 485 at 523, where he says:

'If, as a result of the working of the forces of nature, there is, poised above my land, or above my house, a boulder or a rotten tree, which is liable to fall at any moment of the day or night, perhaps destroying my house, and perhaps killing or injuring me or members of my family, am I without a remedy? . . . Must I, in such a case, if my protests to my neighbour go unheeded, sit and wait and hope that the worst will not befall? If it is said that I have in such circumstances a remedy of going on my neighbour's land to abate the nuisance, that would, or might, be an unsatisfactory remedy. But in any event, if there were such a right of abatement, it would, as counsel for the plaintiffs rightly contended, be because my neighbour owed me a duty. There is, I think, ample authority that, if I have a right of abatement, I have also a remedy in damages if the nuisance remains unabated and causes me damage or personal injury.'

He cites authority for that. So the defendant was not, in my judgment, freed from liability by the possibility that the plaintiffs may have a right of access to abate the nuisance, nor, I think, is she freed from liability by the fact that the actual demolition was carried out with her consent by the local authority when she had herself neglected to comply with the demolition order.

What then was the known risk of damage for which she is liable? Before demolition it was the risk of dry rot coming through the wall. This I think counsel concedes. It was a nuisance which the defendant allowed to spread to no 55. She should have appreciated the risks and could and should have taken steps to prevent the damage. After demolition, the main concern of the plaintiffs is the party wall, as regards its stability, first of all, and, secondly, its weatherproofing and appearance. As I have indicated, the original party wall is still standing but, of course, it was never intended to be an outside wall.

Structural engineers were called on both sides to give evidence as to the strength of the wall. That evidence I found to be of limited helpfulness because the tables and calculations on which they relied were based, I think, on the assumption that a wall would be properly built and it is not an assumption which is justified in the present case. The strength of the party wall is largely a matter of judgment. There is no doubt that at the rear of the main part of no 55 is a large area of wall in the stairwell which has little lateral support. I think that the engineers agreed that the wall was not likely to fall at once, but were not prepared to be so confident of what the position might be in five years' time. If no 53 were still standing and in reasonable repair I am satisfied that the party wall, and no 55 with it, would have had a longer life than that. And, in my judgment, the plaintiffs are entitled to some support in the centre of the wall as well as at the ends.

The engineers agreed that each end of the party wall, the front and the rear, needed building up with brick piers. The dispute was really about the length of wall between. I am satisfied that as far as stability goes work is required. The plaintiffs' experts wanted a new leaf of brickwork supported buttresses. The defendant's expert, as far as stability goes, would have been content with metal ties fixed into the walls and attached to the joists of no 55, but I was not satisfied that in the light of the evidence about the nature of the construction of the party wall that ties into it would be a satisfactory solution and, in my judgment, the support should take the form of buttresses with or without an additional brick leaf over the rest of the wall. The matter is complicated by the fact that both properties have or had large cellars. The cellar of no 53 is now a large hole beside the party wall with a certain amount of earth, rubbish and vegetation in it. The experts agree that, if that hole were to be filled in as, in my opinion, on the evidence would be really inevitable if the site of no 53 were to be redeveloped, then, under the building regulations or some such, this would not be permitted without strengthening of the party wall below ground level as the present approximately 9-inch wall is not, according to modern standards, strong enough to take the pressure from the site of no 53 if the cellar was filled in.

The plaintiffs' experts said that this should be done straight away and claim it as part of the work for which they say the defendant should be made to pay. Mr Parker, the engineer who appeared for the defendant, very frankly said at the end of his evidence that he himself if he lived in no 55 would certainly be happier with a strengthened wall and would not like to rely on the defendant to keep the cellar space of no 53 unfilled. I am satisfied that if no 53 comes to be redeveloped then this wall is something which the developer will have to build, but I think that there is no serious risk to no 55 in the mean time. A certain amount of earth and vegetation may I suppose get into the hole on no 53 but there is, in my judgment, no such present or imminent danger to no 55 as was referred to in *Batty v Metropolitan Property Realizations Ltd* [1978] 2 All ER 455, [1978] QB 554.

That leads me to the question of the finish of the party wall, that is to say to weatherproofing and appearance. Counsel for the defendant referred to *Phipps v Pears* [1964] 2 All ER 35, [1965] 1 QB 76, where the Court of Appeal decided that there is no such easement known to the law as an easement to be protected from the weather. That was a case where a house had been built right against an old house so that the wall of the new house could not be properly pointed on the outside, and then, the old house having been pulled down, damp got into the wall of the new house. There was no question there of support and no question of party walls. If I am right that the plaintiffs are entitled to require the defendant to provide support for the gable wall which I have mentioned they must, in my judgment, be entitled to have the work done to a reasonable specification so as to make good, within reason, the damage done by the defendant's neglect. This includes reasonable steps to prevent a recurrence of the dry rot from no 55 and work on the roof in order to produce a reasonable and permanent finish.

The work suggested by Mr Parker, the defendant's expert, to the roof was not ideal, but might, I think, be considered adequate in the circumstances and would involve a minimal entry into the air space of no 53. On the wall itself I think that rendering and a colouring cement wash would be satisfactory having regard to the age and condition of no 55. I accept the evidence that this could be done without building the retaining wall below the ground level or the additional brick leaf which the plaintiffs contended for. But, as I have said, I think the plaintiffs are entitled to supporting buttresses as indicated on their surveyor's report and plan. That would mean there would be three buttresses in the length of the wall apart from those at either end. They could be rendered with the wall and so would not necessarily be built of facing bricks.

Before any such work is carried out the plaintiffs are, in my judgment, entitled to have the wall treated with dry rot prevention fluid from the outside, the site of no 53. They have obtained an estimate from Rentokil Ltd for doing the work from the inside of no 55 which involves stripping all the plaster on no 55's side of the wall and then irrigating the wall. Then a builder would have to be employed (because Rentokil Ltd do not do it themselves) to put all the plaster back again. I think that the work could be done more cheaply from the outside and that it is only the cost of that for which the plaintiffs can look to the defendant.

As to all these matters there will have to be an inquiry before the district registrar to ascertain the cost of the works which I find to be the liability of the defendant. As regards dry rot penetration before the demolition of no 53 there is no difficulty there. The damages there are, I think, probably the damages in the first action and will amount to the money paid to Rentokil for what they did in 1976 (that was something over £100) and the money subsequently spent by Mr Bradburn in buying materials for work which he did himself. He produced receipts from firms called Armitage & Co (Builders' Merchants) Ltd and Sovereign Chemical Industries Ltd. All those amount to a considerable sum and no 55 is not and never was a very valuable property. I think the plaintiffs are not entitled to more than the difference between the value of no 55 as it would have been if no 53 was still standing (and not amounting to a nuisance) and its present value. This also if it cannot be agreed will have to be the subject matter of an inquiry.

Finally, I have said nothing about the rear wall of no 55 in which there are relatively minor subsidence cracks. These may, to some extent, be attributable to the demolition of no 53 and if they are I have no doubt that the strengthening works which will be carried out will prevent any further movement. In my judgment, however, they are to a very large extent due to the weakening of the rear wall of no 55 by Mr Bradburn in an unskilful building operation in 1972 when he removed a large part of the support for the rear wall in order to insert what is called a picture window, and to the vagaries of the weather thereafter, and I do not propose to award any separate damages under this head.

Judgment for the plaintiffs accordingly.

Solicitors: *Fentons Stansfield & Co*, Stockport (for the plaintiffs); *Bell Hough & Hamnett*, Stockport (for the defendant).

M Denise Chorlton Barrister.

Practice Note

COURT OF APPEAL, CIVIL DIVISION
SIR JOHN DONALDSON MR, DUNN AND PURCHAS LJJ
18 MAY 1983

Court of Appeal – Practice – Documents to be lodged by appellant – Duty to comply with rules and directions as to bundles of documents – Duty to comply with time limits – RSC Ord 59, r 9(1).

SIR JOHN DONALDSON MR made the following statement at the sitting of the court. The purpose of this statement is to remind all concerned that it is the duty of those acting for appellants to ensure that the bundles of documents lodged for the use of the court comply with the relevant rules and directions. It is also their duty to lodge the bundles within the time limit prescribed by RSC Ord 59, r 9(1), as amended. Neglect of these duties may delay the hearing of the appeal or even lead to it being struck out.

Scrutiny of the bundles submitted over the past few months has shown that there are certain errors and omissions which occur very frequently. For that reason attention is drawn in particular to the following requirements. (1) All transcripts lodged (whether of evidence or of the judgment) must be originals. Unofficial copies are not permitted (see *The Supreme Court Practice 1982* vol 1, p 939, para 59/9/2). (2) In cases where there is no official transcript of the judge's judgment (eg county court cases and certain High Court hearings in chambers) either the judge's own note of his judgment must be submitted or, where there is no such note, the counsel or solicitors who appeared in the court below must prepare an agreed note of the judge's judgment and submit it to him for his approval. A copy of the approved note of judgment must be included in each bundle. (3) In county court cases a copy of the judge's notes of evidence must be bespoken from the county court concerned and a copy of those notes must be included in each bundle. (4) Bundles must be clearly paginated and there must be an index at the front of the bundle listing all the documents and giving the page references for each one. (5) All the documents (with the exception of the transcripts) must be bound together in some form (eg ring binder, plastic binder or laced through holes in the top left-hand corner). Loose documents will not be accepted. (6) The transcripts, or judge's notes of evidence, must be bespoken as soon as the appeal is set down. Time limits will be strictly enforced except where there are very good grounds for granting an extension. An extension of time is unlikely to be obtained where the failure to lodge the bundles within the prescribed time limit is due to failure on the part of the appellant's solicitors to start soon enough on the preparation of the bundles.

Frances Rustin Barrister.

R v Maher and others

COURT OF APPEAL, CRIMINAL DIVISION
O'CONNOR LJ, PETER PAIN AND STUART-SMITH JJ
16 NOVEMBER 1982, 15 FEBRUARY 1983

Criminal law – Costs – Order to pay – Costs incurred in or about prosecution – What constitutes costs incurred in or about prosecution – Effect on order of plea of guilty – Effect on order of long term of imprisonment – Necessity for accurate estimate by Crown of costs of prosecution – Costs in Criminal Cases Act 1973, s 4(1)(a).

The 'costs incurred in or about the prosecution' which the Crown Court may order an accused to pay or contribute to, under s 4(1)(*a*)[a] of the Costs in Criminal Cases Act 1973, refers to those costs incurred by the prosecutor which the court can order to be paid out of central funds as the costs of the prosecution under s 3[b] of that Act. Accordingly, although 'costs incurred in or about the prosecution' include such items as counsel's fees, the Director of Public Prosecutions' costs and witnesses' expenses, they do not include such items as jury expenses or the costs of providing security at the trial court or the trial judge's lodgings, since they are not costs incurred by or chargeable to the prosecutor (see p 418 *j* to p 419 *e*, post).

A plea of guilty by an accused is a factor to be taken into account by the Crown Court in deciding whether to make an order against the accused under s 4(1)(*a*) of the 1973 Act, although the weight to be given by the court to a guilty plea must depend on the nature of the case and the stage of the proceedings at which the plea is offered. Furthermore, the nature of the case may make it proper to make an order for costs against an accused on whom a long term of imprisonment is imposed (see p 419 *e* to *h*, post); *R v Mathews* (1979) 1 Cr App R (S) 346 explained.

Where it seems likely that in the event of a conviction the Crown Court may be minded to make an order for costs under s 4(1)(*a*) of the 1973 Act against the accused, it is desirable that the Crown should not overestimate the costs of the prosecution (see p 419 *h j*, post).

Notes
For the award of costs as between parties in proceedings in the Crown Court, see 11 Halsbury's Laws (4th edn) para 784.

For the Costs in Criminal Cases Act 1973, ss 3, 4, see 43 Halsbury's Statutes (3rd edn) 269, 271.

Case referred to in judgment
R v Mathews (1979) 1 Cr App R (S) 346, CA.

Appeals against order for costs
At a trial held from January to July 1981 in the Crown Court at Preston before Heilbron J and a jury the appellants, Andrew Samuel Maher, Frederick Charles Russell and Alexander James Sinclair were found guilty of murder and of conspiracy to import and supply heroin, and the appellant, Leila Constance Barclay, was found guilty of conspiracy to import and supply heroin. The judge, pursuant to s 4(1) of the Costs in Criminal Cases Act 1973, made orders against the appellants to pay costs incurred in the prosecution in the sum of £1m against Sinclair, in the sum of £20,000 against Russell, in the sum of £10,000 against Maher and in the sum of £5,000 against Barclay. Pursuant to leave to appeal against sentence given to each appellant by the full court on 16 November 1982

a Section 4(1), so far as material, is set out at p 418 *j*, post
b Section 3, so far as material, is set out at p 419 *b*, post

the appellants appealed against the orders for costs. The case is reported only on the appeals against the orders for costs. The facts are set out in the judgment of the court. a

Ian Dobkin (assigned by the Registrar of Criminal Appeals) for Maher.
Stuart Shields QC and *Gerald Gouriet* for Barclay.
Stephen Batten for Russell.
Rhys E Davies QC for the Crown.
Sinclair did not appear. b

At the conclusion of the argument the court announced that it would vary the orders for costs by substituting orders to pay in the case of Sinclair of £175,000, in the case of Russell and Maher of £2,000 each and in the case of Barclay of £1,000 and that it would give its reasons later.

15 February. The following judgment of the court was delivered. c

O'CONNOR LJ. On 16 November 1982 we varied orders for costs made against Maher, Barclay, Russell and Sinclair. We give our reasons for doing so.

This case raises important matters for consideration when the Crown is exercising its discretion to make orders for costs pursuant to the Costs in Criminal Cases Act 1973. These appellants, with others, were indicted in an indictment containing three counts: d Maher, Russell and Sinclair for murder, all four for conspiracy to import heroin and conspiracy to supply heroin. Barclay pleaded guilty. Maher pleaded guilty to the two conspiracy counts, and a week after the trial started he pleaded guilty to murder. Russell pleaded guilty to the conspiracy counts, and six weeks into the trial changed his plea to guilty to murder. Sinclair pleaded guilty to the conspiracy to supply heroin and was convicted on the other two counts after a trial lasting six months. e

The heroin conspiracy formed only part of a worldwide trade controlled by Sinclair. The amounts of heroin were large and the judge had evidence that enormous sums of money were involved. Sinclair boasted of being worth £25m. The murder had been committed in order to eliminate a gang member. It was obvious to the judge that the cost of bringing these criminals to justice had been great. She was minded to make an order against some of the defendants that they should contribute to the costs of the f prosecution. The judge made inquiry into the means of the defendants. Sinclair, who had paid for his own defence and that of his girlfriend, a co-accused, said that his assets were all frozen by government order in New Zealand. Maher and Russell, defended on legal aid, said that they had no assets. Barclay, defended on legal aid, had at least £4,000. The judge did not accept these avowals of poverty and in the circumstances of this case we are satisfied that she was fully justified in coming to the conclusion that there was g money in the power of the defendants against whom she made orders for costs, even though it might prove impossible to enforce them. Next the judge asked for an estimate of the costs of the prosecution, and she got an estimate of a minimum of £1,320,000. In the exercise of her discretion, she made orders of £1m against Sinclair, £20,000 against Russell, £10,000 against Maher and £5,000 against Barclay. These orders total £1,035,000, well below the minimum estimate which had been given. h

The first complaint made about these orders for costs is that the estimate given to the judge was erroneous in that it was an overestimate by a factor of six. The extent of the overestimate depends on the meaning of 'costs' in the Costs in Criminal Cases Act 1973. Section 4 provides:

> '(1) Where a person is prosecuted or tried on indictment before the Crown Court, the court may—(*a*) if the accused is convicted, order him to pay the whole or any j part of the costs incurred in or about the prosecution and conviction, including any proceedings before the examining justices . . .'

The problem is best demonstrated by considering an item included in an attempt to justify at least half the estimate, namely £32,000 jury expenses. In one sense payments made to the jury are certainly an expense incurred in or about the prosecution and conviction of the accused, but is this item part of 'the costs'? We are clear that it is not.

'Costs' in the context of litigation, civil or criminal, does not mean 'the cost of' by whomsoever paid. In the section 'incurred' means 'incurred by the prosecutor'. The expense of providing a jury is not incurred by the prosecutor, nor is it chargeable to the prosecutor. It is not 'part of the costs incurred in or about the prosecution'. That this is so is made clear by s 3 of the 1973 Act, which provides, inter alia, for the payment out of central funds of 'the costs of the prosecution'. Section 3(3) provides:

> 'The costs payable out of central funds under the preceding provisions of this section shall be such sums as appear to the Crown Court reasonably sufficient—(*a*) to compensate the prosecutor . . . for the expenses properly incurred by him in carrying on the proceedings, and (*b*) to compensate any witness for the prosecution . . . for the expense, trouble or loss of time properly incurred in or incidental to his attendance.'

Sections 3 and 4 are in the part of the Act headed 'Awards by Crown Court'. We hold that the wording of s 4(1)(*a*) does not permit the Crown Court to order the accused to pay as costs the expense of items which it could not order as costs to be paid out of central funds.

Other suggested items were even more remote: overtime payments to, and travelling expenses of, officers engaged in the investigation, at £300,000. Similar payments for security at Lancaster Castle and the judge's lodgings, another £300,000. None of these items could be charged to the Director of Public Prosecutions and cannot be included in any bill of costs.

The only reliable figures for costs of the prosecution available to us were for counsels' fees, the Director of Public Prosecutions' costs and witnesses' expenses, which together amounted to at least £188,000. It was for this reason that we reduced the order for costs so that the total order amounted to £180,000, made up at to £175,000 against Sinclair, £2,000 against Maher and Russell and £1,000 against Barclay.

The next matter for consideration is the effect of a plea of guilty on the exercise of the discretion. The cases show that a plea of guilty is a factor to be taken into account when deciding whether to make an order. Sometimes the dicta suggest that some special reason is needed before an order for costs is made. Thus in *R v Mathews* (1979) 1 Cr App R (S) 346 an impecunious woman aged 20 had been fined £300 for handling and ordered to pay £50 to the costs of the prosecution. Reducing the fine to £25, Lord Widgery CJ said (at 347): 'Furthermore we do not see any reason why she should pay the costs of the prosecution having regard to the fact that she pleaded guilty.'

We are satisfied that the court was not saying that the discretion to make an order ought not to be exercised in cases where there had been a plea of guilty, save in exceptional circumstances. The case decided no more than, on its facts, no order should have been made. It is well established that orders for costs should not be made which are beyond the means of the accused. The weight to be given to a plea of guilty must depend on the nature of the case and the stage of the proceedings when it is offered. In the present case Barclay pleaded guilty at the earliest opportunity, Maher and Russell during the trial. The pleas of guilty are to their credit, but the nature of the case was such that we are satisfied that it was proper to make orders against all three.

The nature of the case also makes it proper to make orders for costs against accused on whom long terms of imprisonment were imposed.

Before we leave the case we should like to say that in cases where it seems likely that in the event of a conviction the court may be minded to make an order for costs, it is desirable that the prosecution should be in a position to give an estimate of the costs of the prosecution, and that the estimate given should be one that will not be an overestimate.

Appeals allowed.

Solicitors: *Baldwin Mellor & Co* (for Barclay and Russell); *Director of Public Prosecutions.*

April Weiss Barrister.

R v Immigration Appeal Tribunal, ex parte Khan (Mahmud) a

COURT OF APPEAL, CIVIL DIVISION
LORD LANE CJ, ACKNER AND OLIVER LJJ
12, 13 JANUARY 1983 b

Immigration – Appeal – Reasons for decision – Immigration Appeal Tribunal – Appeal against deportation order made on ground that applicant had entered into marriage of convenience – Tribunal dismissing appeal – Reasons for decision not making it apparent, directly or by inference, that tribunal had considered all elements constituting marriage of convenience – Whether failure to give adequate reasons an error of law. c

The applicant, a citizen of Pakistan, married a United Kingdom citizen who was a convicted prostitute. Subsequently the applicant was given indefinite leave to stay in the United Kingdom. He later applied to be registered as a citizen of the United Kingdom, at which stage inquiries were made which raised the suspicion that his marriage was one of convenience and led the Secretary of State to serve a deportation order on the applicant under the Immigration Act 1971. The order stated that, because his marriage was one of d convenience entered into to obtain settlement in the United Kingdom and without the intention of living permanently with the woman he had married, his deportation was conducive to the public good. The applicant appealed against the order to the Immigration Appeal Tribunal, which dismissed the appeal. It was clear from the reasons given by the tribunal that it only considered whether the marriage was entered into to evade the immigration laws and not whether the applicant ever intended to live permanently with e the woman. The applicant applied for certiorari to quash the tribunal's decision and mandamus requiring the tribunal to rehear the appeal, on the ground that the tribunal erred in law in failing to consider whether the applicant ever intended to live permanently with the woman. The judge dismissed the application and the applicant appealed.

Held – The appeal would be allowed for the following reasons— f

(1) A tribunal dealing with immigration matters had to give sufficient reasons for its decision to make it apparent to the parties, directly or by inference, that it had considered the point in issue between the parties, and was further required to indicate the evidence which formed the basis of its decision (see p 423 *a* to *d* and p 424 *a b*, post); dictum of Donaldson P in *Alexander Machinery (Dudley) Ltd v Crabtree* [1974] ICR at 122 applied.

(2) Since in order to establish that a marriage was one of convenience it was necessary g to prove both that the marriage was entered into for the primary purpose of evading the immigration laws and that the parties to the marriage did not intend to live together permanently as man and wife, since it was not directly apparent from the tribunal's decision that it had considered the necessity for the Secretary of State to prove the applicant's lack of intention to live permanently with the woman he had married, and since it could not be inferred from the tribunal's decision that it had considered that h matter (even though the deportation order was before it when it was considering the case), it followed that the reasons for the decision were insufficiently stated and the necessary basis for upholding the decision was absent. Furthermore, the tribunal had not satisfactorily delineated those parts of the evidence it accepted and those parts it rejected. Accordingly, the tribunal's decision would be quashed and the matter remitted for hearing by a differently constituted tribunal (see p 422 *b c* and p 423 *d* to *g* and *j* to p 424 j *b*, post).

Notes

For appeals against a deportation order, and for the procedure before the Immigration Appeal Tribunal, see 4 Halsbury's Laws (4th edn) paras 1019, 1024–1026.

For the Immigration Act 1971, see 41 Halsbury's Statutes (3rd edn) 12.

Cases referred to in judgments

Alexander Machinery (Dudley) Ltd v Crabtree [1974] ICR 120, NIRC.
Norton Tool Co Ltd v Tewson [1973] 1 All ER 183, [1973] 1 WLR 45, NIRC.

Appeal

The applicant, Mahmud Khan, a citizen of Pakistan, appealed against the decision of Stephen Brown J, hearing the Crown Office list, on 20 April 1982 whereby he refused to grant the applicant judicial review by way of (1) an order of certiorari to quash a decision of the Immigration Appeal Tribunal, notified to the applicant on 23 March 1981 and (2) an order of mandamus requiring the tribunal to rehear the appeal according to law. The principal ground of the appeal was that the tribunal erred in law and misdirected themselves in treating a marriage entered into between the applicant and a woman who was a citizen of the United Kingdom as one of convenience. The facts are set out in the judgment of Lord Lane CJ.

John R Macdonald QC and *Kathryn Cronin* for the applicant.
David Latham for the tribunal.

LORD LANE CJ. This is another immigration appeal. It arises from a decision by Stephen Brown J, and concerns a man called Mahmud Khan.

The case is yet another case of alleged marriage of convenience, and the chronology of events leading up to the hearing before the Immigration Appeal Tribunal and thence before Stephen Brown J are these. The applicant married Cynthia Mitchell on 30 June 1975. She was at that time a prostitute with a number of convictions for prostitution and kindred offences in her past. The applicant on 10 September was given indefinite leave to stay in this country. He is a citizen of Pakistan, and he is now some 37 or 38 years of age. In July 1977 he returned to Pakistan and came back to this country on 11 June 1978 with his parents, who were admitted as dependants. Consequently in this country were his father, his mother, his two sisters and their children and his brother, all of them being lawfully here.

On 9 July 1980, as a result of inquiries which had been made, he was served with a deportation order under s 3(5)(*b*) of the Immigration Act 1971. The reasons for the inquiries being made were that he had applied to be registered as a citizen of the United Kingdom. Inquiries followed as a matter of course, and the result of those inquiries, for reasons which will emerge in a moment, were to raise a suspicion, certainly in the mind of the Secretary of State, that this was a man whose presence in the country was not conducive to the public good.

On 21 July 1980 the applicant set out his side of the matter, where the first ground of appeal reads as follows:

> 'That the marriage of Mahmud Khan to Cynthia Mitchell on the 30th June 1975 was not a marriage of convenience, the parties at the time of the marriage intending to live together permanently as man and wife.'

The Secretary of State's grounds for deportation are to be found on the previous page and read as follows:

> 'To Mahmud Khan: The Secretary of State has reason to believe that your marriage to Cynthia Mitchell at Bradford Register Office on 30 June 1975 was one of convenience entered into to obtain your settlement in the United Kingdom with no intention that you should live together permanently as man and wife. Having regard to this the Secretary of State considers it conducive to the public good to make a deportation order against you.'

There you have the Secretary of State setting out accurately and in concise form the two ingredients of a marriage of convenience: first of all, the marriage is entered into for the primary purpose of evading the immigration law and rules, and, second, the necessity of there being no intention, or a lack of intention to live together permanently as man and wife. I emphasise that, if one may so, by drawing attention to the ground of appeal which I have already read, which confines the issue simply to the latter part of the definition of the marriage of convenience, namely no intention to live together permanently as man and wife.

Consequently when, as in due course, the matter came before the appeal tribunal, one would have expected the issue to be perfectly plain and to have been set out perfectly plainly by the tribunal in its reasons. Of course there was only one issue here. It was apparent that the primary reason for the marriage when it took place had been to try to escape from the tentacles of the immigration laws. The real question was, or should have been, whether this marriage was one in which the husband had intended permanently to live with his wife after the marriage had taken place.

We have been referred helpfully by counsel for the applicant, whose submissions have been accurate, helpful and extremely concise, to a decision of Donaldson P in the Industrial Relations Court in *Alexander Machinery (Dudley) Ltd v Crabtree* [1974] ICR 120 and to the following passage (at 122):

> 'We have already said that it is unsatisfactory and amounts to an error of law for a tribunal simply to state the amount of compensation which is to be awarded without showing how that figure has been arrived at: see *Norton Tool Co. Ltd.* v. *Tewson* ([1973] 1 All ER 183, [1973] 1 WLR 45). The basis of this proposition is that in the absence of reasons it is impossible to determine whether or not there has been an error of law. Failure to give reasons therefore amounts to a denial of justice and is itself an error of law. In the present case it is clear that the whole argument which the employers wish to address to us depends upon the tribunal's evaluation of the evidence relating to the reasons for the employee's dismissal and the reasonableness of the employers' conduct in all the circumstances in dismissing him on the basis of those reasons. The tribunal said that they were not satisfied with the reasons set out but gave no detailed explanation of why they were not satisfied. Whilst there can be no appeal from findings of fact, the absence of evidence to support a particular finding is an error of law. Similarly a finding of fact or a refusal to find a fact will involve an error of law if the finding or refusal is a conclusion which no tribunal, properly directing itself, could reach on the basis of the evidence which has been given and accepted by it. I stress the word "accepted" because it is important that tribunals, in reaching findings of fact, should set out in substance what evidence they do or do not accept. When the matter is reconsidered by this tribunal, no further evidence should be called, but the parties will be entitled, if they wish, to elaborate their contentions based on the evidence which has been given. We trust that the tribunal will record those contentions and make all necessary findings of fact in relation to them. The tribunal should also state briefly, if appropriate, why they find or do not find a particular fact—stating, for example, that they are not satisfied in relation to the evidence given by a particular witness, or that they are satisfied, and so on. It is impossible for us to lay down any precise guidelines. The overriding test must always be: is the tribunal providing both parties with the materials which will enables them to know that the tribunal has made no error of law in reaching its findings of fact? We do not think that the brief reasons set out here suffice for that purpose.'

Those final remarks in the last two sentences that I have read are proper guidelines for tribunals dealing with immigration matters.

Speaking for myself, I would not go so far as to indorse the proposition set forth by Donaldson P that any failure to give reasons means a denial of justice and is itself an error of law. The important matter which must be borne in mind by tribunals in the present type of circumstances is that it must be apparent from what they state by way of reasons first of all that they have considered the point which is at issue between the parties, and they should indicate the evidence on which they have come to their conclusions.

Where one gets a decision of a tribunal which either fails to set out the issue which the tribunal is determining either directly or by inference, or fails either directly or by inference to set out the basis on which it has reached its determination on that issue, then that is a matter which will be very closely regarded by this court, and in normal circumstances will result in the decision of the tribunal being quashed. The reason is this. A party appearing before a tribunal is entitled to know, either expressly stated by it or inferentially stated, what it is to which the tribunal is addressing its mind. In some cases it may be perfectly obvious without any express reference to it by the tribunal; in other cases it may not. Second, the appellant is entitled to know the basis of fact on which the conclusion has been reached. Once again in many cases it may be quite obvious without the necessity of expressly stating it, in other cases it may not.

Turning to the circumstances in the present case, there is no necessity for me to read the findings of the tribunal. We have been helped by counsel for the applicant and also by the submissions of counsel on behalf of the tribunal by the concession, which is obvious if one reads the reasons, that the tribunal nowhere states the two legs of a marriage of convenience. It nowhere states that it is addressing its mind to the important leg in this case, namely the necessity to prove that the applicant had no intention of living permanently with the woman Cynthia. Consequently that necessary basis for the upholding of the decision is absent. It cannot be read inferentially from its decision. It is true that both the notice of appeal and the deportation order by the Secretary of State contained the ingredients. It is perfectly true that these two documents would of necessity be before the tribunal when it was considering this matter. But it is by no means certain from the language that it used in its findings that the tribunal considered anything other than the other leg, namely the use of the marriage in an endeavour to evade the provisions of the immigration law and rules. Consequently on that basis alone it seems to me that the appeal should be allowed.

Second, although I am, speaking for myself, less impressed by this ground, it does not satisfactorily delineate those parts of the evidence of the applicant, and indeed of Cynthia, which it accepts and those parts which it does not. The expression that is used is as follows:

> 'We regret to say that there are aspects of the [applicant's] evidence which we are unable to believe—notably that he was unaware of Cynthia Mitchell's character when he married her, and that he had no idea that the marriage would facilitate his remaining in this country.'

But that remark is pregnant with the suggestion that there are other aspects of his evidence, and indeed that of the other witnesses, which it did believe and it does not vouchsafe which is which.

It is arguable, and may very well be the case, that the tribunal, once it came to the conclusion, as it apparently did, that this man knew from the start, certainly before they got married, that this woman Cynthia was a prostitute, considered that to be the end of the matter and that no further discussion was required. That is speculation. I myself am not prepared to base my decision on the assumption that that was so.

Therefore without going any further, it seems to me that these reasons are unsatisfactory. The tribunal's decision should be quashed. It should go back to be dealt with again, either by this tribunal or preferably, one imagines, by a differently constituted tribunal, so that the matter can be reconsidered. One hopes on this occasion the basis of the decision both in law and in fact will be properly expressed one way or the other.

I accordingly would allow this appeal.

ACKNER LJ. I agree.

OLIVER LJ. I also agree.

Appeal allowed. Matter remitted to be heard by a differently constituted tribunal.

Solicitors: *Howard Cohen & Co*, Leeds (for the applicant); *Treasury Solicitor*.

Sepala Munasinghe Esq Barrister.

Lloyds Bank plc v Ellis-Fewster and another

COURT OF APPEAL, CIVIL DIVISION
SIR JOHN DONALDSON MR AND DILLON LJ
28 FEBRUARY 1983

Practice – Summary judgment – Leave to defend – Appeal – Judge giving plaintiffs leave to sign judgment in respect of part of claim but granting defendants unconditional leave to defend as to remainder of claim – Grounds on which Court of Appeal will interfere with exercise of judge's discretion – RSC Ord 14.

In 1978 a company, which carried on business in the motor trade, obtained overdraft facilities from a bank for the sale and lease-back of two cars for the use of the defendants, who were two of the directors of the company. At the bank's request, the defendants both signed unlimited guarantees of the company's liability to the bank, and a second account (the no 2 account) was opened in the name of the company to meet the payments for the leasing of the vehicles. By 1981 the company's liability to the bank exceeded £100,000 and the company went into liquidation. The bank issued a writ against the defendants as guarantors, claiming the full amount of the company's indebtedness and applied for summary judgment under RSC Ord 14. The defendants sought leave to defend, contending (i) that they were entitled to relief since there was a relationship of confidence between the bank and themselves and the effect of the guarantee had not been fully explained to them, alternatively (ii) that they were entitled to rectification of the guarantees since there had been a previous agreement between themselves and the bank that the guarantees were limited to the company's no 2 account only. The judge rejected the defendants' first contention but held that there was an arguable case for rectification. He accordingly ordered the defendants to pay to the bank the sum of £36,500 outstanding in the no 2 account and granted them unconditional leave to defend. The defendants appealed and the bank, by a respondent's notice, claimed judgment, contending that there was no arguable defence by way of rectification.

Held – Where the triability of an issued depended on fact, as opposed to law, the court was unlikely to interfere with the discretion of the judge at first instance. The question whether there was a triable issue as to rectification was a matter for the judge's discretion and he had decided that there was a triable issue, and further that there was no arguable defence to the claim for the sum due on the no 2 account. Accordingly, since there was nothing to indicate that the judge had exercised his discretion wrongly, the court would not intervene and the appeal would be dismissed (see p 426 *f* to *h* and p 427 *a b*, post).

Per curiam. Although a plaintiff may appeal against the grant of unconditional leave to defend, it does not follow that the Court of Appeal will regularly question decisions of

the judge at first instance where leave to defend has been granted on the basis that there
a is a triable issue of fact (see p 426 *g h* and p 427 *b*, post).

Notes

For means by which a defendant may resist an application for summary judgment under RSC Ord 14, see 37 Halsbury's Laws (4th edn) paras 413–415, 419, and for cases on the subject, see 50 Digest (Repl) 410–414, *1183–1227*.

b

Case referred to in judgments

Contract Discount Corp Ltd v Furlong [1948] 1 All ER 274, CA.

Cases also cited

Joscelyne v Nissen [1970] 1 All ER 1213, [1970] 2 QB 86, CA.
c *Lloyds Bank Ltd v Bundy* [1974] 3 All ER 757, [1975] QB 326, CA.

Interlocutory appeals

By a writ issued on 14 December 1981 the plaintiffs, Lloyds Bank plc, claimed against the first defendant, Penelope Letitia Wyvol Ellis-Fewster, the sum of £99,787·33, and against the second defendant, George Ellis Taylor Ellis-Fewster, the sum of £103,783·18,
d together with interest, being the extent of the liability of Carnies of Chelsea Ltd (the company) and being moneys due under a guarantee dated 14 December 1978 and signed by the defendants whereby they jointly and severally guaranteed payment on demand of all moneys and liabilities of the company. On 22 October 1982 Bingham J gave judgment for the bank for £36,500 (being the sum outstanding on the company's no 2 account at the bank's St James's Street branch) but granted the defendants unconditional leave to
e defend as to the balance of the sums claimed. The defendants appealed on the grounds, inter alia, (i) that the bank owed the defendants a fiduciary duty to explain the nature of the guarantee and had failed to do so, and (ii) that having determined that there was an arguable defence for rectification the judge should have left the trial judge to determine the precise sum owing in the event of the defendants succeeding. By a respondents' notice dated 14 December 1982 the bank contended that there was no arguable defence
f for rectification and sought judgment in the full sum. The facts are set out in the judgment of Sir John Donaldson MR.

Geoffrey D Conlin for the first defendant.
John Weeks for the second defendant.
Peter Cresswell for the bank.

g

SIR JOHN DONALDSON MR. We are concerned this morning with three appeals from a judgment of Bingham J given on 22 October 1982 whereby he ordered the defendants to pay the plaintiffs the sum of £36,500 as representing money outstanding on the no 2 account of Carnies of Chelsea Ltd (in liquidation) at the plaintiffs' St James's Street branch to the extent that the account was used for the purpose of leasing Rolls-
h Royce and BMW motor cars for the first and second defendants respectively.

That so stated may be a little incomprehensible. Let me therefore briefly set the scene. The bank was approached by Carnies of Chelsea to provide them with overdraft facilities for their business in the motor trade, including the leasing of motor cars. Mr and Mrs Ellis-Fewster, who had banked with the bank for many years, were interested in Carnies of Chelsea and the activities of that company in two ways. First, they were interested in
j the company. Second, they were interested in using the company as a vehicle for sale and leaseback transactions in connection with the Rolls-Royce and BMW mentioned in the judge's order. They both signed unlimited guarantees of the company's liability to the bank. As is always the case in transactions of this nature which reach the courts, the company was not as successful as all concerned hoped and the overdraft rose and rose, and at the present time a sum of something of the order of £100,000 is owed to the bank.

That was the amount of the claim, subject to a minor adjustment in the case of Mrs Ellis-Fewster who had paid a small sum on account. The bank claimed that sum from the two *a* defendants under the unlimited guarantee when the claim was put forward under RSC Ord 14.

Bingham J decided that there was an arguable case for saying that the guarantee should not be given effect to in its unlimited form, but could possibly be rectified so as to limit it to the no 2 account to the extent that that account was used for the purpose of leasing the Rolls-Royce and BMW motor cars. *b*

The possible justification for that view is to be found principally in a letter of 8 December 1978 in which the bank manager for the plaintiffs writes to Mrs Ellis-Fewster saying:

> 'I am sorry that I was not in when you telephoned yesterday regarding the arrangements for Carnies of Chelsea Limited to have facilities on a No. 2 account in connection with the leasing of your Rolls Royce and Geoff's B.M.W. I am of course *c* perfectly happy to make the facilities available to the Company and I understand that you and Geoff will give a guarantee to cover them.'

There are other letters to a somewhat similar effect, and there is also an internal memorandum dated 8 December 1978 from the manager to a Mr Wells, the manager of the Battle branch (the local branch where the Ellis-Fewsters were going to sign the *d* guarantee), saying:

> 'You will see that I have made the form unlimited and I would explain that the arrangement is for us to provide facilities on a separate account for the Company to pay monthly payments in respect of the lease of two cars for the use of the Ellis-Fewsters.'

e

On the face of those two letters, I can well understand the judge thinking there was a triable issue that this guarantee should be rectified; although, in fairness to the bank, I must make it clear that there is a strong case against it on the basis of failure to reply to various statements made in correspondence and so on.

This was essentially a matter for the judge's discretion. He thought there was a triable issue. In a case where the triability of the issue depends on evidence as opposed to law, I *f* would think it a very surprising situation if the Court of Appeal was prepared to disturb the judge's view. If one judge thinks there is a triable issue, it would be surprising if two or three judges think there is not. It is quite different if you are dealing with a triable issue which arises as a matter of law. When it arises as a matter of evidence and fact, it is most unlikely that the Court of Appeal would interfere with the discretion of the judge below. Of course, it is only recently that it has been possible to appeal at all against the *g* decision of the judge of first instance that there should be unconditional leave to defend. I cannot believe that it was ever intended that the Court of Appeal should move into a new era in which it regularly questions decisions of judges to grant leave to defend on the basis that there is a triable issue of fact. However, for my part I can see no possible grounds for dissenting from the judge's view in this case.

But then it is said by the two defendants, 'Nevertheless there should be unconditional *h* leave to defend because it is quite impossible in the present instance to decide what is due.' Accordingly, in reliance on the decision of this court in *Contract Discount Corp Ltd v Furlong* [1948] 1 All ER 274, the proper order was said to be a judgment for such sum as may be found due on the taking of account. For my part I would like to reserve the question of the lengths to which that decision goes because I do not think it arises in this case. The judge decided in principle that there was no defence to a claim for the sum due *j* on that account in so far as the account was used for the purpose of leasing the two cars. He then turned to counsel and solicitors representing the two parties and said: 'Please work out what that would amount to in figures.' They went away and worked it out. They came back with a figure agreed as being the monetary result of the judge's judgment. It seems to me in the face of that situation that it is quite impossible to cavil at the sum for which judgment has been given. It does not mean to say of course that the whole of the account will not be open for examination in the ultimate trial, but these sums, in so far as they are paid under the judgment, will be treated as payments on account.

The judge exercised his discretion. I can see nothing wrong in the way in which he exercised it. Accordingly I would not intervene either in favour of the defendants or in favour of the plaintiffs.

DILLON LJ. I entirely agree and have nothing to add.

Appeals dismissed.

Solicitors: *Beeney & Co*, Reigate (for the first defendant); *F B Jevons Riley & Pope*, Tonbridge (for the second defendant); *Cameron Markby* (for the bank).

Diana Procter Barrister.

R v Mitchell

COURT OF APPEAL, CRIMINAL DIVISION
PURCHAS LJ, TALBOT AND STAUGHTON JJ
1, 18 FEBRUARY 1983

Criminal law – Manslaughter – Causing death by unlawful act – Dangerous act – Chain of causation – Accused assaulting third party causing him to fall against victim – Victim receiving injuries in fall and later dying as a result of injuries – Whether unlawful and dangerous act must be aimed at victim – Whether unlawful and dangerous act must be a direct attack or impact on victim – Whether accused guilty of manslaughter.

The appellant became involved in an altercation with A. He struck or threw A causing him to fall accidentally against B and both A and B fell to the ground. B was injured in the fall and later died in hospital as a result of her injuries. The appellant was convicted of manslaughter for the unlawful killing of B. He appealed against the conviction contending (i) that to constitute the offence of manslaughter the unlawful and dangerous act had to be aimed at, or involve a direct attack or impact on, the person who died and (ii) that the judge should have directed the jury that the appellant was not guilty if he had not committed the act intentionally.

Held – (1) To establish the offence of manslaughter of the type of which the appellant had been convicted it had to be shown (a) that he had committed an unlawful act, (b) that the act was dangerous in the sense that a sober and reasonable person would inevitably recognise that it carried some risk of harm, (c) that the act was a substantial cause of death and (d) that he intended to commit the act, as distinct from intending its consequences. It did not matter that the act had been aimed at some person other than the victim or that the death had not arisen due to some immediate impact on, or physical contact with, the victim since the primary question was one of causation, i e whether the appellant's act caused the victim's death. Moreover, it was open to the jury on the evidence before them to conclude that it had been the cause of death (see p 429 *e f*, p 431 *h j* and p 432 *d g*, post); *R v Pagett* (1983) Times, 4 February applied.

(2) Furthermore, although a judge should normally direct a jury that the act relied on for an offence of manslaughter must have been a deliberate or intentional act, the judge's failure to give that direction was immaterial since all of the appellant's actions, whether hitting, pushing, grabbing or throwing, were obviously and admittedly deliberate actions. Accordingly the appeal would be dismissed (see p 433 *b* to *e*, post).

Notes

For manslaughter by killing by an unlawful act, see 11 Halsbury's Laws (4th edn) para *a*
1169, and for cases on the subject, see 15 Digest (Reissue) 1137–1140, *9616–9656*.

Cases referred to in judgment

DPP v Newbury [1976] 2 All ER 365, [1977] AC 500, [1976] 2 WLR 918, HL.
R v Church [1965] 2 All ER 72, [1966] 1 QB 59, [1965] 2 WLR 1220, CA.
R v Dalby [1982] 1 All ER 916, [1982] 1 WLR 425, CA. *b*
R v Larkin [1943] 1 All ER 217, CA.
R v Latimer (1886) 17 QBD 359.
R v Pagett (1983) Times, 4 February, CA.

Appeal

The appellant, Ronald James Mitchell, was convicted on 21 July 1982 at the Central *c*
Criminal Court, before his Honour Judge Abdela QC and a jury, of manslaughter (count one) and of assault occasioning actual bodily harm (count two) and sentenced to 27 months' imprisonment on count one and 9 months' imprisonment on count two, to be served concurrently. He applied for leave to appeal against his conviction on count one and against sentence. The facts are set out in the judgment of the court.

d

Rosina Hare QC and *W R Powell* for Mitchell.
Oliver Sells for the Crown.

At the conclusion of the argument the court announced that the appeal would be dismissed for reasons to be given later.

e

18 February. The following judgment of the court was delivered.

STAUGHTON J. Ronald James Mitchell was tried on 19, 20 and 21 July 1982 at the Central Criminal Court, before his Honour Judge Abdela QC and a jury, on an indictment containing two counts, count one was a charge of manslaughter, in that he unlawfully killed Anne Crafts. Count two charged that he assaulted Edward Smith thereby *f*
occasioning him actual bodily harm. It will be noticed that there were two different victims. That is what gives rise to the main problem in this appeal. The appellant was convicted by a majority verdict of eleven to one on count one, and unanimously on count two. He was sentenced to 27 months' imprisonment on count one and to nine months' imprisonment on count two, the sentences to run concurrently.

On 1 February 1983 there were before this court applications for leave to appeal against *g*
conviction and sentence. Leave to appeal against conviction was granted, and the appellant's counsel consented to the application being treated as the hearing of the appeal. But the appeal against conviction was dismissed. Leave to appeal against sentence was refused. The court announced that its reasons would be given at a later date. This we now do.

The facts alleged by the prosecution at the trial were briefly as follows. On 26 March *h*
1981 Mitchell, who was aged 22 at the time, was in a busy post office at Tottenham. An altercation arose when he tried to force himself into a queue or in some other way to be served before those who had been waiting longer than he had. A Mr Edward Smith, who was aged 72, spoke to him about his behaviour. There was some argument, and Mitchell hit Mr Smith in the mouth, causing him to stagger back and hit the back of his head against a glass panel above the post office counter. The glass panel shattered. Mr Smith *j*
recovered and moved forward. Mitchell then either hit Mr Smith again or else threw him, so that he fell into other people who were waiting in the post office. Mr Smith fell against Mrs Anne Crafts, a lady aged 89. Both Mr Smith and Mrs Crafts fell to the ground. Mr Smith suffered a bruise in the back of his head, and his lower lip was cut and swollen. Mrs Crafts suffered a broken femur. She was taken to hospital, and on 31 March

1981 an operation was performed to replace her hip joint. She appeared to make a satisfactory recovery, but on 2 April 1981 she died suddenly. The cause of death was pulmonary embolism caused by thrombosis of the left leg veins, which in turn was caused by fracture of the femur.

Some of those facts were disputed at the trial. There was conflicting evidence as to who struck what blows, and the issue of self-defence was raised. The jury evidently accepted, at least in substance, the facts alleged by the prosecution; they likewise evidently found that self-defence had been disproved. No complaint is made about the summing up or the verdicts in relation to those matters. No ground of appeal is advanced in relation to the conviction for assault occasioning actual bodily harm on Mr Smith. But in relation to count one (manslaughter) it is argued that the learned judge (i) wrongly failed to accede to a defence submission that there was no case to answer, (ii) misdirected the jury in failing to tell them that an unlawful and dangerous act, for the purposes of manslaughter, had to be directed at the victim, that is to say the person whose death was caused, (iii) failed to direct the jury that the unlawful and dangerous act had to be deliberate, in that the accused must be shown to have intended to do the act in question.

Grounds (i) and (ii) raised one and the same point, as counsel for Mitchell agreed. Ground (iii) did not feature in the grounds of appeal, but no objection was taken to its being argued.

What is said on grounds (i) and (ii) is that Mitchell aimed no blow at Mrs Crafts, nor did he hit or touch her. The conviction on count two, of assault occasioning actual bodily harm, showed that he committed an unlawful and dangerous act. But it was argued that to establish manslaughter the unlawful and dangerous act had to be directed at the person whose death was caused.

Both counsel were agreed that there are four elements in this class of manslaughter, as follows: first, there must be an act which is unlawful; second, it must be a dangerous act, in the sense that a sober and reasonable person would inevitably recognise that it carried some risk of harm, albeit not serious harm (that being an objective test); third, the act must be a substantial cause of death; fourth, the act itself must be intentional. No question relating to any other class of manslaughter (such as manslaughter by gross negligence) arose in this case.

The main question argued was whether the person at whom the act is aimed must also be the person whose death is caused. On that question, it was suggested, there is no authority directly in point. Counsel for Mitchell also argued that the act must have been directed at the victim in the sense, as we understand the point, that it must have had some immediate impact on the victim. For that proposition the case of *R v Dalby* [1982] 1 All ER 916, [1982] 1 WLR 425 was said to be authority.

There are cases which apparently support the first part of this argument. Thus in *R v Larkin* [1943] 1 All ER 217 at 219 Humphreys J referred to 'an act which is likely to injure another person, and quite inadvertently [the doer of the act] causes the death of *that* other person.' Similarly in *R v Church* [1965] 2 All ER 72 at 76, [1966] 1 QB 59 at 70 Edmund Davies J said 'the unlawful act must be such as all sober and reasonable people would inevitably recognise must subject *the* other person to, at least, the risk of some harm resulting therefrom, albeit not serious harm.' (My emphasis in both cases.)

However, in neither case was there any question raised of an act, which carried the risk of harm to A, in fact causing the death of B. We cannot treat either case as authority on that question. It is possible that such a question could have been raised in *Larkin*, but it was not.

Nor does any such question appear to have been raised in the leading case of *DPP v Newbury* [1976] 2 All ER 365, [1977] AC 500 although it might have been. There two youths aged 15 were on a railway bridge. One of them pushed part of a paving-stone over the bridge parapet towards an oncoming train. It fell on the driver's cab, killing the guard, who was sitting next to the driver. Both were convicted of manslaughter of the guard. Their convictions were upheld by the House of Lords.

Presumably it could have been said that the act of the two youths was aimed at the driver, if at anyone, or perhaps at the passengers, if there were any; it may be that the guard was the least likely to be injured, unless it were known that he was travelling in the front of the train. However, no argument on those lines appears to have been advanced. The whole contest was as to mens rea. It was argued that the youths themselves had to be proved to have foreseen that they might cause harm to someone. That argument was rejected. Lord Salmon said ([1976] 2 All ER 365 at 366–367, [1977] AC 500 at 506–507):

> 'The learned trial judge did not direct the jury that they should acquit the appellants unless they were satisfied beyond a reasonable doubt that the appellants had foreseen that they might cause harm to someone by pushing the piece of paving stone off the parapet into the path of the approaching train. In my view the learned trial judge was quite right not to give such a direction to the jury. The direction which he gave is completely in accordance with established law, which, possibly with one exception to which I shall presently refer, has never been challenged. In *R v Larkin* [1943] 1 All ER 217 at 219 Humphreys J said: "Where the act which a person is engaged in performing is unlawful, then if at the same time it is a dangerous act, that is, an act which is likely to injure another person, and quite inadvertently he causes the death of that other person by that act, then he is guilty of manslaughter." I agree entirely with Lawton LJ that that is an admirably clear statement of the law which has been applied many times. It makes it plain (a) that an accused is guilty of manslaughter if it is proved that he intentionally did an act which was unlawful and dangerous and that that act inadvertently caused death and (b) that it is unnecessary to prove that the accused knew that the act was unlawful or dangerous. This is one of the reasons why cases of manslaughter vary so infinitely in their gravity. They may amount to little more than pure inadvertence and sometimes to little less than murder. I am sure that in *R v Church* [1965] 2 All ER 72, [1966] 1 QB 59 Edmund Davies J, in giving the judgment of the court, did not intend to differ from or qualify anything which had been said in *R v Larkin* [1943] 1 All ER 217 at 219. Indeed he was restating the principle laid down in that case by illustrating the sense in which the word "dangerous" should be understood. Edmund Davies J said ([1965] 2 All ER at 76, [1966] 1 QB 59 at 70): "For such a verdict [guilty of manslaughter] inexorably to follow, the unlawful act must be such as all sober and reasonable people would inevitably recognise must subject the other person to, at least, the risk of some harm resulting therefrom, albeit not serious harm." The test is still the objective test. In judging whether the act was dangerous, the test is not did the accused recognise that it was dangerous but would all sober and reasonable people recognise its danger.'

He went on to say that juries should continue to be directed in accordance with the law as laid down in *Larkin* and *Church*.

We do not read Lord Salmon as saying that the unlawful and dangerous act must necessarily be aimed at the same other person whose death is caused. No such limitation was contended for in the House of Lords. If it had been, it was at least open to question, as we have suggested, whether the act of the youths was aimed at the guard; and therefore it would have had to be considered whether on that different ground their convictions should be quashed.

Then there is *R v Dalby*. The facts there were that the appellant obtained on prescription some diconal tablets, a class A controlled drug. He supplied some of those tablets to a friend who was also an addict, and each injected himself intravenously. They then parted company for the evening, and the friend, with the assistance of some other person, took two further injections of an unspecified substance. Later the friend died. The prosecution alleged that the supply of diconal caused the friend's death. The appellant was convicted of manslaughter. His appeal was allowed by this court. Waller LJ, delivering the judgment of the court, said ([1982] 1 All ER 916 at 919, [1982] 1 WLR 425 at 428–429):

> 'The difficulty in the present case is that the act of supplying a controlled drug
> a was not an act which caused direct harm. It was an act which made it possible, or even likely, that harm would occur subsequently, particularly if the drug was supplied to somebody who was on drugs. In all the reported cases, the physical act has been one which inevitably would subject the other person to the risk of some harm from the act itself. In this case, the supply of drugs would itself have caused no harm unless the deceased had subsequently used the drugs in a form and quantity
> b which was dangerous ... In the judgment of this court, the unlawful act of supplying drugs was not an act directed against the person of O'Such and the supply did not cause any direct injury to him. The kind of harm envisaged in all the reported cases of involuntary manslaughter was physical injury of some kind as an immediate and inevitable result of the unlawful act, eg a blow on the chin which knocks the victim against a wall causing a fractured skull and death, or threatening
> c with a loaded gun which accidentally fires, or dropping a large stone on a train (see *DPP v Newbury*) or threatening another with an open razor and stumbling with death resulting (see *R v Larkin*). In the judgment of this court, where the charge of manslaughter is based on an unlawful and dangerous act, it must be an act directed at the victim and likely to cause immediate injury, however slight.'

d We shall have to return to this passage later, in connection with the second part of the argument. For the present it is enough to say that this case too was not concerned with an act aimed at A which in fact caused the death of B. The court was there concerned with the quality of the act rather than the identity of the person at whom it was aimed. Again we do not read Waller LJ as saying that the unlawful and dangerous act must be aimed at that very person whose death is caused. If, however, that was what the court
e was saying, then we would, with the greatest respect, hold that it was not part of the ratio decidendi of the case.

The only authority (if such it be) which we have found to be directly in point is *Russell on Crime* (12th edn, 1964) vol 1, p 588 citing the 1839 Commissioners on Criminal Law:

> 'Involuntary homicide, which is not by misadventure, includes all cases where,
> f without intention to kill or do great bodily harm, or wilfully to endanger life, death occurs in any of the following instances: Where death results from any unlawful act or omission done or omitted with intent to hurt the person of another, whether the mischief light on the person intended, or on any other person; where death results from any wrong wilfully occasioned to the person of another; where death results from any unlawful act or unlawful omission, attended with risk of hurt to the person of another; where death results from want of due caution either in doing an
> g act, or neglecting to prevent mischief, which the offender is bound by law to prevent.'

We can see no reason of policy for holding that an act calculated to harm A cannot be manslaughter if it in fact kills B. The criminality of the doer of the act is precisely the
h same whether it is A or B who dies. A person who throws a stone at A is just as guilty if, instead of hitting and killing A, it hits and kills B. Parliament evidently held the same view in relation to the allied offence of unlawful and malicious wounding contrary to s 20 of the Offences against the Person Act 1861: see *R v Latimer* (1886) 17 QBD 359. We accordingly reject the argument of counsel for Mitchell that, because Mitchell's acts were aimed at Mr Smith, it cannot have been manslaughter when they caused the death of
j Mrs Crafts.

The second limb of the argument was based wholly on *Dalby*. It was argued that for manslaughter to be established the act of the defendant must be shown to have caused direct harm to the victim. On that ground, although it would be manslaughter to throw a stone at A which hits and kills B, it was submitted that there was no manslaughter in the present case, because there was no physical contact between Mitchell and Mrs Crafts.

The passage which we have already read from *Dalby* was relied on in support of that argument. In particular, there is this sentence in the judgment of the court ([1982] 1 All a
ER 916 at 919, [1982] 1 WLR 425 at 426–427):

> 'The kind of harm envisaged in all the reported cases of involuntary manslaughter was physical injury of some kind as an immediate and inevitable result of the unlawful act, e g a blow on the chin which knocks the victim against a wall causing a fractured skull and death, or threatening with a loaded gun which accidentally fires, or dropping a large stone on a train (see *DPP v Newbury*) or threatening another b
> with an open razor and stumbling with death resulting (see *R v Larkin*).'

We can well understand, if we may say so, why the court held that there was no sufficient link between Dalby's wrongful act (supplying the drug) and his friend's death. As Waller LJ said ([1982] 1 All ER 916 at 919, [1982] 1 WLR 425 at 427):

> '... the supply of drugs would itself have caused no harm unless the deceased had c
> subsequently used the drugs in a form and quantity which was dangerous ... the supply did not cause any direct injury to him.'

Here however the facts were very different. Although there was no direct contact between Mitchell and Mrs Crafts, she was injured as a direct and immediate result of his act. Thereafter her death occurred. The only question was one of causation: whether her d
death was caused by Mitchell's act. It was open to the jury to conclude that it was so caused; and they evidently reached that conclusion.

Since the conclusion of the argument we have seen a transcript of the judgment of this court in *R v Pagett* (1983) Times, 4 February. This supports the views we have expressed in two respects. Robert Goff LJ, delivering the judgment of the court, said:

> 'If, as the jury must have found to have occurred in the present case, the appellant e
> used Gail Kinchen by force and against her will as a shield to protect him from any shots fired by the police, the effect is that he committed not one but two unlawful acts, both of which were dangerous: the act of firing at the police, and the act of holding Gail Kinchen as a shield in front of him when the police might well fire shots in his direction in self-defence. Either act could, in our judgment ... constitute
> the actus reus of the manslaughter.' f

In the case of the first act mentioned, firing at the police, it could scarcely be said to have been *aimed* at the ultimate victim, Gail Kinchen; nor could it be said by itself to have caused harm to the victim by direct physical contact. We agree that neither requirement exists for manslaughter. Granted an unlawful and dangerous act, the test is one of causation. That is clear from *R v Pagett* where Robert Goff LJ said: g

> 'The question whether an accused person can be held guilty of homicide, either murder or manslaughter, of a victim the immediate cause of whose death is the act of another person must be determined on the ordinary principles of causation ...'

As to ground (iii), it was argued that the judge failed to direct the jury that Mitchell's act had to be a deliberate act, in the sense that he intended to do it. The direction was as h
follows:

> 'You have been told, and told perfectly accurately, what this offence of manslaughter is: it is where an act a person is engaged in is unlawful and if, at the same time, it is a dangerous act and another person is injured, and is injured even through inadvertence, and as a result of an injury death is caused to that other person, then the offence is one of manslaughter. Even if that act is one which is j
> likely to injure another person and it is done quite inadvertently, the offence is one of manslaughter. Again, you have been told, and told quite properly, that it does not matter whether the accused person knows that the act is an unlawful one, or indeed a dangerous one. It does not depend on what he believes to be unlawful or

dangerous. If you came to a conclusion in this case that what this young man, Mitchell, was doing was unlawful, inasmuch as it constituted an assault on Mr Smith, then your consideration would have to be on whether or not it was dangerous at the same time. In judging whether the act is a dangerous act, the test which you apply is not whether the accused recognises that it was a dangerous act, but whether all sober and reasonable people would have recognised it to be dangerous in the circumstances which attain in this particular case: in other words, whether you consider it was dangerous in the circumstances of this case.'

The judge there used the words 'inadvertence' and 'inadvertently'. He was perfectly right to do so, in dealing with the connection between the act and the injury or death. There need not be any intention to injure or kill, or any foresight that injury or death would be caused, provided that all sober and reasonable people would have recognised the act to be dangerous. That is the sense in which Humphreys J used the word 'inadvertently' in *Larkin*.

But it is said that the judge may have conveyed to the jury that the act need not itself have been a deliberate act. Whether he did or not is, in the context of this case, wholly immaterial. All of Mitchell's actions, whether hitting, pushing, grabbing or throwing, were obviously and admittedly deliberate actions. There was no suggestion of inadvertence, or even automation, in any part of his conduct. The issues before the jury, on this aspect of the case, were firstly self-defence and secondly whether he did all the things he was said to have done or only some of them. As we have already observed, there is no appeal against the conviction of assault occasioning actual bodily harm. In many if not most cases the judge should direct the jury that the act relied on for an offence of manslaughter must have been a deliberate or intentional act. Here it was quite unnecessary.

It remains to consider the application for leave to appeal against sentence. Mitchell was, as we have said, a young man of 22 at the time of these offences. He was by no means a man of previous good character; he had been before the courts on nine previous occasions. In 1975 he was sent to a detention centre; in 1977, for burglary, he received a suspended sentence of six months' imprisonment; in September 1980, for theft of a purse, he was conditionally discharged. Even after this offence and before his trial for it, he was on two occasions sentenced to six months' imprisonment. But he has never before been convicted of an offence involving violence.

It is true that the appellant expressed remorse when interviewed by the police. He said: 'I suppose I shouldn't have hit the old man, and I'm sorry the old lady got injured.' But according to one witness he was in a different frame of mind earlier: as Mr Smith went to the ground on top of Mrs Crafts, Mitchell said to him: 'I hope you die there.' The judge said that this offence was at the lower end of the scale of gravity which exists for offences of manslaughter. So indeed it was. But a sentence of 27 months' imprisonment was by no means too long, bearing in mind the gravity with which the public would view such an offence.

Appeal dismissed.

The court refused leave to appeal to the House of Lords but certified, under s 33(2) of the Criminal Appeal Act 1968, that the following point of law of general public importance was involved in the decision: whether, to constitute the offence of manslaughter, the unlawful and dangerous act (1) had to be aimed at the person who died or (2) had to involve a direct attack or impact on the person who died.

Solicitors: *Corkers*, Chingford (for Mitchell); *Director of Public Prosecutions.*

Sepala Munasinghe Esq Barrister.

Coupland v Arabian Gulf Petroleum Co

QUEEN'S BENCH DIVISION
HODGSON J
18, 19, 20, 21 JANUARY 1983

Conflict of laws – Tort – Claim based on tort – Scottish plaintiff employed by Libyan company to work in Libya – Plaintiff suffering personal injuries in course of employment in Libya – Plaintiff bringing action for damages against company in England – Defendant applying for stay of proceedings – Whether cause of action or parties having connection with English law – Whether proceedings should be stayed.

Conflict of laws – Tort – Actionability – Actionability in lex loci delicti – Scottish plaintiff employed by Libyan company to work in Libya – Plaintiff suffering personal injuries in course of employment in Libya – Plaintiff receiving payments under Libyan social security and labour law – Libyan law on damages not deducting social security benefits from assessment of damages – Plaintiff bringing action against Libyan company in England – Whether tort actionable in Libya – Whether claim satisfied under Libyan law by payment of benefits – Approach of court where substantial difference between lex fori and lex loci delicti where issue would be decided differently in the two systems of law.

Conflict of laws – Contract – Proper law of contract – Contract of employment – Libyan company employing Scotsman through agent in London to work in Libya – Contract made in London – Whether proper law of contract English law or Libyan law.

The plaintiff was a maintenance technician living and domiciled in Scotland. The defendants were a nationalised oil company in Libya which was registered in England under Part X of the Companies Act 1948. In January 1978 the plaintiff was employed by the defendants through agents in London to work for them in Libya. The contract of employment having been duly made in London, the plaintiff worked in Libya until December 1978, when he had a serious accident at work. As a result of his injuries, he returned to Scotland and was thereafter paid certain sums under the Libyan social security and labour laws, and also a sum of money under an insurance policy against accidental injury taken out by the defendants. The plaintiff began proceedings against the defendants in England for damages for personal injuries. By their defence the defendants claimed that the proper law applicable to the contract and/or to any obligation owed by the defendants to the plaintiff was Libyan law. The defendants subsequently issued a summons by which they sought, inter alia, to have the claim struck out on the grounds (i) that neither the cause of action nor the parties had any connection with English law and it would be unjust to permit the action to continue, (ii) that the claim was governed by Libyan law and had been satisfied under Libyan law by the payments already made to the plaintiff and accordingly there was no actionable cause of action in Libya. The defendants further sought to have the question of the proper law of the claim determined as a preliminary issue. The master refused the defendants' application to strike out the claim but ordered that a preliminary issue be tried whether the plaintiff's claim was governed by Libyan law and had been satisfied under Libyan law. Under the Libyan Civil Code the law as to tortious liability was the same as English law except as to damages, in respect of which Libyan law provided that social security and labour payments made to a plaintiff by the state were not to be deducted in the assessment of damages. On the trial of the preliminary issue, the defendants sought to have the proceedings stayed under the court's inherent discretionary power.

Held – (1) In order to justify a stay of proceedings the defendant had to satisfy the court that there was another forum to whose jurisdiction he was amenable in which justice

could be done at substantially less inconvenience and expense, and that the stay would
a not deprive the plaintiff of a legitimate personal or juridicial advantage to him in England. On the evidence, there were clear personal and juridical disadvantages to which the plaintiff would be subjected were the proceedings in the English courts to be stayed. Furthermore, there were clear advantages in having the case tried in England, since the witnesses to the accident were English-speaking and the defendants' agents (who had conducted most of the negotiations with the plaintiff) were in England. In any event, it
b was too late for the defendants to seek a stay at such a stage of the proceedings when they should have done so at the start of the proceedings. The stay of proceedings would therefore be refused (see p 442 *d* to *j* and p 448 *b c*, post); *MacShannon v Rockware Glass Ltd* [1978] 1 All ER 625 applied.

(2) On the preliminary issue, the general rule as to bringing a claim in an English court for a tortious act committed in a foreign country was that the tort had to be
c actionable under, and in accordance with, English law, subject to the condition that civil liability in respect of the relevant claim existed between the actual parties under the law of the foreign country (the lex loci delicti). Where those requirements were fulfilled the rule as to the choice of law to be made by the court was that the law of the place where the action was brought (the lex fori) applied. However, where there was a substantial difference between the two systems of law (ie the lex fori and the lex loci delicti), and
d there was an issue which would be decided differently by the two systems of law and which was capable of being segregated, the court could take a flexible approach and decide that the foreign law ought as a matter of policy to be applied in relation to that issue. On the facts, the only issue which could be segregated was the rule in Libyan law that social security and labour benefits were not deductible from an award of general damages. However, because that was a rule for the quantification of damages and not a
e rule dealing with liability for damages, it did not prevent English law from being the law to be applied. It followed that the plaintiff's claim in tort was not governed by Libyan law but by English law and that because the plaintiff's claim was actionable in both England and Libya the plaintiff was entitled to bring his claim in England (see p 443 *e* and *j* to p 444 *a* and *e f*, p 445 *b c e* to *g*, p 446 *e* to *j* and p 448 *b c*, post); dicta of Lord Wilberforce in *Chaplin v Boys* [1969] 2 All ER at 1098, 1100, 1102, 1103–1104 and
f *Church of Scientology of California v Comr of Metropolitan Police* (1976) 120 SJ 690 followed.

(3) On the issue of the proper law of the contract of employment, although there were many factors connecting the contract with England, on balance the fact that the defendants were employing nationals of different nationalities on what were, effectively, the same terms of contract was a connection which ought to prevail. The place where the contract was to be performed was to be, in effect, Libya and the proper law of the contract
g was therefore Libyan law. However that did not prevent the plaintiff from proceeding in tort in England since there was nothing in the contract which would give the defendants any defence to the plaintiff's claim in tort or limit the claim in tort (see p 447 *h* to p 448 *b*, post).

Notes

h For the general rule as to foreign torts and actionability under English law and under the law of the place of the tort, see 8 Halsbury's Laws (4th edn) paras 617–618, and for cases on the subject, see 11 Digest (Reissue) 495–497, *943–953*.

For the Companies Act 1948, Part X, see 5 Halsbury's Statutes (3rd edn) 404.

Cases referred to in judgment

j *Assunzione, The* [1954] 1 All ER 278, [1954] P 150, [1954] 2 WLR 234, CA.
Chaplin v Boys [1969] 2 All ER 1085, [1971] AC 356, [1969] 3 WLR 322, HL.
Chatenay v Brazilian Submarine Telegraph Co [1891] 1 QB 79, [1886–90] All ER Rep 1135, CA.
Church of Scientology of California v Comr of Metropolitan Police (1976) 120 SJ 690, CA.
Jacobs v Crédit Lyonnais (1884) 12 QBD 589, [1881–5] All ER Rep 151, CA.
Machado v Fontes [1897] 2 QB 231, CA.

MacShannon v Rockware Glass Ltd, Fyfe v Redpath Dorman Long Ltd [1978] 1 All ER 625,
[1978] AC 795, [1978] 2 WLR 362, HL. a
Phillips v Eyre (1870) LR 6 QB 1.
Sayers v International Drilling Co NV [1971] 3 All ER 163, [1971] 1 WLR 1176, CA.

Preliminary issue
By a writ issued on 22 September 1980 the plaintiff, John Waugh Frazer Coupland,
brought against the defendants, Arabian Gulf Oil Co (a nationalised corporation in b
amalgamation with Umm Al-Jawaby Petroleum Co SAL), in action for damages for
personal injuries suffered by the plaintiff in the course of his employment with the
defendants in Libya. On 7 November 1980 the defendants served their defence denying
liability and claiming that the proper law of the contract of employment was that of
Libya. By a summons dated 24 July 1981 the defendants applied, inter alia, to have the
claim struck out on the grounds (i) that neither the cause of action nor the parties had c
any connection with English law and it would be unjust to permit the action to continue,
(ii) that the claim was governed by Libyan law and had been satisfied under Libyan law
and accordingly there was no actionable cause of action in Libya, and they further sought
to have the question of the proper law of the claim determined as a preliminary issue.
On 4 December 1981 Master Lubbock refused the defendants' application to strike out
the claim but ordered, inter alia, that a preliminary issue be tried, namely whether the d
plaintiff's claim was governed by Libyan law and had been satisfied. The facts are set out
in the judgment.

Raymond Croxon for the defendants.
V E Hartley Booth for the plaintiff.

e

HODGSON J. The plaintiff in this case is a maintenance technician. He lives and is
domiciled in Scotland. The defendants are a nationalised oil company in Libya. It has a
British residence and is registered under Part X of the Companies Act 1948 in this
country. It is well known that in Arab countries, which with the recently acquired oil
revenue have become possessed of more wealth than their own technology is yet able
properly to service, they recruit in more technically advanced countries experts to assist f
in their oil industry. In order to recruit such people the defendant company employed as
its agents in England Charles R Lister (International) Ltd, which is an English company
licensed by the Department of Employment so to recruit.

In January 1978 that company, on behalf of the defendants, inserted an advertisement
in the Daily Express which came to the notice of the plaintiff. The plaintiff found the
pay and conditions of work adumbrated in that advertisement tempting, and accordingly g
he answered the advertisement and went to London where he saw the representatives of
the agents, and accepted employment with the defendant company.

There has been a good deal of debate in this case as to the precise way in which the
contract of employment which existed between the plaintiff and the defendants came
into being; but, for reasons which I hope will be clear, it does not seem to me to be
necessary to go in detail into that aspect of the case. Suffice it to say that, on the pleadings h
as at present constituted, the contract is admitted to have been made in England.

After the necessary formalities had been concluded in England (such as medical
examination, the preparation of documents giving the plaintiff's qualifications, the
obtaining of a visa and other matters) the plaintiff went to Libya in the capacity of a
senior maintenance technician. He worked in such capacity, with generous periods of
leave in England, until 12 December 1978, when he had a serious accident at work. It is j
not necessary for me to state the facts of the accident in detail. Briefly, the plaintiff was
working on a machine, parts of which (I am told) became very hot in the Libyan sun,
and he had to climb the fencing of a rotating radiator cooling fan. In some way the guard
to that fan had been cut creating a large space, and it was through that space that the
plaintiff's foot slipped as he was descending, as a result of which he suffered a below knee
amputation.

He was immediately flown home to Scotland, and thereafter he has been paid certain sums under Libyan social security and labour laws, and also a sum of money on an insurance policy against accidental injury, taken out by the defendants under the terms of its contract with the plaintiff, the premiums for which policy were paid by the defendants. It is not suggested that that payment of insurance money was accepted otherwise than without prejudice to the plaintiff's claim, and of course the other sums are paid by (in so far as they have been paid) the Libyan state.

By a writ dated 22 September 1980, which had a statement of claim indorsed on it, the plaintiff began proceedings against the defendant company. The writ was served on the defendant company at its English address. By para 2 of the statement of claim the plaintiff averred:

> 'On or about the 20th February, 1978 the Defendant by or through its agents Charles R. Lister International Limited acting as an employment agency licensed by the Department of Employment and operating in England offered the Plaintiff employment with the Defendant in Libya as a Senior Maintenance Technician and the Plaintiff accepted the same. The said contract was made in England and was partly oral and in writing.'

Paragraph 3 alleged the contract of employment and its confirmation.

In para 4 brief details of the accident were set out. It was alleged that the plaintiff suffered injury, loss and damage, and that that injury, loss and damage was caused either by the negligent acts or omissions of the defendant company.

In paras 5 and 6 the plaintiff averred:

> '5. In addition to the Plaintiff's claim referred to in Clause (4) above the Plaintiff claims that the Defendant had failed in its statutory obligation to guard the rotating fan and thereby protect its employees from injuries which would have been expected to have been occasioned as a result of failing to ensure the same.
>
> 6. Further the Plaintiff claims the Defendants are in breach of an implied term in his Contract of Employment that the Defendant would take all steps as were necessary for the safety and well being of the Plaintiff.'

Counsel for the plaintiff pointed out that, though that is not perhaps the usual way of pleading that the claim brought in Libya would be actionable in that country, paras 5 and 6 do contain facts from which that allegation of law can be properly derived.

The defendants entered appearance to that statement of claim. The defence was dated 7 November 1980 and was served on the plaintiff's solicitors. In that defence the defendants admitted para 2 of the statement of claim, and by so doing admitted that the contract had been made in London. Apart from that the defence was in a common form and raised no choice of law or jurisdictional point at all.

The next relevant step in the action (I do not need to refer to the requests for further and better particulars and the notices to admit facts which are in the bundle of pleadings) was a summons taken out by the defendants and dated 24 July 1981. By that summons the defendants sought (1) leave to amend their defence in certain particulars, (2) that the claim be struck out on the grounds that neither the cause of action nor the parties had any connection with English law, and it would be unjust to permit the action to continue, (3) that the claim be struck out in that it is governed by Libyan law and has been satisfied (which I take to be an averment that the second part of the rule in *Phillips v Eyre* (1870) LR 6 QB 1, as amended, could not be satisfied by the plaintiff), (4) what I take to be a request for the trial of a preliminary issue, which read: 'Further or in the alternative to determine the proper Law to be applied to the claim', because I do not think that it was within the master's jurisdiction so to decide, and (5) that the plaintiff give security for costs.

There was on 4 December 1981 a full hearing of that summons, at which hearing the plaintiff was represented by Mr Hartley Booth, who represents him before me today. Unfortunately, it is clear that Mr Croxon (who appears for the defendants before me today) was not at those proceedings, and I know not how they were represented. The amendments sought by the defendants were allowed in part. But at that hearing the master was firmly of the view that no amendment should be allowed to retract the *a* admission as to the plaintiff's contract, and that was made clear by the master. In addition, the master refused the defendants' application to strike out the claim, on either of the grounds alleged in paras 2 and 3 of the summons, and refused to give security.

The amendments that were permitted expanded para 2 of the defence and in para 4 added the words:

> '... and further deny the applicability of the law of negligence and will rely upon *b* the following matters:
>
> (i) That such duty as the Defendants owed to the Plaintiff were contained in a written contract to which reference will be made, if necessary, at the trial as to the terms therein and as to their meaning and effect.
>
> (ii) The proper law applicable to the contract and/or to any other obligation by the *c* Defendants to the Plaintiff, of which none are admitted is Libyan law.'

By para 8 the defendants pleaded:

> 'The Defendants will rely upon the fact that under Libyan law any claim by the Plaintiff for compensation arising out of the aforesaid industrial accident has been satisfied in that he received a lump sum payment of approximately £4,500 and a *d* state pension of 116.822 L.D. [that is, 116 dinars and 822 dirhams] per month for life. In the premises, the Defendants deny that he is entitled to claim any further sums as alleged or at all.'

The pleading in para 8 was no doubt to raise the issue whether the plaintiff could bring himself within the second part of the rule in *Phillips v Eyre*, as amended by the decision of the House of Lords in *Chaplin v Boys* [1969] 2 All ER 1085, [1971] AC 356. *e*

In addition, the master accepted the application of the defendants for the trial of a preliminary issue. In para 4 of the order he said: 'There be a trial of a preliminary issue whether the Plaintiff's claim is governed by Libyan law and has been satisfied ...'

It is that preliminary issue which comes before me.

However, during his opening it became clear that counsel for the defendants had not been told of the amendment as to the place where the contract was made, which he had *f* been advised had not been allowed by the master. He may (I know not) not have been told either that the master had refused to strike out the claim, because if he had been told either of those things he would have advised that the master's order should be appealed. It also became clear that, despite the refusal of the master to strike out the claim on either of the grounds alleged by the defendants, he intended in these proceedings to attempt, in effect, to stop the plaintiff's claim from going further by invoking the power of this *g* court preserved by s 49(3) of the Supreme Court Act 1981 to stay the proceedings.

So far as the place at which the contract was made is concerned (and at the end of the day I doubt whether, either here or if the case goes further, it makes any difference) the defendants in the course of proceedings, and without dissent from the plaintiff's counsel, undertook to make application in proper form to me to extend the time for appealing from the master's decision, and to abridge service on the plaintiff. *h*

I heard that application and I refused it on three main grounds. First, the enormous delay in seeking leave to appeal out of time. The correct time to appeal on that issue, as indeed to appeal the refusal of the master to strike out, was at the time when the master's order was made and not over one year later. Second, on my reading of the documents I personally consider it unarguable that the contract was made anywhere but in England. Third, I doubt the relevance, in any event, of where the contract was made. *j*

So far as the application to stay is concerned I have heard, without dissent by counsel for the plaintiff, full submissions from both sides. Obviously, to reach a decision in this case it was necessary for me to hear evidence as to Libyan law, because the parties clearly did not agree that the presumption that English law is the same as a foreign law would be applicable in this case.

I heard the evidence of an expert called by the defendants (who, by agreement, opened a this case) and an expert called by the plaintiff. At the outset I must say that in helping me to decide, as a matter of fact, what was the relevant Libyan law, I much preferred the evidence of the expert called by the plaintiff. Not only was he, in my judgment, better qualified to assist me than the defendants' expert, but it also seemed to me that he presented his opinion in a more persuasive way, and in a way which seemed to demonstrate that his knowledge of Libyan law was (quite apart from the superiority of b his patent qualifications) fuller and more detailed than that of the defendants' expert.

Before I turn to consider the two main questions in this case, (1) whether I should stay the proceedings under s 49(3) of the 1981 Act, and (2) the actual preliminary issue which comes before me, it will, I hope, be helpful if I outline the facts as to Libyan law and procedure, as I find them.

It was in 1968 that the monarchy in Libya fell and was succeeded by the republic and c its present governing bodies. Prior to 1968 the law of Libya had been codified. Among the codes of Libyan law was the Civil Code. It is not without interest that the plaintiff's expert had taken a part in the drafting of that code, and there is no doubt that after the replacement of the monarchy by the republic that Civil Code remained in force.

I have been provided by both experts with translations of various articles, both in the Civil Code and in the laws relating to social security and labour, to which I shall come in d a moment. Article 2 of the Libyan Civil Code reads as follows:

> '*Repeal of laws*:
> No legislative provision shall be repealed except by subsequent legislation which provides expressly for such repeal, nor which contains a provision which conflicts with the old provision or which regulates anew the subject whose principles have been determined by said legislation . . .'

e The remainder of that article, it was agreed, dealt mainly with any consolidating provision. The plaintiff's expert told me (and I accept) that, as one would expect from time to time, there have been amendments of the Civil Code, but that where there has been any amendment of the Civil Code it has always been done specifically by reference to the article in question.

f Article 166 of the Civil Code, under the heading 'General basis', provides that 'Every wrong which causes injury to others will make the wrongdoer liable to compensation and damages'.

Article 168 provides:

> '*Injury resulting from extraneous cause*
> If the person proves that the injury was caused by an extraneous cause in which g he had no hand, such as sudden accident or force majeure or the fault of the injured person or the fault caused by a third party, then the person will not be liable to compensate for that injury unless there is a text or an agreement to the contrary.'

Article 214 deals with taking reasonable care, and provides:

> '1. In cases where a person undertakes to carry out work and if what is required h of such person is to take care of something given to him or to be administered by him or to take care while carrying out his obligations, then such person will have performed his obligation if he has taken the care an ordinary man would take, even if the intended object has not been attained, unless the law or an agreement specifies otherwise.
> 2. In any case, the person will continue to be liable for any act of fraud or gross j negligence by him.'

Article 219, under the heading 'Contributory Negligence', provides:

> 'The judge may reduce the amount of compensation or damages or may refrain from awarding such compensation or damages if the Defendant, through his fault, has contributed to cause the injury or increased its effect.'

With the possible exception of the power given to the court in art 219 to bar a plaintiff from any damages at all if his fault has contributed to cause the injury or increased its effect, those provisions I am told and I accept (indeed, it seems clear from their wording) amount to precisely the law which would govern this case in England.

There has been controversy in the past whether, if a plaintiff's negligence was so great, he could lose a case altogether, even though there was some breach of statutory duty on the part of the defendant or perhaps some fault on behalf of the defendant. And there are certain cases whereby judges have been able, either through the weapon of causation or in some other way, to exclude a plaintiff altogether from the remedy. But apart from that perhaps very minor difference between the law of England as to tortious liability in these circumstances and the law of the Civil Code, there seems to be no difference. The plaintiff's expert (who is a member of the English Bar and a practising advocate in Libya) told me, in effect, that there was no real difference, and his evidence I accept.

So far as damages are concerned, one has to look at arts 173, 224 and 225. Article 173 provides:

> '*Damages*
> The judge shall estimate the extent of the damages for injury suffered by the injured party in accordance with Articles 224 and 225 taking into consideration surrounding circumstances. If at the time of giving judgment it is not feasible for him to make a final determination of the extent of damages, he may reserve to the injured party the right to ask within a defined period of time for a reconsideration of the estimate.'

Therefore, in so far as the quantification of damages is concerned, the court in Libya would not be limited to a lump sum payment as are we in our less (in this respect) developed jurisprudence.

I ought to read part of art 220, which provides:

> '*Exemption from Liability* . . .
> 3. Any condition providing for exemption from liability arising out of an unlawful act (tort) shall be null and void . . .'

Article 224 provides:

> '*Determination of Damages*
> 1. The judge shall determine the damages if they are not determined in the contract or by a provision of the law. Damages shall include the loss suffered by the creditor and the profits he missed, provided that such shall be the natural result of failure to meet the obligation or the delay in its fulfilment. The injury is deemed a natural result if it was not possible for the creditor to avoid it through the exercise of reasonable effort.
> 2. Nevertheless, if the source of the obligation is contract, the debtor who did not commit fraud or gross fault shall be obligated to compensate only the injury which normally could be expected at the time of making the contract.'

Article 225, which has not been translated, deals with moral damages.

The plaintiff's expert told me (and I accept) that under the Civil Code all heads of damage which would be recoverable in an English court are recoverable in a Libyan court, including damages for pain and suffering and loss of amenity. And the only difference which he said would apply in Libyan law, and not in English law, would be that the social security and labour law payments made to the plaintiff by the state would not be taken into account, by deduction, in the assessment of damages in the Libyan court.

With the advent of the republic the state turned its attention to social security, and in 1970 and 1973 respectively, labour laws and social security laws were passed. Article 1 of the Social Security Law (No 72) reads:

> 'Social security is a right guaranteed by the State in the way specified in this law for all citizens and protection for non-citizens who reside in Libya for the purpose

> of work. Social security will include all [this could be translated as 'every'] regulations or procedures taken in accordance with the law for the purpose of protecting the individual in cases of illness or work injuries or birth or death or disablement or old age or unemployment or disaster and looking after him in taking care of family responsibility or childhood or old age.'

Article 42 of the Labour Law (No 58) reads:

> 'The employee whose sickness or disability is proved shall be entitled to a sick leave during which he shall receive 50% of his pay for the first 60 days, to be increased to 60% for the subsequent one hundred and twenty days in the course of a single year.'

It then goes on to deal with the employee's rights to those payments.

Claims under these two laws are adjudicated on by committees (or tribunals as we know them in this country), to whom the claimant makes his claim and before which there is no representation. There are, as happens in some other jurisdictions, rights in the committee to go against employers for indemnity in certain circumstances, and in what seems a fairly draconian way.

It was this social security and labour law legislation which, in the opinion of the defendants' expert, would have the effect of making any claim by the plaintiff for damages for this accident unactionable in Libya. He told me that the effect of these two bodies of law was to repeal the provisions of the Civil Code so far as actions for tort by an employee was concerned, and perhaps (I know not) for all other actions in tort, and therefore the claim of the plaintiff would not be actionable in the courts in Libya. If that were right, then the plaintiff could not bring himself within the second part of the rule in *Phillips v Eyre* (1870) LR 6 QB 1, and would have to seek his remedy in Libya.

The main plank in this opinion of the defendants' expert was art 26 of the Social Security Law for 1980, which provides as follows:

> '*Civil liability in cases of work injuries*
>
> 1. [An] Injured contributor or his heirs in case of his death, shall be entitled to claim for damages caused by injury he suffered against any person responsible for any such accident, in case he be not the employer or from his employer if the injury took place because of his violation of service or labour laws or regulations or due to his negligence in taking occupational safety precautions . . .'

In para (2) of that article it provides for, in effect, indemnity by the employer or work authority.

What the defendants' expert says is that the fact that in the social security legislation it was necessary to pass that law shows that prior to 1980 the effect of the social security and labour laws has been to repeal the tort provisions in the Civil Code.

But the plaintiff's expert says with total conviction the contrary. He accepts that between 1973 and 1980 it may be that there was some argument on this point and that it was desirable that any doubt should be removed, and that it was primarily for that purpose that art 26 was passed. Secondly, he tells me (and I accept) that the article was necessary because it extended the right in tort to the employee's heirs. Thirdly, he said (and I accept) that it is unthinkable that these important and long-established provisions of the Civil Code should have been repealed or held to be repealed by a side wind. He said that there was no reported decision between 1973 and 1980; only the decisions of the Supreme Court are reported. But, had it been contended that this effect of the social security and labour laws had in fact taken place, he would have expected any such argument (whichever way it went) in a case to have been the subject of a reported decision. Finally, he points to the fact that there is nothing in the social security or labour laws to compare with art 2 of the Civil Code in Libya. Thus, I am left in no doubt whatsoever that the provisions of the Civil Code as to tortious liability subsisted throughout the first 12 years of the republic.

I turn now to consider the procedure in the civil court in Libya. Representation in the civil court, unlike that before the tribunal or committees, is permitted by a lawyer, but there is no way in which a litigant can get a lawyer of his own choice. What he has to do *a* is to apply to the relevant committee of the Ministry of Justice, and they will allot him a lawyer whom they consider in their wisdom to be qualified to conduct his case.

Legal representation is free to a Libyan subject, but an expatriate if he wants to bring proceedings in a Libyan court has to make a substantial deposit, being a percentage of the total amount of his quantified claim, though, in exceptional circumstances, the amount of the deposit can be reduced or, in certain circumstances, provided for by social *b* security payments to which the plaintiff is entitled. It goes without saying that the proceedings in the court are conducted in Arabic.

Libya has exchange control regulations and special permission is required to get money transferred out of Libya. The defendants' expert agreed that achieving that takes longer than would be thought reasonable, and that the procedure is extremely cumbersome because of the bureaucracy in Libya and the inability to divine what particular documents *c* any particular bureaucrat will consider necessary before consent is given.

The plaintiff's own experience, to which he spoke in evidence before me, goes a long way to substantiate these difficulties. He has been entitled to a social security payment from the Libyan state since his accident, but since May 1980 none has been paid despite protracted efforts by his solicitors which continued until June 1981, to persuade the state to make these payments. Whether they have in fact been paid into the defendants' *d* account or whether they have not been paid at all I do not know, but what is clear is that no expatriate is entitled to have a bank account in Libya into which the money could have been paid.

I turn now to consider the question of whether I ought to stay these proceedings at this late stage under s 49(3) of the 1981 Act. Authoritative guidance as to when, in circumstances where it is alleged that the court in which the proceedings are going on is *e* not the convenient forum, that jurisdiction should be exercised is provided in the decision of the House of Lords in *MacShannon v Rockware Glass Ltd* [1978] 1 All ER 625, [1975] AC 795. I need do no more than read the headnote of that case, which concerned Scottish plaintiffs, accidents in Scotland and bringing proceedings in England. The House of Lords held ([1975] AC 795):

> '(1) that the conditions necessary to justify a stay were (a) that the defendant must *f* satisfy the court that there was another forum to whose jurisdiction he was amenable in which justice could be done at substantially less inconvenience and expense and (b) that the stay would not deprive the plaintiff of a legitimate personal or juridical advantage which would be available to him in England . . .'

It seems to me that the matters to which I referred in dealing briefly with the *g* procedure in Libya amount to plain personal and juridical disadvantages to which the plaintiff would be subjected were these proceedings in this court to be stayed. To be added to the equation are what I would have thought plain advantages of having the case tried in this court, namely the witnesses to the accident are English-speaking, and the defendants' agents (who conducted most of the negotiations with the plaintiff) are in England. In any event, to the extent that I have a discretion in the matter it is, in my *h* judgment, far too late for the defendants to seek this remedy. Had they wished to do so, they could have done so at the time when the proceedings were begun. In my judgment, it was too late to do it when they took out their summons before the master, and by so much more is it too late to do so now.

I turn now to deal with the question of the choice of law in tort. Since the decision of the House of Lords in *Chaplin v Boys* [1969] 2 All ER 1085, [1971] AC 356, their *j* Lordships' speeches in that case have provided a field-day for academic writers. I have read during the course of the trial of this action a number of articles by various learned academics, and one must accept that the discovery of the true ratio decidendi of that decision is not without its difficulties. Fortunately, so far as I am concerned, I have had my attention drawn to what is an almost unreported case in the Court of Appeal, the name of which is *Church of Scientology of California v Comr of Metropolitan Police*, the judgments in which were given on 13 July 1976. I believe the case is reported only, and that not fully, in the Solicitors' Journal (120 SJ 690). In my view, it is a case which deserved fuller reporting than it got. Fortunately, I have been provided with a transcript of their Lordships' judgments from the Bar Library, and they make my task in approaching *Chaplin v Boys* very much easier.

The case was concerned with a claim by the plaintiffs that four police officers, acting under the direction and control of the commissioner, published to the West German Federal Police Authority a report defamatory of the Church of Scientology. The publication having been made in Germany, choice of law rules were involved in the case, which came before the Court of Appeal on appeal from the master and the judge, who had held that the defendant had shown that the cause of action pleaded against him was not actionable by German domestic law, and accordingly that it was (because of the second rule in *Phillips v Eyre*) not actionable in this country. The Court of Appeal allowed the appeals, but the importance of the case is that the Court of Appeal came firmly down, with the consent of both counsel, in favour of the ratio decidendi in *Chaplin v Boys* contained in the speech of Lord Wilberforce. Thus, so far as I am concerned, putting an end to controversy.

The passage from the leading judgment of Bridge LJ, which is relevant on this point begins thus:

> 'The whole subject matter of conflict of laws in tort was elaborately considered and reviewed in the House of Lords in 1971 in the case of *Boys v Chaplin*. Counsel before us are both content to proceed on the footing that the effect of the majority decision of their Lordships in the case is to establish the general rule of double actionability. It is most succinctly expressed by Lord Wilberforce ([1969] 2 All ER 1085 at 1102, [1971] AC 356 at 389): "I would, therefore, restate the basic rule of English law with regard to foreign torts with requiring actionability as a tort according to English law, subject to the condition that civil liability in respect of the relevant claim exists as between the actual parties under the law of the foreign country where the act was done." But again it is accepted as the basis of the argument before us that the majority of their Lordships pronounced themselves in favour of a limited exception to that general rule. The second point in this appeal is the question whether it is shown to be plain and obvious that the plaintiffs cannot bring themselves within that limited exception.'

Bridge LJ then considered in detail the exception and the need for flexibility laid down by the House of Lords (and, in particular, by Lord Wilberforce), and concluded:

> 'This is an extremely uncertain subject. The exception to the general rule of double actionability is one newly enunciated by their Lordships in *Boys v Chaplin*. Its true limits will no doubt become clearer as more cases are decided in the courts.'

I cite no further from their Lordships in that case because it seems to me that that case allows me to go, and go alone, to the speech of Lord Wilberforce with which, in these respects, Lord Hodson concurred, and with which Lord Pearson concurred also.

Lord Wilberforce began by considering the existing English law. He said ([1969] 2 All ER 1085 at 1098, [1971] AC 356 at 384–385):

> 'Apart from any revision which this House may be entitled, and think opportune, to make, I have no doubt that this [that is, the existing English law] is as stated in DICEY AND MORRIS ON THE CONFLICT OF LAWS (8th Edn.), r. 158, pp. 919, 920, adopting with minor verbal adaptations, the "general rule" laid down by the Court of Exchequer Chamber in *Phillips* v. *Eyre* ((1870) LR 6 QB 1). This is as follows: "An act done in a foreign country is a tort and actionable as such in England, only if it is both (i) actionable as a tort, according to English law, or in other words, is an act which, if done in England, would be a tort; and (ii) not justifiable, according to the

> law of the foreign country where it was done." I am aware that different interpretations have been placed by writers of authority on the central passage in *a* the judgment of WILLES, J. (LR 6 QB 1 at 28–29), in which the general rule is contained. Like many judgments given at a time when the relevant part of the law was in course of formation, it is not without its ambiguities, or, as a century of experience pehaps permits us to say, its contradictions. And if it were now necessary to advance the law by re-interpretation, it would be quite legitimate to extract new meanings from words and sentences used. Two of the judgments in the Court of *b* Appeal ([1968] 1 All ER 283, [1968] 2 QB 1) have done just this, reaching in the process opposite conclusions. I do not embark on this adventure for two reasons: first, because of the variety of interpretation offered us by learned writers no one of which can claim overwhelming support; secondly, and more importantly, because, on the critical points, I do not think there is any doubt what the rule as stated has come to be accepted to mean in those courts which apply the common law. And it *c* is with this judicially accepted meaning and its applications, that we are now concerned. (a) The first part of the rule—"actionable as a tort, according to English law". I accept what I believe to be the orthodox judicial view that the first part of the rule is laying down, not a test of jurisdiction, but what we now call a rule of choice of law: is saying, in effect, that actions on foreign torts are brought in English courts in accordance with English law. I would be satisfied to rest this conclusion on *d* the words of the rule itself "if done [committed] in England" which seem clear enough to exclude the "jurisdiction" theory but, since the point is important, I give some citations to support it.'

So that there Lord Wilberforce was saying in clear terms that the first rule in *Phillips v Eyre* was a choice of law rule, and that the lex fori should be the law to be applied.

After citation of authorities to support that conclusion, he concluded ([1969] 2 All ER *e* 1085 at 1100, [1971] AC 356 at 387):

> 'I am of opinion, therefore, that, as regards the first part of this rule, actionability as a tort under and in accordance with English law is required.'

He went on to deal with the second rule in *Phillips v Eyre*, which read 'not justifiable according to the lex loci delicti'. Having examined that rule and the case of *Machado v* *f* *Fontes* [1897] 2 QB 231, he then said this ([1969] 2 All ER 1085 at 1100, [1971] AC 356 at 387):

> 'It results from the foregoing that the current English law is correctly stated by DICEY AND MORRIS, it being understood (a) that the substantive law to be applied is the lex fori, (b) that, as a condition, non-justifiability under the lex delicti is *g* required.'

He then asked himself whether that was a satisfactory rule, and came to the conclusion that, in so far as its second part was concerned, it was not. And having considered that, he went on ([1969] 2 All ER 1085 at 1102, [1971] AC 356 at 389):

> 'The broad principle should surely be that a person should not be permitted to *h* claim in England in respect of a matter for which civil liability does not exist, or is excluded, under the law of the place where the wrong was committed. This non-existence or exclusion may be for a variety of reasons and it would be unwise to attempt a generalisation relevant to the variety of possible wrongs. But in relation to claims for personal injuries one may say that provisions of the lex delicti, denying, or limiting, or qualifying recovery of damages because of some relationship of the *j* defendant to the plaintiff, or in respect of some interest of the plaintiff (such as loss of consortium) or some head of damage (such as pain and suffering) should be given effect to. I can see no case for allowing one resident of Ontario to sue another in the English courts for damages sustained in Ontario as a passenger in the other's car, [he is there referring to the "non-liability to passengers" rule which pertains in the State

> of Ontario] or one Maltese resident to sue another in the English courts for damages in respect of pain and suffering caused by an accident in Malta. I would, therefore, restate the basic rule of English law with regard to foreign torts as requiring actionability as a tort according to English law, subject to the condition that civil liability in respect of the relevant claim exists as between the actual parties under the law of the foreign country where the act was done. It remains for me to consider (and this is the crux of the present case) whether some qualification to this rule is required in certain individual cases.'

That, of course, is the rule that there must be actionability in England, that being a choice of law rule; and there must also be actionability in the foreign country.

Lord Wilberforce continued ([1969] 2 All ER 1085 at 1102, [1971] AC 356 at 389):

> 'There are two conflicting pressures: the first in favour of certainty and simplicity in the law, the second in favour of flexibility in the interest of individual justice. Developments in the United States of America have reflected this conflict. I now consider them.'

Lord Wilberforce went on to consider those developments at some length.

He then considered the question whether there should be introduced into English law a concept of the proper law of the tort. And he continued ([1969] 2 All ER 1085 at 1103–1104, [1971] AC 356 at 391–392):

> 'There is force in this [by that he referred to the argument against the contention for a proper law of the tort] and for this reason I am not willing to go so far as the more extreme version of the respondent's argument would have us do and to adopt, in place of the existing rule, one based solely on "contacts" or "centre of gravity" which has not been adopted even in the more favourable climate of the United States. There must remain great virtue in a general well-understood rule covering the majority of normal cases provided that it can be made flexible enough to take account of the varying interests and considerations of policy which may arise when one or more foreign elements are present. Given the general rule, as stated above [and that is the general rule as to actionability in both England and the foreign country, to which I have referred] as one which will normally apply to foreign torts, I think that the necessary flexibility can be obtained from that principle which represents at least a common denominator of the United States decisions, namely, through segregation of the relevant issue and consideration whether, in relation to that issue, the relevant foreign rule ought, as a matter of policy or as WESTLAKE said of science, to be applied. For this purpose it is necessary to identify the policy of the rule, to enquire to what situations, with what contacts, it was intended to apply; whether not to apply it, in the circumstances of the instant case, would serve any interest which the rule was devised to meet. This technique appears well adapted to meet cases where the lex delicti either limits or excludes damages for personal injury; it appears even necessary and inevitable. No purely mechanical rule can properly do justice to the great variety of cases where persons come together in a foreign jurisdiction for different purposes with different pre-existing relationships, from the background of different legal systems. It will not be invoked in every case or even, probably, in many cases. The general rule must apply unless clear and satisfying grounds are shown why it should be departed from and what solution, derived from what other rule, should be preferred. If one lesson emerges from the United States decisions it is that case-to-case decisions do not add up to a system of justice. Even within these limits this procedure may in some instances require a more searching analysis than is needed under the general rule. But unless this is done, or at least possible, we must come back to a system which is purely and simply mechanical.'

He then applied that approach to his instant case, and said ([1967] 2 All ER 1085 at 1104, [1971] AC 356 at 392):

> 'The tort here was committed in Malta; it is actionable in this country. But the law of Malta denies recovery of damages for pain and suffering. Prima facie English *a* law should do the same: if the parties were both Maltese residents it ought surely to do so; if the defendant were a Maltese resident the same result might follow. But in a case such as the present, where neither party is a Maltese resident or citizen, further enquiry is needed rather than an automatice application of the rule. The issue, whether this head of damage should be allowed, requires to be segregated from the rest of the case, negligence or otherwise, related to the parties involved and their *b* circumstances, and tested in relation to the policy of the local rule and of its application to these parties so circumstanced.'

Lord Wilberforce then went on to consider such matters as whether the Maltese state had any interest in applying its special rule to persons outside the state, and concluded that it had not. He then dealt with the question whether the decision as to a head of damage was substantive or adjectival, and he concluded ([1969] 2 All ER 1085 at 1105, *c* [1971] AC 356 at 393):

> 'There certainly seems to be some artifice in regarding a man's right to recover damages for pain and suffering as a matter of procedure. To do so, at any rate, goes well beyond the principle, which I entirely accept, that matters of assessment or quantification, including no doubt the manner in which provision is made for *d* future or prospective losses, are for the lex fori to determine.

None of their Lordships disagreed with that last sentence. Lord Guest based his decision on the point not accepted by the majority: that, in fact, the question whether a head of damage was included was procedural and not substantive.

It is clear that the ordinary rule in tort is that the law of the place where the action is being brought (the lex fori) is the law to be applied. *e*

To find an exception to that rule one has to find an issue, which is decided differently by the two jurisprudences, which is capable of being segregated and which can then be decided by an application of what, in effect by the back door, is the proper law of that issue. But before one can do that one has to have some substantial difference between the two systems of law. In this case (as I have demonstrated) the only possible candidate for segregation would be the rule in Libyan law that social security benefits are not deductible *f* from an award of general damages. But that contention is not advanced by counsel for the plaintiff (and properly so, it seems to me), for that rule is, in my judgment, a rule for the quantification of damage and not a rule dealing with a head of damage. And, if it is a rule dealing with the quantification of damage, then it is for the law of this country to prevail.

In my judgment, there is no doubt that the answer to the preliminary issue which I *g* am asked to decide whether the plaintiff's claim is governed by Libyan law so far as tort is concerned is that it is not, and I am satisfied that the claim in tort is governed by English law. I am further satisfied, as has become clear from my judgment, that the defendants cannot succeed on the second part of the rule in *Phillips v Eyre* (1870) LR 6 QB 1. And I am satisfied that, were the plaintiff to bring a claim against the defendants in Libya on these facts, that claim would be actionable. *h*

Finally, I am asked to decide the proper law of the contract, because the claim is in form brought under both contract and tort. The rules are accurately stated in *Dicey and Morris on the Conflict of Laws* (10th edn, 1980) vol 2, r 145:

> 'The term "proper law of contract" means the system of law by which the parties intended the contract to be governed, [that does not apply in this case] or, where *j* their intention is neither expressed nor to be inferred from the circumstances [and I think it is not in this case], the system of law with which the transaction has its closest and most real connection.'

Sub-rule 3 provides:

> 'When the intention of the parties to a contract with regard to the law governing

> it is not expressed and cannot be inferred from the circumstances, the contract is governed by the system of law with which the transaction has its closest and most real connection.'

In the comment on sub-r 3, under the heading 'The law of the place of performance', *Dicey and Morris* states:

> 'Where all the parties have to perform their contractual obligations in the same country, it is very likely the court will consider the legal system of that country as the one with which the contract is most closely connected. Seen in terms of the modern development of the law, this, it is submitted, is the practical meaning to be attached to the well-known judgment of Lord Esher M.R. in *Chatenay v. Brazilian Submarine Telegraph Co* ([1891] 1 QB 79, [1886–90] All ER Rep 1135) which has always been considered as the principal authority for the *lex loci solutionis*. Great weight will thus be given to the law of the place of performance as being the proper law of the contract, especially where the contract is made in one country but to be wholly performed in another. The important decision of the Court of Appeal in *The Assunzione* ([1954] 1 All ER 278, [1954] P 150) shows that, where both parties have to perform in a country other than that in which the contract was made, the argument in favour of the *lex loci solutionis* is very strong because the contract is almost certain to be more closely connected with the law of the place of performance than with any other law. Where, on the other hand, as in *Jacobs v. Crédit Lyonnais* ((1884) 12 QBD 589, [1881–5] All ER Rep 151), the parties have to perform their obligations in different countries, the court will not normally be able to attach much significance to the place of performance.'

Then the editors go on to point out that it is not conclusive.

A number of cogent reasons have been put forward by counsel for the plaintiff why I should find the proper law of this contract to be English law. I go through them very quickly. The advertisement was in an English newspaper; the negotiations took place in England; the contract, although perhaps conditional, was made in England; there is dicta that it is important in which language the contract is made; English is also the language in which the interview was conducted; the plaintiff's salary was paid in sterling; the defendant company is resident in England; the job was arranged through the company's official agent in England; the witness to the contract was English; all the administration so far as payment was concerned throughout the period when the plaintiff was off sick was completed in this country; the plaintiff was more in England during the period of the contract than in Libya; the plaintiff is a UK taxpayer; the insurance company used by the defendant company was based in London; and throughout the contract of employment the plaintiff was always treated as an expatriate.

These are powerful arguments in favour of the proper law of this contract being the law of England. But, on balance, I think that the fact that the defendant company was employing nationals of different nationalities on what was, effectively, the same terms of contract, really is a connection which ought to prevail. It seems to me that the place where this contract was to be, in effect, performed was Libya, and that the proper law of this contract should be Libyan law.

But I do not think that that decision can make the slightest difference to the way in which this case is decided, because the plaintiff is perfectly entitled to proceed in tort in the courts of this country. There is no suggestion that there is anything in the contract which would give the defendants any defence to the plaintiff's claim in tort, or limit the claim in tort, as there was in one of the cases cited to me (see *Sayers v International Drilling Co NV* [1971] 3 All ER 163, [1971] 1 WLR 1176). Therefore, I do not think my decision, so far as that is concerned, can make the slightest difference to the decision in this case. Indeed, it seems to me, on looking at the Civil Code, that the claim in contract, governed as it would be by Libyan law, would succeed equally easily with the claim in tort in this country. But it cannot make any difference because, although the defendants would be entitled to any defence which it could found on its contract, there is none pleaded and there is no suggestion that there is one. So my decision, which is that Libyan law is the proper law of the contract, cannot in my judgment make the slightest difference to this case.

In those circumstances I answer the preliminary issue by saying that the claim in tort is governed by English law, that the action is actionable in Libya, and that the proper law of the contract between the plaintiff and the defendant company is Libyan law. I refuse to stay the plaintiff's claim, and I have already refused leave to appeal against the master's decision on the place at which the contract was made. Although, of course, in the light of my decision as to the proper law of the contract that question is totally irrelevant.

Order accordingly.

Solicitors: *Dibb & Clegg* (for the plaintiff); *Amhurst Brown Martin & Nicholson* (for the defendants).

K Mydeen Esq Barrister.

R v Morris

COURT OF APPEAL, CRIMINAL DIVISION
LORD LANE CJ, O'CONNOR LJ AND TALBOT J
4 FEBRUARY, 8 MARCH 1983

Criminal law – Theft – Appropriation – Defendant taking articles from shelf in self-service store and attaching price labels taken from lower-priced articles – Defendant paying lower price for articles at check-out point – Whether taking articles from shelf 'appropriation' of articles – Whether taking must be without owner's consent to constitute 'appropriation' – Whether defendant must assume all or only some of owner's rights – Theft Act 1968, ss 1(1), 3(1).

Criminal law – Obtaining property by deception – Defendant dishonestly switching price labels on goods in store and thereby deceiving cashier into charging too low a price – Whether defendant guilty of both theft and obtaining property by deception – Theft Act 1968, ss 1(1), 15(1).

The defendant removed articles from shelves in a self-service store and attached in place of or on top of the correct price labels price labels removed from lower-priced articles in the store. He then paid at the check-out point the lower prices indicated on the false labels. He was charged with theft of the articles contrary to s 1(1)[a] of the Theft Act 1968. The judge directed the jury that the changing of the price labels amounted to 'appropriation' of the articles within s 3(1)[b] of the 1968 Act and that therefore the defendant had committed theft by appropriation within s 1(1). The defendant was convicted. He appealed on the ground of misdirection of the jury.

---

a Section 1 is set out at p 451 *c d*, post
b Section 3(1) is set out at p 451 *f*, post

Held – For the purposes of ss 1 and 3(1) of the 1968 Act the term 'appropriates' meant taking possession of an article and assuming any of the owner's rights in it: it was not necessary for the prosecution to prove that possession was taken without the owner's consent or that the defendant had assumed all the owner's rights. Accordingly, taking an article from a supermarket shelf with a view to carrying it to the check-out was an appropriation of the article for the purposes of s 3(1) since it amounted to the assumption of one of the owner's rights, that of removing the article from the shelf, notwithstanding that the taking would not have been without the owner's consent at the time. It followed that the defendant had appropriated the articles, within s 3(1), when he removed them from the shelves. Moreover, even if he did not have a dishonest intent at the time and had thus come by the articles without stealing them, nevertheless his subsequent switching of the price labels amounted to a 'later assumption of a right to [them] by keeping or dealing with [them] as owner' and therefore an appropriation within s 3(1). The appeal would accordingly be dismissed (see p 453 *j*, p 454 *d g h*, p 455 *b c g* to *j* and p 456 *e f*, post).

Lawrence v Comr of Police for the Metropolis [1971] 2 All ER 1253, *R v McPherson* [1973] Crim LR 191, *Oxford v Peers* (1980) 72 Cr App R 19 and *Anderton v Wish* (1980) 72 Cr App R 23 applied.

Dip Kaur v Chief Constable for Hampshire [1981] 2 All ER 430 and *Eddy v Niman* (1981) 73 Cr App R 237 doubted.

Per curiam. Sections 1(1) and 15(1)[c] of the 1968 Act are not mutually exclusive and therefore a person who dishonestly switches the price label on goods in a store and thereby deceives the cashier at the check-out point into charging too low a price for the goods is guilty of the offences of theft under s 1(1) and obtaining property by deception under s 15(1) (see p 456 *d e*, post).

Notes

For theft, see 11 Halsbury's Laws (4th edn) para 1262, and for what amounts to appropriation, see ibid para 1264.

For obtaining property by deception, see ibid para 1278.

For cases on appropriation in theft, see 15 Digest (Reissue) 1264, 1282, *10831–10832*, *11029–11030*.

For the Theft Act 1968, ss 1, 3, 15, see 8 Halsbury's Statutes (3rd edn) 783, 784, 792.

Cases referred to in judgment

Anderton v Wish (1980) 72 Cr App R 23, [1980] Crim LR 319, DC.
Burnside v Anderton (5 November 1982, unreported), DC.
Dip Kaur v Chief Constable for Hampshire [1981] 2 All ER 430, [1981] 1 WLR 578, DC.
Eddy v Niman (1981) 73 Cr App R 237, DC.
Edwards v Ddin [1976] 3 All ER 705, [1976] 1 WLR 942, DC.
Lacis v Cashmarts [1969] 2 QB 400, [1969] 2 WLR 329, DC.
Lawrence v Comr of Police for the Metropolis [1971] 2 All ER 1253, [1972] AC 626, [1971] 3 WLR 225, HL.
Martin v Puttick [1967] 1 All ER 899, [1968] 2 QB 82, [1967] 2 WLR 1131, DC.
Oxford v Peers (1980) 72 Cr App R 19, DC.
R v Hircock (1978) 67 Cr App R 278, CA.
R v McHugh (1976) 64 Cr App R 92, CA.
R v McPherson [1973] Crim LR 191, CA.
R v Meech [1973] 3 All ER 939, [1974] QB 549, [1973] 3 WLR 507, CA.
R v Skipp [1975] Crim LR 114, CA.

---

c Section 15(1), so far as material, provides: 'A person who by any deception dishonestly obtains property belonging to another, with the intention of permanently depriving the other of it, shall on conviction on indictment be liable to imprisonment . . .'

Cases also cited

Davies v Leighton (1978) 68 Cr App R 4, DC. a
R v Hale (1978) 68 Cr App R 415, CA.
R v Monaghan [1979] Crim LR 673, CA.
R v Pitham, R v Hehl (1976) 65 Cr App R 45, CA.

Appeal

On 23 April 1982 in the Crown Court at Acton before Mr W Thomas sitting as an assistant recorder and a jury the appellant, David Alan Morris, was convicted on two counts of theft contrary to s 1 of the Theft Act 1968. He was fined £50 on each count. He appealed against the conviction. The main ground of appeal was that the trial judge erred in law in directing the jury that the changing of price labels on articles in a store alleged against the appellant amounted to an appropriation of the articles under s 3(1) of the 1968 Act. The facts are set out in the judgment of the court. b c

Neil Denison QC and *Philippa Jessel* (assigned by the Registrar of Criminal Appeals) for the appellant.
David Jeffreys QC and *Laura Harris* for the Crown.

Cur adv vult d

8 March. The following judgment of the court was delivered.

LORD LANE CJ. On 23 April 1982 in the Crown Court at Acton the appellant was convicted on two counts of theft under s 1(1) of the Theft Act 1968 and was fined £50 on each count. A third count laid under s 15 of the 1968 Act, which was alternative to count 2, was left on the file on the usual terms. He now appeals against that conviction. e

The prosecution case, which was clearly accepted by the jury, was that the appellant had, on 30 October 1981, taken articles from the shelves of a self-service store and had at some stage attached to those articles, in place of or on top of the true price labels, labels which he had removed from cheaper articles. At the check-out he was asked for and paid the lower prices. He was then arrested. f

The ground of appeal runs as follows: 'That the learned trial Judge erred in law in directing that the alleged changing of price labels by the appellant in this case amounted to an appropriation under s 3(1) of the Theft Act 1968.'

This matter has been fully argued before us by counsel on behalf of the appellant. It was at our encouragement that he did so, and the arguments which he has placed before the court have proved most helpful. The case raises two principal questions. First, the meaning of the word 'appropriation' in the Theft Act 1968. Súbsidiary to this point is the question of what the effect is in law of a customer in a self-service store changing price labels on an article so as to indicate a sale price lower than the original and true price. The second point is the relationship between s 1 of the Act on the one hand and s 15 on the other. g h

The self-service store, generally speaking, operates as follows. Articles are displayed on racks or shelves or on pegs in the store. The price of each article is or should be marked on it by means, usually, of an adhesive label. Wire trolleys or baskets are provided for the convenience of customers into which they can put the articles which they wish to buy and have therefore taken from the shelves. The articles are then taken to a 'check-out' point where an assistant lists the price of each item, totals them up, usually on a cash till. The customer pays and takes the goods away. j

Looked at from the legal point of view, the articles displayed on the shelves with their price tags constitute an invitation to the customer to take an article or articles for purchase and to pay for them at the check-out. At the check-out the customer offers to buy at the price shown, the cashier accepts and the sale is complete.

When payment is made, the ownership of the articles passes to the customer: *Lacis v*
a *Cashmarts* [1969] 2 QB 400. It should be noted that there is no obligation on the customer to use either a trolley or a basket. Providing the customer takes the article to the check-out and there pays the proper price, it is immaterial what means he uses to get the article to the check-out. However, for reasons which will soon be apparent, if they are not so already, it may be imprudent to use any receptacle other than those provided by the store for taking the articles to the check-out point.

b Self-service stores of this sort and the type of dishonest activity which they seem to engender have caused problems in the criminal courts. These problems arise largely from the difficulty in determining the point at which it can be said that appropriation has taken place, which in its turn is caused by a difficulty in deciding what is meant by appropriation. The area of dispute is a very narrow one. The amount of debate which has resulted is disproportionate to the importance of the issue.

c The relevant provisions of the Theft Act 1968 are as follows:

> '**1.** *Basic definition of theft*—(1) A person is guilty of theft if he dishonestly appropriates property belonging to another with the intention of permanently depriving the other of it; and "thief" and "steal" shall be construed accordingly.
>
> (2) It is immaterial whether the appropriation is made with a view to gain, or is made for the thief's own benefit.
>
> d (3) The five following sections of this Act shall have effect as regards the interpretation and operation of this section (and, except as otherwise provided by this Act, shall apply only for purposes of this section).
>
> **2.** "*Dishonestly*"—(1) A person's appropriation of property belonging to another is not to be regarded as dishonest—(*a*) if he appropriates the property in the belief that he has in law the right to deprive the other of it, on behalf of himself or of a
> e third person; or (*b*) if he appropriates the property in the belief that he would have the other's consent if the other knew of the appropriation and the circumstances of it . . .
>
> (2) A person's appropriation of property belonging to another may be dishonest notwithstanding that he is willing to pay for the property.
>
> **3.** "*Appropriates*"—(1) Any assumption by a person of the rights of an owner
> f amounts to an appropriation, and this includes, where he has come by the property (innocently or not) without stealing it, any later assumption of a right to it by keeping or dealing with it as owner . . .
>
> **5.** "*Belonging to another*"—(1) Property shall be regarded as belonging to any person having possession or control of it, or having in it any proprietary right or interest (not being an equitable interest arising only from an agreement to transfer
> g or grant an interest) . . .'

As to the meaning of the word 'appropriation', there are two schools of thought. The first contends that the word 'appropriate' has built into it a connotation that it is some action inconsistent with the owner's rights, something hostile to the interests of the owner or contrary to his wishes and intention or without his authority. The second
h school of thought contends that the word in this context means no more than to take possession of an article and that there is no requirement that the taking or appropriation should be in any way antagonistic to the rights of the owner. Support can be found for each of those two points of view both in the authorities and also amongst the textbook writers.

The following are the authorities which support the first school of thought.

j In *Eddy v Niman* (1981) 73 Cr App R 237 the defendant and a friend entered a self-service supermarket with the intention of stealing goods from it. Goods were taken from a shelf and put into the trolley supplied by the store with that intention. Thereupon the defendant changed his mind and decided not to carry on with the plan. He left the goods with his friend and went out of the store. He was later arrested. He accepted that the facts were as stated and was charged with theft contrary to s 1 of the 1968 Act. The

justices found that although the defendant had a dishonest intention, there had been no
appropriation by him, because the public were authorised and indeed encouraged by the a
owners of the store to take goods from the shelf and put them in the trolley. The
prosecutor appealed. It was held by the Divisional Court, dismissing the appeal, that for
the prosecution to prove theft, they must show, in addition to a dishonest intention, that
the defendant assumed the rights of an owner. The placing of goods in a receptacle
provided by the store was acting within the store's implied consent, so that such an act
could not amount to appropriation. The court distinguished the decision in *R v McPherson* b
[1973] Crim LR 191, on the grounds that in that case the customer put the articles into
her shopping bag rather than the store's basket, which was an act inconsistent with the
owner's rights.

In *R v Skipp* [1975] Crim LR 114 the defendant was convicted on a count which
charged him with stealing a number of boxes of fruit and vegetables. He had falsely
posed as a genuine haulage contractor and thereby obtained instructions to collect two c
loads of oranges and one load of onions from three different places in London. He was to
deliver these to customers in Leicester. Having collected the goods he made off with
them. It was submitted by him on appeal to the Court of Appeal, Criminal Division that
as he had had the intention to steal the goods from the outset, the count was bad for
duplicity in that there were three separate appropriations. The Court of Appeal dismissed
the appeal on the basis that the different acts constituted parts of one activity and d
consequently the three loads were properly included in the one count. They held that an
assumption of the rights of an owner did not necessarily take place at the same time as an
intent permanently to deprive the owner of the property. There might be many cases in
which a person having formed the intent was lawfully in possession of the goods and
could not be said to have assumed the rights of an owner because he had not done
something inconsistent with those rights. The court took the view that up to the point e
when all the goods were loaded and probably up to the point when the goods were
diverted from their true destinations, there had been no assumption of rights and so
there was only one appropriation.

In *R v Meech* [1973] 3 All ER 939, [1974] QB 549 the defendant cashed a cheque in
accordance with the instructions of the owner. At the moment he received the cash in
exchange for the cheque, he intended to steal the proceeds. It was however held by the f
Court of Appeal, Criminal Division that there was no appropriation by him of the goods
until he divided up the money with two accomplices. All three, Meech and the two
accomplices, had been charged with theft and there was no alternative charge of receiving
in respect of the two accomplices. Consequently, if the theft by Meech had taken place
when he received the money from the bank, the other two men were entitled to be
acquitted. The court held that, although the money was withdrawn with a dishonest g
intention, it was not appropriated by Meech until it was divided at the scene of the faked
robbery which the three men had staged.

In *Dip Kaur v Chief Constable for Hampshire* [1981] 2 All ER 430, [1981] 1 WLR 578 the
appellant had been convicted of theft in the following circumstances. She had selected a
pair of shoes from a rack marked £6·99. One of the shoes, as she observed, was marked
£6·99, the other £4·99. Without concealing either label and intending to pay whichever h
of the two prices might be demanded from her, she proffered the shoes to the cashier and
was charged and paid £4·99. The justices held that the cashier had no authority to accept
payment of £4·99, but since the appellant knew that that was not the correct price, the
contract was void, the goods were in the ownership of the store, the appellant had
appropriated them and since she was dishonest, the offence was made out. The Divisional
Court allowed the appeal on the grounds that the cashier had authority to charge the j
price she did, that a mistake as to price induced by wrong marking was not so
fundamental as to destroy the validity of the contract of sale, but merely rendered it
voidable, and that, accordingly, since the contract had not been avoided by the time the
appellant left the store, property of the shoes passed on payment and the appellant had
not appropriated property belonging to another. It was not in this case argued that the

initial removal of the shoes from the rack was an appropriation. Nor was there any suggestion that the appellant herself had altered the price label.

R v Hircock (1978) 67 Cr App R 278 is another decision to like effect in respect of the alleged theft of a motor car which was the subject of a hire-purchase agreement.

The first school of thought is supported by *Smith on the Law of Theft* (4th edn, 1979) p 15, para 31. Having considered the decisions in *Eddy v Niman* (1981) 73 Cr App R 237, *R v Skipp* [1975] Crim LR 114 and *R v Meech* [1973] 3 All ER 939, [1974] QB 549, he goes on to write:

> 'These decisions raise fundamental questions about the nature of "appropriation". They suggest that "helping oneself" to the property of another is an essential characteristic, that a man does not "assume" the right of an owner if the owner confers those rights on him; and that, notwithstanding the fact that the words "without the consent of the owner" are neither expressed nor implied in the Act, "appropriation" implies something done without the owner's authority. This is far from being an unreasonable interpretation of the words "appropriation" and "assumption"; but there remains an element of doubt whether it is consistent with the decision of the House of Lords in *Lawrence* ([1971] 2 All ER 1253, [1972] AC 626). It is submitted, however, that the better view is that *Skipp, Meech* and *Hircock* in this respect are rightly decided and that *Lawrence* is distinguishable.'

The second school of thought is supported by the decision in *R v McPherson* [1973] Cr LR 191. McPherson and two others were convicted of theft. The others distracted the attention of the manager of the supermarket whilst McPherson took two bottles of whisky from a display stand and put them in her shopping bag. They were then arrested. They appealed on the ground that taking the bottles from the display stand could not amount to an appropriation until the bottles had been taken past the check-out point. This argument was rejected by the Court of Appeal (Lord Widgery CJ, Megaw LJ and Talbot J) on the grounds that since there was an intention to steal when the bottles were taken from the display stand, there was then an appropriation. A commentary on this case in the Criminal Law Review reads as follows:

> 'The removal of the bottles from the shelf in the present case would have been a sufficient "asportation" under the old law of larceny; and, once the dishonest intention was proved, it was clearly a sufficient "appropriation" within section 3(1) of the Theft Act.'

This decision was cited with approval in *Anderton v Wish* (1980) 72 Cr App R 23.

There are other decisions, albeit not in respect of supermarkets, which tend to support the same view. We cite for purposes of completeness *R v McHugh* (1976) 64 Cr App R 92, which was a case involving a self-service petrol station. There is a further decision in *Edwards v Ddin* [1976] 3 All ER 705, [1976] 1 WLR 942. That was another petrol station case but there the petrol was served by an attendant.

This line of argument is supported by the editors of *Archbold on Criminal Pleading Evidence and Practice* (41st edn, 1982) paras 18–13 to 18–15.

It seems to us that these two lines of authorities are not reconcilable by any logical method. Counsel for the appellant was inclined to agree with that proposition. Therefore it becomes necessary for us to examine the matter afresh and try to decide which of the two is the correct approach.

Much of the difficulty which is highlighted by the decisions to which we have made reference arises from the words of s 3(1) of the 1968 Act. That section is only a partial definition of the word 'appropriation'. It is to be noted that any assumption by a person of the rights of an owner is sufficient. It should also not be overlooked that the second half of s 3(1) makes any assumption of a right to the article by keeping or dealing with it as owner also an appropriation. Thus one has first of all the ordinary meaning of 'appropriates', then the meaning of 'any assumption of the rights of an owner', then 'any keeping of the article as owner', and finally 'any dealing with the article as owner'.

We approach the task of determining the meaning of 'appropriates' in a number of different ways. First of all there is the dictionary meaning: the *Shorter Oxford English Dictionary* defines it as 'to take for one's own or to oneself'. That seems to connote some sort of claim being staked to the article. It would not cover, for example, picking up an article in a supermarket simply to examine it before deciding to put it in the basket. It seems to us however that it is apt to describe the actions of the customer who takes an article from the shelf determining to buy it.

Secondly, the object of the first five sections of the Theft Act 1968 was to get rid of the distinctions which existed under the Larceny Act 1916 between simple larceny, larceny as a bailee, larceny by a trick, embezzlement and fraudulent conversion. 'Appropriates' was the word chosen as the key to that operation. It was plainly intended to have a wider meaning than the word 'take' under the 1916 Act. Consequently the observations of Winn LJ in *Martin v Puttick* [1967] 1 All ER 899, [1968] 2 QB 82, where the defendant was charged under the 1916 Act, do not affect the present decision. He said ([1967] 1 All ER 899 at 902, [1968] 2 QB 82 at 89):

> '... the customer does in a physical sense take the article by picking it up and putting it into a basket or shopping bag: that is not such a taking as is contemplated by ... the Larceny Act 1916 ...'

Next it seems to us that in taking the article from the shelf the customer is indeed assuming one of the rights of the owner: the right to move the article from its position on the shelf to carry it to the check-out.

Finally, and this seems to us to be the weightiest argument, is the decision of the House of Lords in *Lawrence v Comr of Police for the Metropolis* [1971] 2 All ER 1253, [1972] AC 626. In that case a taxi driver at Victoria Station told an Italian student that the cost of the journey to his destination would not be covered by the £1 proffered. The student opened his wallet to the taxi driver and the taxi driver took from it a further £5 in notes. The taxi driver then drove the student to his destination. The proper fare was some 10s 6d. The taxi driver was convicted of theft under s 1(1) of the 1968 Act. The House of Lords upheld the conviction as had the Court of Appeal. Viscount Dilhorne, with whose speech the remaining members of the House agreed, based his decision on the fact that all the necessary ingredients to establish the offence of theft were present, that is to say (1) dishonesty, (2) appropriation, (3) property belonging to another and (4) intention permanently to deprive the other of that property. He stated tersely in terms ([1971] 2 All ER 1253 at 1256, [1972] AC 626 at 633):

> 'The first question posed in the certificate was: "Whether Section 1(1) of the Theft Act, 1968, is to be construed as though it contained the words 'without having the consent of the owner' or words to that effect." In my opinion, the answer is clearly No.'

That being the emphatic view of their Lordships, it would, we think, be quite wrong in effect to reimport into the offence the necessity of proving what amounts to absence of consent on the part of the owner by saying that the word 'appropriates' necessarily means some action contrary to the authority or interests of the owner and that that is one of the requirements which the prosecution must prove.

Consequently in our view the taking the article from the shelf with a view to transporting it to the check-out is an appropriation, as *R v McPherson* [1973] Crim LR 191 decides. We are conscious that this casts doubt on other decisions referred to previously in this judgment and in particular on the two supermarket cases, *Eddy v Niman* (1981) 73 Cr App R 237 and *Dip Kaur v Chief Constable of Hampshire* [1981] 2 All ER 430, [1981] 1 WLR 578. If we may respectfully say so, we do not think that the placing of the article in the shopper's bag rather than in the basket belonging to the store is a sufficient ground for distinguishing *R v McPherson*. Such action on the part of a customer may have some relevance to the question of dishonesty but not, for the reasons set out earlier, to the question of appropriation.

As far as *Dip Kaur v Chief Constable of Hampshire* [1981] 2 All ER 430, [1981] 1 WLR 578 is concerned, a decision for which I was at least partly responsible, on the facts as found by the justices theft was plainly made out and our decision was wrong. There was an appropriation when the shoes were taken from the shelf, dishonesty was found as a fact by the justices, the property then belonged to another and the intent to deprive was obvious. In retrospect the real answer to *Kaur* was that what the appellant did was probably not rightly categorised as dishonest.

Turning back to the facts of the instant case, when the appellant removed the articles from the shelf that was an appropriation. If the labels were switched prior to the removal, that was overwhelming evidence that the appropriation was dishonest, even if it was not itself an appropriation (see below). If the labels were switched by him after the removal of the articles from the shelf, that likewise would be evidence on which the jury could have come to the conclusion that the initial appropriation was dishonest.

What if, however unlikely, the jury were not satisfied that at the time of the removal from the shelf the defendant's intention was dishonest? Section 3(1) comes into operation. The defendant has come by the property without stealing it. Has there been a later assumption of a right to it by keeping or dealing with it as owner? The authorities on this point are all one way. *Anderton v Wish* (1980) 72 Cr App R 23, a Divisional Court decision, held that appropriation took place when the customer switched the price labels. That decision was followed in *Oxford v Peers* (1980) 72 Cr App R 19, albeit with hesitation, and in the latest case *Burnside v Anderton* (5 November 1982, unreported), a decision of the Divisional Court. The hesitation in *Oxford v Peers* was due to the commentary on *Anderton v Wish* [1980] Crim LR 320, in which the commentator has this to say:

> 'It is respectfully submitted that the better view of the facts in the present case was that taken by the justices, namely that the act of labelling the brush was a preparatory step towards the offence of obtaining the brush by false pretences but did not amount to theft. The court relies on the wide definition of appropriation in section 3(1) of the Theft Act 1968. This states that "*any assumption* by a person of the rights of an owner amounts to an appropriation," but it does not state that "an assumption by a person of *any* of the rights of an owner amounts to an appropriation," and there is a very important difference. Certainly the defendant was assuming a right of the owner in re-pricing the brush. She was not assuming all of the owner's rights.'

Having heard argument on the matter from both counsel, we have come to the conclusion that it is not necessary for the prosecution to prove that the defendant assumed all the rights of an owner. It is sufficient is he 'deals with' the article as owner. Putting a label on an article indicating the price at which the owner will be prepared to sell is plainly such a dealing.

Consequently, assuming in favour of the appellant that no dishonesty is proved at the moment of taking the article from the shelf, the later dealing with it as owner was an assumption of a right to it and that in its turn was an appropriation.

On the facts of this case the recorder had of course no need to go through the analysis of events as we have felt obliged to do. This is what he said:

> 'It is said that he appropriated each of these articles, and the basis of that allegation is that he took it off the shelf, or the peg, or wherever it was on display, and changed the label on it. That is the conclusion that the Crown invite you to draw from the evidence. It is for you to say whether you do draw it. If he did change the label to a label of much lower value, as the Crown's evidence suggests, it would be open to you to find that he had appropriated goods on that basis. That would amount to an appropriation for the purposes of the law: an appropriation of somebody's else's property; an act inconsistent with the owner's rights.'

That direction was in the circumstances of the case correct.

Counsel for the appellant in his final submission to the court urged us to tackle the whole problem anew, and to restore what he argued is a proper balance between s 1 and s 15 of the 1968 Act. Until the customer reaches the check-out point, he argues, he is *a* acting as agent of the shopkeeper. He is doing what in a conventional shop the shopkeeper would do for himself, namely taking the selected article from the shelf and putting it on the counter to await payment by the customer. Therefore there can be no assumption of the rights of an owner until the point where the sale takes place. On this argument nothing done before the check-out point is reached can be theft. If that approach is adopted there are, it is said, two possibilities. Either the customer walks out without *b* paying, in which case, providing that dishonesty and intent permanently to deprive are proved, that is theft. Alternatively, if the customer has switched price labels or carried out some similar deceit whereby he is charged too low a price, that is the offence under s 15 of obtaining by deception.

Whilst appreciating the simplicity of this approach, we think, for the reasons already set out, that the wording of the Act, coupled with the decision in *Lawrence v Comr of* *c* *Police for the Metropolis* [1971] 2 All ER 1253, [1972] AC 626, does not allow us to adopt this solution.

As we said earlier, this is a problem within a very narrow compass. There will be, one hopes, very few occasions when the suspected thief in a self-service store will be arrested before he passes the check-out point. The idea that the mere failure to use the basket or trolley provided by the store without more is evidence of dishonesty is plainly wrong. *d* Consequently it will be seldom that in the absence of a price-label-switching there will be any evidence of dishonesty before the check-out point is passed.

Finally, we have of necessity dealt with this case on the basis of theft or no theft. It should not be overlooked that a person who is proved to have dishonestly switched price labels and as a result has succeeded in deceiving the cashier at the check-out into charging too low a price for the article of which he intends to deprive the owner permanently is *e* also guilty of an offence under s 15(1) of the Act. Sections 15(1) and 1(1) are not mutually exclusive: see *Lawrence v Comr of Police for the Metropolis* [1971] 2 All ER 1253 at 1256, [1972] AC 626 at 633 per Viscount Dilhorne.

This appeal against conviction is dismissed.

Appeal dismissed. *f*

24 March. The court refused leave to appeal to the House of Lords but certified, under s 33(2) of the Criminal Appeal Act 1968, that the following point of law of general public importance was involved in the decision: if a person substituted on an item of goods displayed in a self-service store a price label showing a lesser price for one showing a greater price, with the intention of paying the lesser price, and then paid the lesser price at the till and took the goods, whether there was at any stage a 'dishonest appropriation' for the purposes of s 1 of the Theft Act 1968 and, if so, at what point such appropriation took place.

5 May. The Appeal Committee of the House of Lords granted the appellant leave to appeal.

Solicitors: *Ferris & Evans*, Ealing (for the Crown).

N P Metcalfe Esq Barrister.

Torminster Properties Ltd v Green and another

COURT OF APPEAL, CIVIL DIVISION
STEPHENSON AND KERR LJJ
7, 17 MARCH 1983

Landlord and tenant – Rent – Review – Rent payable on review to be rent agreed between parties or fixed by arbitration in default of agreement – Rent fixed by arbitration after tenant surrendering lease – Whether surrender before arbitrator's determination discharging tenant's liability to pay new rent – Whether tenant liable to pay new rent even though new rent not determined until after surrender of lease.

By a lease made between the lessor and a company as lessee premises were demised to the lessee for a term of 25 years from 24 June 1973 at a rent of £7,100 a year for the first five years of the term and, under a rent review clause in the lease, for the next five years from 24 June 1978 (the review date) at the same rent or at the open market rent at the review date, whichever was the higher. The rent was payable quarterly in advance on the usual quarter days. Performance of the lessee's covenants, including the covenant to pay rent, was guaranteed by two sureties. The rent review clause provided that if the lessor and the lessee failed to agree the open market rent payable at the review date the rent was to be determined, at the lessee's election, by an independent arbitrator and that, if the arbitrator's determination had not for any reason been published prior to the review date, then the lessee was to pay the old rent for each quarter until the arbitrator made his determination. The rent review clause further provided that if the arbitrator determined a higher rent the difference between the new rent and the actual rent paid at the old rate for the period from the review date until the new rent was fixed was to be a contract debt from the lessee to the lessor payable when the new rent was determined. The parties failed to agree on the open market rent as at the review date and accordingly one quarter's rent at the old rate was paid on behalf of the lessee for the quarter following the review date. On 13 July 1978 the lessee gave notice to the lessor that it required the open market rent to be determined by an independent arbitrator. In November the lessee was wound up. In January 1979 an arbitrator was appointed under the rent review clause. On 4 April 1979 the lessee's liquidator surrendered the lease of the premises. No reference was made in the terms of the surrender, or otherwise, regarding the lessee's liability to pay rent from the rent review date at the rate determined by the arbitrator. On 25 January 1980 the arbitrator determined the open market rent as at the rent review date and in June 1980 the lessor brought an action against the sureties claiming rent at the new rate for the quarterly instalments of rent due in June and September 1978, less the rent at the old rate which had already been paid. The judge held that the sureties, as guarantors of the lessee's obligations, were liable to pay rent at the new rate for the period the lessee had remained in possession after the review date even though the new rent had been determined after the surrender of the lease. The sureties appealed, contending that the surrender of the lease extinguished, discharged or released the lessee's liability to pay the rent under the rent review clause because the obligation to pay that rent had not accrued at the date of the surrender.

Held – A lessee's liability to pay rent in accordance with a rent review clause in his lease was not destroyed or discharged by a surrender of the lease which took place after the rent review date, because where there was a lease containing such a clause the lessee covenanted that he would pay rent determined in accordance with that clause from the rent review date, and thus his obligation under that covenant took effect from the review date. Likewise, the lessor had a corresponding right from that date to sue for a declaration that that was the lessee's obligation. It followed that the lessee's obligation under the lease to pay the rent determined by the arbitrator from the review date, when such rent was determined, accrued on 24 June 1978 (the rent review date) and took effect before the a date of the surrender on 4 April 1979. On the principle that a lessee remained liable for breaches of covenant occurring before the surrender of a lease, the lessee remained liable for rent at the rate determined by the arbitrator in respect of the two quarters payable in June and September 1978, those quarters having expired before the date of the surrender, and since the lessee was unable to pay that rent at the new rate the sureties were liable to pay. Their appeal would therefore be dismissed (see p 462 *b* to *d* and p 463 *g* to p 464 *a*, b post).

Richmond v Savill [1926] All ER Rep 362 and *United Scientific Holdings Ltd v Burnley BC* [1977] 2 All ER 62 applied.

Decision of John Mowbray QC sitting as a deputy judge of the High Court [1982] 1 All ER 420 affirmed on different grounds.

c

Notes

For rent review clauses and for the retroactive effect of such a clause, see 27 Halsbury's Laws (4th edn) paras 215, 217.

Cases referred to in judgments

A-G Cox, Pearce v A-G (1850) 3 HL Cas 240, 10 ER 93.
Bailey (C H) Ltd v Memorial Enterprises Ltd [1974] 1 All ER 1003, [1974] 1 WLR 728, CA. d
Dalton v Pickard (1911) [1926] 2 KB 545, [1926] All ER Rep 371, CA.
Fussell, Re, ex p Allen (1882) 20 Ch D 341, CA.
Grimman v Legge (1828) 8 B & C 324, 108 ER 1063.
Latham, Re, ex p Glegg (1881) 19 Ch D 7, CA.
Morrish, Re, ex p Sir W Hart Dyke (1882) 22 Ch D 410, CA.
Richmond v Savill [1926] 2 KB 530, [1926] All ER Rep 362, CA. e
Slack v Sharpe (1838) 8 Ad & El 366, 112 ER 876.
United Scientific Holdings Ltd v Burnley BC, Cheapside Land Development Co Ltd v Messels Service Co [1977] 2 All ER 62, [1978] AC 904, [1977] 2 WLR 806, HL; *rvsg* [1976] 2 All ER 220, [1976] Ch 128, [1976] 2 WLR 686, CA.
Walker's Case (1587) 3 Co Rep 22a, 76 ER 676.

f

Appeal

The defendants, Clive Edward Green and Adrian Nicholas Kerridge (the sureties), who were guarantors of the obligations of Cadac (London) Ltd, the lessee under a lease of premises dated 18 October 1973, appealed against a judgment of John Mowbray QC sitting as a deputy judge of the High Court ([1982] 1 All ER 420, [1982] 1 WLR 751) whereby he held that the plaintiff, Torminster Properties Ltd (the lessor), was entitled to g £2,947·82 as two quarters of the new rent due from the lessee under a rent review clause in the lease although the amount of new rent was determined under the clause after the lessee had surrendered the lease. The facts are set out in the judgment of Stephenson LJ.

Robert Wakefield for the sureties.
Vivian Chapman for the lessor. h

Cuv adv vult

17 March. The following judgments were delivered.

STEPHENSON LJ. This appeal raises a novel point, the effect of a surrender of a lease on a claim for increased rent fixed after the surrender. The appeal arises out of a lease j made on 18 October 1973 between the respondent, Torminster Properties Ltd (the lessor), of the first part and Cadac (London) Ltd (the lessee) of the second part and the appellants, Green and Kerridge (the sureties), of the third part, demising by cl (1) unto the lessee a factory unit in Harpenden for the term of 25 years from 24 June 1973, yielding and paying during that term the rents set out in the fourth schedule to the lease.

By cl (2) the lessee covenanted to perform the covenants set out in the fifth schedule, including a covenant to pay during the term the rent reserved on the day and in the manner aforesaid.

By cl (4) the sureties covenanted to perform the covenants set out in the seventh schedule, including a covenant that the lessee would pay the rent reserved and in default of such payment the sureties would pay and make good to the lessor all losses thereby arising. There were further provisions for the sureties taking over the lease in the event of the lessee entering into liquidation and the liquidator disclaiming the lease.

The fourth schedule provided as follows:

'Rent

(A) For the first five years of the said term the rent of £7,100

(B) For the next five years of the said term and for each successive period of five years of the said term thereafter either the yearly rent reserved in sub-clause (A) hereof or the open market rental value of the demised premises at the review date or the rental then under review whichever is the higher and in any case the same shall remain constant during the whole period referred to in each of such successive periods of five years

AND the said rents shall in all cases be paid by equal quarterly payments in advance from the usual quarter days in every year without any deduction whatsoever the first payment apportioned in respect of the period from the date hereof to the quarter day next hereafter to be paid on the execution hereof

PROVIDED THAT for the purposes of sub-clause (B) hereof it is hereby agreed that the following definitions and provisions shall apply namely:—

(1) The expression "open market rental value" means the annual rental value of the demised premises in the open market which might reasonably be demanded by a willing landlord on a lease for a term of years certain equivalent in length to the residue unexpired at the review date of the term of years hereby granted with vacant possession at the commencement of the term but upon the supposition (if not a fact) that the Lessee has complied with all the obligations as to repair and decoration herein imposed on the Lessee (but without prejudice to any rights or remedies of the Lessor in regard thereto) and there being disregarded (if applicable) those matters set out in paragraphs (a) (b) and (c) of Section 34 of the Landlord and Tenant Act 1954 and there being disregarded (so far as may be permitted by law) all restrictions whatsoever relating to rent or to security of tenure contained in any statute or orders rules or regulations thereunder and any directions thereby given relating to any method of determination of rent such lease being on the same terms and conditions (other than as to amount of rent and length of term) as this present demise without the payment of any fine or premium:

(2) The expression "review date" means the expiration of the fifth year of the said term or the expiration of the tenth year of the said term or the expiration of each successive period of five years as the context requires for the purpose of ascertainment of the open market value under sub-clause (B) hereof

(3) The open market rental value shall be determined in manner following that is to say it shall be such annual sum as shall be (a) specified in a notice in writing signed by or on behalf of the Lessor and posted in a pre-paid envelope addressed to the Lessee at the demised premises at any time after the beginning of a clear period of six months immediately preceding the review date (and such notice shall be conclusively deemed to have been received by the Lessee in due course of post) or (b) agreed between the parties before the expiration of three months immediately after the date of posting of such notice as aforesaid in substitution for the said sum or (c) determined at the election of the Lessee (to be made by counter-notice in writing served by the Lessee upon the Lessor not later than the expiration of the said three months) by an independent surveyor appointed for that purpose by the parties jointly in writing or upon their failure to agree upon such appointment

within one month immediately after the date of service of the said counter-notice then by an independent surveyor appointed for that purpose on the application of *a* either party alone by the President for the time being of the Royal Institution of Chartered Surveyors and in either case in accordance with the provisions of the Arbitration Act 1950
Delay in rent determination
(4) In the event of failure to agree or of the determination of such independent surveyor not having been published prior to the review date for any reason whatever *b* then in respect of the period of time (hereinafter called the delay period) beginning with the review date or the date or the Lessor's notice under sub-clause 3(a) (whichever shall be the later) and ending on the quarter day immediately following the date on which such determination shall have been agreed or published the Lessee shall pay to the Lessor in manner hereinbefore provided rent at the yearly rate payable immediately before the review date PROVIDED that at the expiration of *c* the delay period there shall be due as a debt payable by the Lessee to the Lessor on demand a sum of money equal to the amount whereby the yearly rent agreed or determined by such independent surveyor shall exceed the yearly rent at the yearly rate aforesaid but duly apportioned on a daily basis in respect of the delay period . . .'

I need not read the rest of the fourth schedule.

Paragraph (B) (5), that is the next paragraph, which I have not read, made time of the *d* essence; para (C) provided for payment by way of further rent of a proportion of, inter alia, insurance and service charges.

On 10 March 1978 the lessor's agents gave the lessee notice under cl (1) and the fourth schedule that they intended to increase the rent to £15,500 per annum. There was no agreement and on 13 July 1978 the lessee's agents gave the lessor notice under para (B)(3)(c) of the fourth schedule that it required the open market rental value of the *e* premises to be determined by an independent surveyor. But the lessee was in financial difficulties, receivers were appointed, and on 25 October 1978 solicitors wrote to the sureties on behalf of the lessor calling on both to pay one quarter's rent in advance, due date 29 September 1978, amount payable £1,775, and insurance, but stating that the total amount of the rent due as from the review date was not shown because it had not been finalised. *f*

On 13 November 1978 a winding-up order was made. The liquidator appointed did not disclaim the lease, but by an exchange of letters dated 4 April 1979 between him and the lessor's solicitors the lessee surrendered the lease to the lessor. On 22 January 1979 the President of the Royal Institution of Chartered Surveyors had appointed an independent surveyor under para (B)(3)(c) of the fourth schedule. On 6 May 1979 the lessor's solicitors wrote to both sureties that as a result of the surrender the lessor was now *g* able to finalise its claim against the sureties and enclosed a statement claiming £2,947·82. That is the sum claimed in this action against the sureties and awarded by Mr John Mowbray QC sitting as a deputy judge of the High Court on 31 July 1981 ([1982] 1 All ER 420, [1982] 1 WLR 751), from whose decision this appeal is brought.

The claim is made up as follows: *h*

'Rent 25th June 1978 to 29th September 1978	£3,375·00
Less amount paid	£1,775·00
	£1,600·00
Rent 30th September to 25th December 1978	£3,375·00
Insurance 1st October 1978 to 25th December 1978	£ 207·50
Service charges for 1978	£ 265·32
	£5,447·82
Less amount received on account	£2,500·00
	£2,947·82'

j

That being the sum which is claimed.

Of the two sums credited, the £1,775 was a quarter's rent at the old rate of £7,100 per annum paid by the sureties (apparently £25 short) and the £2,500 was an occupation fee calculated on the basis of the proposed rent of £13,500 per annum and paid by a company called Candystrope Ltd, which bought the lessee's assets (but not the lease) and occupied the factory unit in 1979.

Though the lessor's notice had specified the increased annual rent as £15,500, the lessor sought from the independent surveyor ex parte a lower figure of £13,500, and £13,500 per annum was the open market rental value on the review date determined by the award of the independent surveyor on 25 January 1980.

The question raised by this appeal is whether the surrender of the lease has extinguished, discharged or released the lessee's liability (and thereby the sureties' liability) to pay two quarterly payments of increased rent for which there would have admittedly been liability if the lease had not been surrendered. The surrender took place after the first review date and during the next five years of the term of the lease, but before the open market rental value of the demised premises at the review date had been determined by an independent surveyor in accordance with the rent review clause in the lease. It is common ground that the sureties are in the same position as the lessee and that there was no reference to liability to pay the increased rent in the terms of surrender and no express agreement as to that liability. The question is therefore one of law depending on the true construction of the terms of the lease and the legal effect of its surrender in the light of authorities which are not directly in point.

There are cogent arguments for and against the judge's view that the sureties are liable to pay the increased rent and charges claimed and that their liability is not extinguished by the surrender of the lease. And the arguments on both sides have been very well put.

Counsel for the sureties submits that the wording of para (B) (4) of the fourth schedule is such as to show that the surrender put an end to liability for any rent. The authority of decided cases shows that a surrender puts an end to the lease itself, not merely to the term of years granted by the lease. All the tenant's liabilities are thereby extinguished except those which have already accrued or have been expressly reserved. There was no reservation in the letters exchanged on 4 April 1979, and the language of para (B)(4) does not preserve an accrued liability or corresponding right to sue but negatives it. Where, as here, there has been a 'delay period' because there has been a failure to agree or the determination of the independent surveyor has not been published prior to the review date, it is (I quote from the fourth schedule) 'at the expiration of the delay period' that 'there shall be due as a debt payable by the Lessee to the Lessor on demand a sum of money equal to the amount whereby the yearly rent agreed or determined by such independent surveyor shall exceed' the previous rent. That means that that excess is not due before the expiration of the delay period, and until then there is no debt due or payable, there is no yearly rent agreed or determined and nothing which can be (I quote again from the schedule) 'duly apportioned on a daily basis in respect of the delay period'. The only accrued right is to have an arbitration, not to be owed or paid a debt. There is no right of action vested in the lessor before the surrender enabling the lessor to sue for the increase.

Counsel for the lessor emphasises the basic obligation of the lessee under cl (1) and the fourth schedule, para (B) to pay as rent for the next five years after the review date the open market rental value of the demised premises at that date by equal quarterly payments in advance; and he contrasts that with the machinery for ascertaining that rent and open market rental value provided by sub-paragraphs including sub-para (4). That basic obligation exists at the review date as an obligation to pay the increased rent when it is determined, like the contractual obligation to pay the price of goods to be fixed by a third party. The debt is due at the review date, though it waits to be payable until the expiration of the delay period and the determination of its amount. It is owed from the review date until surrender, and nothing in para (B)(4) indicates that it is not; after surrender it becomes payable retrospectively and would be so payable without the provisions of para (B)(4). Counsel for the lessor might not be able to say that there was a debt before 25 January 1980; but he does say that there was a liability. Even if the debt does not exist until quantified, the contractual obligation to pay it when quantified does exist from the review date until surrender of the lease, perhaps rather as on an interlocutory judgment for damages to be assessed the judgment 'debtor' is under a present liability to pay unliquidated damages to be assessed in the future. Or, another imperfect analogy, as a party ordered to pay costs to be taxed if not agreed owes a duty to pay them but cannot be sued for them until they are agreed or taxed.

There is authority for the following propositions. (1) Rent payable in arrear which has not accrued or become due at the date of surrender of a lease is not recoverable in full; until the Apportionment Act 1870 it was not recoverable pro rata for so long a time as the tenant occupied the premises before surrender: *Grimman v Legge* (1828) 8 B & C 324, 108 ER 1063, *Slack v Sharpe* (1838) 8 Ad & El 366, 112 ER 876. (2) Rent which has accrued or become due at the date of surrender is recoverable: *Walker's Case* (1587) 3 Co Rep 22a, 76 ER 676, *A-G v Cox, Pearce v A-G* (1850) 3 HL Cas 240 at 275, 10 ER 93 at 106. (3) A surrender of a lease operates only to release the tenant from liability on covenants taking effect after the date of the surrender, leaving him liable for past breaches, eg of repairing covenants: *Dalton v Pickard* (1911) [1926] 2 KB 545, [1926] All ER Rep 371, *Richmond v Savill* [1926] 2 KB 530, [1926] All ER Rep 362, in which the court followed *Dalton's* case, *Walker's Case* and *Cox's* case. Statements in cases of disclaimer of the lease by a trustee in bankruptcy deemed to have been surrendered by s 23 of the Bankruptcy Act 1869, which suggested that the surrender of a lease destroys all its provisions and every liability under it (*Re Latham, ex p Glegg* (1881) 19 Ch D 7, *Re Fussell, ex p Allen* (1882) 20 Ch D 341, *Re Morrish, ex p Sir W Hart Dyke* (1882) 22 Ch D 410) are to be taken as limited to future breaches and rights of action not yet accrued. The proposition derived from them that the mere surrender of a tenancy precludes the landlord from further enforcing against the tenant any of his obligations under the lease, whether those obligations had already accrued before the date of the surrender or had not, was stated to be wrong by this court in *Richmond v Savill*, and does not appear to have been revived since it was laid to rest in 1926. Counsel for the sureties does not seek to revive it.

Now the rent which the lessor has recovered from the sureties is rent payable in advance in respect of two quarterly periods which had in fact expired before the date of surrender. The amount would have been different had the independent surveyor fixed a different open market rental value. If he had found that that value was no higher than £7,100 a year, that would have been the rent for which the lessee would have continued to be liable. And, once the amount of the rent payable for the second period of five years has been determined, it is payable retrospectively from the review date and the start of that period: *C H Bailey Ltd v Memorial Enterprises Ltd* [1974] 1 All ER 1003, [1974] 1 WLR 728, *United Scientific Holdings Ltd v Burnley BC, Cheapside Land Development Co Ltd v Messels Service Co* [1977] 2 All ER 62, [1978] AC 904.

In the *Cheapside Land Development Co* case Graham J had granted the landlords a declaration that the market rent as determined by the valuer for the second and third periods of seven years in a lease for a term of 21 years, if higher than the annual rent payable in arrear on the usual quarter days for the first period of seven years, would be recoverable with effect from the start of the second period at the review date. The Court of Appeal reversed his decision, apparently on the ground that the rent was not, and had to be, certain. The House of Lords restored the order of Graham J, holding that to be distrainable rent had to be certain, that a contractual money payment made by a tenant to his landlord in consideration for the use of the latter's land was rent and that it need not be certain at the date from which it became payable: see the speeches of Lord Diplock, Lord Simon and Lord Fraser ([1977] 2 All ER 62 at 72, 76, 86, 99, [1978] AC 904 at 930, 934–935, 947, 964). (When Lord Fraser speaks of the rent as the contractual sum due which 'need not be certain at the date on which it becomes payable', I think he must mean 'at the date from which it becomes payable when ascertained'.) In the first of these passages Lord Diplock points out ([1977] 2 All ER 62 at 72, [1978] AC 904 at 930):

> 'The determination of the new rent under the procedure stipulated in the rent
> a review clause neither brings into existence a fresh contract between the landlord and the tenant nor does it put an end to one that had existed previously. It is an event on the occurrence of which the tenant has in his existing contract already accepted an obligation to pay to the landlord the rent so determined for the period to which the rent review relates. The tenant's acceptance of that obligation was an inseverable part of the whole consideration of the landlord's grant of a term of years
> b of the length agreed. Without it, in a period during which inflation was anticipated, the landlord would either have been unwilling to grant a lease for a longer period than up to the first review date or would have demanded a higher rent to be paid throughout the term than that payable before the first review date. By the time of each review of rent the tenant will have already received a substantial part of the whole benefit which it was intended that he should obtain in return for his
> c acceptance of the obligation to pay the higher rent for the succeeding period.'

Counsel for the lessor naturally relies on what Lord Diplock there said as supporting his submission that the obligation precedes the surrender and is therefore enforceable once its extent has been determined. So did the deputy judge in support of his statement
d ([1982] 1 All ER 420 at 423–424, [1982] 1 WLR 751 at 755–756):

> 'Here, at the surrender, the landlord was entitled to be paid as a contract debt the difference, if any, between the old rent and the review rent for the period after the review date. It was a present right based on a partly executed consideration ... But it was a present right not yet actionable, to a future payment, because the difference
> e was not payable until the quarter day after the arbitrator fixed the new rent and there might be no difference; but again, the landlord could, apart at least from the surrender, compel the arbitration to be carried through ... It seems to me that the tenant's duty to pay the difference between the old and the review rent for the period after the review date is correlative with the tenant's right to possession during that period and so it should be paid, even though the surrender intervenes before its
> f amount is fixed. As the lessee here continued in possession during the period after the rent review date, it ought to pay the difference between the arbitrator's rent and what the lessor has received for that period.'

He then gave judgment for that rent and the undisputed service and insurance charges claim.

g It may be said that the tenant who pays rent in arrear will have already received when he pays it a substantial part of the benefit of the occupation for which he has agreed to pay it, yet his liability does not survive a surrender. But in my judgment the liability to pay rent determined in accordance with a rent review clause is a liability which is not destroyed or discharged by a surrender after the period for which it will ultimately be paid has started to run. There is, when that period has started, a right to sue, not for the
h as yet undetermined rent but for a declaration that the tenant is liable to pay it when determined, as the *Cheapside Land Development Co* case shows. There is not an antecedent breach of an obligation, indeed there could not be until the quarter day immediately following 25 January 1980; but there is an antecedent obligation accruing before surrender puts an end to the lease. The lessee has no right to occupy the premises after the review date rent-free: he owes a contractual duty to pay at least the initial rent as long
j as he holds the lease, however long the determination of the new rent may be delayed. It is the prior existence of that contractual obligation, that covenanted liability, of the tenant which differentiates such a claim as this from a landlord's claim to recover rent payable in arrear after the date of surrender, for there the tenant is under no obligation or liability to pay any rent before that date.

I would accordingly uphold the lessor's submission, affirm the judgment of the deputy judge and dismiss the appeal.

KERR LJ. I agree; there is nothing I wish to add.

Appeal dismissed.

Solicitors: *Richard Southern* (for the sureties); *Slowes* (for the lessor).

Diana Brahams Barrister.

X AG and others v A bank

QUEEN'S BENCH DIVISION (COMMERCIAL COURT)
LEGGATT J
24, 25, 26, 27 JANUARY 1983

Conflict of laws – Contract – Proper law of contract – Swiss company having account with London branch of New York bank – Relationship between bank and customer commencing in London – Whether proper law of banking contract English law or New York law.

Conflict of laws – Foreign order – Enforcement – New York subpoena – Swiss company having account with London branch of American bank – New York court issuing subpoena against bank to produce documents relating to company held by London branch of bank – Production of documents likely to constitute breach of banking contract and breach of bank's duty of confidentiality – Whether private interest of confidentiality between banker and customer should prevail over duty of disclosure to foreign court – Whether court should restrain bank from disclosing documents.

Injunction – Balance of convenience – Bank – Confidential information between bank and customer – Bank seeking to comply with foreign subpoena to produce in foreign court documents belonging to customer – Disclosure of documents likely to harm customer beyond adequate compensation – Bank fearing it would be liable to proceedings in foreign court for contempt of court if documents not produced – Whether court should grant injunction restraining bank from complying with subpoena.

The plaintiffs, X, a multinational corporation incorporated under Swiss law and based in Switzerland, and Y, an American subsidiary of X incorporated in Switzerland but having a major branch in New York, were both companies concerned in the marketing of oil, metals and fertilizers. X conducted its business wholly outside the United States and all its books and records were kept in Switzerland. Y handled business emanating from and destined for New York, but its other business was operated from Switzerland. Both plaintiffs had accounts with the London branch of the defendant, an American bank, that branch being used for a major part of the plaintiffs' general banking operations. In 1977 investigations were commenced by the United States Department of Justice into the crude oil industry as a result of which the investigators wished to produce before a federal grand jury documents belonging to the plaintiffs. When the plaintiffs refused to produce certain documents, on the ground that they were not subject to the jurisdiction of the United States courts, a subpoena was served on the bank to produce all documents relating to any accounts maintained by the plaintiffs at the bank's London branch. The bank declared its intention to comply with the subpoena, whereupon the plaintiffs sought and were granted injunctions in the High Court to restrain the bank from producing the documents, on the grounds that if the bank were to produce the documents it would thereby be in breach of the duty of confidentiality it owed to the

plaintiffs. An order was then obtained in the New York District Court, ex parte and in
a camera, requiring the bank to comply with the subpoena. In proceedings by the plaintiffs to continue the injunction, the bank conceded that it was under a duty of confidentiality towards the plaintiffs and that disclosure of the documents under the subpoena would constitute a breach of that duty but it claimed that the subpoena required the production of all bank records over which the bank had control regardless of their location and that if the bank failed to comply with the subpoena it would, as a United States corporation,
b be subject to proceedings for contempt of court in the United States. The bank contended (i) that the proper law of the banking contract was New York law and therefore, since New York law governed both the subpoena and the contract, the order of the New York court relating to the subpoena should prevail over the contract, (ii) that, as a matter of law, an English court would not compel performance of, or enforce, a contract if performance of the contract required the doing of an act which violated the law of the
c place of performance, at least where the person required to do the act was resident in or amenable to the law of the place of performance, and therefore, since the contract was to be performed at least partly in New York, an English court would not compel the bank to perform its contractual obligation of confidentiality to the plaintiffs when to do so violated the law of New York, (iii) that an English court would not prevent a party to a contract from doing an act in the place where the contract was to be performed when
d that party was obliged to do that act by the law of that place, and that as a matter of policy an English court should decline to impede legitimate proceedings in other jurisdictions or orders (such as the subpoena) issued in the course of such proceedings when directed to a person within the jurisdiction of the foreign court, and that the primary effect of the United States order was in New York and only incidentally in London, (iv) that the public policy of respecting the order of a foreign court should prevail over requiring a banker
e to preserve confidentiality in relation to his customer's accounts and dealings, and (v) that in any event the subpoena should prevail over the duty of confidentiality because the bank had a genuine and legitimate interest of its own in obeying a subpoena issued under the law of the country to which it was subject and avoiding the genuine and not unreasonable possibility of being held in contempt of court.

f **Held** – (1) Since instructions in relation to the plaintiffs' bank accounts were received and acted on in London, since the relationship of banker and customer was centred in London and since the plaintiffs had contemplated that their transactions with the bank would be governed by English law, it followed that English law was the proper law of the banking contract between the plaintiffs and the bank, not only because the branch with which the contracts were originally made was in London, but because that was
g where the relationship began and where the contract was made in circumstances such that the contract was to be taken to have had English law as its proper law from its inception (see p 474 *h* to p 475 *b*, post).

(2) It did not follow from the fact that the production of the documents had been ordered to be made in New York pursuant to the subpoena that confidentiality on the part of the bank could be said to have been rendered unlawful in New York, because a
h subpoena requiring disclosure was to be contrasted with legislation or a judgment requiring disclosure, since failure to produce the documents might be excused if an adequate excuse was produced and, furthermore, the subpoena and the subsequent order had been obtained without any form of hearing on the merits or inter partes (see p 475 *g* to *j*, p 476 *a* and p 480 *e f*, post).

(3) In determining whether the injunctions should be continued the court had to
j determine the balance of convenience, having regard to (a) the fact that the order of the New York court would take effect in London in breach of both a private interest, namely a contract between a banker and a customer, and the public interest in maintaining the obligation of confidentiality imposed on banks conducting business in the City of London, (b) the effect of the subpoena of the New York court and the fact that under the United States doctrine of foreign government compulsion the New York court would

not hold the bank liable in contempt for complying with an injunction issued by a foreign court (ie the English court) which had jurisdiction over the branch where the a
documents were located (ie London) and would treat the English injunction as being an adequate excuse for the non-production of the documents, (c) the fact that, although the court would not be 'enforcing' a foreign revenue or penal law if the New York subpoena was permitted to be enforced in London, nevertheless the mere fact of not impeding the subpoena would involve a measure of assistance and approbation of the subpoena since, in particular, it would involve the court tolerating a breach of that obligation of b
confidentiality which in the ordinary course it would maintain in the public interest, and (d) the fact that there was no evidence that delay in producing the documents caused by continuing the injunctions would be significant. Accordingly, the balance of convenience was between, on the one hand, impeding the New York court in the exercise in London of powers which, by English standards, were excessive without in so doing causing detriment to the bank, and, on the other hand, causing very considerable c
commercial harm to the plaintiffs by not continuing the injunctions. In the circumstances the balance of convenience clearly favoured the plaintiffs and accordingly the injunctions would be continued (see p 471 *e f*, p 473 *a b d* and *h j*, p 474 *e* to *g*, p 476 *j* to p 477 *b*, p 478 *c* to *e* and *j* and p 479 *a* to *d* and *j* to p 480 *d* and *f g*, post); *American Cyanamid Co v Ethicon Ltd* [1975] 1 All ER 504 applied; *Tournier v National Provincial and Union Bank of England* [1923] All ER Rep 550, *British Nylon Spinners Ltd v Imperial Chemical Industries Ltd* d
[1952] 2 All ER 780, *Regazzoni v K C Sethia (1944) Ltd* [1957] 3 All ER 286, *Rio Tinto Zinc Corp v Westinghouse Electric Corp* [1978] 1 All ER 434 and *British Steel Corp v Granada Television Ltd* [1981] 1 All ER 417 considered.

Notes

For jurisdiction of the court to grant injunctions to restrain enforcement of a foreign e
judgment, see 8 Halsbury's Laws (4th edn) para 730, and for cases on the subject, see 11 Digest (Reissue) 641–642, *1747–1753*.

Cases referred to in judgment

American Cyanamid Co v Ethicon Ltd [1975] 1 All ER 504, [1975] AC 396, [1975] 2 WLR 316, HL. f

British Nylon Spinners Ltd v Imperial Chemical Industries Ltd [1952] 2 All ER 780, [1953] Ch 19, CA.

British Steel Corp v Granada Television Ltd [1981] 1 All ER 417, [1981] AC 1096, [1980] 3 WLR 774, Ch D, CA and HL.

Cable (Lord), Re, Garratt v Waters [1976] 3 All ER 417, [1977] 1 WLR 7.

Kleinwort Sons & Co v Ungarische Baumwolle Industrie AG and Hungarian General Creditbank g
[1939] 3 All ER 38, [1939] 2 KB 678, CA.

NWL Ltd v Woods, NWL Ltd v Nelson [1979] 3 All ER 614, [1979] 1 WLR 1294, HL.

Ralli Bros v Compañia Naviera Sota y Aznar [1920] 2 KB 287, [1920] All ER Rep 427, CA.

Regazzoni v K C Sethia (1944) Ltd [1957] 3 All ER 286, [1958] AC 301, [1957] 3 WLR 752, HL; *affg* [1956] 2 All ER 487, [1956] 2 QB 490, [1956] 3 WLR 79, CA.

Rio Tinto Zinc Corp v Westinghouse Electric Corp, RTZ Services Ltd v Westinghouse Electric h
Corp [1978] 1 All ER 434, [1978] AC 547, [1978] 2 WLR 81, HL.

Tournier v National Provincial and Union Bank of England [1924] 1 KB 461, [1923] All ER Rep 550, CA.

US v First National City Bank (1968) 396 F 2d 897.

Interlocutory applications j

By writs issued on 15 and 22 November 1982, the first plaintiffs, X AG, and the second plaintiffs, Y AG, severally brought actions against the defendants, an American bank, seeking a declaration that by virtue of the contract between the plaintiffs as customer and the branch of the defendants as bank, the defendants owed the plaintiffs a duty of secrecy and confidence in respect of the plaintiffs' accounts with the branch, all transactions thereon, all securities in respect thereof and all documents and information relating thereto, and an injunction restraining the defendants by themselves, their servants or agents or otherwise howsoever from passing to the head office of or to any other office or branch of the defendants or to any person any information or documents relating in any way whatsoever to any accounts maintained by the defendants in the name of the plaintiffs in London, any transactions thereon or connected therewith or any securities in respect thereof. By a writ issued on 19 November 1982 the third plaintiffs, Z Inc, sought an injunction in similar terms. On 25 November 1982 Lloyd J granted ex parte the injunctions sought and on 20 December 1982 they were renewed by Mustill J. The proceedings were adjourned for the hearing of full argument by the parties. The applications were heard in chambers but judgment was given by Leggatt J in open court. The facts are set out in the judgment.

Peter Cresswell and *Ali Malek* for the first and second plaintiffs.
Jonathan Hirst for the third plaintiffs.
Andrew Longmore for the bank.

LEGGATT J. There is before me an application in each of three actions. At the request of the parties, this judgment is given in open court. This is another of those cases in this court in which felicity must give way to celerity, in which the urgency of the matter must outweigh the desirability of reserving judgment in deference to the importance which both sides understandably ascribe to it. I shall refer to each of the plaintiffs by initials, arbitrarily selected, that is to say as the 'X company', the 'Y company' and the 'Z company', and the defendants, who are the same in each of the three applications, I shall refer to as 'the bank'. Although I cannot direct, I shall certainly expect that that anonymity will be preserved in any report of this judgment. The bank has its head office in New York and it is with the London branch of the bank that these applications are immediately concerned. The applications in the three actions have been heard together and all applications are in similar form. In short, they raise the question whether injunctions already issued should be continued to trial so as to prevent obedience by the London branch of the bank to subpoenas issued in New York requiring production by the London branch of documents relating to an account of each of the three plaintiffs, who are customers of the bank, two of the plaintiffs being incorporated in Switzerland and one in Panama. The X company was formed under the laws of Switzerland in the early 1970s. It has over 40 offices located in some 30 different countries throughout the world. The Y company, which is a subsidiary of the X company, is also incorporated in Switzerland and has a major branch in New York. The Z company is a company associated with the X company, incorporated in Panama, but having its headquarters, like the X company, in Switzerland. The X company and its subsidiary, the Y company, are concerned in the marketing of crude oil and oil products, ferrous and non-ferrous ores and metals, and also fertilizers. Both the X company and the Z company conduct their business wholly outside the United States; they have no presence there, that is to say no employees nor any business conducted there, and all the books of both companies, together with their records, are kept in Switzerland. The Y company, on the other hand, handles business emanating from and destined for New York, but its other business is operated from its headquarters in Switzerland and, in particular, through use of its London account with the London branch of the bank. Accounts have been maintained by the plaintiffs with the bank for some time now, in the case of the X company since 1975, of the Y company since 1978 and of the Z company since 1980.

The relationship enjoyed by the X company with the bank is explained in an affidavit by a gentleman who is, in effect, the company secretary of that plaintiff. He asserts that the company did not, in forming its relationship with the bank, contemplate that United States law would govern the banking relationship for the reason that, since that relationship would be centred in London, it was naturally contemplated that it would be subject to English law. It is a relationship which has grown over the years and the London branch of the bank is used by the X company for a major part of its general banking affairs, including loans, deposits, letters of credit, guarantees, confirmations, credit references and presentments. All the instructions from the X company emanate from Switzerland or via an English subsidiary of the X company. The X company uses the London branch as its centre for worldwide dollar denominated banking arrangements and that deponent asserts, in common with those who have sworn affidavits on behalf of the other plaintiffs, that the X company would not have placed any business with the London branch of the bank unless it was confident that its business secrets would remain secure in accordance with the stringent standards observed in London. This is of particular consequence in the context of letters of credit, because the documents held in the London branch in relation to letters of credit would contain instructions received from the X company or its London subsidiary and include—

> 'the application for the credit, the terms and conditions upon which it is to be opened and paid, the terms of the underlying transaction, the buyer, the documentary conditions for the transaction, the place of presentment and expiration, and countless other commercial and proprietary items'.

It is said that the London branch files, that is to say the files of the London branch of the bank, also contain not only instructions concerned with general banking matters, investments and business facilities, but multifold data communicated to and shared with the branch in reliance on what the deponent terms 'the sanctity of the professional and confidential relationship between a customer and a bank carrying on business in London'.

In response to this aspect, an affidavit has been sworn by the general manager of the London branch of the bank. After explaining that the plaintiffs are, like many of the bank's customers, large, multinational corporations, whose banking requirements transcend national boundaries, he explains that the bank provides a co-ordinated worldwide service to its customers through its international department, so as to meet the customers' requirements. This deponent says:

> 'However complex and geographically widespread a customer's requirements may be his banking relationship with [the bank] will be subject to overall direction, co-ordination and control from a relationship manager at one location. The relationship manager is usually based at [the New York office of the bank] or at the particular location of [the bank] where the customer has its head office or main management centre.'

He concludes this passage by saying that, so far as the bank is concerned, its banking relationship with the plaintiffs is centred in New York.

With this passage I must, however, contrast the affidavit of the gentleman who appears to be the relevant relationship manager himself. He says that he is a vice-president of the bank presently assigned to the London branch and he declares: 'I am responsible for managing [the bank's] business relationship with numerous commodity customers at' the London branch, including those of the plaintiffs.

It seems to me that, by way of application of the principles described in the first affidavit sworn on behalf of the bank, it is the second deponent who is to be identified as the relationship manager and he at all events is physically present in London for most of the time, as it would appear. Whatever may be said in the affidavit of the first deponent to the effect that the bank's banking relationship with the plaintiffs is centred in New York, it seems to me that it can only be as a matter of internal administration of the bank and then only in a limited sense which does not detract from the fact that the bank maintains its own relationship manager in London.

In the main affidavit sworn on behalf of the bank, namely that of its first deponent, he says in a later passage that the plaintiffs must be fully aware of the worldwide context in which their English dealings are conducted and of their own and the bank's close connections with New York. He then says:

> 'Unlike a domestic U.K. customer of an English bank in London the plaintiffs (with the possible exception of [the Z company]) must, in my belief, have anticipated

that their dealings with [the bank] would be subjected to the necessary incidents of an overall international relationship having close connections with New York.'

I have some difficulty with that statement. First of all, it appears to me that the reference to the dealings being subject to the necessary incidents of an overall international relationship begs the question of what incidents are to be regarded as necessary, and, second, I am not sure that I understand the meaning of the phrase 'dealings . . . would be subjected to the . . . incidents of an overall international relationship'.

This part of the deponent's affidavit concludes by saying that in the much wider context of dealings between the bank and the plaintiffs—

> 'the bank must, notwithstanding its efforts and obligations to provide a full service to very valued customers, have regard to and comply with the legal obligations of the country in which it is incorporated and in which its head office is based and where its relationship with the plaintiffs is centred.'

Comment about the relationship between the bank and the plaintiffs I have already made; but it is noteworthy that in that passage there is nothing said about the bank having regard to or complying with the legal obligations of the country in which its branch is situated. Nor, indeed, is there any reference to any regard that might be paid to the welfare of the bank's customers, although it is fair to say, and I say it now, that if there may appear in affidavits sworn on behalf of the bank to be a dearth of reference to the bank's concern for the welfare of its customers that may be, having regard to the doctrine which it is said may be material in New York, that the bank must be in a position to show that it has made what are termed 'good faith efforts' to comply with the requirements of the subpoenas served on it and too much concern for the welfare of customers might be misconstrued as a lack of good faith in the efforts being made by the bank to do what the subpoenas require it to do.

The subpoenas are apparently the product of an investigation begun in about 1977 in the United States of the crude oil industry by various agencies there. It does not seem that the X company and its associated companies in the first instance were in any way concerned. Certain it is that no charges in consequences of any investigation undertaken over the years have ever been preferred against any of the plaintiffs. At the end of 1981 the Department of Justice in particular started an inquiry into crude oil trading of the Y company in the United States and one of the plaintiffs, I think the Y company, was served with a subpoena, in pursuance of which some 75,000 documents have been produced to the Department of Justice. But, notwithstanding the production of those documents, there was on 15 April 1982 a subpoena served on the X company, which was thereafter considered by its board. On 1 June 1982 the board, on the advice of Swiss and United States lawyers, decided not to comply with that subpoena. The X company believed that it was not and is not subject to the jurisdiction of the United States and that for the best of all reasons: that it is not conducting any business in the United States. Proceedings were therefore instituted to quash this subpoena. On 25 August the United States District Court for the Southern District of New York refused to quash the subpoena and on 13 September the same court held the X company to be in contempt for its failure to comply with the subpoena. On 15 October X company's appeal against the findings of the District Court was heard, but a decision on that appeal is still awaited. Meanwhile, on 8 October a subpoena had been served on the bank and it is with that subpoena that I am particularly concerned. It was followed by certain correspondence between those acting for the bank and solicitors for the plaintiffs, and, the bank having declared its intention to comply with the subpoena, injunctions were applied for. On 12 November Staughton J granted an ex parte injunction to the X company, restraining the defendants in relation to the X company; on 26 November Lloyd J continued that injunction and granted injunctions in respect of the Y company and the Z company in similar terms; and on 20 December all three injunctions were continued by Mustill J. It seems that on the same day a subpoena was served on the Z company itself, which, for the first time, became directly implicated in the investigation. On 11 January the bank's subpoena or the effect of it was indorsed by an order made on that day by the United States District Court for the Southern District of New York.

It is necessary to look in a little more detail at the terms of the subpoena. It is addressed to the bank, for the attention of 'Any officer or authorised custodian of records', and it commands the person addressed to attend before what is called the Grand Inquest of the body of the people of the United States of America for the Southern District of New York 'to testify and give evidence in regard to an alleged violation' of two Titles of the United States Code, which are specified in the subpoena. I have been told that they relate respectively to conspiracy to commit an offence or defraud the United States and to an attempt to evade or defeat tax. The subpoena requires the person addressed to produce what is then set out in an extensive rider. The rider reads:

> 'For the period of January 1st 1979 through December 31st 1981 [in other words a period of three years] any and all books, records and other documents regarding all accounts (including the known accounts listed below) and transactions of the following companies, to include, but not be limited by, all bank statements (with debit and credit advices), loan documents, letters of credit (including bills of lading, invoices, contracts and other subsidiary documents), correspondence, internal memoranda, signatory and/or authorisation documents'

and there are then specified the account of the X company in London, the account of the Z company in London and the account of the Y company in London, in each case being, presumably, the account of that company held by the bank's London branch. The subpoena concludes by saying in its printed form that 'for failure to attend and produce the said documents you will be deemed guilty of contempt of court and liable to penalties of the law'.

The order of the United States District Court, Southern District of New York, which was made on 11 January was one expressed to be in the matter of a grand jury subpoena directed to the bank, a reference no doubt to the subpoena which I have just recited. The order says that, the bank having been subpoenaed to appear before a federal grand jury to produce various documents and the bank having failed to produce various records maintained in its London branch as a result of a restraining order (as it is called) issued by the High Court of Justice, Queen's Bench Division—

> 'and upon representation that it is necessary for the better enforcement of said Grand Jury subpoena, and the court being satisfied that the production of the documents requested by the subpoena is necessary in the best interests of justice and the Grand Jury investigation, it is hereby ordered and adjudged that [the bank] produce all the documents . . . relating to any accounts [of the X company, the Y company and the Z company] maintained in its London, England, branch.'

I am told that this order was obtained ex parte and in camera and there is no evidence about what material, if any, was available to the district judge when the order was made.

The predicament in which the bank in consequence finds itself is obvious. The subpoena is binding on it. United States law obliges the bank to comply with it. It involves the relevant documents (when I say 'relevant' I mean relevant in the sense of being those documents which are identified in the subpoena) being produced to the court and there is by way of indorsement of the subpoena an express order of the court also binding on the bank. On the other hand, there are now current in this country injunctions prohibiting the bank from obeying that subpoena, being a subpoena supported by the order of a competent court of the United States.

There is no dispute that the bank is subject to a duty of confidentiality. Apparently the nature of the duty is no different in New York from the duty to which it is regarded as subject in London. For convenience, I would describe the duty as arising from an implied term of the contract governing the relationship of banker and customer and as being that, subject to certain qualifications which it may be material to consider, a banker shall not without the consent of the customer disclose to any other person any document or other information obtained by the banker in the course of that relationship.

There is no dispute that disclosure of the documents to the grand jury would constitute or create a breach of that duty. It would be so, as it appears from the evidence, not merely in the technical sense of the grand jury itself constituting a third person to whom disclosure of confidential documents would constitute a breach of that confidentiality, but also in the far wider and more material sense that, as it would appear, there is in practice no secrecy in relation to matters entrusted to grand juries. I have this on the authority of Mr Marvin Frankel, now advising the plaintiffs in New York, who himself has served as a district judge there and is the author of a book entitled *The Grand Jury: An Institution on Trial* (1977). Apart from the fact that that work refers expressly to leaks which are common of material entrusted to grand juries, Mr Frankel refers in his affidavit to disconcerting matters arising in this very case, because he says that the United States attorney—

> 'sought and obtained the District Court's acceptance of a secret affidavit and documentary exhibits, characterised as decisive against [the X company's] motion to quash [the subpoena served on them, but not shown to the X company's attorneys] on the plea that to do so would reveal the government's theory of the case and identity of co-operating witnesses to the possible prejudice of the government's investigation.'

But, says Mr Frankel—

> 'almost immediately following the argument of an appeal in that case ... newspapers at several places in the United States were publishing supposedly secret information about this very matter and attributing the revelations both to identified "secret" witnesses, and, more importantly, to "government sources"'

and he exhibits a copy of an article which in lurid terms contains or purports to contain such revelations.

The other matter which is not in dispute is the nature and the extent of the harm which the plaintiffs would suffer were such breach of confidentiality to occur in this case. The damage which the X company would sustain is described as immediate, irreparable and incalculable, and similar descriptions are given to that which would be suffered by the other plaintiffs in like circumstances.

For the purpose of explaining himself the deponent in relation to the X company takes by way of example letters of credit. He says that for those translations in which the X company—

> 'is the purchaser of commodities, and in which a letter of credit is opened by [the London branch of the bank] for the benefit of [the X company's] supplier, and for those transactions in which [the X company] is the seller, and in which [the London branch of the bank] either confirms a letter of credit opened by [the X company's] customer or collects on a letter of credit under which [the X company] is the beneficiary [the London branch of the bank] receives all of the shipping and title documents including bills of lading and invoices. From these documents the following information may be obtained: (a) the name of [the X company's] supplier or customer; (b) the type of commodity bought or sold; (c) the quantity of the commodity bought or sold; (d) the price at which the commodity was bought or sold; and (e) the relevant shipping information. In many cases it would be possible to determine from such information [the X company's] margin on a particular transaction and, where [the X company] acts as intermediary, to identify the trading parties on both sides of a transaction.'

Engaged in various trades, as the X company is, this would have very serious repercussions. For example, it is said that the X company operates in and trades with countries which are in politically sensitive areas of the world, with the result that their governments or their agencies often prefer to trade through an intermediary in order not to reveal the buying and selling strategies for particular commodities or, in some instances, the fact that the governments or their agencies may have entered into such transactions contrary

to some policy which publicly may have been professed on the governments' behalf. Many transactions, it is said on the X company's behalf, are concluded with governments a
or governmental agencies in countries in which the commodity in question is one of the chief sources of foreign exchange revenue and for that reason alone the details of such transactions are highly confidential. Similarly, damage might well be caused if knowledge of the trading patterns of the X company were to reveal, for example, that there was stockpiling of particular strategic materials by any of the Western customers. There might be revealed a breach of some restriction imposed on particular Middle Eastern, b
Latin American or Iron Curtain countries on the dealing with other particular countries in respect of certain materials. Finally, and perhaps most obviously, disclosure of information of the character held by the London branch of the bank would put the X company at a severe disadvantage in relation to its competitors in that it would allow what the deponent calls 'a window into the X company's commercial secrets'. The X company's suppliers and customers, its pricing decisions, its margins and its delivery c
dates would all be liable to become public knowledge and an analysis of such information would obviously enable competitors to tell much, and, as it may be, all that they need to know, about the X company's operating methods, resources and strategy. That those consequences would be liable to occur is not controverted.

A review of the evidence in this case must include reference in particular to the expert evidence sworn on each side. d

The bank relies on an affidavit of an attorney who is a member of a New York law firm, Mr Connick. After asserting that the federal grand jury subpoena requires the production of all bank records over which the bank has control, regardless of their location, and citing authority for that proposition, the deponent states:

> '[Should the bank] fail to comply with the subpoena it would be subject to proceedings under the Federal Rule of Criminal Procedure 17(g) which reads: e
> "Failure by any person without adequate excuse to obey a subpoena served upon him may be deemed a contempt of the court from which the subpoena issued"...'

He then refers to the leading case of *US v First National City Bank* (1968) 396 F 2d 897, in which the United States Court of Appeals for the Second Circuit dealt with the question of a New York bank's obligation to comply with a grand jury subpoena. He remarks f
that, after balancing certain factors, the court ordered compliance with this subpoena 'despite the apparently conflicting law of the nation where the records were kept, West Germany', and he says that a recent decision of the United States District Court for the Southern District of New York has affirmed the validity of that case with respect to process issued by United States government investigators. The case in which that affirmation was made was one in which the court ordered a Swiss bank to comply with g
informational demands of the Securities and Exchange Commission, despite the possibility of criminal prosecution in Switzerland for such compliance. Conservatively, the deponent remarks that there are some factual differences between those two cases and the present, and he says that, for that reason, as well as the uncertainty of the outcome of the balancing test, it is impossible to predict with certainty what the United States attorney or the federal courts would do should the High Court continue the outstanding h
injunctions against the bank in this matter. However, he says that it is 'entirely possible' that a bank officer in New York would be summoned to appear before the United States District Court and directed to produce the documents, that on the basis of the balancing test the District Court would not recognise the High Court's injunction as an adequate excuse for failure to produce such documents, and that if thereafter the bank refused to produce the documents the District Court would imprison the bank officer and impose j
a daily fine on the bank until the documents were produced. He does, however, end his affidavit by saying:

> 'Should the High Court continue the outstanding injunctions [the bank] would have no choice but to oppose vigorously any contempt proceeding in New York and to incur additional substantial legal expenses toward that end.'

I am bound to say that had the matter ended there I should have been left in very great
a doubt whether the bank stood in any real jeopardy in New York. Although it might have understandable apprehension so long as the subpoena remained outstanding and not complied with, my feeling would stem quite simply from the fact that no suggestion is made how the prohibition of this court on the production of relevant documents would not constitute an adequate excuse for failure by the person to whom the subpoena was addressed to produce the documents in question.

b But the matter does not end there, because a substantial affidavit has been sworn on behalf of the plaintiffs by Professor Lowenfeld, Professor of Law at the Law School of New York University. He is a person of the greatest academic distinction and one of the leading authorities in the particular field of law with which this case is concerned. He is, indeed, an associate reporter of the American Law Institute's current revision of the Restatement of the Foreign Relations Law of the United States. His principal responsibility
c in that capacity is for Part IV of the Restatement, concerning jurisdiction and judgments, and including in particular the sections concerning resolution of conflicting exercises of jurisdiction, which are the subject of the present dispute.

The professor says that he believes it highly unlikely that a United States bank or its officers would be held in contempt for conduct in compliance with the order of a British court in the circumstances stated, that is an injunction restraining the transfer or
d disclosure of records kept in London in respect of a bank account maintained by a non-American corporation at the bank's London branch. He declares himself quite certain 'that no United States court has ever held a bank or other party in contempt in such circumstances', assuming, as he does, that there is no suggestion of wrongdoing by the bank either in transferring overseas records ordinarily kept in New York or in any way assisting the depositor in a scheme of concealment or non-disclosure.

e After reciting the basic rule in the event of conflict between commands of the courts of different jurisdictions, which apparently is that no one is to be put in the position of fearing punishment irrespective of whether he does or does not do an act, the professor cites authority for that proposition.

The authorities include one which it behoves me to mention and that is *British Nylon Spinners Ltd v Imperial Chemical Industries Ltd* [1952] 2 All ER 780, [1953] Ch 19. That
f case is of general importance in this matter for the comments of Evershed MR where he said ([1952] 2 All ER 780 at 783–784, [1953] Ch 19 at 27):

> '... the courts of this country will, in the natural course, pay great respect and attention to the superior courts of the United States of America, but I conceive that it is none the less the proper province of English courts, when their jurisdiction is invoked, not to refrain from exercising that jurisdiction if they think that it is their
> g duty so to do for the protection of rights which are peculiarly subject to their protection. In so saying, I do not conceive that I am offending in any way against the principles of comity ...'

Looking at that case, it is convenient also to mention the comment of Denning LJ ([1952] 2 All ER 780 at 784, [1953] Ch 19 at 28): 'The writ of the United States does not
h run in this country, and, if due regard is had to the comity of nations, it will not seek to run here.'

There is, as would appear from the professor's affidavit, a doctrine in the United States, or at any rate in New York, known as the doctrine of foreign government compulsion, which depends, as he explains, on a prohibition in one state conflicting with a command in another. The professor considers the case mentioned in Mr Connick's affidavit, *US v*
j *First National City Bank* (1968) 396 F 2d 897. He describes how the District Court held that the defence based on German law in that case was speculative, based at most on possible exposure to civil liability or loss of standing in the financial community, and that on appeal the district judge's holding was affirmed, with the court pointing out in detail the distinction between the Swiss bank secrecy law, which was a mandatory law, backed by criminal sanction, and German law, for breach of which there was at most a civil liability.

The professor then proceeds to consider the special rules concerning the discovery of documents. He says that it has been the pattern, although not followed in all cases, for United States courts faced with discovery requests or subpoenas calling for the production of documents located abroad to issue an order to produce and, if a foreign prohibition against production is asserted, to order the party before the court to make a good faith effort to secure release or waiver from the prohibition, but, if no release from the prohibition has been obtained, to dismiss petitions for contempt.

Certain authorities for that proposition are considered, including the other recent case in the United States District Court referred to by Mr Connick, on which the professor comments that the bank there in question was held to have failed to make a good faith effort to comply with the request for production. In addition, the government of the state where the records were kept had not acted to prevent the bank from complying with the subpoena; or, in other words, in that case the bank was not subject to an injunction in the manner that the bank in the present case is. The professor expresses some doubt whether that case was properly decided and summarises the matter by reference to his current draft of para 420 of the Restatement of Foreign Relations Law, which deals specifically with requests for disclosure and foreign government compulsion. Sub-paragraph (2) of that paragraph reads, so far as is material:

> '(a) the person to whom the order is directed may be required by the court to make a good faith effort to secure permission from the foreign authorities to make the information available; (b) the court may not ordinarily impose the sanction of contempt, dismissal, or default on the party that has failed to comply with the order for production, except in cases of deliberate concealment or removal of information or of failure to make a good faith effort in accordance with paragraph (a).'

It has been explained that the restatement is intended to be declaratory of existing law in the United States.

In those circumstances, the professor summarises his conclusion by saying that an injunction by a foreign court having jurisdiction over the branch where the documents are located—

> 'would, I believe, come within the foreign compulsion defence, provided (a) the bank at all times acted in good faith as defined; and (b) disobedience of the injunction would subject the branch and its officers to serious sanction.'

I accept that conclusion. It represents, in my judgment, an accurate summary of the law of New York so far as applicable, from which it follows that the bank, having properly pursued its good faith efforts to relieve itself from the consequences of an injunction in this country, ought not to be held liable for contempt in any proceedings brought to that end in New York.

It is convenient to consider the arguments of counsel addressed to me by reference to these matters by following the structure of counsel's argument for the bank. He was content in offering his propositions of English law to assume at the outset that English law is the proper law. Advocate that he is, he left until the end any suggestion that the proper law should be regarded as being anything other than English law. When he came to it he argued that the law of New York should apply to the transaction as a whole for the reason that that was the law with which, so he bravely asserted, the contract has its closest and most real connection in each case.

I unhesitatingly reject that submission. It seems to me, for such reasons as counsel advanced on behalf of the first and second of the plaintiffs, concurred in by counsel for the third of the plaintiffs, that English law is the proper law, not only because the London branch with which the contracts were initially made is in London, but because that is where the relationship started and where the contract was made in circumstances where that contract must be taken to have had a proper law from its inception. Instructions in relation to the account are received and acted on in London. The reality of the matter, as it appears to me, whatever comments to a contrary effect may be made on behalf of the bank, is that the relationship between banker and customer is in truth centred in London. The plaintiffs all say, and I accept the truth of their assertions, that they contemplated that their transactions with the bank would be governed by English law. For all those reasons, quite apart from the more general description of the contract as being one which has its closest and most real connection with English law, I hold that English law is, indeed, the proper law of the contract.

The first proposition of counsel for the bank was that as a matter of English law an English court will not compel performance of or enforce a contract if performance requires the doing of an act which violates the law of the place of performance, at any rate where the doer is resident in or amenable to the law of the place of performance; nor will an English court prevent a party to a contract from doing an act in the place where the contract is to be performed when he is obliged to do that act by the law of that place.

In pursuing this argument, counsel for the bank contended that the contract cannot be enforced in so far as it requires confidence to be respected in the United States. Thereby he raised the curious concept of confidentiality which no longer was. This seems to me to be a true example, if one were prepared to envisage it, of the curate's egg, that is to say good in parts. The reality of the matter is that once confidence escapes, like air from a punctured tyre, the confidence is no more. But in aid of this argument counsel for the bank relied on *Ralli Bros v Compañia Naviera Sota y Aznar* [1920] 2 KB 287 esp at 290, 299, [1920] All ER Rep 427 esp at 431, 435 per Lord Sterndale MR and Scrutton LJ. That was a case involving a contract which was to be performed partially in Spain and it was held pro tanto to be invalid in the event that performance was unlawful in Spain. The argument is that this contract is to be performed, at least in part, in the United States and, as counsel for the bank characterises it, it requires violation of United States law, by which he means the keeping of confidentiality, with the result that the bank should not be restrained from doing the act of disclosure as being one which it is required to do in the place where the contract is to be performed. In aid of this he relied also on *Re Lord Cable, Garratt v Waters* [1976] 3 All ER 417, [1977] 1 WLR 7, in which it was held that where compliance with an injunction would expose the relevant trustees to serious risk of penal consequence the injunction would not issue.

In opposition to this argument counsel for the first and second plaintiffs relied in particular on *Kleinwort Sons & Co v Ungarische Baumwolle Industrie AG and Hungarian General Creditbank* [1939] 3 All ER 38, [1939] 2 KB 678. That was a case in which an English bank opened an acceptance credit for a Hungarian firm. When the credit expired the Hungarian firm refused to pay in London on the ground that under Hungarian legislation it was illegal for them to remit money abroad. But it was held that this was no defence to the bank's claim. English law was the proper law of the contract, the money was payable in London and the Hungarian law could not affect the legality of a contractual promise in fact governed by Hungarian law but not to be performed in Hungary.

In my judgment it does not follow from the fact that the production has been ordered pursuant to a subpoena that secrecy can be said to have been rendered unlawful, especially in circumstances where it is no doubt the argument, even if perhaps it be only a fiction, that security is still preserved in respect of grand jury proceedings. The fact is that confidentiality is not rendered illegal by a subpoena requiring disclosure, which is to be contrasted with some form of legislation to that end; and I have in mind in particular that from the terms of the relevant procedural rule failure to produce the documents may be excused if the excuse be adequate.

Counsel for the first and second plaintiffs remarked that, since a foreign judgment may be a good defence to an action in England when the judgment is in favour of the defendant and finally conclusive on the merits, he could envisage that an argument might be advanced which sought to equate a subpoena with a judgment; and so, indeed, it proved, because counsel for the bank duly contended that, if need be, he would argue that the subpoena operates as a defence, final and conclusive as it is in the absence of challenge.

It seems to me that there is no analogy for present purposes between a judgment and a subpoena and, in particular, there is no suggestion whatever that the obtaining of this a subpoena or the order which has subsequently indorsed it has involved any form of hearing on the merits. Certainly it has not as yet involved any form of hearing inter partes.

Next, counsel for the bank argued that as a matter of the policy of English law an English court should decline any invitation to impede legitimate proceedings in other jurisdictions and orders such as the subpoena issued in the course of proceedings, b especially where directed to a person within the jurisdiction of the foreign court.

For this he admits that it is difficult to find precise authority. He asserts it as a matter of common sense dictated by international comity, and he seeks to found on the well-established rule of English law that it will not enforce a contract to do something illegal in another country. He relies on *Regazzoni v K C Sethia (1944) Ltd* [1957] 3 All ER 286, [1958] AC 301, which is authority for the proposition that that public policy will avoid c at least some contracts which violate the laws of a foreign state. He says that properly regarded it is wrong to think of this subpoena as being extra-territorial in its effect. At that stage he meets *Rio Tinto Zinc Corp v Westinghouse Electric Corp* [1978] 1 All ER 434, [1978] AC 547, much relied on by counsel for the first and second plaintiffs. That was a case, according to counsel for the bank, which merely affords guidance as to the interpretation of the Evidence (Proceedings in Other Jurisdictions) Act 1975 and, having d regard to the narrow way in which particular comments were expressed, should be regarded as applicable only to attempts made by means having extra-territorial effect to make United Kingdom companies amenable to the investigation of a foreign court. The case was, indeed, concerned with the use that might be made in this country of letters rogatory and a possible conversion of the letters rogatory into a request for evidence for the purposes of a grand jury investigation. Counsel for the bank says that the primary e effect of the United States order in the present case is in New York and only incidentally in London, with the result that it does not represent any invasion of United Kingdom sovereignty and all that is at issue is a matter of private law.

Counsel for the first and second plaintiffs contends that the case is what he terms 'vitally relevant'. He says that it shows how a subpoena is to be regarded here and, in particular, by reference to submissions there made by the Attorney General, what the f attitude would be of the United Kingdom government. In that case the Attorney General had submitted that the government considers that the wide investigatory procedures under the United States anti-trust legislation against persons outside the United States who are not United States citizens constitutes an infringement of a proper jurisdiction of sovereignty of the United Kingdom.

Both counsel read to me with great emphasis a passage from the speech of Lord g Wilberforce where he said ([1978] 1 All ER 434 at 448, [1978] AC 547 at 617):

> 'The intervention of Her Majesty's Attorney-General establishes that quite apart from the present case, over a number of years and in a number of cases, the policy of Her Majesty's Government has been against recognition of United States investigatory jurisdiction extra-territorially against United Kingdom companies. The courts should in such matters speak with the same voice as the executive ... h they have, as I have stated, no difficulty in doing so.'

Counsel for the bank relied on that for its specific application to United Kingdom companies which he said is absent here and counsel for the first and second plaintiffs relied on it as betokening the attitude which Her Majesty's government may be expected to take about the use in this country by the United States of the investigatory jurisdiction j of the relevant character. Counsel for the bank concludes his argument under this head by asserting that if the English law issued a subpoena it would expect what he calls 'credence' to be given to its order and that it must be a matter of discretion whether or not that is accorded to it.

It seems to me that the proper use which I should make of the *Westinghouse* case is to regard it in the circumstances not as definitive either way, but as raising one important factor which I ought to take account of in determining whether this is a case in which the injunction should be continued. The factor that is involved in the exercise of jurisdiction by the United States court in this case is that its order would take effect in London for the production of documents in breach of what might be termed a private interest in the sense that what is directly involved is a contract between banker and customer. But this indubitably is also a matter of public interest, because it raises issues of wider concern than those peculiar to the parties before me.

The third proposition of counsel for the bank is that public policy is not defeated by the rule of private law between banker and customer that the banker should preserve confidentiality in relation to the customer's accounts and dealings. He says that it is not uncommon for confidentiality to be displaced in favour of a higher interest. The bank has to do a balancing act to see whether confidence or the order of a foreign court should take precedence.

It is an argument which he considerably elaborated, starting first with *British Steel Corp v Granada Television Ltd* [1981] 1 All ER 417 at 455, [1981] AC 1096 at 1168–1169, relying in particular on a passage from the speech of Lord Wilberforce where he says:

> '... as to information obtained in confidence, and the legal duty, which may arise, to disclose it to a court of justice, the position is clear. Courts have an inherent wish to respect this confidence, whether it arises between doctor and patient, priest and penitent, banker and customer, between persons giving testimonials to employees, or in other relationships. A relationship of confidence between a journalist and his source is in no different category; nothing in this case involves or will involve any principle that such confidence is not something to be respected. But in all these cases the court may have to decide, in particular circumstances, that the interest in preserving this confidence is outweighed by other interests to which the law attaches importance. The only question in this appeal is whether the present is such a case.'

Counsel for the bank relies on that passage as showing that there is a process of weighing to be undertaken. Counsel for the first and second plaintiffs, on the other hand, points out that it expressly relates to information obtained in confidence, and the legal duty which may arise to disclose it to a court of justice and is, therefore, directly within one of those qualifications to which the obligation of confidentiality is normally treated as subject.

The scope of the obligation was reviewed in *Tournier v National Provincial and Union Bank of England* [1924] 1 KB 461, [1923] All ER Rep 550. To understand the argument in this case it is necessary to read some short passages from the judgments of each of the Lords Justices. First, Bankes LJ considered in a classic passage what the qualifications are of the contractual duty of secrecy implied in the relationship of banker and customer, remarking that there appeared to be no authority on the point. He said ([1924] 1 KB 461 at 473, [1923] All ER Rep 550 at 554):

> 'On principle I think that the qualifications can be classified under four heads: (*a*) Where disclosure is under compulsion by law; (*b*) where there is a duty to the public to disclose; (*c*) where the interests of the bank require disclosure; (*d*) where the disclosure is made by the express or implied consent of the customer.'

In referring in particular to examples of the third class, he mentioned the issue by a bank of a writ claiming payment of an overdraft stating on the face of the writ the amount of the overdraft. In a comparable passage Scrutton LJ gave a similar example (see [1924] 1 KB 461 at 481, [1923] All ER Rep 550 at 558–559), whilst Atkin LJ expressed himself somewhat more widely, saying ([1924] 1 KB 461 at 486, [1923] All ER Rep 550 at 561):

> 'It is difficult to hit upon a formula which will define the maximum of the

obligation which must necessarily be implied. But I think it safe to say that the obligation not to disclose information such as I have mentioned is subject to the qualification that the bank have the right to disclose such information when, and to the extent to which it is reasonably necessary for the protection of the bank's interests, either as against their customer or as against third parties in respect of transactions of the bank for or with their customer, or for protecting the bank, or persons interested, or the public, against fraud or crime.'

Counsel for the bank remarks that this duty is not absolute. He treats the first three of Bankes LJ's qualifications or exceptions as only examples of public policy. He says that the case does not constitute a statute and does not fall to be construed as such, and he says that what are given by the Lords Justices are no more than indications of occasions when the confidence is to be displaced. The contention is that an English court will respect the order of a foreign court. If it finds the order to be in conflict with the private law of confidentiality the English court will, so it is submitted, proceed with caution to uphold the order of the foreign court unless there is compelling reason not to do so.

It seems to me that, even if it be right to regard the exercise which has to be undertaken here ultimately as being a balancing exercise, it must involve an evaluation of the relevant order of the foreign court. It would be necessary for this court in particular to consider the nature, scope, quality and effect of the foreign order and to analyse it with some care, because the fact is that to allow that order to take effect on a bank conducting its business in the City of London would be, as it would appear, to allow a fairly large cuckoo in the domestic nest. But I say 'would be necessary' because the balance with which I am immediately concerned in this interlocutory matter is the balance of convenience and not the performance of that balancing act which counsel for the bank has in mind.

The balancing act which he urges on me he seeks to support by three arguments. The first is that it is in the public interest that affairs of multinational companies should be investigated across borders in a proper case. That must be so, although I would add: with due regard to the public interest in the preservation of banking confidence.

Second, he says that it is no answer for the plaintiffs to point to internal English considerations, as he characterises the basis of the argument, for example, in the *Westinghouse* case [1978] 1 All ER 434, [1978] AC 547, to which I have already referred. He says that that case and those like it only apply to English internal policy, which may have to yield to some of the ways in which a foreign court may govern its own procedures. An English court, so he acknowledges, may have jurisdiction, but in its discretion should not exercise it against the bank. In that way he is able to dispose of difficulties such as are raised by an article of Dr Mann ((1964) 111 Hague Recueil 146), where he said:

'In those cases in which the enforcing state asserts a prerogative right and demands obedience to it abroad, an additional point of some significance is available. The enforcing state . . . cannot achieve respect for its prerogative rights in foreign countries by proceedings taken there. It is precluded, *a fortiori*, from achieving its ends indirectly by having orders made in its own territory, which are to take effect abroad and thus attribute to themselves a power equal to that of an order which the foreign country could, but refuses, to make. The crux of the matter lies in the fact that the enforcing state requires compliance with its sovereign commands in foreign countries where its writ does not run and where it cannot be made to run by clothing it into the form of judgments of courts, whether they be its own or those of the foreign country.'

I consider that, on a true view, the effect of the foreign order is at any rate one factor of which I am entitled to take account in exercising my discretion whether or not to grant or to continue the injunction sought.

Third, counsel for the bank, in contending for the balancing act to be performed by means of gauging the effect of public policy, says that it is natural that the bank should wish to obey the law of the United States, especially since it is quite possible in the light

of the American cases that the bank will be liable for contempt in the United States; and
a he made some limited submissions about the American cases designed merely to show that the bank's fear is not fanciful. But as to that I have considered the evidence of the American lawyers and it appears to me that the reality of the bank's fear is for present purposes a matter for my determination.

Counsel for the bank says that it is irrelevant that the subpoena was made in aid of foreign criminal or revenue matters, because that consideration does not justify any
b impediment being made by English courts to the legitimate processes of United States courts. Although it is true that the English court will not enforce foreign revenue or penal law, he says that the English court is not being invited to undertake enforcement in this case, but merely not to impede; and at the heart of many of the submissions of counsel for the bank is the suggested distinction between enforcement on the one hand and not impeding on the other. He relies, for example, on *Regazzoni v K C Sethia (1944)*
c *Ltd* [1956] 2 All ER 487, [1956] 2 QB 490, which is authority for the proposition that, if two people agree to break the laws of a foreign friendly country, the court will not enforce the agreement, the application being that by implication the parties here, so he contends, have agreed to keep confidential what has been rendered illegal by the law of the place of performance.

I think that this submission is attended by a certain unreality. The fact is that the
d gamekeeper is invited to turn a blind eye whilst the poacher takes a brace of pheasants, or three peasants. In this context, it appears to me that not impeding involves a measure of assistance and, indeed, approbation, because, in particular, it would involve this court tolerating a breach of that obligation of confidentiality which, as I have pointed out, in the ordinary course must be maintained in the public interest.

The fourth argument on which counsel for the bank relies is that, if *Tournier v National*
e *Provincial and Union Bank of England* [1924] 1 KB 461, [1923] All ER Rep 550, to which I have referred, does indeed contain the whole law on the topic without elaboration and public policy is irrelevant, the subpoena should still prevail over the duty of secrecy, because the bank has a genuine and legitimate interest of its own to obey the subpoena since it is issued pursuant to the law of the country to which it is subject and the fear of being held in contempt is genuine and not unreasonable. Suffice to say that the protection
f which the bank seeks appears to me to be different in character from that which was contemplated in the *Tournier* case, where the circumstances before the court were totally different.

Counsel for the bank was not content to accept that *American Cyanamid Co v Ethicon Ltd* [1975] 1 All ER 504 esp at 510, [1975] AC 396 esp at 407–408 per Lord Diplock would necessarily have effect in this case. Alternatively, if it did take effect, he argued that it
g must be with an important cast on it, which he sought to derive from *NWL Ltd v Woods* [1979] 3 All ER 614 at 625, [1979] 1 WLR 1294 at 1306, where Lord Diplock said:

> '... there is the risk that if the interlocutory injunction is granted but the plaintiff fails at the trial the defendant may in the meantime have suffered harm and inconvenience which is similarly irrecompensable. The nature and degree of harm and inconvenience that are likely to be sustained in these two events by the
> h defendant and the plaintiff respectively in consequence of the grant or the refusal of the injunction are generally sufficiently disproportionate to bring down, by themselves, the balance on one side or the other ...'

With an eye to what might occur between this date and the date of trial in the actions out of which these applications arise, I must proceed to consider the matters rendered
j material by the *American Cyanamid* case, with the comment in mind that I have just read from the later speech of Lord Diplock in the *NWL* case.

These being interlocutory applications, I intend to deal with them strictly in conformity with the principles enunciated in the *American Cyanamid* case, whilst taking account, as is implicit in what I have said, of the fact that contempt proceedings, if any be taken, will probably fall to be dealt with before a trial of the present actions and also of the fact that production of any documents to which the grand jury may be entitled and which might prove useful to it would be delayed by my continuing the injunctions sought, although there is no evidence that delay of such a period as would be involved in their review of this particular aspect of the investigation, already running for some time, will prove significant. a

I can summarise in a sentence the balance of convenience as I see it. On the one hand, there is involved in the continuation of the injunction impeding the exercise by the United States court in London of powers which, by English standards, would be regarded as excessive, without in so doing causing detriment to the bank: on the other hand, the refusal of the injunctions, or the non-continuation of them, would cause potentially very considerable commercial harm to the plaintiffs, which cannot be disputed, by suffering the bank to act for its own purposes in breach of the duty of confidentiality admittedly owed to its customers. b

That represents the balance of convenience, against the background that indisputably there is a serious issue to be tried. Damages would not constitute an adequate remedy for the plaintiffs. I am not satisfied that the bank will suffer any detriment, even allowing for the probability that any contempt proceedings that might be brought would be dealt with before the trial of the actions. In those circumstances, it appears to me that the balance of convenience clearly favours the plaintiffs. c

If and in so far as it is necessary for me to pay any regard to the merits of the matter at this stage, I am firmly on the side of the plaintiffs. I have considered the position of the plaintiffs separately, but I am not satisfied that the case is so much stronger against the Y company that I should be justified in distinguishing between it and the other plaintiffs. The circumstances in relation to either that company or the others may change and further evidence may put a different complexion on the matter. d

I would not leave these applications without remarking that I do not see this as a matter of conflict between jurisdictions. I can fully understand that the United States District Court would wish to see where the line is in practice drawn by the courts of this country; but, having been drawn where it has, I find it hard to believe that the bank is in any danger of being held to be in contempt, since the adequacy of the excuse that it makes for non-production of the documents sought is now obvious indeed. Any sanction imposed now on the bank would look like pressure on this court, whereas, as it seems to me, it is for the New York court to relieve against the dilemma, in which it turns out to have placed its own national, by refraining from holding it in contempt if contempt proceedings are issued. e f

For those reasons, I shall continue the injunctions now running against the defendants.

Interlocutory injunctions continued until trial or further order. g

Solicitors: *Allen & Overy* (for the bank); *Simmons & Simmons* (for the first and second plaintiffs); *Norton Rose Botterell & Roche* (for the third plaintiffs).

K Mydeen Esq Barrister.

a R v Eastleigh Borough Council, ex parte Betts and another

COURT OF APPEAL, CIVIL DIVISION
STEPHENSON, GRIFFITHS AND PURCHAS LJJ
24, 25 JANUARY, 3 MARCH 1983

b

Housing – Homeless person – Duty of housing authority to provide accommodation – Person having no local connection with area of housing authority – Applicant not 'normally resident' in authority's area – Normally resident – Authority applying arbitrary or rigid residential qualification of residence for six out of previous twelve months – Whether authority entitled to impose arbitrary residential qualification – Housing (Homeless Persons) Act 1977, ss 5(1)(a),
c *18(1)(a).*

Housing – Homeless person – Duty of housing authority to provide accommodation – Responsibility between housing authorities – Notifying authority wrongly deciding that applicant having local connection with notified authority – Whether notifying authority remaining under primary duty to house applicant – Whether dispute arising between authorities – Whether court precluded from
d *reviewing notifying authority's decision – Housing (Homeless Persons) Act 1977, s 5(1)(a) (7).*

In August 1980 the male applicant obtained a job in Southampton and moved there from Leicester. In October the female applicant and their two children joined him and the family moved into a council house in the area of the respondent council. Shortly afterwards, the male applicant lost his job and fell into arrears with the rent for the
e council house, with the result that the council obtained a possession order in respect of the house. On 6 February 1981 the applicants applied to the council, as the local housing authority, for accommodation under the Housing (Homeless Persons) Act 1977. The council decided that the family were homeless, that they had not become homeless intentionally and that they had a priority need for accommodation (and therefore would normally have been entitled under s 4(5)[a] of the 1977 Act to housing for an indefinite
f period), but the council further decided that the applicants had no 'local connection', as defined by s 18(1)[b] of the 1977 Act, with the council's area because they were not and never had been 'normally resident' in the area but instead had a local connection with another housing authority's area, namely the area of the authority which housed them in Leicester. The council therefore considered that by virtue of s 5(1)(*a*)[c] of the 1977 Act it was relieved of the duty to house the applicants which would otherwise have been
g imposed on it by s 4(5). In deciding that the applicants had no 'local connection' with its area the council relied on a recommendation in a national agreement between housing authorities regarding the implementation of the 1977 Act to the effect that a working definition of 'normal residence' should be residence in the area for at least six out of the previous twelve months. The applicants applied for judicial review of the council's decision. The judge dismissed the application and the applicants appealed.

h

Held – On the ordinary and natural meaning of the phrase 'normally resident' in s 18(1)(*a*) of the 1977 Act a person was normally resident in the area of a housing authority if he was ordinarily resident there and intended to settle there for the time being, in contrast to being resident there in extraordinary, abnormal or unusual circumstances. Accordingly, the question whether a person was 'normally resident' in a
j particular place required the various characteristics, and not just the length, of the residence to be considered. By applying arbitrarily or rigidly the period of residential qualification recommended in the agreement between housing authorities rather than

---

a Section 4(5) is set out at p 484 *e*, post
b Section 18(1) is set out at p 485 *d e*, post
c Section 5(1) is set out at p 484 *f g*, post

considering the particular circumstances of the applicants, the council had misdirected itself. The appeal would therefore be allowed and an order of mandamus issued requiring the council to carry out the duty imposed on it by s 4(5) of the 1977 Act to provide accommodation for the applicants (see p 488 *g* to *j*, p 489 *h j*, p 490 *b* to *e*, p 492 *c d* and *g* to *j*, p 493 *b c* and p 494 *a* to *d* and *g h*, *post*).

Dicta of Somervell LJ in *Macrae v Macrae* [1949] 2 All ER at 36–37, of Widgery J in *Peak Trailer and Chassis Ltd v Jackson* [1967] 1 All ER at 176 and *Shah v Barnet London BC* [1983] 1 All ER 226 applied.

Per Stephenson and Purchas LJJ. Where a housing authority (the notifying authority) wrongly decides under s 5(1)(*a*) of the 1977 Act that a homeless person has a local connection not with its area but with the area of another authority (the notified authority) the court may refer the case back to the notifying authority to reconsider its decision, notwithstanding that s 5(7)[d] requires that any question arising between a notifying and a notified authority regarding the accommodation of a homeless person is to be determined by agreement between the two authorities or in accordance with arrangements made by the Secretary of State, since if the homeless person does have a local connection with the area of the notifying authority that authority remains under the primary duty under s 4(5) to house the homeless person and therefore no question of responsibility between the two authorities arises and s 5(7) does not come into play (see p 491 *h j*, p 492 *b c* and p 494 *c*, post).

Notes

For responsibility for accommodation as between housing authorities, see 22 Halsbury's Laws (4th edn) para 514.

For the Housing (Homeless Persons) Act 1977, ss 4, 5, 18, see 47 Halsbury's Statutes (3rd edn) 318, 319, 330.

Cases referred to in judgments

Associated Provincial Picture Houses Ltd v Wednesbury Corp [1947] 2 All ER 680, [1948] KB 223, CA

Macrae v Macrae [1949] 2 All ER 34, [1949] P 397, CA; *affg* [1949] 1 All ER 290, [1949] P 272, DC.

Peak Trailer and Chassis Ltd v Jackson [1967] 1 All ER 172, [1967] 1 WLR 155, DC.

R v Bristol CC, ex p Browne [1979] 3 All ER 344, [1979] 1 WLR 1437, DC.

R v McCall, ex p Eastbourne BC (29 April 1981, unreported), QBD.

R v Slough BC, ex p Ealing London BC [1981] 1 All ER 601, [1981] QB 801, [1981] 2 WLR 399, CA.

R v Wyre BC, ex p Parr (1982) Times, 4 February, CA.

Shah v Barnet London BC [1983] 1 All ER 226, [1983] 2 WLR 16, HL; *rvsg* [1982] 1 All ER 698, [1982] QB 688, [1982] 2 WLR 474, CA.

Appeal

Ronald Thomas Betts and Vivien Anne Betts applied, with the leave of Woolf J granted on 22 May 1982, for judicial review of a decision of the Eastleigh Borough Council to the effect that they were not under a duty to rehouse the applicants because they had no local connection with the council's area, since they were not normally resident in the area, within ss 5(1) and 18(1) of the 1977 Act. The applicants sought (1) a declaration that they were not intentionally homeless, (2) an order of mandamus requiring the council to carry out their duty under s 4(5) of the 1977 Act to house them, and (3) an injunction restraining the council from executing a warrant for the possession of 85 High Street, Eastleigh, Hants. By a judgment given on 26 October 1982 Webster J, hearing the Crown

d Section 5(7) is set out at p 485 *a*, post

Office list, dismissed the application for judicial review. The applicants appealed. The facts are set out in the judgment of Stephenson LJ.

James W Black QC and *Barrington Myers* for the applicants.
Anthony Scrivener QC and *Graham Stoker* for the council.

Cur adv vult

3 March. The following judgments were delivered.

STEPHENSON LJ. This is an appeal by Mr and Mrs Betts against an order of Webster J made on 26 October 1982 dismissing their application for judicial review. Their application was threefold: (1) for a declaration that they were not intentionally homeless; (2) for an order of mandamus requiring the respondent council to carry out their duty to house them under s 4(5) of the Housing (Homeless Persons) Act 1977; (3) for an injunction restraining the council from executing the warrant for possession of 85 High Street, Eastleigh, Hants.

As to (1), the council have withdrawn long since their allegation that the applicants are intentionally homeless. As to (3), the council obtained in the Southampton County Court an order for possession on 27 October 1981 of the temporary accommodation which they provided for the applicants at 85 High Street in the borough as long ago as 29 September 1981, but have not executed the warrant for possession which they obtained in March 1982 pending the determination of these proceedings. The relief with which these proceedings are really concerned is accordingly (2), the housing of the applicants by the council under the 1977 Act.

The facts which give rise to the application are these. Mr Betts is a man of 36, London born, who since 1973 has worked in various places, including Leicester, where he lived and worked from 1978 to 1980 within the area of the Blaby District Council. He lived with his common law wife, the second applicant, and their two daughters born in 1974 and 1978. Her parents have lived in Leicester for some six years.

In 1980 he got a job with Southern Television as a film processer and on 4 August 1980 he went to live in Southampton. Next month he moved into a houseboat in Southampton where his wife and children joined him. On 9 October 1980 they all moved to 40 Cranmore, Ingleside, Netley Abbey, in the borough of Eastleigh on a six-month tenancy. Not long after, probably in the following month, Southern Television lost their franchise, Mr Betts lost his job, he fell into arrears with his rent, and on 3 February 1981 the council obtained an order for possession of 40 Cranmore and provided him and his family with temporary accommodation at 85 High Street. On 6 February 1981 Mr and Mrs Betts applied to the council for housing accommodation under the 1977 Act.

It is now necessary before completing the history of this matter to refer to the relevant provisions of the 1977 Act:

> '**1.**—(1) A person is homeless for the purposes of this Act if he has no accommodation, and a person is to be treated as having no accommodation for those purposes if there is no accommodation—(*a*) which he, together with any other person who normally resides with him as a member of his family or in circumstances in which the housing authority consider it reasonable for that person to reside with him—(i) is entitled to occupy by virtue of an interest in it or of an order of a court, or (ii) has, in England or Wales, an express or implied licence to occupy . . .
>
> (3) For the purposes of this Act a person is threatened with homelessness if it is likely that he will become homeless within 28 days.
>
> **2.**—(1) For the purposes of this Act a homeless person or a person threatened with homelessness has a priority need for accommodation when the housing authority are satisfied that he is within one of the following categories:—(*a*) he has

dependent children who are residing with him or who might reasonably be expected to reside with him . . . *a*

3.—(1) If—(*a*) a person applies to a housing authority for accommodation or for assistance in obtaining accommodation, and (*b*) the authority have reason to believe that he may be homeless or threatened with homelessness, the authority shall make appropriate inquiries.

(2) In subsection (1) above "appropriate inquiries" means—(*a*) such inquiries as are necessary to satisfy the authority whether the person who applied to them is *b* homeless or threatened with homelessness, and (*b*) if the authority are satisfied that he is homeless or threatened with homelessness, any further inquiries necessary to satisfy them—(i) whether he has a priority need, and (ii) whether he became homeless or threatened with homelessness intentionally.

(3) If the authority think fit, they may also make inquiries as to whether the person who applied to them has a local connection with the area of another housing *c* authority.

(4) If the authority have reason to believe that the person who applied to them may be homeless and have a priority need, they shall secure that accommodation is made available for his occupation pending any decision which they may make as a result of their inquiries (irrespective of any local connection he may have with the area of another housing authority). *d*

4.—(1) If a housing authority are satisfied, as a result of inquiries under section 3 above, that a person who has applied to them for accommodation or for assistance in obtaining accommodation is homeless or threatened with homelessness, they shall be subject to a duty towards him under this section . . .

(5) Where—(*a*) they are satisfied—(i) that he is homeless, and (ii) that he has a priority need, but (*b*) they are not satisfied that he became homeless intentionally, *e* their duty, subject to section 5 below, is to secure that accommodation becomes available for his occupation . . .

5.—(1) A housing authority are not subject to a duty under section 4(5) above—(*a*) if they are of the opinion—(i) that neither the person who applied to them for accommodation or for assistance in obtaining accommodation nor any person who might reasonably be expected to reside with him has a local connection with their *f* area, and (ii) that the person who so applied or a person who might reasonably be expected to reside with him has a local connection with another housing authority's area, and (iii) that neither the person who so applied nor any person who might reasonably be expected to reside with him will run the risk of domestic violence in that housing authority's area, and (*b*) if they notify that authority—(i) that the application has been made, and (ii) that they are of the opinion specified in paragraph *g* (*a*) above.

(2) In this Act "notifying authority" means a housing authority who give a notification under subsection (1) above and "notified authority" means a housing authority who receive such a notification.

(3) It shall be the duty of the notified authority to secure that accommodation becomes available for occupation by the person to whom the notification relates if *h* neither he nor any person who might reasonably be expected to reside with him has a local connection with the area of the notifying authority but the conditions specified in subsection (4) below are satisfied.

(4) The conditions mentioned in subsection (3) above are—(*a*) that the person to whom the notification relates or some person who might reasonably be expected to reside with him has a local connection with the area of the notified authority, and *j* (*b*) that neither he nor any such person will run the risk of domestic violence in that area.

(5) In any other case it shall be the duty of the notifying authority to secure that accommodation becomes available for occupation by the person to whom the notification relates.

(6) It shall also be the duty of the notifying authority to secure that accommodation
a is available for occupation by the person to whom notification relates until it is determined whether subsection (3) or (5) above applies to him.

(7) Any question which falls to be determined under this section shall be determined by agreement between the notifying authority and the notified authority or, in default of such agreement, in accordance with the appropriate arrangements.

(8) The appropriate arrangements for the purposes of this section are any such
b arrangements as the Secretary of State may by order direct.

(9) An order under subsection (8) above may direct that the appropriate arrangements for the purposes of this section shall be—(*a*) arrangements agreed by any relevant authorities or association of relevant authorities, or (*b*) in default of such agreement, any such arrangements as appear to the Secretary of State, after appropriate consultations, to be suitable.

c (10) No order under subsection (8) above shall be made unless a draft of the order has been approved by resolution of each House of Parliament . . .

6.—(1) A housing authority may perform any duty under section 4 or 5 above to secure that accommodation becomes available for the occupation of a person—(*a*) by making available accommodation held by them under Part V of the Housing Act 1957 or Part VII of the Housing (Scotland) Act 1966 or under any other enactment,
d or (*b*) by securing that he obtains accommodation from some other person, or (*c*) by giving him such advice and assistance as will secure that he obtains accommodation from some other person . . .

18.—(1) Any reference in this Act to a person having a local connection with an area is a reference to his having a connection with that area—(*a*) because he is or in the past was normally resident in it and his residence in it is or was of his own
e choice; or (*b*) because he is employed in it, or (*c*) because of family associations, or (*d*) because of any special circumstances . . .'

Section 19(1) provides that unless the context otherwise requires 'local connection' shall be construed in accordance with s 18.

Faced with Mr and Mrs Betts' application, the council were of the opinion that neither
f of them had a local connection with the council's area because they did not qualify under any of the four kinds of local connection required by s 18: (a) they neither were nor had been normally resident in their area; (b) nor were they employed in it; (c) nor had they family association with it; (d) nor were there any special circumstances. The council were also of opinion that they had a local connection with the Blaby District Council's area and notified that housing authority in pursuance of s 5 of the Act.

On 25 February 1981 the chief housing officer of the council wrote and told them so
g in a letter which also offered them, as being homeless and having a priority need, temporary accommodation at 85 High Street, for four weeks from 2 March 1981, the day before the order for possession of 40 Cranmore took effect. The second paragraph of the letter told them this:

'Your homelessness is not regarded as intentional but your application under the
h Act has been notified to Blaby District Council because you have lived in this Borough for less than six months, are not employed in this Borough and do not have any relatives living here. Your rehousing is therefore considered to be their responsibility.'

On 3 April 1981 the estates and recreation officer of the Blaby District Council, as the
j notified authority, wrote informing the applicants that the respondent council had referred their case to that council and asking for confirmation that they were willing to return to the Blaby district. On 27 April Mr Betts replied on behalf of himself and his wife: 'This letter is confirmation that if it is possible we would like to return to the Blaby District.'

On 1 May Blaby District Council replied:

> 'In reply to your letter dated 27th April 1981, I hope to have a property in the homeless unit at Victoria Street, Narborough, in a fortnight or so. The offer will be *a* on a licence and for a limited period until such time as other property becomes available and you have shown your occupation of Victoria Street is satisfactory.'

On 12 May they sent Mr and Mrs Betts the final offer of a two-bedroomed house with this request:

> 'Would you please reply immediately stating your intentions regarding this *b* property as the offer will only be held until the 27th May 1981 and failure to reply before that date will result in the offer being withdrawn.'

Mr Betts signed the form of acceptance at the foot but never returned it.

On 4 June Blaby District Council wrote: '... as the offer has not been taken up, it is now withdrawn.'

Mr Betts explained his reasons for telling Blaby District Council that he wished to *c* return to their district and then changing his mind in two affidavits and in a letter of 1 April 1982 from his solicitors. He had not taken legal advice when Blaby District Council first communicated with him, he accepted the respondent council's view that he was not eligible for housing in Eastleigh because of their contention to that effect and he was desperate to get some permanent accommodation and willing to go anywhere to do so; but by the time the offer came he had obtained temporary work in Southampton and *d* though he would have been willing to give it up, he inspected the cottage offered to him in the Blaby disrict and considered it unreasonable, impracticable and unfair to move from Eastleigh to Blaby. His solicitors later gave a list, stated not to be complete or exhaustive, of eight reasons for his rejecting the offer, including the small size of the accommodation and the excessive amount of the rent required for it.

In 1982 the applicants consulted solicitors, who wrote first to the respondent council *e* on 19 March, and on 29 March they made a further application for council accommodation. On 31 March the council refused the application on the mistaken ground that the applicants were intentionally homeless, an allegation disputed by the applicants' solicitors and withdrawn by the council, whose case before the judge and before us is that they have discharged their duty to the applicants under the Act by transferring their responsibility to Blaby District Council under s 5. *f*

The applicants' case here and below was that the respondent council have not succeeded in transferring their responsibility to Blaby District Council. They can only do that if they were of the opinion that the applicants were not on 6 February 1981 (or before that) normally resident in their area. They formed that opinion by the rigid application of a guideline that normal residence short of six months was not enough to constitute a local connection with their area, and, if they had had regard to matters other than that six *g* months' minimum, they could not properly or reasonably have come to the conclusion that the applicants were not (or had not been) normally resident in their area. So counsel for the applicants submits that the real question for this court is the meaning in their context of the words 'normally resident'.

On the evidence the judge rejected these submissions. The evidence was the evidence of the council's chief housing officer, Mr Grant, in what he swore in an affidavit of 21 *h* June 1982, and what he wrote in the letter of 25 February 1981, from which I have already quoted. Counsel for the council offered to call him, but the judge said it would have been undesirable to call him in proceedings of this kind only to amplify or explain the affidavit which he had sworn, and he was not called. In his affidavit he said:

> '2 ... After considering a report from Mr. Renouf, my Senior Assistant (Estates *j* Management), I decided that the application should be referred to Blaby District Council under Section 5 of the Housing (Homeless Persons) Act 1977 as I considered that the responsibility for housing the Applicants lay with that Council. The decision was taken by me having regard to the wording of the Act together with the recommendations set out in the "Agreement on Procedures for Referrals of the Homeless—Revised 6th June 1979" issued by the Association of District Councils, Association of Metropolitan Authorities and the London Boroughs Association ...

> 3. Upon considering the report of Mr. Renouf, the crucial factor in my decision was that the Applicants did not have a "local connection" with the Borough of Eastleigh, within the meaning of Section 5 of the 1977 Act. The phrase "local connection" is defined in Section 18(1) of the 1977 Act, but as Section 18(1)(b) and Section 18(1)(c) were not applicable, unless the Applicants were "normally resident" in the Borough within the meaning of Section 18(1)(a) or unless any special circumstances applied, a local connection with the Respondent would not be established. In considering the question of "normally resident" I had regard to the revised "Agreement on Procedures for Referrals of the Homeless" which states that a "working definition of 'normal residence' should be that the household has been residing for at least six months in the (Borough) during the previous twelve months"—(clause 2.5). The Applicants having only resided in the Borough for some four months before the date of their application on the 6th February 1981, I considered that a "normal residence" had not been established within the meaning of the Act. The "Revised Agreement on Procedures for Referrals of the Homeless" is in wide use by Housing Authorities when considering a referral under Section 5 of the 1977 Act, and Blaby District Council fully accepted the working definition of normal residencies.
>
> 4. From the report of Mr. Renouf, no special circumstances appeared for consideration and I therefore decided that the Applicants' application should be referred to Blaby District Council in whose area they had resided for the two years prior to taking up accommodation in the Borough of Eastleigh. Blaby District Council accepted responsibility under the Act and made an offer of accommodation to the Applicants which was not accepted by Mr. and Mrs. Betts.'

We admitted without objection an affidavit sworn on 19 January 1983 by Mr Carroll, assistant secretary (housing management) of the Association of District Councils, explaining how the Agreement on Procedures for Referrals of the Homeless came into being, was discussed and approved by the Department of Environment during the passage of the Housing (Homeless Persons) Bill, and was ratified by local authorities on 1 December 1977, who also discussed with the department the draft of the order which is now the Housing (Homeless Persons) (Appropriate Arrangements) Order 1978, SI 1978/69, and which was the subject of a letter from the department dated 26 January 1978, exhibited to Mr Carroll's affidavit.

This nation-wide agreement sets out in cl 1 by way of introduction s 5(7), (8) and (9) of the 1977 Act and proceeds in cl 1.2 to recommend to local authorities agreed arrangements for referrals. Then comes a statement with which the experience of the courts makes it impossible to disagree:

> 'There are, however, considerable areas of possible disagreement and dispute in the interpretation of the Act, and although in the last resort these can only be decided by the courts, the Association are anxious to avoid as far as possible legal disputes between local authorities. They therefore issue this agreement on the procedures and criteria to be followed, and recommend it for general adoption by all their members. It has been revised in the light of experience in the first 12 months of operation and may be revised hereafter as necessary.'

Clause 2 correctly sets out the requirements of s 5, including (in cl 2.4) the requirement that before making a referral, the local authority must be of the opinion that 'no member of the household has any local connection with their own area', and then in cl 2.5 makes the suggestion which has caused all the trouble in this case:

> 'A local connection may be:—That the household is, or in the past was, normally resident in the area. It is suggested that a working definition of "normal residence" should be that the household has been residing for at least 6 months in the area during the previous 12 months, or for not less than 3 years during the previous 5 year period. In this connection, residence up to 6 months under one or more tenancies subject to Case 13 of Schedule 15 of the Rent Act 1977 should be disregarded for the purpose of defining "normal residence".'

Clause 2 concludes with a paragraph (cl 2.8) not cited to us or apparently to the judge, of which the first sentence reads: *a*

> 'Once the local authority has established that the household is homeless, is not intentionally homeless, is in a priority category, and does not have any local connection in its own area, then and only then may it notify another authority under Section 5 of the Act.'

That is enough to support the judge's comment that the agreement confines itself to *b* recommendations and suggestions and I need not quote other clauses (such as cll 2.5 (iv) and 7) which support his further comment that it not only allows for but encourages a certain flexibility in the operation of s 5 of the 1977 Act.

Now nobody can dispute that the working definition of 'normal residence' suggested in the agreement cannot be elevated to the status of a statutory interpretation applicable to every case. The first question is: how did Mr Grant regard it? Did he regard it in the *c* light of a definition to be applied without exception or further consideration, or did he regard it as a guideline when considering all the circumstances of Mr and Mrs Betts? What did he mean by saying, 'I had regard to the revised Agreement' and 'having regard to the wording of the Act together with the recommendations set out in the agreement'?

Unlike the judge, I find no apparent ambiguity in the phrase 'I had regard to', and would consider it by itself to mean 'I took it into account', not 'I had regard to it and to *d* nothing else'; and that is how the judge understood his evidence. He said:

> 'It is true that he did say at the end of the passage: "I considered that a 'normal residence' had not been established within the meaning of the Act." It is also true that, prima facie, by saying that, he was simply applying the recommendation obtaining in the agreement as to the meaning or suggestion of the working definition of the words "normal residence" for the purpose of s 18(1)(*a*). However, I *e* am far from satisfied, on the material before me that he misdirected himself as to that meaning. I am very far from satisfied that he only applied that suggested working definition of the words "normal residence" when deciding whether the applicants were normally resident in the area of his authority. Also, I am far from satisfied that he regarded the decision that he had to make as being fettered in any way by the terms of that agreement. I am far from satisfied that the decision *f* whether or not the applicants were normally resident in the area of the respondent housing authority or in the area of the Blaby District Council was a decision which could not have been reached on the material before him had he properly directed himself.'

I regret to have to differ from the judge's conclusion, and my hesitation in doing so is *g* increased by the fact that Mr Grant did not give his own interpretation, I suspect because the judge had taken (and perhaps indicated) the view of his affidavit evidence which he expressed in the passage which I have read from his judgment. But I feel compelled to differ from the judge's conclusion by the terms of the letter of 25 February 1981, which the judge certainly quoted but without comment or further reference. There the reason and the only reason given by Mr Grant for his decision at the time when he made it is *h* that the applicants had lived in the borough for less than six months; and when I add to that the last sentence in para 3 of his affidavit, which the judge omitted to quote, with its reference to Blaby District Council's acceptance of the agreement's working definition of normal residence, I would have had considerable difficulty in believing Mr Grant if he had said in the witness box that he did not mean what his letter of 25 February to my mind necessarily conveys. I am afraid that he did fetter the council's decision by a rigid *j* application of the suggested definition of normal residence.

If I am right and the judge wrong on this point, the appeal must be allowed, but I doubt very much whether I could accept the second submission of counsel for the applicants that no reasonable housing authority, which had also had regard to all the other circumstances of the applicants' case than the short time they had resided in the council's area, could have decided as the council did, that the applicants were not (and had not in the past been) normally resident in their area. I would have thought the right

course would be that we should remit the application to the council for them to
a reconsider it on all available information about the applicants' tenancy of 40 Cranmore, and in the light of our judgment and of two cases to which counsel referred us: the very recent decision of the House of Lords in *Shah v Barnet London BC* [1983] 1 All ER 226, [1983] 2 WLR 16 on what is meant by 'ordinarily resident' in s 1 of the Education Act 1962, and the decision of this court in *Macrae v Macrae* [1949] 2 All ER 34, [1949] P 397 on the words 'ordinarily resides' in s 6 of the Summary Jurisdiction (Process) Act 1881.

b *Macrae*'s case would appear to have been decided on that section (s 6 of the 1881 Act), though it is nowhere cited in the reports of the case (see [1949] 1 All ER 290, [1949] P 272, DC; [1949] 2 All ER 34, [1949] P 397, CA). But counsel for the applicants relied on the leading judgment of Somervell LJ when he said ([1949] 2 All ER 34 at 36–37, [1949] P 397 at 403):

> 'Ordinary residence is a thing which can be changed in a day. A man is ordinarily
> c resident in one place up till a particular day. He then cuts the connection he has with that place—in this case he left his wife; in another case he might have disposed of his house—and makes arrangements to have his home somewhere else. Where there are indications that the place to which he moves is the place which he intends to make his home for, at any rate, an indefinite period, as from that date he is ordinarily resident at that place.'

d In the *Barnet* case (where counsel for the council tells us he cited *Macrae*'s case, though the reporters omit it) Lord Scarman, with whose speech all their Lordships agreed without qualification, applied the natural and ordinary meaning given to the words in another context by judicial authority to the condition of ordinary residence in this country qualifying immigrant students for grants under the Education Act 1962. What
e he said 'ordinarily resident' meant was this ([1983] 1 All ER 226 at 235, [1983] 2 WLR 16 at 26–27):

> 'Unless, therefore, it can be shown that the statutory framework or the legal context in which the words are used requires a different meaning, I unhesitatingly subscribe to the view that "ordinarily resident" refers to a man's abode in a particular place or country which he has adopted voluntarily and for settled purposes as part
> f of the regular order of his life for the time being, whether of short or long duration ... There are two, and no more than two, respects in which the mind of the propositus is important in determining ordinary residence. The residence must be voluntarily adopted. Enforced presence by reason of kidnapping or imprisonment, or a Robinson Crusoe existence on a desert island with no opportunity of escape, may be so overwhelming a factor as to negative the will to be where one is. And
> g there must be a degree of settled purpose. The purpose may be one or there may be several. It may be specific or general. All the law requires is that there is a settled purpose. This is not to say that the propositus intends to stay where he is indefinitely; indeed his purpose, while settled, may be for a limited period. Education, business or profession, employment, health, family or merely love of the place spring to mind as common reasons for a choice of regular abode. And there may well be
> h many others. All that is necessary is that the purpose of living where one does has a sufficient degree of continuity to be properly described as settled.'

Counsel for the council argued that 'normally resident' means something different from 'ordinarily resident', and hazarded 'usually resident' as its true equivalent. I cannot see much, if any, difference between the three expressions. Nor could Lord Denning
j MR, saying what he did in the passage from his judgment in the *Barnet* case [1982] 1 All ER 698 at 704, [1982] QB 688 at 720, quoted by Lord Scarman ([1983] 1 All ER 226 at 234, [1983] 2 WLR 16). They point the contrast with what is extraordinary or abnormal or unusual. I would accept what Widgery J said in *Peak Trailer and Chassis Ltd v Jackson* [1967] 1 All ER 172 at 176, [1967] 1 WLR 155 at 161 in considering whether an articulated vehicle was 'normally used' for the conveyance of exceptional loads contrary to reg 3 of the Motor Vehicles (Construction and Use) Regulations 1963, SI 1963/1646, as amended:

'In my view the word "normally" has a perfectly ordinary meaning which would be given to it by ordinary people in everyday use as a man might say "I normally get a
to the office every morning at 9.30 but this morning I was delayed by fog and only arrived at 10 o'clock". In using the word "normally", one is referring to something which is in contradistinction to abnormal or exceptional.'

These authorities (and the judge did not have the benefit of considering them) seem to me to show that a person may be normally resident where he intends to settle not necessarily permanently or indefinitely and may have, at different times, more than one b
normal residence. So much is clearly recognised by the wording of s 18(1)(*a*), and we do not have to consider whether a person can be normally, as well as ordinarily, resident in more than one place at the same time. If that follows from the natural and ordinary meaning of the words 'normally resident', I see no reason in their statutory framework or legal context to require a different meaning in s 18(1)(*a*) of the 1977 Act, or in s 1(1)(*a*); and two consequences follow. (1) The working definition suggested in the agreement c
may give valuable guidance for many cases but eliminates from the normally resident in an area any homeless person who had been normally resident there, for however many years, at any time earlier than five years before his application. (2) There was material here on which the council could have been of the opinion that Mr and Mrs Betts were or had been normally resident in their area, according to the natural and ordinary meaning of those words. It seems pretty clear that Mrs Betts and their daughters were persons who d
'normally resided' with Mr Betts as a member of his family within s 1(1)(*a*) of the Act: there may be considerable doubt whether they were not all normally resident in Eastleigh for four months. In considering that question and their intention their later attitude to the offer of the Blaby District Council might have some relevance.

I would therefore send this case back to the council were it not that counsel for the council has asked us not to do that but either to dismiss the appeal or to allow it and grant e
the applicants the order of mandamus which the judge refused. If I understood him aright, what the council, and it may be other housing authorities, want is a decision upholding the 1977 agreement (whatever precisely that may mean) and accepting his submission that the courts cannot question or direct an authority to alter their opinion under s 5(1)(*a*) that a person has no local connection with their area, even if there is nothing to support it except the provisions of the Agreement on Procedures for Referrals f
of the Homeless and no reasonable authority could have formed it.

Counsel was reluctant to go so far as to submit that the courts have no jurisdiction to review a referral under s 5, but that, unless the boldness of his argument has dazzled me, is what I think his submission comes to when he said: 'If two local authorities have made an agreement, you look to the agreement and no further.' The submission is that the question which the applicants have brought to the court to decide is one which is to be g
determined, and determined only, by agreement between housing authorities according to the agreed procedure laid down in s 5 of the 1977 Act and worked out in the 1977 agreement as revised and, in default of agreement, by the person appointed to determine the question in accordance with the directions given by the Secretary of State in the 1978 order.

The argument is based on s 5(7), which I read again. It provides that: h

'Any question which falls to be determined under this section shall be determined by agreement between the notifying authority and the notified authority or, in default of such agreement, in accordance with the appropriate arrangements.'

The Secretary of State has directed the appropriate arrangements by the 1978 order and the requirements of sub-ss (8), (9) and (10) have been fulfilled. Summarising those j
arrangements, the order set out in the schedule to them provides that any question which falls to be determined under s 5 is to be determined either by a person agreed on by the two authorities concerned, or in default by a person appointed from a panel to be drawn up by the three associations who drew up the 1977 agreement (though that agreement is not referred to in the order), by the chairman or chairmen of those associations. His reasoned determination notified in writing shall be final and binding on both authorities: see para 7 of the schedule.

According to counsel for the council it is to be final and binding also on the homeless
a persons who are not parties to the agreement between the notifying and the notified authority or to the 1977 agreement. They are bound by the opinion of the notifying authority, however erroneous, which is the starting point of the referral under s 5. The notifying authority do not have to be satisfied, as under s 3(2) or s 4, or to think fit, as under s 3(3), or to have reason to believe, as under s 3(4). And binding also is the overall agreement made in 1977 between all the authorities which ratified it with ministerial
b approval. The referral of the homeless from one authority to another can safely be left to them. They usually agree the question which authority's area has the closest connection with the homeless applicant and which authority is accordingly to house him and there have been, according to Mr Carroll, only 48 references to the panel since the Act was passed. If they agree between themselves, the homeless appellant has no choice between areas in which he has normally resided. Nor is there any real prejudice to him because
c when accepted by a notified authority he can always invoke s 6 of the Act and require that authority to secure that he obtains accommodation from, e g, the notifying authority. Anyway, counsel for the council submits that the question as to which the notifying authority have to form an opinion, namely whether the homeless person who has applied to them for accommodation has a local connection with their area, is a question which falls to be determined under s 5: see what Templeman LJ said in *R v Slough BC, ex p Ealing*
d *London BC* [1981] 1 All ER 601 at 618, [1981] QB 801 at 817:

> 'In my judgment the only questions which fall to be determined under s 5 are questions which are in doubt under that section, in particular questions which arise as to the local connection of an applicant for housing accommodation.'

I am far from satisfied that an applicant might not be prejudiced by being transferred
e from one authority to another. Mr and Mrs Betts might find it harder to prove against Blaby District Council than against the respondent council that they had failed to do their statutory duty to provide them with appropriate accommodation, in the light of such cases as *R v Bristol CC, ex p Browne* [1979] 3 All ER 344, [1979] 1 WLR 1437 and *R v Wyre BC, ex p Parr* (1982) Times, 4 February. And they might even have difficulty in establishing that a housing authority was a person in the context of s 6: see *R v Bristol CC,*
f *ex p Browne* [1979] 3 All ER 344 at 350, [1979] 1 WLR 1437 at 1442 per Lloyd J. But, however that may be, counsel for the council's submissions seem to me to break down on one cardinal consideration: a housing authority's primary duty to house the homeless in need under s 4(5) is only subject to s 5, and a housing authority are only *not* subject to that primary duty, if they are of the opinion that the applicant for accommodation does not have a local connection with the area (as defined in s 18), not if they are of opinion
g that he has a local connection with their area but a closer connection with another authority's. I agree that s 5 requires the authority to make up their mind whether he has or has not a local connection and, if there is material on which a reasonable authority properly directing themselves and properly interpreting the statute, definition and all, can form the opinion that he has not, the courts will not substitute their opinion for the authority's. But s 5 says nothing about a closer local connection with the notified
h authority than with the notifying authority. If there is plainly a local connection, as defined in the statute correctly understood, s 5 does not come into operation at all and referral to another authority, whether or not there is also a local connection with them, does not get off the ground. The duty remains with the authority who want to notify and cannot be transferred to the authority they want to be notified. As Woolf J said in *R v McCall, ex p Eastbourne BC* (29 April 1981, unreported), where a referee had had to
j arbitrate under s 5(7) between three housing authorities:

> 'The right to notify other authorities is conditional on it being established that the persons concerned have no local connection with the area of the notifying authority.'

If, by 'established' Woolf J meant 'established to the reasonable satisfaction of the notifying authority', I would accept that proposition. It is for the authority to establish that it is not bound by s 4 but can take advantage of s 5. I would not quarrel with the way in which cl 2.8 of the 1977 agreement puts the condition: a

> 'Once the local authority has established that the household . . . does not have any local connection in its own area, then and only then may it notify another authority under Section 5 of the Act.'

It is only when that condition is fulfilled that questions as to the local connection of an applicant with other authorities fall to be determined under that section, and I do not b understand Templeman LJ to have been referring to any questions other than those, in the passage on which counsel for the council relied. It is only between properly notified authorities, not between an improperly notifying authority and those authorities they desire to notify, that any question of the closest local connection can arise.

We have not had the benefit of the judge's view on these submissions for the council because we are told he cut short the argument and disposed of the application on the c grounds set out in his judgment. But we have had the advantage of full argument, at the end of which I have no doubt that the court is not precluded by s 5 on its true construction from entertaining such an application as this and that it ought to be granted for the reasons I have given.

I would allow the appeal and require the respondent council to carry out their duty to house the applicants under s 4(5) of the Housing (Homeless Persons) Act 1977. d

GRIFFITHS LJ. The facts and the statutory framework are to be found set out so fully in the judgment of Stephenson LJ that I can state my own view on what I conceive to be the crucial issue in this appeal quite shortly.

The Betts family were homeless, they had a priority need, and they were not intentionally homeless. The Eastleigh Borough Council therefore had a duty to house e them unless they could pass on that obligation to the Blaby District Council, in whose area the Betts family had lived before they came to Eastleigh: see ss 4(5) and 5(1) of the Housing (Homeless Persons) Act 1977.

Eastleigh could only pass on the obligation to Blaby if they were of the opinion that the Betts family had no local connection with their area: see s 5(1)(*a*)(i). Eastleigh, acting through their housing officer, did form the opinion that the Betts family had no local f connection with their area, and so they passed on the housing obligation to Blaby. If it can be shown that the opinion was arrived at by applying a wrong principle of law, that opinion must be set aside by this court on *Wednesbury* principles (see *Associated Provincial Picture Houses Ltd v Wednesbury Corp* [1974] 2 All ER 680, [1948] KB 223) and the council will remain under a duty to house the Betts family. The Eastleigh Borough Council would of course be free to reconsider their opinion applying the law correctly, but we g understand from counsel for the respondent council that if our decision in this appeal is against the council they intend to house the Betts family.

A local connection is defined by s 18(1) and includes a person who is normally resident in the housing authority's area. I am satisfied that the chief housing officer decided that the Betts family were not normally resident in Eastleigh area because they had not lived there for six months before they applied for shelter under the Act. This is clear from the h terms of his letter dated 25 February 1981, the material part of which reads:

> 'Your homelessness is not regarded as intentional but your application under the Act has been notified to Blaby District Council because you have lived in this Borough for less than six months, are not employed in this Borough and do not have any relatives living here. Your rehousing is therefore considered to be their responsibility.' j

I am also satisfied that the chief housing officer formed his opinion on the question of normal residence by applying the suggested definition of 'normal residence' contained in the revised Agreement on Procedures for Referrals of the Homeless dated 6 June 1979. This agreement was entered into by the majority of housing authorities to govern arrangements between them to share the burden of housing the homeless pursuant to the provisions of s 5 of the Act. The definition reads as follows (cl 2.5):

> 'It is suggested that a working definition of "normal residence" should be that the household has been residing for at least 6 months in the area during the previous 12 months, or for not less than 3 years during the previous 5 year period.'

This may be a good practical starting point to consider the question of normal residence, but it certainly is not a correct definition of normal residence within the meaning of this Act. 'Normal residence' within the meaning of this Act is in my opinion to be construed in the same sense as 'ordinarily resident' was construed by the House of Lords in *Shah v Barnet London BC* [1983] 1 All ER 226, [1983] 2 WLR 16. It requires a consideration of many features of the residence and is not to be decided solely by the application of a six-month rule.

It follows that as the housing officer applied the six-month rule to decide 'normal residence' he misdirected himself in law when forming his opinion on normal residence and thus on whether the Betts family had a local connection with Eastleigh's area; that opinion must be set aside and Eastleigh declared to remain under a duty to house the Betts family pursuant to s 4(5) of the Act.

I therefore agree that this appeal must be allowed.

PURCHAS LJ. The history of events which led to the appellants applying to the respondent council under s 3 of the Housing (Homeless Persons) Act 1977 has been fully described in the judgment of Stephenson LJ already delivered. The council made temporary accommodation available under s 3(4) of the Act while they took steps under an agreement which had been reached on a national basis between the Association of District Councils, the Association of Metropolitan Authorities and the London Boroughs Association dated 6 June 1979. Both the respondent council and the Blaby District Council were parties to this agreement. I wish to repeat only three of the clauses in this agreement:

> '1. INTRODUCTION ...
>
> 1.2 With this in mind [namely, the provisions of s 5 of the Act] the three associations have agreed on arrangements for referrals which they recommend to the local authorities who are primarily concerned with providing for homeless households ...
>
> 2. PROCEDURES FOR DECIDING WHETHER A NOTIFICATION SHOULD BE MADE ...
>
> 2.5 A local connection may be:—(i) That the household is, or in the past was, normally resident in the area. It is suggested that a working definition of "normal residence" should be that the household has been residing for at least 6 months in the area during the previous 12 months, or for not less than 3 years during the previous 5 year period ...
>
> 2.8 Once the local authority has established that the household is homeless ... and does *not* have any local connection in its own area, then and only then may it notify another authority under Section 5 of the Act.'

In accordance with the criteria set out in cl 2.5 of the national agreement Blaby was the authority responsible and to be notified under s 5 of the 1977 Act. Paragraph 3 of an affidavit sworn by the council's housing officer, Mr Renouf, reads as follows:

> '3. As a result of the information given to me by Mr. Betts in the interview, the Applicants were classified as having a "priority need" under Section 2 of the 1977 Act because there were dependent children of the family residing with the Applicants. Accordingly, temporary accommodation was made available to the family at 85, High Street, Eastleigh, but pending referral of this matter under Section 5 of the 1977 Act, and notification of the availability of this accommodation was sent to them by means of letter dated the 25th February ... 4. I then reported my findings to the Chief Housing Officer who confirmed that this application should be referred to the Blaby District Council under Section 5 of the 1977 Act because the Applicants had no local connection with the Respondents, but they had a local connection with the Blaby District Council.'

This affidavit discloses that the council relied on the information given by the applicants to Mr Renouf at the initial interview and immediately determined to refer the matter to Blaby under the agreement. There is no suggestion of any specific or individual consideration of the matters which should be considered before an application is notified to another housing authority under s 5 of the Act. This is confirmed both by the extract from the affidavit of the council's chief housing officer and the letter dated 25 February 1981 quoted by Stephenson LJ.

Although the national agreement purports only to make 'recommendations', if the criteria of cl 2.5(1) are strictly applied to cl 2.8 without more, then in effect the agreement is being used to override the duty imposed on an authority by ss 5(1)(*a*)(i) and 18(1) of the Act to consider each application on its own merits in light, inter alia, of the provisions of s 18(1)(*a*) before forming the opinion that the applicant does not have a local connection with their area. Before an authority can properly form this opinion it is not open to that authority to notify another housing authority within the remaining provisions of s 5 of the Act.

In my judgment, it is not possible to say that the council did more than apply the terms of the agreement to decide that the applicants did not qualify under s 18(1)(*a*). They did not at the time of their application qualify under any other paragraph of s 18(1). In forming this conclusion I find myself regrettably unable to agree with the conclusions reached in the judgment of Webster J.

In considering the meaning of 'normally resident in the district' I can see no mandate for distinguishing between the expression 'normally resident' and 'ordinarily resident'. We have been referred to *Shah v Barnet London BC* [1983] 1 All ER 226, [1983] 2 WLR 16 on the meaning of 'ordinarily resident' in s 1 of the Education Act 1962 and the decision of this court in *Macrae v Macrae* [1949] 1 All ER 290, [1949] P 272 (Divisional Court) and [1949] 2 All ER 34, [1949] P 397 (Court of Appeal) referring to the words 'ordinarily resides' in s 6 of the Summary Jurisdiction (Process) Act 1881. The effect of these authorities has already been reviewed by Stephenson LJ. I will not repeat them except to refer to part of the judgment of Widgery J in *Peak Trailer and Chassis Ltd v Jackson* [1967] 1 All ER 172 at 176, [1967] 1 WLR 155 at 161:

> 'In my view the word "normally" has a perfectly ordinary meaning which would be given to it by ordinary people in everyday use as a man might say "I normally get to the office every morning at 9.30 but this morning I was delayed by fog and only arrived at 10 o'clock".'

Adopting this approach to the instant case, if the applicants had been asked by an inquirer where they were normally living between October 1980 and January 1981 I have little doubt that they would have answered 'in Eastleigh'. In my judgment this would be the normal reaction, as an objective test, of any person in the particular circumstances in which the applicants found themselves at that time.

In the light of these authorities, the adherence to an arbitrary period of residential qualification cannot be the correct approach to s 18(1)(*a*) of the Act. In my judgment in doing this the respondent council failed to comply with the statutory duty placed on them by s 5(1)(*a*)(i) of the Act before notifying Blaby under s 5(1)(*b*). In these circumstances the council did not divest themselves of the duty imposed on them by s 4(5) and, therefore, this appeal should succeed.

Appeal allowed. Order of mandamus as prayed. Leave to appeal to the House of Lords refused.

5 May. The Appeal Committee of the House of Lords granted the council leave to appeal.

Solicitors: *Christopher Green & Partners*, Eastleigh (for the applicants); *R W Read*, Eastleigh (for the respondent council).

Diana Brahams Barrister.

Intpro Properties (UK) Ltd v Sauvel and others

COURT OF APPEAL, CIVIL DIVISION
WATKINS AND MAY LJJ
14, 15, 29 MARCH 1983

Constitutional law – Foreign sovereign state – Immunity from suit – Exceptions – Proceedings relating to interest in or possession of immovable property – Action to enforce obligation under lease – Landlord letting house to French government – House used as residence of diplomatic agent – Whether court having jurisdiction to entertain action by landlord to enter and repair premises – Whether proceedings relating to an interest in or possession of property – Whether property used for purposes of diplomatic mission – Whether French government immune from proceedings – State Immunity Act 1978, ss 6, 16(1)(b).

In August 1971 the plaintiffs let to the French government (represented by the French Consul General in London) certain premises for a term of four years. By a clause in the lease the French government agreed not to use the premises for any purpose other than that of a private dwelling house in the occupation of a named diplomat with the French embassy in London. The French government further agreed to permit the plaintiffs or their agents, with or without workmen, at reasonable times during the lease to enter into and on the premises for the purpose of inspecting and examining the premises and carrying out repairs. The diplomat occupied the premises as a home for him and his family and for use in carrying out his social obligations as a diplomat. In January 1982 dry rot appeared in the house and the plaintiffs instructed contractors to carry out remedial work. However, access to the premises was denied to the workmen by the diplomat. The plaintiffs issued a writ against the diplomat seeking an injunction to restrain him from preventing access to the premises or interfering with the repair work, and damages. The diplomat applied to set aside the writ on the ground that, as a member of the diplomatic staff of the French mission, he was a 'diplomatic agent' within art 1(*e*)[a] of the Vienna Convention on Diplomatic Relations, as set out in Sch 1 to the Diplomatic Privileges Act 1964, and accordingly enjoyed diplomatic immunity. The judge in chambers granted leave to amend the writ to join the French government as a party to the action and adjourned the proceedings for service to be effected on the Consul General. The French government gave notice under RSC Ord 12, r 8 of its intention to contest the proceedings with a view to setting aside the writ on the ground that it could not be impleaded in the English courts. By virtue of s 6(1)[b] of the State Immunity Act 1978 a foreign state was not immune from proceedings relating to 'any interest of the State in, or its possession or use of, immovable property in the United Kingdom' or 'any obligation of the State arising out of its interest in, or its possession or use of, any such property'. However by s 16(1)(*b*)[c] of the 1978 Act that exception from immunity under s 6(1) did not extend to proceedings concerning 'a State's title to or its possession of property used for the purposes of a diplomatic mission'. On the hearing of the diplomat's application to set aside the writ the judge held that because the diplomat was merely the licensee in occupation and the servant of the French government he was not a proper party to the action. He further held that the plaintiffs' action related not just to the French government's use of the premises but also to the rights and obligations arising from its possession of the premises and was therefore an action falling within the exception from immunity set out in s 6(1). However he further held that because the premises were used

---

a Article 1(*e*) provides: 'a "diplomatic agent" is the head of the mission or a member of the diplomatic staff of the mission.'

b Section 6(1) is set out at p 499 *j*, post

c Section 16(1) is set out at p 499 *j* to p 500 *a*, post

by the French government as a residence for one of its officials they were 'used for the purposes of a diplomatic mission' within s 16(1)(*b*) and the French government was a
therefore immune from proceedings. The diplomat subsequently gave up occupation of the premises and the plaintiffs appealed, claiming that they were entitled to damages against the French government for the loss which they had sustained as a result of the French government's refusal to permit the plaintiffs' contractors entry on the premises. The plaintiffs contended that the covenants in the lease constituted obligations on the part of the French government relating to its 'interest . . . in, or its possession or use of, b
immovable property', within s 6(1) of the 1978 Act and that consequently the French government was not immune from the proceedings, and that although by reason of the 1978 Act the plaintiffs could not have obtained relief by way of an injunction or an order for possession against the French government they were not barred from claiming damages for breach of covenant.

c

Held – The appeal would be allowed for the following reasons—

(1) On the true construction of s 16(1)(*b*) of the 1978 Act premises were 'used for the purposes of a diplomatic mission' if they were used for the professional diplomatic purposes of such a mission. It followed that where the premises were used as a private residence by a diplomatic agent, even though incidentally to this position the diplomatic agent had certain social obligations which he carried out on the premises, those premises d
were not used for the purposes of a diplomatic mission within s 16(1)(*b*). Furthermore, the specific reference to the residence of the head of the mission in art 1(*i*)[d] of Sch 1 to the 1964 Act made it clear that residences of other members of the mission could not form part of the premises of the mission (see p 500 *h j*, p 501 *e* to *h* and p 502 *f g*, post).

(2) Whereas s 6(1) of the 1978 Act dealt with a state's interest in, or its possession or use of, immovable property in the United Kingdom, there was no corresponding e
reference to the 'use' of such property in s 16(1)(*b*) of that Act which dealt with proceedings concerning a state's title to or its possession of property. Accordingly, the operation of s 16(1)(*b*) in removing the exception from immunity from proceedings under s 6(1), and thus restoring that immunity, was limited to those proceedings in which a state's title or right to possession in the strict sense was in question. It followed that s 16(1)(*b*) did not apply where the proceedings related to the 'use' of the premises; f
such proceedings remained within the exception from immunity conferred by s 6(1) (see p 500 *d e* and p 501 *j* to p 502 *b f g*, post).

(3) The immunity of foreign states and diplomatic agents to proceedings in the English courts was a matter of procedure and not of substance, and accordingly where that immunity applied it did not erase the cause of action but merely prevented an action being maintained on it. Since the 1964 and 1978 Acts gave full effect by procedural g
means to the physical inviolability of diplomatic premises, by precluding a plaintiff from obtaining an injunction or an order for specific performance in respect of diplomatic premises, that inviolability would not be allowed to operate as a bar to proceedings which were otherwise permitted by the 1964 and 1978 Acts, ie where the relief sought was merely damages for breach of covenant. It followed that the English courts had jurisdiction to hear and determine the action (see p 502 *c* to *g*, post); *Empson v Smith* h
[1965] 2 All ER 881 followed.

Decision of Bristow J [1983] 1 All ER 658 reversed.

Notes

For sovereign immunity from suit, see 8 Halsbury's Laws (4th edn) para 410 and 18 ibid para 1548, and for cases on the subject, see 1(1) Digest (Reissue) 54–59, *358–382*. j

For the Diplomatic Privileges Act 1964, Sch 1, art 1, see 6 Halsbury's Statutes (3rd edn) 1017.

For the State Immunity Act 1978, ss 6, 16, see 48 ibid 92, 99.

---

d Article 1(*i*) is set out at p 501 *c d*, post

Case referred to in judgments

a *Empson v Smith* [1965] 2 All ER 881, [1966] 1 QB 426, [1965] 3 WLR 380, CA.

Cases also cited

Johore (Sultan) v Abubakar Tunku Aris Bendahara [1952] 1 All ER 1261, [1952] AC 318, PC.

Thai-Europe Tapioca Service Ltd v Government of Pakistan, Ministry of Food and Agriculture, Directorate of Agricultural Supplies (Imports and Shipping Wing) [1975] 3 All ER 961,
b [1975] 1 WLR 1485, CA.

Appeal

The plaintiffs, Intpro Properties (UK) Ltd, appealed with the judge's leave against the order of Bristow J ([1983] 1 All ER 658, [1983] 2 WLR 1) made on 26 November 1982 whereby the plaintiffs' action against the first defendant, Dominique Sauvel, the second
c defendant, Danielle D Sauvel, and the third defendant, the government of the Republic of France, was dismissed, and sought, inter alia, an order that the court had jurisdiction to hear and determine the action on the basis that the defendants had no diplomatic immunity. The facts are set out in the judgment of May LJ.

George Newman QC and *Eugene Cotran* for the plaintiffs.
d The defendants did not appear.

Cur adv vult

29 March. The following judgments were delivered.

e **MAY LJ** (giving the first judgment at the invitation of Watkins LJ). This appeal raises a question about the extent of the immunity of a foreign state to proceedings in the English courts. The matter comes before us by way of an appeal from the judgment and order of Bristow J ([1983] 1 All ER 658, [1983] 2 WLR 1) of 26 November 1982 dismissing the plaintiffs' action against the defendants. The judge held the first and second defendants, M and Mme Sauvel, to be immune from the civil jurisdiction of our
f courts by virtue of art 31(1)(*a*) contained in Sch 1 to the Diplomatic Privileges Act 1964. In so far as the third defendant is concerned, the Republic of France, the judge held that that state in its turn was immune from the civil jurisdiction of our courts by virtue of s 1 of the State Immunity Act 1978; although s 6(1) of that Act does in certain circumstances permit actions to be brought against a foreign state, Bristow J held that that subsection did not apply to the present proceedings by virtue of s 16(1) of the 1978 Act. I shall refer
g to the statutory provisions in more detail hereafter.

The action was begun by a writ issued on 4 November 1982, originally against M and Mme Sauvel only. After an ex parte application for an interlocutory injunction, the details of which are no longer material, M and Mme Sauvel issued a summons on 10 November 1982 asking for orders to discharge it and to set aside the writ and its service on them, and also for a declaration that the court had no jurisdiction over them by virtue
h of the various provisions contained in Sch 1 to the Diplomatic Privileges Act 1964.

This came before Comyn J on 11 November, when he stayed the injunction until after the further hearing of the summons and gave the plaintiffs leave to join the Republic of France as third defendant. He ordered service on this defendant to be by way of service on the Consul General and gave the latter liberty to apply to set this aside on 12 hours' notice.

j On 18 November 1982 service was acknowledged on behalf of the French government, who gave notice of their intention to contest the proceedings, so taking the first step under RSC Ord 12, r 8 of the new procedure to set aside a writ and its service on the ground that the English court has no jurisdiction in the suit.

When the summons then came on for full hearing by Bristow J on 26 November 1982, counsel who had earlier represented M and Mme Sauvel before Comyn J told the judge that he no longer had instructions from them and that they were not present in person. Further, no one was instructed to appear on behalf of the French government. By virtue of s 1(2) of the State Immunity Act 1978, to which I shall refer in detail hereafter, it thus became necessary for the court to examine the jurisdiction point of its own motion, although it was able to enlist the aid of counsel who had previously been acting for M and Mme Sauvel as amicus curiae. In the event, as I have said, the judge held all three defendants to be immune from the civil jurisdiction of our courts by virtue of the 1964 and 1978 Acts respectively. It is from this decision that the plaintiffs now appeal.

The plaintiffs' claim in this action is based on a lease dated 8 August 1979 and made between them as landlord and the French government as tenant. For reasons which will appear, the plaintiffs no longer seek any relief in the action from M and Mme Sauvel. Nevertheless they contend that they are entitled to continue to prosecute it against the French government, from whom they claim damages for alleged breaches by the latter of covenants in the lease to which I have referred.

By that lease the plaintiffs let and the French government took the house and garden known as 19 Pelham Crescent, London SW7, together with the fixtures, furniture and household and other effects in or on those premises, more particularly specified in an inventory which was signed by the parties, for a term of four years from 8 August 1979 at a rent of £23,400 for the first year and increasing thereafter to a rent of £31,145 for the fourth year of the term.

The lease was in an entirely usual form. It contained covenants by the French government duly to pay the rent, to keep the interior of the premises and their contents in good repair and condition, to replace articles damaged with articles of a similar kind, and to deliver up to the plaintiffs the premises and their contents in such good condition and complete repair on the expiration or sooner determination of the lease. In addition, it contained usual covenants on the part of the tenant to permit the plaintiffs and their agent to enter the premises for the purpose of examining their state and condition and that of the contents and also for the purpose of carrying out any repairs that were found to be necessary. Finally, there was a covenant not to use the premises for any other purpose than that of a private dwelling house in the occupation of the first defendant and his family.

At all material times M Sauvel, the first defendant, has been the financial counsellor at the French Embassy in London. The demised premises were taken for occupation by him and his family so long as he remained in London. If he ceased to be employed within the Greater London area at any time after the end of the first year of the term, the lease contained a provision whereby on not less than five months' previous notice in writing the French government could determine the term.

Very early in 1982 an outbreak of dry rot was discovered on the premises. It is unnecessary to go into any detail except to say that a number of attempts, some successful, others not, were made to obtain entry for the plaintiffs' contractors to the premises in order to inspect them, to provide estimates for the work of repair, and then to do the necessary work once their estimate had been accepted. In the event, the plaintiffs were unable to obtain entry for themselves or their contractors for these purposes for a considerable period and they accordingly started these proceedings.

At the start of the hearing of this appeal counsel for the plaintiffs showed us a letter from the French Embassy dated 25 January 1983. From this it appears that M and Mme Sauvel gave up their occupation of the premises on 26 November 1982. The French government has also delivered up the keys to the plaintiffs' managing agents, but its representatives have been told that these keys are being held by those agents as trustees, that no surrender of the lease has been accepted and that the plaintiffs' rights thereunder remain unaffected. In addition, there are some arrears of rent which have not yet been paid. The amount of the arrears has been tendered, but only on the basis that it must be accepted in full and final settlement of the plaintiffs' claims and therefore it has been refused.

In all these circumstances the present relief sought by the plaintiffs against the French
a government alone is damages for the loss which they have sustained as a result of the French government's refusal to permit the plaintiffs' contractors entry to the premises. The plaintiffs have already received claims from their contractors for abortive visits to the site. Further, the plaintiffs contend that, as the result of the refusal by the French government to allow the plaintiffs' contractors to do the necessary work, the dry rot has spread and that the cost of remedying it has consequently increased by some £2,500. In
b addition, the plaintiffs are contending that on delivery up of the premises by the Sauvels there are certain items, particularly of furniture and paintings, missing from the premises. There is also the question of dilapidations as a result of the French government's failure to comply with the repairing covenants in the lease. These last claims may have to be made in further proceedings started after M and Mme Sauvel moved out of the premises. Nevertheless, counsel for the plaintiffs submits that the court's decision on the
c points which already arise in the existing litigation will cover similar points which may arise in that further litigation.

As was the situation when this matter was before the judge below, no one appeared before us on the hearing of this appeal on behalf of the French government to argue the various points which arise. I think that this was unfortunate. The result has been that we too have had to examine the question of jurisdiction of our own motion without the
d benefit of the help which counsel instructed on behalf of the French government could no doubt have given us.

As the plaintiffs are no longer pursuing their claim against M and Mme Sauvel, we have been principally concerned with the State Immunity Act 1978. Section 1 of that Act is in these terms:

> '(1) A State is immune from the jurisdiction of the courts of the United Kingdom
> e except as provided in the following provisions of this Part of this Act.
>
> (2) A court shall give effect to the immunity conferred by this section even though the State does not appear in the proceedings in question.'

The other relevant provisions of the 1978 Act are ss 3, 6(1) and 16(1)(*b*). These are in the following terms:

f

> '**3.**—(1) A State is not immune as respects proceedings relating to—(*a*) a commercial transaction, entered into by the State; or (*b*) an obligation of the State which by virtue of a contract (whether a commercial transaction or not) falls to be performed wholly or partly in the United Kingdom.
>
> (2) This section does not apply if the parties to the dispute are States or have
> g otherwise agreed in writing; and subsection (1)(*b*) above does not apply if the contract (not being a commercial transaction) was made in the territory of the State concerned and the obligation in question is governed by its administrative law.
>
> (3) In this section "commercial transaction" means—(*a*) any contract for the supply of goods or services; (*b*) any loan or other transaction for the provision of finance and any guarantee or indemnity in respect of any such transaction or of any
> h other financial obligation; and (*c*) any other transaction or activity (whether of a commercial, industrial, financial, professional or other similar character) into which a State enters or in which it engages otherwise than in the exercise of sovereign authority; but neither paragraph of subsection (1) above applies to a contract of employment between a State and an individual...
>
> **6.**—(1) A State is not immune as respects proceedings relating to—(*a*) any interest
> j of the State in, or its possession or use of, immovable property in the United Kingdom; or (*b*) any obligation of the State arising out of its interest in, or its possession or use of, any such property...
>
> **16.**—(1) This Part of this Act does not affect any immunity or privilege conferred by the Diplomatic Privileges Act 1964 or the Consular Relations Act 1968; and—(*a*) section 4 above does not apply to proceedings concerning the employment of the

> members of a mission within the meaning of the Convention scheduled to the said Act of 1964 or of the members of a consular post within the meaning of the Convention scheduled to the said Act of 1968; (*b*) section 6(1) above does not apply to proceedings concerning a State's title to or its possession of property used for the purposes of a diplomatic mission ...'

Although counsel for the plaintiffs recognised that he might prima facie be able to develop an argument for the plaintiffs against the existence of any immunity for the French government in respect of the claims in these proceedings based on s 3(1)(*b*) of the 1978 Act, he did not press this. He recognised that as the 1978 Act contains both ss 3 and 6 it may well be that on its proper construction s 3(1)(*b*) only applies to contracts properly and solely so called, whereas a lease, although in one sense a contract, nevertheless was concerned more particularly with the respective rights of the parties to it to immovable property, that is to say land, in the United Kingdom and consequently fell more appropriately to be dealt with under s 6 of the 1978 Act. In the light of counsel's approach, I express no concluded opinion on this point.

Counsel for the plaintiffs based his argument in this appeal principally on s 6(1)(*b*) of the 1978 Act. He submitted that the covenants in the material lease constituted obligations of the French government arising out of its interest in or possession of the demised premises, and that consequently the French government was not immune as respects the present proceedings. He accepted that by reason of s 13(2)(*a*) he could not have obtained any relief by way of an injunction or an order for possession against the French government but contended that there was no such bar to his claim for damages for breach of covenant. I agree with the judge below that the plaintiffs are prima facie entitled to rely on s 6(1)(*b*) and that consequently the French government is not entitled to immunity in these proceedings, unless the latter comes within s 16(1)(*b*) of the 1978 Act.

The judge took the view, however, both that the demised premises were 'used for the purposes of a diplomatic mission' and also that the instant proceedings concerned a state's title to or its possession of property used for that purpose and that consequently s 16(1)(*b*) operated to maintain the French government's immunity in the action.

The first submission of counsel for the plaintiffs was that the judge erred in holding that the premises were used for the purposes of a diplomatic mission and that therefore, whatever may be the proper construction of the first part of s 16(1)(*b*), the French government is entitled to no immunity herein. The point is one of mixed fact and law, and in my opinion more particularly one of fact. The evidence in support of the contention that they were used for the purposes of a diplomatic mission is meagre. It comprises, first, the known and agreed facts that M Sauvel was at all material times the financial counsellor at the French Embassy, and that the lease of 8 August 1979 contained the covenant that the demised premises should be used as a private residence for him and his family. Second, there was before the judge an affidavit sworn by a M Roux, first counsellor at the French Embassy, which contained a short passage to the effect that the demised premises were occupied by M and Mme Sauvel also 'for use in carrying out M Sauvel's social obligations as a Senior Diplomatic Agent of the French Government', and that it was for this reason the French consul on behalf of his government took the premises.

With respect to the judge, I do not think that this is sufficient to satisfy a court that the demised premises were 'used for the purposes of a diplomatic mission' within s 16(1)(*b*). First, I think that on its proper construction this phrase contemplates that the premises should be used for the professional diplomatic purposes of such a mission. It is not enough, in my opinion, that the premises are used as a private residence by a diplomatic agent, even though incidentally that diplomatic agent has certain understandable social obligations which he and his wife carry out on the premises. Second, I have no doubt that the relevant provisions of the 1978 Act were in the mind of the draftsman of and deponent to M Roux's affidavit, and, if the demised premises had in truth been used for the purposes of the French mission in this country within s 16(1)(*b*), then I would have expected the affidavit to have condescended to much more precise particulars than it did.

Third, I think that one can obtain substantial assistance about the construction of the whole of s 16(1)(*b*) of the 1978 Act from a consideration of arts 1 and 31 of the Vienna Convention on Diplomatic Relations (Vienna, 18 April 1961; TS 19 (1965); Cmnd 2565), which amongst other articles have the force of law in the United Kingdom by virtue of s 2(1) of and Sch 1 to the Diplomatic Privileges Act 1964. The 1978 Act arose out of the European Convention on State Immunity (Basle, 16 May 1972; Misc 31 (1972); Cmnd 5081) and I have no doubt that the respective draftsmen of both the Act and the convention had the terms of the 1964 Act and the 1961 convention well in mind. The 1964 Act and 1961 convention dealt with the immunities of diplomats; the 1978 Act and 1972 convention dealt with the immunities of the sovereign states which those diplomats represented. At least in so far as civil proceedings in respect of land in the United Kingdom is concerned, I would expect the immunities of the foreign state on the one hand and its diplomats on the other to be at least consistent, if not identical.

The relevant parts of arts 1 and 31 in Sch 1 to the 1964 Act are as follows:

> 'ARTICLE 1. For the purpose of the present Convention, the following expressions shall have the meanings hereunder assigned to them ... (*i*) the "premises of the mission" are the buildings or parts of buildings and the land ancillary thereto, irrespective of ownership, used for the purposes of the mission including the residence of the head of the mission ...
>
> ARTICLE 31. 1. A diplomatic agent shall enjoy immunity from the criminal jurisdiction of the receiving State. He shall also enjoy immunity from its civil and administrative jurisdiction, except in the case of: (*a*) a real action relating to private immovable property situated in the territory of the receiving State, unless he holds it on behalf of the sending State for the purposes of the mission ...'

In her book *Diplomatic Law: Commentary on the Vienna Convention on Diplomatic Relations* (1976) published by the British Institute of International and Comparative Law, Eileen Denza expressed the view that the specific mention of the residence of the head of the mission in this definition made it clear that residences of other members of the mission cannot form part of the premises of the mission. For my part, I respectfully agree. I think that it follows that, if the premises with which we are concerned in this appeal, namely 19 Pelham Crescent, were not part of the premises of the mission for the purposes of the 1964 Act, then had M Sauvel been the tenant and not the French government it could not have been said that he held those premises 'for the purpose of the mission' within art 31(1)(*a*) in Sch 1 to the 1964 Act. If this would be a correct approach if the provisions of the 1964 Act were in issue, then, when we are in fact concerned with the 1978 Act, because the actual tenant of the premises was the French government, I think that almost the same words in s 16(1)(*b*) of the 1978 Act should be similarly construed and not be held to reintroduce the immunity to civil proceedings in respect of 19 Pelham Crescent which the earlier s 6(1)(*b*) had excluded.

Further, the opinions of commentators referred to by the judge on the meaning of the phrase translated as 'real action' from the French master text of the 1961 convention suggest that in so far as real property in England is concerned such an action is one in which the ownership or possession, as distinct from mere use, of such property is in issue. If this is correct, and I believe it to be so, then the similarity between the provisions of art 31(1)(*a*) in Sch 1 to the 1964 Act and those of s 16(1)(*b*) of the 1978 Act is at once apparent.

In addition, as counsel for the plaintiffs further contended, when one looks for assistance on the construction of the phrase 'proceedings concerning a State's title to or its possession of property' in s 16(1)(*b*) of the 1978 Act from within the Act itself, one sees that s 6(1) deals with a state's interest in, or its possession or use of, immovable property in the United Kingdom. There is no corresponding reference to the 'use' of such property in s 16(1)(*b*). Consequently I agree with the submission of counsel for the plaintiffs that the proceedings to which by s 16(1)(*b*) of the 1978 Act s 6(1) of the same Act is not to apply are limited to those in which a state's title to or right to possession of, in the strict *a* sense, is in question. In this respect also, therefore, consistency between the respective 1964 and 1978 provisions is retained.

In my opinion, therefore, the present proceedings against the French government for damages for alleged breaches of covenant are within 6(1)(*b*) of the 1978 Act and are not within s 16(1)(*b*), first, because the relevant premises were not 'used for the purposes of a diplomatic mission', and, in any event, because the proceedings do not concern the *b* French government's title to or its possession of them.

Finally, I should refer to one other point on which this court invited the submissions of counsel for the plaintiffs as we did not have the benefit of counsel arguing the case for the French government against him. By virtue of art 30 in Sch 1 to the 1964 Act, the private residence of a diplomatic agent enjoys the same inviolability and protection as the premises of the mission itself. Thus it would seem clear that M and Mme Sauvel *c* could not in any event have been compelled to permit the plaintiffs or their agents entry into 19 Pelham Crescent notwithstanding the material covenants in the lease. In such circumstances, could an action for damages for breaches of those covenants be maintained?

The submissions of counsel for the plaintiffs in answer to this point were, first, that the immunity of foreign states and diplomatic agents to proceedings in the courts of this country is a matter of procedure and not of substance. The immunity does not erase the *d* cause of action; it merely prevents proceedings being maintained on it. 'It is elementary law that diplomatic immunity is not immunity from legal liability but immunity from suit': per Diplock LJ in *Empson v Smith* [1965] 2 All ER 881 at 886, [1966] 1 QB 426 at 438.

Second, the two Acts do specifically preclude a plaintiff from obtaining an injunction or an order for specific performance in respect of what I can generically call 'diplomatic *e* premises': see art 31(3) in Sch 1 to the 1964 Act and s 13(2) of the 1978 Act. Procedurally, therefore, these provisions give full effect to the physical inviolability of diplomatic premises. Consequently this inviolability should not be allowed to operate as a bar to proceedings otherwise permitted by the statutes where the relief sought is merely damages for breach of covenant. For my part, I think that these submissions effectively deal with this final point which this court raised. *f*

In the result, and in so far as the proceedings against the French government are concerned, I respectfully disagree with the view expressed by the judge below. I would allow this appeal and hold that the English courts do have jurisdiction to hear and determine those proceedings. In the events which have occurred and to give effect to the plaintiffs' expressed intention to proceed only against the French government, I think that the plaintiffs' action against M and Mme Sauvel should continue to stand dismissed. *g*

WATKINS LJ. I agree.

Appeal allowed.

Solicitors: *Philip Conway Thomas & Co* (for the plaintiffs).

Sophie Craven Barrister.

a

R v Bailey

COURT OF APPEAL, CRIMINAL DIVISION
GRIFFITHS LJ, PETER PAIN AND STUART-SMITH JJ
17 FEBRUARY, 11 MARCH 1983

b *Criminal law – Automatism – Self-induced automatism – Availability of defence of automatism – Accused suffering from diabetes – Accused in state of automatism due to hypoglycaemia following failure to eat food after drinking mixture of sugar and water – Accused striking victim with iron bar – Accused charged with wounding with intent, alternatively with unlawful wounding – Whether defence of automatism available to accused – Offences against the Person Act 1861, ss 18, 20.*

c The appellant, who suffered from diabetes for which he received insulin treatment, had lived with his girlfriend for two years, when she left him and formed an association with another man, the victim. Not long afterwards, the appellant went to see the victim. After they had discussed the situation briefly, the appellant told the victim that he felt unwell and took a mixture of sugar and water but ate nothing. Ten minutes later he struck the victim on the head with an iron bar, severely injuring him. Later that day he told the
d police that he had had to hit the victim to teach him a lesson for associating with his girlfriend. He was subsequently charged with wounding the victim with intent to cause him grievous bodily harm, contrary to s 18[a] of the Offences against the Person Act 1861, or, alternatively, with unlawfully wounding the victim, contrary to s 20[b] of that Act. His defence was that he had acted in a state of automatism caused by hypoglycaemia following his failure to take food after drinking the mixture of sugar and water and that,
e accordingly, he had neither the specific intent to cause grievous bodily harm for the purpose of s 18 nor the appropriate mens rea or basic intent for the purpose of s 20. The judge directed the jury that the defence of automatism was not available to the appellant because his incapacity was self-induced. The appellant was convicted of causing grievous bodily harm with intent, contrary to s 18. He appealed.

f **Held** – (1) The judge had misdirected the jury as to the defence of automatism so far as s 18 of the 1861 Act was concerned because the specific intent to cause grievous bodily harm could be negatived even if an accused's incapacity of mind was self-induced (see p 506 *g h*, post); *DPP v Majewski* [1976] 2 All ER 142 applied; *R v Quick* [1973] 3 All ER 347 distinguished.

(2) The judge had also misdirected the jury as to the defence of automatism so far as
g s 20 of the 1861 Act was concerned, because self-induced automatism, other than that due to intoxication from alcohol or drugs, could provide a defence to a crime of basic intent. The question was whether the accused's conduct, in the light of his knowledge of the likely results of his actions or inaction, had been sufficiently reckless to establish the mens rea necessary for the offence. There was no conclusive presumption (as there was in the case of a man who voluntarily took alcohol or drugs) that it was reckless conduct
h for a person to fail, for example, to take food after a dose of insulin. In cases of assault, the prosecution had to establish that the accused knew or appreciated that his actions or inaction might make him aggressive, unpredictable or uncontrolled (see p 506 *j* to p 507 *j*, post); *R v Lipman* [1969] 3 All ER 410, dictum of Lawton LJ in *R v Quick* [1973] 3 All ER at 356 and *DPP v Majewski* [1976] 2 All ER 142 considered.

j

---

a Section 18, so far as material, provides: 'Whosoever shall unlawfully and maliciously by any means whatsoever wound or cause any grievous bodily harm to any person with intent to do some grievous bodily harm to any person . . . shall be guilty of [an offence] . . .'

b Section 20, so far as material, provides: 'Whosoever shall unlawfully and maliciously wound or inflict any grievous bodily harm upon any other person . . . shall be guilty of [an offence] . . .'

(3) However, in all the circumstances and notwithstanding the judge's misdirections, there had been no miscarriage of justice. The appeal would accordingly be dismissed (see a
p 508 *a* to *c*, post).

Notes

For automatism as a defence, see 11 Halsbury's Laws (4th edn) paras 6–7, and for cases on the subject, see 14(1) Digest (Reissue) 15–16, *31–34*.

For the offence of wounding with intent, see 11 Halsbury's Laws (4th edn) paras 1198– b
1199, and for cases on the subject, see 15 Digest (Reissue) 1183–1184, *10096–10127*.

For the offence of unlawful wounding, see 11 Halsbury's Laws (4th edn) para 1200, and for cases on the subject, see 15 Digest (Reissue) 1195–1197, *10263–10276*.

For the Offences against the Person Act 1861, ss 18, 20, see 8 Halsbury's Statutes (3rd edn) 152, 154.

c

Cases referred to in judgment

DPP v Majewski [1976] 2 All ER 142, [1977] AC 443, [1976] 2 WLR 623, HL.
R v Cottle [1958] NZLR 999, NZ CA.
R v Lipman [1969] 3 All ER 410, [1970] 1 QB 152, [1969] 3 WLR 819, CA.
R v Quick, R v Paddison [1973] 3 All ER 347, [1973] QB 910, [1973] 3 WLR 26, CA.

d

Case also cited

A-G for Northern Ireland v Gallagher [1961] 3 All ER 299, [1963] AC 349, HL.

Appeal

On 14 October 1982 in the Crown Court at Bolton before Mr Recorder Wootton and a
jury the appellant, John Graham Bailey, was convicted of wounding Michael William e
Harrison with intent to cause him grievous bodily harm, contrary to s 18 of the Offences against the Person Act 1861. He was sentenced to 18 months' imprisonment, 12 months of which were suspended for two years. He appealed against conviction. The facts are set out in the judgment of the court.

Hugh Laing (assigned by the Registrar of Criminal Appeals) for the appellant. f
Howard Baisden for the Crown.

Cur adv vult

11 March. The following judgment of the court was delivered.

g

GRIFFITHS LJ. The judgment that I am about to read is the judgment of the court and it was written by Stuart-Smith J.

At the Crown Court at Bolton on 14 October 1982 the appellant was convicted of wounding with intent to cause grievous bodily harm, contrary to s 18 of the Offences against the Person Act 1861. The jury were not required to give a verdict on an alternative
count of unlawful wounding contrary to s 20 of that Act. He now appeals against this h
conviction.

The appellant is a diabetic and has been so for some thirty years. He requires to take insulin to control his condition. His defence at the trial was that he was acting in a state of automatism, caused by hypoglycaemia.

In early January 1982 the woman with whom the appellant had been living for the
previous two years left him and formed an association with the victim, Mr Harrison. At j
about 7 pm on 20 January 1982 the appellant, seeming upset, visited Mr Harrison at his home. They had a cup of tea and discussed the matter. After ten or fifteen minutes the appellant said that he felt unwell and asked Mr Harrison to make him some sugar and water, which the appellant drank. About ten minutes later the appellant started to leave. He then said that he had lost his glove and that it might be down the side of the chair on

which he had been sitting. Mr Harrison bent down to look and the appellant struck him *a* on the back of the head with an iron bar, which was a case opener about 18 inches long. The appellant remained there holding the iron bar. Mr Harrison ran from the house. His wound required ten stitches.

The Crown's case was that although it was theoretically possible, from a medical point of view, for there to have been a temporary loss of awareness due to hypoglycaemia, as the appellant claimed, this was not what had happened. On the contrary, it was contended *b* that the appellant, upset and jealous about Mr Harrison's relationship with his girlfriend, had armed himself with the iron bar and gone to Harrison's house with the intention of injuring him. They relied on the evidence of the police to show that this was the case.

At 10.10 pm the appellant was seen by police in a public house. They told him they were making inquiries about the attack on Mr Harrison. He replied: 'Yes, it was me. I hit him with a bar.' He was then cautioned and he said that he was expecting them. *c* While in the police vehicle, the appellant asked after Mr Harrison and said: 'I'm sorry now, but I couldn't stop myself. I had to hit him.' He then added: 'I had to teach him a lesson.' When he was asked what he meant, he said: 'He's been going out with my girlfriend. I went round to sort it out.' He was then asked what the bar was doing in his pocket and he replied: 'It was just there and when I went round to see him I felt it in my pocket. I thought I'd use it to teach him a lesson.' He then described how he had thrown *d* it away out of his van.

When he was at the police station he was again cautioned and was asked if he knew why he was there. He said: 'Yes, it was for hitting Michael with that bar.' He was asked to tell about it and he replied: 'What is there to tell? My life's been turned upside down. I wanted to marry Beatrice and still do. Michael Harrison's just in the way.' Later, in the course of a written statement, he said:

e

> 'About ten to seven I went to see Mike Harrison. I went on the spur of the moment. I knocked on the door and he asked me in. We had a conversation and he admitted that something had been going on between him and Beatrice, more than a platonic relationship. I felt sick inside at this. The conversation meant little to me after that. I told him I was going. I told him I had lost a glove and he looked for it *f* inside an armchair where I had been sitting. As he was getting up from looking on the chair he was half leaning forward. I took out a metal case opener that I had in my pocket which I had taken with me. I held it in my right hand and hit him on the back of the head. I don't know why I did it, but I knew I had to hit him. I then held the bar in my hand against my side and said: "Come and hit me."'

When he gave evidence, the appellant, who was a man of good character, maintained *g* he had no intention of harming Mr Harrison and he had acted in a state of automatism. He said that he had to take two doses of insulin a day and was under his general practitioner and a special clinic. He had arrived home at 5.30 pm and had his insulin and a cup of tea. At 7 pm he decided to go and see Harrison and his account of what took place accorded with that of Harrison up to the point where he asked Harrison to look for his glove. The next thing he could remember was standing with the bar in his hand. He *h* saw that Harrison was injured and he said: 'What the hell am I doing?' He then described how he went home and later to the public house where he was arrested.

The appellant's general practitioner gave evidence. He confirmed that the appellant was a diabetic and received insulin treatment, after which he had to take food within a short period. If he failed to do so, it could produce symptoms of weakness, palpitations, tremor and sweating. He might develop more aggressive tendencies than normal and *j* this could be accompanied by loss of memory. After describing what the appellant had said he had had to eat, he said that the appellant had not had sufficient to counteract and balance the dose of insulin. So far as he was aware, the appellant in 30 years had never developed a condition of coma due to hypoglycaemia. He said that the effect of taking sugar and water in Harrison's house would be to help bring back the sugar level within five or ten minutes. When he was cross-examined he said he thought it unlikely that there could have been the sudden switch-off effect alleged by the appellant and he regarded the likelihood of such a thing happening as being remote if sugar and water a had been taken five minutes before it happened.

It was therefore the appellant's case that the attack had taken place during a period of loss of consciousness occurring due to hypoglycaemia caused by his failure to take sufficient food following his last dose of insulin. Accordingly, it was submitted that he had neither the specific intent to cause grievous bodily harm for the purpose of s 18, nor the appropriate mens rea or basic intent for the purpose of the s 20 offence. b

But the recorder, in effect, told the jury that this defence was not available to the appellant. He said:

> 'One thing is equally clear, members of the jury, that if that state of malfunctioning was induced by any agency or self-induced incapacity, then the defence of automatism does not apply.'

c

It is clear from the rest of the summing up that 'self-induced' in this context meant or included the appellant's failure to take sufficient food after his dose of insulin. The recorder appears to have derived this proposition, which he applied to both counts of the indictment, from *R v Quick* [1973] 3 All ER 347, [1973] QB 910. In that case the appellant, a nurse in a mental hospital, had attacked a patient. Quick was a diabetic and his defence was that he was in a state of automatism at the time due to hypoglycaemia. d The trial judge had ruled that, if established, this amounted to a disease of the mind and could only be relied on in support of a defence of insanity. Following this ruling, Quick pleaded guilty to assault occasioning actual bodily harm.

The Court of Appeal held that this ruling was wrong and that the malfunctioning caused by the hypoglycaemia was not a disease of the mind and that the appellant was entitled to have his defence considered by the jury. Lawton LJ said ([1973] 3 All ER 347 e at 356, [1973] QB 910 at 922):

> 'Such malfunctioning, unlike that caused by a defect of reason from disease of the mind, will not always relieve an accused from criminal responsibility. A self-induced incapacity will not excuse (see *R v Lipman* [1969] 3 All ER 410, [1970] 1 QB 152) nor will one which could have been reasonably foreseen as a result of either f doing, or omitting to do something, as, for example, taking alcohol against medical advice after using certain prescribed drugs, or failing to have regular meals whilst taking insulin. From time to time difficult borderline cases are likely to arise. When they do, the test suggested by the New Zealand Court of Appeal in *R v Cottle* [1958] NZLR 999 is likely to give the correct result, viz can this mental condition be fairly regarded as amounting to or producing a defect of reason from disease of mind?'

g

But in that case, the offence, assault occasioning actual bodily harm, was an offence of basic intent. No specific intent was required. It is now quite clear that, even if the incapacity of mind is self-induced by the voluntary taking of drugs or alcohol, the specific intent to kill or cause grievous bodily harm may be negatived: see *DPP v Majewski* [1976] 2 All ER 142, [1977] AC 443. This being so, as it is conceded on behalf of the Crown, the direction to which we have referred cannot be correct so far as the offence under s 18 is h concerned.

But it is also submitted that the direction is wrong or at least in too broad and general terms, so far as the s 20 offence is concerned. If the passage quoted above from *R v Quick* correctly represents the law, then the direction given by the recorder was correct so far as the second count was concerned, even though the appellant may have had no appreciation of the consequences of his failure to take food and even though such failure may not j have been due to deliberate abstention, but because of his generally distressed condition. In our judgment, the passage from Lawton LJ's judgment was obiter and we are free to re-examine it.

Automatism resulting from intoxication as a result of a voluntary ingestion of alcohol or dangerous drugs does not negative the mens rea necessary for crimes of basic intent, because the conduct of the accused is reckless and recklessness is enough to constitute the necessary mens rea in assault cases where no specific intent forms part of the charge: see *DPP v Majewski* [1976] 2 All ER 142 at 150, 169, [1977] AC 443 at 475, 496 per Lord Elwyn-Jones LC and Lord Edmund-Davies, where the latter quoted from Stroud *Mens Rea* (1914) p 115:

> 'The law therefore establishes a conclusive presumption against the admission of proof of intoxication for the purpose of disproving *mens rea* in ordinary crimes. Where this presumption applies, it does not make "drunkenness itself" a crime, but the drunkenness is itself an integral part of the crime, as forming, together with the other unlawful conduct charged against the defendant, a complex act of criminal recklessness.'

The same considerations apply where the state of automatism is induced by the voluntary taking of dangerous drugs: see *R v Lipman* [1969] 3 All ER 410, [1970] 1 QB 152, where a conviction for manslaughter was upheld, the appellant having taken LSD and killed his mistress in the course of an hallucinatory trip. It was submitted on behalf of the Crown that a similar rule should be applied as a matter of public policy to all cases of self-induced automatism. But it seems to us that there may be material distinctions between a man who consumes alcohol or takes dangerous drugs and one who fails to take sufficient food after insulin to avert hypoglycaemia.

It is common knowledge that those who take alcohol to excess or certain sorts of drugs may become aggressive or do dangerous or unpredictable things; they may be able to foresee the risks of causing harm to others, but nevertheless persist in their conduct. But the same cannot be said, without more, of a man who fails to take food after an insulin injection. If he does appreciate the risk that such a failure may lead to aggressive, unpredictable and uncontrollable conduct and he nevertheless deliberately runs the risk or otherwise disregards it, this will amount to recklessness. But we certainly do not think that it is common knowledge, even among diabetics, that such is a consequence of a failure to take food; and there is no evidence that it was known to this appellant. Doubtless he knew that if he failed to take his insulin or proper food after it he might lose consciousness, but as such he would only be a danger to himself unless he put himself in charge of some machine such as a motor car, which required his continued conscious control.

In our judgment, self-induced automatism, other than that due to intoxication from alcohol or drugs, may provide a defence to crimes of basic intent. The question in each case will be whether the prosecution has proved the necessary element of recklessness. In cases of assault, if the accused knows that his actions or inaction are likely to make him aggressive, unpredictable or uncontrolled with the result that he may cause some injury to others and he persists in the action or takes no remedial action when he knows it is required, it will be open to the jury to find that he was reckless.

Turning again to *R v Quick* and the passage we have quoted, we think that, notwithstanding the unqualified terms in which the proposition is stated, it is possible that the court may not have intended to lay down such an absolute rule. In the following paragraph Lawton LJ considers a number of questions, which are not necessarily exhaustive, which the jury might have wanted to consider if the issue had been left to them. One such question was whether the accused knew that he was getting into a hypoglaecemic episode and, if so, why he did not use the antidote of taking sugar which he had been advised to do. These questions suggest that even if the hypoglycaemia was induced by some action or inaction by the accused his defence will not necessarily fail.

In the present case the recorder never invited the jury to consider what the appellant's knowledge or appreciation was of what would happen if he failed to take food after his insulin or whether he realised that he might become aggressive. Nor were they asked to consider why the appellant had omitted to take food in time. They were given no direction on the elements of recklessness. Accordingly, in our judgment, there was also a misdirection in relation to the second count in the indictment of unlawful wounding.

But we have to consider whether, notwithstanding these misdirections, there has been any miscarriage of justice and whether the jury properly directed could have failed to *a* come to the same conclusion. As Lawton LJ said in *R v Quick* [1973] 3 All ER 347 at 355, [1973] QB 910 at 922, referring to the defence of automatism, it is a 'quagmire of law seldom entered nowadays save by those in desperate need of some kind of defence'. This case is no exception. We think it very doubtful whether the appellant laid a sufficient basis for the defence to be considered by the jury at all. But, even if he did, we are in no doubt that the jury properly directed must have rejected it. Although an episode of *b* sudden transient loss of consciousness or awareness was theoretically possible, it was quite inconsistent with the graphic description that the appellant gave to the police both orally and in his written statement. There was abundant evidence that he had armed himself with the iron bar and gone to Harrison's house for the purpose of attacking him, because he wanted to teach him a lesson and because he was in the way.

Moreover, the doctor's evidence to which we have referred showed it was extremely *c* unlikely that such an episode could follow some five minutes after taking sugar and water. For these reasons we are satisfied that no miscarriage of justice occurred and the appeal will be dismissed.

Appeal dismissed.

d

Solicitors: *David S Gandy*, Manchester (for the Crown).

Raina Levy Barrister.

European Asian Bank AG v Punjab and Sind Bank *e*

COURT OF APPEAL, CIVIL DIVISION
SLADE AND ROBERT GOFF LJJ
7, 8, 9, 10 FEBRUARY, 8 MARCH 1983 *f*

Bank – Documentary credit – Irrevocable credit – Duty of bank – Letter of credit required to be negotiated through defendant bank's agent – Letter of credit in fact negotiated through plaintiff bank – Whether letter of credit permitting plaintiffs to act as negotiating bankers – Whether plaintiffs reasonably entitled to interpret letter of credit as authorising them to act as negotiating bankers – Whether defendants estopped from denying that plaintiffs authorised to negotiate letter of credit. *g*

Practice – Summary judgment – Leave to defend – Appeal – Whether appeal a rehearing – Whether Court of Appeal restricted to reviewing judge's exercise of discretion – RSC Ord 14, r 3(1).

On 14 July 1979 the purchasers, who were based in India, contracted to buy a shipment *h* of cloves from the sellers, who were based in Singapore, for a total price of $US2,250,000 c and f Bombay. Payment was to be made by irrevocable letter of credit payable after 180 days of the date of the bill of lading. On 20 July the defendants, who were the purchasers' bankers, opened a letter of credit and through their agents in Singapore advised the plaintiffs, who were the sellers' bankers, that they had done so. Paragraph 6 of the letter of credit stated that it was to be advised through the plaintiffs and that it 'should be *j* divisionable [and] unrestricted for negotiation'. However, para 9 stated that 'negotiations under this credit are restricted' to the defendants' agents in Singapore. The plaintiffs assumed that the letter of credit authorised them to negotiate with the sellers for early payment at a discounted rate and passed it on to the sellers, who on 7 August presented the plaintiffs with a set of completed documents relating to the transaction and a draft for $US2,250,000 drawn on the purchasers and made payable to the plaintiffs. The plaintiffs indorsed the draft and forwarded it and the documents on to the defendants a with a letter stating that the plaintiffs had negotiated the letter of credit, which they would present on maturity for reimbursement and asked the defendants to 'please advise acceptance'. The defendants forwarded the documents to the purchasers, who accepted them and on 16 August the defendants wrote back stating that the documents had been 'accepted by the party to fall due on [3 February 1980]'. On 20 August the plaintiffs credited the sellers' account with the discounted amount of the letter of credit after b negotiating it with them on that day. In September it transpired that the sellers had acted fraudulently and had had no intention of delivering the goods, with the result that the purchasers instructed the defendants not to make payment under the letter of credit when it fell due on 3 February 1980. The plaintiffs then sued on it and applied for summary judgment pursuant to RSC Ord 14, r 3(1)[a]. On the hearing of the application the defendants contended that the documents had not been negotiated by their agents in c Singapore as required by para 9 of the letter of credit but by the plaintiffs and therefore the precondition for payment under the letter of credit, and for the defendants to be liable, had not occurred. The judge held that triable issues were raised by the plaintiffs' claim and accordingly granted the defendants unconditional leave to defend. The plaintiffs appealed against the judge's order, contending (i) that on its true construction the letter of credit authorised them to negotiate it, so that when they accepted it the d necessary privity existed to create a contract between the defendants as issuing bankers and the plaintiffs as negotiating bankers, (ii) that even if the plaintiffs were not authorised by the letter of credit to negotiate it the ambiguity arising from the conflict between paras 6 and 9 of the letter of credit reasonably entitled the plaintiffs so to interpret it, and (iii) that in any event the defendants were estopped by their conduct from denying that the plaintiffs were entitled to negotiate the letter of credit and therefore could no longer e say that the requirements as to negotiation of the credit had not been complied with. The defendants contended (i) that the court ought not to interfere with the judge's exercise of his discretion to grant leave to defend unless there were very special circumstances and (ii) that since the plaintiffs had acted as agents for the sellers the defendants were entitled to raise against the plaintiffs the triable issue of the sellers' fraud and that was a further reason which had entitled the judge to grant leave to defend.

f

Held – (1) Since RSC Ord 14, r 3(1) clearly set out the circumstances in which the court should give summary judgment for a plaintiff, any discretion conferred on the court by that rule was only of the most residual kind. Accordingly, an appeal from such an order was by way of a rehearing and was not limited to a mere review of the judge's exercise of his discretion. Furthermore, if the appeal raised a point of law the court would hear full g argument and decide it even though by doing so it would determine the outcome of the substantive proceedings (see p 515 *c* and *e* to p 516 *d*, post); dictum of Lord Diplock in *M V Yorke Motors v Edwards* [1982] 1 All ER at 1028 applied; *Wing v Thurlow* (1893) 10 TLR 151 distinguished.

(2) On the facts, it was clear that the plaintiffs were not the agents of the sellers and therefore the issue of the fraudulent sale could not be raised against them (see p 518 *c* to h p 519 *e*, post).

(3) On the true construction of the letter of credit it did not permit the plaintiffs to act as negotiating bankers, since para 6 only permitted unrestricted negotiation for the purposes of transfer by the beneficiary of the letter of credit in whole or in part for the benefit of his own pre-sellers of the goods whereas para 9 restricted negotiation, for the purpose of discounting the letter of credit with a bank in order to obtain immediate j payment, to the defendants' agents. Although the letter of credit was at first sight ambiguous, the plaintiffs could not recover their loss from the defendants, as the issuing bank, on the basis that the plaintiffs had reasonably interpreted the ambiguity as authorising them to negotiate, which they had then acted on to their detriment, since (a) that principle was only applicable to instructions given by a principal to an agent and

a Rule 3(1) is set out at p 515 *d*, post

that relationship had not existed between the parties; nor could it arise between an issuing bank and a negotiating bank, and (b) in any event the ambiguity, being apparent a
on the face of the document, put the plaintiffs on inquiry to ascertain what the defendants had intended the correct interpretation to be. Accordingly, the plaintiffs could not rely on any of those grounds to obtain summary judgment (see p 516 *f* to p 517 *c* and *h* to p 518 *c*, post); *Ireland v Livingston* [1861–73] All ER Rep 585 and *Midland Bank Ltd v Seymour* [1955] 2 Lloyd's Rep 147 distinguished.

(4) However, the defendants were estopped by their conduct and representations from b
denying that the plaintiffs were authorised by them to negotiate the letter of credit, since the defendants had unequivocally represented to the plaintiffs that the defendants recognised that the plaintiffs were entitled to act as negotiating bankers under the letter of credit and that the documents were in order. Accordingly, there was on the face of the documents a liability on the defendants to pay the plaintiffs the sum due under the letter of credit on the due date. Since there was no arguable defence on that issue, the appeal c
would therefore be allowed and judgment entered for the plaintiffs (see p 521 *e* to *h*, post).

Notes

For commercial letters of credit, see 3 Halsbury's Laws (4th edn) paras 131–137, and for cases on the subject, see 3 Digest (Reissue) 665–670, *4114–4137*. d

For what conduct will create an estoppel, see 16 Halsbury's Laws (4th edn) para 1609, and for cases on the subject, see 21 Digest (Reissue) 198–204, *1445–1467*.

Cases referred to in judgment

Bank für Gemeinwirtschaft v City of London Garages Ltd [1971] 1 All ER 541, [1971] 1 WLR 149, CA. e
Cow v Casey [1949] 1 All ER 197, [1949] 1 KB 474, CA.
Gordon v Cradock [1963] 2 All ER 121, [1964] 1 QB 503, [1963] 2 WLR 1252, CA.
Guaranty Trust Co of New York v Hannay & Co [1918] 2 KB 623, [1918–19] All ER Rep 151, CA.
Ireland v Livingston (1872) LR 5 HL 395, [1861–73] All ER Rep 585.
Midland Bank Ltd v Seymour [1955] 2 Lloyd's Rep 147. f
Verrall v Great Yarmouth BC [1980] 1 All ER 839, [1981] QB 202, [1980] 3 WLR 258, CA.
Wing v Thurlow (1893) 10 TLR 151, CA.
Yorke (M V) Motors (a firm) v Edwards [1982] 1 All ER 1024, [1982] 1 WLR 444, HL.

Cases also cited

Brickwoods Ltd v Butler and Walters (1970) P & C R 316, CA.
Commercial Banking Co of Sydney Ltd v Jalsard Pty Ltd [1973] AC 279. g
Jacobs v Booth's Distillery & Co (1901) 85 LT 262, HL.
Ng Chee Chong, Ng Weng Chong, Ng Cheng and Ng Yew (a firm trading as Maran Road Saw Mill) v Austin Taylor & Co [1975] 1 Lloyd's Rep 156.
Rose Hall Ltd v Reeves [1975] AC 411, PC.
Tiverton Estates Ltd v Wearwell Ltd [1974] 1 All ER 209, [1975] Ch 146, CA. h

Appeal

European Asian Bank AG appealed against the order of Staughton J made on 15 October 1982 on an application by the appellants for summary judgment under RSC Ord 14, whereby the judge gave the respondents, Punjab and Sind Bank, leave to defend the action. The facts are set out in the judgment of the court. j

Anthony Grabiner QC and *Rhodri Davies* for the appellants.
John Wilmers QC and *Hilary Heilbron* for the respondents.

Cur adv vult

8 March. The following judgment of the court was delivered.

ROBERT GOFF LJ. This is the judgment of the court on an appeal by the appellants, European Asian Bank AG, against an order by Staughton J under which, on an application by the appellants for summary judgment under RSC Ord 14, he gave the respondents, Punjab and Sind Bank, unconditional leave to defend. The appeal is brought by leave of Staughton J.

Until recently, it was not possible for a plaintiff to appeal against such a decision. As a matter of history, such an appeal was possible until 1894, when it was abolished by statute; that abolition was subsequently incorporated in the Supreme Court of Judicature (Consolidation) Act 1925. However, when the new Supreme Court Act was enacted in 1981, the provision abolishing the right to appeal in such a case was not re-enacted, with the effect that, under the ordinary rules of procedure relating to interlocutory matters, an appeal now lies to the Court of Appeal with leave either of the judge or of the Court of Appeal. We shall have more to say about appeals of this kind when we come to consider the substance of the present appeal.

The plaintiff appellants are a West German bank, who conduct a substantial part of their business in the Far East, including Singapore. The defendant respondents are an Indian bank, with a branch office in London. The appellants' claim in the action is made under a letter of credit. They claim to be negotiating bankers, and say that the respondents, as issuing bankers, are liable to them in the sum of $US2,250,000, being the sum due under the letter of credit. The is not the first time that the matter has been before the English courts. In 1981 the respondents applied to have the appellants' action stayed on the ground that India or Singapore, and not England, was the natural forum for the action. Their application for a stay was dismissed; and its dismissal was, in 1982, affirmed by the Court of Appeal. At the time when the respondents applied to have the action stayed, the appellants had already issued a summons for judgment under RSC Ord 14. That matter was however stood over until after the application for a stay had been dealt with.

The facts underlying the present proceedings were summarised by myself as the judge of first instance in the stay proceedings; and my summary was adopted by the Court of Appeal in the stay proceedings, and by Staughton J. For convenience, we too shall adopt that summary (in which the respondents are referred to as 'the Punjab Bank', and their customers, Jain Shudh Vanaspati Ltd, on whose behalf they opened the relevant letter of credit, are referred to as 'Jain'). We quote from the judgment ([1981] 2 Lloyd's Rep 651 at 653–654):

> 'On July 14, 1979, Jain, an Indian company based in New Delhi, contracted to buy 300 tons of Zanzibar quality cloves from a Singapore company called Bentrex & Co. The price payable for the goods was U.S.$2,250,000·00 c. & f. Bombay, and the contract originally provided for payment 120 days from the date of bill of lading, by irrevocable letter of credit. On July 20, 1979, Jain asked the Punjab Bank in New Delhi to cause a letter of credit to be opened; the initial request was for payment 120 days after bill of lading, but this was later changed (for reasons which have not been explained) to payment 180 days after bill of lading. On the following day, July 21, the Punjab Bank telexed their correspondents in Singapore, the Allgemene Bank Nederland (whom I shall refer to as "A.B.N."), and instructed them to advise Bentrex, through the European Asian Bank, of the opening of the letter of credit; and the Singapore branch of A.B.N. duly advised Bentrex through the European Asian Bank. Subsequently, on Aug. 4, A.B.N. confirmed the letter of credit. The text of the letter of credit before the Court was contained in a telex from the Punjab Bank to A.B.N. It reads as follows: FOR USD 22,50,000/- DT 21.7.79 AT THE REQUEST OF M/S. JAINSHUDH VANASPATI LIMITED, 101- AKASH DEEP BUILDING, 26A BARAKHAWBA ROAD, NEW DELHI-110001 WE ESTABLISH OUR IRREVOCABLE LETTER OF CREDIT NO. IBD/118/8371/79 FAVOURING M/S. BENTREX COMPANY, 6 LORONG MALAYU,

SINGAPORE-14 STP FOR USD 22,50,000/-(USD TWO MILLION TWO HUNDRED FIFTY THOUSAND ONLY) C N F BOMBAY AVAILABLE BY THEIR DRAFTS AT 180 DAYS FROM BILL OF LADING DRAWN ON ACCOUNTEE FOR 100 PERCENT INVOICE COST OF 300M TONNES OF CLOVE ZANZIBAR QUALITY FROM SINGAPORE TO BOMBAY STP DRAFTS ARE TO BE ACCOMPANIED BY THE FOLLOWING DOCUMENTS:—1) YR SIGNED INVOICE IN 6 QUOTING IMPORT LICENCE NO. ITEM NO. 30.3 OF APPENDIX 10 OF OGL OF IMPORT POLICY 79–80 DATED — 6 + CERTIFYING GOODS TO BE OF SINGAPORE ORIGIN STP (SHIPMENT MUST NOT BE MADE PRIOR TO THE DATE OF LICENCE) 2) FULL SET OF CLEAN "ON BOARD" OCEAN-SHIPPING COMPANY'S BILLS OF LADING TO ORDER BLANK ENDORSED OR TO ORDER OF THE PUNJAB NSIND BANK LTD. IBD, 6-SCINDIA HOUSE NEW DELHI AND THE ACCOUNTEE DATED NOT LATER THAN 31.8.79 3) CERTIFICATE TO THIS EFFECT THAT THE COPY OF SHIPPING DOCUMENTS ALONG WITH THE COPIES OF BILL OF LADING CERTIFICATE OF ORIGIN INSURANCE POLICY, INVOICE, QUALITY AND WEIGHT CERTIFICATE INSPECTION CERTIFICATE TO BE AIRMAILED TO BUYER IMMEDIATELY AFTER SHIPMENT 4) DESCRIPTION—300 METRIC TONNES CLOVES ZANZIBAR QUALITY 5) SURVEYORS N CERTIFICATE—WEIGHT AND QUALITY CERTIFICATE TO BE ISSUED BY GENERAL SUPERINTENDENCE CO. OR LLOYDS AT PORT OF LOADING AND THEIR CERTIFICATE TO BE FINAL 6) LETTER OF CREDIT SHOULD BE ADVISED THROUGH EUROPIANASIAN BANK, 50 COLLYER QUAY, SINGAPORE N SHOULD BE DIVISIONABLE N UNRESTRICTED FOR NEGOTIATION 7) PARTIAL SHIPMENTS PERMITTED TRANSHIPMENT NOT PERMITTED THIS CREDIT IS IRREVOCABLE VALID FOR NEGOTIATION AT SINGAPORE UNTIL 15TH SEPT 1979 8) DRAFTS MUST STATE "DRAWN UNDER IRREVOCABLE LETTER OF CREDIT NO. IBD/118/8371/79 OF THE PUNJAB NSIND BANK LTD DT 21.7.79" AND MUST BEAR THE CLAUSE "PAYABLE AT THE BANK'S CURRENT SELLING RATE OF EXCHANGE ON NEW YORK WITH CHARGES AND INTEREST AT THE CURRENT RATE FROM THE DUE DATE OF THIS DRAFT UNTIL THE DATE OF PAYMENT" 9) WE HEREBY ENGAGE WITH THE DRAWERS, ENDORSERS AND BONAFIDE HOLDERS OF DRAFTS DRAWN UNDER AND IN COMPLIANCE WITH THE TERMS OF THIS CREDIT THAT SUCH DRAFTS SHALL BE DULY HONOURED ON PRESENTATION AND DELIVERY OF DOCUMENTS AS SPECIFIED ABOVE STP NEGOTIATIONS UNDER THIS CREDIT ARE RESTRICTED TO ALGEMENE BANK NEDERLAND N V 2 CECIL STREET CORNER 'D ALMEIDA STREET, P.O. BOX 493, SINGAPORE-1 10) ALL CHARGES ARE FOR BENEFICIARY'S ACCOUNT THE NEGOTIATING BANK SHOULD FORWARD TO US THE DRAFTS AND ORIGINAL DOCUMENTS BY AIRMAIL AND DUPLICATE DOCUMENTS BY THE FOLLOWING AIRMAIL STP DOCUMENTS MUST BE PRESENTED FOR NEGOTIATION WITHIN 15 DAYS FROM THE DATE OF SHIPMENT 11) IN NEGOTIATIONS PLS CLAIM REIMBURSEMENT FROM IRVING TRUST CO. ONE WALL STREET NEW YORK ON DUE DATES ONLY THIS L/C IS SUBJECT TO UCP BROCHURE 290 OF ICC 1974 PUBLICATION STP THIS IS AN OPERATIVE INSTRUMENT N NO AIRMAIL CONFIRMATION TO FOLLOW STP. Certain amendments were made to the letter of credit by a telex dated July 27; these amendments, which are not material, were passed on to the European Asian Bank on or shortly after July 30, and by them to Bentrex on the following day. On Aug. 7, Bentrex presented to European Asian Bank a set of documents and a draft for $2,250,000 drawn on Jain and payable to the order of the European Asin Bank. That draft was endorsed by the European Asian Bank, and sent by them with the documents to the Punjab Bank in India; it was then accepted by Jain. In point of fact, the documents presented by Bentrex with the draft did not conform to the letter of credit in two respect—(1) the bills of lading were not the shipping company's bills of lading, but were signed by agents, and (2) the weight certificate was not issued by either of the two surveyors named in par. (5) of the letter of credit. On two occasions, on Aug. 8 and Aug. 11, the European Asian Bank attempted to telex the Punjab Bank, drawing attention to these discrepancies, and requesting authority to pay despite them. However these telexes were in error sent to the wrong telex address—to the telex address of the Punjab National Bank—and the telexes were not received by the Punjab Bank. Nevertheless, on Aug. 13 the European Asian Bank appears to have notified Bentrex and A.B.N. (the confirming bank) that they had negotiated the documents, and on Aug. 20 they credited Bentrex's account. Meanwhile, as I have said, the European Asian Bank had sent the

> documents and the draft to the Punjab Bank in New Delhi. (There was some debate
> a as to whether this was done by airmail or by special messenger; but I can see no
> relevance in this point.) At all events, the draft and documents appear to have been
> received by the Punjab Bank on Aug. 16. They were sent to the Punjab Bank under
> cover of a document which stated that they, the European Asian Bank, had
> negotiated the documents under the letter of credit, and that at maturity they would
> reimburse themselves on Irving Trust of New York; and which concluded with the
> b words "please advise acceptance". On the same day, Aug. 16, the documents were
> either sent or shown to Jain by the Punjab Bank, and the Punjab Bank appears to
> have drawn the attention of Jain to one of the two discrepancies in the documents
> (viz. that the bills of lading had been signed by agents); however, Jain took no point
> on the documents and accepted the draft. The documents have not been returned
> by the Punjab Bank to the European Asian Bank, but have been retained by them.
> c On the same date, Aug. 16, the Punjab Bank wrote to the European Asian Bank,
> stating that the documents had been "accepted by the party to fall due on 3.2.1980".
> The next event in the story is that Jain were informed on Sept. 8, 1979, that the ship
> on which the cloves had been shipped, *Averilla*, had sunk on her voyage, and that
> the consignment of cloves had been lost. Jain, who had insured the goods, then
> notified their underwriters, the New India Assurance Co., and made a claim on
> d them. A few days later, underwriters repudiated liability. Their case, as developed,
> was that there had been a large-scale fraud; and that on this occasion, as on two other
> occasions, there had never been any goods shipped at all, and that the ship in
> question had not sunk and no goods had been lost. On Feb. 2, 1980, just before the
> expiry of the 180 day period specified in the letter of credit, the European Asian
> Bank enquired of Irving Trust, the New York paying bank named in par. (11) of the
> e letter of credit, whether they had been put in funds to honour the credit. Irving
> Trust responded that they had no record of this credit. The European Asian Bank
> then claimed payment direct from the Punjab Bank; but, as will appear in a
> moment, Jain had obtain an injunction in the Indian Courts restraining the Punjab
> Bank from paying under the letter of credit, and the Punjab Bank informed the
> European Asian Bank that in these circumstances they were legally restrained from
> f making any payment. The European Asian Bank then turned to A.B.N., who had
> confirmed the letter of credit; they drew a draft on A.B.N., and claimed that, since
> Irving Trust had declined to pay, A.B.N. as confirming bank were liable to pay.
> However A.B.N. also denied liability.'

g This summary must be amended in one respect, namely that, having regard to one of
the amendments made to the letter of credit, there appears to have been no discrepancy
with regard to the weight certificate; so that the only possible discrepancy on the face of
the documents (which is not accepted by the appellants as being a discrepancy) was that
the bills of lading were signed by agents, a point which was noted by the respondents
and drawn by them to the attention of Jain. Furthermore, on the affidavit evidence
h before the court, the order of events as between the appellants and their customers
Bentrex with regard to the negotiation of the letter of credit was that the documents
were presented by Bentrex on 7 August 1979, and that on 20 August the appellants
negotiated the letter of credit, accepted the documents and credited Bentrex's account
with the discounted amount of the letter of credit, though it could not be said with
absolute certainty whether the appellants had already given Bentrex a firm commitment
j to take up the documents on 13 August. Although it was accepted by the appellants that
there was prima facie evidence of fraud on the part of Bentrex, the respondents have
made no suggestion of fraud, or knowledge of fraud, on the part of the appellants. Lastly,
it is now plain that the documents were taken from Singapore to the respondents in New
Delhi by an employee of Bentrex, acting as a messenger, by arrangement between the
appellants and Bentrex.

Such are the basic facts, though we shall have in the course of this judgment to consider one or two of the documents in some detail. a

The issues in the action may be summarised as follows. (1) Did the letter of credit, on its true construction, permit negotiation by the appellants so as to create privity of contract as between the appellants and the respondents? (2) If not, was the letter of credit so phrased as to be ambiguous and capable of a reasonable interpretation under which the appellants were authorised to act as negotiating bankers, and were the appellants in the circumstances entitled to act on such an interpretation and hold the respondents b liable to them under the letter of credit? (3) If the answer to both the first two questions is in the negative, are the respondents nevertheless estopped, having regard to their conduct and to art 8 of the Uniform Customs and Practice for Documentary Credits of the International Chamber of Commerce (1974 revision) (UCP) incorporated into the letter of credit, from denying that the appellants were entitled to negotiate the letter of credit? (4) In the alternative to the third issue, was there an implied contract as between c the appellants and the respondents, under which the respondents agreed that the appellants should be entitled to negotiate the letter of credit? (5) Were the appellants not, as they allege, a negotiating bank, but mere agents of Bentrex for collection of the sum payable under the letter of credit, so that it was open to the respondents to raise against the appellants the issue of fraud under the sale contract? (6) Even if the appellants were a negotiating bank, could the respondents resist their claim under the letter of d credit on the ground that some of the documents presented under the letter of credit were not merely fraudulent, but were forgeries?

In argument before this court, two of these issues disappeared having regard to concessions made in the course of argument. First, counsel for the appellants abandoned the allegation of an implied contract, recognising that if his clients could not succeed on estoppel they could not establish an implied contract; so issue (4) went. Next, counsel for e the respondents recognised that, having regard to the long-established and well-recognised decision of this court in *Guaranty Trust Co of New York v Hannay & Co* [1918] 2 KB 623, [1918–19] All ER Rep 151, it made no difference, as against a bona fide negotiating bank, whether the documents were forged or merely fraudulent: in neither case would the issuing bank be able to raise the issue of fraud or forgery as against the bona fide negotiating bank. So issue (6) disappeared too. f

The judge approached the matter as follows. He considered that there was a triable issue on the construction of the letter of credit. He rejected the contention that the appellants were agents for collection. That left only issue (3), that of estoppel, which he regarded as the real point in the case. On that point, he considered that there was a triable issue, for two reasons. The first was that a letter from the appellants to the respondents, which accompanied the documents when sent to the respondents, contained a g misrepresentation; the second was that, on the messages sent by the respondents to the appellants, there was a triable issue whether these contained an unequivocal representation by the respondents that the appellants were entitled to negotiate the letter of credit. In those circumstances, he decided to give the respondents unconditional leave to defend but, as we have noted, also gave the appellants leave to appeal to this court.

We wish to preface our consideration of the substance of this appeal with a few h remarks about the appellate jurisdiction now exercisable by the Court of Appeal in cases of this kind. We do so because counsel for the respondents submitted, on the basis of the decision of the Court of Appeal in *Wing v Thurlow* (1893) 10 TLR 151 (a decision made just before the abolition, in 1894, of the right of appeal by a plaintiff to the Court of Appeal where unconditional leave to defend has been given to the defendant), that such an appeal should not be allowed unless very special circumstances are shown. j

We do not consider that it would be right to turn the clock back to 1893, after an interregnum of nearly ninety years during which the courts have not been able to exercise the jurisdiction in question. During that period of time, circumstances have changed. Changes in economic circumstances have rendered it more likely that defendants may have recourse to delaying taxtics (cf *M V Yorke Motors (a firm) v Edwards*

[1982] 1 All ER 1024 at 1028, [1982] 1 WLR 444 at 450, per Lord Diplock), which may affect the attitude of the courts to this particular jurisdiction. Furthermore, the relevant rules of court have changed; for example, in 1893 an appeal in a case of this kind could go through three tiers of courts, first to a judge, then to a Divisional Court and then to the Court of Appeal, and could do so without leave, which could well have motivated the Court of Appeal to discourage appeals to them. Nowadays, the matter can at most have been considered by a master and a judge in chambers; where, as here, the action has been started in the Commercial Court, it will only have been considered by one tribunal, a commercial judge. In all the circumstances it would not, in our judgment, be right to regard a statement such as that in *Wing v Thurlow* as applicable to the jurisdiction which can now be exercised.

In truth, no special principles apply to an appeal to the Court of Appeal against an order giving unconditional leave to defend. It is in form an interlocutory appeal. In the ordinary way, the appeal is by rehearing. Counsel for the respondents submitted that, on the appeal, the court would be reviewing the exercise of the judge's discretion; and so should only interfere with that discretion on the ordinary well-established principles. We have to confess that we feel some doubt about this proposition. Order 14, r 3(1) provides:

> 'Unless on the hearing of an application under Rule 1 either the Court dismisses the application or the defendant satisfies the Court with respect to the claim, or the part of a claim, to which the application relates that there is an issue or question in dispute which ought to be tried or that there ought for some other reason to be a trial of that claim or part, the Court may give such judgment for the plaintiff against that defendant on that claim or part as may be just having regard to the nature of the remedy or relief claimed.'

Now it is true that the words used in the rule are 'the Court *may* give such judgment for the plaintiff . . .', and at first sight the word 'may' could be read as indicating that the court has a discretion. But it is to be observed that the court can only give such judgment if (1) the court has not dismissed the plaintiff's application (presumably for some defect in the application itself, eg that there is no due verification of the claim) and (2) the defendant has not satisfied the court either (a) that there is an issue or question in dispute which ought to be tried or (b) that there ought for some other reason to be a trial. Once these three possibilities are eliminated, it is very difficult indeed to conceive of circumstances where the court should not give judgment for the plaintiff, especially when it is borne in mind that the policy underlying Ord 14 has always been that, on a proper application, if the judge is satisfied that there is no triable issue, he should give judgment for the plaintiff (see *The Supreme Court Practice 1982* vol 1, p 165, para 14/3–4/2, and the cases there cited). The use of the word 'may' in this context is, we strongly suspect, a survival from the days when Ord 14 did not contain the words 'or the defendant satisfies the Court . . . that there ought for some other reason to be a trial . . .' If, having regard to those words, there remains any discretion in the court, once the three possibilities we have referred to are eliminated, to decline to give judgment, it can only be a discretion of the most residual kind. In practice, this court will simply approach an appeal of this kind as a rehearing. In this respect, an appeal such as the present is to be contrasted with an appeal against an order giving leave to defend on terms, pursuant to the power conferred on the court under Ord 14, r 4(3): the exercise of that power is plainly discretionary, and this court treats the hearing of an appeal against such an order like any other appeal where the exercise of a discretion is challenged (see, eg, *Gordon v Cradock* [1963] 2 All ER 121, [1964] 1 QB 503, a decision on the old Ord 14, r 6, the precursor of the present Ord 14, r 4(3)). In the present case, however, the judge has very helpfully given detailed reasons for his decision; and, as will appear, it is plain from his judgment that in considering the appellants' arguments on this appeal we shall in any event be concerned with points of law.

We wish however to conclude with this comment. If the judge has already decided, on the evidence, that there is a triable issue on a question of fact, it must in the very nature of things be unlikely that this court will interfere with his decision and decide *a* that no trial should take place; because, where such a conclusion has already been reached by a judge, this court will be very reluctant to hold that there is no issue or question which ought to be tried. But where the appeal raises a question of law, this court may be more ready to interfere. Moreover, at least since *Cow v Casey* [1949] 1 All ER 197, [1949] 1 KB 474, this court has made it plain that it will not hesitate, in an appropriate case, to decide questions of law under Ord 14, even if the question of law is at first blush of some *b* complexity and therefore takes 'a little longer to understand'. It may offend against the whole purpose of Ord 14 not to decide a case which raises a clear-cut issue, when full argument has been addressed to the court, and the only result of not deciding it will be that the case will go for trial and the argument will be rehearsed all over again before a judge, with the possibility of yet another appeal (see *Verrall v Great Yarmouth BC* [1980] 1 All ER 839 at 843, 845–846, [1981] 1 QB 202 at 215, 218, per Lord Denning MR and *c* Roskill LJ). The policy of Ord 14 is to prevent delay in cases where there is no defence; and this policy is, if anything, reinforced in a case such as the present, concerned as it is with a claim by a negotiating bank under a letter of credit (see *Bank für Gemeinwirtschaft v City of London Garages Ltd* [1971] 1 All ER 541 at 547–548, [1971] 1 WLR 149 at 158, per Cairns LJ, a case concerned with a claim on a bill of exchange by a holder in due course). *d*

We turn now to the substance of the appeal, and we shall consider first issue (1), which is concerned with the construction of the letter of credit. As to that, having heard full argument on the point, which is a pure point of construction, we do not shrink from stating our conclusion which is that we accept the respondents' submissions on the point as correct in law. The argument on construction is concerned primarily with paras (6) and (9) of the letter of credit, which for the sake of clarity we will repeat: *e*

> '(6) Letter of credit should be advised through Europianasian Ban, 50 Collyer Quay, Singapore n should be divisionable n unrestricted for negotiation . . .
>
> (9) We hereby engage with the drawers, endorsers and bona fide holders of drafts drawn under and in compliance with the terms of this credit that such drafts shall be duly honoured on presentation and delivery of documents as specified above STP negotiations under this credit are restricted to Algemene Bank Nederland NV 2 *f* Cecil Street Corner 'd Almeida Street, P.O. Box 493, Singapore 1.'

At first sight, these two paragraphs appear to be irreconcilable. Paragraph (6) appears to state that the letter of credit is unrestricted for negotiation: whereas para (9) appears to state that negotiation was restricted to ABN. However, we have been persuaded by counsel for the respondents that these two apparently inconsistent provisions can be *g* reconciled. The clue is to be found in the fact that para (6) provides that the letter of credit should be divisionable and unrestricted for negotiation. There is no doubt that the word 'divisionable' means 'divisible'; and that that word (although proscribed by art 46 of the UCP) means that the letter of credit is transferable by the beneficiary in whole or in part (this being a letter of credit under which, by virtue of para (7), partial shipments were permitted). The purpose of such a transfer is to enable the beneficiary to use the *h* letter of credit to pay off his own pre-sellers of the goods which are the subject matter of the sale transaction underlying the letter of credit. But if his pre-sellers are to be enabled themselves to draw directly on the issuing bank under the letter of credit (instead of doing so through the beneficiary or a bank entitled to act as a negotiating bank) the letter of credit must so provide; negotiation must be permitted for this purpose, and if the pre-sellers are not identified, such negotiation cannot be restricted to any particular person. *j* Hence the provision in para (6), that the letter of credit should not merely be divisible but also unrestricted for negotiation; and, in the context of para (6) (and bearing in mind para (9)) the words 'unrestricted for negotiation' should be read as meaning unrestricted for negotiation for the purposes of transfer by the beneficiary. Paragraph (9), on the other hand, is concerned with the question whether the beneficiary is entitled, quite apart from transfer, to negotiate the letter of credit, which would ordinarily be for the purpose of discounting the letter of credit with a bank in order to obtain immediate payment. a Under this paragraph, negotiation is restricted to a particular bank, ABN, perhaps because this was a bank with which the respondents had a commercial relationship and so wished to reserve to them the commercial advantage of being able to offer the service to Bentrex of discounting the letter of credit. On this construction, sensible effect can be given to the provisions of both para (6) and para (9).

For the appellants, counsel nevertheless submitted that (1) the letter of credit was b ambiguous; (2) it was open to the reasonable interpretation that the appellants were authorised to act as negotiating bank; and (3) the appellants were entitled in the circumstances to act on that interpretation and hold the respondents to it. This was of course issue (2). Once again, not only do we consider that there was a triable issue on this point: we go further and say, having heard full argument on the point, that it was not open to the appellants on the facts of this case. We do not doubt that this letter of credit c was badly drafted, and that paras (6) and (9) can only be reconciled by resort to the process of construction, on the lines we have indicated. But the two authorities on which counsel relied show that the principle invoked by him is only available in very limited circumstances. The first case was *Ireland v Livingston* (1872) LR 5 HL 395, [1861–73] All ER Rep 585. That case was concerned with the construction of an order placed by a Liverpool merchant on commission agents in Mauritius for the purchase of sugar. It was d held that the letter containing the order was so worded as to be capable of more than one interpretation; and that the commission agents having acted in good faith on one of those two interpretations, the merchant was bound by it and could not repudiate the agents' action as unauthorised even if, on a true construction, the other interpretation was to be preferred. The second case was *Midland Bank Ltd v Seymour* [1955] 2 Lloyd's Rep 147, a case concerned with a letter of credit. The plaintiffs were the issuing bank, e and the defendant was their customer. The plaintiffs paid the sellers against documents presented under letters of credit; but the defendant refused to indemnify the plaintiffs on the ground they had acted outside the instructions which he had given them. Devlin J held that, on a true construction of the relevant documents, the defence failed. But he went on to say (at 153):

> f 'In my judgment, no principle is better established than that when a banker or anyone else is given instructions or a mandate of this sort, they must be given to him with reasonable clearness. The banker is obliged to act upon them precisely. He may act at his peril if he disobeys them or does not conform with them. In those circumstances there is a corresponding duty cast on the giver of instructions to see that he puts them in a clear form. Perhaps it is putting it too high for this purpose to say that it is a duty cast upon him. The true view of the matter, I think, is that g when an agent acts upon ambiguous instructions he is not in default if he can show that he adopted what is a reasonable meaning. It is not enough to say afterwards that if he had construed the documents properly he would on the whole have arrived at the conclusion that in an ambiguous document the meaning which he did not give it could be better supported than the meaning which he did give to it.'

h In our judgment there must be some limit to the operation of this principle. Obviously it cannot be open to every contracting party to act on a bona fide, but mistaken, interpretation of a contractual document prepared by the other, and to hold the other party to that interpretation. If an offer is made by one person to another, the offeree has to make up his mind about the meaning of the offer before accepting it and entering into a binding contract; once he enters into a contract by accepting the offer, he is bound j by its terms, which (in the event of dispute) will fall to be construed objectively. Furthermore, even in the context of agency and other analogous transactions, the principle in these two cases presupposes, in our judgment, that a party relying on his own interpretation of the relevant document must have acted reasonably in all the circumstances in so doing. If instructions are given to an agent, it is understandable that he should expect to act on those instructions without more; but if, for example, the ambiguity is patent on the face of the document it may well be right (especially with the facilities of modern communications available to him) to have his instructions clarified by his principal, if time permits, before acting on them.

Turning to the facts of the present case, the appellants cannot be regarded as an agent of the respondents; nor can a negotiating bank be regarded as an agent of an issuing bank. Strictly speaking, the principle as stated in *Ireland v Livingston* cannot for that reason alone apply to the present case. But even if the principle were capable of applying to a case such as the present, the conflict between paras (6) and (9) was apparent on the face of the letter of credit. Given this state of affairs, and the obvious nature of this conflict, the proper course of any bank, considering whether to act as negotiating bank, would be to inquire of the issuing bank whether it was intended that negotiation should be regarded as unrestricted, or as restricted to ABN. It cannot be right that, on facts such as these, a bank should be able to rely on one part of the document, ignoring another part which is inconsistent, without making any inquiry of the issuing bank, by telex or otherwise. For these reasons we hold that the appellants are not able to invoke the principle in *Ireland v Livingston* in the present case.

That disposes of the first two issues. We turn next for convenience to the fifth issue, which raises the question whether there is a triable issue that the appellants were not negotiating bankers, but merely agents for collection on behalf of Bentrex. On this issue we, like the judge, have formed a clear view that the contention that the appellants were mere agents for collection is, on the evidence, unarguable. The matter is plain on the face of the documents. When Bentrex presented the documents to the respondents on 7 August 1979, they completed a standard form of the respondents which could be used whether the documents were sent for collection, for purchase or for discount. Which of these three purposes was intended by Bentrex was not specified expressly in the document; but a very substantial part of the document designed to be completed where documents were sent for collection was left entirely blank, although nearly all the remainder of the document was completed. The draft presented by Bentrex with the documents was made out to the order of the respondents, not to the order of Bentrex. Thereafter, everything which the appellants did was consistent only with their either being in the process of negotiating the letter of credit or having negotiated it. First, they made inquiries on 8 August, addressed in error to the wrong bank. The purpose of their inquiries was to find out whether, in the light of the two supposed discrepancies in the documents, they might themselves pay, an inquiry inconsistent with their acting only as agents for collection. Next, they wrote to the respondents on 13 August, using what was plainly one of their own standard forms. The form was suitable for use by a bank which had already negotiated a letter of credit: whereas the appellants were at this stage plainly still in the process of negotiation. The document begins with the words: 'We have negotiated documents under your [letter of credit] as follows . . .' It refers to the enclosed documents; and there are then typed in the words (which are the most relevant part of the document): 'At maturity i.e. 3/2/80 we will reimburse ourselves on Irving Trust New York. Please advise acceptance.' This document is wholly inconsistent with agency for collection. It is probable that on the same date (though the relevant letter was misdated 23 August) the appellants informed ABN, by then the confirming bank, that they had negotiated and forwarded the documents to the respondents, and that they reserved the right to claim payment from ABN as confirming bank. There followed the two documents received by the appellants from the respondents dated respectively 16 and 18 August, on which the appellants rely as giving rise to estoppel; we shall refer to these in a moment. Following receipt of these, the documents having been retained by the respondents, the appellants on 20 August credited Bentrex's account with the discounted amount of the letter of credit (allowing for interest at the rate of 13¾% between 20 August 1979 and 4 February 1980, viz 180 days after bills of lading when payment fell due under the letter of credit); and they then permitted Bentrex to draw down on their account, so exposing themselves (the appellants) to the risk of dishonour of the letter of credit. Finally, when payment was not forthcoming, they themselves sued on the letter of credit as principals. On this evidence it is inconceivable, in our judgment, that the appellants were in any other position except either in the process of negotiation, or having actually negotiated the letter of credit.

Faced with this evidence, counsel for the respondents sought to argue that since, when
a the appellants forwarded the documents to the respondents on 13 August to inquire
whether the respondents were ready to accept the documents, they had (on their own
admission) not yet negotiated the letter of credit, therefore they might arguably be agents
for collection at that time. In our judgment, the non sequitur in this argument is
obvious. There is no reason to suppose, merely because the appellants had not yet paid
Bentrex, that they were at any time appointed agents for collection by Bentrex. There is
b in fact not a scintilla of evidence to suggest that the appellants were ever constituted
agents by Bentrex to collect the proceeds of the letter of credit; every single piece of
evidence before the court indicates the contrary. For these reasons we, like the judge,
consider that there is no triable issue on this point.

But we wish to add this. Even if it were a fact that, as at 13 August, the appellants had
been appointed agents for collection by Bentrex, it is beyond question that by 20 August
c the appellants had negotiated the letter of credit, and there is no suggestion that they
acted otherwise than in good faith in so doing. Thereafter, in February 1980, they
claimed payment from the respondents; and this was refused. In our judgment it is not
open to the respondents, on these facts, to say against the appellants that they were
justified in refusing payment on the ground that the documents were fraudulent or even
forged. In our judgment, the relevant time for considering this question is the time
d when payment falls due and is claimed and refused. If, at that time, the party claiming
payment has negotiated the relevant documents in good faith, the issuing bank cannot
excuse his refusal to pay on the ground that at some earlier time the negotiating bank
was a mere agent for collection on behalf of the seller and allege against him fraud or
forgery (if that indeed be the case) on the part of the beneficiary of the letter of credit. It
follows that, even if there were (contrary to our view) a triable issue that for a short time
e in August 1979 the apellants were no more than agents for collection, that would be
immaterial in the present case.

That disposes of the fifth issue; and we turn finally to the issue which we, like the
judge, regard as the real point in the case, viz issue (3), estoppel.

The basis of the appellants' plea of estoppel is as follows. They submitted to the
respondents the documents presented to them, under cover of the letter dated 13 August
f 1979 to which we have already referred. That letter began with the words: 'We have
negotiated documents under your L/C as follows . . .' and the most relevant part of the
letter read: 'At maturity i.e. 3/2/1980 we will reimburse ourselves on Irving Trust New
York. Please advise acceptance.' The letter was sent to the respondents by messenger.
The respondents replied by letter dated 16 August, in which they referred to the
appellants' letter and to the letter of credit and stated: 'We are pleased to inform you that
g the above documents are accepted by the party to fall due on 3.2.1980.' Subsequently, on
18 August, the respondents sent a telex to the appellants which was a tested telex
(probably sent in response to a request that the signature on the respondents' letter dated
16 August be verified), in which they confirmed that 'the documents are accepted by
drawee to mature on 3.2.80'. Thereafter, on the faith of these messages, the appellants
credited Bentrex's account with them with the discounted value of the letter of credit
h and permitted Bentrex to draw down on that account. The respondents meanwhile
retained the documents submitted by the appellants, and indeed have never returned
them.

The appellants also rely on art 8 of the Uniform Customs and Practice, which was
incorporated into the letter of credit. Article 8 provides as follows:

> j 'a. In documentary credit operations all parties concerned deal in documents and
> not in goods. b. Payment, acceptance or negotiation against documents which
> appear on their face to be in accordance with the terms and conditions of a credit by
> a bank authorised to do so, binds the party giving the authorisation to take up the
> documents and reimburse the bank which has effected the payment, acceptance or
> negotiation. c. If, upon receipt of the documents, the issuing bank considers that
> they appear on their face not to be in accordance with the terms and conditions of
> the credit, that bank must determine, on the basis of the documents alone, whether

to claim that payment, acceptance or negotiation was not effected in accordance with the terms and conditions of the credit. d. The issuing bank shall have a reasonable time to examine the documents and to determine as above whether to make such a claim. e. If such claim is to be made, notice to that effect, stating the reasons therefor, must, without delay, be given by cable or other expeditious means to the bank from which the documents have been received (the remitting bank) and such notice must state that the documents are being held at the disposal of such bank or are being returned thereto. f. If the issuing bank fails to hold the documents at the disposal of the remitting bank or fails to return the documents to such bank, the issuing bank shall be precluded from claiming that the relative payment, acceptance or negotiation was not effected in accordance with the terms and conditions of the credit. g. If the remitting bank draws the attention of the issuing bank to any irregularities in the documents or advises such bank that it has paid, accepted or negotiated under reserve or against a guarantee in respect of such irregularities, the issuing bank shall not thereby be relieved from any of its obligations under this article. Such guarantee or reserve concerns only the relations between the remitting bank and the beneficiary.'

The appellants do not rely on art 8 as giving rise to a separate plea, independent of the plea of estoppel. But they say that art 8, especially paras (c) and (e), indicates very clearly the understanding that the issuing bank must, on receipt of documents, determine without delay whether payment will be made in accordance with the credit and, if not, hold the documents at the disposal of the remitting bank or return them. This, they say, reinforces their plea of estoppel on the facts of the present case.

Now there were two points which persuaded the judge that there was a triable issue on estoppel. The first was that the letter from the appellants to the respondents dated 13 August, with which documents were enclosed, contained a misrepresentation, viz that the appellants had already negotiated the documents under the letter of credit. There was no evidence before the judge that the respondents had in any way acted, or failed to act, in reliance on that misrepresentation; indeed the misrepresentation was not even pleaded in the respondents' points of defence. But the judge felt that he should not shut the respondents out from proving, if they could, that they had relied on it.

With all respect to the judge, we do not consider that this was the correct approach. The fact of the representation was known to the respondents in 1981, at the time of the stay proceedings. In his affidavit dated 24 March 1981, the respondents' solicitor stated that it would be necessary to ascertain whether the respondents were misled by it. In their points of defence, served over a year later in July 1982, there is no plea whatsoever founded on this misrepresentation. Before the hearing before Staughton J, further evidence was filed on behalf of the respondents, but none of it related to this point. A misrepresentation is of itself of no relevance in law; and we do not consider it to be right that leave to defend an action should be given to enable a party to hunt around for evidence to show that he has acted on a misrepresentation, especially when he has had over a year to discover that evidence before the summons for judgment is heard. Under Ord 14, r 3(1), it is for the defendant to satisfy the court that there is an issue or question in dispute which ought to be tried or that there ought for some other reason to be a trial. Here, the respondents have on this failed to discharge that burden. We would indeed go further. We cannot conceive of any way in which the respondents could have acted, in any material manner, in reliance on this misrepresentation; because it was a matter of no moment to them whether the appellants had negotiated the documents, or were still in the process of doing so. Certainly, no suggestion was made before us how the respondents might have acted on the misrepresentation; and it is now nearly two years since the respondents became aware of it. In our judgment, the judge erred in law on this point, in that he appears to have proceeded on the basis that, on an issue of this kind on a summons for judgment under Ord 14, no evidence whatsoever need be adduced by the defendant of any reliance on the relevant misrepresentation, in order to establish a triable issue on it. In our judgment, the evidence discloses no such triable issue.

The second point on which the judge considered that there was a triable issue was
a whether the respondents' letter and tested telex dated 16 and 18 August respectively
'were unequivocal statements that they, the bank, would see that the draft was paid
pursuant to the letter of credit at maturity'. He apparently thought that these two
communications might indicate only that Jain had accepted the draft. Here again we
find ourselves in disagreement with the judge. The point is one of construction of the
relevant documents, read in their context. It is true that the communications in question
b should be read as meaning that the documents had been accepted by Jain to fall due, or
mature, on 3 February 1980. But we have no doubt that this was intended to indicate to
the appellants that, the respondents' customers having accepted the documents as being
in order, they, the respondents, acknowledged that payment under the letter of credit
would be made to the appellants as negotiating bankers on the date of maturity. As a
matter of commerce, the appellants could not have had the slightest interest in whether
c Jain, a trading company of whom they knew nothing, were promising to pay on the
draft at maturity. After all, it was obvious that the appellants, as negotiating bankers,
would be discounting the letter of credit and so paying out a very large sum of money
on the faith of these messages. As negotiating bankers, they would be relying on the
undertaking of the issuing bank under the letter of credit. That was the only matter that
they were interested in. Their inquiry dated 13 August was plainly directed to that.
d There could have been no question of the appellants attempting to negotiate drafts
accepted by Jain: commercially, they were not saleable documents. In any event,
consistently with the obvious conclusion that all the appellants were concerned with was
the liability of the respondents under the letter of credit, the respondents retained all the
documents, including the drafts, which were never returned to the appellants. In all the
circumstances, we have no doubt that, on a true construction of the relevant documents,
e the respondents did indeed unequivocally represent to the appellants that they, the
respondents, recognised that the appellants were entitled to act as negotiating bankers
under the letter of credit and that the documents were in order so that there was, on the
face of the documents, a liability on the respondents to pay the appellants the sum due
under the letter of credit on the due date. In our judgment, there is no triable issue on
this point.

f For these reasons we conclude that, on the evidence, there is no issue or question in
dispute which ought to be tried, and that there is no other reason for which there ought
to be a trial of the action or any part of it. Furthermore, we have differed from the judge
on only two points; and we have differed from him on issues of law. Indeed, this is one
of those cases where all the relevant evidence is before the court, and where the crucial
point, viz estoppel, depends entirely on the construction of the relevant documents in
g their context, as to which it is not suggested that any further evidence could be available.
If the matter were to go to trial, all that would happen would be that exactly the same
arguments, at much the same length, on exactly the same evidence, would be advanced
all over again before the trial judge. Having formed a clear view, as we have done, that
there is no arguable defence to this claim, it would be quite wrong to allow it to go to
trial, and no doubt to yet another appeal. In all the circumstances, therefore, we consider
h this to be a case where the Court of Appeal should not hesitate to substitute its own view
for that of the judge. We therefore allow the appeal, and order that judgment be entered
for the appellants against the respondents for the sum claimed.

Appeal allowed. Judgment entered for the appellants in the sum of $US2,250,000. Appellants to have interest from 3 February 1980 until date of payment at the current rate ruling in New York equivalent to the London inter-bank rate. Liberty to apply on the question of interest.

Solicitors: *Coward Chance* (for the appellants); *Norton Rose Botterell & Roche* (for the respondents).

Frances Rustin Barrister.

Udale v Bloomsbury Area Health Authority

QUEEN'S BENCH DIVISION
JUPP J
4, 7, 17 FEBRUARY 1983

Damages – Surgery – Unsuccessful operation – Negligence – Doctor negligently performing sterilisation operation – Unwanted pregnancy subsequently occurring – Assessment of damages – Public policy – Whether damages recoverable for unwanted pregnancy – Whether damages recoverable for pain and suffering and disruption of family finances caused by unwanted pregnancy.

The plaintiff, who was the mother of four children, underwent a sterilisation operation which was carried out by doctors employed by the defendant health authority. The operation was not successful and she subsequently became pregnant. After giving birth to a normal, healthy baby the mother brought an action in negligence against the health authority claiming damages for (i) pain and discomfort including anxiety and distress caused by the unsuccessful operation, (ii) loss of earnings during pregnancy, birth and early rearing of the child, (iii) the cost of enlarging the family home to accommodate the new baby and (iv) the cost of the child's upbringing until the age of 16. The health authority admitted liability but disputed the amount of damages.

Held – It was contrary to public policy to award damages to a mother whose child had been conceived after the mother had undergone a negligently performed sterilisation operation to cover the cost of carrying out necessary extensions to the home and of bringing up the child because (a) it was highly undesirable that the child should learn that a court had declared that his life or birth was a mistake and that he was unwanted or rejected, (b) before making such an award the court would have to deduct an amount for the value of the child's life as perceived by the mother so that an uncaring mother would receive a greater net sum than a loving mother and virtue would go unrewarded, (c) medical practitioners who would otherwise incur liability would be placed under pressure to authorise or carry out abortions and (d) the birth of a healthy, normal baby was a beneficial, not a detrimental, event. However, those principles of public policy did not preclude an award of damages for lost income and also for pain, suffering, inconvenience, anxiety and the disruption to the family's finances caused by the unexpected pregnancy (see p 526 *e f* and p 531 *e* to p 532 *c*, post).

Dicta of Lord Denning MR in *Spartan Steel and Alloys Ltd v Martin & Co (Contractors) Ltd* [1972] 3 All ER at 562, of Lord Wilberforce and of Lord Edmund-Davies in *McLoughlin v O'Brian* [1982] 2 All ER at 303, 308–309 and *McKay v Essex Area Health Authority* [1982] 2 All ER 771 applied.

Harbutt's Plasticine Ltd v Wayne Tank and Pump Co Ltd [1970] 1 All ER 225 distinguished.

Notes

For public policy and the measure of damages, see 12 Halsbury's Laws (4th edn) para 1133.

Cases referred to in judgment

Emeh v Kensington, Chelsea and Fulham Area Health Authority (1983) Times, 3 January.
Harbutt's Plasticine Ltd v Wayne Tank and Pump Co Ltd [1970] 1 All ER 225, [1970] 1 QB 447, [1970] 2 WLR 198, CA.
McKay v Essex Area Health Authority [1982] 2 All ER 771, [1982] QB 1166, [1982] 2 WLR 890, CA.
McLoughlin v O'Brian [1982] 2 All ER 298, [1983] AC 410, [1982] 2 WLR 982, HL.
Mallett v McMonagle [1969] 2 All ER 178, [1970] AC 166, [1969] 2 WLR 769, HL.

Sciuriaga v Powell [1980] CA Transcript 597.
a *Spartan Steel and Alloys Ltd v Martin & Co (Contractors) Ltd* [1972] 3 All ER 557, [1973] QB 27, [1972] 3 WLR 502, CA.

Action

By a writ dated 21 August 1980 the plaintiff, Muriel Yvonne Udale, claimed damages in negligence against the defendants, the Camden and Islington Area Health Authority
b (Teaching), for loss suffered by her resulting from the negligent performance of a sterilisation operation on her by doctors employed by the defendants and the subsequent conception and birth of a male child, David Udale. Pursuant to the order of Master Creightmore dated 15 April 1982 the Bloomsbury Area Health Authority were substituted for the Camden and Islington Area Health Authority (Teaching) as defendants in the action. The defendants admitted liability but contested the quantum of damages.
c The facts are set out in the judgment.

Nicholas Brandt for the plaintiff.
David Latham for the defendants.

Cur adv vult

d

17 February. The following judgment was delivered.

JUPP J. This is a claim for damages for the negligent performance of an operation for sterilisation by a surgeon for whom the defendant health authority accept responsibility. Liability is admitted; the court has only to assess the damages.

e The plaintiff, Mrs Udale, was married in 1963 and by the year 1977 she and her husband had four children, all daughters, the last having been born on 1 May 1974. She and her husband decided not to have any more children. So, after finding contraceptive measures difficult, the plaintiff, on 4 October 1977, underwent the operation for laparoscopic sterilisation. The operation failed its purpose. On 15 June 1978 the plaintiff went to a private hospital and was told she was pregnant. On 27 November 1978,
f fortunately or unfortunately, she gave birth to a normal healthy boy. The phrase 'fortunately or unfortunately' encapsulates the most part of the legal argument which has surrounded the plaintiff's claim for damages.

The surgeon who, in this type of operation, should have placed a metal clip on each Fallopian tube in order to close it in fact placed the right-hand clip not on the Fallopian tube at all but on a nearby ligament. The hospital authority admit that that was negligent.
g It is alleged in the statement of claim that the left-hand clip was not attached at all. This has not been investigated and has not been admitted by the defendants. They admit only the misplacing of the right-hand clip.

The damages fall to be considered under four broad headings. These are: (1) the plaintiff's pain and discomfort, especially her fears and anxieties engendered by the unsuccessful operation; (2) the plaintiff's loss of about a year's earnings, covering the
h pregnancy, birth and early rearing of the boy; (3) the cost of enlarging the family home to accommodate the new baby; (4) the cost of the child's upbringing from birth to age 16.

After their marriage in 1963, Mr and Mrs Udale lived for some time as tenants of a house belonging to a new town corporation. After some time they bought that house as sitting tenants. Towards the end of 1975 they sold it and, with the proceeds and with the
j aid of a £10,000 mortgage, bought their present home in Hemel Hempstead for £15,950. They had, by this time, had their four daughters; the youngest would have been nearly 18 months when they moved. Mr Udale is a heavy goods vehicle driver for Kodak Ltd. He has been with that company for 23 years. For the last 10 years he has been on night shift with alternating weeks of 60 hours and 40 hours. He drives to Wales and back one week and to Tunbridge Wells and back the next. Mrs Udale worked part-time as a

telephonist/receptionist/typist. Her hours were 1 to 5 pm. She was also learning to be a computer operator. She has returned to that same employment since the birth. a

The new house at Hemel Hempstead had many assets. It was situated halfway between Mrs Udale's job and Mr Udale's job, a journey for each of them of about one and a half miles. It was a nice area. The infant, primary and secondary comprehensive schools were all most conveniently sited on ground just opposite. The Udales were a thrifty couple. Their joint earnings went into a bank account. They had another account at the bank, called a budget account, out of which, advised by the bank manager, they paid recurring b bills such as for gas, telephone, water, television licence, as well as small repairs and maintenance to house and furniture. Rates were paid by standing order.

Unfortunately, on 5 December 1975, just after they moved, Mr Udale met with a road accident, which severely, though only temporarily, disabled him. After some time in hospital, his wife had to nurse him at home until he returned to work some ten or eleven months after the accident, in October or November 1976. The accident was Mr Udale's c own fault so, of course, he could not obtain compensation for his injuries. While off work he only drew basic pay, and the loss of overtime pay put a strain on the family finances. But by the time of the operation for sterilisation they had had a year of normal earnings (the two of them) in which to get over that and to put their finances on an even keel.

Soon after the last daughter, Natalie, was born, and, I think, again in connection with d their move, the Udales discussed the question of having further children. They discussed it from all angles: the effect of it on the other children, the financial difficulties, the accommodation available in their new house, and so on. The first and obvious thing was to take contraceptive measures and, a few weeks after the birth of Natalie, Mrs Udale had a coil fitted. It caused pain and discomfort, so she had it changed. However, this was not a success. Nature seemed to reject the coil; and what with infection and attendant pain e and discomfort, poor Mrs Udale spent a good deal of time with the doctors in the spring and summer of 1977 before the operation in the autumn of that year. No one seems to have suggested that Mr Udale should be the one to take contraceptive measures, at least it has not been mentioned in evidence. It seems that when the coil was found irksome the solution considered was Mrs Udale's sterilisation. It was discussed extensively between the husband and the wife and Mrs Udale also discussed it with the doctors, though not f for so long. A hospital note dated 4 August 1977 records Mrs Udale as having a fairly constant nagging pain, presumably from the coil and the infection, for about two years. After setting out details of a physical examination, the note concludes:

> 'Doesn't want to feel that she is irreversibly sterilised but does want to be sterilised. Psychological shock makes her not keen to feel that it couldn't be reversed.'

g

This was the position before the operation. The trouble was that Mrs Udale, who came, herself, from a large and happy family, was only 32 years old. She and her husband discussed things like possible divorce, though there was no cloud of that kind on their horizon at that time, or his being killed in an accident and she wanting to remarry, or one of the children dying or being killed, and so on, making another child desirable. In short, at her age, she was loath to surrender altogether her ability to have children. She h really wanted to use sterilisation as a purely contraceptive measure, was prepared to accept the possibility, of which the doctors warned her, that they might not be able to reverse it, but was hoping that it would not turn out to be so if the occasion arose.

The operation was carried out on 4 October 1977. Since it was unsuccessful the assessment of damages must begin with the pain, discomfort and inconvenience of the operation itself. It was done under general anaesthetic but with no long stay in hospital j and, as I understood it, little pain or discomfort. Unfortunately, however, a great deal of pain followed it. The notes for 10 November 1977 record:

> 'Still complaining of pain in right iliae fossa particularly after intercourse. Discharge, foul smelling, several small vaginal bleeds.'

She had had six weeks of short-wave diathermy and antibiotics without relief. There is *a* no medical evidence to suggest that this has anything whatever to do with the operation for sterilisation. Indeed, the obvious inference is that it is a continuing of the previous trouble, whatever that was.

On 12 January 1978 the notes record: 'Worse—almost unbearable. Inter-menstrual bleeding.' Mrs Udale reported that the pain was going down her right thigh, is there constantly and is worse at night. She was tender wherever touched in her lower parts, *b* except the fornices. Again, no evidence has been called to try to establish that as being the result of the operation, although it was after the operation.

The doctors could not understand it and sent her to a psychiatrist. They clearly did not believe her pain was real. The psychiatrist's notes indicate she had to retire to bed at Christmas because of the pain; she was upset at their not believing her; she got bouts of flushing and near fainting; her inside throbbed like an infected finger. She was getting *c* niggly and irritable and her husband was getting depressed. She put this down to his night driving job; he put it down to his worrying about her.

Now, this was all after the operation but, again, no medical evidence has been called to suggest that it was *caused* by the operation. On might suspect that the exacerbation of pain, if true, had something to do with the sterilisation, but that will not quite do. In the absence of medical evidence, I cannot draw an inference of that kind. I have to assume *d* that it is merely a continuation of the old trouble. Indeed, plaintiff's counsel, faced with this, has not felt able to argue to the contrary.

The visit to the psychiatrist was on 1 March 1978, over four months after the operation. Mrs Udale was almost certainly pregnant by then. Hot flushes and near fainting suggest pregnancy, at any rate to the mere layman, and, again, one is tempted to ascribe the symptoms she was relating to the psychiatrist as due to the pregnancy and hence to the *e* unsuccessful operation. But the facts do not warrant this. Counsel for defendants points out (and counsel for the plaintiff accepts) that the appointment with the psychiatrist was made on 12 January 1978. It is quite impossible to suppose that Mrs Udale was pregnant then. So, again, the whole episode of the psychiatrist must be ascribed to the old trouble, whatever that was.

Mrs Udale had, however, been taking antibiotics and pain-killing tablets prescribed by *f* her general practitioner, as well as tables for blood pressure. She continued to do this, and this is something which is important in regard to the damages, for something like three or three and a half months of the pregnancy. It was only on 15 June 1978 that she decided to take a second opinion. Accordingly, she went to the Trade Union Hospital at Manor House, London NW11 and saw Dr Fox as a private patient. He diagnosed pregnancy and estimated that she was 16 weeks gone. He was wrong, in fact, but through *g* no fault of his. Mrs Udale had made no note of, and was unable to recount, the date of any of the usual signs. Dr Fox really had almost nothing to go on.

I have set all this out in detail because it is now clear, contrary to what I supposed when hearing the plaintiff's evidence, that the pain and discomfort and the visit to the psychiatrist with its implication that her pain was imaginary and her resentment of that are not matters which resulted from the unsuccessful operation, although I would be *h* inclined to think that the very fact of being sterilised at her age was a weight on her mind.

That still leaves the operation itself, which had its element of pain and discomfort, the unpleasantness of the usual symptoms of pregnancy (sickness, flushes, bouts of near fainting and so on) which are matters which must be taken to be the result of the unsuccessful operation. The plaintiff suffered no more than the usual symptoms of *j* pregnancy, but she endured it all for nothing. Moreover, the symptoms of pregnancy must have been alarming to a woman who, not without reason, never ascribed them to pregnancy until she went to Dr Fox. She had then, in all probability, been pregnant for something like three and a half months or more. Up to that point, I deal with her symptoms as if they were *not* due to pregnancy but to injury by the operation.

Mrs Udale described her reaction to the news:

> 'I was shattered, I couldn't believe it. I asked him to write it down. In the following months it took me a number of weeks to accept it. I felt angry because I *a* had been deprived of the choice of child or abortion. [She refers there to the fact that she did not find out about her pregnancy until it was too late for abortion.] The news was out of the ordinary. Physically, I had had the usual sickness but I didn't think it was pregnancy. It was like the other pregnancies otherwise; I just had to get used to the idea. I was worried because I had taken tablets I wouldn't have taken if I'd known I was pregnant. I'd lost faith in everybody and in myself after I'd heard *b* the news.'

I am quite satisfied that it took several weeks for Mrs Udale to get over her sense of frustration and anger before she gradually came to accept that she was going to have another baby. During that time she discussed abortion with the doctors. They told her there was no risk of harm to her or to the baby which would justify it legally. She herself felt it would be on her conscience if she terminated the baby's life. In short, she and the *c* doctors agreed that it was too late. It seems that she would have tried to get an abortion, so long as it was lawful, if she had known early enough that she was pregnant. She was asked at one stage whether, if there were no financial problems, she would have been happy to have another child. Her answer was emphatic: 'A hundred per cent No.'

Now, Mrs Udale is a motherly sort of woman, nice looking but rather overweight and tending, it is clear from the medical notes, to blood pressure. Psychologically, she gave *d* the appearance of being healthy. I suspect that that is what the psychiatrist meant when he wrote in his notes that she 'comes from a large happy family—that is a mystery'. I do not think she has in any way exaggerated her distress over the period so far covered. Accordingly, substantial damages have to be awarded for all she suffered from the time of the operation in October 1977 until quite a long time after she learnt that she was pregnant in June 1978, and it is my view proper to bear in mind that the mental strains *e* were superimposed on the physical suffering which preceded the operation and which continued after it, but which cannot be ascribed to the operation.

It did take, as I have said, some time for Mrs Udale to settle down to the idea of having a baby. But then things began to change. She is not only an experienced mother but, so far as I am able to judge, a good mother, who has all the proper maternal instincts which make her work long and hard to look after her offspring. Her description of her situation *f* at that time is recorded in the psychiatrist's notes: she had four beautiful daughters aged 11, 10, $7\frac{1}{2}$ and $4\frac{1}{2}$. She had a nice house and she and her husband both had good jobs which they enjoyed. Her husband was an only child, whilst she came from a large happy family. Moreover, as she said in evidence, her husband had always wanted a boy and I think she must have wished one of her four children had been a boy.

As the birth approached, I am satisfied Mrs Udale gradually settled into doing all she *g* could for the expected child but she must have been worried about the extra expense and about the difficulty of finding room for the child, once it got beyond the stage of the cradle or carry-cot, in her nice house. It was largely considerations of finance which prompted the decision to limit the family to four. She would have been anxious, too, about the effect on the other children. Even more important, she was, I think, desperately worried about the drugs (antibiotics, blood pressure tablets and pain killers) which had *h* been prescribed and which she had been taking, in all innocence, whilst pregnant. She would not have dreamed of taking them had she known she was pregnant and it is common knowledge, or at least it is a common fear (whether true or not), that drugs can affect the unborn child. This, in my judgment, was a nightmare to her.

Then came the birth. Was it fortunate or unfortunate? It was, at any rate, entirely normal. The child was also an entirely normal boy, healthy and happy. Mrs Udale *j* returned home from hospital after ten days, having been resterilised either two or three days after the birth. The necessity for that must, of course, be included in the damages and that is an operation in which she was, as I understand it, cut open in order for the resterilisation to be effected.

At home the boy (they named him David) was accepted by and became very much **a** part of the family. Mrs Udale was grateful it was a boy, she felt that was her reward at the end of it all. Another girl, she said, would not have been welcome. Of course, the housework was (to use her expression) 'colossal', but she went back to her job, as before, when David was not quite a year old. Mrs Udale, to her credit, made no attempt to play down the fact that here was a son, David, who was happy, healthy and, as it turned out, much loved. One is inevitably reminded of the Gospel (John 16:21): 'A woman when **b** she is in travail hath sorrow, because her hour is come: but as soon as she is delivered of the child, she remembereth no more the anguish, for joy that a man is born into the world.'

However, there were troubles. I must go forward in time a little to mention a further operation which she had to undergo for the removal of a sterilisation clip on the left side. This was done at the Manor House Hospital in September 1982. She was ten days in **c** hospital and her abdomen had to be cut open yet again to get rid of the clip. This operation had nothing whatever to do with the birth, nor is it clear why the clip was not removed when she was resterilised two or three days after the birth, but I am satisfied this second operation was necessary in order to remove the last vestige of the unsuccessful operation. In spite of my having refused leave to amend the statement of claim at the end of the plaintiff's case, I think the plaintiff is entitled, even on the pleadings as they **d** stand, to have this operation included in the damages she can recover.

With one exception, the defendants do not dispute that the plaintiff is entitled to damages for the matters so far dealt with. These are: (1) the original operation, which turned out to be useless; (2) the shock and anxiety of an unwanted pregnancy; (3) the anger at the thwarting of the firm decision she and her husband had taken after careful thought not to have further children; (4) the ordinary symptoms of pregnancy during **e** the first three and a half months, thought by her to be illness or disease, and the taking of quite unnecessary drugs to overcome them; (5) the very real fear, after the pregnancy was diagnosed, that the drugs may have harmed, even deformed, the child; she must have feared a mongol might be born; (6) the operation for resterilisation two or three days after the birth; and (7) the operation in September 1982 to remove the last vestiges of the useless operation. This, as I understand it, is the only item that the defendants **f** dispute. I think, in this particular case, that when these matters were heaped on top of pain and suffering not due to the sterilisation they must have given the plaintiff an extremely miserable time.

One other head of damages is conceded by the defendants, namely the plaintiff's loss of earnings for about eleven months, made necessary by the pregnancy and birth. These are agreed at £1,025·20.

g This was not, however, the end of Mrs Udale's difficulties. The house had three bedrooms. Mr and Mrs Udale slept in the front bedroom; the two elder girls in the back bedroom; the two younger girls had bunk-beds in the third bedroom. This was really only a box-room, 9 ft by 9 ft. The baby has had to go in there to make a third. It is obviously a squash. Downstairs, they had a dining-room, living-room and kitchen. Beside the house stood a flat-roofed garage. The space between house and garage formed **h** a passageway, open to the elements and just over 3 ft wide, along which one could walk to the outside wc at the back of the garage. There was, of course, a bathroom with wc upstairs.

In about April 1979 Mr and Mrs Udale got a building consultant, Mr Bacon, to draw up plans for an extension to the ground floor which would add a single storey extra bedroom on the ground floor, 9 ft 6 in by about 14 ft, and would be at the back of the **j** garage beyond the wc. By roofing over the passage and lining it, Mr Bacon's plan made the passage into an internal corridor, leading from the kitchen to the new bedroom. At the same time, the outside wc was to be demolished and an internal cloakroom constructed in its place. This would consist of wc, shower, wash basin and cupboard for cloaks. The plan also shows an extension into the back garden of the dining room and the building of a conservatory between that extension and the new bedroom. Thus the angle between the projecting new cloakroom and bedroom was usefully filled, and the whole building squared off. This was a sensible plan, but in this action the plaintiff only claims the cost of the work necessary to construct the new bedroom and the new downstairs cloakroom with the internal passage leading to them. The lower of two builder's estimates for this work comes to £11,561. £1,420 of this sum goes to the stripping off and refelting of the garage roof and extending the height of the garage wall so that the level of the roof of the garage and the roof of the new corridor are made to match. This enables arrangements to be made for draining off the rain-water. It seems there is no other way of avoiding this rather expensive change.

The house cost £15,950 in 1975; it is certainly more valuable now, although I have no evidence as to this. Counsel for the plaintiff in argument suggested it might be at least two and a half times that figure now, or even more. The proposed extension would add very considerably to the value of the house, especially if combined with the conservatory and extended dining room. Moreover, as the years go by, the increased value will, itself, increase. I was referred to *Harbutt's Plasticine Ltd v Wayne Tank and Pump Co Ltd* [1970] 1 All ER 225, [1970] 1 QB 447 as authority for the proposition that tortfeasors are not entitled to any allowance for an increase in value of this kind. I do not think the case is authority for so wide a proposition. The defendants in that case destroyed the plaintiffs' building and the plaintiffs had no option but to replace it with a modern building. The modernity of the building was bound to add value to the whole; it could not be avoided. Mr and Mrs Udale had other options. They could, for example, have moved into a larger house. They cannot be criticised for choosing to stay where they were and to build an extension, but in my judgment it would be right to make, in the defendants' favour a deduction in the cost so as to reflect the betterment in the plaintiff's position. She and her husband would have a downstairs cloakroom, which is also a shower room, and a much more valuable house overall. Accordingly, the estimate should be scaled down a little and under this head of damages, if they are awarded, I would award £8,000. The work has not in fact been carried out.

The defendants submit that neither this nor the two further heads of damage are recoverable by the plaintiff. These are (1) the cost of bringing up the new baby to date (he is now a little over 4 years and 2 months old) and (2) the future cost of his upbringing to the age of 16. Mrs Udale put at £500 the cost of what has in evidence been called 'the layette'. This covers the pram, carry-cot, car-seat, pushchair, fireguard, knitted coats and clothes. She had kept none of these things after the birth of the fourth daughter. Then there is four years and nearly two months of food and other things. A family on supplementary benefit would, for such a child, be currently getting £8·75 per week, or £455 per annum in addition to the child benefit. It would have been less four years ago, but I have not been told how much less. One would have to allow for inflation during the period. Working backwards, with the assistance of the table in Kemp and Kemp *The Quantum of Damages* (4th edn, 1975) and assuming, unrealistically perhaps, that supplementary child benefit has kept exactly in pace with inflation, the answer seems in round figures to be about £1,550. This figure, however, overlaps to some extent at least with the layette, and it seems to me that £1,750 would be a reasonable figure, and indeed there was no real dispute in argument ultimately about that figure.

With regard to the future cost of David's maintenance, an auditor, Mr Booth, gave evidence. He had prepared from a publication called *The Money Book* an estimate of the future cost, beginning in mid-January 1983, of bringing up David until he reached the age of 16. Mr Booth does not allow for income tax but that is not likely to infringe very much on the Udales' income because of the five children. He set off the extra child benefits to which they would be entitled and produced a figure of £5,100 as the capital sum required now to fund a stream of outgoings at the rate suggested by the book over the period to David's sixteenth birthday. I accept his evidence that government bonds, in which both capital and income are index linked, are the best method of arriving at the right figure. The method automatically allows for inflation because of the index linking. The figure, using the method suggested in *Mallett v McMonagle* [1969] 2 All ER 178, [1970] AC 166, produced the figure of £3,700. The index-linked bond is a comparatively new phenomenon which came into being long after that case was decided. There could be one variable in the index-linked bond, namely the yield. Mr Booth took 2%, but at 2% his figure would be £4,500. I take the round sum of £5,000 as the proper assessment, bearing in mind Mrs Udale's belief that the basic figures are rather tight and the possibility that income tax may begin to impinge when the older children go out into the world and David gets nearer to 16. Again, this figure, by the end of the argument, had been virtually, I think, agreed.

Now it is disputed that these three items are recoverable. They come to £8,000 for the extension of the house, £1,750 for the cost of David's upbringing up until the trial, including the £500 layette, and £5,000 for the cost of his future upbringing to age 16. Counsel for the defendants challenges these three heads of damage. He submits that as a matter of public policy damages should not be awarded for the birth of a normal, happy, healthy and, as it happens to be in this case, a much loved child. Whilst damages might be claimed if the child was handicapped or deformed, a normal child, says counsel, should as a matter of public policy be regarded as loved and wanted. I pause to emphasise that any decision of mine is not intended to deal one way or the other with an abnormal child. It would be intolerable, he says, if a child ever learned that a court had publicly declared him so unwanted that medical men were paying for his upbringing because their negligence brought him into the world. Our society, the argument runs, is founded on the basic unit of the family and assumes that children are the natural and desirable consequence of marriage and that the child's subsistence is a benefit alike to the child, the parents, the family and to society as a whole. In short, the law must assume that children are a blessing. It is pointed out that to allow claims against doctors to include the cost of bringing up a child would affect medical decisions which they might have to make whilst the child is being carried in the mother's womb. He refers to the judgment of Ackner LJ in *McKay v Essex Area Health Authority* [1982] 2 All ER 771 at 786, [1982] QB 1166 at 1187, where the Lord Justice cites the Law Commission's Report on Injuries to Unborn Children (Law Com no 60, August 1974; Cmnd 5709) para 89:

> 'Such a cause of action, if it existed, would place an almost intolerable burden on medical advisers in their socially and morally exacting role. The danger that doctors would be under subconscious pressures to advise abortions in doubtful cases through fear of an action of damages, is, we think, a real one.'

Counsel for the defendants also submits that it would be invidious to weigh up the benefit of having a child against the cost of bringing it up, and that to give, in effect, a free child to some parents would be invidious. If this kind of damage is recoverable, a court would have to quantify in money the blessings and benefit of having a child and set that sum against the capital cost of the child's upbringing and award the difference if the latter exceeded the former. Plaintiff mothers might be tempted to pretend to a lack of affection for their offspring which ought not to be encouraged.

Finally, counsel for the defendants points to the material advantages that are on the side of having a child. Financial support or assistance, especially perhaps from a son, can be a considerable help to parents in their old age. Daughters often give help with housework, shopping, laundry and the like to their ageing parents. Parents can make a claim in suitable cases under the Fatal Accidents Act 1976 in the event of the child being killed and their losing that support.

In so far as these submissions are based on the *difficulty* of assessing the benefits of parenthood, I do not think they can be right. There is ample authority that courts must, as best they can, assess imponderables of all sorts and value them in money terms. Courts often have to find a figure to represent possible financial and other material benefit, however remote, and also immaterial matters of gain and loss, including emotional matters. But, in so far as it is said it is far more satisfactory for reasons of public policy that such damages should be irrecoverable, the submission has to be examined carefully. There is ample authority, in my judgment, showing that the courts have approached damages in this way: see 12 Halsbury's Laws (4th edn) para 1133. In particular I was referred to passages in *Spartan Steel and Alloys Ltd v Martin & Co (Contractors) Ltd* [1972] 3 All ER 557 at 562, [1973] 1 QB 27 at 37 per Lord Denning MR, *McLoughlin v O'Brian* [1982] 2 All ER 298 at 303, 308–309, [1983] AC 410 at 420, 427 per Lord Wilberforce and Lord Edmund-Davies. It is not necessary to quote these passages. They make it clear that considerations of public policy may have to be applied. The question is only whether there are such considerations, and whether they are so powerful that they should be applied in this particular case. Only last year, the Court of Appeal in *McKay v Essex Area Health Authority* [1982] 2 All ER 771, [1982] QB 1166 rejected a claim based on the birth of a child as being contrary to public policy. It was a case akin, to some extent at least, to the present case and I shall refer to it later.

Counsel have discovered the transcripts of two cases very similar to the present case where the question of public policy could have arisen but, as it turned out, did not fall to be decided. The first is *Emeh v Kensington, Chelsea and Fulham Area Health Authority* (1983) Times, 3 January, a decision of Park J. It was a mother's claim for damages for an operation for sterilisation, which failed through negligence. Park J found as a fact that, after about 16½ weeks of pregnancy, the plaintiff deliberately chose to allow the pregnancy to continue because she wanted to bear another child, and she therefore refused an abortion which she would have been quite prepared to have if her intention had been otherwise. This limited the damages to those 16½ weeks or so. There was a claim for the cost of maintaining the child which was countered by a submission that such a claim would be against public policy. After a brief reference to the authorities, Park J said:

> 'It is not necessary for me to express any view on this part of the claim. If it were held not to be contrary to public policy, the amount to which the plaintiff would be entitled can be calculated from the agreed figures without much difficulty.'

That case, accordingly, does not afford the answer.

The second case is *Sciuriaga v Powell* [1980] CA Transcript 597. The claim was for damages in respect of an abortion which failed to remove the fetus owing to the negligence of the defendant doctor. In the result, a perfectly healthy little boy was born to the plaintiff. Damages were awarded under four heads: (1) plaintiff's loss of earnings up to the date of the trial; (2) plaintiff's future loss of earning capacity; (3) impairment of the plaintiff's marriage prospects; and (4) her pain and distress. It is to be observed that the modest sum of £750 was awarded under this last head. The court was not invited to, and did not, consider any question of public policy and there was no claim for the cost of the child's upbringing. However in saying that he had ignored policy considerations, Waller LJ said:

> 'In doing so I must not be taken as assenting to the view that they would be irrelevant in every case ... I quite see that the incidence of pregnancy and the necessity for Caesarian birth would properly form items of damage for the failure of the operation and, indeed, in this case one of the heads of damage covers this, but, once a woman has given birth to a healthy child without harm to her and the fears of the doctors have been shown to be unfounded, I would not regard it as unarguable in another case that thereafter no more damage would arise.'

So, the question at least remains open. In *McKay v Essex Area Health Authority* [1982] 2 All ER 771, [1982] QB 1166 a mother and her child both claimed as plaintiffs because the child had been born with deformities. Her mother had been in contact in early pregnancy with German measles. One of the child's claims for damages was based on the negligence of the doctors in allowing her, in those circumstances, to be born at all. If they had advised properly, her mother would have had an abortion. The Court of Appeal struck out that claim as disclosing no reasonable cause of action; it did so on the grounds of public policy. The court made no adjudication on the mother's claim to the like effect, except to allow it to proceed to trial. Accordingly, although the case demonstrates quite clearly that considerations of public policy do apply to cases of this type, it does not indicate what considerations govern a claim by a mother (as opposed to one by the child itself) for the birth of her child, nor whether those considerations are sufficient to disallow the claim.

Of the policy considerations mentioned in the judgment, some clearly do not apply to the present case, for example, the impossibility which impressed each member of the court (not the difficulty, be it observed, but the impossibility) of comparing life with nothingness or non-existence: illuc unde negant redire quemquam. How could a judge compare his experience of life and set it against his ignorance of death? However, some considerations mentioned in *McKay's* case may be relevant here. (1) The objection that the courts would be open to claims for maintenance by children against doctors who negligently allowed them to be born. (2) The extra burden this would impose on the medical profession and the danger that doctors would be under subconscious pressure to advise abortions for fear of actions for damages. (3) The social implications in the potential disruption of family life and the bitterness it would cause between parent and child. (4) The sanctity of human life which the law must regard as such that failure to prevent it should not be recognised as a cause of action. In other words, the law will not allow an action based on negligence which caused, or at least allowed, a human life to come into being. (5) There should be rejoicing, not dismay, that the surgeon's mistake bestowed the gift of life on the child.

Mrs Udale's claim does not match the claim which the Court of Appeal disallowed in that case. However, the considerations of public policy there put forward are impressive and are relevant to this case. Together with some of the submissions made by counsel for the defendants, they persuade me to the view that on the grounds of public policy the plaintiff's claims in this case, in so far as they are based on negligence which allowed David Udale to come into this world alive, should not be allowed.

The considerations that particularly impress me are the following. (1) It is highly undesirable that any child should learn that a court has publicly declared his life or birth to be a mistake, a disaster even, and that he or she is unwanted or rejected. Such pronouncements would disrupt families and weaken the structure of society. (2) A plaintiff such as Mrs Udale would get little or no damages because her love and care for her child and her joy, ultimately, at his birth would be set off against and might cancel out the inconvenience and financial disadvantages which naturally accompany parenthood. By contrast, a plaintiff who nurtures bitterness in her heart and refuses to let her maternal instincts take over would be entitled to large damages. In short virtue would go unrewarded; unnatural rejection of womanhood and motherhood would be generously compensated. This, in my judgment, cannot be just. (3) Medical men would be under subconscious pressure to encourage abortions in order to avoid claims for medical negligence which would arise if the child were allowed to be born. (4) It has been the assumption of our culture for time immemorial that a child coming into the world, even if, as some say, 'the world is a vale of tears', is a blessing and an occasion for rejoicing.

I am reinforced in the second of these considerations by the fact that, if I had to award damages to Mrs Udale under the disputed heads, I would have to regard the financial disadvantages as offset by her gratitude for the gift of a boy after four girls. Accordingly, in my judgment, the last three heads of damage are irrecoverable. In that event, counsel for the defendants submits that the plaintiff's damages cease at the birth. I do not accept that submission altogether. It seems to me that it is legitimate, without detracting from the above principles of public policy, to have some regard to the disturbance to the family financies which the unexpected pregnancy causes. One may look at the cost of the layette and the sudden necessity of having to find more ample accommodation in assessing the damages for the unwanted pregnancy, without regarding the child as unwanted. One has to bear in mind here that the child has, up until the age of 4 years 2 months, in fact a lived in that house without the extension. It has not of course been built. Accordingly, in my view, it is proper to increase the award of damages with this in mind when awarding general damages for the pain, suffering, inconvenience, anxiety and the like, mentioned at the beginning of this judgment. I do so by awarding the sum of £8,000 for these matters together.

There will be judgment for the plaintiff, accordingly, for £8,000, together with b £1,025·20 for loss of earnings, a total of £9,025·20.

Judgment for the plaintiff accordingly.

Solicitor: *David Picton & Co*, Bedford (for the plaintiff); *T R Dibley* (for the defendants).

c

K Mydeen Esq Barrister.

d

Polish Steam Ship Co v Atlantic Maritime Co and others e

The Garden City

QUEEN'S BENCH DIVISION (ADMIRALTY COURT)
PARKER J
24, 25 JANUARY, 25 FEBRUARY 1983 f

Shipping – Limitation of liability – Limitation fund – Interest – Shipowner paying into court at commencement of limitation action the limitation figure as at date of payment in plus interest thereon from date of collision to date of payment in – Fund invested – Right of shipowner to limit liability to amount of fund in court established in limitation action – Interest accruing on fund – Whether Admiralty Court having discretion to order payment out to defendant of accrued interest g *on fund in addition to fund itself – Merchant Shipping Act 1894, ss 503(1), 504 – Merchant Shipping (Liability of Shipowners and Others) Act 1958, s 1.*

In 1976 the plaintiff shipowners were held partly to blame for a collision which occurred in 1969 between their vessel and the defendant shipowners' vessel. The collision resulted in the defendants' vessel sinking, with the loss of most of the cargo on board. The claims h of the defendant shipowners and cargo owners exceeded the limit of the plaintiffs' liability under s 503(1)[a] of the Merchant Shipping Act 1894, as amended by s 1[b] of the Merchant Shipping (Liability of Shipowners and Others) Act 1958, and consequently on

a Section 503(1), so far as material, provides: 'The owners of a ship . . . shall not, where all or any of j the following occurrences take place without their actual fault or privity; (that is to say,) . . . (*b*) Where any damage or loss is caused to any goods, merchandise, or other things whatsoever on board the ship . . . be liable to damages beyond the following amounts; (that is to say,) . . . (ii) In respect of such loss, damage or infringement as is mentioned in paragraphs (*b*) . . . of this subsection . . . an aggregate amount not exceeding eight pounds for each ton of their ship's tonnage.'

b Section 1, so far as material, is set out at p 538 *a b*, post.

27 April 1978 the plaintiffs commenced a limitation action under s 504[c] of the 1894 Act
a against both the shipowners and the cargo owners to determine the amount of the plaintiffs' liability. On the following day, 28 April, the plaintiffs paid into court £395,341, representing the limitation figure calculated as at that date in accordance with s 503, plus a further sum of £297,559, representing interest on the limitation figure from the date of the collision to 30 April 1978, making the total sum (the limitation fund) paid into court £692,900. At the plaintiffs' request the fund was placed on short-term investment
b account. In March 1982 judgment was given in the limitation action, under which it was held that the plaintiffs were entitled to limit their liability to the defendants to the amount of the limitation fund in court. By November 1982 the interest which had accrued on the limitation fund amounted to £534,904. On 18 November 1982 the Admiralty registrar ordered that the limitation fund be paid out and distributed among the defendants in specified proportions, but he made no order regarding the accrued
c interest, which remained in court earning further interest. The defendants applied to the Admiralty judge for payment out to them of the whole of the accrued interest in the same proportions as in the case of the limitation fund. The plaintiffs submitted that payment of all the accrued interest to the defendants would involve paying them interest on interest, ie interest on that part of the limitation fund representing interest on the limitation figure.

d

Held – It was the intention of s 1(4) of the 1958 Act that, by making a payment in of the full amount of the limitation figure as at the date of payment in, a plaintiff shipowner in a limitation action could discharge his obligation to the defendant in regard to the limitation figure and thus protect himself against both the risk of an increase in the limitation figure occurring by the date of the decree in the action (because of a fall in the
e value of the pound against the gold franc as the measure of liability), and also against the attendant risk of an increase in the interest payable on the limitation figure. Accordingly, the justice of the case as between the plaintiff and the defendant lay in favour of all interest earned on a limitation fund paid into court being treated as part of the fund. Furthermore, when a plaintiff in a limitation action paid into court both principal and interest thereon, he made the interest part of the principal, so that to pay the defendant
f all the accrued interest on a limitation fund paid into court did not involve paying the defendant interest on interest. It followed that the Admiralty Court in exercising its equitable jurisdiction to award interest could, as a matter of discretion, order that all interest which had accrued on a limitation fund paid into court be paid to the defendant as part of the limitation fund. Moreover, such an order would be consistent with the principle that an award included compensation for being kept out of the award.
g Accordingly, as a matter of discretion, the court would order that the defendants were entitled to payment out to them of the accrued interest on the limitation fund (see p 538 *b c j*, p 539 *a* to *c f* to *j* and p 540 *a* to *c* and *g* to p 541 *d*, post).

The Dundee (1827) 2 Hag Adm 137, *The Abadesa* [1968] 2 All ER 726 and *The Mecca* [1968] 2 All ER 731 applied.

Dicta of Lord Denning MR and of Watkins LJ in *Tehno-Impex v Gebr van Weelde*
h *Scheepvaartkantoor BV* [1981] 2 All ER at 678, 689 considered.

Notes

For interest in shipping limitation actions, see 43 Halsbury's Laws (4th edn) paras 1106, 1117, and for cases on the subject, see 42 Digest (Repl) 1064, *8812–8818*.

j

c Section 504, so far as material, provides: 'Where any liability is alleged to have been incurred by the owner of a British or foreign ship in respect of any occurrence in respect of which his liability is limited under section five hundred and three of this Act, and several claims are made or apprehended in respect of that liability, then, the owner may apply in England and Ireland to the High Court . . . and that court may determine the amount of the owner's liability and may distribute that amount rateably among the several claimants . . .'

For the Merchant Shipping Act 1894, ss 503, 504, see 31 Halsbury's Statutes (3rd edn) 328, 331.

For the Merchant Shipping (Liability of Shipowners and others) Act 1958, s 1, see ibid 647.

Cases referred to in judgment

Abadesa, The, Furness-Houlder Argentine Lines Ltd v Steam Tanker Miraflores (owners) [1968] 2 All ER 726, [1968] P 656, [1968] 3 WLR 492.

Dundee, The (1827) 2 Hag Adm 137, 166 ER 194; *previous proceedings* sub nom *Gale v Laurie* (1826) 5 B & C 156, 108 ER 58; *previous proceedings* (1823) 1 Hag Adm 109, 166 ER 39.

Funabashi, The, Sycamore Steamship Co Ltd v Steamship White Mountain (owners) [1972] 2 All ER 181, [1972] 1 WLR 666.

Jefford v Gee [1970] 1 All ER 1202, [1970] 2 QB 130, [1970] 2 WLR 702, CA.

Mecca, The, United Arab Maritime Co v Blue Star Line Ltd [1968] 2 All ER 731, [1968] P 665, [1968] 3 WLR 497.

Northumbria, The (1869) LR 3 A & E 6; *subsequent proceedings* (1869) LR 3 A & E 24.

Tehno-Impex v Gebr van Weelde Scheepvaartkantoor BV [1981] 2 All ER 669, [1981] QB 648, [1981] 2 WLR 821, CA.

Wallersteiner v Moir (No 2) [1975] 1 All ER 849, [1975] QB 373, 508n, [1975] 2 WLR 389, CA.

Cases also cited

Berwickshire, The [1950] 1 All ER 699, [1950] P 204.

BP Exploration Co (Libya) Ltd v Hunt (No 2) [1982] 1 All ER 925, [1979] 1 WLR 783.

Burdick v Garrick (1870) 5 App Cas 233, HL.

Cremer v General Carriers SA [1974] 1 All ER 1, [1974] 1 WLR 341.

Kong Magnus, The [1891] P 223.

La Pintada Compania Navegacion SA v President of India [1983] 1 Lloyd's Rep 37.

Miliangos v George Frank (Textiles) Ltd (No 2) [1976] 3 All ER 599, [1977] QB 489.

Norseman, The [1957] 2 All ER 660, [1957] P 224.

Shamia v Joory [1958] 1 All ER 111, [1958] QB 448.

Theems, The [1938] P 197.

Summons

Following a collision between the vessel Zaglebie Dabrowskie owned by the plaintiffs, Polish Steam Ship Co, and the vessel Garden City owned by the defendant shipowners, Atlantic Maritime Co, in which the Garden City sank and most of her cargo was a total loss, it was held in a collision action that the Zaglebie Dabrowski and the Garden City were respectively 60% and 40% to blame for the collision and that the Garden City sank as a result of the collision. On 27 April 1978 the plaintiffs commenced a limitation action against the defendant shipowners and against the persons, unnamed, claiming to be entitled to damages for the cargo lost on the Garden City, to determine the amount of the plaintiffs' liability in accordance with s 503 of the Merchant Shipping Act 1894, as amended. On 28 April 1978 the plaintiffs paid into court the sum of £692,900·63 comprising the limitation figure calculated in accordance with s 503 of £395,341·40, and interest thereon of £297,559·23 from the date of the collision to 30 April 1978. The amount paid in, ie the limitation fund, was placed on short-term investment account. On 18 November 1982 the Admiralty registrar ordered that the limitation fund of £692,900·63 be paid out of court on 1 December 1982 and be distributed to the solicitors representing the defendant cargo interests, in specified proportions. By a summons in the Admiralty Court dated 24 November 1982 the defendant cargo interests applied to the Admiralty judge, in chambers, for an order that all interest accrued on the limitation fund of £692,900·63 from the date of the payment in to the end of December 1982 should also be paid to the solicitors representing the defendant cargo interests, in the same proportions as the limitation fund was distributed to them. The summons was heard in chambers but judgment was given by Parker J in open court with the consent of the parties. The facts are set out in the judgment.

Geoffrey Brice QC and *Lloyd Lloyd* for the plaintiffs.
Richard Aikens for the defendants.

Cur adv vult

25 February. The following judgment was delivered.

PARKER J. This summons raises for determination a point of considerable importance which has hitherto not received any consideration by the courts. It arises in this way. On 19 March 1969 a collision occurred in the North Sea between the plaintiffs' vessel Zaglebie Dabrowskie and the defendants' vessel Garden City. The Garden City sank and was a total loss. Most of her cargo was also a total loss.

In 1976 it was held, in a collision action in this court, that the Zaglebie Dabrowskie and the Garden City were respectively 60% and 40% to blame. The issue whether the Garden City sank as a result of the collision was at that time left over. In July 1977 that issue was tried and it was held that the Garden City did sink as a result of the collision. The Garden City claims clearly exceeded by a very considerable amount the limitation figure under s 503 of the Merchant Shipping Act 1894, as subsequently amended, and, as a result, the plaintiffs, on 27 April 1978, just over nine years from the date of collision, commenced a limitation action. On the following day they paid into court the sum of £692,900·63 being, as to £395,341·40, the limitation figure correctly determined as at that date under s 503 as amended, and as to the balance of £297,559·23, interest on that sum from the date of collision to 30 April 1978 at 8·25%, being the mean of the interest rates awarded by this court during the period. The amount paid in was, at the request of the plaintiffs, placed on short-term investment account.

On 2 March 1982, thirteen years after the collision and four years after the limitation action was launched, judgment was given in that action. The plaintiffs successfully established their right to limit. That judgment provided, so far as presently material, (1) that the plaintiffs' liability in respect of the specified claims should not exceed £395,341·40 with interest at 8·25% from 19 March 1969 to 30 April 1978, and (2) that the plaintiffs having on 28 April 1978 paid into court the aforesaid sum with the aforesaid interest, all other actions resulting from the casualty should be stayed.

On 18 November 1982 the registrar ordered that the total amount paid into court by the plaintiffs, ie £692,900·63, be paid out of court on 1 December 1982 and distributed in specified proportions to the solicitors representing the defendants in the action. No order was, however, made with regard to accrued interest, and the present summons is for the purpose of determining to whom such interest shall be paid.

On 30 November 1982 the total interest accrued on the sum paid into court by the plaintiffs was £534,904·76, and that sum has since remained in court earning further interest.

For the defendants it is contended by their counsel that all accrued interest should be paid out to the defendants in the same proportions as the amount paid into court either as a matter of entitlement or as a matter of discretion.

Counsel for the plaintiffs contends that the defendants are only entitled to, or as a matter of discretion should only be awarded, that part of the accrued interest which represents (a) simple interest on the limitation figure from date of payment in until date of decree and (b) short-term investment account interest from date of decree to date of payment out on the total of the amount paid in and simple interest on the limitation figure from the date of payment in until date of decree. At the outset of his argument counsel for the plaintiffs contended that the defendants should only receive simple interest on the limitation figure from date of payment in until final payment out, but later he conceded that as from date of decree the defendants were entitled to, or should as a matter of discretion receive, all interest on the total of that to which they were properly entitled as at that date. a

The submission of counsel for the defendants is in accordance with the practice in limitation actions which has prevailed since the time when, after a long period during which payments into court were never made prior to decree, such payments into court became common. When a distribution order is made the amount paid in (assuming it was correctly calculated), together with all interest earned while in court, has, until the present case, been treated as a single fund and distributed amongst the claimants without b
objection from the plaintiffs.

That, in the present case, dispute has arisen is no doubt due to the fact that the delays were so long that about 42% of the amount originally paid in represented interest and that this, by the date of decree some four years later, had itself earned a large amount of interest.

Before considering the submissions made by the respective parties in support of their c
ultimate contentions it is necessary to consider the history of the shipowner's right to limit his liability in certain circumstances. Although two earlier statutes of limited scope (7 Geo 2 c 15 (Responsibility of Shipowners) and 26 Geo 3 c 86 (Merchant Shipping)) had dealt with the matter, it was not until 1813 that the statute, 53 Geo 3 c 159 (Responsibility of Shipowners) afforded a general right to limit liability for damage occurring without the actual fault or privity of the shipowner, the limit of liability for damage occurring by d
one accident being set at the value of the vessel and freight due. That Act, in addition to creating the limit, dealt in a comprehensive manner with the procedure for obtaining the benefit of the limit and the distribution of the amount of the limit. The basic procedure was that the shipowner who wished to limit his liability could file a bill in equity to ascertain the value of the vessel and for distribution of the amount so ascertained rateably amongst claimants. It was, however, specifically provided that, on filing such e
bill, the plaintiff should apply to the court and obtain an order for liberty to pay into court the value of the vessel as stated in an affidavit which had to be filed with the bill. Unless the court for some special reason ordered otherwise the bill would stand dismissed if payment into court was not made in accordance with the order. It was also specifically provided, by s 13, that if money were paid into court—

f

> 'all Interest and Profit made thereof whilst such money shall remain in Court shall be considered as belonging to the Parties in such Suit, who shall appear to be entitled to the Principal Money or Proportions thereof respectively, and shall be divided and distributed accordingly . . .'

Thus the basic system was that it was a condition of the shipowner's right to pursue his limitation action that he should pay into court at the outset his own sworn estimate of g
the limited amount and, having done so, the fund thereby created, together with all interest and profit, would go to the claimants.

The Act also contained provisions for increasing the amount of the payment in should the value be found to be more than the amount estimated and for the giving of security in lieu of payment in, but these provisions did not affect the basic system. The system applied, however, only where several persons had claims. Where there was but one claim h
the shipowner would raise the question of limitation by way of defence in the suit brought by the injured party. This is what happened in *The Dundee* (1827) 2 Hag Adm 137, 166 ER 194, a case in which the court considered a number of objections to an award of £5,947 against the Dundee at the suit of the owners of the Princess Charlotte. The report itself does not reveal the full history of the action, but this may be ascertained from the reports of the earlier proceedings in the same case (see (1823) 1 Hag Adm 109, j
166 ER 39) and of *Gale v Laurie* (1826) 5 B & C 156, 108 ER 58.

The main dispute between the parties was whether the Dundee's liability was limited to £4,921, which was the value of the vessel including her fishing stores, or whether fishing stores should be excluded, in which case the limitation figure would be £2,685. On this issue the Dundee lost and it was decreed that the plaintiffs should be paid the sum of £4,554, of which £350 was in respect of interest to date of decree with further

interest from the date of report until payment. The owners of the Dundee did not pay
a but embarked on protracted proceedings in the Queen's Bench for prohibition, again asserting that their liability was limited to £2,685. When those proceedings ultimately failed the matter again returned to the High Court of Admiralty where the judge referred to the registrar and merchants the question what further interest was due to the Princess Charlotte. They reported that a further £930 was due, this being interest on the whole of the original amount decreed and thus including interest on the £350 interest already
b decreed. The additional £930, together with certain other amounts, brought the total amount to £5,947. A number of objections were taken to the report, of which two were (i) that interest on interest ought not to be allowed, and (ii) that the additions in any event brought the total beyond the limitation figure.

Both objections failed, the first on the ground that once interest was settled or made up it became part of the principal and could and should bear interest, and the second on
c the general ground that it would be an injustice if the limiting owner could retain the amount without paying interest.

I have dealt with this case at some length for it shows that from the very early days the limitation provisions were held not to prevent an award of interest which would take the total amount payable beyond the limitation figure, and secondly because it is direct authority that in the Admiralty Court interest on interest is permissible in certain
d circumstances. The case, however, does not go further, in terms, than to support interest on interest the payment of which has already been decreed.

The 1813 Act remained in force until it was repealed and replaced by the Merchant Shipping Act 1854 and the Merchant Shipping (Repeals) Act 1854. Although, however, the provision as to limitation of liability was re-enacted in substance without change, the procedural provisions whereby payment into court was a condition of the right to pursue
e a limitation action and whereby the sum paid into court, together with all interest, belonged to the claimants were not re-enacted. They disappeared and have not since reappeared.

No reason for this was suggested to me by either side and I have been unable to find any comment on it in any of the textbooks, even those published shortly after the change had been made. Since claimants whose rights were in any event reduced by the principal
f limitation provisions were, by the repeal of the procedural provisions of the 1813 Act, apparently being deprived of two valuable safeguards for the rights with which they were left, I find this somewhat surprising.

The question of interest, which had been touched on in *The Dundee* (1827) 2 Hag Adm 137, 166 ER 194, came squarely before the court in *The Northumbria* (1869) LR 3 A & E 6. In that case it was contended that the owner's liability could not, even with interest,
g exceed the limitation figure, but it was held that interest could and should be awarded on the limitation figure from the date of collision. This was in accordance with the cases both in the Court of Admiralty and the Court of Chancery. In giving judgment Sir Robert Phillimore said (at 13):

> '... there seems no reason why interest should not accrue on the delay to that limited amount, as well as in the case where the amount is unlimited. Indeed the
> h equity of the thing is the other way, for to refuse this interest would be to diminish still further the natural right of the sufferer to full compensation for the injury which he has sustained.'

After some amendments which it is unnecessary to mention, the Merchant Shipping Act 1854 was repealed by the Merchant Shipping Act 1894, s 503 of which, as
j subsequently amended, contains the present principal limitation provision. Although s 504 gave the court in a limitation action a general power to stay other proceedings or require security as it might think just, there was neither requirement nor incentive for the plaintiff to pay into court and no such incentive appeared until the Merchant Shipping (Liability of Shipowners and Others) Act 1958. Section 1(1) of that Act substituted, for the fixed rates per ton in pounds sterling which had hitherto prevailed, tonnage rates expressed as amounts equivalent to a fixed number of gold francs, and

s 1(3) provided for the sterling amounts to be taken as equivalent to such gold francs to be specified from time to time by statutory instrument. Section 1(4) is in the following *a* terms:

> 'Where money has been paid into court (or, in Scotland, consigned in court) in respect of any liability to which a limit is set as aforesaid, the ascertainment of that limit shall not be affected by a subsequent variation of the amounts specified under subsection (3) of this section unless the amount paid or consigned was less than that *b* limit as ascertained in accordance with the order then in force under that subsection.'

On the face of it this subsection appears to afford the limiting shipowner with means to protect himself against a fall in the value of the pound against the gold franc. If he pays in at the rate prevailing at the time of payment in he will be unaffected by subsequent changes.

This effect does not seem to have been appreciated at the time, but in 1968 two cases *c* were decided, as a result of which the already long-standing practice of making no payment into court until after decree changed. From 1958 until 1967 the sterling equivalent of 1,000 gold francs specified for the purposes of s 1 of the 1958 Act had been £23 13s $9\frac{27}{32}$d, but on 22 November 1967 the Merchant Shipping (Limitation of Liability) (Sterling Equivalents) Order 1967, SI 1967/1725, raised the sterling equivalent to £27 12s $9\frac{1}{2}$d. This was as a result of the devaluation of the pound sterling on 18 *d* November 1967.

In *The Abadesa, Furness-Houlder Argentine Lines Ltd v Steam Tanker Miraflores (owners)* [1968] 2 All ER 726, [1968] P 656 the owners of the Abadesa had, in February 1966, commenced a limitation action in respect of a collision which had occurred in 1963. The Admiralty registrar held in February 1968 that the limitation figure was to be calculated by reference to the 1967 order then currently in force and which produced a limitation *e* amount of £333,885 14s 5d. He also awarded interest at 4%. The plaintiffs appealed on the ground that the limitation figure should be calculated by reference to the order in force at the date of collision or at the date of commencement of the action, which would have produced a limitation amount of £286,161 8s 2d. The defendants cross-appealed on the ground that the rate of interest was too low in that 4% was below prevailing commercial rates. Karminski J held that the registrar had rightly determined that the *f* 1967 order applied but that the rate of interest should be increased to $5\frac{1}{2}$%.

In *The Mecca, United Arab Maritime Co v Blue Star Line Ltd* [1968] 2 All ER 731, [1968] P 665 the same point with regard to limitation calculation arose, and again the question of interest rates was canvassed. Brandon J upheld the interest rate of $5\frac{1}{2}$% and followed, but amplified, the decision in the earlier case. He held that when in any case the court comes to ascertain the limit it should apply the equivalents specified either (1) by such order as *g* was in force at the date when the ascertainment was made, or (2) if at an earlier date a payment into court had been made of not less than the limit as ascertained by the order in force at the date of such payment, then by such order (see [1968] 2 All ER 731 at 734, [1968] P 665 at 669). He observed also ([1968] 2 All ER 731 at 735, [1968] P 665 at 670):

> '... it may well be that, as the effect of the Act of 1958 comes to be appreciated, *h* the practice in limitation actions will change and plaintiffs will seek to pay into court as early as possible and certainly before decree. I am told by the registrar that a payment in before decree in a limitation action was in fact made, for the first time in the last thirty years at any rate, in 1967.'

It is clear from these decisions that the limitation figure can, at the option of the plaintiff, be frozen at the date of payment in. The claimants have no say in the matter. *j* The risk of a fall in the value of the pound can be put on them by the plaintiff. It is important to note that changes in the tonnage rates will or may have, in addition to this direct effect on the limitation figure, very considerable consequential effects. This may be simply illustrated.

In the present case, for example, had the limitation figure, as a result of a new order under s 1 of the 1958 Act, risen by the date of judgment to £450,000, the decree, had

there been no payment in, would have been increased not merely by the £55,000-odd
a difference in the principal amount but by nine years' interest on such difference and four years' interest on the increased amount. The plaintiff thus insulates himself against such eventualities. In so doing, of course, he accepts the risk of the limitation figure falling between payment in and the date of judgment.

It appears to me that the intention inherent in the provisions of the 1958 Act was that a plaintiff shipowner who ultimately established his right to limit and who had paid in
b the full amount of the limitation figure at the date of such payment should be treated as having satisfied his obligation so far as the limitation figure was concerned, and that it follows from this that any interest or profit earned on the money in court is no concern of his and should, as a matter of entitlement or discretion, belong to the claimants as it did from 1813 to 1854.

Unfortunately, however, neither the 1958 Act nor the convention on which it was
c based, nor any of the predecessors to the 1958 Act from 1854 onwards, have taken account of the question of interest, which at least since *The Northumbria* (1869) LR 3 A & E 6 has always been awarded in the Admiralty Court on the principal amount.

Nevertheless from the time when, as a result of the decision in *The Mecca* [1968] 2 All ER 731, [1968] P 665, payments in before decree became common, the usual practice with regard to interest in actions in the Admiralty Registry has followed the intention of
d the 1958 Act with regard to the principal, in that (1) when paying in in a limitation action plaintiff shipowners have paid in not merely the principal amount but interest up to date of payment in or even to the end of the month in which payment in is made and arranged for that sum to be transferred to a short-term investment account, (2) the decree when ultimately pronounced has limited the shipowner's liability to the limitation figure plus interest from the date of the casualty to the date of payment in and has not sought
e to add interest in respect of the period between payment in and decree and which would have been awarded had there been no payment in, and (3) all interest on the amount of the payment in has been distributed to the defendants.

As to (1) above, it shows a recognition that the purpose of the payment in is to create a fund sufficient to discharge the plaintiff owner's full liability as at the date of payment in. As to (2), it shows a recognition by the court that this has been done and that the fund
f so created is then held for the benefit of the defendants so that there is no need to provide for interest thereafter. As to (3), it shows a recognition by plaintiffs that the fund is there for the claimants, for otherwise they would, on decree, have applied for payment out to themselves of all interest save such interest as would have been awarded on the principal amount between payment in and judgment.

That this meets the equity of the situation appears, at any rate at first sight, to be clear.
g The plaintiff, by paying in, puts a final limit on his liability. He will never have to pay out more.

If the limitation figure thereafter increases the defendants will be deprived not only of the benefits of the increase itself but also of interest on the increased amount. There appears to be no justification for saying that, having already had his claim to principal limited by statute, he should suffer this further burden merely because to allow him the
h full interest would involve him receiving interest on interest. This particular objection is, in my judgment, disposed of by *The Dundee* (1827) 2 Hag Adm 137, 166 ER 194, in that when the plaintiff pays in both principal and interest he makes the interest part of the principal just as he does when, having made no payment in prior to decree, he pays in principal and interest after decree.

Counsel for the plaintiffs, however, contends that this cannot be right. A plaintiff is
j not obliged to pay in at all as he was under the 1813 Act; if he does pay in there is no need for him to place the amount on deposit or on short-term investment account and no need for him to notify the defendants and thus enable them to have the amount transferred. If he makes no payment in at all the most that could be awarded against him and the most the defendants could get is the principal amount plus simple interest thereon to date of decree. The defendants cannot or should not get more simply because the plaintiff has paid into court and thereby given them complete security.

None of those arguments appear to me to be of great weight. Once the proper payment in has been made the plaintiff never has to pay more. He has, by so doing, discharged his *a* obligation. The defendants may receive more as the result of the payment in than if there had been none, but so they may if the limitation figure has been reduced between payment in and decree. In such a case, moreover, the plaintiff will have paid more, for had he waited he would have paid less by the amount of the reduction in the principal amount and interest on the difference between the two amounts. The plaintiff has his choice. He may pay in or not. If he does so he faces certain advantages and certain *b* disadvantages, but the justice of the case between the plaintiffs and the defendants lies, in my judgment, plainly in favour of all interest earned being treated as part of the limitation fund and distributed accordingly. Can this then be done or, as counsel for the plaintiffs contended, has the court no power to order payment to the defendants of more than simple interest earned on the principal sum between payment in and decree and thereafter all interest on the total of the amount paid in plus such amount of simple *c* interest?

In *The Funabashi, Sycamore Steamship Co Ltd v Steamship White Mountain (owners)* [1972] 2 All ER 181, [1972] 1 WLR 666 it was held that there was no distinction in principle between interest on a limitation fund and interest on damages for personal injuries, that the rate should be based on the principle that the defendant had kept the plaintiff out of his money and had the use of it, but that there might be cases where by reason of special *d* circumstances the court would, as a matter of discretion, adopt a different criterion.

In *Tehno-Impex v Gebr van Weelde Sheepvaart kantoor BV* [1981] 2 All ER 669 at 678, [1981] QB 648 at 666, a case concerning an arbitrator's power to award interest, Lord Denning MR said:

> 'In any case where interest can be awarded, then it is in the discretion of the *e* arbitrator to award it with yearly or half-yearly rests. That is what banks do on overdrafts. It is what we did in *Wallersteiner v Moir (No 2)* [1975] 1 All ER 849 at 855–856, [1975] QB 373 at 388. I know that it is forbidden by the 1934 Act, but arbitrators are not subject to that Act.'

In the same case Watkins LJ said ([1981] 2 All ER 669 at 689, [1981] QB 648 at 682):

> *f* 'The sole point is not whether the Admiralty Court has retained its inherent jurisdiction but whether this jurisdiction extends to the granting of interest on principal already paid and, as damages, in the circumstances of this case of interest on interest. I cannot understand why that question should be answered otherwise than in the affirmative, seeing that it surely is inequitable nowadays anyway to behave as these charterers did. There are no limitations to the extent of the Admiralty jurisdiction that I can see...' *g*

Although the apparently unlimited width of the above two statements may well be open to question it is, in my view, clear that the Admiralty jurisdiction to award interest is an equitable jurisdiction; secondly, that compound interest can be awarded; thirdly, that in general the basis of an award is that the defendant has had the use of the money and the plaintiff has been kept out of it; and, fourthly, that in special circumstances the *h* court can depart from such principle.

In the present circumstances the question is not one of awarding interest but deciding on the destination of interest in fact earned on money paid into court with the clear intention of discharging the plaintiffs' maximum obligation which could have arisen had there been a decree on the date of payment in. Had that occurred and had the money been promptly paid in there can be no doubt, and it is now conceded, that all interest *j* thereafter should be distributable to the defendants. This being so, and bearing in mind that by the payment the plaintiff protects himself against a possible increase in the limitation figure, with the attendant increase in interest which that would entail, it is, in my judgment, both right in equity and consistent with the general principle that all interest thereafter should accrue to the defendants as it would have done from 1813 to 1854. I say it would be in accord with the general principle for, if the defendants do not receive all the interest, the plaintiffs will retain in part the benefit of money of which the defendants have been deprived. It is true that up to the date of payment in, or at any rate until the commencement of the limitation action the defendants will get simple interest only, but when a shipowner commences a limitation action he is necessarily seeking to deprive the defendants of the full principal amount to which they would otherwise be entitled, and also of interest on the difference between such full amount and the limitation amount. He is entitled to do so, but in my judgment a special situation is thereby created which might well, in cases where there was no payment in, justify the court in awarding interest on the same basis as would have occurred had the plaintiff in fact paid in and had the money put on short-term investment account. This would accord with the system originally provided by statute, would be in accord with what the original statute recognised as being required in equity, and would encourage plaintiffs to pay in and secure fully those whose rights have been truncated by statute. Be that as it may, when a payment in has in fact been made all interest should, in my judgment, be distributed amongst the defendants in the same proportions as the original amount paid in and I so order.

In so doing I proceed on the basis that the fate of the interest is a matter of discretion and that various alternatives as to entitlement put forward on either side fail. Since the award of interest in the first place is discretionary it follows, in my view, that the fate of any interest earned on interest paid into court must also be discretionary.

In conclusion I add only that some reliance was placed by counsel for the plaintiffs on the fact that interest earned on a payment into court under RSC Ord 22 is treated as going to the credit of the defendants (see *Jefford v Gee* [1970] 1 All ER 1202 at 1211, [1970] 2 QB 130 at 150) and on the normal practice in actions for debt or damages that interest shall be paid out to the defendants. This position does not, in my judgment, assist him. The two situations are wholly different. In such actions the defendant can take the money out at once, but in a limitation action this is not, or may not be, so. It may be a very long time before all claims on the fund are in and quantified, and thus a very long time before a distribution order can be made.

Application granted. Leave to appeal.

Solicitors: *Elborne Mitchell & Co* (for the plaintiffs); *Holman Fenwick & Willan* (for the defendant shipowners); *Clyde & Co*, Guildford, and *Waltons & Morse* (for the defendant cargo interests).

N P Metcalfe Esq Barrister.

Practice Direction

CHANCERY DIVISION

Practice – Chancery Division – Applications by post or telephone – Applications which may be made by post or telephone – Issue of writ or originating process – Acknowledgment of service – Issue of summons – Agreed orders – Appeals from masters – Adjournment by consent – Legal aid taxation – Documents – Filing – Office copies – Drawing up of orders.

As a result of the establishment of the Chancery registry and the court file it is necessary to bring up to date the directions relating to communications by post and by telephone.

A. APPLICATIONS BY POST

If an acknowledgment of the receipt of papers is required the papers must be accompanied by a list either written on a stamped addressed postcard or else sent with a stamped and addressed open envelope. The court will not accept responsibility for documents alleged to have been sent unless an acknowledgment is produced. If there is any deficiency in the papers lodged they will be returned to the sender.

The following are the applications which may be made by post.

1. *Issue of writ or originating process*

(1) The following documents should be posted in a prepaid envelope properly addressed to:

Chancery Chambers Registry
Royal Courts of Justice
Strand
London WC2A 2LL

(a) An application by letter duly signed by or on behalf of the solicitor requesting the issue of the writ or originating process (hereinafter called 'the writ'). (b) The original and one copy of the writ together with a further copy for service on every defendant to be served. Each copy of the writ must comply with the provisions of RSC Ord 6 and in the case of an originating summons Ord 7. The copy of the writ intended to be stamped with the fee must be signed by or on behalf of the solicitors. The signature to a statement of claim indorsed on the writ is not sufficient for this purpose. (c) A cheque, postal order or money order for the proper fee (which is now £50), crossed and made payable to HM Paymaster General. In the case of a litigant in person, cash, a postal order or a banker's draft must be sent. (d) A stamped addressed envelope for the return of the relevant documents to the solicitors.

(2) An application for the issue of a writ will be treated as having been made at the date and time of the actual receipt and acceptance of the requisite documents at Chancery Chambers (on a day when Chancery Chambers is open), and for this purpose the date and time of dispatch of the requisite documents will be wholly disregarded.

(3) On receiving the requisite documents and proper fee the officer in Chancery Chambers will affix to the application an official stamp showing the date and time of receipt. If it is in order, he will seal the writ and copies for service and return these to the solicitors by post in the stamped addressed envelope provided. If it is not in order, he will not issue the writ but will return all documents by post to the solicitors making the application.

(4) No responsibility will be accepted for non-delivery to the solicitors of any documents sent by post to the court. The use of these facilities is at the risk of the solicitors concerned, and particular care should be taken when any period of limitation may be involved.

(5) This direction does not apply to an originating summons in the expedited form.

2. *Acknowledgment of service*

An acknowledgment of service as provided in RSC Ord 12, r 3 may be sent to Chancery Chambers by post. Particular care should be exercised in completing the form by inserting the action number, inserting the full names of the defendants, ticking the appropriate box and signing the form.

3. *Issue of summons*

The following documents must be lodged.

(1) The proposed summons or notice of appointment to hear the originating summons, or notice under RSC Ord 25, in duplicate, with the hearing date left blank.

(2) Affidavit of service, if the writ was issued on or after 1 October 1982, and there has been no acknowledgment of service. If the writ was issued before 1 October 1982, there must be an acknowledgment of service, certificate of no acknowledgment of service (if obtained prior to 1 October 1982) or an affidavit of service.

(3) Minutes of any proposed order if the case is complex.

(4) Complete set of pleadings up to date, if required.
a (5) The original grant of probate or letters of administration if required.
(6) Any affidavits not already filed, together with any exhibits.
(7) Copy of any writ issued prior to 1 January 1982.
(8) An estimate of the length of appointment, stating whether counsel will attend.
(9) Stamped adddressed envelope for reply.

b 4. *Agreed orders*

(1) Where the terms of an order are agreed by all parties, the party having the carriage of the order may send either the summons with the date of hearing left blank (if the order is to be made in the terms of the summons) or the minutes of order, in each case indorsed with the consent of the solicitors for each of the parties. The consent of a party in person must be signed by that party personally. The master may make technical or
c verbal adjustments to the draft order or, if he considers that there should be a hearing, he will notify the parties accordingly.

(2) In patent actions, agreed minutes of order on a summons for directions, or any other interlocutory order, must be signed by counsel for all parties. If the parties are not agreed, an application must be made by motion to one of the assigned judges. If on a petition for an extension of the term of an unexpired patent under s 23 of the Patents
d Act 1949 the petitioner wishes to apply for the dismissal of his petition his summons must be indorsed with an undertaking by the petitioner not to present a further petition on that patent.

(3) In legal aid cases, copies of the civil aid certificate should be lodged if the originals were filed at the Central Office prior to 1 October 1982.

e 5. *Appeals from masters*

(1) The following documents must be lodged. (a) Two copies of the notice of appeal in the form PF 114, containing the following information: (i) the name of the master against whose decision the appeal is brought; (ii) the terms of the order appealed against and the date of the order; (iii) the relief sought on the appeal; (iv) the name and address of the party issuing the notice of appeal, and the name and address of each party to whom
f the notice of appeal is addressed, together with their respective telephone numbers and references; and (v) if the appeal is out of time, a request to the judge to extend the time. (b) A cheque, postal order or money order, crossed and made payable to HM Paymaster General for the fee of £5. In the case of a litigant in person, cash, a postal order or banker's draft must be sent.

(2) An appeal will be treated as having been made at the date and time of the actual
g receipt of the requisite documents at Chancery Chambers. No acknowledgment will be sent unless this is requested and a stamped addressed envelope is sent for this purpose.

6. *Adjournment by consent*

Where all parties require the adjournment of the hearing of a summons, a letter of
h consent signed by all parties is required. If the master agrees, the summons will be taken out of the list. Such an application should be made as soon as possible so that the appointment vacated can be used for another hearing.

7. *Legal aid taxation*

Where an assisted person's civil aid certificate has been discharged or revoked and an
j order for taxation is required, no summons is required but an application may be made ex parte to the master or by letter.

8. *Filing documents by post*

The following documents may be filed by sending them by prepaid post to Chancery Chambers.

(1) Affidavits. Affidavits for use at a hearing must be filed either personally or by post at least two days before the hearing. a

(2) Civil aid certificates.

(3) Notices of change of solicitors.

9. *Office copies*

A party wishing to obtain an office copy of an affidavit, order or other filed document may apply by post. The registry will reply by post or telephone, indicating the fee b required, and on receipt of the fee will send the office copy to the party by post.

10. *Drawing up of orders*

If a solicitor has been given leave to draw up an interlocutory order himself, two engrossments of the order proposed may be sent to:

Drafting Section c
Chancery Chambers
Royal Courts of Justice
Strand
London WC2A 2LL

d

B. APPLICATIONS BY TELEPHONE

1. The following applications may be made by telephone.

(1) To restore a summons which has been adjourned generally.

(2) To obtain the file for an ex parte application.

(3) To obtain information about the issue of process and masters' appointments.

e

2. Telephone calls should preferably be limited to the periods 1000 hrs to 1100 hrs and 1600 hrs to 1630 hrs. The telephone number for the Chancery Registry is 01-405 7641, ext 3148 for masters' appointments; for the issue of originating process the extension number is 3642. The action number must always be quoted.

The following Practice Directions are revoked:

Practice Direction of 28 November 1969 relating to the avoidance of delay in interlocutory proceedings ([1970] 1 All ER 11, [1970] 1 WLR 95) f

Practice Direction of 16 March 1971 relating to lodgment of copies of legal aid certificates in chambers ([1971] 1 All ER 1109, [1971] 1 WLR 534)

Practice Direction of 25 October 1973 relating summonses for directions in patent actions ([1974] 1 All ER 40, [1973] 1 WLR 1425, para 2)

Practice Direction of 18 July 1975 relating to advanced hearing of masters' summonses ([1975] 2 All ER 1136, [1975] 1 WLR 1203) g

Practice Direction of 25 March 1977 relating to communications by post or telephone ([1977] 2 All ER 173, [1977] 1 WLR 421)

By direction of the Vice-Chancellor.

EDMUND HEWARD
Chief Master.

24 May 1983

R v Edmonton Licensing Justices, ex parte Baker and another

QUEEN'S BENCH DIVISION (CROWN OFFICE LIST)
WOOLF J
18 NOVEMBER 1982

Licensing – Licence – Grant – Off-licence – Grant subject to undertaking – Undertaking contrasted with condition – Whether justices entitled to grant off-licence subject to undertaking from applicant how he will operate licence – Whether applicant bound to observe undertaking if granted licence – Whether departure from undertaking relevant on objection to renewal of licence – Licensing Act 1964, s 3.

Since a justices' off-licence under s 3[a] of the Licensing Act 1964 has to be an unconditional licence, i e a licence which permits the holder to do all that that type of licence is intended by Parliament to allow, it follows that a legally enforceable undertaking cannot be imposed on an applicant as a condition for the grant of such a licence. However, it is not improper for the justices to ask the applicant for an assurance how he intends to operate the licence and to take that assurance into account in deciding whether to grant or to refuse the licence, so long as the justices bear in mind that the assurance will not be enforceable and there will be nothing to prevent the applicant from departing from the assurance once he has got the licence, although such a departure may be relevant on an objection to the subsequent renewal of the licence (see p 547 *c e* to *g*, p 548 *h* to p 549 *a* and p 550 *a* to *d*, post).

Dictum of Lord Parker CJ in *R v Leicester Licensing Justices, ex p Bisson* [1968] 2 All ER at 353–354 applied.

R v Beesly, ex p Hodson [1912] 3 KB 583 explained.

Notes

For the form of new justices' licences, for exacting undertakings from holders of licences and for the attachment of conditions to licences, see 26 Halsbury's Laws (4th edn) paras 63–66, and for cases on the subject, see 30 Digest (Reissue) 38–40, *281–300*.

For the Licensing Act 1964, s 3, see 17 Halsbury's Statutes (3rd edn) 1062.

Cases referred to in judgment

Oldham Justices v Gee (1902) 86 LT 389, DC.
R v Beesly, ex p Hodson [1912] 3 KB 583, DC.
R v Ipswich County Borough Licensing Justices, ex p Edmondson (25 February 1969, unreported), DC.
R v Leicester Licensing Justices, ex p Bisson [1968] 2 All ER 351, [1968] 1 WLR 729, DC.

Application for judicial review

Lawrence Baker and Amir Kapadia applied, with the leave of McCullough J granted on 3 September 1982, for (i) an order of certiorari to quash as being void, unfair or unworkable, or alternatively in excess of jurisdiction, undertakings not to sell intoxicating liquor other than to persons holding a justices' licence given by the applicants on their being granted a new justices' licence authorising them to sell intoxicating liquor of all descriptions for consumption off the premises at unit 1, Arena Estate, Green Lanes, Haringey, London N4 by the licensing justices of the Edmonton petty sessional division sitting at the Court House, Lordship Lane, Tottenham, London N17 on 26 March 1982, or (ii) alternatively, a declaration that the undertakings were void. The facts are set out in the judgment.

Derrick Pears for the applicants.
The justices did not appear.

---

a Section 3, so far as material, is set out at p 547 *a*, post

WOOLF J. This application arises out of the grant by the licensing justices of the petty sessional division of Edmonton of an off-licence to the applicants, subject to undertakings. *a* It raises an issue of concern to those who deal with licensing matters as to the power of licensing justices to require the giving of undertakings as a term for the grant of an off-licence.

The facts giving rise to the application are shortly as follows. The matter came before the licensing committee for the Edmonton petty sessional division on 16 June 1982. In the normal way, the applicants gave evidence and explained to the justices that they *b* carried on a wholesale warehouse business of a cash and carry nature, using a company known as Lam Cash and Carry Ltd. Their business consisted of selling, on a wholesale basis, to retailers a large category of goods and intoxicating liquor. Up until the time of the grant of the present licence, so far as sales of intoxicating liquor were concerned, this was limited to sales permitted by their wholesale dealers' licence, as described by the Alcoholic Liquor Duties Act 1979. That licence, which permitted them to sell spirits or *c* wine in quantities of not less than 9 litres or one case and beer in not less than 21 litres or two cases, was issued by Her Majesty's Customs and Excise.

What the applicants were seeking was a licence which would enable them to supply alcoholic liquor in smaller quantities, not to ordinary members of the public, but to small retailers who would then sell the liquor which they purchased in the course of their small retail businesses. *d*

The justices, through the chairman of the committee, put an affidavit before the court which explains that they were concerned that if they granted the licence which was being sought what would happen would be that instead of sales of smaller quantities than permitted by the licences issued by Her Majesty's Customs and Excise being purchased for resale they would be purchased for personal use. They felt that there was a danger that if they granted a licence which was unfettered it would result in a use of the *e* licence different from that applied for.

They took the advice of their clerk and he drew their attention to the relevant authorities which are in a state of some confusion and to which I shall refer. But, having considered those authorities, the justices determined that it was a case in which they should seek undertakings before coming to a decision. The applicants were informed that the justices wanted to know whether or not the applicants were prepared to give an *f* undertaking that they would not sell alcohol under the licence otherwise than to the holder of a justices' licence. The applicants considered the matter with their counsel. Although they found it by no means an easy question to answer, ultimately they decided to give the undertaking and the licence was accordingly granted. The licence, which was contained in a printed document, had provision for conditions, but the word 'conditions' has been crossed out, leaving the word 'undertakings'. Under the undertakings, there are *g* the words 'not to sell alcohol otherwise than to the holder of a justices' licence'.

Having been granted that licence, the applicants were concerned whether it would prove to be practical because of the undertaking and they decided to consider the question of an appeal and ask for an extension of time to work out whether or not an appeal would be necessary. In fact they found the licence to be impractical, and the matter was looked into further and the conclusion was reached that the appropriate procedure was not to *h* appeal but to apply to the court for judicial review on the basis that the justices had exceeded their power in requiring an undertaking as a condition for the granting of the licence.

Whether or not it would be possible to appeal has not been argued before me. In order to be able to appeal, it would be necessary for the applicants to show that they were persons aggrieved. I express no view whether they would have such right of appeal, *j* because, as I have said, the matter has not been argued before me. What has been argued before me is that, on the basis of the authorities, the magistrates clearly exceeded their jurisdiction. The problem is referred to in the introduction to *Paterson's Licensing Acts 1982* (90th edn) pp 37 ff.

Before going into what is said by the authors of that well-known book in this field, it is necessary just to refer briefly to the relevant lègislation, which is contained, first of all, in s 3 of the Licensing Act 1964, which provides:

> '(1) Licensing justices may grant a justices' licence to any such person, not disqualified under this or any other Act for holding a justices' licence, as they think fit and proper . . .'

That power is in wide terms and it gives the justices a considerable discretion. Normally, they will take into account, in exercising their discretion in relation to the fitness and propriety of the person concerned, the nature of the premises and whether or not there is a need for the licence in the district where it is being sought. The section applies both to off-licences and to on-licences.

Section 4 of the 1964 Act expressly provides, in the case of on-licences, a power to impose conditions. There is no similar express power in the case of off-licences. In the absence of any such express power, the view is taken, obviously rightly, that in the case of off-licences there is no power to impose conditions as to the grant of off-licences. There is no express power to require undertakings, nor is there any express prohibition on the taking of undertakings in relation to off-licences. However, my attention has been properly drawn to s 12(5) of the 1964 Act, which refers to undertakings. It says:

> 'Where an application is made for the renewal of an old on-licence and the licensing justices ask the applicant to give an undertaking, they shall adjourn the hearing of the application and cause notice of the undertaking for which they ask to be served on the registered owner of the premises and shall give him an opportunity of being heard.'

That subsection presupposes the power to extract an undertaking. As there is no express reference to the power to require such an undertaking, it follows that that is some support for the implication that there is an inherent power in licensing justices to require an undertaking. However, quite apart from the authorities, I would not myself drawn any implication as to the power to require undertakings (when I say 'undertakings', I mean legally binding undertakings) from that subsection in the case of off-licences because, if there is no power to impose conditions, it seems to me that there could be no room for a legal power to require undertakings; because what you are really saying if you grant a licence on an undertaking is that you will grant the licence on condition that the licence holder obeys the undertaking, and it really is no different from a licence subject to conditions, for which Parliament has provided no provision in the case of off-licences.

I now go back to the reference in *Paterson*. Summarising what was said there, it would appear that in fact the practice had existed prior to 1968, up and down the country, of justices in certain cases granting off-licences on undertakings being given to use those off-licences in a limited manner. In particular this applied in relation to chemists' licences, where the chemist might wish to sell medicated wines. On the chemist's undertaking to confine his sales to medicated wines, he would be given a licence which permitted off-sales.

Some support for that practice was said to exist from two cases to which I have referred. The first is *Oldham Justices v Gee* (1902) 86 LT 389. Having looked at that case, I need say no more as I regard it as being of no help on this subject at all. The other case which has provided some assistance is referred to in a passage in *Paterson*. It was also referred to by the justices in their affidavit. It is *R v Beesly, ex p Hodson* [1912] 3 KB 583.

That case, according to the headnote, was dealing with an application for an off-licence. The headnote says:

> 'On an application for a new off-licence justices at a general annual licensing meeting have no power to grant a licence subject to conditions; but they may ascertain from the applicant whether he consents to restrictions, being reasonable and proper restrictions, upon the user of the proposed licence, and they may grant

or refuse the licence unconditionally according as he consents or refuses to submit to the restrictions.' *a*

The headnote really over-simplifies the matter which was before the court. What had happened in that case was that in fact no proper decision had been made at all by the justices and, in the course of his judgment, Lord Alverstone CJ said that there was some doubt about whether the licence had actually been granted at all. He then said (at 586):

> 'Either the justices made a conditional grant of the licence, which they had no *b* power to do, or they have given no decision at all. In either case there has not been a hearing and determination according to law. Their proper course would have been to ascertain from the applicant whether he was ready and willing to comply with such conditions as they thought right to impose, and there and then unconditionally to refuse the licence if he declined to accept, or grant it if he agreed to accept, those terms. *c* In the present case the licence was opposed and the opposing parties are entitled to have the case decided according to law. They may persist in their opposition and contend that the licence ought to be refused even though the applicant is prepared to comply with the conditions offered by the justices. It was contended that a conditional grant was equivalent to a refusal if the conditions were not agreed to, but to accede to that argument would be to countenance the granting of conditional off-licences, *d* which I am not prepared to do. At the same time I by no means say that justices are not entitled to ascertain what restrictions an applicant is willing to submit to, and in granting or refusing an off-licence to take into consideration the hours at which it is proposed to keep the house open. But the licence must be either granted or refused simpliciter by the justices, and as this has not been done the rule must be made absolute for a mandamus.' *e*

Channell J said that he thought, on the facts, there was no concluded hearing and he went on to say (at 586–587):

> 'The justices merely intimated what their views would be in either of two events, namely, that if the applicant gave an undertaking they would grant the licence and that if the applicant did not give the undertaking they would refuse the licence . . . *f* If that is in substance what has happened, there has been no concluded hearing. If on the other hand the licence has been granted only on conditions, that is not a grant according to law. In either view the rule for a mandamus must be made absolute. I agree that justices may ask for an undertaking upon a relevant matter for the purpose of considering whether they will grant or refuse the licence, but not for the purpose of attaching a condition to the licence. *g* It would have been good ground for refusing this licence that it was only required during a portion of the day and that a full day licence was not necessary for the want of the neighbourhood. The hours at which the house is to be open is certainly therefore a relevant matter on which the justices might reasonably demand an undertaking. But such an undertaking would not be legally a part of the licence so as to be punishable if it was broken. There is no power to annex a condition or undertaking to an off-licence.' *h*

Avory J agreed, but with some hesitation (at 587).

Properly understood, what the Divisional Court in that case said, it seems to me, was that there is no power to impose conditions on this type of licence, nor is there power to impose a legally enforceably undertaking. However, while it would not be legally enforceable, there would be nothing wrong in justices asking for an assurance from the *j* applicant for the licence and taking that assurance into account in considering whether or not to grant the licence, recognising, in so doing, that the assurance would only be a statement of intention, that it would not be legally binding and that, if the person concerned did not observe the assurance, it would not affect his existing licence but could give rise to a situation where it might thereafter prove of relevance on an objection to the renewal of the off-licence, because it is only on such an objection that the justices would have the power to refuse the renewal.

The matter next came before the court in *R v Leicester Licensing Justices, ex p Bisson* [1968] 2 All ER 351, [1968] 1 WLR 729. That case was concerned with the situation brought about by the Finance Act 1967. Prior to that Act coming into force, there had been a greater number of kinds of licences which it was possible to obtain. Subsequent to that Act, there were only two types of off-licences which could be obtained: either a licence for liquor of all descriptions or a licence for beer, cider and wine only. Problems arose on renewal of licences which had previously been restricted to a more limited degree than was possible under the 1967 Act.

In that case, it was held that—

> 'the proper course on the application for the renewal was to grant such form of licence authorised by the Finance Act 1967 as was the nearest to the previously existing licence, viz., the form of off-licence for beer, cider and wine, which form was to be regarded as "similar" for the purposes of s. 3(3)(*a*) of the Licensing Act 1964 to the previously existing off-licence . . .'

(See [1968] 2 All ER 351.)

In the course of his judgment Lord Parker CJ said ([1968] 2 All ER 351 at 353–354, [1968] 1 WLR 729 at 732):

> 'Despite the fact that the justices went into this with such care, I have come to the conclusion that what they did here was really the one thing which they had no power to do; and indeed counsel for the respondents, appearing in this court, has not sought to uphold that decision. I say it was the one thing they could not do because by reason of the amendment, the licence granted has to be not only in a form prescribed by the Secretary of State, but also has to be either for intoxicating liquor of all descriptions, or for beer, cider and wine only. It appears that this amendment has given rise to considerable trouble all over the country before licensing justices when renewals of the old licences come up. We have been told that some justices grant a beer, cider and wine only licence in every case, even when the existing licence is limited, say, to beer or to wine; other justices, we are told, attempt to get over the difficulty by exacting undertakings, for instance that if the original licence was for beer only, the applicant for renewal would get the full licence for beer, cider and wine if he undertook not to sell cider and wine; and others have taken the view that it is impossible to deal with these licences by way of renewal and that the proper course is for the existing licensee to apply for a new licence, in which case if the licensing justices decide to grant it, it will be in the form prescribed under the amendment, of beer, cider and wine only. Limiting the possibilities here, it seems to me that any question of exacting an undertaking would be utterly wrong; if Parliament say that the form of the licence is to be for beer, cider and wine only, it would be doing exactly what the Act of 1964 says cannot be done, for the justices to exact undertakings limiting the sale to beer only.'

The other members of the court agreed with that judgment.

Strictly speaking, what Lord Parker CJ said in that case was obiter. It was, however, obviously a matter which was expressed to give guidance to justices generally in the difficulty which they were facing. It was also obviously very carefully considered by the court and is entitled to the greatest of respect. *R v Beesly, ex p Hodson*, to which I have previously referred, decided in 1912, was not however drawn to the attention of the court.

The matter next came before the court in an unreported case, which was also before Lord Parker CJ, this time sitting with Blain and Donaldson JJ. That was *R v Ipswich County Borough Licensing Justices, ex p Edmondson* (25 February 1969). I have been provided with a transcript of the judgment in that case, and it refers to *Bisson*'s case; in particular, it sets out again the reference to undertakings and reiterates the passage which I have already read. *a*

Having regard to the authorities to which I have already referred, it seems to me that the position is this. It is not possible on the grant of off-licences to impose a legally enforceable undertaking as a condition for the grant of that off-licence, but the remarks made by Channell J in *Beesly's* case, in my view, are not inconsistent with what Lord Parker CJ was saying in the two later cases. It seems to me that what Lord Parker CJ was referring to was again legally enforceable undertakings. I do not regard what he said in *b* the two later authorities as being inconsistent with what I said earlier about the propriety of the justices asking an applicant for an assurance how he intends to operate his licence and to take into account that assurance in deciding whether or not to grant the licence, so long as the justices bear in mind that that assurance is not enforceable and that there will be nothing, so far as the law is concerned, to prevent the applicant departing from his assurance once he has got the licence. The licence which he gets, if it be an off-licence *c* under s 3 of the 1964 Act, has to be an unconditional licence, that is to say a licence which permits him to do all that that type of licence is intended by Parliament to allow. Once he has that licence, so far as licensing legislation is concerned, he is not restricted from performing any sales permitted by that licence. Nor can he be restricted by any undertaking extracted by the court. However, if, as here, the court requires an undertaking and the licence is clearly given conditionally on that undertaking, then the *d* question arises whether such a licence has any validity at all.

Although I have not been referred to the authorities on this point, one can envisage a situation similar to that where a planning permission is granted subject to conditions and the question arises whether that planning permission which is granted subject to an invalid condition falls to the ground entirely. It is, however, not necessary for the purposes of my decision in this case to go into such rarified matters of law, because the *e* jurisdiction which I am exercising is a discretionary jurisdiction and it seems to me that it would be wrong in this case, even if it were possible for me to do so as a matter of law, to grant certiorari to quash the undertakings and to leave the licence intact.

The situation is that we do not know, and the justices' evidence makes this point clear, whether or not the licence in fact would have been granted if the undertaking had not been offered. It would be wrong, in my view, for the court in its discretion to allow the *f* applicants to keep the licence but to do away with the undertakings.

I drew this problem to the attention of counsel. He took instructions on the matter and, on those instructions, indicated that, if the alternative was relief or no relief as a matter of discretion, his clients would prefer no licence rather than a licence which was still left with those undertakings, for what they are worth, attached to it.

Having regard to the way the matter has been put to me by counsel on behalf of the *g* applicants, it seems to me that the proper course in this case is to take the view that the justices clearly wrongly exercised their powers in granting the licence subject to an undertaking, that in exercising their discretion whether or not to grant such a licence they took into account an irrelevant consideration, namely that they were attaching to the licence a legally binding undertaking. Having regard to that matter, the proper course in this case is to quash the licence and the matter will have to go back before the *h* justices so that they can reconsider the matter according to the law. They will, I am sure, consider the matter fairly and impartially, untrammelled by what has happened quite inadvertently in relation to the undertakings.

Having heard counsel for the applicants, who appeared on their behalf before the justices, I am quite satisfied that there was certainly no intention on these applicants' parts to, so to speak, seek to obtain advantage by giving an undertaking. They gave the *j* undertaking bona fide, not realising the complications that would result from giving that undertaking. They have in fact made this application bona fide, as indicated by the fact that they would prefer to have no licence at all rather than a licence subject to this unlawful undertaking.

I should also refer to the fact that there was an application for an alternative relief by

way of declaration. That alternative relief would not assist the applicants beyond what I
a have already said, because the relief by way of declaration is also discretionary and, in the circumstances, I would not have been prepared to grant the declaration limited to the undertakings alone.

Accordingly, the application succeeds and I make an order of certiorari as indicated.

Order of certiorari granted to quash licence.

b Solicitors: *Bernard Elliston Sandler & Co*, Willesden (for the applicants).

Sophie Craven Barrister.

c

R v Windsor Licensing Justices, ex parte Hodes

COURT OF APPEAL, CIVIL DIVISION

WALLER, DUNN AND SLADE LJJ

d 7, 23 MARCH 1983

Licensing – Licence – Renewal – Off-licence – Original licence for sale of intoxicating liquor on self-service basis in multiple store – Subsequent change of policy by licensing justices – Justices deciding as matter of policy to renew licences for multiple stores only if store agreeing to sell liquor in supervised area with separate check-out – Notification sent to licensee – Store not complying
e *with policy – Justices objecting to renewal of licence – No other objections to renewal – No reason for justices' objection given on oath – Application for renewal refused without licensee having opportunity of dealing with justices' objection – Whether justices entitled to refuse to renew licence – Licensing Act 1964, s 7(4).*

Licensing – Licence – Renewal – Off-licence – Application for renewal – Guidelines on the
f *approach which justices should adopt.*

In 1975 a justices' off-licence, under the Licensing Act 1964, was granted in respect of premises permitting the display and sale on a self-service basis of intoxicating liquor in the food hall of a multiple store. The licence was renewed each year without any objection and was transferred to the applicant, the store's manager, in 1979. It was
g renewed in 1980 and 1981. In 1979 the justices' clerk wrote a letter to the store telling them that the justices had decided, as a matter of policy, that in future they would grant off-licences to multiple stores only if they operated a separate, fully supervised area for the sale of intoxicating liquor with its own check-out, ie as a shop within a shop. The clerk asked the store to confirm that they were prepared to comply with those requirements and that they would submit plans showing the alterations which they
h intended to make to the premises. In 1981 the clerk sent a further letter detailing what the justices expected to be done. The store informed the clerk that they were not prepared to make the changes required by the justices. When the applicant applied to the justices in 1982 for the further renewal of the licence, he was informed that there was no objection to the renewal other than that of the justices. At the outset of the hearing of the application he reminded the justices that on the renewal of an off-licence they had no
j power under the 1964 Act to impose conditions, either directly or by way of an undertaking. The justices indicated to him that they were not prepared to renew the licence. Then, after the applicant had drawn their attention to s 7(4)[a] of the 1964 Act, which required evidence given on an application for the renewal of a licence to be given

a Section 7(4) is set out at p 559 *a b*, post

on oath, their clerk formally stated on oath that the justices objected to the renewal of the licence, but gave no reasons for their objection. The applicant submitted that, as theirs was the only objection and as there was no evidence in support of it, the justices should renew the licence. The justices refused to do so. The applicant sought a declaration that the justices were wrong in refusing to renew the off-licence, an order of certiorari to bring up and quash their decision and an order of mandamus directing them to hear and properly determine the application for renewal. The application was dismissed on the ground that, inter alia, the statement of objection by the justices' clerk, together with the two letters which he had sent to the store, was sufficient evidence of the grounds of the justices' objection for the purpose of s 7(4) and that the justices were accordingly entitled to refuse to renew the licence. The applicant appealed to the Court of Appeal.

Held – The appeal would be allowed and the applicant granted the relief sought, for the following reasons—

(1) Even if the bare statement on oath by the clerk to the effect that the justices objected to the renewal of the licence constituted an implied reference to the earlier correspondence, that correspondence contained nothing which could be described as a ground of objection but merely stated that the justices were adopting a 'shop within a shop' policy, which in itself was not a valid objection for the purposes of the 1964 Act. Natural justice and s 7(4) of the 1964 Act required that evidence should be given on oath of the reason for the objection so that the applicant could have an opportunity to test, by cross-examination, both its relevance (if any) to the premises which were the subject matter of the application and to adduce evidence of his own in opposition (see p 559 *c* to *h*, p 561 *c*, p 562 *f g* and p 563 *a* and *e*, post).

(2) In any event, the justices were required to exercise their discretion in every case that came before them and could not properly determine an application for the renewal of a licence simply by reference to a preordained policy relating to applications of a particular class. On the evidence it was clear that the justices had not given the applicant's application for renewal of the off-licence the individual consideration on its merits to which it was entitled (see p 557 *d*, p 558 *e f*, p 559 *g*, p 561 *c* and p 562 *j* to p 563 *a* and *e*, post; *Sharpe v Wakefield* [1886–90] All ER Rep 651, *R v County Licensing (Stage Plays) Committee of Flint CC, ex p Barrett* [1957] 1 All ER 112 and *R v Torbay Licensing Justices, ex p White* [1980] 2 All ER 25 considered.

Guidelines on the matters which licensing justices might take into account when considering whether they should renew an off-licence, and observations on the practice of applicants for off-licences giving undertakings to licensing justices concerning the manner in which they will use such a licence (see p 560 *a* to *c* and *g* to *j*, p 561 *c*, p 562 *h j* and p 563 *b* to *e*, post); *R v Edmonton Licensing Justices, ex p Baker* [1983] 2 All ER 545 considered.

Notes

For renewal of licences for the sale of intoxicating liquor, see 26 Halsbury's Laws (4th edn) paras 85–103, and for cases on the subject, see 30 Digest (Reissue) 41, *301–309*.

For the Licensing Act 1964, s 7, see 17 Halsbury's Statutes (3rd edn) 1067.

Cases referred to in judgments

R v Beesly, ex p Hodson [1912] 3 KB 583, DC.
R v County Licensing (Stage Plays) Committee of Flint CC, ex p Barrett [1957] 1 All ER 112, [1957] 1 QB 350, [1957] 2 WLR 90, CA.
R v Edmonton Licensing Justices, ex p Baker [1983] 2 All ER 545.
R v Leicester Licensing Justices, ex p Bisson [1968] 2 All ER 351, [1968] 1 WLR 729, DC.
R v Torbay Licensing Justices, ex p White [1980] 2 All ER 25, DC.
Sharp v Wakefield [1891] AC 173, [1886–90] All ER Rep 651, HL.

Cases also cited

R v Corfield (1922) 128 LT 305, [1922] All ER Rep 376, DC.

R v Dodds [1905] 2 KB 40, [1904–7] All ER Rep 658, CA.

R v Godalming Licensing Committee, ex p Knight [1955] 2 All ER 328, [1955] 1 WLR 600, DC.

R v Ipswich County Borough Licensing Justices, ex p Edmondson (25 February 1969, unreported).

Appeal

Gerald Hodes (the applicant) appealed against an order of Webster J, hearing the Crown Office list, on 19 November 1982, whereby he dismissed an application by the applicant for judicial review by way of (i) a declaration that the respondents, the Windsor Licensing Justices, were wrong in refusing, on 8 March 1982, to renew the justices' off-licence in respect of the premises known as Marks & Spencer plc and situated at 130 Peascod Street, Windsor, Berkshire, (ii) an order of certiorari to bring up and quash the respondents' decision and (iii) an order of mandamus directing the respondents to hear and properly determine the applicant's application for the renewal of the justices' off-licence. The facts are set out in the judgment of Slade LJ.

John Hugill QC and *Jarlath Finney* for the applicant.
Andrew Rose for the respondents.

Cur adv vult

23 March. The following judgments were delivered.

SLADE LJ (giving the first judgment at the invitation of Waller LJ). This is an appeal by Mr Gerald Hodes from a decision of Webster J, hearing the Crown Office list, on 19 November 1982 whereby he refused an application for judicial review arising out of a decision of the licencing justices for the licensing district of Windsor given on 8 March 1982. The applicant is the manager of a store of Marks & Spencer plc at 130 Peascod Street, Windsor ('the premises'). By their decision the justices had refused to renew a justices' off-licence in respect of this store.

A justices' off-licence was first granted in respect of the premises by the Windsor licensing justices in 1975. The application was made and the licence was granted on the basis that the display and sale of intoxicating liquors was to be by self-service methods together with and in the same way as other goods in the food hall in this store. Since 1975 the off-licence had been renewed each year without any objection or opposition. It was transferred to the applicant on 14 May 1979 and subsequently renewed in 1980 and 1981.

On 12 June 1979 the clerk to the licensing justices wrote a letter addressed to Marks & Spencer which referred to the adoption by the justices of a new policy, described in the letter as a 'shop within a shop' policy. The letter read:

> 'My Divisional Licensing Committee has been considering for some time the question of the granting of Off-Licences to stores selling other merchandise as well. On the 6th June they met to discuss the matter again and unanimously decided that in future they would, as matter of policy, grant off-licenses only to premises which were specifically designed as off-licence shops or to multiple shops only if those stores operated a separate controlled area for the sale of intoxicating liquor. This policy is commonly referred to as a "shop within a shop" policy, and has not previously been the policy of the Windsor Divisional Licensing Committee. The Committee appreciate that some stores in Windsor are already operating with an Off-Licence on an open uncontrolled self-service basis, and the Committee expects these stores to comply with their new policy by February, 1981. Those premises are being notified separately. Your store is, of course, one of those affected by this change of policy. I would be grateful if you would confirm that you are prepared to comply with my Committee's requirements and ultimately submit plans showing the alterations you intend to make.'

On 7 September 1981 the clerk to the licensing justices wrote a letter addressed to 'All holders of Off-Licenses'. The letter said that the 'shop within a shop' policy applied specifically to 'shops or stores whose main function is to sell other goods and who wish, in addition, to sell liquor'. It continued:

> 'My Committee feel that you may appreciate having some guidance as to what they expect in Off-Licences and, briefly speaking, they expect you to operate a "shop within a shop" in all cases where any self-service of goods exists. Liquor must not be accessible to any customers in the shop unless the area, being a self-service area, is fully supervised and separate from the shop and has its own check out. If you have any doubts perhaps you would bear in mind that you can attend the Brewster Sessions next February—in fact if your premises are considered not suitable you will be invited to attend—and you can raise any points at that time. This policy applies to all intoxicating liquors for which a Justices' Licence is required.'

Marks & Spencer decided that they did not wish to make the changes in the operation of the food hall at the premises which would have been required by the demands contained in these letters. On 26 January 1982 their solicitors wrote a letter to the clerk to the licensing justices, referring to his circular letter of 7 September 1981, and, so far as material, continuing as follows:

> 'Our Client Company have very seriously considered all that is stated in that letter and it is with regret that we have to inform you that they are unable to accept the operation of an Off-Licence within their Store at the above address on a "shop-within-a-shop" policy. It is the view of our Client Company that the strength of the supervision currently seen to exist within their premises coupled with the staff training which is undertaken on a regular frequent basis that the Food Hall of this Store is a strictly controlled area from which there is a very minimum of undetected stock loss. The Food Hall itself attracts very few unaccompanied youngsters under the age of 18 years and since this licence was originally granted on the 14th July, 1975, there has not to our knowledge been any abuse in the exercise of that privilege. As you are aware, our Client Company do not sell spirits at any of their licensed Branches and in these circumstances intoxicating liquor of the highest value is not available to their customers. In all circumstances, it is the wish of our Client Company to explain in detail to your Licensing Committee the reasons why they find themselves unable to comply with the policy and the steps that have been taken and will be taken to ensure that there is no abuse in any licence which they may be allowed to hold in the future. We were pleased to have the opportunity of discussing the matter informally with your Deputy and understand that there would be no objection to our Clients' application for renewal being adjourned until your next Licensing Meeting on the 8th March next . . .'

On 8th March 1982 Mr F M J Littler, the senior partner in the firm of the applicant's solicitors, appeared before the licensing justices to represent the applicant on his application for renewal of the off-licence in respect of the premises. Mr Littler has given an account of what took place at this hearing in para 6 of an affidavit sworn by him on 19 March 1982. This account reads as follows:

> 'I indicated to the said Licensing Justices that I had seen the letters [of 12 June 1979 and 7 September 1981] and it was confirmed by the Licensing Justices that there was no other objection to the renewal of the said Licence. I reminded the said Licensing Justices that they did not have power to impose conditions either directly or by way of the exaction of undertakings on the renewal of an Off-Licence and informed them that the Applicant was not offering any undertaking. The said Justices indicated that they were not prepared at that stage to renew the licence and wished to hear the application for renewal in detail. I then drew the attention of the said Justices specifically to the relevant parts of the legislation and the notes thereto

in the 90th Edition of Paterson's Licensing Acts, and, in particular, to Section 7(4) thereof which requires evidence given on an application for renewal to be given upon Oath. At that stage the Clerk to the said Licensing Justices gave evidence on Oath that on behalf of the said Licensing Justices he made formal objection to the renewal of the said Off-Licence. He gave no reasons therefor, merely expressing the view that all that was necessary was to state the objection. He was not cross-examined by myself. Thereafter I submitted to the said Justices that the said licence should be renewed there being no evidence of any grounds for objection thereto but the said Justices after retiring indicated that they would not renew the said licence. I then reminded them that, as yet, they had heard no evidence from the Applicant and his witnesses in support of the application for renewal and they then agreed to hear that evidence. It is sufficient for the purposes of these proceedings to say that that evidence dealt in some detail with the method of operation of the said premises in particular and other similar licensed premises operated by Marks & Spencer p.l.c. in general, and informed the Justices that the said premises were operated now as the said Justices had been informed that they would be operated on the original application and as they had been operated ever since. At the close of that evidence I again reminded the said Licensing Justices of my submissions in law, indicated that the Applicant was not prepared to comply with the policy set out in the letter [of 12 June 1979] or submit plans therein required and again submitted that there was no evidence in support of the objection taken by the said Justices to the renewal of the said licence, there had been no abuse in the exercise of the licence, no contraventions of the legislation in respect of it nor any criticism from any of the relevant authorities, including the Police, and invited them to renew the licence notwithstanding the express policy. The said Justices then retired and returned a little later to say that the licence would not be renewed.'

Faced with this refusal, the applicant, having obtained the appropriate leave, applied to the High Court seeking a declaration that the justices were wrong in refusing to renew the justices' off-licence, an order of certiorari to bring up and quash the decision and an order of mandamus directed to them to hear and properly determine the application for renewal.

His application for judicial review was supported by the affidavit of Mr Littler, para 6 of which I have already quoted. Paragraph 7 of that affidavit read as follows:

'In the premises the said renewal was refused because the Applicant was not prepared to comply with the conditions laid down by the said Licensing Justices, conditions which, I respectfully submit, they had no power to seek to impose and I respectfully ask this Honourable Court on behalf of the Applicant to grant the relief sought.'

Mr N H Rundell, who is the clerk to the Windsor licensing justices, swore an affidavit in answer on behalf of the justices. The material parts of this affidavit read as follows:

'(2) I have seen the Affidavit of Mr Frank Michael John Littler, and accept that this is a true record.

(3) On the 8th March 1982 when this matter was heard by the Windsor Divisional Licensing Committee, I advised the Committee, and they took the view, that my evidence stating that they objected to the renewal was sufficient as the Parties had already been served Notice of the Committee's new Policy.

(4) Unless a member of the Committee had been called to give evidence, it seemed to me that this was the only way to comply with Section 7(4) of the Licensing Act 1964.

(5) My Licensing Committee accept that they have no power to impose Conditions on the grant or renewal of an Off Licence. Nevertheless, my Licensing Committee took the view, on my advice, that having published a Policy, they would not renew the Licence.

> (6) On my advice, they drew a distinction between that view and the imposition of a Condition which they knew they could not impose.' *a*

On 19 November 1982 Webster J dismissed the application for judicial review.

Before turning to the merits of the appeal, I will make a few observations as to the pattern of the relevant statute, which is the Licensing Act 1964, as amended, and will refer to a few of the relevant sections. The 1964 Act draws a large number of distinctions between a 'justices' on-licence' (which is defined by s 1(2) as 'a justices' licence authorising sale for consumption either on or off the premises for which the licence is granted') and *b* a 'justices' off-licence' (which is defined as 'a justices' licence authorising sale for consumption off those premises only'). I will mention a few of these distinctions which may be particularly relevant in the present context.

Section 4(1) confers on licensing justices an express general power when granting a new on-licence, other than a licence for the sale of wine alone, to attach to it such conditions governing the tenure of the licence and any other matters as they think proper *c* in the interests of the public. Counsel for the applicant told us, no doubt correctly, that in practice conditions of an infinite variety are attached to the original grants of on-licences. The 1964 Act however confers on the justices no equivalent express power to attach conditions on the grant of a new off-licence. And indeed it is common ground that they have no power to attach conditions either on the grant or on the renewal of an off-licence. *d*

A further material distinction between on-licences and off-licences is to be found in those provisions which indicate the concern of the legislature that premises which are to enjoy the benefit of an on-licence shall be structurally suitable for that purpose. Thus s 4(1) provides that, subject to s 113, licensing justices shall not grant a new on-licence unless the premises are in their opinion structurally adapted to the class of licence required. Section 19(1) provides; *e*

> 'On an application for the renewal of a justices' on-licence the licensing justices may require a plan of the premises to be produced to them and deposited with their clerk, and on renewing such a licence the licensing justices may order that, within a time fixed by the order, such structural alterations shall be made in the part of the premises where intoxicating liquor is sold or consumed as they think reasonably *f* necessary to secure the proper conduct of the business.'

Section 20(1) prohibits certain specified categories of alteration to premises for which an on-licence is in force 'unless the licensing justices have consented to the alteration or the alteration is required by order of some lawful authority'. Section 20(2) provides:

> 'Before considering an application for their consent under this section, the *g* licensing justices may require plans of the proposed alteration to be deposited with their clerk at such time as they may determine.'

The 1964 Act contains no equivalent provisions whatsoever relating to off-licences corresponding with ss 4(1), 19(1) and 20(1) and (2).

The only express requirements for the deposit of plans of the relevant premises in relation to off-licences are to be found in s 6 and Sch 2, para 3, which simply relate to the *h* provisional grant of a new off-licence and have little if any relevance in the present context.

Counsel for the applicant submitted that the reason why the 1964 Act contains no equivalent provisions giving the licensing justices express control over the structural conditions and alterations of off-licence premises is obvious. An off-licence, he submitted, amounts to no more than an authority to sell specified intoxicating liquors in an ordinary *j* shop in the ordinary way; there is no need for the justices to have control over the structural condition or layout of off-licence premises.

The licensing justices in the present case by their letters of 12 June 1979 and 7 September 1981 made it plain to Marks & Spencer that they had adopted the new 'shop

within a shop' policy regarding the grant or renewal of off-licences in respect of, inter
a alia, all self-service stores (such as Marks & Spencer) whose main function is to sell other
goods, but which wish in addition to sell liquor. They made it equally plain that no shops
which were already operating on an open uncontrolled self-service basis could expect to
obtain renewals of their licences unless they were prepared to make the necessary
alterations to the premises. On the face of Mr Rundell's affidavit, there was one reason
and one reason only why the justices refused to renew the applicant's licence at their
b meeting on 8 March 1982. This was because Marks & Spencer had failed to make the
alterations to their premises which had been demanded by the justices and the applicant
offered no assurances that any such alterations would be made in the future.

The power conferred on licensing justices by s 3(1) and (2) of the 1964 Act to grant
justices' licences 'as a new licence or by way of renewal' to such properly qualified persons
'as they think fit and proper' is a power expressed in permissive terms, which is exercisable
c or not at their discretion. The authorities show that this discretion is a very wide one,
both in the case of an original grant and of a renewal: see, for example, *Sharp v Wakefield*
[1891] AC 173, [1886–90] All ER Rep 651. Nevertheless, it is a discretion which must be
exercised according to reason and justice, not in an arbitrary manner (see, for example,
[1891] AC 173 at 179, [1886–90] All ER Rep 651 at 653). It is therefore well established
that licensing justices must exercise their discretion in each case that comes before them
d and cannot properly determine an application simply by reference to a preordained
policy relating to applications of a particular class, without reference to the particular
facts of the application before them. A good example of this principle is to be found in *R
v County Licensing (Stage Plays) Committee of Flint CC, ex p Barrett* [1957] 1 All ER 112,
[1957] 1 QB 350. In that case, for over 50 years the Queen's Theatre in Rhyl had been
continuously licensed for the sale of intoxicating liquor and tobacco. There was no
e suggestion of any misconduct at the theatre. In 1956 application was made, pursuant to
the Theatres Act 1843, for the renewal of the theatrical licence on the same terms and
conditions as before, that is to say without restrictions on the sale of intoxicating liquor
and tobacco. The county licensing committee, having recently granted a theatrical
licence in respect of another theatre in the district subject to restrictions of this nature
(set out in r 3 of the Theatrical Licences Rules), decided that, to be consistent and taking
f into account the fact that there were adequate drinking facilities at licensed premises
nearby, similar restrictions should be placed on the licence of the Queen's Theatre. Its
manager obtained from the Court of Appeal an order of mandamus requiring the
committee to hear and determine the application according to law. The ratio of the
decision is, I think, sufficiently indicated by the following passage from the judgment of
Jenkins LJ in which, having quoted a paragraph from the affidavit of the chairman of
g the licensing committee, he said ([1957] 1 All ER 112 at 122, [1957] 1 QB 350 at 367–
368):

> 'So far therefore para. 9 shows no ground for complaint, but it does seem to me
> to show that regarding the matter as open to them to decide de novo in the exercise
> of their discretion, the committee applied some sort of general principle to the effect
> that a licence without deletion of r. 3 ought not to be granted in any case whatsoever
> h where it could be said that there were adequate facilities for obtaining liquor
> elsewhere. That seems to have been regarded by the committee as a matter of
> general principle. Then they went on to consider that they had already refused the
> application for the Pavilion Theatre on the ground of proximity of other sources of
> supply, and that the Queen's Theatre was an a fortiori case, because the alternative
> supply was even more conveniently situated than the supply in the case of the
> j Pavilion Theatre, and to conclude accordingly that if it was right in the case of the
> Pavilion Theatre to refuse the deletion of r 3, it was a fortiori right to do so in the
> case of the Queen's Theatre, and therefore that the Queen's Theatre licence must
> follow the fate of the Pavilion Theatre licence, because it was essential that the same
> rule should be applied in all cases, or, in other words, that the committee should be

> consistent. I cannot think that that method of approach fulfils the requirements that the matter should be heard and determined according to law. It seems to me it *a* sets up a general principle as to the effect of proximity of other premises where liquor can be obtained when the proper course is to consider each case on its merits. It seems to me that it wrongly pursues consistency at the expense of the merits of individual cases.'

More recently in *R v Torbay Licensing Justices, ex p White* [1980] 2 All ER 25, a case concerning the grant of music and dancing licences, the Divisional Court held that there *b* was nothing wrong with licensing justices adopting a general policy in regard to the grant of such licences. As Wien J pointed out (at 27):

> '... having local knowledge and being acquainted with the conditions prevailing in a particular area, they are fully entitled at times to say that they will lay down a rule of policy, which, one observes in passing, only applies for a period of a year and *c* can be revised at the end of that year.'

On the particular facts of that case, however, each member of the court, in refusing an application seeking orders of mandamus requiring the justices to renew the licences until 2 am, emphasised that, on the evidence, the justices had considered each matter separately and on its merits (at 28, 29, for example). They clearly considered that, even though a *d* general policy had been adopted, such individual consideration was still necessary. As Lord Widgery CJ said (at 28);

> 'It is quite clearly established by authority that justices may adopt of policy provided they give each individual case individual consideration...'

In the present case, counsel for the applicant submitted that the justices were not even *e* entitled to adopt a policy of the nature adopted by them, at least in regard to renewals of licences. I shall briefly revert to this point later. However, assuming that they were entitled to adopt it, I think it clear on the evidence that they did not give the applicant's application for renewal the individual consideration on its merits to which it was entitled, in accordance with the authorities already mentioned.

Earlier in this judgment, I set out in detail the relevant evidence relating to the course *f* of the proceedings before the licensing justices. In my opinion, paras 6 and 7 of Mr Littler's affidavit made it plain that the applicant was asserting in substance that the justices had merely followed their self-determined 'shop within a shop' policy, without giving individual consideration to the merits of the applicant's particular application. The affidavit on behalf of the justices by Mr Rundell, who is himself a barrister, sworn in answer to Mr Littler's affidavit, is thus in my opinion highly significant. He did not *g* suggest that the justices had taken into account any of the particular matters referred to in Mr Littler's affidavit, for example that ever since the original grant of a licence in 1975, the premises had been operated as the justices had been told they would be operated, that there was no evidence in support of the objection taken by the justices, that there had been no abuse in the exercise of the licence, no contraventions of the legislation in respect of it nor any criticism from any of the relevant authorities; '... my *h* Licensing Committee,' Mr Rundell simply said, 'took the view, on my advice, that having published a Policy, they would not renew the Licence.' A clearer indication of closed minds would, I think, be hard to imagine.

It would appear from the judge's judgment that this particular point was not specifically argued before him and indeed I do not think it is specifically reflected in the notice of appeal. Nevertheless, without objection from counsel for the justices, we *j* allowed it to be argued in this court and in my view it must by itself suffice to enable the applicant to succeed on this appeal.

There was however, another, closely allied, point which was argued before the judge and does specifically appear in the notice of appeal, namely that the justices were not entitled to refuse to renew the licence on an objection raised by themselves, when no

evidence had been given on oath in support of the objection. It is common ground that,
a if no notice of objection has been served and no objection is made in open court, justices are bound to renew a licence. In the present case, it is significant that the only objection to the renewal came from the justices themselves. While the making of an objection does not itself have to be on oath, s 7(4) of the 1964 Act requires that 'Evidence given on an application for the renewal of a justices' licence shall be given on oath'. At the hearing before Webster J, the applicant's counsel contended, or, as the judge put it, conceded,
b that the only objection which could have been made was the policy referred to in the above-mentioned correspondence. In these circumstances the judge concluded that—

> 'the statement of the objection by the justices' clerk, taken together with the fact that the justices had earlier said that there was no objection other than that contained in their two letters, constituted at the same time in the particular circumstances of this case the giving of evidence of its grounds so that, in my judgment, the justices
> c were entitled to refuse to renew the licence as they did.'

With respect to the judge, I look at the matter from a rather different point of view. Even if in its particular context the bare statement on oath by the justices' clerk, to the effect that they objected to the renewal, constituted an implicit reference to the earlier correspondence, that correspondence had contained nothing which could be called a
d ground of objection, beyond the bare statement that the justices had adopted the 'shop within a shop' policy. No attempt had been made either in the correspondence or at the hearing to explain that policy, still less to justify its application to these particular premises. For reasons which I have already given, the mere fact of the adoption of the policy is manifestly not a valid objection in law. On any footing therefore it does not seem possible to say that *any* evidence had been given as to *any* ground of objection
e which could be valid in law. Counsel on behalf of the justices explained in argument that the purpose of the 'shop within a shop' policy is to mitigate the risk of persons under the age of 18 acquiring intoxicating liquor. If, however, this was a thought which influenced the justices' mind in objecting to this particular application for renewal, in my judgment natural justice and s 7(4) of the 1964 Act together required them to procure that this ground of objection should be specifically stated on oath, so that the
f applicant should have the opportunity both to test its relevance (if any) in relation to these particular premises by cross-examination and to adduce evidence of his own in opposition. It may well be that the 'shop within a shop' policy can be strongly supported on its merits as a general policy. Nevertheless, there may equally be compelling reasons why it is quite unnecessary to apply this policy to the premises in Peascod Street.

As I have already stated, I regard the arguments based on the justices' failure to consider
g the application on its merits and that based on lack of evidence as closely allied to one another. In my opinion either or both of these arguments must entitle the applicant to succeed on this appeal; no doubt quite unwittingly, the justices have not as yet treated his application fairly.

It is tempting to leave matters at that point in this judgment. If, however, the justices are to be directed to hear and properly determine the application for renewal of the off-
h licence, I think that they will need some further guidance from this court when reconsidering the matter. The arguments before us and the arguments reflected in the judgment of Webster J indicate that this case raises a number of other important points of principle on which I have not yet touched.

One point raised by counsel for the applicant concerned the attitude which justices should adopt in approaching an application for renewal of an off-licence. He submitted
j that, on an application for a renewal (whatever the position might be on an application for an original grant), an objection, if it is to be valid, must relate either to bad conduct on the part of the licensee or to breaches of the existing licence or to some changes in the circumstances of the business since it was originally granted. Correspondingly, he submitted in effect, it can never be right for justices to apply a 'shop within a shop' policy when considering the renewal of licences.

I do not think that he referred us to any authority which specifically supported these propositions and, in the absence of such authority, I would not wish to commit myself to *a* a construction which placed such narrow limits on the justices' discretion. On the face of s 3(1) of the 1964 Act, this discretion is a wide one. I agree with Webster J that the word 'may' in that subsection has the effect that they may take into account any matter which, on a proper construction of the 1964 Act as a whole, is relevant to its objects. Despite the absence of any provisions in the Act corresponding with ss 4(1), 19 and 20 relating to off-licence premises, I am not prepared to say that justices are *never* entitled to take the layout *b* or structural state of premises into account in considering an application for renewal of an off-licence. The House of Lords decision in *Sharp v Wakefield* [1891] AC 173, [1886–90] All ER Rep 651, though relating to earlier legislation, confirms that the grant of a licence by way of a renewal is a matter for the exercise of a discretion no less than an original grant. There could, I think, be cases where the layout of the premises was germane to the exercise of the justices' discretion even on a mere application for renewal. *c*

Nevertheless in the latter case, for easily intelligible reasons, Lord Halsbury LC and Lord Bramwell plainly contemplated that in practice applications for renewal would be more readily acceded to than applications for original grants. Lord Bramwell said that 'The hardship of stopping the trade of a man who is getting an honest living in a lawful trade, and has done so, perhaps, for years, with probably an expense at the outset, may well be taken into consideration' (see [1891] AC 173 at 183, [1886–90] All ER Rep 651 at *d* 655). Likewise, in *R v County Licensing (Stage Plays) Committee of Flint CC, ex p Barrett* [1957] 1 All ER 112 at 122–123, [1957] 1 QB 350 at 368 Jenkins LJ said:

> 'It seems to me that notwithstanding *Sharp* v. *Wakefield*, which shows that the grant of a licence by way of renewal is a matter for the exercise of discretion just as is the grant of an original licence, it cannot be right in this case wholly to ignore, as to all appearances the committee wholly ignored so far as giving any weight to it *e* was concerned, the circumstances that for more than half a century the Queen's Theatre had enjoyed a wholly blameless and useful existence as a theatre licensed for the sale of intoxicating liquor; or to ignore the fact that so far, as appears from the evidence, there has been no relevant change of circumstances whatsoever which could affect the committee's decision in March, 1956, as compared with their decision at an earlier period.' *f*

I have no reason at all to doubt that the justices, in considering the application on 8 March 1982, genuinely and conscientiously reached the decision which they then considered to be the right one. However, without intending to fetter their discretion, I would for my part hope that, when they come to reconsider their decision, they will take into account, together with any other matters that seem to them relevant, the following *g* circumstances, namely that, so far as the evidence shows, (a) this is an application for the renewal, not the original grant, of an off-licence, which has been enjoyed blamelessly according to its terms since 1975, (b) the layout of the relevant part of the premises, which no doubt involved substantial expenditure in 1975, remains unchanged, (c) any change in the layout of the premises to comply with the 'shop within a shop' policy would involve further substantial expenditure, (d) there have been no complaints about *h* the conduct of the premises or about the applicant or his company and no objections from anyone but the justices themselves.

In the light of the authorities which have been cited to us, it is my opinion clear that it could *not* be a proper course for them to purport to renew the off-licence subject either (i) to conditions which purported to place a legally binding obligation on the applicant or Marks & Spencer to carry out works on the premises or (ii) to the giving of an undertaking *j* by the applicant or Marks & Spencer which purported to place a legally binding obligation of this nature on either of them. The recent decision of Woolf J in *R v Edmonton Licensing Justices, ex p Baker* [1983] 2 All ER 545 contains a helpful analysis of the authorities in this context.

In principle I am inclined to agree with Woolf J that, when considering whether or not to grant a first licence, there is no objection to justices asking the applicant for a non-legally binding assurance relating to matters which they can properly take into account in the exercise of their discretion, provided that in so doing they recognise that any such assurance would be no more than a statement of intention, that it would not be legally binding and that failure to observe it could not affect the licence during its currency. I am also inclined to think that, if, since the grant of the original licence, there had been substantial changes of circumstances which necessitated changes in the manner of the future conduct of the business, it might even be justifiable in some cases for justices to ask an applicant for a non-legally binding assurance when considering an application for renewal of his licence. However, I find it difficult to see on what basis the justices could justify a request for such an assurance in the present case when, on the evidence, there has been no relevant change of circumstances whatsoever.

As matters stand, respectfully differing from the judge for the reasons which I have given earlier in this judgment, I would allow this appeal. I would make an order of certiorari to quash the justices' decision refusing to renew the applicant's off-licence and would make an order of mandamus directing the justices to hear and properly determine the application for renewal.

WALLER LJ. This case raises an important point concerning the powers of licensing justices when dealing with the renewal of an off-licence. The powers of licensing justices are different when dealing with off-licences from their powers when dealing with on-licences. By s 4 of the Licensing Act 1964, licensing justices granting a new justices' on-licence may attach to the licence conditions. Furthermore by s 19 of the 1964 Act the licensing justices have the power to require structural alterations on renewal of an on-licence. Apart from this power, however, and the power in certain exceptional cases, eg six-day licences and early closing licences, they do not have the power to impose new conditions on a renewal of an on-licence. The 1964 Act does not give licensing justices any similar powers in relation to off-licences. There is, however, a practice of applicants for licences giving undertakings to licensing justices concerning the manner in which they will use their licence. This practice was considered in *R v Beesly, ex p Hodson* [1912] 3 KB 583. The Divisional Court there made it clear that the undertaking did not form part of the licence. Channell J said (at 587):

> 'It would have been good ground for refusing this licence that it was only required during a portion of the day and that a full day licence was not necessary for the wants of the neighbourhood. The hours at which the house is to be opened is certainly therefore a relevant matter on which the justices might reasonably demand an undertaking. But such an undertaking would not be legally a part of the licence so as to be punishable if it was broken. There is no power to annexe a condition or undertaking to an off-licence.'

In *R v Leicester Licensing Justices, ex p Bisson* [1968] 2 All ER 351 at 353–354, [1968] 1 WLR 729 at 732, a case in which *R v Beesly* was not cited, Lord Parker CJ, when considering the question of licensing justices asking for undertakings, said:

> 'Limiting the possibilities here, it seems to me that any question of exacting an undertaking would be utterly wrong; if Parliament say that the form of the licence is to be for beer, cider and wine only, it would be doing exactly what the Act of 1964 says cannot be done, for the justices to exact undertakings limiting the sale to beer only.'

Woolf J in *R v Edmonton Licensing Justices, ex p Baker* [1983] 2 All ER 545 at 548–549 said:

> 'Properly understood, what the Divisional Court in that case [ie *R v Beesly*] said, it seems to me, was that there is no power to impose conditions on this type of licence, nor is there power to impose a legally enforceable undertaking. However, while it would not be legally enforceable, there would be nothing wrong in justices asking

> for an assurance from the applicant for the licence and taking that assurance into account in considering whether or not to grant the licence, recognising, in so doing, *a* that the assurance would only be a statement of intention, that it would not be legally binding and that, if the person concerned did not observe the assurance, it would not affect his existing licence but could give rise to a situation where it might thereafter prove of relevance on an objection to the renewal of the off-licence, because it is only on such an objection that the justices would have the power to refuse the renewal.' *b*

He took the view that although the earlier case was not cited to the Divisional Court in *R v Leicester Licensing Justices* that what Lord Parker CJ said was consistent with what Channell J was saying in the earlier case, namely that undetakings cannot be made conditions of licences but may be matters which the licensing justices may take into consideration. *c*

But *R v Beesly* was concerned with an application for a new licence and *R v Leicester Licensing Justices* was concerned with a particular situation brought about by the passage of the Finance Act 1967. The present case is concerned with the power of the justices to impose, on an application for a renewal, a new undertaking. In this case the off-licence was granted in July 1975 and was renewed annually up to 1979. In June 1979 the clerk to the justices asked for confirmation that the licensee would be prepared to comply with *d* the change of policy and in September 1981 a further letter was written to which a reply was made that Marks & Spencer had decided not to make changes in the operation of the food hall and at the adjourned licensing meeting on 8 March renewal was refused. The sole objection to renewal was the failure of Marks & Spencer to comply with the licensing committee's change of policy that in multiple shops a 'shop within a shop' policy should be applied for the sale of liquor. The sole evidence before the licensing justices was that *e* the clerk to the justices took the oath and objected. He has by affidavit amplified that objection by saying that on his advice the licensing committee took the view that having published a policy they would not renew the licence.

Section 7(4) of the 1964 Act requires that 'Evidence given on an application for the renewal of a justices' licence shall be given on oath'. This would appear to indicate that on an objection to the renewal of a licence there should be factual evidence to justify the *f* objection and, of course, factual evidence to meet the objector. In this case there was no factual evidence given in support of the objection. The applicant for renewal had no opportunity of dealing with the facts raised in objection to his application. Bearing in mind the provisions relating to off-licences as contrasted with the provisions relating to on-licences I find it very difficult to accept that the justices by a mere change of policy can cause the holder of an off-licence for over four years to make arrangements or *g* alterations to the layout of his shop simply because of that change of policy. If it were an on-licence the justices would have such power under s 19 of the 1964 Act but the internal arrangements of an off-licence are not part of the provisions of the licence. Off-licencees in the ordinary way are free to alter the layout of the shop from time to time and it was pointed out at the bar that most off-licencees alter the layout of their shops in the months immediately before Christmas because it is necessary to do so in order to meet the *h* increased demand. In my opinion, in order to justify an objection to the renewal of an off-licence there must be some change of circumstances: either the circumstances of the manner in which the off-licence is being operated as being such as to cause some particular trouble or because the effect of the off-licence being operated in the way in which it is causes some particular trouble outside the premises. There may be many other changes of circumstances with which the licensing magistrates would be concerned *j* but in this case there was no change of circumstances at all. All that happened was that the magistrates had decided to have a particular policy in relation to self-service stores. It may be that they were perfectly entitled to have such a policy in relation to new applications for off-licences by self-service stores but, in my opinion, it is not sufficient to have a change of policy without more in order to force an off-licence holder to make

changes in a store which has caused no trouble at all in six years of operation as an off
a licence.

DUNN LJ. Having read the judgments of Waller and Slade LJJ in draft I agree with both of them, and only desire to add a few words of my own as to the removal of justices' off-licences. Justices have a wide discretion whether or not to renew such a licence, and the practice of requiring undertakings limiting the terms on which the licence will be
b renewed is a well-established and convenient one, so long as it is understood that such undertakings are not legally enforceable, and the only sanction available to the justices if they are broken is not to renew the licence when application is made for its further renewal. But the discretion is to be exercised judicially and in accordance with law, bearing in mind particularly the differences between on-licences and off-licences reflected in the statutory provisions and referred to by Waller and Slade LJJ. And, in deciding
c whether or not to require any particular undertaking which has the effect of modifying the terms of the original licence, the justices are still exercising a judicial discretion.

The provisions in s 7 of the Licensing Act 1964 for notice by objectors, and for evidence to be given on oath on objection to the renewal of the licence being made, in my judgment indicate that in the absence of objection licenses are to be renewed as of course. I agree with Waller LJ that it is only if there has been a material change of
d circumstances since the original grant of the licence that the justices should refuse the application for renewal. Such circumstances include some change in the conduct of the licensee, or in his conduct of the licence, or some change in the business, or in the needs of the neighbourhood, or considerations of public order. They do not however include a mere change in the policy of the licensing justices unsupported by evidence that the new policy is justified by a genuine change of circumstances.

e I mention these matters only to give guidance to the justices when they consider the application for renewal. I would allow the appeal on the grounds that the justices failed to consider the application for renewal on its merits, and that there was no evidence justifying their refusal to renew the licence.

Appeal allowed; declaration in terms asked for.

f

Solicitors: *Cartwrights*, Bristol (for the applicant); *Lovegrove & Durant*, Windsor (for the justices).

Sophie Craven Barrister.

g

Multinational Gas and Petrochemical Co v Multinational Gas and Petrochemical Services Ltd and others

h COURT OF APPEAL, CIVIL DIVISION
LAWTON, MAY AND DILLON LJJ
11, 12, 13, 14, 17, 18 JANUARY, 16 FEBRUARY 1983

Practice – Service out of the jurisdiction – Action founded on tort committed within jurisdiction – Negligent decisions made by plaintiff company's directors outside jurisdiction – Decisions made on
j *basis of negligent financial information provided by its agent within jurisdiction – Whether action founded on tort committed within jurisdiction – RSC Ord 11, r 1(1)(h).*

Practice – Service out of the jurisdiction – Action properly brought against defendant within jurisdiction – Properly brought – Predominant (but not sole) reason for suing English defendant to enable service of writ on foreign defendant – English defendant unlikely to have funds to satisfy judgment – Plaintiff having good arguable case against English defendant and bringing proceedings in good faith – Whether action properly brought against defendant within jurisdiction – RSC Ord 11, r 1(1)(j).

Practice – Service out of the jurisdiction – Necessary or proper party to action – Action properly brought against a person served within the jurisdiction – Person out of jurisdiction a necessary or proper party to action – Foreign defendant having good defence – Action by liquidator against foreign shareholders and directors of company – Shareholders unanimously approving directors' acts – Whether shareholders owing duty of care to creditors – Whether directors' act becoming acts of company – Whether foreign defendants having good defence to action – RSC Ord 11, r 1(1)(f).

In 1970 three international oil companies, incorporated in the United States of America, France and Japan respectively, entered into a joint commercial venture for the purchase, transportation, storage and sale of liquefied petroleum gas, liquefied natural gas and similar products. The three oil companies contemplated chartering and acquiring suitable tankers for the joint venture, which was to be conducted from London through the plaintiff company, a Liberian corporation formed for the purpose of the joint venture. However, on the advice of tax counsel that the plaintiff company should not carry on business, and that its directors should not hold meetings, within the jurisdiction, the three oil companies formed the first defendant company in the United Kingdom to act as the plaintiff company's agent and, acting as agent, to advise the plaintiff company about business prospects, give it financial information, perform routine management work and put into effect decisions made by the plaintiff company, which in fact had no place of business in the United Kingdom or elsewhere. The three oil companies were the sole shareholders in both companies, the directors of which were employees and nominees of each of the three oil companies appointed with the intent that they should run the two companies for and in the interests of the three oil companies. The plaintiff company's directors held all their relevant board meetings outside the United Kingdom. The plaintiff company began trading in 1971 with a capital of $US25m, mostly represented by vessels or interests in vessels. It ran into financial difficulties and in January 1978 was ordered to be wound up with an estimated deficiency of nearly £114m. As a result, the first defendant also ran into difficulties and was ordered to be wound up with assets of only £34,000. The losses sustained by the plaintiff company were alleged by its liquidator to have been caused by the highly speculative decision made by the plaintiff company's directors to build or acquire six tankers for trade in the spot oil market. The liquidator alleged that the decision in regard to the six tankers could not properly be regarded as falling within the scope of reasonable business judgment. However, the liquidator did not allege bad faith. The plaintiff company brought an action against the first defendant company, and also against its directors, the plaintiff company's directors and the three oil companies (the foreign defendants) claiming damages for negligence and alleging that the first defendant's directors were negligent in preparing inadequate and insufficient budgets, forecasts and information for the plaintiff company's directors, and that the plaintiff company's directors and the three oil companies were in turn also negligent in failing to appreciate those deficiencies as they ought to have done before acting on the basis of the material supplied. Since the only defendants able to satisfy a monetary judgment were the three oil companies and since they and most of their nominee directors of the plaintiff and first defendant companies were resident abroad, the plaintiff applied to serve concurrent writs on those defendants outside the jurisdiction under RSC Ord 11, r 1(1)[a] on the grounds that the action was founded on a tort committed within

a Rule 1(1), so far as material, provides: '... service of a writ, out of the jurisdiction is permissible with the leave of the Court in the following cases ... (*f*) if the action begun by the writ is brought against a defendant not domiciled or ordinarily resident in Scotland to enforce, rescind, dissolve, annul or otherwise affect a contract, or to recover damages or obtain other relief in respect of the breach of a contract, being (in either case) a contract which—(i) was made within the jurisdiction,

(*Continued on p 565*)

the jurisdiction, within r 1(1)(*h*), or that it had been properly brought against a person
a (the first defendant company) duly served within the jurisdiction and the defendants
outside the jurisdiction were proper and necessary parties thereto, for the purposes of
r 1(1)(*j*). The master granted leave but the judge set aside his order. The plaintiff
company appealed.

Held – (1) Applying the principle that in determining for the purposes of RSC Ord 11,
b r 1(1)(*h*) whether the action was founded on a tort committed within the jurisdiction the
task of the court was to look back over the series of events alleged to constitute the tort
and then to decide where in substance the cause of action arose, the plaintiff company's
cause of action arose in substance at the place where the plaintiff company's directors
made the decisions which caused loss to the plaintiff company. Although those decisions
were the end product of negligence which began within the jurisdiction because,
c assuming it could be proved, the directors of the plaintiff company negligently allowed
the first defendant in London to provide them with inadequate financial estimates and
forecasts, nevertheless the decisions themselves had not been made within the jurisdiction
and any loss caused by those decisions had not occurred within the jurisdiction.
Furthermore (per May LJ), the directors of the first defendant owed no duty of care to,
and committed no tort against, the plaintiff company; and it followed that the three oil
d companies were not vicariously liable for any tort committed within the jurisdiction by
the directors of either the plaintiff company or the first defendant. Accordingly, the
plaintiff company, having failed to establish that its action was founded on a tort
committed within the jurisdiction, was not entitled to an order for leave under r 1(1)(*h*)
to serve the writs out of the jurisdiction (see p 570 *b* to *e*, p 573 *f g j* to p 574 *e* and p 582 *f*
to *h*, post); dictum of Lord Pearson in *Distillers Co (Biochemicals) Ltd v Thompson* [1971] 1
e All ER at 700 applied.

(2) On the issue of whether, for the purposes of Ord 11, r 1(1)(*j*), the plaintiff
company's action was 'properly brought' against the first defendant as a person within
the jurisdiction, they were 'properly brought' for the purposes of r 1(1)(*j*) if they were
brought in good faith against the English defendant against whom the plaintiff had a
good arguable case even though any judgment obtained against the English defendant
f might or would not be met because of its insolvency and even though the main or
predominant (but not the only) purpose of suing the English defendant was therefore to
enable the plaintiff to serve parties outside the jurisdiction. Since the first defendant was
so closely involved in the matters out of which the plaintiff company's claim arose, and
since the plaintiff company had both a good arguable claim against the first defendant
and a genuine desire to establish it, the action was properly brought against the first
g defendant (see p 570 *f g j*, p 576 *d e*, p 577 *f g j* to p 578 *b h* to p 579 *b*, p 582 *j* to p 583 *c*
and p 584 *a e f*, post); *Witted v Galbraith* [1893] 1 QB 577, *Sharples v Eason & Son* [1911] 2
IR 436, *Ross v Eason & Son Ltd* [1911] 2 IR 459, *Cooney v Wilson and Henderson* [1913] 2 IR
402 and *Tyne Improvement Comrs v Armement Anversois SA, The Brabo* [1949] 1 All ER 294
considered.

(3) (May LJ dissenting) On the issue of whether, for the purposes of Ord 11, r 1(1)(*j*),
h the foreign defendants were 'proper parties' to the action, a foreign defendant who had a
good defence in law to the plaintiff's claim on facts which were not in dispute could not
be a proper party to the action. Since the three oil companies had acted vis-à-vis the
plaintiff company as shareholders and not as agents and since, as the only shareholders,
they had unanimously required the plaintiff company's directors to make decisions or
later approved what had already been done, it followed that they owed no fiduciary duty

j

(*Continued from p 564*)

or (ii) was made by or through an agent trading or residing within the jurisdiction on behalf of a principal trading or residing out of the jurisdiction, or (iii) is by its terms, or by implication, governed by English law ... (*h*) if the action begun by the writ is founded on a tort committed within the jurisdiction ... (*j*) if the action begun by the writ being properly brought against a person duly served within the jurisdiction, a person out of the jurisdiction is a necessary or proper party thereto ...'

to the plaintiff company, which in turn was bound by anything done intra vires in
respect of it with the unanimous agreement of the shareholders, since in law the acts of a
the shareholders became the acts of the plaintiff company itself and binding on it. By
adopting or approving the acts of the directors of the plaintiff company, the three oil
companies acting as shareholders in agreement with each other made those acts the acts
of the plaintiff company. It followed that the liquidator could not sue the oil companies
because as shareholders they owed no duty to the plaintiff company as a separate entity,
and he could not sue the nominee directors because the oil companies had effectively b
made the acts of the directors acts of the plaintiff company itself. The foreign defendants
were therefore not proper parties to the action and the judge had rightly refused leave to
serve the writs out of the jurisdiction. The appeal would accordingly be dismissed (see
p 570 *h j*, p 571 *c* to *g j*, p 584 *g*, p 585 *h*, p 586 *d* to *h*, p 587 *j* and p 588 a h, post); *Salomon
v A Salomon & Co Ltd* [1895–9] All ER Rep 33, *North-West Transportation Co Ltd v Beatty*
(1887) 12 App Cas 589, *Re Express Engineering Works Ltd* [1920] 1 Ch 466, *Re Duomatic* c
Ltd [1969] 1 All ER 161 and *Re Horsley & Weight Ltd* [1982] 3 All ER 1045 applied; dicta
of Cumming-Bruce and Templeman LJJ in *Re Horsley & Weight Ltd* [1982] 3 All ER at
1055, 1056 distinguished.

Notes

For leave to serve a writ out of the jurisdiction, see 57 Halsbury's Laws (4th edn) paras d
171–172, 179, 181, and for cases on the subject, see 50 Digest (Repl) 336–365, *646–852*.

Cases referred to in judgments

A-G for Canada v Standard Trust Co of New York [1911] AC 498, PC.
Castree v E R Squibb & Sons Ltd [1980] 2 All ER 589, [1980] 1 WLR 1248, CA.
City Equitable Fire Insurance Co Ltd, Re [1925] Ch 407; *affd* [1925] Ch 407, [1924] All ER Rep 485, CA. e
Cooney v Wilson and Henderson [1913] 2 IR 402.
Distillers Co (Biochemicals) Ltd v Thompson [1971] 1 All ER 694, [1971] AC 458, [1971] 2 WLR 441, PC.
Duomatic Ltd, Re [1969] 1 All ER 161, [1969] 2 Ch 365, [1969] 2 WLR 114.
Express Engineering Works Ltd, Re [1920] 1 Ch 466, CA.
Foss v Harbottle (1843) 2 Hare 461, 67 ER 189. f
Hagen, The [1908] P 189, [1908–10] All ER Rep 21, CA.
Horsley & Weight Ltd, Re [1982] 3 All ER 1045, [1982] Ch 442, [1982] 3 WLR 431, CA.
Johnson (B) & Co (Builders) Ltd, Re [1955] 2 All ER 775, [1955] Ch 634, [1955] 3 WLR 269, CA.
Lee Behrens & Co Ltd, Re [1932] 2 Ch 46, [1932] All ER Rep 889.
Massey v Heynes & Co (1888) 21 QBD 330, [1886–90] All ER Rep 996, CA. g
North-West Transportation Co Ltd v Beatty (1887) 12 App Cas 589, PC.
Parker & Cooper Ltd v Reading [1926] Ch 975, [1926] All ER Rep 323.
Pavlides v Jensen [1956] 2 All ER 518, [1956] Ch 565, [1956] 3 WLR 224.
Rosler v Hilbery [1925] Ch 250, [1924] All ER Rep 821, CA.
Ross v Eason & Son Ltd [1911] 2 IR 459.
Russell (John) & Co Ltd v Cayzer Irvine & Co Ltd [1916] 2 AC 298, [1916–17] All ER Rep h 630, HL.
Salomon v A Salomon & Co Ltd [1897] AC 22, [1895–9] All ER Rep 33, HL.
Sharples v Eason & Son [1911] 2 IR 436.
Société Générale de Paris v Dreyfus Bros (1885) 29 Ch D 239; *rvsd* (1887) 37 Ch D 215, [1886–90] All ER Rep 206, CA.
Tyne Improvement Comrs v Armement Anversois SA, The Brabo [1949] 1 All ER 294, [1949] j AC 326, HL.
Witted v Galbraith [1893] 1 QB 577, CA.
Yorkshire Tannery and Boot Manufactory Ltd v Eglinton Chemical Co Ltd (1884) 54 LJ Ch 81.

Cases also cited

Bailey, Hay & Co Ltd, Re [1971] 3 All ER 693, [1971] 1 WLR 1357.

Collins v North British and Mercantile Insurance Co, Pratt v Same [1894] 3 Ch 228.
Diamond v Bank of London and Montreal Ltd [1979] 1 All ER 561, [1979] QB 333, [1979] 2 WLR 228, CA.
Gee & Co (Woolwich) Ltd, Re [1974] 1 All ER 1149, [1975] Ch 52.
Halt Garage (1964) Ltd, Re [1982] 3 All ER 1016.
Houghton & Co v Nothard, Low & Wills [1928] AC 1, [1927] All ER Rep 97, HL.
Hutton v West Cork Rly Co (1883) 23 Ch D 654, CA.
Newman (George) & Co, Re (1895) 1 Ch 674, CA.

Interlocutory appeal

The plaintiff, Multinational Gas and Petrochemical Co (in liquidation), a company incorporated in Liberia, applied for leave to appeal and appealed against the decision of Peter Gibson J on 21 December 1981 whereby he allowed an appeal by nine out of the thirteen defendants named in a writ of summons issued on 25 April 1980 against the order of Master Dyson on 27 February 1981 and discharged the master's order granting the plaintiff leave under RSC Ord 11 to issue concurrent writs and serve them in the United States, Liberia, France and Japan on the nine defendants, namely the fifth to eighth defendants, Phillips Petroleum Co (a company incorporated in the State of Delaware, USA), Philtankers Inc (a company incorporated in Liberia), William Lonnie Phillips and John E Harris Jr (the American interests), the ninth to eleventh defendants, SA de Gérance et d'Armement (a company incorporated in the Republic of France), Stephan Redon and Eric de Rothschild (the French interests), and the twelfth and thirteenth defendants, Bridgestone Liquefied Gas Co Ltd (a company incorporated in Japan) and Chozo Ogishi (the Japanese interests). The first defendant, Multinational Gas and Petrochemical Services Ltd (Services), was not concerned in the proceedings and did not appear. The second, third and fourth defendants, Herman Sauer, Masataka Tamaki and Pierre Daridan were not served and also did not appear. The fourteenth defendant, Michio Dio, died and the plaintiff did not serve notice of the proceedings on his personal representatives. The facts are set out in the judgment of Lawton LJ.

John Chadwick QC and *Martin Keenan* for the plaintiff.
Allan Heyman QC and *Robin Hollington* for the fifth to eighth defendants.
Andrew Bateson QC and *Michael Tugendhat* for the ninth to eleventh defendants.
Donald Nicholls QC and *Richard McCombe* for the twelfth and thirteenth defendants.

Cur adv vult

16 February. The following judgments were delivered.

LAWTON LJ. The issue in this appeal is whether nine out of thirteen defendants named in the writ of summons issued on 25 April 1980 should be served out of the jurisdiction, being resident outside. When the writ was issued there were ten defendants outside the jurisdiction, but one of them, a Mr Michio Dio has died and the plaintiff has not asked for leave to serve his personal representatives.

On 27 February 1981 Master Dyson granted leave to issue concurrent writs in the United States, Liberia, France and Japan against these nine defendants. On 21 December 1981 Peter Gibson J set aside Master Dyson's order and refused the plaintiff leave to appeal. The plaintiff applied to this court for leave to appeal and gave notice of appeal if leave were granted. With the consent of counsel we heard the application and the appeal together. We grant leave to appeal.

The plaintiff was incorporated in Liberia on 14 August 1970. There was evidence before us that the law of Liberia relating to companies is substantially the same as English law. The plaintiff's registered office was in Monrovia. Its existence was due to a decision by three multinational oil companies, Phillips Petroleum Co, a company incorporated in the State of Delaware, USA (Phillips), SA de Gérance et d'Armement (SAGA), a company incorporated in France, and Bridgestone Liquefied Gas Co Ltd (Bridgestone), a company incorporated in Japan. These three oil companies intended to join together in a commercial enterprise for the purchase, transportation, storage and sale of liquefied petroleum gas and liquefied natural gas and similar products. They contemplated chartering and acquiring suitable tankers. So far as Phillips were concerned this aspect of the enterprise was to be conducted by their wholly-owned subsidiary, Philtankers Inc (which was incorporated in Liberia), for the purposes of the joint enterprise. Shares in the plaintiff were allotted 40% to each of Phillips and SAGA and 20% to Bridgestone. The original plan was for these three oil companies to appoint an executive committee to run the plaintiff's business from London. English tax counsel advised, however, that an arrangement of this kind would probably have the result of making the plaintiff's profits, wherever earned, liable to British taxation. In order to avoid this consequence the three oil companies decided to form, and did form in December 1970, a company in the United Kingdom which was to act as the plaintiff's agent. This company was given the name of Multinational Gas and Petrochemical Services Ltd (Services). It had offices in London and as agent advised the plaintiff about business prospects, gave it financial information, performed routine management work and put into effect any decisions made by the plaintiff which had no place of business in the United Kingdom or anywhere else. The members of the plaintiff's executive committee resigned as such in November 1970 and became the first directors of Services. After November 1970 the plaintiff had no formal executive committee. According to the statement of claim (from which I have taken the history of this case up to 1977) the three oil companies from time to time nominated certain of their employees or officers to act as the plaintiff's directors. At the times material to this action the individuals named in the writ after Philtankers Inc were directors. Paragraph 11 of the statement of claim made the following allegation:

> 'Further . . . the Multinational Directors acted at all material times in all relevant matters in accordance with the directions and at the behest of the joint venturers [that is, the three oil companies]; and, accordingly, the powers of directing and managing the affairs of Multinational in relation to the matters hereinafter complained of were vested in and were exercised by the joint venturers . . .'

Save on two occasions, which are irrelevant for the purposes of these proceedings, the plaintiff's directors never met within the jurisdiction of this court to make any decisions. When they did meet it was in New York or Paris or Copenhagen.

The plaintiff started trading in 1971. It had a capital of $US25m but only $1m was in cash, the remainder being represented by vessels or interests in vessels. At first its operations were on a smallish scale for oil companies and ran at a loss; but by 1974 it was making a profit. The plaintiff alleges that between 1973 and January 1975 the directors changed their trading policy. They decided to acquire gas tankers for employment on the spot market. To do this they had to undertake substantial future liabilities which were not offset by forward charters. The market turned against them. They found themselves in financial difficulties. In September 1977 they had to cease trading. On 6 October 1977 the estimated deficiency as regards creditors was shown as £113,853,857. The only assets within the jurisdiction of the court were bank accounts which were in credit to between £300,000 and £400,000. The existence of these assets justified, pursuant to s 399 of the Companies Act 1948, the making of a winding-up order on 25 January 1978. The plaintiff, however, has not suggested that its directors and the three oil companies who told them what to do at any material time knew or suspected that the plaintiff was insolvent.

There has been a financial disaster for the plaintiff's creditors. Those affected by five decisions made by the plaintiff's directors and particularised in para 97 of the statement of claim were alleged to have suffered loss to the extent of about £75,416,000. The three oil companies did not offer to discharge the plaintiff's liabilities. The disaster which befell the plaintiff put Services into difficulties too. That company was ordered to be wound up on 7 February 1978. Its assets were worth about £34,000. We were not told what its liabilities were; but whatever they were, the liquidator of Services was unlikely out of the assets to be able to finance litigation of the kind which was started by the writ issued on 25 April 1980.

During the autumn of 1979 and the early months of 1980 the plaintiff's liquidator consulted accountants and lawyers for the purpose of being advised whether the plaintiff could recover from its directors and the three oil companies the losses, or part thereof, which it had sustained as a result of the unsuccessful trading, particularly during the period November 1973 to January 1975. A substantial proportion of the plaintiff's creditors wanted action taken if a successful outcome was possible.

The liquidator was advised that there was evidence that Services, as the plaintiff's agent, had acted negligently in providing financial information for the plaintiff and that its directors and the three oil companies had negligently failed to appreciate that Services was giving them inadequate financial information and had made decisions negligently. The decisions complained of, so it was alleged, had been highly speculative and could not properly be regarded as falling within the scope of reasonable business judgment. The making of these decisions had caused a large proportion of the losses sustained by the plaintiff.

The liquidator was willing to accept this advice but he seems to have appreciated, at least until 21 April 1980, that there were difficulties in the way of getting any worthwhile result from starting litigation. Services would be unable to satisfy any judgment given against it. In any event leave to commence an action against Services would have to be obtained from the Companies Court and if given there was likely to be the usual condition that no monetary judgment in such action was to be enforced without the leave of the court. All those who would be able to satisfy a monetary judgment were resident out of the jurisdiction. Leave to serve them out of the jurisdiction would not be granted unless the plaintiff could satisfy the court that its claim came within either, or both, RSC Ord 11, r 1(1)(*h*) and (*j*).

On 21 April 1980 there was a meeting between Service's liquidator and solicitor and the plaintiff's liquidator and solicitor. There was a discussion about the need, because of the Limitation Act 1939, to start any litigation, if there was to be any, before 28 April 1980, because the first alleged negligent decision had been made on 29 April 1974. During that discussion someone suggested (it was likely to have been the plaintiff's solicitor) that if a writ was issued against someone who was resident within the jurisdiction there would be no difficulty in joining the non-residents. The plaintiff's solicitor on being questioned by Services' solicitor said that he did not think a successful action would necessarily be of benefit to Services. Services' liquidator was also told by someone representing the plaintiff that its liquidator 'would not actually be looking to Services for any satisfaction'. Before this court the plaintiff, by its counsel, did not suggest that this was not the attitude of the plaintiff's advisers on or before 21 April 1980. It was suggested, however, that between 21 April 1980 and 25 April 1980 those same advisers appreciated better than they had done previously that Services might have some rights against its directors and the three oil companies. Unless those persons and corporations were before the court, Services would have to start third party proceedings against them and as all those worth suing were resident out of the jurisdiction the same problems of service would face Services as have always faced the plaintiff. On 25 April 1980 an application was made by the plaintiff to Mr Registrar Bradburn for leave to commence an action against Services. He was told that Services might have claims against those to whom the plaintiff was looking for relief. The order asked for was made on the usual terms. Services, being within the jurisdiction, was promptly served.

Having considered the relevant affidavits and the exhibits to them I am of the opinion that Services was put into the writ as defendant without the plaintiff having any reasonable expectation of being able to get satisfaction from any judgment which it might obtain against it and for the purpose of being able to submit that the action was properly brought against a person duly served within the jurisdiction. This is one of the grounds on which the plaintiff says it is entitled to an order for service out of the jurisdiction (see Ord 11, r 1(1)(*j*)). The other is that the action which it began by the writ is founded on a tort committed within the jurisdiction (see Ord 11, r 1(1)(*h*)). On whatever grounds the application was founded, the plaintiff had to make sufficiently clear to the court that its claim was a proper one for service out of the jurisdiction under

Ord 11 (see r 4(2)). Peter Gibson J judged that the plaintiff had failed to establish any of the matters which they had to do in order to be given leave. The plaintiff has submitted a
that he misdirected himself in coming to this conclusion.

I start my examination of the plaintiff's case by asking these questions. First, why has the plaintiff started this action? Second, what is the essence of its case? Some of the plaintiff's creditors, acting through the liquidator, wanted to make the oil companies discharge at least some of the plaintiff's liabilities, the plaintiff being their creature. The oil companies, particularly Phillips, and possibly some of their nominee directors on the b
plaintiff's board, had enough assets to do so. They knew, or would have been advised, that the oil companies as the plaintiff's shareholders owed them no duty to ensure that the plaintiff discharged its liabilities. The only way they could get at the oil companies was by alleging that that they and their nominee directors had failed to perform some duty which they owed to the plaintiff. They were not interested in Services, who was just as much a creature of the oil companies as the plaintiff was, save perhaps as a route by c
which they could reach the oil companies. Any worthwhile claim had to be founded on what the oil companies had done. What had they done which caused loss to the plaintiff and through it to the creditors? They had made what were alleged to have been highly speculative decisions which could not properly be regarded as falling within the scope of reasonable business judgment. Those decisions had not been made within the jurisdiction and as far as I can discover from the statement of claim the damage which it is said was d
caused by these decisions did not occur within the jurisdiction. It was submitted that the decisions made outside the jurisdiction were the end product of negligence which began within the jurisdiction in that the plaintiff's directors negligently allowed Services in London to provide (by which was meant prepare) financial estimates and forecasts which were inadequate. Following what Lord Pearson said in *Distillers Co (Biochemicals) Ltd v Thompson* [1971] 1 All ER 694 at 700, [1971] AC 458 at 468 I look back over the series of e
events alleged to constitute the tort and ask myself the question: where in substance did this cause of action arise? The answer is clear: wherever the plaintiff's directors made the relevant alleged decisions. In my judgment, the plaintiff has not established that its action is founded on a tort committed within the jurisdiction.

The question whether, the action having been properly brought against a person duly served within the jurisdiction, as Services was, the parties sought to be served are proper f
parties thereto is more complicated. Our attention has been invited to a long line of authorities, starting with the *Yorkshire Tannery and Boot Manufactory Ltd v Eglinton Chemical Co Ltd* (1884) 54 LJ Ch 81. I do not intend to review them in this judgment. Most of them have been gone over many times before. Nor do I intend to rely on forms of words used in some of the judgments. Lord Porter warned against doing so in *Tyne Improvement Comrs v Armement Anversois SA, The Brabo* [1949] 1 All ER 294 at 299, [1949] g
AC 326 at 340. In my judgment the principles which have to be considered in this case are these. First, that the court should 'be exceedingly careful before it allows a writ to be served out of the jurisdiction': see *The Hagen* [1908] P 189 at 201, [1908–10] All ER Rep 21 at 26 per Farwell LJ. Second, that leave ought not to be given if the sole, or predominant, reason for beginning the action against a party duly served within the jurisdiction is to enable an application to be made to serve parties outside the jurisdiction: h
see *Sharples v Eason & Son* [1911] 2 IR 436. Third, that the *mere* fact that the party within the jurisdiction will be unable to satisfy a judgment does not of itself mean that the action was not properly brought against that person. Fourth, that an action is not properly brought against a party within the jurisdiction if it is bound to fail: see *The Brabo*. All the defendants, being the non-resident parties to whom Master Dyson's order referred, submitted that the plaintiff's claim against them was bound to fail as a matter j
of law. Peter Gibson J was not satisfied that this was so.

On the evidence before him Peter Gibson J found, and in my judgment was right to find, that the predominant reason for bringing the action against Services was to enable an application to be made to serve the defendants out of the jurisdiction. The fact that Services was in liquidation was a factor which he was entitled to take into consideration in coming to this conclusion even if, by itself, it was not conclusive against the giving of leave. This view of the case is enough to dispose of this appeal in favour of the defendants. I consider it advisable, however, to make a finding on the defendants' arguments that the plaintiff's claim against them and against Services was bound to fail.

The submission in relation to the defendants was as follows. No allegation had been made that the plaintiff's directors had acted ultra vires or in bad faith. What was alleged was that when making the decisions which were alleged to have caused the plaintiff loss and giving instructions to Services to put them into effect they had acted in accordance with the directions and behest of the three oil companies. These oil companies were the only shareholders. All the acts complained of became the plaintiff's acts. The plaintiff, although it had a separate existence from its oil company shareholders, existed for the benefit of those shareholders, who, provided they acted intra vires and in good faith, could manage the plaintiff's affairs as they wished. If they wanted to take business risks through the plaintiff which no prudent businessman would take they could lawfully do so. Just as an individual can act like a fool provided he keeps within the law so could the plaintiff, but in its case it was for the shareholders to decide whether the plaintiff should act foolishly. As shareholders they owed no duty to those with whom the plaintiff did business. It was for such persons to assess the hazards of doing business with them. It follows, so it was submitted, that the plaintiff, as a matter of law, cannot now complain about what they did at their shareholders' behest.

This submission was based on the assumption, for which there was evidence, that Liberian company law was the same as English company law and on a long line of cases starting with *Salomon v A Salomon & Co Ltd* [1897] AC 22, [1895–9] All ER Rep 33 and ending with the decision of this court in *Re Horsley & Weight Ltd* [1982] 3 All ER 1045, [1982] Ch 442. In my judgment these cases establish the following relevant principles of law. First, that the plaintiff was at law a different legal person from the subscribing oil company shareholders and was not their agent (see *Salomon v A Salomon & Co Ltd* [1897] AC 22 at 51, [1895–9] All ER Rep 33 at 48 per Lord Macnaghten). Second, that the oil companies as shareholders were not liable to anyone except to the extent and the manner provided by the Companies Act 1948 (see *Salomon v A Salomon & Co Ltd*). Third, that when the oil companies acting together required the plaintiff's directors to make decisions or approve what had already been done, what they did or approved became the plaintiff's acts and were binding on it (see by way of examples *A-G for Canada v Standard Trust Co of New York* [1911] AC 498, *Re Express Engineering Works Ltd* [1920] 1 Ch 466 and *Re Horsley & Weight Ltd*). When approving whatever their nominee directors had done, the oil companies were not, as the plaintiff submitted, relinquishing any causes of action which the plaintiff may have had against its directors. When the oil companies, as shareholders, approved what the plaintiff's directors had done there was no cause of action because at that time there was no damage. What the oil companies were doing was adopting the directors' acts and as shareholders, in agreement with each other, making those acts the plaintiff's acts.

It follows, so it seems to me, that the plaintiff cannot now complain about what in law were its own acts. Further, I can see no grounds for adjudging that the oil companies as shareholders were under any duty of care to the plaintiff. In coming to this conclusion I have kept in mind the doubts expressed by Cumming-Bruce and Templeman LJJ in *Re Horsley & Weight Ltd* [1982] 3 All ER 1045 at 1055–1056, [1982] Ch 442 at 454–456. Their comments were obiter. Both my brethren were thinking of 'misfeasance' which probably does not cover 'an ordinary claim for damages simply': see *Re B Johnson & Co (Builders) Ltd* [1955] 2 All ER 775 at 781, [1955] Ch 634 at 648. Having regard to the long line of authorities to which I have referred and the examples I have mentioned I do not share their doubts.

Counsel for the ninth, tenth and eleventh defendants (the French interests) submitted that the plaintiff's claim against Services was also bound to fail because Services could plead volenti non fit injuria. This submission was based on an allegation in the statement of claim that those responsible for the management and direction of the plaintiff's affairs 'knew or ought to have known' that Services had acted negligently. The argument was that if it knew of negligence it impliedly consented to it. There are three short answers to this submission. First, knowledge of negligence does not necessarily amount to consent to negligence. Second, Services has in its defence denied that it acted negligently as alleged or at all. Third, the volenti defence would not apply to 'ought to have known'.

I would dismiss the appeal.

MAY LJ. Although the substantial number of defendants and the length of the statement of claim make it clear that if and when this action has to be tried it will be an extremely complicated one, I think that for the purposes of this judgment I need refer to very little of the detail.

Multinational Gas and Petrochemical Co, the plaintiff, was incorporated in Liberia for the purpose of the business in which it did thereafter principally engage, namely the worldwide purchase, sale, transportation and passing to and through seaport terminals of liquid petroleum gas, anhydrous ammonia and other light hydrocarbons (including liquid natural gas). It was originally intended that the plaintiff should carry on that business in and from London. For tax reasons the plaintiff's affairs in London were managed by Multinational Gas and Petrochemical Services Ltd (Services), a company which was incorporated in England for that purpose. The board meetings of the plaintiff, however, were for the same reason and in so far as is material always held outside the United Kingdom.

Both these companies were incorporated by the joint venturers, who became and remained throughout the relevant period the sole shareholders in each. Further, the directors of both the plaintiff and Services were employees and the nominees of each of the three joint venturers respectively and were so appointed with the intent that all of them should run each of the two companies for and in the interests of the joint venturers.

In this action it is contended that these respective directors were all of them negligent in their respective capacities, and that for that negligence the joint venturers are vicariously liable. It is said that the directors of Services were negligent in carrying out their duties with the result that budgets, forecasts and information prepared for the directors of the plaintiff, to enable the board of that company to make its decisions in and about carrying on its business, were inadequate and insufficient, at best unreliable and at worst wholly incorrect. It is contended that the directors of the plaintiff were in their turn also negligent in that actually knowing or in circumstances in which they ought to have known of the deficiencies in the material with which they were being provided by Services, they nevertheless failed to appreciate those deficiencies, as they ought to have done and not only failed to require Services to rectify the material, but indeed acted on it when making the five decisions to build or acquire the tankers specified in para (A) of the particulars of damage to para 97 of the statement of claim, which they should not have done had they been properly and efficiently advised by Services and had exercised proper care on their own part. It is finally alleged that as a result of making those five decisions the plaintiff suffered damage to the extent of the net liabilities which their participation in such contracts involved, namely about £75m.

As I have said, Services was an English company, carrying on business in London and has been duly served with the writ in this action within the jurisdiction. We are concerned with whether the plaintiff should have leave to serve notice of the writ on the other defendants out of the jurisdiction of this court.

To obtain such leave, it is common ground that the plaintiff must show both that it can bring its claims against the defendants, other than Services, within one of the sub-paragraphs of RSC Ord 11, r 1(1), and also that in all the circumstances of this case it is a proper one for the court to exercise its discretion and grant the appropriate leave: this last requirement will be found in r 4(2) of the same order. It is also I think common ground that the general approach of the court in these cases should be that set out in the well-known passage from the judgment of Farwell LJ in *The Hagen* [1908] P 189 at 201, [1908–10] All ER Rep 21 at 26:

> 'During these present sittings Vaughan Williams L.J. and myself have on more than one occasion had to consider Order XI., and we have had many authorities discussed and fully considered by the Court, and the conclusion to which the

> authorities led us I may put under three heads. First we adopted the statement of
> a Pearson J., in *Société Générale de Paris* v. *Dreyfus Brothers* ((1885) 29 Ch D 239 at 242), that "it becomes a very serious question, and ought always to be considered a very serious question, whether or not, even in a case like that, it is necessary for the jurisdiction of the Court to be invoked, and whether this Court ought to put a foreigner, who owes no allegiance here, to the inconvenience and annoyance of being brought to contest his rights in this country, and I for one say, most distinctly,
> b that I think this Court ought to be exceedingly careful before it allows a writ to be served out of the jurisdiction". The second point which we considered established by the cases was this, that, if on the construction of any of the sub-heads of Order XI. there was any doubt, it ought to be resolved in favour of the foreigner . . .'

Further, we must remember that sub-para (*j*) of Ord 11, r 1(1) is anomalous, in that, different from the other sub-paragraphs, it is not founded on any territorial connection
c between the claim, the subject matter of the relevant action and the jurisdiction of the English courts. This requires one to look particularly closely at any application founded on this sub-paragraph. As Lord Porter said in his speech in *Tyne Improvement Comrs v Armement Aversois SA, The Brabo* [1949] 1 All ER 294 at 298, [1949] AC 326 at 338:

> 'My Lords, where all the facts necessary for a decision are set out by one side or
> d the other and not contradicted, I think that the tribunal must make up its mind on the hearing of the summons, at any rate where the law is plain. Primarily the jurisdiction of the courts in this country is territorial in the sense that the contract or tort sued on must have some connection with this country or the defendant must be served here. To this principle R.S.C. Ord. 11, r. 1(*g*) [now Ord 11, r 1(1)(*j*)] is an exception and enables foreigners domiciled abroad to be impleaded in this country provided an action is properly brought against someone duly served within the
> e jurisdiction and the party outside the jurisdiction is a necessary or proper party to that action. The rule is not only an exception to, but also an enlargement of, the ordinary jurisdiction of the court and should not, in my opinion, be given an unduly extended meaning. The observation of FARWELL, L.J. in *The Hagen* ([1908] P 189 at 201, [1908–10] All ER Rep 21 at 26), and of LORD SUMNER in *John Russell & Co., Ltd.*
> f v. *Cayzer, Irvine & Co. Ltd.* ([1916] 2 AC 298 at 304, [1916–17] All ER Rep 630 at 632) (both quoted by Scott, L.J.) point out the care which should be taken before the jurisdiction is exercised.'

In the present appeal the appellant plaintiff first relies on r 1(1)(*h*), namely that the action is founded on a tort committed within the jurisdiction. It seems to me quite clear on the facts that if tort or torts there were, these were committed partly within and partly
g outside the jurisdiction of this court. In such circumstances the appropriate approach is that stated by Lord Pearson in the opinion of the Privy Council in *Distillers Co (Biochemicals) Ltd v Thompson* [1971] 1 All ER 694 at 700, [1971] AC 458 at 468 recently applied in this court in *Castree v E R Squibb & Sons Ltd* [1980] 2 All ER 589, [1980] 1 WLR 1248. In the *Distillers* case Lord Pearson said:

> 'The right approach is, when the tort is complete, to look back over the series of
> h events constituting it and ask the question: where in substance did this cause of action arise?'

In the instant case I think that the facts and circumstances as alleged in the statement of claim need careful analysis, remembering the three components of the tort of negligence, namely the existence of a duty of care owed to the plaintiff, a breach of that duty by the defendant and, third, damage to the plaintiff resulting from that breach.
j One must also remember that the joint venturers' liability to the plaintiff (if any) can only be a vicarious one.

Now in my opinion there is no doubt that a director of a limited company owes such a degree of care to that company as a reasonable man might be expected to take in the circumstances on his own behalf. Consequently, the defendants who were directors of the plaintiff owed that duty to that company. The statement of claim pleads and particularises breaches by those directors of that duty to take care and damage to the plaintiff resulting therefrom. Quite clearly, however, all those components of that tort, if in the event it can be shown to have been committed, occurred outside the jurisdiction. a Consequently, in so far as the defendant directors of the plaintiff are concerned, and the joint venturers allegedly vicariously liable for their tort, I am quite satisfied that the plaintiff cannot show any ground for service out of the jurisdiction under sub-para (*h*).

Similarly the directors of Services owed a like duty to it, but I do not think that this is relevant for present purposes because, even if those directors did commit breaches of it and those breaches resulted in some damage, the tort so constituted would have been b committed against Services and not against the present plaintiff.

One then must ask whether there is any question on the material before us that the directors of Services owed any duty of care to the plaintiff. This is not so pleaded in part VI or part VII of the statement of claim and it is noticeable that the negligence complained of in, for instance, para 42 of the statement of claim is that of 'Services, the Multinational directors and the joint venturers'. My opinion is that no duty was owed to the plaintiff at c any material time, if at all, by the directors of Services. It follows that even if the Services directors failed to exhibit the degree of care that a reasonable man might have been expected to exhibit in the circumstances on his own account, this was not a failure of which the plaintiff can take advantage in these proceedings and constituted no component of any tort by Services' directors against the plaintiff. Consequently again, but for a different reason, I do not think that the plaintiff can rely on sub-para (*h*) either in respect d of the directors of Services or, consequently, against the joint venturers vicariously in that connection.

I should add, however, that, if I could be satisfied that the directors of Services had owed a duty of care to the plaintiff, then I would also take the view that there is on the material before us certainly a good arguable case that those directors committed a breach of that duty of care and that that breach caused damage to the plaintiff. Further, in such e circumstances and applying Lord Pearson's test I would have concluded, looking back over the series of relevant events and asking myself where in substance did the cause of action arise, come to the conclusion that it arose in London, within the jurisdiction.

In the result, however, and for the reasons which I have indicated, I do not think that the plaintiff can succeed in this appeal in so far as its application is based on sub-para (*h*).

I turn now to consider the terms of sub-para (*j*) of Ord 11, r 1(1). This provides that f one of the circumstances in which leave can be given to serve a writ out of the jurisdiction is 'if the action begun by the writ being properly brought against a person duly served within the jurisdiction a person out of the jurisdiction is a necessary or proper party thereto'. This sub-paragraph thus requires the court to be satisfied of two matters before any question of the exercise of its discretion under Ord 11, r 4 arises. First, on the assumption that the writ has been duly served on a person within the jurisdiction, that g the action begun by that writ was 'properly brought' against that person so served. Second, that the person out of the jurisdiction sought to be served is 'a necessary or proper party' to the action already begun against the English defendant.

It is not, I think, disputed that there is ample authority in the speeches of the members of the House of Lords in *The Brabo* [1949] 1 All ER 294, [1949] AC 326 that an action is not 'properly brought' against an English defendant if that action is in any event bound h to fail, either on the facts if these are ascertainable by the court hearing the application for leave to serve out of the jurisdiction or on the law. Equally, I think that, if it can be shown that the action would be bound to fail against the potential foreign defendant were he made a party to it, he could be described neither as a necessary nor as a proper party to it. Whether it can be said that this action is bound to fail in either of these two respects as a result, first, of the argument based on general principles of company law to j which I shall refer hereafter, or on the basis that the doctrine of volenti non fit injuria applies, are matters with which I shall have to deal later in this judgment.

Apart, however, from actions which are bound to fail, it was submitted that an action cannot be said 'properly' to be brought against an English defendant if the only or predominant purpose for which that defendant has been joined and served is to found an application under sub-para (*j*) for leave to serve other defendants out of the jurisdiction. In my opinion this submission can be analysed in this way. If one can demonstrate that the action against the defendant within the jurisdiction is bound to fail and that it is on this ground alone that one can say that he was only joined to provide a peg for an application to serve others who are out of the jurisdiction, then of course the action cannot be said to be properly brought for the reason I have already mentioned. Thus, I think that I must then consider this second submission under this head in the context of there being a good arguable case against the English defendant, and an action brought bona fide but in which any judgment obtained against that defendant may or will not be met owing to his lack of funds. In such circumstances, and if the main or predominant purpose of keeping the English defendant in the proceedings is to enable the plaintiff to seek and obtain leave to join and serve persons out of the jurisdiction because they are likely to be able to satisfy a judgment which one may obtain against them, is this a ground for saying that the proceedings are not properly brought in the first place against the English defendant? Of course, if this first question is answered in the negative, it still remains to be determined whether the foreign defendants sought to be joined are necessary or proper parties to the litigation already started, and then finally whether in the exercise of the court's discretion leave ought to be granted.

We were referred to a number of authorities on this point, but I think that it is only necessary for me to mention some of them. The first was *Massey v Heynes & Co* (1888) 21 QBD 330, [1886–90] All ER Rep 996. In that case London ship-brokers were sued for breach of warranty of authority to enter into a charterparty on behalf of Austrian principals. They denied the want of authority with the result that the plaintiffs applied for leave to join the principals and to serve them out of the jurisdiction. This was granted. Of necessity the action had to fail either against the English agents or the foreign principals. The case was principally concerned with whether in such circumstances the latter could be said to be proper parties to the action against the former. However, upholding the grant of leave in the Court of Appeal, Lord Esher MR said (21 QBD 330 at 338, [1886–90] All ER Rep 996 at 1000):

> 'The question, whether a person out of the jurisdiction is a proper party to an action against a person who has been served within the jurisdiction, must depend on this, supposing both parties had been within the jurisdiction would they have been proper parties to the action? If they would, and only one of them is in this country, then the rule says that the other may be served, just as if he had been within the jurisdiction.'

In agreeing Lindley LJ said (21 QBD 330 at 338, [1886–90] All ER Rep 996 at 1000):

> 'When the liability of several persons depends upon one investigation, I think that they are all "proper parties" to the same action, and, if one of them is a foreigner residing out of the jurisdiction, rule 1(*g*) [now r 1(1)(*j*)] of Order XI applies.'

Lopes LJ also agreed on the same basis as Lord Esher MR.

The next case was *Witted v Galbraith* [1893] 1 QB 577. That was an action brought to recover damages for the death of the plaintiff's husband under the Fatal Accidents Act 1846. He had been killed when he fell down a hatchway whilst a stevedore about to take part in the unloading of a ship in Glasgow by a Scots firm. The English defendants were ship-brokers carrying on business in London and all that they had done relevant to the accident was to apply to the dock company in Glasgow to have the vessel unloaded. The writ was served on the brokers within the jurisdiction and the plaintiff then obtained an order giving leave to serve the writ out of the jurisdiction on the shipowners under what was then Ord 11, r 1(*g*) but is now r 1(1)(*j*). The writ was served accordingly, but not surprisingly perhaps the Scottish shipowners took out a summons to set aside the writ and service. The Divisional Court refused to make that order and the shipowners appealed. In the course of his judgment, echoing what had been said in *Massey v Heynes & Co*, Lindley LJ suggested that there was a very easy method of testing whether the case then before the court came within the relevant rule. He said (at 579):

> 'Supposing that both the defendant firms were resident within the jurisdiction, would they both have been joined in the action? I cannot think so; there is no plausible cause of action against the brokers. I come to the conclusion that the

brokers have been brought into the action simply to enable the plaintiff to bring the other defendants within the jurisdiction. It is not a bonâ fide case of an action properly brought against a person who has been served within the jurisdiction. Consequently there is no right to proceed under the order, and the appeal must be allowed.'

Kay LJ agreed that the appeal should be allowed and said (at 579–580):

'Looking at the pleading, as I have done very carefully, it seems to me plain that the pleader felt the very great difficulty of framing a pleading shewing any liability on the part of the brokers. I agree that everything shews that the brokers have been joined as defendants only for the purpose of bringing in the Scotch owners so that they may be sued in these Courts. This is not within the Order, and the appeal must be allowed . . .'

In both judgments, therefore, there are dicta which if read in isolation are to the effect that, where the English defendant is brought into the action simply to enable the plaintiff to apply to join the defendants from outside the jurisdiction, then that is not an appropriate case for the application of the relevant rule. However, both members of the court took the view that there was no plausible or indeed possible cause of action against the brokers, notwithstanding the ingenuity of the pleader, and that the only persons against whom the plaintiff could recover were the Scottish shipowners. In other words, this was also a case in which the claim alleged against the English defendant was bound to fail. I do not find it surprising that in those circumstances the court came to the conclusion that leave ought not to have been given to serve out of the jurisdiction. I do not think that this case is any authority for the proposition that where there does exist a cause of action against the English defendant, but one which is unlikely to be satisfied because of his lack of funds, then the action against the English defendant is not 'properly brought' because the real reason for including that defendant in the proceedings is in order to found an application under the rule. Still less if the desire to be in a position to join defendants out of the jurisdiction is only one of the reasons why the action is brought against the English defendant in the first place.

In *Ross v Eason & Son Ltd* [1911] 2 IR 459 the Irish plaintiff's principal complaint was against the publishers of a newspaper in London in respect of an alleged libel in that newspaper. It is quite clear that there was substantial correspondence between those parties before litigation and ultimately the plaintiff's solicitors asked the proposed English defendants to nominate a solicitor in Ireland to accept service of a writ. The very day on which the plaintiff's solicitors received a reply from the English defendants refusing to do this, the former issued a writ against Eason & Son Ltd, well-known newsagents in Dublin, and then applied and obtained leave to serve the English newspaper out of the jurisdiction. The Irish newsagents were joined without there having been any letter before action and indeed without any communication at all between the plaintiff's solicitors and them. The English defendants applied to set aside the order for service out of the jurisdiction. The Divisional Court set aside the order granting leave and the matter then went to the Court of Appeal. There the Lord Chancellor of Ireland said (at 463):

'We are all of opinion that this appeal must be dismissed. From a consideration of the correspondence which passed between the plaintiff's solicitor and the publishers and printers of the "Winning Post" in London, I am driven to the conclusion that the action instituted against Eason & Son was not a *bona fide* action. The very day on which the plaintiff's solicitor received the letter from the English defendants refusing to nominate a solicitor in Ireland to accept service of a writ on their behalf, and pointing out that the action could only be instituted in England, the plaintiff, without any complaint of the alleged libel, or any intimation of his intention to make them defendants, issued a writ against Eason & Son. In my judgment that was an evasion, an abuse of the rule that should not be sanctioned. On the evidence and the particular facts of this case I have arrived at the conclusion that the action was not one properly brought against Eason & Son within the jurisdiction, and I

> agree with the judgment of the King's Bench Division, on the short ground stated by Mr. Justice Gibson, that the defendants, Eason & Son, were introduced merely for the purpose of bringing the other defendants within the jurisdiction—a judgment which is fully supported by the case of *Witted* v. *Galbraith* referred to during the argument.'

Holmes LJ would have been content to dismiss the appeal on the same basis, namely that Easons were introduced merely for the purposes of bringing the English publishers within the Irish jurisdiction, but as a number of other arguments had been raised in the course of the appeal, namely whether the London publishers were a proper party to the action and whether there was a cause of action against Easons, he dealt with these arguments also. In so far as the latter was concerned I think that it is clear that he had substantial doubts, but he felt that in all the circumstances the matter ought to be left to a jury. His judgment then continued (at 467):

> 'Therefore if the plaintiff's solicitor, when instructed to seek redress for the alleged libel, had at once determined to sue the Irish newsvendors and the London publishers and printers jointly, I should have been prepared to hold that the action was brought against them in good faith, and that, having served the writ on Eason & Son, he was entitled to an order for service on the co-defendants out of the jurisdiction. But the evidence is clear that for some reason—and I assume for a good reason—the solicitor never contemplated making Eason & Son defendants until he found that without joining them he could not sue in the Irish Courts the companies whom he regarded as really responsible; and that Eason & Son were brought into the action simply to enable the plaintiff to bring the other defendants within the jurisdiction. For this reason, and on the authority of *Witted* v. *Galbraith*, I concur in the view taken by Gibson, J.'

Cherry LJ reached the same result by applying the test suggested by Lindley LJ in *Witted v Galbraith*, taking the view that if both the defendants had been resident within the jurisdiction there would have been no question of joining Easons in the proceedings.

It is not clear whether the Court of Appeal's decision in that case was founded on the basis that it was not one within the then equivalent of Ord 11, r 1(1)(*j*), or whether the circumstances in which Easons came to be joined led the court as a matter of discretion to refuse the appropriate leave. In any event it was clearly a case decided on its own facts and cannot I think be any authority for the proposition contended for by the defendants in this appeal. For the purposes of the present argument one must assume that there is a good arguable case against Services, and that there are no mala fides in the sense in which the court in *Ross v Eason & Son Ltd* clearly thought that there were, even though the only or predominant reasons why Services was sued was to enable the plaintiff to apply for leave to join the foreign defendants as parties and as more likely to satisfy any judgment that may be obtained.

In *Sharples v Eason & Son* [1911] 2 IR 436 the facts were that the plaintiff sued Easons in another libel action and having done so obtained leave to join as a second defendant the publisher of a London newspaper in which the alleged libel had been published. But then, on the same day as serving notice of trial on the foreign (in that case, English) defendant, the plaintiff gave Easons notice of discontinuance. It is not surprising that on due application the Court of Appeal in Ireland took the view that the plaintiff by his own act had made it clear that Easons had not been properly joined in the first place. As Holmes LJ said in the course of his judgment (at 449):

> 'The only inference I can draw is that the plaintiff had never any cause of action against Eason & Son, and only sued them for a collateral object, namely, to get the order to serve this defendant resident in London.'

I think that the *Sharples* case underlines the fact that in the cases to which we were referred the substantive basis for setting aside the original leave to serve out of the jurisdiction was that when the matter was investigated there was in truth no plausible cause of action against the defendant originally served. Clearly such a defendant could not be said to be a proper party to the proceedings, or alternatively the court in the a exercise of its discretion in those circumstances was not prepared to grant leave to serve out of the jurisdiction. Viewed in this light, I think that these cases are but tenuous, if any, authority for the proposition that in other circumstances, even though a defendant against whom there is a good cause of action has only been joined in order to enable an appropriate application for leave to serve out of the jurisdiction to be made, this by itself should require the court to refuse leave. b

Cooney v Wilson and Henderson [1913] 2 IR 402 was another case concerning libels on an Irish resident written by an English resident, who employed a bill-poster resident in Ireland to post them there. As the report says: 'Henderson was a working bill-poster, and no mark for damages or costs.' However he was sued and leave was then obtained under the equivalent of Ord 11, r 1(1)(*j*) to serve the English tortfeasor out of the jurisdiction. It was argued that as Henderson, the pauper, was sued merely to found jurisdiction to c grant leave to serve the other defendant out of the jurisdiction, he was a sham defendant and no proper party to the litigation. The Court of Appeal in Ireland, however, accepted the argument of counsel for the plaintiff that notwithstanding Henderson's lack of resources there was a good cause of action against him, that if one applied the test suggested in *Massey v Heynes & Co* the action would have lain against both defendants had each been within the jurisdiction and thus Henderson was a proper party. After d discussing *Ross v Eason & Co Ltd* and saying that in that case the court had been of the opinion that on the evidence there had been no real cause of action against Eason, O'Brien LC ended his judgment (at 407):

> 'If there is a real substantial cause of action against both defendants, it would be most dangerous to hold that the mere fact that the one within the jurisdiction is a pauper can make any difference.' e

The other members of the court took the same view, clearly indicating that the ratio of the earlier decisions in the *Eason* cases was that there had really been no cause of action against them when they were joined. The position in *Cooney*'s case then before them, however, was different and as Cherry LJ said (at 409): 'Principal and agent usually and properly are sued together in such cases as this.' f

Rosler v Hilbery [1925] Ch 250, [1924] All ER Rep 821 was also a different case. Russell LJ refused leave in the exercise of his discretion on the basis that a Belgian court was without question the forum conveniens rather than an English court; in any event he doubted whether any good cause of action existed against the English resident Hilbery. The Court of Appeal took the same view.

As Lord du Parcq said in *The Brabo* [1949] 1 All ER 294 at 306, [1949] AC 326 at 350: g '... I have no intention of paraphrasing in my own language the apparently simple words "properly brought".' One is unlikely to find other words which are precisely synonomous with them, and it is useless to substitute for them words which may have a slightly different meaning. I will confine myself to considering what effect ought to be given to these precise words, in their context, with reference to the present case.

I will accept that at least the predominant reason for suing Services in England was to h provide a ground for applying for leave to pursue litigation in England against the other defendants. In my opinion, however, this consideration is much more relevant, to put it no higher, when the court is considering whether to exercise its discretion under Ord 11, r 4(2) than when it is considering whether an action is properly brought against the English resident and whether the foreign defendants are proper parties; in the present case no question of them being 'necessary' parties arises. Even though that was at least j the predominant reason for suing Services, I think that on the evidence a substantial plausible or arguable cause of action has been shown against Services; indeed, subject to the company law point and the argument on the availability to the defendants of a defence based on the maxim volenti non fit injuria, the contrary was not argued. Further, there is no suggestion of any mala fides in the commencement of this litigation. In my judgment an action brought against an English defendant against whom a substantial plausible, pleadable or arguable cause of action is shown, use whatever epithet one may wish, whom an injured plaintiff is fully entitled to sue, even though any money judgment which he obtains will or may not be satisfied, cannot be described, in the absence of mala fides, as one which has not been properly brought. How can one realistically criticise the plaintiff for suing Services? On the evidence the former's rights against the latter had been under consideration for some time before the writ was issued. In my opinion the fact that Services is a pauper and that the motive for suing it in England is to enable the plaintiff to pursue legitimate litigation against those who cannot be so described are irrelevant to the question whether the action was properly brought against Services.

If, therefore, the plaintiff satisfies the first part of the requirement in sub-para (*j*), are the other defendants sought to be served proper parties to this litigation? Although Lord Porter in *The Brabo* made it clear that the tests suggested by Lord Esher MR in *Massey v Heynes & Co* and Lindley LJ in *Witted v Galbraith* are not of universal application, I think that they are convenient and useful ones to apply in many cases and certainly in the present one. Whichever test one does apply to all the facts and circumstances of the instant case, in my opinion it becomes clear that if the action against Services is properly brought, then the other defendants are proper parties to it.

For my part, therefore, subject to the company law point and to volenti non fit injuria, the plaintiff is able to bring itself within the provisions of Ord 11, r 1(1)(*j*). I will return to consider the question of discretion at the end of this judgment.

I turn now to what has been referred to in the course of the argument as the company law point. The respective contentions of the two sides on this issue are clearly set out by Peter Gibson J in his judgment and I need not repeat them. It is well established by such authorities as *Salomon v A Salomon & Co Ltd* [1897] AC 22, [1895–9] All ER Rep 33 and the many authorities to like effect to which we were referred that a company is bound, in a matter which is intra vires and not fraudulent, by the unanimous agreement of its members or by an ordinary resolution of a majority of its members. However, I do not think that this line of authority establishes anything more than that a company is bound by the legal results of a transaction so entered into: that is to say, for instance, by the terms of contract which is so approved; or that neither it nor for that matter its liquidator can challenge the legal consequences, such as a transfer of title, of a transaction to which its members have agreed to the extent that I have mentioned.

This, however, is very different from saying that where all the acts of the directors of a company, for instance, Services, have been carried out by them as nominees for, at the behest and with the knowledge of all the members of the company, namely the joint venturers, then forever the company as a separate legal entity is precluded from complaining of the quality of those acts in the absence of fraud or unless they were ultra vires. If we assume for the purposes of this argument that the directors of the plaintiff did commit breaches of the duty of care that they owed that company, as a result of which it suffered damage, then I agree with the submission made by counsel for the plaintiff that the company thereby acquired a cause of action against those directors in negligence. The fact that all the members of the company knew of the acts constituting such breaches, and indeed knew that those acts were in breach of that duty, does not of itself in my opinion prevent them from constituting the tort of negligence against the company or by itself release the directors from liability for it. Of course, in the circumstances of the present case, whilst the joint venturers retained effective control of the company they would be extremely unlikely to complain of the negligence of their nominees. But such restraint on their part could not and did not in my opinion amount to any release by the company of the cause of action which ex hypothesi had become vested in it against its directors. *Salomon*'s case and the subsequent authorities make it clear that a limited company is a person separate and distinct from its members, even though a majority of the latter have the power to control its activities so long as it is not put into liquidation and whilst they remain members and a majority. Once, however, the joint venturers ceased to be able to call the tune, either because the company went into liquidation or indeed, though it is not this case, because others took over their interests as members of the company, then I can see no legal reason why the liquidator or the company itself could not sue in respect of the cause of action still vested in it. I a agree with counsel's submission that that cause of action was an asset of the company which could not be gratuitously released in the absence of a substantive object in its memorandum of association unless the two conditions stated by Eve J in his judgment in *Re Lee Behrens & Co Ltd* [1932] 2 Ch 46, [1932] All ER Rep 889 were satisfied, namely (i) was the release reasonably incidental to the carrying on of the company's business and (ii) was it made bona fide for the benefit and to promote the prosperity of the company? b That a shareholder knows that a director has been negligent and yet does nothing about it, or that an act is done by a director with his approval which is later shown to have been negligent, does not preclude the company from then suing in respect of it provided that properly authorised and constituted proceedings can be started in respect of it. I need only mention two or three cases to which we were referred on this particular point. In *Re B Johnson & Co (Builders) Ltd* [1955] 2 All ER 775, [1955] Ch 634 two questions arose: c first, whether a receiver and manager of a company's property appointed by a debenture holder was either an 'officer' of the company within s 455 of the Companies Act 1948 or a 'manager' within s 333; second, whether misfeasance proceedings could be taken in respect of common law negligence under s 333. The first question is immaterial for present purposes. On the second it was held that common law negligence did not fall within the scope of s 333, but the Court of Appeal made quite clear that that section was d merely procedural creating no new causes of action nor, on the other hand, preventing a company or, for instance, its liquidator from enforcing established causes of action outside the scope of s 333 otherwise as the law permitted.

The decision in *Pavlides v Jensen* [1956] 2 All ER 518, [1956] Ch 565 was also relied on by the defendants on this point. In my opinion, however, the claim in that case failed solely on well-known principles in *Foss v Harbottle* (1843) 2 Hare 461, 67 ER 189. e

Finally, although their comments were clearly obiter, I think that in their judgments in *Re Horsley & Weight Ltd* [1982] 3 All ER 1045, [1982] Ch 442 Cumming-Bruce and Templeman LJJ were certainly not ruling out claims by a company against its directors based on negligence in the corporate circumstances which existed in the instant case. I agree with Cumming-Bruce LJ that it would surprise me if the law is to be so understood. In so far as the judgment of Templeman LJ is concerned, I respectfully agree with the f trial judge in our case that the distinction which the former drew between gross and ordinary negligence is not easy to reconcile with the comments of Evershed MR in the *Johnson* case [1955] 2 All ER 775 at 781, [1955] Ch 634 at 648. Be that as it may, I think the correct interpretation to place on the latter part of the judgment of Templeman LJ in the recent case, which concerned a misfeasance summons under s 333 of the Companies Act 1948 is: first, that he took the view that on the facts it was difficult to say that the g directors had been guilty of negligence; second, that it was impossible to hold them guilty of gross negligence on that summons because the allegation had never clearly been made, the directors had not even been so accused by the liquidator and did not give evidence at the hearing of the summons; however, and third, that had it been otherwise proper to find the directors guilty of gross negligence Templeman LJ was not satisfied that they could excuse themselves because they held all the issued shares in the company h and as shareholders had ratified their own gross negligence as directors. I then add that if as a matter of law they could not have ratified their own gross negligence, the position can be no different if one removes 'the opprobrious epithet'.

For the reasons I have given, I do not think that what has been described as the company law point does provide the defendants herein with such a defence to the plaintiff's claims that it can be said that these are bound to fail. Consequently, it cannot j be said on this ground either that the action was not properly brought against Services or that the other defendants are not proper parties to it.

Similarly, in so far as the like argument based on the principle of volenti non fit injuria is concerned, I think that there are a number of reasons why it cannot be said that the plaintiff is bound to fail in these proceedings against the defendants.

First, I stress as did counsel that knowledge alone is not enough: the maxim is volenti non fit injuria not scienti. Second, as is pointed out in *Salmond and Heuston on the Law of Torts* (18th edn, 1981) p 469, the traditional form of the question, namely did the plaintiff assume the risk?, tends to disguise the fact that the burden of proving this defence lies on a defendant. Third, subject to the ultimate question of discretion, it is only if one can say that the defence of volenti is bound to succeed in the circumstances of the present case as we so far know them that it follows that either the action was not properly brought against Services, or that one or more of the proposed foreign defendants are not proper parties thereto, as the case may be, and thus the application to serve out of the jurisdiction cannot succeed to the extent that it is based on Ord 11, r 1(1)(*j*).

If, therefore, one postulates for the purpose of this argument that Services was negligent in preparing the relevant information, advice and recommendations for the plaintiff, that the directors of both companies knew this and that each were the nominees of the joint venturers, the question which had to be asked and answered is whether the only inference to be drawn from all the facts and circumstances of the case is that it was a term of the relationship between the plaintiff and Services that the risk of injury to the former by any misconduct of the latter was required by the latter to be accepted by the plaintiff with no right of recourse against Services and that this risk, without any right of recourse, was in fact accepted by the plaintiff. My answer is that that inference cannot be drawn, let alone is it the only possible inference.

Alternatively, if one considers the plaintiff's claim against its own directors, for the principles embodied in the maxim to provide the latter with a defence one has to postulate a consent to assume the risk being given by the very people who ex hypothesi are committing the material negligence. I confess I find this fanciful in the extreme and indeed, although counsel for the plaintiff did not so contend, I doubt whether the concept of volenti non fit injuria has any reality in the particular circumstances of this litigation.

Finally, the relevant pleas in the statement of claim are that the various defendants 'knew *or ought to have known*' (my emphasis) this or that. If in the ultimate event the plaintiff fails on the first part of these pleas but succeeds on the second, no question of volenti can arise and I for my part am not prepared to speculate about the possibility, canvassed in argument before us and the court below by counsel for the ninth, tenth and eleventh defendants (the French interests), that all the defendants apart from Services might serve defences admitting actual knowledge of all matters complained of against them and pleading volenti. For reasons which it is unnecessary to elaborate, I think that such a course is most unlikely.

I turn finally to the question of discretion. I remind myself that foreigners resident outside the jurisdiction ought only to be impleaded in litigation within our jurisdiction in clear cases. I also remind myself of the limited circumstances in which this court is entitled to interfere with the exercise by a judge of a discretion in cases of this nature. However, with all respect to him I think that it is apparent from his judgment, and indeed when pressed counsel for the twelth and thirteenth defendants (the Japanese interests) was inclined to accept, that the former failed to take into account when exercising his discretion that the underlying agreements between the joint venturers setting up the plaintiff and Services included provisions for arbitration in London. I think that in this he erred and that this was a matter which he ought to have taken into account.

On a related point, I think with respect that the judge was wrong in stating as a fact, which he did take into account, that this action has very little indeed to do with this country. As is clear from the recital of the facts in the judgment of Lawton LJ, at the beginning the joint venturers intended that the plaintiff should carry on business in London. It was merely in an attempt to reduce the incidence of United Kingdom taxation on their operations that they incorporated Services to act as their agents in this country. The plaintiff itself, so far as we know, had no office nor office staff; all that it did, apart from hold board meetings and take decisions at them, it did in London by and through Services. Different from the judge, as I have said, I take the view that the torts alleged against Services and its directors were largely committed by it and them within the jurisdiction. Clearly this litigation ought to be conducted in its entirety in one forum.

When I ask myself whether this should be Japan, I find France and the State of Delaware
coming forward as equal contenders with no more real connection with the events a
sought to be litigated than that these are the jurisdictions within which the international
joint venturers were respectively incorporated. I think that this action does have a
substantial connection with this country. In all the circumstances I do not think that one
can justly criticise the liquidator of the plaintiff for suing and serving Services within the
jurisdiction principally or solely to seek leave to serve the other defendants out of the
jurisdiction. In my judgment, with the great majority of a mass of the relevant b
documents being physically in London, in all the circumstances the latter is the most
convenient and likely to be the most economical forum for these matters to be litigated.
Thus I reach the conclusion that this case is a proper one for service out of the jurisdiction.

For the reasons I have given, whilst differing both regretfully and respectfully from
Lawton and Dillon LJJ, I would allow this appeal.

DILLON LJ. The plaintiff, Multinational Gas and Petrochemical Co, has to establish c
that its causes of action against the foreign defendants fall within one or other of the sub-
paragraphs of RSC Ord 11, r 1(1), and it has further to establish, under Ord 11, r 4(2),
that the case is a proper one for service out of the jurisdiction under Ord 11.

The plaintiff submits that the case is within sub-para (*h*) or sub-para (*j*) of Ord 11,
r 1(1). For sub-para (*h*) to apply it has to be shown that the action is founded on a tort or d
torts committed within the jurisdiction.

The plaintiff is faced, however, with this difficulty, that at a very early stage in its
existence it was advised by leading tax counsel that it should not carry on business itself
within the jurisdiction and its directors should not hold their meetings within the
jurisdiction. As a result of that advice, and in accordance with it, the first defendant,
Multinational Gas and Petrochemical Services Ltd (Services), was incorporated in England e
to carry on the day-to-day running of the business under an agency agreement, the
members of the former executive committee of the plaintiff resigned from the board of
the plaintiff and became directors of Services instead, and the directors of the plaintiff
held all their relevant board meetings, including the three at which the decisions
challenged in this action were taken, outside the jurisdiction.

It is not suggested that Services was a sham or that the corporate veil can be torn aside f
so as to treat the activities of Services as activities of the plaintiff. In the circumstances of
this case, that, as it seems to me, is fatal to the attempt to bring this case within sub-para
(*h*) as against the fifth to the thirteenth defendants. Where the tort relied on is the tort of
negligence the right approach, as Lord Pearson stated in *Distillers Co (Biochemical) Ltd v
Thompson* [1971] 1 All ER 694 at 700, [1971] AC 458 at 468, is to look back over the series
of events constituting the tort and ask the question: where in substance did this cause of g
action arise? To substantially the same effect, the question as put by this court in *Castree
v E R Squibb & Sons Ltd* [1980] 2 All ER 589, [1980] 1 WLR 1248 is: where was the
wrongful act, from which the damage flows, in fact done? So far as the fifth to the
thirteenth defendants are concerned, all their allegedly wrongful acts were done abroad
and the cause of action against each of them substantially arose abroad, in New York or
Paris where the directors met or in the United States, France or Japan where the joint h
venturers (that is to say, the fifth or sixth, ninth and twelfth defendants) reside. Therefore
the attempt to rely on sub-para (*h*) must fail.

As for sub-para (*j*), the plaintiff has duly served the proceedings on Services within the
jurisdiction. To be within sub-para (*j*), therefore, the plaintiff has to show, first, that the
action has been 'properly brought' against Services and, second, that the fifth to the
thirteenth defendants are 'proper' parties, although admittedly not necessary parties, to j
that action against Services. The plaintiff has also to satisfy the court, as I have mentioned,
that the case is a proper one for service outside the jurisdiction. This latter point is a
matter primarily for the discretion of the judge at first instance.

It is well established that an action is not properly brought against a defendant within
the jurisdiction if that defendant has been made a party to the action solely in order to

found an application under what is now sub-para (*j*) of Ord 11, r 1(1), to serve the
a proceedings out of the jurisdiction on foreigners who could not otherwise be sued in the courts of this country. The most common instances are where the plaintiff has as a matter of law or on the undisputed facts no valid claim at all against the defendant within the jurisdiction, as in *Tyne Improvement Comrs v Armement Anversois, SA, The Brabo* [1949] 1 All ER 294 [1949] AC 326 and *Witted v Galbraith* [1893] 1 QB 577. But the decisions of the Court of Appeal in Ireland in the *Eason* cases (*Ross v Eason & Son Ltd* [1911] 2 IR 459
b and *Sharples v Eason & Son* [1911] 2 IR 436) show, as I understand those cases, that even if the plaintiff technically has a cause of action against a defendant within the jurisdiction in circumstances in which the probably successful defence of that defendant depends on facts which would have to be proved by that defendant at the trial, yet the action is not to be regarded as properly brought against the defendant within the jurisdiction for the purposes of Ord 11 if the true inference from all the facts is that the sole reason for suing
c the defendant within the jurisdiction is to found an application under what is now sub-para (*j*) of Ord 11, r 1(1) to join foreign defendants in the action: see the judgment of the Lord Chancellor of Ireland in *Ross v Eason & Son Ltd* [1911] 2 IR 459 at 463.

In the present case there is no doubt that if Services was a solvent company this action would have been properly brought against it. The difficulty is that Services is in compulsory liquidation. Such assets as it has will be entirely exhausted in meeting the
d costs and expenses of liquidation, including its own costs of defending this action. It is therefore frankly admitted that the plaintiff, which is itself insolvent and brings these proceedings by its English liquidator, would not for a moment have contemplated bringing such an action as this against Services if there had been no other potential defendants to this action from whom substantial recovery might be made.

In *Cooney v Wilson and Henderson* [1913] 2 IR 402 where a libel action was sought to be
e brought against the first defendant, the author of the libel who was not within the jurisdiction of the Irish court, as being a proper party to an action properly brought against the second defendant, a bill-poster who had disseminated the libel in Ireland and was resident in Ireland, it was held that the action was 'properly brought' against the second defendant in Ireland, notwithstanding that the second defendant was a pauper. O'Brien LC, the then Lord Chancellor of Ireland, said (at 407) that if there was a real
f substantial cause of action against both defendants it would be most dangerous to hold that the mere fact that the one within the jurisdiction is a pauper can make any difference. Holmes LJ referred to the assertion that the Irish defendant was too poor to pay damages, and expressed the view that that was no reason for holding that the plaintiff was not justified in suing him for what was prima facie a most serious libel, and for joining with him another person equally responsible. Cherry LJ expressed a view similar to that of
g Holmes LJ. It is not clear whether it was a factor in the minds of the court that the plaintiff might reasonably have wanted to sue the second defendant in Ireland despite the latter's poverty, as the most obvious way of clearing the plaintiff's name in Ireland from a very grave libel. Unless, however, the court did have some such factor in mind, I find it difficult to support *Cooney*'s case. Whether an action is properly brought against a particular defendant within the meaning of sub-para (*j*) must surely depend on the
h substance of the matter in the light of all the circumstances, and not on the mere form of the pleading and whether there is technically a cause of action.

It is suggested that, by the time the writ was issued, there was a fresh factor which justified the plaintiff in suing Services in this action, in that it had been appreciated by the liquidator and his advisers that Services might, if sued, bring third party proceedings or serve contribution notices against the fifth to thirteenth defendants or some of them.
j I cannot think that this can assist the plaintiff under sub-para (*j*) because the argument is circular: it comes down to this, that the action is properly brought against Services under sub-para (*j*) so as to enable the foreigners to be made defendants because Services would wish to make claims against the foreigners for which, if they are not made defendants, Services would itself require leave under Ord 11.

Until December 1979 or thereabouts the fifth defendant, Phillips Petroleum Co, was registered as an overseas company under Pt X of the Companies Act 1948. It was thus unnecessary at that stage for the plaintiff to make Services a defendant in order to found jurisdiction against the fifth defendant or any of the other foreign defendants. The evidence shows, however, that from the outset it had been contemplated by the liquidator and advisers of the plaintiff that Services would be a defendant in the proposed action.

By the time the writ came to be issued in April 1980, the fifth defendant had been deregistered, and I have no doubt that the judge was right in his conclusion that by the time the writ was issued the predominant reason why Services was joined as a defendant was not to recover damages from Services but to enable the foreign defendants to be joined in one action in England. The attendance note of Mr Hodge, the assistant to the liquidator of the plaintiff, of a meeting with the liquidator of Services on 21 April 1980, four days before the issue of the writ, contains the following paragraph:

> 'Basically it was necessary to issue a writ for negligence against Mr. Sauer and Services and subsequently to join the directors of Multinational and its shareholders as proper parties to the action and obtain leave to serve a writ outside the jurisdiction. Whilst it was clear that there was no great profit in pursuing litigation against Services for its own sake it was necessary to go this route and sue Services otherwise it would not be possible to join the directors and shareholders and it was from the latter that one expected to make any substantial recoveries.'

The reference to Mr Sauer, the second defendant, does not matter as he has not been served and is now out of the jurisdiction. The very experienced solicitors for the plaintiff would be bound to have had Ord 11 very much in mind.

Nevertheless, it does not follow, in my judgment, that the joining of Services as a defendant in the action was not bona fide or that the action has not been properly brought against Services in this country.

I lay aside, since it has not been relied on in any of the affidavits filed on behalf of the plaintiff, the procedural convenience of being able to obtain discovery against Services in this action, instead of having to bring the equivalent of a bill of discovery against Services, or to claim against Services in separate proceedings to produce all documents which came into its possession as a former agent of the plaintiff.

Bearing in mind, however, how closely Services was involved in all the matters of which complaint is made in the action and bearing in mind the evidence as to the preparation of the plaintiff's claims, I conclude that this action has been brought properly and in good faith against Services. There is a genuine desire to establish the claim against Services.

It is then necessary to consider whether the fifth to the thirteenth defendants are proper parties to the action. By analogy to *The Brabo* they cannot be proper parties who should be hailed before the English court although they owe no allegiance here, if they have a good defence in law to the plaintiff's claim on facts which are not in dispute. In my judgment they have such a defence.

The fifth to the thirteenth defendants were the only shareholders in and the only directors of the plaintiff when the three board meetings of the plaintiff were held, two in New York and one in Paris, on 23 May 1974, 8–9 October 1974 and 28 January 1975, at which the decisions were made, allegedly negligently, to commit the plaintiff to contracts and arrangements for the building, purchase, or chartering on long-term time charter of six ships, carriers of liquid petroleum gas or other gases. The term 'joint venturers' is, as I have mentioned, used in the statement of claim to mean the fifth or sixth, ninth and the twelfth defendants and they at all times held all the issued shares in the plaintiff.

The case against the fifth to the thirteenth defendants is summarised in para 11 of the statement of claim as follows:

> '... the business and affairs of Multinational were, at all times material to this action, under the control of the joint venturers. Further (as is pleaded more particularly in paragraph 32 below) the Multinational Directors acted at all material times in all relevant matters in accordance with the directions and at the behest of

the joint venturers; and, accordingly, the powers of directing and managing the affairs of Multinational in relation to the matters hereinafter complained of were vested in and were exercised by the joint venturers. In the alternative, such powers were vested in and exercised by the Multinational Directors as the employees and nominees of the joint venturers and the joint venturers are liable to answer for the acts or defaults of Multinational Directors in the direction and management of the affairs of Multinational.'

The plaintiff is a Liberian company, but such evidence of Liberian law as is before us indicates that Liberian company law is the same as English and American company law, and for the purposes of this appeal all parties have been content to treat it as the same as English law.

Certain fundamental facts are not in dispute. (1) It is not alleged and could not be alleged that the making of any of the contracts or arrangements authorised at the three board meetings of which complaint is made was ultra vires the plaintiff or in any other way illegal. On the contrary they were well in line with the plaintiff's main objects. (2) It is not alleged that the plaintiff was insolvent when the board meetings were held. On the contrary on the figures pleaded in the statement of claim the plaintiff traded profitably in the calendar years 1973 and 1974 and the forecast, available to the joint venturers and directors, although in the event not borne out and much criticised in the statement of claim, predicted that the plaintiff would continue to make profits in 1975. It is said that the plaintiff suffered a shortage of working capital from and after the end of 1975. (3) It is not alleged that the joint venturers or the directors of the plaintiff acted fraudulently or in bad faith in any way or were guilty of fraudulent trading. What is alleged is that they all acted negligently in that they made five speculative decisions in relation to the six ships, when they knew or ought to have known that they did not have sufficient information to make sensible business decisions. The decisions which they took in good faith went, it is said, outside the range of reasonable commercial judgment.

The heart of the matter is therefore that certain commercial decisions which were not ultra vires the plaintiff were made honestly, not merely by the directors but by all the shareholders of the plaintiff at a time when the plaintiff was solvent. I do not see how there can be any complaint of that.

An individual trader who is solvent is free to make stupid, but honest, commercial decisions in the conduct of his own business. He owes no duty of care to future creditors. The same applies to a partnership of individuals.

A company, as it seems to me, likewise owes no duty of care to future creditors. The directors indeed stand in a fiduciary relationship to the company, as they are appointed to manage the affairs of the company and they owe fiduciary duties to the company though not to the creditors, present or future, or to individual shareholders. The duties owed by a director include a duty of care, as was recognised by Romer J in *Re City Equitable Fire Insurance Co Ltd* [1925] Ch 407 at 426–429, though as he pointed out the nature and extent of the duty may depend on the nature of the business of the company and on the particular knowledge and experience of the individual director.

The shareholders, however, owe no such duty to the company. Indeed, so long as the company is solvent the shareholders are in substance the company. The most commonly cited passage as to the position of the shareholders is in the decision of the Privy Council in *North-West Transportation Co Ltd v Beatty* (1887) 12 App Cas 589 at 593 delivered by Sir Richard Baggallay, who said:

> 'The general principles applicable to cases of this kind are well established. Unless some provision to the contrary is to be found in the charter or other instrument by which the company is incorporated, the resolution of a majority of the shareholders, duly convened, upon any question with which the company is legally competent to deal, is binding upon the minority, *and consequently upon the company*, and every shareholder has a perfect right to vote upon any such question although he may have a personal interest in the subject-matter opposed to, or different from, the general or particular interests of the company.' (My emphasis.)

He went on to contrast the position of a director who owed a fiduciary duty to the company. Thus in *Pavlides v Jensen* [1956] 2 All ER 518 at 523, [1956] Ch 565 at 576, *a* where the directors were alleged to have been guilty of negligence in effecting a sale of a valuable asset of the company at a price greatly below its market value, but there was no allegation of fraud, Danckwerts J was, in my judgment, right when he said that it was open to the company on the resolution of the majority of the shareholders to sell the asset at a price decided by the company in the way the price had been decided. It was also open to the company by a vote of the majority to decide that if the directors by their negligence *b* or error of judgment had sold the company's mine at an undervalue proceedings should not be taken by the company against them. Therefore, on a preliminary issue it was held that a minority shareholder's action, seeking to complain of the negligent sale, was not maintainable and it was dismissed.

Counsel for the plaintiff has submitted that the real analysis of *Pavlides v Jensen* is that the plaintiff's claim was dismissed because it was premature. He ought to have waited *c* until the company had purportedly carried a resolution to absolve the directors and ought then to have challenged that resolution as ultra vires or not passed bona fide in the interests of the company as a whole. But there is no suggestion of that in the judgment of Dankwerts J.

Counsel for the plaintiff has put before us some very interesting submissions on what the shareholders ought to have in mind if they seek to release a director from liability to *d* the company for breach of duty, and the release is not to be ultra vires the company, and as to the extent of knowledge of the facts which the shareholders must have before they can validly release a director from such liability, i e they must know that there is said to have been something wrong with what the director did. It seems to me, however, that in the present case we never get to that point. The case set up is that all the shareholders, the joint venturers, made the impugned decisions at the outset. In so far as the decisions *e* were made at the three meetings in New York and Paris referred to in the statement of claim, it matters not that these meetings were called board meetings, rather than general meetings of the plaintiff: see *Re Express Engineering Works Ltd* [1920] 1 Ch 466. It would equally matter not if the decisions were made by all the shareholders informally and without any meeting at all: see *Parker & Cooper Ltd v Reading* [1926] Ch 975, [1926] All ER Rep 323 and *Re Duomatic Ltd* [1969] 1 All ER 161, [1969] 2 Ch 365. *f*

The well-known passage in the speech of Lord Davey in *Salomon v A Salomon & Co Ltd* [1897] AC 22 at 57, [1895–9] All ER Rep 33 at 51 that the company is bound in a matter intra vires by the unanimous agreement of its members is, in my judgment, apt to cover the present case whether or not Lord Davey had circumstances such as the present case in mind.

If the company is bound by what was done when it was a going concern, then the *g* liquidator is in no better position. He cannot sue the members because they owed no duty to the company as a separate entity and he cannot sue the directors because the decisions which he seeks to impugn were made by, and with the full assent of, the members.

To get out of this difficulty, counsel for the plaintiff points to certain dicta, which he admits were obiter, of Cumming-Bruce and Templeman LJJ in *Re Horsley & Weight Ltd* *h* [1982] 3 All ER 1045, [1982] Ch 442. In that case a company which at the material time had three directors, two of whom held all the issued shares of the company, had with the approval of all three expended a substantial sum of the company's money in buying a pension annuity for the director who had no shares. Subsequently the company went into compulsory liquidation. The liquidator then made claims against the recipient of the pension. The primary claim was that the purchase of the pension for a director was *j* in all the circumstances ultra vires the company. That claim was rejected by the court after examination of a number of decisions at first instance to which I need not refer. The liquidator claimed in the alternative that the taking out of the pension for a director was a misfeasance on the part of the directors which was not cured or validated by the fact that two of the directors were the only shareholders of the company. Buckley LJ took the view that the assent to the transaction of the two directors who held all the shares made it binding on the company and unassailable by the liquidator. He cited the passage to which I have just referred in the speech of Lord Davey, and also *Re Express Engineering Works Ltd* and *Parker & Cooper Ltd v Reading*.

Cumming-Bruce LJ said that the ratification by the shareholders was effective unless the decision of the directors was proved to have been misfeasance on their part. He commented that the evidence fell far short of proof that the directors should at the time have appreciated that the payment for the pension was likely to cause loss to creditors. It was therefore unnecessary to decide whether, had misfeasance by the directors been proved, it was open to them in their capacity as shareholders to ratify their own negligence so as to prejudice the claims of creditors, but he said he would be surprised if it was open to them.

Templeman LJ, while agreeing that the claims of the liquidator failed, held that even in the absence of fraud there could have been negligence on the part of the directors if the company could not afford to spend the relevant sum on the grant of a pension having regard to problems of cash flow and profitability, and there could have been gross negligence amounting to misfeasance if, as I understand what he said, the company was doubtfully solvent and so the expenditure threatened the continued existence of the company. On the facts neither negligence nor gross negligence was made out but Templeman LJ was not satisfied that directors who were guilty of such misfeasance, even without any fraudulent intent, could excuse themselves because two of them held all the issued shares in the company.

Several points arise in relation to these observations of Templeman LJ (and I take it that in his briefer comments Cumming-Bruce LJ meant much the same as Templeman LJ).

In the first place there is in the statement of claim in the present case no allegation of misfeasance against the directors of the plaintiff.

In the second place, Templeman LJ draws a distinction between negligence and what he calls 'gross negligence amounting to misfeasance'. It is only if misfeasance is alleged and proved that he has doubts whether the fact that the delinquent directors are also the shareholders can absolve them. It is clear from the judgment of Evershed MR in *Re B Johnson & Co (Builders) Ltd* [1955] 2 All ER 775 at 781, [1955] Ch 634 at 648 in which Jenkins LJ concurred that a claim based exclusively on common law negligence, an ordinary claim for damages for negligence, is not a claim for misfeasance. That is of course in line with what Templeman LJ said. It is more difficult to discern what he meant by 'gross negligence amounting to misfeasance'. Indeed, in *Re B Johnson & Co (Builders) Ltd* Evershed MR commented that an ordinary claim for negligence is not brought into the field of misfeasance by the mere expedient of adding epithets to it such as 'gross'. The distinction between mere negligence, failure to satisfy a director's duty of care to his company, on the one hand and misfeasance or 'gross negligence amounting to misfeasance' on the other hand, must, I apprehend, lie in the state of mind of the director. It seems to me that what Templeman LJ had in mind when he used the phrase 'gross negligence amounting to misfeasance' was what is often called 'recklessness'. Recklessness, however, which is conduct nearly approaching fraud, is not alleged against any of the defendants in the present case.

In the third place, Templeman LJ's comments are concerned with a situation where directors guilty of misfeasance are themselves or include all the shareholders. In the present case, the shareholders in the plaintiff are the joint venturers who are not directors and owe no duty to the company.

For my part, therefore, I find nothing in the dicta of Cumming-Bruce and Templeman LJJ in *Re Horsley & Weight Ltd* to assist counsel for the plaintiff and I conclude that the plaintiff has failed to make out that the fifth to the thirteenth defendants are proper parties within the meaning of sub-para (*j*) to this action.

It remains to consider the question of discretion.

Had I taken the same view as the judge on the company law point and on the question whether this action was properly brought against Services, I would have agreed with his exercise of his discretion against the granting of leave to serve the foreign defendants outside the jurisdiction, and indeed I would have had no valid ground for interfering with his exercise of his discretion.

Taking a different view from him on the question whether the action was properly brought against Services, I would still exercise discretion against granting leave to serve the foreign defendants outside the jurisdiction.

The factors which favour granting leave under Ord 11 in order that the action may be tried here as between all parties are, as I see them, (1) that by the arrangements with the joint venturers Services, which is at the very heart of the matters in issue, carried on its business in London, with the result that, as we are told, an enormous number of documents relevant, or possibly relevant, to the matters in issue are in London, (2) that the liquidator has been properly constituted to represent the plaintiff in this country, but he has as yet no locus standi to act for the plaintiff in any other jurisdiction, (3) that Liberian company law is the same as English or American company law and so it would be more convenient to decide the issues of law involved in this action in England than in, for instance, France or Japan and (4) that the agreements made by the joint venturers to incorporate the plaintiff and Services provided for the arbitration of disputes in London.

As against these factors, however, it has been often emphasised that the courts should exercise great care before they subject to the jurisdiction of these courts a foreigner who owes no allegiance here. This is, in part at least, for reasons of the comity of nations and to avoid invasion of the sovereignty of the state within which leave to serve is granted. In so far as the reluctance of the courts to bring foreigners before the English courts is also due to a recognition of the inconvenience to the foreigner that would be involved, it has been submitted that the inconvenience is greatly reduced by modern methods of communication. But that argument cuts both ways, in that modern methods of communication would make it much less difficult for the plaintiff to bring this action in any other jurisdiction, eg in that part of the United States where the fifth defendant is resident. I cannot assume that it is impossible for the creditors of the plaintiff to achieve effective representation of the plaintiff in other jurisdictions.

In the next place, even if it is putting it too high to say, as I do, that the company law point provides a complete answer to all the plaintiff's claims and has the effect that the foreign defendants would not be proper parties to be joined in this action, the position must be that to succeed the plaintiff must break new ground in company law. The foreign defendants would therefore be faced with an action in this country involving novel propositions of law as well as lengthy and expensive investigation of the facts. It seems probable that all the principal witnesses, other than accountants investigating ex post facto, would have to come from abroad and would have to remain in this country for many weeks.

The wrongs alleged against the fifth to the thirteenth defendants in the statement of claim were not committed here and in so far as this action is, in substance, a dispute between the creditors of the plaintiff on the one hand and the shareholders and directors of the plaintiff on the other hand, it is, on the information before us, a dispute between foreigners over the affairs of a foreign company.

These factors outweigh, in my judgment, those which would favour granting leave to serve outside the jurisdiction.

I agree that, as such full argument has taken place, the plaintiff should be granted leave to appeal to this court but I would dismiss the appeal.

Leave to appeal granted. Appeal dismissed. Leave to appeal to House of Lords refused.

Solicitors: *Stephenson Harwood* (for the plaintiff); *Freshfields* (for the fifth to eighth defendants); *Jaques & Lewis* (for the ninth, tenth and eleventh defendants); *Linklaters & Paines* (for the twelfth and thirteenth defendants).

Mary Rose Plummer Barrister.

a
WEA Records Ltd v Visions Channel 4 Ltd and others

COURT OF APPEAL, CIVIL DIVISION
SIR JOHN DONALDSON MR, DUNN AND PURCHAS LJJ
12, 13 APRIL 1983

b

Practice – Inspection of property – Property subject matter of action in respect of which question arising – Interlocutory motion – Ex parte application – Appeal against order – Writ seeking injunctions to restrain defendants from producing or selling copies of films and video tapes in breach of copyright – Judge granting injunctions – Defendants complying with order and subsequently seeking to have order set aside – Judge not making order on defendants' motion but
c *granting leave to appeal to Court of Appeal – Whether appeal to Court of Appeal proper course where motion to set aside not heard and determined by judge at first instance – Whether Court of Appeal will hear appeal from ex parte order – Supreme Court Act 1981, s 16(1).*

Practice – Conduct of proceedings – Access to confidential information – Plaintiffs applying for Anton Piller order against defendants – Judge given confidential information which was not
d *revealed to defendants – Whether judge should be given information which could not be disclosed to defendants at a later stage – Whether defendants' solicitors can be excluded from access to information disclosed to court.*

The plaintiffs, who were members of a trade association of owners of copyright in tape recordings and video cassettes, suspected that the defendants were infringing their
e copyright by making or selling copies of films and video tapes. On 26 January 1983 they accordingly made an ex parte application to a High Court judge for an Anton Piller order requiring, inter alia, the defendants to disclose the identity of suppliers of or customers for infringing tapes and to allow the plaintiffs' solicitors to enter the defendants' premises to search for infringing tapes and material used to make them. At the hearing, in addition to relying on other evidence, they revealed to the judge certain information
f which they considered to be so confidential and sensitive that it could not be communicated to the defendants even at a later stage. The judge made the orders sought. The order expressly reserved liberty to the defendants to apply to vary or discharge the order on giving 24 hours' notice. The order was duly served on the defendants and its terms were complied with, as a result of which one of the defendants made various important admissions. Subsequently three of the defendants applied by motion for the
g ex parte order to be set aside on the ground that the judge should not have made the order on the material then available to him. They further sought the return of the goods seized pursuant to the order and claimed that the admissions made in compliance with the order should be declared inadmissible. The motion came before another judge and at the hearing the transcript of the proceedings on 26 January was read in the absence of the defendants and their solicitors, although subsequently the defendants' solicitors were
h allowed to read the transcript. The judge made no order but gave leave to appeal to the Court of Appeal against the order of 26 January.

Held – The appeal would be dismissed, as being an abuse of the process of the court, for the following reasons—

(1) Although the Court of Appeal had jurisdiction under s 16(1)[a] of the Supreme
j

a Section 16(1) provides: 'Subject as otherwise provided by this or any other Act (and in particular to the provision in section 13(2)(*a*) of the Administration of Justice Act 1969 excluding appeals to the Court of Appeal in cases where leave to appeal from the High Court directly to the House of Lords is granted under Part II of that Act), the Court of Appeal shall have jurisdiction to hear and determine appeals from any judgment or order of the High Court.'

Court Act 1981 to entertain appeals from any order made by the High Court on an ex parte application, the Court of Appeal would not hear an application to set aside an ex *a* parte order because ex parte orders were by their nature provisional and it was to be expected that such an order would be revised by the judge who made the order or another High Court judge in the light of subsequent evidence and argument. Furthermore, there was no power which enabled a judge of the High Court merely to adjourn an ex parte application to the Court of Appeal for it to make an original order. It followed that the proper course for an applicant seeking to challenge an ex parte order *b* was to apply to the judge who made the order or to another High Court judge to discharge or vary it, and to appeal to the Court of Appeal only after that application had been heard and determined (see p 593 *f* to p 594 *a d g h* and p 595 a to *d*, post).

(2) Where an ex parte order had been executed but the defendant sought to have it set aside on the ground that it should not have been made, his proper remedy (save where the order was obtained mala fide or by some material non-disclosure) was to proceed *c* against the plaintiff after the trial under the undertaking as to damages given by the plaintiff when the order was first granted. It followed that an application to discharge the order once the defendants had complied with it was misconceived (see p 594 *b* to *d g h* and p 595 *b d*, post).

Per curiam. On an application for an ex parte order it cannot be right for the judge to hear information which cannot by reason of its confidentiality be disclosed to the *d* defendants at a later stage, since the issue is to be considered only on the basis of evidence known to both parties, and where a judge is given other evidence or information he must ignore it. Furthermore, if such a situation arises, it is wrong to exclude the defendant's solicitors from access to such information, since they are officers of the court who are to be trusted to the same extent as counsel and are likewise liable to penalties for breach of that trust (see p 591 *f g*, p 593 *c d*, p 594 *f* and p 595 *b d*, post). *e*

Notes

For the detention, custody, preservation or inspection of property and for Anton Piller orders, see 37 Halsbury's Laws (4th edn) paras 371–372, and for cases on the subject, see 28(2) Digest (Reissue) 1125, *1234–1242*.

f

Cases referred to in judgments

Hallmark Cards Inc v Image Arts Ltd [1977] FSR 150, CA.
Vint v Hudspith (1885) 29 Ch D 322, CA.

Cases also cited

Bestworth v Wearwell [1979] FSR 320.
Harper v Secretary of State for the Home Dept [1955] 1 All ER 331, [1955] Ch 238, CA. *g*

Appeal

By a writ of summons dated 26 January 1983, the plaintiffs, WEA Records Ltd (suing on behalf of themselves and on behalf of and as representing all other members of the Federation Against Copyright Theft Ltd (FACT)), sought as against the defendants, Visions Channel 4 Ltd, Terence Collins, Jeffrey Charles Collins, Jack Wengrow and *h* Rosalyn Wengrow, injunctions, inter alia, prohibiting the defendants from selling pirated tapes or passing off video cassettes as being genuine cassettes of members of FACT, directing the defendants to disclose the names and addresses of customers and suppliers and the addresses of all premises where any illicit goods were being stored, manufactured or packed, directing the defendants to permit the plaintiffs' solicitors to enter the defendants' premises and directing the defendants to hand over to the plaintiffs' solicitors *j* any illicit goods in their possession. On 26 January Mervyn Davies J made an ex parte order granting the injunctions sought. On 3 February Mervyn Davies J stood over the plaintiffs' notice of motion on the defendants giving undertakings, inter alia, not in any way to make or sell, distribute or otherwise part with possession of the goods in their possession or to pass off video cassettes as the genuine products of the plaintiffs. By a notice of motion the first three defendants sought to have the order of 26 January set aside. On 24 February Peter Gibson J made no order on the defendants' motion but gave leave to appeal. The facts are set out in the judgment of Sir John Donaldson MR.

Romie Tager (who did not appear below) and *Philip Kremen* for the defendants.
Mark Potter QC and *John Baldwin* (neither of whom appeared on the ex parte application before Mervyn Davies J) for the plaintiffs.

SIR JOHN DONALDSON MR. In these proceedings the defendants, Visions Channel 4 Ltd, Terence Collins and Jeffrey Collins, seek to appeal against an Anton Piller order made ex parte by Mervyn Davies J on 26 January 1983. The proceedings are important because we are told that both branches of the profession are in doubt whether, in circumstances such as these, a defendant or proposed defendant who objects to the grant of an Anton Piller order should apply to the judge who granted it or, if he is not available, to another High Court judge, asking that it be discharged or varied, or whether he should appeal to this court.

The history of the matter is as follows. The plaintiffs suspected that the defendants were actively engaged in what is popularly known as 'video piracy': making or selling unauthorised copies of films or video tapes in breach of copyright. They made inquiries, including the keeping of observation on certain premises, and came to the conclusion that it was an appropriate case in which to apply ex parte for an Anton Piller order immediately before, or simultaneously with, an application to issue a writ claiming injunctive relief, delivery up of offending material and an inquiry as to damages.

Such was thought to be the urgency of the situation that counsel was asked to appear before Mervyn Davies J armed only with a draft writ and instructions as to the nature and results of the plaintiffs' inquiries. No affidavit evidence was produced, nor had counsel the advantage of being able to produce unsworn draft affidavits.

Thus far the procedure was unusual, but not without precedent in a situation of appropriate urgency. However, we are told that counsel also revealed to the judge certain information which may well have been relevant, but which was so confidential and sensitive that the plaintiffs considered that it could not properly be revealed to the defendants at a later stage.

I do not know what this information was, but I cannot at the moment visualise any circumstances in which it would be right to give a judge information on an ex parte application which cannot at a later stage be revealed to the party affected by the result of the application. Of course there may be occasions when it is necessary, for example, to conceal the identity of informants, but the judge should then be told that this information cannot be given to him and the judge will then have to make up his mind to what extent he is prepared to rely on information coming from anonymous and unidentifiable sources.

Again I do not know to what extent the judge relied on this sensitive information. All that I do know is that he granted an Anton Piller order. The relevant parts of that order read as follows:

> 'UPON . . . the Plaintiff by its Counsel undertaking (1) forthwith to issue a Writ of Summons claiming relief similar to or connected with that hereinafter granted and within 48 hours to file affidavits of Deryk John Cumberland and James Bond (2) To serve this Order upon the Intended Defendants . . . by a Solicitor of the Supreme Court (3) To pay the reasonable costs of any person other than the Defendants to whom notice of this Order may be given in ascertaining whether any assets specified in this Order be within their possession custody or control and (4) to obey any Order this Court may make as to damages if it shall consider that the Defendants shall have sustained any damages by reason of this Order which the Plaintiff ought to pay AND the Solicitors for the Plaintiff by Counsel for the Plaintiff being their Counsel for this purpose undertaking (1) to offer to explain to the persons served with this

> Order its meaning and effect fairly and in everyday language and to inform the Defendants of their right to seek and obtain professional legal advice before *a* complying with this Order provided that such advice is sought and obtained forthwith and (2) that all records tapes equipment documents or other articles obtained as a result of this Order will be retained in their safe custody or to their order until further Order IT IS ORDERED . . .'

and then para 1 contained injunctive relief prohibiting the defendants from selling or offering for sale goods which were described as 'illicit goods', a term which was defined *b* and, loosely, meant pirated tapes, second, from passing off, or attempting to pass off, video cassettes which were not the product of the plaintiffs or other persons associated with the plaintiffs in a trade association as being genuine video tapes, and, third, directly or indirectly informing anyone of the existence of the proceedings.

Paragraph 2 called on the defendants to disclose to the solicitor for the plaintiffs the names and addresses of customers for these tapes and suppliers of them. Paragraph 3 *c* required the defendants to verify that information by affidavit to be produced within four days after service of the Anton Piller order. Paragraph 4 required them to disclose to the plaintiffs' solicitor the identity of all premises and addresses in which any illicit goods were being stored, manufactured or packed. Paragraph 5 required the defendants to permit the plaintiffs' solicitors to enter their premises. Paragraph 6 required the defendants to transfer into the custody of the plaintiffs' solicitors any 'illicit goods' in the *d* sense in which the order had defined the term. Paragraph 7 restrained the defendants in terms of a Mareva injunction, the details of which do not matter. And para 8 called on them to reveal the extent and nature of their assets in aid of that injunction.

The order ended with a very significant paragraph, reading:

> 'AND the Defendants and each of them are to be at liberty to move to vary or *e* discharge this Order upon giving to the Plaintiff's Solicitors 24 hours' notice of their intention so to do.'

The order was duly served on the defendants and, without asking for any time in which to exercise their right to take legal advice and without applying to the judge to vary or discharge the order, they complied with it. They could, if they had wished, have *f* refused immediate compliance and instead have made an urgent application to have the order set aside. This, in my judgment, is implicit in the final paragraph of the order which I have just read. However I must emphasise, as did Buckley LJ in *Hallmark Cards Inc v Image Arts Ltd* [1977] FSR 150, that defendants who take this line do so very much at their peril. If they succeed in getting the order discharged, all well and good. But, if they fail, they will render themselves liable to penalties for contempt of court. If they *g* fail and there is any reason to believe that, in the period between the time when the order has been served on them and the time when they eventually comply with the order, they had taken any steps which were inconsistent with the order, they had, for example, destroyed any records, the consequences to them would be of the utmost gravity.

In part compliance with the Anton Piller order, affidavits were in fact filed by the *h* personal defendants. In the case of Mr Jeffrey Collins, this affidavit involved important admissions.

The injunctive relief, including the Mareva injunction, had been granted until 3 February. Meanwhile, on 1 February, the plaintiffs had filed affidavit evidence in accordance with their counsel's undertaking. The affidavit evidence did not cover the confidential matters which had been disclosed to the judge. On 3 February Mervyn *j* Davies J had before him a motion to continue the prohibitory injunctions until trial, but that motion was ineffective and was stood over on the defendants giving undertakings in terms of the notice of motion.

On 18 February a different motion was listed before Warner J, namely one by the defendants to discharge the Anton Piller order. The judge had insufficient time to hear

it. However he was told that a tape recording existed of the statements made by counsel
a for the plaintiffs when obtaining the ex parte injunction from Mervyn Davies J, and the judge suggested that it be played over to the defendants' counsel on terms that it was for their ears only. This was done on 21 February. On 23 February a transcript was provided to counsel for the defendants on terms that it should be seen by counsel only.

On 24 February the defendants' motion came on before Peter Gibson J and occupied the time of the court throughout the day. The filed evidence was read and, in the absence
b of both the defendants and of their solicitors, the transcript of the proceedings before Mervyn Davies J was read to Peter Gibson J. After the short adjournment, application was made for leave for the defendants' solicitor to attend in court, but not for the defendants to do so. This was granted and the solicitor was then allowed to read the transcript.

I fully appreciate the problem which faced Peter Gibson J when he learned that the
c original order had been granted after Mervyn Davies J had been given confidential information which could not be disclosed to the defendants. I have already said that such a situation should never be allowed to arise. But, it having arisen, there was no possible justification for this information being revealed to the defendants' counsel, but not to their solicitors. Solicitors are officers of the court and are to be trusted to exactly the same extent as counsel. Any breach of that trust would be visited with the direst consequences
d and it is immaterial that the machinery involved might, but would not necessarily, differ according to whether the transgressor was counsel or a solicitor.

When the time came for the court to adjourn, counsel had not completed their arguments. However, it was indicated that whichever way the judge decided the matter there would be an appeal to this court. Furthermore, there was some discussion on whether the appropriate procedure might not be an appeal to this court rather than a
e motion to discharge the ex parte order where, as here, the defendants had filed no evidence other than in compliance with the Anton Piller order and were contending that the ex parte order should never have been granted on the material available to the judge.

In this situation the judge, without I think any discouragement from either party, made no order but gave leave to appeal to this court. The undertakings by the defendants were continued meanwhile.

f In terms of jurisdiction, there can be no doubt that this court can hear an appeal from an order made by the High Court on an ex parte application. This jurisdiction is conferred by s 16(1) of the Supreme Court Act 1981. Equally there is no doubt that the High Court has power to review and to discharge or vary any order which has been made ex parte. This jurisdiction is inherent in the provisional nature of any order made ex parte and is reflected in RSC Ord 32, r 6. Whilst on the subject of jurisdiction, it should also be said
g that there is no power enabling a judge of the High Court to adjourn a dispute to the Court of Appeal which, in effect, is what Peter Gibson J seems to have done. The Court of Appeal hears appeals from orders and judgments. Apart from the jurisdiction (under RSC Ord 59, r 14(3)) to entertain a renewed ex parte application, it does not hear original applications save to the extent that they are ancillary to an appeal.

As I have said, ex parte orders are essentially provisional in nature. They are made by
h the judge on the basis of evidence and submissions emanating from one side only. Despite the fact that the applicant is under a duty to make full disclosure of all relevant information in his possession, whether or not it assists his application, this is no basis for making a definitive order and every judge knows this. He expects at a later stage to be given an opportunity to review his provisional order in the light of evidence and argument adduced by the other side, and, in so doing, he is not hearing an appeal from
j himself and in no way feels inhibited from discharging or varying his original order.

This being the case it is difficult, if not impossible, to think of circumstances in which it would be proper to appeal to this court against an ex parte order without first giving the judge who made it or, if he was not available, another High Court judge an opportunity of reviewing it in the light of argument from the defendant and reaching a decision. This is the appropriate procedure even when an order is not provisional, but is made at the trial in the absence of one party: see RSC Ord 35, r 2 and *Vint v Hudspith* (1885) 29 Ch D 322, to which counsel for the defendants very helpfully referred us this morning.

In the instant case the Anton Piller order is spent in the sense that it has been executed. However, the defendants seek to go back to the beginning of the action saying that, regardless of whether the fruits of the order are such as to show that it was abundantly justified, the judge had insufficient material to justify his action at the ex parte stage. They therefore invite us to set the ex parte order aside and to order the return of the affidavits to the two personal defendants and the seized material to the defendants' solicitors.

I regard this as wholly absurd. The courts are concerned with the administration of justice, not with playing a game of snakes and ladders. If it were now clear that the defendants had suffered any injustice by the making of the order, taking account of all relevant evidence including the affidavits of the personal defendants and the fruits of the search, the defendants would have their remedy in the counter-undertaking as to damages. But this is a matter to be investigated by the High Court judge who is seised of the matter, and only when he has reached a decision can this court be concerned.

I would dismiss this appeal, not on the merits, but on the grounds that it is an abuse of the process of the court. Lest it be thought that that is an opprobrious phrase, let me explain that by that I mean that it is wholly inappropriate for this court to entertain an appeal from the order of Mervyn Davies J made ex parte when not only has it been executed, but the matter has subsequently come back to and is in the process of being considered by other High Court judges.

The parties will, of course, take such further steps as they are advised. However, I would hope that speedy progress would be made with the trial of the action, in which the Anton Piller order was merely an ancillary procedural step.

However that may be, there remains the problem of the confidential information disclosed to Mervyn Davies J and, I think, to Warner and Peter Gibson JJ and eventually, of course, disclosed to the defendants' counsel and solicitors but not to the defendants. Understandably Mervyn Davies J felt difficulty in dealing with the matter further if this information could not be passed to the defendants. Clearly the matter has to be considered solely on the basis of evidence which is known to both parties, and in so far as any judge concerned has other evidence or information he must ignore it. This is a difficult exercise and in the circumstances it may be thought better that some judge other than these three judges be seised of the action for the future. If the transcript of what was said to Mervyn Davies J is considered to be relevant, it should be edited by counsel and solicitors on both sides in order to remove confidential matter which cannot be disclosed to the defendants. If there is any dispute as to the right of the defendants to be informed of any particular matter put before Mervyn Davies J, then this should be decided either by that judge, Warner J or Peter Gibson J, as they already have that information from the transcript.

For those reasons I would dismiss this appeal.

DUNN LJ. I agree for the reasons given by Sir John Donaldson MR that this appeal is misconceived. Even if the appeal did proceed, it seems to me that the issue is a wholly academic one. Whatever information was given orally to the judge, it was accepted that certain attendance notes from inquiry agents were put before him, the contents of which were subsequently put in affidavits which we have read. That evidence, in my view, alone was sufficient to entitle the judge to make the order which he did.

Following the execution of the Anton Piller order, Messrs Terence and Jeffrey Collins swore affidavits. The effect of Terence Collins's affidavit was to admit that certain illicit goods, as defined in the order, were in their possession. It was said on behalf of the defendants that that evidence was irrelevant and inadmissible in any application to review the order either by way of an application to discharge it or by way of appeal, and that on such an application the court should confine itself to the evidence before the judge who made the order. I do not agree with that submission. *Hallmark Cards Inc v*

Image Arts Ltd [1977] FSR 150, to which Sir John Donaldson MR has referred, shows that the court looks at the reality of the situation, including any evidence filed or statement made by counsel by way of admissions after the execution of the Anton Piller order. If consequent on the grant of the Anton Piller order the evidence shows that the order was in fact justified, then the fact that the evidence before the judge was not as strong as it ultimately became does not in my view provide a ground for challenging the order itself. It does not of course affect the situation if the order was obtained mala fide or by some material non-disclosure, but neither of those matters are alleged in this case, and I too would dismiss the appeal for the reasons given by Sir John Donaldson MR.

PURCHAS LJ. I agree with all that has been said in both judgments. By 3 February 1983 the ex parte order against which this appeal is brought had been executed and had expired. The matter was before Mervyn Davies J on that occasion on a fresh motion for further, technically fresh, relief. This was stood over on undertakings given by the defendants which are no longer challenged on this occasion in this court.

This appeal is concerned with the order made on 26 January 1983. For my part I doubt that on an application to set aside an ex parte order which has become entirely spent, even if made to the court which made that order, let alone by way of appeal, the party against whom the order had been made can succeed save only in those very exceptional circumstances to which Sir John Donaldson MR and Dunn LJ have referred. I agree that if and in so far as this motion purports to involve proceedings which took place on 26 January 1983 or on subsequent occasions on those grounds it is misconceived.

For those reasons and for what has already fallen from Sir John Donaldson MR and Dunn LJ I agree that this appeal should be dismissed.

Appeal dismissed. Costs of appeal to be plaintiff's costs in cause.

Solicitors: *Hughmans* (for the defendants); *A E Hamlin & Co* (for the plaintiffs).

Diana Procter Barrister.

Universal City Studios Inc and others v Hubbard and others

CHANCERY DIVISION
FALCONER J
20, 21 JANUARY 1983

Practice – Inspection of property – Property subject matter of action or in respect of which question arising – Privilege against self-incrimination – Exception to rule against self-incrimination – Proceedings for infringement of copyright or passing off – Defendant ordered to hand over to plaintiff relevant documents – Order executed – Plaintiff intending to rely in copyright proceedings on documents obtained – Risk that documents might incriminate defendant of offence unconnected with copyright proceedings – Whether exception to rule against self-incrimination restricted to excepting self-incrimination of infringement of copyright, passing off or similar offences – Whether defendant entitled to claim privilege against self-incrimination – Supreme Court Act 1981, s 72(1)(2)(c)(5)(b).

The plaintiffs, who owned the copyright in certain films, none of which were pornographic, believed that the defendant and others were making counterfeit copies of them on his premises. They issued a writ against the defendant, seeking an injunction restraining him from infringing their copyright. They then obtained, ex parte, an Anton Piller order requiring the defendant to allow them to enter his premises and take any material used or capable of being used for the making of unauthorised copies of the films. After the order had been executed, the plaintiffs applied for interlocutory relief and indicated that at the hearing of the application they would be relying on certain documentary evidence taken from the defendant's premises under the Anton Piller order to support their allegation that he was the ringleader of a gang which was making counterfeit copies. Before the evidence was adduced, the defendant applied for the Anton Piller order to be set aside and for an order directing the plaintiffs to return the documents which they had taken under it and to make no further use of the information contained in them. In his affidavit in support of the application the defendant denied that he was the leader of a counterfeiting gang and stated that the evidence on which the plaintiffs had relied on their application for the Anton Piller order was more consistent with involvement by him in the manufacture and distribution of pornographic films than with involvement in the counterfeiting trade. He submitted that he was entitled to claim privilege against self-incrimination because there was a very serious risk that at the hearing of the plaintiffs' application for interlocutory relief (i) he might incriminate himself (in respect of unlawful activity with regard to pornographic films) if he answered questions about the documents and (ii) that he might be incriminated by the documents themselves. The plaintiffs contended that his claim of privilege was barred by s 72(1) and (2)(*c*)[a] of the Supreme Court Act 1981, which provided that in civil proceedings in the High Court brought to prevent an apprehended infringement of copyright or passing off a person was not to be excused from answering questions put to him in such proceedings on the ground that to do so would tend to expose him to proceedings for 'a related offence', which was defined in s 72(5)(*b*) as being 'in the case of proceedings within [s 72(2)(*c*)] any offence revealed by the facts on which the plaintiff relies in those proceedings'. The defendant submitted that his claim of privilege was not barred by s 72 because 'any offence', within s 72(5)(*b*), was to be restricted to any offence in connection with the infringement of copyright or passing off.

Held – On the true construction of s 72 of the 1981 Act, the words 'any offence' in s 72(5)(*b*) covered any kind of offence revealed by the facts on which the plaintiff relied.

---

a Section 72, so far as material, is set out at p 606 *g* to p 607 *f*, post.

It followed that s 72 provided a complete answer to the defendant's claim of privilege
a and his application would accordingly be dismissed (see p 608 *d* to *g*, post).

Notes

For privilege against incrimination and statutory exceptions thereto, see 13 Halsbury's Laws (4th edn) para 92 and 17 ibid paras 240–242, and for cases on the subject, see 18 Digest (Reissue) 19, 149–152, *97–102, 1195–1246* and 22 ibid 433–437, *4310–4346*.

b For the Supreme Court Act 1981, s 72, see 51 Halsbury's Statutes (3rd edn) 1263.

Cases referred to in judgment

Ashburton (Lord) v Page [1913] 2 Ch 469, [1911–13] All ER Rep 708, CA.
Calcraft v Guest [1898] 1 QB 759, [1895–9] All ER Rep 346, CA.
D v National Society for the Prevention of Cruelty to Children [1977] 1 All ER 589, [1978] AC
c 171, [1977] 2 WLR 201, HL.
Helliwell v Piggott-Sims [1980] FSR 356, CA.
ITC Film Distributors v Video Exchange Ltd [1982] 2 All ER 241, [1982] Ch 431, [1982] 3 WLR 125.
Kuruma, Son of Kaniu v R [1955] 1 All ER 236, [1955] AC 197, [1955] 2 WLR 223, PC.
Norwich Pharmacal Co v Customs and Excise Comrs [1973] 2 All ER 943, [1974] AC 133,
d [1973] 3 WLR 164, HL.
R v Tompkins (1977) 67 Cr App R 181, CA.
Rank Film Distributors Ltd v Video Information Centre [1981] 2 All ER 76, [1982] AC 380, [1981] 2 WLR 688, HL; *affg* [1980] 2 All ER 273, [1982] AC 380, [1980] 3 WLR 487, CA; *rvsg in part* [1982] AC 380, [1980] 3 WLR 487.
Riddick v Thames Board Mills Ltd [1977] 3 All ER 677, [1977] QB 881, [1977] 3 WLR 63,
e CA.

Motion

Peter Hubbard, the first defendant in a copyright action brought by the plaintiffs, (1) Universal City Studios Inc (suing on behalf of themselves and on behalf of and as representing all other members of the Motion Picture Association of America Inc), (2)
f WEA Records Ltd, (3) Go Video Ltd, (4) Guild Home Video Ltd, (5) Home Video Holdings plc, (6) Intervision Video, (7) Precision Video Ltd, (8) RCA/Columbia Pictures UK (a firm), (9) Thorn EMI Video Programmes Ltd, (10) VCL Video Services Ltd, (11) Videomedia Ltd, (12) Videospace Ltd, (13) Embassy Pictures (a firm) and (14) MGM/UA Entertainment Co, applied for an order (i) that an Anton Piller order made by Whitford J on 29 September 1982 be set aside, (ii) that the plaintiffs, by themselves or their
g solicitors, return forthwith to those from whom they took them all documents and other material taken into their possession in the course of execution of the Anton Piller order and (iii) that the plaintiffs, by themselves or their solicitors, destroy on oath all copies made by them of any such documents or other material and make no further use whatsoever of any information contained in such documents or other material. The facts are set out in the judgment.

h

Alastair J D Wilson for the first defendant.
J P Baldwin for the plaintiffs.

FALCONER J. I have before me two motions, and the first is the plaintiffs' motion for interlocutory injunctions and for relief against the first defendant in this action, and the
j second is a motion by the first defendant to discharge an Anton Piller order made against him by Whitford J on 29 September 1982. In this judgment, I am dealing with the first defendant's motion only.

The matter arises in this way. At the start of the hearing of the plaintiffs' motion yesterday, counsel for the plaintiffs opened his motion, outlining the nature of the case and the history of the proceedings to date; but, before going into his evidence, he gave

way, very properly, to counsel for the first defendant to enable him to move his motion, which, as I understand, if successful, will have the effect of excluding at least some of the *a*
material that the plaintiffs seek to adduce in evidence in support of their motion for interlocutory relief.

I should indicate briefly the history of the proceedings as outlined to me and as to which, I understand, as far as I will go there is no dispute, in order to show how the present matter arises. As to the parties in the action, the first plaintiffs, Universal City Studios Inc, as the title of the action indicates, sue on behalf of themselves and all other *b*
members of the Motion Picture Association of America Inc, which I think makes their position and who they represent plain. The second to twelfth plaintiffs inclusive are distributors of cinematograph films in this country, and the thirteenth and fourteenth plaintiffs, as well as being distributors, I understand also produce cinematographic films.

There are now four defendants, the fourth defendant having been added, as it happens, after the execution of the Anton Piller order which counsel for the first defendant seeks *c*
to have set aside as against the first defendant. What appears (and about which I think so far there is no dispute) is that the defendants have been running what counsel for the plaintiffs calls 'in effect a factory' at premises at 8A, and I think 7A, York Parade, Great West Road, Brentford, engaged in what he says is a massive production of counterfeit infringing of films in which the plaintiffs have rights. That is the basis of the plaintiffs' claim, in respect of which counsel for the plaintiffs seeks interlocutory relief. *d*

It appears that, as a result of an initial tip-off, the plaintiffs' solicitors were able to institute inquiries as against the second defendant, who was followed to the premises in question at 8A York Parade; and the first defendant was recognised by an inquiry agent, being seen going to the premises, which were being watched; boxes of video cassettes and so on were seen being taken into and away from the premises. The plaintiffs, who are very much concerned in the present war against the video pirates, have an *e*
arrangement by which they are able to check with the companies who rent video cassette recorders, to obtain information in respect of the renting of such video cassette recorders, particularly when they are rented in relatively large numbers, in other words other than in single instruments. Such inquiries revealed that the first defendant had in fact hired 14 video cassette recorders from one such hire company, and similar inquiries in another direction had indicated that he had purchased what is called a Transcan machine, which *f*
is something which is not in dispute (apparently it is said in the first defendant's own evidence on his own motion) and apparently such machines cost about £26,000. They are capable of manufacturing video cassettes from 16 mm cine film. The first plaintiffs' films (that is to say those that are distributed by the other plaintiffs in this country) come, as indeed I have seen from certain catalogues put in evidence on this motion, in 35 mm and 16 mm films mainly. *g*

As a result of inquiries that were made and the watch that was kept on these particular premises, the application for the Anton Piller order against the first, second and third defendants came before Whitford J on 29 September 1982, when he made an Anton Piller order. As a result of what emerged on the execution of that Anton Piller order, the involvement of the fourth defendant became apparent, and he was joined in the proceedings and on 30 September a similar Anton Piller order was made against him. *h*

The motion return day in those Anton Piller orders was stated to be 6 October; and on 5 October the first defendant, Mr Hubbard, swore two affidavits in the proceedings. On 6 October, the return day, the matter came for the first time before Peter Gibson J for the first hearing of the substantive motion. The first defendant was not prepared to give any undertakings and did not do so. The second, third and fourth defendants offered undertakings which were satisfactory to the plaintiffs. The motion was moved ex parte *j*
against the first defendant, and the judge made an order in the terms asked over 20 October, the order being substantially in the form of the Anton Piller order that had been granted. It included, amongst other things, certain provisions which could be regarded as being in the Mareva injunction form, but I am not concerned with that at the present time.

When 20 October came along and the motion returned into court, it was not ready for hearing; and on that hearing on 20 October the first defendant did give undertakings substantially in the form of the order made against him at the first hearing (that is to say on 6 October) over the hearing of the motion. It came before the court again, as I understand it, on 10 November, and the undertakings of the first defendant were continued. It came before Goulding J again on 16 November, when the plaintiffs' motion was stood over to a date to be fixed, it having become apparent that it was a substantive matter which required to be fixed.

The first defendant launched his motion by notice of motion for 10 November 1982 and that, too, was stood over to come on with the hearing of the plaintiffs' substantive motion, and that is how the matter comes before me today.

The first defendant's notice of motion is for an order that the order of Whitford J made on 30 September (I think that it should be 29 September) be set aside. That was the Anton Piller order. This, as I have explained is a motion by the first defendant only. He then asks:

> '2. That the Plaintiffs, by themselves or their Solicitors, do return forthwith to those from whom they took them all documents and other material taken into their possession in the course of execution of the said Order. 3. That the Plaintiffs by themselves or their Solicitors do destroy upon oath all copies made by them of any such documents or other material, and do make no further use whatever of any information contained in such documents or other material.'

Then there is a paragraph as to costs and a paragraph as to further or other relief.

The effective part of the Anton Piller order made on 29 September 1982 to which the present application is really directed, is in the part which deals with the documents and the material taken into possession by the plaintiffs' solicitors on the execution of the order. After the usual type of order requiring them to disclose certain information about various persons, we have this provision:

> 'AND IT IS ORDERED that the Defendants and each of them (whether by themselves or by any persons appearing to be in charge of the premises hereinafter specified) do permit the person who shall serve this Order upon them together with such persons not being more than 4 in number as may be duly authorised by the Plaintiffs' Solicitors to enter forthwith each of the premises known as [and they are set out and include 8 and 8A York Parade, Great West Road, Brentford, Middlesex, and also 7A York Parade] disclosed to the Plaintiffs' pursuant to the last preceding provision of this Order together with any outhouse or any other building which forms a part of the said premises and any motor vehicles owned or used by the said Defendants and any of them at any hour between 8 o'clock in the forenoon and 8 o'clock in the evening for the purpose of inspecting photographing and looking for and removing into the Plaintiffs' Solicitors' custody (i) any illicit goods (ii) any labels sleeves or other printed or written matter which is for use with any illicit goods (iii) any plates or tapes or video discs or video recording machines or other material used or capable of being used or intended to be used for making illicit goods (iv) all or any documents relating in any way to any of the aforesaid items in (i) (ii) and (iii) above.'

The next part of the order goes on:

> 'AND IT IS ORDERED that the Defendants and each of them do within 48 hours after service of this Order upon them place into the Plaintiffs' solicitors custody any illicit goods as herein defined which may come into their possession.'

For clarity, I should point out that 'illicit goods' are defined a little earlier on in the order as being:

> '(1) Any complete or substantial copy (whether in the form of video cassettes or otherwise) of any film being less than 50 years old and being distributed by the

> Plaintiffs or any of them or any other member of the Motion Picture Association of America Incorporated (MPAA) (a list of whom appears in the schedule hereto) of any film in which copyright is vested in or exclusively licensed to or claimed to be so vested in or licensed to the Plaintiffs or any other member of MPAA not being a copy made by or on behalf of the Plaintiffs or any other member of MPAA. (ii) Any labels sleeves or other printed or written matter which is for use with any illicit goods (iii) Any plates or tapes or other material used or intended to be used for making illicit goods.'

That is effectively the material to which the first defendant's motion is really directed, and I mean in particular the documents, although the order sought is not restricted to documents. It is what is asked for in para 2 of the first defendant's motion, namely 'all documents and other material taken into their possession in the course of execution of the said Order'. Of course in seeking to have the Anton Piller order set aside, those parts dealing with entry and so on have long since been executed and spent.

The reason for the present application is this. Apparently the plaintiffs' evidence on motion makes substantial use of the material seized on the execution of the Anton Piller order against the first defendant. The first defendant in the first of his affidavits in support of his motion, sworn on 8 November 1982, says this, having in the earlier parts referred to the execution of the Anton Piller order and to a change of solicitors, with which I am not concerned:

> '7. My Solicitors were subsequently served with an Affidavit of Mr Cumberland of the Plaintiffs' Solicitors which exhibits a mass of material much of it seized from my home in the course of the Anton Piller raid and some of it my property but found at numbers 7A and 8A York Parade, the counterfeiters base.
>
> 8. The material contains much which the Plaintiffs regard as suspicious. For example, pages 1–4 on exhibit D.J.C.2. is a copy of a notebook seized from my home by the Plaintiffs. This, on page 2, contains a list of numbers and dates together with the name "Curly". "Curly" is the second Defendant herein who has admitted to handling counterfeit films.
>
> 9. As a result of this, and similar documents, together with evidence which indicates that over the past year I have handled rather considerable sums of money, the Plaintiffs consider that I am the ringleader of the counterfeiting gang which they exposed when they raided 7A and 8A York Parade.'

It does not seem to be in dispute that the evidence which the plaintiffs seek to adduce on their motion is indeed, at least to some extent, based on material obtained by their solicitors when they executed the Anton Piller order against the first defendant. It is evidence which of course, I have not yet seen, having regard to this application by the first defendant.

The ground for the present application, as submitted by counsel for the first defendant, is that the evidence on this motion shows that there is a very serious risk that the first defendant may be required to incriminate himself in answering questions about the documents seized in the Anton Piller raid; and further, counsel for the first defendant says, the documents themselves may incriminate the first defendant. That being so, he submits, the first defendant is entitled, having regard to the nature of what the possible incrimination may lead to, to claim privilege against those parts of the Anton Piller order which involves the handing over of the documents and material which he now seeks to have returned, together with any copies which may have been made of it.

Before I go further into that, with regard to how, in so far as the first defendant wishes to put it forward at this stage, that submission was founded, I go back to the same affidavit of the defendant. In para 9 he had pointed out that, as a result of what had been obtained, the plaintiffs consider that he is the ringleader of the counterfeiting gang which they have exposed when they raided 7A and 8A York Parade. He then continues:

> '10. In fact I am not, but I have considerable difficulty explaining the documents

which the Plaintiffs have seized. I do not wish to say in so many words why I have difficulty explaining them, but the reason may perhaps be gathered from the following paragraphs of the Affidavit which set out some of the reasons for which I would respectfully submit the Anton Piller and Mareva Orders should never have been made.

11. The most important evidence against me at the time of the application for the Anton Piller and Mareva Order was a combination of three matters: (i) I had been seen carrying a box into 8A York Parade, the premises where counterfeiting was being carried out. (I should say that I do not admit that I was seen entering those premises. I entered 7A, which is next door, but the point is of no importance since 7A was part of the same business as 8A). (ii) I was alleged to have been the purchaser of a "Transcan" machine for copying 16 mm film onto video cassettes. (I should say here that I was not in fact the owner, but the point is of no importance since I was undoubtedly involved in its purchase by a friend of mine, and I advised on what machine he should get). (iii) That I had hired a substantial number of video recorders from a company called Multi Broadcast. (Again the Plaintiffs had got the details wrong, but it is true that I was connected with a Company which owned a substantial number of video recorders).

12. What the Plaintiffs did not say in their evidence, but what I am sure they must have been well aware of it, is that the Transcan machine is never used for counterfeiting operations . . .'

He then goes into reasons, I need not go into this, why he says that a Transcan machine is suitable only for 16 mm film and says that counterfeiters work from 35 mm films. That matter is in issue on evidence on this motion, but I need not go into that further.

He goes on:

'13. There is, however, another possible use for the Transcan machine. I am quite sure that the Plaintiffs are and were well aware that this is so. This is for the copying of pornographic films onto tape. Pornographic films are available primarily on 16 mm film because they are shown in small dirty cinemas using relatively cheap amateurish equipment.

14. It will thus be appreciated that all the evidence relied on by the Plaintiffs on the application for the Anton Piller and Mareva Order is more consistent with the involvement by me in the manufacture and distribution of pornographic films than with involvement in the counterfeiting trade.

15. Such manufacture and distribution is often a criminal activity, but I was given no real opportunity to claim privilege from producing documents or answering questions at the time the Anton Piller and Mareva Order was enforced. Nor is the criminal nature of the activity merely technical: there has been a great deal of police activity in recent months, directed at cracking down on the manufacture and distribution of pornographic films.

16. I am seriously concerned that I will not be able adequately to answer the Plaintiffs' allegations, now that they have seized the documents referred to above, without incriminating myself.

17. I therefore respectfully ask this Honourable Court to discharge the Anton Piller and Mareva Order on the grounds that it should never have been granted.'

I mention in passing at this stage that it is not in dispute that included in the material which was seized on the execution of the Anton Piller order on the first defendant's premises were a number of films in which the plaintiffs did not have copyright, again there is no dispute about this, because they are pornographic films, with which of course they just say that they are never concerned. As to that particular material, counsel for the plaintiffs agrees, as I understood it, that it should be returned because it is not covered by the material ordered to be taken into custody under the Anton Piller order.

Counself for the first defendant submits that, if he can get the material in question on which some of the plaintiffs' case was based and used in their evidence handed back before the court sees it, it cannot be put before the court; and he says that that part of the Anton Piller order to which I have referred should be set aside and that, in setting aside that part of the order, I should provide in any order that I make on this motion that anything obtained in the course of enforcement of the order should not be made use of by the plaintiffs thereafter. That is covered by paras 2 and 3, but particularly para 3, of the notice of motion. He submits that that is a principle which should apply generally, because an Anton Piller order is, after all, always obtained ex parte and, if it should turn out that the person against whom an Anton Piller order is made and executed is able to establish afterwards that the order should not have been made in respect of some or all of the material in question, that should be the position, that is to say that the person against whom the order is made should be restored to the position as if the order had never been made.

It will be remembered that in *Rank Film Distributors Ltd v Video Information Centre* [1981] 2 All ER 76, [1982] AC 380, which was a case again concerned with an Anton Piller order, again made in a case dealing with video piracy, the plaintiffs in that particular case were owners of copyright in certain films; and, on the basis of evidence that, in breach of that copyright, the defendants were making and selling video cassette copies of those films, the plaintiffs obtained Anton Piller orders requiring, amongst other things, that the defendants should give immediate discovery of relevant documents and answers to interrogatories relating to the supply of infringing copies.

The defendants applied to Whitford J unsuccessfully to have those orders discharged, on the ground, inter alia, that, by disclosing the documents and answering the interrogatories, the defendants might expose themselves to criminal proceedings (see [1982] AC 380). That decision was set aside by a majority decision of the Court of Appeal ([1980] 2 All ER 273, [1982] AC 380), and, on appeal to the House of Lords, the House dismissed the plaintiffs' appeal, holding that the defendants were entitled to rely on privilege against self-incrimination by discovery or by refusing to answer interrogatories, since, if they complied with the orders, there was in the circumstances a real appreciable risk of criminal proceedings for conspiracy to defraud being taken against them. It was also indicated in their Lordships' speeches in the House of Lords, particularly that of Lord Wilberforce, that the mere fact that such a discovery might have resulted in the defendants being prosecuted for breaches of s 21 of the Copyright Act 1956 (which I interpolate is, of course, that provision in the Act which provides for criminal remedies in respect of infringement) was not sufficient reason of itself to enable the privilege against self-incrimination to be relied on.

In the short speech in the House of Lords of Lord Russell, in which he agrees with the speeches of Lord Wilberforce and of Lord Fraser concurring in the dismissal of the appeal, he went on and made a special plea in these terms ([1981] 2 All ER 76 at 86, [1982] AC 380 at 448):

> 'Inasmuch as the application of the privilege in question can go a long way in this and other analogous fields to deprive the owner of his just rights to the protection of his property I would welcome legislation somewhat on the lines of s 31 of the Theft Act 1968; the aim of such legislation should be to remove the privilege while at the same time preventing the use in criminal proceedings of statements which otherwise have been privileged.'

The speeches in the House were given on 8 April 1981. The plea was speedily answered by s 72 of the Supreme Court Act 1981. Counsel for the plaintiffs says that s 72 of that Act is the short answer to the first defendant's present motion; counsel for the first defendant seeks to construe s 72, to which I will come in a moment, narrowly and submits that the present case is outside its ambit and that further he is entitled to claim privilege on the basis of the decision in the *Rank* case.

However, before coming to s 72 of the 1981 Act, I should deal with counsel for the first defendant's submission to which I have already referred, that, if he can pursue his application, get the material back into his hands and obtain the order which he seeks *a* against use of any material or information gained thereby, it cannot thereafter be put before the court as evidence for the plaintiffs in support of their motion or their action.

In his answer to that submission, counsel for the plaintiffs say that, even if he is wrong in his submission that s 72 of the 1981 Act is a complete answer to the defendant's application, nevertheless the court should not order the return of the material or of any copies and should not prevent him from making use of such information as he has *b* gained. He says that the Anton Piller order has been implemented, and he relies on the decision of the Court of Appeal in *Helliwell v Piggott-Sims* [1980] FSR 356. The heading to that report is in these terms:

> '*Admissibility of evidence obtained by plaintiffs in implementation of full Anton Piller Order – Objection taken by defendants – Evidence admitted by trial judge – Defendants' appeal dismissed – No discretion in civil cases to refuse unlawfully obtained evidence.*'

c

I read that because these reports do not, in the ordinary way, provide the usual type of headnote.

Lord Denning MR said this, in giving a short judgment (at 356–357):

> 'This is an aftermath of the recent case in this court of Rank Film Distributors *d* about Anton Piller orders. The majority of the court, although it approved those orders to some extent, nevertheless placed restrictions on them. In our present case a full Anton Piller order was made at the end of 1977 by Fox J. That order was implemented and, as a result, quite a number of documents and other material were found and became available to the plaintiffs in the cause. No application was made to discharge that order, or anything of that kind. The case has come on for trial now before Whitford J. for final determination. In the course of the case the plaintiffs *e* propose to put in evidence which has been obtained as a result of the full Anton Piller order. Objection was made to a lot of that evidence being given because, it was said, in the light of the recent decision in *Rank Film* case in the Court of Appeal, some portions of the evidence were unlawfully obtained. In those circumstances, it is said that the judge ought not to admit it now. He had a discretion to refuse to *f* admit it. Furthermore, he refused to adjourn the case. He said that he was going to admit it, and that he would go on with the case. [Counsel for the defendant] appeals from that decision to this court. It seems to me that there is a very short answer to it. Assuming for a moment that the full order ought not to have been made in the first place in 1977, nevertheless it has been implemented. The evidence is available in the hands of the plaintiffs for them to give in evidence. I do not think that the judge has any discretion to refuse to admit it in evidence. I know that in criminal *g* cases the judge may have a discretion. That is shown by *Kuruma* v. *The Queen* ([1955] 1 All ER 236, [1955] AC 197). But so far as civil cases are concerned, it seems to me that the judge has no discretion. The evidence is relevant and admissible. The judge cannot refuse it on the ground that it may have been unlawfully obtained in the beginning. I do not say that it was unlawfully obtained. It was obtained under an *h* Anton Piller order which was not appealed against. But, even if it was unlawfully obtained, nevertheless the judge is right to admit it in evidence and to go on with the case as he proposes to do. I think this application must be refused.'

Bridge and Oliver LJJ agreed with that short judgment.

However, counsel for the first defendant distinguished that case by pointing out that Lord Denning MR specifically stated that there had been no application in the proceedings *j* to get those documents returned; and counsel for the first defendant then referred me to, and relied on, the decision of Warner J in *ITC Film Distributors v Video Exchange Ltd* [1982] 2 All ER 241, [1982] Ch 431. In view of his reliance on that, I must look at it a little closely. In that particular case, the headnote (see [1982] Ch 431) makes clear that the plaintiffs, who were again companies concerned in the production or distribution of feature films—

> 'brought an action alleging breach of copyright by the defendants, whose business included the management of a club providing facilities in connection with video *a* cassettes. During the course of the hearing of motions in the action on July 31, 1981, the second defendant, C., obtained possession of certain documents belonging to the plaintiffs or their solicitors. He refused to return the documents and exhibited some of them with other documents to a long affidavit sworn on October 1, 1981. The plaintiffs by notice of motion sought, inter alia, an injunction restraining the making of copies of any of the documents without their consent, delivery up of all *b* the documents or copies thereof which were in C.'s possession, and an injunction restraining him from making any use of the documents or copies or of any information contained in them.'

In other words, the relief sought there was very similar to that which is sought by the first defendant in the case before me. The headnote continued:

c

> 'On October 1, Warner J. heard, first, motions brought by C. in which C.'s affidavit with the plaintiffs' documents exhibited was referred to and used for the purpose of cross-examining a witness. The plaintiffs' motion was then heard and, when the judge found as a fact that C. had obtained the documents by a trick, C. consented to an order being made subject to the qualification that he was not deprived of the use of the documents exhibited to his affidavit. The judge made the *d* order as sought by the plaintiffs but, pending further order, subject to a proviso, entitling C. to retain and use, for the purposes of the action only, copies of the documents thus exhibited.'

Then the judge, as I understood it, heard further argument whether the proviso should stand.

In regard to the documents which have not been used in cross-examination and, *e* therefore, answers to which in cross-examination the judge felt he could not thereafter disregard, he refused to make the order, but in respect of documents not up to that stage used, he was prepared to make the order sought by plaintiffs. It is important to realise that the judge had cited to him the *Helliwell* case, on which counsel for the plaintiffs relies.

In his judgment the judge turned to deal with the law, and he said that Mr Chappell, *f* who was the defendant in question—

> 'relies on the general rule that in civil, as distinct from criminal, proceedings the court has no power to exclude relevant evidence, even though that evidence has been unlawfully or improperly obtained; and on the cognate rule that, if the original of a document is privileged, secondary evidence of its contents, such as a copy of it, *g* may if available be adduced. He relies in particular on *Calcraft v Guest* [1898] 1 QB 759, [1895–9] All ER Rep 346 and *Helliwell v Piggott-Sims* [1980] FSR 356. Counsel for the plaintiffs puts his case in two ways. First, he relies on *Lord Ashburton v Pape* [1913] 2 Ch 469, [1911–13] All ER Rep 708. He submits, and I agree, that that was not an isolated decision but is illustrative of a general rule that, where A has improperly obtained possession of a document belonging to B, the court will, at the *h* suit of B, order A to return the document to B and to deliver up any copies of it that A has made, and will restrain A from making any use of any such copies or of the information contained in the document.'

(See [1982] 2 All ER 241 at 244, [1982] Ch 431 at 438.)

Then the judge cited from *Lord Ashburton v Pape* [1913] 2 Ch 469 at 473, 474, 476–477, [1911–13] All ER Rep 708 at 710, 711, 712–713 in the Court of Appeal a passage *j* from the judgment of Cozens-Hardy MR, a passage from the judgment of Kennedy LJ and a passage from the judgment of Swifen Eady LJ. I should point that in the passage cited from the judgment of Kennedy LJ he is quoted as saying:

> 'I agree that the better view seems to me to be that although it is true that the

principle which is laid down in *Calcroft* v. *Guest* must be followed, yet, at the same
a time, if, before the occasion of the trial when a copy may be used, although a copy improperly obtained, the owner of the original can successfully promote proceedings against the person who has improperly obtained the copy to stop his using it, the owner is none the less entitled to protection, because, if the question had arisen in the course of a trial before such proceedings, the holder of the copy would not have been prevented from using it on account of the illegitimacy of its origin. If that is
b so, it decides this case.'

In the passage quoted from Swinfen Eady LJ's judgment, there occurs this passage:

'There is here a confusion between the right to restrain a person from divulging confidential information and the right to give secondary evidence of documents where the originals are privileged from production, if the party has such secondary
c evidence in his possession. The cases are entirely separate and distinct. If a person were to steal a deed, nevertheless in any dispute to which it was relevant the original deed might be given in evidence by him at the trial. It would be no objection to the admissibility of the deed in evidence to say you ought not to have possession of it. His unlawful possession would not affect the admissibility of the deed in evidence if otherwise admissible. So again with regard to any copy he had. If he was unable to
d obtain or compel production of the original because it was privileged, if he had a copy in his possession it would be admissible as secondary evidence. The fact, however, that a document, whether original or copy, is admissible in evidence is no answer to the demand of the lawful owner for the delivery up of the document, and no answer to an application by the lawful owner of confidential information to restrain it from being published or copied.'

e

After citing those passages from the judgment in the Court of Appeal in *Lord Ashburton v Pape* Warner J goes on ([1982] 2 All ER 241 at 246–247, [1982] Ch 431 at 440–441):

'I have little doubt that if, on or before 1 October, the plaintiffs and Messrs Clifford-Turner (for it appears to me that some at least of the documents here in question probably belong to Messrs Clifford-Turner rather than to the plaintiffs) had
f issued a writ against Mr Chappell claiming relief on the lines of that granted in *Lord Ashburton v Pape*, and had on a motion in that action sought an order for such relief, they would have been held entitled to it. But there seem to me to be diffculties in the way of my granting the plaintiffs such relief on the basis of *Lord Ashburton v Pape* now. I need not, however, discuss those difficulties because counsel for the plaintiffs has satisfied me that as regards, at all events the exhibits to Mr Chappell's affidavit
g that I have not yet looked at, he is entitled to succeed on his alternative submission. That submission is in a nutshell that, in the circumstances of this case, I must balance the public interest that the truth should be ascertained, which is the reason for the rule in *Calcraft v Guest*, against the public interest that litigants should be able to bring their documents into court without fear that they may be filched by their opponents, whether by stealth or by a trick, and then used by them in evidence.
h Counsel for the plaintiffs referred me in particular to *Riddick v Thames Board Mills Ltd* [1977] 3 All ER 677, [1977] QB 881, where it was held that a document obtained on discovery in an action could not be used as the basis of a subsequent action. By the same token, said counsel for the plaintiffs, such a document could not be used in evidence in a subsequent action. This case is, counsel for the plaintiffs submitted, a fortiori because in *Riddick v Thames Board Mills Ltd* the document had been lawfully
j obtained in the first place.'

Then there is a citation from the speech of Lord Simon in *D v National Society for the Prevention of Cruelty to Children* [1977] 1 All ER 589 at 607, [1978] AC 171 at 233, and I need not read that; but he goes on, after citing that passage from the speech of Lord Simon, to say:

> 'Counsel for the plaintiffs submits that I should in my turn add the present case to the list [that is the list of exceptions]. I think that the interests of the proper a administration of justice require that I should do so. I do not overlook that for a party to litigation to take possession by stealth or by a trick of documents belonging to the other side within the precincts of the court is probably contempt of court, so that there may be another sanction. But it seems to me that, if it is contempt of court, then the court should not countenance it by admitting such documents in evidence. Nor do I overlook the decision of the Court of Appeal in *R v Tompkins* b (1977) 67 Cr App R 181. But that case proceeded on the footing that the document in question there had come into the possession of the prosecution fortuitously. The relevance of possible impropriety was not discussed.'

I can omit the next paragraph from the judge's judgment, but he concludes in this way:

> 'On the other hand, I do not think it possible for me now to exclude the c documents that I have already looked at. Of course, it often happens that a judge is called on to look at a document in order to see whether it is admissible in evidence. If, having done so, he decides that it is not, he puts its contents out of his mind, even though that is not always an easy mental feat. But here the documents, although perhaps they have not been formally put in evidence, have in fact been used as evidence. It is quite impossible for me, for instance, to ignore the answers given by d Mr Browne when such documents were put to him. I therefore think that the provisos in my order must stand as regards those documents. I draw comfort from the thought that counsel for the plaintiffs could have excluded them if he had opened the present motion on 1 October, instead of inviting me to deal first with Mr Chappell's new motions and then to hear Mr Browne's cross-examination. I do not wish, in saying that, to imply any criticism of counsel for the plaintiffs' conduct e of the case, for which there were no doubt good reasons, but merely to indicate that a different course would have led to a different result.'

In this particular case, of course, the motion by the first defendant to exclude these documents has been brought before they have been made use of in court. I stress that, in coming to that conclusion, Warner J had had cited to him *Helliwell v Piggott-Sims* [1980] f FSR 356. I think that, in view of that decision, if I should conclude that the defendant is not barred by the provisions of s 72 of the Supreme Court Act 1981, I should order the return of the documents concerned and make the order that he seeks, this being a case where the defendant has properly brought proceedings for the return of the documents in the form of the present application, and that before they have been adduced in any form or shape or any evidence based on them has been put before the court.

I therefore turn to consider what is really the main point on the application, and that g is s 72 of the 1981 Act. By sub-s (1), it provides:

> 'In any proceedings to which this subsection applies a person shall not be excused, by reason that to do so would tend to expose that person, or his or her spouse, to proceedings for a related offence or for the recovery of a related penalty—(*a*) from answering any question put to that person in the first-mentioned proceedings; or (*b*) h from complying with any order made in those proceedings.'

I pause there to say that it will be seen that, so far as whatever comes within the term 'related offence' to which I will come in a moment is concerned, that subsection is in effect reversing the effect of the decision in *Rank Film Distributors Ltd v Video Information Centre* [1981] 2 All ER 76, [1982] AC 380.

Subsection (2) provides: j

> 'Subsection (1) applies to the following civil proceedings in the High Court, namely—(*a*) proceedings for infringement of rights pertaining to any intellectual property or for passing off; (*b*) proceedings brought to obtain disclosure of information relating to any infringement of such rights or to any passing off; and

> (*c*) proceedings brought to prevent any apprehended infringement of such rights or
> a any apprehended passing off.'

So that sub-s (1) is limited to those kinds of proceedings.

Subsection (3) provides some protection for the person against whom such an order as an Anton Piller order would operate. It provides:

> 'Subject to subsection (4), no statement or admission made by a person—(*a*) in
> b answering a question put to him in any proceedings to which subsection (1) applies; or (*b*) in complying with any order made in any such proceedings, shall, in proceedings for any related offence or for the recovery of any related penalty, be admissible in evidence against that person or (unless they married after the making of the statement or admission) against the spouse of that person.'

c I pause there to say that that is closely analogous to s 31 of the Theft Act 1968.

Subsection (4) provides:

> 'Nothing in subsection (3) shall render any statement or admission made by a person as there mentioned inadmissible in evidence against that person in proceedings for perjury or contempt of court.'

d Subsection (5) has some definitions, and it provides:

> 'In this section—"intellectual property" means any patent, trade mark, copyright, registered design, technical or commercial information or other intellectual property ..."'

We are concerned in the present case with an action for infringement of copyright.

e Then I come to the important definition, that of 'related offence'. It says:

> '"related offence", in relation to any proceedings to which subsection (1) applies, means—(*a*) in the case of proceedings within subsection (2)(*a*) or (*b*)–(i) any offence committed by or in the course of the infringement or passing off to which these proceedings relate; or (ii) any offence not within sub-paragraph (i) committed in connection with that infringement or passing off, being an offence involving fraud
> f or dishonesty; (*b*) in the case of proceedings within subsection (2)(*c*), any offence revealed by the facts on which the plaintiff relies in those proceedings.'

So far as para (*a*) in that definition of 'related offence' is concerned, that specifically relates back to the type of proceedings which are mentioned in sub-s (2)(*a*) or (*b*), and they are:

> g '(*a*) proceedings for infringement of rights pertaining to any intellectual property [which of course includes copyright]... (*b*) proceedings brought to obtain disclosure of information relating to any infringement of such rights or to any passing off...'

That para (*b*) covers the sort of proceedings that were brought in *Norwich Pharmacal Co v Customs and Excise Comrs* [1973] 2 All ER 943, [1974] AC 133. I need not concern myself
h further with those. The two types of offence under that part of the definition each refers to an offence committed, that is to say, in sub-para (i), an 'offence committed by or in the course of the infringement or passing off...' or, in the case of sub-para (ii), 'any offence not within sub-paragraph (i) committed in connection with that infringement or passing off...'

It is therefore submitted, and I agree, that that part of the definition is dealing with
i offences which have been committed, and it does require that an infringement or a passing off shall have taken place. Sub-paragraph (i) would cover, for instance, an offence, if we are speaking about infringement of copyright, under s 21 of the Copyright Act 1956. I am not intending to be exclusive in giving that example. Under sub-para (ii) we have 'any offence not within sub-paragraph (i) [that is to say an offence 'committed by or in the course of the infringement'] committed in connection with that infringement or

passing off, being an offence involving fraud or dishonesty', and that is just the sort of offence which was being dealt with and considered in *Rank Film Distributors Ltd v Video Information Centre* [1981] 2 All ER 76, [1982] AC 380, that is to say, for example, an offence of conspiracy to counterfeit in order to defraud. Again, it has to be an offence which has been committed in connection with an infringement or with passing off.

But, when one comes to the second part of the definition under sub-para (*b*), we have—

> 'in the case of proceedings within subsection (2)(*c*), any offence revealed by the facts on which the plaintiff relies in those proceedings.'

As far as sub-s (2)(*c*) is concerned, those are proceedings brought to prevent any apprehended infringement of such rights or any apprehended passing off, i e proceedings where the actual infringement or passing off has not yet taken place but is apprehended. That wording covers, in the case of such proceedings, any offence revealed by the facts on which the plaintiffs rely in these proceedings.

As I understand his submission, counsel for the first defendant says that in that definition of 'related offence' in para (*b*) the words 'any offence' have got to be read narrowly and read in the light of the kind of offences which are described or defined in the previous para (*a*). As I understand it, for example, he agrees that under para (*b*), if the facts in question were being relied on by the plaintiffs to establish a future infringement of their copyright, then, if those facts revealed that there had been a conspiracy to effect such infringement, for example, to counterfeit films, that would be caught by that part of the definition, and it would become a 'related offence' for the purpose of s 72. I have no doubt that that part of the definition would cover such an offence, but I see no reason, on the plain language of the statute, to limit it to that. If the legislature had intended that the offence under para (*b*) should be narrowly restricted to the sort of offence which comes under either limb of para (*a*), but on the facts which have occurred although the infringement had not yet been committed, it would have been so simple for the legislature to have so defined and narrowed the definition. The definition in para (*b*) is in striking contrast to the definition of the offence under sub-paras (i) and (ii); and I see no reason whatsoever for limiting the offence in para (*b*) of the definition in the way that counsel for the first defendant seeks to have it construed and limited. The wording 'any offence revealed by the facts on which the plaintiff relies' would, in my judgment, cover any kind of offence, and is not restricted in the way that counsel for the first defendant seeks to have it construed.

That being so, I think the plaintiffs are right in saying that this is a case where the short answer to the first defendant's application on their motion is to be found in s 72, which prevents the first defendant from raising the plea of privilege in that the documents and the material concerned might tend to incriminate him or that he might, in answering question relating to that material, be in danger of incriminating himself.

On that basis, I refuse the first defendant's application made on his motion.

Application dismissed. Leave to appeal granted on terms.

Solicitors: *Michael Davis & Co* (for the first defendant); *A E Hamlin & Co* (for the plaintiffs).

Evelyn M C Budd Barrister.

Re American Greetings Corp's Application

CHANCERY DIVISION
WHITFORD J
20, 29 OCTOBER 1982

COURT OF APPEAL, CIVIL DIVISION
SIR JOHN DONALDSON MR, DILLON LJ AND SIR DENYS BUCKLEY
28, 29 MARCH, 28 APRIL 1983

Trade mark – Registered users – Trafficking in trade mark – Application for registration of trade mark and registration of person as registered user – Proprietor not using or proposing to use mark in connection with goods similar to those to be marketed by licensees – Licence agreements including quality control provisions exercisable by proprietor over licensees' goods – Whether grant of proprietor's applications tending to facilitate 'trafficking' in trade mark – Trade Marks Act 1938, s 28(6).

The applicants, an American company, were the proprietors of a trade mark consisting of the drawing of a fictional character, a little girl, to which the applicants gave the name Holly Hobbie. They used the trade mark in relation to greeting cards and a small range of other goods marketed by them in the USA. The drawing and name were popular with the American public, causing the applicants to engage in the USA in the business of licensing the use of the drawing and name (known as 'character merchandising') to merchants who wished to promote their own ranges of goods by using the trade mark in connection with those goods. The applicants wished to extend the character merchandising aspect of their business to England and to licence licensees in England to use the Holly Hobbie name in connection with a wide variety of goods to be marketed by the licensees. The applicants themselves neither used nor proposed to use the trade mark in connection with those goods. Accordingly, the applicants applied under s 29(1)(*b*)[a] of the Trade Marks Act 1938 to the registrar of trade marks to have the name comprised in their trade mark registered in respect of 12 classes of goods which the applicants' licensees wished to market in association with the name. Each application was supported by a registered user agreement with the relevant licensee and also by an application for the registration of the licensee as a registered user under s 28[b] of the 1938 Act. Each agreement contained comprehensive provisions for the exercise of control by the applicants over the quality of the licensee's goods to be marketed under the applicants' trade name. The assistant registrar refused to grant the applications on the ground that the grant would tend to facilitate 'trafficking' in the applicants' trade mark, contrary to s 28(6) of the 1938 Act. On appeal the judge upheld the registrar's decision. The applicants appealed to the Court of Appeal.

Held – The appeal would be dismissed for the following reasons—

(1) Since the reason for prohibiting 'trafficking' in a trade mark was to protect the public, when it had become accustomed to the trade mark as identifying goods which came from a particular source, against being deceived by the use of the mark on goods which came from a different source, it followed that for the purposes of s 28(6) of the 1938 Act 'trafficking' meant any disposal of a trade mark or the reputation in the name as a marketable commodity in circumstances where there was no trade connection between the proprietor of the mark and the goods or business in respect of which the mark was to be used. Thus, trafficking was not restricted to illegal or similar improper dealing in a trade mark, or to preventing of the outright transfer of a trade mark or to

a Section 29(1), so far as material, is set out at p 618 *c d*, post
b Section 28, so far as material, is set out at p 618 *j* to p 619 *f*, post

preventing the evasion of the restrictions on assignment of a trade mark contained in
s 22[c] of the 1938 Act. Furthermore, the mere fact that a licence granted by the proprietor *a*
to use his trade mark included provisions entitling the proprietor to control the quality
of the licensee's goods marketed under the trade mark did not automatically constitute a
trade connection between the proprietor and the licensee's goods (see p 619 *h*, p 620 *d e*,
p 621 *f g j*, p 622 *d* to *h*, p 623 *c d f* to p 624 *c g h*, post); dicta of Earl Loreburn in *Bowden
Wire Ltd v Bowden Brake Co Ltd* (1914) 31 RPC at 392 and of Cross J in *British Petroleum Co
Ltd v European Petroleum Distributors Ltd* [1968] RPC at 63 applied; dictum of Aickin J in *b*
Pioneer Electronic Corp v Registrar of Trade Marks [1978] RPC at 731 not followed.

(2) Since the applicants intended to dispose of their trade mark as a marketing aid to
the licensees to promote the sale by them of a wide variety of goods in the production
and marketing of which the applicants were to play no part, the purpose of including
quality control provisions in the licences was to protect the trade mark as a marketable
commodity and not to protect the applicants' goods or business. Therefore the quality *c*
control provisions did not constitute a sufficient trade connection between the applicants
and the goods to be marketed by the licensees, and, since the grant of the applications
would tend to deceive and confuse the public regarding the source of goods marketed
under the trade mark, it followed that the grant of the applications would tend to
facilitate trafficking in the trade mark (see p 621 *j* to p 622 *a*, p 623 *c d* and p 624 *d* to *h*,
post). *d*

Notes

For registration of a proposed registered user of a trade mark, see 38 Halsbury's Laws (3rd
edn) 587, para 980.

For the Trade Marks Act 1938, ss 22, 28, 29, see 37 Halsbury's Statutes (3rd edn) 907,
913, 916. *e*

Cases referred to in judgments

Batt (John) & Co's Registered Trade Marks, Re, re Carter's Application [1898] 2 Ch 432; *affd* [1898] 2 Ch 432, CA; *affd* [1899] AC 110, HL.

Bowden Wire Ltd v Bowden Brake Co Ltd (1914) 31 RPC 385, HL.

British Petroleum Co Ltd v European Petroleum Distributors Ltd [1968] RPC 54. *f*

General Electric Co v The General Electric Co Ltd [1969] RPC 418; *rvsd* [1970] RPC 339, CA; *rvsd* [1972] 2 All ER 507, [1972] 1 WLR 729, HL.

Pioneer Electronic Corp v Registrar of Trade Marks [1978] RPC 716, Aust HC.

Radiation Trade Mark, Re (1930) 47 RPC 37.

Sinclair (John) Ltd's Trade Mark, Re [1932] 1 Ch 598, CA.

Cases also cited *g*

'Bostitch' Trade Mark [1963] RPC 183.

Coles (J H) Pty Ltd v J F Need [1934] AC 82.

Pinto v Badman (1891) 8 RPC 181, CA.

Originating motion

By an originating motion dated 13 May 1982 the applicants, American Greetings Corp, a *h*
company incorporated in the State of Ohio, USA, sought an order reversing the decision
of the assistant registrar of trade marks, Mr D G A Myall (acting for the registrar), dated
2 April 1982, refusing 12 applications by the applicants, made pursuant to the Trade
Marks Act 1938, to register the trade mark Holly Hobbie in 12 different classes of the
register of trade marks, on the ground that the grant of the applications would tend to
facilitate trafficking in the trade mark. The principal ground of the motion was that the *j*
assistant registrar was wrong in law and fact in finding that the grant of the applications
would tend to facilitate trafficking in the trade mark. The facts are set out in the
judgment.

c Section 22, so far as material, is set out at p 620 *f g*, post

Robin Jacob QC and *Michael Silverleaf* for the applicants.
Gerald Paterson for the registrar of trade marks.

Cur adv vult

29 October. The following judgment was delivered.

WHITFORD J. American Greetings Corp have made applications to register the words 'Holly Hobbie' as a trade mark in 12 different classes in respect of a very extensive variety of goods.

Trade marks can only be registered by virtue of the provisions of s 17 of the Trade Marks Act 1938. Subsections (1) and (2) of s 17 are in these terms:

> '(1) Any person claiming to be the proprietor of a trade mark used or proposed to be used by him who is desirous of registering it must apply in writing to the Registrar in the prescribed manner for registration either in Part A or in Part B of the register.
>
> (2) Subject to the provisions of this Act, the Registrar may refuse the application, or may accept it absolutely or subject to such amendments, modifications, conditions or limitations, if any, as he may think right.'

Trade Mark Form 2, the application form, accords with the terms of s 17.

There is a provision for defensive registrations where there is in fact no intention to use, but we are not in any way concerned with any question of defensive registrations.

On applications covering such a wide variety of goods the registrar of trade marks may be forgiven for wondering whether the mark was in use by the applicants or whether there was, indeed, any intention on the part of the applicants to use it in respect of all these goods. A letter seeking further information on this point was sent by the registrar to the applicants' agents on 25 October 1979. Other questions arose touching these applications. Many of these questions have, I think, been resolved. I propose first to deal with the main objection argued before me on the appeal. Indeed, there were only two objections that were argued before me. The first was based on the width of the claim to use or proposed use.

The applicants, who have, I gather, long dealt in greetings cards and similar materials, have developed in the United States over the course of the years a rather different business interest. This started when one of their executives saw some drawings by Holly Ulinskas Hobby, which, in the words of the author of their brochure 'A Gallery of Fresh Ideas from American Greetings', 'captured the rustic innocence of her own childhood in water colour paintings of little girls in calico and lace'.

So Holly Hobbie was born. Her name and likeness were first used by the applicants in 1967 on greetings cards and related products; and since then (again, I quote from words to be found in the same brochure) 'through licensing, she's expanded into almost every product area. Now over 412 products manufactured by some 66 companies bear Holly's name'. This brochure is dealing with the American market as the matter stood in 1978. At this date we learn from the brochure that top manufacturers were saying such things as: 'She will establish herself quickly in the jewelry marketplace'; 'She's been a substantial factor in Knickerbocker's growth' (which, I should perhaps add, seems to have been in the toy field rather than that of articles of apparel); 'the consumer is looking forward to Holly Hobbie cakes'; 'We plan to introduce new Holly products regularly'; and so on.

The applicants want to promote the use of the Holly Hobbie trade mark over here in exactly the same way; they want to use the mark on their own fairly limited range of products, and no difficulty arises on registration so far as these are concerned. They also, however, want to license other manufacturers to use the Holly Hobbie mark on any goods for which it may be thought suitable. Over here, as in America, they intend not only to sell their own goods but to sell to others the right to use this mark Holly Hobbie. In respect of the vast majority of goods covered by the present applications for registration, they had never used the mark, nor had they ever had any intention to use it. On the basis of the strict provisions of s 17 of the 1938 Act alone, the case of the applicants on the a applications for registration must accordingly fail.

It is necessary, however, to look a little further. When the trade mark registry was first established by the Registration of Trade Marks Act 1875, it was specifically enacted by s 2:

> 'A trade mark must be registered as belonging to particular goods, or classes of b goods; and when registered shall be assigned and transmitted only in connexion with the goodwill of the business concerned . . .'

It was also provided that a mark should be determinable with the goodwill.

At common law, the right of traders to protect marks distinctive of their goods has long been recognised. It was also recognised that the public had an interest in trade marks in this sense: that, to the purchaser, a mark indicates or should indicate the c genuine goods. For this reason, at common law licensing of a trade mark was held destructive of its validity, and marks were assignable only with the goodwill.

The common law position, which was expressly preserved in relation to registered trade marks by the 1875 Act, continued in this country to be thus preserved until 1938. The Trade Marks Act 1938 had been preceded by an investigation into the law and practice relating to trade marks carried out by a committee set up in 1933, the Goschen d committee. Among its recommendations, the Goschen committee recommended that registered trade marks should be assignable without any assignment of goodwill (see Report of the Departmental Committee on the Law and Practice Relating to Trade Marks (Cmd 4568)). They further recommended that an assignment in respect of some only of the goods the subject of the registration should be permitted, with the safeguard that an assignor should not be allowed to continue to use the mark on goods of the same e description as those for which it was going to be assigned.

It is plain, however (and I shall come further to deal with this), that it must have been suggested to this committee that a relaxation in the rule as to assignment might lead to a 'trafficking' (the word to be considered as notionally being in inverted commas) in trade marks.

The committee was also urged to make provision for some form of licensing. It was f suggested that parent companies should be entitled to license specifically. It was suggested that third persons might be licensed provided that there was some association between the licensor and the licensee; others suggested that there need not necessarily be any restriction of this kind. The committee was not prepared to recommend a system of unrestricted licensing, fearing that it might result in deception and confusion among the purchasing public. They were, however, of the view that in the public interest it would g none the less be possible to allow licensing, which is what traders were seeking, but that the public interest required that there should be strict control. Subject to this, they were of the view that licensing need not be limited to parent-subsidiary or any other especial relationships.

At an earlier stage in the report, the committee turned their mind to a consideration of the definition of a trade mark. At the relevant date, 'trade mark' was defined in s 3 of h the then subsisting Act (the Trade Marks Act 1905) in these terms:

> 'A "trade mark" shall mean a mark used or proposed to be used upon or in connection with goods for the purpose of indicating that they are the goods of the proprietor of such trade mark by virtue of manufacture, selection, certification, dealing with, or offering for sale . . .'

j

The Goschen committee said this in their report (p 8, sub-para (iii)):

> 'Recommendations we make later on (Paragraph 115) for relaxing some of the present restrictions on the assignment of trade marks might, unless precautions are taken, have the effect of encouraging the registration of trade marks by persons who have no intention themselves to use the marks in trade, but register them merely in

order to sell them. We think it advisable to add the words "by the proprietor" after the word "used" where that word occurs for the second time in order to make it clear that an applicant for registration must himself have used or must himself propose to use the trade mark to indicate a connection in the course of the trade between him and the goods. There are, however, two instances in which we think this requirement must be relaxed provided that trafficking in registered trade marks is not thereby facilitated. The first case is that of a person who does not himself trade but desires to register a trade mark to be used only by others under the "registered user" provisions we propose in Paragraph 123. No doubt this case can be met under our "registered user" proposals by registration of the mark in the name of one of the persons who does in fact propose to use it; but it would often be more convenient if the registration could be in the name of a non-trading applicant.'

When Parliament enacted the Trade Marks Act 1938, a rather different definition of 'trade mark' was in fact adopted. Licensing provisions, called in the 1938 Act 'registered user' provisions', were introduced. I must come to s 28, the relevant section touching registered user, but before I come to that (it is perhaps the vital question so far as this present proceeding is concerned) I shall turn briefly to s 29 of the Act, which by sub-s (1) provides:

> 'No application for the registration of a trade mark in respect of any goods shall be refused, nor shall permission for such registration be withheld, on the ground only that it appears that the applicant does not use or propose to use the trade mark . . . (*b*) if the application is accompanied by an application for the registration of a person as a registered user of the trade mark, and the tribunal is satisfied that the proprietor intends it to be used by that person in relation to those goods and the tribunal is also satisfied that that person will be registered as a registered user thereof immediately after the registration of the trade mark.'

The Goschen committee had in fact recommended an amendment of the then application section, s 12, to bring about an effect which was in fact brought about in 1938 by the enactment of s 29(1)(*a*) and (*b*). There was in fact no relevant amendment of the section dealing with the question of applications for registration, s 17.

All the applications in suit were the subject of contemporaneous registered user applications. In the result, of course, the apparent difficulty which might otherwise have arisen under s 17 is overcome.

I come to s 28, and I must read some of the subsections:

> '(1) Subject to the provisions of this section, a person other than the proprietor of a trade mark may be registered as a registered user thereof in respect of all or any of the goods in respect of which it is registered (otherwise than as a defensive trade mark) and either with or without conditions or restrictions. The use of a trade mark by a registered user thereof in relation to goods with which he is connected in the course of trade and in respect of which for the time being the trade mark remains registered and he is registered as a registered user, being use such as to comply with any conditions or restrictions to which his registration is subject, is in this Act referred to as the "permitted use" thereof . . .
>
> '(4) Where it is proposed that a person should be registered as a registered user of a trade mark, the proprietor and the proposed registered user must apply in writing to the Registrar in the prescribed manner and must furnish him with a statutory declaration made by the proprietor, or by some person authorised to act on his behalf and approved by the Registrar, (*a*) giving particulars of the relationship, existing or proposed, between the proprietor and the proposed registered user, including particulars showing the degree of control by the proprietor over the permitted use which their relationship will confer and whether it is a term of their relationship that the proposed registered user shall be the sole registered user or that there shall be any other restriction as to persons for whose registration as registered

users application may be made; (*b*) stating the goods in respect of which registration is proposed; (*c*) stating any conditions or restrictions proposed with respect to the characteristics of the goods, to the mode or place of permitted use, or to any other matter; and (*d*) stating whether the permitted use is to be for a period or without limit of period, and, if for a period, the duration thereof; and with such further documents, information or evidence as may be required under the rules or by the Registrar.

(5) When the requirements of the last foregoing subsection have been complied with, if the Registrar, after considering the information furnished to him under that subsection, is satisfied that in all the circumstances the use of the trade mark in relation to the proposed goods or any of them by the proposed registered user subject to any conditions or restrictions which the Registrar thinks proper would not be contrary to the public interest, the Registrar may register the proposed registered user as a registered user in respect of the goods as to which he is so satisfied subject as aforesaid.

(6) The Registrar shall refuse an application under the foregoing provisions of this section if it appears to him that the grant thereof would tend to facilitate trafficking in a trade mark . . .'

The question is: will the grant of these applications for registered usership facilitate trafficking in the trade mark Holly Hobbie? If it will, the registrar must refuse registration. Subsection (6) is to be contrasted with sub-s (5), where, on a consideration of public interest, in general terms the registrar is left with a discretion. If the registered user applications are not going to succeed, the terms of s 29(1)(*b*) cannot be met and the applications for trade mark registrations must fail on the terms of s 17.

The assistant registrar, in the decision under appeal, sets out in rather more detail the nature of the applicants' activities, as outlined in their own literature and evidence. Setting aside the greetings card side of the business, the side with which we are now concerned was at one stage described by Mr Grant, an agent then acting for the applicants, as 'character merchandising'. Of this, the assistant registrar says in his decision:

'At the rehearing Mr Grant said that the applicants were engaged in two sorts of enterprise, namely as manufacturers and merchants on their own account and as licensors in the business of character merchandising. The phrase "character merchandising" is one of imprecise meaning in this country when it comes to the definition of legal rights, but was explained to me by Mr Grant as one of legitimate exploitation of a character in, for example, a film, play or book by the owner's licensing of its association with the goods of traders who have no other connection with him. However, I informed Mr Grant that it seemed to me that, whatever might be protectable under the copyright laws where a device of such a character is involved (such as is the subject of the applicants' registration no 1,050,652 in class 16 and referred to in my letter of 13 August 1980), no such protection was available to mere names of characters and that, in any event, character merchandising as revealed by these applications tended to facilitate trafficking in a trade mark and so registration of such licensees as registered users was prohibited by s 28(6) of the 1938 Act. Accordingly any licence that could not be brought within s 28 meant that the application under s 29(1)(*b*) based on it must fail. However, I adjourned the hearing to allow Mr Grant to put forward some further general information on the practice of character merchandising before coming to a final decision. The hearing was resumed at Mr Grant's request on 8 February 1982, when he produced the attached copy of an article which appeared in an Australian magazine and is entitled "What is Licensing?" After hearing further argument, I refused to proceed with any of the applications and formal written refusals were issued on 19 February 1982.'

I do not propose to make further reference to the article 'What is Licensing?' I do not think it takes the matter any further, and it was not referred to by counsel when the case was argued.

The assistant registrar was, however, asked for written grounds of refusal; and, having summarised the contents of the applicants' exhibited literature and dealt with the evidence, said in his decision:

> 'In my opinion these items show that the applicants' business is really that of providing a marketing advertising service and is saying, in effect, to any manufacturer of any product whatever that, if they like to get on the bandwaggon, they can use the applicants' trade marks. It seems clear that any Tom, Dick or Harry, in any trade whatever, will be given a licence if he applies for one and that the applicants are, in effect, hawking the trade mark around. Mr Grant did not dissent from this as a description of character merchandising, but submitted that this kind of exploitation of a character is legitimate. He said character merchandising was merely a new term for an old practice, namely licensing, and that it merely exploited the popularity gained in other fields. He instanced Mickey Mouse, which had been used on school writing pads since the 1930s. He said the popularity could be gained as a result of television or films or by reason of prior use in a different product area and that it was in the latter group that his clients' applications fell. Of course I accept that the applicants are engaged in a legitimate activity, but I do not believe it to be one that can be brought within the protection of the Trade Marks Act 1938.'

Considering this passage, it is true, as was pointed out by counsel for the applicants, that the provision of a marketing advertising service, for so the assistant registrar described it, is only a part, though possibly the major part, of the applicants' business in America, and intended perhaps to be the major part of the business in this country. They are, within a limited field, selling or proposing to sell goods. It is also true, as counsel for the applicants pointed out, that not any Tom, Dick or Harry will get a licence; if Tom, Dick or Harry wants a licence, he will have to sign the appropriate registered user agreement. I must, of course, assume for present purposes that, if such registered-userships were granted, no doubt there would be the usual provisions in agreements of this kind for supervision of the quality of products to which the mark is going to be applied by the registered user; I must assume that all obligations, imposed on one side on the proprietors and on the other on the proposed registered users, will be met.

I shall also assume that s 28(5) of the 1938 Act will be met, save to the extent that an objection under s 28(6), which in substance is a particular objection touching the public interest, has got to be considered.

The position is that, if all these applications succeed, the applicants are going to be in a position to do business, selling the right to use the trade mark Holly Hobbie, albeit on terms; and the question is: will this facilitate trafficking in the trade mark Holly Hobbie?

The first definition of the word 'trafficking' in the *Shorter Oxford Dictionary* is, so far as the definitions are relevant: 'In wider sense: the buying and selling or exchange of goods for profit; bargaining; trade.' The *Oxford English Dictionary* also indicates that the word may be used in a disparaging sense of dealings considered improper.

Webster's Dictionary gives us: 'to engage in commercial activity; buy and sell regularly', with as an alternative: 'to engage in an illegal or disreputable business or activity.' The example given in *Webster* is 'began to traffick in army promotions', and I trust that this is now wholly outdated; but it is of course common enough to see references to 'the traffic in drugs' or 'trafficking in drugs', when the word is undoubtedly used in the second sense, that is to say in connection with some illegal or improper activity.

Counsel were unable to refer me to any authority which might assist on the meaning to be given to the word 'trafficking' in the context of the Trade Marks Act 1938. Counsel for the applicants rightly points out that the mere fact that you are applying for a registered user right to be granted to someone who has no connection with you other than that he wants to use your trade mark cannot lead to the conclusion that the grant of that registered usership will facilitate trafficking; and, of course, the question must be considered in relation to each application for registered usership. Counsel for the applicants points to the undoubted fact that character merchandising in the form of the grant of registered-usership covering the right to use, for example, the words 'Mickey Mouse' for a variety of goods has undoubtedly taken place on a not inconsiderable scale in connection with a number of marks popularised in other fields under the provisions of registered user agreements.

Some more up-to-date examples of applications for registrations, where it would, on the face of it, seem unlikely that the applicants are going to use the goods in question, which are, indeed, proceeding under s 29(1)(*b*), are to be found in the documents before the court.

Trafficking, I think, on any basis must involve some payment in cash or kind in connection with a business transaction. Counsel for the applicants did not shrink from the fact that his clients are doing, or want to do, a trade in the trade mark Holly Hobbie for money. To that extent, his position did not alter from the position of Mr Grant before the assistant registrar. His case, again, as was the case of Mr Grant, was that this is a legitimate trade.

A practice permitting the grant of merchandising rights to third parties has, so counsel for the applicants submitted, been established for many years, and there is nothing wrong in it. True it may be that in the past such grants have come from organisations who have made a name popular in a sphere other than trade, in general in the entertainments field; but there is not reason why a name popularised in one field of trade should not be licensed under the registered user provisions to another trader operating in some different field. The word 'trafficking', counsel for the applicants submits, implies a dealing in some illegitimate way, or in some manner contrary to the public interest.

The registrar has to consider the question of public interest in general terms under s 28(5). Parliament has, however, chosen to place a prohibition on the grant of registered user rights if it would 'tend to facilitate trafficking' in the trade mark. In the context of the 1938 Act, this must, in my view, be considered as an activity considered by Parliament to be so contrary to the public interest that nothing should be allowed to be done which might further it. I reject the suggestion that the word 'trafficking' in the context of s 28 should be related only to dealings which are illegal or dubious. If, as is the case here, the registrar becomes aware that what is afoot is not merely the grant of a right to some associated organisation or the grant of a right in a name which has acquired fame elsewhere to a trader whose use of the name is subject to adequate supervision, but an application for a trade mark, or a fortiori a whole series of applications for trade marks, with at the same time registered user applications, the intention being that thereafter the marks will be licensed, albeit on terms and subject to the provisions of the registered user agreements, to any number of traders, the registrar can, in my view, only sensibly conclude that the grant of any one such application, a fortiori the grant of all of them, would tend to facilitate a trade in the relevant mark, or, as it is put in s 28(6), trafficking.

The underlying undesirability of this appears to have been the view that multiple usage and, indeed, the possibility of many changes in usership in relation to particular goods in particular classes due to one registered usership coming to an end and another for the same goods being granted, must lead to confusion and deception among the purchasing public.

In my judgment, the registrar rightly came to the conclusion that the registered user applications must be rejected; and, in the result, the applications for registration, which are supported only on a s 29(1)(*b*) basis, must likewise fail.

In the result which I have reached, the only other point argued before me has become of academic interest only. It centres round the question as to the period of time for which a registered user agreement must be expressed to run, if a s 29(1)(*b*) application supported only by registered usership is to be accepted.

Both counsel for the applicants and counsel for the registrar were agreed that the proposed duration of the registered user agreement must be relevant; indeed, the 1938 Act indicates that as clearly as can be. An agreement expressed to run for 24 hours only might, indeed, excite the suspicions of the registrar. On such argument as I have heard, I would say only this: that the period of time for which a registered user agreement is

intended to run must be a factor relevant to be considered by the registrar, but that it is
a impossible to say that the registrar ought to be satisfied with a period of, let me say, x years. The period may have to be related to other provisions of the agreement and possibly, indeed, other circumstances dealt with in the application.

The appeal, however, will stand dismissed.

Motion dismissed.

b

Evelyn M C Budd Barrister.

Appeal

The applicants appealed.

c *Robin Jacob QC* and *Michael Silverleaf* for the applicants.
Gerald Paterson for the registrar of trade marks.

Cur adv vult

28 April. The following judgments were delivered.

d

DILLON LJ (giving the first judgment at the invitation of Sir John Donaldson MR). This is an appeal by the applicants American Greetings Corp, against a decision of Whitford J given on 29 October 1982. By that decision the judge dismissed an appeal by the present applicants against the refusal by the assistant registrar, Mr Myall, acting for the registrar, on 2 April 1982 of 12 applications by the applicants to register the mark
e 'Holly Hobbie' as a trade mark in classes 3, 8, 11, 14, 16, 18, 20, 21, 24, 25, 27 and 28.

The appeal raises an issue of trade mark law which is both of considerable general importance and to me novel.

The applicants are an American company based in Cleveland, Ohio, who have for many years carried on business as designers and producers of greetings cards. In 1967 one of their designers produced a drawing of a little girl in a patchwork pinafore and
f billowy bonnet to whom they gave the name of Holly Hobbie. The drawing and the name have proved remarkably popular with the American public. They have been used extensively by the applicants on or in relation to their greetings cards and the other goods in a relatively small range which the applicants themselves manufacture or have manufactured for them. It is not in dispute that the applicants are properly entitled to be registered as the proprietors of the mark Holly Hobbie in respect of those goods, but the
g 12 applications with which this appeal is concerned are not in respect of such goods.

The activity known as character merchandising has for many years been common in America and known, if less common, in this country. A person who has a popular fictional character to exploit, for instance a fictional character from a film or television series or book or drawing, does so by granting licences to use the character, its name and relevant copyright material, usually on a royalty basis, to licensees who wish to promote
h their own goods by using the fictional character in association with those goods. The applicants were approached by manufacturers in the fashion trade who wanted to use Holly Hobbie on their products, and so the applicants entered on the activity of character merchandising, and they have been so successful at it that, on their own promotional literature, their licensees now produce over 400 products, from T-shirts and lamps to towels and dolls and other toys and including cakes, biscuits and other foods.

j The applicants desire to have the protection of trade mark registration of the name Holly Hobbie, as a name only without the drawing, in respect of the various classes of goods which the applicants' licensees want to produce. The sense of this from the applicants' point of view is obvious: there is no copyright in the mere name of a fictional character and there are decisions, at any rate at first instance, to the effect that the inventor of a fictional character cannot bring a passing-off action against a person who chooses to use the name of that character to promote his business in some field of commercial activity in which the inventor of the character has never engaged. It is said that there has to be a common field of activity to support a passing-off action. This is the background to the 12 applications which came before the assistant registrar and the question for the court is whether what the applicants want is permissible under trade mark law. The assistant registrar and the judge have held that it is not.

Trade mark law is now governed by the Trade Marks Act 1938. The relevant sections for present purposes are ss 17(1), 22, 28 and 29(1). The 1938 Act involves considerable changes to the previous law. The most relevant changes for present purposes are that by s 22 the previous restrictions on the assignment of trade marks were relaxed, and by s 28 a new system was introduced for the licensing of registered users of trade marks.

By s 17(1) it is provided that any person claiming to be the proprietor of a trade mark used or proposed to be used by him who is desirous of registering it must apply in writing to the registrar in the prescribed manner for registration.

By s 29(1) it is provided, so far as material:

> 'No application for the registration of a trade mark in respect of any goods shall be refused, nor shall permission for such registration be withheld, on the ground only that it appears that the applicant does not use or propose to use the trade mark . . . (*b*) if the application is accompanied by an application for registration of a person as a registered user of the trade mark, and the tribunal is satisfied that the proprietor intends it to be used by that person in relation to those goods and the tribunal is also satisfied that that person will be registered as a registered user thereof immediately after the registration of the trade mark.'

It is common ground that as the 12 applications before this court are all concerned with goods to be made by licensees under the applicants' character marketing activities and not with goods to be made by or for the applicants themselves, the applicants cannot rely on s 17 unaided by s 29(1). The applicants neither use nor propose to use the mark themselves in respect of any of the 12 classes of goods. Each of the 12 applications is therefore supported by a registered user agreement with the relevant licensee and by an application for the registration of the licensee as a registered user under s 28. It is common ground, and here is the nub of the case, that if the registered user agreements fall foul of s 28, and in particular of s 28(6), and cannot be accepted by the registrar, the rejection of the applications for registration of the mark Holly Hobbie in these 12 classes must follow.

The registered user agreements are in substantially common form. Each is terminable on relatively short notice and each contains, in form at least, comprehensive provisions for the exercise by the applicants of quality control over the goods of the licensees marketed under the mark Holly Hobbie. In particular the licensee undertakes to use the mark only so long as the goods are manufactured in accordance with standards, specifications and instructions submitted or approved by the applicants, the applicants reserve the right to inspect the goods on which the trade mark is to be used and the methods of manufacturing such goods, and the applicants have the right to approve all packaging and advertising of such goods and the licensee undertakes to amend any packaging or advertisements which are not approved.

The relevant provisions of s 28 are sub-ss (1), (2), (4), (5) and (6), which are in the following terms:

> '(1) Subject to the provisions of this section, a person other than the proprietor of a trade mark may be registered as a registered user thereof in respect of all or any of the goods in respect of which it is registered (otherwise than as a defensive trade mark) and either with or without conditions or restrictions. The use of a trade mark by a registered user thereof in relation to goods with which he is connected in the course of trade and in respect of which for the time being the trade mark remains registered and he is registered as a registered user, being use such as to comply with

> any conditions or restrictions to which his registration is subject, is in this Act referred to as the "permitted use" thereof.
>
> (2) The permitted use of a trade mark shall be deemed to be use by the proprietor thereof, and shall be deemed not to be use by a person other than the proprietor, for the purposes of section twenty-six of this Act and for any other purpose for which such use is material under this Act or at common law . . .
>
> (4) Where it is proposed that a person should be registered as a registered user of a trade mark, the proprietor and the proposed registered user must apply in writing to the Registrar in the prescribed manner and must furnish him with a statutory declaration made by the proprietor, or by some person authorised to act on his behalf and approved by the Registrar, (*a*) giving particulars of the relationship, existing or proposed, between the proprietor and the proposed registered user, including particulars showing the degree of control by the proprietor over the permitted use which their relationship will confer and whether it is a term of their relationship that the proposed registered user shall be the sole registered user or that there shall be any other restriction as to persons for whose registration as registered users application may be made; (*b*) stating the goods in respect of which registration is proposed; (*c*) stating the conditions or restrictions proposed with respect to the characteristics of the goods, to the mode or place of permitted use, or to any other matter; and (*d*) stating whether the permitted use is to be for a period or without limit of period, and, if for a period, the duration thereof; and with such further documents, information or evidence as may be required under the rules or by the Registrar.
>
> (5) When the requirements of the last foregoing subsection have been complied with, if the Registrar, after considering the information furnished to him under that subsection, is satisfied that in all the circumstances the use of the trade mark in relation to the proposed goods or any of them by the proposed registered user subject to any conditions or restrictions which the Registrar thinks proper would not be contrary to the public interest, the Registrar may register the proposed registered user as a registered user in respect of goods as to which he is so satisfied subject as aforesaid.
>
> (6) The Registrar shall refuse an application under the foregoing provisions of this section if it appears to him that the grant thereof would tend to facilitate trafficking in a trade mark.'

The crucial subsection is sub-s (6). If the registered user agreements fall foul of sub-s (6) as tending to facilitate trafficking in a trade mark, then this appeal must be dismissed, because sub-s (6) is mandatory in its terms. If, however, the registered user agreements do not fall foul of sub-s (6) the 12 applications, which stand or fall together so far as this court is concerned, should be referred back to the registrar for him to consider all outstanding points under sub-ss (4) and (5) of s 28.

Trafficking in a trade mark has from the outset been one of the cardinal sins of trade mark law. But there is no statutory definition of trafficking, and one may suspect that, as with usury in the Middle Ages, though it is known to be a deadly sin, it has become less and less clear, as economic circumstances have developed, what the sin actually comprehends.

Trafficking must involve trading in or dealing with the trade mark for money or money's worth, but it is not all dealing with a trade mark for money that is objectionable, since it has always been accepted that it is permissible to sell a trade mark together with the goodwill of the business in the course of which the trade mark has been used.

Two separate examples of the sin of trafficking do, however, emerge from the early authorities.

The first, exemplified by *Re John Batt & Co's Registered Trademarks* [1898] 2 Ch 432, a decision of Romer J, is where a person has succeeded in obtaining registration as a proprietor of marks which he has no intention of using as trade marks, but only of using as a weapon to obtain money from subsequent persons who may want to use bona fide trade marks in respect of classes of goods in respect of which they find these bogus trade *a* marks, as Romer J calls them, registered. Here the vice is not so much the deception of the public as the damage and inconvenience to the persons who genuinely want to use the marks in the course of their trade and who may be held to ransom. I can see no indication in the 1938 Act of any intention to condone this sort of trafficking. It is not however relevant to what the applicants want to do and I say no more about it.

The second example of trafficking can be seen from the speech of Earl Loreburn in *b* *Bowden Wire Ltd v Bowden Brake Co Ltd* (1914) 31 RPC 385 at 392, where he said:

> 'The object of the law is to preserve for a trader the reputation he has made for himself, not to help him in disposing of that reputation as of itself a marketable commodity, independent of his goodwill, to some other trader. If that were allowed, the public would be misled, because they might buy something in the belief that it was the make of a man whose reputation they knew, whereas it was the make of *c* someone else. All this is elementary . . .'

What was objectionable in the *Bowden* case was that the registered proprietor of the mark had granted an unfettered licence to someone else to use the mark, throughout the currency of the registration, in respect of that other person's goods. The reason why it was objectionable was that the public might be deceived. They had become accustomed *d* to the mark as identifying goods from a particular source, and were now presented with it on similar goods from another source. I cannot think that it was crucial to the decision that the licence had been granted for the whole duration of the registration. The licence would have been as objectionable if granted for a term of years only.

The sin, therefore, was disposing of the reputation in the mark, as of itself a marketable commodity, independent of the goodwill established in the business in which the mark *e* was used. The objection, the reason why it was a sin, was that it would, or might, lead to deception of the public. Consequently, before 1938 a mark could only be sold together with the goodwill of the relevant business.

The law has now been changed by s 22 of the 1938 Act. Subsections (1) and (2) of that section provide:

> '(1) Notwithstanding any rule of law or equity to the contrary, a registered trade *f* mark shall be . . . assignable and transmissible either in connection with the goodwill of a business or not.
>
> (2) A registered trade mark shall be . . . assignable and transmissible in respect either of all the goods in respect of which it is registered . . . or of some (but not all) of those goods.' *g*

These provisions are subject to certain requirements as to advertisement and also to a fundamental requirement in sub-s (4) that a trade mark shall not be assignable or transmissible if, broadly, the effect of the assignment or transmission would be that several people would have independent exclusive rights to use the same, or substantially the same, mark in respect of the same goods, so that the use would be likely to deceive or cause confusion. *h*

Subsection (2) of s 22 is plainly intended to override the decision in *Re John Sinclair Ltd's Trade Mark* [1932] 1 Ch 598 that a trade mark can only be assigned in connection with an assignment of the goodwill of the whole business and not merely a part of the business in respect of which the mark was used. Subsection (1) would permit the assignment of an unused mark by a proprietor, bona fide registered, to another person carrying on a similar business who wanted to use the mark in the course of his business *j* (eg by one motor manufacturer to another motor manufacturer). What further effects s 22 may have is less clear.

So far as s 28 is concerned, it is easy to think of various instances where the granting of a registered user's licence would be convenient and proper. One instance would be to enable a mark to be used by several companies in the same group, something which could to some extent be done even before the 1938 Act, as in *Re Radiation Trademark* (1930) 47 RPC 37. Another instance would be where a foreign proprietor of a mark grants a licence to its UK distributor to use the mark in relation to the distribution of the proprietor's goods. Another instance would be where a proprietor grants franchises to local distributors to market the proprietor's goods under the proprietor's mark or to make up and market under the mark goods according to the proprietor's formula or patent. In the last mentioned cases one would expect the licence agreement to contain provisions enabling the licensor to exercise quality control over the products or packaging of the licensee on which the mark is to be used. In all these cases there would be an obvious trade connection between the licensor and the goods of the licensee on which the mark is used.

In *British Petroleum Co Ltd v European Petroleum Distributors Ltd* [1968] RPC 54 at 63 Cross J made some comments in relation to s 28 which I find helpful. He said:

> 'No doubt if subsections (1) and (2) of that section stood alone, its effect would have been revolutionary since it would have authorised user of the mark in circumstances in which there was no trade connection between the proprietor of the mark and the goods in relation to which the mark was being used; but subsections (4), (5) and (6) show clearly enough that the Registrar ought not to allow the proposed registered user unless there will continue to be a trade connection between the proprietor of the mark and the goods in respect of which the mark will be used under the agreement.'

The phrase 'trade connection' reflects the current definition of a trade mark in s 68(1) of the 1938 Act, viz:

> '... a mark used or proposed to be used in relation to goods for the purpose of indicating, or so as to indicate, a connection in the course of trade between the goods and some person having the right either as proprietor or as registered user to use the mark ...'

By sub-s (2) of s 28 the permitted use of a trade mark by the registered user is to be deemed for the purposes there mentioned to be use by the proprietor thereof; that is one of the advantages of granting a registered user's licence.

I would therefore sum up the position as I see it as follows.

1. Subsection (6) of s 28 shows that trafficking in a trade mark is still a sin and the registration of a user is prohibited if it would tend to facilitate trafficking.

2. Trafficking in this sense means, in Earl Loreburn's words, disposing of the mark or the reputation in the name, as of itself a marketable commodity.

3. Before 1938 this was shown if the mark was disposed of, or a licence was granted, independently of the goodwill of the relevant business of the registered proprietor.

4. Since the 1938 Act has come into force, this last criterion must be relaxed in that s 22 permits assignments of a mark apart from goodwill.

5. On the scheme of the 1938 Act and as trafficking remains prohibited, the criterion now is that there must be a trade connection between the proprietor of the mark and the goods of the licensee on which the mark is to be used.

Counsel for the applicants submits that there is a trade connection in the present case because of the quality control provisions in the licences granted by the applicants. He points to certain observations, particularly of Graham J in *General Electric Co v The General Electric Co Ltd* [1969] RPC 418 at 454–455 to the effect that the quality control provisions exemplified a trade connection. I do not doubt those observations at all in the context of that case; there was there a valid trade connection and the quality control provisions helped to prove it. But it is a very different matter to suggest that the mere inclusion in an agreement of quality control provisions provides automatically a trade connection where otherwise there would be none.

I do not doubt the genuineness of the quality control provisions in the applicants' licence agreements, and I assume that the applicants will endeavour to enforce those

provisions. But the reason why they are required is not to preserve the applicants' business in greetings cards, but to protect the character whom the applicants are a
marketing, i e to protect the mark as of itself a marketable commodity. If goods marketed under the name of Holly Hobbie became known as inferior, or, in the case of foods, unfit for human consumption or tainted in some way, producers of high quality goods would become unwilling to pay for licences to associate their goods with the name.

The position can be illustrated by taking in vain the name of very well-known manufacturers, who no doubt in fact have no thought of such conduct. If Rolls-Royce b
decided to market the well-known Rolls-Royce badge of quality by granting licences for money to use the mark to a wide range of independent manufacturers of, eg lawn mowers, motor boats, wrist watches, bicycles, transistors and other equipment, that would plainly, in my judgment, be trafficking in the mark, and might well lead to the confusion of the public which Earl Loreburn feared. It would not be any the less trafficking and impermissible under s 28(6) if each licence agreement included quality c
control provisions to ensure that the licensed products were not shoddy goods of their kind, shoddy lawn mowers etc.

It may well be that character marketing does not involve any deception of the public. People who see the figure of Mickey Mouse on a T-shirt or a box of biscuits will not assume that Walt Disney Productions have gone into the clothing and food trades. Equally people who see Holly Hobbie on a toy will not be led to buy it because the d
applicants sell good greetings cards: the expertise is different. But as I see it the risk of deception is not an integral part of the definition of trafficking; it is merely the reason why trafficking, which I would define as disposing of the mark, or the reputation in the name, as of itself a marketable commodity in circumstances where there is no trade connection between the proprietor of the mark and the goods or business in relation to which the mark will be used, is objectionable. e

Counsel for the applicants has submitted that the object of the inclusion of sub-s (6) in s 28 with its reference to trafficking is to prevent the evasion of the restrictions on assignment in s 22. I do not accept this. In my judgment the archaic word 'trafficking' is used in s 28(6) to refer to the old sin of trafficking, and not to any new sin arising under s 22. Moreover, if a registered proprietor proffered a registered user licence which the registrar held to be designed to evade either the requirements in s 22 as to advertisement f
or the requirement that there be no assignment of one mark to several people in circumstances which might deceive the public, the registrar would have ample power to deal with this under s 28(5).

Counsel for the applicants submits alternatively that inherent in the old idea of trafficking in trade marks is the notion of outright assignment or disposition of the marks rather than the grant of a licence. I do not see why that should be so. In the *Bowden* g
case what was granted was a licence for the duration of the currency of the mark and not in form an outright assignment. But a licence in the same circumstances for a term of years would have been as objectionable and the initial danger of confusion to the public would have been as great. Moreover, the reference to trafficking in s 28(6) imports at the least that licences can be relevant to the notion of trafficking. Licensing would be an obvious means of trafficking in trade marks and I see no reason why the concept of h
trafficking should be limited to out-and-out assignments.

Counsel for the applicants points finally to the words in s 28(6), 'the grant thereof would tend to facilitate trafficking in a trade mark', and he submits that these words show that the licence cannot itself be trafficking. One answer to that is that the words 'the grant thereof' do not refer to the licence, but to the grant by the registrar of the application for the registration of the registered user. The grant of the application for j
registration would not itself be trafficking, but it would tend to facilitate trafficking by giving validity under the section to the licence to the registered user and, in a case such as the present, by enabling the mark to be registered at all in the relevant classes under s 29(1). The judge put this concisely in a passage in his judgment with which I entirely agree, where he said (at p 616, ante):

> 'If, as is the case here, the registrar becomes aware that what is afoot is not merely *a* the grant of a right to some associated organisation or the grant of a right in a name which has acquired fame elsewhere to a trader whose use of the name is subject to adequate supervision, but an application for a trade mark, or a fortiori a whole series of applications for trade marks, with at the same time registered user applications, the intention being that thereafter the marks will be licensed, albeit on terms and subject to the provisions of the registered user agreements, to any number of traders, *b* the registrar can, in my view, only sensibly conclude that the grant of any one such application, a fortiori the grant of all of them, would tend to facilitate a trade in the relevant mark, or, as it is put in s 28(6), trafficking.'

For the foregoing reasons, I would dismiss this appeal.

I should add that I have no quarrel at all with the Australian decision in *Pioneer* *c* *Electronic Corp v Registrar of Trade Marks* [1978] RPC 716, but with all respect to Aickin J I do not agree with his statement (at 731) that the principal objective of the prohibition on 'trafficking' in the registered user section was to prevent the registered user provisions from being misused so as to avoid or evade the requirements of the Act with respect to assignment.

d

SIR DENYS BUCKLEY. I have had the advantage of reading the judgment which Dillon LJ has prepared, with which I entirely agree. I add only a few observations.

The interpretation of the Trade Marks Act 1938, s 28(6) is, of course, a question of law, but the question whether the grant of registration of a particular application by the registrar under s 28 would tend to facilitate trafficking in the relevant mark is a question *e* of fact for decision by the registrar. The hearing officer who heard the applicants' applications in the registry refused registration of all of them on the ground that they would so tend. The judge affirmed that decision on the same ground. We thus have concurrent findings of fact that the registration of the proposed registered users would tend to facilitate trafficking in the mark Holly Hobbie. This court would not interfere with such findings unless it could be shown that the lower tribunals had misdirected *f* themselves. This the applicants contend that they did by misconstruing the word 'trafficking'.

Counsel for the applicants contends that 'trafficking' involves a transfer of property, whereas, he says, the course which the applicants seek to pursue involves no transfer of any property in the mark, of which the applicants would remain the registered proprietors. Like Dillon LJ, I see no reason for restricting the meaning of the word in *g* this way. The word 'trafficking' is not defined or explained anywhere in the 1938 Act, nor does it seem to have been the subject of any judicial interpretation in this context. In *Re John Batt & Co's Registered Trade Marks* [1898] 2 Ch 432 Romer J used the word to describe the conduct of a registered proprietor of a mark who had secured registration without a genuine intention of using that mark but intending simply to obstruct other traders wishing to use the mark. The judge did not there purport to define the meaning *h* of the word 'tafficking': he was using the word to describe the conduct in question. In my judgment 'trafficking' in s 28(6) extends to any conduct carried out or intended to be carried out in respect of a mark or a proposed mark with a view to commercial gain which is not a bona fide exploitation of that mark in pursuance of the true function of a trade mark, viz its use in relation to goods for the purpose of indicating, or so as to indicate, a connection in the course of trade between the goods and some person having *j* the right either as proprietor or as registered user to use the mark (Trade Marks Act 1938, s 68(1), 'trade mark').

Counsel for the applicants further contended that 'trafficking' imports some sort of illegal or improper dealing, as might be the case if one referred to 'trafficking in drugs'. The word 'trafficking' is, I think, capable of being used in an appropriate context with this kind of pejorative innuendo, but I think that no dictionary suggests that this is the primary sense of the word and I am unable to accept this contention in the present context.

In the present case there is, in my view, ample evidence of an intention on the part of the applicants to use the mark Holly Hobbie not simply as a trade mark but as a part of a marketing aid in conjunction with pictorial representations of the little girl for promoting the sale of a wide variety of goods in the production and marketing of which the applicants will play no part.

Counsel for the applicants has contended that the fact that in each of the proposed permitted user agreements the applicants propose to retain a power to monitor and regulate the quality of the goods dealt in by the permitted user under that agreement affords a sufficient trade connection between the proprietor of the mark (the applicants) and the goods in respect of which the mark will be used by the permitted user to justify registration of the permitted user. This degree of quality control may constitute a sufficient trade connection so far as the existence of some such connection may be necessary for the applicants to secure registration as the proprietor of the mark; it has, in my opinion, no relevance to the question whether the registration of the permitted user would be liable to lead to deception or confusion of the public, which has always been regarded as a cardinal sin in trade mark law, or would tend to facilitate trafficking in the mark.

There was, I think, plentiful evidence available to the hearing officer to indicate that the applicants' intention was to conduct their business in this country with the proposed permitted users on the same lines as their existing 'character merchandising' activities in the United States, that a major element of that business would be to enable the permitted users to exploit the name Holly Hobbie in conjunction with pictorial representations of the little girl (for one without the other would be likely to be much less valuable than the combination) as the main marketing aid for goods dealt in in the course of the merchandising operation, that the mark would be registered for permitted use in respect of a wide variety of goods, extending under these 12 applications alone to 12 distinct and dissimilar classes of those goods which are listed in Sch 4 to the Trade Marks Act 1938, to which further dissimilar goods might quite probably be added hereafter on further applications, and that the applicants would be unlikely to trade in any of the goods in question.

Not all the agreements annexed to the several applications stipulate for a commission or other monetary consideration, but it seems highly unlikely that the applicants would enter on any such transaction without a commercial incentive of some kind.

In these circumstances it seems clear to me that there was ample material available to the hearing officer, acting on behalf of the registrar, to reach the conclusion of fact which he did.

I would dismiss the appeal.

SIR JOHN DONALDSON MR. I have had the advantage of reading in draft the judgments of Dillon LJ and Sir Denys Buckley, with which I am in complete agreement. Accordingly I too would dismiss this appeal.

Appeal dismissed. Leave to appeal to the House of Lords refused.

Solicitors: *Slaughter & May* (for the applicants); *Treasury Solicitor*.

Frances Rustin Barrister.

a # R v Taaffe

COURT OF APPEAL, CRIMINAL DIVISION
LORD LANE CJ, McCOWAN AND NOLAN JJ
14 APRIL 1983

b *Customs and excise – Importation of prohibited goods – Knowingly concerned in fraudulent evasion of prohibition or restriction – Knowingly – Importation of drugs – Cannabis – Defendant carrying cannabis in mistaken belief that it was currency – Defendant mistakenly believing importation of currency prohibited – Whether defendant 'knowingly' concerned with fraudulent evasion of prohibition on importation of cannabis – Customs and Excise Management Act 1979, s 170(2).*

c The defendant was enlisted by a person in Holland to carry a substance, which he believed to be currency, through customs into England and thereby fraudulently evade what he thought was the prohibition on the importation of currency. The defendant was stopped and searched on entry, when it was discovered that the substance was in fact cannabis. He was charged under s 170(2)[a] of the Customs and Excise Management Act 1979 with
d being knowingly concerned in the fraudulent evasion of the prohibition on the importation of cannabis imposed by s 3(1) of the Misuse of Drugs Act 1971. At his trial the judge ruled that even on the defendant's version of events he was obliged to direct the jury to convict because the defendant believed he was importing prohibited goods even though he did not know the precise nature of the goods. The defendant was convicted. He appealed.

e **Held** – The relevant mental element required for a defendant to be convicted of an offence under s 170(2) of the 1979 Act was actual knowledge, and not merely a belief which might or might not have been right, that the goods he was importing were goods subject to a prohibition, although it was not necessary to prove that the defendant knew the precise nature of the prohibited goods. Since the defendant would not have been
f guilty of an offence if the substance he had imported had been currency, the defendant's mistaken belief that he was importing currency and that by doing so he was committing an offence did not turn his actions into the criminal offence of being 'knowingly' concerned in the importation of prohibited drugs within s 170(2) of the 1979 Act. The appeal would therefore be allowed and the conviction quashed (see p 628 *c d h j* and p 629 *b*, post).

g Dictum of Lord Diplock in *Sweet v Parsley* [1969] 1 All ER at 361 applied.

R v Hussain [1969] 2 All ER 1117 and *R v Hennessey (Timothy)* (1978) 68 Cr App R 419 considered.

Notes

For the importation of controlled drugs and assisting in offences abroad, see 30 Halsbury's
h Laws (4th edn) para 745 and 11 ibid para 1098, and for cases on the subject, see 15 Digest (Reissue) 1085–1086, *9186–9193*.

For the Misuse of Drugs Act 1971, s 3, see 41 Halsbury's Statutes (3rd edn) 882.

For the Customs and Excise Management Act 1979, s 170, see 49 ibid 443.

Cases referred to in judgment

j *Bank of New South Wales v Piper* [1897] AC 383, PC.
R v Hennessey (Timothy) (1978) 68 Cr App R 419, CA.

---

a Section 170(2), so far as material, provides: '. . . if any person is, in relation to any goods, in any way knowingly concerned in any fraudulent evasion or attempt at evasion . . . (*b*) of any prohibition or restriction for the time being in force with respect to the goods under or by virtue of any enactment . . . he shall be guilty of an offence under this section and may be detained.'

R v Hussain [1969] 2 All ER 1117, [1969] 2 QB 567, [1969] 3 WLR 134, CA.
R v Tolson (1889) 23 QBD 168, [1886–90] All ER Rep 26, CCR. a
R v Vickers [1975] 2 All ER 945, [1975] 1 WLR 811, CA.
Sweet v Parsley [1969] 1 All ER 347, [1970] AC 132, [1969] 2 WLR 470, HL.

Case also cited
R v Hallam [1957] 1 All ER 665, [1957] 1 QB 569, CCA. b

Appeal
The appellant, Paul Desmond Patrick Taaffe, was charged on indictment with being knowingly concerned in the fraudulent evasion of the prohibition on the importation of a controlled drug contrary to s 170(2) of the Customs and Excise Management Act 1979. At his trial in the Crown Court at Gravesend before Mr Recorder DJ Griffiths and a jury he pleaded not guilty to the charge. The recorder ruled that on the agreed facts, viz (a) c that the appellant was enlisted by a third party in Holland to import a substance from that country into England in fraudulent evasion of the prohibition on its importation and he did so import it, (b) that that substance was in fact cannabis, the importation of which was prohibited by the Misuse of Drugs Act 1971, (c) that the appellant mistakenly believed the substance to be currency, (d) that currency was not subject to any such prohibition and (e) that the appellant mistakenly believed that currency was the subject d of a prohibition against importation, the appellant had no defence to the offence. The appellant thereupon changed his plea to guilty and was convicted and sentenced to 18 months' imprisonment. He appealed against conviction on the ground that the recorder had erred in ruling that the agreed facts did not afford a defence. The facts are set out in the judgment of the court. e

Roy Roebuck (assigned by the Registrar of Criminal Appeals) for the appellant.
Christopher Aylwin for the Crown.

LORD LANE CJ delivered the following judgment of the court. On 18 November 1982 at the Crown Court at Gravesend the appellant was charged under s 170(2) of the f Customs and Excise Management Act 1979 with having, on 12 November 1982, at Sheerness, in relation to a class B controlled drug, namely 3,732 grammes of cannabis resin, been knowingly concerned in the fraudulent evasion of the prohibition on the importation of that substance imposed by s 3(1) of the Misuse of Drugs Act 1971. That section simply prohibits the importation or exportation of controlled drugs, of which cannabis resin is of course one. g

The facts of the case are simple. The appellant drove a car into the green lane of the ferry terminal at Sheerness and told the customs officer who was on duty there that he had nothing to declare. The car was searched. It was noticed that the spare tyre was deflated. An examination was made of that tyre, and inside were found to be five packages containing cannabis resin. Not unnaturally the search then moved to the body of the appellant himself, and strapped to his back and underneath his clothing were h discovered three further packages also containing cannabis resin, the total quantity being that stated in the indictment.

The appellant was cautioned by the customs officer and was asked if he knew what the substances in the packages were. He replied, 'No, I am waiting to find out, because if it is drugs...' and there his reply ended. So the officer then asked him, 'What did you think was in the packages?' and to that he replied simply, 'Money.' j

When arraigned he initially pleaded not guilty. The evidence which the prosecution were proposing to tender was not disputed and the procedure which was adopted in *R v Vickers* [1975] 2 All ER 945, [1975] 1 WLR 811 was then put into operation, and the judge was asked to rule on the question whether the version of events advanced by the appellant, if accepted by the jury, would entitle him to be acquitted. Having heard

arguments from both sides the judge then came to the conclusion that he would be
a obliged, even on the appellant's version of events, to direct the jury to convict. The defendant thereupon, on advice, pleaded guilty and was sentenced to 18 months' imprisonment.

He now appeals against that conviction on the ground that the judge was wrong in law in the ruling which he gave on the question posed before him.

The problem is not difficult to state but, like all problems which are not difficult to
b state, it is not quite so easy of solution. The question is this: on the assumption that the following facts are established, has the alleged offence been committed? These are the facts which, counsel on behalf of the Crown concedes, were the basis of the judge's determination: (1) the appellant was enlisted by a third party in Holland to import a substance from that country into England in fraudulent evasion of the prohibition on its importation and he did so import it; (2) that substance was in fact cannabis, the
c importation of which is prohibited by the Misuse of Drugs Act 1971; (3) the appellant mistakenly believed the substance to be currency; (4) currency is not subject to any such prohibition; (5) the appellant mistakenly believed that currency was the subject of a prohibition against importation.

The material parts of the judge's ruling are as follows:

> d 'It subsequently turned out that they were prohibited goods . . . it is not necessary for him to know precisely what the goods were and I take the view that if he believed, as he must have done, that there was a prohibition, and he was prepared to concern himself with the importation notwithstanding that prohibition, in the way in which it was done . . . then I think that is sufficient for this offence to be made out. The fact that it subsequently transpires that he believed or he thought, and I am saying this for the purpose of this argument and not that it is a fact, that he
> e believed that it was money that he was bringing in, does not afford him a defence.'

One starts with the premise that this is not an offence of absolute liability. It is plain, from the use of the word 'knowingly' in s 170(2), that the prosecution have the task of proving the existence of mens rea, the mental element of guilt. Mens rea in this context means the mental element required by the particular statute on the part of the defendant
f before the prosecution can succeed.

What then in this case was the relevant mental element which s 170(2) required to be proved? It seems to us that it was primarily knowledge that the substance which was being imported was a drug, or certainly was a substance of some sort the importation of which was prohibited. We say 'relevant', because there were no doubt other facets of the mental element which are not here in issue.

g Counsel on behalf of the Crown, seeking to uphold the conviction, relies principally on two cases. The first is *R v Hussain* [1969] 2 All ER 1117, [1969] 2 QB 567, a decision of this court. That was a case where a seaman was charged with the corresponding offence to the instant one, on the basis that he had assisted the prime movers in the importation of a quantity of cannabis by allowing the substance to be hidden in a cabin which he occupied on the ship. He appealed on the ground that the judge had misdirected the jury
h by telling them that they could convict even if they were not satisfied that he knew precisely the nature of the goods. It should be observed that it was not suggested that the defendant in that case believed the goods to be of a nature which were not in fact the subject of prohibition.

The second case was again a decision of this court in *R v Hennessey* (1978) 68 Cr App R 419. In that case the court adopted and applied the reasoning of the decision in *R v*
j *Hussain*. It should equally be observed that in *R v Hennessey* the appellant's stated belief was that the substance which he was importing was not drugs but was obscene films, again matters which he rightly believed to be the subject of prohibition so far as importation was concerned.

We do not think that these cases are helpful in deciding the issue which is before us, and, in order to demonstrate why, it is necessary to read a short passage from *R v Hussain*

[1969] 2 All ER 1117 at 1119, [1969] 2 QB 567 at 571–572, where Widgery LJ had this to say: a

'It seems perfectly clear that the word "knowingly" in s. 304 is concerned with knowing that a fraudulent evasion of a prohibition in respect of goods is taking place. If, therefore, the accused knows that what is on foot is the evasion of a prohibition against importation and he knowingly takes part in that operation, it is sufficient to justify his conviction, even if he does not know precisely what kind of goods are being imported. b It is, of course, essential that he should know that the goods which are being imported are goods subject to a prohibition. It is essential he should know that the operation with which he is concerning himself is an operation designed to evade that prohibition and evade it fraudulently. But it is not necessary that he should know the precise category of the goods the importation of which has been prohibited. Accordingly, in our judgment, there is nothing in that point taken c on behalf of the appellant.'

Counsel for the Crown submits that the word 'know' in the context of that judgment includes the state of mind of a person who mistakenly believes a fact to exist. We respectfully disagree with that contention. It is essential that the defendant should know, in the ordinary sense of the word 'know', that the goods being imported are goods subject d to a prohibition, though on the basis of the decisions in *R v Hussain* [1969] 2 All ER 1117, [1969] 2 QB 567 and *R v Hennessey* (1978) 68 Cr App R 419 he may not know the precise nature of the goods.

The matter can be approached from another angle. We turn to the decision of their Lordships in the House of Lords in *Sweet v Parsley* [1969] 1 All ER 347 at 361, [1970] AC 132 at 163, and to a passage, where Lord Diplock, after citing what Stephen J said in *R v Tolson* (1889) 23 QBD 168 at 187, [1886–90] All ER Rep 26 at 37, put the matter in these e words:

'... even where the words used to describe the prohibited conduct would not in any other context connote the necessity for any particular mental element, they are nevertheless to be read as subject to the implication that a necessary element in the offence is the absence of a belief held honestly and on reasonable grounds in the f existence of facts which, if true, would make the act innocent. As was said by the Privy Council in *Bank of New South Wales* v. *Piper* ([1897] AC 383 at 389–390) the absence of mens rea really consists in such a belief by the accused.'

We say in passing that it is doubtful, in the light of subsequent decisions, whether the words 'on reasonable grounds' should still be included, but it is not necessary for us to g embark on any inquiry as to that.

What then if the jury in the present case had been asked to decide the matter and had come to the conclusion that the appellant might have believed that what he was importing was currency and not prohibited drugs? He is to be judged against the facts that he believed them to be. Had this indeed been currency and not cannabis, no offence would have been committed. Does it make any difference that the appellant thought h wrongly that by clandestinely importing currency he was committing an offence? Counsel for the Crown strongly submits that it does. He suggests that a man in this situation has to be judged according to the total mistake that he has made, both the mistake with regard to the fact of what he was carrying and also mistake of law as to the effect of carrying that substance. We think that that submission is wrong. It no doubt made his actions morally reprehensible. It did not, in our judgment, turn what he, for j the purpose of argument, believed to be the importation of currency into the commission of a criminal offence. His views on the law as to the importation of currency were to that extent, in our judgment, irrelevant.

Counsel for the Crown, by way of argument in terrorem, suggests that if this appeal is allowed, then all importers of prohibited drugs will say that they believed the substance

was money and that we should be inundated by bogus defences, and all sorts of people
a who ought to be severely punished will go free.

As to that we say this. Whether the jury, if the matter had been left to them to decide, would have had any doubt about the appellant's knowledge that the substance he was importing was a controlled drug was another matter altogether, one that we do not have to decide. However, this is not an appropriate case for the application of the proviso, and it has not been suggested that it is. But for the reasons we have endeavoured to give, this
b appeal must be allowed and the conviction quashed.

Appeal allowed; conviction quashed. Crown's application for a venire de novo refused. Leave to appeal to the House of Lords refused.

29 April. The court certified, under s 33(2) of the Criminal Appeal Act 1968, that the following
c *point of law of general public importance was involved in its decision: whether, when a defendant was charged with an offence, contrary to s 170(2) of the Customs and Excise Management Act 1979, of being knowingly concerned in the fraudulent evasion of the prohibition on the importation of a controlled drug, the defendant committed the offence where he (a) imported prohibited drugs into the United Kingdom, (b) intended fraudulently to evade a prohibition on importation, but (c) mistakenly believed the goods to be money and not drugs and (d) mistakenly believed that money*
d *was the subject of a prohibition against importation.*

Solicitors: *Solicitor for the Customs and Excise.*

Sepala Munasinghe Esq Barrister.

e

Wettern Electric Ltd v Welsh Development Agency

f

QUEEN'S BENCH DIVISION
HIS HONOUR JUDGE NEWEY QC SITTING AS A JUDGE OF THE HIGH COURT
2, 3, 4, 8, 15 FEBRUARY 1983

Contract – Implied term – Implication necessary to give business efficacy to contract – Licence to
g *occupy factory– Factory becoming unsuitable and dangerous forcing licensee to relocate and suffer loss – Whether term to be implied in licence that factory fit for purpose required by licensee.*

Contract – Offer and acceptance – Acceptance – Retrospective acceptance – Contractual licence to occupy factory – Licensee occupying and later moving from factory due to licensor's breach before indicating acceptance by prescribed mode – Whether late acceptance constituting contract
h *with effect from date of occupancy thus entitling licensee to bring action for breach – Whether offer and acceptance arising from parties' other actions so as to create contract with effect from date of occupancy.*

Licence – Licence to occupy premises – Contractual licence – Implied term – Fitness for purpose – Licence to occupy factory – Factory becoming unsuitable and dangerous forcing licensee to relocate
j *and suffer loss – Whether term to be implied in licence that factory fit for purpose required by licensee.*

By letter dated 21 June 1979 a regional development agency offered a plastic manufacturing company a licence to occupy a factory unit for 12 months from 25 June 1979 on terms which were all in the agency's favour and which involved an annual fee

payable when the licence expired. In particular, the letter provided that the manufacturers would not acquire 'any legal rights, title or interest in the premises'. The manufacturers a
went into occupation on 25 June without completing the acceptance portion of the letter as required. Soon after occupying the unit, serious structural defects became apparent and by 18 December, after correspondence from the agency requesting formal acceptance of the licence, the unit had become so dangerous that the manufacturers were forced to evacuate it for other premises. They sued the agency for breach of an implied term of the licence contained in the letter that the unit was of sound construction and would be b
reasonably suitable for their purposes. They claimed damages for the consequent loss of production, cost of removal and general disruption. On 19 December, after having relocated and commenced legal proceedings, they returned the completed acceptance portion of the letter to the agency. The agency contended (i) that the manufacturers had not accepted the licence offered on 21 June but instead had become occupants pursuant to a gratuitous permission given by the agency and (ii) that, alternatively, the court c
should not imply a term as to fitness for purpose into a licence to occupy land since it would not do so in the case of contracts for the sale of land or the grant of a lease.

Held – (1) The manufacturers had become occupants under a contract on the terms contained in the letter notwithstanding their late formal acceptance, since (a) by occupying the unit the manufacturers were offering to enter into a contractual licence d
on the terms contained in the letter and, by permitting them to occupy, the agency was accepting their offer, or (b) the occupation of the unit was on the basis of a licence, the terms of which were to be agreed later, and by their correspondence the parties had agreed that the terms were those set out in the letter of 21 June, as well as any other terms which might properly be implied, and would take effect from 25 June 1979 (see p 633 *e* to *j*, post). e

(2) Although the court would not imply terms as to fitness or suitability for purpose into contracts for the sale of land or the grant of a lease, that did not preclude the court from implying such terms into contracts granting a licence to occupy land, whenever such terms were necessary to give business efficacy to the contract, since a contract granting a licence did not confer on the licensee any title to, or interest in, the land. Applying that test, a warranty was to be implied in the licence that the unit was of sound f
construction and reasonably suitable for the purposes required by the manufacturers. The agency was in breach of that implied warranty and accordingly was liable to the manufacturers for the resulting loss (see p 635 *f g*, p 637 *h* to p 638 *a d* to *g*, post); *Francis v Cockrell* (1870) LR 5 QB 501, *The Moorcock* [1886–90] All ER Rep 530, *Maclenan v Segar* [1917] 2 KB 325, *Reigate v Union Manufacturing Co (Ramsbottom) Ltd* [1918–19] All ER Rep 143 and *Liverpool City Council v Irwin* [1976] 2 All ER 39 applied. g

Notes

For terms implied in a contract by court, see 9 Halsbury's Laws (4th edn) paras 355–360, and for cases on the subject, see 12 Digest (Reissue) 746–756, *5371–5420*.

Cases referred to in judgment h

Bentley Bros v Metcalfe & Co [1906] 2 KB 548, CA.
Bottomley v Bannister [1932] 1 KB 458, [1931] All ER Rep 99, CA.
Collins v Hopkins [1923] 2 KB 617, [1923] All ER Rep 225.
Francis v Cockrell (1870) LR 5 QB 501.
Hart v Windsor (1843) 12 M & W 68, 152 ER 1114.
Jones v Just (1868) LR 3 QB 197. j
Liverpool City Council v Irwin [1976] 2 All ER 39, [1977] AC 239, [1976] 2 WLR 562, HL; *affg in part* [1975] 3 All ER 658, [1976] QB 319, [1975] 2 WLR 663, CA.
Maclenan v Segar [1917] 2 KB 325.
Manchester Bonded Warehouse Co Ltd v Carr (1880) CPD 507, [1874–80] All ER Rep 563, DC.

Moorcock, The (1889) 14 PD 64, [1886–90] All ER Rep 530, CA.
a *Randall v Newson* (1877) 2 QBD 102, CA.
Reigate v Union Manufacturing Co (Ramsbottom) Ltd [1918] 1 KB 592, [1918–19] All ER Rep 143, CA.
Robbins v Jones (1863) 15 CBNS 221, [1861–73] All ER Rep 544.
Smith v Marrable (1843) 11 M & W 5, 152 ER 693.
Sutton v Temple (1843) 12 M & W 52, 152 ER 1108.
b *Yeoman Credit Ltd v Apps* [1961] 2 All ER 281, [1962] 2 QB 508, [1961] 3 WLR 94, CA.

Action

By a writ issued on 14 December 1981 the plaintiffs, Wettern Electric Ltd, claimed against the defendants, Welsh Development Agency (a body corporate), damages for breach of an implied term in a licence granted by the defendants to the plaintiffs by a c letter dated 21 June 1979. The facts are set out in the judgment.

Philip Goodenday for the plaintiffs.
Gerald Godfrey QC and *Hywel Moseley* for the defendants.

Cur adv vult

d

15 February. The following judgment was delivered.

HIS HONOUR JUDGE NEWEY QC. In this case Wettern Electric Ltd, the plaintiffs, are manufacturers of electrical junction boxes made of plastic which they sell mainly to purchasers overseas. The Welsh Development Agency, the defendants, were established e by s 1(1) of the Welsh Development Agency Act 1975. Their purposes under s 1(2) of the Act included the promotion of industrial efficiency and international competitiveness and the provision and safeguarding of employment in Wales. Their functions under s 1(3) include the provision of sites, premises, services and facilities for industrial undertakings.

In 1975 the defendants granted to the plaintiffs a lease for a term of 21 years of a f factory with an area of 10,000 sq ft on an industrial estate at Marsh Road, Rhyl, Clwyd. By early 1979 the plaintiffs' business had increased so that they were in urgent need of further accommodation. The plaintiffs approached the defendants, who offered to build a 10,000 sq ft extension to the factory and to let it to the plaintiffs. So that the plaintiffs might have the use of some additional accommodation while the extension was being built, the defendants offered to grant to the plaintiffs a licence for 12 months of a 4,500 g sq ft industrial unit which was itself in the course of construction on the estate. The reason for the defendants offering a licence rather than a lease was to avoid the effect of the Landlord and Tenant Act 1954.

On 31 May 1979 the plaintiffs gave an undertaking in writing, called 'an abortive fees agreement', that should the extension project be abandoned, the plaintiffs would pay to the defendants costs which they had incurred, including sums expended in investigating h and testing the suitability of the land on which it was proposed to construct the extension. On the same day the plaintiffs wrote to the defendants stressing their urgent requirement for storage space and their wish to obtain the 4,500 sq ft unit as temporary accommodation. On 12 June the defendants replied, stating that the target date for occupation of the unit was 18 June, that their construction department had experienced some difficulty with the contractors and that they did not wish to afford the contractors any excuse for delay, j which might result from letting the plaintiffs into occupation before completion of the works.

On 21 June the defendants wrote to the plaintiffs, stating that they were prepared to grant them a licence of the unit known as 'Advance Factory Unit No 7' from 25 June 1979 to 24 June 1980, on specified conditions. The defendants' officers and agents were to be free to visit the unit at any time. The conditions required the plaintiffs to pay

£3,750 at the end of the licence period, to pay all rates and charges, to use the premises for the manufacture of plastics and composite materials only, to make good any damage to the premises, to be responsible for the maintenance and repair of the exterior and interior of the premises and to reinstate them to their original condition at the expiration of the licence, not to carry out structural alterations without consent and to indemnify the defendants against claims arising from the licence. Further conditions provided that the licence should not be deemed to pass to the plaintiffs 'any legal rights, title or interest in the premises', and that if the plaintiffs did not perform or observe any of the conditions the licence might be terminated on seven days' notice in writing. The terms were all in the defendants' favour.

The penultimate sentence in the defendants' letter read:

> 'If you accept this licence on the above terms, will you please complete the acknowledgment and acceptance at the foot of the enclosed copy and return it to us at your earliest convenience.'

A copy of the defendants' letter was enclosed with it, but the plaintiffs did not immediately complete the acceptance on it and return it.

On 25 June the plaintiffs went into occupation of unit 7 and installed plant and machinery in it. They did not carry out any survey of the premises before entering; indeed, there was little opportunity then to do so. On 26 June the plaintiffs wrote to the defendants inquiring whether they would be prepared to include in the licence a stipulation for its extension in the event of the enlargement of their factory not being completed by 24 June 1980. On 27 July the plaintiffs sent a reminder to the defendants. On 30 July the defendants replied, saying that they did not issue licences for longer than 12 months, but should there be a delay in completing the extension, a request for another licence would be sympathetically considered.

In August defects began to appear in unit 7 and gradually became worse. The foundations of the building were inadequate to support the building which became progressively unsafe. Large cracks appeared in the party wall with unit 6 next door and cracks appeared in internal walls. A water storage tank had to be shored up. A flank wall rocked when hand pressure was exerted on it. The ground and upper floors began to sink and part of the upper floor dropped away. Cracks in walls opened up, brickwork around windows began to break up and glass cracked. From about November the unit had ceased to be suitable for the plaintiffs' purposes and eventually became so dangerous that the plaintiffs had to evacuate it.

On 31 October the defendants wrote to the plaintiffs asking for their approval of what they described as the 'draft licence' sent on 21 June. On 14 December the defendants again asked for the completion of the licence document. On 19 December the plaintiffs returned it approved but undated with a covering letter, stating that the original terms of the licence and intention were in order. Between 18 and 21 December the plaintiffs moved from unit 7 to other temporary accommodation provided by the defendants at Bagillt, at a distance of about twenty miles from Rhyl.

On 14 December 1981 the plaintiffs commenced this action. By their amended statement of claim they now alleged in the alternative breach of an implied term in the licence and claim damages for loss of production, cost of removal, additional expense due to having to operate at two widely separated locations, and general disruption. The defendants by their amended defence deny liability and damages.

I do not know who designed unit 7, but, unless the defendants' own staff designed it, they may have causes of action against the designers in contract and/or in negligence. They may also have causes of action against the contractors in contract and/or negligence, and against the building regulations authority in negligence. Possibly the plaintiffs may also have causes of action against the defendants, the designers (if other than the defendants), the contractors and the authority in negligence. So far as I am aware, however, no other proceedings have been commenced.

The first issue which I am asked to decide is whether the plaintiffs went into occupation of unit 7 on the terms of the licence dated 21 June 1979, notwithstanding that they did not return to the defendants their part thereof duly executed until 19 December 1979.

Counsel for the plaintiffs submitted that they must have gone into occupation on the basis of the licence contained in the letter of 21 June. There was no other licence which permitted them to enter. The plaintiffs by their letter of 26 June asked for variation in the licence, which would not have affected existing rights. The defendants' reply of 30 July was written on the premise that a licence for 12 months existed. Since the defendants did not agree to a variation, the original licence continued. Counsel pointed out that until the defendants' defence was amended, it had admitted that the defendants had granted to the plaintiffs a licence on the terms of the letter of 21 June.

In the alternative, counsel submitted that the defendants' letter of 14 December, written after all the defects in unit 7 had shown themselves, was an indication that their offer contained in the letter of 21 June was still open and that the plaintiffs, by sending back the second copy of that letter on 19 December, accepted the offer. The licence took effect from the date when the plaintiffs went into occupation and the defendants were by their conduct estopped from contending the contrary.

Counsel for the defendants submitted that their letter of 21 June was an offer of a licence which was capable of being accepted in the manner prescribed. The plaintiffs went into occupation without accepting. They went in not as tresspassers but as licensees but pursuant to a gratuitous permission, and remained as such.

In the alternative, if the plaintiffs, by returning a copy of the letter of 21 June on 19 December, accepted the defendants' offer, they did so with full knowledge of the state of unit 7 and not insisting on any contractual provision, which might have existed as to its condition.

In my view, the defendants' letter of 21 June was an offer of a licence on terms set out in it and the letter did prescribe the manner in which acceptance should be communicated. The plaintiffs went into occupation on 25 June with the consent of the defendants. Since entry was not the method of communicating acceptance prescribed in the letter of 21 June, it was not therefore an acceptance of the offer contained in that letter. At the time when the plaintiffs occupied unit 7, they and the defendants knew that the terms on which the defendants were willing that the plaintiffs should occupy the unit were those set out in the letter of 21 June. I think that by occupying the plaintiffs were offering to enter into a contractual licence on those terms and that the defendants, by permitting them to occupy, were accepting their offer. In other words, the parties made by conduct a contract for a licence which took effect forthwith.

If I am wrong in the view which I have just expressed, then I think that the plaintiffs went into occupation as licensees, but not simply with the gratuitous consent of the defendants, but on the basis that the licence should be governed from its commencement by terms which, so far as they were expressed, would be agreed subsequently. Obviously the parties always intended that the defendants should receive payment and that other terms should apply. By the defendants' letter of 14 December and the plaintiffs' letter of 19 December, the parties agreed the express terms which had formed part of the licence agreement from its commencement, namely those contained in the letter of 21 June. I think that from 25 June the licence was subject to those terms and any properly to be implied. I do not think that there is any occasion for the plaintiffs to seek to rely on estoppel; nor do I think that by returning the copy of the letter of 21 June on 19 December they intended to or did give up any contractual or other rights which they had at that time. Whether my first view be correct or my second view be correct, the result is the same, namely that from the time when the plaintiffs went into occupation of unit 7, they were bound by the terms of the defendants' letter of 21 June.

The second issue before me is whether the terms on which the plaintiffs went into occupation of unit 7 included an implied term whereby the defendants warranted (a) that unit 7 was of sound construction and reasonably suitable for the purposes required by the plaintiffs, or (b) that unit 7 was in the condition referred to in (a) above save in relation to defects which could not have been discovered by reasonable care and skill on the part of any person concerned in the construction thereof.

All arguments with regard to the second issue were put forward on the assumption that I would reach the conclusion which I have on the first issue. The arguments ranged far and wide and a large number of cases were cited. The substance of counsel for the plaintiffs' submissions were that in commercial contracts the courts will normally, in the absence of express terms to the contrary, imply terms requiring that their subject matters be sound and fit for purpose, that contracts for the sale and leasing of land are exceptions, but contracts for licences to occupy land are not, and that, in any event, such a term is to be implied in this case because it was necessary to give efficacy to the contract and to make it workable.

Counsel for the plaintiffs submitted that the implied term should be held to be a warranty. He said that the defendants existed to provide accommodation for companies such as the plaintiffs, that they knew the purpose for which the plaintiffs wished to use unit 7, and that the plaintiffs would not have a structural survey made of it.

The substance of counsel for the defendants' submissions was that since implied terms as to fitness were not implied in contracts for the sale and leasing of land, it would be absurd if they were to be implied in contracts conferring only rights to occupy land, that the express terms contained in the letter of 21 June excluded the implied term alleged, and that before a court may imply a term, it must be satisfied that the parties would both have agreed it and what precisely that term would have been, but in this case the defendants would never have agreed to a term which might have involved substantial liability and the plaintiffs themselves have alleged terms in the alternative.

Counsel for the defendants said that if, contrary to his submissions, the contract had included an implied term, it would not have been an absolute warranty but simply an obligation to take reasonable care.

The law with regard to implied terms has obviously been the product of a long development. Until the eighteenth century the tendency of the courts was to apply the maxim caveat emptor to all types of contract, but during that century the idea grew that warranties could be implied, first in relation to title, and later, and less completely, in respect of quality: see *Holdsworth's History of English Law*, vol 8 (2nd edn, 1937) pp 69, 70.

In the nineteenth century the courts came to imply certain terms in certain types of contracts on a prima facie or matter of course basis unless the parties had agreed express terms which excluded them. Examples taken from sale of goods are that when a buyer had not had an opportunity of examining goods they should be of merchantable quality (*Jones v Just* (1868) LR 3 QB 197) and that when a buyer had made known to a seller the purpose for which he intended to use the goods so as to show that he relied on his skill and judgment, they should be reasonably fit for that purpose (*Randall v Newson* (1877) 2 QBD 102). Other examples could be taken from hire of goods, work and materials, master and servant, and several other branches of the law. Terms which were normally implied in contracts for the sale of goods came to be codified, with minor amendments, in the Sale of Goods Act 1893.

In contracts for the sale of land and for the grant of leases, the courts, while willing to imply terms as to title and in the case of leases that the lessee should have quiet enjoyment, adopted the general rule that there were no implied terms as to fitness or suitability for purpose. In *Sutton v Temple* (1843) 12 M & W 52, 152 ER 1108 a tenant of pasture land whose cattle had died because of paint which had been spread with manure before the commencement of the tenancy failed in an action against his landlord. In *Hart v Windsor* (1843) 12 M & W 68, 152 ER 1114 a tenant of an unfurnished house, which he found to be infested with bugs, failed against his landlord. Parke B said (12 M & W 68 at 87–88, 152 ER 1114 at 1122):

> 'We are all of opinion . . . that there is no contract, still less a condition, implied by law on the demise of real property only, that it is fit for the purpose for which it is let. The principles of the common law do not warrant such a position . . .'

In *Robbins v Jones* (1863) 15 CBNS 221 at 240, [1861–73] All ER Rep 544 at 547, which concerned a private way let to tenants next to the approach to Waterloo Bridge, Erle CJ

said in the Court of Exchequer that 'fraud apart, there is no law against letting a tumble-
a down house . . .'

In *Manchester Bonded Warehouse Co Ltd v Carr* (1880) 5 CPD 507 at 510, [1874–80] All ER Rep 563 at 565, in which a warehouse had collapsed after flour had been loaded onto one of its floors, Lord Coleridge CJ, giving judgment in the Divisional Court, said:

> '. . . we are of opinion that the plaintiffs are not liable to damages by reason of any
> b implied covenant or warranty by them that the building was fit for the purpose for which it was to be used.'

In this century the Court of Appeal followed the earlier cases in *Bottomley v Bannister* [1932] 1 KB 458, [1931] All ER Rep 99. In that case the purchasers of a new house had been let into possession of it as tenants at will and had died as the result of carbon monoxide poisoning due to a defective boiler. Scrutton LJ said ([1932] 1 KB 458 at 468,
c [1931] All ER Rep 99 at 102):

> 'Now it is at present well established English law that, in the absence of express contract, a landlord of an unfurnished house is not liable to his tenant, or a vendor of real estate to his purchaser, for defects in the house or land rendering it dangerous or unfit for occupation . . .'

d Parke B in *Hart v Windsor* made plain that the court was dealing with 'a demise of real property only'. Where a contract has included the provision of something other than land, the courts have been willing to imply terms. In *Smith v Marrable* (1843) 11 M & W 5, 152 ER 693 the Court of Exchequer held that when a house which had been let furnished was infested with bugs there was a breach of an implied condition that it should be reasonably fit for habitation. In *Bentley Bros v Metcalfe & Co* [1906] 2 KB 548
e the Court of Appeal held that, when a room in a mill had been let on terms which included the provision of a power supply to a machine in the room and the supply had been excessive and caused damage, the landlords were liable for the breach of an implied term that the supply would be reasonably fit for its purpose. *Collins v Hopkins* [1923] 2 KB 617, [1923] All ER Rep 225 was another case of a furnished letting. McCardie J held that there was a breach of an implied warranty that the premises should be reasonably fit
f for habitation at the commencement of the tenancy because they had recently been occupied by a person suffering from an infectious disease, namely tuberculosis.

Licences resemble conveyances of freeholds and leases in that they relate to land, but they differ from them in that licensees do not acquire estates in land nor do they obtain legal possession, although the terms of their licences may entitle them to remain in occupation for specified periods and even to exclude the landowner from entering. An
g important difference between tenancies and licences which often makes licences attractive to landowners is that licensees are not entitled to the special protection conferred on tenants by such Acts as the Landlord and Tenant Act 1954, the Agricultural Holdings Act 1948 and the Rent Act 1977.

No reported case has been cited to me in which a court has held specifically that a term as to suitability for a licensee's purposes should not be implied in a licence. In *Yeoman*
h *Credit Ltd v Apps* [1961] 2 All ER 281 at 291, [1962] 2 QB 508 at 522–523, which concerned a hire-purchase agreement relating to a car with many defects, Harman LJ said:

> 'I take it to be quite clearly the law that the hirer of a chattel does warrant that it is reasonably fit for the purpose for which he hires it—in this case that the motor car shall be a viable motor car. That is the contrast between the hirer of a chattel and
> j the hirer of a piece of realty, or a chattel real: it is well known that the hire of an immovable involves no condition that it is fit or suitable for the purpose for which it is hired.'

Despite Harman LJ's use of the words 'hirer' and 'immovable', I think that it is by no means certain that he had licences in mind. His references to realty and a chattel real point to his thinking only of freeholds and leaseholds. In any event, his words were plainly obiter. a

In *Francis v Cockrell* (1870) LR 5 QB 501 the defendant employed contractors to erect a grandstand overlooking Cheltenham Racecourse and then charged the plaintiff five shillings to sit on it. The stand collapsed and the plaintiff was injured. The Court of Exchequer Chamber held that the defendant has impliedly undertaken that due care had been exercised in the erection of the stand and that it was reasonably fit for its purpose. The word 'licence' was not used in the judgments, but obviously that was what the b plaintiff had. The judges reasons varied. Martin B said (at 510):

> 'Not that I consider the defendant in any way an insurer, and responsible for anything beyond what a man could reasonably be responsible for; but I think that he was responsible for that stand being in a fit and proper condition, in a reasonably fit and proper condition for the purpose for which he took the money and admitted c the person . . .'

In *Maclenan v Segar* [1917] 2 KB 325 the plaintiff, who was occupying a room as a guest in the defendants' hotel, suffered injuries when attempting to escape from a fire in the hotel. McCardie J held that the plaintiff was entitled to succeed. He said (at 332–333):

> d 'Where the occupier of premises agrees for reward that a person shall have the right to enter and use them for a mutually contemplated purpose, the contract between the parties (unless it provides to the contrary) contains an implied warranty that the premises are as safe for that purpose as reasonable care and skill on the part of any one can make them. The rule is subject to the limitation that the defendant is not to be held responsible for defects which could not have been discovered by e reasonable care or skill on the part of any person concerned with the construction, alteration, repair, or maintenance of the premises.'

A person in the position of the plaintiff in either *Francis v Cockrell* or *Maclenan v Segar* would today no doubt rely on the common duty of care under the Occupiers' Liability Act 1957, but the cases are none the less instances of courts holding that there are implied terms as to suitability in licences. f

In the *Francis* and *Maclenan* cases the courts treated the terms which they implied rather as if they were prima facie or common form. Except where that is the correct approach, the circumstances in which the courts would imply a term are limited. In *The Moorcock* (1889) 14 PD 64, [1886–90] All ER Rep 530 the Court of Appeal held that wharfingers who had allowed a vessel to be moored against their wharf in order to discharge its cargo by the use of their cranes on payment were liable to the shipowner g when the tide ebbed and the vessel settled on a ridge in the bed of the River Thames and was damaged. The court held that it was implied that the wharfingers should have taken reasonable care, but Lord Esher MR made plain that that was the least onerous duty which could be implied and not necessarily the whole of the duty (see 14 PD 64 at 67, [1886–90] All ER Rep 530 at 534). Bowen LJ said, in a famous passage, that an implied warranty is in all cases founded on the presumed intention of the parties and will be h drawn only in order to give business efficacy to the transaction (see 14 PD 64 at 68, [1886–90] All ER Rep 530 at 534–535).

In *Reigate v Union Manufacturing Co (Ramsbottom) Ltd* [1918] 1 KB 592 at 605, [1918–19] All ER Rep 143 at 149, a case which concerned agent and principal, Scrutton LJ said:

> 'A term can only be implied if it is necessary in the business sense to give efficacy j to the contract; that is, if it is such a term that it can confidently be said that if at the time the contract was being negotiated some one had said to the parties, "What will happen in such a case", they would both have replied, "Of course, so and so will happen; we did not trouble to say that; it is too clear." '

Liverpool City Council v Irwin [1976] 2 All ER 39, [1977] AC 239 concerned a 15-storey

block consisting of flats let to tenants after they had signed conditions of tenancy prepared
a by the council, and staircases, lifts and rubbish chutes, which were for use by the tenants but which remained in the possession of the council. The documents signed by the tenants did not impose any obligations on the council in respect of the means of access to the flats and, in the Court of Appeal ([1975] 3 All ER 658 [1976] 1 QB 319, Roskill and Ormrod LJJ held that none could be implied. Ormrod LJ commented that since experienced counsel for the tenants had suggested no less than five alternative implied
b terms, it was not unreasonable to suggest that there could be no certainty what the right implied term (if any) was (see [1975] 3 All ER 658 at 672, [1976] QB 319 at 338). Lord Denning MR dissented; he considered that a court should imply a term if it were reasonable to do so.

The House of Lords reversed the Court of Appeal and held that since the conditions of tenancy were incomplete and of a unilateral nature, the court had to complete the
c contract, that there were to be implied easements for the tenants to use the stairs and rights in the nature of easements to use the lifts and chutes, and that there was to be implied an obligation on the council to take reasonable care to keep the means of access in reasonable repair and usability (see [1976] 2 All ER 39, [1977] AC 239). Lord Wilberforce said that there are varieties of implications which the court think fit to make. One of them was, he said ([1976] 2 All ER 39 at 43, [1977] AC 239 at 253)—

d

> 'where there is an apparently complete bargain, the courts are willing to add a term on the ground that without it the contract will not work—this is the case, if not of *The Moorcock* itself on its facts, at least of the doctrine of *The Moorcock* as usually applied. This is . . . a strict test . . .'

Lord Wilberforce did not indorse Lord Denning MR's principle that a court could imply
e terms because they would be reasonable. He thought that a further category or shade of a continuous spectrum was where the parties had not fully stated the terms of the contract. Lord Cross said ([1976] 2 All ER 39 at 47, [1977] AC 239 at 258):

> 'Sometimes . . . what the court is being in effect asked to do is to rectify a particular—often a very detailed—contract by inserting in it a term which the
> *f* parties have not expressed. Here it is not enough for the court to say that the suggested term is a reasonable one the presence of which would make the contract a better or fairer one; it must be able to say that the insertion of the term is necessary to give—as it is put—"business efficacy" to the contract and that if its absence had been pointed out at the time both parties—assuming them to have been reasonable men—would have agreed without hesitation to its insertion.'

g In the present case the licence granted by the defendants to the plaintiffs bore a resemblance to a lease in that it related to land, it was for a fixed period and because many of the terms contained in the letter of 21 June 1979 it resembled covenants usually to be found in leases. The licence differed from a lease in all the important respects in which licences differ from leases and to which I have referred previously. A reason for the defendants having offered the plaintiffs a licence rather than a lease was to prevent the
h plaintiffs from becoming entitled to the protection of the Landlord and Tenant Act 1954.

If the defendants had granted a lease to the plaintiffs, it is clear from *Sutton v Temple* (1843) M & W 52, 152 ER 1108 and subsequent cases that a term as to suitability could not have been implied. Since, however, the plaintiffs were granted a licence, there is no reason why the prohibition of such a term in leases should be applied. *Francis v Cockrell* and *Maclenan v Segar* show that terms as to suitability may be implied in licences. They
j were, however, cases involving personal injuries whereas, fortunately, in the present case no one suffered physical injury.

My view is that it is possible for terms as to fitness for purpose to be implied in licences, but that, except perhaps in relation to safety, there are none which the courts imply prima facie in the way that such terms are implied in sale of goods, hire and the like. If any term as to suitability was to be implied in the contractual licence in this case it must,

I think, be on the application of the test propounded in *The Moorcock*, as clarified by *Reigate v Union Manufacturing Co (Ramsbotton) Ltd* and by *Liverpool City Council v Irwin*, or a
because it is necessary to complete an incomplete contract as in *Irwin*, or both.

The issue asks whether a warranty was to be implied and not a mere obligation to take reasonable care. The warranty proposed in (a) is twofold: namely, that unit 7 should be of 'sound construction' and that it should be 'reasonably suitable for the purposes required by the plaintiffs'. The warranty proposed in (b) is the same as in (a) except that it excludes liability for defects not discoverable by reasonable means. The plaintiffs' reason for b
putting forward (b) as an alternative to (a) is because the term implied by McCardie J in *Maclenan v Segar* was in that qualified form.

In *The Moorcock* and in *Liverpool City Council v Irwin* the terms implied required only that the body held liable should have taken reasonable care, but in the former the river bed was not owned or controlled by the wharfingers and, in the latter, vandals were likely to undo the work of the council at any time. In contrast, unit 7 was owned by the c
defendants, had been built on their instructions, and had only just been completed when the plaintiffs were allowed into occupation. In *Maclenan v Segar* the hotel was an old one and might conceivably have concealed or developed defects which were not discoverable by exercise of reasonable care and skill. The position in the present case was quite different. Unit 7 was completely new and the defendants did or could have employed engineers and architects capable of discovering any defects. d

Asking, as *The Moorcock* test requires, whether it was necessary in order to give efficacy to the licence agreement that the defendant should have warranted as set out in (a) of the issue that unit 7 was of sound construction or reasonably fit for the purposes required by the plaintiffs, namely the manufacture of plastics and composite materials, I think that the answer must be Yes. The sole purpose of the licence was to enable the plaintiffs to have accommodation in which to carry on and expand their business while their existing e
factory was being enlarged. If anyone had said to the plaintiffs and the defendants' directors and executives at the time when the licence was being granted, 'Will the premises be sound and suitable for the plaintiffs' purposes?' they would assuredly have replied, 'Of course; there would be no point in the licence if that were not so.' The term was required to make the contract workable.

The defendants' letter of 21 June 1979 which the plaintiffs were required to approve f
was not unlike the conditions of tenancy which the tenants in *Liverpool City Council v Irwin* were required to sign. In each case the terms provided were one-sided. If I had not thought that a warranty of soundness and suitability for the plaintiffs' purposes was to be implied on the application of *The Moorcock* test, I would have thought that an identical term would have had to be implied in order to complete the contract as the parties must clearly have intended. g

Since I have decided that the defendants gave an actual warranty to the plaintiffs and that it was unqualified, it follows that I give judgment for the plaintiffs on liability with damages to be assessed.

Judgment for the plaintiffs. Damages to be assessed.

h

Solicitors: *Stoneham Langton & Passmore*, Croydon (for the plaintiffs); *Theodore Goddard & Co*, agents for *Morgan Bruce & Nicholas*, Cardiff (for the defendants).

K Mydeen Esq Barrister.

a Data Card Corp and others v Air Express International Corp and others

QUEEN'S BENCH DIVISION (COMMERCIAL COURT)
BINGHAM J
25, 28 MARCH 1983

b

Carriage by air – Damage to baggage or cargo – Limitation of liability – Damage to package forming essential part of consignment – Carrier's liability for loss or damage limited to '250 francs per kilogramme' – Whether liability calculated per kilogramme of total consignment weight – Whether liability calculated per kilogramme of lost or damaged part of consignment – Whether liability calculated per kilogramme of consignment affected by damage to or loss of part – Carriage
c *by Air Acts (Application of Provisions) Order 1967, Sch 2, Pt A, para 3(12).*

Article 22(2)[a] of the unamended Warsaw Convention, as set out in para 3(12) of Pt A of Sch 2 to the Carriage by Air Acts (Application of Provisions) Order 1967, limits a carrier's liability for the loss of, or damage to, a package forming part of a consignment of registered baggage or of cargo to 250 francs per kilogramme of the lost or damaged
d package and not to 250 francs per kilogramme of the total consignment of which the lost or damaged package forms part nor to 250 francs per kilogramme of the part of the total consignment which has its value affected by the loss of or damage to the package (see p 643 *e* to *g* and p 644 *h*, post).

Notes
e
For limitation of liability of carriers of air cargo, see 2 Halsbury's Laws (4th edn) paras 1388–1394, and for cases on the subject, see 8(2) Digest (Reissue) 607–608, 43–48.

For the Carriage by Air Acts (Application of Provisions) Order 1967, Sch 2, Pt A, para 3, see 3 Halsbury's Statutory Instruments (4th reissue) 46.

f **Cases referred to in judgment**
Fothergill v Monarch Airlines Ltd [1980] 2 All ER 696, [1981] AC 251, [1980] 3 WLR 209, HL.
Norwood v American Airlines Inc 1980 US Av R 1854.

Action
g By a writ dated 23 February 1982 the plaintiffs, Data Card Corp, Data Card (UK) Ltd and Jardine Air Cargo (UK) Ltd (formerly Industrial Freight Ltd), sought damages for breach of contract and breach of statutory duty against the first defendants, Air Express International Corp, and damages for breach of duty against the second defendants, Air Express International (UK) Ltd, following damage to a package weighing 659 kg and forming part of a total consignment of eight packages which was the property of the first
h or the second plaintiff. Damage occurred to the package while the consignment was being carried by the first and the second defendants to the third plaintiffs pursuant to a contract of carriage by air between the first and the third plaintiffs and the first defendants. Damages were not sought against the third defendants, British Airways Board, or the fourth defendants, Field Cargo Services Ltd. The first defendants admitted liability and on 15 October 1980 Lloyd J in chambers ordered that judgment be entered
j against them for £6,622·95 plus interest, being damages calculated pursuant to the unamended Warsaw Convention at the sterling equivalent rate of £10·05 per kilogramme

---

a Article 22(2) is set out at p 641 *h*, post

of the damaged package, and further ordered that the balance of damages be assessed by a judge of the Commercial Court. The facts are set out in the judgment.

Geoffrey Kinley for the plaintiffs.
Marcus Edwards for the defendants.

Cur adv vult

28 March. The following judgment was delivered.

BINGHAM J. This is an action brought by the plaintiffs against the defendants claiming damages arising out of damage to cargo during its carriage by air from Minneapolis, in the United States, to this country. On 15 October 1982 Lloyd J entered judgment for the plaintiffs against the first defendant, Air Express International Corp, for £6,622·95 plus agreed interest, and ordered that the balance of damages be assessed by a judge of the Commercial Court.

The matter accordingly comes before me for the assessment of damages. In truth, however, the task is not one of assessing damages but of deciding a point of pure legal principle as to the proper construction of art 22(2) of the unamended Warsaw Convention, which governed the air carriage in question. That unamended convention is set out in the Carriage by Air Acts (Application of Provisions) Order 1967, SI 1967/480, Sch 2. If the defendants' construction of art 22(2) is correct, no further sum is payable to the plaintiffs. If the plaintiffs are correct, they are entitled to receive a further sum. The size of that further sum will depend on which of their alternative arguments succeeds. If successful in their main argument, they will recover more than if they succeed in their subsidiary argument.

Before referring to the convention in detail or recounting the submissions of the parties, it is convenient to turn to the facts. The parties have very helpfully agreed a statement of the relevant facts:

> '1. Pursuant to a contract of carriage by air, made on about 22nd February 1980 between the First Plaintiffs as shippers and the Third Plaintiffs as consignees and the First Defendants as carriers, the First Defendants carried a consignment of cargo from Minneapolis to London. The single Air Waybill issued by the First Defendants in respect of this consignment described it as comprising 8 packages with a gross weight of 3132·5 kilogrammes, the goods being further described as consisting of calendering/embossing machines . . .
>
> 3. During the course of the carriage by air of the said consignment, and whilst it was in the charge of the First Defendants as carriers by air within the meaning of Article 18(2) of the Schedule, part of the consignment was damaged in that during the course of loading the consignment on to road transport at Heathrow Airport, London, 1 of the 8 packages was dropped from a forklift truck, causing the machine contained therein to receive severe damage. The package which was dropped weighed 659 kilogrammes.
>
> 4. The 8 packages listed on the Air Waybill described in paragraph 1 hereof contained 2 complete embossing machine systems. Each system consisted of machinery and ancillary items packed in 4 separate crates for carriage by air. The plaintiffs say that the total weight of each system was 1566 kgs. The Defendants are not yet satisfied as to the exact weight.
>
> 5. The Plaintiffs say that each complete system was designed to operate as a single unit and that none of the individual items separately crated could function on its own. Further each system was designed and constructed by the Plaintiffs to an individual customer's specification and was thus unique as far as its embossing and encoding characteristics were concerned. Without the one damaged item, the whole system was useless to the consignee or anyone else. Accordingly the damage to that one item affected the value of the other items.
>
> 6. The Defendants are not at present satisfied as to the facts set out in paragraph 5

above but before the matter is taken further on the facts, they join with the Plaintiffs in seeking a ruling of the Court as to whether or not the basis contended for in paragraph (b) of the Plaintiffs' Summons is the law.'

I would only add, although this is probably already clear, that the eight packages were included in a single air waybill with a single gross weight, no weight being given for the eight individual packages.

The articles of the convention to which my attention was drawn were:

'CHAPTER II

DOCUMENTS OF CARRIAGE . . .

SECTION 3.—AIR WAYBILL

Article 5

(1) Every carrier of cargo has the right to require the consignor to make out and hand over to him a document called an "air waybill"; every consignor has the right to require the carrier to accept this document . . .

Article 7

The carrier of cargo has the right to require the consignor to make out separate waybills when there is more than one package.

Article 8

The air waybill shall contain the following particulars . . . (*h*) the number of the packages, the method of packing and the particular marks or numbers upon them; (*i*) the weight, the quantity and the volume or dimensions of the cargo . . . (*m*) the amount of the value declared in accordance with Article 22(2) . . .

CHAPTER III

LIABILITY OF THE CARRIER . . .

Article 18

(1) The carrier is liable for damage sustained in the event of the destruction or loss of, or of damage to, any registered baggage or any cargo, if the occurrence which caused the damage so sustained took place during the carriage by air . . .

Article 20

(1) The carrier is not liable if he proves that he and his servants or agents have taken all necessary measures to avoid the damage or that it was impossible for him or them to take such measures.

(2) In the carriage of cargo and baggage the carrier is not liable if he proves that the damage was occasioned by negligent pilotage or negligence in the handling of the aircraft or in navigation and that, in all other respects, he and his servants or agents have taken all necessary measures to avoid the damage . . .

Article 22

(1) In the carriage of passengers the liability of the carrier for each passenger is limited to the sum of 125,000 francs . . .

(2) In the carriage of registered baggage and of cargo, the liability of the carrier is limited to a sum of 250 francs per kilogramme, unless the consignor has made, at the time when the package was handed over to the carrier, a special declaration of the value at delivery and has paid a supplementary sum if the case so requires. In that case the carrier will be liable to pay a sum not exceeding the declared sum, unless he proves that that sum is greater than the actual value to the consignor at delivery . . .

Article 26

(1) Receipt by the person entitled to delivery of baggage or cargo without complaint is *prima facie* evidence that the same has been delivered in good condition and in accordance with the document of carriage . . .

> (3) Every complaint must be made in writing upon the document of carriage or by separate notice in writing despatched within the times aforesaid . . . *a*
>
> CHAPTER V
>
> GENERAL AND FINAL PROVISIONS . . .
>
> *Article* 33
>
> Nothing contained in this Convention shall prevent the carrier either from refusing to enter into any contract of carriage, or from making regulations which *b* do not conflict with the provisions of this Convention.'

The question may now be stated. The plaintiffs contended that damages should be assessed on the basis that, for the purpose of art 22(2) Sch 2 to the Carriage by Air Acts (Application of Provisions) Order 1967, the liability of the air carrier for damage to part of cargo is limited to a sum of 250 francs per kilogramme of the weight of the entire consignment covered by the air waybill, and that that weight is particularised in the said *c* air waybill pursuant to art 8 of Sch 2. This basis has been conveniently referred to in argument as 'the entire weight'. Alternatively the plaintiffs contended that damages should be assessed on the basis that, for the purpose of art 22(2), the liability of the air carrier for damage to part of the cargo is limited to a sum of 250 francs per kilogramme of the actual total weight of such packages of cargo covered by the air waybill as have their value affected by such damage. This basis has been referred to as 'the affected *d* weight'. When the Warsaw Convention was amended at The Hague in 1955 art 22 was amended so as to achieve this result.

The defendants contended that the correct basis was a third one, namely that the limit was determined by the weight of the package lost or damaged, in this case the weight of the package which was dropped. This basis has been called 'the package weight'.

Counsel for the plaintiffs advanced arguments in favour of the entire weight basis *e* under four heads: construction of the article; travaux préparatoires; authority; and academic commentary. I will adopt the same headings, dealing first with his primary argument in favour of the entire weight basis.

Construction

The argument of counsel for the plaintiffs was to this effect. Article 22(2) provided a limit of 250 francs per kilogramme. Kilogramme of what? The answer, he submitted, *f* was to be found in art 8(1) of the unamended convention: 'the weight of the cargo', since that was the only weight which the convention was concerned with, and it was a weight which was particularised in the air waybill. The natural inference was, in his submission, that the weight referred to in art 22(2) was the weight required to be included in the air waybill, that being the total weight of the cargo covered by the air waybill. Of course it was convenient to include a number of packages in a single air waybill, which art 8(*h*) *g* expressly envisaged, but the carrier took the risk in doing so of increasing his total liability in the event of damage. Article 7 enabled a carrier to protect himself by insisting on separate air waybills for each package. Why, asked counsel rhetorically, should art 7 be included unless to give the carrier a right to split up cargo into smaller units of liability?

Counsel for the defendants submitted that art 22(2) was to be read as saying '250 francs *h* per kilogramme per package', not 'per entire consignment', because (1) it is 'per package' by necessary implication, by reason of the words 'the package' later in the same sentence of art 22(2) (2) it is easier to read art 22(2) as 'In the carriage of registered baggage and of cargo, the liability of the carrier is limited to a sum of 250 francs per kilogramme per package, unless the consignor has made, at the time when the package was handed over to the carrier, a declaration . . .', than as 'In the carriage of registered baggage and of *j* cargo, the liability of the carrier is limited to a sum of 250 francs per kilogramme per entire consignment carried on the air waybill, unless the consignor has made, at the time when the package was handed over to the carrier . . .' and (3) it is more natural and reasonable to limit liability to the weight of the object for which the carrier is liable in damages than to limit it to the weight of all other objects which are listed on the air waybill, no matter how many and how heavy they may be and no matter that such other objects have not been damaged and that the carrier is not liable in damages for damage to them. Counsel for the defendants elaborated this last submission by pointing out that the convention increased the responsibility of the carrier by making him absolutely liable to damage to cargo unless exceptionally he could bring himself within art 20. On the other hand the convention allowed him to limit his liability but, quite apart from art 20(1), he had no liability except for goods lost or damaged. He had no liability for goods which arrived safely. It was very odd, counsel submitted, if the limitation of damages had reference to goods for which there was no liability at law anyway. Why should the limit escalate in proportion to the number of undamaged packages? There should be the same limit, no matter how many packages. Counsel for the defendants submitted, fourthly, that on a question of interpretation of commercial law, where there is doubt, it is permissible to look at commercial convenience. If there is doubt in the present case, the plaintiffs' interpretation would obstruct the useful practice in carriage by air of pooling quantities of baggage on one ticket and quantities of packages on one air waybill, because carriers would issue separate tickets or air waybills for each item in order to limit their liability to the minimum sum. This would be inconvenient to passengers, consignors, consignees and their agents as well as to the carriers and their agents. In respect of art 7, counsel submitted that it was an unnecessary article since an air carrier was not a common carrier: see art 33 of the convention. The carrier was therefore free to make any bargain he wished, or to make no bargain, but there were, in counsel's submission, many reasons why a carrier might wish to issue separate air waybills. There might be a number of different consignees; there might be a need to put cargo on different flights; it might be desirable for there to be different air waybills for special cargo of different kinds, and so on. Counsel also drew attention to other parts of the convention where specific reference was made to identified documents of carriage, and submitted that, if art 22(2) had been intended to refer to the goods comprised in a particular air waybill, that would and should have been made clear.

Having heard the submissions of both parties on the construction of art 22(2) in the context of the convention as a whole, I am left in no doubt but that the defendants' submissions on the construction of the article are correct. The words '250 francs per kilogramme' do, I accept, pose the question, 'per kilogramme of what?', but the natural and grammatical answer derived from the clause itself seems to me to be 'per kilogramme of the package which was handed over to the carrier'. A requirement that the limit should be calculated by reference to goods neither lost nor damaged would, as it seems to me, require express language or clear implication which are not to be found in the paragraph. The strongest point in favour of the plaintiffs is, in my view, the anomaly that the limit should be calculated by reference to the weight of a package which need not be, and in this case was not, specified in the air waybill at all. It is, however, for a plaintiff to prove the weight of the package lost or damaged, and in many cases this will be easily calculable by subtracting from the total weight shown on the air waybill the weight of the packages not lost or damaged. Moreover, it seems to me very unlikely that the draftsman of the convention intended carriers to be fully protected by the limitation of liability available to them under the convention only if they went through the bureaucratic, costly and time-wasting procedure of issuing or insisting on separate air waybills for each package of cargo. On these grounds, therefore, I consider the defendants' argument on construction to be preferable.

I can deal with the other heads relied on more briefly.

Travaux préparatoires

In order to demonstrate that art 22(2) was intended to have reference to the entire weight, as he contended, counsel for the plaintiffs, referred me to the minutes of the Paris Conference of 1925, the second and third sessions of the Comité Internationale Technique d'Experts Juridique Aériens in 1927 and 1928, and of the Warsaw Conference of 1929. These documents showed that art 22(2) was originally drafted so that the financial limit was attached to 'the package', that a reference to weight was substituted, that importance was attached to the carrier being able to calculate the total liability to which he was subject and that a proposal made by His Majesty's government (which, if adopted, would have made clear beyond argument that the reference was intended to be to the package weight) was sunk without trace. While, however, English courts are now sometimes prepared to consider the travaux préparatoires which precede the adoption of international conventions, reliance may be placed on such materials only where they contain a clear and indisputable indication of a definite legislative intention: see *Fothergill v Monarch Airlines Ltd* [1980] 2 All ER 696 at 703, [1981] AC 251 at 278 per Lord Wilberforce. The present materials are, as it seems to me, an excellent example of materials which may not be relied on, because, far from containing a clear and indisputable indication of a definite legislative intention, they leave one altogether unclear what was to be intended to be the rule on the point at issue. Perusal of these materials in the present case serves only to highlight the wisdom of the courts' cautious approach to such materials. I do not feel it necessary to make any detailed reference to the documents to which I was referred, interesting though they were, because they did not, in my judgment, begin to offer a solution to this case.

Authority

There was a striking dearth of authority on the point at issue. The only case drawn to my attention was *Norwood v American Airlines Inc* 1980 US Av R 1854, a decision of the Superior Court of the District of Columbia, Small Claims Branch,. The airline in that case was contending that the financial limit of the carrier's liability was to be assessed with reference to the weight of an article stolen, not (as these defendants would contend) the weight of the package from which it was stolen. The airline failed, rightly as I think, and as the present defendants would accept. There are dicta in the decision which support the present plaintiffs' argument that the limit in art 22(2) is set with reference to the total weight of checked baggage per passenger, but I do not think that that conclusion was necessary for decision of the case, and in any event I do not find the reasoning of the judge sufficiently convincing to outweigh the effect of what, as I have indicated, seems to me to be the proper construction of the article.

Academic commentary

My attention was drawn to a work by Professor Drion, of the Netherlands, *Limitation of Liabilities in International Air Law* (1954) and an article by Professor Cheng 'The Law of International and Non-International Carriage by Air' (1964) 61 LS Gaz 37. These writers, alone (it would seem) among academic commentators on international air law, venture to discuss the present problem. I do not, however, find that their discussion, for all its interest, offers any penetrating new insight or impels one towards any solution. In short, I find nothing in their commentary which greatly supports or weakens the conclusion I have reached on the correct construction of the article.

The affected weight

This was, as I have said, the solution adopted by the Hague amendment to the Warsaw Convention. I find nothing whatever in the wording of the unamended Warsaw Convention, in the travaux préparatoires of the Warsaw Convention, in any authority or in any academic writing to suggest that art 22(2) in its unamended form was intended to have the meaning which it later bore after being amended at The Hague. I regard this contention as quite unarguable. In the result, therefore, my acceptance of the defendants' construction of art 22(2) is decisive in favour of 'the package weight'.

It follows that, in my judgment, no further damages are payable by the defendants to the plaintiffs.

Declaration that liability of air carrier limited to 250 francs per kilogramme per package damaged or lost.

Solicitors: *Clyde & Co* (for the plaintiffs); *Ince & Co* (for the defendants).

K Mydeen Esq Barrister.

R v Ewing

COURT OF APPEAL, CRIMINAL DIVISION
O'CONNOR LJ, PARKER AND STAUGHTON JJ
17, 18, 20, 21 DECEMBER 1982, 11 MARCH 1983

Criminal evidence – Handwriting – Comparison of handwriting – Admissibility for comparison with disputed writing – Satisfaction of judge that writing to be admitted genuine – Standard of proof – Whether criminal standard of proof – Whether judge must be satisfied beyond reasonable doubt that writing to be admitted is genuine – Criminal Procedure Act 1865, s 8.

Criminal evidence – Record relating to trade or business – Computer print-out of bank account – Operator who fed information into computer not reasonably to be expected to recollect information he supplied to computer because of lapse of time – Whether computer print-out of account showing payments into account admissible as evidence of payment into account – Whether print-out a 'document' – Whether computer operator a person having personal knowledge of matters dealt with in information supplied – Criminal Evidence Act 1965, s 1(1).

Criminal evidence – Improper conduct of accused on other occasions – Whether desirable in interests of fair trial that judge should know during trial that accused is of bad character.

Section 8[a] of the Criminal Procedure Act 1865, which provides that 'any writing proved to the satisfaction of the judge to be genuine' may be compared with a disputed writing, merely directs that it is the judge and not the jury who is to decide whether writing is genuine and can be admitted in evidence for comparison with a disputed writing, and does not deal with the standard of proof required to satisfy the judge that writing sought to be admitted in evidence for comparison is genuine. Accordingly, the standard of proof is governed by the common law and therefore when s 8 is being applied in a criminal trial it must be shown beyond all reasonable doubt that the writing sought to be adduced for comparison is genuine writing of the accused before it may be admitted in evidence (see p 652 *j* to p 653 *e*, post); *Blyth v Blyth* [1966] 1 All ER 524 applied; *R v Angeli* [1978] 3 All ER 950 disapproved.

Where a bank uses a computer to store information regarding customers' accounts and the Crown seeks in criminal proceedings to establish that a sum of money was paid into a customer's account, a computer print-out of the movements on the account may properly be admitted as evidence, under s 1(1)[b] of the Criminal Evidence Act 1965, of the payments stated in the print-out if it is established that the computer operator who fed into the computer information regarding the customer's account cannot reasonably be expected, having regard to the time which has elapsed after he supplied the information to the computer, to have any recollection of dealing with particular payments into the account, because (i) for the purposes of s 1(1) the computer operator is the person who could give 'direct oral evidence' of the payment into the account, (ii) the print-out is, or forms part of, a 'device by means of which information is recorded or stored', within s 1(4), and is therefore for the purposes of s 1(1)(*a*) a 'document' forming part of a record compiled in the course of the bank's business, and (iii) for the purposes of s 1(1)(*a*) the computer operator is a person who 'supplied' the information and who has personal knowledge of the matters dealt with in the information he supplied (see p 655 *j* and p 656 *b c d e*, post).

In the interests of a fair trial it is desirable that a trial judge should know that a defendant is of bad character, and therefore it is permissible for the judge to have before him during the trial antecedents of a defendant who is of bad character, so that the judge can, for example, then prevent cross-examination of Crown witnesses that will let in the defendant's character (see p 649 *g* to *j*, post).

---

a Section 8 is set out at p 650 *e f*, post
b Section 1, so far as material, is set out at p 655 *f* to *h*, post

Notes

For the comparison of handwriting, see 17 Halsbury's Laws (4th edn) para 91, and for cases on the subject, see 22 Digest (Reissue) 214–215, *1809–1828* a

For the admissibility of evidence of business records, see 11 Halsbury's Laws (4th edn), para 442.

For the Criminal Evidence Act 1865, s 8, see 12 Halsbury's Statutes (3rd edn) 840.

For the Criminal Evidence Act 1965, s 1, see 12 Halsbury's Statutes (3rd edn) 907.

b

Cases referred to in judgment

Blyth v Blyth [1966] 1 All ER 524, [1966] AC 643, [1966] 2 WLR 634, HL; *rvsg* [1965] 2 All ER 817, [1965] P 411, [1965] 3 WLR 365, CA.

Hornal v Neuberger Products Ltd [1956] 3 All ER 970, [1957] 1 QB 247, [1956] 3 WLR 1034, CA.

Preston-Jones v Preston-Jones [1951] 1 All ER 124, [1951] AC 391, HL. c

R v Angeli [1978] 3 All ER 950, [1979] 1 WLR 26, CA.

R v Grimsby Borough Quarter Sessions, ex p Fuller [1955] 3 All ER 300, [1956] 1 QB 36, [1955] 3 WLR 563, DC.

R v Liverpool City Justices, ex p Topping [1983] 1 All ER 490, [1983] 1 WLR 119, DC.

R v Nicholls (1976) 63 Cr App R 187, CA.

R v Pettigrew (1980) 71 Cr App R 39, CA. d

R v Van Vreden (1973) 57 Cr App R 818, CA.

Case also cited

R v Gregory [1972] 2 All ER 861, [1972] 1 WLR 991, CA.

Appeal e

On 20 May 1981 at the Central Criminal Court before his Honour Judge Abdela QC and a jury the appellant, Terence Patrick Ewing, was convicted on 24 counts of an indictment charging seven counts of theft (counts 1, 9, 12, 15, 18, 21 and 24), six counts of forgery of a valuable security (counts 3, 5, 8, 11, 14 and 17), four counts of forgery and uttering forged documents (counts 19, 20, 22 and 23) and one count of forgery (count 25). He was convicted and sentenced on all those counts. He appealed against conviction. The facts are set out in the judgment of the court. f

David Farrington (assigned by the Registrar of Criminal Appeals) for the appellant.
Michael Corkery QC and *John O Haines* for the Crown.

At the conclusion of the argument the court announced that the appeal against conviction on counts 1, 2 and 3 of the indictment would be allowed and the convictions thereon quashed but that the appeal against conviction on all the other counts would be dismissed for reasons to be given later. g

11 March. The following judgment of the court was delivered.

h

O'CONNOR LJ. On 20 May 1982, at the Central Criminal Court, the appellant was convicted on 24 counts of an indictment charging 7 counts of theft, 9 counts of forgery of a valuable security and 8 counts of uttering a forged document. He appeals against conviction on points of law. We concluded the hearing of the appeal on 21 December 1982, having allowed the appeal against conviction on counts 1, 2 and 3 of the indictment and quashed those convictions. We dismissed the appeal against conviction on all other counts. We now give our reasons for so doing. j

The appellant, aged 30, is a fraudsman. The offences charged in this indictment were committed between June 1979 and March 1980. The nature of the offences was very simple. On two occasions he altered the amount on cheques payable to him (forgery) and paid them into a bank account in his name (uttering a forged document) and, in due course, drew out the money. In other cases he stole a cheque, opened a bank account in the name of the payee, paid the cheque into it, sometimes altered the amount payable, and drew the money out.

In December 1979 the appellant was arrested in connection with an offence committed in October 1979, of altering a Paymaster General draft from £30 to £1,130 and obtaining that sum from the Yorkshire Bank in Cheapside. In due course, he was released on bail and he was finally arrested on 13 March 1980 in Reading.

Originally, three indictments came into existence: the first containing two counts, founded on a committal from the Mansion House to the Central Criminal Court on 10 April 1980; the second containing fifteen counts, founded on a committal from the Highbury Corner Magistrates' Court to the Crown Court at Inner London Sessions on 13 June 1980; and, the third containing eight counts, founded on a committal from the Highbury Corner Magistrates' Court to the Central Criminal Court on 4 December 1980. On 10 February 1981 Russell J gave leave to prefer a voluntary bill in order to amalgamate the three indictments into one.

In the course of his career, the appellant has sought to familiarise himself with, and has gained a certain expertise in, those elements of the criminal law and procedure that concern his particular form of criminality. He is ever anxious to demonstrate his skill in both fields; before the trial started, he gave instructions that no admissions whatsoever were to be made under s 10 of the Criminal Justice Act 1967 and that the prosecution were to be put to strict proof of every ingredient of every single count.

Before we continue, we should like to pay tribute to the integrity and skill of Mr Farrington, who conducted this man's defence and argued his appeal. In this court, he refused to argue hopeless points, despite express instructions from his client.

The trial opened on Monday, 6 April 1981. The first eight days were occupied with legal submissions and a trial-within-a-trial. The court adjourned for Easter on 15 April, and the trial was resumed on Wednesday, 22 April 1981, when a jury was sworn. The Crown case lasted 14 working days and finished on Wednesday, 13 May 1981. During that time the jury were sent out on 27 occasions whilst submissions in law were made to the judge. After the normal submissions at the end of the Crown case, the appellant did not give evidence, but made a statement from the dock. The summing up lasted just over a day and after a retirement of 4 hours and 15 minutes, the jury found the appellant guilty on all counts. No criticism is made of the summing up. The grounds of appeal arise out of matters occurring during the trial and the rulings given by the judge.

The first ground of appeal is that the judge was wrong when he refused an application to sever the indictment and order five separate trials in order to avoid prejudice and embarrassment to the appellant and overburdening the jury.

The counts in the indictment were founded on nine cheques, or warrants, and formed a series of offences of a similar character, within r 9 of the Indictment Rules 1971, SI 1971/1253. The judge had a discretion under s 5(3) of the Indictments Act 1915 to order separate trials, but, in our judgment, he was quite correct in ruling that it was proper to try this indictment as a whole. As far as the jury was concerned, there was nothing complex or difficult about the law or the facts, because the reality was that there was no doubt whatever that the cheques and drafts had been forged either by an alteration of the amount payable, or the indorsement, or both. There was no doubt that eight of them had been uttered and there was no doubt that seven of them had been stolen. In the end, the only issue for the jury was whether it had been proved that it was the appellant who was responsible.

The second ground of appeal must be set out in full:

> 'The Learned Judge erred in law in indicating that he was going to rely upon a medical report produced from Brixton Prison during the course of a trial within a trial upon inducements, threats, fear and hope for advantage. The medical report was neither formally proved, nor formally in evidence, nor relied upon by The

> Crown. The Learned Judge indicated that he was taking it into consideration. It is further clear that the Learned Judge placed great weight upon the report, since his a ruling at the end of the trial within a trial was in exact conformity with the said findings of the medical officer at Brixton Prison.'

On 22 April 1981, that is the day the jury was empanelled, counsel for the appellant applied to the judge to release the case for trial by another judge, on this ground. The judge refused the application. Counsel then said to the judge: b

> 'My client instructs me that he wishes to apply to a High Court judge that this case be transferred. I had better not say what has gone on in conference, save to say that I am not prepared to make that application myself, having checked the authorities.'

The factual background to this complaint is that on 21 January 1981 the medical c officer at Brixton Prison sent to the Central Criminal Court a report on the appellant which he had prepared on 23 December 1980. That report reads:

> 'I have interviewed this 27 year old man at the request of the Court. At my invitation he was also examined by a Consultant Psychiatrist from Springfield Hospital. Our medical records indicate that a Section 60 order was made in 1974, and at that time a diagnosis of schizophrenia was made. In the interview situation d he presents as a vague, socially isolated individual, and impresses on the interviewer that he is without love or friendship. He tells me that he is "paranoid" against his neighbours. He also claimed that his solicitors would spoil his case. He did not present with features of any formal psychiatric illness, but rather appeared to be manipulative, demonstrating features of a sociopathic personality disorder. He has been seen by Dr. J. Bolton who reports as follows: "Although in the past he has been e diagnosed as suffering from schizophrenia he has always made a dramatic recovery on admission to hospital. There was some evidence during his last admission that he had deliberately concocted the symptom in order to be put on a hospital order rather than be sent to prison. His symptoms have always been seen when it might be to his advantage to appear mentally ill. He shows no signs of mental illness today and I doubt very much whether his 'mental illnesses' in the past have been genuine. f I see no indication for further psychiatric help as far as any psychotic illness and I would not regard his personality as amenable to change by psychiatric treatment." I agree with this opinion and submit that he is fit for disposal as the Court deems appropriate.'

This document had been placed with the judge's papers and it is plain that he had read g it. During the trial-within-a-trial, before the jury were sworn, the appellant gave evidence. There is no transcript of what took place, but it seems that there came a stage when he was behaving oddly in the witness box, assuming an extravagant Welsh accent. The judge said to the appellant's counsel, who was trying to examine in chief: 'Do you realise I have got a medical report?' This came as a surprise to counsel, who had not seen the report. After it had been handed down to him and he had read it, the judge h apparently said, 'I am going to bear it in mind', or words to the like effect.

The gravamen of the complaint on behalf of the appellant is that at this stage the judge had to decide not only matters of law, but issues of fact, because he had to decide whether the oral answers given by the appellant to the police were voluntary, in the sense that they had not been obtained from him 'by fear of prejudice or hope of advantage, exercised or held out by a person in authority, or by oppression'. It is said that the medical j report should not have been included in the judge's papers, that it contained prejudicial material, opinions about the appellant untested in the witness box, and that in the result the judge was biased.

We were referred to two decisions of the Divisional Court. The first was *R v Grimsby Borough Quarter Sessions, ex p Fuller* [1955] 3 All ER 300, [1956] 1 QB 36. In that case, the court was hearing an appeal against conviction by the magistrates. During the hearing the antecedents of the defendant, which listed 14 previous convictions, were put before the recorder, not to show the convictions, but in order to show that the defendant could not have worked because he was in custody, the charge being vagrancy. Lord Goddard CJ said ([1955] 3 All ER 300 at 303, [1956] 1 QB 36 at 41):

> 'With a few statutory exceptions, unless the accused puts his character in issue his convictions must not be made known to the tribunal which has to decide his guilt or innocence as a matter of fact.'

The court then applied the same test as where bias on the part of a justice adjudicating is alleged and quashed the conviction.

The second decision is the recent case in the Divisional Court of *R v Liverpool City Justices, ex p Topping* [1983] 1 All ER 490, [1983] 1 WLR 119. The applicant was charged with criminal damage to a door. When he appeared before the justices, they were given the court register, in the form of sheets produced through a computer, and those sheets showed not only the charge before the justices, but seven further charges pending against the applicant. His solicitor submitted that the justices should not hear the matter as they might be prejudiced by their knowledge of the other charges. The clerk to the justices advised the justices that the matter had been considered and, in the circumstances pertaining, it had been decided that it would not be prejudicial to the defendant for the justices to know of other pending charges. The chairman then stated that the bench would hear the matter and, in due course, convicted the applicant. The Divisional Court quashed the conviction, the ground for so doing being that the justices themselves had never considered the question and, therefore, had not exercised their discretion at all. But the court posed the question, 'What should be the proper approach of the justices, having learned of previous convictions and/or outstanding charges, to an application made to them not to try the case?' Ackner LJ then reviewed the authorities and concluded that the test to be applied was—

> 'would a reasonable and fair-minded person sitting in court and knowing all the relevant facts have a reasonable suspicion that a fair trial for the applicant was not possible?'

(See [1983] 1 All ER 490 at 494, [1983] 1 WLR 119 at 123.) The court then went on to consider the Liverpool computer system and granted a declaration that it was wrong in law.

In our judgment, the position of the judge working with a jury on a trial on indictment in the Crown Court is different from that of justices trying a case as judges of fact. In the first place, the judge has to decide questions arising on the admissibility of evidence. This he cannot do without hearing the evidence going to the question of admissibility, which may be highly prejudicial to the defendant. If, for whatever reason, the judge rules the evidence out, we have never heard it suggested that the judge cannot continue with the trial because he might appear 'biased' and thus should not sum up to the jury.

Then there are cases where one or more accused plead guilty and their statements blame the defendant. Once again, the fact that the judge has read the papers before arraignment and, therefore, has read those statements, does not disqualify him from trying the defendant.

Should the judge have available the antecedents of a defendant who is of bad character? We consider that, in the interests of a fair trial, it is desirable that the judge should know that the defendant is of bad character so that he can, if necessary, fire a warning shot should it seem that cross-examination of Crown witnesses is following a course that will let the defendant's character in. There are other cases where, for example, it is absolutely necessary for the judge to know where the Crown seek to lead similar fact evidence. The judge must, in order to determine the issue, know much more than will go to the jury in the event of the evidence being rejected.

In the present case, we think that it would have been better if the medical report had not been with the judge's papers. However, the prejudicial element in the medical report was the hearsay assertion that the appellant had feigned mental illness in the past. In fact, a that added nothing to what was already before the judge in the statement of Det Sgt May, dealing with his interview with the appellant (who was well known to him) on Monday, 17 March 1980, where the following interchange of questions and answers took place:

> 'Q. People are going to ask themselves why a man has all these duff accounts, why b he pays all these stolen cheques into them. *A.* I've managed quite well in the past.
> *Q.* What do you mean, with your Mental Health Act nonsense? No one is going to fall for that one again. You conned the doctors last time, but I will not accept that this time. *A.* We'll see, it's worked before.'

In these circumstances, even if the test propounded by Ackner LJ is applied, in our judgment, no reasonable person sitting in court and seised of the matters properly before c the judge could conclude that the medical report could make him 'biased'. Furthermore, although application to release this case to another judge was made on the day the jury were empanelled, no objection was taken by counsel for the appellant when the judge quite rightly informed him that he had seen the medical report, supplied it to him and stated that he would bear it in mind. In our judgment, the fact that the judge had seen the report and stated that he would bear it in mind did not preclude him from ruling on d the trial-within-a-trial or thereafter from trying the case. This ground of appeal fails.

[His Lordship then considered further grounds of appeal relating to the overruling by the trial judge of objections made at the trial to the admissibility of the evidence of a number of police officers, and continued:]

The next ground of appeal is that the judge wrongly held that certain documents used by the handwriting expert for purposes of comparison were in the appellant's e handwriting. Section 8 of the Criminal Procedure Act 1865 provides:

> 'Comparison of a disputed writing with any writing proved to the satisfaction of the judge to be genuine shall be permitted to be made by witnesses; and such writings, and the evidence of witnesses respecting the same, may be submitted to the court and jury as evidence of the genuineness or otherwise of the writing in f dispute.'

In *R v Angeli* [1978] 3 All ER 950, [1979] 1 WLR 26 this court held that the standard of proof under this section was the civil standard; on the balance of probabilities. Having said that it was well established that the criminal standard applied when the judge was ruling on the admissibility of a confession, Bridge LJ said ([1978] 3 All ER 950 at 953, [1979] 1 WLR 26 at 30): g

> 'We are prepared to assume that it is a rule of general application whenever the admissibility of evidence in a criminal trial turns on some issue of fact and depends on a rule of common law, but the vital distinction between the kind of decision which the judge has to make in relation to a disputed confession and the decision which the judge had to make as to the admissibility of disputed writings in this case h is that whereas the confession evidence and its admissibility depend on rules of common law, the admissibility of the disputed writings in this case depended wholly on the application of the 1865 Act. In our judgment all this court has to do here is to consider the Act which the judge was called on to apply, and it is clear that that is all the judge thought that he was doing. Approached in that light we think the answer to the issue which has been canvassed in this appeal is clear beyond j argument. The 1865 Act, as already stated, applied for the first time to courts of criminal jurisdiction the statutory provision which had already been in operation in civil courts since 1854, the Common Law Procedure Act of that year, and applied it without change of statutory language. Section 8 of the 1865 Act simply repeats what had been the rule applicable in civil cases for the previous 11 years. It was

> made applicable to criminal courts by the provisions of s 1 of the 1865 Act which so far as relevant enact: "The provisions of ss 3 to 8 inclusive of this Act shall apply to all courts of judicature." That being the position under the statute, there is in our judgment no ground for construing this provision as having a different application in civil courts from its application in criminal. Whatever was the standard of proof implicit in the words "proved to the satisfaction of the Judge to be genuine" when those words applied in civil courts only, as they did from 1854 to 1865, the same standard became applicable when the self-same provision was made operative in criminal courts by the enactment of the 1865 Act.'

This decision has been criticised by Sir Rupert Cross and Professor Smith on the ground that the court was not referred to the decision of the House of Lords in *Blyth v Blyth* [1966] 1 All ER 524, [1966] AC 643.

Before the judge, counsel for the appellant accepted that he was bound by *Angeli* and that the matter had to be decided on the balance of probabilities. In his ruling in favour of the Crown, the judge said he had done just that. Before us, counsel for the appellant has submitted that *Angeli* was decided per incuriam, in that it cannot stand with *Blyth v Blyth*, and that the criminal standard of proof beyond reasonable doubt is the standard to be applied, and that, in the result, however forgivably, the judge was wrong in law to decide the matter on the balance of probabilities.

In *Blyth v Blyth* the question was whether the civil or criminal standard of proof should be used in deciding whether adultery had been condoned under s 4(2) of the Matrimonial Causes Act 1950. Subsection (2) provides:

> 'If the court is satisfied on the evidence that—(*a*) the case for the petition has been proved; and (*b*) where the ground of the petition is adultery, the petitioner has not in any manner been accessory to, or connived at, or condoned, the adultery, or, where the ground of the petition is cruelty, the petitioner has not in any manner condoned the cruelty; and (*c*) the petition is not presented or prosecuted in collusion with the respondent or either of the respondents; the court shall pronounce a decree of divorce, but if the court is not satisfied with respect to any of the aforesaid matters, it shall dismiss the petition . . .'

The commissioner who tried the suit had found 'on a rather slender balance of probabilities, that the husband did not intend to condone the adultery'. The Court of Appeal held that the word 'satisfied' in the section meant 'satisfied beyond reasonable doubt' (see [1965] 2 All ER 817, [1965] P 411). The majority in the House of Lords held that this view of the meaning of the section was wrong. Lord Denning said ([1966] 1 All ER 524 at 535–536, [1966] AC 643 at 667):

> 'What is the meaning of the word "satisfied" in s. 4 of the Act of 1950? Willmer and Harman, L.JJ. ([1965] 2 All ER 817 at 827, [1965] P 411 at 431–432) have held that it means "satisfied beyond reasonable doubt" and that, on the finding of the commissioner, the evidence in the present case did not come up to that standard. I can well understand how, sitting in the Court of Appeal, the lords justices took that view. Some years ago in 1950 in *Preston-Jones* v. *Preston-Jones* ([1951] 1 All ER 124 at 138, [1951] AC 391 at 417) Lord MacDermott expressed the view that, in respect of a ground for dissolution, the word "satisfied" was not capable of connoting "something less than proof beyond reasonable doubt". Proof beyond reasonable doubt was required. Lord Simonds expressed his concurrence. And in *Hornal* v. *Neuberger Products* ([1956] 3 All ER 970 at 977, [1957] 1 QB 247 at 264), Hodson, L.J. said that the House of Lords had held that the words of the Act of 1925 [ie s 178 of the Supreme Court of Judicature (Consolidation) Act 1925, as amended by the Matrimonial Causes Act 1937, s 4] "produce the same result as the rule in criminal cases". In the present case the lords justices took the next logical step. They said that the word "satisfied" must mean the same throughout s. 4 (2) of the Act of 1950 (see [1965] 2 All ER 817, [1965] P 411). If it means that the petitioner must prove

adultery beyond reasonable doubt, so also it meant that he must prove beyond reasonable doubt that he had not condoned the adultery. The logic of the lords justices is impeccable. The error lies in what LORD MACDERMOTT said in 1950 ([1951] 1 All ER 124 at 138, [1951] AC 391 at 417). It was said obiter and without argument. I cannot think that he would have said it if he had been taken, as your lordships have been, through the other sections of the Act where the word "satisfied" is used. It then becomes plain that the word "satisfied" deals only with the incidence of proof, not with the standard of proof. It shows on *whom* the burden lies to satisfy the court, and not the degree of proof which he must attain. The best example of this is in regard to connivance. The court has to be "satisfied" that the petitioner has not in any manner connived at the adultery. That clearly puts the burden on him to prove a negative—to prove that he was not guilty of connivance—to prove that he was innocent of it. Can anyone seriously suggest that he has to prove his innocence beyond reasonable doubt? Surely it is sufficient if the scales tip the balance in his favour.'

Lord Denning added ([1966] 1 All ER 524 at 536, [1966] AC 643 at 668):

> 'The legislature . . . said *on whom* the burden of proof rested, leaving it to the court itself to decide what standard of proof was required in order to be "satisfed".'

Lord Pearce said ([1966] 1 All ER 524 at 539, [1966] AC 643 at 672–673):

> 'I think Parliament did not intend the section to define the degree of proof which is necessary to satisfy the court. The section merely informs the court what must be proved and by whom to the satisfaction of the court. I cannot accept the argument that the repetition of the word "satisfied" in the various sections is a constant reminder of the great weight of the proof to be attached to such serious matters as those with which the various reliefs contained in the Act are concerned. The word "satisfied" is a neutral word which leaves to the court the duty of assessing its own satisfaction. I would rather regard "satisfied" as expressing a minimum, such as is needed by any court in giving any relief in any interlocutory, procedural or final matter in civil or other proceedings. And it is, I think, to be found in many statutes or rules of court even in trivial matters. It is to the common law and not to the statute that one must look for any authority which binds a judge to be satisfied in certain cases with nothing less than a proof beyond reasonable doubt.'

Lord Pearson, having examined the speeches in *Preston-Jones v Preston-Jones*, said ([1966] 1 All ER 524 at 542, [1966] AC 643 at 678):

> 'This language is consistent with the view that the word "satisfied" does not, as a matter of interpretation, mean "satisfied beyond reasonable doubt", and that the requirement of proof beyond reasonable doubt may be limited to the grounds for dissolution and may not extend to the matters referred to in sub-paras. (*b*) and (*c*).'

The majority of their Lordships decided that as a divorce suit was a civil proceeding, it was the civil standard or proof that applied, but, nevertheless, the degree of proof required to satisfy of adultery was very much higher than the degree of proof required to satisfy of the absence of condonation or connivance.

Section 1 of the Criminal Procedure Act 1865 provides that—

> 'the provisions of sections from three to eight, inclusive, of this Act shall apply to all courts of judicature, as well criminal as all others . . .'

These sections were in precisely similar terms to ss 22 to 27 of the Common Law Procedure Act 1854. Those provisions of the 1854 Act were in due course repealed by the Statute Law Revision Act 1892.

In our judgment, the words in s 8 of the 1865 Act, 'any writing proved to the satisfaction of the judge to be genuine', do not say anything about the standard of proof to be used, but direct that it is the judge, and not the jury, who is to decide, and the standard of proof is governed by common law (see the passage from Lord Pearce's speech in *Blyth v Blyth*). It follows that when the section is applied in civil cases, the civil standard of proof is used, and when it is applied in criminal cases, the criminal standard should be used. Were it otherwise, the situation created would be unacceptable, where conviction depends on proof that disputed handwriting is that of the accused person and where that proof depends on comparison of the disputed writing with samples alleged to be genuine writings of the accused; we cannot see how this case can be said to be proved beyond reasonable doubt, if the Crown only satisfy the judge, on a balance of probabilities, that the allegedly genuine samples were in fact genuine. The jury may be satisfied beyond a reasonable doubt that the crucial handwriting is by the same hand as the allegedly genuine writings, but if there is a reasonable doubt about the genuineness of such writings, then that must remain a reasonable doubt about the fact the disputed writing was that of the accused and the case is not proved.

It is with reluctance, and with all due respect, that we find ourselves unable to agree with the reasoning in the last paragraph of the judgment in *R v Angeli*, which we have quoted. In our judgment, that reasoning is contrary to the decision of the House of Lords in *Blyth v Blyth*, and we are satisfied that it must have been reached per incuriam. We are fortified in our view that different standards of proof must have been envisaged by Parliament when enacting s 1 of the 1865 Act because ss 3 to 8 extended not only to 'all courts of judicature, as well criminal as all others', but also to 'all persons having, by law or by consent of parties, authority to hear, receive, and examine evidence'. We hold that in a criminal trial, where handwriting is to be used for comparison under s 8, it should be proved to the satisfaction of the judge to be genuine, and the standard of proof should be the ordinary criminal standard, namely proof beyond reasonable doubt.

We must now consider whether there is any reasonable doubt that the documents used for comparison purposes were in the handwriting of the appellant.

There is no dispute about the material used by the handwriting expert Mr Welch, for he used the statement written by the appellant in the presence of his solicitor and Det Con Ralph. That evidence only went to one transaction. The dispute is in respect of two of the documents used by Mr Ellen, another handwriting expert. It is as well to remember that he had a large quantity of the appellant's writing, about which there can be no dispute; for example, he had a document which is a handbook for fraudulent operations, setting out 61 different forms of fraudulent operation, covering many pages, all in the appellant's handwriting, as admitted by him. For obvious reasons, this document was never put in front of the jury. He had the appellant's address book; again, a document admitted by the appellant.

The real complaint is about two exhibits (FM/5 and FM/7), also used by Mr Ellen. These two exhibits were found by Det Sgt May, when he searched an upstairs flat at 73 Streathbourne Road, London SW7 on 18 March 1980. This was a flat occupied by the appellant and the police gained access to it with a Yale key found on the appellant. Exhibit FM/5 consists of three typescript letters, the only manuscript writing being the signatures 'Terence Ewing', and on two of them the addition of 'ESQ'. One manuscript letter was signed 'Terence Ewing' and there were a number of sheets of paper in manuscript, all quite obviously in the same hand, including a sheet which contains three draft counts, which might go into an indictment, referring to Terence Patrick Ewing, the other sheets being notes of various cases from law reports. In our judgment, there can be no possible doubt about the genuineness of the manuscript writing in exhibit FM/5.

Exhibit FM/7 consists of a typed sheet, being particulars of a house in Tilehurst, from some estate agents. At the bottom of the page are some manuscript entries, including the name 'Leo Curran' and '30 Pine Road, Birmingham'. This was an address used by the appellant in opening the Leo Curran account with Lloyds Bank in Reading. Once again, there is no reasonable ground for doubting that these entries were made by the appellant. It is to be noted that, in his ruling, the judge was in no doubt about the documents, save that he said of exhibit FM/7 that he thought it was 'highly probable as being in the defendant's writing'.

It is worth noting that in argument (of which we have a transcript) the judge has said of this document: a

> 'Surely the ordinary, natural inference to be drawn from the totality of those circumstances must be such that without some explanation to refute it it must be attributable to him?'

If the judge had directed himself that he should apply the criminal standard of proof, we are in no doubt whatever that he must have said that he was satisfied that these b documents were in the genuine writing of the appellant, and this ground of appeal must fail.

The next ground of appeal is that the judge wrongly admitted a number of documents in evidence which he ought to have rejected, on the ground that the production of the document did not prove the facts recorded on the face of the document. The nature of this complaint is best explained by considering it against individual counts, and we will c consider it in relation to counts 7 and 8 of the indictment. Those are the counts alleging the forging and uttering of the court funds warrant for £30, to which we have referred earlier in this judgment.

For these two counts, the Crown had to prove (1) the drawing and dispatch of the warrant for £30 on 19 October 1979, to the appellant at 615A Holloway Road, London N19 (proved by the witnesses Archibald Martin and Janina Czernecka); (2) that the d warrant had been altered to £1,130 (proved by production of the warrant); (3) that the alteration had been made by the appellant with intent to defraud (forgery, count 7) and that the appellant had uttered the document with intent to defraud (count 8): there was no expert evidence as to the handwritten alterations.

The Crown set out to prove these requirements, by proving (i) that on 22 October 1979 the appellant had opened a bank account (no 20151) in the name of T Ewing of 615 e Holloway Road, London N19, at the Yorkshire Bank, Cheapside, with a deposit of £1; the witness Yvonne Earl proved that this account had been opened by a man she might be able to recognise; (ii) that on 22 October the appellant had paid in the warrant at the National Westminster Bank, Lothbury, by bank giro credit, for his account at the Yorkshire Bank: the transaction was proved by two National Westminster officials, T Poulton and Olive Newsome, who identified her initials on the bank giro credit, which f was produced, but they could not identify the appellant; (iii) that the sum of £1,130 represented by the above bank giro credit had been credited to the T Ewing account at the Yorkshire Bank, Cheapside, and that £1,130 had been drawn out of that account: proved by Richard Addyman, assistant manager of the Cheapside branch, who produced a computer print-out of the account, which was a blank piece of paper with the following on it: 20151 0.00; 23 10 79 CR. 1.00; 24 10 79 B/G 1130.00; 29 10 79 RPD 1130; 1,78 g 1.00.

It is said that the computer print-out was not admissible in evidence; that it should not have been exhibited and, indeed, that Mr Addyman could not use the document to found his evidence. The payment out to the appellant was proved by the witness Paula Ralphs. The technicality of this objection is apparent because all these facts had been expressly admitted by the appellant in the statement which he had made in the presence of his h solicitor and Det Sgt Ralph on 4 December 1979. Nevertheless, there is the problem: could the Crown prove the passage of the sum of £1,130 represented by the bank giro credit, which had undoubtedly reached the Yorkshire Bank, for Mr Addyman produced it into the T Ewing account (no 20151)? The judge admitted the print-out under the Criminal Evidence Act 1965. It is submitted that he was wrong to do so. Counsel for the appellant relied on *R v Pettigrew* (1980) 71 Cr App R 39. We will come to that case in a j moment, but first we must look to see what it is that the computer does.

The evidence was given by Mr Addyman, the assistant manager, who is not a computer expert. We have no transcript of his evidence, but an agreed note by counsel, which we think is more than adequate for the purposes of this case. Mr Addyman said that the bank had a computer at its head office, that it stored information which was put into it by machines at each of the branches. He said the machine was like a keyboard, operated by a machinist. He said:

> 'I think we could ascertain, but with difficulty, and it's not possible to be 100%, who was on the machine on any one day . . . Such an entry as typed out, can be recalled by the computer. The check on the system is done manually.'

The computer can provide a range of services; it can sort out and accept or reject items in a sorting method. He continued:

> 'I do not take information out of the machine, it is done by a computer operator. Therefore, getting the right answer depends on having an accurate machinist.'

The computer print-out was checked at a later date.

The evidence establishes the fact that the computer holds the existence of an account by number in its memory and records movements on that account, doing the arithmetic and, if asked, printing out details of those movements and a balance. The facts in this case further establish, beyond any doubt, that on 22 October Yvonne Earl brought into existence a bank index card and that, in the ordinary course of business, the existence of the new account (no 20151) was fed to the computer by a machine operator at Cheapside, so too the existence of a £1 credit. When the bank giro credit was received at Cheapside, in the ordinary course of business, the information on it, namely to credit account no 20151 with £1,130, would be fed to the computer by an operator. On 29 October, when the cashier paid out £1,130 to the appellant, she took a signed receipt from him and the information on that, namely that account no 20151 was to be debited with £1,130, would be fed to the computer by an operator. Thereafter, as and when the computer was asked for a print-out of the movements and balance on this account, it would be expected that the print-out would read precisely as the print-out does read.

The relevant provisions of the Criminal Evidence Act 1965 are contained in s 1:

> '(1) In any criminal proceedings where direct oral evidence of a fact would be admissible, any statement contained in a document and tending to establish that fact shall, on production of the document, be admissible in evidence of that fact if—(*a*) the document is, or forms part of, a record relating to any trade or business and compiled, in the course of that trade or business, from information supplied (whether directly or indirectly) by persons who have, or may reasonably be supposed to have, personal knowledge of the matters dealt with in the information they supply; and (*b*) the person who supplied the information recorded in the statement in question is dead, or beyond the seas, or unfit by reason of his bodily or mental condition to attend as a witness, or cannot with reasonable diligence be identified or found, or cannot reasonably be expected (having regard to the time which has elapsed since he supplied the information and to all the circumstances) to have any recollection of the matters dealt with in the information he supplied.
>
> (2) For the purpose of deciding whether or not a statement is admissible by virtue of this section, the court may draw any reasonable inference from the form or content of the document in which the statement is contained . . .
>
> (4) In this section "statement" includes any representation of fact, whether made in words or otherwise, "document" includes any device by means of which information is recorded or stored . . .'

The first question is whether the print-out is a document which 'is, or forms part of, a record relating to any trade or business'. The computer is undoubtedly a 'device by means of which information is recorded or stored'. The print-out is part of that device, for there is no other means of discovering the information recorded or stored by the device. The print-out is, therefore, a 'document' within the meaning of sub-s (4). There is no doubt that the document either is, or forms part of, a record relating to the business of the bank and that it was compiled in the course of business. The record has to be compiled—

> 'from information supplied (whether directly or indirectly) by persons who have, or may reasonably be supposed to have, personal knowledge of the matters dealt with in the information they supply . . .'

It will be seen that the record does not have to be compiled by a person who has knowledge of the matters dealt with in the information, so we must return to the earlier part of sub-s (1) to discover what persons we are looking for on whom para (*b*) of subs (1) will bite.

The fact which the Crown was trying to establish was that the £1,130 in the bank giro credit was paid into account no 20151. The person who could give direct oral evidence of that fact would be the operator who put it into the account in the computer, so that (by chance in the present case) the record was compiled by the person who had the information.

We now turn to para (*b*) of sub-s (1). The judge held that the operator who fed the information into the computer could—

> 'not reasonably be expected (having regard to the time which has elapsed since he supplied the information and to all the circumstances) to have any recollection of the matters dealt with in the information he supplied.'

It will be seen that the provisions of the subsection are disjunctive and, on the evidence of Mr Addyman, the judge was quite entitled to hold that the person who fed this information into the computer, whoever he was, could not reasonably be expected to have any recollection of it. There was no need for a search to be made for this person, even though a diligent search might have identified the person or persons who were operating the keyboard at the Cheapside branch at the relevant times.

Counsel for the appellant referred us to a number of cases. In *R v Van Vreden* (1973) 57 Cr App R 818 (the South African Barclaycard case) no attempt was made to use the provisions of the Criminal Evidence Act 1965 and (at 823) Lawton LJ plainly thought that the document in question would have been admissible had the Act been used. In *R v Nicholls* (1976) 63 Cr App R 187 the trial judge ruled the document in under the 1965 Act, at a stage when, apart from the document itself, there was no evidence from which he could reasonably infer that the person supplying the information could not reasonably be expected to have any recollection about the matter. In *R v Pettigrew* (1980) 71 Cr App R 39 the Crown wanted to prove that three new £5 notes found on the defendant were part of the proceeds of a burglary in which £650 had been stolen, by proving that the three notes formed part of a bundle of £5,000 worth of notes dispatched by the Bank of England to Newcastle, from which the victim of the burglary had drawn £650. For this purpose, the Crown sought to rely on a Bank of England computer print-out, listing the serial numbers of a parcel of £5,000 worth of £5 notes dispatched to Newcastle. The machine referred to as a computer had a dual function, one of which was to reject any defective notes fed into it and to record the serial numbers of the notes so rejected. This court held that on those facts, there was no person, or persons, who had personal knowledge of the matters within s 1(1)(*a*) of the Act and, for that highly technical reason, the print-out had been wrongly admitted.

For these reasons, we hold that the print-out of the present appellant's bank account was properly admitted by the judge.

We will deal shortly on this topic with the other counts. Counts 4 and 5 are concerned with a cheque for £100 from Safeways, sent to the appellant on 8 August 1979, altered to read £1,100 and paid in on 15 August at Lloyds Bank, Oxford Street by giro credit, for the credit of an account in the name of 'Terence Ewing' at Lloyds Bank, Kingsway, which had been opened on 14 August, with a deposit of £1. The bank witness, Mr Peacock, produced a computer print-out of the transactions on the Kingsway branch account. The print-out is, for practical purposes, in the same form as that which we have already considered. Mr Peacock does not appear to have given any evidence about the computer, and it was objected that there was no evidence that the computer might not have functions such as the computer in *R v Pettigrew*. The judge, in our judgment rightly, admitted the document, for, on the face of the document itself, it is reasonable to infer that it is of the same nature as the Yorkshire bank print-out. On these two counts, it is to be noted that at the appellant's premises a torn up bank account statement of this account, showing these precise details, was found.

Counts 9 to 11 concerned a cheque for £5,072·63, drawn by the Abbey National Building Society in favour of Altman & Co, and dispatched to them on 7 January 1980. That cheque, indorsed 'A. Willow p.p. Cecil Altman and Co. A. Willow', was paid in on 7 January at Barclays Bank, Oxford Street, by giro credit note, for the credit of the account of A Willow at Barclays Bank, 145 Upper Richmond Road, an account which had been opened with a deposit of £5, on 23 August 1978. £5,000 was drawn out of that account on 14 January 1980. The bank evidence was given by Mr Bashford, who produced a computer print-out which, in the case of Barclays Bank, is in the more familiar form of a bank statement which showed these transactions. Once again, we are satisfied that this document was properly admitted under the Criminal Evidence Act 1965. In this case the handwriting expert was positive that the giro credit slip had been completed in the name of A Willow by the appellant.

[His Lordship dealt with the remaining grounds of appeal, and concluded:]

It remains to give our reasons for quashing the convictions on counts 1, 2 and 3. These counts concerned a cheque for £3,000, drawn by Lustrend Ltd on 5 June 1979, in favour of a payee 'Hilgarde Heating'. Hilgarde Heating never received the cheque, which was dispatched on 5 June 1979 and, on 6 June, it was paid into Barclays Bank at 144 Kings Road, London, for the credit of the account of 'H. Hill', and purported to be paid in by 'H. Hill', endorsed 'p.p. Hilgarde Heating H. Hill for value received H. Hill'. This account had been opened in August 1978 and the only evidence from which it was suggested that the jury could infer (so as to be sure about it) that this account was opened and operated by the appellant was the fact that when the person who opened the account gave an address, he gave '60 Early Road, Reading, Berkshire' and a London address, '70 Flood Street, SW1'. On 13 March 1980 the appellant had tried to explain the non-receipt of a letter from the bank manager in Reading by saying that he had moved to 50 Early Road.

There was no other evidence to connect the appellant with this offence and, although it might appear the appellant's usual method of work, we cannot say that the conviction on this count was safe.

Since the conclusion of the hearing, the appellant has written to the court asking for the case to be relisted, should the court be minded to decide any part of the case by the application of the proviso, on the ground that the possible application of the proviso was not sufficiently argued at the hearing. The short answer is that the matter was considered and we are not prepared to entertain any further argument on the topic.

Appeal allowed in part.

29 June. The court refused leave to appeal to the House of Lords and refused to certify, under s 33(2) of the Criminal Appeal Act 1968, that a point of law of general public importance was involved in the decision.

Solicitors: *D M O'Shea* (for the Crown).

N P Metcalfe Esq Barrister.

Finelvet AG v Vinava Shipping Co Ltd a
The Chrysalis

QUEEN'S BENCH DIVISION (COMMERCIAL COURT)
MUSTILL J
22, 23 NOVEMBER, 15 DECEMBER 1982 b

Shipping – Charterparty – Frustration – War – Vessel under charterparty trapped in Shatt al-Arab river by war between Iran and Iraq – Whether declaration of war between Iran and Iraq automatically frustrating charterparty.

Contract – Frustration – War – Charterparty – Vessel under charterparty trapped in Shatt al- c
Arab river by war between Iran and Iraq – Whether declaration of war automatically frustrating charterparty.

Arbitration – Award – Appeal – Basis on which award may be appealed.

By a time charterparty dated 19 March 1980 on the New York Produce Exchange form d
the shipowners chartered a vessel to the charterers for one trip from North America to the Persian Gulf, following which the vessel was to be redelivered to the shipowners at Muscat. In the course of the charterparty voyage the vessel proceeded to the Persian Gulf and docked at the Iraqi port of Basrah in the Shatt al-Arab river on 14 September 1980. Eight days later, on 22 September, war broke out between Iraq and Iran and the vessel
became one of some sixty ships trapped on the Shatt al-Arab by the war. The vessel e
continued to discharge her cargo and by 1 October was ready to proceed to Muscat to be redelivered to the shipowners. However, the vessel was prevented from leaving Basrah by the Iraqi port authorities and the risk of damage and injury from the hostilities across the Shatt al-Arab. On 14 November the charterers purported to cancel the charterparty and by 24 November it was the view of most informed people in shipping circles that
the obstacles to navigation, including sunken ships, in the Shatt al-Arab were such that f
vessels trapped in the river were unlikely to be able to leave safely for at least several months and probably not for a much longer period. A dispute arose as to when the charterparty was frustrated, the charterers contending that the declaration of war between Iraq and Iran was of itself the frustrating event and that therefore the charterparty was frustrated on 22 September 1980, while the shipowners contended that the charterparty
was not frustrated (and that therefore the charterers continued to be liable to pay hire) g
until 24 November. The arbitrator held that the charterparty was not frustrated until the delay was such that to hold the parties to the contract would have been to impose on them radically different obligations from that which they had undertaken and that that had not occured until 24 November. The charterers appealed.

Held – There was no rule or irrebuttable presumption that a declaration of war prevented h
the performance of, and therefore discharged, a contract on which the war had a direct bearing since, except where the declaration of war made the contract illegal because it would then involve trading with the enemy, it was not the declaration of war but acts done in furtherance of the war which might prevent performance of the contract. Although there was a rebuttable presumption that a state of war, once it arose, would
continue for an indefinite period, it depended on the circumstances whether the effects j
of the war frustrated performance of the contract. Accordingly, the arbitrator was right to hold that the outbreak of war between Iraq and Iran had not automatically frustrated the charterparty. Furthermore, since the arbitrator's choice of date for when the charterparty was frustrated was within the range of permissible dates his award would not be disturbed. The charterers' appeal would therefore be dismissed (see p 668 *d* to *f*, p 669 *e* to *g*, p 670 *b* and p 671 *e*, post).

Geipel v Smith [1861–73] All ER Rep 861, *Horlock v Beal* [1916–17] All ER Rep 81, *Bank*
a *Line Ltd v Arthur Capel & Co* [1918–19] All ER Rep 504 and *Denny Mott & Dickson Ltd v James B Fraser & Co Ltd* [1944] 1 All ER 678 considered.

Observations on the basis of an appeal against an arbitration award (see p 662 *g* to p 664 *g* and p 670 *c* to *h*, post).

Notes

b For frustration of a contract by war, see 9 Halsbury's Laws (4th edn) para 453, and for cases on the subject, see 12 Digest (Reissue) 487–490, *3447–3461*.

For appeal to the High Court from an arbitrator's award, see 2 Halsbury's Laws (4th edn) para 627.

Cases referred to in judgment

c *Akties Nord-Osterso Rederiet v E A Casper, Edgar & Co Ltd* (1923) 14 Ll L Rep 203.
Anglo-Northern Trading Co Ltd v Emlyn Jones & Williams [1917] 2 KB 78.
Bank Line Ltd v Arthur Capel & Co [1919] AC 435, [1918–19] All ER Rep 504, HL.
Davis Contractors Ltd v Fareham UDC [1956] 2 All ER 145, [1956] AC 696, [1956] 3 WLR 37, HL.
Denny Mott & Dickson Ltd v James B Fraser & Co Ltd [1944] 1 All ER 678, [1944] AC 265,
d HL.
Geipel v Smith (1872) LR 7 QB 404, [1861–73] All ER Rep 861.
Horlock v Beal [1916] 1 AC 486, [1916–17] All ER Rep 81, HL.
International Sea Tankers Inc v Hemisphere Shipping Co Ltd, The Wenjiang (No 2) [1983] 1 Lloyd's Rep 400.
Kodros Shipping Corp v Empresa Cubana de Fletes, The Evia [1982] 3 All ER 350, [1982] 3
e WLR 637, HL.
Melville v De Wolf (1855) 4 E & B 844, 119 ER 313.
Pioneer Shipping Ltd v BTP Tioxide Ltd, The Nema [1981] 2 All ER 1030, [1982] AC 724, [1981] 3 WLR 292, HL.
Taylor v Caldwell (1863) 3 B & S 826, [1861–73] All ER Rep 24, 122 ER 309.
Uni-Ocean Lines Pte Ltd v C-Trade SA, The Lucille [1983] 1 Lloyd's Rep 387.

f **Motion**

The appellants, Finelvet AG (the charterers), who were the respondents in an arbitration in which Vinava Shipping Co Ltd (the shipowners) were the claimants, sought by motion dated 8 October 1981 to have the interim award of the arbitrator, R A MacCrindle QC, made on 22 September 1981 varied so as to direct that the shipowners repay to the charterers hire amounting to $US141,537·47 paid by the charterers for the period from
g 1 October until 19 October 1980 in respect of a charterparty concerning the vessel Chrysalis, and that the interim award be further varied to declare that the charterparty was frustrated on 1 October and that the vessel was off-hire from that date. The facts are set out in the judgment.

Anthony Hallgarten QC and *Patricia Phelan* for the charterers.
h *Bernard Eder* for the shipowners.

Cur adv vult

15 December. The following judgment was delivered.

j **MUSTILL J.** This matter is before the court in the shape of an appeal from an interim award made by Mr R A MacCrindle QC in a dispute between Vinava Shipping Co Ltd (the shipowners) and Finelvet AG (the charterers). The appeal is brought, not by virtue of leave granted under s 1(3)(*b*) of the Arbitration Act 1979, but pursuant to an agreement falling within s 1(3)(*a*) of that Act, whereby the parties agreed, before the award was published, that each should have the right to appeal to the High Court 'on any question of law arising out of any award made by the arbitrator'.

The dispute is one of a series which has become familiar to the High Court in recent times. The subject matter of the dispute was a charterparty dated 19 March 1980, whereby the charterers chartered the vessel Chrysalis from the owners for 'one T/C trip via safe port(s) in/out of geographical rotation via S America/US Gulf/USNH/Great Lakes/St Lawrence/Persian Gulf excluding Iran intention grain in bulk to Basrah . . .' The Chrysalis suffered the same fate as some sixty other vessels, being trapped in the Shatt al-Arab river in the course of the conflict between the states of Iran and Iraq. In common with other similar disputes, this particular case raised a number of important and difficult questions of laws, including the following: (a) was the vessel's discharging port (in this case Basrah) a 'safe port'; (b) was the vessel off-hire during the period of detention; (c) was the charterparty frustrated by the war, or by the detention consequent on war; (d) if so, when did the frustration take place? After the award was published, the decision of the House of Lords in *Kodros Shipping Corp v Empresa Cubana de Fletes, The Evia* [1982] 3 All ER 350, [1982] 3 WLR 637 has greatly narrowed the area of potential dispute. It is now quite clear that the warranty of safety contained in these and other charters does not extend so far as to put the charterer in breach simply because the ship is overtaken by misfortune such as the one which happened to the ships trapped in the Shatt al-Arab. Furthermore, it is now treated as common ground that the charterparty was indeed frustrated by reason of the events occurring in the Shatt al-Arab. What does, however, remain in issue is the date on which the frustration occurred. The identification of this date raises a comparatively short issue of law, although the sum of money involved is large.

The facts

As I have said, the vessel was chartered on 19 March 1980 for a trip on time charter terms. Delivery was to be made on dropping outward pilot at Rotterdam, and redelivery was to take place 'on passing Muscat outbound'. In his award, the arbitrator has found that Muscat had for years been a common redelivery point for vessels trading to the Persian Gulf, since whether their next succeeding fixture, when in due course concluded, should require them to load eastwards or westwards of the Gulf, Muscat would inevitably be on the way.

In the main, the charter took the shape which one would have expected of that curious hybrid contract, a fixture for the trip on the New York Produce Exchange charter form. Only cl 42 of the charter calls for special mention. This read as follows:

> 'If the vessel is off hire for more than thirty consecutive days, Charterers have the right of cancelling the remaining period of this time charter, without prejudice to rights sustaining under this Charter Party. Charterers to have the option of adding any off-hire times to the duration of this Charter period.'

The vessel was delivered to the charterers under the time charter on 1 April 1980. After a ballast voyage across the Atlantic she loaded in North America, completing on 1 May 1980, and returned eastbound to the Persian Gulf, arriving at Basrah pilot station on 28 May 1980. On 14 September the vessel finally berthed at Basrah and began to discharge.

Three days later, on 17 September 1980, Iran abrogated a treaty of 1975 between itself and Iraq, whereby Iran had been granted a share in the control of the Shatt al-Arab. The President of Iraq announced that the Shatt al-Arab was now under Iraqi sovereignty. On 22 September the dispute flared into open war between Iraq and Iran. On that day and thereafter there were attacks on vessels in the Shatt al-Arab. The arbitrator has found that navigation of the river by cargo ships would thereafter have been highly dangerous, involving a high probability of loss by the action of the belligerents, and that it effectively ceased on that date. It has not since been renewed. With effect from the same date, vessels and their crews at Basrah were exposed to the risk of damage and injury by reason of the hostility. The arbitrator has found that—

> 'The view of many informed commentators at that time was that the conflict would be short, that the odds were heavily in favour of Iraq, and that, via a victory by Iraq or a settlement in its favour, peace would be restored in a very short time, perhaps a matter of days.'

Meanwhile, with effect from the same date, vessels at Basrah were totally prohibited from leaving by the Iraqi port's administration.

The vessel continued to discharge, and by 1 October 1980 all but approximately 150 tons of her cargo had been delivered. She was then moved off her berth and was required by the Iraqi authorities to wait. On 13 October 1980 the remaining 150 tons were discharged.

The arbitrator has found that, but for the outbreak of war and the events consequent thereon whereby the vessel was delayed at Basrah, she would in the normal course on 1 October 1980 have proceeded, on completion of discharge of all but 150 tons of cargo, to Muscat and there been redelivered to her owners under the time charterparty. This would have taken about sixty hours from completion of such discharge.

Rather than risk distortion by compressing the findings of the arbitrator relative to what happened thereafter, it is convenient to quote in full the material passage from the award. This reads as follows:

> '10. By the third week in October a number of the trapped vessels at Basrah had suffered physical damage from military action. The foreign crew members of them were being repatriated and arrangements were being made for substitute crew members to be placed on board. By then it had become widely felt that there would be no quick victory for either side. The prospects of a settlement also receded, both sides being apparently unyielding if not fanatical. Nevertheless, during the ensuing days and months attempts were made (notably by the U.N. Envoy, Mr Olaf Palme) to negotiate a cease-fire, or at all events the release of the several score foreign vessels trapped in the Shatt-al-Arab. At first hopes of their release were quite high. On 14th October, 1980 it had been reported that Iran had expressed willingness to cooperate in freeing the ships. By 27th October, 1980 Iraq, for its part, appears to have indicated that it would be willing to allow the vessels to leave if they did so under the auspices of the International Red Cross and flying the Red Cross flag (it was not until the end of December that it emerged that the Red Cross were not at that stage willing to lend their support to this).
>
> 11. On 14th November, 1980 the charterers purported without prejudice to the question of frustration to cancel the charterparty under Clause 42. By 24th November 1980 various peace bids had been rejected, and it became clear beyond reasonable doubt that the war would not end rapidly. On that date Mr Olaf Palme expressed the opinion that there would be no rapid end to the war. A struggle of indefinite duration now seemed inevitable. There remained, it is true some possibility that without further inordinate delay the trapped vessels might, despite this, be allowed by the belligerents to depart if they could. They were still precluded from sailing by the Iraqi authorities on any conditions which the vessels were in a position to satisfy. In addition already by that date it had become necessary that the river be dredged and cleared of sunken craft before it could be safely navigated. Whether either side would be willing to undertake this at its own expense, or to allow the other to undertake it, and how long such operations would take, were all wholly uncertain. By 24th November 1980 it was the view of most informed people in shipping circles that the obstacles were such that vessels were unlikely to be able safely to leave for several more months at best, and probably much longer.'

In his award, the arbitrator went on to make findings about events during December 1980 and January 1981, but there is no need to set these out, since neither party has argued for a date of frustration later than 24 November, the date on which, to repeat the arbitrator's finding, 'it was the view of most informed people in shipping circles that the obstacles were such that vessels were unlikely to be able safely to leave for several more months at best, and probably much longer'.

It seems that notwithstanding the outbreak of war, the charterers continued for a time to make payment of hire under the charterparty. The arbitrator has found that they paid hire 'covering the period up to 1730 hours on 19th October 1980, but no later'. Since, by virtue of cl 5 of the charter, hire was payable semi-monthly in advance, it seems that the last payment must have been made on 5 October 1980.

On 14 November 1980, the charterers purported without prejudice to the question of frustration to cancel the charterparty under cl 42.

Other cases

This is not the only Shatt al-Arab dispute in which an arbitrator's award has been before the court.

The Evia [1982] 3 All ER 350, [1982] 3 WLR 637 concerned a time charter for a period of 18 months, two months more or less. By the beginning of October 1980 it had between about six and ten months left to run, depending on how the option would have been exercised. The vessel had completed discharge on 22 November 1980. The arbitrator held that the charter was frustrated on 4 October. The House of Lords declined to intervene.

In *International Sea Tankers Inc v Hemisphere Shipping Co Ltd, The Wenjiang (No 2)* [1983] 1 Lloyd's Rep 400 the charterparty was for 12 months, one month or less, and had four to six months left of the charter period to run at the beginning of October 1980. The arbitrator held that the contract was frustrated on 24 November. An appeal against this decision was dismissed by Bingham J.

Finally, in *Uni-Ocean Lines Pte Ltd v C-Trade SA, The Lucille* [1983] 1 Lloyd's Rep 387 the arbitrators held that the charter was frustrated on 9 December. The contract was a time charter, which had been running since 14 July 1980. It is not clear how long the charter was to continue. The wording of the report suggests that the contract may have been for a time charter trip. Discharge was completed on 23 October. The charterers sought leave to appeal against the award, on the ground that 24 November was too late, and that 23 October was the right date. Parker J declined to grant leave.

The basis of an appeal

The shape of the charterers' argument makes it necessary to begin with certain comments on the manner in which, in the light of the guidance given by the House of Lords in *Pioneer Shipping Ltd v BTP Tioxide Ltd, The Nema* [1981] 2 All ER 1030, [1982] AC 724 and *The Evia*, the courts should approach an appeal under the 1979 Act.

In the first place, it must be kept in mind that quite different considerations apply to the question whether, in the exercise of its discretion, the court should grant leave to appeal under s 3 of the 1979 Act from those which are material when the court comes to hear the appeal itself. The first stage is a filtering process, at which the court gives effect to the policy embodied in the 1979 Act and enunciated in *The Nema*, whereby the interests of finality are placed ahead of the desire to ensure that the arbitrator's decision is strictly in accordance with the law. Some examination of the merits takes place at this stage, because the stronger the applicant's case for saying that the arbitrator was wrong, the better his prospect of obtaining leave to appeal. But the examination of the law is summary in nature, and does not lead to any definite conclusion. The exercise is discretionary throughout, the mesh of the filter is fine, and it must, I think, be recognised that some cases will be caught in the filter which would, if the appeal had been allowed to go forward, result in a decision that the award could not stand.

The position when the appeal itself is heard is quite different. Here there is no discretion. The only issue is whether it can be shown that the decision of the arbitrator was wrong in law. The court must answer this question yes or no, and, if the answer is yes, the appeal must be allowed however finely balanced the issue may be. It is not only unhelpful but positively misleading to introduce at this stage the questions of degree raised by the *Nema* guidelines, such as whether the award is clearly or obviously wrong, *a* for these are material only to the discretionary process of finding out whether the award should be allowed to come before the court for challenge.

Starting therefore with the proposition that the court is concerned to decide, on the hearing of the appeal, whether the award can be shown to be wrong in law, how is this question to be tackled? In a case such as the present, the answer is to be found by dividing the arbitrator's process of reasoning into three stages. (1) The arbitrator ascertains the *b* facts. This process includes the making of findings on any facts which are in dispute. (2) The arbitrator ascertains the law. This process comprises not only the identification of all material rules of statute and common law, but also the identification and interpretation of the relevant parts of the contract, and the identification of those facts which must be taken into account when the decision is reached. (3) In the light of the facts and the law so ascertained, the arbitrator reaches his decision.

c In some cases, the third stage will be purely mechanical. Once the law is correctly ascertained, the decision follows inevitably from the application of it to the facts found. In other instances, however, the third stage involves an element of judgment on the part of the arbitrator. There is no uniquely 'right' answer to be derived from marrying the facts and the law, merely a choice of answers, none of which can be described as wrong.

The second stage of the process is the proper subject matter of an appeal under the *d* 1979 Act. In some cases an error of law can be demonstrated by studying the way in which the arbitrator has stated the law in his reasons. It is, however, also possible to infer an error of law in those cases where a correct application of the law to the facts found would lead inevitably to one answer, whereas the arbitrator has arrived at another; and this can be so even if the arbitrator has stated the law in his reasons in a manner which appears to be correct: for the court is then driven to assume that he did not properly *e* understand the principles which he had stated.

Whether the third stage can ever be the proper subject of an appeal, in those cases where the making of the decision does not follow automatically from the ascertainment of the facts and the law, is not a matter on which it is necessary to express a view in the present case. *The Nema* and *The Evia* show that, where the issue is one of commercial frustration, the court will not intervene, save only to the extent that it will have to form *f* its own view, in order to see whether the arbitrator's decision is out of conformity with the only correct answer or (as the case may be) lies outside the range of correct answers. This is part of the process of investigating whether the arbitrator has gone wrong at the second stage. But once the court has concluded that a tribunal which correctly understood the law could have arrived at the same answer as the one reached by the arbitrator, the fact that the individual judge himself would have come to a different conclusion is no *g* ground for disturbing the award.

Counsel for the charterers has, however, contended that the position is different in the present case, because the parties had agreed in advance that there should be a right of appeal on any question of law. This shows, so it is maintained, that the parties wanted an authoritative ruling on the question of frustration and this they would not get from a mode of appeal which precluded the judge from substituting his own opinion for that of *h* the arbitrator on the 'judgmental' stage of the reasoning process. I am afraid that I cannot read the agreement as showing any such intention. Its obvious purpose was to save the time and expense involved in a contested application under s 1(3)(*b*) of the 1979 Act. I cannot go on to infer that the parties also wished to vary the substantive basis of the appeal, in such a way that the respondent would be more likely to lose than if the appeal had followed on an unsuccessful resistance to an application brought under s 3(1)(*b*). *j* Moreover, I am very doubtful whether, even if this had been the intention, it could validly have been put into effect. The court has no jurisdiction to review the arbitrator's decision otherwise than by an 'appeal' on a 'question of law', and the interpretation given to these expressions in *The Nema* would preclude the court from deciding on any basis other than the one which I have summarised.

I shall therefore proceed by considering first whether there is any principle of law which the arbitrator has incorrectly stated, and then go on to see whether it can be said that he has taken into account something which in law was immaterial, or left out of account something to which he should have attached weight, and then finally inquire whether the date chosen by the arbitrator is within the range of dates from which a properly directed arbitrator could choose, as a matter of personal judgment, for the purpose of reaching his decision.

When carrying out this exercise the court must, I suggest, be careful not to recreate one of the more objectionable features of the special case procedure. Under the former system, the arbitrator was often forced to deal in his award with rival lists of suggested findings of fact, adopting or traversing them all, so as to eliminate the risk of the award being declared incomplete, and remitted for further findings. It was made clear, both before and after the enactment of the 1979 legislation, that the 'reasons' contemplated by s 1 were to be embodied in a document of an altogether simpler and more informal kind than the old-fashioned special case. This being so, the court should not allow itself to be drawn any distance into a process of examining the award to see whether this or that fact or principle has been mentioned by the arbitrator, with a view to seeing whether he has based his exercise of judgment on an imperfect view of what was relevant to it. Otherwise, the arbitrator would be forced to protect himself by identifying everything that he had taken into account, and left out of account, lest some adverse inference be drawn. The result would be a document even more cumbersome than the old special case, which never had to set out any of the arbitrator's reasoning on the law.

Finally, I must refer to the arguments based on a comparison with the decisions in relation to other ships, to which I have already referred. In my judgment, these arguments carry no weight, for two reasons. (1) The terms, durations and unexpired periods of the relevant contracts were not the same as in the present case, so the decisions provide no reliable guidance on the instant dispute: see per Lord Roskill in *The Evia* [1982] 3 All ER 350 at 368, [1982] 3 WLR 637 at 660. (2) The decisions in the previous cases were not to the effect that such and such a date was right, but simply that it could not be said to be in the wrong bracket. The cases do not establish what was the right bracket.

It may, it is true, seem odd at first sight that the courts should appear to be ratifying each of a series of awards, attributing substantially different consequences to what are, in many respects, the same sets of facts. That this will happen from time to time is an inevitable consequence of the shift of policy introduced by the 1979 Act, and by the speeches and judgments which have expounded it. It is impossible to secure uniformity without complete judicial control. The tolerance of some degree of disconformity is the price which has to be paid for a relaxation of judicial control, introduced for the greater benefit of the arbitral process as a whole.

The effect of war

The first argument advanced on behalf of the charterers is that this is one of the cases where the third stage of the arbitrator's reasoning ought to have been purely automatic, involving no element of judgment. It is a rule of law, so they maintain, that a declaration of war frustrates a contract ipso jure, in that it impinges directly on the performance of the contract. If this proposition can be made good, the award must be set aside, for the arbitrator has explicitly proceeded on the basis that the declaration of war did not itself serve to frustrate the contract. There would thus be an error in the arbitrator's reasoning at the second stage, not the third, and there would be nothing to inhibit the court from substituting its own view as to the true position in law.

It is convenient to begin with the authorities on which counsel for the charterers relies as showing that war brings about an automatic discharge.

First, there is *Geipel v Smith* (1872) LR 7 QB 404, [1861–73] All ER Rep 861. This was a charterparty case, argued on demurrer. The plaintiff charterers pleaded in their declaration a charterparty for the carriage of coal to Hamburg, and a renunciation of the contract by the defendant shipowners before the inception of the voyage. Two of the

defendants' pleas to this declaration are relevant for present purposes. The fifth plea
a averred an outbreak of war between France and Germany; a blockade of Hamburg by the French navy; a proclamation by the Queen enjoining all her subjects to maintain strict neutrality; the fact that the defendants were British subjects; and that further performance of the contract became and was illegal. The seventh plea averred the state of war and the blockage and went on to allege that the charterparty could not have been carried out and fulfilled within a reasonable time, except by running the blockade. The
b Court of Queen's Bench held that both pleas were good, Blackburn J expressing some doubt regarding the fifth plea. With regard to the seventh plea, Cockburn CJ held that the blockade fell within the exception of the restraint of princes and went on to say (LR 7 QB 404 at 410–411, [1861–73] All ER Rep 861 at 865):

> 'But then it is said that the exception must be taken to apply to the whole contract, and that, inasmuch as the defendants were bound to sail as soon as wind and weather
> c would permit, that must mean, if there be no such restraint; and if there be, then as soon as wind and weather permit after the restraint is removed. But it would be monstrous to say that in such a case the parties must wait—for the obligation must be mutual—till the restraint be taken off—the shipper with cargo, which might be perishable, or its market value destroyed—the shipowner with his ship lying idle,
> d possibly rotting—the result of which might be to make the contract ruinous. At all events it must be taken that the restraint must cease within a reasonable time, and that the duty of the defendants was to wait only a reasonable time prepared to carry out their contract should the restraint be removed; but the defendants rest their defence on the ground that it was here impossible to expect, from the nature of the circumstances, that the obstacle of the blockade would be removed within a reasonable time. It is a sufficient answer on the defendants' part that it was not likely
> e to be removed within a reasonable time; and assuming that either party was bound to wait a reasonable time to ascertain whether the obstacle would be removed, in point of fact it was not so removed, and the defendants were therefore justified in not attempting to perform their contract.'

Blackburn J said in this respect (LR 7 QB 404 at 413–414, [1861–73] All ER Rep 861 at
f 867):

> '[Counsel for the plaintiffs] says the plea only shews facts which go to reduce the damages to a nominal sum, but affords no answer to the declaration, which says that the defendants refused to sail at all; but this plea, it seems to me, does not only shew that the plaintiffs have suffered no damage, but affords a defence to the action, inasmuch as the contract was still executory, and the defendants say, "We are not
> g going to let our ship sail to the port of loading at all, because you, the plaintiffs, never will be ready and willing to perform your part of the contract." But then it is said, it is possible that blockade might be raised within a reasonable time. No doubt it was possible. But it must be taken on this record that it was not raised within a reasonable time; so if the defendants chose to run the risk, and in the event turn out
> h right, they are in the same position as if they had waited the reasonable time and had then sailed away. Possibly, had they turned out wrong, the plaintiffs would have been entitled to say, "We were ready and willing to put a cargo on board, you chose to take your chance, and have turned out wrong, therefore we have a cause of action against you." But the defendants here were right, and there never was a time when the plaintiffs could say, "We are ready and willing and able to perform our contract".'

j

The two leading judgments did not expressly deal with the fifth plea, and after counsel had raised the matter with the court, Lush J said (LR 7 QB 404 at 414–415, [1861–73] All ER Rep 861 at 867):

> 'The sixth and seventh pleas have been already pronounced to be good. I think the fifth plea may also be treated as valid. It alleges the breaking out of a war

> between France and Germany, and a blockade of the port of Hamburg. If the impediment had been in its nature temporary I should have thought the plea bad; but a state of war must be presumed to be likely to continue so long, and so to disturb the commerce of merchants, as to defeat and destroy the object of a commercial adventure like this. The plea, therefore, seems to me prima facie good.'

The next case relied on was *Horlock v Beal* [1916] 1 AC 486, [1916–17] All ER Rep 81. The plaintiff was a merchant seaman on board a vessel which was caught at Hamburg at the outbreak of the 1914–18 war. He remained on board ship for a time, and was then imprisoned, his detention not having ceased at the time he brought an action for his wages. Four of the five members of the House of Lords held that the claim failed, although there was a difference of opinion whether the contract was discharged immediately on the outbreak of war, or whether, as Earl Loreburn considered, the discharge did not take place until the crew were imprisoned.

The speeches of the three Lords who decided in favour of immediate discharge contain elaborate discussions of the doctrine of frustration, which it would be impracticable to analyse in full. It is sufficient to say the following—

(1) Lord Atkinson held that the doctrine of frustration applied to contracts which were part performed, as well as those which were wholly executory, and that the doctrine extended to what would now be regarded as commercial frustration. In the latter respect, Lord Atkinson quoted from the judgment of Lush J in *Geipel v Smith* that I have already quoted and went on ([1916] 1 AC 486 at 502, [1916–17] All ER Rep 81 at 89):

> 'It is not necessary, therefore, in such a case to wait till the delay has occurred. It is legitimate to come to the conclusion that the delay caused by war will be so long and so disturbing to commerce as to defeat the adventure and to act accordingly at once.'

(2) Lord Shaw said ([1916] 1 AC 486 at 507–508, [1916–17] All ER Rep 81 at 92):

> 'Without fault on the part of either party to the contract of service, law and force combined to stop the prosecution of this voyage; and the adventure was consequently lost. In my humble opinion that stoppage and loss, having arisen from a declaration of war, must be considered to have been caused for a period of indefinite duration, and so to have effected a solution of the contract arrangements for and dependent upon the completion or further continuance of the adventure. I say this advisedly, in consequence of the argument presented to the House, and founded on the possibility that after a declaration of war peace may be concluded within a short time, ships may be released and voyages and shipping adventures be resumed. My Lords, as the cases show, such resumption does of consent take place, and Courts of law pay respect to the terms upon which the resumption was made. But, apart from the private arrangements of parties, the contracts are, in my opinion (and subject to the point as to a period of grace hereafter dealt with), brought to an end by a declaration of war, and all interested are entitled to have affairs settled upon that footing.'

Lord Shaw then went on to say that in any event he should have felt entirely free to hold that the circumstances of the case left no doubt as to the disruption of the contract relations of the parties and the loss of the adventure. Finally, he said ([1916] 1 AC 486 at 510, [1916–17] All ER Rep 81 at 94):

> 'What, in short, during the course of the war or under the stress of circumstances, may happen to this ship, no one can foresee: destruction, confiscation, or return—any of these things may occur; and all are involved in the overwhelming uncertainty both as to time and circumstances which follows from the present state of war. With regard to the effect of a declaration of war there is certainly, however, one presumption. It has been expressed in various decisions, but was clearly stated by Lush J. in *Geipel* v. *Smith*: "a state of war must be presumed to be likely to continue

so long, and so to disturb the commerce of merchants, as to defeat and destroy the object of a commercial adventure like this".'

(3) Lord Wrenbury said ([1916] 1 AC 486 at 526, [1916–17] All ER Rep 81 at 102):

> 'On August 4, 1914, there occurred, in the case of this ship, a supervening cause which resulted in the impossibility of continuing that adventure which was the subject of the seaman's contract of May 21, 1914, and that impossibility has continued for such a time as that its character, which might have proved to be temporary, is now known to be for a time so indefinite and so long that the adventure which was the whole basis of the contract has failed. The case falls, I think, within the principle of *Taylor* v. *Caldwell* ((1863) 3 B & S 826, [1861–73] All ER Rep 24). *Melville* v. *De Wolf* ((1855) 4 E & B 844, 119 ER 313) is a like case. The plaintiff there was taken from his employment and sent home by the order of a Court and, as Lord Campbell C.J. put it, the contract was "dissolved by the supreme authority of the State." The plaintiff was not entitled to wages from the date when he was taken away and his service ceased.'

The next case relied on was *Bank Line Ltd v Arthur Capel & Co* [1919] AC 435, [1918–19] All ER Rep 504, where it was held that a time charter was frustrated by government requisition during 1915. In the present case, reliance was placed on the following passage from the speech of Lord Sumner ([1919] AC 435 at 454–455, [1918–19] All ER Rep 504 at 514):

> 'Bailhache J. [in *Anglo-Northern Trading Co Ltd v Emlyn Jones & Williams* [1917] 2 KB 78 at 84] says that the main thing to be considered is the probable length of the total deprivation of the use of the chartered ship compared with the unexpired duration of the charterparty, and I agree in the importance of this feature, though it may not be the main and certainly is not the only matter to be considered. The probabilities as to the length of the deprivation and not the certainty arrived at after the event are also material. The question must be considered at the trial as it had to be considered by the parties, when they came to know of the cause and the probabilities of the delay and had to decide what to do. On this the judgments in the above cases substantially agree. Rights ought not to be left in suspense or to hang on the chances of subsequent events. The contract binds or it does not bind, and the law ought to be that the parties can gather their fate then and there. What happens afterwards may assist in showing what the probabilities really were, if they had been reasonably forecasted, but when the causes of frustration have operated so long or under such circumstances as to raise a presumption of inordinate delay, the time has arrived at which the fate of the contract falls to be decided. The fate is dissolution or continuance and, if the charter ought to be held to be dissolved, it cannot be revived without a new contract. The parties are free.'

Finally, there was *Denny Mott & Dickson Ltd v James B Fraser & Co Ltd* [1944] 1 All ER 678, [1944] AC 265. The dispute concerned the letting of a timber yard, coupled with a transaction involving mutual obligations as to the supply of timber. Ministerial orders made on and shortly after the declaration of war prevented the timber from being supplied. The House of Lords held that the entire contract was frustrated. In the present case the charterers relied on the following passage from the speech of Lord Wright ([1944] 1 All ER 678 at 685, [1944] AC 625 at 277–278):

> 'It is true that the agreement was for an indefinite time, and that the war might end within a comparatively short period. The position must be determined as at the date when the parties came to know of the cause of the prevention and the probabilities of its length as they appeared at the date of the Order. But subsequent events ascertained at or before the trial may assist in showing what the probabilities really were (as Lord Sumner said in *Bank Line* v. *Capel* ([1919] AC 435 at 454, [1918–19] All ER Rep 504 at 514)). In addition there is to be remembered the principle

stated by Lush, J., in *Geipel* v. *Smith*, that a state of war must be presumed to be likely to continue so long and so to disturb the commerce of merchants as to defeat and destroy the object of a commercial adventure. It is true that Lush, J., was there referring to a single definite adventure, not to a continuous trading. But the real principle which applies in these cases is that business men must not be left in indefinite suspense. If there is a reasonable probability from the nature of the interruption that it will be of indefinite duration, they ought to be free to turn their assets, their plant and equipment and their business operations into activities which are open to them, and to be free from commitments which are struck with sterility for an uncertain future period. Lord Shaw emphasised this principle in the *Bank Line* case ([1919] AC 435 at 449, [1918–19] All ER Rep 504 at 511), and so did Lord Sumner in the same case ([1919] AC 435 at 454, [1918–19] All ER Rep 504 at 514).'

Do these cases establish the proposition that a declaration of war ipso jure discharges any contract on which the war directly bears? Counsel began his submissions for the ship owners by asserting that if the cases ever did ground such a proposition, they may now be disregarded, because wars have changed their character. As recent history shows, improvements in weapons and communications have created the possibility of very short wars: shorter than would be necessary to discharge any ordinary commercial contract. It is no longer justifiable to make any presumptions as to the indefinite duration of a state of war.

While I have sympathy with this argument, it is one which a court of first instance should adopt with caution, in the face of weighty authority. In the event, I do not find it necessary to grasp this particular nettle, because I am of the opinion that the law never did take the shape for which counsel for the charterers contends. In my judgment the true position is as follows. (1) Except in the case of supervening illegality, arising from the fact that the contract involves a party in trading with some one who has become an enemy, a declaration of war does not prevent the performance of a contract; it is the acts done in furtherance of the war which may or may not prevent performance, depending on the individual circumstances of the case. (2) If there is any presumption at all, it relates to the duration of the state of war, not to the effects which the war may have on the performance of the contract. The war itself and its effects on the contract are by no means necessarily coterminous. (3) Any presumption as to the indefinite duration of the war is capable of being rebutted.

These propositions may be tested against the authorities on which counsel for the charterers relied. As to *Geipel v Smith*, it must be noted that the issue which is relevant to the present case is the one which was raised by the seventh plea, the decision on which is one of the foundations of the modern law of frustration. The issue was argued on the pleaded assumption that the blockage would last beyond a reasonable time, a plea which would nowadays be expressed to relate to 'such a time as would not frustrate the commercial object of the adventure'. If the charterers' proposition in the present case were correct, it would follow that the Court of Queen's Bench was looking in entirely the wrong direction. It would have been the war, not the blockage, which mattered. The court need not have concerned itself with the plea of a delay beyond a reasonable time, since the war, presumed to be of indefinite duration, would on its own have been sufficient to found a defence. In my opinion, the general tenor of the judgments is contrary to the sense of the charterers' present submission.

Then, when one comes to look at the fifth plea, in the context of what the court had already said about the seventh plea, the meaning of what Lush J was saying becomes plain. The fifth plea contains no allegation as to the duration of the illegality, and, equally important, there was no replication to the plea. In my opinion, all that Lush J intended to convey was that on the bare pleadings as they stood, the fifth plea was valid. But what if the plaintiff had averred by replication that the sovereigns were at the very moment of the British proclamation on the point of negotiating a settlement of peace, that it was asserted by the sovereigns that there was no longer any impediment to the conclusion of a settlement, that peace was universally believed to be imminent, and that a cessation of the state of war did indeed follow on the next day? Can it really be suggested that on the pleadings so constituted the court would have held that the fifth plea was still good? Surely not. Lush J was postulating the existence of a presumption, not an inflexible rule of law.

As regards *Horlock v Beal*, the passages cited, notably the extracts from the speech of Lord Shaw, do seem at first sight, when read in isolation from the facts with which they were concerned, to support the argument of the charterers in the present case. The context is, however, important. At the time of the declaration of war, nobody could tell what would happen to the ship or the seamen, or for how long the war would last; or indeed know with any certainty what was going on in the enemy camp. By the time the case came on for argument, in the House of Lords, the seamen had already been in prison for more than one year. The war was grinding on with no end in sight. The possibility that the service would be resumed before the end of the war could be disregarded, and there was no sound basis on which it could be maintained that the presumption as to the indefinite duration of the war was rebutted. In these circumstances it is not surprising that, to employ the language of Lord Atkinson, it was 'legitimate' to presume that the contract was discharged from the outset. But I find nothing in the speeches of Lord Atkinson and Lord Wrenbury, and even in that of Lord Shaw, to suggest that in every case, as a matter of law, it will always be legitimate to act on this assumption, no matter what the circumstances might be.

As regards *Bank Line v Capel*, this could not possibly found an argument that war automatically frustrates, since the charterparty was entered into several months after war broke out. The frustrating event was the requisition, being one of the effects of the war. Some assessment of the duration of the war was necessary in order to assess the duration of the requisition. But even in this context, Lord Sumner was not in my judgment expounding any irrebuttable presumption that the war would be of infinite duration; on the contrary, the reasoning of the passage cited points to the conclusion that in this particular situation, as in others where frustration is alleged, the circumstances must be looked at as a whole.

Nor can I accept that the passage from the speech of Lord Wright in *Denny Mott & Dickson Ltd v James B Fraser & Co Ltd* supports the charterers' contention. The reference by Lord Wright to 'a reasonable probability from the nature of the interruption' shows that the period of anticipated delay is to be judged by reference to the circumstances of the individual case, and not according to some presumption which is to apply indiscriminately in every situation.

In these circumstances, I cannot extract from the cases any irrebuttable presumption as to the duration of the war, or as to its impact on the contract. It is reassuring that this should be so, for any other conclusion would in my judgment be contrary to common sense. I derive further reassurance from three sources.

First, the textbooks do not support the suggested argument. The discussion in Lord McNair's work *The Legal Effects of War* (4th edn, 1966) contains no reference to any such principle as the charterers propound. It is inconceivable that the learned author would have discussed the matter in the way in which he did if he had seen any foundation for such a principle. Moreover, in the work by McElroy and Williams *Impossibility of Performance* (1941) p 176 the authors summarise the cases by saying:

> 'Accordingly, when the excepted cause of delay is one which is, in its nature, coterminous with the war itself (as was the case with the blockade in Geipel v. Smith) a presumption of frustration prima facie arises.'

The authors then immediately go on to quote from the speech of Lord Shaw in *Horlock v Beal*.

Nor does the existence of the rule appear to be appreciated by those who have argued and ruled on the more recent cases involving frustration by war or its effects. Thus, for example, if the charterers' argument were right, the passage from the speech of Lord Roskill in *The Evia* [1982] 3 All ER 350, [1982] 3 WLR 637, with which the remainder of the House concurred, on the question whether the award of the arbitrator was open to attack, must be taken to have proceeded per incuriam. It may also be noted that in *The* a *Wenjiang (No 2)* [1983] 1 Lloyd's Rep 400, where the argument was not advanced in the High Court, Bingham J observed that 'the arbitrator did not, quite rightly, accept the view that war itself frustrated the contract'. Finally, there is a passage in the speech of Lord Sumner in *Akties Nord-Osterso Rederiet v E A Casper Edgar & Co Ltd* (1923) 14 Ll L Rep 203, admittedly obiter, which supports the view which I have already expressed.

Accordingly, I conclude that the arbitrator was right in rejecting the charterers' b primary argument of law. Having reached this conclusion, there is no need to examine the question which might otherwise have arisen, as to the effect of the payment of hire after the date of the supposed frustration.

Other grounds of appeal

I now turn to the other grounds on which it is said that the court should interfere. c Two matters must be dealt with at the outset.

First, it is pointed out by the charterers that the arbitrator is not a commercial man, but is instead a lawyer of long experience. Hence, so it is said, the court should be more ready than in many cases to substitute its own view of the correct solution, than if he had, for example, been a shipbroker. I recognise that in the context of some types of dispute there might be force in such a submission. For example, if the issue concerned a d matter of judgment in a field where long practical experience was of the essence, a judge might feel that he was just as well or ill equipped to establish the correct 'bracket' as would be a legally trained arbitrator, whereas he would be much more cautious if the arbitrator himself possessed the necessary experience. In the present case, however, the element of judgment calls for no special expertise. I cannot see that a lawyer sitting as arbitrator is any worse qualified to decide on commercial frustration than the other e persons of divers experience who are called on to perform the same function. The court has the ultimate responsibility of establishing the bracket. Having done so, and having ascertained that the arbitrator's answer lies within the bracket, the court should honour the award, whatever the particular qualifications of the arbitrator who made it.

The second general question relates to the submission made by counsel for the charterers that the award is open to objection because the arbitrator has not given reasons f for what he (the arbitrator) described as his visceral reaction. I cannot accept this at all. From the technical point of view, the argument gets the charterers nowhere, because even if it were right it would at most found an application for further reasons under s 1(5) of the 1979 Act. No such application has been made by the charterers. But, more than this, the argument is, in my view, misconceived. The whole point of the judgmental task performed at the third stage of the arbitrator's process of thought is that it does not g and indeed cannot involve detailed ratiocination and the very reason why the parties choose arbitration is that they prefer the 'hunch' or 'feel' or call it what one will of the arbitrator to that of the court. To force the arbitrator to give reasons for a conclusion which in truth is not reasoned would merely create opportunities for an exercise in spurious logic. The court does, I have said, retain a supervisory control, so as to make sure that the arbitrator's reaction to the problem is not based on a false premise of law. h Beyond this it must not go.

Turning to the individual grounds of complaint, the charterers do not say, nor could they, that the award gives any sign that the arbitrator has misunderstood the relevant general principles of law. After quoting from *Davis Contractors Ltd v Fareham UDC* [1956] 2 All ER 145, [1956] AC 696, the arbitrator restates the principle in his own graphic terms in a way from which I would certainly not dissent. Later he formulates the test for j the date of frustration in a way which, I would respectfully suggest, is entirely correct.

Nor is it said that an error of law is betrayed by the inclusion in the reasons of some factors which ought to have been left out of account. The charterers do, however, maintain that the arbitrator has failed to attach weight to matters which he ought to have brought into the balance, and they say this because the arbitrator has not specifically drawn attention to them in his award. They mention in particular: (1) the fact that the paramount feature of the adventure was a voyage to Basrah, which had already been performed at the time of the war; (2) the fact that, but for the war, less than three days would have remained before the completion of the contract service; (3) the presence in the charter of cl 42 which (so the charterers contend) provides a strong indication of the kind of delay which would strike at the root of the adventure; (4) the fact that the Shatt al-Arab in which the vessel was trapped was itself the casus belli; (5) a gap between the end of September and the middle of October 1980 during which, so far as the evidence goes, there were no grounds for anything but extreme pessimism as regards the release of the ships.

These factors are material to the issue of frustration, although not individually conclusive on it. If it could be shown that the arbitrator had mistakenly ruled them out of account, or simply ignored them, there would be grounds for questioning the validity of his conclusion. I can, however, see no ground for saying that there has been any such error here. The arbitrator had to deal with eight issues of law, some more complex than the one with which this appeal is concerned. To set out every relevant factor on every relevant point would have required a reasoned award of prodigious length. The arbitrator was under no obligation to produce such a document. Instead, he chose to deal shortly with this short point. He cannot be criticised for doing so, nor can his brevity be used to found a suspicion of error. In my judgment, there is no substance in this ground of appeal.

There remains one final step which the reviewing court must take, namely to see whether the answer arrived at by the arbitrator lies outside the range of permissible answers. For this purpose it is unnecessary for the court to stipulate the precise limits of the range, and still less for it to express any view as to the conclusion which it would itself have formed, if it had been for the court, not the arbitrator, to decide the issue. I do not do so, and will simply state that in my judgment the conclusion at which the arbitrator arrived is not outside the permissible range, and that no error of law can be inferred.

Accordingly, the appeal will be dismissed.

Appeal dismissed. Leave to appeal granted.

Solicitors: *Sinclair Roche & Temperley* (for the charterers); *Holman Fenwick & Willan* (for the shipowners).

K Mydeen Esq Barrister.

Practice Direction

FAMILY DIVISION

Ward of court – Parties to proceedings – Ward seeking to make undesirable association with another person – Other person not to be party to originating summons but defendant in summons for injunction or committal – Other person to be given time to obtain representation – Title to proceedings.

In cases in which the ward has formed or is seeking to form an association, considered to be undesirable, with another person, that other person should not be made a party to the originating summons. He or she should be made a defendant in a summons within the wardship proceedings for injunction or committal. Such a person should not be added to the title of the proceedings or allowed to see any documents other than those relating to the summons.

The judges of the Family Division consider that any such person should be allowed time within which to obtain representation and any order for injunction should in the first instance extend over a few days only.

This Direction supersedes that dated 15 December 1961 ([1962] 1 All ER 156, [1962] 1 WLR 61).

Issued with the concurrence of the Lord Chancellor.

B P Tickle
Senior Registrar.

16 June 1983

R v Sullivan

HOUSE OF LORDS

LORD DIPLOCK, LORD SCARMAN, LORD LOWRY, LORD BRIDGE OF HARWICH AND LORD BRANDON OF OAKBROOK

20, 21 APRIL, 23 JUNE 1983

Criminal law – Automatism – Insanity distinguished – Epileptic seizure – Seizure causing total deprivation of understanding and memory – Epileptic inflicting grievous bodily harm during seizure – Whether accused entitled to rely on automatism as a defence – Whether accused's condition during seizure amounting to insanity – Whether proper verdict not guilty by reason of insanity – Trial of Lunatics Act 1883, s 2(1) – Criminal Procedure (Insanity) Act 1964, s 5(1).

The defendant was charged with inflicting grievous bodily harm on P. At his trial he admitted inflicting grievous bodily harm on P, who was a friend, but asserted by way of a defence that he had done so while in the final stage of recovering from a minor epileptic seizure. The undisputed medical evidence at the trial was that the effect on the functioning of the brain of such a seizure was that the epileptic could have no memory, and would not be conscious, of what he had done during the seizure. The trial judge ruled that the defence amounted to one of insanity, rather than a defence of automatism, and that if the jury accepted the defence they would be required to return the special verdict of not guilty by reason of insanity provided for in s 2(1)[a] of the Trial of Lunatics Act 1883, and that in consequence the judge would be required, by virtue of s 5(1)[b] of the Criminal Procedure (Insanity) Act 1964, to order the defendant to be detained in a special hospital. To avoid those consequences the defendant changed his plea to guilty of the lesser offence of assault occasioning actual bodily harm and was convicted of that offence. He was sentenced to probation under medical supervision. He appealed against the conviction on the ground that the judge's ruling was erroneous in law and had deprived him of the opportunity of pleading the defence of automatism to the charge of inflicting grievous bodily harm which would have been likely to result in an acquittal. The Court of Appeal upheld the judge's ruling and dismissed the appeal. The defendant appealed to the House of Lords.

Held – When a defence of insanity was put forward on a criminal charge it remained the case that the accused had clearly to prove, in accordance with the definition of insanity in the M'Naghten Rules, that at the time of committing the criminal act he was labouring under a 'defect of reason' resulting from 'disease of the mind', the term 'mind' being used in the ordinary sense of the mental faculties of reason, memory and understanding. Thus, if the effect of a disease was to impair those faculties so severely as to have the consequence that the accused did not know what he was doing, or, if he did, that he did not know that it was wrong, he was 'insane' in the legal sense. Accordingly, it did not matter whether the cause of the impairment was organic, as in epilepsy, or functional, or whether the impairment itself was permanent or was transient and intermittent, provided it subsisted at the time of commission of the act, since the purpose of the

---

a Section 2(1) provides: 'Where in any indictment or information any act or omission is charged against any person as an offence, and it is given in evidence on the trial of such person for that offence that he was insane, so as not to be responsible, according to law, for his actions at the time when the act was done or omission made, then, if it appears to the jury before whom such person is tried that he did the act or made the omission charged, but was insane as aforesaid at the time when he did or made the same, the jury shall return a special verdict that the accused is not guilty by reason of insanity.'

b Section 5(1), so far as material, provides: 'Where—(*a*) a special verdict is returned . . . the court shall make an order that the accused be admitted to such hospital as may be specified by the Secretary of State.'

legislation relating to the defence of insanity was to protect society against recurrence of the dangerous state, no matter how temporary the duration of the suspension of faculties a
might be. It followed therefore that, if the occurrence of an epileptic fit brought about a temporary suspension of the mental faculties of reason, memory and understanding during the course of which an offence was committed, the special verdict of not guilty by reason of insanity was appropriate. The appeal would therefore be dismissed (see p 677 *h* to p 678 *b g* to p 679 *a*, post).

Dictum of Devlin J in *R v Kemp* [1956] 3 All ER at 253 applied. b

Bratty v A-G for Northern Ireland [1961] 3 All ER 523 considered.

Per curiam. A defence of non-insane automatism, for which the proper verdict would be a verdict of not guilty, may be available in cases where temporary impairment of the mental faculties, not being self-induced by consuming drink or drugs, results from some external physical factor such as a blow to the head causing concusssion or the administration of an anaesthetic for therapeutic purposes (see p 678 *b c h* to p 679 *a*, post). c

Decision of the Court of Appeal [1983] 1 All ER 577 affirmed.

Notes

For the defence of insanity, see 11 Halsbury's Laws (4th edn) para 30, and for cases on the subject, see 14(1) Digest (Reissue) 37–47, *143–218*.

For the Trial of Lunatics Act 1883, s 2, see 8 Halsbury's Statutes (3rd edn) 225. d

For the Criminal Procedure (Insanity) Act 1964, s 5, see ibid 528.

Cases referred to in opinions

Bratty v A-G for Northern Ireland [1961] 3 All ER 523, [1963] AC 386, [1961] 3 WLR 965, HL.

M'Naghten's Case (1843) 10 Cl & Fin 200, [1843–60] All ER Rep 229, 8 ER 718, 4 St Tr NS 847, HL. e

R v Kemp [1956] 3 All ER 249, [1957] 1 QB 399, [1956] 3 WLR 724, Assizes.

R v Quick, R v Paddison [1973] 3 All ER 347, [1973] QB 910, [1973] 3 WLR 26, CA.

Appeal

The defendant, Patrick Joseph Sullivan, appealed pursuant to leave granted by the Appeal f
Committee of the House of Lords on 10 February 1983 against the decision of the Court of Appeal, Criminal Division (Lawton LJ, Michael Davies and Bush JJ) ([1983] 1 All ER 577, [1983] 2 WLR 392) on 9 December dismissing the appeal of the defendant against his conviction on 15 January 1982 at the Central Criminal Court before his Honour Judge Lymbery QC and a jury for an offence of assault occasioning bodily harm. The facts are set out in the opinion of Lord Diplock.

g

Lionel Swift QC and *Bruce Speller* for the appellant.
Stephen Mitchell and *V B A Temple* for the Crown.

Their Lordships took time for consideration.

h

23 June. The following opinions were delivered.

LORD DIPLOCK. My Lords, the appellant, a man of blameless reputation, has the misfortune to have been a lifelong sufferer from epilepsy. There was a period when he was subject to major seizures known as grand mal; but as a result of treatment which he was receiving as an out-patient of the Maudsley Hospital from 1976 onwards, these j
seizures had, by the use of drugs, been reduced by 1979 to seizures of less severity known as petit mal, or psychomotor epilepsy, though they continued to occur at a frequency of one or two per week.

One such seizure occurred on 8 May 1981, when the appellant, then aged 51, was visiting a neighbour, Mrs Killick, an old lady aged 86 for whom he was accustomed to perform regular acts of kindness. He was chatting there to a fellow visitor and friend of his, a Mr Payne aged 80, when the epileptic fit came on. It appears likely from the expert medical evidence about the way in which epileptics behave at the various stages of a petit mal seizure that Mr Payne got up from the chair to help the appellant. The only evidence of an eye-witness was that of Mrs Killick, who did not see what had happened before she saw Mr Payne lying on the floor and the appellant kicking him about the head and body, in consequence of which Mr Payne suffered injuries severe enough to require hospital treatment.

As a result of this occurrence the appellant was indicted on two counts: the first was of causing grievous bodily harm with intent, contrary to s 18 of the Offences against the Person Act 1861; the second was of causing grievous bodily harm, contrary to s 20 of the Act. At his trial, which took place at the Central Criminal Court before his Honour Judge Lymbery QC and a jury, the appellant pleaded not guilty to both counts. Mrs Killick's evidence that he had kicked Mr Payne violently about the head and body was undisputed and the appellant himself gave evidence of his history of epilepsy and his absence of all recollection of what had occurred at Mrs Killick's flat between the time that he was chatting peacefully to Mr Payne there and his returning to the flat from somewehere else to find that Mr Payne was injured and that an ambulance had been sent for. The prosecution accepted his evidence as true. There was no cross-examination.

Counsel for the appellant wanted to rely on the defence of automatism or, as Viscount Kilmuir LC had put in *Bratty v A-G for Northern Ireland* [1961] 3 All ER 523 at 530, [1963] AC 386 at 405, 'non-insane' automatism, that is to say that he had acted unconsciously and involuntarily in kicking Mr Payne, but that when doing so he was not 'insane' in the sense in which that expression is used as a term of art in English law, and in particular in s 2 of the Trial of Lunatics Act 1883, as amended by s 5 of the Criminal Procedure (Insanity) Act 1964. As was decided unanimously by this House in *Bratty*'s case, before a defence of non-insane automatism may properly be left to the jury some evidential foundation for it must first be laid. The evidential foundation that counsel laid before the jury in the instant case consisted of the testimony of two distinguished specialists from the neuropsychiatry epilepsy unit at the Maudsley Hospital, Dr Fenwick and Dr Taylor, as to the pathology of the various stages of a seizure due to psychomotor epilepsy. Their expert evidence, which was not disputed by the prosecution, was that the appellant's acts in kicking Mr Payne had all the characteristics of epileptic automatism at the third or post-ictal stage of petit mal, and that, in view of his history of psychomotor epilepsy and the hospital records of his behaviour during previous seizures, the strong probability was that the appellant's acts of violence towards Mr Payne took place while he was going through that stage.

The evidence as to the pathology of a seizure due to psychomotor epilepsy can be sufficiently stated for the purposes of this appeal by saying that after the first stage, the prodram, which precedes the fit itself, there is a second stage, the ictus, lasting a few seconds, during which there are electrical discharges into the temporal lobes of the brain of the sufferer. The effect of these discharges cause him in the post-ictal stage to make movements which he is not conscious that he is making, including, and this was a characteristic of previous seizures which the appellant had suffered, automatic movements of resistence to anyone trying to come to his aid. These movements of resistence might, though in practice they very rarely would, involve violence.

At the conclusion of the evidence, the judge, in the absence of the jury, was asked to rule whether the jury should be directed that if they accepted this evidence it would not be open to them to bring in a verdict of not guilty, but they would be bound in law to return a special verdict of not guilty by reason of insanity. The judge ruled that the jury should be so directed.

After this ruling, the appellant, on the advice of his counsel and with the consent of the prosecution and the judge, changed his plea to guilty of assault occasioning actual bodily harm. The jury, on the direction of the judge, brought in a verdict of guilty of that offence, for which the judge sentenced him to three years' probation subject to the condition that during that period he submitted to treatment under the direction of Dr Fenwick at the Maudsley Hospital.

My Lords, neither the legality nor the propriety of the procedure adopted after the judge's ruling has been canvassed in this House, nor was it canvassed in the Court of Appeal to which an appeal was brought on the ground that the judge ought to have left to the jury the defence of non-insane automatism which, if accepted by them, would have entitled the appellant to a verdict of not guilty. In these circumstances the present case does not appear to be one in which it would be appropriate for this House to enter into a consideration of the procedure followed in the Central Criminal Court after the judge's ruling, more particularly as it raises some questions that will shortly come before your Lordships for argument in another appeal.

The Court of Appeal held that Judge Lymbery's ruling had been correct (see [1983] 1 All ER 577, [1983] 2 WLR 392). It dismissed the appeal and certified that a point of law of general public importance was involved in the decision, namely:

> 'Whether a person who is proved to have occasioned, contrary to section 47 of the Offences against the Person Act 1861, actual bodily harm to another, whilst recovering from a seizure due to psychomotor epilepsy and who did not know what he was doing when he caused such harm and has no memory of what he did should be found not guilty by reason of insanity.'

My Lords, for centuries, up to 1843, the common law relating to the concept of mental disorders as negativing responsibility for crimes was in the course of evolution, but I do not think it necessary for your Lordships to embark on an examination of the pre-1843 position. In that year, following the acquittal of one Daniel M'Naghten for shooting Sir Robert Peel's secretary, in what today would probably be termed a state of paranoia, the question of insanity and criminal responsibility was the subject of debate in the legislative chamber of the House of Lords, the relevant statute then in force being the Criminal Lunatics Act 1800, an Act 'for the safe custody of Insane Persons charged with Offences', which referred to persons who were 'insane' at the time of the commission of the offence, but contained no definition of insanity. The House invited the judges of the courts of common law to answer five abstract questions on the subject of insanity as a defence to criminal charges. The answer to the second and third of these questions combined was given by Tindal CJ on behalf of all the judges, except Maule J, and constituted what became known as the M'Naghten Rules. The judge's answer is in the following well-known terms (see *M'Naghten's Case* (1843) 10 Cl & Fin 200 at 210, [1843–60] All ER Rep 229 at 233):

> '... the jurors ought to be told in all cases that every man is to be presumed to be sane, and to possess a sufficient degree of reason to be responsible for his crimes, until the contrary be proved to their satisfaction; and that to establish a defence on the ground of insanity, it must be clearly proved that, at the time of the committing of the act, the party accused was labouring under a defect of reason, from disease of the mind, as not to know the nature and quality of the act he was doing; or, if he did know it, that he did not know he was doing what was wrong.'

Although the questions put to the judges by the House of Lords referred to insane delusions of various kinds, the answer to the second and third questions (the M'Naghten Rules) is perfectly general in its terms. It is stated to be applicable 'in all cases' in which it is sought 'to establish a defence on the ground of insanity'. This answer was intended to provide a comprehensive definition of the various matters which had to be proved (on balance of probabilities, as it has since been held) in order to establish that the accused was insane within the meaning of the 1800 Act, which, like its successors of 1883 and 1964, make it incumbent on a jury, if they find the accused to have been 'insane' at the time that he committed the acts with which he is charged, to bring in a verdict neither of guilty nor of not guilty but a special verdict the terms of which have been varied under three successive statutes, but are currently not guilty by reason of insanity.

The M'Naghten Rules have been used as a comprehensive definition for this purpose by the courts for the last 140 years. Most importantly, they were so used by this House in *Bratty*'s case. That case was in some respects the converse of the instant case. Bratty was charged with murdering a girl by strangulation. He claimed to have been unconscious of what he was doing at the time he strangled the girl and he sought to run as alternative defences non-insane automatism and insanity. The only evidential foundation that he laid for either of these pleas was medical evidence that he might have been suffering from psychomotor epilepsy which, if he were, would account for his having been unconscious of what he was doing. No other pathological explanation of his actions having been carried out in a state of automatism was supported by evidence. The trial judge first put the defence of insanity to the jury. The jury rejected it; they declined to bring in the special verdict. Thereupon, the judge refused to put the alternative defence of automatism. His refusal was upheld by the Court of Criminal Appeal of Northern Ireland and subsequently by this House.

The question before this House was whether, the jury having rejected the plea of insanity, there was any evidence of non-insane automatism fit to be left to the jury. The ratio decidendi of its dismissal of the appeal was that the jury having negatived the explanation that Bratty might have been acting unconsciously in the course of an attack of psychomotor epilepsy, there was no evidential foundation for the suggestion that he was acting unconsciously from any other cause.

In the instant case, as in *Bratty*'s case, the only evidential foundation that was laid for any finding by the jury that the appellant was acting unconsciously and involuntarily when he was kicking Mr Payne was that when he did so he was in the post-ictal stage of a seizure of psychomotor epilepsy. The evidential foundation in the case of Bratty, that he was suffering from psychomotor epilepsy at the time he did the act with which he was charged, was very weak and was rejected by the jury; the evidence in the appellant's case, that he was so suffering when he was kicking Mr Payne, was very strong and would almost inevitably be accepted by a properly directed jury. It would be the duty of the judge to direct the jury that if they did accept that evidence the law required them to bring in a special verdict and none other. The governing statutory provision is to be found in s 2 of the Trial of Lunatics Act 1883. This says 'the jury *shall* return a special verdict'.

My Lords, I can deal briefly with the various grounds on which it has been submitted that the instant case can be distinguished from what constituted the ratio decidendi in *Bratty*'s case, and that it falls outside the ambit of the M'Naghten Rules.

First, it is submitted the medical evidence in the instant case shows that psychomotor epilepsy is not a disease of the mind, whereas in *Bratty*'s case it was accepted by all the doctors that it was. The only evidential basis for this submission is that Dr Fenwick said that in medical terms to constitute a 'disease of the mind' or 'mental illness', which he appeared to regard as interchangeable descriptions, a disorder of brain functions (which undoubtedly occurs during a seizure in psychomotor epilepsy) must be prolonged for a period of time usually more than a day, while Dr Taylor would have it that the disorder must continue for a minimum of a month to qualify for the description 'a disease of the mind'.

The nomenclature adopted by the medical profession may change from time to time; Bratty was tried in 1961. But the meaning of the expression 'disease of the mind' as the cause of 'a defect of reason' remains unchanged for the purposes of the application of the M'Naghten Rules. I agree with what was said by Devlin J in *R v Kemp* [1956] 3 All ER 249 at 253, [1957] 1 QB 399 at 407 that 'mind' in the M'Naghten Rules is used in the ordinary sense of the mental faculties of reason, memory and understanding. If the effect of a disease is to impair these faculties so severely as to have either of the consequences referred to in the latter part of the rules, it matters not whether the aetiology of the impairment is organic, as in epilepsy, or functional, or whether the impairment itself is permanent or is transient and intermittent, provided that it subsisted at the time of commission of the act. The purpose of the legislation relating to the defence of insanity, ever since its origin in 1880, has been to protect society against recurrence of the dangerous conduct. The duration of a temporary suspension of the mental faculties of *a* reason, memory and understanding, particularly if, as in the appellant's case, it is recurrent, cannot on any rational ground be relevant to the application by the courts of the M'Naghten Rules, though it may be relevant to the course adopted by the Secretary of State, to whom the responsibility for how the defendant is to be dealt with passes after the return of the special verdict of not guilty by reason of insanity.

To avoid misunderstanding I ought perhaps to add that in expressing my agreement *b* with what was said by Devlin J in *R v Kemp*, where the disease that caused the temporary and intermittent impairment of the mental faculties was arteriosclerosis, I do not regard that judge as excluding the possibility of non-insane automatism, for which the proper verdict would be a verdict of not guilty, in cases where temporary impairment not being self-induced by consuming drink or drugs, results from some external physical factor such as a blow on the head causing concussion or the administration of an anaesthetic for *c* therapeutic purposes. I mention this because in *R v Quick* [1973] 3 All ER 347, [1973] QB 910 Lawton LJ appears to have regarded the ruling in *R v Kemp* as going as far as this. If it had done, it would have been inconsistent with the speeches in this House in *Bratty*'s case, where *R v Kemp* was alluded to without disapproval by Viscount Kilmuir LC and received the express approval of Lord Denning. The instant case, however, does not in my view afford an appropriate occasion for exploring possible causes of non-insane *d* automatism.

The only other submission in support of the appellant's appeal which I think it necessary to mention is that, because the expert evidence was to the effect that the appellant's acts in kicking Mr Payne were unconscious and thus 'involuntary' in the legal sense of that term, his state of mind was not one dealt with by the M'Naghten Rules at all, since it was not covered by the phrase 'as not to know the nature and quality of the *e* act he was doing'. Quite apart from being contrary to all three speeches in this House in *Bratty*'s case, the submission appears to me, with all respect to counsel, to be quite unarguable. Dr Fenwick himself accepted it as an accurate description of the appellant's mental state in the post-ictal stage of a seizure. The audience to whom the phrase in the M'Naghten Rules was addressed consisted of peers of the realm in the 1840s when a certain orotundity of diction had not yet fallen out of fashion. Addressed to an audience *f* of jurors in the 1980s it might more aptly be expressed as: he did not know what he was doing.

My Lords, it is natural to feel reluctant to attach the label of insanity to a sufferer from psychomotor epilepsy of the kind to which the appellant was subject, even though the expression in the context of a special verdict of not guilty by reason of insanity is a technical one which includes a purely temporary and intermittent suspension of the *g* mental faculties of reason, memory and understanding resulting from the occurrence of an epileptic fit. But the label is contained in the current statute, it has appeared in this statute's predecessors ever since 1800. It does not lie within the power of the courts to alter it. Only Parliament can do that. It has done so twice; it could do so once again.

Sympathise though I do with the appellant, I see no other course open to your Lordships than to dismiss this appeal.

h

LORD SCARMAN. My Lords, I agree with the speech delivered by my noble and learned friend Lord Diplock. I would dismiss the appeal.

LORD LOWRY. My Lords, I have had the advantage of reading in draft the speech prepared by my noble and learned friend Lord Diplock. I agree with his conclusions and, *j* for the reasons which he gives, I would dismiss the appeal.

LORD BRIDGE OF HARWICH. My Lords, for the reasons given in the speech of my noble and learned friend Lord Diplock, with which I fully agree, I too would dismiss this appeal.

LORD BRANDON OF OAKBROOK. My Lords, I have had the advantage of reading in draft the speech prepared by my noble and learned friend Lord Diplock. I agree with it, and for the reasons which he gives I would dismiss the appeal.

Order appealed from affirmed. Certified question answered in the affirmative. Appeal dismissed.

Solicitors: *Armstrong & Co*, Forest Hill (for the appellant); *D M O'Shea* (for the Crown).

Mary Rose Plummer Barrister.

Practice Direction

FAMILY DIVISION

Minor – Maintenance – Education or training – Maintenance order including element in respect of school fees – Provision for automatic adjustment to allow for increase in fees – Amount paid direct to school – Tax relief – Form of order – Contract for child's education to be between child and school – Form of contract.

Maintenance orders which contain an element in respect of school fees frequently have to be varied when the school fees increase. This requirement could be avoided if the relevant part of the maintenance order were to be automatically adjusted when the school fees go up.

The Inland Revenue have agreed to this principle. A form of order which they would find acceptable is as follows:

> 'IT IS ORDERED that the petitioner [*or* respondent] do pay or cause to be paid to the child AB as from the day of 19 until he [*or* she] shall attain the age of 17 years [*or* for so long as he [*or* she] shall continue to receive full-time education] or further order periodical payments for himself [*or* herself] (a) of an amount equivalent to such sum as after deduction of income tax at the basic rate equals the school fees [but not the extras in the school bill] [including specified extras] at the school the said child attends for each financial year [by way of three payments on and and] [payable monthly] together with (b) the sum of £ per annum less tax payable monthly in respect of general maintenance of the said child.'

It should be noted that, even if the amount referred to in part (b) is within the current limits of small maintenance payments, it should still be expressed as 'less tax' because the relevant figure for the maintenance order will be the combined total of the two parts.

In such cases the Revenue will require to be satisfied that the payer under the order has no contractual liability for payment of the school fees.

If an order expressed as payable to the child, whether made in this form or in a form which includes an element in respect of school fees for a specific amount, also provides that payment of the element representing school fees should be paid direct to the school (because, for example, it is feared that the other spouse might dissipate it) the Revenue have agreed, subject to the condition hereafter set out, that tax relief will be given on that element. The wording of the order should be:

> 'AND IT IS FURTHER ORDERED that that part of the order which reflects the school fees shall be paid to the headmaster [*or* bursar *or* school secretary] as agent for the said child and the receipt of that payee shall be sufficient discharge.'

The school fees should be paid *in full* and should be paid out of the net amount under the maintenance order after deduction of tax. Certificates for the full tax deduction should continue to be provided by the other spouse (or other person referred to in r 69 of the Matrimonial Causes Rules 1977, SI 1977/344) in the normal way.

It is a condition of such an order being acceptable for tax purposes that the contract for the child's education (which should preferably be in writing) should be between the child (whose income is being used) and the school and that the fees are received by the officer of the school as the appointed agent for the child.

A form of contract which is acceptable to the Inland Revenue is as follows:

> 'THIS AGREEMENT is made between the governors of .... by their duly authorised officer .... (hereinafter called "the school") of the first part .... and the headmaster [*or* bursar *or* school secretary] of the second part and .... (hereinafter called "the child") of the third part.
>
> WHEREAS it is proposed to ask the .... Court to make an order [*or* the .... Court has made an order] in cause number ...... that the father of the child do make periodical payments to the child at the rate of £ per annum less tax until the child completes full-time education [*or as the case may be*] and that that part of the order which reflects the school fees shall be paid to the headmaster [*or* bursar *or* school secretary] as agent for the child and the receipt of that agent shall be a sufficient discharge
>
> 1. the child hereby constitutes the headmaster [*or* bursar *or* school secretary] to be his agent for the purpose of receiving the said fees and the child agrees to pay the said fees to the said school in consideration of being educated there
>
> 2. in consideration of the said covenant the headmaster [*or* bursar *or* school secretary] agrees to accept the said payments by the father as payments on behalf of the child and the school agrees to educate the child during such time as the said school fees are paid.
>
> Dated the day of 19 .'

This Direction supersedes the Registrar's Direction of 10 November 1980 ([1980] 3 All ER 832, [1980] 1 WLR 1441), which is hereby cancelled.

Issued with the concurrence of the Lord Chancellor.

B P TICKLE
Senior Registrar.

16 June 1983

Stokes (Inspector of Taxes) v Costain Property Investments Ltd

CHANCERY DIVISION
HARMAN J
17, 18, 28 MARCH 1983

Income tax – Capital allowances – Machinery or plant – Ownership of machinery or plant – Machinery or plant belonging to taxpayer in consequence of expenditure – Belong – Machinery or plant installed by tenant becoming landlord's fixtures – Whether machinery or plant belonging to tenant – Finance Act 1971, s 41(1).

Income tax – Capital allowances – Machinery or plant – Expenditure on provision of machinery or plant – Expenditure met directly or indirectly by person other than taxpayer – Met – Provision of finance by financier – Whether expenditure 'met' directly or indirectly by financier – Capital Allowances Act 1968, s 84(1).

The taxpayer company installed lifts and central heating equipment in buildings at two sites at which it had undertaken development work. At neither site was the taxpayer the freeholder of the land, but, when the development was completed, it became entitled to a lease or an underlease of both sites. It was common ground that on installation the lifts and central heating equipment, admitted to be machinery or plant, became landlord's fixtures. The taxpayer claimed that the machinery or plant installed in the buildings belonged to it for the purposes of s 41(1)(*b*)[a] of the Finance Act 1971 and that accordingly the expenditure incurred thereon qualified for a first-year allowance. The inspector of taxes rejected the claim on the ground that machinery or plant which had become landlord's fixtures could not properly be said to 'belong' to a tenant, within s 41(1)(*b*). The General Commissioners upheld the taxpayer company's claim. The Crown appealed.

Held – Where a person incurred capital expenditure on the provision of machinery or plant for the purposes of his trade and that machinery or plant became a part of a building of which he was the tenant and thereby became a landlord's fixture, the machinery or plant did not 'belong' to the tenant, for the purposes of s 41(1)(*b*) of the 1971 Act, because a thing could not 'belong' to a person who, although having a right to possession of it, had no right of disposition of the thing possessed by sale, gift or destruction. It followed that the lifts and central heating equipment did not 'belong' to the taxpayer, within s 41(1)(*b*), and the taxpayer was accordingly not entitled to a first-year allowance in respect of the capital expenditure incurred on them. The appeal would therefore be allowed (see p 687 *a* to *c e*, p 688 *b d* and p 690 *d*, post).

Per Harman J. A transaction whereby a financier lends money to meet a taxpayer's bills and as a result a valuable asset is transferred from the taxpayer to the financier cannot appropriately be described as the financier 'meeting' the expenditure of the taxpayer for the purposes of s 84(1)[b] of the Capital Allowances Act 1968 (see p 690 *d*, post).

Notes

For first-year allowances, see 23 Halsbury's Laws (4th edn) para 426.

For expenditure met directly or indirectly by a person other than the taxpayer, see ibid paras 389, 1298.

For the Capital Allowances Act 1968, s 84, see 34 Halsbury's Statutes (3rd edn) 1129.

For the Finance Act 1971, s 41, see 41 ibid 1459.

---

a Section 41(1), so far as material, is set out at p 686 *f g*, post

b Section 84(1), so far as material, is set out at p 688 *d*, post

Cases referred to in judgment

Lupton (Inspector of Taxes) v Cadogan Gardens Developments Ltd, Carlton Tower Ltd v Moore a
(Inspector of Taxes), Carlton Tower Ltd v IRC [1971] 3 All ER 460, CA.

Macsaga Investment Co Ltd v Lupton (Inspector of Taxes) [1967] 2 All ER 930, [1967] Ch 1016, [1967] 3 WLR 333, CA.

Sargaison (Inspector of Taxes) v Roberts [1969] 3 All ER 1072, [1969] 1 WLR 951.

Union Cold Storage Co Ltd v Simpson (Inspector of Taxes) [1939] 2 All ER 94, [1939] 2 KB 440, CA.

b

Cases also cited

Boarland (Inspector of Taxes) v Pirie Appleton & Co Ltd, Stemco Ltd v IRC, Stemco Ltd v Hyett (Inspector of Taxes) [1940] 3 All ER 306n, [1940] 2 KB 491, CA.

Dowson and Jenkins's Contract, Re [1904] 2 Ch 219, CA.

Heritable Reversionary Co Ltd v Millar (M'Kay's Trustee) [1892] AC 598, HL. c

IRC v George Guthrie & Son 1952 SC 402.

Lord (Cyril) Carpets Ltd v Schofield (Inspector of Taxes), Cyril Lord Carpets Ltd v IRC (1966) 42 TC 637, CA(NI).

Wiltshire County Valuation Committee v Marlborough and Ramsbury Rating Authority, Wiltshire County Valuation Committee v Boyce [1948] 1 All ER 694, [1948] 2 KB 125, CA.

d

Case stated

1\. At the meeting of the Commissioners for the General Purposes of the Income Tax
Acts for the division of Second East Brixton, held at 47 Parliament Street, London SW1
on 26 and 27 November 1980, Costain Property Investments Ltd (the taxpayer) appealed
against the following assessments to corporation tax: (i) for the accounting period ended
31 December 1975 in the sum of £375,000; (ii) for the accounting period ended 31 e
December 1976 in the sum of £402,053.

2\. Shortly stated, the questions for decision were whether the taxpayer was entitled to
claim first-year and writing-down allowances in respect of expenditure on certain plant
and machinery comprised in developments at Nicholsons Walk, Maidenhead and at 1
Kennington Road, London.

3\. Mr Denis Aubrey Lucas, a director of the taxpayer, gave evidence before the f
commissioners.

[Paragraph 4 listed the documents proved or admitted before the commissioners.]

5\. The following facts were proved or admitted before the commissioners. (1) The
taxpayer was incorporated in 1957 as a property investment company. (2) The taxpayer
was at all material times a wholly owned subsidiary of Richard Costain Ltd (Costain). (3)
The taxpayer had at all material times carried on business as a property investment g
company and had not carried on any trade.

The development at Nicholsons Walk, Maidenhead

(4) On 19 April 1973 an agreement (the 1973 agreement) was made between the
mayor, aldermen and burgesses of the Borough of Maidenhead (the corporation), Costain h
and the taxpayer concerning the redevelopment project in Maidenhead which formed
phase 2 of the Maidenhead central area redevelopment. Phase 2 comprised shops, offices
and flats at Nicholsons Walk. Part of the site for phase 2 was already owned by the
corporation. Under the 1973 agreement the taxpayer undertook to acquire the remainder
of the site. The corporation granted the taxpayer a licence to go onto that part of the site
belonging to the corporation and the taxpayer undertook to develop the site in accordance j
with agreed plans as shops, offices and flats. On satisfactory completion of the
development the corporation agreed to grant the taxpayer a lease of the development for
99 years at an initial rent of £22,000 per annum subject to review. An agreed form of
that 99-year lease was scheduled to the agreement. (5) On 14 December 1973 the
taxpayer, Costain and Robert Fleming & Co Ltd (Fleming) entered into an agreement

(the Fleming agreement). Under the terms of the Fleming agreement the taxpayer undertook to complete the development of phase 2 and Fleming undertook to pay the cost of the development up to a limit in total of £3,220,000. These costs were to be advanced to the taxpayer by way of loans secured by mortgage over the 1973 agreement. The taxpayer undertook to procure the grant of the lease of phase 2 to Fleming and Fleming agreed to grant an underlease to the taxpayer of phase 2 for a term of 99 years less 10 days. The rent payable under the underlease was a fixed rent equal to the rent payable to the corporation under the headlease plus an additional quarterly rent consisting of the greater of 5·3% of the cost of the development or a fraction of the rents received by the taxpayer from sublettings. Under cl 3 of the mortgage of the 1973 agreement it was provided that, if the taxpayer company satisfactorily completed the development of phase 2, the debt in respect of the development costs was to be discharged. (6) On 30 May 1973 construction of phase 2 was begun. The contractor was Costain Construction Ltd, which carried out the work under a contract made with the taxpayer dated 10 December 1973. Construction was complete by 23 June 1975. The total construction cost was £2,964,049. On 15 September 1975 the corporation granted the headlease to Fleming. Fleming in turn on 16 September 1975 granted an underlease to the taxpayer. On 1 October 1976 the taxpayer sublet the office part of phase 2 to Costain and the remainder of the development, consisting of flats and shops, was sublet to various tenants, the first letting being on 17 March 1975. The headlease from the corporation to Fleming was in the form of a draft lease annexed to the 1973 agreement. (7) Included in the cost of construction of phase 2 was expenditure on plant and machinery consisting principally of lifts and central heating equipment. Costs incurred totalled £456,284. They were all incurred in the taxpayer's accounting period to 31 December 1975. The expenditure incurred on the plant and machinery would have been included on architects' certificates presented to the taxpayer, which were passed to Fleming. Fleming would pay to Costain Construction Ltd the amounts shown on the certificates and the payment would increase the total indebtedness of the taxpayer to Fleming. (8) Mr D A Lucus, a director and the secretary of the taxpayer, had been employed by the Costain group of companies for 18 years. He had been in charge of the permanent funding of the Maidenhead and Kennington developments and had been involved in the funding negotiations with Fleming. Funding arrangements of the type made with Fleming were common. There were two stages. First, the raising of provisional finance to finance the building works and bring the project to fruition. This was a short-term provision of funds. Second, there was the long-term finance. This was a long-term investment decision whereby Fleming put in as a new investment the sum previously advanced.

The Kennington Road development

(9) By an agreement (the Kennington agreement) dated 22 February 1974 the trustees of the charity known as the Christ Church and Hawkstone Hall agreed to grant the taxpayer a 99-year lease of land known as 1 Kennington Road, London SE1 on terms that the taxpayer would first at its own expense erect an office block and church hall on the land according to approved plans. (10) The taxpayer started construction of the office block on 8 February 1974 and incurred expenditure totalling £602,696, of which £50,905 was agreed to be expenditure on plant and machinery. Construction was completed on 30 October 1975. (11) On 29 December 1976 the headlease was duly granted pursuant to the Kennington agreement to the taxpayer. The rent was a fixed rent plus a percentage of rents achieved on underlettings. On the same day the taxpayer underlet the whole development for a term of 25 years at a rent of £46,950 per annum at five-yearly rent reviews. (12) On 30 December 1976 the taxpayer assigned the headlease to the Liverpool Victoria Friendly Society (LVFS) for £388,600. LVFS was obliged under the terms of the assignment to grant an underlease back to the taxpayer for a term of 99 years less 3 days. This underlease was duly granted on 30 December 1976 subject to and with the benefit of the underlease to Costain. The rent payable under the underlease from LVFS to the taxpayer was £30,800 plus the rent payable under the headlease.

The claims to capital allowances

(13) The taxpayer claimed under ss 41(1) and 46(1) of the Finance Act 1971 first-year and writing-down allowances in amounts equal to the whole of expenditure on plant and machinery comprised in the phase 2 development at the Maidenhead and the Kennington Road developments. The total expenditure claimed was: accounting periods ending 31 December 1975 and 1976, £79,994 and £427,195 respectively. (14) The inspector of taxes refused both claims. (15) It was common ground that, if the taxpayer was entitled to the first-year and writing-down allowances, the entitlement arise under s 46(1) of the 1971 Act.

6. It was contended on behalf of the taxpayer that: (1) in the Maidenhead development, expenditure on the plant and machinery was incurred by the taxpayer. It was incontrovertible that there was a loan by Fleming to the taxpayer because of the mortgage dated 14 December 1973 and a loan could not be a direct or indirect method by which Fleming met the expenditure; (2) Fleming funded the cost of the development as a short-term loan; (3) Fleming could have demanded repayment if the development had not been completed; (4) on completion of the development, the taxpayer was indebted to Fleming; (5) Fleming, as a long-term investment decision, then purchased an interest in the development by taking the headlease; (6) that transaction, from the standpoint of the taxpayer, was a sale of the headlease to Fleming and, in consideration, Fleming wrote off a loan which it had already made; (7) that transaction was not one whereby Fleming met anyone's expenditure: it was the sale of an asset; (8) Fleming by, inter alia, cancelling the mortgage and discharging the loan as consideration for the purchase of an interest in the development did not thereby meet the expenditure on the development: it had purchased an interest in the development; (9) in reference to s 84 of the Capital Allowances Act 1968, if Fleming was not entitled to the capital allowance, it was irrelevant that it had met the expenditure; (10) Fleming did not come within s 85 of the 1968 Act because it had not been trading but had been making an investment in property; (11) in the case of both developments, the plant and machinery were fixtures and fittings and thus became part of the lands comprised in the developments; (12) in regard to the Maidenhead development, on 16 September 1975 the taxpayer acquired an underlease in the land for a term of 99 years less 10 days; (13) that interest was one of the two legal estates that could exist in land; (14) accordingly, the plant and machinery being part of the land and the taxpayer having a legal estate in that land, the plant and machinery belonged to the taxpayer at a point in the accounting period to 31 December 1975; (15) the plant and machinery did not have to belong to the taxpayer throughout the accounting period, but just at some time during that period; (16) in considering to whom the plant and machinery belonged in the case of the Kennington development, the same reasoning could be applied as for the Maidenhead development; (17) accordingly, in the case of the Maidenhead development, the expenditure on plant and machinery had been incurred by the taxpayer and had not been met by Fleming within the meaning of s 84(1) of the 1968 Act; (18) in the case of both developments, the plant and machinery belonged to the taxpayer at some time during the accounting period to 31 December 1975; (19) accordingly the taxpayer was entitled under ss 41(1) and 46(1) of the 1971 Act to first-year and writing-down allowances in amounts equal to the whole of the expenditure on plant and machinery comprised in the Maidenhead and Kennington developments.

7. It was contended on behalf of the Crown that: (1) in the case of the Maidenhead development, whether Fleming provided the funds required for the building works as a loan or not, the Fleming agreement provided that Fleming would meet the building expenses, which they did, and the taxpayer was thereby relieved of the capital expenditure and did not therefore incur such expenditure; (2) the funds provided by Fleming were never repaid and it was never intended that they should be; (3) Fleming's ability or inability to claim first-year and writing-down allowances under s 85 of the 1968 Act should be disregarded; no evidence had been heard on behalf of Fleming and, as it was contended by the taxpayer that it could claim the allowances because of Fleming's inability to do so, the taxpayer had to prove affirmatively that Fleming could not have

obtained the allowances; the taxpayer had not discharged that onus of proof; (4) in the case of the Maidenhead and Kennington development, the plant and machinery in question belonged to the party having the highest estate in the land in question, that is to the freeholder; (5) in the context under consideration, the plant and machinery could not belong to several people having different estates in the land to which the plant and machinery was affixed; (6) accordingly, the plant and machinery comprised in both developments had not at any time during the accounting period to 31 December 1975 belonged to the taxpayer; (7) accordingly, the taxpayer was not entitled to first-year and writing-down allowances, in the case of the Maidenhead development, because it had not incurred expenditure on plant and machinery and, even if it had incurred such expenditure, the plant and machinery never belonged to it as a consequence; (8) accordingly, the taxpayer was not entitled to first-year and writing-down allowances, in the case of the Kennington development, because the plant and machinery had never belonged to the taxpayer within the meaning to be ascribed to the word 'belong' in the particular context under consideration.

8. The following authorities were cited before the commissioners: *A-G v Oxford, Worcester and Wolverhampton Rly Co* (1862) 7 H & N 840, 158 ER 709; *affd* (1866) LR 1 HL 1; *Dowson and Jenkins's Contract, Re* [1904] 2 Ch 219, CA; *Heritable Reversionary Co Ltd v Millar (M'Kay's Trustee)* [1892] AC 598; *Lowe (Inspector of Taxes) v J W Ashmore Ltd* [1971] 1 All ER 1057, [1971] Ch 545; *Sargaison (Inspector of Taxes) v Roberts* [1969] 3 All ER 1072, [1969] 1 WLR 951; *Shell-Mex & BP Ltd v Clayton (Valuation Officer)* [1956] 3 All ER 185, [1956] 1 WLR 1198, HL; *Wiltshire County Valuation Committee v Marlborough and Ramsbury Rating Authority* [1948] 1 All ER 694, [1948] 2 KB 125, CA.

9. The commissioners who heard the appeal took time to consider their decision and gave it in writing on 18 December 1980 as follows:

> '(1) At a meeting held at 47 Parliament Street, London, S.W.1, [the taxpayer] appealed against assessments to Corporation Tax made on it for the years to 31 December [1975] and 31 December 1976. (2) The question for our decision was whether [the taxpayer] was entitled to claim under [ss] 41(1) and 46(1) of the Finance Act 1971 first year and writing down allowances in amounts equal to the whole of the expenditure on plant and machinery comprised in Phase 2 of a development at Maidenhead and in a development at Kennington Road. (3) Our decision is: (a) In the Maidenhead case that the alleged "reimbursements" by Fleming against architects' certificates counter signed by [the taxpayer] can be likened to the practice whereby an ordinary bank pays out on behalf of a customer with overdraft facilities, sums against the authority of a cheque. In short, no "reimbursement" took place and Sections 84 and 85 of the Capital Allowances Act 1968 need not be invoked. (b) In both the Maidenhead and the Kennington cases notwithstanding various leases, sub-leases, mortgages and so on, the plant "belonged" to [the taxpayer] in any commonsense view. (4) We conclude from 3(a) and 3(b) above that the requirements of Section 41(1)(*a*) and (*b*) and of Section 46(1) of the Finance Act 1971 have been satisfied and that [the taxpayer] is entitled to first year and writing down allowances in the amounts claimed. (5) Accordingly, we determine the assessments under Appeal in agreed figures as follows:
>
> *Year to 31 December 1976*

Reduce to:	£p.	£p.
Schedule A		224,473
Less Management expenses	120,947	
Charges	103,526	224,473
		NIL'

10. The Crown immediately after the determination of the appeal declared dissatisfaction with the decision as being erroneous in point of law and on 7 January 1981

required the commissioners to state a case for the opinion of the High Court pursuant to s 56 of the Taxes Management Act 1970. a

11. The question of law for the opinion of the court was whether, on the facts found by the commissioners, their decision was correct in law.

Robert Carnwath for the Crown.
Andrew Thornhill for the taxpayer.

b

Cur adv vult

28 March. The following judgment was delivered.

HARMAN J. This is an appeal by the Crown against a decision in favour of a taxpayer by the General Commissioners for Second East Brixton. The taxpayer, Costain Property c Investments Ltd, claimed capital allowances in respect of certain articles (principally lifts and central heating equipment) admitted to be plant and machinery for the purposes of such a claim. The larger amount of the expenditure, £450,000-odd (the precise figures being wholly unimportant), was incurred on lifts and central heating installed in a building development of offices, flats and shops at Maidenhead. The remainder, £50,900-odd, was incurred on similar items installed in an office block developed by and built for d the taxpayer in Kennington Road. At neither building site was the taxpayer the freeholder of the land developed. At both it became entitled when the development was completed to a lease or underlease out of which it granted further sub-terms. At neither, so far as I can determine from the case stated, did the taxpayer go into physical occupation of any part of the development.

The question which arises on both the Maidenhead and the Kennington developments e is whether the plant and machinery built into the buildings, and becoming (as was common ground before me) landlord's fixtures, can properly be said to 'belong' to the taxpayer. That question has to be answered Yes for the taxpayer to qualify under s 41(1) of the Finance Act 1971, which provides (omitting words unnecessary for present purposes):

> '... where—(*a*) a person carrying on a trade incurs capital expenditure on the f provision of machinery or plant for the purposes of the trade, and (*b*) in consequence of his incurring the expenditure, the machinery or plant belongs to him at some time during the chargeable period ... there shall be made to him ... an allowance ...'

The commissioners' decision on this point is not embellished with reasoning, elaborate g or simple. At para 9(3)(b) they simply state that 'in any commonsense view' the plant belonged to the taxpayer and that the varying interests in the land, of which the plant and machinery became part, of freeholder, head lessee and sublessee can be dismissed from consideration.

On the hearing before me Mr Carnwath appeared for the Crown and Mr Thornhill, as he had done below, for the taxpayer. I was taken by counsel for the Crown on an h extended tour, starting in 1878, of varying enactments showing the variations in parliamentary requirements for the obtaining of what are loosely called capital allowances. This learned disquisition, while fascinating, did not in the end enlighten my mind on the point I have to decide. I was reminded, correctly, by counsel for the taxpayer that English real property is never in the absolute ownership of any subject, and that all any subject can have is one of the two legal estates in land. This subtlety of learning, which is j sound and the source of much important thought in English law, I regret to say left me equally unenlightened.

As it seems to me, the question is one of the meaning of a fairly ordinary word in the English language. It was common to both counsel that the term 'belong' was not a word of art; certainly in my judgment it is not a term of the art of conveyancing. I was helpfully reminded by both counsel that the sections or clauses in the various relevant Acts of Parliament have to apply to leases of chattels as well as to leases (or subleases) of land. The various provisions deeming a lessee to be an owner, none of which applies to this case, are thus an imperfect guide to determining whether Parliament has contemplated that a piece of plant or machinery 'belongs' to a lessee of it, whether as the mere hirer of a chattel or as included in the demise to him of a long lease of a building. Such a concept as 'belonging' is, in my judgment, very difficult to justify as appropriate as a matter of English language if one thinks by way of example of the hire of a motor car or lorry (using them merely as examples of what are generally thought of as plant and machinery and ignoring special provisions as to such particular classes of chattels) for a week, a month or even a year. To my mind it would be untrue for me to answer 'Yes' to the question, 'Does that Rolls-Royce belong to you?' when I have merely hired it for the day. It remains untrue even if I have hired that automobile for a whole year, or even longer.

Counsel for the taxpayer submitted that 'belong' could mean, according to the *Shorter Oxford Dictionary*, 'the rightful possession of' whatever the property was. He went on to say that a leaseholder of land is entitled to the rightful possession of all that is part of that land, and thus that the taxpayer could say that the lift and central heating plant belonged to it because it was entitled to the rightful possession of the buildings in which they were installed. Difficult questions arise in English real property law on the concept of possession. Possession can be by receipt of the rents and profits of land, absent any immediate physical possession of the land. In my judgment the *Oxford English Dictionary* reference is to a right to immediate physical possession which might properly, in some cases, be described by saying that the object possessed did 'belong' to the possessor. But as I have already said I do not consider that the word 'belong' is normally satisfied by a right to possession if the possessor has no right of disposition of the thing possessed by sale, gift or destruction.

Both counsel agreed that there was no decision directly in point. Counsel for the Crown referred me to *Union Cold Storage Co Ltd v Simpson (Inspector of Taxes)* [1939] 2 All ER 94 at 102, [1939] 2 KB 440 at 455. There, Clauson LJ asserted that it was obvious that certain plant did not belong to the taxpayer, who held a 21-year term of premises including the plant. The distinction between an owner (to whom one would normally attribute the verb 'to belong') and a lessee was set out by Scott LJ in his judgment ([1939] 2 All ER 94 at 96, [1939] 2 KB 440 at 447–448). It is clear that the observation of Clauson LJ is only a dictum. The point now argued by counsel for the taxpayer was not taken in the *Union Cold Storage* case. He submitted that the assertion was either an oversight by Clauson LJ based on an assumption not tested by argument or was wrong.

I was also reminded of the decision of Megarry J in *Sargaison (Inspector of Taxes) v Roberts* [1969] 3 All ER 1072, [1969] 1 WLR 951. The decision is illuminating and the exposition of thinking helpful, but the case does not closely compare with the language I have to construe in this case. It points slightly against too much regard being paid to the niceties of real property law or to the accurate use of language by parliamentary draftsmen. Various other cases on claims to capital allowances in differing circumstances were cited. Two of them, *Lupton (Inspector of Taxes) v Cadogan Gardens Developments Ltd* [1971] 3 All ER 460 and *Macsaga Investment Co Ltd v Lupton (Inspector of Taxes)* [1967] 2 All ER 930, [1967] Ch 1016, concerned claims to capital allowances in respect of plant installed in buildings. In neither of them was the point now before me raised for decision.

Counsel for the taxpayer demonstrated in argument that very surprising consequences arise if a tenant of a building (a fortiori but not in law relevantly different where the tenancy is for a term of 99 years) who for his own business purposes installs during the term expensive plant which becomes part of the realty and a landlord's fixture cannot claim capital allowances. From the mere perusal of the various statutes no policy was discernible by me. At the end of the argument I asked counsel for the Crown, who argued the case most helpfully and ably, what was the policy lying behind the requirement of belonging. After taking instructions he frankly admitted that he could not explain any policy and that the anomalies seemed to exist. However, as he might have said, this claim seems never to have been raised before, so that in real life tenants do *a* not seem to have suffered by the anomaly; and, as he did say, in the three cases where the point has arisen the freeholder has paid for the plant.

In the end I return to the language. Pace the General Commissioners' assertion as to common sense, it seems to me plain and obvious as a matter of language that property of which a taxpayer has no right of disposition does not belong to him. It follows that plant and machinery which becomes part of the realty and a landlord's fixture does not belong *b* to a tenant of the building. I am comforted to find that what seems obvious to me also seemed obvious to Clauson LJ, and I consider that the taxpayer's point was not argued in the *Union Cold Storage* case because its ingenuity outruns its strength. I say nothing about plant or machinery installed by a tenant in such a way that it remains a tenant's fixture. A machine tool which is fixed down for the better use of it as a machine tool, and not as an improvement of the premises, which machine tool could be removed by the tenant at *c* the expiry of his term and then disposed of by him, may well be said to 'belong' to that tenant. The point does not arise before me and I make no decision on it.

That suffices to dispose of the taxpayer's claim in both appeals. In my judgment the Crown succeeds in respect of both claims and no capital allowances can be claimed by the taxpayer.

However, a quite separate and different point arose in respect of the Maidenhead *d* development. It was alleged that by reason of the financing arrangements made by the taxpayer it did not 'incur' the expenditure, which was 'met directly or indirectly . . . by [a] person other than' the taxpayer within s 84(1) of the Capital Allowances Act 1968. The contention of the Crown was that the taxpayer did not incur the expenditure on the Maidenhead development because Robert Fleming & Co Ltd, well-known merchant bankers, had agreed to finance the project. On this I found the facts stated by the case less *e* than wholly satisfactory. By para 4(c) the commissioners found proved before them a mortgage (exhibit C) dated 14 December 1973, to which it was recited the taxpayer, Fleming, Maidenhead corporation as freeholders and the building firm of Richard Costain Ltd were parties. On referring to exhibit C it was clear that the exhibit had never been stamped, not even with a 50p deed stamp. On my raising this objection to the admissibility in evidence of the document counsel for the taxpayer took careful *f* instructions. It emerged that the so-called mortgage had never been executed by all parties or delivered. It was said that Fleming and the taxpayer had been content so to proceed, conducting their affairs as if the mortgage existed but without any binding document or security. This may well have been because the paying of substantial sums of stamp duty had no attraction for either party. In the circumstances, no effective mortgage can ever have been created. I was invited by both parties to proceed, and did so *g* proceed, on the basis that, in the absence of any mortgage, the parties none the less conducted themselves on the footing that some such arrangement was to be treated as in force between them.

Further in the case stated, at para 5(7), the commissioners found (I quote the second paragraph):

> 'The expenditure incurred on the plant and machinery [at Maidenhead] would *h* have been included on Architect's Certificates presented to [the taxpayer] which were passed to Fleming. Fleming would pay to Costain Construction Limited the amounts shown on the certificates and the payment would increase the total indebtedness of [the taxpayer] to Fleming.'

These statements about what 'would' have happened are thoroughly unsatisfactory in *j* circumstances where the commissioners are the only fact-finding body and evidence is called before them which is not, quite rightly, put in before the court and it is to the case stated alone that any reference can be made.

Counsel for the taxpayer was anxious that no effective point should be taken against him by reason of deficiencies in the case stated. He asserted, and I have no doubt accurately, that elaborate evidence was in fact given to the General Commissioners, although no findings are made by them on the basis of it, as to the exact methods of financing and the exact ways of payment. Counsel for the Crown was reluctant, quite naturally, to have any remission of this matter to the commissioners for the better stating of the case on the basis of evidence already given to them, and we proceeded on the basis that those statements of what would have happened were to be treated as statements of what had happened. They remain jejune in the extreme and surprising in their form, but none the less I must do my best on that factual basis.

The commissioners' conclusion on this point is at para 9(3)(a), where they state:

> '... the alleged "reimbursements" by Fleming against architects' certificates counter signed by [the taxpayer] can be likened to the practice whereby an ordinary bank pays out on behalf of a customer with overdraft facilities, sums against the authority of a cheque.'

I confess to finding the analogy between an architect's certificate and a cheque far-fetched; none the less, one sees the drift of what they are saying, and it may be that the precise machinery whereby Fleming advanced moneys on account of the taxpayer was not precisely determinative.

The argument of counsel for the taxpayer before me was effectively that because the taxpayer agreed to provide a substantial asset as valuable consideration to Fleming it could not be said as a matter of English language that Fleming had 'met directly or indirectly' the expenditure on the development. He argued that the payments by Fleming of the taxpayer's liabilities on the architect's certificates were no more than loans by Fleming. The making of loans to A cannot be said to be the meeting of A's liabilities; the loans merely provide the wherewithal for A to meet his liabilities. The satisfaction of these loans by the transfer of an asset does not change the nature of the loans at the time they were made, and is merely a way of paying off debts. The transfer of the asset does not mean that the transferee has 'met' the expenditure which was the consideration for the agreed transfer.

It is clear on the facts that the taxpayer undoubtedly bore the risk of the cost of the development had there been an overrun in the cost, and, Heaven knows, the courts have seen examples enough of overruns in English building contracts in the last 20 years. The excess of cost over the limit of the moneys which Fleming was liable to provide was entirely to the taxpayer's account. Again, that money might well have been provided on a temporary basis by Fleming, but that money, according to the Fleming agreement, would have had to be repaid by the taxpayer to Fleming in addition to the procurement of the grant of the headlease by Maidenhead corporation on the direction of the taxpayer to Fleming.

Further, the taxpayer undoubtedly bore the risk that if the development were delayed in completion, another matter which was certainly a real risk in England at the time this development took place, it would have to bear the whole cost itself by repaying all the advances to Fleming and would not be able to satisfy the advances by procuring the grant of the headlease to Fleming.

It seems to me that the truth of this matter was that, although the financing arrangements were somewhat odd, there was a genuine incurring of the expenditure by the taxpayer, who was at risk of having to repay the loans, the advances, made from time to time by Fleming by payment of the expenses, and that, had any event occurred which prevented the taxpayer from procuring the grant to Fleming, eventually, of the headlease, plainly and beyond any question the taxpayer would have been liable to repay Fleming all the moneys advanced. In those circumstances it seems to me impossible to say that the moneys advanced by Fleming were in any genuine sense of the words being paid for the work done. Those payments, at the time they were made, were undoubtedly, in my judgment, loans. The loan was discharged by the procuring of the grant of the headlease. In no proper sense did Fleming 'meet' the taxpayer's expenditures. In my judgment the taxpayer's argument is right.

That seems to me to accord with the policy, so far as I can perceive it, of s 84. The section's reference to meeting the expenditure of another is one which is plainly primarily directed to cases of government grants or local authority contributions and such matters. It includes the reference to expenditure being met 'by any person other than' the taxpayer, but that is a tailpiece thrown in to catch any other such meeting of expenditure. The concept as it seems to me of that whole section is of the provision of money to meet expenditure by way of, in effect, bounty. 'Bounty' may be an inappropriate way to describe the grants made by a government department, remembering that the government have no money save what they take from taxpayers and then give back to other taxpayers. None the less, it seems to me that a transaction whereby a financier lends money to meet a taxpayer's bills and as a result a valuable asset is transferred from the taxpayer to the financier is not appropriately described as the financier 'meeting' the expenditure of the taxpayer. He has bought an asset, paid for an asset, or whatever other phrase of the English language one may care to use, but he has not, in my judgment, met the expenditure of the taxpayer in any proper use of that term in the context in which it appears.

In my judgment, had the matter turned on the question of s 84 of the Capital Allowances Act 1968 the taxpayer would on that head have succeeded. However, my decision on the 'belonging' point determines the whole matter against it, and I therefore allow the appeal.

Appeal allowed.

Solicitors: *Solicitor of Inland Revenue*; *R M Freeman* (for the taxpayer).

Edwina Epstein Barrister.

a
The St Anna

QUEEN'S BENCH DIVISION (ADMIRALTY COURT)
SHEEN J
24 FEBRUARY, 1 MARCH 1983

Admiralty – Jurisdiction – Action in rem – Claim arising out of agreement relating to carriage of
b *goods – Claim by charterers to enforce arbitration award under arbitration agreement in charterparty – Whether 'claim arising out of [an] agreement relating to the carriage of goods in a ship' – Whether claim arising out of award itself – Whether Admiralty court having jurisdiction to entertain claim – Supreme Court Act 1981, s 20(2)(h).*

A voyage charter, made between the plaintiffs as charterers and the defendants as owners
c of the chartered ship, contained an agreement to submit disputes arising out of the charter to arbitration. A dispute arose out of the charter in regard to a claim by the plaintiffs for alleged short delivery of cargo, and pursuant to the charter the dispute was referred to arbitration. Had the claim not been submitted to arbitration the plaintiffs could have brought an action in rem against the ship, which was subsequently sold under an order of the court in an action in rem brought by the mortgagees of the ship. The
d proceeds of sale were paid into court. The arbitrators made an award in the plaintiffs' favour but the defendants failed to satisfy the award. The plaintiffs were given leave to enforce the award and issued a writ in rem out of the Admiralty Registry seeking to enforce the award against the proceeds of sale in court. The defendants failed to serve a defence to the plaintiffs' action and the plaintiffs moved for judgment in default of defence. The question arose whether the plaintiffs' action to enforce the award was a
e 'claim arising out of [an] agreement relating to the carriage of goods in a ship', within s 20(2)(*h*)[a] of the Supreme Court Act 1981, so that the Admiralty Court had jurisdiction under s 20(1)(*a*) to entertain the action, or whether the claim arose out of the award itself, in which case it was not an Admiralty matter.

f **Held** – Since in an action to enforce an arbitration award both the arbitration agreement and the award were essential elements in the plaintiff's cause of action, both of which had to be proved, it followed that an action to enforce an arbitration award made under an arbitration agreement in a charterparty was an action which arose out of the charterparty, and not merely out of the award. Accordingly, the plaintiffs' claim to enforce the award against the proceeds of sale was a 'claim arising out of [an] agreement
g relating to the carriage of goods in a ship' within s 20(2)(*h*) of the 1981 Act, and therefore the Admiralty Court had jurisdiction to entertain the claim. The plaintiffs were therefore entitled to judgment on the motion (see p 695 *d* and p 696 *e* to *g*, post).

Bremer Oeltransport GmbH v Drewry [1933] All ER Rep 851 followed.

Dicta of Merriman P and of Scott LJ in *The Beldis* [1935] All ER Rep at 764, 774 not followed.

h

Notes

For the jurisdiction of the Admiralty court in claims relating to a contract of carriage, see 1 Halsbury's Laws (4th edn) para 321, and for cases on the subject, see 1(1) Digest (Reissue) 272–276, *1610–1629*.

j For the enforcement of an arbitration award by action, see 2 Halsbury's Laws (4th edn) para 632, and for cases on the subject, see 3 Digest (Reissue) 311–313, *2106–2121*.

For the Supreme Court Act 1981, s 20, see 51 Halsbury's Statutes (3rd edn) 612.

---

a Section 20, so far as material, is set out at p 694 *c d*, post

Cases referred to in judgment

Beldis, The [1936] P 51, [1935] All ER Rep 760, CA.

Bremer Oeltransport GmbH v Drewry [1933] 1 KB 753, [1933] All ER Rep 851, CA.

Jade, The, The Escherscheim, mv Erkowit (owners) v Ship Jade (owners), mv Erkowit (cargo owners) v Ship Eschersheim (owners) [1976] 1 All ER 920, [1976] 1 WLR 430, HL; *affg* [1976] 1 All ER 441, [1976] 1 WLR 339, CA; *affg* [1974] 3 All ER 307, [1975] 1 WLR 83.

Northcote v Heinrich Bjorn (owners), The Heinrich Bjorn (1885) 10 PD 44, CA; *affd* (1886) 11 App Cas 270, HL.

Termarea SRL v Rederiaktiebolaget Sally [1979] 2 All ER 989, [1979] 1 WLR 1320.

Cases also cited

Stella Nora, The [1981] Com LR 200.

Tasabi, The [1982] 1 Lloyd's Rep 397.

Motion for judgment

The plaintiffs, Upechemical Anstalt of Vaduz, the charterers of the ship St Anna, brought an admiralty action in rem against the defendants, as the owners of the proceeds of sale of the St Anna, seeking to enforce against the proceeds an arbitration award made in the plaintiffs' favour in respect of a dispute between the parties which arose out of the charterparty and which had been referred to arbitration pursuant to an arbitration agreement in the charterparty. In their action the plaintiffs claimed (1) $105,923·87 with interest thereon at 8% from 1 July 1977 to 16 August 1979, alternatively damages, (2) the plaintiffs' costs in the arbitration, alternatively damages, (3) interest on the above sums from 16 August 1979, and (4) the costs of the action. The defendants failed to serve a defence to the action and the plaintiffs moved for judgment in default of defence. On the motion the question arose whether the Admiralty Court had jurisdiction under s 20(1) of the Supreme Court Act 1981 to entertain the plaintiffs' action to enforce the award and therefore whether the court could grant the motion for judgment in default. The facts are set out in the judgment.

Timothy Charlton for the plaintiffs.
The defendants did not appear.

Cur adv vult

1 March. The following judgment was delivered.

SHEEN J. This is a motion for judgment in default of service of a defence. The plaintiffs' claim arises in this way. By a tanker voyage charterparty made in London on 2 June 1977, in a modified Exxonvoy 1969 form, the plaintiffs hired the Greek tanker St Anna (then known as Agnh) from her owners, who were Croydon Corp of Panama, for the carriage of a quantity of fuel oil from one port in northern Europe to one or two ports in Italy.

That charterparty contained the following relevant terms:

> '20 (b) The carriage of cargo under this Charter Party and under all Bills of lading issued for the cargo shall be subject to the statutory provisions and other terms set forth or specified in sub-paragraphs (i) through (vii) of this clause ... (i) CLAUSE PARAMOUNT [which incorporated the Hague Rules, and which I need not set out in full]...
>
> 24 ARBITRATION. Any and all differences and disputes of whatsoever nature arising out of this Charter shall be put to arbitration in the City of New York or in the City of London whichever place is specified in Part I of this charter pursuant to the laws relating to arbitration there in force, before a board of three persons, consisting of one arbitrator to be appointed by the Owner, one by the Charterer, and one by the

> two so chosen. The decision of any two of the three on any point or points shall be
> *a* final.'

Part I specified the place of arbitration to be London.

A dispute arose between the plaintiffs and the defendants in respect of a cargo of fuel oil which the plaintiffs alleged was short-delivered at the discharge port in Sicily. The plaintiffs' claim arising out of the alleged short delivery was a claim which, in the absence of the submission to arbitration, could have been brought by an action in rem in this *b* court provided that the writ was issued within one year of completion of discharge.

On 20 June 1978 solicitors acting on behalf of the plaintiffs appointed Mr R W Reed as arbitrator on behalf of the shipowners as claimants. In due course the defendants appointed Mr Donald Davies as their arbitrator. Those arbitrators did not appoint a third arbitrator. Their failure to do so did not deprive them of jurisdiction (see *Termarea SRL v Rederiaktiebolaget Sally* [1979] 2 All ER 989, [1979] 1 WLR 1320).

c On 16 August 1979 the arbitrators published their final award by which they adjudged that the owners of St Anna, the defendants in this action, forthwith pay to the plaintiffs the sum of $US105,923·87 together with interest at the rate of 8% per annum as from 1 July 1977 to the date of the award. The arbitrators further awarded and adjudged that the shipowners do bear and pay their own and the charterers' costs in the reference and that the owners do bear and pay the cost of the award, which amounted to £580. The *d* defendants have not paid the sums due under that award.

Thus the facts with which I am concerned can be summarised in this way. (1) There was a contract (the charterparty) between the plaintiffs and the defendants for the carriage of oil in the ship St Anna. (2) That charterparty contained an agreement to submit disputes to arbitration. (3) A dispute arose out of the charter. (4) Arbitrators were appointed in accordance with the agreement. Those arbitrators made an award in the *e* plaintiffs' favour. (5) There award has not been satisfied. Indeed, there has been no payment made in respect of it.

For the sake of completeness I should say that on 6 October 1981 Parker J gave leave to enforce the arbitration award dated 16 August 1979 pursuant to s 26 of the Arbitration Act 1950 in the same manner as a judgment or order to the same effect. The award has not been registered as a judgment.

f In recent years many actions in rem have been brought against the ship St Anna. In 1979 mortgagees of St Anna issued a writ in rem, claiming arrears of principal and interest due under the mortgage. St Anna was arrested in Ellesmere Port on 20 July 1979. On 13 August 1979 the vacation judge, Neill J, ordered that St Anna be appraised and sold by the Admiralty Marshal pendente lite. Pursuant to that order St Anna was sold on 16 December 1979.

g The proceeds of sale were brought into court. There is sufficient money in court to satisfy all the claims of which the court has knowledge.

On 24 February 1982 the plaintiffs issued a writ in rem out of the Admiralty Registry against the proceeds of sale of the ship St Anna. The statement of claim indorsed on the writ recites the relevant terms of the charterparty and alleges, correctly in my judgment, that it was an implied term of the arbitration agreement contained in the charterparty *h* that each party would pay to the other any sum found due by the arbitrators appointed in accordance with that agreement. It is further alleged that a dispute arose under the charterparty and that the parties appointed their arbitrators, who found that certain sums were due from the owners of St Anna to the plaintiffs.

All the relevant facts have been proved to my satisfaction. There is no defence to the claim. Why, then, have I no jurisdiction to give judgment for the plaintiffs for the sums *j* due to them, so that they can be paid out of the proceeds of sale of St Anna?

The answer to that question given by the editors of *Russell on Arbitration* (20th edn, 1982) p 350 is:

> 'An action to enforce an award cannot be brought as an action *in rem*, even where the dispute giving rise to the award is such that if it had not been submitted to arbitration the claimant could have proceeded *in rem*.'

The authority cited for that proposition is *The Beldis* [1936] P 51, [1935] All ER Rep 760. Mustill and Boyd *Commercial Arbitration* (1982) expresses the same view, but in words which are challenged by counsel for the plaintiffs. They say (at p 369):

> 'An action on an award made under an arbitration clause in a charterparty or bill of lading is not a "claim arising out of any agreement relating to the carriage of goods in a ship or to the use or hire of a ship", and cannot be brought as an Admiralty action in rem.'

In both books it is said that it may be possible to proceed on the original cause of action in rem and to ignore the unsatisfied award. But that remedy is lost with the expiration of the time limit within which a claim must be brought.

The Admiralty jurisdiction of the High Court is laid down in s 20 of the Supreme Court Act 1981, which provides as follows:

> '(1) The Admiralty jurisdiction of the High Court shall be as follows, that is to say—(*a*) jurisdiction to hear and determine any of the questions and claims mentioned in subsection (2) . . .
>
> (2) The questions and claims referred to in subsection (1)(*a*) are . . . (*h*) any claim arising out of any agreement relating to the carriage of goods in a ship or to the use or hire of a ship . . .'

Counsel for the plaintiffs contends that this action is a claim arising out of an agreement relating to the carriage of goods in a ship. He drew my attention to a number of dicta in *The Jade, The Eschersheim* [1976] 1 All ER 920, [1976] 1 WLR 430, in which judges have expressed their views on the construction of s 1 of the Administration of Justice Act 1956, which then prescribed the Admiralty jurisdiction of the High Court. Brandon J said ([1974] 3 All ER 307 at 318, [1975] 1 WLR 83 at 94):

> '. . . I think that all the paragraphs of s 1(1) of the 1956 Act, including para (*h*), should be construed in the usual way, that is to say by giving the words used their ordinary and natural meaning in the context in which they appear.'

In the Court of Appeal Cairns LJ said ([1976] 1 All ER 441 at 448, [1976] 1 WLR 339 at 348):

> 'In my opinion there is no good reason for excluding from the expression "an agreement for the use or hire of a ship" any agreement which an ordinary businessman would regard as being within it.'

In the House of Lords Lord Diplock said ([1976] 1 All ER 920 at 926, [1976] 1 WLR 430 at 438): 'I see no reason in that context for not giving to them their ordinary wide meaning.' If, in respect of the claim which is the subject matter of this action, one asks the question, 'Does that claim arise out of the agreement relating to the carriage of oil in St Anna?', the answer must be, 'Yes.'

Does the fact that this action is based on the award made by the arbitrators have the effect that it can no longer be said that the claim arises out of an agreement for the carriage of oil in St Anna? To answer that question it is necessary to examine the nature of an action based on an arbitration award. In *Bremer Oeltransport GmbH v Drewry* [1933] 1 KB 753, [1933] All ER Rep 851 a charterparty had been made in London which provided that any dispute arising during the execution of the charterparty should be settled by arbitration in Hamburg. Disputes arose between the parties which were submitted to arbitration in Hamburg. An award was made against the defendant. The plaintiffs issued a writ against the defendant for the amount due under the award, and sought leave to serve it on the defendant in France. The question which arose for decision was whether the action was for the enforcement of a contract made within the jurisdiction, namely the submission to arbitration contained in the charterparty. The Court of Appeal considered the authorities on the question whether in an action on an award the action is founded on the award (which was made in Hamburg) or on the

agreement to submit the differences from which the award results. Slesser LJ said ([1933]
a 1 KB 753 at 764–765, [1933] All ER Rep 851 at 857):

> 'It would appear, therefore, that the greater weight of authority is in favour of the view that in an action on the award the action is really founded on the agreement to submit the difference of which the award is the result ... it is sufficient for the purpose of the plaintiffs here to show that, at any rate, they are entitled to say that on their claim they are suing on the charterparty made in London and more
> b particularly on the submission to arbitration therein contained. The few cases which appear to support the view that an action may be brought upon the award in my view do not exclude in any event an action brought upon the agreement to refer differences and for this purpose, in my view, the submissions are here sufficiently stated to be in the charterparty of November 19, 1929. Without, therefore, finally determining whether an action may or may not be brought on an implied contract
> c in the award itself, I am clearly of opinion that it may be brought upon an agreement containing a term to refer disputes, and that the present claim is properly pleaded as arising from such an agreement. It is, therefore, an action for the enforcement of a contract made within the jurisdiction.'

That decision of the Court of Appeal is clear authority for the proposition that an
d action based on an award is an action for the enforcement of the contract which contains the submission to arbitration. In the instant case that is the charterparty. There can be no doubt that an action for the enforcement of a voyage charter is a claim within the Admiralty jurisdiction of this court.

If that decision of the Court of Appeal were the only relevant authority there would be no doubt that this action is within the Admiralty jurisdiction and has been properly
e brought against the proceeds of sale of St Anna. But the later decision of the Court of Appeal in *The Beldis* [1936] P 51, [1935] All ER Rep 760, in so far as it is relevant to the instant case, does not seem to be consistent with the decision in *Bremer Oeltransport GmbH v Drewry* which was not cited in argument. Brandon J drew attention to this inconsistency in *The Eschersheim* [1974] 3 All ER 307 at 318, [1975] 1 WLR 83 at 94.

In *The Beldis* an action in rem had been brought in a county court against the
f defendants, who were the owners of the Norwegian ship Beldis for money payable by the defendants to the plaintiffs under an arbitrator's award in respect of overpayment of freight under a charterparty relating to another of the defendants' ships, namely the Belfri. The defendants failed to appear and judgment was entered against them by default. Before 1956 in this country an action in rem could not be brought against a 'sister ship' of the particular ship in respect of which the cause of action arose. The
g appellants were mortgagees of the Beldis, who intervened in the action. By agreement an issue was submitted to the county court judge whether the plaintiffs' action in rem against the Beldis was maintainable in view of the fact that the plaintiffs' claim in the action arose out of a charterparty of the Belfri. The county court judge decided in favour of the plaintiffs, relying on a dictum of the Court of Appeal in regard to procedure in rem in *The Heinrich Bjorn* (1885) 10 PD 44 at 54 that 'the arrest need not be of the ship in
h question, but may be of any property of the defendant in the realm'. The Court of Appeal held that the dictum in *The Heinrich Bjorn* was obiter and was erroneous (see [1936] P 51 at 65–66, 84, [1935] ER Rep 760 at 765–766, 775). The court held that the procedure in rem either in the Admiralty Court or in the county court does not permit the arrest of a ship or other property of a defendant unconnected with the cause of action. On that ground alone the appeal would have been allowed. During the course of counsels'
j submissions Merriman P raised the question whether there was any jurisdiction to deal with the matter at all, suggesting that the issue arose under an arbitration (see [1936] P 51 at 56). It is quite clear from the report that neither counsel was ready to deal with this point and, as I have said, the decision of the Court of Appeal in *Bremer Oeltransport GmbH v Drewry* was not referred to. Merriman P in the course of his judgment said ([1936] P 51 at 61–62, [1935] All ER Rep 760 at 764):

> 'There was in fact no evidence before the county court judge as to the nature of the dispute arising under the charterparty of the *Belfri*, but the arbitrator's award a has been put in before us, and I am prepared to assume that both the claim on which he gave his award in favour of the plaintiffs, and the counterclaim which he dismissed, arose in respect of matters relating to the use or hire of the *Belfri* under the charterparty . . . But in my opinion the claim in this action was not based upon that foundation at all. It was an action upon the award. The award does not in fact show upon its face what was the nature of the claim made by the plaintiffs; nor is b there any reason why it should do so, though incidentally it happens to show the nature of the counterclaim which was dismissed. The particulars of the claim contain no reference to the nature of the dispute, or disputes, arising under the charterparty . . . Quite plainly the cause of action is founded, in the summons in this case, upon the award itself, and has no relation to the original dispute which gave rise to the arbitration. That being so, I should not be prepared to hold, even if c the matter were free from authority, that a claim upon an award held under the arbitration clause in a charterparty is a claim arising out of any agreement made in relation to the use or hire of a ship. I think that it is a common law claim upon an award and nothing else.'

Scott LJ put it differently. He said ([1936] P 51 at 82–83, [1935] All ER Rep 760 at d 774):

> 'In my view it would be entirely wrong to hold that an action on an award arising indirectly out of such a maritime contract was included by the words of the above sections.'

(He was referring to sections of the Admiralty Courts Acts 1840 and 1861.)

Scott LJ acknowledged that the action on the award arose indirectly out of the e charterparty. In a discussion about the essential elements of an action on an award Mustill and Boyd *Commercial Arbitration* (1982) p 368 says:

> 'We submit that the better view is that the plaintiff must plead and prove both the arbitration agreement and the award: both are essential elements in his cause of action.' f

If that statement is accurate, as I think it is, then it seems to me that this action arises out of the charterparty. One ground of the decision of the Court of Appeal in *The Beldis* is inconsistent with the decision of the Court of Appeal in *Bremer Oeltransport GmbH v Drewry*. This leaves me free to decide which authority I should follow. As the decision in the latter case was not brought to the attention of the Court of Appeal during argument in *The Beldis*, and as I find myself convinced by the reasoning in the latter case, g I have no hesitation in following it. I therefore hold that this claim is within the Admiralty jurisdiction of this court and I give judgment for the plaintiffs on their claim.

I cannot pretend that it does not give me pleasure to be able to decide this point as I have done, because the result enables this court to do justice in a way which would be denied to it if creditors could not bring proceedings in rem merely because they faithfully honoured their agreement to submit to arbitration a dispute which is clearly within the h Admiralty jurisdiction. I have only heard argument from one side, but that argument was fully and fairly presented by counsel for the plaintiffs, to whom I am indebted.

Judgment for the plaintiffs.

Solicitors: *Clyde & Co*, Guildford (for the plaintiffs).

N P Metcalfe Esq Barrister.

whether that period is the whole or part of the period mentioned in subsection (1) of this section . . .'

In *Jefford v Gee* the court laid down two guidelines as to interest to be awarded on damages for non-economic loss. The first was: that the period for which interest should be awarded was one beginning on the date of service of the writ and ending on the date of judgment. The second was: that the rate of interest should be the same as that which is payable on money paid into court which is placed on short-term investment account, ie the short-term investment account rate.

The guideline as to the date from which interest should be awarded has been followed ever since. It has not been questioned in the instant appeal. There are several considerations that justify the selection of this date rather than the date of the accident in the general run of personal injury cases. Since this guideline has not been attacked and was adopted sub silentio by this House in *Pickett v British Rail Engineering Ltd* [1979] 1 All ER 774, [1980] AC 136, to which I shall be referring, I can state those considerations briefly.

The starting point for any consideration of the inclusion of a sum for interest in an award of damages is the oft-cited statement of Lord Herschell LC in *London, Chatham and Dover Rly Co v South Eastern Rly Co* [1893] AC 429 at 437 expressing his regret that under the Civil Procedure Act 1833 interest could not be included in the judgment in an action claiming an unliquidated amount for what, in that case, was economic loss:

> 'I confess that I have considered this part of the case with every inclination to come to a conclusion in favour of the appellants, to the extent at all events, if it were possible, of giving them interest from the date of the action; and for this reason, that I think that when money is owing from one party to another and that other is driven to have recourse to legal proceedings in order to recover the amount due to him, the party who is wrongfully withholding the money from the other ought not in justice to benefit by having that money in his possession and enjoying the use of it, when the money ought to be in the possession of the other party who is entitled to its use. Therefore, if I could see my way to do so, I should certainly be disposed to give the appellants, or anybody in a similar position, interest upon the amount withheld from the time of action brought at all events.'

Non-economic loss in personal injury cases is not sustained co instanto when the accident takes place. Lord Denning MR said in *Jefford v Gee* [1970] 1 All ER 1202 at 1209, [1970] 2 QB 130 at 147 it is 'spread indefinitely into the future'. The loss is not capable of being quantified then and, when injuries are serious and stabilisation of medical condition slow, some considerable time may have to elapse before it is possible to make an informed estimate of the amount that ought to be awarded. Furthermore, a person can hardly be said to be 'wrongfully withholding' a sum of money owing to another at a time when the amount, if any, that will ultimately be found to have been owing remains unknown and no demand has yet been made for it. In *Jefford v Gee* Lord Denning MR, giving the judgment of the court, did not exclude the possibility that in some cases the appropriate starting point from which interest should run might be the date of the letter before action. But this would be only in the simplest type of case where liability was not seriously in doubt and the medical condition of the plaintiff had by then become stabilised. 'Speaking generally,' said Lord Denning, 'we think that interest on this item (pain and suffering and loss of amenities) should run from the date of service of the writ to the date of trial.' He added the important practical consideration: 'This should stimulate the plaintiff's advisers to issue and serve the writ without delay which is much to be desired.' In *Birkett v Hayes* the Court of Appeal took the occasion to suggest that, where the plaintiff was guilty of unreasonable delay in bringing the action to trial, it would not be inappropriate to make a corresponding reduction in the period for which interest was given.

The second guideline laid down in *Jefford v Gee* relating to rate of interest is that with which your Lordships are particularly concerned. It has had a more chequered history. In *Cookson v Knowles* [1977] 2 All ER 820 at 823, [1977] QB 913 at 921, which was a fatal accident case involving only economic loss, Lord Denning MR giving the judgment of the court made use of the occasion to alter that guideline to take account of the fact that owing to inflation awards of damages for pain and suffering and loss of amenities of life were of a higher nominal sum in the money of the day at the time of trial than the nominal sum that would have been awarded had the trial taken place at the date of service of the writ. He said:

> 'The plaintiff thus stands to gain by the delay in bringing the case to trial. He ought not to gain still more by having interest from the date of service of the writ. We would alter the guideline, therefore, by suggesting that no interest should be awarded on the lump sum awarded at the trial for pain and suffering and loss of amenities.'

Cookson v Knowles went to the House of Lords on the question whether in awarding damages for future economic loss allowance ought to be made for future inflation. The House upheld the decision of the Court of Appeal that no such allowance should be made (see [1978] 2 All ER 604, [1979] AC 556). The House had no occasion to deal with interest on non-economic loss; and it did not do so. The only relevance of the case to the appeal with which your Lordships are now concerned is that, as appears from the speeches in this House, the expert evidence in *Cookson v Knowles* had shown that interest rates obtainable by prudent investment, even in what was a time of high inflation between December 1973 and July 1976, were, very broadly speaking, sufficient to offset the fall in the real value of money due to inflation.

The guideline recommending that no interest be awarded on damages for non-economic loss prevailed during the interval between the date of the judgment of the Court of Appeal in *Cookson v Knowles*, in July 1977, and the decision of this House in November 1978 in *Pickett v British Rail Engineering Ltd*. Although most of the argument and their Lordships' speeches in that case were directed to the question whether damages could be recovered for economic loss during the 'lost years', the House also held that interest *should* be awarded on damages for non-economic loss. Nothing, however, was said about the rate at which interest should be allowed, since this had apparently been the subject of an agreement between counsel.

Lord Wilberforce, Lord Edmund-Davies and Lord Scarman pointed out the fallacy underlying the new 'no interest' guideline propounded by Lord Denning MR in *Cookson v Knowles*. As Lord Wilberforce succinctly put it ([1979] 1 All ER 774 at 782, [1980] AC 136 at 151):

> 'Increase for inflation is designed to preserve the "real" value of money, interest to compensate for being kept out of that "real" value. The one has no relation to the other. If the damages remained, nominally, the same, because there was no inflation, interest would normally be given. The same should follow if the damages remain in real terms the same.'

Lord Scarman, in addition to referring to the fallacy, also relied on the construction of the 1934 Act which makes mandatory the award of interest on damages, or such part of the damages as the court considers appropriate, 'unless the court is satisfied that there are special reasons why no interest should be given in respect of those damages'. He pointed out that inflation is an economic and financial condition of general application. Its impact on any particular plaintiff has been neither more nor less than on everybody else; there is nothing special about it.

My Lords, just as the lump sum of money assessed as being the appropriate compensation for past and future pain and suffering and loss of amenities cannot be other than a conventional figure, since such non-economic loss is not susceptible of measurement in money, so too an award of simple 'interest' on that lump sum as the method of assessing compensation for the temporary loss of the use of it between the date of service of writ and the date of judgment is wholly conventional; but it is the

method that the court is commanded by the statute to adopt. To what use the particular
a plaintiff would have actually put that capital sum during the period for which 'interest'
is to be given is utterly irrelevant. It is most unlikely that if he had received it he would
have invested and kept it in income earning securities throughout that period. Yet that
is the assumption that judges are called on to make; and its artificiality is enhanced by
the fact that, whereas the market rate of interest, at any time, represents the return *after
deduction of tax* that lenders are able to obtain from borrowers for forgoing the use of
b money, interest on damages for personal injuries that is included in a judgment is
exempted from liability to income tax by s 19 of the Finance Act 1971. So one would
expect a lender to accept as compensation for forgoing the use of his money a rate of
interest lower than the market rate, if the interest that he received was free of tax.

My Lords, it has been recognised since medieval times that interest exacted for the
loan of a capital sum of money may comprise two elements: one, a reward for taking a
c risk of loss or reduction of capital; the other, a reward for forgoing the use of the capital
sum for the time being. The former, or risk element, was early recognised in canon law
and the law merchant as legitimate; the latter element was regarded as the sin of usury:
it was visited originally by ecclesiastical sanctions and was the subject of successive
statutory curbs, the history of which is to be found in *Holdsworth's History of the Law of
England*, vol 8 (2nd edn, 1937), pp 100–113.

d This distinction, though not the sanctions that once attached to it, still holds good
today. In times of stable currency the rate of interest obtainable on money invested in
government stocks includes very little risk element. In such times it is, accordingly, a
fair indication of the 'going rate' of the reward for temporarily forgoing the use of
money. Inflation, however, when it occurs, exposes all capital sums of money that are
invested temporarily in securities of any kind instead of being spent at once in tangibles
e to one form of risk, amounting to a certainty that on realising the security there will be
some reduction in the 'real' value of the money received for it, whatever other kind of
risk the security selected for investment may attract.

As was pointed out in *Cookson v Knowles*, that element of risk which is presented by
inflation is taken care of in a rough and ready way by higher rates of interest obtainable
as one of the consequences of it. It cannot be more than rough and ready because, as has
f since been explained in the expert evidence that was called in *Birkett v Hayes*, there are
other factors which have temporary effects on interest rates, notably government policy;
and, in any event, the risk element due to inflation that is reflected in interest rates is not
actual past inflation (as measured by an appropriate index such as the IMF consumer
price index or the UK retail price index), but what it is anticipated the rate of inflation
will be in the future until the date of maturity of the security. Nevertheless, inflation has
g provided over the last few years what is far and away the greatest risk element in the
interest rates obtainable on government stocks and other securities in which other risk
elements are minimal.

If judges carry out their duty of assessing damages for non-economic loss in the money
of the day at the date of the trial, and this is a rule of practice that judges are required to
follow, not a guideline from which they have a discretion to depart if there are special
h circumstances that justify their doing so, there are two routes by which the judge's task
of arriving at the appropriate conventional rate of interest to be applied to the damages
so assessed can be approached. The starting point for each of them is to ascertain from
the appropriate table of retail price indices covering the period between service of writ
and trial what would have been the equivalent of those damages in the money of the day
at the date of service of writ, reckoned in pounds sterling at the higher value that they
j then stood at at the very beginning of the period for which simple interest is to be given.
That figure represents both the real, and also what was then the nominal, value of the
sum of money for the loss of use of which the plaintiff is to be compensated by interest.
Such interest, like the damages on which it is to be given, is to be calculated in the money
of the day at the date of trial, the real value of which has been depreciated by the full
amount of the inflation that has taken place since the date of service of the writ.

The first route by which an informed choice of the appropriate rate of interest can be reached has only been accessible since the United Kingdom government started to issue index-linked (ie inflation-proof) bonds: first, Retirement Bonds, popularly known as Granny Bonds, then, Save-As-You-Earn investments, and, most relevant for present purposes, medium- and long-term, ie 15-year and 25-year index-linked Treasury stock, first issued in 1981. The realisation of an index-linked investment that has been held for a period equivalent to that between service of writ and trial presents the closest analogy in the investment market to an award of damages for personal injuries assessed at a sum of money which takes account of the depreciation in the real value of the pound sterling due to inflation since the date on which the plaintiff is to be treated as having been entitled to a sum which in the money of the day at the date of service of the writ represented the same 'real' value. In effect, he may be regarded as having held an inflation-proof investment between the date of service of the writ and the date of trial; and the rate of interest accepted by investors in index-linked government securities should provide a broad indication of what is the appropriate rate of interest to be awarded him.

Index-linked government securities are of recent origin and comparatively rare; and there are limitations on their acquisition. The other route by which the choice of an appropriate rate of interest may be approached is, first, to see what were the actual rates of interest that were obtainable over the relevant period on various kinds of government or other securities in which the risk element apart from inflation is minimal, next to deduct from the actual rates of interest that were obtainable over the relevant period on various kinds of government or other securities in which the risk element apart from inflation is minimal, next to deduct from the actual rates of interest the rate of inflation over the same period, and then to treat the difference as representing the element in the interest that represents the reward for forgoing temporarily the use of the invested money.

In the instant case no expert evidence on either of these lines of approach was tendered; but it had been given in *Birkett v Hayes* and the relevant periods in respect of which interest was to be awarded were broadly comparable in the two cases. In *Birkett v Hayes* the period was roughly five years ending in July 1981; in the instant case it was roughly four years ending in October 1982. Each of these periods started after the period that was the subject of expert evidence in *Cookson v Knowles* had ended. In the absence of any expert evidence leading to a different conclusion, the trial judge in the instant case considered that the 2% guideline laid down by the Court of Appeal in *Birkett v Hayes* ought to be applied by him.

My Lords, in *Cookson v Knowles* [1978] 2 All ER 604 at 611, [1979] AC 556 at 571, I said:

> 'In times of stable currency the multipliers that were used by judges [ie to estimate the present value of future economic loss] were appropriate to interest rates of four per cent to five per cent whether the judges using them were conscious of this or not.'

It does not follow from this, however, that, in times of highly unstable currency, the part of the interest rate that represents the reward obtained for forgoing the use of money still remains at 4% to 5%. The virtually unchallenged expert evidence that was given in *Birkett v Hayes* goes far to show that it does not. On index-linked securities the rate of return on Retirement Bonds after being held for five years was 0·8% per annum free of tax; on the Save As You Earn investment, it was 1·3% per annum also free of tax; and on the 15-year and 25-year index-linked Treasury stock issued in 1981, it was 2%. In effect subscribers to this stock obtained that 2% free of tax since initially, at any rate, it was only available to gross funds: pension funds, life funds and the like, not liable to income tax; but, subject to limits as to amount, medium- and long-term index-linked issues at 2% or 2½% have latterly been made available to private individuals who, if liable to income tax, obtain a net return of 2% to 2½% less tax, and even now are currently traded at around about par.

The expert's examination of the rate of return obtained on a range of investments that were not inflation proof but in which the risk element, apart from inflation, was small led him to the conclusion that no better return than 2% in excess of the rate of inflation could be expected during that period of recession and inflation as the real reward for forgoing the use of money. The success of the index-linked issue of long-dated Treasury stock carrying 2% interest came after his original report in which he had expressed that conclusion and provided powerful confirmation of it. Although 4% to 5% may again become an appropriate rate to allow for forgoing the use of money if currency becomes stable again, when inflation is rampant and recession has increased the risk of investment in equities, anxiety to preserve the 'real' value of money that is not immediately needed but is saved for future use makes investors willing to accept a much lower 'real' rate of interest; and I see no ground for rejecting, for the time being, the 2% rate adopted by the Court of Appeal in *Birkett v Hayes* as the rate to be used for calculating the conventional 'interest' on an award for damages for non-economic loss that the state requires the court to include in the sum for which judgment is given.

In *Birkett v Hayes* Eveleigh LJ drew particular attention to the artificiality, to which I initially referred, of treating the sum ultimately assessed at the trial as damages for non-economic loss, both that which the plaintiff had sustained by that date and also that which he was likely to sustain thereafter (although no discount for its deferment was made in the lump sum awarded), as if it were a debt for a sum certain of the same 'real' value, payable on the date of service of the writ. Even assuming, as he was prepared to do, that after elimination of the risk element due to inflation the market rate of interest obtainable by investors as a reward for forgoing the use of their money remained at 4% gross before deduction of tax, notwithstanding that the currency was rapidly depreciating, Eveleigh LJ would have regarded it as fair to apply a rate lower than the net rate of 2·8% which represented the gross rate of 4% less tax. The 2% fairly represented an appropriate lower rate.

My Lords, given the inescapably artificial and conventional nature of the assessment of damages for non-economic loss in personal injury actions and of treating such assessment as a debt bearing interest from the date of service of the writ, it is an important function of the Court of Appeal to lay down guidelines both as to the quantum of damages appropriate to compensate for various types of commonly occurring injuries and as to the rates of 'interest' from time to time appropriate to be given in respect of non-economic loss and of the various kinds of economic loss. The purpose of such guidelines is that they should be simple and easy to apply though broad enough to permit allowances to be made for special features of individual cases which make the deprivation caused to the particular plaintiff by the non-economic loss greater or less than the general run of cases involving injuries of the same kind. Guidelines laid down by an appellate court are addressed directly to judges who try personal injury actions; but confidence that trial judges will apply them means that all those who are engaged in settling out of court the many thousands of claims that never reach the stage of litigation at all or, if they do, do not proceed as far as trial will know very broadly speaking what the claim is likely to be worth if 100% liability is established.

The Court of Appeal, with its considerable case-load of appeals in personal injury actions and the relatively recent experience of many of its members in trying such cases themselves is, generally speaking, the tribunal best qualified to set the guidelines for judges currently trying such actions, particularly as respects non-economic loss; and this House should hesitate before deciding to depart from them, particularly if the departure will make the guideline less general in its applicability or less simple to apply.

A guideline as to quantum of conventional damages or conventional interest thereon is not a rule of law nor is it a rule of practice. It sets no binding precedent; it can be varied as circumstances change or experience shows that it does not assist in the achievement of even-handed justice or that it makes trials more lengthy or expensive or settlements more difficult to reach. But, though guidelines should be altered if circumstances relevant to the particular guideline change, too frequent alteration deprives them of their usefulness in providing a reasonable degree of predictability in the litigious process and so facilitating settlement of claims without going to trial.

As regards assessment of damages for non-economic loss in personal injury cases, the
Court of Appeal creates the guidelines as to the appropriate conventional figure by a
increasing or reducing awards of damages made by judges in individual cases for various
common kinds of injuries. Thus, so-called 'brackets' are established, broad enough to
make allowance for circumstances which make the deprivation suffered by an individual
plaintiff in consequence of the particular kind of injury greater or less than in the general
run of cases, yet clear enough to reduce the unpredictability of what is likely to be the
most important factor in arriving at settlement of claims. 'Brackets' may call for alteration b
not only to take account of inflation, for which they ought automatically to be raised,
but also, it may be, to take account of advances in medical science which may make
particular kinds of injuries less disabling or advances in medical knowledge which may
disclose hitherto unsuspected long-term effects of some kinds of injuries or industrial
diseases.

As regards the fixing of the conventional rate of interest to be applied to the c
conventional figure at which damages for non-economic loss have been assessed, the rate
of 2% adopted and recommended as a guideline by the Court of Appeal in *Birkett v Hayes*
covered a period during which inflation was proceeding at a very rapid rate. As I have
already said, I see no ground that would justify this House in holding that guideline to
have been wrong, or to overrule the trial judge's application of it to the instant case.
Although the rate of inflation has slowed, at least temporarily, since the period in respect d
of which the 2% guideline in *Birkett v Hayes* was laid down, no one yet knows what the
long-term future of the phenomenon of inflation will be; and the guideline, if it is to
serve its purpose in promoting predictability and so facilitating settlements and
eliminating the expense of regularly calling expert economic evidence at trials of personal
injury actions, should continue to be followed for the time being at any rate, until the
long-term trend of future inflation has become predictable with much more confidence. e
When that state of affairs is reached, and it would be unrealistic to suppose that it will be
in the immediate future, it may be that the 2% guideline will call for examination afresh
in the light of fresh expert economic evidence, which may show that assumptions that
could validly be made at the time of *Birkett v Hayes* as to what was the current rate of
interest obtainable in the market that was attributable to forgoing the use of money will
have ceased to hold good. But there is no material before your Lordships to suggest that f
the time is yet ripe for this. Accordingly, I would dismiss this appeal.

LORD FRASER OF TULLYBELTON. My Lords, I have had the advantage of reading in draft the speech of my noble and learned friend Lord Diplock. For the reasons given by him I would dismiss this appeal.

g

LORD SCARMAN. My Lords, I have had the advantage of reading in draft the speech delivered by my noble and learned friend Lord Diplock. I agree with it, and for the reasons he gives I would dismiss the appeal.

LORD BRIDGE OF HARWICH. My Lords, for the reasons given in the speech of
my noble and learned friend Lord Diplock, with which I agree, I too would dismiss this h
appeal.

LORD BRANDON OF OAKBROOK. My Lords, I have had the advantage of reading in draft the speech prepared by my noble and learned friend Lord Diplock. I agree with it, and for the reasons which he gives I would dismiss the appeal.

j

Appeal dismissed.

Solicitors: *Pattinson & Brewer* (for the appellant); *M G Baker* (for the respondents).

Mary Rose Plummer Barrister.

Sybron Corp and another v Rochem Ltd and others

COURT OF APPEAL, CIVIL DIVISION
STEPHENSON, FOX AND KERR LJJ
21, 22, 23 FEBRUARY 1983

Master and servant – Duty of servant – Disclosure of fraudulent misconduct – Employee acting fraudulently in conjunction with subordinate employees to detriment of employer – Employee obtaining discretionary pension benefits on retiring before fraud discovered – Payment would not have been made if employer knew of fraud – Whether employee under duty to disclose his misconduct to employer – Whether employee under duty to disclose misconduct of others if disclosure would reveal his own misconduct.

Mistake – Mistake of fact – Money paid under mistake of fact – Employment – Employee acting fraudulently in conjunction with other employees to detriment of employer – Employee obtaining discretionary pension benefits on retiring before fraud discovered – Payment would not have been made if employer knew of fraud – Whether payment recoverable as money paid under mistake of fact induced by employee's breach of duty to disclose his or other's fraud.

The respondent company employed the appellant employee as a manager to oversee its European operations. He was required to report periodically to the company regarding developments within his zone. The employee, who was a member of a pension scheme operated by the company, opted for early retirement on 30 September 1973. The pension scheme provided that an employee taking early retirement was entitled to be repaid immediately his own cash contributions but that the balance of accrued benefits was to be applied entirely at the company's discretion. The company exercised that discretion by paying the employee a lump sum of some £13,200 and purchasing life assurance policies which it held in trust and from which annuities were paid to the employee and his wife as beneficiaries. It was subsequently discovered that the employee had been a party to fraudulent misconduct in conjunction with other employees subordinate to him, and the company sued those involved in the fraud for damages. In particular, the company claimed against the employee and his wife for the return of the lump sum of £13,200 paid to the employee under the pension scheme and also claimed that the company was entitled to the benefit of the policies bought to provide annuities for the employee and his wife. At the trial of the company's action the judge found that there had been a conspiracy, of which the employee was a member, which had resulted in a massive commercial fraud on the company. In regard to the employee and his wife, the judge, after holding that the trusts to provide annuities had been established and the payments therefrom had been made under a mistake of fact induced by the employee's breach of duty, granted a declaration that the company held the policies free of any trust in favour of the employee and his wife and ordered the repayment of all sums paid to them. The employee and his wife appealed, contending that the company could not have the pension arrangements set aside on the grounds of the employee's breach of his duty to disclose the fraud because an employee was under no legal obligation to his employer to disclose breaches by him of his obligations arising out of his employment.

Held – Although the employee had not been under a duty to disclose to his employers his own misconduct, he had been under a duty to disclose the fraudulent misconduct of the subordinate employees with whom he had acted, even though that disclosure would have revealed his own misconduct to his employers, since that duty arose out of the position he had held as a senior manager which required him to report on developments within his zone. His failure to disclose their misconduct constituted a serious breach of his contract of employment and had the company known of the breach when retirement arrangements were made they would have exercised their discretion under the pension scheme by refusing to pay him the lump sum and pension. Accordingly, payment of his lump sum and pension had been made under a mistake of fact induced by his breach of duty. Moreover, since his wife, although not a party to the fraud, was a volunteer she was in no better position than her husband regarding entitlement to payment as a beneficiary under the pension trusts. It followed that the declaration and order had been properly made and that the appeal would accordingly be dismissed (see p 713 *h*, p 714 *j* to p 715 *a*, p 717 *c g h*, p 718 *c* to *h*, p 719 *a e* to *h* and p 720 *b* to *g*, post).

Swain v West (Butchers) Ltd [1936] 3 All ER 261 applied.

Healey v Société Anonyme Française Rubastic [1917] 1 KB 946 and *Bell v Lever Bros Ltd* [1931] All ER Rep 1 distinguished.

Per Kerr LJ. An employee may be under a duty to disclose his own fraudulent misconduct to his employer (see p 720 *c d*, post); *Healey v Société Anonyme Française Rubastic* [1917] 1 KB 946 and *Bell Lever Bros Ltd* [1931] All ER Rep 1 considered.

Cases referred to in judgments

Bell v Lever Bros Ltd [1932] AC 161, [1931] All ER Rep 1, HL; *rvsg* [1931] 1 KB 577, CA and KBD.

Fletcher v Krell (1872) 28 LT 105.

Healey v Société Anonyme Française Rubastic [1917] 1 KB 946.

Ramsden v David Sharratt & Sons Ltd (1930) 35 Com Cas 314, HL.

Swain v West (Butchers) Ltd [1936] 3 All ER 261, CA; *affg*, [1936] 1 All ER 224.

Notes

For misconduct inconsistent with an employee's proper discharge of his duties, see 16 Halsbury's Laws (4th edn) para 642, and for cases on the subject, see 20 Digest (Reissue) 434–444, *3530–3646*.

For recovery of money paid under mistake of fact, see 9 Halsbury's Laws (4th edn) para 665, and for cases on the subject, see 35 Digest (Repl) 158–167, *475–532*.

Appeal

By notice of appeal dated 6 October 1981 the fourth and twelfth defendants, William Seymour Roques and Muriel Roques, appealed against that part of the order made by Walton J on 27 March 1981 at the hearing of the action brought by the first and second plaintiffs, Sybron Corp and Gamlen Chemical Co (UK) Ltd against them and eleven other defendants which (a) declared that the second plaintiffs stood possessed of two policies of assurance and moneys payable thereunder free and discharged from any trust in favour of the fourth and/or twelfth defendants, (b) ordered that the fourth defendant pay the second plaintiff the sum of £13,208·10 plus interest and (c) ordered the fourth and twelfth defendants to pay such portion of the plaintiffs' costs as were properly attributable to the claim made against them. The facts are set out in the judgment of Stephenson LJ.

James Munby for Mr and Mrs Roques.

C A Brodie QC and *Ian Geering* for the plaintiffs.

STEPHENSON LJ. This is an appeal by two out of 13 defendants against three parts of an order made by Walton J on 27 March 1981 and entered on 26 August 1981. That order provided for three things by the only relevant part of it for the purposes of this appeal. The first was a declaration that the second plaintiffs, Gamlen Chemical Co (UK) Ltd 'stand possessed of the two policies of assurance referred to in paragraph 23(D) of the re-re-re-Amended Statement of Claim and the moneys payable thereunder respectively and the full benefit thereof free and discharged from any trust in favour of [the appellants] or either of them'. The second was an order that the appellant Wilfred Seymour Roques, the fourth defendant, 'do pay to [the company] on the 5th February 1981 the sum of £13,208·10 with interest thereon at 10 per cent per annum from the 31st October 1973 until payment'. The third was an order that the appellants, ie Mr Roques and his wife, who is the twelfth defendant, 'do pay to the plaintiffs [ie Sybron Corp as well as Gamlen Chemical Co (UK) Ltd] such of the costs of the Plaintiffs of the Action [taxed if not agreed] as are properly attributable to the issues raised by paragraph 23 of the said re-re-re-Amended Statement of Claim'.

Paragraph 23 is in these terms:

> '(A) Roques was employed by Gamlen UK from 2nd October 1952 until 30th September 1973. During the period of his said employment both Roques as employee and Gamlen UK as employer made payments to the Scottish Widows Fund and Life Assurance Society ("the Society") under a Pension and Life Assurance Scheme ("the Scheme") administered by Gamlen UK. Roques paid contributions to the Scheme amounting in the aggregate to £4,641·90. Under the rules of the Scheme (to which Gamlen UK will at the trial refer for their full terms and true effect) on the retirement of a member such member becomes entitled to a pension payable by the Society or under Rule 11 Gamlen UK may take part or the whole of the benefits for the member in the form of a cash payment to be applied in purchasing an annuity for that member from an insurance company or the member may request Gamlen UK to arrange for a lump sum to be paid to him in lieu of the annuity or part thereof and Gamlen UK may at its discretion arrange accordingly. Under the Scheme the normal retirement age of any member is that member's 65th birthday. Under Rule 8(b) if before his normal retirement date a member leaves the service of Gamlen UK voluntarily or is dismissed for fraud or serious misconduct in connection with the affairs of Gamlen UK he is entitled to the benefit secured by his own contributions towards the premiums due and in respect of his membership of the Scheme and the balance of the benefit secured by such premiums will be dealt with at the discretion of Gamlen UK.
>
> (B) Roques was 62 years of age on the 20th January 1973 and from about February 1973 was desirous of retiring from the service of Gamlen UK before reaching his normal retiring age of 65 under the Scheme.
>
> (C) By virtue of the said Rule 11 of the Scheme in the event of Roques retiring on the 30th September 1973 there would be payable to Gamlen UK by the Society the sum of £49,672.
>
> (D) By an agreement between Gamlen UK and Roques in or about July, August and September 1973 it was agreed:—(i) that Roques should retire on the 30th September 1973; (ii) that Gamlen UK would exercise the option conferred by Rule 11 of the Scheme and claim the sum of £49,672; (iii) that Gamlen UK would add to the sum of £49,672 a further sum of £7,177·14 making an aggregate of £56,849·14; (iv) that Gamlen UK would apply the said sum of £56,849·14 as follows:—(a) by paying £17,850 thereof to Roques; (b) by purchasing in the name of Gamlen UK from the Society a policy of assurance under which the sum of £3,360·12 per annum would be paid to Gamlen UK during the joint lives of Roques and Mrs. Roques and the life of the survivor of them and Gamlen UK would hold such sum upon trust for Roques and Mrs. Roques as in the policy mentioned; (c) by purchasing from the Society a further policy under which the annual sum of £756·36 would be payable to Gamlen UK for the same period and be held on the same trusts as affected the said annual sum of £3,360·12; (v) that Roques would enter into a Consultancy Agreement with Gamlen UK for a period of three years (such Consultancy Agreement to include a covenant against competition with Gamlen UK for a period of three years from the 31st August 1976) in consideration of the sum of £7,500 to be paid in 12 quarterly instalments of £625 each.
>
> (E) Roques retired on the 30th September 1973.
>
> (F) Pursuant to the said Agreement Gamlen UK (1) in or about October 1973 paid to Roques the said sum of £17,850 and (2) effected the said two policies at a total cost of £38,999·14.

(G) Gamlen UK effected the said policies and each of them and made the said payment under or pursuant to a mistake of fact namely that (i) Roques was entitled to his pension rights under the Scheme and that Gamlen UK had no good cause to invoke the provisions of Rule 8(b) on the ground that Roques was liable to be dismissed for serious misconduct in connection with the affairs of Gamlen UK and (ii) that Roques had faithfully and diligently carried out his duties as an employee of Gamlen UK prior to his said retirement.

(H) Gamlen UK had good cause to invoke the provisions of Rule 8(b) on the ground that Roques could have been summarily dismissed for serious misconduct in connection with the affairs of Gamlen UK and Gamlen UK repeats the particulars given under paragraphs 6, 15(1), (2), (3), (4) and 20 hereof. Further or alternatively Roques did not faithfully or diligently carry out his duties as an employee of Gamlen UK prior to his said retirement and Gamlen UK repeats the said particulars.

(I) In the premises the said payment of £17,850 was made under a mistake of fact and Gamlen UK effected the said policies and created the trusts thereof under the same mistake. As regards the sum of £17,850 Gamlen UK is willing to give credit for the sum of £4,641·90 to which Roques would have been entitled under the provisions of Rule 8(b).'

I need read no more of that document.

So the claim to £13,208·10 is a claim for the balance of £17,850 after deducting the £4,641·90 contributed by Mr Roques himself to the scheme. This claim, to be repaid £13,208·10, is a very small part of a very much larger claim for many millions of dollars as damages for conspiracy; it is a claim by two companies for conspiracy against three companies with the name Rochem, and nine others, including Mr Roques, a Mr Bove and other employees; I say nine others and not ten, because Mrs Roques was not a conspirator but simply a beneficiary under the policy and throughout no allegations whatever have been made against that lady and it is her misfortune that the judge has found her husband guilty of the conspiracy to which I shall shortly come.

Mr Roques and all the other defendants, companies and individuals except Mrs Roques and three other defendants against whom the plaintiffs discontinued, were found by the judge guilty of a conspiracy amounting to a massive commercial fraud, after a trial lasting more than 90 days, in a judgment given on 3 and 4 December 1980, of which the transcript runs to 240 pages.

The plaintiff Sybron was described by the judge as 'an American financial conglomerate'. It acquired another American company, called Gamlen Chemical Co Ltd, which specialised in chemicals and equipment for cleaning ships and industrial sludge. On the merger of Gamlen Chemical Co Ltd with Sybron all the subsidiaries of Gamlen Chemical Co Ltd became subsidiaries of Sybron, and those subsidiaries included the second plaintiffs, Gamlen Chemical Co (UK) Ltd, who were reponsible for the activities of the company in the United Kingdom, and also for its activities in Norway and in the Middle East and the Gulf area. Included in those subsidiaries were a French subsidiary, an Italian subsidiary, a German subsidiary and a Dutch subsidiary with a branch in Belgium.

The French subsidiary took an independent line to a considerable extent. In his judgment the judge said:

> 'Leaving, therefore, Gamlen France completely out of the picture for present purposes, the manner in which the Gamlen Division of Sybron, through the former subsidiaries of Gamlen Chemical Co Ltd and the Gamlen Division of Sybron Italia, operated was through a unified European zone, and at all times material for present purposes the no 1 in Europe of this unified zone was the defendant Wilfred Seymour Roques (Mr Roques).'

After 1971 his right-hand man was a United States citizen much younger than he, called Bove; of him and his relationship to Mr Roques the judge said:

> 'On 1 August of that year (1971) he was appointed controller of the European zone; later he became director of operations, European zone. Whatever his official

position may have been designated he was, in effect, throughout this history, Mr Roques's right-hand man. They were respectively no 2 and no 1 in the Gamlen European zone.'

As the judge found, Mr Roques had the power of hiring and firing over the whole of the European zone, including those countries which I have already named. In June of 1970 he used that power to dismiss a Mr Van den Heuval, who was the manager for Germany and Holland. For reasons which are obvious he denied in the witness box his reponsibility for that dismissal but, according to the judgment of the judge, he was caught out in a direct lie in dealing with that dismissal and his denial of responsibility for it was rejected by the judge.

Counsel for Mr and Mrs Roques has conceded that the conspiracy as pleaded in the statement of claim, and indeed all or most of the overt acts there pleaded, were in fact proved to the satisfaction of the judge; and they are admitted for the purposes of this appeal. I can therefore best describe the conspiracy of which Mr Roques, Mr Bove and others were found guilty by reading the way in which it is pleaded in para 6 of the statement of claim:

> 'From a date not earlier than 1971 Roques, Bove, Baldwin and Fletcher and each of them [they were two other English employees of the company] or some one or more of them wrongfully and with intent to injure Sybron and/or Gamlen UK and/or the Relevant Subsidiaries or some one or more of them conspired and agreed together and/or with [and a number of other employees are named] to do the following acts or some one or more of such acts:—(a) (i) To set up in the case of Roques Bove Baldwin and Fletcher while they were respectively employed by the Plaintiffs or one of them and in the case of the other said conspirators while they were respectively employed by a subsidiary of Sybron business organisations (hereinafter called "the New Business") throughout the world including England which would carry on business of the same kind as the said business carried on by Sybron through Gamlen UK and/or the Relevant subsidiaries or one or more of them (hereinafter together called "the said subsidiaries of Sybron"). (ii) To carry on business through the New Business while still employed as aforesaid in competition with and so as to injure the said business of Sybron. (iii) To hide and disguise from Sybron and/or the said subsidiaries of Sybron their respective interests in the New Business during their respective employment by Sybron or the said subsidiaries of Sybron as the case might be.'

That is the 'guts' of the conspiracy; I need read no more of that paragraph.

In effect the judge found that what he called the top management, headed by Mr Roques and Mr Bove, defected, unknown to the plaintiffs, while still employed by the plaintiffs, to these Rochem companies who form three of the defendants to the plaintiffs' action, and worked actively against their employers.

The judge also found that Mr Roques was a party to the conspiracy (reluctant, hesitant it may be, but a party from its inception) doomed, as the judge described it, to dance to the dominant Mr Bove's tune, but nevertheless the judge found that the conspiracy would not have got off the ground if Mr Roques had disclosed to the plaintiffs what, in the judge's view, he ought to have disclosed, namely the activities of his fellow conspirators and fellow employees. He saw to it that nothing was passed to the plaintiffs or to their lawyers; he was not prepared to 'rock the boat', as the judge put it, by doing his duty to report their activities and so to risk losing his pension. In February 1973 he was telling Mr Gamlen that he wanted to retire early, at the age of 62 in January 1974. He was writing what the judge called 'window-dressing letters' to Mr Gamlen in March and in July of that year; I think I should read one or two sentences from the letter of 13 July 1973, which was quoted by the judge. In that letter he expressed his anger at references being made to a product called Roquesite, indicating, as he said in the letter, that 'this might belong to some company of mine. I know you do not need me to assure you I have no company nor do I contemplate such'.

That was written to Mr Gamlen, the son of the founder of the Gamlen Chemical Co Ltd in the United States, by a man who was at that time busy forming a company, or companies, of his own in competition with the plaintiffs. I would spare Mrs Roques's feelings by not going further into the sorry details of Mr Roques's part in this conspiracy, his visits to various lawyers and perhaps in particular his visit to Kuwait, nominally to advance the interests of the plaintiffs but in fact to destroy them.

Common sense might suggest that a man in the responsible position of Mr Roques, which I have outlined, was under a duty to the plaintiffs, his employers, to stop what was going on, to dismiss the perpetrators, or at least to report the perpetrators and what was going on to his employers, the plaintiffs. He did not do any of these things; he did not do any of them because he could not, and he could not do them because he was in the conspiracy himself up to the hilt. Yet it is submitted by counsel on behalf of Mr and Mrs Roques, that Mr Roques owed no duty of the kind which I have suggested common sense might indicate, he did not break any such duty because he did not owe any such duty and, submits counsel for Mr and Mrs Roques, the House of Lords has said so. If he owed no duty, and broke no duty, by being unfaithful in the way in which I have described in outline, he is entitled to keep the £13,000 which his employers have paid him in ignorance, and again the House of Lords has said so. If this is the law, in my judgment there is something very seriously wrong with the law.

Walton J would not accept it as the law, and neither do I. After reading r 8(a) and (b) of the scheme, the judge said:

> 'Based on these rules, the statement of claim reads, in relation to Mr Roques's pension, as I have already indicated, that Gamlen effected the policies, and each of them, and made the payment under or pursuant to a mistake of fact, namely, in substance, that Roques was entitled to his pension rights under the scheme and that Gamlen had no good cause to invoke the provisions of r 8(b), and that Gamlen had been caused to invoke those provisions on the ground that Mr Roques could have been summarily dismissed for serious misconduct. [Counsel for Mr Roques and others] submitted that it was nowhere there alleged that in regard to the negotiations which took place in relation to the pension provisions finally agreed for Mr Roques there had been any fraud, misconduct or misrepresentation by Mr or Mrs Roques. But that even if there had been any such pleaded there was certainly no evidence to support any such allegation. Consequently, he claimed, the matter was concluded in favour of Mr and Mrs Roques by the decision of the House of Lords in *Bell v Lever Bros Ltd* [1932] AC 161, [1931] All ER Rep 1. As will be recalled, that was a case where the respondents, Lever Bros paid two of their employees, Bell and Snelling, considerable sums representing, in effect, damages for premature termination of their service contracts. Unknown to Lever Bros at the time the payments were negotiated they had the right, because of certain breaches of the terms of such contracts which Bell and Snelling had committed, to terminate such contracts without compensation and immediately. On discovering their servants' peccadilloes Lever Bros sued to recover the amount of compensation so paid, alleging fraud. Fraud was, however, completely negatived. So the case was then put on the ground of mistake, both mutual or, alternatively, unilateral, on the part of Lever Bros. The Court of Appeal, agreeing with the trial judge, held that the parties were under a mutual mistake, both of them believing (contrary to the fact) that the one was entitled to, and the other bound to pay, compensation for termination of the agreements (see [1931] 1 KB 557). The Court of Appeal further held that each of them, Bell and Snelling, owed a duty to their employer to disclose their breaches of duty, and that such non-disclosure invalidated the compensation agreements. By one vote the House of Lords reversed this decision. Lord Blanesburgh would have decided the matter on the ground that, after a charge of fraud had been made and negatived, it would not be just to allow the employers to succeed on a ground based on the alternative hypothesis of good faith. But he was content also to agree with

Lord Atkin and Lord Thankerton that the action failed, as to mutual mistake on the ground that the mutual mistake related not to the subject matter of the action but to its quality, and as to unilateral mistake on the ground that the defendants owed no duty to their employers to disclose the impugned transactions.'

I cannot improve on that summary of *Bell v Lever Bros Ltd*, but I would add that I take the judge to mean, when he says that the Court of Appeal further held that each of them owed a duty to their employer to disclose *their* breaches of duty, that each was bound to disclose his own breaches of duty because, as I shall point out, there is nothing in the decision of *Bell v Lever Bros Ltd* which decides what, if any, duty is owed by a servant to disclose to his master breaches of other servants' duty. The judge went on:

'The relevance of that case to the claim against Mr and Mrs Roques is at once apparent: if Mr Roques owed no duty to the plaintiffs to disclose his serious breaches of duty then the settlement of his pension provisions could not, as such, be upset. I say "as such" because it appears to me that, as far as Mr Roques himself is concerned, there might well be arguments for saying that the plaintiffs could recover the costs of such settlement by way of damages for breach of his service agreement. But, whether that is so or not, it would be quite clear that the position of Mrs Roques would remain unaffected, and she would continue to be entitled to the pension provision made for her. [Counsel for Mr Roques and others] pointed out, and I think that his observation is well founded, that the House of Lords in that case made it perfectly clear that, in general, even if the servant has committed a fraudulent breach of the terms of his employment (eg he has stolen from his master), there is no superadded duty on him to report his own dishonesty.'

I make no apology for reading that passage also from the judge's judgment because it contains an admirable statement of the relevance of *Bell v Lever Bros Ltd* and also, I think, of the argument of counsel for Mr and Mrs Roques.

In *Bell v Lever Bros Ltd* [1931] 1 KB 557 at 575 the trial judge, Wright J, did not find it necessary to decide whether these two servants owed a duty to their employers to disclose their own misconduct or breaches of contract, though he clearly indicated that he thought they well might. All the Lords Justices in the Court of Appeal were I think of opinion that there was such a duty, or that there certainly was such a duty in that case, and that they could have put their decision on that ground (see [1931] 1 KB 557 at 586, 593, 599–601, per Scrutton, Lawrence and Greer LJJ). But the House of Lords said No, there was no such duty; and they held, by a majority of three to two, that Bell and Snelling were entitled to retain from their employers the moneys which had been paid to them in spite of their misconduct or breach of contract and their failure to disclose it.

Counsel for Mr and Mrs Roques has, in the course of his admirably presented argument in this court, made some further concessions. First, he has conceded that Mrs Roques, though innocent, can be in no better position than her husband because, though bona fide, she was a volunteer and not a purchaser for value. Second, neither Mr Roques nor Mrs Roques can be in any better position by seeking to argue the matter in trust rather than in contract. I also understand him to concede that the judge's three orders stand or fall together; either the plaintiffs are entitled to their declaration and are entitled to their order for repayment, and I think it must follow that they are entitled to their order for costs, or if they are not entitled to one, they are not entitled to any.

Counsel for Mr and Mrs Roques then made four submissions. (1) In the circumstances of this case the plaintiffs cannot set aside the pension arrangements on the ground of mistake unless they can show either (a) that their mistake was induced by some misrepresentation on the part of Mr Roques or (b) that their mistake was induced by some breach on the part of Mr Roques of a duty of disclosure; for that he relies on *Bell v Lever Bros Ltd.* (2) Neither a servant nor a director is under any legal obligation to his employer or principal to disclose any breaches by him of obligations arising out of their relationship. (3) It makes no difference to the principle just submitted (a) that the servant

or director has in fact had his misconduct present to his mind at the moment when it is said that he ought to have made disclosure; it likewise makes no difference to that a
principle (b) that his wrongdoing is fraudulent; nor (c) that the breach of the obligation was deliberately effected in such a way that it remains secret from the employer; nor (d) that he conceals his breach of obligation by submitting to his employer false and misleading reports, intending to deceive him. Then, says counsel for Mr and Mrs Roques, if all those three submissions are correct, it is puzzling why it never appears to have been considered, if not decided, that Bell might have been under a duty to disclose Snelling's b
breach of contract and Snelling might have been under a duty to disclose Bell's. (4) Fraud in respect of the misconduct not disclosed is irrelevant; there must be fraud specifically in relation to the negotiating and carrying out of the subsequent transaction which gives rise to the mistake on which the employers are relying.

In support of each of those propositions, counsel for Mr and Mrs Roques has referred us to particular passages in the speeches of Lord Atkin and Lord Thankerton in *Bell v* c
Lever Bros Ltd and to the decision and an observation of Avory J in *Healey v Société Anonyme Française Rubastic* [1917] 1 KB 946, and what those two learned Lords said about them.

It is quite plain that Bell's and Snelling's concealment of their misconduct was innocent; that appears clearly from the argument of Mr Schiller KC, leading counsel for the appellant, and from the argument of Sir John Simon KC, the respondents' leading counsel (see [1932] AC 161 at 165, 167), as well as from the jury's answer to the questions d
put to them by Wright J (see [1932] AC 161 at 185–186, [1931] 1 All ER Rep 1 at 12–13) negativing fraud, and finding that neither Bell nor Snelling had his previous misconduct in mind at the time when he claimed compensation for early termination of the contract of employment. It is also reasonably plain, I think, that the headnote (see [1932] AC 161 at 162) is justified in saying that it was the dictum of Avory J in *Healey*'s case, and not merely his decision, which was approved by Lord Atkin and Lord Thankerton (see [1932] e
AC 161 at 228, 231, [1931] 1 All ER Rep 1 at 33, 34). Avory J's decision in *Healey*'s case had already won the approval of Lord Warrington in *Ramsden v David Sharratt & Sons Ltd* (1930) 35 Com Cas 314 at 319. The decision was that a servant who had been dismissed for misconduct was entitled to recover arrears of salary due to him after the time when he committed the misconduct and before the time when his misconduct became known to his employers and he was consequently dismissed. f

The dictum which I think was accepted by their Lordships in *Healey*'s case ([1917] 1 KB 946 at 947) is:

> 'I cannot accept the view that the omission to confess or disclose his own misdoing was in itself a breach of the contract on the part of the plaintiff . . .'

I accept, as I must accept, that by a majority the House of Lords were saying that a g
contract of employment, though often described as creating a relationship of trust between master and servant, is not a contract uberrimae fidei so as to require disclosure by the servant of his own misconduct, either before he is taken into employment as in *Fletcher v Krell* (1872) 28 LT 105 or during the course of his employment as in *Healey*'s or *Bell*'s case. But I find it unnecessary to consider further how far the submissions of counsel for Mr and Mrs Roques, in particular his third submission, are supported by *Bell*'s case or h
are correct, or whether the case pleaded and proved against Mr Roques covers an allegation of payment induced by fraudulent misrepresentation within counsel's fourth submission, because what in my judgment entitles the plaintiffs to recover the £13,000 here is Mr Roques's serious misconduct in breach of contract in failing to report to the plaintiffs the fraudulent misconduct of Bove and other subordinates.

Counsel for Mr and Mrs Roques was forced to concede that if the plaintiffs had known j
of Mr Roques's failure to report that misconduct they would have invoked r 8(b) of the scheme and would not have paid the pension; and, if that failure was a breach of duty because Mr Roques was under a duty to report that misconduct, the plaintiffs were under a mistake of fact which entitled them to recover the £13,000 as money paid under a

mistake of fact, so in those circumstances the judge would be right to make the declaration and the orders which he did.

In *Bell v Lever Bros Ltd* nothing was said about a duty to disclose the misconduct of fellow servants, except by Scrutton LJ in the Court of Appeal and by Lord Atkin in the House of Lords. In the Court of Appeal, Scrutton LJ said ([1931] 1 KB 557 at 586–587):

> 'I do not propose to lay down any general rule for disclosure by servants: I only desire to say that I notice that Wright J. held himself bound by the remark of Avory J. in *Healey* v. *Société Anonyme Française Rubastic* ([1917] 1 KB 946 at 947): "I cannot accept the view that an omission to confess or disclose his own misdoing was, in itself a breach of the contract on the part of the plaintiff." This statement was also accepted, though I think it was not material to his decision, by Lord Warrington in *Ramsden* v. *David Sharratt & Sons, Ld.* ((1930) 35 Com Cas 314 at 319). I must reserve myself liberty to reconsider this as a general rule if it becomes relevant in any subsequent case. I cannot think that a servant who knows his fellow servant is stealing the goods of his employer is under no obligation to disclose this to his employer. If the servant himself has stolen goods, and his employer, finding out the theft, accuses an innocent fellow servant of having committed it, is not the real thief bound to inform his employer of his delinquency? His theft is a vital breach of his contract of employment: is he not bound by his contract of service to inform his employer of acts detrimental to his employer? However, it is not in the present case necessary to lay down any general rule: it is enough to deal with the present case.'

There, as counsel for Mr and Mrs Roques rightly pointed out, Scrutton LJ is, as it were, tacking on what he says about a duty (which he plainly accepted) to disclose a theft by a fellow servant, to his duty to disclose his own theft (which was also accepted by Scrutton LJ and the other Lords Justices but has been negatived by the House of Lords). In the House of Lords, Lord Atkin said ([1932] AC 161 at 228, [1931] All ER Rep 1 at 32):

> 'It is said that there is a contractual duty of the servant to disclose his past faults. I agree that the duty in the servant to protect his master's property may involve the duty to report a fellow servant whom he knows to be wrongfully dealing with that property. The servant owes a duty not to steal, but, having stolen, is there superadded a duty to confess that he has stolen? I am satisfied that to imply such a duty would be a departure from the well established usage of mankind and would be to create obligations entirely outside the normal contemplation of the parties concerned.'

So, there again, what that judge is saying about the duty to report a fellow servant is linked to the question of a duty to report his own wrongdoing, but it is I think significant that Lord Atkin is agreeing that the duty of a servant to protect his master's property 'may involve the duty to report a fellow servant whom he knows to be wrongfully dealing with that property', although Lord Atkin was of the firm view that the servant had no such duty to report his own wrongful conduct. It is, as I have already indicated, puzzling that it never seems to have occurred to counsel or to any of the many judges who dealt with *Bell v Lever Bros Ltd*, that they might have to consider the duty of Bell to report Snelling's misconduct, or Snelling's duty to report Bell's.

But the question was not there considered, let alone decided, and there is the direct authority of a decision of this court, in a case in which *Bell v Lever Bros Ltd* was considered, that there is in certain circumstances a duty to report the misconduct of fellow servants. That case is *Swain v West (Butchers) Ltd* [1936] 1 All ER 224, [1936] 3 All ER 261, reported at first instance and in this court. There the plaintiff was employed for a term of five years as a general manager of the defendant company. His contract of service provided, inter alia, that he would do all in his power to promote, extend and develop the interests of the company. The managing director gave the plaintiff certain unlawful orders, which orders the plaintiff carried out. The matter came to the notice of the chairman of the board of directors who, in an interview with the plaintiff, told the plaintiff that if he gave conclusive proof of the managing director's dishonesty, he would not be dismissed. The plaintiff duly supplied the information required and was then dismissed, the defendants *a* alleging fraud and dishonesty. The plaintiff did not deny the allegations, but he brought an action for breach of contract and wrongful dismissal on the grounds that, under the terms of a verbal agreement between the plaintiff and the chairman, it was not open to the defendants to rely on information given by the plaintiff relating to his own fraud and dishonesty. It was held that it was the plaintiff's duty, as part of his contract of service, to report to the board of directors any acts which were not in the interests of the company; *b* that there was therefore no consideration for the alleged verbal agreement and the defendant company was not prevented from relying on the information received from the plaintiff.

There is an interesting report of an interchange of observations between the Lords Justices and Mr Schiller KC, appearing for the plaintiff Swain, who had, it will be remembered, been leading counsel for the appellant in *Bell*'s case. Mr Schiller is reported *c* as having said ([1936] 3 All ER 261 at 262):

> '*Schiller, K.C.:* In my submission the view of the law upon which the learned judge acted is erroneous. The judge took the view that the chairman was entitled to ask questions of the appellant which were likely to incriminate him.
>
> GREER, L.J.: It was his duty to report the wrong of somebody else and his greater duty when asked to do so. *d*
>
> *Schiller, K.C.:* I do not think there is any authority which says that a servant is under an obligation to report the misdeeds of his fellow-servant.
>
> GREENE, L.J.: As I recollect the decision in *Bell* v. *Lever Bros., Ltd.* . . . the question whether a servant should report the misconduct of a fellow-servant depends upon the circumstances of the particular case.'

e

I am not sure how far that observation of Greene LJ is justified, but Greer LJ's observation is important.

From the judgments of Greer and Greene LJJ I take the following passages. Greer LJ said ([1936] 3 All ER 261 at 264):

> 'It was his duty [ie the duty of the plaintiff] if he knew of acts which were not in the interests of the company to report them to the board. He did not do so.' *f*

After referring to his interview with the chairman, which I have summarised from the headnote, Greer LJ went on:

> 'I find it impossible to come to any other conclusion but that it was the duty of the general manager to find out what he could. In the course of time he did find out and sent in his report. In sending in that report I think he was doing what was his *g* obvious duty as manager of the company to do. I do not decide that in every case where the relation of master and servant exists it is the duty of the servant to disclose, or to disclose upon inquiry, any discrepancies of which he knows of his fellow servants.'

Greene LJ said (at 264–265): *h*

> 'It was submitted to us that there was some general principle of law applicable to contracts of service in general and to this contract in particular that a servant is under no duty to disclose the improper conduct of his fellow servant. I am unable to accept such a proposition. Whether there is such a duty or not must depend upon the circumstances of each particular case . . . If the dishonesty of a fellow-servant came within his notice he should tell the board. The true position in my view is: *j* what are the obligations undertaken in this particular contract? The managing director gave the plaintiff unlawful orders. The plaintiff's duty was to report to his employer that the managing director had endeavoured to persuade him to do something which was dishonest and which would, if carried out, be a breach of his

> duties in controlling the business of the company. If this was his duty it is not altered by the circumstances that he carried out the suggestion made to him. The fact that he carried out the suggestion made it none the less his obligation to inform his directors of the orders which had unlawfully been given to him. He was invited thereafter to give the board details of the complicity of the managing director in these proceedings. He gave a statement of his knowledge of the facts. Can it be said that what he was invited to do was not already his duty to do? His duty to give information to the board arose at the moment when the original improper orders were given to him, and this duty is not lessened by the fact that he obeyed those orders himself.'

I find that case, when considered from the point of view of Mr and Mrs Roques, uncomfortably close to this. I think the passage I have read from Greene LJ's judgment must dispose of the point of counsel for Mr and Mrs Roques that no duty to inform against other fellow servants arises if by so doing you inevitably incriminate yourself. Swain was engaged in carrying out the improper practices (in breach of some Order in Council) which he had been persuaded to carry out by the managing director, and it was of course because he had incriminated himself by admitting his part in the practices that, contrary to what he had been promised by the chairman, he was ultimately dismissed. But counsel for Mr and Mrs Roques seeks also to distinguish *Swain*'s case from this, by the fact, not present in this case, that the plaintiff Swain was asked by the chairman of the board of his employers for the information which he did disclose. But I am afraid that that does not assist him; I cannot accept that that is a valid distinction. The trial judge in *Swain*'s case [1936] 1 All ER 224, Finlay J, found it unnecessary to decide what the position would have been if Swain had volunteered the information, whether there would then have been a duty and whether there would then have been consideration for the agreement; he decided the case on the basis that as Swain was asked to supply the information he was under a duty to supply it. But the passages I have read from what was said by Greer and Greene LJJ, with whom MacKinnon J agreed, I think indicate, all too clearly for counsel's purpose, that the fact that Swain was asked to supply the information created, perhaps, a greater duty, but the duty to volunteer the information was there and the Court of Appeal expressly decided that case on the ground on which Finlay J found it unnecessary to decide it (see [1936] 3 All ER 261).

It follows from that decision, which is consistent with *Bell*'s case and is binding on us, that there is no general duty to report a fellow servant's misconduct or breach of contract; whether there is such a duty depends on the contract and on the terms of employment of the particular servant. He may be so placed in the hierarchy as to have a duty to report either the misconduct of his superior, as in *Swain*'s case, or the misconduct of his inferiors, as in this case. Counsel for Mr and Mrs Roques will not have it that Mr Roques's 'no 2' was subordinate to Mr Roques, or that the other managers involved in the conspiracy were his subordinates or inferiors; but on this point I agree with the judge and I refer, again without apology and with approval, to the way in which he put the matter in his judgment:

> 'I do not think that there is any general duty resting on an employee to inform his master of the breaches of duty of other employees; the law would do industrial relations generally no great service if it held that such a duty did in fact exist in all cases. The duty must, in my view, depend on all the circumstances of the case, and the relationship of the parties to their employer and inter se. I think it would be very difficult to have submitted, with any hope of success, that Bell and Snelling, having been appointed to rescue the affairs of their employers' African subsidiary in effect jointly, ought to have denounced each other.'

That is a reference to the finding that Bell and Snelling were, according to the report of *Bell v Lever Bros Ltd* [1932] AC 161, [1931] All ER Rep 1 in the House of Lords, in joint management and therefore one was not subordinate to the other. The judge continued:

> 'However, where there is an hierarchical system, particularly where the person in the hierarchy whose conduct is called into question is a person near the top who is responsible to his employers for the whole of the operation of a complete sector of the employers' business, here the European zone, then in my view entirely different considerations apply. That the principle of disclosure extends at least as far as I think it extends (and perhaps further, but that is of no consequence for present purposes) has been decided once for all, so far as this court is concerned, by *Swain v West (Butchers) Ltd*, a decision of the Court of Appeal. *Bell v Lever Bros Ltd* was very much in the forefront of everybody's mind in that case, but none of the Lords Justices thought it had any bearing on the case before them.'

After reading, pretty well in full, the judgment of Greene LJ, from which I have read extracts, the judge went on:

> 'This judgment has, if I may respectfully say so, the great merit of common sense. A person in a managerial position cannot possibly stand by and allow fellow servants to pilfer the company's assets and do nothing about it, which is really what [the] submissions [of counsel for Mr Roques and others] would come to when applied to the present type of case. Certainly at all events where the misconduct is serious and the servant is not discharged immediately it must be quite obvious that, as part of his duties generally, the senior employee is under a duty to report what has happened as soon as he finds out, and further to indicate which steps (if any) he has taken to prevent a repetition thereof. Of course, this all depends on the duties of the relevant employee under his contract of service. In the present case there was a well-recognised reporting procedure, whereunder the zone controller, Mr Roques, was expected to make reports as to the state of matters in his zone every month. It may possibly be argued that in such a case the duty to report was not an immediate duty but one to be fulfilled at the next reporting date; so be it, because even if this is correct no such report was ever made by Mr Roques to his superiors. I therefore reach the not very surprising conclusion that Mr Roques was under a duty to report all he knew about the misdeeds of his subordinate employees, commencing with those of Mr Bove, as soon as he found out about them, and that he did not do so, deliberately and fraudulently, because he was one of the conspirators himself. The duty which lay on him was, I repeat, not a duty to report his own misdeeds (this may well be regarded as negatived by *Bell v Lever Bros Ltd*) but to report those of his fellow conspirators.'

Sorry as I am for Mrs Roques, I am happy to find that the law is not so outrageous as to enable Mr Roques to keep the £13,000. What Mr Roques did disentitled him, and I am afraid his wife, from keeping the money, and the plaintiffs are entitled to the declaration and orders for which they have asked, against these two defendants.

I would accordingly dismiss the appeal.

FOX LJ. I agree. In *Bell v Lever Bros Ltd* [1932] AC 161, [1931] All ER Rep 1 Lord Atkin and Lord Thankerton decided, and Lord Blanesburgh, who decided the case on another ground, agreed with them, that there is no contractual duty on a servant to confess to his employer his past misconduct. Lord Atkin said that to imply such a duty would be a departure from the ordinary usage of mankind. Counsel for Mr and Mrs Roques contends, therefore, that *Bell v Lever Bros Ltd* really determines the present matter in his favour so far as breach of duty is concerned.

Bell v Lever Bros Ltd was concerned with breaches of duty by the appellants themselves, which had occurred in the past: they were completed. What we are concerned with in the present case are continuing breaches of duty, not merely by Mr Roques but by other servants of the company. Those breaches were part of a continuing fraudulent design, damaging to the company, which Mr Roques was involved in and of which he was well apprised. Mr Roques, in effect, was in executive control of the European zone. The judge said that he was expected to make reports on the state of the zone every month. It seems to me that by any test of general commercial usage a man in such a position must have been under a duty to report to his superiors on the continuing malpractices of the servants of the company, who were engaged in fraudulent activities designed to maraud the assets of the company.

Authority for that is, in my view, to be found in *Swain v West (Butchers) Ltd* [1936] 3 All ER 261 in this court. I see no reason to suppose, any more than did the court which decided it, that that decision is in any way contrary to *Bell v Lever Bros Ltd*. Counsel for Mr and Mrs Roques points out that Lord Atkin in *Bell v Lever Bros Ltd* [1932] AC 161 at 228, [1931] All ER Rep 1 at 33, after stating his view that a servant has no general duty to disclose his own wrongdoing, says that an employer who wishes to protect himself can question his servant and will then be protected by the truth or otherwise of his answers. Counsel for Mr and Mrs Roques says that in *Swain v West (Butchers) Ltd* it was after the chairman had told the plaintiff, 'If you don't get us the conclusive proof, you are for it—if you do, you can carry on,' that the plaintiff provided the information against the other employee. That is quite true, but the issue in the case was whether there was consideration for the promise to permit the plaintiff to carry on if he provided the information. It was held that it was not. That was because there was, as it seems to me, at all relevant times a duty on the plaintiff to disclose; it did not depend on any obligation arising from the questioning by, or the requirement of, the chairman. Thus Greene LJ said ([1936] 3 All ER 261 at 265):

> 'The plaintiff was responsible for the management of the business and was responsible for seeing that the business was conducted honestly and efficiently by all who came under his control. If the dishonesty of a fellow-servant came to his notice, he should tell the board.'

That applies equally to Mr Roques in the present case. The effect of a disclosure of the activities of the other employees would, of course, have been to disclose Mr Roques's own misconduct. In my view that is not a justification for failure to disclose. As Greene LJ said in *Swain v West (Butchers) Ltd* [1936] 3 All ER 261 at 265:

> 'His duty to give information to the board arose at the moment when the original improper orders were given to him and his duty is not lessened by the fact that he obeyed those orders himself.'

I am not at all saying that an employee has in every case a duty to disclose to his employers any information that he has about breaches of duty by his fellow employees. I can see that ordinary usage is in many respects against such a rule. The matter must depend, I think, on all the circumstances of the case. The important circumstances in the present case are that Mr Roques was in a senior executive position in the group and there was existing a continuing fraud by the employees against the company, of which he was well aware.

In my view Walton J's decision was quite right and, despite the skilful argument of counsel for Mr and Mrs Roques, I too would dismiss the appeal.

KERR LJ. I also agree. In the face of the findings of Walton J, counsel for Mr and Mrs Roques had to make a number of inevitable concessions for the purposes of his argument on these appeals. Firstly, that Gamlen Chemical Co (UK) Ltd had ample grounds for dismissing Mr Roques for fraud and serious misconduct. Secondly, that if they had known this when Mr Roques retired before his normal retiring date, as he did, they would clearly have exercised their discretion adversely to him under r 8(b) of the rules of the pension scheme, and that in not doing so they acted under a mistake. Thirdly, that if this mistake on their part was induced either by a misrepresentation or a breach of duty on the part of Mr Roques, then Gamlen are entitled to rescission of the pension transaction, both in the law of trust and of contract, and to recovery of the sum paid to Mr Roques other than to the extent of his own contribution. Fourthly, that Mrs Roques, for whom one cannot but have sympathy, cannot be in a better position than Mr Roques in this regard. a

Since mistake induced by misrepresentation has not been pleaded, although I think that, in the circumstances of this case, it might well have been, the issue is whether or not Mr Roques was in breach of a duty to his employers which induced the mistake on their part. As to this, it seems to me that there can only be one answer. Mr Roques was throughout in fraudulent breach of a clear duty owed to his employers to put an end to the activities of Mr Bove and the other conspirators, who were engaged in seeking to b destroy the employers' business for their own purposes, and this continuing breach of his duty induced the mistake. His duty was to report the activities of the conspirators in any event, and to dismiss them forthwith in so far as it lay within his powers to do so. Covering up and deliberately concealing their activities, which is what he was doing throughout, was the clearest possible breach of duty for a person in his position, and equally clearly it induced the mistake in question. All that *Bell v Lever Bros Ltd* [1932] AC c 161, [1931] All ER Rep 1 decides in this regard, at most, is that Mr Roques was under no duty to disclose his own misconduct. I say 'at most' because I am far from convinced that *Bell v Lever Bros Ltd* applies, even to this extent, to cases where the concealment is fraudulent, as here, since the absence of fraud was stressed throughout the appellate proceedings in that case, including the speeches of Lord Atkin and Lord Thankerton ([1932] AC 161 at 223, 231, 235; cf [1931] 1 All ER Rep 1 at 30, 34, 36) with which Lord d Blanesburgh agreed. On no view, however, can *Bell v Lever Bros Ltd* be invoked by Mr Roques to a greater extent than this. The fact that compliance by Mr Roques with his duties in this regard would in this case inevitably have revealed his own fraudulent complicity is irrelevant, as shown by the decision of this court in *Swain v West (Butchers) Ltd* [1936] 3 All ER 261; and in my view the approval of the decision of Avory J in *Healey v Société Anonyme Française Rubastic* [1917] 1 KB 946 by the House of Lords in *Ramsden v* e *David Sharratt & Sons Ltd* (1930) 35 Com Cas 314 and in *Bell v Lever Bros Ltd* makes no difference whatever to these conclusions. *Healey*'s case merely decided, as confirmed by *Bell v Lever Bros Ltd* [1932] AC 161 at 228, 231, [1931] All ER Rep 1 at 33, 34, that, at any rate in the absence of fraudulent concealment, there is no continuing duty on an employee to disclose his own misconduct, and that an employer cannot rely on past, and evidently spent, acts of misconduct as a ground for refusing to pay the employee for his f subsequent services.

I therefore do not accept that it makes any difference that the pension arrangements as such were not directly induced by misrepresentation or breach of duty on the part of Mr Roques. What matters is that when these arrangements were concluded and acted on by his employers, he was in clear breach of his duty to his employers, and indeed in fraudulent breach, and that these breaches induced the mistake on their part, which g caused them not to exercise their rights under r 8(b) of the scheme.

Accordingly I agree that these appeals must be dismissed.

Appeal dismissed.

Solicitors: *Douglas Goldberg & Co* (for Mr and Mrs Roques); *Herbert Smith & Co* (for the plaintiffs).

Diana Brahams Barrister.

Attorney General's Reference (No 1 of 1982)

COURT OF APPEAL, CRIMINAL DIVISION
LORD LANE CJ, TAYLOR AND McCOWAN JJ
21, 30 MARCH 1983

Criminal law – Conspiracy – Conspiracy to defraud – Conspiracy to be carried out abroad – Performance of conspiracy would cause economic loss and damage to proprietary rights of company within jurisdiction – Whether conspiracy indictable in England.

Criminal law – Conspiracy – Conspiracy to defraud – Conspiracy to be carried out abroad – Performance of conspiracy would injure person or company in England by causing him or it damage abroad – Whether conspiracy indictable in England.

X Ltd, an English company, were the proprietors of whisky labelled as being distilled by them and the owners of the copyright in the labels. The defendants, the directors of another company which had no business dealings with X Ltd, were charged on indictment with conspiracy to defraud, the particulars of the offence being that they had conspired to defraud X Ltd by causing them to suffer loss through the unlawful labelling, sale, supply or marketing of their products. The prosecution alleged that the defendants had contracted in London to sell L a large quantity of whisky, the ultimate destination of which was the Lebanon, that they had had printed labels imitating those of X Ltd, that the labels had been prepared for transmission to Germany, where they were to be fixed to bottles of the defendants' whisky, prior to the whisky being shipped to the Lebanon and sold as X Ltd's product, and that the defendants' plan would have been implemented if the German police had not intervened and seized the whisky. The prosecution asserted that the conspiracy was indictable in England, even though it was to be performed abroad, because if it was executed, it would cause X Ltd damage in England because X Ltd's own sales of whisky to the Lebanon would be adversely affected and their copyright in the labels would be infringed there. The trial judge ruled that he had no jurisdiction to try the indictment because a conspiracy in England to commit a crime abroad was not indictable in England unless the contemplated crime was one for which an indictment would lie in England. He accordingly directed the jury to acquit the defendants. On a reference by the Attorney General on the question whether persons could be charged on indictment with conspiracy to defraud where the conspiracy was to be carried out abroad, if the performance of the conspiracy would cause economic loss and damage to the proprietary interests of a company within the jurisdiction or would injure a person or company within the jurisdiction by causing him or it damage abroad,

Held – (1) Whether persons could be charged on indictment with conspiracy to defraud when the conspiracy was to be carried out abroad and the conspiracy would cause economic loss and damage to the proprietary interest of a company within the jurisdiction depended on whether the true object of the agreement entered into by the conspirators was to cause economic loss and damage to the proprietary interests of the company within the jurisdiction. Since the true object of the alleged conspiracy had been to defraud potential purchasers of the whisky in the Lebanon by falsely representing that it was X Ltd's whisky, and since damage to X Ltd was only a side effect or incidental consequence of the conspiracy, the conspiracy was not aimed at X Ltd and a charge of conspiracy to defraud the company would not lie (see p 724 *a* to *c* and p 725 *b*, post); *Board of Trade v Owen* [1957] 1 All ER 411, *Scott v Comr of Police for the Metropolis* [1974] 3 All ER 1032, *R v Allsop* (1976) 64 Cr App R 29 and *Rank Film Distributors Ltd v Video Information Centre* [1981] 2 All ER 76 considered.

(2) There were no grounds for holding that a conspiracy in England to be carried out abroad was indictable on proof that its performance would injure a person or company in England by causing him or it damage abroad (see p 725 *b*, post); dictum of Lord Wilberforce in *DPP v Doot* [1973] 1 All ER at 943 applied; dictum of Lord Tucker in *Board of Trade v Owen* [1957] 1 All ER at 422 considered.

Notes

For conspiracy to commit offences abroad, see 11 Halsbury's Laws (4th edn) para 77, and for cases on conspiracy to defraud, see 15 Digest (Reissue) 1398–1401, *12,236–12,272*.

Cases referred to in judgment

Board of Trade v Owen [1957] 1 All ER 411, [1957] AC 602, [1957] 2 WLR 351, HL.
DPP v Doot [1973] 1 All ER 940, [1973] AC 807, [1973] 2 WLR 532, HL.
R v Allsop (1976) 64 Cr App R 29, CA.
Rank Film Distributors Ltd v Video Information Centre [1981] 2 All ER 76, [1982] AC 380, [1981] 2 WLR 668, HL.
Scott v Comr of Police for the Metropolis [1974] 3 All ER 1032, [1975] AC 819, [1974] 3 WLR 741, HL.

Reference

This was a reference by the Attorney General, under s 36 of the Criminal Justice Act 1972, for the opinion of the Court of Appeal, Criminal Division, on two points of law arising in a case where the respondents and others had been acquitted on the direction of the trial judge on an indictment containing one count charging the accused with conspiracy to defraud. The facts are set out in the judgment of the court.

Ann Goddard QC and *P C Ader* for the Attorney General.
Colin Dines for the respondents.

Cur adv vult

30 March. The following judgment of the court was delivered.

LORD LANE CJ. This is a reference by Her Majesty's Attorney General under s 36 of the Criminal Justice Act 1972. The respondents were charged with conspiracy to defraud. The particulars of the offence were that they had conspired together and with others to defraud such companies and persons, and in particular X Ltd, as might be caused loss by unlawful labelling, sale, supply or marketing of whisky purporting to be that of X label products, the said X Co Ltd being the proprietors of the labelled products and owning the copyright in the label.

At the conclusion of the Crown case, the judge upheld submissions on behalf of the respondents that the court had no jurisdiction to try the indictment, because a conspiracy in England to commit a crime abroad is not indictable here unless the crime contemplated is one for which an indictment would lie in England.

The points of law referred for consideration by this court are set out in para 1 of the reference:

> '(i) Whether on a charge of conspiracy to defraud where the conspiracy is to be carried out abroad, it is indictable if its performance will cause economic loss and damage to the proprietary interests of a company within the jurisdiction. (ii) Whether on a charge of conspiracy to defraud where the conspiracy is to be carried out abroad, it is indictable if its performance would injure a person or company here by causing him or it damage abroad.'

The relevant facts are as follows. X Co distil and market whisky. Their registered offices are in England. Two of their brands or labels are world famous. They own the copyright in and claim the exclusive use of those labels. Their labels are protected by trade marks registered in almost all countries, and in particular in England, Germany and the Lebanon. Two of the respondents, A and B, were directors of Y Co. That company had no business dealings with X Co.

The prosecution case was that A and B arranged to sell to L a large quantity of whisky,
a the ultimate destination of which was to be the Lebanon. The contract was concluded in London. The whisky was in Frankfurt. Perforated sheets of labels imitating those of X Co were printed and brought to Y Co in London, where A and B and C (another respondent) prepared them for transmission to Frankfurt, where they were to be fixed to the bottles of whisky, prior to the whisky being shipped to the Lebanon and sold as X Co's product. The German authorities then seized the whisky before the plans could be
b further implemented.

X Co Ltd had appreciable sales in the Lebanon, and it was likely that, if the respondents' whisky, masquerading as that of X Co, had been sold in the Lebanon, X Co would have suffered loss of trade, quite apart from the infringement of their trade marks and possible injury to their reputation generally.

Counsel for the Attorney General asserts that the indictment was drawn with the
c intention of alleging against the respondents a conspiracy to defraud X Co and/or their parent or subsidiary companies. It was not intended, despite its wording, to allege a conspiracy to defraud any possible purchasers of the whisky in the Lebanon. Indeed she expressly disavowed any reliance on a conspiracy to obtain money by deception. Her argument stood or fell on her contention that what was proved here was a conspiracy formed in this country to defraud X Co or their associates by the dishonest use of their
d labels.

Thereafter she advances two separate propositions. Her starting point is, as it must be, the decision of the House of Lords in *Board of Trade v Owen* [1957] 1 All ER 411, [1957] AC 602. That case decided that a conspiracy in England to commit a crime abroad is not indictable in England unless the crime contemplated is one for which an indictment would like in England. On the facts of that case no such indictment would lie, since the
e conspiracy was not to commit a crime but to obtain a lawful object by unlawful means both of which were outside the jurisdiction.

The first argument of counsel for the Attorney General is this. Accepting the test in *Board of Trade v Owen*, although no indictment would lie in England for a substantive crime if this conspiracy were carried out, the conspiracy itself was indictable here because its ultimate object was to injure X Co in England, albeit by acts done abroad. It was a
f conspiracy to defraud X Co in England by infringing their copyright abroad.

Counsel for the Attorney General cited three cases to show that a conspiracy to defraud can exist without deceit, that false representations need not be made, and that the execution of the conspiracy need not involve the commission of a substantive crime. All that is required, she says, is an agreement dishonestly to cause economic loss or prejudice to another.

g In *Rank Film Distributors Ltd v Video Information Centre* [1981] 2 All ER 76, [1982] AC 380 the respondents were suspected of selling pirated video cassettes, thereby infringing the appellants' copyright. Lord Wilberforce said conspiracy to defraud was an 'exact description' of that activity (see [1981] 2 All ER 76 at 80, [1982] AC 380 at 441). Similarly in *Scott v Comr of Police for the Metropolis* [1974] 3 All ER 1032, [1975] AC 819 the indictment charged conspiracy to defraud 'such companies . . . as might be caused loss by
h the unlawful copying and distribution of films the copyright in which and the distribution rights of which belonged to [others]'. The House of Lords ruled that deceit was not a necessary ingredient of a conspiracy to defraud: an agreement by dishonesty to injure some proprietary right of a person was sufficient.

In *R v Allsop* (1976) 64 Cr App R 29 the appellant, a sub-broker for a hire purchase company, falsified the particulars on application forms to induce the company to accept
j applications they may otherwise have rejected. He intended no loss, believing the transactions would ultimately be satisfactory. He was held to have been rightly convicted of conspiracy to defraud, as he had put the company's economic interests in jeopardy by dishonesty even though he did not intend to cause loss.

Counsel for the Attorney General argues that in the present case, whether the conspirators intended it or not, the effect of this dishonesty abroad would have been to injure X Co's economic interest here. She says that was the real object of the fraud. It should however be noted that in the first two cases she cites the owners of the copyright were the intended and only possible victims of the fraud. In *R v Allsop* likewise the hire-purchase company was the intended and only possible victim. The false representations were aimed at the company.

The real question must in each case be what the true object of the agreement entered into by the conspirators? In our judgment, the object here was to obtain money from prospective purchasers of whisky in the Lebanon by falsely representing that it was X Co's whisky. It may well be that, if the plan had been carried out, some damage could have resulted to X Co, but that would have been a side effect or incidental consequence of the conspiracy, and not its object. There may be many conspiracies aimed at particular victims which in their execution result in loss or damage to third parties. It would be contrary to principle, as well as being impracticable for the courts, to attribute to defendants constructive intentions to defraud third parties based on what the defendants should have foreseen as probable or possible consequences. In each case, to determine the object of the conspiracy, the court must see what the defendants actually agreed to do. Had it not been for the jurisdictional problem, we have no doubt that charge against these conspirators would have been conspiracy to defraud potential purchasers of the whisky, for that was the true object of the agreement. Accordingly we reject the first argument.

Counsel for the Attorney General's alternative approach is more bold. She asks us to lay down a different test from that propounded in *Board of Trade v Owen*, which she suggests is inappropriate to the facts of this case. The new test proposed is this. If a conspiracy to defraud, although to be wholly carried out abroad, would cause injury to an individual or company within the jurisdiction, it is indictable here. Counsel for the Attorney General contends that the protection of economic interests in this country against injury by fraud here or abroad is a legitimate and proper function of the criminal law.

The only semblance of support for her proposal is a dictum at the end of Lord Tucker's speech in *Board of Trade v Owen* [1957] 1 All ER 411 at 422, [1957] AC 602 at 634. After stating the general test already cited, he went on:

> 'In so deciding I would, however, reserve for future consideration the question whether a conspiracy in this country which is wholly to be carried out abroad may not be indictable here on proof that its performance would produce a public mischief in this country or injure a person here by causing him damage abroad.'

It is to be noted that Lord Tucker limited the point for consideration to cases where the conspiracy was made in England, and counsel for the Attorney General adopts that limitation. But this could well involve the most technical anomalies, such as were foreshadowed by Lord Wilberforce in *DPP v Doot* [1973] 1 All ER 940 at 943, [1973] AC 807 at 818, where he said:

> 'Often in conspiracy cases the implementing action is itself the only evidence of the conspiracy—this is the doctrine of overt acts. Could it be said, with any plausibility, that if the conclusion or a possible conclusion to be drawn from overt acts in England was that there was a conspiracy entered into abroad, a charge of conspiracy would not lie? Surely not; yet, if it could, what difference should it make if the conspiracy is directly proved or is admitted to have been made abroad? The truth is that, in the normal case of conspiracy carried out, or partly carried out, in this country, the location of the formation of the agreement is irrelevant; the attack on the laws of this country is identical wherever the conspirators happened to meet; the "conspiracy" is a complex, formed indeed, but not severally completed, at the first meeting of the plotters. A legal principle which would enable concerting law breakers to escape a conspiracy charge by crossing the Channel before making their agreement or to bring forward arguments, which we know can be subtle enough, as to the location of agreements or, conversely, which would encourage the prosecution into allegation or fiction of a renewed agreement in this country, all this with no compensating merit, is not one which I could endorse.'

If, on the other hand, Lord Tucker's limitation to conspiracies entered into in England were removed, the new test would be immensely wide. Whenever a fraudulent conspiracy made abroad and to be carried out abroad sent ripples back to England washing over and damaging some economic interest here, an indictment would lie.

We can find no grounds in authority or principle for so holding. If it is necessary to enlarge the present jurisdiction, which we think it is not, then that is a matter for Parliament. Accordingly, we reject counsel for the Attorney General's second argument. Our answer to the points of law posed for consideration in para 1(i) and (ii) of the reference is in each case No.

Declaration accordingly

Solicitors: *Director of Public Prosecutions*; *Alistair Porter & Co* (for the respondents).

N P Metcalfe Esq Barrister.

Astro Exito Navegacion SA v Southland Enterprise Co Ltd and another (Chase Manhattan Bank NA intervening)

The Messiniaki Tolmi

HOUSE OF LORDS

LORD DIPLOCK, LORD KEITH OF KINKEL, LORD SCARMAN, LORD ROSKILL AND LORD BRIDGE OF HARWICH

3, 4 MAY, 23 JUNE 1983

Execution – Instrument – Execution by person nominated by High Court – Jurisdiction – Contract – Contract for sale of vessel – Notice of readiness – Buyer refusing to countersign notice of readiness – Letter of credit in payment of purchase price – Bank refusing to release money secured by letter of credit because notice of readiness not countersigned as required by terms of letter of credit – Seller commencing proceedings for specific performance – Judge ordering buyer to sign notice of readiness by certain date failing which notice to be signed by master – Jurisdiction of court to make order – Whether notice of readiness executed by master binding on parties other than buyer and seller – Whether bank obliged to accept notice of readiness countersigned by master – Supreme Court of Judicature (Consolidation) Act 1925, s 47.

The sellers, a Panamanian company, agreed to sell a vessel to the buyers, a Taiwanese company, in accordance with a memorandum of agreement dated 2 July 1980. The vessel was intended to be broken up by the buyers and the sellers agreed to deliver the vessel to a specified harbour in Taiwan with a valid gas-free certificate and a notice of readiness which was to be countersigned by the buyers. Under the terms of the contract, it was agreed that arbitration of any dispute arising out of the sale was to be in London in accordance with English law. Pursuant to the contract the buyers opened a letter of credit with a bank in Taiwan for payment of the purchase price. The letter of credit was confirmed by a London bank. The sellers duly delivered the vessel to the Taiwan harbour with a gas-free certificate and gave noticed of readiness. The buyers refused to accept the notice on the ground that the gas-free certificate was not valid. They consequently refused to countersign the notice of readiness and purported to cancel the contract. The sellers commenced proceedings in the Commercial Court for specific performance of the contract. The buyers applied for a stay of proceedings pending the outcome of arbitration.

On 24 October 1980 the judge stayed the proceedings but on terms which included by way of interim relief granted to the sellers injunctions directing the buyers (i) to *a*
countersign the notice of readiness by 28 October 1980, failing which the notice was to be signed by a master of the Supreme Court for and on behalf of the buyers, and (ii) to instruct the Taiwan bank to authorise the London bank to release the moneys secured by the letter of credit, the moneys so released to be lodged in the joint names of the parties' solicitors until agreement or further order. The buyers failed to comply with the order on the due date and the notice of readiness was signed by a Supreme Court master and *b*
presented to the London bank with the documents necessary to operate the letter of credit. The London bank refused to release the moneys and the letter of credit expired on 30 October. The buyers issued a notice of appeal against the order of 24 October and on 12 November the sellers commenced proceedings against the London bank in respect of its refusal to pay on the letter of credit. Subsequently the arbitrators awarded damages to the sellers for the buyers' breach of contract. The sellers and the buyers then applied to *c*
the Court of Appeal to withdraw the appeal against the order of 24 October, since it had been overtaken by the arbitrators' award. However, the sellers' claim against the London bank remained alive and the London bank accordingly applied to intervene in the appeal in order to be joined as a defendant so that it could pursue the appeal. In the course of the hearing of the London bank's application the bank was granted leave on 4 March 1982 to intervene as a defendant. On the hearing of the merits of the London bank's *d*
claim that the judge had had no jurisdiction to make the order of 24 October, or if he had that he ought to have exercised his discretion by refusing to make the order, the Court of Appeal held that the judge had had jurisdiction to make the order under his power under s 47[a] of the Supreme Court of Judicature (Consolidation) Act 1925 to order that a document be executed 'Where any person neglects or refuses to comply with a judgment or order directing him to execute [the] document', and further held that the *e*
judge had exercised his discretion correctly in making the order. The London bank appealed, contending, inter alia, (i) that the court's power under s 47 to order the execution of a document was limited to documents necessary to fulfil the requirements of a contract between the parties immediately before the court and did not extend to ordering a 'substitute' signature on a document (such as the notice of readiness) which affected the relationship between third parties (such as the two banks or the London bank *f*
and the sellers), (ii) that, if there was jurisdiction under s 47 to order such a 'substitute' signature, the judge had exercised his discretion wrongly because that section was being used to alter the nature of the obligations assumed both by the London bank and by the Taiwan bank, since absolute compliance with the documentary requirements of the credits was essential, and (iii) that the Court of Appeal should not have affirmed the judge's order because once the letter of credit had expired on 30 October 1980 the sellers *g*
had no longer had a claim for specific performance of the contract but only a claim against the buyers for unliquidated damages and in those circumstances an order in support of the claim for specific performance was only proper up to 30 October while the letter of credit was extant.

Held – On the true construction of s 47 of the 1925 Act there was no limitation either *h*
on the class of document which the court could order to be executed or on the purpose for which a document so executed could be used. Since the court had had jurisdiction over the letter of credit because it was a contract governed by English law, the court had had jurisdiction to order that the notice of readiness required to operate the letter of credit be executed by a Supreme Court master. Furthermore, the exercise by the judge of the jurisdiction under s 47 did not alter the respective obligations of the London bank *j*
and the Taiwan bank, since the order did not compel the London bank to do anything, and the fact that the buyers failed to comply with the order did not entitle the London bank, which was not a party to the contract in relation to which the order was made, to

a Section 47 is set out at p 735 *e*, post

complain about its effect. If the London bank had wished to show that its rejection of the
a documents was justified the appropriate method of doing so was by way of a defence in the proceedings brought against it by the sellers. The appeal would accordingly be dismissed (see p 727 *g* to *j*, p 735 *g* to p 736 *e*, post).

Decision of the Court of Appeal [1982] 3 All ER 335 affirmed.

Notes

b For the execution of documents or instruments by a person nominated by the High Court, see 26 Halsbury's Laws (4th edn) paras 570–571, and for cases on the subject, see 17 Digest (Reissue) 264–265, *295–306*.

For the Supreme Court of Judicature (Consolidation) Act 1925, s 47, see 25 Halsbury's Statutes (3rd edn) 719.

As from 1 January 1982, s 47 of the 1925 Act was replaced by s 39 of the Supreme
c Court Act 1981.

Case referred to in opinions

United City Merchants (Investments) Ltd v Royal Bank of Canada [1982] 2 All ER 720, [1983] AC 168, [1982] 2 WLR 1039, HL.

d **Appeal**

Chase Manhattan Bank NA appealed with leave of the Appeal Committee of the House of Lords granted on 29 July 1982 from an order of the Court of Appeal (Stephenson, Ackner and O'Connor LJJ) ([1982] 3 All ER 335, [1982] QB 1248) dated 5 April 1982 dismissing an appeal by the bank from an interlocutory order of Parker J dated 27 October 1980 in proceedings between the respondents, Astro Exito Navegacion SA (the
e sellers), and Southland Enterprise Co Ltd and Nan Jong Iron and Steel Co Ltd (the buyers). The bank was not a party to the proceedings before Parker J but was given leave by the Court of Appeal to be joined as a defendant in the action for the purpose of enabling them to appeal and thus replace the buyers who withdrew their appeals against the order of Parker J. The facts are set out in the opinion of Lord Roskill.

f *Leonard Hoffmann QC* and *Michael Tugendhat* for the bank.
Nicholas Phillips QC and *Steven Gee* for the sellers.

Their Lordships took time for consideration.

23 June. The following opinions were delivered.

g **LORD DIPLOCK.** My Lords, I have had the advantage of reading in draft the speech of my noble and learned friend Lord Roskill. I agree with it, and for the reasons he gives I would dismiss the appeal.

LORD KEITH OF KINKEL. My Lords, for the reasons given in the speech to be delivered by my noble and learned friend Lord Roskill, which I have had the benefit of
h reading in draft and with which I agree, I too would dismiss the appeal.

LORD SCARMAN. My Lords, I have had the advantage of reading in draft the speech to be delivered by my noble and learned friend Lord Roskill. I agree with it, and for the reasons which he gives I would dismiss the appeal with costs.

j **LORD ROSKILL.** My Lords, the history of the dispute which gives rise to this appeal to your Lordships' House by the Chase Manhattan Bank NA (the bank) is long and complex and must, I fear, be related in some detail in order that the matters for decision can be properly understood, though those matters themselves are not, as I understand all your Lordships to agree, difficult of decision. The appeal arises out of an action (the action) between the respondents, Astro Exito Navegacion SA, a Panamanian company, and Southland, Enterprise Co Ltd, a Taiwanese company. In the action the respondents (I shall call them 'sellers') were plaintiffs and the Taiwanese company (I shall call them 'buyers') were the first defendants. I can ignore the existence of the second defendants in the action. The bank, though now the appellants to your Lordships' House, were not initially parties to the action; indeed it is of great importance to observe at the outset that they were not parties to the contract out of the clear and indeed deliberate breaches of which by the buyers the action arose. The bank applied for and were granted leave to be added as defendants in the action by the Court of Appeal (Stephenson, Ackner and O'Connor LJJ) ([1982] 3 All ER 335, [1982] QB 1248) on 4 March 1982 after the action itself as between the sellers and the buyers had been stayed by Parker J on 24 October 1980. The purpose of that application by the bank was to enable the bank to appeal against other parts of that order which Parker J had then made, an order in which the bank claimed to be interested in circumstances still to be related. After that leave had been given and by the time the bank's appeal was thereafter heard, the buyers, who had themselves on 10 November 1980 initially given notice of appeal against that order, withdrew from proceedings so that, unless the bank were allowed to be joined and to prosecute the appeal, no appeal would have been pursued against the judge's order. Subsequently, on 5 April 1982, the Court of Appeal dismissed the bank's appeal, the judgment of the court being given by Ackner LJ (see [1982] 3 All ER 335 at 344, [1982] QB 1248 at 1264). Leave to appeal was refused, but such leave was later given by your Lordships' House.

My Lords, with that brief introduction to explain how this appeal arises, I turn to consider the history of the dispute. The sellers owned a Greek motor vessel named Messiniaki Tolmi. She was some 51,400 grt, and was built in Norway in 1965. By a written agreement (the sale agreement) dated 2 July 1980, but not signed until 23 July 1980, the sellers agreed to sell and the buyers agreed to buy the vessel for breaking up at Taiwan at the price of $US4,241,575, which your Lordships were told represented a price of $US212.50 per lightweight ton. The sale agreement included the following provisions which it is necessary to set out in full:

> '(1) The vessel is now trading and is to be delivered to the Purchasers inside Kaohsiung Harbour under her own power "as is" safely afloat and substantially intact expected during 1st–30th September, 1980, with 30th September, 1980, cancelling (after discharge of inward cargo, if any) with all her outfit, materials, tackle, apparel and spare gear as on board but with the exception of private effects of Captain, Officers and crew and hired equipment, if any. Should the vessel not be ready for delivery within the 30th September, 1980 cancelling for any reason other than mentioned in Clause 3 hereof, the Purchasers have the option of maintaining or cancelling this Agreement, such option to be declared within 48 hours and in the event of cancellation or the Purchasers' failure to exercise such option, the deposit and Letter of Credit shall be immediately released to the Purchasers in full and this Agreement shall be considered null and void.
>
> (2) The Purchasers shall deposit with the Vendors' Agents, Felicity Navigation Corp., a New Taiwan Dollar Cheque for the equivalent of 10% of the Purchase Price, such deposit to be lodged on signing this Agreement and to be returned to the Purchasers on opening the confirmed irrevocable Letter of Credit as detailed hereunder. The whole of the Purchase Price amounting to U.S. $4,241,575 (say four million, two hundred and forty-one thousand, five hundred and seventy-five United States dollars) shall be paid by a confirmed irrevocable Letter of Credit in terms acceptable to the Vendors and valid until 30th October, 1980, established by a full detailed cable or telex within 15 working days from signing this Agreement, such confirmed irrevocable Letter of Credit to be in favour of the Vendors for the account of Oceanic Finance Corporation Limited (for and on behalf of Astro Exito Navegacion S.A.) with the Royal Bank of Canada, 6 Lothbury Street, London, E.C.2. England, either established direct with the said Bank or through another first-class London

Bank (hereinafter called the "Negotiating Bank"). Immediately upon receipt of the foregoing Letter of Credit and upon acceptance of its terms the Vendors shall forthwith deposit the undermentioned documents with the Negotiating Bank as stakeholders of the documents. (Unless the 10% deposit of this Purchase Price and the irrevocable Letter of Credit are confirmed established and within times herein stipulated, then cancelling time stipulated in Clause 1 to be extended accordingly at Vendors' option. If Letter of Credit is not established with Memorandum of Agreement limits, Sellers option to cancel). 1. Legal Bill of Sale, duly attested by a Notary Public, specifying free from encumbrances, all debts, claims and maritime liens. 2. Signed Commercial Invoice in quadruplicate, setting out the vessel's particulars. 3. The Vendors' written undertaking to cable the Master or their representatives in Taiwan instructing them to physically deliver the vessel to the Purchasers immediately the Purchase Money has been received in full. 4. Certificate of Deletion of the vessel from the Greek Register or the Vendors' written undertaking stating that deletion of registration will be effected as soon as possible but not later than two weeks after the vessel has been fully paid for. 5. Signed Suppliers' Certificate.

Within three business days of the Vendors or their Agents in Taiwan giving notice to the Purchasers by letter or telegram of the vessel's readiness for delivery in accordance with this Agreement and presenting the Gas Free Certificate as per Clause 17, the Negotiating Bank shall be instructed by the Purchasers to release the full Letter of Credit amount to the Vendors forthwith. Such notice of readiness must be countersigned by the Kaohsiung Harbour Master or Lloyd's Agents in Taiwan, confirming safe arrival of the vessel. This document and Gas Free Certificate as per Clause 17 with documents 1–5 as mentioned above shall be sufficient evidence to permit the Negotiating Bank to release the Letter of Credit in full to the Vendors. When the full Purchase Price has been released the aforementioned documents shall be released to the Purchasers. In the event that the confirmed irrevocable Letter of Credit is not established as aforesaid, the 10% (ten per cent) deposit shall immediately be forfeited to the sole use of the Vendors. Any Taiwan legal consular or import fees or taxes or bank charges to be for the Purchasers' account. All bank charges in London in connection with the Letter of Credit, except bank confirmation and opening charges, are for the account of the Vendors.

(3) Should the vessel be unable to enter Kaohsiung Harbour on arrival for any reason other than on account of the weather or for any reason under the Vendors' control the Purchasers are to pay to the Vendors demurrage at U.S. $6,000.00 (say six thousand United States Dollars) per day or pro rata commencing 48 hours after the vessel's arrival off Kaohsiung. The Purchasers' guarantee the availability of a suitable berth immediately upon arrival of the vessel at Kaohsiung outer anchorage, in order that the Vendors can complete necessary pre-hand over formalities. If Purchasers breaking-up berth is either not free or not accessible, then the vessel is to be delivered "as is where is" as near as she can reasonably get to Purchasers breaking-up berth in Master's discretion, and the Purchasers shall arrange a berth, anchorage or buoy, able to accommodate the vessel and same to be available upon vessel's arrival. Should the vessel still be unable to enter Kaohsiung Harbour within 7 business days after arrival then the Vendors shall have the right to cancel this Agreement and in such case the deposit referred to in Clause 2 hereof shall be forfeited to the sole use of the Vendors together with payment of the accrued demurrage or at their option the Vendors have the right to deliver the vessel at Kaohsiung anchorage safely afloat and in this case the full amount of the Letter of Credit will be released to the Vendors as per Clause 4 (subject to the logical amendment in the notice of readiness) and Vendors' crew will be released immediately for repatriation (at Vendors' cost). In addition Purchasers undertake if expired, to extend the validity of the Letter of Credit in order to cover the above period of time.

(4) It shall be a special instruction of the confirmed irrevocable Letter of Credit as referred to in Clause 2 hereof, that in the event that the Purchasers or the Purchasers' Opening Bank in Taiwan fails to despatch a cable or telex to the Negotiating Bank releasing the full Letter of Credit amount to the Vendors within 3 (three) business days of the Vendors or their agents in Taiwan giving the countersigned notice of readiness aforesaid and the Gas-Free Certificate as per Clause 17, to the Purchasers (or their Agents or otherwise as may be stipulated in the Letter of Credit), then the Vendors have the right to negotiate the confirmed irrevocable Letter of Credit by presenting to the Negotiating Bank a copy of the aforesaid countersigned notice of readiness, together with the documents, 1, 2, 3, 4 and 5 as specified in Clause 2 hereof and presentation of such documents alone shall constitute sufficient evidence to permit the Negotiating Bank to release the Letter of Credit amount in full to the Vendors.

(5) The vessel is sold for the purpose of breaking-up only and the Purchasers hereby covenant that they will neither trade the vessel for their own account nor sell the vessel to a third party for any purpose other than breaking-up. The Purchasers undertake to complete breaking-up within nine months from time of delivery to be proved by production of certificate issued by the appropriate Local Authority . . .

(14) Any dispute or difference arising under this Agreement shall be settled by arbitration in London each party choosing one Arbitrator who shall if necessary appoint an Umpire whose decision shall be accepted as final and may be made a Rule of Court. Arbitrators and Umpire are to be commercial men and not lawyers. Such arbitration to be in accordance with the provisions of the Arbitration Act of 1950 or any statutory modifications thereof.

(15) This Agreement is to be construed and take effect as a Contract made in England and in accordance with the Laws of England and shall not only in England but in other countries be interpreted and enforceable in all respects in accordance with the said laws . . .

(17) The vessel will be delivered to the Purchasers with a valid Gas-Free Certificate for hot work, which Certificate to be approved by the Taiwan Authorities. However, if the said Gas-Free Certificate is not approved by the Taiwan Authorities, gas clearance shall be carried out again by the Vendors or their Agents at Vendors expense unless the Vendors are able to deliver the vessel with the Gas-Free Certificate accepted by the Taiwan Authorities the Purchasers will not accept and sign the notice of readiness . . .'

It was common ground that the last date for establishing and confirming the letter of credit was 13 August 1980, but when on that date a letter of credit was established by an issuing bank in Taiwan, it neither complied with the terms of the sale agreement nor was it confirmed by a London bank. However, amendments were made and on 3 September 1980 the bank duly confirmed the letter of credit. The important respect in which the letter of credit did not comply with the sale agreement was in regard to the notice of readiness.

The letter of credit provided:

'. . . A copy of the valid gas-free certificate for hot work, which certificate to be approved by the Taiwan Authorities, together with a copy of the notice of readiness countersigned by the Kaohsiung harbour master or Lloyd's agents in Taiwan (Jardine, Matheson and Co. Ltd., Taipei) confirming safe arrival of the vessel inside Kaohsiung harbour and accepted and signed by the purchasers (Nan Jong Iron and Steel Co. Ltd., Tainan Taiwan on behalf of Southland Enterprise Co. Ltd., Tainan, Taiwan) . . .'

This provision contrasted sharply with the provision of the last paragraph of cl (2) of the sale agreement.

The ensuing events will be found detailed with care and clarity in the reasons annexed to an award dated 30 November 1981 by Mr Kazantzis and Mr Selwyn, the two commercial arbitrators respectively appointed in the arbitration between the sellers and the buyers which followed the stay of the action granted by Parker J on 24 October 1980. I gratefully refer to their narrative in order to avoid unnecessarily lengthening this speech. Suffice it to say that the vessel arrived at Kaohsiung at 0900 hrs on 22 September 1980. Notice of her arrival was telexed to the buyers. A formal notice of readiness was issued by the master at 1530 hrs on 22 September 1980 and indorsed by Lloyd's agents on 25 September 1980. On that day the buyers rejected the notice on the ground that the gas-free certificate presented with the notice of readiness had not been approved by the Taiwan authorities; it followed that the requirement in the letter of credit to which I have just referred that the notice of readiness should be accepted and signed by the buyers was not complied with.

My Lords, the explanation of the buyers' strenuous endeavours to find some excuse for avoiding their contractual obligations to the sellers is to be found in paras 18 to 20 of the arbitrators' reasons. By the end of September the market price of scrap had fallen to around $US190 per lightweight ton. As the autumn progressed so did the market fall, until by December 1980 the market price was $US150 per lightweight ton, at which price the sellers ultimately resold the vessel to Hong Kong.

Meanwhile, events had moved to London. On 9 October 1980 the sellers, doubtless appreciating that the buyers were determined not to fulfil their obligations if they could possibly find some excuse for avoiding them and anticipating the approach of the expiry date of the letter of credit, issued a specially indorsed writ against the buyers in the Commercial Court claiming specific performance of the sale agreement. The prayer in the statement of claim sought, inter alia, a mandatory order on the buyers requiring them to sign the notice of readiness and to cause the deletion of the condition in the letter of credit regarding signature of the notice of readiness to which I have already referred.

On 10 October 1980 the sellers issued a summons in the Commercial Court designed to secure this relief. This summons was heard by Parker J on 24 October 1980. At the same time, no doubt by consent, the judge heard a cross-summons (formally this still had to be issued) by the buyers seeking a stay of the action by reason of the presence of the arbitration clause in the sale agreement. By reason of s 1 of the Arbitration Act 1975 the judge was bound to grant this stay. But he granted the buyers the mandatory relief sought in relation to the notice of readiness and ordered that notice duly signed by the buyers in accordance with his order to be returned to the sellers' solicitors in London by noon of 28 October 1980. Failing compliance with this order, the judge appointed a master of the Supreme Court (by amendment made on 28 October 1980 the master was named as Master Bickford Smith) to sign that notice on behalf of the buyers. He further ordered the buyers to instruct the issuing bank in Taiwan to instruct the bank to release the full amount of the letter of credit, that instruction to be given not later than the same date and time.

Paragraphs 4 and 5 of the judge's order read thus:

> '4. The Plaintiffs do direct the full amount received under the said Letter of Credit to be placed in an interest bearing account in the joint names of the Plaintiffs' and Defendants' Solicitors with Lloyds Bank at 72 Fenchurch Street, London. No sums whatsoever are to be paid out of the said account other than pursuant to an agreement in writing between the Plaintiffs and the Defendants or pursuant to a further Order of this Court.
>
> 5. The First and Second Defendants whether by themselves their servants or agents or otherwise howsoever be restrained and an Injunction is hereby granted restraining them from making use of or dealing with howsoever any of the documents presented by the Plaintiffs under the said Letter of Credit, except with the prior written permission of the Plaintiffs' Solicitors and in accordance with the terms of such permission until further Order of the Court.'

Your Lordships have a brief note taken by counsel of the judge's oral judgment. It is clear from that note and indeed from the terms of the order itself that the judge, having stayed the action, thought (in my view entirely correctly) that the sellers had a strong case for specific performance of the sale agreement and therefore for obtaining the benefit of the letter of credit but that any defence which the buyers might ultimately prove to have could be adequately safeguarded by the provisions of paras 4 and 5 of his order which I have just set out, the proceeds of the letter of credit being meanwhile put into a joint account unless otherwise agreed between the sellers and the buyers or ordered by the court. To this end the judge exacted an undertaking from the sellers that the vessel should not be moved from her then anchorage save with the leave of the court. There is no doubt that in making this part of his order the judge, as indeed he stated, was using the powers given to the High Court by s 12(6) of the Arbitration Act 1950 and in particular by paras (*f*) and (*h*) of that subsection in support of the sellers' claim in the intended arbitration for specific performance. There is also no doubt that, in ordering the notice of readiness to be executed by the buyers or in default by Master Bickford Smith, the judge was purporting to exercise the powers given by ss 45 and 47 of the Supreme Court of Judicature (Consolidation) Act 1925.

The buyers did not comply with the judge's orders either as regards the notice of readiness or the letter of credit. Accordingly, in furtherance of para 2 of the judge's order, Master Bickford Smith executed the notice of readiness on behalf of the buyers. On 29 October 1980 the sellers presented all the documents to the bank including the notice of readiness as altered and signed by Master Bickford Smith, those being the documents said to be necessary to operate the letter of credit in favour of the sellers. The bank rejected the documents. On 30 October 1980 after an ex parte application to the Court of Appeal by the sellers to authorise a minor alteration by Master Bickford Smith to what he had previously written, the documents, including the reamended notice of readiness, were re-presented to the bank and were again rejected. On 30 October the bank had in fact sought authority to pay from the issuing bank in Taiwan but were instructed not to do so (see [1982] 3 All ER 335 at 339, [1982] QB 1248 at 1254 per Ackner LJ). Thus the proceeds of the letter of credit were never paid into the joint account envisaged by Parker J in para 4 of his order. On 30 October 1980 the validity of the letter of credit expired, the bank having by then twice rejected the documents tendered to them. Any hope of the sellers therafter securing specific performance of the sale agreement vanished with the expiry of the letter of credit. Unless the buyers could justify their conduct, as they subsequently sought to do in the arbitration to which I have referred, the sellers were left with a clear claim for damages against them.

Clearly there was no future in the vessel remaining in Taiwan. Accordingly, on 31 October 1980 the sellers sought and obtained from Mocatta J release from the undertaking exacted by Parker J from the sellers on 24 October 1980 that the vessel should not move from her then anchorage. Thereafter the sellers became free to treat the buyers' conduct as a repudiation of the sale agreement and to claim damages on that basis and also to sail the vessel away from Taiwan.

On 12 November 1980 the sellers issued a writ against the bank claiming, inter alia, $US4,241,575, being a sum equal to the purchase price of the vessel under the sale agreement, either as due under the letter of credit or as damages for the wrongful rejection by the bank of the documents. Pleadings in their original form were later exchanged, but those pleadings were subsequently extensively amended and reamended. I shall call this action against the bank 'the bank action'. Subsequently the issuing bank in Taiwan were joined as second defendants in the bank action, the pleadings in which presently extend to almost fifty pages although it would seem that the issues in that action are comparatively simple.

As already stated, the buyers on 10 November 1980 gave notice of appeal to the Court of Appeal against the order of Parker J made on 24 October 1980. On 16 January 1981 the sellers moved the Court of Appeal for an order for security on the grounds that the buyers were in contempt of the order of Parker J by their disobedience to it and further

contending that for that reason the buyers' appeal ought not to be heard. This matter for
a some reason did not come before the Court of Appeal (Lawton, Brandon and Templeman LJJ) until 17 September 1981. That court in reserved judgments delivered on 24 September 1981 dismissed the sellers' appeal and refused the sellers leave to appeal to this House (see [1981] 2 Lloyd's Rep 595).

On 28 September 1981, four days after the sellers' appeal had thus been dismissed, the arbitration proceedings between the sellers and the buyers began and continued until 7
b October 1981. The sellers claimed $US1,501,524·99 as damages for the buyers' wrongful refusal to accept delivery of the vessel and a further $US397,125·00 as demurrage under the sale agreement from 24 September until 29 November 1980. This last date was the date on which the vessel ultimately left Taiwan for Hong Kong. The buyers, one might have thought somewhat optimistically in the circumstances, counterclaimed $US483,912·40 as damages for the sellers' alleged breach of the sale agreement in failing
c to deliver the vessel to the buyers. By their award dated 30 November 1981 the two arbitrators held the buyers to be in breach and dismissed their counterclaim. Questions of quantum were stood over in the hope of agreement being reached but, as no such agreement was reached, the two arbitrators by a further award dated 23 March 1982 awarded not only the two sums above mentioned to the sellers but also a further $US35,240 in respect of overheads and expenses. The total award was for $US1,933,889·99
d together with interest at 16% from 1 December 1980 to 31 March 1982 and costs.

Between the dates of these two awards the bank on 12 January 1982 moved the Court of Appeal to be joined as defendants in the action, adopting the buyers' notice of appeal to which I have already referred and adding some grounds of their own which included the contention that Parker J had no jurisdiction under s 47 of the 1925 Act to make the order which he made on 24 October 1980 or alternatively that he exercised his discretion
e wrongly in making that order. It is to be observed that those grounds do not assert any special interest of the bank as distinct from the interest of the buyers in seeking to be joined as parties to the appeal against Parker J's order.

The buyers having thus dropped out of the proceedings, the sellers not unnaturally resisted the bank's attempt to come in in effect in their own supposed right. But the bank relied on RSC Ord 15, r 6(2) and sought to meet the sellers' contention that the right
f place to advance a challenge to the judge's order was in the bank action and not in the present proceedings by saying that while they could advance the want of jurisdiction argument in the bank action they could not in the bank action advance the contention that if the judge contrary to their contention had jurisdiction he had exercised his discretion wrongly. It was, it seems, this last contention which persuaded the Court of Appeal to allow the bank to be joined (see [1982] 3 All ER 335 at 343, [1982] QB 1248 at
g 1259 per Ackner LJ). The Court of Appeal subsequently heard the bank's appeal and dismissed it for the reasons given in a reserved judgment delivered by Ackner LJ. In substance the reasons were first that the judge had jurisdiction under s 47 to make the order and second that, for the reasons given by Ackner LJ, he had exercised his discretion correctly, especially in view of the remarkable fact, to quote the words of Ackner LJ, that 'the operation of the letter of credit could depend on the will of the buyer' (see [1982] 3
h All ER 335 at 348, [1982] QB 1248 at 1269).

My Lords, at the outset of his submissions to your Lordships' House counsel for the bank accepted that so long as the sellers were seeking specific performance of the sale agreement, as they were at least until 30 October 1980, the judge had jurisdiction under s 12(6)(*h*) of the 1950 Act and possibly also under para (*f*) of that subsection to make an order in aid of the sellers' claim for specific performance in the arbitration. But he
j contended that once, as was inevitable after 30 October 1980, the sellers were restricted to a claim against the buyers for unliquidated damages, the judge's order could not stand in order to support such a claim for, save only in a case appropriate for the issue of a Mareva injunction, a defendant or a respondent in arbitration could not be required to secure a plaintiff's or a claimant's claim for unliquidated damages. The judge had jurisdiction to make this order under the 1950 Act in support of the sellers' primary

right to claim specific performance but not in support of their secondary right to claim damages. The order was only proper so long as the letter of credit was extant, that is *a* down to 30 October 1980, for the letter of credit was the means whereby the sellers would receive payment when the mutual obligations of the sellers of delivery and of the buyers of acceptance of the vessel were performed but was not the means whereby the sellers could enforce any claim for unliquidated damages for non-performance by the buyers of their obligations. Further, counsel for the bank contended that the order was defective because it made no alternative provision for the possibility that the sellers' claim *b* might subsequently become one for unliquidated damages only. In any event, he argued, the Court of Appeal was wrong to have affirmed the judge's order because by the time of its decision the arbitration had been held and the award of damages made.

So far as the order empowering Master Bickford Smith to sign the notice of readiness was concerned, counsel for the bank contended that this part of the order was in any event wrong, because s 47 on its true construction did not entitle the judge to order a *c* 'substitute' signature of a document of this kind affecting the relationship between third parties, that is to say between the bank and the issuing bank and between the bank and the sellers. Any jurisdiction was limited to ordering a 'substitute' signature of a document effective only as between the parties to the proceedings before the court in which the order was made. It was not right, he contended, to order the 'substitute' signature of a document needed to satisfy the requirements of another contract. Alternatively, counsel *d* for the bank contended that, if there were jurisdiction under s 47 to order such a 'substitute' signature, the judge exercised his discretion wrongly because that section was being used to alter the nature of the obligations assumed both by the bank and by the issuing bank, since absolute compliance with the documentary requirements of the credits was essential. A 'just as good' document would not suffice. It must, he contended, be inherently wrong to use powers accorded by a United Kingdom statute in *e* circumstances in which international letters of credit, by no means universally governed by English law, would or might be affected.

My Lords, at the outset of his reply to these submissions counsel for the sellers forcefully pointed out that the inability of the sellers to claim specific performance of the sale agreement arose directly from the bank's refusal to accept the documents twice tendered to them so that the letter of credit expired without payment having been made. *f* It was the bank alone who by their action obliged the sellers to seek damages rather than specific performance. Had the bank paid against documents the proceeds would under para 4 of the order of Parker J have been paid into the joint account, title to the vessel would, conditionally at least, have passed to the buyers on transfer of the bill of sale, the issuing bank would have got their security for what it was worth and the bank would have been free of any further obligations to the sellers. If by any chance the proceeds in *g* the joint account became repayable to the bank rather than to the buyers, any necessary application to that end could have been made to Parker J by the bank. But, instead of looking only to their obligations under the letter of credit, the bank had of their own motion involved themselves in a dispute under a contract the performance of which as between the sellers and the buyers was no concern of the bank. Counsel for the sellers reminded your Lordships of the recent restatement of the position by Lord Diplock in *h* *United City Merchants (Investments) Ltd v Royal Bank of Canada* [1982] 2 All ER 720 at 725, [1983] AC 168 at 183. I venture to quote the whole passage:

> 'Again, it is trite law that ... the seller and the confirming bank, "deal in documents and not in goods" ... If, on their face, the documents presented to the confirming bank by the seller conform with the requirements of the credit as notified to him by the confirming bank, that bank is under a contractual obligation *j* to the seller to honour the credit, notwithstanding that the bank has knowledge that the seller at the time of presentation of the conforming documents is alleged by the buyer to have, and in fact has already, committed a breach of his contract with the buyer for the sale of the goods to which the documents appear on their face to relate that would have entitled the buyer to treat the contract of sale as rescinded and to

reject the goods and refuse to pay the seller the purchase price. The whole commercial purpose for which the system of confirmed irrevocable documentary credits has been developed in international trade is to give to the seller an assured right to be paid before he parts with control of the goods and that does not permit of any dispute with the buyer as to the performance of the contract of sale being used as a ground for non-payment or reduction or deferment of payment.'

Counsel for the sellers submitted that it was this basic principle of commercial law which the bank's actions and indeed their present submissions infringed. The bank, he contended, had no legitimate interest in challenging the order of Parker J, which was made in proceedings between the sellers and the buyers under the sale agreement. They had no legitimate interest in the question whether an order of the specific performance should be made. But, having first rejected the documents and then sought to intervene in a dispute to which they were not parties, the bank took the risk of their rejection of the documents being wrong and were not entitled to seek to pre-empt the decision in the bank action by intervening in the action to disturb an order made some two and a half years ago in proceedings to which they were strangers.

My Lords, before considering these several submissions I will deal briefly with the submission for the bank on s 47 of the Supreme Court of Judicature (Consolidation) Act 1925 on which your Lordships did not find it necessary to hear counsel for the sellers. Section 47 reads:

'Where any person neglects or refuses to comply with a judgment or order directing him to execute any conveyance, contract or other document, or to indorse any negotiable instrument, the High Court may, on such terms and conditions, if any, as may be just, order that the conveyance, contract or other document shall be executed or that the negotiable instrument shall be indorsed by such person as the court may nominate for that purpose, and a conveyance, contract, document or instrument so executed or indorsed shall operate and be for all purposes available as if it had been executed or indorsed by the person originally directed to execute or indorse it.'

Counsel for the bank sought to argue that on the true construction of this section there was no power to order the execution of a document such as the notice of readiness in order to fulfil the requirement of a contract other than the contract between the parties immediately before the court. The signing of the notice of readiness by Master Bickford Smith was not, he argued, the 'execution' of a document of the character referred to in the section. My Lords, with all respect this submission is untenable and I can see no justification for cutting down the plain and wide language of the section in the manner for which counsel for the bank contended. There is no limitation on the class of document in relation to which the powers accorded by s 47 may be invoked. Nor is there any limitation on the purpose for which a document executed in accordance with the powers so accorded may be used. The letter of credit was a contract governed by English law. So, I apprehend, was the contract between the bank and the issuing bank. The English courts clearly had jurisdiction at least over the letter of credit which the bank confirmed and that jurisdiction included power to make an order under s 47. I am of the clear opinion that Parker J had jurisdiction to make this order and, inasmuch as this was, as he rightly thought, a strong case for ordering specific performance in favour of the sellers, I think in his discretion he was entitled to make the order he did.

I have earlier used the phrase 'substituted' signature, a phrase I have borrowed from counsel for the bank. But I do not intend by my use of that phrase to imply that the document possesses any different characteristics from those it would have possessed had the buyers signed the notice of readiness as directed by Parker J. 'Alternative' signature might perhaps be a better phrase. Whether such a document so 'alternatively' signed was a good tender or whether the bank have any other defence in the bank action is not a matter on which it is necessary for your Lordships' House to pronounce in this appeal.

My Lords, I am unable to see how the exercise by Parker J of the jurisdiction accorded by s 47 in any way altered the obligations which had been assumed by the bank or by the issuing bank, as counsel for the bank sought to contend. The order which the judge made did not itself order the bank to do anything. Counsel for the bank accepted that had the buyers complied with the judge's order no problems would have arisen for the bank. The requisite documents would have been presented in the ordinary course of events and the terms of the letter of credit complied with so as to enable the sellers to receive, subject to the terms of the order, the payment of the purchase price which the award of the arbitrators subsequently made plain that the buyers should have procured to be paid to the sellers. That being so, I have found some difficulty in seeing why the bank should be concerned to disturb this order at all, let alone at this very late stage. I am afraid I am unable to see why the buyers' non-compliance with the order entitles the bank, not parties to the contract in relation to which the order was made, now to complain of its effect. Having adopted the stance they did on 29 and 30 October it is for them to show in their defence in the bank action, if they are able to do so, that their two-fold rejection of the documents was justified.

My Lords, it follows that I have no doubt not only that the order of Parker J was correct but that the Court of Appeal was also correct in dismissing the bank's appeal. Though I readily understand why the Court of Appeal allowed the bank to be joined as defendants in the action, I cannot but wonder whether if it had had the benefit of the full argument to which your Lordships have listened it would have granted the bank's application to be joined. I would dismiss this appeal with costs.

LORD BRIDGE OF HARWICH. My Lords, for the reasons given in the speech of my noble and learned friend Lord Roskill, with which I agree, I too would dismiss this appeal.

Appeal dismissed.

Solicitors: *Allen & Overy* (for the bank); *Holman Fenwick & Willan* (for the sellers)

Mary Rose Plummer Barrister.

George Mitchell (Chesterhall) Ltd v Finney Lock Seeds Ltd

HOUSE OF LORDS

LORD DIPLOCK, LORD SCARMAN, LORD ROSKILL, LORD BRIDGE OF HARWICH AND LORD BRIGHTMAN

23, 24 MAY, 30 JUNE 1983

Contract – Fundamental breach – Effect on clause limiting liability – Construction of exclusion clause – Whether exclusion clause inoperative because of fundamental breach.

Sale of goods – Implied condition as to merchantable quality – Exclusion of implied term – Unfair contract term – Whether fair and reasonable for seller to rely on clause limiting liability for supplying goods not of merchantable quality – Whether question of fairness and reasonableness of limitation or exclusion clause to be determined at time contract made or at time of breach – Sale of Goods Act 1979, s 55.

By an agreement made in December 1973 the appellants, who were seed merchants, agreed to supply the respondents, who were farmers who had dealt with the appellants for some years, with 30 lb of Dutch winter cabbage seed at a cost of £201·60. The seed was delivered together with an invoice in a form commonly used over a long period in the seed trade. The invoice contained a clause purporting to limit the liability of the appellants, in the event of the seed proving to be defective, to merely replacing the defective seed or refunding the purchase price thereof, and further purporting to 'exclude all liability for any loss or damage arising from the use of any seeds or plants supplied by us and for any consequential loss or damage arising out of such use . . . or for any other loss or damage whatsoever'. The respondents planted some 63 acres using the seed supplied by the appellants. However, unknown to the respondents and as a result of negligence on the part of a company associated with the appellants, the seed supplied was not of the variety agreed to be supplied and furthermore was, in the event, of inferior quality. The crop was a failure and had to be ploughed in, and consequently the respondents lost a year's production from the 63 acres. The respondents brought an action against the appellants claiming damages of £61,513 for breach of contract. The appellants contended that they were entitled to rely on the clause in the invoice to limit their liability. The respondents contended (i) that the clause did not apply to the breach in question because the seed which had been delivered was not cabbage seed in any accepted sense of the term and (ii) that it would not be 'fair or reasonable' for the appellants to rely on it and therefore, by virtue of s 55[a] set out in para 11 of Sch 1 to the Sale of Goods Act 1979, it was unenforceable. The judge held that the clause could not limit the appellants' liability because it did not apply where what was delivered was wholly different in kind from that ordered. The judge accordingly awarded the respondents the damages sought, plus interest. On appeal by the appellants, the Court of Appeal held, inter alia, that the appellants could not rely on the limitation clause, on the grounds (i) that on its true construction the clause did not apply to the breach either because the loss had resulted from the negligence of the appellants' associate company or because what had been delivered was wholly different in kind from that ordered and (ii) that in any event, applying s 55, it would not in all the circumstances be fair or reasonable to permit the appellants to rely on the clause. The appellants appealed to the House of Lords.

Held – (1) Although a limitation clause was to be construed contra proferentem and had to be clearly expressed, it was not subject to the very strict principles of construction applicable to clauses of complete exclusion of liability or of indemnity. Thus on its true

a Section 55, so far as material, is set out at p 742 *f* to p 743 *b*, post construction the limitation clause was effective to limit the appellants' liability to the replacement of the seeds or the refund of the price paid, since the clause was concerned with 'seed' and the appellants had delivered seed to the respondents, albeit of the wrong variety and of inferior quality. It was only by a process of unacceptably strained construction that the defective seed could be regarded as wholly different in kind from that which was ordered, or that the clause could be read as limiting liability only in the absence of negligence on the part of the appellants. The clause was therefore enforceable at common law (see p 739 *e* to *g*, p 742 *c d* and p 744 *h*, post); *Photo Production Ltd v Securicor Transport Ltd* [1980] 1 All ER 556 and *Ailsa Craig Fishing Co Ltd v Malvern Fishing Co Ltd* [1983] 1 All ER 101 applied.

(2) However, applying s 55 as set out in para 11 of Sch 1 to the 1979 Act, it would not be fair or reasonable to permit the appellants to rely on the clause, because (a) in the past in other cases of seed failure the appellants had negotiated settlement of farmers' claims for damages rather than seeking to rely on the limitation clause, (b) the supply of the defective seed was due to the negligence of the apellants' associate company and (c) the appellants could have insured against claims arising from the supply of defective seed. Accordingly, the appeal would be dismissed (see p 739 *e* to *g* and p 744 *c* to *h*, post).

Per curiam. When determining whether it would be fair or reasonable to permit reliance on a limitation or exclusion clause pursuant to s 55 of the 1979 Act the court is to have regard to the circumstances prevailing at the time of the breach rather than at the time the contract was made (see p 739 *e* to *g*, p 743 *h j* and p 744 *h*, post).

Decision of the Court of Appeal [1983] 1 All ER 108 affirmed.

Notes

For exclusion clauses and statutory provisions, and for exclusion clauses generally, see 9 Halsbury's Laws (4th edn) paras 363–380.

For the Sale of Goods Act 1979, s 55 (as set out in para 11 of Sch 1 to that Act), see 49 Halsbury's Statutes (3rd edn) 1155.

Cases referred to in opinions

Ailsa Craig Fishing Co Ltd v Malvern Fishing Co Ltd [1983] 1 All ER 101, HL.
Canada Steamship Lines Ltd v R [1952] 1 All ER 305, [1952] AC 192, PC.
Photo Production Ltd v Securicor Transport Ltd [1980] 1 All ER 556, [1980] AC 827, [1980] 2 WLR 283, HL.
Smith v UMB Chrysler (Scotland) Ltd 1978 SC (HL) 1.

Appeal

The appellants, Finney Lock Seeds Ltd, appealed with leave of the Appeal Committee of the House of Lords granted on 9 December 1982 against the decision of the Court of Appeal (Lord Denning MR, Oliver and Kerr LJJ) ([1983] 1 All ER 108, [1983] QB 284) on 29 September 1982 dismissing the appellants' appeal from the judgment of Parker J given on 10 December 1980 whereby he awarded the respondents, George Mitchell (Chesterhall) Ltd, damages of £61,513·78 together with interest of £30,756 in the respondents' claim against the appellants for breach of contract. The facts are set out in the opinion of Lord Bridge.

Mark Waller QC, *Mordecai Levene* and *Mark Howard* for the appellants.
Leonard Hoffmann QC and *Patrick Twigg* for the respondents.

Their Lordships took time for consideration.

30 June. The following opinions were delivered.

LORD DIPLOCK. My Lords, this is a case about an exemption clause contained in a contract for the sale of goods (not being a consumer sale) to which the Supply of Goods (Implied Terms) Act 1973 applied. In reliance on the exemption clause the sellers sought to limit their liability to the buyers to a sum which represented only 0·33% of the damage that the buyers had sustained as a result of an undisputed breach of contract by the sellers. The sellers failed before the trial judge, Parker J, who, by placing on the language of the exemption clause a strained and artificial meaning, found himself able to hold that the breach of contract in respect of which the buyers sued fell outside the clause. In the Court of Appeal both Oliver LJ and Kerr LJ, by similar processes of strained interpretation, held that the breach was not covered by the exemption clause; but they also held that if the breach had been covered it would in all the circumstances of the case not have been fair or reasonable to allow reliance on the clause, and that accordingly the clause would have been unenforceable under the 1973 Act. Lord Denning MR was alone in holding that the language of the exemption clause was plain and unambiguous, that it would be apparent to anyone who read it that it covered the breach in respect of which the buyers' action was brought, and that the passing of the Supply of Goods (Implied Terms) Act 1973 and its successor, the Unfair Contract Terms Act 1977, had removed from judges the temptation to resort to the device of ascribing to the words appearing in exemption clauses a tortured meaning so as to avoid giving effect to an exclusion or limitation of liability when the judge thought that in the circumstances to do so would be unfair. Lord Denning MR agreed with the other members of the court that the appeal should be dismissed, but solely on the statutory ground under the 1973 Act that it would not be fair and reasonable to allow reliance on the clause.

My Lords, I have had the advantage of reading in advance the speech to be delivered by my noble and learned friend Lord Bridge in favour of dismissing this appeal on grounds which reflect the reasoning although not the inimitable style of Lord Denning MR's judgment in the Court of Appeal.

I agree entirely with Lord Bridge's speech and there is nothing that I could usefully add to it; but I cannot refrain from noting with regret, which is, I am sure, shared by all members of the Appellate Committee of this House, that Lord Denning MR's judgment in the instant case, which was delivered on 29 September 1982, is probably the last in which your Lordships will have the opportunity of enjoying his eminently readable style of exposition and his stimulating and percipient approach to the continuing development of the common law to which he has himself in his judicial lifetime made so outstanding a contribution.

LORD SCARMAN. My Lords, I have had the advantage of reading in draft the speech to be delivered by my noble and learned friend Lord Bridge. I agree with it, and for the reasons which he gives would dismiss the appeal.

LORD ROSKILL. My Lords, I have had the advantage of reading in draft the speech to be delivered by my noble and learned friend Lord Bridge. I agree with it, and for the reasons which he gives I would dismiss the appeal.

LORD BRIDGE OF HARWICH. My Lords, the appellants are seed merchants. The respondents are farmers in East Lothian. In December 1973 the respondents ordered from the appellants 30 lb of Dutch winter white cabbage seeds. The seeds supplied were invoiced as 'Finneys Late Dutch Special'. The price was £201·60. Finneys Late Dutch Special was the variety required by the respondents. It is a Dutch winter white cabbage which grows particularly well in the area of East Lothian where the respondents farm, and can be harvested and sold at a favourable price in the spring. The respondents planted some 63 acres of their land with seedlings grown from the seeds supplied by the appellants to produce their cabbage crop for the spring of 1975. In the event, the crop proved to be worthless and had to be ploughed in. This was for two reasons. First, the seeds supplied were not Finneys Late Dutch Special or any other variety of Dutch winter white cabbage, but a variety of autumn cabbage. Second, even as autumn cabbage the seeds were of very inferior quality.

The issues in the appeal arise from three sentences in the conditions of sale indorsed on the appellants' invoice and admittedly embodied in the terms on which the appellants contracted. For ease of reference it will be convenient to number the sentences. Omitting immaterial words they read as follows:

> '[1] In the event of any seeds or plants sold or agreed to be sold by us not complying with the express terms of the contract of sale . . . or any seeds or plants proving defective in varietal purity we will, at our option, replace the defective seeds or plants, free of charge to the buyer or will refund all payments made to us by the buyer in respect of the defective seeds or plants and this shall be the limit of our obligation. [2] We hereby exclude all liability for any loss or damage arising from the use of any seeds or plants supplied by us and for any consequential loss or damage arising out of such use or any failure in the performance of or any defect in any seeds or plants supplied by us or for any other loss or damage whatsoever save for, at our option, liability for any such replacement or refund as aforesaid. [3] In accordance with the established custom of the seed trade any express or implied condition, statement or warranty, statutory or otherwise, not stated in these Conditions is hereby excluded.'

I will refer to the whole as 'the relevant condition' and to the parts as 'clauses 1, 2, and 3' of the relevant condition.

The first issue is whether the relevant condition, on its true construction in the context of the contract as a whole, is effective to limit the appellants' liability to a refund of £201·60, the price of the seeds (the common law issue). The second issue is whether, if the common law issue is decided in the appellants' favour, they should nevertheless be precluded from reliance on this limitation of liability pursuant to the provisions of the modified s 55 of the Sale of Goods Act 1979 which is set out in para 11 of Sch I to the Act and which applies to contracts made between 18 May 1973 and 1 February 1978 (the statutory issue).

The trial judge, Parker J, on the basis of evidence that the seeds supplied were incapable of producing a commercially saleable crop, decided the common law issue against the appellants on the ground that—

> 'what was supplied . . . was in no commercial sense vegetable seed at all [but was] the delivery of something wholly different in kind from that which was ordered and which the defendants had agreed to supply.'

He accordingly found it unnecessary to decide the statutory issue, but helpfully made some important findings of fact, which are very relevant if that issue falls to be decided. He gave judgment in favour of the respondents for £61,513·78 damages and £30,756 interest. Nothing now turns on these figures, but it is perhaps significant to point out that the damages awarded do not represent merely 'loss of anticipated profit', as was erroneously suggested in the appellants' printed case. The figure includes, as counsel for the appellants very properly accepted, all the costs incurred by the respondents in the cultivation of the worthless crop as well as the profit they would have expected to make from a successful crop if the proper seeds had been supplied.

In the Court of Appeal, the common law issue was decided in favour of the appellants by Lord Denning MR, who said ([1983] 1 All ER 108 at 113, [1983] QB 284 at 296):

> 'On the natural interpretation, I think the condition is sufficient to limit the seed merchants to a refund of the price paid or replacement of the seeds.'

Oliver LJ decided the common law issue against the appellants primarily on a ground akin to that of Parker J, albeit somewhat differently expressed. Fastening on the words 'agreed to be sold' in cl 1 of the relevant condition, he held that the clause could not be construed to mean 'in the event of the seeds sold or agreed to be sold by us not being the seeds agreed to be sold by us'. Clause 2 of the relevant condition he held to be 'merely a supplement' to cl 1. He thus arrived at the conclusion that the appellants had only succeeded in limiting their liability arising from the supply of seeds which were correctly described as Finneys Late Dutch Special but were defective in quality. As the seeds supplied were not Finneys Late Dutch Special, the relevant condition gave them no protection. Kerr LJ, in whose reasoning Oliver LJ also concurred, decided the common law issue against the appellants on the ground that the relevant condition was ineffective to limit appellants' liability for a breach of contract which could not have occurred without negligence on the appellants' part, and that the supply of the wrong variety of seeds was such a breach.

The Court of Appeal, however, was unanimous in deciding the statutory issue against the appellants.

In his judgment, Lord Denning MR traces, in his uniquely colourful and graphic style, the history of the courts' approach to contractual clauses excluding or limiting liability, culminating in the intervention of the legislature, first, by the Supply of Goods (Implied Terms) Act 1973, and second, by the Unfair Contract Terms Act 1977. My Lords, in considering the common law issue, I will resist the temptation to follow that fascinating trail, but will content myself with references to the two recent decisions of your Lordships' House commonly called the two Securicor cases: *Photo Production Ltd v Securicor Transport Ltd* [1980] 1 All ER 556, [1980] AC 827 and *Ailsa Craig Fishing Co Ltd v Malvern Fishing Co Ltd* [1983] 1 All ER 101.

The *Photo Production* case gave the final quietus to the doctrine that a 'fundamental breach' of contract deprived the party in breach of the benefit of clauses in the contract excluding or limiting his liability. The *Ailsa Craig* case drew an important distinction between exclusion and limitation clauses. This is clearly stated by Lord Fraser ([1983] 1 All ER 101 at 105):

> 'There are later authorities which lay down very strict principles to be applied when considering the effect of clauses of exclusion or of indemnity: see particularly the Privy Council case of *Canada Steamship Lines Ltd v R* [1952] 1 All ER 305 at 310, [1952] AC 192 at 208, where Lord Morton, delivering the advice of the Board, summarised the principles in terms which have recently been applied by this House in *Smith v UMB Chrysler (Scotland) Ltd* 1978 SC (HL) 1. In my opinion these principles are not applicable in their full rigour when considering the effect of conditions merely limiting liability. Such conditions will of course be read contra proferentem and must be clearly expressed, but there is no reason why they should be judged by the specially exacting standards which are applied to exclusion and indemnity clauses.'

My Lords, it seems to me, with all due deference, that the judgments of the trial judge and of Oliver LJ on the common law issue come dangerously near to reintroducing by the back door the doctrine of 'fundamental breach' which this House in the *Photo Production* case had so forcibly evicted by the front. The judge discusses what I may call the 'peas and beans' or 'chalk and cheese' cases, ie those in which it has been held that exemption clauses do not apply where there has been a contract to sell one thing, eg a motor car, and the seller has supplied quite another thing, eg a bicycle. I hasten to add that the judge can in no way be criticised for adopting this approach since counsel appearing for the appellants at the trial had conceded 'that, if what had been delivered had been beetroot seed or carrot seed, he would not be able to rely on the clause'. Different counsel appeared for the appellants in the Court of Appeal, where that concession was withdrawn.

In my opinion, this is not a 'peas and beans' case at all. The relevant condition applies to 'seeds'. Clause 1 refers to 'seeds sold' and 'seeds agreed to be sold.' Clause 2 refers to 'seeds supplied'. As I have pointed out, Oliver LJ concentrated his attention on the phrase 'seeds agreed to be sold'. I can see no justification, with respect, for allowing this phrase alone to dictate the interpretation of the relevant condition, still less for treating cl 2 as 'merely a supplement' to cl 1. Clause 2 is perfectly clear and unambiguous. The reference to 'seeds agreed to be sold' as well as to 'seeds sold' in cl 1 reflects the same dichotomy as the definition of 'sale' in the Sale of Goods Act 1979 as including a bargain and sale as well as a sale and delivery. The defective seeds in this case were seeds sold and delivered, just as clearly as they were seeds supplied, by the appellants to the respondents. The relevant condition, read as a whole, unambiguously limits the appellants' liability to *a* replacement of the seeds or refund of the price. It is only possible to read an ambiguity into it by the process of strained construction which was deprecated by Lord Diplock in the *Photo Production* case [1980] 1 All ER 556 at 568, [1980] AC 827 at 851 and by Lord Wilberforce in the *Ailsa Craig* case [1983] 1 All ER 101 at 102.

In holding that the relevant condition was ineffective to limit the appellants' liability for a breach of contract caused by their negligence, Kerr LJ applied the principles stated *b* by Lord Morton giving the judgment of the Privy Council in *Canada Steamship Lines Ltd v R* [1952] 1 All ER 305 at 310, [1952] AC 192 at 208. Kerr LJ stated correctly that this case was also referred to by Lord Fraser in the *Ailsa Craig* case [1983] 1 All ER 101 at 105. He omitted, however, to notice that, as appears from the passage from Lord Fraser's speech which I have already cited, the whole point of Lord Fraser's reference was to express his opinion that the very strict principles laid down in the *Canada Steamship Lines* *c* case as applicable to exclusion and indemnity clauses cannot be applied in their full rigour to limitation clauses. Lord Wilberforce's speech contains a passage to the like effect, and Lord Elwyn-Jones, Lord Salmon and Lord Lowry agreed with both speeches. Having once reached a conclusion in the instant case that the relevant condition unambiguously limited the appellants' liability, I know of no principle of construction which can properly be applied to confine the effect of the limitation to breaches of *d* contract arising without negligence on the part of the appellants. In agreement with Lord Denning MR, I would decide the common law issue in the appellants' favour.

The statutory issue turns, as already indicated, on the application of the provisions of the modified s 55 of the Sale of Goods Act 1979, as set out in para 11 of Sch I to the Act. The 1979 Act is a pure consolidation. The purpose of the modified s 55 is to preserve the law as it stood from 18 May 1973 to 1 February 1978 in relation to contracts made *e* between those two dates. The significance of the dates is that the first was the date when the Supply of Goods (Implied Terms) Act 1973 came into force containing the provision now re-enacted by the modified s 55, the second was the date when the Unfair Contract Terms Act 1977 came into force and superseded the relevant provisions of the 1973 Act by more radical and far-reaching provisions in relation to contracts made thereafter.

The relevant subsections of the modified s 55 provide as follows: *f*

> '(1) Where a right, duty or liability would arise under a contract of sale of goods by implication of law, it may be negatived or varied by express agreement, . . . but the preceding provision has effect subject to the following provisions of this section . . .
>
> (4) In the case of a contract of sale of goods, any term of that or any other contract exempting from all or any of the provisions of section 13, 14 or 15 above is void in *g* the case of a consumer sale and is, in any other case, not enforceable to the extent that it is shown that it would not be fair or reasonable to allow reliance on the term.
>
> (5) In determining for the purposes of subsection (4) above whether or not reliance on any such term would be fair or reasonable regard shall be had to all the circumstances of the case and in particular to the following matters—(*a*) the strength of the bargaining positions of the seller and buyer relative to each other, taking into *h* account, among other things, the availability of suitable alternative products and sources of supply; (*b*) whether the buyer received an inducement to agree to the term or in accepting it had an opportunity of buying the goods or suitable alternatives without it from any source of supply; (*c*) whether the buyer knew or ought reasonably to have known of the existence and extent of the term (having regard, among other things, to any previous course of dealing between the parties); *j* (*d*) where the term exempts from all or any of the provisions of section 13, 14 or 15 above if some condition is not complied with, whether it was reasonable at the time of the contract to expect that compliance with that condition would be practicable; (*e*) whether the goods were manufactured, processed, or adapted to the special order of the buyer . . .

> (9) Any reference in this section to a term exempting from all or any of the a provisions of any section of this Act is a reference to a term which purports to exclude or restrict, or has the effect of excluding or restricting, the operation of all or any of the provisions of that section, or the exercise of a right conferred by any provision of that section, or any liability of the seller for breach of a condition or warranty implied by any provision of that section . . .'

The contract between the appellants and the respondents was not a 'consumer sale', as b defined for the purpose of these provisions. The effect of cl 3 of the relevant condition is to exclude, inter alia, the terms implied by ss 13 and 14 of the Act that the seeds sold by description should correspond to the description and be of merchantable quality and to substitute therefor the express but limited obligations undertaken by the appellants under cll 1 and 2. The statutory issue, therefore, turns on the words in s 55(4) 'to the extent that it is shown that it would not be fair or reasonable to allow reliance on' this c restriction of the appellants' liabilities, having regard to the matters referred to in subs (5).

This is the first time your Lordships' House has had to consider a modern statutory provision giving the court power to override contractual terms excluding or restricting liability, which depends on the court's view of what is 'fair and reasonable'. The particular provision of the modified s 55 of the 1979 Act which applies in the instant case is of limited and diminishing importance. But the several provisions of the Unfair Contract d Terms Act 1977 which depend on 'the requirement of reasonableness', defined in s 11 by reference to what is 'fair and reasonable', albeit in a different context, are likely to come before the courts with increasing frequency. It may, therefore, be appropriate to consider how an original decision what is 'fair and reasonable' made in the application of any of these provisions should be approached by an appellate court. It would not be accurate to describe such a decision as an exercise of discretion. But a decision under any of the e provisions referred to will have this in common with the exercise of a discretion, that, in having regard to the various matters to which the modified s 55(5) of the 1979 Act, or s 11 of the 1977 Act direct attention, the court must entertain a whole range of considerations, put them in the scales on one side or the other and decide at the end of the day on which side the balance comes down. There will sometimes be room for a legitimate difference of judicial opinion as to what the answer should be, where it will be f impossible to say that one view is demonstrably wrong and the other demonstrably right. It must follow, in my view, that, when asked to review such a decision on appeal, the appellate court should treat the original decision with the utmost respect and refrain from interference with it unless satisfied that it proceeded on some erroneous principle or was plainly and obviously wrong.

Turning back to the modified s 55 of the 1979 Act, it is common ground that the onus g was on the respondents to show that it would not be fair or reasonable to allow the appellants to rely on the relevant condition as limiting their liability. It was argued for the appellants that the court must have regard to the circumstances as at the date of the contract, not after the breach. The basis of the argument was that this was the effect of s 11 of the 1977 Act and that it would be wrong to construe the modified s 55 of the Act as having a different effect. Assuming the premise is correct, the conclusion does not h follow. The provisions of the 1977 Act cannot be considered in construing the prior enactments now embodied in the modified s 55 of the 1979 Act. But, in any event, the language of sub-ss (4) and (5) of that section is clear and unambiguous. The question whether it is fair or reasonable to allow reliance on a term excluding or limiting liability for a breach of contract can only arise after the breach. The nature of the breach and the circumstances in which it occurred cannot possibly be excluded from 'all the circumstances j of the case' to which regard must be had.

The only other question of construction debated in the course of the argument was the meaning to be attached to the words 'to the extent that' in sub-s (4) and, in particular, whether they permit the court to hold that it would be fair and reasonable to allow partial reliance on a limitation clause and, for example, to decide in the instant case that the respondents should recover, say, half their consequential damage. I incline to the view that, in their context, the words are equivalent to 'in so far as' or 'in circumstances in which' and do not permit the kind of judgment of Solomon illustrated by the example. a

But for the purpose of deciding this appeal I find it unnecessary to express a concluded view on this question.

My Lords, at long last I turn to the application of the statutory language to the circumstances of the case. Of the particular matters to which attention is directed by paras (*a*) to (*e*) of s 55(5), only those in paras (*a*) to (*c*) are relevant. As to para (*c*), the respondents admittedly knew of the relevant condition (they had dealt with the appellants b for many years) and, if they had read it, particularly cl 2, they would, I think, as laymen rather than lawyers, have had no difficulty in understanding what it said. This and the magnitude of the damages claimed in proportion to the price of the seeds sold are factors which weigh in the scales in the appellants' favour.

The question of relative bargaining strength under para (*a*) and of the opportunity to buy seeds without a limitation of the seedsman's liability under para (*b*) were interrelated. c The evidence was that a similar limitation of liability was universally embodied in the terms of trade between seedsmen and farmers and had been so for very many years. The limitation had never been negotiated between representative bodies but, on the other hand, had not been the subject of any protest by the National Farmers' Union. These factors, if considered in isolation, might have been equivocal. The decisive factor, however, appears from the evidence of four witnesses called for the appellants, two d independent seedsmen, the chairman of the appellant company, and a director of a sister company (both being wholly-owned subsidiaries of the same parent). They said that it had always been their practice, unsuccessfully attempted in the instant case, to negotiate settlements of farmers' claims for damages in excess of the price of the seeds, if they thought that the claims were 'genuine' and 'justified'. This evidence indicated a clear recognition by seedsmen in general, and the appellants in particular, that reliance on the e limitation of liability imposed by the relevant condition would not be fair or reasonable.

Two further factors, if more were needed, weigh the scales in favour of the respondents. The supply of autumn, instead of winter, cabbage seed was due to the negligence of the appellants' sister company. Irrespective of its quality, the autumn variety supplied could not, according to the appellants' own evidence, be grown commercially in East Lothian. Finally, as the trial judge found, seedsmen could insure against the risk of crop failure f caused by supply of the wrong variety of seeds without materially increasing the price of seeds.

My Lords, even if I felt doubts about the statutory issue, I should not, for the reasons explained earlier, think it right to interfere with the unanimous original decision of that issue by the Court of Appeal. As it is, I feel no such doubts. If I were making the original decision, I should conclude without hesitation that it would not be fair or reasonable to g allow the appellants to rely on the contractual limitation of their liability.

I would dismiss the appeal.

LORD BRIGHTMAN. My Lords, I would dismiss this appeal for the reasons given by my noble and learned friend Lord Bridge.

h

Appeal dismissed.

Solicitors: *Davidson Doughty & Co* (for the appellants); *McKenna & Co* (for the respondents).

Mary Rose Plummer Barrister.

Turner and others v Turner and others

CHANCERY DIVISION
MERVYN DAVIES J
14, 15, 16, 17 FEBRUARY, 1 MARCH 1983

Trust and trustee – Discretionary trust – Non-exercise of discretion – Settlor creating trust giving trustees discretion to appoint members of his family as beneficiaries to receive income or capital – Trustees at settlor's behest appointing all of settlor's children as beneficiaries – Later at settlor's behest trustees revoking appointment of one son as beneficiary and appointing other children – At settlor's behest trustees later purporting to appoint son as beneficiary and transferring trust property to him – Whether any or all appointments a valid exercise of discretionary powers.

By a deed dated 30 March 1967 the settlor established a trust for the benefit of his wife, children, remoter issue and any spouse of such issue. Contrary to legal advice he appointed his father, his sister-in-law and her husband to be his trustees, although none of them had any experience or understanding of trusts. The settlement conferred on the trustees discretionary power to appoint all or any of the beneficiaries to receive capital or income from the trust fund, and by a deed dated 1 June 1967 the trustees exercised the power of appointment in favour of such of the settlor's four children who attained the age of 21. In 1969 the trustees purchased a farm property, which they held on the trusts of the settlement. By a deed dated 9 July 1971 the trustees revoked the appointment to one of the settlor's children appointed in the first deed and appointed the remaining three children as the beneficiaries of the trust funds which the fourth child would have been entitled to. In 1975 the legal executive with the settlor's solicitors who was responsible for the trust affairs retired and another legal executive, who was unaware of the 1971 appointment, assumed responsibility. In 1976 that legal executive prepared, on the settlor's instructions, a conveyance of the farm to the child whose appointment as beneficiary had been revoked by the 1971 deed and that conveyance was duly executed by the trustees. The conveyance was intended both to operate as a beneficial appointment under the settlement and to convey the legal estate in the farm to the child. The trustees throughout had failed to appreciate the nature of a trust or their powers and duties as trustees of a discretionary trust. They had left the decision-making to the settlor and, in the case of each of the 1967, 1971 and 1976 appointments, had executed the documents at the behest of the settlor without understanding that they had a discretion to act. The trustees applied to the court to determine which, if any, of the three appointments were a valid exercise of their powers of appointment.

Held – When exercising their power of appointment the trustees were under a duty to consider the appropriateness of the proposed appointment and, since on each occasion they had not known that they had a discretion, had not read or understood what they were signing and had merely signed when requested without first making a decision to appoint, the trustees had made the appointments in breach of that duty. Accordingly, there had not been a valid exercise of the power to appoint and the three purported appointments would be set aside (see p 752 *f g* and p 753 *e f* and *h*, post).

Dicta of Upjohn LJ in *Re Pilkington's Will Trusts, Pilkington v Pilkington* [1961] 2 All ER at 341, of Cross J in *Re Abrahams's Will Trusts, Caplan v Abrahams* [1967] 2 All ER at 1191, *Re Hastings-Bass (decd), Hastings v IRC* [1974] 2 All ER 193 and dictum of Sir Robert Megarry V-C in *Re Hay's Settlement Trusts* [1981] 3 All ER at 792 applied.

Notes

For the duties of trustees, see 38 Halsbury's Laws (3rd edn) 966–970, paras 1673–1679, and for cases on the subject, see 47 Digest (Repl) 348, *3138–3145*.

Cases referred to in judgment

Abrahams's Will Trusts, Re, Caplan v Abrahams [1967] 2 All ER 1175, [1969] 1 Ch 463, a
[1967] 3 WLR 1198.

Hastings-Bass (decd), Re, Hastings v IRC [1974] 2 All ER 193, [1975] Ch 25, [1974] 2 WLR 904, CA.

Hay's Settlement Trusts, Re [1981] 3 All ER 786, [1982] 1 WLR 202.

Pilkington v IRC [1962] 3 All ER 622, [1964] AC 612, [1962] 3 WLR 1051, HL; *rvsg* sub nom *Re Pilkington's Will Trusts, Pilkington v Pilkington* [1961] 2 All ER 330, [1961] Ch b
466, [1961] 2 WLR 776, CA.

Summons

By an originating summons dated 8 December 1981 the plaintiffs, Lionel Edward Turner, Henry William Nutland and Janet Ida Nutland, being trustees of a discretionary trust created by the fourteenth defendant, John Lionel Turner, by settlement dated 30 c
March 1967, applied, inter alia, to the court to determine which, if any, of the appointments made by deed of appointment dated 1 June 1967, deed of revocation and new appointment dated 9 July 1971 and conveyance dated 30 March 1976 were effective exercises by the trustees of the discretionary power conferred on them by the settlement and which, if any, failed effectively to exercise that power. The first to twelfth defendants and the fifteenth defendant were all discretionary objects of the trust. The Attorney d
General was the thirteenth defendant. The facts are set out in the judgment

Peter Horsfield QC and *Andrew Lloyd-Davies* for the plaintiffs.

Jonathan Henty, W D Ainger and *David A Lowe* for the first to seventh, ninth to twelfth and fourteenth and fifteenth defendants.

The eighth defendant did not appear and the Attorney General took no part in the e
proceedings.

Cur adv vult

1 March. The following judgment was delivered.

MERVYN DAVIES J. This is an originating summons in which the trustees of a f
settlement ask whether all or any of three successive deeds effectively exercised certain powers of appointment created by the settlement. As will appear the circumstances are highly unusual. In 1958 the fourteenth defendant, John Lionel Turner (the settlor) acquired Manor Farm of about 2,000 acres in Winterbourne Stoke, Wiltshire from his father and mother. In May 1966 he considered buying more land but was unable to borrow. An acquaintance suggested that rather than buy more land he should plan to g
save estate duty. The settlor discussed the matter with his legal adviser Mr Edwin William Tipper. Mr Tipper was a legal executive in the firm of Sylvester & Mackett of Trowbridge. The settlor has no clear recollection of what was discussed but it seems that in one way or another the settlor and Mr Tipper had available some documents that they believed had been used by another farmer in the course of an estate duty saving scheme. It was plain that any scheme would involve a settlement and so at an early stage there h
was discussion about who were to be trustees. I understand the settlor was advised to appoint professional trustees but unfortunately that advice was not taken. In a letter of 28 July 1966 Mr Tipper also advised that counsel's advice be taken. But that advice was not accepted. The settlor's father, Mr Lionel Edward Turner, the first plaintiff agreed to be a trustee. This Mr Turner is now 80 years old and resident in Australia. He went there in December 1976. He is a retired farmer and quite unfamiliar with trusts and the like. j
Mr Henry William Nutland, the second plaintiff, also agreed to be a trustee. He farms at Wilsford in Wiltshire just across Salisbury Plain from the settlor's Manor Farm. A little later it was thought wise to have a third trustee and Mrs Janet Ida Nutland, the third plaintiff agreed to act. Mrs Nutland is the wife of Mr Nutland, and the sister of the settlor's wife, the settlor's wife being Mrs Monica Josephine Turner, the fifth defendant.

Mr and Mrs Nutland are, like the Turners, without any experience or understanding of
a trust matters. Mr Tipper in his affidavit evidence said that he prepared four documents: (i) a settlement with discretionary trusts; (ii) a conveyance of Manor Farm to the settlement trustees; (iii) a partnership agreement between the settlor, his wife and his elder son, John Gregory Turner, the first defendant, constituting the partnership of J L Turner & Co; (iv) a tenancy agreement between the settlement trustees and the partners. As I have indicated the plaintiffs are the three trustees, i e Mr Lionel Edward Turner, the
b settlor's father, and the Nutlands. It will be convenient now to mention the defendants. Defendants one to four are the settlor's four children, all of whom are of age. They are John Gregory Turner, Mrs Sarah Tate, Mrs Ruth Turner and Robert Lionel Turner. The fifth defendant is, as I have said, the settlor's wife. The sixth defendant is Frances, the wife of John Gregory Turner. The seventh defendant is Jonathan Philip Herbert Tate, the husband of Mrs Tate. Then as eighth defendant there is Peter Herbert Turner. He is
c now divorced from Mrs Ruth Turner and now has no part in this action. Defendants nine, ten and eleven are the children of Mr and Mrs John Gregory Turner, namely Benjamin John Farrell, Bruce Charles Farrell and Jessica Frances. They are minors as are Rebecca Margaret Clare Tate, the twelfth defendant and Lucy Elizabeth Tate, the fifteenth defendant, the two last named being children of the Tates. The settlor is, as I have said, the fourteenth defendant. The Attorney General is the thirteenth defendant
d by reason of some ultimate charitable trusts in the settlement but I understand that the Attorney General does not desire to take any part. Of course I had the benefit of a family tree which makes the above facts very much more clear.

The draft settlement I have mentioned was before the settlor, the Nutlands and Mr Tipper at a meeting at Manor Farm in or about March 1967. The draft together with the other three drafts mentioned above were executed by those present. Lionel's signature
e was procured at about the same time. The settlement, conveyance and partnership agreement are all dated 30 March 1967. The tenancy agreement is dated 1 April 1967.

By the settlement it is recited that the settlor desired to make such irrevocable settlement as was thereinafter contained for the benefit of the 'Beneficiaries' as thereinafter appeared, and that the settlor had transferred £100 to the trustees to be held by them on the trusts thereinafter declared; and additional property might be transferred to be held
f on like trusts. The settlement then contained a definition clause. There 'The Vesting Day' was said to be the day on which should expire the period of 80 years after the settlement date or such earlier date as the trustees should appoint; 'The Beneficiaries' were said to be the wife, children and remoter issue of the settlor born or to be born before the vesting day, and any spouse or former spouse of any such issue.

Clause 2 of the settlement was in these terms:

g

> 'THE Trustees shall stand possessed of the Trust Fund and the income thereof upon such trusts for the benefit of the Beneficiaries or any one or more of them to the exclusion of the other or others in such shares and proportions and subject to such terms and limitations and with and subject to such provisions for maintenance education or advancement or for accumulation of income during minority or for the purpose of raising a portion or portions or for forfeiture in the event of
h bankruptcy or otherwise and with such discretionary trusts and powers exercisable by such persons as the Trustees shall from time to time by deed or deeds revocable or irrevocable executed before the Vesting Day but without infringing the rule against perpetuities appoint.'

Clause 3 reads as follows:

j

> '(a) IN default of and subject to any such appointment as aforesaid the Trustees shall until the Vesting Day pay or apply the income of the Trust Fund and may in their absolute discretion at any time or times before the Vesting Day pay transfer or apply the whole or any part or parts of the capital of the Trust Fund to or for the benefit of all or such one or more of the Beneficiaries for the time being living in such shares if more than one and in such manner as the Trustees shall in their

absolute discretion think fit. (b) Without prejudice to the generality of the foregoing the Trustees shall have power under the preceding sub-clause hereof to apply income for the benefit of any Beneficiary for the time being living by paying or contributing towards the payment of the premiums or costs of any policy of insurance by the terms of which any sum or sums of money may in any contingency be payable to or applicable for the maintenance education or benefit of such Beneficiary absolutely and to apply income for the benefit of any such Beneficiary who is an infant by appropriating such income to such infant absolutely and investing the same and the resulting income thereof in any of the investments hereby authorised. (c) The Trustees shall apply all or any part of such income not applied or contributed as aforesaid in or towards the discharge of all or any of the incumbrances for the time being affecting the said Trust Fund or any part thereof.'

Then there are cll 4 and 5:

> '4. SUBJECT as aforesaid the Trustees shall stand possessed of the Trust Fund on the Vesting Day in trust as to income and capital for such of the Beneficiaries as shall then be living or any one or more of them and in such shares as the Trustees shall prior to or upon the Vesting Day determine and in default of such determination in trust for such of the Beneficiaries as shall then be living in equal shares absolutely
>
> 5. SUBJECT as aforesaid the Trustees shall stand possessed of the Trust Fund and the income thereof in trust for such charitable purposes as the Trustees shall determine.'

I need not read further.

By the conveyance the settlor conveyed Manor Farm to the trustees on the trusts of the settlement. The conveyance was in consideration of the payment of £500,000.

That sum was paid by the trustees after the settlor had paid them £430,000 and with the aid of a £70,000 overdraft taken by the trustees on an account opened in their names.

With the settlement and other documents so executed there followed the following events.

(1) A deed of appointment dated 1 June 1967 (the 1967 appointment). This was executed by the trustees. Therein the trustees—

> 'hereby revocably appoint and settle that the Trust Fund (as defined in clause 1(ii) (a & b) of the Principal Deed) shall henceforth be held UPON TRUST for such of the above mentioned children of the Settlor who shall attain the age of twenty one years and if more than one in equal shares absolutely.'

The children referred to are all four of the settlor's children. They were then all under 18.

(2) The purchase of another farm, namely Camel Hill Farm by the trustees. By a conveyance dated 24 February 1969 they acquired, on the trusts of the settlement, this farm of about 470 acres in Queens Camel and Sparkford, Somerset for £95,000. There followed on 20 June 1969 a tenancy agreement of the farm in favour of J L Turner & Co. Camel Hill Farm was originally bought by Mr L E Turner. Before it was conveyed to him he agreed that it should be taken by his son, the settlor. As I understood, the settlor was to pay his father £95,000. The settlor then made Camel Hill Farm over to the trustees but the trustees had to borrow £60,000 from the Eagle Star in order to complete the purchase. There is a mortgage deed dated 23 June 1969.

(3) A deed of revocation and new appointment dated 9 July 1971 (the 1971 appointment). This deed recites that it is supplemental to the 1967 appointment and that 'in exercise of the power in this behalf reserved by the [1967 appointment]' the trustees were desirous of revoking the said appointment in favour of John Gregory Turner and of making a new appointment in manner thereinafter appearing. In the 1971 appointment it is then said that the trustees—

> 'revoke and make void all the trusts and interests appointed by the [1967
> a appointment] in favour of the said John Gregory Turner and in lieu thereof in
> exercise of the said powers vested in them by the said Settlement and of every other
> power enabling them in that behalf the [trustees] hereby appoint that the said trust
> funds appointed by the said Deed in favour of the said John Gregory Turner shall be
> held by the Trustees . . . upon trust for the said Sarah Elizabeth Turner Ruth Jane
> Turner and Robert Lionel Turner.'

b (4) On 31 December 1975 Mr Tipper retired and the trust affairs passed into the hands
of Mr J C Lane, another legal executive at Sylester & Mackett. Mr Lane was unaware of
the execution of the 1971 appointment. It was not with the trust papers when he took
over.

(5) A conveyance dated 30 March 1976 (the 1976 conveyance). By this conveyance the
trustees, with the concurrence of Eagle Star (who required some adjustment in the matter
c of life policies), conveyed Camel Hill Farm to John Gregory Turner. The settlor and his
wife joined in the conveyance to confirm their continuing personal liability to Eagle Star
under the mortgage. The trustees conveyed Camel Hill Farm to John Gregory Turner for
no consideration. It was intended, as I understand, that the conveyance should operate
(as well as conveying the legal estate) as a beneficial appointment under the settlement in
favour of John Gregory Turner.

d (6) On 20 May 1977 the trustees bought Eastfield Farm of 141 acres in Cheselbourne,
Dorset for £110,000. The money was borrowed from the National Westminster Bank.
This farm was let to the Tates until its sale on 26 May 1981. The proceeds of sale
£188,729.02 went towards buying Kennel Farm, Clarendon, Salisbury for £195,000.
The Tates are now the tenants of Kennel Farm.

Mr Elliot is the senior partner in Sylvester & Mackett. In 1979 Mr Elliot decided that
e his firm should no longer act in the matter of the settlement. That was principally
because it came to his attention that Mr Lane albeit in good faith had drafted the 1976
conveyance without knowing about the 1971 appointment. Mr Elliot visited the
Nutlands and told them that they should seek separate advice. In evidence Mr Elliot said
that was the only time that he met the Nutlands. He said it was clear to him that they
were quite unaware of their responsibilities and duties under the settlement. By this
f time the third trustee was of course in Australia.

It is this question about the trustees' understanding of their rights, powers and duties
that gives rise to question 1 in the originating summons. Question 1 asks, as respects (i)
the 1967 appointment, (ii) the 1971 appointment and (iii) the 1976 conveyance, whether
or not the trustees effectively exercised their powers of appointment. In effect the
question is whether or not the trustees so far failed to direct their minds to the matter of
g their discretionary powers of appointment that the deeds of appointment ought not to
be regarded as an exercise of the powers of appointment. To see such a question asked is
at first sight surprising but the evidence given in this case shows good reason for it.

I proceed to mention some of the evidence. There was affidavit evidence (apart from
some formal evidence from the trustees' new solicitor) from (i) Mr Nutland, (ii) Mrs
Nutland, (iii) Lionel Edward Turner, (iv) John Gregory Turner, (v) the settlor, (vi) Mr
h Tipper, (vii) Mr Lane. All save Lionel Edward and John Gregory were cross-examined.

It is plain that the Nutlands, unversed entirely in business affairs, became trustees to
oblige the settlor as their friend with a family connection. They had no thought that
they would be expected to do anything at all. It may be that the settlement was in some
sense explained to them by Mr Tipper. They saw Mr Tipper in March 1967 when the
settlement was executed. They did not see Mr Tipper again or have any connection with
j him or his firm until the Elliot visit in 1979. Mr Tipper said that at the 1967 meeting he
explained to the Nutlands and to the settlor the effect of all the documents. He said he
went through the documents clause by clause and explained to the Nutlands what their
duties as trustees were. I accept Mr Tipper's evidence without hesitation. I fully accept
that he went through some form of words with the Nutlands. But I am quite certain

that, whatever he said, the Nutlands did not understand. Mr and Mrs Nutland were clearly to be believed. Mr Nutland said in his affidavit:

> 'I believe that Mr. Tipper went through the Settlement with us, but we were not clear as a result of this what our duties were or what the effect of the Settlement was. We did realise that it was intended to benefit the Settlor's children, but we really thought that our duties would only arise if something happened to the Settlor and his wife, in which case we would be responsible for looking after the interests of their children.'

Mrs Nutland said:

> 'I, like my husband, thought that we would only become concerned in any substantial sense if something happened to the Settlor and his wife, in which case we would be responsible for looking after the interests of the Settlor's family.'

Answers in cross-examination more than confirmed those statements. Mr Nutland said he thought that his signatures were always required as a formality and that he had no business to look into the settlor's affairs. His phrase was that the settlor held the reins. He disagreed with Mr Tipper's statement that Tipper explained to him the nature of the duties of a trustee. Mrs Nutland when questioned spoke precisely to the same effect as her husband, but by no means as an echo. She used her own words.

From the execution of the settlement at the meeting in March 1967 one moves to consider the conduct of the trust affairs. I was shown 11 files of correspondence from the office of Sylvester & Mackett. There was a general file on trust and tax matters from 26 July 1966 to 28 November 1975. The other files related to particular items such as the purchase of Camel Hill Farm, the 1976 conveyance and the sale of various small plots, eg for an electricity substation. It is quite evident from all this correspondence that the Nutlands and Lionel Edward Turner were wholly disregarded for the purpose of any decision making. Mr Tipper wrote to the settlor and it was with him that all decisions were taken. The settlor, not the trustees, was regarded as the client. The signatures of the trustees were required from time to time. These were usually obtained by documents being sent to the settlor. He would obtain the Nutlands' signatures. They would sign without question at his request. Similarly Lionel Edward Turner signed without any question. The settlor said in his evidence: 'I did not discuss anything with the Nutlands. I considered myself captain of the ship'. It is quite clear from the correspondence that the trustees were no more than cyphers. I must consider particularly the three documents that are in question. As to the 1967 appoinntment, Mr Nutland in para 10 of his affidavit said:

> 'In any event neither I nor my wife were concerned in any way with the preparation of the 1967 Appointment and we certainly never gave any instructions to Mr. Tipper or to anyone else at Messrs. Sylvester and Mackett for the preparation of this or any other document connected with the Settlement. I am quite certain that neither of us knew what the document really meant nor appreciated how it might alter the trusts. We would not have concerned ourselves with its effect, since we did not realise at this time that the documents we were executing required any consideration or decision by us. We merely executed the documents which were placed before us by the Settlor because he asked us to do so and because we believed that all decisions in connection with the Settlement were a matter for him.'

Mrs Nutland confirms that statement. No cross-examination affected these statements in the least degree. Lionel Edward Turner's affidavit evidence is to much the same effect. I should add here that there was never ever any meeting between the three trustees, although of course the Nutlands knew Lionel Edward Turner in the locality reasonably well as the father-in-law of Mrs Nutland's sister, ie the settlor's wife. As to the 1971 appointment the evidence shows that the trustees were again cyphers. In para 11 of his affidavit Mr Nutland says (and his wife confirms):

> 'In any event I am confident that neither I nor my wife knew what the document really meant or appreciated how it might alter the trusts, and as I have already explained, we did not at this date realise that any consideration or decision on our part was required or that our signatures were more than a formality.'

Lionel Edward Turner in para 7 of his affidavit said

> 'I have no particular recollection of executing the 1971 Appointment, but I am sure that nobody explained to me what it was for. Certainly I would not have signed it if I had realised that it might have had the effect of cutting my grandson John out of all benefit under the Settlement.'

Speaking of the 1967 and 1971 appointments in his affidavit the settlor said:

> 'It is quite clear that when I obtained the signatures of Mr. and Mrs. Nutland to the Appointments, I would not have endeavoured to explain what the document did; I did not think this was a matter which really concerned them, and I could not have explained the documents anyway. I should add that I cannot think that they would have asked for any explanation of the documents: they never did on any other occasion when I obtained their signatures. I would also add that I do not recall whether they read the documents before they signed, but I think it most unlikely that they would have done so: they never did on any other occasion when I obtained their signatures.'

Mr Tipper can throw little light on the matter of the 1967 and 1971 appointments because as he says in his affidavit after March 1967 that he had no direct contact with the Nutlands. He relied on the settlor to get all documents signed. Mr Tipper said that he explained the appointments to Lionel Edward Turner. It was Mr Tipper who obtained Lionel Edward Turner's signature to the appointments.

The situation as to the 1976 conveyance is not quite the same because all three trustees realised that the purpose of the 1976 conveyance was to make over Camel Hill Farm to John Gregory Turner. In para 12 of his affidavit Mr Nutland said:

> 'I recollect that in 1976 the Settlor told us that he would like his son John to have a farm of his own and that the idea was that Camel Hill Farm should be conveyed to him. My wife and I both thought that this was sensible enough and I recollect that a Conveyance of the Farm to John was subsequently executed by us. I have been shown a letter of the 9th February 1976 from Messrs. Sylvester and Mackett to the Investment Manager of Eagle Star Group (included in bundle "R.S.B. 18" to Mr. Battersby's affidavit) in which it is stated that "the Trustees have consented" to the conveyance of the Farm to John. In fact neither Messrs. Sylvester and Mackett nor the Settlor ever asked for our "consent" or suggested that our "consent" was necessary. As I have already stated, the Settlor mentioned the proposed conveyance to us, but there was no suggestion that the decision was one for us rather that the Settlor himself. On the other hand we had indicated that we thought it a sensible idea and we understood that the document we signed was a conveyance of the Farm to John. We had not previously been consulted in any way about the purchase of Camel Hill Farm or the way in which the purchase money was to be found.'

Mr Nutland confirms what her husband says. Lionel Edward Turner's affidavit states that he had no recollection of executing the 1976 conveyance or of any discussion about it.

In cross-examination Mr Nutland said that at the time he did not appreciate that it was his decision that Camel Hill should go to John Gregory. He thought it was a matter for the settlor, but if he had known it was a matter for him, he would have done the same thing, i e given the farm to John Gregory. But as it was he did not intend to pass the farm to anyone. He had no thoughts on it. Mrs Nutland indicated that she never considered the farm in relation to the other beneficiaries. Mr Tipper was not concerned with the 1976 conveyance. As I have said by that time Mr Lane had taken over. Mr Lane's evidence was that he had no contact with any of the trustees on the matter of the 1976 conveyance. He simply got the settlor to procure the signatures of the trustees.

One is naturally very reluctant to contemplate that documents admittedly executed by persons of intelligence may be ineffective by reason of the fact that the persons executing did not address their minds to the documents signed. To do so makes for uncertainty, confusion and dishonesty. On the other hand here there are two considerations which may justify that course in the particular circumstances of this case. First there is the consideration that all the persons involved in the administration of the trusts have been perfectly frank and are plainly to be believed. There has been no rancour or dispute. No one other than the Turner family and the Nutlands are concerned in the immediate difficulties that have arisen. There has been on all sides a straightforward assertion of misunderstanding and a desire to set right anything that is wrong. The second consideration is that it is not any ordinary document that is being examined but, in the case of all three documents under consideration, a document whereby a discretionary power appears to have been exercised. When a discretionary power is given to trustees they come under certain fiduciary duties. In a context removed from the present case, Sir Robert Megarry V-C said in *Re Hay's Settlement Trusts* [1981] 3 All ER 786 at 792, [1982] 1 WLR 202 at 209 that 'a trustee to whom, as such, a power is given is bound by the duties of his office in exercising that power to do so in a responsbile manner according to its purpose'. Later the Vice-Chancellor said ([1981] 3 All ER 786 at 793, [1982] 1 WLR 202 at 209):

> 'If I am right in these views, the duties of a trustee which are specific to a mere power seem to be threefold. Apart from the obvious duty of obeying the trust instrument, and in particular of making no appointment that is not authorised by it, the trustee must, first, consider periodically whether or not he should exercise the power; second, consider the range of objects of the power; and third, consider the appropriateness of individual appointments. I do not assert that this list is exhaustive; but as the authorities stand it seems to me to include the essentials, so far as relevant to the case before me.'

Accordingly the trustees exercising a power come under a duty to consider. It is plain on the evidence that here the trustees did not in any way 'consider' in the course of signing the three deeds in question. They did not know they had any discretion during the settlor's lifetime, they did not read or understand the effect of the documents they were signing and what they were doing was not preceded by any decision. They merely signed when requested. The trustees therefore made the appointments in breach of their duty, in that it was their duty to 'consider' before appointing, and this they did not do.

It is accordingly necessary to consider what is the effect of a deed of appointment, on the face of it effective, but executed by the appointors in breach of their duty, in so far as they have signed, in all good faith, without ever having given any attention to the contents of the deed. *Pilkington v IRC* [1962] 3 All ER 622, [1964] AC 612 was concerned with the exercise of a power of advancement conferred by s 32 of the Trustee Act 1925. In that case the trustees asked the court whether a proposed advance by way of sub-settlement could be made. So the case differs from this case where one is concerned with an appointment, not an advancement, and with an appointment 'made' and not to be made. However that may be, some observations of Upjohn LJ in the Court of Appeal seem to bear on the present situation (see [1961] 2 All ER 330 at 340–341, [1961] Ch 466 at 488–490). Upjohn LJ's words in the Court of Appeal were approved by Viscount Radcliffe (see [1962] 3 All ER 622 at 632, [1964] AC 612 at 641–642). Upjohn LJ said:

> 'The effect, therefore, of the rule against perpetuities on the proposed settlement is basic; it entirely alters the settlement, and that seems to me to be fatal to this case, for the trustees have never been asked to express any opinion as to whether they would think the proposed settlement, modified by reason of the rule against perpetuities in the manner I have mentioned, is for the benefit of Penelope. That is a matter to which they have never addressed their minds, and, therefore, it cannot

> possibly be justified under s. 32, for it has not been shown that the trustees think that the settlement, as so modified, is for the advancemewnt or benefit or Penelope. On that ground too, therefore, I would think that the transfer to the trustees of this new settlement is entirely beyond the powers of the trustees.'

Those words suggest that when trustees, in the course of exercising a power in a way that they suppose will effect a sub-settlement, fail to appreciate what they are doing in some important respect (in the *Pilkington* case the impact of the perpetuity rule), then the sub-settlement will be void.

Re Abrahams's Will Trusts, Caplan v Abrahams [1967] 2 All ER 1175, [1969] 1 Ch 463 is an instance of the court declaring a settlement wholly void when made in exercise of a power of advancement. The exercise of the power had been made without a due regard to the rule against perpetuities, so that the trustees had not had a right appreciation of their discretion. This case must now be treated as limited in its application: see *Re Hastings-Bass (decd), Hastings v IRC* [1974] 2 All ER 193 at 203, [1975] Ch 25 at 41. However that may be, the words of Cross J in *Re Abrahams's Will Trusts* [1967] 2 All ER 1175 at 1191, [1969] 1 Ch 463 at 485 show that when the facts fit the exercise of a power may be set aside. Those words are:

> 'Here, however, there is no doubt that the effect of the operation of the rule is wholly to alter the character of the 1957 settlement. In my judgment the result of that must be that there never was a valid exercise by the trustees of the power of advancement.'

The authorities I have mentioned, including *Re Hastings-Bass*, permit the inference that, in a clear case on the facts, the court can put aside the purported exercise of a fiduciary power, if satisfied that the trustees never applied their minds at all to the exercise of the discretion entrusted to them. If appointors fail altogether to exercise the duties of consideration referred to by Sir Robert Megarry V-C then there is no exercise of the power and the purported appointment is a nullity. Applying those principles to this case I am satisfied on the evidence that all three purported appointments ought to be set aside. It was urged that the 1976 conveyance stood on a footing apart from the 1967 and 1971 appointments, in that in the case of the 1976 conveyance the trustees knew that their signatures would transfer Camel Hill Farm to John Gregory Turner, and moreover that the trustees thought at the time that it was a 'good idea' to make a transfer to John Gregory Turner, whereas in the case of the earlier appointment they did not know at all what was being done. In my view the 1976 conveyance as an instrument of appointment falls as well as the earlier appointments. At the time of the execution of the 1976 conveyance there was a total failure on the part of the trustees to consider whether or not in their discretion Camel Hill Farm ought to go to John Gregory Turner. They did not appreciate that they had a discretion to exercise.

The 1976 conveyance is of course effective as a conveyance of the legal estate and nothing I say affects the rights of the mortgagees. The 1976 conveyance is set aside in so far as it purports to operate as an exercise of the trustees' powers of appointment under the 1967 settlement. Subject to the mortgagees' rights, John Gregory will hold the legal estate on trust for the trustees of the 1967 settlement. The three appointments are set aside with effect from the dates that they bear. In the circumstances of this case I would have liked to set aside the 1976 conveyance (considered as an appointment) with effect from today. But since I regard the 1976 appointment as wholly void I do not think that that course is open to me.

Order accordingly.

Solicitors: *Burges Salmon*, Bristol (for the plaintiffs); *Drewett Nalder & Co*, Castle Cary, *Jonas & Parker*, Salisbury, and *Osborne Clarke*, Bristol (for the defendants).

Jacqueline Metcalfe Barrister.

Kuwait Minister of Public Works v Sir Frederick Snow & Partners (a firm) and others

COURT OF APPEAL, CIVIL DIVISION
STEPHENSON, FOX AND KERR LJJ
28 FEBRUARY, 1, 2, 3, 17 MARCH 1983

Arbitration – Award – Enforcement – Foreign award – Enforceability – Whether to be enforceable award must post-date foreign state becoming a party to convention – Arbitration Act 1975, s 3.

An arbitration award made in the territory of a foreign state which is a party to the New York Convention on the Recognition and Enforcement of Foreign Arbitral Awards is enforceable in the United Kingdom as a 'Convention award' pursuant to s 3[a] of the Arbitration Act 1975 irrespective of whether that award is published before or after the date on which the foreign state became a party to the convention (see p 754 *j*, p 755 *b*, p 759 *d e* and p 762 *f*, post).

Notes
For arbitration on foreign awards, see 2 Halsbury's Laws (4th edn) paras 634–635, and for cases on the subject, see 3 Digest (Reissue) 303–305, *2040–2044*.
For the Arbitration Act 1975, s 3, see 45 Halsbury's Statutes (3rd edn) 35.

Cases referred to in judgments
Jackson v Hall [1980] 1 All ER 177, [1980] AC 854, [1980] 2 WLR 118, HL.
West v Gwynne [1911] 2 Ch 1, CA.
Yew Bon Tew v Kendaraan Bas Mara [1982] 3 All ER 833, [1983] AC 553, [1982] 3 WLR 1026, PC.

Appeal
The plaintiff, the Minister of Public Works of the State of Kuwait, appealed against the decision of Mocatta J of 19 February 1981 whereby on the trial of preliminary issues he held, inter alia, that the plaintiff could not enforce, pursuant to the Arbitration Act 1975, as a convention award, as defined in the 1975 Act, an arbitration award against the defendant, Sir Frederick Snow & Partners (a firm), and four of the 12 other defendants published in Kuwait on 15 September 1973 on the ground that Kuwait was not a party to the New York Convention until 27 July 1978 and the award could only be enforced pursuant to the Act if it was published after Kuwait had become a party to the convention. The facts are set out in the judgment of Kerr LJ.

Bernard Rix QC and *John Tracy Kelly* for the plaintiff.
Desmond Wright QC and *Nicholas Dennys* for the defendants.

Cur adv vult

17 March. The following judgments were delivered.

STEPHENSON LJ. We have handed down the judgments in this case; the appeal will be allowed. Fox LJ has read the judgment of Kerr LJ in draft; he agrees with that judgment and with the order which we propose.

---

a Section 3, so far as material, is set out at p 758 *f g*, post

KERR LJ. This is an appeal by the plaintiff from a decision of Mocatta J on one of a
a number of preliminary issues in this action which he decided in a judgment delivered as long ago as 19 February 1981 ([1981] 1 Lloyd's Rep 656 at 663–666). It raises an important question on the correct construction of the Arbitration Act 1975, which is described in its long title as 'An Act to give effect to the New York Convention on the Recognition and Enforcement of Foreign Arbitral Awards'. The issue, briefly, is whether *any* award made in the territory of a state which is a party to the New York Convention
b is a 'Convention award' for the purposes of enforcement under the 1975 Act, or whether this is merely so in relation to such awards to the extent that they were made after the accession of the state in question. Mocatta J upheld the latter construction, and the plaintiff is now appealing against that decision.

The time-scale of the dispute and of the proceedings is remarkable and not a good advertisement for the legal process of international arbitrations. In July 1958 a contract
c was concluded between the Minister of Public Works of the Government of Kuwait and the well-known defendant firm, then Frederick S Snow & Partners, for the construction of certain civil engineering works at the airport at Kuwait. Thereafter, when certain defects appeared, evidently cracks in a runway, a dispute arose, and in October 1964 the government terminated the contract. This contained a provision for arbitration in Kuwait, and it appears that the dispute was referred to arbitration in September 1966.
d Thereafter, in the absence of agreement between the parties, an arbitrator, Dr Aziz Ahmed Yassin, was appointed by the Kuwait National Court in May 1972 in accordance with the arbitration clause. The arbitration then proceeded and on 15 September 1973 Dr Yassin published his award. This was in favour of the government and awarded damages and interest against the firm which amounted to the equivalent of about £3½ m in July 1979, the date of the points of claim in the present proceedings. The proceedings
e themselves had been instituted on 23 March 1979 for the purpose of enforcing Dr Yassin's award, about 5½ years after its publication. Apart from the firm itself, there were then ten individual defendants who were alleged to be liable on the award as partners in the firm, as well as the estates of two deceased former partners. The plaintiff at first sought to enforce the award summarily under s 26 of the Arbitration Act 1950, but since the defendants raised a number of issues on the validity of the award, as well as disputing
f its binding effect in relation to most of the defendants, Donaldson J considered that it was not a suitable case for summary enforcement and ordered in November 1979 that the plaintiff should proceed by bringing an action on the award. Then, having regard to the numerous issues between the parties, which appear in the pleadings, on 21 March 1980 Mustill J ordered the trial of four preliminary issues. These were decided by Mocatta J in his judgment of 19 February 1981. The first two concerned the question as
g to which of the defendants, other than the firm itself, had been properly made parties to the proceedings. This involved complex investigations concerning the history of the firm and problems of limitation, and in the result Mocatta J held that of the original 12 defendants, apart from the firm itself, only four individuals could properly be sued on the award. Since then, as we were told, the action has been discontinued against two of these by consent, so that the only remaining defendants are now the firm and two
h individuals. However, the present appeal, about 18½ years since the dispute arose, is not concerned with any of these matters but only relates to the third preliminary issue ordered by Mustill J. This was: 'Whether the award relied on by the plaintiffs is a convention award for the purposes of the Arbitration Act 1975?' The judge answered this question in the negative, and the issue on the present appeal is whether this was correct or not. I will also briefly have to mention the fourth issue, which relates to the
j same topic, but the judge's decision on this in favour of the plaintiff is not the subject matter of any cross-appeal by the defendants.

Having set out the dates concerning the dispute and the proceedings, I must then turn to the chronology concerning the enforcement of foreign arbitral awards which is relevant to the issue on this appeal. This relates primarily to the history of the New York Convention, particularly in the context of the accession to it by the United Kingdom and

Kuwait, but it is convenient to begin with the Geneva Convention on the Execution of Foreign Arbitral Awards of 26 September 1927 (TS 28 (1930); Cmd 3655) to which the United Kingdom, but not Kuwait, was also a party. Statutory effect was given to that convention in this country by the Arbitration (Foreign Awards) Act 1930, but it is now only necessary to refer to the Arbitration Act 1950, which consolidated and repealed the earlier Acts in this field. The Geneva Convention 1927 is set out in Sch 2 to the 1950 Act, and Pt II of that Act deals with the enforcement of awards under it, following on a 'Protocol on Arbitration Clauses' signed at the League of Nations on 24 September 1923 which is set out in Sch 1 to the Act. For present purposes it is convenient to set out s 35 of the 1950 Act, since it has some bearing on the construction of the 1975 Act which we have to consider:

> '(1) This Part of this Act applies to any award made after the twenty-eighth day of July, nineteen hundred and twenty-four—(*a*) in pursuance of an agreement for arbitration to which the protocol set out in the First Schedule to this Act applies; and (*b*) between persons of whom one is subject to the jurisdiction of some one of such Powers as His Majesty, being satisfied that reciprocal provisions have been made, may by Order in Council declare to be parties to the convention set out in the Second Schedule to this Act, and of whom the other is subject to the jurisdiction of some other of the Powers aforesaid; and (*c*) in one of such territories as His Majesty, being satisfied that reciprocal provisions have been made, may by Order in Council declare to be territories to which the said convention applies; and an award to which this Part of this Act applies is in this Part of this Act referred to as "a foreign award".
>
> (2) His Majesty may by a subsequent Order in Council vary or revoke any Order previously made under this section.'

Numerous countries became parties to the Geneva Convention, and a number of Orders in Council were made pursuant to s 35; the latest list of countries will be found set out in Mustill and Boyd *Commercial Arbitration* (1982) pp 639–640.

However, the Geneva Convention proved to be unsatisfactory in a number of respects which it is unnecessary to discuss here. Accordingly, the New York Convention came into force on 7 June 1959, no doubt in the hope that it would largely, and ultimately wholly, supersede the Geneva Convention. The New York Convention adopted a more ambitious approach by being primarily designed for the enforcement of *all* foreign awards, i e all awards made in a state in which enforcement is sought, but with an option to enforce awards only on a basis of reciprocity, i e if they were made in the territories of states which adhere to the convention. This pattern can be seen by setting out most of arts I and VII(2) of the New York Convention (the full text of the convention will be found in *Mustill and Boyd* p 689 and in *Russell on Arbitration* (20th edn, 1982) p 504):

> 'ARTICLE I.
>
> 1. This Convention shall apply to the recognition and enforcement of arbitral awards made in the territory of a State other than the State where the recognition and enforcement of such awards are sought, and arising out of differences between persons, whether physical or legal. It shall also apply to arbitral awards not considered as domestic awards in the State where their recognition and enforcement are sought . . .
>
> 3. When signing, ratifying or acceding to this Convention, or notifying extension article X hereof, any State may on the basis of reciprocity declare that it will apply the Convention to the recognition and enforcement of awards made only in the territory of another Contracting State. It may also declare that it will apply the Convention only to differences arising out of legal relationships, whether contractual or not, which are considered as commercial under the national law of the State making such declaration.'

(For present purposes we are only concerned with the option on the basis of reciprocity and not with the last sentence.)

> 'ARTICLE VII . . .
>
> 2. The Geneva Protocol on Arbitration Clauses of 1923 and the Geneva Convention on the Execution of Foreign Arbitral Awards 1927 shall cease to have effect between Contracting States on their becoming bound and to the extent that they become bound, by this Convention.'

Most, but not all, states who have adhered to the New York Convention appear to have done so on this basis of reciprocity; the United Kingdom did so (TS 20 (1976); Cmnd 6419), and this is also shown by the Arbitration Act 1975, to which I turn in a moment. First, however, I should briefly refer to certain differences, or alleged differences, between the two conventions. There is a difference as regards the burden of proof, but the main differences mentioned in the argument before us relate to the grounds on which enforcement of awards may be refused. These differences can be seen by comparing art 2 of the Geneva Convention as set out in Sch 2 to the 1950 Act with s 5(2) of the 1975 Act. Thus it was pointed out that whereas a refusal was mandatory under the former, such refusal is discretionary under the latter. But I do not think that much is to be gained from such a comparison. Thus, the last paragraph of art 2, as well as art 3, of the Geneva Convention also introduces a measure of discretion; moreover, the grounds for refusal under the New York Convention are wider: see in particular s 5(2)(*c*) of the 1975 Act, which has no counterpart in Sch 2 to the 1950 Act and on which the defendants appear to place particular reliance in this case.

However, on behalf of the defendants it was also submitted that the effect of s 5(1) of the 1975 Act, which provides that enforcement 'shall not be refused except in the cases mentioned in this section', might possibly be to preclude a defence of limitation in relation to the enforcement of awards under that Act, or that the wording of this provision has some other bearing on the problem of construction facing us on this appeal. I feel bound to say that I cannot for one moment accept any argument on these lines. Article III of the New York Convention provides:

> 'Each Contracting State shall recognize arbitral awards as binding and enforce them in accordance with the rules of procedure of the territory where the award is relied upon . . .'

And it is settled law that all issues as to limitation are procedural in their nature. On the aspect of limitation, the enforcement of awards under the 1975 Act pursuant to the New York Convention is, in my view, precisely the same as under Sch 2 to the 1950 Act pursuant to the Geneva Convention. Both Acts must be read in conjuction with what is now s 7 of the Limitation Act 1980, which provides that an action to enforce an award (other than under seal) 'shall not be brought after the expiration of six years from the date on which the cause of action accrued'. The same applies to awards which are merely enforceable at common law. Whatever may be the effect of this provision in the context of any particular case, I cannot accept that problems concerning limitation have any bearing on this appeal.

In the upshot I was accordingly left with the impression that in the present case little, if anything, is likely to turn on any differences in the grounds for refusal of enforcement as between the position at common law and under either of the conventions, and neither party was able to point to any relevant difference for present purposes. However, we nevertheless have to decide this preliminary issue; it is clearly of great importance generally, and, as we were told, an issue to which the Kuwait government attaches importance in relation to other awards.

Before turning to the relevant provisions of the 1975 Act I must then return to the chronology. As already mentioned, the New York Convention came into force on 7 June 1959 as between the first states which adhered to it. The award, as also already mentioned, was published on 15 September 1973. At that time the United Kingdom, but not Kuwait, was a party to the Geneva Convention, and neither was a party to the New York Convention. Accordingly, the award was then enforceable in this country, if at all, only at common law, either summarily in the same manner as a judgment under s 26 of the 1950 Act, or by bringing an action on the award. Both of these remedies are equally available in relation to convention and other awards.

Then, on 23 December 1975, the United Kingdom became a party to the New York Convention and the 1975 Act came into force. This left the position in relation to the present award as before. Then, however, Kuwait also became a party to the New York Convention on 27 July 1978, and thereafter, on 23 March 1979, as already mentioned, the present proceedings were instituted by the plaintiffs to enforce the award as a New York Convention award under the 1975 Act. The Order in Council declaring Kuwait to be a party to the New York Convention was not made until 14 April 1979. The fact that this had not yet happened when the present proceedings were instituted was the point raised by the fourth preliminary issue to which I have already referred. However, Mocatta J held in this respect that, although an Order in Council, once made, and while in force, is 'conclusive evidence' that a state is party to the convention (see s 7(2) of the 1975 Act as set out below), that fact can also be proved by other evidence, and there is no challenge to this conclusion on the present appeal. The issue is whether, after 27 July 1978, when Kuwait became a party to the New York Convention, the United Kingdom already being a party, the award made in Kuwait in 1973 can be enforced as a New York Convention award under the 1975 Act. The judge held that it could not, because on his construction of the Act it only applies to awards made in Kuwait after that date and not before, and it is this conclusion which is challenged before us.

I then turn to the relevant provisions of the 1975 Act, and I think that one can go directly to s 2, under the cross-heading 'Enforcement of Convention Awards', which was clearly designed to give effect to art VII(2) of the New York Convention which I have already cited:

> 2. '*Replacement of former provisions.* Sections 3 to 6 of this Act shall have effect with respect to the enforcement of Convention awards; and where a Convention award would, but for this section, be also a foreign award within the meaning of Part II of the Arbitration Act 1950, that Part shall not apply to it.'

Section 3 deals with the effect of convention awards in the different parts of the United Kingdom, and I only set out the beginning:

> '(1) A Convention award shall, subject to the following provisions of this Act, be enforceable—(*a*) In England and Wales, either by action or in the same manner as the award of an arbitrator is enforceable by virtue of section 26 of the Arbitration Act 1950 . . .'

Then I need not set out ss 4, 5 and 6, though I have already mentioned s 5 ('Refusal of enforcement') by way of comparison with the Geneva Convention, and I can go directly to the crucial interpretation provisions in s 7, omitting the definitions of 'arbitration agreement' and 'The New York Convention', which need not be set out:

> '(1) In this Act . . . "Convention award" means an award made in pursuance of an arbitration agreement in the territory of a State, other than the United Kingdom, which is a party to the New York Convention . . .
>
> (2) If Her Majesty by Order in Council declares that any State specified in the Order is a party to the New York Convention the Order shall, while in force, be conclusive evidence that that State is a party to that Convention.
>
> (3) An Order in Council under this section may be varied or revoked by a subsequent Order in Council.'

Counsel for the plaintiff and counsel for the defendants submitted that the natural meaning of these provisions in s 7 bears out their respective constructions, and both invoked grounds of policy in support of these; there was also a good deal of discussion

about 'retroactivity' in this connection, to which I turn later. Furthermore, since the
a 1975 Act was designed to give effect to an international convention, we were also referred to a good deal of material from other countries bearing on the problem to some extent, viz the legislation which gave effect to the convention in other states, the decisions of foreign courts and learned articles by writers in other countries. Many, but by no means all, of the matters which were canvassed are mentioned below.

I found the point of construction one of considerable difficulty, and my mind wavered
b on it during counsel's skillful arguments. Mocatta J, who of course had to deal with many other, and perhaps even more complex, issues in this case, ultimately decided in favour of the defendants for three brief reasons. First, after referring to a number of authorities dealing with retroactivity in the construction of statutes, he concluded that there was no clear reason, based on the language of the definition of 'Convention award', why this should be given what he regarded as retrospective effect. Second, he preferred a
c 'prospective' construction as being more in accordance with the language of the definition. Third, he said that—

> 'Kuwait could have substantially safeguarded their enforcement position by acceding to the Geneva Protocol and Convention before the award was made and possibly even after it.'

d However, counsel for the defendants did not seek to rely on this, and in my view it cannot assist the defendants. As regards the first two reasons, I have reached the clear conclusion, with great respect, that there is no substance in the 'retroactivity' argument, and on a careful analysis of the Act, whether taken alone or in the context of the convention, I have also reached the conclusion that the plaintiff's construction is correct. I propose to list my reasons for reaching these conclusions, but it is difficult to place them
e in any particular order of logic or importance.

(1) In the ultimate analysis the problem revolves round the question whether the word 'made' in the phrase 'an award made' is to have attached to it some chronological meaning, ie made after the date when a particular state becomes a party to the convention, or whether it is merely to be construed geographically, in the sense that the award must have been made in the territory of a state which is party to the convention
f when the award is sought to be enforced under the Act. Although at first sight the view formed by Mocatta J may well appear to be preferable, I do not think that it follows on a closer reading of the definition. The phrase 'which is a party to the ... Convention' qualifies 'State' and not 'award made'. As pointed out during argument by Fox LJ, this becomes even more clearly apparent if the whole definition of 'convention award' is read into some of the provisions of the Act instead of using the abbreviation, eg if it is read
g into s 3(1) of the 1975 Act set out above. Accordingly, looking at the definition in isolation, I feel that the point is a very open one, and that there is certainly no clear preference for the defendants' construction.

(2) The plaintiff submits that when an award is presented to the court for enforcement under the Act, the definition shows that the court only needs to ask itself two questions, viz (i) in the territory of what state was the award made and (ii) is that state a party to the
h convention? On the wording of the definition the court is not concerned with the date of accession by the state in question, and, when the definition is read together with s 7(2), it is clear that the definition does not envisage that the Orders in Council need or will make any reference to the date of accession. I think that this is right. In saying this, I merely note, but otherwise disregard, that the irrelevance of any date of accession is in fact borne out when one looks at the Orders in Council themselves, which make no
j reference to dates, since counsel for the defendants correctly reminded us that an Act cannot be construed by reference to any subordinate legislation made under it: see *Jackson v Hall* [1980] 1 All ER 177, [1980] AC 854. However, the point on the definition remains: the defendants' construction requires the words 'is a party to the ... Convention' to be read as if there were added words such as 'and was a party when the award in question was made'.

(3) The absence of any reference in the definition to any date relating to awards which qualify the enforcement in my view becomes even more significant when this feature of the 1975 Act is contrasted with the language used in other legislation in this field. Thus, s 35 of the 1950 Act, as set out above, dealing with the enforcement of Geneva Convention awards, provides expressly that Pt II of the Act applies to awards made after 28 July 1924. Similarly, s 1(2)(*c*) of the Foreign Judgments (Reciprocal Enforcement) Act 1933 provides that Pt I applies only to judgments—

> 'given after the coming into operation of the Order in Council directing that this Part of this Act shall extend to that foreign country.'

And in the recent Civil Jurisdiction and Judgments Act 1982 the same course has been adopted: see Sch 1, art 54, and Sch 3, art 34. I think that the omission of any reference to any date, directly or indirectly, and the use of the present tense ('is a party to the . . . Convention') are deliberate and significant. In relation to the latter point counsel for the defendants urged us to bear in mind that, in the reciprocity provision in the first sentence of art I(3) of the convention, the words 'Contracting State' are used, and submitted that 'awards made only in the territory of another Contracting State' can only refer to awards made after a state has become a 'Contracting State', or that these words are at least ambiguous in the present context. However, in my view no weight can be given to this argument. Quite apart from the fact that 'contracting state' is used throughout the convention in every context, the significance of the option as to reciprocity is to confine enforcement to awards made 'only in the territory of another Contracting State' in contrast with the enforcement of *all* foreign awards, wherever made, under art I. As counsel for the plaintiff aptly put it, it is an option relating to geographical and not to chronological limits; there is no indication that the dates of the awards are in any way relevant. And, in so far as the convention may be ambiguous in this respect, the unqualified use in the Act of the words 'award made . . . in the territory of a State . . . which is *a party to the . . . Convention*' (not 'a Contracting State') supports the conclusion that the only relevant factor under the Act is also a geographical one.

(4) Next, there is in my view a fundamental fallacy in the defendants' main line of argument. This bears both on construction and on the plea against 'retroactivity'. Counsel for the defendants repeatedly submitted that an award 'cannot change its character', and, as Mocatta J summarised the submission which he ultimately accepted, 'the award could not change its character on 27 July 1978, nearly four years after it had been published'.

However, it can easily be shown that awards can, and will, 'change their character', in the sense of a change in the basis for their enforcement, by reason of the accession to the New York Convention of the state in which enforcement is sought or of the state in whose territory the award was made. Thus, take the following examples in the context of the United Kingdom. State X was a party to the Geneva Convention; it then acceded to the New York Convention; and an award was then made in its territory. Until 23 December 1975 the award would have been enforceable here under the Geneva Convention. But after 23 December 1975 the award would become enforceable under the 1975 Act by virtue of s 2 set out above. Similarly, if state X had never been a party to the Geneva Convention, but had then acceded directly to the New York Convention, an award made thereafter would, in the United Kingdom only, have been enforceable at common law until 23 December 1975, but would have become enforceable as a 'Convention award' under the 1975 Act thereafter, as counsel for the defendants expressly and rightly conceded. These are 'changes in character' resulting from the accession to the New York Convention of the United Kingdom, the state in which enforcement is sought. Then, take the case of the accession to the New York Convention by state X, the state in which an award is made. Suppose that state X was still only a party to the Geneva Convention in 1977 when an award was made in its territory. The award would then clearly have been enforceable here under the Geneva Convention alone. (The Orders in Council made under the Geneva Convention remain in force: see *Russell on Arbitration* p 477). But, on the accession by state X to the New York Convention in, say, 1978, I think

that the effect of s 2 of the 1975 Act would again clearly be to turn the award into a
a 'convention award' under the 1975 Act, since it would qualify under both conventions. In this case, accordingly, a 'change in the character of the award' would result from the accession of the state in whose territory the award was made.

(5) The defendants' argument which Mocatta J accepted also faces a formidable difficulty of pure construction. As counsel for the plaintiff rightly pointed out, the twice repeated phrase, 'is a party', in s 7(2) must have the same meaning as 'is a party' in the
b definition of 'Convention award' in s 7(1). But, on counsel for the defendants' argument, the meaning of this phrase differs in the following respect. In s 7(2) it clearly means what it says, and the date of accession of the state in question is irrelevant. However, in the definition of 'Convention award' in s 7(1), the same words must be interpreted to mean, in effect, 'is and was a party at the date when the award was made', as pointed out in (2) above.

c (6) I can see no reason of policy, in the sense of the presumed intention of Parliament as expressed in the 1975 Act, which favours the defendants' construction. First, to put it broadly, the interest of the United Kingdom lies in the enforcement by the courts of other contracting states of awards made here, and to that extent we may hope for a wider basis of reciprocity if we enforce all awards made in states which are parties to the New York Convention. Second, the realities can be put more bluntly. Counsel for the
d defendants submitted that the New York Convention is like a club, and that the attitude of the United Kingdom is, in effect: 'Once you have joined the club, we will enforce your awards.' However, this merely begs the question of construction: which awards? All of them? Or only those made thereafter? Furthermore, the convention is not a selective club. Any state can adhere to it. Unless the convention is denounced in toto under art XIII, every adherent must enforce all awards made in the territory of every other
e adherent, past or future. So, why should awards made in Ruritania after Ruritania has chosen to adhere to the convention be any more deserving of enforcement than those made before? In my view, the presumed intention of Parliament, on grounds of policy, does not enter into the question of construction.

(7) Nor do I think that any argument against 'retroactivity' is of any substance. If the illustrations in (4) above imply retroactivity, then to that extent the 1975 Act is inevitably
f retrospective. But, although 'retrospective' is an ugly word in the context of construing a statute, it is often misapplied. Thus, in *West v Gwynne* [1911] 2 Ch 1 this court had to consider a statute which outlawed the right to demand payments, in relation to 'all leases', for the landlord's consent to assignment, etc, and it was argued that the statute should not be construed so as to apply to existing, but only future, leases in order to avoid any retrospective construction. This argument was rejected unanimously.

g Buckley LJ said (at 11–12):

> 'To my mind the word "retrospective" is inappropriate, and the question is not whether the section is retrospective. Retrospective operation is one matter. Interference with existing rights is another. If an Act provides that as at a past date the law shall be taken to have been that which it was not, that Act I understand to be retrospective. That is not this case . . . There is, so to speak, a presumption that it
> h speaks only as to the future. But there is no like presumption that an Act is not intended to interfere with existing rights. Most Acts of Parliament, in fact, do interfere with existing rights.'

There are also many other considerations in this context. Thus, as the judge pointed out ([1981] 1 Lloyd's Rep 656 at 665), the presumption against a retrospective construction
j does not apply to statutes which are procedural in their nature; in relation to procedural statutes the presumption is the other way. However, a statute dealing merely with the recognition or enforcement of prior rights would be classified as procedural under our rules of private international law: see *Dicey and Morris on the Conflict of Laws* (10th edn, 1980) vol 2, pp 1177–1178. Moreover, if all retrospective effect were to be avoided in the present context, then one would logically have to go back beyond the arbitration

agreement itself. Thus, in *Mustill and Boyd* p 375, n 4, the decision at first instance in the present case is summarised as follows: a

> 'An award is not a "Convention award" unless the state in question was a party to the Convention at the date of the award and (*semble*) at the date of the arbitration agreement . . .'

This addition would be logical to bar all retrospectivity, but on any view it is clearly an unwarranted extension of the 1975 Act, and counsel for the defendants' argument rightly b disclaimed it. In any event, as pointed out by Lord Brightman in *Yew Bon Tew v Kendaraan Bas Mara* [1982] 3 All ER 833 at 839, [1983] AC 553 at 563 the term 'procedural' can also be misleading; the question is whether a particular construction would 'impair existing rights and obligations'. However, I do not consider that the defendants ever had anything in the nature of a 'vested right', as they contend, not to have this award enforced against them under the New York Convention, but only at c common law.

(8) I do not think that much assistance is to be gained from the foreign material which counsel for the plaintiff put before us. All of it derives from a long article by Mr Giorgio Gaja in *International Commercial Arbitration* (Oceana, 1979, booklet 2, p 1.A.5) which contains a valuable survey of the legislation and decisions concerning the convention in different countries and a review of the writings about it. The question of 'retroactivity' is d complicated by the fact that in a number of states the legislation giving effect to the convention provided expressly that it was only to apply to awards made thereafter. But, where this has not been the case, the predominant view appears to be that the convention has what would (I think inaccurately) be described as having 'retrospective' effect. However, in my view the material is too disparate to provide any reliable guidance for present purposes under the principle of comity, other than to show that there is nothing e internationally dissonant in the construction of the 1975 Act which I consider to be correct, for the reasons already stated, and that this construction in fact appears to be in line with the law in other New York Convention states.

Accordingly, I would allow this appeal and answer the preliminary issue affirmatively, by holding that the award relied on by the plaintiffs is a convention award for the purposes of the 1975 Act. f

STEPHENSON LJ. I agree and have only this to add. A great part of the time of this court is taken in attempting to discern the meaning of statutes. Much if not most of that time might have been saved if Parliament had added a few words to make its meaning plain. Making allowance for the obstacles which parliamentary procedure may put in the way of clarity, for the political considerations which may sometimes invite ambiguity g and for the impossibility of foreseeing what situations may require consideration of particular statutory provisions, I cannot help thinking that the issue in the present appeal is one which the legislature might have been expected to have saved the parties the trouble and expense of litigating by the simple addition to s 7(1) of the Arbitration Act 1975 of such words as 'whether the award is made before or after that state is a party to that convention'. h

I say this because, as Kerr LJ has pointed out, this legislation is in a realm where the question left open to argument by the language of s 7(1) had already been considered and answered beyond doubt by those who drafted s 35 of the Arbitration Act 1950 and s 1(2)(*a*) of the Foreign Judgments (Reciprocal Enforcement) Act 1933.

Appeal allowed. Leave to appeal to the House of Lords refused. j

Solicitors: *Charles Russell & Co* (for the plaintiff); *Blakeney's* (for the defendants).

Diana Brahams Barrister.

Scandinavian Trading Tanker Co AB v Flota Petrolera Ecuatoriana
The Scaptrade

HOUSE OF LORDS

LORD DIPLOCK, LORD KEITH OF KINKEL, LORD SCARMAN, LORD ROSKILL AND LORD BRIDGE OF HARWICH

11 MAY, 30 JUNE 1983

Shipping – Charterparty – Time charter – Withdrawal – Relief against forfeiture – Default in payment of hire – Right of withdrawal exercised – Whether court having jurisdiction to grant relief against forfeiture.

By a time charter in the Shelltime 3 form the owners chartered a vessel to the charterers for a specified period which was later extended to three years. Payments of hire under the charter were to be made monthly in advance. The charter also provided that if the charterers defaulted in paying the monthly hire instalment by the due date the owners could withdraw the vessel from hire. In July 1979, when the charter had still a year to run, the charterers failed to pay the instalment due on 8 July. On 12 July, the instalment still being upaid, the owners gave notice to the charterers withdrawing the vessel. Tender of the overdue hire was made on the following day but was refused. The parties agreed that the vessel should continue in the service of the charterers while the question whether the owners were entitled to withdraw the vessel was litigated. It was further agreed that, if the court found in favour of the owners, the charterers would pay, from the date of the recharter, hire at the increased market rate rather than at the original contract rate. The owners sought and were granted a declaration that they were entitled to withdraw the vessel for non-payment of hire. The charterers appealed to the Court of Appeal contending, inter alia, that the court had jurisdiction to grant, in appropriate circumstances, the equitable remedy of relief against forfeiture in order to relieve charterers from the consequences of withdrawal for non-payment of hire, and that it would be proper in the circumstances to grant them such discretionary relief. The Court of Appeal dismissed the appeal, holding that the court had no jurisdiction to grant the equitable remedy of relief against forfeiture in such circumstances. The charterers appealed to the House of Lords.

Held – A time charter, unless it was a charter by demise, transferred to the charterer no interest in, or right to possession of, the vessel but was merely a contract for services to be rendered to the charterer by the shipowner through the use of the vessel by the shipowner's own servants (the master and the crew) acting in accordance with such directions as to cargo to be loaded and the voyage to be undertaken as the charterer was entitled to give them under the terms of the charterparty. Since an injunction restraining a shipowner from exercising his right of withdrawal of the vessel, though negative in form, was in effect an affirmative order to the shipowner to perform the contract, it was juristically indistinguishable from a decree for specific performance of a contract to render services, which the court had no jurisdiction to order. It followed that the court had no jurisdiction to grant relief against forfeiture to relieve a time charterer from the consequences of withdrawal of the chartered vessel by the shipowner following non-payment of hire instalments. Furthermore, where the parties bargained on equal terms and made time of the essence for the performance of the primary obligation to pay hire instalments on time, the charterer's failure to perorm that obligation punctually would amount to a breach of a condition of the contract which would entitle the owners to elect to treat the breach as putting an end to all primary obligations under the contract which had not already been performed. Accordingly the appeal would be dismissed (see p 766 *e* to p 767 *a*, p 768 *c* to *j* and p 769 *e* to *j*, post). a

Dictum of Lord Wilberforce in *Shiloh Spinners Ltd v Harding* [1973] 1 All ER at 100 distinguished.

Dictum of Lloyd J in *Afovos Shipping Co AS v R Pagnan & Flli, The Afovos* [1980] 2 Lloyd's Rep 476–480 disapproved.

Dictum of Lord Simon in *Mardorf Peach & Co Ltd v Attica Sea Carriers Corp of Liberia, The Laconia* [1977] 1 All ER at 553 doubted. b

Decision of Court of Appeal [1983] 1 All ER 301 affirmed.

Notes

For relief against forfeiture, see 16 Halsbury's Laws (4th edn) paras 1447–1451, and for cases on the subject, see 20 Digest (Reissue) 898–899, *6695–6703*.

c

Cases referred to in opinions

Afovos Shipping Co AS v R Pagnan & Flli, The Afovos [1980] 2 Lloyd's Rep 469; rvsd [1982] 3 All ER 18, [1982] 1 WLR 848, CA.
A/S Awilco v Fulvia SpA di Navigazione, The Chikuma [1981] 1 All ER 652, [1981] 1 WLR 314, HL.
Clarke v Price (1819) 2 Wils Ch 157, 37 ER 270, LC. d
Lumley v Wagner (1852) 1 De GM & G 604, [1843–60] All ER Rep 368, 42 ER 687, LC.
Mardorf Peach & Co Ltd v Attica Sea Carriers Corp of Liberia, The Laconia [1977] 1 All ER 545, [1977] AC 850, [1977] 2 WLR 286, HL.
Shiloh Spinners Ltd v Harding [1973] 1 All ER 90, [1973] AC 691, [1973] 2 WLR 28, HL.
Stockloser v Johnson [1954] 1 All ER 630, [1954] 1 QB 476, [1954] 2 WLR 439, CA.
Tankexpress A/S v Compagnie Financière Belge des Petroles SA [1948] 2 All ER 939, [1949] e AC 76, HL.

Appeal

The defendants, Flota Petrolera Ecuatoriana (the charterers), appealed with leave of the Appeal Committee of the House of Lords granted on 20 January 1983 against the order of the Court of Appeal (Sir John Donaldson MR, May and Robert Goff LJJ) ([1983] 1 All f
ER 301, [1983] 2 WLR 248) dated 26 November 1982 dismissing the appeal of the charterers from the order of Lloyd J dated 3 July 1981 whereby it was directed that judgment should be entered for the plaintiffs, Scandinavian Trading Tanker Co AB (the owners), in an action commenced by writ issued on 27 February 1980. The facts are set out in the opinion of Lord Diplock.

g

Johan Steyn QC and *A G Bompas* for the charterers.
Kenneth Rokison QC and *Timothy Saloman* for the owners.

Their Lordships took time for consideration.

30 June. The following opinions were delivered. h

LORD DIPLOCK. My Lords, in this appeal between the appellant (the charterers) and the respondent (the owners) of the tanker Scaptrade, your Lordships have heard argument on one question only: has the High Court any jurisdiction to grant relief against the exercise by a shipowner of his contractual right, under the withdrawal clause in a time charter, to withdraw the vessel from the service of the charterer on the latter's failure to j
make payment of an instalment of the hire in the manner and at a time that is not later than that for which the withdrawal clause provides? I call this the jurisdiction point.

Since, at the conclusion of the argument on the jurisdiction point your Lordships were unanimously of opinion that there is no such jurisdiction, it became unnecessary to consider whether Lloyd J, who tried the case at first instance in the Commercial Court and was willing to assume that he did have jurisdiction to grant relief in his discretion, *a* exercised that discretion in a manner that was erroneous in law when he refused to grant relief to the charterers. I call this the discretion point.

The time charter concerned was on the standard printed 'Shelltime 3' form with typed additions that are not material to the question that your Lordships have to decide. This form of charterparty is expressed to be governed by the law of England, and to be subject to the jurisdiction of the English court. The relevant wording of the payment of hire *b* clause, which, as is usual in most standard forms of time charter, incorporated the withdrawal clause was:

> 'Payment of the said hire shall be made in New York monthly in advance . . . In default of such payment Owners may withdraw the vessel from the service of Charterers, without prejudice to any claim Owners may otherwise have on Charterers under this charter.'

c

The charter had become by extension a three-year charter. In July 1979 when it had still a year to run the freight market was rising steeply. The charterers were unfortunate enough, through some slip-up in their own office, to fail to pay on 8 July 1979 the instalment of hire due on that date. Four days later, on 12 July, the owners gave notice to the charterers withdrawing the vessel. Tender of the overdue hire was made on the *d* following day but was refused. After negotiations had taken place, the vessel was rechartered by the owners to the charterers on a 'without prejudice' agreement of the usual kind, the rate of hire (ie charter rate or market rate) to abide the result of litigation, which in the event, came before Lloyd J.

My Lords, the jurisdiction point which your Lordships have to decide is a compact one. In order to deal with it I see no need to mention any more facts than those that I *e* have now stated, although there were other issues that were canvassed at the trial, some of which were canvassed again in the Court of Appeal. That being so, I should like to say how helpful I have found both the typewritten summary of the propositions intended to be developed, and the chronological table of relevant events, that leading counsel for the charterers handed in at the beginning of his oral argument. This response to suggestions that have recently been made in this House has shown how useful it can be in shortening *f* the time needed for the hearing and in concentrating the attention of your Lordships (and of counsel) on those points that are essential to the argument that is being presented.

Lloyd J adopted the course that he had previously adopted in *Afovos Shipping Co AS v R Pagnan & Flli, The Afovos* [1980] 2 Lloyd's Rep 469. He assumed that the jurisdiction point could be decided in the charterers' favour; but on the particular facts he decided against them on the discretion point. The charterers appealed to the Court of Appeal. *g* The Court of Appeal, while expressing doubt as to the adequacy in law of the judge's reasons for refusing to grant relief in the circumstances of the case, if there were vested in him a discretion to grant it, decided against the charterers on the jurisdiction point, and dismissed their appeal (see [1982] 3 All ER 18, [1982] 1 WLR 848).

My Lords, the judgment of the Court of Appeal, delivered by Robert Goff LJ, on the jurisdiction point was the first direct decision by any English court, given after hearing *h* argument, on the question that I have set out at the beginning of this speech. For reasons admirably expressed, and which, for my part, I find convincing, the Court of Appeal held that there was no such jurisdiction (see [1983] 1 All ER 301, [1983] 2 WLR 248). The argument that there was jurisdiction in the court to grant relief against the withdrawal of the vessel from the charterer's service for default in punctual payment of an instalment of hire pursuant to the terms of the withdrawal clause in a time charter could, however, *j* be supported by certain obiter dicta to be found in speeches in this House, in particular that of Lord Simon in *Mardorf Peach & Co Ltd v Attica Sea Carriers Corp of Liberia, The Laconia* [1977] 1 All ER 545 at 553, [1977] AC 850 at 873–874. Since such large sums of money may be at stake when rights to withdraw a vessel under a time charter are exercised at a time of rising freight rates (which, except where insolvency of the charterer is feared, is normally the only time when such rights are exercised), it seemed desirable to the Appeal Committee of this House that leave to appeal should be granted to the charterers, not, I must confess, with any great expectation that fuller consideration would show that on the jurisdiction point the Court of Appeal had got it wrong, but in order that a matter of such practical importance to the shipping world should, by a decision of the highest appellate court, be put beyond reach of future challenge.

Apart from a throw-away sentence in the speech of Lord Uthwatt in *Tankexpress A/S v Compagnie Financière Belge des Petroles SA* [1948] 2 All ER 939 at 949, [1949] AC 76 at 100, in which he said, 'Courts of equity, indeed, in appropriate cases relieve against failure to pay on a stipulated day,' but did not suggest that the operation of a withdrawal clause in a time charter provided a case that was 'appropriate', the origin of what I will, proleptically at this stage, describe as a beguiling heresy, which the Court of Appeal rejected in the instant case, is to be found in Lord Simon's speech in *The Laconia*. In *The Laconia* itself the availability of equitable relief had not been raised in the courts below; and, since it had not occurred to anyone to invite the judge to exercise a discretion to grant relief, the House had ruled that the point could not be taken in argument in the appeal.

I need not cite the passages in Lord Simon's speech that gave encouragement to future charterers to claim equitable relief against withdrawal of the vessel under a withdrawal clause in a time charter, except to note that after referring to a possible analogy to relief against forfeiture for non-payment of rent under leases of real property he says ([1977] 1 All ER 545 at 554, [1977] AC 850 at 874):

> '... in any case, English law develops by applying an established rule of law to new circumstances which are analogous to the circumstances in which the rule was framed ...'

Nor need I cite the passages in the speeches of Lord Wilberforce and Lord Salmon in which the analogy with leases of real property is decried.

A time charter, unless it is a charter by demise, with which your Lordships are not here concerned, transfers to the charterer no interest in or right to possession of the vessel: it is a contract for services to be rendered to the charterer by the shipowner through the use of the vessel by the shipowner's own servants, the master and the crew, acting in accordance with such directions as to the cargoes to be loaded and the voyages to be undertaken as by the terms of the charterparty the charterer is entitled to give to them. Being a contract for services it is thus the very prototype of a contract of which before the fusion of law and equity a court would never grant specific performance: see *Clarke v Price* (1819) 2 Wils Ch 157, 37 ER 270, *Lumley v Wagner* (1852) 1 De GM & G 604, [1843–60] All ER Rep 368. In the event of failure to render the promised services, the party to whom they were to be rendered would be left to pursue such remedies in damages for breach of contract as he might have at law. But as an unbroken line of uniform authority in this House, from the *Tankexpress*, case to *A/S Awilco v Fulvia SpA di Navigazione, The Chikuma* [1981] 1 All ER 652, [1981] 1 WLR 314, has held that, if the withdrawal clause so provides, the shipowner is entitled to withdraw the services of the vessel from the charterer if the latter fails to pay an instalment of hire in precise compliance with the provisions of the charter. So the shipowner commits no breach of contract if he does so; and the charterer has no remedy in damages against him.

To grant an injunction restraining the shipowner from exercising his right of withdrawal of the vessel from the service of the charterer, though negative in form, is pregnant with an affirmative order to the shipowner to perform the contract; juristically it is indistinguishable from a decree for specific performance of a contract to render services; and in respect of that category of contracts, even in the event of breach, this is a remedy that English courts have always disclaimed any jurisdiction to grant. This is, in my view, sufficient reason in itself to compel rejection of the suggestion that the equitable principle of relief from forfeiture is juristically capable of extension so as to grant to the court a discretion to prevent a shipowner from exercising his strict contractual rights under a withdrawal clause in a time charter which is not a charter by demise.

My Lords, Lloyd J who, as counsel for the charterers in *The Laconia* had been prevented

from arguing the point, was enabled to return to the charge when there came before him
a as judge of the Commercial Court *The Afovos*, in which the question of jurisdiction to
grant relief against the operation of a withdrawal clause *was* argued. That case also
ultimately reached this House, where it was decided on the ground that on the true
construction of a 'non-technicality clause' included in a time charter in New York Produce
Exchange form, the shipowner's notice of withdrawal was invalid. This made it
unnecessary to refer in the speeches in this House to that part of Lloyd J's judgment
b where he had discussed the jurisdiction to grant a charterer relief from the operation of a
withdrawal clause. In this House that was a question that was never reached.

In dealing with the jurisdiction point in *The Afovos* Lloyd J, in addition to adopting
Lord Simon's suggested analogy between re-entry on leasehold premises for non-payment
of rent and withdrawal of a ship for non-payment of hire (an analogy which I reject for
the reasons that I have already given), sought to extract from the speech of Lord
c Wilberforce in *Shiloh Spinners Ltd v Harding* [1973] 1 All ER 90, [1973] AC 691 a more
general proposition that wherever a party to a contract was by its terms given a right to
terminate it for a breach which consisted only of non-payment of a sum of money and
the purpose of incorporating the right of termination in the contract was to secure the
payment of that sum, there was an equitable jurisdiction to grant relief against the
exercise of the right of termination.

d My Lords, *Shiloh Spinners Ltd v Harding* was a case about a right of re-entry on leasehold
property for breach of a covenant, not to pay money but to do things on land. It was in a
passage that was tracing the history of the exercise by the Court of Chancery of its
jurisdiction to relieve against forfeiture of property that Lord Wilberforce said ([1973] 1
All ER 90 at 100, [1973] AC 691 at 722):

> e 'There has not been much difficulty as regards two heads of jurisdiction. First, where it is possible to state that the object of the transaction and of the insertion of the right to forfeit is essentially to secure the payment of money, equity has been willing to relieve on terms that the payment is made with interest, if appropriate, and also costs.'

That this mainly historical statement was never meant to apply generally to contracts not
f involving any transfer of proprietary or possessory rights, but providing for a right to
determine the contract in default of punctual payment of a sum of money payable under
it, is clear enough from Lord Wilberforce's speech in *The Laconia*. Speaking of a time
charter he said: 'It must be obvious that this is a very different type of creature from a
lease of land.'

Moreover, in the case of a time charter it is not possible to state that the object of the
g insertion of a withdrawal clause, let alone the transaction itself, is essentially to secure the
payment of money. Hire is payable in advance in order to provide a fund from which
the shipowner can meet those expenses of rendering the promised services to the
charterer that he has undertaken to bear himself under the charterparty, in particular the
wages and victualling of master and crew, the insurance of the vessel and her maintenance
in such a state as will enable her to continue to comply with the warranty of performance.

h This, the commercial purpose of obtaining payment of hire in advance, also makes
inapplicable another analogy sought to be drawn between a withdrawal clause and a
penalty clause of the kind against which courts of law, as well as courts of equity, before
the Judicature Acts had exercised jurisdiction to grant relief. The classic form of penalty
clause is one which provides that on breach of a primary obligation under the contract, a
secondary obligation shall arise on the party in breach to pay to the other party a sum of
j money which does not represent a genuine pre-estimate of any loss likely to be sustained
by him as the result of the breach of primary obligation but is substantially in excess of
that sum. The classic form of relief against such a penalty clause has been to refuse to
give effect to it, but to award the common law measure of damages for the breach of
primary obligation instead. Lloyd J in *The Afovos* attached importance to the majority
judgments in *Stockloser v Johnson* [1954] 1 All ER 630, [1954] 1 QB 476, which expressed

the opinion that money already paid by one party to the other under a continuing contract prior to an event which under the terms of the contract entitled that other party *a* to elect to rescind it and to retain the money already paid might be treated as money paid under a penalty clause and recovered to the extent that it exceeded to an unconscionable extent the value of any consideration that had been given for it. Assuming this to be so, however, it is incapable of having any application to time charters and withdrawal notices. Moneys paid by the charterer prior to the withdrawal notice that puts an end to the contract for services represent the agreed rate of hire for services already rendered, *b* and not a penny more.

All the analogies that ingenuity has suggested may be discovered between a withdrawal clause in a time charter and other classes of contractual provisions in which courts have relieved parties from the rigour of contractual terms into which they have entered can in my view be shown on juristic analysis to be false. Prima facie parties to a commercial contract bargaining on equal terms can make 'time to be of the essence' of the performance *c* of any primary obligation under the contract that they please, whether the obligation be to pay a sum of money or to do something else. When time is made of the essence of a primary obligation, failure to perform it punctually is a breach of a condition of the contract which entitles the party not in breach to elect to treat the breach as putting an end to all primary obligations under the contract that have not already been performed. In the *Tankexpress* case this House held that time was of the essence of the very clause *d* with which your Lordships are now concerned where it appeared in what was the then current predecessor of the Shelltime 3 charter. As is well known, there are available on the market a number of so-(mis)called 'anti-technicality clauses', such as that considered in *The Afovos*, which require the shipowner to give a specified period of notice to the charterer in order to make time of the essence of payment of advance hire; but at the expiry of such notice, provided it is validly given, time does become of the essence of the *e* payment.

My Lords, quite apart from the juristic difficulties in the way of recognising a jurisdiction in the court to grant relief against the operation of a withdrawal clause in a time charter, there are practical reasons of legal policy for declining to create any such new jurisdiction out of sympathy for charterers. The freight market is notoriously volatile. If it rises during the period of a time charter, the charterer is the beneficiary of *f* the windfall which he can realise if he wants to by sub-chartering at the then market rates. What withdrawal of the vessel does is to transfer the benefit of the windfall from charterer to shipowner.

The practical objections to any extension to withdrawal clauses in time charters of an equitable jurisdiction to grant relief against their exercise are so convincingly expressed by Robert Goff LJ in the judgment of the Court of Appeal in the instant case that I can *g* do no better than to incorporate them in my own speech for ease of reference ([1983] 1 All ER 301 at 308–309, [1983] 2 WLR 248 at 257–258):

> 'Parties to such contracts should be capable of looking after themselves; at the very least, they are capable of taking advice, and the services of brokers are available, and are frequently used, when negotiating terms. The possibility that shipowners *h* may snatch at the opportunity to withdraw ships from the service of time charterers for non-payment of hire must be very well known in the world of shipping; it must also be very well known that anti-technicality clauses are available which are effective to prevent any such occurrence. If a prospective time charterer wishes to have any such clause included in the charter, he can bargain for it; if he finds it necessary or desirable to agree to a charter which contains no such clause, he can warn the *j* relevant section of his office, and his bank, of the importance of securing timeous payment. But the matter does not stop there. It is of the utmost importance in commercial transactions that, if any particular event occurs which may affect the parties' respective rights under a commercial contract, they should know where they stand. The courts should so far as possible desist from placing obstacles in the

> way of either party ascertaining his legal position, if necessary with the aid of advice from a qualified lawyer, because it may be commercially desirable for action to be taken without delay, action which may be irrevocable and which may have far-reaching consequences. It is for this reason, of course, that the English courts have time and again asserted the need for certainty in commercial transaction, for the simple reason that the parties to such transactions are entitled to know where they stand and to act accordingly. In particular, when a shipowner becomes entitled, under the terms of his contract, to withdraw a ship from the service of a time charterer, he may well wish to act swiftly and irrevocably. True, his problem may, in any particular case, prove to be capable of solution by entering into a without prejudice argeement with the original time charterer, under which the rate of hire payable in future will be made to depend on a decision, by arbitrators or by a court, whether he was in law entitled to determine the charter. But this is not always possible. He may wish to refix his ship elsewhere as soon as possible, to take advantage of a favourable market. It is no answer to this difficulty that the ship may have cargo aboard at the time, so that her services cannot immediately be made available to another charterer (cf *The Afovos* [1980] 2 Lloyd's Rep 469 at 479 per Lloyd J); for one thing the ship may not have cargo on board, and for another she can be refixed immediately under a charter to commence at the end of her laden voyage. Nor is it an answer that the parties can immediately apply to arbitrators, or to a court, for a decision, and that both maritime arbitrators and the Commercial Court in this country are prepared to act very quickly at very short notice. For, quite apart from the fact that some delay is inherent in any legal process, if the question to be decided is whether the tribunal is to grant equitable relief, investigation of the relevant circumstances, and the collection of evidence for that purpose, cannot ordinarily be carried out in a very short period of time.'

For all these reasons I would dismiss this appeal. I do so with the reminder that the reasoning in my speech has been directed exclusively to time charters that are not by demise. Identical considerations would not be applicable to bareboat charters and it would in my view be unwise for your Lordships to express any views about them.

LORD KEITH OF KINKEL. My Lords, I have had the advantage of reading in draft the speech of my noble and learned friend Lord Diplock, and for the reasons given by him, with which I agree, I too would dismiss the appeal.

LORD SCARMAN. My Lords, I have had the advantage of reading in draft the speech delivered by my noble and learned friend Lord Diplock. I agree with it, and for the reasons he gives would dismiss the appeal.

LORD ROSKILL. My Lords, I have had the advantage of reading in draft the speech delivered by my noble and learned friend Lord Diplock. For the reasons he gives I, too, would dismiss this appeal.

LORD BRIDGE OF HARWICH. My Lords, for the reasons given in the speech of my noble and learned friend Lord Diplock, with which I entirely agree, I would dismiss this appeal.

Appeal dismissed.

Solicitors: *Elborne Mitchell & Co* (for the charterers); *Sinclair Roche & Temperley* (for the owners).

Mary Rose Plummer Barrister.

Garden Cottage Foods Ltd v Milk Marketing Board a

HOUSE OF LORDS

LORD DIPLOCK, LORD WILBERFORCE, LORD KEITH OF KINKEL, LORD BRIDGE OF HARWICH AND LORD BRANDON OF OAKBROOK

12, 13 APRIL, 23 JUNE 1983 b

European Economic Community – Rules on competition – Abuse of dominant position – Remedy – Statutory undertaking sole supplier in England and Wales of bulk butter – Undertaking selling butter to distributors in England and Wales including plaintiff for resale to EEC countries – Undertaking subsequently deciding to limit sale to only four distributors excluding plaintiff – Decision made on commercial grounds – Whether 'abuse . . . of a dominant position within the c *common market' – Whether remedy of injunction available to plaintiff – Whether remedy of damages available – EEC Treaty, art 86.*

The defendant milk marketing board, a statutory body, was the major producer of bulk butter in England and Wales. The board sold bulk butter to distributors in the United Kingdom, including the plaintiff company, who in turn sold it at a profit to purchasers d in countries in the European Economic Community. Between May 1980 and April 1982 the plaintiff purchased 90% of its bulk butter requirements from the board and made 95% of its resales to a single Dutch customer. In March 1982 the board informed the plaintiff that following a review of its sales and marketing strategy it had decided to limit the sale of bulk butter to four other distributors in England and Wales and that in future the plaintiff would have to purchase bulk butter from those distributors. That meant e that the plaintiff would have to pay more for the butter than it had when it had dealt directly with the board and also that it would be unable to compete with the four distributors when reselling to purchasers in the EEC. The plaintiff brought proceedings against the board, claiming that the board's conduct amounted to an 'abuse . . . of a dominant position within the common market' within art 86[a] of the EEC Treaty, and applied for an interlocutory injunction to restrain the board from withholding supplies f of butter from the plaintiff or otherwise refusing to maintain normal business relations with the plaintiff contrary to art 86. The judge refused to exercise his discretion in the plaintiff's favour because, although he held there was a serious issue to be tried, he further held (i) that damages would be an adequate remedy since they could be easily assessed and the board would be able to pay them if the plaintiff succeeded at the trial, (ii) the business of the board and the four distributors would be damaged by the grant of g an injunction and (iii) it would be difficult to frame an injunction in terms which were sufficiently precise to give the relief sought. The plaintiff successfully appealed to the Court of Appeal, which granted an interlocutory injunction on the ground that although the plaintiff had a good cause of action there was some doubt whether that cause of action, based on a breach by the defendants of art 86, sounded in damages at all and that an injunction was the only effective remedy that would be available to protect the h plaintiff. The board appealed.

Held (Lord Wilberforce dissenting) – Article 86 of the EEC Treaty imposed a duty on an undertaking holding a dominant position within the common market or a substantial part of it not to abuse that dominant position in a way which affected trade between member states, and also thereby conferred corresponding rights on individual citizens of j member states of the EEC. Assuming that an individual citizen of the United Kingdom affected by a breach of art 86 could bring an action based on a breach of statutory duty in order to gain redress for loss or damage caused by an undertaking's breach of its statutory duty under art 86, it was unarguable that such a cause of action would not give rise to a

a Article 86 is set out at p 775 *e f*, post

remedy in damages for loss already caused by that contravention but would merely give rise to a remedy by way of injunction to prevent future loss occurring. Furthermore, because the only loss which the plaintiff would suffer would be loss of profits, which could easily be assessed, damages would be an adequate remedy should the plaintiff ultimately succeed at the trial of the action. Since the judge had not misunderstood the law and since he was entitled to conclude that damages would be an adequate remedy, the Court of Appeal was wrong to interfere with the exercise of the judge's discretion and to grant an injunction. Accordingly, the appeal would be allowed and the injunction would be discharged (see p 775 *g* to p 776 *b*, p 777 *g* to p 778 *d* and *j* to p 779 *b*, p 780 *c d* and p 786 *e f*, post).

Belgische Radio en Televisie v SV SABAM [1974] ECR 51, *American Cyanamid Co v Ethicon Ltd* [1975] 1 All ER 504 and *Hadmor Productions Ltd v Hamilton* [1982] 1 All ER 1042 applied.

Per curiam. For the purpose of deciding whether an interlocutory injunction should be granted to preserve the status quo, the status quo is the state of affairs existing during the period immediately preceding the issue of the writ seeking the permanent injunction or, if there is unreasonable delay between the issue of the writ and the motion for an interlocutory injunction, the period immediately preceding the motion (see p 774 *j* to p 775 *a*, p 784 *c* and p 786 *e f*, post); *Texaco Ltd v Mulberry Filling Station Ltd* [1972] 1 All ER 513 overruled.

Decision of the Court of Appeal [1982] 3 All ER 292 reversed.

Notes

For abuse of a dominant market position, see Supplement to 38 Halsbury's Laws (3rd edn) para 185F, and for cases on the subject, see 21 Digest (Reissue) 279–282, *1792–1804*.

For the EEC Treaty, art 86, see 42A Halsbury's Statutes (3rd edn) 1183.

Cases referred to in opinions

American Cyanamid Co v Ethicon Ltd [1975] 1 All ER 504, [1975] AC 396, [1975] 2 WLR 316, HL.

Amministrazione delle Finanze dello Stato v Sas Mediterranea Importazione, Rappresentanze, Esportazione, Commercio (MIRECO) Case 826/79 [1980] ECR 2559, CJEC.

Application des Gaz SA v Falks Veritas Ltd [1974] 3 All ER 51, [1974] Ch 381, [1974] 3 WLR 235, CA.

Belgische Radio en Televisie and Société belge des auteurs v SV SABAM and NV Fonior Case 127/73 [1974] ECR 51, CJEC.

Camera Care Ltd v EC Commission Case 792/79R [1980] ECR 119, CJEC.

Europemballage Corp and Continental Can Co Inc v EC Commission Case 6/72 [1973] ECR 215, CJEC.

Hadmor Productions Ltd v Hamilton [1982] 1 All ER 1042, [1983] AC 191, [1982] 2 WLR 322, HL.

Hoffmann-La Roche (F) & Co AG v Secretary of State for Trade and Industry [1974] 2 All ER 1128, [1975] AC 295, [1974] 3 WLR 104, HL.

Lyons (J) and Sons v Wilkins [1896] 1 Ch 811, CA.

Rewe-Zentralfinaz eG and Rewe-Zentral AG v Landwirtschaftskammer für das Saarland Case 33/76 [1976] ECR 1989, CTEC.

Texaco Ltd v Mulberry Filling Station Ltd [1972] 1 All ER 513, [1972] 1 WLR 814.

United Brands Co and United Brands Continentaal BV v EC Commission Case 27/76 [1978] ECR 207, CJEC.

Valor International Ltd v Application des Gaz SA [1978] 3 CMLR 87, CA.

Interlocutory appeal

The defendants, the Milk Marketing Board, appealed, with the leave of the Appeal Committee of the House of Lords granted on 29 July 1982, against the decision of the Court of Appeal (Lord Denning MR, May LJ and Sir Sebag Shaw) ([1982] 3 All ER 292, [1982] QB 1114) on 18 and 27 May 1982 allowing an appeal by the plaintiff, Garden

Cottage Foods Ltd (the company), discharging an order of Parker J dated 21 April 1982 and granting an interlocutory injunction to the company restraining the board whether by itself or by its servants or agents or otherwise (i) from confining its sales of bulk butter to any particular person or persons or body of persons or any particular organisation or corporate body and (ii) from imposing significantly different terms in relation to the supply of butter to buyers in the bulk butter market, whether as regards price, quantity, credit terms or otherwise, than pursuant to ordinary mercantile and commercial practice, such injunction to remain in force until the trial of the action or further order. The facts are set out in the opinion of Lord Diplock.

John Swift QC, *Derrick Turriff* and *Christopher Vajda* for the board.
David Vaughan QC and *Peter Langdon-Davies* for the company.

Their Lordships took time for consideration.

23 June. The following opinions were delivered.

LORD DIPLOCK. My Lords, although the action in which this interlocutory appeal is brought may, if it is proceeded with, raise interesting and complex questions of European Economic Community law and the remedies available in English law for contravention of the EEC's rules on competition, the only issue which falls for determination by your Lordships at the present stage is whether the Court of Appeal (Lord Denning MR, May LJ and Sir Sebag Shaw) ([1982] 3 All ER 292, [1982] QB 1114) was justified in interfering with the refusal by the commercial judge, Parker J, in the exercise of his discretion, to grant to the plaintiff in the action (the company) an interlocutory injunction against the Milk Marketing Board in either of the alternative terms in which an injunction was sought.

The judge in his judgment (of which only an agreed note which is not a transcript is available) had expressed the view that damages would be an adequate remedy for any loss sustained by the company during the period before the action could be brought to trial, if the company were then to obtain judgment in its favour. It was stated unanimously by this House in *American Cyanamid Co v Ethicon Ltd* [1975] 1 All ER 504 at 510, [1975] AC 396 at 408 that, where this was the case and the defendant would be in a financial position to pay the damages, normally no interlocutory injunction should be granted. Parker J, however, also took into consideration the fact that the injunction applied for would disrupt the business of the board and the businesses of four distributors that it had recently appointed on profit-sharing terms. He also took into account the imprecision and unsuitability of the wording of each of the alternative forms of injunctions asked for.

In an expedited appeal by the company against the judge's refusal to grant an interlocutory injunction, the Court of Appeal delivered an extempore judgment on 18 May 1982, shortly after the publication of the decision of this House in *Hadmor Productions Ltd v Hamilton* [1982] 1 All ER 1042 at 1046, [1983] AC 191 at 220, in which this House took occasion to point out that on an appeal from the judge's grant or refusal of an interlocutory injunction an appellate court, including your Lordships, must defer to the judge's exercise of his discretion and must not interefere with it merely on the ground that the members of the appellate court would have exercised the discretion differently. The function of an appellate court is initially that of review only. It is entitled to exercise an original discretion of its own only when it has come to the conclusion that the judge's exercise of his discretion was based on some misunderstanding of the law or of the evidence before him, or on an inference that particular facts existed or did not exist, which, although it was one that might legitimately have been drawn on the evidence that was before the judge, can be demonstrated to be wrong by further evidence that has become available by the time of the appeal, or on the ground that there has been a change of circumstances after the judge made his order that would have justified his acceding to an application to vary it. Since reasons given by judges for granting or refusing interlocutory injunctions may sometimes be sketchy, there may also be occasional cases where, even though no erroneous assumption of law or fact can be identified, the judge's decision to grant or refuse the injunction is so aberrant that it must be set aside on the ground that no reasonable judge regardful of his duty to act judicially could have reached it. It is only if and after the appellate court has reached the conclusion that the judge's exercise of his discretion must be set aside for one or other of these reasons that it becomes entitled to exercise an original discretion of its own.

My Lords, I have ventured to repeat much of the ipsissima verba of the relevant passage of my speech in *Hadmor Productions Ltd v Hamilton*, which had the considered approval of all the other members of the House, since, from the list of cases reported as having been referred to in the argument at the hearing of the instant case, it would appear the attention of the Court of Appeal was not drawn to it. Certainly there is no hint in any of the judgments that the members of that court considered that they were doing anything other than exercising an independent discretion of their own. Although there was some additional evidence before the Court of Appeal that was not before the judge, no member of the court relied on it or even referred to it; there is no suggestion that the judge misunderstood the evidence before him; and, so far as I can see, the only suggestion that he may have misunderstood the law is that he ought not to have taken it for granted that if the company had a cause of action at all in English law for contravention of art 86 of the EEC Treaty it was one in which a remedy in damages would be available to it. To this suggestion I shall have to revert when I have outlined the facts and referred to the relevant EEC and United Kingdom legislation.

To complete the procedural history of the instant case, the Court of Appeal allowed the company's appeal. It granted the company an interlocutory injunction, not in either of the alternative forms sought by the company in its notice of appeal but in terms suggested by Sir Sebag Shaw in his judgment. These are so unclear as to what conduct by the board would constitute a contempt of court under them, that counsel for the company has not attempted to defend them before your Lordships. Instead he has invited this House to substitute for the injunction set out in the order of the Court of Appeal an injunction in terms not hitherto suggested in either of the courts below and which on examination showed similar defects of clarity and precision. That at least five unsuccessful attempts have been made to draft an interlocutory injunction that would make it clear what the board could do and could not do without committing a contempt of court goes far to vindicate the judge's view, which influenced his exercise of his discretion, that on the present state of the evidence, to the paucity of which I shall be referring shortly, it is not possible to devise an appropriate wording for an interlocutory injunction which would enable the board to know precisely what it is required to do or to abstain from doing.

My Lords, it was this procedural history that induced an Appeal Committee of this House to depart from its usual practice and to grant leave to appeal in an interlocutory matter the decision on which will not be conclusive of the action.

I turn now to such sketchy facts about the nature of the company's business as can be gathered from the available evidence. These are relevant both to the cause of action in English law to which it claims to be entitled against the board and also to the question whether the view taken by Parker J that, in the event of the company succeeding at the trial in establishing its claim, damages would be an adequate remedy for any loss it has sustained while the trial was pending was so untenable that an appellate court would be entitled to disregard it.

The company, which started business in May 1980, operates from the residence of Mr Bunch at Crowborough in East Sussex. Mr Bunch and his wife are its only employees. In effect, it is Mr and Mrs Bunch with limited liability. The only part of its business that is dealt with in the evidence is its purchase and resale of bulk butter. Between May 1980 and the commencement of the action in April 1982 this accounted for 80% of the company's turnover. Of its purchases during that period 90% were from the board, and of its resales 95% were for export to a single purchaser in the Netherlands, J Wijffels BV (the Dutch company). Save that the company purchased bulk butter from the board ex *a* creamery or ex cold store, there is no evidence as to the terms on which it was sold on to the Dutch company or whether the company or the Dutch company itself was responsible for making arrangements for the transport of consignments from creamery or cold store to the Netherlands. Your Lordships may take judicial notice that under the common agricultural policy (CAP) mountainous surpluses of butter are produced in the EEC, for which there is no market for human consumption as such within the member states of *b* the EEC. Some of this surplus, it would appear, goes into the 'bulk butter' market where it is dealt in by private traders as distinct from being purchased by the intervention agency at intervention prices under the CAP; but how this bulk butter market operates and whether it bears any resemblance to other international commodity markets your Lordships can find no inkling in the evidence.

The board is a statutory authority established by the Milk Marketing Scheme 1933, as *c* subsequently amended. The scheme is made under legislation that is now contained in the Agricultural Marketing Act 1958. The board is also subject to the EEC Council Regulation 804/68 on the common organisation of the market in milk and milk products and to a further EEC Council Regulation 1422/78 which authorises the grant to the board, and to other milk marketing boards in Scotland and Northern Ireland, of exclusive rights to purchase milk in those three parts of the United Kingdom respectively, and *d* contains other provisions which on the face of them appear to permit the imposition of restrictions on free competition in milk products. At this stage of the proceedings in the instant case, however, your Lordships are not concerned with any of the detailed EEC regulations relating to the organisation of the market in milk products under the CAP as they affect the operations of the board. It is sufficient to draw attention to the fact that the market is subject to a special regime and the application of the EEC's rules on *e* competition to this regime may well give rise to questions of EEC law of considerable complexity. Factually, the evidence does disclose that the board produces some 75% of the butter produced in England and Wales (not the United Kingdom) and it is reasonable to infer that it is the largest, and maybe by far the largest, producer of bulk butter exported from the United Kingdom for trading in the bulk butter market. The board started to accept tenders from the company for the purchase of bulk butter in August *f* 1980. It continued to do so roughly once or twice a month until May 1981, after which there was a gap until it made a tender that was accepted in August 1981. Thereafter no further tenders were accepted although delivery was continued under earlier forward contracts until the end of 1981. There was, however, no express refusal by the board to do further business in bulk butter with the company until, by letter dated 24 March 1982, it informed Mr Bunch that it had decided to revise its sales and marketing strategy *g* and to appoint four independent distributors (whose names and addresses were given) to handle the sales of its bulk butter for export, with effect from 1 April 1982. Mr Bunch was advised that he should contact those distributors to discuss availability of supplies if the company should require the board's bulk butter for export.

This letter was followed by a meeting between Mr Bunch and a representative of the board at which the latter said that the board was not prepared to reconsider its decision. *h* This refusal triggered off the present action.

The history of the trading relations between the company and the board, as I have outlined them, make it difficult to identify what was the relevant status quo which it was said in the *American Cyanamid* case it is a counsel of prudence to preserve *when other factors are evenly balanced*. The status quo is the existing state of affairs; but since states of affairs do not remain static this raises the query: existing when? In my opinion, the *j* relevant status quo to which reference was made in the *American Cyanamid* case is the state of affairs existing during the period immediately preceding the issue of the writ claiming the permanent injunction or, if there be unreasonably delay between the issue of the writ and the motion for an interlocutory injunction, the period immediately preceding the motion. The duration of that period since the state of affairs last changed must be more than minimal, having regard to the total length of the relationship between the parties in respect of which the injunction is granted; otherwise the state of affairs before the last change would be the relevant status quo.

In *Texaco Ltd v Mulberry Ltd* [1972] 1 All ER 513 at 529, [1972] 1 WLR 814 at 831 Ungoed-Thomas J took as the relevant period for ascertaining what constituted the status quo the period preceding the commencement of the conduct on the part of the defendant in respect of which the action was brought, in that case breaches of covenant. But that decision was before the *American Cyanamid* case and was based on the assumption that a 'strong prima facie' case that the plaintiff would succeed at the trial in obtaining a final injunction had to be made out before an interlocutory injunction would be granted, a requirement which he held to have been satisfied on the evidence that was before him. Now that the necessity for the court to determine that the plaintiff has made out a strong prima facie case for a permanent injunction before granting him an interlocutory injunction has been removed by the decision of this House in the *American Cyanamid* case, this also flaws the reasoning by which Ungoed-Thomas J reached the conclusion that he did as to what constituted the relevant period for determining what is the status quo. In the instant case, however, for reasons that will appear hereafter, I do not think that one ever reaches the stage at which the desirability of maintaining the status quo is brought into the balance of convenience.

The cause of action alleged by the company in its writ issued on 14 April 1982 was contravention by the board of art 86 of the EEC Treaty by withholding supplies of butter from the company or otherwise refusing to maintain normal business relations with it.

Article 86 is in the following terms:

> 'Any abuse by one or more undertakings of a dominant position within the common market or in a substantial part of it shall be prohibited as incompatible with the common market in so far as it may affect trade between Member States. Such abuse may, in particular, consist in: (*a*) directly or indirectly imposing unfair purchase or selling prices or other unfair trading conditions; (*b*) limiting production, markets or technical development to the prejudice of consumers; (*c*) applying dissimilar conditions to equivalent transactions with other trading parties, thereby placing them at a competitive disadvantage; (*d*) making the conclusion of contracts subject to acceptance by the other parties of supplementary obligations which, by their nature or according to commercial usage, have no connection with the subject of such contracts.'

This article of the EEC Treaty was held by the Court of Justice of the European Communities in *Belgische Radio en Televisie v SV SABAM* Case 127/73 [1974] ECR 51 at 62 to produce direct effects in relations between individuals and to create direct rights in respect of the individuals concerned which the national courts must protect. This decision of the Court of Justice as to the effect of art 86 is one which s 3(1) of the European Communities Act 1972 requires your Lordships to follow. The rights which the article confers on citizens in the United Kingdom accordingly fall within s 2(1) of the 1972 Act. They are without further enactment to be given legal effect in the United Kingdom and enforced accordingly.

A breach of the duty imposed by art 86 not to abuse a dominant position in the Common Market or in a substantial part of it can thus be categorised in English law as a breach of a statutory duty that is imposed not only for the purpose of promoting the general economic prosperity of the Common Market but also for the benefit of private individuals to whom loss or damage is caused by a breach of that duty.

If this categorisation be correct, and I can see none other that would be capable of giving rise to a civil cause of action in English private law on the part of a private individual who sustained loss or damage by reason of a breach of a directly applicable provision of the EEC Treaty, the nature of the cause of action cannot, in my view, be affected by the fact that the legislative provision by which the duty is imposed takes the negative form of a prohibition of particular kinds of conduct rather than the positive form of an obligation to do particular acts. Of the many statutory duties imposed on employers under successive Factories Acts and regulations made thereunder, which have provided far and away the commonest cases of this kind of action, some take the form of prohibitions, others positive obligations to do something, yet it has never been suggested that it makes any difference to the cause of action whether the breach relied on was a failure to perform a positive duty or the doing of a prohibited act.

My Lords, when faced with the company's application for an interlocutory injunction, the first task of the judge was to make up his mind whether there was a serious question to be tried. Plainly a number of difficult and doubtful questions would be involved in any trial of the action. The jurisprudence of the Court of Justice of the European Communities, which in this field of law is well settled, indicates that there are three matters that must be proved to constitute a contravention of art 86. First, the contravenor must be in a dominant position in a substantial part of the Common Market, and this involves as a preliminary question the identification of the 'relevant market'; not necessarily an easy task as *Europemballage Corp and Continental Can Co Inc v EC Commission* Case 6/72 [1973] ECR 215 shows. Second, there must be shown an 'abuse' of that dominant position. The particular examples in paras (*b*) and (*c*) of art 86 on which the company principally relies *may* constitute an abuse but do not necessarily do so, and in this connection it may be necessary to take into account the interaction between the EEC rules on competition and the CAP. Third, it must be shown that the abuse affects trade between member states.

My Lords, I express no view as to what is likely to be the answer to any of those questions, save to observe that it would be quite impossible at this stage, and probably at any stage until after a reference under art 177 of the treaty to the Court of Justice of the European Communities, to say on the one hand that the board's behaviour that forms the subject matter of the action is clearly not capable of having any appreciable effect on competition or on trade between member states, or, on the other hand, that there is no doubt of the incompatibility of that behaviour with art 86. I mention this because, your Lordships having been informed that the company, since the judgment of the Court of Appeal, has also made a complaint to the EEC Commission under art 3 of Regulation 17 of 6 February 1962, the judgment of the European Court in the *Belgische Radio* case indicates that it may have some relevance to the future progress of the present action in the High Court.

My Lords, Parker J, having rightly, indeed inevitably, decided that there were serious questions to be tried, next turned, as directed by *American Cyanamid Co v Ethicon Ltd*, to consider whether if the company were to succeed at the trial in establishing its right to a permanent injunction (if a permanent injunction in some appropriate form could be devised) it would be adequately compensated by an award of damages for the loss it would have sustained as a result of the board's continuing to do what was sought to be enjoined between the time of the application for the interim injunction and the time of the trial.

Parker J was of opinion that an award of damages would provide adequate compensation for any such loss if the board's refusal to accept direct tenders from it for bulk butter should be held to be a contravention of art 86. So far as the business of the company, conducted as it was entirely by Mr and Mrs Bunch from their own home, consisted of dealing in bulk butter it appears to have involved no more than acting as a middleman who transferred to traders in the bulk market immediately on delivery by the board of ex creamery or ex cold store consignments of butter that the company had itself bought on seven-day credit terms, and taking its own 'cut' out of the price at which it passed on the consignment to the trader. If it were compelled to buy bulk butter from one or other of four distributors referred to in the letter of 24 March 1982 instead of directly from the board this would be likely to reduce the amount of the company's cut, or even to eliminate the possibility of retaining one, so that the sensible course would be to suspend until trial of the action this part of the company's business. But, if that were the course adopted, all that the company would lose by such suspension of business

would be the opportunity of obtaining the sums of money represented by that cut. There
a could hardly be a clearer case of damages being an adequate remedy unless insuperable difficulties of estimation could be foreseen; but any difficulties of estimation would be greatly reduced by the fact that the company had only one substantial customer, the Dutch company, with whom 95% of the company's business in bulk butter was transacted, and that one customer, as appears from an affidavit of Mr J Wijffels that was before the Court of Appeal, during the period that the company was obtaining butter
b from the board, purchased from the company about one-third of its requirements for bulk butter originating in the United Kingdom.

Difficulties of estimation, however, were not the ground on which the Court of Appeal overruled the judge's opinion that damages would be an adequate remedy. Neither Lord Denning MR nor Sir Sebag Shaw made any mention of this topic; nor does a passing reference by May LJ to possible difficulties of assessment of the proper measure of
c damages 'in cases such as this', without any reference to the special characteristics of the company's business to which I have just drawn attention, appear to play a significant role in his ratio decidendi. It was for an entirely different reason that the Court of Appeal rejected the view of the judge that damages would provide an adequate remedy.

To that reason I must shortly come; but, before doing so, I should refer to another aspect of the difficulty of estimating damages, which the judge also took into account in
d exercising his discretion in favour of refusing to grant an interlocutory injunction. That was the damage that would be caused to the business of the board and the business of the four distributors to whom it had already made commitments. For that disturbance, in the event of the company failing in the action, the board's only remedy would be the recovery of damages from the company under the cross-undertaking which it would be required to give. This is a matter which, it was said by this House in *American Cyanamid*
e *Co v Ethicon Ltd*, a judge ought to take into consideration in deciding how to exercise his discretion. No consideration appears to have been given to it by the Court of Appeal, save that it evoked the procrustean comment from Lord Denning MR ([1982] 3 All ER 292 at 298–299, [1982] QB 1114 at 1125): 'I am afraid that that is a bed of their own making and they must deal with it as best they can.'

The only reason why the Court of Appeal held that the judge was wrong in his view
f that damages would provide an adequate remedy to the company for any interference with its bulk butter business pending the trial of the action appears to have been that each member of the court felt doubt, in varying degrees, whether the company's cause of action sounded in damages at all. Sir Sebag Shaw expressed considerable misgivings whether a remedy in damages lies for a contravention of art 86 of the EEC Treaty. Lord Denning MR thought there was a good deal to be said for there being a remedy in
g damages, but that it was not altogether certain. May LJ, though less doubtful than Lord Denning MR as to the availability of a remedy in damages, considered that the contrary was certainly arguable.

My Lords, in the light (a) of the uniform jurisprudence of the Court of Justice of the European Communities, of which it is sufficient to mention the *Belgische Radio* case (which I have already cited) and the subsequent case of *Rewe-Zentralfinanz eG v*
h *Landwirtschaftskammer für das Saarland* Case 33/76 [1976] ECR 1989, which was to the same effect as respect the duty of national courts to protect rights conferred on individual citizens by directly applicable provisions of the treaty, and (b) of ss 2(1) and 3(1) of the European Communities Act 1972, I, for my own part, find it difficult to see how it can ultimately be successfully argued, as the board will seek to do, that a contravention of art 86 which causes damage to an individual citizen does not give rise to a cause of action in
j English law of the nature of a cause of action for breach of statutory duty; but since it cannot be regarded as unarguable that is not a matter for final decision by your Lordships at the interlocutory stage that the instant case has reached. What, with great respect to those who think otherwise, I *do* regard as quite unarguable is the proposition, advanced by the Court of Appeal itself but disclaimed by both parties to the action, that, if such a contravention of art 86 gives rise to any case of action at all, it gives rise to a cause of

action for which there is no remedy in damages to compensate for loss already caused by that contravention but only a remedy by way of injunction to prevent future loss being a caused. A cause of action to which an unlawful act by the defendant causing pecuniary loss to the plaintiff gives rise, if it possessed those characteristics as respects the remedies available, would be one which, so far as my understanding goes, is unknown in English private law, at any rate since 1875 when the jurisdiction conferred on the Court of Chancery by Lord Cairns's Act, the Chancery Amendment Act 1858, passed to the High Court. I leave aside as irrelevant for present purposes injunctions granted in matrimonial b causes or wardship proceedings which may have no connection with pecuniary loss. I likewise leave out of account injunctions obtainable as remedies in public law whether on application for judicial review or in an action brought by the Attorney General ex officio or ex relatione some private individual. It is private law, not public law, to which the company has had recourse. In its action it claims damages as well as an injunction. No reasons are to be found in any of the judgments of the Court of Appeal and none has c been advanced at the hearing before your Lordships why in law, in logic or in justice, if contravention of art 86 of the EEC Treaty is capable of giving rise to a cause of action in English private law at all, there is any need to invent a cause of action with characteristics that are wholly novel as respects the remedies that it attracts, in order to deal with breaches of articles of the EEC Treaty which have in the United Kingdom the same effect as statutes. d

The notion that it is seriously arguable that a contravention of art 86 may give rise to a cause of action possessing such unique characteristics appears to have been based on a misunderstanding by the Court of Appeal of a cautionary obiter dictum of Roskill LJ in *Valor International Ltd v Application des Gaz SA* [1978] 3 CMLR 87. In a previous decision of the Court of Appeal, *Application des Gaz SA v Falks Veritas Ltd* [1974] 3 All ER 51 at 58, [1974] Ch 381 at 396, Lord Denning MR had stated: 'Articles 85 and 86 are part of our e law. They create new torts or wrongs.' The issue in that case, however, which was one for breach of copyright in a drawing of a tin for holding liquid gas, was whether a defendant could plead breaches by the plaintiff of art 85 or art 86 as a defence to the plaintiff's claim. The court was unanimous in holding that the defendant could so plead but only Lord Denning MR expressed any view whether those articles created new torts or wrongs in English law. It was unnecessary for the purposes of that case to do more f than to decide that it was arguable that those articles could be used as a shield, whether or not they could also be used as a sword; and in the *Valor International* case [1978] 3 CMLR 87 at 100 Roskill LJ, who had been a member of the court in the *Falks Veritas* case, pointed this out and said that there were—

> 'many questions which will have to be argued in this Court or elsewhere in this country or at Luxembourg, before it can be stated categorically . . . that **Articles 85** g and **86** create new torts or wrongs . . .'

The concept of conduct by a plaintiff in legal proceedings that may be relied on by the defendant as a defence to the plaintiff's claim although it *does not* give rise to a cause of action on the part of the defendant against the plaintiff is one with which English law is familiar. Examples of the application of this concept are provided by estoppel and, what h Roskill LJ may have had in mind as presenting the closest analogy to a contravention of art 85 or art 86, the application of the maxim ex turpi causa non oritur actio. There is nothing whatever in his observations to suggest that it had ever crossed his mind that, if art 86 *did* give rise to a cause of action in English private law on the part of an individual citizen who suffered pecuniary loss as a result of another individual's contravention of that article, the resulting cause of action might have the unique and heterodox j characteristics that it gave a remedy by injunction to prevent future pecuniary loss but none in damages for loss that had already been sustained.

To summarise, the Court of Appeal was in my view wrong in suggesting that, if it were established at the trial (a) that the board had contravened art 86 and (b) that such contravention had (i) caused the company pecuniary loss and (ii) thereby given rise to a

cause of action in English law on the part of the company against the board, it was a
a seriously arguable proposition that such cause of action did not entitle the company to a remedy in damages although it did entitle the company to a remedy by injunction. Parker J did not misunderstand the law in this respect. He was entitled to take the view that a remedy in damages would be available and, for the reasons I have stated earlier, that such remedy would be adequate.

I next turn briefly to the difficulty of formulating the terms of any interlocutory
b injunction to which Parker J referred as an additional ground for not granting one. The injunction granted by the Court of Appeal was in the following terms:

> 'there be an injunction herein and an injunction is hereby granted restraining the Defendants whether by themselves or by their servants agents or otherwise from:— (i) confining its sales of bulk butter to any particular person or persons or body of persons or any particular organisation or corporate body; (ii) From imposing
> c significantly different terms in relation to the supply of butter to buyers in the bulk butter market whether as regards price, quantity, credit terms or otherwise, otherwise than pursuant to ordinary mercantile and commercial practice. UNTIL the trial of this action or further order.'

It is sufficient to say of this that counsel for the company conceded that an injunction in
d these terms was indefensible. He submitted to your Lordships an alternative form in which paragraphs (i) and (ii) were replaced by:

> '(i) from refusing to supply the plaintiffs with bulk butter and (ii) in supplying such bulk butter from applying to such supply dissimilar conditions, whether as to price, quantity or credit terms or otherwise, from those applied to equivalent transactions with other traders to whom the defendants supply bulk butter.'

e

This draft, unlike the injunction granted by the Court of Appeal, is at least restricted to restraining the conduct of the board towards the company, but it still suffers from a similar lack of precision as to what the board may and may not do without infringing it.

My Lords, I would accept that, if this action were to proceed to trial before any positive step had been taken by the EEC Commission under Council Regulation 17 of 27 February
f 1962 and the company were to succeed in establishing a continuing contravention by the board of art 86, the High Court would have to do its best to devise a suitable form of words for a permanent injunction; but the court by then would have a great deal more evidence of the operation of the bulk butter market in the EEC and its task, which in the present dearth of detailed evidence I regard as being impossible, would at least be thereby facilitated. As already mentioned, however, your Lordships have been informed that the
g company has made a complaint to the commission under Regulation 17, which will entitle the commission to investigate the behaviour of the board that is complained of and either make an order under art 3 of the regulation requiring the board to bring such behaviour to an end if the commission finds that it constitutes an infringement of art 86 or grant negative clearance under art 2 if the commission finds that there is no infringement. Continuance of the behaviour after an order to cease and desist under art
h 3 may be visited with penalties imposed by the commission under art 15(2)(*b*) of Regulation 17. From decisions of the commission under Regulation 17 there lies an appeal to the Court of Justice of the European Communities.

As was held by the Court of Justice in the *Belgische Radio* case [1974] ECR 51, the initiation of proceedings by the commission under Regulation 17 does not deprive the national court of jurisdiction to continue with an action brought by an individual citizen
j based on the same behaviour that is concurrently the subject of investigation by the commission and, in continuing that action, to refer a request for a preliminary ruling by the Court of Justice of the European Communities under art 177 of the EEC treaty; but it may be worth while quoting two paragraphs of the judgment in the *Belgische Radio* case [1974] ECR 51 at 63, couched in the tactful language in which the Court of Justice habitually refers to the exercise of their functions by national courts:

> 'The fact that the expression "authorities of the Member States" appearing in Article 9(3) of Regulation No 17 covers such courts cannot exempt a court before which the direct effect of Article 86 is pleaded from giving judgment. Nevertheless, if the Commission initiates a procedure in application of Article 3 of Regulation No 17 such a court may, if it considers it necessary for reasons of legal certainty, stay the proceedings before it while awaiting the outcome of the Commission's action. On the other hand, the national court should generally allow proceedings before it to continue when it decides either that the behaviour in dispute is clearly not capable of having any appreciable effect on competition or on trade between Member States, or that there is no doubt of the incompatibility of that behaviour with Article 86.'

So it may be that, as the company is now pursuing also a remedy under Regulation 17, the High Court will be spared the problem of devising a suitable form of words for a permanent injunction if the company is ultimately successful in this action.

For the cumulative reasons given earlier in this speech, I am of opinion that the judgments in the Court of Appeal disclose no ground which would justify an appellate court in interfering with the way in which Parker J had exercised his discretion by refusing to grant an interlocutory injunction in this case; and that the only ground on which the Court of Appeal appears to have relied for doing so is bad in law.

I would accordingly allow this appeal and discharge the order of the Court of Appeal.

LORD WILBERFORCE. My Lords, these proceedings are brought by Garden Cottage Foods Ltd (the company) against the Milk Marketing Board for the following relief:

> '1. An injunction restraining the Defendants whether by themselves or by their servants or agents or otherwise from withholding supplies of butter from the Plaintiffs or otherwise refusing to maintain normal business relations with the Plaintiffs contrary to Article 86 of the Treaty of Rome. 2. Damages.'

Article 86 says:

> 'Any abuse by one or more undertakings of a dominant position within the common market or in a substantial part of it shall be prohibited as incompatible with the common market in so far as it may affect trade between Member States. Such abuse may, in particular, consist in: (*a*) directly or indirectly imposing unfair purchase or selling prices or other unfair trading conditions; (*b*) limiting production, markets or technical development to the prejudice of consumers; (*c*) applying dissimilar conditions to equivalent transactions with other trading parties, thereby placing them at a competitive disadvantage; (*d*) making the conclusion of contracts subject to acceptance by the other parties of supplementary obligations which, by their nature or according to commercial usage, have no connection with the subject of such contracts.'

Garden Cottage Foods Ltd is a company owned and managed by Mr Christopher Bunch and his wife, and its primary business is the purchase and resale of butter in bulk. Mr Bunch was previously employed for six years by another company in the dairy business and has had two years' experience with the company. He claims great expertise in the butter trade. The principal customer of the company is a Dutch company, J Wijffels BV, whose director, Mr Joannes B A Wijffels, testifies that the company is a very efficient and capable organisation and that the services of Mr C R Bunch are of the utmost value to the Dutch company. There is no doubt that the company has a genuine and profitable business but also a precarious one, operating as it does in a highly competitive field with powerful rivals in the UK and outside.

Since commencing business the company has bought considerable quantities of bulk butter from the board:

August 1980 to November 1980	£2,170,257·00
January 1981 to August 1981	£20,126,854·69

Its profits arise from a small margin of sale price over purchase price, and from the maintenance of low overheads. The greater part of its purchases, in fact over 90%, is sold to J Wijffels BV, which specialises in the sale of British butter. About 90% of the company's supplies of bulk butter come from the board.

The board has a statutory monopoly in England and Wales for the purchase and resale of milk. When it has a milk surplus it makes butter. Up to August 1981 it sold butter to the company as the latter required it, but after a period during which no butter was offered to the company, although butter was (by admission of counsel) available for sale, it wrote a letter to the company on 24 March 1982 saying that it was only going to sell bulk butter to four 'independent distributors'. The company was told that if it wanted any bulk butter it should contact the above distributors. It is this decision which the company contends is a breach of art 86 of the EEC Treaty. Having issued a writ on 14 April 1982 asking for (a) an injunction against withholding supplies from the plaintiff company and (b) damages, it applied for interlocutory relief in the form of an injunction, following the terms of the writ until judgment or further order. This relief was refused by Parker J but (subject to the wording of the injunction to which I refer later) was granted by the Court of Appeal (see [1982] 3 All ER 292, [1982] QB 1114).

Evidence was filed to support the company's application. In the interest of speed, this evidence was not presented in a very regular manner. Parker J had before him an affidavit of Mr Bunch showing in some detail the nature of the company's business and the orders it placed with the board. It endeavoured to show that the board holds a dominant position as manufacturers of butter in England and Wales. It gave evidence of inquiries made of the board after August 1981 whether the board had any butter for sale, to which a negative reply was given, and of the letter of 24 March 1982 (see above). It testified that if the company had to go for butter to the four distributors, which are competitors in the same market, it would be unable to compete with them on price when reselling, and 'may be forced out of business as it cannot purchase equivalent supplies from other sources'. An undertaking in damages which might be suffered by the board was offered. On the other side a draft and unsworn affidavit on behalf of the board was before the court. It denied any 'dominant position' and claimed that the company could obtain supplies of butter from elsewhere in the EEC. It denied any 'abuse'. It claimed to have entered into commitments with the four distributors for 1982–83 while admitting that details of an agreement remained to be agreed and that the latter 'can be expected to have entered into forward commitments'. It asserted that, if an injunction were granted, there would be uncertainty as to its application. The company could, in any event, have a claim for damages.

When the case came before the Court of Appeal, further evidence was put in, apparently by agreement, or at least without disagreement, and the Court of Appeal within its powers decided to receive it. We must proceed on the basis of this being evidence in the case. Mr Bunch amplified his previous evidence as to his company's dependence on the board for bulk butter supply. He specified the only alternative sources in the United Kingdom and established, to my mind beyond doubt, that the company could not obtain supplies from them: since trading started it had only had been able to buy 38 tonnes as compared with 11,700 tonnes from the board. He explained that even if the company could obtain butter from EEC sources (which would be difficult if not impossible) this would not be acceptable to J Wijffels BV. He provided figures showing how, if the company had to buy butter from the four distributors, it could not sell to J Wijffels BV so as to make any profit. He dealt explicitly with the suggestion that the company would have an adequate remedy in damages in the following passage, which I quote:

> 'The contention made in paragraph 5 of Mr. C. C. Abram's said affidavit (namely that the Plaintiff Company would have an adequate remedy in damages against the Defendants) is impossible to support. For the reasons explained above, the Plaintiff Company will not be able to make any profit whatsoever and must inevitably make a loss once its overheads are taken into consideration. There is no question in my mind that any remedy which the Plaintiff Company may have in damages would

> be totally inadequate in these circumstances. The fact of the matter is that it will not be able to buy adequate (if any) supplies of butter elsewhere and will not be able *a* to continue trading. It is therefore essential to the Plaintiff Company that, if it is to survive, it is able to continue buying butter direct from the Defendants and that in doing it is not discriminated against by the Defendants.'

He gave further and full evidence as to the practical consequences which would follow if the board were to be prevented from excluding the company from purchasing butter. *b* This affidavit was accompanied by one from Mr J B A Wijffels describing his trading relationship with the company and testifying to its expertise. A final affidavit was sworn on behalf of the board without adding anything material.

On this evidence (including that which was not before the judge) I have, for my own part, no doubt that, subject to consideration of certain points with which I shall deal, a court of equity would regard the case as being one for an interlocutory injunction. If *c* satisfied that a serious case had been made out that the board occupied a dominant position in the relevant market, and was abusing it, the board would then be engaging in a course of action 'prohibited' by the EEC Treaty. By doing so, it would inflict serious injury on the company's business. Every argument including the balance of convenience would seem to fall in favour of maintaining the status quo until determination of the action, which is the normal purpose for which interlocutory injunctions are granted. *d*

In order to satisfy itself that such was the position, the court would, in my opinion, have to give consideration to the following matters. 1. Has the company made out a case, and if so how strong a case, that the board (a) has a dominant position in the common market or in a substantial part of it and (b) is abusing it by the action in question? 2. Is it shown that damages would be (a) available and (b) adequate? 3. Is the balance of convenience in favour of, or against, granting an injunction? 4. Would the board be *e* adequately protected by the company's cross-undertaking in damages? I include this point for completeness, but I do not find any basis for a suggestion that it would not, nor did the board take such a point in their case. Incidentally the order of the Court of Appeal does not (contrary to practice) incorporate any undertaking as to damages, which suggests that this element was not regarded as calling for special consideration. I deal, as briefly as I can, with the other points. *f*

As to the first point, subject to a possible question as to what is the relevant market, it seems to me clear that a strong prima facie case is made on the question of dominance. I am less confident on the issue of 'abuse'. This is a much more difficult question as to which no settled jurisprudence has emerged either in the Court of Justice of the European Communities or in the courts of member states. The main relevant decision of the European Court is *United Brands Co v EC Commission* Case 27/76 [1978] ECR 207, which *g* on the one hand suggests that an abuse may be held to exist in a case such as this (of refusal to supply an established customer who places orders not out of the ordinary) but also shows that difficulties of proof may face the complainant. However, since all four judges who have considered this case below have felt able, though with differing degrees of conviction (Parker J describing the case, on this point, as weak), to conclude that a sufficient case of abuse is made out at this stage, and since I understand that your *h* Lordships do not take a different position, I am able, though with some hesitation, to agree. The preliminary requirement that the company must be able to make out a prima facie, or arguable, case (however one expresses it) is therefore satisfied.

As to the second point, this question, a necessary one which has always to be answered in cases when an interlocutory judgment is sought, has become entangled into some confusion. Argument was devoted, both in the courts below and in this House, to the *j* question whether an action for damages can be brought in the courts of this country in respect of art 86 of the EEC Treaty. The position in English law before the present case was obscure. In *Application des Gaz SA v Falks Veritas Ltd* [1974] 3 All ER 51 at 58, [1974] Ch 381 at 396 Lord Denning MR, by way of obiter dictum, expressed the view that art 86 (as well as art 85) created a tort, namely, in the case of art 86, the tort of abuse of dominant position within the common market. This was not assented to by the other

members of the court. In *Valor International Ltd v Application des Gaz SA* [1978] 3 CMLR
a 87 at 100 (a relevant case since the claim there was for damages for breach of art 86)
Roskill LJ said that many questions would have to be argued, in English courts or at
Luxembourg, before it could be stated categorically that arts 85 and 86 created new torts
or wrongs, ie as must follow, as giving rise to a claim for damages. In the present
proceedings Parker J, citing Lord Denning MR's dictum, expressed the view that an
interlocutory injunction could be granted and later assumed, without supporting
b argument, that damages could be awarded. In the Court of Appeal there was obviously
substantial argument on this point. Lord Denning MR thought that the present was not
the occasion to decide the point; he thought there was a good deal to be said for there
being a remedy in damages, but it was not altogether certain. He thought that the only
effective remedy in such a case was an injunction. May LJ thought that a remedy in
damages in an appropriate case would be damages but 'the contrary is certainly arguable'.
c Sir Sebag Shaw had considerable misgivings whether a remedy in damages lay for a
contravention of art 86.

It can I think be accepted that a private person can sue in this country to prevent an
infraction of article 86. This follows from the fact, which is indisputable, that this article
is directly applicable in member states. The Court of Justice of the European Communities
has moreover decided in *Belgische Radio en Televisie v SV SABAM* Case 127/73 [1974] ECR
d 51 at 62, para 16 in connection with art 86 that it is for the national courts of member
states to safeguard the rights of individuals. Since art 86 says that abuses of a dominant
position are prohibited, and since prohibited conduct in England is sanctioned by an
injunction, it would seem to follow that an action lies, at the instance of a private person,
for an injunction to restrain the prohibited conduct. But can he recover damages? Your
Lordships, I understand, regard the contrary as 'unarguable' or indeed 'quite unarguable',
e a bold proposition in the fact of doubts expressed by the learned Lords Justices and one
whose confidence I do not share. So far as the community is concerned, art 86 is enforced
under Regulation 17 of 27 February 1962 by orders to desist (art 3), and if necessary by
fines (art 15), and the Court of Justice has similar powers on review. Fines are not payable
to persons injured by the prohibited conduct, and there is no way under Community
law by which such persons can get damages. So the question is whether the situation is
f changed, and the remedy extended, by the incorporation of art 86 into our law by s 2 of
the European Communities Act 1972. To say that thereby what is prohibited action
becomes a tort or a 'breach of statutory duty' is, in my opinion, a conclusionary statement
concealing a vital and unexpressed step. All that s 2 says (relevantly) is that rights arising
under the EEC Treaty are to be available in law in the United Kingdom, but this does not
suggest any transformation or enlargement in their character. Indeed the section calls
g them 'enforceable Community rights', not rights arising under United Kingdom law.
All that the relevant cases (*Rewe-Zentralfinanz eG v Landwirtschaftskammer für das Saarland*
Case 33/76 [1976] ECR 1989 and *Amministrazione delle Finanze dello Stato v Sas Mediterranea
Importazione, Rappresentanze, Esportazione, Commercio* (*MIRECO*) Case 826/79 [1980] ECR
2559) tell us is that it is for national laws to designate the appropriate courts having
jurisdiction, and to establish the precedural conditions. Does this enable national laws to
h define the remedy? There is of course nothing illogical or even unusual in a situation in
which a person's rights extend to an injunction but not to damages; many such exist in
English law. Community law, which is what the English court would be applying, is, in
any case, sui generis and the wording used in art 86, 'prohibited' and 'so far as it may
affect trade between Member States', suggest that this may be such a case, the purpose of
this article in the treaty being, so far as necessary, to stop such practices continuing. No
j doubt there are arguments the other way; I am certainly not contending for reverse
unarguability, but I regret that this House should take a position on this point, which
was only skeletally argued in an interlocutory proceeding. It seems to me, with respect,
and I am supported by Lord Denning MR, to deserve consideration in greater depth, and,
if I may invoke *American Cyanamid Co v Ethicon Ltd* [1975] 1 All ER 504 at 510, [1975]
AC 396 at 407 the court should not in an interlocutory proceeding 'decide difficult
questions of law which call for detailed argument and mature consideration'.

If this is right, and the company's right to damages is an uncertain one, that would be, in itself, a strong ground for not leaving the company to recover hypothetical damages *a*
at the trial but for granting an injunction. But I will now consider the position on the assumption that such a right to damages does exist. Should the company be left to this claim? There are here two relevant considerations. In the first place, there can be no doubt that the primary remedy against a prohibited act is an injunction against continuance of it. To allow a defendant to persist in conduct which is prohibited at the price of paying damages is something the court does not countenance. It was precisely *b*
this principle which induced this House in *F Hoffmann-La Roche & Co AG v Secretary of State for Trade and Industry* [1974] 2 All ER 1128, [1975] AC 295, overruling the trial judge's discretionary order, to grant an interim injunction restraining the illegal conduct until trial; the objection would remain, said Lord Reid, if the injunction were refused even on terms, that the law would be disregarded until the case was decided (see [1974] 2 All ER 1128 at 1134–1135, [1975] AC 295 at 342). No doubt, even in such a case, the *c*
balance of convenience (including the desirability of maintaining the status quo) has to be considered (cf *Texaco Ltd v Mulberry Filling Station Ltd* [1972] 1 All ER 513, [1972] 1 WLR 814), but it must be for the defendant to make a strong case why the prohibited conduct should not cease. Secondly, from the point of view of the company, there is in my opinion good reason for not holding that it would be adequately compensated by damages. It is clear from the evidence, and was made clearer by the new evidence before *d*
the Court of Appeal, that the company would not, if the board were allowed to restrict its sales to the four distributors, be able to carry on its business. To depreciate this argument by representing the company's business as acting merely as intermediary through a telephone located at Mr and Mrs Bunch's home, seems to me, with all respect, no part of our task at the present time. Any dealing in commodities, or bullion, or currency, can be so represented, but it remains the case that successfully to operate such *e*
a business requires skill, experience, a nice judgment of market movements, a sound reputation in the market and a willingness to take risks. The evidence shows that the company is such a business. To say to the company that, even if it voluntarily suspends business pending a final decision, it will be able to resume it if it wins together with damages for the period of cessation must ring hollow. The evidence makes, to my mind, a clear case of what is called 'irreparable' damage. Of the many cases in which this has *f*
been held, I will cite only the well-known judgment of Kay LJ in *J Lyons & Sons v Wilkins* [1896] 1 Ch 811 at 827, where he said:

> '... in all these cases of interlocutory injunctions where a man's trade is affected one sees the enormous importance that there may be in interfering at once before the action can be brought on for trial; because during the interval, which may be long or short ... a man's trade might be absolutely destroyed or ruined by a course *g*
> of proceedings which ... may be determined to be utterly illegal; and yet nothing can compensate the man for the utter loss of his business by what has been done in that interval.'

The only substantial argument in favour of refusing an injunction appears to me to be that the judge refused it and that his discretion should not have been interfered with. *h*
This argument has two aspects, formal and substantive. The formal argument is that the Court of Appeal did not in terms refer to the discretionary character of the decision below, nor did it cite a passage from the judgment of this House in *Hadmor Productions Ltd v Hamilton* [1982] 1 All ER 1042 at 1046, [1983] AC 191 at 220. It might, indeed, have been wiser to have done both of these things, but it can and should be said in the court's favour that the *Hadmor Production Ltd* case laid down no new law: it restated, by *j*
way of reminder, in clear and vigorous terms principles long applied to appeals from discretionary decisions, and it is not lightly to be supposed that an experienced Court of Appeal, including Lord Denning MR who heard the *Hadmor Production Ltd* case in that court, was not fully aware of the limits within which such decisions may be reversed. I should certainly suppose, with some confidence, that these limits would have been urged

on it by the very experienced and able counsel who then represented the board and we were assured that this was done. But it is the substance that matters. Did the Court of Appeal properly evaluate the grounds on which the judge's decision was based, and was it justified in finding that these grounds were wrong in law or misapprehended in fact? The critical passage in the judge's judgment was the following, stated after a finding that there was a 'triable issue':

> 'I reject the application for interlocutory relief on two principal grounds which may overlap each other, which come within the balance of convenience. The position is as follows. If no relief is granted the [company] is still able to purchase butter albeit less profitably from four appointed distributors and others. It would therefore appear that a remedy of damages would be available in due course. If relief though is granted the [board] will have to disrupt their business and the business of their distributors. It appears to me therefore that this is a sufficient ground for rejecting this application.'

There follows a passage about the form of the injunction with which I will deal later. We must recognise that this is a report based on notes, and construe it in bonam partem. This passage was criticised by the respondents in five respects: 1. it assumes, without argument, that a remedy in damages lies under art 86; 2. it does not examine at all the questions of adequacy of damages in the circumstances; 3. it does not give recognition to the fact that, in aid of a legislative prohibition, an injunction is the primary remedy; 4. it misapprehends the evidence as to the economic consequences of having to purchase butter from, in effect, the company's own competitors; 5. it does not give recognition to the fact that any dislocation of the board's business would arise from its having chosen to embark on prohibited conduct.

Of these points, the Court of Appeal dealt clearly and explicitly with points 1, 3 and 5. On point 2 its judgments are exiguous, at best a short reference by May LJ, but that of the judge is no more expansive. Point 4 was explicitly dealt with by Lord Denning MR. So I cannot see validity in the argument that the Court of Appeal embarked on a trial de novo and did not examine, as it was entitled to examine, the bases for the judge's discretionary decisions. Was its examination correct, or at least more correct than that of the judge? I will test this by stating the alternatives.

On the judge's view, the board is to be allowed to continue a course of action as to which a case is made that it is prohibited by art 86. This will have, at least, a seriously disruptive effect on the company's business: pending trial it will simply be unable to carry it on. It is faced with the prospect of long and expensive proceedings which may reach this House and/or the Court of Justice of the European Communities against a defendant with unlimited financial resources. At the end of the day, even assuming that the company is held entitled to damages, the quantum must be wholly uncertain and it may not be possible for it to resume business at all. On the decision of the Court of Appeal the status quo is preserved until the trial, ie the board must observe a policy of 'open door' and 'no discrimination'. The plaintiff company's business is preserved; on the hypothesis that it remains profitable, it will be in a position to pay damages to the board if it fails in the action. This course of action is in line with what the European Court thought appropriate in *Camera Care Ltd v EC Commission* Case 792/79R [1980] ECR 119. I cannot avoid the conclusion that the Court of Appeal's order makes for better justice and I see nothing wrong with it in law.

I have left to the end the question of the form of injunction, a problem which has not been satisfactorily solved. It is necessary to distinguish two quite separate arguments. The first is that it is impossible to devise a satisfactory injunction, at least at the interlocutory stage. The second relates to the actual text of an injunction assuming that one is to be granted.

The first argument I emphatically reject. It is a counsel of despair and if accepted would lead to the conclusion that interlocutory injunctions cannot be obtained in cases such as these. There is no greater difficulty (indeed normally there is less) in drafting an

injunction suitable for interim relief than one suitable for perpetual relief and I refuse to
believe that the Commercial Court is less capable than the Chancery Division of framing *a*
a suitable order. In the latter a judge would find no difficulty in so doing. The question
of the actual text is a difficult one and I have felt some perplexity how to deal with it. At
the trial, two alternatives were suggested, both different from what was claimed by the
writ. Parker J felt unable, understandably, to accept either. In the Court of Appeal, Lord
Denning MR and May LJ were in favour of an injunction obliging the board to supply
bulk butter to the company on terms not significantly less favourable, either as to *b*
quantity or as to price, than those normally applied to other persons. Ultimately a draft
in a form suggested by Shaw LJ was commended to the parties. This extended protection
beyond the company to other persons. After some consideration and correspondence, the
board did not raise any question as to this except to suggest (unjustifiably) a provision as
to credit terms which, on reference back to the Court of Appeal, was rejected by that
court. Before this House counsel for the company did not seek to uphold this form of *c*
injunction, though in fact it seems to have worked quite well over the 1982 season, but
instead suggested yet another form which did not attract your Lordships. However, he
must be taken to have maintained the company's claim for some injunctive relief. In
these circumstances, without the benefit of your Lordships' views, I can only express my
own, that the best course would have been to refer the case back to the Commercial
Court to frame an injunction which would prevent the board, until judgment or further *d*
order, from excluding the company from purchases of bulk butter and from treating the
company less favourably as to quantity, price and conditions of sale than other customers.

I would dismiss the appeal.

LORD KEITH OF KINKEL. My Lords, for the reasons given in the speech of my
noble and learned friend Lord Diplock, which I have had the benefit of reading in draft *e*
and with which I agree, I too would allow the appeal.

LORD BRIDGE OF HARWICH. My Lords, I have had the advantage of reading in advance the speech of my noble and learned friend Lord Diplock. I entirely agree with it and for the reasons he gives I too would allow the appeal.

f

LORD BRANDON OF OAKBROOK. My Lords, I have had the advantage of reading in draft the speech proposed by my noble and learned friend Lord Diplock. I agree with it, and for the reasons which he gives would allow the appeal.

Appeal dismissed. Injunction discharged.

Solicitors: *Ellis & Fairbairn*, Thames Ditton (for the board); *Joynson-Hicks & Co* (for the company).

Mary Rose Plummer Barrister.

Stoke-on-Trent City Council v B & Q (Retail) Ltd and other appeals

COURT OF APPEAL, CIVIL DIVISION
LAWTON, ACKNER AND OLIVER LJJ
24, 28, 29, 30 MARCH, 26 APRIL 1983

Shop – Sunday closing – Enforcement by local authority – Promotion or protection of interests of inhabitants of its area – Trader in local authority's area deliberately and flagrantly flouting Sunday closing laws – Fines not acting as deterrent – Local authority applying for injunction to restrain trader from acting in contravention of law – Whether local authority proper plaintiff – Whether proceedings required to be brought by Attorney General – Whether local authority acting to protect interests of inhabitants – Shops Act 1950, ss 47, 71(1) – Local Government Act 1972, s 222(1)(a).

Practice – Parties – Local authority – Promotion or protection of interests of inhabitants of their area – Prevention of deliberate contravention of Sunday trading laws – Local authority seeking injunction to restrain trader from acting in contravention of law – Whether authority bound to sue on relation of Attorney General – Whether local authority entitled to obtain injunction in own name – Shops Act 1950, ss 47, 71(1) – Local Government Act 1972, s 222(1)(a).

The defendant companies (B & Q and Home Charm), which both had chains of retail shops selling 'do-it-yourself' goods, carried on Sunday trading at their shops in breach of s 47[a] of the Shops Act 1950. B & Q had two shops in the area of one local authority (Stoke-on-Trent) and three in the area of another local authority (Wolverhampton), while Home Charm had one shop in the area of another local authority (Barking). The three local authorities (the plaintiffs), in accordance with their duty under s 71(1)[b] of the 1950 Act to enforce the provisions of that Act in their areas, prosecuted the defendants, who were convicted of offences under s 47 and fined. However, the defendants continued to trade unlawfully on Sundays at their shops in the plaintiffs' areas and ignored warnings not to do so. There was no element of public nuisance and no evidence of complaint from any member of the public. In separate actions in which the plaintiffs purported to act pursuant to the power conferred on them by s 222(1)(*a*)[c] of the Local Government Act 1972 to institute civil proceedings in their own name where it was 'expedient for the promotion or protection of the interests of the inhabitants of their area', the plaintiffs issued writs seeking injunctions to restrain the defendants from anticipated unlawful Sunday trading. The plaintiffs also sought interlocutory injunctions in the same terms. The defendants contended that a local authority's power to claim injunctive relief under s 222 of the 1972 Act to restrain anticipated offences was limited to circumstances where the acts complained of were likely to cause a public nuisance, and where that was not the case an action seeking to restrain a breach of the criminal law could only be brought by the Attorney General and then only in exceptional circumstances. In the Stoke-on-Trent and Barking cases the plaintiffs were granted the injunctions sought but in the Wolverhampton case the judge dismissed the local authority's application. The defendants in the Stoke-on-Trent and Barking cases and the plaintiff local authority in the Wolverhampton case appealed. In the Barking case the further issues arose (i) whether the local authority had exercised its discretion at all by considering the requirements of s 222 of the 1972 Act and (ii) if it had, whether the proceedings for injunctive relief were properly authorised.

---

a Section 47 is set out at p 789 *g*, post
b Section 71(1) is set out at p 795 *a*, post
c Section 222, so far as material, is set out at p 795 *g*, post

Held – (1) The power which a local authority had under s 222 of the 1972 Act to institute proceedings in its own name for injunctive relief to restrain anticipated criminal a offences, and in particular breaches of s 47 of the 1950 Act, was not restricted to proceedings where the anticipated offences were likely to cause a public nuisance. Instead, a local authority could apply for, and be granted, injunctive relief in those exceptional cases where prior to 1972 the Attorney General could properly have invoked the relief, which included those cases where an injunction was necessary to restrain an offender who had deliberately and flagrantly flouted the law when the statutory remedies were b inadequate to deter him (see p 796 *h* to p 797 *a* and *d* to *f*, p 800 *g h*, p 802 *j* and p 804 *c* to *h*, post); *Gouriet v Union of Post Office Workers* [1977] 3 All ER 70 applied.

(2) Although a local authority could only institute proceedings under s 222 of the 1972 Act if it was expedient to do so for the promotion or protection of the interests of the inhabitants of its area, the effective prevention of unlawful trading which resulted in unfair competition among local traders fell within the scope of protecting the inhabitants c of the area. In considering whether to institute proceedings under s 222 to prevent unlawful trading the local authority was required to consider the interests of the inhabitants generally, not merely a particular section of the community, and furthermore, having regard to its duty under s 71(1) of the 1950 Act to ensure compliance with that Act, the local authority was not entitled to refuse to take effective action merely because the Act was unpopular in its area. Furthermore, if the authority considered that criminal d proceedings would be ineffective to stop the anticipated offences, it was not required to exhaust its statutory remedies before instituting proceedings under s 222 of the 1972 Act. Where a local authority purported to act for the promotion or protection of the interests of the inhabitants of its area it would be presumed to have done so lawfully pursuant to s 222 and it was for those who asserted unlawfulness on the part of the authority to prove it, but even if the proceedings were improperly initiated because the e local authority was shown not to have considered the criteria in s 222 the proceedings could subsequently be ratified and validated by the local authority (see p 795 *f*, p 797 *a b h*, p 800 *b*, p 801 *a* to *g*, p 802 *a* to *c*, and p 805 *c d* and *j* to p 806 *a* and *e* to *g*, post); *Warwick RDC v Miller-Mead* [1962] 1 All ER 212 and *R v Braintree DC, ex p Willingham* (1982) 81 LGR 70 applied; dicta of Bridge LJ in *Stafford BC v Elkenford Ltd* [1977] 2 All ER at 528 approved. f

(3) Although in the Stoke-on-Trent case the proceedings had been instituted without the council considering the limitation imposed on its power by s 222, the subsequent ratification of the proceedings by the policy committee of the local authority and the fact that the council was justified in concluding that the defendants intended deliberately and flagrantly to flout the law meant that the case was a proper one for the grant of an injunction, and therefore the appeal would be dismissed. In the Wolverhampton case, g since the local authority had purported to act from the outset under s 222 and since the defendants had called no evidence to the contrary, the local authority would be presumed to have exercised its discretion before authorising the proceedings. Furthermore, there was evidence before the local authority that the interests of the inhabitants generally would be prejudiced by unfair competition between the local traders and that the local authority had reasonable grounds for concluding that the defendants would continue h deliberately and flagrantly to flout s 47 of the 1950 Act. It followed therefore that Wolverhampton's appeal would be allowed. In the Barking case, there was no evidence that the council exercised its discretion at all or that any authority was given for instituting civil proceedings and therefore the defendant's appeal would be allowed (see p 797 *j* to p 798 *f*, p 800 *e f*, p 803 *c* to *g* and p 806 *g* to p 807 *b*, post).

Per curiam. Section 71 of the 1950 Act does not authorise local authorities to institute j and carry on civil proceedings for injunctive relief to restrain anticipated breaches of s 47 of that Act (see p 795 *b c*, p 803 *g* and p 807 *b*, post).

Notes

For the power of local authorities to prosecute or defend, see 28 Halsbury's Laws (4th edn) para 1339, and for cases on the subject, see 16 Digest (Reissue) 274–276, *2611–2626*.

For the Shops Act 1950, ss 47, 71, see 13 Halsbury's Statutes (3rd edn) 357, 371.
a For the Local Government Act 1972, s 222, see 42 ibid 1053.

Cases referred to in judgments

Associated Provincial Picture Houses Ltd v Wednesbury Corp [1947] 2 All ER 680, [1948] 1 KB 223, CA.
A-G v Chaudry [1971] 3 All ER 938, [1971] 1 WLR 1614, CA.
b *A-G (ex rel Hornchurch UDC) v Bastow* [1957] 1 All ER 497, [1957] 1 QB 514, [1957] 2 WLR 340.
A-G (ex rel Manchester Corp) v Harris [1960] 3 All ER 207, [1961] 1 QB 74, [1960] 3 WLR 532, CA.
Gouriet v Union of Post Office Workers [1977] 3 All ER 70, [1978] AC 435, [1977] 3 WLR 300, HL.
c *Hampshire CC v Shonleigh Nominees Ltd* [1970] 2 All ER 144, [1970] 1 WLR 865; *subsequent proceedings* sub nom *Shonleigh Nominees Ltd v A-G (ex rel Hampshire CC)* [1971] 3 All ER 473, [1971] 1 WLR 1723; *affd* [1972] 2 All ER 263, [1972] 1 WLR 577, CA; *affd* [1974] 1 All ER 734, [1974] 1 WLR 305, HL.
Kitchener v Evening Standard Co Ltd [1936] 1 All ER 48, [1936] 1 KB 576.
Prestatyn UDC v Prestatyn Raceway Ltd [1969] 3 All ER 1573, [1970] 1 WLR 33.
d *R v Braintree DC, ex p Willingham* (1982) 81 LGR 70, DC.
Solihull Metropolitan BC v Maxfern Ltd [1977] 2 All ER 177, [1977] 1 WLR 127.
Stafford BC v Elkenford Ltd [1977] 2 All ER 519, [1977] 1 WLR 324, Ch D and CA.
Stoke-on-Trent City Council v Saxon Scaffolding Ltd (26 October 1979, unreported), Ch D.
Tottenham UDC v Williamson & Sons Ltd [1896] 2 QB 353, CA.
Warwick RDC v Miller-Mead [1962] 1 All ER 212, [1962] Ch 441, [1962] 2 WLR 284,
e CA; *affg* [1961] 3 All ER 542, [1961] Ch 590, [1961] 3 WLR 737.

Cases also cited

Caldwell v Pagham Harbour Reclamation Co (1876) 2 Ch D 221.
Hammersmith London Borough v Magnum Automated Forecourts Ltd [1978] 1 All ER 401, [1978] 1 WLR 50, CA.
f *Kent CC v Batchelor* [1978] 3 All ER 980, [1979] 1 WLR 213.
Wyre Forest DC v Taylor (22 October 1981, unreported), Ch D.

Conjoined interlocutory appeals

Stoke-on-Trent City Council v B & Q (Retail) Ltd

By a writ issued on 5 May 1982 the plaintiffs, Stoke-on-Trent City Council, brought an g action against the defendants, B & Q (Retail) Ltd, claiming an injunction restraining the defendants until trial of the action or further order, by themselves or their directors or officers, or their servants or agents or otherwise howsoever, from using or permitting to be used premises at Waterloo Road, Burslem, Stoke-on-Trent, Staffordshire (and presently known as B & Q DIY Superstore) and Leek Road, Hanley, Stoke-on-Trent, Staffordshire (presently known as Dodge City Home Improvements and Garden store) as a retail do-it-h yourself and garden centre on Sundays other than for the purposes of carrying out transactions exempted from the operation of the Shops Act 1950 by s 47 of, and Sch 5 to, that Act. By notice of motion dated 6 May 1982 they applied for an interlocutory injunction in the same terms. On 25 June 1982 Whitford J granted their application. The defendants appealed. The facts are set out in the judgment of Lawton LJ.

j

Wolverhampton Borough Council v B & Q (Retail) Ltd

By a writ issued on 13 December 1982 the plaintiffs, Wolverhampton Borough Council, brought an action against the defendants, B & Q (Retail) Ltd, claiming an injunction restraining the defendants, whether by themselves, their directors, agents or servants or otherwise howsoever, from using or causing or permitting to be used their premises at Howard Street, Wolverhampton, and (under the name of Dodge City) at Loxdale Street,

Bilston, Wolverhampton, and at Bushbury Lane, Wolverhampton, as retail do-it-yourself trade or business or as garden centres on Sunday except for the purposes of carrying out transactions exempted from the operation of the Shops Act 1950 by s 47 of and Sch 5 to that Act. By notice of motion dated 13 December 1982 they applied for an interlocutory injunction in the same terms. On 18 January 1983 Nourse J dismissed their application. The plaintiffs appealed. The facts are set out in the judgment of Lawton LJ.

Barking and Dagenham London Borough Council v Home Charm Retail Ltd

By a writ issued on 15 December 1982 the plaintiffs, Barking and Dagenham London Borough Council, brought an action against the defendants, Home Charm Retail Ltd, claiming an injunction restraining the defendants, by themselves, their officers, agents or servants or otherwise howsoever, from opening a shop or causing or permitting others to open a shop for the service of customers on a Sunday at 9–10 Merrielands Crescent, Dagenham or elsewhere in the borough in breach of the Shops Act 1950. By notice of motion served on the same day the plaintiffs claimed an interlocutory injunction in the same terms. On 11 January 1983 Falconer J granted their application. The defendants appealed. The facts are set out in the judgment of Lawton LJ.

John Samuels QC and *Nicholas Davidson* for B & Q in the Stoke-on-Trent case.
Robert Reid QC and *Nicholas Patten* for Stoke-on-Trent and Wolverhampton.
John Samuels QC and *L J West-Knights* for B & Q in the Wolverhampton case.
Konrad Schiemann QC and *Keith Knight* for Home Charm.
Julian Sandys QC for Barking.
Simon D Brown for the Attorney General as amicus curiae.

Cur adv vult

26 April. The following judgments were delivered.

LAWTON LJ. These three appeals raise a common issue. Can local authorities obtain injunctions to restrain shopkeepers from anticipated unlawful Sunday trading contrary to s 47 of the Shops Act 1950? In the Wolverhampton appeal this is the sole issue. In the other two appeals queries arise on the evidence whether the proceedings were ever properly authorised and instituted.

The common issue touches on a matter of general interest and some public controversy. It is common knowledge that the provisions of the Shops Act 1950 about Sunday trading are widely disregarded and that many people want the statutory prohibition against the Sunday opening of shops for many kinds of retail trading repealed. But not all want this. Some local authorities do what they can within their resources to curb unlawful Sunday trading. Others do little, if anything. We were told by counsel for Home Charm, who has an extensive knowledge of local government law and administration, that for a few years now some local authorities have sought and obtained injunctive relief against anticipated unlawful Sunday trading; but not all applications have been successful. In the cases before us, the Stoke-on-Trent and Barking councils got such relief; Wolverhampton did not.

The two companies involved in these appeals are typical defendants. They both have chains of retails shops which sell building materials and tools which are used mostly by individuals for home repairs and improvements, colloquially known as do-it-yourself goods. The sale of these kinds of goods on Sundays is clearly convenient to customers who want to use them during their weekends away from their normal work.

There was some evidence in the Stoke-on-Trent case, which may be typical of what is happening in many areas, that it was the policy of that local authority to proceed by injunction against the bigger retailers and by warnings against the smaller. This alleged policy was criticised as oppressive at first instance but it is, in my opinion, justifiable if it is effective, as it may be, either by warning off the smaller retailers or by making examples of the bigger ones so as to deter the others.

At the outset of this judgment I wish to make clear what I regard as irrelevant considerations: first, that s 47 of the Shops Act 1950 is widely disregarded; second, that many people want it repealed; third, that many people find it convenient to shop for non-exempt goods on Sundays; and, fourth, that with the resources of manpower and money which are available to local authorities many of them could not hope to stop unlawful Sunday trading save on a selective and spasmodic basis which would probably be regarded as unfair and oppressive. My judicial duty is to apply the law as laid down by Parliament, not to change it. Change is the function of Parliament, not of judges. But cases may reveal to Parliament weaknesses and anomalies in the law which call for change. Whether these appeals will have such an effect is for Parliament to decide.

The Wolverhampton appeal

This appeal brings out clearly the main issue in all three appeals. It is uncomplicated by side issues. The defendants, B & Q (Retail) Ltd, have three retail shops in Wolverhampton. In the late spring and summer of 1982 they advertised locally that their shops would be open on Sundays; and they were. On 3 November 1982 they were convicted by the Wolverhampton magistrates of 24 offences under s 47 of the 1950 Act and fined £50 in respect of each, and ordered to pay £120 costs. The offences had been committed on dates between May and July 1982.

On 13 October 1982 the environmental health and control committee of the council met. It was the appropriate one to consider breaches of s 47 of the 1950 Act. It had before it a report from its chief executive and town clerk which stated what B & Q had been doing in Wolverhampton and that they had been convicted in a number of other towns of unlawful Sunday trading. The report also dealt with the unlawful trading of other retailers. It contained the following paragraph:

> 'Since fines are no deterrent, the only effective form of action which can be taken against companies trading in defiance of the Shops Act 1950 is that taken by Stoke City Council, viz: the obtaining of an Injunction. A local authority has power under Section 222 of the Local Government Act 1972 to take such proceedings where they consider it expedient for the promotion or protection of the interests of the inhabitants of their area. This would entail more serious sanctions being applied against the company and its directors and management should they continue to open, and I understand that since the obtaining of the Injunction at Stoke-on-Trent the store of B & Q (Retail) Limited has remained closed.'

The chief executive advised that before starting proceedings B & Q should be sent a warning letter. This advice was accepted. On 19 October a letter was sent to them under the heading 'Shops Act 1950—Sunday Trading':

> 'In response to complaints received by the Council, inspections by officers of the Environmental Health Department have revealed that premises operated by you in Wolverhampton are open on Sundays and are then selling goods outside those contained in the Fifth Schedule to the above Act. This of course, is in clear breach of the law and a report was accordingly submitted to the Environmental Health and Control Committee of the Council last week. The Committee resolved that if the operations in breach of the law did not cease application would be made to the Court for an injunction to compel you to observe the law. I therefore inform you that should your premises in Wolverhampton be open in breach of the Shops Act 1950 next Sunday, 24 October, and subsequently, application will be made to the Court for an injunction without further notice.'

B & Q took no notice. They opened their shops on 24 October and again committed offences against s 47 of the 1950 Act.

On 9 November 1982 the policy and resources committee resolved that the decisions on Sunday trading taken by the environmental health and control committee should be supported. The chief legal officer was authorised to start proceedings for an injunction. He did so. A writ was issued on 13 December 1982 and on the same day the

Wolverhampton council served a notice of motion asking for an injunction to restrain B & Q until trial from using or causing or permitting the use of their premises otherwise a than for lawful Sunday trading. The affidavit in support, sworn by an assistant solicitor in the council's employment, ended as follows:

> '6. I believe that the Defendants have been warned verbally as well as by letter that they are breaking the provisions of the Shops Act 1950 and that the Defendants continue to trade in breach of section 47 of the Shops Act 1950.
>
> 7. The Plaintiffs are under a duty to enforce the provisions of the Shops Act 1950 b and I verily believe that contravention of the legislation will take place if an injunction is not granted.'

In my judgment the council had good grounds for thinking that B & Q would go on committing offences under s 47 unless restrained by injunction. I infer that they would not have been deterred by having had even the maximum fine of £200 imposed on them for each offence. They would have regarded this as the price they had to pay for c Sunday opening and that that price was worth paying having regard to the profits which were likely to be made.

Nourse J heard the motion on 17 December 1982 and on 18 January 1983 he dismissed it. The council have appealed. The judge gave two reasons for his decision. The council had failed to show first, that the proceedings for an injunction were 'expedient for the protection of the interests of the inhabitants of their area' as required by s 222 of the d Local Government Act 1972 and second, that a desire on the part of the council to stop the commission of criminal offences under s 47 of the 1950 Act within their area did not justify their using their powers under s 222. The council have submitted that the judge misdirected himself on both points.

The Stoke-on-Trent case e

In April 1982 it became clear to the city council's officers that a number of retail shops selling do-it-yourself goods in their area intended to trade on Sundays. Observation was kept on them on Sunday, 11 April 1982. A number were found to be unlawfully trading, including two shops belonging to the defendants, B & Q (Retail) Ltd. A written report was put before the council's environmental health sub-committee at its meeting on 15 April 1982. It ended with two recommendations: f

> '1. That in view of the proliferation of contraventions of the Shops Act 1950 legal proceedings be instituted and injunctions be taken out against all the offending companies.
>
> 2. That the Council make a representation to the Association of District Councils in an endeavour to secure an increase in the level of fines which might more adequately serve as a deterrent to potential offenders.' g

The report inaccurately stated that B & Q had been convicted in 1981 of an offence under s 1 of the Shops Act 1950. The sub-committee passed the following resolution:

> 'That, in view of the proliferation of contraventions of the Shops Act, 1950, the Town Clerk be authorised to institute legal proceedings and, where considered appropriate, take out injunctions against the Companies concerned.' h

By letter dated 19 April 1982 the council warned B & Q that legal proceedings might be instituted. They opened their shops again on Sunday, 25 April 1982. By letter dated 27 April 1982 the council warned them that unless they gave an undertaking within 24 hours that they would not open their shops on Sunday, 2 May 1982 an application would be made for an injunction. No undertaking was given. The council issued a writ on 5 j May 1982 asking for an injunction to restrain B & Q from unlawful Sunday trading in their Stoke-on-Trent shops. They served a notice of motion next day, which came before the court on 12 May and was adjourned. B & Q agreed not to open their shops pending a full hearing. They informed the council's lawyers that they intended to question their power to start proceedings for an injunction. On 17 May the council's policy committee met and passed the following resolution:

> 'That this Committee, acting on behalf of the Local Authority and exercising
> a executive powers granted by the City Council, and having read and considered the Report of the Director of Environmental Services submitted to the Environmental Health Sub-Committee on 15th April, 1982 and considering that it is expedient for the promotion or protection of the interests of the inhabitants of the City of Stoke-on-Trent that the provisions of Section 47 of the Shops Act, 1950 should be enforced and in particular that the further breach of those provisions by the Retailers named
> b in the Report of the Director of Environmental Services should be prevented, the Council hereby resolves that pursuant to Section 222 of the Local Government Act, 1972, the proceedings for an injunction in the High Court against B & Q (Retail) Ltd., under title No. 1982 S2111 Chancery Division Group A should be prosecuted and continued and hereby ratifies the same.'

In an affidavit sworn on 26 May 1982 in answer to the motion one of B & Q's regional
c managers made it clear that in addition to opposition on legal grounds B & Q would contend that the proceedings had been commenced without any proper authority given by or any behalf of the council.

The motion was heard by Whitford J on 25 June, 1982. He granted the injunction asked for by the council. He adjudged that the proceedings had been properly authorised and that the council had acted properly pursuant to s 222 of the 1972 Act because 'it
d must be in the general interest of the inhabitants of any area that if there is an open, plain breach of any law all appropriate action may and should be used to ensure compliance'. B & Q have submitted that he was wrong on both points.

The Barking case

The defendants, Home Charm Retail Ltd, own a shop within the area of the London
e borough of Barking and Dagenham. On 11 March 1982 the manager of this shop was warned by one of the council's officers not to open for unlawful Sunday trading. He took no notice. The shop was opened on three successive Sundays thereafter, 14, 21 and 28 March 1982. Informations were laid against Home Charm. On 13 July 1982 they were convicted of offences against s 47 of the 1950 Act and fined £50 for each offence and ordered to pay £25 costs.

f On 15 September 1982 the council's general purposes committee considered a number of cases of alleged unlawful Sunday trading, including 14 involving Home Charm. They had opened their shop on all Sundays during the spring and summer. Minute 757(i) reads as follows:

> 'TRADING STANDARDS
>
> g (i) *Authorisation of proceedings*—We have authorised the institution of legal proceedings subject to the Town Clerk being satisfied with the evidence in the following cases:—[there then followed particulars of offences committed by a number of traders including these appellants].
>
> The Chief Trading Standards Officer reported that the Chairman and Vice-Chairman had, in accordance with Standing Order No. 34, and as a matter of
> h urgency, authorised the institution of legal proceedings subject to the Town Clerk being satisfied with the evidence in the following cases:—[there then followed further references to offences against the Shops Act 1950 committed by traders including these appellants].
>
> The Chief Trading Standards Officer reported that, in addition, the Chairman and Vice-Chairman had agreed to the seeking of injunctions in the High Court
> j restraining the Directors of companies referred to above ... from further contraventions of the Shops Act 1950.'

On 15 December 1982 the council issued a writ to restrain Home Charm from unlawful Sunday trading. They served a notice of motion which was heard by Falconer J on 11 January 1983. Home Charm took the same legal objection as in the other two cases and in addition submitted that the proceedings for an injunction had never been authorised.

This point turned not on the delegated powers of the council's general purposes committee or of its chairman and vice-chairman but on the lack of any reference in the minutes to the exercise of powers under s 222 of the 1972 Act and indications in the evidence that the council thought that they were empowered to start proceedings for injunctive relief by s 71(1) of the 1950 Act. The judge granted the council an injunction. He adjudged that s 71(1) gave them an enabling power to claim injunctive relief in their own name and that on the evidence the council had brought themselves within s 222. Home Charm have appealed against these specific findings as well as on the issue common to all three cases.

The law relating to Sunday trading

According to the legal research undertaken by counsel for Wolverhampton, English law started to prohibit Sunday trading in the reign of King Athelstan. For about two centuries after the Norman Conquest Sunday trading was legal but, according to *Pease and Chitty on the Law of Markets and Fairs* (2nd edn, 1958) p 41, in the thirteenth century the view began to prevail that Sunday marketing was wrong. The Sunday Fairs Act 1448, which was not repealed until 1969, made Sunday trading unlawful. There was, however, an exemption in favour of 'necessary victual' which was the origin of the list of goods which may be sold on Sundays set out in Sch 5 to the Shops Act 1950. The Sunday Observance Act 1677, which remained on the statute book until 1969, by s 1 provided:

> '... noe person or persons whatsoever shall pubklickly cry shew forth or expose to sale any wares merchandizes, fruit, herbs, goods or chattells whatsoever upon the Lord's day or any part thereof...'

Section 3 provided exemptions for the—

> 'selling of meat in inns cookshops or victualling houses for such as otherwise cannot be provided nor to the crying or selling of milke before nine of the clocke in the morning or after foure of the clocke in the afternoone.'

This Act was widely disregarded in parts of London, mostly in the street markets of the East End. Parliament made special provisions in both the Shops (Sunday Trading Restriction) Act 1936 and the Shops Act 1950 (s 54) to legalise such trading. At the end of the nineteenth century Parliament started to pass Acts regulating the conditions under which shop assistants worked. These Acts provided for closing hours and conditions of employment. The 1950 Act was intended to consolidate the Shop Acts 1912 to 1938 and other enactments relating to shops. It is pertinent to remember that when Parliament passed the 1950 Act both the Sunday Fairs Act 1448 and the Sunday Observance Act 1677 were still in force. As recently as 1936 in *Kitchener v Evening Standard Co Ltd* [1936] 1 All ER 48, [1936] 1 KB 576 Atkinson J had given judgment in favour of a common informer suing for penalties pursuant to the Sunday Observance Act 1780. As the 1950 Act allowed the sale of some goods on Sundays (see ss 48 to 56 and Schs 5 to 7), provision had to be made to ensure that such sales were not unlawful under the old Acts. This was done by s 59(2). In 1950 Parliament presumably had regard for what was thought to be the public's attitude towards trading activities on Sundays. Section 47 left no doubt that shops should be closed on Sundays save for serving customers with the goods specified in Sch 5. Local authorities were given limited dispensing powers to deal with special situations: see ss 48, 49, 51, 52, 53 and 54. Section 59 made any contravention of the provisions of the Act relating to Sunday trading a criminal offence punishable in the case of a first offence to a fine of £5 and in the case of a second or subsequent offence to £20. These penalties were later increased to £50 and £200; but were not revised again when Parliament increased the maxima for fines for many offences by the Criminal Law Act 1977 and the Criminal Justice Act 1982.

The duty of enforcement

Parliament thought it prudent to make a special provision for the enforcement of the 1950 Act. Section 71(1) provided:

> 'It shall be the duty of every local authority to enforce within their district the provisions of this Act and of the orders made under these provisions, and for that purpose to institute and carry on such proceedings in respect of contraventions of the said provisions and such orders as aforesaid as may be necessary to secure observance thereof.'

By sub-s (2) it was the duty of local authorities 'For the purpose of their duties under the foregoing subsection' to appoint inspectors and to authorise them to institute and carry on any proceedings under the Act on their behalf. In the Barking case it was submitted by the council and accepted by Falconer J that the word 'proceedings' which is to be found in sub-ss (1), (2) and (4) includes civil proceedings. Before us it was accepted by all counsel, including counsel for Barking, that this word had to be construed in its context as being limited to criminal proceedings and that s 71 did not authorise local authorities to institute and carry on civil proceedings for injunctive relief against anticipated commissions of offences against s 47. What s 71 does make clear, however, is that Parliament intended the prohibition against unlawful Sunday trading to be observed and charged local authorities with the duty of ensuring it was. It seems likely, too, that in 1950 Parliament thought that taking traders before magistrates' courts and fining them would be an adequate deterrent. The facts of these cases and the social and economic changes which have occurred since 1950 show that convictions and the present scale of fines are no deterrent.

Local authorities have to grapple with administrative problems when seeking to perform their duties under s 71. Getting evidence of contraventions of s 47 necessitates their inspectors or other employees keeping observation on shops suspected of unlawful Sunday opening. If contraventions are widespread, as in many parts of England and Wales they are, this means an extensive use of expensive manpower; and if that use is ineffective in securing observance of the 1950 Act time and ratepayers' money are wasted. Further, failure to secure observance of the Act tends to generate complaints of unlawful and unfair competition by traders who do comply with it. If local authorities disregard these complaints, disgruntled traders may try to make them enforce the Act by means of a judicial review. This is what happened in *R v Braintree DC, ex p Willingham* (1982) 81 LGR 70. The Divisional Court adjudged that the council did not have a general discretion to decide whether or not to enforce the 1950 Act, nor to decide whether it would be expensive or desirable to institute proceedings. In my judgment that case was rightly decided. What then is a local authority to do? Clearly some action has to be taken to stop widespread deliberate flouting of the law. The three local authorities involved in these appeals, and others not before the court, have tried to rely on the powers given them by s 222(1) of the 1972 Act, which provides:

> 'Where a local authority consider it expedient for the promotion or protection of the interests of the inhabitants of their area—(*a*) they may prosecute or defend or appear in any legal proceedings and, in the case of civil proceedings, may institute them in their own name . . .'

Enforcement by injunction

Both companies involved in these appeals have submitted that these statutory powers do not enable the plaintiff local authorities to do what they did. If any action needs to be taken, they submitted by their counsel, it should be by the Attorney General and then only in exceptional circumstances. He has, they said, a wide discretion as to when and how the criminal law should and can be enforced. He alone can weigh the considerations whether attempted enforcement would be likely to make the administration of justice unpopular with a large section of the public, thereby undermining respect for the law. They submitted that these were the principles enunciated by the House of Lords in *Gouriet v Union of Post Office Workers* [1977] 3 All ER 70 at 83–84, 90–91, 95, 97–98, 110, [1978] AC 435, 481–482, 489, 491, 495, 498–499, 513 per Lord Wilberforce, Viscount Dilhorne, Lord Diplock and Lord Edmund-Davies. Counsel pointed out that before the passing of the 1972 Act local authorities had no power anyway to institute in their own names proceedings for injunctive relief to restrain anticipated breaches of the criminal *a* law in their areas. They had to persuade the Attorney General either to act ex officio or to allow them to proceed ex relatione: for examples, see *A-G (ex rel Hornchurch UDC) v Bastow* [1957] 1 All ER 497, [1957] 1 QB 514 and *A-G (ex rel Manchester Corp) v Harris* [1960] 3 All ER 207, [1961] 1 QB 74. Section 222 of the 1972 Act did give them a power to sue for such relief in their own names but it was a limited power circumscribed by the words 'expedient for the promotion or protection of the interests of the inhabitants of *b* their area'. In consequence of these limiting words local authorities were not given in their areas the wide discretion which the Attorney General had. Counsel for B & Q submitted further that as a consequence of these limiting words a local authority could only use their powers under s 222 to restrain anticipated offences if the commission of them was likely to cause a public nuisance. This, he said, was how the Sunday market trading cases, such as *Stafford BC v Elkenford Ltd* [1977] 2 All ER 519, [1977] 1 WLR 324, *c* could be justified. Sunday markets do tend to cause public nuisances by attracting large crowds with consequential traffic problems. In the *Stafford* case neither Oliver J at first instance nor the Court of Appeal were asked to consider the limitations on local authorities' powers under s 222. Further, Lord Denning MR's comment ([1977] 2 All ER 519 at 527, [1977] 1 WLR 324 at 329):

d

> 'When there is a plain breach of the act I do not think that the authorities concerned need wait at all for finality anywhere. They can take proceedings in the High Court before any other proceedings are even started'

must be qualified by what was said in *Gouriet*'s case. Before local authorities could institute proceedings for injunctive relief they had to consider the interests of the inhabitants of their areas, which meant the inhabitants generally, not of some of them *e* such as traders who did close their shops on Sundays and complained of unfair or unlawful competition. He invited our attention by way of contrast to s 137(1) of the 1972 Act which limited a local authority's powers to use for the benefit of 'all or some of its inhabitants'.

The answer of counsel for Stoke-on-Trent and Wolverhampton was that the words of *f* s 222 did not limit the exercise of power to the restraining of anticipated public nuisances. Both the House of Lords in *Gouriet*'s case and Bridge LJ in the *Stafford* case had envisaged that the institution of proceedings for injunctive relief to restrain anticipated offences could be used in exceptional cases: see *Gouriet*'s case [1977] 3 All ER 70 at 83, 92, 115, [1978] AC 435 at 481, 491, 519 per Lord Wilberforce, Viscount Dilhorne and Lord Fraser. Exceptional cases included those in which an injunction was necessary to restrain an anticipated criminal act 'where the penalties imposed for the offence have proved *g* wholly inadequate to deter its commission': see *Gouriet*'s case [1977] 3 All ER 70 at 92, [1978] AC 435 at 491. Counsel for Stoke-on-Trent and Wolverhampton pointed out that Bridge LJ, in the *Stafford* case [1977] 2 All ER 519 at 528, [1977] 1 WLR 324 at 330, seemingly in anticipation of what the House of Lords was to decide in *Gouriet*'s case and of the problems which have to be dealt with in these appeals, stated the appropriate *h* approach in these words:

> 'We have been urged to say that the court will only exercise its discretion to restrain by injunction the commission of offences in breach of statutory prohibitions if the plaintiff authority has first shown that it has exhausted the possibility of restraining those breaches by the exercise of the statutory remedies. Ordinarily no doubt that is a very salutary approach to the question but it is not in my judgment *j* an inflexible rule. The reason why it is ordinarily proper to ask whether the authority seeking the injunction has first exhausted the statutory remedies is because in the ordinary case it is only because those remedies have been invoked and have proved inadequate that one can draw the inference, which is the essential foundation for the exercise of the court's discretion to grant an injunction, that the offender is, in the language of Oliver J, "deliberately and flagrantly flouting the law".'

I agree with what Bridge LJ said in this passage; but he did not have to consider, because the point was never taken in the *Stafford* case, what we have to decide in these appeals, namely whether the instituting of proceedings for injunctive relief to restrain anticipated offences against s 47 of the 1950 Act is expedient for the promotion or protection of the interests of the inhabitants of a local authority's area. I accept the proposition of counsel for B & Q that before instituting such proceedings a local authority must consider the interests of the inhabitants generally, not of a particular section of them. I also accept that it is for the Attorney General to take such steps as he deems necessary in his absolute discretion to ensure that the criminal law is enforced in all parts of England and Wales. But Parliament in 1972 entrusted local authorities with limited powers to institute legal proceedings of *all* kinds. These powers are ancillary, as counsel as amicus pointed out, to the discharge of their statutory duty of administering their areas. They must concern themselves with the environment and the enforcement of a number of statutes creating criminal offences of a regulatory kind. They must safeguard their resources and avoid the waste of their ratepayers' money. It is in everyone's interest, and particularly so in urban areas, that a local authority should do what they can within their powers to establish and maintain an ambience of a law-abiding community; and what should be done for this purpose is for the local authority to decide. Members of the public should be confident that the local authority will do all they can to ensure that they will not be sold unwholesome food or given false measure, that goods will not be sold with false trade descriptions, that property will not be used in breach of the planning legislation and that shops will be open on days and at hours regulated by the 1950 Act. In my judgment a local authority is entitled to use their powers for all these purposes. Their power under s 222 of the 1972 Act to institute proceedings for injunctive relief is not limited to restraining public nuisances. Further, as I have already commented, the employment of shop inspectors and other employees Sunday after Sunday to keep observation on shops which advertise that they will open on Sundays is a waste of manpower and money; and the cost of prosecuting offenders is not always covered by any orders for costs made by magistrates. It follows, in my judgment, that all local authorities who give thought to these factors and satisfy themselves on reasonable grounds and on adequate evidence that an injunction is the only way of stopping anticipated offences amounting deliberately and flagrantly to flouting the law may use their powers under s 222 of the 1972 Act to apply for injunctive relief. The Wolverhampton and Barking councils had reasonable grounds for concluding that B & Q and Home Charm would continue deliberately and flagrantly to flout s 47. The evidence in the Stoke-on-Trent case is less clear. I will examine it separately when dealing with that case.

The exercise of discretion

In all three cases the question arises whether before instituting proceedings for injunctive relief the councils did give thought to the limitation of their powers under s 222 of the 1972 Act. In the Wolverhampton case Nourse J adjudged that it was for the council to show that what they did was within s 222. In so deciding, as all counsel accepted in this court, he overlooked the application to the exercise of local authorities' powers of the rebuttable presumption of omnia praesumuntur rite esse acta. It was for B & Q and Home Charm to show, if they could, that the three councils had not given thought to any limitation on the exercise of their powers. In the Wolverhampton case B & Q called no evidence, so the presumption that the council's appropriate committee did exercise their discretion before authorising proceedings applies. There was in fact evidence that their attention was invited to s 222. This was provided by the written report made to them by the council's chief executive to which I have already referred.

The evidence in the Stoke-on-Trent case leads me to infer that that council's environmental health sub-committee did not give thought to the limitations imposed on their council's powers by s 222 but that the policy committee at its meeting on 17 May 1982 did. Their resolution of that date provided that the proceedings against B & Q 'should be prosecuted and continued' and they purported to ratify them. They had,

however, been instituted in the council's own name without thought being given to the statutory limitations on the council's powers. In my judgment the words 'prosecute' and a
'appear' in s 222(1)(*a*) of the 1972 Act are apt to describe what the policy committee did, namely to authorise and ratify what had been started without the proper exercise of discretion. Since 17 May 1982 the council have 'prosecuted' the proceedings, having decided that their continuance was expedient for the statutory purposes. The resolution of 17 May 1982 was an effective ratification.

There remains the question whether on the evidence the conduct of B & Q was such b
as to require restraint by injunction. When the sub-committee resolved to authorise the town clerk to institute legal proceedings B & Q had only committed one offence against s 47 of the 1950 Act in the Stoke-on-Trent area and had not yet been prosecuted for it. But before the writ was issued on 5 May 1982 the council had more evidence of what their intentions were for the future. After having been warned by letter dated 19 April 1982 that proceedings had been authorised in respect of the unlawful openings on 11 c
April 1982, B & Q unlawfully opened their shops on 25 April 1982 and made no reply to the council's request that they should give an undertaking not to do so on 2 May 1982; and they did open on that date. In my judgment the council were justified in concluding the B & Q intended deliberately and flagrantly to flout the law.

The evidence in the Barking case raises two issues. Did that council exercise their discretion at all? If they did, were the proceedings for injunctive relief properly d
authorised? Minute 757 of the meeting of the general purposes committee makes no reference to the matters which had to be considered if proceedings were to be instituted under s 222. I infer that they were not considered. Even had they been there is no evidence that any authority was given for the instituting of legal proceedings for injunctive relief against Home Charm. The references to 'legal proceedings' against Home Charm in their context clearly refer to criminal proceedings to be taken under e
s 71(1) of the 1950 Act. The authorisation of civil proceedings was limited to the directors of the companies referred to, not to the companies themselves. No such proceedings were ever instituted.

I would allow the appeals of the Wolverhampton Borough Council and Home Charm Retail Ltd and dismiss the appeal of B & Q (Retail) Ltd.

f

ACKNER LJ. The common question of law which these appeals raise is the extent to which it is open to a local authority to seek in ther own name injunctive relief in relation to those who infringe the Shops Act 1950 in relation to Sunday trading.

The Shops Act 1950

Section 47 of the Act provides: g

> 'Every shop shall, save as otherwise provided by this Part of this Act, be closed for the serving of customers on Sunday: Provided that a shop may be open for the serving of customers on Sunday for the purposes of any transaction mentioned in the Fifth Schedule to this Act.'

Schedule 5 specifies a variety of transactions for the purposes of which a shop may be h
open in England and Wales for the serving of customers on Sunday. They do not cover the activities of the shops concerned in these appeals, all of which were open for the sale of equipment for use in what is conveniently referred to as 'do-it-yourself' activities particularly related to house decoration and maintenance.

No one suggests that the Act is obsolete. On the contrary, it has been recently under much attack and an attempt to achieve its repeal, by the Shops (Amendment) Bill, failed j
in the House of Commons this year, on 4 February 1983. It is common ground that the penalties provided by s 59 are in themselves quite inadequate to restrain the large organisations, particularly those who operate a chain of shops which find it highly profitable to trade on Sundays. Recent growth, in particular, in leisure activities has made Sunday the next most popular day after Saturday for shopping for many commodities,

including in particular do-it-yourself articles. The penalties provided by s 59 were
a originally £5 in the case of a first offence and £20 in the case of a second or subsequent offence. In 1972 the penalties were increased to £50 and £200 respectively.

In s 71 of that Act, Parliament has imposed a clear obligation on the local authority with regard to the enforcement of the Act. The section provides:

> '(1) It shall be the duty of every local authority to enforce within their district the provisions of this Act and of the orders made under those provisions, and for that
> b purpose to institute and carry on such proceedings in respect of the contraventions of the said provisions and such orders as aforesaid as may be necessary to secure the observance thereof ...'

This section unequivocably obliges the local authority to use the best means they can, having regard to their resources, 'to secure observance' of, inter alia, s 47 of the 1950 Act.
c Prior to 1972, if a trader refused to heed the local authority's warnings in regard to breaches of s 47 of the 1950 Act, then the only direct action which the local authority could take would be to institute criminal proceedings in the hope that the fines that would be imposed for the first or subsequent offences would be enough to dissuade the offender. Where, however, the trader, despite the imposition of fines, persisted in defying the Act, then all that was left to the local authority was to apply to the Attorney General
d for his permission to bring relator proceedings in order to obtain an injunction. They had no power, if they thought summary proceedings afforded an inadequate remedy, to bring proceedings in their own name in the civil courts for injunctive relief (see *Tottenham UDC v Williamson & Sons Ltd* [1896] 2 QB 353). This was so despite the provisions of s 276 of the Local Government Act 1933 which provided:

> 'Where a local authority deem it expedient for the promotion or protection of the
> e interests of the inhabitants of their area, they may prosecute or defend any legal proceedings.'

(See *Prestatyn UDC v Prestatyn Raceway Ltd* [1969] 3 All ER 1573, [1970] 1 WLR 33 and *Hampshire CC v Shonleigh Nominees Ltd* [1970] 2 All ER 144, [1970] 1 WLR 865.)

f *Section 222 of the Local Government Act 1972*

This section replaced s 276 of the Local Government Act 1933. It provides, so far as is material to these appeals:

> '(1) Where a local authority considers it expedient for the promotion or protection of the interests of the inhabitants of their area—(*a*) they may prosecute or defend or appear in any legal proceedings and, in the case of civil proceedings, may institute
> g them in their own name ...'

Thus, there was added to the local authority's armoury in relation to securing the observance of the provisions of s 47 of the Shops Act 1950, the right to bring proceedings in the civil court for injunctive relief.

h *The scope of s 222 of the Local Government Act 1972*

It is common ground that the local authority is not entitled to use the civil courts generally to control criminal conduct; for instance, they would not be entitled to use s 222 to apply for injunctive relief to prevent obscenity occurring in a theatre in their area or the sale of pornography from a local newsagent's shop. The House of Lords in *Gouriet v Union of Post Office Workers* [1977] 3 All ER 70 esp at 83, [1978] AC 435 esp at
j 481 per Lord Wilberforce made it clear that relator actions, which are the exclusive right of the Attorney General to represent the public interest, and in which the assistance of the civil courts is invoked in aid of the criminal law, is a jurisdiction which, although useful on occasions, is one of great delicacy and to be used with caution. In that case, the right of a local authority to invoke the assistance of the civil courts was not in point, but Viscount Dilhorne referred to the section as giving local authorities a 'limited power' to

sue on behalf of the public (see [1977] 3 All ER 70 at 94, [1978] AC 435 at 494). Lord Edmund-Davies observed that whenever public rights are in issue, the general rule is that relief may be sought only by, and granted solely at the request of, the Attorney General subject to the statutory exception created by s 222 'which enables a local authority to institute civil proceedings for the promotion or protection of the interests of the inhabitants of their area' (see [1977] 3 All ER 70 at 110, [1978] AC 435 at 513).

The proper limitation on the entitlement of the local authority to apply in their own name for injunctive relief is to be found in the opening words of the section: 'Where a local authority consider it expedient for the promotion or protection of the interests of the inhabitants of their area ...' A local authority must consider it expedient and there must be material to support that opinion that the civil proceedings may promote or protect the interests of the inhabitants of their area. With respect, I cannot accept the general observation made by Goulding J in *Stoke-on-Trent City Council v Saxon Scaffolding Ltd* (26 October 1979, unreported), when he said:

> '... I conceive that, for the purposes of the section, the inhabitants of any area have a general interest to see that the provisions of Acts of Parliament in force in the area are duly observed.'

However, in relation to Sunday trading, there are some matters that are self-evident. The essential motivation for a trader to keep his shop open on a Sunday is because it is profitable to do so. The trader who refuses to abide by the law with regard to Sunday trading and remains undissuaded from trading on that day by repeated prosecutions is, through his criminal conduct, obtaining a wholly unfair advantage in relation to his competitors. He is not only obtaining the profit which is normally associated with his own activities, but he is obtaining an increased profit, likely to be substantial, by reason of his competitors abiding by the law and keeping their shops closed. He is thus, by his criminal conduct, obtaining part of the profit which would normally have gone to them. It is clearly in the interests of the inhabitants of the area involved that there should be fair competition amongst the local traders. If unfair trading is permitted to exist not only will the commercial interests of the trading community be prejudiced, but so ultimately will those of the inhabitants generally in the area.

Moreover, there is a further point which to my mind is equally self-evident. No one doubts that, once an injunction has been obtained, unlawful Sunday trading will cease. The penalties for contempt of court are likely to dissuade any commercial activity in breach of the law from continuing. In an appropriate case, an injunction is a relatively speedy and inexpensive remedy to obtain. Assuming that the maximum fines that can be obtained will have no deterrent effect on the trader intent on trading on Sunday, ratepayers' money will be wasted by the preparation for, and the institution of, criminal proceedings. It is clearly in the interests of ratepayers generally that public money is not wasted on useless litigation.

I accordingly, with respect, reject as quite unrealistic the submission of counsel for B & Q that breaches of s 47 of the Shops Act 1950 do not in themselves, unless coupled with behaviour which causes a public nuisance, prejudice the interests of the inhabitants of a particular area. I find support for the view which I have expressed in the observations of Sellers LJ in *A-G (ex rel Manchester Corp) v Harris* [1960] 3 All ER 207 at 211, [1961] 1 QB 74 at 86, when he said:

> 'It cannot, in my opinion, be anything other than a public detriment for the law to be defied week by week and the offender to find it profitable to pay the fine and continue to flout the law. The matter becomes no more favourable when it is shown that, by so defying the law, the offender is reaping an advantage over his competitors who are complying with it.'

The discretion of the local authority

(1) I have already referred to the duty imposed on local authorities by s 71(1) of the Shops Act 1950 to enforce the Act, including the Sunday trading provisions. The means of carrying out their duty is essentially a matter for the local authority, bearing in mind

their resources, the nature of the breach and any other relevant factors. No local authority could be criticised for first issuing a warning, when it is established that a breach of the Act has occurred or is being threatened. If that warning is disregarded, then much must depend on the particular circumstances of the case. If satisfied that a successful prosecution may well have the effect of dissuading any repetition of the offence, then, of course, summary proceedings in the local magistrates' court would seem the next appropriate step. However, if the terms in which the warning was rejected, the policy adopted by the offender in regard to Sunday trading in other districts and the likelihood of a conviction and fine for the maximum having no deterrent effect are such, the local authority may well properly decide that criminal proceedings are a waste of time and money. Further, the status in the commercial world of the offender may be such that the speed with which the local authority obtain an effective remedy may make their task of enforcing in their area the provisions of this controversial Act a great deal easier. Each case must be considered on its own merits, but there is no rigid rule which requires a local authority to institute criminal proceedings which are bound, or highly likely, to be ineffectual before moving for injunctive relief (see *Stafford BC v Elkenford Ltd* [1977] 2 All ER 519 esp at 528, [1977] 1 WLR 324 esp at 330 per Bridge LJ).

(2) Having regard to the clear terms of s 71(1) imposing the duty to take such proceedings as may be necessary to secure observance of the Shops Act 1950, the local authority is not entitled to refuse to take effective action because the Shops Act 1950 may be unpopular within their area. They are not entitled to say, 'We have carried out our obligations under s 71(1) by instituting criminal proceedings on a number of occasions, although we fully recognise that such proceedings are quite useless to achieve the observance of the Act.' If such were the attitude of a local authority then they would have laid themselves open to an order of mandamus requiring them to exercise their powers under s 222 and institute civil proceedings (see *R v Braintree DC, ex p Willingham* (1982) 81 LGR 70, a decision of the Divisional Court with which I respectfully agree). I view this as an important constitutional point. If an Act has become so unpopular that it should no longer be enforced, then it is for Parliament to achieve its repeal. So long as it remains on the statute book, containing as it does a positive obligation on the local authority to enforce its provisions, it has to be treated as the still effective manifestation of the will of Parliament. Its demise is not to be achieved by attrition. If it is no longer justifiable to make it a criminal offence for shops generally to open on a Sunday, and accordingly s 47 should be repealed, this will not be achieved by the non-enforcement of its provisions. Quite the contrary. The strength of the public support for a change in the law will only be debilitated if the section is disregarded.

The institution of proceedings

As previously stated, the local authority have under s 222 of the 1972 Act a discretion whether to prosecute or institute civil proceedings in their own name. It is axiomatic that in order validly to exercise this discretion the local authority must apply their minds to whether or not they consider it expedient for the promotion or protection of the interests on the inhabitants of their area to exercise these statutory powers. The exercise of such a discretion must be a real exercise of the discretion. If, in the statute conferring the discretion, there is to be found expressly or by implication matters which the authority exercising the discretion ought to have regard to, then in exercising the discretion they must have regard to those matters (see *Associated Provincial Picture Houses Ltd v Wednesbury Corp* [1947] 2 All ER 680 at 682, [1948] 1 KB 223 at 228 per Lord Greene MR). It is, of course, for those who assert that the local authority have not had regard to the matters which they ought to have considered to establish that proposition (see the *Wednesbury* case). This may often be difficult. However, where a local authority can be shown to have relied on some other but invalid statutory justification for bringing the proceedings and can thus be shown never to have purported to have exercised the discretion given to them by s 222, the local authority would be shown to have contravened the law.

Where the local authority purport to act for the promotion or protection of the interests of the inhabitants of their area, then they will be presumed to have done so lawfully pursuant to s 222: the maxim omnia praesumuntur rite esse acta applies. Again applying the *Wednesbury* decision, it is for those who assert the unlawfulness to prove this by showing that the local authority made their decision on the basis of facts they should not have taken into account, or failed to take into account matters that they ought to have taken into account, or that no reasonable local authority could have reached the decision they reached.

Ratification

The question which next arises is: given that the proceedings under s 222 of the 1972 Act are improperly initiated because the local authority are shown not to have considered the criteria of the section, can those proceedings be subsequently ratified and validated? On the authority of *Warwick RDC v Miller-Mead* [1962] 1 All ER 212, [1962] Ch 441 the answer is in the affirmative. In that case, the statutory power relied on by the local authority was s 100 of the Public Health Act 1936 which placed the local authority in the privileged position of being entitled to sue in respect of a statutory nuisance without the necessity of proving special damage. The section is in the following terms:

> 'If in the case of any statutory nuisance the local authority are of opinion that summary proceedings would afford an inadequate remedy, they may in their own name take proceedings in the High Court for the purpose of securing the abatement or prohibition of that nuisance, and such proceedings shall be maintainable notwithstanding that the authority have suffered no damage from the nuisance.'

The solicitors for the local authority issued a writ against the owner of a caravan site and served notice of motion to restrain him from keeping or maintaining the site in such a state as to be a statutory nuisance contrary to s 92 of the 1936 Act. However, it was only three days later that the local authority in council meeting resolved, 'being of opinion that summary proceedings would afford an inadequate remedy' to take proceedings in the High Court to secure the abatement of the alleged statutory notice. When subsequently Widgery J heard the council's motion for an injunction (see [1961] 3 All ER 542, [1961] Ch 590), the defendant raised the objection that the proceedings were a nullity since, at the date of the issue of the writ, the local authority had not recorded 'its opinion' by resolution, as required by s 100 of the 1936 Act and therefore had no capacity to sue and could not by subsequent resolution ratify the act of its servant in issuing the writ. This objection failed and in this court it was held (Lord Evershed MR and Danckwerts LJ, Willmer LJ dissenting) that by the time the defendant challenged the validity of the council's cause of action promulgated in the indorsement of the writ, the council had by then satisfied the terms of s 100 of the Act. Moreover, I think that counsel for Stoke-on-Trent and Wolverhampton is correct in his submission that an analogy can properly be drawn with the power which has been accepted to exist to convert an ordinary action into a relator action (see *Hampshire CC v Shonleigh Nominees Ltd* [1970] 2 All ER 144 at 154, [1970] 1 WLR 865 at 876, where the action would have been struck out unless the Attorney General was prepared to give his fiat, which fiat was subsequently granted: see *Shonleigh Nominees Ltd v A-G (ex rel Hampshire CC)* [1971] 3 All ER 473, [1971] 1 WLR 1723, CA; [1974] 1 All ER 734, [1974] 1 WLR 305, HL).

The discretion of the court to grant or refuse the injunction sought by the local authority

It is important to have firmly in mind that although the local authority may have acted entirely lawfully in seeking in the exercise of their statutory powers under s 222 of the 1972 Act, injunctive relief against a trader, the court's discretion still exists whether or not to grant the injunction sought. Generally speaking a court will not grant an injunction unless the defendant is deliberately and flagrantly flouting the law. Generally speaking the local authority would have to show that their complaints were unheeded and that subsequent prosecutions, resulting in convictions and fines, had failed to deter the defendant. However, as Bridge LJ recognised in *Stafford BC v Elkenford Ltd*, exceptional cases may exist where the scale of the operation which the defendant is carrying on, or plans to carry on, the extent of the profits likely to be enjoyed, are such that it can be legitimately inferred that the defendant will continue in his operations or plans unless the court orders him to desist. But the court must at all times be alert to ensure that its civil jurisdiction does not oust its criminal jurisdiction as the appropriate means of controlling criminal conduct.

The three appeals

I will now seek to apply the principles which I have endeavoured to set out, to the three appeals before us. In so doing I gratefully accept the facts so succinctly set out by Lawton LJ in his judgment and I shall not therefore repeat them.

The Wolverhampton appeal (1) The local authority purported to act from the outset under s 222 of the 1972 Act. (2) There was ample material to justify the local authority's concluding that the defendant company would continue deliberately and flagrantly to flout s 47. (3) I cannot agree with Nourse J that the material before the council did not point to any particular prejudice to the interests of the inhabitants of their area as distinct from the public in general. For the reasons given, it is in my judgment self-evident that effectively to prevent unlawful trading which results in unfair competition protects the interests of the inhabitants in the area where the law is being disregarded. I too, therefore, would allow the appeal of the local authority.

The Stoke-on-Trent appeal (1) I agree that although the council's environmental health sub-committee did not give thought to the limitations imposed on their council's powers by s 222 of the 1972 Act, the policy committee did do so at its meeting on 7 May 1972 and thereby ratified what had been started without the proper exercise of discretion. (2) That there was material which justified the local authority in concluding that the defendants intended deliberately and flagrantly to flout the law. (3) I accordingly agree with the conclusion of Whitford J that this was a proper case for the grant of an injunction and I too would dismiss this appeal.

The Barking and Dagenham appeal (1) I agree that the proper inference is that the general purposes committee never gave any thought to s 222 of the 1972 Act and therefore never embarked on the consideration of the requirements of the section which are necessary to the valid exercise of the discretion which the section confers. If they gave any thought to the basis of their authority to institute proceedings, they wrongly concluded that it was to be found in s 71 of the Shops Act 1950. (2) I further agree that there is no evidence that any authority was given for the institution of legal proceedings for injunctive relief. (3) I too would therefore allow the appeal of Home Charm Retail Ltd.

OLIVER LJ. Each of the three appeals with which we are concerned has individual features which require consideration, but there are two questions which are common to all three and which are fundamental to the arguments which have been addressed to the court. Although they are, in my judgment, quite distinct questions, they tended to become confused in the course of the argument and it is, I think, important that they be considered separately. The first, which really lies at the threshold of any useful discussion of the subject matter of these appeals, is that of the extent to which it is ever proper to invoke the civil remedy of injunction as an aid to the enforcement of the criminal law in cases where the breach gives rise to no civil right of action in any individual. The second, which assumes the propriety of the invocation of a civil remedy, relates to the circumstances in which proceedings to obtain that remedy can properly be put in motion at the suit, not of the Attorney General, but of a local authority acting under the statutory power conferred on them by s 222 of the Local Government Act 1972.

As has been pointed out by both counsel for B & Q and Home Charm, the decision of

this court in *Stafford BC v Elkenford Ltd* [1977] 2 All ER 519, [1977] 1 WLR 324 and my
own decision at first instance in *Solihull Metropolitan BC v Maxfern Ltd* [1977] 2 All ER a
519, [1977] 1 WLR 127 both preceded the decision of the House of Lords in *Gouriet v
Union of Post Office Workers* [1977] 3 All ER 70, [1978] AC 435, which now represents an
authoritative statement of the circumstances in which it will be proper for the court to
grant the civil remedy of injunction to restrain threatened breaches of the criminal law
which do not also constitute any private wrong. The majority of their Lordships in that
case concurred in expressing the view that this form of proceeding is anomalous and to b
be resorted to only in exceptional circumstances, Lord Wilberforce ([1977] 3 All ER 70
at 83, [1978] AC 435 at 481) observing that in practice it is restricted to cases where an
offence is frequently repeated in disregard of a usually inadequate penalty, as in *A-G (ex
rel Manchester Corp) v Harris* [1960] 3 All ER 207, [1961] 1 QB 74 or cases of emergency
such as *A-G v Chaudry* [1971] 3 All ER 938, [1971] 1 WLR 1614.

Where such proceedings are appropriate, that is where the circumstances are of such c
an exceptional nature, the proper plaintiff, and the only proper plaintiff, is the Attorney
General unless the case can be brought within one of the statutory or common law
exceptions. One such exception is that provided by s 222 of the 1972 Act but, so the
argument runs, that provision does not enlarge the ambit within which such proceedings
may properly be brought: it merely enables a local authority, in a proper case and (and
this is important) subject to satisfying the provisions of the section, to institute d
proceedings in their own name instead of in the name of the Attorney General, as was
necessary prior to 1972.

Thus, it is argued, a local authority suing to enforce by injunction a criminal
prohibition involving no private wrong have to surmount two hurdles. They have first
to show that the case is one where, prior to 1972, it would have been proper for the
Attorney General to proceed in accordance with the principles laid down in *Gouriet*. e
Second, they have to satisfy also the internal requirements of the section.

Counsel for B & Q, indeed, goes further than this, if I understand his argument
correctly. He suggests, I think by analogy with s 100 of the Public Health Act 1936, that
the power of the local authority to institute proceedings is restricted to cases where some
element of public nuisance is involved and that where there is no such element and no
invasion of any private right, a relator action by the Attorney General is still the only f
appropriate proceeding. Speaking for myself, I am unable to accept this submission and
I can see nothing in the history of the legislation or in the structure of the section itself
which leads to the conclusion that the power conferred by it is so restricted.

Nevertheless, I accept entirely the general proposition that the section was not intended
to extend and ought not to be treated as extending the range of cases in which application
can properly be made to a civil court to aid in the enforcement of the criminal law by g
providing a remedy which Parliament itself has not seen fit to provide. It was, as counsel
as amicus curiae had submitted, clearly designed by Parliament to confer a substantial
autonomy on local authorities within their areas to institute proceedings in cases where
they would previously have needed to invoke the assistance of the Attorney General, but
the considerations by which the court should be guided in determining whether or not
to grant injunctive relief remain, in my view, the same. Thus the critical question, h
regardless of the identity of the plaintiffs, is whether the case is an appropriate one for
injunctive relief having regard to the limitations suggested by the *Gouriet* case.

It then has to be considered whether, on the assumption that the case is one in which
the Attorney General could properly have invoked the relief sought, the local authority
can properly assume the role of plaintiff, for s 222 does not give a general and unlimited
power. It is a discretionary power to institute civil proceedings in their own name 'where j
the local authority consider it expedient for the promotion of the interests of the
inhabitants of their area', and this raises two questions which have occupied the bulk of
the argument on these appeals, namely (1) in what circumstances can the enforcement
of the criminal law in general, and s 47 of the Shops Act 1950 in particular, by means
other than those envisaged by Parliament at the time of creating the offences, be

considered to be 'for the promotion of the interests of the inhabitants of their area' and (2) to what extent is it incumbent on the local authority in each case (i) actually to consider and (ii) to prove that they have considered the promotion of those interests.

On the first of these questions several arguments have been advanced. It is not, it is submitted, sufficient to say, as has been said in some cases, simply that it is for the benefit of the inhabitants that the law of the land should be enforced. Section 222 is directed to specifically local interests and it is not, it is suggested, appropriate to use the power conferred by that section for the purpose of general law enforcement, which is for the benefit of the population of the British Isles generally. Thus, the argument runs, one has to look for some more localised interest and where, it is asked forensically, is that to be found? No doubt the closing of all shops on Sunday promotes the interests of those shopkeepers who do not wish to open on Sunday. It promotes the interests of those who have environmental or religious objections to trading on Sundays. But these groups are only sections of the local inhabitants and the section is not referring to the promotion of the interests of 'persons who are inhabitants of their area' but of '*the* inhabitants of their area'. I agree with the submission of counsel for B & Q that this more appropriately refers to the inhabitants generally, so that what one has to look for is some general interest common to the inhabitants taken as a whole, although it may not be the interest of particular individual inhabitants or groups of inhabitants.

There may well, it is argued, be such a general interest where what is sought to be restrained is some generally organised breach of the law which involves public nuisance, traffic congestion, breaches of planning law and the inducement of others to undertake an illegal activity, features which were present in the *Elkenford* and *Solihull* cases. But here, it is submitted, there are no such features. The cases in which the three appeals before the court have arisen are cases of individual traders opening their ordinary shopping premises with no element of conspiracy or public disturbance and no evidence of complaint from any member of the public. True it is that in all three cases, the defendants had indicated beyond doubt their intention of flouting the law, but nevertheless, it is argued, the penalties prescribed by the Shops Act 1950 are those which Parliament has seen fit to provide and which, so it seems, have been deliberately left unaltered despite there having been subsequent opportunities to increase them. There being, therefore, here no element of public nuisance nor evidence of public complaint, the plaintiffs should, it is argued, be content with the exaction of such penalties as Parliament has prescribed, despite its being perfectly clear that those penalties have absolutely no deterrent effect and are totally ineffective to secure compliance with the statute. Now of course I appreciate the argument for restricting enforcement of the statute to the method which Parliament has prescribed and which, therefore, Parliament must presumably have considered to be adequate. But the fact is that, certainly in the Stoke and Wolverhampton cases, the statutory penalties have proved entirely inadequate. Parliament no doubt considered the penalties adequate and was confident that they would be effective. But at the same time, Parliament intended the 1950 Act to be enforced and there cannot, I think, be attributed to it the intention by restricting the statutory penalties to figures which are derisory when compared with the profitability of the prohibited activity, of turning a nation of shopkeepers into a nation of commercial recidivists. Thus the argument based on the non-alteration of the statutory penalties is one which I find less than compelling. There remains, however, the limitation in s 222 of the 1972 Act to the promotion of the interests of the inhabitants of the area and the difficulty of establishing the criteria for determining where those interests lie. I agree that this is a difficult question but it is one which cannot, in my judgment, be segregated from the essential feature which statutorily underlies the approach of the local authority to enforcement of the Shops Act 1950 by whatever means. I do not, for my part, see how the interests of the inhabitants of the area can be treated apart from the statutory duties of the local authority in relation to the area for which they are responsible, and in this context the provisions of s 71 of the 1950 Act are, in my judgment, crucial. That section has already been referred to in the judgments of Lawton and Ackner LJJ and, as has been pointed out, its effect has been the subject matter of a decision of the Divisional Court in *R v Braintree DC, ex p Willingham* (1982) 81 LGR 70 with which I respectfully agree. No a useful consideration of the interests of the inhabitants of the area can be divorced from the background that they are inhabitants of an area the local authority for which is under a specific duty to enforce and to maintain (at the ratepayers' expense) the machinery to enforce the provisions of the Act.

Parliament, for good or ill, has decreed that shops shall not be open on Sunday except for certain specified transactions and it has placed on local authorities a specific duty to b enforce that prohibition in their areas. Argument about whether some or all of the inhabitants think that the existence of that duty serves their interests is irrelevant. The duty exists and has to be carried out and it follows that the local authority best serves the interests of the inhabitants by doing that which it is statutorily obliged to do in the way which it considers most effective and most economical. To put it in a negative way it cannot be in the interests of the inhabitants that an offender should be regularly and c repeatedly brought before the court for the exaction of a statutory penalty which obviously has no deterrent effect whatever, for there ultimately comes a point where so barren a process not only brings the law into disrepute but exposes the prosecuting authority itself to public ridicule. Nevertheless it still has to carry out its duty and it has to continue to expand public funds on maintaining the machinery of enforcement and on repetitive but ineffective proceedings. If this situation arises, or in the exceptional case d if it is clear that such a situation is inevitably going to arise, then enforcement of the prohibition by proceedings for an injunction not only could properly be considered to promote the interests of the inhabitants but would also do so as a matter of fact, for the local inhabitants have to recognise that one of the facts of life with which they have to live is that their local authority is under this inescapable statutory duty.

Turning to the evidential problem, I entirely accept the submissions of counsel for e B & Q and Home Charm that the power under s 222 of the 1972 Act is exercisable only in the circumstances envisaged in the section and that this involves a consideration of whether the action proposed is one which is expedient for the promotion of the interests of the inhabitants. What is less clear to me is how far this involves the consideration of anything beyond the proposition that the action envisaged is the most effective way of carrying out the local authority's statutory duty under s 71. If that is the opinion of the f authority, and that it is is self-evident from the very resolution to institute the proceedings, then that, as it seems to me, subsumes the expediency for the promotion of the interests of the inhabitants, for the reasons given above, and it does not seem to be that it becomes necessary to look for some further and different interest of the inhabitants beyond that of having their local authority carry out their statutory duties as expeditiously, effectively and economically as it considers possible. In any event, I agree respectfully g with what has fallen from Lawton LJ as regards the application of the maxim omnia praesumuntur rite essa acta.

Turning to the facts of the individual cases, the questions which arise in each case are (a) were the proceedings properly authorised and (b) if they were, are they, in any event, proceedings of that exceptional nature envisaged in the *Gouriet* case which justifies the exercise of the court's discretion in granting injunctive relief to restrain the commission h of further offences? As regards the former, the facts have been fully set out in the judgment of Lawton LJ and I respectfully concur with his conclusions. As regards the latter, the Wolverhampton case is beyond argument a case in which, in the absence of an injunction, the defendants openly state that they intend to go on breaking the law, and their counsel has frankly accepted, indeed averred, this on their behalf. That seems to me to be a case plainly within the *Gouriet* principles. As regards Stoke-on-Trent, it is true that j when the proceedings commenced there had not been a course of conduct which could be said to amount to persistent breach of the law. Nevertheless, again, it is entirely clear that, unless the injunction granted by Whitford J is continued, the defendants propose to embark on the same course in Stoke-on-Trent as that on which they have already embarked in Wolverhampton. I can see no useful purpose which would be served by refusing an injunction now merely to enable offences to be committed in the future until they reach the point at which the conduct can be said to be persistent.

Accordingly, I agree that the appeal of the Wolverhampton Borough Council should be allowed and that of the defendants in the Stoke-on-Trent case dismissed. I also agree that the appeal in the Barking and Dagenham case should be allowed for the reason given by Lawton LJ. There simply was, in that case, no proper authority given by the plaintiff council for the institution of the proceedings and it is, I think entirely clear that s 71 of the 1950 Act itself does not confer on the local authority any power to institute proceedings of this nature in their own name.

Stoke-on-Trent case: appeal of B & Q (Retail) Ltd dismissed.
Wolverhampton case: appeal of Wolverhampton BC allowed; injunction granted.
Barking and Dagenham case: appeal of Home Charm Retail Ltd allowed; injunction discharged.
Application by B & Q (Retail) Ltd for leave to appeal to House of Lords refused.

Solicitors: *Hepherd Winstanley & Pugh*, Southampton (for B & Q); *Sharpe Pritchard & Co*, agents for *S W Titchener*, Stoke-on-Trent (for Stoke-on-Trent); *Sharpe Pritchard & Co*, agents for *Michael Duffell*, Wolverhampton (for Wolverhampton); *Laytons* (for Home Charm); *D C J Farr*, Barking (for Barking); *Treasury Solicitor.*

Mary Rose Plummer Barrister.

Richards v Richards

HOUSE OF LORDS
LORD HAILSHAM OF ST MARYLEBONE LC, LORD DIPLOCK, LORD SCARMAN, LORD BRIDGE OF HARWICH AND LORD BRANDON OF OAKBROOK
18, 19 APRIL, 30 JUNE 1983

Injunction – Exclusion of party from matrimonial home – Divorce proceedings pending – Wife having moved out of matrimonial home with children of marriage and living in unsuitable accommodation – Wife applying for order excluding husband from matrimonial home – Wife not having reasonable grounds for refusing to live in matrimonial home with husband but refusing to return while husband living there – Whether grounds for court to exclude husband from matrimonial home – Whether needs of children rather than justice between husband and wife proper test of whether husband should be excluded – Principles to be applied – Matrimonial Homes Act 1967, s 1 – Guardianship of Minors Act 1971, s 1.

The husband and wife were married in 1974 and had two young children. In January 1982 the wife filed a petition for divorce on the ground that the marriage had irretrievably broken down because of the husband's unreasonable behaviour. The allegations in the petition about the husband's behaviour were extremely flimsy and amounted to little more than that the wife had become disenchanted with the husband. The husband wished the marriage to continue and filed an answer denying the wife's allegations and asking for the petition to be dismissed. After filing the petition the wife remained in the matrimonial home for several months performing her duties as a wife and mother, but moved out of the matrimonial bedroom. In June 1982 she left the matrimonial home with the children and went to live temporarily with a woman friend. Each weekend and during the husband's holidays she brought the children back to the matrimonial home where the husband looked after them. The wife intended to set up a permanent establishment with another man but those plans came to nothing and her woman friend asked her to leave by November. The wife made strenuous efforts to find other accommodation for herself and the children but she could only find temporary accommodation in a council caravan which was unsuitable for the children. The wife therefore applied to a judge, in October 1982, for an order excluding the husband from **a** the matrimonial home so that she and the children could return to live there, on the grounds that there was no other suitable accommodation for the children and the wife would not live with the husband. The judge was faced with conflicting authorities in the Court of Appeal to the effect on the one hand that in 'ouster applications' the principle contained in s 1[a] of the Guardianship of Minors Act 1971 applied, namely that the welfare of the children was the first and paramount consideration, and on the other hand **b** that the welfare of the children was just one factor to be considered along with the other criteria specified in s 1(3)[b] of the Matrimonial Homes Act 1967. The judge found that there was nothing in the husband's behaviour to give the wife any reasonable ground for refusing to return to live with him in the matrimonial home; nevertheless, because the wife, who did not want a reconciliation with the husband, would not return to the matrimonial home while the husband was living there, and because it was in the 'public **c** interest' that the children should live in the matrimonial home with the mother, the judge made an order excluding the husband from the matrimonial home, even though he thought it unjust to the husband to do so. The husband appealed against the exclusion order. The Court of Appeal dismissed his appeal on the ground that the needs of the children were paramount and their needs required that they be returned to the matrimonial home with their mother to look after them. The husband appealed to the **d** House of Lords. Since the order made by the Court of Appeal the parties had come to an arrangement whereby the wife occupied the house from Monday to Friday and the husband from Friday to Monday. The children were permanently in the house and were looked after by the parent in occupation. The husband had no difficulty in looking after them, either under that arrangement or when the wife was on holiday, during which time he stayed in the house throughout the week. **e**

Held – The husband's appeal would be allowed for the following reasons—

(1) (Lord Scarman dissenting) The jurisdiction of the High Court and of the county court to make an ouster injunction in pending proceedings between spouses or by way of an originating application was governed exclusively by s 1 of the 1967 Act and accordingly when making such an order the court was obliged to follow the criteria **f** prescribed by s 1(3) of that Act which made it clear that, when exercising the jurisdiction, both the conduct of the spouses and the needs of the children were, with other considerations, matters to which the court was required to have regard and to weigh together so as to produce a just and reasonable result. Moreover, s 1 of the 1967 Act did not require any of the specified matters to be treated as paramount over any of the others, but the weight to be given to any particular matter depended on the facts of each case. **g** The principle enunciated in s 1 of the 1971 Act that the welfare of the children was to be the first and paramount consideration applied only to proceedings in which custody, upbringing or the proprietary jurisdiction implied by s 1(*b*) of the 1971 Act fell to be decided as a matter directly in issue and that principle had no application to ouster proceedings, where those matters arose only incidentally. Since the judge and the Court of Appeal had applied the wrong principle the ouster order would be set aside (see p 814 **h** *j* to p 815 *c* and *h* to p 816 *a* and *f* to p 817 *b* and *e f*, p 824 *b d*, p 829 *h* to p 830 *e* and *j*, p 831 *a* to *c* and p 832 *d e*, post).

(2) (Per Lord Hailsham LC, Lord Diplock and Lord Scarman) The evidence did not justify the making of an ouster order excluding the husband from the matrimonial home, since it was neither just nor reasonable to make the order nor, even if the principle that the needs of the children were paramount applied, was the order needed in the **j** interests of the children. It followed therefore that the judge had erred in the exercise of his discretion in making the order since it was inconsistent with his plainly stated findings of fact (see p 810 *e f*, p 812 *d e*, p 816 *c* to *e*, p 817 *e f* and p 823 *b* to *j*, post).

---

a Section 1 is set out at p 815 *f g*, post

b Section 1 is set out at p 813 *g* to p 814 *h*, post

Per Lord Hailsham LC and Lord Diplock. (1) Where there are two statutory provisions a in force, one of which is general while the other deals in precise detail with the special situation under consideration and was enacted at a time when the general provision already existed, it is not open to litigants to bypass the special Act nor to the courts to disregard its provisions by resorting to procedures under the general Act, thereby choosing to apply a different jurisprudence from that which the special Act prescribes (see p 813 *a* to *c* and p 817 *e f*, post).

b (2) The general jurisdiction to grant or withhold injunctions now contained in s 37[c] of the Supreme Court Act 1981 may be invoked in appropriate cases (eg molestation) for the protection of minors (see p 814 *j* and p 817 *e f*, post).

(3) Whether in a case arising under s 1 of the 1967 Act the 'needs' of children are treated as a relevant factor or their welfare as paramount, the court ought not to confine itself to a consideration of purely material requirements or immediate comforts (see c p 817 *b c e f*, post).

Per Lord Hailsham LC, Lord Diplock, Lord Bridge and Lord Brandon. Observations on the appropriate practice and procedure to be followed in relation to applications under s 1 of the 1967 Act (see p 810 *e f*, p 817 *e f*, p 824 *b* and p 831 *f* to p 832 *d*, post).

Decision of the Court of Appeal [1983] 1 All ER 1017 reversed.

Notes

d For the grant of an injunction excluding a spouse from the matrimonial home, see 13 Halsbury's Laws (4th edn) para 1228, and for cases on the subject, see 27(2) Digest (Reissue) 936, *7549–7559*.

For the Matrimonial Homes Act 1967, s 1, see 17 Halsbury's Statutes (3rd edn) 139.

For the Guardianship of Minors Act 1971, s 1, see 41 ibid 762.

For the Supreme Court Act, s 37, see 51 ibid 632.

e

Cases referred to in opinions

Adams v Adams (1965) 109 SJ 899.
Agar-Ellis, Re, Agar-Ellis v Lascelles (1883) 24 Ch D 317.
Bassett v Bassett [1975] 1 All ER 513, [1975] Fam 76, [1975] 2 WLR 270, CA.
Davis v Johnson [1978] 1 All ER 1132, [1979] AC 264, [1978] 2 WLR 553, HL.
f *Elsworth v Elsworth* (1979) 1 FLR 245, CA.
Gurasz v Gurasz [1969] 3 All ER 822, [1970] P 11, [1969] 3 WLR 482, CA.
J v C [1969] 1 All ER 788, [1970] AC 688, [1969] 2 WLR 540, HL.
McGrath (infants), Re [1893] 1 Ch 143, CA.
Montgomery v Montgomery [1964] 2 All ER 22, [1965] P 46, [1964] 2 WLR 1035.
Myers v Myers [1982] 1 All ER 776, [1982] 1 WLR 247, CA.
g *North London Rly Co v Great Northern Rly Co* (1883) 11 QBD 30, CA.
O'Hara (an infant), Re [1900] 2 IR 232.
Phillips v Phillips [1973] 2 All ER 423, [1973] 1 WLR 615, CA.
Samson v Samson [1982] 1 All ER 780, [1982] 1 WLR 252, CA.
Silverstone v Silverstone [1953] 1 All ER 556, [1953] P 174, [1953] 2 WLR 513.
Spindlow v Spindlow [1979] 1 All ER 169, [1979] Fam 52, [1978] 3 WLR 777, CA.
h *Stewart v Stewart* [1973] 1 All ER 31, [1973] Fam 21, [1972] 3 WLR 907.
Tarr v Tarr [1972] 2 All ER 295, [1973] AC 254, [1972] 2 WLR 1068, HL.
Thain, Re, Thain v Taylor [1926] Ch 676, [1926] All ER Rep 384, CA.
Walker v Walker [1978] 3 All ER 141, [1978] 1 WLR 533, CA.

Interlocutory appeal

j Gordon William Richards (the husband) appealed with leave of the Appeal Committee of the House of Lords granted on 10 February 1983 against the decision of the Court of Appeal (Cumming-Bruce and Dillon LJJ) ([1983] 1 All ER 1017, [1983] 2 WLR 633) on 6 December 1982 dismissing his appeal against an order made by his Honour Judge Pennant sitting as a judge of the High Court in chambers on 8 November 1982 on the

c Section 37, so far as material, is set out at p 812 *h j*, post

application of Christine Norma Richards (the wife) whereby the judge ordered the husband to vacate the matrimonial home at 13 Stoborough Green, Stoborough, Wareham, Dorset on or before 22 November 1982. The facts are set out in the opinion of Lord Hailsham LC.

Joseph Jackson QC and *Simon Levene* for the husband.
Patrick Back QC and *Timothy Coombes* for the wife.

Their Lordships took time for consideration.

30 June. The following opinions were delivered.

LORD HAILSHAM OF ST MARYLEBONE LC. My Lords, I believe that all your Lordships are agreed that this appeal must be allowed. But there is a difference of opinion as to the ground. My noble and learned friend Lord Scarman is content to decide the issue on the ground that the discretionary decision of the judge can be demonstrated to be plainly wrong, broadly because it was inconsistent with his plainly stated findings of fact which established that the wife's application for interlocutory relief never achieved even a prima facie case.

The view of my noble and learned friend Lord Brandon, concurred in, as I understand, by the remainder of your Lordships, is based on a proposition of law, namely that, in an application of the kind under consideration in the instant appeal, the court to which the application is made is bound to follow the principles enunciated in s 1 of the Matrimonial Homes Act 1967, as amended by s 38 of the Matrimonial Proceedings and Property Act 1970 and by ss 3 and 4 of the Domestic Violence and Matrimonial Proceedings Act 1976, and no other. From this point of principle I apprehend my noble friend Lord Scarman dissents.

My Lords, since I have the pleasure in agreeing with the conclusion of my noble and learned friend Lord Scarman that this appeal succeeds independently of the point of principle and with my noble friend Lord Brandon, in his analysis and conclusions on the point of principle itself, after some consideration I have decided to set out at length my reasons for these two concurrent grounds of decision.

There is at least no dispute about the facts of the case and the course of the proceedings up to and including the hearing of the appeal before your Lordships' Committee.

Mr and Mrs Richards were married on 18 November 1974. The matrimonial home is a council house rented from the Purbeck District Council. Mr Richards appears to be the tenant. Mr Richards is a bricklayer, in regular work.

Mr and Mrs Richards have two children, a girl and a boy. The girl, Melanie Jayne, is aged six, having been born on 30 April 1977. The boy, Daniel Gordon, is aged four, having been born on 26 March 1979. The girl is at school and old enough to know, and to say, that she does not wish her parents to be separated.

The marriage was not without its ups and downs. According to the welfare report, Mrs Richards had left Mr Richards on a number of occasions. Other men had been involved. But Mr Richards had always forgiven Mrs Richards and had never referred to these infidelities. These facts were based on Mr Richards's statements to the welfare officer but have not been challenged.

In January 1982 while the parties were still cohabiting, Mr Richards was surprised to receive a divorce petition signed by his wife. It sought, amongst other remedies, dissolution of their marriage. It alleged that their marriage had irretrievably broken down. It sought to establish this by proving that Mr Richards had 'behaved in such a way that the petitioner cannot reasonably be expected to live with the respondent'. Mr Richards denies these allegations. According to the welfare report, his interest centres on his family and his home. He still cannot 'accept the idea of divorce'. The petition is therefore opposed, but without a cross-prayer. It has yet to be heard. According to his Honour Judge Pennant, sitting as a judge of the High Court, the allegations struck the judge as being 'rubbishy'. Mrs Richards's own counsel admitted in the Court of Appeal that they were 'flimsy in the extreme' and described them as 'amounting to no more than that the wife was disenchanted by the husband'.

On receipt of the petition Mr Richards asked his wife whether she still wanted to cook for him and so forth. She said she did. She moved out of their bedroom into one of the children's rooms. Thereafter, the children shared a room. The parties continued under the same roof for some months. Mrs Richards went out a good deal in the evenings. On one occasion she told her husband that she had been seeing a man called David with whom the children got on very well and with whom she was going to live. There is no means of knowing how much of this was true and nothing came of it until June 1982.

At the beginning of June 1982, Mrs Richards left home again. She took the children with her. She went to stay with a Mrs Moore at Mrs Moore's house in conditions admittedly overcrowded. Mrs Moore's house is eight miles away in Swanage. From Friday teatime to Sunday evening Mrs Richards took the children to stay with their father in the matrimonial home. During term she drove the daughter to school. When she was on holiday she took the children to stay with their father. At some time during this period she took the children for a short time to stay with a man called Alan in Hanworthy. This appears to have been during July 1982. She described this as a business arrangement, but, not altogether surprisingly, the judge said that he had more than a suspicion that she had been committing adultery. On 2 August the court welfare officer made the report to which reference has already been made with a view to investigating the possibility of reconciliation or a possible order of custody. The welfare officer reported that in view of the children's need of their father, of the couple's proven ability to co-operate and of concern for the children's security, the court might feel that joint custody was desirable and workable. No order for custody has in fact been made. In his answer to the petition, Mr Richards does not seek care and control.

So matters rested until 15 October 1982. On that date the wife issued a summons making an application intituled in the pending suit from which the present appeal ultimately stems. There was no reference in the heading indicating which jurisdiction the wife was seeking to invoke. It was simply an interlocutory application in the suit. In it, the wife claimed an injunction against molestation and another restricting communication. Both of these were rejected and are not now persisted in. She also sought an order that the husband should quit and deliver up possession of the matrimonial home, and not return thereto. There was an affidavit in support. Both the summons and the supporting affidavit were served on 3 November 1982. On 8 November 1982 the husband filed an affidavit in reply. This was the date of the hearing before Judge Pennant. Both parties gave brief evidence to the judge. Mrs Richards said she could not stay at the house of her friend beyond 22 November, and that, although she had tried to get accommodation from the council, the best they could offer, at least at that moment, was a caravan. She added that she would not return to the matrimonial home while her husband was there. In these circumstances, Judge Pennant was called on to make his decision on the wife's application.

The judge found that Mrs Richards 'has no reasonable ground for refusing to return to live in the same house as her husband', but that the existing accommodation where she was then living was 'overcrowded and not a fit home for the children'. Contrasting the case with *Samson v Samson* [1982] 1 All ER 780, [1982] 1 WLR 252 he said that the wife had told him that she 'could not bear to be in the same house as the husband'. He added: 'The wife is strong-willed and does not wish to be in the same house as her husband and says she cannot bear to be with him. *But it is not true that she cannot*' (my emphasis).

The judge further found: 'I think it is thoroughly unjust to turn out this father, but justice no longer seems to play any part in this branch of the law.' He felt himself constrained to follow *Samson v Samson* rather than *Myers v Myers* [1982] 1 All ER 776, [1982] 1 WLR 247, on the ground that the matrimonial home 'was a house provided by the public as a home for these four people, and that being so, the public interest [sic] is best met by installing the children in that home, which means in practice installing their mother too'. He added:

> 'I find that it is by no means certain that there will be a divorce on the present

grounds, and I have come to the conclusion that although it is unjust to the husband, it seems right to grant the order sought in the interests of the children.'

In the event the judge made an order, not in the terms asked for by the wife but in the following terms:

> 'That the [husband] do vacate the matrimonial home [at] 13, Stoborough Green, Stoborough, Wareham, Dorset on or before the 22nd November 1982.'

There was no order to the effect that he should not return. In the event Mr Richards appealed and by an order dated 8 December 1982 his appeal was dismissed by the Court of Appeal (Cumming-Bruce and Dillon LJJ) who also refused leave to appeal to the House of Lords. By leave of the Appeal Committee the husband now appeals to your Lordships. It is, however, important to point out that what has in fact happened on the ground is, owing to the good sense of the parties, rather different from what the orders of the courts below might have led one to expect. In fact, the wife occupies the house from Monday to Friday, and the husband from Friday to Monday. The children are permanently in the house and are looked after by the parent in occupation. The husband has no difficulty in looking after them either under this arrangement or when the wife is on holiday, when he stays in the house throughout the week. This rather bears out what the welfare officer said in August 1982:

> 'When I asked whether Mr. Richards could manage the children on his own, he was amused, as, he said, he had been in the habit of looking after them.'

As will appear from the above facts and findings, it must now be clear, and I believe that it ought to have been clear all along, that the wife has never made out a case for excluding the husband from the home. If there had been any doubt about this, the matter has now been established by the subsequent events beyond a peradventure. It therefore follows that I entirely accept the reasoning on this point of my noble and learned friend Lord Scarman.

I have now to consider the decision of the Court of Appeal, and the general principles of law involved. The court were quite right in thinking that the previous decisions of the Court of Appeal in this jurisdiction, to mention only *Elsworth v Elsworth* (1979) 1 FLR 245, *Myers v Myers, Samson v Samson* and *Bassett v Bassett* [1975] 1 All ER 513, [1975] Fam 76, appear to conflict. In the event, the court chose to follow *Bassett v Bassett* and *Samson v Samson* and disapprove *Elsworth v Elsworth* and *Myers v Myers*. Since I believe all four to have erred to some extent in principle, though not necessarily on the facts before them, I believe it is right to begin at the beginning and trace back the error to its source.

From the start it struck me as strange that in none of the cases cited before us was the statutory basis of the jurisdiction to grant these ouster injunctions properly discussed or investigated, and, as a result, the criteria which should actuate the court in exercising it were never properly considered or formulated. This is the more strange, since the jurisdiction of the Supreme Court to grant or withhold ouster injunctions is, I believe, based on statute and statute alone, and the criteria which should be applied are now, to my mind, adequately formulated in the relevant statutory provisions.

Prior to 1967, the jurisdiction of the High Court to grant or withhold injunctions, final or interlocutory, was contained in what was then s 45 of the Supreme Court of Judicature (Consolidation) Act 1925. With the omission of the now inappropriate reference to mandamus, the section is now found in s 37 of the Supreme Court Act 1981, the material words of which read:

> '(1) The High Court may by order (whether interlocutory or final) grant an injunction . . . in all cases in which it appears to the court to be just and convenient to do so . . .'

I do not think it necessary to proceed to consider whether, apart from the section, the court has any inherent jurisdiction. If it has, I believe it is indistinguishable in its application to the jurisdiction conferred by the section. I prefer to say that any inherent jurisdiction is absorbed by the section.

Being in general terms, the section is silent as to the criteria to be followed, and since the section applies to all divisions, such criteria had before 1967 been the subject of case law jurisprudence of a wide and multifarious kind. The section is still in force, and still applies in principle to all divisions of the High Court. Nevertheless, and while it is still there in reserve in cases where the special legislation to which I will be referring does not apply, in my opinion, where, as here, Parliament has spelt out in considerable detail what must be done in a particular class of case it is not open to litigants to bypass the special Act, nor to the courts to disregard its provisions by resorting to the earlier procedure, and thus choose to apply a different jurisprudence from that which the Act prescribes.

Any other conclusion would, I believe, lead to the most serious confusion. The result of a particular application cannot depend on which of two alternative statutory provisions the applicant invokes, where one is quite general and the other deals in precise detail with the situation involved and was enacted at a time when the general provision already existed.

The rights conferred by s 37 were however subject to one serious limitation which applies to all equitable remedies of this class, whether statutory or arising from inherent jurisdiction, namely that an injunction could only be used in support of a legal right (and therefore only doubtfully in a number of ouster applications in the matrimonial jurisdiction), and despite statements (mostly obiter) to the effect that the court might apply different principles where the welfare of children was in question (cf *Stewart v Stewart* [1973] 1 All ER 31, [1973] Fam 21 at 23, *Adams v Adams* (1965) 109 SJ 899, *Phillips v Phillips* [1973] 2 All ER 423, [1973] 1 WLR 615) neither the extent of the jurisdiction nor the criteria for its exercise were fully explored. Before the passing of the legislation to which I am about to refer this jurisdiction was also regularly invoked in ouster cases: see e g *Silverstone v Silverstone* [1953] 1 All ER 556, [1953] P 174, *Montgomery v Montgomery* [1964] 2 All ER 22 at 24, [1965] P 46 at 51. There was, indeed, no other basis for its exercise, since the section is wide enough to cover applications for ouster, and all-embracing enough to make any inherent jurisdiction superfluous.

Nevertheless, in my opinion, a new era opened with the passage of the Matrimonial Homes Act 1967, which, however, in *Tarr v Tarr* [1972] 2 All ER 295, [1973] AC 254, proved to contain an important but, in my opinion probably unintentional, casus omissus. This was repaired by s 3 of the Domestic Violence and Matrimonial Proceedings Act 1976, and the jurisdiction was extended by the application of s 4 of the same Act as regards ss 1(3), (4) and (6) of the Matrimonial Homes Act 1967 to joint interests owned by each of two spouses.

In its amended form, which in my view is applicable to, and decisive of, the present proceedings, s 1 of the Matrimonial Homes Act 1967 now reads as follows:

> '*Protection against eviction, etc., from matrimonial home of spouse not entitled by virtue of estate, etc., to occupy it.*—(1) Where one spouse is entitled to occupy a dwelling house by virtue of any estate or interest or contract or by virtue of any enactment giving him or her the right to remain in occupation, and the other spouse is not so entitled, then, subject to the provisions of this Act, the spouse not so entitled shall have the following rights (in this Act referred to as "rights of occupation"):—(*a*) if in occupation, a right not to be evicted or excluded from the dwelling house or any part thereof by the other spouse except with the leave of the court given by an order under this section; (*b*) if not in occupation, a right with the leave of the court so given to enter into and occupy the dwelling house.
>
> (2) So long as one spouse has rights of occupation, either of the spouses may apply to the court for an order declaring, enforcing, restricting or terminating those rights or prohibiting, suspending or restricting the exercise by either spouse of the right to occupy the dwelling house or requiring either spouse to permit the exercise by the other of that right.
>
> (3) On an application for an order under this section the court may make such order as it thinks just and reasonable having regard to the conduct of the spouses in relation to each other and otherwise, to their respective needs and financial resources, to the needs of any children and to all the circumstances of the case, and, without

prejudice to the generality of the foregoing provision,—(*a*) may except part of the dwelling house from a spouse's rights of occupation (and in particular a part used *a* wholly or mainly for or in connection with the trade, business or profession of the other spouse); (*b*) may order a spouse occupying the dwelling house or any part thereof by virtue of this section to make periodical payments to the other in respect of the occupation; (*c*) may impose on either spouse obligations as to the repair and maintenance of the dwelling house or the discharge of any liabilities in respect of the dwelling house. *b*

(4) Orders under this section may, in so far as they have a continuing effect, be limited so as to have effect for a period specified in the order or until further order.

(5) Where a spouse is entitled under this section to occupy a dwelling house or any part thereof, any payment or tender made or other thing done by that spouse in or towards satisfaction of any liability of the other spouse in respect of rent, rates, mortgage payments or other outgoings affecting the dwelling house shall, whether *c* or not it is made or done in pursuance of an order under this section, be as good as if made or done by the other spouse; and a spouse's occupation by virtue of this section shall for purposes of the Rent Act 1977 (other than Part VI thereof and sections 103 to 106) be treated as possession by the other spouse. Where a spouse entitled under this section to occupy a dwelling house or any part thereof makes any payment in or towards satisfaction of any liability of the other spouse in respect of mortgage *d* payments affecting the dwelling house, the person to whom the payment is made may treat it as having been made by that other spouse, but the fact that that person has treated any such payment as having been so made shall not affect any claim of the first-mentioned spouse against the other to an interest in the dwelling house by virtue of the payment.

(6) The jurisdiction conferred on the court by this section shall be exercisable by *e* the High Court or by a county court, and shall be exercisable by a county court notwithstanding that by reason of the amount of the net annual value for rating of the dwelling house or otherwise the jurisdiction would not but for this subsection be exercisable by a county court.

(7) In this Act "dwelling house" includes any building or part thereof which is occupied as a dwelling, and any yard, garden, garage or outhouse belonging to the *f* dwelling house and occupied therewith.

(8) This Act shall not apply to a dwelling house which has at no time been a matrimonial home of the spouses in question; and a spouse's rights of occupation shall continue only so long as the marriage subsists and the other spouse is entitled as mentioned in subsection (1) above to occupy the dwelling house, except where provision is made by section 2 of this Act for those rights to be a charge on an estate *g* or interest in the dwelling house.

(9) It is hereby declared that a spouse who has an equitable interest in a dwelling house or in the proceeds of sale thereof, not being a spouse in whom is vested (whether solely or as a joint tenant) a legal estate in fee simple or a legal term of years absolute in the dwelling house, is to be treated for the purpose only of determining whether he or she has rights of occupation under this section as not *h* being entitled to occupy the dwelling house by virtue of that interest.'

Subsection (9) of this section was added by the Matrimonial Proceedings and Property Act 1970. But the vital subsections of this all-important change in the law affecting the present appeal, are sub-ss (1), (2), (3) and (6).

Of these subsections, sub-s (3) makes it clear that when exercising this jurisdiction, both the conduct of the spouses and the needs of the children are, with other *j* considerations, matters to which the court must have regard and which require to be weighed together so as to provide a just and reasonable result.

I do not for a moment suggest that the general jurisdiction conferred by s 37 of the Supreme Court Act 1981 has been abolished or that it cannot be invoked in appropriate cases (eg molestation) for the protection of minors. But in my view the effect of s 1 of the Matrimonial Homes Act 1967, which was in no way referred to in argument in the Court of Appeal or, so far as I can make out, in any of the reported cases cited, is to codify and spell out, where it is applicable, the jurisdiction of the High Court and county court in ouster injunctions between spouses whether in pending proceedings or by way of originating applications, and the criteria to be applied are those referred to in sub-s (3) and not any other criteria sometimes treated as paramount by reported decisions of the court. I do not know that they differ very much from those developed by the case law evolved prior to 1967 and 1976 as respects the more limited jurisdiction of the court. But in so far as any decisions of the Court of Appeal whether before or after the passing of the Matrimonial Homes Act 1967 (with its amendments and additions) suggest any other criteria than those set out in sub-s (3), particularly any which may claim that one set of criteria are to be treated as prior to, or paramount over, any or all of the others, in my opinion they are not to be regarded as sound law, although I wish to say that most if not all the decisions in which such dicta occur are probably to be justified on the particular facts, and even the general observations when taken in the context of their particular facts, but not out of context, may well be justifiable.

In particular I contrast the language of s 1 of the Matrimonial Homes Act 1967, which I have set out in full above, and especially sub-s (3), with the language of the first and paramount consideration or criterion laid down in s 1 of the Guardianship of Minors Act 1971 which has been the law at least since 1925 but has a different legislative pedigree and covers (in my judgment) a different field from the legislation which I have been endeavouring to describe and is designed to prevent an altogether different 'mischief'. In my view this Act was passed in order to lay to rest once and for all decisions and doubts which had been expressed in proceedings of a limited kind as to the respective rights of the parents inter se and against their children. I regard it as significant and probative of this view that the priority and paramountcy of the principle enunciated by this section is absolute and not qualified, as in the two sections conferring jurisdiction to pronounce interlocutory injunctions, by any requirement that the result should be 'just and reasonable'. Section 1 of the 1971 Act reads as follows (the emphasis when it occurs in the text of the section is, of course, mine):

> '*Principle on which questions relating to custody, upbringing etc. of minors are to be decided* [these words are in a sidenote and do not, of course, form part of the section to be construed]. Where in any proceedings before any court (whether or not a court as defined in section 15 of this Act)—(*a*) the legal custody or upbringing of a minor; or (*b*) the administration of any property belonging to or held on trust for a minor, or the application of the income thereof, *is in question*, the court, *in deciding that question*, shall regard the welfare of the minor as the first and paramount consideration, and shall not take into consideration whether from any other point of view the claim of the father in respect of such legal custody, upbringing, administration or application is superior to that of the mother, or the claim of the mother is superior to that of the father.'

I do not believe that an application for ouster is 'a proceeding' in which 'the legal custody or upbringing of a minor is in question', although of course 'the needs of the children' are expressly required by s 1 of the 1967 Act to be taken into account in an application under that section, and may of course prevail in any given case where it is 'just and reasonable' that they should.

In the Matrimonial Homes Act 1967, the 'needs of the children' are an important and specified, but not in every case first or paramount, consideration to be applied. In the Guardianship of Minors Act 1971, the 'welfare' of the children is the 'first and paramount' consideration. In my view, the Guardianship of Minors Act criterion is to be applied only in the proceedings of the type specified in the section, i e proceedings in which custody, upbringing, or the proprietary jurisdiction implied by s 1(*b*) fall to be decided as a matter directly in issue, and not in cases to which s 1(3) of the Matrimonial Homes Act 1967 is to be applied so as to produce a just and reasonable result, even though in these cases the

interests of the children are directly or indirectly affected, when the various considerations
must be balanced in the light of the particular facts. The same I consider would be true a
of the criteria set forth in s 25 of the Matrimonial Causes Act 1973, another section which
gives rise to poignant and emotionally charged decisions with which the interests of
children may often be directly or indirectly intimately bound up. When Parliament has
told the courts the criteria to be applied in a particular class of case it is not for the courts
either to invent new criteria or to apply new and absolute priorities of their own whether
derived from some other and differing statutory provisions or not. The apparent conflict b
between the rival decisions of the Court of Appeal which have given rise to the
controversy in the present case is due in my view to the failure in repeated instances of
successive divisions of that court to remind itself of the correct legislative framework
within which it should act. It should further be noted that s 1 of the Domestic Violence
and Matrimonial Proceedings Act 1976 conferring jurisdiction on the county court is
expressed to be without prejudice to the High Court jurisdiction here in question, and is c
relevant, if at all, only for purposes of comparison.

It follows, I think, that the present decision cannot be supported either on the grounds
expounded by my noble and learned friend Lord Scarman or the ground of principle on
which my noble and learned friend Lord Brandon founds his opinion. It is plain that
Judge Pennant would not have reached the decision he did if he had not felt himself
constrained by conflicting decisions of the Court of Appeal which he sought vainly to d
reconcile by appeal to the 'public interest', itself not one of the criteria set forth in s 1(3)
of the Matrimonial Homes Act 1967, unless it can be subsumed under the general rubric
'all the circumstances of the case'. It is clear that he did not consider the result 'just and
reasonable' as s 1(3) of the 1967 Act requires and it is clear that it was not so even if the
paramountcy principle were applicable. In any event, for the reason that it no longer
corresponds to what, owing to the good sense of the parties, is now actually happening, e
his order could not stand. For the same reason if no other, the passage in the judgment
of Cumming-Bruce LJ (see [1983] 1 All ER 1017 at 1026, [1983] 2 WLR 633 at 643),
must also fall as being overtaken by events.

It follows also from what I have said that in my view both judgments are vulnerable
to the objection of principle which I have tried to summarise in what I have already said.
I do not think the principle enunciated in the Guardianship of Minors Act 1971 is f
applicable for the following reasons. (1) This application is not and cannot be construed
as being a proceeding in which 'the legal custody or upbringing of a minor or the
administration of any property belonging to or held on trust for a minor, or the
application of the income thereof, is in question', ie to adopt Lord Scarman's phrase, 'is
in issue and has to be decided' in the application, though no doubt legal custody will fall
to be decided in the suit. (2) Although, for the reasons given by my noble and learned g
friend Lord Brandon, it may have been wrongly intituled, the application is one to which
the Matrimonial Homes Act 1967 as amended does apply, and accordingly 'the needs of
the children', although one of the factors to be considered and weighed, is not the only
factor, and to make it the 'first and paramount' consideration is to fly in the face of s 1(3).
This is not, of course, to say that if, on consideration, the 'needs of the children' are so
clamant as in the circumstances of the case require them to be given paramountcy the h
court should not in the proper exercise of its discretion give effect to precisely that. (3)
To come to a different conclusion would be to fly in the face of the express words of
s 1(1)(*a*) of the 1967 Act that a spouse in occupation is not to be evicted 'except with the
leave of the court given by an order under' s 1. The fact that in the instant case the spouse
against whom the ouster order was sought was the spouse entitled to occupy the dwelling
house under 'an estate or interest or contract' is a fortiori to this provision since it cannot j
be supposed that a spouse so entitled is in a worse position than a spouse 'not so entitled'.
(4) So far as regards the cases cited, I am far from saying that *Elsworth v Elsworth*, *Myers v
Myers*, *Samson v Samson*, *Bassett v Bassett* or *Walker v Walker* [1978] 3 All ER 141, [1978] 1
WLR 533 were wrongly decided on their own facts. But their rationes decidendi, if taken
as universal expressions of principle, are inconsistent with one another, and, if so taken,

are wrong in so far as one line of cases purports to subordinate the 'needs of the children' to 'the conduct of the spouses' in every case or vice versa or in so far as an ouster application is said to be treated as a 'housing matter'. I venture to think, however, that the facts in matrimonial proceedings are so varied in their nature that courts should be extremely careful before reading into judgments which are uttered in the context of a particular case universal principles which may have the virtue of simplicity but which if so treated are at variance with the fuller and more appropriate criteria prescribed by Parliament, and in particular with the requirement that the total result should be just and reasonable. (5) I would venture to add that whether one treats the 'needs' of children as a relevant factor or their 'welfare' as paramount, the court ought not to confine itself to a consideration of purely material requirements or immediate comforts. These may have to be given priority in a given case either owing to their urgency or the seriousness of denying them. But it is not necessarily for the interests of children that either parent should be allowed to get away and be seen to get away with capricious, arbitrary, autocratic, or merely eccentric behaviour. It may well be difficult for a court to exercise control. But the difficulty is not rendered less if it is prepared to throw its hand in so readily.

At all events the appeal must be allowed. The order of ouster cannot stand. For myself, I would deprecate the parties taking too much advantage of this. Despite their estrangement which may or may not prove permanent, subsequent events indorse the welfare report as to their ability to co-operate. If either acts unreasonably, the courts are still open. What is now proposed does not deprive the parties of their right to come to a business-like agreement voluntarily or to apply for a suitable order should either act unreasonably.

In the event I agree with my noble and learned friends on both the grounds proposed in their several judgments. The appeal must be allowed, the order appealed from be set aside, and there must be a legal aid taxation of costs on both sides.

LORD DIPLOCK. My Lords, I too would allow this appeal for the reasons given by my noble and learned friends Lord Hailsham LC and Lord Brandon, whose speeches I have had the privilege of reading in advance. Like them and my noble and learned friend Lord Bridge, I find myself unable to accept the view of my noble and learned friend Lord Scarman that the provisions of s 1 of the Guardianship of Minors Act 1971 are applicable to ouster proceedings.

LORD SCARMAN. My Lords, in this appeal the House is called on to determine the principle governing the exercise of a court's discretion where, during the subsistence of a marriage where there are children to be considered, it is invited on application by one spouse to make an order excluding the other spouse from the matrimonial home. The specific question for decision is whether the court must, as a matter of law, treat the interests of the children as the first and paramount consideration.

In the present case, the trial judge in ordering the husband out of the home, and the Court of Appeal in upholding his decision, acted on this principle. The husband, as appellant before your Lordships, submits that they erred in law. It is his submission that, though the interests of the children are always important and often critically important, there is no rule of law which requires the courts, when considering an application to oust a spouse from his home, to give them priority. The court's duty, it is submitted, is to weigh the conflicting interests, to have regard to the needs of all who are affected, and to make an order which is fair, just and reasonable in all the circumstances. He then asks the House to conclude that on the facts it would be unfair, unjust and unreasonable to exclude him from the home.

Two statutes fall to be considered. First in order of date is s 1 of the Guardianship of Infants Act 1925 as now re-enacted and amended by s 1 of the Guardianship of Minors Act 1971, which has itself been amended. I shall refer to this legislation as the Guardianship Act and to the principle there enunciated, as 'the principle of paramountcy'.

The second is the Matrimonial Homes Act 1967 as amended. I shall refer to this legislation as 'the 1967 Act' and to the test it requires as 'the fair and reasonable test'. There is no express reference to either piece of legislation in the judgment below, although the principle of paramountcy of the children's interests emerges clearly as the ground of decision. This omission (for that is what it is) is commonly found in the case law. I do not know of a case where a court invited to make an ouster order has addressed itself to the question of construction of s 1 of the Guardianship Act, though in making ouster orders courts have frequently assumed it applies. Nor do I know of any case in which the court has asked itself whether 'the fair and reasonable test', as set forth in s 1(3) of the 1967 Act, excludes the Guardianship Act 'principle of paramountcy'. This inattention to the statute law explains, I believe, the divergence of views in the case law dealing with the question now in issue before the House, and renders it unnecessary to consider the cases in any detail.

In this appeal the House is concerned with an ouster order granted as interlocutory relief in a pending divorce suit. But there exist other statutory powers to make ouster orders, and it is notable that the case law has tended to pay scant regard to the particular statutory power being invoked. The statutory provision is a hotchpotch of enactments of limited scope passed into law to meet specific situations or to strengthen the powers of specified courts. The sooner the range, scope, and effect of these powers are rationalised into a coherent and comprehensive body of statute law, the better. Briefly, the various jurisdictions are these. (1) The jurisdiction (which the wife invoked in this case) of the divorce court to grant interlocutory relief in pending matrimonial causes: see the Matrimonial Causes Act 1973 and s 37(1) of the Supreme Court Act 1981 re-enacting s 45 of the Supreme Court of Judicature (Consolidation) Act 1925; in this jurisdiction custody is in issue. (2) The jurisdiction conferred on the High Court and county court by the 1967 Act in protection of the spouse who is given by that Act a statutory right of occupancy of the home; the exercise of this jurisdiction does not directly raise the custody issue but it can, and frequently does, have a great impact on the welfare and upbringing of children. (3) The jurisdiction of the county court under s 1 of the Domestic Violence and Matrimonial Proceedings Act 1976; custody is not in issue, but the comment on the 1967 Act power applies here also. (4) The jurisdiction of the magistrates under s 16 of the Domestic Proceedings and Magistrates' Courts Act 1978. The magistrates have extensive powers in respect of the custody, welfare and upbringing of children.

I would make three comments at this stage. The divorce court is able to make an interlocutory order excluding a spouse from the home under the statutory power mentioned above because, as I shall emphasise later, it has an inherent power independent of statute to protect the parties in a pending matrimonial suit and their children. My second comment is that a court exercising the wardship jurisdiction would seem also to have an inherent power to exclude a parent from the matrimonial home: if it has, its discretion would appear to be governed by the Guardianship Act, since wardship in its modern dress is concerned directly with questions as to the custody, care and upbringing of children. Thirdly, the common feature in all these jurisdictions is that the court has a discretion. But only in the case of magistrates is there to be found an express incorporation of the priority conferred by the Guardianship Act in relation to the custody and upbringing of children: see s 15 of the Domestic Proceedings and Magistrates' Courts Act 1978. Is this statutory priority generally applicable wherever and in whatever context the court has to have regard to the welfare of children of a family? Or is it limited? And, if limited, what is the range of its application? More specifically, does it apply in cases in which the spouse making the application possesses the 1967 Act's statutory right of occupation of the matrimonial home?

These questions have, so far as I am aware, never been directly faced by any court exercising any of the jurisdictions listed above. The courts have, understandably, sought to establish a common basis of principle in deciding whether or not to make an ouster order. They have signally failed. Contrast *Myers v Myers* [1982] 1 All ER 776, [1982] 1 WLR 247, where the Court of Appeal allowed a husband's appeal against an ouster order because the judge failed to consider whether the wife's refusal to live with him in the home was reasonable, with *Samson v Samson* [1982] 1 All ER 780, [1982] 1 WLR 252, where another division of the Court of Appeal had regard to the welfare of the children, adopted the principle of paramountcy and upheld the ouster order. The reason for such divergence may well be that the courts have sought to establish a principle independently of the statute law. For myself, I believe a full consideration of the statute law will establish not only that *Samson*'s case was correctly decided but also that the principle of paramountcy does afford a common basis of principle.

It is necessary, however, to have regard not only to the language of s 1 of the Guardianship Act, but also to the law, whether it be statutory provision or the inherent power of the court, conferring the jurisdiction which is being invoked. An illustration of the danger of ignoring the statute law can be found in the way in which the Court of Appeal, in *Spindlow v Spindlow* [1979] 1 All ER 169, [1979] Fam 52, handled an application under s 1 of the Domestic Violence Act. It must be unlikely that the section, though it offers no express guidance, can be applicable unless there be shown violence, or the threat of it, or a reasonable apprehension that the presence of the man (or woman) in the house constitutes a danger to the physical or emotional health or well-being of the woman (or man) and the children: see *Davis v Johnson* [1978] 1 All ER 1132, [1979] AC 264. But whatever be the scope of the section (a question which does not arise in this appeal), the question whether or not to make an order under the section cannot be classified as 'essentially a housing matter, housing for the children' as the Court of Appeal classified it in *Spindlow*'s case [1979] 1 All ER 169 at 173, [1979] Fam 52 at 59 per Ormrod LJ. Yet the Court of Appeal was right to seek a rationalisation of principle covering the whole field of ouster orders under whatever jurisdiction they are made. As Ormrod LJ later observed in *Samson v Samson* [1982] 1 All ER 780 at 781–782, [1982] 1 WLR 252 at 254, an application for an ouster order cannot be considered in isolation from questions as to the custody, care and control of the children. In deciding, therefore, whether to make an order or not, a court must, unless the statute which confers the power is to the contrary effect, bear in mind that it is the will of Parliament expressed in the Guardianship Act that in questions of custody the principle of paramountcy is to be applied.

The Guardianship Act

The development of the law's protection of the welfare of children took a new direction with the enactment of the Guardianship of Infants Act 1886. In 1883 Bowen LJ was able to say that it would be fallacious to accept the recognised test in custody cases of 'the benefit of the infant' as permitting the court, save in exceptional cases, to interfere with the rights of the father: see *Re Agar-Ellis, Agar-Ellis v Lascelles* (1883) 24 Ch D 317 at 337. But by 1893 Lindley LJ, delivering the judgment of the Court of Appeal, could say: 'The dominant matter for the consideration of the Court is the welfare of the child': see *Re McGrath (infants)* [1893] 1 Ch 143 at 148. In 1925 the principle of paramountcy, by now well-recognised by the courts, was fully formulated in s 1 of the Guardianship of Infants Act 1925. Indeed, in *Re Thain, Thain v Taylor* [1926] Ch 676, [1926] All ER Rep 384 the section was said by the Court of Appeal to be declaratory of the existing law. The case law, like the statute law, was concerned with the right of parents to the custody, care and control of the infant; but the law by judicial decision and statutory enactment did proclaim the principle of paramountcy as a principle which could not be said to be irrelevant in other contexts where the welfare of children fell to be considered by a court. It could not be confined, save by the pedantry of literalism, to the issue of custody with such strictness that its guidance was to be rejected in other cases where problems as to the welfare of children and their upbringing fell to be considered.

I turn now to consider the Guardianship Act. The current statutory provision is s 1 of the 1971 Act, as amended. The sidenote is in these terms: 'Principle on which questions relating to custody, upbringing etc. of minors are to be decided'.

The section is as follows:

> 'Where in any proceedings before any court (whether or not a court as defined in section 15 of this Act)—(*a*) the legal custody or upbringing of a minor; or (*b*) the

> administration of any property belonging to or held on trust for a minor, or the application of the income thereof, is in question, the court, in deciding that question, shall regard the welfare of the minor as the first and paramount consideration, and shall not take into consideration whether from any other point of view the claim of the father in respect of such legal custody, upbringing, administration or application is superior to that of the mother, or the claim of the mother is superior to that of the father.'

The term 'legal custody' was substituted for 'custody' by s 36 of the Domestic Proceedings and Magistrates' Courts Act 1978. Its meaning is to be found in s 86 of the Children Act 1975:

> '... unless the context otherwise requires, "legal custody" means, as respects a child, so much of the parental rights and duties as relate to the person of the child (including the place and manner in which his time is spent)...'

Legal custody, therefore, includes the custody, the care and control of a child, and access to him. It embraces all the parental rights and duties in respect of the person of the child.

Two points of construction of the section were settled by your Lordships' House in *J v C* [1969] 1 All ER 788, [1970] AC 688. The first is the universality of the application of its principle of paramountcy. In whatever court and between whatever parties (be they parents, foster-parents, institutions or strangers), if legal custody is in issue, the principle applies. The second point is the meaning of 'first and paramount consideration'. It is a principle not of exclusion but of priority. In *J v C* [1969] 1 All ER 788 at 824, [1970] AC 688 at 715, Lord Macdermott put it thus:

> '3. While there is now no rule of law that the rights and wishes of unimpeachable parents must prevail over other considerations, such rights and wishes, recognised as they are by nature and society, can be capable of ministering to the total welfare of the child in a special way, and must therefore preponderate in many cases. The parental rights, however, remain qualified and not absolute for the purposes of the investigation, the broad nature of which is still as described in the fourth of the principles enunciated by FitzGibbon, L.J., in *Re O'Hara* ([1900] 2 IR 232 at 240).'

'Unimpeachable' is, perhaps, stating an unattainable ideal. 'Good', however, would be a worthy substitute. The reference to *O'Hara*'s case was to the following passage:

> '4. In exercising the jurisdiction to control or to ignore the parental right the Court must act cautiously... acting in opposition to the parent only when judicially satisfied that the welfare of the child requires that the parental right should be suspended or superseded.'

J v C was a ward of court case; and in *O'Hara*'s case FitzGibbon LJ was considering a choice between institutional care and parental care. But the section applies in *any* proceedings in *any* court where legal custody is in question.

It is clear that, as a matter of strict literal construction, the section imposes the principle of paramountcy only where legal custody (or the property of the child) is in issue and has to be decided. But, unless it can be shown to have been excluded by express enactment or by necessary implication, the principle must guide the exercise of a court's discretion in every case in which the court is required to consider the welfare and upbringing of minor children. It would be contrary to the will of Parliament for a court to make an order directly affecting the rights, duties and responsibilities of parents in respect of the personal life of their children without ensuring that its order did not obstruct, or offend against, the principle which must govern judicial decision as to legal custody. On this broad ground I would hold that, unless expressly or by necessary implication excluded by statute, the principle of s 1 of the Guardianship Act applies wherever there are children whose interests must be considered before an order is made excluding one parent from the family home.

It is, however, submitted, and, as I understand, your Lordships accept the submission, that in cases in which the spouse seeking an ouster order has the 1967 Act's right of occupation, the Guardianship Act's paramountcy of the interests of the children is excluded. I turn, therefore, to the Act.

The Matrimonial Homes Act 1967

The Matrimonial Homes Act 1967 confers on a spouse who has no beneficial estate or interest in the matrimonial home a right (a) if in occupation, not to be excluded except by leave of the court given by order, and (b) if not in occupation, a right with the leave of the court so given to enter into and occupy the home: (s 1(1)). Subsection (2) provides for application to the court: so long as one spouse has the statutory right of occupation, either spouse may apply for 'an order ... prohibiting, suspending or restricting the exercise by either spouse of the right to occupy the dwelling house or requiring either spouse to permit the exercise by the other of that right.'

Subsection (3) provides for the manner in which the court is to exercise its discretion on an application for an order under the section:

> '... the court may make such order as it thinks just and reasonable having regard to the conduct of the spouses in relation to each other and otherwise, to their respective needs and financial resources, to the needs of any children and to all the circumstances of the case ...'

The 1967 Act is essentially one which governs the exercise of the property rights of the spouse who enjoys the legal right to the home so as to confer on the other spouse a judicially protected right of occupation. The 1967 Act applies only during the subsistence of the marriage, and only while the other spouse has a legal right of occupation. It has, therefore, no application to the situation which arises on divorce; and none where neither spouse has any property or contractual or statutory right to the matrimonial home, a situation not so improbable as might appear at first sight.

Indeed, most of its provisions are concerned with the adjustment of a spouse's property rights and liabilities to give effect to the statutory right of occupation conferred on the other spouse.

Finally, an application under the 1967 Act may be made either by originating summons in the High Court or by originating application in the county court: see r 107 of the Matrimonial Causes Rules 1977, SI 1977/344 and CCR 1981, Ord 47.

The 1967 Act stands independently, therefore, of other judicial proceedings; it is not tied to a matrimonial cause or any other proceeding. It does apply during the pendency of a divorce suit, but not after decree. The 1967 Act is of general application, I have no doubt, so long as the marriage is in being, ie until death or a decree pronounced in a matrimonial cause.

In an appropriate case, therefore, a wife petitioner in a pending suit will have her right of occupancy under the 1967 Act. But she also has her right under the inherent jurisdiction of the court to be protected with the children of the family in the matrimonial home. I do not construe the 1967 Act as a substitute for the court's inherent power to protect but as conferring an additional right. There may be cases where the 1967 Act cannot be invoked but the court's inherent power to protect the wife and children can, eg where the family is living in premises in which neither has a property right. But there will also be many cases where the protective power cannot be invoked (there being no threat to the wife or children), but the 1967 Act's right of occupation exists.

I accept, of course, the appellant's contention that, where the statutory right of occupancy exists, s 1(3) of the 1967 Act sets out the matters to be considered by the court in deciding whether it is just and reasonable to make an order evicting a husband from the home. But is it necessary to construe s 1(3) as excluding the principle of paramountcy where there are children to whom the principle would apply if custody were being decided?

It would be very strange if it did; for it would mean that in pending divorce proceedings, where custody is in issue and the wife has the right of occupation conferred by the 1967 Act, she would be able to secure an order evicting the husband from the home without regard to the principle of paramountcy which would, but for the 1967 Act, apply. I do not believe for one moment that Parliament intended any result so anomalous as that. When an ouster order is sought in pending divorce proceedings, the court is being invited to intervene at a most critical period in the lives of the children, the relationship between their parents having broken down (possibly irretrievably). The court is seized with the question of their welfare and upbringing. If ever there was a time to apply the principle of paramountcy of their needs and interest, it is in pending divorce proceedings. If the conclusion against its application is compelling on the construction of the statute, so be it. But I would not be persuaded so to hold, unless the language was clear or the implication irresistible. And, even if the Guardianship Act be of limited application, it is open to the courts to accept the principle as relevant when the welfare of the children has to be considered, as it must be before making an ouster order.

But there is, in my view, no inconsistency between s 1(3) of the 1967 Act and s 1 of the Guardianship Act. The principle of paramountcy is a rule of priority, not of exclusion. All the matters which s 1(3) specify can be considered; indeed, they must be. The Guardianship Act excludes none of them but establishes a priority. The 1967 Act is silent on priorities; but silence cannot be construed as exclusion, unless inconsistency emerges so as to make the implication necessary.

It has long been recognised that the divorce court has an inherent power to protect parties and their children by the grant of interlocutory injunctive relief and that the power extends to the granting of an order excluding, if necessary, the husband from the home pending suit. The jurisdiction was recognised by Pearce J in *Silverstone v Silverstone* [1953] 1 All ER 556, [1953] P 174, and by Ormrod J in *Montgomery v Montgomery* [1964] 2 All ER 22 at 24, [1965] P 46 at 51. Statute, however, governs the exercise of this power. Section 45 of the Supreme Court of Judicature (Consolidation) Act 1925, which, of course, consolidated existing law, provided that the High Court may grant an injunction by interlocutory order in all cases in which it appears to the court to be just or convenient so to do. This section has now been replaced in substantially the same terms by s 37 of the Supreme Court Act 1981. There is, however, an important limitation on the power: it can be exercised only if there is a right recognised by law independently of the Act (see *North London Rly Co v Great Northern Rly Co* (1883) 11 QBD 30 at 40). The right in this class of case is to the protection by the court of the right of wife and children to occupy the matrimonial home while matrimonial proceedings are pending. If their occupancy is endangered by the presence of the husband he may be excluded.

Has this right of protection while matrimonial proceedings are pending been superseded by the 1967 Act in cases to which that Act applies? For the reasons already given, I do not so construe the 1967 Act. And the Guardianship Act, in my view, applies either as a matter of construction or because its principle of paramountcy cannot properly be excluded in the exercise of the court's inherent power to protect children. For in divorce proceedings custody of the children of the family is in issue. Indeed, the court cannot make a decree of divorce or nullity absolute or grant a decree of judicial separation unless it is satisfied as to the arrangements for the children: see s 41 of the Matrimonial Causes Act 1973.

Accordingly, I would accept that s 1 of the Guardianship Act establishes a principle of priority to which the court, in this case, was bound to have regard. The courts below were correct to adopt it as their guide. In a pending matrimonial cause custody is in issue and the 1967 Act is no bar to the application of the principle of paramountcy. In other proceedings also for an ouster order, where there are children but custody is not directly in issue, the courts should apply the principle of paramountcy for the reason I have earlier given, namely that the question whether or not to make the order cannot be considered without having regard to the issue of custody. On an application by originating summons under the 1967 Act where there are children to be considered, this will be so as in the other jurisdictions in which ouster orders may be made.

But that is not enough to determine the appeal, for the principle is one of priority, not

exclusion. The husband's case that it was neither just nor reasonable to make the order
a may well succeed, even if the principle does apply. If, for instance, it can be shown that
the ouster order was not needed in the interests of the children, he succeeds. And, in my
view, that is the demonstrable truth in this case. It is the duty of an appellate court to
intervene, where a judge has exercised a discretionary power, not only if he has erred in
law but also if his decision can be demonstrated to be plainly wrong. This is what can be
demonstrated in this case. On his provisional findings of fact (and, of course, they were
b only provisional as the suit was pending and the issues unresolved), the judge went
wrong in finding that it was necessary in the interests of the two children of the family
that their father be excluded from the home. He found that the mother had no reasonable
ground for refusing to return to live in the same house as her husband. 'This wife,' he
said, 'is strong-willed and does not wish to be in the same house as her husband, and says
that she cannot bear to be with him: but it is not true that she cannot.' It was not
c suggested in evidence that the husband was a violent man; indeed, the judge thought
that the allegations of unreasonable behaviour against him were 'rubbishy'. He was an
excellent parent and the elder child had made it plain that she did not want her parents
to separate. The judge recognised that, whatever order he might make, 'the practical
probability' was that the children would continue to live with their mother but that their
father would look after them when he was not working, i e at weekends. And he certainly
d found that the matrimonial home was the place where the children should live. The
accommodation available to mother and children since leaving home was overcrowded.
His conclusion was that—

> 'it is thoroughly unjust to turn out this father, but justice no longer seems to play any part in this breach of the law . . . the public interest is best met by installing the children in that home, which means in practice installing their mother too.'

e

No doubt it did; but on his findings as to future 'practical probability' and the attitude,
will and feelings of the wife towards her husband it by no means followed that in order
to instal mother it was necessary to exclude father. And subsequent events have shown
how right the judge was in his assessment of the future practical probability and how
wrong he was in thinking it necessary to exclude the father from the home. Husband
f and wife have come to a sensible arrangement which on the evidence is clearly in the
best interests of the children. The children are installed in the matrimonial home; their
mother lives with them there from Monday to Friday; their father takes over on Friday
and lives with them there during the weekend. On the facts, therefore, it was neither
just (here I agree with the judge) nor reasonable nor necessary to oust the father. Had no
order been made, the 'practical probability' is that the same result would have been
g reached. If it had not, there might then have arisen a need for the intervention of the
court. The evidence did not justify the making of the order. The needs of the children
did not, on the judge's findings, require the protection of an ouster order.

The Court of Appeal fell into the same error. Both judges misinterpreted the crucial
finding of the judge which was in terms which I make no apology for repeating: 'This
wife is strong-willed . . . and says she cannot bear to be with him, but it is not true that
h she cannot.'

They failed to pay sufficient regard to this finding, or to the evidence of the welfare
officer that the children needed their father, or to the admitted fact that he was a good,
affectionate and loved father.

Notwithstanding, therefore, that I must, regretfully, respectfully but firmly, dissent
from your Lordships on the point of legal principle, I have no doubt that the appeal
j should be allowed. The existing agreed arrangement should, however, continue until
further order. If it is threatened in any way, either spouse can apply to the court to
embody it, or a variation of it, in a formal order.

At the conclusion of his speech my noble and learned friend Lord Brandon makes
certain recommendations as to the future practice and procedure where there are pending
divorce proceedings and the wife has rights under the 1967 Act. It will be obvious that I

do not think the changes which he proposes are either necessary or convenient. Indeed, I think they would obstruct the will of Parliament. If, as is my view, the 1967 Act does not supersede, but does co-exist with the inherent power of the divorce court to protect the wife and children, it would be convenient as well as just and reasonable for the court which has before it the whole family problem arising from the breakdown of the relationship between husband and wife to make whatever order with respect to the matrimonial home is necessary in the family interest.

LORD BRIDGE OF HARWICH. My Lords, I have had the advantage of reading in advance the speech to be delivered by my noble and learned friend Lord Brandon and I entirely agree with it.

For my part, pace my noble and learned friend Lord Scarman, I cannot see how, in proceedings brought by one spouse seeking to evict the other from the matrimonial home (the only proceedings with which this appeal is concerned), there can be any room for the application of the provisions of s 1 of the Guardianship of Minors Act 1971. That section applies only to proceedings in which '(*a*) the legal custody or upbringing of a minor; or (*b*) the administration of any property on trust for a minor, or the application of the income thereof, is in question' and requires the court '*in deciding that question*' (my emphasis) to 'regard the welfare of the minor as the first and paramount consideration.' In 'ouster' proceedings no question as to the custody, upbringing or property of a minor falls to be decided.

I would allow this appeal.

LORD BRANDON OF OAKBROOK. My Lords, this appeal arises in the field of family law and is concerned with what are commonly and not inappropriately described as 'ouster orders'. Such an order takes the form of an injunction granted to one spouse (usually the wife) requiring the other spouse (usually the husband) to vacate the matrimonial home previously occupied by both and not to return to it until further order. An ouster order can be made either in the High Court or in a county court, and its effect on the spouse against whom it is directed will often be extremely serious. This is because such an order involves turning such spouse, usually at very short notice, out of what is in most cases the only home which he or she possesses, and leaving him or her to find, often with great difficulty, alternative accommodation in which to live.

My Lords, I apprehend that it was the potentially serious effect of ouster orders, coupled with a marked divergence of opinion which has arisen between different divisions of the Court of Appeal concerning the principles in accordance with which applications for such orders should be granted or refused, which led the Appeal Committee to give the husband in the present case leave to appeal to your Lordships' House after the Court of Appeal had earlier declined to do so.

My Lords, the essential facts of the present case can be summarised as follows. The husband and the wife were married on 18 November 1974. They have two children, a girl, Melanie, now aged six, and a boy, David, now aged four. Before the wife left the husband in circumstances which I shall describe later the family was, and had been for some time, living in a three-bedroomed council house known as 13 Stoborough Green, Wareham, Dorset.

On 8 January 1982, while the family was still living in that home, the wife presented in the Weymouth County Court a petition for divorce on the ground that the marriage had broken down irretrievably. In support of that case she relied on facts of the kind specified in s 1(2)(*b*) of the Matrimonial Causes Act 1973 namely that the husband had behaved in such a way that she could not reasonably be expected to live with him. The particulars of the husband's behaviour complained of contained no allegation which could be regarded, on paper at any rate, as being at all serious. It was, as it was later described, an extremely thin case.

The service of the petition on the husband shortly after its presentation came as a complete surprise to him. He thought that the marriage was reasonably happy, despite earlier infidelities of the wife which he had forgiven and forgotten, and wished that it should continue. On 8 March 1982 the husband filed an answer to the petition, as a result of which the suit became a defended one and was on that account transferred immediately to the Weymouth District Registry of the High Court. In that answer, subject to certain pleas of confession and avoidance, the husband denied all the wife's allegations about his behaviour, and further denied that the marriage had broken down irretrievably.

Following the service of the petition and answer the wife remained for nearly three months in the matrimonial home. She cooked and performed other wifely duties for the husband, but ceased to share the same bedroom with him. On 1 June 1982 the wife left the matrimonial home, taking the children with her. She did not inform the husband beforehand of her intention to leave, nor did she tell him afterwards where she had gone. She had in fact gone, as the husband later discovered, with the children to a cottage in Swanage belonging to a Mrs Moore, who was a friend of hers. Her intention appears to have been to stay there only temporarily, and then to go to live with the children in a house at Hamworthy belonging to a man called Alan. Although the evidence is not entirely clear, it appears that the wife and children went to Alan's house for a few days in about the middle of July 1982, but that her plan, whatever it was, miscarried, as a result of which she returned with the children to Mrs Moore's cottage in Swanage.

Some three months later, on 15 October 1982, the wife issued in the Weymouth District Registry of the High Court an application headed in the divorce suit for three interlocutory injunctions against the husband: the first restraining him from molesting her; the second restraining him from communicating with her except through her solicitors; and the third requiring him to leave the matrimonial home and not to return to it. The wife's application was heard on 8 November 1982 by his Honour Judge Pennant, sitting as a judge of the High Court. The evidence before him consisted of affidavits and some oral evidence from both spouses, and a court welfare officer's report dated 2 August 1982. At the conclusion of the hearing the judge did not grant either of the first two injunctions sought by the wife, but, in relation to the third injunction sought by her, made an order that the husband should vacate the matrimonial home by 22 November 1982. He did not include in the order a prohibition against the husband returning to the matrimonial home, but no point arises on that omission.

The husband complied with the judge's order and went to live with his elderly father in the latter's two-bedroomed council home in Corfe Castle. Having done so, he lodged notice of appeal to the Court of Appeal against the order. The husband's appeal came before a division of the Court of Appeal consisting of Cumming-Bruce and Dillon LJJ on 6 December 1982 and was dismissed (see [1983] 1 All ER 1017, [1983] 2 WLR 633). As I indicated earlier, the Court of Appeal refused the husband leave to bring a further appeal to your Lordships' House, but such leave was later given to him by the Appeal Committee.

My Lords, Judge Pennant, when he came to give judgment on the wife's application, expressed himself as being in a legal dilemma. He had been referred by counsel for the husband to the decision of one division of the Court of Appeal in *Myers v Myers* [1982] 1 All ER 776, [1982] 1 WLR 247, in which it was held that the judge below had erred in principle in failing to consider whether on the facts before him the wife's conclusion that she was unwilling to return to the matrimonial home while the husband was still there was a reasonable conclusion having regard to the personalities of both the husband and the wife. The judge had also been referred by counsel for the wife to the decision of another division of the Court of Appeal in *Samson v Samson* [1982] 1 All ER 780, [1982] 1 WLR 252, in which it was held that, where there were young children, the first consideration was their welfare, and that the court should not consider whether the wife was justified in leaving and refusing to return to the matrimonial home while the husband was still there or not. The judge, correctly in my view, regarded these two decisions of different divisions of the Court of Appeal as incompatible with each other, and asked himself the difficult question which of them he should follow.

My Lords, so far as the facts of the case are concerned the judge made the following findings: (1) that the practical probability was that the children would continue to live with the wife; (2) that the allegations in the wife's petition relating to the behaviour of the husband were 'rubbishy' and 'very flimsy indeed'; (3) that the elder child, Melanie, did not want her parents to separate; (4) that the wife was living in overcrowded accommodation not fit as a home for the children; (5) that the wife had no reasonable grounds for refusing to return to live in the same house as the husband; and (6) that the wife's assertion that she could not bear to live in the same house as the husband was untrue, the reality being that she was a strong-willed woman who simply did not wish to do so. On these facts he said that he thought that it was thoroughly unjust to turn the husband out, but justice no longer seemed to play any part in this branch of the law. The matrimonial home was a house provided by the public as a home for the four persons concerned, and, that being so, the public interest was best met by installing the children in that home, which meant in practice installing the wife there also. He went on to say that it was by no means certain that there would be a divorce on the existing grounds, and he had come to the conclusion that, although it was unjust to the husband, it seemed right to grant the ouster order sought in the interests of the children. It will be apparent that, in reaching that conclusion, he decided to apply *Samson v Samson* rather than *Myers v Myers*.

My Lords, in his judgment in the Court of Appeal Cumming-Bruce LJ recognised that there was a conflict of authority in that court with regard to the principles on which ouster orders should be granted or refused. According to two authorities, *Elsworth v Elsworth* (1979) 1 FLR 245 and *Myers v Myers*, an ouster order should be refused unless the wife has reasonable grounds for refusing to live in the same house as the husband. According to another authority, *Samson v Samson*, where there are children whose welfare demands that they should be looked after by the wife, the question whether the wife has reasonable grounds for refusing to live in the same house as the husband is irrelevant, the welfare of the children is the first consideration, and the question whether the husband should be ousted or not must be decided by reference to that first consideration. After reviewing a considerable number of authorities in this class of case, the outcome of which necessarily depended on the widely differing facts of each, Cumming-Bruce LJ came to the conclusion that the approach in *Samson v Samson* should be preferred, and that Judge Pennant had been right to apply that decision rather than the conflicting decision in *Myers v Myers*.

Dillon LJ, who also made a careful examination of the authorities, reached the same conclusion as to which should be preferred as Cumming-Bruce LJ. In doing so, he laid stress on the judgment of Geoffrey Lane LJ in *Walker v Walker* [1978] 3 All ER 141 at 143, [1978] 1 WLR 533 at 536. In that case Geoffrey Lane LJ expressed the view that authority was of little value in cases of this kind, and that what the court had to do was to decide what was in all the circumstances of the case fair, just and reasonable, and if it was fair, just and reasonable that the husband should be excluded from the matrimonial home, then that is what must happen. It appears to me, however, that Dillon LJ took that passage from the judgment of Geoffrey Lane LJ in isolation, without regard to the fact that Geoffrey Lane LJ went on to say that, among the circumstances to be regarded, were the behaviour of the husband and the behaviour of the wife. Be that as it may, Dillon LJ was in substantial agreement with Cumming-Bruce LJ that Judge Pennant had applied the right principle to the problem before him, that he had come to the right conclusion, and that the husband's appeal should be dismissed accordingly.

My Lords, I think that it was with growing astonishment, as the citation of the relevant authorities by counsel for the appellant husband proceeded, that your Lordships found that they contained for the most part no reference whatever either to the statutory powers which enable courts to make ouster orders at all, or to the statutory principles which, in most cases arising today, govern the exercise of such powers. It appears to me that, in these circumstances, it falls to your Lordships, in order to determine this appeal and to give guidance for the future, to do what the courts below have signally failed to do, namely to examine, and having examined, to pay proper regard to, the statutory framework within which courts dealing with applications for ouster orders are not only empowered, but also obliged, to operate.

Before 1967 the only power which the High Court had to make an ouster order was the general power to grant injunctions conferred on it by s 45(1) of the Supreme Court of Judicature (Consolidation) Act 1925. That subsection provided, so far as material:

> 'The High Court may grant . . . an injunction . . . by an interlocutory order in all cases in which it appears to the court to be just and convenient.'

The subsection replaced in substantially the same terms s 25(8) of the Supreme Court of Judicature Act 1873, in respect of which it had long been held that, despite the apparently wide words of the subsection, the High Court only had jurisdiction to grant injunctions for the purpose of protecting legal or equitable rights: see *North London Ry Co v Great Northern Ry Co* (1883) 11 QBD 30 at 40 per Cotton LJ. It follows that s 45(1) of the 1925 Act, and s 37(1) of the Supreme Court Act 1981, by which it has now been replaced in substantially the same terms, must be interpreted as subject to the like limitation in their scope.

My Lords, until the radical social changes which have occurred in this country during the last two or three decades, the usual situation with regard to the ownership of a matrimonial home was that the whole estate in it, both legal and equitable, was vested in the husband. It followed from this that most wives could not apply for an ouster order under s 45(1) of the 1925 Act on the ground that they had any legal or equitable interest in the matrimonial home which such an order could protect. However, a wife against whom no disqualifying matrimonial offence had been proved had a common law right to be provided by her husband with a home in which to live, and the High Court regarded itself as having jurisdiction under s 45(1) of the 1925 Act to make an ouster order against a husband in order to protect that right pending suit: see *Silverstone v Silverstone* [1953] 1 All ER 556, [1953] P 174; *Gurasz v Gurasz* [1969] 3 All ER 822, [1970] P 11.

Parliament, however, did not regard this limited right of protection under s 45(1) of the 1925 Act as adequate, as a result of which it passed the Matrimonial Homes Act 1967. Section 1 of the 1967 Act provided, so far as material:

> '(1) Where one spouse is entitled to occupy a dwelling house by virtue of any estate or interest or contract or by virtue of any enactment giving him or her the right to remain in occupation, and the other spouse is not so entitled, then, subject to the provisions of this Act, the spouse not so entitled shall have the following rights (in this Act referred to as "rights of occupation");—(*a*) if in occupation, a right not to be evicted or excluded from the dwelling house or any part thereof by the other spouse except with the leave of the court given by an order under this section; (*b*) if not in occupation, a right with the leave of the court so given to enter into and occupy the dwelling house.
>
> (2) So long as one spouse has rights of occupation, either of the spouses may apply to the court for an order declaring, enforcing, restricting or terminating those rights or regulating the exercise by either spouse of the right to occupy the dwelling house.
>
> (3) On an application for an order under this section the court may make such order as it thinks just and reasonable having regard to the conduct of the spouses in relation to each other and otherwise, to their respective needs and financial resources, to the needs of any children and to all the circumstances of the case . . .
>
> (4) Orders under this section may, in so far as they have a continuing effect, be limited so as to have effect for a period specified in the order or until further order . . .
>
> (6) The jurisdiction conferred on the court by this section shall be exercisable by the High Court or by a county court . . .
>
> (8) . . . a spouse's rights of occupation shall continue only so long as the marriage subsists and the other spouse is entitled as mentioned in subsection (1) above to occupy the dwelling house . . .'

My Lords, experience of the working of the 1967 Act revealed a serious weakness in it. That weakness was that, by reason of the terms of s 1(1), the Act afforded no protection to wives who had an equitable interest in the matrimonial home, as many either had, or at any rate wished to reserve their right to claim that they had. In order to remedy this weakness in the 1967 Act, it was provided by s 38 of the Matrimonial Proceedings and Property Act 1970 that there should be inserted in s 1 of the 1967 Act a new sub-s (9) in these terms:

> '(9) It is hereby declared that a spouse who has an equitable interest in a dwelling house or in the proceeds of sale thereof, not being a person in whom is vested (whether solely or as a joint tenant) a legal estate in fee simple or a legal term of years absolute, is to be treated for the purpose only of determining whether he or she has rights of occupation under this section as not being entitled to occupy the dwelling house by virtue of that interest.'

In 1976 the legislature enacted the Domestic Violence and Matrimonial Proceedings Act of that year in order to deal with the problem of those persons who are commonly called 'battered wives'. Section 1 of the 1976 Act conferred on county courts, without prejudice to the jurisdiction of the High Court, power to grant, on the application of one party to a marriage, injunctions containing one or more of the following provisions: (a) a provision restraining the other party to the marriage from molesting the applicant; (b) a provision restraining the other party from molesting a child living with the applicant; (c) a provision excluding the other party from the matrimonial home or part of the matrimonial home or from a specified area in which the matrimonial home is included; (d) a provision requiring the other party to permit the applicant to enter and remain in the matrimonial home or a part of the matrimonial home.

Section 2 of the 1976 Act empowered judges, when granting certain kinds of injunctions designed to protect one party to a marriage, or a child living with that party, from violence by the other party to the marriage, in certain specified circumstances to attach a power of arrest to such injunctions.

Sections 3 and 4 of the 1976 Act provided:

> '**3.** In section 1(2) of the Matrimonial Homes Act 1967 (which provides for applications for orders of the court declaring, enforcing, restricting or terminating rights of occupation under the Act or regulating the exercise by either spouse of the right to occupy the dwelling house),—(*a*) for the word "regulating" there shall be substituted the words "prohibiting, suspending or restricting"; and (*b*) at the end of the subsection there shall be added the words "or requiring either spouse to permit the exercise by the other of that right."
>
> '**4.**—(1) Where each of two spouses is entitled, by virtue of a legal estate vested in them jointly, to occupy a dwelling-house in which they have or at any time have had a matrimonial home, either of them may apply to the court, with respect to the exercise during the subsistence of the marriage of the right to occupy the dwelling-house, for an order prohibiting, suspending or restricting its exercise by the other or requiring the other to permit its exercise by the applicant.
>
> (2) In relation to orders under this section, section 1(3), (4) and (6) of the Matrimonial Homes Act 1967 (which relate to the considerations relevant to and the contents of, and to the jurisdiction to make, orders under that section) shall apply as they apply in relation to orders under that section; and in this section "dwelling-house" has the same meaning as in that Act.
>
> (3) Where each of two spouses is entitled to occupy a dwelling-house by virtue of a contract, or by virtue of any enactment giving them the right to remain in occupation, this section shall apply as it applies where they are entitled by virtue of a legal estate vested in them jointly.'

The provision in s 3(a) was enacted in order to reverse the effect of the decision of your Lordships' House in *Tarr v Tarr* [1972] 2 All ER 295, [1973] AC 254, in which it had

been held that the expression 'regulating', as used in s 1(2) of the 1967 Act in its original
a form, was not wide enough to include total prohibition or exclusion. Section 4 extended further the process begun by s 38 of the 1970 Act.

A further amendment to s 1 of the 1967 Act was made by s 1(1) of the Matrimonial Homes and Property Act 1981 (as from 14 February 1983), the effect of which was to substitute for the words 'any estate or interest' in s 1(1) of the 1967 Act the words 'a beneficial estate or interest'. This amendment was made to cover the case of matrimonial
b homes held by trustees.

My Lords, the 1967 Act contained in its original form, and still contains in a form extensively amended by subsequent Acts, various provisions relating to the registration as a charge on a matrimonial home of the rights of occupation conferred by it, to the situation arising when a matrimonial home is let on a tenancy to which the Rent Acts apply or on a tenancy made a secure tenancy by the Housing Act 1980, and to
c matrimonial homes subject to mortgages. Save that the matrimonial home in the present case was let to the husband on a tenancy made a secure tenancy by the Housing Act 1980 (a circumstance which is not material to the appeal), none of the matters to which I have just referred arise in the present case, and I shall therefore make no further reference to them.

My Lords, I indicated earlier my view that, in order to determine this appeal and to
d give guidance for the future, it was necessary for your Lordships to examine, and having examined to pay regard to, the statutory framework within which courts to which applications for ouster orders are made are not only empowered, but also obliged, to operate.

Having performed the first part of that task by setting out, or referring to, what appear to me to be the essential statutory provisions applicable, I conclude that it was the
e intention of the legislature, in passing and later amending and extending the scope of the 1967 Act, and in passing the 1976 Act, that the power of the High Court to make, during the subsistence of a marriage, orders relating to the occupation of a matrimonial home, including in particular an ouster order, which had previously been derived from s 45(1) of the 1925 Act, should for the future be derived from, and exercised in accordance with, s 1 of the 1967 Act. In this connection it is to be observed that, in s 1(1) of the 1967 Act
f as originally enacted, it was expressly provided that, where one of the spouses was entitled to occupy the matrimonial home by virtue of any estate, interest or contract, and the other spouse was not so entitled, the latter should have rights of occupation, including a right 'not to be evicted or excluded . . . *except with the leave of the court given by an order under this section*' (my emphasis). If spouse A can only oust spouse B pursuant to an order made under s 1 of the 1967 Act, it must surely follow that spouse B can only oust spouse
g A pursuant to a like order.

I reach a similar conclusion with regard to ouster orders made in a county court, namely that it was the intention of the legislature that the power of a county court to make ouster orders, which had been previously derived from the very general provisions of s 74 of the County Courts Act 1959, should for the future be derived from, and exercised in accordance with, the provisions of the 1967 Act. County courts were given
h an additional power to make ouster orders by s 1 of the 1976 Act, but it seems to me to be a necessary inference that the legislature intended such additional power to be exercised in accordance with the principles laid down in the 1967 Act.

The result of the conclusion which I have reached on these matters, when applied to the facts of the present case, is that the application issued by the wife in the Weymouth District Registry on 15 October 1982, in so far as it sought an ouster order against the
j husband, was in substance, though not in form (a matter to which I shall return later), an application for an order under s 1 of the 1967 Act. The case was one in which, because the requirements of s 1(1) of the 1967 Act as amended were fulfilled, the wife had the rights of occupation given by that subsection, and was therefore entitled to apply to the court for whatever order might be appropriate under s 1(2) and (3).

On the footing that the wife's application was one made under the 1967 Act, the court

to which it was made was obliged to follow the principles relating to such applications
prescribed by that Act. Those principles are contained in s 1(3), the essential parts of a
which I set out earlier. That subsection requires the court to make such order as it thinks
just and reasonable having regard to a number of specified matters. The matters so
specified are these: (1) the conduct of the spouses to each other and otherwise; (2) the
respective needs and financial resources of the spouses; (3) the needs of any children; and
(4) all the circumstances of the case. With regard to these matters it is, in my opinion, of
the utmost importance to appreciate that none of them is made, by the wording of s 1(3), b
necessarily of more weight than any of the others, let alone made paramount over them.
All the four matters specified are to be regarded, and the weight to be given to any
particular one of them must depend on the facts of each case.

My Lords, *Samson v Samson*, which Judge Pennant felt that he should apply in the
present case, proceeds on the basis that it is not relevant, on an application for an ouster
order, to consider whether the applicant wife has reasonable grounds for refusing to c
return to the matrimonial home while the husband remains in it or not. To treat that
matter as irrelevant appears to me to be in direct conflict with the principles laid down
in s 1(3) of the 1967 Act. That subsection, as I have already said, obliges the court to make
such order as it thinks just and reasonable having regard to a number of specified matters;
and the first matter so specified is the conduct of the spouses in relation to each other and
otherwise. The conduct of a wife, who has no reasonable grounds for refusing to return d
to the matrimonial home so long as her husband remains in it but nevertheless asserts
that she will not do so, is clearly 'conduct of the spouses in relation to each other and
otherwise' within the meaning of that expression as used in s 1(3) of the 1967 Act. It
follows that the court, when adjudicating on a wife's application for an order under s 1
of that Act, must have regard to her conduct in this respect, and is not entitled to treat it
as irrelevant to the decision which has to be made. e

My Lords, I do not go so far as to say that the conduct of an applicant wife in the
particular respect under discussion is necessarily and in all cases decisive, in a manner
adverse to her, of the question whether the order for which she has applied should be
made or not. It is, however, an important factor to be weighed in the scales, along with
the other matters specified in s 1(3) of the 1967 Act; and in a substantial number of cases
at any rate it will be a factor of such weight as to lead a court to think that it would not f
be just or reasonable to allow her application. I regard the two cases of *Elsworth v Elsworth*
(1979) 1 FLR 245 and *Myers v Myers* [1982] 1 All ER 776, [1982] 1 WLR 247 as cases
which come into that category. In saying that, I do not overlook the fact that these two
cases were appeals from decisions of county courts relating to applications made otherwise
than under the 1967 Act. In *Elsworth v Elsworth* it appears that the application was made
(erroneously in my view) under the general jurisdiction conferred by s 74 of the County g
Courts Act 1959 to which I referred earlier, while the application in *Myers v Myers* was
clearly made under the 1976 Act. As I have already indicated, however, it was, in my
view, the intention of the legislature that the same principles should govern the making
of ouster orders under the 1976 Act as under the 1967 Act.

The approach adopted in *Samson v Samson* [1982] 1 All ER 780, [1982] 1 WLR 252
comes very near to treating the needs of any relevant children, not just as one of a h
number of matters to which s 1(3) of the 1967 Act requires the court to have regard, but
as a paramount matter overriding all others. That approach would certainly be justified
in a case to which s 1 of the Guardianship of Minors Act 1971 applied, including in
particular a case in which the custody or upbringing of a child was in question. In my
opinion, however, s 1 of the 1971 Act, which re-enacted in like terms s 1 of the
Guardianship of Infants Act 1925, only applies where the custody or upbringing of a j
child is directly in question, and does not apply to a case where such matters are not
directly in question but only arise incidentally in relation to other matters which are
directly in question. In this connection it is to be observed that s 1 of the Guardianship
of Infants Act 1925 was in force when s 1, including in particular sub-s (3) of that section,
was enacted, and the only inference which can, in my view, be drawn is that, in relation

to ouster orders, s 1(3) of the 1967 Act, making the needs of any children only one of a number of factors to be considered, was intended to exclude the paramount status which such needs would have had if s 1 of the 1925 Act were treated as applicable.

My Lords, in the present case Judge Pennant, by applying *Samson v Samson* rather than *Myers v Myers*, failed to have regard to one of the matters which s 1(3) of the 1967 Act required him to have regard to, namely the conduct of the wife in refusing to return to the matrimonial home when there were, as he had found on the evidence before him, no reasonable grounds for such refusal. The Court of Appeal, in affirming his decision, were guilty of the same omission. Both courts having failed, in exercising their discretionary powers under s 1 of the 1967 Act, to have regard to the reasonableness or unreasonableness of the wife's conduct as s 1(3) required them to do, it seems to me that your Lordships have no alternative but to set aside both the ouster order made by the judge on 8 November 1982 and the order of the Court of Appeal affirming that order made on 6 December 1982.

Your Lordships were informed by counsel that, since the order of the Court of Appeal, the two spouses have made an amicable arrangement between them under which the wife occupies the matrimonial home and looks after the children in it from Monday morning to Friday evening, when she leaves and goes to another place which was not disclosed, and the husband then occupies the matrimonial home and looks after the children in it from Friday evening to Monday morning. Your Lordships were further informed that this arrangement have been working well and in a manner satisfactory to both spouses.

My Lords, it does not necessarily follow, if your Lordships' House decides this appeal in the way that I have indicated that I think it ought to be decided, that the arrangement between the spouses to which I have just referred should be disturbed so long as the divorce suit remains pending. An expedited hearing of that suit is clearly required, and it may well be that it would be sensible if no further alterations in the situation with regard to occupation of the matrimonial home were made until that hearing has taken place. Your Lordships would not, however, be justified in compelling the husband, against his wishes, to accept a continuation of the present arrangement.

My Lords, I recognise that your Lordships' House does not, as a general rule, concern itself with questions of practice and procedure, on the ground that such matters are best left for regulation by the Court of Appeal. In the present case, however, it seems to me that there is a good reason why your Lordships should depart from the general rule to which I have referred, and deal with certain questions of practice and procedure relating to applications for orders under s 1 of the 1967 Act. That reason is that, in my opinion, if what I regard as the proper practice and procedure in relation to such applications had been followed in the past, it is unlikely that the courts would over a long period have dealt with applications for ouster orders without any reference to the statutory provisions applicable to them, and in particular the all-important provisions contained in s 1(3) of the 1967 Act.

The practice has grown up, when an application for an ouster order is made during the pendency of a suit, to make it by issuing a summons in that suit. It has further become the practice to ask in such summons for an order requiring the husband to vacate the matrimonial home and not to return to it. These practices may well have the advantage of convenience, but the first seems to me to be in conflict with the relevant rules of court, and the second with the terms of the 1967 Act as amended.

So far as the first practice to which I have referred is concerned, r 107(1) of the Matrimonial Causes Rules 1977, SI 1977/344 provides:

> 'The jurisdiction of the High Court under section 1 of the Matrimonial Homes Act 1967 may be exercised in chambers and the provisions of rule 104 (except paragraph (2)) shall apply, with the necessary modifications, to proceedings under that section as they apply to an application under section 17 of the Act of 1882.'

The reference to the 1882 Act is a reference to the Married Women's Property Act of that year, and r 104, which falls to be incorporated, with the necessary modifications, into r 107, provides in para (1): 'An application to the High Court under section 17 of the Act of 1882 shall be made by originating summons in Form 23 . . .' Form 23, which is to be found in App 1 to the Matrimonial Causes Rules 1977, when used for an application under s 1 of the 1967 Act, carries the following heading: 'In the matter of an application by . . . under section 1 of the Matrimonial Homes Act 1967.'

It follows, in my view that the correct way, and the only correct way, of initiating an application for an order under s 1 of the 1967 Act, whether there is a suit pending or not, is by the issue of an originating summons in Form 23 with the heading which I have just set out. There is no other rule of court which, where a suit is pending, authorises such an application to be made by a summons in that suit. The situation in the county court is similar to that in the High Court: see CCR 1981, Ord 47, rr 4 and 2.

So far as the second practice to which I have referred is concerned, the form of order which should be asked for in an application under s 1 of the 1967 Act should, in my view, be a form which follows, so far as is reasonably practicable, the wording of that section as amended. For instance, if what I have so far described as an ouster order is sought, the form of order applied for should be an order (1) declaring the applicant's rights of occupation of the matrimonial home, and (2) prohibiting the respondent from exercising any right to occupy such home from a specified date and time until further order. In the event of the application then being successful, the order made by the court should, again so far as is reasonably practicable, be in the like form.

That concludes the observations with regard to practice and procedure which it seemed to me appropriate to make in relation to cases of this kind. It only remains for me to say that, for the reasons which I gave earlier, I would allow the appeal and set aside both the order of Judge Pennant dated 8 November 1982 and the order of the Court of Appeal dated 6 December 1982.

Appeal allowed.

Solicitors: *Sharpe Pritchard & Co*, agents for *Edmund Buck & Co*, Swanage (for the husband); *Iliffes*, agents for *Neville-Jones & Howie*, Wareham (for the wife).

Mary Rose Plummer Barrister.

a Dove v Banhams Patent Locks Ltd

QUEEN'S BENCH DIVISION
HODGSON J
10, 11, 14 FEBRUARY, 4 MARCH 1983

Limitation of action – When time begins to run – Actions in tort – Accrual of cause of action –
b *Negligence – Damage – Lapse of time between negligent act and occurrence of damage – Action against burglary prevention specialist for negligent installation of security door – Burglar forcing security door to gain entry – Writ issued more than six years after negligent work completed but less than six years after burglary – Whether limitation period running from date of completion or from date of burglary.*

c In 1967 the defendants, who were burglary prevention specialists, were instructed by the then owners to carry out security work on a property which the plaintiff purchased in 1976. The work included the fitting of a security gate to a basement door. The top of the gate was not affixed directly to the door frame but instead was screwed into a wooden batten which was in turn nailed to the frame. That made the gate less secure and in May 1979 the property was burgled after the burglar gained entry to the house by the
d basement door after forcing the top of the gate. The plaintiff brought an action for damages in negligence against the defendants for the value of the property stolen. The defendants denied that they had been negligent and contended that, in any event, the cause of action arose when the work was carried out and that therefore the proceedings were outside the limitation period.

e **Held** – (1) On the facts, the defendants had been in breach of the duty of care owed to the plaintiff, as subsequent purchaser of the property, when they carried out the installation of the security gate (see p 837 *e*, post).

(2) Furthermore, the action was not time-barred since the cause of action had not arisen at the time the faulty work was completed but when the fault had first manifested itself, ie, when the gate gave way after the burglar applied force to it. Accordingly the
f plaintiff was entitled to judgment and damages for the economic loss consequent on the defective workmanship (see p 840 *a* to *d* and *f*, post); *Cartledge v E Jopling & Sons Ltd* [1963] 1 All ER 341, *Junior Books Ltd v Veitchi Co Ltd* [1982] 3 All ER 201 and *Pirelli General Cable Works Ltd v Oscar Faber & Partners (a firm)* [1983] 1 All ER 65 applied; *Forster v Outred & Co (a firm)* [1982] 2 All ER 753 doubted.

g **Notes**

For limitation periods for actions in tort generally, see 28 Halsbury's Laws (4th edn) paras 679–690 and for cases on the subject, see 32 Digest (Reissue) 503–508, *3842–3869*.

Cases referred to in judgment

Cartledge v E Jopling & Sons Ltd [1963] 1 All ER 341, [1963] AC 758, [1963] 2 WLR 210,
h HL.

Dennis v Charnwood BC [1982] 3 All ER 486, [1982] 3 WLR 1064, CA.

Dutton v Bognor Regis United Building Co Ltd [1972] 1 All ER 462, [1972] 1 QB 373, [1972] 2 WLR 299, CA.

Forster v Outred & Co (a firm) [1982] 2 All ER 753, [1982] 1 WLR 86, CA.

Howell v Young (1826) 5 B & C 259, [1824–34] All ER Rep 377, 108 ER 97.

j *Junior Books Ltd v Veitchi Co Ltd* [1982] 3 All ER 201, [1982] 3 WLR 477, HL.

Miliangos v George Frank (Textiles) Ltd [1975] 3 All ER 801, [1976] AC 443, [1975] 3 WLR 758, HL.

Pirelli General Cable Works Ltd v Oscar Faber & Partners (a firm) [1983] 1 All ER 65, [1983] 2 WLR 6, HL.

Sparham-Souter v Town and Country Developments (Essex) Ltd [1976] 2 All ER 65, [1976] QB 858, [1976] 2 WLR 493, CA. a

Action

By a writ dated 4 August 1980 the plaintiff, Anthony Dove, claimed against the defendants, Banhams Patent Locks Ltd, damages in negligence for the loss suffered by the plaintiff when a burglar gained access to the plaintiff's home at 28 Warwick Square, London, by forcing a security gate which had been negligently installed by the defendants b on the instructions of the previous owner of the property. The facts are set out in the judgment.

John Moxom for the plaintiff.
Adrian Whitfield for the defendants.

c

Cur adv vult

4 March. The following judgment was delivered.

HODGSON J. Number 28 Warwick Square is a pleasant terraced house in fashionable Chelsea. It is tall and narrow and consists of four floors and a basement. There is an d entrance to the basement from the street by means of steps down into an area. From the area one gets into the basement by passing through an outer door into a small enclosed lobby or cubby hole from which a second door leads, via a narrow passage, into the basement.

In 1967 the house belonged to a Mr and Mrs Burton. They consulted the defendants, who are well-established burglary prevention specialists, to advise them on the protection e of the house. The basement approach was an obvious danger spot. The defendants advised that they should have steel sheeting bolted to the outer door and locking bars across to brace the whole door. However, Mrs Burton wanted to be able to leave the outer door open during the day so that tradesmen could leave their goods under cover in the lobby. The defendants, therefore, advised that there should be a security gate fitted to the inner door and that the outer door's defences should be restricted to two rack bolts. f The inner door, therefore, became the main line of defence. If a burglar could reach the inner door (and the outer door defences were, as I have said, limited) he would be able to get to work out of sight of anyone in the street. The defendants also installed two safes, one quite large, one quite small, as well as providing protection of one sort or another for the rest of the house.

In February 1976 the plaintiff, Mr Dove, purchased the house and, after a good deal of g renovation, it became the home of himself and his wife and their two children. Before taking up occupation of the house Mr Dove consulted the defendants and the security in the house was updated, but the defendants were not asked to, nor did they do anything in respect of the basement.

The layout of the house after the Dove family moved in was this. On the top floor the two children slept in a bedroom facing the square, and the nanny slept in the back h bedroom, which she used as her sitting room. On the third floor there was a master bedroom and bathroom for Mr and Mrs Dove. On the second floor there was a large drawing room and on the ground floor a kitchen and dining room. The basement was converted into a guest suite. There was a door at the top of the stairs down to the basement from the first floor.

Miss Morgans was, I think, the first nanny. By May 1979 she had left but still returned j from time to time to look after the children when Mr and Mrs Dove were away. On these occasions she slept in the back bedroom on the top floor. On the landing outside her bedroom there was a telephone.

Mr Dove owned some valuable silver, in particular a large silver gilt rosebowl, two candlesticks and two candelabra which had been presented to his grandfather.

On the weekend of 5 to 7 May 1979 Mr and Mrs Dove went to Paris. There was no
a room in the safe for the rosebowl and two candlesticks. They were left on the dining room table.

Before she left, as was her invariable practice, Mrs Dove went round the house checking that all the bolts on the windows and doors were locked before she left. The keys for the bolts were kept in her bedroom. I am satisfied she checked the rack bolts in the basement door. It is said against her that, as the door was never used, it would have been illogical
b for her to check it, but I am satisfied that it was part of her routine drill. The point taken against her is a valid one, but it was clear to me that, when it was put to her in the witness box, the illogicality of what she did had never entered her head.

On the evening of 6 May the children were asleep. Like most children they would sleep through anything. It was between 10 and 10.30 pm. Miss Morgans decided to telephone her mother. This she did from the landing outside her bedroom door. She
c probably did not put the light on on the landing but used the light from the door to her own bedroom. After making her phone call she went back to continue watching television. Shortly afterwards she remembered that there was something she had forgotten to ask her mother. Her first phone call was after 10 o'clock, her second before 10.30. She would not have phoned her mother after 10.30 as she knew her mother would by then have gone to bed. She again went to the telephone. The line was dead.

d I suppose many people would have thought no more than that something had gone wrong with the phone as, from time to time, we know it does, but Miss Morgans is made of sterner and more intelligent stuff. No doubt after considering the matter for a moment or two, she decided that the line might have been cut by rogues. She therefore turned the lights on and advanced to the third floor, singing in a loud voice 'Onward Christian Soldiers'; arrived at the third floor, she again made as much noise as she could, continued
e her singing and turned the lights on, looking into the master bedroom. She repeated this performance on the second floor and also on the ground floor. She looked in the dining room. The rosebowl and candlesticks were not on the table but, so far as she was concerned, there was no reason why they should have been. It was not a room into which she went. She merely registered the fact that there was nothing on the table. She did not venture further, she had never been in the basement, and she decided it was probably a
f defect in the telephone after all. She went to bed.

The Doves returned on the Monday. Mrs Dove at once noticed that the rosebowl and candlesticks were missing. Investigation showed that the outer and inner doors in the basement had been broken. It also became clear that the burglar or burglars had penetrated as far as the drawing room where some pieces of silver on a desk had been handled and, as well as taking the rosebowl and candlesticks from the dining room, they
g had penetrated the kitchen where the children's boxed silver had also been handled.

The telephone wire had been cut at a point in the lobby above the inner door. It seems to me a clear inference that that was done before operations were begun on the security gate. If that be so it follows that the attack on the security gate began and was completed and the house penetrated to the first floor at least in the short interval between Miss Morgans's two telephone calls. It also seems clear that the intruders were frightened off
h by Miss Morgans's loud and gallant singing. No one will ever know whether there was one or more burglars involved. For the purposes of this case it matters not. My own feeling is that it was one skilled professional thief. But for a burglar, however skilful, to break down a security gate such as this in about ten minutes would, I think, cause anyone at least to question its efficiency.

The outer door had presented no problem. A window in the door frame had been
j broken, an arm inserted, the rack bolts undone and the door forced open. My guess is that the burglar had already 'cased' the outer door and had discovered, by pressing against it, what the situation was.

The security gate as installed by the defendants is shown after it had been forced in the photographs in the two bundles. There are also exhibited the door stop, which was situated at the top of the door and secured to the frame by three cut nails, and the top runner of the gate, which was secured to the bottom of the door stop by three screws. two of these were inserted through the 'top hat'; they were clutch head screws. The distance through the top hat of the runner is one inch, the door stop is half an inch thick, so these screws only penetrated about half an inch into the door frame itself. The third screw did not have to go through the top hat so that it penetrated into the main door frame some one and a half inches. That was at the right-hand side of the door as it faced the intruder; it was at that side that the door was hinged at the top, middle and bottom.

The door stop was a thin length of wood at the top. It was not an integral part of the frame but, as I have said, was merely nailed to the frame with three nails.

I have heard a great deal of evidence as to the precise method used by the intruder to obtain entry. The witnesses have sought to draw inferences from the marks and signs of damage which clearly appear on the photographs. Two things are, I think, clear. First, the overall extent of the damage, considering that entry was made, is really very slight. Second, the top door stop broke in two at a fairly early stage of the onslaught and this greatly facilitated the burglar's task.

I think it is also clear that the first attack was made at the padlock side (the burglar's left) and that, when that proved impregnable, the top of the gate became the focus of attention. I do not think that the damage to that middle hinge or the pulling away of the metal at the left-hand bottom corner (from the burglar's side) was done until the top of the gate was freed by the door stop coming away from the frame. Whether the attack on the door was launched from the front, as is Mr Webber's theory (Mr Webber being an expert called by the defendants), or from the back, as Mr Dodd (the security expert called by the plaintiff) thinks, I cannot be sure. The obvious way would seem to me to be from the front; perhaps both ways were tried. What I think is clear is that the burglar's task was very much easier than it would have been had the gate been screwed direct onto the frame itself. If that had been the problem facing the burglar, I agree with Mr Dodd that it would have taken him a great deal longer and would have made a great deal more noise than it did even if he had eventually succeeded. Mr Dodd doubts whether he would have succeeded. In any event, before he succeeded, he would have been made aware, by the hymn-singing Miss Morgans, that the house was occupied and being, I think, a professional he would then, in all probability, have gone away.

The plaintiff alleges that the defendants were negligent in fixing the gate on top of the door stop. He contends that the proper way to fix this gate in that doorway was to have removed the doorstops and to have screwed the top runner to the frame itself. The whole gate would then have been supported from the door frame.

The defendants deny that they were in breach of their duty. They contended but do so no longer that the plaintiff's wife was negligent in failing to put the silver gilt away in the safe and that she failed to secure the rack bolts on the outer door. I have already held that she did not so fail. By an amendment, for which I gave leave, they now say in addition that the cause of action, if any, against the defendants arose in 1967 when the work commissioned by Mr Burton was completed and that, accordingly, any rights against the defendants are statute-barred. The plaintiff, in an amended reply, relies on s 26 of the Limitation Act 1939 and s 32 of the Limitation Act 1980, as well, of course, as denying that the claim is in any event statute-barred.

It is agreed that the defendants owed a duty of care to the plaintiff but that that duty of care is no greater than the duty owed by the defendants to Mr Burton (the previous owner).

The defendants contend, first, that the gate was just as securely fixed through the door stop as it would have been had it been fixed to the frame itself. That I do not accept. I am quite satisfied that the gate would have been very, very much more secure had its top runner been screwed directly to the frame.

The second way in which the defendants put their case is this. They say that in 1967 it was the general and approved practice to fix security gates to door stops and not to the frame itself. The evidence for this contention comes from the concession made by Mr Dodd that he had seen on occasions gates installed on top of door stops by reputable

firms, although that was a practice of which he strongly disapproved, the evidence of Mr
a Webber, called by the defendants as an expert but as such not impressive though no
doubt an excellent practical man, and the evidence of Mr Bailey, a security consultant
employed by the defendants. He said that many of the defendants' competitors fitted to
stops and that the defendants always did.

Against that there is the evidence of Mr Dodd that at least one of the defendants'
competitors has never followed this practice and that it is in any event a wrong practice
b and has been recognised as such since before 1967.

I do not think that the evidence adduced by the defendants establishes, on a balance of
probabilities, that the practice was, in 1967, generally approved. Had it been, I would
have expected far more cogent evidence than I have had placed before me. I have, indeed,
some doubt whether in fact it is the practice always followed by the defendants. Mr
Bailey went so far as to say this: 'The [defendant] company has said that we must not
c remove door stops. These instructions have been written in the past. It is part of the
training of our fitters.' No written instructions were, however, forthcoming. And I think
it extremely doubtful whether any such instructions were ever given. For consider this:
as I understand it a door stop is fitted to the frame of a door so that the door can fit the
aperture and thus there is no fixed size for a door stop. The one in question was half an
inch thick and, as a result, two of the screws penetrated the frame but half an inch. Had
d the door stop been one inch thick, only one screw at the hinge side would have penetrated
the frame at all and for the rest the gate would have been secured to the frame by but
three nails. No one in their right minds would so fit a gate. In addition, had the
instructions been as Mr Bailey says they were, I should have expected evidence from
someone in authority to tell me so.

In the mean time, accepting as I do the evidence of Mr Dodd in all respects save one
e (to which I shall refer later) that the defendants were in breach of the duty of care which
they owed to Mr Burton and, when he purchased the house, Mr Dove, it follows that,
subject to the limitation defence, the plaintiff is entitled to succeed.

I turn now to that defence. By their amended defence the defendants say that the cause
of action against the defendants arose when Mr Burton was, on completion of the work,
exposed to liability for economic loss in remedying the same. If that is right then Mr
f Dove's action is, it is accepted, statute-barred.

The leading case in this field of the law is undoubtedly now *Pirelli General Cable Works
Ltd v Oscar Faber & Partners (a firm)* [1983] 1 All ER 65, [1983] 2 WLR 6. In that case a
chimney was built in the summer of 1969. Unsuitable material was used. Not later than
April 1970 cracks developed at the top of the chimney. The plaintiffs discovered the
damage in November 1977. With reasonable diligence they could not have discovered it
g before October 1972. In October 1978 the plaintiffs issued their writ claiming damages
for negligent design. I will read from the headnote ([1983] 2 WLR 6):

> '*Held*, allowing the appeal, that the date of accrual of a cause of action in tort for
> damage caused by the negligent design or construction of a building was the date
> when the damage came into existence, and not the date when the damage was
> *h* discovered or should with reasonable diligence have been discovered; that the
> plaintiffs' cause of action therefore accrued not later than April 1970, when the
> cracks occurred in the chimney, and that since that date was more than six years
> before the issue of the writ, the claim was statute barred.'

The issue in the case is clearly stated in Lord Fraser's speech ([1983] 1 All ER 65 at 67,
j [1983] 2 WLR 6 at 8):

> 'All the judge's findings of fact are now accepted by both parties and the sole issue
> between them is on the question of law as to the date at which a cause of action
> accrued. The plaintiffs maintain that the judge came to the right conclusion on that
> matter and that the action is not time-barred. The defendants maintain that the
> cause of action accrued more than six years before the writ was issued. They suggest

three possible dates as the date of accrual. The earliest suggested date is that on which the plaintiffs acted in reliance on the defendants' advice to instal the chimney, which was bound to be defective and eventually to fall down unless previously demolished. They did not fix this date precisely but it must have been between March and June 1969, well outside the limitation period. The second suggested date is that on which the building of the chimney was completed, namely July 1969. The third is that on which cracks occurred, namely April 1970. These three dates are all more than six years before the issue of the writ, which as already mentioned, was 17 October 1978. If any of them is the correct date, the action is time-barred.'

Lord Fraser then considered in detail the decision of the Court of Appeal in *Sparham-Souter v Town and Country Developments (Essex) Ltd* [1976] 2 All ER 65, [1976] QB 858, wherein it had been held that a plaintiff only suffers damage when he discovers, or ought with reasonable diligence to have discovered, damage to the building. Having, in particular, considered the decision of the House of Lords in *Cartledge v E Jopling & Sons Ltd* [1963] 1 All ER 341, [1963] AC 758 he said this of the decision in the *Sparham-Souter* case ([1983] 1 All ER 65 at 69–70, [1983] 2 WLR 6 at 11–12):

'But in *Sparham-Souter* the Court of Appeal took a different view and said that, where a house is built with inadequate foundations, the cause of action does not accrue until such time as the plaintiff discovers that the bad work has done damage, or ought, with reasonable diligence to have discovered it. Lord Denning MR expressly recanted his dictum in [*Dutton v Bognor Regis United Building Co Ltd* [1972] 1 All ER 462, [1972] 1 QB 373]. The limitation question was tried as a preliminary issue, on which the facts as pleaded had to be assumed to be true. The latest act of negligence pleaded was less than six years before the issue of the writ, so that, once again, the observations as to the date on which the cause of action accrued were, strictly speaking, obiter. The main reason for the view of the Court of Appeal was that, until the owner had discovered the defective state of the property, he could resell it at a full price, and, if he did so, he would suffer no damage (see [1976] 2 All ER 65 at 76, 79–80, [1976] QB 858 at 875, 880 per Roskill and Geoffrey Lane LJJ). Geoffrey Lane LJ contrasted the position of the building owner in *Sparham-Souter* with that of the injured person in *Cartledge v Jopling* and said: "There is no proper analogy between this situation [sc the situation in *Sparham-Souter*] and the type of situation exemplified in *Cartledge v E Jopling & Sons Ltd* where a plaintiff due to the negligence of the defendants suffers physical bodily injury which at the outset and for many years thereafter may be clinically unobservable. In those circumstances clearly damage is done to the plaintiff and the cause of action accrues from the moment of the first injury, albeit undetected and undetectable. That is not so where the negligence has caused unobservable damage not to the plaintiff's body but to his house. He can get rid of his house before any damage is suffered. Not so with his body." My Lords, I find myself with the utmost respect unable to agree with that argument. It seems to me that there is a true analogy between a plaintiff whose body has, unknown to him, suffered injury by inhaling particles of dust, and a plaintiff whose house has unknown to him sustained injury because it was built with inadequate foundations or of unsuitable materials. Just as the owner of the house may sell the house before the damage is discovered, and may suffer no financial loss, so the man with the injured body may die before pneumoconiosis becomes apparent, and he also may suffer no financial loss. But in both cases they have a damaged article when, but for the defendant's negligence, they would have had a sound one. Lord Pearce in *Cartledge v Jopling* [1963] 1 All ER 341 at 349, [1963] AC 758 at 778–779 showed how absurd it would be to hold that the plaintiff's knowledge of the state of his lungs could be the decisive factor. He said: "It would be impossible to hold that while the x-ray photographs are being taken he cannot yet have suffered any damage to his body but that immediately the result of them is told to him, he has from that moment suffered damage. It is for the judge or jury to decide when a man has suffered any actionable harm and in borderline cases it is a question of degree." It seems to me that exactly the same can rightly be said of damage to property. I think, with all respect to Geoffrey Lane LJ, that there is an element of confusion between *damage* to the plaintiff's body and latent *defect* in the foundations of a building. Unless the defect is very gross, it may never lead to any damage at all to the building. It would be analogous to a predisposition or natural weakness in the human body which may never develop into disease or injury. The plaintiff's cause of action will not accrue until *damage* occurs, which will commonly consist of cracks coming into existence as a result of the defect even though the cracks or the defect may be undiscovered and undiscoverable. There may perhaps be cases where the defect is so gross that the building is doomed from the start, and where the owner's cause of action will accrue as soon as it is built, but it seems unlikely that such a defect would not be discovered within the limitation period. Such cases, if they exist, would be exceptional. For the reasons I have tried to explain I do not find the distinction between personal injuries and damage to property drawn in the *Sparham-Souter* case convincing. I observe that in *Dennis v Charnwood BC* [1982] 3 All ER 486 at 492, 495, [1982] 3 WLR 1064 at 1071, 1075, Templeman LJ referred to the distinction as "delicate and surprising" and Lawton LJ found reconciling *Sparham-Souter* with the reasoning in *Cartledge v Jopling* as "difficult". I agree.' (Lord Fraser's emphasis.)

Lord Fraser concluded his speech thus ([1983] 1 All ER 65 at 72, [1983] 2 WLR 6 at 14–15):

'Counsel for the defendants submitted that the fault of his clients in advising on the design of the chimney was analogous to that of a solicitor who gives negligent advice on law, which results in the client suffering damage and a right of action accruing when the client acts on the advice (see *Howell v Young* (1826) 5 B & C 259, [1824–34] All ER Rep 377 and *Forster v Outred & Co* [1982] 2 All ER 753, [1982] 1 WLR 86). It is not necessary for the present purpose to decide whether that submission is well founded, but as at present advised, I do not think it is. It seems to me that except perhaps where the advice of an architect or consulting engineer leads to the erection of a building which is so defective as to be doomed from the start, the cause of action accrues only when physical damage occurs to the building. In the present case that was April 1970 when, as found by the judge, cracks must have occurred at the top of the chimney, even though that was before the date of discoverability. I am respectfully in agreement with Lord Reid's view expressed in *Cartledge v Jopling* that such a result appears to be unreasonable and contrary to principle, but I think the law is now so firmly established that only Parliament can alter it. Postponement of the accrual of the cause of action until the date of discoverability may involve the investigation of facts many years after their occurrence (see, for example, *Dennis v Charnwood*) with possible unfairness to the defendant, unless a final longstop date is prescribed, as in ss 6 and 7 of the Prescription and Limitation (Scotland) Act 1973. If there is any question of altering this branch of the law, this is, in my opinion, a clear case where any alteration should be made by legislation, and not by judicial decision, because this is, in the words of Lord Simon in *Miliangos v George Frank (Textiles) Ltd* [1975] 3 All ER 801 at 823, [1976] AC 443 at 480, "a decision which demands a far wider range of review than is available to courts following our traditional and valuable adversary system—the sort of review compassed by an interdepartmental committee." I express the hope that Parliament will soon take action to remedy the unsatisfactory state of the law on this subject. I would hold that the cause of action accrued in spring 1970 when damage, in the form of cracks near the top of the chimney, must have come into existence. I avoid saying that cracks "appeared" because that might seem to imply that they had been observed at that time. The action is, therefore, time-barred and I would allow the appeal.'

Subject to the difficulty I feel as to what is meant by a building being 'so defective as to be doomed from the start', I would have thought that that decision was conclusive against the defendants' case; but it is alleged on their behalf that this gate was 'doomed from the start' because it would fall at the first onslaught of a professional burglar. Therefore, it is said, because damage can consist of pure economic loss consequent on defective workmanship (see *Junior Books Ltd v Veitchi Co Ltd* [1982] 3 All ER 201, [1982] 3 WLR 477), damage occurred in this case when Mr Burton came under a liability at the time that in 1967 the defendants completed defective work such as would require remedial work. If that argument was correct, then it seems to me that the cause of action in *Pirelli* would have been held to arise in the summer of 1969 when the work was completed rather than in 1970 when the cracks appeared. It seems to me that the analogy between the cracks in the chimney and the collapse of this gate is exact.

I confess that I do not understand the qualification as to a building being 'doomed from the start'. It cannot have anything to do with the distinction between latent and patent defect because that would bring back the rejected test of discoverability. It is clear that whatever the circumstances which Lord Fraser had in mind they were such as would be exceptional. It seems to me to be quite impossible to say that this gate was doomed from the start; indeed, had it not been subjected to the onslaught of a professional burglar, it would never have been doomed at all.

Counsel for the defendants also founded an argument on the Court of Appeal decision in *Forster v Outred & Co* [1982] 2 All ER 753, [1982] 1 WLR 86. In that case it was held that the plaintiff's cause of action arose when, because of negligent advice, she executed a mortgage deed which charged her property in favour of a company as security for her son's present and future debts and not when she actually suffered loss, as she did when the company enforced its security. Whether or not the considerations which apply in the case of economic loss of that sort are different from those which have to be taken into account when the negligence relied on is negligence in relation to the building of a house and the damage which is concerned is damage arising because of defects in the house, as Sir David Cairns held in that case, is perhaps open to doubt, and it may be that *Forster v Outred & Co* can no longer stand since *Pirelli*'s case. But, whatever the position in that regard may be, the analogy was advanced between the facts of *Forster*'s case and those of the *Pirelli* case in the *Pirelli* case itself and dealt with in the passage in Lord Fraser's speech which I have already cited.

In my judgment, the defendants' case on the statute of limitations fails. That makes it unnecessary for me to consider the reply to that case by the plaintiff based on ss 26 and 32. However, that does not relieve me of the duty of making one last finding of fact on which that reply was largely based. Mr Dodd gave it as his opinion that a hole in the top right-hand corner of the frame (looking from the outside) had been made by the defendants' workmen when they had removed the door stop in order to accommodate the top hinge pin of the gate and that, when they found that, fixed to the frame, the gate did not fit, they had replaced the stop. I do not accept that, first, because the hole was not drilled, second, because it was not in line with where the pin would be and, last, because the nails were cut nails like those used in the rest of the house and of a type unlikely to be used by the defendants' workmen.

Judgment for the plaintiff.

Solicitors: *Malkin Cullis & Sumption* (for the plaintiff); *Thompson & Co* (for the defendants).

K Mydeen Esq Barrister.

Din and another v Wandsworth London Borough Council (No 3)

QUEEN'S BENCH DIVISION
LLOYD J, SITTING WITH THE CHIEF TAXING MASTER AND MR L J WATMORE AS ASSESSORS
26 APRIL 1983

Legal aid – Certificate – Scope of certificate – Counsel's fees – Certificate to 'brief counsel' – Whether certificate covering counsel's fees for work done before delivery of brief – Whether discretion to allow unauthorised costs incurred in instructing counsel where no party and party taxation – Legal Aid (General) Regulations 1980, regs 60(1), 64(4).

An authority given under reg 60(1)[a] of the Legal Aid (General) Regulations 1980 for 'briefing counsel' covers the brief itself and any necessary consultation on the brief, ie any necessary consultation after delivery of the brief; it does not cover consultations or other work done on instructions prior to the brief. Moreover, where there is no party and party taxation, there is no discretion under reg 64(4)[b] of the 1980 regulations to allow unauthorised costs incurred in instructing counsel (see p 843 *b c* and *g*, post).

Notes
For legal aid taxation of unauthorised costs in instructing counsel, see 37 Halsbury's Laws (4th edn) para 953.

Case referred to in judgment
Din v Wandsworth London Borough [1981] 3 All ER 881, [1981] 3 WLR 918, HL.

Review of taxation
The plaintiffs, Taj Din and Mansura Akther Din, sought a review of the decision of Master Wright on 23 April 1982 whereby, inter alia, he refused to allow certain items included in the plaintiffs' solicitors' bill of costs submitted in connection with an appeal by the plaintiffs to the Court of Appeal whereby that court (Waller and Ackner LJJ, Donaldson LJ dissenting) on 23 June 1981 reversed the decision of his Honour Judge White sitting in Wandsworth County Court on 24 June 1980 giving judgment for the plaintiffs in an action brought by them against Wandsworth London Borough Council. The review was heard in chambers but judgment was given by Lloyd J in open court with the consent of counsel. The facts are set out in the judgment.

Nicholas Blake for the plaintiffs.
The council was not represented.

LLOYD J. This is a summons to review a legal aid taxation under Sch 2 to the Legal Aid Act 1974.

The plaintiffs in the action are Taj Din and Mrs Mansura Din. In December 1979 they made an application to the defendants, the Wandsworth London Borough Council, for housing priority under the Housing (Homeless Persons) Act 1977. On 4 January 1980 their application was refused on the ground that they had become intentionally homeless as defined in s 17 of the 1977 Act. The plaintiffs thereupon brought an action in the Wandsworth County Court claiming damages and a declaration. That action came before his Honour Judge White in June 1980. The plaintiffs succeeded. The local authority then appealed. The Court of Appeal allowed the appeal by a majority. There was then a further appeal by the plaintiffs to the House of Lords. The appeal was dismissed, again

a Regulation 60(1) is set out at p 842 *b c*, post
b Regulation 64(4) is set out at p 842 *c d*, post

by a majority (see [1981] 3 All ER 881, [1981] 3 WLR 918). It was the first case under the 1977 Act to reach the House of Lords.

I need not go into the issues in any detail. It is obvious from what I have already said that this was an important and difficult case.

The present application relates to the plaintiffs' costs in the Court of Appeal. By a civil aid certificate dated 13 August 1980 the plaintiffs' solicitors were authorised to brief leading counsel for the hearing in the Court of Appeal. That authority was given pursuant to reg 60(1) of the Legal Aid (General) Regulations 1980, SI 1980/1894. Regulation 60(1) provides:

> 'Where it appears to an assisted person's solicitor that the proper conduct of the proceedings so requires, counsel may be instructed; but, unless authority has been given in the certificate or by the general committee—(*a*) counsel shall not be instructed in authorised summary proceedings; and (*b*) a Queen's Counsel or more than one counsel shall not be instructed.'

Regulation 64(4) provides:

> 'Where costs are incurred in instructing a Queen's Counsel or more than one counsel, without authority to do so having been given in the certificate or under regulation 60(1), as the case may be, no payment in respect of those costs shall be allowed on any taxation, unless it is also allowed on a party and party taxation.'

Briefs were delivered on 4 June 1981. In fact the plaintiffs' solicitors did not brief leading counsel, but a leading junior counsel, Mr Stephen Sedley. But nothing turns on that. The hearing in the Court of Appeal took place in the same month.

When the plaintiffs' solicitors submitted their bill of costs, it included two items relating to conferences with Mr Sedley in September and October 1980, and instructions to attend on an interlocutory application to expedite the hearing in November 1980, some nine months before the brief was delivered. The taxing master disallowed those items. The plaintiffs lodged objections. The taxing master maintained his refusal to allow the disputed items. He gave his reasons in a decision dated 25 August 1982. I quote the following passage:

> 'The briefs were delivered on 4 June 1981. The solicitors instructed two counsel throughout the Court of Appeal proceedings and did not restrict themselves to instructing two counsel for the hearing and for consultations on the briefs. I took the view that on the wording of the certificate and of reg 15(2) and (7) of the Legal Aid (General) Regulations 1971, SI 1971/62, as amended by SI 1977/1293, and of reg 60(1) of the Legal Aid (General) Regulations 1980 I had no authority to allow any fee to Mr Stephen Sedley prior to 4 June 1981. I disallowed the objections.'

Mr Blake, who appears on the summons, has argued most persuasively that the master was wrong to disallow the objection. He accepts that the question whether the items should be allowed or not depends on the construction of the legal aid certificate. Since the point is one of some general importance in legal aid taxations, and since there is said to be no authority on the point, I am giving this judgment, with counsel's consent, in open court.

The certificate provided:

> 'To defend an appeal to the Court of Appeal from a Judgment given in Wandsworth County Court on 24th June 1980 under Plaint No. 8001524 between T. Din and M. A. Din Plaintiffs -v- The London Borough of Wandsworth Defendants. To include a Respondent's Notice only if so advised by Counsel. To include briefing Leading Counsel, in addition to Junior Counsel, to include any necessary consultation on brief to represent both legally aided Respondents to the Appeal.'

On the face of it that certificate gives the plaintiffs' solicitors authority to brief leading counsel. But what is meant by 'briefing leading counsel'? Counsel argues that it includes

any instructions to leading counsel prior to the brief, and in contemplation of the brief.
a He refers to a definition in *Osborn's Concise Law Dictionary* (5th edn, 1976) p 59, part of which reads as follows: '**brief.** A concise statement. The instructions furnished by a solicitor to a barrister to enable him to represent the client in legal proceedings.'

I cannot accept counsel's argument. It seems to me that there is a well-established and well-understood distinction between a brief, consisting as it does of instructions to counsel to appear at a trial or hearing, and other instructions such as instructions to advise
b in conference or to settle pleadings.

On its true construction, the authority in the present case covers the brief itself and any necessary consultation *on* the brief. That means, I think, any necessary consultation after delivery of the brief. It does *not* cover consultations or other work done on instructions prior to the brief. If counsel's argument were right, it would mean that these items would be allowable even though no brief were ever delivered.

c Counsel says that the difference between a brief and other instructions is purely semantic. In one sense that is right. But in that sense all questions of construction are semantic.

I would therefore uphold the master's disallowance of these items. If the result seems harsh, I would only comment that the whole purpose of Pt VIII of the 1980 regulations is to enable local legal aid committees to exercise control over costs. This can only be
d done if solicitors keep strictly within the authority they have been granted. If there had been any doubt about the extent of their authority, which I do not think there was, the plaintiffs' solicitors could have gone back for amendment of the certificate, or for clarification. But they did not do so.

As for counsel, a copy of the certificate should have been included with his papers: see reg 60(2).

e The construction which I have put on the certificate is not new. In the *Legal Aid Handbook* 1976, p 185 there appears the following passage:

> 'An authority issued by an Area Committee under regulation 15(3) "to brief leading counsel" will cover the brief and any necessary consultation in connection with it, including a consultation on quantum. Written advice on evidence, a written
> f advice on quantum or a consultation or advice on discovery or other interlocutory matters must be specially authorized.'

That statement now reappears in the Fifth Cumulative Supplement to *The Supreme Court Practice 1982* under the notes to para 62/A2/51/52. Master Matthews, the Chief Taxing Master, who has unrivalled experience in this field, observed in the course of the argument that the statement goes back, in his own experience, to at least 1957.

g Counsel had an alternative argument that the master had a discretion to allow these items under reg 64(4), if they would have been allowed on a party and party taxation. But there was no party and party taxation in the present case. That being so, there was no discretion to allow the items. There is nothing in counsel's alternative argument and, to be fair to him, it was not pressed.

I can deal with the other objections very briefly. [His Lordship then dealt with the
h other objections.]

Taxing master's decision upheld.

Solicitors: *Fisher Meredith* (for the plaintiffs).

K Mydeen Esq Barrister.

R v Immigration Appeal Tribunal, ex parte Bastiampillai and another

QUEEN'S BENCH DIVISION (CROWN OFFICE LIST)
GLIDEWELL J
13, 28 JANUARY 1983

Immigration – Appeal – Evidence of facts coming into existence after Secretary of State's decision – Whether adjudicator or appeal tribunal can admit evidence of facts occurring after Secretary of State's decision – Immigration Act 1971, s 14.

Immigration – Leave to enter – Indefinite leave – Dependent parents – Wholly or mainly dependent – Applicants' children all settled in United Kingdom – Applicants without income and living with daughter rent-free – Whether applicants 'wholly or mainly dependent' on child settled in United Kingdom – Whether dependence limited to financial dependence – Whether emotional dependence to be taken into account in determining dependence – Statement of Changes in Immigration Rules (HC Paper (1979–80) no 394), para 48.

Immigration – Leave to enter – Indefinite leave – Dependent parents – Other relatives in their own country to turn to – Applicants' children all settled in United Kingdom – Applicants living with daughter rent-free – Applicants applying for conditions of stay to be removed on ground that they were dependent on children settled in United Kingdom and had no 'other close relatives in their own country to turn to' – Who are 'other close relatives in their own country to turn to' – Statement of Changes in Immigration Rules (HC Paper (1979–80) no 394), para 48.

The applicants, a husband and wife aged 69 years and 58 years respectively, were citizens of Sri Lanka. The husband came to the United Kingdom in 1973 and was joined a few years later by his wife. In 1976 the husband was granted a work permit to work as a trainee accountant conditional on his leaving the United Kingdom on completion of his accountancy training. The husband subsequently obtained employment and the work permit and consent to stay in the United Kingdom were renewed from time to time until 1 June 1979, when it expired. Between the time of his arrival in the United Kingdom and 1979 all three children of the applicants came to the United Kingdom, where they subsequently settled. The applicants lived with one of their daughters rent-free. On 31 May 1979 the applicants applied for the time limit on their stay to be removed on the grounds that they were 'wholly or mainly dependent upon children settled in the United Kingdom' within the then current immigration rules for control on entry of Commonwealth citizens. The Secretary of State refused the application on 12 March 1980 and permission for the applicants to stay in the United Kingdom expired on 9 April 1980. On 25 March 1980 the applicants lodged a notice of appeal to an adjudicator. On 30 March, as a result of the refusal by the Department of Employment to renew his work permit and that of the Secretary of State not to remove the conditions of their stay, the husband ceased work and thereafter his only income was a small pension from Sri Lanka. In March 1981 the appeal to the adjudicator was adjourned so that an application could be made to the Secretary of State to reconsider the matter in the light of the change in the applicants' circumstances, namely the fact that the husband had ceased work, and on 14 April the applicants' solicitors wrote to the Secretary of State asking for the matter to be reconsidered. On 5 June the Secretary of State refused the application on the ground that he was not satisfied that the applicants were 'wholly or mainly dependent' on the daughter with whom they were living or that the applicants were 'without other close relatives in their own country to turn to', as required by para 48[a] of the Statement of Changes in Immigration Rules. On 6 October the applicants' appeal was heard and dismissed by an adjudicator, who held that any change occurring in the applicants'

a Paragraph 48, so far as material, is set out at p 849 *j*, post

circumstances after 12 March 1980 when the Secretary of State initially refused their
a application was irrelevant to the appeal. The applicants' appeal to the Immigration
Appeal Tribunal was also dismissed. The applicants applied for orders of certiorari to
quash the decision of the Secretary of State on 5 June, and the decisions of the adjudicator
and the appeal tribunal, contending, inter alia, (i) that the decisions of the Secretary of
State on 12 March 1980 and 5 June 1981 were effectively a single decision and that
therefore the adjudicator should have taken into account all relevant facts, including the
b change in the applicants' circumstances, occurring up to 5 June 1981, (ii) that 'dependence'
under the rules meant not merely financial dependence but also emotional dependence
and that that had not been taken into account, (iii) that the Secretary of State had
misinterpreted the phrase 'close relatives in their own country to turn to' in para 48 of
the immigration rules, and (iv) that although the husband was still employed on 12
March 1980 nevertheless it was foreseeable at that date that he was likely to cease
c employment in the near future and therefore the adjudicator and the Secretary of State
should have taken that into account in reaching their decision.

Held – (1) The letter of 14 April 1981 from the applicants' solicitors to the Secretary of
State was a second or fresh application by the applicants to remain in the United Kingdom
and not merely a continuation of the original application made on 12 March 1980. It
d followed that (a) because s 14 of the Immigration Act 1971 only permitted an appeal to
be made to an adjudicator and the Immigration Appeal Tribunal against the Secretary of
State's refusal of an application to remain if the application was received during the
period of the applicants' permitted stay, the applicants had no right of appeal against the
Secretary of State's decision of 5 June 1981, since the application of 14 April 1981 was
made after the applicants' permission to stay had expired on 9 April 1980, and (b) the
e adjudicator and the tribunal were right to refuse to take into account any facts or change
of circumstances arising after the date of the Secretary of State's original decision on 12
March 1980 (see p 848 *h* to p 849 *b*, p 850 *c d* and p 852 *a b*, post); *R v Immigration Appeal
Tribunal, ex p Kotecha* [1983] 2 All ER 289 applied.

(2) The requirement in para 48 of the immigration rules that the applicants were
'wholly or mainly dependent' on children settled in the United Kingdom referred
f primarily to financial dependence, although if there was any doubt regarding their
financial dependence other types of dependence (such as emotional dependence) might
also be relevant and might tip the balance in favour of permission to stay being granted.
However, emotional dependence required more than the normal love and affection of a
united family if it was to be relevant. The adjudicator and the tribunal had been entitled
to take the view that since the applicants had each other to depend on there was nothing
g in the nature of emotional dependence on their children beyond the normal desire to be
near them. Accordingly, the adjudicator and the tribunal had not been in error in not
taking into account the applicants' emotional dependence on their children, and certiorari
to quash their decisions would therefore be refused (see p 851 *b* to *g*, post).

(3) Although the Secretary of State's decision of 5 June 1981 was completely
discretionary (since the application of 14 April 1981 had been made after the applicants'
h permission to stay had expired), nevertheless, having regard to the reasons given by the
Secretary of State, his decision was reviewable under the normal principles governing
judicial review. In particular, (a) the phrase 'other close relatives in their own country to
turn to' in para 48 of the immigration rules meant a relative who had the ability to
provide some assistance to the applicants by way of providing a home or financial support
such that it was reasonable to expect the applicants to depend on that relative rather than
j on a child or children in the United Kingdom, and it was not clear that the Secretary of
State had regarded the phrase in that way, and (b) in deciding that he was not satisfied
that the applicants were wholly or mainly dependent on their children in the United
Kingdom the Secretary of State had failed to take into account the material consideration
that by 14 April the applicants had become almost wholly financially dependent on their
daughter because the husband had ceased to work and they had virtually no income of
their own. Accordingly, the Secretary of State's decision would be quashed and the

application remitted to him for reconsideration (see p 852 *d e j* and p 853 *d* to *j*, post); *Associated Provincial Picture Houses Ltd v Wednesbury Corp* [1947] 2 All ER 680 applied. *a*

Notes

For the procedure in immigration appeals, see 4 Halsbury's Laws (4th edn) paras 1016–1026.

For rules governing admission of dependants, see ibid paras 992, 995–996.

For the Immigration Act 1971, s 14, see 41 Halsbury's Statutes (3rd edn) 35. *b*

Cases referred to in judgment

Associated Provincial Picture Houses Ltd v Wednesbury Corp [1947] 2 All ER 680, [1948] 1 KB 223, CA.

Patel (S N) v Entry Clearance Officer, Bombay (21 August 1975, unreported), Immigration Appeal Tribunal. *c*

R v Immigration Appeal Tribunal, ex p Kotecha [1983] 2 All ER 289, [1983] 1 WLR 487, CA.

R v Immigration Appeal Tribunal, ex p Tong (1981) Times, 8 December.

Sharma (Sushila) v Entry Clearance Officer, New Delhi (29 November 1973, unreported), Immigration Appeal Tribunal.

d

Application for judicial review

Swampillai Saverinuttu Bastiampillai and Ruby Benedicta Bastiampillai applied, with the leave of Stephen Brown J granted on 15 October 1982, for, inter alia, an order of certiorari to quash the determination of the adjudicator, E J T Housden Esq, dated 24 September 1981 dismissing the appeal of the applicants against the refusal of the Secretary of State for the Home Department to grant indefinite leave to the applicants to remain in the *e* United Kingdom as dependent parents of their daughters settled in the United Kingdom, an order of certiorari to quash the determination of the Immigration Appeal Tribunal dated 14 May 1982 dismissing the applicants' appeal against the determination of the adjudicator, and an order of certiorari to quash the decision of the Secretary of State for the Home Department dated 5 June 1981 refusing to grant the applicants indefinite leave to remain as the dependent parents of their daughters settled in the United Kingdom. *f* The facts are set out in the judgment.

Ian Macdonald for the applicants.
John Laws for the Secretary of State.

Cur adv vult *g*

28 January. The following judgment was delivered.

GLIDEWELL J. This is an application on behalf of Mr and Mrs Bastiampillai for judicial review. The application seeks three orders: first, an order of certiorari to quash a determination of an adjudicator, Mr Housden, of 24 September 1981 dismissing an *h* appeal to him by the applicants against the refusal of the Secretary of State to grant indefinite leave for them to remain in the United Kingdom; second, an order of certiorari to quash a determination of the immigration appeal tribunal dated 14 May 1982 dismissing an appeal by the applicants against the decision of the adjudicator to which I have just referred; and, third, an order of certiorari to quash the decision of the Secretary of State himself dated 5 June 1981 refusing to grant the applicants indefinite leave to *j* remain in the United Kingdom.

The applicants, Mr and Mrs Bastiampillai are citizens of Sri Lanka. Mr Bastiampillai is now 69 years of age and his wife is just 58. He came to the United Kingdom in 1973 and she came, I think, two or three years later. In 1976 Mr Bastiampillai was granted a work permit to work as a trainee accountant. That permit and consent for him to stay in the

United Kingdom were renewed from time to time until 1979. The consent to stay in the
a United Kingdom expired on 1 June 1979. According to the applicant (and I shall refer to
Mr Bastiampillai as the applicant because in essence the whole of this matter depends on
his position) when he first came to this country he intended at the end of his period as a
trainee accountant to return to Sri Lanka. However, between the time he arrived and
1979 all three children of these two applicants had come to the United Kingdom and all
three of them are now settled in the United Kingdom. Bernadette, who is now Mrs
b Weerasinghe, came here in 1974. Chrisantas, who is the youngest of the three, came here
in 1977. Aimee, who is Mrs Sukumar, came here in 1979.

On 31 May 1979 the applicant wrote to the Under Secretary of State for the Home
Office applying for the time limit on the stay in this country of himself and his wife to
be removed. The basis of the application was that they were living by that time with
Bernadette (Mrs Weerasinghe) and her husband, that they were to a large extent
c dependent on her and that they wished to be allowed to remain in that capacity. The
effect of the Immigration (Variation of Leave) Order 1976, SI 1976/1572, is that
permission for the applicants to stay in the United Kingdom did not expire as it would
otherwise have done on 1 June, but was extended as a result of that application being
made until the Secretary of State made his decision on it and for a further 28 days
thereafter.

d The Secretary of State duly made his decision, which was to refuse the application, on
12 March 1980. The 28 days thereafter and thus the permission for the applicants to stay
in the United Kingdom therefore expired on 9 April 1980. But in the mean time, on 25
March 1980, notice of appeal to the adjudicator against that decision had been entered
under s 14 of the Immigration Act 1971. Again, as a result of the entry of that appeal,
they lawfully remained in this country while that appeal was current. As I have already
e said, at the time of the Secretary of State's decision (that is to say on 12 March 1980) the
applicants were living at the home of their daughter Bernadette Weerasinghe and her
husband. At that time Mr Bastiampillai was working and he was earning about £1,800
per annum. He also had a very small pension from Sri Lanka. The evidence is that they
were living free of charge with their daughter and from time to time both she and the
other daughter gave them occasional gifts of money or clothes or other items. However,
f although he was actually working in March 1980, in the previous month, February 1980,
the Department of Employment had made it clear that it did not intend to renew his
work permit. As a result of that and also, I take it, as a result of receiving the Home
Office decision not to remove the conditions so that he could stay indefinitely, Mr
Bastiampillai ceased work on 30 March 1980. He has not been in paid employment, nor
has he had any earnings, since that time. His only income since then has been the very
g small pension from Sri Lanka.

A year later, on 25 March 1981, the appeal came on for hearing before the adjudicator.
An application was made for an adjournment so that an approach could be made to the
Secretary of State to reconsider the matter, because of the change of circumstances since
12 March 1980, that is to say the fact that Mr Bastiampillai had ceased work. That
application for an adjournment was granted. On 14 April 1981 solicitors on behalf of the
h applicant wrote to the under Secretary of State at the Home Office saying:

> 'We are now writing to you, as promised in an earlier letter, with the detailed background of our application for reconsideration of your decision dated 12th March, 1980, in the light of the change of circumstances which has taken place since then.'

j It then sets out both the facts to which I have shortly referred and also argument whether
or not the applicants' circumstances fell within certain rules in the Statement of
Immigration Rules for the Control on Entry: Commonwealth Citizens (HC Paper (1972–
73) no 79).

On 5 June 1981 the Secretary of State, having considered the application in that letter
of 14 April, refused it. In doing so he said:

> 'Messrs Bates, Wells and Braithwaite [who of course were the solicitors to whom I have referred] have applied on your behalf for indefinite leave to remain in the a
> United Kingdom as the dependant parents of Mr and Mrs Weerasinghe, but the Secretary of State is not satisfied that you are wholly or mainly dependant on Mr and Mrs Weerasinghe nor without close relatives in Sri Lanka to turn to. Furthermore, the Secretary of State is not satisfied that you have honoured a written undertaking to leave the United Kingdom on completion of your accountancy training given in obtaining leave to remain.' b

Following that, on 2 July 1981, the Home Office issued a document described as a supplementary statement to the statement dated 24 November 1980, which was the statement which the Home Office originally served in relation to the appeal against the decision of March 1980. In that statement there is set out the fact that that appeal was adjourned so that the applicants' solicitors could submit a fresh application on their behalf in view of their changed circumstances and there is shortly set out the Secretary of c
State's decision on the later application in the terms to which I have just referred.

On 6 October 1981 the appeal came on for hearing before the adjudicator, Mr Housden, and he dismissed the appeal. During the course of the hearing there was discussion of the question of whether or not the adjudicator should take into account the facts relating to what had happened after 12 March 1980, that is to say the change of circumstances. The adjudicator set out the position as at 12 March 1980 and said: 'I have d
to take the facts as they existed on 12 March 1980.' He then went on to recite certain facts shortly as I have done. He concluded that on the income which Mr Bastiampillai then had he would not necessarily have been wholly or mainly dependent on any or all of this children in the United Kingdom and thus would not meet the fundamental requirement of para 45 of Statement of Immigration Rules for Control after Entry (HC Paper (1972–73) no 80), the rule relating to dependent parents. He then went on to say: e

> 'I accept that after Mr Bastiampillai ceased working for A Maslow & Co he became dependent on his United Kingdom resident daughter, with whom he and his wife have been living for several years without having to contribute to the household expenses.'

I interpolate, that, although he did not use the words 'wholly or mainly dependent' in f
that paragraph, I think it is quite apparent that he meant wholly or nearly wholly. He then said that, for the reasons he had given, the decision of the Secretary of State was in accordance with the law and the immigration rules and he dismissed the appeal. That is not the end of the matter, because he went on: 'Mr Birtles [who appeared for the applicants before the adjudicator] has asked me to make a recommendation to the Secretary of State for the exercise of his discretion outside the rules, so as to enable Mr g
and Mrs Bastiampillai to remain in the United Kingdom with their children.' He considered the matter and decided the circumstances did not warrant him making such a recommendation.

Against that decision the applicants appealed. The Immigration Appeal Tribunal dealt with the matter on 14 May 1982, when they were represented by Mr Macdonald, who had not represented them before the adjudicator. Despite the arguments that he h
presented, the Immigration Appeal Tribunal again dismissed the appeal to them.

I note two points at this stage. There is no right of appeal against the Secretary of State's decision of 5 June 1981. The reason for that is that under s 14 of the Immigration Act 1971 an appeal to an adjudicator, and then if necesary a further appeal to the Immigration Appeal Tribunal, may only be made against the refusal of an application which is received during the period of the applicant's permitted stay. The decision of 12 March 1980 j
satisfies that requirement, because the application was made before the expiry of the permitted stay on 1 June 1979. But, if the application contained in the solicitor's letter of 14 April 1981 was a fresh or second application, then the permitted stay which had been extended as a result of the effect of the Immigration (Variation of Leave) Order 1976 had nevertheless long since expired, namely on 9 April 1980. So, if that was a new application, no appeal lay under s 14 of the 1971 Act against the refusal of it.

The second point is that the refusal of both the adjudicator and the tribunal to base
a their decision on facts arising after the date of the Secretary of State's original decision of 12 March 1980 was in my view entirely correct. The authority for that proposition is the recent decision of the Court of Appeal in *R v Immigration Appeal Tribunal, ex p Kotecha* [1983] 2 All ER 289, [1983] 1 WLR 487, which is an appeal against a decision of my own. To the general rule that appeals to adjudicators and the Immigration Appeal Tribunal may only relate to the facts existing at the time of the decision appealed against
b there is one gloss to which I will refer later, because it forms part of another argument of counsel for the applicants. But, with the exception of that gloss, *Kotecha*'s case is clear authority for the general principle and there is no doubt at all that it applies to the facts of this case.

I turn therefore to the relevant rules for control of immigration. In relation to the decision of the Secretary of State of March 1980, the rules in force were contained in the
c Statements of Immigration Rules for Control on and after Entry: Commonwealth Citizens (HC Paper (1972–73) nos 79 and 80), which I shall refer to as HC 79 and HC 80. HC 80 dealt with control after entry and HC 79 with control on entry. Paragraph 28 of HC 80 reads, so far as is relevant:

> 'When a person who is admitted in the first instance for a limited period has remained here for 4 years in approved employment . . . the time limit on his stay
> d may be removed. Applications for removal of the time limit are to be considered in the light of all the relevant circumstances, including those set out in *paragraph 4* . . . Applications for variation of leave to enter with a view to settlement may also be received from people originally admitted as, for example, visitors; but permission has to be limited to close relatives of people already accepted for settlement. Particulars are set out in *paragraphs 39–46* of the Rules for Control of Entry dated
> e January 1973 (HC79).'

So one turns back to HC 79 and the rule which is relevant here is para 45 which reads:

> '. . . parents travelling together of whom at least one is aged 65 or over [which of course was the case here, because Mr Bastiampillai was 67 in 1980] should be admitted for settlement if wholly or mainly dependent upon children settled in the
> f United Kingdom who have the means to support their parents and any other relatives who would be admissible as their dependants and adequate accommodation for them . . .'

There is no issue here about any other relatives being admissible as dependants, because all the three children are grown up and all are settled here. There is no doubt the
g Weerasinghes have adequate accommodation, there is no doubt the Weerasinghes have the means to support Mrs Weerasinghe's parents, so the issue was: were the applicants wholly or mainly dependent on Mr and Mrs Weerasinghe?

By the time of the Secretary of State's further decision of 5 June 1981, whatever the nature of it for the moment, HC 79 and HC 80 had been replaced by the Statement of Changes in Immigration Rules (HC Paper (1979–80) no 394 (HC 394)). That contains
h paragraphs in similar but not identical terms to those to which I have referred. The equivalent of para 28 of HC 80 is para 119 of HC 394, but I detect no material difference between those paragraphs. The equivalent of para 45 of HC 79 is para 48 of HC 394, which starts off in the same way, that is to say:

> '. . . parents travelling together of whom at least one is aged 65 or over should be admitted for settlement only where the requirements of paragraphs 42 and 43 and
> j the following conditions are met. They must be wholly or mainly dependent upon sons or daughters settled in the United Kingdom who have the means to maintain their parents and any other relatives who would be admissible as dependants of the parents, and adequate accommodation for them . . .'

So far it is the same, but then there is another sentence which is new in HC 394: 'They must also be without other close relatives in their own country to turn to.'

I turn to the arguments of counsel for the applicants. I would like to say that, though I have not found this an easy case, my task has been much assisted by the clarity and cogency with which both counsel advanced their arguments. The first argument of counsel for the applicants is that the decisions of the Home Office of 12 March 1980 and 5 June 1981 were effectively all one decision and that when the appeal to the adjudicator came before him, that is to say on 25 March 1981, it was an appeal against that combined decision. Thus, said counsel, the adjudicator should have taken account of all the facts up to 5 June 1981, establishing the major fact that Mr Bastiampallai was no longer in employment and was no longer in receipt of a salary. He put it in this way: where an appeal is adjourned to enable the Secretary of State to consider new circumstances and the Secretary of State makes a further decision and issues a supplemental statement the further decision is in issue in the appeal and evidence of facts up to the date of the further decision are relevant and admissible. I say at once in relation to that submission, as I indicated at the end of his argument before I asked counsel for the Secretary of State to address me, on that I am against him. In my view the adjournment was requested and was granted so that a new application could be made for a fresh decision to be made, that is a second decision by the Secretary of State. If that decision on the new facts had been in Mr Bastiampillai's favour, then it would of course have been unnecessary to proceed with the appeal.

The fact on which counsel for the applicants places reliance, that the Home Office issued a supplemental explanatory statement, is in my view merely an explanation of the second decision. Counsel did place before me copies of two decisions of the Immigration Appeal Tribunal in *Sushila Sharma v Entry Clearance Officer, New Dehli* (29 November 1973, unreported) and *S N Patel v Entry Clearance Officer, Bombay* (21 August 1975, unreported). I mention them only to say that they seem to me not to be in point, because they were both dealing with second applications which had been made in time while the applicants were still permitted to be in the United Kingdom, so that appeals were laid properly against the second application. That of course is a very different situation from that which arises here.

I therefore come to the second argument of counsel for the applicants. The issue is whether on 12 March 1980 when the Secretary of State made his first decision there was material on which he could properly conclude that the applicants were not wholly or mainly dependent on their daughter, Mrs Weerasinghe. The real issue was whether they were mainly dependent, because clearly they were not wholly dependent since at that time Mr Bastiampillai had an income.

Counsel for the applicants advances two arguments in relation to this matter. The first is that dependence within the rule includes not merely financial dependence, but what has been called emotional dependence. The way he put it was that financial dependence must be the primary matter to be considered, but in a particular case where there is also emotional dependence that may tip the scale in favour of the applicants. In this case, the adjudicator said nothing at all about any question of emotional dependence and thus did not take account of all the relevant considerations.

The second point is that, albeit Mr Bastiampillai was still in employment on 12 March 1980, nevertheless at that date the facts which then existed were such that anybody could have anticipated and should have anticipated that he was likely to cease employment in the very near future and that is a matter which the Secretary of State in the first place and then the adjudicator should have taken into account. In relation to that matter, he referred to another decision of mine, *R v Immigration Appeal Tribunal, ex p Tong* (1981) Times, 8 December. That was a case in which, in order to determine whether it was reasonably likely that a business in which the applicant was engaged would provide sufficient funds to support him, it was necessary at the time of the Secretary of State's decision to make some prognostication about the likely future success or failure of that business. Putting it quite shortly, I took the view that in such circumstances the Secretary of State was entitled or obliged, so to speak, to look forward for a purpose such as that. The issue therefore on that second argument is whether that sort of consideration applies in a case such as the present.

The third argument of counsel for the applicants, if he fails on the second one, relates
a to the Secretary of State's second decision (as I have found it was) of 5 June 1981. Counsel
argues, on *Associated Provincial Picture Houses Ltd v Wednesbury Corp* [1947] 2 All ER 680,
[1948] 1 KB 223, that the Secretary of State has failed to take account of a relevant
consideration in that later decision, namely the fact that by that time Mr Bastiampillai
had ceased work and had almost no income. Counsel, secondly, submits that the Secretary
of State has misdirected himself as to the meaning of the words 'other close relatives . . .
b to turn to' in para 48 of HC 394.

Counsel for the Secretary of State, in relation to the second argument, agrees that in
appropriate circumstances it was right for the Secretary of State, and thus an adjudicator
on appeal, to take emotional dependence into account. But he says that it is very much a
subsidiary matter, that is to say subsidiary to financial dependence. The rule, he argues,
is essentially concerned with persons likely to be financially dependent and if emotional
c dependence is to be taken into account it must mean something more than ordinary
family affection. With that I agree. In my judgment, reference to dependence of parents
on their children primarily means financial dependence. But I can see that, if the
Secretary of State, or the adjudicator on appeal, is in doubt whether an applicant is mainly
dependent on a child financially, then other types of dependence may become relevant
and may tip the balance. I agree with counsel for the Secretary of State that the normal
d love and affection of a united family is not of itself such emotional dependence. It needs
more than that. For instance, and of course this is not comprehensive, suppose one has a
lady who has recently been widowed, who has an adult son or daughter who has been
living close to her and that adult son or daughter comes to the United Kingdom, then
there might well be said in those circumstances to be emotional dependence, because the
lady would have been bereft not merely of her husband, but also of the child to whom
e she would normally have turned for support other than financial support. If in addition
she was in part dependent on that child for financial support then the emotional
dependence in such circumstances might tip the scale in the decision whether or not she
was mainly dependent.

But it seems to me that the adjudicator was perfectly entitled to take the view that the
Bastiampillai family is a good example of a happy united family, and that, since the
f applicants have each other to depend on and are both, one hopes, in good health, there is
nothing in the nature of emotional dependence on their children, albeit one can well
understand their desire to be near their children, a perfectly normal human desire which
all of us have as we get older. Accordingly, in my judgment, the adjudicator was not in
error in not referring to this matter in dealing with the appeal.

As to the second argument on this aspect of the case, whether at 12 March 1980 the
g Secretary of State should have looked forward and anticipated that Mr Bastiampillai was
likely to lose his job, I quote a few words of what I said in *Tong*'s case. They are set out in,
and I am reading them from, the judgment of Lord Lane CJ in the Court of Appeal in
Kotecha's case [1983] 2 All ER 289 at 292, [1983] 1 WLR 487 at 4591, to which I have
already referred. I said that one of the subsidiary points was that—

> 'the adjudicator was obliged to look at the position as it was in May 1978, at the
> h time of the notice of refusal, and in so far as he was entitled to look at anything that
> had happened since he was only entitled to do so as a guide to what could have been
> expected to happen viewed from the standpoint of May 1978. In other words, what
> has actually happened is to be taken into account in deciding what, had one been
> looking forward from two years back, would have been likely to happen. That, I
> think, is right.'

j

Lord Lane CJ, giving the judgment in *Kotecha*'s case [1983] 2 All ER 289 at 293, [1983]
1 WLR 487 at 492, with which the other two members of the court agreed, said:

> 'What that case [another case] and the earlier case of *R v Immigration Appeal*
> *Tribunal, ex p Tong* (1981) Times, 8 December seem to decide is this, that the
> situation may be different where the original decision involves making an inspired
> guess as to the future prospects of, for example, a business. It may be that within a

> very limited sphere it is proper in these limited circumstances to have regard to
> what happened subsequent to the original hearing. That is, as I say, very far from a
> the present case.'

Coming back to this case, it is in my view far from this case too. I do not accept that
there was any obligation on the Secretary of State to look forward or take into account
facts which had not actually arisen at 12 March 1980, and there was no obligation on the
adjudicator to take into account any other facts. In those respects, in my view the decision
of the adjudicator and the Immigration Appeal Tribunal was entirely correct and the first b
two applications therefore fail.

That brings me to the third application which relates to the Secretary of State's decision
of 5 June 1981, which, as I have already said, falls to be treated as a separate decision.
Counsel for the Secretary of State argues that although that decision is framed, that is to
say worded, as though it was a decision made within the immigration rules, when one
considers the matter in detail, that was not so. I go back to the letter of application of the c
applicants' solicitors of 14 April 1981. That application was specifically said to be pursuant
to para 48 of HC 394. But counsel's point is that when one looks at the first paragraph in
HC 394 to which one has to go, namely para 119, one finds that since the application was
made after the permission to enter had expired, para 119 does not apply, because an
application for removal of a time limit can only be made if it is made within the currency d
of the permission to enter, the point I have already referred to. Thus, says counsel for the
Secretary of State, at the time of the further application of 14 April 1981 this applicant
could not bring himself within paras 119 and 48 of HC 394. All he could do was to ask
the Secretary of State to exercise his discretion generally.

So far I agree with counsel for the Secretary of State. It is, however, right to say that
when the Secretary of State came to deal with it, and I have set out the terms on which
he dealt with it on 5 June 1981, the words used were words taken from para 48 of HC e
394. That is relevant to the second point of counsel for the Secretary of State, which is
that a decision of the Secretary of State in those circumstances is wholly a matter for his
discretion and it is itself a matter which counsel submits either is not reviewable at all or
is only reviewable within very limited circumstances. If the circumstances are limited,
counsel submits that the normal *Wednesbury* principles do not apply, although I must
confess I found him at this stage of his argument lacking in his usual clarity when he f
came to say in what respects the *Wednesbury* principles did not apply. In my judgment,
the extent to which such a decision, that is to say a decision of the Secretary of State made
wholly within his discretion, is reviewable depends on the nature of the decision itself.
In many cases such a decision may not be reviewable by the courts at all. For example, if
the Secretary of State is asked to exercise his discretion on compassionate grounds and
decides that the grounds are not sufficiently compelling of themselves that is wholly a g
matter of factual discretion and there is nothing that this court could in my view properly
grasp as a reason for saying that he had not taken into account the right factors.

In this case what the Secretary of State has in effect done in his decision of 5 June 1981
is to indicate the matters he is taking into account. I will read them again, because there
are three and I am adding numbers this time: (1) 'the Secretary of State is not satisfied
that you are wholly or mainly dependant on Mr and Mrs Weerasinghe'; (2) 'nor [that you h
are] without close relatives in Sri Lanka to turn to'; (3) 'Furthermore, the Secretary of
State is not satisfied that you have honoured a written undertaking to leave the United
Kingdom on completion of your accountancy training given on obtaining leave to
remain.' The first two points are direct quotations from para 48 of HC Paper (1979–80)
no 394.

In my view, because the Secretary of State has thought it right to give those reasons, in j
relation to those reasons this decision is reviewable on normal *Wednesbury* principles and
I therefore turn to carry out that exercise shortly. I propose to deal with the reasons in
the reverse order to that in which they are set out.

It is accepted, because it is a clear fact, that Mr Bastiampillai has not left the United
Kingdom and that when he originally arrived he gave an undertaking to leave at the

completion of his accountancy training, I think not when he originally arrived, but back in 1976. He, of course, says: 'I gave that undertaking, but as a result of my children being settled here I applied to have the limitations on my stay removed. In effect what I have asked the Secretary of State to do is to release me from my undertaking.' The fact that he has not carried out the undertaking could be relevant, in two ways. If it were decided that he never intended to leave and thus that he was being untruthful and fraudulent when he gave the undertaking, clearly that would be a ground for refusal of the exercise of further discretion in his favour, because anybody who is going to seek the Secretary of State's discretion must at all times have approached the matter truthfully and honestly. But that is not suggested here. If, as is apparently accepted, he honestly did intend to leave, then in my view the relevance (and it is relevant) is that the applicant, albeit he is still in this country, is to be treated as if he had left and was seeking entry from outside the country under para 48 of HC 394. In itself that is not conclusive against the applicant.

Secondly, 'close relatives . . . to turn to'. The phrase 'to turn to', apart from not coming very well at the end of the sentence (but that is a criticism of the grammar rather than anything else)' obviously qualifies 'close relatives'. Counsel for the Secretary of State suggests that in this matter the test to apply is: was there a person to whom the applicant might reasonably look for some measure of aid and support? Counsel for the applicants accepted that that was a proper test. I agree that a close relative to turn to need not be a relative who is equally able and equally willing to maintain the applicant as is the child who is in this country. But a close relative to turn to must mean a relative who has the ability to provide some assistance to the applicant by way of providing either a home or financial support so as to make it reasonable to expect the applicant to depend on that relative rather than on his child or children in the United Kingdom. It is not clear whether the Secretary of State regarded the phrase in that way. I cannot say he did not, but it is not clear whether he did.

Finally, 'the Secretary of State is not satisfied that you are wholly or mainly dependant on Mr and Mrs Weerasinghe'. I find it difficult to see how the Secretary of State arrived at that decision in 1981, for this purpose thinking only of financial dependence. The applicants, by 1981, were (and still are of course) wholly financially dependent on Mr and Mrs Weerasinghe. They were not only living rent-free with them, but they had no income of their own, save for the very small pension of about £70 a year or something of that nature from Sri Lanka. Counsel for the Secretary of State did not advance any argument on this point. It seems to me that I am justified here in saying that the Secretary of State has overlooked the material consideration, that is to say the change of circumstances in March 1980, when the applicant ceased work.

Counsel for the Secretary of State argues that, even if he fails on that particular aspect of the matter, in order to be allowed to stay the applicant had to satisfy all three tests and that it has only been shown that the Secretary of State was wrong in relation to one aspect. I cannot say what the Secretary of State's decision would have been if he had taken a different view of the first point, the financial dependence. Accordingly, though of course it does not mean that Mr and Mrs Bastiampillai are necessarily going to get a decision in their favour in the end, I think it right to send this matter back again to the Secretary of State for him to reconsider. If, despite having it back again, he says, 'I have taken into account all the relevant matters and I still decide that I am not going to exercise my discretion in his favour,' that is a matter for him, but I have concluded that he should have it back, because I believe that he discounted the change of circumstances after 12 March 1980.

Accordingly, on that limited ground, the application on the third point succeeds and I quash the Secretary of State's decision of 5 June 1981.

Application allowed.

Solicitors: *Bates Wells & Braithwaite* (for the applicants); *Treasury Solicitor.*

Sophie Craven Barrister.

Re a company

CHANCERY DIVISION
VINELOTT J
10, 11 FEBRUARY, 18 MARCH 1983

Company – Compulsory winding up – Just and equitable – Alternative remedy – Company formerly a partnership – Offer to purchase shares of minority shareholder – Whether acceptance of reasonable offer to purchase shares an alternative remedy available to minority shareholder – Whether minority shareholder entitled to have company's assets sold on open market because company was formerly a partnership – Whether just and equitable that company be wound up – Companies Act 1948, s 225(2) – Companies Act 1980, s 75.

A partnership business in which the petitioner and C were the partners was transferred by agreement to a company. The directors of the company were the petitioner, C and subsequently R, each of them being entitled to one-third of the company's issued share capital. The three directors managed the company as joint managing directors and received equal remuneration. The relationship between the petitioner, C and R broke down and the petitioner was excluded from participation in the management of the company. He was not paid any remuneration, although he remained a director, continued to receive the management accounts and was still offered access to the company's books and records. The petitioner stated his willingness to sell his shares to C and R if a fair price could be negotiated taking into account compensation for loss of office and loss of employment. C and R made a counter-offer that the petitioner should give them an option to buy his shares at a fair market value fixed by an independent expert. The petitioner rejected that proposal and, as he had threatened to do throughout, presented a petition for the compulsory winding up of the company. The petitioner contended that it would be just and equitable to wind up the company because (i) as a minority shareholder who was unfairly excluded from participation in the company's affairs by the majority shareholders he was entitled, by analogy with the dissolution of a partnership, to have the company's assets sold on the open market to ensure that full value was received for them and (ii) a winding up would enable the liquidator to investigate the conduct of the business by C and R and if necessary bring an action against them for misfeasance. C and R applied to strike out the petition on the ground that under s 225(2)[a] of the Companies Act 1948 winding up the company was only an appropriate form of relief 'in the absence of any other remedy' and that the petitioner had available to him the remedy of applying to the court for a direction under s 75[b] of the Companies Act 1980 that C and R purchase his shares at a fair value. C and R submitted that for the purposes of s 225(2) the petitioner was 'acting unreasonably in seeking to have the company wound up instead of pursuing that other remedy [under s 75]' and that therefore the court was not entitled to make a winding-up order.

Held – (1) Section 225(2) of the 1948 Act contemplated the making of a winding-up order under s 225 only if the continuance of the company would cause the petitioner an injustice which could not be remedied by any other step reasonably open to him. If any other remedy, and not just the statutory remedy of a court direction under s 75 that the petitioner's shares be purchased by the other shareholders, was reasonably available to the petitioner a winding-up order under s 225 would not be made. It followed that if the offer by C and R to purchase the petitioner's shares was a reasonable offer the petitioner's acceptance of that offer would be 'some other remedy' reasonably available to him to redress any injustice done to him and in those circumstances the court would not make a winding-up order (see p 860 *a* to *c*, post).

(2) Furthermore, even if the petitioner had been unfairly excluded by the majority

a Section 225(2) is set out at p 858 *h j*, post.
b Section 75, so far as material, is set out at p 859 *d e*, post.

shareholders from participating in the company's affairs he was not entitled to have the company's assets sold on the open market in the same way that occurred on the dissolution of a partnership, since the legal nature of a company was different from that of a partnership. If a partnership was superseded by a company the partnership assets became the property of the company and, instead of the presumptive right which a partner had that if the common intention that all partners should participate in the partnership was frustrated the partnership assets should be sold and divided up, all that a minority shareholder could do in similar circumstances was to apply to the court to have the company wound up on the ground that the majority shareholders' conduct made it just and equitable to do so, in which case the court was required to consider whether the minority shareholder had unreasonably refused an offer by the majority shareholders to acquire his shares (see p 861 *g* to p 862 *a*, post); dictum of Lord Wilberforce in *Ebrahimi v Westbourne Galleries Ltd* [1972] 2 All ER at 500 applied.

(3) In all the circumstances, in particular having regard to the terms of the offer to purchase the petitioner's shares, the petitioner had acted unreasonably in rejecting the offer. Accordingly, the court was not entitled to make a winding-up order on the petition (see p 860 *d* to *j*, p 862 *c* to *f* and p 863 *e* to *j*, post).

Notes

For compulsory winding up on the ground that it is just and equitable to do so, see 7 Halsbury's Laws (4th edn) paras 1000–1001, 1029, and for cases on the subject, see 10 Digest (Reissue) 914–928, 5344–5407.

For the Companies Act 1948, s 225, see 5 Halsbury's Statutes (3rd edn) 295.

For the Companies Act 1980, s 75, see 50(1) ibid 167.

Cases referred to in judgment

Bryanston Finance Ltd v de Vries (No 2) [1976] 1 All ER 25, [1976] Ch 63, [1976] 2 WLR 41, CA.

Darby v Darby (1856) 3 Drew 495, 61 ER 992.

Ebrahimi v Westbourne Galleries Ltd [1972] 2 All ER 492, [1973] AC 360, [1972] 2 WLR 1289, HL.

Stevenson (Hugh) & Sons Ltd v Aktiengesellschaft für Cartonagen-Industrie [1917] 1 KB 842, CA; *affd* [1918] AC 239, [1918–19] All ER Rep 600, HL.

Syers v Syers (1876) 1 App Cas 174, HL.

Cases also cited

Fildes Bros Ltd, Re [1970] 1 All ER 923, [1970] 1 WLR 592.

Tito v Waddell (No 2) [1977] 3 All ER 129, [1977] Ch 106.

Motion to strike out winding up petition

By a petition dated 18 May 1982, No 002567 of 1982, the petitioner, T, a contributory of the company, sought the winding up of the company on the ground that it was just and equitable that the company should be wound up. The respondents to the petition, C and R, the other two contributories of the company, applied, by notice of motion dated 6 July 1982, to strike out the petition on the ground that an alternative remedy to winding up the company was available to the petitioner. The facts are set out in the judgment.

Gavin Lightman QC and *R J Powell-Jones* for the respondents.
Alan Steinfeld for the petitioner.

VINELOTT J. This is a motion to strike out a petition for the winding up of a company. The petition was presented on 28 June 1982. The motion to strike out was launched on 6 July. The company was incorporated on 1 January 1967. Its name was changed on 1 June 1972. As the petition has not been advertised I will not refer to the company's present name and I will refer to the petitioner and the respondents where appropriate by initials.

Shortly before the company changed its name, which was on 28 March 1972, the petitioner, T, entered into a partnership agreement with one of the respondents, C. *a* Under that agreement, they agreed to carry on in partnership together the business of manufacturing jewellers, previously carried on by C. The partnership was to be an equal partnership. It was to be a trial partnership and to be superseded, after a year's trial, by the transfer of the business to the company. Also on 28 March 1982 the petitioner, T, and C entered into a further agreement. It was recited that they had entered into the partnership agreement, that each held 50% of the shares of the company, the name of *b* which had not then been changed, and that they intended to transfer the partnership business to the company on 10 June 1973. The agreement then set out terms on which the business was to be transferred, in particular terms as to the amounts of loans to be made by each partner to the company.

The business was duly transferred to the company. T and C became directors and, as I have said, each held an equal number of shares. The business of the company was *c* managed by them jointly in the same way as the partnership had been. Thus, the company was a classic example of a quasi-partnership and, unusually, had its origin in, and reproduced within the corporate structure, an actual partnership.

Later, T's and C's respective wives were also appointed directors. In 1976 R, a partner in the company's auditors, joined the venture. Thereafter, the issued share capital of the company comprised 300,000 £1 ordinary shares, 100,000 being issued to each of the *d* participators. R was appointed a director. The business of the company was managed jointly by the three directors who participated equally in the affairs of the company. Each was employed as managing director and all were paid the same amount of remuneration.

The relationship broke down in August 1980. It is said in the petition that on 14 August C told T that he wanted to buy T's interest and that T replied that he would be *e* willing to sell if a proper price could be agreed. The matter was discussed further on the same day with R, who said that he would prepare a valuation with a view to negotiating a price. Later on the same day, C and R told T that they wanted to remove him as a director. A notice convening an extraordinary general meeting to remove T and Mrs T as directors was handed to T on 15 August. In the event, he was not removed as a director, although Mrs T was. *f*

Although T has continued to be a director, he has, since 1 September 1980, been excluded from any participation in the management of the business of the company and he has not been paid any remuneration. Before 1 September each director was receiving £30,000 a year by way of remuneration. Between 1 September 1980 and November 1981 T received nothing and C and R each received £20,000 per annum. In November 1981 C's and R's remuneration was restored to £30,000 per annum. *g*

It is said in the petition that virtually all the profits have been absorbed in directors' remuneration. That is the case made in the petition.

Between 1 September 1980 and the presentation of the petition there were negotiations between the parties as to the price to be paid for T's shares. Both sides instructed solicitors. There was initially some dispute whether, pending agreement on the price to be paid, T should be restored to his position as managing director and entitled to the same level of *h* remuneration as the others. I do not need to delay further to describe that aspect of this case. On 5 September T's solicitors, Bernard Oberman & Co, which I will abbreviate to Obermans, wrote to R informing him that they had had a conference with counsel—

> 'who has advised that in his opinion the court is likely to make a winding up order on the grounds that it is just and equitable to do so having regard to what has happened. I, therefore, ask you once again whether you will confirm that it is the *j* intention to buy out Mr. [T's] shares at a fair price and I would request you in any event to let me have up to date figures preferably with your valuation and offer so that if such offer is not immediately acceptable to Mr. [T] he can instruct his accountant to enter into negotiations with you without any delay. As I have said, counsel has advised that we are quite justified in presenting a petition now to wind

up the company; alternatively, we could wait until section 75 of the 1980 Companies Act comes into force, probably later this year, and under which the court could grant alternative relief.'

Later, on 17 September, writing to C and R's solicitors, David Alterman & Sewell (Altermans), Obermans said:

> 'You and I now know that the intention must be that Messrs. [C] and [R] will buy our client's shares in the company at a price to be agreed and this can also take into account compensation for the loss of office and for loss of employment.'

On 5 October R put forward an offer of £13,000. In replying to that offer Obermans said that they thought it was absurdly low, but they suggested a meeting when figures supporting the offer could be examined by them. They repeated the threat that either there would have to be an acceptable offer for their client's shares or there would be a petition to wind up the company. Obermans then sought advice from accountants and they, the accountants, put an off-the-cuff value on T's shares of £200,000. That was on 20 November 1980. Between 20 November and 15 December negotiations about other matters, in particular the release of T from a guarantee to the company's bankers, took priority over the negotiations as to the price to be paid for the shares. On 15 December Altermans, writing to Obermans, said that R and C would be happy to sell their shares to T for £200,000 each and commented:

> 'This is subject to both the shareholdings being sold together and you will appreciate that as this would be a majority shareholding it is, therefore, more saleable and more valuable than your client's shareholding.'

Disputes continued on other matters for some time without reference to the price to be paid for T's shares, until on 14 May 1981 Obermans wrote to Altermans to say that as negotiations had not produced results—

> 'We write to inform you that we have received our client's instructions to send the papers herein back to counsel with a view to the presentation of a petition to wind up the company. If your clients would prefer to deal with the matter by way of a realistic offer to purchase our client's shares at a fair price, please do so as quickly as possible.'

With the reply of Altermans on 9 June matters took a new turn. In their reply, Altermans, on behalf of C and R, put forward a suggestion that T should give them an option to buy his shares at a fair market value to be determined by an independent expert and that in default of acceptance by them within 28 days the parties should co-operate in putting the company into liquidation. That offer was rejected on the same day on the ground that it was one-sided in that C and R would not be bound to buy if the price was too high. It was also suggested that the valuation should be made by an arbitrator rather than an expert.

On 11 June Altermans replied to this letter to say that they would consider with their clients a proposal under which, if the price was unacceptable to T, he would not be bound to sell but that if he decided not to sell, he would agree not to press for the winding up of the company. That term was also rejected by Obermans in a letter dated 14 July, again on the ground that it was too one-sided. In rejecting the proposal, Obermans said that T would accept £80,000, part of the price to be paid by instalments. That offer was rejected by Altermans on 26 August when they offered to arrange a meeting with T's accountant to discuss the financial position of the company.

Although there was thereafter further correspondence on other matters, nothing more was said about the proposal for ascertaining a value of the shares by an agreed machinery. As I have said, the petition was presented on 28 June 1982. It was presented with no prior warning.

In an affidavit in support of the motion to strike out the petition, R says that he and C are gravely concerned at the cost and delay that would be involved in a contested petition in which the costs might exceed the net asset value of the company and that while they recognise T's right to have his shareholding bought at a fair valuation or to a winding up, they have endeavoured to meet this by making the offers to which I have referred.

In his affidavit in reply, T makes a number of criticisms of the proposal that his shares should be acquired at a valuation. They are, briefly, as follows. (a) He objects to the proposal that the value of the shares should be made by an expert on the ground that the only way in which the value of the company's assets can be ascertained with any certainty is for the company to be wound up and for the assets to be sold by a liquidator, either as a going concern or on a break-up basis, it being for the liquidator to choose which is the more likely to produce the maximum value. (b) It is said that the proposal in the letter of 9 June, as modified in the letter of 11 July, would put T at a disadvantage in that if the valuation were less than he expected and if C and R were content with it, he would be faced with the alternative of accepting an offer which he thought too low or being locked into the company, whereas C and R if they thought the offer was too high, could simply reject it and have the company wound up. (c) It is said that a valuation of T's shares, if valued as a minority holding, would not fully reflect the value of a one-third share of the assets of the company. (d) Lastly, it is said that since October 1980 T has been excluded from practical participation in the affairs of the company and does not know, in consequence, what transactions have been entered into. He claims that he is entitled to have the company wound up compulsorily so that a liquidator can investigate the way in which the business of the company has been conducted and, if necessary, launch misfeasance proceedings against C and R. No specific allegation of misconduct is made. T draws attention to the fact that there appears to have been a substantial deterioration in the net assets of the company and that at a recent meeting of the board of directors a resolution was passed authorising the company to oppose the petition, a resolution which, he says, might have the effect of throwing the whole cost of the proceedings onto the company.

In an affidavit in reply, R meets the objections summarised in (b), (c) and (d). As to (b), C and R are now prepared to undertake to purchase T's shares at the value placed on them by the expert or arbitrator. As to (c), he states that he and C are willing to purchase T's shares at a value equal to one-third of the value of the company's net assets. As to (d), he says that he and C are willing that the expert or arbitrator should have access to all information he thinks necessary and that he should take into account any claim which he thinks a liquidator could have made against R or C or any third party and that no deduction should be made in respect of any costs incurred by the company in this litigation.

He also says that since October 1980, T has opened his own retail jewellery shop, whereas he and C have been engaged full-time in managing the company's business, which is their sole source of livelihood. That is all I need say about the facts of this case.

Section 225(1) of the Companies Act 1948 provides that on the hearing of a winding-up petition the court may dismiss it or adjourn the hearing conditionally or unconditionally or make any interim order or any other order it may think fit. It is well settled that the powers so conferred on the court give the court the widest discretion. I should read s 225(2) in full:

> 'Where the petition is presented by members of the company as contributories on the ground that it is just and equitable that the company should be wound up, the court, if it is of the opinion—(*a*) that the petitioners are entitled to relief either by winding up the company or by some other means; and (*b*) that in the absence of any other remedy it would be just and equitable that the company should be wound up; shall make a winding-up order, unless it is also of the opinion both that some other remedy is available to the petitioners and that they are acting unreasonably in seeking to have the company wound up instead of pursuing that other remedy.'

The effect of sub-s (2) is that if a petitioner can make out a case of compulsory winding up on the ground that, disregarding the existence of any other remedy, it is just and equitable that the company should be wound up, then a winding-up order should be made unless the court is of the opinion both that the petitioner has another remedy and that he is acting unreasonably in not pursuing that remedy in preference to the winding-up order.

It is common ground in this case that the facts alleged in the petition would establish a case of unjustified exclusion of T, a shareholder entitled to play an equal part, together with the other shareholders, in the management of the company and to participate in the income generated from its business activities by receiving fair remuneration within the principle established by *Ebrahimi v Westbourne Galleries Ltd* [1972] 2 All ER 492, [1973] AC 360.

Counsel who appears for C and R submits that in this case T has another remedy under s 75 of the Companies Act 1980 (which came into force after October 1980 but before the winding-up petition was presented) which remedy, it is said, T ought to pursue in preference to a winding-up petition. Under s 75 the court can, as an alternative to making a winding-up order, direct one member to purchase the shares of another member at what the court considers to be a fair value.

Counsel for T takes the preliminary objection that T cannot, on the facts of this case, bring himself within s 75. He points out that in *Ebrahimi v Westbourne Galleries Ltd* [1972] 2 All ER 492 at 505, [1973] AC 360 at 385, the facts of which are, for practical purposes, the same as in the instant case, Lord Cross said that the petitioner could not bring himself within s 210 of the 1948 Act because the conduct of the majority shareholders in excluding him from participation in the management of the company did not affect his rights as shareholder. Counsel points out that the opening words of s 75 of the 1980 Act—

> 'Any member of a company may apply to the court by petition . . . on the ground that the affairs of the company are being or have been conducted in a manner which is unfairly prejudicial to the interests of some part of the members (including at least himself) . . .'

reflect and are similar to the opening words of s 210 of the 1948 Act:

> 'Any member of a company who complains that the affairs of the company are being conducted in a manner oppressive to some part of the members (including himself) . . .'

He submits that the substitution of the words 'unfairly prejudicial' for 'oppressive' cannot affect the principle, well established by the authorities on s 210 and restated by Lord Cross in the passage I have mentioned that a member can only bring himself within the section if the conduct complained of affects his rights as a shareholder. Counsel for C and R points out that the language of s 210 of the 1948 Act differs also in that the conduct complained of under s 75 of the 1980 Act may be unfairly prejudicial to the *interests* of some of the members, whereas under s 210 it has to be oppressive to *some part* of the members. He submits that in a case where what is alleged is unfair exclusion from the management of the affairs of the company the interest of the minority shareholder under the agreement, express or implied, that he will be allowed to participate and to be paid remuneration is affected, though his strict rights as a shareholder may not be.

I can see considerable force in this submission. It seems to me unlikely that the legislature could have intended to exclude from the scope of s 75 of the 1980 Act a shareholder in the position of Mr Ebrahimi in the *Westbourne Galleries* case, notwithstanding that, as Lord Cross pointed out in that case ([1972] 2 All ER 492 at 505, [1973] AC 360 at 385):

> 'What the minority shareholder in cases of this sort really wants is not to have the company wound up—which may prove an unsatisfactory remedy—but to be paid a proper price for his shareholding.'

However, I do not need to decide this question and I do not do so. In my judgment there are in the instant case two answers to the objection of counsel for T.

First, I do not think that it is necessary for the respondent to a petition to show that the petitioner has some other statutory remedy available to him, that is that he has a remedy under s 210 of the 1948 Act, or now, s 75 of the 1980 Act. What s 225(2) of the 1948 Act contemplates is, I think, a situation in which the continuance of the company would be unjust to the petitioner and where that injustice cannot be remedied by any step reasonably open to the petitioner. If an offer is made to purchase his shares he is thereby provided with an alternative course; the question is whether he is acting unreasonably in rejecting it.

Second, the jurisdiction of the court under s 225 is discretionary. The court would be at least entitled to refuse to make an order if satisfied that the petitioner is persisting in asking for a winding-up order and that it would be unfair to the other shareholders to make that order, having regard to any offer they have made to the petitioner to meet his grievance in another way. If that is right, then the question I have to consider is whether T is acting unreasonably in refusing to accept the respondents' offer to purchase his shares at a valuation. I should add in this connection that it is common ground that in answering this question I have to look at the situation as it is today and not merely the situation as it was when the petition was presented. It is as much an abuse of the process of the court to persist in a petition which, because of a subsequent offer, is bound to fail as it would be to present a petition which, on the facts existing at the time of the petition, is bound to fail: see *Bryanston Finance Ltd v de Vries (No 2)* [1976] 1 All ER 25 at 35, [1976] Ch 63 at 77 per Buckley LJ.

In answering this question I must, of course, assume that all the averments in the petition will be established at the hearing. I must also have regard to the terms of the offer that has now been made.

Two objections are made by T to the offer made by C and R. The first (reflected in his affidavit) is that in a winding up a liquidator would be able to investigate the conduct of the company's affairs since October 1980 and if he thought fit to commence misfeasance proceedings. I have already referred to R's offer that a valuer should have power to take into account any claims which he thinks the company may have against himself or C. Even apart from that offer, T's objection to the respondent's proposals is, in my judgment, wholly misconceived. There is no evidence whatever to suggest that the respondents have been conducting the affairs of the company, in which, of course, they each of them have a one-third interest, otherwise than in the company's interests.

T refers in his evidence to a deterioration in the net asset position of the company since October 1980. That is not of itself evidence of misconduct or evidence which founds even a suspicion of misconduct. There is nothing sinister in the fact that at a time of slump a luxury trade should suffer losses both in day-to-day trading and in the value of its stock and other assets. T relies on the fact that C and R, as the majority of the board, have passed a resolution authorising the company to defend the petition. The claim, as I understand it, is that it was misconduct on their part to expose the company to a possible liability in costs. If anything, it was the launching of the petition to which the company is a necessary party which gave rise to that risk. However, the costs of the petition are always in the discretion of the court and, in the ordinary course, if the petition succeeded the costs of defending it would fall on the opposing shareholders and not on the company.

As against these complaints, it is clear that T, who remains a director, has received management accounts and has been offered access to the company's books and records. In view of the respondents' offer, the terms of the appointment of a valuer or arbitrator can confer on him wide powers to call for information and to investigate the way in which the company's affairs have been conducted. In these circumstances there is, in my judgment, no substance whatever in this objection.

Second, it is said that a minority shareholder unfairly excluded from participation in the affairs of a company should be entitled, like a partner, to have the assets of the company sold on the open market so that he can be confident that full value is obtained for them. It is, of course, well settled that in the case of a partnership the general, though not the invariable, rule is that on dissolution one partner is not entitled to purchase the shares of the other partners at a valuation. The assets of the partnership must be realised by a sale; a partner who wishes to continue the business must apply to the court for leave to bid at an auction: see *Lindley on Partnership* (14th edn, 1979) p 199 and *Hugh Stevenson* a *& Sons Ltd v Aktiengesellschaft für Cartonagen-Industrie* [1917] 1 KB 842 and compare *Syers v Syers* (1876) 1 App Cas 174.

Counsel for T relied on a passage in the speech of Lord Wilberforce in *Ebrahimi v Westbourne Galleries Ltd* [1972] 2 All ER 492 at 500, [1973] AC 360 at 379–380, where, having summarised the factors which made it just and equitable in that case for the company to be wound up, he said:

b

> 'It is these, and analagous, factors which may bring into play the just and equitable clause, and they do so directly, through the force of the words themselves. To refer, as so many of the cases do, to "quasi-partnerships" or "in substance partnerships" may be convenient but may also be confusing. It may be convenient because it is the law of partnership which has developed the conceptions of probity, good faith and mutual confidence, and the remedies where these are absent, which become c relevant once such factors as I have mentioned are found to exist: the words "just and equitable" sum these up in the law of partnership itself. And in many, but not necessarily all, cases there has been a pre-existing partnership the obligations of which it is reasonable to suppose continue to underline the new company structure.'

However, in the words immediately following Lord Wilberforce emphasised that the d analogy with a partnership is not a perfect match. He continued:

> 'But the expressions may be confusing if they obscure or deny that that the parties (possibly former partners) are now co-members in a company, who have accepted, in law, new obligations. A company, however small, however domestic, is a company not a partnership or even a quasi-partnership and it is through the just and e equitable clause that obligations, common to partnership relations, may come in.'

Kindersley V-C pointed out in *Darby v Darby* (1856) 3 Drew 495 at 503, 61 ER 992 at 995, in a passage cited in the Court of Appeal in the *Hugh Stevenson* case [1917] 1 KB 842 at 846, that the rule that on dissolution of a partnership all the assets must be sold and the net proceeds divided is a rule inherent in the very contract of partnership. The rights f of the partners inter se are governed by contract express or implied and by the obligations superimposed on that contract by the principles of equity. Fairness and good faith require that in the absence of some special provision for the purchase by one partner of the shares of another or of special circumstances, such as were present in *Syers v Syers*, on dissolution one partner is not entitled to claim the partnership business as his own and to exclude the other partners and to compensate them only by a sum arrived at by valuation. All g must be treated alike. But when partners transfer their business to a company, they accept a new legal structure with different rights and liabilities, albeit that equitable principles will govern the way in which those rights are exercised. While the partnership continues, the partners own the partnership assets, each is entitled to require that those assets are employed in the partnership business and that they are realised by a sale when that business comes to an end. If the partnership is superseded by a company the h partnership assets become the property of the company. The partners take in exchange shares of the company which, unlike an interest in a partnership, are capable, subject to restrictions in the articles, of being transferred or transmitted, though in the case of a minority holding the full value may not be realisable on sale. It seems to me impossible to say that despite this change in the relationship between the former partners, each shareholder has the same presumptive rights, if the common intention that all should j participate in the affairs of the company is frustrated, to have the company wound up and its assets realised on sale, a course which, I should add, is likely to prove far more damaging to the shareholders than the appointment of a receiver and the sale of a partnership business is to the partners. What each quasi-partner is entitled to do is to apply to the court to have the company wound up on the ground that the conduct of the majority makes it just and equitable to do so. In deciding whether to make an order the court must consider whether, having regard to, amongst other things, any offer to acquire the petitioner's shares, he is acting unreasonably in seeking a winding-up order.

Counsel for T submitted that if T is denied the remedy of a winding-up order on the ground that the respondents have made a reasonable offer to purchase his shares, the court will, in effect, expose any minority shareholder in a company of this kind to the hazard that the majority will be able to exclude him from participation in the affairs of the company, contrary to the understanding which underlay the formation of the company and then compulsorily acquire his shares, notwithstanding the absence of any power in the articles to do so.

I do not think that this consequence follows. Whether, if T had made it clear in August 1980 that he was not willing to sell his shares at any price but would insist on a winding up of the company and had presented a petition forthwith, it would have been right to make a winding-up order notwithstanding the offer that has now been made, I do not find it necessary to decide. That is not what happened in this case. At the time when T was first excluded from participation in the affairs of the company he was willing to sell his shares to his co-shareholders if a fair price could be negotiated. Negotiations having proved unfruitful, his co-shareholders now offer to acquire his shares at a value reached by a machinery which, in my judgment, meets all T's reasonable objections. In insisting on a winding-up order he is, in effect, asking that the respondents should either buy out his shares at the price he chooses to place on them or face the disruption of a winding-up order, and that notwithstanding the fact that at least until July 1982 they continued to run the company in the expectation that a price, or a fair machinery for ascertaining the price, could be agreed and exposed themselves to a continuing liability under a guarantee to the company's bankers in order to do so. In these circumstances, in my judgment, T is not entitled to the order he seeks. However, I think it would be wrong to dismiss the petition forthwith with the possible consequence that if some unforeseen difficulty arises in formulating a detailed agreement governing the machinery for ascertaining the value of the shares, T will have to start all over again. I will, therefore, stand over this petition to enable the parties to agree the terms of a submission to arbitration or to an expert; in the mean time all further proceedings on the petition will be stayed. The matter can be mentioned to me if an agreement can be reached and at that stage the petition will be dismissed. If there is any disagreement as to the terms of the submission I will hear further argument on that question.

18 March. **VINELOTT J**, having heard argument on the terms of submission to arbitration or to an expert, delivered the following judgment. I gave judgment in this case on 11 February 1983. I decided that in the light of an offer to purchase the petitioner's shares made in the respondents' evidence the petitioner was not entitled to the winding-up order sought in the petition. However, I did not dismiss the petition or strike it out then in order that, if unforeseen difficulties arose in formulating a detailed agreement for the way in which the value of the shares was to be ascertained in an arbitration, the petitioner would not be put in a position where he would have to start a fresh petition.

A difficulty has arisen. It is this. Should the value of the business, one-third of which is to be attributed to T's one-third of the shares, be ascertained at the date of submission to arbitration, or in September 1980 when T was excluded from participation in the affairs of the company? Counsel for T has argued as always very persuasively in favour of the view that the valuation should relate back to September 1980, and he submits that that would be a date which the court could fix in the case of a petition under s 75 of the Companies Act 1980. He intimated that if necessary he would seek leave to amend the petition so as to invoke s 75. I do not think any amendment is necessary but if it were I would doubt very much whether at this stage I should allow it to be made. It is unnecessary because it seems to me that in considering whether the terms of the offer are fair (and it is only if they are fair that it would be right to dismiss the petition) I am entitled to weigh the question whether the valuation should be current or retrospective. I can conceive of many cases where, in an application under s 75 or where a valuation is offered in the face of a winding-up petition, fairness would require that the valuation should relate back to an earlier date such as, in this case, the exclusion of T. I do not think that that would be the right course in this case. My reasons are shortly as follows.

As long ago as 9 June 1981 the respondents made an offer in these terms, that T's shares should be valued by an expert and that they should be given an option to purchase T's shares at the value attributed to them by the expert; and that if they did not exercise the option within a brief period they would join with T in winding up the company. That was rejected as one-sided. A further modified offer, under which T was similarly given the right to reject an offer to purchase his shares at the price arrived at by the expert or an arbitrator, but on the basis that if he did so the company would not be wound up, was also rejected as one-sided.

In my judgment the claim that these offers were one-sided is wholly misconceived. What the respondents were doing on 9 June 1981 was in effect to say to T, 'You may have the full value of your shares, ascertained by an independent expert, if that is a price which we find we are able and willing to pay; and, if not, the company will have to be wound up because that is the only other way in which your complaint can be met.' It was, as it happens, precisely the effect of the order made by the House of Lords in *Syers v Syers* (1876) 1 App Cas 174, on which counsel for T heavily relied.

That offer having been rejected, nothing happened until May 1982, when this petition was launched. Throughout the course of the petition, in the evidence and in argument, the case of T has been that notwithstanding the offers made, he is entitled to have the company wound up. In a winding up of the company he would get one-third of the net value of the assets of the company ascertained on sale rather than by valuation. Why (if I may put the point rhetorically), if he is paid out by valuation instead of by sale, should he seek to make the valuation retrospective?

What I think has happened in this case is that T has rejected what to my mind was a fair offer in order to use the threat of winding up to exact from the respondents what he considers to be the fair value of his shares. It may be that there were deficiences in the original offer but I have no doubt myself that if the criticisms later made had been made at the time they would have been answered in the way they have been answered; in particular, by making it clear that the value to be attributed to T's shares would be one-third of the value of the net assets of the company, so that any discount attributable to a minority holding would be avoided.

It seems to me that in the light of that history it would be wrong to allow T now to go back to a valuation at an earlier date. It may well be that if he had made it clear initially that he was willing to sell at a valuation ascertained in this way and if that offer had been refused by the respondents, they would have been compelled, if they were to avoid a winding up, to accept a valuation on that basis. But that is not this case.

The point that has troubled me is that T has been excluded, with the consequence that he has not shared in the profits of the company. The profits have all been paid out by way of remuneration to the respondents. It seems at first sight unfair that, having been, at least on the face of it, wrongly and unfairly excluded from the profits of a joint venture, he should not be compensated. But again, this consequence is, it seems to me, a result of his own failure to accept a fair offer as long ago as 9 June 1981. If he had negotiated then he might well have been able to secure agreement both to the valuation relating back to October 1980 and to an arrangement under which interest would be paid at the proper rate on what was ascertained to be his share. But it is, I think, now impossible, in the light of events as they have unfolded, for T to ask to participate in that income. There is, in particular, no evidence, indeed, no claim in the evidence, that the remuneration paid to the respondents was not remuneration which would have had to have been paid to secure the services they provided so that it would, even in the case of a partnership, fall to be deducted in ascertaining the profit to the partnership. Any feeling of anxiety I might have had on this score has been to some extent allayed by the fact that T has made a claim for unfair dismissal, which has yet to be heard. I understand that it is agreed that that claim is to be disregarded by the arbitrator but that if it succeeds the respondents will only be asked to be paid two-thirds of the amount awarded.

The other question is, of course, the costs of the petition. It will be apparent from what

I have said that in my judgment T was wrong to issue his petition without exploring further the terms of the offer in the letter of 9 June 1981, in particular in relation to the a matters which have since been resolved by agreement by the respondents. That being so, I think he must pay the costs of the petition up to and including today, to be taxed on the usual basis.

Order accordingly.

Solicitors: *Bernard Oberman & Co* (for the petitioner); *David Alterman & Sewell* (for the b respondents).

Jacqueline Metcalfe Barrister.

c

Amin v Entry Clearance Officer, Bombay

COURT OF APPEAL, CIVIL DIVISION
ORMROD, DUNN LJJ AND WATERHOUSE J
5 JUNE 1981 d

HOUSE OF LORDS
LORD FRASER OF TULLYBELTON, LORD KEITH OF KINKEL, LORD SCARMAN, LORD BRANDON OF OAKBROOK AND LORD BRIGHTMAN
25, 26, 27 APRIL, 7 JULY 1983

e *Commonwealth immigrant – Appeal – Appeal against refusal to issue special voucher admitting United Kingdom passport holder to United Kingdom – Whether right of appeal from entry clearance officer's decision – Whether special voucher an 'entry clearance' – Whether voucher evidence of eligibility for entry – Immigration Act 1971, ss 13(2), 33(1).*

Commonwealth immigrant – Special voucher scheme – Sex discrimination – Refusal to issue f *special voucher to married woman who was not head of a household – Whether special voucher scheme unlawful sex discrimination – Sex Discrimination Act 1975, ss 1, 29(1).*

The appellant, an Asian woman, was a citizen of the United Kingdom and Colonies and the holder of a United Kingdom passport. In 1976 she applied to the entry clearance officer in Bombay, where she lived with her husband who was an Indian citizen, for a g special voucher on her own account to enable her to settle in the United Kingdom. The special voucher scheme was a non-statutory scheme under which entry vouchers were issued to Commonwealth citizens who held British passports but who were prevented by the provisions of the Commonwealth Immigrants Act 1968 from entering and settling in the United Kingdom. As a matter of administrative discretion special vouchers were only issued to heads of households who were under pressure to leave their country of h residence. The appellant's father, who lived in Tanzania, had previously obtained a special voucher for himself, his wife and his unmarried children but had not included the appellant in his application. The appellant's application was refused on the ground that she was not the head of a household and therefore not eligible to apply for a special voucher. The appellant applied for judicial review of the entry clearance officer's refusal of her application, seeking a declaration that she had a right of appeal to an adjudicator j under s 13(2)[a] of the Immigration Act 1971 because a special voucher was 'an entry clearance' as defined in s 33(1)[b] of that Act. The Divisional Court and, on appeal, the Court of Appeal refused to grant judicial review. The appellant appealed to the House of

a Section 13(2) is set out at p 866 *h*, post
b Section 33(1), so far as material, is set out at p 867 *h*, post

Lords, contending further that in so far as the special voucher scheme discriminated between husbands and wives it was unlawful under ss 1[c] and 29(1)[d] of the Sex Discrimination Act 1975.

Held (Lord Scarman and Lord Brandon dissenting) – The appeal would be dismissed for the following reasons—

(1) A special voucher was not a 'document which [was] to be taken as evidence of a person's eligibility . . . for entry into the United Kingdom' and therefore not an entry clearance as defined in s 33(1) of the 1971 Act, because the issue of a special voucher depended on the exercise of an administrative discretion rather than on proof of facts establishing eligibility. Since a special voucher was not an entry clearance it followed that a refusal to issue a special voucher was not appealable under s 13(2) of the 1971 Act (see p 870 *c* to *e*, p 873 *e* to *g* and p 883 *c* to *j*, post).

(2) Although the special voucher scheme was by its nature discriminatory against women, that discrimination was not unlawful under s 29 of the 1975 Act, because s 29 as a whole applied to the direct provision of facilities and services and not to the mere grant of permission to use those facilities, and the entry clearance officer in Bombay had not been providing a service for would-be immigrants but performing his duty of controlling immigration (see p 871 *c e g* to *j*, p 872 *e*, p 873 *e* to *g* and p 883 *h j*, post); *Kassam v Immigration Appeal Tribunal* [1980] 2 All ER 330 and *Home Office v Commission for Racial Equality* [1981] 1 All ER 1042 approved; *Savjani v IRC* [1981] 1 All ER 1121 distinguished.

Decision of the Court of Appeal p 866, post, affirming decision of the Divisional Court of the Queen's Bench Division sub nom *R v Entry Clearance Officer, Bombay, ex p Amin* [1980] 2 All ER 837, affirmed.

Notes

For what constitutes entry clearance, and for the special voucher system, see 4 Halsbury's Laws (4th edn) paras 981, 991.

For sex discrimination generally, see 16 ibid para 771:2.

For the Commonwealth Immigrants Act 1968, see 4 Halsbury's Statutes (3rd edn) 60.

For the Immigration Act 1971, ss 13, 33, see 41 ibid 34, 52.

For the Sex Discrimination Act 1975, ss 1, 29, see 45 ibid 227, 248.

Cases referred to in opinions

Applin v Race Relations Board [1974] 2 All ER 73, [1975] AC 259, [1974] 2 WLR 541, HL.

Associated Provincial Picture Houses Ltd v Wednesbury Corp [1947] 2 All ER 680, [1948] 1 KB 223, CA.

Chief Constable of the North Wales Police v Evans [1982] 3 All ER 141, [1982] 1 WLR 1155, HL.

Home Office v Commission for Racial Equality [1981] 1 All ER 1042, [1982] QB 385, [1981] 2 WLR 703.

Kassam v Immigration Appeal Tribunal [1980] 2 All ER 330, [1980] 1 WLR 1037, CA.

Savjani v IRC [1981] 1 All ER 1121, [1981] QB 458, [1981] 2 WLR 636, CA.

Appeal

Mrs Bhadrabala Arvindbhai Amin appealed against the decision of the Divisional Court of the Queen's Bench Division (Lord Lane CJ, Griffiths and Webster JJ) ([1980] 2 All ER 837, [1980] 1 WLR 1530) on 30 June 1980 dismissing her application for judicial review of a decision of the respondent, the entry clearance officer at Bombay, that she was not entitled to a special voucher enabling her to enter the United Kingdom and that there was no right of appeal under s 13(2) of the Immigration Act 1971 against the decision. The facts are set out in the opinion of Lord Fraser (see p 866, post).

K S Nathan for the appellant.
David Latham for the respondent.

---

c Section 1, so far as material, is set out at p 871 *a*, post
d Section 29(1) is set out at p 872 *a b*, post

ORMROD LJ. This is an appeal by the applicant, Mrs Amin, against a decision of the Divisional Court of the Queen's Bench Division given on 30 April 1980 and contained in a a judgment by Lord Lane CJ, with whom the other two members of the court, namely Griffiths and Webster JJ, agreed (see [1980] 2 All ER 837, [1980] 1 WLR 1530).

We have listened with interest to the submissions of counsel for the appellant in this court which reproduced in substance the submission which he made to the Divisional Court and, while taking the points that he has made, I think it only necessary to say this, that the argument which he seeks to put forward, namely that under the Immigration b Act 1971, s 13(2) the applicant in this case has a right of appeal against the refusal to grant her what is called a 'special voucher', is answered shortly. There is no conceivable means by which any form of appellate body could adjudicate on that issue because whether or not a special voucher is granted appears to be (and there are no rules about it) wholly a matter of practice and discretion. All I can say is that I agree with the judgment of Lord Lane CJ and would dismiss this appeal. c

DUNN LJ. I agree.

WATERHOUSE J. I agree.

Appeal dismissed. Leave to appeal to the House of Lords refused. d

Appeal
The appellant appealed to the House of Lords with the leave of the Appeal Committee granted on 12 October 1981.

Sir Charles Fletcher-Cooke QC and *K S Nathan* for the appellant. e
Simon D Brown and *David Latham* for the respondent.

Their Lordships took time for consideration.

7 July. The following opinions were delivered.

f

LORD FRASER OF TULLYBELTON. My Lords, this appeal raises two questions, one under the Immigration Act 1971 and the other under the Sex Discrimination Act 1975. The question under the 1971 Act concerns the status of what are called 'special vouchers', sometimes also called 'special quota vouchers', which are issued in certain circumstances to persons who are citizens of the United Kingdom and Colonies and holders of a United Kingdom passport. The appellant is a citizen of the United Kingdom g and Colonies who holds a United Kingdom passport. She is a woman of Asian origin. The appeal was presented on the footing that she had applied for a special voucher and that her application had been refused. That is not a strictly accurate description of what occurred, but, for reasons that will appear later, I propose to assume that it is correct. The appellant now claims to be entitled to appeal to an adjudicator against the refusal of a special voucher. Her claim is founded on s 13(2) of the 1971 Act, which provides: h

> 'Subject to the provisions of this Part of this Act, a person who, on an application duly made, is refused a certificate of patriality or an entry clearance may appeal to an adjudicator against the refusal.'

The appellant contends that a special voucher is an entry clearance within the meaning of that subsection. Her contention is denied by the respondent. In order to explain the j rival contentions, it is necessary to refer briefly to the origin of special vouchers. Before 1968 holders of British passports were, generally speaking, free to enter and settle in the United Kingdom without restriction. From about 1965 onwards the governments of certain East African states, formerly British colonies, adopted a policy of excluding persons who were not citizens of their state from trading or taking employment there.

The consequence was that persons who did not hold local citizenship of the East African state in which they were living were virtually obliged to leave it. Many of them came to the United Kingdom, as they were then entitled to do, but the influx became difficult to absorb. The Commonwealth Immigrants Act 1968 therefore extended immigration control, which had previously applied only to persons not holding British passports, to apply also to citizens of the United Kingdom and Colonies holding British passports unless they had certain prescribed connections with the United Kingdom. Difficulties then arose because many holders of British passports, particularly Asians living in East Africa, found themselves obliged to leave the countries where they had been living and with nowhere else to go because they were not allowed into the United Kingdom. To ease their position, the British government in 1968 introduced the special voucher scheme, whereby vouchers are issued to heads of households, who are holders of British passports, and who are under pressure to leave their countries of residence. The scheme has no express statutory basis and no rules have been published defining the conditions on which special vouchers will be issued. The reason is that the scheme is intended to be flexible and is operated by the exercise of administrative discretion, according to the needs of particular individuals and to the circumstances prevailing in their country of residence at the time. It is subject to an overall ceiling of 5,000 special vouchers per annum. The ceiling applies to the number of heads of families, but the number of persons actually admitted to the United Kingdom as a result of the scheme is much larger than that as dependants, including children up to 25 years old provided they are unmarried and dependant on the voucher holder, are allowed to accompany the head of the family to the United Kingdom if they have entry clearance.

Special vouchers were at first issued at the discretion of the British High Commissioners in East Africa, but some are now issued at the discretion of entry clearance officers in India, including the entry clearance officer at Bombay who is the respondent to this appeal.

In 1973 the appellant's father applied for a special voucher. He was a citizen of the United Kingdom and Colonies and held a British passport but he was living in Tanzania. He was granted a special voucher for himself, and entry clearance was also given to his wife and two unmarried children. At that date the appellant was already married to an Indian national and was living with him in India. Her father therefore did not include her in his application, although he was still supporting her financially. In 1976 the appellant, who was still living in India, applied for a special voucher on her own account. Her application was refused on the ground that she was not the head of a family. She then initiated the present proceedings for judicial review directed to the (British) entry clearance officer at Bombay. Her application for judicial review was refused by the Divisional Court (Lord Lane CJ, Griffiths and Webster JJ) ([1980] 2 All ER 837, [1980] 1 WLR 1530) and on appeal by the Court of Appeal (Ormrod, Dunn LJJ and Waterhouse J) (see p 866, ante).

The whole question in this part of the case is whether a special voucher is an entry clearance in the sense of s 13(2) of the 1971 Act. 'Entry clearance' is defined in s 33(1) of that Act as follows:

> '"entry clearance" means a visa, entry certificate or other document which, in accordance with the immigration rules, is to be taken as evidence of a person's eligibility, though not patrial, for entry into the United Kingdom (but does not include a work permit).'

Clearly a special voucher is not a visa or an entry certificate but the appellant contends that it is an 'other document' of the type described in that definition. I agree with both the courts below that it is not. I reach that opinion for two reasons.

First, as Ormrod LJ said in the Court of Appeal, there is no basis on which any appellate body or person could properly adjudicate on an appeal against refusal of a special voucher. An applicant has no right to be granted a special voucher and he could not show that an entry clearance officer had erred in law by refusing his application. The grant or refusal of a special voucher is a matter of administrative discretion, depending on the circumstances of the individual applicant and, as it is subject to an overall ceiling, it may involve weighing the needs of one applicant against those of others who are in competition with him. In my opinion, accordingly, a right of appeal would be unworkable in practice, and I would only be disposed to decide that it had been conferred by the 1971 Act if the Act contained an unambiguous provision to that effect. The only part of the Act said to have that effect is the definition of entry clearance in s 33(1) which I have just quoted and to which I shall return later.

Before I consider that definition, I should mention that counsel for the respondent conceded (rightly in my opinion) that, although the discretion of the administrative officer responsible for issuing special vouchers is unrestricted, its exercise is always subject to judicial review on the principles which were stated by Lord Greene MR in the well-known case of *Associated Provincial Picture Houses Ltd v Wednesbury Corp* [1947] 2 All ER 680 at 682, [1948] 1 KB 223 at 228. But that concession does not in any way imply that there is a right of appeal on the merits against an administrative decision. Judicial review is concerned not with the merits of a decision but with the manner in which the decision was made. No abuse of authority or unfair treatment such as would call for judicial review is alleged here, where the appellant's case rests simply on an assertion of a legal right of appeal. Judicial review is entirely different from an ordinary appeal. It is made effective by the court's quashing an administrative decision without substituting its own decision, and is to be contrasted with an appeal, where the appellate tribunal substitutes its own decision on the merits for that of the administrative officer. The difference was explained in this House recently in *Chief Constable of the North Wales Police v Evans* [1982] 3 All ER 141, [1982] 1 WLR 1155 and I need not repeat what was said there. Section 19 of the 1971 Act directs adjudicators as to their duties when hearing appeals (see, for example, s 19(3)) but it throws no light on the question of whether there is a right of appeal such as the appellant now asserts. Its only possible relevance to the present question is the reference to discretion in s 19(1), which provides, inter alia:

> '... an adjudicator on an appeal to him under this Part of this Act—(*a*) shall allow the appeal if he considers ... (ii) where the decision or action involved the exercise of a discretion by the Secretary of State or an officer, that the discretion should have been exercised differently ...'

The adjudicator's power under s 19(1)(*a*)(ii) applies to cases where matters of discretion arise in the course of an appeal which is otherwise admissible, but it does not in my opinion have the effect of making an appeal admissible in a case such as the present which depends entirely on the unrestricted discretion of an administrative officer.

For these reasons I consider it highly unlikely that refusal of a special voucher is intended to be subject to the right of appeal under s 13(1) of the 1971 Act.

I return now to the definition of entry clearance in s 33(1) of the 1971 Act. It includes a reference to an 'other document' which fulfils a double qualification, viz one which (1) 'in accordance with the immigration rules' (2) 'is to be taken as evidence of a person's eligibility ... for entry into the United Kingdom'. 'Immigration rules' are defined in s 33(1) to mean 'the rules for the time being laid down as mentioned in section 3(2) above'. Section 3(2) provides:

> 'The Secretary of State shall from time to time (and as soon as may be) lay before Parliament statements of the rules, or of any changes in the rules, laid down by him as to the *practice* to be followed in the *administration* of this Act for regulating the entry into and stay in the United Kingdom of persons required by this Act to have leave to enter ...'

The rules accordingly have parliamentary approval but they are not contained in statutory instruments and they do not have the force of law. The rules which applied to the appellant's case are set out in the Statement of Immigration Rules for Control on Entry: Commonwealth Citizens (HC Paper (1972–73) no 79) ordered by the House of

Commons to be printed on 25 January 1973 (hereinafter referred to as 'HC 79'). It is also necessary to have regard to the corresponding Statement of Immigration Rules for Control on Entry: EEC and other Non-Commonwealth Nationals (HC Paper (1972–73) no 81) ordered by the House of Commons to be printed on 25 January 1973 (HC 81). The only mention of a 'special voucher' in HC 79 is in r 38, which provides:

> 'Where the passenger is a citizen of the United Kingdom and Colonies holding a United Kingdom passport, and presents a special voucher issued to him by a British Government representative overseas (or an entry certificate in lieu), he is to be admitted for settlement, as are his dependants if they have obtained entry certificates for that purpose and satisfy the requirements of *paragraph* 39; but such a passenger who comes for settlement without a special voucher or entry certificate is to be refused leave to enter.'

If that rule stood alone it might well be considered to be ambiguous on the question of whether a special voucher was an entry clearance or not. The rule is quite consistent with the respondent's contention that the whole point of a special voucher is to authorise the admission to the United Kingdom of persons who are *not*, under the rules, 'eligible' for entry into the United Kingdom, and that it is not evidence of eligibility. The difference is not merely verbal. It is substantial in this respect: a document which is evidence (but not 'conclusive evidence') of eligibility for entry (or of any other external fact) will be ineffective if other evidence shows that the eligibility (or other external fact) does not exist, whereas the effectiveness of a special voucher does not depend on the existence of any fact external to itself. It is in itself authority for admission. On the other hand, a special voucher is not absolutely conclusive authority for admission because, as counsel for the respondent conceded, the holder of a special voucher may still be refused leave to enter under rr 59 to 63 of HC 79, that is to say on medical grounds, or because he has a criminal record or is subject to a deportation order, or because his exclusion is conducive to the public good.

But r 38 has to be read in the context of the other rules and of the definition of entry clearance in s 33(1). According to the definition entry clearance means three things. First, there is a visa. This is a form of entry clearance which is required by non-Commonwealth immigrants, and in terms of r 10 of HC 81 it is 'to be taken as evidence of the holder's eligibility for entry to the United Kingdom'. It therefore falls exactly within the definition in s 33(1). Second, there is an entry certificate, which corresponds, in the case of a Commonwealth citizen, to a visa for others. Rule 12 of HC 79 provides that entry certificates 'are to be taken as evidence of the holder's eligibility for entry to the United Kingdom, and accordingly accepted as "entry clearances" within the meaning of the [1971] Act'. It also falls exactly within the definition in s 33(1). Third, there is an 'other document' which complies with the definition. An example of such an other document is a 'Home Office letter of consent', which is referred to in r 10 of HC 81 and which is also to be 'taken as evidence etc'. It also falls exactly within s 33(1).

But there is no provision in the rules that a special voucher is to be 'taken as evidence of a person's eligibility for entry to the United Kingdom'. It therefore does not literally comply with the definition in s 33(1), unlike all the other documents which I have mentioned, which do. In my opinion the proper conclusion is that a special voucher is not evidence of eligibility, but is itself authority for entry, and supersedes the necessity for eligibility. The words which occur in brackets in r 38 of HC 79 ('or an entry certificate in lieu') do not in my opinion indicate that a special voucher and an entry certificate are to be treated as equivalent. On the contrary, they recognise that the two things are different. The reason for the words having been inserted is that, as Lord Lane CJ mentioned in the Divisional Court, in some cases what is really a special voucher has been wrongly called an entry certificate (see [1980] 2 All ER 837 at 839–840, [1980] 1 WLR 1530 at 1533). That can easily happen because, as we were informed by counsel for the respondent, there is no document called a special voucher. When a special voucher is granted all that happens is that the words 'special voucher' are written or stamped in the passport of the holder to whom the voucher has been granted, and occasionally the words 'entry certificate' are written in error. In this very case we have seen a photographic copy of the appellant's father's passport which is stamped 'entry certificate' and which also bears the words 'special voucher' written in ink underneath. Apparently the words 'entry certificate' have been stamped in error and should have been deleted.

The difference between a special voucher and the documents which fall within the definition of entry clearance in s 33(1) of the 1971 Act is emphasised by r 10 of HC 79 and the corresponding r 8 of HC 81. Rule 10 of HC 79 provides:

> 'A Commonwealth citizen who wishes to ascertain in advance whether he is *eligible for admission* to the United Kingdom can apply to the appropriate British representative in the country in which he is living for the issue of an entry certificate. This procedure is of particular value when the claim to admission depends on *proof of facts* entailing enquiries in this country or overseas.'

That rule, and the corresponding r 8 of HC 81, shows that eligibility for admission and therefore entitlement to the issue of an entry certificate may depend on proof of external facts. But neither that nor any other rule suggests that advance application might usefully be made for a special voucher. The reason, I think, is that the issue of a special voucher does not depend on proof of facts establishing eligibility but on an exercise of administrative discretion.

The result of this consideration of the definition in s 33(1) and of the rules is to satisfy me that a special voucher is truly something special, outside the ordinary rules, and that it does not fall within the definition of an entry clearance. It follows that it is not appealable under s 13(2) of the 1971 Act. That conclusion confirms the opinion I had formed against the appealability of refusal, on the ground that an effective appeal would be impracticable.

Before leaving this part of the case I should refer briefly to the relief that is sought by the appellant. The proceedings were begun after the appellant had applied on 19 April 1976 to the deputy British High Commissioner, Bombay for 'the necessary forms for an entry certificate voucher that entitles for permanent settlement in the United Kingdom'. In that letter she said that she had a husband and one child. She received a reply from the entry clearance officer in Bombay dated 3 May 1976 which after acknowledging her letter proceeded as follows:

> '"Special Quota Voucher"s are normally issued to United Kingdom passport holders who are heads of households. I understand that, in your case, the head of household is a citizen of India. I therefore regret to inform you that you are not eligible to apply for a special quota voucher.'

Further correspondence followed and eventually the present proceedings were raised, the relief sought being stated thus:

> 'An Order of Mandamus directed to the Entry Clearance Officer British High Commission, Bombay to entertain the Applicant's application for an Entry Clearance Document namely a "Special Quota Voucher."'

That relief evidently rests on the assumption that the entry clearance officer has refused to entertain the appellant's application for a special quota voucher, and not that he had considered the application and refused it. It was only in the notice of appeal from the Divisional Court to the Court of Appeal that there appears for the first time, as ground 3 of the appeal, the contention that 'upon refusal of a Special Quota Voucher [the appellant] ought to have been granted a right of an appeal to an Adjudicator under Section 13(2) of the Immigration Act 1971'. The Court of Appeal rejected her appeal because, as Ormrod LJ explained in the only reasoned opinion, it considered that she had no right of appeal. Before your Lordship's House this part of the case was argued on the basis that the appellant's application for a special voucher had been refused and that she was now asserting a right of appeal under s 13(2). I have therefore dealt with the case on that basis.

The second part of the appeal arises under the Sex Discrimination Act 1975. That Act
a is divided into eight parts. Part I defines the discrimination to which the Act applies. Section 1(1) provides:

> 'A person discriminates against a woman in any circumstances relevant for the purposes of any provision of this Act if—(*a*) on the ground of her sex he treats her less favourably than he treats or would treat a man . . .'

b Section 5, which is also in Pt I of the 1975 Act, provides:

> '(1) In this Act—(*a*) references to discrimination refer to any discrimination falling within sections 1 to 4; and (*b*) references to sex discrimination refer to any discrimination falling within section 1 or 2, and related expressions shall be construed accordingly . . .'

c In my opinion the entry clearance officer who dealt with the appellant's application for a special voucher did discriminate against the appellant on the grounds of her sex. He had to do so because the special voucher scheme is in its nature discriminatory against women. The evidence in the case includes an affidavit from a principal in the Immigration and Nationality Department of the Home Office. Paragraph 4 of the affidavit is in these terms:

d
> 'There is no discrimination on the ground of sex. A woman holding a United Kingdom passport is eligible for consideration for the grant of a special voucher if she is widowed or single and a head of household or if she is married and obliged to take on all the responsibilities of the head of household owing to her husband's long-term medical disability. In 1977 over 24% of the special voucher holders arriving in the United Kingdom were women.'

e
The assertion in the first sentence of that paragraph that there is no discrimination on the ground of sex is in my opinion shown by the later part of the paragraph to be erroneous. The special voucher scheme proceeds on the assumption that in a household which consists of, or includes, a married couple the husband is normally the head of household. Only in exceptional circumstances, where the husband suffers from long-term medical
f disability, is the wife regarded as the head of household. That may be perfectly reasonable, in accordance with the general understanding in the United Kingdom and elsewhere, but it seems to me plainly discriminatory against women. Test it in this way. If the applicant for a special voucher had been, not the appellant in this case, but a brother of hers, who had married an Indian woman and gone to live in India, he would have been treated as head of his household (assuming that he was not disabled) and, as such, entitled
g to apply for a special voucher. I see no answer to the argument that he would have been treated in that respect more favourably than the appellant, and that the only reason for his more favourable treatment would have been his sex. I do not accept the suggestion that, for the purposes of the special voucher scheme, headship of a household is a fact which is independent of sex. That might be correct if inquiry was made in each case into such matters as whether the husband or the wife is the financial provider of the household
h or whether he or she makes the most important decisions; but such inquiries would be impracticable. The practice therefore is that the husband is assumed to be the head of household in a normal case. Accordingly, I consider that there was sex discrimination in this case.

But not all sex discrimination is unlawful. Part I of the 1975 Act merely defined discrimination and it contains no provision for making it unlawful. Discrimination is
j only unlawful if it occurs in one of the fields in which it is prohibited by Pt II, III or IV of the Act. The decision of the Court of Appeal to that effect in *Kassam v Immigration Appeal Tribunal* [1980] 2 All ER 330, [1980] 1 WLR 1037 was in my opinion correct, and I reject the argument by the appellant's counsel that that case was wrongly decided. The alternative contention by counsel for the appellant, if *Kassam*'s case was rightly decided, was that the discrimination involved in the special voucher scheme was rendered

unlawful because it fell within the provisions of s 29, which is in Pt III of the Act. Section 29 provides:

> '(1) It is unlawful for any person concerned with the provision (for payment or not) of goods, facilities or services to the public or a section of the public to discriminate against a woman who seeks to obtain or use those goods, facilities or services—(*a*) by refusing or deliberately omitting to provide her with any of them, or (*b*) by refusing or deliberately omitting to provide her with goods, facilities or services of the like quality, in the like manner and on the like terms as are normal in his case in relation to male members of the public or (where she belongs to a section of the public) to male members of that section.
>
> (2) The following are examples of the facilities and services mentioned in subsection (1)—(*a*) access to an use of any place which members of the public or a section of the public are permitted to enter; (*b*) accommodation in a hotel, boarding house or other similar establishment; (*c*) facilities by way of banking or insurance or for grants, loans, credit or finance; (*d*) facilities for education; (*e*) facilities for entertainment, recreation or refreshment; (*f*) facilities for transport or travel; (*g*) the services of any profession or trade, or any local or other public authority . . .'

It was said that the granting of special vouchers for entry into the United Kingdom was the provision of facilities or services to a section of the public, and that the wide general words of sub-s (1) of s 29 were not cut down by the examples given in sub-s (2), which are only 'examples' and are not an exhaustive list of the circumstances in which the section applies. Reliance was also placed on para (*g*) of s 29(2), which expressly refers to the services of a public authority and which has been held to apply to the Inland Revenue: see *Savjani v IRC* [1981] 1 All ER 1121, [1981] QB 458.

My Lords, I accept that the examples in s 29(2) are not exhaustive, but they are, in my opinion, useful pointers to aid in the construction of sub-s (1). Section 29 as a whole seems to me to apply to the direct provision of facilities or services, and not to the mere grant of permission to use facilities. That is in accordance with the words of sub-s (1), and it is reinforced by some of the examples in sub-s (2). The example in para (*a*) is 'access to *and use of* any place' and the words that I have emphasised indicate that the paragraph contemplates actual provision of facilities which the person will use. The example in para (*d*) refers, in my view, to the actual provision of schools and other facilities for education, but not to the mere grant of an entry certificate or a special voucher to enable a student to enter the United Kingdom in order to study here. The example in para (*g*) seems to me to be contemplating things such as medical services, or library facilities, which can be directly provided by local or other public authorities. So, in *Savjani v IRC* [1981] 1 All ER 1121 at 1126, [1981] QB 458 at 467 Templeman LJ took the view that the Inland Revenue performed two separate functions: first a duty of collecting revenue and, second, a service of providing taxpayers with information:

> 'As counsel submitted on behalf of the commissioners, the board and the inspector are performing duties, those duties laid on them by the Act which I have mentioned, but, in my judgment, it does not necessarily follow that the board and the inspector are not voluntarily or in order to carry out their duty also performing services for the taxpayer. The duty is to collect the right amount of revenue; but, in my judgment, there is a service to the taxpayer provided by the board and the inspector by the provisions dissemination and implementation of regulations which will enable the taxpayer to know that he is entitled to a deduction or a repayment, which will enable him to know how he is to satisfy the inspector or the board if he is so entitled, and which will enable him to obtain the actual deduction or repayment which Parliament said he is to have.'

In so far as that passage states the ground of the Court of Appeal's decision in that case, I agree with it. If Lord Denning MR intended to base his decision on wider grounds (see [1981] 1 All ER 1121 at 1124–1125, [1981] QB 458 at 465–466), I would respectfully

disagree with him. In the present case the entry clearance officer in Bombay was in my
a opinion not providing a service for would-be immigrants; rather he was performing his duty of controlling them.

Counsel for the appellant sought to draw support for his contention from s 85(1) of the 1975 Act, which provides:

> 'This Act applies—(*a*) to an act done by or for purposes of a Minister of the Crown or government department, or (*b*) to an act done on behalf of the Crown by a
> b statutory body, or a person holding a statutory office, as it applies to an act done by a private person.'

That section puts an act done on behalf of the Crown on a par with an act done by a private person, and it does not in terms restrict the comparison to an act *of the same kind* done by a private person. But in my opinion it applies only to acts done on behalf of the
c Crown which are of a kind similar to acts that might be done by a private person. It does not mean that the Act is to apply to any act of any kind done on behalf of the Crown by a person holding statutory office. There must be acts (which include deliberate omissions: see s 82(1)) done in the course of formulating or carrying out government policy which are quite different in kind from any act that would ever be done by a private person, and to which the 1975 Act does not apply. I would respectfully agree with the observations
d on the corresponding provision of the Race Relations Act 1976 made by Woolf J in *Home Office v Commission for Racial Equality* [1981] 1 All ER 1042 at 1048, [1982] 1 QB 385 at 395. Part V of the Sex Discrimination Act 1975 makes exceptions for certain acts including acts done for the purpose of national security (s 52) and for acts which are 'necessary' in order to comply with certain statutory requirements (s 51). These exceptions will no doubt be effective to protect acts which are of a kind that would otherwise be
e unlawful under the 1975 Act. But they do not in my view obviate the necessity for construing s 29 as applying only to acts which are at least similar to acts that could be done by private persons.

For these reasons I would dismiss the appeal on both grounds. The appellant must pay the respondent's costs of the appeal.

f **LORD KEITH OF KINKEL.** My Lords, I have had the advantage of reading in draft the speech of my noble and learned friend Lord Fraser, and that to be delivered by my noble and learned friend Lord Brightman. I agree with the reasoning and conclusions expressed by both of them on the issue concerned with the nature and effect of a special voucher, and also with the opinion of my noble and learned friend Lord Fraser regarding the issue which arises under the Sex Discrimination Act 1975. Accordingly, I too would
g dismiss the appeal.

LORD SCARMAN. My Lords, the appeal raises two difficult points of statutory construction. In logical order, though not in the order in which the appellant's counsel argued her case, the first is a point as to the true construction of the Immigration Act 1971 and the second a point as to the true construction of the Sex Discrimination Act
h 1975. The appellant's counsel took the course of arguing the second point first for the excellent reason that unless they can show that they have at least an arguable case of unlawful discrimination against the appellant on the ground of her sex there is nothing but a hollow victory in establishing (if they can) that the appellant has a right of appeal under the Immigration Act 1971. Indeed, there is a third issue which, though not argued at length in the appeal, may not be ignored. If the appellant succeeds on her two points
j of construction, has she established a case for the court's intervention?

As I understand the substance of her ill-formulated written application and accompanying statement, the appellant seeks judicial review of the refusal by the entry clearance officer, Bombay to entertain her application for a voucher enabling her to enter the United Kingdom for settlement. She seeks a declaration that she is entitled to appeal to an adjudicator against his refusal and an order directing him to take the necessary steps

(by service of the appropriate notice under the Immigration Appeals (Notices) Regulations 1972, SI 1972/1683) to enable her to exercise her right of appeal. If this be the correct a
view, as I believe it to be, of the true nature of her case, the three issues to which I have already briefly referred fall to be considered by the House. All three issues arise under the law as it was prior to the 1983 change in the immigration rules and to the enactment of the British Nationality Act 1981. The relevant immigration rules are the Statements of Immigration Rules for Control on Entry: Commonwealth Citizens (HC Paper (1972–73) no 79) and EEC and Non-Commonwealth Nationals (HC Paper (1972–73) no 81). b
The issues are concerned with the special voucher scheme under which certain United Kingdom passport holders who are neither patrial nor otherwise eligible for entry into the United Kingdom may be admitted into the country for settlement.

The appellant applied in Bombay for the grant of a special voucher so that she might enter the United Kingdom for settlement. The entry clearance officer by letter dated 3 May 1976 refused her application on the ground that, being a woman married to a c
citizen of India, she was not eligible to be considered for the grant of a voucher. She applied to the Divisional Court for review of his decision but her application was dismissed. The Court of Appeal upheld the decision of the Divisional Court.

The three questions which are raised by her in these proceedings may be formulated as follows: (1) whether a special voucher under the scheme is an 'entry clearance' as defined in s 33(1) of the Immigration Act 1971; if it is, it follows that the appellant has a d
right of appeal to an adjudicator against the entry clearance officer's decision under s 13(2) of that Act, and she succeeds on her Immigration Act point; (2) whether the restriction of the scheme to heads of household and their dependants is by its discrimination between men and women in the meaning it gives to 'head of household' unlawful as being in breach of the Sex Discrimination Act 1975; the point turns on the interpretation of s 29 of that Act; (3) whether, even if the appellant establishes error in e
law on the part of the entry clearance officer, the court ought to exercise its discretion to grant her relief, and, if it should, the nature of that relief.

Before considering these questions it is necessary to state the facts and to describe the scheme. The appellant holds a United Kingdom passport. She was until the passage into law of the British Nationality Act 1981 a citizen of the United Kingdom and Colonies. She was born in East Africa, a member of an Asian family settled there. The family were f
citizens of the United Kingdom and Colonies. They hold United Kingdom passports, and, prior to the enactment of the Commonwealth Immigrants Act 1968, they enjoyed the right of unrestricted entry into the United Kingdom. The effect of that Act was to deprive them of their right of entry and to subject them to immigration control if they, or any of them, should seek to enter the United Kingdom. Today they are, by reason of the British Nationality Act 1981, British Overseas Citizens. g

It was recognised by the British government that the 1968 Act imposed very great distress on certain United Kingdom passport holders resident in East Africa, who were under pressure to quit their countries of residence but had nowhere to go. The special voucher scheme was devised as an administrative expedient to relieve that distress while retaining control over the numbers of those anxious to migrate to the United Kingdom.

A voucher under the scheme confers no legal right of abode such as the patrial possesses h
under s 1(1) of the 1971 Act but does qualify the holder for admission to settle under the immigration rules: see para 38 of HC 79. A voucher holder remains in the class specified by s 1(2) of the Act as one who 'may live, work and settle in the United Kingdom by permission', and is subject to immigration control. The scheme is on a quota basis, which entails that an applicant may be eligible for a voucher and yet not be granted one. It has no express statutory basis but, if challenged, could be defended (at least since the j
enactment of the Immigration Act 1971) as an exercise by the Secretary of State of his power and duty to establish the practice to be followed for regulating the entry into and stay in the United Kingdom of persons required by the immigration laws to have leave to enter: see s 3(2) of the 1971 Act.

The scheme is described in the evidence before the House in these terms:

> 'The scheme allows heads of . . . households and their families into this country for settlement on an annual quota basis notwithstanding the fact that they may be otherwise ineligible for entry under the immigration rules. The great majority of the special vouchers have always been allocated in East Africa, where United Kingdom passport holders have experienced the greatest difficulties.'

A woman holding a United Kingdom passport is eligible for consideration for the grant of a special voucher 'if she is widowed or single and a head of household or if she is married and obliged to take on all the responsibilities of the head of household owing to her husband's long-term medical disability'. A woman married to a husband who is not suffering from a long-term medical disability cannot under the scheme be a head of household. Unless the husband can show he is eligible for a voucher, she is not eligible to enter the country: her eligibility depends on whether her husband can as head of the household obtain a special voucher.

To return to the history, the appellant went with her mother and other children of the family to India in 1964. Her father, who continued to support them, remained in East Africa. The appellant married a farmer in India. In 1973 her father applied for a special voucher for himself as head of household and for entry certificates for his wife and two of their sons to accompany him as his dependants. He did not include his daughter, the appellant, in his application because she was married. The application was successful and on 7 May 1975 he, his wife and two sons were admitted into the United Kingdom for settlement. On 19 April 1976 the appellant applied for a special voucher for herself with the result already mentioned. She described herself as a housewife married to a farmer in India and as the mother of one child.

The Immigration Act 1971 point

The point is a short one. If a special voucher is an entry clearance, the appellant had a right of appeal against the refusal by the entry clearance officer to treat her as eligible for consideration for a grant of a voucher, for s 13(2) of the 1971 Act provides that a person who is refused an entry clearance may appeal to an adjudicator.

'Entry clearance' is defined in s 33(1) as follows:

> 'For the purposes of this Act, except in so far as the context otherwise requires . . . "entry clearance" means a visa, entry certificate or other document which, in accordance with the immigration rules, is to be taken as evidence of a person's eligibility, though not patrial, for entry into the United Kingdom (but does not include a work permit).'

Entry clearances are issued by British representatives overseas. Their purposes is to enable Commonwealth citizens and others to ascertain in advance whether they are eligible for admission to the United Kingdom: see paras 10 to 13 of HC 79 and paras 8 to 13 of HC 81. In some cases, for example dependants of a head of household entering under a special voucher (in which case an entry certificate must be obtained (see para 38 of HC 79)) and 'visa nationals' (who must produce a current visa (see para 8 of HC 81)), an entry clearance must be produced at the port of entry and, if it is not, the immigration officer is to refuse leave to enter. In these cases a visa or entry certificate, each of which is an entry clearance, is as much a condition for the grant of leave to enter as is a special voucher in cases where one is required.

I confess that I do not understand how the words of the statutory definition of entry clearance can be restricted so as to exclude a special voucher.

An entry clearance is exactly what a voucher is. It is a document which, in accordance with the immigration rules, ie para 38 of HC 79, is to be taken as evidence of the eligibility for entry into the United Kingdom of a person who is not a patrial, ie of a person who does not have the right of abode or the freedom to come and go into the United Kingdom but is subject to immigration control. The voucher is a permission granted under an administrative scheme regulating the entry into and stay in the United

Kingdom of a certain class of persons who are required under the 1971 Act to have leave to enter. A voucher does not, and in my judgment cannot, confer a right of entry but only an eligibility. The basic structure of the 1971 Act with its separation of patrials who have the right of entry and abode from all others who require leave to enter denies the possibility of any view of a special voucher other than as a document evidencing a person's eligibility for entry. And, if it be necessary to look for confirmation of this view, it may be found in Pt VI of HC 79, which confers power on an immigration officer in certain circumstances to refuse leave to those who qualify for admission under the rules (this includes special voucher holders entering under para 38 of the rules).

The case for the respondent is that a voucher is not evidence of eligibility but it itself a document of title. In the words of Lord Lane CJ giving the judgment of the Divisional Court ([1980] 2 All ER 837 at 840, [1980] 1 WLR 1530 at 1534): 'It is a document which dispenses with the necessity of such evidence [ie evidence of eligibility] . . .' The fallacy in this reasoning is in holding that it is not evidence of eligibility merely because no further evidence than its presentation to the immigration officer is required. The document is itself sufficient evidence; that is why no further evidence is needed. The true question is whether it is evidence of title or of permission to enter. We are, therefore, driven back to a consideration of the 1971 Act's basic structure, under which, as I have endeavoured to show, the holder of a voucher has not a right but only a permission or leave to enter.

A further argument was advanced against this view of a special voucher. It was said that there is no basis on which any appellate body or person can properly adjudicate on an appeal against refusal of a voucher. Grant or refusal is a matter of administrative discretion, the exercise of which is in no way guided by the immigration rules. An adjudicator, it is said, would have no guidance in the exercise of the appellate power conferred on him by s 19(1) of the 1971 Act. As Ormrod LJ put it in the Court of Appeal (see p 866, ante):

> 'There is no conceivable means by which any form of appellate body could adjudicate on [the] issue because whether or not a special voucher is granted appears to be (and there are no rules about it) wholly a matter of practice and discretion.'

Of course, if an issue is unappealable, it is not difficult to infer that no right of appeal exists. And I would agree that an adjudicator on an appeal against the refusal of a special voucher cannot investigate the exercise of the discretion by the entry clearance officer so as to substitute his discretion for that of the officer. This is because the immigration rules, though they require an immigration officer to give leave to enter for settlement to the holder of a voucher unless there are 'Part VI' grounds for refusing leave, do not themselves offer any guidance as to eligibility for the grant of a voucher. The adjudicator does not have the material to enable him to exercise the power which he does have under s 19 to substitute his discretion for that of the immigration authority.

But this is not decisive. The powers of an adjudicator on an appeal are to be found in s 19 of the 1971 Act. They are not limited to a review of discretion. The section provides, inter alia, that an adjudicator shall allow the appeal if he considers that the decision under appeal 'was not in accordance with the law or with any immigration rules applicable to the case': see s 19(1)(*a*)(i). If, therefore, it is clear on the record that the entry clearance officer erred in law, the adjudicator can, and indeed must, intervene to allow the appeal. And this is exactly what the appellant alleges in this case. She says that it is clear from the entry clearance officer's letter refusing to treat her as eligible for a voucher that he proceeded on the basis that it was lawful for the scheme to discriminate against married women; and her submission is that on the true construction of the Sex Discrimination Act 1975 the scheme's discrimination against married women is unlawful. It is a point of law arising on material all of which is, or can easily be made, available to an adjudicator, as indeed it has been made available to the courts below and to the House in these proceedings. The point which the appellant wishes to raise on appeal is, therefore, justiciable and appealable.

For these reasons, therefore, I would hold that the appellant did have a right of appeal
a against the decision of the entry clearance officer. It is accepted that he did not comply with the Immigration Appeals (Notices) Regulations 1972, SI 1972/1683. The appellant has, therefore, made out a case which at least raises the question whether the court's discretion ought to be exercised in favour of judicial review. If she has no case under the Sex Discrimination Act 1975, it would be pointless to make an order in her favour, for the appeal would be bound to fail. But, if she has a good, or even an arguable case, of
b unlawful discrimination against her on the ground of her sex, a very different situation will arise for consideration.

The Sex Discrimination Act 1975 point

Part I of the Sex Discrimination Act 1975 describes the discrimination to which the Act applies. So far as material to this appeal, s 1(1) provides:

c 'A person discriminates against a woman in any circumstances relevant for the purposes of any provision of this Act if—(*a*) on the ground of her sex he treats her less favourably than he treats or would treat a man . . .'

I do not doubt that the effect of the restrictive meaning given under the special voucher scheme to a head of household is to discriminate against a woman in the way
d described by the subsection. Merely because she is a woman, a wife is treated under the scheme less favourably than a husband. Had one of her brothers married in India, he would have remained a United Kingdom passport holder eligible as a head of household for consideration for the grant of a voucher. But his married sister is not, because she is a woman.

However, not every discrimination against a woman is unlawful. Part II of the 1975
e Act specifies the discrimination which is unlawful in the employment field. Part III specifies the discrimination which is unlawful in other fields: education and the provision of goods, facilities, services and premises. Part IV particularises other actions and practices which are made unlawful by the 1975 Act. Part V makes a number of general exceptions in respect of actions or practices which would otherwise constitute unlawful discrimination under the 1975 Act.

f It has been held, correctly in my judgment, by the Court of Appeal in *Kassam v Immigration Appeal Tribunal* [1980] 2 All ER 330, [1980] 1 WLR 1037 that Pts II to IV of the 1975 Act are exhaustive of the circumstances in which sex discrimination is unlawful. The appellant, therefore, has to bring her case within a field of activity covered by the Act. She seeks to do so by relying on s 29, which is to be found in Pt III of the Act.

Section 29, so far as material, is as follows:

g '(1) It is unlawful for any person concerned with the provision (for payment or not) of goods, facilities or services to the public or a section of the public to discriminate against a woman who seeks to obtain or use those goods, facilities or services—(*a*) by refusing or deliberately omitting to provide her with any of them, or (*b*) by refusing or deliberately omitting to provide her with goods, facilities or services of the like quality, in the like manner and on the like terms as are normal
h in his case in relation to male members of the public or (where she belongs to a section of the public) to male members of that section.

(2) The following are examples of the facilities and services mentioned in subsection (1)—(*a*) access to and use of any place which members of the public or a section of the public are permitted to enter; (*b*) accommodation in a hotel, boarding house or other similar establishment; (*c*) facilities by way of banking or insurance or
j for grants, loans, credit or finance; (*d*) facilities for education; (*e*) facilities for entertainment, recreation or refreshment; (*f*) facilities for transport or travel; (*g*) the services of any profession or trade, or any local or other public authority . . .'

It is her submission that by the special voucher scheme the Secretary of State provides a facility to a section of the public, namely those United Kingdom passport holders who

are neither patrial nor otherwise eligible to enter the country. The facility provided is, it
is said, access for voucher holders to the United Kingdom for settlement. a

United Kingdom passport holders, however attenuated their rights may have become
in recent years, are a section of the public; their slender link with the United Kingdom
must at least be strong enough to entitle them to be so regarded. I agree with the view
expressed in *Kassam*'s case [1980] 2 All ER 330 at 334, [1980] 1 WLR 1037 at 1042 that
immigrants applying for leave to enter the country are a section of the public.

Entry into the United Kingdom for study, a visit or settlement is certainly a facility b
which many value and seek to obtain. And it is one which the Secretary of State has it in
his power under the Immigration Act 1971 to provide: see s 3(2) of that Act. The special
voucher scheme which he has introduced does provide to some this very valuable facility,
namely the opportunity to settle in this country.

On the literal meaning of the language of s 29(1), I would, therefore, construe the
subsection as covering the special voucher scheme provided by the Secretary of State. c

It is, however, said that the kind of facilities within the meaning of the subsection are
essentially 'market-place activities' or activities akin to the provision of goods and services,
but not to the grant of leave to enter under the Immigration Act 1971. Reliance is placed
on sub-s (2) as an indication that this was the legislative intention of the section and on
the decision of the Court of Appeal which interpreted the section in this way in *Kassam*'s
case. d

In *Kassam*'s case [1980] 2 All ER 330 at 334, [1980] 1 WLR 1037 at 1042 Stephenson
LJ found the submission, which is now made to the House in this case, namely that in
giving leave to immigrants to enter the country and to remain here the Secretary of State
provides a facility to a section of the public, so plausible that he was tempted to accede to
it. I agree with him so far. I have yielded to the temptation, if that is a fair description of
selecting a sensible interpretation of a statutory provision. He, however, did not. He e
appears to have accepted the submission that s 29 was concerned with 'market-place
activities'. If he did not restrict the section to the full extent of that submission, he
certainly took the view, which was also expressed by Ackner LJ and concurred in by Sir
David Cairns, that the section applies only to facilities which are akin to the provision of
goods and services. Ackner LJ held that 'facilities' because of its juxtaposition to goods
and services must not be given a wholly unrestricted meaning but must be so confined. f

I reject this reasoning. I derive no assistance from sub-s (2) in construing sub-s (1) of
s 29. I can find no trace of this House accepting any such assistance when in *Applin v Race
Relations Board* [1974] 2 All ER 73, [1975] AC 259 (the 'foster-parent' case) this House had
to consider the directly comparable provision in s 2(1) and (2) of the Race Relations Act
1968. Section 29(2) does no more than give examples of facilities and services. It is
certainly not intended to be exhaustive. If some of its examples are 'market-place g
activities' or facilities akin to the provision of goods and services, others are not; I refer,
in particular, to the examples in paras (*a*), (*d*) and (*g*). And, if the subsection cannot, as I
think it cannot, be relied on as a guide to the construction of sub-s (1), one is left only
with Ackner LJ's point as to the juxtaposition of goods, facilities and services in sub-s (1).

This is too slight an indication to stand up to the undoubted intention of Parliament
that the Act is to bind the Crown. Section 85(1) provides: h

> 'This Act applies—(*a*) to an act done by or for purposes of a Minister of the Crown
> or government department, or (*b*) to an act done on behalf of the Crown by a
> statutory body, or a person holding a statutory office. as it applies to an act done by
> a private person.'

An attempt was made in reliance on the concluding three words of the subsection to j
argue that in its application to the Crown the 1975 Act is limited to the sort of acts which
could be done by a private person, eg 'market-place activities' or the provision of facilities
akin to the provision of goods and services. I do not so read the subsection. It means, in
my judgment, no more and no less than that the Act applies to the public acts of
ministers, government departments and other statutory bodies on behalf of the Crown

as it applies to acts of private persons. It would be inconceivable that the generality of sub-s (1)(*a*) and (*b*) could be restricted by words which in drawing a distinction between two classes of act are intended to show that the distinction is immaterial. I cannot accept that so short a tail can wag so large a dog.

Section 52 also is consistent with the view that the 1975 Act has a wide cover in respect of acts of the Crown. It is designed to ensure that nothing in Pts II to IV of the 1975 Act (which include s 29) shall render unlawful an act done for the purpose of safeguarding national security.

Accordingly, I think that on this point *Kassam*'s case was wrongly decided. In my view, the granting of leave to enter the country by provision of a special voucher or otherwise is the provision of a facility to a section of the public. Indeed, I have no doubt that some see it as a very valuable facility. It is certainly much sought after. Section 29(1) is wide enough, therefore, to cover the special voucher scheme which, in my judgment, is properly described as offering a facility to some members of the public, ie United Kingdom passport holders, who seek access to this country for the purpose of settlement but have no lawful means of entering other than by leave.

In the course of argument, your Lordship's attention was drawn to the Court of Appeal's decision in *Savjani v IRC* [1981] 1 All ER 1121, [1981] 1 QB 458, in which it was held that by putting the plaintiff because of his ethnic origin to a higher standard of proof of his entitlement to a tax relief than is normally required of a claimant the Revenue had unlawfully discriminated against him in the provision of services to the public within the meaning of s 20(1)(*b*) of the Race Relations Act 1976. The decision was, I am satisfied, correct and is certainly consistent with the approach which I would hold that the courts should adopt to s 29(1) of the Sex Discrimination Act 1975. But it was a different case on its facts from this case in that the Revenue did provide, however informally, an advisory service to taxpayers seeking guidance on their problems.

For these reasons I would hold that the special voucher scheme in so far as it discriminates between wives and husbands is unlawful under ss 1 and 29(1) of the Sex Discrimination Act 1975. Even if there should be doubt, I would certainly say that the appellant has an arguable case which she could reasonably take to appeal before an adjudicator, namely that the entry clearance officer had erred in law in refusing to treat her as eligible for a special voucher. The third issue remains. I can take it very shortly. So much time has elapsed, so many fresh circumstances may have arisen since the refusal of her application in May 1976 that I would not order mandamus to go to the entry clearance officer. But the appellant is entitled to a declaration that his refusal to entertain her application for the reason which he gave was contrary to law. This would enable her, if so advised, to submit a further application. If she should again be met by a refusal, she has her right of appeal; and, if she succeeds on appeal, the adjudicator has power under s 19(3) of the Immigration Act 1971 to give directions or make recommendations to the Secretary of State.

Accordingly, I would allow the appeal.

LORD BRANDON OF OAKBROOK. My Lords, I have had the advantage of reading in draft the speech prepared by my noble and learned friend Lord Scarman. I agree entirely with his conclusions on each of the two questions of law raised by this appeal, and with the reasons on which he has based those conclusions. It follows that I too would allow the appeal.

LORD BRIGHTMAN. My Lords, I approach this case by endeavouring to ascertain the scheme of the Immigration Act 1971 and the rules made thereunder.

Part I of the 1971 Act is concerned with the regulation of entry into the United Kingdom, and stay after entry. Section 2 confers a right of abode on certain citizens of the United Kingdom and Colonies, and other. Such persons are described as 'patrial'. They have complete freedom to come and go. Under s 3(1) persons who are not patrial are precluded from entering the United Kingdom unless given leave to do so in accordance with the Act. Subsection (2) requires the Secretary of State to lay before Parliament statements of the rules laid down by him as to 'the practice to be followed in the administration of this Act for regulating the entry into and stay in the United Kingdom of persons required by this Act to have leave to enter'. The content of these rules (which are called in the Act 'the immigration rules') appears to be in the discretion of the Secretary of State. Though laid before Parliament, the immigration rules are not subject to any annulment procedure. If, however, a statement of the rules is disapproved by either House within a time limit, the Secretary of State is under a duty to make such changes thereto as appear to him to be required in the circumstances. Under sub-s (9), a person seeking to enter the United Kingdom and claiming to be patrial is, in certain circumstances, required to prove the fact by means of a certificate of patriality under the immigration rules.

Under s 4, the power to give or refuse leave to enter the United Kingdom is to be exercised by immigration officers, while the power to give leave to remain in the United Kingdom is to be exercised by the Secretary of State.

Part II of the 1971 Act is concerned with appeals. Section 13(1) provides that a person who is refused leave to enter the United Kingdom may appeal to an adjudicator (a) against the decision that he requires leave or (b) against the refusal of leave. Under sub-s (2) a person who is refused (a) a certificate of patriality or (b) an entry clearance may appeal to an adjudicator against the refusal. This is the first use of the expression 'entry clearance'. Under the interpretation section (s 33), except in so far as the context otherwise requires, an 'entry clearance' means—

> 'a visa, entry certificate or other document which, in accordance with the immigration rules, is to be taken as evidence of a person's eligibility, though not patrial, for entry into the United Kingdom (but does not include a work permit).'

The expression 'entry certificate' is not, I think, again used in the 1971 Act.

In January 1973 the Secretary of State laid before Parliament a 'Statement of Immigration Rules for Control on Entry: Commonwealth Citizens' (HC Paper (1972–73) no 79), pursuant to s 3(2) of the 1971 Act. This statement was an amended version of earlier immigration rules. A corresponding statement was made at the same time relating to EEC and other non-Commonwealth nationals (HC Paper (1972–73) no 81). These were the rules in force at the relevant time. They were later amended, and subsequently amalgamated into a single statement which was laid before Parliament in February 1983. The current version of the rules is not relevant to this appeal.

The Commonwealth immigration rules apply to a Commonwealth citizen or British protected person who is required by the 1971 Act to have leave to enter (except a crew member of a ship, aircraft or hovercraft). He is called in the rules a 'passenger'. The rules, as required by s 3(2) of the 1971 Act, regulate both entry and stay.

Paragraphs 10 to 13, headed 'Entry clearances', contain an introduction to the system of entry clearances. Under para 10, a Commonwealth citizen who wishes to ascertain in advance whether he is 'eligible for admission' to the United Kingdom is advised to apply to the appropriate British representative abroad for the issue of an 'entry certificate'. Paragraph 11 provides that a person seeking admission as a wife, child or other dependant of a person settled in the United Kingdom, or of a person admitted for employment, or as the husband or fiancé of such a person must hold a current entry certificate issued for that purpose. Paragraph 12 provides that entry certificates 'are to be taken as evidence of the holder's eligibility for entry to the United Kingdom, and accordingly accepted as "entry clearances" within the meaning of the Act'. Paragraph 12 also provides that a person who holds a duly issued current 'entry clearance' is not to be refused leave to enter save in special circumstances, such as concealment of material facts.

To sum up the position so far, except where otherwise provided by the rules a Commonwealth citizen, who is required by the 1971 Act to have leave to enter, has a choice. He may present himself to an immigration officer at the point of entry, establish that he is eligible under the rules for entry into the United Kingdom and seek leave to enter accordingly; alternatively, he may apply, in advance, for an 'entry certificate' which, if granted, will be prima facie evidence of his eligibility for entry; but in some instances it is expressed to be mandatory to apply in advance for an 'entry certificate'. Paragraph 11 is an example. An entry clearance is, by definition, a document which, in accordance with the immigration rules, is to be taken as 'evidence of eligibility' for entry into the United Kingdom. One species of entry clearance is an 'entry certificate'. Under the comparable immigration rules for EEC and other non-Commonwealth Nationals there are two other species of entry clearances, the visa and the Home Office letter of consent: see rr 8, 9 and 10; these again 'are to be taken as evidence of the holder's eligibility for entry to the United Kingdom': see r 10 of the non-Commonwealth rules.

The code of eligibility for Commonwealth citizens is set out in Pts II, III and IV of the Commonwealth immigration rules. Part II defines eligibility for entry of a person who seeks entry as a temporary visitor, or for private medical treatment, or as a student, or as an 'au pair'. It is apparent, particularly from paras 18 to 21, that such a person may either take the risk of satisfying the immigration officer at the point of entry, or apply in advance for an entry certificate. These paragraphs refer, in fact, to an 'entry clearance', which is perfectly accurate, but the form which the entry clearance will take, if sought in advance, will (presumably) be an 'entry certificate'.

Part III of the immigration rules defines the eligibility for entry of a person who seeks entry for employment, or as a businessman, or as a person of independent means, or as a self-employed person, or as the wife or young child of any such person so admitted. A person so seeking to enter the United Kingdom may present himself at the point of entry with no prior clearance and seek to satisfy the immigration officer of his eligibility, or he may provide himself with an entry clearance in advance. This emerges clearly in r 35 (persons of independent means) and r 36 (self-employed persons). It is implied in other rules.

Part IV of the rules contains a code of eligibility for persons who come to the United Kingdom for settlement. It starts with para 38. This is the paragraph, and the only paragraph, which refers to 'special vouchers' and it contains the problem with which your Lordships are faced. The remaining paragraphs of Pt IV are straightforward. It is, I think, easier to understand para 38 if one goes first to the later paragraphs. They all deal with the eligibility for entry into the United Kingdom for settlement of persons who are dependent on, or associated with, persons already settled or about to be settled. Paragraphs 39 to 46 deal with the admission for settlement of dependants of persons already in the United Kingdom or being admitted. Under these paragraphs it must be shown that the person already settled, or about to be settled, in the United Kingdom is able and willing to support and accommodate his dependants without recourse to public funds, except in the case of a wife or young child of a Commonwealth citizen who is patrial, or was settled in the United Kingdom on the coming into force of the 1971 Act. Paragraph 40 provides that a person seeking admission as a dependant under Pt IV must 'hold a current entry clearance granted to him for the purpose'; cf para 11 to exactly the same effect. In other words, such a dependant must prove his eligibiltiy in advance of presenting himself to the immigration officer at the point of entry. Paragraphs 41 and 42 deal with the eligibility of a wife of, or woman living in permanent association with, a person already settled or about to settle in the United Kingdom. Paragraphs 43 and 44 deal with the eligibility of young children whose parent, or parents, are settled or about to settle. Paragraph 45 defines the eligibility of parents and grandparents of a person settled in the United Kingdom. Paragraph 46 defines the eligibility of a distressed relative of a brother, sister, aunt or uncle of a person settled in the United Kingdom. In each of these cases the paragraph is expressed to be subject to para 40, so that the person seeking entry must provide himself or herself in advance with an 'entry clearance' as evidence of eligibility. Paragraphs 47 to 50 define the eligibility of a husband, fiancé or fiancée of a person already settled in the United Kingdom, and similarly require that the person seeking entry shall hold a current entry clearance issued for that purpose. Paragraphs 51 to 53 define the eligibility for entry into the United Kingdom for settlement of a person who has live here before. These last paragraphs envisage that the application will be dealt with at the point of entry by an immigration officer, but presumably the passenger can, if he chooses, apply for an entry clearance in advance in the form of an entry certificate.

I return now to para 38. It relates to the case of a person who is a citizen of the United Kingdom and Colonies and holds a United Kingdom passport. The event supposed is that the passenger presents a special voucher issued to him by a British government representative overseas (or an entry certificate in lieu). In that event the passenger is to be admitted for settlement. The paragraph continues with the words:

> 'as are his dependants if they have obtained entry certificates for that purpose and satisfy the requirements of *paragraph 39*; but such a passenger who comes for settlement without a special voucher or entry certificate is to be refused leave to enter.'

So the passenger seeking to be admitted for settlement must either present a special voucher, or, if he is a dependant (or the like), an entry clearance, which will presumably be in the form of an entry certificate. I attach no significance to the reference to an 'entry certificate in lieu' of a special voucher, nor did counsel in their addresses to this House.

It emerges from the form of the rules that an entry certificate is a travel document which is issued to an intending passenger for the purpose of providing him with prima facie evidence that he is eligible for entry into the United Kingdom, because he satisfies the rules which apply to a visitor, student, au pair, worker for employment, businessman, person of independent means, self-employed person or dependant or the like. All such persons, if they do not wish or under the rules are not allowed to prove their eligibility at the point of entry, must prove that they come within the rules by obtaining an entry clearance in the form of an entry certificate.

I turn to the 'special voucher'. Its nature is not explained in the immigration rules. Unquestionably it is not the same as an entry certificate. It is not expressed to be a document provided to a passenger in advance of his journey as prima facie evidence that he comes within any rule contained in the immigration rules. The evidence before your Lordships as to the nature of the special voucher is contained in the affidavit of Mr Wingfield of the Home Office, and may be summarised as follows:

> 'The Special Voucher Scheme was introduced following the Commonwealth Immigrants Act 1968 . . . Special Vouchers . . . are primarily intended for people who are subject to pressure in their countries of residence and who have nowhere else to go. The scheme allows heads of . . . households and their families into this country for settlement on an annual quota basis notwithstanding the fact that they may be otherwise ineligible for entry under the immigration rules.'

I think that the words 'and their families' should be qualified to this extent; it is clear beyond argument from paras 38, 40, and 41 ff of the immigration rules that a family is admitted, not because the members have been presented with special vouchers, but because they are in possession of current entry clearances (entry certificates) granted for that purpose, which they can obtain as dependants of a person 'who is on the same occasion given indefinite leave to enter': see rr 39 and 40.

I turn now to reconsider the definition of 'entry clearance' in s 33 of the 1971 Act, and the inclusion of that expression in s 13(2) dealing with the right of appeal. Whatever may be the technical form of the appellant's application, the real issue as it has developed is whether a special voucher is an entry clearance within the meaning of the Act so that its refusal is subject to the appeal procedure in s 13.

Section 13(1) gives a right of appeal to a person against a decision that he requires leave to enter or against the refusal of leave to enter. Subsection (2) gives a right of appeal to a person who is refused a certificate of patriality (under s 3(9)) or is refused an entry clearance. The second limb of sub-s (1) is to be contrasted with the second limb of sub-s (2). Subsection (1) is dealing with a refusal of leave to enter at the point of entry, and sub-s (2) is dealing with the refusal of an entry clearance in advance of entry. Only the second limb of sub-s (2) is in point in this appeal.

An entry clearance is a defined expression. It does not mean any document which lets the holder past the immigration officer. It is confined to—

> 'a . . . document which, in accordance with the immigration rules [ie, by definition, the rules laid down under s 3], is to be taken as evidence of a person's eligibility, though not patrial, for entry into the United Kingdom . . .'

For example, a document proving the eligibility of a dependant under any of paras 39 to 46, or proving the eligibility of a student under paras 18 to 20, or proving the eligibility of a person coming for employment under para 29, or proving the eligibility of a businessman under paras 32 and 33, or proving the eligibility of a person of independent means under para 35, or proving the eligibility of a self-employed person under para 36. All those persons, if intending entrants, may apply for an entry clearance which they can produce to the immigration officer as evidence that they fall within the rules.

A special voucher is entirely different. Its purpose is not to provide prima facie evidence that the holder is eligible under the rules. That is the purpose of an entry certificate, in the case of a Commonwealth passenger, and of a visa or Home Office letter, in the case of a non-Commonwealth passenger. There is no rule compliance with which is evidenced by a special voucher. No immigration rule has been promulgated under s 3(2) which defines eligibility for the grant of a special voucher. Its issue is not a matter of eligibility and its object is not to provide evidence of compliance with any rules. There is a temptation to regard an entry clearance as a document which clears the holder for entry into the United Kingdom. I think that it has a narrower meaning. It is a certificate (in neutral terms) which signifies to an immigration officer that the holder has produced, in advance, to the British representative at the passenger's place of residence the evidence which otherwise he would have to produce to the immigration officer at the point of entry in order to satisfy the officer that he should be given leave to enter. The expression 'entry clearance' in the 1971 Act comes into use mainly in connection with appeals, and it is altogether sensible that the appellate procedure should be confined to cases where there are defined rules of entry.

The view which I have sought to express is no more than an extended version of the reasoning in the judgment of Lord Lane CJ, which was accepted by the other two members of the Divisional Court, and also by the three Lords Justices on appeal. It is a view which initially I did not espouse because I thought it too narrow. But, on reflection, I think that the opposite view fails to give weight to the words 'which, in accordance with the immigration rules, is to be taken as evidence of a person's eligibility, though not patrial, for entry . . .' The immigration rules abound with instances where an entry clearance is requisite or desirable as evidence of the fulfilment of conditions. If the appellant's argument is correct, the words I have quoted might as well be replaced by the words 'which permits entry . . .'

In the result, although the appellant is entitled to apply for an entry certificate, and to appeal if her application is refused, she has no right to appeal against the refusal of a special voucher, which is not an 'entry clearance' within the specialised meaning of that expression in s 33.

The conclusion on this first issue reached by the majority of your Lordships is sufficient to dispose of the matter. I desire, however, to add that I am in agreement with the views expressed by my noble and learned friend Lord Fraser on the application of the Sex Discrimination Act 1975.

I would dismiss this appeal.

Appeal dismissed.

Solicitors: *Suchak & Kanji*, Wembley (for the appellant); *Treasury Solicitor*.

Mary Rose Plummer Barrister.

Amin Rasheed Shipping Corp v Kuwait Insurance Co
The Al Wahab

HOUSE OF LORDS
LORD DIPLOCK, LORD WILBERFORCE, LORD ROSKILL, LORD BRANDON OF OAKBROOK AND LORD BRIGHTMAN
16, 17, 19 MAY, 7 JULY 1983

Conflict of laws – Contract – Proper law of contract – Insurance policy – Marine insurance – Lloyd's SG form – Kuwaiti insurance company insuring vessel owned by Liberian company resident in Dubai – Policy based on Lloyd's standard marine insurance policy – Policy not specifying proper law of contract – Policy issued and to be performed in Kuwait – Liberian owners seeking to bring proceedings in England against Kuwaiti insurers – Owners seeking leave to serve writ on insurers out of jurisdiction – Whether English law to be inferred as proper law from use of Lloyd's policy – Whether court should grant leave to serve writ out of jurisdiction – RSC Ord 11, rr 1(1)(f)(iii), 4(2).

The plaintiffs, a Liberian company resident in Dubai, owned a vessel which they insured with the defendants, a Kuwaiti insurance company. The policy, which was based on the Lloyd's SG form as set out in Sch 1 to the Marine Insurance Act 1906, insured the vessel against war and marine risk. The policy was issued in Kuwait and provided for claims to be paid in Kuwait although the currency specified was expressed in sterling. In 1980 the vessel was seized by the Saudi Arabian authorities and the plaintiffs claimed under the policy for constructive loss of the vessel. The defendants rejected the claim and the plaintiffs sought leave in the English courts to serve proceedings against the defendants under RSC Ord 11, r 1(1)(*f*)(iii)[a], which empowered the court to give leave to serve proceedings out of the jurisdiction if the action was brought to recover damages for breach of a contract which was 'by its terms, or by implication, governed by English law'. The judge refused leave on the ground that the proper law of the contract was Kuwaiti law, not English law. The judge further held that, even if English law was the proper law of the contract, he would nevertheless have exercised his discretion under Ord 11, r 4(2)[b] by refusing to give leave to serve the proceedings outside the jurisdiction. The Court of Appeal dismmissed an appeal by the plaintiffs. The plaintiffs appealed to the House of Lords.

Held – (1) Since the court had jurisdiction only if the contract was governed by English law, the court had to determine what legal system was applicable by ascertaining the system of law which the parties had by express terms or by necessary implication intended should apply to govern the interpretation and enforcement of the contract or, in the absence of a clear intention, by determining from the terms of the contract and the relevant surrounding circumstances which system of law had the closest and most real connection with the contract. Applying that test, little assistance could be derived, in all the circumstances, from a consideration of the place where the contract was made or performed. However, it was clear that the parties had intended the contract to be governed by English law, since (a) at the time the contract was made Kuwait was without a commercial code dealing with contracts of marine insurance and the courts in Kuwait would have no difficulty in applying the law of another state, namely England, to marine insurance contracts concluded in Kuwait, and (b) without recourse to the 1906 Act, which was a codifying Act, and to judicial interpretation of that code it was not possible to interpret the policy. Accordingly, the court had jurisdiction to grant leave for the writ to be served out of the jurisdiction (see p 888 *a* to *c* and *j* to p 889 *f*, p 890 *a b g*, p 891 *c d*,

a Rule 1(1) is, so far as material, set out at p 886 *g*, post
b Rule 4(2) is set out at p 886 *h*, post

p 892 *f* to *j*, p 893 *j* to p 894 *a* and p 895 *f* to p 896 *a* and *f* to *j*, post); dicta of Lord Atkin in *R v International Trustee for the Protection of Bondholders Akt* [1937] 2 All ER at 166, of Lord Wright in *Vita Food Products Inc v Unus Shipping Co Ltd* [1939] 1 All ER at 526–527, of Lord Simonds in *Bonython v Commonwealth of Australia* [1951] AC at 219 and *Compagnie d'Armement Maritime SA v Compagnie Tunisienne de Navigation SA* [1970] 3 All ER 71 applied.

(2) However, since the jurisdiction conferred on the court by RSC Ord 11, r 1(1)(*f*)(iii) was exorbitant, in that the English jurisdiction was being sought to be forced on an unwilling defendant and an English court would only recognise that a foreign court had the same jurisdiction if a treaty conferring it was in existence, the court would normally exercise its discretion under Ord 11, r 4(2) by refusing to grant a plaintiff leave to serve the proceedings out of the jurisdiction unless he satisfied the court that justice could not be obtained if proceedings were taken in the alternative legal system or could only be obtained with excessive cost, delay or inconvenience. The plaintiffs had failed to satisfy the judge that there were sufficient grounds to compel the defendants to submit to the jurisdiction of the English courts and the court would not interfere with the exercise of the judge's discretion against the plaintiff. Accordingly, the appeal would be dismissed (see p 891 *e* to *g*, p 893 *b* to *g* and p 896 *c* to *e* and *h j*, post); *Hadmor Productions Ltd v Hamilton* [1982] 1 All ER 1042 applied.

Per curiam. The fact that the standard form of English marine policy is widely used in insurance markets throughout the world does not make it an international or floating contract unattached to any system of law. Likewise the fact that many foreign litigants voluntarily resort to the Commercial Court in London for the resolution of commercial disputes does not make that court an international court and not simply a national or domestic court of England (see p 890 *j* to p 891 *c*, p 892 *j*, p 893 *f*, p 895 *e* and p 896 *g* to *j*, post).

Decision of the Court of Appeal [1983] 1 All ER 873 affirmed.

Notes

For the determination of the proper law of a contract, see 8 Halsbury's Laws (4th edn) paras 583–591, and for cases on the subject, see 11 Digest (Reissue) 458–459, 760–776.

For the Marine Insurance Act 1906, Sch 1, see 17 Halsbury's Statutes (3rd edn) 882.

Cases referred to in opinions

Aratra Potato Co Ltd v Egyptian Navigation Co, The El Amria [1981] 2 Lloyd's Rep 119, CA.
Bonython v Commonwealth of Australia [1951] AC 201, PC.
Compagnie d'Armement Maritime SA v Compagnie Tunisienne de Navigation SA [1970] 3 All ER 71, [1971] AC 572, [1970] 3 WLR 389, HL.
Hadmor Productions Ltd v Hamilton [1982] 1 All ER 1042, [1983] AC 191, [1982] 2 WLR 322, HL.
Helbert Wagg & Co Ltd, Re [1956] 1 All ER 129, [1956] Ch 323, [1956] 2 WLR 183.
Miller (James) & Partners Ltd v Whitworth Street Estates (Manchester) Ltd [1970] 1 All ER 796, [1970] AC 583, [1970] WLR 728, HL.
R v International Trustee for the Protection of Bondholders Akt [1937] 2 All ER 164, [1937] AC 500, HL.
Torni, The [1932] P 78, [1932] All ER Rep 374, CA.
Vita Food Products Inc v Unus Shipping Co Ltd [1939] 1 All ER 513, [1939] AC 277, PC.

Interlocutory appeal

The plaintiff, Amin Rasheed Shipping Corp (the assured), appealed with leave of the Court of Appeal against the decision of the Court of Appeal (Sir John Donaldson MR, May and Robert Goff LJJ) ([1983] 1 All ER 873, [1983] 1 WLR 228) on 15 December 1982 dismissing an appeal by the assured against an order made by Bingham J ([1982] 1 WLR 961) dated 30 March 1982 which set aside the order of Robert Goff J dated 22 May 1981 granting leave to the assured to issue a writ out of the jurisdiction and to serve notice of the writ on the defendants, Kuwait Insurance Co (the insurers). Bingham J set aside the order of Robert Goff J on the grounds that the court had no jurisdiction to grant leave under RSC Ord 11, r 1(1)(*f*)(iii) to serve proceedings out of the jurisdiction. The facts are set out in the opinion of Lord Diplock.

Colin Ross-Munro QC and *Barbara Dohmann* for the assured.
Adrian Hamilton QC and *R J Thomas* for the insurers.

Their Lordships took time for consideration.

7 July. The following opinions were delivered.

LORD DIPLOCK. My Lords, the plaintiff/appellant (the assured) is a shipping company incorporated in Liberia, but having its head office and carrying on its business in Dubai. It is the owner of a cargo vessel of the landing craft type, the Al Wahab (the vessel) which, at the relevant time, traded in Arabian Gulf waters only. In these proceedings, the assured seeks to litigate in the English Commercial Court its claim against the defendants/respondents (the insurers) for a constructive total loss of the vessel which was insured under a hull and machinery policy of insurance against marine and war risks (the policy) that had been issued in Kuwait by the insurers who have their head office there and branch offices elsewhere in the Gulf, including Dubai, but have no office or representative in England.

The policy was on the insurers' standard printed form of hull policy. It was in the English language only. The wording followed meticulously (with minor and in my view immaterial omissions of express references to London) that of the Lloyd's SG policy scheduled to the Marine Insurance Act 1906, but adapted by typewritten insertions for use as a time, instead of a voyage, policy, and excluding references to goods and merchandise. It incorporated in the body of the policy the usual f c and s clause from what at that time was the 'Standard Form of English Marine Policy'; but, by a typewritten insertion, was expressed to be 'Subject to Institute War and Strikes Clauses Hulls dated 1.10.70 as attached'; and a print of those clauses without any additions or amendments was attached to the policy. The policy was expressed to be issued in Kuwait on 28 April 1979 and claims (if any) expressed to be payable in Kuwait.

In order to achieve its object of pursuing its claim against the insurers in the English court, rather than a Kuwaiti court, the assured had two obstacles to overcome.

First, it had to bring the case within RSC Ord 11, r 1(1) in order to obtain leave to serve a writ on the insurers out of the jurisdiction. Although the assured had originally asserted that the contract of insurance had been made on its behalf by an agent trading in England, this failed on the facts; and in this House the only provision of r 1(1) that was relied on by the assured was that contained in para (*f*) of which the relevant wording is:

> 'if the action begun by the writ is brought against a defendant not domiciled or ordinarily resident in Scotland to enforce ... a contract ... being ... a contract which ... (iii) is by its terms, or by implication, governed by English law.'

I will call this first obstacle the jurisdiction point.

The second obstacle is that the assured must satisfy the requirements of Ord 11, r 4(2) which provides:

> 'No such leave shall be granted unless it shall be made sufficiently to appear to the Court that the case is a proper one for service out of the jurisdiction under this Order.'

I will call this second obstacle the discretion point.

Leave to issue and serve the writ on the insurers in Kuwait was initially granted ex parte by Robert Goff J. A summons by the insurers to set aside this ex parte order came before Bingham J on 4 March 1982. He held against the assured on the jurisdiction point, but in case on appeal he should be held to be wrong on that, he also gave full consideration to the discretion point and held against the assured on that point too. He accordingly ordered the issue and service of the writ to be set aside.

On appeal to the Court of Appeal (Sir John Donaldson MR, May and Robert Goff LJJ) ([1983] 1 All ER 873, [1983] 1 WLR 228), the Master of the Rolls held in favour of the assured on both the jurisdiction point and the discretion point. May LJ found in favour of the assured on the jurisdiction point, but against it on the discretion point. Robert Goff LJ found against the assured on the jurisdiction point but (regrettably as I think) refrained from expressing any opinion on the discretion point, despite the fact that his two brethren were divided on it. So we are left without any majority ratio decidendi in the Court of Appeal.

In the result, although the assured failed all along the line, in the course of doing so it gave rise to considerable diversity of judicial reasoning. Sir John Donaldson MR and May LJ held that there was jurisdiction to grant leave to serve the writ out of jurisdiction; while Robert Goff LJ and Bingham J held that there was no such jurisdiction. May LJ and Bingham J were of opinion that, given jurisdiction (which May LJ thought there was), the discretion should be exercised against leave being granted; the Master of the Rolls took the opposite view that the discretion should be exercised in favour of granting leave, and Robert Goff LJ expressed no opinion on the point.

The jurisdiction point on which judicial opinion in the courts below was evenly divided is one which is of considerable importance in transnational commercial contracts, and the approach in modern times to the exercise of the discretion in cases falling within Ord 11, r 1(1)(*f*) is also deserving of re-examination. So, in spite of the unanimity of the result in both courts below, leave to appeal from the decision of the Court of Appeal was given by that court.

The jurisdiction point

My Lords, the jurisdiction point is one that falls to be determined by English law and by English law alone. The relevant rules to be applied to its determination are the English rules of conflict of laws, not the conflict rules of any other country, which may or may not be the same as those of England. In particular, so far as the jurisdiction point itself is concerned, it is immaterial whether the courts of the only obvious rival forum, a Kuwaiti court, would take the same view as an English court as to what was the proper law of the policy. The relevance of this only arises if and when one reaches the discretion point.

The applicable English conflict rules are those for determining what is the 'proper law' of a contract, i e the law that governs the interpretation and the validity of the contract and the mode of performance and the consequences of breaches of the contract: *Compagnie d'Armement Maritime SA v Compagnie Tunisienne de Navigation SA* [1970] 3 All ER 71 at 91, [1971] AC 572 at 603. To identify a particular system of law as being that in accordance with which the parties to it intended a contract to be interpreted, identifies that system of law as the 'proper law' of the contract. The reason for this is plain; the purpose of entering into a contract being to create legal rights and obligations between the parties to it, interpretation of the contract involves determining what are the legal rights and obligations to which the words used in it give rise. This is not possible except by reference to the system of law by which the legal consequences that follow from the use of those words is to be ascertained. In *Vita Food Products Inc v Unus Shipping Co Ltd* [1939] 1 All ER 513 at 526–527, [1939] AC 277 at 298 Lord Wright said in a passage cited by Upjohn J in *Re Helbert Wagg & Co Ltd* [1956] 1 All ER 129 at 135–136, [1956] Ch 323 at 341:

> 'There were certain differences between that case [*The Torni* [1932] P 78, [1932] All ER Rep 374] and the present. One was that the bills of lading had a clause that they were "to be construed in accordance with English law", not, as in the present case "shall be governed by English law". In their Lordships' judgment that distinction is merely verbal and is too narrow to make a substantial difference. The construction of a contract by English law involves the application to its terms of the relevant English statutes, whatever they may be, and the rules and implications of the English common law for its construction, including the rules of the conflict of laws. In this sense the construing of the contract has the effect that the contract is to be governed by English law.'

My Lords, Ord 11, r 1(1)(*f*)(iii) states as the test that is relevant to the jurisdiction
point in the instant case that the policy is by its terms, or 'by implication, governed by *a*
English law'. English conflict rules accord to the parties to a contract a wide liberty to
choose the law by which their contract is to be governed. So the first step in the
determination of the jurisdiction point is to examine the policy in order to see whether
the parties have, by its express terms or by necessary implication from the language used,
evinced a common intention as to the system of law by reference to which their mutual
rights and obligations under it are to be ascertained. As Lord Atkin put it in *R v* *b*
International Trustee for the Protection of Bondholders Akt [1937] 2 All ER 164 at 166, [1937]
AC 500 at 529:

> 'The legal principles which are to guide an English court on the question of the
> proper law of a contract are now well settled. It is the law which the parties intended
> to apply. Their intention will be ascertained by the intention expressed in the
> contract, if any, which will be conclusive. If no intention be expressed, the intention *c*
> will be presumed by the court from the terms of the contract and the relevant
> surrounding circumstances.'

Lord Atkin goes on to refer to particular facts or conditions that led to a prima facie
inference as to the intention of the parties to apply a particular system of law. He gives as
examples the lex loci contractus or lex loci solutionis, and concludes ([1937] 2 All ER 164 *d*
at 166, [1937] AC 500 at 529):

> 'But all these rules only serve to give *prima facie* indications of intention: they are
> all capable of being overcome by counter indications, however difficult it may be in
> some cases to find such.'

There is no conflict between this and Lord Simonds's pithy definition of the 'proper *e*
law' of the contract to be found in *Bonython v Commonwealth of Australia* [1951] AC 201 at
219 which is so often quoted, ie 'the system of law by reference to which the contract
was made or that with which the transaction has its closest and most real connection'. It
may be worth while pointing out that the 'or' in this quotation is disjunctive, as is
apparent from the fact that Lord Simonds goes on immediately to speak of 'the
consideration of *the latter question*' (my emphasis). If it is apparent from the terms of the *f*
contract itself that the parties intended it to be interpreted by reference to a particular
system of law, their intention will prevail and the latter question as to the system of law
with which, in the view of the court, the transaction to which the contract relates would,
but for such intention of the parties, have had the closest and most real connection, does
not arise.

One final comment on what under English conflict rules is meant by the 'proper law' *g*
of a contract may be appropriate. It is the substantive law of the country which the
parties have chosen as that by which their mutual legally enforceable rights are to be
ascertained, but excluding any renvoi, whether of remission or transmission, that the
courts of that country might themselves apply if the matter were litigated before them.
For example, if a contract made in England were expressed to be governed by French
law, the English court would apply French substantive law to it notwithstanding that a *h*
French court applying its own conflict rules might accept a renvoi to English law as the
lex loci contractus if the matter were litigated before it. Conversely, assuming that under
English conflict rules English law is the proper law of the contract, the fact that the
courts of a country which under English conflict rules would be regarded as having
jurisdiction over a dispute arising under the contract (in casu Kuwait) would under its
own conflict rules have recourse to English law as determinative of the rights and *j*
obligations of the parties, would not make the proper law of the contract any the less
English law because it was the law that a Kuwaiti court also would apply.

I can state briefly what Lord Atkin refers to as the relevant surrounding circumstances,
at the time the policy was issued, before I come to deal with its actual terms; since
although the policy contains no express provision choosing English law as the proper law
of the contract, nevertheless its provisions taken as a whole, in my opinion, by necessary
implication point ineluctably to the conclusion that the intention of the parties was that

their mutual rights and obligations under it should be determined in accordance with the English law of marine insurance.

a The policy was the second renewal of similar policies on the vessel of which the first was issued on 29 April 1977. The assured by 1977 carried out the insurance of its ships through the London office of an English company that was a member of the Rasheed Group. As brokers for this purpose it used J H Minet & Co Ltd (Minet) who also acted as reinsurance brokers for the insurers. Premiums were paid to Minet in London, policies b were issued by the insurers in Kuwait and sent on by them to Minet who passed them on in London to the English company. Claims, though expressed by the policies to be payable in Kuwait were in practice settled in running accounts in sterling in London between Minet and the insurers and between Minet and the assured.

I mention, in passing, that, in these days of modern methods of communication where international contracts are so frequently negotiated by telex, whether what turns out to be the final offer is accepted in the country where one telex is situated or in the country c where the other telex is installed is often a mere matter of chance. In the result the lex loci contractus has lost much of the significance in determining what is the proper law of contract that it had close on fifty years ago when Lord Atkin referred to it in the passage that I have cited. As respects the lex loci solutionis the closeness of the connection of the contract with this varies with the nature of the contract. A contract of insurance is d performed by the payment of money, the premiums by the assured, claims by the insurers, and, in the case of marine insurance, very often in what is used as an international rather than a national currency. In the instant case, the course of business between the insurers and the assured established before the policy now sought to be sued on was entered into, ignoring, as it did, the provision in the previous policies that claims were payable in Kuwait, shows how little weight the parties themselves attached to the lex loci solutionis.

e The crucial surrounding circumstance, however, is that it was common ground between the expert witnesses on Kuwaiti law that at the time the policy was entered into there was no indigenous law of marine insurance in Kuwait. Kuwait is a country in which the practice since 1961, when it began to develop as a thriving financial and commercial centre, has been to follow the example of the civil law countries and to f embody the law dealing with commercial matters, at any rate, in written codes. In Kuwait there had been in existence since 1961 a Commercial Code dealing generally with commercial contracts but not specifically with contracts of marine insurance. The contract of marine insurance is highly idiosyncratic; it involves juristic concepts that are peculiar to itself such as sue and labour, subrogation, abandonment and constructive total loss, to give but a few examples. The general law of contract is able to throw but little g light on the rights and obligations under a policy of marine insurance in the multifarious contingencies that may occur while the contract is in force. The lacuna in the Kuwaiti commercial law has since been filled in 1980 by the promulgation for the first time of a code of marine insurance law. This code does not simply adopt the English law of marine insurance; there are significant differences. However, it did not come into operation until 15 August 1980, and it is without retrospective effect. It does not therefore apply to h the policy which was entered into at a time before there was any indigenous law of marine insurance in Kuwait.

I add here, in parenthesis, that this does not mean that before the Marine Insurance Code was promulgated Kuwaiti courts were disabled from trying cases involving contracts of marine insurance, any more than the Commercial Court in England is disabled from trying a case involving a contract whose proper law is French law. A j number of claims under marine insurance policies were in fact tried in Kuwaiti courts before the Kuwaiti code of marine insurance came into effect. The courts were able to undertake this task because the legal system of Kuwait includes a Code of Conflict of Laws. This incorporates art 59 which deals with determining the proper law of a contract. The article provides that in the case of a transnational contract it—

> 'shall, from the standpoint of the substantive conditions governing it and the effects ensuing from its conclusion, be subject to the law of the state . . . where the

> contract is concluded . . . unless the contracting parties agree to the application of another law or *circumstances suggest that another law is the one contemplated for* a
> *application.*' (My emphasis.)

This article expressly recognises the duty of the Kuwaiti courts to give effect to the substantive law of some state other than Kuwait even where the contract is concluded in Kuwait if circumstances suggest that the law of that other state was the one contemplated for application; and, as will be seen when I come to the discretion point, a relevant circumstance in the case of contracts of marine insurance entered into in Kuwait before b
the promulgation of the Kuwaiti Marine Insurance Code was the non-existence in Kuwait of any indigenous marine insurance law.

Turning now to the terms of the policy itself, the adoption of the obsolete language of the Lloyd's SG policy as scheduled to the Marine Insurance Act 1906 makes it impossible to discover what are the legal incidents of the mutual rights and obligations accepted by the insurers and the assured as having been brought into existence by the contract, unless c
recourse is had not only to the rules for construction of the policy contained in Sch 1 of the 1906 Act, but also to many of the substantive provisions of the Act which is (accurately) described in its long title as 'An Act to codify the law relating to Marine Insurance'. To give some examples: the policy is a valued policy; the legal consequences of this in various circumstances are prescribed by ss 27, 32, 67 and 68. The policy contained two typewritten insertions, 'Warranted Lloyd's class to be maintained d
throughout the policy period' and 'Warranted trading in Arabian Gulf Waters only'; the legal consequences of the use of these expressions in a policy of insurance is laid down in ss 33 to 35. On the other hand, the printed words include the so-called memorandum: 'N.B.—The Ship and Freight are warranted free from Average under Three pounds per Cent. unless general, or the Ship be stranded, sunk or burnt', where 'warranted' is used in a different sense; to ascertain the legal effect of the expression in this context recourse e
must be had to ss 64 to 66 and 76. The legal effect of the sue and labour clause included in the policy is laid down in s 78. These are but a few examples of the more esoteric provisions of the policy of which the legal effect is undiscoverable except by reference to the Marine Insurance Act 1906; but the whole of the provisions of the statute are directed to determining what are the mutual rights and obligations of parties to a contract of marine insurance, whether the clauses of the contract are in the obsolete language of the f
Lloyd's SG policy (which, with the f c and s clause added, is referred to in the Institute War and Strikes Clauses Hull-Time as 'the Standard Form of English Marine Policy'), or whether they are in the up-to-date language of the Institute War and Strike Clauses that were attached to the policy. Except by reference to the English statute and to judicial exegesis of the code that it enacts it is not possible to interpret the policy or to determine what those mutual legal rights and obligations are. So, applying, as one must in deciding g
the jurisdiction point, English rules of conflict of laws, the proper law of the contract embodied in the policy is English law.

How then did it come about that two such experienced commercial judges as Robert Goff LJ and Bingham J came to the conclusion that the contract embodied in the policy was *not* governed by English law? There was evidence, and even in the absence of evidence your Lordships could I think take judicial notice of the fact, that the standard h
form of English marine policy, together with the appropriate Institute Clauses attached, was widely used on insurance markets in many countries of the world, other than those countries of the Commonwealth that have enacted or inherited statutes of their own in the same terms as the Marine Insurance Act 1906. The widespread use of the form in countries that have not inherited or adopted the English common law led both Bingham J and Robert Goff LJ to conclude that the standard form of English marine policy and the j
Institute Clauses had become internationalised; the 'lingua franca' and the 'common currency' of international insurance were the metaphors that Bingham J used to describe it; while Robert Goff LJ identified what he described as the basic fallacy in the argument of counsel for the assured as being—

> 'that, although the historical origin of the policy may be English, and although English law and practice may provide a useful source of persuasive authority on the

> construction of the policy wherever it may be used, nevertheless the use of a form which has become an international form of contract provides of itself little connection with English law for the purpose of ascertaining the proper law of the contract.'

(See [1983] 1 All ER 873 at 888, [1983] 1 WLR 228 at 249.)

My Lords, contracts are incapable of existing in a legal vacuum. They are mere pieces of paper devoid of all legal effect unless they were made by reference to some system of private law which defines the obligations assumed by the parties to the contract by their use of particular forms of words and prescribes the remedies enforceable in a court of justice for failure to perform any of those obligations; and this must be so however widespread geographically the use of a contract employing a particular form of words to express the obligations assumed by the parties may be. To speak of English law and practice providing a useful source of *persuasive* authority on the construction of the policy wherever it may be used begs the whole question: why is recourse to English law needed at all? The necessity to do so is common ground between the experts on Kuwaiti law on either side; it is because in the absence of an indigenous law of marine insurance in Kuwait English law was the only system of private law by reference to which it was possible for a Kuwaiti court to give a sensible and precise meaning to the language that the parties had chosen to use in the policy. As the authorities that I have cited earlier show, under English conflict rules, which are those your Lordships must apply in determining the jurisdiction point, that makes English law the proper law of the contract.

In agreement with Sir John Donaldson MR and May LJ I would accordingly decide the jurisdiction point in favour of the assured.

The discretion point

My Lords, the jurisdiction exercised by an English court over a foreign corporation which has no place of business in this country, as a result of granting leave under Ord 11 r 1(1)(*f*) for service out of the jurisdiction of a writ on that corporation, is an exorbitant jurisdiction, ie it is one which, under general English conflict rules, an English court would not recognise as possessed by any foreign court in the absence of some treaty providing for such recognition. Comity thus dictates that the judicial discretion to grant leave under this paragraph of Ord 11, r 1(1) should be exercised with circumspection in cases where there exists an alternative forum, viz the courts of the foreign country where the proposed defendant does carry on business, and whose jurisdiction would be recognised under English conflict rules. Such a forum in the instant case was afforded by the courts of Kuwait.

In order to decide whether a Kuwaiti court, as well as having jurisdiction, is also a forum conveniens for the dispute, one must start by seeing what are likely to be the issues between the parties in the proposed action. The assured's claim is for a constructive total loss of the vessel in circumstances briefly narrated by Bingham J ([1982] 1 WLR 961 at 964–965):

> 'On February 28, 1980, the vessel entered Ras Al Khafji, a small port in Saudi Arabia, just south of Kuwait. The master and crew were seized by the Saudi Arabian authorities and imprisoned. The crew were released in August 1980 and the master in April 1981. The vessel remained where it was with no crew on board, apparently confiscated. It appears, although the evidence is scant and the Saudi Arabian decision as translated in evidence before me is somewhat opaque, that the master was thought to be using the vessel to try and smuggle diesel oil from Saudi Arabia to the United Arab Emirates. This accusation is strongly denied by [the assured] and the truth of it is likely to be a central issue in the action. Neither [the assured] nor, it would seem [the insurers], feel it prudent to visit Saudi Arabia to inspect the vessel or investigate the matter. [The assured] gave notice of abandonment of the vessel to [the insurers] on October 31, 1980, and again on April 28, 1981. On each occasion [the insurers] rejected the notice but agreed to treat the case as if a writ had been issued on that date.'

The central issue in the litigation, as the judge points out, would appear to be one of fact: was the vessel engaged in smuggling when she was seized by the Saudi Arabian authorities? If she was, the loss was excluded by the exception in cl 4(1)(*e*) of the Institute War and Strikes Clauses attached to the policy: 'arrest, restraint or detainment . . . by reason of infringement of any customs regulations.' Whether she was or not is a question of fact, which involves Saudi Arabian law. The principal witnesses as to what the vessel was doing, and whether what happened after it was seized amounted to a constructive total loss, would be those who were the master and crew of the vessel at the time of her seizure. They are Indian and Bangladeshi nationals and on release by the Saudi Arabian authorities they were repatriated to their native countries where, it appears, they now are. Other principal witnesses would be the Saudi Arabians who seized and detained the vessel and Saudi Arabian officials; they are in Saudi Arabia. Kuwait being on international air routes between Europe and India and the Far East is readily accessible to those potential witnesses and to the only potential witnesses who are said by the assured to be in England: the persons between whom it is said an oral charter of the vessel had been entered into which she was performing at the time of the seizure.

Bingham J was of opinion that the factual question could be determined as well in Kuwait as in England, possibly better, and with no clear overall balance of convenience. His own view that the proper exercise of his discretion would be to refuse leave to serve the writ out of the jurisdiction, even if the proper law of the policy were English law, was influenced largely by the fact that the jurisdiction sought to be invoked by the assured is an exorbitant jurisdiction, and that he had 'been given no reason to doubt that a Kuwaiti judge would set himself thoroughly and justly to determine the truth in this case'. To this I myself would add that a Kuwaiti judge would be likely to have greater familiarity even than the Commercial Court in England with the sort of thing that goes on in purely local trading in the Arabian Gulf, to which the vessel was by express warranty confined.

Although the issues would appear to be primarily issues of fact, questions of law will also be involved relating to notice of abandonment and constructive total loss which are governed by ss 60 to 63 of the Marine Insurance Act 1906. But, as already mentioned, it is common ground between the expert witnesses on Kuwaiti law that Kuwaiti judges in deciding those questions would, under the Kuwait Code of Conflict of Laws, apply English law as the proper law of any policy of marine insurance entered into in Kuwait before 15 August 1980, if it were in the terms of the standard form of English marine policy with Institute War and Strike Clauses attached. Like Bingham J, I see no reason why a Kuwaiti court should find any difficulty in applying the relevant English law to the facts once they had been found.

My Lords, it was urged on this House, as it had been urged on the courts below, that since Kuwait is one of those countries whose courts adopt the practice and procedure that is followed in countries whose legal systems are derived from the civil law and not from the English common law, the ability of a Kuwaiti court to decide matters of disputed fact is markedly inferior to that of the Commercial Court in England. None of the judges in the courts below accepted this invitation to embark on the invidious task of making a comparison of the relative efficiency of the civil law and common law procedures for the determination of disputed facts. In my opinion, it would have been wholly wrong for an English court, with quite inadequate experience of how it works in practice in a particular country, to condemn as inferior to that of our own country a system of procedure for the trial of issues of fact that has long been adopted by a large number of both developed and developing countries in the modern world. So a natural prejudice in favour of a procedure with which English lawyers are familiar is not a consideration to which any weight ought to be given in determining whether a Kuwaiti court or the Commercial Court in England is the forum conveniens for the present litigation.

Nor, with respect, can I accept the suggestion of Sir John Donaldson MR ([1983] 1 All ER 873 at 882, [1983] 1 WLR 228 at 240) that, for the purposes of the application by national courts of the doctrine of comity between one national court and another, the Commercial Court in London is 'far more than a national or domestic court; it is an international commercial court' and that Bingham J erred in regarding it otherwise.

True it is that either directly through a choice of forum clause in commercial contracts or indirectly through an English arbitration clause, the Commercial Court in London is much resorted to by foreign nationals for resolution of disputes; and true it is that its judges have acquired unrivalled expertise in such matters, including marine insurance where that insurance is governed by English law. The latter fact no doubt accounts for the popularity of the court with foreign litigants, but their submission to its jurisdiction in the case of contracts which contain such clauses is voluntary and not, as in the instant case, sought to be forced on an unwilling defendant in the exercise by an English court of what can be classified only as an exorbitant jurisdiction which it does not recognise as possessed by foreign courts.

My Lords, the onus under Ord 11, r 4(2) of making it 'sufficiently appear to the Court that the case is a proper one for service out of the jursidction under this Order' lies on the would-be plaintiff. Refusal to grant leave in a case falling within r 1(1)(*f*) does not deprive him of the opportunity of obtaining justice, because ex hypothesi there exists an alternative forum, the courts of the country where the proposed defendant has its place of business where the contract was made, which would be recognised by the English courts as having jurisdiction over the matter in dispute and whose judgment would be enforceable in England.

The exorbitance of the jurisdiction sought to be invoked where reliance is based exclusively on r 1(1)(*f*)(iii) is an important factor to be placed in the balance against granting leave. It is a factor that is capable of being outweighed if the would-be plaintiff can satisfy the English court that justice either could not be obtained by him in the alternative forum; or could only be obtained at excessive cost, delay or inconvenience. In the instant case, the assured failed to satisfy Bingham J that any of these factors in favour of granting leave to compel the insurers to submit to the exorbitant jurisdiction of the English court were of sufficient moment to satisfy the onus. May LJ, applying the principles laid down by this House in *Hadmor Productions Ltd v Hamilton* [1982] 1 All ER 1042, [1983] AC 191, saw no grounds for interfering with the way in which Bingham J had said that he would exercise his discretion, but May LJ added that if he had thought that he himself had an independent discretion he too would have exercised it in the same way (see [1983] 1 All ER 873 at 885, [1983] 1 WLR 228 at 244).

I too see no reason for differing from Bingham J on the discretion point; while, for reasons I have given, I think that Sir John Donaldson MR was wrong in supposing that Bingham J erred in failing to regard the Commercial Court in London as an international commercial court and not simply a national court of England. I would therefore dismiss the appeal.

LORD WILBERFORCE. My Lords, the question in this appeal is whether service of a writ on the insurers outside the jurisdiction of the English courts should be set aside. The provision which is relied on as justifying such service is that contained in RSC Ord 11, r 1(1)(*f*)(iii), which requires, in the case of an action being brought to enforce a contract, that the contract 'is by its terms, or by implication, governed by English law'. The contract in question is a policy of marine insurance, dated 28 April 1979, between the assured and the insurers, and the first question is, therefore, whether this contract comes within the quoted words. If it is held so to do, so that the court has jurisdiction to order service of the writ in Kuwait, a second question arises whether it should do so in the circumstances of the case.

It has been generally accepted, in my opinion rightly, that the formula used in para (*f*)(iii) is equivalent to a requirement that the proper law of the contract should be English law. This involves treating the words 'by implication' as covering both the situation whether the parties' mutual intention can be inferred and the situation where, no such inference being possible, it is necessary to seek the system of law with which the contract has its closest and most real connection. Although these situations merge into each other, I regard this case as falling rather within the latter words since I can find no basis for inferring, as between the parties to this contract, an intention that the contract should be governed either by English law or by the law of Kuwait. (I should add here that, as was indicated during the hearing, we cannot, consistently with recent authority, have regard to the conduct of the parties subsequent to the making of the contract, here the original policy of 1977.) The court's task must be to have regard objectively to the various factors pointing one way or the other and to estimate, as best it can, where the preponderance lies.

The search is for the 'proper law': the law which governs the contract and the parties' obligations under it; the law which determines (normally) its validity and legality, its effect, and the conditions of its discharge. It is clear that, as regards this contract, there are only two choices, English law and the law of Kuwait.

It is worth considering at the outset what these alternatives involve.

The Lloyd's SG form of policy, which the policy in this case is with insignificant departures, with its obsolete and, in parts, unintelligible language, is one which has been used for centuries, almost without change. The Marine Insurance Act 1906, a codification Act, passed after 12 years of gestation, which schedules the Lloyd's SG policy as a permissible form of policy, also provides in the schedule a number of definitions. These definitions may be regarded as a form of glossary based on established law, and the substantive provisions in the Act (binding by statutory force only if the proper law is English) as evidence of the established and customary law of marine insurance. I think that we can accept that if Kuwaiti law were regarded as the proper law, it would resort to the definitions and would have regard to commercial custom as, inter alia, manifested by the Act. The expert evidence, in my opinion, establishes so much in relation to the relevant law of Kuwait prior to 1980 when Kuwait introduced its own insurance legislation. Thus, whether English or Kuwaiti law is the proper law, the terms of the contract would be given the meaning ascribed to them by English statute, custom, and decisions.

There is nothing unusual in a situation where, under the proper law of a contract, resort is had to some other system of law for purposes of interpretation. In that case, that other system becomes a source of the law on which the proper law may draw. Such is frequently the case where a given system of law has not yet developed rules and principles in relation to an activity which has become current, or where another system has from experience built up a coherent and tested structure, as, for example, in banking, insurance or admiralty law, or where countries exist with a common legal heritage such as the common law or the French legal system. In such a case, the proper law is not applying a 'conflicts' rule (there may, in fact, be no foreign element in the case) but merely importing a foreign product for domestic use.

There is evidence before us that in relation to insurance, and in particular to cases where Lloyd's SG policies are used, courts in Europe do this, and that the courts in Kuwait would act in a similar way, resorting, as to a source of their own domestic law, to English law directly or indirectly via Turkish law.

So returning to the choice before us, it is between the proper law being English law, or the proper law being Kuwaiti law, drawing in part at least on English interpretations. This analysis, if correct, thus early in the discussion calls in question the validity of one line of argument used to support the assured's case (that the governing law is English law). That argument is simply (I am tempted to say simplistically) that since this contract is in English language and form and embodies many technical expressions which can only be explained by resort to English law, that shows that the proper law, the law governing the contract, must be English law.

There are three reasons why this cannot be correct. (1) As a matter of reasoning it inverts the process which has to be followed. Instead of arguing from the proper law to that which governs interpretation it does the reverse. The form of the contract may indeed be a factor to be considered in the search for the proper law; it is so here, and an important one, but one to be considered with other factors. (2) It is inconsistent with authority, including that of this House. In *James Miller & Partners Ltd v Whitworth Street Estates (Manchester) Ltd* [1970] 1 All ER 796, [1970] AC 583 the question for decision was whether the proper law was that of England or of Scotland. The contract was on an English RIBA form which has 'many connections with English law' (see [1970] 1 All ER 796 at 801, [1970] AC 583 at 606 per Lord Hodson). It had, in fact, been built up and amended from time to time as the result of English decisions. The decision, by a scarcely

discernible majority, was that the proper law was English, but this decision was arrived
a at by a careful weighing of factors, including the nature and origin of the form. There
can be little doubt that on either view, whichever the proper law was held to be, the
contract would have fallen to be interpreted according to English law, but this
circumstance alone was not regarded as decisive. Similarly, in *Compagnie Tunisienne de
Navigation SA v Compagnie d'Armement Maritime SA* [1970] 3 All ER 71, [1971] AC 572
the use of an English form of charter was regarded as a factor to be considered, and the
b decision was that the proper law was French. Reliance was place on some observations of
Lord Wright in the Privy Council case of *Vita Food Products Inc v Unus Shipping Co Ltd*
[1939] 1 All ER 513 at 526–527, [1939] AC 277 at 298. The passage is quoted in part by
my noble and learned friend Lord Diplock. But, as I understand him, Lord Wright was
concerned only with the difference in terminology between that case and *The Torni*
[1932] P 78, [1932] All ER Rep 374. I do not read his observations as equating the law
c governing construction with the proper law; if they were so intended, I could not, with
respect, agree with them. (3) The simple proposition that because a form of contract has
to be interpreted in accordance with English rules, or even decisions, the proper law
must be English law would have very unfortunate consequences. It is well known, and
not disputed, that this Lloyd's SG policy is widely used, not only in the British
Commonwealth, or in countries under British influence, but elsewhere, including
d countries in Europe. It is regularly used in the Middle East and in the Arabian Gulf. It is
a strong thing to say that, in the absence of an express choice of law clause, the proper
law of all such policies is to be regarded by an English court as English.

The wide use made of this form of policy calls, on the contrary, for a careful
examination in each case of the question what proper law is appropriate, the English
form or derivation of the form being an (important) factor.

e I do not believe, with respect, that this argument, which both Bingham J and Robert
Goff LJ regarded as important, can be disposed of by describing it as contending for an
internationalised, or floating, contract, unattached to any system of law: to do so does not
do it justice. The argument is that the Lloyd's SG form of policy is taken into a great
number of legal systems, sometimes by statute, as in Australia, sometimes as a matter of
commercial practice, as in Belgium or Germany, or in the Arabian Gulf, and that in such
f cases, though their legal systems may, and on the evidence do, resort to English law in
order to interpret its terms, the contract may be regarded as an Australian, Belgian,
German etc contract. What has to be done is to look carefully at all those factors normally
regarded as relevant when the proper law is being searched for, including of course the
nature of the policy itself, and to form a judgment as to the system of law with which
that policy in the circumstances has the closest and most real connection.

g In my opinion, therefore, the classic process of weighing the factors must be followed,
with all the difficulties inherent in the process. They are well and clearly listed in the
judgment of Sir John Donaldson MR. I agree with him that the majority of the
ingredients said to connect the policy with English law are irrelevant or lacking in
weight: these include payment of premiums in sterling in London and the use of J H
Minet & Co Ltd, London brokers. The significant factors remain: (1) the use of this form
h of policy expressed in the English language and requiring interpretation according to
English rules and practice; (2) the nationality of the parties, the insurers being
incorporated and carrying on business in Kuwait and the assured being Liberian and
resident in Dubai (ie neither in England nor in Kuwait); (3) the use of English sterling as
the money of account; (4) the issue of the policy in Kuwait: this I regard as of little
weight; (5) provision for claims to be paid in Kuwait. This, too, is of minor consequence
j in view of the practice, established at the time of contracting, of settling claims in
London. I think also, for myself, that it is not without importance that the policy
contains no choice of law clause. With a policy in a form so essentially English, the
absence of such a factor leaves the form and language, as a pointer towards English law,
without what one would consider as its natural counterweight. I agree that omission of
the Lombard Street or Royal Exchange or London clause is insignificant, but I regard the
incorporation of the Institute Clauses, with express reference to English law provisions,
as important. With no great confidence, and reluctantly differing as to the ultimate

conclusion from Bingham J and Goff LJ, whose reasoning in principle I approve and follow, I have reached the conclusion that English law is the proper law of this particular *a* contract.

That makes it necessary to decide whether, even so, service of this writ outside the jurisdiction should be allowed to stand. RSC Ord 11, r 1(1) merely states that, given one of the stated conditions, such service is permissible, and it is still necessary for the plaintiff (in this case the assured) to make it 'sufficiently to appear to the Court that the case is a proper one for service out of the jurisdiction under this Order' (RSC Ord 11, r 4(2)). The *b* rule does not state the considerations by which the court is to decide whether the case is a proper one, and I do not think that we can get much assistance from cases where it is sought to stay an action started in this country, or to enjoin the bringing of proceedings abroad. The situations are different (compare the observations of Stephenson LJ in *Aratra Potato Co Ltd v Egyptian Navigation Co, The El Amria* [1981] 2 Lloyd's Rep 119 at 129). The intention must be to impose on the plaintiff the burden of showing good reasons why *c* service of a writ, calling for appearance before an English court, should, in the circumstances, be permitted on a foreign defendant. In considering this question the court must take into account the nature of the dispute, the legal and practical issues involved, such questions as local knowledge, availability of witnesses and their evidence and expense. It is not appropriate, in my opinion, to embark on a comparison of the procedures, or methods, or reputation or standing of the courts of one country as *d* compared with those of another (cf *The El Amria* per Brandon LJ). In this case, Bingham J, having first decided there was no jurisdiction to order service in Kuwait, then proceeded, after a review of the factors, to express the opinion that, if there was jurisdiction, he would not consider that it should be exercised. This in my opinion was a substantive decision on the point, viz an alternative ground of decision of the case before him, not a mere obiter dictum. It is, of course, appealable and was considered, without *e* definitive result, by the Court of Appeal. Having weighed the factors involved and having the benefit of the analysis of them by my noble and learned friend Lord Diplock, I have come to the conclusion that his decision on this point was right.

For this reason I would dismiss the appeal.

LORD ROSKILL. My Lords, I do not find it surprising that this case should have given rise to such a marked difference of judicial opinion and I confess that for a considerable *f* part of the hearing of this appeal I was disposed to accept the view on the jurisdiction point which appealed both to Robert Goff LJ and to Bingham J, in substance for the reasons given in their respective judgments. But on further consideration and having had the advantage of reading in draft the speech of my noble and learned friend Lord Diplock I have ultimately reached the same conclusion as he.

On the discretion point I have no doubt that Bingham J reached the correct conclusion, *g* as did May LJ. With all respect to Sir John Donaldson MR I cannot accept his view that the Commercial Court is far more than a national or domestic court. It is not, even though much of the work which is undertaken by that court is international in character. It was this view which I think led him to reach the contrary conclusion on the discretion point. For the reasons given by my noble and learned friend on the discretion point also, *h* I would reject the appellants' arguments and dismiss this appeal.

LORD BRANDON OF OAKBROOK. My Lords, I have had the advantage of reading in draft the speech prepared by my noble and learned friend Lord Diplock. I agree with both his reasoning and his conclusions and would dismiss the appeal accordingly.

LORD BRIGHTMAN. My Lords, I also am in agreement with my noble and learned *j* friend Lord Diplock both on the question of the proper law of the policy and on the question of how the discretion conferred by RSC Ord 11, r 4(2) should be exercised, and would dismiss the appeal.

Appeal dismissed.

Solicitors: *Constant & Constant* (for the assured); *Ince & Co* (for the insurers).

Mary Rose Plummer Barrister.

R v Poole Justices, ex parte Fleet

QUEEN'S BENCH DIVISION (CROWN OFFICE LIST)
FORBES J
5 MAY 1983

Rates – Distress for rates – Imprisonment in default of distress – Warrant of commitment to prison – Inquiry as to means before issue of warrant of commitment – Rating authority applying for warrant of commitment – Magistrates inquiring into means of defaulting ratepayer and postponing issue of warrant subject to payment of arrears by instalments – Defaulting ratepayer not complying with condition as to payment – Magistrates issuing warrant without making further inquiry whether ratepayer's failure to pay instalments was due to wilful refusal or culpable neglect – Whether issue of warrant unlawful – General Rate Act 1967, s 103(1)(a).

A distress warrant was issued against the applicant for non-payment of rates. When insufficient goods or chattels were found on the applicant's premises on which to levy distress the rating authority applied to the magistrates for a warrant of commitment to prison. Before issuing the warrant the magistrates, as required by s 103(1)(*a*)[a] of the General Rate Act 1967, made inquiry as to the applicant's means, as a result of which they decided to fix a term of imprisonment but postponed the issue of the warrant on condition that the applicant paid the sum due at the rate of £50 per week. The applicant paid the first few instalments but then wrote to the magistrates' clerk stating that he could not keep up the instalments because of financial difficulties. The magistrates decided that they were bound to issue the warrant of commitment because of the applicant's failure to comply with the conditions for its postponement and accordingly issued the warrant without making further inquiries as to the applicant's means. The applicant applied for orders of certiorari to quash the warrant and mandamus to direct the magistrates to inquire into the applicant's means before issuing a new warrant, on the ground that the magistrates were required by s 103(1)(*a*) to inquire whether his failure to pay the instalments was due to his wilful refusal or culpable neglect before the warrant was actually issued.

Held – In the case of an order for the payment of unpaid rates, magistrates could not issue a warrant committing a ratepayer to prison for failure to comply with conditions for the postponement for the warrant unless the rating authority renewed its application for the issue of the warrant and proved that the ratepayer had failed to comply with the conditions. At the hearing of the renewed application the magistrates were required, by s 103(1)(*a*) of the 1967 Act, to inquire, in the ratepayer's presence, whether his failure to pay was due to his wilful refusal or culpable neglect. Since the magistrates had failed to do that certiorari and mandamus would be granted (see p 900 *b* to *g*, post).

R v Chichester Justices, ex p Collins [1982] 1 All ER 1000 distinguished.

Notes

For imprisonment for default in payment of a fine, see 29 Halsbury's Laws (4th edn) paras 454–455, and for cases on the subject, see 33 Digest (Reissue) 172–173, *1351–1354*.

For issue of warrant for commitment for distress for rates, see 13 Halsbury's Laws (4th edn) paras 415, 422–425.

For the General Rate Act 1967, s 103, see 27 Halsbury's Statutes (3rd edn) 194.

Cases referred to in judgment

Forrest v Brighton Justices, Hamilton v Marylebone Magistrates' Court [1981] 2 All ER 711, sub nom *Re Hamilton, Re Forrest* [1981] AC 1038, [1981] 3 WLR 79, HL.
R v Chichester Justices, ex p Collins [1982] 1 All ER 1000, [1982] 1 WLR 334, DC.

---

a Section 103(1) is set out at p 898 *g*, post

R v Clerkenwell Stipendiary Magistrate, ex p Mays [1975] 1 All ER 65, [1975] 1 WLR 52, DC. a
R v Dudley Magistrates' Court, ex p Payne [1979] 2 All ER 1089, [1979] 1 WLR 891, DC.
R v Gateshead Justices, ex p Tesco Stores Ltd [1981] 1 All ER 1027, [1981] QB 470, [1981] 2 WLR 419, DC.

Application for judicial review

Derek Arthur Lucas Fleet applied, with the leave of Stephen Brown J granted on 1 b February 1983, (i) for an order of certiorari to quash a decision of the Poole justices on 12 January 1983 to issue a warrant of commitment of the applicant under s 102 of the General Rate Act 1967 and (ii) for an order of mandamus directing the justices to make inquiry in the presence of the applicant as to his means in accordance with s 103 of that Act. The facts are set out in the judgment.

c

John Bryant for the applicant.
The respondents did not appear.

FORBES J. In this case counsel for the applicant moves for an order of certiorari d quashing the issue by the Poole justices of a warrant of commitment to prison of the applicant and an order of mandamus directing the justices to make inquiry in the presence of the applicant as to his means in accordance with the provisions of s 103 of the General Rate Act 1967.

The 1967 Act makes provision for the execution of a warrant by justices if somebody does not pay his rates and for the rating authority to make the application. The Act also e provides that, if on the execution of the warrant there is an insufficient return, the person charged with the execution of the warrant under s 102 of the Act makes a return to the magistrates' court to that effect. On that being done, the section goes on to provide that a magistrates' court may, if it thinks fit, and subject to the provisions of s 103 of the Act, (a) issue a warrant of commitment against that other person or (b) fix a term of imprisonment and postpone the issue of the warrant until such time and on such f conditions, if any, as the court thinks just.

Section 103(1), as amended, provides:

> 'Section 102 of this Act shall have effect subject to and in accordance with the following provisions:—(*a*) on the application for the issue of a warrant for the commitment of any person, the magistrates' court shall make inquiry in his presence as to whether his failure to pay the sum to which he was rated and in respect of g which the warrant of distress was issued was due either to his wilful refusal or to his culpable neglect; (*b*) if the magistrates' court is of opinion that the failure of the said person to pay the said sum was not due either to his wilful refusal or to his culpable neglect, it shall not issue the warrant or fix a term of imprisonment.'

So that the situation is that on the application for the issue of a warrant an inquiry as h to means must be made by the magistrates' court.

In this case the situation was that such an inquiry was made on the application for the issue of a warrant of committment and the magistrates did go into the means of the applicant. I need not go into that any further save to say this. Largely because the applicant offered to pay £50 per week off the arrears, the magistrates did not issue a warrant straight away. Instead, they fixed a term of imprisonment and postponed the j issue of the warrant on condition that the applicant went on paying £50 a week off the arrears. It so happened that, although the applicant paid off that sum for some time, he then got into even more serious financial difficulty and it is quite clear from his affidavit that he is wholly unable to pay the £50 a week which he offered and was able to pay at the time he offered it.

When the question of the postponement of the issue of the warrant was being
a considered, the applicant wrote to the justices' clerk explaining the position and the clerk, in an affidavit which I have before me, although neither the justices nor the rating authority are represented in this matter, point out that in his view the matter is covered by two cases, *R v Chichester Justices, ex p Collins* [1982] 1 All ER 1000, [1982] 1 WLR 334, and *R v Clerkenwell Stipendiary Magistrate, ex p Mays* [1975] 1 All ER 65, [1975] 1 WLR 52. Reference is also made in the *Chichester Justices* case to *Forrest v Brighton Justices* [1981]
b 2 All ER 711, [1981] AC 1038. At first sight I was disposed to take the view that I was bound to follow the decision of the *Chichester Justices* case and that it was impossible to distinguish the present case from that case. I need not go into the details of the *Chichester Justices* case. It was a decision of the Divisional Court consisting of Ormrod LJ and Woolf J, the judgment of the court being given by Woolf J. Having referred to *Forrest v Brighton Justices* and *R v Clerkenwell Stipendiary Magistrate* Woolf J took the view, if I can paraphrase
c it, that, while it was necessary that a person on the principles of *R v Gateshead Justices, ex p Tesco Stores Ltd* [1981] 1 All ER 1027, [1981] QB 470 should have notice of what was being said against him and adequate opportunity to be heard before any judicial order was pronounced against him, the issue of a warrant following its postponement on conditions was not a judicial order but a mere judicial act and, in those circumstances, he took the view, and Ormrod LJ concurred, that the position was that there was no necessity
d in the operation of the principle of the *Gateshead Justices* case to allow any opportunity for the person affected by the judicial act, as opposed to the judicial order, to have his say.

Woolf J referred to the dissenting judgment of Robert Goff J in *R v Dudley Magistrates' Court, ex p Payne* [1979] 2 All ER 1089 at 1093, [1979] 1 WLR 891 at 897, a passage which was expressly approved of by Lord Fraser in the *Forrest* case. Robert Goff J said:

e 'The offender may have been ill or may have lost his job in the meantime. If that be the case, the court may well think it just not to issue a warrant. But how can it even consider that question unless notice is given to the offender, so that he can then draw the circumstances to the attention of the court? It would be extraordinary if the warrant should be issued automatically in every case where a term of imprisonment has previously been fixed without giving the offender the opportunity
f to draw such matters to the attention of the court.'

Despite that, the court in the *Chichester Justices* case took the view it did.

Counsel for the applicant makes this distinction. Whereas under the Magistrates' Courts Act 1980, s 77(2) (which is in virtually the same terms as the important part of s 102 of the General Rate Act 1967) one is dealing with a case of payment of fines, or
g something of that sort, in the general rates situation there is this difference, that the money, the payment of which was one of the conditions of the postponement of the issue of the warrant, was paid not into the magistrates' court but to the rating authority. The words of s 82(5) of the Magistrates' Courts Act 1980 make it plain that one is there dealing with the sums adjudged to be paid on the conviction. The subsection states:

h 'After the occasion of an offender's conviction by a magistrates' court, the court shall not, unless—(*a*) the court has previously fixed a term of imprisonment under section 77(2) above which is to be served by the offender in the event of a default in paying a sum adjudged to be paid by the conviction . . .'

The scheme under the 1980 Act is quite clearly aimed at dealing with a situation
j where the magistrates have in fact imposed some kind of a fine, or some other sum adjudged to be paid, and adjudged to be paid not to anybody but paid into the magistrates' court. The result is that the court is in no difficulty in discovering whether or not the conditions under which it postpones the issue of a warrant have been satisfied. That is an easy process and is the process which it appears Woolf J had in mind in the *Chichester Justices* case [1982] 1 All ER 1000 at 1004, [1982] 1 WLR 334 at 339 when he said:

> 'In these circumstances, although it will be necessary for the court to satisfy itself that the conditions of postponement have not been complied with before the warrant is issued, the process is not one to which the general principle referred to by Lord Fraser in the passage cited [from *Forrest v Brighton Justices* [1981] 2 All ER 711 at 714, [1981] AC 1038 at 1045] applies.'

As I say, I concede that that applies forcibly to the situation where there is nothing further to be proved by any adversary to the person who is the subject of the postponed warrant. If the court has only got to look up its records to discover whether money had been paid or not, then no further intervention by anybody else is required. But where, as under the General Rate Act 1967, it is encumbent on the rating authority to lay before a magistrates' court or its clerk evidence that the condition has not in fact been complied with, I would take the view that in those circumstances there must be an opportunity to be heard, otherwise the position is wholly contrary to natural justice. There may have been some error, the rating authority may in fact have had the money and due to some error (no doubt on a computer or something else) it has not turned up, or something of that kind; it seems to me to be wholly wrong that, if the issue of the warrant depends on adequate proof to the justices, as it must, that the conditions on which the issue of the warrant is postponed have not been complied with and that proof is necessary from some other source than merely the court records, then the general principle referred to by Lord Fraser is one which ought to apply. In those circumstances, one can only read s 103 as requiring a rating authority, in a case where the issue of a warrant has been postponed, to apply for the issue of that warrant. What other procedure would there be for the warrant to be issued other than an application by the person whose duty it is to satisfy the justices that the conditions have not been complied with?

If that is so, then it seems to me to be a duty on the justices, on such an application under s 103(1)(*a*) of the General Rate Act 1967 to inquire in the applicant's presence whether his failure to pay was due to wilful refusal or culpable neglect. I take the view that there is sufficient difference in the situations which arise under the 1967 Act from those which arise under the Magistrates' Courts Act 1980 conditions to cause one to hold that the principles enunciated in the *Chichester Justices* case do not apply to the General Rate Act situation.

In those circumstances, it seems to me that this application should succeed and that certiorari should go to quash the issue of the Poole justices' warrant and that an order of mandamus should go to cause them to make not merely an inquiry in the presence of the applicant but to proceed only if the rating authority makes an application to issue the suspended warrant. That is the procedure, it seems to me, which should be adopted. It is not, in other words, merely a question of whether the applicant has the means, it is a question of the rating authority first proving that he has not complied with the conditions under which the warrant was suspended. In those circumstances, the order should go.

Application granted.

Solicitors: *Metson Cross & Co*, agents for *Triggs Turner & Co*, Guildford (for the applicant).

Sophie Craven Barrister.

a Enfield London Borough Council v Mahoney

COURT OF APPEAL, CIVIL DIVISION
WATKINS AND MAY LJJ
21 MARCH 1983

Contempt of court – Committal – Breach of court order – Period of custody – Contemnor sentenced b *to two years' imprisonment for breach of court order – Severity of sentence intended to coerce contemnor into complying with order – Application for order for release of contemnor after he had served 12 months of his sentence – Evidence that sentence having no coercive effect – Whether court should order contemnor's release.*

Costs – Official Solicitor – Order for costs against Official Solicitor – Official Solicitor applying in c *his official capacity for release of contemnor from custody – Application dismissed – Whether proper to order Official Solicitor to pay costs.*

The defendant found a cross, which was believed to be of great value, on a local authority's land. The local authority maintained that the cross belonged to them and, on the defendant's refusal to surrender it to them, brought an action against him to recover it. d The court made an order requiring him to deliver up the cross. On his failure to comply with the order, the local authority applied to the judge for an order committing the defendant to prison for contempt of court. At the hearing of the application the defendant told the judge that he would not hand over the cross because of unrelated and imagined grievances he had. The judge committed him to prison for two years, the maximum period allowed under s 14(1)[a] of the Contempt of Court Act 1981, because he considered e that the defendant's refusal to comply with the court order was a serious contempt and because he thought that the severity of the sentence might coerce the defendant into changing his mind. After serving nearly 12 months of his sentence, the defendant showed no inclination to purge his contempt and to obtain his release. His obduracy and the novelty of the subject of it were meanwhile attracting the attention of the press and television. The Official Solicitor, in the exercise of his duty to review all cases of persons f committed to prison for contempt of court and to take such action as he deemed necessary, applied to the court for the discharge of the defendant before the expiry of the fixed term on the grounds that 12 months' imprisonment was sufficient punishment for the contempt and that, as it was apparent that the defendant would not change his mind about complying with the order, no purpose would be served by keeping him in prison any longer. The judge found that the defendant was using his possession of the cross to g draw attention to himself but dismissed the application on the ground that, as the defendant was still firmly resolved not to purge his contempt, he should not order his discharge. The judge further ordered the Official Solicitor to pay the costs of the hearing, on the basis that his position was no different from that of anyone else whose application had failed. The Official Solicitor appealed against the judge's refusal to order the defendant's release and against the order for costs.

h

Held – (1) There were two reasons for committal to custody for a civil contempt of the court: to punish the contemnor for disobedience of an order of the court and to attempt to coerce him to comply with the order. In the circumstances, the defendant had been sufficiently punished for his disobedience by having served 12 months' imprisonment. Moreover, it was clear that further imprisonment would have no coercive effect but j would only enable him to exploit his situation in order to draw further attention to his imagined grievances; prison was not, however, to be used for such a purpose and neither were the court's orders to be so abused. The appeal would accordingly be allowed and the

---

a Section 14(1) is set out at p 904 *d e*, post

defendant's immediate release from prison would be ordered (see p 904 *d e*, p 906 *c d* and *h* to p 907 *a* and *h* to p 908 *e* and *g*, post); *Re Barrell Enterprises* [1972] 3 All ER 631 a
applied.

(2) In applying for the defendant's release, the Official Solicitor had been performing one of his official functions and it would be wrong to inhibit him in performing that function by making an order for costs against him, whether his application succeeded or not, unless there had been some impropriety or lack of justification. Since there was no suggestion that the Official Solicitor had acted with other than absolute responsibility, b
his appeal against the order for costs would also be allowed (see p 907 *d* to *f* and p 908 *e* to *g*, post).

Notes

For discharge by court order from custody of persons committed for contempt of court, see 9 Halsbury's Laws (4th edn) para 120, and for cases on the subject, see 16 Digest c
(Reissue) 122–128, *1267–1336*.

For the duty of the Official Solicitor on behalf of persons committed, see 9 ibid para 107 and 10 ibid para 950, and for a case on the subject, see 16 Digest (Reissue) 247, *2410*.

For the exercise of the discretion to award costs, see 37 Halsbury's Laws (4th edn) para 714.

For the Contempt of Court Act 1981, s 14, see 51 Halsbury's Statutes (3rd edn) 507. d

Case referred to in judgments

Barrell Enterprises, Re [1972] 3 All ER 631, [1973] 1 WLR 19, CA.

Cases also cited

Churchman v Joint Shop Stewards' Committee of the Workers of the Port of London [1972] 3 All e
ER 603, [1972] 1 WLR 1094, CA.

Davies, Re (1888) 21 QBD 236, DC.

G (a minor) (wardship: costs), Re [1982] 2 All ER 32, [1982] 1 WLR 438, CA.

Jennison v Baker [1972] 1 All ER 997, [1972] 2 QB 52, CA.

Morris v Crown Office [1970] 1 All ER 1079, [1970] 2 QB 114, CA.

f

Interlocutory appeal

The Official Solicitor appealed against the order of Croom-Johnson J dated 26 January 1983, whereby the judge (i) dismissed an application by the Official Solicitor for an order that Derek Victor Mahoney be released from the custody of the governor of HM Prison at Highpoint and (ii) awarded the costs of the hearing of the application to Enfield London Borough Council (the local authority). The facts are set out in the judgment of g
Watkins LJ.

Lionel Swift QC and *Nicholas Medawar* for the Official Solicitor.
Richard Mawrey for the local authority.
Mr Mahoney appeared in person.

h

WATKINS LJ. This is an appeal by the Official Solicitor against an order made by Croom-Johnson J on 26 January 1983. He had before him a motion of the Official Solicitor acting in pursuance of his official duties for an order that Derek Victor Mahoney, then and now in Her Majesty's Prison at Highpoint, be released from the custody of the governor of that prison. Croom-Johnson J dismissed the Official Solicitor's application for the release of Mr Mahoney and proceeded on the application of Enfield London j
Borough Council, on whom the notice of motion had been served, to award the costs of the hearings before him to the local authority, as I shall call them henceforth.

The Official Solicitor appeals to this court not only against the judge's decision to refuse to release Mr Mahoney from prison, but also against the award he made of costs in favour of the local authority.

The circumstances which brought the Official Solicitor to act on behalf of Mr Mahoney are rather unusual. As long ago as 30 March 1982, Taylor J had an application before him made by the local authority that Mr Mahoney, the defendant to those proceedings, should deliver up to the local authority a valuable object called the Glastonbury Cross. This is said to be a lead object of great historical interest and of intrinsic value. The cross has been examined at the British Museum; the experts there have not, up to the present moment, decided whether it is the original Glastonbury Cross brought into existence in the days of King Arthur in the sixth century, or whether it is an imitation of the original made in either the seventeenth or eighteenth century. Even if it be an imitation of the original, it remains of considerable historical interest and intrinsic value.

The local authority maintain that the cross belongs to them. Not very long ago the local authority were dredging a lake within the boundaries of their jurisdiction in an estate called Forty Hall, where landscaping works were to be carried out. The fact that they intended to carry out this work excited the interest of the local archaeological society. They applied to the local authority for permission to allow two or three members of the society at a time to observe the excavations of the lake. The members of the society felt that objects of interest might be found in the silt or other deposits taken out of the lake. The local authority were only too pleased, seemingly, to give their consent to the society for that purpose.

Accordingly from that time henceforward two or three members of the society regularly kept observation as arranged. They noted various items of interest to them; they and servants of the local authority observed that there was another observer on occasions on the scene. He was a stranger to them. The likelihood is that it was Mr Mahoney for, as he has acknowledged, it was he who came into possession of what I shall call the Glastonbury Cross. He found it on the estate while excavations were going on. He kept it. He had been a member of the local archaeological society himself some years previously but by this time his membership had lapsed.

Realising, presumably, the significance of his find, he got in touch with the British Museum. Correspondence passed between the interested officers at the museum and Mr Mahoney, one result of which was that he paid a visit to the museum taking the cross with him. It was on that occasion that a preliminary examination was carried out with the result I have already described. Mr Mahoney would not allow the museum to retain the cross even overnight. He took it away with him. The local authority got to know of his possession of the cross and demanded it from him. He refused to give it to them.

The museum and the local authority communicated over the matter. The attitude of the museum was perfectly clear; it could not cause Mr Mahoney to hand over the cross to the local authority but it was perfectly willing to act as the holder of the cross if it was given into its safe-keeping whilst the right to possession of it was established in court. No such arrangement as that could be contrived because Mr Mahoney defeated all attempts to bring it about.

So the local authority brought an action against him claiming the cross to be their property and asserting that the defendant was wrongly withholding it from them. It was consequent on that action that Taylor J made the order already referred to with which Mr Mahoney refused to comply. He has never complied with it.

I should interpolate at this point that Mr Mahoney has a brother who is a qualified engineer. Mr Mahoney himself is an engineer. He has been unemployed for some while. The two brothers live with their mother in North London. The brother has a grievance against a man who was a solicitor and a member of the Law Society. He was struck off the roll in or about the year 1973. That grievance is shared by Mr Mahoney and their mother. The origins of it seem to lie in some kind of transaction which the brother had with the solicitor before he was struck off the roll which concerned an estate agent. It was said that money was given to the solicitor for which he did not account thereafter. This incident has aroused in the family the most extraordinary hostility to anyone who endeavours to bring some common sense into the issue of the ownership of the Glastonbury Cross.

Mr Mahoney admits that, whilst he does not, being in prison, possess in the physical sense this valuable thing, he exercises control over it. He maintains that he has buried it in a place, the whereabouts of which are well known to him. He will not hand it over because, he says, law and order in this country has virtually broken down. He has asserted as much to the United Nations but that international body seems to have taken little or no interest in him. But his attitude of mind remains unchanged.

Returning now to the procession of court appearances which followed, one comes to Mr Mahoney's first appearance before Croom-Johnson J. Because he refused to obey the order of Taylor J, the local authority moved to have him committed for contempt. On 1 April 1982 the judge came to the conclusion that the refusal of Mr Mahoney constituted a contempt of the nature of a refusal to obey an order of the court, and committed the contemnor, as he then became, to prison for two years. The judge had in mind, when so acting, the provisions of s 14(1) of the Contempt of Court Act 1981, which provides:

> 'In any case where a court has power to commit a person to prison for contempt of court and (apart from this provision) no limitation applies to the period of committal, the committal shall (without prejudice to the power of the court to order his earlier discharge) be for a fixed term, and that term shall not on any occasion exceed two years in the case of committal by a superior court, or one month in the case of committal by an inferior court.'

It is clear from those provisions that the judge imposed the maximum sentence available to him for this contempt. He did it for two reasons. He came to the conclusion that the contempt was a serious one meriting severe punishment and that by imposing the maximum sentence he would, by that punishment, coerce Mr Mahoney into changing his mind and into co-operating with those who were endeavouring to ensure that there be a proper investigation into the right to possession of the Glastonbury Cross.

The order that he be imprisoned had no effect on Mr Mahoney. He has, we are told, been in every way a model prisoner. He has shown no marked desire to go home. His stay in prison has excited the interest of newspapers and television. His obduracy, and of course the novelty of the subject of this obduracy, has prompted articles to be written about him and his struggle to keep this cross, and for television programmes to be made about him.

His brother has been invited to assist in order to introduce some change of attitude of Mr Mahoney, but the brother is wholly disinclined to do anything of the sort because he feels much the same about the attempt to take the cross away from Mr Mahoney as he does.

Mr Mahoney is a man of good character. He has never been known, before now, to show any kind of contempt for the law, still less to break it. Why then should he suddenly behave in what would apparently seem to be a wholly irrational way? He has been examined by a psychiatrist and by the medical officer at the prison. His own doctor has endeavoured to assist by providing his opinion about the mental state of Mr Mahoney. Not one of those gentleman can find any form of mental illness. It occurred to at least two of them that a diagnosis of one or other of two well-known mental illnesses might be driving him to do what he does but their ultimate conclusions are that he is not the subject of any kind of illness of that nature.

What is he then? Apparently he is an eccentric; if not a genuine eccentric, he is behaving in a very eccentric way and so is his brother and so is his mother. The whole family is subject to this manifestation, as it is referred to in one of the reports, of eccentricity arising out of a whole constellation of ideas which are shared in this family.

There is no doubt in my mind that Mr Mahoney is prepared to stay in prison until doomsday, so fixed is his determination that any desire to reclaim his cross is thwarted.

It occurred to the Official Solicitor that he ought to do something about Mr Mahoney, who refuses for reasons which I have endeavoured to explain, to help himself to become free again.

The Official Solicitor is encouraged to act on behalf of persons such as this contemnor.

By a direction dated 29 May 1963 Lord Dilhorne LC directed that:

> a '... the Official Solicitor to the Supreme Court of Judicature do review all cases of persons committed to prisons for contempt of court, do take such action as he may deem necessary thereon and do report thereon quarterly on the 31st day of January, the 30th day of April, the 31st day of July and the 31st day of October in every year.'

b We have been referred to a number of cases where the Official Solicitor has, in pursuance of that direction, brought the court's attention to the plight of contemnors in prisons. So in this case the Official Solicitor caused the contemnor to be brought once again before Croom-Johnson J, who was enabled consequently to examine the situation surrounding the continued incarceration of the contemnor at that time. He first heard counsel on behalf of the Official Solicitor on 12 January 1983. On that occasion the judge, c obviously dismayed at the resolution of the contemnor not to purge his contempt, endeavoured to persuade him to change his mind. He was unsuccessful, so he decided that he would adjourn the hearing for another 14 days in the hope that some wisdom might overcome the contemnor in the meanwhile.

On 26 January following, the parties were before him again, by whom I mean the Official Solicitor, the local authority and the contemnor himself. A thorough examination d of the up-to-date position was made by the judge. Several passages from the transcript of those proceedings have been read out here. He used every endeavour to change the contemnor's mind, again without any success at all. So the judge came to the conclusion that the contemnor should stay in prison. The judge expressed himself in this way:

> 'It is quite clear that your attitude about this, although you say it is "I can't," is simply " I won't." You are simply using the possession of the cross which you have e in a way in order to call attention to your brother's grievance. But neither you nor your brother seems to be taking any steps at all to resolve whatever his grievance may be, and indeed it is very hazy as to what steps you have taken in the past in order to relieve your brother's grievance. In view of your attitude and in view of the terms of the Contempt of Court Act I do not think that this is the time at which you should be released from prison.'

f During the course of this hearing we invited counsel for the Official Solicitor to inform us as well as he felt able about the foundation, if there was any, for this grievance. Those instructing him have made inquiries today. There would appear to be no doubt that the solicitor was struck off at the time I have already mentioned for some form of misconduct. There is, however, so they have discovered, no record either at the Law Society or the g insurers who would have dealt with any claim against that solicitor of any claim being made on him with regard to clients' money, especially by a client by the name of Mahoney.

As I have already said it is at the refusal of the judge to allow the contemnor to be released that this appeal is brought. What are the powers of this court in circumstances of this kind? What, among other things, s 14 provided for was a maximum term of h imprisonment for the offence of contempt. It also saved the power of the court to order the earlier discharge of a contemnor than the expiration of a fixed term of imprisonment imposed on him by order of the court. For a long time past it has been well established that, in cases of imprisonment for contempt, this court has an inherent power to release from prison a contemnor at any time including, in such a case, a time before the date of the expiration of a fixed term of imprison imposed on him by the court below. Before j s 14 was enacted, I should add, there was no maximum term of imprisonment for the commission of contempt.

It is submitted to us that the imposition in the present case of a maximum term was probably unnecessary. This was not in the circumstances one of the most serious of cases of contempt which can be envisaged or which has happened in the past. There is not here and never has been any threat to the life or liberty of anybody, nor even of personal injury. In other contempt cases known to the court consequences, and serious consequences, of that kind have been known and published. It would therefore have been, so counsel for the Official Solicitor says, more appropriate if a much shorter period of imprisonment had been chosen by the judge to be the subject of his order.

He has referred us to a number of instances where short terms of imprisonment have been imposed for deliberate flouting of the orders of the court. An example of this is provided by *Re Barrell Enterprises* [1972] 3 All ER 631, [1973] 1 WLR 19. This however, as he himself emphasised, is not an appeal against a sentence of imprisonment imposed by the judge. It is an appeal, and this cannot be too strongly underlined, against the order of the judge by which he refused to bring about the release of a contemnor in prison. He urges us to interfere with that order, in which behalf he submits that, seeing that we have undoubtedly the power to do so, no useful purpose in any connection whatsoever is going to be served by this man being kept in prison.

Of the two elements of the punishment inflicted by the original order, one has by now surely been served, namely that of punishment for the contempt itself. All that remains now of the order, so it is asserted, is that part of the period of two years which can only be said to relate to the coercive effect which it was hoped by the judge the sentence would impose on him. It being obvious to everyone now that no form of coercion, including no matter how long a stay in prison, is going to cause this man to change his mind; it is pointless to keep him where he is.

Counsel for the Official Solicitor refers to what was said by Russell LJ in *Re Barrell Enterprises* [1972] 3 All ER 631 at 640, [1973] 1 WLR 19 at 27 in relation to the problem of deciding when a person in contempt should be released from prison:

> 'If we thought it at all likely that the dismissal of all the appellant's applications to this court and the continuance of her incarceration for some reasonable period would lead to her producing the securities or enabling them to be recovered by the Official Receiver then we would be in favour of refusing her application for release. We cannot accept a proposition that a person committed for failure to obey a mandatory order should never be released so long as he continues in disobedience.'

Earlier on he had stated ([1972] 3 All ER 631 at 639–640, [1973] 1 WLR 19 at 27):

> 'With regard to punishment it is necessary to remember that the conduct being punished was that of failing to produce the documents in obedience to the court's order and not any dishonest mishandling of the documents . . . This does not mean that the act of disobedience was not in this case one of considerable gravity. In weighing its seriousness it is right to take into account that the papers in question were of a value running into many thousands of pounds.'

Counsel for the local authority has endeavoured to persuade this court that the power which we have to order the release of the contemnor is a discretionary power which we should exercise with very considerable care. We should exercise it in favour of an applicant for release from prison, be he here on his own motion or that of the Official Solicitor so as to bring about his release, only if it is plainly demonstrated that he has purged his contempt. I cannot subscribe to that view. There must be many circumstances in which this court, in reviewing the order of the judge below to keep a contemnor in prison, will come to the conclusion that they compel the court to order release.

What is there here by way of a change of circumstances which would entitle this court, in the exercise of its discretion, to order the release of this contemnor? It seems to me to be abundantly plain that Mr Mahoney is quite content to stay where he is and, because of his eccentricity and stubborness, will never move of his own accord to be released. But in the mean while he takes satisfaction from the fact that his predicament, if such it can be called, is receiving the notice which I have already described from the press and television. This seems to please him and I venture to think that he hopes that this will go on. But prison is not to be used for such a purpose; neither are orders of the court to be abused for such a purpose. That is a change of circumstances which weighs with me in coming to the conclusion that it is high time that the prison service was rid of this man.

When one also concludes, as I do, that there is no coercive effect left in the sentence imposed by Croom-Johnson J, that feeling is reinforced.

For those reasons I venture respectfully to disagree with this very experienced judge. I would order the release of this contemnor forthwith, and to that extent I would allow this appeal.

I now turn to the question of costs. This is an important matter. I see no need to refer to various provisions which enable the court to make orders for costs, including the reference which was brought to our attention as to the role of the Official Solicitor. Suffice it to say that he is unique within the system of the administration of justice. There is no one and nothing else like him. He comes on the family scene to help the court in very sensitive matters. He enters on other scenes in innumerable ways (this case provides an example of them) involving the languishing in prison of people who, having been found in contempt, do not themselves seek release.

It is for that reason that Lord Dilhorne LC issued his directive in the public interest. He was obviously anxious to find some person, some means, of bringing the position of those people to the attention of the courts so that a review could be made and decisions taken whether the prison service need be any longer troubled with their presence.

The judge adopted the understandable attitude when the local authority made an application for costs against the Official Solicitor that, since he, the Official Solicitor, had moved for the failed application, he was in no different position from anyone else, such as a solicitor acting for that person, in which event costs always follow the event.

Counsel for the local authority argues powerfully for the maintenance of that consequence here. But I think it would be a positive disservice to the outstanding services which the Official Solicitor can and does render to the courts to bring any possible form of dissuasion to him from acting in cases of this and other similar kinds. If the Official Solicitor, acting of his own volition, as he very often feels called on to do, felt that at the end of the day his services in the public interest were going to be condemned in costs, then one can easily envisage that there would be a number of cases where he might be disinclined to act in pursuing some cause or other in the interests of justice.

It is right to say, however, that, what I have said notwithstanding, the Official Solicitor should not regard himself as always being immune from an order for costs being made against him. If he should be found to have acted with impropriety or wholly unreasonably, he cannot but expect an order for costs to be made against him. In this case the Official Solicitor in my view has acted with absolute responsibility. The order for costs I would set aside and allow that appeal too.

MAY LJ. Before the Contempt of Court Act 1981 came into force the High Court had the power to imprison a contemnor for a civil contempt either for an indefinite period or for a fixed term. After the 1981 Act came into force, if the court is minded to visit a civil contemnor with the penalty of imprisonment, that must now be for a fixed term. The reason for the change is clear: Parliament took the view that anyone put into prison for contempt should know the maximum period for which he is liable to be kept in custody.

The High Court's inherent power to release a person in contempt during that period of custody, however, remains and indeed the words in brackets in s 14(1) of the 1981 Act clearly recognise the existence of that power.

As this court made clear in *Re Barrell Enterprises* [1972] 3 All ER 631, [1973] 1 WLR 19, to which Watkins LJ had referred, the reasons for a committal to custody for a civil contempt are twofold: first, to punish the contemnor for disobedience of an order of the court and second, to attempt to coerce him to comply with the order. Once a contemnor has been sufficiently punished for disobeying a court order he should not, in my judgment, be punished further for continuing to do the same thing, even though in a sense this shows that he is continuing to be contumacious. Given therefore that the court should not punish twice for the same offence, when an application is made for a contemnor to be released during the fixed term of custody imposed, the first question for the court must be whether the contemnor has been punished enough for the

contempt for which he was sent to prison. If, in the view of the court, he has not, then
probably the court will not release him. If, on the other hand, at the time of such an a
application the court takes the view he has been punished enough for the original
contempt, then the only remaining justification for continuing to keep him in custody
is that this may still have a coercive effect and make him comply with the original order.
If it is quite clear that he is not going to comply however long he stays in custody, then
provided, as I say, that he has been punished enough there is in my view no justification
for continuing to keep him in prison. b

The essential factor underlying this reasoning which I think tends on occasions to
become obscured is that although in one sense the contempt is continuing, in that the
contemnor is refusing to obey the order of the court day after day, in another sense, and
I think the proper one, there is only one contempt, namely the refusal to obey the court's
order. Once this contempt has been adequately punished the contemnor should not be
punished further for what is effectively the same contempt. c

If one then seeks to apply those principles to the facts of the present case, the position
is that Mr Mahoney has now served nearly 12 months' imprisonment, that is to say the
equivalent of an 18-month prison sentence. In my opinion, without seeking to specify
what would have been the appropriate period to punish him for his particular contempt,
that period has by now been served. I therefore ask myself whether continuing custody
in so far as he is concerned will have any coercive effect. I think that it is quite clear, as d
Watkins LJ has said, that it will not, and that any further imprisonment of Mr Mahoney
in this case will only enable him and his family to continue to exploit the existing
situation to their misguided and selfish benefit.

In those circumstances I agree with Watkins LJ that it is desirable that Mr Mahoney
should now be released and in that respect I respectfully disagree with the view taken by
the judge below. e

In so far as the question of costs is concerned, I entirely agree with Watkins LJ's
judgment. The Official Solicitor holds a very special office. He is a servant of the court
and may at any time be called on by a judge to carry out an investigation and to assist the
court to see that justice is done between the parties. One of his special obligations is that
to which Watkins LJ has referred in the direction of Lord Dilhorne LC, namely to bring
to the court's notice the situation of persons committed to prison for civil contempt. f

In my judgment the Official Solicitor should in no way be inhibited in performing
that function and indeed his other functions by any financial consideration. When the
Official Solicitor acting pursuant to his powers makes such an application as this, then
whether it succeeds or not it would in my opinion be wrong to make an order for costs
against him unless there has been some impropriety or lack of justification. No such
contention has been or can be made in the circumstances of this case. g

For these reasons I agree also that the order for costs made by the judge below was
wrong. Consequently I think that this appeal should be allowed on both issues.

Appeal allowed. Order for costs set aside. Contemnor to be released from prison forthwith. Costs on solicitor and own client basis.

Solicitors: *Official Solicitor*; *Wilfred D Day*, Enfield (for the local authority).

Sophie Craven Barrister.

Walker v Walker

COURT OF APPEAL, CIVIL DIVISION
CUMMING-BRUCE, GRIFFITHS LJJ AND SIR ROGER ORMROD
3 MAY 1983

Divorce – Financial provision – Military pay, pensions etc – Avoidance of assignment of, or charge on, military pay, pensions etc – Army resettlement grant – Husband receiving resettlement grant on discharge from army – Registrar ordering Paymaster General to pay grant into court pending outcome of wife's application for ancillary relief – Whether order directing payment 'to another person' – Whether order facilitating a 'charge' on the grant – Whether court precluded from making order – Army Act 1955, s 203(1)(2).

On 24 March 1982 the wife and the husband, who was then in the army, were divorced on the wife's petition. In the petition the wife applied for ancillary relief by way of financial provision in the form of a lump sum and periodical payments. On 1 April 1982 the husband was discharged from the army with an entitlement to a resettlement grant of £2,436 in respect of his army service. On 2 April the wife applied under s 37 of the Matrimonial Causes Act 1973 for an order preserving the grant for her benefit. On 5 April the registrar ordered, inter alia, that if the grant had not been paid to the husband the Paymaster General should pay the grant into court until trial of the wife's application for ancillary relief. The Ministry of Defence, on behalf of the Paymaster General, objected to the order and the registrar transferred the wife's application to enforce the order to the High Court. The judge held that the particular prohibition in s 203(2)[a] of the Army Act 1955 against the court directing 'payment [of the grant] to another person' did not apply because the grant would remain the husband's property while it was in court. However, he further held that the court was precluded by s 203 from making the order sought, because the only purpose of the payment into court was to make possible the alienation of the grant to which the husband was entitled by ordering payment out to the wife. The judge accordingly discharged the order. The wife appealed.

Held – The appeal would be dismissed for the following reasons—

(1) An order directing the Paymaster General to pay into court any sum specified in s 203(1) of the 1955 Act, including a grant payable in respect of army service, was an order directing payment 'to another person', namely the official to whom the payment into court had to be made, and as such was prohibited by s 203(2) of the 1955 Act (see p 913 *j* and p 914 *a* to *f* and *h*, post).

(2) Furthermore, because s 203(1) of the 1955 Act expressly made void any 'charge' on any grant payable to a person in respect of his army service and because the order for payment into court of the husband's grant was designed to facilitate the wife's obtaining a charging order against the grant in the event of her obtaining judgment in the ancillary proceedings, it followed that the order for payment was itself contrary to the intention of s 203(1) and was therefore void (see p 913 *h* to p 914 *b* and *f* to *h*, post).

Notes

For assignment of service pensions, see 33 Halsbury's Laws (3rd edn) 1055, para 1764.

For the Army Act 1955, s 203, see 29 Halsbury's Laws (3rd edn) 306.

For the Matrimonial Causes Act 1973, s 37, see 43 ibid 584.

Case referred to in judgments

Lucas v Harris (1886) 18 QBD 127, CA.

---

a Section 203, so far as material, is set out at p 912 *c d*, post

Appeal

The petitioner wife, Mrs Diane Walker, appealed from that part of an order of Sheldon J made in chambers on 29 July 1982 discharging an order made by Mr Registrar Elliott on 5 April 1982, as formally amended by Mr Registrar Le Mesurier the following day, ordering Her Majesty's Paymaster General to pay into court, pending the trial of the wife's application for ancillary relief, the army resettlement grant payable to the husband, Gerald Walker, on his discharge from the Army, in the event that it had not already been paid to him; and dismissing the wife's summons dated 23 April 1982 seeking to enforce the order. The facts are set out in the judgment of Cumming-Bruce LJ.

Joseph Jackson QC and *Nicholas Mostyn* for the wife.
E James Holman for the Ministry of Defence.

CUMMING-BRUCE LJ. This is an appeal by the petitioner wife in matrimonial proceedings against the order of Sheldon J when he discharged two parts of an order made by Mr Registrar Elliott in the Bedford County Court, dated 5 April 1982 and amended by another registrar the next day. This appeal is only concerned with those orders made by the registrar in so far as orders were made imposing the duty of compliance on Her Majesty's Paymaster General for the regimental payments. The short point raised on the appeal is the question whether the judge was right in his view that the effect of s 203 of the Army Act 1955 was to put it outside the powers of the court to make the orders that the registrars made on 5 and 6 April 1982.

I begin by turning to the order of Mr Registrar Elliott dated 5 April 1982. The orders sought were pursuant to an ex parte application on behalf of the petitioner wife, supported by the affidavit of the petitioner dated 2 April 1982, and that affidavit in terms stated that the application was made under s 37 of the Matrimonial Causes Act 1973. On 5 April Mr Registrar Elliott made the following orders:

> '1. In the event of Her Majesty's Paymaster General not having accounted and paid to the Respondent or his agents or otherwise such monies as are due to him by way of a re-settlement grant or otherwise following upon his service with Her Majesty's Armed Forces or any monies due to him he do pay such sum or sums into this Court to remain in Court until the trial of the issues relating to ancillary relief for the Petitioner and the children of the family or further order.
>
> 2. In the event of Her Majesty's Paymaster General having paid such sum or sums as set out in Clause 1 hereof to the respondent or his agent at the date of service upon Her Majesty's Paymaster General the Respondent to pay such sum or sums into this Court until the trial of the issues relating to ancillary relief for the Petitioner and the children of the family or further order.'

The amendment made the following day added to the registrar's order, after the words 'Her Majesty's Paymaster General', which appeared in both orders, the words 'and/or The Regimental Paymaster'.

The judge, for the reasons which he stated in his judgment, decided that by virtue of the provisions of s 203 of the Army Act 1955, there was no power in the court to make the order made by the registrar in so far as it sought to bind Her Majesty's Paymaster General to deal with moneys payable to the respondent in the ways stated.

In this court there is no appeal on behalf of the respondent personally against that part of the orders made by the judge and the registrar which imposed on the respondent a duty to pay the moneys into court. The only appeal with which this court is concerned is the appeal by the petitioner wife whereby counsel on her behalf submits that the judge was wrong in discharging the order made by Mr Registrar Elliott, as amended the next day by the addition to which I have referred, imposing on the Paymaster General that, in the event of his not having accounted and paid to the respondent moneys due by way of a resettlement grant or otherwise, such moneys should be paid into court and stay in court until the trial of the issue. In those circumstances it is unnecessary for this court to make any observation on that part of the order made by the judge against which there is no appeal and it is important that I should make it plain that nothing in this judgment relates in any way to that part of the judge's order which is not before this court as an order subject to appeal. I am careful to say nothing about that order and I will not mention it again in the course of this judgment. I address myself to the only order subject to the jurisdiction of this court on the notice of appeal.

It is only necessary, in order to make this judgment intelligible, to make a brief extract of certain dates because, in so far as the facts are material, they are all sufficiently to be found in the judgment of the judge and as this court is concerned only with the question of construction, the reasoning of the judgment will not be clarified by reference to examination of the detailed facts.

The skeleton facts to which I refer are these. On 3 April 1976 the husband and wife were married. There were three children of the family. On 22 May 1981 there was a separation. On 26 June 1981 the wife petitioned for dissolution, in reliance on s 1(2)(*b*) of the Matrimonial Causes Act 1973. On 26 October 1981 the wife filed her form giving notice of application for financial provision and the relevant applications for the purposes of the instant proceedings are her applications for periodical payments and for a lump sum. The wife inquired on 26 October 1981, while her husband was still a serving soldier, whether his prospective resettlement grant could be preserved by consent. On 4 January 1982 the registrar gave directions in the ancillary proceedings, including a direction that the husband should file an affidavit of means. He did not comply. On 4 March 1982 the husband left the army on terminal leave. On 24 March 1982 there was a decree nisi. On 1 April 1982 the husband was discharged from the army with an entitlement, by way of resettlement grant, of £2,436. His entitlement arose under the provisions of the royal warrant and not otherwise.

On 2 April, as I have earlier stated, the wife applied under s 37 of the Matrimonial Causes Act 1973 for preservation of the fund, to wit the £2,436 to which her husband was entitled pursuant to the royal warrant. On 5 April 1982 the registrar made a further direction and made the injunctions to which I have already referred, including the injunction against Her Majesty's Paymaster General and the regimental paymaster.

On 13 April 1982 the Ministry of Defence on behalf of the Crown raised objection to the order in so far as it affected them. The registrar transferred the application to the High Court and in his judgment the judge deals with the machinery of that matter, which is not material for the purposes of this appeal.

On 6 May 1982 there was a decree absolute, the wife having issued a summons under s 37 of the 1973 Act a fortnight before. On 21 May 1982 the respondent's solicitors took themselves off the record and the order of the judge was made on 29 July. Since the respondent's solicitors were taken off the record, he has taken no part in these proceedings.

The judge, for reasons stated in his judgment, decided that s 203 of the Army Act 1955 precluded the court from making the order which the registrar had made, ordering the Paymaster General to pay the resettlement grant moneys into court in the event of their not already having been paid to the respondent personally. In the part of his judgment which dealt with that issue, he was satisfied that the resettlement grant was a grant, and though there was at one time an issue about it, counsel for the petitioner takes no point about it now that he knows the accurate facts about the entitlement of the respondent to the moneys.

The judge expressed the view that the proposed order would not in itself have the effect of directing payment of the gratuity to another person, because the money while in court would legally become the respondent's, although subject to a restraint on his power to dispose of it. But the judge went on to say that clearly the sole purpose of such an order is to enable the court, if it could do so, to order that some part or all of the money thus paid into court should, in due course, be paid to the petitioner. The judge said:

> '... in my opinion, it would be wholly unrealistic and incorrect to treat that second order as distinct from the first and to suggest (if I have correctly understood the argument of counsel for the wife) that the whole is unimpeachable because the first part did not direct payment of the gratuity to another person and because the

> second part, although not a direction for the payment of the sum in question to "another person" was a direction which related to a sum which had been "paid" a
> (albeit into court) and therefore was no longer "payable" within s 203 of the 1955 Act. The same objection, moreover, in my opinion, applies to a further submission made by counsel that the court should order that the gratuity should be paid to a receiver who, although holding it as the respondent's agent, would do so on the terms that he did not part with it otherwise than in accordance with some further order of the court.' b

The judge referred to *Lucas v Harris* (1886) 18 QBD 127 and relied on it.

When one comes to s 203 of the 1955 Act it is necessary to examine the first two subsections in order to determine the intention of the legislature:

> '(1) Every assignment of or charge on, and every agreement to assign or charge, any pay, military award, grant, pension or allowance payable to any person in c
> respect of his or any other person's service in Her Majesty's military forces shall be void.
>
> (2) Save as expressly provided by this Act, no order shall be made by any court the effect of which would be to restrain any person from receiving anything which by virtue of this section he is precluded from assigning and to direct payment thereof to another person.' d

Subsections (3) and (4) are not in point.

It is clear that the mischief against which s 203(1) was directed was to prevent the potential recipients of moneys to which they were entitled, having the character of moneys specified in the subsection, from losing the benefit thereof in advance by way of any assignment or charge. This was consistent with those provisions of the 1955 Act which have been re-enacted over a period of nearly a century, which provided that there e
should be a strict control over military pay, and by this section also, over grants, pensions or allowances. It is expressly provided that any agreement to charge such moneys shall be void.

Then when one comes to s 203(2) it reads:

> 'Save as expressly provided by this Act, no order shall be made . . . the effect of f
> which would be to restrain any person from receiving anything which by virtue of this section he is precluded from assigning . . .'

Pausing there, in my judgment the words 'anything which by virtue of this section he is precluded from assigning' have been included by the draftsman simply in order to identify the particular moneys and property to which sub-s (2) applies. The effect of those g
words is to identify the moneys which come within the ambit of sub-s (2) and have no other effect. The further words of the subsection, 'and to direct payment thereof to another person', have to be given their full force and effect so that sub-s (2) prohibits the making of an order the effect of which will restrain any person from receiving anything and to direct payment to another person.

Counsel for the petitioner's first submission is that, when sub-s (2) is considered, an h
order for payment of money into court (which is the order in question) is not an order which directs payment to another person. The court is not a person, he submits, and it would be an unusual draftsman's technique to include in the phrase, 'to direct payment . . . to another person', an order for payment into court. When one looks at the provisions of r 22 of the Supreme Court Funds Rules 1975, SI 1975/1803, one finds that, when a payment into court is ordered, the banker's draft or the cheque shall be made payable to j
Her Majesty's Accountant General. Looking at it from the point of view of a person subject to an order for payment into court, he is thereby ordered to make out a cheque, or other payable order, to Her Majesty's Accountant General. At that stage the payer is paying another person, namely the Accountant General. Counsel for the petitioner submits that that is not enough to bring the payment within s 203(2) of the 1955 Act, because when money is paid into court no other person immediately has the right to

claim beneficial enjoyment of that money. Until some other order is made, on the facts of this case, as between the petitioner and the respondent, the money is the money of the respondent. It certainly is not the money of the petitioner until some other order is made, and so, he submits, it would be an unusual technique of drafting to interpret the words 'to direct payment thereof to another person' as contemplating the particular and special kind of payment which takes place when an order is made that money is to be paid into court. Counsel submits that that would be to stretch the words of the section much further than they should go.

The judge accepted counsel's submission but, by the respondent's notice filed in this court pursuant to leave given, counsel for the Ministry of Defence raises the additional ground that the judge was wrong in holding that the proposed order would not in itself have the effect of directing payment of the gratuity to another person and that the money, while in court, would legally become the respondent's.

That ground was a different ground to the judge's ground. The judge held that the court ought not to attempt to circumvent the express provisions of s 203 of the 1955 Act by making an order whether for payment into court or for the appointment of a receiver, of which the only purpose could be the alienation of a sum of money to which the respondent, by statute, is entitled.

In relation to that ground of the judge, I think it is useful to consider the machinery of the payment into court which was necessary in order to complete the operation of the exercise of payment into court in order to give it any effect. The only effect of the order for payment of money into court must have been to enable the wife, if successful on her application for financial provision, then to obtain payment out to her, or to her solicitor, of the whole or such part of the moneys in court as were necessary in order to satisfy the court's order for financial provision in her favour. But this was not a payment into court of the kind contemplated by the Rules of the Supreme Court, whereby money is paid into court stating on the face of the notice of payment in that it is paid in respect of satisfaction, or part satisfaction, of moneys claimed in an action. There could be no such notice in the instant case and I am not at present satisfied that, on the petitioner successfully obtaining judgment in her ancillary proceedings for a sum equal to or greater than the sum of the resettlement grant, she would simply by producing that judgment be able to obtain an order for payment out of the moneys in court. I cannot see that there is any rule that would enable her to do so. What she would be able to do would be to obtain a charging order, charging any moneys of the respondent, including moneys of the respondent presently in court, pursuant to an order of the court or otherwise. On the presentation and proof of such charging order, she would then have established a right to payment out of the moneys held in court as being moneys otherwise to be credited to the respondent personally. But how would that fit with the scheme in s 203? The first subsection of that section in terms makes void any charge on, or any agreement to charge any moneys having the character of the moneys with which the instant appeal is concerned, so that if the petitioner succeeded in obtaining an order equal to or greater than the amount of the resettlement grant, and if she then obtained or sought to obtain a charging order on such money, such charging order would be void by virtue of the provision of sub-s (1). Therefore, in so far as the order for payment into court can only be given a rational effect by preserving the fund in court pending the petitioner obtaining a charging order on it, any such charging order would be void and any such procedure by way of payment into court designed to facilitate such a charging order would itself, in my view, be clearly contrary to the intention of the statute.

This leads me to my conclusion, and I prefer to put my reasoning on two grounds. Either a cheque payable by the Ministry of Defence to Her Majesty's Accountant General by way of payment into court of the sum representing the entitlement of the former soldier to his resettlement grant was payable to another person pursuant to the order of the court that the money be paid into court, in which case such order for payment into court would be contrary to the express terms of s 203(2) of the 1955 Act, or alternatively, if that is wrong, the order for payment into court is itself bad, because the only explanation or reason for such an order would be to circumvent the prohibition in

s 203(1) which prohibits any charge on the grant in question. I am content to hold that
the order for payment into court made by the county court, making the order against a
Her Majesty's Paymaster General, was bad, either because the Paymaster General, on
paying this cheque to the Accountant General was paying to another person, which is
prohibited, or if he was not, then what he was ordered to do was to take the step which,
to have any valid or useful effect for the benefit of the petitioner, must involve at some
stage a restraint or charge on the grant, which itself is prohibited by sub-ss (1) and (2).

On those grounds I would uphold the judge's order and move that the appeal be b
dismissed.

GRIFFITHS LJ. The object of sub-s (1) of s 203 of the Army Act 1955 is to ensure that
a soldier will receive in his hands his pay or the other analogous sums payable by the
Crown such as pensions, grants and so forth, so that he can then dispose of them as he
wishes, and to this end it is expressly provided that any previous assignment or charge
on the pay or other emolument is void. I read sub-s (2) as directed towards the same end. c
It is to provide that no court shall make any order which would impose a restraint on his
pay, or other emolument, which would prevent him receiving it into his hand to be
disposed of as he then wishes. It is, however, subject to certain statutory exceptions which
are not relevant to this appeal. I would construe an order to the Paymaster General by a
court to pay a soldier's emolument into court as an order directing the Paymaster General
to make payment to another person. I think the words 'another person' are wide enough d
to cover the making of a cheque payable to the appropriate official when money is paid
into court, or in the somewhat exceptional circumstances when money is paid in over
the counter, if it were a small sum, the payment of actual cash to the counter-clerk who
receives it into court. In my view the direction to the court in sub-s (2) that it must not
make any order to restrain the soldier from receiving his pay must be read together with
the direction to the court that it must not direct payment to any other person, because if e
the court can direct payment into court, it renders meaningless the protection prohibiting
it from restraining the soldier from receiving his pay. Accordingly, in my view, a
direction to make this payment into court is a direction to make a payment to another
person within the meaning of sub-s (2).

If I were wrong in this view, I would still follow the judge's line of reasoning. It is f
manifest that the judge could not, under sub-s (2), make an order that this money should
be paid direct to the wife because on any view that would be an order directing payment
to another person, which he is not entitled to do. It seems to me that it would be quite
wrong to construe the subsection as enabling him to achieve this same end in two steps,
namely by first ordering the money to be brought into court and then, by a further
order, seeing that it fell into the hands of the wife. That was the judge's approach and, as
I say, if I were wrong in my first approach, I would fall back and adopt the judge's g
approach.

For these reasons, I would dismiss this appeal.

SIR ROGER ORMROD. I agree and I agree in terms with the judgments which have
just been delivered. I only wish to add my caveat to what Cumming-Bruce LJ said in the
course of his judgment. Nothing in our judgments in this case can be used in argument h
on the applicability, or otherwise, of s 37 of the Matrimonial Causes Act 1973 to the facts
of this case, or as to the practice, as we understand it to be, in the Brentford County Court
of ordering payments into court in certain circumstances in cases arising under the 1973
Act. Whether there is in fact jurisdiction to make those orders may have to be considered
some day. I only wish to make it clear that we are not deciding that the order made
against the respondent in this case by the judge was, or was not, a valid order. j

Appeal dismissed. Application for ancillary relief transferred back to the county court.

Solicitors: *Giffen Couch & Archer*, Leighton Buzzard (for the wife); *Treasury Solicitor*.

Patricia Hargrove Barrister.

R v Bow Street Stipendiary Magistrate, ex parte Commissioner of Police of the Metropolis

QUEEN'S BENCH DIVISION (CROWN OFFICE LIST)
GLIDEWELL J
10 SEPTEMBER 1982

Licensing – Occasional licence – Grant – Circumstances in which occasional licence may be granted – Applicant forgetting to renew on-licence for premises – Applicant holder of on-licence for other premises – Whether magistrate entitled to grant occasional licences for purpose of allowing liquor to be sold lawfully until application for late renewal of on-licence heard – Whether 'occasional licence' can only be granted for a particular event or function – Licensing Act 1964, s 180(1)(2).

The licensee was the holder of a justices' on-licence for each of two sets of premises. One of those licences expired on 4 April 1982 but the licensee forgot to apply for a renewal, although if he had it would have been granted unopposed. When the licensee discovered the failure to apply for renewal of the licence and that in consequence the sale of liquor on the premises had become unlawful, he made an application for late renewal of the on-licence and in the mean time, to enable the lawful sale of liquor on the premises pending the hearing of that application, he applied to the justices under s 180[a] of the Licensing Act 1964, as the holder of an on-licence elsewhere, for an occasional licence in respect of the premises for a period of three weeks. The stipendiary magistrate granted him two occasional licences for the premises under s 180(1), each of three weeks' duration, to run consecutively. The police applied for a declaration that the magistrate's decision was wrong in law, contending that an 'occasional licence' under s 180(1) could only be granted in respect of a particular event or function.

Held – The words 'occasional licence' in s 180(1) of the 1964 Act and 'occasion' in s 180(2) referred to the existence of circumstances which gave rise to the need for a licence to sell liquor at premises other than those for which the applicant held a valid on-licence, and did not refer only to a particular event or function for which a licence was required. Accordingly, where an applicant who was the holder of an on-licence elsewhere had forgotten to apply for a renewal of an on-licence for premises, circumstances existed which entitled the justices to grant an occasional licence for those premises since an occasional licence was necessary to make the sale of liquor on the premises lawful until the on-licence was renewed. It followed that the magistrate had been entitled to grant the occasional licences and the application for a declaration would accordingly be dismissed (see p 920 *a* to *c* and *f g*, post).

Dictum of Upjohn J in *R v Bath Licensing Justices, ex p Chittenden* [1952] 2 All ER at 705 applied.

Notes

For the grant of occasional licences, see 26 Halsbury's Laws (4th edn) para 20, and for cases on the subject, see 30 Digest (Reissue) 85–87, 642–650.

For the Licensing Act 1964, s 180, see 17 Halsbury's Statutes (3rd edn) 1209.

Cases referred to in judgment

R v Bath Licensing Justices, ex p Chittenden [1952] 2 All ER 700.
Tidd, Ex p [1962] Crim LR 705, DC.

---

a Section 180, so far as material, is set out at p 917 *f g*, post

Application for judicial review

The Commissioner of Police of the Metropolis applied, with the leave of Glidewell J granted on 16 July 1982, for (1) an order of certiorari to quash the decision of Mr W E C Robins, a metropolitan stipendiary magistrate sitting at Bow Street Magistrates' Court on 11 June 1982, granting two occasional licences to Mr John Paul under s 180 of the Licensing Act 1964 for the purpose of allowing intoxicating liquor to be sold lawfully in formerly licensed premises until an application for late renewal of a justices' on-licence for the premises could be made and (2) a declaration that the magistrate's decision was wrong in law. The facts are set out in the judgment.

Vivian Robinson for the police.
Gerald Gouriet for Mr Paul.
David Barnard as amicus curiae.

GLIDEWELL J. This is an application by the Commissioner of the Metropolitan Police for judicial review by way of a declaration that the decision of Mr Robins, a metropolitan stipendiary magistrate sitting at Bow Street Magistrates' Court on 11 June 1982, to grant to Mr John Paul two occasional licences under s 180 of the Licensing Act 1964 for consecutive periods, one of three weeks beginning on the following day and one for the following period up to 20 July, was wrong in law and on the facts.

When application for leave was originally made on paper, McCullough J seems to have had no doubt about it, because he refused leave saying, 'I see nothing to have prevented the magistrate from doing what he did'. When the matter came before me on oral argument I did not find myself in such a certain position and I thus granted leave. I am very happy to have done so, because it has given me the pleasure of listening to argument of the highest quality from all three counsel who appeared before me, despite the fact that all of them have been as brief as they possibly could. Secondly, it has meant that I can endeavour to tackle a point which I am told is exercising the minds of courts throughout the country from time to time and thus may be of some modest importance.

The facts of this matter are in no doubt at all. Mr Paul was until April 1982 the licensee, together with another gentleman, of a justices' on-licence, authorising him to sell intoxicating liquor at premises known as Tokyo Joe's, at 85 Piccadilly, London W1. No suggestion is made that there is anything about those premises or about the conduct of them to which there is the slightest objection and, if an application had been made in due course for the renewal of the licence which expired on 4 April 1982, there can be virtually no doubt that that renewal would have been granted unopposed. Indeed, when an application was made late on 20 July 1982 for that licence to be renewed, it was renewed.

The matter that arises concerns the steps taken to enable Tokyo Joe's and Mr Paul to continue to sell intoxicating liquor legally in those premises during the intervening period. It is quite clear that Mr Paul and those acting on his behalf simply forgot to apply for the renewal of the licence, and thus at the licensing sessions in the spring of 1982 no application for renewal was on the list and the licence was not renewed. As I have said the former licence terminated on 4 April.

Wholly unconscious of the failure to renew the licence, those running Tokyo Joe's continued to open the premises and to sell intoxicating liquor for some six weeks, until on 19 May two police officers visited the premises and found people drinking there peacefully and respectfully. The other gentleman, Mr Maestri, was in charge, and he expressed what is said in the affidavit of one of the police officers to have been surprise (I imagine it was rather deeper emotion) when he was told that he was not licensed and was breaking the law. Mr Maestri promptly rushed off to his solicitors, and the following morning they took two steps. First of all they set in train an application for a late renewal. At one time they hoped it might be heard at the beginning of June but that did not prove possible, and, as I said, it was heard and granted on 20 July.

Secondly, and materially for my purposes, they also wrote a letter dated 19 May to the clerk to the licensing justices, saying:

> '... we would advise you that yesterday evening the Licensee discovered that the Justices on Licence granted on the 10th February 1981, to Mr John Paul and Mr Luciano Maestri had not been renewed and had accordingly expired on the 4th April 1982 ... We have accordingly enclosed two Notices, one in respect of the Transfer Session to be held on the 8th June and the other in respect of a Transfer Session to be held on the 20th July, should Mr Bowerman decide that it is not possible for our client's late renewal Application to be included in the list for hearing on the 8th June.'

They also sent on the same day another letter saying: 'We should be obliged if you could treat this letter as Application for an occasional Licence in respect of the above premises ...' They name the applicant, Mr Paul, they name the premises, and then they say, 'The period for which the Applicant requires the Occasional Licence to be in force is three weeks and the hours to be specified in the Occasional Licence please, are 6.30 p.m. to 3.00 a.m.' They made it clear that Mr Paul held another justices' licence at premises in King's Road, Chelsea and they also made clear what could happen. They said:

> 'Unfortunately in respect of the latter premises [ie Tokyo Joe's] which are of course the subject of the Occasional Licence Application, the Licensees have forgotten to make Application for renewal of their Justices Licence although an Application for late renewal has already been submitted ...'

They sent a copy of that letter with a covering letter to the Chief Commissioner of Police of the Metropolis.

That is the application which resulted in Mr Robins granting the two occasional licences to which I have referred, and the point that is taken is that there is no power to grant an occasional licence under s 180 of the Licensing Act 1964 in these circumstances. I therefore turn to consider the wording of that section, as it now reads, because it has been amended by the Finance Act 1967:

> '(1) Justices of the peace may, on the application of the holder of a justices' on-licence, grant him a licence (in this Act referred to as an "occasional licence") authorising the sale by him of any intoxicating liquor to which his justices' on-licence extends at such place other than the premises in respect of which his justices' on-licence was granted, during such period not exceeding three weeks at one time, and between such hours, as may be specified in the occasional licence ...
>
> (2) Subject to the following provisions of this section, the justices shall not hear an application for an occasional licence unless satisfied that the applicant has served on the chief officer of police at least twenty-four hours' notice of his intention to apply for it, stating the name and address of the applicant, the place and occasion for which it is required, the period for which he requires it to be in force, and the hours to be specified in it ...'

The real question I have to consider is: what is the meaning, in the context of that section, of the words 'occasion' in sub-s (1) and 'occasional' in sub-s (2)?

There is no doubt at all, and it is the experience of all counsel whom I have heard as well as my own so far as my experience of these matters goes, that in the vast majority of cases a licence under this section, or its predecessor, is a licence granted for the sale of intoxicating liquor at or on the occasion of some event or function, such as a sporting event, a festival, a dance or a dinner. The event or function, it is clear, may take place only on one day or may extend over a number of days, that matters not. But that the occasion in such circumstances can be described as relating to or as being the event or function I have no doubt. What I have to decide is whether the words are restricted in their meaning to events or functions, or whether the words have a somewhat wider meaning.

Counsel for the police contends that 'occasional' means referable to an occasion of some sort, and in effect, though I think not until his final reply, in terms he submits an occasion of some sort means an event or function. Both counsel who appears for Mr Paul and counsel who at my request appears as amicus curiae submit that the words have a wider meaning, that they mean the circumstances which give rise to the need for the grant of a licence to a person who already holds a justices' on-licence elsewhere, which can be interpreted more shortly as being 'the reason'.

The authorities which have been cited to me, and those which are cited in that well-known textbook, *Paterson's Licensing Acts*, are, I think I am right in saying, without exception authorities where what was in question was an event or a function, and most of them, though I have found them interesting and helpful to look at, really do not bear on the question I have to consider.

There are, however, two which to some extent do. One is the decision of the Divisional Court, in *Ex p Tidd* [1962] Crim LR 705. That was an application in circumstances which had arisen not unlike the present circumstances, an application for leave to apply for mandamus. The report reads:

> 'A club failed to apply for registration under the Licensing Act, 1961, and thus became unable lawfully to supply and sell liquor. To "keep the club alive" until registration could be effected a licence was applied for under section 148 of the Licensing Act, 1953, for an occasional licence for three weeks.'

I break off to say that s 148 of the Licensing Act 1953 is the predecessor, in effect, of s 180 of the 1964 Act. I say 'in effect', because formerly legislation was to be found both in the Licensing Acts and in the Customs and Excise Acts, but that is the predecessor in the Licensing Act. The report continues:

> 'The magistrate refused the application on the ground that the occasional licence could only be granted in regard to a particular function or special occasion. The licensee applied for leave to apply for mandamus directing the magistrate to hear and determine the application according to the provisions of section 148 of the Act of 1953. It was contended on his behalf that an occasional licence was not limited to a "special occasion", but could be applied for on any occasion. It was conceded that the application sought would be valueless unless expedited and heard during this term, but contended that the case would be a test case for many other clubs in a similar position. *Held*, that leave would be refused.'

I make two comments about that. First, I must confess that I do not fully understand the briefly reported argument that what was needed was to look for a special occasion, because this section does not use the adjective 'special' in relation to an occasion, nor did s 148 of the 1953 Act. Though it may be that that is mere semantics, what in effect was there being said is what counsel for the police is here saying, that occasion means an event or function. Second, of course, I do not have the benefit of any judgment. Although leave was refused, I do not know whether leave was refused because the court decided that the magistrate was right, or whether it was refused as a matter of discretion or precisely why it was refused. If I did know, I would of course be bound by the court's decision.

The second authority is a decision of Upjohn J sitting as vacation judge almost exactly 30 years ago, in *R v Bath Licensing Justices, ex p Chittenden* [1952] 2 All ER 700. Under the legislation then in force, which was the Licensing (Consolidation) Act 1910, occasional licences could only be granted for three days, not three weeks. In this case the justices had granted four occasional licences, each to succeed one another to cover a period of 12 days. There was no doubt that the 12 days taken together constituted a function or event, namely the Festival of Bath. So the point I have to consider essentially was not in issue. The point that was under consideration was whether there had to be a gap between each occasional licence, and his Lordship held that there need not.

Right at the end of his judgment, which is helpful, Upjohn J said (at 705):

a 'Although the word "occasional", which occurs throughout licensing law but is nowhere defined, has, apparently, given rise to the view that the grant of an occasional licence must be for a separate and independent occasion only, that, in my view, is not its normal meaning, and I have been referred to no authority to show that the use of the adjective "occasional" connotes that necessity before the justices can give consent. They have to consider the matters set out in s. 13 of the Act of
b 1862 and all other matters properly raised before them. If they come to the bona fide conclusion that the circumstances of the case are appropriate to the grant of an occasional licence, although one of a series, as in this case, in my judgment, there is nothing to prevent them giving their consent.'

Counsel appearing as amicus curiae places some reliance on that as showing apparently
c that it was Upjohn J's view that the proper definition of the word 'occasion' was wider than a particular event and related to the circumstances of the case.

Those authorities apart, counsel are united in their view that I have to approach the matter unchallenged by authority and there is no clear decision of the course in point.

Counsel for Mr Paul and counsel as amicus curiae argue two points. First, that the meaning of the words 'occasion' and 'occasionally', as I have already said, have reference
d to the circumstances which give rise to the application, rather than to an event and counsel as amicus curiae has taken me to the dictionary definition in support of that. Although I accept that it is a matter that I have to decide, a matter of ordinary English usage, it is helpful to go to the dictionary, and it is right to see that the *Shorter Oxford English Dictionary* gives the second main definition of the word 'occasion', as 'necessity or need arising from a juncture of circumstances' and as the third meaning, 'a juncture of
e circumstances', followed by 'an event, incident, circumstance'.

When one looks back at the wording of s 180 itself, one sees that the principal subsection, sub-s (1), does not limit the scope of the justices' discretion in any way: 'Justices . . . may, on the application of the holder of a justices' on-licence, grant him a licence . . . authorising the sale by him of any intoxicating liquor . . .' It is only in parenthesis that the licence is described as 'an occasional licence', and the use of the word
f 'occasion', as I hope I have already made clear, in sub-s (2) is not in relation to the definition of the licence itself, but in that part of the section which requires notice to be given to the police.

Counsel for Mr Paul, as his second argument, distinguishes s 180 from s 74 of the 1964 Act. Section 74 deals with what are now called 'exemption orders', which may be special or general. Whereas occasional licences granted under s 180 are licences authorising a
g person who holds an on-licence for one set of premises to sell intoxicating liquor at other premises, s 74 covers the situation of somebody who wishes to sell liquor at premises in respect of which he already holds a licence in hours outside those he is normally permitted to sell and there are a number of such circumstances covered by the section.

But the point which counsel for Mr Paul makes is that in sub-s (4) of s 74 it is provided:

h 'Justices of the peace may—(*a*) on an application by the holder of a justices' on-licence for any premises . . . make an order (in this Act referred to as a special order of exemption) adding such hours as may be specified in the order to the permitted hours in those premises on such special occasion or occasions as may be so specified.'

Counsel for Mr Paul argues that a 'special occasion' does mean some particular event or circumstances which gives rise to the desire to sell liquor for a longer period of time and
j is to be distinguished from 'an occasion' in s 180.

I have been referred to the sections which form the genesis of both s 74 and s 180 and I have been taken through the intervening legislation, a process which I found helpful but to which I do not propose to refer save to say this, that originally both what are now known as 'exemption orders' and 'occasional licences' were called 'occasional licences'. It was obviously found by 1910 that that was somewhat confusing and the nomenclature 'exemption orders' appeared in the 1910 Act for the first time. But that does not detract from the point which counsel for Mr Paul made.

In the end it seems to me that this is largely a matter of impression. As I have said, there is nothing in sub-s (1) of s 180 which limits the discretion which the magistrates may exercise, and I have come to the conclusion that the principal argument advanced by counsel for Mr Paul and counsel as amicus curiae is correct. In other words 'occasion' is to be defined in relation to s 180 as meaning the circumstances which give rise to the need, or the alleged need, for the sale at premises other than those for which the applicant holds an on-licence of intoxicating liquor.

If that be right, as in my judgment it is, then the magistrate in this case was entitled to do as he did, and the application for a declaration must therefore fail.

However, there are two subsidiary points about which I should say something briefly. First, it was suggested initially by me, and counsel reinforced the suggestion, that the letter of 19 May, which was an application to the court, a copy of which went to the police, did not really satisfy s 180(2), because it did not in terms specify the occasion for which the licence was required, and there was some debate how that defect should have been made good. I am not going to rule whether it did or did not. It is quite clear that the solicitors in the letter made all the facts entirely clear. They said quite frankly that the licensees forgot to make application for the renewal of the justices' licence, and it could well be that might be held sufficient to meet the requirement of s 180(2). But, if I am right in my view on the meaning of 'occasion' and 'occasionally', then some such wording as that suggested by counsel for Mr Paul, namely 'the occasion is the occasion of having failed or forgotten to apply for a renewal of the licence', would indeed satisfy the subsection. What is needed of course is to tell the police why the application is being made at all.

The second matter is this: to an extent all counsel placed arguments before me based on policy. I have not sought to base my decision one way or another on policy. But I will say this, that I am dealing with a case in which, I emphasise, there is no question of objection to this applicant, Mr Paul, of any sort whatever. Nobody suggested for a minute that he was not conducting his premises properly. If there were objection, it would be a totally different case. The police would be entitled to object and the justices would be justified in refusing the licence. But, where there is no objection, the only purpose for which the annual on-licence is required to be renewed is really a revenue-gathering purpose. And, if it is relevant to consider policy, then there is a lot to be said for the argument that it is to be assumed that Parliament intended some provision to be made for circumstances where the applicant has forgotten to apply for a renewal. Whether Parliament indeed has considered this in terms, I know not. What I have found is that the wording that Parliament has chosen to use in s 180 is wide enough to cover that situation.

Accordingly I so hold and I decline to grant the declaration sought.

Application refused.

Solicitors: *D M O'Shea* (for the police); *Amhurst Brown Martin & Nicholson* (for Mr Paul); *Treasury Solicitor.*

Sepala Munasinghe Esq Barrister.

Greek City Co Ltd and another v Demetriou (trading as Spectron Electronics) and another
Greek City Co Ltd v Athanasiou (trading as Alpha Alpha Electrical Contractors)

CHANCERY DIVISION
GOULDING J
7, 8, 9 MARCH 1983

Practice – Dismissal of action for want of prosecution – Delay – Delay in delivering statement of claim – Plaintiff applying for interlocutory relief before serving statement of claim and obtaining undertakings from defendant until trial of action – Plaintiff failing to serve statement of claim within prescribed time – Defendant applying for order to dismiss action – Whether mere failure to observe time limit in rules equivalent to disobedience of peremptory order – Whether court can dismiss action for failure to serve statement of claim in time without considering nature of delay – Whether court should dismiss action where delay inordinate and inexcusable but not contumelious and plaintiff likely to issue fresh writ within limitation period – RSC Ord 18, r 1, Ord 19, r 1.

The plaintiffs commenced two actions for infringement of copyright. Immediately after the issue of the writs the plaintiffs applied for and were granted interlocutory injunctions against the defendants under which the defendants in both actions gave certain undertakings which restricted their trading activities. In the first action the undertakings were given until the trial of the action or further order, while in the second action the undertakings were given only until the hearing of the interlocutory proceedings or further order. The affidavits relied on by the plaintiffs in the interlocutory proceedings did not make it clear whether the plaintiffs were suing as copyright owners or as exclusive licensees. In both actions the defendants served notice of intention to defend but the plaintiffs failed to serve statements of claim within the time prescribed by RSC Ord 18, r 1[a]. The defendants applied for orders under Ord 19, r 1[b] to dismiss the actions because of the plaintiffs' failure to serve statements of claim within the prescribed time. At the date of the hearing of the applications the limitation period for the actions had not expired and it was likely that if the actions were dismissed for want of prosecution the plaintiffs would issue fresh writs within the limitation period.

Held – (1) The mere failure to observe a time limit in the rules of court for taking a step in an action, such as failing to serve a statement of claim in time, was not to be treated as equivalent to disobedience of a peremptory order of the court, nor was it a default which was to be treated as intentional and contumelious and thus an abuse of the court's process. Accordingly, before the court could dismiss an action under RSC Ord 19, r 1 for failure to serve a statement of claim within the time prescribed by Ord 18, r 1, the court had first to consider whether the plaintiff's delay had been inordinate and inexcusable and whether it would give rise to a substantial risk of an unfair trial or was likely to cause prejudice to the defendant. Moreover, where the limitation period had not expired and the plaintiff was likely to issue a fresh writ if his pending action was dismissed for want of prosecution, that was generally a conclusive reason against dismissal (see p 925 *b* to *f* and p 926 *j* to p 927 *e*, post); *Birkett v James* [1977] 2 All ER 801 applied; *Hytrac Conveyors Ltd v Conveyors International Ltd* [1982] 3 All ER 415 explained; *Janov v Morris* [1981] 3 All ER 780 distinguished.

a Rule 1 is set out at p 922 *h*, post
b Rule 1 is set out at p 922 *j*, post

(2) In all the circumstances the plaintiffs' delay in serving statements of claim had been inordinate and inexcusable and the delay was likely to cause the defendants a prejudice. However, because there had been no peremptory order which the plaintiffs had disobeyed and their conduct had not amounted to an abuse of the process of the court, and because the limitation period had not run and it was likely that the plaintiffs would issue fresh writs if the actions were dismissed, and in the circumstances it would not be an abuse of the process of the court for the plaintiffs to issue fresh writs, the court would not, in the exercise of its discretion under Ord 19, r 1, dismiss the existing actions b but would direct that the time for delivering the statements of claim in the actions be extended (see p 927 *j* to p 928 *c* and *g* to *j* and p 929 *a b d e*, post).

Notes

For dismissal of actions for delay, see 37 Halsbury's Laws (4th edn) para 449.

c

Cases referred to in judgment

Allen v Sir Alfred McAlpine & Sons Ltd [1968] 1 All ER 543, [1968] 2 QB 229, [1968] 2 WLR 366, CA.

Birkett v James [1977] 2 All ER 801, [1978] AC 297, [1977] 3 WLR 38, HL.

Hytrac Conveyors Ltd v Conveyors International Ltd [1982] 3 All ER 415, [1983] 1 WLR 44, [1983] FSR 83, CA. d

Janov v Morris [1981] 3 All ER 780, [1981] 1 WLR 1389, CA.

Motions to dismiss actions

By notices of motion dated 14 and 17 January 1983 issued in an action between the plaintiffs, Greek City Co Ltd and Pavlos Theodorou, and the defendants, Andreas Athanasiou (trading as Alpha Alpha Electrical Contractors) and Themis Demetriou e (trading as Spectron Electronics), in which the plaintiffs alleged infringement of copyright in respect of video cassettes, the defendants applied under RSC Ord 19, r 1 for an order dismissing the action on the ground that the plaintiffs had failed, within the time limit prescribed in RSC Ord 18, r 1, to serve a statement of claim in the action. In a further, similar, action between Greek City Co Ltd as sole plaintiff and Mr Athanasiou as sole defendant, Mr Athanasiou issued a similar notice of motion dated 14 January 1983 f seeking an order dismissing that action on the ground that the plaintiff had failed to serve a statement of claim within the prescribed time limit. The facts are set out in the judgment.

W Bruce Spalding for Mr Demetriou.
Nicolas Bragge for Mr Athanasiou. g
J E Rayner James for the plaintiffs.

GOULDING J. RSC Ord 18, r 1 provides as follows:

> 'Unless the Court gives leave to the contrary or a statement of claim is indorsed on the writ, the plaintiff must serve a statement of claim on the defendant or, if h there are two or more defendants, on each defendant, and must do so either when the writ is served on that defendant or at any time after service of the writ but before the expiration of 14 days after that defendant gives notice of intention to defend.'

The consequences of failure to comply with that command are prescribed in RSC Ord 19, r 1, which provides: j

> 'Where the plaintiff is required by these Rules to serve a statement of claim on a defendant and he fails to serve it on him, the defendant may, after the expiration of the period fixed by or under these Rules for service of the statement of claim, apply to the Court for an order to dismiss the action, and the Court may by order dismiss the action or make such other order on such terms as it thinks just.'

I have before me three applications made under that last-recited rule, based in each case on failure by a plaintiff to serve a statement of claim within the 14-day period prescribed by Ord 18, r 1. The applications are made in respect of two different actions, in both of which the plaintiffs allege infringement of copyright in respect of video cassettes containing films whereof the sound material is in the Greek language. The first of the actions concerned I shall refer to as 'the 1981 action'. That is an action between two plaintiffs, Greek City Co Ltd and Pavlos Theodorou, and two defendants, one called Demetriou and the other called Athanasiou. Each defendant there has made a separate application to dismiss the action. The other action with which I am concerned I shall refer to as 'the 1982 action', and that was brought by one of the plaintiffs in the 1981 action, namely Greek City Co Ltd, as sole plaintiff, against one of the defendants in the 1981 action, Mr Athanasiou, as sole defendant. There Mr Athanasiou applies to dismiss the action.

I will state the sequence of events in relation to each of the three applications. As regards the 1981 action, so far as concerns the defendant Demetriou, the writ was issued on 20 July 1981. The plaintiffs immediately applied for interlocutory injunctions. On 24 July the defendants gave undertakings expressed to last until judgment in the action or further order in the mean time. Mr Demetriou gave notice of intention to defend on or about 3 August, that is to say after the beginning of the long vacation, and accordingly a statement of claim ought to have been served on him on or about 16 October. However, negotiations were taking place between the plaintiffs and Mr Demetriou. They appear to have ended by the end of November 1981. There was then, so far as regards him, a period of inactivity by the plaintiffs until on or about 19 January 1983, when Mr Demetriou notified the plaintiffs that he was applying to dismiss the action. That did not immediately produce a satisfactory response, but when I began to hear the motions on 7 March 1983, two days ago, a proposed statement of claim was served on Mr Demetriou.

The course of events as regards the defendant Athanasiou in the 1981 action will take a little longer to narrate. There was the same writ issued on 20 July 1981. Mr Athanasiou joined with Mr Demetriou in giving undertakings until trial on 24 July. His notice of intention to defend was given on or about that day, 24 July, and accordingly I suppose that a statement of claim ought to have been served on him a little earlier, at about 13 or 14 October. The exact date does not matter. The defendant Athanasiou was, through his solicitors, clearly concerned to get a statement of claim. By a letter of 26 August 1981 his solicitors asked the plaintiffs' solicitors for some indication when a statement of claim would be forthcoming. By another letter of 5 October 1981, still within the time for service of the statement of claim, the defendant's solicitors pointed out that the allegations made by the plaintiffs were not yet formulated in a statement of claim. So far as Mr Athanasiou was concerned, negotiations seem to have gone on rather longer than in the case of Mr Demetriou; they did not cease until about February 1982.

However, the plaintiffs still did not serve any statement of claim. What they were concerned with was an alleged breach by Mr Athanasiou of his undertakings given in July 1981. That complaint was first raised towards the end of April 1982. After some correspondence a motion, which has still not been disposed of, was served on or about 26 July 1982 to commit Mr Athanasiou to prison for breach of undertakings. There was some pressure by the plaintiffs' solicitors to get Mr Athanasiou to put in his evidence on the committal motion and on another motion to which I need not refer at the moment, and there may have been some negotiations in the summer of 1982.

By a letter of 20 October 1982 the plaintiffs gave notice of intention to proceed with the action to Mr Athanasiou's solicitors and promised a statement of claim, but none came. It was not until after the application to dismiss the action had been made and indeed, as in the case of Mr Demetriou, it was not until the hearing of the application before me that the proposed statement of claim was produced, namely on 7 March 1983.

The 1982 action was against Mr Athanasiou alone. There the writ was issued on 23 July 1982. Again an immediate application was made by the plaintiffs for an interlocutory injunction, and an undertaking was given by Mr Athanasiou on 29 July 1982. That differed in certain respects from the undertaking given in the 1981 action (and in particular, in my judgment, it is less difficult for Mr Athanasiou to be sure that he is complying with it) but the important difference for my present purposes is that the undertakings were not until the trial of the action, but only until judgment on the motion or further order in the mean time, as Sir Robert Megarry V-C, before whom this initial motion came on 29 July, did not effectively dispose of it. He simply accepted undertakings until the hearing of the motion and stood it over.

The notice of intention to defend was given on 29 July 1982. The statement of claim would have been due on or about 13 October. From time to time the undertakings have been renewed on applications by Mr Athanasiou for more time for evidence. Therefore the initial motion was still pending when Mr Athanasiou served notice of intention to strike out the action for want of a statement of claim. There was a letter of 20 October 1982 in which a statement of claim had been promised, but none was forthcoming until 7 March, as in the other cases. It is fair to say that, as regards the motion, Mr Athanasiou in the 1982 action acknowledges that the delay in disposing of it lay at his door rather than that of the plaintiffs.

Those being briefly the facts in the three applications which I have it found it convenient to state together at the outset, I now have to decide how to exercise the discretion given to the court by Ord 19, r 1. That has involved the consideration and reconciliation of two authorities, both quite well known, one in the House of Lords and a later one in the Court of Appeal.

The authority in the House of Lords is *Birkett v James* [1977] 2 All ER 801, [1978] AC 297, where the most comprehensive speech was made by Lord Diplock, and it will be sufficient for my purposes to refer to certain passages therefrom. In the beginning of his opinion Lord Diplock made some general observations about applications to dismiss actions for want of prosecution, using that phrase in its widest sense. I will read part of what he said ([1977] 2 All ER 801 at 804–805, [1978] AC 297 at 318):

> 'Although the Rules of the Supreme Court contain express provision for ordering actions to be dismissed for failure by the plaintiff to comply timeously with some of the more important steps in the preparation of an action for trial, such as delivering the statement of claim, taking out a summons for directions and setting the action down for trial, dilatory tactics had been encouraged by the practice that had grown up for many years prior to 1967 of not applying to dismiss an action for want of prosecution, except on disobedience to a previous peremptory order that the action should be dismissed unless the plaintiff took within a specified additional time the step on which he had defaulted.'

I pause there to remark that the phrase 'peremptory order' is used in some of the cases on this subject without express definition, but I take it to mean what Lord Diplock says there, an order that the action should be dismissed unless the plaintiff takes a step within a specified time. Lord Diplock continued:

> 'To remedy this High Court judges began to have recourse to the inherent jurisdiction of the court to dismiss an action for want of prosecution even where no previous peremptory order had been made, if the delay on the part of the plaintiff or his legal advisers was so prolonged that to bring the action on for hearing would involve a substantial risk that a fair trial of the issues would not be possible.'

Lord Diplock referred to certain reported cases. Then his Lordship said that *Allen v Sir Alfred McAlpine & Sons Ltd* [1968] 1 All ER 543, [1968] 2 QB 229 was a case in which 'the Court of Appeal laid down the principles on which the jurisdiction has been exercised ever since'. Those principles are set out, said Lord Diplock, in the note to RSC Ord 25, r 1, in *The Supreme Court Practice 1976* vol 1, pp 424–427. Lord Diplock then said:

> 'The power should be exercised only where the court is satisfied either (1) that the default has been intentional and contumelious, eg disobedience to a peremptory order of the court or conduct amounting to an abuse of the process of the court; or (2)(a) that there has been inordinate and inexcusable delay on the part of the plaintiff

> or his lawyers, and (b) that such delay will give rise to a substantial risk that it is not possible to have a fair trial of the issues in the action or is such as is likely to cause or to have caused serious prejudice to the defendants either as between themselves and the plaintiff or between each other or between them and a third party.'

That divides the cases in which the power to dismiss an action for want of prosecution can properly be exercised into two classes that have been referred to in argument as class or type (1) and class or type (2), the first being exemplified, perhaps not exhaustively, by disobedience to a peremptory order or conduct amounting to an abuse of process, and the second being a case where those grave elements do not exist but where the delay is both inordinate and inexcusable and prejudicial in its effect.

A question that arose in *Birkett v James* was whether the court ought in general, and particularly in that case, to exercise its jurisdiction to dismiss an action for want of prosecution where it was open to the plaintiff to issue a fresh writ without being met by a defence of a statute of limitation, and the conclusion of the House of Lords on that point was quite clear. Lord Diplock gave his own view in these words ([1977] 2 All ER 801 at 808, [1978] AC 297 at 322):

> 'For my part, for reasons that I have already stated, I am of opinion that the fact that the limitation period has not yet expired must always be a matter of great weight in determining whether to exercise the discretion to dismiss an action for want of prosecution where no question of contumelious default on the part of the plaintiff is involved; and in cases where it is likely that if the action were dismissed the plaintiff would avail himself of his legal right to issue a fresh writ, the non-expiry of the limitation period is generally a conclusive reason for not dismissing the action that is already pending.'

Later Lord Diplock repeated the conclusion (see [1977] 2 All ER 801 at 810, [1978] AC 297 at 325). He stated what he there called the general principle—

> 'that where the limitation period has not expired and the plaintiff is likely to issue a fresh writ if his pending action is dismissed for want of prosecution, this is a conclusive reason against dismissal.'

That decision in the House of Lords was followed by a case in the Court of Appeal, *Hytrac Conveyors v Conveyors International Ltd* [1982] 3 All ER 415, [1983] 1 WLR 44. I propose to use the alternative report in the Fleet Street Reports ([1983] FSR 63) because it contains certain additional material to which I wish to refer. That case was founded on infringement of copyright and breach of confidence. It was a case in which the plaintiffs had obtained an Anton Piller order, executed it and issued a writ, but failed to serve a statement of claim within 14 days. There was an application for interlocutory relief, and some interlocutory relief was obtained in consequence of the execution of the Anton Piller order, but a statement of claim was not forthcoming. The writ having been issued on 30 April 1982, Whitford J dismissed the action on 22 July. I do not think I need read very much of his judgment, but there is one passage that I ought to read. It appeared that at the time of Whitford J's judgment instructions had been given by the plaintiffs to counsel to prepare a statement of claim but it had not yet been served. What his Lordship said is this ([1983] FSR 63 at 67):

> 'It is not right, in my judgment, that the plaintiffs should start an action apparently not in a position even to know what form of statement of claim they should make until possibly after an *Anton Piller* order has been secured and the evidence upon an application for an interlocutory injunction has been taken through to the end. It is in my judgment particularly important where questions of infringement of copyright are concerned and where questions of confidence are concerned that in the clearest possible terms the exact ambit of the plaintiffs' claim in these regards should be made known.'

It is apparent that Whitford J not only took the view that the plaintiff had failed to deliver a statement of claim within the time limited, but also thought that the plaintiff did not really know what his allegations were going to be and in effect was using the Anton Piller order for fishing purposes.

In the Court of Appeal the reasoned judgment was given by Lawton LJ, with whom the other two Lords Justices, Templeman and Fox LJJ, simply agreed without amplifying their views. Lawton LJ said this in the course of his judgment ([1982] 3 All ER 415 at 417, [1983] 1 WLR 44 at 47):

> 'We have been told by counsel that there has grown up in the Chancery Division a practice that, when an application is made for an interlocutory injunction, a statement of claim is not served. It may be that an application for an interlocutory injunction is a good reason why the court should give an extension of time, but it is not a good reason why the rules of court should be disregarded.'

He said later ([1982] 3 All ER 415 at 417–418, [1983] 1 WLR 44 at 47):

> 'In this case, as a result of the attempt to get an interlocutory injunction before the delivery of the statement of claim, weeks passed and by the middle of July still no statement of claim had been delivered ... As a result of pressure put on the plaintiffs by the defendants, the plaintiffs asked at long last for extension of time in which to deliver a statement of claim. By this time the first seven defendants had applied under Ord 19, r 1 for the action to be dismissed on the ground of inordinate delay. Whitford J granted that application.'

Lawton LJ then read from a note he had of the judge's judgment which is in part the passage I have just read. He then said ([1982] 3 All ER 415 at 418, [1983] 1 WLR 44 at 47–48):

> 'For my part, I agree with that approach. It has to be remembered by all concerned that we do not have in this country an inquisitorial procedure for civil litigation. Our procedure is accusatorial. Those who make charges must state right at the beginning what they are and what facts they are based on. They must not use Anton Piller orders as a means of finding out what sort of charges they can make. They must deliver their statement of claim within the time specified in the rules, unless the court orders otherwise. I would refuse this application.'

Accordingly, the Court of Appeal refused leave to appeal from Whitford J's order.

The next day (see [1983] FSR 63 at 71–72) counsel who had been unsuccessful in the application to the Court of Appeal came back and apologised to the Court of Appeal for not having referred it to *Birkett v James* [1977] 2 All ER 801, [1978] AC 297. I think he would have been inviting them, had he been allowed to do so, to have a look at it then, but Lawton LJ replied: 'We are not unfamiliar with that case.' Counsel then went on to ask for leave to appeal to the House of Lords, which was refused, but in the course of the reported debate between counsel and the Lords Justices, after a reference by Lawton LJ to Ord 19, r 1, and by counsel to Ord 25, r 1(4), which gives a similar power to dismiss where the plaintiff does not take out a summons for directions, Templeman LJ said this: 'But as we mentioned yesterday, things are different entirely when you have *Anton Piller* orders. I do not accept that all your costs are thrown away if you start another action.'

This is the position. The Court of Appeal clearly was aware of *Birkett v James* when deciding *Hytrac Conveyors Ltd v Conveyors International Ltd*, and, as it had not been cited, it did not think it necessary to deal with it expressly. It is for me to see how, for the purposes of the applications before me, the two cases can be combined.

Counsel for the defendant Demetriou, supported by counsel for the defendant Athanasiou, suggests in the first place that Ord 19, r 1 gives a special jurisdiction on its own, saying in terms that where a statement of claim is not delivered at the proper time the court may by order dismiss the action, and that, he suggested in one of his submissions, really takes this particular jurisdiction right outside the general observations in *Birkett v James*. I cannot accept that at all. It is quite clear that at the beginning of his speech Lord Diplock referred to the express powers given where there is default in delivering a statement of claim, taking out a summons for directions or setting down for trial, and said that judges had been relying more on the inherent jurisdiction because those specific provisions had not proved powerful enough against indolent plaintiffs. The speeches in *Birkett v James* generally appear to me to be as perfectly applicable to each of those three specific rules as to the general jurisdiction. I find it quite impossible to think that such considerations as prejudice to the defendant or the existence of a possible second action within the limitation period need not be taken into account under Ord 19, r 1, if that indeed was what counsel was submitting.

Alternatively counsel for the defendant Demetriou, supported by counsel for the defendant Athanasiou, says this: that where you have an express time limit with a power to dismiss the action if it is not observed, as you have in relation to the service of the statement of claim that is the equivalent of a peremptory order and therefore it is within class (1) of Lord Diplock's taxonomy, a case where the default has been intentional and contumelious, and it is not necessary to consider the requirements under class (2), the requirements of inordinate and inexcusable delay, and prejudicial effects. That again I cannot accept. When one reads the speeches in *Birkett v James* it is to my mind abundantly clear that their Lordships did not regard mere failure to observe a date required by the Rules of the Supreme Court as equivalent to disobedience to a peremptory order as defined by Lord Diplock. Therefore those submissions on the part of the defendants fail and I have to consider how I am really to give effect to both authorities.

Counsel for the plaintiffs submits (and I think he is right) that a mere failure to serve a statement of claim in time is not, within the language used in *Birkett v James*, a case where the default has been intentional and contumelious; accordingly, one has to see whether there has been inordinate and inexcusable delay and whether the delay will either give rise to substantial risk that it is not possible to have a fair trial or is likely to cause or to have caused serious prejudice to the defendant. But how, it may be asked, if that is right, can the *Hytrac* case be reconciled with *Birkett v James*? Counsel for the plaintiffs points out that at the end of Lawton LJ's judgment, which in effect is the judgment of the Court of Appeal, he stated three requirements which evidently in his view the plaintiffs in the *Hytrac* case had failed to satisfy: first, those who make charges must state right at the beginning what they are and what facts they are based on; second, they must not use Anton Piller orders as a means of finding out what sort of charges they can make; and, third, they must deliver their statement of claim within the time specified in the rules, unless the court orders otherwise. Counsel for the plaintiffs did not differ from me when I suggested that the first and third of those are normally the same, because the statement of claim is the way of stating one's charges and the facts on which they are based. He submitted that disregarding those requirements would not of itself take the case outside Lord Diplock's class (2). However, to use Anton Piller orders as a means of finding out what sort of charges the plaintiff can make, a fishing expedition, to take the common term used in these courts, is in the submission of counsel for the plaintiffs conduct amounting to an abuse of the process of the court which brought the *Hytrac* case within class (1) of Lord Diplock's classification. With that I agree, and all the more so since Whitford J had particularly observed in the passage I have cited, and with which the Court of Appeal evidently agreed, that the plaintiffs were not in a position even to know what form of statement of claim they should make until possibly after the Anton Piller order had been secured and the evidence on interlocutory application taken to the end.

Accordingly, although I think it possible that Lawton LJ might have expressed himself more fully had *Birkett v James* been read to the Court of Appeal, it seems clear that there is no inconsistency between the two decisions and that the *Hytrac* case is properly explained as a case falling within class (1) of Lord Diplock's scheme because the use made of an Anton Piller order amounted to an abuse of the process of the court.

Let me now come back to the present case. As I have indicated, I cannot see anything in the facts on any of the three applications that brings the conduct before me within class (1). As to class (2), I am satisfied that in all three cases the delay has been inordinate and inexcusable, and although I heard a good deal of argument about it I remain of opinion that it is likely to have inflicted and may continue to cause prejudice to the *a* defendants. For one thing, the undertakings which the defendants have given to avoid the interlocutory injunctions which would probably have been imposed on them, whether the plaintiffs in the end are found to be right or wrong, are of a character to restrict the trading of the defendants as dealers in Greek language video films. Further, the presumptions on which a plaintiff can rely in interlocutory proceedings by virtue of s 20 of the Copyright Act 1956 apply until a defendant puts the question of title in issue, *b* and no defendant can satisfactorily do that until he has a statement of claim and knows exactly and formally on what the plaintiff relies. Thirdly, on seeing the affidavits relied on by the plaintiffs, it is not altogether clear whether they sue in respect of various films as copyright owners or as exclusive licensees, and for procedural purposes a defendant is under difficulties because of s 19 of the 1956 Act until he knows the plaintiff's position clearly in that respect. *c*

Accordingly, I would be minded to consider these as proper cases for dismissing the actions were it not for the point on which great stress is laid in *Birkett v James*, that the limitation period has not run and the plaintiffs, I should think, would not be at all unlikely to issue fresh writs if I dismissed these actions. Counsel for the defendant Demetriou, in an address by way of reply, pressed me with a case in the Court of Appeal, *Janov v Morris* [1981] 3 All ER 780, [1981] 1 WLR 1389. Here it was pointed out to the *d* Court of Appeal that the Law Lords who expressed their opinions in disposing of *Birkett v James* were not entirely of one mind, so far as one can judge from obiter dicta, as to the position of a plaintiff who, having had his action struck out for want of prosecution, issues a second writ. Is it or is it not open to the court, within the period of limitation, to stay or dismiss that second action as an abuse of the process of the court? In *Janov v Morris* the first action had been dismissed for breach of a peremptory order whereby the master *e* had ordered the action to be struck out unless a summons for directions was served by a specified date. It was not served and the master struck the action out. The plaintiff then started a second action. The Court of Appeal, after careful consideration of *Birkett v James*, held that, where there had been a failure by a litigant to comply with a peremptory order of the court in a previous action, the court had a discretion to dismiss the action or not. They thought that the judge below had erred in thinking that he had not got that *f* discretion, and in the particular case before them they said that they must uphold the principle that peremptory orders were made to be complied with and not to be ignored. Therefore they dismissed the second action.

It does not appear to me that that decision affects my view in the present case for reasons I have already given. I do not think that there has here been any peremptory order within the meaning of that term as used in the cases and expressly defined by Lord *g* Diplock, nor do I think the plaintiffs' conduct has amounted to an abuse of the process of the court in the sense in which that phrase has been used in the authorities. Accordingly the case is not within class (1) of Lord Diplock's classification. On reading all the dicta in *Birkett v James*, I cannot think that in a class (2) case there is anything in general to make it an abuse of the process of the court to issue a fresh writ. That it is not in general such an abuse seems to me to be really the foundation of the decision of the House of Lords *h* with regard to the limitation point in *Birkett v James*. Accordingly I think that I ought not to dismiss either the 1981 action or the 1982 action.

However, in the *Hytrac* case, even when explained in the way I have proposed, the Court of Appeal made it strongly apparent that in the absence of an extension agreed between the parties or allowed by the court, a statement of claim must be delivered within the specified time, and of course Ord 19, r 1 gives the court a discretion to make *j* any other order than dismissal on such terms as it thinks just.

As regards the 1981 action, the plaintiffs obtained undertakings from the defendants immediately after the issue of the writ by means of a motion for an injunction to endure until the trial of the action. It is elementary in the High Court that a party who seeks the equitable remedy of injunction before questions of right and wrong have been tried between him and the defendant has to exert diligence and promptness. It happens every day that a plaintiff's application for interlocutory relief is refused because he has not come to the court quickly enough. Logically it appears to me that, if he is given relief until the trial of the action, he is under a special obligation to get on with the action speedily because the defendant is restrained, it may be justly or it may be unjustly, but that cannot be known until the trial. The plaintiff undertakes in damages in the usual form, but everyone who has practised in these courts knows that those undertakings do not always provide easy or adequate relief where the court at the trial finds in the defendant's favour.

Accordingly, as regards the 1981 action I propose (I gathered from what was said in reply that this would be desired as an alternative remedy by the defendants) forthwith to release the defendants from the undertakings which they have given in the order that was made on 24 July 1981.

The 1982 action is in a rather different position because there the relief given was only until the disposal of the motion, and the defendant frankly concedes that it is at his instance that that process has taken longer than it otherwise might have done. Accordingly I do not think it would be right for me to now release Mr Athanasiou from the undertakings he gave in the 1982 action, but it will be open to counsel of course when that motion comes to be heard to submit as one of the matters to be taken into account (it can be no more than that as there may be many other matters) in deciding whether such restraints are to be continued until the trial of the action, that the plaintiff has been guilty of this default in prompt service of the statement of claim.

As I am not dismissing the actions I must in each action extend the time for delivery of the statement of claim.

[After discussion with counsel his Lordship extended the time over that day.]

Order accordingly. Application by first defendant for leave to appeal refused.

Solicitor: *Shindler & Co*, Golders Green (for the defendant Demetriou); *Redstone Kirschel & Bray* (for the defendant Athanasiou); *Gordon Dadds & Co* (for the plaintiffs).

Evelyn M C Budd Barrister.

Re R (a minor) (child in care: access)

COURT OF APPEAL, CIVIL DIVISION
SIR JOHN DONALDSON MR AND PURCHAS LJ
9 MAY 1983

Divorce – Custody – Access – Committal of child to care of local authority – Jurisdiction of court to give directions regarding treatment of child while in care – Local authority deciding to refuse father access to child – Father applying to court for direction that he should have access – Whether court's jurisdiction to give directions merely jurisdiction to review local authority's decision – Whether jurisdiction merely an appellate jurisdiction – Whether court having original jurisdiction to give directions for child's benefit – Matrimonial Causes Act 1973, s 43(5).

In custody proceedings regarding a child whose parents were divorced and whose mother was living with a violent man the judge, acting pursuant to s 43[a] of the Matrimonial Proceedings Act 1973, made an order committing the child into the care of the local authority, which was then entitled to exercise the powers which it had under the Child Care Act 1980 in regard to the treatment of the child while he was in care, although by virtue of s 43(5) of the 1973 Act the exercise of those powers was 'subject to any directions given by the court'. The local authority placed the child with foster parents and decided, in accordance with its powers under the 1980 Act, to refuse the father access to the child

a Section 43, so far as material, is set out at p 933 e, post

on the ground that the child was very disturbed and the father's behaviour was erratic. The father applied to the judge for a direction under s 43(5) of the 1973 Act that he *a* should be given access to the child. The judge held (i) that his jurisdiction under s 45 was limited to reviewing the exercise by the local authority of its discretion, in accordance with the well-established principles applicable to the review of the exercise of an administrative discretion, and that it had not been established that the local authority had acted contrary to those principles, and (ii) alternatively, that on the basis that, if his jurisdiction was appellate in nature, the evidence showed that the local authority had *b* taken a properly informed decision in the child's best interests. The father appealed.

Held – The jurisdiction which the court had under s 43(5) of the 1973 Act to give directions where a child had been committed into care under s 43(1) was an original jurisdiction under which the court retained overall power to give any proper direction which was for the child's benefit, and was not merely a review jurisdiction. However *c* (per Sir John Donaldson MR), if the local authority acted bona fide in the child's interest in reaching a particular decision, that was a factor to be taken into account by the court. Although, therefore, the judge had had jurisdiction to make a direction giving the father access the judge had been right not to make such a direction because the local authority's decision refusing the father access was a properly informed decision which was in the child's best interests. The appeal would accordingly be dismissed (see p 932 *j*, p 933 *d* to *d* *g* and p 934 *a* to p 935 *b*, post).

Dictum of Ormrod LJ in *Re Y (a minor) (child in care: access)* [1975] 3 All ER at 354 explained.

Notes

For power to commit a child to the care of a local authority in custody proceedings, see *e* 13 Halsbury's Laws (4th edn) para 929.

For the Matrimonial Causes Act 1973, s 43, see 43 Halsbury's Statutes (3rd edn) 591.

For the Child Care Act 1980, see 50(1) ibid 1054.

Cases referred to in judgments

A v Liverpool City Council [1981] 2 All ER 385, [1982] AC 363, [1981] 2 WLR 948, HL. *f*

Associated Provincial Picture Houses Ltd v Wednesbury Corp [1947] 2 All ER 680, [1948] 1 KB 223, CA.

Y (a minor) (child in care: access), Re [1975] 3 All ER 348, [1976] Fam 125, [1975] 3 WLR 342, CA.

Interlocutory appeal *g*

On 2 December 1981 his Honour Judge Tibber sitting in the Edmonton County Court made an order under s 43(1) of the Matrimonial Causes Act 1973 giving interim care of a young child to the London Borough of Merton (the local authority). The local authority decided not to allow the father access to the child. The father applied to the court for a direction under s 43(5) of the 1973 Act giving him access to the child. On 3 February 1983 the judge refused to give a direction under s 43(5) on the ground that the court *h* could not override the local authority's decision regarding access unless it was established that the decision was unreasonable or was reached without the authority properly informing itself. The father appealed. The facts are set out in the judgment of Purchas LJ.

Cherie Booth for the father. *j*

Ian Peddie for the local authority.

PURCHAS LJ (delivering the first judgment at the invitation of Sir John Donaldson MR). This is an appeal from a judgment of his Honour Judge Tibber and an order made by him on 3 February 1983. The order was made on an application by the father seeking a direction from the court to the intervener, the London Borough of Merton (the local

authority), that they should accord access to him, the father, to his son, to whom I will
a refer as Jason.

Jason was born on 18 February 1977, so we are dealing with a small boy of now a few months over six years of age. He did not have a very happy start in life. For the first two years, his mother was working and he seems to have spent long times with daily child-minders.

In February 1979 the marriage broke down. The mother left the father (who is the
b appellant in this case), and Jason went to his maternal grandparents in the North. In March 1979 the father left for Australia and stayed there for a considerable time. In May 1979 Jason returned to his mother, who had then set up a home with a man, to whom I shall refer as C. C was clearly a man of violence. Although the custody of Jason had been committed to the mother in the divorce proceedings, in which a decree nisi had been pronounced on 3 June 1980, Jason suffered physical abuse and assaults at the hands of C
c to the extent that he clearly became thoroughly disturbed; indeed, as the judge found in his judgment, Jason still carries the scars of that early experience.

It is sad that the real fault here lies with neither of the parents. But the mother had taken up with this man, and her loyalties were clearly split. At one stage, during one of a number of hearings, it was apparently accepted by the judge that there was no question of C and the mother separating. On the other hand, when he was considering this matter
d at an earlier stage Judge Tibber was of the view that the mother ought to have the custody of the child if only C was not on the scene.

So it was that in July 1980 the father returned from Australia and discovered what was going on.

Jason was made a ward of court by the mother, because she was afraid that the father would arrive from Australia and remove Jason. Subsequently and before the instant
e proceedings Jason was dewarded. Then eventually, as I say, the father came back, in the summer of 1980, and had occasional access when Jason was visiting his aunt (the father's sister). That access stopped because the aunt was no longer on the scene. The father was enjoying his access, but the mother was clearly anxious so she stopped the visits to the aunt in December 1980. The father had meanwhile applied to the court in September 1980 seeking the custody of Jason; that application was adjourned for welfare reports.

f The father's solicitors had referred the matter to the local authority, and on 5 December 1980 Jason was placed on the 'at risk' register because of possible non-accidental injury. On 26 June 1981 a place of safety order was granted in respect of Jason who, without burdening this judgment with a lot of detail, had showed signs of obvious non-accidental injury over a considerable period of time.

There were further proceedings; the important one with which I should deal, quite
g shortly, is when the matter came before the court in July 1981 on the custody hearing at Edmonton County Court. The judge was not available, and the matter was adjourned.

In the mean while, in November 1981, the father became seriously ill, and that fact influenced Judge Tibber on the adjourned hearing on 2 December 1981. It was clear to the judge then that the solution of allowing Jason to remain with his mother while C was on the scene was not a viable solution. So the judge dismissed an application for
h custody made by the mother and made an order giving interim care of Jason to the local authority. The father's application was adjourned, and some access then ensued.

The matter came again before the judge on 23 February 1982, on the father's application, when there was a long hearing and a great deal of evidence. We have before us a note of the judgment on that occasion; it is not necessary to deal with it in detail but the result, at the end of the day, was that the judge accepted the evidence of the consultant
j psychiatrist that Jason was by then a very disturbed child requiring psychotherapy, so the judge continued the order keeping Jason in the care of the local authority.

Then there was a further difficulty about access. The judge in fact expressed the view that there should be some access for the father if that could be arranged. In correspondence which is exhibited to two affidavits there is disclosed the history of the attempts made by the local authority to arrange some degree of access.

In the early stages, Jason was placed with short-term foster-parents of very considerable experience, Mr and Mrs K. They had had a series of different children in short-term fostering. Then, after the first judgment in 1982, the situation changed because Mr and Mrs K became increasingly attached to Jason and indicated that they would be pleased to continue being his foster-parents on a longer-term basis. That was a change in circumstances which had occurred between the hearing in 1982 and the hearing from which this appeal is brought.

In the mean while, the question of access does not show the father in altogether an advantageous light. Perhaps, I hope not unfairly, it can be summarised in this way: the father refused the initial suggestions by the local authority and clearly was out to get as much access as he thought he could, by placing pressure on those responsible for the management of the child and, as Sir John Donaldson MR mentioned during argument, he was not above using presents to achieve the furthering of the greatest degree of access he could achieve. It was only when he suddenly discovered that he was not making any progress that he then came round to indicating that he would accept the original offer made by the local authority. By this time (as is disclosed in the affidavit of the social worker involved) it had been explained to Jason that the father was not going to be having access; the social worker very properly, if I may say so, said, 'Well, I am not going to allow this child, who is still very disturbed, to be subjected to the changes and whims of the father, who is manoeuvring.' I may be doing a disservice to the social worker, but that is the way I really interpret her attitude towards the situation; and, if I may say so, a very proper attitude it was. Even then, some telephone contact was maintained between Jason and his father, but that was not satisfactory.

The present position as it came before the judge was, as I have said, that the father is now seeking some specific order for access. It is to be noted that in 1982 it was not access he was seeking, it was full custody for the purpose of placing Jason with a relative. It is not necessary to go into details here, but one glance at the background of the family into which the father had intended Jason to go shows that it would have been a quite unsuitable home for a disturbed child, as the judge found on the earlier occasion.

On this occasion (23 February 1982) the judge again gave a careful and reasoned judgment. It is, in fact, in two stages. It demonstrates the care with which he was approaching his task in this case which, like all cases of this sort, is never without some difficulties.

I now turn to the notice of appeal, which attacks the judgment, stating that the judge had considered himself unduly fettered by an interpretation which he placed on part of the judgment of Ormrod LJ in *Re Y (a minor) (child in care: access)* [1975] 3 All ER 348 at 353–354, [1976] Fam 125 at 140–141. Judge Tibber in his judgment said:

> 'I take the view that when Ormrod LJ says that it is wrong for the court to override the local authority's views about access unless the local authority's views cannot be supported, what is meant, bearing in mind that the child's needs are paramount, is that the court must have in mind that if the court is satisfied that the local authority has made an informed decision, having taken proper advice and not acted vindictively or otherwise wrongly, it is not for the court to override the decision of the local authority.'

The judge then went on to recite that the local authority had relied on an experienced social worker, and had consulted a doctor. He indicated that he felt there was a heavy onus on the father to be discharged in support of his application for an order for access under s 43 of the Matrimonial Causes Act 1973, namely to show some error of a fundamental jurisdictional nature, as one has to consider in the *Wednesbury* case (see *Associated Provincial Picture Houses Ltd v Wednesbury Corp* [1947] 2 All ER 680, [1948] 1 KB 223), before it was open to him to make an order relating to access in this case.

For my part, I do not read the judgment of Ormrod LJ as saying anything of the sort. *Re Y* was an entirely different case. It was an appeal from Arnold J and concerned orders made under s 7(2) of the Family Law Reform Act 1969 in wardship, and although there are similarities between the provisions of that section and s 43 of the 1973 Act, in particular s 43(5), they are different statutory provisions. The judge also seems to have been influenced by the speeches in the House of Lords in *A v Liverpool City Council* [1981] 2 All ER 385, [1982] AC 363. But that case again involved an entirely different state of affairs, namely the attitude of the High Court where a child is placed in care under s 1 of the 1969 Act in relation to arrangements made for access. That again is an entirely different consideration.

Turning to *Re Y*, Ormrod LJ was in fact indicating that under s 7 of the 1969 Act the court did not abandon its power to make orders in the future. Ormrod LJ said ([1975] 3 All ER 348 at 354, [1976] Fam 125 at 141):

> 'Of course, in 99 cases out of 100, the court will leave the question of detailed access to the good sense and judgment of the local authority, and that is how it should work and no doubt does work. It is quite another matter when a court is confronted with a challenge to its powers, and local authorities need not be surprised at the court's reaction to such a challenge.'

In any event, all Ormrod LJ was saying was that the court will be slow to make orders (in that case, of course, under the 1969 Act) where a responsible local authority, acting properly, has come to a decision in accordance with the law under which it exercises its powers under what was then Part II of the Children Act 1948 (see now the Child Care Act 1980). But that is not a matter whether the court has power to intervene; it is a question of whether a court will in practice question an administrative action by the local authority which is properly in line with the dictates of the statutory provisions under which it works. It was no more than a comment how the system should work, and certainly it did not go to matters of jurisdiction.

The position of the court under s 43 of the Matrimonial Causes Act 1973 is in fact stronger, if anything, than its position under the 1969 Act. In sub-s (5) of s 43 it is specifically stated that the application of Part II of the Children Act 1948 'shall be subject to any directions given by the court'. So there is no question of the provisions of Part II of the 1948 Act (and now the provisions of the 1980 Act) in any way impinging on the power of a court to give any proper directions as to the management of a child which has been placed for the time being in the care of a local authority. If one seeks any further assurance about this, it is to be found in s 43(7) of the 1973 Act, which provides:

> 'The court shall have power from time to time by an order under this section to vary or discharge any provision made in pursuance of this section.'

So there cannot be any doubt that Parliament intended that an order made under s 43 should not in any way restrict or confine the court's overall powers to make appropriate orders for the welfare of the child under that section. So to that extent this appeal would have succeeded.

But the judge, very properly, continued his judgment on the basis that he was wrong in his assessment of the law. It is on this part of his judgment that counsel for the local authority strongly relies. He has not sought to support the question of law raised in the first part of the judgment. But he has not been called on to argue the merits as set out in the second part of the judgment; again, I can deal with those very briefly.

The real issue here concerns a boy aged six, in contact with his mother but only by way of visiting access (we are not given any details about that), aware of the existence of his natural father (the appellant), but who is recovering from the damage done during his younger years, and the disputes which have taken place since then. It is sometimes overlooked that merely presenting before the court an application for custody, as opposed to access (which was done in 1982 in this case), is sometimes a disturbing feature in a child's life. However careful the parents or adults involved may be, for my part I have never yet met a case in which the child does not somehow or other find out that there is a threat to its stability. In this case, Jason showed over the years a serious disturbance. The doctor deals with this in his reports. Any threat to the stability which he had achieved in the home of Mr and Mrs K must be a retrograde step affecting his recovery from the damage which he has suffered. This really was the burden both of the recommendations of the social worker and of the doctor, which the judge accepted. I quote from the passage in the judgment, where the judge refers to the change of attitude of Mr and Mrs K in accepting the role of long-term foster-parents: a

> 'Jason is able to stay with them and be brought up by them in a caring and very loving relationship. These matters have left their scars on Jason so much so that he has for the last eight months attended the department of child psychiatry at St George's Hospital for weekly sessions of psychotherapy. Jason is a child who has caused concern because he has shown friendly contact with adults which is beyond what children would normally show. The reason for this can be bad parenting or b too much association with too many adults causing Jason difficulty in forming selective bonding, that is he has not formed a close enough relationship with a limited number of adults and this shows itself by over-friendly contact with too many adults. This bodes ill for Jason's future relationships. The doctor is anxious to see that this is put right before there is too much contact with other adults [I interpose at this stage to say that that clearly includes the father]. Jason is close to Mr c and Mrs K and has a relationship with his mother whom he sees regularly, for the moment that is enough until Jason is more secure. It is not right for Jason to have another bond at this stage. Jason has enough contact at this stage although this will be kept under review. The doctor is anxious to see a relationship with his father if conditions are right in the future. For these reasons, it is not right for there to be contact at the moment.' d

The judge goes on to deal with further details and the case presented by the parties. But in that paragraph are to be found, first of all, findings which the judge was not only able to reach but, in my judgment, really had no other alternative but to reach. Those are findings which themselves indicate that the only safe course to adopt in relation to Jason (who is, as I have said earlier in this judgment, on the path of recovery from e disturbance) was that taken by the judge, namely to withhold contact with his father at the moment, and that is all that this judgment is about. For my part, I have gone into some detail about it, out of respect for the submissions ably made by counsel for the husband. But so far as that paragraph of the judge's judgment is concerned, I would be content to adopt that as my own judgment and would have felt very little need to say much else as regards the proper approach to the solution for the time being of this very f sad and not easy case with which the judge was faced.

For those reasons, I would dismiss this appeal.

SIR JOHN DONALDSON MR. I think that the judge was mistaken in the view which he took of the nature of his jurisdiction under s 43(5) of the Matrimonial Causes Act 1973. He appears to have thought that it was a review jurisdiction; in other words, g that his task was simply to review the decision of the local authority. Consistently with that view, he applied the *Wednesbury* test, that is to say he considered whether no reasonable local authority could have reached this particular decision. He also considered the matter on the alternative basis that he was entertaining an appeal from a decision of the local authority.

My own view is that neither of those approaches is correct. The court has original h jurisdiction to resolve disputes which arise between a local authority and others interested in the welfare of a child, normally parents. The decision of the local authority, in my view, merely precipitates the dispute and is not the subject matter of either review or appeal.

But having said that, these cases are always difficult, and, if the local authority has applied its collective mind bona fide to the problem in the interests of the child and j reached a particular decision, this is a factor which the court has to take into consideration in deciding whether or not it should give a specific direction under the section. That, I think, is all that Ormrod LJ meant when, in *Re Y (a minor)* [1975] 3 All ER 348 at 351, [1976] Fam 125 at 137, he said that there must be co-operation between the court and the local authority who have to administer any access ordered by the court, and that it would be wrong for the court to override the views of the local authority on access unless it is satisfied that the local authority's view cannot be supported. That is different from a review jurisdiction. It is taking account of the local authority's views as an important factor, but only one factor, in the equation.

For those reasons, in addition to those given by Purchas LJ, I too would dismiss the appeal.

Appeal dismissed.

Solicitors: *Allan Jay & Co* (for the father); *G J Norris*, Wimbledon (for the local authority).

Diana Procter Barrister.

Neumann v Bakeaway Ltd and another (Ghotli, claimant)

COURT OF APPEAL, CIVIL DIVISION
MEGAW, GEOFFREY LANE LJJ AND SIR JOHN PENNYCUICK
19 JANUARY 1977

Execution – Sheriff – Protection – Action by third party in respect of wrongful execution against his goods – Exercise of court's discretion to make protective order barring action by third party – Necessity for third party to show arguable case that he has substantial grievance against sheriff – Action for conversion – Whether sale by sheriff at auction of third party's goods at an undervalue amounting to substantial grievance against sheriff – Whether terms of writ of fieri facias protecting sheriff in regard to seizure of all or any goods at premises whether or not belonging to judgment debtor – RSC Ord 17, r 8.

The judgment debtor, a company, leased premises to the claimant, who took possession of the premises and carried on business there. The judgment debtor fell into arrears with the rent under his headlease from the execution creditor. In October 1974 the execution creditor obtained judgment for the arrears against the judgment debtor. Although the judgment was later set aside by a master, the sheriff was never informed of that fact and, acting under a writ of fieri facias which instructed the sheriff to enter the premises and seize in execution 'the goods, chattels and other property of [the judgment debtor] authorised by law to be seized in execution' and which also stated that the judgment debtor was a limited company and carried on business at the premises, the sheriff's officer, without any misconduct or negligence on his part, seized equipment on the premises which in fact belonged to the claimant and not to the judgment debtor. The equipment was sold by the sheriff at auction in December 1974 and realised approximately £429. Up to the date of the sale the claimant, even though he was aware of what was happening, made no claim to the equipment and it was not until November 1975 that he asserted a claim, and also asserted that the equipment had been sold at the auction at a substantial undervalue. The sheriff, pursuant to RSC Ord 17, r 2, issued interpleader proceedings to determine who was entitled to the proceeds of sale and also seeking a protective order barring an action against him by the claimant in respect of the seizure and sale of the equipment. Before the master, the claimant failed to produce any evidence and the master accordingly made a protective order, under Ord 17, r 8[a], that, although the sheriff should withdraw from possession of the proceeds of sale, no action

a Rule 8 is set out at p 938 *f*, post

was to be brought against him in respect of the execution he had levied against the equipment. The claimant appealed against the protective order, contending (i) that if a a sheriff, acting pursuant to a writ of fieri facias, sold goods which in fact did not belong to the judgment debtor but to a third party then, however innocently the sheriff had acted in levying the execution, he was nevertheless liable in conversion to the third party, and (ii) that the court should only make a protective order in the sheriff's favour barring an action for conversion by the third party where the third party did not have a substantial claim or grievance against the sheriff, such as where the goods had been sold at auction b at a substantial undervalue. On the appeal the claimant was given leave to adduce evidence as to the value of the goods seized and sold but, although he adduced evidence as to the cost of the goods when purchased, he failed to adduce any evidence to show their value as at the date of auction.

Held – (1) The terms of the writ of fieri facias did not direct the sheriff to seize all or c any business goods on the premises whether or not they belonged to the judgment debtor, and therefore under the terms of the writ the sheriff was only protected in regard to the seizure of goods belonging to the judgment debtor. It followed that the sheriff was liable to an action for conversion by the claimant in respect of the seizure and sale of his equipment (see p 939 *e* to *j* and p 943 *b* and *f*, post); *Jelks v Hayward* [1905] 2 KB 460 applied. d

(2) The discretion which the court had under RSC Ord 17, r 8 to make a protective order barring proceedings for conversion against a sheriff by a claimant whose goods had been wrongly taken in execution would be exercised only if, in the light of all the relevant facts surrounding the execution, including the value of the goods seized, the claimant did not have any real and substantial grievance against the sheriff, the quality of the sheriff's wrong in seizing the claimant's goods being the relevant factor in e determining whether the claimant had a real and substantial grievance. Assuming that an owner of goods had a substantial grievance against a sheriff where he had an arguable case that the sheriff had sold them at an undervalue, nevertheless, having regard to all the circumstances and in particular the facts that the claimant had been dilatory in advancing his claim to the equipment and had failed to adduce sufficient evidence that the sale at the auction was at a substantial undervalue, the master had properly exercised f his discretion under Ord 17, r 8 in making the protective order. The appeal would accordingly be dismissed (see p 941 *e* and p 942 *g* to p 944 *g*, post); *Cave v Capel* [1954] 1 All ER 428 applied; *London Chatham and Dover Rly Co v Cable* (1899) 80 LT 119 considered.

Notes

For a sheriff's interpleader relief, see 25 Halsbury's Laws (4th edn) paras 1005–1006, for g a sheriff's duties and liabilities generally, see 17 ibid para 429, for third parties' claims against goods taken in execution, see ibid, paras 485–486, and for cases as third parties' claims against a sheriff, see 21 Digest (Reissue) 384, 401–403, 409–410, *2806–2807, 2994–3015, 3076–3085*.

Cases referred to in judgments h

Cave v Capel [1954] 1 All ER 428, [1954] 1 QB 367, [1954] 2 WLR 325, CA.
Dean v Whittaker (1824) 1 C & P 347, 171 ER 1225, NP.
Jelks v Hayward [1905] 2 KB 460, DC.
London Chatham and Dover Rly Co v Cable (1899) 80 LT 119, DC.
Manders v Williams (1849) 4 Exch 339, [1843–60] All ER Rep 545, 154 ER 1242.
Smith v Ashforth (1860) 29 LJ Ex 259. j
Smith v Critchfield (1885) 14 QBD 873, CA.
Winter v Bartholomew (1856) 11 Exch 704, 156 ER 1013.

Appeal

The plaintiff, Moshe Marcel Neumann, having obtained against the defendant, Bakeaway Ltd, judgment for arrears of rent under a lease of 482 Chiswick High Road, London W4 made between the plaintiff and the defendant, obtained a writ of fieri facias directing the Sheriff of Greater London to seize goods and chattels at 482 Chiswick High Road. The sheriff, pursuant to the writ, seized goods at those premises which belonged to the claimant, Manocher Afshar Ghotli, and not to the defendant, and sold the goods at auction. When the claimant asserted his claim to the goods the sheriff issued interpleader proceedings under RSC Ord 17, r 7 to determine who was entitled to the proceeds of sale and seeking a protective order barring the claimant from bringing an action for conversion against him. On 16 July 1976 Master Creightmore ordered (i) that the sheriff should withdraw from possession of the proceeds of sale and that no action be brought by the claimant against the sheriff and (ii) that the sheriff should pay to the claimant's solicitors the net proceeds of sale of the goods after deducting the sheriff's charges. The claimant appealed against the order that no action should be brought against the sheriff. The ground of the appeal was that a protective order ought not to have been made by the master because the claimant had a substantial grievance and a substantial claim against the sheriff which he should be allowed to pursue. The facts are set out in the judgment of Geoffrey Lane LJ.

Robert Reid for the claimant.
Geoffrey Shaw for the sheriff.

GEOFFREY LANE LJ (delivering the first judgment at the invitation of Megaw LJ). On 3 May 1973 Mr Neumann, the plaintiff in this matter, let his shop at 482 Chiswick High Road, London W4 to a limited company called Bakeaway Ltd (the defendant company) for a term of 20 years at an initial annual rent of £2,200. On 18 July 1973 that company granted an underlease, for 20 years again, to date from 3 May 1973, at the same rent, to a Mr Ghotli. Mr Ghotli duly took possession. He took possession under the terms of what is called a franchise, which he held of Bakeaway Ltd, to sell their cooked foods. He carried on that business on those premises until some time in May of the following year, 1974. Mr Ghotli, who is the claimant in these proceedings, continued to live above the shop until about July 1974. On 23 July 1974 a writ was issued by the plaintiff Neumann against the defendant company and a man called Pinney, who was a guarantor of the lease. On 24 October 1974 the plaintiff obtained judgment for £550 arrears of rent and for a sum in respect of mesne profits, and costs. That judgment, on 11 November 1975 (that is to say some thirteen months later), was set aside by Master Lubbock on grounds which are not altogether clear in these proceedings. But what is clear is that the execution creditor never informed the sheriff of the fact that that judgment had been set aside; and indeed the solicitors appearing for the plaintiff, the execution creditor, seem throughout to have maintained a diplomatic silence despite all the letters which were addressed to them. However (and this is the nub of the present proceedings) in between the time when judgment was obtained in October 1974 and the time when that judgment was set aside in November 1975 the sheriff had been instructed to levy execution on the goods and chattels of the defendant company.

The terms of the writ, in so far as they were material, were these:

> 'WE COMMAND YOU that You enter the said land and cause MOSHE MARCEL NEUMANN [the plaintiff] to have possession of it. AND WE ALSO COMMAND YOU that of the goods, chattels and other property of BAKEAWAY LIMITED in your County authorised by law to be seized in execution you cause to be made the sums of [and so on] until payment . . .'

Then there are the final words:

> 'The Defendant is a limited Company and carries on business at 482 CHISWICK HIGH ROAD, LONDON W4.'

Those words have a materiality which will become apparent at a later stage.

Unfortunately, a quantity of the goods which were seized by the sheriff in purported execution of that writ belonged, not to the defendants, but to Mr Ghotli, the claimant. The goods were seized so we are told, in December 1974, and they were sold by auction a on 25 April 1975. Up to that time no claim had been made to the goods by anyone, certainly not by the claimant, though he was to some extent, it seems, aware of what was likely to be going on in the light of a letter which apparently was written on his instructions or on his behalf on 22 January 1975.

The goods were sold, as I say, at auction, and realised the sum of £429-odd, from which the sheriff's costs of the sale were deducted, leaving something over £200 net as b the proceeds of the goods.

The claimant has two complaints. His first complaint is that the goods were seized and sold when they were his goods and not the goods of the defendant company and, also, that those goods were worth much more than the £429 which in fact they realised. His second complaint, the main complaint in these proceedings, is that the master, when the matter came before him on interpleader proceedings, made an order which protected c the sheriff from proceedings which might be brought against him by Mr Ghotli, the claimant.

What happened was this. The plaintiffs' solicitors, as I say, refused to answer letters. They refused to say whether they disputed the claims of the claimant which by this stage had been made. So the sheriff issued interpleader proceedings under RSC Ord 17, r 2. The plaintiff was on one side, so to speak; the claimant was on the other; and the sheriff d was in the middle, waiting for the outcome of the decision of the master.

The matter came before Master Creightmore on 16 July 1976. The claimant was represented by a solicitor, Mr Janisch. The under-sheriff appeared to represent the sheriff's office. The order that was made, in so far as it is material, reads as follows:

> 'IT IS ORDERED that the Sheriff withdraw from possession of the proceeds of sale of goods seized and sold by him under the writ of fieri facias herein and claimed by e the Claimant that no action be brought.'

That is the imprecise, somewhat unsatisfactory jargon which indicates that the master is making an order under Ord 17, r 8 protecting, as I say, the sheriff from proceedings in conversion or trespass in respect of the goods of the claimant which had been seized. The wording of Ord 17, r 8 is as follows: f

> 'Subject to the foregoing rules of this Order, the Court may in or for the purposes of any interpleader proceedings make such order as to costs or any other matter as it thinks just.'

There is ample authority for the contention (which is indeed not disputed) that under that order it is open to the master, in a proper case, to make the protective order which g in fact he did.

That order is, in these proceedings, contested by way of appeal by the claimant, through his counsel who, if I may say so, has put forward his case with clarity, brevity and precision. He submits that in the circumstances of this particular case that order, directing that no action should be taken, should not have been made. It seems (and speaking for myself I understand it) that Mr Janisch, the plaintiff's solicitor, was h somewhat taken by surprise when this protective order was made. Possibly (there is no reason to believe the contrary) he was not as experienced as he might have been in this particular type of proceeding, which is somewhat recondite; and the result was that he had not sufficiently prepared the evidence to meet the possibility of the protective order being made. Consequently, before this court an application was made by counsel for the claimant that he be permitted to adduce further evidence which was not before the j master. This court gave leave for an affidavit from Mr Janisch, dealing with the proceedings before the master, to be admitted; but we reserved our decision on the question whether the further affirmation from the chairman, in additional to the one which was before the master, should be admitted before this court. We now give leave for that further affirmation to be used as evidence here.

The propositions put forward by counsel for the claimant are as follows. First of all, he submits that, if the sheriff sells goods that in fact do not belong to the judgment debtor but belong to some third party, he is liable in conversion, however innocently he may have been acting. For that proposition he cites the authority of *Jelks v Hayward* [1905] 2 KB 460. There is a passage in the judgment of Lord Alverstone CJ to which he refers and which runs as follows (at 465):

> 'After considering the authorities dealt with by the county court judge in his judgment, I have come to the conclusion that in this Court, at any rate, we must hold that if the high bailiff sells goods, of which the owner is entitled at the time of sale to retake possession, he is liable in trover. It is unnecessary for me to deal at length with the string of cases cited, beginning with *Dean* v. *Whittaker* ((1824) 1 C & P 347, 171 ER 1225), because the county court judge fully recognises that, if it were a mere question of seizing the goods and holding them, the high bailiff might be protected, inasmuch as up to a certain point the owner of the goods was not entitled to possession . . . To my mind, the effect of the decision in [*Manders v Williams* (1849) 4 Exch 339, [1843–60] All ER Rep 545] is that, if at the time of the sale the owner is entitled to take possession, the sale is an act of conversion as against him, and I am unable to see that the right to sue in trover depends upon any notice given to the sheriff or high bailiff. It is a branch of the general law that the sheriff seizes and sells goods at his peril, and I see no reason why a county court bailiff is in that respect in any better position than the sheriff.'

That proposition is challenged by counsel on behalf of the sheriff. His submission is this. He says that the court should have regard to the words of the sheriff's writ to which I have made reference, and, in particular, to the last words which appear on the writ, those stating, 'The Defendant is a limited Company and carries on business at 482 CHISWICK HIGH ROAD, LONDON W4.' His argument proceeds in this way. Those words are new: they did not until recently appear on this form of writ; consequently, submits counsel, there must have been an intention to change the effect of the writ. It is, he says, accepted law that the sheriff is protected by his writ, and, he goes on to submit, those words indicate that the sheriff is being directed to seize any business goods found on those premises. Consequently, he says, if the sheriff does seize any goods found on those premises, the wording of the writ protects him even though those goods are not the property of the judgment debtor but are the property of some third person.

Speaking for myself, that is a contention which I am unable to accept. To start with, it seems to me very doubtful that the Rule Committee would have the power, by this sort of alteration, to make such a radical change in the effect of the law; and, secondly, the suggested operation of those words seems to be in direct contradiction to the words contained earlier in the writ on the first page, which run as follows:

> 'WE COMMAND YOU that you enter the said land and cause MOSHE MARCEL NEUMANN to have possession of it. AND WE ALSO COMMAND YOU that of the goods, chattels and other property of BAKEAWAY LIMITED in your County authorised by law to be seized in execution . . .'

Those words, in my judgment, plainly limit the ambit of the later words to which I have made reference and render the argument of counsel for the sheriff in this respect untenable.

The next proposition put forward by counsel for the claimant is that the fact that the sale is by auction is no defence. For that he cites the decision in *Smith v Ashforth* (1860) 29 LJ Ex 259. That proposition is not disputed on behalf of the sheriff. The sheriff concedes that the auction price is not conclusive of the value of the goods. But he points out, correctly, that the sheriff is, subject to any order to the contrary being made, under a statutory duty to sell by auction. Counsel for the sheriff contends that the sheriff's only duty is not to sell at a gross undervalue, and points out that he is not bound to get the best price available.

But the main contention of counsel for the claimant, on which his argument principally turns, is this: that the court should and will only give protection to the sheriff, in circumstances of this type, if there is no substantial claim against the sheriff. For that proposition he relies, first of all, on a decision of the Queen's Bench Divisional Court in *London Chatham and Dover Rly Co v Cable* (1899) 80 LT 119, the Gas Light and Coke Co being the claimants. That was an appeal by the claimants from the county court judge at Wandsworth. What had happened was that the high bailiff of the county court, at the instance of the execution creditors, had seized on the premises of the debtor two gas stoves, which belonged to the Gas Light and Coke Co. Those stoves were exempted from distress by the Gas Light and Coke Company's Act 1861. The stoves were sold for £1 14s od but their value was no less than 18 guineas. The claimants, therefore, claimed the proceeds of sale, and, further, damages, against the high bailiff. The county court judge gave judgment for the high bailiff with costs on the question of damages, because no misconduct or negligence was alleged against him; and he ordered the proceeds of sale to be paid out to the claimants. The Gas Light and Coke Co appealed against that order to the Divisional Court. In the judgment of the court, first of all Lawrance J said that he thought that the county court judge should have made an order giving damages. Channell J said (at 120):

> 'It is quite clear that the only question on the interpleader summons as to the barring of a claim for damages, is the staying of any action brought in respect of such a claim or of any damage arising out of the execution, and as to the barring of any claim for trespass where the claimant has got back his goods and has suffered no substantial grievance. But here there was a substantial grievance suffered. Now, the goods of a third party cannot be taken in execution, even when on the premises. That is the law as to distress only. The claimants were entitled to damages.'

As against that, counsel for the sheriff submits that the court should only protect the sheriff if the claimant has no 'substantial grievance'; and he submits that it is not enough that the *claim*, namely the difference between the value of the goods and the price realised, is 'substantial': the *grievance* must be 'substantial'. Speaking for myself, I find it very difficult to see the distinction between those two matters. But there is the proposition. There is no doubt that that case, decided in the Divisional Court, is authority for saying that where there is a great difference between the value of the goods and the price realised that may on some occasion be a ground for not granting protection to the sheriff.

The situation in the present case with regard to the value of the goods and the price realised is this. In the first affirmation of the claimant, namely that which was available before the master when he considered the matter, the claimant sets out that the goods realised at auction £429 gross, and then in the next paragraph says: 'The cost to me of such goods when I purchased them in 1973 was about £3,600.' That, of course, is a statement of little or no value when one is endeavouring to ascertain the value of the goods at the date when they were sold by auction, because some goods may maintain their value while other goods may drop sharply in value directly they leave the shop and are delivered to the purchaser.

There is no doubt that Mr Janisch realised, after the hearing before the master, that further evidence on that particular point would be vital if this court was to allow the appeal from the master's decision; and so, in the further affirmation which we have given leave to be adduced, the following statement by the claimant appears: 'The cost of the equipment was £4,366·85 exclusive of VAT (which I paid but later recovered).' That obviously refers to the value added tax. He goes on:

> 'two letters from Bakeaway Ltd. to me dated respectively 8th and 14th May, 1973, which confirm this are now produced and shown to me in bundle marked "M.A.G.3".'

When one turns to those documents, one finds that the first document, dated 8 May 1973, is a list of equipment set out by Bakeaway Ltd sent to the claimant, and with the prices of the various items alongside, totalling £4,276-odd, plus value added tax, giving a total of £4,704-odd. Then they set out the terms of supply and so on; and at the bottom, in manuscript (we have not been told in whose writing this is) appear the words, '£1,000 was paid by cheque on 23/5/73. £225 to Bakeaway at same time.'

The next document is another letter from Bakeaway Ltd dated 14 May 1973 (which it is to be observed comes before 23 May, the date of the alleged payment), saying:

> 'Dear Mr. Afshar [which is the alias of the claimant],
>
> Further to our telephone conversation yesterday the price of the Bakeaway illuminated sign has been confirmed as £210. This will alter my quotation of the 8th May, 1973, as follows: Total £4,336 . . .'

Then he adds the VAT, making a total of £4,770, less deposit £1,225, and the balance outstanding is set out as £3,545. The letter continues:

> 'Thank you for your two cheques made payable to Barbequipment and Bakeaway for £1,000 and £225. The cheque for Barbequipment has to-day been passed to the company to enable production of your machinery to commence.'

It is, perhaps, a little unfortunate, in view of the specific reasons for which this evidence was prepared after the hearing before the master, that there is no further evidence from the suppliers as to the payment of any money. But, much more important, there is no evidence as to the value, or estimated value, of this equipment at the date when the auction took place. That is the material date. The result is that, although a comparison may be drawn between the cost of the goods which was allegedly paid by the claimant to the suppliers on the one hand and the amount which was realised at auction on the other, and although there is undoubtedly a substantial difference between those two figures, speaking for myself I am by no means satisfied that there is here any proper reliable evidence as to the true value of those goods at the date of the auction on 25 April.

But before reaching any conclusion in the matter it is desirable that one should look at the most recent decision of this court relating to this type of case. That is the decision in *Cave v Capel* [1954] 1 All ER 428, [1954] 1 QB 367. The facts there were that a sheriff's officer seized a caravan, which was the property of a third party and not of the judgment debtor, erroneously believing it to belong to the judgment debtor, and removed it, with the judgment debtor's mother inside, to the judgment creditor's farm, and locked it in a barn there. Under those circumstances the court, perhaps not surprisingly, refused the sheriff protection, under what was then Ord 57, r 16A, from an action by the mother.

There are passages in the judgment of Somervell LJ to which I should like to refer. First of all, citing passages from the judgment in *Smith v Critchfield* (1885) 14 QBD 873, Somervell LJ says ([1954] 1 All ER 428 at 431, [1954] 1 QB 367 at 371):

> 'It was held by the court that: "Where the sheriff in the execution of a fi. fa. enters the premises of a person other than the execution debtor and there seizes goods believing erroneously that such goods belong to the execution debtor, the sheriff may, upon interpleader proceedings, be protected against an action for trespass to the land as well as against an action for seizure of the goods, if no substantial grievance has been done to the person whose premises are wrongfully entered." It is quite clear from the judgment that those last words are not meant to qualify solely the protection against trespass but are necessary if relief is to be given at all. Sir William Brett, M.R., said (at 878): "It is not, of course, in every case that the judge will protect the sheriff. He will be protected when he has only made an honest mistake in executing the process of the court, and but for such mistake everything that he has done would have been justified by the writ." He then considered whether the sheriff was to be protected against a necessary trespass as well as the seizure. Then he said: "It seems to me that the sheriff is entitled to protection in respect of the whole of the act which through error he has wrongfully done under

> the writ, that is, in respect of his having entered the house and seized the goods." He then referred to *Winter* v. *Bartholomew* ((1856) 11 Exch 704, 156 ER 1013) and a approved what was said there and he put it in his own words: "... it is said that the sheriff may be protected in such a case as this in respect both of the trespass to the land and that to the goods where no real grievance has been sustained by the claimant. It is obvious that that cannot mean where there is no legal wrong, because by the hypothesis a tortious act must have been committed. It is clear, therefore, that by 'no real grievance' is meant no substantial grievance beyond the mere entry b and seizure of the goods, such as might exist if the sheriff's officer were guilty of insolent or oppressive conduct in excess of his duty, and not justified by the writ." BOWEN, L.J., referred (at 881) to *Winter* v. *Bartholomew*, and again he reiterated the phrase "no substantial grievance". He then quoted PLATT, B., in *Winter* v. *Bartholomew* and said: "PLATT, B., said that s. 6 of the Act [of 1831] authorised the judge to make such decision as should appear to be just according to the circumstances of the case, c and that nothing could be more just than to prevent the sheriff being harassed by an action in which no more than nominal damages could be recovered. MARTIN, B., said '... If indeed the sheriff in execution of the writ has committed any real grievance the court will allow the injured party to bring an action, but if he has done no real wrong the court will stay proceedings against him'."'

d

I wish in addition to quote simply the short judgment of Upjohn J. He said ([1954] 1 All ER 428 at 433, [1954] 1 QB 367 at 375):

> 'Order 57, r. 16A, confers on the court a valuable discretionary power to protect sheriffs who have wrongfully seized goods under a writ of fi. fa. The order that the court may make is "such order as may be just and reasonable." That is the test we have to apply. In my judgment, those words mean that the order must be just and e reasonable, not only from the point of view of the sheriff, but also from that of the claimant (in this case the plaintiff). It may well be just and reasonable to make an order in the ordinary case where the plaintiff or claimant has suffered no real grievance and whose only claim is for nominal damages. I do not propose to refer to the facts, but it is clear that this is not the ordinary case, and, in my judgment, it would be neither just nor reasonable to preclude the plaintiff, from pursuing such f remedies at law as she may have against the sheriff. I agree that the order of the master should be restored.'

In so far as the decision in that case, *Cave v Capel*, is inconsistent with the earlier decision of the Divisional Court in the *London Chatham and Dover Rly* case, the later case must, of course, take precedence. It seems to me in the present case that had the claimant successfully proved that there was this sharp difference between the value of the goods at g the time of the auction sale and the price in fact realised, it may very well have been that this would have amounted to a 'substantial grievance' felt by him, and a substantial reason for not affording to the sheriff the protection which the master did in fact afford him. But, for the reasons which I have endeavoured to indicate, the claimant has failed, in my judgment, to produce that necessary evidence. Not only that; but one has, in the h light of the judgments in *Cave v Capel*, to look at all the relevant facts surrounding the execution and, in the light of all those facts, including the value of the goods, to see if there was a 'real and substantial grievance' properly felt by the claimant. It is the quality of the sheriff's admitted wrong which is relevant. There are a number of matters here which the master no doubt had in mind. There was the somewhat odd behaviour of the claimant himself. One would have expected a little more interest to be exhibited by him in this very valuable equipment which undoubtedly was on the premises where he had j carried on his business. That is the sort of thing to which the master was entitled to have regard, and to which we are entitled to have regard. Taking all those matters into account, I am unable to say that, had I been in the position of the master, I should have come to any different conclusion from that which he in fact reached. In my judgment the master was correct in the conclusion which he reached. He was correct in holding that these were proper circumstances in which his power to protect the sheriff under Ord 17, r 8 should be exercised.

It only remains to say this. An argument was propounded by counsel for the sheriff that s 15 of the Bankruptcy and Deeds of Arrangement Act 1913 applied in this case so as to protect the sheriff. It is not, in the light of the decision which I have already made clear, necessary to reach a conclusion one way or the other on that proposition.

In my judgment, this appeal must be dismissed.

SIR JOHN PENNYCUICK. I agree. I have no doubt, on the authorities, that the act of the sheriff in selling these goods belonging to the claimant represented a wrongful conversion of the goods by the sheriff. I do not accept the argument of counsel for the sheriff to the contrary on this point. Further, I will assume in favour of the claimant that in the present connection the owner of goods has a 'substantial grievance' where the sheriff wrongfully, but without misconduct, sells the goods at a great undervalue. I abstain from expressing a concluded view as to the meaning and scope of the expression 'substantial grievance'. The authorities cited to us on this question do not seem to me wholly easy to reconcile. Given this assumption in favour of the claimant, it would not be right to preclude the claimant from bringing an action for conversion against the sheriff if the claimant had advanced his claim promptly and had adduced sufficient prima facie evidence of sale at an undervalue. But in truth the claimant omitted to assert his claim until November 1975, long after the sale in April 1975. Moreover, the claimant's evidence of value is, as pointed out by Geoffrey Lane LJ, unsatisfactory to a high degree.

It seems to me that, taking into account these and all the other relevant facts, the master, by inserting the words 'that no action be brought', exercised his judicial discretion properly and that this court should not interfere. I will only observe in conclusion that on the hearing of the interpleader summons the master had before him only the interpleading sheriff and the claimant. The explanation for the absence of the execution creditor is, I imagine, that the judgment had by then been set aside. I would dismiss this appeal.

MEGAW LJ. I agree. RSC Ord 17, r 8 provides that in interpleader proceedings of this sort the court 'may . . . make such order . . . as it thinks just'. The question is whether it was appropriate in this present case to make an order debarring proceedings by the claimant against the sheriff.

I am prepared to assume for the purposes of this appeal that it would constitute 'a substantial grievance', within those words as they have been used in the number of cases which have been cited to us, if there were material on which it could be said to be fairly arguable that the sheriff, having, without any misconduct or negligence on his part, seized and sold goods which did not in fact belong to the judgment debtor, had sold them at a price which was substantially less than their true value at the date when they were thus sold. Making that assumption, then I ask myself first the question whether, when this matter came before the master and he made the order that he did, there was material before him on which he could regard that proposition as being arguable in the present case. To my mind the answer to that is No. The nearest that the evidence before him came to it was para 7 of the original affirmation by the claimant, which reads: 'The cost to me of such goods when I purchased them in 1973 was about £3,600.' As has been stressed in the judgment of Geoffrey Lane LJ, that does not begin to give any indication of what was the fair or true value that could be expected to be realised for those goods when they were sold in April 1975. The further negative factor in the evidence before the master at that stage, which may well have influenced his mind, and which could perfectly properly have influenced his mind, was the absence of any explanation, which certainly could have been expected, on the part of the claimant how it came about that when these goods, his goods, were seized in December 1974, and were not sold until April 1975, the first intimation that was made to the sheriff, or anybody representing the sheriff, of any claim in respect of those goods was in November 1975. The solicitor representing the claimant at the hearing before the master was, indeed, as Geoffrey Lane LJ has suggested, probably taken by surprise; and for myself also I would not regard that as something which was in itself surprising. He could indeed at that stage have applied for an adjournment of the summons, if he had fully realised what the position was, in order that he might seek to supplement any gaps that there were in the evidence in order to show the existence of 'a substantial grievance'. Again, I would not blame him for not having made that application at the time, having regard to the circumstances. I think that in those circumstances it was right and proper that this court should do as it has done, that is to say to allow the fresh evidence to be given, in spite of the fact that the ordinary principle is that the evidence would not be admitted in this court when it could have been adduced in the court below. In the circumstances here, speaking for myself, I should at any rate have been very unhappy that that evidence should not have been available to this court. The evidence having been put before this court, we are then in the position in which the master would have been to make his decision if an application had been made to him to adjourn for fresh evidence and if the fresh evidence which the claimant wished to put forward had been put forward. That fresh evidence having been put forward, presumably after careful consideration without the necessity for any hurry involving any possibility of omissions, it is, in my judgment, for the reasons given by Geoffrey Lane LJ, entirely insufficient to fill the gaps to which I have referred, and entirely insufficient to lead the court to the conclusion that there has been here anything that can be properly described as 'a substantial grievance' in relation to the price at which these goods were sold when they were sold by auction by the sheriff.

I would also take into account (as I think, on the basis of the decision in *Cave v Capel* [1954] 1 All ER 428, [1954] 1 QB 367, the court is entitled to take into account) other facts of the particular case. It is a question what is the just order to make. The discretion, on the face of it, is absolute, and the court is entitled to take into account all relevant circumstances. Another relevant circumstance which bears on my mind here, in addition to the lack of proper evidence of the sale being below the true value of the goods, is the continued absence of any explanation how it came about that the sheriff had no claim made to him on behalf of the claimant. If, of course it was within the knowledge of the claimant before the date when the sale took place, he could then, no doubt, have successfully prevented any such loss as that in respect of which he now claims by himself simply giving notice to the sheriff at that stage of his claim in that regard. Whether or not the claimant knew of the facts before that sale took place, we simply do not know: we are left in the dark; and as the claimant has not seen fit to inform us on that matter that is another reason why I think that it would be quite wrong, in the circumstances, to say that the discretion has here been wrongly exercised.

I agree that the appeal should be dismissed.

Appeal dismissed.

Solicitors: *J Tickle & Co* (for the claimant); *Burchell & Ruston* (for the sheriff).

Diana Procter Barrister.

Observer Ltd v Gordon (Cranfield and others, claimants)

QUEEN'S BENCH DIVISION
GLIDEWELL J
9, 17 FEBRUARY 1983

Execution – Sheriff – Protection – Action by third party in respect of wrongful execution against his goods – When action by third party against sheriff should be allowed to proceed – Action for conversion – Action should be allowed to proceed where fairly arguable that third party's claim overrides sheriff's defences under statute or at common law – What constitutes 'notice' or 'reasonable inquiry' showing that goods seized were not property of execution debtor – Whether sheriff protected at common law from action by third party if third party having substantial grievance against sheriff – Whether third party having substantial grievance where his goods are sold by sheriff at substantial undervalue – Whether fact that sale is by auction conclusive that sale not at undervalue – Bankruptcy and Deeds of Arrangement Act 1913, s 15 – RSC Ord 17, r 2(4).

The execution debtor carried on the business of reconditioning pianos for their owners and of selling pianos which either the debtor had bought and reconditioned for sale or which belonged to other persons and were being sold by the debtor on commission on a sale or return basis. Accordingly, at any given time, the pianos at the execution debtor's premises (which consisted of a showroom and workrooms) included pianos owned by the debtor and pianos owned by other persons. Writs of fieri facias were issued to the sheriff to levy execution on pianos at the debtor's premises to cover the value of the execution creditor's debt, and pursuant to the writ the sheriff seized a number of pianos at the premises and subsequently sold them at public auction. At all times up to the auction the sheriff believed that all the pianos at the debtor's premises belonged to the debtor, because nobody had suggested the contrary to him, either at the time he levied the execution or on previous occasions when he had attended the premises to levy execution, and because there were no markings on the pianos to indicate whether or not they belonged to the debtor. Consequently, when the sheriff levied the execution he made no inquiries whether the pianos belonged to other persons. The claimants, who owned some of the pianos on which the execution was levied, claimed to be entitled to the proceeds of sale of those pianos; they also wished to bring an action for conversion against the sheriff. The claimants adduced no more than hearsay evidence that the sheriff and his officers had been told when removing the pianos in the course of the execution that some of them did not belong to the execution debtor. The sheriff issued an interpleader summons under RSC Ord 17, r 2[a] applying, inter alia, for an order restraining the claimants from bringing an action against him on the grounds (i) that he had a good defence under s 15[b] of the Bankruptcy and Deeds of Arrangement Act 1913, because he had no 'notice', and even by 'making reasonable inquiry' would not have ascertained, that the pianos in question were not the property of the execution debtor, and (ii) that he also had a good defence at common law to the claimants' claim. The execution creditor conceded that the pianos belonged to the claimants. The master, pursuant to Ord 17, r 2(4), made a protective order that no action be brought by the claimants against the sheriff in respect of the execution levied against the claimants' pianos. The claimants appealed to the judge.

Held – (1) Where, having levied execution against goods in the execution debtor's possession which belonged to another person (the claimant), a sheriff applied under RSC

a Rule 2, so far as material, is set out at p 947 *f*, post
b Section 15, so far as material, is set out at p 949 *j* to p 950 *a*, post

Ord 17, r 2(4) for a protective order that no action be brought by the claimant against him on the ground that he had a good defence to such a claim under s 15 of the 1913 Act *a*
or at common law, the test to be applied by the court in determining whether the claimant should be allowed to proceed with his action was whether the claimant had shown that it was fairly arguable that his claim against the sheriff overrode the sheriff's defences under s 15 of the 1913 Act or at common law (see p 949 *b* to *f*, post); dictum of Megaw LJ in *Neumann v Bakeaway Ltd (Ghotli, claimant)* (1977) [1983] 2 All ER at 943 followed. *b*

(2) Since the sheriff would only have had 'notice', within s 15 of the 1913 Act, that the pianos he had seized were not the execution debtor's property if he had either known or been informed that they were not the debtor's property, and since the only evidence that the sheriff knew that the pianos in question were not the execution debtor's was the hearsay evidence adduced by the claimants, on which, in all the circumstances, the court could not rely, it followed that the sheriff did not have sufficient 'notice' that the pianos *c*
in question were not the execution debtor's property. Furthermore, in all the circumstances it had been reasonable for the sheriff not to make inquiries about the ownership of the pianos, but even if he had it was unlikely that he would have ascertained the ownership of the pianos within a reasonable time. It followed that it was not fairly arguable that the claimants' claim would override the sheriff's defence under s 15; on the contrary, the sheriff had a good defence under s 15. Accordingly, the appeal would be *d*
dismissed (see p 950 *b c e f*, p 951 *e f* and p 952 *g*, post).

Per curiam. (1) At common law a sheriff is not protected from an action by a claimant in respect of the claimant's goods taken in execution where the claimant has a substantial grievance against the sheriff. A substantial grievance against the sheriff may exist where the sheriff's officers have been insolent or guilty of oppressive conduct or where the claimant's goods are sold by the sheriff at an undervalue. The fact that the goods are sold *e*
by the sheriff at auction is not conclusive that they have not been sold at an undervalue and the court will hear evidence as to the value of the goods to determine whether they were in fact sold at an undervalue (see p 951 *g h* and p 952 *c* to *g*, post); *Neumann v Bakeaway Ltd (Ghotli, claimant)* (1977) [1983] 2 All ER 935 applied.

(2) An appeal to a judge from a protective order made by a master under RSC Ord 17, r 2(4) is by way of a hearing de novo (see p 949 *g h*, post). *f*

Notes

For a sheriff's interpleader relief, see 25 Halsbury's Laws (4th edn) paras 1005–1006, for a sheriff's duties and liabilities generally, see 17 ibid para 429, for third parties' claims against goods taken in execution, see ibid paras 485–486, and for cases on third parties' claims against a sheriff, see 21 Digest (Reissue) 384, 401–403, 409–410 *2806–2807, 2994–* *g*
3015, 3076–3085.

For the Bankruptcy and Deeds of Arrangement Act 1913, s 15, see 3 Halsbury's Statutes (3rd edn) 18.

Cases referred to in judgment

Cave v Capel [1954] 1 All ER 428, [1954] 1 QB 367, [1954] 2 WLR 325, CA. *h*
London Chatham and Dover Rly Co v Cable (1899) 80 LT 119, DC.
Neumann v Bakeaway Ltd (Ghotli, claimant) (1977) [1983] 2 All ER 935, CA.
Smith v Ashforth (1860) 29 LJ Ex 259.

Appeal

In an action by the plaintiffs, Observer Ltd, against the defendant, Mrs Reeva Gordon, *j*
trading as Gordon Pianos, claiming £3,868·50 as the balance due for the cost of advertisements placed by the defendant in the plaintiffs' newspaper, the plaintiffs obtained judgment, and writs of fieri facias were issued to the Sheriff of Greater London requiring him to seize in execution goods on the defendant's premises to cover the judgment debt. After the sheriff had seized certain goods on the defendant's premises and sold them pursuant to the writs, eight persons claimed that they owned certain goods

seized and sold and claimed to be entitled to the proceeds of their sale. They also wished
a to bring proceedings for conversion against the sheriff in respect of the execution levied on their goods. The sheriff issued an interpleader summons dated 23 November 1981 to determine whether the plaintiffs or the claimants were entitled to the proceeds of the sale and sought an order that in the mean time all further proceedings against him be stayed. On 9 July 1982 Master Bickford-Smith ordered that no action be brought by the claimants against the sheriff in respect of the execution levied against the claimants'
b goods. The first, second and seventh claimants, respectively Mr J W Cranfield, Mr Sean Parsons and Mr Wolf Ruskin, appealed from the master's order. The appeal was heard in chambers but judgment was given by Glidewell J in open court at the request of the parties. The facts are set out in the judgment.

Nicholas Stadlen for the first, second and seventh claimants.
c *John A Sabine* for the plaintiffs.
Andrew Caldecott for the sheriff.

Cur adv vult

17 February. The following judgment was delivered.

d

GLIDEWELL J. Although I heard this matter, over parts of two days, in chambers I am giving judgment in open court as I was requested to do by both parties.

This is an appeal against the decision of Master Bickford-Smith that 'No Action' may be brought by the claimants against the sheriff in respect of their claim to the proceeds of the sale of goods seized and sold by the sheriff under a writ of fieri facias.

e The order made by Master Bickford-Smith was made, I believe, under RSC Ord 17, r 2(4). Order 17, r 2 deals with claims to goods taken in execution. Rule 2(1) provides that a person making a claim to money, goods or chattels taken in execution must give notice of his claim to the sheriff. By r 2 the sheriff then gives notice to the execution creditor and the execution creditor must then say whether he admits or disputes the claim and, if there is a dispute between the execution creditor and the claimant, the
f sheriff may apply for relief, that is to say for that dispute to be resolved by the court. By r 2(4):

> 'A sheriff who receives a notice from an execution creditor under paragraph (2) admitting a claim made under this rule shall withdraw from possession of the money, goods or chattels claimed and may apply to the Court for relief under this Order of the following kind, that is to say, an order restraining the bringing of an
> g action against him for or in respect of his having taken possession of that money or those goods or chattels.'

As an alternative, it may be that the order was made under the more general terms of Ord 17, r 8, which provides:

> 'Subject to the foregoing rules of this Order, the Court may in or for the purposes
> h of any interpleader proceedings make such order as to costs or any other matter as it thinks just.'

I indicated during the hearing that it seemed to me that the earlier rule was appropriate.

The facts, as disclosed by the affidavits before me, can be summarised as follows. Mrs Gordon, the defendant, ran a business of reconditioning and selling secondhand pianos
j at premises in Camden Town. She was assisted (or it may be that it is more accurate to say that the business was managed for her) by her father, Mr L Ruskin. The seventh claimant, Mr Wolf Ruskin, is her brother. It seems from the affidavits, and I gather that it is now accepted by the sheriff, that the business comprised three different aspects. First, the defendant bought secondhand pianos, reconditioned them and resold them, second, sometimes she simply reconditioned pianos for their owners and, third, sometimes she sold pianos on commission or on sale or return for the owners, usually after she had

reconditioned them. The premises comprised a saleroom and workshop. At any one time some of the pianos, in both parts of the premises, were owned by the defendant and some were not. I find, however, that the sheriff, until the matter came to his attention as a result of the claims made by the claimants, did not know that any of the pianos in the premises were owned by any person other than the defendant.

In the summer of 1981 the business was in financial difficulties. Creditors, including Observer Ltd, issued, or had issued, a number of writs and obtained judgments against the defendant. At that stage both the defendant and her father died within a few weeks of each other. The defendant died on 17 June and her father on 6 July 1981.

On previous dates, starting in December 1980 and after the two deaths up to August 1981, a number of writs of fieri facias were issued to the sheriff requiring him to take in execution goods covering amounts totalling some £12,000. By August something over £4,000 had been paid against those total debts. On 19 August 1981 the sheriff's officers were instructed to proceed with the execution of the writs which were still outstanding. They went to the defendant's premises and they found them locked and unoccupied. With the help of a locksmith the premises were entered and the officers removed a number of pianos. Within two weeks they were sold at public auction by Harvey's Auction Ltd, in Covent Garden. The sale was on 2 September. The proceeds of the sale sufficed to meet the amounts in the various writs of fieri facias and the sheriff's costs.

Shortly afterwards the under-sheriff received a number of inquiries from persons who claimed that they owned pianos at the defendant's premises, and it transpired that some of these pianos were amongst the pianos seized and sold by the sheriff. In particular, the three present appellants (although there were eight claimants there are now only three appellants) had pianos in that category. The first claimant had arranged for the defendant to sell a Blüthner grand piano for him on commission, and it was at her premises awaiting sale. The second claimant had purchased a Blüthner grand piano from the defendant but had not taken delivery of it and in 1981 it was being stored on his behalf at her premises. The seventh claimant was storing a Boyd upright piano at the premises. These three pianos were amongst those taken by the sheriff, and the plaintiffs in this action. Observer Ltd, have conceded that they were owned by the respective claimants.

Now I turn, with that relatively brief recital of the facts, to say something about the legal position of the sheriff. I have a very full note of Master Bickford-Smith's judgment, and it seems to me that I cannot do better than start by reading the beginning of the judgment. He said:

> 'The sheriff is an officer of the Crown whose chief remaining duty is to execute the judgments of the High Court in obedience to the writs directed to him; in particular he may be directed by the writ of fieri facias to seize the goods of a judgment debtor and sell them to satisfy the judgment. If he neglects to perform this duty he may be proceeded against by the judgment creditor and may be punished as for a contempt of court. It may often happen that the sheriff, who, in practice, entrusts the performance of his duties in relation to execution to the under-sheriff and to officers acting under the under-sheriff's direction, seizes goods which belong to a third party, not to the judgment, debtor.'

And that, of course, breaking off from his judgment, was the position here.

If the claim or claims are received from claimants claiming that the goods are theirs while the goods are still held by the sheriff then, of course, he may invoke the interpleader procedure in Ord 17 and, as I have already indicated, the judgment creditor, the plaintiff in the action, may accept, as they did here, that the goods are indeed those of the claimant or, alternativelly, if there is an issue between them, it can be set down to be tried. But if, as here, the goods have already been sold when the claim is received then interpleader can, if necessary, determine whether the judgment creditor or the claimant is entitled to be paid the proceeds of sale by the sheriff. If, of course, the judgment creditor withdraws his claim then the proceeds of sale can go to the claimants, and that is what happened here. But the claimant may have said that the sheriff should not have seized the goods at all and is liable to be sued for conversion.

Now, prima facie, there has, in these circumstances, been conversion of the goods
a because the sheriff, without right or title to do so, being required by the writ to seize the goods of the judgment debtor, has seized the goods of some other person or persons. But in his special position the sheriff has two lines of defence to such an action. The first is under s 15 of the Bankruptcy and Deeds Arrangement Act 1913 (I will come to the relevant terms of that section) and, secondly, he has a defence at common law which is not open to other persons.

b The purpose of the procedure under Ord 17, r 2(4) or r 8 is to protect the sheriff and his officers in cases in which they are entitled to the benefit of either defence by preventing any action being brought against them.

Two preliminary points were considered before me and I think it is right I should say something about them. First of all, what is the proper approach of the court to an application on behalf of the sheriff that the court should order 'No Action' be brought?
c The court, in this sense, means the master in the first instance and, on appeal, the judge. In my view one can properly draw the analogy of Ord 14 proceedings in reverse, i e to be allowed to proceed with his action it is for the claimant to show that he has a real chance of defeating both defences available to the sheriff. If he does show this, a 'No Action' order should not be made and the claimant should be allowed to continue with his action. Counsel for the sheriff submitted to me that the claimant has to show a reasonable
d chance of success. That is to say, that he has more than an arguable case. But, in *Neumann v Bakeaway Ltd (Ghotli, claimant)* (1977) [1983] 2 All ER 935 at 943 Megaw LJ said:

> 'I am prepared to assume for the purposes of this appeal that it would constitute "a substantial grievance", within those words as they have been used in the number of cases which have been cited to us, if there were material on which it could be said
> e to be fairly arguable that the sheriff, having, without any misconduct or negligence on his part, seized and sold goods which did not in fact belong to the judgment debtor, had sold them at a price which was substantially less than their true value at the date when they were thus sold.'

In other words, Megaw LJ was there suggesting that the proper test was whether it was
f 'fairly arguable' that the claimant had a claim which overrode both defences. I propose to adopt 'fairly arguable' as the proper test.

Second, there was discussion before me as to what are the powers of the judge on appeal from the master. The matter arises because, I was told, this is the first appeal to a judge from a decision of a master under this particular provision. The reason for that is that until 1978 an appeal of this sort went straight from the master to the Court of
g Appeal. But in that year, by an amendment to the Rules of the Supreme Court, what was para (*c*) of Ord 58, r 2(1) was deleted and that had the effect of taking this procedure out of the provision relating to appeals going straight to the Court of Appeal and meant that it simply became yet another form of appeal to a High Court judge: In my judgment it is now like any other appeal from a master to a High Court judge; it comes before the court de novo. That, in many cases, will raise the question whether further evidence, not
h before the master, can properly be put in before the judge. I do not need to decide that because no further evidence was put in before me. What is clear to me is that, while, of course, I give full weight to the master's views, since I am hearing this matter de novo I can properly, if I think right, differ from his conclusions, and I could make a finding of fact on the evidence which differed from the finding of fact which he had made.

I turn, therefore, to consider the defences open to the sheriff. Firstly, the statutory
j defence. The relevant words of s 15 of the Bankruptcy and Deeds of Arrangement Act 1913 read as follows:

> 'Where any goods in the possession of an execution debtor at the time of seizure by a sheriff . . . are sold by such sheriff . . . without any claim having been made to the same . . . no person shall be entitled to recover against the sheriff . . . for any sale of such goods . . . unless it is proved that [he] had notice, or might by making

> reasonable inquiry have ascertained that the goods were not the property of the execution debtor . . .' a

And so the issue that has to be decided is whether it is arguable either that the sheriff had notice or that he might, by making reasonable inquiry, have ascertained that the goods were not the property of the execution debtor.

Counsel for the claimants (the appellants before me) submits that the sheriff has notice if he knows of facts which should cause him to make inquiries, which inquiries would reveal the true ownership of the goods. Counsel for the sheriff, on the contrary, submits b
that the words mean what they say. The sheriff only has notice if he knows or is informed that the goods are not the property of the execution debtor. On this point I agree with counsel for the sheriff. So interpreting the phrase 'has notice' the only evidence before me that the sheriff or any of his officers had notice is contained in two affidavits, that of the eighth claimant, Miss Ward, not an appellant before me, and an affidavit of the second claimant, Mr Parsons, sworn on 7 April 1982. In Miss Ward's affidavit she said: c

> 'Further enquiries early in November 1981 led me to a Mr. Smith of Challons Pianos, 13 Selous Street, who told me that several pianos had been taken from Mrs. Gordon's business to be sold. Mr. Smith related to me a conversation which he had had with the removers at that time. He told them that the pianos did not belong to Mrs. Gordon but to individuals. The man Mr. Smith spoke to told him that this was d
> not his concern because there was not enough time . . . I asked Mr. Smith whether he would be willing to appear in Court to relate his story. He told me he was old and did not wish to become involved . . . [I] telephoned him again and he said that as he could not see how this would benefit our case he was still unwilling to even repeat our conversation in writing.'

Mr Parsons, in his affidavit, says much the same about the conversation he had with e
Mr Smith.

Now, if what Mr Smith said was true clearly it would have been possible to obtain an affidavit from him or to bring him to court on subpoena. His unwillingness, even to put his story on paper, casts the greatest doubt on its accuracy. That hearsay, secondhand, evidence does not justify allowing the action to proceed against the sheriff.

The more difficult question is: might the sheriff or his officers, by making reasonable f
inquiry, have ascertained that some of the pianos were not the defendant's property? It is clear from the affidavit sworn by Mr Alistair Black, the under-sheriff of Greater London, on 1 April 1982, that the sheriff and his officers believed and assumed at all times, before the auction sale on 2 September 1981, that all the pianos in the defendant's premises were her property. Thus he made no inquiries at all to ascertain whether this was correct. g

There are thus two questions, both of which the master considered. First, was it reasonable for the sheriff not to make any inquiries? If not, second, might reasonable inquiries have revealed that some of the pianos were owned by third parties?

As to the first question, the master commented:

> 'A sheriff would be ill-advised to seize without inquiry the goods on the premises h
> of a tradesman whose business was the repair of other persons' goods: a cobbler or a motor repairer. An ordinary retail shop would be quite different.'

With that I entirely agree. The evidence available to the sheriff at the time of seizure was, first, that the premises comprised a showroom and a workroom; the workroom would be necessary to recondition the pianos bought for resale by the defendant and there was no notice or mark on any of the pianos to indicate that they had been sold or j
were not her property. Second, on previous occasions the sheriff's officers had attended to levy execution at the premises and on each occasion a sufficient payment had been made, if not to meet the debt, at any rate to stave off the execution. But the important point is that on those occasions nobody, neither the defendant nor her father nor anybody else, had ever suggested that any of the pianos were owned by third parties.

There was a further piece of information available to the sheriff, though he had not, in fact, seen it. As obviously follows from the fact that the writ in this case was by Observer Ltd for unpaid advertising charges, there had been a series of advertisements for the business in the Observer. The sheriff had not in fact seen the advertisements but, if he had done so, he would have found that they advertised reconditioned pianos for sale. They were, in my view, entirely neutral as to the ownership of the reconditioned pianos. The sheriff having got it into his head that they were owned by the defendant, there was nothing in the advertisements that would lead him to believe that this was not necessarily the case. There was equally nothing to lead him to believe that they were owned by the defendant.

In addition to the contrary arguments to which the master referred in his judgment, that the workshops should have suggested the possibilities that other people's pianos were repaired and that piano dealers do sometimes sell on commission, counsel for the claimants submitted to me that the fact that the defendant was in financial difficulties should itself have suggested to the sheriff that some of the pianos might not be hers. Moreover, he pointed out that the evidence shows that there was on the premises a card index which, if examined, showed who owned each piano that was in the premises.

On the second question, on what reasonable inquiries might have revealed, it is important to remember that each of the claimant deponents knew that he owned his or her piano and thus he started from the knowledge that the defendant had in her possession at least one piano that was not hers and it was, of course, a reasonable inference that she might well have other pianos which were not hers. For the sheriff, who did not know this, the difficulties were much greater. He did not even know that the defendant was dead. Even if he had ascertained this, no member of the family had taken out letters of administration and if he had made inquiries of the defendant's brother, Mr Wolf Ruskin, he would probably not have received any or much assistance. Indeed when, in November 1981, Mr Black's firm wrote to Mr Ruskin about his own claim, Mr Ruskin replied that he did not wish to be named as having any connection with his sister's affairs.

On both questions the master had to consider under this head, I agree with his decision. In my view, in the circumstances, there was nothing which should have caused the sheriff to make inquiries about the ownership of the pianos, and if he had made such inquiries it is most unlikely that, within a reasonable time, he would have gained any useful information. I say 'within a reasonable time' because I remind myself, as the master did, that he is under a duty to execute the writ and that doubtless did place him under a time constraint.

This concludes the appeal in favour of the sheriff. But lest I should be wrong on the statutory defence I have gone on to consider the alternative defence at common law. The most recent decision on this branch of the law is that of the Court of Appeal in *Neumann v Bakeaway Ltd (Ghotli, claimant)* (1977) [1983] 2 All ER 935, to which I have already referred. That decision establishes that the sheriff is not protected from an action against him if the claimant has a substantial grievance against him, the words 'substantial grievance' being a direct quotation from the judgment. Such a grievance may arise if the sheriff's officers are guilty of insolence or oppressive conduct, which is not suggested here, or if, having seized the goods, they are sold at a gross undervalue. Of course, the reason for that is that if they are sold for anything approaching a proper value then the claimant, as here, gets the value for which they were sold and to that extent his grievance is met. Geoffrey Lane LJ said (at 940):

> '... counsel for the sheriff submits that the court should only protect the sheriff if the claimant has no "substantial grievance"; and he submits that it is not enough that the *claim*, namely the difference between the value of the goods and the price realised, is "substantial": the *grievance* must be "substantial". Speaking for myself, I find it very difficult to see the distinction between those two matters. But there is the proposition. There is no doubt that that case, decided in the Divisional Court, is authority for saying that where there is a great difference between the value of the

goods and the price realised that may on some occasion be a ground for not granting protection to the sheriff.' (Geoffrey Lane LJ's emphasis.) a

The case to which he was referring is *London Chatham and Dover Rly Railway Co v Cable* (1899) 80 LT 119. Later in his judgment Geoffrey Lane LJ said (at 942), having referred to *Cave v Capel* [1954] 1 All ER 428, [1954] 1 QB 367:

'In so far as the decision in that case, *Cave v Capel*, is inconsistent with the earlier decision of the Divisional Court in the *London Chatham and Dover Rly* case, the later b case must, of course, take precedence. It seems to me in the present case that, had the claimant successfully proved that there was this sharp difference between the value of the goods at the time of the auction sale and the price in fact realised, it may very well have been that this would have amounted to a "substantial grievance" felt by him, and a substantial reason for not affording to the sheriff the protection which the master did in fact afford him.' c

The question therefore is, or would be if I had not found against the claimants on the statutory defence, whether there is evidence that the sheriff sold at a gross undervalue.

Counsel for the sheriff argues that the sheriff is obliged by law to sell the goods by auction and provided that he chooses an appropriate auctioneer and an appropriate date and place for the auction it cannot be said that the goods have been sold at an undervalue. That argument was, in my view, advanced to the court in *Neumann* but was rejected by d that court, that is to say that the fact of sale by auction is conclusive against the proposition that the goods have been sold at an undervalue. Indeed, Geoffrey Lane LJ makes it clear that in *Neumann* the point was not disputed on behalf of the sheriff. He said (at 939):

'The next proposition put forward by counsel for the claimant is that the fact that the sale is by auction is no defence. For that he cites the decision in *Smith v Ashforth* e (1860) 29 LJ Ex 259. That proposition is not disputed on behalf of the sheriff.'

And, of course, I am bound by that, though one sees the logic of the argument.

Is there then evidence that the goods have been sold at a gross undervalue? If I had not found for the sheriff on the statutory defence, I would not have found myself able to say that either the first claimant or the second claimant did not have an arguable case. In other words, I would have said that on the common law defence the order 'No Action' f should not have been made against them. Their evidence as to value might persuade a court that the goods were sold at a gross undervalue; it is not for me, of course, to decide that it would so convince a court. The seventh claimant is, however, in a different position. The only evidence as to value in his affidavit is his own estimate. That is not sufficient, in my view. Even if the statutory defence were not available in his case I would agree with the master that the order 'No Action' should have been made. g

It follows, for the reasons I have sought to give, that the appeals of all three claimants fail and they are dismissed.

Appeal dismissed. Leave to appeal.

Solicitors: *P R Wright-Morris & Co* (for the first, second and seventh claimants); *Blyth Dutton Holloway* (for the plaintiffs); *Burchell & Ruston* (for the sheriff).

K Mydeen Esq Barrister.

a
Graham v Dodds

HOUSE OF LORDS

LORD DIPLOCK, LORD KEITH OF KINKEL, LORD SCARMAN, LORD ROSKILL AND LORD BRIDGE OF HARWICH

9, 10 MAY, 30 JUNE 1983

b
Fatal accident – Damages – Multiplier – Date at which multiplier to be determined – Four years elapsing from date of death until trial of action – Whether multiplier to be determined at date of death or at date of trial.

The plaintiff brought an action in Northern Ireland against the defendant for damages under the Fatal Accidents (Northern Ireland) Order 1977 for herself and her two
c dependent children following the death of her 41-year-old husband in a road accident in December 1977. The defendant admitted liability at the trial in January 1982 and the judge directed the jury when summing up that they could, in addition to making an award of special damages for the period between the date of death and the date of trial, award damages for the dependants' future loss from the date of trial, by analogy to the assessment of loss suffered by a surviving plaintiff in a personal injury case. He suggested
d to the jury that in all the circumstances a reasonable multiplier for the purpose of calculating the future loss would be between 11 and 14, or a little more or less than that. The jury awarded the plaintiff damages of just over £100,000, including special damages. The defendant appealed unsuccessfully to the Court of Appeal in Northern Ireland and then appealed to the House of Lords, contending that the judge's suggestion as to the correct multiplier was erroneous since it was based on a calculation from the date of trial,
e instead of from the date of death, which meant that an erroneously large multiplier had been applied by the jury and that an excessively large award had been made. The plaintiff contended (i) that the multiplier should be calculated from the date of trial, (ii) that even if the judge's direction had been erroneous so that the jury had consequently applied in effect a multiplier of 18 (being the judge's suggested maximum of 14, plus 4 for the years between the death and the trial) that figure was not excessive in relation to a fatal accident
f victim aged 41 at the date of death, and (iii) that in any event the actual quantum of damages was not excessive.

Held – The appeal would be allowed for the following reasons—

g (1) In assessing the future loss of dependency in a fatal accident claim the multiplier was to be calculated from the date of death and not the date of trial (as in a personal injury case where the injured person survived until trial), because there was no certainty what might have happened to the deceased if he had lived after the date of death, and there would otherwise be the undesirable anomaly that the dependants would recover more merely by delaying the date of trial. Accordingly, the judge had erred in law in
h basing his direction to the jury regarding the appropriate multiplier on the considerations appropriate in the award of future loss of earnings to a surviving plaintiff in a personal injury case and in treating the pre-trial loss as special damage; instead the multiplier was to be selected as at the date of death and the number of pre-trial years for which special damages were awarded was then to be deducted from the multiplier (see p 954 *f* to *j* and p 958 *e* to p 959 *a*, post); *Cookson v Knowles* [1978] 2 All ER 604 applied.

j (2) Moreover, a multiplier of 18 was excessive in relation to a deceased who was aged 41 at his death, since it assumed that he would have continued to make the same contribution to the support of his family without interruption right up to retirement age without taking into account the vicissitudes of life (see p 954 *f* to *j* and p 959 *h* to p 960 *a*, post); dictum of Brett LJ in *Phillips v London and South Western Rly Co* [1874–80] All ER Rep at 1180–1181 applied.

(3) Furthermore, the quantum of damages could not be upheld on the basis that it was an award which a reasonable jury could have made, because it was impossible to *a*
avoid the conclusion that the award was vitiated by the judge's invitation to apply an excessively high multiplier (see p 954 *f* to *j* and p 960 *b c* and *f g*, post).

Notes

For assessment of damages under the Fatal Accidents Act 1976, see 34 Halsbury's Laws (4th edn) para 98, and for cases on the subject, see 36(1) Digest (Reissue) 360–365, *1456–* *b*
1483.

The Fatal Accidents (Northern Ireland) Order 1977 corresponds to the Fatal Accidents Act 1976. For the 1976 Act, see 46 Halsbury's Statutes (3rd edn) 1115.

Cases referred to in opinions

Cookson v Knowles [1978] 2 All ER 604, [1979] AC 556, [1978] 2 WLR 978, HL; *affg* *c*
[1977] 2 All ER 820, [1977] QB 913, [1977] 3 WLR 279, CA.

Mallett v McMonagle [1969] 2 All ER 178, [1970] AC 166, [1969] 2 WLR 767, HL.

Phillips v London and South Western Rly Co (1879) 5 CPD 280, [1874–80] All ER Rep 1176, CA.

Appeal *d*

The defendant, John Dodds, appealed from the order of the Court of Appeal in Northern Ireland (Gibson and O'Donnell LJJ, Jones LJ dissenting) dated 5 October 1982 dismissing the defendant's appeal and affirming the judgment entered in favour of the plaintiff, Iris Pauline Graham, on 22 January 1982 in an action for damages brought under the Law Reform (Miscellaneous Provisions) Act (Northern Ireland) 1937 and the Fatal Accidents (Northern Ireland) Order 1977, SI 1977/1251, and tried before Lord Lowry LCJ and a *e*
jury in the High Court in Northern Ireland. The facts are set out in the opinion of Lord Bridge.

W P McCollum QC and *M A Morrow* (both of the Northern Ireland Bar) for the defendant.
R C Hill QC and *G E J Simpson* (both of the Northern Ireland Bar) for the plaintiff.

f

Their Lordships took time for consideration.

30 June. The following opinions were delivered.

LORD DIPLOCK. My Lords, I have had the advantage of reading in draft the speech of my noble and learned friend Lord Bridge. I agree with it, and for the reasons he gives *g*
I would allow the appeal and order a new trial.

LORD KEITH OF KINKEL. My Lords, I have had the benefit of reading in draft the speech to be delivered by my noble and learned friend Lord Bridge. I agree with it, and for the reasons he gives I too would allow the appeal and order a new trial.

h

LORD SCARMAN. My Lords, I have read in draft the speech to be delivered by my noble and learned friend Lord Bridge. For the reasons he gives I would allow the appeal, and I assent to the orders which he proposes for a new trial and in respect of costs.

LORD ROSKILL. My Lords, I have had the advantage of reading in draft the speech to be delivered by my noble and learned friend Lord Bridge. I entirely agree with it and *j*
for the reasons he gives I would allow this appeal.

LORD BRIDGE OF HARWICH. My Lords, this is an appeal brought by leave of the Court of Appeal in Northern Ireland from an order of that court made on 5 October 1982 which, by a majority (Gibson and O'Donnell LJJ, Jones LJ dissenting), dismissed an appeal from a judgment of the High Court in Northern Ireland given on 22 January 1982 by Lord Lowry LCJ awarding the plaintiff £103,562·10 damages. The plaintiff's husband was killed on 30 December 1977 in a road accident for which full liability was admitted at the trial on behalf of the defendant. The plaintiff claimed damages under the Law Reform (Miscellaneous Provisions) Act (Northern Ireland) 1937 and, on behalf of herself and her two daughters, under the Fatal Accidents (Northern Ireland) Order 1977, SI 1977/1251. The action came on for trial before Lord Lowry LCJ and a jury on 20 January 1982 and the trial extended over three days. The jury assessed the total damages to be awarded under the Fatal Accidents Order in the sum of £103,300·00. It is the quantum of that award alone which is challenged on behalf of the defendant in this appeal. Nothing turns on the apportionment of damages as between the plaintiff and her daughters or on the Law Reform Act award.

Joshua Graham was born on 25 August 1936. He married the plaintiff in 1962. Their two daughters were born on 25 February 1964 and 18 January 1967 respectively. For the first six or seven years of the marriage the husband, who was the holder of a diploma in theology from a Baptist theological college, worked for the Irish Baptist Mission in Donegal and Northern Ireland. He then worked for about two years in advertising. His next venture was to set up in business on his own account as a haulage contractor. He obtained the capital for this from the sale of two bungalows which he and the plaintiff owned. Unfortunately, in 1975 the business foundered. After a short period of employment with another haulage contractor, the husband, in May 1976, obtained employment with Texaco Ltd, the well-known oil company, as a tanker driver operating from their Carrickfergus depot. This employment continued until his death. The Texaco drivers worked on different shifts. Throughout his employment the husband's shift was from 7 pm to 3 am. A vacancy for a driver on this shift was the only vacancy offered to him when the employment began. In addition to basic pay, workers on this shift earned a shift bonus of 25% to compensate them for their unsocial hours of work. The husband also worked some overtime.

At the time of the husband's death he and the plaintiff, with their daughters, were living in rented local authority accommodation. The husband's average net pay in his employment with Texaco was about £66 per week. The plaintiff was a trained nurse. She was also in employment earning net about £33 per week. The family were saving to buy a house (no doubt with the aid of a mortgage) and to this end the plaintiff paid from her earnings about £100 per month into a building society account. The plaintiff also received a mileage allowance for the use of a car in her work and in fact used the family car in the daytime, while the husband used it to go to work at night.

At the time of the trial, more than four years later, the plaintiff, having gained a further qualification, was in more remunerative employment and was earning between £300 and £390 per month net inclusive of mileage allowance. She was buying a house on mortgage. The elder daughter was almost 18. She was in her last year at school, intending to take A levels, and had been provisionally accepted for university entry. The younger daughter was just 15 and intended to stay at school a further three years. Her future beyond that was naturally uncertain.

In addition to the facts so far related, there was, I think, substantial agreement as to what the plaintiff's husband's net pay would have been at the date of the trial had he survived and continued in the identical employment with Texaco. But beyond this almost everything relevant to the assessment of damages under the Fatal Accidents Order was very much in dispute. The matters principally in issue were the following. 1. What value was to be attributed to various fringe benefits enjoyed by Texaco drivers? 2. What proportion of the husband's notional net earnings was to be attributed to the dependency (a) in calculating the loss from the date of death to the date of trial and (b) in calculating the multiplicand on which to base the estimate of future loss? 3. What value was to be put on the husband's services at home such as car maintenance, home decorating, and even cooking and housework? 4. How, if at all, was the calculation of dependency affected by the plaintiff's earnings from which the husband, if surviving, would have continued to benefit? 5. What account should be taken in the assessment of a nation-wide productivity agreement which was confidently expected to be concluded between Texaco and the husband's union shortly after the date of trial? 6. What multiplier should be applied to the appropriate multiplicand in assessing damages for future loss?

The resolution of these issues depended, in the main, not on the determination of disputed primary facts, but on matters of inference and assessment. In spite of this, however, the issues were extensively canvassed with the witnesses, including an accountant, in examination and cross-examination as well as by learned counsel in speeches to the jury of which your Lordships have a full transcript. Widely divergent calculations were recommended to the jury by opposing counsel as the basis for a fair assessment.

My Lords, I find it difficult to suppose that at the end of the evidence and argument the jury were not thoroughly confused. What is certain is that Lord Lowry LCJ faced a daunting task in summing up. If I may say so respectfully, he took the eminently sensible view that, as well as giving directions in law and on matters of general principle, he ought to give the jury a lead in some detail on the figures. He introduced this part of his summing up as follows:

> 'I may be in danger of being too precise, because if there is one thing that I'm still suffering from on the third day of this case, it is uncertainty, even about some figures that might perhaps be capable of being reduced to clearer proportions, but I think I must try and give you a bit of help, and I want to warn you that when I am talking figures I don't want to take your job over, you can regard my figures as examples, you can regard them as fairly reliable, but don't regard them as telling you what verdict you are to bring in this afternoon.'

I will attempt to summarise very briefly the suggestions he then put to the jury, with frequent reminders that his views were not binding on them. He recommended 80% of the husband's notional total contribution to the family budget as representing the dependency for the period from the date of death to the date of trial, when both daughters would have remained fully dependent. In assessing future loss, however, having regard to the ages of the daughters, he recommended 75%. He suggested a figure of £18,000 as representing the husband's notional contribution to the family budget from the date of death to the date of trial, to which the application of 80% yielded a figure of £14,400 as representing the dependants' pre-trial loss. He then went in detail through the figures to arrive at an estimate of the notional annual contribution of the husband to the family budget as at the date of trial (earnings net of tax, fringe benefits, and services at home), arriving at a total of £6,400, with a resulting figure, representing the suggested 75% dependency, of £4,800. He substantially discounted the relevance of the plaintiff's own earnings. The effect of the prospective productivity agreement for Texaco drivers he treated as relevant not to the multiplicand but to the multiplier to be used in calculating future loss.

The crucial directions in the summing up on which this appeal essentially turns relate to the multiplier to be applied in assessing the future loss of dependency. Lord Lowry LCJ said: 'Now, I personally would take between 11 and 14 as the multiplier, according to what you think.' He then explained that the choice of multiplier depended on the jury's assessment of the weight of various 'plus factors' or 'good points' set against the 'minus factors' or 'bad points'. Having reviewed the 'plus factors' he said that they 'could make you think that you should go a little higher still [ie than the suggested multiplier of 14], but I think only a little higher would be justified'. Having reviewed the 'minus factors' he concluded as follows:

> 'Frankly, I don't think there are too many bad points there, but this is where the jury comes in, this is really the part of the case, more than anything else I think, where you have got to make up your own mind what is the sensible approach, and I have suggested, rather putting my head on the block, I think, as far as counsel are concerned, somewhere from 11 to 14. You could just possibly fall below 11, you could, slightly more credibly, get just above 14, in my opinion.'

At the conclusion of the summing up counsel for the defendant challenged the propriety of the judge's direction with respect to the basic multiplier, saying, inter alia:

> 'I would respectfully submit that on the auhorities, and on the views generally
> a held, a 14-year multiplier would be about appropriate for a man of 41 at the present time, and therefore he is getting a four year lapse since the accident which makes it an 18-year multiplier of the overall loss averaged out, and I would respectfully submit that that is too high . . .'

Lord Lowry LCJ's reply was to say:

> b 'Well, I think I will have to stick with 14 . . . but I am going to tell them something, which is that they can only get to the top of this scale probably if they think all the good points are good and the bad points aren't there at all.'

Lord Lowry LCJ then recalled the jury and reviewed once more the factors affecting the multiplier. This review did not, perhaps, put the matter quite in the way the answer to counsel for the defendant had suggested, but certainly sounded a note of caution against
c the danger of taking too high a multiplier.

The only issue arising in this appeal which is strictly one of law is whether, in assessing damages for loss of dependency arising from a fatal accident, the multiplier or number of years' purchase should be calculated from the date of death or from the date of trial. Counsel for the defendant has contended for the former. Counsel for the plaintiff has throughout contended for the latter and this view prevailed with Lord Lowry LCJ and
d the majority of the Court of Appeal. The judge, in a short note appended to the transcript in his report of the trial, said this:

> 'I took the view that there is no legal principle that the number of years of purchase (in this case I suggested 11 to 14) should be automatically reduced having regard to the number of years' special damage since the death of the deceased and
> e that the contrast sometimes made with personal injury cases is not a sound one.'

On this issue the majority of the Court of Appeal examined the speeches in your Lordships' House in *Cookson v Knowles* [1978] 2 All ER 604, [1979] AC 556 and reached the conclusion that Lord Diplock and Lord Fraser had expressed opposite and irreconcilable opinions. Gibson LJ illustrated his understanding of the supposedly conflicting doctrines by indicating how they would apply in assessing the dependency of
f the widow of a young man killed at the age of 21, in the following terms:

> 'Should the action not come to hearing until five years had elapsed Lord Fraser would assess at death the multiplier, which I take at say 18, and he would then allow five years' special damage and 13 years as the multiplier of future loss. Lord Diplock on the other hand, would also give five years' special damage and then fix the
> g multiplier on the assumption of the death of the deceased at the age of 26 years, which [counsel for the plaintiff] conceded could not be appreciably less than the original figure of 18.'

On the basis of such a conflict, Gibson and O'Donnell LJJ held themselves free to choose which of the two doctrines they preferred and both came down in favour of the view they attributed to Lord Diplock.

h It is to be observed that in *Cookson v Knowles* Viscount Dilhorne, Lord Salmon and Lord Scarman all expressed their agreement with the speeches of both Lord Diplock and Lord Fraser. Gibson LJ recognised this and described it as a 'confusing feature' of the case. It would indeed be astonishing that such a radical conflict should have escaped the attention of the three concurring members of your Lordships' House, but still more astonishing that neither Lord Diplock nor Lord Fraser should have said a word to indicate any
j awareness that they were disagreeing with each other on a matter of fundamental principle.

My Lords, I have to say, with all respect, that the majority of the Court of Appeal based their decision in this case on a misunderstanding of the decision in *Cookson v Knowles*. In that case the widow's claim under the Fatal Accidents Acts 1846 to 1959 arose from the death of her husband at the age of 49. The trial judge took 11 years' purchase from the

date of death as the appropriate multiplier. But he applied it to the estimated annual dependency at the date of trial, $2\frac{1}{2}$ years after the date of death, to arrive at a single capital a
sum of damages on which he awarded interest at 9% from the date of death to the date of trial. The Court of Appeal reduced the capital award by estimating the dependency in two parts, (a) from the date of death to the date of trial, (b) from the date of trial onwards, and allowed interest on the first part of the award only at a reduced rate. For the purpose of the capital assessment, the trial judge's figure of 11 years' purchase from the date of death had to be divided; $2\frac{1}{2}$ was applied in calculating the pre-trial loss, $8\frac{1}{2}$ in calculating b
the future loss. But the propriety of calculating the overall multiplier from the date of death was not questioned (see [1977] 2 All ER 820, [1977] QB 913). In the unanimous decision of this House affirming the Court of Appeal, Lord Fraser dealt with the last point expressly in the following passage ([1978] 2 All ER 604 at 614–615, [1979] AC 556 at 575–576):

> 'In the present case the deceased was aged 49 at the date of his death and the trial c
> judge and the Court of Appeal used a multiplier of 11. That figure was not seriously criticised by counsel as having been inappropriate as at the date of death, although I think it is probably generous to the appellant. From that figure of 11, the Court of Appeal deducted $2\frac{1}{2}$ in respect of the $2\frac{1}{2}$ years from the date of death to the date of trial, and they used the resulting figure of $8\frac{1}{2}$ as the multiplier for the damages after the date of trial. In so doing they departed from the method that would have been d
> appropriate in a personal injury case and counsel for the appellant criticised the departure as being unfair to the appellant. The argument was that if the deceased man had had a twin brother who had been injured at the same time as the deceased man was killed, and whose claim for damages for personal injury had come to trial on the same day as the dependants' claim under the Fatal Accidents Acts, the appropriate multiplier for his loss after the date of trial would have been higher e
> than $8\frac{1}{2}$. On the assumption, which is probably correct, that that would have been so, it does not in my opinion follow that the multiplier of $8\frac{1}{2}$ is too low in the present claim under the Fatal Accidents Acts where different considerations apply. In a personal injury case, if the injured person has survived until the date of trial, that is a known fact and the multiplier appropriate to the length of his future working life has to be ascertained as at the date of trial. But in a fatal accident case the multiplier f
> must be selected once and for all as at the date of death, because everything that might have happened to the deceased after that date remains uncertain. Accordingly having taken a multiplier of 11 as at the date of death, and having used $2\frac{1}{2}$ in respect of the period up to the trial, it is in my opinion correct to take $8\frac{1}{2}$ for the period after the date of trial. That is what the Court of Appeal did in this case.'

g

If I may say so respectfully, I find the reasoning in this passage as cogent as it is clear. But, what is perhaps more important, I can find nothing in the speech of Lord Diplock which conflicts in any way with Lord Fraser's reasoning or with his conclusion. The two passages cited by Gibson LJ from Lord Diplock's speech dealing with the assessment of the dependants' future loss from date of trial are not directed to the question of the appropriate multiplier and certainly lend no support to the doctrine that this can be h
calculated on the assumption that the deceased, if he had survived the accident, would certainly have remained alive and well and in the same employment up to the date of trial. Such a doctrine, ignoring the uncertainty which, as Lord Fraser pointed out, affects everything that might have happened to the deceased after the date of his death, is clearly contrary to principle and would lead to the highly undesirable anomaly that in fatal accident cases the longer the trial of the dependants' claims could be delayed the more j
they would eventually recover.

Accordingly, in so far as Lord Lowry LCJ based his directions to the jury with respect to the multiplier to be applied in assessing future loss on the considerations appropriate in awarding damages for future loss of earnings to a surviving plaintiff in a personal injury case aged 45 (the age the plaintiff's husband would have attained at the date of trial if he had survived) and treated the pre-trial loss as 'special damage', and in so far as the majority of the Court of Appeal approved the directions given on that basis, they erred in law.

But that is not the end of the matter. Gibson LJ in the Court of Appeal proceeded, in the alternative, to approve the directions given to the jury on the footing that a multiplier of 18 was not excessive in assessing dependency in relation to the victim of a fatal accident aged 41 at the date of death. To understand his reasoning, it is only fair to cite in full the passage in which he justifies this conclusion, as follows:

> 'The table of awards set out in *Kemp and Kemp on the Quantum of Damages* vol 1 (4th edn, 1982) pp 247–252, tables I–IV, illustrate that the ceiling multiplier which has been accepted, lacking any special circumstances, is about 18. I therefore assume that a multiplier of 18 is at or very close to the maximum which should be used. Up to what age of a deceased at death should that figure be applied assuming a steady, regular employment with no particular hazards or risks of redundancy or reduced working? So long as current interest rates stand at a level which is appreciable, the value of any deferred estate in property diminishes with each year of deferment until ultimately the value becomes negligible for practical purposes. It is for this, among other reasons, that in fatal accident cases the multiplier reaches a generally recognised maximum figure beyond which, irrespective of the further number of years which the deceased would have been expected to earn, there is no increase in the multiplier. The question is, up to what age at death will a deceased command the maximum multiplier? As a general rule it seems to me that one could say that a dependency which is deferred for more than 25 years may be ignored in deciding the multiplier. If one assumes that employment and therefore dependency continues until the age of 65 years, it would follow that the maximum multiplier would, on that assumption, apply to any deceased wage earner who had at least 25 years' anticipated working life. This would mean that until the age of 40 years at death the dependants could in favourable circumstances claim to qualify for the maximum multiplier. Applying that working rule to the present case, two conclusions emerge. First, the deceased was at death aged 41 and so his dependants are on the very border of qualifying in that respect for the maximum multiplier. Secondly, the circumstances of his employment and mode of life were both favourable for assessing a maximum multiplier for a person of his age. Can it be said that the sum of 4 plus 14, namely 18 years is clearly excessive? It is certainly at or near the upper limit. But both the evidence and the charge would have warranted the jury in concluding that the measure of damages should go to the limit.'

I leave aside the question whether Gibson LJ was justified in preferring a maximum multiplier of 18 derived from the table of awards in *Kemp and Kemp* to the figure 16 years' purchase which Lord Diplock in *Mallett v McMonagle* [1969] 2 All ER 178 at 191, [1970] AC 166 at 177 suggested was 'seldom exceeded' for the convincing reasons which he demonstrated by reference to annuity values at different rates of interest. Assuming the premise that a multiplier of 18 applied in assessing the dependency of the family of a breadwinner killed between the age of 20 and 30 could not be disturbed on appeal, I cannot accept the conclusion that the same considerations govern the assessment in the case of a breadwinner killed at the age of 41. The fallacy of the reasoning on which Gibson LJ proceeds is that, in the case of the older man, it assumes as certain that he would have continued without interruption to make as valuable a contribution, in real terms, to the support of his family as he was making at the date of death right up to retiring age. It allows no discount for the vicissitudes of life which might have falsified that assumption. In *Phillips v London and South Western Rly Co* (1879) 5 CPD 280 at 291, [1874–80] All ER Rep 1176 at 1180–1181, dealing with loss of future earnings in a personal injury case, Brett LJ said:

> 'With regard to subsequent time, if no accident had happened, nevertheless many circumstances might have happened to prevent the plaintiff from earning his previous income; he may be disabled by illness, he is subject to the ordinary

> accidents and vicissitudes of life; and if all these circumstances of which no evidence can be given are looked at, it will be impossible to exactly estimate them; yet if the a jury wholly pass them over they will go wrong, because these accidents and vicissitudes ought to be taken into account.'

Exactly the same principle, mutatis mutandis, is applicable here.

It is right to remember that the assessment of damages in every case, including such a case as this, is ultimately a question of fact. Accordingly, it will normally be permissible to set aside a jury's award on appeal only if it can be shown to be manifestly inadequate b or excessive. But a different principle must, I think, apply when the jury have been invited by the judge in summing up to choose from a range of multipliers in assessing the future loss, of which the upper limit exceeds the maximum which the tribunal of fact could reasonably apply. This is a misdirection not of law but of fact. In such a case, I would accept that it is open to the party seeking to uphold the award to show that, despite the misdirection, there has been no miscarriage of justice. Indeed, counsel for the plaintiff c has sought to persuade your Lordships of just that by arguing that, on an analysis of the evidence, the jury's award falls comfortably within the bracket of figures reasonably open to them. I find it impossible to accept this argument.

In a further note included in his report of the trial, Lord Lowry LCJ said:

> 'The verdict returned by the jury appears to be very close to the figures mentioned d in my charge if one makes most of the reasonable assumptions in favour of the plaintiff.'

I confess to a difficulty in understanding this. If one takes the judge's suggested figure of £14,400 for the pre-trial loss and subtracts it from the jury's award of £103,300, the remainder is £88,900. Taking then the judge's suggested figure of £4,800 as the multiplicand in the assessment of future loss, it requires a multiplier exceeding 18 to e achieve the product of £88,900. Testing the figures in the converse way, dividing £88,900 by 15 (the judge's figure of 14 plus 1 for pension rights) gives a quotient of £5,926. This seems to me to reach, if not to exceed, the maximum figure which any reasonable jury could have extracted from the evidence as the annual value of the dependency at the date of trial. Perhaps the most probable explanation of the jury's award is that they took, as they were entitled to do, more generous figures than those f recommended to them by the judge either for the pre-trial loss or for the annual dependency at the date of trial or both, and then pushed up the multiplier from 15 (14 plus 1) to 16 or 17 in response to the judge's invitation to 'go a little higher still'. However that may be, it is impossible to avoid the conclusion that the jury's award was vitiated by the judge's invitation to apply an excessively high multiplier. I would accordingly allow the appeal, set aside the judgment and order a new trial. g

On the question of costs, the plaintiff is entitled to retain the benefit of the order in her favour for the costs of the trial. In the Court of Appeal the plaintiff was not legally aided. The case for the defendant was less fully argued in the Court of Appeal than it has been in your Lordships' House, where important new points have been canvassed. Moreover, the issues arising in the case have a significance for the well-known insurance company standing behind the defendant which goes beyond the sum of money in h dispute in the case. I would propose that there be no order in respect of the costs in the Court of Appeal or in this House.

Appeal allowed.

Solicitors: *Hextall Erskine & Co*, agents for *Vincent P Fitzpatrick & Co*, Belfast (for the defendant); *Robin Thompson & Partners*, agents for *Francis Hanna & Co*, Belfast (for the plaintiff).

Mary Rose Plummer Barrister.

Eton College v Bard and another

COURT OF APPEAL, CIVIL DIVISION
OLIVER AND SLADE LJJ
14 APRIL, 17 MAY 1983

Landlord and tenant – Leasehold enfranchisement – Long tenancy – Tenancy for term of years certain – Tenancy granted by housing association – Tenancy granted for term of years exceeding 21 years 'or until this Lease shall cease . . . to be vested in a Member of the Association' – Tenant becoming and remaining a member of the association – Tenant claiming right to acquire freehold – Whether tenancy for a 'term of years certain' – Whether tenancy a 'long tenancy' – Leasehold Reform Act 1967, s 3(1).

The defendant had been the lessee by assignment of a leashold house from 25 September 1974 under a sub-underlease granted to his predecessor in title by a housing association for a term from 17 November 1969 until 24 June 2063 'or until the Lease shall cease (otherwise than by death or bankruptcy) to be vested in a Member of the Association (whichever shall be the earlier) . . .' On 29 August 1980 the defendant, who was a member of the association, served on the plaintiff, the freehold owner of the property, a notice claiming the right to acquire the freehold under the Leasehold Reform Act 1967. The plaintiff disputed the claim and issued a summons to have determined the question, inter alia, whether the tenancy was a 'long tenancy', within s 3(1)[a] of the 1967 Act, which defined a long tenancy as 'a tenancy granted for a term of years certain exceeding twenty-one years, whether or not the tenancy is (or may become) terminable before the end of that term by notice given by or to the tenant or by re-entry, forfeiture or otherwise . . .' The plaintiff contended that the tenancy was not a long tenancy because it was not granted for 'a term of years certain', within the meaning of s 3(1), since the lease expressly provided for the term to be brought to an end if it ceased to be vested in a member of the association and that a term of years determinable before the expiration of the time for which it was limited was 'certain' for the purposes of s 3(1) only if its termination could be brought about by acts of the parties, because the word 'terminable' was used in the sense of 'liable to be terminated', ie by notice, re-entry or forfeiture, the words 'or otherwise' being construed ejusdem generis therewith. The defendant contended that the only effect of that provision was to render the tenancy 'terminable before the end of that term . . . otherwise' within the meaning of the subsection so that the term did not fail to qualify as a 'a term of years certain exceeding twenty-one years'. The judge held that the tenancy was 'a long tenancy' within the subsection and the plaintiff appealed.

Held – The words 'term of years certain' in s 3(1) of the 1967 Act, in the context of the subsection as a whole, included a term which might become 'terminable' before the maximum duration of the term, the word 'terminable' being applicable equally to a liability of the lease to be determined by an act of one or more of the parties to the lease as to its liability to terminate or come to an end by the happening of an event on which the lease was limited to determine before the expiration of the maximum stated duration of its term. It followed that, subject to a premature termination of the term occurring through the defendant ceasing to be a member of the association or purporting to assign to a person who was not a member or through other events entitling the lessors to forfeit the lease, the defendant was entitled to remain tenant until 24 June 2063, ie for more than 21 years from the date the tenancy was granted, and accordingly his tenancy was a 'long tenancy' within s 3(1) of the 1967 Act. The appeal would therefore be dismissed (see p 965 *c* to *f* and *j* to p 966 *a c d* and *f* to *j*, p 967 *c* and p 968 *j* to p 969 *b*, post).

---

a Section 3(1), so far as material, is set out at p 963 *j* to p 964 *a*, post

Notes

For meaning of 'long tenancy' for purposes of right to acquire the freehold or an extended lease of premises, see 27 Halsbury's Laws (4th edn) para 1008. a

For the Leasehold Reform Act 1967, s 3(1), see 18 Halsbury's Statutes (3rd edn) 638.

Cases referred to in judgments

Lace v Chantler [1944] 1 All ER 305, [1944] KB 368, CA.

Orman Bros Ltd v Greenbaum [1954] 3 All ER 731, [1954] 1 WLR 1520; *affd* [1955] 1 All ER 610, [1955] 1 WLR 248, CA. b

Roberts v Church Comrs for England [1971] 3 All ER 703, [1972] 1 QB 278, [1971] 3 WLR 566, CA.

Appeal

The plaintiff, the King's College of Our Lady of Eton Beside Windsor, otherwise called Eton College, appealed against so much of the order of Whitford J made on 8 October 1981 as declared that a lease dated 17 November 1969 and made between Eton Housing Association Ltd of the one part and James Ralph McCarthy of the other part and which had since vested in the second defendant, Peter St John Hevey Langan, was, on its true construction and in the events which had happened, a long tenancy within the meaning of s 3(1) of the Leasehold Reform Act 1967. The first defendant, Mrs Shoshana Bard, took no part in the proceedings. The facts are set out in the judgment of Slade LJ. c d

Julian Byng for the plaintiff.
The second defendant appeared in person.

Cur adv vult e

17 May. The following judgments were delivered.

SLADE LJ (giving the first judgment at the invitation of Oliver LJ). This is an appeal by Eton College from part of a judgment of Whitford J given on 8 October 1981. It raises the question whether a lease dated 17 November 1969 and relating to a property known as 29 Fellows Road, London NW3 is a 'long tenancy' within the meaning of s 3(1) of the f Leasehold Reform Act 1967. Part I of that Act has the effect of conferring on the tenant of a leasehold house, occupying the house as his residence, a right to acquire the freehold of the premises, where certain conditions are fulfilled. Among other conditions, the tenant for this purpose has to show that his tenancy is a 'long tenancy', as defined by s 3(1), and that it is at a 'low rent', as defined by s 4(1).

The lease in question was granted by Eton Housing Association Ltd as sub-underlessor g to Mr J R McCarthy as sub-underlessee. The freehold of the property is vested in Eton College, which is the plaintiff in the proceedings. According to the evidence there is no connection between the plaintiff and Eton Housing Association Ltd, notwithstanding the name of the association.

Since 25 September 1974 the interest of the lessee under the lease has been vested, either jointly or solely, in Mr Peter Langan QC. He is the second defendant in the h proceedings and on this occasion we have had the pleasure of hearing him appearing in person. The first defendant is a Mrs Bard. She has taken no part in the proceedings in this court or the court below.

On 29 August 1980 Mr Langan served notice of a claim to acquire the freehold of the property under the 1967 Act. The plaintiff disputed this claim and on 22 January 1981 issued a summons to have determined two questions, namely: (a) whether the lease is 'a j long tenancy' within the meaning of s 3(1) of that Act; (b) if the answer to question (a) is in the affirmative, whether the lease is a tenancy 'at a low rent' within the meaning of s 4(1).

Whitford J answered question (a) in the affirmative, but question (b) in the negative. The effect of his decision was thus to leave Mr Langan with no immediate right to acquire the freehold. Nevertheless, Mr Langan does not seek to challenge the judge's decision on question (b) because certain subsequent events, which need not be related, have now occurred; and he considers that they may or will enable him to assert that, notwithstanding that decision, his tenancy has become one 'at a low rent' in the relevant sense. Question (a), on which the plaintiff seeks to challenge the judge's decision, is thus the only issue before this court.

The summons is supported by an affidavit sworn by Mr Lockhart, a partner in the firm of the plaintiff's solicitors. There is exhibited to this affidavit a full statement of facts which had been agreed between him and Mr Langan. I need not refer to many of these facts. The property forms part of an estate known as the Chalcots Estate at Hampstead of which the freehold has been vested in the plaintiff for over 400 years. By a lease dated 4 January 1965 (the headlease), the plaintiff demised a part of the estate, which included the land on which the property is situated and is referred to in the statement of facts as 'the housing association area', to the metropolitan borough of Hampstead for 99 years from 29 September 1964. Following the enactment of the London Government Act 1963, the headlease became vested in the London borough of Camden, which, by an underlease of 20 December 1967, demised the housing association area to the association for 97¼ years less 10 days from 24 June 1966.

On 17 November 1969 the association granted to Mr McCarthy the lease of the property which is in issue in the present case. The habendum clause to the lease (cl 1) began with the following words:

> 'In consideration of the rents and the Members covenants hereinafter reserved and contained The Association DEMISES unto the Member the premises (including the rights demised therewith) described in the First Schedule hereto (hereinafter called "the Unit") with the exceptions and reservations specified in the Second Schedule hereto TO HOLD the premises from the 17th day of November One thousand nine hundred and sixty-nine until the Twenty-fourth day of June Two thousand and sixty-three or until this Lease shall cease (otherwise than by death or bankruptcy) to be vested in a Member of the Association (whichever shall be the earlier) and subject to the provisions for determination hereinafter contained YIELDING AND PAYING therefor during the said term . . .'

Clause 1 of the lease then set out a number of provisions in regard to the payment of rent and additional rent. I need not refer to them or to any other provisions of the lease save, perhaps, to the covenants in cl 2(9) and (10) which permit the lessee to assign the lease of the whole property to a member of the association, but otherwise preclude him from assigning, subletting or parting with possession of all or any part of the property.

The effect of the provisions of the lease to which I have referred is to oblige a person to become a member of the association before he can become qualified to take an assignment of the lease. Mr Langan became a member of the association shortly before 25 September 1974 and has remained a member ever since.

Mr Lockhart's affidavit exhibited a copy of the rules of the association. They have, I understand, since been amended, but it is common ground that these amendments are not material to the legal issue now before the court; the rules in force at the date of the lease are the relevant ones. I do not find it necessary to make more than a passing reference to the contents of these rules. It suffices to say that r 12 provided for the cessation of a member's membership of the association in a number of contingencies and r 15 gave the other members certain express rights to expel a member for conduct 'detrimental to the interests of the Association'.

Having first become a member of the association and then taken an assignment of the lease, Mr Langan served the notice of 29 August 1980 which gave rise to the present proceedings. I now turn to consider the legal position.

Section 3(1) of the 1967 Act, so far as material for present purposes, states as follows:

> 'In this Part of this Act "long tenancy" means, subject to the provisions of this section, a tenancy granted for a term of years certain exceeding twenty-one years,

whether or not the tenancy is (or may become) terminable before the end of that term by notice given by or to the tenant or by re-entry, forfeiture or otherwise, and includes a tenancy for a term fixed by law under a grant with a covenant or obligation for perpetual renewal unless it is a tenancy by sub-demise from one which is not a long tenancy...'

There then follow certain provisos to the subsection to which I need not refer, since it has not been suggested that they assist the determination of the question now before the court.

The judge dealt with this question succinctly in the following passage of his judgment:

'Certainly this is, on the face of it, a tenancy granted for a term of years exceeding 21 years. But is it for a term of years certain exceeding 21 years? It is a lease which will cease if it becomes vested in somebody who is not a member of the association. Mr Langan is of course a member of the association. However improbable it may seem, it would appear that, according to the rules of the association, he might be expelled from the association. Although the requirement so far as he is concerned if he were to desire to part with his interest is that he should only part with it to a member of the association, he might, I suppose, purport not so to do. But the words which I have read indicate that what one has to consider when one is considering whether one is dealing with a long tenancy is whether it is granted for a term of years certain exceeding 21 years whether or not the tenancy is or may become terminable before the end of that term by notice given by or to the tenant or by re-entry, forfeiture or otherwise. This is, as I understand the terms of the lease, a lease for a term of years certain exceeding 21 years which may become terminable in certain circumstances, which I have already indicated. I think for myself that, so far as question 2(a) is concerned, which is whether or not the relevant lease is on its true construction a long tenancy within the meaning of s 3(1), that question must be answered in the affirmative.'

The first ground on which counsel, for the plaintiff attacks this part of the judgment is that the term under the lease held by Mr Langan is not a 'term of years certain' within the meaning of s 3(1) of the 1967 Act. In these circumstances, in his submission, it is unnecessary to consider whether the lease was one of a term 'exceeding twenty-one years' or whether the tenancy was or might become 'terminable' in the manner mentioned in the subsection.

For the purpose of this submission the crucial word is 'certain'. The 1967 Act contains no definition of this word, but counsel for the plaintiff submits that useful guidance to its construction is to be found in s 205(1)(xxvii) of the Law of Property Act 1925, which, for the purposes of that Act, defines 'term of years absolute' as meaning:

'a term of years (taking effect either in possession or in reversion whether or not at a rent) with or without impeachment for waste, subject or not to another legal estate, and either certain or liable to determination by notice, re-entry, operation of law, or by a provision for cesser on redemption, or in any other event (other than the dropping of a life, or the determination of a determinable life interest); but does not include any term of years determinable with life or lives or with the cesser of a determinable life interest, nor, if created after the commencement of this Act, a term of years which is not expressed to take effect in possession within twenty-one years after the creation thereof where required by this Act to take effect within that period; and in this definition the expression "term of years" includes a term for less than a year, or for a year or years and a fraction of a year or from year to year.'

The wording of this particular definition thus indicates a clear dichotomy between a term of years which is 'certain' and one which is 'liable to determination by notice, re-entry, operation of law, or by a provision for cesser on redemption, or in any other event ...' A term of years which falls into the latter category was clearly not regarded as 'certain' by the draftsman of the latter Act.

Counsel for the plaintiff submits by analogy that the habendum to the lease by its very words defines a term of years of uncertain rather than certain duration, because it expressly provides for the term to cease before 24 June 2063 if the lease (otherwise than by death or bankruptcy) ceases to be vested in a member of the association. He points out that having regard to r 12 and 15 of the association's rules, as they subsisted at the grant of the lease, there were a number of contingencies in which the lessee could thereafter cease to be a member of the association. In these circumstances, he submits that Mr Langan cannot say that he has a 'tenancy granted for a term of years certain exceeding twenty-one years', that Mr Langan thus fails at this first hurdle and that it is unnecessary to consider the remaining words of the subsection.

This submission, though attractive in its simplicity, is not in my judgment well founded. No doubt, if the phrase 'for a term of years certain exceeding twenty-one years' stood alone in the subsection, there would be much to be said for the view that a tenancy could not qualify unless the term must of necessity last for more than 21 years. In my opinion, however, one cannot properly attempt to construe and apply this phrase in isolation from the second limb of the definition (beginning with the words 'whether or not . . .') which immediately follows and qualifies it. In my opinion, it is obvious that the purpose which the legislature intended to achieve by the addition of the second limb was to make it clear that a term which would *otherwise* qualify as a 'term of years certain exceeding twenty-one years' shall not fail to qualify *merely* because the tenancy is or may become terminable before the end of that term in the manner mentioned. Thus, in my opinion, the legislature in s 3(1) was attributing to the phrase 'term of years certain' a sense quite different from the sense in which it was used in s 205(1)(xxvii) of the Law of Property Act 1925.

In the present case, Mr Langan points out that, but for the provision in the habendum to the lease which brings the term to an end if it ceases to be vested in a member of the association (otherwise than by death or bankruptcy), the term would indisputably be a term of years certain exceeding 21 years enduring until 24 June 2063. He submits that the only effect of the last-mentioned provision is to render the tenancy 'terminable before the end of that term . . . otherwise', within the meaning of the subsection. In these circumstances he submits that, having regard to the second limb of the subsection, this provision does not cause his term to fail to qualify as a 'term of years certain exceeding twenty-one years'.

In my judgment this submission is well founded. Counsel for the plaintiff sought to counter it, first, by submitting that the word 'terminable' in s 3(1) of the 1967 Act means no more than 'capable of being terminated by the act of one or more of the parties to the lease or their successors in title'. In this context he invoked one of the alternative definitions of the word 'terminable' to be found in the *Shorter Oxford English Dictionary*: 'Capable of being or liable to be terminated'.

He cited *Orman Bros Ltd v Greenbaum* [1954] 3 All ER 731 at 732, [1954] 1 WLR 1520 at 1522, in which Devlin J had to construe the word 'terminated' in s 24(1) of the Landlord and Tenant Act 1954 (which provides that a tenancy to which Pt II of that Act applies shall not come to an end unless 'terminated in accordance with this Part of this Act') and construed it as referring to the instrument or act which was the terminating factor and not to the effluxion of time. That was, however, a decision on the particular wording of a subsection which, as Devlin J pointed out, appeared to draw a distinction between a tenancy 'coming to an end' and a tenancy being 'terminated'. I therefore find the decision of little assistance in the present case. Nor do I derive much assistance from the dictionary definition of the word 'terminable'. The same dictionary shows that the word 'terminate' is capable of bearing a transitive or intransitive meaning, according to the context. The word 'terminable' in my opinion can likewise bear a transitive or intransitive meaning (or both meanings at once) according to the context. It is interesting to note that the word 'determination' clearly bears both a transitive and an intransitive sense in s 205(1)(xxvii) of the Law of Property Act 1925.

For these reasons, I cannot accept that the word 'terminable' in s 3(1), when read in isolation, prima facie bears the exclusively transitive sense attributed to it by counsel for the plaintiff. To discover its proper meaning in its context, one has in my opinion to study the immediately succeeding words of the subsection.

Counsel for the plaintiff proceeded to submit that, in these succeeding words, the phrase 'or otherwise' must be construed ejusdem generis with re-entry and forfeiture and is not apt to include the mere happening of an event (as opposed to the act of an interested party) on which the lease is limited to determine. He submitted that the common characteristic possessed by re-entry and forfeiture, which constitutes them a 'genus', is that each involves an act by one or more of the parties to the relevant lease or their respective successors in title, which has the effect of ending the lease.

I was initially attracted by this submission but am not in the end convinced by it. If re-entry and forfeiture can properly be said to constitute a 'genus' at all, then that genus can in my opinion only comprise acts of *the landlord* which bring the lease to an end; acts of the tenant which have this effect are of an essentially different category. It is, however, difficult to think of acts of the landlord which could bring the lease to an end without involving a re-entry or forfeiture. In these circumstances, it seems to me that the words 'or otherwise' must have been intended to refer to acts or events *other than* acts by the landlord, which would have the effect of bringing the lease to an end before the expiration of the maximum stated duration of the term. Accordingly the words 'or otherwise' are in my opinion apt to include, and do include, the happening of any event on which the lease is limited to determine before such expiration.

This conclusion is I think fortified when one considers the probable intentions of the legislature. Let it be supposed that the habendum to the lease in the present case had been drafted so as to express the term as one enduring until 24 June 2063 (simpliciter), but the lease had then contained a covenant by the lessee to the effect that the benefit of the lease should at all time remain vested in a member of the association, and had given the lessors an express right of re-entry if this covenant were broken. On these hypothetical facts, the rights of the lessee against the lessors (statute apart) would for practical purposes have been the same as they are now; yet I would have thought it clear almost beyond argument that the tenancy would have constituted a 'long tenancy' within the relevant statutory definition. It hardly seems likely to have been the intention of the legislature that the substantive rights of the tenant should be drastically affected by drafting points of this nature.

Anomalies of this kind are avoided if one attributes to the word 'terminable' in the context of s 3(1) a both transitive and intransitive sense, which I think it is well capable of bearing, and to the word 'otherwise' a sense wide enough to include the happening of an event on which the lease is limited to determine, before the expiration of the maximum stated duration of its term, which again I think the word is well capable of bearing.

If, as I think, this is the correct meaning to attribute to the succeeding words which qualify the phrase 'term of years certain exceeding twenty-one years', it may fairly be asked: what is the force of the word 'certain' in that phrase? On this footing, is not the word 'certain' otiose? I accept that this construction of the succeeding words does involve attributing to the phrase something other than its natural meaning, which is I conceive a fixed term that must *of necessity* last longer than 21 years. Nevertheless, I think that the draftsman of the subsection has made plain his intention that the phrase should bear a somewhat artificial sense, extended beyond its natural meaning, just as the draftsman of s 205(1)(xxvii) of the 1925 Act made clear his intention that the phrase 'term of years absolute' might include a tenancy which was neither a 'term of years' nor 'absolute', according to the ordinary meaning of words (for example, a monthly tenancy liable to forfeiture on non-payment of rent). In my judgment, the word 'certain' need not be regarded as otiose, even if the definition of a 'long tenancy' in s 3(1) of the 1967 Act is capable of including a lease such as that in the present case. For the word serves to make it plain that a tenancy will not fall within this definition unless *a fixed maximum duration of the term* has been specified. It thus makes it clear that a tenancy from year to year is not included within the definition, even though it is well capable of lasting for more than 21 years and is a 'term of years absolute', within the definition of that phrase already cited.

Furthermore, the word 'certain' makes it clear that, in calculating the length of the term
a for which a tenancy has been granted, for the purposes of s 3(1) an option to take a tenancy for a further term is to be disregarded; sub-s (4) contains special provisions covering tenancies granted with a covenant or obligation for renewal. The word 'certain' thus does still serve a purpose.

Counsel for the plaintiff referred to *Roberts v Church Comrs for England* [1971] 3 All ER 703 at 706, [1972] 1 QB 278 at 284, where Russell LJ suggested a test for determining
b whether a tenant can bring himself within the statutory definition:

> '... to fulfil the definition a tenant must at some point of time be, or have been, in a position to say that, subject to options to determine, rights of re-entry and so forth, he is entitled to remain tenant for the next 21 years ...'

Mr Langan is in my opinion in a position to say that, subject to a premature
c termination of the term occurring through his ceasing to be a member of the association or purporting to assign it to a person who is not a member or through other events entitling the lessors to forfeit the lease, he is entitled to remain tenant for more than the next 21 years. This in my judgment suffices to bring his tenancy within s 3(1).

For these reasons I think that the judge reached the correct conclusion on question (a) raised by the summons and I would dismiss this appeal.

d

OLIVER LJ. This appeal raises a short but interesting point on the construction of s 3(1) of the Leasehold Reform Act 1967, an Act which is described in its long title as one 'to enable tenants of houses held on long leases at low rents to acquire the freehold or an extended lease'. Section 1(1) confers the right to acquire the freehold or an extended lease on a tenant of a leasehold house which he occupies as his residence where, inter alia, 'his
e tenancy is a long tenancy at a low rent'. 'Long tenancy' is defined by s 3(1) as—

> 'a tenancy granted for a term of years certain exceeding twenty-one years, whether or not the tenancy is (or may become) terminable before the end of that term by notice given by or to the tenant or by re-entry, forfeiture or otherwise ...'

The three critical words of this definition in the context of the instant case are 'certain',
f 'terminable' and 'otherwise'.

I need not repeat the facts which have already been set out in the judgment of Slade LJ. As he there mentions, the habendum of the relevant lease is, so far as material, in these terms:

> '... TO HOLD the premises from the 17th day of November One thousand nine hundred and sixty-nine until the twenty-fourth day of June Two thousand and
> g sixty-three or until this Lease shall cease (otherwise than by death or bankruptcy) to be vested in a Member of the Association (whichever shall be the earlier) ...'

There is a covenant in the sub-underlease prohibiting assignment to anyone other than a member of the association and the document includes the usual proviso for re-entry on breach of covenant. The only other relevant document for present purposes consists of
h the rules of the association in force at the date of the grant of the sub-underlease. Rule 10 requires a member on being notified by the committee of the association within one month to enter into an agreement in respect of a house and r 11 enables a member before being required to enter into such agreement to withdraw from the association on giving three months' notice.

The circumstances in which a member may cease to be a member are dealt with in
j r 12 and are (i) failing to enter into an agreement when required under r 10, (ii) failing to subscribe and pay for loan stock in accordance with r 18, (iii) withdrawal under r 11, (iv) expulsion under r 15, (v) determination of the agreement entered into under r 10, (vi) death, (vii) cessation of membership of a joint member.

The provisions of r 18 require loan stock to be taken up before entering into an agreement and the non-assignment clause in the sub-underlease provides for assignment of any loan stock vested in the assigning member to the assignee member.

Rule 15 is concerned with expulsion, which is effected by resolution in general meeting and effectively is limited to expulsion for conduct detrimental to the interests a
of the association.

Relating these rules to the habendum, effectively the only circumstances in which the term can come to an end prematurely are expulsion and, possibly, purported assignment to a non-member. Death and bankruptcy are expressly excluded as relevant and cessation of membership by determination of agreement involves the lease having been brought to an end in any event, it being an agreement within the meaning of the rules. b

The other grounds for cessation of membership in r 12 are grounds which, relating as they do to events leading up to the grant of a lease, must have ceased to be applicable once the lease has been granted.

The primary submission of counsel for the plaintiff is that a term of x years or so long as the lease remains vested in a member of the association, whichever is the shorter, is not a term of years 'certain' within the meaning of s 3(1) of the 1967 Act. c

He points out that in s 205(1)(xxvii) of the Law of Property Act 1925, which defines a term of years absolute, a distinction is drawn between a term of years 'certain' and a term of years 'liable to determination by notice etc'. But, as Mr Langan points out, that subsection is concerned with the definition of what is a term of years absolute (ie a legal estate under the 1925 Act). Counsel for the plaintiff has drawn our attention to the following passage from the judgment of Russell LJ in *Roberts v Church Comrs for England* d
[1971] 3 All ER 703 at 706, [1972] 1 QB 278 at 284:

> 'In the course of the argument I ventured to suggest a test, which is that to fulfil the definition a tenant must at some point of time be, or have been, in a position to say that, subject to options to determine, rights of re-entry and so forth, he is entitled to remain tenant for the next 21 years, whether at law or in equity.'

e

Speaking for myself, however, I do not derive much guidance from this in the very different context of the instant case, for it begs the question that has to be decided here in the qualification 'subject to options to determine, rights of re-entry and so forth'. In effect, as it seems to me, the lease creates a term of years determinable on failure of a condition, namely that it shall remain vested in a member of the association, and counsel's construction would, as it seems to me, lead to the conclusion not merely that there was f
no term certain but that the lease did not even create a legal estate (see *Lace v Chantler* [1944] 1 All ER 305, [1944] KB 368).

His argument, if valid at all, must in any event rest on the proposition that a term of years determinable before the expiration of the time for which it is limited is 'certain' within the meaning of the subsection only if its termination can be brought about in certain limited ways, which he broadly defines as 'acts of the parties'. Thus, the argument g
runs, 'terminable' is used not in the sense of 'liable to come to an end' but in the sense of 'liable to be terminated' and the section goes on to exemplify ways in which this may occur: notice, re-entry or forfeiture.

Now it is true that these methods of termination are all acts which are in the control of one or other party to the lease and from this counsel for the plaintiff seeks to deduce two consequences, which are in fact interrelated. The first is the construction mentioned h
above which he attributes to the word 'terminable' and the second, which really follows from the first, is that the word 'otherwise' falls to be construed ejusdem generis with what has gone before, the genus being, as he contends, an act of one or other party to the lease and not an event limited by the lease itself as one on which the term will determine. I find myself unimpressed by either of these points. 'Terminable', as it seems to me, is a word which is applicable equally to a liability to be determined as to a liability to j
terminate or come to an end. Nor do I find it easy to ascribe any identifiable genus to notice, re-entry or forfeiture. If, indeed, one has to look for an act of a party to the lease, one in fact finds it, as Mr Langan has pointed out. An assignment to a non-member can only be at the instance of the tenant himself, and expulsion can be effected only by the association. Counsel for the plaintiff meets the latter point by suggesting the possibility

of the association assigning the leasehold reversion and thus ceasing to be the landlord. I am unimpressed by this. 'The Association' is defined by the lease as including the successors in title not to 'the landlord' but to the association and the clear contemplation, as it seems to me, is that the reversion is to remain vested in some body that is a housing association and that the sub-underlease will remain vested in that body.

Despite the clear and able argument of counsel for the plaintiff, I remain unconvinced that the judge came to the wrong conclusion. For the reasons given above and for those stated in the judgment of Slade LJ, I agree that the appeal should be dismissed.

Appeal dismissed. Leave to appeal to the House of Lords refused.

Solicitors: *Peake & Co* (for the plaintiff).

Mary Rose Plummer Barrister.

Lloyd and others v Wright
Dawson v Wright

COURT OF APPEAL, CIVIL DIVISION
EVELEIGH AND DUNN LJJ
26, 27 JANUARY, 23 FEBRUARY 1983

Arbitration – Continuation of proceedings – Continuation after commencement of court proceedings – Dispute referred to arbitration – Writ subsequently issued in High Court by claimant in arbitration seeking substantially same relief – Step taken in court proceedings after arbitrator giving directions to respondent in arbitration proceedings – Claimant in arbitration proceedings applying for court order requiring respondent to comply with arbitrator's directions – Whether application could be entertained – Whether arbitration proceedings terminated as soon as step taken in court proceedings.

In 1982 the appellant and the respondents submitted to arbitration five disputes which had arisen between them. Then, on 20 August 1982, the respondents issued a writ against the appellant in the High Court seeking substantially the same relief as they claimed in the arbitration proceedings. On 7 October the arbitrator consolidated the five arbitrations, gave directions to the appellant regarding discovery of documents and fixed 4 January 1983 as the date for the hearing. On 28 October 1982 the appellant applied to have the High Court proceedings stayed, but, on 25 November, he withdrew the application. With the consent of all the parties an order was made extending, until 20 December, the time for the service of the appellant's defence. On 26 November an application by the respondents for an order requiring the appellant to comply with the arbitrator's directions of 7 October came before a master of the Supreme Court. He dismissed the application on the ground that as the court was already seised of the dispute no order could be made in respect of the arbitration proceedings as the arbitrator was by then functus officio. The respondents notified the appellant that they intended to appeal against the master's decision but, on 17 December, they discontinued the High Court proceedings. On 20 December a judge allowed the respondents' appeal against the master's decision. The appellant appealed to the Court of Appeal, asking that the master's decision be restored. He contended that, since it was the practice of the courts to assume paramount jurisdiction over disputes which were submitted to the courts and to arbitration, the arbitration proceedings had been terminated once the writ in the High Court proceedings had been issued and a step in the action taken, and accordingly that the master had had no power on 26 November to order him to comply with the arbitrator's directions. a

Held – The arbitration proceedings had not ceased to exist once the jurisdiction of the High Court had been invoked and a step in the action taken. The two sets of proceedings continued concurrently, but while the action subsisted it had to be taken into account in deciding what steps, if any, were to be taken in the arbitration proceedings. So long as the court was seised of the dispute the arbitrator could not make an effective award b without the consent of the parties, but he could give directions and, if he did, the parties were bound to comply with them. It followed that the appeal would be dismissed because the master had had power on 26 November to order the appellant to comply with the arbitrator's directions of 7 October and the judge had accordingly been right to allow the respondent's appeal (see p 974 *c* to *e* and p 975 *a* to *e*, post).

Doleman & Sons v Ossett Corp [1912] 3 KB 257 explained. c

Tradax Internacional SA v Cerrahogullari TAS, The M Eregli [1981] 3 All ER 344 considered.

Observations on the relationship between court proceedings and arbitration proceedings (see p 972 *f* to *h* and p 975 *e*, post).

Notes d

For arbitration proceedings as ousting the court's jurisdiction, see 2 Halsbury's Laws (4th edn) paras 555–557, and for cases on the subject, see 3 Digest (Reissue) 57–62, *305–332*.

Cases referred to in judgments

Doleman & Sons v Ossett Corp [1912] 3 KB 257, CA.

SL Sethia Liners v Naviagro Maritime Corp, The Kostas Melas [1981] 1 Lloyd's Rep 18. e

Tradax Internacional SA v Cerrahogullari TAS, The M Eregli [1981] 3 All ER 344.

Cases also cited

City Centre Properties (ITC Pensions) Ltd v Tersons Ltd [1969] 2 All ER 1121, sub nom *City Centre Properties (ITC Pensions) Ltd v Matthew Hall & Co Ltd* [1969] 1 WLR 772, CA. f

Heyman v Darwins Ltd [1942] 1 All ER 337, [1942] AC 356, HL.

Kaye (P & M) Ltd v Hosier & Dickinson Ltd [1972] 1 All ER 121, [1972] 1 WLR 146, HL.

Rederi Kommanditselskaabet Merc-Scandia IV v Couniniotis SA, The Mercanaut [1980] 2 Lloyd's Rep 183.

Vawdrey v Simpson [1896] 1 Ch 166.

g

Interlocutory appeal

Ian McDonald Wright appealed against the judgment of Drake J given on 20 December 1982 whereby he held that Master Grant had erred in deciding on 26 November 1982, on hearing an application by the respondents, Hugh Richard Rowland Meirion Lloyd, John Jeremy Howorth, Timothy Workman, Malcolm John Tanner, Jeremy Nicholas Dawson and David Anthony Kempton, for an order that the appellant comply with h certain directions given by the arbitrator in arbitration proceedings between the parties, that the arbitration proceedings could not be the subject of any further directions and that the arbitrator was functus officio. The facts are set out in the judgment of Eveleigh LJ.

Esyr Lewis QC and *David H J G Powell* for the appellant. j

Anthony Scrivener QC and *Ian Croxford* for the respondents Lloyd, Howorth, Workman, Tanner and Kempston.

David Ritchie for the respondent Dawson.

Cur adv vult

23 February. The following judgments were delivered.

EVELEIGH LJ. The appellant is the senior partner in a firm of solicitors. The respondents are the other partners. Disputes between the appellant and his partners led to five submissions to arbitration. On 7 October 1982 the arbitrator made orders in the arbitrations. He consolidated all five. He ordered the appellant within 21 days to serve lists of documents, and to give further and better particulars of defences in the fourth and fifth arbitrations. The respondents were also required to serve lists of documents. On 20 August 1982 the respondents served on the appellant a writ with a statement of claim in which they claimed an order for the dissolution of the partnership. For the purposes of this judgment I can assume that the statement of claim was a repetition of the points of claim in the arbitration, although the respondents would, if necessary, argue that there were minor differences. There were further claims for relief in the arbitrations in addition to a claim for dissolution, but again for the purposes of my judgment I attach no significance to this.

On 28 October the appellant took out a summons to stay the action. On 25 November before Master Gowers the appellant withdrew his application and, with the consent of all parties, an order was made extending the appellant's time to serve his defence until Monday, 20 December; but on 17 December the respondents discontinued the Chancery action. Before that, however, the following matters occurred. As a result of summonses issued on 12 and 19 November, the parties appeared before Master Grant on 26 November. He refused the respondents' application for an order compelling the appellant to comply with the directions of the arbitrator made on 7 October, on the grounds that, as an action had been commenced in which a step had been taken, the arbitrator was functus officio in accordance with the decision of the Court of Appeal in *Doleman & Sons v Ossett Corp* [1912] 3 KB 257. On 20 December Drake J allowed an appeal against Master Grant's decision. The appellant now asks that the decision of the master be restored.

By the first ground of appeal it is submitted that the judge erred in law in holding that the steps taken by the respondents in applying before Master Gowers for an order requiring the appellant to deliver a defence in the Chancery proceedings did not amount to an election not to proceed with the arbitration proceedings. This argument was advanced before the judge on another basis also, namely that the respondents expressly or by inference repudiated the arbitration agreement and the appellant accepted such repudiation. Before us, this ground has not been pursued with enthusiasm. The respondents had commenced their action as they were in doubt whether the arbitrator had power to order a dissolution in addition to the other relief asked for in the arbitration proceedings. They did not make their intentions clear. However, it is apparent that on 7 October all the parties were accepting that the arbitration was still alive, for, in addition to the other directions given by the arbitrator on that date, a date for hearing, namely 4 January 1983, was fixed. Furthermore, after the hearing on 25 November, when all parties were aware that the summons before Master Grant was to be heard the following day, there was an argument between counsel after the hearing before Master Gowers whether or not the arbitrator was functus officio. I agree with the judge that the respondents had not repudiated the arbitration proceedings or elected to abandon them.

By his second ground the appellant submits that, on the authority of *Doleman & Sons v Ossett Corp*, the issue of the writ followed by a step in the action brought the arbitration proceedings to an end. This argument was also put in another form, namely that it is the practice of the courts to assume paramount jurisdiction over disputes submitted simultaneously to them and to arbitration.

In *Doleman*'s case the contract between the parties contained a provision for reference to arbitration to a named arbitrator who should be competent to enter on the subject matter of disputes between the parties without formal reference or notice to the parties. Subsequently to the commencement of the respondents' action claiming damages, the arbitrator, without giving notice to the parties and without the knowledge or consent of the respondents, made an award purporting to decide the matters which were the subject

of the action. The appellant pleaded this award in bar to the respondents' claim in the action. It was held that it was not competent for the arbitrator to determine the matters a
in question pending the action, and therefore the award was no bar. Counsel for the appellant referred to the judgment of Fletcher Moulton LJ, where he said ([1912] 3 KB 257 at 269):

> 'If the Court has refused to stay an action, or if the defendant has abstained from asking it to do so, the Court has seisin of the dispute, and it is by its decision, and by its decision alone, that the rights of the parties are settled. It follows, therefore, that b
> in the latter case the private tribunal, if it has ever come into existence, is functus officio, unless the parties agree de novo that the dispute shall be tried by arbitration, as in the case where they agree that the action itself shall be referred. There cannot be two tribunals each with the jurisdiction to insist on deciding the rights of the parties and to compel them to accept its decision. To my mind this is clearly involved in the proposition that the Courts will not allow their jurisdiction to be c
> ousted. Their jurisdiction is to hear and decide the matters of the action, and for a private tribunal to take that decision out of their hands, and decide the questions itself, is a clear ouster of jurisdiction. Therefore to hold that the private tribunal is still effective after the dispute has come before the Court would be to say that, in all cases in which s. 4 of the Arbitration Act, 1889, applies, the defendant may still force on an arbitration and, by obtaining an award from the arbitrators, oust the d
> jurisdiction of the Courts to decide the question they have in hand. In each case where the Court has decided that it will retain in its own hands the decision of the case, there would thus be a race between it and a private tribunal which should be the first to give a decision in the matter. The learned judge has decided that, if during the pendency of the action an award is obtained from the arbitrator, it can be pleaded in bar to the action, or, in other words, the decision of the arbitrator, and e
> not that of the Court, decides the rights of the parties. If this were good law, there would in every case be the race between the public and private tribunals which I have described, and the decision of the speediest would prevail. This would be ousting the jurisdiction of the Court in a most ignominious way.'

The principle that the court will not allow its jurisdiction to be ousted is at the root of f
the appellant's argument. However, the court does not claim a monopoly in deciding disputes between parties. It does not, of its own initiative, seek to interfere when citizens have recourse to other tribunals. The court exercises its jurisdiction when appealed to. Until then, the court is not conscious of ignominy if an arbitrator decides a question with which the court is competent to deal. Furthermore, the court will not refuse to allow the subject matter of an action already begun to be referred to arbitration, if the parties so g
agree, as Fletcher Moulton LJ makes clear in the above passage. The court, however, will not permit its assistance to be denied to a party who has invoked it except by that party's consent or by its own ruling. If the defendants in *Doleman*'s case had been able to plead the award in bar, the principle thus stated would be breached. In my opinion, the judgments in *Doleman*'s case show that the court was not seeking to assert a wider principle than this. h

Referring to the Common Law Procedure Act 1854 and the Arbitration Act 1889, Fletcher Moulton LJ said (at 268):

> 'Prior to these statutable provisions the Court could not refuse to settle any such dispute which was brought before it, because it not only had the jurisdiction but also the duty to decide that dispute *if called upon so to do*.' (My emphasis.) j

It is clear that the court has no burning desire of its own to retain the settlement of a dispute in its own hands. Farwell LJ said (at 272–273):

> 'It is also clear that any binding agreement between the parties settling all the disputes raised in the action made after writ is a good defence as a plea puis darrein

continuance (now pleaded under Order xxiv.), whether such agreement is a direct settlement between the parties themselves, or made by means of a third person to whom they have referred the dispute after writ, or by means of an award made after writ in an arbitration existing before writ, if both parties subsequent to writ carry on the arbitration, and agree to an award being made notwithstanding the action. But this is because it is always open to litigants to settle their differences after writ as they please. The case is quite different if there is no such agreement after writ.'

The reference to 'an award made after writ in an arbitration existing before writ' is not intended, in my opinion, to be qualified by adding 'provided neither party has taken any further step in the action'. I take those words to refer to an award made at any time with the agreement of the parties. While Farwell LJ refers to the agreement of the parties subsequent to writ, it is significant that he envisages the arbitration as existing before writ. He clearly does not regard the arbitration as being extinguished by the writ.

Farwell LJ said (at 273):

> 'The plaintiffs cannot be deprived of their right to have recourse to the Court when the agreement is a mere agreement to refer, unless the Court makes an order to that effect under s. 4 of the Arbitration Act. They can, of course, deprive themselves of such right by their own act after writ, as for example by going on with the arbitration and obtaining an award . . .'

Again, he does not regard the arbitration as being at an end; but, of course, he makes it clear that the existence of arbitration proceedings will have no effect on the court's power to decide the question which the plaintiff asks it to decide, unless it entertains an application under s 4 of the Act.

The reference by Fletcher Moulton LJ to the private tribunal being 'functus officio' is not necessarily inconsistent with the passages which I have quoted from the judgment of Farwell LJ. Whether or not Fletcher Moulton LJ intended to say that the arbitration must be treated as being at an end, he was contemplating the position where an action was proceeding. However, I do not think that he was saying that the arbitration was dead. I regard him as saying that the arbitrator was not in a position to make an effective award without the agreement of the parties.

In *Tradax Internacional SA v Cerrahogullari TAS, The M Eregli* [1981] 3 All ER 344 there were two proceedings issued by the plaintiff charterers: a writ and an application for summary judgment under RSC Ord 14 for dispatch money, and an application for extension of time under s 27 of the Arbitration Act 1950 to validate the appointment of an arbitrator which was made out of time. The defendant submitted that the plaintiffs were barred from applying for the extension of time because the courts were already seised of their claim in an action, and they relied on *Doleman*'s case. Kerr J said (at 351):

> 'All that the case decided, I think, as correctly stated in the first paragraph of the headnote, is that, when the court is seised of a dispute in an action, an arbitrator cannot (in effect) oust the jurisdiction of the court by purporting to make a final award in a concurrent arbitration, and that any award so made cannot be a defence to the action before the court.'

He went on to say:

> 'In my view the legal position is clear. The fact that arbitration proceedings are pending between parties is clearly not in itself any ground for preventing the courts from becoming seised of the same dispute in an action. Conversely, as it seems to me, the concurrent existence of an action should not preclude an application under s 27 of the Arbitration Act 1950, to remove the time bar to a claim imposed by an arbitration clause. The contrary conclusion would be highly inconvenient and make little sense in practice. It would mean that a claimant or plaintiff would have to pursue his possible remedies consecutively instead of concurrently, perhaps even to the extent of having to discontinue his action, obtain relief under s 27, and then

start a fresh action in order to apply for summary judgment on a claim which is then no longer barred and which may be indisputably due. I think that the practice of this court shows that the formal requirements of the law do not go as far as this. Claims which are covered by an arbitration clause, but which are said to be indisputable, are nowadays frequently put forward in an arbitration, but then also pursued concurrently by an attempt to obtain summary judgment in the courts. In effect, a claimant can, and in my view should be able to, obtain an order for payment in such cases by either means, and the coexistence of both avenues towards a speedy payment of an amount which is indisputably due was recently referred to in this court by Robert Goff J in *The Kostas Melas* [1981] 1 Lloyd's Rep 18 at 27. It was there held that, as an alternative to an application for summary judgment under Ord 14 in an action, there was jurisdiction to make an interim award for an indisputable part of the claim in an arbitration; which also shows, incidentally, the misconception of the plaintiffs' first submission in the present case with which I have already dealt.'

In my judgment, therefore, it is wrong to treat the arbitration proceedings as having ceased to exist once a step was taken in the Chancery action. The existence of the action will no doubt be a relevant consideration in determining what steps shall be taken, if any, in the arbitration proceedings. Certainly an award without the consent of both parties would have no effect. We are not concerned to decide what precise orders Master Grant might have made. In my opinion, however, he did have jurisdiction to entertain the application which was before him. By the time the matter came before the judge the action had been discontinued and so no longer remained a consideration in deciding whether or not to make the order.

I therefore would dismiss this appeal.

DUNN LJ. The question of law which arises in this appeal is: what is the effect on arbitration proceedings if, during the currency of those proceedings, one of the parties to the arbitration issues a writ claiming similar relief to that claimed in the arbitration?

It was not seriously suggested in this court that the judge was wrong in holding that the issue of a writ by the respondents, coupled with an application for directions to Master Gower on 25 November 1982, constituted a repudiation of the arbitration agreement itself. What was said was that, once the respondents had taken a step in the action by applying for directions, then the court was seised of the dispute, and the arbitrator became functus officio. Thereafter the arbitration could only be revived by a further reference, so that the fact that the action was discontinued on 17 December was irrelevant because the arbitrator had been functus officio since 25 November.

This submission was based on the judgments of the majority, and in particular on certain dicta of Fletcher Moulton LJ in *Doleman & Sons v Ossett Corp* [1912] 3 KB 257. The facts in that case were very different to the facts in this appeal. In that case an action was commenced on a contract which contained an arbitration clause providing for reference of all disputes between the parties to the defendants' engineer. The defendants did not apply for a stay of the action, but the engineer, without giving notice to the parties and without the knowledge or consent of the plaintiffs, made an award purporting to decide the matters which were the subject of the action. The defendants pleaded the award in bar to the plaintiffs' claim in the action. It was held that the award was no bar to the plaintiffs' claim. In the course of his judgment, Fletcher Moulton LJ made the general observations cited by Eveleigh LJ but, like him, I do not read those observations as meaning that the arbitration was dead. I understand them to mean that, notwithstanding the existence of the arbitration, the plaintiffs had a right of recourse to the court, subject to its power to order a stay. This view is consistent with the judgment of Farwell LJ when he said (at 273):

'They [the plaintiffs] can, of course, deprive themselves of such right by their own act after writ, as for example by going on with the arbitration and obtaining an award; but, when nothing has been done by them since writ, and the only matter relied upon is an award made since writ without their knowledge or consent, under an agreement antecedent to the action, the plea is in fact and in truth a plea of the agreement, because there is no act of the plaintiffs subsequent to the writ on which reliance can be placed, and is bad.'

In the instant case, the arbitration was already in existence when the writ was issued. I ask: why, on principle, should the arbitration and the action not proceed side by side? To maintain the action is not a contempt of court (see per Vaughan Williams LJ, whose dissent did not cover this point in *Doleman*'s case [1912] 3 KB 257 at 262), and the court has ample powers to restrain further proceedings in the arbitration by an injunction, or to refuse a stay of the action if the appropriate applications are made to it. In those circumstances, there can be no question of a race between the arbitration and the court proceedings. The court retains control throughout, if it is asked to do so. In the absence of any such application and in the absence of any intervention by the court. I can see no reason why the arbitration should not continue, and so long as the arbitration continues the parties to the reference are bound to comply with the requirements of the arbitrator (see s 12(1) of the Arbitration Act 1950).

Fletcher Moulton LJ referred in *Doleman*'s case to the arbitrator becoming 'functus officio' apparently because the court was seised of the dispute. With great respect to Fletcher Moulton LJ, he must have been using that expression in a different sense to that in which it is used now. The expression 'functus officio' in relation to arbitrators is used nowadays to describe the position of an arbitrator once he has made his award. Until then he has the power and the duty to deal with any application which is made to him in the arbitration, notwithstanding the existence of a concurrent action.

The position in this case therefore was, in my judgment, that the arbitration continued notwithstanding the existence of the action, that the arbitrator was not functus officio and that this situation existed on 17 December when the action was discontinued. Thereafter, the court was no longer seised of the matter. This view of the law was the one adopted by Kerr J in *Tradax Internacional SA v Cerrahogullari TAS, The M Eregli* [1981] 3 All ER 344.

For those reasons and for the reasons given by Eveleigh LJ, I would dismiss this appeal.

Appeal dismissed.

Solicitors: *Woodroffes* (for the appellant); *Oswald Hickson Collier & Co* (for the respondents Lloyd, Howorth, Workman, Tanner and Kempton); *Collyer-Bristow* (for the respondent Dawson).

Henrietta Steinberg Barrister.

Gubay v Kington (Inspector of Taxes) a

COURT OF APPEAL, CIVIL DIVISION
SIR JOHN DONALDSON MR, DILLON LJ AND SIR DENYS BUCKLEY
23, 24 MARCH, 15 APRIL 1983

*Capital gains tax – Disposal of assets – Husband and wife – Married woman living with her
husband – Wife not resident in United Kingdom in year of assessment – Husband resident in* b
*United Kingdom for part of year of assessment – Whether husband resident in United Kingdom
'for year of assessment' – Finance Act 1965, s 45(3), Sch 7, para 20(1) – Income and Corporation
Taxes Act 1970, s 42.*

On 4 April 1972 the taxpayer's wife left the United Kingdom for the Isle of Man. The
taxpayer and his wife were not separated but the taxpayer remained in the United c
Kingdom, visiting his wife at weekends, until 28 October 1972, when he joined his wife.
From that date they lived at various places outside the United Kingdom, so that from 4
April in the case of the wife and from 28 October in the case of the taxpayer neither of
them was resident or ordinarily resident in the United Kingdom. On 7 July 1972 the
taxpayer transferred a large number of shares in a company to his wife. The taxpayer was
assessed to capital gains tax for the year 1972–73 on the gain deemed to have accrued to d
him on the disposal of the shares to his wife. The taxpayer appealed against the
assessment, claiming that the disposal did not give rise to any chargeable gain by virtue
of para 20(1)[a] of Sch 7 to the Finance Act 1965. The Revenue contended that the
taxpayer's wife was not 'living with her husband' within para 20(1) by virtue of s 45(3)[b]
of the 1965 Act, which provided that references to a 'married woman living with her
husband' were to be construed 'in accordance with section 42(1)(2)[c] of the Income and e
Corporation Taxes Act 1970'. It was common ground that by applying only s 42(1) of the
1970 Act the taxpayer's wife would be treated as living with her husband. The Revenue
however contended that, while the taxpayer's wife was not resident in the United
Kingdom for the year 1972–73, the taxpayer was, and accordingly by virtue of s 42(2)(*a*)
of the 1970 Act the taxpayer's wife was not to be treated as living with her husband for
the purpose of para 20(1) of Sch 7 to the 1965 Act. The taxpayer contended that s 42(2)(*a*) f
did not apply since the expression 'for a year of assessment' in that section meant
'throughout the year of assessment'. The Special Commissioners accepted the Revenue's
contention and dismissed the taxpayer's appeal. An appeal against their decision was
dismissed by the judge. The taxpayer appealed, contending that, in construing para 20(1)
of Sch 7 to the 1965 Act, s 42(2) of the 1970 Act had no application as it was not a
construction provision. g

Held (Sir Denys Buckley dissenting) – (1) On the true construction of s 45(3) of the 1965
Act reference was to be made to both sub-s (1) and sub-s (2) of s 42 of the 1970 Act in
order to construe references to 'a married woman living with her husband' for capital
gains tax purposes; sub-s (1) related to deemed reconciliations between certain husbands
and wives who were not in fact living together, whereas sub-s (2) related to deemed h
separations between certain husbands and wives who were living together. It followed
that a married woman was for capital gains tax purposes not to be treated as living with
her husband either if she was actually separated from him in the circumstances covered
by s 42(1)(*a*) or (*b*) or if she was to be treated as separated from him in the circumstances
covered by s 42(2)(*a*) or (*b*) (see p 982 *b* to *f* and p 984 *a* to *d*, post).

(2) In the context of fiscal legislation 'resident in the United Kingdom for a year of j
assessment' was a natural way of describing a person who had the status or quality for the

a Paragraph 20(1) is set out at p 978 *f*, post
b Section 45(3) is set out at p 978 *g*, post
c Section 42 is set out at p 978 *h* to p 979 *b*, post

purpose of liability to tax of being so resident for the year of assessment, and therefore included a person who was resident for part of the year. Furthermore, if Parliament had intended the references only to describe a person who was resident in the United Kingdom throughout the whole of a year of assessment it would have said so, as it had in s 42(2)(*b*) in relation to a person being absent from the United Kingdom throughout the period. It followed that, for tax purposes, the taxpayer had been resident in the United Kingdom for the year of assessment 1972–73 while his wife had not been so resident. Accordingly, by virtue of s 45(3) of the 1965 Act and s 42(2)(*a*) of the 1970 Act, the wife was not to be treated as living with her husband for that year, and para 20(1) of Sch 7 to the 1965 Act did not apply to the disposal of the shares. The appeal would therefore be dismissed (see p 983 *b* and *f* to *j* and p 984 *e* to *g*, post).

Notes

For the treatment of disposals between husbands and wives for capital gains tax purposes, see 5 Halsbury's Laws (4th edn) paras 126, 128, 181.

For the Finance Act 1965, s 45, Sch 7, para 20, see 34 Halsbury's Statutes (3rd edn) 916, 961.

For the Income and Corporation Taxes Act 1970, s 42, see 33 ibid 79.

With effect from 6 April 1979 s 45(3) of and para 20 of Sch 7 to the 1965 Act were replaced by ss 155(2) and 44 respectively of the Capital Gains Tax Act 1979.

Cases referred to in judgments

Inchiquin (Lord) v IRC (1948) 31 TC 125, CA.
Nugent-Head v Jacob (Inspector of Taxes) [1948] 1 All ER 414, [1948] AC 321, HL.

Cases also cited

Back (Inspector of Taxes) v Whitlock [1932] 1 KB 747, [1932] All ER Rep 241.
Elmhirst v IRC [1937] 2 All ER 349, [1937] 2 KB 551.
Levene v IRC [1928] AC 217 [1928] All ER Rep 746.
Mitchell v IRC (1951) 33 TC 53.
Neubergh v IRC [1978] STC 181.

Appeal

Albert Gubay appealed against the decision of Vinelott J ([1981] STC 721) dated 6 July 1981 dismissing his appeal by way of case stated (set out at [1981] STC 722–730) from the determination of the Commissioners for the Special Purposes of the Income Tax Acts confirming an assessment to capital gains tax for the year of assessment 1972–73 in respect of the transfer of certain shares by Mr Gubay to his wife. The facts are set out in the judgment of Sir Denys Buckley.

James Holroyd Pearce QC and *Robert Venables* for Mr Gubay.
Robert Carnwath for the Crown.

Cur adv vult

15 April. The following judgments were delivered.

SIR DENYS BUCKLEY (giving the first judgment at the invitation of Sir John Donaldson MR). This is an appeal by a taxpayer, Mr Gubay, from the dismissal by Vinelott J ([1981] STC 721) of his appeal from a decision of the Special Commissioners for Income Tax on an assessment made on him for capital gains tax for the year of assessment 1972–73. Mr Gubay had been assessed to capital gains tax for that year in a sum of £7,250,000. The Special Commissioners affirmed that assessment but in an agreed reduced sum of £1,399,965. It was from that decision that Mr Gubay appealed.

The appeal came before Vinelott J in the form of a case stated by the Special
Commissioners under the Taxes Management Act 1970, s 56. a

The facts, which were not in dispute, are set out in para 3 of the commissioners'
decision annexed to the case. They are also summarised in the judgment of the judge. I
need not set them out in any detail, but to render this judgment more easily understood
I may summarise them as follows.

Mr Gubay and his wife were both of them resident and ordinarily resident in the
United Kingdom and living together until 4 April 1972. Mrs Gubay then ceased to be b
resident or ordinarily resident in the United Kingdom and so continued throughout the
year of assessment 1972–73. She was absent from the United Kingdom throughout that
year. Mr Gubay continued to be resident or ordinarily resident in the United Kingdom
until 28 October 1972, when he left the United Kingdom and was neither resident nor
ordinarily resident there for the remainder of the year of assessment 1972–73; but
throughout the period from 4 April to 28 October 1972 he made frequent visits to Mrs c
Gubay in the Isle of Man, where she then resided. At all relevant times Mr and Mrs
Gubay were living together in the common acceptance of that expression. At all relevant
times from and after 28 October 1972 Mr Gubay was physically absent from the United
Kingdom.

On 7 July 1972 Mr Gubay transferred to his wife by way of gift 479,638 shares of
Kwik Save Discount Group Ltd. It is this disposal which gives rise to the claim to tax d
which is in question in this case.

By virtue of the Finance Act 1965, s 20(1), capital gains tax (which was a new tax
imposed for the first time by that Act and regulated by the provisions contained in Pt III
of the Act) is chargeable in respect of any capital gain accruing to a person in a year of
assessment during any part of which he is resident in the United Kingdom or during
which he is ordinarily resident in the United Kingdom. Mr Gubay was resident or e
ordinarily resident in the United Kingdom during part of the year of assessment 1972–
73 and accordingly is liable to capital gains tax in respect of the disposal in question if it
gave rise to a chargeable gain. This it did, unless the case falls within para 20(1) of Sch 7
to the 1965 Act, which provides as follows:

> 'If, in any year of assessment, and in the case of a woman who in that year of f
> assessment is a married woman living with her husband, the man disposes of an
> asset to the wife, or the wife disposes of an asset to the man, both shall be treated as
> if the asset was acquired from the one making the disposal for a consideration of
> such amount as would secure that on the disposal neither a gain or a loss would
> accrued to the one making the disposal.'

Section 45(3) of the 1965 Act provides as follows: g

> 'References in this Part of this Act to a married woman living with her husband
> should be construed in accordance with section 361(1)(2) of the Income Tax Act 1952.'

Section 361 of the Income Tax Act 1952 has been replaced in identical terms by the
Income and Corporation Taxes Act 1970, s 42, which reads thus:
h

> '(1) A married woman shall be treated for income tax purposes as living with her
> husband unless—(*a*) they are separated under an order of a court of competent
> jurisdiction, or by deed of separation, or (*b*) they are in fact separated in such
> circumstances that the separation is likely to be permanent.
>
> (2) Where a married woman is living with her husband and either—(*a*) one of
> them is, and one of them is not, resident in the United Kingdom for a year of j
> assessment, or (*b*) both of them are resident in the United Kingdom for a year of
> assessment, but one of them is, and one of them is not, absent from the United
> Kingdom throughout that year, the same consequences shall follow for income tax
> purposes as would have followed if, throughout that year of assessment, they had
> been in fact separated in such circumstances that the separation was likely to be

permanent: Provided that, where this subsection applies and the net aggregate amount of income tax falling to be borne by the husband and the wife for the year is greater than it would have been but for the provisions of this subsection, the Board shall cause such relief to be given (by the reduction of such assessments on the husband or the wife or the repayment of such tax paid (by deduction or otherwise) by the husband or the wife as the Board may direct) as will reduce the said net aggregate amount by the amount of the excess.'

Neither para (*a*) nor para (*b*) of sub-s (1) of that section is applicable to the circumstances of the present case. Consequently, subject to sub-s (2), if it is applicable, Mrs Gubay was a married woman living with her husband in the year of assessment 1972–73. That section is imported by s 45(3) of the 1965 Act into Pt III of that Act for purposes of construction only, that is for interpreting references in Pt III to 'a married woman living with her husband'. Section 42(1) is not in conventional form a definition clause but it does make clear in what circumstances a woman is to be regarded for income tax purposes as living with her husband. Section 42(2) is couched in different terms. It first postulates that the woman in question is a married woman living with her husband and goes on to provide that in two distinct contingencies set out in paras (*a*) and (*b*) of the subsection certain consequences shall follow for income tax purposes, viz the same consequences as would have followed if the the case had fallen within sub-s (1)(*b*).

Mr Gubay was permitted by leave of this court to amend his notice of appeal so as to introduce an additional ground of appeal to the effect that, in construing para 20 of Sch 7 to the 1965 Act, s 42(2) of the 1970 Act (formerly s 361 of the 1952 Act) has no application as it is not a construction provision and as its effect is to ensure that certain consequences shall flow in certain circumstances for income tax purposes, but not for capital gains tax purposes. The point was not taken before the judge.

Section 361 of the 1952 Act (like its successor s 42 of the 1970 Act) comprised only two subsections. The language of the proviso, I think, makes clear that that proviso forms part of sub-s (2). Accordingly, the reference in s 42(3) of the 1965 Act to 'section 361(1)(2)' of the 1952 Act is a reference to the whole of that section. What reason can the draftsman have had for specifically mentioning the two subsections? No doubt a court of construction, when attempting to construe a reference to 'a married woman living with her husband' in Pt III of the 1965 Act, must look not merely at sub-s (1) of s 361 of the 1952 Act or of s 42 of the 1970 Act, but also at sub-s (2) to see what guidance he can obtain from the whole section; but, if sub-s (2) affords no guidance on construction, the court can, in my judgment, have no alternative to treating the reference to sub-s (2) as surplusage. Having regard to the express reference to sub-s (2) one should, no doubt, make a valiant effort to find some guidance in sub-s (2). As I have already remarked, the subsection postulates that in any case to which it applies the lady in question is a married woman living with her husband. The subsection enacts that, notwithstanding that fact, she shall in some circumstances be treated for certain fiscal purposes as though she were not a married woman living with her husband. So read and understood, and I can see no other way of reading it or understanding it, the subsection, in my judgment, gives no guidance or assistance as to how the expression 'a married woman living with her husband' is to be interpreted. It follows that, in my judgment, no part of s 42(2) has any bearing on the present case. So the primary proposition of s 42 that a married woman shall be treated as living with her husband remains in unabated force in the instant case and Mrs Gubay was at all relevant times to be treated as a married woman living with her husband.

I turn now to para 20(1) of Sch 7 to the 1965 Act. In the court below counsel for Mr Gubay submitted that on the true construction of this clumsy sentence the words 'and in the case of a woman who in that year of assessment is a married woman living with her husband' are applicable only to a case in which the disponor is the wife. Counsel has not pursued that argument in this court and, in my view rightly, has conceded that the words in question are operative whether the disponor be the husband or the wife. If the

conclusion which I have reached about the way in which s 42 of the 1970 Act operates in this case is correct, the condition contained in the words in para 20(1) now under a
consideration is satisfied and the disposal must be treated as having been made for a consideration of such an amount that the disponor makes neither a gain nor a loss on the disposal in question. So, if my conclusion on s 42 is correct, this appeal succeeds. I should, however, consider what the outcome of this appeal should be if my conclusion on s 42 is not correct. This involves considering the words in s 42(2):

> 'Where a married woman is living with her husband and either—(*a*) one of them b
> is, and one of them is not, resident in the United Kingdom for a year of assessment, or (*b*) both of them are resident in the United Kingdom for a year of assessment, but one of them is, and one of them is not, absent from the United Kingdom throughout that year'

and particularly the words '*for* a year of assessment'. Counsel for Mr Gubay contends that c
these words should be interpreted as meaning 'throughout' or 'for the whole of' a year of assessment. Counsel for the Crown on the other hand submits that the words mean 'for the purposes of' or 'in respect of', and that they apply in any case in which a propositus is amenable to United Kingdom tax legislation by reason of residence in the United Kingdom during any part of a relevant year of assessment.

The expression 'resident for' some particular period is not, I think, a term of art in d
income tax or capital gains tax legislation. It must be construed in any particular context in that context, and may have different significations in different contexts. I consequently do not get any assistance for present purposes from language used in charging provisions in the relevant statutes under which a person who has been resident in the United Kingdom during part only of a year of assessment is chargeable to tax on his income or chargeable gains accruing during the whole of that year. Section 42 of the 1970 Act is concerned with e
the circumstances in which the incomes of a husband and a wife should be aggregated. The policy of the group of sections dealing with this subject seems to be that the incomes should be aggregated so long as the parties are married and 'living together'. One would expect that aggregation would cease so soon as the husband and wife should cease to be 'living together'. Under s 42(1), if a formal separation takes place, the wife is thereupon no longer to be treated as living with the husband (see s 42(1)(*a*)). If no formal separation takes f
place but the parties are in fact living separately in such circumstances that the separation is likely to be permanent, the parties are no longer to be treated as living together (see s 42(1)(*b*)). Section 42(2) equates with this last situation the situations described in s 42(2)(*a*) and (*b*). It seems to me that Parliament by using the language of s 42(2) must have had in contemplation a significant interruption of the parties living together in an untechnical sense of that expression. g

As I understand the Crown's argument, if either the husband or the wife were resident for tax purposes in the United Kingdom for any part of a year of assessment, however small, and the other were not so resident for any part of that year, s 42(2)(*a*) would apply; and, if each of them were resident for tax purposes in the United Kingdom for some part, however small, of a year of assessment but one of them were physically absent from the United Kingdom throughout (ie during the whole of) that year whereas the other of them h
was 'not absent from the United Kingdom throughout that year', s 42(2)(*b*) would apply. On the facts Mrs Gubay was not resident in the United Kingdom for any part of the assessment year 1972–73 but Mr Gubay was so from 6 April 1972 to 28 October 1972. Consequently, according to the Crown's argument, Mrs Gubay was not, but Mr Gubay was resident in the United Kingdom 'for' the assessment year 1972–73 within the meaning of s 42(2)(*a*). The result would have been the same if Mr Gubay had ceased to be resident in j
the United Kingdom on 7 April 1972, although there might in that case have been no significant interruption in the parties living together.

On Mr Gubay's argument, on the other hand, s 42(2)(*a*) would only have applied if, contrary to the facts, Mr Gubay had been resident in the United Kingdom throughout the assessment year 1972–73 and Mrs Gubay had, as was the case, not been resident in the

United Kingdom during any part of that year; in other words, s 42(2)(*a*) could only apply
a if the facts were such that one of the parties was resident in the United Kingdom whereas the other was resident out of the United Kingdom for at least twelve months, so that there must have been at least a year's interruption of the parties actually living together.

A person may be resident in the United Kingdom for tax purposes during all or part of a year of assessment notwithstanding that he or she may be physically absent from the United Kingdom during all or some part of that period. Section 42(2)(*b*) of the 1970 Act
b can apply only if one or other of a married couple, who are living together and both of whom are resident in the United Kingdom 'for a year of assessment', is absent from the United Kingdom throughout that year and the other of them is not absent from the United Kingdom throughout that year. Mrs Gubay was not physically present in the United Kingdom at any time during the year of assessment 1972–73; nor was she resident or ordinarily resident in the United Kingdom at any time after 4 April 1972, that is at any
c time during the year of assessment 1972–73. So, whether Mr Gubay was or was not resident in the United Kingdom 'for' that year of assessment, s 42(2)(*b*) cannot apply to the present case because Mrs Gubay was not resident in the United Kingdom at any time during that year. But let me suppose for the sake of argument that Mrs Gubay, although she was physically absent from the United Kingdom for the whole of the assessment year 1972–73, had remained technically resident in the United Kindom until 7 April 1972 or
d until 5 April 1973 for tax purposes. In neither of these cases could s 42(2)(*b*) apply because Mr Gubay was not absent from the United Kingdom throughout the assessment year 1972–73. The expression 'is not absent from the United Kingdom throughout that year' is an equivocal one, capable of meaning either 'is present in the United Kingdom during at least some part of that year' or 'is throughout that year in a state of not being absent from (ie of being present in) the United Kingdom'. The words 'and one of them is not absent
e from the United Kingdom throughout that year' cannot, in my judgment, seriously be supposed to be capable of applying to a case in which the party in question was absent from the United Kingdom for 364 days of the relevant year but not the 365th. If the subsection were susceptible of that meaning the married couple in question might fall to be treated as if throughout the year in question they were in fact separated in such circumstances that the separation was likely to be permanent, notwithstanding that they might have spent
f 364 days of that year in matrimonial harmony outside the United Kingdom.

Although the question what construction of s 42(2)(*b*) should be preferred does not arise for decision in this case, I am inclined to think that the latter of the two suggested constructions (ie Mr Gubay's) is to be preferred. If so, s 42(2)(*b*) must require the husband and wife to be physically separated throughout the year in question in such a way that there would be a significant interruption in their living together. Consequently, although
g the expression 'for a year of assessment' and 'throughout' that year are both used in s 42(2), I do not regard this as significant. The draftsman seems to have regarded the one form of words as appropriate to residence and the other as appropriate to absence, but I find it hard to suggest why. These considerations relating to s 42(2)(*b*) do not appear to me to help to discover how the expression 'for a year of assessment' should be construed in s 42(2)(*a*).

For the reasons which I have given earlier in this judgment I prefer Mr Gubay's
h construction of s 42(2)(*a*) to that of the Crown.

Accordingly, in my judgment, this appeal succeeds either for the reasons I have given earlier for regarding s 42(2) as mere surplusage for the purpose of construing the expression 'a married woman living with her husband' or, if I am wrong about that, for the later reasons set out in this judgment.

I would allow this appeal.

j

DILLON LJ. The appellant, Mr Gubay, has taken two points on this appeal.

The first point, taken by leave of this court and not argued in either of the lower courts, is that as s 45(3) of the Finance Act 1965 merely provides that 'References . . . to a married woman living with her husband should be construed in accordance with section 361(1)(2) of the Income Tax Act 1952' (now s 42(1)(2) of the Income and Corporation Taxes Act

1970) the effect is merely to import s 361(1), now s 42(1), into the capital gains tax legislation and not s 361(2), now s 42(2). *a*

The second point is that if s 42(2) is applicable at all then it only applies where one of the spouses is resident in the United Kingdom for the whole of a year of assessment, from 6 April to the following 5 April, because that is the natural meaning of the words 'resident in the United Kingdom for a year of assessment', and so it cannot apply to the year from 6 April 1972 to 5 April 1973, since neither spouse was resident in the United Kingdom for the whole of that year. *b*

As to the first point, I regret that I am unable to concur in the conclusion which Sir Denys Buckley has reached.

In s 45(3) of the 1965 Act Parliament has, in clear terms, imported into the capital gains tax legislation both sub-ss (1) and (2) of s 361 of the 1952 Act, now s 42 of the 1970 Act, which were originally only concerned with income tax. In my judgment this must involve a greater reliance on sub-s (2) than merely looking at it to see that it is not concerned with *c* construction and therefore disregarding it altogether.

Section 42(1) provides that a married woman shall be treated for income tax purposes as living with her husband unless they are separated in the circumstances indicated in paras (*a*) and (*b*). It is common ground that those circumstances did not apply to Mr and Mrs Gubay. Subsection (2) then provides that in certain other circumstances indicated in paras (*a*) and (*b*) the same consequences shall follow for income tax purposes as would have *d* followed if they had been separated in circumstances in effect within sub-s (1)(*b*). The effect of this is that in the given circumstances they are to be deemed for tax purposes to be separated and not living together. Since therefore s 45(3) of the 1965 Act expressly refers to sub-s (2) as well as sub-s (1) of s 361, now s 42, I have for my part no doubt that a married woman is for capital gains tax purposes not to be treated as living with her husband if either she is actually separated from him in the circumstances covered by para (*a*) or para *e* (*b*) of sub-s (1) of s 42 or she is to be treated for tax purposes as separated from him in the circumstances covered by para (*a*) or para (*b*) of sub-s (2) of s 42. I do not think that this conclusion places any undue weight on the word 'construed' in s 45(3). I would therefore reject this point taken by Mr Gubay.

I turn to the second question, namely whether in para (*a*) of sub-s (2) the phrase 'resident in the United Kingdom for a year of assessment' means resident throughout the whole *f* year from 6 April to the following 5 April, or means resident for tax purposes for the year, i e resident in any part of the year.

We are told that the original statutory predecessor of s 42 was introduced to change and clarify the law in the light of the decision of the House of Lords in *Nugent-Head v Jacob (Inspector of Taxes)* [1948] 1 All ER 414, [1948] AC 321. That information does not, however, help very much since that was a case where both the spouses were resident in the *g* United Kingdom for a year of assessment, but one of them was and one of them was not, absent from the United Kingdom throughout that year. That is the case now covered by para (*b*) of sub-s (2) of s 42 and it therefore does not indicate why it was thought desirable to include para (*a*) in the enactment as well. One may conjecture that the draftsman, having in mind to deal with a de facto situation where both spouses were resident in the United Kingdom but one was absent, thought it logical to deal also with the situation *h* where one was resident and one was not but that conjecture does not cast much light on the meaning of 'resident for a year of assessment'.

It is conceded by the Crown that the term 'resident in the United Kingdom for a year of assessment' is not a term of art in tax law. Because of this I have not found any assistance in citations where these or similar words happen to have been used in judgments or statutory provisions concerned with other aspects of tax law. In particular I have not found *j* any help in *Lord Inchiquin v IRC* (1948) 31 TC 125, where the statutory provision under consideration was concerned with any person who could prove that 'for any year he is resident in the Irish Free State and is not resident in Great Britain or Northern Ireland'.

Counsel for Mr Gubay contends that the phrase in sub-s (2) 'resident in the United Kingdom for a year of assessment' means resident for the whole year. So far as para (*a*) is concerned, this, whether correct or not, is an intelligible conception in relation to the spouse who is resident in the United Kingdom. But it raises an ambiguity as to the spouse who is not resident in the United Kingdom for the whole year of assessment. Is it sufficient, to satisfy para (*a*), if that spouse was resident in the United Kingdom for a part of the year in question but not resident for the whole year, or does that spouse have to have been non-resident for the whole year? On the natural meaning of the words, I would adopt the former alternative, viz that it is enough if one is resident for part of the year but non-resident for the rest of the year. That would however give a bizarre result in relation to Mr and Mrs Gubay in that (i) they would not be assessed separately for the year of assessment from 6 April 1972 to 5 April 1973 since neither of them was resident in the United Kingdom for the whole of that year, but (ii) they would be assessed separately, as spouses separated from each other, for the year of assessment from 6 April 1971 to 5 April 1972 because, though Mr Gubay was resident in the United Kingdom throughout the whole of that year, Mrs Gubay was only resident for a part of the year, viz from 6 April 1971 to 4 April 1972.

If, contrary to my preferred view, not resident in the United Kingdom for a year of assessment means non-resident throughout the whole year, there would still be possible anomalies. Paragraph (*a*) would not apply at all unless there was a year of assessment throughout which one spouse was resident and one was continually non-resident (eg if Mrs Gubay had gone abroad on 4 April 1971 instead of 4 April 1972). But, even if para (*a*) did apply for one year of assessment, it would cease to apply for the following year if, for example the spouse who had been resident ceased to be resident in the course of the following year of assessment as Mr Gubay did in October 1972. Thus, on assumed facts that Mrs Gubay ceased to be resident on 4 April 1971 but Mr Gubay remained resident until October 1972, their incomes, though assessed separately for the year of assessment from 6 April 1971 to 5 April 1972 would have been aggregated for tax purposes for the year of assessment from 6 April 1972 to 5 April 1973 since neither was resident in the United Kingdom throughout the whole of that year.

These difficulties and anomalies are, in my judgment, avoided by the construction for which the Crown contends, viz that resident for the year of assessment means resident for tax purposes for that year, ie resident for any part of the year. The contention can be rephrased in various ways, eg resident in relation to the year or in respect of the year. The object of such paraphrasing is, of course, to bring out and underline the differences between the rival contentions, each of which is said by its proponent to be the sole natural meaning of the simple wording used in the statute, not to suggest that either contention requires an alteration of the wording actually used in the statute.

I agree with Vinelott J that in the context of a fiscal statute the expression 'resident in the United Kingdom for a year of assessment' is a natural way of describing a person who has the status or quality for the purposes of liability to tax of being so resident for the year of assessment. It therefore includes the person resident for part of the year. If the draftsman had intended by these words only to describe a person who was resident in the United Kingdom throughout the whole of the year of assessment, he would naturally have said 'resident in the United Kingdom throughout the year of assessment' both in para (*a*) and in para (*b*) of sub-s (2), just as in para (*b*) he referred to a person being absent from the United Kingdom throughout the year.

For these reasons, albeit with no little hesitation as Sir Denys Buckley takes a different view on both points, I would dismiss this appeal.

SIR JOHN DONALDSON MR. I would dismiss this appeal, but since we are divided I will express my reasons in my own words, albeit briefly, the facts and arguments having been deployed in the judgments of my brethren.

Section 45(3) of the Finance Act 1965

The essence of the interpretation of statutes is an earnest seeking after the intention of Parliament or perhaps, more accurately, the deemed intention of Parliament. Parliament or perhaps, sometimes more accurately, parliamentary counsel make the task more difficult on some occasions than on others as this appeal well illustrates. A reference to 'section 361(1)(2) of the Income Tax Act 1952' invites the reaction that there must have been a typographical omission between '(1)' and '(2)', and when you discover that the section has only two subsections the mystery deepens. The explanation, which in my judgment has in the end to be accepted, is that Parliament's instruction was to construe the phrase 'a married woman living with her husband' in accordance with both sub-ss (1) and (2), but not to take account of the proviso which contains a direction to the Board to grant a statutory concession in the circumstances contemplated by sub-s (2). There is a measure of logic in this approach, since the fact that the proviso does or does not apply has no obvious bearing on who is to be considered as 'a married woman living with her husband'.

Whilst I appreciate that the two subsections employ different phraseology, I am not convinced that sub-s (1) is more of an interpretation provision than sub-s (2). The difference stems, I think, from the fact that sub-s (1) is designed to produce a deemed reconciliation between certain husbands and wives who are not in fact living together, whereas sub-s (2) is designed to produce a deemed separation between certain husbands and wives who are so living. Whether this be right or wrong, the mandate contained in s 45(3) of the 1965 Act seems to me to be clear: for capital gains tax purposes the concept of a married woman living with her husband has to accord with both sub-s (1) and sub-s (2) of s 361 of the 1952 Act, now s 42 of the Income and Corporation Taxes Act 1970.

Section 42(2) of the 1970 Act

Like Dillon LJ I have not derived any assistance from the authorities cited to us, save to note with interest that para (*b*) was probably introduced as a result of the unusual circumstances revealed in *Nugent-Head v Jacob (Inspector of Taxes)* [1948] 1 All ER 414, [1948] AC 321. Nor have I derived any assistance from citations from statutory provisions concerned with other aspects of tax law.

Being resident in the United Kingdom may be a status or a fact. Where it is a status, it is something which is either enjoyed (if that be the right word) or not enjoyed for a whole tax year, subject perhaps to an exception in the case of a woman who marries and ceases to be resident on her wedding day. Where it is a fact, residence can be for the whole or any fraction of a tax year.

If the statute was intended to refer to factual residence, I should have expected it to make it clear whether residence or non-residence was required for the whole or only part of a year, particularly since the draftsman has used appropriate words, 'throughout that year of assessment', where the factual length of absence was material. I therefore have no doubt that what is referred to is status as a resident or, as the case may be, non-resident for fiscal purposes in relation to a particular year of assessment.

Appeal dismissed. Leave to appeal to the House of Lords granted.

Solicitors: *Rooks Rider & Co* (for Mr Gubay); *Solicitor of Inland Revenue.*

Edwina Epstein Barrister.

a

Adsett v West

QUEEN'S BENCH DIVISION
McCULLOUGH J
20, 21, 24, 25, 26, 27 JANUARY, 18 FEBRUARY 1983

Fatal accident – Damages – Loss of future earnings – Survival of claim for benefit of estate –
b *Deceased a single man of 26 without dependants – Deceased having close friendship with girl before death – Assessment of surplus available after deduction of living expenses from earnings – Basis of assessment where deceased a single man without dependants – Whether prospect of marriage to be taken into account in assessing surplus – Law Reform (Miscellaneous Provisions) Act 1934, s 1.*

c *Fatal accident – Damages – Loss of investment income – Survival of claim for benefit of estate – Deceased a single man of 26 without dependants – Deceased having income from investments – Whether loss of investment income to be assessed on same basis as loss of future earnings – Approach to be taken where capital still producing income after death of deceased – Whether award of damages to be balanced against gain from investment income on year by year basis or whether to be balanced at date of award – Law Reform (Miscellaneous Provisions) Act 1934, s 1.*

d

Fatal accident – Damages – Loss of prospect of inheritance – Survival of claim for benefit of estate – Deceased a single man of 26 without dependants – Deceased likely to inherit capital on death of father – Whether loss of inheritance to be taken into account when assessing surplus – Law Reform (Miscellaneous Provisions) Act 1934, s 1.

e The deceased was a single man of 26 when he was killed in a motor accident as a result of the admitted negligence of the defendant. The deceased was the only son of the plaintiff, who was a successful businessman. The deceased was in partnership with the plaintiff and before his death had a substantial income consisting partly of his earnings from his work in the family business and partly of income from capital investments. He was also likely to inherit a considerable amount of capital on the death of the plaintiff. The
f plaintiff brought an action under s 1[a] of the Law Reform (Miscellaneous Provisions) Act 1934 claiming, inter alia, damages (i) for loss of the deceased's anticipated earnings during the lost years, (ii) for loss of income from the capital of which he died possessed and (iii) for loss of income from such further capital as he would have been likely to inherit. The plaintiff contended that, in assessing the amount of damages to be awarded, the deceased was to be treated as a married man, since he had had a close friendship with a girl whom
g he was likely to have married in the near future.

Held – (1) It was well established that in a claim under the 1934 Act the deceased's estate was entitled to damages on account of his anticipated earnings in the lost years, but that loss was not to be awarded in full since the cost of the deceased's own living expenses and pleasures were to be deducted from his earnings before arriving at a surplus as a basis for
h the calculation of damages. Furthermore, where the court was considering a claim for the lost years in respect of a single man (particularly if he was without dependants), the surplus would be very much smaller than that of a married man since, without a wife or children to provide for, most of a single man's income would be devoted to his own maintenance and enjoyment and all that would remain would be that which he either would have saved or would have spent on or given to others (see p 988 *a* to *d* and *j* to
j p 989 *c*, post); *Pickett v British Rail Engineering Ltd* [1979] 1 All ER 774 and *Gammell v Wilson* [1981] 1 All ER 578 considered.

(2) The surplus was to be calculated on the assumption that the deceased would have

---

a Section 1, so far as material, is set out at p 996 *b*, post

remained single during the lost years, except in so far as there were compelling reasons
to do otherwise. While each case depended on its own facts, it was to be borne in mind a
that a single man's surplus was generally treated as a low percentage of lost income. Any
increase to take account of the likelihood that the deceased would have married would
be very modest, having regard to the fact that to predict the financial circumstances of
the deceased in the event of his marriage would involve a high degree of speculation (see
p 992 *j* to p 993 *g*, p 994 *g h* and p 995 *h*, post); *Pickett v British Rail Engineering Ltd* [1979]
1 All ER 774, *Kandalla v British Airways Board* [1980] 1 All ER 341, *Gammell v Wilson* b
[1981] 1 All ER 578 and *White v London Transport Executive* [1982] 1 All ER 410
considered.

(3) When calculating damages for loss of income in the lost years, earned income was
to be distinguished from income yielded from capital of which the deceased died
possessed because, whereas the deceased's earning capacity died with him, his capital and
its ability to yield income survived. Where the deceased died possessed of both an earning c
capacity and capital, the damages, if any, to be awarded for loss of the surplus in the lost
years would only be such as would be required to provide for the balance of his surplus
over the income yielded by the capital which survived him. Further, since the award of
damages was to be made in one sum, the court had to strike a balance once and for all,
rather than year by year, and any excess of such investment income over the surplus in
one year was to be used to offset any deficiency in another year (see p 996 *j*, p 997 *a b d* d
and p 1000 *b* to *g*, post); *Skelton v Collins* (1966) 115 CLR 94, *Pickett v British Rail Engineering
Ltd* [1979] 1 All ER 774, *Kandalla v British Airways Board* [1980] 1 All ER 341 and *Gammell
v Wilson* [1981] 1 All ER 578 considered.

(4) Since there was no difference in principle between the loss of the prospect of
earnings from work in the lost years and the loss of the prospect of income from an
inheritance likely to be acquired, the loss of the prospect of the inheritance would be e
taken into account with moderation (see p 1000 *j* to p 1001 *b* and *f* to *j*, post).

(5) On the assumption that the deceased was to be regarded as a single man throughout
the lost years the appropriate surplus during that period was 15%. However, in all the
circumstances it was proper to increase the surplus to 25% to take account of the
likelihood that the deceased would have married. That would have resulted in a total
award for loss of surplus in the lost years of £31,800. However, since the income during f
the lost years yielded by the capital of which the deceased died possessed was to be valued,
by an equivalent calculation, at £44,698, there would be no award for loss of surplus in
the lost years and the only damages to be awarded would be for funeral expenses and loss
of expectation of life (see p 1003 *h j*, p 1004 *c* to *h* and p 1005 *a*, post).

Notes

For damages for loss of future earnings under the Law Reform (Miscellaneous Provisions) g
Act 1934, s 1, see 12 Halsbury's Laws (4th edn) para 1154.

For the Law Reform (Miscellaneous Provisions) Act 1934, s 1, see 13 Halsbury's Statutes
(3rd edn) 115.

By virtue of the Administration of Justice Act 1982, s 4(2), as from 1 January 1983
s 1(2)(*a*) of the 1934 Act was substituted, with the result that any damages recoverable h
for the benefit of a deceased person's estate shall not include any damages for loss of
income in respect of any period after that person's death.

Cases referred to in judgment

Ashley v Vickers (1983) Times, 18 January.
Benham v Gambling [1941] 1 All ER 7, [1941] AC 157, HL. j
Benson v Biggs Wall & Co Ltd (1980) [1982] 3 All ER 300.
Cattle v Stockton Waterworks Co (1875) LR 10 QB 453, [1874–80] All ER Rep 220, DC.
Clay v Pooler [1982] 3 All ER 570.
Gammell v Wilson, Furness v B & S Massey Ltd [1981] 1 All ER 578, [1982] AC 27, [1981] 2
WLR 248, HL; *affg* [1980] 2 All ER 557, [1982] AC 27, [1980] 3 WLR 591, CA.
Harris v Empress Motors Ltd [1982] 3 All ER 306, [1983] 1 WLR 65.

Kandalla v British Airways Board (formerly British European Airways Corp) [1980] 1 All ER
a 341, [1981] QB 158, [1980] 2 WLR 730.
Lawrence v John Laing Ltd (5 May 1982, unreported), QBD.
Liesbosch, Dredger (owners) v SS Edison (owners) [1933] AC 449, [1933] All ER Rep 144, HL.
Pickett v British Rail Engineering Ltd [1979] 1 All ER 774, [1980] AC 136, [1978] 3 WLR 955, HL.
b *Rooke v Higgins and Stevenson* (4 July 1980, unreported), QBD.
Skelton v Collins (1966) 115 CLR 94, Aust HC.
Solomon v D & A Transport Ltd (26 February 1981, unreported), QBD.
White v London Transport Executive [1982] 1 All ER 410, [1982] QB 489, [1982] 2 WLR 791.
Willshire v Gardner (6 December 1979, unreported), QBD.

c

Action

The plaintiff, Stanley Arthur Adsett, as administrator of the estate of Richard Stanley Adsett deceased issued a writ against the defendant, Ian Edward West, claiming damages for the benefit of the deceased's estate under the Law Reform (Miscellaneous Provisions) Act 1934 in respect of injuries resulting in the death of the deceased when he was
d involved in a road accident as a result of the defendant's admitted negligence. The facts are set out in the judgment.

Anthony Machin QC and *Christopher Sumner* for the plaintiff.
Piers Ashworth QC and *Andrew Prynne* for the defendant.

e *Cur adv vult*

18 February. The following judgment was delivered.

McCULLOUGH J. The plaintiff is the administrator of the estate of Richard Stanley
f Adsett, his only son, who was killed in a road traffic accident on 8 March 1980 as a result of the admitted negligence of the defendant. The action is brought for the benefit of his estate under the Law Reform (Miscellaneous Provisions) Act 1934.

Richard Adsett was 26, unmarried and without dependants. No claim is made under the Fatal Accidents Act 1976. There is a claim for funeral expenses of £399·34 (which is admitted) and for loss of expectation of life for which I award the conventional sum of
g £1,250.

The plaintiff is a successful businessman and from the age of 17 Richard Adsett worked in one or other of his three businesses, each of which was run as a partnership. Over the years Richard Adsett acquired a capital share in each partnership. His not inconsiderable income derived in part from his work and in part from this investment. It is said that had he lived his father would have been likely to pass to him, either in his lifetime or on
h his death, his own much larger share in the two businesses which survive.

Although not engaged to be married, he had a close friendship with a Miss Pope, who was a year or two younger and it is possible that they would have married. Richard Adsett spent a good deal of time with her and must have spent a certain amount of money on her. He had various other interests, mostly sporting and these took much of his income.

j The case is unusual in that it calls for a decision not just as to the damages to be awarded on account of the deceased's inability to earn money by working in the 'lost' years but whether any, and if so what, damages are to be awarded on account of his inability to enjoy the interest on the capital which he had already acquired in his lifetime and on such further capital as he might have acquired from his father.

There are other issues. Some are fact and figures. The principles on which damages in cases of this type should be assessed are the subject of contention in three respects in particular: (a) what is the correct interpretation to be put on the word 'surplus' which is used in *Pickett v British Rail Engineering Ltd* [1979] 1 All ER 774, [1980] AC 136 and a *Gammell v Wilson, Furness v B & S Massey Ltd* [1981] 1 All ER 578, [1982] AC 27; (b) what is the relevance of the degree of probability that the deceased would have married; and (c) when does a matter for legitimate forecasting on the basis of probabilities shade into something involving a degree of speculation which the court ought not to embark on?

It is well established that in a case such as this the deceased's estate is entitled to damages on account of the loss of his earnings in the 'lost' years. This loss is not to be b awarded in full. There must be deducted a sum to represent what was variously described in the House of Lords in *Pickett v British Rail Engineering Ltd* [1979] 1 All ER 774 at 782, 784, 798, 792, [1980] AC 136 at 151, 154, 171, 163 as the victim's 'living expenses' (per Lord Wilberforce, Lord Salmon and Lord Scarman) and as 'the total sum which [he] would have been likely to expend on himself' (per Lord Edmund-Davies) and in *Gammell v Wilson* [1981] 1 All ER 578 at 583, 588, 593, [1982] AC 27 at 65, 71, 78 as 'the amount c he would have spent . . . on his own living expenses and pleasures' (per Lord Diplock), 'the cost of maintaining himself' (per Lord Fraser) and 'the cost of his living at a standard which his job and career prospects at the time of death would suggest he was reasonably likely to achieve' (per Lord Scarman).

There can be no doubt that the cost of the victim's pleasures must also be deducted. This follows from the decision in *Furness v B & S Massey Ltd.* Although Lord Diplock d was alone in referring to the victim's pleasures (see [1981] 1 All ER 578 at 583, [1982] AC 27 at 65), Tudor Evans J had at first instance deducted what he estimated the deceased would have spent both in maintaining himself and on enjoying life and in the House of Lords he was held to have made no error of principle (see [1981] 1 All ER 578 at 587, 588, 594–595, [1982] AC 27 at 71, 72, 80 per Lord Edmund-Davies, Lord Fraser and Lord Scarman). e

Nor I think can it any longer be doubted that, in the case of a married man with dependants, the calculation is to be made according to the same principles as would apply to a claim under the Fatal Accidents Act 1976: see *Benson v Biggs Wall & Co Ltd* (1980) [1982] 3 All ER 300 per Peter Pain J, *Clay v Pooler* [1982] 3 All ER 570 per Hodgson J, *Harris v Empress Motors Ltd* [1982] 3 All ER 306, [1983] 1 WLR 65 per McCowan J and *Lawrence v John Laing Ltd* (5 February 1982, unreported) per Cantley J. f

Mr B A Hytner QC sitting as a deputy judge in the Queen's Bench Division in *Gammell v Wilson* had said:

> 'What then has to be considered where a man has dependants? It seems to be, as in Fatal Accidents Act cases, the net earnings after tax and the sum, as it were, saved by the death. In practical terms this means those sums spent solely by the deceased on himself, whereas sums spent on the family—such as rent, rates and so on—are g not deducted from the net wage. However personal living expenses, that is: his own food, clothing and entertainment are deducted.'

(See *Kemp and Kemp on the Quantum of Damages* vol 1, para 26–004 at p 26009.) Mr Hytner's judgment came under close scrutiny both in the Court of Appeal and the House of Lords and, although these remarks were not essential to his decision, it seems unlikely h that none of the eight judges who read them would have said so had they believed them to be wrong. Megaw LJ (whose dissent was on a different and more fundamental point) took the same view as Mr Hytner and said that he had made no error of principle (see [1980] 2 All ER 557 at 567–568, [1982] AC 27 at 40–41). Brandon LJ agreed in terms (see [1980] 2 All ER 557 at 570, [1982] AC 27 at 44). Lord Fraser said the same and Lord Scarman said that he had directed himself correctly in law (see [1981] 1 All ER 578 at j 588, 594, [1982] AC 27 at 72, 79). His assessment was upheld by all eight judges.

In general the bulk of a married man's income benefits his dependants and the proportion spent for his own benefit alone is small. In the case of the ordinary wage earner the customary calculations and estimations which have been made for many years in Fatal Accidents Acts cases generally reveal that the deceased would have spent only

about a quarter or a third of his income on himself alone. If it be right (and it generally
a is) to assume that any money he would have saved would have been for the benefit of his dependants as much as his, the element of savings will be part of the dependency. These, as I understand them, are the reasons why the 'surplus' for Law Reform Act purposes will in the case of a married man generally be the same as the dependency for Fatal Accidents Acts purposes and will usually be of the order of two-thirds or three-quarters.

Where, however, the court is considering a 'lost years' claim in respect of a single man
b (particularly if he is without dependants) the 'surplus' will be very much smaller because the cost of maintaining his house, like the cost of his food, clothes, motoring, holidays and other pleasures, must first be deducted. All that will remain will be that which would have been saved and that which he would have spent on, or given to, others. Even then there is room for argument whether the full amount of these sums should be regarded as 'surplus'; if a young man takes a girl out for the evening is not this a pleasure,
c and if he saves for his retirement is he not, to an extent at least, setting aside money for his future living expenses?

These considerations demonstrate why in the present case counsel for the plaintiff submits that I ought to treat as 'surplus' whatever the deceased spent on his girlfriend, and why counsel for the defendant submits that much of it should not be so regarded. There is a similar difference between them over the approach which I should adopt to
d such income as he would have been likely to leave in the business over and above that which he would have been likely to draw out.

But the major and much the most important difference between the parties is, understandably, over the assumption which I should make whether or not he would have married. Counsel for the plaintiff invites me to hold he probably would have married Miss Pope in the summer of 1981 and that, for the reasons I have already given,
e I should find that there would have been a 'surplus' of two-thirds or three-quarters. Counsel for the defendant submits that the question is conjectural, that the assumption should not be made and that decided cases establish that I should not make it. He relies in addition on the statements of principle to the effect that the damages to be awarded in this type of case should be moderate and he points to the generally low level of awards which have been made in cases covering men who were single.

f To some extent these questions overlap and in considering the authorities it is convenient to take them together. This will involve looking at the statements of general principle in *Pickett v British Rail Engineering Ltd* and the eight cases to which my attention has been drawn which concerned unmarried victims, namely *Gammell v Wilson, Furness v B & S Massey Ltd* [1981] 1 All ER 578, [1982] AC 27, *Kandalla v British Airways Board (formerly British European Airways Corp)* [1980] 1 All ER 341, [1981] QB 158, *Willshire v*
g *Gardner* (6 December 1979, unreported) per Griffiths J, *Rooke v Higgins and Stevenson* (4 July, 1980, unreported) per Chapman J, noted in *Kemp and Kemp on the Quantum of Damages* vol 1, p 26018, *Solomon v D & A Transport Ltd* (26 February 1981, unreported) per McNeill J, noted in *Kemp and Kemp* vol 1, p 26015, *White v London Transport Executive* [1982] 1 All ER 410, [1982] QB 489 per Webster J and *Ashley v Vickers* (1983) Times, 18 January per Croom-Johnson J.

h In *Pickett v British Rail Engineering Ltd* [1979] 1 All ER 774 at 781, [1980] AC 136 at 150 Lord Wilberforce said:

'My Lords, in the case of the adult wage earner with or without dependants who sues for damages during his lifetime, I am convinced that a rule which enables the "lost years" to be taken account of comes closer to the ordinary man's expectations
j than one which limits his interest to his shortened span of life. The interest which such a man has in the earnings he might hope to make over a normal life, if not saleable in a market, has a value which can be assessed. A man who receives that assessed value would surely consider himself and be considered compensated; a man denied it would not. And I do not think that to act in this way creates insoluble problems of assessment in other cases. In that of a young child (cf *Benham v Gambling*

> [1941] 1 All ER 7, [1941] AC 157) neither present nor future earnings could enter into the matter; in the more difficult case of adolescents just embarking on the a
> process of earning (cf *Skelton* v *Collins* (1966) 115 CLR 94) the value of "lost" earnings might be real but would probably be assessable as small.'

Lord Salmon said ([1979] 1 All ER 774 at 784, [1980] AC 136 at 153–154):

> 'Damages for the loss of earnings during the "lost years" should be assessed justly and with moderation. There can be no question of these damages being fixed at any b
> conventional figure because damages for pecuniary loss, unlike damages for pain and suffering, can be naturally measured in money. The amount awarded will depend on the facts of each particular case. They may vary greatly from case to case. At one end of the scale, the claim may be made on behalf of a young child or his estate. In such a case, the lost earnings are so unpredictable and speculative that only a minimal sum could properly be awarded. At the other end of the scale, the claim c
> may be made by a man in the prime of life or, if he dies, on behalf of his estate; if he has been in good employment for years with every prospect of continuing to earn a good living until he reaches the age of retirement, after all the relevant factors have been taken into account, the damages recoverable from the defendant are likely to be substantial. The amount will, of course, vary, sometimes greatly, according to the particular facts of the case under consideration.' d

The first claim under the Law Reform (Miscellaneous Provisions) Act 1934 which called for the application of these principles was *Gammell v Wilson*, which was tried by Mr Hytner in July 1979. The facts are important; so is his judgment as a whole, because, as I have already said, his assessment of the damages was upheld both in the Court of Appeal and in the House of Lords and he was said to have made no error of principle. His judgment appears in *Kemp and Kemp* vol 1, p 26004. e

The case concerned a 15-year-old gipsy boy who had been working for a year. Prior to his death he was earning £20 per week, out of which he paid his mother £5 for his keep. He wanted to become an antique dealer and was saving up for a van. His father, who was 54, was in poor health and did not work; he had a short expectation of life. The possibility that the son would have helped his father financially in future years led Mr Hytner to assess his Fatal Accidents Act dependency at £250. Although the deputy judge recognised f
that there would have been a substantial risk of the son meeting with financial disaster if he had embarked on his intended career and that he would probably have become an itinerant worker doing a variety of unskilled labouring jobs, there was some chance of his being reasonably financially successful and he had no doubt that if his mother had fallen on hard times he would have supported her. He assessed the mother's dependency at £1,750. In reaching this figure he took account of the fact that the boy would probably g
have married and have had children of his own to keep (see p 26006).

Turning to the question of the 'lost years' he said (at p 26010):

> 'If the principle of deducting from the net wage only the living expenses solely referable to the earner himself were to be applied to this claim the sum awarded would be very considerable. The probability, as I find, is that this young man would h
> have married in his early twenties and had children. This is statistically so and there were no contra indications given in evidence to undermine it. Thus, projecting forward, it is hardly vague speculation to assume that only the smaller portion of his future earnings over the years would have been attributable to his own sole personal expenditure. Such an assessment in the case of this youth who had just embarked on his working life seems, however, to be out of line and in conflict with j
> other observations in *Pickett*, which it seems to me I ought, if possible to follow.'

He then cited the passages from the speeches of Lord Wilberforce and Lord Salmon in *Pickett v British Rail Engineering Ltd* which I have already set out and he continued (at p 26011):

> 'It is possible to reconcile the need to restore the dependants' position to a realistic

level with the clear indication given by Lord Wilberforce and Lord Salmon, that in cases such as the instant one the damages should be moderate. In my judgment the reconciliation lies in what I would call the joint expenses. In the case of a youth, unmarried at the time of his death, it seems to me that I ought initially to regard all of his true living expenses as deductible, and that I ought not to speculate at all as to whether in the lost years others might have had joint use of part of those expenses and part of the remainder. Taking a multiplier of 16 for the lost years and an overall average surplus of £8 per week over that period, which is, in fact, but a small proportion of the net national average wage and bearing in mind, as I do, that the early years weigh more heavily in the average than the later years, I assess the capital value of this claim at £6,656.'

The £8 must have included an appropriate figure to represent what the boy would have devoted to his parents' dependency on him. The remainder must have been a very small proportion indeed of what he would have been likely to earn in adult life. Even so, to one of their Lordships the award seemed high (see [1981] 1 All ER 578 at 588, [1982] AC 27 at 72 per Lord Fraser).

Since this approach was approved it must follow that the House of Lords approved the calculation of the surplus on the assumption that the boy would have remained single, despite the finding that it was probable that he would have married.

The facts of *Furness v B & S Massey Ltd* and the judgment of the trial judge, Tudor Evans J, are important for the same reasons, for, as I have already said, he too was held to have made no error of principle. Mr Furness was a 22-year-old miller who would have been earning £4,063 pa net by the date of trial. He lived at home and did not go out with girls. He had many other interests and the judge found that his pleasures probably used up a fair proportion of his income.

Both counsel agreed that the fact that he would probably have married should be disregarded when assessing the Law Reform Act claim.

The judge valued his surplus at one-third while he was at home and one-quarter thereafter. These figures must have taken account of the fact that at the date of his death he was contributing to the support of his parents and would have done so to the extent of £468 a year between the date of the trial and his leaving home. If this is taken out of the one-third, the remaining surplus in that period is reduced to rather less than one-quarter of his assumed net income, that is roughly the same proportion as in the later period.

Although the award was not upset, all four members of the House of Lords who commented on its size thought it was high (see [1981] 1 All ER 578 at 581, 588, 588, 594, [1982] AC 27 at 62, 71, 72, 80 per Lord Diplock, Lord Edmund-Davies, Lord Fraser, Lord Scarman).

Two further cases concerning single victims had been decided before *Gammell v Wilson* reached the Court of Appeal and it is convenient to consider them now. The first was *Kandalla v British Airways Board* [1980] 1 All ER 341, [1981] QB 158, in which Griffiths J decisively rejected the submission that he should assume that two female doctors of 27 and 31 would have married and that their 'surplus' would then have risen to 40% of their incomes. He said ([1980] 1 All ER 341 at 352, [1981] QB 158 at 173):

> 'If I did this it would mean that I was speculating whether they would marry, speculating whether they would have children and then awarding a sum of money the only social justification of which is to provide support for husbands and children when in fact no such dependants do or can exist. This seems to me to be an absurdity.'

In *Willshire v Gardner* (6 December 1979, unreported) Griffiths J was considering the claim of a man of 23 who died in January 1978. For two years he had been engaged to a Miss Brooker, a fully qualified midwife who gave evidence. They had planned to marry on 1 April 1978. They had both been saving and had contributed equally to a building society account. They had already bought a house in their joint names and had taken possession of it the day before the accident. The judge calculated the 'surplus' in the way

I believe he would have done had the marriage already taken place. It is significant that, while he assumed that the marriage would have taken place, he made only the smallest allowance for the fact that the couple might have had children. And this despite Miss Brooker's evidence (which there is no indication that he doubted) that they were anxious to have children as soon as they could. He said:

> 'Had children been born to them no doubt some of the money which was currently being spent on themselves would have been applied to caring for and bringing up the children. However, there is no certainty that they would have had children, although one hopes of course they would. It is therefore an unrealistic exercise to calculate the damages on the basis that they might have had children who would have needed support, when, unhappily, such an event can never take place.'

Having arrived at a figure of £21,700, he said:

> 'I increase that sum by a modest amount for the speculative possibility of children and increased earnings by the deceased. I do not think it is right, particularly in this class of case, to make any great increase and I round the figure up to £23,000.'

He then added a further £1,950 which I think must have been on account of the period between death and trial.

In the case of a married man the effect of his having children is usually to increase the dependency on him from about two-thirds to about three-quarters of his net income. This is a modest amount: about 8% of his net income.

In *Willshire v Gardner* the dependency of the deceased's wife was assumed to have been lower than it otherwise would have been because of her own earning capacity. To have children she would have had to give up work, at any rate for some time, and may only thereafter have worked part-time. Thus, in her case, had children been assumed, one would have expected them to have made a greater increase in the dependency. Griffiths J's increase of £1,300 (or £93 pa) represented only about 2% of the deceased's assumed net income of £5,600 pa, a modest increase indeed, particularly when it is remembered that it also took account of the possibility that the deceased's earnings would have increased.

This, like *Gammell v Wilson*, is another instance where an occurrence, which must have been probable, and indeed very probable, was regarded as speculative and was almost wholly discounted.

One further case was decided before *Gammell v Wilson* reached the House of Lords and, although it was not there referred to, I mention it now. This was *Rooke v Higgins*, noted in *Kemp and Kemp* vol 1, p 26018, a decision of Chapman J on 4 July 1980.

The deceased was 19; he would have become engaged in three months and would have married within two years. Counsel for the defendant, reading from a transcript of the judgment, which I have not seen, tells me that the young woman whom he would have married gave evidence and that the judge found that he had no doubt that he could accept that marriage on her eighteenth birthday in May 1978 was 'on the balance of probability pretty well a foregone conclusion'. By the date of the trial the deceased would have been earning £5,000 net pa. A post-trial multiplier of 12 was applied to £1,250 (that is to 25% of the net income) and then £5,600 was deducted for uncertainties. This would have had the effect of reducing the £1,250 to £783 pa (just over 15% of the net income). Such a figure cannot have included the cost of a house in the surplus and I can only assume that, despite his findings about the likelihood of marriage, Chapman J assessed the loss on the basis that the deceased stayed single.

When *Gammell v Wilson* and *Furness v B & S Massey Ltd* [1981] 1 All ER 578 at 593, [1982] AC 27 at 78 were heard in the House of Lords, Lord Scarman, speaking of the principles to be applied in the assessment of damages in lost years cases, said:

> 'The correct approach in law to the assessment of damages in these cases presents,

> my Lords, no difficulty, though the assessment itself often will. The principle must be that the damages should be fair compensation for the loss suffered by the deceased in his lifetime. The appellants in *Gammell*'s case were disposed to argue, by analogy with damages for loss of expectation of life, that, in the absence of cogent evidence of loss, the award should be a modest conventional sum. There is no room for a "conventional" award in a case of alleged loss of earnings of the lost years. The loss is pecuniary. As such, it must be shown, on the facts found, to be at least capable of being estimated. If sufficient facts are established to enable the court to avoid the fancies of speculation, even though not enabling it to reach mathematical certainty, the court must make the best estimate it can. In civil litigation it is the balance of probabilities which matters. In the case of a young child, the lost years of earning capacity will ordinarily be so distant that assessment is mere speculation. No estimate being possible, no award, not even a "conventional" award, should ordinarily be made. Even so, there will be exceptions: a child television star, cut short in her prime at the age of five, might have a claim; it would depend on the evidence. A teenage boy or girl, however, as in *Gammell*'s case may well be able to show either actual employment or real prospects, in either of which situation there will be an assessable claim. In the case of a young man, already in employment (as was young Mr Furness), one would expect to find evidence on which a fair estimate of loss can be made. A man, well-established in life, like Mr Pickett, will have no difficulty. But in all cases it is a matter of evidence and a reasonable estimate based on it.'

Thus there is a band of possible circumstances. At one end lie those where the making of forecasts would be pure speculation and must therefore be avoided. At the other end a fair estimate of loss can be made. In between are cases where a claim is, at any rate, assessable; *Gammell* was such a case. Where does the assessable shade into the purely speculative? The question is incapable of any more satisfactory answer than that it must be a matter for the judgment of the tribunal of fact.

In the field of personal injury litigation one quickly becomes used to making estimates of what would probably have happened had a man not been injured and what will probably happen now that he has been. His wages might have risen for one reason or another, they might have fallen for other reasons, the likelihood of which is neither more nor less capable of estimation. It may be impossible to say to what extent they would have fallen, if they had, or to what extent they would have risen, if they had. So one assumes that they would have remained the same, and goes on to consider the next set of imponderables. He may or may not develop osteo-arthritis. What are the chances? Thirty per cent. So that is built into the forecasting. If it does develop will he need an operation? If so, when? How long would he be away? What work could he do afterwards? What would he earn? And so on. It is, in a sense, all speculation; yet it is done all the time. The most complimentary description of it is a process of imprecise averaging.

Almost all of the important aspects of life can be forecast on the basis of probability: that a child will reach maturity, that he will be fit enough to work, that he will probably obtain employment, probably marry and probably have children. Where the range of options is wide resort can be had to averages, such perhaps as an 88% chance of being in employment and a national average wage of so much per year.

But, because it *can* be done, is it the sort of exercise that *should* be done in cases of this kind? This, essentially, was the question Mr Hytner asked himself in the passage which I first quoted from his judgment. Basing himself on what Lord Wilberforce and Lord Salmon had said in *Pickett* he decided not; and his approach was upheld.

I have carefully considered whether the passage which I have last cited from Lord Scarman's speech in *Gammell* requires me to adopt a less restrictive approach. I have come to the conclusion that it does not. Had Lord Scarman thought that it was unreasonable to ignore what Mr Hytner had found to be the probability of marriage, he would surely have said so. He did not; on the contrary he regarded Mr Hytner's approach as reasonable (see [1981] 1 All ER 578 at 594, [1982] AC 27 at 79).

Lord Diplock clearly regarded the exercises which both Mr Hytner and Tudor Evans J had had to conduct as containing a great deal of speculation, as the following passage a shows ([1981] 1 All ER 578 at 583, [1982] AC 27 at 65):

> 'My Lords, if the only victims of fatal accidents were middle-aged married men in steady employment living their lives according to a well-settled pattern that would have been unlikely to change if they had lived on uninjured, the assessment of damages for loss of earnings during the lost years may not involve what can only be matters of purest speculation. But, as the instant appeals demonstrate and so do b other unreported cases which have been drawn to the attention of this House, in cases where there is no such settled pattern (and this must be so in a high proportion of cases of fatal injuries) the judge is faced with a task that is so purely one of guesswork that it is not susceptible of solution by the judicial process. Guesses by different judges are likely to differ widely, yet no one can say that one is right and another wrong.' c

Lord Edmund-Davies, who perhaps came nearer to Lord Scarman in this, said ([1981] 1 All ER 578 at 588, [1982] AC 27 at 71):

> 'More cogent is the further criticism that "any assessment is at best speculative, usually pure guesswork, and where there is any basis for making a calculation such a basis is frequently unreal". It is true that the task confronting Tudor Evans J was d difficult, but, even so, there was available to him the sort of exiguous material which frequently has to be dealt with in the courts.'

Lord Fraser said ([1981] 1 All ER 578 at 588, [1982] AC 27 at 71–72):

> 'It is particularly difficult to justify the law in cases such as the present, in each of which the deceased was a young man with no established earning capacity or settled e pattern of life. In such cases it is hardly possible to make a reasonable estimate of his probable earnings during the "lost years" and it is, I think, quite impossible to take the further step of making a reasonable estimate of the free balance that would have been available above the cost of maintaining himself throughout the "lost years", and the amount of that free balance is the relevant figure for calculating damages. The process of assessing damages in such cases is so extremely uncertain that it can f hardly be dignified with the name of calculation: it is little more than speculation. Yet that is the process which the courts are obliged to carry out at present.'

Lord Russell said that what was involved in cases like *Gammell* and *Furness* was the 'almost grotesque embodiment of estimates or rather guesses' (see [1981] 1 All ER 578 at 590, [1982] AC 27 at 74). g

There are, of course, variations in emphasis in these passages. What is constant is that no member of the House thought that Mr Hytner had either departed from the spirit of *Pickett* or erred in the principles to be applied in a case where the victim had died. I regard myself as bound to adopt a similar approach, making due allowance, of course, for the fact that each case depends on its own facts.

This accords with the approach of Griffiths J in *Kandalla v British Airways Board* in h relation to the possibility of marriage and, more significantly, with his approach to the possibility of children in *Willshire v Gardner*. The same can be said of the next two cases to which I must refer.

The first is *Soloman v D & A Transport Ltd*, noted in *Kemp and Kemp* vol 1, p 26015, where McNeill J in February 1981 was considering the case of a 22-year-old driver who lived with his mother, who was dependent on him. The judge adopted a 'just and j moderate' approach and said that caution should be used. He divided the total multiplier of 16 into three periods of 2, 3 and 11 years in respect of which he assessed the 'surplus' at 40%, 30% and 20% respectively. The third period represented the time after he would have left home for marriage or other reasons. In the first two periods he was assumed to be living at home and during this time it must be assumed that the surplus would have included his mother's dependency on him.

So here again is a case where statistically there must have been a high probability of
a marriage; yet a figure of only 20% was taken. The probability must have been ignored.

In *White v London Transport Executive* [1982] 1 All ER 410, [1982] QB 489 Webster J was dealing with a claim in respect of a single man of 25. Having reviewed the speeches in detail in both *Pickett* and *Gammell* he said ([1982] 1 All ER 410 at 418, [1982] QB 489 at 499):

> 'Although it seems to me in some ways artificial to do so, for reasons I have
> *b* already given it appears that he is to be treated for this purpose as an eternally single man, on the principle, I suppose, that the money he in fact spends on his family, if he has one, or if it is likely that he will have one, is money which would be available after making provision for all the matters I have referred to, to be spent in other ways if he so desired, that is to say if he were to prefer to spend it in other ways rather than to have a family. If he is to be treated in this way it must follow that,
> *c* although the House of Lords, as I have mentioned, said that the award of damages should be moderate, his notional surplus must be large enough to cover at least a not insubstantial part of the cost of maintaining a family, for although in the case of a man in the deceased's circumstances it can be regarded as probable in normal circumstances that his wife, if he were to marry, would do some paid work from time to time, it cannot be supposed that she alone would pay for the housing and
> *d* maintenance of the children.'

Counsel for the plaintiff is critical of this passage. He submits that Webster J was wrong to treat the deceased as an eternally single man, and he submits that the judge fell into further error in equating the situation of a man who left home to live on his own with that of a man who left home to live with a wife (see [1982] 1 All ER 410 at 419,
e [1982] QB 489 at 500–501).

I do not accept these criticisms. As to the first, *Gammell* establishes that Webster J was right. The same had been done in *Rooke v Higgins* (which was cited to him) and in *Solomon v D & A Transport Ltd* (which was not cited to him), and it had been conceded (by counsel for the plaintiff) in *Furness v B & S Massey Ltd*. If this passage signifies any departure from what had gone before, it was to give rather more, not less, recognition to the factor
f of marriage by saying that it was to be borne in mind when quantifying the surplus. The second passage was not, I think, meant to be read in isolation. It comes in the middle of a section containing arithmetical calculations, not all of which I follow, and I will say no more about it.

The last case is the most recent, *Ashley v Vickers* (1983) Times, 18 January, a decision of Croom-Johnson J. It is so briefly reported that I do not think I can usefully draw any
g conclusion from it, though it is right to note that it was said that 'The prospect of marriage of the deceased had to be taken into account, as on marriage many of a bachelor's expenses were directed into supporting the wife and family'. To what extent the judge took it into account does not appear.

Having considered the authorities as a whole, I am satisfied that I must be moderate in my approach and that, because the deceased was single at the date of his death, I should
h regard him as such for the purposes of the lost years except in so far as there are compelling reasons to do otherwise. While each case depends on its own facts, it is useful to bear in mind the generally low percentages of lost income which have been treated as surpluses in the decided cases relating to single men.

I turn next to the question of what attention is to be paid to the fact that a proportion of the income which the deceased would have enjoyed in the lost years would have been
j earned by capital of which he died possessed. Counsel for the plaintiff submits that no distinction can be drawn between it and the income which he would have earned by work; he lost the opportunity to deal with and dispose of the one as much as the other. The fact that it is now in the hands of his estate, which happens to be suing in his place, is immaterial. Counsel for the defendant submits that to take it into account would be to compensate for a loss which has not occurred: the deceased is dead; his earning capacity died with him, but his capital lives on; it has been earning interest ever since, and will

continue to do so, just as if he had lived. The deceased and his estate are one and the same.

There is no authority on the point and the matter must be considered on general principles.

I start with s 1(1) of the Law Reform (Miscellaneous Provisions) Act 1934. So far as material, it says this:

> 'Subject to the provisions of this section, on the death of any person . . . all causes of action . . . vested in him shall survive . . . for the benefit of, his estate . . .'

Section 1(2) and in particular s 1(2)(*c*), which fell for consideration in *Gammell*, has, as the parties agree, no application to this question. The loss for which the plaintiff claims damages is not a 'loss' within the meaning of s 1(2)(*c*); nor are the damages he claims a 'gain'.

When counsel for the defendant says that the deceased and his estate are one and the same, he may be right, but this entices one onto dangerous ground. I have no doubt that counsel for the plaintiff is right in saying that the loss must be considered as it would have been in the assumed moments between the commission of the tort and the occurrence of death. What has to be quantified is not the loss to the estate consequent on the death: it is the loss to the deceased. It is his cause of action which survives.

Counsel for the plaintiff submits that it follows from the decisions in *Pickett* and *Gammell* that loss of investment income must be taken into account. In particular he relies on the following passages from the speech of Lord Wilberforce in *Pickett* [1979] 1 All ER 774 at 781, 780, 781, 782, [1980] AC 136 at 150, 149, 150, 151:

> 'Future earnings are of value to him in order that he may satisfy legitimate desires . . .'
>
> 'To the argument that "they are of no value because you will not be there to enjoy them" can he not reply, "Yes they are; what is of value to me is not only my opportunity to spend them enjoyably, but to use such part of them as I do not need for my dependants, or for other persons or causes which I wish to support. If I cannot do this, I have been deprived of something on which a value, a present value, can be placed"?'
>
> 'My Lords, in the case of the adult wage earner with or without dependants who sues for damages during his lifetime, I am convinced that a rule which enables the "lost years" to be taken account of comes closer to the ordinary man's expectations than one which limits his interest to his shortened span of life. The interest which such a man has in the earnings he might hope to make over a normal life, if not saleable in a market, has a value which can be assessed. A man who receives that assessed value would surely consider himself and be considered compensated; a man denied it would not.'
>
> '. . . the amount to be recovered in respect of earnings in the "lost" years should be that amount after deduction of an estimated sum to represent the victim's probable living expenses during those years. I think that this is right because the basis, in principle, for recovery lies in the interest which he has in making provision for dependants and others, and this he would do out of his surplus.'

Although Lord Wilberforce in each passage confined himself to 'earnings', all these passages, submits counsel for the plaintiff, are as true of investment income as of earned income.

To my mind there is a clear factual distinction, which the 'ordinary man' would at once appreciate, between earned income and investment income. Immediately before he dies the deceased has lost his earning capacity, but his capital remains and with it its capacity (not his) to produce investment income. All that is common to the two is that he has lost the opportunity to use each *as and when they accrue* and he has lost the enjoyment of doing so.

As I read Lord Wilberforce's remarks in the last of the passages that I cited, what he thought significant was the victim's loss of opportunity to use his earnings. In his opinion 'the basis, in principle, for recovery lies in the interest which he has in making provision for dependants and others . . .'

By dying, a man loses the opportunity to provide for his dependants and others out of future earnings from work, but he does not lose the opportunity to provide for them out of income earned by capital of which he dies possessed. This he can achieve by suitable testamentary disposition, if this is required. The only opportunity which has gone is the opportunity to change his will, or to make one if he has not done so already.

Lord Wilberforce, like Lord Salmon and Lord Edmund-Davies, referred throughout to loss of earnings, never to loss of income or loss of financial expectation. In the light of Lord Russell's dissenting opinion which dealt with financial expectations other than earnings, and of which I assume they had advance intimation, it must follow that none of the three wished his opinion to be taken as extending beyond loss of earnings.

I see nothing in Lord Wilberforce's speech which requires me to hold that the submission of counsel for the plaintiff is correct; on the contrary the indications are the other way.

Lord Salmon said that it would be grossly unjust to the plaintiff and his dependants if the law were to deprive him from recovering for the loss of his earnings during his lost years (see [1979] 1 All ER 774 at 783, [1980] AC 136 at 152). But there is no such injustice in excluding a claim of the type which counsel for the plaintiff makes here, for a man can, as I have said, provide for his dependants from the capital of which he dies possessed. It is no answer that he may devise it elsewhere; so may he his Law Reform Act damages.

Lord Salmon's conclusion was reinforced by the judgments in *Skelton v Collins* (1966) 115 CLR 94, the Australian case, and he selected for citation that part of the judgment of Windeyer J (at 129) which said that a man should be compensated for the destruction or diminution in his *capacity* to earn money (see [1979] 1 All ER 774 at 788, [1980] AC 136 at 158). The same passage appealed to and was cited by Lord Edmund-Davies (see [1979] 1 All ER 774 at 792, [1980] AC 136 at 162). I can detect nothing in the speeches of either Lord Salmon or Lord Edmund-Davies to suggest that they would not have regarded the capacity of a man's capital to earn money after his death, particularly when allied with his testamentary capacity, as constituting an important distinction.

Lord Russell, who dissented, dealt expressly with consequential problems which he foresaw in cases involving victims who had lost the opportunity to enjoy unearned income.

Counsel for the plaintiff submits that his argument is supported by this passage in Lord Russell's speech ([1979] 1 All ER 774 at 794, [1980] AC 136 at 165):

> 'I have stated the problem without confining it to earnings in the lost years. Suppose a plaintiff injured tortiously in a motoring accident, aged 25 at trial, with a resultant life expectation then of only one year. Suppose him to be life tenant of a substantial settled funds. If the lost years are to be brought into assessment of damages presumably allowance must be made for that part of the life interest which he would have received but will not receive. So also if he had a reversionary interest contingent on surviving a life in being then aged 60: he will have been deprived of the probability of the funds coming to him during the lost years. Again he might at the trial be shown to be the sole beneficiary under the will of a rich relation whose age made it probable that the testator would die during the lost years, and whose testimony at the trial was that he had no intention of altering his will. In such cases presumably an allowance in damages would require to be made for the lost, and may be valuable, spes successionis, unless the testator was an ancestor of the plaintiff and the plaintiff was likely to have children surviving him (see s 32 of the Wills Act 1837).'

I am grateful to counsel for the defendant for pointing out that the reference to s 32 of the 1837 Act should have been printed as a reference to s 33.

Counsel for the plaintiff argues that the passage indicates that Lord Russell could see no distinction between loss of private income and loss of earnings. However, as counsel for the defendant has shown, in each of the three examples chosen by Lord Russell no capital sum would pass to the estate. Hence the all-important exception of the situation *a* covered by s 33 of the 1837 Act. I infer that he specifically chose examples of this type because it never occurred to him that, even if the view of the majority were accepted, it would follow that damages might be recovered for loss of income from capital which had passed from the deceased to his estate. Contrary to counsel for the plaintiff's submission, I think that Lord Russell also supports counsel for the defendant. *b*

Lord Scarman agreed with Lord Wilberforce, Lord Salmon and Lord Edmund-Davies (see [1979] 1 All ER 774 at 795, [1980] AC 136 at 166). Dealing with what he called Lord Russell's fourth objection, namely that 'if damages are recoverable for the loss of the prospect of earnings during the lost years, must it not follow that they are also recoverable for loss of other reasonable expectations, eg a life interest or an inheritance?' he said that he did not regard this consequence as objectionable (see [1979] 1 All ER 774 at 797, *c* [1980] AC 136 at 169–170). After reciting from the *Report on Personal Injury Litigation—Assessment of Damages* ((1973) Law Com no 56, para 90) he said ([1979] 1 All ER 774 at 798, [1980] AC 136 at 170):

> 'For myself, as at present advised (for the point does not arise for decision and has not been argued), I would allow a plaintiff to recover damages for the loss of his financial expectations during the lost years provided always the loss was not too *d* remote.'

Paragraphs 90 and 91 of the report read as follows:

> '90. We are also of the opinion that, in line with the reasoning of the Australian High Court in *Skelton v. Collins*, the Plaintiff should be entitled to compensation for other kinds of economic loss referable to the lost period. A person entitled by will *e* to receive an annuity for his life would, if his life were shortened by the Defendant's fault, lose the capacity to receive the annuity during the lost period, no less than he would lose his earning capacity. There seems to be no justification in principle for discrimination between deprivation of earning capacity and deprivation of the capacity otherwise to receive economic benefits. The loss must be regarded as a loss of the Plaintiff; and it is a loss caused by the tort even though it relates to moneys *f* which the injured person will not receive because of his premature death. No question of the remoteness of damage arises other than the application of the ordinary foreseeability test.
>
> 91. A Plaintiff's income may, however, come from dividends paid on capital assets and, as these assets will themselves, subject to death duties, be able to pass, on his death, to his dependants, we consider the Court must have a discretion to ignore *g* such lost income in the lost period in its assessment of damages. (See the proviso to Clause 2(2)(b)).'

Each party seeks to interpret Lord Scarman's speech favourably to him after reference to these paragraphs. Counsel for the defendant draws attention to the fact that the words immediately before the part of para 90 which Lord Scarman cited were a further example *h* of a situation where the capital would not pass to the estate; it is therefore to be inferred that he was not contemplating a situation such as the present. For the plaintiff it is argued that, in the light of what Lord Russell had said, it is remarkable that, if Lord Scarman disagreed with para 91, he did not go on to say so. I am therefore asked to infer that he did agree with para 91. I do not think it would be right to draw either inference. What is clear is the Lord Scarman was deliberately leaving the whole question of unearned *j* financial benefits for another day.

Before leaving Lord Scarman's speech I should cite a further passage ([1979] 1 All ER 774 at 798, [1980] AC 136 at 170):

> 'The plaintiff has lost the earnings and the opportunity, which, while he was

living, he valued, of employing them as he would have thought best. Whether a
a man's ambition be to build up a fortune, to provide for his family, or to spend his
money on good causes or merely a pleasurable existence, loss of the means to do so
is a genuine financial loss. The logical and philosophical difficulties of compensating
a man for a loss arising after his death emerge only if one treats the loss as a non-
pecuniary loss, which to some extent it is. But it is also a pecuniary loss: the money
would have been his to deal with as he chose, had he lived.'

b This passage starts with a reference to loss of earnings, not to loss of financial benefits
in general, and it may well be that in it Lord Scarman was considering only loss of
earnings. But, whether this be so or not, the last sentence does not, I believe, lend the
support to counsel for the plaintiff which might at first appear. Once dead it would no
longer be open to a victim to deal as he chose with the income which accrued after his
c death from the capital of which he died possessed, but he could, before death, choose
how he wished it to be used after his death. And I note that Lord Scarman too cited the
same passage from the judgment of Windeyer J which referred to the capacity to earn
(see [1979] 1 All ER 774 at 796–797, [1980] AC 136 at 169).

There is little in the speeches in *Gammell* which touches on this part of the case. Lord
Fraser referred in passing to 'loss of earnings or other income' (see [1981] 1 All ER 578 at
d 588, [1982] AC 27 at 71), but that is all and I draw no conclusion from this. Lord Scarman
indicated that loss of an annuity ceasing on death would be recoverable (see [1981] 1 All
ER 578 at 592, [1982] AC 27 at 77). I have already said that this is another example, like
the three of Lord Russell's, where the victim would have been unable to provide in his
will how the financial benefits which he would have enjoyed had he lived were to be
used after his death. I do not regard this passage as conflicting with the view which I
e have formed, which is that there is nothing in either *Pickett* or *Gammell* which suggests
that I should accept counsel for the plaintiff's submission and that there is a good deal
which suggests I should not.

Counsel for the plaintiff submits that there is a passage in *Kandalla v British Airways
Board* [1980] 1 All ER 341 at 349, [1981] QB 158 at 169 which indicates that Griffiths J
must have been of the view which he submits is correct. It is this:

f '... consider the position of a very high earner of 38 years of age who is also
possessed of a large fortune. Suppose he is contributing £10,000 per annum to the
support of his wife and family during his lifetime and on his death leaves them an
estate of, say, £500,000. The interest on the estate is more than adequate to replace
the dependency of £10,000 per annum and so the accelerated benefit from the
estate extinguishes any Fatal Accidents Acts claim. But if the estate can bring a claim
g for the "lost years" the family will in fact recover a further large sum, say £150,000,
being 15 years purchase of £10,000 per annum. Perhaps in this illustration it will
be truer to say that the defendant will have to pay the extra £150,000 rather than
the family will recover it, for a large slice of it may be destined to the Revenue via
capital transfer tax.'

h I do not believe that in choosing the figures for the point he wanted to make, Griffiths
J was assuming that the £10,000 pa dependency was being provided by the £500,000-
worth of capital. He was speaking of a 'very high earner'. A dependency of £10,000 pa
for the wife and family of such a man is the sort of sum that one would have expected to
come from his earnings.

Finally counsel for the plaintiff relies on the fact that in claims brought under the 1934
j Act, unlike those under the Fatal Accidents Act 1976 for the benefit of dependants,
deductions for what passed from the deceased to his estate are never made when damages
are calculated. Almost anything, he argues, has a value. Take the deceased's half share in
his boat. It could have been sold and the proceeds invested in income-bearing stock.

But there is a simple answer to this. The value of the boat in such a case is not taken

into account because, at the moment before the death of the victim, it has lost none of its value. To deny that there has been a loss is not to set a gain to the estate against a loss to a
the deceased. The deceased has suffered no loss other than that of enjoying his boat, which is taken into account in the award of damages for loss of expectation of life, the £1,250.

Counsel for the plaintiff would have been on firmer ground if he had been able to show that where a man died owning a boat, or indeed a house, it was the practice for the Law Reform Act claim for the lost years to include the assumed rental value of the boat b
and the assumed rental value of the house, for these are benefits capable of evaluation in pecuniary terms which the deceased would have enjoyed in the lost years had he lived, just as much as he would have enjoyed the dividends from his shares.

The reason why all these claims do not lie, and why they have not, so far as I know, been made before this case, is the same: they involve no loss to the deceased.

Accordingly I reject the submissions of counsel for the plaintiff on this part of the case c
and in approaching the loss of income for the lost years I shall ignore the income which would have resulted from the capital which the deceased already owned at death.

This decision leads to two consequential questions. The first is best explained by illustration. Suppose that during the lost years a deceased would have earned £5,000 pa net from work and £5,000 pa net from investments and would have had a surplus of £3,000 pa. Does the £5,000 which survives extinguish the lost £3,000 pa as counsel for d
the defendant argues? Or, as counsel for the plaintiff submits, is only half to be extinguished, on the argument that his surplus would have derived (so far as one can tell) as much from his earned as from his unearned income?

In my judgment, the answer is to be obtained not by asking which part of his income enabled him to save but by considering the position of the deceased immediately before he died. He would then be deprived of his ability to earn £5,000 pa from work. And he e
would be deprived of the need for £7,000 pa to enable him to live and have his pleasures. Since £5,000 pa would remain, and since this would more than provide for his surplus, his surplus would remain intact. The tort would not have taken it away. Therefore, I conclude the £5,000 pa should be deducted in full.

The next question is: when comparing the surplus with the investment income which remains, does one strike a balance year by year or once overall, so that any excess in one f
year may be offset by a deficiency in another?

I have some to the conclusion that, since an award of damages is an award of one sum, the balance should be struck once. I see no logical reason why a gain in one year should not be used to offset a loss in another.

I come now to the final point of law in contention. What, if any, attention is to be paid to the fact that the deceased, had he lived, may have inherited some or all of his father's g
share in the two surviving partnerships?

Counsel for the plaintiff has expressly made no claim for the loss of the opportunity to inherit the capital value of these shares. He limits his claim to the loss of income which they would have produced. Nor does he make any claim in respect of any other asset which the deceased might have inherited from his father.

This presents a different problem from that which I have just been considering, h
because, whereas he had the opportunity during his lifetime to make provision after his death for his dependants and others out of the capital which he already possessed, the same is not true of the capital which he had not yet inherited.

[His Lordship then considered whether, on the pleadings, the plaintiff was entitled to rely on the evidence that he would on his death or earlier have passed his interest in the two remaining partnerships to his son, thereby substantially increasing his son's income. j
Having held that the plaintiff was entitled to pursue the issue, his Lordship continued:]

Counsel for the plaintiff submits that there can be no difference between the loss of the prospect of earnings from work in the lost years and the loss of the prospect of income from an inheritance likely to be acquired in the lost years. On the face of it and in the light of the reasons I have given for rejecting his submission about income from capital already acquired, I think this submission is good. I can see no distinction between being deprived of the opportunity to use the income from the one and being deprived of the opportunity to use the income from the other. And I see nothing in *Pickett* or *Gammell* which suggests that counsel for the plaintiff is wrong.

Against this counsel for the defendant advances four arguments. His first is that there are two causes of the loss of inheritance: the death and the fact that the deceased had a rich father; and the loss of the inheritance he attributes to the latter. That cannot be right. One might as well say that, if a young plaintiff is given a car by his father and a defendant negligently collides with it, the loss of the car was caused by the fact that the plaintiff had a father who could afford to give him a car.

Secondly he submits that this type of damage was not foreseeable. I see no reason why it should be any less foreseeable than that the plaintiff whose finger is permanently stiffened as a result of a minor road accident occasioned by the defendant's negligence is a concert pianist.

Thirdly he submits that this head of damage is too remote. It can never be recovered. Clearly there will be some circumstances in which the loss of the prospect of an inheritance would depend on one or more occurrences which are so improbable that the loss should be left out of account, but he has advanced no reason which satisfies me that every loss of inheritance should be ruled irrecoverable.

Fourthly he relies on the wording of s 4 of the Administration of Justice Act 1982. This substitutes (with effect from a date too late to affect this claim) a new paragraph for s 1(2)(*a*) of the 1934 Act, which has the effect of preventing the recovery of any damages for loss of *income* in respect of any period after a person's death. (The Act preserves the right of a *living* plaintiff to recover such damages.)

It would be anomalous if the right to recover damages for loss of income in the lost years were to be abolished, but the right to recover for the loss of the inheritance of capital were to be maintained. This tends to suggest that Parliament did not think that there was any right to recover for loss of the inheritance of capital or it would have been abolished too. Of the various arguments of counsel for the defendant this has attracted me most. Although the plaintiff's claim is not described as a loss of a prospect of the inheritance of capital, that effectively is what it is: he claims for the loss of income over a period of about half a lifetime, which income would have been derived from the inheritance of capital. However, I am driven back on my inability to see any fundamental difference between the loss of the opportunity to earn income by work in the lost years and the loss of the opportunity to receive income by way of interest on an inheritance expected in the lost years.

That any award should be made in this case is repugnant to one's overall sense of justice, because the person from whom the inheritance would have come is the plaintiff and the persons to whom any damages awarded will go are the plaintiff and his wife, who will take under the rules of intestacy. But I am satisfied that the coincidence must, on principle, be ignored. The destination of the deceased's estate is irrelevant.

I derive no assistance from either *Cattle v Stockton Waterworks Co* (1875) LR 10 QB 453, [1874–80] All ER Rep 220 or *Dredger Liesbosch (owners) v SS Edison (owners)* [1933] AC 449, [1933] All ER Rep 144, to which counsel for the defendant referred me and I reject his submission.

I shall therefore take the loss of the prospect of this inheritance into account but will do so with moderation.

I can now turn to my consideration of the extent to which forecasts for the future can realistically, and should properly, be made in this case. This, inevitably, involves making assessments about the personality, character, abilities, life-style and relationships of a man who I have not seen, a man who through no fault of his own was tragically killed at the age of 26. Not only is the exercise difficult, it is invidious and I approach it with a sense of its impropriety.

The plaintiff, who is now 70, is a successful businessman with interests in partnerships in which his son also held shares. Much the most successful was a furniture business a called Lenleys for which his son was not then working but in which he held a share of approximately one-twelfth. At the time of his death the deceased was working for two other family partnerships known as the Cathedral Gate Hotel and Restaurant and Stanards, a health food shop and restaurant. In these he held shares of one-twelfth and one-quarter respectively. They also contributed to his income. Thus, part of his income resulted from his work and part from the investment of his capital. At the time of his b death his capital in the three partnerships was valued at £33,000.

[His Lordship then considered in detail the business, family and financial circumstances of the plaintiff and the deceased and how they would have been likely to alter had the deceased lived. His Lordship continued:]

I regard 16 as a suitable multiplier in this case. Three years have already passed, leaving thirteen to represent the future. To reflect the lower level of income from capital which c I think it is right to assume in later years, I propose to divide the thirteen years into three periods (A, B and C) to represent respectively the first five years, the next five years and the remainder of the deceased's working life. I shall discount them respectively to 3, 2½ and 7½. The latter will include retirement.

Having assumed a true earning capacity of £6,000 pa gross for period A, I shall make the same assumption for the whole of the deceased's working life. In doing so I recognise d that neither his abilities nor his earning capacity had been tested in the open market; he had worked only for his father. On the other hand it is likely that if he had survived he would have acquired some measure of experience in the hotel business. I shall take lower figures in periods B and C for the income attributable to his capital. Were Lenleys to prosper the deceased, had he lived, would, like other partners, probably have been required to leave a proportion of his future earnings in the business. This would have e increased his capital and in turn would have increased his earnings. However, I propose to ignore this feature in my calculations. Future inflation and the need to finance future expansion are probably the chief reasons why the partners might not have been allowed to withdraw all of their emoluments. I must ignore the first and I am not prepared to assume the second. When, in this part of my judgment, I speak of capital or of unearned income, I mean such capital as the deceased possessed in his lifetime and the interest it f would have yielded in the lost years.

I reduce the unearned income in period B from £6,000 to £4,000 pa, and in period C to £2,000 pa. Even this is speculative, but I think it would be too harsh to assume that it simply disappeared, particularly when one bears in mind that even if Lenleys were to cease to trade there would presumably be some sort of surplus which the deceased could have reinvested. g

The gross income for periods A, B and C thus become £12,000, £10,000 and £8,000 respectively pa. The equivalent net figures are £8,400, £7,000 and £5,600 respectively. Since the net income attributable to work in period A is £4,200 pa, I shall assume this to be so in periods B and C. Thus the net income attributable to capital in periods A, B and C respectively is £4,200, £2,800 and £1,400 pa.

It may be useful to set this out in tabular form: h

Years	Gross Earned	Gross Unearned	Gross Total	Net Total	Net Earned	Net Unearned
1			14,084	12,556	6,278	6,278
2			12,376	8,240	4,120	4,120
3	6,000	6,000	12,000	8,400	4,200	4,200
A	6,000	6,000	12,000	8,400	4,200	4,200
B	6,000	4,000	10,000	7,000	4,200	2,800
C	6,000	2,000	8,000	5,600	4,200	1,400

j

The plaintiff told me that he would have left his son his share of his house (which his

counsel agrees I am to ignore) and his share in Lenleys and Cathedral Gate, and that he
a might well have given him a proportion somewhat earlier, for example on his marriage.
I have already said that I expect the plaintiff might have found himself somewhat more
reluctant than he believes to release his control over Lenleys, particularly when, as I think
likely, his son would have been playing no part in its management. I think that whatever
he left to his son by way of his share in Lenleys would have come later rather than sooner.
The plaintiff is at an age when the average expectation of life of a man is about ten years
b and, although I think it somewhat more likely that he would have been prepared to
release his interest in Cathedral Gate a little earlier, this was the less important business,
and I propose to assume that any inheritance would have come in about ten years' time,
i e at the start of period C.

What would the plaintiff's testamentary wishes have been then? Who can say?
Circumstances may have changed. It may very well have become more desirable to
c divide his interest in Lenleys equally between his three children. In my judgment there
is an insufficient basis for making any other assumption.

Death, at least, is inevitable and I am satisfied that had the deceased survived his father,
he would have inherited some of his father's share in Lenleys, if it then survived, or of
some other investment if it did not.

I have already assumed that after the tenth year (that is in period C) the son's
d investment income should be taken as £2,000 pa. This would derive from his one-
twelfth share in Lenleys and his one-quarter share in Cathedral Gate or, if he withdrew
his money from these, form some other investment. His father presently has a one-
quarter share in Lenleys and a one-quarter share in Cathedral Gate. (I am ignoring the
effect of the advent on these proportions of Mr Chapman, who was admitted as a partner
on 1 May 1979.) I will assume that the deceased would have received the other quarter
e in Cathedral Gate but only one-third of his father's share in Lenleys, in other words, one-
twelfth. This would, on the assumptions I am making, roughly double his private
income in period C. I propose to ignore any slight alterations to the figures attributable
to the possibility that the share in Cathedral Gate might have been passed on before that
in Lenleys.

For these reasons I will increase the income figures in period C to those in period B.

f What would the deceased's 'surplus' have been in these various periods, first on the
assumption that he remained single throughout? [His Lordship then reviewed the facts
material to this question and continued:] I estimate that to date he would have left in the
business a total of £8,000. This £8,000 would have been in the nature of savings but, for
reasons I have given elsewhere, it would have had an element of the personal about it as
well as of 'surplus'. So some deduction may be called for. However, I shall not make it
g because even the most extravagant bachelor will spend some of his drawings on others,
and this is a factor which tends the other way. So I find that the 'surplus' in the three
years to date is £8,000.

What of the future? I am sure that as a single man he would have continued to draw
out all that he could. The acquisition of the boat may have been an exceptional expense,
but when a young man is used to spending large sums of money on himself, one
h exceptional expense is apt to follow another. In any event when he moved into the
converted stable his household expenses would have been increased form virtually nil to
a significant figure. For reasons which I have already given I ignore the possibility that
he would have left further sums in the business in the years ahead. I think the fairest
estimate which I can make of the deceased's 'surplus' on the assumption that he is to be
treated as a single man is 15% over the whole post-trial period which I have to consider.

j What increase, if any, should I make to this figure on account of the likelihood of
marriage? Counsel for the defendant says none. Counsel for the plaintiff says that
marriage in 1981 should be assumed. The one relies on the approach in *Gammell v Wilson*
[1981] 1 All ER 578, [1982] AC 27, the other on that in *Willshire v Gardner* (6 December
1979, unreported). The facts of this case lie in between.

The plaintiff told me that his son and Miss Pope were planning to marry in February

1981. However, the deceased was not formally engaged and I was a little surprised that Mr and Mrs Adsett could not tell me more about her. I have no doubt that she was deeply attached to him. After he died she abandoned her intention to take her final examination; and the plaintiff gave her his son's half share in the boat. But it would not be right to assume that they would necessarily have married, let alone at the time I was told.

Most, though not all, unmarried men of 26, for much of the time at any rate, have a girlfriend whom they see frequently and for whom they have a strong attachment. But they do not all marry and life shows that they by no means always marry the girl that they have taken out for the longest or with whom they appeared to be the closest.

That the deceased would probably have married I have no doubt, but whom and when are questions I cannot answer. Would his wife have had an earning capacity? Would she have used it full-time? Part-time? For how long? People tend to marry those from their own background. Would she have had some private income of her own and the hope or expectation of an inheritance, like the deceased and his sisters? What then would the 'surplus' have been? All this is the purest speculation.

Should I ignore it or should I added some very modest figure to the 15%, as Griffiths J did to take account of the speculative possibility that Mr Willshire would have had children. Having read and reread the speeches in both *Pickett* and *Gammell* I think I would be wrong if I were to make no increase. I shall add something, but not very much. I shall increase the 15% to 25%. I find therefore the 'surplus' to be 25% of the deceased's total net income in each of the periods A, B and C.

When the assumed inheritance is taken into account this leads to the following figures: in the first three years from death to trial the surplus is £8,000. In period A the total net income is £8,400 pa; one-quarter of this is £2,100 pa and when multiplied by 3 leads to £6,300. In period B the total net income is £7,000 pa. One-quarter is £1,750 pa. I apply a multiplier of $2\frac{1}{2}$; that leads to £4,375. In period C again the total net income, once the inheritance has been taken into account, is £7,000 pa. So once again the surplus is £1,750 pa. I apply a multiplier of $7\frac{1}{2}$ and get £13,125. That evaluates the total surplus (pre-trial and post-trial), after appropriate discounts, at £31,800.

Against this must be set the income which would have been (and will be) earned by the capital of which he died possessed. This would produce very slightly less by way of net income after death than before because the personal allowance would no longer be given. But I ignore this.

The net income attributable to capital owned at death is as follows. Year 1, £6,278; year 2, £4,120; year 3, £4,200; total for the pre-trial period, £14,598. Of the periods ahead, period A, £4,200, multiplied by 3 makes £12,600; period B, £2,800 multiplied by $2\frac{1}{2}$ makes £7,000; period C, £1,400 multiplied by $7\frac{1}{2}$ makes £10,500; total £44,698.

This sum exceeds the £31,800. There will therefore be no award for loss of 'surplus' in the lost years. What it comes to is this. At the moment before the deceased died there remained in existence capital which he owned and which would, after his death, continue to earn more money than would have been needed to provide his 'surplus' had he lived. His death obviated the expenditure of that part of his total income which he would have devoted to his own living expenses and pleasures; as a result more 'surplus' money became available in the 'lost years', not less.

In this judgment I have set out in detail the reasoning and figures which have led me to my conclusion. I have been conscious throughout of Lord Scarman's injunction that mathematical calculations are out of place and that a judge must simply make the best estimates he can. I have, nevertheless, done what I have for three reasons. First, I wanted to check the overall impression which I had formed on the evidence that, looking at the case in the round, there has been no true loss. Second, if I had simply said as much it might have been assumed that I had failed to take account of various aspects of the evidence. Third, if my views about the various matters of law should be held to be wrong, the sum which I would have awarded had I not fallen into error can be discovered. This, I hope, would obviate any need for the case later to be remitted for damages to be assessed on a different basis.

In the result there will be damages for the plaintiff for the funeral expenses of £399·40 plus £1,250 for loss of expectation of life, that is for £1,649·40.

Judgment for the plaintiff accordingly.

Solicitors: *Mawby Barrie & Scott*, agents for *Gardner & Croft*, Canterbury (for the plaintiff); *Joynson-Hicks & Co* (for the defendant).

K Mydeen Esq Barrister.

Elliott v C (a minor)

QUEEN'S BENCH DIVISION
ROBERT GOFF LJ AND GLIDEWELL J
5, 6, 20 MAY 1983

Criminal law – Damage to property – Recklessness whether property would be destroyed or damaged – Recklessness – Whether risk of damage or destruction of property must be obvious to a reasonably prudent man although not obvious to accused by reason of his age, lack of understanding, lack of experience or exhaustion – Criminal Damage Act 1971, s 1(1).

On the true construction of s 1(1)[a] of the Criminal Damage Act 1971 an accused may be convicted of the offence of 'being reckless as to whether ... property [belonging to another] would be destroyed or damaged' if the risk of damage or destruction of the property must have been obvious to a reasonably prudent man, even though the particular accused had not thought of the risk, and by reason of some factor such as his age, lack of understanding, lack of experience or exhaustion it would not have been obvious to him had he thought of it. Thus, if a 14-year-old girl sets fire to a shed by pouring white spirit onto the shed floor and throwing a lighted match onto the spirit, she is guilty of an offence under s 1(1) of the 1971 Act notwithstanding that because of her age and lack of experience in dealing with inflammable liquid she would not have appreciated the risk that the shed and its contents would be destroyed if she had given thought to the matter (see p 1008 *e f*, p 1009 *a b*, p 1010 *a b*, p 1011 *b* and p 1012 *a* and *j*, post).

R v Caldwell [1981] 1 All ER 961, *R v Lawrence* [1981] 1 All ER 974 and *R v Miller* [1983] 1 All ER 978 applied.

Notes

For the offence of destroying or damaging property, see 11 Halsbury's Laws (4th edn) para 1306, and for cases on the subject, see 15 Digest (Reissue) 1439–1440, *12,690–12,693*.

For the Criminal Damage Act 1971, s 1, see 41 Halsbury's Statutes (3rd edn) 409.

Cases referred to in judgments

R v Briggs [1977] 1 All ER 475, [1977] 1 WLR 605, CA.
R v Caldwell [1981] 1 All ER 961, [1982] AC 341, [1981] 2 WLR 509, HL.
R v Lawrence [1981] 1 All ER 974, [1982] AC 510, [1981] 2 WLR 524, HL.
R v Majewski [1976] 2 All ER 142, [1977] AC 443, [1976] 2 WLR 623, HL.

---

a Section 1(1) provides: 'A person who without lawful excuse destroys or damages any property belonging to another intending to destroy or damage any such property or being reckless as to whether any such property would be destroyed or damaged shall be guilty of an offence.'

R v Miller [1983] 1 All ER 978, [1983] 2 WLR 539, HL.
R v Pigg [1982] 2 All ER 591, [1982] 1 WLR 762, CA.
R v Stephenson [1979] 2 All ER 1198, [1979] QB 695, [1979] 3 WLR 193, CA.

Case stated

Norman Elliott appealed by way of case stated by the justices for the County of Kent acting in and for the petty session division of Canterbury and St Augustine in respect of their adjudication as a magistrates' court sitting as a juvenile court at Canterbury on 28 September 1982. On 17 August 1982 an information was preferred by the appellant, a police officer of the Kent Constabulary against the respondent, C, a minor, that on 16 June 1982 she without lawful excuse destroyed by fire a shed and contents valued together at £3,206 belonging to Walter Davies, intending to destroy such property or being reckless whether such property would be destroyed, contrary to s 1(1) of the Criminal Damage Act 1971. The magistrates found the respondent not guilty of the charge and dismissed the information. The questions for the opinion of the High Court were (i) whether properly directing themselves and on the true construction of s 1(1) of the 1971 Act the magistrates were correct in their interpretation of the meaning of reckless, namely that a defendant should only be held to have acted recklessly by virtue of his failure to give thought to an obvious risk that property would be destroyed or damaged where such risk would have been obvious to him had he given any thought to the matter, and (ii) whether properly directing themselves on the evidence the magistrates could properly have come to the decision that the respondent had acted neither intentionally nor recklessly in destroying by fire the shed and its contents. The facts are set out in the judgment of Glidewell J.

Alan Moses for the appellant.
Geoffrey Nice for the respondent.

Cur adv vult

20 May. The following judgments were delivered.

GLIDEWELL J (giving the first judgment at the invitation of Robert Goff LJ). This is an appeal by way of case stated from the justices for the Petty Sessional Division of Canterbury and St Augustine in the County of Kent, who on 28 September 1982 found the respondent, C (a minor), not guilty of a charge and dismissed an information which alleged that she on 16 June 1982 without lawful excuse had destroyed by fire a shed and its contents, intending to destroy such property or being reckless whether such property would be destroyed, contrary to s 1(1) of the Criminal Damage Act 1971.

The shed was the property of a Mr Walter Davies, of 1 Glebe Way, Whitstable, Kent. It was a large wooden shed, and stood at the bottom of the garden of Mr Davies's home. In it he stored tools, various paints, and turpentine or white spirit.

The respondent was a schoolgirl who had reached the age of 14 years in May 1982. She lived with her foster mother and was in a remedial class at school. On the evening of 15 June 1982 the respondent went out with an older girl friend. She hoped to stay the night at the friend's home, but was not able to do so. The respondent did not return to her own home but stayed out all night, not sleeping for the whole night.

At about 5 am on 16 June 1982 the respondent entered Mr Davies's garden shed. She found the white spirit in its plastic container. She poured white spirit onto the carpet on the floor of the shed and threw two lighted matches onto the spirit, the second of which ignited it. The fire immediately flared up out of control and the respondent left the shed.

A Mr Hubbard, who was delivering milk in the area, saw the respondent in the vicinity at about 5.40 am, and a few minutes later saw the shed on fire and raised the alarm.

The police arrested the respondent at her home at 8 am on 16 June 1982 on suspicion of arson and two offences of burglary. She was cautioned in the presence of her foster mother and made no reply. She was taken to Whitstable police station and placed in the cells, where she slept until about 3 pm on the afternoon of the same day.

At 3 pm on 16 June 1982 the respondent was interviewed by two police officers in the presence of her foster mother. After caution she admitted that she had entered the shed, put spirit on the floor and set fire to it. She said that she did not know why she had set fire to the shed and that she had 'just felt like it'. She said that she had had the matches with her when she entered the shed and that after she had set fire to the shed she had run out into the road and had been seen by the milkman. She agreed to make a written statement under caution in which she admitted entering the shed and setting fire to it.

Although the wording of the information, following the wording of s 1(1) of the Criminal Damage Act 1971, alleged that the respondent destoyed by fire the shed 'intending to destroy such property or being reckless as to whether such property would be destroyed', at the hearing before the magistrates the contention on behalf of the appellant, the prosecutor, was not that the evidence proved an intention to destroy the property but that it did prove that the respondent was reckless whether the property would be destroyed. The magistrates accepted that the definition of recklessness which they must accept was that given by Lord Diplock in *R v Caldwell* [1981] 1 All ER 961, [1982] AC 341.

In *Caldwell* the relevant offence charged was of destroying property by fire, intending to damage the property and intending to endanger life or being reckless whether life was endangered, contrary to s 1(2) of the 1971 Act. At his trial, the defendant said that when he started the fire he was so drunk that the thought that there might be people whose lives might be endangered by the fire never crossed his mind. It was contended on his behalf that his drunkenness had the effect not merely of making him incapable of forming the intention to endanger life, but was also relevant to the question whether he was reckless. If, it was argued, his drunkenness resulted in him not thinking about the risk to the lives of others, then he was not reckless. By a majority of three to two, the House of Lords rejected this last contention. Lord Diplock, with whose speech Lord Keith and Lord Roskill agreed, said that 'reckless' must be given the same meaning in sub-ss (1) and (2) of s 1 of the 1971 Act (see [1981] 1 All ER 961 at 964, [1982] AC 341 at 350). Lord Diplock said ([1981] 1 All ER 961 at 967, [1982] AC 341 at 354):

> 'In my opinion, a person charged with an offence under s 1(1) of the 1971 Act is "reckless as to whether or not any property would be destroyed or damaged" if (1) he does an act which in fact creates an obvious risk that property will be destroyed or damaged and (2) when he does the act he either has not given any thought to the possibility of there being any such risk or has recognised that there was some risk involved and has none the less gone on to do it. That would be a proper direction to the jury; cases in the Court of Appeal which held otherwise should be regarded as overruled.'

When *Caldwell* was decided the most recent decision in the Court of Appeal on the meaning of 'reckless', on which the recorder in *Caldwell* had based her direction to the jury, was *R v Stephenson* [1979] 2 All ER 1198 at 1203, [1979] QB 695 at 703. Geoffrey Lane LJ giving the judgment of the court in that case said: 'A man is reckless when he carries out the deliberate act appreciating that there is a risk that damage to property may result from his act.'

That was, in essence, the view shared by the minority in the House of Lords in *Caldwell*.

As I have said, the magistrates accepted that they were bound to follow the 'model direction' of Lord Diplock which I have read. It was, however, argued before them, and again before us by counsel for the respondent (to whom, and to counsel for the appellant, the court is much indebted for their arguments) that when, in the first part of his test, Lord Diplock referred to 'an act which in fact creates an obvious risk that property will be destroyed or damaged', he meant a risk which was obvious to the particular defendant. This argument was accepted by the magistrates and is set out by them in the following passages in para 7 of the case stated:

'H. That while the respondent had realised that the contents of the bottle which contained white spirit were possibly inflammable, she had not handled it before and had not appreciated how explosively it would burn and immediately become out of her control, thereby destroying the shed and contents and also placing her own life at risk.

I. That the respondent had given no thought at the time that she started the fire to the possibility of there being a risk that the shed and contents would be destroyed by her actions. That in the circumstances this risk would not have been obvious to her or been appreciated by her if she had given thought to the matter.

J. We were unable to form any conclusion on the question why she had started the fire.

K. That in reaching our findings set out herein we had due regard to the age and understanding of the respondent, her lack of experience of dealing with inflammable spirit and the fact that she must have been tired and exhausted at the time.

L. That we accepted the interpretation of the effect of the decision in the case of *R v Caldwell* put forward on behalf of the respondent.

M. That in particular we found it implicit in the decision in that case that a defendant should only be held to have acted recklessly by virtue of his failure to give any thought to an obvious risk that property would be destroyed or damaged, where such risk would have been obvious to him if he had given any thought to the matter.

N. Accordingly having regard to our findings set out above we found the respondent not guilty of the charge and dismissed the information.'

Before us, counsel for the appellant has argued forcefully that the magistrates were wrong to adopt that interpretation of the decision in *Caldwell*. He submits that the phrase 'creates an obvious risk' means that the risk is one which must have been obvious to a reasonably prudent man, not necessarily to the particular defendant if he or she had given thought to it. It follows, says counsel, that if the risk is one which would have been obvious to a reasonably prudent person, once it has also been proved that the particular defendant gave no thought to the possibility of there being such a risk, it is not a defence that because of limited intelligence or exhaustion she would not have appreciated the risk even if she had thought about it.

It is right to say, as counsel for the appellant pointed out to us, that there are passages in the speech of Lord Diplock in *Caldwell* which suggest that his Lordship was indeed using the phrase 'creates an obvious risk' as meaning, 'creates a risk which was obvious to the particular defendant.' Thus, his Lordship said ([1981] 1 All ER 961 at 964, [1982] AC 341 at 351):

'Among the words [Professor Kenny] used was "recklessness", the noun derived from the adjective "reckless," of which the popular or dictionary meaning is "careless, regardless, or heedless of the possible harmful consequences of one's acts". It presupposes that, if thought were given to the matter by the doer before the act was done, it would have been apparent to him that there was a real risk of its having the relevant harmful consequences . . .'

Speaking of another earlier decision of the Court of Appeal, in *R v Briggs* [1977] 1 All ER 475, [1977] 1 WLR 605, he said ([1981] 1 All ER 961 at 965, [1982] AC 341 at 353): '. . . even though the risk is great and would be obvious if any thought were given to the matter by the doer of the act.'

He said ([1981] 1 All ER 961 at 967, [1982] AC 341 at 355):

'So, in the instant case, the fact that the respondent was unaware of the risk of endangering the lives of residents in the hotel owing to his self-induced intoxication would be no defence if that risk would have been obvious to him had he been sober.'

The last passage was based on the earlier decision of the House of Lords in *R v Majewski* [1976] 2 All ER 142, [1977] AC 443, a decision relating to the effect of self-induced intoxication on intent. But, quite apart from the *Majewski* test, the decision of the

majority in *Caldwell* that intoxication, even if it resulted in the defendant not thinking
a at all whether there was a risk that property or life would be endangered, nevertheless did not take him out of the state of mind properly described as 'reckless' is only consistent in my view with their Lordships meaning by the phrase 'creates an obvious risk' creates a risk obvious to the reasonably prudent person.

That the submission of counsel for the appellant is correct is to my mind, however, put beyond a peradventure by two later decisions of the House of Lords. Firstly, in *R v*
b *Lawrence* [1981] 1 All ER 974, [1982] AC 510, a decision on the meaning of the word 'recklessly' in s 1 of the Road Traffic Act 1972 (as substituted by s 50 of the Criminal Law Act 1977), the members of their Lordships' House unanimously adopted the view of the majority in *Caldwell* as to the meaning of 'reckless' and thus 'recklessly'. In his speech in that case, Lord Diplock said ([1981] 1 All ER 974 at 981, [1982] AC 510 at 525):

> 'In ordinary usage "recklessly" as descriptive of a physical act such as driving a
> c motor vehicle which can be performed in a variety of different ways, some of them entailing danger and some of them not, refers not only to the state of mind of the doer of the act when he decides to do it but also qualifies the manner in which the act itself is performed. One does not speak of a person acting "recklessly", even though he has given no thought at all to the consequences of his act, unless the act is one that presents a real risk of harmful consequences which anyone acting with
> d reasonable prudence would recognise and give heed to.'

Again, his Lordship said ([1981] 1 All ER 974 at 982, [1982] AC 510 at 526):

> 'Recklessness on the part of the doer of an act does presuppose that there is something in the circumstances that would have drawn the attention of an ordinary prudent individual to the possibility that his act was capable of causing the kind of
> e serious harmful consequences that the section which creates the offence was intended to prevent, and that the risk of those harmful consequences occurring was not so slight that an ordinary prudent individual would feel justified in treating them as negligible. It is only when this is so that the doer of the act is acting "recklessly" if, before doing the act, he either fails to give any thought to the possibility of there being any such risk or, having recognised that there was such risk, he nevertheless
> f goes on to do it.'

R v Miller [1983] 1 All ER 978, [1983] 2 WLR 539 was another decision on s 1(1) of the Criminal Damage Act 1971, in relation to a charge of arson. Lord Diplock, with whose speech the remainder of their Lordships agreed, said ([1983] 1 All ER 978 at 982, [1983] 2 WLR 539 at 544):

> g '... where the state of mind relied on is "being reckless", the risk created by the physical act of the accused that property belonging to another would be damaged must be one that would be obvious to anyone who had given his mind to it at whatever is the relevant time for determining whether the state of mind of the accused fitted the description "being reckless whether such property would be damaged": see *R v Caldwell* [1981] 1 All ER 961 at 965, [1982] AC 341 at 352; see
> h also *R v Lawrence* [1981] 1 All ER 974 at 982, [1982] AC 510 at 526 for a similar requirement in the mental element in the statutory offence of reckless driving.'

In the light of these last two authorities, we are in my judgment bound to hold that the word reckless in s 1 of the Criminal Damage Act 1971 has the meaning ascribed to it by counsel for the appellant. It is only fair to the magistrates in the present case to say
j that it seems that they were not referred to the decision in *R v Lawrence*, and *R v Miller* had not, when they reached their decision, been heard by the House of Lords.

The questions posed by the case are:

> '1. Whether properly directing ourselves and upon a true construction of section 1(1) of the Criminal Damage Act 1971 we were correct in our interpretation of the meaning of reckless, namely, that a defendant should only be held to have acted recklessly by virtue of his failure to give any thought to an obvious risk that property

> would be destroyed or damaged, where such risk would have been obvious to him if he had given any thought to the matter? a
>
> 2. Whether properly directing ourselves on the evidence we could properly have come to our decision that the respondent had acted neither intentionally nor recklessly in destroying by fire the shed and contents?'

I would answer No to both questions, and allow the appeal.

ROBERT GOFF LJ. I agree with the conclusion reached by Glidewell J, but I do so b simply because I believe myself constrained to do so by authority. I feel moreover that I would be lacking in candour if I were to conceal my unhappiness about the conclusion which I feel compelled to reach. In my opinion, although of course the courts of this country are bound by the doctrine of precedent, sensibly interpreted, nevertheless it would be irresponsible for judges to act as automatons, rigidly applying authorities without regard to consequences. Where therefore it appears at first sight that authority c compels a judge to reach a conclusion which he senses to be unjust or inappropriate, he is, I consider, under a positive duty to examine the relevant authorities with scrupulous care to ascertain whether he can, within the limits imposed by the doctrine of precedent (always sensibly interpreted), legitimately interpret or qualify the principle expressed in the authorities to achieve the result which he perceives to be just or appropriate in the particular case. I do not disguise the fact that I have sought to perform this function in d the present case.

I start of course with the facts of the case, which have been set out with clarity by the magistrates. For present purposes, the salient features are these: (1) the respondent, a 14-year-old schoolgirl, set fire to a shed by pouring white spirit onto a carpet on the floor of the shed and throwing two lighted matches onto the spirit, the second of which ignited it; (2) while she realised that the contents of the bottle which contained the white spirit e was possibly inflammable, she had not handled it before and had not appreciated how explosively it would burn and immediately become out of control, thereby destroying both the shed and its contents; (3) she gave no thought at the time when she started the fire to the possibility of there being a risk that the shed and its contents would be destroyed; (4) this risk would not have been obvious to her or have been appreciated by her if she had given thought to the matter. f

I add that these conclusions were reached by the magistrates, having regard to the age and understanding of the respondent, her lack of experience of dealing with inflammable spirit, and the fact that she must have been tired and exhausted at the time.

I turn next to the crime with which she was charged, viz that she without lawful excuse destroyed by fire the shed and contents, intending to destroy such property or being reckless whether such property would be destroyed, contrary to s 1(1) of the g Criminal Damage Act 1971. The case advanced against her was not that she intended to destroy the property, but that she was reckless whether the property would be destroyed.

Plainly, she did destroy the shed and its contents by fire; plainly, too, she did so without lawful excuse. But was she reckless whether the shed and it contents would be destroyed? Here I turn, as Glidewell J has done, to authority; and in the decision of the House of Lords in *R v Caldwell* [1981] 1 All ER 961, [1982] AC 341 I find an authority, h binding on this court, which was concerned with the interpretation of the word 'recklessness' as used in the very subsection under which the respondent was charged. In that case, although the House was divided, the ratio decidendi of the decision of the House is to be found in the speech of Lord Diplock, with which both Lord Keith and Lord Roskill agreed. Lord Diplock analysed the word 'reckless' as used in this subsection, and his analysis culminated in the conclusion which reads as follows ([1981] 1 All ER j 961 at 967, [1982] AC 341 at 354):

> 'In my opinion, a person charged with an offence under s 1(1) of the 1971 Act is "reckless as to whether or not any property would be destroyed or damaged" if (1) he does an act which in fact creates an obvious risk that property will be destroyed or damaged and (2) when he does the act he either has not given any thought to the

possibility of there being any such risk or has recognised that there was some risk
a involed and has none the less gone on to do it. That would be a proper direction to the jury; cases in the Court of Appeal which held otherwise should be regarded as overruled.'

Now, if that test is applied literally in the present case, the conclusion appears inevitable that, on the facts found by the magistrates, the respondent was reckless whether the shed
b and contents would be destroyed; because first she did an act which created an obvious risk that the property would be destroyed, and second she had not given any thought to the possibility of there being any such risk.

Yet, if I next pause (as I have done, in accordance with what I conceive to be my proper function) and ask myself the question: would I, having regard only to the ordinary meaning of the word, consider this girl to have been, on the facts found, *reckless* whether
c the shed and contents would be destroyed, my answer would, I confess, be in the negative. This is not a case where there was a deliberate disregard of a known risk of damage or injury of a certain type or degree; nor is it a case where there was mindless indifference to a risk of such damage or injury, as is expressed in common speech in the context of motoring offences (though not, I think, of arson) as 'blazing on regardless'; nor is it even a case where failure to give thought to the possibility of the risk was due to
d some blameworthy cause, such as intoxication. This is a case where it appears that the only basis on which the accused might be held to have been reckless would be if the appropriate test to be applied was purely objective: a test which might in some circumstances be though justifiable in relation to certain conduct (eg reckless driving), particularly where the word 'reckless' is used simply to characterise the relevant conduct. But such a test does not appear at first sight to be appropriate to a crime such as that
e under consideration in the present case, especially as recklessness in that crime has to be related to a particular consequence. I therefore next ask myself the question whether I can, consistently with the doctrine of precedent, sensibly interpreted, legitimately construe or qualify the principle stated by Lord Diplock in *Caldwell* so as to accommodate what I conceive to be the appropriate result on the facts of the present case, bearing in mind that those facts are very different from the facts under consideration by the House
f of Lords in *Caldwell*, where the defendant had set fire to a hotel when in a state of intoxication.

Here again, it would be unrealistic if I were to disguise the fact that I am well aware that the statement of principle by Lord Diplock in *Caldwell* has been the subject of comment, much of it critical, in articles written by jurists; and that I have studied certain of these articles with interest. I find it striking that the justices, in reaching their
g conclusion in the present case, have done so (no doubt in response to an argument advanced on the respondent's behalf) by imposing on Lord Diplock's statement of principle a qualification similar to one considered by Professor Glanville Williams in his article 'Recklessness Redefined' (1981) 40 CLJ 252 at 270–271. This is that a defendant should only be regarded as having acted recklessly by virtue of his failure to give any thought to an obvious risk that property would be destroyed or damaged, where such
h risk would have been obvious *to him* if he had given any thought to the matter. However, having studied Lord Diplock's speech, I do not think it would be consistent with his reasoning to impose any such qualification. I say that not only because this qualification does not appear in terms in his conclusion which I have already quoted, but also because, when considering earlier in his speech Professor Kenny's definition of recklessness (which he rejected as being too narrow), Lord Diplock expressly adverted to the fact that that
j definition presupposed that 'if thought were given to the matter by the doer before the act was done, it would have been apparent *to him* that there was a real risk of its having the relevant harmful consequences . . .' (see [1981] 1 All ER 961 at 964, [1982] AC 341 at 351; my emphasis). It seems to me that, having expressly considered that element in Professor Kenny's test, and having (as I think) plainly decided to omit it from his own formulation of the concept of recklessness, it would not now be legitimate for an inferior court, in a case under this particular subsection, to impose a qualification which had so

been rejected by Lord Diplock himself. It follows that for that reason alone I do not feel able to uphold the reasoning of the magistrates in the present case. But I wish to add that, for my part, I doubt whether this qualification can be justified in any event. Where there is no thought of the consequences, any further inquiry necessary for the purposes of establishing guilt should prima facie be directed to the question why such thought was not given, rather than to the purely hypothetical question of what the particular person would have appreciated had he directed his mind to the matter.

We were referred to the decision of the Court of Appeal in *R v Pigg* [1982] 2 All ER 591, [1982] 1 WLR 762, a case decided after *Caldwell* and the related decision of the House of Lords in *R v Lawrence* [1981] 1 All ER 974, [1982] AC 510, but concerned not with s 1(1) of the Criminal Damage Act 1971 but with s 1 of the Sexual Offences (Amendment) Act 1976. The defendant had been convicted of rape; and one ground of appeal was concerned with a direction given by the judge to the jury on the question whether he knew that the complainant did not consent to intercourse or was reckless as to whether she consented or not. The judgment of the Court of Appeal was delivered by Lord Lane CJ. He referred to the decisions of the House of Lords in *Caldwell* and in *Lawrence*, and quoted extensively from the speeches of Lord Diplock in both cases. He then said ([1982] 2 All ER 591 at 599, [1982] 1 WLR 762 at 772):

> 'Of course it is plain that that opinion cannot, so to speak, be lifted bodily and applied to rape. There has to be a modification in certain of the matters which are there dealt with. But, in the end, it seems to us that in the light of that decision, so far as rape is concerned, a man is reckless if either he was indifferent and gave no thought to the possibility that the woman might not be consenting in circumstances where if any thought had been given to the matter it would have been obvious that there was a risk she was not or he was aware of the possibility that she might not be consenting but nevertheless persisted regardless of whether she consented or not.'

Now it cannot be disguised that the addition of the words 'was indifferent and' constituted a gloss on the definition of recklessness proposed by Lord Diplock in *Caldwell*. Furthermore, if it were legitimate so to interpret Lord Diplock's speech in relation to a case arising not under s 1 of the Sexual Offences (Amendment) Act 1976 but under s 1(1) of the Criminal Damage Act 1971, the effect would be that the second question posed by the magistrates in the case now before this court would be answered in the affirmative, and the appeal would be dismissed, because there is no finding of fact that the respondent in the case before us was indifferent to the risk of destruction by fire of the shed and its contents. This is an approach which I would gladly adopt, if I felt that I was free to do so. However, I do not consider that it is open to this court, in a case arising under the very subsection to which Lord Diplock's speech was expressly directed, to impose this qualification, which I feel would in this context constitute too substantial a departure from the test proposed by him.

Both these possible avenues are, I believe, closed to the court in the present case. I have considered anxiously whether there is any other interpretation which the court could legitimately place on Lord Diplock's statement of principle in *Caldwell*, which would lead to the conclusion which I would prefer to reach, that the respondent was not reckless whether the shed and contents would be destroyed by fire. I have discovered none which would not involve what I would regard as constituting, in relation to the relevant offence, an illegitimate departure from that statement of principle.

In these circumstances, I agree that the questions must be answered as proposed by Glidewell J, and that the appeal must be allowed.

Appeal allowed. Leave to appeal refused.

Solicitors: *Sharpe Pritchard & Co*, agents for *Richard A Crabb*, Maidstone (for the appellant); *Girling Wilson & Harvie*, Canterbury (for the respondent).

Sepala Munasinghe Esq Barrister.

Waite v Government Communications Headquarters

HOUSE OF LORDS

LORD FRASER OF TULLYBELTON, LORD KEITH OF KINKEL, LORD SCARMAN, LORD BRIDGE OF HARWICH AND LORD TEMPLEMAN

13, 14 JUNE, 21 JULY 1983

Unfair dismissal – Right not to be unfairly dismissed – Restriction on right where employee reaches normal retiring age or specified age – Normal retiring age – Determination – Employee's contract providing for compulsory retirement at minimum age of 60 unless employer deciding to keep him on until he was 65 – Employee compulsorily retired at 60½ – Employee alleging unfair dismissal – Whether contractual retiring age conclusively fixing normal retiring age – Whether tribunal having jursidiction to entertain claim – Trade Union and Labour Relations Act 1974, Sch 1, para 10(b).

In December 1961 the appellant, a retired army officer, became a temporary civil servant in the respondent department with the grade of higher executive officer. In March 1967 he became established in that grade and subject to the terms and conditions contained in the Civil Service Pay and Conditions Code. The code provided that the minimum retiring age for a person in the appellant's position was 60, although the department had discretionary power to keep him on in his position until the age of 65. On 30 April 1978 the appellant, then aged 60½, was compulsorily retired before he had completed the 20 years' reckonable service to qualify for a full pension and was immediately re-employed in a lower grade as a clerical officer. On a complaint by the appellant to an industrial tribunal that he had been unfairly dismissed the department contended that the tribunal had no jurisdiction to entertain the claim because the appellant had reached 'the normal retiring age' before his employment was terminated and therefore was precluded by para 10(*b*)[a] of Sch 1 to the Trade Union and Labour Relations Act 1974 from making a complaint of unfair dismissal. The industrial tribunal held that it had jurisdiction to entertain the complaint and that the appellant had been unfairly dismissed. The department appealed to the Employment Appeal Tribunal, which upheld the department's contention that the tribunal had no jurisdiction to hear the complaint. The appellant appealed unsuccessfully to the Court of Appeal and then appealed to the House of Lords, contending (i) that the expression 'normal retiring age' in para 10(*b*) meant that age at which persons holding his position generally retired in the normal course of events, (ii) that the contractual retiring age, if any, was irrelevant, (iii) that if there was no practice to establish a usual retiring age, because the employees retired at various different ages, then there was no normal retiring age and the alternative provided by para 10(*b*), namely the age of 65 for men and 60 for women, applied, and (iv) that the effect of a provision in the code that an officer who had not completed 20 years' reckonable service 'should' be allowed to continue gave him a right to be kept on. The department contended that the contractual retiring age for employees holding the appellant's position conclusively fixed their normal retiring age and that any departure from it in practice was irrelevant.

Held – The contractual retiring age laid down in the employee's terms and conditions of employment did not conclusively fix the 'normal retiring age' for the purposes of para 10 of Sch 1 to the 1974 Act. However, although where there was a contractual retiring age applicable to nearly all the employees holding the position which the appellant held, a rebuttable presumption arose that the contractual retiring age was the normal retiring age for the group. In determining what was the normal retiring age the proper test was

a Paragraph 10, so far as material, is set out at p 1015 *h j*, post to ascertain what would be the reasonable expectation or understanding of the employees holding the position of the appellant at the relevant time. Since the evidence did not establish that there was any practice whereby, such employees were permitted to retain their office after attaining the minimum retiring age of 60 and since the provision in the Civil Service code the employees who had not completed the full period of pensionable service should be allowed to continue was merely discretionary and did not give an employee any right to be kept on, it followed that the minimum retirement age and the contractual retiring age of officers such as the appellant was the age of 60 and accordingly that the industrial tribunal did not have jurisdiction to entertain the claim. The appeal would therefore be dismissed (see p 1016 *a* to *c*, p 1017 *j* to p 1018 *c* and *f* to *j* and p 1019 *e* to p 1020 *b*, post).

Dicta of Bridge LJ in *Post Office v Wallser* [1981] 1 All ER at 673, of Lord Denning MR in *Howard v Dept of National Savings* [1981] 1 All ER at 678 and *Duke v Reliance Systems Ltd* [1982] ICR 449 approved.

Ord v Maidstone and District Hospital Management Committee [1974] 2 All ER 343 distinguished.

Nothman v Barnet London Borough [1979] 1 All ER 142 considered.

Notes

For an employee's exclusion from compensation for unfair dismissal because of age, see 16 Halsbury's Laws (4th edn) para 620.

For the Trade Union and Labour Relations Act 1974, Sch 1, para 10, see 44 Halsbury's Statutes (3rd edn) 1794.

As from 1 November 1978 para 10 of Sch 1 to the 1974 Act was replaced by s 64(1) of the Employment Protection (Consolidation) Act 1978.

Cases referred to in opinions

Duke v Reliance Systems Ltd [1982] ICR 449, EAT.

Howard v Dept of National Savings [1981] 1 All ER 674, [1981] 1 WLR 542, CA.

Nothman v Barnet London Borough [1978] 1 All ER 1243, [1978] 1 WLR 220, CA; *on appeal* [1979] 1 All ER 142, [1972] 1 WLR 67, HL.

Ord v Maidstone and District Hospital Management Committee [1974] 2 All ER 343, NIRC.

Post Office v Wallser [1981] 1 All ER 668, CA.

Secretary of State for Trade v Douglas [1983] IRLR 63, CA.

Appeal

Lt Col John Albert Waite appealed with leave of the Court of Appeal against the decision of the Court of Appeal (Waller, Ackner and Purchas LJJ) on 20 December 1982 dismissing the appellant's appeal from a decision of the Employment Appeal Tribunal (May J, Mr R J Hooker and Mr J G C Milligan) dated 7 May 1981 allowing the appeal of the respondents, the Government Communications Headquarters, against the decision of an industrial tribunal (chairman Dr L V L Blair) sitting at Gloucester on 10 April 1980 and 22 January 1981 whereby the tribunal determined that it had jurisdiction to entertain the appellant's complaint of unfair dismissal against the respondents and that the appellant had been unfairly dismissed. The Court of Appeal held that the industrial tribunal had no jurisdiction to entertain the appellant's application, on the ground that he had attained normal retiring age within the meaning of the Trade Union and Labour Relations Act 1974, Sch 1, para 10(*b*) and was consequently precluded from pursuing a claim for unfair dismissal. The facts are set out in the opinion of Lord Fraser.

Eldred Tabachnik QC and *Elizabeth Slade* for the appellant.
Simon D Brown and *David Blunt* for the respondents.

Their Lordships took time for consideration.

21 July. The following opinions were delivered.

a **LORD FRASER OF TULLYBELTON.** My Lords, the main question raised in this appeal concerns the proper construction of the expression 'the normal retiring age' where it occurs in the Trade Union and Labour Relations Act 1974, Sch 1, para 10. The expression was used in the same context in s 28 of the Industrial Relations Act 1971, which was repealed, and re-enacted with amendments which are not here relevant, by b the 1974 Act. The 1974 Act itself has now been repealed by the Employment Protection (Consolidation) Act 1978. Section 64 of the 1978 Act re-enacts para 10 of Sch 1 to the 1974 Act with further amendments. The 1974 Act was the legislation in force at the time which is material for this appeal, and I shall refer only to it.

A subsidiary question as to the proper construction of certain Civil Service regulations is also raised.

c The appellant, Lt Col Waite, was born on 30 October 1917. He had a distinguished career in the army and attained the rank of lieutenant colonel in the Royal Signals Regiment. In 1961 he left the army in order to take up employment with the respondents' predecessors, the London Communications Electronic Security Agency, who were then advertising for officers with practical experience of telecommunications. His employment with them began on 4 December 1961, when he became a temporary civil servant with d the grade of higher executive officer. On 13 March 1967 he became an 'established' civil servant with pension rights. The appellant now accepts that the contractual terms and conditions of employment applicable to him from and after 13 March 1967 were those contained in the Civil Service Pay and Conditions of Service Code, amplified in some respects by the departmental policy of his employing department. Before the Court of Appeal the appellant had argued that the age at which he could be compelled to retire e depended on the terms of his original employment as a temporary civil servant but the Court of Appeal, and the tribunals, decided against that contention and he now accepts their decision on that issue.

On 30 April 1978 the appellant was compulsorily retired. On that date he was aged $60\frac{1}{2}$ years. He had not completed the 20 years of reckonable service with the respondents and their predecessors necessary to qualify for a full pension. He had in fact completed f slightly over sixteen years of service reckonable for pension. On his retirement he was immediately re-employed in a lower grade as a clerical officer; in the technical language of the department he 'regressed'. Thereafter he worked as a clerical officer, without prejudice to his contention that the respondents had had no power to compel him to retire on 30 April 1978. In July 1978 the appellant complained to an industrial tribunal that he had been unfairly dismissed. The respondents at first denied that his dismissal g had been unfair, but they no longer maintain that denial. They also took, and still maintain, the preliminary point that the industrial tribunal had no jurisdiction to entertain the appellant's application, on the ground that, before the date on which his employment was terminated, he had attained the normal retiring age for an employee holding the position which he held. For that point they rely on para 10(*b*) of Sch 1 to the 1974 Act. Paragraph 10 is in Pt II of the schedule which is the part dealing with 'unfair h dismissal'. Paragraph 4 which is also in Pt II provides that in every employment to which it applies every employee shall have the right not to be unfairly dismissed by his employer, and that the remedy of an employee who is unfairly dismissed is by way of complaint to an industrial tribunal. Paragraph 10 provides as follows:

> 'Subject to paragraph 11 below, paragraph 4 above does not apply to the dismissal of an employee from any employment if the employee—(*a*) was not continuously j employed for a period of not less than 26 weeks ending with the effective date of termination, or (*b*) on or before the effective date of termination attained the age which, in the undertaking in which he was employed, was the normal retiring age for an employee holding the position which he held, or, if a man, attained the age of sixty-five, or, if a woman, attained the age of sixty ...'

The 'effective date of termination' in relation to an employee whose contract of

employment is terminated by notice means the date on which the notice expires: see
para 5(5)(*a*) of the schedule. 'Position' is defined in s 30 of the Act as follows: *a*

> '"position", in relation to an employee, means the following matters taken as a whole, that is to say, his status as an employee, the nature of his work and his terms and conditions of employment.'

For reasons which I shall explain when I come to consider the subsidiary question, I
am of opinion that the retiring age laid down in the terms and conditions of the *b*
appellant's employment (which I shall call the 'contractual retiring age') for a person
holding his position was 60. The respondents had power, in their discretion, to retain
him in his position after he had attained the age of 60 and until he reached the age of 65,
and they did in fact retain him until he was 60½ in order to carry out a particular task,
but he had no right under the terms of his employment to be retained after attaining the
age of 60. Such retention was entirely a matter for the respondents' discretion. *c*
Nevertheless the appellant contends that on 30 April 1978, when he was dismissed, he
had not attained the normal retiring age for an employee in his position, and therefore
the industrial tribunal had jurisdiction to consider his complaint. Counsel for the
appellant in opening the appeal naturally put his contention at its highest, and he
submitted that the expression 'normal retiring age' in para 10(*b*) simply meant the usual
retiring age, or the age at which persons holding the position generally retired in the *d*
normal course of events, and that the contractual retiring age, if any, was irrelevant. He
said that if there is no practice sufficient to establish a usual retiring age, because
employees retire at various different ages, then there is no normal retiring age and the
alternative provided by para 10(*b*), namely the age of 65 for a man or 60 for a woman,
will apply, in accordance with the decision of this House in *Nothman v Barnet London*
Borough [1979] 1 All ER 142, [1979] 1 WLR 67. The respondents' original contention *e*
was that the contractual retiring age for employees holding the appellant's position
conclusively fixed their normal retiring age, and that any departure from the contractual
retiring age in practice was irrelevant. Between these extreme contentions, various
intermediate positions were explored in the course of argument.

Considering that the expression 'normal retiring age' in its present legislative context
dates only from 1971, it has been the subject of judicial exposition to an extent which is *f*
remarkable both in amount and in variety. I must refer to some of the authorities. In
Ord v Maidstone and District Hospital Management Committee [1974] 2 All ER 343 at 346, a
case which counsel for the appellant described as the sheet anchor of the appellant's case,
Donaldson P, in the National Industrial Relations Court, expressed the opinion that the
ordinary meaning of the words 'normal retiring age' is 'the age at which the employees
concerned usually retire'. But that was a case where there was no contractual retiring age
for the group of employees to which the appellant belonged, namely mental health *g*
officers. In that respect the case is distinguishable from the present.

Donaldson P's definition of 'normal retiring age' was disapproved by the Court of
Appeal in *Nothman v Barnet London Borough* [1978] 1 All ER 1243, [1978] 1 WLR 220
where the employee was a woman teacher. The contracts of employment of all teachers,
men and women, provided for automatic retiral at age 65, with no power to the *h*
employers to grant any extension. The teacher concerned was dismissed when she was
aged 61. The Court of Appeal (reversing the Employment Appeal Tribunal) held that
the normal retiring age in any particular profession was the age at which the employees
in that profession 'must retire or should retire' in accordance with their contracts (see
[1978] 1 All ER 1243 at 1245, [1978] 1 WLR 220 at 227 per Lord Denning MR). Lawton
LJ said that counsel for the employers had submitted that there was no normal retiring *j*
age for their assistant teachers. The Lord Justice then said ([1978] 1 All ER 1243 at 1247–
1248, [1978] 1 WLR 220 at 229):

> 'He [counsel] alleged before us, but did not call any evidence before the industrial tribunal to establish that this is so, that the authority's assistant teachers retire at all ages, some after 65, others well before that time. This submission may have been

> founded on the definition of "normal retiring age" which Sir John Donaldson P gave
> a in *Ord v Maidstone and District Hospital Management Committee* [1974] 2 All ER 343 at 246.'

Lawton LJ then quoted the definition and proceeded:

> 'I do not accept Sir John Donaldson P's definition as being correct. I construe the word "retiring" in the phrase "the normal retiring age" as having gerundial qualities
> b so as to give it the sense of "must" or "should". It follows that the normal retiring age of teachers employed by the authority is the age at which they would have to retire unless their service was extended by mutual agreement. This age was 65. The conditions of employment said so.'

Accordingly, that case is authority for the proposition that the normal retiring age for an employee is to be found by looking exclusively at the conditions of employment
c applicable to the group of employees holding his position.

When *Nothman*'s case came on appeal to your Lordships' House, it was decided on another point, and the only reference to the weight to be given to the contractual retirement date was made by Lord Salmon who appears to have assumed that it was conclusive (see [1979] 1 All ER 142 at 143, 145–146, [1979] 1 WLR 67 at 69, 71–72). But as the point was not argued in this House I do not regard anything said here as indicating
d the considered view of the House or any of its members.

The decision of the Court of Appeal in *Nothman*'s case has stood until the present time though not without some judicial criticism, especially in *Howard v Department of National Savings* [1981] 1 All ER 674, [1981] 1 WLR 542 from Ackner and Griffiths LJJ and in *Secretary of State for Trade v Douglas* [1983] IRLR 63 from Lord McDonald.

In *Post Office v Wallser* [1981] 1 All ER 668 the Court of Appeal held that the normal
e retiring age was a matter of evidence and did not depend exclusively on the relevant contract of employment. Some of the observations in that case are not altogether easy to reconcile with what had been said in *Nothman*'s case but I respectfully agree with the view expressed by Bridge LJ as follows (at 673):

> 'I agree with the broad proposition that the normal retiring age within the
> f meaning of [para 10 of Sch 1 to the 1974 Act] is not necessarily to be discovered in the contract of employment of the group of workers with whom the court or tribunal is concerned, but it does seem to me that when contractual terms and conditions of employment do govern the age of retirement of the relevant group, those terms provide the best evidence which will prevail to determine what is the normal age of retirement, *unless effectively contradicted by other evidence*'. (My emphasis.)

g

In *Howard v Dept for National Savings* the Court of Appeal reverted to the view that the contractual retiring age, express or implied, conclusively fixed the normal retiring age, and they also said that unless a contractual retiring age is either expressed or to be implied, it is impossible to establish that there is any normal retiring age. But in *Duke v Reliance Systems Ltd* [1982] ICR 449, where there was no express contractual retiring age,
h the Employment Appeal Tribunal took a more flexible view. Browne-Wilkinson J, delivering the judgment of the tribunal, first held that no contractual retiring age could be implied, and then proceeded to consider whether there was evidence of practice which established a normal retiring age. In my opinion that was the correct approach.

I have reached the opinion that the Court of Appeal in *Nothman*'s case stated the law in terms which were too rigid and inflexible. If the normal retiring age were to be
j ascertained exclusively from the relevant contract of employment, even in cases where the vast majority of employees in the group concerned do not retire at the contractual age, the result would be to give the word 'normal' a highly artificial meaning. If Parliament had intended that result, it would surely not have used the word 'normal' but would have referred directly to the retirement age specified as a term of the employment. Moreover, in a case where, unlike *Nothman*'s case, the contract provides not for an

automatic retiral age but for a minimum age at which employees can be obliged to retire, it would be even more artificial to treat the minimum age as fixing the normal age, as a
the respondents would have us do, even in a case where the minimum age has become a dead letter in practice. By no means all contracts of employment specify the age, or the minimum age, of retirement; indeed, outside of large organisations like the Civil Service it is probably exceptional for the age of retirement to be specified. So, if the normal retiring age can be ascertained only from the terms of the contract, there will be many cases in which there is no normal retiring age and in which the statutory alternative of b
65 for a man and 60 for a woman will automatically apply, although some other age may be well established and recognised in practice. If that were the law it might operate harshly in the case of women employees over the age of 60, as they would never be entitled to complain to the industrial tribunal of unfair dismissal unless they could establish that they were subject to a contractual retiring age higher than 60.

I therefore reject the view that the contractual retiring age conclusively fixes the c
normal retiring age. I accept that where there is a contractual retiring age, applicable to all, or nearly all, the employees holding the position which the appellant employee held, there is a presumption that the contractual retiring age is the normal retiring age for the group. But it is a presumption which, in my opinion, can be rebutted by evidence that there is in practice some higher age at which employees holding the position are regularly retired, and which they have reasonably come to regard as their normal retiring age. d
Having regard to the social policy which seems to underlie the Act, namely the policy of securing fair treatment, as regards compulsory retirement, as between different employees holding the same position, the expression 'normal retiring age' conveys the idea of an age at which employees in the group can reasonably expect to be compelled to retire, unless there is some special reason in a particular case for a different age to apply. 'Normal' in this context is not a mere synonym for 'usual'. The word 'usual' suggests a purely e
statistical approach by ascertaining the age at which the majority of employees actually retire, without regard to whether some of them may have been retained in office until a higher age for special reasons, such as a temporary shortage of employees with a particular skill, or a temporary glut of work, or personal consideration for an employee who has not sufficient reckonable service to qualify for a full pension. The proper test is, in my view, not merely statistical. It is to ascertain what would be the reasonable expectation or f
understanding of the employees holding that position at the relevant time. The contractual retiring age will prima facie be the normal retiring age, but it may be displaced by evidence that it is regularly departed from in practice. The evidence may show that the contractual retirement age has been superseded by some definite higher age, and, if so, that will have become the normal retiring age. Or the evidence may show merely that the contractual retiring age has been abandoned and that employees retire at g
a variety of higher ages. In that case there will be no normal retiring age and the statutory alternatives of 65 for a man and 60 for a woman will apply.

In the present case the evidence does not establish that there was any practice whereby employees holding the position which the appellant held were permitted to retain their office after attaining the minimum retiring age of 60. The figures for the six years 1973 to 1978 inclusive show that a total of 41 officers holding the same position as the appellant h
retired. I use 'retired' to include some who 'regressed'. Of that total, 30 retired or regressed at the age of 60. Eleven were retained after they had attained age 60, but we know nothing of the reasons for their retention. The fact that just over one-quarter of the relevant group of officers were retained after they had attained age 60 falls far short of showing that the contractual retiring age had been abandoned or departed from. If the case had been a narrow one on its facts, one in which a tribunal might reasonably j
have taken the view that the contractual age had been abandoned, your Lordships might have thought it right to remit the case to an industrial tribunal to come to a decision on the facts. But in my view no tribunal applying the law correctly could find that the contractual retiring age had been departed from in this case. Accordingly, I consider that the appellant has failed to show that the industrial tribunal had jurisdiction to consider his complaint.

The subsidiary question which I have already mentioned concerns the meaning of one
a paragraph, para 10442, of the Civil Service Pay and Conditions of Service Code. In order to appreciate that paragraph it is necessary to refer to some of the other paragraphs on the same subject as follows:

> '*The Minimum Retirement Age*
>
> 8572 The minimum retirement age is the earliest possible age at which a civil
> b servant can retire of his own volition and become entitled to immediate payment of pension benefits; this for most civil servants is age 60 . . .
>
> *Continuation of Employment After Retirement Age*
>
> 8575 Provided his department is prepared to retain him, it is not necessary for a civil servant to retire at the minimum retirement age . . .
>
> c
>
> *Age of retirement*
>
> 10441 An officer may on age grounds retire at his own wish or be retired at the instigation of his department. In either case, retirement may be effected when the officer has reached his minimum retirement age, or at any time thereafter. The date of retirement of any officer who is being retired is a matter entirely within the
> d discretion of the head of each department.
>
> 10442 An officer who has not completed 20 years' reckonable service on reaching age 60 should, provided he is fit, efficient and willing to remain in service, be allowed to continue until he has completed 20 years' reckonable service or has reached age 65, whichever is the earlier. Officers with short service generally have special claims to retention.'

e The argument for the appellant on this part of the case is that the effect of the provision in para 10442 that an officer who has not completed 20 years' reckonable service 'should' be allowed to continue gives him a right to be retained. That involves reading the word 'should' as if it were 'must' and in my view there is no justification for reading it in that way. The same argument was presented on behalf of the appellant in *Howard v Dept of National Savings* [1981] 1 All ER 674 at 678, [1981] 1 WLR 542 at 545. Lord Denning
f MR said:

> 'The word "should" has been canvassed before us. It was suggested that it means "must". I do not agree. I think it means should normally be allowed. It still leaves the compulsory retirement age at 60, with a potential extension.'

I respectfully agree.

g Paragraph 10442 appears to me to be addressed to the officer in each department who has the responsibility of deciding whether to retain officers who attain age 60 or not. It is intended as an instruction to him on the general policy to be applied, and not to create rights in officers who attain age 60. That view is reinforced by the second sentence of para 10442. The reference there to officers with short service generally having 'special claims' to retention is in my view entirely inconsistent with the suggestion that they
h have a contractual right to be retained.

I am accordingly of opinion that the minimum retirement age, and the contractual retirement age of officers such as the appellant is age 60.

I would dismiss the appeal,

As success on the main question of law was divided, and as the appeal was to some extent a test case I would make no order for costs in this House or in the Court of Appeal.

j

LORD KEITH OF KINKEL. My Lords, I have had the benefit of reading in advance the speech of my noble and learned friend Lord Fraser. I agree with it, and for the reasons he gives I too would dismiss the appeal.

LORD SCARMAN. My Lords, for the reasons given in the speech of my noble and learned friend Lord Fraser, with whom I agree, I too would dismiss this appeal. I also agree that no order should be made as to costs in this House or the Court of Appeal. a

LORD BRIDGE OF HARWICH. My Lords, for the reasons given in the speech of my noble and learned friend Lord Fraser, with which I entirely agree, I too would dismiss the appeal.

LORD TEMPLEMAN. My Lords, for the reasons given in the speech of my noble b and learned friend Lord Fraser, I too would dismiss the appeal.

Appeal dismissed.

Solicitors: *Simmonds Church Rackham* (for the appellant); *Treasury Solicitor.*

c

Mary Rose Plummer Barrister.

Practice Note d

QUEEN'S BENCH DIVISION
LORD LANE CJ AND BINGHAM J
21 JULY 1983

Practice – Uncontested proceedings – Crown Office list – Criminal causes or matters – Disposal – Disposal without attendance. e

Practice – Crown Office list – Applications outside London – Urgent matters – Proceedings to be continued in London.

Judicial review – Delay – Reasons for delay – Application to set out reasons for delay – Extension of time – Consent of proposed respondent – Application by proposed respondent to set aside leave or direction given – RSC Ord 53, r 4. f

LORD LANE CJ gave the following direction at the sitting of the court.

Uncontested applications in criminal causes or matters g

The Practice Direction of 11 June 1982 ([1982] 2 All ER 704, [1982] 1 WLR 979) deals with the disposal of uncontested civil proceedings entered in the Crown Office list (including applications for judicial review) without the attendance at the court of the parties or their legal advisers where the parties are agreed as to the terms on which the proceedings could be disposed of and an order of the court is required to put the terms into effect. The same practice will from now on apply to criminal causes or matters h entered in the Crown Office list, save that, where a judge is satisfied that the order can be made, the proceedings will be listed for hearing in open court before a Divisional Court, rather than a single judge, without the parties or their representatives having to attend. Parties are reminded of the importance of complying with the requirements of the earlier direction, since the objects of saving time and the cost of attendance at court can only be achieved if the court is given sufficient information to enable a decision to be j made whether or not to make the order.

Applications made outside London

Proceedings which are required to be entered in the Crown Office list should, wherever practicable, be commenced in London. Where the urgency makes it necessary for an application in respect of such proceedings to be made outside London, the Crown Office should be consulted prior to making the application, if necessary by telephone, and the application should be made in accordance with any arrangements made by the Crown Office for its hearing outside London. The application should be confined to those matters which have to be dealt with urgently and, as soon as the application has been dealt with, the proceedings should be continued in London and further applications should be heard and directions given in London.

Delay in applying for leave to apply for judicial review

Where an application for leave to apply for judicial review under RSC Ord 53 is not made promptly and in any event within three months from the date when grounds for the application first arose as required by Ord 53, r 4, the application should set out the reasons for the delay.

If the consent of a proposed respondent to an extension of time has been obtained, such consent should be submitted with the application. If a proposed respondent has not consented to an extension, he shall, on notice to the applicant, have the right to apply promptly in open court to set aside any leave or direction which is given. Such an application to set aside will not always be necessary, since in any event on the substantive hearing a respondent will be entitled to rely on delay in making the application as a ground for opposing the grant of relief.

N P Metcalfe Esq Barrister.

Backer v Secretary of State for the Environment and another

QUEEN'S BENCH DIVISION (CROWN OFFICE LIST)
DAVID WIDDICOMBE QC SITTING AS A DEPUTY JUDGE OF THE HIGH COURT
16, 25 MAY 1983

Town and county planning – Development – Material change of use – Use for stationing residential caravans – Caravan – Structure designed or adapted for human habitation – Adapted for human habitation – Motor vehicle – Motor vehicle not designed for human habitation – Whether to be 'adapted' for human habitation vehicle requires physical alteration – Whether sufficient to constitute vehicle a caravan as being 'adapted' for human habitation if vehicle furnished to make it suitable for human habitation – Caravan Sites and Control of Development Act 1960, s 29(1).

A motor vehicle is not 'adapted' for human habitation so as to constitute it a 'caravan' within s 29(1)[a] of the Caravan Sites and Control of Development Act 1960 unless it has been physically altered in some way for human habitation. Accordingly a vehicle is not 'adapted' for human habitation within s 29(1) merely because by some means short of physical alteration, such as furnishing it with a bed and other furniture, it is made suitable for human habitation. It follows that a Commer van (not being a vehicle 'designed' for human habitation within s 29(1)) is not 'adapted' for human habitation within s 29(1) merely because it is stationed on land, furnished with a bed etc and is being lived in, and therefore it is not a caravan and its use for human habitation on land which is not a caravan site does not constitute a material change in the use of the land (see p 1023 *g h* and p 1024 *e* to *h*, post).

Dictum of Lord Reading CJ in *French v Champkin* [1920] 1 KB at 79, *Taylor v Mead*

a Section 29(1), so far as material, is set out at p 1023 *a*, post

[1961] 1 All ER 626, *Maddox v Storer* [1962] 1 All ER 831, *Burns v Currell* [1963] 2 All ER 297 and *Wurzal v Addison* [1965] 1 All ER 20 considered.

Notes
For control of caravan sites, see 37 Halsbury's Laws (3rd edn) 402, para 512.
For the Caravan Sites and Control of Development Act 1960, s 29, see 24 Halsbury's Statutes (3rd edn) 166.

Cases referred to in judgment
Burns v Currell [1963] 2 All ER 297, [1963] 2 QB 433, [1963] 2 WLR 1106, DC.
French v Champkin [1920] 1 KB 76.
Maddox v Storer [1962] 1 All ER 831, [1963] 1 QB 451, [1962] 2 WLR 958, DC.
Taylor v Mead [1961] 1 All ER 626, [1961] 1 WLR 435, DC.
Wurzal v Addison [1965] 1 All ER 20, [1965] 2 QB 131, [1965] 2 WLR 131, DC.

Appeal
Anthony Ernest Peter Backer appealed, pursuant to s 246 of the Town and Country Planning Act 1971, against the decision of the first respondent, the Secretary of State for the Environment, dated 25 June 1982, dismissing Mr Backer's appeal against an enforcement notice dated 3 December 1982 served on him by the second respondent, Wealden District Council, seeking an order that the decision be remitted to the Secretary of State for reconsideration on the ground that the decision was erroneous in law because it held that a Commer van stationed on land had been 'adapted' for human habitation within s 29(1) of the Caravan Sites and Control of Development Act 1961 and was therefore a caravan. The facts are set out in the judgment.

Andrew Bano for Mr Backer.
Simon D Brown for the Secretary of State.
The second respondent did not appear.

Cur adv vult

25 May. The following judgment was delivered.

DAVID WIDDICOMBE QC. On 3 December 1982 the Wealden District Council made an enforcement notice under s 67 of the Town and Country Planning Act 1971 in respect of an alleged breach of planning control on certain land known as Cullinghurst Wood, Colestock Green, Cowden, East Sussex. The development alleged to have taken place was 'a material change in the use of the land to use for the purposes of stationing residential caravans (including a converted Commer Van) thereon', and the notice called for cessation of the use and the removal of the caravans.

The owner of the land, Anthony Ernest Peter Backer, appealed against the enforcement notice to the Secretary of State for the Environment, the Secretary of State appointed an inspector to determine the appeal on his behalf and the inspector, after an inquiry and an inspection of the site, dismissed the appeal and upheld the enforcement notice. From that decision Mr Backer now appeals to this court pursuant to s 246 of the 1971 Act, but only in respect of the Commer van. An appeal lies only on a point of law.

The appeal raises the short, but not unimportant, question of whether the Commer van is a 'caravan' as defined in s 29(1) of the Caravan Sites and Control of Development Act 1960. This point does not appear in the original notice of motion, which is a manuscript document written, and it appears drafted, by Mr Backer himself, but it does appear in a subsequent notice of motion lodged on his behalf by his solicitors. No objection was taken by the Secretary of State to the point being raised in this way and I would have allowed an amendment of the original notice of motion had that been necessary.

'Caravan' is defined by s 29(1) of the 1960 Act to mean:

> 'any structure designed or adapted for human habitation which is capable of being moved from one place to another (whether by being towed, or by being transported on a motor vehicle or trailer) and any motor vehicle so designed or adapted, but does not include—(*a*) any railway rolling stock which is for the time being on rails forming part of a railway system, or (*b*) any tent.'

This definition operates for the purposes of Pt I of the 1960 Act, which relates to the licensing of caravan sites. It is not a definition for the purposes of the Town and Country Planning Act 1971, although 'caravan site' is defined in the same terms in the 1960 Act and the 1971 Act, so the definition of 'caravan' appears to be incorporated indirectly in the 1971 Act. Be that as it may, everyone concerned with this case has assumed that when the enforcement notice says 'caravan' it means 'caravan' as defined in the 1960 Act, and I am satisfied that that was the meaning the local planning authority intended for the term when they used it in the enforcement notice.

The inspector's decision letter of 25 June 1982, so far as it is relevant to the Commer van, reads as follows:

> '5. When I visited the site, I found it to be partially cleared of coppice behind a belt of matured trees on the west and south. Immediately inside the main access were some 18 vehicles in various states of repair with some tools, and some stocks of scaffold poles timber beams and assorted materials; there were on the site a number of stocks of cut logs and poles. Also on the site were 2 touring caravans, an old unlicensed ambulance and an unlicensed Commer Van (KMF 181B). One touring caravan was in residential use; one touring caravan and the ambulance were in use for storage of tools and materials; the Commer Van contained a bed, valor stoves, cupboards and a filing cabinet, and clothes on hangers, as well as tins of oil etc. The inquiry is only concerned with the caravans and the Commer Van.'

I pass to para 8 and I need only read the last sentence: 'Your client is living in the Commer Van on site at present.' Then para 13 reads:

> 'As regards the appeals on grounds (b) and (c), your client accepted that the Commer Van which he lived in, and a touring caravan in residential use had been stationed on the site for at least 2 years. In my view, after my inspection, the Commer Van is rightly to be regarded as a motor vehicle, which can be towed, and which has been adapted for human habitation; therefore this van is a caravan within the meaning of the Act. Hence, development has occurred as alleged, for which no planning permissions have been given.'

Then the inspector dismissed the appeal and upheld the notice.

Counsel for Mr Backer contended that the Commer van was not a motor vehicle 'designed or adapted' for human habitation so as to come within the second limb of the definition. He said that 'adapted' in the phrase 'designed or adapted' means physically altered in some way. He pointed out that the criteria in the definition, and also in the further definition of 'twin-unit' caravans in s 13 of the Caravan Sites Act 1968, were all physical, and he referred to cases under vehicle licensing law and the Road Traffic Acts where 'adapted' has been held to mean 'altered'. He said that there was no evidence before the inspector that the van had been altered in any way, and that the inspector had therefore erred in law in finding that it was a caravan.

Counsel for the Secretary of State contended that the term 'adapted' could be satisfied without physical alteration. He said that it meant 'fit and apt, or suitable, intrinsically so' or, alternatively, 'made suitable by some efforts short of physical alteration, for example by furnishing it'. He said that the cases cited by counsel for Mr Backer were distinguishable, because they were not concerned with the phrase 'designed or adapted'.

The contention of counsel for Mr Backer that there was no evidence before the inspector of any physical alteration of the Commer van was not disputed by counsel for the Secretary of State, and I accept it. Paragraph 5 of the decision letter, which I have quoted above, records what the inspector saw on his view, and I am satisfied that if he had found a physical adaptation of the van he would have recorded it. I think the a inspector was satisfied that the fact he found in para 5, ie the fact that the van was equipped for living purposes, was sufficient to render it 'adapted' for human habitation. Mr Backer appeared in person at the inquiry and there is no indication in the decision that he put the legal meaning of 'caravan' in issue. It appears that that has only been raised on this appeal.

So what does 'adapted for human habitation' in the phrase 'designed or adapted for b human habitation' mean in the 1960 Act? 'Adapted' in the phrase 'constructed or adapted for use . . . solely for the conveyance of any goods' in the context of vehicle licensing has been held to mean 'altered': see *French v Champkin* [1920] 1 KB and *Taylor v Mead* [1961] 1 All ER 626, [1961] 1 WLR 435. In the former case, Lord Reading CJ said (at 79):

> 'The justices seem to have treated the word "adapted" as if it were synonymous with "suitable" or "apt", whereas it must be construed as meaning altered so as to c make the vehicle apt for the conveyance of goods.'

But in two Road Traffic Act cases it was held that where the word 'adapted' appears by itself it means merely apt, fit or suitable: see *Maddox v Storer* [1962] 1 All ER 831, [1963] 1 QB 451 and *Wurzal v Addison* [1965] 1 All ER 20, [1965] 2 QB 131. In yet another Road Traffic Act case, *Burns v Currell* [1963] 2 All ER 297, [1963] 2 QB 433, it was said d obiter that 'adapted' in the phrase 'intended or adapted for use on roads' means merely 'apt or fit'.

I think the argument of counsel for Mr Macker does gain strength from these cases. There is obviously a parallel between the phrase 'constructed or adapted' in the vehicle licensing cases and the phrase 'designed or adapted' in the definition of caravan. But this is not conclusive. The phrases are not identical and the cases were under a different e statute. What has to be determined here is the meaning of the phrase 'designed or adapted' in the context of the 1960 Act.

During the argument of the case I was inclined to think that the approach of counsel for the Secretary of State was more in line with the purpose of the Act, but on mature consideration I have come to the opposite conclusion. In my judgment, it is important to remember that the definition operates for the purpose of Pt I of the 1960 Act, which f deals with the licensing of caravan sites. 'Caravan site' is defined in s 1(4) of that Act to mean 'land on which a caravan is stationed for the purposes of human habitation'. To constitute a caravan site, the caravans do not have to be in use for human habitation, and indeed counsel for the Secretary of State did not contend that 'adapted' means 'used'. Part I of the 1960 Act provides for the control and regulation of caravan sites and aims to set standards for their use and occupation. I find it hard to believe that these provisions were g aimed at motor vehicles, such as this Commer van, which were not designed for living in, but which merely happen to be capable of it if someone puts a bed and a cooking stove in the back. It seems to me more consistent with these elaborate provisions for regulating sites to adopt counsel for Mr Backer's meaning, and to say that motor vehicles are not caravans unless they are either designed for human habitation or have been physically altered in some way for that purpose and I so hold. h

It follows that the inspector erred in law and the decision must be remitted to the Secretary of State in so far as it relates to the Commer van. No doubt, when the Secretary of State reconsiders the matter, he will bear in mind his powers to correct or vary the notice. That possibility has not been canvassed in court and I express no view whether the use of such powers would be appropriate.

The matter will therefore be remitted to the Secretary of State to reconsider in the j light of the opinion of this court.

Appeal allowed. Case remitted to Secretary of State for reconsideration. Leave to appeal granted.

Solicitors: *Myers Ebner & Deaner*, Hammersmith (for Mr Backer); *Treasury Solicitor*.

Sepala Munasinghe Esq Barrister.

E V Saxton & Sons Ltd v R Miles (Confectioners) Ltd

CHANCERY DIVISION
HIS HONOUR JUDGE JOHN FINLAY QC SITTING AS A JUDGE OF THE HIGH COURT
23 FEBRUARY 1983

Company – Voluntary winding up – Creditors' voluntary winding up – Notice of meeting at which winding-up resolution to be proposed – Failure to give seven days' notice of meeting – Members' consenting to only one day's notice of meeting – Resolution for voluntary winding up passed – Validity of resolution – Companies Act 1948, s 293(1)(7).

A company failed to satisfy a judgment debt and, on 12 January 1982, at the request of the judgment creditor, a writ of fieri facias was issued. On 20 January an extraordinary general meeting of the company was convened for 21 January for the purpose of considering an extraordinary resolution to wind up the company voluntarily and to appoint a liquidator. Although a creditors' voluntary winding up was contemplated, no meeting of creditors was called at the same time, as was required by s 293(1)[a] of the Companies Act 1948 which provided that notwithstanding any power of the members of the company to waive any other requirement of the Act or the company's articles with respect to the period of notice to be given of any meeting of the company, 'the company shall give at least seven days' notice of the meeting of the company at which the resolution for voluntary winding up is to be proposed'. On 21 January the sheriff's officials, acting under the writ of fieri facias, seized goods from the company's premises. The goods were subsequently sold. At 3 pm on 21 January the members of the company, having accepted less than the statutory length of notice of the extraordinary general meeting, passed the extraordinary resolution for the voluntary winding up of the company and for the appointment of a liquidator. Both the liquidator and the judgment creditor claimed the proceeds of the sale of the seized goods. The judgment creditor sought, inter alia, a declaration that the extraordinary resolution was invalid and ineffective on the ground that the company had not complied with s 293(1). The judgment creditor submitted that the company's failure to give at least seven days' notice of the meeting was not saved by s 293(7)[b] of the 1948 Act which provided that failure to give seven days' notice of a meeting of a company at which a resolution for voluntary winding up was to be proposed 'shall not affect the validity of any resolution passed or other thing done at that meeting which would be valid apart from [s 293(1)]', because s 293(7) saved only resolutions and other things of a character different from resolutions for the voluntary winding up of a company (with which alone s 293(1) was concerned) which would, notwithstanding s 293(1), be valid and effective.

Held – On its true construction s 293(7) of the 1948 Act saved anything done at a meeting convened for the purpose of passing a resolution for the voluntary winding up of a company, provided that the only ground on which the thing done would otherwise be invalid was the failure of the company to give the seven days' notice of the meeting required by s 293(1). Since there was no other ground for invalidating the resolution passed at the meeting on 21 January 1982 than the failure to give seven days' notice of the meeting, it followed that the resolution was saved by s 293(7) and was effective to place the company in a creditors' voluntary winding up. The liquidator, and not the judgment creditor, was accordingly entitled to the proceeds of the sale of the seized goods (see p 1030 *f g* and p 1031 *a* to *c*, post).

Re Centrebind Ltd [1966] 3 All ER 889 considered.

---

a Section 293(1) is set out at p 1027 *d*, post
b Section 293(7) is set out at p 1027 *g*, post

Notes

For the Companies Act 1948, s 293(1) and (7) (as respectively substituted and added by the Companies Act 1981, s 106), see 51 Halsbury's Statutes (3rd edn) 353.

Case referred to in judgment

Centrebind Ltd, Re [1966] 3 All ER 889, [1967] 1 WLR 377.

Summons

By a summons dated 2 November 1982 the plaintiff, E V Saxton & Sons Ltd (Saxton) sought (i) a declaration that an extraordinary resolution passed at a general meeting of the defendant, R Miles (Confectioners) Ltd (Miles), held on 21 January 1982 was rendered void and of no effect by s 106 of the Companies Act 1981, (ii) a declaration that a sum standing to the credit of Miles in the Companies Liquidation Account at the Bank of England was payable as to £2,548 to Saxton and as to the balance to Miles or as the court might otherwise direct, and (iii) further or other relief. The facts are set out in the judgment.

Ralph Instone for Saxton.
Miles was not represented.

HIS HONOUR JUDGE JOHN FINLAY QC. This is an application by judgment creditors of the respondent company which raises a novel point, and one not without difficulty, as to the construction of the new sub-s (1) of s 293 of the Companies Act 1948 which was substituted for the original sub-s (1) by s 106(1) of the Companies Act 1981.

The context in which the question as to the construction of that subsection arises is this. On 7 January 1982 the applicant company, E V Saxton & Sons Ltd (which I shall call 'Saxton') recovered judgment for a sum of £10,735·47, plus interest and costs, against the company which is the respondent to this application, R Miles (Confectioners) Ltd (to which I shall refer as 'Miles').

On 12 January 1982 a writ of fi fa was issued by Saxton and on 21 January 1982 the sheriff's officers cleared the premises of Miles of goods but, before these goods were sold, which subsequently happened, there was held at 3.00 pm on that same day, 21 January 1982, a meeting of the company, Miles, in which were passed a resolution that the company be wound up and a further resolution appointing Miss Savill as liquidator of the company.

As I have indicated, execution, at that juncture, had not been completed by payment to the creditors; but the goods seized were subsequently sold and, by reason of the appointment of the liquidator under the provisions of s 325 of the Companies Act 1948, the proceeds of sale were handed over to the liquidator and are now in an account with the Bank of England. Whether the proceeds go to Saxton or to the liquidator turns on whether the resolution to wind up was invalid or valid.

Because of doubts raised as to the validity of the resolution to wind up, a meeting of creditors was held at which Mr Cook was appointed in place of Miss Savill as liquidator of the company, but subsequently, because of these like doubts, Mr Cook resigned as liquidator. There is now, therefore, no liquidator of Miles, the respondent company. Miles has indicated that it does not wish to be represented at this hearing and neither does the Bank of England or the Department of Trade and Industry.

The difficulty which arises by reason of the provisions of s 293(1) arises in this way. The meeting held on 21 January 1982 was convened by a notice dated the preceding day, 20 January 1982, and that notice called the meeting for 3 o'clock on the afternoon of 21 January and stated that the meeting was convened—

> 'for the purposes of considering and if thought fit passing the following Extra Ordinary Resolution: That the Company be wound up voluntarily and that Delya Savill F.C.A. . . . be appointed Liquidator for the purposes of such winding up . . .'

No notice was given to the creditors of Miles and accordingly there was a failure to
a comply with the provisions of s 293(1) of the 1948 Act. As originally enacted that subsection provided:

> 'The company shall cause a meeting of the creditors of the company to be summoned for the day, or the day next following the day, on which there is to be held the meeting at which the resolution for voluntary winding up is to be proposed, and shall cause the notices of the said meeting of creditors to be sent by post to the
> b creditors simultaneously with the sending of the notices of the said meeting of the company.'

Had s 293 not been amended by the substitution of the new subsection there would therefore have been a failure to comply with its provisions by reason of the complete lack of any notice being given to the creditors of the company. But the substituted subsection
c contains an added requirement that the notice should be of a minimum length of seven days and consequently there was the additional failure to comply with that new requirement. The new sub-s (1) is in these terms:

> 'Notwithstanding any power of the members, or of any particular majority of the members, to exclude or waive any other requirement of this Act or the company's articles with respect to the period of notice to be given of any meeting of the
> d company, the company shall give at least seven days' notice of the meeting of the company at which the resolution for voluntary winding up is to be proposed; and the company shall in addition—(*a*) cause a meeting of the creditors of the company to be summoned for the day, or the day next following the day, on which the said meeting of the company is to be held; and (*b*) cause the notices of the said meeting of the creditors to be sent by post to the creditors simultaneously with the sending
> e of the notices of the said meeting of the company.'

The reference to the 'power of the members, or of any particular majority of the members, to exclude or waive any other requirement of this Act or the company's articles with respect to the period of notice' is, so far as the statutory provisions are concerned, a reference to the joint effect of s 141 of the Companies Act 1948, which deals with the
f nature and statutory requirements of extraordinary resolutions and special resolutions, and s 133 of that Act, which deals with the length of notice required for the calling of meetings and, in sub-s (3) of that section, with the powers which the members of a company, or in certain cases a majority holding not less that 95% in nominal value of the shares giving a right to attend and vote, have to waive the statutory requirement as to the length of notice of the meeting.

g In addition to the substitution of the new sub-s (1) of s 293, s 106 of the Companies Act 1981 provides, in sub-s (2) thereof, that there shall be added at the end of s 293 the following new subsection, sub-s (7), and that is in these terms:

> 'Failure to give notice of the meeting of the company mentioned in subsection (1) above as required by that subsection shall not affect the validity of any resolution passed or other thing done at that meeting which would be valid apart from that
> h subsection.'

On 22 December 1981 s 106 of the 1981 Act was brought into operation, so that by the time of the meeting held on the afternoon of 21 January 1982 it was the new sub-s (1) and the additional sub-s (7) of s 293 which determined the validity, operation and effect of resolutions passed on that afternoon.

j I have indicated the nature of the rest of the notice by which the meeting on 21 January was convened. Notwithstanding the fact that the notice referred to the 'passing of an extraordinary resolution that the company would be wound up voluntarily' (which appears to indicate an intention to pass a resolution in accordance with s 278(1)(*c*) of the 1948 Act) the terms of the proposed resolution are expressed in language more apt to indicate an intention to act under para (*b*) of sub-s (1) of that section. The minutes of the meeting show that the secretary of the company having reported that the company could not, by reason of its liabilities, continue its business and that it was advisable to wind up (a report which echoes the wording of s 278(1)(*c*)) it was then resolved that the company be, and was thereby, wound up under s 278(1)(*b*). Pursuant to the statutory provisions notice of that resolution, the notice being in a printed form, was duly given and lodged. a

The question of construction which arises in relation to the resolution to wind up concerns the meaning and effect of the new sub-s (7) of s 293 of the 1948 Act. Counsel for the applicant company has submitted that there are two possible constructions to be given to the words at the end of that sub-s (7), namely 'which would be valid apart from that subsection', that these words mean, on the one hand, 'notwithstanding that subsection', that is to say notwithstanding sub-s (1) or, alternatively, on the other hand, mean 'in the absence of that subsection' or, to put it another way, 'were it not for subsection (1)' or, indeed, to put it in a third manner, 'if subsection (1) had not been enacted'. b c

I have not had the advantage of hearing adversarial argument on this question of construction but I do not think I have suffered any real disadvantage from that because counsel for the applicant company has placed the arguments for and against the two constructions before me with that amplitude and fairness which one would expect. He submits that the arguments for what he calls the 'substantive' construction, that is the construction which would invalidate the resolution to wind up, are three in number. Before I turn to them, let me put, in different terms, the construction which has the effect of invalidating the resolution to wind up. Subsection (7), which I will read again, provides: d

> 'Failure to give notice of the meeting of the company mentioned in subsection (1) above as required by that subsection shall not affect the validity of any resolution passed or other thing done at that meeting which would be valid apart from that subsection.' e

The substantive construction is that that saving provision is intended to save those resolutions, other than a resolution for the voluntary winding up of the company (which is the resolution with which sub-s (1) is concerned), which would, notwithstanding the provisions of s 293(1), be valid and effective, and in a case of a meeting called at such short notice as one day or even less such resolutions could be valid and effective where, as for example, in the present case, the only two shareholders in the company both attend the meeting and, as was done in this case, agree to waive the requirement of 14 or, as the case might require, 21 days' notice. f

The 'substantive' construction of sub-s (7) is that the words 'would be valid apart from that subsection' mean 'which would be valid notwithstanding sub-s (1)', so that the validation or saving provision applies only to resolutions other than the resolution for voluntary winding up, with which alone sub-s (1) deals. By implication the effect is that the resolution for voluntary winding up is not saved or validated by sub-s (7) and the substantive construction of s 293(1) has the result that the resolution has not been effectively passed. g

The other construction is that sub-s (7) is not limited in its effect to resolutions of a particular category passed at the meeting in question but applies to anything done at that meeting including the resolution for voluntary winding up and validates any resolution passed or other thing done at that meeting which would be valid if sub-s (1) in its new form had not been enacted. Counsel for the applicant company referred to that as the 'procedural' construction. h

The arguments in favour of the substantive construction are, he submitted, three in number. The first, he submitted, is that on the face of it there would not be very much point in prescribing a minimum period of notice if the only consequence of non-compliance with that provision were the imposition of fines which are provided for by sub-s (6) of s 293. j

The second submission is that there can be no doubt that the mischief at which the

new sub-s (1) was directed was that which was highlighted by a decision in 1966, a
a mischief which indeed now takes its name from the title of the matter in which that decision was made, the decision being *Re Centrebind Ltd* [1966] 3 All ER 889, [1967] 1 WLR 377 (in company jargon the mischief is called 'centrebinding'). In that case the shareholders in the company had accepted short notice of an extraordinary general meeting which was held on the following day and at which an extraordinary resolution for winding up the company was passed and the applicant in the matter was appointed
b as liquidator. There had been no compliance with the provisions of s 293(1), as it then stood, in that there had been no convention of a meeting of creditors, and Plowman J held that, notwithstanding the failure to comply with the requirement that the company should 'cause a meeting of the creditors of the company to be summoned for the day, or the day following the day, on which the resolution to wind up was intended to be passed', the liquidator had, nevertheless, been effectively appointed. He said ([1966] 3 All ER 889
c at 890, [1967] 1 WLR 377 at 379):

> 'I take the view that where a meeting of the members has nominated or appointed a liquidator and no meeting of creditors had been held, nevertheless until something is done about it at the instance of the creditors, the person nominated or appointed as liquidator by the members at their meeting is the liquidator of the company . . .'

d The submission, as I understand it, in this regard is that, that being the operation and effect of the former sub-s (1), the necessity to amend it to obviate the possibility that shareholders could set on foot a winding up and appoint their own liquidator without giving creditors a chance to substitute their own nominee was a mischief which could only be effectively countered if the new sub-s (1) had the effect of invalidating the resolution for winding up passed at a meeting of which adequate (that is statutory) notice
e had not been given and, indeed, invalidating the resolution passed at a meeting where the company had failed to cause a meeting of the creditors to be summoned as the statute requires.

The third submission is that, as I understand it, the words that occur at the end of sub-s (7), ie the words 'which would be valid apart from that subsection', are otiose if any construction other than the substantive construction is the proper construction to be
f placed on the subsection, because the same result could have been achieved by making the subsection finish when it said 'failure to give notice . . . shall not affect the validity of any resolution passed or other thing done at that meeting'.

In favour of the contrary construction, the procedural construction, it is submitted, in the first argument, that if it were intended to invalidate the resolution for voluntary winding up passed at a meeting where there had been a failure to comply with the
g provisions of sub-s (1) then there is a simple and unambiguous formula which is found in another provision of the Act which would have achieved that result with no dubiety whatsoever. That formula is to be found in s 142 of the Companies Act 1948, which deals with resolutions requiring special notice and provides that where special notice is required of a resolution—

> h 'the resolution shall not be effective unless notice of the intention to move it has been given to the company not less than twenty-eight days before the meeting at which it is moved . . .'

And there follow other provisions. So that the formula 'the resolution shall not be effective unless' certain conditions are complied with is one that would have been open to the draftsman to employ in sub-s (7) if it had been intended to invalidate the resolution
j for voluntary winding up unless there had been compliance with the statutory requirements.

The second argument in favour of the procedural construction is this. Suppose that the whole of sub-s (7) had been omitted, then the effect of sub-s (1) would be that a resolution for voluntary winding up passed at a meeting of which the requisite seven days' notice had not been given, or passed at a meeting at which the company had failed to comply with the additional requirements of causing a meeting of creditors to be summoned, would be a resolution which had been passed otherwise than in accordance with the statute and accordingly would, prima facie, be invalid. So that the provisions of sub-s (7) would not be necessary to achieve that result. To put it another way. On the face of it the fact that there is a sub-s (7) does not indicate that the resolution for voluntary winding up would be invalid if the statutory requirements had not been complied with but indicates a need to validate it and other things done at the meeting which, by virtue of sub-s (1) would, but for sub-s (7), be invalid.

The third submission is this: that the wording 'which would be valid apart from that subsection', in contradistinction to other alternative forms of wording which occur to one's mind, for example 'which would have been invalid' or 'which is invalid', indicates that the wording 'which would be' implies that 'apart from' means 'if subsection (1) had not been enacted'.

The two possible constructions are, I think, to be distinguished in this way. If the intention of sub-s (7) is to invalidate the resolution for voluntary winding up if the statutory requirements have not been complied with but to validate other things done at the meeting in question, then the amendments effected by s 106 have done not one thing in relation to the old s 293 but two quite different things. In the first place, they have imposed a minimum period of notice that is required and cannot by any means be waived in relation to a resolution for voluntary winding up and, in the second place, they have introduced a new and different sanction to compel observance of this new statutory requirement and, indeed, of the requirements that are on the same lines as those imposed by the original sub-s (1) of s 293.

If, on the other hand, the procedural construction is the correct construction then the amendments make, in effect, one alteration to the form of provision. They insert the requirement that there shall be a minimum period of notice of the meeting, but leave unaffected the operation and effect of the sanctions by way of imposition of a fine which one found in s 293 as originally enacted. That second construction necessitated the introduction of the new sub-s (7) because whereas the old sub-s (1) dealt merely with the company's obligation to cause a meeting of creditors to be summoned, and did not impose a minimum time limit for the notice of the meeting of the company, there was no need in relation to the original sub-s (1) to validate what was done at a meeting which was called otherwise than in compliance with the statutory provisions.

I have come to the clear conclusion that the reason for sub-s (7) is that the legislature has thought fit to validate not only the resolution for voluntary winding up but anything else that is done at a meeting convened for the purpose of passing such a resolution, notwithstanding the fact that there has been a failure to give that notice of the meeting of the company of the length required by the new sub-s (1), provided there is no other ground of invalidity. I am fortified in my view that that is the true construction not only by the considerations, which I have indicated were put before me by counsel for the applicant company, but by this additional point: that sub-s (7) refers to failure to give notice of the meeting of the company but makes no reference to failure to comply with the other requirements of sub-s (1) as to causing a meeting of the creditors of the company to be summoned, as set out in the subsection, or to cause to be posted notices to those creditors in accordance with the statutory provisions. It would be curious if a failure to comply with the time limitation were to give rise to the total invalidity of the resolution to wind up and yet the validity of the resolution would be unaffected by a failure to comply with the other statutory provisions as to giving notice to creditors.

The object of the new subsection appears to me to have been, by imposing a minimum time limit for the notice calling the meeting, to ensure that creditors, if there is compliance with the provisions about notifying them, have a reasonable opportunity not only to attend the meeting but to consider the course of action which they intend to adopt. That object can, in my judgment, be achieved by the imposition of the statutory requirements, with the sanction of fines and penalties if there is default in compliance with them, and I do not find that the effect of sub-s (7) is to add the additional sanction of rendering a resolution for voluntary winding up invalid if there is a failure to comply with the time provisions now imposed.

I would only say finally that the construction which I have placed on sub-s (7) is, I think, the construction which one would arrive at, as a matter of first impression, because the reference in the subsection is to the validity of *any* resolution passed or other thing done at that meeting and that reference appears to me clearly to connote not only resolutions of a character different from resolutions for voluntary winding up but clearly also to include the resolution for voluntary winding up which is the purpose of calling the meeting. In my judgment the validity of the resolution for voluntary winding up which is passed at the meeting is not affected by the failure to give notice in compliance with the new sub-s (1) if the resolution would be valid apart from sub-s (1), that is to say if sub-s (1) had not been enacted. The resolution in question, although passed at a meeting of which only one day's notice had been given, was, I find, an effective and valid notice, apart from the provisions of s 293(1) as substituted by the 1981 Act, in that the shortness of notice was waived by all the members of the company and accordingly the resolution was, in my judgment, effective.

Declaration that extraordinary resolution passed at general meeting of Miles on 21 January 1982 effective to place Miles in creditors' voluntary winding up.

Solicitors: *Sharman & Trethewy*, Bedford (for Saxton).

Hazel Hartman Barrister.

Gloucestershire County Council v Farrow and others

CHANCERY DIVISION
GOULDING J
12, 13, 14, 15, 18, 19, 20, 21, 22, 25 APRIL, 3 MAY 1983

Highway – Dedication – Presumption – Public use for prescribed period – Existing private right not asserted in derogation of highway during prescribed period – Manorial market right – Land originally dedicated subject to market right – Whether user for prescribed period without assertion of market right effecting rededication free from market right and extinguishing right – Highways Act 1980, s 31(1).

A lord of the manor owned an ancient market franchise under royal charter which entitled him to hold a weekly market in a market square owned by him. By the late nineteenth century the square had been dedicated as a highway in connection with the market and in consequence a public right of way had been created over the square, subject to the lord of the manor's right to use the square for the weekly market. The surface of the square, being a highway maintainable by the public at large, became vested in the local highway authority. In about 1900 the weekly market ceased to be held and since then had never been held. In August 1979 the lord of the manor leased his market rights and privileges to a company which wished to revive the weekly market. The highway authority brought an action against the lord of the manor and the company claiming (i) a declaration that because the square was a highway they were not entitled to obstruct it by exercising the manorial market right, and (ii) an injunction restraining them from doing so. The highway authority alleged that the square had been continuously enjoyed as a highway by the public as of right for a period of over 20 years, during which period the right to hold the market had not been asserted, and therefore

by virtue of s 31(1)[a] of the Highways Act 1980 the public had a right of way over the square unqualified by the manorial market right, which was in effect extinguished by a
s 31(1). The defendants submitted that s 31 was not intended to deprive a landowner of the right to exercise on his own land a subsisting legal privilege vested in him such as the market right.

Held – Since s 31 of the 1980 Act, like s 34 of the Highways Act 1959 which it replaced, was enacted to avoid the need for lengthy and expensive investigation of ancient rights b
when highway rights were called in question, s 31 was to be given a broad interpretation. Accordingly, even though the original dedication of the square as a highway had been made subject to the manorial market right and the vesting in the highway authority of the square had not of itself taken away that right, the effect of s 31(1) was that the subsequent period of 20 years' uninterrupted public enjoyment of the square as a highway without the assertion of the manorial market right resulted in the presumption, c
which had not been rebutted, that the square had been rededicated as a highway free from the market right, and thus the market right had been extinguished. It followed that the declaration and injunction would be granted (see p 1035 *e f*, p 1036 *c d*, p 1037 *b c f g* and p 1038 *b* to *e*, post).

Notes d

For the statutory presumption of dedication of a way over land as a highway, see 21 Halsbury's Laws (4th edn) para 78, and for cases on the subject, see 26 Digest (Reissue) 472–475, *3190–3198*.

For the Highways Act 1980, s 31, see 50(1) Halsbury's Laws (3rd edn) 497.

Cases referred to in judgment e

A-G v Honeywill [1972] 3 All ER 641, [1972] 1 WLR 1506.
A-G v Horner (1885) 11 App Cas 66, HL; *affg* (1884) QBD 245, CA.
Beckett v Leeds Corp (1872) 7 Ch App 421, LJJ.
Copestake v West Sussex CC [1911] 2 Ch 331.
Doe d Clayton v Williams (1843) 11 M & W 803, 152 ER 1029.
Newcastle (Duke) v Worksop UDC [1902] 2 Ch 145, [1900–3] All ER Rep 549. f
Tunbridge Wells Corp v Baird [1896] AC 434, HL.
Willmott v Barber (1880) 15 Ch D 96; *on appeal* (1881) 17 Ch D 772, CA.

Cases also cited

A-G v Beynon [1969] 2 All ER 263, [1970] Ch 1.
A-G v British Museum Trustees [1903] 2 Ch 598. g
A-G v Hanmer (1858) 27 LJ Ch 837.
A-G v Horner (1884) 14 QBD 245, CA.
A-G v Horner (No 2) [1913] 2 Ch 140, CA.
Brandon v Barnes [1966] 3 All ER 296, [1966] 1 WLR 1505, DC.
Fairey v Southampton CC [1956] 2 All ER 834, [1956] 2 QB 439, CA.
Lewis v Thomas [1950] 1 All ER 116, [1950] 1 KB 438, CA. h
Lockwood v Wood [1841] 6 QB 31, 115 ER 12.
Tithe Redemption Commission v Runcorn UDC [1954] 1 All ER 653, [1954] Ch 383, CA.

Action

By a writ issued on 17 September 1979 and statement of claim dated 17 April 1980 the plaintiff, Gloucestershire County Council, claimed against the defendants, Michael j
Farrow, trading as Stow-on-the-Wold Market Co, Kenneth de Courcy and Bisbey Properties Ltd (1) a declaration that the land known as Market Square, Stow-on-the-Wold constituted a highway within the meaning of the Highways Act 1959; (2) a declaration

---

a Section 31, so far as material, is set out at p 1036 *j* to p 1037 *b*, post

that the defendants were not entitled either jointly or severally to exercise or to cause or permit to be exercised on the said highway in the Market Square any weekly Thursday market rights derived from any franchise granted under the terms of any royal charter; and (3) an order restraining the defendants and each of them whether by themselves, their servants or agents or otherwise howsoever from causing, permitting, aiding or abetting the holding on the highway, at the Market Square, of a weekly Thursday market so as to obstruct the right of the public to pass and repass and to park their vehicles on the said highway or otherwise to interfere with the rights of the public to the use and enjoyment of the highway or so as to cause a public nuisance. The facts are set out in the judgment.

Michael Burke-Gaffney QC and *G S Lawson Rogers* for the council.
C I Howells for the defendants.

Cur adv vult

3 May. The following judgment was delivered.

GOULDING J. In this action the plaintiff, Gloucestershire County Council, sues for declarations and an injunction. The plaintiff council's object is to prevent the revival of a weekly Thursday market in the place called the Market Square, or often simply the Square, at Stow-on-the-Wold. Such a market began before the commencement of legal memory, having been granted to the Abbey of Evesham by a charter of King Henry I. It is common ground that it ceased about the year 1900, but no evidence has been adduced of the exact date at which it was last held nor of the circumstances of its desuetude. The council sues in the character of local highway authority, and its right to maintain the action in its own name has not been challenged.

The second defendant, Mr de Courcy, claims to be Lord of the Manor of Stow, and owner of the market franchise, as also of a franchise granted to the same abbey in the reign of King Edward IV, to hold a fair in Stow twice yearly, namely in May and October. For the purposes of this action, the plaintiff admits those claims. I shall nevertheless, in a different connection, have to examine the second defendant's title in the course of this judgment. The third defendant, Bisbey Properties Ltd, has a lease dated 3 August 1979 of the second defendant's market rights and privileges, for a term of seven years from 20 September 1979. The company desires to revive the weekly market. The first named defendant, Mr Michael Farrow, is a director of the company, and was described by counsel who appeared for all the defendants as its moving spirit.

The parties have mutually refrained from taking objections to the admissibility of proffered evidence and have not sought to hold one another rigorously to their pleadings, so that the trial assumed the character of an inquiry rather than of a game played by strict rules. Accordingly, I have perused a great deal of documentary material of varying importance and credibility. I have heard viva voce evidence from Mr David Roy Jones, an officer in the surveyor's department of the council. He has made a close study of the pertinent facts, and it is common ground that his evidence on matters within his knowledge is to be believed. I have also had the advantage of viewing the Market Square in the company of counsel, and subsequently of perambulating it alone.

The Square is an open space in the central part of Stow-on-the-Wold. It is about 500 feet long from north to south and of varying breadth, at its widest about 200 feet, from east to west. A street called High Street leads out of the north-western part of the Square and shortly joins a very ancient main road, the Foss Way. Two narrower streets, Church Street and Digbeth Street, respectively connect the south-western and south-eastern corners of the Square with the main road that leads in one direction to Cheltenham and in the other to Chipping Norton. A group of buildings stands in the midst of the southern half of the Square, as does also a restored market cross. In the north-eastern part of the Square is a small green, about 130 feet long and 50 feet wide. Stow-on-the-Wold

Parish Council caused this tract of land to be registered as a town or village green pursuant to the Commons Registration Act 1965. No other claimant having come forward, the a parish council was in due course registered as owner of the land under s 8(3) of the Act.

For the sake of brevity I shall in this judgment use the term 'the market place' to describe the whole of the Square with the exclusion of the buildings and cellars within and surrounding it and of the registered town or village green.

The history of the market place requires examination from three different points of view, first as to the ownership of the soil, second as to the exercise within the market b place of the franchises of a market and two fairs to which I have already referred, and third as to the existence there of a public highway.

Regarding the ownership of the soil, in my judgment the market place was originally waste of the Manor of Stow. I draw that inference from the whole body of documentary evidence which I have perused. I mention, in particular, a decree of the Court of Exchequer dated 18 October 1621, a conveyance of certain land in the Square dated 24 c April 1879, the minutes of the former Stow local board of health and of its successor the urban district council of Stow-on-the-Wold (notably those dated 10 January 1873, 20 December 1921 and 31 October 1922), and a lease of fair rights dated 24 September 1929 made by a Mrs Hewitt to the urban district council. This inference from the documents is supported by the fact that the twice-yearly fair has been continuously held in whole or in part on the market place, until the present time, by the authority of the lord of the d manor or his lessee. On the ordinary civil test of a preponderance of probabilities I think that the indications of a manorial title to the market place, coupled with its great breadth in comparison with an ordinary street, clearly rebut any presumption that the soil belongs to the owners of adjoining tenements usque ad medium filum viae: cf *Beckett v Leeds Corp* (1872) 7 Ch App 421. It will be necessary to mention in a moment the effect on the lord of the manor's title to the market place of the vesting provisions as to e highways contained in the Public Health Act 1875 and later statutes. Subject to the operation of that legislation my inference from the evidence is that the market place remained united with the Manor of Stow until after a conveyance dated 29 October 1945 whereby the manors or Lordships of Stow and of Maugersbury, together with a house, park, and other lands containing approximately 1,656 acres, were assured to Suburban and County Shops Trust Ltd. The following day the last-named company conveyed the f two manors to the second defendant and it is under that conveyance that he claims ownership of the market place for the purposes of the present action. It is, however, an unsatisfactory instrument in two respects. First of all, it contains no mention of the two charges by way of legal mortgage which Suburban and County Shops Trust Ltd had executed on its purchase of the property on the previous day and which certainly, in my opinion, comprised the manors. There is no evidence regarding the discharge or other g history of those encumbrances. Secondly, the description of the parcels conveyed is very puzzling. It is in these terms:

> 'ALL THOSE the Manors or Lordships of Stow-on-the-Wold and Maugersbury in the County of Gloucester but not including in the Conveyance hereby made any land hereditaments and premises comprised in the recited Conveyance other than the said Manors or Lordships. . .' h

The 'recited Conveyance' is that of 29 October in favour of the company.

The council maintains, and the defendants deny, that this form of words prevented any manorial waste from passing under the conveyance, and various arguments have been put forward to interpret the rigmarole in one way or another. No one has suggested that the second defendant was intended to take no more than the bare feudal superiority j of freehold estates, and it is highly unlikely that anyone would have thought of so limited a transaction in 1945. Counsel who represented the council at the trial argued that the conveyance was so expressed as to grant to the second defendant the incorporeal hereditaments appendant or appurtenant to the manors, while reserving all corporeal property. I cannot accept this submission, for such an intention could be very easily expressed in plain words, and I think it inconceivable that a draftsman so minded would have used the phrase 'land hereditaments and premises' in the words of exception. The most favourable interpretation for the council that I can stomach is that the obscure phraseology of the parcels was designed to exclude the operation of s 62(3) of the Law of Property Act 1925, so that only such property passed as would have been carried by a conveyance of specified manors or lordships made before 1882. On that construction I turn at once to the judgment of the Court of Exchequer in *Doe d Clayton v Williams* (1843) 11 M & W 803, 152 ER 1029. The question there was whether certain buildings claimed to have been erected on former waste of a certain manor or to be part of the demesne thereof passed under a grant of several 'manors or lordships, or reputed manors or lordships'. Lord Abinger CB said (11 M & W 803 at 807, 152 ER 1029 at 1030):

> 'Now, although the wastes and demesnes will pass by a conveyance of the manor, if nothing more be said, yet, if the manor be lost, and have become only a manor by reputation, there is no case which I am aware of that goes the length of deciding, that, under the words "reputed manor", the freehold interest in wastes, or in any specific tenement that is possessed by the grantor, will pass.'

The court consequently ordered a new trial to determine whether there was a manor in existence at the date of the grant or not. In the conveyance of 30 October 1945, no references is made to a reputed manor, and although the statement of claim does not admit the second defendant's claim to be Lord of the Manor of Stow, counsel for the council conceded it (for the purposes of this action) in his opening. Accordingly, again for the purposes of this action, I hold that the market place belongs to the second defendant, except to the limited extent and for the limited purposes to and for which it may be vested in the council as highway authority under the legislation now contained in s 263 of the Highways Act 1980. The character of the highway authority's statutory title is explained in several reported cases. It is enough for me to mention the observations of Lord Herschell in *Tunbridge Wells Corp v Baird* [1896] AC 434 at 442. In my judgment, any vesting of the highway in the council did not of itself take away any right of the lord of the manor to hold the market in the market place.

To show that I have not overlooked a point, which I think to be of no practical importance, I add that I do not find sufficient evidence to hold that the site of a small building formerly erected on part of the Square and demolished many years ago has ever ceased to be manorial property.

I turn to the history of the market place as regards the market and fairs. At the present day, part of the twice-yearly fairs, namely the amusement section, is held in the market place, the sale of animals being conducted on grounds just outside the built-up part of the town. It seems tolerably clear that the whole or part of each fair has always been conducted in the market place and I have seen no evidence to suggest the contrary. I am satisfied, and feel sure, that the Thursday market was also held in the market place, although specific positive evidence of the fact is scarce. The name 'Market Square' is an old one: certainly it appears on the ordnance survey map of 1885. The appearance of the Square is similar to that of open spaces in very many English country towns where weekly markets have long been, and still are, held. The presence of a market cross is an important part of that recognisable character of the place. One of the public houses in the Square still has an inscribed brass plate affixed to its wall which, as interpreted by oral tradition, testifies to the regular existence of a corn market outside. If the weekly market were *not* held in the Market Square, the fact would be remarkable and I should expect it to have been revealed by the exhaustive researches undertaken for the purposes of the present action. There is one, though so far as I have observed, only one, solid piece of positive demonstration on the point. It is both direct and strong. On 21 June 1886 the then local government board made a return to an order of the House of Commons dated 26 February in the same year. The order required a return showing, among other things, in respect of each local government district in England and Wales, whether any market was held in the district, to whom the market rights belonged, and whether the markets were held in the streets of any place in the district. The return as regards Stow-on-the-Wold showed that the market rights belonged to the lord of the manor, the tolls being at *a* the time leased, and that the market was held 'in market square'.

Third, as to the character of the market place as highway. At a late stage in the trial the defendants conceded that the whole of the market place is, and has been beyond memory of persons now living, a public highway. Counsel for the defendants was in the end driven to this admission by the mounting weight of the council's evidence, and in particular by the ordnance survey map of 1885, which shows the whole of the market *b* place (except the site of a building then standing and since demolished) coloured as metalled road, and by the evidence of Mr Jones as to the maintenance of the surface.

The effect therefore of my findings about the history of the market place is that in the late nineteenth century the whole of the market place was a highway, that the lord of the manor was entitled to the soil thereof except to the limited extent and for the limited purposes to and for which the market place was vested in the highway authority, and *c* that a Thursday market was held there pursuant to the ancient franchise likewise vested in the lord of the manor. Under those circumstances I am of opinion that I ought to infer that what was being done was being lawfully done. Accordingly, if the question had been raised before a court at that time, I would expect the court to have held that the market place was dedicated as a highway in connection with the market and with a view to utilising the franchise, and that consequently the dedication created a public right of *d* way subject to the right of the lord of the manor to use the market place for a market and fairs. The House of Lords reached a similar conclusion regarding a modern highway in *A-G v Horner* (1885) 11 App Cas 66. I have seen no evidence which would enable the court to limit the inference to any particular part of the market place.

That, however, is not the end of the matter because it comes to be litigated not in the latter part of the nineteenth century but in the latter part of the twentieth century. *e*

How has the legal situation of a hundred years ago been affected by the practical cessation of the Thursday market? It is well settled that a franchise is not extinguished by failure to exercise it over even a long period, although non-user may afford grounds for proceedings by the Crown to repeal the relevant charter. Moreover, I have held that the lord of the manor still retains a sufficient interest in the soil of the market place. Counsel for the council nevertheless puts forward two arguments either of which, if *f* accepted, will preclude the revival of the weekly market.

One of them asserts an equitable estoppel along the lines defined by Fry J in *Willmott v Barber* (1880) 15 Ch D 96 at 105–106. I am not convinced by that argument. In the first place, having regard to the knowledge available to its members and officers, I doubt whether it can rightly be said that the council laboured under a mistake as to the continuing existence of a right in the lord of the manor to hold a weekly market in the *g* market place. I have particularly in mind some minutes of the council's general purposes sub-committee dated 9 December 1946. Assuming that point however in favour of the council (as counsel for the defendants himself was disposed to do), it has not in my judgment been demonstrated that the council has incurred expenditure, or otherwise altered its position for the worse, on the faith of its mistaken belief. Market or no market, the council as highway authority has been obliged to maintain the market place from *h* time to time according to its actual condition and the changing needs of the people. The testimony of Mr Jones showed that material expenditure not hitherto incurred will be necessary if the market is revived, but it did not (to my mind) prove that any substantial money or work will have been wasted by that turn of events or would not have been undertaken had it been foreseen.

The other contention of counsel for the council is more formidable. The statement of *j* claim bases the council's case firmly on s 34 of the Highways Act 1959, since replaced by s 31 of the Highways Act 1980 without significant alteration so far as this case is concerned. The first two subsections of s 31 are as follows:

> '(1) Where a way over any land, other than a way of such a character that use of it by the public could not give rise at common law to any presumption of dedication,

> has been actually enjoyed by the public as of right and without interruption for a full period of 20 years, the way is to be deemed to have been dedicated as a highway unless there is sufficient evidence that there was no intention during that period to dedicate it.
>
> (2) The period of 20 years referred to in subsection (1) above is to be calculated retrospectively from the date when the right of the public to use the way is brought into question, whether by a notice such as is mentioned in subsection (3) below or otherwise ...'

The council in the statement of claim alleges that the market place has been continuously used and enjoyed by the public as of right and without interruption as a highway for all purposes for a full period of over 20 years before 6 July 1979, alternatively 10 May 1973, more particularly since at least the year 1900. That allegation has, in my judgment, been established, and I will at once make four comments thereon.

(1) No date has been suggested as that on which, for the purposes of the Highways Acts, the right of the public to use the way was brought into question, except the two proposed by the council, namely 10 May 1973 or 6 July 1979, being the dates of two letters of complaint or claim addressed by the second defendant to the council and to the Chief Constable of Gloucestershire respectively.

(2) The May and October fairs cannot be relied on as interruptions of public enjoyment for the purposes of the Highways Acts. I need not and do not pronounce on their legitimacy in this action, but on the evidence before me they are to be justified by a qualified dedication of the highway, subject to the franchise rights of the lord of the manor.

(3) The fairs on the one hand and the weekly market on the other have to be considered as the subject of independent rights, since they were granted by distinct charters more than three centuries apart and are incapable of merger: see *Duke of Newcastle v Worksop UDC* [1902] 2 Ch 145 at 155–156, [1900–3] All ER Rep 549 at 552–554. The continued holding of the fairs neither preserves nor impairs any right to revive the weekly market.

(4) No attempt has been made to negative the intention to dedicate the market place as a highway during the relevant 20-year period except by admitting and asserting that it was dedicated long before any such period began. The second defendant did not give evidence at the trial.

Counsel for the council maintains that the 20-year enjoyment envisaged by the statute confers on the public a right of way limited and qualified only by such limits or qualifications as in actual fact restricted the public enjoyment during the statutory period. A private right that could be, but is not, asserted in derogation of the highway is in effect extinguished, so far as the highway is concerned, by the passing of 20 years.

Counsel for the defendants says that the language of the Highways Act 1980 does not warrant counsel for the council's submission. Section 31 presumes a dedication, but not necessarily a wholly unqualified dedication. To suppose that Parliament meant by the section to deprive a landowner of the right to exercise on his own land a subsisting legal privilege vested in him and duly granted by the Crown, to deprive him moreover without compensation, is, in counsel for the defendants' submission, to pervert the intention of the Act.

These arguments raise a question of some difficulty on the construction of the section and the answer to the question will determine the result of the action in this court. I much regret that I have to decide it without direct guidance from reported authority. Counsel for the council has drawn my attention to the observations of Parker J in *Copestake v West Sussex CC* [1911] 2 Ch 331 at 340, to the effect that—

> 'any presumption as to the extent of a public right of way ought to be drawn with reference to all the circumstances existing at the time when the question as to the extent of the public right arises ... But it would not, in my opinion, be right to raise a presumption from a state of circumstances proved to have existed thirty or fifty years ago, ignoring all that has happened since.'

That, however, was a case concerning the presumed dedication of particular land to increase the width of the highway and the judge had no such question in mind as that with which I am now concerned. Counsel for the council also mentioned *A-G v Honeywill* [1972] 3 All ER 641, [1972] 1 WLR 1506, where s 34 of the Highways Act 1959 was successfully invoked to show that an established footpath was also a carriageway. In his judgment, Bristow J said ([1972] 3 All ER 641 at 644, [1972] 1 WLR 1506 at 1510):

> 'It is not disputed, and I take it to be clear law, that if a right of way was originally dedicated for use on foot it can subsequently be dedicated for use with vehicles as well.'

Similarly, urges counsel for the council, a highway originally dedicated subject to the right to use the land for a periodic market, can subsequently be dedicated free from that reservation, and that is what the 1980 Act compels one to presume in this case. Counsel was, however, unable to point to any instance in which such a rededication of land used under a franchise had occurred, or to explain the means by which it would be effected.

Thus I am left to decide the matter as best I can on principle alone. On the whole I am of opinion that Parliament enacted s 31 of the Highways Act 1980, and its statutory predecessor, in order to avoid the need for lengthy and expensive antiquarian investigations when highway rights are called in question. That being so, I ought to give the section a broad interpretation and to accept the submission on the effect of 20 years' user which (though framed in my own language) I just now attributed to counsel for the council. Accordingly, I must hold that the manorial right to have a weekly market in the market place has been lost by the lapse of a 20-year period without such market being held.

I am satisfied by the evidence of Mr Jones that the holding of a market on any part of the market place would be a substantial interference with the highway as now enjoyed. Accordingly, I grant the two declarations and the injunction prayed by the statement of claim. I dismiss the counterclaim of the second defendant and also that of the third defendant. The second declaration counterclaimed by the third defendant is indeed in accordance with my view of the facts but it could lead in the circumstances to no consequential relief, and would be misleading, as the demise fails of its purpose. Moreover, persons who are not parties to the action may possibly have claims to the market place or part thereof. Therefore I do not think fit to make such a declaration.

The counterclaim of the first defendant is not really a counterclaim at all but an assertion that he is not a proper party to the action. That point has been fully argued and it is convenient that I should decide it before hearing any argument as to costs. In my view it was reasonable for the council to sue the first defendant in the first instance, but it became clear from an affidavit sworn by the first defendant on 1 October 1979 that the market rights had been leased to the third defendant alone and that the first defendant was only concerned as a director of the company. He was thus not a necessary party to the action, but so far as I know he made no application by summons or motion for a stay of proceedings, simply taking the point by his pleading. I will deal later with questions of costs. All I decide regarding the first defendant at this point is that the injunction is pronounced against the other two defendants only.

Declarations and injunction accordingly.

Solicitors: *Field Fisher & Martineau* agents for *D A Dean*, Gloucester (for the council); *Barretts* (for the defendants).

Evelyn M C Budd Barrister.

a

Buckley v Law Society and another

CHANCERY DIVISION
SIR ROBERT MEGARRY V-C
28, 29 APRIL, 10 MAY 1983

Solicitor – Dishonesty – Intervention by Law Society in solicitor's practice – Discovery of
b *documents – Law Society suspecting solicitor of being dishonest and failing to comply with accounting rules – Council of Law Society passing resolution vesting in Society moneys held by solicitor – Notice of resolution served on solicitor – Solicitor applying by originating summons for withdrawal of notice – Solicitor applying for discovery of Law Society's internal documents relating to its resolution – Whether order for discovery should be made – Solicitors Act 1974, Sch 1, paras 1(2), 6(4)(5) – RSC Ord 24, r 7, Ord 106, r 6(1).*

c

The Council of the Law Society, acting pursuant to its powers under Sch 1[a] to the Solicitors Act 1974 to intervene in the conduct of a solicitor's practice, passed a resolution vesting in the Society all moneys held by a particular solicitor or his firm in connection with his practice or under any trust of which he was a trustee, on the ground that the council had reason to suspect the solicitor of dishonesty and were satisfied that he had
d failed to comply with the Solicitors' Accounts Rules 1975. The Society gave the solicitor notice of the resolution as required by Sch 1 to the 1974 Act. By an originating summons issued in the Chancery Division pursuant to para 6(4)[b] of Sch 1 and RSC Ord 106, r 6(1)[c], the solicitor applied for an order directing the Society to withdraw the notice and for consequential relief in regard to the moneys that had become vested in the Society. By a notice of motion in those proceedings under Ord 24, r 7(1)[d] the solicitor sought an order
e for discovery by the Society of certain documents relating to the council's resolution, including interdepartmental memoranda, minutes and draft minutes and working papers of the Society. The Society objected to the order sought, on the grounds (i) that the exercise of its public function of intervening in a solicitor's practice could only be questioned in an application for judicial review and not in an ordinary action, and (ii) that if discovery were to be ordered it should be restricted to documents which provided
f factual evidence which tended to show the solicitor's honesty and should not extend to documents containing expressions of opinion or which showed the Society's internal thinking.

Held – The order for discovery would be made, for the following reasons—

(1) Since a solicitor who sought withdrawal of a notice served on him under Sch 1 to
g the 1974 Act did not have the option of proceeding either by way of an ordinary action or by way of judicial review but was required by para 6(4) of Sch 1 and RSC Ord 106, r 6 to proceed by way of originating summons in the Chancery Division, the originating summons was properly brought. Furthermore, the wide jurisdiction which the court

---

a Schedule 1, so far as material, is set out at p 1041 *d e*, post

h b Paragraph 6, so far as material provides:

> '... (4) Within 14 days of the service of a notice under sub-paragraph (3), the person on whom it was served, on giving not less than 48 hours' notice in writing to the Society and (if the notice gives the name of the solicitor instructed by the Society) to that solicitor, may apply to the High Court for an order directing the Society to withdraw the notice.
>
> (5) If the court makes such an order, it shall have power also to make such other order with respect to the matter as it may think fit ...'

j c Rule 6(1) provides: 'Proceedings in the High Court under Schedule 1 to the [Solicitors Act 1974] shall be assigned to the Chancery Division.'

d Rule 7(1) provides: 'Subject to rule 8, the Court may at any time, on the application of any party to a cause or matter, make an order requiring any other party to make an affidavit stating whether any document specified or described in the application or any class of document so specified or described is, or has at any time been, in his possession, custody or power, and if not then in his possession, custody or power when he parted with it and what has become of it.'

possessed by virtue of para 6(5) of Sch 1 meant that the court had jurisdiction to set aside
the notice if the resolution preceding the notice ought never to have been passed (see a
p 1043 *e* to *j*, post); *O'Reilly v Mackman* [1982] 3 All ER 1124 distinguished.
(2) Even though the Law Society was exercising a public function when intervening
in a solicitor's practice under Sch 1 to the 1974 Act, that did not exempt the Society from
the process of discovery in ordinary litigation. Since the Society's objections to discovery
did not outweigh the public interest in making disclosure of the documents in the
interests of justice, it followed that the Society would be ordered to disclose all documents, b
including the Society's internal documents, which tended to show any grounds, whether
existing when the resolution was passed or subsequently, for suspecting the solicitor's
dishonesty or which indicated that he was not dishonest, subject to any claim that
particular documents were privileged from discovery (see p 1043 *j* to p 1044 *a* and *d* to *f*,
post); dictum of Cross J in *Coni v Robertson* [1969] 2 All ER at 615 and *Williams v Home
Office* [1981] 1 All ER 1151 applied. c

Notes

For intervention in a solicitor's practice, see 44 Halsbury's Laws (4th edn) paras 338–342.
For discovery in proceedings begun by originating summons, see 13 ibid para 10, and
for cases on the subject, see 18 Digest (Reissue) 12–16, 66, *48–76*, *453–460*.
For withholding documents on the ground of public interest, see 13 Halsbury's Laws d
(4th edn) paras 86–91, and for cases on the subject, see 18 Digest (Reissue) 154–160,
1265–1301.
For the Solicitors Act 1974, Sch 1, para 6, see 44 Halsbury's Statutes (3rd edn) 1560.

Cases referred to in judgment

Borthwick, Re [1948] 2 All ER 635, [1948] Ch 645, CA. e
Compagnie Financiere et Commerciale du Pacifique v Peruvian Guano Co (1882) 11 QBD 55,
CA.
Coni v Robertson [1969] 2 All ER 609, [1969] 1 WLR 1007.
Heywood v Hull Prison Board of Visitors [1980] 3 All ER 594, [1980] 1 WLR 1386.
O'Reilly v Mackman [1982] 3 All ER 1124, [1982] 3 WLR 1096, HL; *affg* [1982] 3 All ER
680, [1982] 3 WLR 604, CA. f
Williams v Home Office [1981] 1 All ER 1151.

Motion for discovery

By an originating summons dated 23 November 1982 as amended the plaintiff, a
solicitor, sought as against the defendants, the Law Society and Margaret Mason its agent,
the following relief: (1) an order that the Law Society should withdraw a notice it served g
on the solicitor, pursuant to para 6(4) of Sch 1 to the Solicitors Act 1974, of a resolution
passed by the council of the Society to vest in the Society all moneys held by or on behalf
of the solicitor or his firm in connection with his practice or under any trust of which he
was formerly a trustee on the ground that the council suspected the solicitor of dishonesty
and were satisfied that he had failed to comply with the Solicitors' Accounts Rules 1975;
(2) a consequential order that the Law Society should take all proper steps to withdraw its h
agent, the second defendant, from the management and control of the affairs of the
solicitor's practice and vest the same in the solicitor as beneficial owner of the practice;
(3) an order directing the Law Society to hold all moneys, property, papers and books
relevant to the practice, save for the moneys held on clients' account, on trust for the
solicitor and to hold the moneys in the clients' account on trust for the person beneficially
entitled to them; (4) an inquiry as to who including the solicitor was entitled to the funds j
in the clients' account; (5) further or other consequential relief. On 20 January 1983
Master Cholmondeley Clarke made an order under RSC Ord 24, r 7 requiring the
defendants to file an affidavit disclosing certain categories of documents which were or
had been in their possession. The defendants failed to comply with that order. By a
notice of motion in the proceedings by originating summons the solicitor applied under
Ord 24, r 7 for an order of discovery against the Law Society in respect of certain
categories of documents under nine heads, relating to the council's resolution, including

reports, interdepartmental memoranda, minutes, statements of witnesses, working
a papers and correspondence. The Law Society objected to production of those documents
on the ground that production would be injurious to the public interest, or alternatively
that production of documents which showed the internal thinking of the Law Society
ought not to be ordered. The motion was heard in chambers but judgment was given by
Sir Robert Megarry V-C in open court with the parties' consent. The facts are set out in
the judgment.

b *E S Cazalet QC* and *Ian McCulloch* for the solicitor.
J P Whittaker for the defendants.

Cur adv vult

10 May. The following judgment was delivered.

c **SIR ROBERT MEGARRY V-C.** This is a motion in proceedings under the Solicitors
Act 1974. Under s 35 of and Sch 1 to the 1974 Act the Council of the Law Society are
given important powers of intervention in the conduct of a solicitor's practice. Part I of
Sch 1 sets out the circumstances in which the council may intervene, and Pt II sets out
the powers which the council may exercise. In this case the grounds on which the council
d exercised their powers were those set out in para 1(1) of the schedule. These grounds are
as follows:

> '(*a*) the Council have reason to suspect dishonesty on the part of—(i) a solicitor, or
> (ii) an employee of a solicitor, or (iii) the personal representatives of a deceased
> solicitor, in connection with that solicitor's practice or in connection with any trust
> of which that solicitor is or formerly was a trustee . . . (*c*) the Council are satisfied
> e that a solicitor has failed to comply with rules made by virtue of section 32 or
> 37(2)(*c*) . . .'

These sections relate to client's accounts and to insurance. Paragraph 1(2) provides that
the powers under Part II can only be exercised in respect of para 1(1)(*c*) if the Law Society
has given the solicitor notice in writing that the council are satisfied of his failure to
f comply with the rules specified in the notice and that the powers are accordingly
exercisable in his case. Under para 6, where the powers are exercisable under para 1, the
council may resolve that all sums of money held by or on behalf of the solicitor or his
firm in connection with his practice or any trust of which he is or formerly was a trustee
shall vest in the Society, and thereupon such moneys vest in the Society on trust to
exercise its powers under the schedule and subject thereto on trust for the persons
g beneficially entitled to the moneys. Such a resolution in effect puts a solicitor out of
practice by taking over all the funds of the practice. The Society must serve on the
solicitor a certified copy of the resolution and a notice prohibiting the payment out of
any of the sums of money: see para 6(3).

What happened in this case was that on 17 August 1982 the Law Society wrote to the
solicitor saying that—

> h 'the Council have resolved that they have reason to suspect dishonesty on your
> part and are satisfied that you have failed to comply with the Solicitors' Accounts
> Rules 1975.'

The letter stated that the council had further resolved to vest in the Society all moneys
referred to in para 6(2)(*a*) of the schedule, and to require the solicitor (under para 9(1)) to
i deliver to their agent all documents in his possession in connection with his practice or
with any controlled trust. The letter enclosed a certified copy of the council's resolution
(in accordance with para 6(3)), which shows that it had been made on 29 July 1982 by
the professional purposes committee of the council under delegated powers: no question
now arises on the power to delegate. The delay in putting the resolution into effect was
due, it seems, to the time taken to find a suitable agent able and willing at that time of
the year to act on behalf of the council.

By para 6(4) of the schedule, within 14 days of the service of a notice of such a resolution the solicitor may apply to the High Court for an order directing the Society to withdraw the notice; and by para 6(5), if the court makes such an order, the court may make such other orders in the matter as it thinks fit. By RSC Ord 106, r 6, proceedings under the schedule are to be assigned to the Chancery Division, and the application is to be made by originating summons. The solicitor accordingly issued an originating summons claiming this and other relief. (The copy of the originating summons put before me is dated 23 November 1982, and so is out of time, but no point has been taken on this; I think that there was a reissue of the summons.) By para 15 of the schedule, any application to the High Court under the schedule may be disposed of in chambers. I was requested to sit in chambers for the hearing of this motion, and I took the view that the provision for sitting in chambers applied not only to the hearing of the substantive originating summons but also to any motion or other application under the originating summons. I therefore heard the motion in chambers. In view of the apparent absence of any authority on the operation of the schedule, it seemed appropriate to deliver judgment in open court, with appropriate anonymity. To this both the solicitor and the Law Society assented, save that the solicitor then said that he wanted no anonymity.

I can now turn to the motion before me. The notice of motion seeks leave to amend the originating summons in the manner shown in a draft. On behalf of the Law Society counsel said that there was no objection to the amendment, provided that it was understood that the Law Society reserved all rights of challenge at the hearing. On that understanding I give leave to make the amendment. The notice of motion also seeks directions as to the hearing of the originating summons, and in particular the date. On this, the parties are in substantial agreement, and at the conclusion of this judgment I shall consider how far I can give effect to their wishes. That leaves the one real matter in dispute. That matter is whether the Law Society should be ordered (the notice of motion says under RSC Ord 24, r 7) to make discovery of certain categories of documents set out in a letter dated 17 March 1983 exhibited to an affidavit dated 25 April 1983 filed on behalf of the solicitor. This letter sets out under nine heads a wide range of documents relating to the resolution of the council, including reports, interdepartmental memoranda, minutes and draft minutes, statements of witnesses, working papers, correspondence and so on.

The relief sought by the originating summons is that the Law Society should withdraw the notice of 17 August 1982 which was served on the solicitor, with consequential relief. At one time the position under an originating summons (as distinct from a writ) was that discovery would be ordered only in special circumstances: see *Re Borthwick* [1948] 2 All ER 635, [1948] Ch 645. However, the rules have been changed. The provision for automatic discovery after the close of pleadings (Ord 24, r 1) applies only to actions by writ; but orders for discovery may be made under Ord 24, r 3 in any cause or matter, whether begun by writ, originating summons or otherwise; and Ord 24, r 7, under which this application is made, also applies to any cause or matter. Under the latter rule, an application may at any time be made for what is often called 'specific discovery', requiring the litigant to make an affidavit stating whether any specific document or class of documents is or has been in his possession, and so on.

Counsel for the Law Society put forward a variety of objections to the order sought by the solicitor. First, he accepted and asserted that the acts of the Law Society in such matters were subject to judicial review. He then contended that in some way *O'Reilly v Mackman* [1982] 3 All ER 1124, [1982] 3 WLR 1096 had the effect of precluding the court from making the order for discovery sought by the solicitor, or at least showed that the court ought to exercise its discretion to refuse to make such an order. He said that the Law Society was exercising a public function when it took action under the schedule, and that discovery should no more be ordered against the Law Society in the exercise of such functions than it would be exercised against a bench of magistrates or a coroner. In this connection counsel cited *Heywood v Hull Prison Board of Visitors* [1980] 3 All ER 594 at 598, [1980] 1 WLR 1386 at 1391, where Goulding J referred to discovery as not being compatible with the free and proper discharge of the public functions of prison visitors. This was not, counsel said, a case of ordinary adversarial litigation, for there was no issue

between the solicitor and the Law Society, but merely an exercise by the Law Society of
a its statutory powers, in accordance with its public duty, which the solicitor was
challenging. He emphasised that what the court had to determine under the schedule
was not whether the resolution had rightly been made, but whether the notice should
now be withdrawn. Any challenge to the resolution itself should be made fair and square
by judicial review, and not otherwise.

After some discussion of these contentions, counsel for the Law Society fell back on a
b second line of defence in case his first line failed to hold. He said that, subject to all
questions of documents that were privileged or should be excluded on the score of
confidentiality, he would not oppose the discovery of any documents which tended to
show the honesty of the solicitor by providing factual evidence, as distinct from mere
expressions of opinion. To this, he added the further qualification that the court ought
not to force the Law Society to disclose documents which showed the internal thinking
c of the Law Society. Counsel for the solicitor controverted most of these submissions, and
emphasised the serious consequences for the solicitor. He sought the full order for
discovery, but accepted that questions of public interest privilege or confidentiality
might arise and, on the point being taken, certain documents might then be excluded
from the process.

First, I do not think that *O'Reilly v Mackman* and that line of cases has anything to do
d with what I have to decide; and even if it did, proceedings by way of judicial review do
not prevent an order for discovery being made (see [1982] 3 All ER 1124 at 1131–1132,
[1982] 3 WLR 1096 at 1107, citing Ord 53, r 8). *O'Reilly v Mackman* shows (and I put it
broadly) that where a remedy is sought under public law, and under Ord 53 proceedings
for judicial review may give the remedies sought, it is not open to the plaintiff to frame
his case as an ordinary action for a declaration or other ordinary remedy and so escape the
e safeguards which Ord 53 gives for proceedings for judicial review but not for ordinary
actions. To allow an ordinary action to proceed in such circumstances would be an abuse
of the process of the court. In other words, the litigant's apparent option to proceed either
by ordinary action or else by judicial review is not a true option. In the present case, no
option is given. Statute confers a particular jurisdiction on the High Court, and the Rules
of the Supreme Court require that the jurisdiction is to be exercised by originating
f summons in the Chancery Division. The applicant is not seeking to avoid the safeguards
of Ord 53 by bringing an ordinary action, but is applying to the court in obedience to
particular statutory provisions; and how it could be an abuse of the process of the court
to do this instead of attempting to proceed in some other way I cannot see.

Second, the points to be decided by the court under para 6(4) and (5) of Sch 1 to the
1974 Act are whether the Society should be directed to withdraw the notice, and what
g other orders (if any) should be made with respect to the matter. The jurisdiction is
plainly very wide. There may be all sorts of reasons why the notice should be withdrawn.
Supervening events may show that although the council were perfectly right to make
the resolution in the first place, it would be quite wrong to allow the order to remain in
force. On the other hand, investigation may show that the order never should have been
made, and that there is no ground for continuing it in force. It would be remarkable
h indeed if the statutory jurisdiction could be exercised in the first case, but in the second
the applicant had to be told, as I think counsel for the Law Society would tell him, that
any attack on the original validity of the resolution could only be pursued by way of
judicial review, so that in the statutory proceedings it could not be relied on as a collateral
part of the process of showing that the order should be withdrawn.

Third, nothing has been put before me which satisfies me that the Law Society should
j in these matters be exempt from the process of discovery. As was accepted on all hands,
the procedure under the schedule is entirely distinct from the disciplinary process before
the Solicitors' Disciplinary Tribunal. The Council of the Law Society are not adjudicating
in contested proceedings but are exercising a statutory power to take executive action to
avoid possible financial defaults by solicitors. In detaining and controlling prisoners the
Home Secretary is undoubtedly exercising public functions some of them under statutory
instruments; yet subject to claims for public interest privilege and so on, it seems clear

that in ordinary litigation he is subject to the process of discovery: see, for example, *Williams v Home Office* [1981] 1 All ER 1151. I do not think that the Law Society is in any better position in proceedings under the schedule.

Fourth, there is Ord 24, r 8, a rule to which Ord 24, rr 3 and 7 are both expressly made subject. This runs as follows:

> 'On the hearing of an application for an order under rule 3, 7 or 7A the Court, if satisfied that discovery is not necessary, or not necessary at that stage of the cause or matter, may dismiss or, as the case may be, adjourn the application and shall in any case refuse to make such an order if and so far as it is of opinion that discovery is not necessary either for disposing fairly of the cause or matter or for saving costs.'

Of this rule, Cross J said that it 'shows that discovery will be ordered unless there is some good reason why it should not be ordered': see *Coni v Robertson* [1969] 2 All ER 609 at 615, [1969] 1 WLR 1007 at 1015. I was not referred either to the rule or to the case during the argument, and so, if requested by either side, I shall direct that the order should not be drawn up until there has been an opportunity for further submissions on the point. Subject to that, these authorities seem to me to point to an order for discovery being made. I cannot see what there is in the objections of counsel for the Law Society which outweighs the public interest in making disclosure in the interests of justice.

I do not propose to work my way through the long and varied list of documents for which discovery is sought as set out in the letter dated 17 March 1983. Counsel agreed that if I decided the motion in principle, that would suffice. They would then probably be able to agree the documents, subject to any dispute being brought before me under the liberty to apply which I now give. It seems to me that the Society should make discovery of all documents which tend to show any grounds for suspecting the solicitor's dishonesty in connection with his practice or any trust of which he was a trustee or any grounds which indicate that he was not dishonest. These grounds should include any grounds existing when the professional purposes committee of the Law Society passed its resolution on 29 July 1982 and at all subsequent times. I do not think any documents should be excepted merely because they are internal documents, for the question is one of there being reason to suspect dishonesty on the solicitor's part, and internal documents may show how much or how little reason there was for the suspicion. I feel some hesitation about draft minutes, as distinct from the minutes themselves, but I do not think that I can say, in the classic words of Brett LJ in *Compagnie Financiere et Commerciale du Pacifique v Peruvian Guano Co* (1882) 11 QBD 55 at 63, that these might not 'fairly lead' the solicitor 'to a train of inquiry' which may advance his case or damage that of the Society. Naturally, any order for discovery is subject to all claims that may be made that any particular document is privileged or otherwise exempt from discovery on some ground.

Finally, I should say this. I have abstained from discussing the facts of the case, on the footing that this is merely an application for discovery, and the less I say about what is in issue between the parties under the originating summons the better: that will all be discussed when the originating summons is heard. However, I do not think that it would be fair to the solicitor if I did not say that there is considerable evidence to the effect that his financial difficulties are at least in part due to certain acts by a partner of his (who is now dead) in relation to the deposit in a conveyancing transaction. Documents in the possession of the Society might well be expected to throw some light on this matter, and in particular how far there was, and still is, 'reason to suspect dishonesty' on the part of the solicitor.

Order for discovery.

Solicitors: *Simpson Silvertown & Co*, agents for *Betesh & Co*, Manchester (for the solicitor); *Hempsons* (for the defendants).

Vivian Horvath Barrister.

R v Immigration Appeal Tribunal, ex p Enwia and others
R v Immigration Appeal Tribunal, ex p AS

COURT OF APPEAL, CIVIL DIVISION
STEPHENSON AND O'CONNOR LJJ
20, 21, 22 APRIL, 20 MAY 1983

Immigration – Appeal – Deportation – Appeal to tribunal from adjudicator – When leave must be granted – Direction that person is to be removed to country where he fears persecution – Is to be removed – Iraqi citizen required to leave United Kingdom – Applicant fearing persecution if he returned to Iraq – Whether applicant to be treated as a person 'to be removed' to Iraq – Whether applicant having right of appeal from adjudicator to tribunal – Immigration Act 1971, s 14(1) – Immigration Appeals (Procedure) Rules 1972, r 14(2)(b).

The applicant, AS, was an Iraqi citizen who was given leave to enter the United Kingdom for a limited period as a student. In the course of his stay the applicant applied to the Secretary of State to remain in the United Kingdom on the ground that he would be persecuted if he returned to Iraq. His father had been executed by the regime in power in Iraq. The Secretary of State refused his request and required the applicant to leave the United Kingdom by a specified date. The applicant appealed to an adjudicator under s 14[a] of the Immigration Act 1971 against the Secretary of State's refusal to vary the conditions of his leave to enter. The adjudicator found that although the applicant's fear of persecution in Iraq was well founded that fear was not for any of the reasons specified in the immigration rules and further found that he would not have to go back to Iraq. He therefore dismissed the appeal. The applicant applied to the Immigration Appeal Tribunal for leave to appeal from the adjudicator's decision but the tribunal refused leave. The applicant then applied for judicial review of the tribunal's refusal to grant leave. The judge held that although a deportation order had not been made against the applicant he was to be treated as a person who 'is to be removed' to a country to which he was 'unwilling to go owing to the fear of being persecuted' and therefore had a right of appeal, under r 14(2)(*b*)[b] of the Immigration Appeals (Procedure) Rules 1972, to the tribunal so that the question of whether the applicant was entitled to political asylum could be determined once and for all. The judge granted certiorari to quash the tribunal's refusal and mandamus requiring the tribunal to grant leave and hear the applicant's appeal. The tribunal appealed. At the hearing of the appeal a similar appeal was also heard.

Held – A person was 'to be removed' to a country, for the purposes of having a right of appeal to, inter alia, an immigration tribunal under r 14(2)(b) of the 1972 rules, only if directions had been given for the removal of that person from the United Kingdom to a fixed destination, being a country where he feared persecution. Accordingly, an applicant was only entitled to leave to appeal under r 14(2)(*b*) if he was appealing under s 17(1)[c] of the 1971 Act against directions for his removal to a specified country where he feared persecution. Since the applicant had been merely required to leave the United Kingdom, from which he could go to a country of his choice, and had not yet been directed to be deported to Iraq, r 14(2)(*b*) did not apply and the tribunal was not bound by that rule to grant leave to appeal. The grant of leave was accordingly a matter for the tribunal's discretion and since, on the facts, the tribunal had come to a reasonable decision the court

---

a Section 14, so far as material, is set out at p 1049 *a b*, post
b Rule 14 is set out at p 1050 *h* to p 1051 *a*, post
c Section 17(1) is set out at p 1049 *j* to p 1050 *a*, post

would not interfere with its decision to refuse to grant leave to appeal from the adjudicator (see p 1055 *a* to *c*, p 1056 *b* to *d* and p 1057 *g h*, post). a

Notes

For the procedure on appeal to the tribunal from an adjudicator, see 4 Halsbury's Laws (4th edn) para 1025.

For the Immigration Act 1971, ss 14, 17, see 41 Halsbury's Statutes (3rd edn) 35, 38.

For the Immigration Appeals (Procedure) Rules 1972, r 14, see 2 Halsbury's Statutory Instruments (4th Reissue) 31. b

Cases referred to in judgment

Chief Constable of the North Wales Police v Evans [1982] 3 All ER 141, [1982] 1 WLR 1155, HL.

Mohammed Taj and Mohammed Riaz v Immigration Appeal Tribunal (30 June 1982, CA Unbound Transcript 572). c

R v Immigration Appeal Tribunal, ex p Mehmet [1977] 2 All ER 602, [1977] 1 WLR 795, DC.

R v Leyland Justices, ex p Hawthorn [1979] 1 All ER 209, [1979] 2 QB 283, [1979] 2 WLR 28, DC.

R v West Sussex Quarter Sessions, ex p Albert and Maud Johnson Trust Ltd [1973] 3 All ER 289, [1974] QB 24, [1973] 3 WLR 149, CA. d

Ridge v Baldwin [1963] 2 All ER 66, [1964] AC 40, [1963] 2 WLR 935, HL.

Appeals

R v Immigration Appeal Tribunal, ex p Enwia and others

Yousif Isaac Enwia, Varginia Daood Gerges Enwia, Ubert Enwia and Meshaid Enwia e applied, with the leave of McNeill J granted on 16 March 1982, for (1) an order of certiorari to quash the determination of the Immigration Appeal Tribunal dated 17 August 1981 refusing them leave to appeal from the determination of an adjudicator dated 6 July 1981 dismissing their appeal under s 14 of the Immigration Act 1971 from the refusal of the Secretary of State to vary the first applicant's leave to enter the United Kingdom and to grant him asylum in the United Kingdom, and (2) an order of f mandamus directing the tribunal to grant the applicants leave to appeal and to hear the first applicant's appeal. On 26 May 1982 Comyn J, hearing the Crown Office list, quashed the tribunal's determination and issued an order of mandamus directing the tribunal to grant leave and to hear the first applicant's appeal on the grounds, inter alia, that the tribunal did not give the applicants an oral hearing, and that by virtue of r 14(2)(*b*) of the Immigration Appeals (Procedure) Rules 1972 the tribunal was bound to grant the g applicants leave to appeal. The tribunal appealed on the grounds, inter alia, that the judge erred in law in deciding that the tribunal was bound to grant the applicants leave to appeal. The facts are set out in the judgment of the court.

R v Immigration Appeal Tribunal, ex p AS

AS applied, with the leave of Stephen Brown J given on 22 October 1982, for (1) an h order of certiorari to quash the determination of the Immigration Appeal Tribunal dated 22 June 1982 refusing him leave to appeal from the determination of an adjudicator dated 12 May 1982 dismissing his appeal under s 14 of the Immigration Act 1971 against the Secretary of State's refusal to vary his leave to enter the United Kingdom and to grant him asylum, and (2) an order of mandamus directing the tribunal to grant leave to appeal and to hear the appeal. On 23 March 1983 Woolf J, hearing the Crown Office list, j quashed the tribunal's determination and issued an order of mandamus directing the tribunal to grant leave to appeal and to hear the appeal, on the ground that under r 14(2)(*b*) of the Immigration Appeals (Procedure) Rules 1972, the tribunal was bound to grant AS leave to appeal. The tribunal appealed on the ground that the judge erred in law in deciding that the tribunal was bound to grant AS leave to appeal. The facts are set out in the judgment of the court. The case is reported for the issue which arose in AS's appeal.

Andrew Collins for the tribunal.
Sir Charles Fletcher-Cooke QC and *K S Nathan* for the Enwia family.
Anthony Scrivener QC and *K S Nathan* for AS.

Cur adv vult

20 May. The following judgment of the court was delivered.

STEPHENSON LJ. These five respondents were refused leave to appeal by the appellant tribunal against determinations by adjudicators of their appeals under s 14 of the Immigration Act 1971. Their appeals have one point in common and we have therefore heard them together. On 26 May 1982 Comyn J quashed the tribunal's determination, dated 17 August 1981, refusing the first four respondents leave to appeal, and on 23 March 1983 Woolf J quashed the tribunal's determination dated 22 June 1982 refusing the fifth respondent leave to appeal. Under the orders made by those judges on a judicial review of the tribunal's determinations the respondents' cases must go back to the tribunal for their appeals to be heard, orally in the case of the first respondent. Counsel for the tribunal submits that they should not be sent back or heard, because leave to appeal was rightly refused in each case.

The first four respondents are a family, father, mother and two sons, all of Iraqi citizenship. Their appeals are from the same determination, and we shall refer to them collectively as Enwia. The fifth respondent is an Iraqi citizen, unconnected with the others, whom we shall refer to for his own protection, as he has successfully requested, as AS. His appeal is from a different determination, unconnected with the Enwia determination, though by the same member of the tribunal. Enwia and AS are persons who are not patrial. Both were given leave to enter the United Kingdom for a limited period under s 3(1)(*b*) of the 1971 Act, Enwia in August 1979 for six months as a visitor, AS in October 1974 for 12 months as a student, extended from time to time to October 1981.

Each applied to the Secretary of State to vary his leave by removing the limit on its duration under s 3(3)(*a*), Enwia in February 1980 as a self-employed businessman, AS in September 1980 while still a student. Enwia wrote to the Home Office on 18 February 1980:

> 'I would be very grateful, if you kindly grant me Business Permission as "Self-Employed", as I wish to invest and deal with the Export Business, to promote the sales of the British products in the Middle East. I am trying to get all my money out of Iraq to invest them in this country, as I have no more chance to invest them in Iraq because of Government nationalization and discrimination of races and religion by the Governing party, as we are Christians and from Assyrian nation. My father has worked for the British R.A.F. Army in Iraq as a Sergeant Major for 15 years.'

AS wrote to the Home Office on 22 September 1980:

> 'I write to ask if consideration could be given to this application to remain in this country. I am still studying at Brighton Polytechnic, but owing to unforseen and very tragic circumstances connected with my late father in Iraq it will not be possible for me, either at the conclusion of my studies or even for holidays, to return to my country... My position is extremely difficult, as I have been advised from high sources in Iraq that I should not return to that country.'

His father had in fact been executed in Iraq for alleged bribery in connection with the business of an English company. Each raised the question of asylum in this country, Enwia as a subsidiary ground for extending his leave. Each was interviewed by the Home

Office, and had his application refused by the Secretary of State. His decision of 17 February 1981 informed Enwia: a

> 'You have applied for leave to remain as a self employed businessman but you were not admitted for this purpose and it is a purpose for which an entry clearance obtained before arrival is necessary. Further you have applied for leave to remain on the grounds that if you return to Iraq you will be persecuted, as you are an Assyrian Christian but the Secretary of State is not satisfied that your fears of persecution are well-founded. The Secretary of State therefore refuses your application. Under the b Immigration (Variation of Leave) Order 1976, your stay has been extended to 17th March 1981. If you do not wish to appeal, you should leave the United Kingdom by that date. You are entitled to appeal against this decision under section 14(1) of the Immigration Act 1971 to the independent appellate authorities established under that Act. If you wish to appeal you should complete the attached form and return it to the Under Secretary of State, Home Office (Appeals Section), Lunar House, c Wellesley Road, CROYDON CL9 2BY, TO ARRIVE NOT LATER THAN 14 DAYS AFTER THE DATE OF THIS NOTICE. The Home Office will transmit your notice of appeal to the appellate authorities. The United Kingdom Immigrants Advisory Service, a voluntary organisation independent of the Government, will advise you, if you wish, about the decision which has been taken against you and on whether to exercise your right of appeal. If you decide to appeal, the Service can also help you to prepare your d appeal and to present it to the appellate authorities. These services are provided free of charge.'

His decision of 9 November 1981 informed AS:

> 'You have applied for leave to remain in the United Kingdom on the grounds that if you are required to leave you would have to go to Iraq where you fear persecution e but the Secretary of State is not satisfied that your fear of persecution is well founded. The Secretary of State therefore refuses your application. Under the Immigration (Variation of Leave) Order 1976, your stay has been extended to 7 December 1981. If you do not wish to appeal, you should leave the United Kingdom by that date.'

AS was then given the same further information about appealing. f

Each appealed to an adjudicator. Enwia's appeal was dismissed on 6 July 1981, AS's on 20 May 1982. Each applied to the tribunal for leave to appeal. The tribunal refused Enwia leave on 17 August 1981, and AS leave on 22 June 1982. Judges of the Divisional Court have declared both those refusals wrong. Counsel for the tribunal appeals to this court to uphold the tribunal's refusals on the ground which was given by the tribunal for refusing AS's application, though it was not the ground it gave for refusing Enwia's g application.

Comyn J's main reason for allowing Enwia's appeal was that he had not been given an oral hearing. But he also rejected a submission, not considered by the tribunal but made in support of its decision by counsel for the tribunal, that leave to appeal to the tribunal was required, and held that Enwia had a right of appeal under r 14(2)(*b*) of the Immigration Appeals (Procedure) Rules 1972, SI 1972/1684. Woolf J allowed AS's appeal h on the second point, which was considered and decided by the tribunal, namely that AS had a right of appeal under that rule. On these appeals by the tribunal we have to consider whether those judges were right in their interpretation and application of r 14(2)(*b*), and whether Comyn J was right to quash the tribunal's determination of Enwia's application for leave to appeal because he was not given an oral hearing; and on AS's cross-notice whether if r 14(2)(*b*) did not apply to AS's case, the tribunal should j nevertheless have given him leave to appeal because the adjudicator's decision was one which no reasonable adjudicator could have reached or because his case might require a further oral hearing.

It now becomes necessary to consider the statutory provisions governing immigration appeals. They are contained in Part II of the 1971 Act and in the 1972 rules, of which r 14 is one. There are two 'appellate authorities', adjudicators and the Immigration Appeal Tribunal: see s 12 and r 2(1). There are appeals to an adjudicator against exclusion

from the United Kingdom by persons refused leave to enter: see s 13. Appeals against
a variations of leave and refusals to vary it by persons who have limited leave to enter or remain are provided by s 14, sub-s (1) of which reads:

> 'Subject to the provisions of this Part of this Act, a person who has a limited leave under this Act to enter or remain in the United Kingdom may appeal to an adjudicator against any variation of the leave (whether as regards duration or conditions), or against any refusal to vary it: and a variation shall not take effect so
> *b* long as an appeal is pending under this subsection against the variation, nor shall an appellant be required to leave the United Kingdom by reason of the expiration of his leave so long as his appeal is pending under this subsection against a refusal to enlarge or remove the limit on the duration of the leave.'

It is by virtue of this section that Enwia and AS appealed to adjudicators.
c Section 15(1) provides:

> 'Subject to the provisions of this Part of this Act, a person may appeal to an adjudicator against—(*a*) a decision of the Secretary of State to make a deportation order against him by virtue of section 3(5) above . . .'

Section 15(2) provides:

d
> 'A deportation order shall not be made against a person by virtue of section 3(5) above so long as an appeal may be brought against the decision to make it nor, if such an appeal is duly brought, so long as the appeal is pending. . .'

No decision to make a deportation order has yet been made in respect of Enwia or AS, but each is 'liable to deportation', as well as being guilty of a criminal offence (s 24(1)(*b*)(i))
e unless his appeal to be allowed to remain here is successful; for s 3(5) provides:

> 'A person who is not patrial shall be liable to deportation from the United Kingdom—(*a*) if, having only a limited leave to enter or remain, he does not observe a condition attached to the leave or remains beyond the time limited by the leave. . .'

Once liable to deportation an immigrant may expect to have a deportation order made
f against him. By s 5(1):

> 'Where a person is under section 3(5) or (6) above liable to deportation, then subject to the following provisions of this Act the Secretary of State may make a deportation order against him, that is to say an order requiring him to leave and prohibiting him from entering the United Kingdom; and a deportation order against a person shall invalidate any leave to enter or remain in the United Kingdom
> *g* given him before the order is made or while it is in force.'

Section 5(5) provides:

> 'The provisions of Schedule 3 to this Act shall have effect with respect to the removal from the United Kingdom of persons against whom deportation orders are in force and with respect to the detention or control of persons in connection with
> *h* deportation.'

and para 1(1) of Sch 3 provides alternative destinations:

> 'Where a deportation order is in force against any person, the Secretary of State may give directions for his removal to a country or territory specified in the directions being either—(*a*) a country of which he is a national or citizen; or (*b*) a
> *j* country or territory to which there is reason to believe that he will be admitted.'

Appeals are given against directions for a person's removal by s 16, where they are given on the ground that he is an illegal entrant or has entered in breach of a deportation order, and under s 17 on any one of three grounds set out in sub-s (1), which provides:

> 'Subject to the provisions of this Part of this Act, where directions are given under this Act for a person's removal from the United Kingdom either—(*a*) on his being

refused leave to enter; or (*b*) on a deportation order being made against him; or (*c*) on his having entered the United Kingdom in breach of a deportation order; he may a appeal to an adjudicator against the directions on the ground that he ought to be removed (if at all) to a different country or territory specified by him.'

The section goes on in sub-ss (2) and (3) to provide that where a person appeals under s 13(1) on being refused leave to enter, or under s 15 against a decision to make a deportation order against him and has notice that any directions which may be given for his removal will be for his removal to a specified country or territory or one of several b specified countries or territories, he may on that appeal object and claim that he ought to be removed (if at all) to a different country or territory specified by him.

Section 19(1) lays down an adjudicator's duties on an appeal and provides that:

'Subject to sections 13(4) and 16(4) above, and to any restriction on the grounds of appeal, an adjudicator on an appeal to him under this Part of this Act— (*a*) shall c allow the appeal if he considers—(i) that the decision or action against which the appeal is brought was not in accordance with the law or with any immigration rules applicable to the case; or (ii) where the decision or action involved the exercise of a discretion by the Secretary of State or an officer, that the discretion should have been exercised differently; and (*b*) in any other case, shall dismiss the appeal.'

Section 20 provides for appeals to the tribunal from his determination: d

'Subject to any requirement of rules of procedure as to leave to appeal, any party to an appeal to an adjudicator may, if dissatisfied with his determination thereon, appeal to the Appeal Tribunal, and the Tribunal may affirm the determination or make any other determination which could have been made by the adjudicator.'

Section 22 gives the Secretary of State power, exercisable by statutory instrument, to e make rules of procedure relating to appeals and he has made the 1972 rules in exercise of that power.

Part II of those rules contains the rules for appeal to an adjudicator or the tribunal at first instance, Part III the rules for appeals from an adjudicator to the tribunal. In Part II the only rule referring to appeals under s 14(1) is r 4(5) giving a time limit for appealing, but there are references to appeals under s 17(1) against directions for removal in rr 4(10) f and 9.

Rule 12 deals generally with the determination of appeals at first instance, whether by adjudicators or by the tribunal, without a hearing, and its relevant provisions are:

'An appellate authority may determine an appeal without a hearing if—(*a*) no party to the appeal has requested a hearing; or ... (*d*) the appellate authority is g satisfied that no matter arises on the appeal other than an objection by the appellant to removal to a particular country or territory or a claim by him that he ought to be removed (if at all) to a different country or territory and is of opinion that matters put forward in support of the appeal in pursuance of Rule 9 do not warrant a hearing ...'

Part III contains the all-important r 14, which provides: h

'(1) An appeal shall lie only with the leave of the adjudicator or of the Tribunal where it is from a determination by an adjudicator—(*a*) on an appeal under any provision of the Act other than section 14 (appeals against conditions); (*b*) on an appeal under section 14 which was dismissed on the determination of such a preliminary issue as is referred to in Rule 11, or (*c*) on an appeal under section 14(1), j by a person who has a limited leave under the Act to enter or remain in the United Kingdom, against a refusal to vary that leave.

(2) In addition to the circumstances in which leave to appeal must be granted by virtue of section 22(5) of the Act (existence of certificate of patriality or entry clearance), an appellate authority to whom application for leave to appeal as aforesaid is duly made shall grant it—(*a*) if the authority is satisfied that the determination of the appeal turns upon an arguable point of law; or (*b*) where an adjudicator has

> dismissed an appeal by a person who is in the United Kingdom, if the authority is
> a satisfied that the country or territory to which he is to be removed is one to which he is unwilling to go owing to the fear of being persecuted there for reasons of race, religion, nationality, membership of a particular social group or political opinion.'

Rule 16 provides for notice of appeal or an application for leave to appeal being given or made on Form 2, which is scheduled to the rules; the grounds of either may be varied (r 4(3)); r 16 (5) provides that 'an application for leave to appeal shall be disposed of
b without hearing unless the adjudicator or, as the case may be, the tribunal considers that the special circumstances render a hearing desirable'.

Rule 40 requires an appellate authority to cause a summary or record of the proceedings before it to be taken, and r 18 gives the tribunal power 'in its discretion' to 'receive or decline to receive further evidence of which notice has been given' than the summary or record of any evidence received by the adjudicator; and if the tribunal decides to receive
c further evidence 'it shall be given, as the tribunal may direct, either (i) orally . . . or (ii) in writing . . .' By r 20 'The Tribunal may dispose of an appeal without a hearing if—(*a*) no party to the appeal has requested a hearing . . .'

There are many references in later rules to a hearing, which indicate that it is an oral hearing: see rr 24, 28, 32, 35, 36, 37. Rule 18 would appear to apply to appeals, not to applications for leave to appeal, though that may not be the effect of its references to 'any
d party to the appeal' and 'any proceedings on an appeal' in paras (2) and (3). And r 28 may also be so limited by its references to 'each party to the appeal', as may be r 35 by its reference to 'on an appeal'. Rule 35 provides for summary determination of appeals in these terms:

> '(1) Subject to the provisions of paragraph (2) below, where it appears to an
> e appellate authority that the issues raised on an appeal have been determined—(*a*) in the case of an appeal before an adjudicator, by the same or another adjudicator or by the Tribunal, or (*b*) in the case of an appeal before the Tribunal, by the Tribunal, under Part II of the Act or the former appeal provisions, in previous proceedings to which the appellant was a party, on the basis of facts which did not materially differ from those to which the appeal relates, the authority may forthwith determine the
> f appeal without a hearing.
>
> (2) Before an appellate authority determines an appeal without a hearing in accordance with paragraph (1) above, the authority shall give the parties an opportunity of making representations to the effect that the appeal ought not to be so determined.
>
> (3) Where an appeal is determined without a hearing in accordance with
> g paragraph (1) above, the appellate authority shall give written notice to the parties that the appeal has been so determined, and any such notice shall contain a statement of the issues raised on the appeal and specify the previous proceedings in which those issues were determined . . .'

Rule 32 does provide that '*any* hearing by an appellate authority shall take place in
h public' (my emphasis), with certain immaterial exceptions, and that would include, perhaps by inadvertence, the hearing of an application. We have, however, no doubt that a power to receive oral evidence on the hearing of an appeal must carry with it the power to receive that evidence de bene esse on an application for leave to appeal, if it is necessary to help the tribunal to decide whether to grant or refuse leave.

Of these rules, four provide for proceedings 'without a hearing': rr 12, 16(5), 20 and
j 35.

Against that background of legislation we now consider the points raised by these appeals and the cross-notice of the respondent AS.

1. The first point to be decided is whether Enwia is entitled to have the tribunal's refusal of his application for leave to appeal quashed because he had no oral hearing.

Unlike AS, he had no oral hearing of his appeal to the adjudicator, and the tribunal has not given him an oral hearing either. Under r 12 the adjudicator was entitled to determine his appeal without a hearing if he did not request a hearing, or if the

adjudicator was satisfied that no matter arose on the appeal other than his objection to
removal to Iraq and that the matters he had put forward in support of his appeal did not
warrant a hearing. Under r 16(5) the tribunal was bound to dispose of his application for a
leave to appeal without a hearing unless it considered that special circumstances rendered
a hearing desirable. Rule 20 had no application to Enwia, except in so far as, on his
application for leave to appeal, the tribunal might have to consider any request for a
hearing of his appeal if his application for leave to appeal was granted. Rule 35 had no
application to his case. b

The reason why he was not granted an oral hearing of his appeal to the adjudicator is
not far to seek: he did not ask for one. Indeed, a counsellor of the United Kingdom
Immigrants Advisory Service wrote on 1 June 1981 asking the adjudicator to determine
the appeal without a hearing.

[The court considered the facts relating to Enwia's failure to ask for an oral hearing
before the adjudicator and the tribunal. The court stated that Comyn J had found that c
the tribunal reached its determination on the wrong assumption that Enwia did not
want to give oral evidence before the adjudicator or the tribunal and that the judge had
held that because the tribunal's determination was reached on that fundamental false
assumption he, Comyn J, could interfere with the determination by way of judicial
review. Accordingly, Comyn J had quashed the determination. The court then went on
to consider the question whether, on the basis that Enwia wanted an oral hearing before d
the adjudicator and the tribunal, the remedy of judicial review was available to quash the
determination because he had not been given an oral hearing. On that question, the
court said:]

Counsel for the tribunal has submitted on its behalf first that there was no basis in fact
for Comyn J's finding that Enwia always wanted to be heard in person, and second that
even if there were, the remedy of judicial review would not be available because there e
was no error of law on the tribunal's part or on the adjudicator's part, or on the part of
the Secretary of State, in not giving him an oral hearing. Counsel for Enwia has, on the
other hand, submitted first on the facts that the judge was entitled to find that the United
Kingdom Immigrants Advisory Service acted without authority in agreeing that there
should be no oral hearing of Enwia's case before the adjudicator (though there was a
hearing of the Secretary of State's case), that he did request a 'hearing' in his notice of f
application for leave to appeal of 17 July 1981, and that there were special circumstances
which should have led the tribunal to hear him on his application for leave, or to have
granted him leave in order that he, and perhaps other evidence, might be heard. Second,
on the law there was here a denial of natural justice in that the principle audi alteram
partem had not been complied with.

On the second question, we have considered what Lord Reid said in *Ridge v Baldwin* g
[1963] 2 All ER 66 at 71, [1964] AC 40 at 64–65 about the importance of proceeding
fairly when the procedure may lead to a decision seriously affecting the subject of it, and
what Slynn J said in *R v Immigration Appeal Tribunal ex p Mehmet* [1977] 2 All ER 602 at
608, [1977] 1 WLR 795 at 804–805 of the need to interpret special circumstances widely
in another of these immigration rules.

We have considered also the four or five categories of case to which judicial review h
applies, which counsel for the tribunal submits, contrary to the judgment of Comyn J,
are exhaustive, and the possibility that they may be extended in a proper case to cover
errors in law, not only of the decision-making body, but of the other party, for which *R
v Leyland Justices, ex p Hawthorn* [1979] 1 All ER 209, [1979] 2 QB 283 is an authority,
and even of the party complaining of the decision by way of judicial review, for which
there is no authority. Bearing in mind the judgments of Orr and Lawton LJJ in *R v West* j
Sussex Quarter Sessions, ex p Albert and Maud Johnson Trust Ltd [1973] 3 All ER 289 at 298–
299, 301, [1974] QB 24 at 39, 42, and of Lord Hailsham LC and Lord Brightman in *Chief
Constable of the North Wales Police v Evans* [1982] 3 All ER 141 at 143–144, 155, [1982] 1
WLR 1155 at 1160–1161, 1174–1175, we can see that it might be permissible to quash a
decision seriously affecting a person who by mistake or misunderstanding due to his own
defects or those of his advisers was deprived of the opportunity of being fully heard
before the decision was reached.

However, we find it unnecessary and undesirable to decide whether judicial review would lie in such a case, because we are clearly of opinion that this is not such a case. With the greatest respect to the judge and his commendable desire to ensure that no injustice was done to a party in the position of Enwia and his family, we cannot see what material he had on which to base his conclusion that Enwia had always wanted an oral hearing.

[The court reviewed the facts and continued:] Moreover, we do not accept the submission of counsel for Enwia that in every case where asylum is claimed, unless the claim is obviously unfounded or the applicant has had an oral hearing before the adjudicator, there are 'special circumstances' within r 16(5) because the tribunal must answer the question whether the applicant has a subjective fear of being persecuted in the country to which he is unwilling to go, however well- or ill-founded objectively his fear may be. It may be generally desirable that an applicant refused asylum should be heard at some stage of the appeal process; but the existence of special circumstances allowing (not requiring) a hearing of the application for leave to appeal against the adjudicator's refusal of asylum must depend on all the facts of the particular case.

For these reasons we reject the judge's main reason for quashing the tribunal's refusal of leave.

2. The next point is one common to the appeals of Enwia and AS. Was the tribunal bound to grant leave to appeal to Enwia and AS because they came within r 14(2)(*b*) of the 1972 rules? Each was a person in the United Kingdom whose appeal had been dismissed by an adjudicator; each was unwilling to go to Iraq, and it is to be assumed for the purpose of this point each was 'unwilling to go owing to the fear of being persecuted there for reasons of race, religion, nationality, membership of a particular social group or political opinion'. Ought the tribunal to have been satisfied that Iraq was 'the country or territory to which he is to be removed'? Or was each and is each still not, not yet, in that situation?

We have found this a much more difficult question to answer. Counsel for the tribunal contends that the words of r 14(2)(*b*) should be given their plain natural meaning, and if they are, they do not apply to a person appealing against a refusal of leave to remain under s 14, but to a person appealing against directions for removal under s 17; and possibly (though he expressed doubts about the alternative raised in his notices of appeal) to a person appealing against a decision to make a deportation order under s 15 'when as a matter of fact it was established that the particular appellant would, if deported, be removed to a country or territory to which he was unwilling to go for fear of persecution on the grounds referred to in r 14(2)(*b*)'. There can be no doubt that a person is to be removed to that country, say to Iraq, when the Secretary of State has given directions for his removal from the United Kingdom on a deportation order being made against him. Then he has his appeal under s 17 and the tribunal (or the adjudicator) must grant him leave to appeal against the adjudicator's dismissal of his appeal. The same would be true if directions for removal had been given for the removal of a person who came within s 16 of the Act. But neither Enwia nor AS has been given a direction to be removed. All that has happened is that he has been refused leave to remain here and informed by the notice of refusal that if he does not wish to appeal he should leave the United Kingdom by the date to which his stay has been extended.

At this stage there are various options open to the immigrant. He may decide to leave for a country of his choice, perhaps in Enwia's case the United States of America, where his brother and sister are, and in AS's case Switzerland, where most of his money is. The Secretary of State may decide not to deport him, eg on compassionate grounds, and to allow him to stay. It is uncertain whether he will have to be removed to any country, and still less certain whether he will be removed to the particular country where he faces persecution. The Statement of Changes in Immigration Rules (HC Paper (1979–80) no 394) laid before Parliament on 20 February 1980 draws the distinction between asylum at the stage of variation of leave to enter or remain (Pt X) and deportation (Pt XI). After pointing out in para 64 (in Pt VI) that—

'Special considerations arise when the only country to which a person *could be*

> *removed* is one to which he is unwilling to go owing to well-founded fear of being persecuted for reasons of race, religion . . .' [then follow the words of r 14(2) (*b*) of the 1972 rules]

the rules, by para 120 in Pt X, provide:

> 'A person may apply for asylum in the United Kingdom on the ground that, *if he were required to leave, he would have to go* to a country to which . . .' [using the same words]

and para 150 in Pt XI provides:

> 'In accordance with the provisions of the Convention and Protocol relating to the Status of Refugees, a deportation order will not be made against a person if the only country to which *he can be removed* is one to which . . .' [using the same words].

(My emphasis throughout.)

An immigrant who has been refused leave to remain and told he should leave this country by a particular date has clearly been 'required to leave', and could be removed to the country he fears, and would have to go there, if, liable to deportation, he is later the subject of a decision to make a deportation order to that particular country and no other and, on the making of the deportation order, directions are given for his removal to that country and no other; and he has a right of appeal against the removal directions on that ground (see HC Paper (1979–80) no 394, para 154). Whatever the position may be under s 15 after a decision to deport has been made, it cannot be said that he is to be removed to a particular country when he has merely been required to leave this country. It is not until his destination has been fixed as that country that it can be said that that is the country 'to which he is to be removed', and then he has his appeal to the tribunal under s 17 because he must be granted leave to appeal by virtue of r 14(2)(*b*).

Both Comyn J and Woolf J refused to give that effect to the rule, and held that it could and should be construed to apply to Enwia and AS when appealing under s 14. Comyn J dealt with the point shortly in a manner which we find some difficulty in following. He said:

> '[Counsel for the tribunal] suggested to me in one argument of his that the situation envisaged in r 14(2)(*b*) had not yet arisen, because there was no assignment or consignment of this applicant to any country, much less to Iraq. I would have been more attracted to that argument had not the proceedings before the adjudicator and the tribunal plainly gone on the footing that removal to Iraq was the essential matter. I have therefore rejected that argument.'

He went on to say that it seemed to him 'pre-eminently desirable that in a case relating to r 14(2)(*b*) oral evidence from the applicant should be heard', apparently because the test of the applicant's fear was subjective, and only by seeing and hearing him could the appellate authority be satisfied that he could establish that his fear was real, reasonable (which must have meant something different from 'well-founded' in HC Paper (1979–80) no 394, paras 120 and 150), genuine and substantial.

Woolf J dealt with counsel for the tribunal's argument rather differently. While counsel for the tribunal conceded that it would be practical to read the rule as in effect giving AS a right of appeal 'because it would enable the tribunal, on the first series of appeals, to determine once and for all the issue whether or not the applicant was entitled to political asylum', he pointed out that there was no question of his being removed at this stage. But the judge, after underlining the words 'to be removed', went on to conclude that although the rule refers to the word 'removed' it should not be confined to that situation:

> 'It should apply to all three series of appeals, although the matter would not have to be gone into on three occasions. I say that because I think any other result is so undesirable that it cannot be attributed as being the intention of those responsible for making the rules.'

We confess that our difficulty in following these two decisions stems not from the use

of the word 'removed' but from the use of the words 'is to be removed'; not from any
a doubt as to the desirability of the issue of entitlement to asylum or of removal to Iraq being decided once at an early stage, but from the ordinary meaning of the language used. We find great difficulty in interpreting 'is to be removed' as the gerundive 'is meet to be removed' (as the Latin used to be translated by schoolboys), or 'is fit to be removed', or 'is liable to be removed'. From the moment that there is a refusal to extend a limited leave the immigrant is on risk of being removed, may be removed, and in the ordinary
b course of things is very much more likely to be removed, to the country to which he is unwilling to go. But until his case proceeds as far as deportation, there is no 'must be removed' about it. The day of judgment, 'quando caeli movendi sunt et terra'. has not yet come, and we would think that counsel for the tribunal was right in submitting that he is not 'to be removed' to that country until that day comes and there is a direction 'Thou shalt go there', unless there is no reasonably possible purpose in giving the words
c of the rule their natural meaning.

Counsel for AS has elaborated many arguments, some stronger than others, which counsel for Enwia was content to adopt, in support of the judges' decisions. He called attention to some paragraphs in the handbook on Procedures and Criteria for Determining Refugee Status for their emphasis on the subjective element in fear of persecution; but this may explain why r 14(2)(*b*) imposes the duty to grant leave, and opens the door to a
d further appeal and perhaps an oral hearing, without helping to determine at what stage the applicant for leave comes within the rule.

More to the point is the consequence of supposing that he does not come within the rule until he appeals under s 17; for then he may have had two appeals already, each with two stages, to an adjudicator and then to the tribunal, under ss 14 and 15, followed by a further appeal, to the adjudicator under s 17, before he can demand leave from the
e tribunal under the rule. And not only is that undesirable, as the judges have pointed out, but it exposes an applicant to the risk of having each appeal determined summarily under r 35 of the 1972 rules, for fresh evidence will not help an applicant if it relates to basic facts not materially different from those on which the issues raised have been previously determined: see *Mohammed Taj and Mohammed Riaz v Immigration Appeal Tribunal* (30 June 1982), an unreported decision of this court.

f Furthermore, if r 14(2)(*b*) is confined to an appellant under s 17, who has been directed to be removed to the country where he fears persecution, the rule could have said so, either by inserting the word 'directed' into the phrase 'is to be removed', or by introducing a reference to 'under s 17' after the word 'appeal'. If the rule is limited as counsel for the tribunal contends, it could and must have read 'where an adjudicator has dismissed an appeal *under s 17* . . . if the authority is satisfied that the country or territory to which he
g is *directed* to be removed . . .' or with one of those simple additions, or, to be clear beyond argument, with both a reference to s 17 and the phrase 'to which *he has been directed* to be removed'. We cannot regard the words 'appeal as aforesaid' in the opening sentence of r 14(2) as referring either to 'an appeal under any provision of the Act' within r 14(1)(*a*), or to an appeal under s 14 or s 14(1) within r 14(1)(*b*) or (*c*), because whatever else r 14(2)(*b*) covers it must cover an application for leave to appeal under s 17.

h The argument against what counsel for AS picturesquely termed a 'pyramid of appeals' has force, and so has his submission that its prospect might encourage an immigrant to overstay his leave and commit a criminal offence against s 24, rather than appeal straightaway against a refusal to extend his leave.

There are, however, many cases in which an appeal under s 17 by an applicant in fear of persecution will be his first appeal—if, for instance, he has asked for asylum on entry
j into the United Kingdom, or has been recommended by a court for deportation on being convicted of an offence, or for any reason has decided not to appeal under s 14. If an immigrant has a right of appeal under ss 14 and 15 and chooses to exercise it, he will not be in danger of the discretionary remedy of summary determination being exercised against him, because although his unwillingness to go to a particular country for fear of persecution is properly raised at each stage of the appeal process, the issues are not the same, being whether the Secretary of State was entitled under s 14 to refuse to vary the limited leave, under s 15 to decide to make a deportation order, and under s 17 to direct

his removal. Counsel for the tribunal frankly and rightly concedes that the earlier an immigrant can have the issue whether he is unwilling to go to a particular country owing a to a well-founded fear of persecution decided the better; and that in most cases a refusal to extend such a person's limited leave leads to a deportation order and his removal to the country to which he is unwilling to go. But he submits, to our minds convincingly, that there is nothing improbable or unreasonable in providing a 'long stop' measure to prevent anyone being sent back to a particular country without an appeal: and that is a reasonably possible purpose of the rule given its natural meaning. b

On the best consideration we can give to r 14(2)(*b*) we conclude with reluctance and regret that although there is much to be said for the interpretation of it by the judges in the Divisional Court, there is more to be said for the construction of it by one Immigration Appeal Tribunal which counsel for the tribunal asks us to accept on behalf of both. The purpose of the rule as expressed in its language is to give a right of appeal to those, and only those, whose destination has been fixed as the country or territory to c which they are to be removed. There is no country to which the immigrant is to be removed until then. We would accordingly allow these appeals, including the appeal in the case of AS, unless the decision of Woolf J giving him leave to appeal to the tribunal ought to be upheld notwithstanding that his decision on the application of r 14(2)(*b*) cannot be affirmed.

3. The remaining point is whether the adjudicator's determination of AS's appeal itself d required the tribunal to give him leave to appeal against it. His is, as counsel for the tribunal admitted, a strong case for asylum on the merits. Woolf J said that if it had been his decision he would have granted leave. But he went on to say that he could find no error of law in the determination of the adjudicator, and the argument that it was perverse was not begun to be made out. We agree with him.

The grounds on which the respondent's notice relies are: e

> '1. That there were reasonable grounds for contending that the Adjudicator had failed to direct himself properly as to the proper interpretation of H.C.394 para. 120 and/or had reached a decision which no reasonable Adjudicator could have reached having given himself proper directions in that the Applicant's 'well founded fear of being persecuted' arose because of his political opinions. f
>
> PARTICULARS
>
> (a) The Applicant had refused when asked to join the Ba'ath political party in Iraq.
> (b) By reason of the said refusal he was liable to be imprisoned.
> (c) Further by reason of the said refusal he was liable to be the victim of false accusations which could be used as an excuse for imprisoning him. g
> (d) ther by reason of the said refusal he would have no protection under the legal system in Iraq.
>
> 2. Alternatively, that since the matters upon which the Tribunal had to be satisfied under H.C. 94 para. 120 depended in part upon the assessment of the Applicant's subjective fears the Tribunal should have given leave and considered further an application to hear oral evidence from the Respondent.' h

AS has had a sympathetic oral hearing before the adjudicator, whose determination and reasons are set out in 17 detailed paragraphs: (1) he found that AS had a fear of being persecuted if he had to go to Iraq; and indeed he allowed the hearing of his appeal to be conducted in private; (2) he assumed that AS's fear was well-founded; (3) he found however that that fear was not for any of the reasons specified in para 120 of HC Paper (1979–80) no 394 (now replaced by a new rule in the same terms), but for the reason that j he lacked confidence in the judicial process of Iraq and his fear could not be considered to be of a social or political nature; (4) he did not find that he would have to go back to Iraq.

On the third finding he was bound to dismiss the appeal. Counsel for AS submits that no reasonable adjudicator would have made that finding, and so determined the appeal, even if the fourth finding was correct, being perhaps justified by his having money in

Switzerland and land in Lebanon. But we agree with Woolf J that it was not a perverse finding, and there was evidence to support it. Counsel for AS submits that the reason why AS lacked confidence in the judicial process of Iraq was that he had refused to join the Ba'ath party, and that although the rest of his family were not being persecuted in Iraq, he was accordingly liable to be persecuted, on any pretext such as a false charge of bribery, after what had happened to his father. But the adjudicator found that his refusal to join the Ba'ath party was of relatively minor significance. And we agree with the judge that that was a finding of fact which involved no misunderstanding of the case or error of law, because it was a rejection of AS's case which was open to the adjudicator.

As to the tribunal's refusal of leave, counsel for AS submitted that it was the duty of the tribunal to decide whether an appellant's case was hopeless when looked at broadly and with regard to the summary of the proceedings supplied under para 40 of the 1972 rules and to the need for an oral hearing in an asylum case; and that unless it was hopeless, and if there was a case to argue, the tribunal ought to grant leave.

We cannot accept that view of the tribunal's duty under rr 14 and 16. Having stated, in our opinion correctly, that r 14(2)(*b*) had no application 'because at the moment it is not proposed to remove the appellant to Iraq' the tribunal expressed its opinion on the merits in this way:

> 'In the opinion of the tribunal there was sufficient evidence to support the adjudicator's findings of fact, which were not unreasonable, and he does not appear to have misdirected himself in any way as to the law or immigration rules. In the opinion of the tribunal, the determination of this appeal does not turn on any arguable point of law and there are no other circumstances which would merit the granting of leave to appeal. Leave to appeal to the tribunal is refused.'

That opinion also was, in our judgment, correct. There may be special reasons for AS not being deported to Iraq, as the adjudicator indicated, but there were no special reasons for granting him a second hearing, for which he asked in his written grounds. On the only other grounds in his notice of application, relating to the adjudicator's finding about his refusal to join the Ba'ath party and his failure to prove a political reason for his fear of persecution, the tribunal was right to hold that the findings were not unreasonable and involved no misdirection as to the law or immigration rules: see s 19(1)(*a*)(i) of the 1971 Act which I have read. The adjudicator was entitled to determine that the decision to refuse AS leave to remain here was in accordance with the law and para 120 of HC Paper (1979–80) no 394 and the tribunal's determination to refuse leave to appeal was an exercise of its statutory discretion which had to be erroneous in law or plainly wrong before the court could interfere with it on appeal. This is not an appeal but an application for judicial review, and on an application for judicial review it is the process by which the determination was reached which must be wrong before the court can quash it.

We cannot find anything wrong with the process by which these applications for leave to appeal were refused, or that there was anything unfair in the manner in which they were conducted by the appellate authorities. These appeals are important to the respondents because, although only concerned with refusals of leave to appeal, those refusals exhaust their rights of appeal to the appellate authorities. But there remains the possibility that they will not have to return to Iraq, and we hope that nothing said or decided in this court will affect that possibility. However, for the reasons we have given we allow the tribunal's appeals in both cases, setting aside the orders of Comyn J and Woolf J and restoring the orders of the tribunal.

These appeals will be allowed, with the consequences that are set out in the judgment of the court which has been handed down.

Appeals allowed. Leave to appeal to the House of Lords refused.

Solicitors: *Treasury Solicitor* (for the tribunal); *Egerton Sandler Summer & Co* (for Enwia); *Camerons*, Harrow (for AS).

Diana Brahams Barrister.

R v Seymour

a

HOUSE OF LORDS
LORD DIPLOCK, LORD FRASER OF TULLYBELTON, LORD ROSKILL, LORD BRIDGE OF HARWICH AND LORD TEMPLEMAN
7 JUNE, 21 JULY 1983

Road traffic – Reckless driving – Causing death by reckless driving – Charge of manslaughter – Proper direction to jury b

Where manslaughter is charged when the victim was killed as a result of reckless driving by the defendant on a public highway, the trial judge should give the jury the direction laid down as appropriate in a case of causing death by reckless driving, while also pointing out that to constitute the offence of manslaughter the risk of death being caused by the c manner of the defendant's driving must be very high, and omitting if necessary any reference to there being a risk of damage to property if that is irrelevant (see p 1059 *b* to *d*, p 1063 *a b* and p 1066 *b* to *d*, post); *R v Lawrence* [1981] 1 All ER 974 adopted.

Although the legal ingredients of the common law offence of manslaughter and the statutory offence of causing death by reckless driving contrary to s 1[a] of the Road Traffic Act 1972 are identical they should not be joined in the same indictment, one count d alleging manslaughter and another alleging the statutory offence, because the degree of recklessness required for conviction of the statutory offence is less than that required for conviction of manslaughter and a jury ought not to be required to assess differing degrees of turpitude when determining a defendant's guilt or innocence, since the degree of turpitude is a matter relevant to sentence rather than conviction (see p 1059 *b* to *d* and p 1065 *c* to p 1066 *d*, post). e

Notes

For trial for manslaughter by causing death by reckless driving, see 33 Halsbury's Laws (3rd edn) 624, para 1050.

f

Cases referred to in opinions

Andrews v DPP [1937] 2 All ER 552, [1937] AC 576, HL.
Dunn v HM Advocate 1960 JC 55.
HM Advocate v Earnshaw 1982 SLT 179.
Jennings v United States Government [1982] 3 All ER 104, [1983] AC 624, [1982] 3 WLR 450, HL; *rvsg* [1982] 3 All ER 104, [1982] 1 WLR 949, DC.
R v Caldwell [1981] 1 All ER 961, [1982] AC 341, [1981] 2 WLR 509, HL. g
R v Church [1965] 2 All ER 72, [1966] 1 QB 59, [1965] 2 WLR 1220, CCA.
R v Lawrence [1981] 1 All ER 974, [1982] AC 510, [1981] 2 WLR 524, HL.
R v Lowe [1973] 1 All ER 805, [1973] QB 702, [1973] 2 WLR 481, CA.
R v Pigg [1982] 2 All ER 591, [1982] 1 WLR 762, CA; *rvsd* [1983] 1 All ER 56, [1983] 1 WLR 6, HL,

h

Appeal

On 15 January 1982 the appellant, Edward John Seymour, was convicted at the Crown Court at Northampton before Bush J and a jury of manslaughter by unlawfully killing Iris Ada Burrows on 30 April 1981 by his reckless driving on a public highway. The appellant was sentenced to five years imprisonment and disqualified from holding or j obtaining a driving licence for a period of six years. He appealed against his conviction to the Court of Appeal, Criminal Division (Watkins LJ, Lawson and Stephen Brown JJ) which dismissed his appeal on 12 January 1983. On 26 January 1983 the court certified under s 33(2) of the Criminal Appeal Act 1968, on the application of the appellant, that a

a Section 1, so far as material, is set out at p 1061 *h j*, post

point of law of general public importance was involved in the decision to dismiss the appeal and refused leave to appeal to the House of Lords. On 17 March 1983 the Appeal Committee of the House of Lords gave the appellant leave to appeal against the decision. The facts are set out in the opinion of Lord Roskill.

Michael Connell QC and *John Cartwright* for the appellant.
Graeme Hamilton QC and *Conrad Seagroatt QC* for the Crown.

Their Lordships took time for consideration.

21 July. The following opinions were delivered.

LORD DIPLOCK. My Lords, I have had the advantage of reading in draft the speech of my noble and learned friend Lord Roskill. I agree with it, and for the reasons he gives I would dismiss this appeal.

LORD FRASER OF TULLYBELTON. My Lords, I have had the advantage of reading in draft the speech of my noble and learned friend Lord Roskill. I agree that, for the reasons stated by him, the appeal should be refused.

But I wish to refer to the difference which the appeal has brought to light between the practice in the courts of England and Wales and that in the courts of Scotland with regard to prosecutions for causing death by reckless driving of motor vehicles, in cases which are regarded as particularly bad. In England and Wales the practice is to prosecute the driver on a charge of manslaughter, but not to charge the statutory offence of causing death by reckless driving, contrary to the Road Traffic Act 1972, s 1, as amended by the Criminal Law Act 1977, s 50. In Scotland the practice is to prosecute on one charge of culpable homicide, or alternatively of the statutory offence, leaving the jury (if it decides to convict) to decide whether to do so on the first or second alternative. The fact that there is such a difference between the procedure in the two jurisdictions is perhaps surprising, as there is no relevant difference between the crimes of manslaughter and culpable homicide, and the statutory offence is laid down by the same Act in both countries.

Lord Roskill has explained the logical reasons why the English practice, at least since the passing of the Criminal Law Act 1977, has been to prosecute only for one or other of the common law or the statutory offences. I have no intention of criticising the English practice, as it is applied in England, but there are in my opinion good reasons why the Scottish practice should continue as it is in Scotland.

The Scottish practice was settled in *Dunn v HM Advocate* 1960 JC 55 where the accused had been tried on an indictment which charged culpable homicide and the statutory offence as alternatives, and had been convicted of culpable homicide. At that time, the statutory offence was that created by the Road Traffic Act 1956, s 8(1) (driving 'recklessly or at a speed or in a manner which is dangerous to the public'). As the degree of negligence which constitutes dangerous driving is less that that which constitutes reckless driving, the statutory offence in that form was clearly less serious than the common law crime of culpable homicide, which requires recklessness. But it is plain that neither the trial judge (Lord Guest) nor the Lord Justice-Clerk (Thomson), who delivered the only reasoned opinion in the High Court of Justiciary, based the distinction on the use of the word 'dangerous'. Accordingly, the amendment made by the Act of 1977, which deleted dangerous driving from the statutory offence leaving it consisting only of driving recklessly, has not affected the practice, which continues to be that in cases which appear to the prosecutor to be particularly bad cases, culpable homicide and the statutory offence are charged alternatively. At least one case has been prosecuted in that way since 1977: see *HM Advocate v Earnshaw*, tried at Ayr on 22 May 1981 (reported only on another point on appeal in 1982 SLT 179).

The Scottish practice can, in my view, be justified on the ground that, when Parliament created the statutory offence of reckless driving, it left the common law crimes of culpable homicide, and manslaughter, in existence. This House decided in *Jennings v United States Government* [1982] 3 All ER 104, [1983] AC 624 that the crime of manslaughter had not been impliedly repealed and the decision is in principle applicable *a* to culpable homicide in Scotland. But in *Jennings* [1982] 3 All ER 104 at 117, [1983] AC 624 at 644–645 Lord Roskill said that 'the ingredients of the statutory offence are co-extensive with the ingredients of the . . . common law offence of manslaughter', and it is suggested that the effect of that statement is that any attempt to distinguish between the two offences according to their respective degrees of gravity, or indeed on any other *b* ground, is illogical and wrong. It is said that they are not two offences but only one offence with two names. I do not accept that argument. Although the ingredients of the two offences are the same, the degree of recklessness required for conviction of the statutory offence is less than that required for conviction of the common law crime. That is why the maximum sentence for the statutory offence (five years' imprisonment) is less than the maximum sentence for culpable homicide or manslaughter (imprisonment for *c* life). That is also why, in cases such as that which is the subject of the instant appeal, which the prosecutor considers to be very grave, it is thought appropriate to prosecute for the common law crime.

But then it is said to be wrong for the jury to be concerned with assessing the different degrees of turpitude between one case and another. It is of course the law in Scotland, as in England, that the decision on sentence is for the judge alone, but the jury's decision to *d* convict of culpable homicide rather than of the statutory offence does not oblige the judge to impose a sentence of more than five years' imprisonment. It merely makes it possible for him to do so, by increasing the range of punishments within which he can select that which he considers appropriate. Since the common law crime and the statutory offence continue to exist together, and since (as is agreed) the distinction between the two depends on the degree of wickedness exhibited by the accused, it seems to me to be *e* perfectly proper (to put it no higher) that the duty of assessing the degree of wickedness should be performed by the jury in order to decide which offence (if any) he has committed. That view has the overwhelming advantage in practice that it avoids the risk, which existed in the instant appeal, that a person who is accused only of manslaughter or culpable homicide may be acquitted of that charge and may then go unpunished, although he would have been convicted of the statutory offence if it had *f* been charged as an alternative. Such a result would not, in my view, be in the interests of justice and I would be sorry to see the risk of its occurring being introduced into Scottish procedure where at present it does not arise. If it became necessary for the judge, in answer to questions from the jury, to refer to the question of sentence, I think that a jury is well able to understand the difference between selecting the *actual* sentence (which is the duty of the judge) and selecting the offence which carries a *maximum* sentence at least *g* adequate to cover what is required in the circumstances of the case (which is the effect of the jury's decision between culpable homicide and the statutory offence). If the choice is between leaving the jury with a poor impression of the trial process, on the one hand, and risking allowing a guilty motorist to escape wholly unpunished because of some supposed technical difficulty in bringing alternative charges against him, on the other hand, I would have no hesitation in preferring the former.

h I would only add that the number of cases in which, either in Scotland or in England, it will be appropriate to prosecute a motorist on a charge of culpable homicide or manslaughter must be very small, as it is extremely rare for conviction on such a charge to result in a sentence in excess of five years' imprisonment. In the instant appeal, and also in the *Earnshaw* case, where the accused was convicted of culpable homicide, sentences of five years' imprisonment were imposed. *j*

With regard to the certified question in this appeal, the submission of counsel for the appellant that the direction suggested in *R v Lawrence* [1981] 1 All ER 974, [1982] AC 510 should not be given in its entirety where the charge is one of manslaughter, is not, in my opinion, well founded. If any modification of the '*Lawrence* direction' is appropriate in a case where manslaughter alone is charged, it would be to add a warning to the jury that before convicting of manslaughter they must be satisfied that the risk of death being

caused by the manner of the accused's driving was very high. Such a direction will, of
a course, always be necessary where the common law crime and the statutory offence are charged alternatively, but where, as in this case, the common law crime is charged alone, it may be unnecessary and inappropriate. In the present case I think it was unnecessary.

I would dismiss the appeal.

LORD ROSKILL. My Lords, this appeal arises from the dismissal on 12 January 1983
b by the Court of Appeal, Criminal Division (Watkins LJ, Lawson and Stephen Brown JJ) of the appellant's appeal against his conviction on 15 January 1982 for manslaughter after a trial at the Crown Court at Northampton before Bush J and a jury. The Court of Appeal, Criminal Division granted the appellant a certificate to the terms of which I will later refer. Leave to appeal was refused by the court but was later given by your Lordships' House.

c The Crown's case which was accepted by the jury was that the appellant had killed Mrs Ada Burrows by his reckless driving on a public highway of an 11 ton lorry. The allegation was that on 30 April 1981 following a quarrel between the appellant and Mrs Burrows, with whom the appellant had been living, the appellant met Mrs Burrows driving a Vauxhall car in the opposite direction from that in which he was driving the lorry. There was a slight collision. Mrs Burrows got out of the Vauxhall car and
d approached the lorry. He, allegedly intending only to push her car out of the way, drove his lorry up against the car. He did so so violently that the car was moved some ten to twenty feet and one of its tyres was forced off. In the course of so doing Mrs Burrows was crushed between the two vehicles. Her injuries were such that, in the words of an ambulance driver who gave evidence as quoted by the judge in his summing up, 'had the ambulance driver picked her up in the normal way as ambulance drivers do, she
e would have broken in two.' She died about a week later on 6 May 1981.

The jury accepted those facts as established without hesitation for they unanimously convicted the appellant in just over three-quarters of an hour. It was an extremely grave case of 'motor-manslaughter' to use the popular phrase, a view which the trial judge clearly took since he passed a sentence of five years' imprisonment on the appellant and your Lordships were told that there was no appeal to the Court of Appeal, Criminal
f Division against that sentence.

My Lords, in recent years, and indeed since the enactment of s 8 of the Road Traffic Act 1956 when the statutory offence of causing death by reckless or dangerous driving was first created, charges of 'motor manslaughter' have been comparatively rare. It is common knowledge that the statutory offence was created carrying a maximum penalty of five years' imprisonment because of the extreme reluctance of juries to convict
g motorists of manslaughter. After 1956 when the statutory offence was created, the practice in England and Wales was to charge the offence of causing death by dangerous driving only and not by reckless driving.

The subsequent legislative history of this offence has recently been twice discussed in your Lordships' House, first, in the speech of my noble and learned friend Lord Diplock in *R v Lawrence* [1981] 1 All ER 974, [1982] AC 510 and, second, in my speech in *Jennings*
h *v United States Government* [1982] 3 All ER 104, [1983] AC 624 and requires no further repetition. Suffice it to say that by reason of the enactment of s 50 of the Criminal Law Act 1977, the former provisions of s 8 of the 1956 Act, which by 1977 had become s 1(1) of the Road Traffic Act 1972, were replaced by a new s 1 which provided: 'A person who causes the death of another person by driving a motor vehicle on a road recklessly shall be guilty of an offence.'

j This enactment in due course gave rise to two questions. First, what was the meaning of the word 'reckless' in this new section? Or, to put the same point in other words, what was the proper direction for the trial judge to give to a jury as to the test to be applied in determining whether or not a person charged under this section was guilty of the offence charged? Second, and in particular having regard to the speech of Lord Atkin in *Andrews v DPP* [1937] 2 All ER 552 at 557, [1937] AC 576 at 584, did the common law offence of manslaughter by reckless driving of a motor vehicle survive the enactment of s 50 of the

1977 Act, for if it did so survive there would be two offences, one at common law and
the other by statute which, since the ingredients of each were indistinguishable, would a
be co-extensive, though one carried the maximum penalty of imprisonment for life, and
the other of five years' imprisonment only.

The meaning of the words 'reckless' and 'recklessly' came before your Lordships' House
in two cases, namely *R v Caldwell* [1981] 1 All ER 961, [1982] AC 341 and *R v Lawrence*
to which I have already referred. The former case arose out of the Criminal Damage Act
1971. The latter was a tragic case arising under s 1 of the Road Traffic Act 1972, as b
amended in 1977, of causing death by reckless driving.

The decisions in this House, in the former case by a majority and in the latter
unanimously, made it plain what the words 'reckless' or 'recklessly' meant in these
statutes, and in the latter case what the proper direction to the jury was in a case of
causing death by the reckless driving of a motor vehicle. In *R v Lawrence* [1981] 1 All ER
974 at 982, [1982] AC 510 at 526–527 my noble and learned friend Lord Diplock, in a c
speech with which all my noble and learned friends then sitting agreed, said:

> 'In my view, an appropriate instruction to the jury on what is meant by driving
> recklessly would be that they must be satisfied of two things: first, that the defendant
> was in fact driving the vehicle in such a manner as to create an obvious and serious
> risk of causing physical injury to do some other person who might happen to be
> using the road or of doing substantial damage to property; and, second, that in d
> driving in that manner the defendant did so without having given any thought to
> the possibility of there being any such risk or, having recognised that there was
> some risk involved, had none the less gone on to take it. It is for the jury to decide
> whether the risk created by the manner in which the vehicle was being driven was
> both obvious and serious and, in deciding this, they may apply the standard of the
> ordinary prudent motorist as represented by themselves. If satisfied that an obvious e
> and serious risk was created by the manner of the defendant's driving, the jury are
> entitled to infer that he was in one or other of the states of mind required to
> constitute the offence and will probably do so; but regard must be given to any
> explanation he gives as to his state of mind which may displace the inference.'

As to the second question, there had been, as Watkins LJ said in giving the judgment f
of the Court of Appeal, Criminal Division in the present case, a body of opinion which
thought that the common law offence of manslaughter by the reckless driving of a motor
vehicle must be taken to have been impliedly repealed by s 50 of the 1977 Act, or
possibly earlier. That view was taken by the Divisional Court in *Jennings* [1982] 3 All ER
104, [1982] 1 WLR 949. But your Lordships' House in that case unanimously held
otherwise. The argument founded on implied repeal was rejected for the reasons given g
in my speech (see [1982] 3 All ER 104 at 113–117, [1983] AC 624 at 639–644) which I
will not repeat. But I added:

> 'No doubt the prosecuting authorities today would only prosecute for
> manslaughter in the case of death caused by the reckless driving of a motor vehicle
> on a road in a very grave case.'

My Lords, *Jennings* was decided on 29 July 1982, over a year after Mrs Burrows's death h
and some six months after the appellant's trial at Northampton Crown Court. This trial
also preceded the hearing of *Jennings* in the Divisional Court. As already stated, the
appellant was charged only with manslaughter, no doubt because of the view which the
prosecuting authorities took of the gravity of the case. Your Lordships were told that a
plea of guilty to the statutory offence, had that also been charged, was proffered but was j
rejected by counsel for the Crown. I agree with the view of the Court of Appeal that this
was an entirely proper course for counsel for the Crown to have adopted. The jury was,
of course, unaware of this fact.

After the close of the evidence, counsel for the appellant invited the judge not to give
the jury what I will call for brevity the '*Lawrence* direction' simpliciter, arguing that that
direction was applicable only where the statutory offence was charged. He submitted

that where the common law offence of manslaughter was charged, the jury should be
a directed that the Crown must further prove that the appellant recognised that some risk was involved and had none the less proceeded to take that risk.

The judge rejected the submission and gave the *Lawrence* direction subject only to the omission of any reference to the 'obvious and serious risk . . . of doing substantial damage to property': see *R v Lawrence* [1981] 1 All ER 974 at 982, [1982] AC 510 at 526. In my view, he was entirely right not to refer to damage to property, a reference to which was
b irrelevant in this case and might well have confused the jury. His admirably clear direction not only properly reflected the decision of this House in *R v Lawrence* but also Lord Atkin's speech in *Andrews v DPP*. I quote the relevant passage:

> 'The second question you have to decide: was the driving that caused those injuries reckless? If so, then it is manslaughter. If you are not satisfied that it was reckless, then the verdict is not guilty. To amount to reckless driving mere
> c negligence is not enough. His conduct must go beyond the question of compensation between citizens and amount to, in your view, criminal conduct requiring punishment. You have to be satisfied on the question of recklessness that he drove in such a manner as to create an obvious and serious risk of causing physical harm to some other person who might happen to be using the road at the time . . . Once you are satisfied that the manner of his driving was such as to create an obvious and
> d serious risk of causing physical harm to a person using the road at the time, you also have to be satisfied that driving in that manner he did so without having given any thought to the possibility of there being any such risk, or alternatively, having recognised that there was some risk involved, none the less went on to take it; in other words, he was reckless. He reckoned not of the consequences. In determining the quality of his driving, you apply the standards of the ordinary reasonable
> e motorist. You, of course, take into account all the evidence including his explanation.'

As already stated, the appellant was convicted. He appealed and his appeal to the Court of Appeal was dismissed. By the date of the appeal *Jennings* had been decided in your Lordships' House. The reasons given for the dismissal of his appeal were in substance,
f that since your Lordships' House had held that the ingredients of the common law and statutory offences were identical, the *Lawrence* direction, which was appropriate when the statutory offence was charged, must be equally appropriate when the common law offence of manslaughter was charged. The Court of Appeal, Criminal Division granted the appellant a certificate in the following terms:

> 'Where manslaughter is charged and the circumstances of the offence are that the
> g victim was killed as the result of the reckless driving of the defendant on a public highway; should the trial Judge give the jury the direction suggested in *R v Lawrence* in its entirety; or should the direction be that only a recognition by the defendant that some risk was involved and he had none-the-less gone on to take it would be sufficient to establish the commission of the offence?'

h In his able submissions on behalf of the appellant, counsel accepted, as he was indeed bound to accept, that the common law and statutory offences co-existed but he challenged that it necessarily followed that the same direction was appropriate in both cases. He founded on the phrase 'aggravating circumstances', a phrase used by Mr Littman QC, counsel for the respondent in *Jennings*, and adopted in the last paragraph but two of my speech. Counsel for the appellant urged that the reference to 'aggravating circumstances'
j showed that there might be different degrees of recklessness in the different cases. He also urged that what I had said regarding the ingredients of the two offences being identical was obiter and should not be followed, especially as there had been no argument that knowledge of the risk involved was a prerequisite to conviction for manslaughter though not for the statutory offence. He also challenged as obiter the sentence (see [1982] 3 All ER 104 at 116, [1983] AC 624 at 644) that 'the offence of causing death by reckless driving of a motor vehicle on a road is still manslaughter by the law of England . . .',

saying that the sentence should have read only 'is still capable of being manslaughter . . .'

My Lords, I have carefully considered these criticisms but I am unable to accept any of them as valid. In *Jennings* [1982] 3 All ER 104 at 113, [1983] AC 624 at 639 I had listed the four prerequisites to a successful application for the extradition of the respondent of which the first was that the crime charged in California was properly described in England as manslaughter. The argument was that it was not properly so described because of the suggested implied repeal of the relevant part of the law of manslaughter. That argument was rejected for the reasons given at length (see [1982] 3 All ER 104 at 113–117, [1983] AC 624 at 639–644). The criticised sentence was the last sentence of that part of my speech setting out those reasons. It states the conclusion to which the reasoning had led and is not obiter.

As to the passage in the last paragraph but two of my speech, this was directed to the fourth prerequisite. Since for the reasons given the two offences co-existed and the ingredients were thus the same, there was no room for Mr Littman's argument on 'aggravating circumstances'. This passage was also not obiter but was essential to the reasoning leading to the rejection of Mr Littman's argument in connection with the fourth prerequisite.

Counsel for the appellant also submitted that if the *Lawrence* direction were given in manslaughter cases and a conviction followed, the trial judge when considering sentence would not know whether the jury took the view that the defendant had deliberately taken a risk of which he was aware or not. My Lords, juries do not and should not be asked to explain their verdicts. It is by no means unusual for a guilty verdict to be properly founded for a number of reasons and it is for the judge, who is the person best placed to assess the degree of turpitude involved in the light of the evidence and the jury's verdict, to pass such sentence as he thinks right in all the circumstances. That sentence is of course always open to review if necessary.

My Lords, I would accept the submission of counsel for the Crown that once it is shown that the two offences co-exist it would be quite wrong to give the adjective 'reckless' or the adverb 'recklessly' a different meaning according to whether the statutory or the common law offence is charged. 'Reckless' should today be given the same meaning in relation to all offences which involve 'recklessness' as one of the elements unless Parliament has otherwise ordained. That this has been so in the past is shown by the respective decisions of the Court of Criminal Appeal and the Court of Appeal, Criminal Division in *R v Church* [1965] 2 All ER 72 at 75, [1966] 1 QB 59 at 68 and *R v Lowe* [1973] 1 All ER 805 at 808, [1973] QB 702 at 708, to neither of which was the attention of this House drawn in either *R v Caldwell* or *R v Lawrence*. This was also clearly the view taken by the Court of Appeal, Criminal Division in *R v Pigg* [1982] 2 All ER 591 esp at 597–599, [1982] 1 WLR 762 esp at 770–772 per Lord Lane CJ, with all of whose reasoning I respectfully agree.

In truth, the argument of counsel for the appellant is an attempt to overcome an anomaly resulting from the amendment of the law in 1977, an amendment made not for the purpose of effecting a reform of substantive law but, as my noble and learned friend Lord Diplock pointed out in his speech in *R v Lawrence* [1981] 1 All ER 974 at 980–981, [1982] AC 510 at 524, in connection with the redistribution of criminal business between the Crown Court and magistrates' courts. The very difficulty which counsel for the appellant encountered in trying to distinguish between a defendant who gave no thought to a risk to which he was indifferent and who even if he had thought of that risk would have acted in precisely the same way and a defendant who gave no thought to a risk because it never crossed his mind that the risk existed is eloquent of the need to prescribe a simple and single meaning of the adjective 'reckless' and the adverb 'recklessly' throughout the criminal law unless Parliament has otherwise ordained in a particular case. That simple and single meaning should be the ordinary meaning of those words as stated in this House in *R v Caldwell* and in *R v Lawrence*.

Parliament must however be taken to have intended that 'motor manslaughter' should be a more grave offence than the statutory offence. While the former still carries a maximum penalty of imprisonment for life, Parliament has thought fit to limit the

maximum penalty for the statutory offence to five years' imprisonment, the sentence in
a fact passed by the trial judge on the appellant on his conviction for manslaughter. This difference recognises that there are degrees of turpitude which will vary according to the gravity of the risk created by the manner of a defendant's driving. In these circumstances your Lordships may think that in future it will only be very rarely that it will be appropriate to charge 'motor manslaughter': that is where, as in the instant case, the risk of death from a defendant's driving was very high.

b My noble and learned friend Lord Fraser drew the attention of counsel for the Crown to the decision of the High Court of Justiciary in *Dunn v HM Advocate* 1960 JC 55, a case decided before the change in the law in 1977. It is clear from that decision and from other cases decided in Scotland since 1977 that the practice in Scotland has been to charge both culpable homicide, an offence identical with manslaughter in English law, and the statutory offence and to leave both charges with the jury for their determination
c according to their view of the gravity of the offence proved. I have had the advantage of reading the speech of my noble and learned friend on the practice which has prevailed in Scotland.

My Lords, there was some debate before your Lordships whether in England and Wales it should, since the decision in *Jennings*, be permissible to join in the same indictment one count alleging manslaughter and another alleging the statutory offence,
d it now being clear law that these offences co-existed and their ingredients were identical in point of law.

I know of nothing in the Indictments Act 1915 or the Indictment Rules 1971, SI 1971/1253 to preclude such joinder but in my view there are considerable practical difficulties in permitting it arising from the fact that, as I have just endeavoured to explain, though the legal ingredients of the two offences are the same, the degrees of turpitude may vary
e greatly between one case and another. Under the practice in England and Wales the assessment of differing degrees of turpitude between one case and another is not a matter relevant to the determination by jury of a defendant's guilt or innocence of the particular offence charged. It is a matter relevant to the determination by the judge of the appropriate penalty to be inflicted on a defendant found guilty of the offence with which he has been charged. Yet a jury if required to make a choice between convicting a
f defendant of motor manslaughter at common law and convicting him of the less grave statutory offence would have to be told what criteria they should apply in determining on which side of the boundary line between the two offences the case against the defendant falls. The only criterion that Parliament has laid down is that the statutory offence does not merit a punishment exceeding five years' imprisonment while the common law offence of motor manslaughter may. To tell the jury this, whether they be
g told it in the speech of counsel for the defence or in answer to a question that a justifiably puzzled jury might well put to the judge, would make it difficult to avoid leaving them with the impression that only if they think that what the defendant did deserved to be punished by more than five years' imprisonment should they find him guilty of motor manslaughter. If the judge were then to sentence him to five years (as in the present case) or less, as well he might, the jury would be left with a very poor impression of the trial
h process.

In England and Wales it is for the prosecution and not for the court to decide what charge or charges should be made against a particular defendant. The prosecution is entitled to consider all the circumstances of the case before so deciding. In the instant case the prosecution properly charged manslaughter and manslaughter alone. In doing so the prosecution took the risk that a jury might have refused to convict the appellant
j of that crime though on the evidence it is difficult to see how any reasonable jury could have acquitted him of that offence. But had he been acquitted he would have gone unpunished even though the jury might have convicted him of the statutory offence had that been charged.

In my opinion that consideration cannot justify the joinder of both charges in a single indictment. In future if in any case in England and Wales any such joinder should occur I think it must behove the trial judge to require the prosecution to elect on which of the two counts in the indictment they wish to proceed and not to allow the trial to proceed on both counts. This may result in a different practice prevailing in England and Wales from that which has prevailed in Scotland, a part of the United Kingdom over which no criminal jurisdiction is exercised by this House. But since it is clear that the substantive law is the same in both countries, differences in practice may be thought to be not of great importance.

I would therefore answer the certified question as follows: 'Where manslaughter is charged and the circumstances are that the victim was killed as a result of the reckless driving of the defendant on a public highway, the trial judge should give the jury the direction suggested in *R v Lawrence* but it is appropriate also to point out that in order to constitute the offence of manslaughter the risk of death being caused by the manner of the defendant's driving must be very high.'

I would dismiss this appeal.

LORD BRIDGE OF HARWICH. My Lords, for the reasons given in the speech of my noble and learned friend Lord Roskill, with which I agree, I would dismiss the appeal.

LORD TEMPLEMAN. My Lords, I have had the advantage of reading in draft the speech of my noble and learned friend Lord Roskill. I agree with it, and for the reasons he gives I would dismiss this appeal.

Appeal dismissed.

Solicitors: *Sharpe Pritchard & Co* (for the appellant); *Director of Public Prosecutions.*

Mary Rose Plummer Barrister.

Practice Direction

FAMILY DIVISION

Contempt of court – Release of contemnor – Application for release of contemnor – Contemnor to be present in court – Exception in case of mental health patients.

The President has directed that on applications for the release of a contemnor from prison the contemnor should be present in court to hear the outcome of the application.

The only exception to this practice is in those cases in which the provisions of the Mental Health Act 1959 apply and it is considered by the solicitor conducting the application that in the particular circumstances it would not be desirable for the contemnor to attend.

Issued with the concurrence of the Lord Chancellor.

B P TICKLE
Senior Registrar.

25 July 1983

a Amherst v James Walker Goldsmith & Silversmith Ltd

COURT OF APPEAL, CIVIL DIVISION
LAWTON, ACKNER AND OLIVER LJJ
15, 16, 30 MARCH 1983

b

Landlord and Tenant – Rent – Review – Failure to comply with time limits – Delay in serving assessment notice to initiate rent review – Time not of the essence in serving notice – Whether delay, however unreasonable, precluding landlord from relying on notice.

The tenants were the lessees of business premises under a lease for a term of 28 years
c from 24 June 1961 at a rent of £2,500 a year for the first 14 years of the term and, under a rent review clause in the lease, £2,500 a year or the market rent, whichever was the higher, for the second half of the term. The rent review clause provided that the rent review was to be initiated by the landlord submitting to the tenants on or before 25 December 1974 his assessment of the market rent and that if the tenants failed to agree that rent the assessment was to be made by an independent surveyor, time being of the
d essence in the appointment of the surveyor. The landlord failed to serve his assessment by 25 December 1974 and on 25 January 1975 wrote to the tenants seeking an extension of time and requesting that the rent review be referred to an independent surveyor. The tenants refused his request. After taking legal proceedings to assert his right to serve notice initiating the rent review (in which it was held that time was not of the essence in initiating the rent review) the landlord, on 10 May 1979, served a notice on the tenants
e specifying his assessment of the market rent as £16,000 a year and on 10 October 1980 issued an originating summons claiming a declaration that the tenants were required to pay the market rent as determined by an independent surveyor. The judge granted the declaration. The tenants appealed, contending (i) that the landlord's delay in serving the notice was such that he ought to be deemed to have abandoned his right to serve it, and (ii) that the delay was in any event unreasonable and invalidated the notice.

f

Held – Where time was not of the essence in serving a landlord's notice for a rent review under a lease, mere delay by the landlord in serving notice, however lengthy and even if coupled with hardship to the tenant, did not of itself destroy the contractual right which the landlord had to serve the notice. In order to show that the landlord was precluded from exercising his right to serve the notice despite delay, the tenant had to show that
g the lease or the agreement relating to the review of rent had been abrogated by mutual agreement or that the contract had been repudiated by the landlord or that the landlord's conduct was such that he was estopped from exercising his right to serve notice. Since time was not of the essence of the rent review clause and nothing had occurred between 25 December 1974 when the landlord's notice should have been served and 10 May 1979 when the notice was actually served which disentitled the landlord from relying on the
h notice it followed that the notice was a valid and effective initiation of the rent review process. The appeal would accordingly be dismissed (see p 1074 *d* to p 1075 *g*, p 1076 *a b e* to *j* and p 1077 *c* and *f* to p 1078 *b*, post).

Dictum of Slade LJ in *London and Manchester Assurance Co Ltd v G A Dunn & Co* (1982) 265 EG at 135 applied.

Telegraph Properties (Securities) Ltd v Courtaulds Ltd (1980) 257 EG 1153 overruled.

j Dicta of Lord Salmon in *United Scientific Holdings v Burnley BC* [1977] 2 All ER at 89, 93 not followed.

Notes

For time being of the essence of a rent review clause, see 27 Halsbury's Laws (4th edn) para 216.

Cases referred to in judgments

Accuba Ltd v Allied Shoe Repairs Ltd [1975] 3 All ER 782, [1975] 1 WLR 1559.
Bailey (C H) Ltd v Memorial Enterprises Ltd [1974] 1 All ER 1003, [1974] 1 WLR 728, CA. a
Cornwall v Henson [1900] 2 Ch 298.
Farrant v Olver (1922) 91 LJ Ch 758, [1922] All ER Rep 783.
James v Heim Gallery (London) Ltd (1980) 41 P & CR 269, CA.
Kenilworth v Industrial Sites Ltd v E C Little & Co Ltd [1974] 2 All ER 815, [1974] 1 WLR 1069; *affd* [1975] 1 All ER 53, [1975] 1 WLR 143, CA. b
Kirkland Properties Ltd v GRA Developments Ltd (4 May 1978, unreported), Ch D.
London and Manchester Assurance Co Ltd v G A Dunn & Co (1982) 265 EG 39, 131, CA.
MEPC Ltd v Christian-Edwards [1978] 3 All ER 795, [1978] Ch 281, [1978] 3 WLR 230, CA; *affd* [1979] 3 All ER 752, [1981] AC 205, [1979] 3 WLR 713, HL.
Mills v Haywood (1877) 6 Ch D 196, CA.
Raineri v Miles [1980] 2 All ER 145, [1981] AC 1050, [1980] 2 WLR 847, HL. c
Stickney v Keeble [1915] AC 386, [1914–15] All ER Rep 73, HL.
Telegraph Properties (Securities) Ltd v Courtaulds Ltd (1980) 257 EG 1153.
United Scientific Holdings Ltd v Burnley BC [1977] 2 All ER 62, [1978] AC 904, [1977] 2 WLR 806, HL.
Woods v Mackenzie Hill Ltd [1975] 2 All ER 170, [1975] 1 WLR 613.

d

Cases also cited

Grice v Dudley Corp [1957] 2 All ER 673, [1958] 1 Ch 329.
Lloyd v Collett (1793) 4 Bro CC 469, 29 ER 992.
Lock v Bell [1931] 1 Ch 35.

Appeal

The defendants, James Walker Goldsmith & Silversmith Ltd (the tenants), appealed e against an order made by John Mowbray QC sitting as a deputy judge of the High Court on 12 October 1981 declaring that on the true construction of a lease dated 29 August 1961 made between the plaintiff, William John Amherst (the landlord), and Walton Hassell and Port Ltd, the predecessors in title of the tenants, the landlord was entitled to receive from the tenants as from 24 June 1975 rent at such rate as might be determined f by an independent surveyor appointed by the President of the Royal Institute of Chartered Surveyors notwithstanding the fact that the landlord did not submit to the tenants a written assessment of rent for approval on or before 25 December 1974 in pursuance of the terms of the lease but submitted such assessment on or about 10 May 1979. The facts are set out in the judgment of Oliver LJ.

Michael Rich QC and *Richard Moshi* for the tenants. g
John Hamilton for the landlord.

Cur adv vult

30 March. The following judgments were delivered. h

OLIVER LJ (giving the first judgment at the invitation of Lawton LJ). This is an appeal from an order made by Mr John Mowbray QC, sitting as a deputy judge of the High Court, on 12 October 1981, declaring that on the true construction of the lease referred to below and in the events which have happened the plaintiff landlord is entitled to receive from the defendant tenants as from 24 June 1975 rent at such rate as may be j determined by an independent surveyor nominated in accordance with the lease notwithstanding the failure of the landlord to serve a notice of assessment of rent on the tenants prior to 25 December 1974.

This is yet another rent review clause case, but the history here is an unusual one. The tenants are the lessees by assignment of certain commercial premises, 449 High Road,

Wembley, demised by a lease dated 29 August 1961 and made between the landlord of
a the one part and Walton Hassell and Port Ltd of the other part for a term of 28 years from 24 June 1961. The original rent reserved was a sum of £2,500 for the first 14 years of the term and thereafter a rent of £2,500 or such higher sum as should be ascertained under the subsequent provisions of the lease. The proviso to the reddendum, which is the only part of the lease that matters for present purposes, is (so far as material) in the following terms:

b 'PROVIDED ALWAYS AND IT IS HEREBY AGREED that the yearly rent payable by the Lessee during the second fourteen years of the term hereby granted (hereinafter called "the second period") shall be the yearly sum of Two thousand Five hundred pounds aforesaid or such yearly sum representing the rental value of the demised premises in the open market on a Lease for fourteen years certain on the assumption that the premises are available for letting with vacant possession and without the
c payment of a premium whichever shall be the higher such assessment of the second period rent to be made in the following manner, that is to say: *(a)* Such assessment shall be made in the first instance by the Lessor and submitted to the Lessee for approval in writing on or before the Twenty fifth day of December One thousand nine hundred and seventy four . . .'

d There follow certain provisions about what is to happen if the assessment is not agreed. If they fail to agree the assessment before 25 December 1974 (time being of the essence for this agreement) then the matter is to be referred to an independent surveyor appointed by the parties, but if they fail to agree on his appointment by 25 January 1975 (in respect of which, again, time is of the essence) then the independent surveyor is to be appointed by the President of the Royal Institution of Chartered Surveyors.

e The clause is a slightly unusual one, since it prescribes expressly that time is to be of the essence for the two subsequent stages of the review machinery but does not so prescribe in relation to the initiating assessment under sub-para *(a)*.

In fact the landlord, or, to be more accurate, the solicitors then acting for him, allowed 25 December 1974 to pass without serving the triggering assessment. They woke up to that omission fairly shortly afterwards and on 25 January 1975 they wrote seeking an
f extension of time and asking for the matter to be referred to an independent surveyor. Perhaps not altogether surprisingly, in the light of the law as it then stood, the tenants declined to entertain either of these suggestions. Nothing daunted, the landlord nevertheless, on 10 February 1975, approached the President of the Royal Institution of Chartered Surveyors to make an appointment but, after some correspondence, he, having learned that the appointment was opposed by the tenants' solicitors, declined to act in the
g matter. That was in March 1975 and thereafter nothing further was done and, indeed, nothing further could then have been done unless the landlord was sufficiently handy to start proceedings and litigate the matter to the House of Lords. There the matter rested until 1978. In March 1977 the House of Lords gave their decision in *United Scientific Holdings Ltd v Burnley BC* [1977] 2 All ER 62, [1978] AC 904. The landlord's then solicitors then wrote to the tenants' solicitors on 2 June 1978 calling on them to withdraw their
h objection to the appointment of an independent surveyor. That received the perhaps predictable answer that, whatever may have been the position in the *United Scientific* case, the clause in the instant case was one where time *was* of the essence and that accordingly, there having been no triggering notice within time, the subsequent machinery never came into operation. After some further correspondence up to the end of July 1978, the landlord, on 12 October 1978, issued an originating summons seeking, in effect,
j declarations (a) that time was not of the essence with regard to the initiation of a rent review and (b) that the tenants were not entitled to object to the appointment of an independent surveyor.

Evidence was duly filed on that summons which came on for hearing in May 1979 before his Honour Judge Mervyn Davies. He held that in the light of the *United Scientific* case and on the true construction of the lease, time was not of the essence of the review clause but that the occasion for the appointment of an independent surveyor had not yet arisen since the letter of 25 January 1975 was merely a request for an extension of time a and was not the landlord's assessment of rent required to trigger the operation of the review clause. Thus he granted the landlord the first declaration sought but refused the second. The point that the 25 January letter did not operate as the necessary trigger does not seem to have occurred to the landlord or his advisers until the hearing and on 10 May 1979 a belated attempt was made to rectify the omission by serving a notice which specified a market rent of £16,000 per annum. The judge declined to rule on the validity b of that notice. He expressed a view that there had been unreasonable delay in serving it and that if that had resulted in prejudice to the tenants such prejudice might invalidate it, but since the tenants had not come to court to meet a case of an ex facie valid notice and therefore had not been given the opportunity to adduce any evidence of prejudice, he felt himself unable to deal with the matter. The tenants appealed to the Court of Appeal against the judge's declaration that time was not of the essence and on 18 January c 1980 that appeal was dismissed. Thereafter the President of the Royal Institution of Surveyors was persuaded to make an appointment but the surveyor so appointed was, perhaps not unnaturally, reluctant to enter on a determination while there was still a dispute about whether the notice which triggered the clause was a valid notice.

Accordingly, on 1 October 1980, the landlord issued a further originating summons claiming a declaration that the landlord is entitled to receive from the tenants such rent d as is determined by the surveyor appointed despite the failure to serve a notice of assessment prior to 10 May 1979. That summons came before Mr Mowbray QC in October 1981 and the sole question which fell to be argued before him was whether the delay which had occurred since 25 December 1974 in serving the triggering notice was such as to invalidate the notice of assessment. The tenants did not rely on any point of estoppel nor did they seek to adduce any evidence to show that they had suffered any e prejudice as a result of the delay. The sole questions before the deputy judge were (a) whether the delay amounted to an abandonment of the landlord's right to serve a notice and (b), assuming no abandonment, whether the delay (i) was unreasonable and (ii) of itself invalidated the notice.

The deputy judge found that the delay which had occured was unreasonable. He gave no independent reasons for this finding but adopted the reasoning of Judge Mervyn f Davies on the previous summons which was, in effect, that the landlord ought to have served his assessment notice before the issue of the first originating summons (on 12 October 1978) and that failure to serve between then and 10 May 1979 constituted unreasonable delay. He held, however, that such delay, although unreasonable, did not invalidate the assessment notice as a matter of law because *mere* delay, without proof of prejudice to the tenant, does not prevent a landlord from relying out of time on a rent g review clause where time is not of the essence. He went on to hold, on the facts, that the delay which had occurred was not evidence of abandonment. He accordingly granted the landlord the declaration sought.

It is against that declaration that the tenants now appeal and in this court counsel for the tenants has not sought to found any argument on abandonment, but has been content to confine himself to two propositions: (a) that the delay which took place was h unreasonable and (b) that unreasonable delay, without more, and, in particular, without any evidence of prejudice or hardship to the tenant, is fatal to the landlord. Thus this case raises directly for decision a question which has been touched on in a number of previous cases but answered, or ar least arguably answered, in only one of them, that being the decision of Foster J in *Telegraph Properties (Securities) Ltd v Courtaulds Ltd* (1981) 257 EG 1153, a case explained by the deputy judge on the ground that the delay there under j consideration was so extensive as to constitute an abandonment of the landlord's rights.

In approaching the problem the convenient course will, I think, be first to consider some of the previous authorities in which there has fallen to be considered the question of the effect of delay where time is not of the essence of the contract. The question was touched on briefly by Lord Denning MR in *C H Bailey Ltd v Memorial Enterprises Ltd*

[1974] 1 All ER 1003 at 1007, [1974] 1 WLR 728 at 732 and it seems to have been his
a view that mere delay would not affect the landlord's right unless it had, in some way, induced the tenant to act to his detriment so as to amount to an equitable estoppel. He observed:

> 'It was said: suppose the landlord did not apply for the rent revision for months or years after the date when he became entitled to it. Would not this operate unfairly on the tenant? In most cases it would not do so . . . But, if there was a case where the
> b delay of the landlord did prejudice the tenant, then I should think the tenant might well pray in aid the principle of equitable estoppel to hold up the increase. It is to be remembered, too, that it is always open to the tenant himself to take steps to ascertain the increased rent.'

On the other hand, Megarry J in *Kenilworth Industrial Sites Ltd v E C Little & Co Ltd*
c [1974] 2 All ER 815 at 818, [1974] 1 WLR 1069 at 1072 seems to have entertained the view that mere delay might be fatal. He said:

> 'No doubt, as counsel for the landlord accepted, the landlord could not wait for several years after the first five years had run, and then demand what in effect would be a retrospective increase for the whole of the second five years . . .'

d However, in a subsequent passage in the judgment, he expressly disclaimed any decision as to the effect of a notice not served within a reasonable time.

Both these cases were cited by Goff J in his judgment in *Accuba Ltd v Allied Shoe Repairs Ltd* [1975] 3 All ER 782, [1975] 1 WLR 1559 where he had to deal directly with the question of unreasonable delay simpliciter. What he said was, I think, strictly obiter, because he decided on the facts that the delay in the case before him was not unreasonable.
e Nevertheless, it seems clear that he was accepting in principle that the landlord's right to operate a clause of this sort in a case where time is not of the essence can be defeated simply by unreasonable delay. He said ([1975] 3 All ER 782 at 787, [1975] 1 WLR 1559 at 1564):

> 'The submission for the tenants is that the landlord has a reasonable time and no more and that was exceeded. Counsel for the landlords contends that notice could
> f be given at any time before the tenants gave notice making time of the essence which they never did. I think the latter contention is too narrow: see *Farrant v Olver* (1922) 91 LJ Ch 758 at 759, [1922] All ER Rep 783 at 784 where Sargant J said: "It is not necessary that time should be made of the essence of the contract when the defendant had so persistently and for so long refused to perform the contract". Sargant J there referred to refusal, but it was not a case of positive refusal, rather of
> g failure to perform.'

The *Accuba* case was referred to by their Lordships in the *United Scientific* case but this particular point was not commented on and, indeed, Lord Salmon appears to have been of the view that mere delay, however prolonged, was not of itself fatal unless accompanied by prejudice to the tenant. He observed ([1977] 2 All ER 62 at 89, [1978] AC 904 at 951)
h that the provisions for rent review, in general, were directory only, adding: 'Nevertheless any unreasonable delay caused by the landlords and which is to the tenants' prejudice would prevent the rent being revised after the review date'. That is reflected in a further passage in his speech (see [1977] 2 All ER 62 at 93, [1978] AC 904 at 956).

This passage from the speech of Lord Salmon was adopted by Slade J in *Kirkland Properties Ltd v GRA Developments Ltd* (4 May 1978, unreported). He expressed the view
j that delay would defeat the exercise of the right of review only if it caused hardship to the tenant or if it amounted to abandonment by the landlord of his right. This, again, however, was obiter, since in the case before him he held that time was of the essence.

In *James v Heim Gallery (London) Ltd* (1980) 41 P & CR 269 the matter of abandonment was very briefly touched on by Buckley LJ in his judgment but without expressing any view about whether, in fact, a right could be defeated in this way and the only reported

direct decision on the effect of delay is that of Foster J in *Telegraph Properties (Securities)*
Ltd v Courtaulds Ltd (1981) 257 EG 1153. There something over six years had elapsed a
between the date fixed by the lease for giving notice and the date on which notice was
actually given. Foster J rejected any suggestion that the defeasance of the right in the case
before him was attributable to a promissory estoppel. He said (at 1154):

> 'In my judgment the plaintiff has been guilty of such a delay as to make it
> unreasonable for it to call on the defendant for a rent review and to do so would be
> of necessity unfair to the defendant ... I therefore need not go into the facts in b
> regard to the matters which have been put in evidence as to the effect both on the
> plaintiff and the defendant if the notice is not held to be good.'

Thus the judge clearly there was adopting what seems to have been the view of Goff J in
the *Accuba* case and rejecting the suggestion implicit in the speech of Lord Salmon in the
United Scientific case that prejudice or hardship to the tenant is essential before delay can c
operate to defeat the landlord's right. Counsel for the tenants naturally prays this decision
in aid in the instant case and it is certainly consistent with the argument which he has
advanced before this court. The deputy judge took the contrary view, because he
regarded Foster J's decision as being consistent only with his having formed the view that
the landlords in that case had abandoned their rights. I do not, for my part, find the
decision explicable on that ground and, as appears hereafter, I have the gravest reservation, d
despite dicta to the contrary, whether any such concept as unilateral abandonment can
exist. In my judgment Foster J's decision was a direct decision of the point in favour of
counsel for the tenants and the question which has to be squarely grasped in this court is
whether it was correct.

Counsel for the tenants, in a most skilful and persuasive argument, has submitted that
it was and his reasoning may be summarised as follows: (1) A stipulation as to time in a e
contract is a term of the contract just like any other term and it means exactly what it
says. (2) If, therefore, the party who is obliged under the contract to perform by a certain
time, fails to do so, he is in breach of contract and the other party is prima facie entitled
to treat himself as discharged from the performance of *his* obligation. (3) Prior to the
Supreme Court of Judicature Act 1873, however, a court of equity would nevertheless
still decree specific performance at the instance of the party in default, and indeed would f
restrain an action at law based on the failure to perform, if, in all the circumstances, it
was equitable to do so. Instances of it being inequitable to do so would be, for instance,
cases where the parties themselves had in terms agreed that the time stipulation was to
be essential or cases where the nature of the property was such as to indicate that time
was of critical significance. (4) The effect of s 41 of the Law of Property Act 1925 is
merely that in all contracts stipulations as to time are to be treated as governed by the g
equitable rule, that is to say, it has to be asked in each case whether it would be equitable
for the contract to be specifically enforced notwithstanding that the stipulated timetable
has not been adhered to. (5) In answering that question the court has simply to apply the
ordinary rules of equity and if, therefore, the other party shows that there is some ground
on which specific performance should be refused, the party in default will not be entitled
to enforce the contract. (6) Delay in applying for the remedy of specific performance is h
one ground on which the remedy may be refused. Accordingly, in a case where a rent
review date has been allowed to pass and where unreasonable delay has taken place in
seeking to invoke the clause, the court should, by analogy, hold that the right to rely on
it has been lost.

It is, counsel for the tenants submits, only by an analysis along these lines that it is
possible to explain the references by Lord Salmon in the *United Scientific* case and by Slade j
J in the *Kirkland Properties* case to hardship to the tenant, for if, as a matter of construction
of the contract, the stipulation as to time is effectively deleted, save as fixing the earliest
date at which the given event may occur and the date after which the other party may
call for performance if he requires it, then hardship cannot come into the matter. These
references show, therefore, he submits, that after the contractual date has passed there is

an alteration of the contractual right. It becomes a right which can only be exercised
a under the control of the court and in exercising its control the court will have regard to the ordinary principles applicable to specific performance actions, one of which is that prolonged delay, of itself and by itself, may operate as a bar to specific performance, without regard to any consideration of whether it causes unfairness or hardship to the other party. In support of this proposition counsel for the tenants relies on Cotton LJ's statement in *Mills v Haywood* (1877) 6 Ch D 196 at 202 that 'a party cannot call upon a
b Court of Equity for a specific performance unless he has shewn himself ready, desirous, prompt, and eager' and on the decision of Sargant J in *Farrant v Olver* (1922) 91 LJ Ch 758 at 759, [1922] All ER Rep 783 at 784 where he is reported as having held that 'It is not necessary that time should be made of the essence of the contract when the defendant has so persistently and for so long refused to perform the contract'.

While not doubting the proposition that prolonged and unexplained delay in seeking
c specific performance may, in a proper case, be a ground for refusing that relief, I doubt in fact whether it emerges from that particular decision, where in fact a notice to complete had been given and the only question was whether the plaintiff, having elected to sue for specific performance with an alternative claim for rescission, could, in default of defence, opt for the alternative relief at the hearing.

In my judgment, however, the analogy which counsel for the tenants so persuasively
d urges on us is itself fallacious, and for several reasons. First and foremost, although no doubt the practice of courts of equity to grant specific performance forms the historical basis for the rule that time is not of the essence of the contract, it is, in my judgment, a fallacy to test the rights arising under a contract as a matter of construction by reference to what the consequences would be in a hypothetical action for specific performance if such an action were appropriate. Second, even if that were the proper approach, I am not
e sure that I see any logical reason why the equitable principles governing the circumstances in which the court may withhold the remedy of specific performance where it is needed to enforce the mutual rights and obligations arising out of a contract should necessarily be applied to the rather different question of whether a unilateral privilege reserved by one party to a contract has been extinguished. Third, the argument, in my judgment, involves a confusion between the initial construction of the contract and the remedies
f which may be available for its breach. It assumes that the moment that the date specified in the contract is past the party who has allowed it to pass is seeking an indulgence which he can only get through the intervention, notional or actual, of the court. That may have been true in 1872 but it does not, in my judgment, accurately reflect the position today.

It seems to me that the argument of counsel for the tenants seeks to revive and to perpetuate the very error which Lord Diplock, in the *United Scientific* case, was seeking to
g lay to rest. In his speech in that case ([1977] 2 All ER 62 at 67, [1978] AC 904 at 924) he points out that when one speaks of time being 'of the essence' of a contract, one is speaking of a stipulation compliance with which is to be treated as a condition precedent to performance of the contract by the other party, so that default may itself be treated as a repudiation by the party in default of his obligations: and he rejects specifically the contention (based on a passage from the speech of Lord Parker in *Stickney v Keeble* [1915]
h AC 386 at 417, [1914–15] All ER Rep 73 at 82) that in each case one has to inquire whether prior to the Judicature Act a court of equity would have granted relief (see [1977] 2 All ER 62 at 69, [1978] AC 904 at 926–927). In his speech he draws attention to the danger involved in treating the expression 'the rules of equity' as anything more than a description of the source from which the current rules of substantive or adjectival law are derived (see [1977] 2 All ER 62 at 69–70, [1978] AC 904 at 927). Section 41 of the
j Law of Property Act 1925 provides in terms:

> 'Stipulations ... as to time ... which according to the rules of equity are not deemed to be or to have become of the essence of the contract, are also construed and have effect at law in accordance with the same rules.'

Essentially, as it seems to me, the question is one of construction, not of remedies, and

what one has to ask is whether, as a matter of construction of the contract, compliance
with the time stipulation is so essential to the contract that any failure to comply with it a
entitles the other party, without more, to treat the contract as repudiated. Of course, that
does not mean either that the contract is to be treated for all purposes as if the time had
never been mentioned or that, when it comes to exerting any remedies for breach of
contract, the ordinary rules of specific performance are suspended or abrogated. Thus,
albeit the contract is not to be construed as if time were essential, damages may still be
obtained for failure to comply with the fixed date for completion if damage can be b
shown (see *Raineri v Miles* [1980] 2 All ER 145, [1981] AC 1050).

Equally where, as a matter of construction, time is not of the essence, it does not follow
that the party in default may not, by extensive delay or other conduct, disentitle himself
from having it specifically performed (see, eg *Cornwall v Henson* [1900] 2 Ch 298; *MEPC
Ltd v Christian-Edwards* [1978] 3 All ER 795, [1978] Ch 281).

But the question of how the contract should be construed and the question of whether c
a party in default may have deprived himself of a right to rely on the contract must now,
in my judgment, be treated as logically distinct and separate questions, whatever may be
the historical origin of the rule of construction.

The submission of counsel for the tenants treats the service of a renewal notice after
the time stipulated as a submission to the court of the issue whether or not the contract
should be performed. But the landlord, in serving notice, is not invoking the aid of the d
court to perform the contract. He is exercising the right which the contract, as properly
construed, confers on him. If it is to be construed in the sense that time is of the essence,
he has no right to serve the notice. If it is not, then the right subsists, unless the tenant
can show either that the contract, or that part of the contract, has been abrogated or that
the landlord has precluded himself from exercising it. He may do that by showing that
the contract has been repudiated, for instance where he has served a notice calling on the e
landlord to exercise his right within a reasonable time or not at all and such notice is
ignored, or that some event has happened which estops the landlord from relying on his
right. But I know of no ground for saying that mere delay, however lengthy, destroys
the contractual right. It may put the other party in a position where, by taking the
proper steps, he may become entitled to treat himself as discharged from his obligation;
but that does not occur automatically and from the mere passage of time. I know of no f
authority for the proposition that the effect of construing a time stipulation as not being
of the essence is to substitute a fresh implied term that the contract shall be performed
within a reasonable time and even if such a term is to be substituted the passage of a
reasonable time would not automatically abrogate the contract. It is, I think, important
to distinguish between that which entitles a party to treat the contract as at an end and
that which entitles the party not in default to enforce it. No one contests that, once the g
stipulated date is passed, proceedings may be instituted to enforce the agreement (see, eg
Woods v Mackenzie Hill Ltd [1975] 2 All ER 170, [1975] 1 WLR 613), but that is quite a
different question.

Counsel for the tenants warns us against the dangers which, he suggests, lie in the
notion that the effect of construing a time clause as not being of the essence is, in effect,
to write the clause out of the contract altogether. I see no such danger. As has been h
pointed out on more than one occasion the remedy of the party who feels he may be
prejudiced by delay lies in his own hands.

In my judgment, therefore, the deputy judge was right in the conclusion at which he
arrived, although I would in fact go further and suggest that, despite what Lord Salmon
said in the *United Scientific* case, even delay plus hardship to the tenant would not disentitle
the landlord to exercise the right which he has, on the true construction of the contract, j
unless the combination amounted to an estoppel. In my judgment, the contractual right
continues to exist unless and until it is abrogated by mutual agreement or the contract is
discharged by breach or, to adopt the example of Lord Diplock in the *United Scientific*
case, by the obligor being substantially deprived of the whole benefit that it was intended
that he should have (which I take to be a reference, in effect, to frustration or failure of

consideration and which I cannot envisage as arising in this sort of case). Apart from these circumstances, the only way in which I can envisage the landlord as being precluded from relying on the clause is by an estoppel and I think that that must have been what Lord Salmon had in mind in the passages to which I have referred.

In particular, I cannot, speaking for myself, see how the right can be lost by 'abandonment'. So far as I am aware, this is not a term of art but I take it to mean the unilateral signification of an intention not to exercise the contractual right in question. If that is right, then I cannot see how it could bind the landlord save as a promise (promissory estoppel) or as a representation followed by reliance (equitable estoppel) or as a consensual variation of the agreement or as a repudiation accepted by the other party. I know of no ground for importing into the law of contract the notion that mere non-exercise of a contractual right is to be treated as analogous to an abandonment of chattels or of an appurtenant right such as an easement. It follows that, in my judgment, the *Telegraph Properties* case, in so far as it rests (as I believe that it does) on simple delay or, alternatively, on abandonment, was wrongly decided.

Finally, I should add that I am not, for my part, persuaded that in fact the instant case is one where 'unreasonable' delay has occurred. The expression 'unreasonable delay' does, I think, require some definition. It must, I think, mean something more than 'prolonged delay' and it may, I suppose, be used to express the notion either of delay for which no acceptable reason can be advanced or delay which no reasonable man would incur acting in his own interest. But if this is its meaning then the absence of reason has no necessary relation to duration. If on the other hand, as I suspect, the phrase is used to describe such delay as it would not in the circumstances be reasonable to expect the other party to put up with, then it seems to me that it contains within it, by necessary implication, the notion of hardship or prejudice, for how otherwise is the other party harmed by it?

In the instant case certainly no prejudice is shown nor does it seem to me that there has been any substantial delay which is not perfectly rationally accounted for. The landlord's solicitors tried to rectify their omission within a month of the contract date and they can hardly be blamed, in the state of the law as it then stood, for not pursuing the matter further prior to 1978. If, thereafter, they had appreciated that their original letter did not, in fact, comply with the lease not only as to date but in point of form also, they could, no doubt, have issued a fresh notice before issuing the first originating summons, so that all matters could be dealt with in one set of proceedings. That they did not do so may be unfortunate, but it has been extremely beneficial to the tenants who got a further uncovenanted reprieve; but I cannot, speaking for myself, regard their failure to do so as 'unreasonable'.

Finally, I am encouraged to find that the view that I have formed as to the way in which this type of problem should be approached coincides (save in the one respect of the possibility of abandonment as a separate legal concept) with the views expressed by Slade LJ in the recent decision of this court in *London and Manchester Assurance Co Ltd v G A Dunn & Co* (1982) 265 EG 39 at 135 where he said:

> 'In the absence of binding authority compelling a different conclusion, I am satisfied that delay on its own, even if unreasonable, will not in general disentitle a landlord from invoking a rent review clause in a case where time has not been made of the essence of the contract. There is, I think, no general principle of the law of contract that *mere* delay in the enforcement of a contractual right, or in the performance of a contractual duty, by one party to a contract ("A") will entitle the other part ("B") to regard himself as discharged from the obligation to recognise such right or from the contract as a whole (as the case may be). If in such circumstances A has been guilty of unreasonable delay, then, ordinarily, the prudent and proper course for B to adopt, if he wishes to bring matters to a head, will be to serve a notice on A fixing a reasonable period within which A must exercise his right (if at all) or must perform his part of the contract (as the case may be). In some circumstances, of course, the delay on the part of A may be so gross and inexplicable

> as to make it so clear that he does not intend to exercise his right or to perform his part of the contract that any such notice is unnecessary. But, ordinarily, it will be necessary for B to serve a notice on A or at least to have some communication with him before he can properly and safely regard himself as being absolved.'

It is true that in the circumstances of that case what Slade LJ said was obiter, but it forms part of a carefully reasoned analysis which I gratefully adopt.

In my judgment, the appeal fails and should be dismissed.

ACKNER LJ. The rent review clause in this lease, which was for a term of 28 years, enabled the landlord to ensure that for the second half of the term, viz 14 years, he received the rent reserved in the lease, £2,500, or the market rent for the premises, whichever was the higher. Since the clause could only enure for his benefit, understandably the trigger mechanism, as it is conveniently called, could only be operated by him. The lease provided that the rent review for the second period was to be initiated by an assessment made by the landlord of the market rent, such assessment to be submitted in writing on or before 25 December 1974 to the tenants for their approval. It made further provision should the tenants not approve the landlord's assessment.

Once it was established, by an appeal heard in this court in January 1980, that, following the decision in *United Scientific Holdings Ltd v Burnley BC* [1977] 2 All ER 62, [1978] AC 904, time was not of the essence in relation to operating the trigger mechanism, the resolution of this dispute seems relatively simple. The landlord having not lost his opportunity to implement the rent review clause by not serving a written notice of his assessment of the rent on or before 25 December 1974, the question is, has anything occurred thereafter to disentitle him from invoking the clause? Counsel for the tenants contended that the landlord was obliged to give the notice of the assessment within a reasonable time after 25 December 1974, and having failed so to do, he has thereby lost the right given to him under the lease. But what is a reasonable time is a question of fact to be determined in the light of all the circumstances, and the circumstances of this case are most unusual. If a reasonable time had elapsed the tenants could have given a notice fixing a time for performance. This must itself be reasonable, notwithstanding that, ex hypothesi, a reasonable time for performance had, in the view of the tenants, already elapsed. Such a notice would operate as evidence that the tenants considered that a reasonable time for performance had elapsed by the date of the notice and as evidence of the date by which they considered it reasonable for the notice to be given. In such a situation the tenants would have been saying: 'Unless you give your notice of assessment by such and such a date we shall treat your failure as a refusal to invoke the clause' (see the observations of Lord Simon in the *United Scientific* case [1977] 2 All ER 62 at 85, [1978] AC 904 at 946). However, the tenants never gave such or any notice. They were content to let matters be until the landlord took the initiative. In such circumstances it cannot lie in the tenants' mouth to contend that the landlord has refused to exercise his rights.

In this appeal the tenants have not sought to suggest that the landlord waived or abandoned his entitlement to invoke the clause. Moreover, they have not sought to contend either that the landlord's delay in ultimately giving the notice of assessment amounted to an express or implied representation that the landlord accepted that the rent for the second period should remain at £2,500. Nor have the tenants sought to argue that they have in any way been prejudiced by the delay described by Oliver LJ. On the contrary, it has to be accepted that they have gained by such delay, because their obligation to pay the market rent, which one may assume to be higher than the rent reserved in the lease, has been delayed several years and they have had the use of that money in the meantime. Thus no possible question of an estoppel can arise.

In such circumstances, there seems to me to be no basis on which the tenants could effectively claim that the landlord has lost his right to invoke the rent review clause.

I too would accordingly dismiss this appeal.

LAWTON LJ. During the hearing of this appeal there were many references to 'the rules of equity' and to 'equitable relief'. The use of these phrases obscured the issue. In *United Scientific Holdings Ltd v Burnley BC* [1977] 2 All ER 62 at 67–79, [1978] AC 904 at 924–927 Lord Diplock pointed out that nowadays perpetuating a dichotomy between rules of equity and rules of common law is conducive to erroneous conclusions as to the ways in which the law of England has developed in the last hundred years. I do not intend in this judgment to use either of these phrases.

The question whether the plaintiff landlord's rent assessment notice given on 10 May 1979 operated to start the rent review procedure provided for in the lease made on 29 August 1961 can only be answered by construing it. Neither the landlord nor the tenants had any rights or obligations towards one another save those which were given or imposed by the lease itself. What these rights and obligations were depended on the terms of the lease when construed in accordance with the ordinary canons of construction and the provisions of s 41 of the Law of Property Act 1925. In my judgment there is no justification for reading into the lease an implied term that if the landlord did not serve a rent assessment notice on or before 25 December 1974 he had to do so within a reasonable time thereafter. Such an implied term would not have been necessary to give business efficacy to the lease. The landlord would not have wanted it and the tenants benefited by not having it. Any delay on the landlord's part would mean that the tenants went on paying the original rent until such time as the landlord did serve a notice. If for any reasons of their own, such as a general fall in rental values, they had wanted the landlord to come to a decision about the service of a rent assessment notice they themselves could have served what has come to be known, inaccurately, as a notice 'making time of the essence of the contract': see *Stickney v Keeble* [1915] AC 386, [1914–15] All ER Rep 73 and the *United Scientific* case.

By the judgment given on 18 January 1980 this court adjudged that on its true construction time was not of the essence of the rent review provisions in this lease. It followed that the landlord's failure to deliver a rent assessment notice on or before the stipulated date did not bring the lease to an end. The tenants continued to be bound by it. They had taken benefits under it and had agreed to pay an increased rent if the landlord did serve a rent assessment notice, even though it was not served on or before the fixed date. On 10 May 1979 the landlord did serve a rent assessment notice. As the tenants were still bound by the lease, they continued to be subject to the obligations contained in it, one of which was to pay a higher rent in the specified circumstances. They could only be relieved of this obligation in a way known to the law. One way was by agreement with the landlord. There was no such agreement in this case. Another way of their getting relieved of their liability to pay a higher rent would have arisen if they could have shown that the landlord's conduct had been such that he was estopped from relying on the rent assessment notice which he did serve. He would only have been estopped if the tenants could have proved that by his words or conduct he had represented that he did not intend to ask for the payment of a higher rent and in reliance on that representation they had altered their position to their prejudice. In my judgment nothing short of estoppel would have relieved the tenants from their liability to pay a higher rent. The concept of abandonment has been referred to in some of the rent review cases. I do not regard it as a term of art apt to describe a defence to a landlord's claim for a higher rent. If a landlord by his words or conduct leads his tenant reasonably to infer that he did not intend to claim a higher rent he makes a representation to that effect so that the foundation of an estoppel is laid; but the landlord will not be estopped unless the tenant has acted on the representation to his prejudice. A landlord who over a long period makes no attempt to set a rent review procedure in motion may be adjudged to have represented that he did not intend to exercise his rights; but whether he did would be a matter of inference from the circumstances in which the delay had occurred, not from the mere fact of the delay. I can see no reason why mere delay, not amounting to a representation, can be a bar to a landlord in this kind of case claiming a higher rent. He has his contractual rights to a higher rent and the tenant has an obligation to pay it unless

he can prove that there is some good reason why he should not. Mere delay would not
be a good reason. On the facts of this case, as counsel for the tenants admitted when a
opening the appeal, there was no evidence which would have founded an estoppel.

In this judgment I have tried to deal with the issue from principle as enunciated in the
United Scientific case. I had the advantage of reading in draft the judgment which Oliver
LJ has delivered. He has examined and commented on all the relevant cases. I agree with
what he has said. I too would dismiss the appeal.

Appeal dismissed. Leave to appeal to the House of Lords refused. b

Solicitors: *Bulcraig & Davis* (for the tenants); *Macdonald Stacey*, agents for *Thorne &
Thorne*, Minehead (for the landlord).

Mary Rose Plummer Barrister. c

d

Mason and others v Farbrother and others

CHANCERY DIVISION AT MANCHESTER
HIS HONOUR JUDGE BLACKETT-ORD V-C SITTING AS A JUDGE OF THE HIGH COURT
1, 2 MARCH 1983

e

*Variation of trusts – Variation by the court – Investment clause – Extension of powers of
investment – Pension fund – Enlargement of fund due to inflation – Co-operative Society's
employees' pension fund – Different views existing as to proper construction of investment clause
but parties not in dispute – Whether court having power under inherent jurisdiction to confer on
trustees wide modern power of investment – Whether court having statutory jurisdiction to vary
trust and give trustees wider investment powers – Whether range of investments sanctioned must* f
be limited to those permitted under Trustee Investments Act 1961 – Trustee Act 1925, s 57(1).

By a trust deed executed in 1929 the Co-operative Society established a pension and death
benefit scheme for members of the society and set up a fund to finance the scheme. The
trust deed contained an investment clause giving the trustees of the scheme only a
limited power of investment of the fund, namely power to invest principally in the g
society itself and subject thereto in authorised trustee securities. In 1929 that was an
adequate power of investment in relation to the size of the fund and was in accord with
the principles of the Co-operative movement. By 1982, however, because of inflation,
the size of the fund had increased to some £127m, of which £6m was invested in the
society and the balance in securities permitted under the Trustee Investments Act 1961.
The trustees were uncertain whether on the true construction of the investment clause h
they were required to invest the whole of the fund either with the society or in securities
authorised by the 1961 Act. Furthermore the trustees considered that the permitted
range of investments under the 1961 Act was inadequate for so large a fund and wished
to have the wide power of investment considered appropriate for modern pension funds.
Accordingly, the trustees applied to the court seeking its sanction to a variation of the
trust deed by the insertion, in substitution for the existing investment clause, of a j
modern type of investment clause giving the trustees wide powers of investment. The
trustees submitted that the court had power to sanction such a variation of the trust deed,
because (i) disputed questions existed regarding the proper construction of the existing
investment clause which were required to be resolved by compromise and under its
inherent jurisdiction to approve a compromise of the disputed questions the court could

sanction the variation of the deed by the insertion of a wider investment clause, and (ii)
a alternatively, the court had jurisdiction to vary the trust deed by extending the trustees' investment powers under s 57(1)[a] of the Trustee Act 1925. The trustees adduced evidence that the insertion in the trust deed of such a wide power of investment would be for the benefit of present and future members of the society, and the defendants, who represented those members, supported that view. The society was also made a defendant to the application.

b

Held – (1) The court had inherent jurisdiction to vary the terms of a trust by approving the compromise of disputed rights even though there was not a contested dispute between the parties, since the existence of genuine points of difference which were required to be settled by compromise was sufficient to give the court jurisdiction. The questions regarding the construction of the existing investment clause in the society's
c scheme, arising from the relationship between the express power of investment in the clause and the statutory power of investment under the 1961 Act imported into the clause, gave rise to genuine points of difference which were required to be settled by compromise, and therefore the court could vary the trust deed under its inherent jurisdiction. However, even though in exercising that jurisdiction the court did not always have to produce a compromise which lay somewhere between the opposing
d views, namely in the instant case between the view that under the existing clause the whole of the fund had to be invested with the society or alternatively had to be invested in securities authorised by the 1961 Act, it was doubtful whether the court could under its inherent jurisdiction substitute an entirely new investment clause for the existing investment clause in the trust deed. For that reason the court would not under its inherent jurisdiction sanction the variation of the trust deed (see p 1085 *c* to p 1086 *c*,
e post); *Chapman v Chapman* [1954] 1 All ER 798, *Re Rider's Will Trusts, Nelson v Rider* [1958] 3 All ER 135 and *Re Burke, Burke v Burke* [1908] 2 Ch 248 applied; *Re Powell-Cotton's Re-settlement, Henniker-Major v Powell-Cotton* [1956] 1 All ER 60 distinguished; dictum of Evershed MR in *Re Powell-Cotton's Re-settlement, Henniker-Major v Powell-Cotton* [1956] 1 All ER at 62 considered.

(2) However, where the court considered that it was expedient for the management
f or administration of trust property that the trustees should have wider powers of investment than existed under the trust, the court had jurisdiction under s 57(1) of the 1925 Act to substitute a wider investment clause for the existing clause. Furthermore, where there were special circumstances the wider investment clause did not have to be restricted to the range of investments permitted under the 1961 Act. The effect of inflation and the fact that the pension fund was in the nature of a public fund rather than
g a private trust were special circumstances which entitled the court, in exercising its jurisdiction under s 57(1) of the 1925 Act, to sanction the insertion in the deed of the wide modern investment clause sought by the trustees, even though the power of investment thereunder would be wider than that permitted under the 1961 Act. The application would accordingly be granted (see p 1086 *g* to p 1087 *b*, post); *Re Shipwrecked Fishermen and Mariners' Royal Benevolent Society Charity* [1958] 3 All ER 465 applied; *Re*
h *Cooper's Settlement, Cooper v Cooper* [1961] 3 All ER 636 and *Re Kolb's Will Trusts, Lloyd's Bank Ltd v Ullmann* [1961] 3 All ER 811 considered.

Notes

For trustees' power to invest, see 38 Halsbury's Laws (3rd edn) 987–1001, paras 1710–1725.

j For variation of trusts under the Trustee Act 1925, see ibid 1027–1029, para 1771, and for cases on the subject, see 47 Digest (Repl) 328–332, 2970–2992.

For the Trustee Act 1925, s 57, see 38 Halsbury's Statutes (3rd edn) 180.

For the Trustee Investments Act 1961, s 1, see ibid 228.

---

a Section 57, so far as material, is set out at p 1086 *d e*, post

Cases referred to in judgment

Burke, Re, Burke v Burke [1908] 2 Ch 248.

Chapman v Chapman [1954] 1 All ER 798, [1954] AC 429, [1954] 2 WLR 723, HL. a

Coates' Will Trusts, Re [1959] 2 All ER 51, [1959] 1 WLR 375.

Cooper's Settlement, Re, Cooper v Cooper [1961] 3 All ER 636, [1962] Ch 826, [1961] 3 WLR 1029.

Kolb's Will Trusts, Re, Lloyd's Bank Ltd v Ullmann [1961] 3 All ER 811, [1962] Ch 531, [1961] 3 WLR 1034. b

Powell-Cotton's Re-settlement, Re, Henniker-Major v Powell-Cotton [1956] 1 All ER 60, [1956] 1 WLR 23, CA.

Rider's Will Trusts, Re, Nelson v Rider [1958] 3 All ER 135, [1958] 1 WLR 974.

Shipwrecked Fishermen and Mariners' Royal Benevolent Society Charity, Re [1958] 3 All ER 465, [1959] Ch 220, [1958] 3 WLR 701.

c

Originating summons

By an originating summons dated 26 January 1983 the plaintiffs, James Mason, Robert Chillcott, Robert Michael Grindrod, Douglas William Heydon, Graham John Melmoth, Joseph William Parker, Frank Peel, William Quentin Russell, Frederick Douglas Galbraith, Joseph Howard Perrow and Alan Henry Billinge, the trustees of the Co-operative Wholesale Society's Employees' Pension and Death Benefit Scheme, constituted d by a trust deed dated 19 April 1929, sought the following relief: (1) Determination of the question whether on the true construction of the trust deed and in the events which had happened the plaintiffs (a) were bound to deposit with the fourth defendant to the application, the Co-operative Wholesale Society Ltd, the whole of the moneys comprised in the fund constituted by the scheme requiring to be invested or (b) were required merely to invest such moneys in accordance with the provisions of the Trusteee e Investments Act 1961 or (c) were required to invest such moneys otherwise. (2) In the alternative, the approval of the court of a compromise of the above-mentioned question whereby the trust deed thenceforth should be read and construed and take effect as if it had contained a power of investment in the terms set out in the schedule to the plaintiffs' application, in lieu of the powers of investment contained in cll 5 and 6 of the deed. (3) In the further alternative, an order under s 57 of the Trustee Act 1925, or alternatively f under s 1 of the Variation of Trusts Act 1958, approving on behalf of all persons (other than the parties to the application) who were or might hereafter become entitled to any beneficial interest under the trusts of the scheme, an arrangement whereby the trust deed should be varied so as to substitute the power of investment set out in the schedule for the existing powers contained in cll 5 and 6 of the deed. (4) That the following representation orders be made, namely (a) the first defendant, Roger Gordon Farbrother, g to represent all contributing members of the scheme; (b) the second defendant, Richard Foster, to represent all persons entitled to a pension or other benefits under the scheme and (c) the third defendant, Albert Gordon Dalgleish, to represent all persons who might in future become members of the scheme or otherwise become entitled to benefits under the scheme.

The power of investment set out in the schedule was as follows: h

'(1) The Trustees may invest any moneys comprised in the Fund and available for investment in the purchase of any investments or property of any sort either real or personal and whether or not being investments or property authorised by the general law for the investment of trust funds or upon loan upon the security of any property of any description or without security and may also from time to time j vary such investments. (2) Moneys comprised in the Fund which the Trustees do not think fit immediately to invest may be deposited at any bank. (3) In relation to land whether freehold or leasehold the Trustees may exercise all the powers of management or improvement which could be exercised by an absolute owner holding the land beneficially. (4) Without prejudice to the generality of the

foregoing the Trustees may deposit any moneys comprised in the Fund with the
a Society at such rate of interest thereon as shall be agreed with the Society from time to time.'

The facts are set out in the judgment.

Charles Sparrow QC and *D B Mallard* for the plaintiffs.
P W Watkins for the first defendant.
b *Peter B Keenan* for the second defendant.
Adrian Kirsten for the third defendant.
L J Porter for the society.

HIS HONOUR JUDGE BLACKETT-ORD V-C. The plaintiffs in this application are the present trustees of the Co-operative Wholesale Society's Employees' Pension and
c Death Benefit Scheme constituted by a trust deed dated 19 April 1929. I will call them the trustees. I will call the scheme, the scheme.

There are four defendants: a Mr Farbrother, who is an employee of the society and a member of the scheme, so he hopes for a pension in the future; a Mr Foster, who is a retired employee and has paid in the past but who is now getting it back again; and a Mr Dalgleish, who is also a member and an employee, but who has been joined to represent
d all persons who in the future may become members of the scheme or who may otherwise become entitled to benefits under it. The fourth defendant is the society, that is the Co-operative Wholesale Society Ltd which set up the scheme.

The essential facts are conveniently obtained from the first affidavit of Mr James Mason, the first plaintiff, who is vice-chairman of the board of the society, as well as being the chairman of the trustees of the scheme. He says that the society was formed in
e 1863 to provide wholesale facilities for the Co-operative Movement, and I will now read some of what he states, starting at para 3 of his affidavit:

'The growth of the Co-operative Movement in the United Kingdom owed much to two of its central principles: first, that members of a retail distributive society should qualify for dividends on their purchases, and secondly, that the capital they
f invested in the society should earn interest at relatively low rates. The retention by members of dividend on share account, together with unappropriated surplus, funded societies' additional working capital requirements. A large number of retail societies came into being during the middle of the nineteenth century and in 1863 they combined to create the CWS for the purpose of procurement, wholesaling and manufacture.'

g In para 4 he says:

'The Scheme was constituted by the above mentioned Trust Deed dated 19th April, 1929 (hereinafter called "the 1929 Deed") at a time of virtually no inflation. By then, the CWS had enjoyed more than sixty years of phenomenal growth and, in addition to its extensive manufacturing and wholesale interest, had assumed the
h role of main banker and insurer for the Co-operative Movement.'

He then deals with the 1929 deed and I can go on reading what he says:

'5. By the 1929 Deed after reciting that the CWS was desirous of establishing a superannuation scheme for the benefit of employees of the CWS, and after having provided by Clause 1 thereof that there should be established a Superannuation
j Fund (thereinafter called "the Fund") for the benefit of employees of the CWS to which the CWS and the employees should contribute, it was provided by Clauses 5 and 6 thereof as follows reading from the 1929 Deed:

5 (a) Moneys comprised in the Fund shall be deposited with the Society so long as (i) the Society shall during each of the ten years last past before the date of the deposit have paid a dividend or interest at a rate of not less than 3 per cent on its

> ordinary shares and (ii) all moneys so deposited are secured by a charge on the whole or part of the assets of the undertaking of the Society. *a*
>
> (b) Where moneys are so deposited the Society shall allow interest on the average amount of the Fund in each half year at such a rate as after deducting income tax at the standard rate leaves a net rate of 4½ per cent per annum or at such other rate as shall be equal to the highest rate of interest paid by the Bank Department of the Society on special deposits . . .'

and I do not think I need read the rest of cl 5(b). *b*

Clause 5(c) provides:

> 'Interest shall be credited half-yearly on the second Saturday in January and second Saturday in July.'

I do not need to read cl 5(d). Then there is cl 6, which provides as follows:

> 'Subject as aforesaid money requiring investment shall be invested in such *c* securities authorised by law for the investment of Trust Funds as the Trustees shall think fit.'

That is all that Mr Mason quotes from the deed, and he goes on in his affidavit at para 6:

> 'It was further provided by Rule 11 in Part 1 of the Schedule to the 1929 Deed *d* that the CWS might on six months notice terminate its liability to contribute to the Scheme. The CWS has never given any such notice and indeed has from time to time made additional contributions to the Scheme over and above the amounts prescribed by the Rules.'

I can add to that, for completeness, that the original r 34 (which I think has now got a different number) provided that if notice was given by the society terminating its *e* liability, then there was to be convened a meeting of the persons entitled to any interest in the scheme in order to decide what to do, whether to wind it up or not.

Mr Mason then deals with certain attempted variations of the deed of 19 April 1929, made in 1937 and later, and says that he is advised that they were ineffective to alter the trusts of the 1929 deed because it contained no provision within itself for its alteration.

But a deed dated 1 March 1937, which I think was the first attempted alteration, *f* purported to delete any reference to 4½% pa in cl 5(b) and then to insert a new cl 6(a) as follows:

> 'The Society undertakes that if in any half year the amount of the interest or dividends upon the deposits, investments or securities for the time being constituting the Trust Fund, after making allowance for the repayment of any income tax which *g* may be reclaimable shall be less than a sum equivalent to interest at the rate of four per centum per annum upon the average amount of such Fund in such half year, the Society will pay to such Fund a sum equivalent to the amount of such difference.'

Mr Mason says that the trustees are advised that that clause had a contractual effect; it may not have altered the trusts of the deed, but it was a contract by the society to make the income of the fund up to 4½% pa if it fell short of it. *h*

Mr Mason then goes on to say that from 1929 until 1968 the assets of the fund were deposited with the society and that from 1968 (and I think he implies as a result of consideration of the Trustee Investments Act 1961 which extended the investment powers of trustees, notably as regards investment in industrial ordinary shares) new money was invested outside the society in accordance with the provisions of the 1961 Act, half in narrower range and half in wider range investments. And the deposit with *j* the society, of what might be called old money, was progressively withdrawn. He says in para 16 of his affidavit:

> 'The total funds in the Scheme as at 3rd April 1982 amounted to £127,221,000 of which £6,166,000 were invested in the CWS and the balance of £121,055,000

were invested outside the CWS in narrower and wider range securities in accordance with the provisions of the Trustee Investments Act 1961 . . .'

I propose to read para 17 of Mr Mason's affidavit, and the five following paragraphs. Paragraph 17 reads:

'Since the Trustee Investments Act 1961 was passed over 20 years ago much more sophisticated forms and opportunities for investment have arisen than those prescribed in the Act, particularly in regard to land and in overseas securities, and the Plaintiffs are concerned about their present limited powers of investment. The Plaintiffs have noted the opinion of the Law Reform Committee that the present statutory powers of investment contained in that Act are inadequate. I refer to a print of the 23rd Report of the Law Reform Committee which is now produced and shown to me marked "JM6". The Plaintiffs believe and respectfully submit that there are good grounds for the Committees opinion and that such grounds are relevant to this application. The Plaintiffs believe that the funds in the Scheme are so large that they may reasonably be allowed a greater degree of flexibility in investment than if the funds were small. They are also aware that most large modern pension funds, such as the Clergy Pensions Fund, have wider investment powers than those set out in the Trustee Investments Act 1961. Likewise most modern statutory pension funds have wider investment powers than those in the 1961 Act. There is moreover the possibility that had the Scheme enjoyed wider investment powers over the last 20 years the return on investments may have been higher than it has been. The Plaintiff's beliefs aforesaid are based on the expert opinion and evidence contained in the affidavits of Messrs. Bird, Bridgford, Herbert, Ives, James, Johnson, Malnick, Oldfield and Thackray . . .'

whose affidavits, the burden of which I will return to, have indeed been filed.

Mr Mason's affidavit continues:

'18. However the Plaintiffs are further advised that a question of difficulty arises in regard to the extent of their present investment powers, that is to say, whether they are obliged to deposit with the CWS the whole of the moneys comprised in the Scheme requiring to be invested or whether they are duty bound under the Trustee Investments Act 1961 to invest all such moneys in accordance with the provisions of that Act.

19. In view of the difficulty and importance of the question of construction aforesaid and the amount of moneys at stake, the Plaintiffs respectfully submit to this Honourable Court that it is proper that the same should be compromised, and accordingly the Plaintiffs propose, subject to the approval of this Honourable Court, that by way of compromise there should be substituted for the existing powers of investment of the Plaintiffs contained in Clauses 5 and 6 of the 1929 Deed a power of investment in the terms set forth in the Schedule to the Originating Summons herein whereby the Plaintiffs would have a wide investment power in a modern form, basically the same as that which the Clergy Pensions Fund presently enjoys, but with in addition a discretionary power to deposit such part of the moneys in the Scheme as the Plaintiffs think fit with the CWS at such rate of interest as shall be agreed with the CWS from time to time. The Plaintiffs believe that such compromise will be in the interests of all present and future members of the Scheme and other persons now or hereafter entitled to benefit thereunder who will benefit from an enlargement of the Plaintiffs investment powers and the anticipated improved performance of the pension fund which should result therefrom. The Plaintiffs believe also that the compromise is in the interest of CWS who will benefit from having an improved pension fund for their employees and also the prospect that some part of the pension moneys available for investment may still be placed on deposit with CWS instead of being wholly invested outside the CWS in accordance with the provisions of the Trustee Investments Act 1961.

> 20. Alternatively the Plaintiffs seek the approval of this Honourable Court to such substituted power of investment by way of variation of the 1929 Deed under *a* the provisions of Section 57 of the Trustee Act 1925 or alternatively under the provisions of Section 1 of the Variation of Trusts Act 1958.
>
> 21. The Plaintiffs' records show that as at 3rd April 1982 there were 19,361 contributing members of the Scheme. The Defendant Roger Gordon Farbrother is one of such contributing members. He commenced employment with the CWS on 30th June 1969 and joined the Scheme on or about the same date. He is currently *b* the Group Personnel Manager of the CWS Stationery and Packaging Group.
>
> 22. As at 3rd April 1982 there were 12,140 persons in receipt of pensions or other benefits under the Scheme of whom the Defendant Richard Foster is one. He commenced his employment with CWS on the 14th October 1974 when he also joined the Scheme and he retired on 3rd May 1981 from his then position as Head of Security.'

c

The first three defendants have each sworn an affidavit, I suppose in their personal capacities, saying that they support the proposal to insert a modern investment clause in the trust deed, though the first and second defendants have, I am told, made no attempt to consult the other persons whom they purport to represent. There are obviously practical difficulties to this, in view of the large numbers, though the rules of the society do contemplate meetings in certain circumstances, and there is, I trust, no question of *d* uncertainty as to who these two categories of subscribers and pensioners are; but this question of an investment clause is a technical matter on which it may well be thought that many members would not have very clear views.

The plaintiffs have filed a great deal of expert evidence including representations from Lazards and Warburgs (who between them have advised on the investment of the fund) including evidence showing that a large number of big pension schemes have wide *e* investment clauses, as perhaps one would have supposed.

I am told and I accept that the scheme which I have to consider was relatively early in the field and, as Mr Mason says in his evidence, was set up at a time of little or no inflation and that the narrower field of investment which it allowed was considered appropriate at the time and was in accordance with the principles of the Co-operative Movement.

However, the burden of the expert evidence is summarised in the first sentence of para *f* 4 of Mr Johnson's affidavit. Mr Johnson is the actuary of the scheme, and he says:

> 'In my opinion—and I believe this to be the general view of those who have the task of advising on the financial aspects of pension funds—it is in the interests of the existing and prospective beneficiaries of pension funds set up under deeds of trust that the trustees should have wide powers of investment of the moneys in their *g* care.'

Mr Mason also referred to the Law Reform Committee's twenty-third report, *The Powers and Duties of Trustees* (Cmnd 8733), which was presented to Parliament in October 1982 and which commented on the Trustee Investments Act 1961. That Act was passed to liberalise to some extent the powers of investment of trustees which previously had been confined to gilt-edged securities, taking that in a fairly wide sense, and it permitted *h* the division of trust funds into halves, one to be invested in a narrower range of investments and the other in a wider range of investments, which included equities, with complicated provisions for the balance between the two. It also, of course, provided for a special range where special types of investment are authorised by a trust deed, but the details are not relevant to the present situation.

The Law Reform Committee says that the provisions of the 1961 Act have largely *j* been ignored by the draftsmen of subsequent documents who almost always insert wider powers of investment than are provided for by the statute, and in para 3.17 of the report of the Law Reform Committee the third sentence says this:

> 'However, a cautious approach was taken in the new provision, investment in

equities being considered to be somewhat speculative. The Act has proved to be
a tiresome, cumbrous and expensive in operation with the result that its provisions are now seen to be inadequate. Furthermore, careful investment in equities is perhaps more likely in the long run to protect and benefit both income and capital beneficiaries than is investment in fixed-interest securities. In our view, therefore, the present statutory powers are out of date and ought now to be revised.'

b Apart from para 18 in Mr Mason's affidavit (which I have read) there is nothing in any of the evidence, including the evidence filed on behalf of the defendants, about any question of difficulty having actually arisen in the construction of cll 5 and 6 of the 1929 deed. The emphasis is entirely on the benefits of a new investment clause, and it is perfectly clear to me that what the parties are seeking is the insertion of such a clause in the trust deed. It is also perfectly clear to me that such an insertion will be for the benefit
c of all parties, that is to say, the trustees, the potential and actual beneficiaries, and the society itself.

The question that I have to decide is whether such an insertion can be validly sanctioned by the court, because it is perfectly clear that apart from statute and apart from certain clear exceptions, the court has no inherent jurisdiction to vary the terms of a trust simply because it is, or the court thinks it is, beneficial to do so. The authority for
d that is *Chapman v Chapman* [1954] 1 All ER 798, [1954] AC 429. It is also clear from the same case that one of the exceptions is that the court has jurisdiction to approve the compromise of disputed rights. And the matter has been laid before me primarily on this footing.

It is clear that the relationship between express and statutory investment powers can give rise to difficulties, and I refer to *Re Burke, Burke v Burke* [1908] 2 Ch 248, and *Re*
e *Rider's Will Trusts, Nelson v Rider* [1958] 3 All ER 135, [1958] 1 WLR 974; and I refer also to s 1(3) of the Trustee Investments Act 1961 itself, which seems to me almost to invite confusion. I am satisfied that cll 5 and 6 of the 1929 deed do indeed give rise to questions both between the trustees and the society and between the trustees and the members and I do not think there need be open warfare before the court may approve a compromise, provided that there are genuine points of difference requiring determination
f or settlement. There is therefore room for compromise in this case.

To that extent I can distinguish the case of *Re Powell-Cotton's Re-settlement, Henniker-Major v Powell-Cotton* [1956] 1 All ER 60, [1956] 1 WLR 23. That case had something in common with the present case; there was an old-fashioned investment clause but in a family settlement; there was a point of obscurity in it, but it was a much smaller point; and the parties purported to compromise the question of the meaning of the investment
g clause (which had not in fact given rise to any difficulty) by striking it out entirely and putting in a modern clause. Danckwerts J and the Court of Appeal both considered that there was really nothing to compromise and that the proposals were therefore beyond the jurisdiction of the court. In the present case, in my judgment, there is something to compromise. But what is proposed in the present case is very much what was sought to be done in *Re Powell-Cotton's Re-settlement* ie to sweep the old away and substitute the
h new.

It has been suggested by counsel for the first defendant that once it is found that there is some point to be compromised, then the terms of the compromise are at large. Against that it is said that if the opposing views in the present case are that under the present clauses either all the funds of the society ought to be invested in the society or, alternatively, all the funds of the society ought to be invested in accordance with the
j Trustee Investments Act 1961, then the compromise should be something between the two. I accept that that need not always be the case. But in *Re Powell-Cotton's Re-settlement* (see [1956] 1 All ER 60 at 62, [1956] 1 WLR 23 at 26) Danckwerts J took both points, not only that there was nothing to compromise, but also that if there had been, the proposals before him were not such that the court should approve. When the matter got to the Court of Appeal, Evershed MR, after saying how useful was the jurisdiction of the

Chancery judges in connection with the execution of trusts, said ([1956] 1 All ER 60 at
62, [1956] 1 WLR 23 at 27): a

> 'Bearing that in mind, I for my part prefer to base my own conclusion in rejecting
> this appeal on the second ground which I have stated. If it could be said that a
> question was being compromised, nevertheless I would feel quite unjustified in
> interfering with the view which the learned judge in his discretion took, that it was
> not the right way to go about it to substitute an entirely new modern investment
> clause, for that which was found in the settlement.' b

All Evershed MR there was doing in terms was refusing to interfere with the exercise of
the judge's discretion. But he seems to me to be indicating certain views and, with that
in mind, I turn to consider the alternatives put forward in the originating summons by
reference to the statutory enactments.

First, in the alternative, an order is sought under s 57 of the Trustee Act 1925 or, c
second, under s 1 of the Variation of Trusts Act 1958, approving on behalf of all persons
who may or hereafter become entitled under the trusts, an arrangement to vary the trust
deed so as to put in the new power of investment.

The matter of the Variation of Trusts Act 1958 has not been pursued, because perhaps
of difficulties in connection with the representative parties. That leaves s 57 of the
Trustee Act 1925, which provides, so far as is relevant, in sub-s (1): d

> 'Where in the management or administration of any property vested in trustees,
> any sale, lease, mortgage, surrender, release, or other disposition, or any purchase,
> investment, acquisition, expenditure, or other transaction, is in the opinion of the
> court expedient, but the same cannot be effected by reason of the absence of any
> power for that purpose vested in the trustees by the trust instrument, if any, or by
> law, the court may by order confer upon the trustees, either generally or in any e
> particular instance, the necessary power for the purpose, on such terms, and subject
> to such provisions and conditions, if any, as the court may think fit...'

That power was exercised by Danckwerts J in a charity case, *Re Shipwrecked Fishermen
and Mariners' Royal Benevolent Society Charity* [1958] 3 All ER 465, [1959] Ch 220, so as to
extend the investment powers of the trustees. f

Shortly afterwards, in *Re Coates' Will Trusts* [1959] 2 All ER 51, [1959] 1 WLR 375,
the view was put forward by Harman J that the proper way to proceed where trustees
wished to obtain extended investment powers was by way of an application under the
Variation of Trusts Act 1958, and that advice, in my experience, was acted on and many
applications were made under that Act; but the law as laid down by Danckwerts J in *Re
Shipwrecked Fishermen and Mariners' Royal Benevolent Society Charity* has not been overruled, g
and I am satisfied that where in the management or administration of trust property it is
in the opinion of the court expedient, I have the power to authorise the substitution for
cll 5 and 6 of the 1929 deed of the sort of investment clause which is being put forward
here.

The next question to be considered is whether there is any reason why this should not
be done, based on the Trustee Investments Act 1961. I have indicated that after 1959 a h
great many applications were made by trustees of trusts under the Variation of Trusts
Act 1958 to obtain wider investment powers, but Parliament then passed the 1961 Act
extending investment powers of trustees and in two later cases, namely *Re Cooper's
Settlement, Cooper v Cooper* [1961] 3 All ER 636, [1962] Ch 826, and *Re Kolb's Will Trusts,
Lloyd's Bank Ltd v Ullmann* [1961] 3 All ER 811, [1962] Ch 531, Buckley J and Cross J
respectively expressed the view that in the light of such a recent expression of the views j
of Parliament, it would not be right for the courts to continue to extend investment
clauses with the enthusiasm with which they had done up to date; and for many years
few applications, if any, were made.

But the rule was not an absolute one; it was said to apply in the absence of special
circumstances, and the special circumstances in the present case are manifest: in a word,

inflation since 1961. And also of course the fact that the trust is an unusual one in that it is not a private or family trust but a pension fund with perhaps something of a public element in it.

In my judgment, therefore, there is no reason why in a proper case an application such as the present one should not be acceded to under s 57 of the Trustee Act 1925. And it seems to me on the evidence that it is (in the words of the section) 'expedient' that the application should succeed. Therefore, the way that I think it is proper to deal with the application is by making an order under s 57 of the 1925 Act, and this I will do.

The form of investment clause sought is set out in the schedule to the originating summons and it carries with it the odour of sanctity in that it is that now applicable to clergy pensions under the Clergy Pensions Amendment Measure 1982, with consequential amendments, and with the addition of a power for the trustees to deposit any moneys comprised in the fund with the society at such rate of interest as shall be agreed, a power which, I am bound to say, I feel is of perhaps more sentimental than practical value. However, there it is.

In agreeing to the proposals, two of the defendants have put forward suggested additions. First, Mr Farbrother says that he would like to be assured that the trustees will take professional advice before deciding on their investments and has put forward a suggested para (5) (there are four paragraphs to the clause in the original proposal) which is based on s 6 of the Trustee Investments Act 1961. This is accepted by the trustees and the other defendants.

The second defendant, Mr Foster, puts forward his para (6) dealing with three different topics: first, insurance; second, the power to appoint nominees; third, the power to borrow money. The trustees accept it in principle but not all the details.

In the first sub-paragraph dealing with insurance, it is proposed that the trustees should have the power to insure against certain specified risks up to the market value or the full replacement value. It does not say 'whichever is the greater', but perhaps we do not need to go into that. Then there is a proviso that 'it shall be the duty of the trustees to insure in all the circumstances in which an ordinary and prudent man of business would so insure . . .' I accept the views of the trustees that it is undesirable to complicate matters by bringing in the man on the Clapham omnibus and I propose to delete that proviso and simply leave it to the trustees to insure.

In the second sub-paragraph, dealing with the power to appoint a nominee or nominees, there is a proviso about a nominee being a bank or something like that. But in my view that is an undesirable complication. I will simply authorise the trustees to appoint a nominee or nominees to hold any investment in the fund. That is a power that the trustees can exercise in proper circumstances and if they misuse it, they will be liable.

Finally there is the provision relating to borrowing money. It has been said that it is not a trustee's business to borrow money. However, for a fund of this size I think such a power is obviously desirable and I authorise that.

So the clause which will be substituted for cll 5 and 6 is that which is set out in the schedule to the originating summons, together with para (5) which was put forward by counsel for the first defendant and para (6) put forward by counsel for the second defendant, but with the omission of those two provisos.

Order accordingly under s 57 of the Trustee Act 1925.

Solicitors: *W A Shawdon*, Manchester (for the plaintiffs); *Croftons*, Manchester (for the first, second and third defendants); *W A Shawdon*, Manchester (for the Society).

M Denise Chorlton Barrister.

Practice Direction

FAMILY DIVISION

Husband and wife – Matrimonial home – Rights of occupation – Practice – Declaration of rights of occupation – Injunction prohibiting exercise of rights of occupation – Heading of summons – Transfer to High Court of pending divorce proceedings in county court – Procedure – Matrimonial Causes Act 1967, s 4 – Domestic Violence and Matrimonial Proceedings Act 1976, s 1 – Matrimonial Homes Act 1983, ss 1, 9 – RSC Ord 90, r 17 – Matrimonial Causes Rules 1977, rr 104, 107.

Matrimonial Homes Act 1983

Where relief is sought under the Matrimonial Homes Act 1983 the application must be made by originating summons. The procedure in the High Court is set out in r 107 of the Matrimonial Causes Rules 1977, SI 1977/344, which applies r 104, with the necessary modifications. The summons should be headed 'In the matter of an application under section 1 [*or* section 9] of the Matrimonial Homes Act 1983'. The affidavit in support of the application should contain evidence of the applicant's rights of occupation of the matrimonial home and the circumstances in which the application is made. The form or order applied for should be an order (1) declaring the applicant's right of occupation of the matrimonial home and (2) if ouster is sought, prohibiting the respondent from exercising any right to occupy such home from a specified date and time until further order.

The registrar's direction dated 21 December 1973 (unreported) in so far as it relates to an initial hearing for directions will not apply to applications under s 1 (or s 9) of the Matrimonial Homes Act 1983 for ouster injunctions.

The Principal Registry has no jurisdiction in relation to ouster injunctions under the Matrimonial Homes Act 1983 except in the High Court. Where there are pending divorce proceedings in the Principal Registry which are treated as pending in a divorce county court under the provisions of s 4 of the Matrimonial Causes Act 1967, and a party to those proceedings applies in the Principal Registry for ouster relief under s 1 (or s 9) of the Matrimonial Homes Act 1983, a registrar or the judge hearing the s 1 (or s 9) application should be asked that the cause be transferred to the High Court.

RSC Ord 90, r 17

Applications in the Principal Registry for relief analogous to that available under s 1 of the Domestic Violence and Matrimonial Proceedings Act 1976 must also be made by originating summons in the High Court. The procedure to be followed is set out in RSC Ord 90, r 17. The originating summons should be headed 'In the matter of an application within the meaning of section 1 of the Domestic Violence and Matrimonial Proceedings Act 1976'.

[Until 9 August 1983, when the Matrimonial Homes Act 1983 comes into force, references to ss 1 and 9 of that Act should be construed as being respectively s 1 of the Matrimonial Homes Act 1967 and s 4 of the Domestic Violence and Matrimonial Proceedings Act 1976.]

B P TICKLE
Senior Registrar.

28 July 1983

R v Ball and another

COURT OF APPEAL, CRIMINAL DIVISION
LORD LANE CJ, McCULLOUGH AND LEONARD JJ
13 MAY 1983

Criminal law – Handling stolen goods – Undertaking or assisting in retention etc – Doctrine of recent possession – Whether inference that defendant knew goods were stolen can be made in offence of handling by assisting in dealing with recently stolen goods – Theft Act 1968, ss 22(1), 27(3).

A quantity of citizens' band radios was stolen from a store in Stourbridge. Some 48 hours later the police found in a car parked in Exeter boxes containing citizens' band radios. The occupants of the car were G, his girlfriend W, and another man B. G was charged with burglary of radios from the store in Stourbridge and W and B with handling the stolen radios by dishonestly undertaking or assisting in their retention, removal, disposal or realisation for the benefit of another, knowing them to be stolen, contrary to s 22(1)[a] of the Theft Act 1968. At the defendants' trial the Crown adduced clear evidence that the radios in the car had been stolen from the store in Stourbridge some 48 hours before they were found in the car. None of the defendants gave evidence. The trial judge directed the jury that the doctrine of recent possession applied to the offence of handling stolen goods by assisting in dealing with them, contrary to s 22(1), so that in the absence of an innocent explanation by the handler of his contact with recently stolen goods the jury were entitled to infer that he knew that the goods were stolen. The judge did not direct the jury on the element of dishonesty in the offence of handling stolen goods but he gave a clear direction on the need for the jury to be sure that the defendants knew or believed that the goods were stolen. G was convicted of burglary of the radios and W and B were convicted of handling the stolen radios by assisting in dealing with them. W and B appealed against their conviction, on the grounds (i) that the doctrine of recent possession only applied to the s 22(1) offence of handling stolen goods by dishonestly receiving them and not to the other s 22(1) offence of handling by dishonestly assisting in dealing with stolen goods, and (ii) that the judge ought to have directed the jury on the element of dishonesty in the offence of handling.

Held – The appeal would be dismissed for the following reasons—

(1) The doctrine of recent possession applied to both handling offences under s 22(1) of the 1968 Act and therefore applied to the offence of handling stolen goods by assisting in dealing with them, since there was no reason why it should be permissible to draw the inference of guilty knowledge that goods were stolen in the case of a defendant charged with handling by receiving recently stolen goods if it were not also permissible to draw the same inference where the charge was handling by assisting in dealing with recently stolen goods. Moreover, that view was supported by s 27(3)[b] of the 1968 Act which provided that the inference of guilty knowledge which could have been drawn in cases of receiving stolen goods under the Larceny Act 1916 where certain facts existed could also be drawn in all cases of handling under the 1968 Act where those same facts existed. Accordingly, the trial judge's direction on the applicability of the doctrine of recent possession had been correct (see p 1093 *f g* and p 1094 *d* to *j*, post); dictum of Roskill J in *R v Sloggett* [1971] 3 All ER at 267 not followed.

(2) Since the defendants must in all the circumstances have been acting dishonestly, a direction on the element of dishonesty in the offence of handling had not been necessary, but even if such a direction had been necessary, the failure to give it would not have been a material misdirection (see p 1094 *j* to p 1095 *a*, post).

---

a Section 22(1) is set out at p 1093 *d e*, post
b Section 27(3) is set out at p 1094 *f* to *h*, post

Notes

For handling stolen goods, see 11 Halsbury's Laws (4th edn) para 1289, and for cases on the subject, see 15 Digest (Reissue) 1362–1363, *11900–11904*.

For the Theft Act 1968, s 22, see 8 Halsbury's Statutes (3rd edn) 796.

Case referred to in judgment

R v Sloggett [1971] 3 All ER 264, [1972] 1 QB 430, [1971] 3 WLR 628, CA.

Appeal and application

On 13 May 1982 in the Crown Court at Wolverhampton before his Honour Judge John Lee and a jury the appellant, Michael Anthony Ball, and the applicant, Rosanna Jayne Winning, were convicted of handling stolen goods contrary to s 22(1) of the Theft Act 1968 by dishonestly undertaking or assisting in the retention, removal, disposal or realisation of 30 citizens' band transceivers knowing them to be stolen. Ball was ordered to do 160 hours of community service. Winning was given a conditional discharge for 12 months. Ball appealed pursuant to a certificate granted by the trial judge that the case was fit for appeal on the question whether his direction to the jury that the doctrine of recent possession could be applied to a defendant like Ball who was charged with dishonestly undertaking or assisting in the retention, removal, disposal or realisation of stolen goods knowing them to be stolen where the evidence established that he had physically handled recently stolen property by transferring it from one vehicle to another in company with the thief and by accompanying the thief on an expedition to sell the stolen property for the purpose of taking care of the money obtained from the sale. Accordingly, Ball appealed on the grounds (1) that the judge was wrong to direct the jury that physical contact with recently stolen property was enough to justify the inference of his guilt, (2) that the judge was wrong to direct the jury that proof of legal possession of the goods was not necessary for the doctrine of recent possession to apply, and (3) that the judge omitted dishonesty from his definition of the offence charged when directing the jury. Winning applied for leave to appeal against her conviction on the the grounds (1) that the judge omitted dishonesty from his definition of the offence charged when directing the jury, (2) that the only relevant evidence against her was her presence in a car with the recently stolen citizens' band transceivers and (3) that although the Crown said she obtained the citizens' band transceivers in suspicious circumstances, the circumstances were normal in relation to the trade in illicit citizens band radios.

The facts are set out in the judgment of the court.

Peter de Mille (assigned by the Registrar of Criminal Appeals) for Ball and Winning.
Malcolm Lee QC for the Crown.

McCULLOUGH J delivered the following judgment of the court. On 13 May 1982 in the Crown Court at Wolverhampton Winning and Ball were convicted of the offence of handling stolen goods. Winning was conditionally discharged for 12 months and Ball was ordered to undertake 160 hours of community service. A man called Gordon was convicted of burglary in the same trial.

Ball now appeals against conviction by right, the trial judge having granted a certificate that the case is fit for appeal. Winning applies for leave to appeal against conviction on the same ground.

The indictment contained three counts, but in the event count 2 was withdrawn from the jury. Count 1 charged Gordon with burglary. It alleged that on a day unknown between 26 and 29 October 1981, having entered as a trespasser a building known as 16 Lawnswood Road, Wordsley, Stourbridge, he stole therein 122 citizens' band transceivers. Count 3 alleged that Ball and Winning on a day unknown between the same dates dishonestly undertook or assisted in the retention, removal, disposal or realisation of certain stolen goods, namely 30 citizens' band transceivers, by or for the benefit of another, knowing or believing the same to be stolen.

The prosecution evidence in summary was as follows. A man called Hartland, who *a* was a butcher, had a shop in Stourbridge. He bought and sold citizens' band transceivers. He had a large stock. At the time such trading was illegal. By Saturday, 24 October 1981, his stock was in one of his cold stores. Gordon visited the premises that evening and saw it.

On Wednesday, 28 October, at 12.30 pm Hartland found that the padlock on this store was missing and that all the transceivers had gone. The burglary must have taken *b* place some time after 6 pm the previous evening when the padlock had last been seen in position.

On Friday, 30 October, at 2.45 am, in other words during the Thursday night, police officers went to a Ford Escort estate car which was then on the car park of a motorway service station near Exeter. Gordon was in the driving seat. Winning, who was his girlfriend and was living with him, was beside him. Ball was in the back seat. It was a *c* hired car. The police said to Gordon that they believed it was carrying a load of 'CB rigs', which they alleged he was 'pushing out cheap to local breakers'. Gordon was asked to open a trunk. Under some blankets numerous boxes containing citizens' band transceivers were found. Gordon said that he had bought them from a dealer in Birmingham. He was unable to produce any receipt. After this the car and its three occupants were taken to a local police station. There Gordon was interviewed. The evidence of what he said to *d* the police was not admissible against the other two, and I shall not refer to it.

The boxes were found to contain 30 citizens' band transceivers, all new. These were later shown to Hartland. He had no record of the serial numbers of those stolen from him, but he said that the types of those found in the car corresponded with the types which he had had stolen. He put the price of the 30 found in the car at just under £3,000.

e Gordon, Winning and Ball were all taken back to the West Midlands and they were interviewed separately at Brierley Hill police station on the Friday evening. Ball was asked how he came to be in possession of these stolen CBs, as the police described them. At first he said that he did not know that they were in the vehicle. He said that he was in Exeter with Gordon because Gordon had asked him to keep him company. The police officer suggested this was nonsense as Gordon had his girlfriend with him, whereupon *f* Ball changed his account and said, 'Honest, I didn't know they were nicked'. He went on to explain that Gordon had told him the previous day that Winning had bought them.

Later in the same interview he said, 'O K then, this is the truth. I was in the yard yesterday afternoon. Martin Gordon comes in, he's got all these CBs, and he asked me to go to Exeter with him to sell them.' He said that he and Gordon had then moved the transceivers from Gordon's Jaguar car into the Escort, which Gordon had borrowed *g* 'because the Jag was no good'. He was asked 'Where did you think the CBs were from?' He said 'Didn't ask, don't want to know, do I?' At the end of the interview he was asked 'Why did you have to go to Exeter?' He said 'Once the CBs were sold we were going to have quite a bit of bread, weren't we? I was there to look after the money.'

When Winning was asked how she had come by the rigs she said, 'I bought them. A man came to the house and I bought them.' Who was he?' she was asked. I don't know'. *h* How much did they cost you?' She said '£1,500.' 'Where did you get £1,500?' 'In the house, money I had saved for the kitchen.' 'How many did you buy?' 'I cannot remember. It was £1,500 for the lot.' The officer asked 'I presume you bought them to resell?' She said 'Yes.' The officer asked 'At a profit?' Then she replied 'I thought Martin would be able to sell them.' Then the officer put to her, 'Before you pay out £1,500 you want to know what you are buying. You must know how many were offered for sale?' She said, *j* 'I never counted them.' She said that they had come to her house in a van. She had not thought to ask for a receipt. Then she said that she had heard about them on her CB when a man from Birmingham who used the name Street Walker on the CB said that he got them to sell. So she had called him up and asked how much he wanted. He said £1,500. She said she would have them if he brought them round. They were delivered about 3 pm that day.

She was told that Gordon said the £1,500 was his. She replied 'Yes, it was, but it was for the kitchen.' She said that when Gordon heard what she had done he went mad. a
Then the police put to her, 'They were only stolen on Tuesday night, Wednesday morning. It would be too rash for the thief to advertise them for sale on the Wednesday afternoon on the local CB.' To that, as she was entitled to do, she made no reply. Asked 'Why go all the way down to Exeter to sell them?' she replied 'There is a market for CBs down there. There isn't any market round here.'

At the trial the prosecution witnesses were cross-examined by the defence to suggest b
that Hartland could not be relied on when he said that the transceivers found in the estate car at Exeter were some of those which had been stolen from his premises.

None of the three defendants gave evidence. The only evidence called for the defence was a man called Rolfe, who referred to dealings he had had with Hartland, the purpose of which was apparently to cast doubt on the assertion that the transceivers found at Exeter had been stolen from Hartland. c

Thus there was clear evidence before the jury that the transceivers in the car at Exeter had been stolen in the burglary at the cold store and if, as would be likely, the burglary took place during Tuesday night, the three defendants had some of the stolen property with them 48 hours later. The jury, as I have said, found Gordon guilty of burglary. There was clear evidence that each of the other two was at the least assisting in the disposal of stolen goods for Gordon's benefit. There was evidence from which a jury d
might properly infer that Winning had lied about how she came to be dealing with them. Ball, as he admitted, had certainly lied.

Counsel who appears for both Winning and Ball submits that the judge misdirected the jury in a passage which runs as follows:

> 'What about the handling charge so far as the other two are concerned? Members of the jury, a similar principle applies. If a defendant is found handling stolen e
> property in the sense that he is in possession of it or in control of it or in physical control or has physical contact with it, assisting somebody else who has got possession of it to dispose of it for instance, as in this case the prosecution allege, very soon after the property is stolen, you may again think and the law thinks that may call for an explanation. It is entirely for you, but in the absence of some innocent explanation you are entitled to infer against those people charged with handling what the law f
> calls guilty knowledge; in other words, that they knew or believed the property they were dealing with was stolen property.'

Counsel for Winning and Ball referred also to a later passage, but the substance of the misdirection which he alleges is contained in the passage which I have just read.

His submission shortly is this, that common sense suggests that a person in control of g
recently stolen goods should be asked to account for his possession, and an adverse inference should be drawn as to his state of mind should he give no credible explanation; that such an inference should not be drawn against a person who merely has physical contact with such goods and is acting under the direction of someone who has them in his possession. In short the so-called doctrine of recent possession should apply only to those whom the jury find to be in possession of recently stolen property and should not h
apply to those who are merely assisting other people to retain, remove, dispose or realise such property.

There is no direct authority on the submission which counsel for Winning and Ball makes, save for one short passage in *R v Sloggett* [1971] 3 All ER 264, [1972] 1 QB 430, to which I shall refer. None of the texts to which reference is ordinarily made in such cases deals with the submission, save for Griew *The Theft Acts 1968 and 1978* (4th edn, 1982) j
p 184, para 13–23 in a passage to which I shall refer. The question has to be considered on principle and logic.

The so-called doctrine of recent possession is misnamed. It has nothing to do with goods recently possessed. It concerns possession of goods recently stolen. It is not even a doctrine. It is in fact no more than an inference which a jury may, or may not, think it right to draw about the state of mind of a defendant who is dealing in goods stolen not long beforehand. It is based on common sense.

Stolen goods frequently pass quickly from hand to hand. Many of those who deal in them knowing or believing them to be stolen tell lies when they are asked to explain how the goods came into their possession. Others prefer to give no explanation. That has been the experience of the courts for generations. So when a defendant is found to have been in possession of goods recently stolen and either gives no explanation of how he came to acquire them innocently or gives an explanation which is patently untrue, it is the practice of judges to tell juries that they may, if they think it right, infer that he acquired them knowing or believing that they were stolen. The innocent man has nothing to fear from this. He has no need to lie. He will, as a rule, be only too willing to give his explanation. It is, in any event, an inference which a jury will only draw if they think it right to do so.

Before the Theft Act 1968 came into force on 1 January 1969, there was no offence of handling stolen goods. The governing provision was s 33 of the Larceny Act 1916, which made it an offence for a person to receive stolen property knowing that it had been stolen. Receiving meant receiving property into his possession or control. Section 22 of the Theft Act 1968 created the offence of handling. This provision is wider than the old one. It embraces two kinds of handling: the first is essentially the old offence of receiving and the second is what I shall call, for brevity, assisting.

The words of s 22(1) are as follows:

> 'A person handles stolen goods if (otherwise than in the course of the stealing) knowing or believing them to be stolen goods he dishonestly receives the goods, or dishonestly undertakes or assists in their retention, removal, disposal or realisation by or for the benefit of another person, or if he arranges to do so.'

Inevitably every case in which the question arose prior to 1969 was a case of receiving, and many of these cases therefore touched on, or turned on, the question of whether it could be said that the goods passed into the possession or control of the defendant.

There is, in the view of this court, no reason in logic or justice why, since 1969, it should be permissible to draw the inference where the defendant has received recently stolen goods into his possession, but impermissible to draw it when he is merely assisting somebody else to deal with such goods. The distinction between the two types of handling lies in the relationship between the defendant and the goods. In each his state of mind is the same, and it is in relation to his state of mind that the jury may think it right to draw the inference.

Griew in the passage to which I have already referred, says this:

> 'On a charge under the old law of receiving stolen goods knowing them to have been stolen, if the prosecution proved that D received the goods and that they were *recently* stolen, it was proper to direct the jury that they could convict if they heard from D no innocent explanation of his possession which they thought might reasonably be true ... A similar direction remains appropriate under the Act in a case of receiving (and no doubt also in a case of arranging to receive). But it would not be right to use such a direction in relation to all modes of handling. Mere porterage is not on a par with the acquisition of exclusive control when it comes to considering the probability that the handler knew the history of the goods ...'

He then refers to *R v Sloggett* [1971] 3 All ER 264, [1972] 1 QB 430.

No doubt a receiver of recently stolen goods who knows or believes that the goods are stolen may sometimes enlist the assistance of someone without such knowledge or belief. Such a person is not in peril from the inference. If the innocent receiver has nothing to fear from it, nor, a fortiori, has the innocent assistant. It is, as I have already said, an inference which a jury will only draw if they think it right to do so.

Any view other than that to which the court has come would lead to a wholly artificial position where, as is sometimes the case, a defendant faces alternative counts of handling by receiving and handling the same goods by assisting. The jury would have to be told that it was open to them to draw the inference in relation to the one count but not in *a* relation to the other. Were the two types of receiving to be referred to in the same count, as would be possible in certain circumstances, the position would be even more ridiculous.

The material passage in *R v Sloggett* [1971] 3 All ER 264 at 267, [1972] 1 QB 430 at 433–434 expresses a contrary view. Roskill J giving the judgment of the court, said this:

> 'A more serious criticism is that in a passage immediately following this statement of the law, the chairman introduced the doctrine of recent possession which, with *b* respect, had nothing to do with count 2, although it was or at least might have been relevant to count 1. [Count 1 had charged handling stolen goods by receiving them and count 2 charged handling stolen goods by dishonestly assisting their retention.] If this topic had to be introduced at all it should have been introduced earlier in the summing-up. In juxtaposition to a passage dealing with count 2, there may have been some confusion in the jury's mind as to its relevance. But even so the chairman *c* at the end of this criticised passage made it plain that this doctrine had no relevance unless the defendant was in fact first shown to be in actual possession of the stolen goods, this being of course relevant only to count 1 and in no way to count 2.'

It appears to us that the opinion there expressed was not necessary to the decision. No reasoning for it was given. Having endeavoured to reason the matter for ourselves and *d* with all due respect to the court in *R v Sloggett* we prefer our own conclusion.

There is a further consideration. Under the legislation in force prior to 1968, s 43(1) of the Larceny Act 1916 permitted the inference of guilty knowledge to be drawn in a case of receiving from two facts: first, 'the fact that other property stolen within the period of twelve months preceding the date of the offence charged was found or had been in his possession', and second, 'the fact that within the five years preceding the date of the *e* offence charged he was convicted of any offence involving fraud or dishonesty.' There followed a proviso that notice had to be given to the defendant of the intention to prove such a conviction.

This provision has been re-enacted in essentially the same form in the Theft Act 1968, s 27(3) of which says:

> *f* 'Where a person is being proceeded against for handling stolen goods (but not for any offence other than handling stolen goods), then at any stage of the proceedings, if evidence has been given of his having or arranging to have in his possession the goods the subject of the charge, or of his undertaking or assisting in, or arranging to undertake or assist in, their retention, removal, disposal or realisation, the following evidence shall be admissible for the purpose of proving that he knew or believed the goods to be stolen goods:—(*a*) evidence that he has had in his possession, or has *g* undertaken or assisted in the retention, removal, disposal or realisation of, stolen goods from any theft taking place not earlier than twelve months before the offence charged; and (*b*) (provided that seven days' notice in writing has been given to him of the intention to prove the conviction) evidence that he has within the five years preceding the date of the offence charged been convicted of theft or of handling stolen goods.' *h*

Thus the inference which might be drawn in cases of receiving under the old legislation may now be drawn from the same facts in *all* cases of handling under the new legislation, exactly as one would expect if our reasoning is correct. This lends support for the view to which the court has come.

In the judgment of this court the trial judge was right to direct the jury about the *j* inference in the way that he did.

Counsel for Winning and Ball takes a second point which is that at no stage did the judge tell the jury that one of the essentials of the offence of handling was the element of dishonesty. In the circumstances of this case it is inconceivable that the defendants' minds could have been anything other than dishonest if they knew or believed that the

goods were stolen. The contrary was not even suggested. There was the clearest direction
a on the need for the jury to be sure that each individual defendant did know or believe that the goods were stolen. We take the view that a direction on dishonesty was not necessary. If it was, the failure to give it was certainly not a material misdirection. Accordingly this submission also fails.

Ball's appeal is dismissed and Winning's application for leave to appeal is refused.

b *Ball's appeal dismissed. Winning's application refused.*

Solicitors: *I S Manson*, Birmingham (for the Crown).

N P Metcalfe Esq Barrister.

c

d
Mallalieu v Drummond (Inspector of Taxes)

HOUSE OF LORDS
LORD DIPLOCK, LORD ELWYN-JONES, LORD KEITH OF KINKEL, LORD ROSKILL AND LORD BRIGHTMAN
30 JUNE, 27 JULY 1983

e *Income tax – Deduction in computing profits – Expenditure wholly and exclusively laid out or expended for purposes of trade – Purpose of expenditure – Barrister's clothing – Female barrister's court clothes – Whether expenditure incurred in replacing, cleaning and laundering clothes deductible – Income and Corporation Taxes Act 1970, s 130(a).*

The taxpayer was a practising barrister. During the year 1976–77 she spent some £564
f on the replacement, cleaning and laundering of certain items of clothing which she wore in court, and sought to deduct that sum when computing the profits of her profession as being expenses 'wholly and exclusively . . . expended for the purposes of [her] profession' within s 130(*a*)[a] of the Income and Corporation Taxes Act 1970. The inspector of taxes disallowed the deduction and the taxpayer appealed to the General Commissioners. The commissioners found, as facts, that the taxpayer had ample other clothing for the
g purposes of warmth and decency, that she would not have purchased any of the disputed items had it not been for the requirement of her profession that she should be so clothed, that she only wore those clothes in connection with her work, that she bought the disputed items only because she would not have been permitted to appear in court if she did not, when in court, wear them or similar clothes, and that the preservation of warmth and decency was not a consideration in her mind when she bought them. The
h commissioners considered that, notwithstanding that the taxpayer's sole motive in choosing the particular clothes was to satisfy the requirements of her profession and that had she been free to do so she would have worn different clothes, the expenditure had a dual purpose, the professional one of enabling her to earn profits in her profession and the non-professional one of enabling her to be properly clothed while engaged in her professional activity. They therefore held that, because of that dual purpose, the taxpayer
j was not entitled to the deduction claimed. On an appeal by the taxpayer, the judge held

a Section 130, so far as material, provides: 'Subject to the provisions of the Tax Acts, in computing the amount of the profits or gains to be charge under Case I or Case II of Schedule D, no sum shall be deducted in respect of—(*a*) any disbursements or expenses, not being money wholly and exclusively laid out or expended for the purposes of the trade, profession or vocation . . .'

that there was no evidence to support the commissioners' conclusion that the taxpayer had a dual purpose in mind, but only evidence to conclude that the expenditure on the *a* disputed items was incurred by the taxpayer solely for the purpose of carrying on her profession, and that the benefits of warmth and decency which she would enjoy while wearing the clothes were purely incidental to the carrying on of her profession. Accordingly, he held that the expenditure was deductible and allowed the appeal. The Crown appealed unsuccessfully to the Court of Appeal and further appealed to the House of Lords. *b*

Held (Lord Elwyn-Jones dissenting) – In determining whether an expense was wholly and exclusively expended for the purposes of the taxpayer's profession within s 130(*a*) of the 1970 Act, the conscious motive of the taxpayer at the moment of expenditure, although of vital significance in determining the object of the expenditure, was not conclusive of the matter, and the finding that the taxpayer's conscious motive for making *c* the expenditure was exclusively for the purposes of her profession did not preclude the commissioners from finding that the expenditure also satisfied other objects apart from professional purposes. The expenditure by the taxpayer on the maintenance of clothing which conformed to the dress requirements of her profession was made not only for professional purposes but also for personal purposes, namely so that she could be warmly and decently clothed. Accordingly, the commissioners were correct in concluding that *d* the expenditure had a dual purpose, one professional and the other non-professional. It was irrelevant that non-compliance with the dress requirements of her profession would have prevented the taxpayer from earning her living, since other professional people also faced various sanctions, albeit less damaging, if they did not conform to the dress code of their particular profession and the right of deduction should not depend on the degree of the sanction, and moreover s 130(*a*) of the Act was not concerned with the necessity of *e* the expenditure. Furthermore, there was no distinction between a barrister, whether male or female, and any other self-employed person when determining the right to claim a deduction under s 130 of the 1970 Act for expenditure on the maintenance of a complete wardrobe of clothing used only at work or for travel to and from work. The appeal would therefore be allowed (see p 1097 *e*, p 1098 *e*, p 1102 *h* to p 1103 *c* and *f* to *h* and p 1104 *a* to *h*, post). *f*

Dicta of Lord Davey in *Strong & Co of Romsey Ltd v Woodifield (Surveyor of Taxes)* [1904–7] All ER Rep at 956, of Lord Greene MR in *Norman v Golder (Inspector of Taxes)* [1945] 1 All ER at 354, of Lord Morton and Lord Reid in *Morgan (Inspector of Taxes) v Tate & Lyle Ltd* [1954] 2 All ER at 416, 423, and *Prince v Mapp (Inspector of Taxes)* [1970] 1 All ER 519 and *Hillyer v Leeke (Inspector of Taxes)* [1976] STC 490 applied.

Decision of the Court of Appeal [1983] 1 All ER 801 reversed. *g*

Notes

For deduction of expenditure laid out wholly and exclusively for the purposes of a trade or profession, see 23 Halsbury's Laws (4th edn) paras 295, 305–306, and for cases on the subject, see 28(1) Digest (Reissue) 141–158, *421–505*.

For the Income and Corporation Taxes Act 1970, s 130, see 33 Halsbury's Statutes (3rd *h* edn) 182.

Cases referred to in opinions

Bentleys Stokes & Lowless v Beeson (Inspector of Taxes) [1952] 2 All ER 82, CA.

Caillebotte (Inspector of Taxes) v Quinn [1975] 2 All ER 412, [1975] 1 WLR 731.

Hillyer v Leeke (Inspector of Taxes) [1976] STC 490. *j*

Morgan (Inspector of Taxes) v Tate & Lyle Ltd [1954] 2 All ER 413, [1955] AC 21, [1954] 3 WLR 85, HL.

Norman v Golder (Inspector of Taxes) [1954] 1 All ER 352, CA.

Prince v Mapp (Inspector of Taxes) [1970] 1 All ER 519, [1970] 1 WLR 260.

Robinson (Inspector of Taxes) v Scott Bader Co Ltd [1981] 2 All ER 1116, [1981] 1 WLR 1135, CA; *affg* [1980] 2 All ER 780, [1980] 1 WLR 755.

Strong & Co of Romsey Ltd v Woodifield (Surveyor of Taxes) [1906] AC 448, [1904–7] All ER
a Rep 953, HL.

Appeal

The Crown appealed against the judgment of the Court of Appeal (Sir John Donaldson MR, Kerr LJ and Sir Sebag Shaw) ([1983] 1 All ER 801, [1983] 1 WLR 252) dated 14 December 1982 affirming the decision of Slade J ([1981] STC 391) given on 12 March
b 1981 whereby he allowed an appeal by way of case stated (set out at [1981] STC 392–397) by Ann Mallalieu (the taxpayer) against the determination of the Commissioners for the General Purposes of the Income Tax for the Division of the Middle Temple in the City of London dismissing the taxpayer's appeal against an assessment made on her under Case II of Sch D for the year of assessment 1977–78 in respect of her claim to be entitled to deduct in computing the profits of her profession as a barrister the sum of £564·38
c expended on the replacement, cleaning and laundering of certain items of clothing used by her for the purposes of her profession. The facts are set out in the opinion of Lord Brightman.

Andrew Park QC and *David C Milne* for the taxpayer.
Peter Millett QC, Robert Carnwath and *Michael Hart* for the Crown.

d

Their Lordships took time for consideration.

27 July. The following opinions were delivered.

LORD DIPLOCK. My Lords, I have had the advantage of reading in draft the speech
e of my noble and learned friend Lord Brightman. I agree with it, and for the reasons he gives I would allow this appeal.

LORD ELWYN-JONES. My Lords, the issue in this appeal is whether the disbursements of the appellant taxpayer in the relevant years on replacements, laundering
f and cleaning the clothes she wore during the practice of her profession of barrister were 'wholly and exclusively laid out or expended for the purposes of her profession': see s 130 of the Income and Corporation Taxes Act 1970.

As stated in para 4 of the case stated, the General Commissioners found, after hearing oral testimony from the appellant which their findings indicate they accepted, that: (1) the appellant would not have incurred any of the expenditure on the items of clothing
g in question had it not been for the requirement of her profession that she should comply when appearing in court with the notes for guidance of the Bar Council (which are quoted in the speech of my noble and learned friend Lord Brightman); (2) at all material times she had a private wardrobe of clothes and shoes which were amply sufficient to keep her clothed and shod in comfort and decency; (3) the preservation of warmth and decency was not a consideration which crossed her mind when she bought the disputed
h items; (4) she bought the items only because she would not have been permitted to appear in court if she did not wear them when in court, or other clothes like them.

It was common ground that the relevant time for determining what were the taxpayer's purposes and what was in her mind when the expenditure was incurred was at the moment the expenditure was made.

The General Commissioners did look into the taxpayer's mind (as far as humans can
j look into the minds of others) and found that 'when [the taxpayer] laid out money on clothes for wearing in court her purpose in making that expenditure was to enable her to earn profits in her profession and also to enable her to be properly clothed during the time she was on her way to chambers or to court and while she was thereafter engaged in her professional activity' (see [1981] STC 391 at 396). This apparently is in fact what she said and their findings of fact indicate that they believed her.

The test as to why the expenditure was incurred is subjective. As Romer LJ stated in

Bentleys Stokes & Lowless v Beeson (Inspector of Taxes) [1952] 2 All ER 82 at 84: 'The sole question is . . . what was the motive or object in the mind of the [individual] . . . in a
question.'

This proposition was affirmed by Walton J in *Robinson (Inspector of Taxes) v Scott Bader Co Ltd* [1980] 2 All ER 780, [1980] 1 WLR 755 and by the Court of Appeal ([1981] 2 All ER 1116, [1981] 1 WLR 1135).

Applying that test I respectfully agree with the conclusions of Slade J and the Court of Appeal that the commissioners' findings of fact in this case led inevitably to the conclusion b
that the taxpayer's expenditure was expended wholly and exclusively for the purposes of her profession.

It was in my view not open to the commissioners in view of their findings of fact as to the appellant's purposes to conclude that as in this case the clothing was suitable for private as well as for professional use, one of her purposes must have been to spend money on the clothing for her private use. This in my view was to disregard the evidence c
which they accepted as to her actual motive and purpose. This they have found was to enable her to carry on her profession. Other benefits derived from the expenditure, namely that the clothing also provided her with warmth and decency, were purely incidental to the carrying on of her profession in the compulsory clothing she had to wear.

I am naturally diffident in disagreeing with my noble and learned brethren but I find d
the conclusions arrived at by Slade J and the Court of Appeal inescapable in view of the commissioners' findings of the primary facts in this case. I would dismiss the appeal.

LORD KEITH OF KINKEL. My Lords, for the reasons given in the speech to be delivered by my noble and learned friend Lord Brightman, which I have had the opportunity of reading in draft and with which I agree, I too would allow the appeal. e

LORD ROSKILL. My Lords, I have had the advantage of reading in draft the speech to be delivered by my noble and learned friend Lord Brightman. For the reasons he gives I too would allow this appeal.

LORD BRIGHTMAN. My Lords, the immediate issue in this appeal concerns the f
right of a female barrister, in computing the profits of her profession, to deduct the cost of upkeep of a wardrobe of clothes of a design and colour suitable to be worn under her gown during court appearances. But during the course of the argument this issue was found to resolve itself into a far more general and fundamental question: whether any person carrying on a trade, profession or vocation on his own account is entitled to a similar deduction if he chooses to set apart clothes, underclothes and footwear for use g
only at his place of work, and when proceeding to and from his place of work.

The taxpayer is a member of the junior Bar with a busy court practice. When appearing in open court she is obliged, with a few exceptions, to wear a gown over her ordinary clothing, and a wig. When not in open court but in the chambers of a judge, master or registrar, she would (or could) appear in her ordinary clothes without wig or gown. What sort of clothes a barrister should wear in court (I include chambers) is a matter of good h
taste and common sense, the criterion being that they should be appropriate to the dignity of the occasion. However in recent years some brief rules have been laid down or authoritative guidance given as to what is the appropriate clothing to be worn by barristers appearing in court. So far as I am aware no official guidance was ever thought necessary until about 60 years ago. A barrister conformed as a matter of course to the sartorial standards of his colleagues. By 1922 the ranks of the Bar began to be enriched j
by the entry of women barristers, who had no precedents or comparisons to draw on. Rules were accordingly issued by the Lord Chief Justice, and amended in 1968. The 1968 rules have now been replaced by brief notes for guidance on dress in court, which apply to barristers of both sexes. These notes were formally approved by the Bar Council and received the assent of the Lord Chief Justice. The notes for the most part reflect the

requirements of common sense. They are short, and so far as relevant for present purposes provide as follows:

> '1. The dress of barrister appearing in court should be unobtrusive and compatible with the wearing of robes. 2. Suits and dresses should be of dark colour. Dresses or blouses should be long-sleeved and high to the neck . . . Shirts and blouses should be predominantly white or of other unemphatic appearance. Collars should be white and shoes black.'

There are no other rules relating to the clothes to be worn by a female barrister under her court gown.

The taxpayer bought clothes in conformity with those requirements. The initial cost of purchase was a capital expense, and therefore not material for present purposes. However, she needed to clean and renew them from time to time and in the accounting period for the 1977–78 year of assessment she spent some £500 on replacements, laundering and cleaning. This sum is claimed as a deduction in computing the profits of her practice chargeable under Sch D. To qualify as a deduction, the expenditure must fall outside the prohibition contained in s 130 of the Income and Corporation Taxes Act 1970. The relevant paragraph of the section is para (*a*) but para (*b*) should perhaps be read with it as it was referred to in argument:

> '130. Subject to the provisions of the Tax Acts, in computing the amount of the profits or gains to be charged under Case I or Case II of Schedule D, no sum shall be deducted in respect of (*a*) any disbursements or expenses, not being money wholly and exclusively laid out or expended for the purposes of the trade, profession or vocation, (*b*) any disbursements or expenses of maintenance of the parties, their families or establishments, or any sums expended for any other domestic or private purposes distinct from the purposes of the trade, profession or vocation . . .'

The effect of para (*a*) is to exclude, as a deduction, the money spent by the taxpayer unless she can establish that such money was spent exclusively for the purposes of her profession. The words in the paragraph 'expended *for the purposes* of the trade, profession or vocation' mean in my opinion 'expended *to serve the purposes* of the trade, profession or vocation', or as elaborated by Lord Davey in *Strong & Co of Romsey Ltd v Woodifield (Surveyor of Taxes)* [1906] AC 448 at 453, [1904–7] All ER Rep 953 at 956 'for the purpose of enabling a person to carry on and earn profits in the trade, &c.' The particular words emphasised do not refer to 'the purposes' of the taxpayer as some of the cases appear to suggest. They refer to 'the purposes' of the business which is a different concept although the 'purposes' (ie the intentions or objects) of the taxpayer are fundamental to the application of the paragraph.

The effect of the word 'exclusively' is to preclude a deduction if it appears that the expenditure was not only to serve the purposes of the trade, profession or vocation of the taxpayer but also to serve some other purposes. Such other purposes, if found to exist, will usually be the private purposes of the taxpayer: see for example *Prince v Mapp (Inspector of Taxes)* [1970] 1 All ER 519, [1970] 1 WLR 260.

To ascertain whether the money was expended to serve the purposes of the taxpayer's business it is necessary to discover the taxpayer's 'object' in making the expenditure: see *Morgan (Inspector of Taxes) v Tate & Lyle Ltd* [1954] 2 All ER 413 at 416, 423, [1955] AC 21 at 37, 47. As the taxpayer's 'object' in making the expenditure has to be found, it inevitably follows that (save in obvious cases which speak for themselves) the General Commissioners need to look into the taxpayer's mind at the moment when the expenditure is made. After events are irrelevant to the application of s 130 except as a reflection of the taxpayer's state of mind at the time of the expenditure.

If it appears that the object of the taxpayer at the time of the expenditure was to serve two purposes, the purposes of his business and other purposes, it is immaterial to the application of s 130(*a*) that the business purposes are the predominant purposes intended to be served.

The object of the taxpayer in making the expenditure must be distinguished from the effect of the expenditure. An expenditure may be made exclusively to serve the purposes *a* of the business, but it may have a private advantage. The existence of that private advantage does not necessarily preclude the exclusivity of the business purposes. For example a medical consultant has a friend in the South of France who is also his patient. He flies to the South of France for a week, staying in the home of his friend and attending professionally on him. He seeks to recover the cost of his air fare. The question of fact will be whether the journey was undertaken solely to serve the purposes of the medical *b* practice. This will be judged in the light of the taxpayer's object in making the journey. The question will be answered by considering whether the stay in the South of France was *a* reason, however subordinate, for undertaking the journey, or was not a reason but only the effect. If a week's stay on the Riviera was not an object of the consultant, if the consultant's only object was to attend on his patient, his stay on the Riviera was an unavoidable effect of the expenditure on the journey and the expenditure lies outside the *c* prohibition in s 130.

There is no dispute between the parties as to the true meaning of s 130(*a*), and it is common ground that the principles which I have outlined are those which fall to be applied. The appeal before your Lordships is basically concerned with the distinction between object and effect. The inspector of taxes disallowed the deduction claimed by the taxpayer, with the result that she appealed to the General Commissioners against the *d* assessment made on her. The General Commissioners, who had themselves been in practice at the Bar, confirmed the assessment subject to a small adjustment on which there was agreement. The taxpayer successfully appealed to the High Court, and the decision of the Chancery judge was upheld on appeal. The inspector of taxes now appeals to this House with the leave of your Lordships.

The primary facts found by the General Commissioners are contained in para 4 of the *e* printed case and para 8 of the decision (see [1981] STC 371 at 392–395). The clothes which the taxpayer maintained for professional purposes were, broadly speaking, worn by her only in connection with her work. That is to say, she travelled in them to her chambers or directly to court, wore them throughout the day and changed out of them when she arrived home at the end of her working day. There were odd occasions on which the taxpayer might find it convenient to remain in her working clothes after her *f* work was done. But no point is taken by the Revenue in relation to such occasions nor is any point taken that the clothes were worn not only at work but also when travelling to and from work.

The critical findings of fact as set out in paras 4 and 8 of the case are these ([1981] STC 391 at 393, 395):

> '4 . . . (c) The rules for guidance are . . . normally complied with and it would be *g* virtually impossible for a lady barrister to practice unless she complied with the rules laid down . . . (f) At all material times the taxpayer had a private wardrobe of clothes and shoes which was amply sufficient to keep her clothed and shod in comfort and decency, without having to resort to any of the disputed items. She would not have purchased any of the disputed items had it not been for the *h* requirement of her profession that she should comply with the notes for guidance when appearing in court . . . (j) . . . She bought such items only because she would not have been permitted to appear in court if she did not wear, when in court, them or other clothes like them. Similarly the preservation of warmth and decency was not a consideration which crossed her mind when she bought the disputed items. (k) The white blouses and black clothing bought by the taxpayer were items of *j* ordinary civilian clothing readily available for purchase by anyone at many clothing stores . . .
>
> 8. We consider that the evidence shows that when she bought the clothes she bought them to wear in court and that she would not have bought them but for the exigencies of her profession . . .'

In addition there are certain statements in a proof of evidence of a senior executive of Marks and Spencer Ltd. These were accepted by the taxpayer as accurate statements of fact. They are summarised in the commissioners' decision in the following terms:

> '(i) that it is important for a major retail outlet to design garments likely to have a broad popular appeal, (ii) that the colours in which garments are produced must necessarily be what are called "safe" colours, including black, (iii) that a black velvet jacket is a perennial favourite, and (iv) that black clothing is always acceptable whether it is a fashion colour or not and always represents a proportion (which he put at over 10%) of sales in ladies' outerwear.'

I refer to this evidence only to emphasise the point that the clothing in question consists of perfectly ordinary articles of apparel which many ladies wear from choice. On the basis of those findings of fact the commissioners had to draw an inference and decide whether or not the taxpayer had expended money on her professional wardrobe exclusively to serve the purposes of her business, or alternatively to serve both purposes of her business and her own private purposes. The inference drawn by the commissioners and the determination reached by them are contained in the second part of para 9 of their written decision, which reads as follows ([1981] STC 391 at 395):

> 'We consider, in the present case, that when [the taxpayer] laid out money on clothes for wearing in court her purpose in making that expenditure was to enable her to earn profits in her profession and also to enable her to be properly clothed during the time she was on her way to chambers or to court and while she was thereafter engaged in her professional activity, and in the other circumstances indicated in para 2. We do not consider that the fact that her sole motive in choosing the particular clothes was to satisfy the requirements of her profession or that if she had been free to do so she would have worn clothes of a different style on such occasions altered the purpose of the expenditure which remained the purpose of purchasing clothes that would keep her warm and clad during the part of the day when she was pursuing her career as well as the purpose of helping her to earn profits in that career. We think, therefore, that the expenditure had a dual purpose, one professional and one non-professional . . .'

The commissioners accordingly concluded that the taxpayer had two objects in making the expenditure, to serve the purposes of her business, and to serve her own purposes by enabling her properly to be clothed. Since there is no appeal from the commissioners on a question of fact, the only question before your Lordships is whether the findings of primary fact were such as to entitle them to draw that inference.

It is, I think, clear that Slade J was, to use his own words, 'driven to the conclusion that the relevant expenditure in the present case was incurred by her solely for the purpose of carrying on her profession' because he took the view that the so-called subjective approach to the application of s 130(*a*) led inexorably to the conclusion that the conscious objects or reasons of the taxpayer making the expenditure were decisive. (See [1981] STC 391 at 406.) All that mattered was what was actually in her conscious mind when the expenditure was made:

> '. . . it is common ground that, in determining whether these expenses have been wholly and exclusively laid out or expended for the purpose of [the taxpayer's] profession of a barrister, it is necessary to ascertain what purpose or purposes was or were *in her mind* at the date when they were incurred . . . The ultimate question for my decision here will, I think, be whether, having regard to their primary findings of fact as set out in para 4 of the case stated, there was evidence to support the inference ultimately drawn by the commissioners that the expenditure was incurred by the taxpayer with dual purposes *in mind*' (My emphasis.)

(See [1981] STC 391 at 399, 400.)

As the taxpayer according to the undisputed evidence had nothing in her mind except
the etiquette of her profession on the several occasions when she spent money on the
upkeep of her wardrobe of working clothes, and 'had no thought of warmth and decency', *a*
it inevitably followed that the money was spent exclusively to serve the purposes of her
business. The provision of clothing as such, it was held, was nothing more than an
incidental, although no doubt welcome, effect of her one and only object. The approach
of the Court of Appeal was similar. After summarising the General Commissioners'
findings of fact, Sir John Donaldson MR continued ([1983] 1 All ER 801 at 806, [1983] 1
WLR 252 at 258): *b*

> 'From those findings of fact there is in my judgment only one reasonable
> conclusion to be drawn, namely that the taxpayer's sole purpose in incurring the
> expenditure was a professional purpose, any other benefit being purely incidental.'

Kerr LJ reasoned along the same lines ([1983] 1 All ER 801 at 808, [1983] 1 WLR 252 at
261): *c*

> 'In the present case, as it seems to me, the primary findings of fact are wholly
> exceptional in the sense that they are conclusive in the taxpayer's favour. In
> particular, para 4(f) and (j) of the case stated and para 8 of the decision (see [1981]
> STC 391 at 393, 395) contain unqualified findings to the effect that the taxpayer's
> sole purpose in incurring the expenditure for the clothes in question was that she *d*
> had to have them in order to exercise her profession and that she had no need for
> them, nor any other purpose, when she acquired them . . . By these findings they
> have, in effect, stated themselves out of court so far as any ultimate conclusion to
> the contrary is concerned. All that remains can only be incidental effect; there is no
> room for a conclusion that there was a dual purpose.'

e

The brief judgment of the late Sir Sebag Shaw was to the same effect.

I think, with respect, that Kerr LJ's paraphrase of paras 4(f) and (j) and 8 goes further
than the findings warrant. The sense of the General Commissioners' findings of fact is
that the taxpayer did not have any object *in her mind*, that is to say, any *conscious* motive,
when she incurred the expenditure, except that she needed the clothes in order to exercise
her profession. *f*

Before I seek to examine the conclusions reached by the High Court and the Court of
Appeal, I return to my opening observations that the issue involved in this appeal has
inevitably opened up a far wider and more fundamental point, namely the right of any
self-employed person to maintain, at the expense of his gross income and therefore partly
at the expense of the general body of taxpayers, a wardrobe of everyday clothes which are
reserved for work. I find myself at odds with Slade J when he says 'I accordingly *g*
emphasise that this is a decision on the particular facts of the present case' a remark
which, though accurate, implies that there is something exceptional about the case (see
[1981] STC 391 at 407). In the first place, counsel for the taxpayer disclaimed any reliance
on the fact that his client disliked dark clothing, never purchased it for private use, and
therefore was not in a position to resort to her private wardrobe to answer the
requirements of her profession. This disclaimer was rightly made. It would be absurd to *h*
suppose that there exists one law for the blonde barrister who lacks a wardrobe of dark
clothes, and another law for the brunette barrister whose wardrobe of everyday clothes
contains many dresses suitable for court appearances. It therefore inevitably followed, as
counsel conceded, that the taxpayer was arguing that if a barrister, male or female, chose
to establish a wardrobe of clothes exclusively for working purposes, he or she would be
entitled to deduct the cost of its upkeep. The question then arose whether this beneficent *j*
state of affairs would apply to other professional persons, such as solicitors, accountants,
medical practitioners, trades people and persons in all other walks of self-employed life,
and if not why not. The only distinction that could be drawn was that a barrister who
wore unacceptable clothes would find himself barred from pleading in court, as well as
risking the loss of the goodwill of his clients, while other professional persons might be
subject only to the latter sanction. It did not seem logical that the right of deduction

should depend on the degree of the sanction which induced the professional person to
a equip himself with subdued clothing. Furthermore, 'necessity' is not part of the formula
in s 130(*a*), and therefore the existence of a sanction was wholly immaterial. So there was
no reason for concluding that the tradesman would be debarred from maintaining his
own wardrobe of clothes for working days if the taxpayer's argument were correct.
Finally, there could be no distinction between top clothes and underclothes and other
articles of wearing apparel. The position was ultimately reached that there was no
b distinction to be drawn between the position of male and female barristers, or between
the position of barristers and practitioners of every other trade, profession and vocation,
or between top clothes, underwear and footwear. So, at the end of the day, if the
argument for the taxpayer is right, it will be open to every self-employed person to set
against his gross income the cost of the upkeep of a complete wardrobe of clothes, so long
as he reserves such clothes strictly for use only at work, or when proceeding to and from
c his work. Counsel for the taxpayer did not shrink from this conclusion. I mention this
wider aspect of the problem only to emphasise once again that there is nothing
exceptional about the facts of this case.

I return to the question for your Lordships' decision whether there was evidence which
entitled the commissioners to reach the conclusion that the object of the taxpayer in
spending this money was exclusively to serve the purposes of her profession, or was also
d to serve her private purposes of providing apparel with which to clothe herself. Slade J
felt driven to answer the question in favour of the taxpayer because he felt constrained
by the commissioners' finding that, in effect, the only object present in the mind of the
taxpayer was the requirements of her profession. The conscious motive of the taxpayer
was decisive. The reasoning of the Court of Appeal was the same. What was present in
the taxpayer's mind at the time of the expenditure concluded the case.

e My Lords, I find myself totally unable to accept this narrow approach. Of course the
taxpayer thought only of the requirements of her profession when she first bought (as a
capital expense) her wardrobe of subdued clothing and, no doubt, as and when she
replaced items or sent them to the launderers or the cleaners she would, if asked, have
repeated that she was maintaining her wardrobe because of those requirements. It is the
natural way that anyone incurring such expenditure would think and speak. But she
f needed clothes to travel to work and clothes to wear at work, and I think it is inescapable
that one object, though not a conscious motive, was the provision of the clothing that she
needed as a human being. I reject the notion that the object of a taxpayer is inevitably
limited to the particular conscious motive in mind at the moment of expenditure. Of
course the motive of which the taxpayer is conscious is of a vital significance, but it is not
inevitably the only object which the commissioners are entitled to find to exist. In my
g opinion the commissioners were not only entitled to reach the conclusion that the
taxpayer's object was both to serve the purposes of her profession and also to serve her
personal purposes, but I myself would have found it impossible to reach any other
conclusion.

It was inevitable in this sort of case that analogies would be canvassed; for example,
the self-employed nurse who equips herself with what is conveniently called a nurse's
h uniform. Such cases are matters of fact and degree. In the case of the nurse, I am disposed
to think without inviting your Lordships to decide, that the material and design of the
uniform may be dictated by the practical requirements of the art of nursing and the
maintenance of hygiene. There may be other cases where it is essential that the self-
employed person should provide himself with and maintain a particular design of
clothing in order to obtain any engagements at all in the business that he conducts. An
j example is the self-employed waiter, mentioned by Kerr LJ, who needs to wear 'tails'. In
his case the 'tails' are an essential part of the equipment of his trade, and it clearly would
be open to the commissioners to allow the expense of their upkeep on the basis that the
money was spent exclusively to serve the purposes of the business. I do not think that
the decision which I urge on your Lordships should raise any problems in the 'uniform'
type of case that was so much discussed in argument. As I have said, it is a matter of
degree.

The case before your Lordships is indistinguishable in principle from *Hillyer v Leeke (Inspector of Taxes)* [1976] STC 490. That case arose under Sch E, but the ratio of the first ground of decision is equally applicable to Sch D. The taxpayer was a computer engineer. His work involved travelling to the establishments of his firm's customers. His employers required him to wear a suit. When present on a customer's premises he might be called on to assist the customer's engineer at short notice without an opportunity to change into overalls or a boiler suit. The taxpayer therefore maintained two working suits which he wore only for the purposes of his work. He claimed a deduction of £50 for their upkeep. This was disallowed by the inspector. The commissioners confirmed the assessment. I read the following passages from the judgment of Goulding J which seem to me to be correct and in point ([1976] STC 490 at 492–493):

> 'The truth is that the employee has to wear something, and the nature of his job dictates what that something will be. It cannot be said that the expense of his clothing is wholly or exclusively incurred in the performance of the duties of the employment ... In the case of clothing, the individual is wearing clothing for his own purposes of cover and comfort concurrently with wearing it in order to have the appearance which the job requires ... Does it make any difference if the taxpayer chooses, as apparently the taxpayer did, to keep a suit or suits exclusively for wear when he is at work? Is it possible to say, as Templeman J said about protective clothing in the case of *Caillebotte (Inspector of Taxes) v Quinn* [1975] 2 All ER 412, [1975] 1 WLR 731 that the cost of the clothing is deductible because warmth and decency are merely incidental to what is necessary for the carrying on of the occupation? That, of course, was a Sch D and not a Sch E case, but the problem arises in a similar way. The answer that the Crown makes is that where the clothing worn is not of a special character dictated by the occupation as a matter of physical necessity but is ordinary civilian clothing of a standard required for the occupation, you cannot say that the one purpose is merely incidental to the other. Reference is made to what Lord Greene MR said in *Norman v Golder (Inspector of Taxes)* [1945] 1 All ER 352 at 354. That was another case under Sch D, but again, in my judgment, applicable to Sch E cases, where Lord Greene MR said, referring to the food you eat and the clothes that you wear: "But expenses of that kind are not wholly and exclusively laid out for the purposes of the trade, profession or vocation. They are laid out in part for the advantage and benefit of the taxpayer as a living human being." In my judgment, that argument is conclusive of the present case, and the expenditure in question, although on suits that were only worn while at work, had two purposes inextricably intermingled and not severable by any apportionment that the court could undertake.'

The judge then founded on a second argument turning on the word 'necessarily', to which I need not refer as that requirement only exists in the case of a Sch E computation.

I find myself in complete agreement with Goulding J and I regard his observations as appropriate in their entirety to the case before your Lordships.

So, my Lords, I respectfully differ from the conclusion reached by Slade J and by the members of the Court of Appeal. I would allow this appeal.

Appeal allowed.

Solicitors: *Solicitor of Inland Revenue*; *Penningtons* (for the taxpayer).

Mary Rose Plummer Barrister.

Young v Secretary of State for the Environment and another

HOUSE OF LORDS

LORD FRASER OF TULLYBELTON, LORD ELWYN-JONES, LORD LOWRY, LORD ROSKILL AND LORD BRIGHTMAN

5, 6, 27 JULY 1983

Town and country planning – Enforcement notice – Effect – Reversion to earlier lawful use – Purpose for which land may be used without planning permission – Purpose for which land could lawfully have been used if development enforced against had not been carried out – Use immediately preceding that enforced against unlawful – Whether person on whom enforcement notice served can follow planning history back to earlier lawful uses in order to revert to use which land lawfully used – Whether person on whom enforcement notice served only able to revert to use immediately preceding that enforced against provided that use was lawful – Town and Country Planning Act 1971, s 23(9).

From 1912 until 1969 a large building was used as a laundry, the use being that of a general industrial building within class IV of the Schedule to the Town and Country Planning (Use Classes) Order 1972. In 1969 there was a change of use when the building was used for food processing, the use being that of a light industrial building within class III of the Schedule. Although the change from use as a general to a light industrial building was a material change of use, it was a change which was permitted without the need for specific planning permission and accordingly the change of use was a permitted development and the use for food processing a lawful use. In 1970 there was a change of use back to use as a laundry for which planning permission ought to have been obtained but was not, and therefore the change from food processing (light industrial) to laundry (general industrial) was not lawful. From 1977 the building was used by the appellant for his business as an insulating contractor, that use being use as a light industrial building, but that was not a lawful use because the immediately preceding use as a laundry had been unlawful and any change from it required planning permission. The appellant failed to seek or obtain planning permission for the change in 1977 and in 1980 an enforcement notice was issued by the local planning authority, in pursuance of their powers under the Town and Country Planning Act 1971, alleging that there had been a breach of planning control in that the land had been developed by making a material change of use without the grant of planning permission. The appellant appealed to the Secretary of State denying that there had been any breach of planning control. A public inquiry was held and the appeal was dismissed. The appellant appealed to the High Court against the decision of the Secretary of State but his appeal was dismissed. He further appealed to the Court of Appeal who also dismissed the appeal. The appellant then appealed to the House of Lords, contending that by virtue of s 23(9)[a] of the 1971 Act, which provided that where an enforcement notice had been served in respect of any development 'planning permission was not required for the use of the land for the purpose for which ... it could lawfully have been used if that development had not been carried out', he was entitled to revert to the use to which the land was last lawfully put, namely as a light industrial building (when it was used for food processing). The Secretary of State contended that under the provisions of s 23(9) the only use following the enforcement notice that could be made of the land without obtaining fresh planning permission was use for the purpose for which it could have been used immediately before the use struck at by the enforcement notice, i e as a laundry, provided that that use was itself lawful, which on the facts it was not.

---

a Section 23(9) is set out at p 1107 *b*, post

Held – On the true construction of s 23(9) of the 1971 Act a person on whom an enforcement notice had been served alleging a breach of planning permission by making a a material change in the use of the land, could revert to the use immediately preceding that enforced against, provided that use was lawful, but could not follow the planning history back through its earlier uses in order to revert to the use for which the land was last lawfully used. When the land was being used as a laundry during the period 1970 to 1977 any change of use back to use for food processing would have required planning permission, because although it would have been a change from general to light industrial b use, which would not otherwise have required planning permission, the general industrial use on which such a change would have been based was itself unlawful. It followed that the appellant could not revert to light industrial use after a further unlawful change of use in 1977 and accordingly he was not entitled to go back beyond the immediately preceding use in order to rely on a previous lawful use. Furthermore, the provisions of s 23(9) were not ambiguous and their meaning was not to be distorted in c order to mitigate any element of hardship. The appeal would accordingly be dismissed (see p 1108 *j* to p 1109 *g* and *j* to p 1110 *h*, post).

Dictum of Cairns LJ in *LTSS Print and Supply Services Ltd v Hackney BC* [1976] 1 All ER at 317 approved.

Notes d

For development for which planning permission is required, see 37 Halsbury's Laws (3rd edn) 269–272, para 370, and for cases on the subject, see 45 Digest (Repl) 335–340, *33–55*.

For the Town and Country Planning Act 1971, s 23, see 41 Halsbury's Statutes (3rd edn) 1608.

For the Town and Country Planning (Use Classes) Order 1972, SI 1972/1385, see 21 e Halsbury's Statutory Instruments (3rd reissue) 111.

For the Town and Country Planning General Development Order 1977, SI 1977/289, art 3, Sch 1, see ibid 197, 219.

Cases referred to in opinions

Balco Transport Services Ltd v Secretary of State for the Environment (1981) 45 P & CR 216. f
Blenkinsopp v Secretary of State for the Environment (unreported) 28 January 1983.
LTSS Print and Supply Services Ltd v Hackney BC [1976] 1 All ER 311, [1976] QB 663, [1976] 2 WLR 253, CA.

Appeal

By an enforcement notice dated 11 February 1980, the London Borough of Bexley, the g second respondents, required the appellant, John Anthony Young, to cease to use the premises at 24/25 Woodside Crescent, Sidcup, Kent, for the purpose of carrying out a business of an insulating contractor, on the ground that there had been a breach of planning control by the making of a material change in the use of the premises without the grant of planning permission. The appellant appealed to the Secretary of State for the Environment, the first respondents, and following a public inquiry the appeal was h dismissed on 21 November 1980. By a notice of motion dated 10 December 1980 the appellant appealed to the High Court and on 7 April 1982 Forbes J dismissed the appellant's appeal. The appellant appealed to the Court of Appeal and on 7 February 1983 the Court of Appeal (Lord Lane CJ, Watkins LJ and Sir Roger Ormrod) dismissed the appeal. The appellant then appealed with leave of the Appeal Committee of the House of Lords granted on 5 May 1983 from the order of the Court of Appeal. The facts are set j out in the opinion of Lord Fraser.

Nigel MacLeod QC and *Stephen Bickford-Smith* for the appellant.
Simon D Brown and *Andrew Collins* for the first respondents.
The second respondents were not represented.

Their Lordships took time for consideration.

a 27 July. The following opinions were delivered.

LORD FRASER OF TULLYBELTON. My Lords, this appeal raises a question of construction of s 23(9) of the Town and Country Planning Act 1971. That subsection provides:

b '(9) Where an enforcement notice has been served in respect of any development of land, planning permission is not required for the use of the land for the purpose for which (in accordance with the provisions of this Part of this Act) it could lawfully have been used if that development had not been carried out.'

The issue raised in the appeal is whether s 23(9) enables a person, on whom an c enforcement notice has been served alleging a breach of planning control by making a material change in the use of land, to revert to the use to which the land was last lawfully put, or only to revert to the use immediately preceding that enforced against, provided that such use was itself lawful. The appellant contends for the former alternative, the first respondent for the latter. The first respondent was the only respondent who was represented before this House, and I shall refer to him hereafter as 'the respondent'.

d Part III of the 1971 Act, which includes s 23, deals with general planning control. It provides by s 22(1) that 'development' of land means the making of any material change in the use of any buildings or other land. That general rule is qualified by sub-s (2) of s 22 which provides that a change from one use to another use in the same class, as defined in an Order by the Secretary of State, shall not be taken for the purposes of the Act to involve development. Section 23 provides that any development of land, with certain e specified exceptions, requires planning permission. Section 23 so far as relevant to this appeal provides as follows:

'23(1) Subject to the provisions of this section, planning permission is required for the carrying out of any development of land.

(2) Where on 1st July 1948 (in this Act referred to as "the appointed day") land was being temporarily used for a purpose other than the purpose for which it was f normally used, planning permission is not required for the resumption of the use of the land for the last-mentioned purposes before 6th December 1968 . . .

(5) Where planning permission to develop land has been granted for a limited period, planning permission is not required for the resumption, at the end of that period, of the use of the land for the purpose for which it was normally used before the permission was granted.

g (6) In determining, for the purposes of subsection (5) of this section, what were the purposes for which land was normally used before the grant of planning permission, no account shall be taken of any use of the land begun in contravention of the provisions of this Part of this Act or in contravention of previous planning control . . .'

h On 11 February 1980 an enforcement notice was issued by the second respondents to the appellant in respect of development of land at Woodside Crescent, Sidcup, Kent. The land in question consists of a large building, which is used by the appellant to process, store and distribute insulating materials. It is surrounded by a residential area. The enforcement notice was issued by the respondents in pursuance of their powers under s 87(1) of the 1971 Act. It alleged that there had been a breach of planning control in that j the land had been developed by the making of a material change of use without the grant of planning permission which was required. The appellant appealed to the Secretary of State, under s 88(1) of the Act, denying that there had been any breach of planning control. A public inquiry was held and on 21 November 1980 the appellant's appeal to the Secretary of State was dismissed (subject to a slight extension of the time allowed by the enforcement notice for ceasing to use the land and removing his materials from it).

Section 88(7) provides that when such an appeal is brought the appellant is deemed to have applied for planning permission for the development to which the notice relates. *a*
This deemed application was refused.

The appellant appealed to the High Court under s 246(1) of the Act, and on 7 April 1982 his appeal was dismissed by Forbes J. On 2 February 1983 the Court of Appeal (Lord Lane CJ, Watkins LJ and Sir Roger Ormrod) dismissed the appellant's appeal and affirmed the judgment of Forbes J.

Before your Lordships' House, counsel for the appellant accepted that the enforcement *b*
notice was valid and well founded in fact. His argument was confined to the question of its effect, under s 23(9), on the footing that it was valid. In order to appreciate the contentions of the parties it is necessary to refer to the planning history of the land. It was as follows.

(a) From 1912 until 1969 the building was used as a laundry. This was use as a general industrial building within class IV of the Schedule to the Town and Country Planning *c*
(Use Classes) Order 1972 SI 1972/1385 (the Use Classes Order 1972).

(b) In 1969 there was a change of use to use for food processing. This was use as a light industrial building within class III of the Schedule to the Use Classes Order 1972. The change from use as a general to use as a light industrial building was a material change of use, but it was a change which was permitted without the need for specific permission from the local planning authority or the Secretary of State: see art 3(1) of the Town and *d*
Country Planning General Development Order 1977 SI 1977/289, and Sch 1, Class III. Planning permission for such a change is given by the order. Accordingly the change of use in 1969 was permitted development and the use for food processing was a lawful use.

(c) In 1970 there was a change of use back to use as a laundry. This change from food processing (light industrial) to laundry (general industrial) was not lawful because planning permission ought to have been obtained for it but was not. Accordingly the use *e*
as a laundry from 1970 onwards was not a lawful use of the building.

(d) Since 1977 the building has been used by the appellant for his business as an insulating contractor, mainly for storing and processing materials. This is use as a light industrial building but it is not a lawful use because the immediately preceding use as a laundry having been unlawful, any change from it required planning permission. But planning permission was not sought or obtained for the change of use in 1977. This *f*
change of use was the development in respect of which the enforcement notice was issued.

It is apparent from that history that the purpose for which the land was last lawfully used before the use struck at by the enforcement notice was for food processing (light industrial) from 1969 to 1970. The appellant contends that, by virtue of s 23(9) of the 1971 Act, he is entitled to revert to using it as a light industrial building. There is no *g*
dispute that use for storage for the purposes of his business is use as a light industrial building. The result of that contention, if it is correct, is that the enforcement notice is futile because use of the land as a store, although unlawful in the sense that it was begun without the requisite planning permission, is rendered lawful by s 23(9).

The respondent contends that the meaning of s 23(9) is that, following on the enforcement notice, the only use that can be made of the land without obtaining fresh *h*
planning permission is use for the purpose for which it could have been used immediately before the use struck at by the enforcement notice, i e as a laundry, provided that use was itself lawful. But it is common ground that the use as a laundry from 1970 to 1977 was not lawful. So, if the respondent is right, there is, in practice, no purpose for which the land can now be used without obtaining planning permission. I say 'in practice' because there are some purposes, such as agriculture (see s 22(2)(*e*) of the 1971 Act), for which it *j*
could lawfully be used without planning permission, but they are unlikely to be practical possibilities.

The argument of the respondent prevailed in the Court of Appeal and in my opinion it is well founded. I reach that opinion on construction of s 23(9) itself and especially of the last few words in the subsection. Where an enforcement notice is issued in respect of any development, what the subsection authorises without planning permission is use for the purpose for which the land could lawfully be used 'if *that development* had not been carried out'. Accordingly one has to assume that the development consisting of the change of use in 1977 had not been carried out, and see what would have been the state of affairs on that assumption. Clearly if that development had not been carried out, the land would have continued to be used as a laundry, as it was from 1970 to 1977. But admittedly it was not 'lawfully' so used during that period. The appellant claims to be entitled to follow the planning history of the land further back through its earlier uses until he gets back to the last lawful use, which in this case was use as a light industrial building for food processing in 1969 to 1970. But the process of following the history back would in my view not be consistent with the hypothesis of sub-s (9) of s 23 which is that only the development of 1977 had not been carried out. The appellant's argument would involve reading the subsection as if it referred to the purpose 'for which the land could *last* lawfully have been used *before* that development had been carried out'. Such a reading would materially alter the sense of the subsection and is in my view unwarranted. Moreover I agree with Watkins LJ who said, when this case was in the Court of Appeal, that it was—

> 'inconceivable that the [recipient] of an enforcement notice was intended to be allowed to search the history of the use of the relevant land and, on discovery of a ... lawful use, no matter how long ago ... claim the benefit of that use without planning permission.'

The construction of the subsection which appears to me correct is consistent with the general scheme of the Act. During the period 1970 to 1977, when the land was being used as a laundry, any change of use back to use for food processing would have required planning permission, because, although it would have been a change from general to light industrial use, the general industrial use was unlawful. That was disputed by the appellant at an earlier stage of the appeal, but he no longer contends that he was entitled to change from general to light industrial use, if the former was unlawful. It would be strange if the appellant was in a better position now, after a further unlawful change of use in 1977 than he, or his author, would have been during the period 1970 to 1977.

Counsel for the appellant argued that the reference in s 23(9) to 'the use' of land for the purpose for which it could lawfully have been used etc suggested that there was a presumption that there probably was a purpose for which it could lawfully have been used, and thus entitled one to look back beyond the immediately preceding use. Even if it be accepted that some such presumption is implied, I do not see why it should entitle one to look back beyond the immediately preceding use, and in any event I do not consider that it could possibly be strong enough to overcome the words later in the subsection to which I have already referred. Counsel also presented a plea ad misericordiam to the effect that, if s 23(9) was construed in the way for which the respondent contends, it would operate harshly in his case. He pointed out, rightly, that if the enforcement notice had been issued during the period between 1970 and 1977, when the land was being used unlawfully as a laundry, planning permission would not have been required to revert to the immediately preceding use for food processing, because that was a lawful use. It would be harsh, counsel said, if the appellant were to lose that right because, instead of continuing to use the land as a general industrial building (a laundry), he had changed to using it as a light industrial building, which by definition is less objectionable (see Use Classes Order 1972, art 2(2)). Counsel also presented an alternative argument based on hardship to the effect that, had the use as a laundry not been interrupted for the short period of about a year in 1969 to 1970 by the use for food processing, it would have been lawful and he could have reverted to it now under s 23(9). Finally counsel urged your Lordships to regard the provisions of s 23(9) as ambiguous, and to construe them in the way that would cause least hardship to the appellant. I have some sympathy for the appellant, but I am unable to accept the submission that the provisions of s 23(9) are ambiguous, or that their meaning should be distorted in order to mitigate any element of hardship. It must in my view be accepted that, in the application of a detailed statutory code such as that in the 1971 Act, or those which are commonly found in fiscal legislation, a measure of hardship may in some cases be unavoidable.

We were referred to the case of *LTSS Print and Supply Services Ltd v Hackney BC* [1976] 1 All ER 311 at 317, [1976] 1 QB 663 at 673 where Cairns LJ said in the Court of Appeal that the effect of s 23(9) was that—

> '... when an enforcement notice had been served reverter should be allowed only to the use which was current immediately before the development the subject of the enforcement notice, and if that use was not lawful in accordance with that part of the Act, then planning permission would be required for any use it was proposed to adopt.'

Glidewell J in *Balco Transport Services Ltd v Secretary of State for the Environment* (1981) 45 P & CR 216 at 222 after saying he regarded that observation by Cairns LJ as obiter, expressed the view that it was not correct. But in a subsequent unreported case (*Blenkinsopp v Secretary of State for the Environment* (28 January 1983)) Glidewell J recanted that view. Whether the observation of Cairns LJ was obiter or not, I am respectfully in agreement with it for the reasons that I have tried to explain. Some reference was made by the Lord Justice to the effect of sub-ss (5) and (6) of s 23 and counsel for the appellant sought to found an argument on a comparison between those sub-sections and sub-s (9) of s 23. Counsel for the respondents did not accept that the meaning attributed to sub-ss (5) and (6) by Cairns LJ was correct. The provisions of those subsections are materially different from the provisions of sub-s (9) and I do not find them to be of any assistance in construing the latter subsection. I therefore express no opinion on the meaning of sub-ss (5) and (6) or on the correctness or otherwise of anything said about them by Cairns LJ in the *LTSS* case.

I would dismiss this appeal.

LORD ELWYN-JONES. My Lords, I agree with the draft speech prepared by my noble and learned friend Lord Fraser, and for the reasons he has given I would dismiss this appeal.

LORD LOWRY. My Lords, I have had the advantage of reading in draft the speech prepared by my noble and learned friend Lord Fraser. I agree with his conclusions and, for the reasons which he gives, I would dismiss the appeal.

LORD ROSKILL. My Lords, I have had the advantage of reading in draft the speech to be delivered by my noble and learned friend Lord Fraser. I agree with it and for the reasons which he gives I too would dismiss the appeal.

LORD BRIGHTMAN. My Lords, I would dismiss this appeal for the reasons given by my noble and learned friend Lord Fraser.

Appeal dismissed.

Solicitors: *Ward Bowie* (for the appellant); *Treasury Solicitor*.

Mary Rose Plummer Barrister.

a Eastleigh Borough Council v Betts and another

HOUSE OF LORDS

LORD FRASER OF TULLYBELTON, LORD WILBERFORCE, LORD EDMUND-DAVIES, LORD ROSKILL AND LORD BRIGHTMAN

b 12, 27 JULY 1983

Housing – Homeless person – Duty of housing authority to provide accommodation – Person having no local connection with area of housing authority – Applicant not 'normally resident' in authority's area – Normally resident – Authority applying arbitrary or rigid residential qualification of residence for six out of previous twelve months – Whether authority entitled to
c *impose arbitrary residential qualification – Housing (Homeless Persons) Act 1977, ss 5(1)(a), 18(1)(a).*

In August 1980 the male applicant obtained a job in Southampton and moved there from Leicester. In October the female applicant and their two children joined him and the family moved into a council house in the area of the respondent council. Shortly
d afterwards, the male applicant lost his job and fell into arrears with the rent for the council house, with the result that the council obtained a possession order in respect of the house. On 6 February 1981 the applicants applied to the council, as the local housing authority, for accommodation under the Housing (Homeless Persons) Act 1977. The council decided that the family were homeless, that they had not become homeless intentionally and that they had a priority need for accommodation (and therefore would
e normally have been entitled under s 4(5)[a] of the 1977 Act to housing for an indefinite period), but the council further decided that the applicants had no 'local connection', as defined by s 18(1)[b] of the 1977 Act, with the council's area because they were not and never had been 'normally resident' in the area but instead had a local connection with another housing authority's area, namely the area of the authority which housed them in Leicester. The council therefore considered that by virtue of s 5(1)(*a*)[c] of the 1977 Act
f it was relieved of the duty to house the applicants which would otherwise have been imposed on it by s 4(5). In deciding that the applicants had no 'local connection' with its area the council relied on a recommendation in a national agreement between housing authorities regarding the implementation of the 1977 Act to the effect that a working definition of 'normal residence' should be residence in the area for at least six out of the previous twelve months. The applicants applied for judicial review of the council's
g decision. The judge dismissed the application and the applicants appealed to the Court of Appeal which allowed the appeal on the grounds that the applicants had a local connection with the council's area merely by being normally resident there, however short the period of residence, and that the council had misdirected itself by arbitrarily or rigidly applying the period of residence contained in the agreement between housing authorities. The council appealed to the House of Lords.

h

Held – On the true construction of ss 5(1)(*a*) and 18(1) of the 1977 Act the test of whether an applicant for accommodation under the 1977 Act had a 'local connection' with the area of a particular housing authority was not merely whether the applicant had any local connection with the area nor even whether he was normally resident or employed in, or had family associations or special circumstances connecting him with, the area, but
j whether those factors of residence, employment, family associations or special

a Section 4(5) provides: 'Where—(*a*) they are satisfied—(i) that he is homeless, and (ii) that he has a priority need, but (*b*) they are not satisfied that he became homeless intentionally, their duty, subject to section 5 below, is to secure that accommodation becomes available for his occupation.'

b Section 18(1) is set out at p 1114 *h*, post

c Section 5(1), so far as material, is set out at p 1114 *c* to *e*, post

circumstances, referred to in s 18(1), were sufficient to build up and establish in real
terms a local connection with the area. Thus, although it was possible for an applicant to a
be 'normally resident' in an area after living there for only a day that would not show
that the applicant had built up a local connection with the area because of his residence
there. Furthermore, in determining whether an applicant's residence was of sufficient
duration to establish a local connection a housing authority were entitled to operate a
policy and establish guidelines applicable to all applications made to them, provided they
did not close their mind to the particular facts of each individual case. Since the council b
had not misdirected itself in reaching its opinion that the applicants did not have a local
connection with its area because they had lived there for less than six months the council
were not under a duty to house the applicants permanently under s 4(5) of the Act. The
council's appeal would therefore be allowed (see p 1112 *j* to p 1113 *c*, p 1118 *g* to
p 1119 *a* and *d* to *j* and p 1120 *b* to *e*, post).

Shah v Barnet London BC [1983] 1 All ER 226 distinguished. c

Decision of the Court of Appeal sub nom *R v Eastleigh BC, ex p Betts* [1983] 2 All ER 481 reversed.

Notes

For responsibility for accommodation as between housing authorities, see 22 Halsbury's
Laws (4th edn) para 514. d

For the Housing (Homeless Persons) Act 1977, ss 4, 5, 18, see 47 Halsbury's Statutes (3rd edn) 318, 319, 330.

Cases referred to in opinions

British Oxygen Co Ltd v Minister of Technology [1970] 3 All ER 165, [1971] AC 610, [1970] 3 WLR 488, HL. e

IRC v Lysaght [1928] AC 234, [1928] All ER Rep 575, HL.

Levene v IRC [1928] AC 217, [1928] All ER Rep 746, HL.

Macrae v Macrae [1949] 2 All ER 34, [1949] P 397, CA.

Shah v Barnet London BC [1983] 1 All ER 226, [1983] 2 WLR 16, HL.

f

Appeal

Eastleigh Borough Council appealed with leave of the Appeal Committee of the House
of Lords granted on 5 May 1983 against the decision of the Court of Appeal (Stephenson,
Griffiths and Purchas LJJ) ([1983] 2 All ER 481, [1983] 1 WLR 774) on 3 March 1983
allowing an appeal by the respondents, Ronald Thomas Betts and Vivien Anne Betts (the
applicants), against the judgment of Webster J hearing the Crown Office list given on 26 g
October 1982 whereby he dismissed an application by the applicants for judicial review
of a decision of the appellant council to the effect that the council were not under a duty
to rehouse the applicants because they had no local connection with the council's area
since they were not normally resident in the area within ss 5(1) and 18(1) of the Housing
(Homeless Persons) Act 1977. The facts are set out in the opinion of Lord Brightman.

h

Anthony Scrivener QC and *Graham Stoker* for Eastleigh Borough Council.

James W Black QC and *Barrington Myers* for the applicants.

Their Lordships took time for consideration.

27 July. The following opinions were delivered. j

LORD FRASER OF TULLYBELTON. My Lords, I have had the advantage of reading in draft the speech of my noble and learned friend Lord Brightman. I agree with it, and for the reasons stated in it I would allow this appeal.

LORD WILBERFORCE. My Lords, I have had the advantage of reading in draft the a speech by my noble and learned friend Lord Brightman. I agree with it and for the reasons he gives I would allow the appeal.

LORD EDMUND-DAVIES. My Lords, I have had the advantage of reading in draft form the opinion prepared by my noble and learned friend Lord Brightman, and I concur in the reasoning which has led him to the conclusion that this appeal should be b allowed.

LORD ROSKILL. My Lords, I have had the advantage of reading in draft the speech to be delivered by my noble and learned friend Lord Brightman. For the reasons he gives I too would allow this appeal.

c **LORD BRIGHTMAN.** My Lords, the Housing (Homeless Persons) Act 1977 entitles a homeless person to apply to a housing authority for accommodation. If the housing authority to whom application is made considers that the applicant has no local connection with the area of that authority, the authority may be in a position to transfer the statutory responsibility to another housing authority with whose area the applicant has a local connection. The respondents to this appeal, Ronald Thomas Betts and Vivien d Anne Betts, became homeless through no fault of their own at a time when they were living in the area of the appellants, the Eastleigh Borough Council (Eastleigh), in Hampshire. They applied to Eastleigh for accommodation. Mr and Mrs Betts had formerly lived in the area of the Blaby District Council (Blaby) in Leicestershire. Both Eastleigh and Blaby are in agreement that the responsibility for housing Mr and Mrs Betts properly belongs to Blaby. Mr and Mrs Betts, who wish to remain in the area of e Eastleigh, seek to challenge that decision by way of judicial review. They were successful before the Court of Appeal (see [1983] 2 All ER 481, [1983] 1 WLR 774).

Mr Betts is 37 years of age. He was born in London, and in his early years worked there. In 1973 he lived and worked in Dunstable. In the following year he moved to Milton Keynes and commuted to work in London. Thereafter he lived and worked abroad for a while. In 1978 he secured a job in Leicester and went to live in a council f house in the Blaby area. In the meantime Mr and Mrs Betts' two daughters had been born, the elder being now aged nine and the younger nearly five.

In August 1980 Mr Betts left his family temporarily in order to take up employment with Southern Television as a film processor at their studios in Southampton. In October he secured rented accommodation in the Eastleigh area, and Mrs Betts and their daughters joined him there. He gave up his Blaby council house, regrettably without giving the g council any notice and with arrears of rent outstanding. Unfortunately Southern Television lost their franchise shortly afterwards and as a result Mr Betts lost his employment. He again fell into arrears with his rent. On 3 February 1981 an order for possession was made against him, to take effect on 3 March. On 6 February he was given an interview with Mr Renouf, a senior assistant in the estates management department of Eastleigh, and he applied under the 1977 Act for accommodation.

h The immediate result of that application was that Eastleigh became under a statutory duty to make inquiries to satisfy themselves that Mr and Mrs Betts were in fact homeless, and to ascertain whether they had a 'priority need' for accommodation by reason of dependent children and whether they had become homeless 'intentionally' within the meaning of the 1977 Act: see s 3(1) and (2). Furthermore, Eastleigh became entitled, if they thought fit, to make inquiries whether the applicants had 'a local connection with j the area of another housing authority': see s 3(3). Eastleigh also became under a duty to secure that temporary accommodation was made available for occupation by Mr and Mrs Betts pending any decision which Eastleigh might make as a result of their inquiries: see s 3(4). Eastleigh has performed the duty of securing temporary accommodation for Mr and Mrs Betts by making a dwelling house available for them at 85 High Street, Eastleigh.

As a result of inquiries, Mr Grant, the chief housing officer of Eastleigh had satisfied himself by 25 February 1981 that Mr and Mrs Betts were homeless, had a priority need for accommodation, and were not homeless intentionally. Eastleigh thereby became under a duty under s 4(5) of the 1977 Act, replacing their previous duty under s 3(4), to secure that (permanent) accommodation became available for Mr and Mrs Betts subject however to s 5. Section 5 defines responsibility as between different housing authorities, and it is with this section that this appeal is concerned. In his letter of 25 February Mr Grant added:

'... your application under the Act has been notified to Blaby District Council because you have lived in this Borough for less then six months, and are not employed in this Borough and do not have any relatives here. Your rehousing is therefore considered to be their responsibility,'

This assessment of the situation is accepted by Blaby, but not by Mr and Mrs Betts.

I turn now to the provisions of s 5. If that section does not apply, Eastleigh accept that the responsibility is theirs under s 4(5) to secure accommodation for Mr and Mrs Betts. So far as relevant, s 5 reads as follows:

'(1) A housing authority are not subject to a duty under section 4(5) above—(*a*) if they are of the opinion—(i) that neither the person who applied to them for accommodation or for assistance in obtaining accommodation nor any person who might reasonably be expected to reside with him has a local connection with their area, and (ii) that the person who so applied or a person who might reasonably be expected to reside with him has a local connection with another housing authority's area ... (*b*) if they notify that authority—(i) that the application has been made, and (ii) that they they are of the opinion specified in paragraph (*a*) above.

(2) In this Act "notifying authority" means a housing authority who give a notification under subsection (1) above and "notified authority" means a housing authority who receive such a notification.

(3) It shall be the duty of the notified authority to secure that accommodation becomes available for occupation by the person to whom the notification relates if neither he nor any person who might reasonably be expected to reside with him has a local connection with the area of the notifying authority but the conditions specified in subsection (4) below are satisfied.

(4) The conditions mentioned in subsection (3) above are—(*a*) that the person to whom the notification relates or some person who might reasonably be expected to reside with him has a local connection with the area of the notified authority ...

(7) Any question which falls to be determined under this section shall be determined by agreement between the notifying authority and the notified authority or, in default of such agreement, in accordance with the appropriate arrangements.

(8) The appropriate arrangements for the purposes of this section are any such arrangements as the Secretary of State may by order direct ...'

Section 19(1) of the 1977 Act provides that unless the context otherwise requires 'local connection' shall be construed in accordance with s 18, which enacts as follows:

'(1) Any reference in this Act to a person having a local connection with an area is a reference to his having a connection with that area—(*a*) because he is or in the past was normally resident in it and his residence in it is or was of his own choice; or (*b*) because he is employed in it, or (*c*) because of family associations, or (*d*) because of any special circumstances.'

Subsections (2) and (3), which I need not read, explain when residence is not of a person's own choice, and when a person is not to be considered as employed in an area.

It is obvious that time-consuming and expensive disputes might arise between housing authorities as to the existence of a 'local connection'. Such disputes are not in the interest either of housing authorities or of homeless persons. The purposes of the 1977 Act demand speedy solutions to questions of doubt. To avoid such disputes, and to settle them quickly and cheaply if they arise, certains steps have been taken on behalf of housing authorities. First, in order to facilitate agreements between notifying authorities and notified authorities as required by s 5(7) a national 'Agreement on Procedures for Referrals of the Homeless' was negotiated between the Association of District Councils, the Association of Metropolitan Authorities and the London Boroughs Association at the time when the Bill was being considered by Parliament. This agreement has been adhered to by the majority of housing authorities. Second, by the Housing (Homeless Persons) (Appropriate Arrangements) Order 1978, SI 1978/69 the Secretary of State for the Environment, in exercise of his powers under sub-s (8) has established the 'Appropriate Arrangements' set out in the schedule to the order for the purpose of settling unresolved disputes between housing authorities. These arrangements are in a form which was agreed by the three associations who negotiated the agreement on procedures. They provide for any disputed question under s 5 to be determined speedily either by a person agreed on by the authorities concerned or by a person chosen from a panel. These arrangements came into operation on 21 January 1978, that is to say, a few weeks after the 1977 Act came into force. There is evidence that the agreement on procedures has worked well, and that as a result there have only been about 50 references under the order since the 1977 Act came into force.

The agreement on procedures does not purport to impose a legally binding code on housing authorities who adhere to it. It is merely a policy document. Its tone is set by para 1.2 which reads as follows:

> 'With this [sub-ss (7) ff of s 5] in mind the three associations have agreed on arrangements for referrals which they recommend to the local authorities who are primarily concerned with providing for homeless households. Section 5 of the Act lays down the general procedure to be followed where it appears that a local authority other than the authority to whom application is made by a homeless household . . . should be made responsible. There are, however, considerable areas of possible disagreement and dispute in the interpretation of the Act, and although in the last resort these can only be decided by the courts, the Associations are anxious to avoid as far as possible legal disputes between local authorities. They therefore issue this agreement on the procedures and criteria to be followed, and recommend it for general adoption by all their memebers . . .'

After intermediate paragraphs, the agreement then picks up the statutory expression 'local connection' and gives guidance on 'normally resident', 'employed', 'family associations' and 'special circumstances'. The guidance on 'normal residence' is in the following terms (para 2.5):

> '*A local connection may be*: (i) That the household is, or in the past was, normally resident in the area. It is suggested that a working definition of "normal residence" should be that the household has been residing for at least 6 months in the area during the previous 12 months, or for not less than 3 years during the previous 5 year period. In this connection, residence up to 6 months under one or more tenancies subject to Case 13 of Schedule 15 of the Rent Act 1977 should be disregarded for the purposes of defining "normal residence" . . .'

The exclusion of certain Rent Act lettings relates to winter and holiday lettings.

With this explanation of the statutory background, I return to the narrative of events. Following on the chief housing officer's letter of 25 February 1981 informing Mr and Mrs Betts that their application had been notified to Blaby, Blaby duly offered accommodation to Mr and Mrs Betts within their area. This was not acceptable to Mr and Mrs Betts. Eastleigh then obtained an order for possession of 85 High Street, Eastleigh, where Mr and Mrs Betts had been provided with temporary accommodation pursuant to s 3(4). This order is not being enforced pending the result of these proceedings. On 1 April 1982 Mr and Mrs Betts' solicitors informed Eastleigh of their clients' intention to apply to the High Court for judicial review of Eastleigh's decision.

Later that month Mr Betts obtained full-time employment as a warehouseman in the Eastleigh area, and shortly afterwards Mrs Betts secured contract work with British Rail. On 23 June 1982 Mr and Mrs Betts moved for judicial review. There was at that time an assertion on the part of Eastleigh that Mr and Mrs Betts were intentionally homeless as a result of their refusal of Blaby's offer of accommodation. This assertion, if correct, would have relieved both housing authorities of the major obligation imposed by the 1977 Act. The relief originally sought by the notice of motion accordingly included a declaration that Mr and Mrs Betts were not homeless intentionally. However, this point is no longer pursued by Eastleigh, and the only relief outstanding is an order of mandamus requiring Eastleigh to carry out their supposed duty under s 4(5). As I have already indicated the existence of that duty is not in dispute if Eastleigh are unable to rely on s 5. Accordingly, an injunctive order against Eastleigh would not be appropriate if their reliance on s 5 is misplaced.

The attack on Eastleigh hinges on the chief housing officer's letter of 25 February 1981, and the inference to be drawn from his statement that 'your application under the Act has been notified to Blaby District Council because you have lived in this borough for less than six months.' The evidence in relation to that letter is somewhat brief, but is not challenged by Mr and Mrs Betts. Mr Renouf deposed that after he had reported to Mr Grant, the chief housing officer, the result of his preliminary inquiries, Mr Grant—

> 'confirmed that this application should be referred to the Blaby District Council under section 5 of the 1977 Act because the applicants had no local connection with the respondents but they had a local connection with Blaby District Council.'

This was elaborated by Mr Grant in his own affidavit in the following terms:

> 'The Applicants' application for accommodation came before me on the 23rd February 1981 when I had to give a decision as to whether they should be offered accommodation. After considering a report from Mr. Renouf, my Senior Assistant (Estates Management), I decided that the application should be referred to Blaby District Council under Section 5 of the Housing (Homeless Persons) Act 1977 as I considered that the responsibility for housing the Applicants lay with that Council. The decisionwas taken by me having regard to the wording of the Act together with the recommendations set out in the "Agreement on Procedures for Referrals of the Homeless—Revised 6th June 1979" issued by the Association of District Councils, Association of Metropolitan Authorities and the London Boroughs Association ... Upon considering the report of Mr. Renouf, the crucial factor in my decision was that the Applicants did not have a "local connection" with the Borough of Eastleigh, within the meaning of Section 5 of the 1977 Act. The phrase "local connection" is defined in Section 18(1) of the 1977 Act, but as Section 18(1)(b) and Section 18(1)(c) were not applicable, unless the applicants were "normally resident" in the Borough within the meaning of Section 19(1)(a) or unless any special circumstances applied, a local connection with the Respondent would not be established. In considering the question of "normally resident" I had regard to the revised "Agreement on Procedures for Referrals of the Homeless" which states that a "working definition of normal residence" should be that the household has been residing "for at least six months in the (Borough) during the previous twelve months" (clause 2.5). The Applicants having only resided in the Borough for some four months before the date of their application on the 6th February 1981, I considered that a "normal residence" had not been established within the meaning of the Act. The "Revised Agreement on Procedures for Referrals of the Homeless" is in wide use by Housing Authorities when considering a referral under Section 5 of the 1977 Act, and Blaby District Council fully accepted the working definition of normal residences.'

The motion came before Webster J in October 1982. The decision made by Eastleigh was attacked on three grounds, but two were abandoned. The ground which survived related to the meaning of "normally resident" in s 18(1)(*a*) of the 1977 Act. Counsel

contended that (1) Eastleigh had misdirected themselves as to the meaning of those
a words, or (2) they had fettered their discretion in deciding how to apply those words to the facts before them, or (3) their decision as to the question of whether the applicants were normally resident in the Eastleigh area was a decision which no authority properly directing themselves could have reached on the facts before them.

After considering the affidavit evidence the judge said that he was not satisfied that the chief housing officer had misdirected himself as to the meaning of normal residence;
b or that he had confined himself to the suggested working definition of that expression in para 2.5 of the agreement on procedures; or that he had regarded the decision which he had to make as being fettered in any way by the terms of that agreement; or that his decision that the applicants were not normally resident in the Eastleigh area was one which could not have been reached on the material before him had he properly directed himself. The motion was accordingly dismissed.

c In December 1982 your Lordships' House gave judgment in *Shah v Barnet London BC* [1983] 1 All ER 226, [1983] 2 WLR 16. This case was thought by the applicants to open up new horizons. In *Shah*'s case certain immigrant students who had no right of abode in the United Kingdom claimed to qualify for mandatory awards under the Education Act 1962. Under s 1 of that Act and regulations made thereunder it was the duty of every local authority, in certain circumstances, to bestow awards on persons who 'are ordinarily
d resident in the area of the authority', and had been so resident for the three preceding years, and possessed the requisite educational qualifications.

Lord Scarman, with whom all their Lordships agreed, stated the problem and answered it in the following terms ([1983] 1 All ER 226 at 232–233, [1983] 2 WLR 16 at 23):

> 'Two questions of statutory interpretation, therefore, arise. The first is: what is the natural and ordinary meaning of "ordinarily resident ... in the United
> e Kingdom" ...? The second is: does the statute in the context of the relevant law against the background of which it was enacted, or in the circumstances of today, including in particular the impact of the Immigration Act 1971, compel one to substitute a special, and, if so, what, meaning to the words "ordinarily resident in the United Kingdom"? For the reasons which I shall endeavour to develop I answer the two questions as follows. The natural and ordinary meaning of the words has
> f been authoritatively determined in this House in two tax cases reported in 1928 (*Levene v IRC* [1928] AC 217, [1928] All ER Rep 746 and *IRC v Lysaght* [1928] AC 234, [1928] All ER Rep 575). To the second question my answer is No. The 1962 Act and the regulations are to be construed by giving to the words "ordinarily resident in the United Kingdom" their natural and ordinary meaning.'

g The natural and ordinary meaning of the words 'ordinarily resident', as laid down in those tax cases, is explained with complete clarity in the different speeches of your Lordships' predecessors, the key phrases being 'residence in a place with some degree of continuity and apart from accidental or temporary absences': see *Levene v IRC* [1928] AC 217 at 225, [1928] All ER Rep 746 at 750 per Viscount Cave LC; 'The regular order of a man's life, adopted voluntarily and for settled purposes': see *IRC v Lysaght* [1928] AC 234
h at 243, [1928] All ER Rep 575 at 580 per Viscount Sumner; 'According to the way in which a man's life is usually ordered': see *Levene v IRC* [1928] AC 217 at 232, [1928] All ER Rep 746 at 754 per Lord Warrington. Lord Scarman's general conclusion, therefore, was ([1983] 1 All ER 226 at 235, [1983] 2 WLR 16 at 26):

> 'Unless, therefore, it can be shown that the statutory framework or the legal context in which the words are used requires a different meaning, I unhesitantly
> j subscribe to the view that "ordinarily resident" refers to a man's abode in a particular place or country which he has adopted voluntarily and for settled purposes as part of the regular order of his life for the time being, whether of short or long duration.'

The instant case came before the Court of Appeal in January 1983. The argument there, as also before your Lordships, was that Eastleigh could not properly transfer their responsibility to Blaby unless they were of the opinion that the applicants were not, on 6 February 1981, normally resident in the Eastleigh area; that they formed that opinion by the rigid application of a guideline that normal residence short of six months was not enough to constitute a local connection with the Eastleigh area; and that the real question for the court was the meaning in the context of the words 'normally resident'. After reviewing the evidence, Stephenson LJ reached the conclusion that the chief housing officer 'did fetter the council's decision by a rigid application of the suggested definition of normal residence' in the agreement on procedures. Stephenson LJ then considered the authorities on 'ordinary residence' to which he was referred by the applicants' counsel, including not only *Shah v Barnet London BC* but also *Macrae v Macrae* [1949] 2 All ER 34 at 36, [1949] P 397 at 403 where Somervell LJ pointed out, in the context of a matrimonial cause, that 'ordinary residence can be changed in a day'. These authorities, said Stephenson LJ ([1983] 2 All ER 481 at 490, [1983] 1 WLR 774 at 785), showed that 'a person may be normally resident where he intends to settle not necessarily permanently or indefinitely ...' The judgment of Griffiths LJ was to the same effect ([1983] 2 All ER 481 at 493, [1983] 1 WLR 774 at 788):

> '"Normal residence" within the meaning of this Act is in my opinion to be construed in the same sense as "ordinarily resident" was construed by the House of Lords in *Shah v Barnet London BC* [1983] 1 All ER 226, [1983] 2 WLR 16. It requires a consideration of many features of the residence and is not to be decided solely by the application of a six-month rule. It follows that as the housing officer applied the six-month rule to decide "normal residence" he misdirected himself in law when forming his opinion on normal residence and thus on whether the Betts family had a local connection with Eastleigh's area ...'

Finally, Purchas LJ said ([1983] 1 All ER 481 at 494, [1983] 1 WLR 774 at 790):

> '... if the applicants had been asked by an inquirer where they were normally living between October 1980 and January 1981 I have little doubt that they would have answered "in Eastleigh". In my judgment this would be the normal reaction, as an objective test, of any person in the particular circumstances in which the applicants found themselves at that times. In the light of these authorities, the adherence to an arbitrary period of residential qualification cannot be the correct approach to s 18(1)(*a*) of the Act.'

My Lords, in my respectful view the manner in which the applicants have approached this case, and were successful in persuading the Court of Appeal to approach it, is misconceived. Eastleigh are relieved of their obligations under s 4(5) if they are 'of the opinion' specified in s 5(1)(*a*)(i) and (ii). The requisite 'opinion' is that the applicants do not have (in the present tense) a local connection with the Eastleigh area but do have a local connection with the Blaby area. 'Local connection' is not a defined expression in the sense that it means, inter alia, that the applicant 'is or in the past was normally resident in [the area] and his residence in it is or was of his own choice'. Section 18(1) does not entitle the reader to construe s 5(1)(*a*) by substituting 'is or was normally resident in', or 'is employed in', or 'has family associations with' for the words 'has a local connection with'. What s 18(1) does is to say that a reference to a person having a local connection with an area is a reference to his having such a connection because he is, or in the past was normally resident there, or because he is employed there, or because he has family associations with that area or because there are special circumstances. Section 18 specifies those factors alone on which the local connection is to be founded. A local connection not founded on any of the four stated factors is irrelevant. The fundamental concept of s 5(1)(*a*) is local connection, not any local connection, but a local connection having any of the origins described in s 18(1). The opinion which has to be formed by a notifying housing authority in a residence case is not whether the homeless person is now or was in the past normally resident in the area of the notifying authority, but whether the applicant has now a local connection with either area based on the fact that he is now or was in the past normally resident in that area.

The approach of the applicants is very different. They ask the question, are they now normally resident in the Eastleigh area? They answer that question affirmatively and then claim as a result, by definition, a local connection with Eastleigh which invalidates the opinion reached by Eastleigh under s 5(1)(*a*). This erroneous approach emerges with clarity from the terms of their notice of appeal to the Court of Appeal, the first ground of which contains the following:

> '... the fundamental question was what is meant in Section 18(1)(*a*) of the said Act by the term "normally resident"...'

Stephenson LJ accepted that definition of the issue which was thought to be before the court when he said ([1983] 2 All ER 481 at 486, [1983] 1 WLR 774 at 780):

> 'The applicants' case here and below is that the respondent council have not succeeded in transferring their responsibility to Blaby District Council. They can only do that if they were of the opinion that the applicants were not on 6 February 1981 (or before that) *normally resident* in their area.' (My emphasis)

My Lords, that is not the fundamental question. The fundamental question is the existence of a 'local connection'. In construing s 5 it is only to be expected that the emphasis falls on 'local connection', and not on past or present residence or current employment, etc. The 1977 Act is one which enables a homeless person in certain circumstances to jump over the heads of all other persons on a housing authority's waiting list, to jump the queue. One would not expect any just legislation to permit this to be done unless the applicant has in a real sense a local connection with the area in question. I accept that 'residence' may be changed in a day, and that in appropriate circumstances a single day's residence may be enough to enable a person to say that he was normally resident in the area in which he arrived only yesterday. But 'local connection' means far more than that. It must be built up and established; by a period of residence; or by a period of employment; or by family associations which have endured in the area; or by other special circumstances which spell out a local connection in real terms.

I return to the agreement on procedures. Faced with s 5 of the 1977 Act, a housing authority is involved, not with the question whether the applicant is or was normally resident, etc in the area in question, but whether the applicant has a local connection with that area. Has the normal residence of the applicant in the area been of such a duration as to establish for him a local connection with the area? To answer that question speedily it is sensible for local authorities to have agreed guidelines. I see nothing in the least unreasonable with a norm of six months' residence during the previous 12 months, or three years' residence during the previous five years. Seeing that the section is concerned with a subsisting, and not with a past, local connection, it is also reasonable to work on the basis that, after five years have gone by, no local connection based on residence is likely to have any relevance.

So I start my conclusions on this appeal by expressing the view that para 2.5 of the agreement on procedures is eminently sensible and proper to have been included in the agreement. Although 'an opinion' formed by a housing authority under s 5(1) must be concluded by reference to the facts of each individual case, there is no objection to the authority operating a policy or establishing guidelines, for reasons which the authority may legitimately entertain, and then applying such policy or guidelines generally to all the applications which come before them, provided that the authority do not close their mind to the particular facts of the individual case. There is ample authority that a body which is charged with exercising an administrative discretion is entitled to promulgate a policy or guidelines as an indication of a norm which is intended to be followed: see, for example, the speech of Lord Reid in *British Oxygen Co Ltd v Minister of Technology* [1970] 3 All ER 165, [1971] AC 610.

As regards the meaning of 'normally resident' in the context of s 18(1)(*a*), this will take its colour from the fact that residence of any sort will be irrelevant unless and until it has a
been such as to establish a local connection with the area in which such residence subsists or has subsisted. I doubt whether in these circumstances any elaborate attempt at a definition of 'normally resident' will be profitable. They are ordinary English words, which in many contexts will mean what this House said 'ordinarily resident' meant in *Shah v Barnet London BC*. But they are only a subsidiary component of the formula which a housing authority will be applying under s 5 of the Act. If the residence of an applicant b
has been of a sufficient duration to create a local connection, no difficulty is likely to arise in deciding whether such residence was normal. But if it were necessary to decide such a point in a particular case, I do not think that the housing authority would be wrong if they applied to the words 'normally resident' the meaning which in *Shah*'s case was attached to the words 'ordinarily resident', remembering that the real exercise will be to decide whether the normal residence has been such as to establish a subsisting local c
connection.

That leaves me with a single question, which is the ultimate one in this appeal; whether Eastleigh misdirected themselves in reaching the opinion that the applicants did not have a local connection with the Eastleigh area. The onus of establishing this is on the applicants. They rely principally on the wording of the letter of 25 February 1981 which says that Blaby have been notified 'because you have lived in this Borough for less d
then six months'. The question before Eastleigh being whether the applicants had a local connection with the Eastleigh area as a result of residence, I see nothing whatever wrong with the decision by Eastleigh that as the applicants had lived in the area for less than six months, it was considered that they did not have a local connection with that area. It is true that the letter does not expressly refer to the absence of a local connection, only to the briefness of the residence, but it is to be observed that in his affidavit of 21 June 1982 e
which I have quoted, Mr Renouf attributes the decision under s 5 to lack of a local connection, which is the correct approach.

In my opinion the applicants have not made out any ground for attacking the validity of the opinion formed by Eastleigh under s 5(1). Eastleigh therefore are not under a duty under s 4(5) of the 1977 Act to house the applicants. I would allow this appeal.

f

Appeal allowed.

Solicitors: *Sharpe Pritchard & Co* agents for *R W Read*, Eastleigh (for Eastleigh Borough Council); *William Charles Crocker*, agents for *Christopher Green & Partners*, Eastleigh (for the applicants).

Mary Rose Plummer Barrister.

End of Volume 2